THE WORD FINDER

THE

The Word Finder

Compiled and edited by J. I. RODALE

With the collaboration of KINGSBURY M. BADGER, M. A.

THEODORE G. EHRSAM, M. A. MABEL E. MULOCK, B. S.

EDWARD J. FLUCK, Ph. D.

Rodale Books, Inc.
EMMAUS, PENNSYLVANIA

Printed in U.S.A.
344
Twentieth Printing — June 1978

PREFACE

What is the WORD FINDER? Is it a new kind of thesaurus? The answer is emphatically "no"! In a thesaurus one looks for substitutes for the word he has in mind. If he wishes to say "large," reference to a thesaurus will supply him with a better word such as "spacious." The WORD FINDER, on the other hand, does not merely yield a substitute word but produces an augmentative word, one to embellish and add to the idea. Thus, in the WORD FINDER by referring to the adjective *large* the user is taught to describe "how large?" by a selected list of words such as *incalculably*, *incredibly*, *preposterously*, *overwhelmingly*, *prodigiously*, *inordinately*, etc.

The WORD FINDER has been created to improve a writer's style by adding to the bare, essential words of a sentence. A thesaurus does not do that. It merely assists the user to change such a sentence as "This business had a loss" to some such variant as "This trade suffered a reversal." The WORD FINDER, however, teaches one that "business *droops*, *expires*, *falters*, *founders*, *simmers* and *succumbs*," simply by referring to the noun *business*. And if none of these adjuvant words is precisely what the writer has in mind to describe a languishing trade, the WORD FINDER will tell him, also under the heading *business*, to see *occupation*, *trade*, *concern*, *enterprise*, *industry*, *work*, *commerce*, etc.

Nouns, verbs, and adjectives are listed, alphabetically arranged, and in connection with each such word a list of "augmentatives" is given, that is, words that can be used to condition such a noun, verb, or adjective. In the case of *hill*, for example, the WORD FINDER will furnish either adjectives, such as *gleaming*, *emerald*, *moon-swept*, *verdured*, *radiant*, *shadowed*, *naked*, *pastoral*, *defiant*, or verbs, as *hills dot*, *encroach*, *flank*, *greet*, *interpose*, etc. In the case of the verb *hinder* we are told that a thing can hinder us *unendurably*, *insurmountably*, *irritatingly*, *irksomely* or *burdensomely*, as well as that we should also consult the synonym entries, *retard* and *obstruct*.

It is a simple type of book to use, and immediate results follow in the form of vigorous and deft variety, essential to the creation of a literary style. By studying any particular word in the WORD FINDER along with its coupling expressions and synonyms, the user is enabled to develop a concept and build a thought in such a way that intricate sentences can be evolved from the study of that word. He will find that whatever particular idea he has in mind will rise to fluent proportions under the leavening influence of the WORD FINDER's associated words, that his vocabulary has been increased and his powers of self-expression immeasurably improved.

For example, the sentence, "His cheerful character charmed me very much," contains the adjective *cheerful*, the noun *character*, the verb *charmed*, and the adverbs *very* and *much*. Though it is grammatically correct and genial in thought, it is sadly lacking in specific statement and colorful diction. What exactly are the elements in a *character* that *charm?* And what are the suggestive ingredients of being *cheerful?*

On pages 182-183 of our WORD FINDER the noun *character* has grouped with it a selected list of adjectives that explain and describe it. After studying the columns of epithets descriptive of our word while bearing in mind that this is a *character* that *charms*, we reap a rich harvest of modifiers. Depending on the nature of the characteristics that charm us, we can depict our character as *fabulous*, *munificent*, *steadfast*, *liberal*, *intense*, *frivolous*, *gallant*, *chivalrous*, *artistic*, *elusive*, *exotic*, *gentle*, *jovial*, *airy*, *gay*, *sympathetic*, *magnanimous*, *many-sided*, *jaunty*, *bizarre*, *racy* and *whimsical*, to cite only a few of the appropriate words that will expand our idea. Thus, if we admire the fay, will-o'-the-wisp facets of a certain personality, we may say, "His elusive character charmed me very much," and we have started on our quest for the specific and the well-delineated. We have, of course, substituted *elusive* for *cheerful*, but *cheerful* and *charmed* are faintly synonymic anyhow, and our purpose is to show what a plenitude of ideas related to our original sentence may be found in the WORD FINDER, rather than merely to adorn the flimsiness of that original sentence.

Since the original modifier of *character* was *cheerful*, what can we learn about ways of modifying that adjective in our book? Words which describe adjectives, verbs, or other adverbs are known as adverbs. On page 189 we find a choice list of such adverbs in association with the word *cheerful*. If we wish to express what we feel about this charmingly elusive character, we can readily avail ourselves of the most pertinent of these modifiers for *cheerful* and transfer it to *elusive*. Thus, we should choose from some such qualifying words as *habitually*, *blithely*, *casually*, *oddly*, or *perplexingly*, if, let us say, we were charmed by the casually elusive character of a Britisher.

The verb of our original thought was *charmed*, and it was described by the barren, inexpressive adverbial phrase *very much*. On page 185 we find the noun *charm* with its cluster of associated adjectives, among which we note our selection for character, namely *elusive;* this confirms our concept that an elusive character can be charming. On page 186, however, appears the verb *charm*, marked (v) as are all the verbs in this book. Browsing among its adverbs and choosing a few of the most applicable, we find that we can say with import that an elusive character charms *subtly*, *mysteriously*, *hauntingly*, *inexplicably*, *piquantly*, or *irresistibly*.

As we reflect over all the words associated with *character*, *cheerful*, and *charm*, which three alone we have studied, we find that from that glittering galaxy of modifiers we can create innumerable combinations relevant to our original thought, but more sumptuously expressed; for an instance, "His piquant charm was of a perplexingly elusive character, haunting, subtle; yet its very intensity was irresistible." From the delicate contours of a silhouette our character has been projected full-featured.

Only words that are evocative, that stimulate and unfurl the wings of the imagination, are of real assistance to the aspiring writer. These are the words that avoid the flat surface of the cliché, that give dimensional depth to the picture we are creating. We believe such words to be found in hitherto unprecedented numbers in this book. They are the ones which, starting from a single unit in combination with another word, will, as they round a phrase, multiply and burgeon into a complete thought, while at the same time often yielding an unlooked-for but brighter image.

The editors sincerely trust that all students of this book will succeed in sending *winged words* on far-flung odysseys to Fame.

EDWARD J. FLUCK, PH. D.

PREFACE

To The Original Adjective-Finder

Adjectives have been excellently defined as "the words of our language that make everything clearer, plainer, more beautiful or more dreadful." Oral or written expression without any adjectives at all would be meager, monotonous, utterly drab and colorless. The word *adjective* comes from the Latin *adjectivus,* meaning "that is added." The only part of English speech to which an adjective may be added is of course a noun. (That is why, in this volume, nouns have been listed alphabetically, with fitting adjectives appended to each noun).

Adjectives are as life blood to the language. William Freeman, in his book *Plain English,* says, "One can't embark upon any type of narrative, from embittered conversation to the conventional post-card, without turning to the adjective for help." For this reason adjectives may be described as the paints with which one brightens and vivifies the scenes and events behind the printed words, and lends fascinating hues to what might otherwise be prosaic and deadly dry.

No matter what writers turn their attention to, they must draw upon the adjective. Of course in certain types of narrative there is less need of the descriptive paint-brush than in others. An interesting study of the actual use of adjectives in various fields of writing has recently been made by Dr. David P. Boder, head of the department of psychology at Lewis Institute. His study—which he has termed the A. V. Q. (Adjective-Verb Quotient)—is a measure of the ratio of adjectives to verbs employed by writers. For example, an A. V. Q. of 20 means that a writer uses 20 adjectives for every 100 verbs he employs. (For a discussion of the verb, see the introduction to THE VERB-FINDER). Dr. Boder has found that of the four principal fields of writing, drama has the fewest adjectives, with an average A. V. Q. of 11. Laws are next, with an A. V. Q. of 20. Fiction has an A. V. Q. of 35; scientific writing, 75. Business letters, according to Dr. Boder's findings, show a relative paucity of adjectives, with only 19 to every 100 verbs. Private letters by inexperienced writers have on an average but 22 adjectives to a hundred verbs. Advertisements, on the other hand, are lavish of adjectives, with an A. V. Q. of 78. Theses written by candidates for the Ph. D. degree are loaded with even more adjectives than are advertisements—88 to 100 verbs! Poetry has what is perhaps a golden mean for proportion of adjectives to verbs—an A. V. Q. of 36. Dr. Boder's studies in this field make it clear that writers use more adjectives than speakers do. The reason for this is not far to seek; writers closeted with their thoughts have unlimited time in which to select appropriate adjectives while those who express themselves orally and extemporaneously do not.

Adjectives suffer, as any part of speech is bound to, if not properly employed. And adjectives, perhaps more than any other part of our language, are subject to wide-spread misuse. The adjective, of all the parts of English speech, is the most recklessly overworked. Both inexperienced and half-educated writers use far too many, and use them far too loosely. The amateur tends to use the first adjective that enters his mind, though that adjective may be shoddy and threadbare from excessive use, or though it may not express exactly what he wishes to say. Wesseen, in his *Dictionary of English Grammar,* calls this *adjectivitis* (a coined word meaning the habit of using many adjectives, especially big ones.)

Poor writers and beginners obscure their meaning by weighting their sentences with too many adjectives. Dr. Boder found in the course of his researches that the fewer the adjectives, the easier any writing is to read. With experience and practice the writer learns to substitute for makeshift, trite adjectives others which express his meaning exactly and vividly. Daniel Webster, as a young man, was bombastic in his speeches, but it did not take him long to discover that the power of a sentence lies chiefly in its meaning, and that forceful writing is that which is most direct. Upon making this discovery Webster became "a great eraser of adjectives," and used only the plainest in his addresses. Yet he won immortality for his eloquence. "You will find," he said, "in my speeches to juries, no hard words, no Latin phrases, no *fieri facias;* and that is the secret of my style, if I have any."

Because the adjective is of all parts of speech the most frequently abused and misused, it has come to be regarded with a suspicious eye by many a worker in words. The late columnist, Arthur Brisbane, termed the adjective the enemy of the noun. Many years before Brisbane's time Voltaire meant exactly the same thing when he said that adjectives are frequently the greatest enemies of the substantives.

"An adjective is, indeed, an addition," wrote William Matthews, in his book, *Words; Their Use and Abuse.* "But, he concludes, "an addition may be an incumbrance, as even a dog finds out when a kettle is tied to his tail. Generally the weakness of a composition is just in proportion to the frequency with which this abused class of words is introduced."

Ernest Weekley, a well-known authority on words, expressed irritation because of the wide-spread tendency to overwork the adjective. For example, some years ago, after an attempt had been made upon the life of Mussolini, the President of the Irish Free State congratulated the Italian dictator upon his "providential escape" from an "odious attack," and sent his "earnest wishes" for a "speedy recovery" from the "infamous attempt" which had caused "utmost indignation."

This sort of thing—with reason—goads Mr. Weekley to exasperation, and in an essay on the adjective he has been led to condemn it as being perhaps our least essential part of speech. But neither Mr. Weekley nor any other worker in words worth his salt scorns the adjective in actual practice. For example, Mr. Weekley, in his book *Cruelty to Words,* speaks of "linguistic absurdities perpetrated by contemporary authors," and "a small leavening of peptonized uplift and dilettante pornography." Here are adjectives a-plenty, and employed by an authority who has declared the adjective the least important part of our language! And though Arthur Brisbane termed the adjective the enemy of the noun, a study of Brisbane's writings reveals that the columnist used approximately 42 adjectives to every 100 verbs he employed.

The adjective has come to have a somewhat unsavory reputation, then, not because there is anything inherently bad about it, but because it is the one part of speech first seized upon and worked to death by novices and inferior writers.

When properly used, however, the adjective is an indispensable tool in the hands of all who would communicate with their fellow men by means of words. Employed with discrimination and restraint it becomes a source of tremendous power. Selection of the exact adjective to convey their meaning has done as much as anything to lend beauty and strength to the writings of men whose names have long since become household words wherever English is spoken. Thomas De Quincy, for example, famed for his style, was a master of the adjective. A single sentence from the pen of the man who wrote *The Confessions of an English Opium Eater* serves to show this:

"His diction blazed up into a sudden explosion of prophetic grandeur."

Had De Quincy used an adjective in connection with the word "diction," this fine sentence would have been spoiled.

Just as an adjective thoughtlessly or carelessly placed can wreck an otherwise excellent sentence, so a fitting adjective inserted at just the proper place can build magic into a sentence. The William

Saroyan play, *Love's Old Sweet Song,* offers an interesting example. Walter Huston, in the role of the leading male character, approaches an ornamental stone lion and in expressing disgust with the situation in which he finds himself, gestures toward the figure, referring to it not as "That lion!" but rather, as "That Abyssinian lion!" The adjective Abyssinian, as the author intended, brings a roar of laughter from the audience.

The danger in using adjectives lies in employing overworked and "tired" adjectives, or adjectives unsuited to the noun with which they are joined. That is the *raison d'etre* for the present volume. In the following pages a host of adjectives, each group appended to the noun modified, offers the user of this book a wide choice in the words so vital to memorable writing.

Very simple adjectives have been avoided except where their use in connection with certain nouns appears to be somewhat unusual. This point is worth a second glance—for quite simple adjectives have frequently aided authors in the moments of their greatest genius. Ernest Hemingway, in describing one of his characters, writes:

"His face was small and white and he had tight lips."

How simple are these adjectives: "small," "white," tight!" And yet they enable one to see that character immediately—and not only to see him, but to be on guard against him.

Indeed, Hemingway is famed for the simplicity of his style. At the other extreme there are writers who do not hesitate to use three words where one would suffice. Rufus Choate, the famous American statesman and orator, was such a man. So prodigal he was of adjectives that it was said that he "drove a substantive-and-six" whenever he spoke. When Chief-Justice Shaw, before whom Choate frequently pleaded, heard that a new edition of *Worcester's Dictionary* was off the press and that it contained 2,500 new words, he cried out, "For heaven's sake, don't let Choate get hold of it!"

Perhaps Choate frightened those who knew him with his verbiage, but he was so skilled in the use of words that he succeeded in spite of an overloaded style. A person of less experience or skill is almost certain to fall disastrously into the octopus arms of elaborate language. And curiously enough, it frequently happens that the amateur writer seeks to express himself in a more or less highly ornamented manner, usually with sad results.

The student, and even the practiced writer, cannot be advised too strongly against the use of long, unusual words. The urge to show off to the reader must be kept down. Not only will the worker in words —if he would possess a clear, vigorous style—guard against employing too many adjectives, but he will avoid the pitfalls and detours and handicaps that are likely to be encountered through the use of excessively elaborate adjectives. The simple adjective is almost always preferable to the unusual adjective.

Of course an adjective not met every day may be employed with profit if it expresses the author's thought better than any other word could, but in general the student—in using the present volume—will find it to his advantage to select such simple and yet vivid adjective-noun combinations as "casual visitor," "speechless agony," "misty diplomacy," "liquid gurgle," "giddy intoxication," and "silvery laughter."

Remember that adjectives—like visitors—become a nuisance only when there are too many of them. The adjective is never the enemy of of the noun until the adjective—like a drowning swimmer—drags down and strangles the noun.

J. I. RODALE.

PREFACE

To The Original Verb-Finder

THE POWER OF VERBS

There is an old saying that "fine words butter no parsnips." But of course they do, and always will—whenever the words have been fine enough. Words act. Think of the information, the insight, the entertainment that words provide through books, plays, radio programs, and sound motion pictures. Words are practical, practical even in the narrowest American sense; that is, they bring in money, support life. Let us be clearer by being more definite.

From the days when Anglo-Saxon and medieval minstrels earned their board by entertainment in mead-hall and castle, to modern times, word-craftsmen have moved and delighted their audiences by telling stories or by expressing thoughts, emotions, and aspirations at once personal and common to all people. In modern times such authors as Kipling, Shaw, Wells, Barrie, Masefield, and Bennett, to mention only a few, have achieved literary eminence by the power of fine words. They, like many other writers, not only have woven bright tapestries in poetry or prose, but also have buttered many a delicious parsnip. Robert Frost found the pen more powerful than the plow—even if he did have to go to England to make sure of it. Edgar Lee Masters wrote himself clear of the stifling influence of the small mid-western town. Edwin Arlington Robinson kept the wolf from his door for years by retelling for the modern world some of the most enchanting of the old romances, as well as by painting satirical portraits of New England townspeople. Arnold Bennett, through a tremendous amount of diligent work—he loved to gloat over the number of words he turned out every day—succeeded in becoming both a first-rate literary "merchant," as he liked to call himself, and one of the best novelists of his time. He lived zestfully by the power of words, and even realized his great desire to own a yacht.

Many other persons, perhaps no more gifted than we, have also succeeded. Although they have not profited greatly in a financial way, or become famous by their ability to write well, they have, nevertheless, shared with the eminent one satisfaction—that of expressing themselves adequately, of communicating their emotions, their thoughts, their opinions, attitudes, and ideals. By the power of well-wrought language they have achieved self-expression and have succeeded in rising from the buried life of a solitary organism to the rich life of communion with their fellows. Such satisfaction, such success is within the reach of all of us.

"But show us the road," people say. "What is the secret? Which way?" There is no one way, of course, for writing is a many-sided, complex art. Nor is there any formula for us to follow, for art is creative and imaginative, by no means a matter of slavish imitation or of scientific procedure. We need not despair, however,—not so long as we have the will to write. A close examination of what good writers produce, cannot fail to reveal to us something about how those works were produced, to give us some hints toward improvement. Arnold Bennett, whose improvement in style was due in large measure to his careful study of other writers, realized that the best novelists were word-conscious, that they sought constantly for strength, for clarity, precision. Incidentally, a good craftsman in writing must always be more than grammatically correct, and he will do well to keep ever in mind those three cardinal principles: strength, clarity, and precision. Bennett, by comparing and examining passages of equal length in the works of a great many novelists, discovered that the better artists—and the better merchants—chose lively adjectives and lively verbs. He discovered, furthermore, that adjectives, unless used charily, overornament; that nouns, unless cut down to a minimum, tend to overweight; but that verbs, if well chosen and skillfully handled, invigorate one's style.

We can see this for ourselves. Every day writers strive vainly to ornament and enrich their expression before they have learned to animate and strengthen it. The result of their striving is too often mere prettiness with no vigor beneath it, writing that is all sweetness and flourishes, a meal of all pastry, a beauty with no grain in it. This is a common fallacy among amateur writers, and even professional writers. They fail to see that ornamental adjectives often blur and obscure their meanings and that too many nouns, especially learned nouns—scientific, psychological, technical terms—bog it down. Expression demands life, not merely the trappings of life; vigor, not merely glitter. The sword must be keen that it may cut and thrust as well as glitter in the sun.

The true knight fought valiantly in battle; he did not spend most of his time strutting about with his plume, spear-pennant, and lady's scarf rippling in the breeze. The modern athlete, if he would excel on the field of competition, must display strength, agility, and sportsmanship, not merely a good sun-tan, bulging muscles, and his college or club colors. It is not enough that cathedrals be magnificently adorned with tapering spires and beautiful storied windows; they must be firmly braced and buttressed. Likewise, our written or oral expression must be keen-edged, powerful and agile, and well buttressed at the walls. Without a large number of carefully selected verbs, these essentials are impossible; moreover, selection, which is one of the cardinal principles of all art, is far more important than numbers.

Now, after so many generalizations, it is high time we substantiated what we have said about verbs by referring to particular passages in the writing of particular authors, for surely one good illustration is worth at least sixty generalizations.

Perhaps the most obvious use for verbs is to express physical action. In order to illustrate not a mere piling-up but a skillful selection of verbs, let us examine an action-scene from one of John Masefield's poems, *Dauber.* The poet transports his reader immediately to the deck of a clipper. The ship's painter, the "Dauber," and Si, the apprentice, stood by the rail while the swift ship "*tore*" on, "*straining*" her sheets and "*whitening*" her trackway.

> Her **clacking** tackle **tugged** at pins and cleats,
> Her great sails **bellied** stiff, her great masts **leaned:**
> They watched how the seas **struck,** and **burst,** and **greened.** *

On she sailed toward Cape Horn through snow and hail, her spars straining as she was tossed on the toppling billows. Just before she reached the cape, polar snow came "*tumbling*" and "*wavering*" down, "*furring* the ropes with white, *casing* the mast." At the cape all hands were called on deck to combat the storm, and the Dauber was sent aloft to furl one of the sails. As he lay out on the yardarm, "*gripping*" hard and "*clutching*" at the jack, he was sickened by the vast space that yawned just below his feet, where birds were "*mewing*" and "*wheeling.*" He felt the wind "*hurl*" the ship on her side, and

> . . . . .darkness **speared**
> At her with wind; she **staggered,** she **careened,**
> Then down she lay. The Dauber felt her go;
> He saw the yard **tilt** downwards. Then the snow
> **Whirled** all about—dense multitudinous, cold—*

It was a terific storm, one that "*whiffled* out men's tears" and put to a severe test their courage and endurance.

---

* Quoted by special permission of the publishers, The Macmillan Company, from *Poems* by John Masefield, 1935. (The boldface and italics are the editor's.)

While we are considering action and the sea, we recall those vigorous lines in Shakespeare's *HENRY V* in which the poet describes the effect of the blast of war on man, ending up with a fine picture of the sea drenching the rocks on the coast.

Then lend the eye a terrible aspect;
Let it **pry** through the portage of the head,
Like the brass cannon; let the brow **o'erwhelm it,**
As fearfully as doth a **galled** rock
O'erhang and **jutty** his **confounded** base,
Swilled with the wild and wasteful ocean.

Here the imagery of the sea and the coast is employed by the poet, not as the setting of a narrative poem, but to describe the appearance of man when the horrible spirit of war distorts his features. We recall, also, those famous lines from *MACBETH*. Macbeth is hounded by guilt and every noise "*appals*" him. He finds that all Neptune's ocean cannot wash the blood from his hands but that

"............this my hand will rather
The multitudinous seas **incarnadine.**"

Thousands of such powerful lines could be culled from Shakespeare's works. A rereading of some of the famous passages reveals his chary use of lively adjectives, his strong contempt for mere prettiness, for what he called "silken terms" and "taffeta phrases," and his consummate mastery in the use of verbs. Reread, for example, Hamlet's advice to his players, or his soliloquies; Gloucester's speech in the opening scene of *Richard III;* Jacques' description of the seven ages of man, in *As You Like It;* the description of Cleopatra in her barge; Portia's mercy speech; Falstaff's witty lines, especially in *Henry IV* (Part I); or the splendid songs and sonnets. Cull a few phrases such as these:

Absent thee from felicity awhile
Godlike reason **to fust** in us unus'd
Lilies that **fester**
Struts and **frets** his hour
Thoughts **people** this little world
I am **unking'd** by Bolingbroke
Let the **galled** jade **wince**, our withers are **unwrung.**
Screw your courage to the sticking place
The cliff that **beetles** o'er his base
Paragon description
Beggars description
Native resolution **sicklied** o'er with the pale cast of thought
Daffodils that come before the swallow **dares**

Shakespeare's use of the verb *dares* is an excellent example of the selection of a verb that is neither long nor rare but singularly apt. How better could he have distinguished the daffodil from other flowers or suggested the venturesome nature of the swallow than in these lines?

"........................... daffodils
That comes before the swallow **dares**, and take
The winds of March with beauty................."

Another excellent example of fine selection is to be found in Ophelia's beautiful lament for Hamlet, in which she says,

"Now see that noble and most sovereign reason,
Like sweet bells **jangled**, out of tune and harsh."

"Sweet bells jangled." What a perfect phrase to suggest the contrast between noble reason and madness! On one side of the word *bells* we have the adjective *sweet,* and on the other side the verbal adjective, or participle, *jangled.*

So we might continue to quote from Shakespeare and other poets, from Shelly and Byron, Wordsworth and Coleridge, Tennyson and Browning, Keats, and many others. We recall the sound effects in the skating scene in Wordsworth's *Prelude* and in the scene toward the end of Tennyson's *Morte d'Arthur* in which Sir Bedevere carries Excalibur down to the edge of the mere. We remember, also, the remarkable description of storm-clouds in *The Testament of Beauty,* by Robert Bridges. Mention of Keats calls to mind many lines, especially those in his ode *To Autumn* in which he says of the bees, "Summer has *o'er-brimmed* their clammy cells." But since we must stop quoting somewhere, why not with this exceptionally fine example from Keats? Now let us turn to a consideration of the power of verbs in prose. It really makes little difference here whether we speak of poetry or prose, except that poetry is usually more concise and, consequently, more suitable for illustration. Certainly the need and selection of verbs is much the same.

In pure nature description one might not expect to find much action, certainly not so much as in an action-scene such as that quoted from *Dauber* or in any similar action-scene in prose. One might expect to find far fewer verbs than adjectives. Good description of nature, however, is never flat, static, motionless, but always alive. In his story, "The Lagoon," Conrad heightens an effect of stillness and immobility by emphasizing what action there is. Although the lagoon was "*bewitched* into an immobility perfect and final", the paddlers found themselves in a world not entirely devoid of motion. "The *churned-up* water *frothed* alongside with a *confused* murmur," the cry of a bird, "discordant and feeble, *skipped* over the smooth water," the voices of the paddlers "*reverberated* between the walls of vegetation," and "darkness *oozed* out from between the trees." In Mary Webb's novel, *Gone To Earth,* we find description that is surpassingly beautiful. Notice how much life she expresses in these two sentences, both of which describe Undern, a farm in Shropshire, England:

> Even in May, when the lilacs **frothed** into purple, **paved** the lawn with shadows, **steeped** the air with scent; when soft leaves **lipped** each other consolingly; when blackbirds sang, **fell** in their effortless way from the green height to the green depth, and sang again—still, something that **haunted** the place set the heart **fluttering.**
>
> In winter the yews and firs were like **waving** funeral plumes and **mantled,** headless goddesses; then the giant beeches would **lash** themselves to frenzy, and, **stooping,** would **scourge** the ice on Undern Pool and the **cracked** walls of the house, like beings **drunken** with the passion of cruelty. *

Here we have description that is alive, alive with suggestive and vigorous words, many of which are verbs.

Poets, novelists, historians; military leaders and peace-makers; statesmen, diplomats, lawyers; journalists, advertisers, and business men—all are men of action, wielders of words, wielders of verbs. Powerful words spurred Napoleon's men to push on over the Alps and down onto the fertile plains of Italy, just as, later, powerful words spurred the Italian army in its conquest of Ethiopia. No little eloquence was required to pass the Great Reform Bill of 1832 in England, or to free negro slaves in America. Salesmen cannot sell, business men cannot transact, diplomats cannot negotiate, lawyers can neither prosecute nor defend without forceful, convincing language. Without words our personalities become feeble and defunct; with words they spring into life. To express ourselves is to live—and where there's a will there's a word.

GUIDE TO THE USE OF VERBS

1. The Contents and Arrangement of the Thesaurus

Every workman requires the special tools, materials, and technique of his particular trade, and it is the function of the VERB-FINDER to provide the word-craftsman with these requisites. We must first go to the lumberyard and mill to see what materials and machinery we have with which to construct the furniture of our thoughts. In addition we must learn the technique of building.

The Arrangement of the Verbs

The Thesaurus consists of verbs, or action-words, listed alphabetically under nouns. These nouns are the subjects of our sentences, and they, together with the verbs listed below them, form the nuclei or cores of the sentences. Immediately below each noun a number of verbs are listed alphabetically with dashes following them, and under this list other verbs are arranged with dashes preceding them. The

* Quoted by special permission of the publishers, E. P. Dutton and Company, Inc., from *Gone To Earth,* by Mary Webb. (The boldface is the editor's.)

dashes are used to avoid needless repetition of the nouns. Notice that the verbs in the first list act upon the nouns, and that those in the second list carry out the action of the noun; that is, in the first list the noun is the receiver of the action, usually the object of the verb, and in the second list the doer of the action, or the subject of the verb. For example, under the noun *fire* you will find these two lists and these two relationships between noun and verb.

Fire

feed — (*Fire* is the object and receiver of action)
— crackles (*Fire* is the subject and doer)

Verb Forms

Obviously, not all forms of the verbs can be included in the lists, any more than all sizes and shapes of boards can be piled in the lumberyard. The carpenter must select suitable boards of approximately the right size and then shape them to his needs. Consequently, in the first list under each noun, that in which the verb precedes the dash, you will find the infinitive form of the verb (with the *to* omitted), which is exactly the same form as that of the first person singular of the present indicative. In the second list under each noun, that in which the dash follows the verb, you will find the third person singular or plural form of the present indicative, to agree with the noun preceding. For example:

Fish

prepare — (*Prepare* means *to prepare* or *I prepare*)
— squirms (*Squirms* means *It squirms*)

Brick

build with —s (*Build* means *to build* or *I build*).
—s crumble (*Crumble* means *They crumble*)

No verbals are listed. However, verbals and their value in writing will be discussed in another section of the "Guide."

2. How to Build Sentences

In the Thesaurus you will find thousands of sentences and suggestions for sentences right at hand. Given any thought or feeling that you want to express, all you have to do is to find the one best word to express the action that you want. The sentence is a unit of thought or predication containing a subject and predicate. Given a subject, you can easily find here the other element, the word to set it into motion, to make it alive—the verb.

Selecting the Verb

Let us assume that you hear a bell ringing, and that you wish to communicate to us the sound that you hear and exactly how that sound affects you. It is not enough to say, "I hear a bell ringing." That communicates little, for there are all sorts of bells and all sorts of ringing sounds. *Bell* is your subject, however, and *rings* your action, at least tentatively. Now run your finger down the second column of verbs under *bell* and find a better verb. Perhaps you will choose *chimes, clangs, reverberates, sings,* or *tinkles.* It makes considerable difference. Or suppose you want to describe the way a bird moves through the sky. It is not enough to say "The bird moves," or even "The bird flies." Look down the list under *bird* until you come to a verb that will make the bird *dart, hover, float, wheel,* or what you will. This is the way to find your verb, whether you want a verb that will sell a shirt or one of the latest novels, or a verb that will make a poem magical. The same method enables you to find a verb that acts upon a noun used as its object. To express the idea of disposing of an argument, for example, run your finger down the first column under *argument* until you come to a verb, say *refute.* You now have your sentence: "I will refute the argument."

Cross References

If the procedure described above fails to provide you with the verb you are after, you can search elsewhere. At the foot of the verb lists you will usually find a number of guide words or cross references. "See" leads us, through these words, to other lists of verbs. We refer to these other lists in the following ways: from the generic to the specific word, from the specific to the generic, from synonym to synonym, and from the word listed to a word related but not synonymous. Let us explain.

(*a*) *Generic To Specific*

Suppose you have been trying to find a verb to express the sound (song or other sound) that a bird makes. Suppose that *bird,* although it has many such words listed, does not have the right one. Turn, then, to a specific kind of bird, such as *lark, nightingale,* or *grouse.* You will find that different and more specific verbs are listed under these headings to describe the characteristic sounds and actions of these very different birds. A few examples of this generic to specific reference are:

poetry—See *sonnet*
profession—See *teaching, law*
gem—See *diamond, ruby*

(*b*) *Specific To Generic*

This is, of course the exact opposite. Some examples are:

diamond—See *gem*
painting—See *art*
bee—See *insect*
musician—See *artist*
law—See *profession*

It is well, if possible, to choose the word you want in the first place; that is, not to be talking vaguely about birds if you mean robins or about art if you mean painting. Nevertheless, you will often find it necessary and profitable to refer from the generic to the specific and from the specific to the generic word.

(*c*) *Synonym To Synonym*

Often you will find synonyms among your guide words. You will do well to use them. For example, after looking in vain for a verb to go with *courage,* you can easily and quickly turn to *bravery, fortitude,* or *valor.* Incidentally, in addition to finding the verb you are after, you may decide that *fortitude,* not *courage,* is the noun that you want.

(*d*) *The Related Word*

If you refer from *hand* to *claw,* which is not exactly a synonym, you will find good verbs for a claw-like hand. Likewise, if you refer from *anvil* to *bell* or from *art* to *artist* you will find verbs related to your subject. Sometimes you might well refer to a word whose meaning is directly opposite, to an antonym. Many verbs, for example, are used interchangeably with such pairs of words as the following:

Summer and *Winter, comparison* and *contrast, poetry* and *prose.*

3. How to Build Better Sentences

The best way to explain how to build better sentences is to build a few. Below you will find a series of sentences which, although grammatically correct, can stand considerable improvement:

> The red embers sent a strong and ruddy glow from the chimney. Dom Nicholas, the Picardy monk, stood before it. He pulled up his skirts and bared his fat legs to the comfortable warmth. His large shadow appeared in the middle of the room. The firelight shone on either side of his broad person, and in a little pool on either side of his feet, which were spread out. His face had the beery appearance of the continual drinker's, and it was bruised. It was covered with a network of veins, which were purple in ordinary circumstances, but were now violet. He had his back to the fire, but he was cold on the other side.

This is badly written. Why? In the first place, the style is monotonous and choppy because every sentence begins with the subject followed immediately by the verb; secondly, most of the verbs are weak or commonplace; and thirdly, there are too many verbs. If we substitute *diffused* for "*sent*", *straddled* for "*stood*", *picked* for "*pulled*", *escaped* for "*shone*", and *cut the room in half* for "*appeared in the middle of the room,*" we will sharpen the picture by the use of stronger verbs. If we recast the second sentence by combining it with the third and by beginning it with a prepositional phrase, instead of with the usual subject-verb combination, we will create a much more compact sentence and relieve the paragraph of some of its monotony. We might write it this way:

> Before this straddled Dom Nicholas, the Picardy monk, with his skirts picked up and his fat legs bared to the comfortable warmth.

Thus, in combining the two sentences, we have used two participles instead of the two verbs, *picked* and *bared.* Participles often help us to condense and vary our sentences; moreover they add life to a sentence when used in place of commonplace adjectives. For example, if we place *arched* before "*chimney*" in the first sentence, *dilated* in place of "*large*" in the fourth, and *outspread* before "*feet*" in the fifth, we will greatly enhance the power of the description. Notice the unnecessary clause in the fifth sentence—"which were spread out". By rewriting the sentence with the participle *outspread* before "*feet,*" we eliminate a whole clause, and thus condense the writing without losing any of the meaning. We see now that sentences can be improved in several ways: by substituting strong, precise, colorful, accurate verbs for weak, indefinite, colorless, and inaccurate verbs; by recasting sentences so as to vary, condense, and strengthen their structure by either adding verbals or converting verbs into verbals. Following these principles, we have transformed a crude paragraph into a remarkably fine paragraph. Here it is exactly as R. L. Stevenson wrote it in his story, "A Lodging for the Night:"

> A great pile of **living** embers **diffused** a strong and ruddy glow from the **arched** chimney. Before this **straddled** Dom Nicholas, the Picardy monk, with his skirts **picked** up and his fat legs **bared** to the comfortable warmth. His **dilated** shadow **cut** the room in half; and the firelight only **escaped** on either side of his broad person, and in a little pool between his **outspread** feet. His face had the beery, **bruised** appearance of the continual drinker's; it was covered with a network of **congested** veins, purple in ordinary circumstances, but now pale violet, for even with his back to the fire the cold **pinched** him on the other side. His cowl had half fallen back, and made a strange excrescence on either side of his bull neck. So he **straddled, grumbling,** and **cut** the room in half with the shadow of his portly frame. *

* Quoted by special permission of the publishers, Charles Scribner's Sons, from *New Arabian Nights,* by R. L. Stevenson. The editor wrote the first version for the purpose of showing how poor writing can be transformed into good writing. (The boldface is the editor's.)

What a striking portrait this is! Notice the use of the sharp verb *pinched* in place of *was* and of the participles *congested* and *grumbling.*

Since the paragraph above contains no infinitives—it is difficult to find any one selection that will illustrate everything—something remains to be said about the use of this type of verbal. The following words, uttered by Napoleon before his army in Milan, serve as a fine illustration of the effective use of infinitives:

> **To re-establish** the Capitol, **to set up** there the statues of the heroes, **to awaken** the Roman people which for centuries have been paralyzed by servitude—that is the fruit of your victories, that will amaze posterity.

What eloquent words—no matter what our feelings about war and peace—from this man of action! Take out the infinitives and you emasculate the sentence. How comparatively feeble it is when we rewrite it like this:

> The re-establishment of the Capitol, the erection of the statues of the heroes, the awakening of the Roman people which for centuries have been paralyzed by servitude—that is the fruit of your victories, that will amaze posterity.

Observe how heavy and academic this last version is. If you look at these two sentences, one above the other as they stand, you cannot fail to see the power of the infinitive.

4. Diction

A few words should be said about good and bad usage in verbs, for often we find ourselves uncertain as to whether or not a word has been generally accepted as good English. How can we be sure? The VERB-FINDER should help us here. To avoid unnecessary verbiage and confusion, the editors have arranged the verbs in the Thesaurus as simply as possible. You will find only three classifications: slang, colloquialism, and general usage.

Slang

Slang expressions, although sometimes extremely forceful, are often limited in use to a small locality or to a small number of people, to the college campus, to the Southwest, or to baseball, for example. Consequently, outside of its own little sphere it may mean nothing. Moreover slang is often too indefinite, too vague in meaning, to be of much value. For these reasons, when you see a verb listed with quotation marks around it, take care to avoid it in formal writing and to use it informally only where it will be understood. If, however, you feel that the word is sufficiently definite and more vigorous than any other you can think of, use it—but always with quotation marks to indicate that you know exactly what sort of word you are using. Although the word may some day be accepted as respectable, at present it must be regarded as questionable.

Colloquialisms

These words, if a bit more respectable than slang, are to be avoided in formal writing, because they are usually peculiar to one section of the country. However, authors often, and rightly, use colloquialisms in dialogue, for which the spoken word rather than the written or literary word is more appropriate.

Good Usage

We are correct when we say that usage determines what is right or wrong in language. Certainly usage is the power behind the dictionary. But we must qualify our statement, for not every word in common usage is the best word or even a good word. The standard for good usage is the standard set by the language customs of the better writers and speakers. In general, the most intelligent, the best educated, the most highly cultured, the most expressive people attain to the most effective and most beautiful expression. On the other hand, in general, persons of lesser intelligence, education, and culture use poorer language; they tend toward the mediocre and the trite, and even fall into barbarisms, improprieties, clumsiness, and confusion. We might make a table like this:

Good Usage (Formal)

Choice Diction (the best)
Good Diction (superior)
Fair Diction (tending toward the mediocre and trite)

Good and Bad Usage (Informal)

Slang
Colloquialisms

Bad Usage (Inexcusable)

Archaisms
Vulgarisms or Barbarisms
Improprieties or Malapropisms
Affection and Pedantry

If we keep in mind some such distinctions in diction we can be liberal and flexible without being uncertain and inconsistent. The VERB-FINDER concerns itself with the first two categories only. The greater part of the Thesaurus is devoted to the first, but the second, because of the good in it, cannot be ignored.

5. The Verb-Finder As a Source of Information

In addition to performing its chief function, that of aiding us in expressing ourselves, The VERB-FINDER also furnishes encyclopedic information. By consulting the verb lists we can obtain valuable information about many subjects and can even construct fairly good dictionary definitions. Certainly a good way to characterize or define a person or thing is to state what that person or thing does, what its actions are. How, for example, can we define a snob, except by stating how a snob acts? What is a snob? The VERB-FINDER tells us that the snob *apes, affects, pretends, cringes, worships, swaggers, overbears,* etc. Do not such verbs characterize this sort of person through his actions? Here is the definition of *snob* given in Funk and Wagnall's unabridged *DICTIONARY*:

> A person who vulgarly **affects** gentility, or **pretends** to a superiority he does not possess; one who **apes** and **cringes** to his superiors and is **overbearing** to those upon whom he looks as beneath him; one who regards wealth or position rather than character. *

In the same way we could find out a great deal about the habits of birds or termites or horses; about the nature and function of literature or sculpture or biology; about the characteristics of salesmen, artists, fools, clowns, sages, philosophers, lovers, or thieves.

KINGSBURY M. BADGER

---

*The boldface, which does not appear in the dictionary, is the editor's.

A

ABANDON

adjectives

delightful; gleeful; unconscious; passionate; drunken; increasing; intoxicated; idolatrous; hilarious; airy; fanatical; reckless; artistic; dissolute; emotional; melodramatic; universal; insane; humorous; bird-like; wild; childish; desolate; mystic; sensual; cruel; wanton; natural; boyish; typical; joyful; delirious; carefree; ecstatic.

ABANDON (v)

adverbs

shamelessly; ingloriously; regretfully; dramatically; definitely; recklessly; simultaneously; reluctantly; prudently; despairingly; eventually; inhumanly; cravenly; wantonly; childishly; temporarily; pusillanimously; faint-heartedly; pitiably; haplessly; remorsefully; ruefully; sullenly; woefully; wretchedly; contritely; dejectedly; dolefully; mournfully; dispiritedly; mirthlessly; tragically.

(See repudiate, forsake, waive, surrender.)

ABANDONED (a)

adverbs

delightfully; gleefully; hilariously; airily; recklessly; emotionally; insanely; crazily; ridiculously; wantonly; childishly; boyishly; ludicrously; lamentably; pitiably; unblushingly; provokingly; totally; shamefully; widely; maliciously; regretfully.

ABANDONMENT

adjectives

courageous; inhuman; introspective; hasty; moral; spontaneous; shameless; inglorious; melodramatic; notorious; cowardly; reluctant; prudent; despairing; criminal; crazy; odd.

ABASE (v)

adverbs

disgracefully; degradingly; humiliatingly; shamefully; mortifyingly; ruinously; brutally; belittlingly; calumniously; traducingly; mortifyingly; dishonorably; slanderously.

(See humiliate, degrade, disgrace.)

ABASEMENT

adjectives

servile; mortifying; humiliating; cruel; wilful; total; ultimate.

ABBE

adjectives

infidel; pleasure-loving; gay; witty; dissolute; dull; aristocratic.

ABBREVIATION

adjectives

offensive; delicate; apt; cryptic; unintelligible; suggestive; recognizable; remote; felicitous.

ABDICATE (v)

adverbs

altruistically; willingly; voluntarily; dramatically; ignominiously; unaccountably; cravenly; enforcedly; pusillanimously; submissively; shrewdly; pliantly; tractably; passively.

(See abandon, forsake, surrender, repudiate.)

ABDICATION

adjectives

dramatic; ignominious; unaccountable; altruistic; precipitate; unprecedented; reckless; voluntary; enforced.

ABDOMEN

adjectives

ample; protruding; protuberant; pendulous; flaccid; lean; monstrous; sagging.

verbs

develop—; distend—; enlarge—; exercise—; flatten—; knead—; massage—; relax—; rest on—; subject—; support—; thrust forward—; —is bounded by; —is composed of; —is lined; —juts out; —sags.

(See stomach, intestines, paunch, belly.)

ABDOMINAL

misc.

—surgery; —distress; mobilize the—contents.

ABERRATION

adjectives

vulgar; isolated; philosophic; abhorrent; dangerous; spiritual; noteworthy; marked; human; apparent; mental.

ABHOR (v)

adverbs

passionately; unqualifiedly; deeply; uncontrollably; vindictively; undyingly; vigorously; smoulderingly; malignantly; diabolically; vengefully; inimically; satanically; malevolently; misanthropically; disdainfully.

(See detest, scorn.)

ABHORRENCE

adjectives
unqualified; modern; cold; hard-headed; justified; passionate; rational; uncontrollable; utmost; inexpressive; well-organized; sullen; deadly; respectful; furious; fierce; stealthy; holy; professed; burlesqued.

ABHORRENT

adverbs
excruciatingly; loathsomely; impossibly; utterly; completely; horribly; terribly; abominably; odiously; repulsively; detestably; hatefully; shockingly; unspeakably.

ABIDE (*v*)

adverbs
faithfully; religiously; staunchly; temporarily; permanently; trustworthily; stoutly; steadfastly; diligently; persistently; unabatingly; deathlessly; enduringly; unfalteringly; firmly; constantly; assiduously.

ABILITY

adjectives
unexcelled; superior; transcendent; surpassing; brilliant; eminent; distinguished; commanding; promising; superb; never-failing; proved; rare; unique; marked; conspicuous; discernible; pronounced; obvious; manifest; undeniable; surprising; amazing; astounding; extraordinary; remarkable; phenomenal; superhuman; inherent; innate; intrinsic; natural; vast; immense; limited; mediocre; middle; cold-blooded; uncanny; eerie; latent; administrative; artistic; executive; forensic; histrionic; linguistic; organizing; oratorical; recuperative; selective; story-telling; mature; mystifying; embryonic; intuitive; sensitive; supposed; sheer; versatile; productive; respectable; slender; professional; superlative; dramatic; acquired; individual; strategic; recognized; peculiar; wonted; potential; striking; crafty; constructive; singular; conscienceless; overrated; intellectual; humble; undoubted; uncommon; critical; technical; variant; creative; doubtful; adroit; vocalistic; practical; enhanced; discontented; melodic; universal; conscious; humble.

verbs
analyze—; ascertain—; attribute—; bow to—; bluster about—; confer—; demonstrate—; destroy—; determine—; develop—; diminish—; display—; distrust—; donate—; endow with—; enhance—; estimate—; evince—; exhibit—; increase—; invest with—; lack—; make use of—; manifest—; mistreat—; outstrip—; outweigh—; pool—; possess—; presume—; prove—; register—; test—; vitiate—; weigh—; —develops; —enables; —enhances; —falls short; —redeems; —undergoes.

(See talent, capability, capacity, faculty, power, skill.)

ABJECT

adverbs
inconceivably; hopelessly; mournfully; pitiably; incurably; basely; incredibly; piteously; horribly; tragically; unbelievably; singularly; miserably; comically; ridiculously; ostensibly; ostentatiously; glumly; dismally; disconsolately; moodily; heavily; ludicrously.

ABLE

adverbs
tremendously; extremely; wonderfully; adequately; marvelously; uncommonly; extraordinarily; astonishingly; brilliantly; superbly; surprisingly; amazingly; remarkably; particularly; consciously.

ABLUTION

adjectives
sacred; ordinary; daily; outward; unwonted; ritualistic.

ABNEGATION

adjectives
manly; unselfish; absolute; subtle; apostolic; heroic; inspired; unsparing.

ABNORMAL

adverbs
grotesquely; distressingly; painfully; pitiably; noticeably; hideously; undoubtedly; positively; emotionally; markedly; patently; harmlessly; mildly; slightly; entirely; admittedly; grievously; repulsively; shockingly.

ABNORMALITY

adjectives
distressing; emotional; allied; fancied; imperceptible; marked; noticeable; hideous; incredible; patent.

ABODE

adjectives
lonely; peaceful; august; blissful; ancient; eternal; Elysian; sheltered; inaccessible;

dolorous; lasting; obscure; desolate; ancestral; claustral; comfortless; indispensable; serene; fit; fixed; permanent; primitive; sequestered; sybaritic; transient; immortal; ramshackle; dreadful; disconcerting; abandoned; secure; blest; troglodytic; unostentatious; luxurious; phantasmal; damp; dreary; perilous; abhorred; melancholy; mean; soft; eremitic; dread.

verbs
choose—; disdain—; make—with; retire to —; seek—; take up—; welcome to—.

ABOLISH (v)

adverbs
ultimately; effectually; virtually; universally; legally; permanently; entirely; dictatorially; tyrannically; destructively; obliteratingly; deleteriously.

(See annul, repeal.)

ABOLITION

adjectives
projected; forcible; universal; virtual; effectual; ultimate; immediate; instantaneous; gradual.

ABOMINABLE

adverbs
incredibly; intolerably; unbelievably; hatefully; utterly; completely; maliciously; oppressively; brutally; flagrantly; detestably; perniciously; viciously; deplorably; diabolically; execrably; noxiously; lamentably; hatefully; villainously; woefully; odiously; abhorrently; repulsively; invidiously; despicably.

ABOMINATION

adjectives
heathenish; hideous; dark; whitewashed; nondescript; loathsome; indescribable; foul; monstrous; gross.

verbs
behold—; cast away—; commit—; delight in—; work—; multiply—; overspread—; perpetrate—; provoke to—; turn away from —.

(See squalor, wickedness, aversion.)

ABORTION

adjectives
cruel; criminal; sterility-inducing; inadvisable; mutilating; illegal; wanton.

verbs
advise an—; anticipate—; avert—; balk at —; bring about—; cause—; contribute to—; expose to—; frustrate—; have—; impose an—; indicate—; induce—; indulge in—; instruct about—; justify—; lead to—; legalize—; perform—; permit—; precede—; prevent—; procure—; produce—; prove—; provoke into—; resort to—; stop—; submit to—; terminate in—; tolerate—; treat—; undergo—; weaken by—; yield to—; —arises from; —occurs; —results.

(See miscarriage, failure, operation.)

ABOUND (v)

adverbs
plentifully; luxuriantly; astonishingly; endlessly; naturally; primevally; multitudinously; munificently; swarmingly; throngingly; monstrously; boundlessly; excessively; generously.

(See swarm.)

ABRUPT

adverbs
unpardonably; rudely; roughly; instinctively; unconsciously; unfortunately; startlingly; whimsically; intentionally; astonishingly; amusingly; offensively; ridiculously; inexcusably; unforgivably; unexpectedly; unreasonably; momentarily; habitually; unintentionally.

ABRUPTNESS

adjectives
embarrassed; off-hand; startling; uncompromising; whimsical; wolfish; characteristic; brusque; brisk; easy.

ABSCESS

adjectives
hidden; internal; monstrous; fatal; pestilent; cankerous; gnawing; tentacle-like.

verbs
confine—; develop into—; drain—; dress—; evacuate—; exude from—; give rise to—; incise—; inflame—; irritate—; lance—; poultice—; swab out—; —arises; —attains size; —becomes embedded; —bulges; —bursts; —destroys; —develops; —discharges; —forms; —grows; —infiltrates; —inflames; —occurs; —opens; —re-forms; —ruptures; —spreads; —swells.

(See sore, ulcer, tumor, boil.)

ABSCOND (v)

adverbs
villainously; faithlessly; vilely; treacherously; unexpectedly; basely; knavishly; mysteriously; monstrously; nefariously; odiously; lawlessly; mendaciously.

(See flee.)

ABSENCE

adjectives
utter; cautious; restful; prolonged; total; unaccounted; trying; oppressive; frequent; momentary; undutiful; perilous; considerable; striking; enforced; protracted; continued; pleasing; unauthorized; comparative; apparent; voluntary; everlasting; occasional; intermittent (pl).

verbs
attend—; bear—; berate—; bewail—; deplore—; dote on—; endure—; lament—; mourn—; presuppose—; regret—; support by—; take advantage of—; wail—; grant—; yield to—; —diminishes; —draws; —grows; —increases; —kills; —lessens; —quickens.

ABSENT
(*in mind or in person*)

adverbs
conspicuously; unfortunately; unaccountably; frequently; irritatingly; apparently; voluntarily; inexcusably; noticeably; purposely; inexplainably; mysteriously; carelessly; usually; provokingly.

ABSOLUTION

adjectives
general; priestly; just; rapturous; timely; insincere; virtual; conscientious; serene; blissful.

ABSOLVE (*v*)

adverbs
religiously; entirely; wholly; thoroughly; certainly; partly; freely; leniently; placably; sympathetically; forbearingly; compassionately; palliatively.

(See free, pardon, release.)

ABSORB (*v*)

adverbs
incessantly; wholly; passively; profoundly; partially; racially; nationally; intelligently; intellectually; physically; studiously; hurtfully; mentally; accretively; electively; vocationally; bibulously; crapulently; cannibalistically; edaciously; intemperately; ghoulishly.

(See monopolize, engross.)

ABSORBED

adverbs
ridiculously; tragically; utterly; profoundly; shamelessly; mentally; wholly; deeply; completely; rapturously; ecstatically; tensely; eagerly; anxiously; gloomily; ludicrously; foolishly; fatuously; amazingly.

ABSORBENT

adverbs
extraordinarily; scarcely; completely; gradually; quickly; remarkably; marvelously; notably; wonderfully; exceptionally; genuinely; astonishingly; unusually; unfailingly; singularly; particularly; unbelievably; highly.

ABSORPTION

adjectives
bookish; omnivorous; profound; tragic; unflattering; shame-faced; poetic; gradual; mental; tense; detached; droll; indecent; stolid; passive; demoniac; vigorous.

ABSTAIN (*v*)

adverbs
cautiously; perniciously; carefully; systematically; firmly; voluntarily; austerely; religiously; totally; wilfully; narrowly; wholesomely; cautiously; prudently; discreetly; circumspectly; scrupulously; squeamishly; judiciously; economically; frugally; parsimoniously; sparingly; penuriously; chastely.

(See refrain, withhold.)

ABSTEMIOUS

adverbs
ascetically; piously; wholly; strictly; austerely; rigorously; proudly; awkwardly; fanatically; ridiculously; absurdly; carefully; abominably; cautiously; correctly; habitually; warily; ostentatiously; inconspicuously; glaringly; conspicuously; reluctantly; unctuously; smugly; grimly.

ABSTEMIOUSNESS

adjectives
ascetic; austere; stern; rigorous; calculated; proud.

ABSTINENCE

adjectives
bigoted; excessive; prolonged; total; rash; systematic; forced; holy; marked; firm; strict; self-enforced; austere; cautious; pernicious; absolute; recurrent; partial; half-hearted; protracted; extreme; habitual.

ABSTRACT

adverbs
academically; infinitely; immeasurably; uncomfortably; abstrusely; indefinitely; illusively; remotely; undeniably; obscurely; completely; terribly; entirely; sheerly; thoroughly; immaterially; undefinably; immutably; vaguely; fantastically; chimerically;

extravagantly; eternally; evanescently; transcendentally; unverifiably; preternaturally; spiritually; mystically; conceptually; palpably; patently; speculatively; intuitively; ideologically; empirically; occultly; visionarily; doctrinally; hypothetically.

ABSTRACTION

adjectives
mysterious; intense; subtle; hazy; sublime; unquiet; meaningless; thoughtful; dreamy; noble; mythical; shadowy; gloomy; statistical; far-off; eerie; stony; melancholy; moody; tight-lipped; deep; dull; pernicious; wistful; lengthy; grandiose; grave; wonted.

ABSTRUSE

adverbs
disagreeably; unfortunately; vexatiously; remotely; obscurely; profoundly; extremely; unreasonably; unnecessarily; needlessly; foolishly; absurdly; foggily; senselessly; stupidly; inexpediently; enigmatically; annoyingly; heavily; injudiciously; incomprehensibly; highly; unwisely; preposterously; confusingly; bewilderingly; perplexingly; indiscreetly.

ABSURD

adverbs
palpably; perniciously; nakedly; impudently; ludicrously; manifestly; fantastically; quaintly; grotesquely; patently; tragically; comically; perversely; detestably; pathetically; ignominiously; ridiculously; monstrously; grossly; unreasonably.

ABSURDITY

adjectives
palpable; pernicious; unfathomable; essential; naked; impudent; ornithological; ludicrous; moral; manifest; fantastic; quaint; reigning; infantine; grotesque; patent; tragic; perverse; colossal; detestable; inadequate; pathetic; ignominious; cumulative (pl); assorted (pl); ridiculous; monstrous; wholesome; gross; intrinsic; raucous; unreasonable.

verbs
atone for—; behold—; condone—; excuse—; expose—; father—; grieve over—; perpetrate—; smile at—; —destroys; —falls away; —impairs; —saps; —undermines.
(See folly, foolishness, nonsense.)

ABUNDANCE

adjectives
copious; uninterrupted; lavish; unbelievable; natural; flowing; laudable; culinary; theoretical; coveted; peculiar; careless; needless; wasteful; economic; sheer.

verbs
bless with—; conserve—; diminish—; endow with—; groan under—; inherit—; lavish—on; partake of—; pile up—; pour —; sate with—; satiate with—; squander—; surround by—; tap—; weaken by—; —flows; —lies; —melts away.
(See plenty.)

ABUNDANT

adverbs
overwhelmingly; marvelously; happily; fortunately; lavishly; naturally; profusely; uncommonly; unusually; remarkably; ravishingly; staggeringly; surprisingly; unbelievably; incredibly; voluptuously; wonderfully; particularly; amazingly; astonishingly; extraordinarily; fabulously; immeasurably; incalculably; indisputably; inexpressibly; alarmingly.

ABUSE

adjectives
political; unintelligible; intemperate; personal; treasonable; alarming; existing; scurrilous; sore; glaring; triumphant; abundant; filthy; scandalous; pernicious; tyrannical; alleged; disastrous; noisy; humorous; false; indiscriminate; stupid; mighty; virulent; intolerable; horrible; obscene; vicious; violent; flagrant; inhuman; profane; foul; notorious; barefaced; arrogant; shameful.

verbs
brook—; check—; condone—; correct—; cry out at—; curb—; direct—against; drive to —; eliminate—; exchange—; heap—; incur —; pour—; prevent—; reckon up—; remedy —; shovel—on; spare—; spy into—; stumble on—; subject to—; thunder—; tolerate —; wipe out—; —blackens; —damns; —prevails; —s are rife; —s reckon up.
(See perversion, invective.)

ABUSE (v)

adverbs
profanely; notoriously; foully; arrogantly; barefacedly; grossly; scandalously; shamefully; intemperately; treasonably; indiscriminately; alarmingly; scurrilously; perniciously; tyrannically; stupidly; virulently; mightily; obscenely; viciously; violently; inhumanly; flagrantly; heinously; malevolently; malignantly; noxiously; tempestuously; truculently; atrociously; hellishly; roughly.
(See misuse, injure, violate.)

ABUSIVE

adverbs
inexcusably; tragically; absurdly; painfully; scathingly; blisteringly; scandalously; alarmingly; ferociously; noisily; intolerably; pugnaciously; truculently; inhumanly; foully; diabolically; inconceivably; incredibly; obscenely; cruelly; scurrilously; unpardonably; unforgivably; unreasonably; immoderately; virulently; rashly; criminally; preposterously; unbelievably; recklessly; terribly; humiliatingly; profanely; disgracefully; shamefully; insanely; crazily; appallingly; maliciously; lamentably; violently; destructively; rancorously; blasphemously; spitefully; wickedly; revoltingly; illegally; direly; deliriously; horribly.

ABYSS

adjectives
immovable; nethermost; awful; blossoming; unfathomed; threatening; watery; dolorous; howling; moral; infernal; financial; yawning; void; profound; desolate; murky; bottomless; sunless; horrible; widening; black; unavoidable; breath-taking; gaping; immeasurable; hellish; hideous; Stygian.

ACADEMIC

adverbs
incurably; consistently; abstrusely; formally; formidably; illusively; evasively; impracticably; idealistically; impractically; remotely; uselessly; patently; frankly; uncomfortably; completely; dangerously; intrinsically; vaguely; fantastically; unfortunately; dreamily; unserviceably; worthlessly.

ACCEDE (v)

adverbs
heartily; speedily; willingly; unconditionally; amicably; rationally; gladly; genially; grudgingly; boorishly; tacitly; affably; benevolently; courteously; complaisantly; civilly; chivalrously; deferentially.

(See agree, concur, comply.)

ACCELERATE (v)

adverbs
tremendously; expectedly; abruptly; naturally; foolhardily; thoughtlessly; mechanically; intemperately; instantaneously; promptly; hurriedly; startlingly.

(See hasten, quicken.)

ACCELERATION

adjectives
whirling; considerable; impressive; impetuous; swift; easy; breath-taking; faulty; smooth; effortless.

ACCENT

adjectives
joyous; respectful; tender; well-bred; practiced; unctuous; affected; ornamental; mincing; vicious; blighting; coarse; peremptory; deliberate; icy; imperative; mocking; taunting; hurried; quivering; thick; clipped; mutilated; lingering; guttural; musical; silvery; mellow; pedantic; bell-like; clarion; insinuating; pleasant; droning; persuasive; melancholy; pitying; agonized; oratorical; professional; plebeian; objectionable; awed; faltering; half-impertinent; dispassionate; searching; trembling; gracious; mûsing; hushed; sober; measured; warning; meek; bluff; terrible; charming; feeble; soothing; compassionate; audible; smart; distinct; hollow; uncouth; haughty; ringing; honeyed; emphatic; nautical; swaggering; furious; mingled; tearful; crystal; pained; ecclesiastical; hesitant; wistful; authentic; melodious; sonorous; Teutonic; flippant; perceptible; provincial; circumflex; hesitating.

verbs
affect—; betray—; brook—; miss—; muffle —; reiterate in —s; —breaks; —echoes; —weakens.

(See stress, emphasis.)

ACCENT (v)

adverbs
nicely; pedantically; unctuously; joyously; tenderly; affectedly; mincingly; coarsely; deliberately; mockingly; tauntingly; quiveringly; lingeringly; musically; mellowly; insinuatingly; persuasively; falteringly; dispassionately; charmingly; soothingly; uncouthly; haughtily; emphatically; hesitantly; wistfully; melodiously; sonorously; flippantly; haltingly.

(See stress.)

ACCEPT (v)

adverbs
graciously; frankly; unreservedly; grudgingly; lifelessly; courteously; readily; cheerfully; fatalistically; passively; cautiously; phlegmatically; elatedly; enthusiastically; universally; bravely; casually; consciously; eagerly; generally; peacefully; credulously; thankfully; reluctantly; gratefully; reasonably; willingly; unhesitatingly; implicitly; philosophically; good-naturedly; slavishly; glibly; skeptically; impulsively, stoically; magnanimously; complacently.

(See approve.)

ACCEPTABLE

adverbs
unquestionably; charmingly; wholly; delightfully; genuinely; joyously; happily; providentially; luckily; gratifyingly; tragically; comically; vastly; duly; profoundly; admittedly; puzzlingly; infinitely; incalculably; immeasurably; particularly; personally; absolutely; frankly; socially; politically; officially; conventionally; widely; universally; locally.

ACCEPTANCE

adjectives
happy; warm; joyous; incoherent; complacent; wholesale; unanimous; fearless; impulsive; stoical; resigned; public; frank; modified; glib; skeptical; slavish; loathsome; unquestioning; ready; belated; simulated; good-natured; pacific; philosophic; reluctant; social; implicit; relieved; gracious; grudging; fatalistic; passive; phlegmatic; appreciatory; wide; delayed; patient; ironical; cheerful; general; unreserved; universal; credulous; grave; grandiloquent.

verbs
authorize—; coax—; confirm—; elicit—; find—; guarantee—; meet with—; presuppose—; —displays; —precludes.
(See agreement, assent.)

ACCESS

adjectives
impregnable; casual; unrestricted; momentary; exclusive; strange; convenient; direct; expeditious; easy.

verbs
bar—; deny—to; desire—to; disdain—; give—; grant—; seek—; procure—; shut off—; stop up—; survey—; throng—.
(See approach, admittance.)

ACCESSIBLE

adverbs
conveniently; easily; instantly; directly; serviceably; handily; immediately; instantaneously; casually; imperceptibly; inconspicuously; unobtrusively.

ACCESSORY

adjectives
agreeable; scenic; fashionable; cultured; gracious; impressive; colorful; distinctive; exquisite; decorative; tawdry; indispensable; unwilling; criminal.

ACCIDENT

adjectives
unlucky; capricious; untoward; melancholy; singular; unfortunate; comical; happy; felicitous; merest; incalculable; inescapable; preventable; frightful; pure; deplorable; subversive; divine; haphazard; perverse; monstrous; trivial; sheer; malignant; regrettable; vexing; inexplicable; minor; heart-breaking; curious; ghastly; providential; incredible; stupid; dreadful; fatal; predictable.

verbs
answer for—; barring—; breed —s; curb —s; excuse—; fake—; incapacitate by—; subject to—; trace to—; —befalls; —forces; —happens; —occurs; —oppresses; —places.
(See event, mishap.)

ACCIDENTAL

adverbs
scarcely; obviously; presumably; luckily; purposely; wholly; comically; inexplicably; curiously; mysteriously; certainly; undoubtedly; admittedly; undeniably; ludicrously; purportedly; evidently; supposedly; awkwardly; tragically; plainly; rarely.

ACCLAIM

adjectives
critical; tumultuous; public; boisterous; deafening; wide-spread; enthusiastic; spontaneous; immeasurable; resounding; joyous; jubilant; riotous; grandiloquent; noisy; righteous; deserved; universal.

ACCLAIM (v)

adverbs
riotously; grandiloquently; enthusiastically; noisily; tumultuously; boisterously; deafeningly; spontaneously; resoundingly; jubilantly; joyously; obstreperously; thunderously; persistently; turbulently; vociferously; sepulchrally; blatantly; clamorously; flamboyantly.
(See applaud, approve, cheer.)

ACCOMMODATE (v)

adverbs
effectually; appreciatively; easily; nobly; amiably; freely; generously; beneficently; benignly; graciously; impartially; magnanimously; altruistically; benignantly; legally; legitimately.
(See favor, oblige.)

ACCOMMODATING

adverbs
ingratiatingly; amiably; delightfully; ob-

sequiously; ostentatiously; pompously; profusely; helpfully; fawningly; cordially; pretentiously; courteously; habitually; unusually; ominously; grudgingly; willingly; significantly; heartily; civilly; servilely; loftily; exceedingly; gravely; graciously; charmingly; freely; gruffly; politely; bluntly; splendidly; magnificently; surprisingly.

ACCOMMODATIONS

adjectives
luxurious; superior; splendid; modern; complete; princely; excellent; cheery; spacious; genial; straitened; pacific; dismal; comfortable; overnight; transient; capacious; commodious; sorry; mean; ordinary; slender; wretched.

ACCOMPANIMENT

adjectives
regrettable; picturesque; harmonic; supernatural; deprecatory; violent; aesthetic; invariable; undulating; confused; fearful; running; pleasurable; inharmonious; unsuitable; inevitable; throbbing; spirited; vague; faint; discordant; splendid; sinister; satiric; verdant; fiendish; bewitching; fitting; orchestral; indispensable; competent; riotous; listless; unhappy; staccato.

ACCOMPANY (*v*)

adverbs
listlessly; inevitably; invariably; delightedly; unhappily; fearfully; confusedly; harmoniously; unsuitably; spiritually; intelligently; discordantly; bewitchingly; competently; skillfully; dexterously; gaily; gladly; blissfully; rejoicingly; mirthfully; rapturously; dutifully.

(See escort, follow, attend.)

ACCOMPLICE

adjectives
menial; principal; provocative; vigilant; criminal; unwitting; dastardly; secret; willing; assiduous; inept; perfidious.

ACCOMPLISH (*v*)

adverbs
effectively; boastfully; deliberately; adequately; culturally; indefatigably; ultimately; substantially; peacefully; divinely; signally; impressively; skillfully; meritoriously; energetically; invincibly; irresistibly.

(See achieve, perform, execute.)

ACCOMPLISHED

adverbs
brilliantly; wonderfully; unusually; marvellously; cleverly; incredibly; undoubtedly; distinctly; expertly; thoroughly; consummately; remarkably; politely; elegantly.

ACCOMPLISHMENT

adjectives
germinant; cultural; mental; limited; fatiguing; glittering; ultimate; substantial; brilliant; peaceful; divine; signal; human; impressive; creative; infinite (pl); successful; superb; scrupulous; notable; worthy; effete; versatile; effective; deliberate; boastful.

verbs
appraise —s; awe by—; credit with—; dwarf—; echo with—; enrich with—; gird oneself for—; hail—; lack—; marvel at—; praise—; strive for—; sum up —s; want (lack)—; —pales; —taunts.

(See achievement, action, deed feat.)

ACCORD

adjectives
complete; mutual; enthusiastic; technical; sweet; voluntary; sensual; solid; simple; superficial; perfect; generous; hearty; tumultuous; universal; widespread; peaceful; temporary; lasting; harmonious.

ACCORD (*v*)

adverbs
generously; universally; genially; voluntarily; willingly; grudgingly; superficially; beneficently; gladly; intelligently; benevolently; reasonably; magnanimously; graciously; impartially; altruistically; benignly.

(See agree, conform.)

ACCOST (*v*)

adverbs
cordially; genially; jovially; graciously; familiarly; rudely; roughly; heartily; acrimoniously; bitterly; bluffly; drunkenly; blithely; gleefully; mirthfully; vivaciously; exultantly; ecstatically; conceitedly; cheerily.

(See greet, address.)

ACCOUNT

adjectives
elaborate; detailed; full; minute; lengthy; analytical; concise; brief; condensed; picturesque; magnificent; beautiful; hackneyed; inspired; felicitous; scanty; fragmentary; sketchy; rambling; inadequate; exact; accurate; veracious; precise; factual; personal; intimate; unaffected; sincere; straightforward; biased; impartial; prejudiced; sober; childish; intelligible; cap-

able; continuous; straight-running; chimerical; absurd; amusing; humorous; whimsical; facetious; thrilling; breath-taking; hair-raising; blood-curdling; lurid; ambiguous; conflicting; contradictory; amazing; disquieting; alarming; ribald; sordid; sprawling; incoherent; statistical; romantic; syllogistic; proselytizing; ironical; informative; lusty; rigorous; indignant; delirious; articulate; uninhibited; charming; fascinating; delightful; absorbing; striking; graphic; vivid; animated; leisurely; belated; garrulous; circumstantial; exhaustive; specific; inferential; synthetic; punctilious; glowing; exaggerated; superficial; singular; unrhetorical; contemporary; profuse; inspired; gloomy; harrowing; technical; wire-drawn; conjectural; malicious; farcical; biographical; voluble; prosaic; racy; awful.

verbs
balance—; boost—; fabricate—; juggle —s; revel in —s; render—; settle—; tally up—; treble the—; attach to your—; call to—; give—of; open—; place to—; take—of; take into—; enliven—; favor with—; furnish—; launch upon—; peruse—; ramble through—; deny—; sum up—; supplement —; thrill to—; —amuses; —bores; —depicts; —differs; —entertains; —maneuvers; —wearies.

(See reckoning, bill, notice, history, report, record, narrative.)

ACCOUNTABLE

adverbs
personally; legally; entirely; wholly; scarcely; officially; morally; partially; solely; admittedly; seriously; terribly; unofficially; really.

ACCRETION

adjectives
scholastic; formalistic; enormous; elaborate; slow-forming; cumulative; natural; hidden; gradual.

ACCUMULATE (v)

adverbs
uselessly; painstakingly; laboriously; toilsomely; eccentrically; penuriously; cautiously; judiciously; prudently; close-fistedly; frugally; parsimoniously; economically; conservatively.

(See collect, gather.)

ACCUMULATION

adjectives
periodic; slow; colossal; perpetual; laborious; appalling; dangerous; insistent; useless; unsmiling; prodigious; ponderous; contorted; massive.

ACCUMULATIVE

adverbs
laboriously; ingeniously; peculiarly; unaccountably; painstakingly; instinctively; irresponsibly; habitually; dangerously; suspiciously; unsmilingly; laughingly; openly; furtively; surreptitiously; cleverly; cunningly; frankly; delightfully; deliriously; whimsically; garrulously; sincerely; unaffectedly; leisurely.

ACCURACY

adjectives
absolute; dependable; historical; businesslike; substantial; precise; unrivaled; scrupulous; tolerable; measurable; predictable; muscular; unfailing; blunt; remarkable; strict; deadly; guaranteed; mechanical; clock-like; excellent; uncanny; timed; impeccable; apparent; unctuous; machine-like; relentless; meticulous; unerring; horrible; photographic; sensitive; nautical; perfect; infinite; rhythmic; diabolical; humdrum; monotonous.

verbs
ascertain—; concede—; depend upon—; reveal—; scout—; test—; vouch for—; —fosters; —sustains

(See precision.)

ACCURATE

adverbs
absolutely; dependably; awfully; terrifyingly; scrupulously; tolerably; unfailingly; remarkably; strictly; uncannily; meticulously; monotonously; veritably; disturbingly; nakedly; essentially; unimpeachably; rigidly; mathematically; scientifically; carefully; particularly; astonishingly; insatiably; avidly; impartially; ostentatiously; punctiliously.

ACCUSATION

adjectives
frivolous; unfounded; monstrous; plaintive; vulgar; horrible; tearful; vague; rash; unanswerable; recurrent; merciless; mock; human; public; groundless; menial; eloquent; positive; keen; railing; sarcastic; indignant; constant; trumped up; nonsensical; sharp; determined; wild; unjust; false; cruel; revolting; wholesale (pl); grave; scurrilous; slanderous; violent; sensational; hasty; playful; vitriolic; villainous.

verbs
balk at—; bring—; clear—; contradict—;

counteract—; defend against—; deny—; disprove—; face—; headline—; heap —s; hurl—; level—at; parry—; refute—; resist —; roar —s; secure against—; set—; splutter—; uncover—; weigh—; withstand—.
(See charge, complaint.)

ACCUSE (v)

adverbs
publicly; consistently; unjustly; deliberately; scurrilously; falsely; sternly; vainly; frivolously; monstrously; plaintively; vulgarly; tearfully; vaguely; rashly; mercilessly; groundlessly; eloquently; indignantly; sarcastically; triumphantly; determinedly; wildly; cruelly; revoltingly; libellously; slanderously; sensationally; ruinously.
(See blame, charge.)

ACHE

adjectives
strange; dull; continual; yearning; maddening; hungry; trifling; brief; cold; numbing; throbbing; muscular; angry; bodily; intolerable; murderous; unbearable; agonizing; intermittent (pl).

verbs
aggravate—; allay—; alleviate—; assuage —; charm—; distress with—; fill with —s; harry by —s; hide—; increase—; mitigate —; mollify—; soothe—; subdue—; tantalize by—; torture by—; —abates; —contracts; —develops; —diminishes.
(See pain, agony, anguish, misery.)

ACHE (v)

adverbs
intolerably; dully; maddeningly; agonizingly; throbbingly; bitterly; sorely; mentally; dismally; tormentingly; torturingly; sharply; interminably; incessantly; monotonously; ceaselessly; periodically.
(See pain, suffer.)

ACHIEVE (v)

adverbs
unbelievably; secretly; laboriously; lastingly; consistently; tirelessly; honorably; gloriously; spiritually; conspicuously; momentously; splendidly; monumentally; superhumanly; signally; creatively; magnificently; spectacularly; breath-takingly; impressively; memorably; heroically; illustriously; valorously; fabulously; significantly.
(See accomplish, gain, acquire.)

ACHIEVEMENT

adjectives
solid; practical; lasting; remarkable; scientific; human; technological; metaphysical; civic; routine; happy; courageous; difficult; universal; authentic; fantastic; consistent; tireless; honorable; laureate; glorious; noble; conspicuous; spiritual; major; momentous; monumental; superhuman; signal; sublime; phenomenal; noteworthy; worthwhile; meritorious; creditable; praiseworthy; creative; constructive; colossal; vast; stupendous; magnificent; artistic; picturesque; rare; unparalleled; unique; spectacular; culminating; breath-taking; stirring; supreme; crowning; Homeric; impressive; memorable; heroic; valorous; illustrious; unfading; poetic; precocious; fabulous; laborious; subtle; immortal; significant; epoch-making; irreproachable.

verbs
belittle—; conceive—; denote—; disparage —; enhance—; facilitate—; hedge about—; laud—; meditate on—; mock at—; plan—; praise—; proclaim—; question—; reaffirm —; rejoice in—; strive toward—; —contributes to; —distinguishes; —goes unrecognized; —mocks.
(See accomplishment, action, deed, feat.)

ACID

adjectives
pungent; aromatic; biting; insidious; corrosive; baneful; mineral; powerful; fatal; astringent; violent; fuming.

verbs
immerse in—; isolate—; neutralize—; treat with—; —bites; —burns; —cauterizes; —corrodes; —dissolves; —eats; —etches; —evaporates; —meets; —penetrates; —scars; —sears; —seeps off.
(See chemical.)

ACID (a)

adverbs
bitterly; maliciously; viciously; purposely; unnecessarily; uncontrollably; hatefully; insidiously; sharply; cynically; spitefully; resentfully; venomously; intentionally; designedly; cunningly; insinuatingly; sarcastically; incisively; shrewdly; antagonistically; needlessly; unwisely.

ACKNOWLEDGE (v)

adverbs
gratefully; appreciatively; tacitly; thankfully; obsequiously; grudgingly; pusillanimously; handsomely; tardily; instinctively; cheerfully; profusely; indulgently; exuberantly; restrainedly; warmly; characteristically; graciously; jocosely; belatedly; glum-

ly; obstreperously; boisterously; taciturnly; incoherently.
(See admit, confess.)

ACKNOWLEDGMENT

adjectives
profuse; indulgent; exuberant; restrained; polite; conventional; frank; warm; characteristic; humiliating; enthusiastic; grateful; public; gracious; jocose; courteous; grim; belated; thankful; obsequious; tacit; grudging; handsome; tardy; appreciative.

ACQUAINT (v)

adverbs
intimately; minutely; partially; familiarly; imperfectly; mutely; affectionately; eagerly; reluctantly; entirely; affably; amiably; charitably; amicably; loyally; politely; piously; complacently.
(See tell.)

ACQUAINTANCE

adjectives
vast; mutual; desirable; intimate; eventful; favorable; brilliant; charitable; prosperous; common; conventional; casual; stray; select; congenial; slight; valued; ingenious; inaccurate; preliminary; fair; imperfect; superficial; extensive; critical; tolerable; nodding; astounding; injudicious; chance; passing; temporary; broad; well-born; garrulous; good-humored; varied (pl); amiable; numerous (pl); bowing; renewed; promiscuous; protracted; professional; informal; cursory; first-hand; incomplete.

verbs
bless with—; boast—; crave—; dim—; estrange—; exploit—; greet—; hold—; lend—; pursue—; put away—; renew—; resume—; strangle—; strike up—; urge—; —creeps; —is estranged; —widens.
(See intimacy, friendship, association, friend.)

ACQUAINTED

adverbs
intimately; slightly; favorably; unhappily; fortunately; unluckily; auspiciously; personally; directly; indirectly; well; happily; familiarly; casually; superficially; thoroughly; closely; generally; absolutely; naturally; remotely; barely; insufficiently; hardly; scarcely.

ACQUIESCE (v)

adverbs
grudgingly; silently; reluctantly; feelingly; pleasantly; cheerfully; tepidly; carelessly; stolidly; sullenly; dignifiedly; cravenly; phlegmatically; grumblingly; tacitly; amiably; passively; candidly; complacently; fatalistically.
(See agree, assent, submit.)

ACQUIESCENCE

adjectives
stolid; tepid; agreeable; sullen; silent; dignified; polite; craven; unanimous; wise; courageous; phlegmatic; grumbling; delighted; tacit; stupid; amiable; passive; desperate; compulsory; candid; reluctant; fatalistic; cheerful; complacent; grudging; grim.

verbs
arrive at—; attain—; draw into—; signify —; soften into—; urge—; wheedle into—.
(See submission, agreement, compliance.)

ACQUIESCENT

adverbs
courteously; willingly; reluctantly; gruffly; grudgingly; graciously; cheerfully; necessarily; unwillingly; happily; pliantly; blithely; devotedly; wholly; glumly; halfheartedly; stolidly; timidly; stupidly; blindly; politely; passively; wisely; tacitly; complaisantly; sullenly; amiably; cunningly; shrewdly; casually; apparently; restrainedly; indifferently.

ACQUIRE (v)

adverbs
righteously; readily; patiently; instinctively; innocently; painfully; unjustly; gloriously; sensibly; ultimately; brutally; systematically; dictatorially; vigorously; ruthlessly; villainously; cruelly; treacherously; barbarously; legally; scientifically.
(See learn, master, attain.)

ACQUIREMENT

adjectives
scientific; glorious; systematic; consequent; linguistic; unrighteous; instinctive; innocent; painful.

ACQUISITION

adjectives
painful; noteworthy; desirable; permanent; eternal; arduous; exciting; superior; territorial; profitless; erudite; patient; mental; valuable; perfunctory; forcible; peaceful; cherished; long-sought.

ACQUISITIVE

adverbs
inordinately; insanely; avidly; eagerly; in-

curably; indiscriminately; universally; peculiarly; incorrigibly; distressingly; gloriously; happily; instinctively; painfully; embarrassingly; systematically; irreclaimably; hopelessly; promiscuously; vexatiously; shamelessly; perpetually; laboriously; insistently; appallingly.

ACQUIT (*v*)

adverbs
unhesitatingly; legally; unexpectedly; unanimously; generously; triumphantly; entirely; constitutionally; legitimately; tolerantly; graciously; licitly; condescendingly; acquiescently; deferentially.
(See absolve, justify, pardon.)

ACQUITTAL

adjectives
prompt; triumphant; unexpected; honorable; disquieting; undeserved; trumped-up.

verbs
advance toward—; argue for—; ballot for —; beg for—; concede—; decide on—; demand—; deny—; deserve—; direct—; earn —; effect an—; entreat for—; expect—; gain—; hope for—; justify—; merit—; move for—; order—; plead for—; produce —; provoke—; refuse—; request—; secure —; seek—; solicit—; vote on—; win—; —carries; —exonerates; —follows.
(See pardon.)

ACREAGE

adjectives
valuable; vast; fruitful; expansive.

ACRES

adjectives
wooded; impoverished; scant; unworked; well-fenced; paternal; suburban; airy; broad; rolling; broken; untilled; scrubby; verdant; denuded; cultivated; dead; ill-acquired.

ACRIMONIOUS

adverbs
pithily; dryly; sharply; tartly; pungently; wilfully; remorselessly; mercilessly; deliberately; ominously; obnoxiously; malignantly; destructively; roughly; bitterly; pertly; insolently; churlishly; crustily; snarlingly; bitingly; banefully; rancorously; quietly; unsparingly; chronically; unrelentingly; viciously; unnecessarily; hatefully; insidiously; venomously; cunningly; needlessly.

ACROBAT

verbs
—amuses; —arches his back; —awes; —balances; —clowns; —contorts; —dances; —dazzles; —displays; —dives; —executes; —flexes; —flies; —flips; —folds; —frolics; —gyrates; —hangs; —hurtles; —leaps; —manipulates; —postures; —pyramids; —rebounds; —recovers; —relaxes; —revolves; —rolls; —soars; —somersaults; —spins; —swings; —thrills; —throws himself; —tumbles; —twirls; —twists; —vaults; —waddles; —whirls; applaud—; gape at—; gasp at—; marvel at—.

ACT

adjectives
virtuous; generous; gracious; unspeakable; self-confident; aggressive; dastardly; ruthless; loathsome; detestable; horrific; barbarous; ignominious; brutal; wilful; rash; servile; cowardly; militant; hostile; mutinous; lawless; illicit; churlish; unknown; condescending; reprehensible; compromising; unfortunate; suspicious; ungallant; unwise; impulsive; thoughtless; childish; gauche; dauntless; hardy; hazardous; official; ritualistic; conspicuous; overt; inopportune; voluntary; unremembered; well-planned; expressive; benevolent; needless; oppressive; conscientious; exasperating; arbitrary; sublime; amusing; incongruous; valid; symptomatic; disadvantageous; adumbrative; heroic; authenticated; meritorious; unfeeling; decisive; instinctive; valiant; beneficent; disinterested; crowning; innumerable (pl); offensive; daring; energetic; lugubrious; touching; specific; governmental; noble; salutary; impolitic; disdainful; violent; dishonorable; ferocious; generous; cogitative; unpopular; infamous; creative; atrocious; dreaded; mischievous; imposing; inexpiable; illogical; egotistic; compulsive; overbold; unwarrantable; disgraceful; unauthorized; superfluous; defensible; treasonable; climactic; derisive; craven; irrevocable; impudent.

verbs
achieve—; applaud—; behold—; betray—; bring to pass—; catch in the—; commend—; commit—; condemn—; derive from—; dispense with—; incite—; inspire—; perform —; provoke—; pursue—; smile upon—; take in—; urge in—; view—; visualize—; —abides; —blurs; —commences; —denotes; —overtakes; —unfolds; embody—in; frustrate—; galvanize into—; goad into—; govern—.

ACT
(*statute*)

abolish—; abrogate—; annul—; broaden—; design—; disallow—; invalidate—; invoke

—; make void—; outlaw—; proclaim—; put an end to—; repeal—; resurrect—; set aside—; supersede—; suspend—; term—; violate—.

(See bill.)

ACT (*v*)

adverbs

ignominiously; shamefully; disgracefully; irrationally; impulsively; impetuously; vengefully; abnormally; irregularly; generously; cautiously; coldly; officially; officiously; erratically; superfluously; adversely; involuntarily; admirably; imprudently; ostensibly; mercifully; independently; recklessly; detrimentally; impecuniously; deliberately; frivolously; graciously; viciously; self-confidently; aggressively; unspeakably; ruthlessly; detestably; brutally; wilfully; servilely; mutinously; churlishly; compromisingly; condescendingly; gallantly; impulsively; dauntlessly; disinterestedly; offensively; disdainfully; atrociously; illogically; treasonably.

(See behave, feign.)

ACTING

adjectives

immobile; technical; robust; allegorical; iridescent; extravagant; resolute; creditable; unnatural; effective; apt; adequate; inspired; imitative; wooden; facile; listless; pantomimic; sluggish; unconvincing.

ACTION

adjectives

intelligent; noble; efficient; authoritative; authenticated; sober; riotous; furious; hair-raising; intense; virile; vigorous; muscular; courageous; aggressive; direct; resolute; determined; independent; bold; gallant; heroic; positive; affirmative; decisive; vitalizing; tumultuous; perfidious; impetuous; lively; right; stimulating; frenzied; fervent; glorious; justifiable; regrettable; passionate; unrelated (pl); pointless; spectacular; futile; indiscreet; thoughtless; ill-advised; impulsive; commonplace; immoral; uncontrolled; desperate; contemptible; rash; unhesitating; ruthless; unsocial; negative; destructive; infernal; unconventional; drastic; menial; shameful; distressing; implacable; hysterical; mob; maternal; unprecedented; vivid; pending; coordinated; definite; prompt; preliminary; simultaneous; concerted; collective; selective; absurd; dramatic; restrained; involuntary; organized; unified; isolated; strenuous; mechanical; casual; singular; unguarded; unpremeditated; instinctive; punitive; admirable; favorable; laudable; unselfish; virtuous; righteous; conscientious; irritant; unscrupulous; individual; cordial; arbitrary; precipitate; abrasive; ill-considered; disinterested; excited; physiological; spirited; sweeping; chivalric; soothing; unopposed; insolent; pantomimic; rebellious; radical; postponed; vicious; incessant; automatic; emotional; enlightened; summary; ceaseless; engrossing; self-contained; lightning; distinguished; feverish; morbid; convulsive; vehement; uncertain; purgative; igneous; reflex; public-spirited; unobstrusive; meritorious; functional; dynamic; clannish; crude; awkward; insane; poisonous; reciprocal; inspired; adventurous; unheralded; unobserved; habitual; significant; deleterious; epic; atrocious; persistent; effectual; perturbative; accelerating; deplorable; trifling; magical; vacillating; prohibited; unholy; unforeseen; spontaneous; sporadic; headlong; logical.

verbs

accelerate—; account for—; advise—; affirm—; atone for—; authenticate—; authorize—; bare—; behold—; burst into—; call into—; chafe for—; classify—; clog—; concentrate—; condemn—; construe—; contemplate—; contrive—; control—; counterfeit—; crystallize—; embark on—; emulate—; enhance—; enter upon—; expedite—; dignify—; diminish—; disguise—; dwarf—; embody—in; frustrate—; galvanize into—; goad into—; govern—; hail—; hamper—; hasten—; hinder—; identify with—; imitate—; impede—; increase—; induce—; influence—; initiate—; intensify—; interpret—; introduce—; justify—; kindle into—; maintain—; motivate—; nullify—; paralyze—; perform—; pledge to—; postpone—; prescribe—; prod into—; produce—; put into—; quicken—; repeat—; repudiate—; restrain—; retard—; revel in—; reverse—; ripen into—; rue—; shame into—; snap into—; spring into—; spur to—; stimulate—; stint—; sum up—; support—; swing into—; threaten—; throw light on—; time—; underprop—; utilize—; weigh—; yield to—; —belittles; —betrays; —blasts; —centers; —confers; —contrives against; —conveys; —divorces from; —predominates; —proceeds from; —rends; —tires; —yields.

(See motion, gesture, act, operation.)

ACTIVE

adverbs

tremendously; keenly; perpetually; enormously; nervously; appallingly; seldom; terribly; amicably; despicably; charitably; helpfully; vitally; dramatically; ostentatiously; shamelessly; absurdly; villainously; ridiculously; admirably; efficiently; pompously; socially; ludicrously; perpetually; politically; singularly; habitually; uncommonly; infernally; vexatiously; suspiciously; subversively; constructively; excitedly; impudently; presumptuously; ardently; rebelliously; obtrusively; insanely; significantly; gravely; persistently.; disturbingly; noisily; amazingly; annoyingly; tirelessly; normally; surreptitiously; restlessly; furtively; openly; boldly; incessantly.

ACTIVITY

adjectives
intellectual; bustling; political; characteristic; extra-curricular; charitable; unavailing; elemental; intense; supporting; spasmodic; mischievous; feverish; exaggerated; volitional; sustained; pedagogical; commercial; unrivaled; spontaneous; volcanic; essential; potent; gastric; peculiar; mental; disquieting; productive; suspicious; erotic; cultural; infantile; unfettered; creative; mercantile; hampered; cataclysmic; magnetic; hive-like; fruitful; beneficent; unparalleled; throbbing; fiendish; functional; social; subversive; publicized; philanthropic; outstanding; recreational; buoyant; prodigious; ceaseless; energetic; incessant; tireless; editorial; violent; unedifying; frivolous; manifold; literary; accustomed; stunning; physiologic; purposeless; destructive; influential; malignant; cooperative; inspirational; painful; irresponsible; aesthetic; earthly; kaleidoscopic; zealous; wholesome; morbid; constructive; normal; disciplined; fascinating; dexterous; nefarious; frantic; surreptitious; clandestine; deficient; tortuous; expanding; multiple; conglomerate (pl); diversified; teeming; widespread; innumerable (pl); multifarious; incredible; nervous; passionate; eager; restless; strident; humming; hilarious; fertile; instigated; prosaic; bizarre; vicarious; villainous.

verbs
accompany—; administer—; boil with—; camouflage—; center—; chart—; condemn —; confine—; constitute—; contemplate—; control—; cramp—; cripple—; curb—; dedicate—; deliberate on—; diffuse—; direct —; display—; edge out—; embrace—; engage in—; examine—; focus—; frustrate—; guide—; hamper by—; hum with—; immerse in—; induce—; inhibit—; initiate—; interrupt—; involve—; kindle—; leap into —; limit—; link—; maintain—; motivate —; nag into—; overshadow—; participate in—; pursue—; regulate—; restrict—; resume—; rouse—; seethe with—; spring into —; spur—; supervise—; undertake—; witness—; —abates; —defeats; —ebbs and flows; —excites; —flares into; —reigns; —stimulates.
(See action.)

ACTOR

adjectives
daring; conspicuous; tragic; eminent; gesticulating; diligent; impulsive; distinguished; celebrated; obscure; godlike; prominent; inimitable; popular; expert; unschooled; recalcitrant; "ham"; strolling; itinerant; persuasive; consummate; competent; forthright; character; skilled.

verbs
applaud—; greet—; key up—; prompt—; —acquits; —administers; —affects; —apes; —blunders through; —burlesques; —conforms to; —appears; —evokes; —executes; —forces; —gesticulates; —impersonates; —interprets; —mimics; —narrates; —parrots; —performs; —personifies; —radiates; —recites; —spouts; —suggests; —wails.
(See player, performer.)

ACTRESS

adjectives
gifted; distinguished; competent; charming; brilliant; subtle; exotic; fascinating; indomitable; obscure; hardened; stately; naturalistic; mediocre; energetic; spirited.

ACUMEN

adjectives
critical; philosophical; rare; financial; intellectual; penetrative; business; distinguished; acute.

ACUTE

adverbs
unwontedly; keenly; actually; remarkably; apparently; astonishingly; unexpectedly; surpassingly; shrewdly; cleverly; uncommonly; fairly; profoundly; thoughtfully; politically; sharply; discriminatingly; naturally; subtly; restlessly; prophetically; reassuringly; penetratingly; craftily.

ACUTENESS

adjectives
consummate; vicious; tense; native; unwonted; proverbial; incredible; godlike; rare; apparent.

ADAGE
adjectives
favorite; familiar; classic; oft-quoted; apt; well-phrased; clumsy; appropriate.

verbs
accept—; call to mind—; conceive—; disprove—; grasp—; interpret—; lean against —; paraphrase—; reiterate—; verify—; — expresses.

(See proverb, maxim, saying.)

ADAMANT
adverbs
wilfully; indomitably; bitterly; unyieldingly; obdurately; pitilessly; unrelentingly; unrepentantly; inexorably; stubbornly; obstinately; mulishly; doggedly; perversely; fanatically; pig-headedly; contumaciously; bigotedly.

ADAPT (v)
adverbs
admirably; skilfully; eminently; artistically; mentally; physically; intellectually; professionally; ingeniously; mechanically; adroitly; dexterously; aesthetically; craftily; competently; consummately; deftly; matchlessly; cleverly; efficaciously; factitiously; gracefully; scientifically; diplomatically; inventively; ingeniously; peerlessly; incomparably.

(See adjust, conform.)

ADAPTABILITY
adjectives
ready; wide-awake; facile; quick.

(See adaptation.)

ADAPTABLE
adverbs
complaisantly; hardly; readily; intelligently; graciously; easily; ingeniously; comfortably; moderately; scarcely; willingly; quickly; dexterously; cleverly; wisely; diplomatically; sagaciously; sympathetically; mercifully; affably; courteously; civilly; companionably; amiably; discreetly; judiciously; wisely.

ADAPTATION
adjectives
judicious; exquisite; conscious; functional; deliberate; scenic; terrestrial; approximate; stereotyped; passive; studious; agile; unfulfilled; inexpensive; ingenious; errant.

ADD (v)
adverbs
fondly; facetiously; significantly; intelligently; wearily; dreamily; sorrowfully; passionately; thoughtfully; mildly; parenthetically; frowningly; hopefully; bluntly; decisively; soothingly; carelessly; regretfully; stridently; hurriedly; unobtrusively; contemptuously; tremulously; doubtfully; self-reproachfully; wistfully; breathlessly; impressively; haughtily; needlessly; falteringly; graciously; tentatively; briskly; generously; coolly; cryptically; slyly; speedily; accurately; erratically; mentally; alternately; materially; freely; jerkily; vertically; diagonally; horizontally.

(See annex, join.)

ADDICT
adjectives
passionate; miserable; confirmed; incurable; depraved; pitiful.

ADDICTED
adverbs
miserably; unfortunately; hopelessly; tragically; incurably; ridiculously; pitifully; irreparably; comically; fatally; incorrigibly; lamentably; unhappily; absurdly; unluckily; distressingly; pathetically; laughably; unreasonably; strangely; curiously.

ADDICTION
adjectives
pedantic; stubborn; tiresome; conspicuous; learned; hopeless; desultory; violent; favorite.

ADDITION
adjectives
incongruous; anachronistic; desirable; simultaneous; pleasing; necessary; costly; significant; worthy; astonishing; dubious; immediate; unprofitable; meager; valuable; substantial; imaginative; gratuitous; indispensable; distinctive; popular.

ADDLED
adverbs
hopelessly; comically; strangely; disastrously; slightly; completely; sweetly; horribly; delightfully; indescribably; visibly; manifestly; uproariously; foggily; vociferously; dazedly; rosily; brokenly; incurably; pathetically; palpably.

ADDRESS
adjectives
impromptu; flattering; impending; emphatic; passionate; pithy; temperate; grave; inaugural; intuitive; masterly; graphic; soldier-like; moving; fervid; insinuating; il-

luminating; commemorative; laudatory; radical; carefully-worded; sensational; post-prandial; lengthy; stirring; inspiring; rousing; keynote; eloquent; amatory; ardent; affectionate; lucid; preliminary; charming; naive; stumbling; halting; extempore; incoherent.

ADDRESS (speech)

verbs
alter—; charge—with; compose—; concoct —; condense—; curtail—; expand—; grind out—; organize—; pour forth—; reel off—; thunder—.

(See speech, oration, sermon, lecture, discourse.)

ADDRESS (v)

adverbs
informally; cordially; intimately; affectionately; indiscriminately; pretentiously; exclusively; mournfully; passionately; extemporaneously; temperately; fervidly; insinuatingly; stirringly; inspiringly; rousingly; eloquently; ardently; lucidly; intelligently; pugnaciously; pointedly.

(See lecture, discourse.)

ADEPT

adverbs
expertly; scarcely; palpably; undoubtedly; cleverly; ingeniously; incredibly; marvellously; clearly; remarkably; smartly; unimaginably; surprisingly; dangerously; alarmingly; exceptionally; subtly; fearfully; comparatively; confidently.

ADEQUATE

adverbs
completely; excellently; pleasantly; delightfully; remarkably; providentially; sufficiently; scarcely; essentially; suitably; wholly; admirably; quite; satisfactorily; wonderfully; gratifyingly; fortunately; luckily.

ADHERE (v)

adverbs
rigidly; tenaciously; doggedly; staunchly; passionately; strictly; perversely; pertinaciously; scrupulously; unflinchingly; undeviatingly; formally; steadfastly; stubbornly; obstinately; blindly; unalterably; intractably; militantly; contentiously; cantankerously; incorrigibly; immovably; impassively; insistently; bigotedly; sullenly; waywardly, strenuously; religiously; moderately.

(See stick, cling.)

ADHERENCE

adjectives
lingering; firm; strict; scrupulous; unflinching; passionate; undiscriminating; rigid; undeviating; formal; steadfast; stubborn; obstinate; exact; staunch; apparent; blind; unalterable; inborn; tenacious; dogged; pertinacious; devout; perverse; rash; vigorous; unwise; smug; unswerving; ardent.

ADHERENT

adjectives
staunch; unquestioning; zealous; pious; numbered (pl); faithful; deluded; superstitious; loyal; devout; close; spirited.

ADIEU

adjectives
courtly; final; graceful; gentle; mute; sublime; fearful; silent; grave; painful; brash; condescending; disdainful; despairing; wistful.

ADIPOSE

adverbs
incredibly; irremediably; unfortunately; disagreeably; incurably; unacceptably; distressingly; absurdly; ridiculously; needlessly; ludicrously; damagingly; lamentably; sadly; dangerously; heavily; admittedly; unreasonably.

ADJECTIVE

adjectives
qualifying; explosive; unfactual; decorative; severe; impressive-sounding; apt; augmenting; glowing; sonorous; obsolete; laudatory; rapturous; nauseous; overworked; uncomplimentary; unfavorable; commendatory; descriptive; flattering; inept; obvious; appropriate; exact; distinctive; moving; brilliant; breezy; racy; lurid; lush; picturesque; suggestive; well-chosen; precise.

verbs
accompany by—; adorn with—; allot—; arrange—; attach—; avoid—; bandy—; choose—; classify—; compare—; depend on —; derive—; eliminate—; eschew—; exhaust—; group —s; indulge in —s; juggle —s; lavish —s on; overwork—; pile up —s; reject—; strike out—; stuff with —s; supply with —s; swamp with —s; transpose —s; —answers; —colors; —conveys; —defines; —denotes; —describes; —disappears; —explains; —expresses; —forms; —implies; —interprets; —limits; —modifies; —occurs; —s pad; —points out; —presents; —qualifies; —springs from; —supplies.

(See word.)

ADJUNCT

adjectives
impressive; non-essential; inevitable; external; unusual; absurd; impedimental; artificial.

ADJUST (*v*)

adverbs
delicately; improperly; satisfactorily; accurately; eventually; fortunately; happily; languidly; harmoniously; nervously; peaceably; enduringly; elaborately; amply; subtly; magnanimously; equitably; mathematically; minutely; precisely; punctiliously; specifically; exactly.
(See settle, fit.)

ADJUSTABLE

adverbs
amicably; easily; instantly; comfortably; necessarily; wisely; conveniently; fortunately; luckily; amazingly; extraordinarily; cunningly; cleverly; naturally; serviceably; handily; peaceably; sensibly.

ADJUSTMENT

adjectives
necessary; temporary; ultimate; long-awaited; peaceful; visual; constant; artistic; enduring; honorable; felicitous; elaborate; studied; rightful; immediate; patriotic; corresponding; ample; scientific; preliminary; harmonious; sensible; subtle; economic; discreet; enforced; poetical; complex; delicate; heart-rending; mental; compensating; calm; prompt; partial; compromised; amicable.

verbs
adopt—; advocate—; challenge—; effect—; honor—; postpone—; recommend—; reject—; stimulate—; submit to—; —obviates; —pleases; —prevents; —satisfies; —settles.
(See regulation, arrangement, settlement.)

ADMINISTER (*v*)

adverbs
efficiently; steadily; faithfully; methodically; internally; cautiously; economically; corruptly; benignly; wholesomely; incompetently; satisfactorily; formally; ecclesiastically; conventionally; customarily; domestically; wontedly; ethically; vigorously.
(See manage, regulate, settle.)

ADMINISTRATION

adjectives
successful; businesslike; memorable; subservient; corrupt; economical; incapable; filial; benign; stormy; incumbent; spiritual; contemporary; centralized; unified; communal; careful; incoming; civil; eventful; efficient; wholesome; bureaucratic; incompetent; judicial; provincial; internal; stern; progressive; partisan.

verbs
backbite—; consolidate—; dominate—; entrust with—; facilitate—; flout—; hamper—; repudiate—; set up—; —comes into power; —contemplates; —defends; —draws to a close; —justifies; —plows under; —refutes; —relegates to; —vindicates; —wields.
(See government.)

ADMINISTRATIVE

adverbs
capably; stormily; benignly; thoroughly; nonchalantly; conscientiously; patriarchally; paternally; ably; cleverly; sternly; severely; strictly; judiciously; wisely; tolerantly; wholesomely; busily; fussily; majestically; pompously; simply; arrogantly; officiously; laxly; loosely; democratically; dogmatically; tyrannically; sagely; affably; fairly; honestly; incorruptibly.

ADMIRABLE

adverbs
genuinely; virtuously; correctly; laudably; truly; really; unexpectedly; consciously.

ADMIRAL

adjectives
mustachioed; famed; stern; plucky; renowned; redoubtable; capable; undaunted.

ADMIRATION

adjectives
heartfelt; affectionate; ecstatic; whole-hearted; rapturous; unbounded; cordial; genuine; undying; profound; unstinted; grateful; modest; effusive; wistful; unfeigned; passionate; intense; open; frank; enthusiastic; reluctant; waning; grudging; fictitious; perverse; patriotic; youthful; girlish; wondering; amazed; hushed; puzzled; unabashed; sneaking; ardent; mirthful; self-contained; inexpressible; repressed; blind; mute; envious; reiterated; deluded; mutual; unmitigated; critical; loquacious; unrestrained; clamorous; passing; complacent; prolonged; smiling; unwilling; universal; ineffable; impersonal; respectful; astonished; reverent; calculating; noisy; untutored; outspoken; undisguised; unlimited; sympathetic; reciprocal; excessive; maudlin; rapt;

half-envious; magnanimous; indulgent; pitying; healthy; speechless; momentary; enhanced.

verbs
arouse—; challenge—; command—; draw—; elicit—; evoke—; excite—; express—; fill with—; inspire—; lose in—; mirror—; modify—; obtain—; profess—; reap—; reserve—; retain—; season—; strike with—; suppress—; temper—; utter—; win—; —abates; —beams; —buzzes; —cools; —haunts; —moves; —seizes; —wanes; —waxes.

(See amazement, wonder, astonishment, love, respect.)

ADMIRE (v)

adverbs
universally; prodigiously; immensely; gushingly; passionately; cordially; legitimately; tremendously; ardently; ecstatically; wholeheartedly; rapturously; effusively; profoundly; wistfully; intensely; mutely; unrestrainedly; loquaciously; complacently; clamorously; ineffably; reverently; outspokenly; frankly; undisguisedly; unboundedly; magnanimously; 'indulgently; unceasingly; fervently; legitimately; perfunctorily.

(See approve, appreciate.)

ADMIRER

adjectives
idolatrous; credulous; soft; ardent; fervent; enthusiastic; irresponsible; discriminating; solemn; passionate; devoted; staunch; countless (pl); sole; persistent; injudicious; quondam; appreciative; reluctant; blind; over-enthusiastic; fond; rival; well-bred; zealous; hearty.

verbs
abuse—; discourage—; displease—; humor —; indulge—; —acclaims; —adores; —amuses; —applauds; —deifies; —eulogizes; —fawns; —flatters; —glorifies; —gratifies; —idolizes; —lauds; —pays tribute; —pleases; —puffs; —renounces; —reveres; —s throng; —toasts; —worships.

(See favorite, follower, lover.)

ADMISSION

adjectives
grudging; heartfelt; inexorable; damaging; fatal; flattering; virtual; certain; tacit; frank; candid; liberal; naive; irreparable; plain-faced; blunt; obvious; rueful; reluctant; unguarded; brash; arrogant; gracious; ineluctable; quaint; final.

effusively; duly; solemnly; tearfully; parentally; cautiously; gently; paternally; prophetically; frantically; urgently; maternally; stingingly; harshly; bitterly; brutally; sternly; sensibly; ceremoniously; formally; puritanically; scrupulously; rigorously; stringently.

(See reprove, warn.)

ADMONITION

adjectives
soft-voiced; tearful; intensified; plain-spoken; parental; judicious; condescending; moral; cautious; stimulating; gentle; poetical; solemn; prophetic; grave; parting; frantic; urgent; forcible; affectionate; respectful; classical; discouraging; paternal; stinging; whispered; effusive; suave; bold; brazen; prosaic; tedious; beautiful.

verbs
cluck —s; elude—; heed—; merit—; —demoralizes; —distorts; —distracts; —repels; —scorches; —softens.

(See caution, warning, advice.)

ADOLESCENCE

adjectives
uneventful; painful; self-conscious; callow; awkward; gawky; supersensitive; vain; joyous; feverish; shy; coy; brash; brusque; carefree.

verbs
apply for—; authorize—; begrudge—; demand—; insure—; refuse—; win—.

(See entrance.)

ADMIT

adverbs
remorsefully; brashly; candidly; universally; reluctantly; arrogantly; ruefully; grudgingly; privately; semi-officially; willingly; graciously; equably; laughingly; knowingly; tacitly; humbly; formally; dubiously; unreservedly; savagely; unfeelingly; naively; bluntly; unguardedly.

(See acknowledge, confess, concede, grant.)

ADMITTANCE

verbs
buy—; crave—; deny—; desire—; gain—; grant—; request—; seek—.

(See entrance, admission.)

ADMONISH (v)

adverbs

ADOLESCENT

adverbs
delightfully; glowingly; dully; painfully; awkwardly; gawkily; sensitively; feverishly; shyly; joyously; obviously; incurably; alluringly; exuberantly; inexpressibly; unbelievably; markedly; radiantly; vividly; excitably.

ADOPT (*v*)

adverbs
gratefully; dogmatically; advantageously; ostensibly; unanimously; prudently; voluntarily; solemnly; vigorously; obstreperously; judiciously; arbitrarily; ultimately; frankly; deceitfully; apparently; formally; ceremoniously; prudishly; skilfully; tactfully; strategically.

(See espouse, support, maintain.)

ADOPTION

adjectives
solemn; vigorous; obstreperous; timely; judicious; grateful; dogmatic; ostensible; prudent; voluntary; ready.

ADORABLE

adverbs
mysteriously; utterly; altogether; delightfully; confoundedly; bewilderingly; amazingly; wondrously; unexpectedly; unimaginably; miraculously; graciously; coolly; warmly; radiantly; glowingly; joyously; unbelievably; consciously; contentedly.

ADORATION

adjectives
ecstatic; idolatrous; inarticulate; solemn; shy; passionate; young; breathless; unswerving; servile; filial; fervent; boyish; maternal; doglike; restrained; impassioned; cold; soft; silent; rapturous; mad; hushed; quiet; poetic; unlimited; deprecatory.

verbs
bestow—; fall in—; rear in—; repel—; yield to—; —buoys; —captivates; —enslaves.

(See worship, love, prayer, reverence.)

ADORE (*v*)

adverbs
blindly; angelically; ecstatically; inarticulately; solemnly; shyly; passionately; breathlessly; servilely; filially; fervently; restrainedly; boyishly; worshipfully; impulsively; wantonly; vehemently; warmly; carnally; ruttishly; meretriciously; faithfully; intensely; excessively; fondly; soulfully.

(See worship, reverence.)

ADORN (*v*)

adverbs
lavishly; sumptuously; elaborately; expensively; attractively; richly; architecturally; ceremonially; lustrously; artistically; triumphally; splendidly; decoratively.

(See decorate, ornament, embellish, gild.)

ADORNMENT

adjectives
lavish; extraneous; expensive; sculptural; architectural; curious; feminine; personal; lustrous; rich; sumptuous; elaborate; garish; gaudy; tasteful.

ADROIT

adverbs
marvellously; cleverly; incredibly; admirably; artfully; remarkably; dangerously; palpably; suspiciously; neatly; matchlessly; craftily; masterfully; wonderfully; uncommonly; consummately; innately; constitutionally; instinctively; inherently.

ADROITNESS

adjectives
masterly; neat; witty; technical; skilled; swift; matchless; wily; manual.

ADULATE (*v*)

adverbs
extravagantly; prodigally; servilely; vociferously; amorously; abjectly; indiscriminately; fulsomely; humbly; shrewdly; deceitfully.

(See praise, flatter.)

ADULATION

adjectives
tribal; hysterical; prodigal; vociferous; amorous; servile; abject; unnatural; fulsome; indiscriminate.

verbs
bask in—; deluge with—; enjoy—; expose to—; feast upon—; indulge in—; relish—; sicken by—; yield to—; —fatigues.

(See flattery, extravagance, praise, compliment.)

ADULATORY

adverbs
abjectly; fawningly; coquettishly; flatteringly; servilely; tribally; hysterically; politically; sycophantically; unctuously; officiously; ostentatiously; subtly; speciously; openly; disagreeably; disgustingly; blatantly; offensively; fulsomely; lavishly.

ADULT (a)

adverbs
surprisingly; completely; fully; obviously; fairly; precociously; prematurely; undeniably; wisely; mysteriously; emotionally; intellectually; uncommonly; buxomly; indescribably; consciously; appallingly; terribly; suddenly; unquestionably.

ADULTERY

verbs
commit—; condone—; forgive—; indulge in—; justify—; revel in—; take in—.
(See unfaithfulness.)

ADVANCE

adjectives
striking; logical; unflinching; subsequent; economic; orderly; general; sharp; courageous; intellectual; triumphant; successive; perpetual; incessant; definite; studious; haughty; unprecedented; spectacular; prodigious; dizzy; substantial; marked; distinct; material; noteworthy; trifling; modest; tenacious; reconnoitering; arduous; implacable; cautious; glacial; faltering; pugnacious; jaunty; ominous; bold; persistent; menacing; notable.

verbs
characterize—; check—; constitute—; discourage—; facilitate—; fear—; hinder—; mark—; pioneer in —s; reject —s; smile at—; —culminates; —terminates.
(See progress.)

ADVANCE (v)

adverbs
aggressively; cautiously; boldly; jauntily; ominously; menacingly; reluctantly; tremblingly; pugnaciously; progressively; ungracefully; simultaneously; hesitantly; secretly; persistently; hopelessly; inexorably; eagerly; notably; triumphantly; timidly; fearfully; compactly; materially; impulsively; awkwardly; unflinchingly; unprecedentedly; spectacularly; substantially; markedly.
(See progress, promote, enhance.)

ADVANCEMENT

adjectives
revolutionary; material; technical; significant; professional; cultural; economic; scientific; industrial; corresponding; spiritual; signal; long-sought; respective (pl).

verbs
contribute to—; deserve—; desire—; hope for—; note—; promote—; strike a blow to—; strive for—.
(See promotion, progress.)

ADVANCES

adjectives
tender; lover-like; friendly; surreptitious; tactless; unwelcome; old-fashioned; formal; vigorous; amoristic; bold; boorish; bestial; intimate; circumspect.

ADVANTAGE

adjectives
irretrievable; vile; inevitable; inescapable; obvious; patent; remote; trifling; marked; private; educational; pecuniary; fallacious; immediate; inestimable; enduring; appreciable; unfair; hidden; incidental; underestimated; permanent; contingent; manifold; accidental; worldly; material; human; revolutionary; worth while; practical; unique; physical; substantial; undue; reciprocal; temporary; compensating; theoretical; reasonable; invaluable; surreptitious; matchless; graceless; definite; decisive; adventitious; base; hard-earned; initial; momentary; actual; cultural; exclusive; strategic; shameless; frail; selfish; perishable; unparalleled; mutual; overwhelming; hygienic; unsurpassed; decided; tangible; numerical; signal; partisan; insurmountable; incalculable; ineluctable; irresistible.

verbs
buy with—; cite—; confer—; contemplate—; derive—; discern—; embody—; enjoy—; forbear—; forego—; gain—; hold—; hold forth on the —s of; jeopardize—; lack—; let pass—; offset—; pay back with—; press—; press home—; reap—; sacrifice—; seize upon—; set—against; shear off—; stress—; surrender—; turn to—; use—; vouchsafe—; —accrues; —achieves; —is connected with; —feeds; —slips.
(See profit, victory, benefit.)

ADVANTAGEOUS

adverbs
politically; obviously; essentially; undoubtedly; suspiciously; practically; financially; eventually; immensely; socially; highly; materially; personally.

ADVENT

adjectives
illustrious; early; imposing; spectacular; exciting; miraculous; pretended; anticipated; long-awaited.

ADVENTURE

adjectives
lunatic; divers (pl); romantic; pioneering; nocturnal; foolish; intriguing; blithe; maritime; amusing; gustatory; prodigious; dramatic; weird; preposterous; boisterous; fascinating; glorious; royal; gallant; flagrant; healthful; spiritual; pleasurable; remarkable; scientific; desperate; petty; vicarious; glamorous; ludicrous; aesthetic; perilous; disgusting; intellectual; wearisome; terrifying; profitless; formidable; calamitous; extraordinary; countless (pl); notorious; stupendous; sensational; fruitful; curious; rambling; peaceful; gay; audacious; epic; colorful; picturesque; sparkling; piquant; joyous; sentimental; diverting; exuberant; chivalrous; colossal; uproarious; unprecedented; hazardous; astounding; extravagant; sordid; banal; indecorous; untoward; foolhardly; promiscuous; trying; unbelievable; singular; fantastic; fearful; incredible; curious; stimulating; stirring; hectic; mad; daring; breath-taking; strenuous; pathetic; amorous; mental; fearsome; quixotic; unique; exotic; stark; erotic; piscatory; disconcerting; picaresque; alcoholic; engrossing; comic; tragic; void; equivocal; agile.

verbs
achieve—; crown with—; dare—; dishonor—; dread—; embark on—; encounter—; expose to—; go in quest of—; hanker after—; hazard—; imperil—; mingle among —s; plunge into—; recount—; ride forth to—; risk—; search for—; seek—; set out upon—; thirst for—; thrill with—; urge to—; weave—; yearn for—; —awakens; —befalls; —diverts; —edges; —enlivens; —grips; —lurks; —sweeps over one; —thrills.
(See quest.)

ADVENTURE (*v*)

adverbs
amorously; haphazardly; romantically; nocturnally; intriguingly; blithely; prodigiously; dramatically; preposterously; boisterously; gloriously; gallantly; vicariously; glamorously; perilously; breath-takingly; strenuously; fearsomely; quixotically; exotically; erotically.
(See dare, venture, happen.)

ADVENTURER

adjectives
venal; intrepid; astute; adroit; unscrupulous; reckless; ambitious; rapacious; martial; noisy; impudent: colossal; hardy; dauntless; despondent; amorous; born; charming; calculating; worthless; thieving; hard-bitten; lusty; penniless; unprincipled; sordid.

ADVENTUROUS

adverbs
madly; boldly; avidly; bravely; timidly; rashly; innately; daringly; carefully; crazily; recklessly; gloriously; notoriously; audaciously; romantically; dramatically; vicariously; courageously; foolishly; terribly; eagerly; inherently; joyously; colossally; foolhardily; singularly; breath-takingly; tragically; youthfully; fantastically; madly; boyishly; disconcertingly; incredibly; alarmingly; discreetly; constitutionally; extravagantly; hazardously.

ADVERSARY

adjectives
shallow; maimed; underrated; vanquished; doughty; imaginary; stubborn; stony; formidable; proud; courteous; intangible; hostile; vigorous; resolute; worthy; generous; stout; reluctant; well-matched; stalwart; sinister; deadly; harassed; venomous.

verbs
abash—; avenge one's—; battle with—; challenge—; combat—; conquer—; embrace—; fight against—; frustrate—; harass—; heckle—; mock at—; oppose—; overcome—; overpower—; overrule—; overthrow—; overwhelm—; provoke—; quell—; resist—; shake—; stir up—; summon—; take vengeance on—; terrify—; triumph over—; weed out —s; wrestle with—; —conquers; —defeats; —delivers; —fights; —gives battle; —rages; —strives; —struggles.
(See antagonist, enemy, opponent, foe.)

ADVERSE

adverbs
bitterly; fundamentally; persistently; openly; outspokenly; frankly; traditionally; formidably; irreconcilably; strangely; unaccountably; unfortunately; unhappily; powerfully; unmistakably; unmitigatedly; immoderately; unflaggingly.

ADVERSITY

verbs
acquaint with—; afflict with—; assay one's—ies; bruise with—; cast down by—; cross with—; deliver from—; distress by—; embrace—; endure—; redeem out of—; rejoice in—; smite with—; stand against—;

struggle against—; suffer—; withstand—; wound with—; —crosses; —tests; —threatens; —thwarts; —tries.

(See misfortune, disaster, trouble, affliction, calamity.)

ADVERTISE (v)

adverbs

consistently; effectively; dramatically; blatantly; extensively; intelligently; widely; truthfully; nationally; spectacularly; legally; enormously; limitedly.

(See announce, declare, publish, proclaim.)

ADVERTISEMENT

adjectives

circus; powerful; posthumous; gaudy; effective; urgent; fantastic; modest; glowing; spectacular; fraudulent; deceptive; blatant; shrill; prefatory; alluring; truthful; current; consistent; astute; dubious; adequate; seductive; dignified; exaggerated; misleading; objectionable; competitive; skilful; plaguy; unsharpened; productive.

verbs

accent—; alter—; analyze—; approve—; beautify—; believe—; belittle—; change—; complete—; creep into —s; criticize—; decorate—; discard—; follow through—; form—; heed—; identify—; illustrate—; insert—; issue—; launch—; lay out—; lengthen—; limit—; order—; overestimate —; overlook—; point up—; prepare—; purge—; react to—; recognize—; regulate —; respond to—; run—; scan—; solicit—; spoil—; survey—; turn to —s; underestimate—; weaken—; write—; —admonishes; —announces; —concentrates; —extols; —informs; —infuriates; —misleads; —represents; —warns.

(See announcement, notice, publication.)

ADVERTISING

verbs

abuse—; apply—; believe—; benefit by—; blame—; broaden—; buy—; campaign for —; charge for—; circularize—; clarify—; concentrate—; condemn—; continue—; contract for—; credit—; delineate—; display —; dissect—; disseminate—; eliminate—; emphasize—; employ—; exaggerate—; expend for—; experiment with—; exploit—; flash—; guide—; hail—; immunize to—; insist on—; intensify—; inveigh against—; issue—; judge—; learn—; mail—; minimize—; mislead by—; necessitate—; oppose—; overdo—; pay for—; parallel—; peruse—; post—; pound away with—; prepare—; praise—; prolong—; promote with —; rate—; require—; resist—; revolutionize—; schedule—; segregate—; sell—; solicit—; specialize in—; spurn—; supplement —; survey—; teach—; time—; uphold—; undertake—; utilize—; value—; wage—; warn by—; welcome—; withhold—; —accomplishes; —advances; —appeals; —attracts; —builds; —colors; —embraces; —familiarizes; —features; —fosters; —increases; —influences; —informs; —infringes upon; —inspires; —invites attention; —markets; —merits; —ministers to; —offends; —organizes; —pays; —persuades; —popularizes; —profits; —promotes; —publicizes; —rewards; —sells; —speeds up; —standardizes; —stimulates; —stirs up; —succeeds; —suggests; —trade-marks; —transcends; —transforms; —urges.

(See announcement, notice, advertisement.)

ADVICE

adjectives

interested; sage; facetious; determinative; wholesome; admirable; rash; hasty; parental; urgent; salutary; serious; dissimilar; competent; authentic; unadulterated; old-fashioned; practical; shrewd; hard-headed; requisite; customary; proffered; medical; appropriate; moderate; supplemental; unprejudiced; concentrated; superfluous; brusque; disconcerting; unselfish; matrimonial; pregnant; brutal; subtle; impartial; conservative; canny; intelligent; expert; explicit; pertinent; dreary; resented; overweening; recurrent; interjected; cautionary; voluntary; unheeded.

verbs

adopt—; bombard with—; burst with—; consider—; consult—; counsel—; deliberate over—; disregard—; drum—into; adopt—; follow—; grind out—; hark to—; heap—; heed—; honor—; ignore—; impart—; judge —; lack—; modify—; ooze—; plan—; ponder—; profit by—; reckon—; regard—; relish—; seek—; shun—; solicit—; subscribe to—; supplant—; swallow up—; volunteer—; weigh—; —aids; —hinders; —leaks out.

(See counsel, instruction, information.)

ADVISABLE

adverbs

undoubtedly; scarcely; financially; discreetly; practically; profoundly; morally; urgently; politically; usually; selfishly; solidly; undeniably; particularly; honestly.

ADVISE (v)

adverbs

earnestly; briefly; urgently; unhesitatingly; fatally; needlessly; rightly; strenuously; coolly; sagely; rashly; shrewdly; moderately; wisely; incompetently; brusquely; disinterestedly; unselfishly; impartially; brutally; solemnly; subtly; explicitly; pertinently; drearily; overweeningly; intelligently; cleverly; cautiously.

(See admonish, counsel, inform.)

ADVISER

adjectives

competent; confidential; ill-humored; technical; conservative; sympathetic; prudent; facetious; spiritual; sagacious; influential; unscrupulous; resourceful; invaluable; altruistic; experienced.

ADVOCATE

adjectives

conspicuous; disinterested; benevolent; keen; stalwart; ardent; earnest; pioneer; militant; unselfish; persistent; distinguished; zealous; uncompromising; prominent; enthusiastic; sincere; warm; strenuous; erudite; adroit; exclusive; ingenious; notorious; active; argumentative; fearless; courageous; competent; aggressive; ironic; staunch; resourceful; idealistic; eloquent; loyal; tactful; obstinate; timorous; vigilant; virile; impassioned; able.

ADVOCATE (v)

adverbs

emphatically; disinterestedly; ostensibly; passionately; absurdly; warmly; fanatically; ardently; characteristically; openly; stalwartly; earnestly; militantly; unselfishly; persistently; zealously; uncompromisingly; eruditely; adroitly; ingeniously; notoriously; fearlessly; competently; idealistically; eloquently; obstinately; timorously; truculently.

(See defend, support.)

AERONAUT

adjectives

adventurous; ardent; intrepid; daring; seasoned; war-worn; accomplished; barnstorming; globe-circling; dashing.

AEROPLANE

verbs

ballast—; bank—; capture—; charter—; christen—; equalize—; experiment with—; explore with—; fabricate—; design—; ground—; herd in—; horse down—; hover in—; kick—into a spin; kite—; land—; lift —; modify—; navigate—; nose in—; overload—; "pancake"—; pilot—; propel—; revolutionize—; salvage—; shelter—; spiral —; stabilize—; stall—; sustain—; tilt—; underpower—; —alights; —attacks; —banks; —bombs; —cartwheels; —circles; —s compete for; —s convoy; —dashes; —dives; —drones; —flattens out; —folds up; —gleams; —glides away; —gyrates; —hovers; —loops; —manoeuvers; —pierces the sky; —pivots; —propels; —rains gas; —rises; —roars; —rolls; —scoots; —sheds its wings; —skids in; —skims the turf; —slips into the sky; —soars; —swirls; —swoops; —takes off; —taxies out; —throbs; —trundles on the field; —tumbles down; —twirls; —twists; —wings its way; —wings over; —winnows its way; —zooms; —floats down.

(See balloon, plane.)

AFFABILITY

adjectives

gracious; smiling; kindly; offensive; sardonic; rare; dry; dull; heartfelt; cordial; generous; insincere; pleasing; unwonted.

AFFABLE

adverbs

unaffectedly; courteously; comfortably; enthusiastically; pleasantly; placidly; unfailingly; graciously; smilingly; considerately; sincerely; genuinely; cordially; usually; singularly; quietly; remarkably; ostentatiously.

AFFAIR

adjectives

Gargantuan; spiritual; delicate; practical; multifarious; tumultuous; domestic; conventional; financial; droll; disagreeable; pressing; internal; personal; celebrated; complicated; instructive; public; petty; weighty; vast; grave; ecclesiastical; monotonous; corporate; clandestine; passing; quiet; prim; sublunary; uninteresting; intimate; detestable; charitable; masculine; elaborate; dramatic; vigorous; rustic; unsettled; momentous; foolish; flimsy; insignificant; wearisome; troublous; warlike; multitudinous (pl); provocative; secret; temporal; risky; supernatural; deplorable; fatal; community; wretched; barbarous; rollicking; primitive; hasty; reputable; gay; charming; harmless; enchanting; colorful; profitable; resplendent; spectacular; pretentious; colossal; rueful; painful; freakish; sordid; unsavory; tragic; diabolic; disreputable; absurd; distasteful; scandalous; iniquitous; sanguinary; ferocious; blundering; dismal; apathetic; frail-looking; terrestial; academic; amorous; intricate; drawn-out; complex; droll; flippant; bewildering; laborious; different.

verbs
absorb in —s; administer —s; be conversant with—; carry on—s; change—s; characterize—; commit—to; con —s; scan—; conclude—; conduct—; connect—; control —; deal with —s; debate —s; detach from —s; dispute —s; embroil with —s; emerge from—; entangle in —s; expatiate —s; extricate from —s; grapple with —s; grasp —s; guarantee—; guide —s; hinder—; indulge in —s; intrude in —s; jumble up —s; manage —s; meddle in —s; muddle —s; operate —s; order —s; parallel—; persevere in—; pertain to—; picture—; place at the head of —s; pry into —s; shirk —s; snow under with —s; supervene in —s; support—; transact —s; travel from one—to another; undertake—; veil—; weather—; wind up —s; —drags; —intrigues; —prospers; —recurs; —rests; —ripens.
(See business, matter.)

AFFECT (v)

adverbs
gravely; materially; profoundly; visibly; powerfully; indirectly; strongly; detrimentally; vexatiously; adversely; vitally; poignantly; deeply; fundamentally; frequently; primarily; invariably; seriously; painfully; considerably; appreciably; enormously; variously; pleasantly; sensibly; injuriously; intimately; definitely; undoubtedly; differently; unconsciously; peculiarly.
(See touch, melt, incline.)

AFFECTED

adverbs
conceitedly; foppishly; pretentiously; sentimentally; stiltedly; mincingly; simperingly; stagily; abominably; absurdly; ridiculously; ludicrously; disgustingly; pathetically.

AFFECTION

adjectives
true-hearted; dramatic; warm; enthusiastic; filial; reciprocal; hysterical; nervous; natural; tepid; responsive; divine; purest; maternal; tender; intense; spasmodic; inordinate; domestic; dutiful; crushed; subtle; heartwarming; admiring; paternal; overflowing; sympathetic; ludicrous; disappointed; unreciprocated; mutual; demonstrative; indiscriminating; mature; pious; wifely; unrequited; pastoral; temperate; inflammatory; untried; brotherly; peremptory; tempestuous; rabid; conjugal; well-grounded; doglike; overbrimming; sweet-toned; grateful; impulsive; healthful; involuntary; rational; perishable; playful; forced; respectful; ancient; concrete; trustful; overstrained; passionate; connubial; hollow; vulgar; vile; pretended; boundless; irrepressible; delirious; lasting; tacit; disinterested; sound; profound; nobler; generous; unreasoning; gleeful; coarse; tolerant; doubtful; confessed; foolish; blighted; wavering; long-suffering; stifled; sincere; beautiful; intimate; thoughtful; extreme; sheer; naive; frank; chaste; physical; unbounded; proud; tenacious; priceless; violent; immortal; sworn; zealous; sublime; sweet; sentimental; critical; undying; revived; ephemeral; embedded; calm; chilled; obvious; airy; childish; fastidious; quaint; aristocratic; stiff; awkward; disagreeable; languid; teasing; absurd; spruce; showy; deliberate; injudicious; comical; patent.

verbs
advert to—; alienate—; analyze—; arouse —; attach—to; awaken—; bear—; betoken —; bind by—; bless with—; blind by—; breed—; capture—; chain with—; coerce—; compel—; contain—; crave—; deflect—; demand—; denote—; desire—; detect—; disclose—; display—; earn—; eat up—; elicit —; enforce—; engage—; exempt from—; express—for; feed upon—; force—; gain—; impair—; impress by—; influence—; inspire with—; join in—; kindle—; lend—; manifest—; meet the demands of—; motivate by —; object to—; oppose—; overrule by—; pledge—; pour forth—; preserve—; pretend to—; produce—; promote—; regain—; regard with—; remove—; restrain—; reveal—; scatter—; sense—; shun—; speak—; starve for—; steal—; swear—; temper—; tender—; thwart—; transfer—; transplant —; uproot—; wean from—; weigh—; wrestle with—; —alternates; —bursts out; —ceases; —gets out of bounds; —grows; —links together; —prevails; —spreads; —springs from; —strays; —sways; —thickens; —turns; —warms; —wavers.
(See attachment, love, feeling, emotion.)

AFFECTIONATE

adverbs
enthusiastically; deeply; extremely; dutifully; heart-warmingly; tempestuously; gratifyingly; warmly; sincerely; temperately; im-

pulsively; playfully; naturally; paternally; respectfully; innately; essentially; confessedly; beautifully; sweetly; frankly; devotedly; apparently; incongruously; professedly; hypocritically; openly; sentimentally; truly; pretentiously; inherently; intensely; ludicrously; moderately; passionately; consistently; ostentatiously; maternally; spasmodically; obviously; steadily; tacitly; foolishly; intimately; proudly; furtively.

AFFILIATION

adjectives
growing; cosmopolitan; party; cultural; intimate; tender; undesirable.

verbs
arrange—; ascertain—; benefit by—; block —; deny—; destroy—; determine—; establish—; impute—with; maintain—; preclude —; recognize—; sponsor—; suspend—; wangle—; —aims at; —complicates; —engenders.

(See association, connection, relationship.)

AFFINITY

adjectives
peculiar; commercial; elective; natural; uncanny; temperamental; secret.

AFFIRM (*v*)

adverbs
plausibly; solemnly; plainly; distinctly; facetiously; venomously; categorically; definitely; significantly; constantly; vigorously; smilingly; glaringly; nonchalantly; gravely; splendidly; boldly; brazenly; swiftly; readily.

(See assert, state.)

AFFIRMATION

adjectives
smiling; glaring; nonchalant; grave; splendid; bold; brazen; ready; swift.

AFFLICT (*v*)

adverbs
distressingly; suddenly; desperately; irremediably; bitterly; poignantly; sharply; undeservedly; recurringly; harshly; fatally; brutally; temporarily.

(See persecute, scourge, harass, trouble.)

AFFLICTED

adverbs
distressingly; direly; tragically; unnecessarily; unfortunately; sadly; miserably; incurably; painfully; agonizingly; wretchedly; grievously.

AFFLICTION

adjectives
respiratory; corporal; irremediable; desperate; bitter; poignant; mute; sharp; undeserved; recurring; rending; harsh; fatal; brutal; palsied; temporary.

verbs
ameliorate—; amend—; bear—; bind in—; break with—; carry—; comfort—; conceal —; deliver—; diagnose—; endure—; grant refuge from—; purify by—; shake off—; visit in—; —bites; —follows; —grows; —persists; —prevents; —refines; —softens; —threatens.

(See trouble, tribulation, distress, grief, misfortune.)

AFFLUENCE

verbs
attain—; bask in—; enjoy—; glitter in—; manifest—; raise to—; reduce from—; revive—; wallow in—.

(See wealth, riches, abundance, plenty.)

AFFLUENT

adverbs
gorgeously; enormously; comfortably; fortunately; pleasantly; agreeably; serenely; snugly; enviably; complacently; sufficiently; smugly; graciously.

AFFORD (*v*)

adverbs
undoubtedly; scarcely; indiscriminately; abundantly; inadvertently.

(See furnish, yield, produce.)

AFFRAY

adjectives
murderous; nocturnal; head-punching; fierce; bloody; violent.

AFFRONT

adjectives
rude; personal; sacrilegious; deliberate; unmerited; unintentional; intolerable; vile; unnecessary; brutal; boorish; ill-mannered; brazen.

AFFRONT (*v*)

adverbs
impudently; brazenly; rudely; personally; sacrilegiously; deliberately; unmeritedly; unintentionally; intolerably; vilely; unnecessarily; brutally; boorishly; ill-manneredly.

(See insult, aggravate.)

AFFRONTED

adverbs

easily; definitely; slightly; quickly; increasingly; unreasonably; foolishly; senselessly; absurdly; unjustly; unfairly; deeply.

AFRAID

adverbs

superstitiously; timidly; childishly; queerly; curiously; dreadfully; horribly; perpetually; oddly; strangely; starkly; mysteriously; faint-heartedly; cautiously; timorously; extraordinarily; unquestionably; secretly; terribly; mortally; foolishly; frightfully; constantly; cravenly; temperamentally; distressingly; unwontedly; unusually; incredibly; shudderingly; surprisingly; unutterably; incomprehensibly; obviously; genuinely; suspiciously; idiotically; nervously.

AFTERMATH

adjectives

disastrous; psychological; barren; confused; melancholy; unfortunate; sordid; troublesome; hectic; sorry.

AFTERNOON

adjectives

inspiring; brilliant; dismal; gloomy; ghastly; cheerless; dull; restless; raw; fragrant; serene; wintry; rain-washed; humid; sunless; breezeless; tropical; drowsy; clement; drear; golden; rosy; rain-soaked; darkling; declining; showery; sweltering; formal; glamorous; sultry; miserable; fervid.

verbs

beguile—; devote—; fritter away—; nap away—; pass—; shadow—; tarry till—; while away—; —advances; —pales; —pauses; —pushes forward; —spends itself; —takes wing; —unrolls; —vanishes; —wanes; —wears on.

(See evening.)

AGE

adjectives

pastoral; comfortable; endless; bygone; primitive; seasoned; abominable; imponderable; distant; crabbed; prehistoric; gray-grown; infidel; enlightened; feeble; unnumbered (pl); glorious; relative (pl); countless (pl); paleozoic; prolific; venerable; immemorial; aesthetical; barbarous; Pliocene; dim-lit; embittered; susceptible; infinite; green; polished; deathless; heroic; jostling; remote; pre-chromo; realistic; frostless; advancing; ripe; patriarchal; responsive; besotted; waning; historic; prudish; hoary; blissful; geologic; energetic; fabulous; middle; streamlined; advanced; receptive; decrepit; retirement; earnest; unregarded; tender; dingy; glamorous; roistering; marriageable; approaching; homely; renowned; rosy; honored; critical; heartless; prescribed; masquerading; electric; discreet; weak; dull; contented; mature; rotting; ambitious; exorbitant; muddled; revolutionary; live; unresting; premature; credulous; pre-scientific; weary; degenerate; fabled; classical; sententious; hectic; dateless; material; iron-bound; licentious; ruthless; flourishing; indeterminate; haggish; adolescent; sedate; debutante; disillusioned; discretionary; vast; eligible; unhonored; mellowed; inventive; withered; golden; machine; raucous; tabloid; pagan; graceless; robust; sordid; decayed; ripened; unorthodox; practical; vanished; leisurely; stalwart; toddling; primeval; hoary; talking; shallow; successive (pl); sentimental; dangerous; undiscriminating; independent; buried; innumerable (pl).

verbs

advance in—; attain—; clothe—in glory; come of—; decay with—; defy—; denote—; dim with—; enfeeble with—; ensnare with—; exempt from—; honor old—; incapacitate with—; increase with—; judge—; knock at the door of—; limit—; renew—; reveal—; scoff at old—; serve—; stoop with—; succumb to old—; —accounts for; —adorns; —s average; —cracks; —decays; —deposits; —diminishes; —dispels; —enfeebles; —honors; —impairs; —measures; —mellows; —prevails; —privileges; —retards; —shrivels; —steals on; —strikes; —wears; —withers; —wrinkles; —yellows; attribute to—; belong to—; classify —s; corrupt—; denounce—; designate—; divide into—; epitomize—; excel—; fade into —s; gild—; glorify—; mark—; mechanize—; outlive—; pervade—; proclaim—; represent—; symbolize—; terminate—; usher in—; —s behold; —recognizes.

(See maturity, era, epoch, generation.)

AGED

adverbs

prematurely; terribly; tragically; pathetically; patriarchally; dingily; ridiculously; mournfully; uncommonly; desolately; contentedly; rosily; datelessly; lamentably; comfortably; crabbedly; hoarily; feebly; incredibly; wondrously; mellowly; honorably.

AGENCY

adjectives

effective; volcanic; ordained; secret; external; conservative; all-sufficient; subtle; sole; appropriate; divine; supernatural; regulative; luciferal; technical; bureaucratic; bargaining; ubiquitous; organized; conducive; charitable; law-enforcing; mitigating; curative; myriad (pl).

verbs

administer—; assume—; consolidate—; develop—; create—; employ—; exclude from —; license—; obtain—; operate—; register with—; require—; squeeze (colloq.)—; terminate—; weld —s into a unit; —acts for; —advocates; —authorizes; —charges; —commissions; —functions; —handles; —offers; —places; —promotes; —recommends; —stimulates; —surrenders functions.

AGENT

adjectives

dominant; consular; imaginative; enterprising; remedial; unscrupulous; catalytic; cleansing; stimulating; diplomatic; publicity; purchasing; fiscal; coloring; trustworthy; energetic; physical; involuntary; recruiting; confidential; vigilant; corrosive; superfluous; purifying; accredited; cajoling; advance; rapacious.

verbs

appoint—; authorize—; commission—; delegate to—; deliberate—; discredit—; employ —; endow—; evade—; exert—; direct—; frustrate—; hearten—; rely upon—; remunerate—; request—; vest in—; yield to—; —accounts for; —acts for; —agitates; —assists; —bickers; —conducts; —contrives; —deliberates; —distributes; —enforces; —exerts; —implies; —negotiates; —operates; —profits; —represents; —slumbers; —solicits; —stipulates; —transacts; —vanishes.

(See representative, operator, factor.)

AGGRAVATE (v)

adverbs

arrogantly; brutally; continually; obviously; detrimentally; unceasingly; painfully.

(See intensify, irritate, provoke.)

AGGREGATION

adjectives

enormous; notable; glamorous; indefinable; congenial; simple; continuous.

AGGRESSION

adjectives

wanton; wilful; jealous; conscienceless; fiery; brisk; ruthless; merciless; destructive; ill-timed.

verbs

anger by—; anticipate—; avenge—; bear—; bulwark against—; check—; crush with—; denounce—; dread—; encounter—; oppose —; protest against—; provoke—; renounce —; resent—; resist—; save from—; submit to—; surrender to—; wear out by—; —flourishes; —saps; —staggers; —undermines.

(See assault, attack, intrusion, invasion.)

AGGRESSIVE

adverbs

boldly; offensively; truculently; bluntly; presumptuously; impertinently; unbecomingly; unwarrantedly; daringly; courageously; fearlessly; calmly; steadily; persistently; incurably; gallantly; pluckily; heroically; confidently; doggedly; criminally; savagely; indomitably.

AGGRESSIVENESS

adjectives

male; crocodilian; dynamic; sullen; forced; predatory; war-like; unthinking; brutal.

AGGRESSOR

verbs

agitate against—; badger—; blockade—; curse—; defend against—; denounce—; disconcert—; disorganize—; mobilize against —; punish—; repel—; —assails; —assaults; —depresses; —encroaches; —invades; —provokes; —seizes; —sets upon; —sweeps; —attacks.

(See intruder, trespasser.)

AGGRIEVE (v)

adverbs

mortally; painfully; brutally; bitterly; deeply; heartlessly.

AGHAST

adverbs

utterly; wanly; amazingly; amazedly; astoundingly; wonderingly; blankly; staringly; breathlessly; wordlessly; indescribably; stupidly; tremulously; fearfully.

AGILE

adverbs

nimbly; gracefully; unusually; swiftly; briskly; actively; alertly; surprisingly;

youthfully; slenderly; clumsily; unexpectedly; quickly; dangerously; mentally; physically; smartly; light-footedly; spryly; fleetly; trippingly; lightly

AGILITY

adjectives
graceful; grotesque; sailor-like; astonishing; spidery; acrobatic; unsurpassed; feline; tigerish; apish; rare; unusual.

AGITATE (v)

adverbs
convulsively; considerably; indescribably; fiercely; greatly; gently; violently; internally; nervously; feverishly; vigorously; incessantly; recurrently; destructively; visibly; intellectually; markedly.

(See disturb.)

AGITATION

adjectives
revolutionary; indescribable; gentle; violent; profane; internal; nervous; legitimate; gloomy; feverish; throbbing; vigorous; indignant; preliminary; incessant; convulsive; recurrent; destructive; inner; student; bewildered; smothered; visible; intellectual; marked; wearying; unflinching; wholesale; righteous; wide-spread.

verbs
accustom to—; admire—; allay—; cease—; discuss—; flutter in—; infect with—; introduce—; keep in—; kindle—; menace by—; express—; produce—; provoke—; resume—; stir—; set up—; understand—; witness—; —arises; —arouses; —disorganizes; —disturbs; —excites; —ignites; —impassions; —moves; —perturbs; —stirs; —terrifies; —unsettles.

(See emotion, commotion, disturbance.)

AGITATOR

adjectives
veteran; headstrong; unscrupulous; earnest; didactic; deft; extreme; sincere; dangerous; willing; adept.

AGONY

adjectives
profound; envenomed; tearless; inglorious; mute; unattended; vulgar; unconquerable; mortal; delirious; fiery; nervous; crowning; supreme; keen; blank; dying; childless; nameless; final; convulsive; hot; thudding; acute; multitudinous (pl); cowardly; utter; rending; loathsome; internal; remittent; prolonged; heartfelt; mental; frightful; exquisite; stern; superstitious; unspeakable; piercing; secret; prophetic; scathing; ill-fated; amorous; helpless; concentrated; cold; excruciating; human; unendurable; spiritual; indescribable; invisible; throbbing; last; speechless; intensified; impotent; bitter; blinding; benumbing; timeless; relentless.

verbs
alleviate—; convulsed in—; distort with—; efface—; endure—; face—; impose—; prolong—; relish—; shriek in—; stir with—; strive in—; struggle in—; wrench in—; writhe in—; —abates; —clutches; —confuses; —despairs; —distresses; —shoots.

(See distress, pain, anguish, torture.)

AGREE (v)

adverbs
pleasantly; universally; tacitly; gravely; solemnly; heartily; voluntarily; magnanimously; cheerfully; listlessly; cordially; completely; meekly; mutually; fervently; blandly; wholly; accordingly; passively; unanimously; comfortably; reluctantly; privately; definitely; amicably; pacifically; tentatively; sensibly; politely; reassuringly; fatuously; verbally; voluntarily; vehemently; emphatically; unhappily; authoritatively; benignly.

(See accord, acquiesce, comply, grant.)

AGREEABLE

adverbs
consistently; obviously; openly; frankly; sweetly; essentially; warmly; gratifyingly; extremely; unaffectedly; courteously; comfortably; pleasantly; placidly; gravely; unfailingly; generously; graciously; smilingly; considerately; sincerely; cordially; quietly; remarkably; ostentatiously; charmingly; singularly; genuinely; happily.

AGREEMENT

adjectives
substantial; stringent; mutual; diplomatic; tacit; loose; amicable; pacific; unanimous; working; preliminary; undisclosed; tentative; moratory; provisional; corrupt; sensible; effective; water-tight; polite; blissful; conscientious; hearty; reassuring; noncommittal; fatuous; despotic; verbal; voluntary; vehement; emphatic; unhappy; compromising; iron-clad; binding; enforced; authoritative.

verbs
accept—; assent to—; avow—; breach of—;

bring to—; cement—; come to—; conform with—; consent to—; consolidate—; construct—; consummate—; declare—; default—; deny—; disregard—; dissent from—; enter into—; execute—; express—; formulate—; fulfill—; illustrate—; imply—; "junk"—; negotiate—; perfect—; prescribe—; reach—; repudiate—; sanction—; scrap—; set forth in—; shape into—; subject to—; tie down with—; violate—; —cements; —consolidates; —expires; —manifests; —reveals; —stands.

(See contract, compact, bargain.)

AGRICULTURAL

adverbs
seriously; playfully; spasmodically; seasonably; showily; enthusiastically; presumptuously; ridiculously; professionally; amateurishly; preachily.

AGRICULTURE

adjectives
scientific; crude; experimental; diversified; mechanical; variegated.

verbs
administrate—; appropriate—; classify—; commercialize—; conduct research in—; control—; cooperate in—; crystallize—; depress—; devastate—; develop—; doom—; educate—; employ in—; encourage—; exploit—; extend—; extend credit to—; feed—; foster—; grant to—; improve—; industrialize—; inflate—; instruct in—; insure—; isolate—; manage—; mechanize—; modernize—; nationalize—; organize—; pertain to—; promote—; protect—; regulate—; replenish—; reshape—; restrict to—; revolutionize—; subsidize—; subsist on—; supervise—; survey—; systematize—; teach—; —benefits from; —domesticates; —economizes; —experiments; —flourishes; —markets; —prospers; —rises; —succumbs to; —suffers; —unfolds; —yields.

(See industry.)

AID

adjectives
material; mutual; quickening; self-denying; welcome; preternatural; vigorous; positive; substantial; prompt; efficient; generous; invaluable; all-important; sovereign; practical; inconspicuous; artificial; fictitious; dubious; healthful; supernatural; gloomy; adventitious; reluctant; priceless; functional; loyal; extraneous; potential; enlightened; specific; vital; essential; sustaining; necessary.

verbs
abolish—; afford—; apply for—; apportion—; assist with—; assure—; avail of—; award—; call upon—; condone—; contribute—; deserve—; dispatch—; distribute—; enlist—; extend—; grant—; howl for—; interpose—; invoke—; lack—; lend—; limit—; march to—; offer—; pledge—; proffer—; prompt—; render—; require—; seek—; speed up—; subsidize—; support with—; swear—; trust in—; volunteer—; withhold—; —arrives; —disappears; —preserves; —redeems; —saves.

(See help, assistance, relief, cooperation, succor, subsidy.)

AID (v)

adverbs
gladly; secretly; modestly; materially; unquestionably; unobtrusively; treacherously; substantially; self-denyingly; vigorously; positively; promptly; efficiently; generously; invaluably; practically; inconspicuously; dubiously; gloomily; reluctantly; loyally; potentially; specifically; essentially; necessarily.

(See help, assist, foster.)

AILMENT

adjectives
neurotic; minor; correctible; physical; incurable; hereditary; emotional; imaginary; pernicious; childish; dreaded; mysterious; vague; mythical; chronic; feminine; nervous; obscure; grave.

verbs
complain of—; cure—; diagnose—; disregard—; ignore—; neglect—; relieve—; rout—; —indisposes; —springs from.

(See malady, illness, sickness, disease.)

AIM

adjectives
instructive; principal; lofty; undeviating; murderous; intelligible; unerring; ultimate; personal; heroic; apparent; conscious; poetic; unselfish; generous; fictitious; ulterior; illusory; deadly; deliberate; laudable; ambitious; elevated; unattainable; logical; altruistic; devotional; basic; sole; cherished; confessed; wild; sordid; infallible; sinister; paltry; futile; frustrated; irrelevant; altered; modest; fundamental; kindred; radical; novel; immediate; primal; vain; impracticable; double; sober; impossible.

verbs
applaud—; attain—; baffle—; cast out—; define—; design—; disguise—; dissipate—;

embrace—; encourage—; endorse—; fulfill —; picture—; promote—; propose—; realize—; restrict—; sanction—; set forth—; sum up—; wander from—; —conflicts; —elevates; —succeeds; —tends; affect—; avoid—; calculate—; direct—; estimate—; guide—; hinder—; lead—; level—; mark —; miss—; point—; take—; train—; —errs.

(See object, end, aspiration, purpose, direction.)

AIM (v)

adverbs
uselessly; deliberately; primarily; instructively; immediately; principally; loftily; undeviatingly; murderously; unerringly; apparently; heroically; consciously; poetically; unselfishly; generously; fictitiously; laudably; ambitiously; elevatedly; unattainably; logically; altruistically; basically; solely; confessedly; futilely; frustratedly; irrelevantly; modestly; fundamentally; radically; vainly; soberly; impossibly.

(See aspire, desire.)

AIMLESS

adverbs
lamentably; invariably; unfortunately; carelessly; happily; blithely; deplorably; unluckily; unhappily; moodily; gloomily; deliberately.

AIR

adjectives *(atmosphere)*
crisp; healthful; bracing; balmy; salt; mountain; vitalizing; tingling; invigorating; pungent; exhilarating; sparkling; scented; lofty; comfortable; luminous; polluted; vapory; unbreathed; troublous; sultry; jocund; frosty; ambient; stifling; glittering; precipitant; pernicious; darkened; shadowed; vital; dusky; misty; hushed; viewless; frigid; salubrious; tepid; muffled; wholesome; vibrant; vacant; raw; impalpable; thin; strangling; nocturnal; atmospheric; rarefied; enervating; delicious; genial; cleft; unjaded; foggy; fermenting; heavy; nipping; chilled; vivifying; interlunar; brisk; emerald; buoyant; singing; deoxidized; dewy; trackless; stinking; fetid; starry; caressant; scorching; tranquil; spiced; sharp; soothing; health-giving; circulating; conditioned; compressed; illimitable; translucent; moon-struck; wanton; sulphurous; pellucid; miasmic; penetrating; oppressive; desolate; pale; filtered; humidified; twilight; windless; tempest-charged; electric; upper; sanctified; cloudless; greedy; wholesome; dreamy; mineral; limpid; startled; sun-sweetened; purgatorial; inclement; pestilential; highland; laughing; murky; soul-sustaining; heaven-high; infected; mellow; free; summering; mouldy; impregnated; vitiated; toxic; acrid; moontide; dust-scented; crystalline; smoke-saturated; balsam-laden; forest-scented; rainswept; clammy; roseate; lifeless; aromatic; ruffled; buxom; clinging; glimmering; pleasant; tropic; perfumed; empyreal; luscious; blue; stagnant; spreading; eddying; transparent; yielding.

verbs
admit—; ascend into—; bask in—; beat—; blacken—; bore through—; build in—; change—; charge—; choke—with dust; compose—; compress—; condition—; consume—; cool—; dance in—; darken—; dart through—; deprive of—; detect in—; diffuse —; disappear into thin—; dissipate into—; distribute—; drink—; embalm—with; embrace—; exhale—; exhaust—; expel—; expose to—; fan—; float through—; flush—; hallow—; heave into—; hurtle through—; impregnate—; infect—; inflame—; inhale —; inject—; liquidize—; load—; lope into —; melt into thin—; mix with—; mount into—; navigate—; penetrate—; perfume —; permeate—; pervade—; pierce—; purge —; purify—; pursue in—; putrefy—; ravish —; remove from—; rend—; ride—; ripple —; rise into—; rule—; sail in—; saturate —; scent—; seep into—; shelter from—; smite—; sniff—; split—; stir—; subject to —; support in—; surge into—; suspend in —; sweep—; taint—; tinge—; vanish into —; vitiate—; warm—; —blows; —circles; —circulates; —consists of; —conveys; —diffuses; —expands; —fans; —lulls; —murmurs; —palpitates; —reeks; —resounds; —reverberates; —rings; —ripples; —rushes by; —scintillates; —seeps in; —sighs; —singes; —stirs; —surges in; —surrounds; —swirls; —thickens; —throbs; —trembles; —whispers; —whistles.

(See atmosphere, wind, breeze, ether.)

AIR

adjectives *(attitude)*
racy; ironical; professional; coquettish; hesitating; surly; monastic; elegant; proud; condescending; saucy; insouciant; youthful, carefree; confident; joyous; buoyant; hospitable; grotesque; perky; deliberate; abstracted; mystic; druid-like; prehistoric; unctuous; becoming; serious; protecting; perplexed; ardent; businesslike; inquiring; passionate; prosperous; dolorous; pathetic;

discomfited; prophetic; judicial; desperate; peculiar; proprietary; confidential; indefinable; plaintive; dejected; distant; self-confident; rustic; cold; patient; fantastical; lackadaisical; pouting; well-bred; encouraging; calm; sweet; polished; devilish; dashing; unaffected; imposing; disappointed; striking; distinguished; excited; tragic; undaunted; artless; pompous; shamed; furtive; playful; genteel; wheedling; pensive; citified; injured; sedate; wanton; roguish; insulted; contrite; womanly; virginal; frivolous; feline; jaunty; meditative; bewitching; sinister; forbidding; portentous; sagacious; riotous; appreciative; courteous; unapologetic; candid; youthful; pitiless; voluptuous; simple; languid; reserved; threatening; imperious; intellectual; reminiscent; glib; deprecating; intolerant; patronizing; passionless; composed; comic; engaging; celestial; virtuous; elegant; exquisite; masterful; aggressive; knowing; shrewd; appraising; sophisticated; elaborate; obedient; tranquil; staid; quizzical; enigmatic; lofty; supercilious; possessive; matter-of-fact; nonchalant; detached; insolent; ominous; dissipated; moody; irrational; belligerent; calculating; obstinate; irritating; scandalized; dogged; harassed; martyred; injured; distraught; shrinking; crestfallen; disconcerted; motherly; suave; exotic; masculine; incorrigible; colloquial; cherubic; critical; indulgent; salubrious; appreciative; deferential; disarming; sly; accommodating; grandiose; spiritual; majestic.

verbs
acquaint with—; address with—; adopt—; affect—; ape—; assume—; bear—of; communicate—; describe—; draw up with—; feign—; give —s to; invest with—; manifest—; treat with—; unfold—; —excites; —pleases.

(See manner, mien, appearance, demeanor, expression.)

AIR

adjectives (*tune*)
wizard; stirring; martial; light; melancholy; flippant; patriotic; lilting; mournful; plaintive; persistent; haunting; nostalgic; memorable; heartfelt; militant.

verbs
accompany—; arrange—; chorus—; compose—; harmonize—; hum—; play—; recognize—; sing—; spoil—; synchronize—; whistle—; —charms; —cheers; —enchants; —expresses; —gladdens; —moves; —stirs.

(See melody, tune.)

AIRPLANE

adjectives
multi-engined; droning; adventitious; obsolete; commercial; fleet; metal; transcontinental.

AIRY

adverbs
gracefully; exquisitely; boyishly; youthfully; lightly; cheerfully; inexpressibly; racily; blithely; gaily; elegantly; saucily; proudly; carelessly; joyously; confidently; buoyantly; mystically; prophetically; proprietarily; fantastically; devilishly; dashingly; imposingly; artlessly; playfully; wantonly; roguishly; jauntily; bewitchingly; engagingly; elegantly; superciliously; nonchalantly; suavely; smoothly; indulgently; disarmingly; slyly; fashionably; stagily; conceitedly; refreshingly; racially.

AISLE

adjectives
shadowy; cathedral; winding; grassy; gloomy; long-drawn; teeming; pillared; silent; narrow; raucous; leafy; forest; cloistered; slender; gorgeous; moldering.

verbs
amble down—; arch—; block—; bound down—; build—; divide into—; drift down—; extend—; flank—; form—; indicate—; labor up—; negotiate—; obstruct—; open—; pace—; separate by —s; speed down—; tear up—; traverse—; trip down—; walk down—; widen—; —bisects; —divides; —extends; —leads; —runs; —swallows one up.

(See passage.)

ALACRITY

adjectives
marvelous; gladsome; incredible; peculiar; sparkling; unequalled; comical; momentary; light-footed; nimble; feigned; eager; warlike; rhythmic; enthusiastic; headlong; keen; noteworthy; nervous.

ALARM

adjectives
serious; groundless; vague; superstitious; unnecessary; high; nocturnal; perpetual; tremulous; faint; profound; spectral; manifest; shrill; evident; grave; imminent; scandalized; unfounded; painful; imbecile; grim; mute; abrupt; midnight; uneasy; sounding; friendly; grisly; deadly; incessant.

verbs
answer—; bewilder by—; blow—; broadcast—; burden with—; check—; chime—; cry—; discourage undue—; excite—; exclaim in—; give rise to—; incite—; occasion—; peal—; produce—; recoil in—; respond to—; shake with—; shudder in—; signal—; sound—; strike—; suppress—; take—; transmit—; —awakens; —clangs; —demoralizes; —dismays; —disturbs; —notifies; —signifies; —spreads; —startles; —steals over one; —subsides; —summons; —surprises; —vanishes; —warns.
(See terror, fright, consternation, apprehension, panic, dismay, fear, dread, warning, signal.)

ALARM (v)

adverbs
sincerely; fearfully; seriously; astoundingly; exceedingly; groundlessly; unnecessarily; vaguely; superstitiously; perpetually; faintly; profoundly; manifestly; gravely; painfully; abruptly; incessantly.
(See terrify, frighten, scare.)

ALCOHOL

verbs
abstain from—; apply—; banish—; bloat with—; clean with—; concentrate—; condemn—; consume—; contain—; crave—; denature—; detect—; dilute—; dissolve in—; distill—; dose with—; ferment into—; formulate—; heat with—; indulge in—; injure with—; manufacture—; methylate—; power with—; prod with—; purvey—; redistill—; reduce to—; reek with—; reinforce by—; resist—; respond to—; restrict—; saturate with—; solace with—; stain with—; steep in—; stimulate with—; taint with—; utilize—; vaporize—; —accelerates; —contracts; —deadens; —depresses; —derives from; —dulls; —expands; —flames; —inebriates; —influences; —intoxicates; —menaces; —occurs in; —penetrates; —plays a role; —poisons; —preserves; —ravages; —retards; —soothes; —stimulates.
(See wine, liquor, whiskey, ale, etc.)

ALE

adjectives
nut-brown; home-brewed; spicy; unlimited; earth-cooled; bubbling; foam-flecked; gurgling; spirited; heaven-sent; sparkling; cheery; tempting; joyous.

verbs
appreciate—; brew—; consume—; deal in—; drink—; ferment into—; fill with—; flavor—; gulp down—; guzzle—; hop up—; imbibe—; medicate—; pour—; process—; revel in—; set up to a drink of—; swill—; warm with—; —inebriates; —intoxicates; —matures; —pacifies; —ripens; —sours; —stupefies.
(See beer, liquor.)

ALERT

adverbs
guardedly; extremely; wisely; resolutely; diabolically; eternally; zealously; embarrassingly; cautiously; suspiciously; terribly; comically; capably; amazingly; inordinately; passably; incessantly; mentally; nervously; uncommonly; keenly; coolly; warily; sharply; suavely; briskly; swiftly; signally.

ALERTNESS

adjectives
practical; mental; nervous; paradoxical; keen; fierce; flea-like; scientific; cool; quick; wary; sharp; sly; suave; brisk; swift; signal; undervalued.

ALIBI

adjectives
dubious; unquestioned; plausible; unbreakable; incontestable; air-tight; fantastic; faked; unprovable; admirable.

verbs
allege—; build—; concoct—; dispense with—; establish—; fabricate—; furnish—; introduce—; manufacture—; offer—; perjure—; pose—; prove—; regard—; resort to—; scrutinize—; set up—; snarl—; substantiate—; support—; tender—; verify—; —acquits; —bewilders; —confounds; —disconcerts; —proves.
(See plea, excuse.)

ALIEN

adjectives
unwashed; pseudo-intellectual; criminal; invading; objectionable; well-meaning; spying; unpatriotic; harmless.

verbs
admit—; appoint—; bilk—; comfort—; confuse—; defend—; define—; defraud—; delude—; dominate—; dupe—; exclude—; expel—; exploit—; hinder—; hoodwink—; incite—; legislate against—; naturalize—; outwit—; prejudice against—; restrict—; smuggle—; subsidize—; succor—; tolerate—; —agitates; —consumes; —demolishes; —domiciles; —immigrates; —rends; —resides; —sojourns in; —thwarts.
(See stranger, foreigner.)

adverbs
intrusively; irrelevantly; outlandishly; undeniably; ostentatiously; palpably; essentially; obviously; disagreeably; inimicably; inconceivably; unconcernedly; disinterestedly; relatively; discordantly; impertinently; fantastically; exotically; discordantly; incidentally; multifariously; remotely; strangely; unconformably; extraneously; exceptionally; inadmissably; objectionably; harmlessly; unpatriotically; unquestionably.

ALIENATE (v)

adverbs
irretrievably; completely; irreconcilably; temporarily; permanently; successfully; finally; spitefully.

(See transfer, separate.)

ALIENATION

adjectives
mental; complete; temporary; irreconcilable; permanent.

ALIMONY

verbs
appoint—; approve of—; award—; consent to—; decrease—; entitle to—; fall behind in—; imprison for—; lapse—; reward with—; seek—; settle—on; sue for—; win —; —supports.

(See allowance.)

ALIVE

adverbs
gaily; blithely; barely; resolutely; completely; eagerly; energetically; fortunately; happily; surprisingly; beamingly; briskly; industriously; alertly; animatedly; bustlingly; actively; diligently; friskily; restlessly; strenuously; gloriously; joyously; delightedly; rapturously.

ALLEGATION

adjectives
oft-repeated; prevailing; pointless; irrelevant; unsubstantiated; unsupported; insistent.

verbs
affirm—; blurt out—; declare—; deny—; disprove—; dispute—; disregard—; excuse —; hurl—; justify—; moderate—; overthrow—; persevere in—; plead—; propound —; protest—; prove—; refute—; reprove —; state—; voice—; —condemns; —effects; —supports; —validates; —warrants.

(See assertion, declaration, plea, statement.)

ALLEGE (v)

adverbs
emphatically; repeatedly; pointlessly; irrelevantly; insistently; heatedly.

(See state, maintain.)

ALLEGIANCE

adjectives
ill-defined; supreme; unflinching; unfaltering; passionate; vague; firm; absolute; self-sacrificing; divided; faithful; half-hearted; enthusiastic; constrained.

verbs
abandon—; affirm—; begrudge—; bid for —; cease—to; confer—; declare—; desert —; disavow—; dissolve—; exact—; follow with—; free from—to; gain—; imply—; pledge—; profess—; render—; renounce—; repudiate—; seek—; supplant—; swear—; throw off—; violate—; vow—; withdraw—; —binds; —comforts; —continues; —ties.

(See loyalty, devotion, fidelity, obedience.)

ALLEGORICAL

adverbs
abstrusely; openly; frankly; cleverly; disguisedly; ostensibly; ironically; typically; far-fetchedly; obtusely; complexly; incomprehensibly; palpably; evidently; thinly.

ALLEGORY

adjectives
horrid; tremendous; apt; philosophical; pompous; hidden; inappropriate; far-fetched.

ALLEVIATE (v)

adverbs
cheerily; markedly; tremendously; remarkably; slightly; apparently.

(See relieve, lighten, reduce, lessen.)

ALLEY

adjectives
blind; medieval; inclosing; labyrinthian; squalid; grimy; malodorous; slimy; unpromising; filthy; twisting; green; rat-infested.

verbs
approach—; border—; cower in—; lurk in —; saunter through—; skulk in—; slink through—; strike into—; —crawls with; —reeks; —resembles; —slumbers; —teems with; —turns; —twists; —winds.

(See street, passage, path, walk, way.)

ALLIANCE

adjectives
suspicious; entangling; defensive; amazing; long-desired; dubious; firm; treacherous; political; unholy; unspeakable; tribal; intimate; loose; epoch-making; bizarre; dissolved; prosperous; unhappy; matrimonial; iniquitous; extraneous; staunch; fitting; corrupt; unsurpassed; nuptial; accursed; formidable.

verbs
achieve—; acquire—; adhere to—; alter—; combine in—; conclude—; connect with—; contract—; contribute to—; defend—; deny —; disapprove of—; dissolve—; enhance —; entangle in —s; form—; found—; knit —; maintain—; preserve—; revise—; revoke—; sanction—; seek—; solidify—; stipulate—; terminate—; unite in—; —augments; —concludes; —crumbles; —discriminates against; —empowers; —enables; —enriches; —entangles; —fortifies; —insures; —knits; —maintains; —preserves; —promises; —reanimates; —reinforces; —rejuvenates; —revives; —solidifies; —stiffens; —stipulates; —sustains.

(See league, union, federation, coalition, relationship.)

ALLIGATOR

verbs
conserve —s; corner—; despatch—; exterminate —s; harpoon—; preserve—; prey upon—; prod—; spy on—; stock with —s; stuff—; —s abound; —attacks; —attains a length; —basks; —bellows; —burrows; —charges; —crawls; —crunches; —crushes; —deposits eggs; —devours; —draws his prey; —emits odors; —flips his tail; —floats; —frequents; —glides; —grunts; —hatches; —hibernates; —inhabits; —lashes; —lies in wait; —makes off with; —matures; —measures; —nips; —retreats; —roars; —slips into the water; —snaps; —splashes; —submerges; —suns; —surges; —swarms; —swings its tail; —tends its young; —thrashes about; —twists; —writhes.

(See reptile, crocodile.)

ALLOT (*v*)

adverbs
fairly; equitably; unjustly; unfairly; satisfactorily; magnanimously; impartially.

(See apportion, distribute, divide.)

ALLOW (*v*)

adverbs
ultimately; generously; grudgingly; graciously; subsequently; tacitly; reluctantly; liberally; handsomely; munificently; reasonably; lavishly; regularly; intermittently; impartially.

(See permit, consent, tolerate.)

ALLOWABLE

adverbs
expressly; always; scarcely; socially; officially; legally; obviously; evidently; patently; unconditionally; reportedly; apparently; unquestionably; indubitably; undoubtedly; manifestly; definitely; explicitly; palpably.

ALLOWANCE

adjectives
liberal; generous; handsome; munificent; reasonable; meager; due; tolerable; lavish; modest; regular; intermittent; niggardly; kingly; stated.

verbs
admit—; allot—; apportion—; award—; concede—; continue—; deduct from—; draw from—; exhaust—; husband—; laud—; limit—; oppose—; pledge—; restrict—; sanction—; spurn—; tolerate—; —astounds; —shrinks; —staggers.

(See salary, wages, amount.)

ALLUDE (*v*)

adverbs
publicly; poetically; indelicately; pointedly; superciliously; jocosely; sarcastically; distinctly; crudely; obscurely; perplexingly; scripturally; casually; playfully; metaphorically; slyly; sneeringly; disdainfully; contemptuously; monotonously; personally; irreverently; subtly; timidly; blasphemously; insultingly; condescendingly; scurrilously; jocularly; abstrusely; respectfully.

(See hint, intimate, refer.)

ALLUREMENT

adjectives
economic; taunting; entrancing; delightful; exquisite; siren; agreeable; overpowering; female.

ALLURING

adverbs
mysteriously; utterly; delightfully; disturbingly; designedly; intentionally; confoundedly; diabolically; bewilderingly; amazingly; unquestionably; wondrously; unexpectedly; surprisingly; coolly; radiantly; joyously; quietly; consciously; unconsciously; tauntingly; tormentingly; overwhelmingly; provokingly.

ALLUSION

adjectives
happy; distinct; obscure; incidental; scholarly; crude; contemporary; sarcastic; pointed; topical; perplexing; scriptural; casual; facile; parting; playful; metaphorical; delicate; sly; biverbal; sneering; disdainful; contemptuous; literary; monotonous; personal; indecent; stray; well-timed; irreverent; laudatory; hidden; subtle; mythological; rambling; timid; blasphemous; insulting; condescending; scurrilous; jocular; abstruse; respectful.

verbs
accept—; discern—; endure—; explain—; insert—; sport with—; weave in —s; —s abound; —s clutter; —s crowd; —encumbers; —enriches; —implies; —suggests; —weighs down.
(See reference, hint, suggestion.)

ALLY

adjectives
ancient; formidable; constant; treacherous; invaluable; powerful; brilliant; faithful; indispensable; perfidious; distrustful; illustrious; staunch; natural; sturdy; vigorous; sympathetic; unmanageable; lifelong.

verbs
abuse—; alienate—; combine with—; consult—; defend—; forsake—; outrage—; seek—; take for—; unite with—; welcome —; —collapses; —concurs; —s connive; —contributes; —cools down; —forfeits.
(See colleague, friend, partner.)

ALLY (*v*)

adverbs
closely; inseparably; exclusively; treacherously; invaluably; faithfully; indispensably; perfidiously; staunchly; naturally; sturdily; sympathetically; vigorously.
(See join, associate.)

ALMS

verbs
allot—; bestow—; contribute—; dole out—; donate—; entreat for—; merit—; ministrate —; pilfer—; provide—; relieve with—; scatter—; scorn—; solicit—; support by—.
(See charity, dole, gift.)

ALOOF

adverbs
coldly; proudly; shyly; timidly; arrogantly; superciliously; intellectually; naturally; dreamily; discourteously; deliberately; resolutely; unsocially; impenetrably; ponderously; inscrutably; mysteriously; maddeningly; becomingly; gruffly; gravely; augustly; imposingly; absurdly; magnificently.

ALOOFNESS

adjectives
natural; sweet; drowsy; dignified; dreamy; dainty; unbending; icy; mystic; abstract; courteous; silent; defensive; impenetrable; absent-minded; Olympian; detached; despairing; pardonable; ponderous; inscrutable; effective; becoming.

verbs
attain—; enshroud in—; maintain—; preserve—; withdraw from—; wrap in—; —dehumanizes; —indicates; —induces; —inhibits; —leads to; —results in; —starves.
(See reserve.)

ALTAR

adjectives
garlandless; dreaded; cold; smokeless; nuptial; honored; glowing; conjugal; auspicious; idolatrous; brazen; impious; favored; lofty; sacrificial; venerable.

verbs
accept on—; adorn—; attend—; bow before —; burn at—; cast down—; consecrate—; dedicate at—; desecrate—; disparage—; elevate—; encrust—; enshrine on—; erect —; hang on—; inscribe on—; lure to—; offer on—; perform at—; raise—; rear—; repose on—; sacrifice at—; stagger to—; swear by—; vow at—; worship before—; —fumes with incense; —graces; —rises; —stands.
(See platform, bier.)

ALTER (*v*)

adverbs
placidly; ridiculously; radically; appreciably; considerably; materially; profoundly; conspicuously; extremely; subsequently; invariably; frankly; significantly; sensibly; quantitatively; mysteriously; extensively; basically; subtly; markedly; seriously; intangibly; indefinably.
(See vary, change, transform.)

ALTERABLE

adverbs
frankly; conveniently; easily; extensively; fortunately; unfortunately; always; happily.

ALTERATION

adjectives
frank; significant; sensible; trifling; quanti-

tative; mysterious; basic; suggested; extensive; observable; subtle; marked; serious; intangible; indefinable.

verbs
detect—; dispute—; effect—; employ—; indicate—; modify—; ponder—; substitute —; yawn at—; —charms; —displeases; —effects; —enchants; —invalidates; —occurs; —offends; —pleases; —satisfies; —is wrought.
(See modification, change, variation.)

ALTERCATION

adjectives
monstrous; lurid; bitter; gesticulatory; high-pitched; wordy; domestic; deadly; unprovoked; violent; acrimonious.

ALTERNATION

adjectives
mad; periodical; endless; rapid; unconscious; intermittent; infinite.

ALTERNATIVE

adjectives
painful; pleasant; admirable; desperate; intolerable; unthinkable; dire; impossible; practicable; subtle; ghastly; grim; vague; contradictory; undesirable; inescapable; serious.

verbs
arrive at—; bewilder with—; conceive—; confront with—; countenance—; endorse—; explore—; extend—; mystify by—; propose —; reject—; request—; suggest—; —circumscribes; —curbs; —lies open; —limits; —puzzles; —remains.
(See option, preference.)

ALTITUDE

adjectives
bleak; dizzy; infinite; considerable; starlit; moderate; healthful; breezy; breath-taking; excessive; unbelievable; unattainable.

verbs
ascertain—; compute—; elevate—; exceed —; fix—; forfeit—; gain—; gauge—; heighten—; level off at—; maintain—; register—; rise to—; scale—; soar to—; —dazzles; —increases.

ALTRUISM

adjectives
genuine; noble; philanthropic; lofty; feeble; non-existent.

ALTRUISTIC

adverbs
sincerely; fanatically; pompously; vaingloriously; publicly; ostentatiously; extremely; instinctively; characteristically; truly; genuinely; amazingly; essentially; quixotically.

ALUMNUS

adjectives
distinguished; valuable; brother; successful; staunch; dependable; rabid; generous.

verbs
appeal to—; browbeat—; organize—; —associates; —i build; —celebrates; —i constitute; —i convene; —endows; —fosters; —i gather; —i nourish; —pledges; —relives; —i reunite; —revisits; —i stand behind.
(See graduate.)

AMALGAMATION

adjectives
compulsory; racial; ethnic; subtle; industrial; necessary; advantageous; vital.

AMATEUR

adjectives
persistent; enterprising; enthusiastic; complacent; inexperienced; deplorable; superficial; distinguished; literary; gifted.

verbs
bar—; brand as—; close to —s; define—; deride—; distinguish—; encourage—; exempt—; govern—; handicap—; outdistance —; purge —s; repudiate—; restrict —s; rule —s; safeguard—; sanction—; vindicate —; —aspires to; —attains; —barters; —competes; —cultivates; —devotes; —engages in; —participates; —preserves his status; —stresses.
(See novice.)

AMATEURISH

adverbs
hopelessly; youthfully; admittedly; eagerly; fancifully; fantastically; ambitiously; avidly; fervidly; enthusiastically; comically; pathetically; inexpertly; deplorably; unexpectedly.

AMAZE (v)

adverbs
perfectly; absolutely; ludicrously; indignantly; honestly; utterly; unboundedly; mutually; bewilderedly; unutterably; speechlessly; blankly; raptly; helplessly; ineffably; dumbfoundedly; haughtily; unconcealedly; senselessly; horribly.
(See astonish, surprise, astound.)

AMAZEMENT

adjectives

sheer; indignant; fond; honest; stupid; starry-eyed; stupefied; utter; mute; unbounded; rising; mutual; bewildered; half-incredulous; mocking; unutterable; speechless; critical; dawning; blank; rapt; wide-eyed; shocked; helpless; dumbfounded; ineffable; freezing; justifiable; startled; horrified; petrified; haughty; agonized; unconcealed; hurt; smothering; open-mouthed; uneasy; senseless.

verbs

augment—; confound with—; evince—; eye with—; feign—; overwhelm with—; paralyze with—; peer with—; petrify with—; smite with—; stupefy with—; —bewilders; —divulges; —manifests itself; —reveals; —seizes; —stuns.

(See astonishment, confusion, surprise, admiration, awe, bewilderment, perplexity, wonder.)

AMBASSADOR

verbs

accredit—; assign—; authorize—; charge —with; commission—; confer with—; delegate—; dismiss—; dispatch—; empower—; entrust—with; exchange —s; exclude—; exempt—; immunize—; induct—; install—; invest—with; maintain—; nominate—; ordain—; oust—; raise to the rank of—; recall—; retract—; suspend—; turn out—; unfrock—; —abrogates; —arbitrates; —arms with; —carries on; —conveys; —develops; —entreats; —has access to; —intercedes; —mediates; —ministers; —negotiates; —represents; —repudiates; —transmits.

(See agent, minister, official.)

AMBER

adjectives

limpid; pale; rich; clear; electrified; honey-colored; translucent; opaque.

AMBIGUITY

adjectives

unfortunate; verbal; apparent; subtle; disturbing; deliberate; undesirable.

verbs

admit—; brush away—; burden by—; clear away—; cling to—; develop—; disentangle —; dissolve—; distinguish—; express—; obscure with—; oppress with—; reduce—; remove—; —clouds; —deludes; —occurs; —puzzles; —vanishes.

(See uncertainty, obscurity.)

AMBIGUOUS

adverbs

unfortunately; disturbingly; deliberately; undesirably; evasively; obscurely; distressingly; offensively; suspiciously; undeniably; quibblingly; equivocally; perplexingly; obscurely; mysteriously; vexatiously; seriously; irritatingly; vaguely; disagreeably; insidiously; stupidly; unwisely; objectionably; unacceptably; cunningly.

AMBITION

adjectives

forceful; unbounded; misplaced; personal; warring (pl); criminal; abstracted; reasonable; social; ancestral; uninstructed; worthy; unquenchable; industrial; average; grandiose; sole; thick-sighted; racial; lofty; cherished; lifelong; thwarted; worldly; vaulting; vain; conflicting (pl); daring; unprincipled; insane; intense; unbridled; noisy; darling; foiled; primary; disquieting; peculiar; fierce; humble; honorable; wandering; moderate; sensible; imperial; kingly; persistent; mad; tremendous; sublime; soaring; disappointed; desultory; insatiable; absurd; unreined; corrupt; beastly; misdirected; undying; healthy; satisfied; blind; august; youthful; vulgar; inordinate; life-ruling; troublous; sinister; irreconcilable; political; odious; crushed; tacit; impassioned; private; unscrupulous; persevering; senile; exalted; praiseworthy; modern; resolute; aggressive; consuming; gnawing; spurring; boastful; indiscreet; petty; visionary; conceited; dictatorial; egotistical; dynastic; abjured; hypertrophied; latent; innate; undeviating; tempered; boundless; distempered; focalized.

verbs

achieve—; attain—; badger—; balk—; betoken—; breed—; characterize—; cherish —; chill—; choke with—; commend—; control—; credit—; cultivate—; derive—; devour with—; direct—; display—; dose with —; drop—; dwarf—; endow with—; enslave—; entertain—; exaggerate—; extinguish—; feed with—; fire with—; fling away—; frustrate—; fulfill—; further—; gratify—; hamper—; honor—; humor—; infect with—; inflame with—; inspire—; master—; nurse—; overleap—; placate—; realize—; reawaken—; rein—; relinquish —; restrain—; satisfy—; scoff at—; scotch —; stifle—; stimulate—; subordinate—; temper—; thwart—; whet—; —burns; —s conflict; —emboldens; —lures; —overleaps itself; —pushes; —soars; —suffers; —vaults.

(See aspiration, desire, eagerness.)

AMBITIOUS

adverbs
socially; extremely; unspeakably; inordinately; profoundly; mercilessly; unscrupulously; politically; ruthlessly; odiously; laudably; properly; dangerously; admirably; industriously.

AMBLE (*v*)

adverbs
joyously; industriously; gently; languorously; lazily; impudently; lackadaisically.

(See walk.)

AMBUSH

verbs
assault from—; attack from—; capture by —; conceal in—; draw into—; elude—; employ—; encounter—; hide in—; lay—; lie in—; lurk in—; perish in—; post in—; set up—; station in—; suspect—; tempt into—; walk into—; waylay in—; —arises; —succeeds; —surprises.

(See trap.)

AMEN

adjectives
hearty; hasty; solemn; sincere; throaty; husky; heavenly.

AMENABLE

adverbs
pleasantly; personally; entirely; wholly; scarcely; seriously; terribly; directly; agreeably; accommodatingly; willingly; satisfactorily; sufficiently; fortunately; happily.

AMENDMENT

adjectives
belated; rash; drastic; pending; beneficent; continual.

verbs
abandon—; abrogate—; adopt—; allow—; alter—; complete—; concur with—; deliberate—; disagree with—; discuss—; dismiss —; initiate—; insert—; oppose—; propose —; ratify—; reject—; repeal—; resolve—; subject to—; substitute—; veto—; violate —; —adjusts; —alters; —betters; —compensates; —corrects; —deprives; —expiates; —gives birth to; —modifies; —overthrows; —provides; —reforms; —remedies; —removes; —restricts; —stands.

(See change, improvement, correction.)

AMENITY

adjectives
ancient; social; hard-won; nonsensical; accepted; expected.

AMERICAN

adjectives
dashing; chauvinist; adventurous; eminent; loud; red-blooded; level-headed; intellectual; sensitive; liberal; stout-hearted; rapid-fire; virile; swift-moving; industrial-minded.

adverbs
loyally; thoroughly; completely; independently; dauntlessly; proudly; consciously; resolutely; ostentatiously; ridiculously; adventurously; bravely; essentially; obviously; distinctively; characteristically; insistently; consistently; persistently; dashingly; steadily; coolly; charmingly; informally; violently; volubly; restrainedly; serenely; confidently; unmistakably; undeniably; loudly; quietly; palpably; evidently; level-headedly; stoutly; invincibly.

AMERICANISM

verbs
adhere to—; ally with—; appeal to—; assault—; assert—; assimilate—; awaken—; cherish—; cite—; cultivate—; defend—; develop—; deviate from—; embrace—; endow with—; establish—; explore—; express —; federate—; hearten by—; inculcate—; ingrain—; insure—; interfere with—; laud —; menace—; molest—; motivate by—; pledge to—; proclaim—; promote—; resist—; retain—; retreat to—; ripen—; safeguard—; surround by—; sympathize with—; tamper with—; threaten—; unite in—; uphold—; verse in—; vest in—; —converges with; —embraces; —flounders; —flourishes; —forges through; —fosters; —languishes; —progresses; —promotes; —signifies; —survives.

(See patriotism.)

AMIABILITY

adjectives
impassioned; delightful; sincere; disconcerting; utmost; gushing; easy-going; placid; unwonted; native; condescending; rarefied.

AMIABLE

adverbs
charmingly; unfailingly; always; sincerely; unaffectedly; calmly; serenely; happily; cheerily; naturally; bewitchingly; softly; gently; enchantingly; unwontedly; unusually; habitually; incomparably; modestly;

winningly; ineffably; genuinely; becomingly; refreshingly; wonderfully; sweetly; graciously; frankly.

AMITY

adjectives
godlike; cordial; ghastly; mutual; rough; genial; generous; feigned; jealous.

verbs
abide in—; bind in—; cultivate—; despise —; disrupt—; found upon—; knit in—; link in—; promote—; radiate—; restore—; swear—; unite in—; —conduces; —fosters; —insures.

(See friendship, harmony, good-will, peace.)

AMMUNITION

verbs
assign—; cap—; cast—; consume—; contract for—; discharge—; exhaust—; furnish—; fuse—; guard—; handle—; ignite —; insert—; jacket—; project—; protect—; ration out—; replenish—; safeguard—; secrete—; stack—; store—; transport—; —detonates; —embraces; —saves; —shatters; —undergoes improvement.

(See explosives, shells.)

AMOROUS

adverbs
ardently; erotically; tenderly; lovingly; excessively; ostentatiously; fervidly; adoringly; idolatrously; infatuatedly; passionately; rapturously; yearningly; coquettishly; excitedly; flirtatiously; sweetly; philanderingly; seductively; enchantingly; winningly; wooingly; devotedly.

AMOUNT

adjectives
sufficient; excessive; stipulated; immense; cumulative; dangerous; exhausting; vast; exorbitant; fabulous; incredible; gigantic; indecent; unreasonable; prodigious; unprecedented; fantastic; appalling; colossal; ruinous; incalculable; goodly; sizable; average; traditional; stated; strategic; proportionate; lucrative; harmonious; comfortable; infinite; negligible; inexhaustible; inadequate; moderate; insignificant; undue; maximum; requisite; definite; appreciable; trifling; minimum; perceptible; preponderant; staggering; unheard-of.

verbs
aggregate—; anticipate—; calculate—; compute—; diminish—; discount—; estimate—; expend—; forecast—; gauge—; indicate—; magnify—; register—; sum up—; total—; view—; withdraw—; —dwindles; —exceeds; —recedes; —reverts; —rises.

(See quantity, total, sum.)

AMOUNT (v)

adverbs
collectively; sufficiently; excessively; immensely; cumulatively; dangerously; exhaustingly; vastly; exorbitantly; fabulously; incredibly; gigantically; indecently; unreasonably; prodigiously; unprecedently; fantastically; appallingly; colossally; ruinously; incalculably; sizably; proportionately; lucratively; harmoniously; infinitely; comfortably; inexhaustibly; moderately; insignificantly; definitely; appreciably; perceptibly; staggeringly.

(See reach, extend.)

AMOUR

adjectives
scandalous; classic; innocent; juvenile; delicate; passionate; fanciful; restless; discreet.

AMPHITHEATER

adjectives
Gargantuan; vast; immense; natural; wooded; colossal; sylvan; shaded; massive; florid; shadowy; splendid.

AMPLE

adverbs
generously; extensively; abundantly; liberally; amazingly; overwhelmingly; gratifyingly; astonishingly; capably; enormously; hugely; voluminously; immeasurably; immensely; magnificently; stupendously; splendidly; wastefully; boundlessly; illimitably; immoderately; incredibly; surprisingly; excessively; preposterously.

AMUSE (v)

adverbs
unconsciously; constantly; superficially; inwardly; genuinely; mightily; whole-heartedly; powerfully; secretly; libidinously; vociferously; considerably; indescribably; falteringly; undisguisedly; obviously; grimly; jovially; highly; impersonally; unspeakably; obscurely; good-humoredly; tolerantly; contemptuously; harmlessly; idly; endlessly; intimately; deliriously; detachedly; cynically; maliciously; puerilely; discreetly; ironically; benevolently; magnificently; haughtily; vaguely; wistfully; unconcealedly; emptily; sophisticatedly; insipidly; sheepishly; meretriciously; irritatingly; wholesomely; child-

ishly; intriguingly; fashionably; sparklingly; barbarously.

(See entertain, divert, please.)

AMUSED

adverbs

highly; slightly; definitely; postively; mildly; uproariously; unusually; tremendously; ingeniously; cleverly; constantly; greatly; gaily; indescribably; unspeakably; secretly; tolerably; heartily; idly; grimly; suitably; vaguely; foolishly; oddly; properly; fashionably; conventionally.

AMUSEMENT

adjectives

impersonal; unspeakable; obscure; good-humored; tolerant; worldly; contemptuous; harmless; favorite; abundant; hearty; secret; elegant; solitary; idle; puzzled; after-dark; racy; traditional; endless; intimate; delirious; detached; cynical; malicious; puerile; costly; discreet; innocent; sarcastic; healthy; ironic; benevolent; magnificent; mocking; mild; considerable; grim; undisguised; haughty; round-eyed; vague; wistful; unconcealed; empty; suppressed; sophisticated; scornful; wry; ribald; sly; reminiscent; facile; sheepish; heightened; meretricious; insipid; irritating; wholesome; childish; passing; intriguing; idle; fashionable; time-killing; sparkling; barbarous; evident.

verbs

absorb in—; afford—; attend with—; betray —; contrive—; crave—; cultivate—; dedicate to—; devise—; excite—; fall into—; indulge in—; revel in—; seek—; tickle with—; vary—; —affords; —attracts; —beguiles; —detains; —distracts; —diverts; —engages; —entertains; —grows out of; —invigorates; —relaxes.

(See diversion, entertainment, pastime, sport, pleasure.)

ANACHRONISM

adjectives

ineffective; moral; unconscious; flagrant; painful; bold; impossible.

ANAESTHETIC

verbs

absorb—; administer—; apply—; breathe—; confine—; discover—; dope with—; doze under—; drug with—; employ—; experiment with—; inhale—; inject—; introduce —; localize—; numb with—; relieve with —; sniff—; spray—; undergo—; —allays; —alleviates; —benefits; —benumbs; —comforts; —deadens; —depresses; —dulls; —freezes; —induces; —paralyzes; —relieves; —renders insensible; —restricts.

(See ether, chloroform.)

ANALOGOUS

adverbs

relatively; proportionally; approximately; closely; exactly; nearly; ridiculously; truly; interestingly; strikingly; internationally; remarkably.

ANALOGY

adjectives

striking; ironic; obvious; classic; intellectual; palpable; mysterious; astonishing; exaggerated; secret.

ANALYSIS

adjectives

scientific; flawless; exact; brilliant; learned; careful; thorough; logical; painstaking; vivid; keen-sighted; cautious; sound; cogent; revealing; trenchant; penetrating; rigorous; profound; probing; searching; minute; critical; intensive; microscopic; tortuous; shallow; abstruse; absorbing; unsparing; arbitrary; inadequate; illuminating; erroneous; obscure; involved; ruthless; merciless; complex; devastating; scathing; complete; frank; straightforward; philosophic; metaphysical; auditory; primary; legal; chemical; financial; exhaustive; elaborate; compact; comprehensive; thoroughgoing; grueling; final; interrelated; deliberate; cold; accurate; subtle; pedagogic; lucid; fine-spun; perspicacious; detailed; provocative; dispassionate; uncompromising; acute; ingenious; rational; intensive; tragic; patient; forceful; skilful.

verbs

answer with—; apply—; carry out—; clarify—; defy—; descend to—; display—; elude—; employ—; examine—; exhibit—; explain by—; introduce—; involve—; proceed by—; study—; submit to—; suggest—; summarize—; tabulate—; withstand—; yield to—; —assays; —breaks up; —concludes; —correlates; —cultivates; —decomposes; —defines; —determines; —differentiates; —discovers; —identifies; —precedes; —produces; —reduces; —resolves into; —restricts; —results in; —reveals; —separates; —solves; —teaches; —traces; —uncovers; —unearths.

(See investigation, examination.)

ANALYTIC

adverbs

brilliantly; learnedly; carefully; painstakingly; skilfully; cautiously; trenchantly; rigorously; profoundly; searchingly; minutely; critically; intensively; abstrusely; ruthlessly; mercilessly; scathingly; philosophically; primarily; exhaustively; tiresomely; coldly; offensively; accurately; impersonally; patiently; uncompromisingly.

ANALYZE (*v*)

adverbs

fully; scarcely; scientifically; adequately; exhaustively; flawlessly; exactly; brilliantly; learnedly; carefully; thoroughly; logically; painstakingly; vividly; skilfully; cautiously; soundly; cogently; penetratingly; rigorously; profoundly; probingly; searchingly; minutely; critically; intensively; microscopically; tortuously; shallowly; abstrusely; unsparingly; inadequately; involvedly; ruthlessly; mercilessly; devastatingly; scathingly; dispassionately; frankly; straightforwardly; philosophically; metaphysically; legally; chemically; financially; exhaustively; elaborately; comprehensively; finally; accurately; subtly; pedagogically; lucidly; perspicaciously; provocatively; dispassionately; uncompromisingly; ingeniously; rationally; patiently; forcefully.

(See discriminate, resolve.)

ANARCHIST

adjectives

moral; intellectual; communistic; theoretical; unthinking; rabid.

verbs

accuse—; apprehend—; combat—; condemn —; denounce—; disperse —s; execute—; expel—; take measures against—; —advocates; —blasts; —conceives; —denies; —disregards; —endeavours; —escapes; —executes; —maintains; —masses; —orates; —plunders; —promotes disorder; —rises; —rules; —scorns; —shatters; —struggles; —theorizes; —violates.

(See communist, terrorist.)

ANARCHISTIC

adverbs

ungovernably; dangerously; alarmingly; naively; youthfully; heedlessly; hatefully; enthusiastically; lamentably; deplorably; openly; actively; defiantly; insurgently; seditiously; restively; insubordinately; mutinously; rebelliously; violently; tumultuously; incorrigibly; persistently; obstinately; treasonably.

ANARCHY

adjectives

multitudinous; malignant; emulous; lawless; social; dormant; practical; moral.

verbs

abandon—; bear—; cast into—; conceive—; confuse—; control—; cope with—; crash into—; curse—; degrade by—; drift towards —; exclude—; expel—; fall under—; overthrow—; proclaim—; realize—; revive—; subject to—; suppress—; —abolishes; —advocates; —agitates; —appeals; —conflicts with; —confuses; —connotes; —degrades; —denounces; —destroys; —disorders; —dominates; —emancipates; —frees; —hurls back; —overlaps; —overthrows; —rages; —relates to; —repudiates; —resorts to; —strikes; —threatens; —violates.

(See revolution, confusion, chaos.)

ANATHEMA

adjectives

dire; violent; involuntary; incoherent.

ANATOMY

verbs

advance—; approach—; consult—; develop —; dissect—; practice—; protect—; rely on—; reveal—; segregate—; shrink—; shrivel—; sketch—; wither—; —admits; —analyzes; —applies to; —considers; —deals with; —defines; —denotes; —details; —detects; —develops; —dissects; —investigates; —produces; —rejects; —signifies; —specializes; —teaches; —traces; —treats of.

(See science.)

ANCESTOR

adjectives

rude; far-away; august; pious; dim; divine; symbolical; barbaric; martial; devout; renowned; remote; illustrious; cave-dwelling; heroic; primitive; forgotten; venerable; respected; roistering; adventurous; astute; seafaring; contemporary; solitary-minded; immortal; tainted; prehistoric; talented; frugal; lineal; immigrant; blue-blooded; aristocratic; benighted.

verbs

address—; anger—; bury with—; descend from—; hark back to—; honor—; idealize —; idolize—; inherit from—; invoke—; propitiate—; renounce—; revere—; sleep with—s; swear by—; trace—; venerate—; worship—; —bequeaths; —blesses; —counsels; —fades; —foreruns; —influences; —precedes; —vouchsafes.

(See father.)

ANCESTRY

adjectives

dubious; pre-human; illustrious; revolutionary; mixed; remote; rustic; insignificant; select; healthy; hard-working; shabby; spiritual; far-renowned.

ANCHOR

verbs

back—; cast—; cat—; come to—; drag—; drop—; fasten—; fish—; forge—; foul—; free from—; grapple with—; ground—; haul up—; heave up—; hoist—; hook—; let fall—; let go—; lie at—; lift—; load—; loose—; moor—to; raise—; rest—; ride at —; shackle—; shoe—; stow—; sweep for —; throw out—; tow—; weigh—; —bites bottom; —branches; —comes home; —drags; —entangles; —fixes itself to; —fouls; —holds; —moors; —resists; —rusts; —secures; —settles; —sinks; —slides down; —stabilizes; —strikes; —takes hold.

ANECDOTAL

adverbs

interestingly; racily; risquily; graphically; sentimentally; boisterously; insipidly; fruitily; drolly; ineptly; dismally; sparklingly; ponderously; edifyingly; endlessly; childishly; pertinently; entertainingly; startlingly; shockingly; amusingly; surprisingly.

ANECDOTE

adjectives

traditional; minute; chatty; amusing; sentimental; familiar; insipid; startling; authentic; childhood; trite; pertinent; fruity; long-buried; small-town; pointed; ponderous; sparkling; endless; harmless; edifying; illustrative; droll; badly-told; touching; gossipy; trifling; dismal; antique; inept; apt; satirical.

verbs

apply—to; avoid —s; collect —s; compile —s; dispel by means of —s; edit —s; elaborate—; enrich with —s; launch into—; manufacture—; narrate—; refer to—; reject—; relate—; retail —s; spice with —s; swell —s; venture—; weaken—; —betrays; —deals with; —entertains; —interests; —treats of.

(See story, narrative, incident.)

ANGEL

adjectives

ministering; painted; household; hovering; expectant; tutelary; accursed; avenging; light-invested; grave; rapturous; cheering; ancient; compassionate; invisible; bewitching; fallen; sensuous; rude; naughty; lugubrious; attendant; sorrowing; accusing; luminous; wrathful; flame-robed; benign; pearl-colored.

verbs

cast out—; conduct—; defy—; degrade—; deify—; etherealize—; exalt—; personify —; pray to—; summon—; transform into—; worship—; —appears; —ascends; —attends; —bears; —blesses; —descends; —exemplifies; —flutters; —guards; —hovers above; —ministers to; —proclaims; —represents; —salutes; —serves; —tends; —watches; —weeps.

(See God, cherub.)

ANGER

adjectives

murderous; sullen; slow; revengeful; momentary; disheartened; fatal; clamorous; fierce; hot; uneasy; headlong; savage; proud; righteous; wholesome; controlled; loyal; strident; terrified; tolerant; inordinate; unjust; unreasoning; merciless; dull; cold; stern; carnal; blistering; ferocious; injurious; mute; violent; implacable; assumed; well-feigned; sham; dumb; speechless; suppressed; smouldering; futile; white; pale; impotent; subdued; kindling; seething; blazing; scorching; consuming; flaring; whirlwind; devouring; passionate; incipient; latent; oblivious; quivering; cooling; frenzied; jealous; parental; black-browed; senseless; restrained; impetuous; uncharitable; genuine; uncontrollable; boisterous; arrogant; icy; savage; contemptuous; insane; confused; concentrated; puzzled; craven.

verbs

analyze—; blind with—; bristle with—; burn with—; cast—upon; cherish—; coddle —; control—; defer—; detour—; disarm—; exhibit—; expostulate in—; flash—; flush with—; incite—; kindle—; manifest—; pacify—; pale in—; project—; provoke—; rage in—; rebuke in—; repent—; revive—; scream in—; slay in—; sting with—; strike in—; swallow—; swell with—; unleash—; upbraid in—; vent—; vex with—; visit—upon; voice—; —abates; —blazes; —boils; —burns; —bursts out; —congeals; —consumes; —dies; —distresses; —exasperates; —falls; —flames; —flares up; —floods; —grieves; —inflames; —melts; —over-excites; —rages; —rises; —ruffles; —simmers; —startles; —subsides; —throbs; —wanes; —waxes.

(See fury, rage, wrath, exasperation, ire,

animosity, resentment, vexation, pique, frenzy.)

ANGER (v)

adverbs
violently; murderously; sullenly; slowly; revengefully; momentarily; fatally; clamorously; fiercely; hotly; savagely; inordinately; righteously; unjustly; unreasoningly; mercilessly; ferociously; injuriously; violently; implacably; speechlessly; futilely; impotently; passionately; frenziedly; jealously; senselessly; genuinely.
(See irritate, displease, offend, provoke.)

ANGLE

adjectives
salient; rakish; technical; astonishing; intricate; remote; projecting; peculiar; social; unfortunate; legal; odd; divergent (pl); elevated; oblique; obtuse; acute; precise; humanitarian.

verbs
bisect—; derive—; draw—; figure—; form—; increase—; inscribe—; maintain—; measure—; proceed from—; produce—; reckon—; trisect—; —adjoins; —corresponds.

ANGLER

adjectives
enthusiastic; insatiable; beginning; ardent; jubilant; expert; practiced; bungling; awkward; skilled; proficient; able.

ANGRY

adverbs
senselessly; sullenly; intolerably; hotly; obviously; righteously; foolishly; ridiculously; dangerously; icily; genuinely; uncontrollably; passionately; violently; sternly; implacably; unjustly; inordinately; insanely; naturally; ludicrously; unnaturally; curiously; strangely.

ANGUISH

adjectives
nameless; unspeakable; excessive; bodily; nauseating; dumb; mental; excruciating; keen; maddening; intolerable; sheer; startled; mortal; hopeless; indescribable; frightful; unbearable; bitter; profound; acute; tearless; soul-piercing; occult; strangling; perpetual; fierce; insufferable; universal; maternal; jealous; subdued; transient; dull; stifling; short-lived; audible; intimate; unuttered; grim; heart-rending; despairing; spiritual; killing; sickening; dark; abrupt; amazed; insupportable; passionate; sensational.

verbs
burst with—; choke with—; consume with—; cry out in—; endure—; escape—; heal—; hearken to—; heed—; lessen—; overwhelm with—; soothe—; strike with—; suffer—; tremble with—; vent—; wring the mind with—; waste one's soul in—; writhe in—; —oppresses; —rends; —splits; —tears; —wrings.
(See distress, pain, anxiety, agony, misery, torture.)

ANGULAR

adverbs
forbiddingly; unattractively; raw-bonedly; repulsively; stiffly; absurdly; awkwardly; gawkily; pathetically; ludicrously; ridiculously; youthfully; painfully; pitifully; wretchedly; distressingly; crookedly.

ANGULARITY

adjectives
solid; raw-boned; stiff; absurd; awkward.

ANIMAL

adjectives
bold; pugnacious; ferocious; uncongenial; stiff-legged; indigenous; alpine; envenomed; elusive; heroic; familiar; social; patient; malignant; sensual; sentient; domesticated; performing; herbivorous; meek; rational; predatory; carnivorous; outlandish; articulate; restive; balky; well-groomed; ignoble; prowling; hunted; elusive; preternatural; reasoning; hoofed; pampered; white-sterned; emaciated; ruminant; noble; vigorous; throwing; marine; native; diabolical; graminivorous; frugivorous; armorial; agile; grotesque; docile; burly; aquatic; water-loving; amphibious; savage; invertebrate; porcine; devoted; thin-skinned; intelligent; responsive; affectionate; tractable; sagacious; helpless; magnificent; sleek; stunning; reclining; trapped; tethered; wounded; careening; stricken; harassed; fretting; snorting; panic-stricken; squealing; recalcitrant; maddened; infuriated; snarling; blood-thirsty; enraged; depraved; gregarious; prowling; omnivorous; albino; lower; furry; unshod; gaunt; catlike; thick-skinned; sure-footed; nervous; stray; castrated; cautious; fabulous; marsupial; mangy; pachydermatous; oviparous; refractory.

verbs
breed—s; cage—; classify —s; clutch—;

conserve —s; corral —s; cross —s; decoy —; derive from—; discover—; distinguish —; domesticate—; dominate—; educate—; encounter—; ensnare—; exhaust—; exhibit —; experiment with—; exploit—; exterminate—; feed—; fondle—; groom—; harness —; improve—; infuriate—; inspect—; mate —; pat—; protect—; raise—; reproduce—; revert to—; search for—; stalk—; suffocate —; track—; train—; wheel—; —charges; —s cluster; —curls up; —feeds; —forages; —gestates; —gnaws; —hibernates; —hunts; —migrates; —s multiply; —occurs in; —perishes; —rages; —ranges; —reproduces; —roars; —scurries; —senses; —sniffs; —succumbs; —suckles.

(See beast, creature, brute.)

(See also specific animals, such as bear, cat, lion, etc.)

ANIMATE (v)

adverbs
impiously; fascinatingly; gladly; garrulously; characteristically; vividly; dazzingly; delightfully; picturesquely; mechanically; preternaturally.

(See stimulate, rouse.)

ANIMATED

adverbs
delightfully; eagerly; garrulously; excitedly; nervously; happily; rapturously; ecstatically; unusually; hilariously; gleefully; merrily; lightly; joyously; cheerfully; blithely; sparklingly; pleasingly; playfully; racily; energetically; vigorously; restlessly; resolutely; determinedly.

ANIMATION

adjectives
fascinating; glad; suspended; perspiring; garrulous; contagious; social; characteristic; vivid; dazzling; delightful; playful; transient; picturesque; returning; intense; mechanical; preternatural.

verbs
attain—; behold—; bestow—upon; buoy up with—; breathe out—; burst into—; counterfeit—; enliven with—; evince—; feign—; fire with—; impart—; incite to—; inject—; inspire with—; instil—; manifest—; provoke to—; recite with—; restore—; revive —; sparkle with—; suspend—; vitalize with —; woo with—; —enlivens; —fatigues; —flags; —flares up; —jades; —wearies.

(See vivacity, life, gayety.)

ANIMOSITY

adjectives
intensified; personal; sullen; jealous; ecclesiastical; rancorous; deep-seated; vindictive; savage; deadly; implacable; partisan; smouldering; relentless; emotional; bitter.

verbs
arouse—toward; bear—; break out into—; effect—; excite—; feed—; feel—; incite—; incur—; inherit—; manifest—; nurse—; regret—; revive—; stir up—; tend toward —; unveil—; —alienates; —breaks up; —damages; —disrupts; —exists between; —hinders; —wavers.

(See rancor, hatred, enmity.)

ANKLE

adjectives
delicate; generous; fragile; beefy; bony; wrenched; swollen; immaculate; slender; aristocratic; well-turned.

ANNALS

adjectives
dramatic; fabulous; mythic; factual; voluminous; priceless; ancestral; contemporary; tragic; fragmentary; historic; literary; bloodstained; ancient; gossipy; racy.

ANNEX (v)

adverbs
formally; swiftly; utterly; forcefully; readily; craftily; partially.

(See take.)

ANNIHILATE (v)

adverbs
utterly; surely; swiftly; mercifully; unprecedentedly; craftily.

(See destroy.)

ANNIHILATION

adjectives
utter; sure; swift; terrible; bloody; merciful; beastly; unprecedented; crafty.

ANNIVERSARY

verbs
anticipate—; applaud—; commemorate—; dramatize—; fete—; institute—; observe—; disregard—; stamp—; —follows; —is marked by; —recurs.

(See observance, celebration, day, event.)

ANNOUNCE (v)

adverbs
flatly; vociferously; oracularly; mercifully; sententiously; paternally; clamorously; explicitly; pompously; publicly; simultaneously; reluctantly; solemnly; arrogantly; virtuously; ostentatiously; formally; blandly;

abruptly; jokingly; officially; unreservedly; significantly; jubilantly; gleefully; authoritatively; blithely; flatteringly; finally; mournfully; dramatically; haltingly; brazenly; prematurely; tersely; gayly; briskly.
(See proclaim, advertise, publish.)

ANNOUNCEMENT

adjectives
lurid; flattering; calamitous; conciliatory; final; implicit; successive (pl); encouraging; initial; mournful; drastic; dramatic; droning; halting; formal; brazen; devastating; pending; dire; premature; exclusive; vain-glorious; formidable; post-prandial; terse.

verbs
broadcast—; cheer—; confirm—; declare—; deliver—; dispatch—; disseminate—; misconstrue—; notify by—; reiterate—; rise at—; substantiate—; —astounds; —bursts upon; —gives notice; —proclaims; —publicizes; —overtakes; —takes by surprise.
(See proclamation, advertisement, notice.)

ANNOY (v)

adverbs
blusteringly; obviously; sorely; intensely; greatly; positively; unduly; temporarily; mildly; savagely; markedly; jealously; frivolously; unavoidably; excessively.
(See trouble, aggravate.)

ANNOYANCE

adjectives
petty; unconcealed; prolonged; unique; undue; shocked; temporary; intense; mild; savage; internal; mock; marked; aristocratic; impotent; sharp; repressed; obvious; inhospitable; nervous; dangerous; jealous; frivolous; unavoidable; private.

verbs
avoid—; condemn—; dislike—; flush with —; frown with—; generate—; molest with —; occasion—; plague with—; rumble in —; temper—; tolerate—; vent—; —disgusts; —injures; —persists; —returns; —troubles; —vexes.
(See vexation, irritation.)

ANNOYING

adverbs
mischievously; accidentally; disastrously; devilishly; diabolically; intentionally; outrageously; painfully; teasingly; persistently; unintentionally; purposely; defiantly; revengefully; abominably; exceptionally; characteristically; wretchedly; tormentingly; maliciously; unbecomingly; increasingly; senselessly; unspeakably; deliberately.

ANNUL (v)

adverbs
virtually; wisely; quickly; unthinkingly; promptly; shrewdly.
(See abolish, reverse.)

ANOINT (v)

adverbs
sacrificially; religiously; perfunctorily; daily; occasionally.
(See smear.)

ANOMALY

adjectives
monstrous; dreadful; curious; noble; racial; peculiar.

ANONYMITY

adjectives
scrupulous; illegitimate; heartless; carefully-preserved; politic; necessary; defensive; desperate; cowardly; enforced.

verbs
bury in—; clothe in—; disguise in—; ensconce in—; hide in—; lend—; maintain —; mystify with—; preserve—; prowl in—; remain in—; resort to—; retire from—, skulk in—; slink in—; steal into—; surround with—; veil in—; write in—; —cloaks; —conceals; —impresses; —masks.
(See secrecy.)

ANONYMOUS

adverbs
mysteriously; naturally; obviously; necessarily; securely; safely; forever; scrupulously; legitimately; politically; defensively; timidly; bashfully; shyly; unaccountably; evasively; hopelessly; irretrievably; astonishingly; vaguely; perplexingly; undecipherably; unfathomably; enigmatically.

ANSWER

adjectives
definite; clinching; efficient; contemptuous; indignant; accurate; concrete; requisite; affirmative; negative; disconsolate; evasive; categorical; magnanimous; flippant; consenting; authoritative; verbal; comprehensive; bewildered; favorable; impatient; economical; unconsidered; worthy; doleful; enigmatical; discouraging; meaningless; deft; admissible; explicit; perfect; memorable; quavering; stubborn; sufficient; ready; boorish; cryptic; measured; boun-

tiful; definitive; vague; vehement; imperious; impertinent; oral; candid; argumentative; haughty; laconic; convincing; soul-sufficing; admirable; casual; amazing; proud; skilful; scorching; rash; incoherent; intelligible; insulting; fit; apt; indulgent; practical; animated; reassuring; respectful; impressive; comforting; satisfactory; courteous; illuminating; logical; conclusive; cool; pertinent; surly; equivocal; irritable; insolent; scathing; lame; harsh; dilatory; unorthodox; uninteresting; relevant; prodigal; disquieting; sardonic; pungent; sharp; exultant; dramatic; breathless; crushing; partial; tentative; cautious; inevitable; instantaneous; simultaneous; ultimate; rueful; unconscious; impromptu; time-honored; prescribed; mechanical; mollified; confident; significant; broken; impetuous; impulsive; fateful; matter-of-fact; irrefutable; agnostic; mild.

verbs
address—; appeal for—; approve—; bark —; bind to—; confine—; constitute—; defend—; deliver—; draw—from; echo—; entreat—; evade—; evolve—; exhort—; express—; extort—; fire back—; fling back —; frame—; fumble—; glean—; hang on —; hit upon—; justify—; marvel at—; merit—; mock—; muffle—; owe—; petition—; protest—; reject—; respond with—; signal—; snap—; stir to—; supply—; sustain—; sweeten—; tabulate —s; tear—from; volunteer—; word—; wrench—from; —accuses; —arises; —charges; —claims; —clamors; —contradicts; —implies; —informs; —invalidates; —pleases; —pledges; —rebuts; —reveals; —satisfies; —solves; —states.

(See reply, retort, response, defense.)

ANSWER (v)

adverbs
gruffly; candidly; haughtily; uncomfortably; energetically; evasively; bluntly; darkly; breathlessly; sulkily; affectionately; sagely; casually; volubly; listlessly; persistently; yawningly; carelessly; pointedly; enigmatically; stubbornly; proudly; definitely; tartly; hysterically; reluctantly; sadly; falteringly; unconcernedly; gravely; doggedly; directly; sententiously; completely; triumphantly; hoarsely; brusquely; laughingly; stolidly; cautiously; curtly; impatiently; nervously; desultorily; affirmatively; visibly; faithfully; bitterly; obstinately; thoughtfully; impetuously; effectually; guardedly; evasively; bravely; readily; distinctly; candidly; respectfully; emphatically; squeamishly; ponderingly; surlily; coherently; challengingly; cynically; bashfully; knowingly; passionately; petulantly; hotly; non-committally; rancorously; instantly; simply; affirmatively; monosyllabically; laconically; directly; excitedly; evasively; indignantly; civilly; mechanically; fantastically; meekly; scoffingly; confusedly; definitely; pathetically; pertinaciously; wistfully; accurately; soothingly; tremulously; peevishly; disconsolately; evasively; categorically; verbally; comprehensively; bewilderedly; economically; worthily; dolefully; enigmatically; deftly; explicitly; perfectly; quaveringly; cryptically; measuredly; vehemently; imperiously; scorchingly; rashly; fitly; aptly; indulgently; animatedly; uninterestingly; relevantly; prodigally; disquietingly; sardonically; partially; tentatively; ruefully; matter-of-factly; mildly.

(See reply, respond, concede.)

ANSWERABLE

adverbs
personally; awfully; painfully; seriously; undoubtedly; terribly; officially; directly.

ANT

adjectives
antenna-manipulating; assiduous; destructive; exemplified; ever-questing; eternally-constructing; encroaching; frugal; formic-producing; garnering; gregarious; greedy; hoarding; harvesting; industrious; persistent; swarming; scurrying; sugar-seeking; store-collecting; troublesome; unpopular; wise.

verbs
burden—; combat —s; consider—; cultivate —s; disturb —s; examine—; exhibit —s; exterminate —s; fall victim to —s; infest with —s; go to —s; observe —s; purge of —s; spray —s; study—; teem with —s; —s abound; —accomplishes; —achieves; —accumulates; —s adapt themselves; —s amass; —ascends; —attacks; —bites; —bores into; —s build; —bustles; —s capture; —s collect; —s colonize; —s consolidate; —s construct; —s contend for; —s converge upon; —crawls; —s crowd; —defends; —s denude the area; —s deposit eggs; —descends; —despoils; —destroys; —s devastate; —devours; —digs; —dissects; —dominates; —dwells; —s eddy from; —emerges; —endures; —s enslave; —entombs; —excavates; —explores; —exudes; —s find their way; —s flit about; —s fly; —forages; —gathers; —gorges; —guards; —harvests; —hastens; —hatches; —heaps; —hibernates; —s hol-

low out; —hustles; —imprisons; —s insinuate themselves; —s invade; —labors; —lays up food; —mates; —s migrate; —s nest; —s nurse their young; —occupies; —s organize; —performs; —s pillage; —s preserve; —s pour in; —races; —s raid; —s ravage; —reconnoiters; —regurgitates; —roams; —roves; —rushes; —scouts; —scurries; —secretes; —seizes; —s share; —shears; —s socialize; —stings; —stores; —stows; —s stream up; —struggles; —s surge out; —survives; —s swarm; —s throng; —transports; —trudges; —utilizes; —vanishes; —wars.

(See insect, termite.)

ANTAGONISM

adjectives

political; bitter; surly; heartfelt; overwhelming; violent; subtle; mutual; professional; recurring; stiffening; fundamental; religious; bristling; deep-seated; social; sectional; persistent; racial; pronounced; ingrained; unrelenting; outspoken; vindictive; implacable; lofty; subdued; traditional; compromising; monosyllabic.

verbs

accentuate—; adjust—; balance—; conquer—; create—; develop—; express—; heighten—; increase—; mark—; oppose—; rack by—; risk—; rouse—; soften—; stimulate—; struggle with—; topple—; weaken—; —thwarts; —weakens.

(See opposition, hostility, resistance.)

ANTAGONIST

adjectives

legitimate; formidable; potential; appointed; contemptible; implacable; dreaded; defeated; crafty; redoubtable; irreconcilable; fallen; wary; agile; relentless; acrid.

verbs

admonish—; belittle—; best—; daunt—; defeat—; fence with—; overcome—; overpower—; overwhelm—; —argues; —assails; —battles; —collapses; —contends; —contests; —counteracts; —disputes; —languishes; —opposes; —relaxes; —slumps; —springs up.

(See opponent, rival, assailant, foe, adversary.)

ANTAGONISTIC

adverbs

violently; bitterly; subtly; fundamentally; persistently; racially; socially; politically; openly; outspokenly; vindictively; traditionally; formidably; unreasonably; irreconcilably; relentlessly; utterly; strangely; inexplicably; essentially; palpably; undeniably; basically; alarmingly; unaccountably.

ANTAGONIZE (v)

adverbs

derisively; politically; bitterly; overwhelmingly; violently; professionally; recurringly; fundamentally; religiously; socially; sectionally; persistently; racially; outspokenly; vindictively; implacably.

(See oppose, hinder.)

ANTECEDENT

adjectives

mental; worthy; historic; dwarfish; undeniable; necessary; grammatical.

ANTHEM

adjectives

pealing; eternal; blessed; doleful; joyous; heavenly; resounding.

ANTIC

adjectives

unconscious; infantile; puerile; capricious; ridiculous; glib; sterile; gay; exuberant; mad; absurd; droll; small-boy; mechanical; erratic; drunken; boisterous.

ANTICIPATE (v)

adverbs

curiously; fondly; reasonably; pessimistically; confidently; mentally; ecstatically; gleefully; joyously; originally; pleasurably; eagerly; passionately; blissfully; gloatingly; hungrily; ardently; impatiently; avidly; tremblingly; greedily; reasonably.

(See expect, apprehend.)

ANTICIPATION

adjectives

unhesitating; sensitive; charming; bright; daring; joyful; mysterious; pleasurable; eager; greedy; sanguine; exhilarating; passionate; picturesque; lascivious; tingling; heightened; lively; thrilling; blissful; undefined; morose; gloating; hungry; ferocious; keen; alert; ardent; impatient; avid; trembling; crushing; panic-stricken; reasonable; quivering.

verbs

beam with—; delight in—; look forward with—; pardon—; resist—of; restrain—; revel in—; rob—; toil in—of; tremble in—; —cheers; —enhances; —excites; —gladdens; —incites; —stimulates.

(See expectation, hope.)

ANTICIPATORY

adverbs
joyously; mysteriously; pleasurably; excitedly; hysterically; passionately; thrillingly; hungrily; unreasonably; avidly; impatiently; ardently; keenly; hopefully; eagerly; charmingly; joyfully; mischievously; hastily; incontinently; fervently; anxiously; greedily; impetuously; crazily; madly; feverishly; nervously.

ANTIDOTE

adjectives
specific; effective; cursed; pungent; stupefying; vile.

ANTIPATHY

adjectives
blind; cordial; mortal; unaccountable; mutual; invincible; deep-rooted; natural; rational; bigoted; tacit; peculiar.

verbs
admit—; be born of—; date—; display—; dispose toward—; dwell in—; excite—; hold—; imply—; introduce—; mark—; remove—; rouse—; saturate with—; turn from—; —blazes; —burns; —manifests; —melts; —originates from; —prejudices; —puzzles; —restricts; —takes root.
(See aversion, enmity, dislike.)

ANTIQUARY

adjectives
ardent; musical; distinguished; honorary; eminent; passionate; shallow; classical; hoary; curious.

ANTIQUE

adjectives
charming; spurious; rare; valuable; precious; genuine; colorless; fraudulent.

adverbs
genuinely; expensively; unquestionably; authentically; truly; actually; veritably; really; pricelessly; richly; decoratively; garishly; gorgeously; gaudily; ornamentally; deceptively; fraudulently; cheaply; showily; smartly; trickily; foolishly; flimsily; absurdly; beautifully; unbelievably; spuriously.

ANTIQUITY

adjectives
unknown; remote; honorable; pagan; venerable; traceable; hoar; classical; quaint; dead; historical; respectable; solemn; remote; fabulous; feudal; fascinating; observable.

ANTISEPTIC

adjectives
powerful; intestinal; efficient.

verbs
act as—; advise—; apply—; bathe in—; compare—; develop—; dilute—; discard—; dust with—; embalm in—; employ—; expose to—; glaze with—; immerse in—; impregnate with—; inject—; introduce—; operate with—; paint with—; soak in—; sterilize with—; surround with—; swab with—; wash with—; wrap in—; —acts; —aids; —aims at; —arrests; —burns; —cleans; —combats; —counteracts; —destroys; —exercises; —fulfils; —functions; —influences; —inhibits; —insures; —irritates; —kills; —preserves; —prevents; —protects; —purifies; —reaches; —relieves; —removes; —renders; —replaces; —restrains; —restricts; —retards; —rids of; —serves; —sterilizes; —thwarts.

adverbs
genuinely; effectively; valuably; infallibly; powerfully; extremely; heroically; mildly; perfectly; soothingly; correctively; specifically; simply; safely; beneficially; beneficently; advantageously; commendably; highly; essentially.

ANTITHESIS

adjectives
vile; complacent; inharmonious; striking; complete; false.

ANTLERS

adjectives
budding; branching; cresting; clashing; defiant; deciduous; graceful; gouging; fathom-wide; interlocking; lordly; massive; menacing; pronged; palm-tree (moose); periodically-shed; regal; sail-like (moose); self-entrapping; tined; velvety; vigorously-beating; wicked.

verbs
adorn with—; bear—; brandish—; carry—; decorate with—; form—; gore with—; impale on—; lock—; mount—; ornament with—; renew—; shed—; snag—; solidify—; spear—; spike—; sprout—; stunt—; toss—; weaken—; —branch out; —develop; —fork; —menace; —pierce; —protrude; —rend; —stab; —threaten.
(See horn.)

ANVIL

adjectives
clanging; crude; fiery; harsh; hammer-worn; historic; mighty; massive; steely; spark-emitting; shaping; transforming; traditional; invincible; proving; resistant; unvarying; unyielding; Vulcan-symbolizing.

verbs
balance on—; beat on—; bend on—; clink on—; crack on—; fashion on—; flatten on—; forge on—; hammer on—; harden on —; jangle on—; shape on—; strike—; twist on—; —clashes; —resounds; —rings; —sustains.

(See bell.)

ANXIETY

adjectives
touching; breathless; irrepressible; excessive; torturing; slight; supreme; utmost; undue; considerable; deep; vague; absorbing; unsatisfied; paternal; indescribable; fretting; gnawing; indeterminate; haggard; unceasing; infinite; unavoidable; financial; perceptible; predominant; tender; insufferable; connubial; excited; feverish; brooding; trembling; pious; deep-seated; maternal; agonizing; bated; flushed; mortal; worldly; cruel; morbid; devastating; betrayed; hysterical; nerve-racking; frantic; breath-taking; mental; domestic; motherly; painful; intense; unjust; sleepless; poignant; sick; grueling; heart-broken; keen; acute; soul-searing; gratuitous; relieved; drab; unwarranted; common; unspoken; hidden; repressed; troublesome; throbbing; annoying; sudden; subconscious; discernible; undeceived; human; suppressed; wearisome; impatient.

verbs
accompany with—; betray—; burden with —; create—; disturb by—; evince—; free from—; gaze with—; harass with—; increase—; manifest—; overshadow with—; reveal—; seize by—; shake with—; strain with—; trouble with—; wear to shreds with—; —agitates; —clouds; —constricts; —depresses; —disturbs; —etches; —prevails; —seizes; —vexes.

(See solicitude, apprehension, worry, fear, care, misgiving.)

ANXIOUS

adverbs
over; unnaturally; painfully; laughably; ridiculously; pathetically; lamentably; curiously; eagerly; abnormally; naturally; touchingly; supremely; unduly; deeply; indescribably; perceptibly; tenderly; suspiciously; excitedly; frantically; frenziedly; inexplicably; nervously; timidly; terribly; keenly; pitiably; miserably.

APARTMENT

adjectives
luxurious; sumptuous; modern; bachelor; tawdry; gorgeous; immaculate; dignified; old-fashioned; impressive; swanky; spacious; cooped-up; dusty; dingy; squalid; isolated; unpersonalized; ground-floor; terraced; doll-size; private; commodious; magnificent; dirty; immense; whitewashed; dimly-lighted; home-like; shabby; imposing; distinctive; charming; elegant; well-ordered; ill-furnished; communal.

verbs
assign to—s; billet in —s; divide into —s; ensconce in—; fit out—; occupy—; wreck —.

(See room, house.)

APATHETIC

adverbs
stupidly; dully; strangely; abnormally; alarmingly; weakly; heavily; stolidly; vacantly; ridiculously; unnaturally; singularly; oddly; curiously; unaccountably; irritatingly; shockingly; callously; coldly; carelessly; hopelessly; unpardonably.

APATHY

adjectives
selfish; weary; dream-like; despairing; stagnant; incredible; dull; immovable; resigned; settled; curious; growing; strange; enveloping; political; unaffected; accustomed; complete.

verbs
denote—; disturb—; encounter—; engender —; escape—; free from—; forsake—; master—; overcome—; produce—; result in—; rouse from—; signify—; sink into—; suffer —; suppress—; tolerate—; —chills; —paralyzes; —prevails; —signifies.

(See indifference, lethargy.)

APE

adjectives
grotesque; lumbering; chattering; soot-colored; restless; anthropoid; man-like; monstrous.

verbs
descend from—; —chatters; —clambers; —claws; —crouches; —dances; —drops to earth; —gallops off; —imitates; —leaps;

—lodges in; —lumbers; —mimics; —plucks; —resembles; —screams; —springs; —sways; —swings; —yelps.

(See monkey, animal.)

APE (v)

adverbs
comically; sedulously; grotesquely; lumberingly; chatteringly; restlessly; monstrously; shamelessly; ludicrously.

(See imitate, mimic.)

APERTURE

adjectives
narrow; barred; grated; half-moon; yawning; ungarnished; ragged; circular; limiting.

APHORISM

adjectives
favorite; pregnant; cynical; resounding; sparkling; hackneyed; abominable; pithy; selfish.

APOLOGETIC

adverbs
awkwardly; humbly; sincerely; nervously; slavishly; hastily; instantly; preposterously; disgustingly; unnecessarily; skillfully; sufficiently; reluctantly; profoundly; deeply; tearfully; pathetically; incoherently; sheepishly; half-heartedly; confusedly; honestly; openly; generously; embarrassingly; miserably; eagerly.

APOLOGY

adjectives
practical; humble; voluble; metrical; nervous; groveling; abject; handsome; awkward; universal; hasty; muttered; cynical; preposterous; skillful; suitable; sufficient; sincere; rapturous; profound; exaggerated; strongly-worded; pathetic; pitiful; tearful; murmured; mumbled; incoherent; obscure; sheepish; mute; half-hearted; amazed; mental; public; automatic.

verbs
acknowledge—; attack—; attempt—; convey—; elicit—; express—; favor with—; imply—; indulge in—ies; plead for—; refuse—; shame into—; stammer—; tender—; trouble with—; wave aside—; —alters; —atones; —excuses; —vindicates.

(See defense, confession, excuse, plea, alibi.)

APOLOGY (v)

adverbs
meekly; pitifully; gruffly; profusely; humbly; volubly; nervously; abjectly; grovelingly; awkwardly; cynically; exaggeratedly; suitably; skillfully; pathetically; tearfully; incoherently; sheepishly; half-heartedly; automatically.

(See justify, defend, vindicate.)

APOSTLE

adjectives
current; intrepid; inspired; non-ecclesiastical; ordained; recalcitrant; self-appointed; subsequently-commissioned; specifically-chosen; treacherous; virtuous; world-denouncing.

verbs
alienate —s; bar —s; call —s; commission —s; delegate—; elect—; gain —s; gather —s; hail—s; initiate—; lead—s; martyr —s; ordain —s; persecute —s; quote—: regulate —s; select —s; send forth —s; —accompanies; —administers; —advocates; —executes; —leads; —performs miracles; —preaches; —proclaims; —records; —scatters.

(See witness.)

APPALLING

adverbs
grievously; sorely; bitterly; painfully; distressingly; excruciatingly; hauntingly; gruesomely; horridly; piercingly; tormentingly; torturingly; deplorably; disastrously; dreadfully; execrably; fearfully; frightfully; insufferably; insupportably; intolerably; odiously; oppressively; pathetically; ruefully; shockingly; woefully; touchingly; unbearably; terrifically.

APPARATUS

adjectives
dust-collecting; elaborate; abundant; scientific; perceptive; sentient; makeshift; curative; simple; intricate; complicated; ghastly; imperfect; digestive; inefficient; ingenious; culinary; new; ponderous; expensive; thinking; hefting; spectroscopic; murderous; solemn.

verbs
adapt—; adjust—; apply—; demonstrate—; design—; employ—; equip with—; evolve —; experiment with—; gear—; guard—; invent—; manipulate—; modernize—; provide—; put—in motion; set up—; simplify—; tinker with—; toy with—; —facilitates; —functions.

(See device, machine, tool.)

APPAREL

adjectives
glorious; superfluous; trim; homely; fashionable; smart; coarse; becoming; gorgeous; exquisite; ceremonious; luxurious; decorous; flamboyant; plain.

verbs
adorn in—; array in—; attire in—; behold —; change—; clothe in—; deck in—; don —; embroider—; equip with—; fashion—; fit—; furnish—; ornament—; outfit with—; prepare—; provide with—; rig with—; snatch at—; —beautifies; —conceals; —enhances; —proclaims.

(See clothing, dress, raiment.)

APPARENT

adverbs
plainly; conspicuously; downright; undeniably; clearly; definitely; flagrantly; glaringly; notoriously; openly; constantly; easily; strikingly; reasonably; shamefully; outrageously; dangerously; plaguedly; perilously.

APPARITION

adjectives
false; glorious; formidable; celestial; enchanting; distinguished; impatient; frightful; phenomenal; monstrous; intruding; startling; soulless; personal; exquisite; grisly; blushing; unpleasant; bloody; fantastic; overwhelming; ill-omened; black; ghostly; miraculous; horrid; singular; continuous.

verbs
authenticate—; believe in —s; disprove—; divine—; exhibit—; generate—; imagine—; occasion—; perceive—; produce—; shroud —; summon—; —s abound; —appears; —comes forth; —groans; —haunts; —lures; —suspends; —vanishes; —warns.

(See specter, ghost, phantom, illusion.)

APPEAL

adjectives
effective; universal; pathetic; emphatic; overt; contagious; impassioned; dramatic; modern; sorrowful; mute; unwitting; infinite; frail; sudden; potential; lamentable; eternal; frantic; mournful; diversified; rude; artless; inharmonious; constant; visible; urgent; boisterous; manifest; felicitous; irresistible; self-respecting; gastronomic; singular; persistent; troubled; popular; manly; matchless; unconscious; skillful; powerful; agonizing; unanswerable; eloquent; psychological; despairing; qualified; humanitarian; tragic; genuine; lasting; sad; unspoken; pitiable; speechless; crushing; fiery; piteous; tender; shrill; plaintive; hypnotic; sensuous; unavailing; habitual; emotional; enticing; alluring; joyous; visual; wonderful; deafening; logical; lovable; warm; convincing; devout; childish; rare; luxurious; stirring; lusty; courageous; challenging; feminine; public; delicate; artistic; magic; poetic; world-wide; human; timid; hurt; solemn; abject; weak; vague; adventurous; whimsical; strange; sensational; animated; electrifying; magnetic; tremendous; spectacular; imploring; wistful; timely; poignant; demagogical; superficial; panic-stricken; vain; inflammatory; dumb; admirable; olfactory; savory; mysterious; abnormal; sporadic; prophetic; distinct; comprehensive; gripping; unique; strong; intense; spontaneous; overbearing; sympathetic; strident; truculent; blatant; unvoiced.

verbs
abandon—; address—; admit—; afford—; bolster—; broadcast—; claim—; decline—; deny—; desist in—; discourage—; disregard—; enact—; exercise—; file—; give notice of—; grant—; institute—; invoke—; involve—; justify—; lose—; merit—; modify—; nullify—; present—; prevent—; privilege to—; prosecute—; provide—; provide security for—; question—; refuse—; regulate—; rely on—; render—; renew—; resist—; respond to—; review—; rule—; schedule—; stir by—; subject to—; submit to—; succumb to—; support—; voice—; whine—; yield to—; —engrosses; —fails; —reverses.

(See entreaty, petition, application, request, prayer.)

APPEAL (v)

adverbs
strangely; frantically; directly; strongly; confidently; constantly; irresistibly; forcibly; specially; powerfully; perpetually; effectively; dramatically; sorrowfully; mutely; strongly; mournfully; artlessly; rudely; urgently; boisterously; eloquently; tragically; piteously; tenderly; emotionally; shrilly; deafeningly; logically; stirringly; warmly; lustily; courageously; publicly; abjectly; wistfully; stridently; truculently; blatantly; outspokenly; mysteriously; grippingly; uniquely; sympathetically.

(See entreat, invoke.)

APPEAR (v)

adverbs
conspicuously; malignantly; impressively; presently; portentously; perpetually; tardily; distinctly; substantially; simultaneously;

miraculously; hesitatingly; posthumously; anonymously; manifestly; commandingly; mysteriously; astoundingly; exotically; flamboyantly; phlegmatically; demurely; ethereally; slovenly; ferociously; unhealthily; obtrusively; majestically; spectrally; inscrutably.

(See emerge, seem, look, resemble.)

APPEARANCE

adjectives
august; pompous; distinguished; stately; austere; noble; commanding; charming; cordial; worthy; antiquated; venerable; comfortable; immaculate; sleek; well-fed; quaint; luscious; artistic; dainty; lovely; comely; gorgeous; untidy; uncouth; angular; ungainly; forlorn; shabby; genteel; plaintive; somber; mysterious; weird; eerie; astounding; arresting; striking; singular; sprightly; grotesque; rakish; massive; robust; rugged; emaciated; deceitful; cadaverous; unearthly; desolate; quarrelsome; offending; miserable; sullen; disgusting; ungraceful; incongruous; gross; flamboyant; resentful; jaded; phlegmatic; grim; physical; youthful; nautical; grave-like; nun-like; orderly; unkempt; park-like; rabbit-like; clerk-like; mournful; exotic; ethereal; leonine; tolerable; ludicrous; poverty-stricken; fragile; casual; contrite; slovenly; dismaying; unfortunate; disjointed; sunken; bedraggled; animated; faint; diaphanous; picturesque; slothful; worm-eaten; contradictory; stern; benevolent; wretched; vulgar; dilapidated; external; promising; visual; ducal; inviting; ideal; squalid; sedate; outward; greasy; attractive; distinctive; ursine; demure; decorative; satanic; fearful; vacant; independent; portentous; beneficent; dignified; mottled; studious; stupid; timid; opalescent; ferocious; prepossessing; sickly; festive; reconciliatory; tawdry; impoverished; voluntary; scattered; deserted; prosperous; famished; thumb-worn; unhealthy; reverential; respectable; swing-like; school-teacherish; unobtrusive; weedy; natty; frank; antediluvian; genuine; brave; flattering; material; palatial; battered; dressy; individual; variegated; watered; majestic; spectral.

verbs
come into—; detect—; disclaim—; discredit —; disfigure—; display—; involve—; greet —; judge by—; observe—; parade—; perceive by —s; present an—; preserve —s; put in—; ruffle—; transfigure—; transform —; —arrests; —belies; —repels.

(See aspect.)

APPEASE (*v*)

adverbs
inadequately; lightly; painstakingly; fully; completely.

(See pacify, calm, reconcile, propitiate.)

APPELLATION

adjectives
equivocal; false; incongruous; inappropriate; ill-mannered; heathenish; phantom; elegant; jocose; permanent; trite; hated; affectionate.

APPENDIX (*anatomy*)

verbs
drain—; excise—; freeze—; incise—; inflame—; locate—; perforate—; remove—; —adheres; —bursts; —infects; —poisons; —ravages; —suppurates; —swells.

APPENDIX (*book*)

adjectives
derogatory; contributory; complementary; concomitant; accessory; essential; explanatory; prolonged; solemn; supernumerary; superfluous; statistical.

verbs
advise by—; affix—; consult—; insert—; refer to—; relate in—; review in—; —concurs; —contributes; —directs; —guides; —introduces.

(See addition.)

APPERTAIN (*v*)

adverbs
unquestionably; undoubtedly; certainly; solely; exclusively.

APPETITE

adjectives
unmanageable; eager; inordinate; ravenous; cavernous; voracious; squeamish; keen; jaded; gluttonous; rude; depraved; abnormal; unappeased; phenomenal; prodigious; robust; natural; sharpened; vicious; eccentric; enormous; monstrous; gross; gigantic; sensitive; coarse; languid; sponge-like; pampered; devouring; herbivorous; rude; husky; boundless; leaden; capricious; perverted; obscene; unashamed; sleepy; sensual; catholic; brutish; perennial; inactive; lusty; insatiate; animal; satisfied; fleshy; overpowering; irrational; beastly; hearty; unreasonable; diseased; postponed; demoniac; surfeited.

verbs
acquire—; allay—; animate—; appeal to—; appease—; bury—; cloy—; comply with—;

curb—; delight—; deprave—; depress—; digest with—; express—; gorge—; govern —; gratify—; humor—; impair—; indulge —; obey—; pamper—; pervert—; preserve —; quench—; quicken—; raise—; reduce —; regulate—; relish—; revive—; sate—; satiate—; satisfy—; sharpen—; sicken—; staunch—; stimulate—; stir—; suffice—; suit—; yield to—; whet—; woo—; —anticipates; —diminishes; —drives; —dwindles; —gnaws; —grows; —increases; —languishes; —lessens; —returns; —sleeps.

(See desire, hunger, passion.)

APPLAUD (v)

adverbs

riotously; vociferously; warmly; valiantly; equally; tumultuously; spontaneously; hungrily; thunderously; deafeningly; lavishly; enthusiastically; uproariously; vigorously; wildly; irrepressibly; furiously; vehemently; clamorously; frantically; sycophantically.

(See cheer, laud, praise, admire.)

APPLAUSE

adjectives

spontaneous; thunderous; general; deafening; lavish; boisterous; kindly; willing; tumultuous; enthusiastic; whirlwind; uproarious; widespread; rapturous; intelligent; well-directed; vigorous; wild; hearty; irrepressible; furious; delirious; unqualified; vehement; rolling; sporadic; murmuring; rippling; prolonged; forced; warm; courteous; commendatory; heavy-handed; derisive; unbounded; mocking; frantic; vociferous; wondrous; controlled; inordinate; generous; singular; sycophantic; grateful; sarcastic; hollow; malicious; serious; clamorous; ecstatic; scattered.

verbs

acclaim by—; anticipate—; appreciate—; bask in—; chant—; clap—; commend—; demonstrate—; drink up—; echo—; envy—; express—; gain—; huzza—; laugh out—; long for—; love—; manifest—; merit—; murmur—; pronounce—; raise—; reap—; relish—; rock with—; shake with—; snap —; thunder—; trick into—; voice—; win —; —ascends; —breaks out; —bursts out; —crackles; —delights; —encourages; —gratifies; —interrupts; —lessens; —reverberates; —rings from.

(See cheers.)

adjectives

smooth; polished; firm; cool; full-juiced, red-cheeked.

verbs

blight—; blow down—; bob for —s; bore into—; bruise—; bud —s; chip—; chop—; core—; crate —s; crop —s; crunch—; cultivate—; devour—; dice—; ferment —s; freeze—; gather —s; graft —s; harvest —s; hoard —s; market —s; munch —; palm—; pare—; plant —s; pluck —; preserve —s; press —s; propagate —s; quarter —; redden —s; scrape—; seed—; spray —s; store —s; taste—; vend —s; —s canker; —s ferment; —matures; —rots; —tempts; —s thrive.

(See fruit.)

APPLIANCE

adjectives

approved; base; complicated; suitable; adroit; crude; ingenious; rude; primitive.

APPLICANT

adjectives

gentle; clamorous; qualified; hopeful; admissible; profitable.

verbs

eliminate—; expose—; mortify—; place—; repulse—; —declares; —petitions; —qualifies.

(See candidate.)

APPLICATION

adjectives

diligent; intelligent; conscientious; rigid; assiduous; sedulous; steadfast; utmost; rigorous; concrete; fascinating; platonic; practical; universal; adroit; progressive; broad; specific; thorough; dynamic; degrading; perfunctory; strenuous; steadfast; presumptuous; unflinching; educated; continuing; pertinent; quantitative; undue; formalistic; correct; professional; ceaseless; industrial; systematic; repeated; inviting; ingenious; influential; superior; fruitful; admirable; economic; dexterous; unfriendly; timely.

verbs

attach—; consider—; cure with —s; demand —; detail—; justify—; petition for—; postpone—; present—; reconsider—; reject—; require—; solicit—; —eases; —kills; —modifies; —pends; request—.

(See use, request.)

APPLY (v)

adverbs

assiduously; indiscriminately; skilfully; ten-

, diligently; ingeniously; extensively; incorrectly; dex- arbitrarily; consciously; compre- vely; advantageously; artificially; rigorously; directly; usefully; necessarily; promiscuously; adroitly; perfunctorily; professionally; ceaselessly; systematically; admirably; literally; liberally; scientifically; practically; universally.

(See use, utilize, practice, adapt.)

APPOINT (v)

adverbs
providentially; celestially; tentatively; publicly; clandestinely; arbitrarily; voluntarily.

(See establish, ordain, assign, allot.)

APPOINTMENT

adjectives
tentative; lifetime; public; onerous; clandestine; absolute; arbitrary; formal; voluntary.

verbs
assign—; benefit by—; cancel—; confirm—; decline—; decree—; designate—; direct—; dispose of—; engineer—; establish—; fix—; grant—; miss—; order—; perform—; ratify—; shuffle—; stipulate—; thrill by—; wangle—; —confers; —pays; —stands; —vests in one.

(See meeting.)

APPOINTMENTS

adjectives
luxurious; elegant; sumptuous; modernistic; dignified.

APPORTION (v)

adverbs
equitably; equally; fairly; justly; wisely; thoughtfully.

(See allot, distribute, grant, share.)

APPRAISAL

adjectives
silent; objective; luminous; shrewd; searching; rational; cool; desperate; intelligent; nimble; careful; adequate; critical; acute; technical; enlightening; scientific; convincing; prolonged; independent.

APPRAISE (v)

adverbs
critically; covertly; judiciously; conceitedly; knowingly; silently; objectively; shrewdly; rationally; coolly; intelligently; adequately; scientifically; independently.

(See judge, estimate.)

APPRECIATE (v)

adverbs
highly; adequately; justly; deeply; properly; particularly; readily; fully; correctly; sympathetically; mutually; genuinely; heartily; whole-heartedly; passionately; aesthetically; belatedly; artistically; profoundly.

(See esteem, prize.)

APPRECIATION

adjectives
intense; genial; detached; sympathetic; respectful; delicate; impersonal; laughing; bashful; mutual; poetic; innocent; definite; full; critical; hearty; high; true; genuine; discreet; wide; sensitive; wholehearted; clearer; deep; heightened; passionate; stunted; aesthetic; anticipated; patriotic; brilliant; cordial; amazed; generous; affectionate; splendid; reluctant; belated; keen; warmhearted; unsolicited; complete; proper; sensuous; fine; vivid; total; marked; flashing; humorous; expressed; emotional; rarefied; scant; supreme; increased; childish; sincere; oppressive; growing; loyal; hard-driven; rare; radiant; tentative; direct; intellectual; spiritual; alleged; artistic; enthusiastic; profound; youthful.

verbs
differ in—; drink in with—; evoke—; increase—; perceive with—; promote—of; recognize with—; stamp—; —grows; —increases; —rises.

(See esteem.)

APPRECIATIVE

adverbs
genially; sympathetically; laughingly; wholly; definitely; heartily; truly; genuinely; wholeheartedly; deeply; highly; passionately; discriminatingly; cordially; amazingly; pathetically; splendidly; keenly; warmly; completely; properly; childishly; sincerely; increasingly; oppressively; radiantly; delightfully; enthusiastically; gratifyingly; profoundly.

APPREHEND (v)

adverbs
readily; imperfectly; clearly; distinctly; nervously; tremblingly; fearfully; vaguely; acutely; undisguisedly; gnawingly.

(See dread, fear.)

APPREHENSION

adjectives
slumbering; uneasy; maternal; troublesome; nervous; wistful; sickening; sensitive; clammy; hazy; ghostly; trembling; frenzied;

lingering; quivering; fearful; shivering; fickle; rational; feigned; lively; vague; acute; undisguised; suppressed; gnawing; constant; religious; dismal; gloomy; ill-defined; cruel; despondent; remorseful; uncomfortable; foreboding; alarming; abject; distinct; unrelieved; sad; breathless; anguished; piteous; idle; grave; continuous; professed; indignant; daily; delighted; dread; warm; groundless; serious; vain; ever-present; nameless; instant; goading; painful; affected; supreme; right; puerile; terrible; mortal; cowardly; tempered; utmost; murky; miraculous.

verbs
allay—; arouse—; rise above—; becloud —; clear—; crystallize—; deny—; dull—; express—; free of—; ingrain—; look about with—; obtain—; profess—; rejoice in—; remove—; rest on—; sense with—; shake with—; strengthen—; torment by—; warrant—; wear out with—; —assails; —flames; —possesses; —seizes.
(See fear, dread, anxiety, distrust.)

APPREHENSIVE

adverbs
uneasily; nervously; fearfully; vaguely; acutely; constantly; occasionally; dismally; gloomily; cruelly; uncomfortably; alarmingly; distinctly; piteously; idly; gravely; professedly; groundlessly; seriously; namelessly; painfully; supremely; childishly; superstitiously; curiously; strangely; inexplicably; suddenly.

APPRENTICE

adjectives
idle; bright; haughty; hand-picked; drunken; able; practiced; clumsy.

verbs
abuse—; bind—; burden—; chastise—; contact—; dismiss—; employ—; engage—; enroll—; fledge—; instruct—; regulate—; remove—; retain—; school—; serve as—; teach—; —binds himself to; —gathers; —learns; —masters; —practices; —serves; —trains.
(See beginner, novice, student.)

APPRENTICESHIP

adjectives
weary; devious; tedious; long; arduous; strict; sordid; faithful.

APPROACH

adjectives
hackneyed; single; sociological; novel; organic; traditional; inevitable; oblique; tentative; obvious; impressive; immediate; logical; flanked; insidious; common-sense; majestic; tactful; critical; methodological; natural; simple; wary; galloping; fair; hushed; original; insinuating; wistful; cautious; illuminating; subtle; indirect; shamefaced; stealthy; boisterous; chic; affable; experimental; tolerable; warm; mutual; soft; ample; casual; rapid; cunning; active; timid; gradual; intimate; sympathetic; distant; tumultuous; extraordinary; speedy; hostile; irresolute; ironical.

verbs
bar—; betoken—; construct—; cover—; discover—; discuss—; disguise—; divert—; examine—; foresee—; herald—; hinder—; linger over—; obstruct—; reconstruct—; repel—; restore—; sense—; shun—; watch —; —bodes; --leads.
(See access, way, entrance.)

APPROACH (v)

adverbs
penitently; hilariously; noiselessly; devoutly; remotely; diffidently; cautiously; perilously; sinuously; stealthily; unwarily; dexterously; delicately; humbly; reluctantly; leisurely; suppliantly; obsequiously; blushingly; circumspectly; obliquely; irresolutely; casually; confidentially.
(See advance.)

APPROBATION

adjectives
individual; startled; enthusiastic; unmeasured; modest; full; audible; virtuous; general.

verbs
bestow—; concur in—; declare—; enjoy—; entertain—; express—; mark with—; meet with—; merit—; quote with—; receive—; revoke—; seal in—; voice—.
(See commendation, encouragement, admiration, approval, praise.)

APPROPRIATE (v)

adverbs
selfishly; unceremoniously; thievishly; eagerly; doubtfully; reverently; solely; wastefully; adequately; fraudulently; extravagantly; lavishly.
(See take, assume.)

APPROPRIATION

adjectives
wasteful; blind; adequate; permanent; con-

tinuing; ruthless; fraudulent; extravagant; lavish; excessive; passive; meager.

verbs
assign—; authorize—; bar—; bequeath—; carry on with—; default—; designate—; diminish—; draw—; economize on—; employ—; enact—; exceed—; expend—; finance—; grant—; legislate—; necessitate—; pass—; pinch—; reserve—; restrict—; set apart—; shave—; specify—; transfer—; triple—; —aids; —allows; —enables; —provides; pay—.

(See fund, tax.)

APPROVAL

adjectives
affectionate; highest; delighted; private; priceless; overwhelming; unqualified; monotonous; marked; reiterated; vigorous; patent; warm; unanimous; sage; genuine; condescending; frank; complete; roaring; tacit; maternal; hapless; loud; excited; free; world-wide; unrestrained; languid; partial; social; hearty; widespread; abject; masculine; enthusiastic; grudging; expressed; perfect; denominational; popular; surprised; intense; voiceless; unconscious; distant; reluctant.

verbs
authorize—; bask in—; beam—; clamor—; consent to—; imply—; insure—; intimate—; meet with—; nod—; roar—; sanction—; secure—; stamp with—; trick into—; win—; —encourages; —greets; —heartens.

(See approbation, sanction, commendation, indorsement, ratification.)

APPROVE (v)

adverbs
heartily; warmly; thankfully; strongly; unanimously; instinctively; deliberately; indifferently; condescendingly; cordially; unconditionally; thoughtlessly; entirely; unqualifiedly; rapturously; delightedly; privately; vigorously; sagely; completely; condescendingly; tacitly; partially; enthusiastically; grudgingly; reluctantly; overwhelmingly.

(See commend, sanction, favor.)

APPROXIMATION

adjectives
progressive; well-bred; thematic; urbane; close; clear; definite.

APRON

adjectives
gingham; ridiculous; filthy; frilled; generous; snowy; tiny; flowered; humble; voluminous; diminutive; coarse; greasy; billowy; prophylactic; womanish.

APT

adverbs
adroitly; cleverly; specially; dexterously; felicitously; expertly; intelligently; practically; technically; ably; artistically; capably; cunningly; deftly; handily; ingeniously; proficiently; scientifically; shrewdly; remarkably; unusually.

APTITUDE

adjectives
natural; intellectual; remarkable; judicial; military; special; mechanical; oratorical; hidden; artistic; singular; curious; high; unusual; characteristic; musical; surprising; versatile.

AQUEDUCT

adjectives
subterraneous; ancient; spacious.

ARAB

adjectives
tall; graceful; grave; dressed; big; powerful; surly; harmless; wiry; black-bearded; black-browed; courteous; hawk-faced; fine-looking; excited; fierce-looking; chivalrous; filthy; ragged; imperturbable; amorous.

ARABESQUE

adjectives
elfin; exquisite.

ARBITER

adjectives
unprejudiced; just; trembling; implacable.

ARBITRARY

adverbs
overwhelmingly; extraordinarily; despotically; domineeringly; intolerably; paternally; patriarchally; dictatorially; imperiously; presumptuously; harshly; strictly; severely; tyrannically; oppressively; cruelly; haughtily; obdurately; positively; relentlessly; sternly; neatly; unreasonably; excessively; unbelievably; offensively; dangerously; alarmingly.

ARBITRATION

adjectives
compulsory; bloody; impartial; friendly.

verbs
abide by—; accept—; adopt—; advocate—; ascertain by—; compel—; conduct—; control by—; decide by—; discuss—; employ—;

obtain—; put to—; renounce—; respect—; seek—; submit to—; —adjusts; —adverts; —avoids; —awards; —conciliates; —considers; —determines; —judges; —negotiates; —referees; —results in; —settles; —succeeds.
(See decision.)

ARBOR

adjectives
rustic; flowering; sequestered; private; moving; gigantic; latticed; conical; bowery; sultry.

ARC

adjectives
deadly; skyward; graceful; fiery; luminous; friedelite; speed-blurred; controlling; unthinkable; zooming; ethereal; splendid; deficient; recurrent; flaming.

ARCADE

adjectives
blind; massive; sheltered; garish.

ARCH

adjectives
dignified; old; majestic; steel-trussed; artistic; echoing; horizontal; darkened; graceful; vast; livid; rustic; crumbling; leafy; peaked; magnificent; triumphal; subtle; elliptical; boundless; crystal; culminant; groined; successive; massive; shadowy; proscenium; titanic; accursed; rainbow; emerald; dazzling; topsy-turvy; inverted; cragged; shallow; stupendous; squashed; overworked; collapsed; glistening; flowery; melancholy; starry; tendriled; brazen; rising; interlacing; dim; somber; fretted.

verbs
adorn—; assemble—; cap—; construct—; crown—; develop—; employ—; erect—; form—; point—; span—; vault—; —carries; —commemorates; —curves; —gives way; —graces; —spans; —spreads; —strides over; —supports.
(See curve.)

ARCH (*v*)

adverbs
servilely; solidly; deeply; majestically; artistically; gracefully; magnificently; triumphally; massively.

ARCHAEOLOGIST

adjectives
distinguished; spectacular; venerable.

ARCHAEOLOGY

verbs
delve into—; derive from—; owe to—; study—; —absorbs; —accomplishes; —attempts; —attracts; —authenticates; —brings to light; —catalogues; —classifies; —collects; —compares; —concerns; —concludes; —conserves; —deals with; —deciphers; —decodes; —designates; —digs; —discovers; —disputes; —excavates; —fills in; —influences; —investigates; —marks; —misleads; —portrays; —preserves; —progresses; —recognizes; —reconstructs; —records; —rejects; —relates; —restores; —reveals; —scratches; —searches; —seeks; —sheds light upon; —surveys; —traces; —uncovers; —unravels.
(See science.)

ARCHAIC

adverbs
hopelessly; entirely; poetically; obviously; admittedly; veritably; venerably; traditionally; respectably; genteelly.

ARCHITECT

adjectives
philandering; eminent; self-constituted; consultant; ingenious; known; cunning; celebrated; fledgling; uninterested; creative; imaginative; successful; general; practical; exuberant; contemporary; admirable; lavish; discreet; romantic; symmetry-loving.

ARCHITECTURAL

adverbs
elaborately; chastely; unmistakably; charmingly; poetically; impressively; elegantly; tastefully; traditionally; nobly; ornately; rustically; historically; ecclesiastically; intricately; fantastically.

ARCHITECTURE

adjectives
primitive; diverse; ornate; semi-classic; elaborate; gilded; garbled; symphonic; charming; curious; rustic; organic; naval; noble; plastic; surrounding; historic; repellent; stodgy; colonial; editorial; ecclesiastical; florid; massive; distinctive; domestic; fantastic; traditional; impressive; intricate; tasteful; incrusted; elegant; incomparable; internal; diverse; rambling; poetic.

verbs
acquaint with—; adorn—; apply—; appreciate—; apprentice to—; build—; characterize—; conceive—; consider—; construct—; create—; crystallize—; decorate—; design

—; desolate—; destroy—; develop—; dress —; embellish—; embody in—; emphasize —; encourage—; enrich—; exhibit—; imitate—; immortalize—; practise—; preserve —; produce—; proportion—; raise—; regard—; regulate—; restore—; resuscitate —; revivify—; —adorns; —arises; —arranges; —consists; —designs; —details; —enables; —evolves from; —flourishes; —implies; —includes; —involves; —ornaments; —requires; —solves; —tends toward; —trains; —transfigures.
(See building, art.)

ARCHIVES

adjectives
historical; secret; incriminating; inexhaustible; enriched; treasured; indestructible; national; enduring.

verbs
burn—; conserve in—; deposit in—; preserve in—; record in—; register in—; rummage through—; store in—; superintend—; unlock—; —document; —include; —preserve; —record; —relate.
(See records, documents.)

ARCHWAY

adjectives
grated; sunken; ancient; ponderous; shining.

ARCTIC

adverbs
frigidly; frostily; rigorously; horribly; shiveringly; bleakly; coldly; freezingly; glacially; inclemently; piercingly; pinchingly; nippingly; rawly; intolerably; killingly; stiffly; frozenly; unbelievably; unbearably.

ARDENT

adverbs
youthfully; brightly; indiscreetly; amazingly; warmly; tenderly; generously; instinctively; impetuously; furiously; poetically; passionately; mutually; hastily; impulsively; irrepressibly; ingenuously; irresistibly; fervently; fervidly; anxiously; avidly; fondly; affectionately; devotedly; hungrily; yearningly; ambitiously; breathlessly; eagerly; insatiably; wistfully; sincerely; rapturously; ecstatically; racily; glowingly; feverishly; earnestly; emotionally; acutely; deeply.

ARDOR

adjectives
clean; bright; open-hearted; indiscreet; fiery; youthful; beauteous; amazing; cooled; revolutionary; tender; generous; characteristic; instinctive; inexplicable; impetuous; furious; sacrificial; covert; renewed; dampened; fastidious; poetic; passionate; mutual; tedious; professional; new-born; obsessing; war-like; wandering; hasty; impulsive; ready; redoubled; irrepressible; intrepid; exaggerating; emulous; heroic; ingenious; martial; patriotic; lyrical; military; submissive; irresistible; fervent.

verbs
burn with—; confine—; dampen—; effulge with—; electrify with—; extinguish—; fire with—; flame with—; heat with—; intensify—; pursue with—; radiate—; spend—; —abates; —swells; —wanes; —warms; —waxes.
(See eagerness, zeal, fervor, enthusiasm, warmth.)

ARDUOUS

adverbs
relatively; tremendously; overwhelmingly; formidably; unbelievably; supremely; gravely; seriously; administratively; physically; obviously; naturally; peculiarly; necessarily; unpleasantly; conspicuously; alarmingly; dishearteningly; incredibly; intricately; embarrassingly; perplexingly; complexly; desperately; perversely; occasionally.

AREA

adjectives
immense; unexplored; swampy; suburban; consolidated; misty; outlying; considerable; combined; vast; interior; populated; arid; scenic; circumscribed; stagnant; marshy; interstitial; limited; treeless; straggling; gale-swept; huge; enormous; bewildering; prolific; petty; devastated; inconspicuous; decreasing; unobstructed; forest; hazardous; widening; cultivable; superficial; diminished; liberal; super-productive; pestilential; varying; cleared; enveloping; trading; unpeopled; restricted; restoration; stone; faunal.

verbs
apply to—; approach—; bound—; cover—; cultivate—; define—; denude—; determine —; distinguish—; encircle—; enclose—; erect on—; excavate—; fence in—; give access to—; infest—; level—; limit—; measure—; reclaim—; remove from—; scatter over—; vacate—.
(See space, tract, portion, ground, yard.)

ARENA

adjectives
fit; conspicuous; commercial; frenzied; bloody; foggy; diplomatic.

verbs
combat in—; conflict in—; contend in—; display in—; emerge from—; enclose in—; flood—; jam—; perform in—; plunge into —; strew—; surround—; throng—.
(See space, field.)

ARGUE (v)

adverbs
persuasively; placatingly; elusively; understandingly; thoughtfully; drawlingly; fallaciously; rationalistically; preposterously; sensibly; captiously; lamely; fairly; roughly; impressively; profoundly; affirmatively; excitedly; hypercritically; vainly; irrationally; indefatigably; wisely; logically; adversely; scientifically; sophistically; deviously; contentiously; cantankerously; discursively; priggishly; clumsily; pettishly; hypothetically; ingeniously; crushingly; exhaustively; lucidly; formidably; tellingly; irrefutably; fruitlessly; acrimoniously; equivocally; irritatingly; stubbornly; superfluously; abusively; circuitously.
(See plead, remonstrate, discuss, dispute.)

ARGUMENT

adjectives
ingenious; powerful; affirmative; reasonable; sound; winning; crowning; notable; crushing; logical; acceptable; exhaustive; irresistible; conclusive; weighty; strong; favorable; effective; broad; doughty; truthful; unanswerable; cogent; forceful; basic; substantial; formidable; lucid; imaginative; eager; precious; matchless; intensive; illuminating; flawless; clear-cut; telling; close-knit; irrefutable; practical; heated; forensic; sonorous; eloquent; vehement; revolutionary; bitter; fiery; sharp; impassioned; ferocious; stale; fallacious; insidious; spurious; old; painful; futile; nervous; confused; specious; needless; feeble; conflicting; fruitless; influential; nation-wide; mild; half-playful; solemn; mathematical; typical; endless; extended; editorial; interminable; constant; protracted; final; prolific; deliberate; persistent; lengthy; wordless; delightful; good-selling; long-standing; widespread; impetuous; inevitable; rapid; brilliant; well-rounded; acrimonious; theistic; undeniable; utilitarian; scientific; moral; inconsiderable; violent; lofty; bloody; dispassionate; solid; grave; vulgar; absent; craven; staple; personal; positive; labored; rational; earnest; commonplace; hair-splitting; ampler; penetrating; embodied; outspoken; equivocal; irritating; convincing; coarse; adverse; timid; stubborn; wearisome; wretched; judicious; superfluous; honest; enticing; slender; abusive; keen; potent; concise; odd; maternal; clear; close.

verbs
admit—; advance—; anticipate—; arm with —; arrange—; attack—; base—; bolster—; bolt—; bring forth—; burnish—; clinch—; color—; combat—; construct—; counter with —; debate—; deduce—; demolish—; derive —from; destroy—; dispense with—; dispute —; dread—; drive home—; employ—; engage in—; enumerate—; explain—; fashion —; force—; found on—; ground upon—; indulge in—; invalidate—; kindle—; maintain—; marshal —s; meet—; open—; oppose—; permit of—; premise—; proffer—; propose—; prove—; provoke—; pursue—; push—; qualify—; question—; rebut—; reduce to—; refute—; reiterate—; remove—; resume—; scorn—; settle—; sift—; steel with—; stir—; substantiate—; support—; weigh—; —appeals; —confounds; —depends on; —drones on; —fades away; —implies; —impresses; —infers; —involves; —rages; —rests on; —s simmer down; —s wax hot.
(See reason, proof, debate, discussion, dispute, controversy.)

ARGUMENTATIVE

adverbs
sagaciously; readily; disagreeably; hotly; sagely; offensively; cleverly; adroitly; ingeniously; reasonably; irresistibly; obstinately; pesteringly; abusively; stubbornly; convincingly; mulishly; irritatingly; dispassionately; earnestly; violently; acrimoniously; brilliantly; impetuously; interminably; endlessly; playfully; solemnly; fruitlessly; mildly; feebly; needlessly; nervously; insidiously; unnecessarily; ferociously; bitterly; significantly; foolishly; intelligently; astutely; shrewdly; vigilantly.

ARID

adverbs
dessicatingly; terribly; rainlessly; horribly; intolerably; unbearably; unproductively; wildly; fruitlessly; treelessly; dustily; insufferably; hopelessly; desperately; bitterly; malignly; pestiferously; agonizingly; heartbreakingly; destructively; murderously; joylessly; desolately; insupportably; dolorously.

ARISE (v)

adverbs
involuntarily; energetically; automatically;

spontaneously; pretentiously; incessantly; majestically; strenuously; readily; imperceptibly; irresistibly; hastily.

(See rise, ascend, mount, proceed.)

ARISTOCRACY

adjectives

odious; genuine; true; privileged; effete; heaven-descended; remarkable; gilded; canine; feudal; landed; moribund; pampered; devout; old; dominant; hereditary; high; admitted; recognized; idle; proud; democratic; industrial; sword-girt; phantasmal; martial.

verbs

attain—; break down—; choose from—; compose—; denote—; distinguish—; imperil —; oppose—; overthrow—; pervert—; privilege—; rank among—; strengthen—; vest in—; weaken—; —abuses; —administrates; —conforms; —degenerates; —develops from; —enlists; —fosters; —governs; —lolls; —predominates; —rules; —wields.

(See nobility, peerage, class, government.)

ARISTOCRAT

adjectives

bloated; proud; ante bellum; wealthy; exiled; hot-tempered; born; disgraced; snobbish; cosmopolitan; country; liberal; embryo; impoverished; stripling; emigrant; soft-voiced.

ARISTOCRATIC

adverbs

proudly; genuinely; truly; admittedly; tenaciously; inherently; innately; fantastically; snobbishly; nobly; actually; elegantly; unaffectedly; avowedly; unquestionably; palpably; essentially; stubbornly; ostentatiously; conspicuously; eminently; grandly; imposingly; magnificently.

ARK

adjectives

doveless; guarded; grounded.

ARM

adjectives

beautiful; tapering; superb; perfect; sculptured; marble-smooth; shaped; spiritual; graceful; delicate; slim; daisy-white; slender; golden; tender; soft; fragile; brawny; muscular; steel; iron; terrifying; strong; powerful; stout; tremendous; muscle-corded; firm; capable; sinewy; enormous; massive; mighty; bony; puny; thin; snaky; frail; lean; plump; thick; rounded; chubby; flabby; awkward; clumsy; grisly; profaning; threatening; offending; degraded; shattered; wounded; wasted; molded; numb; aching; bruised; limp; drowsy; languid; listless; waving; gesticulating; beckoning; outstretched; clutching; outflung; extended; proffered; hanging; rigid; outspread; wide-open (pl); reaching; classical; uplifted; imploring; dangling; upraised; crossed (pl); wan; throbbing; swaying; swinging; linked; shaking; silken; jeweled; uniformed; khaki-clad; veiled; soapy; bare; powdered; hirsute; overlong; fearful; willing; sheltering; protecting; pacifying; combined (pl); engulfing; encircling; supporting; wandering; longing; waiting; accusing; thankful; reluctant; yearning; affectionate; reassuring; flailing; nerveless; tremulous; developed; incredible; ineffective; enthusiastic; detaining; wriggling; reinforcing; impulsive; derisive; forging; bewildered; rapturous; whirlwind; alabaster; movable; crooked; potent; swirling; remorseless; glittering; generous; unsuspected; mutual; temporal; swordless; disposing; gigantic; resplendent; large; fetching; elephantine; revengeful; pendent; lithe; barren; seraphic; twining; motherly; impatient; fearsome; restful; despised; unwieldy; braving; stiffened; sausage-like; unloaded; gilded; speckled; gnarled; angular; hungry; aching; dingy; cautious; protesting; victorious; desolate; almighty; grotesque; ponderous; rebellious; shaggy; puissant; steadying; poetic; enticing; conjugal; wrathful; sustaining; furbished; oft-bended; pleached; dimpled; grounded; sinuous; shining; dazzling; figured; artificial; feeble; gross; snowy; loving; withered; impeccable; mailed; restful; troublesome; gorgeous; fondling; out-reaching; restraining; springy; naked; lascivious; locked (pl); municipal; amputated; freckled; unreasoning; chapel-like; dusky; official; embracing; unhallowed; burnished; alien; faith-clad; waxen; needful; hairy-fibred; sturdy; akimbo (pl); strangling; glowing; lily; secular; bandaged; steel-strong; dissonant; puffy; boneless; broken; stalwart; whirring; blazoned (pl); branching (pl).

verbs

amputate—; attach—to; bare—; bind—; cast —s around; clasp in —s; cradle in —s; cross —s; dangle on—; develop—; drive—through; embrace in —s; encircle in —s; encumber —s; enfold in —s; entwine in —s; extend —s; extricate —s; flap —s; fling—around; fold —s; gather in —s; hail

with open —s; hang on —s; leap into —s; lend—; lock —s; impair the use of —s; open —s; paralyze —s; proffer—; pluck from —s; recline on—; rotate —s; sling —s; stretch out —s; strip from —s; support in —s; tear from —s; uncover —s; wave —s; wind in —s; wound—; wrap in—; wreathe in —s; —bleeds; —s cling around; —s dandle; —hangs; —projects.
(See limb, wrist.)

ARM (v)

adverbs
imperfectly; impenetrably; superbly; powerfully; mightily; threateningly; incredibly; ineffectively; puissantly; sturdily; stalwartly.

ARMADA

adjectives
air; huge; mighty; ponderous; impressive; death-dealing.

ARMAMENT

adjectives
unchecked; formidable; excessive; national; increased; vaunted; enormous; splendid; considerable.

verbs
appropriate for—; discard—; equip with—; limit—; outlaw—; produce—; rebuild—; reduce—; rehabilitate—; replace—; scale down—; strip of—; —s collapse; —s exceed.
(See force, guns.)

ARM-CHAIR

adjectives
palatial; chintz-covered; cushioned; shabby; restful; spacious; luxurious.

ARMISTICE

adjectives
unspoken; assumed; undeclared; disregarded.

ARMOR

adjectives
adamantine; customary; shining; sunbright; noticeable; virginal; magic; mortal; radiant; incongruous; elaborate; tough; chain; safest; steel-plated; jointless; impenetrable; protective; defensive; invisible; golden; horny; inviolate; spiritual; battered; granite; celestial.

verbs
buckle on—; burden with—; burnish—; c'ad in—; clothe in—; collect—; cover with —; defend in—; design—; discard—; employ—; enclose in—; furnish—; harness in —; pad—; pierce—; plate with—; scar—; scour—; sheathe in—; stain—; strip off—; swagger in—; —clashes; —gives way; —hampers; —jingles; —protects; —resists; --shields.
(See steel.)

ARMS
(weapons)

adjectives
purposeful; puny; ruthless; skilfully-handled; unfriendly.

verbs
abate—; abolish—; bear—; burnish—; call to—; chastise with—; defend with—; display—; draw—; engage with—; excel in—; exploit with—; fire—; force with—; furnish —; groove—; invent—; lack—; lay down —; leap to—; march in—; notch—; order —; present—; rally to—; rattle—; repel with—; resist with—; rise in—; shoulder —; smuggle—; surrender—; take by force of—; take up—; throw away—; train in—; wield—; win with—; —clash; —run out.
(See weapons.)

ARMY

adjectives
bristling; cleverly-concealed; cold-staring; death-dealing; destruction-spilling; flashing; sullen; grim-looking; grisly; havoc-playing; malignant; murderous; make-shift; exalted; exultant; invincible; indefatigable; gallant; superb; glorious; determined; splendid; formidable; magnificent; picked; distressed; retreating; doomed; ragged; unpaid; disgruntled; decimated; demoralized; domestic; defeated; pathetic; tarnished; recalcitrant; standing; motor-camping; contending; organized; modern; vast; surging; invading; beleaguering; besieging; heterogeneous; overwhelming; furtive; ravishing; enraged; respective; heathen; cooperating; dwindling; fraternal; opposing; immense; precious; powerful; half-famished; dispersed; concentrated; rude; innumerable (pl); incompetent; victorious; scattered; solid; flying; compact; well-commanded; self-reliant; enthusiastic; principal; desolating; provisional; starry; wrangling; succoring; allied; obstinate; barefoot; omnipotent; shattered; phantom: insurgent; faithful; melancholy; deplorable; routed.

verbs
call out—; clothe—; command—; conscript into—; consolidate—; dash at—; defy—; demobilize—; disband—; discharge—; discipline—; dishearten—; dismiss—; disperse

—; double—; drill—; encompass—; engage—; enlist in—; equip—; evacuate—; furlough—; harry—; hire—; impress into—; improvise—; increase—; join—; mechanize—; mobilize—; motorize—; muster—; organize—; pledge—; provide—; provision—; raise—; recruit—; regiment—; route—; serve in—; supply—; support—; transport—; turn—to flight; —assembles; —blockades; —charges; —converges on; —crusades; —encamps; —intercepts; —mutinies; —pillages; —plunders; —retires; —retreats; —rumbles; —rushes in; —storms; —strikes; —swarms; —wages war.

(See troops, soldiers, forces.)

AROMA

adjectives

fruity; exquisite; peculiar; offensive; fragrant; spicy; pungent; delicious; pleasant; remote; earthly; preprandial; tempting; lingering; sickly; intoxicating; faint; ineffable; questionable; delicate; luscious; quick; penetrating.

verbs

breathe in—; dissipate—; exhale—; imitate—; send forth—; —escapes; —floats; —pervades.

(See perfume, fragrance, odor.)

AROMATIC

adverbs

pleasantly; spicily; fragrantly; redolently; sweetly; pungently; arrestingly; refreshingly; pleasingly; definitely; strongly; delicately; exquisitely; enchantingly; charmingly; drowsily; faintly; overpoweringly; delectably; softly; intoxicatingly; lingeringly; richly; attractively; exotically.

AROUSE (v)

adverbs

thoroughly; seditiously; instantaneously; antagonistically; suddenly.

(See excite, rouse, animate, stimulate.)

ARRAIGNMENT

adjectives

harsh; eloquent; appalling; incredible.

ARRANGE (v)

adverbs

dramatically; delicately; becomingly; temptingly; alphabetically; elaborately; admirably; systematically; beautifully; sensibly; exquisitely; harmoniously; ideally; felicitously; obviously; cleverly; efficiently; hideously; crudely; clumsily; finally; previously; complexly; artistically; mechanically; methodically; ostensibly; confidentially; painfully.

(See classify, dispose, devise, contrive.)

ARRANGEMENT

adjectives

balanced; careful; impeccable; admirable; ideal; pleasant; impromptu; serene; formal; elaborate; desirable; skilful; felicitous; fair; obvious; regular; clever; cordial; efficent; divine; empty; attractive; devious; inequitable; hideous; crude; clumsy; final, judgmatical; fiscal; temporary; previous; spacious; preconcerted; incompatible; defensive; complex; dinette; cunning; provident; inconsistent; due; pleasure-principle; special; dilapidated; artistic; compensatory; mechanical; disconcerting; free-wheeling; line; practical; rectilinear; methodical; curious; graceful; established; fairest; simple; credit; harmonious; picturesque; traditional; fitting; domestic; ostensible; existing; unnatural; systematic; complicated; unsatisfactory; municipal; judicious; ingenious; charming; reciprocal; habitual; old-fashioned; dexterous; cumbrous; confidential; countermanded; painful; spacious.

verbs

adapt—; adjust—; adopt—; cancel—; criticize—; declare—; design—; desire—; determine—; devise—; dispute—; elaborate—; enter into—; furnish—; improvise—; insure—; negotiate—; order—; prepare—; prevent—; reach—; register—; repudiate—; standardize—; style—; welcome—; —conforms to; —disposes of; —prevails.

(See contract, understanding.)

ARRAY

adjectives

formidable; imposing; glorious; impressive; prodigious; rich; colorful; fascinating; enticing; neat; disordered; unsightly; stubborn; bristling; bridal; superb; abounding; motley; glittering; formal; endless; giddy; heterogeneous; bewildering; astonishing; comprehensive; superficial; hostile; confused; gorgeous; meek; gallant; militant; vivid; festival; flimsy; tranquil; immense; bright; terrible; meteor-eclipsing; incomparable; undisciplined; loose; vast; inexhaustible; noble; scattered; threatening; ragged; magnificent; grand; feudal; symmetrical; complete; awful; martial; chaste; white; stern; cold; battle; goodly; wild; flowering.

verbs
attire in—; break—; challenge—; deck in —; display—; draw up—; gaze at—; impose—; loose—; order—; outfit in—; rank in—; renew—; review—; stand in—; —impresses; —stretches.
(See display, exhibition.)

ARRAY (v)
adverbs
tastefully; gloriously; handsomely; formidably; impressively; richly; colorfully; fascinatingly; enticingly; superbly; formally; bewilderingly; superficially; vividly; gorgeously; incomparably; nobly.
(See arrange, marshal.)

ARREST
adjectives
arbitrary; capricious; frequent; summary; indiscriminate; wrongful; friendly; dreamy; injudicious; inspired; resisted; abrupt.

verbs
authorize—; charge with—; compel—; declare—; decree—; defend against—; delay —; demand—; dispense with—; effect—; enforce—; execute—; facilitate—; force to —; immunize against—; interfere with—; obtain—; order—; justify—; place under—; procure—of; release from—; resist—; restrain from—; result in—; secure—of; stop —; subject to—; warrant—; —deters; —s outnumber; —prevents.
(See imprisonment.)

ARREST (v)
adverbs
arbitrarily; unjustly; capriciously; summarily; indiscriminately; wrongfully; abruptly; injudiciously.
(See apprehend, stop, check, restrain.)

ARRIVAL
adjectives
mysterious; initial; late; speedy; unheralded; modest; merry; unconventional; noisy; bustling; timely; impending; abstract; successful; adventitious; seasonable; welcome; opportune; brilliant; unexpected; imminent; dread; anticipated.

ARRIVE (v)
adverbs
jubilantly; ultimately; punctually; incessantly; tardily; mysteriously; unconventionally; bustlingly; adventitiously; seasonably; opportunely; abruptly; expeditiously; slumberously.
(See come.)

ARROGANCE
adjectives
haughty; hard; cool; wounded; odd; splendid; stupid; vulgar; small; aesthetic; hot; unresponsive; tactless; desperate; despotic; supercilious; misstyled; unamiable; masculine; intellectual; tempered; monstrous; cynical; intolerable; meddlesome; ruffling; crested; burgher; blustering; brash; brusque; brisk; bristling; unbridled.

verbs
abandon—; disdain—; endure—; feed—; humble—; loathe—; purge the soul of—; satirize—; —causes; —indicates; —offends; —repels; —vexes.
(See assumption, assurance.)

ARROGANT
adverbs
intolerably; justifiably; noticeably; smugly; insolently; proudly; coolly; offensively; condescendingly; irritatingly; purposely; rudely; unpardonably; incurably; ridiculously; laughably; splendidly; oddly; stupidly; brashly; deplorably; uncivilly.

ARROW
adjectives
poisoned; fiery; answering; strong-shot; vengeful; ultimate; barbed; ineffectual; envenomed; burning; rankling; twanging; buried; eagle-plumed; crafty; featherless; swift; blunt; deadly; death-dealing.

verbs
aim—; barb—; bear—; discharge—; draw —; drop—; feather—; fire—; imbed—; lash—; let fly—; loose—; mark with—; notch—; pierce with—; pinch—; place—; point—; poison—; pour —s; release—; secure—; send—; shape—; shoot—; slay with —; smite with—; string—; throw off—; tip—; wound with—; —carries; —describes an arc; —glances off; —goes to the mark; —leaves; —passes; —penetrates; —pierces; —quivers; —reaches; —rides; —slips; —speeds; —wings.
(See dart, shaft.)

ART
adjectives
elaborate; consummate; undying; pleasurable; delicate; gentle; analogous; remarkable; serious; subtle; new; wonderful; ingenious; experienced; sophisticated; noblest; superb; ripe; gracious; obliging; unsurpassable; fine; tedious; glowing; profound; proficient; great; simple; sincere; glorious; pure; epic; meticulous; surpassing; graphic;

snubbed; aristocratic; modernistic; plastic; decorative; landscape; ancient; rustic; epistolary; contemporary; poetic; constructive; modern; applied; dramatic; elegant; antiquated; pyrotechnic; seeming; inscrutable; suave; finished; vanishing; fine; mystical; living; enviable; esoteric; replaced; cultured; lost; symbolic; fancy; hidden; servile; musical; colorless; blandishing (pl); kindred; perfidious; vital; culinary; fascinating; healing; peaceful; unpremeditated; specious; inventive; cunning; brain-spattering; baneful; fickle; windpipe-slitting; flawless; matchless; structural; virile; indigenous; superhuman; dreadful; tonsorial; imitative; classicizing; black; inharmonious; recreational; canonic; piscatorial; sunny; fertilizing; sublime; instrumental; regal; enrapturing; rational; idealistic; acquired; substantial; representative; lenient; vagrant; agile; equestrian; fearful; grotesque; public; deathless; prosperous; evasive; memorial; coarse; spiritual; abominable; inventive; exalted; mechanical; mortuary; histrionic; indifferent; vicious; living; coactive; quaint; empirical; irregular; incomprehensible; demoniacal; jealous; new-invented; loftier; orthodox: commercial; medical; ceramic; unhallowed: athletic; subservient; florid; classic; exquisite; practical; perishable; spontaneous; immature; elevated; patented; etched; menial; poor; low; voluptuous; illustrative; unlawful; rare; piquant; conspicuous.

verbs
animate—; apply—; appreciate—; attain—; awaken—; become—; breed—; caricaturize —; characterize—; choke—; compose—' comprehend—; conceive—; contrive by—; counterfeit—; cultivate—; dabble in—; deem —; devise—; devote to—; discriminate in —; display—; educate in—; elaborate—. embellish—; encourage—; etch—; evolve—; exaggerate—; execute—; exercise—; facilitate—; further—; glorify—; illustrate—- imitate—; inaugurate—; influence—; interpret—; limit—; master—; murder—; originate—; ply—; practise—; preserve—; produce—; purge—; pursue—; refine—; school in—; stifle—; supplement—; sustain —; systematize—; take refuge in—; trace—; verse in—; wed to—; —achieves; —assists; —attains; —builds; —conceals; —depicts; —derives from; —dies away; —disguises; —embodies; —enlightens; —evolves from; —excites; —expresses; —feigns; —flourishes; —functions; —imitates; —lags; —languishes; —ornaments; —portrays; —reflects; —remains; —reproduces; —reveals. (See literature, science.)

ARTERY

adjectives
pulsating; hardened; tiny; petty; spiritual; emotional.

verbs
block—; circulate in —s; drain—; expel from—; flow through—; incise—; involve —; ligate—; live in—; lodge in—; nourish —; obstruct—; pump through—; rupture—; sever—; terminate—; —s anastomose; —s ascend; —s branch; —s carry; —s contract; —s deteriorate; —s distribute; —s divide; —s empty; —s function; —s harden; —s join; —s spurt; —s supply; —s thicken; —s throb; —s unite.

ARTFUL

adverbs
instinctively; characteristically; slyly; craftily; subtly; insidiously; stealthily; smoothly; shrewdly; fiendishly; maliciously; astoundingly; astutely; cunningly; insinuatingly; trickily; habitually; adroitly; manifestly; openly; undeniably; knowingly; suavely; ingratiatingly; speciously; expertly; dangerously.

ARTICLE
(writing)

adjectives
respective; undesirable; perfunctory; subsequent; able; valuable; detailed; forceful; inflammatory; unrelated; editorial; antiquarian; foregoing; explanatory; abusive; preliminary; hysterical; noteworthy; famous; fascinating; occasional; thought-provoking; enlightening; hypocritical; exasperating; comprehensive; arresting; lurid; delightful; frivolous; authentic; unusual; informative; striking; disturbing; sane; well-reasoned; sensible; condensed; inspired; vituperative; amusing; recent; fiery; stodgy; leading; stimulating; provocative; well-considered; critical; descriptive; proposed.

verbs
abolish—; administrate—; alter—; amend —; approve—; break—; combine —s; compose—; design—; dismiss—; dispute—; ease out—; emit—; enact—; entreat—; excerpt —; fashion—; form—; found upon—; invoke—; peruse—; point out—; prefix—; promote—; promulgate—; provide—; ratify—; reject—; revise—; rewrite—; sanction—; submit—; summarize—; swerve from—; transgress—; —asserts; —author-

izes; —binds; —compels; —concerns; —denotes; —effects; —exposes; —expostulates; —governs; —guarantees; —impeaches; —indicts; —libels; —regulates; —slanders; —specifies; —stipulates; —treats of.
(See detail, item, clause, editorial, essay.)

ARTICLE

adjectives (an object)
proprietary; admirable; charming; befrilled; practical; previous; metallic; objectionable; bloated; inferior; humblest; aggressive; cardinal; minutest; tempting; conspicuous; distinctive; cumbersome; superior; conceivable; forbidden; ancient; bulky; expensive; flimsy; showy; adulterated; intimate; plated; useful; novel; remarkable; superfluous; indispensable; harsher; inanimate; patented; preceding; fulminated; fugitive; non-durable; particular; obnoxious; important; suitable; necessary; principal; existing; resplendent; forbidden; unmistakable; toilet; serviceable; staple; unsightly; ornamental.

ARTICULATE (a)

adverbs
clearly; particularly; distinctly; emphatically; finely; especially; wonderfully; powerfully; unmistakably; cruelly; meticulously; precisely; exactly; easily.

ARTICULATE (v)

adverbs
precisely; faintly; meticulously; whisperingly; breathlessly; clearly.
(See speak.)

ARTICULATION

adjectives
supple; well-remembered; appreciative; meticulous.

ARTIFICE

adjectives
amazing; shallow; harmless; debasing; delicate; petty; plotted; ingenious; fictional; honest; dazzling; wicked.

ARTIFICER

adjectives
deft; cunning; fierce; sly; suave.

ARTIFICIAL

adverbs
subtly; stiffly; crudely; inelegantly; crassly; grotesquely; gracelessly; ponderously; highly; pretentiously; flashily; floridly; laughably; ridiculously; awkwardly; offensively; outlandishly; affectedly; coquettishly; simperingly; mincingly; stagily; smoothly; slyly; cleverly; adroitly; ingeniously.

ARTILLERY

adjectives
active; coastal; defiance-roaring; doom-sounding; death-propelling; deafening; concerted; effective; earth-shaking; enormously-heavy; funeral-voiced; fierce-stabbing; incessant; liberal; offensive; reverberating; silenced; threatening; tumultuous; well-placed.

verbs
assign—; blast with—; capture—; command—; concentrate—; detail—; discharge—; disperse—; elevate—; employ—; encamp—; fear—; forge—; fortify—; improve—; introduce—; mechanize—; mount—; project—; reenforce with—; shelter from—; transport—; —attacks; —batters; —bears; —bombards; —breaks down; —concentrates on; —counters; —demolishes; —deploys; —destroys; —deteriorates; —devastates; —discharges; —fires; —forms; —handles; —harasses; —inflicts; —launches; —manoeuvers; —marches; —masses; —moves up; —occupies; —pounds; —projects; —pushes forward; —ranges; —reassembles; —repulses; —shells; —smashes; —supports; —thunders; —withdraws.
(See cannon, arms.)

ARTISAN

adjectives
tramping; skilled; capable; indolent; impatient; swarthy; humble; subordinate; simple; adroit.

ARTIST

adjectives
capable; excellent; first-rate; gifted; accomplished; competent; versatile; consummate; instinctive; true; creative; unerring; purposive; brilliant; conscientious; authentic; supreme; exquisite; cosmopolitan; keen-eyed; indefatigable; illustrious; great; cynical; world-famous; noted; distinguished; dissipated; weedy; sophisticated; temperamental; dissolute; adverse; melancholy; despairing; sought-after; pandering; unbusiness-like; impecunious; struggling; harassed; ragged; persecuted; misunderstood; detestable; sensitive; human; local; jealous; collaborating; fastidious; contemporary; eminent; eccentric; egotistic; excitable, fashionable; talented; outraged; accomplished; vulgar; scenic; native; mature; skilled;

well-known; inimitable; musical; liberal; unique; successful; sincere; decorative; technical; modern; renowned; interpretative.

verbs
confound—; encourage—; endow—; extol —; imitate—; inspire—; mark—; patronize —; remunerate—; revere—; —accomplishes; —apprehends; —attempts; —conceives; —contributes; —conveys; —creates; —cultivates; —designs; —displays; —elevates; —embodies; —employs; —endeavors; —entertains; —eschews; —executes; —expresses; —forges; —imbibes; —imitates; —opposes; —paints; —patterns; —portrays; —practises; —presents; —pursues; —renders; —reproduces; —reveals; —scorns; —sketches; —struggles with; —typifies; —unearths; —unfolds; —verses himself in.
(See sculptor, painter, musician, writer, poet, creator.)

ARTISTIC

adverbs
superbly; magnificently; delicately; actually; genuinely; indubitably; consummately; vividly; lustily; carefully; deftly; exultantly; studiedly; naturally; colorfully; richly; chastely; virginally; traditionally; radically; nostalgically; instinctively; inherently; innately; learnedly; creatively; unerringly; brilliantly; spontaneously; conscientiously; authentically; exquisitely; keenly; notably; temperamentally; sensitively; fastidiously; eminently; fashionably; inimitably; elegantly; gorgeously; magnificently; splendidly; radiantly; sublimely; bonnily; curiously; dazzlingly; passably; prettily; quaintly; showily; ingeniously; intrinsically; imitatively; academically; readily; correctly; easily; neatly; unaffectedly; crudely; ponderously; adroitly; cleverly; dexterously; intelligently; proficiently; skilfully; deftly; expertly; handily; critically; discriminatingly.

ARTISTRY

adjectives
superb; genuine; consummate; lusty; vivid; infinite; careful; deft; exalted; transcending; sheer; traditional; studied; fanatical.

ARTLESS

adverbs
unaffectedly; delightfully; refreshingly; sincerely; naively; touchingly; wondrously; manifestly; charmingly; ravishingly; exquisitely; deliciously; surprisingly; unbelievably; graciously; ingenuously; alluringly; adorably; innocently.

ASCEND (*v*)

adverbs
magically; majestically; simultaneously; directly; unwaveringly; lazily; leisurely; personally.
(See mount.)

ASCENDANCY

adjectives
inherent; moral; intellectual; growing; fatal; odious; papal; commercial; personal; complete.

ASCENDANT

adverbs
significantly; prominently; interestingly; materially; substantially; emphatically; chiefly; firmly; cardinally; markedly; primarily; remarkably; signally; vitally; influentially; preponderantly; prevalently; dominantly; authoritatively; absolutely; supremely; blessedly; happily; luckily; unfortunately; adversely; unluckily.

ASCENT

adjectives
marked; breakneck; preliminary; formidable; continual; toilsome; gentle; gradual; measureless; feasible; elevated; winding; tortuous; sheer; interminable; perilous.

verbs
accomplish—; attempt—; fear—; grade—; overcome—; schedule—; top—; —fatigues; —slopes; —tires; —wearies.
(See climb.)

ASCERTAIN (*v*)

adverbs
accurately; distinctly; dimly; instantaneously; vaguely; unhesitatingly.
(See discover.)

ASCETIC

adverbs
austerely; exceptionally; completely; incomprehensibly; obviously; excessively; terribly; remarkably; innately; naturally; puritanically; rigidly; rigorously; strictly; severely; harshly; arbitrarily; despotically; tyrannically; prudishly; haughtily.

ASCRIBE (*v*)

adverbs
unanimously; vaguely; openly; modestly; unsparingly; deliberately; unhesitatingly; villainously; frankly.
(See attribute, assign, impute.)

ASHEN

adverbs
pallidly; neutrally; coldly; colorlessly; dingily; dully; faintly; muddily; wanly; pearly.

ASHES

adjectives
quenchless; fallen; gossamer-like; glowing; whitening; lifeless; dreamless; smouldering; sparkless; venerated; charred; damped; cold; livid; vile; volcanic; blackened; dead; humble; feeble.

verbs
collect—; exhaust into—; flick—; gather—; grovel in—; heap—; mix with—; powder —; pulverize—; reduce to—; scorch to—; sift—; sprinkle with—; strew with—; throw out—; —char; —flame; —glow; —pirouette down; —remain; —rest; —settle; —smoulder.

(See cinders, remains, residue.)

ASK (*v*)

adverbs
courteously; equably; genially; discreetly; vaguely; pointedly; cannily; unctuously; spitefully; specifically; evasively; incredulously; querulously; swiftly; bluntly; huskily; contemptuously; relentlessly; persuasively; listlessly; compassionately; placidly; critically; guardedly; grouchily; shrewdly; brusquely; involuntarily; guilelessly; insistently; delicately; piteously; beseechingly; impressively; audaciously; plaintively; ironically; deadly; tremulously; naively; belligerently; provisionally; quizzically; socratically; apprehensively.

(See inquire, question, beg.)

ASPECT

adjectives
interesting; practical; picturesque; attractive; encouraging; smiling; humorous; prepossessing; pleasing; romantic; charming; benevolent; calm; noteworthy; absurd; sinister; ominous; accusing; contradictory (pl); dismal; diabolical; grim; forbidding; jaded; ludicrous; sensual; cynical; unnatural; maddening; gloomy; ridiculous; woebegone; volatile; evanescent; odd; grisly; irrational; controversial; shocking; ethical; ceremonial; physical; legal; psychic; religious; psychological; moral; genetic; scientific; obvious; broad; eternal; suggestive; original; fresh; superficial; ingratiating; beneficent; harsh; astonished; intimate; emotional; national; economic; conventional; unique; grave; formal; ferocious; haggard; drawn; staring; piteous; forsaken; melancholy; wan; miserable; pallid; repulsive; formidable; enticing; cheery; weather-beaten; propitious; feminine; appealing; many-sided; festival; material; transitional; cadaverous; ironic; appalling; dark; interrelated (pl); insinúating; benignant; spiritual; unreal; artificial; unlovely; gloomy; tragic; mournful; neglected; mysterious; reverend; stern; belligerent; bleak; legal; aesthetic; incoherent; deserted; rustic; malign; utilitarian; forlorn; sanguine; primitive; alarming; supernatural; stunned; impressive; imposing; inspiring; weird; rigorous; chilling; intangible; classic; foreign; multiform; cultivated; settled.

verbs
accentuate—; adorn—; afford—; assume—; bear—; behold—; bend—; cloud—; color—; contemplate—; contrast—; dominate—; dramatize—; dwell on—; extol—; gaze at —; intensify—; meet—; muzzle—; regard —; stress—; take on—; turn—; view—; wear—; —speaks.

(See appearance, view, scene, expression, mien, look.)

ASPERSIONS

adjectives
obsolete; hasty; casual; thinly-veiled; bitter; subtle.

verbs
bespatter with—; cast—; let fall—; resort to—; vindicate from—; —besprinkle; —damage; —enrage; —infuriate; —soil; —stain.

(See slander, scandal, calumny.)

ASPIRANT

adjectives
baffled; literary; defeated; penitent; conscientious; judicial.

ASPIRATIONS

adjectives
generous; lofty; noble; national; boundless; passionate; vague; artistic; intellectual; glowing; elegant; pure; awakened; dictatorial; spiritual; unlimited; greedy; earnest; forgotten; exalted; exquisite; long-cherished; fond; sacred; speculative; political; moral; musical; social; scrupulous; secretive; rebuffed; undirected; ladylike; thwarted; professional; humdrum; poetic; determined; enthusiastic.

verbs
cherish—; deride—; dignify—; embody—;

fan with—; further—; give force to—; long with—; nurse—; realize—; restrain—; sigh with—; swamp—; thwart—; —is bounded by; —lifts him; —ripens; —soars.
(See ambition, desire, aim.)

ASPIRE (v)

adverbs
invariably; loftily; nobly; boundlessly; generously; passionately; artistically; intellectually; spiritually; earnestly; socially; professionally; poetically; determinedly; enthusiastically.
(See desire.)

ASS

adjectives
preposterous; incompetent; slow-gaited; conceited; affected; insignificant; arrant; pretentious; patient; gibbering; portentous; egregious; pompous.

verbs
act as—; brand—; breed —es; burden—; call—; corral —es; domesticate —es; employ —; harness—; overtake—; plow with —es; procure—; saddle—; shelter—; stall—; yoke —; —balks; —bears; —brays; —flees; —plods; —roams; —sniffs the wind; —strays; —subsists on.
(See animal.)

ASSAIL (v)

adverbs
abusively; fearlessly; unjustly; vituperatively; untruthfully; vaguely; furiously; keenly; constantly; perpetually; unrelentingly; doughtily; blood-thirstily; rudely; vociferously; audaciously; formidably; boldly.
(See attack.)

ASSAILANT

adjectives
fierce; quick; skillful; deadly; doughty; unrelenting; potent; unwary; blood-thirsty; rude; violent; savage; vociferous; audacious; powerful; bold; formidable; deceased.

ASSASSIN

adjectives
foiled; fiendish; jealous; vile; doomed; cool; professional; cowardly; terrorizing; wolfish; mercenary; well-meaning.

verbs
evade—; execute—; hire—; martyrize—; reward—; subdue—; —attacks; —conspires; —knifes; —lurks; —murders; —slays; —stabs; —terrorizes.
(See murderer.)

ASSASSINATE (v)

adverbs
treacherously; fiendishly; vilely; coolly; tragically.
(See kill.)

ASSASSINATION

adjectives
cold-blooded; murderous; foul; villainous; predatory.

verbs
accomplish—; aim at—; applaud—; attempt —; avert—; execute—; finish—; foment—; loathe—; pay for—; plot—; revenge—; witness—; —kindles.
(See murder, killing.)

ASSAULT

adjectives
intermittent; rude; meditated; critical; damnable; aggravated; gallant; fresh; feeble; furious; formidable; anonymous; salutary; murderous; vigorous; mock; contemplated; desperate; boisterous; drunken; base; vain; magnificent; counter; general; unprovoked; concentrated; criminal; inexplicable; destructive; terrific; simultaneous; felonious; courageous; vicious; serious; determined; savage; wicked; shrewd; frenzied; devastating; thorough-going.

verbs
aggravate—; bear—; carry by—; commit —; constitute—; counter—; defy—; fortify against—; gain by—; incur—; inflict—; intend—; make—upon; overthrow—; parallel—; project—; punish—; renew—; repeat —; repulse—; resist—; rush to—; scorn—; threaten with—; win by—; withstand—; —destroys; —produces; —weakens.
(See attack, charge, invasion, onslaught.)

ASSAULT (v)

adverbs
outrageously; violently; rudely; critically; damnably; gallantly; feebly; murderously; furiously; formidably; vigorously; desperately; boisterously; drunkenly; basely; vainly; magnificently; unprovokedly; criminally; inexplicably; destructively; simultaneously; feloniously; frenziedly; devastatingly.
(See attack, assail.)

ASSEMBLAGE

adjectives
vast; matchless; international; dazzling; brilliant; striking; immense; gracious; ad-

miring; hapless; motley; confused; popular; learned; glittering; melancholy; ludicrous; riotous; dreary; solemn; pitiful; plutocratic; chattering; variegated; august; hushed; listless; inattentive; public.

ASSEMBLE (v)

adverbs

elaborately; festively; tumultuously; confusedly; glitteringly; riotously; drearily; solemnly; pitifully; chatteringly; listlessly; publicly; inattentively.

(See congregate, gather, meet.)

ASSEMBLY

adjectives

fair; stormy; provincial; propitious; august; primary; legislative; glorious; numerous; gay; venerable; representative; illustrious; staid; significant; deliberative; electrified; distinguished; religious; truculent; uncongenial; periodical (pl); artless; orderly; polite.

verbs

address—; appoint to—; call—; compose—; convoke—; dismiss—; gather—; haunt—; lead—; organize—; pervade—; petition—; remodel—; salute—; set—against; unite in —; —abolishes; —adjourns; —annuls; —collects; —communes; —condemns; —congregates; —convenes; —decides; —decrees; —deliberates; —enforces; —excludes; —frames; —invests; —limits; —resolves; —suppresses.

(See meeting, congregation, council, conference.)

ASSENT

adjectives

unqualified; wordless; unanimous; preoccupied; spiritless; reluctant; deep-throated; provisional; silent; rational; requisite; cordial; vague; mournful; universal; callous; intellectual; placid; ready; brief; rapturous; smiling; rough; demure; enthusiastic; perfunctory; deliberate.

verbs

approve—; confess—; declare—; engage—; gain—; gesture—; imply—; mutter—; necessitate—; nod—; obtain—; promise—; purchase—; read—; require—; stir to—; vote—; vow—; win—; withdraw—; withhold—; yield—; —emanates; —signifies.

(See agreement, acquiescence, consent.)

ASSENT (v)

adverbs

grudgingly; appreciatively; graciously; solemnly; benevolently; ironically; indifferently; wordlessly; unanimously; unqualifiedly; spiritlessly; reluctantly; silently; cordially; vaguely; mournfully; callously; demurely; placidly; briefly; rapturously; enthusiastically; perfunctorily; deliberately.

(See concur, acquiesce, yield.)

ASSERT (v)

adverbs

positively; incredibly; blasphemously; unanimously; courageously; peremptorily; persistently; strenuously; dogmatically; emphatically; erroneously; eloquently; lustily; judicially; ignorantly; aggressively; boastfully; truculently; blandly; stalwartly; irresponsibly; autocratically; despotically; arbitrarily; fallaciously; contradictorily; presumptuously; vaingloriously; groundlessly; unequivocally; gratuitously.

(See affirm, state, say, declare.)

ASSERTION

adjectives

ignorant; lofty; vigorous; hare-brained; aggressive; emphatic; blundering; boastful; truculent; reiterated; extravagant; prior; impudent; audacious; wild; bland; complete; incredible; dogmatic; complimentary; intense; loud; incensed; controversial; irresponsible; sweeping; absolute; stalwart; astounding; autocratic; despotic; arbitrary; brutal; blustering; erroneous; pharisaical; fallacious; monstrous; disputable; contradictory; vainglorious; random; groundless; florid; deliberate; colorful; presumptuous; unequivocal; gratuitous.

verbs

affirm—; aver—; conclude—; contest—; contradict—; controvert—; credit—; declare —; defend—; flinch under—; justify—; maintain—; protest—; prove—; qualify—; refute—; sponsor—; support—; —contradicts; —elicits from; —liberates; —persuades; —sets free; —vindicates.

(See statement, declaration.)

ASSERTIVE

adverbs

loftily; aggressively; emphatically; boastfully; truculently; extravagantly; impudently; insolently; audaciously; arrogantly; blandly; confidently; dogmatically; irresponsibly; sweepingly; astoundingly; autocratically; despotically; imperiously; brutally; monstrously; vaingloriously; floridly; presumptuously; preposterously; unequivocally; heedlessly; rashly; brusquely; blatantly.

ASSESS (v)

adverbs
equitably; unjustly; annually; repeatedly.
(See rate.)

ASSET

adjectives
dubious; distinct; domestic; inestimable; stupendous; valuable; perdurable; tangible; priceless; frozen; unassailable; paramount; strategic; scenic; compelling.

verbs
assess—s; bear—; capitalize on—; claim—; collect—s; dissolve—; distribute—s; earn —s; falsify—; fix—; freeze—; include—; inflate—s; inherit—; liquidate—; market—; note—; omit—; possess—; reduce—; represent—; salvage—; take over—; trade—; undervalue—; water—; work—; —s appear; —s increase; —s shrink; convert into —s; deduct from—; defer—.
(See property, resources, effects, possessions.)

ASSEVERATE (v)

adverbs
repeatedly; hotly; continually; sincerely; persistently; whole-heartedly; coldly; pleasantly.
(See declare.)

ASSIDUITY

adjectives
attentive; persevering; unremitting; discriminating; devastating; relentless; parental; bee-like; well-meaning.

ASSIDUOUS

adverbs
conscientiously; painfully; perseveringly; dependably; unremittingly; energetically; industriously; reliably; faithfully; amazingly; unusually; remarkably; loyally; uncomplainingly; unwaveringly; invariably; uniformly; persistently; constantly.

ASSIGN (v)

adverbs
subsequently; precisely; rigorously; pedagogically; frequently; unthinkingly.
(See allot, apportion, appoint.)

ASSIGNMENT

adjectives
elaborate; roving; precise; glamorous; charming; pedagogical; rigorous; impossible; difficult.

verbs
accept—; administer—; advance—; allot—; alter—; appoint to—; apportion—; authorize—; block—; botch—; bungle—; create —; designate—; determine—; dispose of—; earn—; exempt from—; free from—; fulfill—; interest in—; merit—; muff—; nominate for—; pass—; point out—; reject—; relieve of—; set to—; share—; specify—; transfer—; wangle—; —consists of; —denotes; —pays.

ASSIMILATE (v)

adverbs
actively; readily; unhesitatingly; spiritually; painfully; whole-heartedly; easily.
(See absorb.)

ASSIMILATION

adjectives
ready; spiritual; difficult.

ASSIST (v)

adverbs
industriously; chivalrously; materially; cordially; officiously; vigorously; effectively; financially; invaluably; charitably; generously; medically; professionally; scientifically; voluntarily; temporarily; mechanically; indispensably; skillfully; mutually; vicariously.
(See help, aid.)

ASSISTANCE

adjectives
masculine; armed; pecuniary; financial; material; invaluable; ineffectual; extraneous; charitable; generous; medical; scientific; voluntary; professional; temporary; mechanical; outside; indispensable; skilled; additional; tactful; mutual.

verbs
accept—; afford—; contribute—; crave—; disdain—; entreat—; furnish—; further with—; lend—; limit—; present—; procure—; rely upon—; render—; requisition —; solicit—; swear—; win by—; —enables; —encourages.
(See aid, relief, cooperation, help, support.)

ASSISTANT

adjectives
capable; patient; faithful; self-sacrificing; esteemed; untrained; temporary; fledgling; green-eyed; detached; ambidexterous; qualified; voluble; clinical; able; scholarly.

verbs
advance—; appoint—; choose—; dispatch —; —accompanies; —aids; —cooperates; —endeavours; —practices; —stands by.
(See partner.)

ASSOCIATE

adjectives
habitual; blithe; old-time; ill-looking; dignified; daring; vulgar; confidential; barbarian; cherished; hardened; crafty; literary; business; questionable; unsavory; droll; gallant; close; intimate.

verbs
applaud —s; exile —s; idolize —s; prevail upon —s; —s accompany; —s ally with; —s belong; —s cooperate; —s share; —s unite.
(See companion, colleague, partner.)

ASSOCIATE (*v*)

adverbs
inalienably; intimately; indissolubly; inseparably; profoundly; fraternally; indelibly; habitually; vulgarly; daringly; confidentially; craftily; questionably; drolly; closely.
(See connect.)

ASSOCIATION

adjectives
intimate; gloomy; ancestral; disparate; incidental; promiscuous; philanthropic; mournful; obscure; historical; tenuous; scandalous; polite; charitable; congenial; unpleasant; childish; cherished; tender; undefinable; endearing; memorable; haphazard; obligatory; natural; exclusive; ghastly; imperious; voluntary; indissoluble; subtle; casual; facile; aesthetic; unanalyzed; curious; struggling; unsavory; venerable; daily; picturesque; legendary; democratic; classic.

verbs
admit to—; affiliate with—; awaken—; combine in—; conceive—; confederate into —; conjure up —s; connect with—; deal with—; disband—; disorganize—; disrupt —; distinguish—; endow—; establish—; exclude from—; expel from—; father—; found—; frequent—; immortalize—; incorporate—; laud—; league into—; manage—; nurse—; oppose—; organize—; outlaw—; quarter at—; revive—; support—; terminate—; unite in—; vouch for—; —aims at; —classifies; —s combine; —confers upon; —flourishes; —fosters; —rivals; —sets forth; —springs up.
(See alliance, fellowship, affiliation, connection.)

ASSORTMENT

adjectives
imposing; varied; appealing; hideous; heterogeneous; distinguished; tangled; remarkable; excellent; amazing; complete; exceptional; motley; disintegrated; outstanding; vast; crude; comprehensive; diversified; odd; generous; extensive; incongruous; confused; conglomerated; concentrated; balanced; weird.

ASSUME (*v*)

adverbs
presumptuously; gradually; voluntarily; dogmatically; hypothetically; commonly; vigorously; unconsciously; unlawfully; tacitly; boastfully; superciliously; playfully; theatrically; irritatingly; erroneously; gratuitously; whimsically; groundlessly; complacently; fallaciously; blandly; smugly; ungraciously; baselessly; traditionally; fundamentally; falsely; imperturbably; candidly; placidly; fatuously; humorously; viciously; unpardonably; arrogantly; innocently.
(See undertake, presume, accept, usurp.)

ASSUMPTION

adjectives
tacit; boastful; supercilious; theatrical; sweeping; charitable; playful; irritating; erroneous; verbal; gratuitous; transparent; whimsical; preposterous; groundless; natural; complacent; calm; wearied; unparallelled; fallacious; unwarranted; commonplace; absurd; precarious; mute; hereditary; bland; smug; ungracious; critical; baseless; plausible; traditional; fundamental; reckless; false; imperturbable; candid; gross; placid; random; shallow; unconcealed; fatuous; humorous; vicious; unproved; undue; gentlemanly; unpardonable; arrogant; innocent.

verbs
accept—; adopt—; anticipate—; contest—; grant—; guide by—; lay bare—; limit—; pardon—; predicate upon—; proceed upon —; steer clear of—; sustain—; take up—; throw out—; verify—; warrant—; weigh —; —holds; —implies; —leads.
(See supposition.)

ASSURANCE

adjectives
gracious; positive; easy; lavish; pleasant; solemn; full; happy; sincere; serene; unqualified; mute; respectful; modest; delicate; advance; dispassionate; tender; sufficient; renewed; calm; comforting; blissful; counterfeit; diplomatic; vain; insolent;

convincing; serious; limitless; reciprocal; mutual; characteristic; uncomfortable; ineffable; lukewarm; well-founded; disbelieved; inner; loquacious; inspiriting; exquisite; disheartening; definite; false; absolute; emphatic; melodious; tranquil; dampening; ponderous; smiling; gentle; cool; diminishing; considerable; significant; bland; waning; professional; swaggering; ineradicable; unwavering; infallible; magnificent; smug; defiant; blunt; insensitive; brassy.

verbs
breed—; confirm—; convey—; establish—; flash—; guarantee—; handle with—; inspire—; pledge—; procure—; promise—; renew—; rest in—; secure—; smile—.
(See confidence, conviction, trust.)

ASSURE (v)

adverbs
virtually; solemnly; diligently; indolently; secretly; vaguely; reasonably; positively; lavishly; serenely; unqualifiedly; mutely; respectfully; modestly; tenderly; diplomatically; insolently; convincingly; reciprocally; mutually; characteristically; absolutely; emphatically; tranquilly; blandly; professionally; swaggeringly; unwaveringly; infallibly; defiantly; bluntly.

ASTONISH (v)

adverbs
sublimely; rousingly; amazingly; silently; profoundly; inconceivably; utterly; unboundedly; inexpressibly; blankly; palpably; unmistakably; intensely; unaffectedly; ludicrously; dramatically.
(See amaze, astound, stagger.)

ASTONISHMENT

adjectives
respectful; amused; tempestuous; unrestrained; affronted; silent; rapturous; whimsical; fat; pure; feigned; involuntary; mute; profound; initial; inconceivable; liveliest; unspeakable; utter; unbounded; swift; indignant; delighted; ever-increasing; inexpressible; horrified; dull; dawning; contemptuous; blank; palpable; sardonic; unmistakable; puzzled; intense; fond; breathless; wordless; annoyed; unaffected; acute; uncomfortable; curious; faint; open-mouthed; petrified; bitter; wide-eyed; stupefied; ludicrous; dramatic; sheer; hurt; shocked; bored; bald.

verbs
benumb with—; blink with—; confuse—; elicit—; excite—; express—; feign—; gasp with—; move to—; numb with—; paralyze with—; pretend—; quell—; restrain—; seize with—; stagger with—; stupefy—; supersede—.
(See amazement, surprise, wonder.)

ASTOUND (v)

adverbs
utterly; amazingly; thoroughly; completely; tremendously; dramatically; inexpressibly.
(See astonish, amaze, stagger.)

ASTUTE

adverbs
cleverly; keenly; sagaciously; sagely; wisely; craftily; cunningly; invariably; habitually; unfailingly; adroitly; customarily; discerningly; artfully; manifestly; undeniably; intelligently; shrewdly; deftly; ingeniously; insidiously; judiciously; learnedly.

ASTUTENESS

adjectives
habitual; strategical; devious; native; editorial; customary.

ASYLUM

verbs
abolish—; afford—; attend—; cast into—; claim—; commit to—; deliver up to—; devote to—; escape from—; establish—; flee from—; force into—; found—; guarantee—; grant—; harbor in—; huddle in—; incarcerate in—; invade—; limit—to; maintain—; maltreat in—; preside over—; provide—; refuse—to; remove from—; reside in—; restrict to—; retreat to—; sanctify—; seek—; support in—; torture in—; violate—; —accumulates; —cares for; —deals with; —protects; —shelters.
(See retreat, sanctuary, refuge, institution.)

ATHEISM

adjectives
uncompromising; overt; aggressive; militant; downright; courageous; swaggering.

verbs
cast off—; charge with—; clothe in—; countenance—; despise—; disprove—; destroy—; disapprove—; eradicate—; exhibit—; fall into—; incline toward—; inculcate—; justify—; mourn—; overthrow—; practice—; prate about—; pretend to—; proclaim—; recognize—; reject—; replace—; substitute—; support—; thunder—; unloose—; voice—; —acknowledges; —appears; —captivates; —conceives; —denies;

—disbelieves; —exists; —flounders; —grips; —grows; —lacks; —organizes; —philosophizes; —protests; —quiets down; —startles.
(See skepticism, disbelief.)

ATHEIST

adjectives
passionate; impious; positive; extreme; practical.

verbs
convert—; convince—; —arises; —confuses; —defames; —denies; —disbelieves; —discourses; —disregards.
(See skeptic, heretic.)

ATHEISTIC

adverbs
bigotedly; horribly; irreverently; impiously; perversely; fanatically; avowedly; sacrilegiously; profanely; heart-breakingly; grievously; tormentingly; obstinately; stubbornly; unhappily; irrationally; unreasonably; profoundly; irrevocably; immovably; obdurately; openly; essentially.

ATHLETE

adjectives
tall; wiry; well-built; fleet-legged; husky; energetic; lithe; young; scintillant; distinguished; professional; promising; splendid; all-around; barrel-chested.

verbs
address —s; applaud—; coach—; coddle—; condition—; debar—; develop—; commercialize—; exhaust—; experience—; fete—; fit—; govern—; honor—; inspire—; key up —; league —s; match—; oppose—; privilege—; proselyte—; provide for—; solicit—; stimulate—; strain—; subsidize—; time—; —accomplishes; —combats; —competes; —contends; —contests; —endures; —excels; —exhibits; —leaps; —overhauls; —strives; —surpasses; —trains; —vaults; —vies; —wrestles.
(See contestant, player.)

ATHLETIC

adverbs
splendidly; stoutly; noisily; sturdily; healthily; devotedly; robustly; heartily; vigorously; wholesomely; healthfully; magnificently; whole-heartedly; stockily; brawnily; ardently; assiduously; zealously; energetically; gravely; seriously.

ATHLETICS

verbs
bar—; bar from—; coach—; compete in—; create—; develop—; dip into—; dispel—; draft into—; embrace—; encourage—; engage in—; enter into—; establish—; excel in—; favor—; further—; go in for—; improve—; interest in—; pertain to—; practise—; promote—; referee—; score—; skill in—; subordinate—; succeed in—; support —; teach—; train for—; undertake—; utilize—; witness—; —builds; —develops; —occupies; —stirs; —thrills.
(See game, exercise.)

ATMOSPHERE

adjectives
radiant; genial; congenial; rosy; general; ideal; blessed; refreshing; exhilarating; free; invigorating; gentle; homelike; calm; pure; enervating; charming; genteel; mirthful; enchanting; quiet; restful; exquisite; bracing; serene; cordial; genuine; healthful; happy; buoyant; delightful; queenly; hospitable; wholesome; agreeable; jolly; rare; admirable; weird; uncanny; indescribable; electric; amazing; spooky; exciting; creepy; gloomy; stratified; brutal; criminal; dingy; severe; restricted; unhappy; air-cooled; sinister; dire; hostile; uneasy; chilling; insidious; polluted; murky; smoky; terrible; fetid; soggy; sour; nauseous; poisonous; dim; small-town; rural; frozen; human; political; learned; adventurous; poetic; slumbrous; fairylike; cosmopolitan; humid; sultry; close; windless; stuffy; living; changed; sheltered; realistic; distinctive; intangible; unfathomable; essential; inimical; apprehensive; thunderous; balmy; swift-moving; colorful; unreal; cool; ethereal; misty; special; enveloping; natural; intoxicating; characteristic; refined; clean; correct; luxurious; pleasant; distinguished; cheerful; ambient; suffocating; limpid; burning; steaming; faint; foul; rayless; grim; tense; vapory; bell-clear; venomous; contagious; quivering; artistic; musical; charged; consistent; intimate; straitened; infective; spiritual; hot; scintillating; transparent; stagnant; ruffling; lucid; rosy; uninteresting; agitated; nervous; romantic; artificial; unearthly; fierce; factitious; sleepy; metropolitan; easy; controlled; surcharged; depressing; lost; medieval; continental; stilted; decorous; respectable; social; intellectual; dewy; drear; summer; frightening; intimate; choked; rich; subtle; unindividual; exciting; clarified; dense; ladylike; dismal; troublous; emotional; roseate; oil-reeking; picturesque; somber; country; sentimental; hallowed; poetic; humid; damp; burdensome; scientific; dust-

less; quivering; reactionary; provincial; pellucid; unconventional; thrilling; livable; indoor; germ-laden; putrid; festive; impersonal; disloyal; elastic; sun-warm; crystal; lifeless; mutual; beamless; evening; tranquil; emerald; precious; furnace-heated; authentic; oppressive; concentrated; uncongenial; wet; commonplace; rarefied; burning; impassive; remote; ever-stormless.

ATMOSPHERE
(air)

verbs
absorb in—; adulterate—; analyze—; combine with—; compose—; constitute—; contaminate—; cool—; befoul—; cleanse—; erupt into—; escape into—; gain access to —; illuminate—; inhale—; invade—; filter —; float in—; mix in—; occupy—; pervade —; pump from—; rarify—; refresh—; release into—; smother in—of; surcharge—; —reeks.

(See air.)

ATMOSPHERE
(element or influence)

verbs
achieve—; break—; breathe—; capture—; charge—; create—; dispel—; dissipate—; distill—; drink in—; electrify—; enhance—; evoke—; indicate—; inform—; leaven—; load—; shatter—; surround—; —hinders; —inspires; —lends; —lures; —mingles; —promotes; —vivifies.

(See influence, environment.)

ATOM

adjectives
primordial; golden; pungent; intrusive; paltry; jarring; meditative; quenchless; homogeneous; gaseous; tormented; intelligent; throbbing; phosphorescent.

ATONE (*v*)

adverbs
fully; peacefully; heroically; bitterly; finally; vicariously; solemnly; sorrowfully; humbly.

(See pay.)

ATONEMENT

adjectives
heroic; final; least; bitter; vicarious; solemn; innocent.

verbs
emphasize—; make—; modify—; offer—; preach—; punish—; purify by—; refuse—; reject—; repent in—; reward—; sacrifice in—; set at—; —amends; —appeases; —dawns; —expiates; —reconciles; —redeems; —repairs; —restores; —satisfies; —saves; —vindicates.

(See reparation, satisfaction.)

ATROCIOUS

adverbs
scandalously; outrageously; glaringly; notoriously; horribly; monstrously; inhumanly; harshly; ruthlessly; wickedly; abominably; savagely; barbarously; pitiably; remarkably; incredibly; unbelievably; inexpressibly; inconceivably.

ATROCITY

adjectives
Victorian; lugubrious; unbelievable; monstrous; unprovoked; barbaric; utter; cold-blooded; out-of-the-way.

verbs
attend with—; avenge—; commit—; defend from—; deserve—; expiate—; hide—; inflict—upon; revenge—; subject to—; —horrifies; —shocks; —stupefies.

(See outrage, crime, cruelty, wickedness, blunder.)

ATTACH (*v*)

adverbs
passionately; unfeignedly; exclusively; violently; devoutly; gratefully; justly; indissolubly; sentimentally; ardently; unashamedly; romantically; hopelessly; insanely; incestuously; uniformly; tenderly; fervidly; emotionally; recklessly; conjugally; avowedly; cynically; excessively; momentarily.

(See annex, fasten.)

ATTACHMENT

adjectives
sentimental; passionate; warped; ardent; violent; deep; affectionate; unashamed; romantic; hopeless; boundless; invisible; insane; warm; incestuous; altruistic; disinterested; uniform; prior; tender; honest; steady; unrequited; fervid; special; emotional; underlying; reckless; filial; conjugal; marked; lasting; growing; lukewarm; serious; avowed; cynical; excessive; momentary.

verbs
absorb by—; affect—; apprehend—; authorize—; cement—; command—; connect—; decree—of; deepen—; deprecate—; devote to—; divide—; enforce—; execute—; fasten —; further—; grant—; process—; recover by—; regulate—; secure—; seize in—; sympathize with—; tack on—; warrant—;

—binds; —perishes; —persists; —survives; —withstands.

(See affection, devotion.)

ATTACK

adjectives

smashing; savage; murderous; fiery; bold; homicidal; ripping; bulldog; tearing; deadly; devastating; ruthless; angry; fierce; brutal; reckless; terrific; treacherous; scathing; hurricane; severe; damaging; formidable; desperate; prolonged; diplomatic; merciless; literary; hand-to-hand; journalistic; verbal; demagogic; vehement; unrestrained; incessant; determined; inexorable; rapid; zestful; impetuous; correct; serious; unexpected; direct; surprise; resounding; logical; vague; mysterious; provocative; sudden; well-organized; sustained; widespread; subtle; persisting; counter; organized; vigorous; withering; open; pulmonary; precipitate; simultaneous; scientific; bitter; damaging; crushing; unprovoked; whirlwind; strategic; oblique; furious; hysterical; peculiar; systematic; secular; outside; ordered; infantry; desultory; threatened; blasphemous; lawless; decisive; barbarous; noisy; seditious; premature; subsequent; convulsive; contemplated; nocturnal; burglarous; unjust; insidious; unfortunate; indiscriminate; ill-natured; abrupt; outrageous; immediate; tumultuous; abortive; violent; ignoble; frontal; satirical; tireless; sagacious; spasmodic; censurable; epileptoid; premeditated; venomous.

verbs

anticipate—; avert—; block—; blunt—; carry—; change—; characterize—; conceive—; concentrate—; consolidate—; counter—; cure of—; defy—; desist from—; direct—; dislodge—; divert—; double—; foresee—; forestall—; guard against—; head off—; immunize against—; induce—; initiate—; intensify—; launch—; mass for—; mount to—; plan—; precipitate—; predispose to—; prepare for—; presage—; pretend—; proceed with—; proclaim—; recover from—; re-enforce—; repel—; repudiate—; repulse—; satirize—; shift—; soften—; subdue—; succeed in—; succumb to—; suppress—; survive—; sustain—; terminate—; throw off—; time—; unite in—; unleash—; usher in—; wind up—; —abates; —arises; —coincides; —defames; —excites; —impends; —injures; —occurs; —overthrows; —recurs; —seizes; —subsides; —succeeds; —sways; —swerves; —swings.

(See invasion, siege, attempt.)

ATTACK (v)

adverbs

ardently; simultaneously; bitterly; scurrilously; fiendishly; virulently; libelously; savagely; anonymously; ridiculously; characteristically; sorely; energetically; vehemently; criminally; unscrupulously; smashingly; murderously; devastatingly; ruthlessly; scathingly; treacherously; verbally; incessantly; determinedly; inexorably; impetuously; venomously; scientifically; unprovokedly; obliquely; blasphemously; decisively; barbarously; prematurely; insidiously; satirically.

(See assail, invade, combat.)

ATTAIN (v)

adverbs

ultimately; cheaply; effectually; artistically; modestly; legally; intellectually; profitably; educationally; singularly; ultimately; scientifically; technically; astronomically; linguistically; incomparably; rarely.

(See achieve, gain, acquire.)

ATTAINMENTS

adjectives

remarkable; artistic; desirable; modest; legal; mental; distinguished; unusual; intellectual; profitable; scholarly; educational; singular; ultimate; ornamental; eminent; scientific; technical; astronomical; linguistic; incomparable; rare.

ATTEMPT

adjectives

sincere; valiant; memorable; sympathetic; serious; honest; admirable; successful; elaborate; ingenious; ambitious; eloquent; careful; kindly; enlightened; reasonable; well-meaning; ill-directed; slow-witted; weak; faltering; feeble; sorry; slightest; bashful; ineffectual; unavailing; half-hearted; laughable; grotesque; hopeless; vain; unfortunate; clumsy; futile; stupid; foolish; fruitless; farcical; mock; foolhardy; despairing; inept; pitiful; nugatory; maladroit; murderous; outrageous; mad; disastrous; dreary; infamous; superhuman; bold; daring; heroic; spectacular; systematic; repeated; definite; organized; long-heralded; vituperative; obvious; belated; freest; picturesque; covert; blind; passionate; abortive; miscarried; unappreciated; curious; numerous; pretentious; early; labored; major; hurried; unsteady; involuntary; extreme; rash; remarkable; creditable; impious; patriotic; rude; youthful; vigorous; embarrassed; misguided; cramplike; isolated; memorable; inconsiderate; arduous; coquettish; ignoble; forcible; deliberate; laudable; forlorn; torturing; charitable; unconstitutional; wicked; complicated; brutal; discouraging; direct; previous; mimic; exorbitant; murderous; strange; unorganized; perpetual; chimerical; excellent; traitorous; premature; uncouth; half-satirical; despicable; inauspicious; villainous; experimental; bare.

verbs
acclaim—; afford—; applaud—; commence—; commit—; complete—; constitute—; defeat—; deter from—; discern—; essay—; evade—; fail in—; fall short in—; foil—; glorify—; honor—; indict for—; interpret—; justify—; oppose—; overcome—; put forth—; recognize—; repel—; repudiate—; restrain—; suffer from—; stimulate—; thwart—; undertake—; warrant—; —blinds; —confounds; —triumphs; —wearies; interrupt—.

(See trial, endeavor, effort, attack.)

ATTEMPT (*v*)

adverbs
desperately; amateurishly; repeatedly; strenuously; previously; feebly; inadvertently; valiantly; memorably; sincerely; ingeniously; eloquently; reasonably; enlightenedly; falteringly; ineffectually; unavailingly; half-heartedly; grotesquely; futilely; fruitlessly; farcically; ineptly; maladroitly; murderously; outrageously; odiously; hazardously; disastrously; infamously; superhumanly; heroically; spectacularly; daringly; systematically; vituperatively; obviously; picturesquely; covertly; abortively; pretentiously; laboriously; unsteadily; involuntarily; creditably; impiously; patriotically; misguidedly; memorably; arduously; coquettishly; ignobly; forcibly; laudably; forlornly; charitably; unconstitutionally; brutally; exorbitantly; prematurely; uncouthly; half-satirically; despicably; inauspiciously; villainously.

(See endeavor, strive, undertake.)

ATTEND (*v*)

adverbs
diligently; faithfully; habitually; punctually; consistently; patiently; strictly; frequently; numerously; successively; expertly; rarely; invariably; assiduously; casually; nightly; compulsorily; unavailingly; properly; medically; overflowingly; scantily; professionally; defectively; suitably; stolidly; unceremoniously; devotedly; cheerfully; intermittently.

(See guard, heed, listen.)

ATTENDANCE

adjectives
assiduous; casual; interminable; nightly; compulsory; constant; unavailing; unrelaxing; agitated; proper; medical; overflowing; increased; scanty; professional; slovenly; defective; suitable; stolid; unceremonious; regular; unasked; devoted; cheerful; surpassed; intermittent.

verbs
advise—; await—; charge for—; command—; compel—; continue—; dance—; delay—; engage—; exact—; expect—; gather in—; increase—; minister in—; order—; resume—; wait in—; win—; —dwindles; —falls off; —grows; —increases; —manifests.

(See audience, congregation.)

ATTENDANT

adjectives
faithful; trained; black-robed; courteous; general; unobtrusive; gaudy; official; mercenary; nervous; chattering; spectacled; skilled; constant; flustered; experienced; obsequious; diligent; brave; dissolute; whispering; excited; inspiring; inseparable; obliging; fez-covered.

ATTENTION

adjectives
gentle; popular; eager; favorable; considerate; respectful; flattering; courteous; charming; gracious; delicate; faithful; thoughtful; keen; interested; undisguised; open-mouthed; undivided; rapt; riveted; absorbed; precise; painstaking; critical; persistent; assiduous; meticulous; scrutinizing; scrupulous; particular; strict; studious; unremitting; unceasing; wide-eyed; skilled; intellectual; pusillanimous; unwavering; obsequious; irritating; odious; casual; unappreciated; scant; trifling; idle; surface; slight; wandering; excessive; concentrated; individual; general; underground; wide; alert; spurious; prompt; special; country-wide; final; increased; considerable; cursory; rival; calm; acute; anxious; unobtrusive; tactful; sharp; serious; deliberate; emphatic; sufficient; abstracted; frowning; ample; enwrapped; unreasoning; ungrudging; momentary; minute; precious; nocturnal; faintest; strained; vague; uninterrupt-

ed; polite; unwonted; willing; careful; admirable; well-meant; irksome; solitary; bland; impersonal; edifying; ill-omened; best; tense; languid; profound; watchful; painful; summary; supreme; deepest; unfatigued; hesitating; manual; undue; reluctant; early; marked; feigned; unwelcome; parental; benumbed; whole-souled; funny; startled; minimum; indifferent; exclusive; breathless; sour; statistical; forced; vital; rational; unflagging; close; listless; animated; universal; insensible; fawning; unmeasured; conscientious; uncaressing; vigilant; affectionate; mournful; cheap; fascinated; earnest; cataleptic; wifely; public.

verbs
absorb—; acquire—of; arouse—; arrest—; bestow—upon; bring to—; call—to; capture —; center—; chide into—; claim—; clamor for—; come to—; command—; compel—; compete for—; concentrate—; confine—; crave—; demand—; desire—; devote—; dictate—; direct—; dispose—; distract—; distribute—; divert—; draw—; enforce—; engage—; engross—; enlist—; escape—; exact—from; excite—; exercise—; exhaust —; exhibit—; fasten—; favor with—; fix —; flash—; focus—; gain—; garner—; hold in—; increase—; influence—; lavish —upon; lend—; load with—; locate—; maintain—; mark with—; merit—; monopolize—; object to—; observe with—; occupy —; pay—; provoke—; reap—; recall—; reduce—; register—; reject—; relax—; require—; resume—; rivet—; secure—; stand at—; stimulate to—; straighten up in—; strike—; strive for—; subject to—; summon—; sustain—; train—upon; turn—toward; warrant—; win—; yield—; —embarrasses; —flags; —lies in; —wanders; —wanes; attract—.

(See gaze.)

ATTENTIVE

adverbs
absorbingly; steadily; intently; alertly; critically; analytically; closely; remarkably; astoundingly; suspiciously; guardedly; mildly; noticeably; intelligently; breathlessly; eagerly; engrossingly; raptly; carefully; considerately; thoughtfully; scrupulously; deferentially; respectfully; obsequiously; decorously; immensely; favorably; courteously; charmingly; graciously; assiduously; unwaveringly; flatteringly; idly; excessively; generally; finally; calmly; anxiously; unobtrusively; tactfully; sharply; politely; earnestly.

ATTEST (v)

adverbs
explicitly; unequivocally; duly; sincerely; authoritatively; freely.

(See confirm, indorse, corroborate.)

ATTIC

adjectives
stuffy; dusty; cobwebby; unused.

verbs
betake oneself to—; climb to—; confine to—; construct—; decorate—; design—; designate to—; enclose—; insulate—; lock in—; lodge in—; modernize—; relegate to—; renovate —; rumble around—; rummage in—; scour —; seclude in—; store in—; utilize—; ventilate—; —contains; —covers; —extends; —holds.

(See garret, room, cellar.)

ATTIRE

adjectives
bedizened; elaborate; motley; disreputable; informal; injudicious; fit; scandalous; crumpled; male; hunting; gala; quaint; drab; fairest; elegant; gay; evening; holiday; unaccustomed; scanty; showy; absurd; feminine; careful; splendid; mourning; unceremonious; picturesque; ornamented; exquisite; tawdry; ostentatious; festal; negligent; substantial; wild; coarse; abbreviated; gaudy.

verbs
acquire—; adorn in—; array in—; checker —; costume in—; deck in—; decorate in—; don—; dress in—; equip with—; flash—; gear in—; outfit in—; pin on—; shroud in—.

(See dress, clothing, apparel, costume.)

ATTIRE (v)

adverbs
somberly; impeccably; fantastically; faultlessly; modishly; scrupulously; superbly; disreputably; informally; fittingly; scandalously; quaintly; drably; elegantly; scantily; unceremoniously; picturesquely; exquisitely; ostentatiously; negligently; coarsely; gaudily.

(See dress.)

ATTITUDE

adjectives
firm; oblivious; listless; denunciatory; truculent; philanthropic; apathetic; scrupulous; unsisterly; composed; studied; absolutory; pathetic; impassive; civilized; rebellious; disconsolate; misanthropic; sensible; figura-

tive; contemptuous; hostile; lukewarm; egotistical; endless; assiduous; subtle; depressive; mental; indolent; contemplative; motionless; orientated; threatening; ridiculous; forlorn; political; basic; insidious; exulting; swaying; slouching; stoical; bellicose; favorable; submissive; positive; procrastinating; fearless; lofty; charming; gallant; gorgeous; piquant; reverent; exalted; resolute; cool; unbending; courageous; affirmative; adamantine; uncompromising; optimistic; light-hearted; complacent; cordial; self-sufficient; devil-may-care; overindulgent; carefree; depressed; serious; morose; sound; healthy; sane; natural; quiet; firm; eager; dignified; obliging; respectful; sympathetic; jubilant; conciliatory; enlightened; cultivated; timid; tolerant; cautious; generous; perfunctory; arrogant; supercilious; self-centered; disdainful; unsympathetic; condescending; patronizing; censorious; lordly; imperious; deprecatory; antagonistic; pugnacious; alien; militant; menacing; detestable; vengeful; devastating; preposterous; catastrophic; treasonable; unfriendly; transient; impolite; resentful; flippant; drooped; unfortunate; irreconcilable; condemnatory; suspicious; callous; pessimistic; dejected; ironical; overconfident; balanced; objective; unconventional; sudden; mature; fluid; familiar; injured; pragmatic; necessary; passive; watchful; worshipful; free; set; easy; quiescent; menial; annoying; defensive; condoning; sentimental; typical; talkative; realistic; various; restrained; destructive; ignorant; moral; ostrich; nonchalant; depreciatory; historical; nervous; benevolent; mutual; constrained; praiseworthy; infantile; graceful; belligerent; consistent; peculiar; suppliant; non-aggressive; defiant; untrammeled; presumptuous; judicial; helpless; negligent; characteristic; unsatisfactory; unpleasant; heroic; charming; strutting; comical; righteous; despondent; wholesome; unjust; hard-boiled; anachronistic; unlike (pl); crouching; fashionable; abnormal; chivalrous; discreet; penitential; peering; hypocritical; business-like; suggestive; forensic; fundamental; rigid; habitual; bipolar; ungraceful; tender; nonsensical; erect; resigned; traditional; warlike; emotional; mute; romantic.

verbs
abandon—; acquire—; adopt—; advocate —; analyze—; assume—; behave in—; breed—; choose—; color—; condemn—; define—; denote—; deplore—; discount—; distort—; dominate—; dramatize—; embrace —; emphasize—; encourage—; exalt—; examine—; exhibit—; explain—; expound—; express—; fall into—; gesture—; give rise to—; hold—; illuminate—; implant—; imply—; inculcate—; indicate—; ingrain—; interpret—; justify—; maintain—; manage —; manifest—; modify—; move to—; obsess with—; overcome—; persist in—; pervert—; portray—; posture—; preserve—; project—; reflect—; regard—; relax—; repose in—of; resent—; revere—; reverse—; sense—; stand in—; study—; —antagonizes; —applies; —implies; —menaces; —prejudices; —prevails; —reveals; —robs; —survives; —warns.

(See position, idea.)

ATTORNEY

adjectives
shyster; sneaking; incompetent; eminent; scurrilous; fashionable; prosecuting; well-tried; wealthy; astonished; illiterate; uneducated; brilliant.

verbs
appoint—; bar—; betray—; bind—; commission—; confer with—; confide in—; consult—; criticize—; delegate—; disbar—; discipline—; dispatch—; employ—; endorse —; engage—; ordain—; procure—; refer to—; reimburse—; retain—; train —s; —acknowledges; —acts; —administers; —advocates; —argues; —assails; —attacks; —bickers; —contracts for; —counsels; —cross-examines; —defames; —defends; —discusses; —examines; —exerts; —exposes; —formulates; —influences; —intercedes; —manages; —objects; —orates; —performs; —pleads; —practices; —prepares; —promotes; —prosecutes; —quibbles; —represents; —solicits; —sues for; —tries; —s wrangle.

(See lawyer.)

ATTRACT (*v*)

adverbs
instinctively; adroitly; romantically; magnetically; commandingly; irresistibly; profoundly; inescapably.

(See draw, engage, induce.)

ATTRACTION

adjectives
supreme; irresistible; queer; sweet; rare; natural; voluptuous; defective; dreadful; morbid; tragic; uncomfortable; fierce; insidious; unrivaled; loudly-heralded; dazzling; outstanding; overwhelming; principal; unusual; foremost; notable; cosmopolitan; physical; manifold; tidal; sexual; pastoral;

scenic; sartorial; historic; instant; growing; current; fleeting; scant; mutual; indefinable; obvious; chief; personal; myriad (pl); time-mellowed; casual; added; unspoken; spiritual; powerful; material; instinctive; clouded; poetical; limitless (pl); specific; resultant; acute; gratuitous; magnetic; electrostatic; hideous; fatal; permanent; feature; secret; coquettish; specious; mysterious; reciprocal; innumerable (pl); intellectual; accelerative; divine; enormous; sylvan; intrinsic; varying; imperious; conjugal; subtle.

verbs
admit—; augment—; cause—; center—; confess to—; exert—; force—; form—; illustrate—; yield to—; —adheres; —allures; —develops; —diminishes; —draws; —enhances; —fades; —lures; —recedes; —unsettles.
(See charm, fascination.)

ATTRACTIVE

adverbs
radiantly; irresistibly; rarely; sweetly; dazzlingly; overwhelmingly; indefinably; divinely; mysteriously; unutterably; powerfully; singularly; charmingly; alluringly; uncommonly; engagingly; undeniably; beautifully; bewitchingly; enchantingly; delightfully; exquisitely; interestingly; daintily; smartly; jauntily; bewilderingly; exotically; tormentingly.

ATTRACTIVENESS

adjectives
varied; bright; inevitable; annoying; physical; unusual; singular.

ATTRIBUTE

adjectives
supernatural; desirable; priceless; fundamental; fantastic; fearful; feminine; senseless; wonderful; detestable; recognizable; splendid; striking; peacock; literary; time-honored; chief; mistaken; characteristic; essential; accessory; homely; moral; intellectual; unalterable; judicial; human; highest; universal; gracious; noble; specific; conventional; sacred; productive; lofty; infinite; known; hereditary; striking; armorial; vacillating; diverse; sovereign; modified.

verbs
ascribe—to; credit with—; determine—; discover—; distinguish—; dramatize—; endow with—; enlarge—; estimate—; eulogize—; honor—; invest with—; limit—; manifest—; mark—; possess—; recognize—; ridicule—; shed all —s; value—; —enhances.
(See characteristic, symbol, quality, property.)

ATTRIBUTE (v)

adverbs
invariably; solely; entirely; modestly; skilfully; chiefly; basely; falsely; absurdly; innocently; supernaturally; fantastically; senselessly; graciously; nobly; specifically; conventionally.
(See impute, ascribe.)

AUDACIOUS

adverbs
disconcertingly; dauntlessly; rashly; indiscreetly; injudiciously; hot-headedly; foolishly; impudently; incredibly; recklessly; serenely; amazingly; overbearingly; shamelessly; tragically; singularly; strangely; innately; crazily; notoriously; dramatically; terribly; inherently; colossally; foolhardily; breath-takingly; fantastically; alarmingly; offensively; constitutionally; temperamentally.

AUDACITY

adjectives
incredible; utmost; reckless; characteristic; rapid; serene; gay; gorgeous; winning; amazing; sheer; insolent; cynical; cool; unfailing; unparalleled; vigorous; indelicate; heroic; harmless; human; inward; personal; dissolute; splendid; unnecessary; supreme; brilliant; operative; adventurous; unheard-of; aggressive; masculine; magnificent.

verbs
admire—; assume—; cool—; counterfeit—; depart from—; encourage—; exhibit—; relapse from—; reprimand—; shame by—; tame—; thrill at—; venture forth with—; —affronts; —engenders; —perturbs; —shocks; disregard—.
(See recklessness.)

AUDIENCE

adjectives
intelligent; sympathetic; understanding; appreciative; meager; sophisticated; attentive; interested; discerning; approving; imposing; vociferous; distinguished; admiring; enchanted; happy; democratic; meticulous; hilarious; enthusiastic; frenzied; vast; crowded; wide; undetermined; large; huge; fair; capacity; slender; tense; hushed; expectant; whispering; breathless; startled; astonished; mystified; chilled; bewildered; hard-boiled; wayward; cynical; hostile;

critical; ribald; unprecedented; unseen; reading; special; famished; invited; dull; applauding; nightly; respectable; imaginary; apathetic; suspicious; technical; motley; martial; impromptu; select; laughing; legislative; eager; delighted; dead-struck; enormous; gloomy; indiscriminate; polished; tragic; absorbed; satisfied; circular; pitying; listless; reasonable; added; dreary; prospective; elect; stupid; unresponsive; advertent; haughty.

verbs
accustom to—; admit—; appeal to—; assemble—; break up—; command—; convulse—; crave—; delight—; dismiss—; draw—; enslave—; enthuse (colloq.)—; exhort—; grant—; harangue—; hypnotize —; inflame—; lend—; lure—; overwhelm —; panic—; scan—; seek—; survey—; sway —; vouchsafe—; win—; —acclaims; —applauds; —cheers; —claps; —demands; —detects; —gapes; —gasps; —groans; —hisses; —howls; —laughs; —listens; —melts away; —packs; —pays; —responds; —roars; —rustles; —sobs; —stamps; —swells; —thrills; —throngs; —weeps.
(See hearing, interview, conference, gathering.)

AUDITOR

adjectives
skilled; bated; confounded; enchanted.

AUDITORIUM

adjectives
tight-packed; seething; huge; crowded; firetrap.

verbs
assemble in—; fill—; hire—; jam—; occupy —; receive in—; reverberate through—; throng—; —accommodates; —echoes; —holds; —resounds; —rings with; —seats.
(See building, hall, arena.)

AUGMENT (*v*)

adverbs
currently; incredibly; scarcely; tremendously; indefinitely; continually.
(See swell, increase.)

AUGURY

adjectives
favorable; evil; happy; reassuring; fearful; grim; heathen; sinister.

AUNT

adjectives
thin; sallow; unflagging; gaunt; sophisticated; worldly; ancient; strait-laced; maiden; pious.

AURA

adjectives
healthful; vague; flashing; evil; invidious; shimmering; tangible; smoky.

AUSPICES

adjectives
authoritative; pleasant; responsible; cordial; favorable; present; flattering; charitable.

AUSPICIOUS

adverbs
highly; opportunely; properly; suitably; happily; fairly; favorably; fortunately; luckily; providentially; remarkably; unusually; duly; consistently; gratifyingly; pleasantly; agreeably; fittingly; delightfully.

AUSTERE

adverbs
gravely; starkly; sombrely; monastically; harshly; puritanically; severely; rigorously; rigidly; uncompromisingly; inflexibly; unsparingly; arbitrarily; tyrannically; sternly; oddly; unfashionably; haughtily; soberly; odiously; unmitigatedly; unbendingly; unrelentingly.

AUSTERITY

adjectives
tempering; neat; wholesome; geometric; beautiful; dark; unrelieved; dignified; seeming; monastic; prayerful; natural; gentle; harsh; unyielding; famous; mild; hoar.

AUTHENTIC

adverbs
undeniably; unquestionably; admittedly; avowedly; unchallengedly; assuredly; professedly; palpably; obviously; evidently; apparently; absolutely; positively; categorically; genuinely; incontestably; indisputably; manifestly; unmistakably.

AUTHENTICITY

adjectives
doubtful; absolute; stylistic; altered; unmistakable; unquestioned; unforgettable.

verbs
accept—; command—; confirm—; dispute—; doubt—; entitle to—; insure—; profess—; prove—; question—; satisfy with—; stamp with—; testify to—; value—; verify—; —holds up; —stands.
(See accuracy.)

AUTHOR•

adjectives
veteran; competent; wild; versatile; accomplished; important; successful; prolific; eminent; favorite; distinguished; famous; modern; esteemed; engaging; amiable; vivacious; charming; noble; ardent; cheerful; well-meaning; inspiring; sane; disputatious; capricious; irresponsible; untrained; whimsical; perplexed; budding; unknown; putative; sentimental; dogmatic; forgotten; judicious; elusive; nascent; anonymous; irate; gregarious; antique; disillusioned; gifted; recent; alleged; striving; fearless; venerable; aspiring; delightful; remote; contemporary; cunning; neglected; profound; classical; agitated; anxious; vain; juvenile; comic; bigoted; superstitious.

verbs
acclaim—; acquaint with—; animate—; appreciate—; challenge—; criticize—; dishonor—; disturb—; employ—; engage—; enthuse (colloq.)—; exhaust—; frustrate—; honor—; inspire—; laud—; persecute—; plague—; rouse—; slander—; —bewitches; —casts about; —characterizes; —colors; —compels; —compiles; —composes; —creates; —cultivates; —dabbles; —declares; —dedicates; —describes; —devotes; —divines; —dreams; —edits; —exploits; —foreshadows; —gloats; —improvises; —indicates; —instigates; —labors; —languishes; —libels; —moralizes; —motivates; —objects; —originates; —philosophizes; —pirates; —plagiarizes; —produces; —pursues; —retires; —shapes; —soliloquizes; —translates; —voices; discuss—.

(See writer, poet.)

AUTHORITATIVE

adverbs
impressively; eminently; unquestionably; undisputedly; distinctly; reliably; responsibly; dependably; infallibly; highly; supremely; competently; expertly; peerlessly; imposingly; abundantly; respectably; quietly; learnedly; famously; deftly; academically; locally; legally; mildly; magisterially; uncompromisingly; pompously; imperially; condescendingly; truculently; brutally; studiously; specifically; directly; dogmatically; smoothly; suavely; conventionally; solemnly; delicately; finally; venerably; despotically; officially; divinely; habitually; undeniably; proudly; gently; unmistakably; cruelly; ostentatiously.

AUTHORITY

adjectives
leading; unimpeachable; acknowledged; accredited; recognized; renowned; eminent; unquestioned; well-known; undisputed; distinguished; reliable; responsible; dependable; prominent; infallible; high; foremost; supreme; unchallenged; competent; peerless; imposing; abundant; famous; respectable; quiet; learned; interesting; superior; deft; academic; civil; shocked; local; apostolic; outstanding; parental; legal; mild; arrogated; deputed; magisterial; uncompromising; constituted; imperial; sacred; express; crushing; appointed; condescending; revered; truculent; unique; adequate; humiliating; studious; practical; outraged; shadowy; specific; direct; limited; established; dogmatic; smooth; legitimate; apocryphal; mystic; coordinate; unbounded; sundry; conventional; solemn; centralized; concurrent; sufficient; executive; actual; delicate; minor; harassing; censorial; musical; administrative; standard; venerable; serious; delegated; ecclesiastical; parliamentary; despotic; base; brief; oracular; paramount; spiritual; dissolving; firm; provincial; far-distant; disciplinary; excellent; conferred; all-persuasive; scientific; territorial; governmental; antenatal; coercive; private; discretionary; ministerial; coequal; worn-out; military; provisional; ascertained; mellow; habitual; inspired; sovereign; central; weighty; grammatical; consular; divine; unassailable; sanctified.

verbs
abuse—; accept—; act with—; appeal to—; appoint to—; arm with—; aspire to—; assert—; attain—; boast—; carry—; challenge—; claim—; clothe with—; command—; confer—upon; confirm—; consult—; declare—; decree—; defy—; delegate—; derive—; desire—; discredit—; enforce—; entrust—; establish—; esteem—; execute—; exercise—; extend—; fetter—; flout—; grant—; heighten—; ignore—; inspire—; invest with—; lend—; limit—; mark with—; obey—; possess—; preserve—; pronounce—; question—; quote—; rebel against—; regard with—; register—; reject—; relinquish—; rely upon—; respect—; restrain—; revere—; revolt against—; ridicule—; speak with—; squelch—; submit to—; support—; uphold—; usurp—; weaken—; weigh—; wield—; wink at—; wrest—; yield to—; —s arrest; —s intervene; —s jockey; —melts away; —s speculate.

(See right, jurisdiction, influence, power.)

AUTHORIZE (v)

adverbs
specifically; confidentially; responsibly; infallibly; respectably; locally; magisterially; expressly; practically; specifically; directly; limitedly; legitimately; ecclesiastically; despotically; basely; governmentally; divinely; unassailably; grammatically.
(See confirm, justify.)

AUTOBIOGRAPHICAL

adverbs
honestly; inadvertently; factually; probably; possibly; embarrassingly; amusingly; lightheartedly; blithely; gaily; solemnly; revealingly; lustily; radiantly; indecently; decorously; selectively; happily; lustily; gustily; gloriously; delightfully; unexpectedly; helpfully; analytically; critically; literally.

AUTOBIOGRAPHY

adjectives
factual; honest; intimate; embarrassing; lusty; amusing; accurate; unbelievable.

AUTOCRACY

adjectives
malignant; church; incompetent; pernicious; monstrous.

AUTOCRAT

adjectives
rival; irresponsible; absolute; vigorous; beneficent; ruthless; ancient.

AUTOCRATIC

adverbs
imperiously; tyrannically; unyieldingly; inflexibly; hatefully; meanly; arbitrarily; insolently; arrogantly; overbearingly; openly; brazenly; audaciously; jauntily; teasingly; regally; offensively; obnoxiously; deplorably; intolerably; lamentably; unfortunately.

AUTOGRAPH

adjectives
interesting; stateliest; boldest; facsimile.

AUTOMATIC (n)
(gun)

adjectives
wicked; mean-looking; flashing; blue-nosed; compact; sputtering; deadly.

AUTOMATIC (a)

adverbs
entirely; conveniently; amazingly; optionally; originally; luckily; ingeniously; cleverly; smoothly.

AUTOMOBILE

adjectives
ancient; dusty; long; swerving; lean; unidentified; obsolete; two-seated; rusty; rattlesome; undependable; sleek; streamlined.

verbs
climb into—; construct—; crank—; demolish—; design—; develop—; enclose—; engage—; equip—; improve—; insure—; license—; pilot—; pour out of—; power—; salvage—; —careens; —chugs; —climbs; —crawls; —creaks; —cruises; —descends; —flashes by; —flits by; —hauls; —hurtles; —joggles; —jolts; —lumbers; —moans; —noses; —pants; —pokes; —quivers; —roars; —skids; —slips by; —snarls; —snorts; —spins; —squeaks; —s swarm; —swoops; —transports; —travels; —trundles; —whines; —whirs; —whizzes; —zooms.
(See wagon, train.)

AUTOPSY

adjectives
unfavorable; warmly controverted; ghastly; inevitable; long-drawn-out; purely experimental; gruesome; ensuing; consequent; co-incidental.

verbs
carry on—; complete—; conclude by—; consent to—; consider—; consult—; diagnose by—; dispense with—; evidence by—; examine by—; hold—; inspect—; observe—; order—; perform—; permit—; record—; refuse—; report on—; request—; require —; seek—; subject to—; testify to—; urge —; witness—; —confirms; —determines; —discloses; —discovers; —reveals; —verifies.
(See examination.)

AUTUMN

adjectives
first; radiant; rank; meek; eventful; distributed; colorful; ambient; bounteous; dreary; everlasting; sere; paradisaical; chill.

verbs
enter—; hail—; welcome—; —advances; —basks; —beams; —burnishes; —bursts; —clamors; —colors; —decays; —decks; —declines; —descends; —embellishes; —extends from; —fades; —flames; —flushes; —follows; —garners; —gleams; —harvests; —haunts; —heralds; —lavishes; —matures; —meditates; —merges; —mocks; —paints; —pierces; —pours; —precedes; —presses near; —reaps; —resigns; —ripens; —rushes

in; —rustles; —scatters; —shackles; —spreads; —sweeps in; —thwarts; —upbraids; —violates; —warns; —wreathes; —yields.
(See fall.)

AUXILIARY

adjectives
warlike; unexpected; disaffected; thundering.

AUXILIARY (*v*)

adverbs
patronizingly; officially; officiously; legally; cooperatively; helpfully.

AVAIL (*v*)

adverbs
freely; promptly; continually; unobtrusively; scarcely; covertly; openly; slyly; villainously; brutally.
(See use.)

AVAILABLE

adverbs
easily; instantly; immediately; presumably; always; undoubtedly; obviously; evidently; apparently; unquestionably; scarcely; seldom.

AVALANCHE

adjectives
hoofed; blinding; deep; startling; rocky; appalling; impending; sun-awakened; stupendous.

verbs
beat—; endure—; evade—; loose—; perish in—; precipitate—; protect against—; roll down in—; —crashes; —denudes; —descends; —destroys; —endangers; —gathers force; —masses; —occurs; —overwhelms; —plunges; —pours by; —roars; —rushes by; —suffocates; —swallows; —sweeps past; —washes along.

AVARICE

adjectives
besetting; anxious; sullen; pecuniary; insatiable; gripping; cruel; greedy.

verbs
decry—; deplore—; detest—; display—; evince—; gather with—; grovel in—; hoard in—; staunch—; take up with—; —acquires; —eats; —shrieks.
(See greed.)

AVARICIOUS

adverbs
incurably; avidly; insanely; peculiarly; incorrigibly; distressingly; painfully; embarrassingly; irreclaimably; hopelessly; shamelessly; appallingly; terribly; horribly; churlishly; sordidly; rapaciously.

AVENGE (*v*)

adverbs
horribly; sufficiently; fiercely; self-appointedly; blood-thirstily; cruelly; finally; primarily; satisfactorily.
(See punish, revenge, vindicate, retaliate.)

AVENGER

adjectives
fierce; blood-stained; unblamed; ordained; avowed; self-appointed.

AVENUE

adjectives
fine; moonlit; glittering; ignominious; trim; tidy; intersecting; cobble-stoned; open; fashionable; principal; diagonal; spacious; densely-shaded; leafy; dwarfish; continuous; noble; tree-lined; gorgeous; melancholy.

verbs
amble down—; approach—; border—; circle—; enter—; gain access to—; light—; litter—; locate on—; mark—; promenade —; shade—; shadow—; stroll down—; venture up—; —crosses; —extends; —leads to; —parallels.
(See road, thoroughfare, way, approach, street.)

AVERAGE

adjectives
well-gauged; inversely-proportioned; adjusted; stalwart; standardized; skeptical; unvarying; prevailing; weighted; weighty; timely.

verbs
adjust—; arrive at—; ascertain—; better —; compare—; compile—; derive—; determine—; diminish—; distribute over—; divide—; estimate—; evolve—; hit—; lower —; model on—; obtain—; propose—; reckon —; record—; refer—; reveal—; strike—; suggest—; yield—; —amounts to; —compares; —falls; —ranges; —rises; —varies; —yields.
(See amount.)

AVERSE

adverbs
persistently; unreasonably; ineradicably; unnaturally; innately; openly; avowedly; unrelentingly; tenaciously; immovably; inflexibly; headily; arbitrarily; mulishly; stubbornly; obstinately.

AVERSION

adjectives
persistent; marked; ineradicable; strong; unnatural; staunch; unconquerable; inherent; thorough; instinctive; deep-rooted; instantaneous; utter; hereditary; loathing; inexpressible; proportionate; decided; favorite; extreme; separate; marked; mutual; cold; feminine; undisguised; developed; unreasonable; deadly.

verbs
augment—; cement—; fix—; intimate—; produce—; purge of—; recollect with—; rid of—; side-track—; strengthen—; voice—; —estranges.

(See antipathy, dislike, hatred.)

AVERT (*v*)

adverbs
cleverly; happily; coldly; swiftly; thoughtfully; dexterously; skilfully; painstakingly; scarcely.

(See prevent.)

AVIATOR

adjectives
daring; illustrious; famous; amateur; imaginative; intrepid; fearless; skilled.

verbs
exhaust—; inform—; license—; overtake—; strain—; test—; —accomplishes; —achieves; —ascends; —attempts; —circles; —controls; —descends; —dips; —endures; —lands; —loops; —manipulates; —navigates; —operates; —perceives; —pilots; —somersaults; —speeds; —takes off; —transports; —views; —zooms.

(See flier, airplane.)

AVID

adverbs
childishly; unnaturally; fatally; obviously; extraordinarily; excessively; anxiously; ardently; breathlessly; hungrily; fantastically; impetuously; zealously; madly; curiously; fervently; queerly; insatiably; sedulously.

AVOCATION

adjectives
ecstatic; pleasant.

AVOID (*v*)

adverbs
zealously; openly; studiously; industriously; contemptuously; scrupulously; cautiously; purposely; persistently; honorably; sedulously; decorously; involuntarily; totally; vigilantly; absolutely.

(See parry, evade, shun, elude.)

AVOIDANCE

adjectives
total; vigilant; lazy; absolute.

AVOW (*v*)

adverbs
brutally; simply; enthusiastically; bluntly; plainly; ardently; ostentatiously; boldly; energetically; unequivocally; manfully; gratefully; daringly; commonly; sincerely; savagely; secretly.

(See acknowledge, admit, profess.)

AVOWAL

adjectives
brutal; simple; enthusiastic; blunt; plain; ardent.

AWAIT (*v*)

adverbs
tensely; anxiously; silently; impatiently; apprehensively; informally; excitedly; tremblingly; breathlessly; courageously.

(See look, wait.)

AWAKE (*v*)

adverbs
rudely; shudderingly; accidentally; muscularly; singularly; breathlessly; consequently; hauntingly; blissfully; manifestly; spiritually; mechanically.

(See wake.)

AWAKENING

adjectives
rude; first; startled; innocent; new; blissful; moral; consequent; modest; manifest; stormy; spiritual.

AWARD

adjectives
long-coveted; grudging; merited; carefully-computed; just; princely; bounteous; inconsequent.

verbs
adjudicate—; applaud—; arbitrate—; assign—; capture—; consider—; decide—; deliberate—; dispute—; earn—; embody—; examine—; furnish—; grant—; institute—;

judge—; merit—; please with—; praise—; pronounce—; provide—; submit—; win—.
(See decision, verdict, judgment.)

AWARE

adverbs
sensitively; painfully; acutely; vividly; sharply; keenly; curiously; psychically; subconsciously; sorely; uncomfortably; wretchedly; pleasingly; happily; rapturously; fully; intensely; suddenly; poignantly; astutely; wholly; neurotically; powerfully; perfectly; desperately; dimly; scarcely; barely; breathlessly.

AWARENESS

adjectives
neurotic; powerful; increased; sensitized.

AWE

adjectives
superstitious; deep; deferential; mysterious; simulated; joyous; strange; cringing; profound; candid; ineffable; vague; devout; tender; respectful; salutary; reverential; meaningful; undefined; fearful; slavish; unwilling; sacred; restraining; inspiring; trembling; adoring; mystic; silent; religious; hideous; inexpressible; supernatural; pious; rapt; ecstatic; dumb.

verbs
approach with—; awake—; bask in—; bind in—; breed—; command—; conduce—; create—; deepen—; develop—of; entertain —of; excite—; eye with—; fill with—; flock round in—; hold in—of; inspire with —; keep in—of; learn with—; mingle with —; oppress with—; overcome with—; remove—; shake with—; stand in—of; strike with—; —afflicts; —arises; —breeds; —overcomes; —shakes; —smites; —stirs; —strikes.
(See amazement, fear, reverence.)

AWKWARD

adverbs
clumsily; ungracefully; bashfully; shyly; gawkily; self-consciously; painfully; embarrassingly; ludicrously; laughably; ridiculously; intentionally; adorably; unconsciously; charmingly; affectedly; momentarily; remarkably; flutteringly; clownishly; amusingly; pathetically; lamentably; unfortunately; helplessly; hopelessly.

AWKWARDNESS

adjectives
adorable; fumbling; mirth-provoking; pleased; unconscious; involuntary; slight; obvious; charming; blundering; affected; bristling; momentary.

verbs
begin in—; bungle with—; disperse—; encounter—; laugh at—; rebuke—; scorn—; —adheres; —embarrasses; —inconveniences.
(See clumsiness.)

AWNING

adjectives
luxuriant; striped; woven; rotting; shady; gaudy; ordinary; ready-made; gaily-colored.

AXE

adjectives
keen; lusty; glittering; gallant; rude; sounding; devastating; biting; consecrated.

verbs
apply—; chop with—; clasp—; cleave with —; condemn to—; cool—; execute with—; fashion—; fell with—; forge—; grind—; hack with—; heave—; helve—; hew with —; lay on—; resist—; scar—; shaft—; shape—; sharpen—; slay with—; stroke—; swing—; temper—; turn—; wedge—; whip —; wield—; yield to—; —chips; —cleaves; —decapitates; —falls; —gleams; —glitters; —hacks; —hews; —resounds; —rings; —rusts.
(See hatchet.)

AXIOM

adjectives
simple; religious; moral; accepted; fundamental; irrefutable; educing; settled; divine; intricate; established.

AZURE

adjectives
kindling; greenish; vivid; intense; clear; glowing; cold; cloudless; ambient; smiling; dazzling; beauteous; palpitating.

B

BABBLE

adjectives
charming; ceaseless; drunken; foolish; incoherent; literary; senseless; perpetual; meaningless; idle; excited; irrelevant; soothing; childish; idiotic; pleasant; prattling; confused.

BABBLE (v)

adverbs
drunkenly; grievously; ecstatically; idiotically; weirdly; ingeniously; charmingly; ceaselessly; incoherently; perpetually; meaninglessly; irrelevantly; confusedly.
(See murmur, prattle.)

BABE

adjectives
innocent; unmothered; speechless; maiden; starving; wailing; nursing; testy; naked; unborn.

BABOON

adjectives
malevolent; bouncing; dog-faced; patriarchal; chattering; grotesque; gaping; smirking.

BABY

adjectives
healthy; fat; angelic; grown-up; pallid; sickly-looking; unweaned; peaceful; bewitching; sturdy; squalling; new-born; lonesome; pitiful; wriggling; cunning; squeaking; babbling; sticky; petulant; strong-lunged; appealing; featureless; blithesome; staring; mewling; rosy-cheeked; tousled; clamorous; stubborn; disobedient; delicate; inopportune; undisciplined.

verbs
comfort—; cradle—; croon to—; fondle—; indulge—; lull—; mother—; quiet—; rear—; suckle—; swaddle—; tend—; train—; treat as—; wean—; —babbles; —coos; —creeps; —crows; —drools; —moans; —pukes; —plains; —teethes; —toddles; —weeps; —whimpers.
(See infant.)

BABYISH

adverbs
entrancingly; ridiculously; disgustingly; utterly; beamingly; angelically; sturdily; cunningly; appealingly; rosily; delicately; helplessly; clingingly; shyly; absurdly; adorably; completely; artlessly; boisterously; irresistibly; lovably; warmly; lustily; magically; mysteriously; excitedly.

BACHELOR

adjectives
virtuous; level-headed; arrant; vagrant; typical; sexagenary; impeccable; desolate; austere; dashing; predestined; crusty; cynical; solitary; elusive; confirmed; lonely; gruff; perennial; wary; indignant; perpetual.

BACK

adjectives
expressive; prosperous; narrow; wiry; slender; straight; innocent-looking; broad; benevolent; roomy; rigid; brawny; powerful; aching; inexorable; lovely; lithe; obtrusive; bent; naked; cringing; arched; agile; discreet; wrenched; deliberate; lacerated; burly; indiscriminate; stiffening; hairy; ramrod; contemptuous; incurious.

verbs
arch—; bear on—; bow—; buckle on—; clamor at—; huddle on—; hump—; mount—; pluck from—; prick—; recline on—; ride—; set upon—; strip—; sway—; upheave—; —arches; —creaks.

BACK (v)

adverbs
stealthily; consistently; obtrusively; cringingly; agilely; discreetly; deliberately; contemptuously.
(See support, indorse.)

BACKGROUND

adjectives
psychological; Puritan; political; historical; rich; Quakerish; botanical; proletarian; intellectual; educational; cultural; moral; monotheistic; inherited; pictorial; blurred; neutral; changeless; realistic; scenic; unwonted; stereotyped; garish; dense; serrated; meager; complex; star-flecked; shimmering; kaleidoscopic; broad; effective; financial; conspicuous; attractive; authentic; religious; fitting; immaterial; plain; harmonious; rocky; precipitous; theatrical; social; domestic; appropriate; technical; fascinating; vivid; lush; convincing; serene; striking; unforgettable; imaginative; glamorous; enchanting; admirable; impressive; shabby; sinister; cluttered; bizarre; weirdest.

verbs
blend into—; broaden—; enhance—; fade

into—; form—; maintain—; melt into—; paint—; screen—; set into—; weave—; —blends; —brightens; —contrasts; —enhances; —looms; —sets off.

(See setting.)

BACON

adjectives

crisp; tender; tasty; mouldy; crackling; rank; sizzling; tempting.

BACTERIA

adjectives

antagonistic; classified; disease-producing; friendly; gram-positive; harmful; infectious; invading; injurious; lethal; minute; multitudinous; overwhelming; poisonous; secondary; succulent; swarming.

verbs

absorb—; activate—; annihilate—; attack—; class—; combat—; cultivate—; culture—; destroy—; discover—; disperse—; distribute—through; dose with—; examine—; filter—; group—; identify—; immunize against—; inhale—; inoculate with—; investigate—; isolate—; observe—; produce—; propagate—; protect against—; raise—; resist—; separate—; study—; treat—; —behave; —cause; —course through; —disturb; —enter; —form; —increase; —infect; —invade; —irritate; —multiply; —poison; —reproduce; —secrete; —split; —spoil; —survive; —swarm; —dwell.

(See organism, germs.)

BAD

adverbs

flagrantly; destructively; infinitely; harmfully; dangerously; mischievously; violently; vilely; irretrievably; inconceivably; poisonously; abominably; accursedly; perniciously; viciously; basely; deplorably; detestably; diabolically; disastrously; dreadfully; exceptionably; grievously; hatefully; malignantly; obnoxiously; venomously; virulently; manifestly; scandalously; irremediably; irrevocably; immeasurably.

BADGE

adjectives

corrupt; distinctive; decorative; decorous; distinguished; emblematic; glittering; heraldic; identifying; imperial; pompous; pretentious; tarnished; tawdry.

verbs

bear—; blazon with—; flash—; flaunt—; merit—; ornament—; wear—; work—; —betokens; —distinguishes; —heralds; —honors; —indicates; —marks; —signifies.

(See device, emblem.)

BADGER

adjectives

belligerent; biting; aggressive; defensive; fierce; hibernating; ungainly; moody.

verbs

bait—; snare—; trap—; —s abound; —burrows; —charges; —claws; —digs; —dives in; —dwells; —excavates; —flattens out; —growls; —haunts; —hisses; —leaps; —lumbers; —mines; —plunges; —purrs; —retreats; —robs; —rushes; —senses; —seizes; —snarls; —sniffs; —squats.

(See animal.)

BADINAGE

adjectives

lazy; giddy; banal; good-natured; teasing; gay; cheap; frivolous; merciless; untimely.

BAFFLE (v)

adverbs

hopelessly; completely; genuinely; scarcely; continually; shrewdly; slyly; plainly.

(See thwart, frustrate.)

BAFFLING

adverbs

mysteriously; irritatingly; bewilderingly; unaccountably; disturbingly; genuinely; strangely; surprisingly; astonishingly; indescribably; fearfully; disappointingly; utterly; insuperably; dishearteningly; incommodiously; discouragingly; depressingly; terribly; vexatiously; seriously; alarmingly; perfectly; absolutely; incomprehensibly; inconceivably.

BAG

adjectives

sealed; sanitary; shiny; travel-worn; soggy; cloth-covered; bottomless; diminutive; bulky; pendulous.

verbs

bind in—; dip into—; purloin—; rifle—; seal—; secure in—; snatch—; stow—; trap in—; —bulges; —dangles; —emits; —hangs; —sags; —slides; —slips.

(See wallet, satchel.)

BAGGAGE

adjectives

unnecessary; hand, superfluous; mental; multitudinous; clumsy; ponderous; weighty.

verbs

abandon—; attend with—; convey—; dispatch—; encumber with—; lighten—; retrieve—; splotch—; stow—; transport—; tuck—away; —encumbers; —weighs.

(See satchel.)

BAGPIPE

adjectives
awesome; blood-chilling; dominant; droning; ear-splitting; eerie; fiercely-screaming; lamenting; long-winded; screeching; triumphant; victory-sounding; vengeful.

verbs
adjust—; blow upon—; compress—; elbow —; embrace—; esteem—; finger—; inflate —; introduce—; muffle—; press—; puff up —; regulate—; —bawls; —bellows; —chants; —cries; —drones; —emits; —expands; —groans; —harmonizes; —heaves; —labors; —mourns; —pipes; —proclaims; —rouses; —shrills; —sighs; —stirs; —swells; —wails; —whistles.

BAIL

adjectives
appointed; certified; forfeited; generous; responsible; specified; superficial; trifling; enforced; heavy; necessary; substantial.

verbs
admit to—; allow—; apply for—; assure—; bind with—; collect—; default—; demand —; deny—; designate—; dispense with—; enter—; exempt from—; fix—; forfeit—; furnish—; give—; grant—; gauge—; guarantee—; hold to—; insure by—; justify—; liberate on—; pledge—; post—; procure—; provide—; put up—; raise—; receive—; refund—; release on—; require—; risk—; satisfy with—; set—; set free on—; surrender—; —obligates; —releases.

(See security.)

BAIT

adjectives
tempting; dainty; false; seductive; coveted; treacherous; pernicious; alluring.

verbs
devour—; expose—; feed—; hold out—; proffer—; swallow—; —allures; —ensnares; —entices; —lures; —tempts; —traps.

(See lure, inducement, temptation.)

BALANCE

adjectives
unexpended; fabulous; unnatural; proper; delicate; subtle; artistic; comfortable; unpaid; neutral; sentimental; smooth; floating; adverse; peculiar; precarious; normal; miraculous; economic; trifling; workable; unfavorable; scrupulous; logical; physiological; trembling; accurate.

verbs
achieve—; adjust—; arrange—; attain—; augment—; bear—; bequeath—; control—; deflect—; determine—; disturb—; equalize —; even—; exhaust—; hang in—; hold—; lay in—; maintain—; measure—; reach—; readjust—; recover—; restore—; strike—; supply—; suspend on—; sway—; test—; tip —; totter in—; turn—; upset—; weigh in —; —turns.

(See scales, equilibrium.)

BALANCE (v)

adverbs
precariously; equally; ultimately; harmoniously; unskillfully; exactly; accurately; systematically; uncomfortably; cautiously; dexterously; eventually.

(See poise.)

BALCONY

adjectives
exquisite; overhanging; latticed; moon-drenched; screened; high-perched; vine-clad; narrow; grilled; delicate; frail.

verbs
crowd—; gain—; occupy—; overlook—; peer from—; rail—; salute from—; view from—; —encompasses; —overhangs; —projects; —swarms.

(See gallery.)

BALD

adverbs
shinily; fatly; rosily; hopelessly; nakedly; ruddily; ghastly; ridiculously; laughably; gracelessly; grossly; haggardly; hideously; unashamedly; odiously; shockingly; smilingly.

BALEFUL

adverbs
perniciously; terribly; venomously; malignantly; undeniably; villainously; exceptionally; sadly; grievously; deplorably; lamentably; woefully; shockingly; cruelly; detestably; infernally; irremediably; atrociously; malevolently; incorrigibly; brutally; unpardonably; incredibly; shamefully; iniquitously.

BALK (v)

adverbs
continually; cruelly; particularly; recalcitrantly; exasperatingly; pettishly; provokingly; irritatingly.

(See thwart, frustrate, baffle, disappoint.)

BALKY

adverbs
astonishingly; surprisingly; naturally; in-

corrigibly; wonderfully; unexpectedly; tormentingly; vexatiously; embarrassingly; stubbornly; obstinately; temperamentally; characteristically; abnormally; habitually; usually; uncompromisingly; invariably; consistently; inherently; innately; blithely; unreasonably; provokingly; unaccountably.

BALL

adjectives (dance)
inauguration; carnival; rustic; impromptu; magnificent; birthday; anniversary; annual; masquerade.

BALL

adjectives (object)
gilded; glowing; gleaming; bouncing; glittering; devil-guided; luminous; swift; gelatinous; fungous.

BALL

adjectives (sport)
back-firing; catapulting; foul; fair; ricocheting; trenchant; tangential; sodden; speeding; bombastic; refractory.

verbs
bat—; bobble—; bunt—; chuck—; club—; control—; cover—; drive—; feed —s; fling —; foul—; fumble—; grip—; heave—; hurl —; inflate—; juggle—; lob—; loft—; muff —; pass—; pole—; pop—; project—; pursue—; release—; round into—; smash—; snare—; spear—; strike—; top—; toss—; trap—; waggle at the golf—; whip—; zip —; —bounds; —curves; —hops; —zooms.

BALLAD

adjectives
woeful; doleful; ribald; odious; patriotic; vigorous; dramatic; celebrated; tawdry; rude; merry; scurrilous; tender; lewd; blasphemous; interminable; vulgar; sentimental; brisk; ringing; homely; dolorous; obscene; raucous.

verbs
accompany—; carol—; characterize—; classify—; compose—; measure—; narrate—; print—; revive—; traduce—; translate—; wail—; —celebrates; —deals with; —exploits; —narrates; —relates; —survives; —swells.
(See poem, song.)

BALLET

adjectives
gaudy; glittering; dainty; sumptuous; exquisite; fairylike.

BALLOON

adjectives
gigantic; invisible; floating; lifeless; air-filled; gaseous.

verbs
anchor—; attach to—; ballast—; blow—; burst—; check—; command—; dispatch—; cut away—; deflate—; elevate—; experiment with —s; fire—; guide—; improve—; inflate—; liberate—; lift—; lighten—; man —; navigate—; power—; propel—; steady —; suspend—; swell—; —ascends; —circles; —collapses; —descends; —drifts; —expands; —explodes; —floats; —journeys; —kites; —rises; —sallies; —soars; —spins; —tosses; —wallows.
(See bladder, aeroplane.)

BALLOT

adjectives
approved; adopted; computed; disputed; fatal; political; polled; open; reformed; secret.

verbs
accede by—; acknowledge by—; agree by—; arrange—; assent by—; broadcast—; cast —; circulate —s; choose by—; deposit—; draw up—; employ—; hinge on—; inspect —; introduce—; record—; reform—; reject —; satisfy with—; stuff —s; tabulate —s; tally —s; tamper with —s; —acquits; —affirms; —ascertains; —condemns; —decides; —elects; —eliminates; —installs; —proclaims.
(See vote, ticket.)

BALLROOM

adjectives
huge; improvised; dimly-lit; crowded; decorated.

BALM

adjectives
soothing; fragrant; golden; philosophic; blissful; healing; temperate; assuaging; precious; unguentary; icy.

verbs
anoint with—; exude—; soothe with—; steep in—; yield—; wash off—; —assuages; —charms; —eases; —heals; —mitigates; —soothes; —trickles.
(See ointment, salve.)

BALMY

adverbs
soothingly; refreshingly; softly; comfortingly; curatively; quietly; coolly; gently; mild-

ly; blandly; healingly; gratifyingly; satisfactorily; remarkably; tenderly; mercifully; pleasantly; especially.

BALUSTRADE

adjectives
granite; terrace; sandstone; marble; graceful; wrought-iron; exquisite; carved; shining; quaint; twisting; serpentine; monstrous.

BAMBOO

adjectives
delicate-leaved; pliant; plaited; feathery.

BAN

adjectives
authoritative; blasphemous; cruel; common; harsh; inhibitory; legal; maledictory; proclamatory; senseless; tyrannical; unjust.

verbs
announce—on; command—on; contradict—; curse—; decree—; end—; enforce—; exempt from—; impose—; lift—; proclaim—; publish—; reaffirm—; remove—; renew—; send—; —deprives; —forbids; —offends; —outlaws; —prohibits.

(See notice, taboo, edict, proclamation, excommunication.)

BANAL

adverbs
monotonously; tritely; tiresomely; boringly; disagreeably; drearily; unceasingly; invariably; triflingly; vapidly; inanely; insipidly; intolerably; trivially; unbearably; exhaustingly; wearily; tediously; frivolously; senselessly; vacuously; insufferably; habitually; prosily; uninterestingly.

BANALITY

adjectives
routine; easy; preliminary; gross; unpleasant; boring; dreary; repetitious.

BANANA

adjectives
tempting; sun-hungry; lush; ripened.

BAND

adjectives (company)
aimless; diminished; detached; ferocious; foraging; gladsome; hunted; hapless; march-worn; pillaging; rapine; rollicking; straggling; vandalistic; victorious.

verbs
arm—; associate with—; attach to—; banish from—; bind in a holy—; captain—; collect—; compose—; disperse—; divide into —s; enlist in—; muster—; scatter—; summon—; unite in—; wander in—; —attacks; —invades; —pillages; —plunders; —pursues; —roves; —shrinks.

(See company, group, gang, troop.)

BAND

adjectives (fetter, tie)
ring-stacked; quivered; artful; swaddling; unrelieved; restraining; flexible; iridescent; metallic.

verbs
break asunder the—s; cancel—s; chain in —s; dissolve—; link in —s; release from —s; rend —s; strengthen —s; twist —s; untie —s; untwine —s; weaken—; —s bind; —s encircle; —s fetter; —s shackle.

(See tie, cord, bond, fetter, belt, bandage, chain.)

BAND

adjectives (group)
infuriated; angelic; cycling; alabaster; ruthless; scarlet; riotous; massed; melancholy; marauding; adverse; servile; devoted; encircling; colic; baleful; eager; doomed; notorious; peaceful; full; unbroken; bloody; amiable; swirling; murderous; numberless; resplendent; scattered; reckless; chosen; shadowy; formidable; violent; apathetic; restless; defiant; eternal; itinerant; enthralling; wandering; guerilla; fantastic; sullen; glittering; expectant; valiant; considerable; predatory; snail-like; gallant; mirth-breathing; heroic; enormous; mute; ghastly; scanty; boisterous; prying; mirthful; devoted; adventurous; ambitious; imperious; fairy; social; scattering; brazen; nondescript; partisan; thin; doughty; fierce; worn; insignificant; rival; small; well-armed; thundering; wild; howling; heretical; shabby; unkempt; conspicuous; feeble; mighty; unconquerable; inexhaustible; laborious; invading; brave.

BAND

adjectives (instrumental)
tuneful; stirring; gorgeously-arrayed; regimental; swing; jazz; competent.

verbs
assemble—; compose—; conduct—; engage —; group—; maintain—; organize—; pitch —; strike up—; supervise—; —arouses; —blares; —blasts on; —encourages; —harmonizes; —honors; —marches; —parades;

—performs; —renders; —serenades; —toots; —troops.
(See orchestra.)

BANDAGE

adjectives
crimsoned; filthy; swathing; emergency; bloodstained; saving.

verbs
apply—; attach—; border with—; change —; discard—; fasten—; loose—; replace—; sew—; sterilize—; stitch—; stripe with —s; swathe in —s; tighten—.
(See band.)

BANDIT

adjectives
famous; amiable; cold-blooded; ferocious; ruthless; wily; out-and-out; dark-visaged; bold; outrageous; notorious; reckless; tantalizing; enraged; burly; restless; lawless.

verbs
defend—; execute—; grant sanctuary to—; hire—; hunt—; imprison—; infest with —s; organize—; outlaw—; seclude—; slay—; —harries; —marauds; —s pillage; —s plunder; —s terrorize.
(See robber, burglar.)

BANDY (v)

adverbs
mercilessly; repeatedly; continuously; freely; haphazardly; thoughtlessly.
(See toss.)

BANG

adjectives
loud; emphatic; thudding; resounding; ear-splitting.

BANG (v)

adverbs
fitfully; resoundingly; loudly; emphatically; terrifically; crashingly; tremendously; explosively; thunderously; furiously.
(See thump, resound.)

BANISH (v)

adverbs
utterly; effectually; everlastingly; perpetually; dishonorably; eternally; inescapably; deservedly; ultimately; reluctantly; cruelly.
(See dismiss, expel.)

BANISHMENT

adjectives
timely; everlasting; perpetual; honorable; deadly; eternal; inescapable; deserved.

verbs
compel—; consent to—; decree—; doom to —; order—; repeal—; reside in—; return from—; suffer—.
(See exile, expulsion.)

BANJO

adjectives
melodious; melancholy; tuneless; twanging; plunking; soul-fathoming; heart-voicing; unstrung; voodoo-charming.

verbs
compose for—; employ—; excel at—; finger —; fret—; harmonize with—; introduce—; peg—; perform on—; pick—; pluck—; strike —; string—; strum—; twitch—; —expresses; —lulls; —registers; —serenades; —sings; —twangs; —vibrates.
(See instrument, music.)

BANK

adjectives (finance)
shiftless; leading; unthrifty; local; financial; depleted; impoverished; badly-managed; safe; insured.

verbs
borrow from—; charter—; conduct—; consult—; deal with—; deposit in—; draw upon—; equip—; loot—; patronize—; plunder—; run on—; wreck—; —acquires; —advances; —advises; —amasses; —appropriates; —authorizes; —branches; —cashes; —charges; —collapses; —consolidates; —discounts; —dominates; —drafts; —expands; —finances; —flourishes; —guards; —handles; —incorporates; —insures; —invests; —issues; —loans; —manages; —mortgages; —negotiates; —operates; —profits; —rates; —regulates; —sanctions; —serves; —transacts.
(See banker, firm, company, corporation.)

BANK

adjectives (land)
naked; oozy; perpendicular; shagged; grassy; wooded; precipitous; steep; slippery; tottering; glorious; flowering; rocky; river; mud; sloping; mossy; willow; sheltering; forested; shelving; placid; tossing; pine-clad; green-wooded; rugged; dirt; overhanging; miry; gentle; weedy; curving; rain-gullied; clay; eroding; tree-lined; heavily-wooded; glistening; caving; mosquito-infested; rabbit-riddled; willow-tufted; low-lying; unlimited; enormous; smothering; noisy; frequented; fringed; deep; impassable; unmolested; storm-shaken; weary; embroidered; permanent; high; bramble-

covered; primrose; cnalk; starred; settled; craggy; stifled; ash; wasted; picturesque; marshy; swampy; rugged; herbless; upland; tawny; bounding; beauteous; verdant; calm; rounding; porcelain; encompassing; lonesome; craggy; fraudulent; puddled; never-withering; glittering; blossom-laden.

verbs
bask on—; bound by —s; couch on—; fortify —s; overflow —s; scramble up—; shadow—; support—; swell over—; teeter on —; —encircles; —s rise.
(See ridge, pile.)

BANKER

adjectives
conservative; prosperous; resourceful; foremost; international; sophisticated; tall; dignified; mustached; gray-haired; trusted; rich; mean; bearded; cautious; private; leading; upstate; honest; hard-headed; prominent; defaulting; metropolitan; sagacious; astute; expert; established; benevolent; shortsighted; unscrupulous.

verbs
denounce—; envy—; protect—; —absconds; —collects; —contracts; —credits; —deals; —defaults; —embezzles; —executes; —investigates; —proffers; —provides; —refunds; —reimburses; —remits; —safeguards; —secures; —swindles; —traffics in.

BANKRUPT

adverbs
frequently; unfortunately; unhappily; profitably; conveniently; adroitly; inevitably; morally; irretrievably; unaccountably; mysteriously; surprisingly; seriously; temporarily; expediently; smartly; ingeniously; pitiably; dishearteningly; grievously; ruinously; touchingly; hopelessly; heartbreakingly.

BANKRUPTCY

adjectives
inevitable; economic; honest; moral; voluntary; irretrievable.

verbs
adjudge—; administer by—; administrate in —; annul—; arrange for—; arise from—; assent to—; authorize—; avoid—; commit to—; contract—; declare—; decree—; defer —; delay—; discharge from—; drift into—; effect—; embarrass into—; enter—; evade —; examine for—; face—; force into—; head for—; incur—; investigate—; involve —; liquidate in—; petition for—; record—; reduce to—; relieve by—; save from—; seize in—; settle—; surrender to—; terminate in—; threaten with—; verge on—; —deprives; —divests; —solves; —threatens.
(See failure.)

BANNER

adjectives
bloodless; darkling; tattered; starry; spangled; elastic; prosperous; flaunting; murky; insurgent; bright-colored; gaudy; mimic; emblematical; superb; barbarous; gorgeous; unfurled; horse-tail; hostile; flapping; gay; flamboyant; victorious; appropriate; clustered; sinister; bloodstained; triumphant; rippling; holy; silken; star-faced; faded; historic; impalpable; crimsoned; ragged.

verbs
adopt—; bear—; flaunt—; flout—; gather round—; hail—; hang out—; hoist—; lift —; rally round—; serve—; spread—; stretch out—; unfurl—; unroll—; wave—; —dances; —droops; —flies; —flutters; —inspires; —rises into the air; —streams; —symbolizes; —undulates.
(See flag, standard, ensign.)

BANQUET

adjectives
unpretentious; sumptuous; diplomatic; delicious; fantastical; open-air; luxurious; artistic; unending; exotic; artificial; voluptuous; good-will; Lucullan; elaborate; stately; philanthropic.

BANTER

adjectives
familiar; good-natured; brilliant; delicate; contemptuous; gay; slow; facetious; witty.

verbs
assail with—; chide with—; engage in—; exchange—; indulge in—; pass for—; ridicule with—; turn to—; —entertains; —floats about.
(See ridicule, derision, mockery, repartee.)

BANTER (v)

adverbs
vivaciously; familiarly; brilliantly; delicately; contemptuously; gaily; facetiously; wittily; good-naturedly; slyly; cleverly; satirically.
(See jest, chaff.)

BAR

adjectives
unfeeling; resonant; colossal; extemporized;

statutory; invidious; anticipatory; inexorable; sullen; dissolving; alternating (pl); corporeal; multitudinous (pl); legal; oaken; drink-laden.

BAR

adjectives (law)
lofty; magisterial; inviolable; relentless; arraigning; ruling; invincible.

verbs
accuse at—; address—; admit to—; appear before—; arraign before—; beseech—; bring to—; cajole—; call to—; defend at —; disagree with—; elect to—; expel from —; influence—; pass—; plead before—; reproach—; resign from—; solicit—; station at—; summon to—; —administers; —advises; —criticizes; —directs; —disciplines; —encourages; —establishes; —exercises; —governs; —grants; —orders; —privileges; —rules.
(See tribunal, law.)

BAR

adjectives (obstruction)
basic; formidable; frowning; impassable; protective; forbidding; impenetrable; unscalable.

verbs
beat —s; cut —s; escape —s; fence in with —s; strengthen —s; —creates a barrier; —excludes; —hinders; —impedes; —obstructs; —prevents; —prohibits; —restrains.
(See barrier, obstruction, obstacle.)

BAR (*v*)

adverbs
strongly; unfeelingly; invidiously; inexorably; sullenly; corporeally; legally; determinedly; harshly; ultimately; utterly; unkindly; treacherously.
(See exclude, hinder, obstruct, restrain.)

BARBARIAN

adjectives
ferocious; sanguinary; tumultuous; idolatrous; lusty; obstinate; suspicious; bestial.

verbs
civilize—; conquer—; crush—; culture—; dominate —s; overcome—; quell—; repress —; subdue—; vanquish—; —imitates; —s overthrow; —pillages; —plunders; —subjugates; —sacks.
(See brute, savage, monster.)

BARBARISM

adjectives
medieval; colloquial; unenlightened; dark; heathen; unavoidable.

verbs
brand—; crash into—; degrade to—; descend to—; enslave by—; fall to—; rise from—; stave off—; succeed—.
(See brutality, anarchy.)

BARBARITY

adjectives
execrable; shocking; vulgar; calculated; legal; deliberate; indecent.

BARBAROUS

adverbs
fiercely; savagely; shockingly; deliberately; outlandishly; rudely; inhumanly; brutally; indecently; unforgivably; inherently; instinctively; heathenishly; triumphantly; vauntingly; mercilessly; fiendishly; oddly; uncouthly; bizarrely; grotesquely; cruelly; blatantly; flagrantly; incredibly.

BARD

adjectives
love-stricken; saturnine; high-dreaming; didactic; epic; merry; subtle; pied; mercenary; gifted.

BARE

adverbs
starkly; nakedly; pitiably; shamelessly; distressingly; skimpily; scantily; stingily; pathetically; austerely; painfully; grievously; unfortunately; wretchedly; miserably; cheerlessly; horribly; surprisingly; desolately; dismally; hopelessly; deplorably; utterly; unnecessarily.

BARGAIN

adjectives
mammoth; amazing; selfish; outstanding; remarkable; vaunted; sensational; sharp; fair; sordid; impious.

verbs
agree upon—; bind to—; buy a—; close a —; consider—; contract for—; discuss—; drive a—; enter into—; fulfill—; gobble up —; jump at—; maintain—; propose—; refuse—; release from—; rue—; seal—; search for —s; seize—; settle—; stipulate in—; strike—; strive for—.
(See transaction, contract.)

BARGAIN (*v*)

adverbs
collectively; indigently; amazingly; selfish-

ly; remarkably; sensationally; sharply; fairly; sordidly; impiously; cleverly; shrewdly; stupidly; astutely.

(See agree, contract, stipulate.)

BARGE

adjectives

imperial; ungainly; gorgeous; state; abandoned; sluggish; dingy; gaily-painted; clumsy.

verbs

adorn—; anchor—; board—; christen—; command—; control—; convoy—; cushion—; decorate—; design—; dock—; equip—; escort—; fit out—; land—; lash—; launch—; license—; moor—; navigate—; pilot—; power—; propel—; rig—; shift—; stow—; straddle—; tow—; —coasts; —conveys; —discharges; —drifts; —journeys; —plies; —sails; —slips past; —trades; —transports; —tugs.

(See boat.)

BARK
(boat)

adjectives

venturous; perfidious; passing; stranded; swift-winged; lofty; fragile; floating; deep-drawing; foundering; proud; flying; frail; enchanted; storm-tossed.

BARK
(dog's)

adjectives

snappish; harsh; fiendish; welcoming; irritated; short; sharp; wild; eager; thundering; swaggering; acute; agonized; imperative; gay; high-pitched; teasing; expressive; ferocious; frenzied; staccato; frantic; furious; deafening; ecstatic; jubilant; ringing; desolate; muffled; defiant; confident; playful.

BARK
(tree)

adjectives

sapless; gnarled; rugged; indigenous; silvery; bruised; corrugated; peeling.

BARK (v)

adverbs

imperiously; lustily; inopportunely; explosively; joyously; injuriously; snappishly; harshly; fiendishly; welcomingly; irritatedly; sharply; wildly; eagerly; agonizedly; imperatively; teasingly; expressively; ferociously; frenziedly; frantically; deafeningly; jubilantly; desolately; defiantly; confidently; playfully.

(See shout.)

BARN

adjectives

substantial; commodious; solitary; comfortable; cool; tumble-down; ruinous; dilapidated; rickety; rambling; ramshackle; abandoned; neglected; decaying; well-filled; bulging.

verbs

construct—; equip—; erect—; fire—; forage in—; frame—; gather into—; house in—; install in—; remodel—; stable in—; stake out—; store in—; —collapses; —harbors; —shelters.

(See building.)

BAROMETER

adjectives

alternating; disconcerting; steadily-rising; unvarying; vacillating; threatening; faltering.

verbs

adjust—; affect—; compensate—; correct—; depend on—; devise—; employ—; equip with—; experiment with—; expose—; govern—; influence—; learn from—; read—; record—; rely on—; seal—; sheathe—; steady—; test—; throw off—; vouch for—; —assists; —climbs; —demonstrates; —determines; —falls; —fluctuates; —forecasts; —graduates; —indicates; —measures; —oscillates; —predicts; —records; —registers; —represents; —rises; —shows; —sinks; —soars; —threatens; —warns.

(See meter, thermometer.)

BARON

adjectives

medieval; villainous; cattle; feudal; despotic; coal; monocled; proud; impetuous; monstrous.

BARRACKS

adjectives

bleak; disciplinary; grim; cheerless; orderly; solid.

verbs

advance toward—; allot to—; arouse—; arrange for—; assault—; assign to—; censor—; command—; concentrate in—; confine to—; construct—; convert into—; dispatch to—; encamp in—; equip—; extend to—; file into—; fire on—; fortify—; guard—; invade—; protect—; quarter in—; repair to—; report to—; restrict to—; retire to—; sanitize—; station in—; superintend—; survey—; threaten—; —accommodate; —collapse; —house; —lodge; —resound; —spring up.

(See quarters, shelter, building.)

BARRAGE

adjectives
gigantic; advertising; incessant; verbal; rolling; murderous; leaden; shrapnel; deadly; fatal; vicious; violent.

verbs
advance under—; approach—; beat down —; concentrate—; create—; curtain with—; defend against—; defy—; denounce—; disperse—; establish—; extend—; invade—; lay down—; penetrate—; prolong—; reduce —; resist—; restrict—; retreat from—; strengthen—; sweep through—; —cuts off; —holds up; —obstructs; —parries; —protects; —surprises; —threatens.

BARREL

adjectives
dilapidated; hoopless; cobwebbed; moss-grown; sagging; scarred; slimy; stout; warped.

verbs
bung—; measure—; pipe—; pump from—; roll—; store in—; stove in—; tap—; valve —; —bulges; —reeks; —resounds; —thuds; —thunders; —tumbles.

BARREN

adverbs
monotonously; treelessly; desolately; endlessly; infinitely; alarmingly; frightfully; indescribably; immeasurably; comfortlessly; formidably; blankly; inhospitably; illimitably; boundlessly; terrifyingly; perilously.

BARRICADE

adjectives
verdant; feeble; defensive; disputed; stone; bristling; human; effective.

verbs
advance toward—; approach—; assault—; capture—; defend—; denounce—; entrench behind—; erect—; extend—; invade—; pile up—; strengthen—; support—; survey—; sweep through—; threaten—; withdraw—; —annoys; —bars; —blocks; —collapses; —confines; —cuts off; —defends; —fortifies; —parries; —prevents; —protects; —resists; —restricts; —withholds.

(See barrier, obstruction.)

BARRIER

adjectives
golden; external; sufficient; insuperable; material; formidable; subjective; effective; feeble; obstinate; intervening; screening; conventional; fancied; invisible; insurmountable; stair-like; impassable; airy; serried; moss-draped; dismal; ancient; irregular; surf-beaten; absolute; stout; invincible; powerful; unconquerable; mighty; impenetrable; awesome; lofty; serious; eternal; natural; legal; psychological; economic; cultural; vast; lowered; inadequate; stubborn; artificial; puerile; indefinable; pitiless; traditional; countless (pl); imagined.

verbs
beat—; build—; burst—; confine by—; create—; cross—; erect—; flatten against—; follow—; form—; hurdle—; hurl against—; jump—; rail in with —s; smash—; step over —; strengthen—; surmount—; tear down—; vault—; —bounds; —hinders; —isolates; —limits; —looms; —obstructs; —prevents; —supports; —thwarts.

(See obstruction, barricade.)

BARRISTER

adjectives
conscientious; ambitious; overworked; struggling; smug; briefless; infant; sneering; brilliant; competent.

BASE

adjectives
substantial; solidified; tottering; commodious; crumbling; flattering; immutable; firm; circular.

verbs
advance to—; attach to—; break from—; build on—; challenge—; communicate with —; construct—; create—; decorate—; dump at—; enlarge—; establish—; gather at—; hollow—; issue from—; mould—; protect—; puncture—; rest on—; separate from—; set on—; situate at—; spread on—; store at—; —projects.

(See foundation, basis, bottom.)

BASE (a)

adverbs
intolerably; meanly; ignobly; obscurely; contemptibly; abjectly; unbecomingly; undisguisedly; shamefully; glaringly; flagrantly; unmistakably; palpably; nakedly; brazenly; shamelessly; flauntingly; sorrily; brutishly; rudely; fawningly; obsequiously; cringingly; sneakily; subtly.

BASE (v)

adverbs
primarily; wholly; unsoundly; substantially; totteringly; firmly; immutably.

(See depend.)

BASEBALL

verbs

blacken—; condemn—; destroy—; rebuke—; sponsor—; spread—; welcome—; —animates; —breeds; —engenders; —enlivens.

(See game.)

BASEMENT

adjectives

sunless; dark; stone; historical; excavated; dungeon-like; dank; damp; airless; musty; rat-infested.

verbs

climb from—; consist of—; drain—; excavate—; floor—; flood—; form—; relegate to—; rummage in—; well from—.

(See cellar.)

BASENESS

adjectives

inherent; forced; unconfinable; adroit; despicable; apparent; undisguised.

BASHFUL

adverbs

awkwardly; uneasily; boyishly; self-consciously; embarrassingly; uncomfortably; painfully; engagingly; charmingly; peculiarly; strangely; unwontedly; becomingly; naturally; modestly; timidly; fearfully; clumsily; foolishly; distressingly; ridiculously; pitiably; touchingly; adorably; comically; absurdly.

BASHFULNESS

adjectives

uneasy; maiden; engaging; virgin; childish; boyish; graceful; captivating; peculiar; shamefaced.

verbs

feign—; mask in—; shrink in—; —disturbs; —inhibits; —melts; —overcomes; —unfits.

(See modesty, shyness, diffidence.)

BASIC

adverbs

scientifically; fundamentally; essentially; indispensably; admittedly; emphatically; prescriptively; usually; ordinarily; officially; obviously; palpably; conspicuously; explicitly; positively; definitely; unavoidably.

BASIN

adjectives

remarkable; treeless; shallow; vast; starlit; drainage; rock-bottomed; tidal; empty; volcanic; gigantic; pitlike; lacustrine; rustic; beautiful; incrusted; weedy; marshy; natural; fan-shaped; broad; spacious; sumptuous.

BASIS

adjectives

psychological; moral; social; military; commission; logical; scientific; voluntary; geographical; tangible; potential; essential; sustaining; concrete; apperceptive; experimental; daily; hypothetical; structural; universal; simplified; sound; economic; well-established; sensible; rationalized; secure; efficient; profitable; firm; prosperous; indispensable; healthy; solid; equitable; liberal; substantial; broad; possible; false; unsatisfactory; narrow; slippery; temporary; vast; meager; factual; ample; permanent; tenuous; inevitable; reliable; pecuniary; corporative; practical; immovable; flimsy; philosophical; physical; monarchical; creditable; feudal; mechanical; theoretical; dubious; imperishable; fantastic; enduring; lowest.

verbs

build upon—; establish a—; explain on—; form—; found on—; meet on—of; obtain—; place on—; rest on—; rise from—of; shake —; support on—; win a higher—; —consists.

(See foundation, base.)

BASK (*v*)

adverbs

obviously; torpidly; cozily; lazily; drowsily; blissfully; comfortably; sleepily; pleasantly; restfully.

(See luxuriate.)

BASKET

adjectives

enormous; rustic; severe; round; shallow; inexhaustible; wicker; huge; garlanded; split-oak; cup-shaped; upturned; filigree.

verbs

charge—; coil—; convey in—; cram in—; design—; fashion—; lattice into—; load—; measure in—; net—; provision—; stuff—; twine—; weave—.

(See case, chest, box.)

BASKING

adverbs

luxuriously; comfortably; buoyantly; joyously; prosperously; happily; warmly; radiantly.

BASS

adverbs

thunderingly; resonantly; deeply; breezily; boomingly; awfully; mightily; magnificently; toweringly; enormously; stupendously.

BASS (fish)

adjectives
game; scrappy; small-mouthed; stern; skittish.

BASS (voice)

adjectives
thunderous; resonant; bawling; masculine; profound; growling; deep; unruly; swelling; mellow; breezy.

BASTION

adjectives
sparkling; absurd; massive; futile; sloping; tower-like; coral.

BAT (baseball)

adjectives
firm-resounding; decisive; sturdy; uncompromising; stout; spindly; threatening; relentless.

verbs
balance—; choose—; fling—; fondle—; grip—; oil—; paw—; release—; sandpaper—; scrape—; select—; shave—; shorten—; shoulder—; split—; swish—; tape—; weight—; wield—; —cracks; —flies; —slips; —splits.
(See club.)

BAT (mammal)

adjectives
insectivorous; gloomy; grisly; monstrous.

verbs
attract—; disturb—; ensnare—; entice—; loose—; pursue—; strike—; trap—; —s abound; —clings; —flits; —hibernates; —lurks; —preys upon; —shuns; —sucks; —swoops; —terrorizes; —wheels; —whirls; —whirs; —wings.
(See animal, bird, insect.)

BATH

adjectives
chemical; imperceptible; ice; cold; Diocletian; perfumed; steaming; reducing; discomforting; relaxing; refreshing; portable; warm; soapy; splashing; freezing; medicated; involuntary; tepid; open-air; sun; modern; finely-appointed; immaculate; world-famous; well-equipped; radio-active; mud; matutinal.

verbs
administer—; arrange—; cure by —s; drain—; enter—; immerse in—; lather in—; loll in—; medicate—; perspire in—; rub in—; scald in—; sponge in—; steam in—; treat in—; vaporize—; —enervates; —exhilarates; —refreshes; —relaxes.
(See water.)

BATHE (*v*)

adverbs
actually; chemically; steamingly; discomfortingly; comfortingly; refreshingly; soapily; splashingly; freezingly; involuntarily; tepidly; immaculately; daily; matutinally; thoroughly.
(See wash.)

BATHER

adjectives
ecstatic; adventurous; timid; floundering; inept; expert.

BATHING

adjectives
unexcelled; luxurious; indiscriminate; clear; clean; surf; safe; ocean.

BATON

adjectives
authoritative; commanding; directing; gilt; guiding; silencing; silver-tipped; suspended.

verbs
carry—; conduct with—; cudgel with—; dash—; direct with—; flourish—; lead—; mark with—; point—; signal with—; strike—; swing—; tap—; wave—; wield—; —guides.
(See wand, sceptre.)

BATTALION

adjectives
repulsed; puny; assaulting; steel-clad; potential; defending; staunch; sturdy; stalwart.

BATTER

adjectives
alert; deftly-moving; eagle-eyed; able-armed; wary; splendid; famous.

verbs
fan—; strike out—; —bats; —bunts; —crashes; —doubles; —drives; —flies; —fouls; —hits; —loops; —pops; —singles; —steals; —triples; —walks.

BATTERY

adjectives
sensitive; galvanic; pointed; discharged; weakened.

BATTLE

adjectives
bitter; hard-fought; furious; terrific; fierce;

raging; frantic; desperate; hot; bloody; savage; gory; gallant; sanguinary; thrilling; glorious; mighty; valiant; decisive; ceaseless; brief; impending; arduous; incessant; strenuous; historic; bloodless; inglorious; exhausting; hopeless; undercover; stiff; ironic; silent; pitched; fateful; phantom; life-long; offensive; parliamentary; dramatic; unrighteous; perpetual; discouraging; hereditary; nameless; memorable; earthly; childish; verbal; crashing; hand-to-hand; immediate; never-ending; weird; raging; naval; puny; intellectual; disastrous; losing.

verbs
arouse a—; clash in—; climax—; conflict in—; contend in—; create—; distinguish in —; doom to—; encounter in—; engage in—; finance—; gain in—; gird for—; give—; honor in—; join—; light the fuse of—; manoeuver—; offer—; overcome in—; pit in—; pitch—; precipitate—; premeditate—; provoke—; pursue—; slay in—; stay—; strive in—; subsist in—; sway—; triumph in—; wage—; —depends on; —ensues; —flashes; —presses; —rages; —rings; —swirls.
(See conflict, encounter, combat, fight, contest.)

BATTLE (v)

adverbs
fiercely; doggedly; invincibly; manfully; heroically; furiously; terrifically; desperately; gallantly; thrillingly; gloriously; valiantly; decisively; ceaselessly; briefly; arduously; incessantly; strenuously; hopelessly; exhaustingly; silently; fatefully; perpetually; childishly; verbally; intellectually; disastrously.
(See fight, encounter, combat.)

BATTLEFIELD

adjectives
immense; immortal; stupendous; rolling; ill-fated; scarred; silent; bloody; bone-strewn; glorious; memorial.

verbs
abandon on—; advance on—; assault on—; campaign on—; clash on—; concede on—; concentrate on—; encounter on—; enmesh on—; exhaust on—; fell on—; mass on—; occupy—; overthrow on—; perish on—; redden—; relinquish—; replace on—; slay on —; suffer on—; surprise on—; surrender on —; test on—; —lies; —reaps a harvest; —reeks; —stretches.
(See field, plain.)

BATTLELINE

adjectives
wavering; bent; far-flung; crushed; crumbling; tottering.

BATTLEMENTS

adjectives
frowning; massive; time-scarred; dim; castellated; crackling; imperial; haunted; escarped; cloud-capped; shining; narrow; gilded; tottered.

BAUBLE

adjectives
ingenious; gilt; worthless; imperial; silken; gorgeous; gleaming; heavy.

BAWD

adjectives
wicked; powdered; notorious; infamous; lewd; libidinous.

BAWL (v)

adverbs
hoarsely; plaintively; pitifully; intermittently; fitfully; loudly; wailingly.
(See cry.)

BAY

adjectives
land-locked; craggy; shallow; native; tranquil; yawning; eddying; noble; silvery; curving; regal; extensive; deep; protective; roaring; billowy; treacherous; glassy; squally; distant; sheltered; whispering; shimmering; murky; shark-infested; broadening; magnificent; protected; misted.

verbs
anchor in—; break on—; dredge—; drop into—; embark at—; enter—; put into—; recede into—; ride—; surround—; —eddies; —extends; —lashes the beach; —narrows; —widens.
(See ocean, river, gulf, harbor.)

BAYONET

adjectives
gleaming; pointless; glistening; fixed; bared; flashing; pitiless; ruthless; slanting; slashing; gory; grisly; merciless; murderous.

verbs
arm with—; attach—; charge with —s; clasp —; clutch—; connect—; defend with—; drive home—; equip with—; fix—; impale on—; insert—; jab with—; juggle—; raise —; repulse with—; rush with—; sheathe—; shield from—; spar with—; stab with—;

struggle with—; thrust—; vanquish with—; wield—; withdraw—; —catches; —flashes; —gores; —gouges; —pierces; —sticks.
(See dagger, weapon.)

BAZAAR

adjectives
straggling; languorous; Oriental; romantic; gay; grubby; modern; noisy.

BEACH

adjectives
artificial; accessible; secluded; clean; sloping; crescent; sandy; curving; private; sun-warmed; beautiful; commodious; gay; bright; fascinating; golden; rocky; pebbly; silvery; brilliant; sun-swept; gleaming; silent; desolate; shelving; surf-smoothed; windless; mosquito-infested; ancient; calcareous; foamy; private.

verbs
batter—; break on—; dawdle along—; drift on—; lash against—; pound—; ripple on—; roam—; run aground on—; settle on—; sprawl on—; stagger onto—; strand on—; strew—; throw up on—; —extends; —gleams; —stretches.
(See shore.)

BEACON

adjectives
eternal; indubitable; towering; revolving; long-distance; visual; dangerous; spiritual; gleaming; rebel; warning.

verbs
operate—; provide—; set—; —aids; —blazons; —circles; —directs; —guides; —identifies; —illuminates; —indicates; —leads; —lights; —marks; —notifies; —rotates; —shines; —signals; —swings; —warns.
(See fire, light, signal.)

BEADS

adjectives
wired; shining; iridescent; pale; gleaming; coiled; garish; many-colored; greasy; wooden; pea-sized; unstrung; cheap.

verbs
barter with—; color—; count—; crush—; dye—; facet—; fashion—; grind—; mould—; mount—; ornament with—; perforate—; pray with—; shape—; space—; string—; suspend—; trade—; trim with—; —glisten; —sparkle.
(See diamond, ornament, drop, jewel.)

BEAK

adjectives
curled; relentless; ravening; golden; brazen; Wellingtonian; lifelike; twisted; hooked; powerful; crooked; tuneless.

BEAM

adjectives (light)
quivering; hazy; dulled; transient; sunny; noonday; blessed; invisible; silvery; chaste; stray; steady; unwinking; eternal; creeping; intermittent; half-extinguished; bright; pallid; guiding; fervid; virgin; naked; feeble; divergent; crimson; intellectual; belated; transverse; kindly; slanting; piercing; horizontal; penetrating; weird; leaf-entangled; genial; blinding; sunny; burning; effulgent; gracious; glancing; refracted.

verbs
clothe in —s; emit—; enwreathe with —s; flash—; fling—; focus—; follow—; furnish—; gild with —s; isolate—; outshine—; play—upon; radiate—; shade—; shed—; shoot—; spot—; throw—; —blazes; —blinds; —brightens; —creeps up; —dazzles; —directs; —emanates from; —glitters; —guides; —penetrates; —pierces; —reflects; —scorches; —shines; —shoots forth; —slants; —sweeps.
(See ray, gleam.)

BEAM

adjectives (wood)
sagging; massive; uncovered; metal-weighted; rough; hand-hewn; exposed; blackened; tarred.

verbs
arch—; center—; cross —s; fell—; lay—; saw—; set—; split—; suspend from—; warp—; —connects; —extends; —projects; —strengthens; —supports.
(See timber.)

BEAM (v)

adverbs
affably; vaguely; benevolently; radiantly; hazily; transiently; sunnily; unwinkingly; chastely; steadily; eternally; intermittently; pallidly; fervidly; nakedly; intellectually; feebly; belatedly; slantingly; horizontally; penetratingly; weirdly; genially; blindingly; effulgently; graciously.
(See gleam, shine, glitter, glisten.)

BEAMING

adverbs
radiantly; joyously; fairly; delicately; beautifully; becomingly; bonnily; curiously; unconsciously; gorgeously; prettily; rosily;

smilingly; laughingly; ridiculously; foolishly; ruddily; sparklingly; mischievously; openly; innocently; girlishly; shyly; modestly; frankly; happily; brightly.

BEAR

adjectives
ponderous; huge; crafty; burly; brindled; fearless; monstrous; murderous; menacing; untamed; vicious; playful.

verbs
ambush—; bait—; cage—; chain—; confine—; exterminate —s; fatten—; harass—; madden—; roast—; skin—; stalk—; tame —; tether—; trap—; —attacks; —burrows; —charges; —claws; —climbs; —clowns; —dances; —flourishes; —forages; —gambols; —growls; —grunts; —hibernates; —hugs; —lumbers; —lurks; —migrates; —multiplies; —paws; —pounces on; —preys on; —ravages; —roars; —sheds; —shuffles; —whelps.

(See animal.)

BEAR (*v*)

adverbs
patiently; manfully; oppressively; prematurely; extremely; stiffly; valiantly; coldly; stoically; recklessly; philosophically; heavily; hurriedly.

(See endure, stand, tolerate.)

BEARD

adjectives
sheaved; vigorous; spreading; bushy; tawny; curly; peaked; dripping; comic; incipient; wiry; rippling; full; tangled; mangy; grizzled; downy; matted; filthy; forked; crisp; trim; close-cropped; well-clipped; Oriental; venerable; unshorn; hoary; foolish; overgrown; silken; military; telescopic; verdant; patriarchal; Mephistophelian.

verbs
acquire—; adorn with—; attain—; clip—; comb—; curl—; dignify with—; disguise by—; distinguish by—; drag by—; part—; paw—; pluck off—; pull—; run down—; scratch—; seize by—; shave—; singe—; smooth—; stroke—; style—; take by—; trim —; twitch—; waggle—; weep in—; —bristles; —blooms; —covers; —glistens.

(See hair, whiskers.)

BEARD (*v*)

adverbs
boldly; fearlessly; manfully; foolhardily; playfully; exasperatingly; foolishly; valiantly.

(See defy, oppose, encounter.)

BEARING
(manner)

adjectives
modest; timid; manly; noble; courteous; polished; dignified; tranquil; unpretentious; unostentatious; imperial; austere; regal; lofty; haughty; patrician; godlike; majestic; jaunty; lively; gay; contemptuous; disdainful; martial; soldierly; military; clerkly; grave; staid; courteous; queenly; gallant; graceful; intimate; alarming; humble; courageous; worthy; unbridled; steadfast; chivalrous; heroic; imperious; rollicking; straightforward; immitigable.

BEARING
(meaning)

adjectives
intimate; immediate; favorable; happy; vital; frank; tragic; popular; external; direct; mutual.

BEAST

adjectives
skulking; brutish; ingenious; ravenous; wily; unfriendly; elusive; slippery; wild; driveling; boisterous; unruly; unsavory; massive; infuriated; ill-trained; bloody; savage; grisly; predatory; formidable; monstrous; maddened; outlandish; venomous; grotesque; fabulous; cross-grained; beauteous; malicious; cowardly; sanguine; sulky; unkempt; jaded; voracious; undisciplined; squealing; nocturnal; four-footed; noble; lordly; cruel; murderous; ferocious; relentless; marauding; prowling; hostile; enraged; screaming; snarling; cornered; charging; frantic; restless; stamping; crouching; sagacious; cunning; well-bred; gaunt; hairy; stolid; plodding; shaggy; rugged; graceless; diminutive; foolish; prehistoric; sleek.

verbs
cage—; chase—; constrain—; depict—; flay —; hunt—; mount—; pen up—; shelter—; skin—; slash—; slaughter—; spare—; subdue—; track—; transform into—; —bays; —cries; —forages; —growls; —grunts; —prowls; —roams; —subsists; —yelps.

(See brute, monster, animal.)

BEAT

adjectives
receding; impatient; dynamic; incessant; steady; rhythmic.

BEAT (*v*)

adverbs
unmercifully; continuously; impatiently; in-

cessantly; rhythmically; languidly; mercilessly; boisterously; joyously; youthfully; manifestly; pleasantly; proportionately; regularly; audibly; unpitifully; unreasonably; horribly; uncontrollably; thoroughly; strenuously; burningly; merrily; lazily; lightly.
(See hammer, smite, strike, chasten.)

BEATIFIC

adverbs
ethereally; mysteriously; divinely; happily; ecstatically; gloriously; rapturously; mystically; devoutly; fervently.

BEATING

adjectives
merciless; tumultuous; fierce; unjust.

verbs
administer—; chastise with—; deserve—; endure—; flatten out with—; punish—; suffer—; throb from—; —intimidates.
(See drubbing, defeat, blows.)

BEATING
(sound)

adjectives
loud; insistent; barbaric; tumultuous; staccato.

BEATITUDE

adjectives
infinite; limitless; insouciant.

BEAU

adjectives
ardent; fascinating; devoted; distant; cool.

BEAUTIFUL

adverbs
gloriously; ethereally; dazzlingly; elusively; unearthly; fatally; fleetingly; intangibly; mysteriously; magnificently; fabulously; charmingly; radiantly; exquisitely; matchlessly; fiercely; surprisingly; exotically; sullenly; poignantly; bloomingly; naturally; simply; lustrously; languidly; compellingly; opulently; richly; wondrously; duskily; cruelly; stormily; vitally; singularly; vividly; gracefully; flawlessly; harmoniously; calmly; graciously; serenely; sweetly; childishly; unforgettably; innocently; imposingly; surpassingly; disdainfully; daintily; proudly; wildly; ineffably; triumphantly; ravishingly; weirdly; unconsciously; sternly; devastatingly; darkly; resplendently; robustly; infinitely; pensively; faultlessly; divinely; quietly; vivaciously; glamorously; glitteringly; glowingly; alluringly; unspeakably; adorably; startlingly; chastely; regally; terribly.

BEAUTY

adjectives
glorious; guarded; sable; animal; dazzling; uncultivated; moral; unearthly; distinctive; luscious; inexhaustible; famous; mortal; fleeting; iridescent; passionate; sensuous; gleaming; talented; mysterious; perpetual; mystic; homely; all-pervading; picturesque; infantile; notable; fabulous; radiant; exquisite; unmatched; haughty; reigning; stately; insistent; fierce; surprising; changeful; indescribable; celestial; sullen; naked; blooming; antique; poignant; morose; abstracted; delicate; poetic; unparalleled; mocking; unrivaled; natural; lustrous; wistful; ideal; rare; polished; perennial; languid; indefinable; compelling; opulent; rugged; matronly; rich; wondrous; original; verdant; dusky; cruel; peculiar; marvelous; stormy; despoiled; masculine; singular; indestructible; substantiated; transfigured; intellectual; graceful; harmonious; bedizened; unforgettable; luxurious; surpassing; sacred; evanescent; pictorial; breathless; crystal; excelling; considerable; spiritual; peerless; creative; dainty; speckled; wild; triumphant; weird; celebrated; impersonal; vaunted; plastic; blemished; stern; angelic; dismal; dark; earthly; comprehensible; robust; ripe; melodic; supernal; pensive; tragic; divine; intrinsic; vivacious; glittering; mellow; soul-awakening; tanned; alluring; exclusive; haunting; chaste; bridal; somber; unadorned; fadeless; geometric; impassioned; terrible; regal; majestic; voluptuous; sculptured; artistic; traditional; unexampled; rustic; enhanced; startling; unspeakable; glowing; patrician; pristine; tonic; glamorous; superlative; ornate; quiet; nymph-like; faultless; gnarled; debased; garnished; infinite; midnight; filmy; feathery; refined; gossamer; sheer; resplendent; impalpable; devastating; ravishing; beguiling; unique; lavish; ineffable; intoxicating; commanding; proud; lofty; disdainful; scornful; awesome; imposing; inherent; innocent; restful; unconscious; unspoiled; child-like; lyrical; ethereal; exotic; eerie; serene; calm; colorful; riotous; flawless; nonpareil; vivid; vital; lucid; transcendant; deathless; Grecian; statuesque; rural; odorous; pastoral; colonial; scenic; buxom; pagan; Botticellian; lush; creamy; elusive; fatal; still; sepulchral; guileless; proverbial; unattainable; unveiled; shroud-

ed; stage; intoxicating; sylvan; intangible; consummate.

verbs
achieve—; approve of—; array in—; awaken—; bathe in—; bless with—; build—; capture—; commend—; deface—; depict—; desire—; desolate the—; drink up—; enamour of—; enhance—; envy—; excel in—; favor with—; gladden by—; glorify—; hanker for—; heighten—; hunger for—; hypnotize by—; impair—; lust for—; maintain—; mar—; outrage—; perfect—; praise —; preserve—; recapture—; rejoice in—; restore—; seek—; smother—; soften—; stain—; surrender—; tinge with—; trample —; unfold—; unmask—; veil—; vouchsafe —; worship—; —abounds; —attracts; —captivates; —charms; —decays; —departs; —enchants; —endures; —enraptures; —entrances; —excites; —fades; —fascinates; —glows; —shines; —stabs; —withers.

(See perfection, charm, loveliness, grace, harmony.)

BECKON (v)

adverbs
significantly; enticingly; captivatingly; smilingly; quaintly; repeatedly; imperceptibly.

(See wave.)

BED

adjectives
soft; snowy; luxurious; comfortable; lovely; quaint; chilly; four-poster; carved; musty; damp; ghoulish; spotless; wretched; pendent; curtained; sagging; painful; rocky; wholesome; cursed; barren; lustful; wormy; pensive; restless; regal; naked; sickly; fruitful; odorous; peaceful; creaking; makeshift; lumpy; hallowed; pebbly; nuptial; feverish; dying; sandy; virgin; sleepless; inviting; aching; pious; tumbled; weary; woeful; spectral; turfy; unhallowed; incestuous.

verbs
canopy—; cast upon—; clamber into—; confine to—; convey to—; couch in—; deck—; decorate—; defile—; enclose—; flop into—; fold—; glide into—; hang from—; heave from—; hurl out of—; kneel beside—; lay out in—; loll on—; lounge on—; mattress—; pillow in—; prop in—; recline in—; repose in—; retire to—; roll in—; rouse from—; sink into—; slumber in—; spring from—; squirm in—; stagger from—; stow in—; strike—; toss in—; toss into—; tuck in—; usurp—; warm—.

(See cot, couch, mattress.)

BED (v)

adverbs
softly; luxuriously; quaintly; comfortably; mustily; damply; nightly.

(See rest.)

BEDECK (v)

adverbs
gaily; gorgeously; fabulously; lavishly; grandly; attractively; picturesquely; gloriously.

(See ornament.)

BEDLAM

adjectives
clamorous; dreadful; foul; frantic; mind-sundering; raging; unsubdued.

verbs
lead into—; subject to—; —abates; —breaks out; —confuses; —deranges; —roars.

(See confusion, noise.)

BEDROOM

adjectives
gaudy; banal; voluptuous; charming; airy; dismal; silent; gloomy; ill-ventilated; dreary; diminutive.

verbs
air—; dash into—; deny—; emerge from —; furnish—; repair to—; retire to—; —contains.

(See room, apartment.)

BEE

adjectives
swarming (pl); laden; anxious; straggling; sucking; noontide; murmuring; stingless; maudlin; industrious; voluptuous; blunt-faced; sexless; restless; marauding; buzzing; bustling; busy.

verbs
handle—; keep —s; —alights on; —breeds; —bristles; —chases; —collects; —colonizes; —darts; —deposits; —dozes; —flits; —forages; —gathers; —gorges; —hibernates; —hums; —impregnates; —s issue; —labors; —mumbles; —murmurs; —nests; —oviposits; —perforates; —plies; —pollinates; —regurgitates; —secretes; —sips; —stings; —stores; —s swarm; —swoops down; —s throng; —tunnels; —wings its way.

(See insect.)

BEECH

adjectives
russet; stalwart; giant; leafy; serpent-rooted.

BEER

adjectives
authentic; stout; frothy; pale; foamy; powerful; drowsy.

verbs
abstain from—; addict to—; annihilate—; age—; bottle—; brew—; concoct—; consume—; de-alcoholize—; down—; extract —; gulp—; guzzle—; hop up—; lap up—; manufacture—; market—; process—; quaff —; sample—; sip—; steep in—; stock—; stow away—; strengthen—; swill—; tap —; weaken—; —bubbles; —ferments; —flows; —foams; —froths; —glistens; —intoxicates; —quenches; —thickens; —winks.
(See ale, liquor.)

BEETLE

adjectives
noisome; infuriated; drowsy; iridescent; carnivorous; obscurely-colored; glistening.

verbs
armor—; attack —s; control —s; crush—; exterminate —s; infest with —s; plague with —s; sheathe—; spray—; —bites; —captures; —chews; —destroys; —devastates; —feigns; —forages; —gnaws; —menaces; —s ravage; —scurries along; —tears out; —tumbles along.
(See insect.)

BEFALL (*v*)

adverbs
occasionally; preposterously; happily; unaccountably; auspiciously; inadvertently; inexplicably.
(See happen.)

BEG (*v*)

adverbs
solicitously; ingratiatingly; deprecatingly; appealingly; importunately; urgently; embarrassedly; impudently; clamorously; reproachfully; whiningly; fawningly; grimacingly; piteously; pestiferously; professionally; earnestly.
(See beseech, implore, ask.)

BEGGAR

adjectives
sturdy; amiable; jolly; disciplined; filthy; whining; gloomy; worthless; disgraced; greedy; blind; wandering; monkish; implacable; stalwart; unclean; bareheaded; crippled; loathsome; fawning; grimacing; piteous; penniless; tattered; pestiferous; hideous; impudent; professional; formidable.

verbs
contribute to—; corrupt—; die a—; ease—; feast—; foster—; lodge—; reduce to—; relieve—; repel—; revive—; sink to—; spurn —; —s band together; —complains; —desires; —entreats; —implores; —intrudes; —loafs; —petitions; —pleads; —roams; —shirks; —starves; —struggles; —tramps along.

BEGIN (*v*)

adverbs
jerkily; resentfully; methodically; mechanically; earnestly; hesitatingly; ostensibly; clumsily; euphemistically; sarcastically; argumentatively; oracularly; surreptitiously; savagely; wistfully; eventually; contemporaneously; ecstatically; romantically; insidiously; auspiciously; appealingly; rapturously.
(See commence, originate.)

BEGINNER

adjectives
awkward; anxious; fearful; mere; overconfident; zealous; untried.

verbs
bestow on—; condition—; describe to—; educate—; encourage—; foster—; induce—; pit against—; reveal to—; school—; sponsor—; stimulate—; suggest to—; train—; trouble—; —acquires; —advances; —applies; —contacts; —copes with; —crams; —demands; —embarks on; —emerges; —errs; —experiences; —learns; —plunges into; —questions.
(See novice, apprentice, amateur.)

BEGINNING

adjectives
remote; slow; tentative; crude; auspicious; recorded; amateurish; nebulous; unworkable; humble; long-deferred; promising; simple; tragic; ambitious; mandatory; microscopic; substantial; inconspicuous; modest; casual; sweet; indestructible; unpropitious; unlimited; significant.

verbs
celebrate—; commemorate—; declare—; honor—; initiate—; mark—; proceed from —; read from—; trace—; —introduces; —leads off.
(See origin.)

BEGRUDGE (*v*)

adverbs
habitually; selfishly; unfeelingly; implac-

ably; cruelly; odiously; remorselessly; frowningly.

(See deny.)

BEHAVE (v)

adverbs

unchastely; abhorrently; alluringly; treacherously; erratically; abominably; indifferently; unsociably; diabolically; errantly; debonairly; gawkily; ridiculously; prudently; uncouthly; proverbially; boisterously; obtusely; ludicrously; conclusively; theatrically; drably; courteously; jocularly; artlessly; imposingly; lasciviously; austerely; capriciously; speciously; decorously; callously; irreverently; obstreperously; generously; admirably.

(See act, bear.)

BEHAVIOR

adjectives

artless; imposing; offensive; lascivious; distant; picturesque; humorous; demonstrative; objective; portentous; genetic; outward; baffling; tormenting; prudential; austere; blunt; infantile; rude; stupid; loutish; unfilial; capricious; unparalleled; highhanded; emotional; ungracious; specious; courteous; ingenious; mild; odd; cruel; frantic; despicable; unbecoming; cowardly; disgusting; deferential; creditable; wanton; displeasing; suitable; individualistic; disheartening; noble; unique; odious; decorous; erratic; shameful; senseless; outrageous; shocking; riotous; mysterious; instinctive; decent; manly; intelligent; exceptional; reasonable; circumspect; polite; unmaidenly; childish; detestable; inhuman; callous; irreverent; egocentric; annoying; insulting; abominable; eccentric; obstreperous.

verbs

condone—; dignify—; interpret—; simulate —; soften—; —implies; —improves; —infuriates; —pleases.

(See demeanor, conduct, manner, action.)

BEHEAD (v)

adverbs

publicly; cruelly; wantonly; outrageously; heartlessly; shockingly; abominably; detestably.

(See execute.)

BEHOLD (v)

adverbs

gladsomely; earnestly; unblinkingly; respectfully; rapturously; tremblingly; blankly.

(See contemplate, gaze, look, observe.)

BEING

adjectives

sovereign; invisible; sinful; ungrateful; stormy; neurotic; faulty; inner; loathed; human; transformed; wayward; puny; delusive; reasonable; rare; radiant; rational; uninhibited; amiable; jovial; lively; lovely; sentimental; reasoning; semidivine; supernatural; mythological; legendary; unearthly; exalted; supreme; superior; forceful; intrepid; corporeal; unfortunate; self-conscious; unsheltered; despicable; ominous; intellectual; mysterious; rebellious; subtle; wild; immortal; created; wondrous; incomprehensible; countless; deluded; satanic-looking; helpless; finite; enchanted; malevolent; celestial; terrestrial; infernal; articulate; moral; responsible; spiritual; conscious; unnatural; tame; passionless; progressive; humble; supernal; incarcerated; physical; transcendent.

verbs

corrupt—; eat into—; insinuate into—; oppose—; reject—; subjugate human —s; —s differ.

(See individual.)

BELABOR (v)

adverbs

soundly; cruelly; wantonly; heartlessly; persistently; grossly; unfeelingly; murderously.

(See beat.)

BELCH

adjectives

nauseating; embarrassed; resounding.

BELIEF

adjectives

comforting; sincere; inspiring; venerable; sustaining; profound; cherished; traditional; calm; dispassionate; widespread; ingenuous; indestructible; unshakable; unswerving; staunch; rock-bound; deep-rooted; unwavering; overpowering; long-established; settled; personal; persistent; thoroughgoing; time-honored; inescapable; unquestioning; poetic; fantastic; weird; romantic; quaint; crazy; fanatical; blind; senile; heretical; fatuous; illogical; widely-varying; theosophical; medieval; atheistic; religious; general; common; dogmatic; tottering; badly-shaken; pathetic; childlike; implicit; tacit; supernatural; pragmatical; ancient; serious; exacting; slow; rising;

important; indisputable; eager; unavoidable; prevailing; ineradicable; immemorial; confident; gross; unconscious; contrary; reasonable; theoretic; generous; universal; unassailable; vast; pious; ethical; fundamental; credulous; intellectual; old-fashioned; traditional; discreet; doctrinal; lingering; instinctive; cherished; unflattering; strange; irrational; adorable; spiritualistic; erroneous; grotesque; uncomprehending; popular; stubborn; independent; rote-learned; fatalistic; indomitable; unfounded; growing; stout; superstitious; honest; unstable; rooted; purposive; current; obstinate; divine; peremptory; vague; hoary; dangerous; prevalent; desirable; uncompromising; systematized; battered; consequent; conflicting (pl).

verbs
abandon—; allay—; alter—; annihilate—; apprehend—; arise from—; asphyxiate—; banish—; battle for—; bolster—; blot out—; break down—; cast out—; cherish—; cling to—; comfort in—; confide—; confirm—; conquer—; consider—; contradict—; convict on—; create—; credit—; delude into—; derive—; designate—; destroy—; dispel—; dissipate—; doubt—; draw—; drop—; embody—; embrace—; encourage—; endorse —; entertain—; establish—; evolve—; excite—; expel—; explain—; explode—; expound—; express—; favor—; fetter—; fix —; found upon—; free from—; imply—; incline to—; include—; indoctrinate—; influence—; inherit—; inspire—; justify—; labor under—; lend weight to—; manifest —; master—; nourish—; obliterate—; originate—; outgrow—; perpetuate—; persist in—; persuade in—; present—; profess—; realize—; reject—; relapse into—; relinquish—; repose—in; represent—; repudiate —; rest upon—; retain—; reverse—; rid of —; ripen into—; scotch—; share—; strengthen—; stress—; subdue—; submerge—; support—; surmise—; subscribe to—; trust in —; value—; vindicate—; voice—; waive—; wallow in—; warrant—; witness—; wound —; —s conflict; —decays; —dies; —disappears; —emerges from; —expires; —functions; —intrudes; —melts; —obsesses; —rests on; —springs from; —tempts; —totters; —vanishes; —wanders; —wanes; —waxes low.

(See faith, conviction, persuasion, assurance, doctrine, dogma, creed, opinion, view.)

BELIEVE (v)

adverbs
erroneously; candidly; passionately; frankly; ingenuously; assertively; infallibly; conscientiously; currently; popularly; deliberately; ardently; mournfully; instinctively; dispassionately; unshakably; unswervingly; staunchly; unwaveringly; persistently; unquestioningly; fatuously; illogically; religiously; dogmatically; pathetically; implicitly; tacitly; indisputably; immemorially; reasonably; fundamentally; irrationally; uncomprehendingly; obstinately; unfoundedly; fatalistically; superstitiously; uncompromisingly.

(See suppose.)

BELIEVER

adjectives
devout; ardent; passionate; true; firm; conscientious; tremendous; frantic; lifelong; unquestioning; consummate; fervent; enthusiastic; rapt.

BELITTLE (v)

adverbs
scoffingly; maliciously; subtly; justifiably; surreptitiously; obstreperously; venomously; insidiously; invidiously.

(See reduce.)

BELITTLEMENT

adjectives
malicious; subtle; justifiable.

BELL

adjectives
peaceful; enchanted; clinking; muffled; tinkling; gentian; chiming; mellow; shimmering; deep; oracular; old; cracked; twilight; clear-toned; insistent; tremulous; sullen; ponderous; clanging; gold-rimmed; discordant; warning; ringing; rankling; sleigh; jingling; pealing; rich-toned; musical; resonant; glittering; dazzling; brass; bronze; doleful; melancholy; drowsy; monotonous; jangling; feeble; faint; rusty; antique; little; clapping; sobbing; vesper; shrilling; sonorous; salvage; sweet; cracked; midnight; mournful; heavy-hanging; tolling.

verbs
adorn—; answer—; bear away—; bless—; cast—; clap—; coat—; consecrate—; crack —; fashion—; flare—; found—; gain—; hallow—; invert—; jangle—; lose—; mould —; muffle—; rattle—; recast—; rivet—; shake —s; shape—; silence—; strike—; swing—; trill—; tune—; —alarms; —assembles; —booms; —calls; —carols; —chimes; —clangs; —clashes; —ding-dongs; —heaves; —honors the dead; —invites; —knells; —marks the hour; —notifies; —

peals; —punctuates; —records; —reverberates; —rolls; —screams; —shrieks; —signals; —sings; —speaks; —strikes; —summons; —taunts; —tinkles; —tolls; —ushers in; —vibrates.
(See instrument, anvil.)

BELLE

adjectives
merciless; waltzing; ballet; faded; traditional; brilliant; raging.

BELLICOSE

adverbs
habitually; constitutionally; inherently; naturally; hopelessly; aggressively; truculently; atrociously; barbarously; brutally; cruelly; fiercely; hatefully; hard-heartedly; maliciously; obdurately; rancourously; resentfully; spitefully; uncharitably; venomously; relentlessly; ruthlessly; outrageously; churlishly; invidiously; fiendishly.

BELLIGERENT

adverbs
naturally; habitually; inherently; incorrigibly; lamentably; incurably; racially; inveterately; intrinsically; fanatically; customarily; admittedly; contentiously; wranglingly; quarrelsomely; malevolently; cruelly; cold-heartedly; irreconcilably; disturbingly; riotously; aggressively; irretrievably; hopelessly.

BELLOW

adjectives
inflated; mysterious; bleating; righteous; forty-acre; overpowering; epochal; hearty; ludicrous; untuneful; cataclysmal; angry; summoning; resonant; stupendous; ear-shattering; huge; tempestuous; inhuman; fantastic; wonder-provoking; throaty; hoarse; terrified; subterranean; hollow.

BELLOW (*v*)

adverbs
tumultuously; gloomily; piercingly; pleasedly; lustily; bleatingly; heartily; ludicrously; untunefully; resonantly; inhumanly; throatily; subterraneanly; hollowly; barbarously.
(See roar.)

BELLY

adjectives
remorseless; wrinkled; vile.

verbs
band—; belt—; constrict—; fill—; grovel on—; inflate—; stuff—; swell—; thrust into —; —aches; —bulges out; —contains; —hungers; —protrudes; —swells; —vibrates.
(See abdomen, paunch.)

BELONG (*v*)

adverbs
remotely; infinitely; notoriously; legally; tacitly; anonymously; permanently; patriotically; temporarily; indefinitely; perpetually.

BELONGINGS

adjectives
countless; diminished; age-hoarded; scanty; scattered; pathetic; vestigial.

verbs
carry—; cherish—; endow with—; increase —; injure—; possess—; retrieve—; value —.
(See possessions, property.)

BELT

adjectives
tarnished; studded; endless; embroidered; green-fringed; unbuckled; impenetrable; surrounding; inimitable; controversial; safety; gentian; fertile; swaying; sequoia; flashing.

verbs
adorn with—; apply—; bind with—; carve —; design—; emboss—; flap—; hang at—; inlay—; join —s; load—; loose—; notch—; pattern—; secure with—; strap—; tense—; tighten—; tool—; unclasp—; —borders; —confines; —conveys; —encircles; —girdles; —restrains; —stretches; —supports; —surrounds.
(See band.)

BEMOAN (*v*)

adverbs
miserably; piteously; sobbingly; gently; chronically; unspokenly; tremulously; wailingly; wretchedly.
(See lament, bewail, deplore.)

BENCH

(furniture)

adjectives
slab; roughly-carved; pew-like; crude; sun-dried; high; dry; disfigured; secluded; notched; Sheraton; offending; judicial; rustic; sympathizing; elevated.

verbs
adorn—; decorate—; design—; display—; indicate—; model—; occupy—; provide—; reserve—; squat on—; tilt—; utilize—; work at—; —affords; —serves; —supports; —topples.
(See seat, table, furniture, chair.)

BENCH

adjectives (legal)

dignified; exalted; honorable; judicial; learned; triumvirate; upper.

verbs

appoint to—; bring before—; elect to—; esteem—; occupy—; preside at—; resign from—; retire from—; return to—; serve at—; vacate—; —accepts; —affects; —approves; —ascertains; —charges; —conducts; —deems; —derives; —exemplifies; —fines; —fixes; —fulfills; —imposes; —judges; —pronounces; —sentences.

(See court.)

BEND

adjectives

distant; graceful; alternate; convex; keen; sharp; magisterial; sudden; tender; tolerant.

BEND (v)

adverbs

feebly; impulsively; confidentially; inextricably; mournfully; solicitously; alternately; magisterially; tenderly; tolerantly.

(See turn, curve.)

BENEDICTION

adjectives

low; gentle; healing; apologetic; silver; short; pontifical; perpetual; celestial.

verbs

accompany with—; apply—; attend—; bestow—upon; bless at—; implore—; kneel for—; perform—; pray at—; pronounce—; receive—; seek—; serve at—; shower —s upon; speak—; visit—upon; wreathe in—; —closes; —encourages; —inspires; —opens.

(See prayer, blessing.)

BENEFACTION

adjectives

unknown; gracious; admirable; notorious.

verbs

appeal for—; appreciate—; begrudge—; bestow—upon; cloak—; confer—; contribute—; demand—; expose—; imply—; influence—; judge—; launch—; menace—; offer—; owe to—; publicize—; reduce—; secure—; surprise by—; thwart—; volunteer—; withhold—; —elates; —redeems; —satisfies; —succors.

(See charity.)

BENEFACTOR

adjectives

anonymous; modest; silent; elderly; leading; munificent; life-long; potent.

verbs

appeal to—; betray—; burden—; depend on—; devote to—; distinguish—; employ—; flourish under—; inherit from—; —aids; —bequeaths; —cares for; —comforts; —counsels; —demands; —endows; —establishes; —finances; —fosters; —inquires; —institutes; —lavishes; —patronizes; —profits; —relieves; —retains; —satisfies; —shapes; —succors; —tempts; —volunteers.

BENEFICENCE

adjectives

magical; embodied; leading; heedless; iridescent.

BENEFICENT

adverbs

altruistically; amiably; benignly; charitably; considerately; generously; generally; good-naturedly; kindly; mercifully; sympathetically; tenderly; unselfishly; warmly; bountifully; graciously; indulgently; maternally; paternally; modestly; gently; anonymously; magnificently; simply; unassumingly.

BENEFICIAL

adverbs

permanently; desirably; cumulatively; particularly; reciprocally; mutually; enormously; surprisingly; extraordinarily; satisfactorily; gratifyingly; appreciably; economically; politically; internationally; ultimately; eventually; immensely; essentially; peculiarly; tolerably; generally; universally; absolutely; socially; financially.

BENEFIT

adjectives

permanent; community; important; practical; substantial; lasting; visible; far-reaching; anonymous; persuasive; sweet; merited; accrued; transforming; material; fixed; particular; cumulative; reciprocal; unsurpassed; mutual; enormous; inestimable; overwhelming; extraordinary; incalculable; remarkable; international; economic; educational; tolerable; especial; peculiar; corresponding; patriotic; public; conferred; positive; admitted; innumerable (pl); secluded; essential; immense; desirable; full; doubtful; immediate; surprising; unintended; ultimate; hazardous.

verbs

abolish—; acquire—; attend with—; bequeath —s; bestow—upon; claim—; con-

cede—; confer—upon; defend—; demand—; deprive of—; derive—; disable—; embrace —; enumerate —s; finance—; grant—of; load with —s; mark—; merit—; nullify—; proffer—; reap—; render—; reveal—; secure—; share—; stress—; yield —s; —s accrue; —occurs; —s proceed from.
(See profit, advantage, service, favor.)

BENEFIT (v)

adverbs
questionably; directly; substantially; visibly; anonymously; materially; particularly; cumulatively; reciprocally; unsurpassedly; mutually; inestimably; incalculably; internationally; economically; educationally; peculiarly; correspondingly; admittedly; essentially; unintentionally; ultimately.
(See help, avail.)

BENEVOLENCE

adjectives
unexpected; winged; remarkable; defective; private; expansive; factitious; tolerant; vague; world-wide; significant; muscle-loosening; red-blooded; social; despotic; easy; universal; dominant; sympathetic; amused; innate.

verbs
assist through—; assure one of—; contribute—; depend upon—; disguise—; dispense with—; encourage—; endow with—; exercise—; exploit—; expose—; flourish under —; manifest—; practice—; promote—; reform by—; rejoice in—; rouse—; support with—; surprise by—; withhold—; —aids; —consoles; —delights; —relieves; —shines.
(See bounty, charity, generosity.)

BENIGNANT

adverbs
graciously; invariably; consistently; tenderly; notably; amiably; big-heartedly; mildly; simply; warmly; tolerantly; gently; courteously; smoothly; generously; complacently; genially; thoughtfully; considerately.

BENIGNITY

adjectives
politic; hopeful; inexpressible; suave; soothing; gentle.

BENT

adjectives
artistic; philosophical; natural; immediate; practical.

BEQUEATH (v)

adverbs
mutely; subsequently; generously; acceptably; munificently; extravagantly; liberally; miraculously; unsparingly.
(See transmit.)

BEQUEST

adjectives
subsequent; munificent; acceptable; final; generous; scanty.

BERATE (v)

adverbs
morosely; abusively; furiously; heatedly; indignantly; vociferously; venomously; drunkenly; privately; desperately; deplorably; monstrously.
(See upbraid, reprimand, censure.)

BEREAVEMENT

adjectives
irreparable; personal; domestic; mitigated; intolerable; unforgettable.

BERRIES

adjectives
fresh-picked; luscious; delicious; bunched; packaged; frozen; helpless; scarlet.

verbs
consume—; crate—; crush—; cultivate—; devour—; enjoy—; feast on—; hull—; market—; pluck—; preserve—; relish—; wreathe with—; yield—; —crackle; —flourish; —redden; —ripen; —suspend from; —thrive.
(See fruit, vegetable, flower.)

BESEECH (v)

adverbs
unfeignedly; weepingly; vainly; piteously; charmingly; graciously; guilelessly; exquisitely; sentimentally; fanatically; piously; humbly.
(See beg, entreat, implore.)

BESIEGE (v)

adverbs
ineffectually; resolutely; foolhardily; miraculously; overwhelmingly; vigorously; ragingly; persistently; intermittently; intensively; desultorily.
(See surround, attack.)

BESIEGER

adjectives
arrogant; merciless; infuriated; intrepid; importunate; relentless; tireless; unreasoning; wrathful.

verbs
arm —s; take —s by surprise; taunt —s; —s advance; —s assail; —s assault; —s beleaguer; —s blockade; —s capture; —s hem in.
(See fighter, soldier, troops.)

BESTIAL

adverbs
coarsely; horribly; brutally; fiercely; grossly; indecently; ribaldly; shamelessly; unbelievably; abusively; obscenely; evilly; brutishly; violently; abominably.

BESTOW (v)

adverbs
gratuitously; felicitously; improperly; equally; facetiously; unwittingly; philanthropically; munificently; grudgingly.
(See grant.)

BET

adjectives
fatal; reckless; shrewd; timely; underhanded; unfair; unfortunate.

verbs
arouse—; balance—; cancel—; cover—; encourage—; forfeit—; hedge—; instigate—; insure—; lay—; stake—; support—; —stands; —surprises.
(See wager, stake.)

BETRAY (v)

adverbs
grossly; deliberately; hideously; vilely; viciously; virtually; infrequently; treacherously; incautiously; bluntly; subtly; heartlessly; venomously; emotionally; mentally.
(See reveal, disclose.)

BETRAYAL

adjectives
gross; deliberate; grave; hideous; vile; vicious.

verbs
avenge—; charge—; commit—; fume at—; lead into—; —divulges; —exposes; —violates.
(See treason, treachery, exposure.)

BETRAYER

adjectives
accidental; circumspect; disloyal; shameless; subtle; treacherous; unwitting.

verbs
accuse—; confront—; denounce—; dishonor—; execute—; vindicate—; —deserts; —discloses; —flees.

BETROTH (v)

adverbs
gladsomely; diplomatically; religiously; contemptuously; sordidly; inappropriately; beatifically.
(See give.)

BETROTHAL

adjectives
enforced; happy; opposed; favored; proclaimed; prolonged; signalized; unduly influenced.

verbs
compact—; compound—; consecrate—; consummate—; contract—; dissolve—; fulfill—; honor—; promote—; ritualize—; sanction—; solemnize—; violate—; —affiances; —binds; —couples; —engages; —promises.
(See engagement.)

BETTERMENT

adjectives
permanent; material; economic; moral; human; spiritual; lasting; civic.

BEVERAGE

adjectives
intoxicating; wholesome; fermented; distilled; seductive; beguiling; customary; exhilarating; soothing; mild; constant; limpid; refreshing; invigorating; fragrant; thirst-quenching.

verbs
brew—; carbonate—; consume—; devise—; dispense—; dissolve into—; draw off—; formulate—; infuse—; ladle—; medicate—; quaff—; sip—; tap—; treat—with; weaken—; —cools; —effervesces; —ferments; —foams; —induces; —intoxicates; —percolates; —relieves; —satisfies; —warms.
(See drink, liquor, wine, beer, coffee, etc.)

BEWAIL (v)

adverbs
sepulchrally; mournfully; heartbrokenly; blatantly; vigorously; hoarsely; stentoriously; stormily; fearfully; inarticulately; raucously.
(See bemoan.)

BEWILDER (v)

adverbs
confusingly; completely; perplexingly; inscrutably; spiritually; pitifully; naively; tragically; childishly.
(See confuse, perplex, mystify.)

BEWILDERED

adverbs
strangely; suddenly; hopelessly; helplessly; mysteriously; alarmingly; gravely; seriously; tragically; disastrously; completely; horribly; terribly; indescribably; obviously; manifestly; dazedly; brokenly; pathetically; laughably; ridiculously; foolishly; undeniably; significantly; painfully; confusedly; embarrassingly; ludicrously; bashfully; modestly; piteously; awkwardly; confoundedly; disturbingly; timidly; vaguely; dangerously; overwhelmingly; unluckily; miserably; wretchedly; indefensibly; ineptly.

BEWILDERMENT

adjectives
blank; growing; vague; dazed; helpless; elated; stunned; weary; hurt; spiritual; disgusted; pitiful; naive; added; incredulous; cross; seeming; sheer; complete; deep; suspicious; dazzling; tragic; childish.

verbs
extricate from—; hide—; lose in—; meet with—; stray in—; tangle in—; wander in —; —confuses; —grows; —perplexes.
(See confusion.)

BEWITCHING

adverbs
dangerously; enchantingly; charmingly; radiantly; indescribably; indefinably; marvelously; startlingly; fatally; ineffably; inexplicably; utterly; delightfully; designedly; diabolically; surprisingly; quietly; consciously; tauntingly; overwhelmingly; provokingly; tormentingly; youthfully; irresistibly; unconsciously.

BIAS

adjectives
distorting; grossest; racial; political; natural; beneficial; theoretic; considerable; economic; favorable; moral; elemental; personal.

verbs
deliver from—; free from—; —clouds; —crops up; —distorts; —inclines one toward; —influences; —leans; —misleads; —prejudices; —rejects; —slopes; —swerves; —warps.
(See prejudice.)

BIBLE

adjectives
consoling; dignified; family-recording; mutilated; treasured; time-honored; oft-perused; woe-comforting.

verbs
adopt—; advance—; blaspheme—; commend—; conflict with—; dethrone—; embellish—; embrace—; esteem—; execute—; inscribe in—; interpret—; misconceive—; mutilate—; preserve—; reject—; spread—; undermine—; —aims at; —appeals; —authorizes; —condemns; —decrees; —endures; —impresses; —inspires; —presents; —reveals; —sets forth; —stirs; —teaches; —unites; —veils.
(See book, scriptures.)

BIBLIOGRAPHY

adjectives
extensive; sketchy; elaborate; speculative; heavy; selective; analytical; complete; annotated; comprehensive; critical.

BICKER (*v*)

adverbs
constantly; cantankerously; perpetually; unappetizingly; pettishly; undiplomatically; uncharitably; blatantly; repulsively; incompatibly.
(See dispute.)

BICKERING

adjectives
unseemly; perpetual; unappetizing; petty; diplomatic; international.

adverbs
eternally; spitefully; ill-naturedly; nervously; feverishly; incessantly; tempestuously; fussily; intolerably; quarrelsomely; forever; habitually; ill-temperedly; unnecessarily; shrewishly; continually.

BID

adjectives
subtle; foolhardy; feathery; maddest; miraculous; casual; curt; collusive; contemptuous.

verbs
advance—; dispose of —s; double—; govern—; ignore—; pass—; rattle off —s; redouble—; reject—; retract—; run up—; shout—; submit—; withdraw—; —astounds; —s compete; —s pour in; —suffices.
(See proposal, offer.)

BID (*v*)

adverbs
mockingly; artfully; graciously; regretfully; shrewdly; imperiously; subtly; foolhardily; madly; casually; curtly; contemptuously.
(See offer, order, direct, ask.)

BIDDABLE

adverbs
graciously; astonishingly; miraculously; devotedly; pliantly; amiably; indifferently; apparently; cunningly; shrewdly; grudgingly; necessarily; glumly; stolidly; stupidly; passively; complacently; wisely; politely; suavely; cheerfully; blindly; blithely; unthinkingly; foolishly.

BIDE (*v*)

adverbs
patiently; habitually; naively; perpetually; ephemerally; transiently; independently; pensively.
(See inhabit, abide, endure.)

BIER

adjectives
watery; beckoning; hasty; hallowed; senseless; wretched; blazing.

verbs
array before—; deck—; decorate—; deposit on—; expose on—; file before—; kneel before—; mourn at—; repose on—; surround —; venerate—; weep at—; worship at—.
(See coffin, frame, grave, altar.)

BIGAMY

adjectives
defiling; forbidden; law-evading; ostracised; perfidious; shameful; titled; wretched.

verbs
charge with—; commit—; condone—; define—; imprison for—; live in—; loathe—; outlaw—; practice—.
(See crime.)

BIGOT

adjectives
fierce; intelligent; splendid; self-satisfied; pernicious; vicious; unsparing.

BIGOTED

adverbs
intolerably; fanatically; narrow-mindedly; obdurately; obstinately; incurably; persistently; hopelessly; offensively; arbitrarily; doggedly; incorrigibly; mulishly; inflexibly; perversely; pig-headedly; stubbornly; intractably; perniciously; wilfully; narrowly; dogmatically; arrogantly; imperiously.

BIGOTRY

adjectives
puritanical; sordid; religious; inveterate; unthinking; patent.

BILE

adjectives
abounding; acrid; complex; reactivated; yellow-green.

verbs
expel—; secrete—; store—; —collects; —converts; —flows; —reacts; —trickles.
(See fluid.)

BILL
(invoice)

adjectives
preposterous; inevitable; exorbitant; unexpected; modest; staggering; delusive; long-unpaid.

BILL
(law)

adjectives
substitute; pending; mandatory; feasible; amended; revised; comprehensive; militia; drafted; pork-barrel.

BILL
(legislation)

adjectives
adopted; accepted; amended; contested; discussed; defeated; dismissed; parliamentary; petitionary; true; revised.

verbs
act on—; advocate—; challenge—; confer on—; confront with—; contest—; deliberate—; draft—; draw—; denounce—; enact —; frame—; hurry—through; incorporate in —; kill—; modify—; originate—; railroad —; reject—; retain—; slap through—; smother—; sponsor—; veto—; urge—; —entails; —looms; —provides; —sets forth; —stipulates.
(See law, legislation.)

BILL
(money)

adjectives
limp; dejected; worn; crumpled; charitable; elusive; proud; defaced; carefully-fondled; ragged; crisp; faded; crinkled.

BILL
(statement of account)

adjectives
adjusted; dunning; final; lavish; harassing; paltry; peccant; padded; uncollected; overwhelming.

verbs
deduct—; deliver—; discount—; draw up—; enter—; file—; foot—; forward—; pad—; render—; scale—; tuck—away; —itemizes; —overcharges; —s pour in; —s rain in.

BILLBOARD

adjectives
blatant; blazing; huge; glaring; inappropriate; inartistic.

verbs
censor—; crusade against —s; employ —s; greet with —s; plaster on—; post on—; rebel against —s; —blares; —campaigns; —coaxes; —s dot the highways; —informs; —s line; —s mar; —pictures; —promotes.
(See advertisement.)

BILLOW

verbs
bear on—; beset by—; cleave—; produce—; steer through—; swell into —s; swim through—; —beats; —breaks; —crests; —dances; —endangers; —foams; —overwhelms; —rages; —rears up; —roars; —rolls; —silvers; —surges; —sweeps on; —swells; —tosses up; —tumbles.
(See wave, breaker.)

BILLOW (*v*)

adverbs
softly; tumblingly; restlessly; dashingly; furiously; advancingly; foamingly; wrathfully; seethingly; multitudinously; glitteringly; darkly; crestedly.
(See pound.)

BILLOWS

adjectives
inky; heaving; crested; vibrant; slanting; wild-roaring; rocking; undulating; glittering; high; multitudinous; dark; solemn; breaking; proud; unreposing; tawny; ruffian; surging; unblended; foaming; unawakened; rolling; tempestuous; seething; wrathful; dancing; curling; building; ridgy; wafting; advancing; dashing; obedient; sleepless; furious; resistless; cruel; immense; endless; tumbling; glimmering; restless.

BIND (*v*)

adverbs
indubitably; beautifully; closely; exquisitely; intimately; firmly; conveniently; infinitely; eternally; irrevocably; inextricably.
(See fasten, tie, restrict, restrain.)

BINDING

adjectives
neat; original; practical; imperishable; ornate; exquisite; excellent; worn; mildewed; embossed; leather; drab; linen; luxurious.

BINDING (*a*)

adverbs
legally; morally; onerously; embarrassingly; awkwardly; laboriously; perplexingly; formidably; desperately; dreadfully; outrageously; distressingly; vexatiously; uncomfortably; appallingly; alarmingly; unquestionably; definitely; positively; absolutely; securely; cruelly; truly; inescapably; conclusively; oppressively.

BIOGRAPHER

adjectives
distinguished; veracious; worthy; eulogistic; skilled; faithful; enthusiastic; pedestrian; debunking; ecclesiastical; iconoclastic.

BIOGRAPHICAL

adverbs
palpably; unmistakably; blatantly; evidently; undisguisedly; apparently; openly; flagrantly; accurately; historically; clearly; nakedly; pleasantly; slightly; pseudo-; cruelly; completely; purportedly; intentionally; carelessly.

BIOGRAPHY

adjectives
full-fledged; fascinating; literary; splendid; noble; notable; dignified; readable; compelling; painstaking; vital; rhapsodic; exuberant; fictionalized; authoritative; official; comprehensive; iconoclastic; miniature; definitive; pretentious; sensational; previous; informal; inclusive; reliable; remarkable; famous; picturesque; best-selling; meritorious; colorless; satisfactory; magnified; racy; critical; dull; drab; musty; hero-worshipping.

verbs
acquaint with—; attempt—; cultivate—; illuminate—; interpret—; launch—; live—; record in—; —accounts; —appeals; —attributes; —catalogues; —chronicles; —"debunks"; —defames; —delights; —details; —distorts; —enchants; —eulogizes; —exaggerates; —extols; —fires; —informs; —lauds; —narrates; —pictures; —portrays; —reveals; —sketches; —treats of; —twists; —unfolds.
(See life.)

BIRCHES

adjectives
superb; slim; silver; delicate; colored; snow-hung.

BIRD

adjectives
carrion; landward; flitting; red-breasted; homeward; chattering; fluttering; honey-sucking; soaring; stuffed; widowed; songless; stripe-winged; glowing; ruffled;

choleric; captive; nesting; melodious; succulent; rapacious; flippant; full-throated; chirping; unclean; ominous; insolent; feathered; sober; morbid-looking; migratory; aquatic; timorous; joyful; frightened; grand-limbed; restless; gold-flecked; bewildered; caged; nest-deserted; reckless; human-hearted; singing; fledgling; unhappy; babbling; solemn; cruel; furtive; night; huge; deserted; callow; blind; bright-winged; predatory; cheerful; brooding; herald; unscared; dapple-breasted; silly; ragged; riotous; noxious; pigmy; tropical; sable; striking; raucous; contented; brilliant; ravenous; monstrous; bewildered; imprisoned; mateless; rare; unusual; strange; valuable; roosting; circling; wingless; timid; tenderest; startled.

verbs
breed —s; cage—; capture—; cripple—; dislodge—; encage—; exterminate—; fall prey to —s; flush—; kill off —s; peg—; scatter —s; stuff —s; teem with —s; —s anthem; —ascends; —babbles; —breeds; —broods; —builds; —calls; —carols; —chants; —cheeps; —cheers up; —chirps; —chitters; —s chorus; —s clamor; —s congregate; —croons; —s copulate; —crouches; —cuddles; —darts; —descends; —disgorges; —disports; —drifts; —dwells; —s enliven; —feeds; —fledges; —flits; —floats; —s flock; —flutters; —frequents; —gorges; —gossips; —gushes; —hatches; —haunts; —hovers; —inhabits; —lays; —lights upon; —mates; —migrates; —molts; —mounts; —nests; —s orient themselves; —s pair; —pecks; —perches; —pierces sky; —pipes; —pirouettes; —plaints; —plumes himself; —plunges; —pours out his song; —preens; —preys upon; —probes; —prunes; —s quarrel; —s race; —ranges; —rears; —s roost; —s ruffle their plumage; —s scatter; —s scold; —screams; —scuds; —scurries; —serenades; —shoots; —shuns; —sips; —skips; —soars; —sputters; —s stridulate; —s swarm; —sweeps; —swoops down; —taxies; —traces a circle in the air; —trills; —s troop; —twitters; —unfolds; —vanishes; —wanders; —warbles; —wheels; —whirls about; —whistles; —wings his way; —zooms.
(See animal, fowl.)

BIRTH

adjectives
checkered; illustrious; multiple (pl); doubtful; restless; mystic; abhorred; prodigious; timeless; visible; high; noble; royal; immortal; declining; exotic; heavenly; unnatural; approaching; violent; promiscuous; mortal; majestic; wondrous; adulterated; hallowed; painful; miraculous; princely; portentous; abortive; vernal; unexceptional; worthy; monstrous; ill-starred; fated; celebrated; virgin.

verbs
announce—; assist at—; attend at—; celebrate—; extol—; foretell—; govern—; herald—; honor—; manifest at—; preside over—; record—; register—; rejoice at—; restrict —s; travail in—; —s decline; —occurs.
(See beginning, origin, renaissance.)

BIRTHDAY

adjectives
happy; sad; romantic; memorable; unsung.

verbs
commemorate—; document—; endow on—; fete on—; honor on—; memorialize—; observe—; register—; trace—; —approaches.
(See anniversary.)

BIRTHPLACE

adjectives
forsaken; humble; remembered; sterile.

BIRTHRIGHT

adjectives
unattainable; unbound; bitter; unwhipped; unburned; unchained; separated; precious; inalienable; undeniable.

verbs
claim—; forfeit—; honor—; pawn—; retain—; rob of—; salute—; sell—; sway to—; —entitles; —privileges.
(See privilege, inheritance.)

BISCUITS

adjectives
delicious; crumbly; crisp; brown; golden-topped; delicate.

BISHOP

adjectives
affable; resident; pompous; dignified; massive; dutiful; esoteric; eccentric.

BISON

adjectives
attacked; watered; labored; tamed; horned; roaming; vagrant; herded; captured; slaughtered; conquered; hunted; skinned; galloping; thundered; inhabited; restricted; protected.

verbs
corral—; exterminate—; herd—; shelter—; yoke—; —abound; —bellows; —charges; —grazes; —pastures; —ranges; —roams; —roars; —sheds; —stampedes; —vanishes.
(See ox, buffalo, animal.)

BIT

adjectives
needful; tempting; savory; checked; insignificant; fluffy; bright; picturesque; unrelated; choice; fragmentary; imaginary; premature; fantastic; mute; tuneless; disquieting; impossible; brilliant; incredible; dainty; demoralized; charred; flimsy.

BIT

adjectives (mouthpiece of bridle)
double; chain; cruel; champed; curbing; excruciating; maddening; torturous; vexing.

verbs
accustom to—; adjust—; attach to—; callous to—; champ at—; choke on—; control with —; cough out—; fight against—; jerk at—; respond to—; ride—; run away from—; saw at—; shy at—; slaver—; spit out—; stop with—; swallow—; take—between teeth; veer from—; yank at—; —chafes; —clamps tongue; —curbs; —restrains; —slackens; —subdues; —tames; —tortures.

BITE

adjectives
crisp; short; crunching; vicious; murderous; prodigious; good-sized; furious; agonizing; hurried; hasty.

verbs
down—; gulp—; inflict—; —cuts; —heals; —pierces; —wounds.

BITE (v)

adverbs
savagely; impetuously; unmercifully; unexpectedly; annoyingly; passionately; viciously; daintily; crunchingly; murderously; agonizingly; hurriedly; hastily.
(See nibble, chew.)

BITING (a)

adverbs
sarcastically; bitterly; viciously; venomously; insidiously; hatefully; mercilessly; deliberately; churlishly; unsparingly; crustily; insolently; obnoxiously; captiously; censoriously; caustically; acrimoniously; perversely; contumaciously; snappishly; peevishly; uncivilly; ungraciously; abusively.

BITTER

adverbs
maliciously; shrewdly; enviously; viciously; purposely; unnecessarily; uncontrollably; insidiously; invidiously; sharply; cynically; sarcastically; spitefully; jealously; intentionally; cunningly; ironically; insinuatingly; incisively; cruelly; brutally; unwisely; atrociously; malevolently; tauntingly; caustically; diabolically.

BITTERNESS

adjectives
thwarted; rancorous; profound; political; unserviceable; chill; quiet; corrosive; smiling; intense; loathsome; speculative; secret; pent-up; sarcastic; extreme; sectional; unsparing; contradictory; personal; sardonic; unrelenting; acrid; partisan; increased; concealed; concentrated; unspoken; undying; chronic.

verbs
be devoid of—; brush aside—; erase—; evoke—; fan—; intensify—; persecute with —; taste—; temper—; —creeps into; —develops; —flames; —gnaws; —heats; —vexes.
(See malice, rancor.)

BIVOUAC

adjectives
picturesque; solemn; miserable.

BLACK (n)

adjectives
solemn; rusty; pitchy; stark; shining; blistered; exploited; wicked; natural; dense; lustrous; inky; midnight; conservative; rich; dense; impenetrable; oppressive; sable; ominous; heavy; palpable; murky; humid; thick.

BLACK (a)

adverbs
rustily; dingily; deeply; lugubriously; formidably; gloomily; duskily; murkily; pitchily; sombrely; richly; pallidly; dunly; faintly; dully; coldly; unearthly; sepulchrally; mournfully; glossily; glassily; smoothly; astonishingly; incredibly; unspeakably.

BLACKBIRD

adjectives
combative; chuckling; glinting; saucy; scolding; sooty; squabbling; planing; winging; windy; timid.

verbs
—chatters; —chants; —claws; —flaps; —

flutes; —hovers; —migrates; —nests; —plasters; —preys on; —raids; —ravages; —sails off; —warbles.
(See bird.)

BLACKGUARD

adjectives
dissipated; turbulent; foreign; drunken; brutal.

BLACKNESS

adjectives
inky; impenetrable; oppressive; pitchy; soft; sable; ominous; murky; cold; drizzling; unsociable; palpable; heavy; humid; piercing; peculiar; dripping; appalling; corrugated; musty; absolute; quivering; menacing; comforting; Cimmerian; Stygian.

verbs
engulf in—; grope through—; lose in—; peer into—; steer through—; —envelops.
(See darkness.)

BLACKSMITH

adjectives
rural; gnarled; sinewy; mighty; brawny.

BLADDER

verbs
control—; dilate—; distend—; empty—; govern—; inflame—; regulate—; swell—; —bursts.

BLADE (grass)

adjectives
trembling; springing; wind-rippled; dewy.

BLADE (man)

adjectives
blushing; foppish; gay; desperate; roistering; brilliant; flashy; overdressed; jolly; generous.

BLADE (sword)

adjectives
flashing; glittering; whirling; bright; heavy; broad; double-edged; sharp; dull; penetrating; rapier; projecting; fiery; lean; delicate; blameful; bloody; dripping; burnished; avenging; dry; scanty; polished; troublesome; flexible; unwithering; tremulous; freshly-springing; fratricidal; bayleaf-shaped; deadly; reddened; shining; scythe-shaped; trenchant; trusty; unsheathed; well-tempered; worthy.

verbs
carve with—; draw—; drive in—; flash—; forge—; grasp—; heave—; lash with—; redden—; send—home; sheathe—; temper—; withdraw—; —glances off; —lacerates; —pricks.
(See knife.)

BLAMABLE

adverbs
partially; lamentably; unhappily; deplorably; unquestionably; entirely; seriously; directly; indirectly; morally; sinfully; deservedly; completely; personally; atrociously; criminally; enormously; outrageously; censurably; exceptionally; reprehensibly; unbelievably.

BLAME

adjectives
high-repented; worthy; moral; sinful; specific; small; ill-placed; complete; deserved; directed; heavenly.

verbs
absolve of—; account for—; accuse of—; allocate—; attach—to; avoid—; bear—; censure in—; charge with—; conceal—; deflect—; deserve—; devise—; expose to—; free from—; impute—to; incur—; lay—to; merit—; reproach with—; share—; stamp with—; trace—; vindicate one of—.
(See censure, reproach, condemnation.)

BLAME (*v*)

adverbs
unjustly; morally; sinfully; specifically; completely; deservedly; prejudicially; unthinkingly; narrow-mindedly; puritanically.
(See censure, reproach.)

BLAMELESS

adverbs
clearly; innocently; exceptionally; altogether; wholly; consciously; truly; undoubtedly; impeccably; virtually; artlessly; virtuously; happily; essentially; palpably; patently; indisputably; incontestably; indubitably; positively; absolutely; spotlessly; unquestionably.

BLAND

adverbs
inscrutably; gently; politely; mysteriously; amiably; civilly; complacently; courteously; genteelly; good-temperedly; obsequiously; suavely; urbanely; suspiciously; sweetly; affably; cordially; graciously; ingratiatingly; habitually; unfailingly; surprisingly; essentially.

BLANDISHMENT

adjectives
spider-like; sordid; paternal; artless; suave; sneering; oily.

BLANDNESS

adjectives
inscrutable; confidential; amazing; acquired; pretended.

BLANKET

adjectives
dripping; lovely; soaked; gaudy; bright-colored; impenetrable; shaggy; government; smelly; ragged; invisible; undulating; stretched; osier; sulphur; tasseled; warming; comfortable.

verbs
air—; clothe in—; divest of —s; double —s; envelop in —s; fold in—; immerse in—; pattern—; shelter with—; snuggle in—; tuck—in; weave—; wrap in—; —comforts; —consoles; —protects; —shields; —shrouds; —smothers.
(See robe.)

BLANKNESS

adjectives
oblivious; utter; lurid; strange; complete; devastating; overwhelming; inescapable; dire.

BLARE (*v*)

adverbs
steadfastly; vigorously; furiously; shrilly; howlingly; fearfully; cuttingly; startlingly; penetratingly; brassily; warningly; echoingly.
(See bellow.)

BLASPHEME (*v*)

adverbs
scandalously; fearfully; soul-searingly; abominably; raucously; mutteringly; luridly; crudely; shockingly; ominously.
(See swear.)

BLASPHEMOUS

adverbs
scurrilously; luridly; startlingly; horribly; unspeakably; soul-searingly; abominably; hideously; shrilly; raucously; noisily; inarticulately; mutteringly; unutterably; impiously; irreverently; brazenly; openly; wilfully; profanely; perversely; sacrilegiously; fanatically; scoffingly; desecratingly; irreligiously; cynically; intolerably; unbearably; terrifyingly; unregenerately; godlessly; unforgivably; diabolically; ruthlessly; implacably; criminally; indefensibly; inexcusably; unpardonably; flagrantly; iniquitously; scandalously; wickedly; offensively; accursedly; indecorously; infamously; nefariously; obdurately; unconscionably; villainously.

BLASPHEMY

adjectives
loud; lurid; startling; horrible; unspeakable; soul-searing; abominable; willful; hideous; shrill; vast; raucous; intricate; illimitable; half-inarticulate.

BLAST

adjectives
overwhelming; vigorous; short; fierce; furious; golden; hoarse; challenging; unbroken; scorching; stentorian; summoning; shrill; chilling; stinging; icy; polar; startling; passing; careening; suffocating; howling; putrid; eddying; tremulous; stirring; modulated; bitter; spasmodic; heated; bleak; fearful; wintry; pitiless; furnace-like; roaring; infernal; scornful; woeful; cutting; unruly; nightly; parching; wailing; foul; stormy; raging.

verbs
blow—; loose—; prepare for—; set off—; shiver in—; shrink from—; spit out—; time —; unloose—; —bites; —bolts; —decapitates; —displaces; —envelops; —frees; —forces; —raves; —rends; —resounds; —rises; —roars; —rocks; —shakes; —shatters; —shocks; —startles; —unearths; —uproots; —vibrates; —withers.
(See explosion, discharge.)

BLAST (*v*)

adverbs
terrifically; overwhelmingly; vigorously; suffocatingly; thunderously; stunningly; tremendously; dynamically.
(See smite, destroy, frustrate.)

BLATANT

adverbs
clamorously; vociferously; cheeringly; uproariously; screamingly; stentoriously; offensively; unnecessarily; asininely; blunderingly; brainlessly; arrogantly; extravagantly; foolishly; heavily; ineptly; obtusely; senselessly; weakly; awkwardly; boorishly; lustily; indecorously; loudly; ribaldly; obstreperously; tawdrily; coarsely; cheaply; vulgarly; oddly; unwontedly; hoydenishly; monstrously; clownishly; outlandishly.

BLAZE

adjectives
ghastly; solstitial; supersolar; hospitable; fruitful; crimson; mellowed; meridian; fierce; brilliant; torrid; departed; passionate; leaping; flaring; cheery; unclouded; quenchless; final; distant; wondrous; continuous; garish; radiant; far-beaming; careless; sullen; comforting; noontide; bright; splendid; golden; hungry; glowing.

verbs
burst into—; confine—to; diffuse—; extinguish—; feed—; smother—; —beams; —flares up; —illumines; —ravages; —roars; —scorches; —sears; —springs up.
(See flame, fire, light.)

BLAZE (*v*)

adverbs
magnificently; spectacularly; terrifically; intensely; defiantly; crimsonly; torridly; passionately; flaringly; garishly; radiantly; sullenly; glowingly.
(See flame.)

BLAZONED

adjectives (also emblazoned)
gloriously; goldenly; ceremoniously; glitteringly; grandly; magnificently; pretentiously; colourfully; punctiliously; properly; ritualistically; ceremonially; spectacularly; splendidly; fancifully; fantastically; ostentatiously; flamingly; garishly; gaudily; gaily; majestically; sumptuously; theatrically; noteworthily; deservedly; lustrously; distinctively; honorably; famously; sublimely; immortally; memorably; exaltedly; surpassingly; deathlessly; imperishably; prominently; proudly; imposingly.

BLAZONRY

adjectives
rich; barred; glorious; blood-red; historic; age-old; aristocratic; meaningful.

BLEAT (*v*)

adverbs
frantically.

BLEATING

adjectives
incessant; piteous; high-pitched; squeaky; helpless; ineffectual.

BLEED (*v*)

adverbs
internally; sorely; profusely; copiously; continually; excessively; fatally; terrifyingly; unexpectedly; intermittently.
(See exude.)

BLEEDING

adjectives
continuous; excessive; fatal; forced; arrested.

verbs
arrest—; benefit from—; check—; coagulate—; combat—; control—; dread—; eliminate—; encourage—; impair by—; induce—; plug—; recover from—; reduce—; result in—; retard—; staunch—; suffer from—; tourniquet—; treat—; witness—; —ceases; —confines; —endangers; —enervates; —impoverishes; —increases; —irrigates; —saps; —shocks; —weakens.
(See hemorrhage.)

BLEMISH

adjectives
superficial; facial; physical; unsightly.

verbs
detect—; discern—; eradicate—; result in—; —blots; —disfigures; —flaws; —impairs; —marks; —mars; —scars; —slurs; —stains.
(See defect, fault, imperfection, flaw.)

BLEND (*v*)

adverbs
softly; intimately; pleasantly; indistinguishably; cunningly; curiously; skillfully; delicately; inextricably; mildly; expertly; exquisitely; amazingly; incredibly; magically; miraculously; mysteriously.
(See merge, combine, mix, assimilate.)

BLENDING

adjectives
extraordinary; delightful; special; uncopiable; mild; expert; discreet; mellow; master; subtle; delicate; rare; happy; strange; colossal; exquisite.

BLESS (*v*)

adverbs
sanctimoniously; benignly; spiritually; devoutly; reverently; graciously; silently; eternally; providentially.

BLESSED

adverbs
blissfully; happily; infinitely; richly; unquestionably; gratefully; ecstatically; gloriously; eternally; divinely; magically; mystically; endlessly; tenderly; devoutly; profoundly; fervently; sincerely; devotedly; reverently; immeasurably; warmly; thankfully.

BLESSING

adjectives
unexampled; greatest; inestimable; countless (pl); infinite; fervent; plural (pl); apostolic; unmitigated; needful; earthly; mutual (pl); manifold (pl); priestly; substantial; redeeming; unfelt; silent; certain; rich; supernatural; heavenly; abundant; guttural; over-cordial; unimpaired; unclouded; sundry (pl); unequivocal; endless; providential; choicest; valueless; lasting; lifelong; eternal.

verbs
abound with —s; bestow—upon; cherish—; consecrate with—; crown with —s; inherit —; invoke—; pour —s upon; pronounce—; prove—; realize—; render—; wish—upon; —s attend; —consoles; —descends upon; —s flow from; —hallows; —redeems; —thrills.
(See benediction, favor.)

BLIGHT

adjectives
devastating; mouldy; cruel; venomous; visible; premature; swarming.

BLIND

adverbs
falsely; defiantly; wilfully; mercifully; besottedly; heart-rendingly; wretchedly; pitiably; totally.
(See obscure.)

BLINDNESS

adjectives
obstinate; approaching; helpless; innocent; ultimate; mortal; burning; perspicacious; willful; social; pedantic.

BLINDS

adjectives
copper; painted; window; genteel; dilapidated; secret; shut; much-used.

BLINK (*v*)

adverbs
solemnly; approvingly; sleepily; drowsily; somnolently; shrewdly; sagaciously; dazedly; incessantly; intermittently.
(See wink, disregard, overlook.)

BLISS

adjectives
truest; rapturous; idiotic; unutterable; hysterical; mortal; conjugal; winged; ecstatic; endless; unforgettable; perennial; purest; youthful; dissolving; ambiguous; matchless; unclouded; virgin; visioned; perfect; connubial; extreme; dreamy; unearthly; ineffable; immortal; highest; domestic; private; perpetual; tranquil; coming; sensual; dead; inward; candid; nameless; eternal; transporting; audacious; mantling; faded; departed; foreshadowed; capricious; passive; paralyzed; everlasting; human; heavenly; imaginary; enormous.

verbs
abide in—; anticipate—; attain—; augment —; dampen—; deluge—; diffuse—; dwell in —; experience—; merit—; reign in—; renounce—; sever from—; share in—; violate —; wither—.
(See rapture, happiness, ecstasy.)

BLISSFUL

adverbs
delightfully; supremely; rapturously; gladly; happily; ravishingly; beatifically; joyously; transportedly; charmingly; joyfully; luxuriously; thrillingly; exquisitely; deliciously; incredibly; fascinatingly; blessedly; truly; idiotically; unforgettably; conjugally; amorously; enormously; eternally; dreamily; ineffably; perfectly; matchlessly; endlessly; youthfully; innocently; ecstatically.

BLISTER

adjectives
benign; dark; burning; malignant; tiny; suppurating; prurient; purulent; unsightly; watery.

verbs
absorb—; acquire—; apply to—; cover with —s; drain—; heal—; infect—; inflame to —; open—; paint—; plague with —s; puff into—; raise—; remove—; rub into—; suffer from—; swell into—; treat—; —annoys; —appears; —burns; —bursts; —inconveniences; —irritates; —pains; —drains.
(See ulcer, sore, boil.)

BLITHE

adverbs
infectiously; charmingly; cheerfully; gaily; healthily; contagiously; habitually; airily; exuberantly; heedlessly; carelessly; nimbly; affectionately; bewitchingly; teasingly; bewilderingly; childishly; girlishly; youthfully; wholeheartedly; enticingly; irresistibly; exhilaratingly; animatedly; gleefully; hilariously; friskily; bonnily; exultingly; happily; jauntily; jovially; joyously; jubilantly; joyfully; laughingly; merrily; mirthfully; playfully; rollickingly; spiritedly; vivaciously; trickily; winsomely.

BLIZZARD

adjectives

biting; dense; muffled; roaring; driving; raging; terrible; insect; blinding; numbing; howling; merciless; swirling.

verbs

dread—; forecast—; forewarn of—; perish in—; precede—; predict—; shelter from—; —blasts; —blinds; —freezes; —rages; —rattles; —redoubles its force; —rises; —shrieks; —suffocates; —tears; —wheels; —whines; —whirls.

(See wind, disaster, storm.)

BLOCK

adjectives

riveted; clanking; creaking; dedicated; bloody; lifeless; vertical; city.

BLOCKADE

adjectives

never-ending; actual; patriotic; economic; dilatory; menacing; complete; vertical; partial; inescapable; innumerable (pl).

verbs

break—; comply with—; cut off by—; denounce—; detail—; effect—; enforce—; engage in—; foil—; force—; impose—; insure—; maintain—; notify of—; patrol in —; penetrate—; proclaim—; raise—; relieve—; resort to—; retaliate for—; run—; slip out of—; smuggle through—; storm—; subject to—; succumb to—; surrender to—; sustain—; terminate—; undertake—; —binds; —checks; —compels surrender; —confiscates; —denies; —detains; —distresses; —endangers; —interrupts; —isolates; —obtructs; —prohibits; —shuts off; —starves.

(See embargo.)

BLOCKHEAD

adjectives

babbling; inconceivable; prattling; idling; complete; accomplished; practiced; genial; harmless; silly; fond.

BLONDE

adjectives

blithe; fine; sandy; honey-colored; flamboyant; debonair; strident; incurable; brilliant; robust; vivacious; appealing; feather-headed; ravishing; pretty; irresponsible; peroxide; raucous; platinum; stringy; petite; insolent; attractive; natural; bleached; wistful.

BLONDE

adverbs

alluringly; rapturously; heavenly; divinely; seductively; naturally; artificially; goldenly; sandily; ruddily; tawnily; flamboyantly; stridently; brilliantly; vivaciously; bleachedly; attractively; provocatively; stringily; irresponsibly; prettily; ravishingly; featherheadedly; appealingly; irresistibly; enchantingly; refreshingly; winsomely; fascinatingly; daintily; felicitously; pleasantly; satisfyingly; tormentingly; disturbingly; grievously; inordinately; bewitchingly.

BLOOD

adjectives

distinguished; vigorous; fighting; chivalrous; tainted; foul; fraternal; stale; rank; polluted; dangerous; feverish; tingling; pounding; pulsing; oozing; flowing; mingled; foreign; human; hot; caked; dried; frozen; chilled; sluggish; innocent; spattered; quick; living; turbulent; bereaved; sacred; hostile; young; drowsy; precious; patriot; malapert; rushing; ebbing; jellied; trading; frolicsome; atoning; molten; violent; daring; kindred; nutrient; swift; basic; true; gummy; martyred; heretic; faultless; systolic; wicked; generous; pale; coursing; royal; aspiring; frothy; haughtiest; sanguine; congealed; arrested; excellent; noble; rare; sweet; comfortable; nomadic; corrupt.

verbs

aerate—; baptize in—; bathe in—; besmear with—; blend —s; chill—; cleanse—; congeal—; contaminate—; convey—; cool—; curdle—; defile with—; dilute—; dip in—; draw—; drip—; dye with—; effuse—; enrich—; expel—; fertilize—; flush with—; forfeit—; foul—; freeze—; go down in—; impoverish—; infect—; infiltrate—; infuse —; inhabit—; inoculate—; inure to—; invigorate—; issue from—; let—; oxygenate —; paint with—; poison—; pollute—; purge —; purify—; redden with—; seal with—; secrete—; shed—; soak in—; spill—; splash with—; spout—; stain with—; staunch—; steep in—; stimulate—; stir—; suck—; suffuse with—; swill—; taint—; taste—; thirst for—; transfuse—; wallow in—; win with —; write in—; yield—; —accumulates; —boils; —clots; —coagulates; —courses; —creeps through; —dribbles out; —flows; —gushes; —issues forth; —jets out; —leaps; —oozes; —palpitates; —pours from; —pulsates; —reabsorbs; —rises; —runs; —rushes through; —shoots forth; —spurts; —

stagnates; —streams; —surges; —tinkles; —throbs; —wells up.

BLOOD PRESSURE

adjectives
alarming; apoplectic; choleric; devastating; mounting; tremendous.

verbs
lower— —; normalize— —; relieve high— —; — —descends; — —drops; — —endangers; — —rises; — —startles; — —threatens.
(See barometer.)

BLOODSHED

adjectives
wanton; continued; unspeakable; needless; callous; ruthless.

verbs
attend with—; conquer without—; denounce —; die in—; ease—; end in—; free from—; instigate—; involve—; precipitate—; provoke—; result in—; revel in—; steep in—; suffer—; terminate in—; win through—.
(See massacre, slaughter.)

BLOODTHIRSTINESS

adjectives
bestial; reckless; ghoulish; vampire; leech-like; insatiable.

BLOODTHIRSTY

adverbs
insatiably; recklessly; criminally; bestially; cruelly; abominably; inhumanly; atrociously; brutally; infamously; iniquitously; knavishly; profligately; scandalously; viciously; incorrigibly; lawlessly; nefariously; sinfully; wickedly; horribly; unspeakably; amazingly; systematically; inherently; savagely; ferociously; diabolically; feloniously; fiendishly; flagitiously; foully; vilely; villainously.

BLOOD VESSEL

adjectives
bulging; bursting; flexible; heated; attenuated; overworked; straining; fragile.

verbs
block— —; burst— —; circulate through— —; clog— —; contract— —; course through — —; dilate— —; distend— —; disturb— —; engorge— —; flex— —; harden — —s; infect— —; line— —s; lodge in— —; narrow— —; puncture— —; retract— —; rupture— —; sever— —; staunch— —; tear— —; thin— —; twist— —; conveys — —; — —pulsates; — —shrivels up; — —s spring from; — —throbs; — —yields.
(See artery, vein.)

BLOOM

adjectives
gorgeous; glossy; girlish; delicate; lusty; fragrant; glorious; lingering; artificial; short-lived; semi-tropic; abundant; natural; sweet; faded; bell-like; wonted; youthful; overflowing; renovated; hopeful; welded; roseated; manifold; definite; luxuriant; virgin; citrus; petaled; vivid; vernal; prolific; radiant; amethystine; braided; sensational; plenteous; bunchy; precious; exotic; hidden; perfumed; wholesome; primeval; straying; ethereal.

verbs
blast—; blight—; break into—; exalt—; nip —; smother—; take—off; —colors; —culminates in; —exudes; —floresces; —flourishes; —flushes; —glows; —pales; —promises; —sparkles; —springs from; —tints.
(See blossom, vigor, flower.)

BLOOM (*v*)

adverbs
unchangingly; abundantly; magnificently; lustily; gorgeously; glossily; youthfully; overflowingly; luxuriantly; prolifically; vernally; exotically; wholesomely; primevally; ethereally.
(See blossom.)

BLOSSOM

adjectives
gorgeous; exquisite; cheerful; bright; fabulous; pure; almond; varicolored; lace-like; fragrant; golden; bursting; myriad; pendulous; showy; petaled; wholesome; marsh; bloodlike; colorful; holy; peach; tender; blazing; curious; living; blighted; pomegranate; sunlit; gaudy; meek; conical; embowering; faded; minute; brimstone; evanescent; odorous; latent; beauteous; topmost; phantom; vernal; winking; barren; mimic; loveliest; storm-beaten; flaming; proud.

verbs
bear—; burst into—; clip—; cover with —s; nip—; press—; produce—; put forth —s; scatter —s; shed —s; shower down —s; trim—; yield—; —buds; —dances; —fades; —flowers; —flutters down; —grows; —opens; —promises; —unfolds; —withers.
(See bloom, flower.)

BLOSSOM (*v*)

adverbs
magnificently; simultaneously; luxuriantly; fabulously; gorgeously; pendulously; colorfully; curiously; gaudily; conically; eva-

nescently; odorously; vernally; winkingly; flamingly.

(See bloom, flower, prosper, thrive.)

BLOT

adjectives
unsightly; tarnished; shadowy; foul; indelible; wrinkled; messy; adulterate.

BLOT (v)

adverbs
remorselessly; indelibly; blackly; permanently; finally; eventually; carelessly; frequently.

(See spot, efface, obliterate.)

BLOTCH

adjectives
sickly; shadowy; ugly; pale; bloody.

BLOTCHY

adverbs
painfully; disagreeably; incurably; unpleasantly; dingily; obnoxiously; disgustingly; repulsively; distressingly; unbecomingly; hopelessly; embarrassingly; disconcertingly; mortifyingly; alarmingly; fearfully; strangely; oddly.

BLOUSE

adjectives
gaudy; flowered; sheer; soft; warm; padded; diaphanous.

BLOW

adjectives
powerful; hammer-like; heavy; severe; fatal; irresistible; lethal; nasty; cruel; treacherous; descending; resounding; percussive; menaced; serious; decisive; frightful; painful; crushing; aggressive; perennial; threatened; echoless; irreparable; doughty; well-directed; staggering; breathless; final; sharpest; faithless; severe; swashing; annihilating; solid; hollow; drunken; amorous; vicious; impending; dull; dexterous; tetchy; ineradicable; heartless; sacrilegious; accusative; death-wind; implacable; ineffective.

verbs
administer—; aim—; break—; breast—; deal—; encounter—; evade—; exchange —s; execute—; experience—; fall to —s; interchange —s; parry—; rain —s upon; reel under—; strike—; stun with—; survive—; thrust—; trade —s; —descends upon; —resounds; —shatters; —smashes; —stretches one out.

(See stroke.)

BLOW (v)

adverbs
adversely; ceaselessly; placidly; gustily; violently; shrewdly; languorously; keenly; incessantly; spasmodically; irresistibly; resoundingly; lethally; aggressively; annihilatingly; viciously; implacably.

(See howl, sigh, swirl.)

BLOWZY

adverbs
ruddily; healthily; sturdily; rosily; attractively; coarsely; blatantly; noticeably; carelessly; showily; floridly; sunnily; pleasantly; roughly; captivatingly; interestingly; wholesomely.

BLUDGEON

adjectives
crude; effective; honest; critical; rough; swift; devastating.

BLUE

adjectives
heavenly; silent; mermaid; exquisite; canonical; dim; celestial; iceberg; indigo; bright; cadmium; intense; sky; glamorous; turquoise; sapphire; brilliant; ordinary; deep; chalcedony; larkspur; limpid; cobalt; delicate; crystal; anemic; illimitable; somber; opalescent; glossy; boundless; uniform; unbroken; dusty; remotest; wood-smoke; cornflower; purest; periwinkle; light; luminous; royal; aquamarine; aerial; tropic; pallid; sulphurous; frost.

BLUE

adverbs
ineffably; deeply; divinely; heavenly; unspeakably; indescribably; pleasantly; coldly; steely; affectionately; exquisitely; dimly; brightly; intensely; brilliantly; limpidly; delicately; sombrely; boundlessly; dustily; uniformly; remotely; purely; lightly; luminously; royally; frostily.

BLUEBIRD

adjectives
ever-welcome; flitting; glorious; luck-bearing; joyful; memory-haunting; merry-whistling.

verbs
—cheers; —pipes; —speeds; —warbles; —whispers.

(See bird.)

BLUFF
(cliff)

adjectives
barren; wind-swept; somber; bare; grass-

grown; bold; low; hazy; fine; sand; scarped; rock-reared.

BLUFF

adjectives (lie)
unadulterated; superb; magnificent; brazen; bold; preposterous.

BLUFF

adjectives (speech or manner)
deceptive; frightening; hearty; imposing; offhanded; pretentious; surly; cruel.

verbs
attempt—; bet against—; boast—; call—; carry out—; get away with—; maintain—; —blinds; —deceives; —deters; —excuses; —frightens; —hoodwinks; —induces; —influences; —serves.
(See lie.)

BLUFF

adverbs
churlishly; rudely; captiously; discourteously; disrespectfully; ill-manneredly; impudently; uncivilly; mischievously; moodily; morosely; perversely; insultingly; impertinently; bitterly; bluntly; boorishly; coolly; grimly; harshly; peevishly; pertly; ruggedly; naturally; characteristically; unpardonably; inexcusably; unpleasantly; playfully; teasingly; tormentingly; nonsensically; disagreeably; unnecessarily; sarcastically; ironically; sourly; unceremoniously; tartly; sullenly; vulgarly; unintentionally; deliberately; indefensibly.

BLUFF (*v*)

adverbs
unnecessarily; superbly; brazenly; preposterously; boldly; magnificently; characteristically; inevitably; grossly; incredibly; unpardonably; faithlessly.
(See frighten, intimidate.)

BLUFFING

adjectives
brilliant; multifarious; inevitable; characteristic; unexpected.

BLUNDER

adjectives
unhappy; colossal; fateful; irretrievable; astounding; disastrous; egregious; political; awful; brave; absurd; idiotic; tactical; ill-judged; sad; marketing; glorious; gross; serious; irreparable; extravagant; incredible; recent; sorry; idiomatic; curious; unpardonable.

verbs
aggravate—; atone for—; commit—; denounce—; fall into—; redeem —s; repair —s; —confounds; —confuses; —disturbs; —troubles.
(See error, mistake.)

BLUNDER (*v*)

adverbs
grossly; ludicrously; chimerically; ineptly; awkwardly; colossally; fatefully; irretrievably; disastrously; egregiously; politically; idiotically; irreparably; incredibly; idiomatically; grammatically; unpardonably.
(See bungle.)

BLUNDERER

adjectives
inept; impudent; awkward; supposed; chagrined; finished.

BLUNDERING

adjectives
hopeless; bureaucratic; forward; silly; understandable; impudent.

BLUNT

adverbs
stupidly; boorishly; ignorantly; unintentionally; deliberately; sullenly; unceremoniously; ironically; unnecessarily; disagreeably; unpardonably; inexcusably; insolently; unpleasantly; characteristically; ruggedly; honestly; pertly; peevishly; sternly; severely; harshly; doggedly; rudely; captiously; discourteously; uncivilly; ungraciously; moodily; morosely; perversely; bitterly; coolly; clumsily; ineptly; exasperatingly.

BLUNTNESS

adjectives
occasional; astringent; exasperating; characteristic; righteous; permissible; ugly; accentuated; clumsy; bludgeoning; inept.

BLUR

adjectives
confused; dim; pale; ineffectual; misted; pensive; wavering; shapeless; golden; retreating; vague.

BLUSH

adjectives
soft; crimson; deep; modest; rare; palest; contagious; piteous; guilty; delicate; scarlet; hot; burning; suffusing; lovely; rising; bright; charming; gracious; guileless; west-

ern; innocent; telltale; pure; vivid; quick; eloquent; mellow; sudden; unseen; fleeting; short; boyish; puzzled; witching; unborrowed; exquisite.

verbs
color with—es; flash—; hide—; redden with —es; result in—; suffuse with—; —beautifies; —embarrasses; —glows; —heats; —inflames; —warms.
(See flush.)

BLUSH (v)

adverbs
furiously; miserably; coyly; elatedly; synthetically; disdainfully; ingenuously; modestly; delicately; eloquently; exquisitely; witchingly; easily.
(See flush, redden.)

BLUSTER (v)

adverbs
furiously; thunderously; fearsomely; tremendously; terrifically; ceaselessly; monotonously; wrathfully; heatedly; vigorously; vainly.
(See storm, rage, fume.)

BOAR

adjectives
urchin; snouted; angry; chafing; blunt; bloody; hideous; monstrous.

BOARD

adjectives (commission)
nonpartisan; expert; efficient; glowing; political; mirthful; superior; ancient.

BOARD

adjectives (official body)
assembled; directing; executive; governing; advisory; high; honorable; local.

verbs
abolish—; admit to—; bring before—; control—; create—; elect to—; enlarge—; entrust to—; establish—; organize—; provide —; refer to—; set up—; staff—; —administers; —adopts; —advises; —authorizes; —agrees; —arbitrates; —condemns; —convenes; —develops; —disposes of; —effects; —elects; —enacts; —enforces; —exercises; —investigates; —modifies; —operates; —outlines; —performs; —promotes; —provides; —reforms; —regulates; —relieves; —reports; —stimulates; —supports; —votes.
(See commission, committee.)

BOARD

adjectives (wood)
resplendent; stray; reeking; creaking; uncarpeted; shot-scarred; glistening; cypress; trophy-laden; decaying; rough-hewn; original; grub; sparing; wine-filled; ugly; sturdy; flimsy; scanty; groaning; festive; plenteous.

verbs
adjust—; burnish—; case with —s; cast upon —s; cover with —s; encase in —s; enclose in —s; finish off—; fit—; frame with —; hew—; measure—; patter over —s; plane—; preserve—; reinforce —s; sand—; scurry over —s; warp—; —bars; —creaks; —extends; —groans; —rots; —splinters; —splits; —warps.
(See table, stage.)

BOAST

adjectives
absurd; playful; empty; foolish; truthful; proudest; ordinary; unique; unadulterated; vapid; peerless; ignoble; honest; sentimental; fanatic; airy; childish; frantic; prattling; noisy; vain.

BOAST (v)

adverbs
justly; blatantly; unmitigatedly; exuberantly; arrogantly; intoxicatedly; hollowly; overweeningly; whimsically; vainly; egotistically; vapidly; ignobly; fanatically; prattlingly.
(See brag, vaunt.)

BOASTFUL

adverbs
extravagantly; absurdly; playfully; foolishly; proudly; vapidly; airily; childishly; boyishly; noisily; blatantly; egotistically; fantastically; grotesquely; palpably; manifestly; essentially; ludicrously; ridiculously; laughably; offensively; unpleasantly; egregiously; ignobly; ineffectually; inanely; senselessly; idiotically; preposterously; dexterously; adroitly; cleverly; indiscreetly; imprudently; feebly; flimsily; wishfully; stupendously; magnificently; splendidly; vaingloriously; blindly; blissfully.

BOASTING

adjectives
egotistical; vain; cursed; extravagant; blustering; bold; blatant.

verbs
glory in—; indulge in—; make good—; occasion—; speak in—; utter—; —extols; —

menaces; —occasions; —terrifies; —threatens.
(See display.)

BOAT

adjectives
crude; wooden; staunch; frail; uptilted; racing; comfortable; sunken; excursion; distant; tiny; fishing; plying; crowded; plunging; fragile; light; portable; lazy; vile; cheap; whirling; driving; moored; outward-bound; crewless; colossal; iron; vanished; half-beached; clumsy; swift; weather-beaten; well-manned; unanchored; pavilioned; worn-out; illuminated.

verbs
alight from—; anchor—; bail—; becalm—; capsize—; caulk—; detail—; fire up—; fit out—; heave to—; moor—; paddle—; pole —; propel—; punt—; push off—; reserve—; swamp—; —churns; —cleaves the water; —dances; —flops; —flounders; —founders; —glides; —grounds; —nuzzles; —outsails; —pitches; —plies; —ploughs; —sneaks; —swings; —touches at.
(See vessel, ship, canoe, launch, schooner, barge, tugboat.)

BOATMEN

adjectives
wrangling; grizzled; inexperienced; skillful.

BOB

adjectives
ravishing; tawny; smooth; smart; shoulder-length.

BOBOLINK

adjectives
joy-swelling; migratory; coy; rice-seeking; reed-swinging; throaty; questing.

verbs
—boasts; —broods; —chirps; —laughs; —prattles; —rattles.
(See bird.)

BOBWHITE

adjectives
covert; dun-colored; misleading; nature-sheltered; shy; sly; wary.

verbs
—bursts out; —calls; —darts; —displays; —feathers; —feigns; —fights; —flushes; —huddles; —preens; —preys on; —puffs out; —sails; —struts; —swells; —trots; —twitters; —whirrs; —whistles; —wings.
(See quail, partridge, bird.)

BODEMENT

adjectives
tremendous; horrid; accurate; uncanny; precise.

BODICE

adjectives
slim; fitted; jeweled.

BODY

adjectives (group)
aggregate; august; responsible; disinterested; official; governing; obscure; civil; picturesque; upstanding; formidable; deliberative; eminent; hasty-witted; public; legislative; virtuous; specialized; illustrious; ecclesiastical; unsympathetic; artistocratic; insensate; permanent; obstructive; impartial; intermediary; heterogeneous; pigmy; arbitrating; expansive; elastic; appropriating; unfathomable; long-established; anxious; consulting; sensible; seeming; well-regulated; confirming; alterable; irresistible; distinct; reckless; contemptible; inanimate; numerous.

BODY

adjectives (substance)
clumsy; angular; boyish; deformed; dangling; hurtling; jerking; squatting; quivering; slouched; struggling; trembling; wan; palpitating; human; paralyzed; mummified; hairy; wrinkled; ruddy; compact; drenched; sodden; bleeding; jarred; relaxed; collapsed; huddled; slumped; sagging; defiant; swaggering; dainty; small-boned; shapely; graceful; delicate; striking; quick; wiry; supple; lithe; sturdy; swift; strong; heavy-muscled; hard; rugged; sinewy; young; vigorous; healthy; sound; vibrant; sensuous; amorous; yielding; passionate; stocky; weightless; stunted; shrunken; emaciated; meager; bronzed; slim; stiffened; taut; lethargic; slack; immovable; prone; lifeless; couchant; motionless; prostrate; huge; overgrown; vast; obese; mountainous; lanky; unclean; ragged; neglected; unshaven; detestable; overworked; meek; fear-driven; weary; worn; exhausted; charred; sick; strangled; ailing; poverty-weakened; disfigured; bruised; torn; jerking; swooning; soulless; negroid; paralyzed; covered; blanketed; relaxed; frozen; dense; unworthy; well-defended; minute; fever-stricken; anemic; religious; misshapen; pierced; organic; transparent; sovereign; inanimate; subterranean; visible; recumbent; influential; spontaneous; rotund; drowned; tattooed; inert; interlaced; uni-

cellular; statuesque; squirming; convivial; flaccid; defunct; astral; adjacent; contradictory; segregated; idle; capable; cheerful; fluid; qualified; bigoted; unsound; chaste; branching; decent; convulsing; cigar-shaped; erect; twitching; Spagnuoled; decomposed; uncoffined; jovial; exhausted; plump; filiform; weazened; undivided; rubicund.

verbs
adapt—; anoint—; array—; attune—; bare —; batter—; bow—; bury—; cast out—; chill—; cleanse—; cling to—; commit—; consecrate—; consume—; contract—; deck —in; defile—; deplete—; discern—; dismember—; dispose of—; drag—; dwarf—; ease—; edify—; emaciate—; embrace—; endanger—; exhilarate—; expose—; exult in—; fetter—; floor—; gloat over—; govern—; incline—; inflict upon—; inter—; introduce into—; invest—; invigorate—; mangle—; pelt—; pommel—; preserve—; reconstruct—; relieve—; reproduce—; rid —of; saturate—; splatter—; sponge—; stiffen—; sustain—; tenant—; torture—; transmit through—; triumph over—; twist—; vitalize—; waste—; wrap—in; —decomposes; —disintegrates; —festers; —flops; —gleams; —glides; —putrefies; —quivers; —rebels; —reigns; —responds; —slumps; —sprawls; —twitches; —vibrates; —wriggles; —writhes.

(See form, frame, carcass, corpse.)

BOG

adjectives
filthy; logical; sinking; swanky; sphagnous; treacherous; dangerous.

BOG (*v*)

adverbs
hopelessly; filthily; logically; treacherously; dangerously; fatally; irresistibly; obscurely; unprecedentedly; miserably.

(See fail.)

BOGGY

adverbs
muddily; plashily; squashily; quaggily; swampily; softly; unpleasantly; unhealthfully; unfortunately; pestiferously; undesirably; irrecoverably; irremediably; hopelessly; unluckily; deplorably; disturbingly; plaguedly; impracticably.

BOIL

(tumor)

adjectives
erupting; festering; hideous; throbbing; rest-robbing; purplish.

verbs
absorb—; cut—; dissect—; extirpate—; incise—; lance—; paint—; puncture—; —buds; —comes to a head; —disappeared; —forms.

(See abscess.)

BOISTEROUS

adverbs
broadly; intolerably; noisily; clamorously; uproariously; vociferously; turbulently; obstreperously; blatantly; fussily; breezily; convivially; festively; jovially; genially; happily; joyously; joyfully; wildly; madly; crazily; drunkenly; merrily; coarsely; crudely; pugnaciously; discordantly; angrily; excusably; childishly; rudely; Rotarily; uncontrollably; foolishly; fatuously; socially; perpetually; heedlessly; carelessly; thoughtlessly; deliberately; unpardonably; inexcusably; understandably; naturally; affectionately; fraternally.

BOISTEROUSNESS

adjectives
boyish; loud; unrestrained; broad; raucous.

BOLD

adverbs
offensively; audaciously; impudently; rashly; wantonly; indiscreetly; injudiciously; hotheadedly; foolishly; recklessly; presumptuously; amazingly; shamelessly; tragically; singularly; ridiculously; inexplicably; dramatically; inherently; fantastically; alarmingly; temperamentally; dangerously; courageously; adventurously.

BOLDNESS

adjectives
unprecedented; characteristic; decent; self-respecting; uncanny; prodigious; sublime; astonishing; pious; persistent; singular; ill-timed; ridiculous; easy; frank; habitual; felicitous; generous; extreme; foolish.

BOLE

adjectives
twisted; opalescent; resinous; hoary; bossy.

BOLT

adjectives
tremendous; heavy; flimsy; sulphurous; sharp; avenging; death-dealing; heaven-sent.

verbs
adjust—; apply—; clamp on—; connect—; discharge—; drive—; employ—; extract—; fasten—; forge—; heat—; hurl—; manipu-

BOMBAST

late—; rivet—; screw—; secure with—; shackle in —s; shoot—; sink—; snap—; strip—; stud—; thread—; tighten—; turn —; undo—; —bars; —expands; —fastens; —locks; —pins; —prevents; —rivets; —safeguards; —seals; —secures; —shrinks; —unties; —withstands.

(See bar.)

BOLT (v)

adverbs

hungrily; avidly; ferociously; grossly; hoggishly; brutishly; barbarously; unrestrainedly; sottishly; permanently.

(See gulp.)

BOMB

adjectives

unsuccessful; exploding; gas; incendiary; volcanic; time.

verbs

bombard with—; clock—; detonate—; direct—; discharge—; drop—; eject—; encase—; examine—; fill—; fire—; fling—; fuse—; hurl—; ignite—; project—; rain —s; release—; set—; shower with —s; time —; toss—; —batters; —bursts; —dynamites; —explodes; —s fly; —hammers; —hums; —plows through; —ruins; —scatters; —shatters; —ticks; —uproots.

(See projectile, shell.)

BOMB (v)

adverbs

cold-bloodedly; unsuccessfully; inhumanly; volcanically; ruthlessly; fiendishly; callously; devilishly; soullessly.

(See attack.)

BOMBARDMENT

adjectives

preliminary; serious; desultory; persistent; intermittent; intensive; aerial; constant; threatened.

verbs

assail with—; command—; concentrate—; conduct—; counter—; defend against—; direct—; flee from—; fortify against—; inflict—; plan—; prepare for—; resort to—; shatter with—; shelter from—; shudder under—; slacken—; unleash—; ward off—; —assails; —attacks; —batters; —damages; —demolishes; —demoralizes; —destroys; —disables; —disheartens; —dispirits; —injures; —reduces; —routs; —rumbles; —scatters; —thunders; —uproots.

(See attack, assault.)

adjectives

oratorical; studied; stilted; rhetorical; empty; loud; pedantic; ranting.

BOMBASTIC

adverbs

magnificently; absurdly; playfully; foolishly; proudly; inanely; vapidly; airily; noisily; childishly; blatantly; fantastically; joyously; ludicrously; ridiculously; laughably; offensively; unpleasantly; ineffectually; senselessly; idiotically; clownishly; preposterously; stupendously; splendidly; blissfully; intolerably; rudely; fatuously; deliberately; crudely; merrily; crazily; convivially; vociferously; uproariously.

BOND

adjectives (certificate or debenture)

corporation; government; interest-bearing; matured; municipal; negotiable; transferable; utility.

verbs

advise on —s; borrow on —s; cash —s; float —s; inherit —s; investigate —s; issue —s; liquidate—; market —s; number —s; print —s; recommend —s; register —s; repudiate —s; sell —s; serialize —s; transfer —s; —accumulates interest; —matures; —promises.

BOND

adjectives (investment)

dubious; crinkly; unimpeachable; funding; highly-secured; gilt-edged.

BOND

adjectives (tie)

textual; unbreakable; inescapable; economic; financial; confidential; cruel; weak; tacit; everlasting; powerful; tenacious; imperishable; invisible; sympathetic; secret; strong; invariable; delusive; indissoluble; indestructible; intellectual; countless (pl); subtle; artistic; single; merry; harmonious; conventional; natural; oppressive; fraternal; eternal; marriage; enduring; close.

verbs

burst —s; contract—; dissolve—; enter—; liberate from—; link with —s; loose —s; maintain—; pledge—; seal—; shatter—; snap —s asunder; tighten—; —cements; —confines; —connects; —constrains; —endures; —enslaves; —fetters; —imprisons; —manacles; —obligates; —restrains; —shackles.

(See band, tie, fetter, obligation, promise.)

BOND (v)

adverbs
indissolubly; unbreakably; inescapably; financially; tenaciously; imperishably; invisibly; conventionally; eternally; oppressively.

BONDAGE

adjectives
infantine; solemn; sweet; petted; deep; hereditary; deadly; commercial; intermittent; mysterious; improvised; voluntary; brittle; tolerable; wholesome; hard; magic; roseate; economical.
verbs
abolish—; bring into—; deliver from—; enforce—; enslave in—; escape from—; free from—; hold in—; impose—; pledge into —; reduce to—; return to—; rid of—; sell into—; serve out—; subject to—; tie in—; —degrades; —warps.

(See slavery, servitude, captivity, subjugation.)

BONE

adjectives
joint; marrow; gaunt; jutting; crumbling; bleached; ravaged-looking; dry; mighty; dismal; poor; tired; aching; trivial; massive; storm-chilled; unsightly; toothsome; aged; blanching; unrememberable; dissevered; aligned; queer-shaped; earthly; chivalric; delicate; distorted; empty; honored; sturdy; white-sown; sound; mastoid; unburied; grilled; uncoffined; shining; petrified; carious; honest; moldering; livid; weary; piteous; cowardly; frontal; pliable; marsupial; steely; brittle; immense; pulsant; femoral; prominent; canonized; spiced; high; saucer-like.

verbs
adhere to—; adjust —s; affect—; assemble —s; bend—; bleach —s; breed in —s; bruise —; cement—; crack—; crush—; cut to—; deform—; dislocate—; distort—; dry—; excavate —s; expose—; fertilize with —s; fracture—; freeze to—; gnaw—; graft—; grind —s; harden —s; heal—; infect—; inflame—; injure—; inter —s; knit—; lengthen—; operate on—; pick—; pierce—; plate —; protect—; rattle —s; realign—; reveal —; scatter —s; set—; shake—; soften—; splinter—; treat—; twist—; unite—; waste —s; wire—; wrap up —s; x-ray—; —s ache; —s creak; —s form; —s frame; —hinges; —s join; —s mature; —s remain; —rots.

BONFIRE

adjectives
solitary; glowing; tremendous; rejoicing.

BONNET

adjectives
dark; coquettish; delicate; starched; battered; flattened; sun; gigantic; hearse-plumed; amazing; poke; durable; dangling; orange-tawny.

BONNY

adverbs
blithely; airily; beautifully; buxomly; rosily; prettily; wholesomely; cheerfully; buoyantly; merrily; jestingly; gaily; lightly; winsomely; joyously; ecstatically; rapturously; simply; dearly; adorably; charmingly; enchantingly; bewitchingly; lovably; irresistibly; tormentingly; teasingly.

BONY

adverbs
awkwardly; fantastically; grotesquely; amusingly; pathetically; complacently; unbelievably; distressingly; angularly; terribly; horridly; oddly; touchingly; grievously; unthinkably; ludicrously; ridiculously; deplorably; lamentably; strangely; queerly; singularly; drolly.

BOOK

adjectives
vade-mecum; reference; glorified; guide; handy; narrow; thin; black; unacademic; unpretentious; amazing; disturbing; terrifying; strange; vital; dynamic; pregnant; monogrammed; original; incisive; passionate; ancient; worn; musty; dusty; littered; moldy; coverless; written; translated; polished; elegant; cynical; illustrated; inferior; painful; heartbreaking; obscure; condemned; ungraceful; dull; tedious; rejected; inadequate; incomplete; fuliginous; obscene; degrading; suggestive; immoral; dreadful; spectacular; shocking; devastating; ill-natured; cursed; blasphemous; seditious; banned; deliberate; quarrelsome; posthumous; sacred; unsigned; anonymous; educative; formidable; scientific; talking; racial; devotional; serious; realistic; truest; provocative; important; notable; warlike; venerable; sophisticated; wise; mature; delicate; learned; informative; readable; clever; agreeable; comprehensive; detailed; popular; best-selling; famous; hilarious; painful; funny; amusing; stimulating; quaint; priceless; rare; difficult; massive; well-made; clear; rich; authentic; factual; authoritative; absorbing; astonishing; ac-

cursed; bewitching; clarifying; diverting; enthralling; exhilarating; extraordinary; first; feminine; forthright; glamorous; glorious; heroic; human; hair-raising; irresistible; intimate; magnificent; practical; perfect; remarkable; readable; stirring; superb; scholarly; strangest; sensitive; timely; splendid; unique; vital; witty; grand; ephemeral; melancholy; useful; thought-provoking; valuable; exercise; scrambling; profitable; memorandum; stormy; edifying; musty; indecent; salable; lewd; elementary; illiterate; lucid; enjoyable; commonplace; censored.

verbs
adapt—; admire—; base on—; belittle—; clutch—; con—; cram—; dedicate—; depreciate—; disparage—; distort—; dive into —; edit—; elaborate—; enshrine—; fling —; illustrate—; label—; launch—; mutilate —; permeate—; peruse—; plot—; plunge through—; pour over—; preface—; propagate—; recommend—; resort to—; review —; revise—; ridicule—; satirize—; scan—; search—; slander—; succumb to—; summarize—; thumb—; tilt—; vend—; —abounds in; —breathes; —charms; —defiles; — details; —depresses; —disturbs; —documents; —embodies; —enchants; —enthralls; —inspires; —meanders; —oppresses; —ranks; —shocks; —sparkles; —surges; —transports.

(See volume, novel, fiction, story, biography.)

BOOKCASE

adjectives
bamboo; elegant; built-in; expensive.

BOOKISH

adverbs
hopelessly; learnedly; ostentatiously; arrogantly; proudly; unfortunately; quaintly; amusingly; complacently; colossally; tediously; monotonously; inordinately; obviously; studiously; ardently; unintelligently; vacuously; inanely; showily; blindly; pedantically; superficially; shrewdly; proverbially; profoundly; eruditely; consciously; academically; omnisciently.

BOOKKEEPER

adjectives
provincial; timid; expensive; overworked; lazy; ambitious.

BOOKLET

adjectives
descriptive; illustrated; attractive; authoritative; fascinating; explanatory; valuable; informative; dainty; interesting; constructive; pictorial.

BOOM

adjectives (activity or prosperity)
amazing; exciting; fortune-rolling; gigantic; rapidly-subsiding; tidal-wave; overnight.

verbs
accelerate—; advance into—; buoy up by—; burst into—; daze by—; delay—; denote—; follow by—; foretell—; launch—; prepare for—; provoke—; revel in—; revive—; stimulate—; work up—; —advances; —bounds; —cheers; —collapses; —crashes; —encourages; —exhilarates; —fades; —follows; —induces; —prospers; —retards; —roars; —sets in; —swells.

(See prosperity, development.)

BOOM

adjectives (business)
postwar; periodic; unprecedented; glorious; fantastic.

BOOM

adjectives (noise)
dwindling; penetrating; deep; disturbing; muffled; incalculable; subdued.

BOOM (*v*)

adverbs
hollowly; deafeningly; penetratingly; disturbingly; muffledly; subduedly; sonorously; dully; monotonously; musically; thuddingly; resoundingly; intermittently.

(See roar.)

BOOMING

adjectives
hollow; sonorous; dull; perpetual; deep-toned; monotonous; musical.

BOON

adjectives
inestimable; priceless; immortal; unspeakable; delusive; blissful; greater; floral; choicest; smaller.

verbs
accord—; beseech—; bestow—; command —; confer—upon; court—; deny—; entreat —; favor with—; grant—; petition—; pray for—; request—; yield—.

(See blessing, advantage, favor, gift.)

BOOR

adjectives
sottish; churlish; ill-bred; insensible; ignor-

ant; thick-necked; rustic; lascivious; horny-handed; drunken.

BOORISH

adverbs
awkwardly; fantastically; inordinately; offensively; contemptibly; amusingly; unconsciously; unwittingly; artlessly; deliberately; morbidly; prodigiously; colossally; tediously; detestably; bluntly; insufferably; intolerably; unbearably; rudely; abominably; crudely; intentionally; carelessly; shockingly; stupidly; innately; churlishly; ignorantly; drunkenly; impudently; uncivilly; moodily; perversely; insultingly; bitterly; harshly; ruggedly; inexcusably; disagreeably; sourly; unceremoniously; sullenly; indefensibly; outrageously.

BOOTH

adjectives
gaudy; little; secluded; vine-covered; mushroom-topped; rustic; impermanent; miserable; demonstration.

verbs
assemble in—; conduct—; conduct to—; construct—; cover—; erect—; exhibit in—; huddle in—; lead to—; lodge in—; provide —; refresh at—; shelter in—.
(See shelter, stand.)

BOOTS

adjectives
squeaking; shining; swaggering; varnished; spurred; heavy; patched; elaborate; flat-soled; faultless; creaking; lustrous; lacquered; immaculate; fancy; neat; soft; studded; tight; high-heeled; close-fitting; dilapidated; clumsy; shapeless; patent-leather; elastic-sided; cavalier; flappy; muddy.

BOOTY

adjectives
hidden; magnificent; honeyed.

BORDER

adjectives
remote; rickety; dusky; inscribed; gaudy; beauteous; eternal; secluded; variegated; terraced; populous.

verbs
adjust—; broaden—; define—; enlarge—; establish—; extend—; fortify—; illustrate —; mark—; mass at—; menace—; pass through—; patrol—; post at—; ravage—; safeguard—; skirt—; touch—; widen—; —bounds; —limits; —margins; —outlines.
(See edge, limit, boundary, frontier.)

BORE

adjectives
deadly; highest; dreadful; everlasting; colossal; ignorant; ceaseless; veritable; incomparable; intimate; fearful; unmitigated; amiable; horrid; practiced.

BORE (*v*)

adverbs
faintly; heartily; dreadfully; everlastingly; colossally; ceaselessly; incomparably; unmitigatedly; horridly; agonizingly.
(See annoy, tire, trouble, vex.)

BOREDOM

adjectives
exasperated; intolerable; sinister; petulant; languid; passionless; unbearable; barren; solitary; sheer; genteel; gentlemanly; profound; drowsy; well-bred.

verbs
bear—; chase away—; consign to—; drug into—; endure—; experience—; free from —; pierce—; relieve—; sink into—; succumb to—; threaten with—; —annoys; —gnaws.
(See ennui, annoyance.)

BORESOME

adverbs
intolerably; profoundly; tiresomely; tediously; monotonously; irksomely; uniformly; terribly; inordinately; feebly; exhaustively; dully; mortally; prosily; disgustingly; unbearably; wearily; flatly; stupidly.

BORN (*v*)

adverbs
royally; posthumously; lowly; painlessly; humbly; legitimately; nobly.

BORROW (*v*)

adverbs
infrequently; constantly; boldly; shamelessly; persistently; frequently; habitually; cheerfully.
(See obtain, acquire.)

BORROWER

adjectives
solvent; would-be; shameless; infinite; unfortunate.

BOSOM

adjectives
ample; abundant; massive; extensive; capacious; expanded; capital; lovely; warm; flat; weak; aching; bare; maternal; austere; quickened; heaving; corseted; covert; jaded; melancholy; contented; placid; chill-

ed; plenteous; peaceful; brinish; immortal; faithless; complete; genial; tranquil; transparent; virginal; brassy; nectared; sad; blushing; sunburnt; sluggish; inconstant; soft-pleated; undefiled; quivering; virile; bloodless; hard; nursing; murmuring; glassy; palpitating; rock-ribbed; shieldless; agonized; fragrant; chaste; simple; writhing.

verbs
agitate—; assail—; bare—; beat—; chamber in—; cherish in—; clasp to—; cleanse—; embrace—; incense—; live in—; lurk in—; nestle in—; nurse in—; pacify—; pain—; perturb—; plant in—; pluck from—; shelter in—; soothe—; stir—; tear from—; vent—; warm—; wrestle in—; —burns; —heaves; —swells.
(See breast.)

BOSS
adjectives (colloq.)
political; nervous; high-strung; dominant; invisible; corrupt; arrogant; powerful; level-headed; department; egomaniac; brazen; bilingual; militant; argumentative.

verbs
anger—; esteem—; promote to—; —dictates; —discharges; —employs; —fires; —lashes; —leads; —manages; —masters; —orders.
(See manager, employer, politician.)

BOSS (v)
adverbs
dreadfully; politically; nervously; dominantly; arrogantly; brazenly; argumentatively; dictatorially; highhandedly; imperiously; swaggeringly.
(See direct, dominate.)

BOSSY
adverbs
disagreeably; ludicrously; infinitely; amusingly; officiously; ridiculously; despotically; tyrannically; pompously; characteristically; inherently; arrogantly; superciliously; loftily; clownishly; insistently; persistently; sharply; curtly; efficiently; offensively; detestably; shockingly; naturally; unreasonably; foolishly; excessively.

BOTHERSOME
adverbs
unduly; disagreeably; intolerably; annoyingly; vexatiously; incessantly; persistently; incorrigibly; incurably; offensively; detestably; shockingly; unreasonably; foolishly; noisily; pestiferously; tediously; stupidly; mortally; inordinately; terribly; disgustingly; cantankerously; unmanageably; insufferably; unendurably.

BOTTLE
adjectives
beautiful; shining; labeled; exquisite; spherical; grotesque; unique; ancient; flamboyant; reliable; venerable-looking; narrow-mouthed; half-empty; crown; coveted; unisonant (pl); unfinished.

verbs
brandish—; case —s; charge—; clink—; cluster —s; convey in—; cork—; drain—; drink—; invert—; manipulate—; pour into —; prepare—; produce—; proffer—; quaff from—; smash—; store in—; strain—; transfer to—; transport in—; —carries; —s clink; —contains; —crashes.
(See glass.)

BOTTLE (v)
adverbs
effectively; exquisitely; reliably; permanently; temporarily; securely; skilfully; perpetually.

BOTTOM
adjectives
noble; shallow; luxuriant; sandy; sieve; fertile; blind; leaky; rugged.

verbs
anchor to—; drag—; dredge—; flounder on —; gauge to—; list at—; lower to—; plunge to—; probe to—; recede to—; rest on—; sink to—; transfix to—.
(See base, foundation.)

BOUDOIR
adjectives
scented; perfumed; luxurious; frivolous; beautiful; alluring; enticing; sumptuous; beckoning.

BOUGH
adjectives
pendent; blossoming; projecting; breathless; fruited; pampered; untrimmed; feathery; colored; drooping; stony; topmost; shelving; unpeeled; majestic; prodigal; thick; snow-laden; fluttering; withered; naked; raven; arching; interlaced (pl); long; snow-hung; unwaving; sinewy; barren; fragrant; untrustworthy; clustering (pl); fresh; disenchanted; gnarled; splintered; hanging; billowy (pl); willing; treacherous; reluctant; nodding; denuded; springy;

mossy; stirring; ragged; beechen; innumerable (pl); dripping.

BOULDER

adjectives
fern-covered; huge; scattered; mighty; sun-warmed; tremendous; mossy; sheltering; flat-topped; great; loosened; granite, steel; ancient; glacial.

BOULEVARD

adjectives
spacious; crowded; engirdling; wintry; gay; bright; lighted; festive.

BOUND (*v*)

adverbs
joyously; gallantly; gracefully; exquisitely; superbly; lithely; sportively; animatedly; freely.
(See leap, spring, dance, frisk.)

BOUNDARY

adjectives
fairy; historical; established; frontier; opposite; outer; definite; geographical; intangible; material; titular; ill-defined; political; utmost.

verbs
break—; dispute—; disregard—; encroach upon—; enlarge—; extend—; fortify—; hang on—; hover over—; indicate—; limit —; line—; mark—; perceive—; reside on —; station at—; transcend —ies; widen—.
(See border, limit, barrier, edge, line.)

BOUNDS

adjectives
abolished; vaulting; narrow; visible; stone-troubled; mad; vulgar; utmost; firm; elastic; graceful; earthly

verbs
appoint—; break—; confine to—; extend—; hurdle—; infringe on—; leap—; narrow—; overleap all—; prescribe—; set—; transcend —; widen—.
(See boundary.)

BOUNTY

adjectives
beneficent; endless; essential; extravagant; munificent; questionable; reckless.

verbs
bestow—; collect—; deserve—; distribute —; earn—; merit—; pay—; proclaim—; reward with—; scorn—; share—; spread—; taste—; value—; —encourages; —excels.
(See gift, favor, fee.)

BOUQUET

adjectives
lavish; huge; enormous; absurd; farewell; conventional; nightly; enchanting; exquisite; intriguing; distinctive; superb; animated; sumptuous; tasteful.

verbs
adorn with—; affix—; arrange—; bunch—; clasp—; clip—; cut—; display—; garnish with—; gather—; inhale—; lavish —s upon; pay tribute with—; sniff—; surrounded by —s; tie up—; toss—; wrap—; —cheers; —compliments; —conveys; —enhances.
(See flowers.)

BOURGEOIS

adverbs
obscurely; barbarously; humbly; boorishly; churlishly; roughly; savagely; snobbishly; flauntingly; obviously; manifestly; basely; evidently; indubitably; unquestionably; ignobly; meanly; sorrily; confessedly; admittedly.

BOURGEOISIE

adjectives (pl)
dispossessed; unconverted; all-pervading; prosperous; ambitious; wealthy; enfranchised; bloated; mercantile.

verbs
address—; besiege by—; class among—; clout (colloq.)—; control—; depend on—; despise—; distinguish—; enslave—; exclude —; familiarize with—; inveigh against—; mingle with—; rank among—; restrain—; tread on—; —arise; —cheer; —congregate; —decay; —gather; —resent; —revolt; —storm; —support; —surround; —triumph.
(See proletariat.)

BOUT

adjectives
match; stiff; humiliating; distressing; winding; dressing; wassail; exciting; boring.

verbs
cancel—; engage in—; indulge in—; stage —; take part in—; time—; witness—; —attracts; —draws; —thrills.
(See contest, conflict, battle.).

BOVINE

adverbs
stolidly; dully; ineptly; absolutely; stupidly; apathetically; calmly; serenely; indifferent-

ly; complaisantly; agreeably; blockishly; doltishly; heavily; idly; obtusely; simply; vacantly; witlessly; prosaically; ridiculously; reposefully; mildly; tranquilly; placidly; tamely; unconcernedly.

BOW

adjectives
noiseless; courteous; flourishing; profound; sweeping; chilly; polite; continuous; Oriental; ceremonious; unbent; mechanical; masculine; formal; conventional; hospitable; drowsy; serious; ironical; garish; humid; humble; grateful; obsequious; sycophantic; inimitable; magnificent; barbaric; sawing; whanging; romantic; historical; burlesque; mischievous; silent; amiable; exaggerated; sardonic; society; manly; valedictory; smashing; frigid; stiff; scarlet; prodigious; liberal; majestic; ethereal; transparent; unctuous.

BOW
(archery)

adjectives
ashen; carefully-adjusted; curiously-fashioned; crude; pliant; servile; trusty; twanging.

verbs
arm with—; bend—; curve—; draw—; employ—; fashion—; form—; joint—; level—; release—; ripple from—; set—; shape—; shoot with—; spring—; string—; tense—; twang—; unleash—; —projects; —quivers; —retracts; —wavers.
(See arrow.)

BOW (*v*)

adverbs
discriminately; involuntarily; prematurely; languidly; ornately; gallantly; ironically; instinctively; profoundly; gravely; unctuously; passively; distantly; obsequiously; cringingly; formally; mockingly; deferentially; debonairly; submissively; desolately; haughtily; profoundly; dejectedly; Orientally; sweepingly; ceremoniously; drowsily; mechanically; sycophantically; sardonically; majestically.
(See incline, nod, yield, stoop.)

BOWELS

adjectives
lazy; lithe; firm-muscled; engorged; surfeited; stubborn.

verbs
clean out—; clear—; constipate—; dilate—; distend—; ease—; empty—; evacuate—; infect—; inflame—; inject into—; insert in—; introduce into—; irritate—; line—; move—; open—; perforate—; purge—; regulate—; relax—; stimulate—; —move; —respond.
(See intestines.)

BOWER

adjectives
complete; myrtle; noontide; bloomless; wavy; heavenly; inmost; comfortless; leafy; over-arching; consecrated; moonlit; sylvan; pleached; native; roseate; apricot-silk; secluded; ravaged; amaranth; pleasant; lyric; noisome; blissful; fragrant; glimmering; newly-woven; close; enchanted; virgin; sequestered.

verbs
canopy with —s; cover—; dwell amid —s; entertain in—; entice into—; hide in—; idealize—; inhabit—; plant with—; shade—; steal into—; —droops; —shades; —thickens.
(See recess, cottage.)

BOWL

adjectives
unmingled; capacious; leathern; meager; ambrosial; flowing; enormous; sealed; pewter; lovely; cloisonne; shallow; flowered; fat; priceless; low; translucid; smooth; shining; adorned; brimming; nut-brown; coarse; coppery; hospitable; friendly.

BOX

adjectives
capacious; dreadful; cumbersome; spacious; stuffed; cozy; convenient; jolly; satin; alabaster; screened; unfurnished; pasteboard; triangular; poetical; wooden; gaudy; proscenium; uncompromising; sunken; hectagonal; oblong; tin; oversize.

verbs
collect in—; encase in—; hide in—; lock—; occupy—; partition—; restore to—; save in —; seal—; search—; shelter in—; —clatters; —contains; —yawns.
(See case, chest, basket.)

BOX (*v*)

adverbs
firmly; securely; clumsily; cumbersomely; conveniently; hectagonally; tastefully; sumptuously.
(See tie, enclose.)

BOX (*v*)
(prize fight)

adverbs
invincibly; vigorously; violently; dexterously; nimbly; uncompromisingly; superbly.
(See slap.)

BOY

adjectives
stalwart; remarkable; inexperienced; unequipped; boastful; unruly; dissolute; precocious; clean-cut; nestling; disobedient; thoughtless; reckless; flint-hearted; peevish; starved; shelterless; amorous; military; irrecoverable; stocky; round-faced; apple-cheeked; rollicking; red-haired; conscripted; sundry; dull; jolly; good-natured; laughing; active; fun-loving; handsome; radiant; lively; loving; good-looking; sturdy; absurd; lanky; chubby; honest; mischievous; lubberly; aggrieved; vociferous; barefoot; cool; silent; frantic; disappointed; irresponsible; incorrigible; devoted; taciturn; moody; thoroughbred; errant; waggish; flattering; well-grown; pestiferous; ungrateful; beautiful; fair; musing; ragged; cocksure; grinning; pernicious; lawless; criminal; medalled; sheepish; bold; sanguine; quick; forward; capable; penitent; ruddy; sleeping; rare; rude; sympathetic; leprous; unbridled; unthinking; wayward; budding; white-headed; thin-faced; black-aproned; black-eyed; scornful; lascivious; patient; tender; serviceable; scrubbed; aristocratic; peevish; rascally; vigorous; enamored; swarthy; brilliant; wild; weedy; daring; tiresome; nonsensical; turbaned; sordid; dreamy; wanton; winning; sassy; sportive; insolent; headstrong; ardent; healthy; robust; sedulous; aggressive; chivalrous; paltry; insipid; feeble-minded; stolid; clever; pugnacious; problem; gloomy; lonely; fragile; timid; impetuous; boisterous; fiery; heavy-hearted.

BOYCOTT

adjectives
fair; hampering; hostile; personal; private; protective; retaliatory; rigid; unwarranted; universal.

verbs
adopt—; approve—; assail—; coerce by—; counter—; discard—; formulate—; incur—; inflict—; instigate—; institute—; justify—; lift—; organize—; patronize—; prepare for —; proclaim—; punish with—; secure against—; shelter from—; stand firm on—; support—; sweep through—; threaten with —; urge—; warrant—; yield to—; —demoralizes; —deprives; —incites; —injures; —outrages; —persecutes; —prevents; —protects; —reduces; —starves.
(See embargo.)

BOYISH

adverbs
delightfully; remarkably; sturdily; stoutly; adventurously; daringly; good-naturedly; impetuously; grinningly; happily; joyously; coaxingly; energetically; vigorously; refreshingly; inextinguishably; vividly; irresistibly; robustly; ungovernably; hilariously; facetiously; blithely; cheerfully; buoyantly; merrily; triumphantly.

BOYLIKE

adverbs
refreshingly; charmingly; irresistibly; utterly; inexpressably; ineffably.

BRACE

adjectives
arching; auxiliary; extended; movable; strengthening; sustaining.

verbs
buckle on—; discard—; loosen—; regulate —; strap on—; —clasps; —connects; —holds; —pinches; —presses; —secures; —supports; —suspends; —tightens.
(See support, belt.)

BRACELET

adjectives
flaming; jingling; massive; jeweled; glittering; diamond; flashing; glancing.

BRAG (*v*)

adverbs
immodestly; alcoholically; heartily; swaggeringly; idly; shamelessly; unrestrainedly; bullyingly; insolently; immoderately.
(See boast, vaunt.)

BRAGGADOCIO

adjectives
swaggering; hearty; idle; alcoholic.

BRAGGART

adjectives
strutting; cowardly; insolent; debonair; bullying; unscarred.

BRAID

adjectives (stripe, ornament)
beaded; encrusting; curiously-patterned; glittering; intricately-woven; silken; embroidered; tarnished.

verbs
adorn with—; attach—; deck in—; decorate with—; display—; embroider in—; entwine in—; envelop in—; exhibit—; flaunt—; interweave —s; knit in—; untwine—; wind

—; —binds; —denotes; —honors; —represents; —slips.

(See ornament.)

BRAID (*v*)

adverbs
skillfully; dexterously; nimbly; radiantly; verdantly; lustrously; heavily; intricately; curiously.

BRAIDS

adjectives
stubby; heavy; lustrous; jetty; shining; long; twisted; verdant; treble; radiant; glossy.

verbs
confine in—; do up in—; knot—; loose—; plait into—; snip—; tangle—; trim—; twist into—; uncoil—; —fly; —stream from.

(See hair.)

BRAIN

adjectives
editorial; reeling; sobering; inquisitive; clamoring; budding; shrinking; plotting; soothed; human; fevered; maddened; fabulous; boiled; whirling; busy; fertile; comprehensive; excited; dissolving; overseeing; keenest; overheated; immature; distempered; fruitful; logical; teeming; troubled; benumbed; sunburnt; tortured; tired; half-awakened; haunted; seething; rapt; bastard; dying; fatigued; maudlin; loyal; dull; cunning; drunken; scheming; throbbing; bewildered; heavily-taxed; misshapen; feverish; visioning; pure; devious; requisite; burning; addled; callow; young; confused; uncertain; grosser; amiable; brute; disordered; ruthless; maggoty; whisky-addled; flighty; emotive; calculating; celestial; erring; infernal; artless; shrewd; stifled; forging; cool; overtasked; wandering; vacant; sagacious; collective.

verbs
addle—; ballast—; bewilder—; clog—; confuse—; connect with—; craze—; cudgel—; dart through—; dash out—; emanate from—; endow with —s; force—; lash —s; nourish—; overtax—; perplex—; pound through—; prey upon—; rack—; rowel—; sear—; tax—; twist—; weigh upon—; —burns; —conceives; —devises; —fails; —functions; —invents; —lumbers; —races; —weaves; —whirls.

(See mind, intellect.)

BRAINLESS

adverbs
utterly; manifestly; feebly; heavily; blithely; cheerfully; obtusely; fatuously; blatantly; vacuously; incoherently obviously; evidently; oddly; crazily; unfortunately; lamentably; deplorably; admittedly; oafishly; loutishly.

BRAINY

adverbs
acutely; exceptionally; cleverly; astutely; profoundly; solidly; unusually; perspicaciously; reasonably.

BRAKE (*n*)

adjectives
dusky; shrieking; grinding; tricky; rasping; serviceable; shrill; inadequate; hissing.

verbs
adjust —s; apply—; clamp on—; contact—; depend on—; depress—; devise—; draw—; employ—; exercise—; fit with—; free—; jam on—; operate—; pedal—; press on—; regulate—; release—; tighten—; utilize—; —acts; —arrests; —checks; —controls; —fails; —grips; —locks; —reduces; —safeguards; —screams; —shrieks; —squeals.

BRAMBLES

adjectives
straggling; thorny; neglected.

BRANCH (division)

adjectives
collateral; subordinate; subsequent; specialized; rudimentary; purifying; despised; architectural; itinerant; local.

verbs
combine —es; consist of —es; corrupt—; diverge into —es; establish—; flourish in all —es; foster—; invest in—; manage—; propose—; separate into —es; spread out into —es; subdivide into —es; subordinate —es; —affiliates with; —booms; —flourishes; —represents; —springs up; —transacts.

(See department, division.)

BRANCH (tree)

adjectives
waxen; soft; wide; spreading; prominent; overhanging; gigantic; interlaced (pl.); rushing; grown; curving; circumstantial; fragrant; blazing; arching; swaying; murmuring; springy; moss-set; peaceful; long; pendulous; feathery; gnarled; picturesque; independent; coordinate; simpler; towering;

tasseled; gigantic; umbrageous; intruding; flowery; greenwood; nodding; flexible; loaded; heavy; somber; lopped; crackling; beauteous; stirring; thick-leaved; legitimate; plumy; luxurious; virgin; low-bent; delicate; shapely; shattered; phantom; profound; hoary; beauteous; obstructing; isolated; fatal; erect; verdant; flattened; crossing; covered; superfluous; naked; strong; thick; overambitious; luscious; knotted.

verbs
bow—; clip—; crash through—; gnarl—; graft—; hew—; lop off—; perch on—; rock—; trim—; —arches; —s cluster; —decays; —dips; —droops; —drops off; —flowers; —hangs low; —springs out; —supports; —tosses; —withers.
(See twig, limb.)

BRAND

adjectives
competitive; impious; petty; ensanguined; advertised; popular; faithful; largest-selling; reliable; searing; offensive; gloomy; smoldering; casual; blurred; wasted; glimmering; obscure; crooked; standard.

BRAND (v)

adverbs
epigrammatically; impiously; pettishly; popularly; offensively; casually; stigmatically; shamefully.
(See mark.)

BRANDISH (v)

adverbs
ferociously; victoriously; eloquently; proudly; heroically; gloriously; heatedly; furiously; exuberantly.
(See wave.)

BRANDY

adjectives
powerful; vile; cheap; canteen; aromatic; mulled; life-restoring.

verbs
age—; bottle—; distill—; entertain with—; flavor—; imbibe—; import—; mix with—; regale on—; sip—; tax—; —burns; —flavors; —intoxicates.
(See liquor, whiskey.)

BRASH

adverbs
impulsively; thoughtlessly; indiscreetly; touchily; testily; waspily; peevishly; fretfully; irascibly; rashly; foolhardily; incautiously; carelessly; giddily; wildly; hotheadedly; precipitately; daringly; heedlessly; headily; jauntily.

BRASS

adjectives
unenduring; lusterless; winking; carved; glittering; burnished; time-stained; gorgeous; barbaric; tarnished.

BRASSY

adverbs
arrogantly; audaciously; flippantly; insolently; haughtily; impertinently; impudently; petulantly; saucily; shamelessly; terribly; dictatorily; presumptuously; bumptiously; superciliously; swaggeringly; intolerably; offensively; vexatiously; provokingly; unpleasantly.

BRAT

adjectives
furtive; howling; brawling; ill-mannered; ugly; puny; dirty; unwanted; cheeky; sweet; angelic; unruly; ungrateful; unteachable.

BRAVADO

adjectives
unmanly; soaring; humorous; polished; sheer; pure; pitiable; shallow; ferocious; speechless.

BRAVE (n)

adjectives
vanquished; murderous; sensible; aged; venerated; tremulous; reckless; selected; gifted; itinerant.

BRAVE (a)

adverbs
physically; indomitably; nobly; conspicuously; inherently; unflinchingly; heroically; magnificently; uncommonly; eminently; gallantly; resolutely; steadily; essentially; confidently; pluckily; valorously; valiantly; remarkably; unbelievably; sublimely; quietly; patiently; exceedingly.

BRAVE (v)

adverbs
defiantly; fearlessly; tremulously; recklessly; stalwartly; unselfishly; nobly; passionately; haughtily; staunchly; patriotically.
(See defy, dare.)

BRAVERY

adjectives
personal; shining; physical; insolent; sex-

ual; drunken; indomitable; reckless; flawless; noble; audacious; conspicuous; stupid; witless; inherent; unflinching; heroic; magnificent; outrageous; glittering; uncommon; fearful; unsurpassed.

verbs
act in—; add to—; admire—; display—; exhibit—; marvel at—; put on—; saturate with—; swagger in—; —amazes; —includes; —lies.
(See courage, heroism.)

BRAWL

adjectives
disreputable; drunken; street; friendly; desperate; private; coarsest.

verbs
approach—; batter in—; brook—; cause—; engage in—; force—; incite—; squabble in —; —clamors; —conflicts; —noises; —upsets.
(See quarrel, wrangle, row.)

BRAWNY

adverbs
extremely; indomitably; mightily; overpoweringly; stoutly; sturdily; vigorously; unbelievably; clumsily; awkwardly; admirably; amazingly; exceedingly; incredibly; undeniably; sufficiently.

BRAY (v)

adverbs
hideously; hoarsely; intermittently; solemnly; agonizingly; terrifyingly; idiotically; repeatedly; huskily.
(See howl.)

BRAZEN

adverbs
monstrously; shamelessly; daringly; boldly; presumptuously; unbecomingly; unsuitably; jauntily; airily; arrogantly; impudently; irreverently; disagreeably; ridiculously; offensively; detestably; hatefully; obnoxiously; excessively; foolishly; nauseatingly; indecently; insolently; incredibly; unwarrantably; atrociously; odiously.

BREACH

adjectives
formidable; continual; unpardonable; social; incurable; deplorable; irreconcilable; perceptible; dreadful; momentary; temporary; general; absolute; religious; flagrant; unhealed; monstrous; meditated.

verbs
excuse—; produce—; repair—; smooth over —; suffer—; widen—; —damages; —disrupts; —fractures; —infracts; —infringes upon; —injures; —outlaws; —ruptures; —separates; —violates; —widens.
(See gap, violation, infringement, infraction.)

BREAD

adjectives
warm; stiff; frozen; daily; gnawed; moldy; sacred; rising; substantial; living; rain-soaked; wheaten; insipid; elfin; unleavened; bitter; blessed; broken; sliced.

verbs
apportion—; beg—; blacken—; break—with; brown—; consume—; cram with—; crave—; crumb—; deprive of—; devour—; dispense —; display—; divide—; earn—; knead—; munch—; nibble—; offer—; partake of—; prepare—; process—; provide—; ration—; restrict to—; sell for—; shape—; sustain with—; tax—; vend—; win—; —nourishes; —satiates; —stales; —strengthens.
(See food.)

BREADTH

adjectives
enormous; bare; unmoved; lyrical; viewless; diverse; endless; scant; epical; rippling; glassy; immoderate; spacious; ample; impassable.

BREAK

adjectives
appreciable; notable; numerous (pl.); unhappy; fatal; final; distinct; sharp; complete; agreeable; unhindered.

BREAK (v)

adverbs
eventually; unwarily; theoretically; treacherously; subsequently; deliberately; violently; unreasonably; forcibly; gratuitously; grimly; incoherently; intentionally; threateningly; advisedly; perilously; hilariously; fatally; distinctly; completely.
(See smash, shatter, burst, demolish.)

BREAKDOWN

adjectives
nervous; moral; universal; disastrous; incipient; mental; practical.

BREAKER

adjectives
foaming; ponderous; rising; swelling; ceaseless; never-silent; immense; wicked; enormous; tumbling; reasonless.

land among —s; warn of —s; —booms; —
verbs
crashes; —crushes; —dashes; —destroys; —flies in; —foams; —lashes; —murmurs; —passes over; —pounds; —rolls in; —subdues; —swells; —tumbles.
(See wave, billow.)

BREAKFAST

adjectives
sophisticated; substantial; hurried; magnificent; wedding; cheerful; gobbled; belated; hearty; impromptu; leisurely; gloomy; abstemious; hospitable; pleasant; supplementary; wholesome.

verbs
adjourn to—; announce—; attack—; beckon to—; bolt—; entertain at—; fast until—; furnish with—; gobble—; gulp—; miss—; partake of—; prepare—; provide—; relish —; rush—; serve—; snatch—; take—; —appeases; —replenishes; —satiates.
(See meal, dinner, supper, food.)

BREAST

adjectives
defenceless; heaving; secret; cavernous; beautiful; gloomy; dauntless; billowy; brooding; snowy; throbbing; dolorous; tortured; rounded; large; tight; swollen; repentant; vast; soothing; barren; sanguine; suckling; happy; glossy; greasy; watery; inspired; boiling; bloody; obedient; elongated; half-tamed; calm; martyr; maternal; well-developed; laboring; hideous; hollow-swelling; feathered; torpid; shuddering; fragrant; woolly; sunken; ample; misshapen; tumultuous; grief-filled; responsive; troubled; palpitating; spotted; peaceable; haughty; silent; careworn; panting; unconscious; pious; guileless; gentle; patriotic; bare; careless; distended; vice-polluted; faultless; oppressed; tawny; speckled; stimulated; supporting; snow-cold; tender; infinite; spangled; uplifted; wanton; sagging; scourged; protruding; mailed; unwary; rugged; stormy; emaciated; full; dulled; immeasurable; harmless; devoted.

verbs
adorn—; bare—; beat—; boil in—; clasp to—; cling to—; crush to—; distend—; disturb—; dry up—; ease—; exhaust—; expand —; fold on—; harbor in—; inflame—with; inflate—; infuse—with; inhabit—; lock in —; lodge in—; nurse at—; penetrate—; pillow on—; plant in—; rend—; smite—; soothe—; strain to—; thunder in—; torment —; trouble—; warm—; —burns with; —flutters; —heaves; —secretes; —throbs.
(See bosom, chest, heart.)

BREASTWORK

adjectives
serpentine; substantial; gingerbread; military.

BREATH

adjectives
fiery; venomous; struggling; aimless; bated; extinguished; unsavory; delighted; sweet-scented; fragrant; idle; ryhthmic; vulgar; warbling; unwholesome; morning; fearful; quivering; foul; blessed; uneasy; snowy; expiring; lightest; infant; untroubled; stifled; stertorous; fetid; dumb; transitory; quick; furtive; tender; ambient; delicate; meager; surprised; hard; wicked; fluttering; damp; sobbing; quivering; dulcet; common; harmonious; maiden; tremulous; full; relieving; divine; clean; soft; rose-laden; wine-laden; smoking; fugitive; bad; cosmic; scorching; delicate; invisible; duteous; fleeting; deadly; rude; consuming; sour; painful; blasting; feverous; spiritual; tempestuous; undying; vital; icy; frightened; clear; cool; warm; natural; gasping; miserable; transient; poisonous; cankering; frosted; panting; rattling; ebbing; infantile; golden; applausive; difficult; sugary; free; audible; suspended; transparent; sharp; worthless; royal; wanting; stinking; fatal; passionate; hot; balsam; contagious; tobacco; scandalous; blighting; sulphurous; meditative; unanimous; offensive; prophet; scant; pestilential; holy; failing; vile.

verbs
animate by—; bate—; catch—; discharge—; draw—; exhale—; exhaust—; frost—; gasp for—; inhale—; labor for—; lose—; murmur—; pen up—; poison—; puff out—; recover—; regain—; release—; revive—; sigh—; smother—; stifles—; struggle for—; suck in—; waste—; —emanates; —reeks.
(See air, respiration, breathing.)

BREATHE (v)

adverbs
stertorously; irregularly; assiduously; audibly; rhythmically; expiringly; uneasily; untroubledly; transitorily; flutteringly; sobbingly; gaspingly; failingly.
(See inhale, pant, gasp.)

BREATHING

adjectives
cumbered; heavy; light; soft; shallow; audible; regular; labored; peaceful; fervent;

placid; ryhthmical; tender; noisy; fluttered; holy; distressful; steady; abundant; hoarse; hurried; quickened; convulsive; alcoholic; long; quiet.

verbs
arrest—; choke—; correct—; ease—; hamper—; impede—; induce—; interfere with —; labor—; lessen—; obstruct—; restore —; smother—; stimulate—; train—.
(See respiration, breath.)

BREATHLESSNESS

adjectives
induced; parenthetical; distressing.

BREECHES

adjectives
tight; leather; drab; torn; baggy; muddy; tweed; nankeen.

BREED

adjectives
ancient; sporting; selective; unsocial; truer; elastic; pure-blooded; reckless; fabulous; recognized; superior; coarser; irritable; voracious.

verbs
adhere to—; ally—; characterize—; combine—; cross—; defile—; degenerate—; despise—; develop—; display—; distinguish —; domesticate—; examine—; exhaust—; exhibit—; exterminate—; generate—; improve—; mingle—; mix—; originate—; perpetuate—; preserve—; procreate—; propagate—; recognize—; strain—; —competes for; —overruns.
(See race.)

BREED (*v*)

adverbs
prodigiously; intelligently; luxuriantly; deiicately; fabulously; superiorly; selectively.
(See multiply, rear, train.)

BREEDING

adjectives
artificial; exquisite; noble; gentle; courteous; virtuous; soft; tender; essential.

BREEDING

adjectives (animals)
straight-line; selective; fertile; aristocratic.

BREEZE

adjectives
sobbing; varying; desultory; increasing; favorable; roving; blessed; subtle; night; summer; scented; playful; rising; steadying; native; faint; wayward; rude; slumbering; imperceptible; cooling; voluptuous; sportive; tonic; telltale; dying; sea; balmy; spicy; healthful; blistering; murmuring; chilling; southerly; fresh; blowing; sweeping; unsatisfied; zephyr; sluggish; nimble; ruffling; searching; western; fitful; sacred; wafting; whispering; treacherous; lightest; caressing; languorous; noiseless; lingering; river; lusty; passing; savage; crooning; tantalizing; penetrating; stray; pungent; stinging; vagrant; mild; raw; westerly; hovering; wanton; genial; odorous; vernal; polar; perfumed; salt-laden; lazy; casual; smoky; increasing; swift; uncontrollable; propitious; peaceful; refreshing; ocean; constant; soft; billowing; woodland; stirring; invigorating; tender; sweet; dependable; tantalizing; bracing.

verbs
bask in—; catch—; float in—; head into—; nod in—; rock with—; rustle in—; scent—; tremble in—; wave in—; —billows; —brushes; —caresses; —dies; —fans; —flutters; —freshens; —kisses; —lulls; —pauses; —ruffles; —rumples; —rustles; —scuds by; —sighs; —steals through; —stirs; —sweeps down; —tousles; —wafts; —wanders; —whistles.
(See wind, current.)

BREEZY

adverbs
delightfully; joyously; buoyantly; jovially; irresponsibly; gaily; vivaciously; brightly; wholesomely; heartily; irresistibly; flippantly; merrily; happily; gleefully; laughingly; rapturously; cheerfully; foolishly; childishly; youthfully; pleasantly; charmingly; exquisitely; daintily; agreeably; habitually.

BRETHREN

adjectives
dreamy; venerable; erring; cloudy; luckier; weak; civilized; wicked; twin-souled; speculative; fortunate; renegade; amiable; literary.

BREVITY

adjectives
laconic; pregnant; voluble; algebraic; tabloid; reassuring cynical; businesslike; curt; characteristic; voluminous; fallacious; laudable.

BRIBE

adjectives
base; timely; unworthy; innocent; custom-

ary; efficient; costly; enormous; extravagant; unclenched; septennial.

verbs
administer—; buy with—; condemn—; consent to—; consider—; exact—; extort—; forfeit—; offer—; pay—; pocket—; procure—; refuse—; surrender to—; tender—; yield to —; —abuses; —corrupts; —entraps; —induces; —influences; —offends; —perverts; —purchases; —purloins; —tempts.
(See inducement, graft.)

BRIBERY

adjectives
barefaced; corrupt; covert; daring; flagrant; offensive; open; surreptitious; vile.

verbs
accuse of—; achieve by—; acquit of—; arrest for—; charge with—; conceal—; convict of—; detect—; frustrate—; gain by—; obtain by—; practise—; punish—; purchase by—; remove for—; solicit—; yield to—; —flourishes; —motivates; —procures; —scandalizes; —sways; —tends to.
(See robbery, plunder.)

BRICK

adjectives
mellow; tawny; warm-toned; Georgian; adobe; harsh; sliding; smoke-blackened; enameled; soft; hard; front.

verbs
bake —s; base on —s; build with —s; cart —s; chisel—; construct of—; cut into—; dry —s; face with —s; fireproof —s; front with —s; harden into —s; heave —s; hem in with —s; inlay with —s; inscribe —s; knead into —s; lay —s; measure —s; pave with —s; prepare —s; pyramid —s; reinforce with —s; shape into —s; strain —s; toss —s; trowel —s; wall in with —s; —s collapse; —s crumble; —endures; mold into —.
(See stone.)

BRIDE

adjectives
peerless; prospective; insatiate; passionless; fastidious; virgin; beloved; blooming; perjured; pretty; bonny; first-made; affianced; gallant; truant; contraband; blushing; vivacious; country.

verbs
act as—; announce—; array—; assemble round—; attend—; bestow upon—; capture —; choose—; confuse—; congratulate—; costume—; dress—; drink to—; endow—; fete—; give away—; greet—; indulge—; kiss—; pledge—; proclaim—; purloin—; serenade—; shower—; toast—; welcome—; win—; yearn for—; —blushes; —pales; —trembles.
(See queen, sweetheart.)

BRIDEGROOM

adjectives
destined; embarrassed; fickle; sturdy; youthful; happy; busy; shy; recreant; bold; brisk.

BRIDGE

adjectives
substantial; indigenous; antiquated; well-constructed; picturesque; rude; covered; mighty; famous; sturdy; swinging; massive; arched; iron; railroad; rustic; medieval; hideous; battered; spiritual; wooden; commodious; fortified; trembling; wide; narrow; rambling; portable; draw; proud; trussed.

verbs
arch—; block—; chain—; construct—; cross —; design—; destroy—; draw—; engineer —; flow under—; fortify—; gird—; imperil —; load—; lower—; overhaul—; patrol—; pattern—; plan—; strain—; suspend from —; sweep away—; —arches; —collapses; —connects; —conveys; —links; —spans; —supports; —surmounts; —totters; —unites.
(See span, support, structure.)

BRIDGE (v)

adverbs
successfully; picturesquely; massively; medievally; spiritually; proudly; tremblingly; diplomatically.
(See connect, link.)

BRIEF

adjectives
apostolic; honest; argumentative.

BRIEF (a)

adverbs
ridiculously; delightfully; agreeably; pitifully; disappointingly; tragically; mercifully; humanely; unreasonably; dramatically; smartly; inexcusably; characteristically; remarkably; satisfactorily; surprisingly; pleasantly; compactly; laconically; conveniently; curtly; commendably; strikingly; sensibly; wisely; prudently; tersely.

BRIEF CASE

adjectives
bulging; dog-eared; important-looking; mys-

terious; over-stuffed; resplendent; secret-charged; shabby; shiny; streamlined.

verbs
clasp— —; cram into— —; dig into— —; extract from— —; fasten— —; pack in— —; strap— —; stuff— —; whip open— —; — —bulges.
(See bag, satchel.)

BRIGADE

adjectives
advancing; combined; battle-toughened; favored; heroic; invincible; thundering.

verbs
command—; compose—; divide—; drill—; enlist in—; enroll—; form—; inspect—; instruct—; make up—; organize—; train—; transfer to—; transport—; —charges; —forages; —hunts; —marches.
(See gathering, regiment, troops, army.)

BRIGAND

adjectives
ferocious; ruthless; fugitive; veritable.

BRIGHT

adverbs
indescribably; dazzlingly; miraculously; ingeniously; amazingly; splendidly; magnificently; unbelievably; unusually; wonderfully; marvellously; artificially; scintillatingly; starrily; intolerably; painfully; bewilderingly; blindingly; unwontedly; suspiciously; crystally; luminously; radiantly; splendidly; unbearably; intensely; gaudily.

BRIGHTEN (v)

adverbs
intensely; momentarily; perceptibly; vividly; dazzlingly; artificially; bewilderingly; superficially; blindingly; unnaturally; intellectually; matchlessly.
(See cheer, illuminate.)

BRIGHTNESS

adjectives
tranquil; dazzling; artificial; scintillant; starry; shifting; shining; superficial; painful; intolerable; transcendent; bewildering; enlivening; unfathomed; expansive; glowing; gradual; sharp; windy; steely; rising; cold; blinding; unmoving; burning; unwonted; fiery; suspicious; poisonous; crystal.

BRILLIANCE

adjectives
youthful; mental; stylistic; dazzling; scintillating; roseate; intellectual; utmost; epigrammatic; feverish; crystal; signal; magnificent; polished; matchless; daring; spontaneous; eye-aching; uncanny; solemn; inevitable; lustrous.

verbs
boast—; hide—; impress with—; intensify—; polish into—; radiate—; shade—; shine in—; sing of—; sparkle with—; strike with—; —amazes; —dazzles; —overpowers; —pervades.
(See splendor.)

BRILLIANCY

adjectives
unnatural; dreamlike; exquisite; sufficient; solar; heightened; blinding; imposing; strange; ivory-like; technical; irregular; sparkling; superhuman.

BRILLIANT

adverbs
scintillatingly; miraculously; cleverly; ingeniously; notably; amazingly; signally; socially; intellectually; dazzlingly; smartly; inexpressibly; indescribably; surprisingly; splendidly; undoubtedly; incredibly; unusually; wonderfully; ostentatiously.

BRIM

adjectives
sparkling; medium-sized; huge; picot; glancing; rolling.

BRINE

adjectives
restless; bitter; mid-sea; rushing; audacious; fragrant; rolling; hoary; fateful; eye-offending; first-made; desolate; level; glassy; hissing.

BRING (v)

adverbs
lightly; finally; rarely; slyly; festinately; constantly; painfully; accordingly; vividly; inevitably; continuously; obviously; ultimately; simultaneously; vaguely.
(See carry, conduct, convey.)

BRINK

adjectives
plashy; dim; breezy; chilling; eternal; shadowy; rushy; precipitous; utmost; abrupt; sandy; giddy.

BRINY

adverbs

bitterly; brackishly; acridly; hotly; pungently; toughly; saltily; spicily; sharply; unsavorily; strongly; disagreeably; unpleasantly; horribly; aromatically; perceptibly; pleasingly; subtly; odoriferously; sufficiently; magnificently; properly.

BRISK

adverbs

tremendously; apallingly; helpfully; efficiently; singularly; habitually; excitedly; noisily; restlessly; nimbly; gracefully; energetically; cheerfully; actively; alertly; vivaciously; surprisingly; youthfully; capably; unexpectedly; quickly; dangerously; smartly; spryly; fleetly; trippingly; lightly; busily.

BRISKNESS

adjectives

keen; flavored; characteristic.

BRISTLE (*v*)

adverbs

defiantly; horridly; furiously; pugnaciously; militantly; bellicosely; belligerently; vindictively.

(See argue.)

BRITISH

adverbs

incurably; stolidly; loyally; sensibly; respectably; obstinately; stubbornly; proudly; unconditionally; obviously; manifestly; essentially; securely; permanently; urbanely; imperturbably; serenely; soundly; stoutly; devotedly; ardently; staunchly; punctiliously; incorruptibly; correctly; virtuously; shrewdly.

BRITISHER

adjectives

sound; solid; sensible; usual; well-fed; obstinate; muddling.

BRITTLE

adverbs

unfortunately; regrettably; exceedingly; smartly; delicately; crisply; lamentably; deplorably; deceptively; unexpectedly; surprisingly; slightly; highly; overly; extremely; evidently; unprofitably; unserviceably; inconveniently; impracticably.

BROAD

adverbs

splendidly; magnificently; illimitably; extensively; spaciously; liberally; boundlessly; infinitely; immensely; admirably; amply; adequately; grandly; majestically; expansively; inexpressibly; capaciously; roomily; extremely; enormously; endlessly; epically; immoderately; unbelievably.

BROADCAST

adjectives

commercial; unsponsored; regional; nationwide.

BROADCAST (*v*)

adverbs

grandiloquently; commercially; regionally; universally; temporarily; professionally; annually; popularly.

(See speak.)

BROADCLOTH

adjectives

bullet; lava; popular; shantung.

BROADEN (*v*)

adverbs

marvelously; appreciably; tremendously; noticeably; immeasurably; imperceptibly; abruptly; gradually.

(See enlarge, expand.)

BROADSIDE

adjectives

genuine; fearful; death-dealing; thundering; tremendous; crashing.

BROCADE

adjectives

jeweled; ancient; gorgeous; stiff; correct; bright; exquisite; historic.

BROCHURE

adjectives

innocent; artistic; modern; intimate; expensive; slender; rare.

BROGUE

adjectives

adorable; quaint; little; soft; clouted; brisk; Irish.

BROIL

adjectives

murderous; internal; prolonged; fierce.

BROKER

adjectives

disreputable; dummy; staid; loose-living; middle-aged.

BRONZE

adjectives

precious; valuable; burnished; enduring; immortal; inimitable; monumental; lined.

BRONZE (a)

adverbs

richly; tawnily; deeply; elaborately; strangely; incongruously; sumptuously; splendidly; magnificently; shimmeringly; ruddily; beautifully; superbly.

BROOD

adjectives

callow; straggling; lowering; hideous; unmanageable; erring; enormous; hapless; late-begotten; human; successive; spurious; shameful; dusky; hateful; writhing; silver; bastard; erratic; gorgeous; infernal; venomous; boreal; heavenly; noisy; viperous.

verbs

bring forth—; cherish—; cultivate—; exhibit—; gather—; give birth to—; hatch—; hover over—; incubate—; mother—; nest —; nourish—; nurse—; nurture—; orphan —; rear—; select—; tend—; tolerate—; warm—; —clucks; —follows; —originates from.

(See offspring, race, flock.)

BROOD (v)

adverbs

solitarily; somberly; vacantly; enviously; mournfully; reverently; haplessly; humanly; bitterly; maternally; superstitiously; fruitlessly; drearily; despondently.

(See ponder, meditate.)

BROODING

adjectives

subsequent; bitter; melancholy; constant; maternal; superstitious; concentrated; fruitless; dreary; despondent.

BROOK

adjectives

sluggish; delectable; south-sloping; unreposing; rapid; boisterous; wandering; brawling; glassy; careless; shallow; hidden; sedgy; rain-full; thirst-inviting; defiled; rippling; weedy; gushing; tumbling; mazy; copious; unsunned; struggling; babbling; gurgling; glittering; limpid; unseen; patient; peaceful; passionless; rushing; shrunken; inland; reedy; swift-running; crisped; hurrying; rushy; pellucid; happy; murmuring; narrow; silver; bisecting; cool; meandering; sweet; perennial; dancing; transparent; rocky; mountain; sparkling; companionable; pebbly; winding; wild; clear; woodland.

verbs

bog in—; bound—; bridge—; cast into—; frequent—; haunt—; pass over—; splash in—; swell—; wade in—; —babbles; —bubbles; —bursts forth; —chatters; —dances; —flows on; —frolics; —groans; —gurgles; —gushes; —murmurs; —races along; —rambles; —ranges; —sings; —swells; —whirls.

(See stream.)

BROOM

adjectives

careless; coarse; ever-questing; immaculate; industrious; lopsided; restless; rude.

verbs

apply—; brandish—; employ—; fill—; peddle —s; tie into—; trim—; twist—; wield —; —brushes; —collects; —delves; —gathers; —raises; —removes; —renews; —routs; —unearths.

(See brush.)

BROTH

adjectives

comforting; stomach-fortifying; satisfying; substantial; tasteless; watery.

verbs

ladle—; sip—; spoon—; strain—; test—; —nourishes; —simmers; —steams; —warms.

(See soup.)

BROTHER

adjectives

kind; indulgent; gentle; arbitrary; fiendish; cruel; illustrious; amorous; truant; healthful; affectionate; poor; unworthy; unemotional; new; distinguished; sworn; loftier; recreant; admirable; manly; ecclesiastical; true; foster; lost; ungrateful; renowned; awe-stricken; heroic; neglected; harrowed; malleable; rebellious; dismal; elder; serious; devoted; erring; unseemly; eligible; aristocratic; obvious; undeniable; slow-witted; indubitable; heavy-going; paretic; blood; model; imperial; puissant.

BROTHERHOOD

adjectives

bristly; critical; human; great; blood; subtle; meritable; idealized; diplomatic; close; cordial; indissoluble; spontaneous; sworn.

verbs

address—; ally with—; associate with—; band into—; cherish—; create—; devote to —; establish—; fraternize with—; fuse in —; head—; join—; league in—; obey—;

organize—; protect—; persecute—; regale —; resign from—; rupture—; salute—; support—; sustain—; tie to—; unite—; —acts; —aids; —arrays against; —convenes; —declines; —equalizes; —flourishes; —instructs.

(See society, fellowship.)

BROTHERLY

adverbs

extremely; heart-warmingly; hardly; affectionately; cordially; intimately; sincerely; sympathetically; amicably; heartily; benevolently; benignly; charitably; considerately; lovingly; unselfishly; tenderly; accommodatingly; good-naturedly; graciously; warm-heartedly; adoringly; devotedly; fondly; adorably; charmingly; admirably; helpfully; companiably; congenially; surprisingly; unexpectedly.

BROUGHAM

adjectives

cozy; little; well-appointed; shiny.

BROW

adjectives

handsome; delicate; beautiful; illumined; bland; amiable; fair; classical; lofty; manly; noble; social; lily; triumphant; low; white; clouded; black; heavy; straight; dark; blonde; rosy; sunburned; freckled; bushy; shaggy; roughened; grizzled; thick; puckered; ruffled; knotted; furrowed; wrinkled; corrugated; contracted; drawn; sad; troubled; overcast; mournful; brooding; swarthy; interrogative; scowling; frowning; stormy; startled; puzzled; plucked; painted; fine; pencilled; arched; whimsical; thin; peaked; curved; meeting (pl.); beetling; well-carved; prominent; level; lifted; placid; tranquil; damp; perspiring; fevered; heaving; crotchety; ironical; pimpled; elderly; austere; intelligent; glistening; deplorable; massive; haughty; dusky; livid; thoughtful; withered; innocent; craggy; calm; angry; weather-beaten; clammy; thorn-pierced; healthful; callow; serene; high; cold; shadowy; intellectual; gloomy; heated; royal; guilt-steeled; scarred; infant; sacred; surly; purpled; upturned; snowy; unaltered; crownless; throbbing; pensive; broiling; olive-tinctured; thunder-blasted; burning; imperious; sun-kissed; barbarian; hopeless; relaxed; rugged; imperial; bewitching; pale; amiable; unsullied; bent; immense; blue-veined; threatening; unkind; pain-knotted; laurel-laden; impenetrable; deep-pent; channeled; ingenuous; contemptuous; stately; conquest-branded; inky; triumphant; wreathed; pedantic; pitying; kindred; profulgent; wizard; animated; stunned; mild; milky; crescent; haggard; earnest; broad; gracious; bared; hooded; bloodless; aching; youthful; dreamy; overhanging; polished; pallid; worn; drooping; godlike; candid; transparent; bald; anxious; smarting; bent; pretty; unsullied; mummied; unwritten; warlike; ensanguined; resigned; sober; compressed; regent; dauntless; overwhelming; spiritual; hazel; burthened; projecting; mobile; airy; averted; peaceful; bronzed; careworn.

verbs

arch—; contract—; crown—; elevate—; flush—; furrow—; gild—; harden—; kiss —; knit—; lift—; mop—; plait—; pluck —s; pucker—; purse—; quirk—; shadow —; singe—; smite—; smooth—; uplift—; wrinkle—; —s bridge; —darkens; —menaces; —s struggle together; —throbs.

(See forehead, eyebrow, countenance.)

BROWBEATEN

adverbs

submissively; shamefully; meekly; disgracefully; humiliatingly; disconsolately; humbly; abjectly; frightfully; horribly; terribly; fearfully; unhappily; incredibly; astoundingly; alarmingly; coweringly; tremulously; dreadfully; nervously; portentously; unforgivably; evidently; visibly; indefensibly.

BROWN

adjectives

lustrous; vehement; russet; unsightly; golden; country; dainty; mellow; shining; turf; ruddy; crisp; curious; grayish; glossy; twilight; yellowish; chestnut; pinkish; autumnal; gleaming; sedate.

BROWN (a)

adverbs

ruddily; lustrously; deeply; richly; gloriously; curiously; crisply; lightly; tawnily; sumptuously; splendidly; superbly; shimmeringly; magnificently.

BROWSE (v)

adverbs

phlegmatically; contentedly; intellectually; placidly; happily; abstractedly; absently.

(See nibble, feed, graze.)

BRUISE

adjectives

livid; marring; hurting; vast; innocent; cruel.

verbs
apply to—; bandage—; heal—; incur—; inflict —s; produce—; receive—; salve—; soothe—; treat—; —dents; —disables; —discolors; —disfigures; —hurts; —infects; —injures; —lacerates; —mangles; —mars; —swells; —weakens.
(See injury, contusion.)

BRUISE (v)

adverbs
ineradicably; severely; agonizingly; disfiguringly; horribly; temporarily; villainously; mercilessly.
(See injure, hurt.)

BRUNETTE

adjectives
small; vivacious; indeterminable.

BRUNETTE (a)

adverbs
wondrously; gloriously; adorably; strikingly; petitely; vivaciously; piquantly; irresistibly; charmingly; saucily; startlingly; captivatingly; fascinatingly; distinctly; radiantly; glowingly; darkly; provocatively; astonishingly; starrily; artificially; naturally; skilfully; enchantingly; bewitchingly.

BRUSH

adjectives
deft; burnishing; illuminating; frugal; obliterating; purging; scavenging; sweeping.

verbs
apply—; attach—; cleanse with—; dust with —; employ—; paint with—; scrub with—; shape—; shine with—; smooth over with—; spread with—; stroke—; sweep with—; wipe with—; —refreshes; —renews; —revives.
(See broom.)

BRUSH (artist)

adjectives
potent; profound; lavish; fragrant; skillful.

BRUSH (plant)

adjectives
leafy; stunted; ragged; meager; aboriginal; sage; alert; tangled; fringing; rabbit; icy; dangerous; flaming; scrawny; crackling.

BRUSH (v)

adverbs
aimlessly; haughtily; hastily; tenderly; effectively; vivaciously; skillfully; interminably; monotonously.
(See wipe.)

BRUSQUE

adverbs
dashingly; fussily; hurriedly; impetuously; hastily; precipitately; urgently; expeditiously; fitfully; boisterously; furiously; outrageously; roughly; uproariously; violently; excitedly; stormily; extravagantly; ostentatiously; hysterically; uncontrollably; irrepressibly; turbulently; wildly; rampageously.

BRUTAL

adverbs
abominably; terribly; unspeakably; villainously; systematically; needlessly; inherently; harshly; sharply; savagely; coarsely; ferociously; nefariously; detestably; indecently; obtrusively; ostentatiously; foully; insolently; caustically; venomously; perversely; incorrigibly; inhumanly; cruelly; atrociously; obdurately; truculently; maliciously; intentionally; treacherously; outrageously; ruthlessly; stonily; barbarously; virulently; diabolically; invidiously; blatantly; flagrantly; openly; resolutely.

BRUTALITY

adjectives
quaint; sacrificed; horrible; primitive; suave; frantic; unspeakable; blind; amazing; unintelligent; villainous; continued; systematic; noisy; downright; needless; inherent; harsh; sharp; ugly; savage; coarse; ferocious; sheer.

verbs
appall by—; breed—; expose—of; imbue with—; inculcate—; indulge in—; refrain from—; subject to—; teach—; treat with—; —cuts; —degrades.
(See cruelty.)

BRUTE

adjectives
shy; perverse; treacherous; conscious; unfeeling; perfect; nasty; polite; ferocious; tawny; horrid; goaded; barbarous; hardy; lustful; grazing; repulsive; drunken; noxious; greedy; innocent; bristling; savage; ponderous; cowardly; self-confessed; surly; dangerous; ruffian; untamed; lowest; husky; sulky; selfish; canny; accursed; exhausted; avenging; cold-blooded; menacing; maddened; bulky; foul; bestial; blundering; evil; designing; ugly; meanest; villainous; merciless; gross; dissipated; burly; callous.

verbs
bring out—; charm—; ensnare—; hypnotize —; polish—; quell—; silence—; slay—;

tame—; worship—; —bolts; —charges; —rends; —survives; —thunders.
(See animal, beast.)

BUBBLE

adjectives
headed; ascending; crystalline; iridescent; innumerable (pl.); lazy; broken; pricked; intoxicating; soothing; pretty; sparkling; flimsy; flattened; beaded; wandering; empty.

verbs
agitate into —s; blow —s; cover with —s; delude with —s; emit —s; produce —s; send forth —s; —amuses; —dances; —dissipates; —drifts; —escapes; —explodes; —fascinates; —floats; —rises; —scintillates; —springs from; —swells.
(See balloon.)

BUBBLE (v)

adverbs
gayly; effervescently; hissingly; foamingly; exhilaratingly; joyously; sputteringly.
(See flow, whirl.)

BUCK (v)

adverbs
spiritedly; suddenly; abruptly; belligerently; spitefully; venomously; wildly.
(See prepare, plan.)

BUD

adjectives
springing; kindling; swaying; bloomless; sluggish; tender; dejected; bursting; fadeless; unexpanded; flower-enfolding; sweetest; masked; dripping; wayside; sulking; terminal; leaf-enfolded; axillary.

verbs
blast—; blight—; clip—; form—; frost—; graft—; kill—; nip—; sprout —s; —s appear; —breaks into bloom; —bursts forth; —s cluster; —s crowd together; —decorates; —develops; —expands; —flowers; —glistens; —matures; —multiplies; —produces; —projects; —promises; —prospers; —reveals; —sprouts; —swells; —unfolds.
(See flower, plant, bulb.)

BUDGET

adjectives
biennial; admirable; bearskin; balanced; moderate; scanty; heart-shaking; ordinary; family; tentative; extraordinary.

verbs
balance—; institute—; jeopardize—; promulgate—; prune—; reduce—; shape—; slash—; stagger under —s; swell—; tax—.
(See estimate, plan.)

BUDGET (v)

adverbs
impecuniously; meticulously; biennially; admirably; annually; tentatively; shrewdly; dexterously; wisely; conservatively.

BUFF

adjectives
rich; golden; glowing.

BUFFALO

adjectives
aggressive; belligerent; bellowing; charging; furious; grunting; humping; powerful; possessive; primitive; prairie-lording; stampeding; roaming.

verbs
domesticate—; exterminate—; farm with—; herd—; overrun with—; plough with —s; protect—; pursue—; stampede—; tame—; teem with—; water—; yoke—; —gores; —grazes; —grunts; —lumbers; —ranges; —roams; —wallows in mud.
(See bison, ox, animal.)

BUFFETINGS

adjectives
reminiscent; repeated; merciless; unkind; intermittent.

BUFFOON

adjectives
enormous; gluttonous; ordinary; stammering; pantomime.

BUFFOONERY

adjectives
exhibitionist; engaging; wanton; mad.

BUG

adjectives
annoying; encroaching; gregarious; insidious; invincible; inoffensive; obnoxious; over-companionable; persevering; patrolling; pestiferous; shelter-seeking; shrilly-serenading; undaunted; diminutive; droning; hovering; jeweled; predatory; piping; snug; vagrant; villainous; vigorous; wiggling.

verbs
destroy—; dissect—; exterminate —s; observe—; spray—; swat—; —s blight; —s bore; —s breed; —s lurk; —stings; —sucks.
(See insect.)

BUGLE

adjectives
blaring; bold; dominant; duty-calling; invocative; piercing; silence-shattering; rousing; sonorous; lamenting; peace-lulling.

verbs
assemble at—; awaken by—; march to—; overblow—; rally to—; respond to—; retire to—; scale—; sound—; —alarms; —arouses; —blares; —blasts; —calls; —declares; —echoes; —orders; —signals; —summons; —trumpets; —wails; —wakens; —warns.

(See instrument, horn, trumpet.)

BUILD

adjectives
elephantine; slender; sinewy; enduring; curious; heroic; gigantic; warlike; sturdy; ascetic; proportional.

BUILD (*v*)

ostensibly; impregnably; simultaneously; airily; irrevocably; variously; intelligently; synthetically; stoutly; expressly; sturdily; magnificently; substantially; enduringly; proportionally; secularly; incomparably; ecclesiastically; shabbily.

(See erect, construct, raise.)

BUILDER

adjectives
timid; prominent; independent; empire; sturdy; hard-working; ambitious; wonderful; body; pioneer; home; prospective; vigorous; devastating.

verbs
—alters; —bids; —commissions; —constructs; —contracts for; —designs; —determines; —develops; —directs; —draws; —employs; —erects; —establishes; —estimates; —excavates; —fireproofs; —guarantees; —initials; —leases; —operates; —profits; —remodels; —renovates; —specifies; —submits; —undertakes.

(See carpenter.)

BUILDING

adjectives
imposing; magnificent; attractive; palatial; rich; adorned; handsome; spacious; wonderful; beautiful; pretentious; fine; substantial; comfortable; monster; mammoth; giant; towering; commercial; Gargantuan; ancient; antiquated; century-old; grim; obsolescent; vestigial; solid; massive; great; stone; immense; gawky; ramshackle; barnlike; flimsy; rickety; rambling; straggling; squatting; cluttered; dirty-looking; sour; dingy; grimy; false-fronted; smoke-stained; bleak; gloomy; wretched; ugly; forlorn; sinister; peculiar; somber; severe; white-walled; red-roofed; multicolored; gaunt; red-bricked; weathered; ivy-grown; long; flat; low; clustered; silent; gilt-domed; unique; sun-flooded; commodious; consistorial; barrack-like; pagan; secular; combustible; oppressive; aggressive; impertinent; tame; uninteresting; proposed; dismal; conventual; tumble-down; unpretentious; heterogeneous; detached; ill-looking; conservative; irregular; opulent; profane; speculative; old-fashioned; well-constructed; extensive; monumental; decayed; moss-covered; useful; ghostlike; worthy; notable; beggarly; ruinous; eccentric; contemporaneous; flanking; arsenal-like; murky; unoccupied; sleepy; deserted; shabby; admonitory; elegant; dilapidated; ecclesiastical; capacious; incomparable; proud; drab.

verbs
clutter up—; demolish—; design—; dominate—; enlarge—; erect —s; evacuate—; extend—; inhabit—; lodge in—; modernize—; raze—; renovate—; restore—; revolutionize—; segregate into—; separate—; throng through—; —looms; —pierces; —straddles; —towers.

(See edifice, structure, house, barn.)

BULB (light)

adjectives
feeble; electric; flickering; unveiled; rarefied; myriad (pl.); inanimate.

BULB (plant)

adjectives
spring; early-flowering.

verbs
bury—; cultivate—; insert—; market—; raise—; sow—; uproot—; —blossoms; —buds; —bursts; —develops; —dilates; —flowers; —nourishes; —radiates; —sends off roots; —stores; —takes root; —tides over.

(See flower, plant, bud.)

BULGE

adjectives
inquisitive; disconcerting; noticeable; awkward.

BULGE (*v*)

adverbs
roundly; awkwardly; disconcertingly; noticeably; inquisitively; prominently; pro-

trudingly; enormously; horribly; abnormally; grotesquely.
(See swell, protrude.)

BULK

adjectives
grotesque; enormous; huge; tremendous; great; black; haughty; proper; mastodonic; insufficient; surging; tawny; cumbrous; low; broad; shadowy; imposing; shaggy; massive; shattered; considerable; vast; languid; full; voluptuous; overgrown; ugly; wavering; helpless; insufficient; ponderous; credent; colossal; crude; patched; bluff; terrifying; faceless; non-irritating; Amazonian; flying; clean-limbed; portly; physical; crushing; overwhelming; threatening.

BULK (*v*)

adverbs
enormously; heavily; cumbrously; overwhelmingly; threateningly; ponderously; terrifyingly; portentously.

BULKY

adverbs
enormously; awkwardly; immensely; massively; mightily; monstrously; crudely; inelegantly; lumpishly; stupendously; grotesquely; queerly; strangely; imposingly; overwhelmingly; ponderously; suspiciously; clumsily; unnecessarily; laughably; ridiculously; deceptively; ludicrously; grossly; delusively.

BULL

adjectives
incorrigible; snorting; mad; infuriated; rumbling; fretful; savage; raging; veritable.

verbs
bait—; brand—; breed—; bring—to bay; castrate—; chafe—; combat—; enrage—; exhibit—; infuriate—; jab—; market—; mistreat—; outnumber —s; plague—; rope —; slaughter—; slay—; torment—; torture —; —bellows; —butts; —charges; —collapses; —emerges; —gores; —grazes; —leaps; —paws; —perspires; —rages; —retires; —rushes; —snorts; —vaults; —wearies; raise—.
(See animal, cattle.)

BULLDOG

adjectives
hideous; squirming; pedigreed; ferocious.

BULLET

adjectives
moaning; well-directed; paper; answering; shrieking; ricocheted; caroming; whistling; spattering; soft-nose; flattened; harmless; powder; telltale; whining; whizzing; fiery; screaming; thudding; dum-dum; explosive.

verbs
cap—; design—; hail —s; jacket—; mold —s; project—; riddle with —s; shower —s; squirt —s; stream —s; —attains a speed; —s buzz by; —careens; —glances off; —grazes; —s hammer; —s patter; —penetrates; —pierces; —ricochets; —s spatter; —speeds toward; —swerves; —wavers; —whines; —whistles by; —s wing past.
(See shot, projectile.)

BULLETIN

adjectives
confidential; monotonous; public.

BULLY

adjectives
beastly; blustering; loutish; strutting; prostrate.

BULLY (*v*)

adverbs
mildly; blusteringly; loutishly; struttingly; overbearingly; diplomatically; pertly; flatly; endlessly; securely; firmly.
(See intimidate.)

BULWARK

adjectives
sturdy; mighty; everlasting; broken; seaward; riddled; splintered; heaven-sustaining; granite; eternal; flimsy; invulnerable.

BUMP

adjectives
dull; heavy; inadvertent.

BUMPKIN

adjectives
small-town; awkward; city; country; overgrown.

BUMPTIOUS

adverbs
aggressively; offensively; disagreeably; absurdly; impertinently; ridiculously; egotistically; presumptuously; pretentiously; vainly; boastfully; ostentatiously; priggishly; unblushingly; brazenly, ludicrously; laughably; quaintly; comically; stupidly; boyishly; fantastically; immensely; complacently; foolishly; senselessly; extravagantly.

BUN

adjectives
delectable; indigestible; round; flat; plump.

BUNCH

adjectives
scattered; beautiful; horrible.

BUNDLE

adjectives
withered; compact; parti-colored; ribboned; exceptional; fine; emaciated; darkish; unwieldy; swaddled; inert; flat; sodden; queer-shaped; precious; muddy; helpless; numerous (pl.); cached; wrinkled; endless; malevolent.

verbs
bind in—; collect in—; contain in—; disorder—; encumber with —s; fasten in—; gather—; group in —s; load down with —s; shift —s; untie—.

(See parcel, package.)

BUNDLE (*v*)

adverbs
unceremoniously; compactly; inertly; flatly; endlessly; securely; firmly; unceremoniously.

(See bind, tie, roll.)

BUNGALOW

adjectives
rose-clad; richly-furnished; swanky; luxurious; screened; rustic; rambling; dark; unpretentious; beloved; picturesque.

BUNGLE (*v*)

adverbs
tragically; atrociously; characteristically; repeatedly; ineptly; generally; idiotically; diplomatically; strategically.

BUNGLING

adjectives
general; inept; patient; characteristic; repeated.

BUNGLING (*a*)

adverbs
awkwardly; clumsily; boorishly; loutishly; shyly; bashfully; ineptly; inexpertly; unskilfully; self-consciously; incompetently; vexatiously; hopelessly; diffidently; timidly; pitifully; helplessly; pathetically; plaintively; outlandishly; pitiably; miserably; sorrily; sadly; grievously.

BUOY

adjectives
dancing; heaving; ringing; rocking; warning.

BUOYANCY

adjectives
reckless; supreme; glad; youthful; virile; unutterable; natural; positive.

BUOYANT

adverbs
positively; joyously; affectedly; naturally; supremely; happily; suddenly; excitedly; unexpectedly; blithely; gleefully; rapturously; lightly; airily; gaily; hilariously; jovially; warmly; delightfully; delightedly; briskly; cheerily; jauntily; jubilantly; lightheartedly; disarmingly; merrily; playfully; irrepressibly; laughingly; smilingly; engagingly; irresistibly; confidently; enthusiastically; fervently; hopefully.

BURDEN

adjectives
grievous; financial; intolerable; painful; unwomanly; deadly; increasing; mutual; fragrant; double; various (pl); accumulated; racking; enticing; unnecessary; venerable; drowsy; precious; fatal; sinister; clattering; unescapable; never-lifted; serious; economic; appropriate; perpetual; fiery; passive; insufferable; monstrous; secret; baneful; oppressive; onerous; corresponding; expensive; equivalent; sweet; heavy; clerical; sheer; melancholy; aggravating; grim; common; unequal; unjust; dangerous; inevitable; cold; prodigious; ever-growing; staggering; crushing; unendurable; unbearable; cumbersome; over-heavy; dreadful; terrific; gruesome; undue; unusual; strange; pitiful; manifold (pl).

verbs
absorb—; ameliorate—; assume—; bear—; bend under—; chafe at—; deliver of—; ease—; groan under—; hamper with—; impose—; labor under—; lay on—; lighten —; load with—; overwhelm with—; shift —; shoulder—; stagger under—; suffer under—; support—; sustain—; unload—; —bows one down; —crushes.

(See load, cargo, weight, oppression, encumbrance.)

BURDENSOME

adverbs
grievously; financially; socially; intolerably; painfully; increasingly; unnecessarily; inescapably; seriously; economically; insuffer-

ably; monstrously; really; oppressively; aggravatingly; vexatiously; irritatingly; unequally; unjustly; dangerously; prodigiously; unendurably; dreadfully; terrifically; unduly; unusually; strangely; pitifully; calamitously; disastrously; unfortunately; tragically; gravely; cumbrously; embarrassingly.

BUREAU

adjectives
topographical; time-blackened; well-organized; devoted; legal; complete; self-supporting.

BUREAUCRACY

adjectives
smug; Teutonic; decadent; hardhearted; centralized.

BUREAUCRATIC

adverbs
complexly; unfortunately; portentously; ominously; dangerously; smugly; comfortably; democratically; autocratically; dictatorially; dominantly; imperiously; administratively; absolutely; arbitrarily; undeniably; hopelessly; irresistibly; terribly; unluckily; fairly; justly; unjustly; surprisingly; increasingly; overwhelmingly.

BURGLAR

adjectives
apprehensive; cautious; cunning; conscientious; felonious; stealthy; unscrupulous; chagrined; amateur; bungling; professional.

verbs
absolve—; accuse—; acquit—; apprehend—; condemn—; convict—; denounce—; detect—; imprison—; investigate —s; jail —s; protect against—; shield—; slay—; vindicate—; wound—; —alarms; —arouses; —invades; —plunders; —sacks; —terrorizes.
(See robber, highwayman, bandit.)

BURIAL

adjectives
obscure; golden; forgotten; Christian; interesting; hasty; premature; decent; respectable; proper; reverent; dismal; pagan.

verbs
assist at—; attend—; authorize—; commend to—; conceal by—; consecrate at—; console at—; draw out—; embalm for—; entitle to—; eulogize at—; notify of—; preach at—; preside over—; solemnize—; superintend—; uncover—; —disposes of.
(See death, funeral.)

BURLESQUE

adjectives
credible; polite; modified; exuberant; profane; farcical; vulgar; risque.

BURLESQUE (*a*)

adverbs
broadly; racily; absurdly; comically; cleverly; ludicrously; bombastically; caustically; sarcastically; ironically; satirically; extravagantly; cuttingly; adroitly; drolly; farcically; politely; profanely; coarsely; laughably; monstrously; ridiculously; refreshingly; delightfully; oddly; bizarrely; preposterously; unpardonably; whimsically; quizzically; uproariously; clownishly; chaffingly; scurrilously; derisively; scoffingly; exquisitely; deftly; expertly.

BURLESQUER

adjectives
hilarious; sheer; apt; clever; practiced.

BURN (*v*)

adverbs
destructively; smolderingly; luridly; noisily; mortally; inwardly; radiantly; shockingly; ruddily; intensely; steadfastly; dimly; sullenly; fitfully; ardently; distressfully; miraculously; inadvertently; glowingly.
(See scorch, consume.)

BURNING

adjectives
senseless; everlasting; endless.

BURRO

adjectives
dusty; dirty; shaggy; lop-eared; lazy; baldfaced; bobbing; munching.

BURST

adjectives
instant; passionate; indignant; convulsive; periodical; dreadful; sudden; fresh; unexplained; fiery; ungovernable; resplendent; scented; spontaneous.

BURST (*v*)

adverbs
turbulently; spontaneously; impetuously; appallingly; scornfully; involuntarily; hoarsely; ceaselessly; indignantly; periodically; ungovernably; resplendently.
(See break.)

BURTHEN

adjectives
breathless; delicate; sad; weighty; sorry.

BURY (v)

adverbs
quietly; reverentially; worshipfully; solemnly; splendidly; impecuniously; shabbily; awesomely; spectacularly.

(See hide, conceal.)

BUS

adjectives
shrieking; steady; dependable; rumbling; lantern-hung; lumbering; gaudy; sight-seeing.

verbs
board—; enter—; jam—; route—; station —; —conducts; —crawls along; —disgorges passengers; —flounders; —jolts; —rolls along; —rumbles; —snorts; —traverses.

(See automobile.)

BUSH

adjectives
tough; elder; laurel; sickly; interminable; towering; rose; fiery; projecting; elderberry; pathless; silent; clustering; naked; sheltering; berried; whortleberry; embracing; sparse; spiny; flourishing; jessamine; spreading; secret; scrubby; gnarled; stiff; stunted; woody; flowering; scraggly; unkempt; mesquite; indigo; patient; blooming; broad; pyramidical; gorse; vase-shaped; irregular; curious; round-topped; twiggy; shriveled; stumpy; sodden.

verbs
conceal in—; cultivate—; dwell in—; grow over with—es; hide in—; lie in—; lose in—; nest in—; nestle in—; prune—; pry in—; shroud in—; skirt—; spring from—; take to —; tangle in—; wind in and out among—es; —blooms; —blossoms; —branches; —flourishes; —protects; —screens; —spreads; —tangles; —yields.

(See shrub, thicket.)

BUSINESS

adjectives
queer; fateful; ugly; hypothecary; mercantile; intelligent; stirring; fascinating; centralized; stiff; ungentle; bloody; snug; unpleasant; keyhole; curious; suspended; profitable; complicated; awkward; terrible; remunerative; weary; rationalized; wretched; unreasonable; sordid; ethical; vengeful; phenomenal; tidy; bustling; superfluous; reputable; flourishing; dangerous; serious; reliable; shameful; discouraging; dubious; late-afternoon; ecclesiastical; villainous; dreadful; dreary; executive; temporal; poor; single; roaring; delightful; toilsome; prosperous; urgent; abstract; illegal; deplorable; unsound; definite; rascally; foul; weighty; stern; solemn; unavoidable; congenial; tedious; momentous; rural; legitimate; extensive; fiery; scratchy; urgent; civil; thriving; swift; blistering; risky; petty; competitive; extended; ordinary; solvent; brisk; lifelong; arduous; tangled; sorry; scurvy; delectable; unscrupulous; dirty; fast-growing; perfunctory; uncrowded; paramount; timely; weighty; subnormal; domestic; miserable; chancy; piratical; prodigious; nefarious; litigated; experimental; well-managed; urgent; hazardous; irrational; creative; exclusive; detailed; ruined; illustrious; muddled; tranquil; reckless; speculative; banking; primary; astounding; fecund; roundabout; essential; menaced; dull; drab; trivial; slack; stupid; pure; unmitigated; heartbreaking; backbreaking; brusque; honest; successful; sound; interesting; lucrative; blessed; rushing; gigantic; immense; tremendous; colossal; modern; increasing; dismal; shady; distasteful; degrading; unsavory; despicable; dark; knavish; damnable; cruel; fearful; ugly; tedious; distressing; nervy; nasty; sad; tiresome; unconstructive; stable; droll; ticklish; queer; silly; increasingly-profitable; substantial; amazing; ever-increasing; secure; ready-made; dependable; troublesome.

verbs
absorb—; accommodate—; adjust—; administer—; badger—; blast—; bolster—; charge with—; confess to—; corrupt—; debate—; democratize—; depress—; derive—; disorganize—; dispose of—; disrupt—; dominate —; drum up—; embark into—; employ in —; endanger—; envelop in—; establish—; evolve—; expedite—; exploit—; foster—; increase—; interfere with—; liquidate—; make inroads into—; meddle in—; mess up —; nurse—; plunge into—; quit—; regulate —; restrict—; resurrect—; revivify—; shift —; slow down—; speed up—; stabilize—; stimulate—; suspend—; swallow up—; symbolize—; tie up—; transact—; undertake—; underwrite—; wrap up in—; —booms; —bounds up; —branches out; —climbs; —droops; —expands; —expires; —falters; —flourishes; —flows; —founders; —lags; —looms; —nets; —simmers; —succumbs.

(See occupation, trade, matter, affair, interest, concern, enterprise, duty, industry, work, commerce.)

BUSINESSLIKE

adverbs
insistently; consistently; briskly; cheerfully;

alertly; keenly; intelligently; curiously; terribly; unreasonably; delightfully; urgently; definitely; positively; absolutely; thriftily; competently; competitively; thoroughly; ordinarily; ardently; scrupulously; astoundingly; essentially; dully; brusquely; honestly; successfully; soundly; immensely; tremendously; tediously; drolly; comically; amazingly; dependably; actively; assiduously; devotedly; eagerly; energetically; industriously; officiously; vigilantly; notably; smartly; zealously; shrewdly; courteously; methodically; craftily; astutely; cleverly; uniformly; capably; ingeniously; felicitously.

BUSINESSMAN

adjectives
average; hard-boiled; shrewd; prudent; substantial.

BUST

adjectives
laurel-crowned; glowing; imperial; negligible; animated; portrait-like; protuberant; resurrected; placid; sculptured.

BUSTLE

adjectives
empty; heroic; sudden; feverish; indescribable; silent; hospitable; intervening; noisy.

BUSTLE (v)

adverbs
valorously; heroically; feverishly; indescribably; hospitably; noisily; officiously; clamorously; indignantly.
(See stir.)

BUSTLING

adverbs
restlessly; fitfully; eagerly; zealously; inefficiently; noisily; happily; affectionately; fondly; vexatiously; everlastingly; ceaselessly; cheerily; moodily; hastily; ardently; actively; energetically; industriously; assiduously; diligently; earnestly; enthusiastically; nervously; excitedly; impetuously.

BUSY (v)

adverbs
hurriedly; interferingly; noisily; officiously; irritatingly; animatedly; industriously; ambitiously; casually; perfunctorily.

BUSY (a)

adverbs
agreeably; delightfully; ceaselessly; charmingly; briskly; cheerfully; intelligently; constantly; curiously; unreasonably; competently; ordinarily; astoundingly; tremendously; comically; amazingly; actively; eagerly; zealously; energetically; smartly; ostentatiously; craftily; cleverly; capably; boyishly; noisily; happily.

BUSYBODY

adjectives
gifted; interfering; old; free lance; gaping; nosy.

BUTCHER

adjectives
benevolent; inexorable; unfeeling; latent; mortal; skilled.

BUTCHER (v)

adverbs
indiscriminately; dexterously; inexorably; unfeelingly; mortally; professionally; methodically; heartlessly; cruelly; wantonly; atrociously.
(See slaughter, kill.)

BUTCHERY

adjectives
horrible; atrocious; deadly; murderous; wartime.

BUTLER

adjectives
impassive; peremptory; perfect; shrinking; hovering; worried; excellent; solemn; diminutive; competent; grizzled.

BUTTER

adjectives
rancid; molten; honeyed.

verbs
adulterate—; cart—; churn into—; color—; crock—; daub with—; deal in—; draw—; exude—; flavor—; grease—; lay on—; market—; melt—; mould—; pot—; ration out—; ripen—; separate—; solidify—; spread—; stir in—; test—; thicken—; work—.

BUTTER (v)

adverbs
sufficiently; goldenly; lavishly; liberally; scantily; meagerly; penuriously; politically.

BUTTERFLY

adjectives
painted; giddy; ingenious; chromatic-winged; bright; honey-sipping; social; gilded; quivering; sipping; marrying; blossom-like; slim; jet; loppy-winged; admired; gaudy; lazy; dainty; fluttering; poising.

verbs
attract—; distinguish—; frame—; hurt—; identify—; preserve—; pursue—; —beautifies; —ies cluster; —flits about; —flutters; —ies gather; —ies hibernate; —lays eggs; —migrates; —mimics; —pollinates; —spins; —sports; —twinkles.
(See moth.)

BUTTON

adjectives
saucer; shining; blue-jerkined; glittering; showy; blazing; fantastic.

verbs
adorn with —s; attach—; card —s; decorate with —s; drill —s; fondle—; grind —s; mold —s; ornament with —s; perforate —s; polish—; press out —s; sew on—; sort —s; stamp out —s; stud with —s; undo—; —affixes; —decorates; —fastens; —signifies.
(See knob, ornament.)

BUXOM

adverbs
agreeably; cheerfully; delightfully; attractively; genially; gaily; hilariously; noisily; lightly; merrily; joyously; charmingly; entrancingly; seductively; captivatingly; fascinatingly; humorously; vivaciously; bonnily; cheerily; gleefully; heartily; jauntily; jovially; jubilantly; playfully; sportively.

BUY

adjectives
exceptional; special; extraordinary.

BUY (*v*)

adverbs
secretly; eagerly; dearly; methodically; recklessly; exceptionally; extraordinarily.
(See purchase.)

BUYER

adjectives
reluctant; unintelligent; reckless; unwilling; avid; adept; ultimate; discriminating; prospective; timorous.

verbs
cater to—; coax—; coddle—; commission—; employ—; forewarn—; petition—; —bargains; —dickers; —obtains; —s pour in; —purchases.
(See customer.)

BUYING

adjectives
hand-to-mouth; cash; unintelligent; abnormal; collective; curtailed.

BUZZ

adjectives
humming; roaring; somnolent; baleful.

BUZZ (*v*)

adverbs
violently; roaringly; somnolently; balefully; monotonously; grindingly; painfully; repeatedly; intermittently; raucously; irritatingly.
(See hum, murmur.)

BUZZARD

adjectives
eternal; circling; watchful; carrion-feeding; waiting; patient.

verbs
—dips; —flaps his wings; —hovers; —soars.
(See bird, fowl.)

BUZZING

adjectives
loud; melancholy; repeated; intermittent; raucous.

BY-PRODUCT

adjectives
dubious; usual; unforeseen.

BYSTANDERS

adjectives
casual; innocent; mere; fascinated; inoffensive-looking; pathetic; sympathetic; superstitious.

verbs
collide with—; entertain—; regale—; strike —; —boo; —cheer; —gather; —hoot; —recognize; —threaten; —witness.
(See spectator, crowd.)

BYWAY

adjectives
deserted; dark; bowered; romantic.

C

CAB

adjectives
dilapidated; high; ridiculous; dejected; creaking; hansom; ramshackle.

CABIN

adjectives
malodorous; ruined; dreary-looking; little; sweet; deserted; primitive; ugly; tumble-down; abandoned; friendly; roomy; windowless; stuffy; spacious; airy; adobe; rustic; frontier; willow; dilapidated; dismal; second-class; unventilated; sanitary; lonely; embowered; remote; populous; tourist.

verbs
allot—; approach—; confine to—; coop in—; crawl into—; dwell in—; huddle in—; inhabit—; lodge in—; occupy—; situate—; thatch—; —flames; —shelters.
(See hut, house, compartment, cottage.)

CABINET

adjectives
quaint; treasure; lacquered; sound-proof; bedstead; canopied; moist; drunken; medicine; reliable; antiquated.

CABINET (governmental)

adjectives
austere; absolute; didactic; dictatorial; disorganized; resolute; united; unsympathetic; vacillating; weak-kneed.

verbs
address—; appoint to—; call—; consult—; convoke—; corrupt—; dismiss—; dissolve—; elect to—; represent in—; summon—; —administers; —advises; —confers; —consists; —convenes.
(See committee, council, ministry.)

CABLE

adjectives
heavy; electric; steel-wire; enormous; light; underground; overhead.

verbs
insulate—; lay—; reclaim—; reenforce—; sheathe—; snap—; solder—; stretch—; —communicates; —connects; —rusts; —transmits.
(See rope, line, chain, conduit, pipe.)

CACKLE

adjectives
sickly; vacant; occasional; sociable; foolish; prodigious.

CACKLE (*v*)

adverbs
obstreperously; sociably; harshly; prodigiously; raucously; stridently; disagreeably; triumphantly; proudly; jubilantly; exuberantly.
(See laugh, chatter, babble.)

CACTUS

adjectives
spiny; mammoth; massive; hardy; scraggly; fantastic; prickly; succulent; large.

CAD

adjectives
sensual; slimy; rotten; brutal; discreet; elderly; ineffable.

CADAVEROUS

adverbs
horribly; forbiddingly; frightfully; spectrally; foully; grimly; gruesomely; hideously; haggardly; monstrously; odiously; shockingly; stiffly; uncannily; fearfully; alarmingly; incredibly; dreadfully.

CADENCE

adjectives
self-possessed; monotonous; odd; singsong; calm; deep; mimic; best-measured; tinkling; merry; queer; wild; sardonic; nasal; minor; rollicking; weird; hideous; entreating; slightest; slurred; strange; rhythmic; musical; affectionate; lingering; effective; gentle; elegant; exotic; passionate; varied; soul-like; plagal; pathetic; pleading; enchanting; sorrowful.

CAFE

adjectives
innumerable (pl); continental; eccentric; gaudy; dingy; sumptuous; garish; gay; air-conditioned; pleasant; obscure; modest; smart; modern.

CAFFEINE

adjectives
unfriendly; stimulating.

CAGE

adjectives
subterranean; quarantined; awful; gilded; bamboo; wire; delicate; adjourning; wicker; pretty.

verbs
bar—; beat—; burst—; chain—; confine in —; convey in—; coop in—; escape from—; fetter in—; flit from—; hoist—; house in—; imprison in—; muffle in—; release from—; seal—; thrive in—; transport in—; wire in —.
(See prison.)

CAKE

adjectives
huge; fluffy; stale; abominable; peatlike; fresh; big; luscious; ancestral; oaten; incalculable; sacrificial; decomposed; fatal; successful; election; rich; moist; tender; smooth; white; pound; futile.

verbs
celebrate with—; crust—; decorate—; feast on—; flavor—; frost—; ice—; knead—; mix—; moisten—; mold—; munch on—; ply with—; regale with—; relish—; shape —; share—; spice—; squash—; sweeten—; yearn for—; —appeals; —appeases; —attracts; —crumbles; —falls; —rises; —stales.
(See bread.)

CALAMITY

adjectives
sudden; near; appalling; frightful; dire; staggering; tremendous; universal; public; painful; evident; undeserved; national; family; inevitable; crowning; impending; ominous; dreadful; absurd; mysterious; natural; inexhaustible; grotesque; unspeakable; ultimate; extraordinary; surrounding; bitter; colossal; temporal; undisguised.

verbs
afflict with—; avert—; avoid—; bear—; beset with—ies; drive to—; free from—; inflict with—; investigate—; involve—; laugh at—; mourn—; overcome—; restore from—; rush to—; save from—; survive—; —arises; —confounds; —damages; —descends; —distresses; —foreshadows; —injures; —menaces; —recurs; —smites; —threatens; —troubles.
(See misfortune, disaster, adversity.)

CALCULABLE

adverbs
easily; accurately; obviously; analytically; rationally; fairly; exhaustively; arithmetically; scientifically; precisely; exactly; laboriously; imposingly; impressively.

CALCULATE (v)

adverbs
mentally; abstractly; arithmetically; shrewdly; convincingly; precisely; astronomically; mathematically; slavishly; systematically; perpetually; strikingly; nicely; artfully.
(See compute, reckon.)

CALCULATION

adjectives
abstruse; optimistic; hasty; mental; abstract; pragmatic; intricate; colorless; chill; arithmetical; trained; shrewd; barren; imposing; convincing; rough; mental; unsettling; hard; stupendous; easy; moderate; absurd; deliberate; prudent; precise; laborious; memorable; astronomical; elaborate; vain; mathematical; calm; monotonous; craniometrical; cool; systematic; slavish; perpetual; reasonable.

verbs
adjust—; adopt—; arrange—; average—; check—; cite—; compute—; denounce—; err in—; estimate—; facilitate—; frame—; perform—; prove—; reckon—; speed—; tabulate—; think out—; upset—; —deceives; —determines; —fits; —indicates; —results in.
(See computation, reckoning.)

CALDRON

adjectives
seething; spiteful; great; live; bubbling; ancestral; hellish; boiling; monstrous; magic.

verbs
agitate—; cook in—; cool—; fry in—; steep in—; —boils; —bubbles; —overflows; —pours out; —seethes; —simmers; —steams.
(See kettle, pot.)

CALENDAR

adjectives
proposed; universal; unscriptural; modern; present; scientific.

verbs
appear on—; count on—; designate on—; introduce—; judge by—; keep—of; pencil —; readjust—; reckon by—; regulate—; revise—; scratch out of—; —computes; —denotes; —determines; —s differ; —groups; —indicates; —measures; —serves; —signifies.
(See list, schedule.)

CALF

adjectives
capering; soft-eyed.

verbs
beget—; corral—s; fatten—; fetter—; groom—; infect—; lasso—; offer—; pasture—; pet—; rend—; sacrifice—; slaughter—; stable—; —bawls; —browses; —grazes; —kicks; —shies; —suckles; —whines.
(See animal.)

CALF
adjectives (leg)
well-turned; unwearying; aching; pretty.

CALIBER
adjectives
high; stern; rare; meager; spectacular; mental; various.

CALL
adjectives
urgent; impatient; hurried; frantic; startled; strenuous; amazing; mystic; persistent; insistent; ceaseless; gallant; thrilling; voiceless; feeble; muffled; strong; canny; joyous; ringing; strident; clarion; screeching; staccato; calm; melodious; loud; musical; excited; effectual; pitiful; petulant; stirring; incoming; home-coming; solemn; doleful; providential; skyward; languid; vigorous; cheering; quavering; inconsiderate; bugle; emphatic; clamorous; person-to-person; night; echoing; high-pitched; immediate; impassioned; immortal.

verbs
evade—; ignore—; register—; respond to —; rise at—; trumpet—; whistle—; yield to—; —beckons; —bursts forth; —deludes; —drifts; —gladdens; —saddens.
(See shout, cry, summons, invitation.)

CALL
adjectives (visit)
deathless; enormous; unending; ceremonious; emergency; neighborly; unexpected; convenient; innumerable (pl); close; honorable; hasty; protracted; reliable; bewildering; personal.

CALL (v)
adverbs
insistently; urgently; frantically; persistently; feebly; ringingly; stridently; screechingly; melodiously; musically; pitifully; petulantly; dolefully; languidly; passionately; vigorously; quaveringly; clamorously; emphatically; echoingly; irresistibly; officially; severely; alternately; bluntly; facetiously; despairingly; technically; irreverently; extemporaneously; plaintively; mysteriously; familiarly; delicately; subsequently; indifferently; timorously; imperiously; cordially; tauntingly; cautiously; virtually; proverbially; unconscionably; sportively; graciously; lustily.
(See summon, bid, invite.)

CALLER
adjectives
white-haired; talkative; bedraggled; irate; bashful; unexpected; disappointed.

CALLING
adjectives
suitable; honorable; money-making; effectual; incessant; primordial; gainful; lawful.

verbs
answer—; awake to—; bend to—; consider —; continue in—; exalt—; exercise—; feel —; follow—; give up to—; heed—; profess to—; succeed in—; surrender to—; —bids; —invites; —invokes; —summons.
(See vocation, occupation, trade, profession.)

CALLOUS (a)
adverbs
coldly; unfeelingly; stolidly; senselessly; obtusely; apathetically; strangely; abnormally; weakly; heavily; vacantly; singularly; oddly; curiously; unaccountably; irritatingly; vexatiously; coolly; unpardonably; inexcusably.

CALLOUSNESS
adjectives
extreme; bitter; cruel; harsh; icy; incurred; repellent; brutal; self-imposed; criminal.

verbs
breed—; develop—; display—; expose to—; immunize to—; relapse into—; —blinds; —forms; —grows; —prevents; —ridicules.
(See callous, cruelty.)

CALLOW
adverbs
crudely; intolerably; uncompanionably; insufferably; rawly; youthfully; unintelligently; rudimentally; coarsely; thoughtlessly; heedlessly; vacuously; fatuously; surprisingly; awkwardly.

CALLUS (n)

adjectives
burning; carefully-tended; horny; leathery; reducible; stubborn; thickening; toil-worn; cushiony; cracked; shell-like.

verbs
apply to—; cut—; expose—; form—; pad—; peel—; press on—; rub into—; salve—; scrape—; slice—; soften—; soothe—; treat —es; wear —es; —aches; —burns; —hardens; —indurates; —irritates; —pains; —thickens.
(See callousness.)

CALM

adjectives
imperturbable; equable; deathly; reproachful; ominous; unutterable; desolate; sullen; philosophic; mental; studied; sensual; false; somber; solemn; classic; customary; comparative; jaded; forced; alert; secretive; unnatural; dovelike; delightful; unbroken; untroubled; restful; flawless; concentrated; hallowed; inmost; underlying; Sabbath; delicious; sweet; bitter; disciplined; stately; unalterable; shimmering; breathless; expressionless; succeeding; prosaic; windless; splendid; night; rigid; eternal; perfect; disquieting; outward; threatening; mysterious; legislative; passionless; remote; lucid; constant; serene; professional; melancholy; colossal; awful; inward; solid; habitual; unapologetic; sad; sacred; stolid; maddening; level; shuddering; kindred; dead; planetary; everlasting; propitious; apparent; judicial.

verbs
agitate—; break—; bring—; disturb—; end —; maintain—; preserve—; retain—; shatter—; suspend—; —bewitches; —delays; —detains; —enchants; —endures; —irritates; —rests; —settles on; —soothes.
(See tranquillity, stillness, serenity.)

CALM (a)

adverbs
pleasantly; delightfully; comfortingly; comfortably; habitually; sweetly; imperturbably; serenely; equitably; ominously; unutterably; philosophically; unnaturally; restfully; inwardly; unalterably; splendidly; mysteriously; perfectly; maddeningly; apparently; suddenly; strangely; pathetically; judicially; indulgently; coolly; placidly; gravely; passively; patiently; quietly; soberly; tranquilly; deliberately; silently; amicably; gently; smoothly; mildly; nonchalantly.

CALM (v)

adverbs
ominously; philosophically; falsely; somberly; soberly; mentally; comparatively; unnaturally; expressionlessly; prosaically; outwardly; mysteriously; passionlessly; professionally; serenely; propitiously; judicially; apparently.
(See lull, appease, hush.)

CALMNESS

adjectives
perfect; deathlike; icy; irritating; tense; sleepy; sudden; terrible; deliberate; strange; stony; peculiar; solitary; intrepid; honest; dreadful; collected; pathetic; fierce; unwonted; unmerciful; dreamy; judicial; proud; displeasing; settled; cold; imperturbable.

CALORIES

adjectives
accumulated; actinic; beneficial; burdening; life-sustaining; stored-up.

verbs
burden with—; calculate—; contain—; define—; determine—; express in—; govern —; increase—; lessen—; measure—; obtain —; regulate—; require—; supply—; vary—; —suffice.
(See unit.)

CALUMNIATORY

adverbs
criminally; scandalously; grossly; wilfully; flagitiously; dangerously; substantially; veritably; avowedly; abominably; detestably; extremely; illegally; nefariously; unfortunately; unluckily; openly; deliberately; maliciously; venomously; libelously; scurrilously; foully; slanderously.

CALUMNIOUS

adverbs
deliberately; inherently; naturally; habitually; unfortunately; unpleasantly; disagreeably; detestably; abominably; hatefully; malignantly; maliciously; poisonously; venomously; viciously; insinuatingly; slyly; subtly; scandalously; wilfully; dangerously; extremely; openly; foully; unforgivably.

CALUMNY

adjectives
gross; frequent; willful; barbarous; backwounding; transparent; private; flagitious; hideous; popular; superstitious.

verbs
accuse of—; asperse with—; characterize

by—; charge with—; diffuse—; invent—; propagate—; raise—; repudiate—; subject to—; utter—; —blights; —defames; —detracts; —imputes to; —injures; —libels; —misrepresents; —slanders.
(See slander, aspersion, accusation.)

CALVINISTIC

adverbs
rigidly; soundly; strictly; unyieldingly; inflexibly; faithfully; scrupulously; unbendingly; loyally; puritanically; chastely; punctiliously; literally; precisely; rigorously; unaffectedly; unimpeachably; frankly; openly; avowedly; sincerely; obstinately; stubbornly; obdurately; intolerantly; proudly.

CAMARADERIE

adjectives
careless; spirited; joyous.

CAMEL

adjectives
gloomy-eyed; crouching; fast; cream-colored; browsing; patient; fleet; miserable; baggage; fine-riding; beautiful; prodding; magnificent; kneeling; swift; sure-footed.

verbs
domesticate—; load—; mount—; train—; water—; —bolts; —consumes; —fasts; —gurgles; —jolts; —kneels; —nibbles; —rages; —roars; —shakes; —stores; —sweats; —thrives.
(See animal.)

CAMEO

adjectives
exquisite; precious.

CAMERA

adjectives
television; candid; clicking; heavy; leveled.

verbs
adjust—; arm with—; besiege with —s; conceal—; focus—; insert in—; level—; load—; operate—; pose before—; regulate—; sit before—; utilize—; —aids; —captures; —catches; —copies; —enlarges; —espies; —grinds out; —obtains; —pictures; —records; —registers; —reproduces.

CAMOUFLAGE

adjectives
pleasant; pious; shallow; discreditable; impenetrable; foolish.

CAMP

adjectives
hostile; dismantled; horrible; concentration; deserted; aboriginal; circumvallating; permanent; temporary; picturesque; fortified; turbulent; peaceful; comfortable; armed; spacious; attractive; modest; thriving; selected; opposite; lawless; antagonistic; divided; nightly; luxurious; chaotic.

verbs
arouse—; beleaguer—; besiege—; command—; concentrate—; conduct—; conduct to—; divide into —s; escort to—; pitch—; proclaim—; put out of—; quarter at—; split into —s; strike—; —busies; —buzzes; —hums; —rises; —swarms.
(See barracks.)

CAMP (v)

adverbs
ostentatiously; conveniently; permanently; temporarily; turbulently; lawlessly; nightly; luxuriously; strategically.

CAMPAIGN

adjectives
triumphant; ill-fated; successful; whispering; perfunctory; systematic; demographic; vigorous; anti-crime; collective; energetic; fruitless; gubernatorial; brilliant; tremendous; aggressive; virulent; victorious; independent; indiscriminate; plausible; preliminary; piratical; comprehensive; subtle; long; tedious; bloody; doggerel; wearisome; approaching; powerful; persistent; perfidious; journalistic; deliberate; devouring; lulled; preceding; critical; anti-feminist; amatory; mighty; brilliant; thrilling; world-wide; far-flung; intense; thorough; guerrilla; national; educational; money-raising; recruiting; secret; quiet; off-stage; complete; exacting; sanguinary; haphazard; extraordinary.

verbs
broaden—; carry on—; conduct—; embark on—; feature—; focus—; foster—; inaugurate—; initiate—; inspire—; intensify—; launch—; map out—; participate in—; plan—; plot—; promote—; push—; stir—; sway—; swing—; transcend—; wage—.
(See operation, contest, appeal.)

CAMPAIGN (v)

adverbs
vigorously; triumphantly; ill-fatedly; vaingloriously; perfunctorily; systematically; energetically; fruitlessly; brilliantly; gubernatorially; aggressively; virulently; independently; indiscriminately; perfidiously; comprehensively; tediously; educationally; extraordinarily; haphazardly.
(See operate.)

CAMPAIGNER

adjectives
agitated; ogling; leering; scheming; artful; active; seasoned.

CAMPER

adjectives
scattered (pl); unsuspecting.

CAMPFIRE

adjectives
forsaken; gleaming; rosy; flickering; bright; glowing; tiny; cozy; smoking; central.

CAMPUS

adjectives
dignified; attractive.

CAN

adjectives
highly-colored; discarded.

verbs
cap—; dent—; deposit in—; dump —s; grade—; heap —s; label—; litter with —s; manufacture—; package —s; penetrate—; put up in—; save in—; seal—; shape—; shelve—; —preserves; —protects; —rusts.
(See cup.)

CANADIAN

adverbs
staunchly; stoutly; shrewdly; indomitably; loyally; dauntlessly; stolidly; generously; cannily.

CANAL

adjectives
shining; picturesque; slender; enchanting; stagnant; inland; crude; sluggish; beautiful; tree-lined; intestinal; vast; network; practicable; intracoastal; alimentary; auditory; winding; lotus-paved; irregular; pestiferous; tortuous; marble-lined; glittering; terrestrial; ribbonlike; semicircular; shadowed; vestigial.

verbs
bank—; block—; border by—; bridge—; circle—; construct—; drain—; dredge—; fortify—; lay out—; line—; lock—; navigate —; obstruct—; project—; tow through—; —communicates; —connects; —conveys; —irrigates; —retains; —shortens; —unites.
(See channel, duct, passage.)

CANARD

adjectives
base; preposterous.

CANARY

adjectives
ephemeral; fluffy; fragile; gladsome; green-gold; restless; song-bursting; twittering.

verbs
—carols; —peeps; —trills; —tweets.
(See bird.)

CANCER

adjectives
malignant; hereditary; inoperable.

verbs
ascribe to—; control—; detect—; diagnose —; discover—; engraft—; examine for—; excise—; indicate—; lecture on—; localize —; recognize—; reveal—; sacrifice to—; suffer from—; suspect—; treat for—; —advances; —appears; —courses through; —develops; —disables; —eats away; —extends; —lodges; —lurks; —results; —spreads.
(See tumor, disease.)

CANCEROUS

adverbs
hopelessly; lamentably; malignantly; incurably; irremediably; morbidly; painfully; distressingly; inoperably; sorely; agonizingly; grievously; horribly; dolorously; frightfully; pitiably; woefully; tragically.

CANDELABRA

adjectives
myriad; tall; bronze; brilliant; huge; silver.

CANDENT

adverbs
glowingly; whitely; tropically; lambently; scintillatingly; flamingly; smolderingly; incalescently; intensely; fiercely; sulphurously; overpoweringly; intolerably; unendurably; incredibly.

CANDESCENT

adverbs
blazingly; dazzlingly; effulgently; brightly; radiantly; intolerably; gloriously; luminously; refulgently; resplendently; splendidly; magnificently; garishly; lustrously; vividly; genially; mildly; exceedingly; surprisingly; gratefully; agreeably; magically.

CANDID

adverbs
utterly; openly; honestly; innocently; simply; sincerely; artlessly; deliberately; resolutely; roughly; directly; downright; frankly; ingenuously; naively; naturally; plainly; unflatteringly; delicately; nakedly; soberly;

palpably; evidently; manifestly; truthfully; veraciously; bluntly; indulgently; particularly; scrupulously; unaffectedly; unnecessarily; inexcusably; faithfully; unreservedly; respectfully; incorruptibly; crudely; painfully; gaily; unfeelingly; characteristically; habitually; amazingly; humorously; unexpectedly; engagingly; alarmingly; charmingly.

CANDIDACY

adjectives
insurgent; unsuccessful.

verbs
announce—; avow—; back—; boost for—; campaign for—; criticize—; decide—; discuss—; interest in—; offer for—; promote—; propose—; protest—; reject—; rob of—; select for—; support—; work for—.

CANDIDATE

adjectives
potential; gubernatorial; legitimate; senatorial; aspiring; glamorous; receptive; prospective; rejected; unexceptionable; proper; eligible; formidable; leading; opposing; passive; alternative; presidential.

verbs
choose—; doom—; endorse—; favor—; groom—; handicap—; honor—; idealize—; squelch—; uphold—; —aspires to; —offers; —orates; —"slings mud"; —stumps; —thunders; —triumphs.
(See contestant.)

CANDIED

adverbs
deliciously; delectably; lusciously; richly; densely; thickly; indissolubly; substantially; sweetly; fruitily; generously; agreeably; palatably; deceptively.

CANDLE

adjectives
dumb; newfangled; paraffin; shining; beeswax; flickering; brief; gigantic; guttering; meek; neglected; tall; ghastly; blessed; diminutive; melancholy; flaring; spent; cabbage-headed; half-burned; lighted; sputtering; waning; snuffed; long-wicked.

verbs
dip —s; extinguish—; mould —s; snuff—; —decorates; —drips; —flickers; —gutters; —illuminates; —melts; —shadows; —shines; —shrinks; —sputters; —stains; —tapers.
(See light, lamp.)

CANDLESTICK

adjectives
squat; slender; graceful.

CANDOR

adjectives
crude; unfailing; ingenuous; shameless; maidenly; winning; half-rebellious; friendly; perfect; pervading; utmost; gay; transparent; unwonted; incomparable; painful; dignified; unfeeling; fresh; apparent; characteristic; piercing; brotherly; stainless; endearing; illuminating; violent; good-humored; unashamed; unsuggestive; uncompromising; amazing; wholesome; spiritual; direct; heartfelt; vigorous; humorous; unexpected; courageous; perfect; devastating; engaging; openhearted; rustic; unruly; alarming; comical.

verbs
acclaim—; boast—; discourse with—; dispose toward—; express—; feign—; honor—; judge with—; radiate—; —brightens; —frees; —shines; —shocks; —strains; —surprises.
(See frankness, impartiality, fairness, sincerity.)

CANDY

adjectives
silk; atrocious; hard; lime; delicious; tempting; nutritious.

verbs
bribe with—; congeal into—; consume—; decorate—; feast on—; flavor—; hanker for—; immerse—in; inspissate—; proffer—; regale with—; thicken—; —appeals; —crystallizes; —sickens; —stales; —vanishes.
(See cake.)

CANE

adjectives
lithe; long; ebony; ivory-headed; silver-headed; Malacca; gold-headed; slender; impenetrable; light; flexible; leaded; jewelled; silver-topped; beribboned.

verbs
beat with—; brandish—; carve—; enamel—; flex—; flog with—; flourish—; jab with—; joint—; lean on—; notch—; poise—; sheathe—; tap with—; utilize—; —supports.
(See stick, staff, whip.)

CANINE

adjectives
affectionate; luckless.

CANINITY

adjectives
groveling.

CANKER

adjectives
vengeful; gnawing.

verbs
banish—; infect with—; slough—; spray—; —consumes; —corrupts; —decays; —depraves; —destroys; —develops; —devours; —discharges; —diseases; —eats; —envelops; —gnaws; —grows; —indisposes; —poisons; —pollutes; —rusts; —spreads; —tarnishes.
(See cancer, ulcer, sore.)

CANKEROUS

adverbs
increasingly; injuriously; poisonously; corrosively; blightingly; irremediably; incurably; painfully; distressingly; troublesomely; pitiably; unfortunately.

CANNED

adverbs
perfectly; exquisitely; expertly; faultlessly; irreproachably; hygienically; scientifically; soundly; carefully; well; safely; home; prophylactically; guardedly.

CANNIBALS

adjectives
gigantic; raging.

CANNON

adjectives
least-accessible; monstrous; small; academical; clumsy; ugly; yawning; widely-sloping; terraced; prostrate; grumbling; booming; brazen-throated; improvised; boulder-choked; distant; useless; breaching; spiked; roaring; frowning; lateral; brazen; belching; thundering; hostile.

verbs
capture—; charge—; discharge—; level—; load—; man—; mount—; sight—; silence—; train—upon; —batters; —blazes away; —booms; —emits; —explodes; —menaces; —pounds; —recoils; —revolves; —roars; —rolls; —salutes; —throws; —thunders; —vollies.
(See gun, weapon.)

CANNONADE

adjectives
tremendous; sullen.

CANNY

adverbs
astonishingly; shrewdly; weirdly; uncommonly; infinitely; suavely; smoothly; adroitly; cleverly; diplomatically; artfully; subtly; cunningly; naturally; craftily; guilelessly; astutely; foxily; deeply; knowingly; politically; discreetly; intelligently; sharply; wisely; sagely; sagaciously; alertly; smartly.

CANOE

adjectives
stealthy; canvas-covered; capsized; frail; careening; racing; dug-out; birchen; lonely.

verbs
ballast—; capsize—; cruise in—; fashion—; guide—; handle—; launch—; level—; model—; navigate—; overturn—; propel—; race in—; right—; rig up—; sail—; stabilize—; steer—; trim—; twist—; waterproof—; weight—; —dips; —glides; —outsails; —rocks; —slips.
(See boat.)

CANOEIST

adjectives
seasoned.

CANON

adjectives
hospitable; highest; continent; aesthetic; worthy; obtrusive; waterless; metrical.

CANONICAL

adverbs
strictly; highly; conformably; obtrusively; ecclesiastically; monastically; pontifically; illustriously; conventionally; formally; habitually; ordinarily; regularly; acceptably; rigidly; typically; uncompromisingly; evangelically; sacredly; prophetically; inviolably; expressly.

CAN OPENER

adjectives
maligned.

CANOPY

adjectives
moon-proof; damask; shifting; irremovable; drooping; arched; orb-like; moth-flitted; overhead; luminous; oblique; skyey; silken; flowery; crimson; celestial; velvet; azure; somber; verdant; umbrageous.

verbs
bracket—; couch under—; embroider—; hang out—; spread—; support—; suspend—; —circles; —covers; —decorates; —

hangs over; —hoods; —projects; —protects; —shades; —shelters; —surmounts.
(See pavilion, tent.)

CANT

adjectives
specious; traditional.

CANTER

adjectives
clumsy; brisk; undeniable; preliminary.

CANTER (*v*)

adverbs
clumsily; briskly; carelessly; steadily; spiritedly; half-heartedly; unevenly; monotonously; jouncingly; pleasurably; lazily.
(See trot.)

CANVAS

adjectives
mute; melancholy; billowing; snowy; smoke-darkened; gigantic; towering; shimmering; famous; important; dark-colored; mighty; somber; rickety; defiled; broad; idly-flapping; mimic; remarkable; inflammable.

verbs
bleach—; daub—; depict on—; display on—; dye—; execute on—; garment in—; line with—; live under—; portray on—; retain on—; spread—; surface—; transfer to—; weave—; —blinds; —filters; —protects; —screens.
(See cloth, sail, tent, picture, painting.)

CANVASS

adjectives
frantic; extensive; national; house-to-house; thorough; misleading; hotly-contested; electoral; industrious; effective.

CANYON

adjectives
deepening; lowland; tributary; carved; narrow; sharp; shallow; dreaded; deserted; winding; mile-deep; color-flaming; hollow; bare; hard; blind; frowning; weird; wind-swept; somber; snow-clad; treeless; mist-filled; nave-like; mystic; rocky-bottomed; grand.

verbs
carve—; collect in—; delve in—; enter—; erode into—; explore—; flow through—; stream through—; traverse—; widen—; —beautifies; —extends; —narrows; —skirts; —traverses; —widens.
(See gorge, valley.)

CAP

adjectives
rakish; coon-tail; checked; grimy; shabby; demure; bulging; peaked; close-fitting; visored; tall; shako-like; thin; plumed; gauze; paltry; flaring; jaunty; blue-tasseled; night-spangled; frilled; perforated; traditional; funnel-shaped; lace; muslin.

verbs
adjust—; admire—; appear in—; clap—on; crown with—; don—; fashion—; fling—; hurl—in air; line—; pattern—; peak—; —balloons; —blows off; —covers; —distinguishes; —fits; —perches; —protects; —shades; —shields; —surrounds; —warms.
(See hat, cover.)

CAPABILITIES

adjectives
ultimate; brilliant; admitted; generous; endless.

verbs
admit—; apprehend—; ascertain—; boast of—; confirm—; convince of—; demand—; destroy—; display—; discover—; doubt—; drain—; enlarge—; establish—; evince—; examine—; exhibit—; gift with—; investigate—of; perceive—; possess—; recognize—; reward—; strike one with—; trust in—of.
(See ability, capacity, skill.)

CAPABLE

adverbs
unusually; brilliantly; remarkably; normally; generally; immensely; naturally; highly; notably; efficiently; sufficiently; incredibly; exceptionally; energetically; potentially; influentially; adroitly; cleverly; dexterously; deftly; discreetly; expertly; ingeniously; indefatigably; tirelessly; intelligently; practically; skilfully; proficiently; felicitously; handily; neatly; pleasantly; willingly; thoroughly; technically; shrewdly; entirely; gratifyingly; prepossessingly; agreeably.

CAPACIOUS

adverbs
unusually; incredibly; extensively; extremely; sweepingly; magnificently; broadly; splendidly; grandly; superbly; unbelievably; wonderfully; marvellously; illimitably; infinitely; admirably; majestically; roomily; enormously; remarkably; notably; famously; renownedly; formidably; singularly; uncommonly; particularly.

CAPACITY

adjectives
imitative; business; temporal; assimilative; remarkable; absorptive; negative; productive; private; normal; functional; boundless; superior; reserve; carrying; immense; phenomenal; histrionic; unbounded; equestrian; bestowed; fruitful; partisan; sovereign; native; fatal; individual; narrowest; physical; psychological; proper; everlasting; increasing; cubical; wage-earning; reputed; creative; intellectual; interpretative; notable; productive; automatic; honorary; earning; predatory; constitutional; dignified; uncommon; extensive; aggregate; daily; destructive; magical; executive; exceptional; innate; latent; automatic; enlarged; varying; inexhaustible; bear-like; extraordinary; tremendous; ultimate; human; seating; consulting; mental; social; official; business; threefold; spiritual; prehensile; advisory; endless; singular; considerable; utmost; marked; unique; stunted; amazing; unparalleled; infinite; limitless; incredible; strange; cold-blooded; meanest; inherent; natural; fertile; implanted; expert; unsuspected; sufficient; demonstrated; flexible; inborn; benevolent; hidden; varied; contrasted; formidable.

verbs
cultivate—; delineate—; demonstrate—; develop—; endow with—; engender—; enlarge—; exceed—; exert to—; expand—; gauge—; impair—; increase—; limit—; measure—; nourish—; overestimate—; reduce—; sharpen—; —dwindles; —wanes.

(See ability, talent, power, space, position, office.)

CAPE
(clothing)

adjectives
dark; all-enveloping; velvet; cloth; dusky; ghostly; chestnut; graceful; small; fluttering.

CAPE
(land)

adjectives
stupendous; huge; rocky; famous; grassy.

CAPER

adjectives
wild; queer; prancing; droll; weird; drunken; inexplicable.

verbs
cut —s; dance in—; execute—; frolic in —s; jump in —s; leap in —s; perform—; prance in—; run into—; skip in—; sport in—; twist in—.

(See prank, trick, leap, spring.)

CAPERING

adjectives
gleeful; lamb-like; idle.

CAPITAL
(city)

adjectives
seething; delightful; mad; hospitable; national; inland; stricken; remote; proud; brilliant; sophisticated; intellectual; financial; provincial; faraway; critical; highland; ancient; gilded; sculptured; flowery; peerless.

CAPITAL
(financial)

adjectives
ample; slender; insufficient; borrowed; local; surplus; invested; ready; maximum; accumulated; potential; enchanting; embellished; tolerable; available; abundant; organized; skittish; enlightened; unproductive.

verbs
accumulate—; amass—; calculate—; contribute—; convert into—; distribute—; employ—; exploit—; favor—; fix—; float—; furnish—; gain—; guarantee—; impair—; increase—; insure—; invest—; organize—; produce—; protect—; subscribe—; withdraw—; —earns; —finances.

(See money, wealth, stock.)

CAPITALISM

adjectives
regenerated; decadent; imperialistic; monopolist.

verbs
abuse—; attack—; base on—; berate—; condemn—; creep upon—; denounce—; deplore—; favor—; oppose—; overthrow—; prejudice against—; rebuild—; reform—; reject—; revive—; support—; vindicate—; —collapses; —concentrates; —evolves from; —exploits; —flourishes; —promotes; —possesses; —retards; —rules; —speeds up; —topples; —tyrannizes.

CAPITALIST

adjectives
foolish; old-style; hard-boiled; new-risen; timid; satanic; retired; world-famed; local; noted; universal; desirable; unregenerate; designing.

CAPITULATION

adjectives
dishonorable; unexpected; so-called; careful; generous.

CAPRICE

adjectives
cruel; revolting; monstrous; swift; boyish; accidental; magnificent; slightest; youthful; expensive; sudden; unaccountable; feminine; passing; innocent; common; irresistible.

verbs
act on—; depend on—; humor—; lead by—; leave to—; restrain—; subject to—; —determines; —fancies; —fixes; —forms; —governs; —guides; —turns.
(See whim, fancy, notion.)

CAPRICIOUS

adverbs
waywardly; whimsically; wantonly; playfully; captiously; unreasonably; amusingly; ridiculously; delightfully; irresistibly; strikingly; extravagantly; senselessly; humorously; cruelly; childishly; irresponsibly; unaccountably; girlishly; incorrigibly; intractably; curiously; foolishly; preposterously; nonsensically; drolly; comically.

CAPSULE

adjectives
compact; dehiscent; formidable; gelatine; handy; metallic; portable; soluble; transparent; unappetizing.

verbs
administer—; cover with—; dissolve—; dose with —s; enclose in—; form in—; heat—; medicate—; melt—; perforate—; seal in—; swallow—; —bursts; —contains; —cures; —envelops; —opens; —sheathes; —surrounds.
(See case.)

CAPTAIN

adjectives
turbulent; portly; doughty; gallant; dauntless; resourceful; inspiring; imperturbable; wily; bluff; honest; naval; brutal; steady; reliable; plump; rubicund; grave; calm; wigged; staff; blustering; youthful; sagacious; usurping; triumphant; modish; unwilling; unapproachable; senior; russet-coated; victorious; mutinous; self-sufficient; spectacular; valiant.

verbs
beseech—; betray—; commission—; commune with—; dread—; elect—; elevate to—; entreat—; promote to—; rank as—; raise to—; —assigns; —authorizes; —commands; —heads; —leads; —orders; —roars; —survives; —thunders; —upbraids.
(See leader, commander.)

CAPTIOUS

adverbs
disagreeably; offensively; irritatingly; needlessly; groundlessly; wilfully; unpleasantly; truculently; cantankerously; capriciously; whimsically; irresponsibly; provokingly; fitfully; contrarily; uncomfortably; excitably; petulantly; intolerably; unpardonably; irascibly; irritably; fretfully; inexplicably; fractiously; sarcastically; woefully.

CAPTIVE

adjectives
illustrious; beautiful; sullen-eyed; barbaric; slaughtered; hopeless; hapless; delighted; luckless; trapped; defenseless; willing; unhappy; devoted; cowardly; shamed; spent; princely; august.

verbs
acquit—; bind—; cage—; carry away—; chain—; deliver—; detain—; enslave—; exchange —s; fetter—; free—; humble—; liberate—; mutilate—; restore—; slaughter —s; struggle with—; subdue—; take—; torture—.
(See prisoner.)

CAPTIVITY

adjectives
killing; limitless; perpetual; weakening; prolonged.

verbs
bring into—; cancel—; carry into—; counsel in—; dash into—; deliver from—; desolate in—; detain in—; dwell in—; enforce—; escape from—; feel—; hold in—; incarcerate in—; languish in—; lead into—; pine in—; resign to—; sell into—; shut in—; sink into—; subject to—; submit to—.
(See bondage, slavery.)

CAPTURE

adjectives
final; violent; rich; gallant; important; nefarious; imminent.

CAPTURE (*v*)

adverbs
triumphantly; previously; brilliantly; finally; violently; gallantly; nefariously; shrewdly; skillfully; dexterously; slyly; viciously; cruelly; wantonly.
(See apprehend, arrest, seize.)

CAR

adjectives
spectral; rheumatic; unobtrusive; high-

toned; high-priced; heavenly; short-lived; sumptuous; rushing; antiquated; magnificent; fast; refrigerator; private; outmoded; jangling; streamlined; swift; horse; electric; dull; faded; forward; triumphal; airborne; pellucid; impressive; frivolous; ill-smelling; clanging; luxurious; excellent; appointed; fine-looking; gay; resplendent; ancient; battered; touring; rattling; scraggly; ramshackle; decrepit; small; shabby; disreputable; armored; torpedo-shaped; queer; coffin-shaped; showy; motor; gaudy; rakish; spectral; death; twisted; crippled; expensive; charging; oncoming; hurtling; roaring; pursuing; departing; passing; jolting; bouncing; purring; lurching; brilliant; swinging; mud-splashed; full-length; close-parked; halted; gleaming; massive; roomy.

verbs
check—; convey in—; crowd—; crush beneath—; demolish—; draw—; fuel—; grease —; guide—; jaunt in—; load—; polish—; power—; proceed in—; ride in—; scramble from—; smash—; tow—; transport in—; tumble from—; wheel—; —backfires; —s collide; —s file by; —glides; —glistens; —groans; —hums; —purrs; —rattles; —serves; —skids; —skims; —speeds; —traverses; —whizzes by.
(See automobile.)

CAR
(railroad)

adjectives
clanking; gliding; heavily-laden; obdurate; rattling; runaway; swaying; unmanned; unwieldy; weighty; trundling; creaking; brawling.

verbs
attach—; brake—; couple —s; derail—; design—; dispatch—; electrify—; equip—; gear—; haul—; hook on—; light—; load—; model—; number—; refrigerate—; shunt—; signal—; station—; streamline—; switch—; transport in—; —chugs along; —s collide; —rattles by; —rumbles past; —rusts.
(See coach.)

CARAVAN

adjectives
innumerable (pl); floating; assembled; angelic; formidable; long-winding; slow-crawling; trekking; vast; imposing; lonely; patriarchal; stately; sluggish.

verbs
arm—; attack—; burden—; convoy—; encounter—; engage—; equip—; guard—; guide—; halt—; head—; hire—; lead—; route—; set upon—; tour in—; —assembles; —marches; —perishes; —sets forth; —starves; —travels; —traverses; —treks; —troops by; —wanders.
(See company, cart, wagon.)

CARAVANSARY

adjectives
frivolous; huge; pretentious; courtyard.

CARBOHYDRATES

adjectives
essential; tissue-building; fortifying; vital; woody.

verbs
analyze—; burn up—; characterize—; class as—; consist of—; consume—; contain—; depend on—; distribute—; form—; induce —; lack—; —benefit; —energize; —fuel; —occur in; —produce; —reveal; —serve as.
(See compound.)

CARBON

adjectives
amorphous; crystallized; free; elemental; ebon; smudgy; uncombined.

verbs
anaylze—; clean—; combine with—; compound with—; crystallize—; deposit—; filter with—; free—; give off—; illuminate —; produce—; reduce to—; —blackens; —condenses; —decolors; —joins with.
(See element.)

CARCASS

adjectives
bloodstained; bovine; flaccid; gross; swarming; fresh-bitten; floating; putrefying; snake-bitten; swollen; miserable; mutilated; handsome; lifeless; rascally; partly-devoured; warm; bleeding; frozen; corrupt; bloody.

verbs
bury—; cast out—; drape—; drop—; glut —; hide—; mutilate—; prostrate—; rend —; reveal—; scatter —s; suspend—; tear —; tread upon—; —decays; —decomposes; —disintegrates; —putrefies; —rots.
(See body, frame.)

CARD
(calling)

adjectives
ill-judged; official; engraved; neatly-typed; attention-compelling.

CARD
(playing)

adjectives
best; false; winning; shuffled; precious; worn; greasy; stacked.

verbs
arrange —s; box —s; cheat at —s; draw —; flash—; gather —s; introduce —s; mark —s; pack —s; perforate—; shuffle —s; stack —s; stake —s; stencil —s; throw up —s; trump—; wager on —s; —s allot; —designates; —slides; —slips; —warrants.

CARDINAL

adjectives (bird)
brilliant-plumaged; crested; flitting; music-flooding; regal; scarlet-flashing; sun-reflecting; pine-homing.

verbs
cage—; tame—; —plumes; —whistles.
(See bird.)

CARE

adjectives
scientific; secret; degrading; unhappy; reverential; dull; business; public; sincere; harassing; artistic; dismal; ill-reputed; wasting; fastidious; considerate; domestic; humbler; stimulating; carping; patient; unquiet; paternal; medical; ministering; nice; meanest; gigantic; thoughtful; bounteous; sharp; fatherly; elaborate; watchful; timely; indefatigable; peculiar; jealous; anxious; cankering; institutional; painstaking; tender; sufficient; chary; honest; reverent; fearful; scrupulous; rankling; loving; never-ceasing; heavy; sleepless; grisly; meticulous; considerable; fostering; wrinkled; persistent; efficient; extreme; municipal; telltale; providential; sympathetic; ignoble; wearying; warlike; chief; overpowering; conscientious; earth-born; practical; untuned; unremitting; apparitional; scrutinizing; eating; arduous; fevered; conquered; alliterative; preventive; utmost; prodigious; perpetual; silent; commonplace; judicious; self-intrusted; mortal; same; knowing; vexing; heavy; particular; gnawing; magnificent; altruistic; reverent; pale; touching; loving; consumptive; excellent; shallow; pastoral; intrusive; daintiest; prudent; exaggerated; vigilant; infinite; special; unusual; foreboding; exacting; sinful; late; surgical; maternal; miserable; sheltering; sordid; rigid; pitying; colossal; intensive; queenly; distracting; peremptory; ancient; religious; studious; sedulous; solicitous; protective; hospitable; exquisite; admirable; tender; expert; rooted; squalid; searing; wrinkling; stern; ageless; minute;. tireless; human; pressing; deliberate; visible; foolish; constant; inevitable; unctuous; inadequate; masterly; incessant; patriarchal.

verbs
abolish—; banish—; bend with—; bestow —upon; brood with—; charge with—of; choke with—; conduct with—; delegate—of; demand—; deride—; devote—to; discharge —s; disclaim—; drive away—; droop with —; drown—; dull with—; ease—; escape —; exempt from—; exercise—; foster with —; free from—; fret with—; harass with —; heal —s; intrust—of; kill —s; lavish—upon; lay aside—; lift —s; load with—; lose —s; merit—; observe—; oppress with —; overcome with—; perform with—; redouble—; relax—; release from—; rest from —; rout—; shake off—; share —s; soothe —s; sour with—; twist with—; unload —s; wash away—; waste with—; weigh down with—; wrack with—; wring with—; yoke with—; —ceases; —s chafe; —s consume; —s linger; —perplexes; —pursues; furrow with—.
(See concern, anxiety, worry, caution.)

CARE (*v*)

adverbs
particularly; hardly; assiduously; violently; chiefly; scientifically; reverentially; artistically; patiently; paternally; medically; bounteously; indefatigably; jealously; anxiously; painstakingly; tenderly; sufficiently; scrupulously; never-ceasingly; meticulously; efficiently; conscientiously; unremittingly; arduously; magnificently; providently; touchingly; prudently; exaggeratedly; surgically; maternally; religiously; studiously; sedulously; solicitously; hospitably; exquisitely; expertly; patriarchally; domestically.
(See worry.)

CAREER

adjectives
decent; brilliant; military; creative; sterile; medical; hard-working; subsequent; honorable; prosperous; notable; checkered; literary; wasted; remarkable; tremulous; serene; cinematic; philanthropic; ill-starred; unblemished; generous; victorious; adequate; kind; unsentimental; stormy; eventual; buoyant; editorial; distinguished; definite; uninterrupted; artistic; academical; parliamentary; changed; rough; terrible; desperate; horrible; riotous; laboring; dignified; forceful; wandering; martial; theatrical; inglorious; unwearied; conjugal; pale; rollicking; joyous; diplomatic; coarse; low; anti-social; recognized; remorseless; official; political; placid; dazzling; wild; agitated; tragic; unscrupulous; clerical; independent; legal; triumphant; mercantile; honest; pro-

fessional; obscure; shameful; disastrous; unadvanced; unswerving; irresistible; journalistic; heavenly; active; normal; marvelous; termagant; bloody; picturesque; celibate; hapless; saintly; inspiring; fluctuating; celebrated; astonishing; story-book; startling; extraordinary; exceptional; amazing; incredible; meteoric; budding; illustrious; clean; vivid; noted; imposing; sensible; fine; assured; magnificent; promising; serious; versatile; invincible; famous; portentous; spectacular; dramatic; sensational; eventful; colorful; breathless; adventuresome; exciting; arduous; quick; tempestuous; mad; extravagant; challenging; tumultuous; controversial; erratic; servile; turbulent; disturbed; revolutionary; happy; rollicking; blithe; disappointing; lonely; hopeless; lively; active; busy; vicious; infamous; strange; tormented; brutal; enigmatic; seafaring; forensic; golfing; burdened; moneymaking; pleasurable; public; scholastic; college; peripatetic; discomforting; scientific; posthumous; brief; true; indecorous; sufficient; chosen; diverging; material; limited; glittering; fixed; fortuitous; penitential; subsequent; prone.

verbs
achieve—; aspire to—; blast—; carve out —; checker—; close—; commence—; crown —; date—; embark on—; embrace—; endanger—; enter upon—; enthrall by—; further—; jeopardize—; litter—; mar—; mark —; pursue—; renounce—; smash—; stunt —; terminate—; unfold—; wreck—.

(See achievement, course, life, profession.)

CAREFUL

adverbs
prudently; vigilantly; alertly; attentively; meticulously; extremely; particularly; intelligently; scrupulously; conscientiously; decorously; dutifully; obediently; admirably; thoughtfully; deliberately; ridiculously; significantly; comfortingly; considerately; warily; cautiously; absolutely; energetically; definitely; discreetly; wisely; singularly; strangely; sagaciously; expertly; nervously; unduly; characteristically; naturally; usually; laughably; uneasily; elaborately; unobtrusively; satisfactorily; exaggeratedly; habitually; fastidiously; solicitously; sedulously; unusually; infinitely; lovingly; prodigiously; indefatigably.

CARELESS

adverbs
inexcusably; nonchalantly; casually; gaily; airily; indecently; recklessly; wantonly; vexatiously; irritatingly; amusingly; laughably; imprudently; indiscreetly; dangerously; perilously; significantly; noticeably; heedlessly; thoughtlessly; deliberately; indifferently; inconsiderately; unwarily; irresponsibly; absolutely; lazily; idly; unaccountably; inexplicably; impossibly; listlessly; languidly; defiantly; rebelliously; ostentatiously; flauntingly; stupidly.

CARELESSNESS

adjectives
aristocratic; criminal; elaborate; assumed; habitual; inveterate; idle; lovable; studied; superb; unpardonable; willful; culpable; deliberate.

verbs
berate—; breed—; condone—; countenance —; decry—; denounce—; inculcate—; inveigh against—; neglect in—; occasion—; punish—; regret—; resent—; utter in—; warn against—; wear an air of—; —disturbs; —worries.

(See neglect.)

CARESS

adjectives
condescending; complacent; fond; final; gentle; hasty; haughty; impulsive; impassioned; perfunctory; sympathetic; mesmeric; bitter-sweet; adolescent; dizzying; monotonous; turbulent; vicarious; exploratory; casual; mellowing; playful; sustained; infinite; indescribable; fierce; pussy-cat; rude; vague.

verbs
bestow —es on; cherish —es; countenance —es; delight in —es; encourage —es; favor with —es; fondle—; hunger for —es; intermix with —es; invite —es; long for —es; overwhelm with —es; ward off —; welcome —; —es allure; —es burn; —es cheer; —es endear; —es offend; —es soothe.

(See embrace, kiss, flattery.)

CARESS (v)

adverbs
endearingly; ecstatically; adoringly; sympathetically; warmly; lovingly; roughly; thrillingly; imploringly; affectionately; blissfully.

(See embrace, kiss, court.)

CAREWORN

adverbs
irritably; distressingly; intolerably; uncomfortably; dejectedly; sadly; anxiously; wretchedly; grievously; miserably; pitiably;

horribly; sorely; sorrily; heartbreakingly; unbearably; piteously; bitterly; dismally; hopelessly; unutterably; tragically; extremely; incredibly; gravely; outrageously; indescribably.

CARGO

adjectives
guarded; guilty; indifferent; precious; smuggled; surreptitious; undeclared; worthless.

verbs
burden with—; dampen—; discharge—; disinfect—; haul—; hoist—; import—; inspect—; insure—; land—; levy on—; load—; salvage—; ship—; tax—; transport—; underwrite—; —ballasts; —weighs.
(See freight, load, burden.)

CARNAL

adverbs
loosely; sensually; intemperately; luxuriously; voluptuously; grossly; shamelessly; wantonly; rakishly; bestially; erotically; indecently; self-indulgently; dissipatedly; intemperately; licentiously; coarsely; unbelievably; obscenely; evilly; sinfully; vilely; detestably; odiously.

CAROL

adjectives
gay; haunting; joyous; lively; merry; rustic; round; ancient; swelling; warbled.

verbs
bellow—; bless in—; burst into—; celebrate with —s; chorus—; compose—; dance to—; exercise—; flute—; hallow—; join in—; listen to —s; practise—; praise—; revive—; scream—; warble—; —cheers; —encourages; —expresses; —rings out; —sounds; —survives; —warms.
(See song, hymn.)

CAROUSE (*v*)

adverbs
hilariously; drunkenly; sordidly; squalidly; riotously; viciously; rollickingly; tumultuously; turbulently; wildly.
(See drink, celebrate.)

CARPENTER

adjectives
village; rare; retired; veteran.

verbs
employ—; hire—; —bevels; —chisels; —constructs; —designs; —frames; —hammers; —joins; —labors; —levels; —measures; —molds; —mortises; —notches; —s organize; —pins; —rules; —sands; —saws; —smooths; —tenons; —tails; —wedges.
(See worker, workman.)

CARPET

adjectives
sumptuous; grassy; mossy; wind-woven; flaunty; matted; frayed; brilliant; swampy; varicolored; taupe; worn; dusty; odorous; dirty; heavy; gay; stair; soft; suspended; treacherous; patternless; fiber; deep-pile; thick; handsome; bright; eye-offending.

verbs
dance on—; design—; dust—; fringe—; kneel on—; litter—; market—; match—; patch—; prostrate on—; scour—; shampoo—; shred—; spread on—; strew on—; tack down—; warp—; weave—; —beautifies; —covers; —decorates; —protects; —shields; —slides.
(See fabric, rug.)

CARRIAGE

adjectives (manner)
military; dashing; haughty; vigorous; graceful; violent; reckless; frank; toiling; unbending; indifferent; picturesque; internal; fierce; unpretentious; gentle; courteous; reverend; elegant; exquisite; superb; certain; sedate; fine; dignified; stately; soldierly; upright; erect; insolent; intelligent; swaggering; unwieldly; faulty; obstinate; headstrong; peculiar; sanctimonious.

CARRIAGE

adjectives (vehicle)
imperial; rough; decent; elegant; horseless; lumbering; travelling; countless; handsome; heavy; painted; lurching; wooden-wheeled; ramshackle; musty; moldy; rickety.

verbs
bar—; burden—; dispatch—; draw—; fashion—; guard—; guide—; harness—; load—; ornament—; provide—; tow—; wheel out—; —accommodates; —bounces; —conveys; —jolts; —rattles; —rocks; —rolls; —rumbles; —sways; —transports; —winds its way.
(See car, vehicle, coach.)

CARRION

adjectives
foolish; unsavory; putrefied.

CARRY (*v*)

adverbs
imperfectly; occasionally; triumphantly;

habitually; surreptitiously; imperceptibly; valiantly; ultimately; infallibly; delicately; laboriously; unfalteringly; accommodatingly; unconsciously; jauntily; continuously; unanimously; infallibly; slavishly; penitently; ostentatiously.
(See convey, bear, transport.)

CART

adjectives
creaking; retreating; fatal; ungainly; heavy; laden; shabby; jaunty.

verbs
direct—; draw—; grease—; harness to—; harvest with—; license—; load—; mount—; operate—; peddle on—; pile in—; provide—; team—; traverse by—; wheel—; —clatters; —conveys; —creaks; —jolts; —looms; —pitches; —progresses; —rumbles; —wheels.
(See vehicle, truck.)

CARTOON

adjectives
animated; completed; contemporary; much-remarked.

CARTOON (v)

adverbs
derisively; animatedly; sarcastically; satirically; diplomatically; viciously; humorously; blisteringly.
(See picture, design.)

CARTOONIST

adjectives
ribald; clever.

verbs
—attacks; —caricatures; —characterizes; —colors; —conceives; —contributes; —copies; —crystallizes; —denotes; —designs; —distorts; —draws; —engages in; —exaggerates; —executes; —illustrates; —implies; —indulges in; —irritates; —lampoons; —misrepresents; —mocks; —offends; —prints; —qualifies; —represents; —sets forth; —supplies; —sways; —wields.
(See artist.)

CARTRIDGE

adjectives
blank; buck-shot; cylindrical; deadly; highly-charged; inflammable; trusty; hoarded.

verbs
arm with —s; belt —s; box —s; case —s; distribute —s; fit—; form into—; ignite—; insert—; load with—; provide—; replenish —s; shape—; store—; —bursts; —detonates; —explodes; —penetrates.

CARVE (v)

adverbs
curiously; richly; marvelously; elaborately; skillfully; exquisitely; delicately; ornately; cunningly; ingeniously; fantastically; medievally; wearily.
(See sculpture, engrave, fashion.)

CARVING

adjectives
elaborate; fantastic; relief; grotesque; intricate; salvaged; weatherworn; delicate; splendid; flat; ornamental; hand; exquisite; artistic; ill-favored; medieval.

verbs
adorn with—; auction off—; destroy—; discover—; display—; embellish with—; exhibit—; fret with—; ornament with—; skill in—; unearth—; —hardens; —lasts; —illustrates.
(See sculpture, art.)

CASCADE

adjectives
foaming; perpetual; shimmering; feathery; pearly; motionless; veritable; gushing; showy; dazzling; musical; enthusiastic; blonde; roaring; tossing; magnificent.

verbs
lose in—; surmount—; sweep over—; —churns; —descends; —erodes; —falls; —foams; —pours over; —roars; —rumbles; —thunders.
(See waterfall.)

CASCADE (v)

adverbs
sibilantly; foamingly; perpetually; shimmeringly; gushingly; dazzlingly; roaringly; magnificently; awesomely; spectacularly.

CASE
(box)

adjectives
huge; packing; worn; oblong; odd-shaped; platinum; ponderous; concrete; jeweled; venerable-looking; tarnished.

verbs
buckle on—; ease—; frame in—; loose—; peel off—; strap on—; strip off—; unclasp—; —covers; —protects; —shields.
(See sheath, box, chest.)

CASE
(legal term)

adjectives
arguable; trying; contested; noted; curious; pending; simple; celebrated; criminal; collateral; disputed; brilliant; trivial; hope-

less; analogous; unaccountable; hardened; pathetic; exceptional; idiopathic; inexplicable; celebrated; pressing.

verbs
advise upon—; assign to—; bring—to trial; clinch—; conduct—; confer on—; contend with—; dispose of—; expedite—; fashion—; frame—; handle—; injure—; judge—; peruse—; plead—; prejudice—; present—; prove—; recount—; rest—; reverse—; review—; support—; sway—; testify in—; try —; unravel—; —hangs fire; —proves.

CASE

adjectives (medical term)
virulent; incurable; chronic; grave; critical; abnormal; dangerous; surgical.

verbs
cure—; diagnose—; encounter—; improve —; isolate—; protract—; relieve—; remedy —; succumb to—; treat—; —occurs; —recovers; —yields.
(See disease.)

CASE

adjectives (situation)
flattering; excellent; exceptional; important; striking; clear; conspicuous; rare; factual; difficult; intricate; severe; complicated; overwhelming; diverse; notable; eminent; necessitous; simplified; weird; inevitable; outrageous; analagous; stubborn; notorious; absurd; inevitable; insoluble; unpardonable; convincing; speculative; twisted; discussed; common; definite; desperate; recent; important; laughable; isolated; sole; parlous; pathetic; extreme; unforeseen; aggravated; deceptive; illustrative; lamentable; specific; evident; authentic; perplexing; superfluous; blessed; parallel; handsome; falsified; battle-scarred; imaginary; unrecognized; well-prepared; remarkable; mournful; special; pitiful; innumerable (pl); suppositious; sporadic; selective (pl); extraordinary; meritorious; multifarious (pl).

CASEMENT

adjectives
clasping; ivied; shaded; rattling; glimmering; ill-shut; oriel; wide; magic.

CASH

adjectives
evanescent; ample; pitiless; unquestionable; predatory; leaking; safe; cold; ambrosial; immediate.

verbs
amass—; appropriate—; check—; convert into—; demand—; discount for—; forward —; guard—; hoard—; involve—; register —; release—; secure—; transact with—; turn into—; —circulates; —flows through; —pours in.
(See coin, currency, money.)

CASKET

adjectives
precious; handsome; bronze; wrought; imposing; leaden; contrary; inlaid; glorious; draped; guiltless; scaly.

verbs
bank—; bless—; cache—; conceal—; decorate—; discover—; encrust—with; enrich—with; entrust—to; file past—; inter in—; lay in—; lower—; mourn at—; penetrate —; rob—; unearth—; unlock—; value—; —reveals.
(See box, chest, coffin.)

CAST

adjectives (drama)
capable; supporting; remarkable; insignificant; mythical; revengeful; fiery; fantastic; medieval; morbid; heterogeneous; desperate; undramatic; frivolous; stony.

verbs
allot to—; annoy—; applaud—; assemble —; assign to—; bestow on—; bring together —; choose—; coach—; congratulate—; direct—; dismiss—; dominate—; introduce—; manipulate—; provide—; recruit—; ruffle —; scan—; select—; train—; try out for—; —bows; —disbands; —impresses; —justifies; —mutilates; —performs; —produces; —rehearses; —renders.
(See actors.)

CAST

adjectives (glance)
pensive; pinkish; determined; wistful; meditative; wonted; somber; pale; mirthful; changeful.

CAST (*v*)

adverbs
rashly; humbly; weakly; demurely; bluntly; pensively; determinedly; wistfully; meditatively; somberly; mirthfully.
(See hurl, throw, fling.)

CASTANETS

adjectives
clicking; distant; jittering; rhythmic; noisy.

CASTAWAY

adjectives
lonely; assembled (pl); starving; lean; cadaverous; despairing; frantic; gaunt.

CASTE

adjectives
learned; distinct; priestly; inconvenient; sacerdotal; perpetual; ethic; transparent; time-honored.

verbs
ally with—; define—; distinguish—; forfeit —; form—; found—; isolate—; loathe—; organize—; preside over—; privilege—; qualify for—; restrict—; revile—; unite—; weld—; —aggregates; —collects; —confines to; —excludes; —groups; —practices; —inhabits; —resembles; —serves; —succumbs.
(See class, rank.)

CASTIGATION

adjectives
heartening; malicious; soul-deadening; deserved.

CASTLE

adjectives
ruined; haughty; baronial; ancient; Moorish; huge; grim; serviceable; razed; shimmering; inconvenient; ancestral; dream; medieval; moated; fairy; grandiose; princely; formidable; bastioned; ruined; cloud; stuccoed; enchanted; moldering; stupendous.

verbs
abide in—; assail—; bar—; besiege—; dominate—; dwell in—; fly to—; force—; ransack—; sack—; storm—; undermine—; —crumbles; —decays; —quakes; —shadows; —topples; —yields.
(See fortress, stronghold, mansion, building.)

CASTOR OIL

adjectives
disgusting; disguised; healing; malignant; nauseating; stomach-turning; skillfully-administered; repulsive; viscous.

verbs
administer— —; capsule— —; decoct— —; dose with— —; employ— —; express— —; inject— —; — —aggravates; — —cleans; — —induces; — —loosens; — —lubricates; — —nauseates; — —purges; — —relieves.
(See oil.)

CASUAL

adverbs
charmingly; nonchalantly; habitually; coolly; presumably; indeterminately; usually; provokingly; vexatiously; vaguely; perplexingly; unfortunately; undoubtedly; absolutely; positively; heartbreakingly; insufferably; intolerably.

CASUALNESS

adjectives
charming; practiced; hushed; lacerating; easy.

CASUALTY

adjectives
unforeseen; distressing; unlooked-for.

CAT

adjectives
clawing; long; tawny; enigmatic; gaunt; watchful; two-faced; ubiquitous; stray; sleek; despicable; huge; Persian; sinuous; predatory; singed; staid; spitting; plump; slinking; suspicious; cold; slow-witted; round-eyed; mewing; quick; harmless; contented; calculating; tiger; musing; lemon; sheltered; homeless; foiled; prudent.

verbs
pet—; stroke—; —arches; —claws; —climbs; —clutches; —darts; —devours; —laps; —leaps; —licks; —meows; —paws; —purrs; —preys on; —slinks; —sniffs; —sprawls; —springs; —washes.
(See animal, kitten.)

CATACOMB

adjectives
vaulted; literary; secret; large.

CATALOGUE

adjectives
descriptive; endless; illustrated; dry; melancholy; amplest; technical; diabolical; wearying; complete; seasonal; beautiful.

verbs
choose from—; clarify—; compile—; edit—; enter in—; index—; insert in—; issue—; list in—; order from—; prepare—; print —; publish—; set up—; —advertises; —confuses; —describes; —enumerates; —explains; —fascinates; —features; —lists; —offers; —pictures; —prices; —registers; —systematizes.
(See list, record.)

CATAPULT

adjectives
deadly; powerful; regulated; vicious; well-aimed.

verbs
discharge—; draw—; fire—; gear—; invent—; lay siege with —s; manipulate—; release—; storm with —s; —batters; —bombards; —damages; —harms; —hurls; —overcomes; —propels; —stones.
(See cannon.)

CATARACT

adjectives
shining; superb; sounding; roaring; earthquaking; fiery; remorseless; smoky; pouring; opaque; tireless; foaming.

verbs
lose in—; spout —s; stem—; view—; —churns; —crashes; —dashes down; —descends; —falls; —flashes; —foams; —leaps; —pours over; —precipitates; —roars; —rumbles; —rushes over; —surges; —sweeps down; —wears away.
(See waterfall, flood, cascade.)

CATASTROPHE

adjectives
tremendous; awful; imminent; historical; welcome; dire; impending; tragic; inevitable; general; calamitous; world-wide; ironical; picturesque; national; unexpected; crowning; unavertable; overwhelming; breath-taking; dreadful; unforeseen.

verbs
avert—; culminate in—; experience—; inflict with—; mourn—; plunge into—; result in—; rush to—; suffer—; survive—; —distresses; —looms; —overwhelms; —shocks; —threatens.
(See disaster, misfortune.)

CATASTROPHIC

adverbs
tragically; unmitigatedly; disastrously; extremely; ruinously; ominously; significantly; appallingly; deplorably; staggeringly; unspeakably; extraordinarily; shockingly; absolutely; unfortunately; unluckily; calamitously; incredibly; gravely; direly.

CATCH

adjectives
meager; passionate; little; obstinate; remarkable; maximum; uncommon; attractive.

CATCH

adjectives (fishing)
boasted; briny; exaggerated; gleaming; meager; modest; silvery; scaly; thrilling; traditional.

verbs
acquire—; bait—; devour—; display—; ensnare—; exhibit—; lure—; market—; net —; prepare—; prize—; relish—; scale—; transport—; value—; —amazes; —disappoints; —impresses; —increases.

CATCH (*v*)

adverbs
unceremoniously; impulsively; instinctively; convulsively; mechanically; red-handedly; charmingly; inadvertently; essentially; unerringly; passionately; obstinately; remarkably.
(See seize, clasp, clutch.)

CATCHER

adjectives (baseball)
adroit; alert; courageous; clumsy; befuddled; dependable; fumbling; unpredictable.

verbs
—blocks; —covers; —encourages; —fumbles; —misses; —muffs; —recovers; —signals; —steadies; —tags.

CATCHING

adverbs
highly; easily; dangerously; epidemically; pestilentially; unfortunately; acutely; widely; perilously; seriously; extremely; decidedly; unquestionably; astonishingly; frightfully; absolutely; remarkably; alarmingly; curiously; awfully; critically; definitely; fatally; positively.

CATCHY

adverbs
irresistibly; sweetly; indefinably; mysteriously; luckily; unutterably; powerfully; singularly; charmingly; engagingly; undeniably; bewitchingly; enchantingly; delightfully; daintily; smartly; jauntily; youthfully; tormentingly; teasingly; hauntingly; unexpectedly; surprisingly; genuinely; miraculously; luckily; unprecedentedly.

CATEGORICAL

adverbs
positively; undeniably; avowedly; broadly; certainly; emphatically; explicitly; formally; markedly; peremptorily; solemnly; reliably; authentically; axiomatically; evidently; manifestly; undoubtedly; indisputably;

irrefutably; solidly; soundly; unmistakably; uncomfortably; conclusively; gratefully; cheeringly; disturbingly; dogmatically.

CATEGORY

adjectives
amiable; poetic; astonishing; definite; separate; neat; depressing; reasonable; odious; scholastic.

verbs
add to—; bring into—; disagree with—; discard—; exclude from—; express in—; group in—; interest in—; list in—; recognize—; reduce to—; regard—; relegate to —; understand—; upset—; —consists of; —deals with; —derives from; —differs from; —includes; —represents.

(See class, division, condition, predicament.)

CATER (*v*)

adverbs
exclusively; delectably; democratically; professionally; amiably; commonly; stealthily; unaccountably.

(See provide, supply, furnish.)

CATERPILLAR

adjectives
bristly; evil-horned; fuzzy; harmless; inching; plushy; sojourning; whither-bent.

verbs
combat —s; cultivate —s; examine—; exterminate—; infest with —s; observe—; spray —s; teem with —s; —s abound; —s attack; —s bore into; —s collect; —crawls; —despoils; —devours; —emerges; —s gather; —hibernates; —s invade; —s molt; —s ravage; —secretes; —spins a cocoon.

(See insect.)

CATHEDRAL

adjectives
Gothic; Doric; staid; sleepy; dim; mystic; peaceful; medieval; miniature; quaint; magnificent; majestic; unfinished; elaborate; spacious; Roman.

verbs
approach—; congregate in—; construct—; design—; erect—; explore—; found—; glory in—; hallow—; install in—; preside over —; pour from—; raise—; revere—; worship at—; —awes; —echoes; —impresses; —induces; —inspires; —looms; —shadows; —towers.

(See church, tabernacle.)

CATHOLIC

adverbs (general sense)
broadly; comprehensively; unusually; prevalently; magnanimously; remarkably; liberally; comfortably; generally; decently; sagaciously; intelligently; admirably; reasonably; generously; dependably; charitably; intellectually; discerningly; perceptively; obviously; manifestly; nobly; unselfishly.

CATTLE

adjectives
blooded; grazing; crazed; unkempt; roving; peaceful; scraggy; weak; driven; fine; drowsy; stolen; bedded; wild; long-horned; bartered; mottled; reclining; tainted; lazy; sweltered; murrained; domesticated; meanest; draught; thin.

verbs
corral—; dehorn—; exchange for—; infect —; market—; raise—; slaughter—; stampede—; tend—; tether—; —bellow; —freeze; —graze; —huddle; —low; —pasture; —plod; —roam; —stagger.

(See animal.)

CAUSATION

adjectives
natural; eternal; inevitable.

CAUSE

adjectives (agent or reason)
abundant; scattered (pl); obnoxious; specific; proximate; predisposing; pressing; apparent; fundamental; hopeless; unavoidable; immediate; prolific; duplicating; rational; dreadful; effective; underlying; mighty; noble; just; sacred; worthy; legitimate; endless; redeeming; supernatural; spectacular; apparent; assignable; faltering; secondary; physical; universal; growing; innocent; predominant; remote; unknown; scandalous; sensational; plausible; permanent; transient; fatal; potential; weighty; assignable; prominent; internal; erroneous; contributory; subjective; temperance; amorous; glorious; breaking; eternal; ultimate; paramount; unconscious; frequent; princely; philosophical; natural; mistaken; malignant; alleged; latent; discreditable; recorded; celebrated; sordid; economic; primeval; mitigating; constitutional; sensible; ennobling; determining; mechanical; infallible; propelling; hated; secondary; obvious; habitual; minute; idiotic; antecedent; justifiable; primal; creative; irritating; efficient; unkind; notable; unwitting; extraneous; lawful; unaccountable; identical; ex-

citing; worthy; immoral; functional; vanquished; multifarious (pl); impious; trivial; sublunary; artificial; ridiculous; everlasting; similar; righteous.
verbs
acquaint with—; advance—; allege—; appraise—; approach—; ascertain—; ascribe —to; assign—; attach—; attribute—to; concern with—; cure—; deal with—; debate—; declare—; define—; demonstrate—; determine—; discover—; display—; dwell upon —; eliminate—; eradicate—; estimate—; explain—; fathom—; inquire into—; judge —; laugh at—; obliterate—; obviate—; overcome—; perceive—; procure—; regard —; relieve—; remand—; remove—; report —; reveal—; reverse—; rue—; seek—; serve as—; state—; strike at—; suggest—; surmise—; suspect—; trace—to; weigh—; —prevails; —resides in.
(See reason, motive, source, origin.)

CAUSE

adjectives (aim, principle, movement)
adopted; alien; championed; espoused; glorious; lost; noble; sacred; undying.

verbs
adopt—; advocate—; approve—; betray—; bolster—; bow to—; champion—; cleave to —; contribute to—; defame—; desert—; devote to—; die for—; do ill to—; embrace —; encourage—; engage in—; enlist in—; espouse—; favor—; forsake—; further—; guide—; harm—; injure—; interpret—; justify—; labor for—; maintain—; misinterpret—; pay tribute to—; persecute—; plead—; praise—; promote—; rally to—; scorn—; serve—; speak for—; sponsor—; spurn—; struggle for—; suffer for—; sunder—; support—; transgress—; tread—under foot; unbraid—; vindicate—; withdraw from—; —perishes; —prospers; —suffers; —triumphs.
(See aim, principle, movement.)

CAUSE (v)

adverbs
inadvertently; noxiously; specifically; fundamentally; apparently; unavoidably; rationally; legitimately; supernaturally; spectacularly; physically; universally; predominantly; fatally; potentially; subjectively; eternally; ultimately; philosophically; malignantly; allegedly; mechanically; infallibly; unaccountably; artificially; righteously.
(See induce, effect.)

CAUSTIC

adverbs
bitterly; unpardonably; unreasonably; mildly; maliciously; hatefully; sharply; acrimoniously; cruelly; brutally; atrociously; resentfully; venomously; ominously; needlessly; incisively; sarcastically; ironically; cunningly; mercilessly; churlishly; unsparingly; perversely; abusively; uncivilly; intolerably; captiously; obnoxiously; unbearably; tauntingly; unwisely; malevolently; unwontedly; habitually; unwarrantably; disagreeably; unpleasantly.

CAUTION

adjectives
superfluous; common; vast; habitual; infinite; singular; subtle; inborn; abominable; timid; commendable; puerile; conscientious; wonted; just; extraordinary; prudent; preliminary; unholy; philosophic; extreme; losing; intended; vigilant; necessary; worldly; superior; redoubled; stealthy; reverent; niggardly; beneficent; utmost; curious; patriotic; friendless.

verbs
advise—; deaden—; exercise—; heed—; indicate—; inspire—; lessen—; motivate by —; necessitate—; perform with—; proceed with—; sound a note of—; throw—to the winds; —safeguards; —wanes.
(See prudence, care.)

CAUTIOUS

adverbs
discreetly; prudently; wisely; significantly; ludicrously; suspiciously; habitually; singularly; unnecessarily; timidly; extraordinarily; alertly; stealthily; curiously; strangely; oddly; outlandishly; sagaciously; expertly; deftly; foolishly; unwontedly; nervously; excitedly; idiotically; incomprehensibly; queerly; cravenly; faintheartedly; genuinely; unduly; inexplicably; laughably; characteristically; gravely; uneasily; extravagantly; elaborately; quietly; unobtrusively; undoubtedly; inherently.

CAVALCADE

adjectives
straggling; grim; martial; scampering; gorgeous; furbished; infinite; brilliant; large.

CAVALIER

adjectives
attentive; boyish; tall; gallant; bold; comely; free; sprightly; deformed; stout-hearted; effeminate; high-spirited; trusty; plumed; pretentious; victorious; arrogant; broken-down; gay; impecunious.

CAVALRY

adjectives
bedizened; best-mounted; thundering; foaming; dismounted; exploiting; dashing; irregular.

CAVE

adjectives
lonely; lovely; moonlit; dark; damp; stalactite; virtual; glistening; unexplored; enormous; ice; magical; winding; abandoned; unlighted; shore-cliff; fretted; destined; toothless; coral; forlorn; shadowy; unfathomed; tiny; deep; cold; yawning; unimagined; sapphire; vaulted; low-browed; monstrous; dewy; gloomy; spacious; coastal.

verbs
abandon—; bar—; block—; bury in—; crawl into—; creep into—; discover—; dwell in —; grope in—; harbor in—; inhabit—; issue from—; lodge in—; retire to—; roll from—; scoop out—; seal—; shelter in—; —echoes; —resounds.
(See hole, recess.)

CAVERN

adjectives
fairy-like; verdurous; dark; beautiful; marvelous; mysterious; ghostly; enormous; notchy; desolate; crystal; unfathomed; smudged; obscure; glaucous; horrid; smoky; dusky; ominous; spacious; tongueless; rifted; sparry; precipitous; gloomy; gelid; mossy; inaccessible; scorched; murmuring.

CAVERNOUS

adverbs
darkly; dimly; vastly; mysteriously; alluringly; deeply; dangerously; alarmingly; irresistibly; fantastically; gloomily; obscurely; duskily; murkily; sombrely; astonishingly; marvellously; frighteningly; indistinctly; strangely; terribly; hideously; formidably; awfully.

CAVITY

adjectives
dark; dungeon-like; hideous; conical.

verbs
cap—; dilate—; drain—; drill—; empty—; fill—; grind—; irrigate—; line—; obliterate —; tap—; treat—; —contains; —weakens.
(See hole, cave, hollow, excavation.)

CAVORT (*v*)

adverbs
blithely; friskily; gaily; spiritedly; joyously; sportively; grotesquely; gracefully; idiotically; pleasingly.

CEASE (*v*)

adverbs
functionally; abruptly; presently; suddenly; definitely; temporarily; prematurely; entirely; eventually.
(See discontinue, stop, refrain.)

CEDAR

adjectives
spicy; stunted; gray-sheathed; pyramiding; tall; slim; fantastic; distorted; stately; lordly; vast; majestic; somnolent; dark; mighty; drooping.

CEDE (*v*)

adverbs
superfluously; entirely; willingly; temporarily; outwardly; prematurely; partially.
(See surrender, relinquish, grant.)

CEILING

adjectives
beamed; frescoed; gorgeous; lofty; gilded; festooned; clouded; vault-like; fallen; damp; stained; crumbling; grimy; dirty; arched; slanting; sagging; dingy; domelike; moulded; ornamented; pictured; sloped; mirrored; reflecting.

CELEBRATE (*v*)

adverbs
hilariously; painfully; pompously; traditionally; obstreperously; appropriately; dissolutely; justly; discreetly; jubilantly; enthusiastically; dramatically; elaborately; barbarously; deliberately; raucously; gorgeously; nationally.
(See commemorate, observe.)

CELEBRATED

adverbs
locally; justly; universally; eminently; notably; illustriously; nationally; genuinely; rightfully; appropriately; brilliantly; remarkably; exceptionally; fitly; especially; particularly.

CELEBRATION

adjectives
discreet; jubilant; enthusiastic; centenary; forthcoming; final; dramatic; flourished; bicentenary; misconstrued; elaborate; decennial; gaudy; monster; roaring; barbarous; deliberate; raucous; gory; gorgeous.

verbs
arrange for—; climax—; deserve—; disturb —; enter—; extol—; fete with—; hold—; indulge in—; launch—; observe—; plan—; retain—; —commemorates; —exhausts; —honors; —overjoys; —surprises.
(See observance.)

CELEBRITY

adjectives
half-forgotten; rare; permanent; cosmopolitan; revered; glittering; dead; contemporary; available; innumerable (pl); continental; immediate; literary; envious; frustrated; fastidious; world-wide; posthumous.

CELERITY

adjectives
swift; amazing; deft; surprising; indescribable; dramatic; magical; characteristic; reckless; miraculous; incredible; rounded; admirable; ingenious.

CELERY

adjectives
crunchy; crisp; green; curled.

CELL

adjectives
fungal; transition; sylvan; poor; mossy; dermal; reflective; solitary; overcrowded; photo-electric; filthy; drafty; narrow; tiny; whitewashed; dingy; cement-floored; steel; quiet; dreary; dismal; naked; cloistered; eremitic; waxen; monastic; longitudinal; convent; inmost; uncouth; unused; ambrosial; functional; albumenoid; wretched; semi-transparent; prophetic; gloomy; uncomfortable; wind-rocked; message-sending; tender; solemn; primordial; dungeon-like.

verbs
bind in—; brood in—; cloister in—; confine in—; dwell in—; ensconce in—; force—; gain—; imprison in—; lodge in—; pour from—; range in—; remand to—; retire to —; share—; store in—; track to—.
(See room, cavity, chamber.)

CELL (biological)

adjectives
amoebic; detached; enlarged; enemy; floating; gelatinous; malignant; normal; structural.

verbs
build —s; destroy —s; feed —s; motivate —s; nourish —s; protect —s; regenerate —s; renew —s; stimulate—; —s adhere to; —s degenerate; —fulfills; —s increase; —s multiply; —s perform; —shrivels; —specializes; —s store; —s work.
(See unit, compartment, blood.)

CELLAR

adjectives
dark; reeking; damp; fire-stopped; verminous; spacious; nether; dry; shallow; rat-infested.

verbs
carpet—; convert—; cool in—; dampen—; descend to—; drain—; emerge from—; enter by—; flood—; grope in—; inhabit—; illumine—; lodge in—; stock in—; store in —; —conceals; —extends.
(See basement, vault, room.)

CELLULOID

adjectives
brittle; explosive; flimsy; highly-inflammable; inexpensive; pretentious; shining; showy.

verbs
compose of—; derive from—; employ—; encase in—; manufacture—; mould—; polish —; press—; season—; shape—; stain—; turn—; utilize—; —covers; —cracks; —imitates; —protects; —serves as; —shields; —shrivels.
(See material.)

CEMENT

adjectives
crack-proof; grayish; impenetrable; marble; plastic; protecting; resisting; tested; unyielding.

verbs
apply—; blast—; bore into—; calcine—; coat with—; compact—; compound—; crush —; grind—; lay—; mix—; slake—; surface with—; —adheres; —binds; —clinkers; —crumbles; —dehydrates; —glues; —hardens; —secures; —sets; —solidifies; —walls in.
(See mortar, plaster.)

CEMENT (v)

adverbs
firmly; securely; fixedly; perpetually; eternally; enduringly; permanently.
(See join, fasten.)

CEMETERY

adjectives
walled; tiny; bleak; dismal; weed-grown; desolate; neighboring; pauper.

CENSER

adjectives
floral; coveted; gilded; flame-like; smoking.

CENSOR

adjectives
royal; strict; sternest; formidable; official; prejudiced; incompetent.

verbs
assign to—; elect—; escape —s; moderate for —s; offend —s; submit to —s; —approves; —bans; —bars; —blames; —clamps down; —condemns; —criticizes; —cuts out; —examines; —exercises; —guards; —grants; —inquires; —inspects; —investigates; —judges; —preserves; —prohibits; —reviews; —slashes; —supervises; —torments.

(See critic.)

CENSORIOUS

adverbs
sharply; mercilessly; ominously; destructively; needlessly; venomously; invidiously; viciously; unsparingly; churlishly; snappishly; obnoxiously; unpleasantly; disagreeably; remorselessly; relentlessly; dryly; roughly; rudely; cleverly; spitefully; sarcastically; maliciously; malevolently; bitterly; ruthlessly; uncompromisingly.

CENSORSHIP

adjectives
moralistic; strict; recent; rigid; vague; effective; religious; powerful; insidious; official; actual; iron; voluntary; rigorous.

verbs
announce—; clamp down—; concoct—; enforce—; establish—; exercise—; impose—; indicate—; institute—; pass—; practise—; submit to—; tighten—; —cuts; —militates; —outlaws; —prevails; —slashes; —supervises; —suppresses.

(See superintendence, revision, criticism, censure.)

CENSURABLE

adverbs
seriously; unquestionably; exceptionally; lamentably; deplorably; deservedly; justly; avowedly; properly; strictly; fairly; unfortunately; unhappily; unluckily; obviously; manifestly; plainly; conspicuously; grievously.

CENSURE

adjectives
moral; heavy-handed; violent; declamatory; implicit; critical; reluctant; ecclesiastical; perpetual; just; erroneous; undeserved; awful; lewd; implied.

verbs
avoid—; cringe under—; endure—; escape —; incur—; smart under—; wag one's tongue in—; —abates; —looms; —repels; —threatens.

(See blame, disapproval, criticism, revision, censorship.)

CENSURE (*v*)

adverbs
morally; violently; critically; reluctantly; ecclesiastically; perpetually; undeservedly; impliedly; scornfully; gravely; captiously; freely; scathingly.

(See reprove, rebuke, upbraid.)

CENSUS

adjectives
national; biennial; previous; rough; partial.

CENTER

adjectives
musical; inspiring; nervous; spiritual; cultural; permanent; intellectual; exclusive; allied; important; residential; veritable; principal; information; overpopulated; dead; banking; distributing; key; trading; financial; industrial; bustling; civic; business; urban; railroad; unique; metropolitan; important; steamship; legislative; exact; religious; commercial; smart; creative; harmonious; congested; prosperous; subtle; dazzling; storm; enlightened; fashionable; remote; accessible; strategic; tessellated; eternal; relative.

verbs
balance at—; collect at—; converge toward —; diffuse from—; draw to—; emerge from —; fall toward—; form in—; gravitate toward—; group in—; intersect at—; move toward—; occupy—; proceed from—; radiate from—; revolve around—; root in—; throw off—.

(See middle.)

CENTRAL

adverbs
conveniently; acceptably; appropriately; diplomatically; advantageously; exactly; comfortably; satisfactorily; relatively; approximately; strategically; practically.

CENTRALIZATION

adjectives
elaborate; rigorous; bureaucratic; political; absorbing; hierarchical.

CENTURY

adjectives
populous; modern; countless (pl); tempestuous; romantic; untold; preceding; myriad (pl); glorious; previous; unborn; hoary; present; noiseless; stormy; arduous; brilliant; successive (pl); amusing; senile.

verbs
endure for —ies; fade into —ies; gild—; measure in —ies; span —ies; roll into—; —abounds in; —creeps past; —draws to an end; —elapses; —unwinds.

CEREAL

adjectives
nourishing; tempting; whole-grain; steaming; golden-wheat; farinaceous.

verbs
bleach—; combine—with; consume—; cultivate—; diet on—; exploit—; moisten—; prepare—; produce—; refine—; steam—; sweeten—; —comprises; —flourishes; —furnishes; —nourishes; —provides; —stimulates; —strengthens; —supplies.
(See grain.)

CEREBRUM

adjectives
divided; convalescent; convoluted; boiling; membrane-wrapped; throbbing; overlapping.

verbs
affect—; injure—; penetrate to—; —compacts; —comprises; —consists of; —controls; —files away; —forms; —is divided into; —is enveloped in; —presides over; —occupies; —overlaps; —regulates.
(See brain.)

CEREMONIAL

adjectives
voodoo; elaborate; fitting; impressive; quaint; stately; insignificant; rich; tiresome; pompous; compulsive; enormous; insulting; cumbrous; wailing; magnificent; frivolous; burdensome; overpowering; curious.

CEREMONIOUS

adverbs
admirably; devoutly; elaborately; meticulously; punctiliously; appropriately; highly; decorously; reverently; traditionally; properly; conventionally; magnificently; splendidly; royally; barbarically; impeccably; reverentially; beautifully; irreproachably; majestically; extravagantly; wondrously; superbly.

CEREMONY

adjectives
preparatory; customary; lawful; scant; whimsical; decent; curious; fetish-like; anointing; approaching; diabolical; bloody; dedicatory; solemn; picturesque; ancient; hazardous; occult; impressive; religious; elaborate; tedious; appalling; venerable; appropriate; outrageous; stately; somber; reverent; enforced; time-consecrated; incongruous; peculiar; inauguration; imposing; formal; august; notable; gracious; futile; melancholy; fantastic; colorful; calm; dignified; punctilious; grim; savage; icy; painful; superstitious; primitive; undue; funeral; final; outward; ritualistic; appointed.

verbs
beautify—; bore with—; endure—; enrich—; observe—; officiate at—; preserve—; ritualize—; shorten—; stand on—; wed with—; —commemorates; —drags; —entails; —honors; —ruffles.
(See rite, form, solemnity, formality, sacrament.)

CERTAIN

adverbs
actually; definitely; positively; absolutely; undeniably; assuredly; solidly; substantially; decisively; categorically; incontestably; irrefutably; conclusively; officially; plainly; indisputably; acceptably; unfortunately; unhappily; fortunately; luckily; humiliatingly; terribly; reasonably; comfortably; authoritatively.

CERTAINTY

adjectives
absolute; inevitable; old; humiliating; terrible; established; polite; painful; perfect; ultimate; unbreakable; considerable; simple; comfortable; practical; swift; astounding; reasonable; atrocious; dark; inevitable; instant; instinctive; automatic; positive; boyish; monumental; fierce; unerring; dead; towering.

verbs
accept as—; authenticate—; be born of—; confirm—; demonstrate with—; destroy—; inform of—; neglect—; postulate as—; ques-

tion—; surrender to—; venture on—; verge on—; —relieves; —satisfies.

(See confidence, assurance, conviction, fact, truth.)

CERTIFICATE

adjectives

gilded; original; engraved; baptismal; round; marriage; laudatory; authenticated; sales.

verbs

attest by—; bear—; collect —s; confirm—; counterfeit—; dispense—s; esteem—; forge —; furnish with—; garner—s; issue—; register—; revoke—; seal—; suspend—; witness—; —assures; —authorizes; —certifies; —guarantees; —licenses; —restricts; —specifies; —testifies.

(See declaration, document, testimony.)

CERTITUDE

adjectives

reasonable; fresh; inward.

CESSATION

adjectives

sudden; entire; instant; negative; good-humored; gradual; complete; premature.

CHAFF

adjectives

mocking; antiquarian; absurd.

verbs

bear up—; beat out—; drive away—; fan—; flay out—; gather—; pick from—; scatter—; separate from—; sift out—; weed out—; winnow—; wipe away—; —flies away.

(See straw.)

CHAFF (v)

adverbs

banteringly; unmercifully; considerably; mockingly; excessively; humiliatingly; boisterously; bitterly; coquettishly; hostilely; enigmatically; frivolously.

(See banter, ridicule, jest.)

CHAGRIN

adjectives

natural; evident; universal; jealous; bitter; secret.

verbs

arouse—; conceal—; devour by—; display —; excite—; feel—; meet with—; observe —; profess—; smile away—; steep in—; touch with—; —daunts; —fumes away; —suffuses; —waxes.

(See mortification, vexation, humiliation, confusion.)

CHAIN

adjectives

linked; secular; leash; endless; indissoluble; unbroken; firm; lengthening; household; ponderous; rattling; long-worn; mesh; nocturnal; clanking; winding; golden; flowery; galling; resplendent; multitudinous (pl); massive; continuous; impressive; feudal; adamantine; ascending; everlasting; dangling; countless (pl); gleaming; indivisible; bolted; door; bloody; glittering; rosy; trembling; human; roaring; shrieking; howling; jingling; hateful; shameful; curious; will-forged; stout; giant; relentless; binding; restraining; damaging; mental; intangible.

verbs

affix—; bind in —s; bolt—; burst—; condemn to —s; dally with—; deliver from —s; drag in —s; draw—; encircle with—; encompass in—; fasten—; file—; hedge —s about; knit—; link in—; loose —s; manacle in —s; pluck off —s; shake off —s; smite at—; strive in —s; tangle—; tighten —; unravel—; untwist—; wreathe in —s; —clanks; —engirdles; —falls off; —fetters; —rattles; —yields.

(See bond, shackle.)

CHAIN (v)

adverbs

ingloriously; secularly; indissolubly; unbrokenly; firmly; ponderously; everlastingly; indivisibly; stoutly; bindingly; relentlessly; restrainingly; intangibly.

(See restrain, fasten.)

CHAIR

adjectives

rocking; lounge; slim; worm-eaten; leather; pillowed; straight; glowing; prominent; swinging; covered; over-stuffed; cane-seated; long-legged; solitary; classic; rickety; capacious; proffered; marble; cushioned; inhospitable; mahogany; rigid; magisterial; split-bottomed; professorial; confessional; narrow; Morris; substantial; dangling; exiguous; ornamental; adjustable; high; triumphal; anatomical; editorial; rustic; fragile; carved; tipped-back; mural; gilt; lower; vacant; cozy; heavy; upholstered; soft; comfortable; club; arm; formidable; easy; roomy; favorite; noble; battered; faded; untrustworthy; worn; invalid; dilapidated; uncertain; overturned; adjoining;

groaning; clattering; reversible; swivel; basket; wing; Windsor; hideous; creaking; wicker; walnut; hickory; iron; horsehair; rattan; curule-back; expectant.

verbs
accept—; advance to—; appropriate—; bound from—; descend from—; drop into—; ensconce in—; hoist from—; jerk out of—; loll back in—; monopolize—; motion to—; occupy—; offer—; perch on—; plump into —; resign—; retire to—; shift in—; shrink back in—; sink in—; slump in—; snuggle in—; splinter—; sprawl all over—; straddle—; throne in—; tip—back; uprear in—.
(See seat, bench.)

CHAIRMAN

adjectives
temporary; anecdotal; prosy.

verbs
—adjourns; —bangs; —conducts; —delegates; —dismisses; —exercises; —occupies; —opens; —performs; —presides; —vetoes.
(See president.)

CHALICE

adjectives
cup-like; poisoned; silver; exuberant; sacred.

CHALLENGE

adjectives
visual; roguish; hoarse; loud; singing; heroic; silent; singular; provocative; sonorous; contemptuous; roistering; gay; feeble; stormy; direct; unsuccessful; peremptory; demoniac; concentrated; insolent; manifest; artistic; chivalrous; pert; mocking; puny; derisive; laughing; flippant; devil-may-care; malicious; sinister; menacing; truculent; fierce; wanton; snarling; angry; sharp; strident; stern; riotous; sweeping; tremendous; formidable; ringing; constant; perpetual; high-pitched; subtle; stimulating; reasonable; vague; unvoiced; startling; blue; definite; objective; hysterical.

verbs
arouse—; blaze—; cringe before—; debate —; defy—; deliver—; fling—; howl—; hurl —; ignore—; meet—; open to—; point—; read—; refuse—; ridicule—; scorn—; take up—; whistle—; —echoes; —rings; —resounds; —withers.

(See defiance, objection, exception, accusation, charge.)

CHALLENGE (v)

adverbs
egotistically; gruffly; justly; promptly; insolently; bravely; provocatively; sonorously; directly; peremptorily; demoniacally; pertly; mockingly; sinisterly; sternly; stridently; formidably; hysterically; definitely; startlingly; fiercely; wantonly; snarlingly.
(See defy, dare, brave.)

CHAMBER

adjectives
conjugal; aspiring; well-guarded; underground; silent; sordid; desolate; bare; nuptial; operating; comfortable; antique; mean; solitary; echoing; sepulchral; voluptuous; subterranean; subaqueous; privy; mystic; chill-looking; glorious; airy; accursed; ducal; treasure; mutilated; respective; chilling; uppermost; gloomy; dismal; unstable; haunted; untenanted; noble; repulsive; empty; crumbling; grimy; dusty; vault-like; lethal; burial; inner; low-ceilinged; tiny; circular; unexplored; spacious; lofty; gilded; confined; packed.

verbs
abide in—; array in—; attend—; build—; carve—; convey into—; dress up—; empty —; gather in—; hie to—; invite to—; retire to—; seal—; seep into—; withdraw into —; —echoes.
(See room, cell, hall.)

CHAMPAGNE

adjectives
effervescent; brisk; excellent; cool; dashing; sparkling; tingling; convivial; atmospheric; gurgling; winking.

verbs
age—; blend into—; bucket—; cask—; characterize—; christen with—; consume—; cork—; drown in—; flavor—; foul—; ice —; lose in—; mature—; mix—; produce—; proffer—; revel in—; sip—; steep in—; support by—; swill—; tap—; toast with—; uncork—; urge on with—; —arouses; —bubbles; —effervesces; —exhilarates; —ferments; —fizzes; —glitters; —inspires; —intoxicates; —matures; —numbs; —sparkles; —unsteadies.
(See wine, liquor.)

CHAMPION

adjectives
undistinguished; formidable; invincible; undoubted; avowed; opposing; proper; ardent; conspicuous; valiant; illustrious; celebrated; sturdy; solitary; devoted; victori-

ous; doughty; undaunted; energetic; stalwart; lusty; redoubtable; brave; resolute; determined; unswerving; uncompromising; foremost; self-admitted; noble; gaunt; royal; prospective; fanatical; loyal; strange; defeated; fearless; resistless.

verbs
acclaim—; applaud—; challenge—; combat—; condition—; crown—; defeat—; defy—; develop—; disable—; dispute—; fear—; hail—; laud—; overthrow—; present—; proclaim—; protect—; provide—; —appears; —competes; —contends; —defends; —engages; —maintains; —performs; —renders; —represents; —teaches; —trains; —upholds; —vanquishes.

(See defender, winner, hero, conqueror.)

CHAMPIONSHIP

adjectives
intrepid; intemperate; conjugal; hyper-enthusiastic; vigorous; notable.

CHANCE

adjectives
slim; fluctuating; lost; opening; opportune; miraculous; lifetime; calculable; divine; slight; desperate; matrimonial; sporting; robust; limited; faint; ironical; impossible; evil; unforeseen; additional; mere; slender; golden; reasonable; fighting; undue; exceptional; brilliant; precious; main; endless; favorable; fortunate; magnificent; good-sized; fair; happy; unlooked-for; convenient; pure; barest; slightest; remote; small; equal; unfortunate; desperate; fatal; frustrated; awful; unfair; hazardous; repeated; fortuitous; amazing; timely; unlimited; glamorous; impartial; full; incorruptible; individualized; complicated.

verbs
advance—; await—; blast —s; brood over —; dispose of—; forfeit—; grab at—; grasp —; imperil —s; intercept by—; invite—; jump at—; leap at—; lessen —s; mind—; muff—; obviate—; rush for—; scoff at—; seize—; shun—; spy by—; stake on—; subject to—; yield to—; —begets; —controls; —detains; —determines; —dies; —fades; —fails; —governs; —guides; —leads.

(See fortune, luck, possibility, hazard, risk, probability.)

CHANCELLOR

adjectives
great; fallen; iron.

CHANDELIER

adjectives
cut-glass; crystal; interesting; central; dazzling; immense; prism-fringed; brilliant; glistening.

CHANGE

adjectives
singular; momentous; subtle; logical; ministerial; definite; threatened; healthful; indescribable; amazing; innovational; perceptible; incestuous; personal; far-reaching; periodical; remarkable; random; striking; varying; gradual; fluctuant; refreshing; incessant; vindictive; rhythmic; continual; rapid; industrial; tragical; stupendous; extraordinary; infinitesimal; withering; physiological; molecular; fine; hideous; enjoyable; radical; ceaseless; generating; appreciable; agreeable; constant; profound; prelusive; frequent; cunning; coincidental; instantaneous; delicate; fearful; acceptable; painful; pathetic; alarming; implied; essential; numerous (pl); eternal; intermediate; never-ending; distressing; partial; genuine; far-reaching; healing; startling; elaborate; drastic; magical; notable; wholesome; comprehensible; monotonous; revolutionary; unaccountable; permanent; consolidating; accumulated; progressive; astonishing; unimportant; political; social; economic; structural; miraculous; obliterative; corresponding; desirable; succeeding; fundamental; constant; violent; geophysical; asthmatic; marked; sudden; degenerative; inexpedient; miserable; extensive; solar; mortal; impending; metamorphic; observable; electrical; agreeable; flattering; malignant; pathological; valuable; secular; lightning-like; fermentative; welcome; seasonal; noticeable; decided; verbal; pleasing; ceaseless; convulsive; panoramic; periodic; beneficent; numerable (pl); realized; much-needed; alleged; abrupt; necessary; sly; wide; complex; enduring; practical; problematic; undeniable; unvarying; tangible; quiet; kindliest; peaceful; noteworthy; magical; refreshing; propitious; vital; tactful; serious; dramatic; vast; thrilling; epoch-making; cataclysmic; arbitrary; doleful; terrific; saddening; inevitable; visible; kaleidoscopic; psychic; psychological; adolescent; bodily; daily; physical; technical; natural.

verbs
accomplish—; advance—; advise—; advocate—; anticipate—; await—; bemoan—; beset by —s; bless—; compel—; concede—; confirm—; contemplate—; debate—; deplore

—; destine for—; dread—; effect—; execute —; exhort—; fathom—; frown upon—; hinder—; impart—; inaugurate—; indicate—; induce—; mourn—; occasion—; oppose—; perceive—; prescribe—; promise—; pronounce—; prophesy—; propose—; report—; stir to—; suffer—; undergo—; warrant—; work—; —accompanies; —arises from; —equalizes; —modifies; —occurs; —perplexes.

(See variation, alteration, transition.)

CHANGE (*v*)

adverbs

accordingly; singularly; momentously; logically; definitely; healthfully; indescribably; amazingly; perceptibly; personally; refreshingly; incessantly; industrially; tragically; stupendously; infinitesimally; molecularly; radically; appreciably; profoundly; instantaneously; acceptably; partially; eternally; genuinely; drastically; momentously; magically; notably; wholesomely; permanently; progressively; economically; miraculously; desirably; fundamentally; electrically; pathologically; seasonally; undeniably; noticeably; unvaryingly; tangibly; propitiously; vitally; arbitrarily; chemically; climatically; technically.

(See alter, shift, reform.)

CHANGEABLE

adverbs

bewilderingly; vexatiously; curiously; characteristically; constantly; impulsively; provokingly; giddily; fitfully; capriciously; inexcusably; wantonly; recklessly; carelessly; injudiciously; ridiculously; fantastically; temperamentally; dramatically; inconsiderately; selfishly; rashly; indiscreetly; unstably; outrageously; unbelievably; tactlessly; unwisely; shiftily; erratically; restlessly; nervously; weakly; timidly; irresolutely; irresponsibly; unreliably; unfortunately; deplorably; wilfully.

CHANNEL

adjectives

correct; proper; earthly; turbulent; precipitous; somber; legitimate; inconsequent; subterranean; intricate; dreaming; transparent; colossal; destined; practical; devious; manifold; diplomatic; regular; sound; conservative; productive; selfish; fortuitous; tranquil; oozy; funnel-like; free-flowing; foaming; tortuous; contorted; rock; unmapped; river; slender; deepened; narrow; burrowed; boiling; miniature; uncounted; noisier; personal; ample; powerful; smiling; artistic; sequestered.

verbs

deepen—; dredge—; explore—; flow into —; narrow—; obstruct—; pilot through—; slide into—; sound—; stray into—; swell —; trench—; turn into—; waft across—; —extends; —widens.

(See canal, avenue, route, stream.)

CHANNEL (*v*)

adverbs

deeply; subterraneously; intricately; deviously; diplomatically; contortedly; narrowly; mysteriously.

CHANT

adjectives

intoned; low; deep-toned; barbaric; monotonous; fragmentary; musical; frenzied; rhythmical; sonorous; rude; solemn; wild; pathetic; droning; mellow; melancholy; triumphant; virginal; wailing; aspirated; joyful; impassioned; antiphonal; liturgic; Gregorian; weird; doleful; guttural; nasal; funeral; ominous; intellectual; wordless; outlandish; obstreperous; pagan; tribal; lachrymose; eerie.

verbs

accompany—; answer with—; compose—; intone—; introduce—; mock—; mourn—; recite—; respond with—; sing—; take up—; throw off—; troll—; uplift—; utter—; warble—; —celebrates; —consists of; —haunts; —influences; —praises; —resounds.

(See song, melody.)

CHANT (*v*)

adverbs

angelically; barbarically; musically; monotonously; rhythmically; sonorously; solemnly; pathetically; mellowly; triumphantly; wailingly; impassionedly; antiphonally; gutturally; ominously; outlandishly; obstreperously; lachrymosely.

(See intone.)

CHAOS

adjectives

stagnant; aboriginal; conquered; formless; barren; shapeless; revolutionary; dark; living; wonderful; glaring; resulting; fierce; cluttered; Stygian; boundless; black; idiotic; financial; human; approaching; turmoiling; whirring; tumultuous; leaden; primeval; unintelligible; blank; entertaining; stimulating; appalling; ghastly; stricken; smothering; gloomy; hopeless; pathetic; bewildering; jumbled; indescribable; cultural; social; economic; industrial; political; primordial; age-long; blind; temporary; strident; ancient.

verbs
beset by—; build out of—; free from—; kindle—; plunge into—; produce—; resolve —; restore from—; rise out of—; survey—; swim through—; —arises; —confounds; —distresses; —overwhelms; —reigns; —roars; —rules; —threatens.

(See confusion, disorder.)

CHAOTIC

adverbs
fiercely; lamentably; uproariously; riotously; noisily; wildly; hysterically; tumultuously; turbulently; hopelessly; madly; distressingly; disturbingly; ominously; alarmingly; threateningly; perplexingly; confusedly; confusingly; indescribably; bewilderingly; pathetically; appallingly; idiotically; senselessly; needlessly; deplorably; unreasonably; unjustifiably; inconceivably; absurdly; perversely; unhappily.

CHAP

adjectives
wild; expensive; likable; sturdy; little; queer; good-looking; affable; lovable; facetious; fortunate; engaging; nice; clear-eyed; clever; capable; bully; jolly; handsome; slender; peaceable; decent-looking; shrewd; stout-hearted; sensible; fastidious; plucky; quiet; reserved; harmless; taciturn; undecided; irresolute; steady; unimpressive; callous; burly; massive; disappointed; solemn; roguish; belligerent; stocky; contriving; smirking; seagoing; oldish; well-mannered; polite; charming.

CHAPEL

adjectives
dimly-lighted; wattled; bare; dreary; lofty; exquisite; fragrant; ivied; unimposing; nonconformist; encircling; compulsory; ancient; carved; gilded; brown-tiled; quaint; old-fashioned; lapis lazuli; private; quiet; forgotten, white-spired; shabby.

verbs
consecrate—; dedicate—; enlarge—; establish—; found—; frequent—; gather at—; grant to—; install in—; maintain—; occupy —; perform in—; revere at—; summon to —; worship in—; —accommodates; —awes; —beckons; —enshrines; —serves; —solaces.

(See church.)

CHAPERON

adjectives
seedy; glowering; inadequate.

CHAPERON (v)

adverbs
conscientiously; inadequately; willingly; cheerfully; nominally; perfunctorily.

(See protect.)

CHAPTER

adjectives
tedious; individual; interesting; brilliant; stimulating; thrilling; solemn; miserable; immortal; spacious; singular; striking; morbid; unwritten; subsequent; supplementary; vivid; crisp; pleasant; debonair; racy; vivacious; fascinating; profoundly-illuminating; surprising; flaming; remarkable; crucial; satirical; provocative; circumspect; concluding; gloomiest; analogous; staccato; explanatory; didactic; drifting; detailed; secret.

verbs
arrange in—s; branch into—s; constitute—; contradict—; divide into—s; head—; introduce—; organize—; pen—; record in—; refer to—; section into—s; touch up—; —deals with; —depicts.

(See category, paragraph, story.)

CHARACTER
(quality, personality)

adjectives
vexatious; illustrious; first-rate; exceptional; celebrated; sheer; toothsome; prosy; composite; parasitic; private; fabulous; axiomatic; positive; nefarious; negative; munificent; salient; deleterious; stern; tempting; formal; reflective; sturdy; undecided; durable; substantial; apoplectic; cabalistic; melodramatic; provisional; indifferent; unscrupulous; vindictive; steadfast; estimable; personal; central; religious; fictional; finite; grasping; hollow; peculiar; composite; intrinsic; amiable; honest; uncelebrated; analogous; distinctive; intellectual; roving; liberal; alarming; feeble; notorious; pedestrian; sad; unspotted; moral; high-toned; daring; intense; diverse; frivolous; startling; half-obliterated; august; gallant; chivalrous; amazing; odious; elevated; heterogeneous; unwieldly; ridiculous; artistic; refulgent; elusive; absorbing; wanton; depraved; timid; trembling; unstable; virtuous; unsullied; robust; arduous; singular; dynamic; determinate; contrasting; beautiful; historical; vicious; interesting; inviolate; seductive; romantic; chameleon-like; miscellaneous; eccentric; arbitrary; powerful; clerical; defective;

murderous; unworthy; pristine; anecdotic; ferocious; sterling; spontaneous; ardent; presumptuous; headstrong; appealing; irresolute; lofty; sinister; luminous; feminine; extraordinary; contrary; eminent; acquired; general; goblin; complimentary; cold; passionless; checkered; obliterated; suspicious; unpractical; public; philological; simplest; primitive; prominent; unpleasant; minor; capricious; voluptuous; nobler; double; outward; antiquated; native; patriotic; deadly; improvident; accursed; external; ungainly; admirable; urgent; dubious; gloomy; melancholy; haughty; imperious; odd; domestic; massive; unique; dry; hard; assumed; fraudulent; heart-rending; exotic; self-reliant; bucolic; pacific; tempestuous; rightful; fictitious; random; complete; exhaustive; timely; idealistic; moral; unemotional; vigorous; epigrammatic; joyous; gentle; sacred; dissolute; flawless; reckless; genial; indelible; reigning; seasoned; lovable; indigenous; predominating; subordinate; unsavory; clean; natural; jovial; shallow; uninspiring; blackened; loquacious; homophonic; physiognomic; hermit; sensational; utilitarian; disturbing; hard-bitten; dwarfish; degrading; flabby; authoritative; jellyfish; picturesque; theocratic; tragic; fluctuating; literary; airy; modish; coquettish; desperate; incidental; colorful; irreproachable; vulgar; veritable; rugged; decorative; compendious; undefined; implacable; pontifical; imperfect; articulate; antithetical; legendary; opaque; tranquil; true; arid; mysterious; commanding; historical; surreptitious; observing; current; grandiose; gay; sympathetic; charming; functional; apathetic; vain; lyrical; nondescript; zigzag; explicit; inherited; statuesque; well-established; trivial; national; contemptible; hurried; hostile; material; accidental; vicious; doubtful; motley; congratulatory; enigmatical; prerogatived; external; abandoned; inviolable; vehement; monochromatic; uncommon; poisonous; sensuous; dicrotic; magnanimous; coherent; positive; semi-divine; normal-sized; strenuous; affectionate; ethereal; disfiguring; irregular; forceful; idealistic; poetical; constipating; spiritual; grave; biographico-historical; proud; lying; submissive; many-sided; dutiful; upright; worthless; homely; humorous; insignificant; imperishable; gentlemanly; useful; abusive; decorous; indecisive; cosmopolitan; vague; dangerous; treasonable; atrocious; half-paternal; factitious; unsteady; shadowy; rude; wooden; impassioned; villainous; yielding; architectural; gross; specific; conscientious; firm; hereditary; unimpeachable; sporting; harmonious; strong; contrasting; unnatural; dominant; special; bright; emphatic; desert; clear-cut; defined; handsome; stainless; collective; corporate; speculative; critical; eclectic; savory; loose; resolved; nebulous; advanced; impeccable; authentic; unblemished; rare; chosen; sophisticated; celestial; saint-like; docile; creditable; cute; attractive; virile; adamantine; curious; idiosyncratic; jaunty; bizarre; adventurous; comic; fantastic; silent; methodical; satisfied; staid; solidified; reticent; dull-witted; timorous; infantile; saturnine; soft; phlegmatic; vacillating; planless; traditionless; varied; racy; infamous; base; notorious; vengeful; unscrupulous; mercenary; obstinate; preposterous; racial; Mephistophelean; Puritan; hieroglyphic; seditious; quasi-public; figurative; youthful; semi-private; artificial; grave; cursive; specialized; representative; confidential; voluntary; individual; composite; intimate; interpolated; unequivocal; abnormal; unified; holy; incidental; deepest; ironic; realistic; abstract; contemporary; secondary; well-rounded; famous; well-known; picaresque; functionless; minor; queer; well-conceived; bygone; rough; Brobdingnagian; deliberate; light; splendid; principal; credible; ambitious; memorable; leading; burlesque; whimsical; quaint; flamelike.

verbs
alter—; analyze—; behold—; besmirch—; blacken—; brand—; breathe—; clear—; debase—; defend—; degrade—; denote—; detract from—; disclose—; display—; elevate—; embody—; emulate—; estimate—; express—; mask—; mold—; paint—; purify—; redeem—; reflect—; rehabilitate—; respect—; reveal—; slur—; traduce—; transform—; undermine—; warp—; —achieves; —breaks down.

(See constitution, nature, personality, temperament.)

CHARACTER
(*role in drama or literature*)

adjectives
biblical; dramatic; heroic; historic; legendary; mythological; fictional; personated; comic; tragic; contemporary.

verbs
assume—; compound—; conceive—; delineate—; depict—; differentiate—s; display—; distort—; draw—; interpret—; in-

troduce—; invent—; juggle—s; merge into—; play—; portray—; produce—; roll into—; unfold—; —impresses; —represents; —symbolizes.

CHARACTERISTIC

adjectives
distinctive; prevalent; hereditary; congenial; essential; distinguishing; dominant; marked; personal; cheering; salient; general; diffusive; artistic; definite; admirable; farseeing; attractive; familiar; striking; swampy; psychical; unfailing; outstanding; individual; unmitigated; rife; recurring; external; commanding; visible; fundamental; praiseworthy; unsuspected; social; unique; national; spiritual; physical; emotional; peculiar; graceful; common; commendable; prudent; conspicuous; habitual; desirable; major; endearing; whimsical; useful; vicious; vulpine; supposed; reprehensible; tiresome; fictitious; radical; fatal; changeable; facial; group; racial; mental; climactic; local; rudimentary; tell-tale; complex; noticeable; great; unavoidable; inclusive; conceivable; differentiated.

verbs
abolish—; conceal—; disclose—; feign—; interpret—; manifest—; normalize—s; —appeals; —condemns; —differs; —distinguishes; —enhances; —heightens; —persists; —resembles.

(See trait, feature, attribute, quality, idiosyncrasy.)

adverbs
distinctly; particularly; superbly; singularly; specifically; specially; racially; inherently; definitely; typically; essentially; genuinely; truly; normally; significantly; notoriously; notably; touchingly; indelibly; intrinsically; substantially; practically; markedly; supposedly; presumably; ordinarily; naturally; fundamentally.

CHARACTERIZATION

adjectives
masterly; subtle; dramatic; first-rate; cursory; striking; curious; essential; accurate; contemptuous; intimate; convincing; appreciative; hopeful; delicate; musical; beneficent; genial; humorous; fine; readable; delightful; amazing; short; pithy; tricky; finely-etched; vivid; naive; exhaustive; spirited; shrewd; vigorous; sympathetic; penetrating; sharp; amusing; superb; hard-boiled.

CHARACTERIZE (*v*)

adverbs
justly; frivolously; positively; nefariously; negatively; substantially; provisionally; indifferently; amiably; honestly; distinctively; feebly; odiously; absorbingly; voluptuously; nobly; fraudulently; exotically; tempestuously; fictitiously; unsparingly; authoritatively; colorfully; irreproachably; vulgarly; sympathetically; charmingly; enigmatically; saturninely; villainously; seditiously; confidentially; intimately; ironically; realistically; credibly; whimsically; abnormally; quaintly; timorously; timidly; dynamically; romantically.

(See distinguish.)

CHARGE

adjectives
false; bayonet; untrue; competent; reiterated; swift; avaricious; substantiated; needy; specific; piebald; unlucky; excessive; gallant; ridiculous; unexpected; baleful; sensational; grievous; galloping; calumnious; tremendous; insulting; bloody; injudicious; precious; ignoble; generous; emotional; nominal; desperate; undiscriminating; exorbitant; modest; moderate; blasphemous; extortionate; spectacular; cruel; swift; impetuous; unburned; roaring; disgraceful; fluctuating; sole; typical; scrupulous; disputed; express; insurance; fair; immediate; humiliating; frivolous; warlike; motherly; boisterous; monstrous; quoted; atrocious; warehousing; bitter; additional; preposterous; ungrateful; unmerited; unnecessary; serious; mighty; cynical; horrible; defamatory; grotesque; homicide; criminal; dissenting; formal; groundless; trivial; indirect; swaggering; startling; accusing.

CHARGE (*accusation*)

adjectives
absurd; civil; criminal; false; lying; specific; preposterous; unfounded; unjust; unsupported; unwarranted; substantial.

verbs
advance—; answer—; brand with—; brush aside—; conclude—; convey—; couch—; deny—; drone—s; fire—at; frame—against; incur—; justify—; lessen—s; level — at; lodge—s against; motivate—; prefer—s against; protest—; squash—s; refute—; repudiate—; splutter—s; spring—; suppress—; vindicate from—; voice—; —arises from; —rifles; —vexes; —wanes.

(See accusation, complaint.)

CHARGE
(*duty, trust*)

adjectives
burdensome; entrusted; costly; difficult; doubtful; inevitable; trying.

verbs
assign—; commit to—of; comprehend—; ease—; execute—; fail in—; fulfill—; impose—upon; obey—; perform—; release from—; resign—; shirk—; tend—.
(See duty, trust, custody, care, responsibility, management.)

CHARGE
(*rush*)

adjectives
driving; furious; concerted; blind; headlong; fruitless; onslaughting.

verbs
ambush—; block—; command—; cut down in—; dodge—; hasten to—; hinder—; lead—; precipitate—; rush to—; succumb to—; —conquers; —overcomes; —overwhelms; —succeeds; —surges; —surprises.
(See attack, assault.)

CHARGE (*v*)

adverbs
temporarily; strictly; bluntly; excessively; falsely; reiteratedly; specifically; ridiculously; unexpectedly; sensationally; calumniously; injudiciously; ignobly; exorbitantly; spectacularly; unscrupulously; bitterly; humiliatingly; unmeritedly; criminally; accusingly; groundlessly; startlingly; indirectly.
(See effort, impose, assault.)

CHARGEABLE

adverbs
conveniently; easily; indubitably; definitely; morally; officially; unquestionably; positively; absolutely; unfortunately; unluckily; inopportunely; legally; equitably; incontestably; explicitly; certainly; justly; properly; legitimately.

CHARGER

adjectives
foaming; wearied; stamping; restless.

CHARIOT

adjectives
black-lacquered; fiery; colliding; triumphal; colossal; four-horse; glossy; flaming; visionary; sumptuous; fierce.

verbs
arm—; depict—; display—; guide—; mount—; ornament—; rein—; —clanks; —conveys; —mows down; —overturns; —s parade; —rolls by; overthrow—.
(See vehicle, carriage.)

CHARITABLE

adverbs
humanely; amiably; benevolently; considerately; generously; lovingly; philanthropically; sympathetically; tenderly; unselfishly; bounteously; complaisantly; mercifully; blessedly; liberally; graciously; freely; tolerantly; unsparingly; munificently; bountifully; astonishingly; admirably; superbly; dependably; genuinely; sincerely; truly.

CHARITY

adjectives
moral; tender; intellectual; remedial; precarious; sniffing; gracious; truest; indiscriminate; princely; spasmodic; grudging; blessed; uncommanded; impulsive; abused; mutual; easy-going; voluntary; unwise; pious; unpublished; natural; aggressive; casual; deadened; superb; neighborly; learned; false; estimable; impressive; endless; confining; rigid; forbidden; tender.

verbs
administer—; appeal to—; assist through—; beseech—; bind with—; contribute to—; entitle to—; influence—; interest in—; lack —; necessitate—; pour forth—; relieve through—; remove from—; subject to—; subscribe to—; temper with—; —alleviates; —ameliorates; —declines; —enables; —grows; —heals; —revives; —suffers from.
(See love, benevolence, tolerance, alms.)

CHARLATAN

adjectives
preying; industrial; accomplished; ingenious; barred; shameless; ambitious.

CHARM

adjectives
flattering; awakened; glittering; soothing; outward; unusual; rare; quiet; distinct; untitled; healing; substantial; paltry; artless; haunting; subtle; inexplicable; personal; awful; lovely; mysterious; indescribable; celestial; imputed; wintry; forbidden; central; veiling; increasing; unique; insinuating; lyric; melodious; superficial; irresistible; heathenish; zestful; home-like;

traditional; distinguished; peculiar; wonder-working; soul-subduing; terrible; inscrutable; voluptuous; conversational; unspeakable; immortal; fictitious; native; unholy; substantial; compact; nostalgic; understanding; piquant; ineffable; delicious; grave; sensitive; vast; inimitable; compelling; indefinable; feminine; quaint; extraordinary; unmodish; seductive; individual; radiant; unfailing; poetic; flirtatious; fastidious; genuine; literary; changeable; reigning; essential; vocal; chief; haunting; quieting; inherent; serene; external; insouciant; modest; striking; incommunicable; inexhaustible; naturalistic; lasting; singular; stately; appropriate; rugged; intrinsic; crowning; restful; picturesque; decorative; elfin; ripening; definite; ideal; sovereign; softening; alluring; nameless; ethereal; inner; dishevelled; potent; spontaneous; simple; flying; material; exotic; unflagging; bitter-sweet; rose-tinted; fatal; suffocating; wild; astonishing; graphic; piquant; varied; recognized; original; perennial; captivating; superlative; brilliant; peaceful; magic; wistful; shy; magnetic; elusive; merry; fleeting; revealing; compensating; persuasive; devastating; certain; ardent; innate; indigenous; unusual; florid; sedate; mature; ancient; lasting; unhurried; lazy; languorous; unsuspected; vexing; thoughtless; ugly; thwarted; melancholy; flexible; chemical; immortal; historic; gala; dimpling; professional; youthful; topographical; provocative; auroral; scenic; domesticated; infantile; old-fashioned; boyish; naive; languorous.

verbs
apply—; attain—; eclipse—; emanate—; enchant with—; endow with—; enhance—; exercise—; loose—; lend—; radiate—; reflect—; resist—; retain—; savor—; survey—s; underrate—; win with—; —appeals; —conquers; —disarms; —dissolves; —enslaves; —fades; —melts; —pervades; —wanes.

(See fascination, beauty, spell, incantation, attraction.)

CHARM (v)

adverbs
delectably; bewitchingly; artlessly; outwardly; angelically; hauntingly; inexplicably; subtly; uniquely; mysteriously; indescribably; celestially; lyrically; melodiously; superficially; irresistibly; peculiarly; conversationally; genuinely; essentially; vocally; inherently; insouciantly; modestly; strikingly; alluringly; ethereally; spontaneously; exotically; unflaggingly; seraphically; piquantly; perennially; captivatingly; superlatively; magnetically; elusively; devastatingly.

(See fascinate.)

CHARMING

adverbs
indescribably; delightfully; bewilderingly; amazingly; unquestionably; wondrously; surprisingly; radiantly; ineffably; wholly; joyously; blithely; consciously; tormentingly; overwhelmingly; provokingly; unimaginably; mysteriously; graciously; gravely; youthfully; exotically; alluringly; downright; exquisitely; genuinely; ingenuously; incomparably; irresistibly; rapturously.

CHART

adjectives
imperfect; neat; workman-like; cosmographical; authoritative; unusual; tattered; triumphal; fever; mystic; customary.

verbs
ascertain by—; calculate by—; compile—; consult—; depend on—; issue—; publish—; refer to—; scan—; stud—with; survey—; utilize—; —assists; —benefits; —directs; —furnishes; —indicates; —informs; —outlines; —plans; —reveals; —supplements; —sustains.

(See map, charter.)

CHART (v)

adverbs
unobtrusively; imperfectly; invisibly; vaguely; neatly; cosmographically; customarily; professionally; expertly; skillfully.

CHARTER

adjectives
accepted; approved; disputed; adopted; granted; grand; rejected; ratified; restored; submitted; revitalized.

verbs
abolish—; grant—; issue—; renew—; revoke—; —allows; —expires; —legalizes; —permits; —privileges.

(See deed, document, lease, agreement, contract, right, immunity.)

CHARY

adverbs
thriftily; stingily; selfishly; closely; parsimoniously; penuriously; frugally; providently; unreasonably; prudently; singularly; superfluously; curiously; needlessly;

unpleasantly; coolly; discreetly; cautiously; guardedly; warily; meanly; sordidly; greedily; cannily.

CHASE

adjectives
spirited; exciting; invisible; emulous; piteous; desultory; vague; dull; panting; delicious; wild-goose; fruitless; protracted; mad; perpetual; hectic; stern; blissful; grim; hard; desperate; cruel; lengthy; weary; heartbreaking; frenzied; thrilling.

verbs
follow—; forsake—; plan—; prolong—; pursue—; refrain from—; swerve from—; undertake—; —ensues; —fatigues.
(See pursuit, hunt.)

CHASE (*v*)

adverbs
spiritedly; madly; perpetually; excitingly; desperately; cruelly; heartbreakingly; thrillingly; remorselessly; grimly.
(See pursue, track, hunt.)

CHASM

adjectives
bloody; fearful; unfathomable; infinite; azure; brazen; billowy; bottomless; immense; fateful; watery; formidable; chalk; sunlit; unaccountable; Alpine; narrow; roaring; remarkable; wide; rock-walled; wonderful; dizzy; precipitous.

verbs
break into—; bridge—; cross—; disrupt into—; hollow—; open into—; rend—; rut with—s; span—; —breaches; —divides; —extends; —gapes; —interrupts; —resounds; —slants; —yawns.
(See gulf, gap, opening.)

CHASTE

adverbs
delicately; artistically; architecturally; virtuously; incomparably; beautifully; modestly; incorruptibly; unaffectedly; tastefully; classically; supremely; marvellously.

CHASTEN (*v*)

adverbs
amply; awfully; unnecessarily; physically; publicly; ruthlessly; brutally; fiendishly; triumphantly; soullessly; odiously; lawfully; legally.
(See punish, whip, correct.)

CHASTISEMENT

adjectives
awful; earthly; unnecessary; literary; physical; maternal; public.

CHASTITY

adjectives
sacred; constant; spotless; cold; enforced; fruitless; habitual; pure; stainless; incomparable.

verbs
affect—; blemish—; dedicate to—; despoil—; enforce—; honor—; impose—upon; laud—; mar—; practice—; pretend—; seduce from—; suspect—of; testify to—; violate—; —extends; —prescribes.
(See purity, virtue.)

CHAT (*v*)

adverbs
vivaciously; confidentially; mirthlessly; desultorily; emptily; pleasantly; informally; comfortably; loquaciously; frivolously; incessantly; jovially; aimlessly; absurdly; nervously; garrulously; carelessly; constantly; superficially; inconsequentially; amiably.
(See talk, gossip.)

CHATEAU

adjectives
imposing; dilapidated; turreted; ruined.

CHATTER

adjectives
rapid; mirthless; empty; convulsive; frothy; furious; confidential; pleasant; informal; short; comfortable; lively; neighborly; slipshod; unexpected; vivacious; social; friendly; loquacious; backstairs; mere; idle; egotistical; gay; joyous; competent; frivolous; merry; subdued; precocious; incessant; jovial; aimless; absurd; nervous; irresponsible; rattle-brained; garrulous; careless; constant; superficial; indignant; inconsequential; unfailing; bootless.

CHATTER (*v*)

adverbs
exuberantly; incessantly; complacently; volubly; monotonously; blithely; woefully; excitedly; affably; obstreperously; vivaciously; querulously; unrestrainedly; perplexingly.
(See chat, talk, gossip.)

CHATTY

adverbs
interminably; sociably; hospitably; heartily; genially; cordially; intimately; casually;

happily; companionably; affably; cosily; gregariously; fluently; gabbily; garrulously; nonsensically; glibly; harmlessly; revealingly; cheerfully; dangerously; indiscreetly; venomously; maliciously; indiscriminately.

CHAUFFEUR

adjectives
recommended; liveried; fur-clad; peaceful; sleeping; uniformed; wary; practiced; able; expert.

CHAUVINISTIC

adverbs
pretentiously; bombastically; flauntingly; triumphantly; swaggeringly; magniloquently; boastfully; brassily; highly; obviously; absurdly; foolishly; vapidly; noisily; ostentatiously; blatantly; fantastically; ludicrously; ignobly; inanely; stupendously; splendidly; vaingloriously; airily; blithely; manifestly; impudently.

CHEAP

adverbs
absurdly; unreasonably; contemptibly; indifferently; miserably; pitifully; ridiculously; laughably; worthlessly; unspeakably; incredibly; amazingly; attractively; undoubtedly; indubitably; tolerably; passably; really.

CHEAT (v)

adverbs
perpetually; infernally; villainously; flagrantly; scandalously; vilely; cleverly; shrewdly; diplomatically.

(See defraud, trick.)

CHEATING

adjectives
infernal; villainous; tyrannical; risky; disguised; cowardly; flagrant; glorious; freeboot.

verbs
amount to—; associate with—; bar for—; condone—; convict of—; depose for—; dispose toward—; implicate in—; indict for—; obtain by—; practice—; tolerate—; —affects; —besmirches; —blemishes; —dishonors; —lowers; —mars.

(See fraud, deception, imposition, delusion.)

CHECK

adjectives
bank; thief-proof; signed; gigantic; cancelled; reversible; formidable; sublime; indispensable; distinct; invaluable; generous; salutary; health-giving; contrasting; wholesome; constitutional; temporary; perceptible; accurate; worn; pallid; deplorable; effective; absolute.

CHECK (v)

adverbs
cleverly; fortunately; powerfully; abruptly; temporarily; effectively; formidably; systematically; constitutionally; perceptibly; accurately; absolutely.

(See impede, curb, restrain.)

CHEEK

adjectives
apple-red; crimson; cherry-colored; ruddy; ruddled; flushed; burning; fat; flaming; glowing; pretty; scarlet; blushing; fevered; blazing; rosy; incarnadining; pale; tranquil; sallow; livid; pasty; pallid; ashen; death-like; wan; triangular; lean; sunburnt; tanned; mottled; ebony; smudged; singed; painted; downy; smooth; boyish; placid; fresh; cold; sweet; firm; amiable; withered; weather-beaten; wrinkled; leathery; haggard; careworn; wizened; wasted; darkened; hollowed; cavernous; sunken; emaciated; bony; heavy; forged; rough; unshaven; flabby; jelly-like; puffed; comfortable; plump; soft; sleep-flushed; icy; droopy; hard; marble; freckled; pockmarked; scarred; smarting; tremulous; pendent; upturned; unresponsive; windfreshened; consumptive; sweat-damp; infantile; peachy; delicate-rounded; high; warm; transparent; wide; strong; protruding; mangy; prominent; sinister; bronzed; tender; sinewy; distended; damask; blanched; dimpled; unprofaned; marked; veined; unworthy; straining; melting; pellucid; brown; tear-stained; mantling; placid; waning; quivering; faded; smiling; furrowed; smutted; tear-sodden; pinched; rubicund; glowing; lank; clear; pink; flaccid; swarthy; untasted; shrunken; shaded; blanched; cracking; languid; bloodless; emaciated; waxen; virgin; harlot; kissing; delicate; changing; inflamed; sunny; white; yellow-cowslip; childish; worn; proud; jutting; silver; drawn; amiable; animated; peony-colored; pinched; haggard; unreluctant; blooming; freshening; massive; lifeless; purplish-mottled; carmine-colored.

verbs
blanch —s; brighten —s; color —s; cool —s; corrugate —s; daub —s; dimple —; empurple —s; fan —; flame —s; flush —s;

hollow —; lean on —; moisten —s; paint —s; pat —; puff —s; redden —s; smite —; stain —s; stream down —; swell —s; tint —; varnish —; waste —; wrinkle —; —s blush; —s burn; —s fade; —s glisten; —s glow; —s hang; —s pale.

(See **face.**)

CHEEKY

adverbs

pertly; brassily; insolently; impertinently; insufferably; offensively; impudently; brazenly; flippantly; shamelessly; unpleasantly; disagreeably; saucily; swaggeringly; arrogantly; audaciously; provokingly; terribly; odiously; ridiculously; presumptuously; daringly; detestably; abominably; unwarrantably; jauntily; unbecomingly.

CHEER

(shout of applause)

adjectives

national; tumultuous; ironical; forced; admiring; hysterical; loud; rousing; shrill; hearty; panting; frenzied; rippling; irrepressible; patient; thunderous; incomparable; immense; blithe; lofty; pathetic; heart-strengthening; daily; mingled; answering; encouraging; sunny; lusty; universal; undaunted; wedding; unanimous; ringing; triumphal; measureless; traditional; good; intimate; massive; whooping; vociferous; solemn; silvery; evil; melancholy; uncertain.

verbs

celebrate with —s; depart with —s; draw —; echo—; grudge—; hail—; incite to —s; judge by —s; kill —; lessen —s; participate in —; raise —; rejoice in —; thunder —; — abates; — ceases; — dies; — fades; — greets; —rouses; — sweeps; — wanes.

(See applause, cheering.)

CHEER (v)

adverbs

raucously; rabidly; lustily; wildly; vociferously; enthusiastically; heartily; jovially; mirthfully; tumultuously; hysterically; rousingly; shrilly; frenziedly; irrepressibly; thunderously; incomparably; encouragingly; undauntedly; unanimously; triumphantly.

(See praise, applaud.)

CHEERFUL

adverbs

habitually; pleasantly; naturally; irrepressibly; immensely; blithely; vociferously; placidly; serenely; vivaciously; charmingly; refreshingly; youthfully; casually; calmly; hilariously; maddeningly; vexatiously; merrily; jauntily; airily; exuberantly; heedlessly; bewilderingly; surprisingly; unexpectedly; strangely; oddly; unwontedly; exhilaratingly; contentedly; lightly; gladly; complacently; tolerably; genially; jovially; jubilantly; briskly; smilingly; winsomely; noticeably; perplexingly; unbelievably; extraordinarily.

CHEERFULNESS

adjectives

unabated; placid; imperturbable; undiminished; sparkling; consistent; weary; hysterical; natural; charming; growing; healthy; infectious; contagious; uncomplaining; pensive; constrained; forced; renewed; spasmodic; affected; perennial; usual; weird; desperate.

verbs

animate with—; conceal—; denote—; diffuse—; dispose toward—; exhibit—; exude—; feign—; fight with—; free with—; inspire—; invade with—; reflect—; regain—; restore—; revive—; season with—; temper with—; welcome—; —comforts; —eases; —encourages; —exhilarates; —pervades; —stimulates.

(See optimism, buoyancy.)

CHEERING

adjectives

earnest; frenzied; fresh; unusual; loud; vociferous.

verbs

accelerate—; conduct—; direct—; drown in—; encounter—; join—; lead—; promote—; repress—; —acclaims; —animates; —compliments; —dies down; —echoes; —encourages; —heartens; —enlivens; —gladdens; —greets; —indicates; —overwhelms; —resounds; —stimulates; —subsides; —swells; —welcomes.

(See applause, ovation, cheer.)

CHEERING

adverbs

reasonably; brightly; definitely; encouragingly; reassuringly; propitiously; comfortingly; helpfully; positively; unusually; finally; tolerably; moderately; fairly; somewhat; downright; wholly.

CHEERLESS

adverbs
dismally; grievously; unhappily; sorely; sadly; unpleasantly; disturbingly; utterly; horribly; drearily; piteously; woefully; deplorably; pathetically; needlessly; discouragingly; dishearteningly; hopelessly; desolately; oppressively; extremely; undeniably; unutterably; wretchedly; peculiarly; cruelly.

CHEERY

adverbs
sturdily; resolutely; brightly; consistently; charmingly; healthily; infectiously; ;contagiously; professionally; philosophically; spontaneously; loudly; serenely; placidly; courageously; confidently; reassuringly; hearteningly; encouragingly; valiantly; gallantly; refreshingly; pleasantly; cordially; attractively; delightfully; calmly.

CHEESE

adjectives
milk; pyramided; vintage; large; ripe; stale; mouse-eaten; rancid; dry.

verbs
coagulate into—; consume—; enclose—in; grate—; import—; introduce—; loaf—; manufacture—; market—; mix—; pack—; process—; refrigerate—; roll—; slice—; spread—; sprinkle with—; toast—; turn into—; —moulds; —ripens.

adverbs
achieve with—s; analyze—s; apply—s; compose of—; concentrate—; devise—; employ—; evaluate—; extract—; force by—s; impregnate with—; involve—; mix—; obtain—; precipitate—; prepare—; produce—; resist—; synthesize—; —accomplishes; —acidizes; —acts; —alkalizes; —alters; —attracts; —catalyzes; —s combine; —converts; —counteracts; —depends on; —neutralizes; —poisons; —preserves; —reacts; —transforms.
(See substance.)

CHEMICALS

adjectives
injurious; common; inexpensive; mixed; synthetic.

CHEMIST

adjectives
renowned; brilliant; ruthless; analytical; alleged.

CHEMISTRY

adjectives
agricultural; pure; applied; industrial; theoretical.

CHERISH (*v*)

adverbs
secretly; mutually; innocently; piously; tenderly; reverently; fondly; unconsciously; vociferously; tenaciously.
(See protect.)

CHERISHED

adverbs
carefully; affectionately; absurdly; highly; sentimentally; tenderly; reverently; ardently; fondly; ridiculously; stoutly; passionately; truly; sincerely; genuinely; whimsically; lovingly.

CHERRY

adjectives
fermented; fiery; ripened; blushing; pale.

CHEST
(*part of body*)

adjectives
stalwart; barrel; bulging; professional; corded; massive; out-muscled; superb; self-confident; thick; plump; brawny; skinny; cadaverous; cavernous; puny; meager; bony; unathletic; feeble; narrow; broad; pigeon; deep-sprung; expanded; wizened; sagging; crushed; collapsed; heaving; hollow; battle-scarred; inflated; hairy; soldierly; portentous; chubby; excessive; vainglorious; ample; laboring; decorated; tattooed.

verbs
blow out—; contract—; crush—; deflate—; deform—; develop—; expand—; flatten—; inflate—; lock up in—; loosen—; massage—; pierce—; puff out—; rend—; seal in—; stretch—; thump—.

CHEST
(*receptacle*)

adjectives
lopsided; crammed; treasure; battered; scarred; wooden; nail-studded; rivet-bound; stout; oaken; ironbound; corded; roped; brass-mounted; refrigerating; musty; capacious; ornate; plenteous; sacred; fireproof; ample.

CHEW (*v*)

adverbs
viciously; contentedly; placidly; hungrily; vigorously; continuously; tranquilly; normally; restrainedly; noisily; crushingly.
(See nibble, munch, crunch.)

CHIC

adverbs

distinctly; smartly; fashionably; exceptionally; dramatically; fabulously; demurely; cleverly; artistically; stylishly; slenderly; effectively; correctly; trimly; conservatively; sparklingly; brilliantly; barbarically; expensively; conventionally; habitually; elegantly; quietly; handsomely; becomingly; intriguingly; appropriately.

CHICKADEE (*titmouse*)

adjectives

black-capped; cheerful; lisping; flocking; lusty; evergreen-loving.

verbs

—carols; —chats; —chirps; —clings; —flits; —frolics; —hops; —preys on; —shrills; —somersaults; —whistles.

(See bird.)

CHICKEN

adjectives

cackling; snowy; browned; fragrant; smoking; drawn; rudimentary.

verbs

behead—; breed—; dine on—; excite—; exhibit—; fatten—; infest—; pen up—; prey on—; relish—; roast—; savor—; spice—; stuff—; —clucks; —flutters about; —gobbles up; —invades; —lays; —molts; —pecks; —perches; —scratches; —scurries; —squawks; —struts.

(See fowl, bird.)

CHICKENHEARTED

adverbs

notably; laughably; ridiculously; ludicrously; constitutionally; unwontedly; timorously; avowedly; shamefully; effeminately; dastardly; basely; solicitously; appallingly; astoundingly; wonderfully; amazingly; surprisingly; inexplicably; shockingly; fearfully; tenderly; obviously; disgracefully; outrageously; infamously; incurably.

CHIDE (*v*)

adverbs

scowlingly; mildly; severely; reprovingly; moderately; kindly; harshly; embarrassingly; vociferously; violently; sharply; shyly; intelligently; churlishly; mercilessly; legitimately; sternly.

(See admonish, censure, scold.)

CHIDING

adjectives

churlish; stormy; gallant; meaningful.

CHIEF

adjectives

indulgent; revered; supreme; prominent; gangster; powerful; local; native; usurping; polygamous; picturesque; murderous; mountain; desert; brigand; hereditary; indignant; deputed; reticent; patriarchal; despotic; venerable; artful; descendant; influential; kind; uncrowned; tribal; dominating; brave-hearted; gentle; generous; formidable; independent; invincible; responsible; crimson-stained.

verbs

advance to—; depose—; execute—; forsake—; guard—; hail—; hang—; idolize—; name—; oppose—; patronize—; rank as—; restore—; serve—; swerve from—; torture—; —commands; —inveighs; —leads; —orders; —rejoices.

(See head, leader, commander, captain.)

CHIEFTAIN

adjectives

feudal; bearded; putative; simple; desert; venerable; bandit; lifeless.

CHIFFON

adjectives

multitone; bright; filmy; sinuous.

CHILD

adjectives

delightful; charming; dutiful; cherubic; enchanting; divine; brilliant; bright; rosy; nice; capable; contented; accomplished; gifted; intelligent; respectable-looking; well-bred; supernatural; fun-loving; eager; exemplary; affectionate; studious; lovable; responsive; winsome; wistful-eyed; misty-eyed; golden-haired; fair-skinned; well-formed; comely; prepossessing; immaculate; prim; unnatural; normal; typical; average; growing; obedient; meek; humble; tactful; old-fashioned; subdued; repentant; contrite; tractable; tranquil; absorbed; silent; reflective; problem; sensitive; bewildered; shy; shrinking; artistic; emotional; unreasonable; nervous; high-strung; neglected; adorable; confused; sickly; delicate; frail; rickety; ragged; spindling; colorless; nondescript; angular; ugly; brutal; beastly; wretched; impertinent; rebellious; spoiled; spiteful; petted; precocious; audacious; impetuous; headstrong; heartbroken; prostrate; unhappy; miserable; forlorn; terrified; adored; admired; afflicted; frightened; greedy; wayward; unruly; exasperating; foolish; grown-up; offensive; refractory; obstreperous; monstrous; stubborn; obdurate; burdensome; unwitting; artless; retarded; stolid; annoying; slow-growing; defective; stupid; sturdy; pot-bellied; lean-faced; leggy; plain; thin; big-eyed; sallow; chubby-faced; regretful; toddling; prattling; wailing; screaming; sobbing; play-loving; beauty-loving; staring; frail; convalescing; engrossed; mere; weeping; casual; innocent; puzzled; venturesome; quizzical; adventurous; riotous; finicky; changeling; romantic; cockney; vaudeville; aristocratic; infant; drowsy; rash; loathed; unflinching; defective; culpable; pouting; petulant; conscientious; minor; wanton; dazed; eloquent; sanguine; forward; reticent; gallant; virtuous; vixenish; beaten; delightful; impious; crippled; exceptional; precious; churlish; talented; robust; engrossed; roguish; heaven-obscuring; loyal; turbulent; houseless; nurtured; tender; unborn; adolescent; simple; sole; heavenborn; cherished; complaining; blind; foolish; vagrant; comparative; scampering; weakest; credulous; guileless; merciless; illegitimate; sacred; fractious; proud; vivacious; burnt; pampered; abused; ambidextrous; healthy; unruly; passionate; undisciplined; self-willed; posthumous; fretful; imitative; melancholy; untutored; docile; migratory; princely; lily-shining; cunning; secretive; unmanageable; victorious; bewitching; sad-looking; riotous; unquenchable; wondrous; slumbering; veritable; eccentric; imaginative; flaxen-haired.

verbs
attend—; awaken—; bear—; befriend—; beget—; bereave—; bring forth—; build-up—; burden—; chastise—; cherish—; circumcise—; comprehend—; conceive—; correct—; debilitate—; deliver—; develop—; discipline—; disinherit—; dispossess ; educate—; emaciate—; embrace—; encourage—; exhort—; expose—; father—; fondle—; forsake—; govern—; harden—; inspire—; lull—; lure—; name—; nourish—; nurse—; oppress—; punish—; rear—; reassure—; remain—; restrain—; revive—; scold—; sire—; spoil—; teach—; tempt—; train—; trust—; understand—; wean—; whip—; —babbles; —clambers; —clamors; —contracts a disease; —disobeys; —heeds; —moans; —pines; —rebels; —skips; —sobs; —strays; —struggles; —thrives; —wails; —weeps.

(See offspring, son, daughter, descendant, boy, girl, infant.)

CHILDHOOD

adjectives
earliest; amazing; seeming; narrow; nightmare-ridden; neglected; sheltered; imaginative; distorted; light-hearted; bleak; lonely; cheerless; spindle-legged; pathetic; precocious; inconsiderate; captious; mysterious; docile; blooming; unappreciative; serene; satisfied; joyous; humble; meditative; healthy; ripe; passive.

verbs
acquire in—; affect—; care for during—; conceive in—; dominate—; form during—; govern—; inculcate in—; learn in—; mould during—; preserve in—; recall—; rejoice in—; reminisce about—; restrict—; revert to—; teach in—; train in—; —contributes; —flees; —lapses; —ripens into; —strays.

(See infancy, youth.)

CHILDISH

adverbs
foolishly; disagreeably; utterly; unpleasantly; unexpectedly; shamefully; dreadfully; inexplicably; deliberately; unreasonably; ill-temperedly; pathetically; unbearably; wretchedly; senselessly; unaccountably; stubbornly; obstinately; horridly; ridiculously; sullenly; flagrantly; awkwardly; gawkily; unhappily; indecorously; outlandishly.

CHILDLIKE

adverbs
innocently; delightfully; simply; artlessly; guilelessly; naively; radiantly; joyously; charmingly; rosily; contentedly; lovably; meekly; adorably; foolishly; chubbily; wonderfully; bewitchingly; irresistibly; appealingly; utterly; touchingly; alluringly; unaffectedly; ingenuously; frankly; sweetly.

CHILDREN

adjectives
passive; fidgety; hostile; supersensitive; refractory; shy; obtrusive; irresponsible; prison; native; illegitimate; semi-hypnotized; bickering; gawky; mercurial; wondering; stoical; egotistical; unimaginative; pampered; promising; bright; worthy; wholesome; angelic; charming; marvel-

lous; carefully-bred; blithe; laughing; rollicking; smiling; audacious; happy; playful; prankish; romping; sturdy; robust; lusty; noisy; clamoring; clattering; frantic; screaming; unkempt; ragged; verminous; unwashed; wide-eyed; stocky; golden-haired; long-legged; quaintly-garbed; chubby; enormous; gayly-dressed; tiny; naked; half-grown; thick-legged; growing; underweight; undernourished; sickly; imperfectly developed; abandoned; heartbroken; frightened; radiant; desolate; trembling; pale; unloved; uncared-for; hungry; homeless; irresponsible; healthy; syphilitic; motherless; restless; squabbling; homespun; true; shivering; bedazed; vagrant; heartless; degenerate; crippled; unruly; earnest-hearted; vexing; starry; promising; natural; unreasonable; unbridled; fiery-blooded; outcrying; myriad; notorious; ill-bred; vulgar; ill-favored; exquisite; fresh; white-faced; silent; insolent; smutty; hovering; pert; dirty; squalling; fretful; sycophantic; mischievous; destitute; glorious-eyed; maddened; strumous; garrulous; hilarious; delinquent; violent; erring; handicapped; unlettered; vociferous; cruel; neglected; veritable; vigorous.

CHILL

adjectives
horrid; penetrating; biting; shrinking; severe; mental; violent; curious; embarrassing; noticeable; hopeless; sharp; congestive; sudden; inexplicable; slight; damp; timid; dry; icy; bone-penetrating; deathly; vault-like; bitter; uncomfortable; balmy; growing; cold; increasing; dreadful; comfortless; shaking.

verbs
blow—; chatter with—s; experience—; expose to—; overcome by—; produce—; prolong—; quiver with—; run—; seize with—; sense—; shake with—; shiver with —; shudder with—; strike with—; survive —; treat for—; —accompanies; —affects; —creeps in; —depresses; —injures; —numbs; —penetrates.

(See sensation, cold.)

CHILL (*v*)

adverbs
bitingly; severely; violently; hopelessly; noticeably; sharply; suddenly; inexplicably; bitterly; increasingly; dreadfully; mortally; painfully.

CHILLY

adverbs
suddenly; inexplicably; curiously; slightly; uncomfortably; dreadfully; alarmingly; keenly; tremulously; visibly; uncommonly; unendurably; strangely; unaccountably; unpleasantly; dangerously; unusually; unwontedly; inexcusably; indefensibly.

CHIME

adjectives
musical; pathetic; dolorous; silvery; sweet-toned; unhurried; clear; jubilant; silver; soothing; unvaried; religious; faint; heavenly.

CHIME (*v*)

adverbs
drowsily; harmoniously; mischievously; dolorously; unhurriedly; jubilantly; soothingly; religiously; faintly; heavenly; musically, clearly.

(See ring.)

CHIMERICAL

adverbs
strangely; fantastically; grotesquely; wildly; eccentrically; erratically; quaintly; curiously; baselessly; foolishly; exceptionally; peculiarly; extraordinarily; unaccountably; extravagantly; preposterously; fabulously; dreamily; fancifully.

CHIMNEY

adjectives
rotten; smoking; natural; stubborn; ample; curious; spiraled; defective; tottering; stumpy; low; ungainly; blackened; ghostly; clustering; open-throated; sparkless; disused.

verbs
block—; blow down—; clean—; connect—; construct—; convey through—; dampen—; decorate—; design—; escape through—; extend—; fire—; inspect—; lodge in—; muffle—; obstruct—; pass through—; suck up—; support—; —breathes; —carries off; —diffuses; —discharges; —draws off; —exhales; —fumes; —leaks; —reeks; —smokes; —topples; —tumbles.

(See passage.)

CHIN

adjectives
out-thrust; curious; jutting; determined; provocative; elongated; significant; prominent; dominant; fighting; obstinate; aggressive; protruding; stubborn; molded;

prognathous; rounded; square; retreating; bulldog; cleft; portly; dimpled; daintily; shaped; clean-cut; aristocratic; triangular; pointed; strong; rounded; sensitive; delicate; demure; quivering; protesting; scrubby; stubbled; unshaven; bristly; sunken; curbed; callow; tremulous; weak; girlish; bevelled; unflinching; lowered; firm; heavy; mutinous; marred; bruised; impudent; receding; arrogant; trembling; dumpy; formless; patrician; slack-set; full; granite; gray-bearded; seamy; witching; clean-shaven; sagging; generous.

verbs
box—; caress—; chafe—; dimple—; dip—; double—; furrow—; guard—; hollow—; pillow—on; razor—; roughen—; smooth—; strike on—; stroke—; stubble—; tickle—; —juts out.
(See jaw.)

CHINA (country)

adjectives
ancient; colorful; present-day; famine-cursed; tasteful.

CHINA (dish)

adjectives
atrociously-patterned; colorful; decorated; egg-shell; fragile; glazed; mongrel; ancestral; mended; imported; lustered; lustrous; treasured; superb; rare; delicate; magnificent; glorious; exquisite; dainty.

verbs
bake—; carve—; decorate—; design—; exhibit—; fire—; glaze—; inherit—; lithograph—; manufacture—; model—; mold—; paint—; preserve—; print—; process—; produce—; trace on—; trim—; turn—; vitrify—; —attracts; —sparkles.
(See porcelain.)

CHINAMAN

adjectives
slant-eyed; sinister; innocent; cryptic.

CHIP (counter or disk in game)

adjectives
accumulated; cashed-in; clicking; ivory; ominous; nested; red-and-blue; rattling; plastic; stacked.

verbs
accumulate—s; amass—s; ante—; calculate—; cash—s; mark—s; pile up—s; revalue—; toss in—; wager—; —s rattle; —s represent.

CHIP (v)

adverbs
laboriously; unweariedly; characteristically; disfiguringly; hurtfully; disastrously; idiotically; carelessly.

CHIPMUNK

adjectives
burrowing; chipping; conspicuous; beautifully-striped; darting; free-roving; fence-travelling; gleaming; marauding; scampering.

verbs
—chirps; —emerges; —ranges; —scurries; —stores.
(See squirrel, animal.)

CHIPPER

adverbs
blithely; heartily; gaily; cheerily; wholesomely; briskly; actively; ably; laughingly; light-heartedly; sunnily; smartly; alertly; energetically; happily.

CHIPS (fragments)

adjectives
infinitesimal; coarse; falling; scattered; shapeless; raw; valueless.

verbs
break into—; chisel into—; chop into—; cut into—; fly into—; gather—; hack into —; hew into—; piece into—; separate into—; split into—; —accumulate; —clutter up; —fly; —gather; —strike.
(See fragment, piece.)

CHIRP (v)

adverbs
shrilly; disdainfully; rapturously; ecstatically; joyously; contentedly; obstreperously; cheerfully; maddeningly; noisily; incessantly; obtrusively; deafeningly; unendingly; subduedly; discordantly.
(See twitter.)

CHIVALRIC

adverbs
patriotically; loyally; fanatically; devotedly; fantastically; bigotedly; faithfully; chauvinistically; unnecessarily; showily; ostentatiously; genuinely; sacrificially; pi-

ously; religiously; ardently; zealously; uncompromisingly; impulsively; sincerely; sublimely; martially; fiercely; incorruptibly; staunchly; inviolably; excessively.

CHIVALROUS

adverbs
delicately; devotedly; politely; generously; magnanimously; innately; inherently; traditionally; racially; suavely; gallantly; civilly; pleasantly; ardently; fervently; courteously; extremely; gently; urbanely; smoothly; obsequiously; amiably; ceremoniously; attentively; blandly; ingratiatingly; pleasingly; tactfully.

CHIVALRY

adjectives
morbid; belated; unsullied; old-fashioned; rekindled; deficient; fantastical; poetic; latent; knightly; gay; misplaced; exaggerated; distant; feudal; religious; delicate; loyal; medieval; undaunted; vaulted; celestial; youthful; generous.

verbs
affect—; attend with—; attribute to—; awaken—; bend toward—; blind by—; celebrate—; charge with—; commend for—; confer on—; dispense with—; educate for —; encounter—; equip for—; institute—; knight for—; reward—; —constitutes; —decays; —dies; —flourishes; —flowers; —prevails; —survives.

(See gallantry, courtesy, bravery.)

CHLOROFORM

adjectives
colorless; ethereal-odored; insidious; penetrating; pungent; sickish-sweet; sleep-producing.

verbs
administer—; anesthetize with—; dissolve in —; dose with —; expose —; gelatinize —; inhale —; melt —; overcome with —; sniff —; solidify —; subject to —; — acts; — boils; — decomposes; — dissolves; — dulls; — eases; — lessens.

(See anaesthetic.)

CHOCK-FULL

adverbs
generously; utterly; satisfactorily; inconveniently; dangerously; sloppily; carefully; calculatedly; accurately; happily; luckily; absolutely; surprisingly; gratifyingly; entirely; brimmingly; nicely.

CHOCOLATE

adjectives
thick; creamy; burning; sugary; tasty; bitter; rancid; delicious.

CHOICE

adjectives
inevitable; sensible; indefensible; ideal; hasty; shrewd; ultimate; emotional; distinguished; alternate; definite; conscious; free; happy; mistaken; unlimited; fortunate; sympathetic; logical; wise; moral; wide; important; half-humorous; unrestricted; endless; arbitrary; uncorrupted; critical; unessential; irrelevant; nonsensical; ideal; solicitous; scrupulous; ghastly; admirable; satisfactory; premium; perfect; sturdy; bitter; loathed; boundless; random; unaccountable; injudicious; intelligent; first; deliberate; perfect; haphazard; excellent; doubtful; mercenary; dazzling; appropriate; resolute; righteous; prudent; haughty.

verbs
abide by —; applaud —; bind to —; commend —; conceal —; contend with —; delight in —; determine —; encourage —; envy —; extend —; favor —; guard —; indicate —; justify —; leave —; overrule —; regulate —; restrict —; widen —; yield to —.

(See alternative, option, preference, election.)

CHOICE

adverbs
unusually; exquisitely; valuably; indubitably; unquestionably; evidently; manifestly; incomparably; inimitably; singularly; particularly; inestimably; invaluably; exceptionally; alluringly; temptingly; exotically; incalculably; immeasurably; imposingly; infinitely; sumptuously; inexpressibly; utterly; absolutely.

CHOIR

adjectives
soothing; plumed; enraptured; chantry; surpliced; cathedral; full-throated; extraordinary; immortal; starry; constellated; matin; white-robed; angelic; sweet-voiced; ritual; dusky; captive; silent; mystic; pausing; shining; winged; invisible.

verbs
accompany —; coach —; compose —; conduct —; direct —; employ —; establish —; garb —; invite —; organize —; pitch —; regulate —; retain —; stimulate —; support

—; train —; — answers; —anthems; — carols; — chants; — croaks; — croons; — devotes; — invokes; — is situated; — performs; — practises; — rehearses; — renders; — resounds.
(See chorus, singers.)

CHOKE (v)

adverbs
horribly; fiendishly; murderously; hellishly; painfully; furiously; fatally; mortally; partially; savagely.
(See strangle, throttle.)

CHOLERA

adjectives
Asiatic; devastating; dread; horrible; life-snuffing; malignant; pestilential; spreading; impartially-dealing; ravaging.

verbs
afflict with —; arrest —; attack with —; cause —; control —; distinguish —; expose to —; inoculate against —; overcome —; prevent —; protect against —; quarantine —; recognize —; recover from —; resemble —; scourge with —; stamp out —; subdue —; subject to —; suffer from —; treat for —; — affects; — infects; — invades; — irritates; — occurs; — prevails; — ravages; — spreads; — subsides; — travels; — visits.
(See disease, epidemic.)

CHOLERIC

adverbs
inveterately; terribly; extremely; excitedly; irascibly; habitually; touchily; cantankerously; exceptionally; intolerably; dangerously; hotly; petulantly; restively; incorrigibly; inherently; incurably; alarmingly; irritatingly; unbearably; unreasonably; senselessly; miserably; unfortunately; ill-temperedly; plaguedly; waspishly; querulously.

CHOOSE (v)

adverbs
promiscuously; precisely; deliberately; unanimously; inevitably; fastidiously; invariably; sedulously; universally; constitutionally; tactfully; tastefully; unselfishly; sensibly; shrewdly; ultimately; emotionally; definitely; mistakenly; sympathetically; logically; morally; unrestrictedly; arbitrarily; critically; irrelevantly; nonsensically; scrupulously; admirably; unaccountably; injudiciously; haphazardly; appropriately; resolutely; righteously; prudently; instinctively; finally; discreetly; speedily.
(See select, prefer.)

CHOP

adjectives
breaded; congealed; dripping; double; evenly-browned; fat; juicy; oozing; bony; shriveled.

verbs
broil —; butter —; devour —; digest —; dine on —; enjoy —; garnish —; grill —; heat —; pepper —; preserve —; relish —; roast —; salt —; savor —; season —; trim —; — burns; —simmers; — sizzles; — steams.
(See meat.)

CHOP (v)

adverbs
savagely; vigorously; ambitiously; hurriedly; leisurely; grimly; regularly; ineffectively; monotonously; continuously.

CHORAL

adverbs
melodiously; harmoniously; lyrically; fundamentally; originally; essentially; tunefully; euphoniously; symphoniously; orchestrally; effectively; splendidly; magnificently; sweetly; primarily; simply; elaborately; complicatedly.

CHORD

adjectives
harmonic; emotional; sympathetic; tender; responsive; peremptory; compassionate; triumphant; thunderous; preliminary; opening; impromptu; maddening; wailing; noisy; closing; sobbing; dreamy; dashing; nerve-racking; rare; vibrant; responsive; strong; broad; determined; familiar; answering; conscious; throbbing; susceptible; airy; sonorous; breaking; plenteous; liquid; sensitive; dominant.

verbs
pluck —; sound —; twang —; — charms; — shivers; — thrills; —trembles.
(See tendon, string.)

CHORE

adjectives
old-fashioned; bitter; small; domestic; weary.

verbs
dispatch —s; do —s; perform —s; plan —; —s bind; —s devolve on; —s occupy; —s settle on.
(See job, duty, task.)

CHORISTER
adjectives
impatient; poor; supercilious; monotonous.

CHORUS
adjectives
noisy; welcoming; general;-angry; fearful; jangling; affirmative; derisive; obtrusive; hallelujah; exhausted; tender; deafening; hoarse; booming; familiar; whispering; pessimistic; eerie; intricate; mighty; hair-raising; shrill; musical-comedy; shrieking; unending; recurrent; tuneful; abusive; masterly; jubilant; echoing; universal; horrendous; solemn; jolly; deep; screaming; hideous; vernacular; subdued; unprecedented; dirge-like; clamorous; wild; unfaltering; multitudinous (pl); seasonable; seditious; blasphemous; bibulous; mumbling; gleeful; meaningless; ranting; discordant.

verbs
accompany —; coach —; collect —; conduct —; constitute —; flow from —; join in on —; laugh in —; manage —; organize —; pitch—; regulate—; repeat—; take up —; train —; transpose —; utter —; whine in —; — breaks out; — chants; — executes; — harmonizes; — imitates; — practices; — rehearses; — renders; — reports; — resounds; — revels; — revives; — shrills; — spreads; — swells.
(See choir, song, refrain.)

CHRIST
adjectives
agonized; crucified; unheralded; infallible; merciful; glorious; death-triumphant; purple-robed; sorrowing; thorn-crowned; unconquerable; comforting.

verbs
acknowledge —; apprehend —; beseech —; bless —; bow before —; conform with —; consecrate to —; contemplate —; deny —; discern —; endow with —; esteem —; fight for —; follow —; forsake —; herald —; interpret —; preach —; preserve —; protect —; receive —; reject —; unveil —; uphold —; — ascends; — bears; — heals; — passes; — prophesies; — redeems; — represents; — rises; — rules; — suffers; — teaches; — toils.
(See God, Jesus.)

CHRISTIAN
adjectives
sincere; misguided; professing; preeminent; heartfelt; genuine.

CHRISTIAN
adverbs
devoutly; sincerely; ardently; fervently; devotedly; faithfully; humbly; meekly; piously; religiously; sanctimoniously; beatifically; joyously; blessedly; reverently; solemnly; benignly; honestly; genuinely; benevolently; mercifully; tolerantly; humanely; charitably; obviously; unmistakably; plainly; evidently; openly; avowedly; professedly.

CHRISTIANITY
adjectives
admirable; dogmatic; muscular; mysterious; primitive; sustained; sympathetic; profound.

verbs
conceive —; convert to —; cut off from —; denote —; embrace —; exalt —; extirpate —; follow —; found —; illustrate —; implant —; inculcate —; live in —; lose faith in —; manifest —; obscure —; persecute —; plant —; preach —; profess —; regard —; reject —; restore —; spread —; support —; teach —; trace —; — concerns; — embodies; — grows; — progresses; — redeems; — saves; — transcends; — triumphs.
(See religion, faith.)

CHRONIC
adverbs
avowedly; incurably; unfortunately; finally; obstinately; stubbornly; lingeringly; mildly; firmly; deplorably; grievously; pitiably; indubitably; manifestly; evidently; palpably; obviously; unquestionably; distinctly; plainly; incontrovertibly; unmistakably.

CHRONICLE
adjectives
sensuous; pagan; commonplace; objective; calm; gay; fascinating; detailed; lively; scandalous; stirring; heroic; racy; salty; wistful; tender; humorous; courageous; mocking; faithful; vivid; massive; memorable; poignant; unique; gripping; incomparable; lofty; moving; human; vigorous; episodic; broad-spoken; tedious; zestful; medieval; tattered; factual; dusty; fast-moving; personal; sententious; intimate.

verbs
accumulate in —; arrange —; compare —; compile —; complete —; compose —; devote — to; examine —; forge —; keep —; preserve —; recite —; refer to —; skeletonize —; — consists of; — contains; — contradicts; — conveys; — disposes; — determines; — embraces; — presents; — recollects; — registers; — reveals; — sets down; — treats of.

(See record, account, narrative, diary, history.)

CHRONICLER

adjectives
matter-of-fact; scandal-loving; contemporaneous.

CHRONOLOGICAL

adverbs
accurately; carefully; meticulously; fussily; absolutely; dependably; tolerably; infallibly; scrupulously; strictly; uncannily; unimpeachably; avidly; punctiliously.

CHRONOLOGY

adjectives
dismal; distilled; condensed; meaningful; mouldering; simple; uneventful; unvarnished; verified.

verbs
arrange —; ascertain —; base — on; check —; compare — with; correlate —; develop —; explain —; fix —; interest in —; preserve —; reckon —; settle —; telescope —; verse in —; — classifies; — computes; — depends on; — enumerates; — includes; — indicates; — measures; — provides; — records; — reveals; — survives; — traces.

(See science, time.)

CHRYSANTHEMUM

adjectives
huge; tawny; bronze; brave; pink; golden; great; pale; shaggy; yellow; calm.

CHUBBY

adverbs
adorably; sweetly; cheerily; buxomly; huskily; rosily; pleasantly; happily; cheerfully; sturdily; healthily; stoutly; laughably; ridiculously; lovably; admirably; ludicrously; stupidly; heavily; laughingly; gaily; blithely; bonnily; winsomely; handsomely; terribly.

CHUCKLE

adjectives
appreciative; affectionate; naive; long; delicious; humorous; benevolent; sepulchral; melancholy; mirthless; low; little; slow; deep; noiseless; vicious; gloating; evil; sneering; irreverent; exultant; gratuitous; ghastly; unpleasant; eerie; soft; childish; crazy; husky; shrewd; mild; elfish; asthmatic; inward; dry; communicative; contagious; cruel; palpitating; suppressed; sly; insulting; bitter; inward; prolonged; coarse; fearful; tremulous; joyous; grim.

CHUCKLE (v)

adverbs
inaudibly; casually; maliciously; gruffly; waggishly; inwardly; fearfully; hollowly; appreciatively; affectionately; naively; humorously; benevolently; sepulchrally; mirthlessly; noiselessly; gloatingly; sneeringly; irreverently; exultantly; gratuitously; unpleasantly; huskily; elfishly; contagiously; asthmatically; insultingly; bitterly; tremulously; joyously; grimly.

(See laugh.)

CHUMMY

adverbs
delightfully; helpfully; devotedly; intimately; sympathetically; companionably; affectionately; cordially; warmly; sincerely; heartily; amicably; affably; wonderfully; frankly; graciously; loyally; distinctly; enthusiastically; congenially; marvellously; unselfishly; staunchly; generously; steadfastly; courageously.

CHURCH

adjectives
venerable; impressive; calm; dignified; simple; famous; historical; imposing; ancient; hoary; handsome; exquisite; fashionable; enormous; frescoed; small; gray; loopholed; ivy-clad; colonial; belfry-towered; country; white-washed; fly-bitten; square-towered; parabolic; village; parish; dismal; silent; superfluous; competing; huddling; dedicated; pillaged; dissenting; buttressed; belfried; cathedral; sumptuous; ornate; friendly-looking; tremendous; dominating; ambitious; primitive; prosaic; barnlike; uncouth; spireless; gloomy; established; conservative; olive-green; sandstone; decent; remote; comprehensive; self-denying; laborious; unwearied; ancient.

verbs
assemble in —; baptize in —; christen in —; confirm in —; consecrate —; deface —; drift away from —; enrich —; establish —; esteem —; file into —; forsake —; gather in —; hie to —; interpret —; laud —; liberalize —; neglect —; orient —; present to —; ransack —; respect —; salute —; unite —; wed in —; worship in —; — absolves; — inspires; — molds; — moulders; — wanes.

(See temple, cathedral, chapel, tabernacle, sanctuary, congregation.)

CHURCH-GOERS

adjectives
austere; backbiting; backsliding; devout; earnest; dogmatic; fervent; grave; heaven-aspiring; hypocritical; morose; long-faced; puritanical; salvation-seeking.

verbs
appeal to —; appoint —; join —; patronize —; prevail on —; respect —; witness —; — abandon; — attend; — authorize; — band; — commune; — conform; —congregate; — contribute; — control; — convene; — criticize; — endow; — flow by; — grow; — ignore; — organize; — provide; — rally; — sneer; — stream past; — support.

(See congregation.)

CHURCHY

adverbs
devoutly; hypocritically; ostentatiously; sententiously; unctuously; devotedly; fashionably; unwearyingly; pompously; dramatically; dutifully; properly; appropriately; adequately; meticulously; punctiliously; obediently; piously; sentimentally; obsequiously; pharisaically; sanctimoniously; conscientiously; righteously; pretentiously.

CHURL

adjectives
drunken; seditious; sturdy; vulgar; brash; brazen.

CHURLISH

adverbs
inordinately; bluntly; sullenly; stupidly; basely; ruggedly; fantastically; awkwardly; offensively; unconsciously; unwittingly; artlessly; deliberately; colossally; detestably; insufferably; intolerably; unbearably; rudely; crudely; abominably; intentionally; shockingly; innately; boorishly; ignorantly; harshly; disagreeably; outrageously; indefensibly; vulgarly; brazenly; coarsely; brashly; brassily; contemptibly; shamefully.

CHURN (*v*)

adverbs
irrationally; viciously; vigorously; wildly; impressively; awesomely; grimly; tumultuously; thunderously; deafeningly.

CIDER

adjectives
piercing; tangy; aromatic; acid.

CIGAR

adjectives
smooth; mild; mellow; vile; unlighted; butted; disheveled; half-smoked; aromatic; excellent; villainous; rank; rough; exotic; inevitable; refreshing.

verbs
box —; chew on —; clip —; clutch —; crave —; display —; extinguish —; flick —; grade —; import —; inhale —; insert —; manufacture —; mold —; object to —; pocket —; point —; produce —; proffer —; puff on —; pull at —; roll into —; shape —; smoke —; wave —; wrap —; yearn for —; — appeals; — burns; — glows.

CIGARETTE

adjectives
disconsolate; soggy; indispensable; lightly-fingered; monogrammed; bungled; unlighted; blended; acrid; quashed; dangling; proffered; pasty; formless; customary.

verbs
blend —s; carton —s; choke on —; consume —s; cough on —; discard —s; fumble for —; grade —; inhale —; mentholize —; moisten —; package —; perfume —; proffer —; purvey —; tip —; toast —; turn out —; wave —; — dies; — dries out; — fumes; — glows; — smoulders; — stales.

CIMMERIAN

adverbs
gloomily; darkly; vastily; expansively; extensively; terrifyingly; frightfully; luridly; sunlessly; tenebriously; umbrageously; obscurely; dimly; shadily; murkily; sombrely; stupendously; appallingly; hideously.

CINDERS

adjectives
besieging; blinding; blazing; cruel; drifting; catapulting; dusty; feathery; gritty; inky; murky; smudgy; sooty; sharp; stinging.

verbs
arrest —s; deposit —s; eject —s; form —s; pile —s; quench into —s; rake —s; reduce to —s; sift —s; throw off —s; turn to —; — die; — fly; — glow; — lodge; — pop; — sear; — smoulder.
(See coal, residue, ashes.)

CIPHER

adjectives
valueless; inextricable; constant.

CIRCLE

adjectives
conversational; social; illustrious; exclusive; gilded; artistic; political; aristocratic; literary; fashionable; wealthy; financial; wide; brilliant; well-bred; bigoted; select; limited; cheery; charmed; real; ideal; convivial; erratic; perfect; dim; pale; iron; eddying; disintegrated; blurred; broken; enclosing; great; sweeping; sturdy; charmed; intimate; executive; solemn; predestined; concentric; cosmopolitan; bizarre; widening; charred; ceremonial; ringing; collapsed; ever-enlarging; original; vicious; agricultural; splendid; decorative; leading; influential; distinguished; smartest; elastic; pleasant; closed; petty; educational; esoteric; polished; interior; operatic; ultrafashionable; awkward; extended; deep; ruddy; vast; walled; uninterrupted; conservative; privileged; noisy; wavering; pallid; giddy; curious; deft; professional; diplomatic.

verbs
accomplish —; assemble in —; bar from —; circumscribe —; cleave —; complete —; cut —; disband —; emit from —; form —; flutter in —; guard —; hallow —; inscribe —; insert in —; join —; lead into —; narrow —; pour in —; revolve —; round —; spin in —; swell —; trace —; — disintegrates; — widens.

CIRCLE (*v*)

adverbs
demurely; erratically; solemnly; wideningly; ceremonially; viciously; awkwardly; noisily; waveringly; curiously; treacherously.
(See surround.)

CIRCLED

adverbs
darkly; ominously; closely; gloriously; radiantly; strangely; completely; hopelessly; fatally; alarmingly; perplexingly; unexpectedly; suddenly; roseately.

CIRCUIT

adjectives
respectful; due; electric; unbroken; annual; elliptical; tedious; irregular; spacious; voltaic; short.

verbs
administer —; appoint to —; attach to —; complete —; discontinue —; divide into —s; enclose within —; form —; plug into —; regulate —; remodel —; retain —; ride —; supervise —; travel —; visit —; — comprises; — consists of; — prevails; — transmits.
(See district, course.)

CIRCUITOUS

adverbs
exasperatingly; terribly; needlessly; tediously; wearisomely; monotonously; vexatiously; undesirably; unsuitably; extremely; hopelessly; endlessly; sadly; tortuously; intricately; crookedly; deviously; disturbingly; distressingly; dangerously; suspiciously; obscurely; alarmingly; astonishingly; bewilderingly; wretchedly; unduly.

CIRCULAR

adjectives
inviting; descriptive; confidential; brief; significant; sluggish.

verbs
announce by —; display —; distribute —; lay out —; request —; shower —s; subscribe to —; summon by —; — advertises; — colors; — describes; — explains; — informs; — proclaims; — propagates.
(See communication, publication, letter.)

adverbs
perfectly; absolutely; symmetrically; artistically; ceremonially; originally; decoratively; significantly; smartly; fashionably; curiously; brokenly; naturally; elliptically; impressively; architecturally; theatrically; harmoniously.

CIRCULATE (*v*)

adverbs
immediately; greedily; continually; widely; extensively; briskly; industriously; limitedly; considerably; enormously; sluggishly; periodically; selectively; inadequately; effectively; normally.
(See disseminate, diffuse.)

CIRCULATION (blood)

adjectives
abnormal; adequate; aroused; deficient; defective; engorged; impaired; lax; hindered; over-stimulated; rapid; sluggish; simulated; tonic.

verbs
aid —; carry on —; check —; constrict —; depress —; increase —; impair —; impede —; improve —; maintain —; obstruct —; overtax —; promote —; quicken —; quiet —; relieve —; restore —; speed up —; stimulate —; throw into —.

CIRCULATION (newspaper, magazine, etc.)

adjectives
amazing; limited; considerable; vast; enormous; select; huge; extensive; sluggish; periodical; suspended; defective; repressed; throttled; inadequate; effective; brisk; normal.

verbs
augment —; boost —; build —; double —; fix —; heighten —; increase —; lose —; maintain —; promote —; reduce —; — climbs; — drops; — gains; — jumps; — sags; — spurts; — wanes.

(See distribution, number, quantity.)

CIRCUMFERENCE

adjectives
extensive; vast; extreme; luminous.

CIRCUMJACENT

adverbs
closely; influentially; contributively; advantageously; interestedly; actively; importantly; anxiously; indivisibly; inseparably; consequentially; momentously; potently; authoritatively; closely; cooperatively; helpfully; serviceably; opportunely; concernedly; sympathetically; watchfully; warily; providently; alertly; heedfully.

CIRCUMLOCUTORY

adverbs
tiresomely; tediously; unnecessarily; amateurishly; monotonously; maddeningly; vexatiously; impossibly; undesirably; ineptly; unsuitably; extremely; excessively; incurably; incorrigibly; insistently; pedantically; pedagogically; academically; hopelessly; digressively; ramblingly; sadly; inexcusably; inefficiently.

CIRCUMSCRIBE (v)

adverbs
narrowly; severely; precisely; closely; rigorously; definitely; clearly; specifically.

(See confine, defense, limit.)

CIRCUMSPECTION

adjectives
exact; utmost; administrative; continual; pious; sly.

CIRCUMSTANCE

adjectives
dominant; antecedent; analogous; formal; favorable; encouraging; exceptional; fortunate; imagined; extenuating; mitigating; accompanying; hurried; external; altered; similar; actual; existing; ensuing; diverse; subsequent; attendant; concomitant; accessory; contingent; manifold; contributory; leading; collateral; expeditious; unfortunate; equivocal; droll; adventitious; novel; romantic; auspicious; pitiful; fortuitous; identical; peculiar; incredible; unsafe; interesting; faulty; minute; formidable; easy; irritable; providential; ridiculous; encumbered; isolated; painful; affluent; present; disastrous; striking; arduous; discouraging; obsolete; momentary; incidental; dreadful; unforeseen; unpropitious; disquieting; untoward; promiscuous; straitened; forgotten; extraordinary; mysterious; uncontrollable; suggestive; singular; suspicious; sordid; curious; comfortable; accidental; unbelievable; peculiar; unlucky; delicate; unpromising; adverse; differing; historical; accidental; evanescent; inexplicable; potent; varying (pl); ignoble; probable; embarrassing; trying; sordid; intellectual; advantageous; astonishing; iniquitous; distressing; trifling; disheartening; agreeable; brutal; reduced; domestic; precarious; impressive; remarkable; frivolous; perplexing; dramatic; diametric; moderate; prevailing; complicated; sensational.

verbs
ascribe to —; attend with —; depend on —; detail —; engender —; impress with —; meet —; overcome by —; ponder —; recount —; relish —; respond to —; rest on —; shape —; stress —; struggle against —; weigh —; — accompanies; — alarms; — alters; — arises; — determines; — forces; — hampers; — imputes; — prevents; — surrounds; — wavers; — yields.

(See condition, incident, cause, occurrence, situation, feature, environment.)

CIRCUMSTANTIAL

adverbs
sensationally; remarkably; insignificantly; trivially; favorably; temporarily; extenuatingly; aggravatingly; coincidentally; fortuitously; unpropitiously; unfavorably; suspiciously; adversely; adventitiously; critically; incidentally; contradictorily; corroboratively; reasonably; plausibly; speciously; credibly.

CIRCUS

adjectives
Jacksonian; bloody; tented; political; traveling; tinseled; three-ring.

verbs
admit to —; "ballyhoo" —; operate —; perform at —; stage —; yearn for —; — amuses; — blares; — displays; — engages; — enlivens; —entertains; — exhibits; — parades; — roams; — tours; — travels; — troups.
(See show.)

CITADEL

adjectives
celebrated; straw-built; unguarded; ancient; social; aerie; capitulated; impregnable; pensile; undefended.

verbs
attack —; bar from —; command —; construct —; erect —; establish —; evolve —; fortify —; man —; pour from —; retreat to —; scale —; siege —; storm —; — contains; — defends; — defies; — guards; — protects; — rises; — stores; — towers; — withstands.
(See fortress.)

CITATION

adjectives
corroborated; ample; apt; ludicrous; partial.

CITE (*v*)

adverbs
earnestly; partially; amply; aptly; accurately; authoritatively; relevantly; sensationally; fortuitously; strikingly.
(See quote, mention.)

CITIZEN

adjectives
belligerent; busy; esteemed; perspicacious; small-salaried; luckless; prosperous; distinguished; patched; individual; prejudiced; plodding; enlightened; enthusiastic; indefinite; unworthy; substantial; intelligent; god-fearing; ordinary; peaceable; law-abiding; unoffending; disillusioned; callous; staid; home-loving; ornamental; defenseless; competent; simple; plain-speaking; public-spirited; conscious; active; conspicuous; callous; vile; half-starved; influential; venerable; indignant; average; private; generous; illustrious; cultivated; grave; respectable; admirable; eminent; cloaked; reputable; representative; loyal; worthy; useful; law-abiding; duteous; bespectacled; patriotic; well-known; honorable; lamented; mutinous; plain; simple; quiet; easygoing; innocent; tight-lipped; august; pugnacious; disgruntled; beleaguered; iron-bellied; wistful; regretful; ordinary; humble; average; mere; prosaic; typical; able-bodied; courageous; husky; young; stalwart; bibulous; sanguine; careless; selfish; blind; serious-minded; straight-thinking; reckless; conscientious; high-minded; foremost; valued; wealthy; prominent; leading; outstanding; revered; self-sacrificing; hard-working; progressive; zealous; loyal; kindly; honest; decent; cultured; altruistic; worthy; well-meaning; stolid; solid; independent; untrammeled; noble; exemplary.

verbs
conscript —s; disfranchise —; entitle as —; harangue —s; interview —; oppress —; privilege —; protect —; regiment —s; register as —; tax —; wheedle —s; —s assemble; —s demand; —s elect; — enjoys; — possesses; — protests; —s rally; —s vote; — vows.
(See individual, inhabitant.)

CITIZENRY

adjectives
outraged; humble; contented; greasy; dignified.

CITIZENSHIP

adjectives
national; commonplace; robust; conscientious.

verbs
accept —; acquire —; admit to —; apply for —; cancel —; confer — upon; declare —; deprive of —; desire —; divest of —; drop —; establish —; forfeit —; obtain —; refuse—; renounce—; revoke—; — confers; — entitles; — privileges; — protects.

CITY

adjectives

throbbing; bustling; seething; hustling; thriving; growing; brutal; busiest; wealthiest; progressive; unperturbed; huge; teeming; headlong; glorious; rushing; stirring; energetic; modern; flourishing; busy; enterprising; gay; laughing; lighthearted; sleeping; dead; quiet; wicked; free; sin-stained; wilted; worth-while; corrupt; ruined; content; intolerant; fanatical; smoldering; dull; murky; grimy; congested; drab; squalid; ugly; commonplace; worse-lit; widespreading; outermost; rich; influential; prosperous; conservative; trading; selfsame; shimmering; noble; thronged; unruly; cathedraled; melancholy; mighty; breathless; ruinous; humming; resplendent; coastal; swarming; fascinating; inspiring; sunken; deserted; gilded; distinguished; diversified; hopeful; distracted; mirthful; opulent; queer; glittering; long-shaped; peaceful; friendly; shivering; glamorous; lamplit; rock-built; annihilated; joyous; menacing; elegant; youthful; mansion-decked; ambitious; nether; imperial; titanic; restless; enchanted; pagan; pleasure; tropical; typical; slumbering; prospective; maritime; clustering; affrighted; melancholy; earth-commanding; advertised; drowned; wondrous; gorgeous; hard-boiled; powerful; awakened; isolated; industrious; ancient; crooked; tortuous; snakelike; rising; unhappy; undefended; cursed; commercial; voluptuous; plague-stricken; congested; wailing; spacious; vast; helpless; holocaust; pest-ridden; torpid; passive; dejected; garrisoned; well-washed; appreciative; ruined; constricted; thriving; decayed; masterful; wrought; luxurious; well-ordered; spirited; advancing; altar-decked; silenced; crowded; provincial; beleaguered; cordial; death-stricken; verdureless; once-famous; heathen; attractive; jeweled; well-watered; eternal; plague-stricken; negligent; vice-laden; spire-adorned; sin-compassed; rogue-haunted; monolithic; hapless; besieged; materialistic; nebulous; commercial; sin-burdened; austere; sunless; unrivalled; futuristic; enthralling; delightful; majestic; marvelous; fabulous; aspiring; great; lovable; desirable; coveted; fascinating; benignant; scintillating; proud; bright; fairest; naughty; impregnable; beautiful; staid; silent; moonlit; dream; lovely; colorful; gray-blue; snow-white; unique; grand; mysterious; adventurous; glittering; dying; buried; bombarded; monotonous; muffled; agate; polyglot; golden-doomed; appealing; infant; native; cosmopolitan; royal; tourist; shipbuilding; lake-girted; guardian; prehistoric; alabaster-like; holy; flat-roofed; oriental-looking; walled; medieval; legendary; industrial; pontifical; celestial; exotic; homogeneous; lurid; confused; incredible; burning; meticulous; leading; principal; vibrant; far-flung; populous; fortified; conquered; well-kept; ever-growing; sun-baked; parched-brown; gentle-mannered.

verbs

abide in —; adjoin —; annihilate —; approach —; assault —; banish from —; besiege —; burn —; congregate in —; corrupt —; crowd —; deface —; defend —; deluge —; depopulate —; desolate —; destroy —; doom —; encompass —; erect —; establish —; flank —; harbor in —; haunt —; huddle in —; impoverish —; inhabit —; inundate —; issue from —; lay siege to —; lay waste to —; march through —; migrate to —; mold —; oppress —; pen up in —; pillage —; pollute —; raze —; rule —; sack —; scatter through —; shake —; stake out —; steal over —; strike —; survey —; swallow up in —; take —; tarry in —; tax —; terrorize —; veer toward —; wall in —; war on —; warn —; — acclaims; — basks; — decays; — expands; — flourishes; — forges ahead; — hums; — reeks; — roars; — simmers; — sprouts; — straggles; — towers.

(See town, community.)

CITYLIKE

adverbs

extraordinarily; significantly; unexpectedly; surprisingly; undeniably; meticulously; deliberately; artificially; naturally; disagreeably; agreeably; discordantly; ostentatiously; inharmonoiusly; superciliously; arrogantly; pathetically; ludicrously; ridiculously; foolishly; awkwardly; busily; enterprisingly; prosperously; proudly; fashionably; grandly; incongruously.

CIVIL

adverbs

smoothly; coolly; correctly; properly; appropriately; scarcely; politely; affably; warmly; graciously; sweetly; fawningly; idly; nonchalantly; unexpectedly; suddenly; carefully; officiously; unctuously; blandly; obligingly; complacently; obsequiously; ingratiatingly; tactfully; diplomatically; sagaciously; wisely; necessarily; condescendingly; urbanely; decorously; fashionably;

punctiliously; meticulously; admirably; conventionally; stiffly; demurely; primly; precisely; cautiously; warily.

CIVILIAN

adjectives
meddlesome; covenanted; humdrum; conceited; wretched.

CIVILITY

adjectives
unforced; sad; cold; sweet; creeping; fawning; base; chill; ancient; restrained; interchanged (pl); impetuous; idle; unmeaning.

verbs
accept with —; act with —; answer with —; breed —; cherish —; conform to —; consider —; employ —; deny —; lack —; oblige with —; observe —; occasion —; preserve —; respect —; teach —; train in —; treat with —; want —; — befits.
(See courtesy, politeness.)

CIVILIZATION

adjectives
brutalized; luminous; distinctive; potential; perished; private; primitive; ancient; increasing; vast; varied; overvaunted; bloated; progressive; sophisticated; troubadour; moral; decadent; earthly; ordered; material; contemporary; turbulent; strange; advancing; complex; indigenous; mechanical; passionate; refined; higher; saturated; enlightened; decent; perilous; sick; alien; technical; crumbling; disintegrating; effete; bygone; older; long-vanished; artistic; archaic; forgotten; unique; extraordinary; so-called; cracked; industrial; megalopolitan; superficial; luxurious; urban; domestic; barbaric; aboriginal; agrarian; national; crude; fastidious; majestic; unrecorded; belligerent; chivalrous; selfish; solid; positive; pernicious; prosy; modern; curious; attendant; perfected.

verbs
blot out—; break down—; contribute to—; court—; cradle—; destroy—; doom—; extol—; flout—; found—; fuse—s; infect—; menace—; promote—; raise—; shame—; standardize—; threaten—; —advances; —asserts itself; —decays; —declines; —enslaves; ;—falls; —inflicts; —mars; —perishes; —progresses; —reverts to type; —sweeps onward; —wanes.
(See enlightenment, progress, refinement, advancement, culture.)

CLAD

adverbs
richly; elaborately; gaudily; wretchedly; fully; scantily; shabbily; raggedly; poorly; luxuriously; carefully; carelessly; recklessly; absurdly; fashionably; ridiculously; ludicrously; grotesquely; honorably; unfashionably; garishly; wantonly; laughably; clownishly; seductively; gaily; gorgeously; glamorously; awkwardly; incongruously; outlandishly; expensively; cheaply; smartly; handsomely; drably; extravagantly; economically; tastefully.

CLAD (*v*)

adverbs
decorously; symbolically; grossly; imperfectly; fittingly; partially; scantily; scarcely; heavily; warmly; harmoniously.
(See dress.)

CLAIM

adjectives
additional; faint; ardent; extenuating; misleading; exaggerated; extravagant; curative; substantiated; indisputable; enormous; groundless; confidential; bitter; exclusive; plausible; intellectual; unquenchable; notorious; complacent; intolerable; advertising; hereditary; unjustifiable; unprophetic; slender; peculiar; sales; fraudulent; rhetorical; accumulating; valid; remaining; worthless; reproachful; respectable; illegal; embroidered; time-honored; extortionate; suitable; contested; obsolete; conflicting (pl); imperial; inexorable; insistent; professional; modest; abiding; prior; rival; inflated; fanciful; questionable; incredible; preposterous; unsavory; false; pecuniary; parental; royal; special; implacable; imperative; unusual; difficult; depreciating; relative.

verbs
adjust—; annul—; assert—; attest to—; base—on; cede—; combat—; confirm—; consider—; contradict—; debate—; defy—; demolish—; denounce—; deny—; dismiss —; dispose of—; dispute—; doubt—; establish—; exempt from—; expose—; forfeit—; honor—; iron out—s; justify—; lay—to; offset—; press—; protest—; reconcile—; record—; refute—; renounce—; retain—; shatter—; smile at—; stake out—; stultify—; substantiate—; support—; surrender—; verify—; waive—; —s diminish; —s dissolve.
(See pretension, demand. title. right.)

CLAIM (*v*)

adverbs

persistently; strenuously; confidently; assuredly; adroitly; falsely; boldly; vociferously; exorbitantly; ardently; exaggeratedly; groundlessly; unjustifiably; reproachfully; fraudulently; extortionately; inexorably; professionally; insistently; incredibly; legitimately; validly; fancifully; preposterously; implacably; imperatively.

(See assert, affirm, maintain.)

CLAIRVOYANT

adverbs

remarkably; unmistakably; mysteriously; unquestionably; marvelously; prophetically; mesmerically; hypnotically; naturally; extraordinarily; undeniably; absolutely; indisputably; incontestably; traditionally; inherently; palpably; infallibly; conclusively; phenomenally; triumphantly; evidently; manifestly; obviously; incredibly; astonishingly; astoundingly; startlingly.

CLAMBER (*v*)

adverbs

aimlessly; bravely; laboriously; ceaselessly; clumsily; unsteadily.

(See climb.)

CLAMMY

adverbs

unpleasantly; disagreeably; horridly; horribly; loathsomely; disgustingly; offensively; repulsively; hatefully; necessarily; distastefully; manageably; stickily; adhesively; cohesively; coldly.

CLAMOR

adjectives

full-voiced; ghastly; noisy; tremendous; hideous; hellish; impatient; violent; nerve-straining; deafening; general; mournful; never-ceasing; heart-warming; popular; raucous; frenzied; turbulent; orchestral; sudden; staccato; venomous; savage; ministerial; excited; wretched; smothered; deplorable; loud; ignorant; exacting; blind; vulgar; universal; confirmatory; persistent; dismal; querulous; fulsome; vague; virile; impertinent; muffled; uncontrollable; petty; frightful; selfish; national; thunderous.

verbs

cease—; ease—; fill with—; harken to—; lose in—; prolong—; raise—; vent—; —abates; —bursts forth; —deafens; —drowns; —peals; —rings; —rumbles; —thickens; —wanes; —waxes.

(See uproar, tumult, din, racket.)

CLAMOR (*v*)

adverbs

dissentingly; noisily; vociferously; obstreperously; shrilly; hideously; hellishly; mournfully; raucously; frenziedly; turbulently; venomously; wretchedly; deplorably; persistently; dismally; querulously; fulsomely; impertinently; thunderously; uncontrollably.

(See bawl, roar.)

CLAMOROUS

adverbs

noisily; impatiently; surlily; angrily; happily; eagerly; hungrily; deafeningly; madly; frenziedly; suddenly; excitedly; wretchedly; blindly; persistently; anxiously; querulously; vaguely; uncontrollably; selfishly; restlessly; explosively; alarmingly; menacingly; hysterically; enthusiastically; ungovernably; significantly; fanatically; boisterously; jubilantly; joyously; shrilly; uproariously; ominously; importunately; appallingly; impressively; extraordinarily; unwontedly; urgently.

CLAN

adjectives

critical; prolific; original; feudal; clamorous; sturdy; romping; murderous; visionary; hostile; rival.

verbs

assemble—; associate with—; connect with —; descend from—; dissolve—; father—; found—; grace—; join—; lead—; muster —; organize—; prohibit—; represent—; rule—; trace—; unify—; —gathers; —marauds; —pillages; —plunders; —terrorizes.

(See tribe.)

CLANDESTINE

adverbs

romantically; furtively; sordidly; inviolately; strictly; necessarily; unhappily; guiltily; subtly; curiously; unsavorily; evasively; stealthily; slyly; skulkingly; terribly; miserably.

CLANG

adjectives

imperious; fearful; warning; horrid; windy; glad; melancholy; lingering; hollow; ecstatic; nonchalant; resounding; harsh; discordant; metallic; muffled; funereal; brassy; vibrating.

CLANG (v)

adverbs
discordantly; infernally; resonantly; imperiously; fearfully; horridly; hollowly; ecstatically; vibratingly; metallically; funereally; dismally.

CLANGOR

adjectives
mad; sudden; merry; deafening; reverberative; impatient.

CLANGOROUS

adverbs
madly; terrifyingly; violently; riotously; horribly; jubilantly; cheeringly; mournfully; funereally; sadly; alarmingly; warningly; menacingly; joyously; happily; joyfully; stirringly; thunderously; sweetly; softly; harmoniously; deeply; deafeningly; sonorously; melodiously; mellifluously; heartily; hearteningly.

CLANK

adjectives
steady; metallic; tiny; tinkling.

CLANNISH

adverbs
incurably; delightfully; loyally; incorrigibly; eternally; characteristically; inherently; sturdily; stoutly; noisily; quietly; devotedly; staunchly; dependably; truly; racially; locally; provincially; intrepidly; indomitably; intrinsically; dangerously; alarmingly; actively; definitely; vigorously.

CLANNISHNESS

adjectives
unconquerable; enforced.

CLAP

adjectives
friendly; frightful; genial.

CLAP (v)

adverbs
conclusively; vigorously; dutifully; noiselessly; unobtrusively; frightfully; thunderously; genially; enthusiastically; freely; monotonously; liberally; appreciatively; sympathetically; gratefully; welcomingly; ceaselessly.
(See applaud.)

CLARIFY (v)

adverbs
successfully; intellectually; admirably; miraculously; satisfactorily; completely; partially; painstakingly; generally; notably.
(See illumine, clear.)

CLARITY

adjectives
intellectual; painful; interpretative; unsurpassed; sparkling; aching; diamond-like; enervating; sickening; miraculous; admirable; fragrant; intense; sunlit; irrefutable; quiet; cold; crystal.

CLASH

adjectives
furious; threatened; explosive; angry; contemporaneous; rude; syncopated; sharp; memorable; initial; street; recurrent; joyous; violent; naval; brisk; soundless; bloody; metallic; muffled; inter-racial.

verbs
attack with—; avoid—; collide with—; embroil in—; engage in—; incite—; produce—; recoil from—; recount—; result in—; strike with—; —conflicts with; —echoes; —peals; —resounds; —shocks; —thunders; —warns.
(See crash, collision, opposition, noise.)

CLASH (v)

adverbs
unpleasantly; antagonistically; explosively; rhythmically; furiously; angrily; rudely; sharply; initially; recurrently; violently; muffledly; thunderously; intermittently; instinctively.
(See hurtle, crash, disagree.)

CLASHING

adverbs
unfortunately; unhappily; hostilely; inimically; contradictorily; unpropitiously; constantly; pugnaciously; truculently; ill-naturedly; contentiously; quarrelsomely; unnecessarily; ill-advisedly; hastily; antagonistically; foolishly; irritably; unreasonably; senselessly; miserably; hotly; frightfully; pathetically; vexatiously; bitterly; rudely; violently; frequently; furiously; crudely; sharply.

CLASP

adjectives (*embrace*)
conventional; dewy; impulsive; uncoercive; warm; comforting; gentlemanly; gentle; confiding; cruel; lingering; eager; cold; firm; frantic; healthy; strong.

CLASP (*fastener*)

adjectives
gilt; ornate; clicking.

CLASP (*general*)

verbs
affix—; brace—; buckle—; cleave—; connect—; fit—; fumble with—; furnish with—; gird with—; hook—; join—; strain—; —bars; —embraces; —encircles; —fastens; —grasps; —insures; —interlocks; —overlaps; —secures.
(See hook, embrace, lock.)

CLASP (*v*)

adverbs
convulsively; deliberately; fondly; unprofitably; familiarly; sensually; hungrily; severely; frantically; impulsively; comfortingly; confidingly; cruelly; lingeringly; coldly; firmly; despairingly.
(See grasp, grapple, clutch.)

CLASS (*school*)

adjectives
academic; attending; assembled; bespectacled; diligent; elementary; fixed; grade; grouped; graduating; freshman; intermediate; lecture; overworked; primer; primary; advanced; subdivided; unlimited.

verbs
address—; admit to—; attend—; change —es; conduct—; divide into—es; examine —; lecture—; limit—; promote—; raise—; rate—; unite—; —answers; —assembles; —choruses; —competes; —graduates; —recites; —reviews; —sings; —studies.

CLASS (*social*)

adjectives
arrogant; unclaimed; ruthless; vast; emergent; ruling; history-conscious; leisure; spurious; laboring; useful; humble; technical; servile; degraded; generic; social; diversified; privileged; conflicting; piratical; consistent; submerged; collected; represented; traditional; dole-receiving; peaceful; better; vicious; inarticulate; dominant; rapid; various (pl); exclusive; despised; venal; conspicuous; liberated; opulent; irresponsible; possessionless; obnoxious; corresponding; lower; agrarian; distinct; noticeable; exploiting; vulgar; inferior; irreconcilable; wealthy; cultured; upper; cultivated; best; preferred; conservative; industrial; intellectual; proletarian; illiterate; submerged; artisan; contented; prosperous; working; object; odious; mediocre; truant; rising; central; middle-aged; indivisible; appointive; chivalrous; holy; iron-bound; vigorous; skeptical; unimpassioned; economic.

verbs
arouse—; bow to—; consort with—; do away with—es; educate—; elevate—; enslave—; fix—; free—; level—; liberate—es; lower—es; separate—; stifle—; —es arise; —es gravitate; —idolizes; —predominates; —rebels.
(See caste, rank, order.)

CLASSIC

adjectives
perfumed; bristling; venerable; favorite; beloved; noblest; unforgettable; purest; intellectual; juvenile; immortal; rare.

CLASSICAL

adverbs
superbly; acceptably; admittedly; elegantly; easily; gracefully; readily; academically; artistically; chastely; correctly; felicitously; naturally; unaffectedly; modestly; unpretentiously; undoubtedly; deservedly; avowedly; pleasingly; aptly; appropriately; commendably; deservedly; admirably; laudably; universally; uniformly.

CLASSICISM

adjectives
capricious; cold; ethical.

CLASSICS

verbs
accept—; acquaint with—; assimilate—; associate with—; bar—; criticize—; delve into—; discuss—; edit—; educate in—; familiarize with—; favor—; forsake—; instruct in—; introduce to—; model on—; pertain to—; place among—; prefer—; quote—; regard—; revel in—; tabulate—; verse in—; —exemplify; —guide.
(See literature, history, biography, religion.)

CLASSIFICATION

adjectives
racial; minute; inexact; detailed; price; misleading; occupational; moral; lucid; compendious; social; principal; broad; fixed.

verbs
allocate—; arrange—; assign—; assume—; attempt—; confirm—; correct—; distinguish—; employ—; exclude—; exhaust—; formulate—; head—; lead—; observe—; place in—; question—; recognize—; reduce—; retain—; separate into—; subordinate—; systematize—; —allows; —orders; —permits.
(See arrangement, group.)

CLASSIFY (v)

adverbs
carefully; ignorantly; conveniently; racially; minutely; exactly; misleadingly; lucidly; compendiously; socially; broadly.
(See arrange.)

CLASSMATE

adjectives
erstwhile; condescending; fun-loving; heckling; parasitic; superiority-inflicting; snubbing; snobbish; unapproachable; whilom.

verbs
compete with—s; enroll with—s; hail—s; prompt—s; recognize—s; reunite with—s; tutor—; —advances; —chooses; —s clash; —cribs (colloq.); —disenrolls; —s elect; —fails; —"flunks"; —graduates; —s honor; —recites; —vacations.
(See member, student, companion, friend.)

CLASSROOM

adjectives
grimy; gloomy; stuffy; modern; noisy.

verbs
absent from—; "barge" into—; bustle into —; buzz through—; clutter up—; congregate in—; dismiss from—; disorder—; equip—; illuminate—; preside over—; retain in—; rule—; scurry through—; survey—; —clamors with; —hums.
(See room.)

CLATTER

adjectives
prodigious; city-bred; glib-tongued; authoritative; confused; subsided; metallic; hideous; delectable; rousing; ringing; harsh; sudden; rhythmic; wild; hysterical; swift; reverberating; castanet.

CLATTER (v)

adverbs
recklessly; dissonantly; prodigiously; confusedly; metallically; hideously; ringingly; harshly; wildly; hysterically; furiously; excitingly; rudely.
(See tramp.)

CLAUSE

adjectives
complicated; misleading; expatiatory; particular; introductory; compensatory; sweeping; glacial; insidious; qualifying; solemn; independent; appended; ambiguous; flexible; limiting; adjective; adverbial; noun; appositional; descriptive; secret; hidden.

verbs
actuate—; condemn—; cudgel—; denounce—; evade—; "fake"—; frame—; insert—; insist on—; introduce—; kill—; legalize—; motivate—; occasion—; order—; ponder—; question—; sacrifice—; rule against—; unearth—; violates—; —bars; —cedes; —denotes; —embodies; —governs; —guards against; —joins; —provides; —stipulates; —varies; —wills.
(See provision, article, part.)

CLAW

adjectives
grimy; hooded; bloody; scarifying; holy; ominous; nipping; powerful; burrowing; slimy; acute; prehensile; scaly; sheathed; quivering; dirt-encrusted; feeble; invisible.

verbs
arm with—s; clip—s; clutch in—s; grapple with—s; grasp in—s; grip in—s; hook in —s; lay hold with—s; pare—; seize in—; sharpen—s; snip off—s; strike with—s; try —s on; —s flash by; —s lacerate; —s miss; —s rend; —s rip; —s scrape; —s scratch; —s snatch; —s tear.
(See talon, nail, clutch, hand.)

CLAW (v)

adverbs
wildly; fiercely; bloodily; ominously; feebly; voraciously; hungrily; viciously; hatefully; fiendishly; frantically; frightfully; sadistically.
(See scratch.)

CLAY

adjectives
clammy; cradling; humble; barren; encumbering; painted; sun-baked; impure; rebellious; uncoffined; tenacious; senseless; fruitful; unconsecrated; well-trodden; unconscious; breathless; human; eventful; sodden; reddish; brittle; damp.

verbs
cart—; cast—; chisel—; cleave—; color—; compound—; daub with—; dry—; fashion of—; fire—; form of—; line with—; mix—; moisten—; mould—; paint—; plaster with

—; prepare—; refine—; rise from—; seal with—; shape with—; soil with—; temper —; tread into—; —cements; —hardens; —moulders; —pastes; —resists; —sinks; —succumbs; —wears.

CLEAN

adverbs
hygienically; immaculately; neatly; spotlessly; stainlessly; tidily; trimly; sweetly; refreshingly; satisfactorily; punctiliously; meticulously; fragrantly; wholesomely; healthily; fastidiously; exquisitely; scrupulously; surgically; personally; shiningly; glowingly; delightfully; gratefully; comfortably; perfectly; faultlessly; impeccably; consummately; neatly; sprucely; radiantly; superbly; incredibly; finically; fussily; fanatically; daintily; sturdily; acceptably; passably; indifferently; presumably; appreciably.

CLEAN (v)

adverbs
immaculately; scrupulously; ambitiously; superficially; fussily; diligently; indifferently; ostentatiously; industriously; scientifically; passably; thoroughly; generally; fastidiously; exquisitely; enviably; orally; spotlessly; surgically; aridly.
(See wash.)

CLEANING

adjectives
distinctive; scientific; effective; exclusive; passable; spasmodic; thorough; general.

CLEANLINESS

adjectives
sterile; sweet; life-saving; fastidious; exquisite; notable; enviable; oral; scrupulous; spotless; personal; surgical; nice; general; arid; sinewy.

verbs
advise —; emphasize —; enjoin —; extol —; honor —; lack —; maintain —; necessitate —; preach —; respect —; sacrifice —; teach —.
(See hygiene.)

CLEAR

adverbs
explicitly; intelligibly; definitely; graphically; unmistakably; beautifully; crystally; unsurpassably; remarkably; unequivocally; decisively; startlingly; essentially; terribly; extraordinarily; easily; smoothly; positively; definitely; absolutely; unquestionably; obviously; plainly; categorically; incontestably; happily; comfortingly; satisfactorily.

CLEAR (v)

adverbs
tolerably; auspiciously; systematically; substantially; crystally; dramatically; poetically; unequivocally; limpidly; essentially; admirably; partially; annoyingly.
(See clarify, elucidate, explain.)

CLEAR-HEADED

adverbs
shrewdly; naturally; subtly; extremely; alertly; consciously; intentionally; discreetly; unexpectedly; infallibly; precociously; coldly; penetratingly; singularly; astoundingly; cleverly; astutely; craftily; profoundly; discriminatingly; manifestly; obviously; significantly; dangerously; alarmingly; perspicaciously; unwontedly.

CLEARING

adjectives
eloquent; unproductive.

CLEARNESS

adjectives
unaccustomed; ever-increasing; unsurpassable; agonizing; masterly; noonday; crystal; remarkable; sufficient; dramatic; admirable; diminished; poetic; crystalline; unequivocal; decisive; limpid; startling; essential; burning; horrible; nauseous; eerie; abominable; impulsive; calculating.

CLEATS

adjectives
longitudinal; transverse; rubber; football; leather; damaging; dangerous.

CLEFT

adjectives
unsunned; mossy; deep; gaping; vertical; narrow; steep.

CLEMENCY

adjectives
executive; merciful; benignant; gracious; bountiful; charitable; magnanimous.

verbs
allow —; beg —; display —; dispose toward —; exercise —; exhibit —; forgive in —; grant —; incline toward —; insure —; offer —; oppose —; promise —; recommend —; soften with —; suggest —; temper with —; — adds; — spares.
(See forbearance, mercy.)

CLEMENT

adverbs
mercifully; sympathetically; tolerantly; moderately; mildly; compassionately; humanely; understandingly; unexpectedly; piteously; charitably; ruthfully; sagaciously; wisely; discerningly; generously; benevolently; shrewdly; magnanimously.

CLENCH (v)

adverbs
convulsively; tightly; firmly; unrelentingly; severely; agonizingly; hopelessly; unceasingly; hysterically; tremblingly; abruptly; fearfully; genially; characteristically; appallingly; deftly; painfully.
(See clutch.)

CLERGY

adjectives
modest; fashionable; regional; corrupt; parochial; reverend; fanatical.

verbs
benefit by —; connect with —; distinguish —; divide —; exempt —; oust from —; persecute —; robe —; set apart —; support —; unfrock —; — advocates; — authorizes; — consecrates; — devotes; — embraces; — engineers; — ministers; — preaches; — privileges.
(See clergyman, minister.)

CLERGYMAN

adjectives
worthy; ordained; well-informed; influential; leading; superannuated; fussy; distinguished; eminent; disgraced; spineless; diffident; respected; deserving; unsuccessful; welcome; elderly; purring.

verbs
abide by —; bar —; confess to —; confide in —; delude —; ordain —; persecute —; qualify as —; revere —; — beseeches; — blesses; — delivers; — endeavors; — intones; — orates; — pleads; — preaches; — teaches; — voices; — waxes.
(See minister.)

CLERIC

adjectives
minor; prim; devout; righteous; exhorting; mild; inoffensive; shepherding; soul-directing.

CLERICAL

adverbs
monotonously; fastidiously; punctiliously; tediously; importantly; primarily; modestly; humbly; pompously; primly; precisely; fanatically; comically; unsuitably; slavishly; humbly; elegantly; gently; mildly; unassumingly; unpretentiously; ostentatiously; flauntingly; worthily; influentially; fussily; sedately.

CLERK

adjectives
shabby; confidential; delicate; officious; trustworthy; discreet; minor; embarrassed; assessing; unsympathetic; dispensing; efficient; obsequious; hard-working; quick-witted; gouging; small; studious; wise; lynx-eyed; vigilant; plodding; sneering; genial; generous; courteous; diligent; satisfactory; busy; conscientious; meticulous; orderly; dapper; impecunious.

verbs
advance —; discharge —; ordain —; promote —; retain —; — accounts; — announces; — collects; — corresponds; — documents; — enters; — greets; — rates; — records; — sells.
(See employee.)

CLEVER

adverbs
notably; strikingly; consummately; diabolically; slyly; fiendishly; peculiarly; artfully; marvellously; adroitly; incredibly; admirably; remarkably; dangerously; palpably; obviously; undeniably; suspiciously; neatly; matchlessly; craftily; masterfully; wonderfully; constitutionally; innately; instinctively; inherently; subtly; cunningly; capably; competently; proficiently; deftly; discreetly; handily.

CLEVERNESS

adjectives
notable; insolent; insinuating; satiric; striking; meretricious; considerable; consummate.

verbs
accompany with —; deceive with —; display —; envy —; exhibit —; market —; necessitate —; perform with —; question —; reward —; shed —.
(See skill, ingenuity.)

CLICK

adjectives
faint; whispered; resolute; dry; animated; soulless; jarring; indignant; responsive; metallic; sharp; hollow; emphatic; mysterious; mechanical; significant.

CLICK (v)

adverbs
teasingly; faintly; animatedly; indignantly; metallically; jauntily; gaily; significantly; spontaneously; mechanically; repeatedly; intermittently.

(See sound.)

CLIENT

adjectives
trembling; desirable; gilded; prospective; fair; courtroom; stolid; indifferent; obstinate; timid; whilom; unfortunate; parasitical; rich; likely; uninvited; much-injured; oppressed; distinguished.

CLIENTELE

adjectives
discriminating; conservative; distinguished; congenial; refined; select; restricted; discerning; diversified; financial; desirable; exacting; influential; fine.

CLIFF

adjectives
smooth; vertical; lofty; abrupt; ebony; frowning; iron-stained; black; distant; ochre; scarped; hoary; jutting; fringing; treacherous; honeycombed; populous; inaccessible; naked; formidable; perpendicular; snowy; desolate; picturesque; precipitous; ragged; rude; radiant; unexpected; perilous; buttressed; stupendous; abrupt; craggy; majestic; impending; fearful; steep; frosty; sheer; rugged; overhanging; reeking; implacable; cloudy; haughty; cloud-encircled; broken; great; colossal; lofty; gigantic; tremendous; high; mighty; towering; giant; barren; bald; bare; wild; tinted; tortuous; weathered; wind-worn; crumbling; jagged; crude; sinister; grotesque; fantastic; limestone; granite; rocky; thorn-clad; narrow; iron-walled; ferny; orchard-crowned; heavily wooded; forest-covered; icebound; broad; bold; receding; sculptured; sloping.

verbs
clamber up —; climb —; fall from —; overhang —; peer from —; reconnoiter —; scale —; skirt —; slither over —; suspend from —; throw from —; tumble from —; — looms up; — rises; — sinks.

(See crag, precipice.)

CLIMATE

adjectives
dry; marvelous; summer; outdoor; world-famous; incomparable; mild; kindly; inviting; pleasant; enervating; rugged; healthful; bracing; life-prolonging; gracious; superb; gentle; beneficent; maligned; semitropical; oppressive; delicious; glowing; balmy; invigorating; divers (pl); burning; listless; villainous; various (pl); boreal; hyperequatorial; bland; trying; exhausting; arctic; dry; sultry; severe; trick; tropical; exhilarating; salubrious; temperate; genial; frowning; delightful; subduing; smiling; perfect; year-round; propitious; equable; fittest; tranquil; ocean; lovely; stern; excellent; unbearable; bitter; forbidding; rigorous; harsh; rotten; poisonous; arid; high; wonderful; winter; southern; atmospheric; variable; capricious; altered; seasonal; coldest; humid; torrid; damp; changing.

verbs
accustom to —; adapt to —; ascribe to —; chart —; malign —; record —; seek —; succumb to —; — affects; — batters; — braces; — depends on; — destroys; —devastates; — discourages; — invigorates; — irritates; — enlivens; — prevails; — ravages; — restores; — revives; — sickens; — stimulates.

(See weather.)

CLIMAX

adjectives
characteristic; appalling; fit; momentous; glorious; culminant; unforgettable; sad; dramatic; exquisite; progressive; prepared; surprising; approaching; autumnal; frolicsome; disgraceful; ingenious; horrifying; grandstand; poignant; emotional; proper; unexpected; thunderous; oratorical; inevitable; marvelous; stupendous; glowing; inescapable; pulsating; deft; unsatisfactory; lightninglike.

verbs
abate at —; ascend to —; culminate in —; deduce —; delay —; delight in —; foreshadow —; hurtle to —; lax after —; postpone —; prelude —; prepare for —; rise to —; — dies; — excites; — interests; — occurs; — surprises.

(See culmination, extreme.)

CLIMAX (v)

adverbs
inevitably; appallingly; momentously; gloriously; unforgettably; dramatically; exquisitely; disgracefully; horrifyingly; poignant-

ly; emotionally; unexpectedly; oratorically; marvelously; stupendously; tragically; comically.
(See finish.)

CLIMB

adjectives
lewd; beastly; upward; breezy; steady; wonderful; sporty; muscle-racking; long; hard; uphill; winding; persistent; plodding; blistering; dizzy.

verbs
accomplish —; ascend —; attain —; boast of —; cease —; enjoy —; gird for —; mount to —; negotiate —; prepare for —; reconnoiter for —; scale —; spur to —; toil up —; — excites; — exhausts; — exhilarates; — fatigues; — thrills; — wearies.
(See ascent.)

CLIMB (*v*)

adverbs
nimbly; perversely; strenuously; reluctantly; desperately; lamely; steadily; ploddingly; dizzily; dexterously; skillfully; laboriously; unceasingly; determinedly.
(See clamber, scale.)

CLIMBER

adjectives
expert; social; respectable; superior; snobbish; repulsed; wonderful; ambitious; intrepid; mountain; indefatigable; aggressive.

CLIMBING

adjectives
hot; venturous; exhausting; tedious; fruitless; arduous.

CLIME

adjectives
serene; inclement; cloudless; delightful; sunless; inhospitable; blissful; celestial; rougher; torrid; pleasant; eastern; drear; hostile; sunny; glorious; radiant; changeful; distant; genial; unknown; capricious; fair; happy; scenic; southern; rigorous.

CLING (*v*)

adverbs
adhesively; tenaciously; desperately; blindly; credulously; firmly; faithfully; purposefully; heavily; persistently; timorously; affectionately; endearingly; invariably; exhaustingly.
(See hang.)

CLINIC

adjectives
public; impersonal; domestic; courtesy; private; convenient; indispensable.

verbs
admit to —; attach to —; attend —; conduct —; contribute to —; endow —; establish —; extol —; install —; institute —; maintain —; practise in —; subsidize —; support —; visit —; — adjusts; — administers; — advises; — cures; — diagnoses; — discovers; — investigates; — observes; — records; — specializes; — surveys; — tabulates; — treats.
(See school, instruction, institution.)

CLIP (*v*)

adverbs
fantastically; closely; raggedly; dexterously; evenly; painfully; skillfully; roughly.
(See trim.)

CLIPPER

adjectives
lofty; heavy; sparred; lean; graceful; swift.

CLIQUE

adjectives
irresponsible; campus; mutinous; ruling; esoteric; secret; nominating.

CLOAK

adjectives
leopard-skin; hooded; constitutional; badfitting; ludicrous; tattered; snatched; feathery; dusky; frieze; cardinal; ungathered; shimmering; girlish; sodden; voluminous; long; sweeping; tinseled; mantled; impervious; full.

verbs
bear under—; bury in—; drape—about; draw—; envelop in—; fashion—; fasten—; garment in—; line—; loose—; pluck off—; raise—; spread—; stain—; wrap in—; —conceals; —covers; —disguises; —hides; —hoods; —mantles; —masks; —protects; —secretes; —shelters; —warms.
(See coat, mask, garment, disguise.)

CLOAK (*v*)

adjectives
constantly; completely; ludicrously; shimmeringly; voluminously; sweepingly; imperviously; snugly; warmly; comfortably; parsimoniously.
(See conceal, mask.)

CLOCK

adjectives
brass-bound; clanging; unvarying; vigilant; ingenious; tall; glowing; synchronous; illuminated; noisy; chiming; solemn; dignified; pine; delirious.

verbs
read—; set—; wind—; —alarms; —chimes; —clangs; —s disagree; —fools; —gains; —heralds; —indicates; —knells; —lies; —misses; —rings; —strikes; —ticks off; —tolls; —trembles; —vibrates; —warns.
(See watch.)

CLOD

adjectives
finite; loamy; frozen; wormy; icy; kneaded; sluggish; plow-cloven.

CLOISTER

adjectives
shady; open; solemn; personal; dilapidated; mournful; monkish; restful; beautiful.

CLOISTERED

adjectives
conventionally; monastically; happily; willingly; voluntarily; perpetually; consecratedly; religiously; inviolably; piously; holily; devoutly; reverently; fervidly; eagerly; blessedly; prayerfully; securely; unassailably; safely.

CLOSE

adjectives
summary; speedy; rapid; long-expected; official; bloody; glorious; victorious; tragic; rollicking; undramatic.

CLOSE (*v*)

adverbs
securely; peremptorily; lazily; reluctantly; abruptly; grimly; instantly; spasmodically; virtually; unexpectedly; wistfully; hermetically; discreetly; summarily; officially; victoriously; tragically.
(See terminate, end.)

CLOSENESS

adjectives
furtive; essential; unwinking.

CLOSET

adjectives
well-filled; portable; glazed; stuffy; cedar; hall; dark; tiny; shallow; obscure.

verbs
air—; conceal in—; creep from—; crowd—; deposit in—; enclose in—; force—; hide in—; imprison in—; invade—; lock in—; occupy—; recess in—; repose in—; retire into—; retreat into—; rummage in—; seclude in—; secrete in—; shut in—; store in—; unlock—; ventilate—.
(See chamber, room, recess.)

CLOSE-TONGUED

adverbs
discreetly; prudently; wisely; judiciously; sagely; quietly; thoughtfully; reflectively; unusually; habitually; philosophically; astutely; cleverly; laconically; reticently; safely; invariably; cautiously; warily; circumspectly; loyally; smartly; consistently; shrewdly.

CLOT

adjectives
convenient; cohesive; fibrous; embolic; gelatinous; hardened; semisolid; stubborn.

verbs
coagulate in—; cohere in—; congeal into—; dissolve—; form—; mass in—; mat with —s; melt—; —cements; —checks; —hardens; —lumps; —stems.

CLOTH

adjectives
worsted; patented; irreproachable; beautiful; nonshrinkable; sturdy; long-fibred; handsome; silver-striped; imported; rugged; soft; subdued; fine-textured; rich; dressy; quality; cool; smart; suave; silky; smooth-textured; wool; long-wearing; summer; unfinished; featherweight; zephyrweight; superlative; firm; striped; two-ply; knife-edge; durable; baize; painted; elegant; hair; spotless; brocaded; coarse; fluttering; thin; cotton; vile; greasy; trailing; polishing; draped; snowy; immaculate.

verbs
adorn—; bias—; cast—over; darn—; emerge from—; finger—; gather—; saturate—; shroud in—; spin—; strain through—; weave—; wrap in—; —adorns; —hangs; —indicates.
(See fabric, wool, silk, cotton, drapery, material.)

CLOTHE (*v*)

adverbs
comfortably; miserably; profusely; uniformly; irreproachably; beautifully; handsomely; coolly; smartly; suavely; spotless-

ly; coarsely; immaculately; vilely; seductively; temptingly; ravishingly; glamorously; appropriately; faultlessly; inappropriately; incongruously; formally; ordinarily; voluminously; hideously; drablv

(See dress, attire.)

CLOTHED

adverbs

richly; elaborately; gaudily; wretchedly; fully; scantily; shabbily; raggedly; luxuriously; carefully; elegantly; carelessly; recklessly; absurdly; fashionably; ridiculously; ludicrously; honorably; unfashionably; garishly; laughably; gaily; seductively; gorgeously; glamorously; rakishly; awkwardly; incongruously; outlandishly; expensively; cheaply; smartly; handsomely; drably; extravagantly; economically.

CLOTHES

adjectives

gay; seductive; feminine; tempting; gorgeous; ravishing; glamorous; bright; fluttering; sensible; fresh; clean; appropriate; harmonized; picture-book; well-cut; ready-made; fashionable; faultless; evening; unkempt; dusty; bedraggled; ragged; patched; town; shiny; stained; dirty; cast-off; inappropriate; lanky; ill-fitting; loose-hanging; awkward; free; incongruous; horrible; dreadful; deplorable; bizarre; rakish; gaudy; nobby; vivid; outlandish; astonishing; everyday; working; riding; queer; country; shabby; summer; immaculate; disordered; ordinary; patriarchal; expensive; swaddling; drenched; bespattered; mud-covered; formal; voluminous; Easter; foolish; smart; dependable; famous; individualized; well-tailored; fine; hand-tailored; comfortable; hideous; baggy; dowdy; string-colored; advertised; pepper-and-salt; drab.

CLOTHING

adjectives

ragged; tailored; travel-stained; indispensable; fastidious; tattered; cast-off; sad; nondescript; complicated; soiled; frayed; legal; dreadful; russet; mortal; small; scant; flashy; drenched; ruined; seedy; personal.

verbs

alter—; array in—; bare of—; cast off—; closet—; design—; discolor—; display—; divest of—; doff—; don—; fashion—; lack—; launder—; model—; outwear—; penetrate—; purvey—; refurbish—; rend —; renew—; saturate—; store—; strip off—; style—; swaddle in—; tailor—; tatter—; vest in—; —allures; —belies; —chafes; —denotes; —expresses; —flutters; —masquerades.

(See dress, raiment, apparel.)

CLOUD

adjectives

slate-colored; puffy; snow-white; gray-blue; mauve; silver; opaline; dense; glittering; golden; crisp; hazy; bluish; sun-filled; dazzling; thin; misty; drifting; passing; hurrying; scattering; rolling; racing; soaring; flying; scudding; broken; rifted; wild; black; frayed; breaking; gritty; paunchy; blood-colored; bulbous; swollen; cumulus; dark; darkening; endless; sullen; rolling; disastrous; angry; menacing; thunder; lowering; heavy; shapeless; curtain; exemplary; leaking; massed; low-hanging; opaque; distant; tangible; unvarying; tiniest; wind-spun; mysterious; mountain; smoke; desolate; incandescent; moon; crimson; flitting; flaky; eternal; sanguine; wind-driven; mantling; dangerous; glimmering; wrinkled; coifing; airy; veiling; purple; fugitive; pasturing; delicate; radiant; coppery; eddying; foggy; melting; lachrymose; mournful; embattled; scattered; perpetual; thick; sun-rimmed; sacred; chariot; sunset; darksome; rainy; luminous; vast; severing; bursting; downpouring; sullen; brilliant; serrate; smothered; lurid; dull; restless; sundering; envious; massive; gilded; fleecy; flowing; hovering; fat; clammy; perturbed; poisonous; westward-stationed; murmurous; suffocating; interwoven; tear-laden; battlemented; dripping; many-folded; perceptible; pillared; inky; irrevocable; feathery; dusking; orange; infernal; sulphurous; amber; canvas; cinerous; wondrous; rosy; billowy; soft-gray; sable.

verbs

ascend to—s; aspire to—s; bivouac in—; checker with—s; cleave—s; clothe in—; curtain with—s; deck with—; descend from —; fan off—; float in—; gild—; lose in—; penetrate—; pierce—; ride upon—; sail on—; slip into—; vanish into—; withdraw into—; wreathe in—; —billows; —blankets; —blots out; —creeps up; —curls; —darkens; —descends; —dims; —discharges; —disperses; —drenches; —drifts; —flees; —freaks; —gushes; —hides; —hovers; —hurries; —lifts; —melts;

—menaces; —mottles; —mounts; —musters; —obscures; —obstructs; —overcasts; —overshadows; —s part; —s pockmark the sky; —races; —rebuffs; —s scatter; —screens; —scurries; —shrouds; —smoulders; —soars; —s stream by; —sweeps down; —swirls up; —threatens; —vanishes; —veils; —wanders; —weeps; —whitens; —wings by.

CLOUD (v)

adverbs
heavily; densely; hazily; mistily; rollingly; scuddingly; blackly; sullenly; disastrously; mysteriously; foggily; mournfully; sulphurously; luridly.
(See shade.)

CLOUDLESS

adverbs
gloriously; beautifully; brightly; brilliantly; dazzlingly; radiantly; sunnily; garishly; refulgently; pitilessly; mercilessly; hotly; breathlessly; happily; luckily; fortunately; joyously; splendidly; magnificently; enchantingly; pleasantly; delightfully; ravishingly; pleasurably; refreshingly; cheeringly; enjoyably; utterly.

CLOUDY

adverbs
mistily; darkly; rosily; densely; hazily; thinly; thickly; completely; partly; occasionally; wildly; gloomily; sullenly; dismaly; angrily; windily; mysteriously; suddenly; delicately; foggily; perpetually; brokenly; luridly; fleecily; suffocatingly; surprisingly; hopelessly; ominously; menacingly; discouragingly; faintly; muggily; dunly; distressingly; disturbingly.

CLOVER

adjectives
incarnate; scented; sweet-smelling; blooming; nodding; bee-calling.

CLOWN

adjectives
sweet; bungling; loutish; sad; yawning; brokenhearted; roguish; impudent; grimacing; rollicking; whimsical; appreciated.

verbs
play—; —antics; —burlesques; —caricatures; —entertains; —farces; —frolics; —grimaces; —jigs; —mimics; —pantomimes; —portrays; —somersaults; —taunts.
(See fool.)

CLOWN (v)

adverbs
professionally; hilariously; divertingly; sophisticatedly; loutishly; roguishly; impudently; grimacingly; rollickingly; whimsically.
(See jest.)

CLOWNISH

adverbs
roguishly; impudently; whimsically; comically; madly; foolishly; provokingly; everlastingly; incurably; teasingly; irresistibly; boorishly; waggishly; jocosely; roughly; innocently; merrily; blithely; joyously; boyishly; entertainingly; rowdily; indecorously; unbecomingly; extravagantly; horridly; amusingly; unwontedly; hilariously; habitually; delicately; deliberately; unceasingly; incessantly; tiresomely.

CLUB
(society)

adjectives
influential; literary; luxurious; attractive; sumptuous; social; enthusiastic; industrial; exclusive; permanent; flourishing; musical.

verbs
affiliate with—; associate with—; bar from—; "blackball" from—; charter—; contribute to—; form—; found—; house—; organize—; pledge to—; preside over—; —assembles; —benefits from; —convenes; —elects; —springs up.
(See organization, association.)

CLUB
(weapon)

adjectives
mossy; powerful; formidable; threatening; respect-inspiring; sturdy; purposeful.

verbs
arm with—; bat with—; batter with—; bear—; brandish—; carve—; clutch—; cudgel with—; exercise—; extend—; flog with—; flourish—; hurl—; rule with—; strike with—; subdue with—; submit to—; threaten with—; whirl—; wield—; yield to—.
(See cudgel, bat.)

CLUBFOOTED

adverbs
unfortunately; hopelessly; irremediably; crookedly; monstrously; hideously; slightly; pathetically; unmistakably; noticeably;

grotesquely; fantastically; outlandishly; miserably; wretchedly; helplessly; strangely; pitiably; woefully.
(See crippled.)

CLUCK (v)

adverbs
busily; anxiously; industriously; maternally; absorbedly; endlessly; cheerfully; fondly; pleasantly; unrestrainedly.
(See chatter.)

CLUE

adjectives
inescapable; priceless; vital; suggestive; recondite; fancied; elusive; definite; flawless; tangible; exhausted; magnificent; startling; surprising; bewildering; slender.

verbs
discover—; divulge—; efface—; follow up—; join—s; muddle up—; produce—; recognize—; scatter—s; strike upon—; tackle—; thread—s together; trace—; track down—; uncover—; unearth—; unravel—; yield—; —convicts; —crumbles; —guides; —indicates; —perplexes; —puzzles; —solves; —warns.
(See intimation, hint.)

CLUMP (v)

adverbs
aimlessly; monotonously; painfully; laboriously; tiredly; woefully; miserably; desolately; lachrymosely; loutishly; rudely.
(See thump.)

CLUMSINESS

adjectives
grotesque; intolerable; wasteful; massive; inexcusable; wanton; marked.

verbs
accentuate—; attend with—; decry—; display—; feign—; lack—; perform with—; ridicule—; simulate—; —annoys.
(See awkwardness.)

CLUMSY

adverbs
childishly; awkwardly; gawkily; inexpertly; adorably; provokingly; vexatiously; unconsciously; involuntarily; obviously; charmingly; ludicrously; ridiculously; laughably; cheerfully; momentarily; naturally; objectionably; unnecessarily; foolishly; unluckily; ungraciously; hopelessly; helplessly; bashfully; shyly; painfully.

CLUSTER

adjectives
superb; globular; kindling; luscious; indefatigable; delicate; shining; drowsy; dense; vivid; telltale; peaceful; gleaming; grapelike; many-branched; rich.

verbs
assemble in—; cultivate—; emerge from—; form in—; gather in—; group in—; halve—; join—; pluck—; swarm in—; tear—; unite in—; —collects; —droops.
(See group.)

CLUSTER (v)

adverbs
gayly; abundantly; luxuriously; lusciously; lovingly; globularly; delicately; gleamingly; richly; darksomely.
(See crowd.)

CLUTCH

adjectives
detaining; fibrous; ungainly; evil; frantic.

verbs
avoid—; clasp in—es; draw into—es; escape—; evade—; fasten—es; free from—; grasp in—es; grip in—; lock in—es; seize in—; snatch from—es; strive in—es; struggle in—es; trap in—es; wrench from—es.
(See grasp, grip, hold.)

CLUTCH (v)

adverbs
frantically; conclusively; desperately; instinctively; covetously; rapaciously; nervously; unconsciously; detainingly; vigorously; fiercely; fanatically.
(See grasp, grip.)

COACH

adjectives
ponderous; gilded; lazy; decayed; liveried; rolling; hackney; rumbling; gilt; clumsy; deserted; ancient; motor; imperial; rattling; elaborate; dingy; passenger; lurching.

verbs
alight from—; attend—; carve—; convey in—; draw—; gild—; hire—; jog along in—; journey in—; ornament—; travel in—; upset—; —approaches; —careens; —jolts; —jounces; —rumbles; —speeds on; —traverses.
(See carriage.)

COACHMAN

adjectives
superannuated; ridiculous; stiff; dignified; glossy; supercilious; liveried; crest-emblazoned.

COADJUTANT

adverbs
willingly; profitably; politically; conveniently; favorably; suspiciously; heartily; voluntarily; reluctantly; cheerfully; agreeably; confessedly; admittedly; avowedly; acquiescently; contentedly.

COAL

adjectives
dull; burning; glowing; red; roseate; glimmering; living; dying; soft; purloined; hard.

verbs
bake on—s; char—; devour—; fire—; fuel with—; heave—; ignite—; kindle—; lay on—s; power by—; quench—; rake—; scuttle—; transport—; —darkens; —emits gas; —glows; —soils.
(See carbon, ember.)

COALESCENT

adverbs
actually; easily; monotonously; valuably; scientifically; fortunately; probably; amazingly; surprisingly; indistinguishably; homologously; convertibly.

COAL FIELDS

adjectives
bleak; dreary; grime-shrouded; honeycombed; exhausted; abandoned; producing; pit-fallen; valuable; wealth-yielding; worked-out; anthracite; bituminous; lignite.

verbs
capture— —; cede— —to; conserve— —; control— —; dominate— —; employ in— —; exhaust— —; exploit— —; inherit— —; invade— —; replenish from— —; transport from— —; utilize— —; value— —; work— —; — —boom; — —extend; — —range; — —supply.

COALITION

adjectives
favorable; fresh; genuine; lasting; instantaneous; political; superfluous; tardy.

verbs
ally in—; blend in—; federate—; form—; fuse in—; improvise—; support—; unite in—; —aids; —connects; —forces; —insures; —offers.
(See alliance, union.)

COARSE

adverbs
disagreeably; abominably; intolerably; unbearably; basely; bluntly; carelessly; hideously; unutterably; stupidly; pathetically; odiously; blatantly; insufferably; awkwardly; boorishly; intentionally; deliberately; unpardonably; barbarously; indecorously; ribaldly; tawdrily; vulgarly; hoydenishly; rowdily; shockingly; heavily; horridly; monstrously; obtrusively; outlandishly; impossibly.

COARSENESS

adjectives
crass; disgusting; homely; hopeless; innate; gorgeous; humiliating; savage; revolting; provincial; vulgar; unvarying.

verbs
acquire—; alleviate—; display—; exhibit —; modify—; pardon—; polish off—; refine—; retain—; sand away—; smooth—; —embarrasses; —inflames; —irks; —irritates; —rasps; —vexes.
(See rudeness, vulgarity.)

COAST

adjectives
unguarded; rock-bound; frequented; desolate; craggy; foggy; adjacent; perilous; eerie; crystal; lowly; bold; sea; sandy; high; verdant; pathless; imperfect; shining; chalk; viny; inhospitable; picturesque; trimmed; rectangular; fateful; misty; extended; iron-bound; remarkable; rebelling; melancholy; weather-beaten; forlorn; murky; azure; colorful; historic; rough; deserted; irregular; dangerous; harborless; barren; indented; shallow; flat; tranquil; elongated; sun-kissed.

verbs
abide on—; batter—; blockade—; border —; depart from—; enlarge—; expel from —; fortify—; guard—; invade—; land on—; move up—; patrol—; pebble—; scout—; skirt—; spy—; travel along—.
(See shore, beach.)

COAT

adjectives
tattered; greasy; dirty; damaged; dusty; shiny; comfortable; dinner; expensive; heavy; shapeless; buttoned; tawny; rhythm-

ic; striped; outer; flimsy; cloth; pajama; sopping; laced; collarless; soft; fleecy; fresh; clean; distinguished; simple; boxy; tailored; custom-made; threadbare; protective; stunning; immaculate; voluminous; enticing; frogged; magic; russet; fetching; fustian; holiday; shabby; smartest; useful; raglan.

verbs
clothe in—; design—; discolor—; divest of—; dry-clean—; embroider—; encase in—; fray—; gird with—; jacket in—; model—; peel off—; press—; provide—; ruin—; seam—; split—; strip off—; style —; tailor—; tatter—; weave—; —envelops; —glitters; —protects; —warms.
(See garment, overcoat.)

COAT-TAIL

adjectives
dangling; elongated; formal; flippant; funereal; restless; tentaculate; twisting; sweeping.

verbs
alter—; cling to—; embroider—; fray—; hoist—; line—; press—; rend—; shorten—; soil—; suspend from—; tatter—; tread on—; wrinkle—; —covers; —drags; —protects.
(See coat.)

COAX (*v*)

adverbs
irresistibly; tantalizingly; endearingly; slyly; treacherously; lewdly; sweetly; angelically.
(See persuade.)

COBWEB

adjectives
dusty; patterned; glittering; hanging; iridescent.

verbs
abound with—s; brush away—; capture in—; dart from—; elude—; enmesh in—; ensnare in—; entangle in—; entwine in—; evade—; fringe with—; lace with—; spin—; strain in—; struggle in—; weave —; —s gather; —hangs from; —traps.
(See web, net, snare, network.)

COCK

adjectives
belligerent; bullying; cavalier; calcarate; defiant; domineering; clarion-sounding; game; strutting; spur-brandishing; vainglorious; vanquishing; victorious.

verbs
breed—s; excite—; —announces the morn; —battles; —crows; —heralds the dawn; —pecks; —perches; —rages; —scurries; —struts.
(See fowl, bird, rooster.)

COCKNEY

adverbs
unmistakably; markedly; rowdily; frankly; honestly; loyally; toughly; helpfully; sturdily; stoutly; idly; unaffectedly; heartily; healthily; humbly; chaffingly; churlishly; sorrily; originally; raffishly; menially; clownishly.

COCKROACH

adjectives
defiant; glistening; horned; invading; inexpugnable; scurrying; ubiquitous; crackling; reddish-brown; filthy; vile; obscene; offensive; nasty; foul; abominable; beastly; repulsive; immodest.

verbs
abound with—es; bait—; crush—; detest—; exterminate—; plague with—; poison—; rid of—; spray—; —infests; —multiplies; —scuds; —scurries; —wanders.
(See insect.)

COCK-SURE

adverbs
calmly; confidently; deeply; professedly; unshakably; arrogantly; egotistically; positively; provokingly; determinedly; doggedly; happily; vainly; insolently; loquaciously; tranquilly; blandly; foolishly; swaggeringly; magnificently; smugly; brassily; brazenly; heedlessly; cavalierly; importantly; blusteringly.

COCKTAIL

adjectives
aromatic; relaxing; reassuring; shudder-producing; stimulating; sticky; welcome.

verbs
chill—; concoct—; dispatch—; down—; drain—; flavor—; ice—; join in—; level—; mix—; partake of—; soak up—; tolerate—; vary—; water—; —exhilarates; —intoxicates; —quickens; —stimulates; —warms.
(See drink, liquor, whiskey.)

COCOON

adjectives
dainty; clumsy; fragile; silken; bark-powdered; suspended; swinging; silver-grey; ovate; webby.

verbs
burst from—; emerge from— encase in—; enclose in—; envelop in—; flutter from—; raise from—; spin—; swathe in—; tend—; weave—; —expels; —flowers; —hatches.

(See envelop, case.)

CODE

adjectives
changing; rigid; moral; unwritten; ambitious; voluminous; detailed; accepted; logical; traditional; ruthless; peculiar; lasting; ancient; true; rigorous; artificial; strict; odious; professed; sexual; chivalrous; elaborate; social.

verbs
decipher—; draft—; elaborate—; enforce—; formulate—; guard—; honor—; impose—; intercept—; interpret—; jeopardize—; observe—; preserve—; protect—; relay—; respect—; sanction—; subject to—; translate—; —amends; —restricts; —systematizes.

(See system, law, legislation.)

COEFFICIENT

adverbs
clannishly; collusively; concertedly; unanimously; fraternally; companionably; collectively; jointly; amazingly; surprisingly; remarkably; notoriously; supremely.

COEQUAL

adverbs
evenly; symmetrically; adaptably; broadly; generously; good-humoredly; amiably; cooperatively; affably; placidly; serenely; scrupulously; carefully; contentedly; apparently; notoriously; easily.

COERCION

adjectives
vulgar; parental; ruthless; painstaking; deliberate; wily.

verbs
advocate—; apply—; bar—; control by—; drive to—; employ—; exercise—; gain by—; govern by—; irk by—; oppose—; rebel at—; resist—; resort to—; restrain by—; retain by—; separate by—; submit to—; —antagonizes; —inflames; —intimidates.

(See compulsion, force, restraint, constraint.)

COERCIVE

adverbs
illegally; substantially; disagreeably; officially; brutally; martially; enforceably; necessarily; forcibly; violently; inexorably; irresistibly; peremptorily; ruthlessly; cruelly; intolerably; authoritatively; unjustly; outrageously; unreasonably; unlawfully; unjustifiably; inauspiciously; injudiciously; openly; furtively; slyly; actually.

COFFEE

adjectives
steaming; strong; savory; weak; adulterated; delicious; best; morning; aromatic; muddy-looking; tepid; syrupy; finest; selected; black; rancid.

verbs
brew—; cultivate—; grind—; gulp down—; ice—; imbibe—; market—; percolate—; pound—; roast—; serve—; sniff—; sweeten—; tend—; tin—; wash down with—; yield—; —refreshes; —rouses; —stales; —stimulates; —wakens; —weakens.

(See tea, drink.)

COFFER

adjectives
depleted; hoarded; mouldy; grudging; opulent; overflowing; well-guarded.

verbs
bind—; burden—; burst—; bury in—; deposit in—; enrich—; force—; hoard in—; lay up in—; line—; ornament—; plunder—; preserve in—; ransack—; seal—; secure—; stuff—; suck—dry; swell—; treasure in—; —yields.

(See treasury.)

COFFIN

adjectives
insignificant; sumptuous; unlowered; precious; naked; flaming; rude; hard; misshapen; stately; large.

verbs
attend—; bear—; confine in—; decorate—; disinter—; encase in—; inter in—; mourn at—; remove from—; rest in—; rob—; seal—; sleep in—; stand around—; trail—; transport—; view—; weep at—; —receives; —sinks.

(See casket, case.)

COGITATE (v)

adverbs
gravely; deeply; absorbedly; perplexedly; abstrusely; abstractedly; studiously; frowningly; fixedly.
(See meditate, think.)

COGITATION

adjectives
gloomy; matrimonial; fragmentary; groping; manifold.

COIFFURE

adjectives
rustling; waved; elaborate; charming; conservative; monstrous; ingenious; gleaming; eccentric; affected; severe; elegant; sculptured.

COIL

adjectives
adamantine; tortured; lustrous; ceaseless; flat; irregular; steel; long; snakelike; hideous; opal; cumbrous; temporal; brilliant; mortal; collapsed; limp; shining; twisting.

COIL (v)

adverbs
lavishly; ceaselessly; flatly; irregularly; hideously; cumbrously; limply; twistingly; intricately.
(See twist.)

COIN

adjectives
fair; bogus; deceptive; well-worked; unadulterated; glittering; nimble; ancient; valuable; artificial; rare.

verbs
assort—s; collect—s; convert into—; counterfeit—; deposit—; devaluate—; fashion —; hoard—s; melt—; mold—; mutilate—; pocket—; press—; stamp—; treasure—; uncover—; unearth—; value—; —circulates; —clinks; —depreciates; —represents; —wears thin.
(See cash, money, metal.)

COINCIDE (v)

adverbs
exactly; oddly; strangely; sardonically; singularly; amazingly; romantically; happily; fortunately; curiously; minutely; unexpectedly; tragically; occasionally; extraordinarily; crazily; closely.
(See agree.)

COINCIDENCE

adjective
strange; odd; singular; sardonic; happy; horrible; cruel; amazing; romantic; lucky; mere; crazy; curious; minute; unexpected; accidental; unusual; overdone; tragic; occasional; extraordinary; powerful; unfortunate; uncomfortable; suggestive.

verbs
discern—; discuss—; evidence—; illustrate—; involve—; marvel at—; report—; strike—; witness—; wonder at—; —amazes; —blends; —confounds; —occurs; —startles.
(See correspondence, agreement.)

COLD

adjectives *(illness)*
harrassing; head; chest; bronchial; miserable; stubborn.

verbs
dispose toward—; down by—; engender—; expose to—; guard against—s; indispose by—; nurse—; predispose to—; resist—; subject to—; —lowers resistance; —strikes; —subsides; —weakens.
(See. sickness.)

COLD
(weather)

adjectives
hostile; icy; intense; biting; deadly; stinging; cruel; casual; arctic; deathlike; encroaching; inescapable; bitter; paralyzing; freezing; wondrous; immense; retreating; purifying; interminable; midnight; piercing; stubborn; extreme; troublesome; ambient; heavy; penetrating; Stygian; monstrous.

verbs
blanket against—; brave—; chatter with—; endure—; expose to—; huddle in—; inure to—; paralyze by—; resist—; stem—; —abates; —bites; —blasts; —creeps in; —freezes; —nips; —persists; —pinches; —refreshes.
(See winter.)

COLD

adverbs
uncomfortably; intolerably; unfortunately; impossibly; frigidly; bitingly; piercingly; icily; wintrily; disagreeably; inconveniently; unpleasantly; uninvitingly; unluckily;

terrifically; dreadfully; frightfully; unnecessarily; dangerously; intensely; cruelly; penetratingly; increasingly; freezingly; nippily; perilously; unbearably.

COLD-HEARTED

adverbs
bitterly; unpleasantly; disturbingly; relentlessly; cruelly; outrageously; inhumanly; unsympathetically; terribly; dreadfully; incurably; habitually; temperamentally; constitutionally; obviously; manifestly; shamefully; unbelievably; astonishingly; actually; selfishly; naturally; inexplicably; fearfully; inexorably; uncharitably; unfortunately.

COLDNESS

adjectives
dewy; incisive; still; sudden; faithless; superficial; wintry; relentless; increasing; contemptuous; supreme; lofty; studied; mortified; intellectual; selfish; fancied; disdainful.

COLLABORATE (*v*)

adverbs
unreservedly; successfully; harmoniously; artfully; skilfully; imaginatively; superbly; brilliantly; startlingly; enthusiastically.
(See work, cooperate.)

COLLABORATION

adjectives
direct; efficient; permanent; enduring; spiritual.

COLLAPSE

adjectives
moral; constant; painful; cataclysmic; progressive; widespread; nervous; complete; disgraceful; simulated; eventual; imminent; inevitable; pretended; subsequent; tragic; alleged; disastrous.

verbs
fall into—; guard against—; hasten—; insure—; predict—; shrink in—; sink into—; verge on—; —discourages; presage—.
(See exhaustion, failure, ruin.)

COLLAPSE (*v*)

adverbs
utterly; invariably; tragically; partially; fatally; completely; ruinously; disastrously; fearfully; wretchedly; dramatically.
(See fall.)

COLLAPSIBLE

adverbs
conveniently; laughably; comically; dangerously; perilously; easily; cleverly; cunningly; neatly; handily; ingeniously; tidily; quickly; instantly; disastrously; momentarily; tragically.

COLLAR

adjectives
ermine; greasy; soft; fur; oppressive; enormous; clerical; obdurate; snug; upstanding; celluloid; muzzle; resplendent; faultless; diminutive; onerous.

verbs
crane at—; engrave—; fumble with—; harness in—; insert in—; jewel—; pleat—; ring with—; slip out of—; split—; strain at—; suspend from—; tug at—; —bands; —binds; —chains; —chokes; —encircles; —encompasses; —fetters; —ornaments; —restrains; —shrinks; —wreathes; —yields; —yokes.

COLLEAGUE

adjectives
word-compelling; melancholy; congressional; conscientious; efficient; critical; turbulent; immediate; peripheral; redoubtable; ardent; gifted; pagan; older; experienced; artful; disgruntled; atrabilious; professional; distinguished.

verbs
aid—; ally with—; assemble—s; associate with—; bow to—; cooperate with—; debate with—; emulate—; enjoin—; favor—; inveigle—into; lead—; sever from—.
(See associate, accessory, ally.)

COLLECT (*v*)

adverbs
painlessly; systematically; haphazardly; eagerly; privately; scientifically; gloriously; remarkably; exclusively; posthumously; dramatically; actively; cantankerously; indiscriminately; laboriously; sedulously; periodically; assiduously.
(See accumulate, group.)

COLLECTION

adjectives
wonderful; arresting; suggestive; pretentious; rare; attractive; ponderous; complete; expensive; priceless; weird; heterogeneous; haphazard; motley; vague; private; interesting; useful; fair; authentic; miscellaneous; entertaining; tolerable; ave-

rage; classified; individual; comprehensive; annotated; voluminous; scientific; varied; hideous; exciting; representative; enticing; adequate; imaginative; brilliant; extensive; world; superb; spring; advanced; copious; incongruous; considerable; notable; vast; glorious; remarkable; exclusive; thrilling; posthumous; original; magnificent; active; dramatic; infinite; zoological; cantankerous; startling.

verbs
accumulate—; amass—; delay—; display—; equal—; examine—; exhibit—; herd—; insure—; join—; lead—; mass—; prize—; raise—; rifle—; speed—; suspend—; treasure—; uncover—; unearth—; value—; yield—; —depicts; —symbolizes.
(See heap, group.)

COLLECTIVE

adverbs
effectively; efficiently; agreeably; typically; officially; undeniably; comprehensively; indivisibly; unanimously; substantially; broadly; indefinitely; locally; significantly; representatively; startlingly; surprisingly.

COLLECTIVE BARGAINING

adjectives
conciliatory; deferred; haggled; generalized; tactless; tolerant; prolonged; summary.

verbs
abolish— —; acclaim— —; achieve through — —; acquire— —; activate— —; base on— —; criticize— —; demand— —; discuss— —; drift into— —; employ— —; enjoy— —; exercise— —; forbid— —; object to— —; oblige by— —; oppose— —; organize— —; prohibit— —; recognize— —; restrict— —; support— —; — —enables; — —functions; — —improves; — —insures; — —involves; — —recognizes; — —secures; — —upholds.
(See negotiation.)

COLLECTOR

adjectives
ardent; modest; assiduous; insatiable; advanced; passionate; entranced; curious; enthusiastic; worthy; unceasing; discriminating; prominent; budding.

verbs
avoid—; evade—; rob—; waylay—; —accumulates; —acquires; —amasses; —assembles; —classifies; —compiles; —displays; —embezzles; —evades; —exhibits; —prizes; —recovers; —solicits; —sues; —values.

COLLEGE

adjectives
aggressive; liberal; commercial; general; aspiring; rival; venerable; electoral; denominational; junior; endowed.

verbs
administer—; attach to—; bar from—; charter—; enroll at—; establish—; father —; found—; incorporate—; invest—with; pursue in—; register at—; reopen—; respect—; restrict—; staff—; suspend from—; —accommodates; —conducts; —confers; —expels; —honors; —instructs; —lodges; —offers; —prepares.
(See school, university.)

COLLEGIATE

adverbs
ostentatiously; airily; knowingly; smartly; ridiculously; pompously; clannishly; arrogantly; thoroughly; strictly; proudly; determinedly; resolutely; correctly; faintly; laughably; properly; academically; actively; becomingly; unimpeachably; respectably; admirably; satisfactorily; duly; responsibly.

COLLISION

adjectives
fierce; monstrous; inevitable; chance; actual; violent; personal; fatal; frequent; successive; clear; serious; menacing; exciting; amusing; sudden; sharp; fateful; imminent; expensive.

verbs
avoid—; foresee—; insure against—; result in—; swerve from—; warn against—; —batters; —dashes; —destroys; —entangles; —impairs; —necessitates; —rends; —upsets.
(See clash, impact, conflict, encounter, shock.)

COLLOQUIAL

adverbs
informally; easily; admissibly; chattily; provincially; pleasantly; frankly; agreeably; comfortably; familiarly; sociably; ingenuously; childishly; simply; naturally; unceremoniously; unconventionally; recklessly; candidly; artlessly.

COLLOQUY

adjectives
prolonged; fruitful; serious; peaceful.

COLLUSIVE

adverbs
shrewdly; dangerously; illegally; astutely; fraudulently; surreptitiously; subtly; cleverly; craftily; cunningly; incontrovertibly; undeniably; unluckily; unfortunately; openly; abominably; unwisely; dishonestly; palpably; manifestly; essentially; substantially; deplorably; unhappily; artfully; inauspiciously; openly.

COLON
(*part of body*)

adjectives
distended; inactive; inflamed; impacted; sluggish; varicose.

verbs
abscess—; accumulate in—; block—; constrict—; distend—; drain—; excise—; flush—; force from—; incise—; inflame—; irrigate—; lubricate—; oil—; purge—; ulcerate—; wash—; irritate—.
(See intestine, bowel.)

COLONEL

adjectives
crusty; old; courtly; benign; gallant; cultured; rum-rotten.

COLONIAL

adverbs
strictly; authentically; architecturally; characteristically; distinctly; respectably; acceptably; accurately; admirably; attractively; boldly; originally; gallantly; charmingly; pleasantly; hospitably; spaciously; formally; beautifully; markedly; significantly; remarkably; conspicuously; faithfully; loyally; generously; broadly.

COLONIST

adjectives
pacific; early; hardy; patriotic; affluent; desperate; original; God-fearing; ever-encroaching.

COLONY

adjectives
abandoned; congenial; agricultural; depressing; independent; outlying; foreign; smart; wealthy; summer; colorful; wrangling; unique; devoted; robust; exempted; hale; dusky; tropical; proprietary; flourishing; inheriting; remote; suburban; wretched; pretty; conquering; segregated; feeble; adjacent; dependent.

verbs
administer—; ban from—; cede to—; defend—; evict from—; free—; govern—; immigrate to—; launch—; maladministrate—; seize—; set up—; transfer to—; —flounders; —founders; —prospers; —rebels; —revolts; —riots; —smoulders; —wars on.
(See settlement.)

COLOR

adjectives
gorgeous; enchanting; rich; shining; clear; dazzling; uniform; subdued; gleaming; unheroic; quiet; faded; reticent; dull; canary; natural; artificial; exuberant; youthful; spirited; vibrant; kaleidoscopic; iridescent; full; lavish; live; vague; harmonious; piebald; sensuous; emotional; crude; raw; delicate; fragile; soft; false; basic; popular; rising; watery; gaudy; daring; welcome; flashy; isolated; normal; clean; complementary; solid; delightful; unwonted; radiant; dulled; hectic; thick; fatty; varied; dark; deep; decorative; brilliant; flying (pl); lustrous; subtle; intermediate; grimy; instrumental; tremendous; local; hideous; detestable; festive; staring; prismatic; heightened; glowing; incredible; warm; flickering; grinding; reassuring; unusual; new; water; factitious; equatorial; autumn; mellow; rapturous; ethereal; tender; faint; sickly; superb; crowded (pl); somber; profuse; motiveless; bright; exuberant; jumbled (pl); sleek; flamboyant; livid; solemn; sad; agreeable; riotous; pastel; summer; prominent; conventional; gay; seasonal; bold; plain; fluctuating; vigorous; orchestral; exquisite; dirty; garish; impregnated.

verbs
abhor—; accentuate—; alter—; array in—; assume—; bathe in—; bedeck with—; blend—; brush on—; burnish—; clothe in—; convey—; dash with—; deck in—; deprive of—; dim—; dip in—; disguise—; enamel with—; exhibit—; flush with—; grade—; indulge in—; invest with—; lend—; lose—; mix—; overcharge with—; paint in—; portray in—; retain—; shade—; sprinkle—; steal—from; subdue—; sully—; tone—; touch with—; vary—; —arrests; —dazzles; —distinguishes; —ebbs; —emanates from; —enhances; —flames; —flow-

ers; —glares; —glows; —harmonizes; —heightens; —mingles; —mounts; —predominates; —runs rampant; —sickens; —soothes; —sparkles; mask—.
(See hue, blush.)

COLOR (*v*)

adverbs
amusingly; distinctly; faintly; unevenly; angrily; painfully; brilliantly; synthetically; violently; conspicuously; obscurely; exquisitely; highly; gorgeously; enchantingly; uniformly; vibrantly; iridescently; lavishly; emotionally; crudely; fragilely; gaudily; daringly; normally; decoratively; harmoniously; festively; incredibly; factitiously; flamboyantly; conventionally; exquisitely; garishly.
(See tint, tinge.)

COLORFUL

adverbs
gorgeously; strikingly; beautifully; garishly; gaudily; remarkably; famously; bizarrely; barbarically; incredibly; delicately; daintily; pleasantly; agreeably; artistically; splendidly; brilliantly; magnificently; superbly; flashily; gaily; cheerfully; strangely; impressively; extraordinarily; riotously; outlandishly; fantastically; extravagantly.

COLORING

adjectives
illusive; youthful; fanciful; mustard; vivid; admirable; tender; somber; warm; luxurious; genuine; motley; special; clear; mellow; rich; artificial; musical; radiant; gorgeous; deep; lustrous; neutral; delightful; flawless; appropriate.

COLORLESS

adverbs
monotonously; dully; cheerlessly; wanly; pallidly; neutrally; dismally; drearily; discouragingly; grievously; sorely; sadly; utterly; piteously; deplorably; pathetically; cruelly; wretchedly; singularly; oppressively; hopelessly; dishearteningly; needlessly; horribly; unpleasantly.

COLT

adjectives
frolicking; uncomely; dark; unhandled; youthful; awkward; wanton; unbroken; rough; handsome.

verbs
corral—; curb—; groom—; exercise—; loose—; mount—; stable—; —balks; —frisks; —gallops off; —grazes; —hurdles; —neighs; —pastures.
(See animal, horse.)

COLUMN (*architectural, military, etc*)

adjectives
twisting; resistless; ascending; noble; tall; solid; marble; sturdy; dusty; massive; huge; vast; soaring; classic; stark; interpretative; warlike; somber; shattered; steel-clad; venerable; marching; flowered; lucrative; attacking; airy; perpendicular; crystal; slender; parallel; surging; monumental; vertebral; isolated; lofty; unending; advancing; ivory-shaped; vaporous; rostral; fragile; majestic; internal; spouting; graceful; gigantic; fantastic; glittering; luminous; rising; fluted; copulated; clustered.

verbs
ambush—; attach to—; construct—; destroy—; encircle—; erect—; file in—; head—; join—; line up in—; reinforce—; rule into—; shake—; shape—; shatter—; shield—; —crumbles; —marks; —supports; —swerves; —tapers; —vibrates; —winds.
(See line, post, shaft.)

COLUMN (*journalistic*)

adjectives
mercurial; exciting; fascinating; informative; interpretative; hackneyed; inspiring; authoritative.

verbs
caption—; condense—; dash off—; devour—; edit—; evolve—; excerpt—; feature—; head—; limit to—; print—; publish—; rewrite—; syndicate—; title—; —berates; —conveys; —demeans; —interests; —inveighs against; —libels; —prejudices; —scandalizes.
(See writing, editorial.)

COMA

adjectives
deathlike; glassy-eyed; mild; rigid; trancelike; wide-staring.

verbs
affect with—; arouse from—; awake from—; emerge from—; fail in—; fall

into—; lapse into—; mutter in—; relieve—; sink into—; succumb to—.
(See unconsciousness, lethargy.)

COMB (animal)

adjectives
cresting; crimson; defiant; flaunting; proudly-borne; imperial; nodding; superbly-curving; waggish.

verbs
adorn with—; curry—; develop—; ruffle—; serrate—; —crests; —matures; —protrudes; —waves.
(See crest.)

COMB (v)

adverbs
sleekly; briskly; dreamily; languidly; dexterously; effectively; left-handedly; gently.
(See brush.)

COMBAT

adjectives
frequent; ensuing; single; fierce; blood-stirring; aerial; chivalric; imaginable; beauteous; armed; hourly; historic; isolated; sportful; savage; noiseless; gladiatorial; primeval; mortal; feminine; caveman; merry; exciting; pitched; mimic; open-air; close; rude.

verbs
challenge in—; clash in—; collapse in—; crave—; dare—; disdain—; engage in—; face—; gird for—; heat—; incite to—; join in—; lay low in—; offer—; pledge to—; prick to—; view—; ward off—; —burns; —devastates; —rages; —seethes.
(See contest, battle, struggle, bout, contention.)

COMBAT (v)

adverbs
continually; effectively; fiercely; aerially; mortally; historically; savagely; gladiatorially; fatally; rudely; overwhelmingly; victoriously; thunderously; surgingly.
(See fight, struggle.)

COMBATANT

adjectives
successful; colossal; effective; unpropitious.

verbs
distinguish—; engage—; face—; fence with—; beat—; irk—; join—; lock with—; oppose—; overwhelm—; surround—; triumph over—; unsnarl—s; —contends; —vanquishes; —wins.
(See contestant, fighter.)

COMBATIVE

adverbs
absurdly; ferociously; foolishly; noisily; unreasonably; immoderately; truculently; pugnaciously; irresponsibly; blatantly; insolently; openly; challengingly; daringly; teasingly; vexatiously; offensively; lamentably; unfortunately; quickly; boyishly; egotistically; vaingloriously; conceitedly; boldly; unpleasantly; disagreeably.

COMBINATION

adjectives
charming; rare; wonderful; striking; perfect; lovely; pretty; extraordinary; amazing; unusual; curious; grotesque; strange; foolish; occasional; lucky; strategic; simplest; unbeatable; agricultural; mental; brilliant; intricate; intellectual; exclusive; special; ecstatic; positive; possible; seasonable; solemn; subtle; gigantic; magnificent; extensive; weird; nutritive; synergistic; inexplicable; incongruous; pleasing; industrial; vigorous; ingenious; color; skillful; equilibrious; pernicious; bright; bold; distasteful; dramatic; compelling; illegal; fortunate; roomy; irresistible; unholy; dextrous.

verbs
achieve—; attain—; balk at—; capture—; conceal—; guard—; hide—; join—; justify—; lock in—; reveal—; seal—; warn against—; weld—; —conflicts; —strengthens; evolve—.
(See union, alliance, league, coalition.)

COMBINE (v)

adverbs
intricately; successfully; euphoniously; felicitously; skillfully; dexterously; chemically; wisely; shrewdly; gorgeously; charmingly; extraordinarily; strategically; grotesquely; agriculturally; mentally; intellectually; subtly; weirdly; inexplicably; incongruously; industrially; ingeniously; perniciously; dramatically; legally; irresistibly; unfortunately.
(See unite, merge.)

COMBUSTIBLE

adverbs
readily; dangerously; unfortunately; perilously; easily; alarmingly; dreadfully; unhappily; conveniently; temptingly; hazard-

ously; appallingly; advantageously; distressingly; unluckily; disastrously; sadly; direly; sorely; deplorably; inauspiciously; spontaneously; instantaneously; explosively.

COMBUSTION

adjectives
fitful; spontaneous; resultant; dire; disastrous; chemical; destructive.

verbs
accompany with—; destroy by—; excite to—; kindle to—; prevent—; produce—; protect against—; reduce by—; resist—; result in—; save from—; support—; throw into—; —consumes; —devours; —eats; —generates; —heats; —rages.
(See outbreak, disturbance.)

COME (*v*)

adverbs
laboriously; reluctantly; decently; prosaically; richly; undeniably; vividly; argumentatively; inevitably; fitfully; steadily; intermittently; confidently; rarely; voluntarily; briskly; warily; peaceably; archly; spasmodically; vehemently; distinctly; unquestionably; drunkenly; rapidly; silently; hopefully; swiftly; hesitatingly; deliberately; monotonously; sporadically; obliquely; seasonably; drowsily; wondrously; indiscriminately; assiduously; ponderously; slyly; jauntily.
(See arrive, approach.)

COMEDIAN

adjectives
eminent; slapstick; popular; audacious; acrobatic; facile.

COMEDIENNE

adjectives
eccentric; apt; world-renowned; clever; scintillating.

COMEDY

adjectives
brilliant; pleasing; charming; restrained; intelligent; rich; social; suave; earnest; ironic; clever; satirical; light; sardonic; fluffy; riotous; farcical; roaring; buoyant; high; tiresome; wry; ineffective; sickly; alleged; fantastic; absurd; lamentable; tragic; mournful; burlesque; macabre; amateur; romantic; artificial; plain; fancy; veritable; crisp; wary; lascivious; admirable; sentimental; slapstick; optimistic; frivolous; robust; complicated; poetic; eccentric.

verbs
applaud—; conclude—; dramatize—; enact—; indulge in—; perform—; present—; produce—; revel in—; write—; —burlesques; —characterizes; —delights; —depicts; —enlivens; —entertains; —lightens; —relishes; —satirizes.
(See play, drama, representation.)

COMELY

adverbs
altogether; sufficiently; surprisingly; bloomingly; rosily; ruddily; roughly; singularly; vividly; serenely; innocently; proudly; unconsciously; robustly; quietly; unspeakably; admirably; unexpectedly; charmingly; pleasantly; gracefully; jauntily; smartly; tidily; specially; pleasingly; attractively.

COMET

adjectives
splendid; wandering; refulgent; vagrant; thunder-toned.

verbs
analyze—; calculate—s; control—; describe—; discover—; distinguish—; — examine—; expel—; focus on—; identify—; interested in—; observe—; recognize—; regard—; separate from—; study—; witness—; —approaches; —burns; —deviates; —diminishes; —emits; —excites; —flashes; —influences; —speeds; —travels; —wanes.

COMFORT

adjectives
blessed; genial; gentle; thoughtful; priceless; bracing; cold; increased; dubious; poor; scant; miserable; physical; plush; velvety; spiritual; knee-deep; old-fashioned; modern; intellectual; home; comparative; measurable; smug; temporary; ordered; necessary; summer; easy; great; shirtsleeve; refreshing; jaunty; ideal; constant; breezy; smart; luxurious; every; physical; whispering; quiet; superior; social; superb; cheerful; supreme; extra; genuine; continental; casual; suffused; melancholy; rural; restful; urban; heavenly; untold; heating; scantiest; maximum; perpetual; swinish; joyous; fireside; filthy; mysterious; dispensing; material; exclusive; blissful; indisputable; needed.

verbs
afford—; augment—; delight in—of; deprive of—; derive—from; draw—from; fill with—; insure—; maintain in—; mini-

ster to—; rear in—; refuse—; restore—; scorn—; subsist in—; take—from; withhold—.

(See ease, solace, consolation, encouragement.)

COMFORTABLE

adverbs

altogether; pleasantly; utterly; finally; increasingly; physically; comparatively; immeasurably; snugly; happily; easily; refreshingly; luxuriously; quietly; socially; supremely; genuinely; mysteriously; blissfully; serenely; contentedly; unexpectedly; immensely; definitely; deliciously.

COMFORTER

adjectives

effectual; wayside; despairing; gorgeous; sympathetic; placating.

COMICAL

adverbs

absurdly; pleasantly; brilliantly; cleverly; ironically; riotously; uproariously; tiresomely; tediously; highly; effectively; fantastically; complexly; eccentrically; intentionally; deliberately; daintily; dazzlingly; hilariously; mercilessly; bitterly; fatuously.

COMMA

adjectives

checking; favored; interfering; interspersed; omitted; perfunctory; setting-off; indispensable; jutting; obstructing.

verbs

designate by—; dot with—s; invert—; mark with—; pause at—; punctuate with—; —clarifies; —denotes; —indicates; —interrupts; —punctuates; —separates.

(See mark, interval, pause, delay.)

COMMAND

adjectives

brisk; snarled; definite; sharp; stern; brusque; crisp; curt; despotic; peremptory; absolute; authoritative; unconditional; tyrannical; facile; supreme; independent; imperious; iron; deathless; masterly; fluent; unconcerned; stentorian; low-voiced; shouted; spoken; hoarse; shrill; raucous; sole; unified; urgent; last; hurrying; prompt; effective; divine; implied; incisive; suggestive; rudimentary; consequential; shaky; tactful; phenomenal; incomparable; geographical; instant; cold; lawful; unique; disguised; renewed; vigorous; immediate; irregular; enthusiastic; instinctive; military; snapped; fierce; unlimited; laudable; pernicious; admirable; stifled; long-desired; rapturous; strenuous; intermingling; respective; just.

verbs

assume—; attend—; await—; bear—; boast—; comply with—; condescend to—; constitute—; defy—; execute—; fulfill—; lose—; obey—; release from—; relieve from—; relinquish—; respond to—; send forth—; stand ready at—; sway by—; thunder—; transgress—; understand—; waive—; —confuses; —enrages; —rings; —splits the air; —startles.

(See order, charge, mandate, authority, leadership, control.)

COMMAND (*v*)

adverbs

imperiously; authoritatively; intellectually; impatiently; laughingly; peremptorily; petulantly; definitely; brusquely; crisply; curtly; despotically; unconditionally; tyrannically; independently; stentorianly; hoarsely; shrilly; raucously; urgently; promptly; effectively; incisively; tactfully; phenomenally; incomparably; vigorously; immediately; enthusiastically; instinctively; fiercely; laudably; perniciously; justly.

(See order, direct.)

COMMANDER

adjectives

trusted; plucky; dashing; able; spectacular; immediate; insulted; victorious; regimental; immovable; illustrious; panic-stricken; fiery; respected; half-clad; venerable; renowned; indomitable.

verbs

appoint to—; exalt—; obey—; raise to—; rank as—; —assigns; —assumes; —authorizes; —campaigns; —controls; —directs; —disposes of; —exercises; —grants; —overrules; —pensions; —plans; —rules.

(See master, officer, captain, leader.)

COMMANDING

adverbs

harshly; fussily; sternly; briskly; definitely; sharply; crisply; curtly; despotically; peremptorily; authoritatively; imperiously; hoarsely; shrilly; raucously; urgently; incisively; tactfully; coldly; vigorously; enthusiastically; insultingly; offensively.

COMMANDMENT

adjectives
harsh; fussy; express; stern; abrupt; strait; unwritten; divine.

verbs
annul—; charge with—; delight in—; deliver—; disregard—; forbid by—; forsake—; fulfill—; hearken to—; neglect—; rebel against—; reject—; send forth—; transgress—; tremble at—; violate—; urge—.
(See command, precept, law, order, warning.)

COMMEMORATE (*v*)

adverbs
jubilantly; appropriately; fitly; justly; splendidly; gloriously; annually; royally; simply; serenely; privately; publicly; passionately; sincerely.
(See celebrate.)

COMMEMORATIVE

adverbs
tenderly; reverently; publicly; appropriately; affectionately; permanently; nobly; deeply; triumphantly; faithfully; perpetually; graciously; worthily; adequately; suitably; gratefully; humbly; lastingly; enduringly; splendidly; magnificently; fittingly; beautifully; especially; impressively; felicitously.

COMMENCE (*v*)

adverbs
ceremoniously; busily; prosperously; daily; accustomedly; jocosely; meticulously; amiably; comfortably; conventionally; shrewdly.
(See begin, start.)

COMMENCEMENT

adjectives
elementary; prosperous; propitious; belated; annual; current.

COMMEND (*v*)

adverbs
grandiloquently; strongly; extravagantly; chiefly; emphatically; warmly; meritedly; flatteringly; heartily; fulsomely; boundlessly; scantily; meagerly.
(See recommend.)

COMMENDABLE

adverbs
altogether; especially; meritoriously; emphatically; particularly; eminently; unusually; unimpeachably; gloriously; admirably; worthily; highly; markedly; uncommonly; definitely.

COMMENDATION

adjectives
sorry; emphatic; extravagant; warm; merited; well-meant; gentle; widespread; worthy; hearty.

verbs
bestow—upon; consider—; convey—; deliver—; deserve—; discharge from—; express—; favor with—; flatter with—; gain—; regard—; respect—; silence—; solicit—; still—; value—; welcome with—; —abates; —ceases; —extols; —graces; —lauds; —praises; —recedes.
(See approbation, approval, praise, recommendation.)

COMMENSURATE

adverbs
exactly; appropriately; approximately; suitably; undeniably; properly; adjustably; tolerably; remarkably; meticulously; essentially; mathematically; scrupulously; carefully.

COMMENT

adjectives
favorable; approving; polite; appreciative; triumphant; grateful; important; significant; interesting; persuasive; sane; civilized; fretful; intelligent; shrewd; laconic; enlightening; cultured; prosaic; inappropriate; characteristic; dry; stumbling; trivial; bewildered; incoherent; wild; trite; open; gloomy; dubious; direct; vigorous; crisp; daring; pungent; scathing; sharp; penetrating; humorous; witty; jesting; facetious; upstart; quick; running; spontaneous; disgruntled; constant; exquisite; philosophic; speculative; editorial; cartoon; pamphleteering; country-wide; local; mental; printed; verbal; moralizing; censorious; detailed; curious; whispered; audible; casual; passing; critical; wistful; rare; contemporary; inane; enthusiastic; playful; cheerful; cynical; caustic; unsympathetic; perverse; churlish; uncomplimentary; endless; sour; abundant; cheering; quain; considerable; public; analytic; needless; inconsequential; musical; stupid; jocular; introductory; prophetic; skeptical; authoritative; enlivening; lavish; vulgar; resentful; acrimonious.

verbs
analyze—; arouse—; attach—; bear—; betray into—; challenge—; conceal—; cram with—; deride—; elicit—; evince—; evoke—; excite—; issue—; lavish—on; occasion—; provoke—; subject to—; underline—; —criticizes; —disconcerts; —elucidates; —enlightens; —flatters; —illuminates; —illustrates; —interprets; —penetrates; —squelches.
(See remark, observation, explanation.)

COMMENT (v)

adverbs
grumblingly; haughtily; admiringly; dryly; audibly; grimly; favorably; approvingly; politely; appreciatively; gratefully; significantly; interestingly; sanely; fretfully; intelligently; shrewdly; laconically; prosaically; inappropriately; characteristically; tritely; gloomily; dubiously; vigorously; crisply; pungently; scathingly; penetratingly; humorously; facetiously; spontaneously; philosophically; speculatively; editorially; locally; mentally; verbally; inanely; wistfully; playfully; cheeerfully; cynically; caustically; endlessly; sourly; cheeringly; quaintly; publicly; analytically; inconsequentially; stupidly; jocularly; drolly; flatteringly; prophetically; skeptically; authoritatively; lavishly; vulgarly; resentfully; acrimoniously; pityingly.
(See remark, observe.)

COMMENTARY

adjectives
significant; brilliant; sad; ironic; biting; pure; dazzling; binding; striking; authentic; curious; philosophic; keen; critical; rollicking; satiric; stressed; subtle; whimsical; penetrating; ludicrous; panoramic.

COMMENTATOR

adjectives
genial; philosophical; dramatic; unknown; hostile; political; inelegant; unseen.

COMMERCE

adjectives
nascent; enlarged; far-flung; unsullied; peaceful; flourishing; lawless; enhanced; expanding; international; vast; increasing; interstate; long-established; petty.

verbs
blockade—; derange—; develop—; encourage—; engage in—; hinder—; imperil—; insure—; interchange—; invade—; join in—; levy on—; negotiate—; open—; profit by—; protect—; regulate—; restrict—; route—; safeguard—; stimulate—; stint—; subsidize—; traffic in—; —dwindles; —flourishes; —transports; —wanes.
(See trade, business, intercourse, traffic, communication.)

COMMERCIAL

adverbs
sordidly; blatantly; profitably; readily; thrivingly; flourishingly; prosperously; productively; unaccountably; satisfactorily; fairly; openly; frankly; avowedly; uninterestingly; brilliantly; insistently; briskly; cheerfully; keenly; terribly; competently; thoroughly; dully; tediously; comically; actively; successfully; assiduously; energetically; shrewdly; craftily.

COMMERCIALISM

adjectives
blatant; camouflaged; high-powered.

COMMISERATION

adjectives
exaggerated; false; gentle; tender; light; regretful; sincere.

verbs
act in—; assist out of—; attend with—; behold in—; conceal—; defy—; deserve—; disdain—; distress with—; excite—; express—; feign—; lack—; pretend—; succumb to—; tear with—; tender—; wrack with—; wring with—.
(See compassion, pity, sorrow.)

COMMISSION

adjectives
perilous; permanent; promised; glorious; royal; simple; delicate; accredited; illicit; flattering; nonpartisan; legislative; eminent; joint; mixed; innocent; imaginary; unspoken; gabbling; much-desired.

verbs
accept—; appoint to—; assume—; authorize—; buy—; charge with—; confer—upon; delegate to—; deliver—; devise—; discharge—; dispatch—; empower—; entrust with—; execute—; tender--; undertake—; warrant—; —empowers; —instructs; —orders; —ranks; —specifies.
(See mission, delegation, errand, trust.)

COMMISSIONER

adjectives
imperial; mouth-dripping; perfunctory; supercilious; unbending; bribe-swallowing; porcine.

COMMIT (*v*)

adverbs
consciously; irrevocably; unconsciously; habitually; sinfully; wilfully; rarely; solemnly; vilely; deliberately; unreservedly; fearlessly; criminally; treacherously; shrewdly; mysteriously; antagonistically; swiftly; veritably; vulgarly.

(See assign, entrust.)

COMMITMENT

adjectives
careless; imaginary; solemn; revealed; judicial; official.

COMMITTEE

adjectives
advisory; influential; corresponding; reception; adjuvant; self-constituted; associational; intractable; select; prudential; vigilance; chagrined; strong; supreme; grand; advisory; special; executive; proper; socialistic; pacific; utilization.

verbs
appear before—; appoint to—; arm—; corral—; dominate—; hamstring—; head—; invent—; preside over—; set up—; taunt—; —advises; —bans; —bars; —condones; —denounces; —evinces; —favors; —functions; —proclaims; —retorts.

(See group, board.)

COMMODIOUS

adverbs
sufficiently; adequately; advantageously; expediently; handily; serviceably; valuably; luckily; conveniently; pleasantly; appropriately; fortunately; splendidly; completely; excellently; spaciously; cheerily; comfortably; capaciously; extremely; admirably; roomily; particularly; suitably; uncommonly; exceptionally.

COMMODITY

adjectives
precious; agricultural; respected; unwanted; unctuous; valuable; opposite; essential; leading; vital; industrial; prized; necessary.

COMMONPLACE

adjectives
culinary; evasive; vapid; conventional; tedious.

verbs
beautify—; enrich—; exalt—; express—; sink into—; soar above—; utter—; —bores; —fails to impress; —tires; —wearies.

(See platitude, remark.)

adverbs
undeniably; insignificantly; trivially; indifferently; particularly; ridiculously; negligibly; cheaply; contemptibly; immaterially; miserably; pitifully; shabbily; wretchedly; distinctly; laughably; remarkably; surprisingly; stupidly; monotonously; prosaically.

COMMON-SENSE

adjectives
practical; supreme; salty; shrewd; courageous; hard-headed.

verbs
accept as— —; argue with— —; characterize by— —; demand— —; derive by— —; develop— —; display— —; endow with— —; evince— —; exhibit— —; forsake— —; judge with— —; lack— —; override— —; perceive with— —; require— —; violate— —; — —prevails.

(See judgment, understanding.)

COMMONWEALTH

adjectives
corrupted; co-operative; precarious; ancient; native; advanced; free; industrial; individual.

COMMOTION

adjectives
nervous; subdued; hurried; violent; sudden; faint; diurnal; inner; economic; mysterious; sad; strong; tremendous.

verbs
engage in—; excite—; quell—; quiet—; still—; throw into—; —agitates; —bristles; —confuses; —disorders; —irritates; —perturbs; —rages; —recurs; —rises;—stirs; —subsides; —terrifies.

(See agitation, excitement, tumult, disturbance, turmoil, riot, stir.)

COMMUNE (v)

adverbs
spiritually; intimately; immortally; rapturously; ineffably; wordlessly; mentally; intellectually; constantly; socially; devoutly; worshipfully; divinely.
(See confer, converse.)

COMMUNICABLE

adverbs
highly; easily; perilously; alarmingly; dangerously; scarcely; freely; openly; secretly; rapidly; slyly; electrically; directly; conveniently; instantly; fearfully; frightfully; hardly; mysteriously; quickly; expeditiously; advantageously; expediently.

COMMUNICATE (v)

adverbs
duly; unknowingly; felicitously; thrillingly; formally; efficiently; gracefully; uniquely; swiftly; economically; rapidly; constantly; continuously; belligerently; garrulously; crudely; slyly; telepathically; directly; anonymously; sympathetically; confidentially; treacherously; conveniently; unreservedly; spiritually; clandestinely; telegraphically; precariously; domestically.
(See impart, transmit.)

COMMUNICATION

adjectives
efficient; sincere; graceful; rich; unique; swift; economical; rapid; easy; constant; continuous; belligerent; inarticulate; garrulous; profane; flimsy; crude; covert; sly; underhanded; world; visual; electrical; papal; aerial; interstate; telepathic; unrestricted; telltale; articulated; direct; anonymous; sympathetic; confidential; treacherous; depressing; convenient; unreserved; spiritual; slow-moving; pregnant; clandestine; evil; friendly; mercantile; unlimited; secure; radio; telegraphic; privileged; pretended; domestic; precarious.

verbs
break—with; contrive—; cut off—; deliver—; draw—; establish—with; exchange—s; interfere with—; reestablish—; relay—; scatter—; set up—with; stimulate—; —conveys; —expresses; —imparts; —informs; —proceeds from; —purports to; —requests.
(See intercourse, conference, correspondence, message, letter.)

COMMUNION

adjectives
immortal; rapturous; ineffable; friendly; wordless; mental; intellectual; intimate; untroubled; constant; social.

COMMUNISM

adjectives
lawless; isolated; outright; iconoclastic; jealous; possessive; intolerant.

verbs
advocate—; aspire to—; bow to—; combat—; decry—; denounce—; draw the line against—; embrace—; envision—; eradicate—; espouse—; flirt with—; incite to—; riddle with—; seethe with—; spread—; storm toward—; suppress—; taint with—; war on—; —abolishes; —derives from; —destroys; —equalizes; —menaces; —levels; —reconstructs; —undermines; —idealizes.
(See socialism.)

COMMUNIST

adjectives
subtle; unadulterated; rabid; confirmed; covert; active.

verbs
ban—; bar—; condemn—; denounce—; deport—; evict—; forbid—; harbor—; organize—s; recognize—; regulate—; reproach—; shelter—; style as—; —advocates; —agitates; —antagonizes; —exhorts; —expresses; —dreams; —influences; —opposes; —orates; —practices; —proclaims; —s riot; —struggles; —supports; —undermines; —vows.
(See socialist.)

COMMUNISTIC

adverbs
honestly; dangerously; sincerely; intrepidly; daringly; audaciously; enthusiastically; actively; furtively; slyly; openly; obviously; convincingly; absurdly; alarmingly; recklessly; inherently; appallingly; bitterly; outright; downright; thoroughly; entirely; subtly; deceptively; startlingly; surreptitiously.

COMMUNITY

adjectives
benighted; enlightened; forward; average; model; decent; beautiful; ideal; prideful; ambitious; busiest; enterprising; self-respecting; progressive; aggressive; sturdy; self-sustaining; comfortable; isolated; much-maligned; antagonistic; sprawl-

ing; ecclesiastical; overcrowded; treeless; civilized; closely-knit; urban; country; laboring; alien; polyglot; quiet; residential; pioneer; rural; sacred; tropical; industrial; monastic; conservative; organized; homogeneous; composite; enormous; fortress-like; curious; moral; congenial; guileless; self-supporting; hostile; opulent; veritable; seafaring; serene; drainageless; expanding; sober; scattered.

verbs
acquaint with—; beautify—; burden—; confine to—; dominate—; dwell in—; elevate—; establish—; expel from—; filter into—; forsake—; govern—; offend—; organize into—; pervade—; present to—; represent—; rule—; unite in—; —elects; —fosters; —levies; —shares; —supports.
(See city, town, village, public, society, association, people.)

COMPACT

adjectives
convenient; social; indissoluble; comfortable; voluntary; earthly; unwritten; imaginary; binding; favorable.

verbs
admit to—; authorize—; compose—; confirm—; contract—; draw up—; frame—; fulfill—; gather in—; join—; knit in—; plan—; ratify—; seal—; sign—; solemnize—; weld in—; —aids; —allies; —consolidates; —insures; —protects; —strengthens; —supports.
(See covenant, agreement, pact, treaty, contract.)

COMPANION

adjectives
beloved; wonderful; alluring; pleasant; charming; gentle; beautiful; popular; trusted; genial; attractive; true; faithful; devoted; wonted; burly; happy; thoughtful; useful; fit; illustrious; bosom; constant; intimate; inseparable; indefatigable; daily; gayest; jolly; jocose; meticulous; amiable; agreeable; lively; entertaining; droll; emaciated; pale; slim; young; feeble; stocky; lithe; rough; double-crossing; profligate; undesirable; sneering; doubtful; fickle; morose; weak; pitiable; gloomy; craven; irate; dispirited; tense; shrinking; prostrate; intellectual; drinking; mysterious; familiar; unsuspecting; grave; normal; authentic; eager; boon; ardent; engaging; quaking; environed; ghastly; polite; unique; troublesome; disappointing; lifelong; blithe; confederate; friendly (pl); semi-conscious; equivocal; spruce; subsidiary; often-tried.

verbs
associate with—; consort with—; engage—; entertain—; hire—; join—; lack—; lead—; long for—; reproach—; reunite with—; seek—; share with—; sway—; vie with—; —entertains; —escorts.
(See comrade, associate, ally.)

COMPANIONABLE

adverbs
pleasantly; agreeably; always; charmingly; unusually; genially; truly; faithfully; happily; thoughtfully; gaily; amiably; comfortably; entertainingly; curiously; politely; delightfully; inestimably; congenially; distinctly; unobtrusively; quietly; cheerfully; sociably; cosily; chattily.

COMPANIONSHIP

adjectives
genial; noble; voluntary; coarse; revered; endeared; creative; neighborly; thoughtful; indiscriminate; intimate; delightful; human; dull; honorable; dark; inestimable; mutual; helpful; satisfactory; refined; sympathetic; loving; mysterious; loyal; gay; humorous; pleasant; exclusive; friendly.

verbs
avoid—; break—; conceal—; crave—; delight in—; denounce—; desire—; hunger for—; invite—; join in—; lack—; limit—; lose—; maintain—of; object to—; seek—; win—; withdraw from—.
(See association, company, intimacy, fellowship, society.)

COMPANY
(*association, companionship*)

verbs
crave—; cultivate—; curse—; delight in—of; detest—; forbid—; forsake—; grace with—; miss—; placate—; refrain from—; regain—of; request—; sever from—; thrust into—of; woo—; —amuses; —bores; —departs; —dwindles; —entertains; —straggles in.
(See companionship.)

COMPANY
(*corporation*)

verbs
absorb—; bankrupt—; buy up—; charter—; consolidate—; defraud—; embezzle from—;

found—; incorporate—; manage—; merge —; reorganize—; ruin—; —branches out; —recovers; —profits; —survives.
(See corporation, firm.)

COMPANY (general)

adjectives
subsidiary; lightheaded; respectable; assembled; scanty; ubiquitous; jocund; devout; treasonable; select; panic-stricken; choice; trading; merry; congenial; licentious; loathsome; saintly; high-born; agreeable; mysterious; villainous; ennobling; distinguished; defunct; brilliant; pleasant; enterprising; cosmopolitan; animated; suspecting; enchanting; glamorous; immortal; great; picturesque; unobtrusive; sympathetic; jovial; buoyant; refined; talented; detestable; rascally; infernal; wild; chartered; generating; transmission; gigantic; aggressive; forward-looking; reputable; commissary; projected.

COMPANY (military division)

verbs
ambush—; assign to—; command—; desolate—; discontinue—; dispatch to—; divide into—ies; enlist in—; evolve—; forge—; head—; manoeuvre—; overtake—; partition—; separate—; spy on—; train—; —retreats; —traverses.
(See army, troops.)

COMPARABLE

adverbs
invidiously; scarcely; highly; easily; definitely; analogously; proportionally; relatively; homogeneously; interestingly; pertinently; distinctly; curiously; significantly; favorably; deservedly; worthily; excellently; appropriately; suitably; fittingly; properly; decently.

COMPARE (v)

adverbs
invidiously; egotistically; unavoidably; faithfully; favorably; unintentionally; approvingly; challengingly; odiously; metaphorically; significantly; caustically; classically; drolly; poignantly; dismayingly; conscientiously; directly; accurately; unfavorably; brutally; inevitably; aptly.
(See observe.)

COMPARISON

adjectives
vigorous; productive; challenging; odious; cost; metaphorical; insignificant; self-invited; curious; outworn; caustic; retrospective; classic; droll; poignant; dismaying; conscientious; direct; accurate; momentary; invidious; hateful; significant; unfavorable; brutal; strained; inevitable.

verbs
attempt—; bear—; belittle—; consider—; despair of—; despise—; disdain—; draw—; fail in—; flaunt—; illustrate—; institute—; invite—; judge—; lend to—; lose by—; place beyond—; ridicule—; scoff at—; stand—; subject to—; suffer by—; —brings out; —emphasizes; —measures; —parallels; —suggests.
(See illustration, simile.)

COMPARTMENT

adjectives
separate; concealed; rear; public; watertight.

verbs
coil in—; couch in—; decorate—; design—; distribute in—; divide in—; dwell in—; lay out—; occupy—; ornament—; panel—; partition into—s; prepare—; retain—; seal—; separate into—s; space—s; widen—; —accommodates; —adjoins; —allows; —permits.
(See section, chamber, part, division.)

COMPASS

adjectives
narrow; golden.

verbs
attract—; box—; manipulate—; navigate with—; observe—; plan with—; plot with—; suspend—; trust—; chart—; —describes; —deviates; —directs; —guides; —indicates; —informs; —leads; —limits; —marks; —measures; —pilots; —records; —routes; —safeguards; —surveys.
(See instrument.)

COMPASSION

adjectives
pitying; proud; deep; sincere; involuntary; august; womanly; delicate; angelic; bleeding; intolerable; melancholy; infinite; chivalrous; moving; affectionate; protective; scornful; profound; hurried; infallible; tender; faint; sweet; bored; dying; divine.

verbs
act in—; arouse—; conceal—; consume with—; contain—; display—; excite—; express—; feign—; fill with—; melt in—; minister with—; mourn in—; move to—; plead for—; pretend—; reveal—; stir to—; succor in—; take—upon; touch with—; weep in—; wrack with—; wring with—; —humanizes; —tempers.
(See commiseration, pity, sympathy, mercy.)

COMPASSIONATE

adverbs
keenly; sympathetically; understandingly; charitably; graciously; leniently; humanely; mercifully; pityingly; tenderly; disarmingly; softly; utterly; gently; tolerantly; indulgently; mildly; magnanimously; comfortingly; effectively; deeply; sincerely; delicately; infinitely; chivalrously; affectionately; profoundly; divinely.

COMPATIBLE

adverbs
easily; happily; felicitously; fortunately; unusually; harmoniously; amiably; agreeably; pleasantly; joyously; obviously; essentially; manifestly; supremely; famously; gracefully; opportunely; auspiciously; comfortably; amicably; extremely; unquestionably; unaccountably; surprisingly; fundamentally; notably.

COMPATRIOT

adjectives
assumed; grateful; affected.

COMPEL (*v*)

adverbs
flatly; ultimately; adroitly; reluctantly; strategically; artfully; slyly; politely; subtly; indirectly; truculently; legally; privately; troublesomely; economically; mysteriously; aggressively.
(See make, force.)

COMPENDIOUS

adverbs
remarkably; surprisingly; pleasingly; compactly; amazingly; laconically; tersely; conveniently; exceedingly; expertly; inexpressibly; faultlessly; commendably; laudably; extraordinarily; strikingly; sensibly; prudently; synoptically; concisely; neatly; cleverly; adroitly; agreeably; usefully; helpfully; advantageously.

COMPENDIUM

adjectives
astonishing; encyclopedic; similar.

COMPENSATE (*v*)

adverbs
adequately; amply; partially; grudgingly; sufficiently; satisfactorily; financially; tolerably; pecuniarily; ultimately; abundantly; solemnly; fully; barely; genially; nobly; voluntarily; loyally.
(See pay, replace.)

COMPENSATION

adjectives
adjusted; ample; satisfactory; dwindling; eternal; objective; financial; reassuming; tolerable; pecuniary; abundant; fixed; heartless; solemn; reasonable; adequate; dynamic; ultimate.

COMPENSATORY

adverbs
satisfactorily; safely; securely; luckily; happily; allowably; considerately; honorably; calculatingly; accurately; remuneratively; retroactively; highly; cleverly; acceptably; soundly; sensibly; wisely; adjustably; amply; financially; tolerably; generously; reasonably; adequately; ultimately; prudently; sufficiently.

COMPETE (*v*)

adverbs
hotly; hilariously; unrestrainedly; unrestrictedly; freely; spectacularly; constructively; legitimately; ruinously; destructively; bitterly; actively; intensely; keenly; strenuously; effectively; formidably; unprecedentedly; meaninglessly; individually; internally; domestically; internationally; critically; primarily; unfairly; unequally; aggressively; benevolently; basely; dishonorably; ruthlessly; hopefully; triumphantly.
(See contend, strive.)

COMPETENCE

adjectives
notable; cold; easy technical; hard; unruffled; modest; financial; mental; utmost; professional; decent; occupational; bare; sufficient.

verbs
allot—; amass—; bestow—upon; enlarge—; exhaust—; fritter away—; furnish—; in-

herit—; insure of—; lack—; live off—; provide—; require—; rob of—; run through—; secure—; —dwindles; —suffices.
(See wealth.)

COMPETENT

adverbs
thoroughly; remarkably; highly; brilliantly; exceptionally; influentially; deftly; ingeniously; intelligently; proficiently; excellently; capably; discreetly; smartly; shrewdly; consummately; prepossessingly; undoubtedly; unquestionably; manifestly; completely; perfectly; notably; modestly; sufficiently.

COMPETITION

adjectives
unrestrained; unlimited; unrestricted; utterly unbridled; free; full; spectacular; unregulated; constructive; legitimate; ruinous; destructive; bitter; active; intense; keen; severe; sharp; heavy; strenuous; serious; effective; unprecedented; formidable; meaningless; puny; individual; world; internal; native; water-power; utility; truck; domestic; socialistic; international; critical; interstate; adjudicable; tangled; unwanted; constant; increased; enhanced; primary; counter; supplantive; unfair; unequal; hampering; foreign; savage; eager; formidable; pecuniary; marginal; benevolent; consequent; base; dishonorable; aggressive; harsh; ruthless; anarchical; hopeful; triumphal.

verbs
cripple—; curb—; discourage—; eliminate—; exclude—; face—; nurture on—; obliterate—; offer—; overcome—; promote—; reduce—; sharpen—; squelch—; stamp out—; stimulate—; suppress—; survive—; sustain—; —abates; —eases; —enlivens; —grinds; —steels; —tempers; —threatens.
(See rivalry, contention, strife.)

COMPETITIVE

adverbs
bitterly; actively; enthusiastically; brutally; ruinously; intensely; keenly; sharply; strenuously; formidably; primarily; savagely; appealingly; contentiously; pugnaciously; destructively; stimulatingly; rousingly; dangerously; cruelly; barbarously; desperately; mischievously; trickily; cunningly; shrewdly; deceptively; unfairly.

COMPETITOR

adjectives
insurgent; easygoing; formidable; alert; dangerous; cruel; honest; lame; veteran; motor; throat-cutting; husky; local; direct; active.

verbs
bankrupt—; defeat—; dispose of—; eliminate—; engage—; equal—; harass—; judge—; mass—s; outdistance—; outstrip—; rival—; suppress—; vanquish—; vie with—; —contests; —endeavors; —gains; —objects; —s organize; —retires; —stimulates.
(See contestant, opponent, rival, antagonist.)

COMPILATION

adjectives
intelligent; magnificent; handy; voluminous; exact; wretched; unoriginal; subsequent; important; systematic; hasty; valuable.

COMPLACENCY

adjectives
philosophical; bland; cynical; benign; pleased; yielding; melancholy; smug; superb; amiable; pleasant; light; foolish; placid; meek; oily; agreeable; affectionate.

verbs
announce with—; approach with—; breathe—; breed—; characterize—; display—; dwell in—; exhibit—; gain—; jolt out of—; observe with—; puncture—; rebuke—; receive with—; regard with—; resent—; satirize—; shake—; shock out of—; smile with—; —reigns.
(See satisfaction, serenity.)

COMPLACENT

adverbs
oddly; serenely; calmly; placidly; maddeningly; smugly; conceitedly; arrogantly; incredibly; imperturbably; vexatiously; pleasantly; comfortably; affably; blandly; gently; graciously; composedly; tranquilly; sedately; contentedly; cheerfully; entirely; good-humoredly; curiously; resolutely; admirably; justifiably.

COMPLAIN (*v*)

adverbs
shrewishly; bitterly; sorrowfully; dismally; audibly; feelingly; grievously; drawlingly; drearily; vehemently; respectfully;

peevishly; humorously; angrily; constantly; unjustly; ignorantly; pathetically; formally; jealously; frivolously; vexatiously; chronically; vigorously; dolefully.
(See grumble, murmur.)

COMPLAINT

adjectives
infantile; troublesome; vehement; loud; private; belated; frequent (pl); timid; alarming; mournful; loathsome; rash; angry; incipient; constant; fatal; unjust; prevalent; ignorant; fond; quavering; pathetic; distressing; formal; jealous; frivolous; dysenteric; pulmonary; vexatious; unintelligible; irritating; wailing; individual; public; chronic; paternal; vigorous; hoarse; well-founded; well-formed; pleasant; bitter; doleful; defensive; frenetic; praiseful; threnodic.

verbs
amend—; burden with—; complicate—; contract—; develop—; dismiss—; ease—; investigate—; issue—; lodge—against; mourn—; murmur—; pour out—; propogate—; renew—; rid oneself of—; set forth—; suffer—; swallow—; terminate—; usher in—; utter—; whisper—; withdraw —; —irritates; —s rain in; —recurs; —saddens; —wanes; —waxes.
(See grievance, lamentation, ailment, accusation, disease.)

COMPLAISANCE

adjectives
ready; affectionate; discreet; supple; sad; veiled.

COMPLAISANT

adverbs
amiably; benignly; kindly; warm-heartedly; indulgently; good-humoredly; benevolently; considerately; tenderly; accommodatingly; obligingly; sweetly; unaffectedly; comfortably; pleasantly; gravely; generously; happily; graciously; quietly; unobtrusively; remarkably; charmingly; gallantly; gently; urbanely; gracefully.

COMPLEMENTARY

adverbs
unusually; fortunately; remarkably; usefully; serviceably; happily; luckily; auspiciously; delightfully; pleasantly; absolutely; completely; entirely; thoroughly; mutually; opportunely; profitably; advantageously; conveniently; astonishingly; ingeniously.

COMPLETE

adverbs
absolutely; finally; happily; fortunately; luckily; satisfactorily; remarkably; unbelievably; magnificently; splendidly; extraordinarily; ideally; actually; delightfully; ceremonially; royally; formally; legally; officially; really.

COMPLETE (*v*)

adverbs
rapidly; swiftly; partially; gradually; skillfully; conventionally; finally; respectably; absolutely; delightfully; entirely; satisfactorily; casually; determinedly; superbly.
(See finish, perfect.)

COMPLETENESS

adjectives
unapproached; exhaustive; ethical; frightful; conventional; ruthless; respectable; final; round; absolute; firm; delightful.

COMPLETION

adjectives
apparent; advanced; divine; glorious; malevolent; plentiful; prophetic; stony; timely; unexpected; premature.

verbs
accomplish—; achieve—; attain—; await—; celebrate—; commemorate—; consent to—; desire—; expedite—; predict—; speed—; time—; —exhausts; —tires.
(See accomplishment, fulfillment, conclusion, end.)

COMPLEX

adjectives
repressed; haunting; sadistic; exceeding; flourishing; superior; vague; parlor; calamity; familiarity; modern; unreconciled; knitting; permanent; inferiority; narcissistic.

verbs
affect by—; analyze—; attribute to—; banish—; comprehend—; develop—; disentangle—; form—; indicate—; interpret—; involve—; nurture—; psychoanalyze—; relieve—; remove—; subject to—; understand—; unravel—; —chains; —consumes; —fetters; —seeks an outlet; arm with—.
(See complication, fear, influence.)

adverbs
bewilderingly; disturbingly; irritatingly; needlessly; seriously; embarrassingly; ambiguously; evasively; strangely; oddly; exceedingly; vaguely; astonishingly; bafflingly; unintelligibly; unnecessarily; tiresomely; painfully; harassingly; impossibly; intricately; perplexingly; confusingly; confoundedly; plaguedly; disconcertingly.

COMPLEXION

adjectives
flawless; clear; transparent; creamy; ivory; putty; sallow; apoplectic; pale; long; faded; unflushed; sanguine; fresh; ruddy; healthy; port-wine; choleric; beery; sunburnt; olive; sandy; swarthy; unnatural; delicate; dazzling; pleasant; muddy; blotchy; pretty; dark; ruined; shadowed; private; country; embrowned; coarse; variable; rubicund; jealous; florid; leaden; tanned; pallid.

verbs
beautify—; blemish—; blot—; change—; clear—; coarsen—; darken—; discolor—; dot—; inflame—; mar—; paint—; praise—; redden—; smirch—; tan—; tinge—; wither —; wrinkle—; —brightens; —freckles; —glows; —shines.
(See character, color, hue.)

COMPLEXITY

adjectives
astonishing; endless; infinite; ever-growing; abstract; ornate; serried; political; extraordinary; exciting; amazing; bewildering; differentiated; cosmic; baffling; increasing; technical.

verbs
attend with—; comprehend—; confine—; delve into—; disintegrate—; dispose of—; dissolve—; embrace—; evolve—; extricate from—; investigate—; involve—; reduce—; regard—; result in—; simplify—; solve—; sweep away—; —amazes; —discourages; —puzzles; —vanishes.
(See intricacy, complication, entanglement.)

COMPLIANCE

adjectives
immediate; faithful; servile; suave; entreating; implicit; infantile; calm; strict.

verbs
balk at—; betoken—; bow in—; coerce into—; demand—; desire—; enforce—; fall into—with; gain—; move to—; necessitate —; press for—; profess—; propose—; refuse—; request—; signify—; utter—; yield—.
(See submission, concession, acquiescence.)

COMPLIANT

adverbs
obligingly; gently; readily; willingly; vexatiously; slavishly; obsequiously; pleasantly; meekly; timidly; obediently; supinely; spinelessly; weakly; devotedly; passively; submissively; deferentially; affectionately; faithfully; loyally; unwillingly; rebelliously; sweetly; gladly; implicitly; childishly; calmly.

COMPLICATED

adverbs
hopelessly; senselessly; foolishly; necessarily; purposely; seriously; dangerously; ominously; sadly; perplexingly; embarrassingly; unavoidably; queerly; strangely; alarmingly; interestingly; disconcertingly; bafflingly; astonishingly; unintelligibly; ridiculously; confusingly; bewilderingly; desperately; painfully; plaguedly.

COMPLICATION

adjectives
serious; unseen; interesting; threatening; sad; annoying; embarrassing; military; endless; ingenious; delicate; everlasting; perplexing; indispensable; annoying; constant; dangerous; simple; psychological; dizzying; fresh; queer; added; social; imaginative; international; unforeseen.

verbs
avoid—; bar—; catch in—; develop—; free from—; guard against—; induce—; involve—; prevent—; result in—; solve—; suffer—; —abates; —arises; —endangers; —occurs.
(See complexity, entanglement, intricacy, confusion.)

COMPLICITY

adjectives
potential; secret; treacherous; eager; energetic; guilty; deceptive.

verbs
accuse of—; act in—with; charge with—; clear of—; convict of—; deal in—; free of—; imprison for—; involve in—; suspect of—; vindicate of—.
(See guilt.)

COMPLIMENT

adjectives
genial; pleasant; admirable; handsome; rare; high; generous; apt; polite; fervid; sincerest; respectful; justified; honest; delicate; smooth-tongued; high-flown; flowery; stilted; grudging; left-handed; fulsome; dubious; youthful; peculiar; unphilosophical; noncommittal; questionable; erudite; abstracted; subtle; appropriate; gentle; awkward; indirect; feminine; gratifying; truculent; stipulated; supreme; piquant; munificent; bombastic; professional; superlative; gallant; ephemeral; deferential; mawkish; double-barreled; formal; undeniable; sugared; two-edged; exaggerated; idle; well-turned; tactful; novel;affectionate; ghastly; hyperbolic.

verbs
accept—; acknowledge—; allow—; bestow—; deliver—; disdain—; expect—; extend—; favor with—; greet with—; imply—; pay—; present—; receive—; return—; turn—; —commends; —flatters; —pleases; —praises; —soothes.

(See greeting, remembrance, congratulation, praise.)

COMPLIMENT (*v*)

adverbs
warmly; genially; admirably; handsomely; rarely; highly; generously; aptly; fervidly; sincerely; justifiedly; delicately; stiltedly; grudgingly; fulsomely; dubiously; eruditely; subtly; appropriately; awkwardly; indirectly; gratifyingly; bombastically; supremely; piquantly; professionally; superlatively; gallantly; deferentially; mawkishly; formally; undeniably; exaggeratedly; idly; affectionately; hyperbolically.

(See praise.)

COMPLIMENTARY

adverbs
delightfully; flatteringly; gallantly; charmingly; politely; exaggeratedly; absurdly; smilingly; chivalrously; adoringly; pleasingly; highly; sincerely; appropriately; affectionately; truly; honestly; grudgingly; dubiously; questionably; subtly; gently; indulgently; pompously; supremely; deferentially; handsomely; lovingly.

COMPLY (*v*)

adverbs
promptly; strictly; willingly; gladly; partially; slavishly; humbly; irritably; nonchalantly; bitterly; sourly; grimly; carelessly.

(See agree, consent.)

COMPONENT

adjectives
essential; necessary.

adverbs
fundamentally; essentially; necessarily; indispensably; unavoidably; constitutionally; organically; vitally.

COMPOSE

adverbs
nominally; identically; wholly; partly; artistically; largely; simultaneously; incessantly; luckily; prolifically; abundantly; charmingly; picturesquely; didactically; pretentiously; ludicrously; vilely; monstrously; allegorically; monumentally; orchestrally; historically; fantastically; chorally; crudely; elaborately; vitally; gravely; dramatically; humorously; gracefully; creatively; realistically.

(See lull, calm.)

COMPOSER

adjectives
native; brilliant; voluminous; contemporary; eminent; operatic; productive; talented; anxious; instinctive; ultramodern; best-known; foremost; outstanding; exuberant; modernist; versatile; pharisaical; famous; hack; master; deft; practiced.

COMPOSITION

adjectives
decorative; didactic; careless; pretentious; ludicrous; tragic; vile; dishonorable; artistic; unwieldy; monstrous; secular; monumental; reposeful; allegorical; touching; fugitive; orchestral; historical; intensive; feminine; studied; capricious; fantastic; motley; choral; essential; elaborate; crude; important; vital; grave; dramatic; humorous; graceful; striking; aesthetic; creative: realistic.

verbs
adjust—; alter—; arrange—; compound—; deliver—; fashion—; form—; frame—; interpret—; order—; polish—; prepare—; print—; release—; reshape—; score—; toss off—; transpose—; versify—; vocalize—; —involves.

(See essay, story.)

COMPOSURE

adjectives
perfect; kind; gentle; magnificent; incomparable; unruffled; flintlike; utmost; splendid; absolute; unimpaired; astonishing; solemn; curious; labored; grave; hard; horrible; contemptuous; reticent; equable; uncanny; airy; mournful; melancholy; marble; seeming; insolent; extraordinary; austere; inflexible; strained; undisturbed; dogged; comparative; amiable; cruel; unshakable; affected.

verbs
blemish—; break—; enjoy—; feign—; handle with—; maintain—; mar—; meet with—; preserve—; recover—; regain—; settle in—; shake—; shock out of—; view with—; —disarms; —follows.
(See equanimity, serenity.)

COMPOUND

adjectives
hypothetical; monstrous; metallic; disastrous; ferrous; utmost; rankest; argenteous; thermoplastic; harmonious; complicated; deliquescent; linguistic; tantalizing; elaborate; ingenious; chemical; incongruous.

verbs
absorb—; analyze—; break down—; characterize—; combine in—; derive—from; devise—; dissolve—; form—; heat—; indicate—; make up—; meet—; mix—; prescribe—; stir—; stimulate—; unite in—.
(See mixture, combination.)

COMPREHEND (*v*)

adverbs
fully; perfectly; readily; rightly; intelligently; discriminatingly; partially; scientifically; deeply; accurately; generally; dispassionately; tardily; masterfully; instinctively.
(See grasp, understand.)

COMPREHENSION

adjectives
conspicuous; intelligent; calm; infant; social; absent; discriminating; untrained; perfect; martial; vast; human; growing; enlightened; scientific; deeper; accurate; easy; imaginative; adequate; general; faithful; quick; dispassionate; gathering; complete; unparalleled; tardy; masterly; instinctive; dawning.

verbs
achieve—; affect—; attain—; attempt—; benumb—; enlarge—; exhibit—; extend—; feign—; go beyond—; grasp—; include in—; lack—; listen with—; simulate—; stagger—; view with—; warp—; —dawns; —results in.
(See understanding, apprehension, knowledge.)

COMPREHENSIVE

adverbs
wonderfully; broadly; unusually; fortunately; cogently; liberally; tolerantly; tolerably; fairly; extremely; luckily; purposely; explicitly; advantageously; generously; admirably; delightfully; superbly; conspicuously; nobly; strikingly; unquestionably; impressively; astonishingly.

COMPRESS (*v*)

adverbs
firmly; severely; savagely; bitterly; tightly; angrily; powerfully; dramatically.
(See crowd.)

COMPROMISE

adjectives
expensive; unworthy; lean; sensible; timid; tolerable; workable; proposed; wise; self-sufficient; practical; judicious; tacit; occasional; dignified; negotiated; imaginable; ineffectual; prudent; pitiful; strange; cowardly; ultimate; wretched; curious; scorning.

verbs
accept—; achieve—; agree upon—; announce—; arrange—; arrive at—; attempt—; come to—; conclude—; consent to—; draw up—; effect—; extend—; maintain—; offer—; result in—; risk—; —adjusts; —decides; —recommends; —reconciles; —settles; —soothes.
(See agreement, settlement, promise.)

COMPROMISING

adverbs
unfortunately; possibly; alarmingly; leniently; sensibly; reasonably; opportunely; fearfully; timidly; timorously; bravely; courageously; senselessly; scandalously; recklessly; indiscreetly; curiously; indubitably; injudiciously; awkwardly; unluckily; evasively; unhappily; unwisely; shockingly; appallingly; rashly; appeasingly.

COMPULSION

adjectives
silent; irresistible; subtle; fascinated; armed; legal; restraining; unrecognized; physical; sad; temperamental; moral; strong; inescapable.

verbs
accept under—; act in—; appear under—; commit under—; confess under—; develop by—; devise by—; exercise—; involve—; obey under—; rebel at—; resist—; restrain by—; submit under—; wring out by—; —exculpates; —forces.

(See coercion, force, necessity, restraint, obligation.)

COMPULSORY

adverbs
disagreeably; hatefully; substantially; significantly; dangerously; disturbingly; implicitly; strictly; rigidly; hideously; flagrantly; wisely; sensibly; cruelly; detestably; odiously; wickedly; irksomely; arbitrarily; officially; locally; inescapably; fortunately; annoyingly; tediously; prosily; vexatiously; needlessly; ineffectively; irresistibly; silently; subtly; sadly; inexorably; stringently; peremptorily; terrifyingly; actually; authoritatively; absolutely; dominantly; imperiously; originally; sternly; necessarily.

COMPUNCTION

adjectives
slight; severe; grievous; motherly; evident; mathematical; natural; bitter.

COMPUTATION

adjectives
careful; sardonic; arithmetical; subsequent; moderate; impressive; ridiculous.

verbs
calculate—; check—; correct—; corroborate—; employ—; err in—; estimate—; fail in—; fall short of—; find by—; increase—; inspect—; prove—; reach by—; reckon—; scorn—; —accounts for; —differs; —helps; —indicates.

(See calculation, reckoning.)

COMPUTE (*v*)

adverbs
accurately; sketchily; carefully; arithmetically; mathematically; geometrically; impressively; ridiculously; statistically; scientifically.

(See calculate, estimate.)

COMRADE

adjectives
worthy; fastidious; gallant; benevolent; wounded; self-denying; placid; hackneyed; suffocated; inseparable (pl); little; garrulous; abiding; agreeable; wonder-loving; intellectual; exhausted; needy; sensible; merry; conforming; loyal; bickering; gluttonous.

verbs
aid—; applaud—; assist—; associate with—; betray—; forsake—; fraternize with—; gain—; march with—; protect—; share with—; shield—; treasure—.

(See companion, associate, mate.)

COMRADELY

adverbs
loyally; devotedly; sympathetically; cordially; warmly; helpfully; heartily; amicably; affably; frankly; distinctly; congenially; unselfishly; staunchly; generously; courageously; gallantly; agreeably; faithfully; gaily; comfortably; entertainingly; curiously; unobtrusively; quietly; sociably; chattily.

COMRADESHIP

adjectives
happy; warm; flattering; unconditional; spiritual; impossible; ceaseless; genuine; kindly; pleasant; tragic; deep-hearted; constant; simple; rare; international; lifelong; sympathetic; unspeakable.

CONCEAL (*v*)

adverbs
cleverly; effectually; criminally; partially; instinctively; feloniously; dexterously; deliberately; stupidly; ignorantly; guiltily; conscientiously; fearfully; scrupulously.

(See hide, suppress.)

CONCEALMENT

adjectives
expedient; ignorant; stupid; coarse; juggling; ladylike; watery.

verbs
appear from—; attempt—; disclose—; divulge—; effect—; intend—; lay bare—; necessitate—; offer—; place in—; reveal—of; seek refuge in—; suspect—; uncover—; veil in—; wrap in—.

(See secretion, seclusion, privacy.)

CONCEDE (v)

adverbs

deferentially; completely; unexpectedly; apologetically; willingly; generally; tactfully; frankly; generously; tamely; gently; freely; liberally.

(See yield, admit.)

CONCEIT

adjectives

devastating; quaint; mere; whimsical; colossal; comical; solemn; peculiar; lessening; sanguine; keen; erroneous; piteous; stupid; rational; boyish; staple; enigmatic; graceful; profound; doubtful; partial; presumptuous; lively; ingenious; gallant; noble; true; innocent; earthy; gross; fantastic; literary; passing; imperious; self-centered; melancholy; artificial; sickening; modest; fabulous; false; platonic; vain; immense.

verbs

bare—; cloud with—; deplore—; devour with—; display—; fill with—; humor—; puff up with—; rebuke—; shatter—; soak in—; swallow up by—; tickle—; wallow in—; ween—; —disgusts; —exaggerates; —inflames; —overestimates; —overvalues; —prejudices; —robs; —twists.

(See egotism, pride, vanity.)

CONCEITED

adverbs

harmlessly; ludicrously; solemnly; piteously; ridiculously; arrogantly; intolerably; stupidly; gracelessly; presumptuously; innocently; grossly; fantastically; offensively; imperiously; sickeningly; immensely; disgustingly; foolishly; inordinately; contemptibly; amusingly; ingenuously; artlessly; complacently; prodigiously; colossally; unconsciously; unwittingly; awkwardly; foppishly; simperingly; stagily; abominably; laughably; pathetically; noisily; theatrically; transparently; unreasonably; loftily; grandly; undeniably; extremely; palpably; remarkably; incredibly.

CONCEIVABLE

adverbs

scarcely; possibly; readily; easily; fantastically; reasonably; sensibly; hardly; barely; obscurely; oddly; grotesquely; faintly; ridiculously; probably; presumably; romantically; preposterously; theoretically; fancifully; appallingly.

CONCEIVE (v)

adverbs

wondrously; hastily; chastely; humbly; craftily; admirably; distinctly; harshly; instantly; empirically; artistically; ingeniously; effectually; erroneously; majestically; nobly; inspiringly; popularly; narrowly; uniquely; morally; politically; cynically; definitely; puerilely; sentimentally; liberally; nebulously; intellectually; romantically; unchristianly; traditionally; previously; exaltedly; dramatically; subjectively; aesthetically; musically; competitively; peculiarly; erroneously; vitiatedly; incongruously; spontaneously; idealistically; judicially; crudely; grandly; divinely; immaculately; sympathetically.

(See understand, imagine.)

CONCENTRATE (v)

adverbs

swiftly; mentally; logically; intensely; fruitfully; protractedly; deliberately; achingly; devoutly; exhaustively; grimly; intently; desperately; incessantly; persistently; passionlessly; impassionedly; carefully; ambitiously; wholly.

(See focus.)

CONCENTRATION

adjectives

mental; intense; logical; zestful; vague; dreamy; undue; fruitful; physical; protracted; deliberate; agonized; aching; devout; exhausting; grim; perpetual; desperate; implacable; administrative; deadly; intent; desired; completed; incessant; persistent; pronounced; impassioned; careful; gigantic.

verbs

affect—; cultivate—; direct—; gain by—; gather in—; lose in—; necessitate—; produce—; require—; strive for—; —collects; —empowers; —enables; —intensifies; —strengthens; —unifies.

(See condensation, contraction.)

CONCEPT

adjectives

cynical; ethereal; social; major; permanent; simple; beneficent; fundamental; negative; petty; platonic; economic; emotional; rational; mystical; anthropopsychic; consonant; abstract; steady; liberal; heroic; ridiculous; idiotic.

verbs
accept—; build up—; discard—; express—; form—; guard—; hallow—; idealize—; join in—; lose—; master—; produce—; reshape—; reverence—; symbolize—; —develops; —disappears; —fades; —grows.
(See idea, conception, thought, notion.)

CONCEPTION

adjectives
majestic; noble; lofty; proud; inspiring; popular; beautiful; imperial; powerful; daring; profound; accurate; just; coherent; ingenious; undiluted; curious; unique; narrow; haziest; raw; immature; moral; military; brilliant; mental; political; cynical; definite; puerile; sentimental; novel; liberal; fixed; abstract; easy; inward; general; nebulous; artistic; imaginative; intellectual; evolutionary; theologic; ethical; romantic; freer; objective; movie; arabesque; unchristian; utopian; traditional; previous; exalted; true; delicate; grotesque; distinguished; gross; crude; dramatic; sensuous; wildest; essential; subjective; aesthetic; musical; dynamic; faintest; fickle; competitive; physical; adequate; theoretical; ancient; poetic; original; admirable; peculiar; erroneous; vitiated; serviceable; advanced; incongruous; spontaneous; idealistic; hysterical; cherished; judicial; fabulous; dim; vague; crude; gracious; rival; radiant; grand; different; proper; divine; immaculate; sordid; dominant; sympathetic; continental.

CONCEPTION

verbs
accept—; acquire—; attain—; base—; blur—; broaden—; clarify—; classify—; color—; confuse—; derive—; destroy—; disrupt—; divorce from—; embody—; endow—; enlarge—; envisage—; exalt—; expound—; fulfill—; gain—; give—; implant—; inherit—; justify—; perfect—; ponder—; reflect—; rest on—; revise—; school in—; set aside—; translate—; —exists; —denotes; —forms; —prevails.
(See idea, notion, concept, impression, imagination.)

CONCERN (*business*)

adjectives
pioneer; long-established; competing; successful; dominating; settled; private; commercial; ultra-respectable; prospective; pretentious.

CONCERN (*feeling*)

adjectives
sweet; kindly; tender; mild; affectionate; anxious; eager; charitable; intense; human; sympathetic; pitying; agonizing; real; honest; deep; serious; grave; consuming; jealous; secondary; irritable; superfluous; dramatic; suprasensual; primary; personal; lifelong; general; vital; ever-pressing; mutual; patent; complex; terrestrial; interior; materialistic; temporal; immediate; flourishing; pressing; extreme; disquieting; ethical; soft; menial; waking; paramount; nonchalant; hypochondriacal.

verbs
cause—; contemplate with—; create—; demonstrate—; detect—; ease—; engage—; excite—; feel—; feign—; frown with—; involve—; lift—; manifest—; neglect—; plead—; pretend—; question—; regard with—; relate with—; share—; throw into—; trouble with—; —vexes.
(See anxiety, care.)

CONCERN (*v*)

adverbs
feverishly; intelligently; intimately; immensely; intensely; principally; solely; tenderly; mildly; affectionately; humanly; anxiously; eagerly; charitably; sympathetically; gravely; consumingly; jealously; dramatically; mutually; patently; materially; disquietingly; ethically; passionately.
(See worry.)

CONCERNED

adverbs
deeply; anxiously; financially; nationally; personally; appallingly; vitally; scandalously; curiously; excitedly; nervously; strangely; unaccountably; justly; responsibly; unfortunately; uneasily; importantly; heavily; solicitously; inseparably; undeniably; painfully; seriously; gravely; primarily; materially; surreptitiously; secretly.

CONCERT

adjectives
classical; orchestral; spiritual; thrilling; indoor; monster; basic; charitable; home; impromptu.

CONCERTED

adverbs
effectively; influentially; efficiently; strongly; irresistibly; favorably; clannishly; irrepressibly; invincibly; alertly; thoughtfully; resolutely; vigilantly; guardedly; securely;

legally; legitimately; warrantably; justifiably; formidably; confidently; ably; authoritatively; adaptably.

CONCESSION

adjectives
radical; scandalous; surprising; trivial; veritable; voluntary; momentary; mutual; temporary; secret; valuable; unconscious; generous; dignified; minor; gracious; reciprocal; commercial; vital; unwise; unlimited; cowardly; benevolent; original; liberal; sufficient; pencil-making; political; unusual; unworthy.

verbs
accept—; allot—; allow—; appreciate—; claim—; demand—; exact—; execute—; exploit—; force into—; grant—; obtain—; receive—; refuse—; scorn—; submit to—; warrant—; yield—; —admits; —ameliorates; —fails; —infers; —mitigates.
(See privilege, right, favor, allowance.)

CONCILIATION

adjectives
harmonious; promoted; predetermined; unattainable; replete; voluntary; amiable; tender; lenient.

verbs
accept—; achieve—; attempt—; bring into—; declare—; dispute—; effect—; hope for—; offer—; open avenues of—; promote—; recommend—; strive for—; tease into—; welcome—; win—; —harmonizes; exhibit—.
(See reconciliation.)

CONCILIATORY

adverbs
hopefully; possibly; presumably; properly; justly; wisely; sagaciously; favorably; sensibly; reasonably; soundly; fairly; profoundly; craftily; subtly; shrewdly; deceptively; fortunately; decently; respectfully; generously; honestly; appropriately; judiciously; impressively; moderately.

CONCISE

adverbs
gratifyingly; remarkably; satisfactorily; surprisingly; pleasingly; pleasantly; briefly; compactly; crisply; laconically; tersely; conventionally; conveniently; exceedingly; curtly; pointedly; inexpressibly; faultlessly; commendably; laudably; extraordinarily; strikingly; necessarily; sensibly; wisely; prudently.

CONCLUDE

adverbs
sorrowfully; erroneously; inevitably; cynically; peremptorily; definitely; abruptly; pessimistically; tartly; amicably; summarily; jocosely; confidently; coolly; officially; triumphantly; contemptuously; reasonably; legitimately; brilliantly; theoretically; logically; humiliatingly; despairingly; irresistibly; obviously; rationally; preposterously; statistically; ultimately; fallaciously; tragically; hypothetically; misleadingly.
(See end, close.)

CONCLUSION

adjectives
official; generalized; conducive; triumphant; intelligible; contemptuous; doubtful; still; strict; legitimate; practical; definite; inevitable; vile; languid; painful; speculative; spiritualistic; solid; meager; practiced; satisfactory; reasonable; brilliant; virtuous; lurid; adventurous; foregone; theoretic; suitable; logical; compulsory; negative; ungracious; erroneous; murdering; palpable; bloody; humiliating; consolatory; dreary; preliminary; impotent; happy; sterile; demonstrated; scientific; auspicious; pregnant; valuable; horrible; devastating; despairing; portentous; irresistible; victorious; trivial; obvious; rational; abrupt; preposterous; statistical; ultimate; farcical; astonishing; surprising; fallacious; lame; subversive; opposite; tragic; hypothetical; critical; spooky; necessary; tricky; misleading.

verbs
accept—; admit—; arrive at—; base—on; bias—; bring to—; build—; carry to—; confirm—; crown—; deduce—; delude—; divine—; draw—; enunciate—; escape—; establish—; formulate—; induce—; influence—; jump to—; lead to—; march to—; perceive—; prejudice—; reach—; refute—; reinforce—; seek—; set down—; shake—; shape—; strengthen—; substantiate—; support—; sustain—; tolerate—; weigh—; win—; —fades; —follows.
(See decision, determination, deduction, completion.)

CONCLUSIVE

adverbs
satisfactorily; officially; doubtfully; legally; definitely; painfully; reasonably; ungraciously; positively; absolutely; decisively; arbitrarily; dogmatically; incontestably;

categorically; tyrannically; unmistakably; brutally; hopelessly; firmly; disagreeably; peremptorily; unconditionally; finally; uncannily; unalterably; happily.

CONCOCTION

adjectives
promoting; bitter; delicious; fatal; philanthropic; potent.

CONCOMITANT

adverbs
usually; habitually; naturally; presumably; probably; inevitably; recurrently; occasionally; reasonably; definitely; ordinarily; assuredly; undoubtedly; apparently; evidently; unavoidably; inescapably; painfully; unfortunately; strangely; miraculously; always; providentially; significantly; luckily; deliberately; designedly.

CONCORD

adjectives
never-ending; everlasting; universal; perfect; gentle; sweeping; jarring.

CONCOURSE

adjectives
fortuitous; gallant; immense; abusive; vast; numerous (pl); divine; affected; orderly; deep.

CONCRETE

adverbs
convincingly; satisfactorily; actually; explicitly; expressly; objectively; substantially; sensibly; perceptibly; representatively; appreciably; unequivocally; unmistakably; demonstrably; intelligently; decisively; intelligibly; comprehensibly.

CONCUR (*v*)

adverbs
entirely; amiably; directly; heartily; halfheartedly; diplomatically; affably; casually; tentatively; provisionally; privately; unboundedly; tranquilly.
(See agree.)

CONCUSSION

adjectives
hearty; fearful; tremendous; momentary; enormous.

CONDEMN (*v*)

adverbs
unjustly; unmercifully; irrevocably; universally; intentionally; mildly; mercilessly; unhesitatingly; petulantly; emphatically; unanimously; bitterly; publicly; unqualifiedly; unhesitatingly; blindly; severely; drastically; indignantly; barbarously; formally.
(See censure, blame.)

CONDEMNATION

adjectives
bitter; unqualified; sharp; public; critical; sweeping; unhesitating; blind; severest; vigorous; censorious; sorrowful; active; reverberating; drastic; unhesitating; iniquitous; unanimous; cruel; scornful; indignant.

verbs
announce—; deserve—; fall into—; judge —; launch—; merit—; procure—of; pronounce—; repent—; reproach with—; spare—; steep in —; —blames; —censures; —inflames; —libels; —slanders.
(See denunciation.)

CONDENSATION

adjectives
amazing; conjoined; hasty; literal; moderate; sensible; viscous.

verbs
effect—; hasten—; —compresses; —concentrates; —converts; —crowds; —eliminates; —hardens; —intensifies; —purifies; —reduces; —thickens; —vaporizes; —heats.
(See contraction.)

CONDESCEND (*v*)

adverbs
urbanely; graciously; ostentatiously; hypocritically; patronizingly; haughtily; languidly; stiffly; benignantly; amusingly; gently; amiably; magnanimously.
(See yield.)

CONDESCENSION

adjectives
gradual; ostentatious; hypocritical; patronizing; lofty; haughty; languid; stiff; graceful; benignant; edifying; condoling; infinite; good-natured; familiar; awful; terrifying; presidential; amusing; gentle; utmost; amiable; degrading.

CONDITION

adjectives
excellent; perfect; satisfactory; ideal; pathological; prepossessing; happy; blissful; remarkable; unusual; stringent; robust; righteous; tumbled; primitive; dilapidated; neglected; unsanitary; crowded; miserable; terrible; deplorable; woeful; pitiful; gloomy; below par; demoralized;

alarming; untidy; fatigued; distracted; productive; senile; mental; unsettled; financial; gaseous; ultimate; permanent; natural; relaxed; garrulous; hard; analogous; harsh; proper; normal; correct; genial; glamorous; inspiring; delectable; humane; contemporary; dangerous; chaotic; changing; temporal; local; grim; corrupt; pleasant; evil; unfavorable; quiet; working; early; stipulated; defined; varying; existing; hazardous; severe; embryonic; calamitous; operating; parlous; servile; underlying; rational; peculiar; degraded; wretched; degenerate; interesting; flowing; discouraging; artificial; erotic; fluctuating; adverse; slight; disabled; neglected; ill; molten; outward; altered; poisoned; responsive; ameliorated; inferior; industrial; abject; starving; infamous; foot; expressed; optical; grievous; flourishing; inchoate; ultimate; top-notch; depraved; unsightly; unbailed; distressing; threatening; unsatisfactory; disturbed; semi-barbarous; undated; prolonged; chronic; stagnant; delicate; incompatible; belligerent; vapory; hopeless; molecular; rigid; fluid; atmospheric; frightful; impaired; moribund; aeronautical; helpless; critical; social; intellectual; established; humblest; embarrassed; bruised; political; drooping; prostrate; arid; thriving; ragged; dreadful; introverted; muddy; complicating; traffic; subgrade; unique; cheeky; destitute; nourishing; visceral; taut; contrasting; inflammatory; amorphous; surrounding; climatic; hypnotic; healthy; antecedent; clogged; encumbered; sober; lamentable; crippled; acute; pecuniary; opposing; ignoble; temporary; famishing; incurable; elastic; seraphic; upset; identical; light; irritated; anguished; tubercular; gruelling; convulsive; befuddled; unhygienic; defenseless; spasmodic; morbid; equivalent; special; cold; heterogeneous; disordered; atomic; perilous; habitable; succulent; certain; unbearable; deterrent; cataleptic; humbler; prevailing; linguistic; odd; sophisticated; desolate; quick; ruinous; exhausted; disastrous; bewildering; desiccated; foolish; precise; replenished; humble; itching; depleted; slovenly; idyllic; impassable; negative; perplexed.

verbs
abolish—; accept—; accustom to—; adapt to—; affect—; aggravate—; alter—; ameliorate—; analyze—; appraise—; avoid—; benefit by—; better—; cavil—; check—; comply with—; comprehend—; conquer—; consider—; contribute to—; convert—; cope with—; create—; depend on—; designate—; diagnose—; discover—; elucidate—; embrace—; encounter—; enter on—; eradicate—; exaggerate—; exemplify—; exempt from—; foresee—; fulfill—; govern—; heal—; ignore—; impose—; improve—; inform of—; investigate—; judge—; manifest—; mark—; neglect—; obviate—; portray—; prophesy—; protest—; recognize—; rectify—; regard—; regulate—; rejuvenate—; relieve—; remedy—; restore—; rule—; scorn—; simulate—; stabilize—; stipulate—; subject to—; submit to—; taint—; thrive on—; treat—; ward off—; welcome—; yield to—; —arises; —attends; —characterizes; —culminates in; —embitters; —ensues; —evolves; —indicates; —permits; —persists; —prevails; —provokes; —recurs; —reflects; —shifts; —spreads; springs from—; —threatens; —vanishes; —warrants; —yields to.

(See state, plight, situation.)

CONDITIONAL

adverbs
wisely; definitely; stringently; deplorably; properly; unfortunately; explicitly; reasonably; ungraciously; tersely; curtly; offensively; repugnantly; humiliatingly; auspiciously; trivially; favorably; rationally; surprisingly; trickily; equivocally; provokingly; treacherously; deviously; perplexingly; unacceptably; fantastically.

CONDONE (*v*)

adverbs
sentimentally; magnanimously; freely; sanctimoniously; unqualifiedly; humanely; broad-mindedly; intelligently; tenderly; affectionately; willingly; absolutely.

(See pardon.)

CONDUCIVE

adverbs
actually; essentially; significantly; distinctly; fundamentally; valuably; originally; splendidly; meritoriously; superbly; indubitably; definitely; expressly; enduringly; surprisingly; virtually; actively; serviceably; indispensably; profitably; indescribably; indisputably.

CONDUCT

adjectives
private; meritorious; exemplary; commendable; efficient; high; sane; civilized; plausible; consistent; circumspect; chivalrous; gallant; lazy; mannerless; unmanly; un-

ruly; annoying; indecorous; flagitious; instinctive; rebellious; licentious; abstemious; intemperate; editorial; criminal; theatrical; active; shameless; cruel; precipitate; fraudulent; inexplicable; barbarous; unyielding; daring; ungenerous; dishonest; peaceful; angelic; perverse; questionable; refractory; intolerable; neutral; patriotic; discreditable; irreproachable; disloyal; flagrant; flighty; analytical; unruly; outrageous; flamboyant; unethical; forward; arbitrary; obstreperous; bearish; boorish; courteous; perceptive; irascible; mad; depraved.

verbs
approve—; better—; correct—; decry—; denounce—; deprecate—; elevate—; emulate—; guide—; improve—; impugn—; influence—; interpret—; loathe—; pursue—; restrain—; shape—; —agitates; —conforms.
(See behavior.)

CONDUCT (*v*)

adverbs
inelegantly; rigidly; honorably; intelligently; prudently; improvidently; solemnly; marvelously; diligently; privately; secretly; commendably; efficiently; circumspectly; indecorously; rebelliously; licentiously; meritoriously; intemperately; editorially; criminally; theatrically; shamelessly; precipitately; fraudulently; barbarously; inexplicably; unyieldingly; daringly; dishonestly; peacefully; perversely; questionably; irreproachably; disloyally; analytically; unethically; arbitrarily; obstreperously; boorishly; courteously.
(See escort, lead.)

CONDUCTOR (*electric*)

adjectives
central; extended; brass; faulty; fixed; insulated; metallic; prime; water-tight.

verbs
ground—; insulate—; pass through—; shield—; tape—; —carries; —conveys; —shocks; —transmits.

CONDUCTOR (*escort or guide*)

adjectives
gifted; orchestral; philharmonic; natural; theatrical; amiable; poor; talented; celebrated.

verbs
tip—; uniform—; —accompanies; —collects; —directs; —escorts; —leads; —lectures; —motions; —signals; —guides.
(See guide, leader, escort.)

CONDUIT

adjectives
earthen; flood; secret; circuitous; transmitting; subterranean; water.

verbs
block—; bury—; clog—; connect—; drain—; force through—; issue from—; obstruct—; paint—; pipe through—; pour from—; pump through—; run through—; spout from—; —channels; —communicates; —conveys; —distributes; —freezes; —irrigates; —leads; —leaks; —protects; —rusts; —spouts; —transmits; —channels.
(See channel, canal, pipe, passage.)

CONE

adjectives
long; slender; truncated; symmetrical; veritable.

CONFECTION

adjectives
tasteless; mystic; sundry; delightful; cooked; appetizing; delicate.

CONFEDERATION

adjectives
absolute; powerful; vigorous; active; loyal.

CONFER (*v*)

adverbs
secretly; ostentatiously; freely; proposedly; hurriedly; briefly; privately; personally; officially; nationally; informally; ominously; endlessly; amicably; annually; softly; treacherously; rebelliously.
(See give, consult.)

CONFERENCE

adjectives
friendly; all-night; midnight; afternoon; dinner; proposed; rapid; hurried; whispered; brief; private; personal; long; wearisome; fateful; remarkable; regional; diplomatic; astronomical; family; official; arms; plenipotentiary; national; sad; radical; recent; emergency; worth-while; informal; preliminary; secret; ominous; homespun; amicable; endless; intended; extraordinary; soft; affable; casual; overheard; annual.

verbs
adjourn—; address—; break off—; bring before—; buckle down to—; close—; demand—with; dissolve—; gather in—; herald—; meet in—; preside over—; represent at—; resume—; sponsor—; urge—; —assembles; —collapses; —convenes; —discusses; —elects; —ensues; —formulates; —governs; —honors; —outlaws; —passes; —resolves; —rules.

(See consultation, assembly, meeting, council.)

CONFESS (*v*)

adverbs
ruefully; subsequently; truthfully; naively; timorously; hesitatingly; blushingly; penitently; candidly; gaily; blankly; humbly; frankly; affectionately; artlessly; shamefully; indiscreetly; unavailably; tacitly; touchingly; reciprocally; mortifyingly; abjectly; tearfully; belatedly; mysteriously; sincerely.

(See acknowledge, admit.)

CONFESSION

adjectives
tender; precious; eloquent; hopeful; naive; humble; honest; frank; full; complete; difficult; horrifying; shameful; deadly; indiscreet; voluptuous; phlegmatic; unavailing; liberal; honorable; tacit; plenary; revealing; bashful; touching; pitiful; reciprocal; soft; mortifying; abject; sham; constant; ecclesiastical; tearful; cool; belated; unconscious; mysterious; derisive; sincere; youthful; unsworn.

verbs
acknowledge—; beat out—; demand—; deny—; dictate—; drag out—; evidence—; force—; pour out—; record—; render—; repudiate—; rescind—; secure—; sign—; urge—; witness—; —absolves; —alleviates; —amends; —humbles; —humiliates.

(See statement.)

CONFIDANT

adjectives
intimate; faithful; special; ever-receptive; sympathetic.

CONFIDE (*v*)

adverbs
tearfully; languidly; apologetically; falteringly; timidly; loyally; genially; divinely; joyously; blithely; serenely; placidly; patriotically; arrogantly; spiritually; intellectually; unhesitatingly; profoundly; utterly; tactlessly; implicitly; tranquilly; pathetically; personally; charmingly; unsuspectingly; absolutely; unboundedly; complacently; wistfully.

(See trust. commit.)

CONFIDENCE

adjectives
gentle; sublime; fine; loyal; supreme; soft; wedded; divine; marvelous; ecstatic; gay; genial; joyous; blithe; touching; cheerful; certain; perfect; fullest; resolute; complete; boundless; utmost; limitless; inviolable; serene; calm; placid; sorry; silent; sober; patriotic; popular; renewed; immovable; easy; abiding; stern; arrogant; thrusting; spiritual; intellectual; infinite; presumptuous; invincible; unhesitating; sordid; utmost; assumed; strict; obliging; overweening; profound; veiled; restored; undiminished; buoyant; fullest; sincerest; utter; vanished; inspired; mutual; tactless; quiet; secure; fulsome; sketchy; unusual; industrial; heart-rending; tranquil; prophetic; pathetic; liberal; devilish; strong; superb; robust; shaken; animated; personal; imposing; charming; public; reminiscent; radiant; humble; preternatural; unsuspecting; absolute; unlimited; innocent; celebrated; unbounded; harassed; habitual; complacent; unreasonable; loving; admiring; snaring; heartfelt; unbroken; implicit; tender; childish; exaggerated; curious; sufficient; eager; wistful; vigorous; community; aboriginal.

verbs
beget—; betray—; blend in—; break—; breed—; buttress—; destroy—; dull—; dwell in—; earn—; enjoy—; establish—; evince—; evoke—; exchange—; express—; found in—; gravitate into—; honor with—; inspire—; interchange—; justify—; merit—; misplace—; mistrust—; reek—; regain—; register—; reject—; rejoice in—; renounce—; repose—in; restore—; root—in; shake—; share—; stimulate—; swear—; treat in—; undermine—; violate—; warrant—; weaken—; win—; —prevails; —soars; —wavers.

(See trust, faith, assurance, reliance.)

CONFIDENT

adverbs
absolutely; unreasonably; justifiably; egotistically; blatantly; extravagantly; gravely; seriously; shrewdly; assuredly; assuringly;

comfortably; comfortingly; sublimely; loyally; marvellously; genially; joyously; blithely; cheerfully; completely; calmly; placidly; quietly; serenely; imperturbably; sternly; presumptuously; overly; foolishly; fully; securely; unusually; tranquilly; impressively; charmingly; innocently; radiantly; unsuspectingly; habitually; complacently; curiously; encouragingly; courageously; egregiously; preposterously; rashly; absurdly; unjustifiably; unwarrantably; groundlessly; erroneously; profoundly.

CONFIDENTIAL

adverbs
strictly; necessarily; solemnly; terribly; mysteriously; portentously; ominously; seriously; vitally; stupendously; scrupulously; inviolately; momentously; significantly; essentially; intimately; sacredly; impressively; formidably; extremely; supremely.

CONFIGURATION

adjectives
geographical; tortured; certain; edifying; fundamental; classic.

CONFINE (v)

adverbs
exclusively; undeservedly; prudently; inexorably; mainly; remorselessly; necessarily; sedulously; comparatively; narrowly; continuously; irksomely.
(See restrict, restrain.)

CONFINEMENT

adjectives
solitary; respectful; prolonged; comparative; narrow; continuous; feverish; rigid; instant; irksome.

CONFIRM (v)

adverbs
speedily; stirringly; rapidly; strikingly; miraculously; unanimously; explicitly; concretely; abundantly; singularly; unexpectedly; instantaneously; amply; particularly.
(See affirm.)

CONFIRMATION

adjectives
complete; concrete; documentary; supplemental; splendid; singular; unexpected; instantaneous; unconscious; unexamined; fresh; particular; ample.

verbs
add the weight of—; ascertain—; authenticate—; dread—; establish—; inspect—; investigate—; maintain—; rejoice in—; sanction—; settle—; strengthen—; —assures; —convinces; —corroborates; —encourages; —fortifies; —legalizes; —proves; —ratifies; —removes doubt; —supports; —verifies.
(See ratification, proof.)

CONFLAGRATION

adjectives
frequent; devastating; disastrous; brilliant; nation-wide; mounting; enormous; widespread; delightful; amorous; raging; perpetual.

verbs
battle—; beat down—; contend with—; fight—; fan—; kindle—; prevent—; quell—; smother—; —blazes; —bursts out; —consumes; —deforests; —denudes; —dies; —envelops; —extends to; —menaces; —rages; —razes; —roars; —spreads; —threatens.
(See fire, blaze.)

CONFLICT

adjectives
triumphant; gigantic; stupendous; long; arduous; amorous; constant; eternal; ceaseless; sensational; heroic; dramatic; deliberate; determined; serious; severe; sharp; irrepressible; terrible; bitter; wasteful; violent; fierce; wanton; emotional; moral; general; visible; notorious; open; direct; external; coming; local; unfortunate; inevitable; sanguinary; approaching; irreconcilable; internal; civilized; irritating; unexpected; enormous; hopeless; impending; obstinate; fighting; deadly; desperate; immediate; disastrous; conscientious; earnest; class; bloody; obvious; unrelenting; savage; decisive; fiery; trying; mental; territorial; genial; protracted; brutal; decorous; tragic; linguistic; hopeless; commercial; hideous; armed; tumultuous; selfish; subjective; periodic; uncertain; psychic; intestinal.

verbs
avert—; avoid—; draw into—; elude—; end—; engage in—; experience—; explode in—; foment—; precipitate—; prolong—; provoke—; raise—; run into—; —bobs up; —bursts out; —consumes; —engulfs; —rages; —rends.
(See strife, battle, antagonism.)

CONFLICT (v)

adverbs
amorously; arduously; eternally; ceaselessly; sensationally; heroically; dramatically; deliberately; irresponsibly; violently; terribly; wantonly; emotionally; notoriously; morally; externally; locally; inevitably; irreconcilably; obstinately; desperately; disastrously; conscientiously; unrelentingly; savagely; decisively; mentally; commercially; tumultuously; subjectively.
(See interfere.)

CONFLUENCE

adjectives
riotous; harmonious; thickest; torrential; raging; seething; undistinguishable; peaceful; grateful.

CONFORM (v)

adverbs
tactfully; placidly; pusillanimously; complacently; docilely; strictly; entirely; rigidly; inflexibly; artistically; artificially; legally.

CONFORMATION

adjectives
athletic; peculiar; well-sculptured.

CONFORMITY

adjectives
complacent; pusillanimous; docile; strict; rigid.

CONFOUND (v)

adverbs
eternally; mysteriously; inexplicably; unspeakably; fathomlessly; gropingly; helplessly; inextricably
(See confuse.)

CONFRONT (v)

adverbs
bravely; indignantly; furiously; impudently; boldly; fearlessly; carelessly; brazenly; dramatically; theatrically; vociferously.
(See face, oppose.)

CONFUSE (v)

adverbs
paradoxically; wildly; deliberately; intricately; endlessly; inextricably; disastrously; emotionally; momentarily; infinitely; significantly; chaotically; intellectually; indescribably; feignedly; mentally; feverishly; socially; psychologically; mysteriously; purposely.
(See perplex, embarrass.)

CONFUSED

adverbs
delightfully; mysteriously; vaguely; perplexingly; hopelessly; strangely; comically; disastrously; completely; horribly; indescribably; visibly; manifestly; palpably; uproariously; tipsily; foggily; dazedly; rosily; brokenly; happily; incurably; pathetically; laughably; ridiculously.

CONFUSION

adjectives
joyous; cheerful; honest; orderly; multiple; endless; inextricable; strange; disastrous; hideous; sad; raging; wildest; lusty; deliberate; emotional; slight; flushed; misty; crimson; seeming; impersonal; peaceful; complete; topographical; blissful; momentary; deepening; infinite; picturesque; sweet; chaotic; irretrievable; tense; inextricable; hopeless; perpetual; crystalline; bosky; horrid; general; utter; utmost; ominous; significant; seeming; gibbering; dire; considerable; delightful; pretty; dreadful; studied; intellectual; speculative; indescribable; handsome; indistinct; tremendous; bubbling; multiform; feigned; visible; musical; whirling; mental; metaphysical; apparent; dusty; feverish; social; psychological; mysterious; manifold; crazy; melancholy; uproarious; disturbing; advertized; puzzling; commodious; vociferous; smiling.

verbs
afflict with—; boil with—; cover—; create—; deliver to—; eliminate—; embroil with—; fall into—; fill with—; flounder in—; grapple with—; heap—; lose in—; provoke—; retire in—; subdue—; subject to—; throw into—; weather—; work—; —aggravates; —ensues; —rises; —surrounds.
(See tumult, consternation, disorder, commotion, agitation, distraction.)

CONGEAL (v)

adverbs
instantaneously; readily; perfectly; partially; entirely; ultimately; normally; swiftly; rapidly; completely.
(See freeze.)

CONGENIAL

adverbs
completely; pleasantly; unusually; agreeably; charmingly; entertainingly; jovially; truly; happily; amiably; comfortably; curiously; delightfully; inestimably; distinctly;

unobtrusively; quietly; cheerfully; sociably; cosily; highly; exceedingly; unexpectedly; affably; unpretentiously; unaffectedly; artlessly.

CONGESTED

adverbs
hopelessly; inconveniently; dangerously; inordinately; needlessly; desperately; irremediably; impossibly; horribly; alarmingly; purposely; intentionally; stupidly; foolishly; senselessly; inextricably.

CONGESTION

adjectives
plethoric; cerebral; abnormal; prolonged; urban; slight; permanent.

verbs
accumulate—; clear—; heap in—; increase—; relieve—; —retards; —bars; —blocks; —crowds; —disorders; —hampers; —hinders; —impairs; —masses; —obstructs; —overcomes; —produces; —spreads; —weakens.
(See confusion.)

CONGLOMERATE

adverbs
ingeniously; heterogeneously; democratically; unmistakably; undeniably; utterly; curiously; interestingly; bewilderingly; confusedly; kaleidoscopically; staggeringly; internationally; unintelligibly; confusingly; diffusely; outlandishly; bizarrely; barbarically; inimitably; noisily; astoundingly; extravagantly; oddly; strangely.

CONGLOMERATION

adjectives
kaleidoscopic; multitudinous; staggering; curious; imperial.

CONGRATULATE (v)

adverbs
civilly; warmly; cordially; sincerely; dutifully; ceremoniously; facetiously; humbly; genially; volubly; effusively; solemnly; heartily; fulsomely; fiendishly.
(See sympathize.)

CONGRATULATIONS

adjectives
dutiful; abortive; ceremonious; facetious; humble; warmest; genial; voluble; solemn; heartiest.

verbs
acknowledge—; appreciate—; beam—; convey—; deliver—; deserve—; dismiss—; exchange—; express—; extend—; flood with—s; offer—; pay—; rejoice in—; return—; shower—; telegraph—; warrant—; wave away—; —gratify.
(See felicitation, sympathy.)

CONGRATULATORY

adverbs
pleasantly; dutifully; filially; grudgingly; ceremoniously; facetiously; happily; joyously; heartily; warmly; genially; jovially; jocosely; waggishly; proudly; solemnly; blessedly; rapturously; ecstatically; coolly; civilly; courteously; officially; politely; perfunctorily; obsequiously; unctuously; sententiously.

CONGREGATE (v)

adverbs
temptingly; silently; conservatively; piously; scantily; annually; triumphantly; sorrowfully; formally; diplomatically; dutifully.
(See gather.)

CONGREGATION

adjectives
motley; cultivated; dissolving; silent; dissenting; pious; foul; dispersing; scanty; sunburned; shaggy; staid; conservative.

verbs
assemble—; bless—; break up—; call—; come into—; cut off from—; distract—; gather—; offer to —; preach to—; rile—; sanctify—; separate from—; —breaks into song; —issues forth; —responds; —worships.
(See assembly, gathering.)

CONGRESS

adjectives
chaotic; international; bicameral; complaisant; musical; unique; legislative; filibustering.

verbs
discipline—; elect to—; empower—; importune—; prevail upon—; prod—; represent in—; seat in—; storm—; sway—; —adjourns; —appropriates; —assembles; —authorizes; —confers on; —confirms; —convenes; —debates; —deliberates; —designates; —dissolves; —frames; —func-

tions; —interviews; —lags; —legislates; —meets; —rebels; —reforms; —regulates; —rejects; —revises; —suspends; —taxes.
(See assembly, conference, legislature.)

CONGRESSMAN

adjectives
conspicuous; humorless; accomplished; grandiloquent; rabble-rousing; argumentative; glorified.

verbs
appeal to—; berate—; bribe—; criticize—; elect—; invite—; petition—; rally to—; reserve for—; run for—; select—; support—; —addresses; —men assemble; —men convene; —declines; —deliberates; —discusses; —filibusters; —introduces; —issues; —orates; —proposes; —protests; —questions; —represents; —signs; —withdraws.
(See legislator, senator, member.)

CONGRUITY

adjectives
separate; manifest; apparent; gratifying; practical; theoretical.

CONGRUOUS

adverbs
wholly; wonderfully; appropriately; nicely; exactly; accurately; entirely; aptly; adroitly; studiously; carefully; considerately; thoughtfully; becomingly; pertinently; relatively; agreeably; altogether; duly; happily; felicitously; opportunely; superbly; extraordinarily.

CONJECTURE

adjectives
whispered; frail; simple; stimulating; vague; languid; rational; bewildered; shrewd; right; straining; probable; plausible; sanguine; hurried; vacillating; speculative; half-hinted; serious; wild; cynical; fruitless; premature; alarming; vague.

verbs
absorb in—; base on—; cast—; conclude from—; form—; gather from—; infer from—; inject—; judge on—; offer—; propose—; scoff at—; scorn—; throw—; —guesses; —puzzles; —surmises.
(See guess, hypothesis, surmise, supposition, inference.)

CONJUNCTION

adjectives
successive; particular; clumsy; covert; helpful.

CONJUNCTURE

adjectives
fortunate; frequent; prodigious; delicate; straight; critical.

CONJURATION

adjectives
detestable; measured; spirited; inviolable; occult; mystic.

CONNECT (v)

adverbs
closely; organically; intimately; indissolubly; collaterally; innocently; eminently; honestly; inseparably; originally; exclusively; subtly; physiologically; remotely; unconsciously; persistently; matrimonially; adequately; lucratively; harmoniously; intellectually; surreptitiously; invisibly; uniformly; rigidly; profitably; vitally; perniciously; internationally.
(See join, link.)

CONNECTION

adjectives
reciprocal; physiological; closest; definite; remote; natural; intimate; unfathomable; unconscious; persistent; unbroken; illicit; valuable; influential; apparent; multifarious; judicious; matrimonial; fragmentary; uninterrupted; shameless; casual; obvious; adequate; touching; apparent; numerous; lucrative; remote; inevitable; mercantile; harmonious; manifold; intellectual; surreptitious; invisible; sole; florid; uniform; rigid; profitable; neat; positive; irregular; plausible; vital; pernicious; direct; deep-water; international; brief; genetic.

verbs
block—; break—; contract—with; disclaim —; dissolve—; establish—; fasten—; invalidate—; join in—with; link in—with; maintain—; mark—; mention in—with; prevent —; prohibit—; rend—; repudiate—; run in —with; sever—; snap—; —binds; —ties.
(See union, alliance, relationship, affiliation, association.)

CONNECTIVE

adjectives
social; iconoclastic; ineffectual; sturdy; tried.

CONNIVING

adjectives
petty; treasonable; clever; skillful; foxy; selfish.

CONNOISSEUR

adjectives
appreciative; true; profound; ogling; dramatic; amateur.

CONNOTATION

adjectives
biological; original; conventional; proper; sentimental; hazy.

CONQUER (*v*)

adverbs
technically; triumphantly; intellectually; eventually; honorably; personally; ultimately; romantically; basely; scientifically; partially; irresistibly.

(See **win.**)

CONQUEROR

adjectives
ultimate; sottish; roving; indigenous; vulgar; rapacious; satiate; daunted; virile; invisible; illustrious; single-handed; lesser.

verbs
hail—; herald—; honor—; overthrow—; proclaim—; welcome—; —acquires; —attains; —campaigns; —defeats; —enslaves; —gains; —invades; —masters; —overcomes; —pursues; —retreats; —subdues; —subjugates; —vanquishes; —wars.

(See **hero, army.**)

CONQUEST

adjectives
intellectual; territorial; illusory; unprovoked; honorable; vainglorious; continental; shameful; prophetic; industrial; imperial; personal; doubtful; amatory; remote; ultimate; easy; dazzling; barren; adventurous; romantic; material; barbarian; complete; base; air; unbroken; momentary; perpetual; fresh; hard-won; social; scientific; partial; furtive; rapid; notorious; feminine; irresistible; radical.

verbs
achieve—; acquire by—; crown—; effect—; enjoy the fruits of—; frustrate—; gain by—; herald—; inspire—; plunge into—; reap—; repel—; revel in—; revenge—; spread—; subdue by—; threaten—; win—; —captivates; —falters; —subdues; —subjugates; —succeeds; —stifles.

(See **victory, triumph.**)

CONSCIENCE

adjectives
smooth; haunting; latent; intellectual; padded; inflexible; insufferable; awakened; strenuous; quickening; guilty; drugged; beaten; stoned; sensitive; reproachful; artistic; obsessed; national; tender; obtuse; uneasy; straightforward; delicate; vast; floating; scientific; sensitive; capricious; filial; indulgent; fastidious; individual; obdurate; seared; well-seasoned; masterful; stricken; resolved; struggling; agonizing; heavy; unsilenced; proscriptive; renewed; peaceful; corrupted; condemning; fierce; judicial; worrying; ethical; aesthetic; perverse; poor; wounded; high; mute; alarmed; keen; free; super-developed; healthy; supreme; determined; clear; untroubled; twinging; aching; writhing; elastic; sluggish; bomb-proof; democratic; prickly; literary; celebrated; puritan; political; approving; private; childish.

verbs
alarm—; appeal to—; arouse—; cauterize—; compromise—; defile—; disburden—; ease—; examine—; fetter—; free—; invoke—; muffle—; offend—; pad—; purge—; quiet—; rectify—; rule by—; salve—; sear—; shake—; sour—; square—; suppress—; torment—; wake—; weaken—; wound—; wring—; —assails; —blames; —condemns; —convicts; —impels; —reproaches; —plagues; —prompts; —reproves; —slumbers; —tortures; —troubles; —twinges; —upbraids; —whispers.

(See **judgment.**)

CONSCIENTIOUS

adverbs
terribly; puritannically; extremely; rigorously; sternly; austerely; deeply; painfully; rigidly; stiffly; decorously; properly; unimpeachably; irreproachably; becomingly; stringently; dutifully; amenably; respectably; scrupulously; incorruptibly; courageously; lamentably; uncomfortably; ostentatiously; unnecessarily; carefully; foolishly.

CONSCIENTIOUSNESS

adjectives
exemplary; deep; historical; magnificent; stubborn; commendable; heroic.

CONSCIOUS

adverbs
fully; acutely; painfully; vividly; sharply; altogether; keenly; curiously; tinglingly; psychically; sorely; happily; uncomfortably;

wretchedly; pleasantly; rapturously; intensely; suddenly; poignantly; astutely; wholly; partially; slowly; wearily; actually; bitterly.

CONSCIOUSNESS

adjectives
full; private; inner; drowsier; ennobling; waking; joyous; veiled; guilty; perverted; bitter; instinctive; ever-abiding; susceptible; dawning; dim; proud; individual; well-founded; disagreeable; acute; living; unadmitted; amiable; gloomy; pleased; uplifting; mortifying; vivid; present; dreadful; despotic; widened; glad; glowing; impersonal; ineffable; half-bewildered; wordless; religious; glimmering; astonishing; sudden; joyful; intense; demure; collective; profound; transitory; shamefaced; lucid; reviving; inward; shaky; disintegrated; beatific; humble; native; growing; diffused; human; continental; pained; financial; class; political; social.

verbs
bestow—; bring to—; develop—; display—; drag to—; enfold—; indicate—; jar into—; lose—; obscure—; obsess—; percolate—; possess—; precede—; retain—; rub into—; seize with—; thrust into—; vanish from—; waken to—; —brings; —evolves.
(See sensation, feeling, intuition.)

CONSCRIPTION

adjectives
ruthless; established; legislated; mandatory; selective; indiscriminative.

CONSECRATE (v)

adverbs
specially; religiously; ceremoniously; hallowedly; reverently; formally; fittingly; impressively.
(See dedicate, hallow.)

CONSECRATED

adverbs
divinely; ecclesiastically; eternally; sacredly; early; devoutly; devotedly; faithfully; humbly; reverently; splendidly; conspicuously; avowedly; deeply; practically; notably; eminently; heroically; illustriously; piously; solemnly; gloriously; signally.

CONSECRATION

adjectives
immortal; pathetic; tragic; perpetual; ecclesiastical.

CONSECUTIVE

adverbs
conveniently; endlessly; monotonously; meticulously; punctiliously; carefully; accurately; impressively; rarely; handily; painstakingly; comfortably; accommodatingly; appropriately; properly; tediously; invariably; methodically; systematically; exactly; significantly; actually.

CONSENT

adjectives
unanimous; magnanimous; particular; ardent; tacit; grudging; reluctant; common; hard; general; cringing; mutual; unwilling; formal; personal; passive; generous; grumbling; effective; mournful; gracious.

verbs
announce—; batter into—; blush—; crave—; deny—; desire—; extend—; nod—; serve with—; suffer—; swear—; win—; wink—; write—; yield—.
(See acquiescence, compliance, approval, agreement.)

CONSENT (v)

adverbs
reluctantly; unwittingly; tacitly; handsomely; gloomily; instantly; sulkily; cheerfully; wisely; legally; unanimously; ardently; magnanimously; grudgingly; cringingly; mutually; unwillingly; formally; personally; passively; generously; mournfully; graciously; blandly.
(See agree, concur.)

CONSEQUENCE

adjectives
natural; territorial; eventual; disastrous; cruel; tremendous; necessary; self-evident; dramatic; dire; logical; inevitable; direct; lurking; ambushed; far-reaching; political; educational; perilous; unavoidable; permanent; favorable; momentous; sensational; serious; instantaneous; important; natural; surprising; paramount; probable; horrible; evil; debasing; fruitful; deplorable; certain; fatal; utmost; ethical; awful; unexpected; deepest; unforeseen; equivalent; temporal; invisible; viewless; heavy; mechanical; mischievous; injurious; dreadful; remoter; unshunned; catastrophic; desirable; possible; incalculable; wretched;

disagreeable; appalling; wonderful; beneficent; brilliant; obvious; patent; inescapable; vital; enormous; tragic; devastating; demoralizing; calamitous; unhappy; embarrassing; ultimate; physiological; emotional; social; financial; moral; risky; comical; small; foolish; involved; detailed; legal.

verbs
abide by—; appreciate—; avert—; balk at—; conceal—; dread—; deter by—; escape—; face—; ignore—; portray—; realize—; shun—; suffer—; torment by—; —ensues; —follows; —results in.
(See issue, result, outcome, importance, distinction, consideration.)

CONSEQUENTIAL

adverbs
evidently; ludicrously; ridiculously; arrogantly; pompously; stupidly; gracelessly; presumptuously; impressively; ostentatiously; grossly; fantastically; grotesquely; immensely; inordinately; amusingly; complacently; colossally; awkwardly; stagily; foppishly; laughably; theatrically; loftily; extremely; unbelievably; absurdly.

CONSERVATISM

adjectives
zealous; sprightly; stubborn; passionate; industrious; extreme; moderate; innate; disillusioned; smug; hearty; emotional.

verbs
abolish—; admire—; characterize by—; embody—; engender—; enliven—; epitomize—; hinder by—; practice—; preserve—; prod—; produce—; satisfy—; school in—; shrink from—; swerve from—; swing toward—; —crops up; —fears; —retains; —safeguards.
(See stability, conventionality.)

CONSERVATIVE

adjectives
uncompromising; extreme; staunchest; gruesome; obstinate; grim; sturdy; born; honest; cynical; stuffy; hidebound.

adverbs
incurably; tenaciously; consistently; obstinately; stubbornly; half-heartedly; permanently; solidly; stiffly; unchangeably; fixedly; firmly; immovably; resolutely; irrevocably; steadfastly; unalterably; inactively; quietly; passively; zealously; passionately; smugly; contentedly; pertinaciously; temperamentally.

CONSIDER (v)

adverbs
intrinsically; impartially; tenderly; duly; carnally; prospectively; lightly; maturely, accordingly; politically; honestly; anxiously; tentatively; dispassionately; seriously; previously; arithmetically; erroneously; respectfully; matrimonially; rationally; theoretically; belatedly; paternally; philosophically; delicately; momentously; sympathetically; unselfishly; posthumously; temporarily; shallowly; economically; sordidly; morally; optionally.
(See ponder, contemplate.)

CONSIDERABLE

adverbs
seriously; worthily; assuredly; notably; prominently; essentially; substantially; critically; imposingly; gravely; materially; remarkably; significantly; signally; vitally; momentously; impressively.

CONSIDERATE

adverbs
courteously; thoughtfully; tenderly; officiously; politely; deferentially; respectfully; appropriately; unusually; obsequiously; deliberately; generally; astutely; keenly; shrewdly; tenderly; mercifully; tolerantly; benevolently; charitably; generously; carefully; prudently; providently; hospitably; alertly; vigilantly; scrupulously.

CONSIDERATION

adjectives
theoretic; paternal; belated; distinguished; favorable; humanitarian; ethical; vital; special; tedious; individual; secondary; close; palpable; philosophic; calm; striking; delicate; tremendous; seeming; abstract; solemn; gracious; serious; momentous; indisputable; respectful; monetary; sympathetic; elusive; salient; important; unselfish; quiet; melancholy; ostensible; due; prime; obvious; mature; practical; minor; limited; partial; long; sedate; candid; fuller; posthumous; unspeakable; distracted; chivalrous; remote; keen; theoretical; various (pl.); confidential; thoughtful; reasoned; dominant; scanty; unhurried; careful; fatherly; triumphant; temporal; elaborate; predominant; common; ultimate;

judicial; weighty; practical; conscientious; difficult; half-hesitating; half-assenting; exclusive; enlarged; grateful; weightier; rational; unpleasing; regrettable; forego-ing; strategical; valuable; distinguished; momentary; urgent; scant; earnest; fair; fascinating; finer; grave; profoundest; pragmatic; marked; primary; careful; tender; prudent; dispassionate; cool; logic-al; intelligent; sordid; false; shallow; sel-fish; money; economic; material; moral; liberal; collateral; painful; constant; im-mediate; accumulated; optional; theoretical; rough; personal.

verbs
analyze—; bar—; compel—; dally with—; demand—; extend—; fade from—; gain—; increase—; merit—; quit—; stifle—; view with—; —actuates; —impresses; —sways.
(See thought.)

CONSIGN (v)

adverbs
everlastingly; formally; customarily; tacit-ly; solemnly; definitely; willingly; commer-cially.
(See command, commit.)

CONSISTENCY

adjectives
muddy; smoothest; possible; fatal; un-wavering; foolish; religious; external; un-broken; theoretical; chewy; conscious.

verbs
boil into—; depart from—; disrupt—; doubt—; establish—; give—to; induce—; practise—; preach—; preserve—; pro-fess—; pursue with—; remain in—; return to—; sacrifice—; stand on—; vary in—; —habituates; —harmonizes.
(See harmony.)

CONSISTENT

adverbs
admirably; dependably; conscientiously; imperturbably; undisturbedly; invariably; equitably; monotonously; conformably; pro-saically; agreeably; regularly; habitually; usually; uncompromisingly; queerly; un-failingly; properly; relatively; obstinately; unreasonably; reliably; altogether; coura-geously; unpleasantly; vapidly; extra-ordinarily; virtuously.

CONSOLATION

adjectives
bitter; inexpressible; profound; hollow; proudest; infallible; homely; tangible; mean; supreme; perfunctory; divine; sub-stantial; wonderful; ironic; religious; orthodox; clumsy; feeble; abiding; inward; infinitesimal.

verbs
admit of—; convey—; derive—; dismiss—; dispense with—; grant—; impart—; offer —; rejoice in—; seek —; secure—; take— from; —ameliorates; —cheers; —com-forts; —encourages; —mitigates; —recom-penses; —relieves; —solaces; —soothes.
(See solace, comfort, relief, support.)

CONSOLE (v)

adverbs
profoundly; hollowly; infallibly; perfunc-torily; divinely; substantially; ironically; religiously; clumsily; feebly; inwardly; infinitesimally; precipitately.
(See cheer, sympathize.)

CONSONANT

adjectives
concurring; mute; nasal; unaspirated; slur-red; elided; rumbling; jarring; harsh; true.

CONSORT

adjectives
ill-fated; gentle; sovereign; hovering; poor; feeble; wasted.

CONSPICUOUS

adverbs
highly; creditably; distinctly; gloriously; intentionally; disagreeably; unpleasantly; vainly; personally; eminently; exaltedly; arrogantly; absurdly; foolishly; unwisely; politically; deliberately; elaborately; fash-ionably; garishly; gaudily; loudly; noisily; officiously; unfortunately; shamefully; awk-wardly.

CONSPIRACY

adjectives
rebel; domestic; tacit; abortive; awkward; finespun; well-contrived; criminal; frater-nal; elaborate; organized; ravishing; pur-ported; irresistible; monstrous; political; dark; infamous; grim; pleasing; silent; popular; crackbrained; malevolent; nation-wide; alley; fatal.

verbs
block—; charge with—; combine in—; conceal—; contrive—; convict of—; disclose—; discover—; excite—; foil—; hatch—; incite—; indict for—; instigate—; intrigue in—; involve in—; plot—; punish—; strengthen—; uncover—; unearth—; —brews; —damages; —fails; —flourishes; —injures; —ripens; —succeeds.
(See plot, intrigue.)

CONSPIRATOR

adjectives
resident; audacious; crafty; baffled; chief; uneasy.

CONSPIRATORS

adjectives
capricious; criminal; fearful; illegal; implicated; fellow; mercenary; reprehensible; treasonable; plotting; seditious.

verbs
arm—; charge—; convict—; disclose—; execute—; expose—; foil—; hang—; join—; punish—; shield—; —chortle; —combine; —contrive; —devise; —engage; —intrigue; —plan; —plot.
(See plotter.)

CONSTABLE

adjectives
discomfited; discredited; learned; unskilled; blustering; rural; overmaligned.

verbs
appoint—; arm—; authorize—; commit to—; consign to—; deputize—; elect—; empower—; enroll—; escape—; overrule—; rank—; serve as—; uniform—; —administers; —arrests; —enforces; —fines; —imprisons; —quells; —sells.
(See officer, police.)

CONSTANCY

adjectives
infatuated; dangerous; unremitting; inviolable; unchangeable; admirable; true; inflexible; invincible; wonted.

verbs
admire—; amaze at—; attack—; attend with—; bear with—; boast of—; break—; commend—; conduct with—; endure with—; esteem—; exhibit—; inspire—; justify—; laud—; maintain—; occasion—; persist in—; praise—; require—; test—; tolerate with—; value—.
(See faithfulness, stability, fidelity.)

CONSTELLATION

adjectives
golden; arched; bright; brilliant; shimmering.

verbs
appear in—; describe—; distinguish—; dominate—; examine—; form—; name—; obscure—; observe—; steer by—; stud with—; study—; treat of—; —awes; —burns; —embodies; —guides; —illuminates; —mystifies; —portrays; —reveals; —symbolizes.
(See stars.)

CONSTERNATION

adjectives
unseen; general; overwhelming; considerable; mournful; visible; silent; inexpressible; comprehensible; unutterable; momentary; frightened.

verbs
betray—; feign—; fill with—; manifest—; overwhelm with—; prostrate with—; recover from—; shock into—; suppress—; terrify with—; terrorize with—; throw into—; —amazes; —confounds; —dismays; —falls; —incapacitates; —surprises.
(See fear, terror, alarm, panic.)

CONSTIPATION

adjectives
intractable; chronic; stubborn; recurring; harrowing; drug-induced.

verbs
afflict with—; alleviate—; cure of—; doctor for—; dose for—; ease—; flush away—; intensify—; overcome—; produce—; relieve—; remedy—; treat—; warn against—; —hints at; —irks; —necessitates; —obstructs; —sets in.
(See disease.)

CONSTITUENCY

adjectives
large; urban; foremost; urgent; enthusiastic.

CONSTITUENT

adjectives
enraptured; characteristic; parsimonious; material; chemical; valuable; necessary; saline; primal; eternal; colored; approved; irreducible; soluble; youthful; enlightened; influential.

verbs
analyze—; assemble—s; authorize by—s; break into—s; determine—s; discern—; distinguish—; gather—; lose—; obey—; represent—s; —s assist; —s complain; —s compose; —s diminish; —elects; —s represent.
(See part, element, ingredient.)

CONSTITUTE (v)

adverbs
singularly; legally; fairly; splendidly; remarkably; amorphously; magnificently; physically; morally; peculiarly; delicately; intellectually; undeniably.
(See compose, establish.)

CONSTITUTION (general)

adjectives
frail; splendid; diseased; amorphous; healthy; remarkable; strong; loose-jointed; robust; magnificent; physical; moral; iron; peculiar; vigorous; delicate; oligarchical; paper; emotional; consolidated; rugged; well-knit; feeble; glorious; powerful; provisional; permanent; liberal; imperial; intellectual; ancient; sickly.

CONSTITUTION (governmental)

adjectives
amended; consolidated; hammered-out; botched-up; intrenched; framed; liberal; oligarchical; standardized.

verbs
abandon—; abide by—; abuse—; adopt—; alter—; amend—; clarify—; construe—; defend—; draft—; embody in—; establish—; flaunt—; form—; found—; frame—; improve—; interpret—; modify—; nullify—; ordain—; organize—; preserve—; ratify—; ruin—; stabilize—; tamper with—; twist—; violate—; —abolishes; —decrees; —defines; —grants; —guides; —limits; —prescribes; —prohibits; —provides; —regulates; —sets forth; —totters.

CONSTITUTION (physical)

adjectives
amorphous; emotional; frail; iron; magnificent; powerful; robust.

verbs
benefit—; brace—; build up—; disturb—; enervate—; exercise—; improve—; inherit—; invigorate—; overtax—; renew—; revitalize—; revivify—; run down—; shatter—; strain—; strengthen—; undermine—; weaken.
(See physique, structure. temperament, character.)

CONSTRAIN (v)

adverbs
unquestionably; unnaturally; artificially; severely; rigidly; commercially; embarrassedly; tyrannically; bitterly; formally;; mercilessly.
(See compel, oblige.)

CONSTRAINT

adjectives
tyrannous; bitter; evident; mute; gloomy; sorrowful; curious; formal; sharp; awkward; merciless; heavy; slight.

verbs
act under—; exercise—; lessen—; manifest—; occasion—; pale under—; prevent—; produce—; resist—; speak with—; subdue—; tug at—; —binds; —checks; —confines; —prohibits; —represses; —tightens; —voices.
(See force, compulsion, pressure, restraint, restriction.)

CONSTRICT (v)

adverbs
rigorously; harmfully; icily; painfully; automatically; physiologically; partially; insufferably; intellectually.
(See compress, contract.)

CONSTRICTION

adjectives
harmful; icy; oppressive; deep; hampering; morbid; marked; express.

CONSTRUCT (v)

adverbs
hastily; diaphanously; patiently; rudely; variously; studiously; ingeniously; dramatically; bizarrely; artistically; ruggedly; flawlessly; primitively; durably; majestically; musically; substantially; solidly; legitimately; technically; scientifically; rudely; crudely; enduringly; flimsily.
(See build, manufacture.)

CONSTRUCTION

adjectives
complicated; unsurpassed; improved; patented; rigid; rugged; initial; complex; flawless; exclusive; superb; famous; primitive; ingenious; harmonic; durable; imperfect; majestic; sublime; riveted; mistaken; institutional; pithy; exquisite; immediate; superior; flattering; constitutional; artful; custom-built; excellent; evasive; strained; questionable; peculiar; musical; dependable; substantial; shrewd; sturdy; malicious; dramatic; contemplated; solid; recent; steel-truss; highway; engineering; correct; worst; wrong; strict; illegitimate; charitable; technical; crude.

CONSTRUCTIVE

adverbs
helpfully; critically; definitely; remarkably; valuably; significantly; magnificently; sensibly; fundamentally; essentially; liberally; splendidly; creatively; clearly; saliently; strikingly; explicitly.

CONSTRUE (*v*)

adverbs
variously; maliciously; confusedly; shrewdly; erroneously; charitably.
(See interpret.)

CONSUL

adjectives
dignified; autocratic; duly-appointed; officiating; protective; prudent; self-important; artful; wily; fastidious.

verbs
appeal to—; appoint—; authorize—; beseech—; charge—with; choose—; elect—; name—; present—; recall—; receive—; retain—; slay—; withdraw—; —advises; —anticipates; —holds office; —promotes; —promulgates; —proposes; —protects; —rejects; —reports; —represents.
(See magistrate, representative, counselor.)

CONSULT (*v*)

adverbs
selfishly; philosophically; confidentially; timidly; vainly; distressingly; solemnly; informally; anxiously; earnestly; gravely; deliberately; privately; frequently; protractedly.
(See deliberate, discuss.)

CONSULTATION

adjectives
solemn; whispered; hasty; informal; mature; anxious; actual; serious; religious; rapid; timely; earnest; vociferous; short; grave; deliberate; private; frequent; brief; protracted; muffled.

verbs
advise—; assist at—; call—; confer in—; deliberate in—; demand—; follow—; go into—; meet in—; secure—; seek—; —advises; —concludes; —decides; —ensues; —exposes; —guides; —results in.
(See conference, council.)

CONSUME (*v*)

adverbs
annually; ravenously; leisurely; utterly; relatively; ultimately; unwarily; industrially; ferociously.
(See burn, destroy.)

CONSUMER

adjectives
desirable; hard-working; mortgaged; ultimate; humble; general; unorganized (pl.); unprotected; unwary; trusting; duped.

CONSUMMATION

adjectives
desirable; relentless; harmonious; supreme; fitting.

CONSUMPTION

adjectives
needful; cold; languorous; melancholy; domestic; laryngeal; pulmonary; equitable; conspicuous; old-fashioned; annual; food; slackening; residential; industrial; diminishing.

verbs
afflict with—; consume with—; contract—; cure—; infect with—; inherit—; predispose to—; smite with—; suffer with—; tend towards—; treat for—; waste away with—; —atrophies; —attacks; —decomposes; —destroys; —invalids; —lingers; —preys on; —rots; —takes a toll; —wreaks.
(See tuberculosis, disease.)

CONTACT

adjectives
friendly; richest; effective; stimulating; intimate; personal; close; casual; fleeting; intermittent; brief; abrupt; superficial; bitter; difficult; banal; brutish; human; nation-wide; diplomatic; domestic; pro-

longed; mere; necessary; constant; alert; accidental; sonorous; immediate; direct; uninterrupted; unrestricted; terrible; intellectual; social; osculatory; slight; unclean; extensive; miscellaneous; spontaneous; careless; rude; proffered; lawless; responsible.

verbs
abolish—; approve of—; balk at—; bring into—; conceal—; defile by—; enter into—; establish—; favor—; harbor—; join in—; lose—; maintain—; modify—; negotiate—; oppose—; profit by—; reestablish —; renew—; uncover—; vary—.
(See connection.)

CONTAGION

adjectives
rigid; terrible; deadly; delicious; virulent.

verbs
check—; convey by—; engender—; expose to—; guard against—; harbor—; isolate—; propagate by—; quarantine—; restrain—; spread—.
(See pestilence, plague. infection.)

CONTAGIOUS

adverbs
highly; dangerously; pestilentially; unfortunately; acutely; widely; perilously; seriously; extremely; exceedingly; decidedly; unquestionably; frightfully; absolutely; remarkably; alarmingly; curiously; awfully; critically; definitely; fatally; positively; notoriously.

CONTAIN (*v*)

adverbs
virtually; fully; partially; entirely; fittingly; snugly; amazingly; completely; substantially.
(See hold.)

CONTAINER

adjectives
transparent; airtight; offsize; metal; standardized; smart; huge.

CONTEMPLATE (*v*)

adverbs
objectively; actually; soberly; vaguely; philosophically; consciously; listlessly; curiously; absorbedly; dreamily; serenely; profoundly; rapturously; complacently; severely; plaintively.
(See meditate.)

CONTEMPLATION

adjectives
frowning; ravishing; precocious; listless; passing; will-less; curious; celestial; absorbed; deep; hopeless; cold; solitary; mystic; dreamy; serene; wondering; academic; narrow; unfettered; profound; continued; sundry; comprehensive; silent; lofty; spiritual; complacent; zealous; rapturous; lonely; steadfast; habitual; pleasurable; melancholy; selfish; leaden; severe.

verbs
absorb in—; arouse from—; drift in—; engross in—; hold in—; fall into—; lose in—; meditate in—; molest in—; rejoice in—; soar in—; steep in—; swathe in—; wrap in—; —beholds; —colors; —pictures; —reflects; —stirs.
(See reflection, thought, meditation.)

CONTEMPLATIVE

adverbs
deeply; thoughtfully; reminiscently; prophetically; studiously; closely; ponderingly; abstractedly; intelligently; philosophically; sagely; wisely; leisurely; thoroughly; habitually; pensively; anxiously; eagerly; curiously; queerly; oddly; coldly; academically; zealously; loftily; mysteriously; calmly.

CONTEMPORARY

adjectives
admirable; poetic; fiendish; celebrated; unanimous; skeptical; disillusioned; eminent; cheery; erudite; wholesome; northern; smaller; male.

adverbs
conveniently; embarrassingly; undeniably; obviously; certainly; unquestionably; evidently; curiously; admittedly; presumably; probably; possibly; supposedly; oddly; incontrovertibly; authentically; actually; categorically; authoritatively; ironically.

CONTEMPT

adjectives
inexplicable; beautiful; impersonal; concentrated; dignified; undisguised; supercilious; exaggerated; inexpressible; reckless; fierce; lofty; veiled; half-compassionate; uncharitable; faint; deprecating; emphatic; cynical; spendthrift; withering; utmost; considerable; unreasoning; infinite; ineffable;

indiscriminate; bitterest; thorough; profound; uncompromising; notable; alternate: characteristic; deep-rooted; loud; ironical; arrogant; irrepressible; supreme; utter; habitual; geniune; biting; absolute; irrevocable; noisy; blighting; ineffable; unequivocal; notable; paternal; grand; magnificent; eloquent; smiling; good-natured; factitious; unfeigned; ardent; courageous; illimitable; aristrocratic; lofty; cavalier; holy; highbred; cold; stern; skeptical; icy; scornful; gloating; exasperating; shocked; keen; apparent; thundering; hereditary; growing; sudden; shattering; inherited; sweeping; high-nosed; friary.

verbs
admit—; awake—; bear—; breed—; convey—; deserve—; disdain—; entertain—; excite—; fill with—; foster—; gesture—; hurl—; imply—; place in—; pour out—; profess—; provoke—; regard with—; shield from—; sigh with—; smile—; spurn—; tinge with—; treat with—; veil—; wither with—; —arises; —deepens; —dies; —flickers; —infuriates; —terrifies; —shrivels up.

(See disdain, scorn, derision.)

CONTEMPTIBLE

adverbs
abominably; odiously; detestably; hatefully; shockingly; unspeakably; despicably; invidiously; woefully; lamentably; noxiously; execrably; flagrantly; intolerably; incredibly; disgustingly; utterly; outrageously; horribly; inexpressibly; notoriously; infamously; glaringly; monstrously; wickedly; remarkably.

CONTEND (*v*)

adverbs
pedantically; strenuously; incredulously; physically; laboriously; forcefully; narrowly; fiercely; boldly; stoutly; optimistically; senselessly; shrewdly; ridiculously; acrimoniously; ironically; undeviatingly; vigorously.

(See oppose.)

CONTENT

adjectives
sufficient; scholarly; organic; prescribed; sociological; trusting; universal; infinite; spacious; final; anti-religious; deepest; intimate; nestling; incongruous; supreme; wondrous; wise; greedy; drowsy; dreamy; measureless; immortal; blissful; cubical; infantile; scrutinized; radiant; adequate; muddy; gorgeous; endless; significant; melodic; shrewd; fluid; flinty; fermented; logical; corrupt; imbecile; unaggressive; protein; perfect; physical; sweet; scented; quiet; intellectual.

CONTENTION

adjectives
stout; brave; optimistic; bloody; senseless; ridiculous; fierce; unnatural; ravishing; rival; critical; acrimonious; basic; general; ironical.

verbs
abandon—; cast out—; contest—; dispute—; endorse—; illustrate—; justify—; match—; raise—; refute—; rend with—; support—; —lingers; —upsets.

(See strife, conflict, struggle, dispute, argument, dissension.)

CONTENTIOUS

adverbs
characteristically; incorrigibly; disagreeably; loftily; shrewdly; intelligently; stupidly; doggedly; foolishly; bitterly; unnecessarily; testily; mildly; impetuously; violently; mulishly; stolidly; abusively; unreasonably; habitually; hotly; offensively; absurdly; pretentiously; brazenly.

CONTENTMENT

adjectives
inward; homelike; childish; stolid; rapturous; sweet; complete; thoughtless; perfect; placid; domestic; rare; abiding; happy; odd; new; supreme; drowsy; ineffable; sleepy; sinking.

verbs
achieve—; attain—; bathe in—; desire—; destroy—; feign—; fill with—; pretend—; purr—; realize—; relax in—; resign in—; result in—; seek—; sigh in—; sink into—; smile with—; strive for—; struggle for—; swathe in—; view with—; yearn for—; —evades; —proceeds from.

(See satisfaction, happiness, gratification.)

CONTENTS

adjectives
valuable; varied; lively; treasurable; illuminating; deadly; gruesome; nauseous; horrific; strange; discursive; golden; heterogeneous; problematical; sluggish; terse.

verbs
add to—; assimilate—; dehydrate—; discharge—; eject—; empty—; expel—; gut of—; imbibe—; master—; pound—; rob of—; stir—; —escape.
(See ingredients.)

CONTEST

adjectives
unequal; remarkable; obstinate; decisive; interstate; animated; bloody; deadly; dread; formal; sanguinary; passionate; inevitable; pending; civic; naked; spirited; frightful; ceaseless; violent; diplomatic; jarring; dramatic; tremendous; culminating; emotional; costly; tedious; amicable; bitter; mighty; audacious.

verbs
attend—; "ballyhoo"—; cheer—; debate—; develop into—; dispute—; emerge from—; enter—; invite to—; lose—; prepare for —; relish—; renew—; strive in—; struggle in—; vie in—; win—; witness—; —awards; —excites; —proceeds.
(See tournament, competition, dispute, dissension.)

CONTEST (*v*)

adverbs
fiercely; energetically; gallantly; bitterly; unequally; remarkably; obstinately; decisively; animatedly; bloodily; passionately; inevitably; ceaselessly; violently; diplomatically; dramatically; amicably; audaciously.
(See oppose, dispute.)

CONTESTANT

adjectives
feeble; leading; vindicated; keen; rival; earnest; obstinate; invincible; indefatigable.

verbs
equip—; reduce—s; —achieves; —applies; —battles; —competes; —contends; —endures; —gains; —overcomes; —races; —rivals; —strains; —strives; —struggles.
(See competitor, rival.)

CONTINENCE

adjectives
absolute; vowed; eternal; inordinate; lofty; ascetic; monastic; impenetrable; inviolable.

CONTINENT

adjectives
rich; new; powerful; remote; sunken; commanding; unexhausted; sunny; undiscovered; virgin; unborn; unmapped; orbed; infinite.

verbs
abound on—; bound—; communicate with —; cover—; discover—; divide—; explore—; exploit—; govern—; inhabit—; populate—; rule—; sail for—; span—; speed across—; study—; tranquilize—; travel—; traverse—; wage on—.
(See land, country.)

CONTINGENCY

adjectives
remote; various (pl); fatal; imaginable; impossible; dangerous; unforeseen; future.

verbs
admit—; conceive—; consider—; contemplate—; exempt from—; expose to—; foresee—; forestall—; fortify against—; free from—; involve—; prepare for—; regard—; subject to—; —befalls; —occurs; —requires.
(See chance, possibility, accident, hazard.)

CONTINGENT

adjectives
various (pl); assorted (pl); fresh; obligatory; unlimited; valuable; denominated; incidental.

adverbs
accidentally; unexpectedly; fortuitously; unfortunately; presumably; casually; unluckily; advantageously; possibly; remotely; imaginably; gravely; distantly; presciently.

CONTINUANCE

adjectives
further; simultaneous; perpetual; dogged; indefinite.

verbs
balk at—; bore by—; detest—; forswear—; hinder—; insure—; lapse—; prohibit—; shrink from—; speed—; stay—; urge—; —adds; —confirms; —engulfs; —improves; —inculcates; —irks; —oppresses; —perfects; —preserves; —renders.

CONTINUATION

adjectives
sketchy; mirthful; interminable; ruthless; casual; fluent; moderate.

CONTINUE (*v*)

adverbs
presumptuously; relentlessly; calmly; uncomplainingly; dauntlessly; voluntarily; passionately; stealthily; triumphantly; obstinately; jerkily; thoughtfully; facetiously; affably; mercilessly; hopefully; defiantly; imperturbably; treacherously; blandly.
(See persevere.)

CONTINUITY

adjectives
historic; unbroken; inexplicable; long-sighted; strict; general; agreeable; grim.

CONTINUOUS

adverbs
maddeningly; providentially; monotonously; tiresomely; intolerably; incredibly; grimly; dangerously; indescribably; unbearably; alarmingly; frightfully; crazily; insufferably; solemnly; ruthlessly; appallingly; cleverly; dismally; noisily; provokingly; automatically.

CONTORT (*v*)

adverbs
misshapenly; facilely; inanely; horribly; capriciously; drolly; spasmodically; frantically; sinisterly; agilely; facially; sneeringly.
(See twist, wrench.)

CONTORTION

adjectives
deprecatory; wonderful; frightful; spasmodic; joyful; frantic; sneering; sinister; unsystematic; slight; facial; agile.

CONTOUR

adjectives
delicate; vertical; bodily; inviting; ground; vague; pleasing; facial; rugged; muscular; hard; skeletal; cranial; childish; chubby; snug; effeminate; pronounced; rounded; sharp; youthful; wasted; swinging; voluptuous; pert; harsh; smooth; girlish; sagging; exquisite.

CONTRABAND

adjectives
confiscated; exported; proclaimed; prohibited; seized; smuggled.

verbs
ban as—; carry—; confiscate—; deal in—; declare as—; destroy—; export—; forbid as—; forfeit—; import—; list as—; proclaim as—; prohibit as—; seize as—; smuggle—; supply—; traffic in—.
(See arms, supplies.)

CONTRACT

adjectives
fat; solemn; valid; conjugal; stamped; workable; favorable; vowed; true; signed; nullified; binding; huge; definite; gilt-edged; legal; repudiated; direct; airtight; substantial; advantageous; invariable.

verbs
abandon—; amend—; breach—; cancel—; celebrate—; cleave to—; depart from—; dispense with—; execute—; forfeit—; fulfill—; interpret—; jockey over—; jump—; land—; modify—; rebel at—; revoke—; term—; terminate—; violate—; void—; waive—; win—; —binds; —discloses; —expires; —holds; —implies; —specifies; —stipulates.
(See compact, agreement, arrangement, bargain, promise.)

CONTRACT (*v*)

adverbs
violently; vigorously; bindingly; definitely; legally; advantageously; substantially; physically; spasmodically; intermittently; solemnly.
(See narrow, shrink.)

CONTRACTION

adjectives
muscular; inevitable; continuous; sharp; deep; nervous; concentric.

verbs
allow for—; produce—; regulate—; tend toward—; —abbreviates; —apostrophizes; —condenses; —confines; —diminishes; —draws; —hampers; —lames; —limits; —narrows; —reduces; —restricts; —shortens; —shrinks.
(See condensation.)

CONTRACTOR

adjectives
certain; labor; alert; scheming; enriched; resourceful; purloining.

CONTRADICT (v)

adverbs

expressly; violently; inexplicably; constantly; embarrassingly; fatuously; flagrantly; mutually; bewilderingly; curiously; logically; extravagantly; vulgarly; boorishly; curtly; ill-manneredly; explicitly; directly.

(See say.)

CONTRADICTION

adjectives

violent; inexplicable; constant; embarrassing; slight; irreconcilable; moral; breathtaking; productive; idealistic; disruptive; imaginary; self-corroding; fatuous; accumulated; social; flat; absurd; apparent; flagrant; painful; notable; mutual; bewildering; amazing; curious; logical; affectionate; extravagant.

verbs

affirm—; brook—; claim—; deny—; discern—; encompass with—; endure—; forbid—; indulge in—; involve—; object to—; offset—; press—; profess—; prove—; reconcile—; solve—; sustain—; utter—; —irritates; —perplexes; —proposes; —yawns.

(See opposition, paradox, inconsistency.)

CONTRADICTORY

adverbs

strangely; oddly; naively; subtly; blatantly; inexplicably; embarrassingly; irreconcilably; disruptively; absurdly; flagrantly; pugnaciously; truculently; amazingly; curiously; apparently; obviously; palpably; illogically; bewilderingly; flatly; fiercely; directly; fatally; unbecomingly; defiantly.

CONTRAPTION

adjectives

happy; pleasing; refreshing; delicious; charming; excellent; attractive; pleasant; effective; interesting; encouraging; true; striking; vivid; marked; sharp; pronounced; momentous; notable; smashing; amazing; astounding; unbelievable; startling; surprising; puzzling; quaint; odd; curious; cruel; violent; prosaic; dismal; amusing; abrupt; ludicrous; deft; precise; tremendous; instructive; dramatic; intense; singular; gratifying; possible; ghastly; artificial; obvious; favorable; crazy; delightful; subtle; melancholy; piquant; gloomy; contemporaneous.

verbs

contemplate—; contrive—; design—; destroy—; devise—; employ—; extricate from—; immerse in—; interest in—; invent—; mesh in—; plan—; set up—; test—; work out—; —attracts; —envelops; —puzzles.

(See device.)

CONTRAST

adjectives

clear; exciting; flattering; bitter; brilliant; remote; poignant; startling; unfavorable.

verbs

accentuate—; cap—; disclose—; emphasize—; mark—; place in—; present—; resent—; revel in—; serve as—; strike—; study—; vow—; —glares; —grows; —interests.

(See comparison.)

CONTRAST (v)

adverbs

vividly; sharply; strangely; whimsically; bitterly; strikingly; violently; picturesquely; invidiously.

(See compare.)

CONTRIBUTE (v)

adverbs

materially; unceasingly; indirectly; voluntarily; considerably; cheerily; altruisticly; willingly; liberally; simultaneously; singularly; gloomily; voluminously; conspicuously; effectively; powerfully; notably; anonymously; originally; technically; fundamentally; uniquely; meritoriously; formidably; permanently; characteristically.

(See give, furnish.)

CONTRIBUTION

adjectives

important; notable; anonymous; epoch-making; significant; distinctive; voluminous; august; practical; passionate; magnificent; literary; original; technical; fundamental; valuable; unique; varying; copious; charming; worthy; liberal; heartfelt; generous; sole; fascinating; splendid; superb; meritorious; formidable; serious; permanent; solid; genuine; enduring; tangible; priceless; cultural; private; statesmanlike; creative; cooperative; definite; negligible; phantom; invigorating; timely; characteristic; startling; immediate.

verbs
begrudge—; collect—; deluge with—s; favor with—; gather—s; offer—; sacrifice—; solicit—; squeeze—out of; —exemplifies; —s pour in.
(See alms.)

CONTRIBUTOR

adjectives
distinguished; prolific; occasional; prospective; sparkling; anonymous; forgotten; flourishing; industrious; scholarly; well-remembered; frequent.

verbs
advertise for—s; appeal to—s; approach—s; back by—s; pay—; promise—; satisfy—; seek—s; serve as—; —aids; —endows; —furnishes; —raises; —rallies; —responds; —supports; —writes.
(See supporter.)

CONTRIBUTORY

adverbs
helpfully; advantageously; liberally; commercially; cooperatively; charitably; economically; encouragingly; generously; harmoniously; jointly; obligingly; originally.

CONTRITION

adjectives
veritable; authentic; apparent; heartfelt; warm; mock; pitiful; sudden; blind.

verbs
afflict with—; arise from—; break with—; bruise with—; display—; dissolve in—; exhibit—; languish in—; melt in—; pray in—; reduce to—; repent in—; sow—; strike with—; suffer—; wear with—; weep in—; —softens.
(See sorrow, remorse.)

CONTRIVANCE

adjectives
clumsy; mechanical; various (pl); discarded; ingenious; kindred; well-fitted; curious; perfect; mysterious; fun-making; excitement-arousing; dumpy; rickety; admirable; mock; peculiar; delightful; tricky; intricate; labor-saving; quaint; malignant.

CONTRIVE (*v*)

adverbs
ingeniously; cunningly; sedulously; curiously; cleverly; providentially; indirectly; scientifically; mechanically; mysteriously; intricately; malignantly; maliciously; viciously; bitterly; revengefully.
(See scheme, invent.)

CONTROL

adjectives
powerful; menial; supervisory; easy; heroic; thought; political; centralized; mysterious; transcending; absolute; repressive; automatic; effective; determined; collective; benevolent; inadequate; virtual; irremissible; remote; autonomous; inventory; democratic; effortless; rigorous; working; parental; precise; undisputed; production; autocratic; perfect; substantial; self-assumed; immediate; hypnotic; arbitrary; excellent; iron; firm; entire; permanent; complete; full; supreme; exclusive; nominal; limited; partial; hectic; craven; hateful; sinister; degrading; systematic; ordered; social; ancestral; merchandising; unjust; civilian; traffic; nerve; scientific; strong; external; silent; boundless; planned; private; growing; critical; steady.

verbs
acquire—; assume—; attest to—; centralize—; concentrate—; demonstrate—; divorce—; endanger—; entrust with—; establish—; exempt from—; exercise—; exert—; fight—; gain—; grab—; lose—; maintain—; manifest—; release—; respond to—; seek—; seize—; settle in—of; teach—; trick into—of; vest—in; win—; —changes hands; —rests with.
(See regulation, restraint, domination, command.)

CONTROL (*v*)

adverbs
absolutely; imperiously; arbitrarily; powerfully; heroically; politically; mysteriously; dictatorially; automatically; determinedly; benevolently; adequately; virtually; democratically; effortlessly; rigorously; autocratically; hypnotically; exclusively; nominally; partially; privately; critically; steadily.
(See regulate, restrain.)

CONTROVERSIAL

adverbs
highly; unfortunately; temptingly; inevitably; religiously; violently; tediously; painfully; excitably; vehemently; stupidly; obstinately; endlessly; bitterly; intricately; dangerously; traditionally; diplomatically; perplexingly.

CONTROVERSY

adjectives
perplexing; pending; long-standing; religious; violent; acrimonious; vehement; tedious; frequent; painful; external; important; bitter; political; sectarian; ferocious; exciting; pending; contemptible; heated; long; warm; drawn-out; endless; intricate; arduous; acrid; terrific; lively; scorching; threatening; dangerous; ancient; long-forgotten; legal; economic; international; diplomatic; clerical; parlor; silly; unfortunate; unexpected; waning.

verbs
appraise—; arouse—; avoid—; carry on—; clarify—; cut through—; dismiss—; engage in—; entangle in—; involve in—; judge—; occasion—; perpetuate—; plunge into—; precipitate—; shrink from—; stir up—; suppress—; sway by—; unleash—; view—; wage—; —arises from; —blasts; —convulses; —fizzles; —flares; —rages; —spits.
(See dispute, contention, debate, feud.)

CONTUMACIOUS

adverbs
stubbornly; stiffly; defiantly; hotly; tempermanentally; habitually; insufferably; intractably; unmanageably; uncontrollably; foolishly; ridiculously; mutinously; violently; restlessly; lawlessly; seditiously; ungovernably; openly; formidably; irreconcilably; alarmingly; dangerously; unaccountably; obstreperously; inveterately; malevolently; distressingly.

CONTUMELIOUS

adverbs
blatantly; absurdly; airily; egotistically; unpardonably; fantastically; insufferably; extremely; audaciously; flippantly; saucily; shamefully; bumptiously; brassily; offensively; provokingly; unpleasantly; disagreeably; intolerably; arrogantly; haughtily; unreasonably; senselessly; idiotically; unwisely; indiscreetly; imprudently.

CONTUSION

adjectives
severe; fatal; painful; serious; violet-hued; predominant.

verbs
acquire by—; anoint—; bandage—; cure—; dress—; infect—; inflame—; irritate—; produce—; relieve—; suffer—; treat—; —bruises; —crushes; —enervates; —heals; —incapacitates; —injures; —swells.
(See bruise, injury.)

CONUNDRUM

adjectives
stock; baffling; fascinating; improvised; stale; original.

CONVALESCENCE

adjectives
tolerable; hard-won; adequate; drowsy; slow; uncertain; maddening.

verbs
affect—; delay—; doze through—; discharge from—; ease through—; interrupt—; nurse through—; regain during—; revive in—; shorten—; strengthen in—; treat during—; visit during—; while away—; —advances; —cures; —overcomes; —proceeds.
(See recovery, improvement.)

CONVALESCENT

adjectives
petulant; selfish; irritable; impatient; implacable; whining; whimsical.

adverbs
happily; fortunately; securely; finally; contentedly; easily; tolerably; slowly; painfully; actually; pleasantly; luckily; gratefully; thankfully; affably; normally; definitely; apparently; blessedly; cheerfully; charmingly; truly; presumably; undoubtedly; decisively.

CONVENIENCE

adjectives
domestic; timesaving; greater; money-saving; every; ultra-fashionable; incidental; notable; modern; homelike; foresighted; admirable; earliest; consequent; passing; delightful; added; safe; metropolitan; undoubted; tremendous; general.

verbs
adopt—; afford—; allow—; appreciate—; avail oneself of—; await—of; enjoy—; extend—; lack—; marry for—; offer—; pay for—; permit of—; possess—; require—; —comforts; —eases; —saves.
(See comfort, ease, opportunity.)

CONVENIENT

adverbs
particularly; comfortably; highly; properly; acceptably; admirably; marvelously; tremendously; safely; delightfully; exceptionally; perfectly; completely; incredibly; wholly; extraordinarily; singularly; suitably; duly; unusually; ingeniously.

CONVENT

adjectives
suppressed; measureless; once-famous; secluded; peaceful; cloistered.

CONVENTION (*custom*)

adjectives
timid; operatic; faith-healing; classic; universal; social; civic; restricting; rigid; facile; poetic.

CONVENTION (*meeting*)

adjectives
radical; national; projected; provincial; famous; cheap; wide-open; labor; advertising.

verbs
appoint to—; assemble in—; boycott—; brand—; cavort at—; control—; denounce—; elect at—; emanate in—; hold—; join—; meet in—; open—; preside at—; represent at—; run away with—; stage—; —abolishes; —adjourns; —alters; —bestows; —considers; —convenes; —nominates; —prepares; —proclaims.

(See meeting, conference, congress, council, assembly.)

CONVENTIONAL

adverbs
properly; formally; strictly; habitually; naturally; normally; ordinarily; positively; usually; uncompromisingly; typically; rigidly; stiffly; consistently; absurdly; needlessly; carefully; arrogantly; affectedly; shyly; bashfully; ostentatiously; pretentiously; pompously; meticulously; insistently.

CONVENTIONALITY

adjectives
pleasant; sterile; frigid; precise; ceremonious; cutting; supreme.

verbs
accept—; adhere to—; base on—; beat down—; blind by—; breach—; break—; break away from—; buttress by—; challenge—; contradict—; defer—; defy—; discard—; disregard—; drop—; flout—; follow—; hamper—; hate—; heed—; obey—; overthrow—; ridicule—; sacrifice to—; satirize—; shatter—; shelter—; smash—; subject to—; violate—; wall in by—; —allows; —determines; —hampers; —permits; —recognizes; —sanctions; —settles; —supports; —upholds.

(See custom, usage, habit, rule, form, practice.)

CONVERGE (*v*)

adverbs
sharply; suddenly; gradually; obviously; abruptly; unexpectedly; consequently; fatally; tragically; significantly.

(See approach.)

CONVERSANT

adverbs
thoroughly; intimately; slightly; fortunately; luckily; auspiciously; expertly; liberally; deeply; profoundly; shrewdly; reportedly; supposedly; reputably; ingeniously; cleverly; intelligently; capably; advantageously; consummately; perfectly.

CONVERSATION

adjectives
desultory; sedate; forcible; vapid; whispered; exquisite; subsequent; inane; trivial; informal; temporary; difficult; frank; touching; calm; natural; cheerful; animated; private; bristling; preliminary; thoughtful; philosophical; savory; embellished; unspecific; mysterious; idyllic; interminable; earnest; measured; gossip-riddled; filthy; reminiscent; considerable; agreeable; subdued; hurried; distracting; energetic; gentle; frivolous; sparkling; undertoned; low-voiced; real; heavenly; pleasant; enchanting; fascinating; egotistic; previous; appreciative; personal; direct; tumultuous; memorable; vivacious; amiable; improbable; intelligent; offhand; comfortable; inmost; casual; serious; bold; liberal; idle; scattered; curious; apparent; ribald; spicy; extravagant; delightful; interesting; sustained; passing; dramatic; diligent; sublimated; piquant; rational; select; easy; graceful; protracted; intimate; eager; edifying; mercurial; running; sportive; open; sociable; antiquarian; inimitable; brilliant; clear; persuasive; sympathetic; sane; coherent; amicable; enthralling; luminous; famous; witty; aphoristic; hilarious; amusing; bantering; facetious; smiling; light; explosive; spirited; lively;

sprightly; negligible; everyday; ordinary; aimless; drifting; languishing; flickering; scattered; intermittent; halting; jerky; wandering; lagging; jumbled; fitful; indefinite; elusive; spiritless; extended; inconclusive; timorous; wearisome; fatuous; insipid; lazy; lackadaisical; muttered; bold; impractical; pert; leery; hidebound; loud; superfluous; irate; embattled; hideous; concerting; coarse; obscene; illiterate; successful; dinner table; eyebrow; traveled; healthy; emotional; quiet; cultured; confidential; startled; amazing; conspicuous; condensed; brief; rapid; promiscuous; unblushing; spontaneous; sudden; chatty; general; developed; simple; polite; absorbed; imaginary; uninterrupted; harmless; dutiful; plausible.

verbs
address—to; conduct—with; connive at—; direct—; divert—; drag into—; dull—; engage in—; essay—; forego—; guide—; infuse into—; interrupt—; key—; lead into—; narrate—; nurture—; open—; overhear—; plunge into—; prolong—; refrain from—; rush into—; shatter—; shift—; shoulder—; snatch at—; suspend—; swing—back to; transcribe—; —breaks out; —drifts on; —evolves from; —flames; —flows; —languishes; —lapses; —palls; —precedes; —rambles; —ranges; —scintillates; —skips from; —streams away; —stumbles upon.

(See dialogue, intercourse, communication, conference, talk.)

CONVERSATIONAL

adverbs
amiably; stiffly; sociably; affably; pompously; garrulously; provincially; gruffly; laconically; informally; calmly; naturally; cheerfully; jovially; helpfully; unwontedly; agreeably; eagerly; gently; brilliantly; enchantingly; illuminatingly; fascinatingly; vivaciously; intelligently; comfortably; casually; seriously; idly; curiously; spicily; ribaldly; drunkenly; convivially; interestingly; dramatically; gracefully; intimately; graciously; wittily; amusingly; facetiously; happily; luckily; intermittently; abstractedly; fitfully; inconclusively; yawningly; insipidly; lazily; loudly; blatantly; noisily.

CONVERSATIONALIST

adjectives
fluent; elegant; absorbing; gifted; interesting; brilliant.

CONVERSE

adjectives
earnest; eager; grave; sagacious; purposeful; covert.

CONVERSE (v)

adverbs
vivaciously; fluently; freely; interestingly; agreeably; courteously; affably; desultorily; acrimoniously; sedately; inanely; trivially; informally; temporarily; frankly; touchingly; animatedly; privately; brilliantly; philosophically; mysteriously; distractedly; curiously; ribaldly; piquantly; rationally; dramatically; gracefully; mercurially; inimitably; persuasively; sympathetically; coherently; amicably; enthrallingly; hilariously; banteringly; aimlessly; pointlessly; intermittently; jerkily; laggingly; fitfully; indefinitely; fatuously; insipidly; timorously; superfluously; irately; emotionally; confidentially; promiscuously; spontaneously; politely; absorbedly; uninterruptedly; harmlessly; pointedly.

(See talk, chat.)

CONVERSION

adjectives
spiritual; infinite; romantic; tardy; religious; abrupt; imminent; vivid.

CONVERT

adjectives
proposed; immovable; enthusiastic; docile; devout; irrevocable.

verbs
baptize—; direct—; gather—s; guide—; lead—s; make—; preach to—; —accepts; —acknowledges; —changes; —embraces; —falls from grace; —forsakes; —gains; —professes; —rallies; —substitutes; —transfers.

(See disciple, follower.)

CONVERT (v)

adverbs
religiously; frequently; enthusiastically; sincerely; passionately; conscientiously; irresistibly; intellectually; rationally; unalterably; solemnly.

(See apply, use.)

CONVERTIBLE

adverbs
readily; easily; handily; economically; quickly; conveniently; instantly; serviceably; instantaneously; advantageously; ingeniously; deftly; dexterously; fortunately;

luckily; accommodatingly; adaptably; providentially; promptly; profitably; altogether; unquestionably; happily.

CONVEY (v)

adverbs
naturally; forcefully; exquisitely; imperceptibly; delicately; competently; peculiarly; luxuriously; privately; diplomatically; tactfully; ceremoniously.
(See carry, transport.)

CONVEYANCE

adjectives
miserable; competent; shaky; tenantless; impossible; peculiar; ornamental; creditable; luxurious; available; modern; private; usual.

verbs
construct—; convoy—; design—; draw—; drive—; escort—; guide—; lead—; load—; lubricate—; mechanize—; model—; pull—; power—; restrain—; transport in—; trust—; upset—; —rattles; —rumbles; —transmits.
(See carriage, vehicle.)

CONVICT

adjectives
political; pardoned; vital; wily; shivering; rat-faced; horrified; fear-dazed; filthy; degraded; villainous.

verbs
apprehend—; chain—; deliver—; execute —; expose—; free—; pardon—; parole—; punish—; rehabilitate—; reprieve—; sentence—; train—; transfer—; try—; —breaks jail; —confesses; —escapes; —invades; —offends; —prowls; —rebels; —reforms; —serves.
(See criminal, culprit, prisoner.)

CONVICT (v)

adverbs
invariably; circumstantially; insidiously; politically; villainously; sternly; intellectually; positively; unmistakably; deliberately; solemnly; theoretically; swiftly; secretly; overwhelmingly; legally.
(See condemn.)

CONVICTION

adjectives
arresting; passionate; humbling; doubtful; historic; conscientious; true; firm; perverse; random; instantaneous; stern; indefeasible; youthful; profound; rapturous; frail; unsettled; irresistible; unshaken; widespread; deep; popular; honest; intellectual; inbred; esteemed; fixed; religious; coessential; subjective; sincere; rational; unalterable; vivid; calm; reasonable; extravagant; remote; positive; instinctive; unmistakable; steel; thorough; moral; antagonistic; internal; jocular; definite; persistent; deliberate; paternal; tried; innermost; solemn; intimate; unspoken; well-known; theoretic; extreme; socialistic; immediate; unutterable; prophetic; perfect; earnest; sober; clear; accepted; assured; lively; joyous; thrilling; exhilarating; lasting; steadfast; stubborn; ineradicable; unassailable; unsullied; unquestioning; independent; heroic; fierce; strong; intense; absolute; personal; individual; horrible; torturing; unaccountable; disagreeable; wild; grim; unfortunate; weary; pathetic; humanitarian; aesthetic; increasing; growing; light; odd; swift; overwhelming; comfortable; latent; naive; dawning; instinctive; secret.

verbs
accept with—; awaken to—; bring—; carry—; cherish—; develop—; express—; fire—; form—; guide by—; indoctrinate—; ingrain—; justify—; lack—; lay down with—; lead to—; profess—; reiterate—; rouse—; share—; stand by—; —accrues; —burdens; —deserts; —grows; —restrains; —springs; —wavers.
(See faith, belief.)

CONVINCE (v)

adverbs
demonstratively; despairingly; rationally; solemnly; reluctantly; unalterably; profoundly; stubbornly; firmly; thoroughly; passionately; conscientiously; irresistibly; honestly; intellectually; religiously; reasonably; positively; theoretically; overwhelmingly; secretly.
(See satisfy.)

CONVIVIAL

adverbs
warmly; extremely; hospitably; sociably; fraternally; cosily; gregariously; entertainingly; chattingly; hilariously; waggishly; uproariously; pleasantly; merrily; gaily; blithely; affably; highly; agreeably; sportively; facetiously; boisterously; noisily; obstreperously; jovially; lovingly; festively; heartily.

CONVIVIALITY

adjectives
dried; dead; joyous; infectious; communicable; sparkling.

CONVOCATION

adjectives
jocund; ecclesiastical; heterogeneous; noble; clamorous; political; incessant.

CONVOKE (*v*)

adverbs
legitimately; legally; formally; annually; flagrantly; solemnly; ceremoniously; perfunctorily.
(See call, gather.)

CONVOY

adjectives
lumbering; speeding; rushing; protective; unwelcome; sequestering.

CONVULSION

adjectives
popular; perilous; suicidal; gleaming; rare; burnished; hammered; tarnished; public; hysterical; spasmodic; passionate; sardonic; civic; fearful; ghastly; strong; horrid; freakish; dreadful; moral; amiable; seething; mighty; mad.

verbs
attend with—; pass through—; produce—; quiet—; shake with—; stiffen in—; treat for—; writhe in—; —arises from; —recurs; —seizes.
(See spasm, fit, paroxysm.)

COO (*v*)

adverbs
plaintively; murmurously; softly; romantically; gently; lovingly; affectionately; delicately.
(See whisper.)

COOING

adjectives
soft; melancholy; subdued; mournful; gentle; lullabied; hushed.

COOK

adjectives
outlandish; splendid; superb; excellent; peerless; lusty; furious; surprised; sleepy-eyed; excited; pious; covetous; studious; cursed.

COOK (*v*)

adverbs
excellently; arduously; outlandishly; superbly; peerlessly; unsurpassingly; appetizingly; deliciously; exotically; delicately; tastefully; experimentally.
(See prepare.)

COOKERY

adjectives
master; tasty; experimental; unpalatable; hopeless; praiseworthy.

COOKIES

adjectives
delicious; stale; fresh; newly-baked; holiday; refrigerator.

COOKING

adjectives
delicate; unsavory; hygienic; casual; indifferent; superb; incomparable.

verbs
delight in—; plan—; practise—; provide—; relish—; school in—; skill in—; teach—; turn to—; —invites; —tempts.

COOL

adverbs
refreshingly; comfortably; uncomfortably; suddenly; unusually; gratefully; sufficiently; extremely; somewhat; moderately; unexpectedly; surprisingly; luckily; unfortunately; unluckily; terribly; beautifully; delightfully.

COOL (*v*)

adverbs
rapidly; sufficiently; scientifically; nocturnally; professionally; autumnally; abnormally; mechanically.
(See chill.)

COOL-HEADED

adverbs
quietly; calmly; equably; dispassionately; gravely; imperturbably; moderately; patiently; wisely; serenely; stoically; tolerantly; judiciously; sensibly; habitually; temperamentally; luckily; provokingly; sanely; extremely; superbly; astutely; admirably; amazingly; cautiously; warily; discreetly.

COOLNESS

adjectives
alluring; masterful; grateful; soft; admirable; nocturnal; cynical; obstinate; pro-

fessional; smooth; twinkling; utmost; undisturbed; slumberous; dim; correct; apparent; matchless; welcome; sudden; autumnal; inhuman; sneering; delicious.

COOPERATE (v)

adverbs
alternately; enthusiastically; gladly; consciously; respectably; willingly; harmoniously; courteously; advantageously; wholesomely; benevolently; mechanically; agriculturally; heartily; voluntarily; sympathetically; spontaneously; successfully.
(See help, unite.)

COOPERATION

adjectives
peaceful; matchless; loyal; genuine; courteous; close; harmonious; wise; generous; advantageous; wholesome; benevolent; municipal; unwavering; active; constant; cordial; constructive; munificent; emotional; agricultural; merchandising; public; international; pontifical; hearty; voluntary; stabilizing; spontaneous; sympathetic; immense; universal; conscious; indispensable; successful; powerful.

verbs
act in—with; advocate—; balk at—; court—; develop—; display—; dispose toward—; effect—; enlist—; exhibit—; foster—; lack—; necessitate—; pledge—; practise—; result in—; stress—; teach—; urge—; work in—with; —helps; —overcomes; —produces; —saves.
(See action, participation.)

COOPERATIVE

adverbs
wonderfully; serviceably; ardently; energetically; intelligently; zealously; actively; overwhelmingly; ingeniously; skilfully; willingly; grudgingly; instantly; loyally; genuinely; wisely; generously; advantageously; benevolently; unwaveringly; cordially; munificently; heartily; spontaneously; immensely; indispensably.

COORDINATE (v)

adverbs
logically; rationally; physically; functionally; excellently; delicately; mentally; muscularly; exactly; definitely; skilfully.

COORDINATION

adjectives
rational; physical; functional; excellent; delicate; mental; local; muscular.

verbs
arrange—; display—; hamper—; impair—; improve—; involve—; lose—; obstruct—; perform with—; proceed in—; regulate with—; require—; study—; supervise—;

—effects; —pleases.
(See harmony.)

COP

adjectives
strutting; hidebound; bullying; pompous; brass-buttoned; mace-brandishing; dictatorial; obliging; humanitarian.

COPE (v)

adverbs
successfully; bravely; heroically; continually; prevailingly; stalwartly; fearlessly; surprisingly.
(See strive.)

COPIOUS

adverbs
overwhelmingly; lavishly; naturally; needlessly; amply; luxuriantly; abundantly; aboundingly; exuberantly; affluently; inexhaustibly; overpoweringly; prodigally; handsomely; excessively; wantonly; unreasonably; remarkably; inexpressibly; fabulously; extraordinarily; astonishingly; amazingly; particularly; wonderfully; staggeringly; surprisingly; unbelievably; marvellously; fortunately; profusely.

COPPER

adjectives
shining; old; burnished; simmering; gleaming; hammered; tarnished.

verbs
alloy—; coat with—; dissolve—; grub out—; heat—; line with—; mine—; mold—; oxidize—; process—; produce—; purify—; refine—; sheathe in—; smelt—; work in—; —conducts; —insulates; —occurs; —oxidizes; —resists.
(See metal.)

COPSE

adjectives
woven; thick; rambling; summer; luxuriant.

COPY
(*general*)

adjectives
spirited; modified; examined; literal; certified; advance; drab; uninteresting; exact; laborious; attested; feeble; unique; mimeographed; photostatic; burlesque; fair; fragmentary; engrossed; virtuous; identical; pale; lame; stray; questionable; fraudulent; plaster; unexpurgated.

COPY
(*journalism*)

adjectives
badly-typed; blue-penciled; interlined; intelligible; transcribed; thumb-worn; sadly-deleted; smudgy.

verbs
arrange—; butcher—; deride—; damage—; edit—; enliven—; expand—; improve—; lengthen—; outline—; overbalance—; overdo—; point up—; read—; rearrange—; review—; set—; shorten—; simplify—; tone up—; write—.
(See advertisement.)

COPY
(*reproduction*)

adjectives
authentic; accurate; flattering; pathetic; preposterous; sketchy; veritable.

verbs
alter—; attest—; bequeath—; change—; collect—ies; distribute—ies; embellish—; forward—; garnish—; guard—; mail—; pattern—; refer to—; retain—; rewrite—; sign—; transcribe—; translate—; witness—; —appears; —exemplifies; —imitates; —reproduces.
(See imitation, duplicate, pattern.)

COPY (*v*)

adverbs
accurately; silently; extensively; uninterestingly; literally; exactly; laboriously; uniquely; photostatically; fairly; fragmentarily; identically; fraudulently; faithfully.
(See reproduce, imitate.)

COPYRIGHT

adjectives
popular; valid; world-wide; ineffective; disregarded.

verbs
apply for—; assign—to; defeat—; grant—; infringe on—; invalidate—; reconvey—; renew—; take out—; violate—; —expires; —protects; —secures.
(See right, patent.)

COQUETRY

adjectives
spasmodic; childish; unconquerable; open; feeble; modest; shy; clumsy; graceful; unconscious; native.

COQUETTE

adjectives
laughing; cold-blooded; superannuated; natural; insolent; typical; attractive; little.

COQUETTE (*v*)

adverbs
saucily; laughingly; insolently; attractively; modestly; shyly; slyly; gracefully; endearingly; lovingly; temptingly; irresistibly; naturally; precociously; shamelessly.
(See flirt.)

COQUETTISH

adverbs
charmingly; shamelessly; wantonly; enchantingly; irresistibly; unconsciously; deliberately; intentionally; effectively; laughingly; coolly; defiantly; inherently; naturally; awkwardly; shyly; incorrigibly; incurably; gracefully; attractively; typically; provokingly; openly; shamefully; clumsily; exquisitely; consciously; demurely; adorably; captivatingly; bewitchingly; reprehensibly; ardently; zealously.

CORAL

adjectives
pearl-hued; polished; blushing; branching; intricately-structured; imperishable.

verbs
abound in—; bedeck in—; deposit—; distribute—; employ—; fashion of—; fish for—; form—; inlay with—; market—; obtain—; polish—; procure—; secrete—; tint—; touch with—; trade—; trim with—; utilize—; value—; —attaches to; —covers; —crusts; —decorates; —flourishes; —ornaments; —grows; prize—.

CORD

adjectives
long; dangling; spinal; tense; frayed; durable; vital; hempen; subtle; sensitive; encircling; creaking; tangled; silver; penny; taut.

verbs
attach by—; bind with—; bite—; break—; cast away—; cut asunder—; draw—; gnaw at—; knit—; lengthen—; loop—; loose—; pull—; sever—; sterilize—; strengthen—; tie—; wind—; —binds; —snaps.
(See string, chain.)

CORDIAL

adjectives
best; exhilarating; warming; stimulating; animating; revivifying.

adverbs
eagerly; spontaneously; graciously; sincerely; warmly; heartily; genially; politely; courteously; unwontedly; ostentatiously; obviously; unusually; pleasantly; agreeably; indulgently; civilly; affectionately; devotedly; intimately; quietly; sympathetically; freely; openly; amicably; frankly; gallantly.

CORDIALITY

adjectives
genial; apparent; unexpected; pleasing; intoxicating; unaffected; great; condescending; businesslike; warm; utmost; loud; unofficial.

verbs
display—; doubt—; exhibit—; fraternize with—; greet with—; hate with—; lack—; resent—; respect—; return—; strive in—; —beckons; —bespeaks of; —cheers; —comforts; —exhilarates; —induces; —warms.
(See sincerity, ardor, affection.)

CORE

adjectives
inmost; putrefied; burning; endearing; festering; hidden; vibrant.

verbs
bore into—; cut from—; destroy—; dig to—; eat at—; extract—; feed upon—; fill to—; imbed at—; loosen—; pare to—; putrefy at—; remove—; rot at—; sheathe —; stab to—; surround—; taste to—; touch to—; wring to—; —contains; —disintegrates; —remains; discard—.
(See heart.)

CORK

adjectives
popping; large; leaking; obstinate; unbudging.

CORN

adjectives
military; starving; unsickled; sprinkled; bounteous; strengthening; bladed; scanty; lusty; golden; bruised; dry; pungent; waving; tall; ripening; thriving; rustling.

verbs
blast—; consume—; feed on—; furrow—; gather—; grind—; harvest—; husk—; market—; parch—; pluck—; prepare—; reap—; sack—; scatter—; shell—; shock—; sift—;sow—; stack—; store—; strip—; thrash—; tread out—; wither—; wreathe in—; —blossoms; —ripens; —rustles; —shoots up; —sustains; —sways; —waves.
(See cereal, grain.)

CORNER

adjectives
favorite; accessible; comfortable; cozy; tranquil; quiet; hintermost; secluded; sheltered; sunny; shaded; obscure; murky; isolated; removed; remote; vine-covered; grassy; theological; neglected; wickedest; overstuffed; coolest; tight; ill-smelling; outward; twisting; propitious; genteel; adjacent; inconspicuous; awkward; unexpected; arbored; hooded; hazardous; farthest; dim; dark; squalid; somber; cooperative; unpretentious; neighboring; idle.

verbs
bevel—; cower in—; crouch in—; droop in—; dwell in—; emerge from—; fall in—; hinge—; move to—; obscure in—; pray in—; round—; sharpen—; sit in—; sulk in—; sweep in—; tuck in—.
(See niche.)

CORNFIELD

adjectives
waving; swaying; sweltering; immense; dense; luxuriant; exuberant; discouraged; struggling.

CORNICE

adjectives
ornamental; hand-wrought; elaborate; top-heavy; scrolled; jutting; overhanging.

CORNUCOPIA

adjectives
generous; filled; flowing; bounteous; redolent; replete; plenteous; expansive; well-assorted; full-variety; assuring.

COROLLARY

adjectives
necessary; reasonable; definite; consequent; maintained; sustained; abrupt; inevitable; eventual; invariable.

CORONATION

adjectives
earthly; princely; poetical; seraphic; triumphant; glorious; climacteric.

CORONET

adjectives
vast; jeweled; braided.

CORPORAL

adjectives
insignificant; stately; impressive; awkward; imposing; exacting; domineering.

CORPORATION

adjectives
prosperous; civil; remarkable; bloated; modern; soulless; giant; moneyed; world-renowned; flourishing; dummy; tremendous; prominent; large.

verbs
bankrupt—; build up—; charter—; combine in—; constitute—; control—; dominate—; form—; found—; head—; join in—; outlaw—; preserve—; rule— unite in—; —advertises; —branches out; —develops; —employs; —grows; —undersells.
(See company, firm, association.)

CORPS

adjectives
diplomatic; detached; meager; well-tried; judiciary; terrible; executive; attacking; admirable; celebrated.

verbs
assign to—; captain—; command—; enlist in—; form—; join—; lead—; organize—; quarter—; station—; uniform—; —assembles; —attacks; —charges; —combats; —encamps; —marches; —patrols.
(See army.)

CORPSE

adjectives
poor; little; galvanized; sundried; good-looking; bleeding; dripping; handsome; desiccated; mangled; unrecovered; mutilated; disfigured; peaceful; lovely; charred; shriven; bloated.

verbs
animate—; attend—; bear—; bury—; collect—s; desert—; destroy—; discover—; disinter—; dismember—; dispose of—; drag for—; exhume—; grapple for—; hide—; hunt—; identify—; inter—; lament—; lay out—; mourn—; preserve—; recognize—; regard—; restore—; strew with—s; stumble on—; trip over—; view—; —decays; —decomposes; —disintegrates; —putrefies.
(See remains, carcass.)

CORPULENT

adverbs
unfortunately; incredibly; unhappily; incurably; comfortably; contentedly; distressingly; absurdly; ridiculously; ludicrously; lamentably; sadly; blithely; joyously; dangerously; heavily; gracefully; admittedly; funnily; unreasonably; incorrigibly; irremediably; complacently; mournfully; dramatically; complainingly.

CORPUSCLE

adjectives
bulbous; life-bearing; oxygen-supplying; scavenging; striving; surging; vitally-laden.

verbs
divide into—s; furnish with—s; increase—s; lower—s; study—; tear down—; —acts; —attacks; —bursts; —destroys; —envelops; —immunizes; —provides; —reproduces; —resists; —splits; —wanders about.

CORRAL

adjectives
rickety; shabby; flaming; palisaded; guarded; over-crowded; incarcerating; confining.

verbs
accept—; acknowledge—; devise—; allow—; authorize—; counteract—; direct—; follow—; fumble for—; invite—; judge—;

modify—; need—; offer—; perform—; print—; refuse—; rejoice in—; resent—; subject to—; substitute—; superintend—; —amends; —improves; —neutralizes; —revises.

(See punishment, discipline.)

CORRECT

adverbs
strictly; formally; fashionably; habitually; ordinarily; positively; uncompromisingly; rigidly; stiffly; insistently; absurdly; carefully; arrogantly; affectedly; ostentatiously; pretentiously; pompously; meticulously; punctiliously; dependably; scrupulously; infallibly; uncannily; disturbingly; unimpeachably; mathematically; insatiably; avidly.

CORRECT (v)

adverbs
painstakingly; constructively; helpfully; sufficiently; harshly; courteously; agreeably; adequately; reasonably; grammatically; infallibly; tactfully; rudely; crudely; curtly; sincerely; obnoxiously.

(See right, reprove.)

CORRECTION

adjectives
courteous; agreeable; autograph; strong; uranographical; adequate.

verbs
accept—; acknowledge—; advise—; allow—; authorize—; counteract—; direct—; follow—; fumble for—; invite—; judge—; modify—; need—; offer—; perform—; print—; refuse—; rejoice in—; resent—; subject to—; substitute—; superintend—; —amends; —improves; —neutralizes; —revises.

(See punishment, discipline.)

CORRECTNESS

adjectives
reasonable; superb; grammatical; irreproachable; lavish; infallible; tactical; rigid.

CORRELATE (v)

adverbs
mutually; definitely; significantly; properly; seriously; exactly; statistically.

(See correspond.)

CORRELATION

adjectives
definite; significant; proper; serious; exact; high; statistical.

CORRESPOND (v)

adverbs
confidentially; exactly; extensively; commonly; spiritually; relatively; curiously; prominently; obviously; superficially.

(See correlate.)

CORRESPONDENCE

adjectives
extensive; poetical; contraband; mutual; clandestine; spurious; noteworthy; seditious; mere; frank; subsequent; spicy; voluminous; lifelong; irresponsible; varied; intimate; diplomatic; heated; imperishable; amatory; objectionable; spiritual; copious; cipher; empirical; commercial; glorious; ungrammatical; vivacious; indiscreet; desultory; relative; curious; sympathetic.

verbs
answer—; conduct—with; enter into—with; establish—with; express—with; file—; influence—; interchange—; invite—; maintain—; manage—; neglect—; open—with; receive—; renew—; return—; safeguard—; treat—; —communicates; —enlightens.

(See communication, intercourse, letter.)

CORRESPONDENT

adjectives
humble; prominent; eavesdropping; sympathetic; flattered; international; energetic; special; active; reliable; diplomatic; warshy; persistent; punctilious.

CORRIDOR

adjectives
vaulted; angling; lengthened; spacious; interminable; golden; gloom-shrouded; dreamland; solitary; labyrinthine; tortuous; majestic; deserted; dusty; footworn; myriad (pl); curtained; endless; sloping; bleak; thronged; polished; resounding; murky; circular; concrete; black; eerie.

verbs
brighten—; clatter in—; cross—; darken—; glimmer through—; guard—; light—; line—; narrow—; pass through—; patrol—; run through—; scrub—; shuffle along—; stroll in—; sweep—; traverse—; watch—; widen—; —connects; —joins; —links; —opens into; —resounds with; —unites.

(See gallery, passage, hall.)

CORRIGIBLE

adverbs
submissively; meekly; humbly; wisely; sensibly; sensitively; fortunately; luckily; happily; easily; willingly; reasonably; intelligently; impressibly; moderately; actually; genuinely; tolerably; surprisingly; unusually; probably; presumably.

CORROBORATE (*v*)

adverbs
substantially; partially; reliably; fully; undeniably; undoubtedly; convincingly; authentically.
(See confirm, support.)

CORROBORATIVE

adverbs
wholly; entirely; partially; satisfactorily; scarcely; collusively; unfortunately; shamefully; unhappily; completely; circumstantially; exactly; generally; authentically; absolutely; warrantably; intrinsically; significantly; impressively; precisely; authoritatively; credibly; inferentially; terribly; fortunately; substantially.

CORRODE (*v*)

adverbs
perniciously; morally; detrimentally; psychically; permanently; fatally; irreparably; irremediably.
(See consume.)

CORROSIVE

adverbs
poisonously; terribly; destructively; irreparably; injuriously; harmfully; wastefully; hopelessly; dangerously; perniciously; rankly; banefully; detrimentally; disastrously; ruinously; irremediably; undoubtedly; seriously; unquestionably; positively.

CORRUGATION

adjectives
delicate; microscopic; faint; threadlike; fluted; transverse; deep; shallow; intense; decided.

CORRUPT

adverbs
incredibly; loathsomely; utterly; infamously; secretly; notoriously; officially; politically; perniciously; basely; generally; grossly; crassly; abominably; shamelessly; openly; admittedly; detestably; odiously; execrably; scandalously; outrageously; darkly; maliciously.

CORRUPT (*v*)

adverbs
flagrantly; undesignedly; dishonorably; profoundly; incredibly; wondrously; loathsomely; utterly; infamously; notoriously; perniciously; basely; generally; systematically; satanically.
(See spoil, debase.)

CORRUPTION

adjectives
chronic; mercenary; medieval; chill; unparalleled; dishonorable; profound; incredible; wondrous; loathsome; utter; infamous; hidden; unhappy; ensuing; glossy; political; foulest; civic; official; business; notorious; pernicious; base; miry; monetary; general.

verbs
attend with—; befoul with—; charge with—; conceive in—; cripple by—; defend from—; deliver from—; denounce—; fall into—; fatten on—; feast on—; infect with—; loathe—; perish in—; practise—; preserve from—; rot with—; sow—; subject to—; taint with—; —blemishes: —breaks up; —contaminates; —decomposes; —depraves; —despoils; —destroys; deteriorates; —disintegrates; —dissolves; —extends to; —perverts; —putrefies; —undermines; —violates.
(See perversion, pollution, demoralization, dishonesty, decay.)

CORSET

adjectives
armor-plated; confining; curve-restricting; corrective; breath-expelling; gusseted; hampering; health-destroying; torturing; ironclad; stout; tightly-laced.

verbs
discard—; divest of—; encircle in—; fit—; lace—; loose—; pierce—; squeeze into—; tighten—; —binds; —covers; —molds; —narrows; —protects; —shapes; —stiffens; —smooths; —strangles; —straps; —supports.

COST

adjectives
trifling; nominal; moderate; inflated; minimum; enormous; appalling; excessive; prodigious; huge; average; comparative; fearful; spiritual; low; relative; ultimate; superfluous; prevailing; exorbitant; admini-

strative; prime; inevitable; extra; classical; operating; additional; insignificant; evident; initial; proper; increasing; outrageous; haulage; aggregate.

verbs
absorb—; avoid—; bear—; calculate—; defray—; forfeit—; heighten—; incur—; maintain—; omit—; prate about—; rate—; reckon—; shave—; shoulder—; spare—; whittle down—; —astounds; —piles up; —soars; —varies; recoup—.
(See price, expense, loss.)

COSTLY

adverbs
enormously; appallingly; unreasonably; fearfully; outrageously; unusually; exorbitantly; absurdly; gorgeously; unwarrantably; senselessly; wickedly; elegantly; flagrantly; unbelievably; extremely; inestimably.

COSTUME

adjectives
charming; brilliant; fetching; clever; intriguing; perfect; gorgeous; colorful; nativity; ornamented; elaborate; unconventional; indelicate; inappropriate; convict-like; native; flamboyant; ballet; bizarre; theatrical; local; allegorical; crepe-paper; abbreviated; authentic; gala; billowing; stiff; characteristic; gaudy; lavish; fantastic; lugubrious; variegated; rhetorical; exquisite; daring; singular; mournful; picturesque; old-fashioned; grotesque; embroidered; quaint; antique; swagger; flattering; jacketed; capricious.

verbs
array in—; attire in—; change—; deck in—; design—; devise—; disguise in—; divest of—; don—; embroider—; fashion—; launder—; mend—; model—; parade in—; pose in—; recognize—; tailor—; trim—; —dazzles; —enhances; —interprets; —symbolizes.
(See dress, garment, clothing.)

COSY

adverbs
comfortably; snugly; luxuriously; entertainingly; pleasurably; gratefully; refreshingly; sweetly; hospitably; cheerfully; companionably; heartily; intimately; socially; easily; confidentially; agreeably; pleasantly; truly; curiously.

COT
(*cottage*)

adjectives
hurdled; weed-inwoven; chimneyed; cozy; overgrown; rose-thatched; sheltered; unpretentious; picturesque; ivied; tenanted.

COT
(*bed*)

adjectives
iron; lowly; downy; snug; sleep-forbidding; lumpy; miserable; untidy; tumbled.

verbs
erect—; pounce on—; slumber on—; throw oneself upon—; toss on—; —creaks.
(See bed, couch.)

COTERIE

adjectives
half-serious; playful; philosophical; select; exclusive; cabal; formidable; numerous; assembled.

COTTAGE

adjectives
thatched; attendant; prim; peaceful; coquettish; straggling; green-shuttered; nestling; squat; smoke-grimed; vine-clad; secluded; luxurious; abandoned; modest; dim-lit; enchanted; attractive; cozy; ancient; rustic; authentic; pert; suburban; eerie; mysterious; gray; small; tidy; weathered; low; lovable; dream; midget.

verbs
abide in—; adorn—; brighten—; construct—; dot with—s; dwell in—; erect—; forsake—; furnish—; inhabit—; lease—; lodge in—; rent—; repair to—; shade—; shelter—; —cheers; —invites; —s line; —secludes.
(See house, hut, cabin, lodge.)

COTTON

adjectives
speckled; glorified; striped; absorbent; excellent; lovely; sheer; snowy; fe·thery.

verbs
apply—; bale—; clean—; clothe in—; cultivate—; dye—; export—; gin—; market—; pack with—; pad with—; pick—; prey on—; print on—; raise—; saturate—; sterilize—; swab with—; thread—; twist—; wad—; weave—; wrap in—.
(See cloth, thread.)

COUCH

adjectives

frosty; hollow; narrow; unruffled; fiery; uncurtained; rushy; slippery; nuptial; tortured; stony; bridal; resplendent; sumptuous; festal; luxurious; be-tumbled; eastern; rude; restless; soft; broad; low; big; grassy.

verbs

clamber on—; defile—; ensconce on—; exalt —; fling upon—; lie on—; recline on—; rest on—; roll off—; sprawl on—; stretch upon—; stuff—; upholster—; —invites; —tempts.

(See bed, sofa.)

COUCH (*v*)

adverbs

cautiously; gracefully; flatteringly; tactfully; fastidiously; expressively; diplomatically.

(See express.)

COUGH

adjectives

bad; monotonous; persistent; sinister; low; irritable; slight; little; sharp; tremendous; sepulchral; muffled; hectic; distressing; hacking; dubious; apologetic; troublesome; churchyard; shattering; discreet; annoyed; wheezing; timid; dismal; hollow; smothered; premonitory.

verbs

affect with—; afflict with—; bark—; characterize by—; contract—; dose—; ease—; relieve—; stifle—; subdue—; suffer with—; —attacks; —disturbs; —drowns; —expels; —expresses; —indicates; —irritates; —persists; —strangles; —warns; —weakens.

COUGH (*v*).

adverbs

incessantly; huskily; heavily; significantly; discreetly; agonizingly; apologetically; monotonously; persistently; sinisterly; sepulchrally; muffledly; hectically; hackingly; distressingly; troublesomely; exhaustingly; wheezingly; dismally.

(See sound.)

COUNCIL

adjectives

local; advisory; official; ecclesiastical; church; intermediate; undecided; lawful; executive; general; private; separated; motley; municipal; imposing; irresponsible; elective; legislative; wicked; common; maiden.

verbs

admit to—; appoint—; assemble—; bar from—; call—; command—; dismiss—; dissolve—; frame—; gather—; hear—; herald—; sit in—; summon—; —advocates; —bans; —condemns; —decrees.

(See assembly, cabinet.)

COUNSEL
(*advice*)

adjectives

profound; wise; simple; humane; sane; sweet; gratuitous; anxious; politic; grave; external; insidious; weighty; sworn; heartsome; friendly; erroneous; paternal; vigorous; stout-hearted; medical; expert; wholesome; diffident; ill; intelligible; divided; prudent; crooked; unanimous; lenient; spiritual; senseless; psychiatric; valorous; sage; distracted; appealing; infernal; misguided; financial.

verbs

accept—; amend—; ask—; bestow—; condemn—; decree—; denounce—; engage—; enter—; examine—; execute—; follow—; hearken unto—; hint—; implore—; lack—; lend—; mislead—; plead—; prize—; propose—; receive—; reject—; seek—; speak—; take—; —displeases; —guides; —prevails; —sways; deliver—; forsake—.

(See advice, admonition, consultation.)

COUNSEL
(*attorney*)

adjectives

opposing; experienced; prosecuting; leading; clever; learned; adroit; defending; burly.

COUNSEL (*v*)

adverbs

earnestly; sternly; wisely; simply; humanely; sanely; gratuitously; gravely; insidiously; weightily; erroneously; paternally; medically; expertly; prudently; senselessly; leniently; sagely; misguidedly; financially.

(See advice, admonish.)

COUNSELOR

adjectives

civil; general; prime; private; prophetic; worthy.

verbs
confer with—; confide in—; empower—; entrust with—; heed—; praise—; retain—; —advises; —advocates; —charges; —cross-examines; —deliberates; —demands; —devises; —insinuates; —instructs; —orates; —perjures; —persuades; —pleads; —plots; —practises; —proposes; —recommends; —schemes; —summarizes; —sums up.
(See lawyer, attorney.)

COUNT

adjectives
grieved; amorous; fraudulent; noble; bona-fide; unctuous; bogus.

COUNT (*v*)

adverbs
definitely; clearly; confidently; silently; legally; partially; entirely; trustingly; basically.
(See compute.)

COUNTENANCE

adjectives
pleasing; amiable; romantic; happy; polite; reverent; smiling; reckless; oval; sturdy; ponderous; eager; grotesque; alert; lugubrious; dejected; long; solemn; rueful; pathetic; idiotic; dull; expressionless; vacant; haughty; frank; serious; gracious; open; thin; simpering; bleeding; battered; convulsed; astute; ingenuous; keen; livid; pale; roseate; dark; clouded; impassive; smug; bland; remote; soft; ordinary; homely; harsh; rumpled; haggard; worn; savage; dirty; hated; evil; stern; brazen; truculent; sullen; grim; frowning; fearful; holy; large; patient; mobile; eloquent; moist; heavy; serenest; rubicund; cheerful; blooming; half-startled; vivacious; menacing; sardonic; animated; colorless; tragic; beaming; austere; whimsical; withered; undue; shiny; discontented; speaking; princely; saturnine; meager; changed; wan; melancholy; reserved; humorous; tranquil; placid; commanding; ruddy; striking; interesting; uncomely; troubled; pallid; malignant; incensed; scandalized; shriveled; truthful; overcast; saddened; branded; joyous; swarthy; repulsive; priestly; unveiled; hueless; watchful; elevated; triumphant; graceful; angry; ferocious; meditative; villainous; mottled; scarred; bloated; tragic; independent; apathetic; spirit-sighted; benignest; puzzled; sculptured; resolute; angelic; household; horror-stricken; familiar; belligerent; blandest; quiet; sleepy; florid; meek; distorted; philosophic; martial; infantile; undenoted; piteous; ashen; marble; courageous; plain; superior; flushed; sallow; rueful.

verbs
agitate—; avert—; behold—; bury—in; change—; darken—; distress—; flush—; lift up—; pale—; sadden—; scan—; study—; unmask—; wrinkle—; —beams; —glares; —glowers; —glows; —rebukes; —resembles; —sharpens; —shines; —wavers.
(See face, appearance.)

COUNTERFEIT

adjectives
gross; specious; notorious; worthless; plausible; ostensible; cheap; clever; apish; vulgar; ingenious; tawdry.

verbs
accept—; beguile with—; circulate—; discover—; expose—; fashion—; forge—; identify—; mark—; pass—; reproduce in—; scout as—; stamp—; transform—; withdraw—; work—; —assumes; —copies; —deceives; —defrauds; —differs; —disguises; —imitates; —pretends; —resembles; —simulates.
(See imitation, copy.)

adverbs
grossly; speciously; notoriously; worthlessly; obviously; cleverly; adroitly; deftly; perfidiously; deceptively; cunningly; craftily; unscrupulously; artfully; skilfully; dexterously; ingeniously.

COUNTERMAND (*v*)

adverbs
dramatically; severely; unjustly; legally; treacherously; unexpectedly; rebelliously; effectively.
(See contradict, oppose.)

COUNTERPART

adjectives
precise; painful; unworthy; institutional; modern; earthly; exclusive; emotional; feminine; dense; stooped; elaborate; shrunken.

COUNTRY

adjectives
beloved; enchanting; interesting; advanced; aristocratic; conservative; quaint; small; peaceful; diminutive; weak; underdeve-

loped; backward; crude; great; mesa; plain; broken; art-producing; flourishing; mountainous; picturesque; cultivated; unrevealed; continental; twilight; desolate; extensive; open; nightmare; exotic; surrounding; drowsy; outlying; inefficient; dun; solitary; barren; sterile; inaccessible; agricultural; wasted; undulating; fainting; familiar; roadless; pine; principal; competing; swampy; illustrious; standardized; gracious; adoptive; thinly-settled; mysterious; semi-pastoral; neighboring; ravaged; habitable; promising; useless; indissoluble; watered; wooded; unexplored; rolling; songless; primitive; modern; poor; parsimonious; unhappy; secluded; peaceful; virgin; unspoiled; exquisite; rugged; arid; dry; dead; deserted; prairie; landscape; imperiled; proud; timbered; droll; level; populous; self-lifted; alpine; respective; lonesome; prosperous; fresh; civilized; undiscovered; fragrant; invaded; overcrowded; thankless; farming; ungraded; hard; unoffending.

verbs
assault—; benefit—; bleed—; bombard—; conquer—; depart from—; desolate—; despoil—; devastate—; distress—; dominate—; dumbfound—; exploit—; fortify—; free—; govern—; honor—; invade—; lay waste—; love—; march through—; plunge —into war; ravish—; repair to—; reverence—; return—; rouse—; ruin—; saddle —; salute—; scurry about—; serve—; travel—; unify—; —endures; —protects; —seethes; —tries.

(See territory, region, nation, state, kingdom, republic.)

COUNTRYMAN

adjectives
seditious; unpolished; rapacious; unhappy; erring; well-fed; suffering; petitionary; humble.

verbs
aid—; appeal to—; elevate—; entertain—; greet—; invite—; mold—; repatriate—; school—; subject—; unite—; uplift—; welcome—; —men aid; —men assemble; —men congregate; —men gather; —men rally; —rejoices.

(See citizen, farmer, peasant.)

COUNTRYSIDE

adjectives
remote; lonely; rolling; charming; picturesque; gossiping; peaceful; pleasant; suburban.

verbs
beautify—; defile—; denude—; depict—; describe—; devastate—; dot—; eulogize—; familiarize with—; haunt—; invade—; landscape—; paint—; plague—; preserve—; prowl about—; range—; roam—; scour—; storm—; terrorize—; unite against —; —abounds with; —echoes; —teems with.

(See country, land, farm, region.)

COUPLE

adjectives
sober; strolling; loving; inseparable; devoted; curious; ill-assorted; delectable; stately; venerable; plump; amorous; retiring; worthy; withered; happy; struggling; prudent; moneyless; elderly.

verbs
attach—; betroth—; bless—; conjoin—; connect—; dance in—s; divide—; divorce—; engage—; eye—; fasten—; halve —; join—; knit—; leash—; link—; loose—; pair—s; rend—; sever—; split—; tie—; troop in—s; unite—; yoke—.

(See partners.)

COUPLE (*v*)

adverbs
inevitably; normally; abnormally; hideously; logically; shrewdly; generally; poetically.

(See connect, joint.)

COUPON

adjectives
detachable; hoarded; interest-bearing; neatly-clipped; prepayment; significant; worthless; separable.

verbs
bear—; cash—; clip—; count—s; date—; detach—; identify—; issue—; present—; rate—; register—; save—; snip—; value—; —certifies; —claims; —promises; —represents.

(See certificate, ticket.)

COURAGE

adjectives
splendid; noble; peerless; sublime; superb; ardent; joyous; proud; frank; quiet; simple; patient; dogged; hot; fiery; fighting; wavering; oozing; rising; swelling; stony; unwonted; creative; philosophic; hereditary; moral; ratlike; steadfast; careless; impetuous; indomitable; shamed; unsurpassed; blended; brute; unflinching;

matchless; rare; moral; desperate; pitiful; undiminished; reawakening; husbanded; conscious; exalted; tremendous; tried; reviving; immortal; reckless; abundant; intelligent; ancient; stubborn; personal; devoted; unshaken; passive; sublime; incredible; admirable; habitual; steady; romantic; undismayed; drooping; magnificent; foolhardy; hopeful; animal; exceptional; imperious; placid; dignified; conspicuous; stand-up; renewed; native; undaunted; obdurate; revolutionary; worn; sober; knightly; unfailing; adamantine; audacious; heroic; passive.

verbs

acclaim—; applaud—; blend with—; boast—; bolster—; cultivate—; daunt—; equip with—; exhibit—; extol—; gain—; imbue with—; instill—; lose—; maintain—; manifest—; muster—; plant—; pluck up—; raise—; reflect—; renew—; require—; reveal—; rouse—; screw up—; shake—; shatter—; stiffen—; stimulate—; stir up—; strain—; strengthen—; strut with—; summon—; take—; temper—; whistle up—; —droops; —endures; —flags; —mounts; —rises; —runs high.

(See bravery, fortitude, heroism, valor.)

COURAGEOUS

adverbs

dangerously; rashly; temperamentally; alarmingly; fantastically; foolhardily; colossally; breath-takingly; terribly; admirably; dramatically; notoriously; crazily; strangely; singularly; amazingly; recklessly; unbelievably; foolishly; romantically; heroically; youthfully; boyishly; disconcertingly; extravagantly; splendidly; nobly; superbly; proudly; quietly; patiently; doggedly; enduringly; morally; steadfastly; impetuously; consciously; stubbornly; devotedly; personally; sublimely; habitually; magnificently; calmly.

COURSE
(*direction*)

adjectives

splendid; admirable; sedate; sagacious; reasonable; sensible; serpentine; winding; sinuous; dizzy; desultory; twisting; circuitous; irregular; roundabout; sanguinary; rich; airy; resistless; dangerous; extreme; disagreeable; meteoric; advisable; straight; secretive; indefensible; devious; speedy; politic; heedless; prudent; fixed; middle; needful; unexplored; comfortable; unenvious; erratic; alternative; traditional; lenient; stupid; evil; dreary; fatal; mild; tortuous; endowed; systematic; peevish; indirect; frail; zigzag; feverish; rigorous; magnanimous; decisive; stony; immutable; desperate; exemplary; circular; natural; prescribed; luminous; unsilent; prolonged; headlong; initiatory; arduous; hereditary; extreme; strange; motley; conquering; skyward; unscrupulous; uniform; impetuous; tangential; precarious; profligate; tardy; basalt; tearless; curvilinear; lusty; coercive; orderly; ambiguous; long; shady; rapid; endless; wheeling; intermitting; destined; practical; furious; fair; bloody; normal; excellent; spherical; tranquil; doubtful; victorious; aimless; uneventful; peculiar; respective; contrary; irresistible; economical; diurnal; swift; precipitate; majestic; preparatory.

verbs

advance—; alter—; appoint—; bend—; blow off—; chart—; check— commend—; conceal—; condemn—; continue in—; cut off from—; decide on—; denote—; determine—; dictate—; direct—; disturb—; drift in—; embark on—; fix—; follow—; hinder—; hold—; illumine—; impede—; interrupt—; lead—; leave to—; map—; mark—; modify—; order—; outrun—; persevere in—; pervert—; plot—; praise—; pursue—; rebuke—; resolve on—; return to—; reverse—; run—; set—; settle on—; shape—; shun—; steer—; stem—; stick to—; subdue—; swerve from—; travel—; tread—; turn—; upbraid—; veer from—; wander off—; wing—; —fluctuates; —runs; —shifts; —winds; —zigzags.

(See direction, line, conduct.)

COURSE
(*study*)

adjectives

advanced; logical; pedagogic; technical; rigorous; difficult; condensed.

verbs

abandon—; change—; choose—; complete—; comprise—; conduct—; cut—; deride—; divide into—s; elect—; emphasize—; establish—; evaluate—; finish—; flunk (colloq.)—; follow—; fulfill—; initiate—; model—upon; pursue—; renew—; revise—; set up—; speed up—; —equips; —intends to; —prepares.

COURSE (v)

adverbs
tortuously; swiftly; windingly; circuitously; sinuously; irregularly; deviously; erratically; impetuously; tranquilly; irresistibly; precipitately.
(See travel.)

COURT (enclosed yard)

adjectives
cobbled; gravelly; dusty; muddy; noisy; paved; tiled; rubbish-filled; neglected; sunless; gloomy; discouraging.

verbs
approach—; besiege—; build—; cross—; fill—; guard—; measure—; pace—; retire to—; roof—; shut up in—.

COURT (law)

adjectives
vested; open; stuffy; instituted; hospitable; primitive; voluntary; spiritual; temporal; silent; petrified; superior; imperial; gloomy; papal; punctilious; murky; merciless; respectable; sapient; strict; corrupt; packed; primitive; competent; inferior; international; circuit; criminal.

verbs
adjourn—; adjudicate in—; beseech—; blockade—; call into—; coerce—; defy—; dismiss—; exploit—; hale into—; haul into—; liberalize—; override—; overrule —; pack—; petition in—; preside over—; reform—; rejuvenate—; remake—; resort to—; revamp—; strangle—; submit to—; sway—; tamper with—; vow in—; —awards; —convenes; —fines; —grants; —impounds; —judges; —recognizes; —renders a decision; —restrains; —upholds.
(See tribunal, judge.)

COURT (royal)

adjectives
ceremonious; tavern; ostentatious; revolutionary; dilapidated; ecclesiastical; spacious; cloistered; envious; weedy; pontifical; assiduous; ambitious; magnolia; pompous; gloomy; admirable; sportive; untidy; dripping; bosky.

verbs
break up—; dispatch to—; entertain at—; establish—; fete at—; forsake—; hold—; honor at—; join—; muster—; open—; present at—; preside at—; station at—; —flourishes; —glories in.

COURT (v)

adverbs
lustfully; assiduously; steadfastly; absurdly; ostentatiously; subtly; romantically; devotedly; shyly; masterfully; wildly; incessantly; languidly; impetuously.
(See attract, woo.)

COURTEOUS

adverbs
exquisitely; deeply; quietly; deferentially; perfunctorily; thoughtfully; extravagantly; tenderly; formally; naturally; dangerously; scarcely; scantily; traditionally; languidly; lazily; grimly; cordially; outwardly; genuinely; provokingly; gracefully; particularly; charmingly; gravely; loftily; meticulously; punctiliously; unfailingly; inherently; reverently; suspiciously; unexpectedly; especially.

COURTESY

adjectives
matchless; perfect; fine; gentle; exquisite; spiritual; deep; quiet; understanding; deferential; insinuating; decent; stately; dignified; perfunctory; thoughtful; extravagant; strained; serious; benevolent; stolid; dissembling; unclean; tender; formal; condescending; studied; national; natural; dangerous; official; gracious; scant; neighborly; poor; traditional; senatorial; caressing; straining; languid; special; grim; pressing; obvious; common; cordial; outward; intolerable; particular; graceful; charming; impersonal; doubtful; princely; international; oily; obliging; grave; last; lofty; wayward; patient; rigid; genuine; meticulous; unfailing; cold; automatic; southern; foreign; mickle; inherent; utmost; unusual; sacred; measured; novel.

verbs
accord—; air—; allow—; deny—; deserve—; disdain—; greet with—; imbue with—; misplace—; offer—; overstrain—; praise—; respect—; return—; scorn—; show—; strain—; stress—; temper with—.
(See politeness.)

COURTIER

adjectives
hovering; splendid; decrepit; senile; veteran; garrulous; subtle; shrewd; wary; pompous; vainglorious; sapient; extrava-

gant; absolute; gallant; dissipated; smirking; expectant; avaricious; eulogizing; gaudiest.

COURTSHIP

adjectives
strange; careful; subtle; devoted; romantic; shy; masterful; wild; long; gradual; unhappy; customary; incessant; orthodox; languid; harassed.

verbs
attend in—; chaperon—; conduct—; delight in—; flatter during—; involve in—; lengthen—; pay—; pledge in—; prolong—; pursue with—; reject—; respond to—; revel in—; rush—; sway by—; verse in—; —ends; —expires; —flags; —softens.
(See friendship.)

COUSIN

adjectives
worthy; philological; valiant; capricious; stalwart; pious; enormous; gentle; favorite; distant; pallid; bloody; aristocratic; impecunious; remote; loutish.

COVE

adjectives
fascinating; shallow; sunlit; quiet; wooded; eddying; drowsy; snug.

COVENANT

adjectives
sacred; solemn; binding; common; perpetual; broad; eternal.

verbs
agree upon—; alter—; annul—; break—; confirm—; declare—; defile—; destroy—; draw up—; ensure—; enter into—; establish—; forsake—; invert—; mind—; obey—; profane—; record—; respect—; sever—; stabilize—; stipulate in—; swear to—; transgress—; void—.

COVER

adjectives
fairest; ephemeral; glazed; dewy; precious; enameled; soiled; coarse; garish; friendly; illuminated; excellent; practical; floor; protective; grassy; underdone; loathsome; reversible; detachable; flimsy; inmost; frail; weedy; sorry; luxuriant; ghostly; variegated; conical.

verbs
attach—; clap on—; form—; improvise—; lift—; ornament—; raise—; remove—; screw on—; slide—on; take to—; wrap in—; —clothes; —conceals; —defends; —encloses; —envelops; —hides; —hinges; —overlays; —overspreads; —projects; —protects; —rests upon; —screens; —shelters; —surfaces.
(See case, lid, canopy, roof, spread, shelter.)

COVER (*v*)

adverbs
instinctively; adequately; grotesquely; insufficiently; inadequately; exhaustively; partially; garishly; protectively; loathsomely; flimsily; frailly; luxuriantly; conically.
(See conceal, hide.)

COVET (*v*)

adverbs
burningly; obviously; lustfully; jealously; bloodthirstily; sinfully; viciously; insanely; instinctively; economically; vulgarly; basely; detestably; infamously.
(See crave.)

COVETED

adverbs
eagerly; highly; passionately; enviously; wickedly; earnestly; excitedly; justifiably; sinfully; fondly; impatiently; keenly; hungrily; greedily; desirously; wishfully; wistfully; insatiably; avidly; madly; ambitiously; rabidly; invidiously; jealously; yearningly; ardently; curiously; fervently.

COVETOUSNESS

adjectives
excited; justifiable; bloodthirsty; unholy; inordinate; eager; rapacious.

COW

adjectives
serene; spotted; fat; milch; gentle; gaunt; fractious; ambitious; sad; mooing; contented.

verbs
breed —s; feed —s; herd —s; infect —; inspect —; raise —; slaughter —; test —; —s graze; —s huddle; —s leap; —s lumber; —s pasture; —s plod; —s roam; —s trail.
(See cattle, animal.)

COWARD

adjectives
thrasonical; arrant; vulgar; miserable; hulking; base; egotistic; contemptible; mannish; notable; faithless; detestable; abject; conscienceless; crafty; blaspheming; blatant; devout; infernal; pale; infamous.

verbs
bar —; brand as —; denounce —; designate as —; develop into —; intimidate —; ostracize —; proclaim —; regale —; reproach —; slay —; sneer at —; stigmatize as —; taunt —; — faints; — falters; — fears; — flees; — pales; — pleads; — protects; — shakes; — shies; — slanders; — slinks; — trembles; — whimpers; — yields.

COWARDICE

adjectives
empty; servile; moral; ineffable; vilest; abject; unexpected; palpable; strange.

verbs
banish —; brand with —; breed —; charge with —; conceal —; curb —; denounce —; display —; exhibit —; feign —; flaunt —; flee in —; hide —; loathe —; mark —; overcome —; protest —; rage at —; soil with —; vindicate of —; — defiles; — demoralizes; — shames.

(See timidity.)

COWARDLY

adverbs
abjectly; unexpectedly; vilely; feebly; shamefully; suddenly; basely; miserably; contemptibly; hideously; detestably; abominably; pitiably; notoriously; infamously; secretly; pathologically; helplessly; hopelessly; embarrassingly; pathetically; irremediably; consciously.

COWBELL

adjectives
jangling; battered; brassy; silvery; tinkling; musical; matutinal; vespertine.

verbs
attach—; hang on—; respond to—; tie on—; —clangs; —clanks; —dangles; —directs; —echoes; —greets; —jangles; —suggests; —sways; —swings; —tinkles; —tolls.

(See bell.)

COWBIRD

adjectives
attending; herd-following; hoarsely-commenting; perching.

verbs
—crowds out; —gurgles; —intrudes; —warbles.

(See bird.)

COWBOY

adjectives
elemental; daredevil; equestrian; bright; crooning; weather-beaten; saddle-hardened; hard-riding.

verbs
employ—s; quarter—s; —brands; —breaks horses; —breaks loose; —charges; —corrals; —drives; —herds; —lassoes; —mounts; —punches cattle; —ropes; —rounds up; —rustles; —stampedes; —trails; —whoops; —wrangles.

COWER (v)

adverbs
gloomily; weakly; shrinkingly; ignobly; basely; abjectly; servilely; palpably; pusillanimously; spinelessly.

(See crouch, squat.)

COY

adverbs
timidly; diffidently; shyly; modestly; retiringly; bashfully; blushingly; humbly; nervously; demurely; primly; pleasantly; adorably; uneasily; engagingly; gracefully; captivatingly; delightfully; sweetly.

COYOTE

adjectives
gaunt; night-prowling; howling; sneaking; sly; wary; pusillanimous.

verbs
frighten by—s; trap—s; —s abound; —s attack; —s bark; —burrows; —s carry off; —cries; —destroys; —digs; —gallops; —hides; —howls; —infests; —inhabits; —laps; —lurks; —mangles; —prowls; —ranges; —screams; —scurries; —slinks; —sneaks; —s surround; —wails; —yaps; —yips; —yowls.

(See animal.)

CRAB

adjectives
roasted; reluctant; soft-shelled; luscious; invading; semi-transparent; side-walking; scurrying; sodden; swiftly-moving.

verbs
broil—; capture—; catch—; devil—; roast —; steam—; —claws; —crawls; —weighs.

CRABBED

adverbs
bitterly; unnecessarily; unwarrantably; vexatiously; sourly; perplexingly; natural-

ly; innately; horribly; detestably; abominably; persistently; obnoxiously; unpleasantly; constantly; permanently; incurably; unreasonably; intractably; stubbornly; plaguedly; discourteously; rudely; uncivilly; tactlessly; coolly; pertly; obtrusively; snarlingly.

CRACK (blow)

adjectives
sharp; smart; mannish; punitive; admonitory; disciplinary; surreptitious; vindictive; solar plexus; resounding.

CRACK (fissure)

adjectives
shallow; minute; widening; seamy; ragged; fearful; devastating.

verbs
close—; fill—; peer through—; seal—; seep through—; shine through—; squeeze into—; stretch out—; trace—; widen—; —breaks; —bursts; —damages; —endangers; —gapes; —opens; —separates; —weakens; —widens; —yawns.
(See chasm, gap, opening.)

CRACKLE

adjectives
snapping; faint; sickening; brittle; cheery; warning; ominous; starchy; silken.

CRACKLE (v)

adverbs
cheerily; fiercely; industriously; faintly; sickeningly; furiously; threateningly.
(See sound.)

CRADLE

adjectives
tiny; earthen; equatorial; leafy; stony; hollow; procreant; clumsy; swaddling; unostentatious; animal-skin; rocking.

verbs
attend—; bar—; carry in—; decorate—; deck—; discard—; dream in—; fall from—; jig—; lull in—; mount—; nurture in—; repose in—; rest in—; rock—; shelter in—; sleep in—; snatch from—; stifle in—; sway—; swing—; unveil—; watch over—.
(See bed.)

CRADLE (v)

adverbs
comfortingly; endearingly; maternally; cozily; domestically.
(See bed.)

CRAFT (boat)

adjectives
stately; leaky; weatherly; ponderous; ghostly; frail-looking; multitudinous (pl); tidy; ill-equipped; clumsy; unseaworthy; aging; tiny; speedy; graceful; small; trim; little; slow; toiling; disabled; staunch; makeshift; slender; strange-looking; waterlogged; ridiculous.

CRAFT (skill)

adjectives
hellish; inexhaustible; vulpine; consummate; purloined; mechanical; extraordinary; manual; devilish; elfin; earthly; astonishing; slippery; subtle; inveterate; intervening; peaceful; ancient; coy; crude; indolent; pleasurable; strange-looking; diabolical; contentious; waterlogged.

verbs
apply—; beguile with—; counterfeit—; devote to—; display—; exhibit—; follow—; learn—; master—; perform with—; pursue—; skill in—; study—; trick with—; verse in—; —deceives; —occupies; —thrives.
(See skill, trade.)

CRAFTINESS

adjectives
uncanny; cold; weird; deft; astounding; practiced.

CRAFTSMAN

adjectives
expert; skilled; master; trained; seasoned; meticulous; experienced; sincere; able; erudite; polished; thoroughgoing; wandering; sedentary.

CRAFTSMANSHIP

adjectives
rare; unusual; exquisite; delicate; centuries-old; superb; authentic; progressive; skilled; custom.

CRAFTY

adverbs
suavely; subtly; urbanely; artfully; designingly; dangerously; commercially; alarmingly; suspiciously; extremely; singularly;

profoundly; unexpectedly; deftly; astutely; inscrutably; habitually; warily; cautiously; wisely; invariably; politically; deliberately; shamefully; fiendishly; expertly; horribly.

CRAG

adjectives

stupendous; bare; massive; far-distant; gray; lofty; inaccessible; steep; tottering; yellow; weathered; sustaining; overhanging; dense-wooded; fantastic; impregnable; rocky; mountain; shaggy; slippery; shrubless; jagged; splintered; accumulated; bald; jutting; morselled; whinstone; descendent; beetling; giant-snouted; lichen-covered; dizzy; gaunt; lordly; shredded; precipitous; storm-washed; airy.

verbs

ascend—; batter—; beat—; blow from—; catch on—; clasp—; cling to—; expose—; peer from—; precipitate from—; scale—; scan—; storm—; strand on—; swing from—; topple from—; —hinders; —juts out; —menaces; —slopes; climb—.

(See cliff, rock.)

CRAM (*v*)

adverbs

completely; reputedly; fully; intellectually; enormously ;swellingly; hoggishly; bestially.

(See crowd, squeeze.)

CRAMP

adjectives

agonizing; distressing; hindering; muscle-fettering; paralyzing; torturing; violent.

verbs

affect with—; alleviate—; cause—; contract with—; ease—; massage—; predispose to—; produce—; rack with—; seize with—; take with—; —agonizes; —attacks; —benumbs; —constricts; —extends; —incapacitates; —knots; —numbs; —pains; —paralyzes; —pinches; —restrains; —stiffens; —tortures.

(See pain.)

CRANE (*bird*)

adjectives

eerie-sounding; frog-questing; mournful; shadowy; ungainly; voracious; eternally-wading.

verbs

—alights; —antics; —circles; —clowns; —croaks; —dances; —drifts down; —evades; —hops; —leaps; —skips; —stalks over; —trumpets; —wades; —whoops.

(See bird.)

CRANK

adjectives

ridiculous; complete; usual; veritable; unenviable; decided.

CRANK (*v*)

adverbs

laboriously; sweatingly; difficultly; stiffly; energetically; spiritedly.

(See turn.)

CRASH

adjectives

ominous; incessant (pl); reverberating; thunderous; dazzling; successive (pl); hideous; simultaneous (pl); fearful; confused; heavy; blinding; railroad; grinding; tremendous; almighty; tumultuous; occasional; mighty; light; rolling; heart-shaking; impending; vicious; loud; fatal; resounding; dull; heavy; smashing; distant; disastrous; terrific; rending; ear-splitting; dangerous; sudden; hollow; rhythmic; splintering.

verbs

avert—; avoid—; escape—; produce—; witness—; —breaks; —bursts; —crushes; —dashes; —resounds; —ruins; —shatters; —shivers; —shocks; —smashes; —splinters; —thunders.

(See noise, collapse, ruin, failure.)

CRASH (*v*)

adverbs

sickeningly; haphazardly; ominously; incessantly; reverberatingly; thunderously; simultaneously; heavily; grindingly; tumultuously; rollingly; fatally; resoundingly; disastrously; terrifically; rendingly; ear-splittingly; hollowly; splinteringly.

(See collapse, smash.)

CRASSNESS

adjectives

unutterable; despicable; undescribable; hopeless; irritating; inane.

CRATER

adjectives

extinct; ancient; gaping; active; grass-covered; weed-grown; smoking; exhausted; submerged; cindery; cuplike; thundering; roaring; seething.

verbs
fly over—; form—; run from—; —boils; —bubbles; —discharges; —disgorges; —ejects; —emits; —erupts; —forms; —furrows; —hardens; —pours out; —roars; —rumbles; —seethes; —simmers; —smokes; —spouts; —throws up.
(See volcano.)

CRAVAT

adjectives
unknotted; voluminous; unkempt; nice; well-chosen; correct; becoming; flowing; resplendent.

verbs
admire—; color—; display—; knot—; purchase—; purvey—s; spot—; tie—; —adorns; —blazes; —encircles; —harmonizes; —muffles; —ornaments; —protects; —shields; —shocks.
(See tie, necktie.)

CRAVE (*v*)

adverbs
irresistibly; humbly; instinctively; insatiably; inordinately; intensely; earnestly; unappeasingly; incessantly; uncontrollably; violently; persistently; abnormally; vaguely; maternally; erotically; spiritually; insensately.
(See desire, want.)

CRAVEN

adjectives
stricken; confessed; marked; cowering; fearful; cringing; crass.

CRAVING

adjectives
intense; earnest; unappeasable; eager; incessant; uncontrollable; violent; persistent; tenacious; unbeautiful; spasmodic; frivolous; abnormal; maternal; unsatisfied; mysterious; endless; forbidden; sporadic; instinctive; premature; erotic; insatiable; cruel; vague; mastered; spiritual; insensate; intermittent.

verbs
annul—; appease—; conceal—; dispatch—; ease—; frown on—; harbor—; indulge—; master—; quell—; repress—; resist—; satisfy—; still—; stir up—; sublimate—; —overpowers; —seizes.
(See passion, appetite, hunger, desire, longing, leaning, entreaty.)

CRAWL (*v*)

adverbs
interminably; sluggishly; softly; wearily; tortuously; bestially; dejectedly; sorrowfully; toilingly; determinedly.
(See grovel, creep.)

CRAZE

adjectives
fashionable; dull; amusement; midsummer; newest; freakish; passing; temporary.

verbs
adopt—; denounce—; despise—; develop into—; fancy—; follow—; ignore—; inaugurate—; overcome—; succumb to—; —affects; —attracts; —dies; —fades; —flashes; —seizes; —spreads.
(See mania, caprice.)

CREAK (*v*)

adverbs
stridently; irritatingly; monotonously; continually; disturbingly; intermittently; rhythmically.
(See sound.)

CREAKING

adjectives
strange; cautious; imperceptible; massive; ear-teasing; inaudible.

CREAM

adjectives
rich; pure; oily; stainless; intellectual; vanishing; rejuvenating; penetrating; superb; cosmetic; dulcet; soothing; massage; unguent.

verbs
add—; anoint with—; apply—; beat—; churn—; convert—; dilute—; filter—; form—; gather—; mature—; mix—; moisten with—; pasteurize—; purify—; rub in—; separate—; serve—; skim—; sour—; spread—; stir—; sweeten—; whip—; —foams; —froths; —greases; —mantles; —rises.

CREAMERY

adjectives
spotless; inviting; appetizing; efficient; germ-proof; hermetic; ship-shape.

CREASE (*v*)

adverbs
deftly; readily; disgustingly; offensively; intolerably.
(See wrinkle.)

CREATE (v)

adverbs

obviously; artistically; unconsciously; independently; unexpectedly; painstakingly; artificially; fantastically; specially; fancifully; complicatedly; permanently; forcibly; harmoniously; uniquely; individually; abstractly; brilliantly; imaginatively; inferiorly; gigantically; intellectually; sublimely; beneficently; ceaselessly; figuratively; literally.

(See make, produce.)

CREATION

adjectives

huge; fantastic; special; foreordained; artistic; fanciful; witty; reflective; grave; complicated; primal; permanent; sculpturesque; forcible; surrounding; psychological; brute; harmonious; unique; individual; abstract; brilliant; dormant; pedigreed; rhythmical; coordinating; visible; ungainly; imaginary; human; various; wide-reaching; evolutionary; artificial; immediate; divine; patented; rejuvenated; pendulous; previous; inferior; gigantic; poetical; violent; splendid; serio-comic; aboriginal; false; aerial; memorable; intellectual; infinite; approved; bountiful; special; sublime; beneficent; genial; warm; inanimate; travailing; catastrophic.

verbs

abolish—; behold—; condemn—; contradict —; counterfeit—; curse—; grasp—; illustrate—; improve—; inspire—; mar—; understand—; —collapses; —reflects.

(See world, universe.)

CREATOR

adjectives

responsible; unworthy; rival; benevolent; conscious; omnipotent.

verbs

betray—; consecrate to—; eulogize—; honor —; praise—; revere—; spring from—; worship—; —animates; —decrees; —divines; —empowers; —fashions; —grants; —moulds; —ordains; —originates; —produces; —reveals; —rules; —works.

(See God, inventor.)

CREATURE

adjectives

rare; likable; upstanding; honest-looking; lovable; admirable; brilliant; luscious; docile; glorious; winning; fine; great-hearted; fascinating; gentle; amiable; demure; marvelous; shy; thin; shortsighted; anemic; limitary; tiny; spiritless; forlorn; obscure; slipshod; ravishing; frugal; despicable; smitten; archaic; perennial; little; dull; yellowish-white; faithful-looking; foolish; struggling; furry; rational; perfect; smooth; pretty; plausible; absurd; doll-like; finite; delicate; sentimental; divine; web-footed; insensible; industrious; drugging; stricken; nasty; ill-bred; inconsequent; voracious; carnivorous; graceful; effeminate; singular; crawling; eyeless; fictitious; overflowing; threadbare; fantastic; bewildering; amphibious; pusillanimous; sensitive; hideous; perverse; desperate; inquisitive; silly; helpless; dependent; brutal; faithful; charming; loathsome; formidable; clear-eyed; harmless; fiery; frail; overgrown; carnal; phlegmatic; unhappy; purest; plainest; kind-hearted; magnanimous; artless; predatory; ever-interesting; nervous; timorous; blunt; pleasant; clambering; monstrous; indigenous; affectionate; sensible; cordial; loving; sweetest; dearest; stealthy; gregarious; insignificant; decrepit; two-fold; strenuous; easy; anxious; poor; unteachable; writhing; tortured; piteous; strange; romantic; sickly; faded; kindly; stout; untidy-looking; flowery; harlequin-like; ridiculous; glorious; foul; infinitesimal; hapless; reasonable; amendable; worthy; horned; love-maddened; coarse-grained; unwashed; flexible; noxious; hairless; diminutive; beastly; poor-spirited; unpolished; veiled; healthy-looking; governmental; discouraged; mendacious; precious; paltry; good-humored; vile; sagacious; dismal-looking; vagrant; nomadic; ferocious; primest; stupid; exquisite; grotesque; exotic; miserable; intellectual; irascible; insufferable; silk-clothed; obliging; goodly; inarticulate; new-made; natural; crooked; shameless; fawn-eyed; gigantic; bewitching; non-aggressive; fickle; thoughtful; grave; wistful; tolerable; human; fearful; sincere; cherubic; yearling; dainty; tallowy; slight; girlish; dawdling; beautiful; ravenous; injudicious; timid; sinful; driven; sweated; magnificent; doe-eyed; clinging; frenzied; heartless; ferocious-looking; impudent; fairest; mongrel; dying; wasted; vivid; earnest; grasping; sylphlike; fine-looking, gorgeous-looking; pretty; dark-eyed; spirited; handsome; elegant; dazzling; furtive; crafty; scheming; wily; baffling; uncanny; wise; cunning; uncouth; spineless; affrighted; gentle; meek-spirited; weak; weary; luckless; poor; humble; long-legged; gaunt; gangling; angular; ragged; emaciated; loose-jointed; lanky; cadaverous-faced; weird; strange; odd-looking; stodgy; porkish; kind; plump; flabby; huge; muscular; poised; self-confident; vital; energetic; big; forthright; hearty; blithe; buxom; sprightly; flippant; self-assured; capricious; sad; ugly; humdrum; stunted; strong-willed; stubborn; obstinate; queer-looking; humpbacked; passive; senseless; idiotic; silliest-looking; star-eyed; sinuous; beady-eyed; slim; bird-like; yellow-striped; half-wild; shy; feathered; migratory; feline; screeching; aquatic; lone; marsh; biting; crawling; forest; pathological; merry; wild; thankless; winged; troublesome; bloodthirsty; mangy-looking; broken; disintegrated; dirty; disheveled; unshorn; emaciated; filthy; ragged; detestable; menacing; primitive; worthless; undesirable; vicious-looking; tarnished; distressing; careless; wretched; half-blind; tottering; imaginary; mythical; fastidious; talkative; plain; huddle; two-legged; newly-evolved; vehement; gaudy; unvapory.

verbs
cage—; curse—; despise—; distress—; eye—; feed—; hunt—; hurt—; kill—; loathe—; oppress—; slay—; tame—; torture—; trap—; —echoes; —senses; —stirs; —walks.
(See being, animal.)

CREDENCE

adjectives
qualified; ready; partial; definite; unwarranted.

CREDENTIALS

adjectives
required; college; personal; time-tested; intellectual; valid; sufficient.

verbs
accept—; arm with—; bear—; check—; display—; doubt—; falsify—; forge—; forward—; honor—; investigate—; lose—; present—; provide with—; sign—; —attest to; —entitle; —reveal.
(See testimonial.)

CREDIBLE

adverbs
deeply; implicitly; actually; presumably; reliably; soberly; conceivably; certainly; assuredly; possibly; positively; impressively; fairly; reasonably; plausibly; probably; speciously; potentially; peradventurously; haply; obviously; unreservedly.

CREDIT

adjectives
unlimited; tentative; threatened; retirement; weakening; unquestioned; everlasting; cooperative; implicit; highest; fullest; personal; moral; comparative; small; unfailing; exhausted; practical; rescinded; domestic; long-term; foreign; extended.

verbs
accept—; accumulate—; ascribe to—; bolster up—; claim—; deserve—; expand—; extend—; favor with—; honor—; obtain —; redound—; rehabilitate—; secure—; share—; strain—; warp—.
(See confidence, trust, faith, prestige, influence.)

CREDIT (v)

adverbs
conveniently; ignorantly; tentatively; everlastingly; implicitly; fully; personally; morally; unfailingly; practically; locally; formally; unhesitatingly.
(See believe.)

CREDITABLE

adverbs
highly; altogether; admirably; becomingly; deservedly; duly; richly; splendidly; notably; eminently; conspicuously; remarkably.

CREDITOR

adjectives
importunate; inexorable; sourest; bloody; persistent; detaining; unfeeling.

verbs
avoid—; cajole—; dismiss—; escape—; evade—; hold off—; pay—; satisfy—; settle with—; —s rise; —assails; —demands; —depends; — descends upon; —s dwindle; —forces; —harasses; —importunes; —menaces; —stands; —sues; —threatens; —trusts.

CREDULITY

adjectives
good-natured; popular; heretical; human; great; unfathomable; reluctant; common; ignorant; curious; scornful; emotional; unshakable; grave; innocent.

verbs
appeal to—; assume—; attack—; bless with—; clothe in—; disguise—; invite—; lose—; preserve—; produce—; register—; remove—; strain—; tax—; transcend—; value—; —accepts; —aids; —astounds; —expires.
(See faith, belief.)

CREDULOUS

adverbs
good-naturedly; reluctantly; instantly; readily; gullibly; foolishly; thoughtlessly; unthinkingly; boyishly; eagerly; enthusiastically; fondly; blindly; innocently; gravely; stupidly; superstitiously; idiotically; laughably; guilelessly; artlessly; ingenuously; childishly; ardently; ignorantly.

CREED

adjectives
everlasting; common; rigid; narrow; respective (pl); noble; vulgar; delicious; confused; fashionable; senseless; rebellious; especial; ancient; healthful; soulless; hopeful; dominant; creative; polemic; cynical; procreative; strange; primeval; adopted; universal; heavenly.

verbs
accept—; adopt—; advance—; alter—; bind to—; displace—; fix—; follow—; formulate—; instill—; institute—; learn—; scoff at—; shake—; support—; subscribe to—; tangle—; teach—; —decays; —summarizes.
(See belief, faith.)

CREEK

adjectives
brawling; briny; winding; log-jammed; silvery; yearning; cheery; echoing; tortuous; emerald; dry; dirty; ice-fringed; dimpled; swollen; fresh-water; unruly; hidden; muddy; scanty; cool; pebbled; tiny; whispering; roaring.

verbs
bridge—; dam—; explore—; fish—; follow —; navigate—; paddle down—; span—; wade in—; —babbles; —bends; —branches off; —dances; —drenches; —gurgles; —harbors; —irrigates; —joins; —overflows; —penetrates; —sings; —twists; —widens; —winds.
(See brook, stream.)

CREEP (v)

adverbs
slyly; mechanically; noiselessly; timidly; cautiously; blindly; stealthily; piteously; meekly; invisibly; mysteriously; ultimately.
(See crawl, grovel.)

CREEPER

adjectives
blooming; luxuriant; spiky; parasitic; interlacing; indigenous; deciduous; poisonous; woody.

CREPE

adjectives
sheer; rayon; tailored; trim; crinkly; clinging; webby.

CRESCENDO

adjectives
rending; sudden; deafening; wild; gradual; muffled.

CRESCENT

adjectives
silvery; paling; sardonic; delicate; sharp; black; stormy.

verbs
adopt—as; attach—; carry—; carve—; decorate with—; design—; employ—; form —; mold—; ornament with—; rest upon—; shape—; trace—; —embellishes; —fades; —glimmers; —signifies; —symbolizes.

CRESS

adjectives
matted; mantling; pungent; tasty; crisp; fresh.

CRESSET

adjectives
blazing; burning; hanging; pendent; swinging; polished; shining; glowing.

CREST

adjectives
ferny; higher; snow-streaked; silver; flamelike; fire-tipped; glittering; ancestral; blazing; upturned; haughty; snowy; kindled; polished; gory; uncontrolled; crimson; golden; bald; towering; glimmering; turret; flaming; stainless; overhanging; compassed; princely; confused; proud; slide-scarred; knife-edged; cloven; tranquil; hissing; lofty; whitening; windy; cockatoo; mountain; jagged; distant.

verbs
affix—; bear—; brighten—; dance on—; elevate to—; erect—; fix—; helmet with—; let fall—; mount to—; plate with—; recognize—; seal with—; strike—; —bristles; —crowns; —droops; —ornaments; —plumes; —signifies; —symbolizes; —undulates; —waves; —wreathes.

(See comb, crown.)

CREVICE

adjectives
barren; rock; narrow; winding; snug; sunken; distant; mysterious.

CREW

adjectives
rollicking; skulking; pestilent; fiendish; motley; vulgar; lachrymose; revolutionary; enthusiastic; marauding; rebellious; persevering; well-organized; worthless; mumbling; rough-and-ready; scribbling; numerous; humorous; back-biting; unhallowed; horrid; dilapidated; whining; besotted; stammering; dispirited; oriental-looking; strange; gaunt; merry; mutinous; gay; adventurous; rugged; coarse-fibred; indigent; stout; burly; handy; unruly; sleepy; ground; marooned; insubordinate; changing; sullen; annihilated; rascal; tiring; nefarious; madcap; banished.

verbs
address—; arouse—; assemble—; augment —; banish—; bestir—; captain—; capture —; command—; consult—; control—; curse—; direct—; dissemble—; engage—; enlarge—; exclude—; gather—; hire—; order—; organize—; oversee—; quarter—; rescue—; rule—; —accomplishes; —boards; —conspires; —embarks; —mans; —mutinies; —rebels; —revels.

(See crowd, company.)

CRIB

adjectives
lace-ruffled; comfortable; safeguarded; padded; wicker; swinging; basket.

CRICKET

adjectives
lusty; creaking; humming; chirping; drumming; incessant.

verbs
plague with—s; —chirps; —fiddles; —rubs; —sings; —shrills.

(See insect.)

CRIME

adjectives
cherished; wretched; horrible; nameless; consummate; atrocious; conspicuous; inhuman; futile; prevailing; heinous; juvenile; unmilitary; sexual; solitary; hideous; unpardonable; darkest; inexplicable; absolute; flagitious; imputed; dreadful; reiterated; malicious; enormous; grave; legalized inexpiable; foul; dastardly; monstrous; locutionary; godless; devastating; cloistered; subsequent; gory; imaginable; heathenish; organized; earthly; unknowing; successful; petty; blackest; heart-crazing; flagrant; diversified; gloomy; aboriginal; perfect; crowning; greedy; calculated; cunning; unnatural; nefarious; infamous; barbarous; abominable; obscene; grisly; violent; gruesome; scandalous; brutal; fiendish; cowardly; ungrateful; hair-raising; unpunished; unsolved; unprevented; serious; professional; modern; vocal; attempted; conceivable; pitiful; incredible.

verbs
abet—; accuse of—; allege—; alleviate—; assail—; atone for—; avenge—; avoid—; betray—; breed—; cancel—; charge with —; check—; cloak—; condone—; contemplate—; contrive—; cover—; detect—; diminish—; divulge—; eradicate—; expiate —; extenuate—; fatten on—; grapple with —; hatch—; impute—to; involve in—; mark with—; perpetuate—; plot—; predispose to—; prosecute—; punish—; reconstruct—; restrain—; sentence for—; smash—; sully with—; suspect of—; taint with—; uncover—; urge—; witness—; —flourishes; —stains; —thrives.

(See offense, misdeed, sin, wrong.)

CRIMINAL

adjectives
irreclaimable; petty; condemned; roving; professional; notorious; dangerous; vicious; utter; conscienceless; piratical; organized (pl); runaway; calculating; confirmed; willful; visible; timorous; skulking; bloody; blackjacked; ruthless; hypothetical; potential; clever; perfect; experienced; frenzied; hardened; desperate; miserable; unfortunate; parricidal; adult; cinematographic; self-confessed; grotesque; incipient; enterprising; habitual; elusive; courageous; fleeing; daring.

verbs
apprehend—; arrest—; charge—; close in on—; coddle—; convict—; detain—; develop into—; harbor—; infest with—s; involve—; lash—; mark—; parole—; penalize—; point out—; pounce upon—; prosecute—; punish—; rehabilitate—; restrain—; retrieve—; round up—; sentence —; shame—; thwart—; —commits; —s congregate; —defies; —habituates; —haunts; —indulges; —plots; —reforms; —repents; —rifles; —schemes; —stalks; —swindles.
(See culprit, prisoner.)

adverbs
shockingly; outrageously; brutally; grossly; basely; iniquitously; despicably; abominably; pestilentially; accursedly; damnably; diabolically; infernally; noxiously; vilely; virulently; preposterously; corruptly; atrociously; viciously; profligately; scurvily; scandalously; heinously; fiendishly; incorrigibly; irreclaimably.

CRIMSON
adjectives
deepest; angry; dull; burning; fever; richest; russet; clear; glowing; spiritual.

CRINGE (v)
adverbs
humbly; servilely; slavishly; menially; brokenly; defeatedly; grotesquely; timorously.
(See cower, fawn.)

CRINKLE
adjectives
crisp; pleasant; laughing; traitorous; effacing; merry; mischievous.

CRIPPLE
adjectives
neglected; wealthy; awful; hopeless; deformed; grotesque; drab; grizzled; ragwrapped; whining.

CRIPPLED
adverbs
hopelessly; helplessly; pitiably; deplorably; tragically; permanently; temporarily; crookedly; slightly; terribly; fearsomely; incredibly; pathetically; pitifully; cruelly; horribly; brutally; deliberately; curiously; strangely; sadly; painfully; dreadfully; indescribably.

CRISIS
adjectives
mighty; momentous; great; tremendous; supreme; fearful; serious; grave; domestic; legislative; intense; emotional; economic; agricultural; unprecedented; spiritual; psychological; political; industrial; national; moral; recurring; financial; banking; favorable; naive; interminable; contemporary; unquiet; distressing; religious; commercial; deplorable; revolutionary; majestic; peculiar; tragical; approaching; memorable; nervous; over-estimated; exciting; sternest; rapid; diplomatic; noisy; striking; desperate.

verbs
aggravate—; avert—; confront with—; cope with—; face—; handle—; improve—; lead up to—; mark—; precipitate—; provoke—; reach—; suffer—; toil over—; weather—; —besets; —grips; —grows; —indicates; —occurs; —passes; —wears off.
(See emergency, exigency.)

CRISP
adverbs
delicately; crunchily; frailly; deliciously; tastily; neatly; concisely; curtly; pithily; crumbly.

CRISPNESS
adjectives
buttery; crunchy; blanched; pleasant; refreshing; airy; invigorating; icy.

CRITERION
adjectives
economic; post-factum; inadequate; surer; whimsical; corresponding.

verbs
admit as —; allow as —; award on —; base on —; conclude by —; decide by —; distinguish as —; establish —; estimate by —; gauge by —; judge by —; mark —; measure by —; present —; produce —; reach —; represent —; test by —.
(See standard, rule, law, test.)

CRITIC
adjectives
superficial; facetious; astute; dramatic; generous; literary; interpretative; levelheaded; penetrating; routine; quibbling; shortsighted; ingenious; unsparing; carping; exacting; fastidious; contemporary; music; unperceived; unknown; crabbed; inimitable; bitter; theatrical; vigorous; judicious; inimical; celebrated; fair-mind-

ed; aggressive; arrogant; opinionated; over-subtle; ignorant; self-constituted; amateur; thoughtful; passionate; clumsy; educational; creative; penetrating; textual; profound; robust; vicious; haughty; persistent; radical; alert; fearless; toilsome; impartial; snarling; invidious; discriminating; unfriendly; surly; grave; primitive; captious; malevolent; merciless; conscientious; competent; sincere; pure; serious; sober; sanguine; enthusiastic; tolerant; disinterested; keen; ablest; authoritative; master; indisputable; first-rate; leading; eminent; noted; outstanding; caviling; jaundiced; befuddled; sarcastic, cynical; pious; caustic; hostile; pertinacious; belligerent; gloomy; ill-disposed; lethargic; incipient; typical; exaggerating; blatant; incessant; thoroughgoing.

verbs
confound —s; silence —s; — appraises; — assails; — asserts; — attacks; — belittles; — blames; —s chatter; — disparages; — exalts himself; — gauges; — gloats; — interprets; — inveighs; — lauds; — opposes; — praises; — pronounces; — rails; — shuns; — snipes at; — weighs.

(See judge, censor.)

CRITICAL

adverbs
facetiously; astutely; generously; penetratingly; ingeniously; unsparingly; exactingly; fastidiously; crabbedly; bitterly; vigorously; judiciously; aggressively; ignorantly; thoughtfully; clumsily; gracelessly; creatively; viciously; haughtily; persistently; constructively; alertly; fearlessly; courageously; impartially; gravely; captiously; mercilessly; malevolently; conscientiously; keenly; authoritatively; tolerantly; ably; caustically; disagreeably; obnoxiously; unpleasantly.

CRITICISM

adjectives
adverse; favorable; brief; hostile; inductive; malevolent; shallow; argumentative; satisfactory; eerie; comparative; dramatic; querulous; harsh; exacting; withering; reverential; hazy; reprobative; numberless (pl); carping; sophistical; irritating; mordant; metaphysical; trenchant; depressing; cold; merciless; absurd; captious; comprehensive; loud; eager; detailed; negative; audible; severe; social; benevolent; injurious; rational; gentle; satiric; ungenerous; prejudiced; spasmodic; unintended; vigilant; frank; dispassionate; scathing; watchful; cheery, acute; unsparing; sweeping; philosophical; loving; implicit; impartial, outside; caustic; sustained; literary; praiseless; biting; stimulating; musical; acrimonious; premature; qualifying; energetic; stupid; reflected; skeptical; unkind; affected; epigrammatic; candid; careful; intelligent; lucid; searching; healthy; salutory; expert; constructive; justified; corrective; witty; ironic; acrid; barbed; endless; lengthy; copious; vehement; stormy; murderous; libelous; bitter; faultfinding; peculiar; slurring; boorish; small-minded; sullen; stringent; factional; journalistic; partisan; aesthetic; presumptuous; subjective; implied; snobbish; retrogressive.

verbs
base — on; bow to —; chafe at —; dispense with —; distort —; draw —; elicit —; endure —; evoke —; expose to —; heap —; hurl —; indulge in —; justify —; pour forth —; provoke —; refrain from —; squelch —; stifle —; subject to —; welcome —; — cites; — confounds; — marks; — stirs; — takes root.

(See censure, judgment, examination.)

CRITICIZE (v)

adverbs
adversely; editorially; harshly; constructively; scoffingly; constantly; insidiously; fiercely; severely; rationally; malevolently; querulously; witheringly; reprobatively; irritatingly; trenchantly; depressingly; mercilessly; captiously; comprehensively; injuriously; impartially; caustically; acrimoniously; prematurely; energetically; candidly; stupidly; intelligently; searchingly; expertly; correctively; ironically; acridly; copiously; vehemently; libelously; slurringly; boorishly; presumptuously; subjectively; snobbishly.

(See censure, reprove.)

CRITIQUE

adjectives
elaborate; exquisite; instructive; poetical; preliminary; commendatory.

CROAK

adjectives
prophetic; monotonous; booming; empty; bellowing; rusty; harsh; discordant.

CROAK (v)

adverbs
tunelessly; roughly; discordantly; inauspiciously; prophetically; monotonously; sinisterly; nocturnally.
(See sound, complain.)

CROCKERY

adjectives
coarse; crudely-shaped; garishly-decorated; homely; humble; over-glazed; paunchy; porous.

verbs
advertise —; bake —; collect —; crack —; craze —; decorate —; display —; exhibit —; glaze —; mould —; paint —; place —; polish —; rattle —; shelve —; smash —; store in —; unearth —.
(See porcelain, china.)

CROCODILE

adjectives
rabbit-footed; slow-living; armored; slimy; stealthy; tearful; preying; slithering; death-dealing.

verbs
— ambles; — bathes; — cracks; — crunches; — crushes; — dives; — floats; —s herd; — invades; — lashes; — slithers; — snaps; — snorts; — splashes; — suns itself; — swims; — whips its tail.
(See reptile.)

CROCUS

adjectives
fatted; lusty; blooming; gay; adventurous; winter-defying; pioneer; spring-bannered.

CRONE

adjectives
withered; gaunt; old; haggard-visaged; dried-up.

CRONIES

adjectives
familiar; odious; bridge-playing; coarse-mouthed; illiterate; race-track; philandering.

CROOK

adjectives
dirty; filthy; loathsome; ordinary; obsequious; terrible; artificial; international; sneaking; whitecollar; capable.

CROOKED

adverbs
unstably; sinuously; jaggedly; darkly; indirectly; implicitly; covertly; cunningly; craftily; strategically; profoundly; diplomatically; shiftily; bafflingly; bewilderingly; insidiously; unscrupulously; disgracefully; perfidiously; treacherously; infamously; contemptibly; scurvily; disloyally.

CROON

adjectives
cheerful; plaintive; melodic; heart-touching; depth-sounding; hollow-ringing; weird; savage.

CROON (v)

adverbs
soothingly; harmoniously; comfortingly; pleasingly; gently; pathetically; sentimentally; romantically; maternally; cheerfully; plaintively; melodiously; touchingly.
(See sing.)

CROP

adjectives
catch; fateful; encouraging; anticipated; bumper; unmanufactured; ungathered; varied; abundant; sprouting; diminished; mildewed; uncertain; agricultural; plenteous; bountiful; scanty; customary; fast-ripening; phenomenal; profitable; huge; staple; immense; luxuriant; tender; supreme; worthless; superior; lavish; fodder; teeming; unfailing; annual; stunted; newly-planted; increased.

verbs
affect —; blast —; blight —; devastate —; devour —; harvest —; injure —; pluck —; produce —; reap —; salvage —; trample —; yield —; — fails; — flowers; —matures; — rustles; — shrivels; — sprouts; — withers.
(See harvest, fruit.)

CROSS

adjectives
customary; blazoned; glimmering; absolving; shameful; abhorred; momentary; reeking; planted; sunken; pastoral; radiant; scarlet; ebony; patient; cold; marble; enameled.

verbs
award —; bear —; curse —; deliver one to —; deny —; embrace —; endure —; erect —; fight for —; glory in —; hallow —; idolize —; kneel before —; mark with —; nail to —; plant —; sign with —; take up —; trust in —; uphold —; vow by —; wear —; worship at —; — leads; — saves; — signifies; — symbolizes.

adverbs
petulantly; perpetually; unreasonably; habitually; disagreeably; sullenly; morosely; gloomily; unbearably; pathetically; tragically; shockingly; waywardly; restively; glumly; crustily; cantankerously; brutally; sternly; forbiddingly; needlessly; gracelessly; unpardonably.

CROSS (v)

adverbs
freely; laterally; obliquely; boldly; accommodatingly; rapidly; devoutly; diagonally; inevitably; cautiously.

(See pass.)

CROSS-EXAMINATION

adjectives
merciless; extraordinary; lengthy; wearisome; pointless; inquisitive; three-cornered.

CROSSING

adjectives
memorable; deserted; careful; transpolar; smooth.

CROSSNESS

adjectives
accustomed; habitual; infectious; morbid; ascetic; acid; bitter; morose.

CROUCH (v)

adverbs
menacingly; sullenly; squatly; tensely; servilely; odiously; threateningly; alertly; aggressively.

(See squat, cringe.)

CROUPIER

adjectives
impassive; efficient; tight-lipped; spidery; inscrutable; grim.

CROW

adjectives
wandering; feeble; poaching; carrion; saucy; heavy-winged; boisterous; amazing; bold; startled; predatory; noisy; ragged; shrill.

verbs
domesticate —; hood —; snare —; tame —; throttle —; — annoys; — caws; — clamors; — claws; — fights; —s flock; — harms; — imitates; — isolates; — quarrels; —ravages; — robs; — roosts; — scours; — shrieks; —s swarm; — thieves; — uproots; — wrangles.

(See bird.)

CROW (v)

adverbs
triumphantly; derisively; harshly; loudly; feebly; saucily; boisterously; boldly; shrilly; monotonously; repeatedly; discordantly.

(See vaunt, brag.)

CROWD

adjectives
discordant; noisy; sportive; yelling; cosmopolitan; shouting; odd; oppressive; silent; rushing; eager; gaping; interminable; boisterous; passing; thick-pressed; promiscuous; voluble; madding; unreasonable; dark-robed; mercenary; miserable; streaming; heartless; hurrying; trembling; unabashed; mingled; surrounding; luckier; gossipy; village; horrid; gloomy; strangling; sympathetic; whispering; assembled; moving; motley; curious; excited; talented; discharged; enthusiastic; threatening; starry; tremendous; seething; scurrying; supper-hungry; still; gentlemanly; jocund; vulgar; dull-faced; self-controlled; dispersing; distinguished; colorful; indiscreet; serried; unfeeling; anxious; quiet; applauding; swirling; weary; malicious; tumultuous; buffeting; raucous; unnumbered; scattered; unhesitating; thickening; impatient; baser; patriotic; good-sized; advancing; watching; awful; jeering; gesticulating; angry; dense; outraged; idle; giddy; well-bred; debauching; surging; thinned; pitying; excited; laughing; unworthy; worthwhile; picturesque; ignoble; cheering; fickle; gazing; prostrate; reformed; exulting; incoming; thoughtless; visionary; sacrificial; virile; idealistic; helpless; ribald; wild-scrambling; myriad-tongued; thronging; dignified; merry; spiteful; purblind; suffering; brilliant; animated; somber; preoccupied; gay; drunken; handsome; glittering; friendly; well-behaved; orderly; healthy; complacent; awed; admiring; acclaiming; morbid; reverent; interested; sober-faced; tranquil; devout; convivial; attentive; hilarious; half-tipsy; roistering; thirsty; rollicking; mirthful; merry-making; congenial; jubilant; good-natured; vivacious; whimsical; smart; sophisticated; well-dressed; expensive; screaming; obstreperous; hooting; queer; enormous; hushed; tatterdemalion; hard-looking; tough; suspicious; quick-acting; realistic; bargaining; heterogeneous; listening; waiting; strolling; murmuring; chattering; milling; swarming; elbowing; lurching; shoving; swaying; eddying; writhing; turbulent; hustling; indifferent; bustling; hostile; challenging; troublesome; pes-

tering; victorious; restless; blood-mad; quarrelsome; frenzied; frightened; wavering; panicky; bibulous; bourgeois; casual; residential; exultant; modern; ubiquitous; famished; impoverished; gaudy; vigorous; powerful; unreflective; increasing; critical; slow-moving; thawing.

verbs
bewilder —; bore —; cater to —; disassociate from —; disperse —; draw —; excite —; harangue —; key up —; plunge into —; steal among —; tower above —; wait with —; — assembles; — clusters; — collects; — dissolves; — gapes at; — gathers; — groans; — hoots; — jams; — jeers; — jostles; — lionizes; — mills about; — mutters; — packs into; — pours from; — presses; — retreats; — scurries; — seethes; — speculates; — stares; — storms; — surges; — swarms; — swerves; — throngs; — wavers.
(See multitude, throng, mob, horde.)

CROWD (v)

adverbs
uncomfortably; amiably; perplexingly; alertly; warmly; thickly; odiously; abundantly; desperately; discordantly; oppressively; boisterously; promiscuously; maddeningly; volubly; unreasonably; horridly; curiously; enthusiastically; vulgarly; colorfully; indiscreetly; tumultuously; buffetingly; raucously; impatiently; gesticulatingly; giddily; animatedly; somberly; complacently; admiringly; acclaimingly; morbidly; roisteringly; hilariously; rollickingly; mirthfully; congenially; vivaciously; obstreperously; suspiciously; listeningly; murmuringly; chatteringly; turbulently; indifferently; bustlingly; victoriously; exultantly; ubiquitously.
(See swarm.)

CROWN

adjectives
silken; crimson; golden; glittering; olive; thorny; kingly; giddy; accursed; treacherous; fruitless; glorious; admired; tufted; starry; molten; embellished; hemispherical; woven; brilliant; rejected; glistening; fadeless; celestial; hoary; clustering; bloomless; flaming; imperial; dread; piercing; blessed; laurel; tiny; jeweled; caplike; magnificent; discarded; pointed; long-expected; unused.

verbs
anoint —; aspire to —; bear —; bequeath —; blemish —; bless —; cast away —; claim —; conform to —; corrupt —; deliver up —; deprive — of; deprive of —; disgrace —; disown —; encompass by —; gild —; inherit —; lay aside —; lift off —; merit —; offer —; pawn —; profane —; raise —; ransom —; refuse —; reject —; remove —; renounce —; repossess —; resign —; revere —; sear —; serve —; shave —; spurn —; tear off —; wear —; weave —; wreathe —; yield to —; yield up —; — flourishes; — rules; — shines.

CROWN (v)

adverbs
visibly; fittingly; spiritually; goldenly; glitteringly; gloriously; brilliantly; celestially; imperially; magnificently.
(See complete.)

CROWNING

adjectives
glorious; gorgeous; colorful; victorious; jubilant.

CRUCIFIX

adjectives
great; gaunt; ghastly; little.

CRUCIFY (v)

adverbs
miserably; horribly; barbarically; brutally; fiendishly; morally; literally; figuratively.
(See punish.)

CRUDE

adverbs
crassly; gracelessly; harshly; stiffly; awkwardly; barbarously; offensively; ignorantly; bashfully; intolerably; unluckily; baldly; unfortunately; offensively; coarsely; roughly; shiftlessly; quaintly; unsophisticatedly; ill-manneredly.

CRUDENESS

adjectives
honest; blunt; crass; vulgar; elemental; unsavory; natural; primitive.

verbs
abhor —; affect —; alter —; breed —; characterize by —; convert — into; correct —; cure of —; develop —; display —; exhibit —; loathe —; lose —; produce —; recoil from —; regard —; silence —; temper —; work —; — alarms; — annoys; — detracts; — shocks.

CRUDITY

adjectives
jocular; stylistic; frontier; obvious; careless; obsolete; sincere.

CRUELTY

adjectives
blood-smeared; organized; unsparing; abysmal; complacent; fiendish; devouring; inhuman; strange; reckless; super-rogatory; amiable; wanton; lawless; innate; stern; execrable; ruthless; tyrannic; sinister; sovereign; hellish; ignorant; atrocious; thriving; intolerable; apparent; abominable; hideous; savage; existing; peculiar; dull; unimaginable; indescribable; unnecessary; foul; barbarous; malevolent; official; violent; devastating; seeming; narrow; incestuous; lecherous; unavenged; social; callous; irrational; insensate; instinctive; moody; excessive; insidious; unbridled; merciless; monotonous; shameful; needless; brutal; persistent; increasing; petty; continuous.

verbs
batter with —; boast of —; delight in —; display —; dispose to —; encounter —; exhibit —; govern with —; impose —; inflict —; manifest —; mask —; master with —; mitigate —; perpetuate —; practise —; prompt —; protect from —; provoke —; repent—; repress—; reproach for—; revel in —; revenge —; subject to —; suffer from —; tolerate —; yield to —; — distresses; — oppresses; — pains; —surpasses.

(See brutality, tyranny.)

CRUISE

adjectives
intrepid; involuntary; world; enchanting; southern; successful; rest-giving; romantic; difficult; strenuous; notable; delightful; varied; premier; attractive; wonderful.

verbs
anticipate —; direct —; embark on —; enjoy —; entertain on —; escort —; leave on —; navigate —; observe on —; operate —; organize —; plan —; promote —; relax on —; sail on —; travel on —; — accommodates; — attracts; — consists of; — embraces; — enthralls; — envelops; — furnishes; — includes; — inspires; — invigorates; — provides; — rests; — thrills.

(See voyage, journey, trip.)

CRUISER

adjectives
vigilant; protected; submersible; mighty; sojourning; tourist-laden.

CRUMB

adjectives
occasional; forsaken; paltry; stale; mouldy; hoarded; grudging; life-sustaining.

verbs
accept —; beg —; break into —s; brush away —; catch —; cover with —s; dress with —s; dry —; fall into —s; finger into —s; gather —s; mouth —s; pick up —; prepare with —s; reduce to —s; step on —; sweep away —s; thicken with —s; throw away —s; toss —s to.

CRUMBLE (*v*)

adverbs
coarsely; gradually; completely; totally; disastrously; fatally; finely; unexpectedly; thoroughly; partially.

(See decline, decay.)

CRUMBLING

adjectives
gradual; complete; ear-splitting; total; erosive; timely; pathetic.

CRUMPLE (*v*)

adverbs
viciously; rudely; roughly; destructively; pathetically; carelessly; hideously; slatternly.

(See smash.)

CRUNCH

adjectives
distinct; audible; sickening; clear; sharp; decisive; monotonous.

CRUNCH (*v*)

adverbs
hungrily; viciously; furiously; bestially; rapaciously; eagerly; greedily; distinctly; audibly; sickeningly; sharply.

(See eat.)

CRUSADE

adjectives
perennial; lifesaving; insane; emotional; organized; humanitarian; noble; pathetic; anti-crime.

verbs
assemble—; bless—; champion—; direct—; endorse—; engage in—; expedite—; inspirit—; instigate—; launch—; lead—; oppose—; organize—; plan—; prepare for —; support—; wage—; —advances; —

campaigns; —conquers; —crushes; —defeats; —defends; —endeavors; —realizes; —revives; —succeeds; —undertakes; —wrestles with.

(See enterprise, movement, warfare.)

CRUSADE (v)

adverbs

vaingloriously; actively; religiously; perennially; insanely; emotionally; nobly; pathetically; gallantly; zealously; victoriously; inspiredly.

CRUSADER

adjectives

gallant; overzealous; anti-vice; young; medieval; valiant.

CRUSH (v)

adverbs

perfectly; deliberately; tenderly; softly; completely; painfully; carelessly; nervously; rigorously; spiritually; overwhelmingly; finally.

(See smash.)

CRUST

adjectives

favoring; scanty; stony; overpublicized; upper; fruitful; flaky; external; treacherous; shallow; brittle; well-browned; flimsy; hardened; fluted.

verbs

beg for—; break—; coat with—; compose—; contract into—; cover with—; deposit—; dissolve—; dry into—; feed—; form—; gnaw—; harden into—; hide under—; line with—; mass into—; munch—; penetrate—; puncture—; render—; scrape—; season—; slice—; —crumbles; —forms; —hardens.

(See casing, shell.)

CRUTCHES

adjectives

badly-worn; needed; helpful; tapping; supporting; betraying; stout; taped.

CRY

adjectives

raucous; feeble; painful; melancholy; guttural; heartsick; cornered; shrill; sharp; solitary; importunate; hoarse; choking; satirical; earnest; furious; thrilling; unanimous; pathetic; protesting; strident; peevish; battle; human; broken; triumphant; warning; petulant; wailing; plaintive; bootless; simultaneous; responsive; similar; distinct; suppressed; avenging; defiant; boastful; inspiring; drunken; pitiful; long-drawn; careless; passionate; supreme; piercing; unending; desolate; discordant; vociferous; prayerful; exultant; half-suppressed; half-demoniac; funeral; answering; terrified; inharmonious; impious; aspiring; yapping; plausible; premature; inevitable; harsh; ugly; shivering; stifled; strangled; joyous; wild; unearthly; despairing; clamorous; sharp; hissing; death-dealing; maniacal; piteous; amazed; comfortable; weird; impassioned; startling; rallying; unceasing; solitary; untenable; delirious; admiring; wrathful; everlasting; universal; prevailing; farthest-sounding; shuddering; inarticulate; gurgling; long; half-hysterical; dirgelike; loud; incoherent; perpetual; distressing; wrenching; sobbing; agonizing; brief; happy; smothered; full-mouthed; drawling; peculiar; fearful; fierce; ribald; far-resounding; odious; ineffable; continuous; mocking; supplicating; terrible; patriotic; noisy; dismal; expostulating; welcoming; ghastly; mutual; exulting; jubilant; ecstatic; joyful; delighted; gladdening; naive; inspiriting; wistful; stimulating; high; soft-noted; insistent; clarion; squeaky; rasping; clangorous; heart-chilling; babyish; heartbroken; dismayed; solemn; whimpering; breathless; stricken; important; frenzied; frantic; gulping; muffled; wanton; insulting; contemptuous; groaning; derisive; murder; fiendish; horror-stricken; anguished; spiteful; barbaric; sighing; yearning; low; appealing; hysterical; entreating; ominous; involuntary; frightened; haunting; elfin; sporting; familiar; asinine; wheezy; wordless; destructive; fluttering; incessant; scattered; hurtling; penetrating; vibrating; soul-shaking; dolorous; mournful; provocative; revolutionary; multitudinous (pl).

verbs

echo—; flee at—; force out—; give ear to—; hearken to—; heed—; let slip—; mock—; raise up—; repeat—; roar—; take up—; utter—; voice—; wring—from; —arouses; —awakens; —bursts forth; —disturbs; —fills; —jars; —resounds; —reverberates; —rises; —scares; —shatters; —wanes.

(See outcry, exclamation, scream, shriek, howl, lamentation, wail, plaint, yell.)

CRY (v)

adverbs

discordantly; querulously; reproachfully; jealously; hoarsely; earnestly; inarticulate-

ly; heartbrokenly; dishearteningly; flippantly; vehemently; enthusiastically; persistently; piteously; sternly; passionately; jovially; tempestuously; haughtily; indignantly; incoherently; irritably; energetically; contemptuously; exultantly; reprovingly; ringingly; gaily; disconsolately; unrestrainedly; tauntingly; feverishly; peremptorily; tantalizingly; falteringly; mirthfully; spontaneously; sympathetically; stormily; unanimously; petulantly; wailingly; drunkenly; passionately; piercingly; agonizingly; vociferously; jubilantly; ecstatically; inspiritingly; solemnly; spitefully; sighingly; hysterically; involuntarily; ominously; wordlessly; incessantly; dolorously; yearningly; bitterly; inwardly.
(See wail, weep.)

CRYING

adjectives
harsh; endless; irrational; awkward; bitter; remorseful; stormy; furious.

CRYPT

adjectives
mournful; venerable; quiet; mossy; dismal; mouldy; time-honored; ancestral.

CRYPTOGRAM

adjectives
magic; involved; difficult; mysterious; puzzling; baffling; tortuous.

CRYSTAL

adjectives
shimmering; transparent; pellucid; celestial; strange; fluffy; slow-frozen; gleaming; stinging; flashing; ice; diaphanous; needlelike; lambent; glittering; perilous; quartz; tempting; tremulous; fragile; long; jagged; tiny; irregular.

verbs
adorn with—; aggregate into—; clear—; concentrate in—; congeal into—; delve for—; dig out—; discover—; dissolve—; drip—s; freeze into—; gaze into—; mass into—; melt—; quaff—; search—; —adheres to; —beams; —darkens; —shines; —sparkles.
(See glass.)

CUB

adjectives
self-willed; young; modest; helpless; clumsy; awkward; closely-watched.

CUCKOO

adjectives
cowled; domineering; echoic; masterful; unmaternal; melancholy; ravenous; usurping; vehement.

verbs
—calls; —chucks; —deposits; —ejects; —flits; —mocks; —shrills; —shies away; —surveys; —wheels.
(See bird.)

CUDDLE (*v*)

adverbs
cozily; snugly; comfortably; lovingly; fondly; maternally; gently; affectionately; tenderly.
(See nestle.)

CUDGEL

adjectives
short; heavy; thick; bloody; bludgeoning; murderous.

verbs
attack with—; awe with—; beat with—; belabor with—; brandish—; combat with—; cross—s; defend with—; resist—; scar with—; shake—; smite with—; strike with—; swing—; take up—; terrify with—; wave—; wield—; —descends; —fells; —stuns.
(See club.)

CUE
(*billiards*)

adjectives
ash-wood; leather-tipped; nicely-balanced; pliant; well-seasoned; tapering; graceful.

verbs
aim—; bridge—; chalk—; crack—; draw with—; indicate with—; point—at; rest—on; retip—; score with—; skill with—; slide—; tip—; —slides; —bends; —slips; —strikes; —warps.

CUE
(*braid*)

adjectives
carefully-braided; bristling; coiled; limp; genteel; powdered; protruding; scrupulous.

verbs
braid into—; clip—; cut—; exhibit—; fashion—; plait—; powder—; roll—; tie into—; twist into—; —dangles; —grows.

CUE (*signal*)

adjectives
cryptic; answering; guiding; secret; suggestive; politic; strategic.

verbs
answer—; begin on—; enter on—; forget —; heed—; hint with—; mind—; miss—; muff—; pronounce—; remember—; speak —; signal with—; wait for—; whisper—; —arrives; —comes; —enables; —warns.
(See hint, suggestion, intimation.)

CUFF (*sleeve*)

adjectives
sheer; possible; transparent; organdy; starched; immaculate; chafing; frilled.

CUISINE

adjectives
local; national; appetizing; exceptional; world-famous; perfect; excellent; tempting; distinctive; wholesome; unsurpassed; distinguished; tasty; matchless; splendid; finest; delicious; unrivaled; superlative; renowned.

CULMINATION

adjectives
over-ripe; dizzy; fitting; probable; ultimate; untimely.

verbs
ascend to—; attain—; bask in—; crown—; develop to—; display—; encourage—; establish—; form—; herald—; look forward to—; reach—; rise to—; speed—; take pride in—; urge—; —occurs; —takes place.
(See end.)

CULPRIT

adjectives
wretched; miserable; shameful; apprehended; confessed.

CULT

adjectives
capricious; ridiculed; emotional; diverse; aesthetic; sweet; love; sentimental; idiotic; nudist; moribund; moral; eminent; logical; exclusive; religious; bizarre; unconventional; secret; sinister.

verbs
adopt—; denounce—; despise—; develop—; embrace—; inaugurate—; join—; organize—; perpetuate—; succumb to—; take up—; —affects; —attracts; —believes; —devotes; —fades; —interests; —practices; —spreads; —worships.
(See belief, system, ritual.)

CULTIVATE (*v*)

adverbs
diligently; extensively; sedulously; passionately; intensively; freely; generously; assiduously; fastidiously; systematically; intellectually; profitably; continuously.
(See work.)

CULTIVATION

adjectives
proper; intensive; fictional; continuous; hot-house; forced.

CULTIVATOR

adjectives
prosperous; sensible; practiced; apt; skilled; trained.

CULTURE

adjectives
snob; diligent; literary; rational; spiritual; high; musical; splendid; unprecarious; profound; virile; brilliant; superior; natural; substantial; polite; simple; harmonious; pronounced; untrammeled; mellow; older; mature; age-old; traditional; borrowed; inherited; acquired; vulgar; inferior; dangerous; national; warmed; raw; wide; universal; abundant; vast; considerable; intellectual; indigenous; cruel; pagan; autonomous; alien; civil; rounded; religious; exhilarating; prescriptorial; petty; nascent; curious; active.

verbs
absorb—; acquire—; assimilate—; attain—; borrow—; disparage—; fetter—; flout—; imbibe—; lack—; perpetuate—; propagate —; relegate—; retard—; shed—; spread —; stifle—; —broadens; —enhances; —enlightens; —improves; —polishes; —raises; —refines.
(See refinement, enlightenment, education.)

CULTURE (*v*)

adverbs
laboriously; diligently; naturally; abundantly; indigenously; spiritually.

CULTURED

adverbs
elaborately; ostentatiously; laboriously; diligently; painfully; highly; profoundly;

brilliantly; naturally; inherently; innately; widely; curiously; delightfully; consciously; obviously; unquestionably; tastefully; genuinely; unaffectedly; bookishly; aimlessly; methodically; scholastically; generally.

CUMBERSOME

adverbs
bulkily; ponderously; gravely; awkwardly; ungracefully; embarrassingly; unmanageably; vexatiously; impossibly; clumsily; massively; stiffly; grotesquely; fantastically; heavily.

CUNNING

adjectives
giddy; diabolical; cordial; tough; stalwart; gentle; sly; fiendish; premeditated; malicious; devilish; peculiar; infinite; instinctive; unconscious; revengeful; stealthy; artful; swift.

verbs
acquire through—; apply—; beguile with—; calculate with—; cheat with—; check—; cover—; deceive by—; devise by—; display—; dispose to—; employ—; entrap by—; excel in—; exercise—; exhibit—; expose—; frame with—; impart—; puff up with—; school in—; trick by—; work—; —hides; —deceives.

(See craft, deceit, trickery, skill, ingenuity.)

adverbs
diabolically; slyly; fiendishly; maliciously; adroitly; cleverly; adeptly; artfully; subtly; insidiously; dangerously; commercially; extremely; astoundingly; profoundly; deliberately; sagaciously; cautiously; carefully; invariably; habitually; incurably; astutely; customarily; ordinarily.

CUP

adjectives
bitter; enameled; verdant; tulip-tinted; silver; red; lacquer; lordly; gold-encrusted; pink-sprigged; intoxicating; crowning; delicate; inebriating; consecrated; lustrous-petaled; sapphire; thin; large; thimble-like; quivering; graceful; odd; vicious; little; demure; coveted; fragile; impersonal; hygienic; invigorating.

verbs
burnish—; drain—; drink—; fill—; finger—; overflow—; partake of—; pour—; quaff—; sip—; share—; steep in—; swell over—; taste—; wash—; win—; —contains; —flows; —runs over; —sparkles; —steams.

CUPID

adjectives
wrestling; painted; devilish; effective; love-darting.

CUPIDITY

adjectives
native; personal; marked; avaricious; expressive.

CUPOLA

adjectives
gigantic; spherical; delicate; gilded; triumphant; towering; opulent.

CUR

adjectives
mean; mongrel; crooked; ragamuffin; contemptible; treacherous; bedraggled; crouching; worthless; cruel-hearted; impenetrable; mangy; carnal; half-starved; yelping.

CURATE

adjectives
perpetual; narrow; egotistical; impecunious; up-to-date; shuffling; pleasant; genial.

CURATIVE

adverbs
effectively; eventually; soothingly; pleasantly; safely; powerfully; speedily; valuably; mythically; infallibly; originally; rarely; expensively; heroically; strangely; miraculously; mysteriously; permanently; remarkably; fraudulently.

CURB (v)

adverbs
intentionally; beneficently; spasmodically; stringently; sternly; harshly; brutally; dictatorially; tyrannically.

(See stop.)

CURE

adjectives
renowned; timely; single; simple; sovereign; contemptuous; radical; drastic; fascinating; little; strange; natural; permanent; jagged; miraculous; efficacious; impersonal; so-called; immediate; alleged; prospective; instant; remarkable; sordid; accurate; elaborate; deepest; fraudulent.

verbs
accelerate—; accomplish—; advocate—; applaud—; apply—; approve—; effect—; hasten—; indicate—; perform—; produce —; proffer—; render—; seek—; trust—; work—; —follows; —results.
(See treatment, remedy.)

CURE (*v*)

adverbs
sufficiently; radically; permanently; miraculously; efficaciously; impersonally; immediately; remarkably; fraudulently; professionally; medically; presumably; partially; temporarily.
(See help.)

CURIOSITY

adjectives
high; sympathetic; logical; healthy; frank; profound; sublime; respectful; natural; reverent; indifferent; lively; breathless; instant; insatiable; passionate; intense; intelligent; vague; sedate; pregnant; half-ironic; mingled; eager; oblique; romantic; ardent; unhealthy; heartless; inflamed; intellectual; jealous; ethnological; indefatigable; laboratory; half-cunning; sheer; calculating; impertinent; kind; latent; amused; overwhelming; excited; persevering; overpowering; vacant; tremulous; typographical; rude; beneficial; blunt; morbid; prying; laudable; irresistible; imperious; unenvious; enlightened; gluttonous; languid; anthropological; idle; discontented; unobtrusive; innocent; frightened; contemptuous; unquenchable; ghoulish; sullen; regretful; literary; kindred; weak; mutual; obtrusive; ill-bred; endless; sharp; delighted; vulgar; childlike; indolent; unsated; gratified; evident; noble; unallayed; baffled; passionate; geographical; prejudiced; piqued; chastened; reluctant; persistent; polite; burning; malicious; cordial; professional; importunate; considerable; great; rampant; immense; inordinate; widespread; untiring; undiminished; penetrating; unappeased; quenchless; devouring; itching; momentary; passing; detached; mild; waning; small; faint; stirring; lazy; undisguised; growing; vast; objective; troubled; worried; timid; nervous; furtive; covetous; indecent; greedy; gruesome; avid; prurient; burdensome; leering; sinister; forbidden; impious; perverse; eclectic; visual; disoriented; titillating; gaping; startled; sudden; scared.

verbs
admit—; arouse—; awaken—; blame—; burst with—; cater to—; develop—; devour with—; display—; evince—; excite—; exhibit—; experience—; feed—; gratify —; manifest—; move by—; overcome—; pique—; practice—; prompt by—; repel—; repress—; satisfy—; seize with—; spur on by—; steam with—; —grows; —impels; —motivates; —prevails.
(See interest, thirst.)

CURIOUS

adverbs
incurably; meanly; inquisitively; intellectually; daringly; crassly; offensively; frightfully; gracelessly; grossly; maliciously; malevolently; unbearably; odiously; roughly; childishly; innocently; wonderingly; impertinently; impudently; unpardonably; inexcusably; hatefully; coarsely.

CURL

adjectives
soft; radiant; salt-wet; shining; drenched; sawdust; flat; vine; floating; countless (pl); short; upturned; sweeping; treasured; thick; mustache; twisted; moistened; lustrous; streaming; falling; disordered; luxuriant; clustering; smoky; stray; sunny; mutinous; glossy; careless; burnished; soft; copious (pl); copper-colored; white; blond; fluffy; gold; silky; black; brown; nut-brown; wire-gold; resolute; blue; massive; willful; protruding; tossing; doubtful; tight; glossy; loose; impracticable; tumbled; stubborn; fluttered; strange; powdered; damp; superabundant (pl); straggling; crisp; rolled; knotted; short; flaxen; corkscrew; dark; riotous; raven; unruly; fuzzy; dishevelled; dusty; gleaming; puffy.

verbs
admire—s; adorn with—s; assume—; arrange—s; clip—s; dress in—s; finger—s; fondle—s; form—s; promote—s; ribbon—s; shake—s; sun—s; tangle—s; tie into—s; twist into—s; wind into—s; —s attract; —s run riot; —s stream; —s wave.
(See hair.)

CURL (*v*)

adverbs
deftly; gracefully; riotously; indolently; systematically; scornfully; disdainfully;

charmingly; lustrously; luxuriantly; mutinously; carelessly; copiously; loosely; dishevelledly.
(See twist.)

CURRENCY

adjectives
spurious; immediate; auxiliary; new; crisp; special; separate; weak; universal; valueless; tropical.

verbs
accept—; adopt as—; coin—; counterfeit—; debase—; deflate—; depreciate—; exchange for—; guard—; honor—; inflate—; issue—; legalize—; rate—; recall—; stabilize—; stamp out—; tender—; value—; —changes; —wobbles.
(See money, coin.)

CURRENT

adjectives
friendly; irresistible; dangerous; treacherous; gentle; perilous; tricky; mighty; powerful; terrific; swift; racing; shifting; swirling; churning; weltering; streaming; air; glacial; tidal; descending; broad; undulating; steady; smooth; pulling; noiseless; skeptical; romantic; vital; philosophical; social; subtle; stinging; buoyant; fluvial; crystal; atmospheric; arduous; swollen; silver; favoring; conflicting; eddying; ceaseless; contrary; plunging; gushing; descending; mealy; clean; sweeping; lessening; warm; life; haze-enveloped; brown; greasy; running; rippling; time-tossed; smooth; moisture-bringing; genial; wild; dreamy; alternating; unbroken; great; strengthened; brinish; galvanic; nauseous; cool; vicious; mazy; low-voiced; prattling; mysterious; permeating; fruity; twisting; lucent; contagious; intellectual; artistic; unseen; integrated; fatal.

verbs
allay—; attune to—; chart—; dam—; defile—; deviate from—; escape—; impede—; oppose—; retard—; ruffle—; stem—; —absorbs; —drives; —forces; —glides; —jets; —originates at; —pushes; —rolls on; —runs on; —shatters; —shifts; —springs from.
(See stream, movement, course.)

CURRICULUM

adjectives
rational; traditionary; academic; narrow; rigid; daily.

verbs
approve—; arrange—; balance—; complete—; constitute—; consult—; contemplate—; decide on—; detail—; fix—; investigate—; load—; offer—; outline—; pursue—; recommend—; regulate—; reject—; run through—; secure—; select—; supervise—; work out—; —covers; —embraces; —entails; —equips; —instructs in; —prepares for; —requires; —satisfies; —trains; —provides.
(See course, study.)

CURSE

adjectives
sobbing; vile; futile; snarling; unintelligible; fervent; dazzling; exasperated; muttered; bitter; great; hot; muffled; steamy; primal; intolerable; irritable; cunning; deep; valiant; haunting; sterile; well-hurled; dread; inevitable; long-forgotten; unutterable; sardonic; primeval; murmuring; blaspheming; shrieking; canceled; smothered; latent; fiendish; furious; primordial; abiding.

verbs
annul—; bait with—; blast—at; breathe—; bring—upon; cast—; croak—; dread—; endow with—; growl—; heap—s upon; hurl—at; mutter—; pronounce—; redeem from—; remove—; shake off—; smite with —; speak—; stifle—; swear—; taunt with —; voice—; wish—; woo—; —bodes ill for; —falls upon; —s pour out; —prevails; —stings.
(See denunciation, imprecation, oath.)

CURSE (v)

adverbs
endlessly; furiously; wrathfully; persistently; belligerently; bitterly; jovially; vulgarly; coarsely; blasphemously; unintelligibly; fervently; exasperatedly; hotly; intolerably; irritably; fiendishly.
(See swear.)

CURTAIL (v)

adverbs
sharply; considerably; drastically; harmfully; detrimentally; abruptly; unexpectedly; nominally; promptly.
(See reduce.)

CURTAILMENT

adjectives
prompt; drastic; unparalleled; harmful; sharp; detrimental.

CURTAIN

adjectives
falling; flapping; wavering; honey-colored; hotel-red; roseate; dirty; mud-brown; cloudless; azure; sinister; black; accordion-pleated; ruffled; embroidered; jeweled; gingham; crisp; bright; chintz; organdie; cretonne; gaily-colored; heavy; felt; wry; old; rich-toned; cheerful; skimpy; hanging; triangular; strong; final; gray; cloudy; dimity; wadded; clinging; billowy; improvised; sunshiny; undrawn; jonquil; silk; blue; light-pierced; dusky; exasperating; crimson; luminous; dazzling; impalpable; tawdry; convenient; sun-lace; formless; tattered.

verbs
adjust—; close—; draw—; drop—; emerge from—; fade behind—; hide behind—; lift—; lower—; peep through—; spread—; stretch out—; —flutters; —protects; —quivers; —shades; —sways.

(See drapery.)

CURTNESS

adjectives
semi-growling; autocratic; sudden; unfeeling; brusque; harsh; perfunctory.

CURTSY

adjectives
majestic; mock; graceful; delicate; practiced; bobbing; deferential.

CURVE
(bend as of a highway)

adjectives
gradually-descending; magnificent; unprotected; precipitous; graceful; sinuous; hairpin; wide-swung; continuous.

verbs
approach—; assume—; bank—; collide on—; crowd at—; dart around—; eliminate—; negotiate—; round—; screech around—; turn over on—; upset on—; warn of—; whiz round—; —confronts; —endangers; —hazards; —menaces; —obscures; —represents; —slants.

CURVE
(general)

adjectives
seductive; sensuous; luscious; ardent; entrancing; magnificent; graceful; exquisite; winsome; dizzy; dazzling; sweeping; bold; wide; scraped; scornful; disdainful; fleshy; opulent; slim; dignified; sensitive; close-coiled; easy; concave; sheltering; irregular; flat; hairpin; downward; lax; convex; subtle; symmetrical; gigantic; sheltered; painted; wavering; drooping; phosphate; additional; cuspidated; majestic; continuous; caustic; lineless; living; epicycloidal; precipitous; prudish; luxurious; aquiline; flowing; gracile; ceaseless; rich; tender; sweeping; alluring; yielding; self-sought; exquisite; glimmering.

CURVE
(line of deviation on a graph)

adjectives
double; reverse; reciprocal; transcendental; mechanical; radical; radial; peculiar.

verbs
construct—; describe—; generate—; interest in—; intersect—; obtain—; study—; trace—; transform—; —corresponds to; —degenerates; —envelops; —falls; —indicates; —recedes; —represents; —sinks.

(See deviation, line.)

CURVE (v)

adverbs
perceptibly; seductively; sensuously; entrancingly; magnificently; exquisitely; winsomely; sweepingly; boldly; abruptly; dangerously; sinuously.

(See bend.)

CUSHION

adjectives
pillow; rustling; elastic; silken; multicolored; bright-hued; thin; downy; soft; velvet; damask; faded; reclining; convertible; form-fitting; slippery; loose-seat; padded; ample; natural.

verbs
conceal with—; cover—; embroider—; fringe—; furnish with—; kneel on—; lay on—; loll on—; offer—; place—under; relax against—; repose on—; rest on—; sit on—; stuff—; —decorates; —eases; —graces.

(See pillow.)

CUSPIDOR

adjectives
stately; ill-placed; fanciful; vulgar; avoided; obstreperous; spattered.

CUSTODIAN

adjectives
possible; official; sole; faithless; temporary; definite.

CUSTODY

adjectives
safe; protective; temporary; court; jealous; zealous; watchful.

verbs
accept—of; acknowledge—of; advise—of; authorize—of; commit to—of; confine to—of; direct—of; preserve—of; resent—of; retain—of; subject to—of; —amends; —improves; —neutralizes; —protects; —rectifies; —restrains; —superintends.
(See care, imprisonment.)

CUSTOM

adjectives
august; precious; gracious; venerated; pleasant; sentimental; quaint; bizarre; effete; mutable; ancient; immemorial; time-honored; convenient; prudent; barbaric; pagan; primitive; yearly; native; austere; civilized; tribal; nightly; family; social; old-fashioned; southern; administrative; religious; accepted; wild; gay; universal; innocent; disinterested; reprehensible; contrasting; established; observed; prevailing; casual; frequent; habitual; recognized; classic; homogeneous; antiquated; unwonted; barbarous; charming; burial; pious; genteel; blind; stupid; laudable; national; long-continued; kingly; transient; excellent; preserved; ludicrous; prescribed; early; depraved; usual; infuriating; political; traditional; obsolete; enlightened; invariable; offensive; salutary; idiotic; well-known; uniform; familiar; reverent; exuberant; discrepant; monastic; praiseworthy; queer.

verbs
adhere to—; break—; cherish—; cling to—; conform to—; corrupt—; defend—; defer —; defy—; deprecate—; develop—; discharge—; establish—; esteem—; extenuate —; flout—; honor—; impose—; inaugurate —; maintain—; mar—; mock—; observe—; overlap—; overwhelm by—; respect—; retain—; reverence—; revert to—; revive —; run counter to—; stamp out—; —demands; —dictates; —governs; —intimidates; —narrows; —runs back to; —springs from; —stales; hamper by—.
(See usage, conventionality, practice, habit.)

CUSTOMARY

adverbs
scarcely; quaintly; queerly; graciously; pleasantly; conveniently; charmingly; stupidly; infuriatingly; idiotically; amusingly; locally; racially.

CUSTOMER

adjectives
potential; quondam; gay; prospective; tough; favored; fussy; cautious; flighty; lavish; famous; resident; difficult; hard; hideous; soldier; quick; hungry; capricious; disgruntled; excellent; grumpy; dark; lathered; noble; open-aired; profitable; residential; favored; satisfied; admiring; discriminating; picnic; slippery; famished; potential; passing; steady; destructive.

verbs
approach—; bargain with—; beckon to—; deal with—; encourage—; entice—; furnish —; guarantee to—; mulct—; refund to—; round up—s; satisfy—; seek—; smirk at—; tempt—; urge—; —bickers; —complains; —orders; —purchases; —responds; —selects; —s support; —s troop in.
(See purchaser, buyer.)

CUT

adjectives
sharp; sincere; substantial; long; ragged; vile; inelegant; vertical; tremendous; duck-bellied; delicate; fearful; whimsical.

verbs
bandage —; bathe —; bleed —; cleave —; disinfect —; dress —; incise —; infect —; inflict —; open —; salve —; sew —; stitch —; suffer —; suture —; treat —; wound with —; — divides; — heals; — pains; — penetrates; — removes; — separates; — severs.
(See wound.)

CUT (*v*)

adverbs
completely; exquisitely; cruelly; violently; deliberately; effectively; diagonally; summarily; snobbishly; obliquely; transversely; keenly; generously; heartlessly.
(See gash.)

CUTLASS

adjectives
gleaming; dripping; naked; sturdy; heavy; serviceable; dangling; undimmed.

verbs
arm with —; brandish —; carve with —; chop with —; dull —; flourish —; furnish with —; hew with —; sever with —;

sharpen —; shield from —; thrust —; wave —; wield —; work —; yield to —; — menaces; — pierces; — slashes; — slays.
(See sword, weapon.)

CUTLERY

adjectives
flashing; steely; keen-edged; ivory-handled; adaptable; concealed; cleverlv-applied; sundering.

verbs
clean —; dent —; employ —; glaze —; grind —; harden —; inspect —; manipulate —; manufacture —; monogram —; place —; plate —; polish —; provide with —; require —; scour —; sharpen —; spread —; stain —; temper —; utilize —; — clatters; — glistens; — jingles; — resists.
(See instrument, tool.)

CYCLE

adjectives
irregular; uncharted; business; elemental; repetitious; past; never-failing; comprehensive; pleasant; distinct; imaginary; endless; unvarying; normal.

verbs
approve —; avert —; complete —; compute —; continue in —; end —; form —; move in —; obviate —; pass through —; recognize —; recur during —; regain during —; resume —; revolve in —; span —; study —; — gauges; — indicates; — possesses; — promises; — represents.
(See period.)

CYCLONE

adjectives
human; lurking; impending; destructive; periodic; seasonable; threatening; rumbling; whirling.

CYLINDER

adjectives
metal; stubby; rotary; inscribed; clay; reciprocating; wicker; unsymmetrical.

verbs
bolt —s together; bore —; compress in —; construct —; design —; employ —; grind —; insert in —; operate —; — circles; — contracts; — expands; — lags; — leaks; — revolves; — rolls; — rotates; — turns.

CYMBAL

adjectives
tinkling; brazen; clashing; vibrating; jubilant; sounding; heartful.

CYMBALS

adjectives
bronzed; clashing; tinkling; empty-sounding; gypsy; triumphant; traditional.

verbs
cast —; clash —; crash —; play on —; rub —; sound —; strike —; — clash; — echo; — quiver; — resound; — ring; — tinkle.

CYNIC

adjectives
unfeeling; bitter; cold-blooded; licentious; ferocious; unmoved; wandering; cruel; irreverent; sensual; intolerable; sated; singular; imperturbable; consistent; decided; admirable; cheery: depressed; despairing.

CYNICAL

adverbs
bitterly; harshly; gloomily; contemptuously; derisively; scornfully; sneeringly; disdainfully; morosely; witheringly; superciliously; pitifully; censoriously; abusively; scandalously; outrageously; dryly; cuttingly; disparagingly; insufferably; pompously; arrogantly; bumptiously.

CYNICISM

adjectives
prevalent; abstract; consummate; immeasurable; meretricious; searing; cold-blooded; bitter; new-found; grinning; smooth; ugly; sinister; unbearable; rough; infamous; arid; appalling; polished; selfish; philosophical; repellent; analytical; thin; querulous; apparent; disdainful; genial.

verbs
adopt —; attain —; base on —; clothe in —; condemn —; criticize —; dethrone —; display —; dispose of —; don —; exhibit —; exercise —; fall into —; fetter with —; imply —; indulge in —; ingrain —; mask —; provoke —; regard with —; ridicule —; uphold —; — cloaks; — develops; — emphasizes; — evolves; — flourishes; — outrages; — seeps in.
(See contempt, sarcasm, distrust, pessimism.)

CYPRESS

adjectives
towering; gigantic; bearded; hoary; patriarchal.

CZAR

adjectives
absolute; perturbed; grieved; obstinate; mighty; omnipotent; craven; ruthless.

CZARINA

adjectives
masterful; frantic; neurotic; vainglorious; pride-eaten; ambitious; power-driven.

D

DAFFODIL

adjectives
giant; yellow; nodding; flaunting; vernal; coquettish.

DAGGER

adjectives
bloody; bronze; gold-hilted; curved; flint; short; heavy; gleaming; well-sharpened.

verbs
attack with —; blunt —; brandish —; conceal —; draw —; dull —; edge —; flourish —; hack with —; nuzzle —; pare with —; pluck with —; point —; reel under —; run — through; sharpen —; sheathe —; shoot —; speak —s; stab with —; threaten with —; thrust —; wave —; wield —; — inflicts; — nicks; — penetrates; — slays; — wounds.
(See knife, weapon.)

DAILY

adjectives (newspaper)
conservative; provincial; radical; yellow; blatant; local; syndicated.

DAINTINESS

adjectives
exquisite; fastidious; unwonted; inimitable; inborn; personal; superlative; luxurious; preening; faultless.

DAINTY

adjectives
carefully-prepared; prized; coveted; diet-robbing; sugared; tempting; toothsome.

verbs
allure by —; crave —; desire —; feed on —; pamper with —; prepare —; promise —; provide —; relish —; reward with —; share —; spice —; store —; surrender to —; — appeals; — delights; — pleases.
(See food.)

adverbs
fastidiously; exquisitely; subtly; extremely; gracefully; charmingly; girlishly; personally; faultlessly; fashionably; meticulously; primly; demurely; delicately; particularly; scrupulously; pleasingly; immaculately; sweetly; fragrantly.

DAISY

adjectives
white; buttercup-hued; English; innocent; unabashed; golden-hearted; question-eyed; love-telling.

verbs
adorn with —; arrange —ies; bear —ies; chain —ies; cultivate —ies; disclose —ies; gather —ies; grow —ies; pin —ies; pluck —ies; scatter —ies; trim with —ies; — blooms; — blossoms; —ies deck; —ies dot; — flowers; — folds; — lurks; — opens; — sleeps; —ies sprinkle; — winks.
(See flower.)

DALE

adjectives
smiling; piny; flowery; wooded; dark; fragrant; shadow-dappled.

verbs
abandon —; bedeck —; bloom in —; grow in —; haunt —; hide in —; inhabit —; retreat to —; roam in —; scatter through —; situate in —; speed over —; wander in —; — invites; — protects; — shelters; — slopes; — winds.
(See valley, dell, vale.)

DALLIANCE

adjectives
pleasant; silken; delightful; primrose; lunar; playful; gentle.

DALLY (v)

adverbs
dangerously; carelessly; playfully; indifferently; procrastinatingly; seductively.
(See delay, trifle.)

DAM

adjectives (water)
gracious; milky; restless; undermined; log; earth-filled; broken; frothy; noisy; gushing; beaver.

verbs
bank —; burst —; construct —; install —; level —; overflow —; pipe from —; reinforce —; sweep away —; — bars; — blocks; — breaks; — bridges; — confines; — controls; — discharges; — halts; — impounds; — irrigates; — leaks; — obstructs; — preserves; — prevents; — protects; — restrains; — supplies.
(See barrier.)

DAMAGE

adjectives
moral; irreparable; considerable; inestimable; permanent; malicious; substantial; sudden; serious; material; pecuniary; noticeable; characteristic; infinite; unspeakable; accidental; consequent; enormous; hidden; resultant; unliquidated; willful; unmistakable; punitive.

verbs
account for —; compute —; counteract —; countervail —; distress by —; forestall —; guard against —; inflict —; measure —; mitigate —; offset —; pay —s; receive —; recoup —; recover —; reveal —; survey —; sustain —; — flows from; — impairs.
(See destruction, injury, harm.)

DAMAGE (*v*)

adverbs
seriously; morally; irreparably; inestimably; permanently; maliciously; substantially; materially; noticeably; characteristically; infinitely; unspeakably; accidentally; unconsequently; enormously; resultantly; unmistakably; punitively; wilfully; revengefully; woefully; unscrupulously; savagely.
(See injure. hurt.)

DAMASK

adjectives
heavy; silk; crimson; mingled; traditional; imported; luxurious; gorgeous.

DAME

adjectives
coquettish; scented; imperious; high-nosed; resolute; fairest; rawboned; admiring; glowing; ruffled; peerless; keen-eyed; beauteous; antiquated; sinful; blooming; handsome; disdainful; solicitous; chaste; tissued; wanton; affrighted.

DAMNABLE

adverbs
utterly; odiously; completely; horribly; shockingly; profoundly; venomously; infernally; consummately; unnaturally.

DAMNATION

adjectives
eternal; relentless; utter; deep; everlasting; irretrievable; consummate.

DAMP

adjectives
murk; occidental; death; soothing; uncheerful; choking; senseless; sickly.

adverbs
slightly; clammily; chillingly; penetratingly; rawly; stuffily; noxiously; foggily; depressingly; inescapably; pestilentially; mistily; mysteriously; coldly; smotheringly; muggily; soggily; soddenly; icily; piercingly; frigidly.

DAMPNESS

adjectives
clammy; chilling; penetrating; stuffy; unctuous; consistent.

DAMSEL

adjectives
pulchritudinous; beauteous; young; calm-eyed; dainty; efficient; demure; frank; attractive; shrieking; lovelorn; stout; faery; comely; flounced; frail; frolicsome; officiating; citified; rubicund; haggling; distressed; dashing; misguided; hapless.

verbs
attend—; avow to—; captivate—; cherish —; court—; dishonor—; distress—; misuse—; nurture—; protect—; win—; woo—; —attracts; —blushes; —curtsies; —dreams; —droops; —faints; —frolics; —simpers; —twitters; —yearns.
(See woman, girl.)

DANCE

adjectives
rhythmic; divine; ingenious; frantic; wild; passionate; pulse-quickening; queer; eccentric; weird; mazy; absurd; freak; astonishing; grotesque; shambling; classic; old-fashioned; curious; square; folk; ritual; holiday; religious; moonlight; native; exotic; reveling; intricate; pompous; judicious; ballet; risque; characteristic; monopolized; fading; confident; scandalous; Moorish; bewitching; quaint; impish; carnal; exquisite; naked; overture; languid; fairy; mystic; howling; murdering; eternal; evening; amusing; sporadic; erotic; sunset; slow; serene; mirthful; astronomical; revolving; barbaric; spectacular; yearlong.

verbs
accompany—; assemble at—; attend—; blend with—; burst forth in—; contort in—; dress for—; embrace in—; escort to—; grace—; invite to—; join in—; lead off—; leave—; master—; open—; perfect—; perform—; polish—; popularize—; rejoice in—; render—; revel in—; study—; survey—; take part in—; vary—; weary of—;

—breaks; —circles; —enchants; —expresses; —interprets.
(See waltz, minuet.)

DANCE (v)

adverbs
frivolously; bewitchingly; gracefully; divinely; exquisitely; violently; vivaciously; solemnly; triumphantly; angelically; strenuously; eccentrically; grotesquely; picturesquely; seductively; wantonly; gleefully; incessantly; rhythmically; ingeniously; religiously; weirdly; shamblingly; ritually; exotically; quaintly; impishly; carnally; exquisitely; serenely; mirthfully; barbarically; spectacularly; skillfully; zestfully.

DANCE FLOOR

adjectives
deserted; pretentious; polished; gleaming; inviting; seductive; mirror-smooth.

DANCE HALL

adjectives
common; tawdry; overcrowded; revolting; frivolous; forcibly-gay.

verbs
assemble at— —; attend — —; congregate in— —; crowd— —; file into— —; frequent — —; gather at— —; introduce to— —; popularize— —; supervise— —; wander around— —; — —appeals; — —breeds; — —corrupts; — —offers; — —swarms with; — —swelters.

DANCER

adjectives
merry; good; superb; delightful; graceful; light; rhythmic.

verbs
applaud—; fete—; fire—; inspire—; train —; —awes; —delights; —entertains; —executes; —exercises; —exerts; —expresses; —interprets; —flies; —flutters; —frisks; —glides; —s jostle; —leaps; —performs; —personifies; —pirouettes; —pivots; —practises; —prances; —s promenade; —quivers; —registers; —springs; —suggests; —wheels; —whirls.
(See acrobat.)

DANCING

adjectives
outlandish; outrageous; exquisite; convulsive; titillating; rhythmic; habitual; acrobatic; furious.

DANDELION

adjectives
straggling; common; autumnal; late-blown; frost-braving; starry; fairy-seeded; omnipresent; humble.

DANDY

adjectives
amiable; professional; hypocritical; dapper; ingratiating; surreptitious; superficial; perfumed; silk-stockinged.

DANGER

adjectives
ever-impending; imminent; looming; hidden; gathering; unseen; unknown; fancied; mythical; inevitable; unceasing; vile; imaginary; indefinite; miserable; acute; extreme; august; constant; remote; significant; undiluted; discernible; obvious; immediate; overwhelming; inherent; grave; pretended; apparent; approaching; potential; future; unavoidable; recurring; spicy; unexampled; real; countless (pl).

verbs
admit—; avert—; avoid—; beset by—; blind to—; brave—; confront with—; court —; create—; demonstrate—; duck—; eliminate—; emphasize—; entail—; exaggerate —; exempt from—; expose to—; face—; flee—; foresee—; foretell—; free from—; guard against—; harbor—; ignore—; increase—; incur—; indicate—; induce—; involve—; laugh at—; lessen—; lie in—; minimize—; overcome—; pluck from—; ponder—; realize—; recognize—; remain in—; risk—; scoff at—; scorn—; sense—; shield from—; state—; stem—; taste—; underestimate—; visualize—; weigh—; wink at—; woo—; —attends; —impends; —looms; —lurks; —subsides.
(See peril. hazard, risk.)

DANGEROUS

adverbs
secretly; imminently; mythically; inevitably; miserably; acutely; extremely; remotely; obviously; overwhelmingly; gravely; potentially; unavoidably; critically; ominously; terribly; incredibly; horribly; palpably; openly; manifestly; conspicuously.

DANGLE (v)

adverbs
mockingly; loosely; tantalizingly; irritatingly; erotically; teasingly; playfully.
(See hang.)

DAPPER

adverbs
effeminately; sartorially; extremely; elegantly; absurdly; smartly; importantly; expensively; brightly; exquisitely; trimly; sprucely; neatly; nimbly; alertly; gracefully; jauntily; nattily; consciously; swankily; sleekly; becomingly; ornamentally.

DARE (v)

adverbs
impiously; virtuously; dauntlessly; boisterously; foolhardily; courageously; impetuously; bravely; unhesitatingly.
(See defy, challenge.)

DAREDEVIL

adjectives
reckless; lovable; hopeful; invincible; adventure-seeking; conquering; amiable.

DARING

adjectives
moon-faced; virtuous; dauntless; remorseless; speculative; boisterous; foolhardy; harmonic.

adverbs
dangerously; rashly; temperamentally; fantastically; alarmingly; foolhardily; breathtakingly; colossally; terribly; dramatically; notoriously; crazily; strangely; singularly; shamefully; amazingly; recklessly; incredibly; unbelievably; foolishly; boldly; avidly; bravely; audaciously; romantically; vicariously; courageously; youthfully; boyishly; disconcertingly; extravagantly.

DARK

adjectives
perilous; fierce; haunted; shuddering; leafy; lugubrious; frosty; shadowed; impenetrable; ambrosial; silent; abysmal; peaceful; fragrant; creeping; intricate; tinkling.

adverbs
mysteriously; impenetrably; perilously; shudderingly; lugubriously; peacefully; abysmally; dismally; fragrantly; suddenly; appreciably; blessedly; fearfully; frightfully; alarmingly; intensely; totally; utterly; pitchy; eerily; unnaturally; bewilderingly; oppressively; increasingly; uneasily; thickly.

DARKEN (v)

adverbs
obscurely; opaquely; murkily; partially; gloomily; unaccountably; perceptibly; inauspiciously; nocturnally; totally; utterly; unnaturally; bewilderingly; increasingly; bafflingly; prematurely; comparatively; mysteriously; generally; devouringly; fatefully; mercifully.
(See shade. obscure.)

DARKENING

adjectives
sudden; gradual; appreciable; perceptible; fathomless; ominous; unprecedented.

DARKNESS

adjectives
blank; blessed; friendly; cozy; deep; hampering; intense; total; opaque; utter; black; somber; pitchy; eerie; unnatural; bewildering; baffling; breathless; preternatural; environing; enveloping; oppressive; choking; stabbing; formless; deepening; increasing; reverberating; howling; Stygian; dense; dripping; silvery; velvety; scented; barbaric; leafy; mental; gross; eternal; uneasy; quiet; serene; abrupt; heavy; muffling; premature; comparative; outer; silent; chilly; blessed; mysterious; general; feudal; blind; lifting; gathering; stormy; horrible; abiding; smooth; fetid; midnight; regnant; fateful; cavernous; dumb; inmost; perennial; wormy; circumambient; thick; devouring; looming; brooding; revolutionary; gay; hot; desert; shadowy; fearful; horrid; merciful; hilltop; windy; marble; healing; unfathomed; priestly; chaotic; abysmal; impending; inwoven; double; lustrous; embarrassing.

verbs
abide in—; accustom to—; beam in—; burnish by—; burrow into—; cast into—; conceal in—; descend to—; disappear into—; discern in—; dispel—; distinguish in—; dread—; dwell in—; encompass by—; encounter—; engulf in—; enlighten—; glow through—; grope in—; haunt—; illumine—; keep in—; lapse into—; laugh at—; lose in—; peer into—; pierce—; plunge into—; prowl in—; pursue in—; remain in—; roam in—; scatter—; shine in—; sink into—; sparkle in—; stumble in—; survey—; toil in—; tread in—; wander in—; wrap in—; yield to—; —approaches; —blinds; —blots out; —broods; —deepens; —depresses; —descends; —devours; —eclipses; —embalms; —embraces; —encompasses; —en-

dures; —enfolds; —ensues; —falls; —flees; —folds over; —gathers; —grows; —hides; —mantles; —melts; —obscures; —prevails; —robes; —shadows; —shrouds; —spreads; —steals upon; —surrounds; —swallows up; —terrifies; —thickens; —veils.

(See gloom, obscurity, shadow.)

DARKY

adjectives
rollicking; superstitious; stalwart; ragged; ingenious; septic-looking; magic-footed; tattered; greasy; cringing; blissful; wool-thatched.

DARLING

adjectives
spunky; plucky; extravagant; spoiled; over-indulged; pampered.

adverbs
utterly; adorably; sweetly; lovably; seductively; charmingly; captivatingly; enchantingly; bewitchingly; tenderly.

DART

adjectives
fiery; false; envenomed; swift; imperceptible; slender; sudden; goading; bullet-like; lightning; dribbling; sickening; spirit-quelling; singing; flaming; shining.

verbs
aim—; blunt—; blow—; brandish—; dash—; defend with—s; envenom—; feather—; flash—; interpose; remove—; poison—; polish—; shake—; shield from—; shoot—; spear—; tip—; thrust—through; —hisses by; —soars; —strikes; —whizzes by; —wounds.

(See missile, spear, shaft, weapon, arrow.)

DASH

adjectives
final; blind; despairing; fiery; flying; headlong; inadvertent; tremendous; meaningful; splendid; giddy; joyous; brilliant; surreptitious; eloquent; refreshing; gallant; rosy.

DASH (v)

adverbs
gently; aimlessly; turbulently; hurriedly; immediately; madly; blindly; inadvertently; despairingly; splendidly; joyously; gallantly; eagerly; anxiously; furiously; victoriously; unrestrainedly; violently.

(See hurl.)

DASHING

adverbs
showily; jauntily; gallantly; pretentiously; proudly; vainly; gorgeously; dramatically; theatrically; spectacularly; sumptuously; boldly; rashly; valiantly; pluckily; stoutly; audaciously; dauntlessly; confidently; fashionably; stylishly.

DATA

adjectives
curious; strange; one-sided; accompanying; available; existing; latest; relative; interesting; relevant; fascinating; convincing; accurate; basic; factual; important; significant; extensive; erroneous; obscure; modern; corrective; research; programmed; official; scientific; technical; merchandising; precise; recorded; necessary; incomplete; impeccable; authentic; intimate; historical; biographic.

verbs
accept—; accumulate—; analyze—; attest by—; authenticate—; catalogue—; collect—; elaborate—; furnish—; gather—; improve—; present—; produce—; study—; survey—; synthesize—; track down—; —indicate; —measure; —prove; —reveal; —show.

(See fact, information.)

DATE

adjectives
ineffective; arbitrary; fixed; exact; recent; ancient; prescribed; decisive; closing; historical; equivalent; significant; future; remote; immediate; memorable; subsequent; calamitous; lasting; endless; tentative; dark; dividing; equinoctial.

verbs
ascribe—to; assign—to; bear—; calculate—; cancel—; confirm—; denote—; determine—; extend—; fix—; forestall—; inscribe—; insert—; jot down—; limit to—; mark with—; reckon—; refer to—; require—; set—; specify—; —denotes; —expires.

(See time, duration.)

DATE (v)

adverbs
variously; significantly; recently; historically; tentatively; unquestionably; subsequently.

(See record.)

DAUB

adjectives
unsightly; wretched; pitiful; artless; spattered; colorful.

DAUB (*v*)

adverbs
wretchedly; hideously; hatefully; amateurishly; carelessly; halfheartedly.
(See smear, soil.)

DAUGHTER

adjectives
loyal; considerate; true; dutiful; self-sacrificing; stubbornly-devoted; tiny; plump; brisk; pretty; beautiful; hardhearted; militant; rebellious; errant; irreconcilable; sedate; tomboy; virginal; debutante; spoiled; idolized; virtuous; modern; outspoken; tender; chaste; marriageable; repentant; gay; beldam; buxom; blithe; debonair; short; untutored; fragile; mangled; abominable; peerless; loving; expiring; flighty; uncultured.

verbs
adopt—; adore—; bear—; berate—; betroth—; bring forth—; chastise—; cherish —; conceive—; confer on—; delight in—; fondle—; long for—; market—; marry off—; mold—; pamper—; preach to—; present with—; nurse—; rear—; rebuke—; rejoice in—; reprimand—; seduce—; woo —; —elopes; —graces; —inherits; —pleads; —shames; —shocks.
(See child, girl, person, woman.)

DAUNTLESS

adverbs
heroically; courageously; recklessly; rashly; resolutely; splendidly; superbly; joyously; proudly; fiercely; morally; carelessly; impetuously; stubbornly; magnificently; exceptionally.

DAVENPORT

adjectives
sagged; restful; upholstered; comfortable; dumpy; deep.

DAWDLE (*v*)

adverbs
perversely; idly; languidly; tantalizingly; calmly; everlastingly; lightly; somnolently; lazily; lackadaisically; irritatingly; aimlessly.
(See dally.)

DAWDLING

adjectives
calm; everlasting; lackadaisical; nonchalant; idle; purposeless.

DAWN

adjectives
black; crawling; opalescent; dirty; gray; thick; crimson; golden; pitiless; pearl; cool; false; dismal; cheerless; wet; pale; perfect; premature; faint; hushed; slow; tropical; clear; stormy; countless (pl); roseate; autumnal; northern; waking; hazy; kindling; crude; softly-breaking; radiant; wintry; savage; streaked; low; dappled; amorous; reddest; tender; noonday; bashful; tempestuous; joyful; azure; unmellowed; crepuscular; smothering; melancholy.

verbs
behold—; foretell—; front—; herald—; journey till—; precede—; rise at—; usher in—; wait for—; wake with—; warn of—; —arouses; —ascends; —blazons; —blushes; —breaks; —cheers; —creeps on; —flares; —flees; —flushes; —glimmers; —pierces; —ripens into day; —surges; —surprises; —steals over; —verges with.
(See daylight.)

DAWN (*v*)

adverbs
finally; abruptly; clearly; brilliantly; incisively; eerie; troubled; gorgeous; antiphonal; hazy; phosphorescent.
(See lighten.)

DAY

adjectives
adventurous; agreeable; arduous; alternate; anxious; auspicious; beautiful; brilliant; buoyant; broiling; blowing; bitter; bloody; blank; bygone; blissful; brave; burning; bright; bustling; boyhood; bountiful; battering; commendable; chaotic; cloudy; cool; crisp; calm; coronation; courageous; clear; checkered; capricious; cheerless; catechizing; corsair (pl); credulous; colorful; crowded; careless; canicular; vivid; carefree; dim; dayless; decisive; declining; dying; dull; disastrous; dismal; dramatic; drab; drizzling; dedicated; diviner; domestic; degenerate; dangerous; decadent; delightful; depression (pl); dark; dragging; dreary; dusty; despairing; distracting; dead; dumb; drowsy; dancing; eventful; empty; epochal; endless; expiring; everlasting; ensuing; eternal; enchant-

ed; enlightened; exciting; evil; exceptional; fateful; first; fatiguing; fatal; funeral; flourishing; former; festal; fragrant; fairy; frosty; foul; gentle; glorious; grinding; gloomy; gushing; garish; gallant; garden; golden; gay; glamorous; gambling; hectic; hot; holy; happy; hopeful; halcyon; honest; historic; humid; homesick; happy-go-lucky; innocent; illustrious; indelible; intercalary; ideal; idle; irretrievable; irreclaimable; interleaving; judgment; jocund; joyous; laborious; late; luckless; long; lively; lazy; limpid; lagging; lifeless; memorable; mysterious; miserable; melancholy; motionless; magnificent; monastic; muted; medieval; momentous; opulent; northern; noisy; newborn; natal; nuptial; neophyte; overbusy; old; opal-colored; proverbial; piercing; peevish; present; prosperous; preceding; proud; perfect; pretty; pleasant; pessimistic; pre-medieval (pl); postwar (pl); planless; phlegmatic; primitive; parsimonious; pilgrim; palmy; quondam; restful; rainy; recurring; reckoning; rosy; romantic; regal; raucous; roisterous; red-letter; ruminant; righteous; splendid; sultry; sunless; silent; soggy; silver; strenuous; summer; somnolent; sorry; smiling; sullen; sinking; sodden; scornful; solitary; serene; superb; solar; sordid; short; simple; somber; sinister; supplementary; sizzling; scorching; tiresome; slumberous; topsy-turvy; tumultuous; toil-stained; triumphal; tedious; temperamental; visionary; torrid; unreal; untroubled; unremembered; vanished; campaigning; victorious; vagabond; vacant.

verbs
appoint—; await—; bemoan—; behold—; bless—; busy—; cap—; cloud—; contemplate—; crown—; curse—; decree—; denounce—; dispose of—; divide—; drag out —s; ease—; enliven—; endure—; grace—; herald—; honor—; keep—; kill—; lament —; lose—; mar—; measure—; name—; observe—; peak—; record—; regret—; rejoice—; reminisce of—s; rest by—; rue—; rule—; save—; solemnize—; waste—; win—; —advances; —affords; —approaches; —breaks; —cheers; —closes; —comforts; —darkens; —dawns; —dazzles; —declines; —decreases; —dies; —drags by; —s elapse; —is born; —lags; —mounts; —oppresses; —peers forth; —races by; —saddens; —s shorten; —unfolds; —vanishes; —wanes; —waxes; —wears off.

(See time. age, generation.)

DAYBREAK

adjectives
glimmering; resplendent; glorious; joyous; gratifying; welcome; salutary; golden.

DAYLIGHT

adjectives
fading; burning; broad; wintry; sick; gray; haggard; dying; garish; partial; glimmering; adequate; diffused; beautiful; blessed; obscure; unnatural; scented; yellow; primrose.

verbs
employ—; keep in—; let in—; surrender to—; —appears; —approaches; —arouses; —breaks; —burns; —dawns; —dazzles; —dies; —diffuses; —discloses; —envelops; —fades; —filters through; —floods; —illumines; —pours in; —promises; —seeps in; —shines; —suffuses; —unfolds; —vanishes; —wanes.

(See day, light. dawn.)

DAZE

adjectives
fatuous; open-mouthed; sodden; staggering; effacing; somnambulistic.

DAZED

adverbs
stupidly; unaccountably; genuinely; disturbingly; strangely; indescribably; fearfully; insuperably; depressingly; terribly; alarmingly; unreasonably; vaguely; uncomfortably; inexplicably; awkwardly;; extremely; helplessly; pitifully; tragically; sadly; hopelessly; dangerously.

DAZZLE (v)

adverbs
suddenly; glamorously; resplendently; purposely; bewilderingly; awesomely; blindingly; fatuously; hopelessly; fatally.

(See blind, bewilder.)

DEACON

adjectives
dutiful; long-faced; solemn; ruling; parsimonious; funereal-looking; sleek-haired; sin-denouncing.

adverbs
appoint—; elect—; ordain—; unfrock—; —administers; —admonishes; —advises; —assists; —attends; —awes; —baptizes; —christens; —collects; —disperses; —dis-

tributes; —performs; —prays; —preaches; —provides; —reproves; —serves; —supervises; —visits.

(See minister, elder, officer.)

DEAD

adjectives

stricken; unseen; illustrious; beloved; pitiful; humble; heroic; war; ghastly; gallant; moldering; enduring; sainted; venerable; imponderable; silent; turbaned; decaying; ungathered; coffined; spectral; pestilential; unconscious; restless; mighty; dearest; honorable; untimely; vulgar; faithful; precious; passionless; floating.

verbs

awaken—; bemoan—; blaspheme—; bury —; commemorate—; consort with—; curse —; defile—; disinter—; embalm—; entomb—; honor—; judge—; mourn—; number—; record—; reincarnate—; remember—; revive—; rise from—; rob—; —sleep on; —wither.

(See carcass, corpse.)

DEADLOCK

adjectives

hopeless; partial; growing; convenient; relentless; quarterless; fatal.

DEADLY

adverbs

disastrously; noxiously; virulently; exceptionally; irremediably; woefully; execrably.

DEAF

adverbs

totally; insufferably; irritatingly; vexatiously; annoyingly; pitiably; slightly; utterly; deplorably; lamentably; unfortunately; stubbornly; callously; deliberately; unhappily; pitifully; tragically; forlornly; desperately; moodily; lonesomely.

DEAL

adjectives

neighborly; momentous; shady; dirty; legitimate; ill-savored; unprotected; square; devised; financial; business; backstairs; important; great; vast; infinite; complete; skin; wandering; famished; sensational; new; tremendous; parlor; wonder; made-to-order; timed-to-the-minute; combination; bargain; smashing; pace-setting; thrilling.

verbs

arrange—; bargain—; benefit by—; carry on—; clinch—; close—; concoct—; disclose—; engage in—; engineer—; engross in—; enter—; involve in—; participate in—; put over—; transact—; unfold—; —fizzles (colloq.); —promises.

(See transaction.)

DEAL (v)

adverbs

ceremoniously; promptly; ruthlessly; bountifully; primarily; heedlessly; discreetly; severely; summarily; zestfully; scientifically; munificently; adequately; rigorously; gratuitously; momentously; legitimately; financially; sensationally; thrillingly; persuasively; exclusively; competently; plainly; brilliantly.

(See negotiate, distribute.)

DEALER

adjectives

opulent; persuasive; ignorant; unscrupulous; keen; double; individual; antique; honest; retail; exclusive; plain; implement; competent.

DEALINGS

adjectives

hard; plain; decent; gracious; unauthorized; shrewd; double; quick; sharp; satisfactory; dishonest; high-minded; generous; rough; hazardous; strenuous; undiplomatic; wanton; unscrupulous; fair; nefarious; punctilious; extensive; business; wise; patient; highhanded; furtive; ruthless.

DEAN

adjectives

callous; pompous; incompetent; meticulous; impeccable; impinging; smug.

DEAR

adverbs

infinitely; adorably; admirably; delightfully; affectionately.

DEARTH

adjectives

barren; deplorable; notable; absolute; sickening; hapless; agreeable.

DEATH

adjectives

brave; beautiful; happy; glorious; heroic; gentle; gallant; calm; romantic; tranquil; painless; swift; reasonable; merciful; natural; appropriate; deliberate; certain; sure; untoward; early; premature; melancholy; tragic; baleful; lamented; instantaneous; quick; sudden; vicious; grappling; grisly; grim; horrible; ghastly; dreadful; beastly;

ignominious; slow; lingering; physical; spiritual; temporal; somatic; cool; enfolding; tearful; sleeping; silent; long; unified; inflexible; ensuing; imbecilic; latent; cruel; intellectual; partial; honorable; immediate; recent; deplored; radiant; shadow-like; diverse(pl); mysterious; uniform; delicious; ugly; moral; fearful; drowning; threatened; awful; gradual; merited; devouring; foreboding; impending; immortal; stalking; unlooked-for; tardy; covetous; bright; unspeaking; heartening; atrocious; disgraceful; adulterate; direful; slaughtering; humane; engrossing; sacrificial; unsubstantial; bloody; maternal; helpless; poetic; violent; affronted; unregretted; flaming; unnoticed; instant; sacred; everlasting; manly; glowing; timeless; malignant; agonizing; eternal; obscure; placid; present; golden; ultimate; approaching; protracted; unrewarded; subsequent; tithed; untimely; distressing; hideous; watery; senseless; dusty; accidental; sequent; tuberculous; occasional (pl); ominous; excruciating; voluptuous; shameful; dramatic; pale; wasted; miserable; princely; paralyzing; drier; opportune; delaying; stony; self-abased; sulphurous; overshadowing; unanticipated; propagating; strong; shrouded; scurvy; treacherous; fierce; unavoidable; unseen; mellow; loathsome; temporal; living.

verbs
administer—; announce—; apprise of—; avert—; bore to—; brood on—; cause—; cheat—; condemn to—; confirm—; contemplate—; dance with—; deliver from—; deserve—; designate—; devise—; dramatize —; endure—; evade—; exact—; experience —; expiate—; face—; feign—; frighten to —; gamble with—; give up to—; guard till; —harass to—; harry to—; hasten—; hunger for—; induce—; join in—; laugh at—; long for—; mete out—; mock—; mourn—; overcome—; persecute unto—; poise at the brink of—; pour—on; predestine to—; prepare for—; preserve from—; quail before—; recoil from—; repose in—; repulse—; rescue from—; result in—; revenge—; scorn—; seal with—; send to—; sentence to—; snatch from—; spare from—; spell—; spurt—; stay—; struggle against —; submit to—; suffer—; symbolize—; threaten with—; triumph over—; usher in—; ward off—; warrant—; welcome—; wreak—; yield to—; —alters; —claims; —clamors; —concludes; —dances; —dawns; —devours; —dogs; —embitters; —engulfs; —ensues; —follows; —grieves; —grins; —harvests; —humbles; —intervenes; —invades; —lurks; —menaces; —parts; —reveals; —shades; —shadows; —spreads; —stalks among; —stings; —supervenes; —swallows up; —terminates; —triumphs; —vanquishes; —walks; —strikes.

(See extinction, destruction, slaughter, mortality.)

DEBASE (*v*)

adverbs
obscenely; miserably; shamefully; tragically; ruinously; unavoidably; irrevocably; irreparably; tyrannically.

(See degrade, humiliate.)

DEBASED

adverbs
grossly; abjectly; morally; perfidiously; treacherously; disgracefully; darkly; infamously; arrantly; vilely; contemptibly; shamefully; bestially.

DEBATABLE

adverbs
highly; unquestionably; definitely; obviously; profoundly; endlessly; turbulently; violently; critically; dangerously; excitingly; hotly; amusingly; readily; easily; reasonably; rationally; concretely; equivocally; hypothetically; precariously; speciously; logically.

DEBATE

adjectives
stormy; profound; mental; inward; parliamentary; foul; keen; acrimonious; notable; instructive; picayune; animated; interrupted; open; free; public; obstructive; lively; endless; prolix; fierce; impassioned; mock; lifelong; extemporaneous; considerable; political; epistolary; vigorous; newspaper; turbulent; organized; heated; disorderly; spirited; exciting; familiar; long-winded; noisy; hot; brotherly; amusing; teleological; loud; dialetical.

verbs
admit to—; assemble for—; climax—; contend during—; deliberate on—; draw into —; engage in—; enter into—; indulge in—; involve in—; judge—; practise—; prepare —; resolve into—; settle—; subject to—; welcome—; wrangle during—; —concludes; —discusses; —revolves about.

(See dispute, controversy, combat, contest, discussion.)

DEBATE (v)

adverbs
abundantly; extensively; futilely; inwardly; profoundly; mentally; instructively; animatedly; openly; publicly; endlessly; fiercely; impassionedly; extemporaneously; considerably; politically; vigorously; turbulently; heatedly; spiritedly; noisily; hotly; amusingly; loudly; dialectically; acrimoniously; shrewdly.
(See argue, discuss.)

DEBATER

adjectives
cogent; convincing; tight-lipped; ready; interlocutory.

verbs
coach—; judge—; prepare—; train—; verse—; —argues; —assembles; —asserts; —assures; —cajoles; —concludes; —contends; —convinces; —declares; —discusses; —disputes; —engages; —gestures; —illustrates; —informs; —points out; —refers to; —refutes; —registers; —shouts; —voices.
(See speaker.)

DEBAUCH

adjectives
veritable; riotous; rudimentary; prolonged; unwonted; limitless; grisly; abnormal; drunken; secret; fictional.

DEBAUCHED

adverbs
pitiably; grossly; terribly; horribly; shamelessly; abjectly; lamentably; openly; shamefully; morally; disgracefully; infamously; notoriously; arrantly; vilely; contemptibly; bestially; voluptuously; wildly; dissolutely; brutishly; indecently.

DEBAUCHERY

adjectives
brutal; sensual; profligate; titled; coarse; truant; corrupt; perverse.

DEBILITY

adjectives
languid; attendant; general; extreme; congenital; nervous; spectral; physical.

DEBRIS

adjectives
accumulated; rock; floating; chaotic; fragmentary; sad; littered; hopeless.

verbs
emerge from—; crumble to—; fall amidst —; rise from—; scatter—; search—.
(See ruins, remains, fragments, rubbish.)

DEBT

adjectives
common; enormous; stale; ancestral; crushing; credit; impaired; recoverable; petty; immeasurable; incalculable; heavy; tremendous; huge; lawful; honest; long-standing; mounting; urgent; floating; discharged; everlasting; terrible; dubious; regulating; desperate; profound; gambling; unpayable, joint; countless; paltry.

verbs
abolish—; acknowledge—; amass—; assume —; cancel—; clear—; confront with—; contract—; die in—; discharge—; dissolve —; encumber with—; free from—; harass with—; incur—; overwhelm with—; plunge into—; repay—; repudiate—; scale down—; smart under—; swell—; unload—; wipe away—; —jumps; —rises; —soars.
(See obligation, liability.)

DEBTOR

adjectives
prodigal; luckless; shabby; insolvent; grateful; broken.

verbs
accommodate—; bind—; bond—; demand of—; die—; harass—; harry—; hound—; imprison—; insure—; jail—; limit—; oblige—; press—; release—; subject—; sue —; —abolishes; —appeals to; —borrows; —discharges; —falls delinquent; —promises; —reduces.

DEBUT

adjectives
operatic; successful; daring; startling; notable; eventual.

DEBUTANTE

adjectives
pretty; awkward; career-seeking; altar-bound; dazzling; successfully-launched; expensive; luxury-seeking.

DECADE

adjectives
present; recent; stormy; independent; successive; mauve; ironical; past; coming; prosperous; legendary.

verbs
approach—; celebrate—; include in—; infuse in—; form in—; recall —s; recognize—; survive—; vanish with—s; —advances; —elapses; —ensues; —envelops; —flourishes.
(See period, time.)

DECADENCE

adjectives
pale; sentimental; brilliant; passionate; pathetic; fragrant; vegetating; mouldy.

verbs
abandon to—; arouse from—; awake from —; crumble into—; fall into—; incur—; lapse into—; prevent—; produce—; resist —; result in—; rise out of—; slide into—; steep in—; suffer—; threaten with—; —approaches; —beckons; —girdles; —sleeps in.
(See deterioration, decay.)

DECADENT

adverbs
cankerously; decrepitly; effetely; corrosively; corruptibly; irreparably; incurably; irremediably; lamentably; deplorably; pitifully; viciously; degenerately; corruptly; unbelievably; astoundingly; pitiably; hopelessly.

DECAY

adjectives
inevitable; melancholy; symbolic; premature; elegant; slow; mental; swift; physical; flamboyant; approaching; common; perpetual; integral; picturesque; unperceived; sensible; dry; gradual; inexorable; fatal; lichened.

verbs
accelerate—; arrest—; attack by—; bar—; conceal—; delay—; doom to—; exempt from—; fall into—; presage—; preserve from—; reek of—; resist—; subject to—; suffer—; —bores into; —sets in.
(See deterioration, decomposition, corruption.)

DECAY (*v*)

adverbs
fearfully; disastrously; inevitably; symbolically; prematurely; mentally; swiftly; physically; picturesquely; sensibly; inexorably; gradually; fatally; obviously; partially; invisibly.
(See rot, disintegrate.)

DECEIT

adjectives
charming; dreamlike; dear; radiant; adored; coquettish; remorseful; blind; beguiling; unprincipled; fatal.

verbs
abhor—; avoid—; breed—; commit—; conceal—; contrive by—; depart from—; dispose to—; dwell in—; indulge in—; intend—; nourish—; quit—; redeem from —; shroud—; suspect—; unearth—; utter —; wallow in—; work—; annoys; —counters; —falsifies; —flourishes; —harms; —irks; —misleads; —pricks; —tricks; reprove—.
(See fraud, deception. trick, stratagem, cheating.)

DECEITFUL

adverbs
inherently; naturally; habitually; characteristically; temperamentally; subtly; shrewdly; astutely; carefully; deliberately; insidiously; smoothly; fiendishly; maliciously; astoundingly; deftly; dangerously; insinuatingly; horribly; abominably; shamefully; daringly; surprisingly; unexpectedly; expertly.

DECEIVE (*v*)

adverbs
deliberately; grossly; palpably; bitterly; eternally; prodigiously; blackly; mightily; heartlessly; systematically; basely; purposely; vilely; villainously; treacherously.
(See mislead.)

DECEIVER

adjectives
systematic; heartless; gracious; seductive; gay; artful; politic; insidious; crafty.

DECENCY

adjectives
ordinary; sheer; conventional; common; mere; enforced; requisite; wanton; political; true; social; eminent; respectable; temperate; native; disregarded.

verbs
breed in—; conform to—; dress in—; dwell in—; execute with—; expect—; inject into—; insist on—; maintain—; manage with—; observe—; perform with—; practise—; pretend—; violate—; —befits; —flourish; —requires; outrage—.
(See propriety, modesty, decorum.)

DECENT

adverbs
decorously; utterly; entirely; honestly; modestly; admirably; habitually; conventionally; eminently; innately; inherently; notably; chastely; suitably; naturally; appropriately; unobtrusively; superbly; remarkably; essentially; palpably; obviously; extraordinarily; unaffectedly.

DECEPTION

adjectives
palpable; gross; downright; swaggering; detestable; obvious; systematic; pious; venial; innocent; intentional; harmless; inevitable; economic; relative; facial; deliberate; refined; universal.

verbs
apply—; avoid—; commit—; conceal—; devise—; dispose to—; expose—; fall into —; fear—; form—; imagine—; impose— upon; justify—; perform—; produce—; practice—; suspect—; unearth—; unfold—; —harms; —injures.

(See deceit, craft, cunning, trickery, fraud.)

DECEPTIVE

adverbs
palpably; grossly; detestably; obviously; cruelly; systematically; methodically; intentionally; purposely; maliciously; harmlessly; deliberately; childishly; innocently; teasingly; criminally; cleverly; astutely; adroitly; expertly; carefully; meanly; despicably; contemptibly; disgracefully; terribly.

DECIDE (*v*)

adverbs
adversely; conclusively; discreetly; positively; affirmatively; irrevocably; authentically; impartially; wisely; tentatively; peremptorily; glumly; confusedly; arbitrarily; simultaneously; impulsively; virtually; unanimously; eventually; conspicuously; grudgingly; favorably; magnanimously; sensibly; temperately; resolutely; unalterably; authoritatively; haphazardly; prematurely; precipitately; tactically; emphatically; spectacularly; promptly; theoretically; academically; technically; politically; speedily.

(See determine, resolve.)

DECISION

adjectives
favorable; comforting; sagacious; well-considered; careful; correct; perfect; practical; magnanimous; sensible; unfettered; unbought; accurate; straightforward; just; calm; temperate; final; irreparable; irrevocable; invincible; expectant; inexorable; peremptory; sweeping; important; resolute; unflinching; firm; unmistakable; unalterable; unchanged; authoritative; unbiased; weighty; momentous; august; arbitrary; vacillating; haphazard; premature; abrupt; precipitate; rapid; instant; hasty; intuitive; quick; swift; hair-trigger; dangerous; desperate; ruinous; illegal; adverse; judicial; critical; temporal; ticklish; major; iniquitous; unanimous; last-moment; applauded; perplexing; tactical; controlling; definite; profitless; cryptic; tentative; overt; successive; prompt; emphatic; due; unbalanced; disastrous; solemn; demurred; spectacular; supreme; indolent; instant; practical; ruling; belated; blamable; strict; impartial; theoretical; calculated; epoch-making; heart-searching; resolute; sudden; daring; executive; tremendous; resounding; academic; unwise; crushing; initiatory; technical; adverse; political; rumored; sundry (pl).

verbs
abide by—; accept—; acclaim—; adhere to—; analyze—; circumvent—; confirm—; contest—; dictate—; enforce—; execute—; greet—; hail—; hand down—; influence—; obey—; prejudice—; reach—; render—; reverse—; stiffen—; subject to—; submit to—; swing—; voice—; weigh—; —embroils; —favors; —foreshadows; invalidates; —takes place; —wavers.

(See settlement, conclusion, verdict.)

DECISIVE

adverbs
alarmingly; conclusively; definitely; scarcely; mercifully; fortunately; happily; favorably; comfortingly; practically; justly; irrevocably; inexorably; sweepingly; importantly; firmly; unmistakably; unalterably; authoritatively; authentically; weightily; augustly; intuitively; swiftly; desperately; critically; iniquitously; solemnly; tremendously; politically.

DECK

adjectives
hurricane; forward; promenade; white-scoured; bright; snowy; spotless; glistening; holystoned; sloping; inclining; reeling; pitching; slippery; slimy; unscrubbed; shattered; spacious; blazing; cluster-lighted; splinter-strewn; awninged; watery;

crowded; ghostly; creamy; tapered; wind-swept; ocean; long; great; open; comfortable; gay; sun; broad; shot-torn; shuddering; wave-set; steamer; stricken; bloody; unobstructed; wreckage-laden.

verbs
batter—; burst—; clear—; cover—; dash on—; glimmer on—; keep above—; lash—; lie on—; pace—; scatter on—; shatter—; splinter—; sprawl on—; stand on—; sun on —; toss on—; tramp—; view from—; wave from—; —extends; —runs.
(See platform. floor.)

DECLAMATION

adjectives
rhetorical; strident; stuttering; insipid; passionate; empty; facetious; sounding.

verbs
alter—; burst into—; compose—; dispute—; influence—; inspire—; publish—; render—; repeat—; set forth—; stir up—; thunder—; utter—; —embodies; —exacerbates; —expresses; —proves; —shocks; —stirs.
(See speech. oration, oratory.)

DECLAMATORY

adverbs
absurdly; effusively; unnecessarily; foolishly; ridiculously; ludicrously; amusingly; bombastically; pompously; arrogantly; pretentiously; stridently; passionately; fervently; emptily; facetiously; sententiously; laughably; piously; grandiloquently; floridly; preachily; pedantically; frothily; flashily; flamboyantly; blatantly.

DECLARATION

adjectives
culminating; remarkable; far-echoing; formal; droll; insulting; emphatic; public; appalling; passionate; blunt; voluntary; candid; downright; bold; determining; significant; official; profound; strong; solemn; superior; positive; vehement; frequent; rigid; important; absolute; distinct; undisguised; open; customary; fierce; friendly; supplementary; bitter; passionate; abasing; unmistakable.

verbs
adopt—; announce—; belie—; constitute—; decry—; dispute—; expound—; immortalize—; inspire—; introduce—; issue—; present—; proclaim—; publish—; set forth—; —contradicts; —embodies; —influences; —pleads; —proves; —shocks.
(See assertion, statement.)

DECLARATORY

adverbs
plainly; comfortingly; reassuringly; explicitly; clearly; analytically; broadly; substantially; literally; honestly; simply; significantly; intelligibly; authoritatively; formally; emphatically; bluntly; officially.

DECLARE (v)

adverbs
vociferously; formally; publicly; emphatically; passionately; bluntly; candidly; boldly; significantly; officially; solemnly; vehemently; absolutely; distinctly; openly; fiercely; bitterly; unmistakably; conceitedly; enthusiastically; pedantically; petulantly; grimly; virtually; impatiently; contemptuously; stoutly; hypocritically; privately; haltingly; inconclusively; antagonistically; formally; shamelessly; speciously; archly; hotly; earnestly; rapturously; severely; wrathfully; repeatedly; unanimously; solemnly.
(See affirm, state.)

DECLINE

adjectives
marked; considerable; general; ultimate; lingering; terrific; unquestionable; alarming; social; drastic; prolonged; accelerated; sad; subsequent; premature; short; dreary; unaccountable; hopeless; marked; incipient; ominous; partial; unprecedented; indubitable.

DECLINE (v)

adverbs
peremptorily; repeatedly; progressively; blandly; spinelessly; respectfully; steadily; gently; invariably; bluntly; querulously; rapidly; gravely; firmly; quietly; majestically; ultimately; alarmingly; socially; acceleratedly; subsequently; prematurely; drearily; unaccountably; hopelessly; ominously; partially; indubitably; unprecedentedly.
(See languish, bend.)

DECLIVITY

adjectives
slight; dread; gentle; abrupt; steep; obstructing.

DECOMPOSITION

adjectives
chemical; spontaneous; painful; tedious; rapid; erosive; timely.

verbs
crumble into—; fall into—; incur—; lapse into—; object to—; prevent—; produce—; resolve into—; result in—; slide into—; suffer—; threaten with—; undergo—; —abates; —continues; —distributes; —separates.
(See disintegration, decay.)

DECORATE (v)

adverbs
elaborately; exquisitely; profusely; picturesquely; garishly; inelegantly; charmingly; lavishly; gaudily; quaintly; splendidly; tastefully; mournfully; superfluously; sumptuously; superbly; festively; gorgeously; pictorially; richly; tastefully; delicately; ornately; ostentatiously; characteristically; formally; realistically; murally; scenically; fantastically; architecturally; grotesquely.
(See adorn, embellish.)

DECORATION

adjectives
coveted; incidental; pictorial; simulated; profuse; mistaken; disturbing; quiet; rich; new; superb; modern; regal; tasteful; delicate; contemporary; delightful; ornate; ostentatious; personal; excessive; last-moment; characteristic; silver; detailed; glaring; formal; realistic; eye-filling; sense-curdling; painted; elaborate; polychrome; mural; casual; sober; religious; lateral; lavish; unobtrusive; sparkling; scenical; stupendous; sculptural; simple; fantastic; costly; lifeless; colorless; architectural; molded; grotesque; subordinated.

DECORATIVE

adverbs
delicately; incidentally; properly; quietly; richly; superbly; regally; tastefully; delightfully; ornately; excessively; formally; elaborately; casually; soberly; lavishly; unobtrusively; pleasantly; agreeably; appropriately; graphically; picturesquely; romantically; unusually; beautifully.

DECORATOR

adjectives
prominent; competent; resourceful; professional; amateur; over-ambitious; aspiring; over-nice; classically-inclined.

DECOROUS

adverbs
becomingly; modestly; essentially; socially; strictly; scrupulously; carefully; invariably; habitually; ordinarily; dependably; politely; fashionably; punctiliously; conventionally; civilly; respectfully; reverentially; deferentially; ceremoniously; decently.

DECORUM

adjectives
external; stately; perfect; naughty; social; artistic; strict; pallid; unyielding; scrupulous; grave; public.

verbs
adhere to—; act with—; behave with—; cling to—; clothe in—; hedge by—; maintain—; mantle in—; nourish—; observe—; preserve—; require—; safeguard—; shed —; shock—; wallow in—; —lapses; —prevails; —restrains.
(See politeness, decency, propriety.)

DECREASE

adjectives
sagging; marked; dripping; noticeable; proportional.

DECREASE (v)

adverbs
imperceptibly; immeasurably; relatively; markedly; proportionally; noticeably; amazingly; astonishingly; tragically; fatally; woefully.
(See diminish, reduce.)

DECREE

adjectives
judgment; repealing; castigatory; omnipotent; law; august; tyrannical; eternal; emergency; royal; unalterable; unfathomable; divine; imperial; established; stern; oppressive; changeless; pitiless; unexecuted; irreversible; obnoxious; generous; paternal; laconic; primeval; absolute; extemporary.

verbs
adjust—; affirm—; alter—; annul—; bow to—; break—; carry out—; condemn—; confirm—; contest—; declare—; delay—; enforce—; favor—; issue—; mold—; obey—; oppose—; overleap—; proclaim—; promulgate—; repeal—; resist—; reverse —; revoke—; shape—; sign—; submit to—; sustain—; trample upon—; —banishes; —bans; —conscripts; —disposes of; —prohibits.
(See law, edict, mandate, ordinance, decision, rule.)

DECREE (v)

adverbs
irrevocably; tyrannically; legislatively; formally.
(See enact.)

DECREPIT

adverbs
helplessly; prematurely; dangerously; pitiably; hopelessly; pathetically; terribly; deplorably; heartbreakingly; hoarily; dodderingly; feebly; totteringly; crazily; incurably; weakly; lamentably; pitifully.

DECREPITUDE

adjectives
premature; dangerous; helpless; hampering; fretful; onrushing; subtle.

DEDICATE (v)

adverbs
pompously; respectfully; tacitly; solemnly; chiefly; wholeheartedly; sincerely; humbly; flatteringly; appreciatively; modestly; arrogantly; worshipfully.
(See consecrate, devote.)

DEDICATION

adjectives
handsome; nauseating; flattering; honorary; memorable; cursory; nominal.

DEDUCE (v)

adverbs
psychologically; rationalistically; unscientifically; logically; immediately; daringly; legitimately; profoundly; modestly; shrewdly.
(See conclude.)

DEDUCTIBLE

adverbs
immediately; legitimately; legally; logically; naturally; liberally; fortunately; ultimately; deceptively; possibly; unquestionably; inferentially; authentically; authoritatively; generously; substantially.

DEDUCTION

adjectives
immense; entomological; immediate; pure; sound; unverified; daring; trifling; logical; legitimate; profound; liberal; analogical; ultimate; false; bibulous; dipsomaniacal; modest; sagest; possible; hazardous; labored; spurious; genuine.

verbs
allow—; arrive at—; bear out—; claim—; confirm—; contemplate—; contradict—; debate—; decide on—; deny—; derive—; draw—; err in—; form—; reach—; reason —; secure—; —confuses; —follows.
(See demonstration, proof, inference.)

DEED
(*general*)

adjectives
sundry (pl); good; glorious; worthy; wise; brilliant; maniacal; meritorious; glamorous; notable; unforgettable; momentous; brave; courageous; heroic; mighty; doughty; rash; evil; dangerous; terrible; dishonest; desperate; inhuman; dirty; brutal; treacherous; violent; bloodthirsty; unholy; harsh; vainglorious; atrocious; silly; tacit; valiant; contemplated; passionate; unnatural; charitable; shameful; cursed; radiant; rueful; conspicuous; piteous; peaceful; wicked; hideous; masterful; execrable; heinous; bloody; lustful; chivalric; honorable; long; traitorous; virtuous; foulest; selfish; corrupt; unjust; steadfast; tragic; dastardly; magnanimous; historic; pious; truculent; knightly; disgraceful; manful; irrevocable; dragon; untried; lovely; sculptured; fiendish; lawless; persistent; deathless; fell; amazing; kindred; hazardous; darkest; venturous; stern; ill; unostentatious; precious; baleful; title; daring; horrible; barbarous; fearful; evil; remorseless; blazing; kind; sublime; caitiff; generous; wholesome; human; reckless; vile; abhorrent; loyal; pure; kingly; senseless; undying; grander; impeachable; noble; despicable; myriad (pl).

verbs
acclaim—; achieve—; answer for—; applaud—; ascribe to—; attempt—; bear out—; belittle—; blame—; bless—; boast of—; celebrate—; commemorate—; commend—; commit—; consent to—; contrive —; dare—; die in—; dignify—; dispense with—; dread—; emulate—; enshrine—; execrate—; glory in—; govern—; hallow—; honor—; incite to—; judge—; justify—; match—; noise—; perform—; please by—; proclaim—; promote—; recompense—; record—; relate—; resent—; render—; repent—; report—; reprove—; reward—; rue—; serve in—; shudder at—; sing of—s; spur to—; spurn—; void—; vouch for—; —awes; —flames; —indicates; —lives; —shames.
(See act. feat, performance, reality, exploit, achievement.)

DEEP

adjectives
restless; violet; uncomprehensible; overbrimming; mystic; uncreated; populous; airy; avenging; waveless; unfathomable; glimmering; laughing; lonely; vasty; waiting; blue; windless; lethal; boundless; lower; muffled; sunnier; sacred; regal; quiet; lampless; charmed; wind-obeying; shuddering; dreary; tranquil; unsounded; dangerous; mid-sea; transparent; unclosing; immeasurable; presumptuous; unnatural; tempest-wrinkled; dark-blue; innumerable (pl); murmuring; voiceless; remorseless; finny; unapparent.

verbs
abound in—; ambush from—; cast into—; conceal in—; delve in—; draw into—s; fill—; gaze at—; hide in—; lower to—; pierce—; pursue through—; recede into—; thunder in—; venture from—; —engulfs; —resounds.

adverbs
abysmally; inscrutably; mysteriously; unfathomably; quietly; immeasurably; profoundly; immensely; dangerously; hideously; prodigiously; wondrously; obviously; enormously; astonishingly; marvellously; unutterably; fabulously; curiously; amazingly.

DEEPEN (*v*)

adverbs
insensibly; sufficiently; unconsciously; unfathomably; boundlessly; shudderingly; immeasurably; unnaturally; remorsefully.
(See intensify.)

DEEP-SEATED

adverbs
intrinsically; inherently; stubbornly; obstinately; incurably; intensely; traditionally; customarily; racially; frequently.

DEER

adjectives
shy; brown; agile; astonished; stricken; shadowy; wounded; tame; antlered; plentiful; exquisite; graceful; sobbing; sleek; truant; fleet; swift.

verbs
chase—; follow—; herd—; lasso—; shelter—; skin—; rouse—; wound—; —bounds; —darts; —frequents; —haunts; —leaps; —roams; —sheds; —shies; —shuns; —treads; —treks.
(See animal.)

DEFACED

adverbs
rustily; unrecognizably; terribly; hopelessly; unpardonably; inexcusably; irreparably; irremediably; frightfully; grimly; horribly; grossly; odiously; shockingly.

DEFAME (*v*)

adverbs
libelously; viciously; revengefully; wantonly; hatefully; treacherously; illegally; spitefully; ruinously.
(See slander.)

DEFAULT

adjectives
glaring; notorious; serious; infinitesimal; covert; punishable.

verbs
arrest—; commit—; convict of—; expect—; expose—; force—; impose—; mend—; occasion—; pardon—; penalize—; practise—; punish—; record—; urge—; —deprives; —occurs.
(See neglect, omission, failure, deficiency.)

DEFEAT

adjectives
avowed; acknowledged; tremendous; crushing; graceful; overwhelming; shameful; ignoble; humiliating; signal; bitter; gory; ugly; rudest; inevitable; ultimate; impending; intellectual; trivial; unconditional; vain; stinging; unwilling; serious; sheer; later; subsequent; disheartening; crowning; humble; expensive; insignificant; final; inglorious; decisive; utter; undisguised; damned; ignominious; logical; ridiculous; unexpected; smashing; dreadful; heartbroken; averted; telling; encompassed; paralyzing; creditable; pet; disastrous; spiritual; dispirited; irretrievable.

verbs
acknowledge—; administer—; bear—; brand with—; brood over—; contribute to—; court—; destine to—; doom to—; emerge from—; foredoom to—; foresee—; gesture—; go down in—; invite—; involve—; meet—; pave the way for—; suffer—; thrive upon—; visualize—; writhe at—; —encompasses; —shakes.
(See repulse, loss, ruin.)

DEFEAT (*v*)

adverbs
incessantly; absolutely; successively; decisively; utterly; subsequently; exultantly;

crushingly; overwhelmingly; effectually; gloriously; shamefully; ignobly; humiliatingly; signally; bitterly; inevitably; ultimately; unconditionally; finally; ignominiously; logically; paralyzingly; disastrously; spiritually.

(See whip, thrash.)

DEFECT

adjectives

basic; vital; grave; serious; glaring; important; dominant; simple; secondary; minor; flagrant; fatal; unfortunate; psychic; functional; mental; mechanical; characteristic; uncorrected; possible; qualitative; latent; undeniable; structural; fair; abominable; constitutional; aggravated; concealed; palpable; inconspicuous; unexpected; temporary; manifold; serious; surface; complementary (pl); immense; obvious; capital; woeful; postural; inherent; radical; glaring; poetical; perilous; speculative.

verbs

analyze—; compensate for—; discover—; eliminate—; judge—; indicate—; make up for—; minimize—; produce—; rectify—; remedy—; shackle by—; spot—; stamp—; suffer from—; supply—; —impairs; —taints.

(See imperfection, blemish, fault, foible. flaw, shortcoming.)

DEFECTIVE

adverbs

unacceptably; unfortunately; grossly; carelessly; crudely; objectionably; provokingly; vexatiously; definitely; altogether; shamefully; outrageously; obviously; perceptibly; palpably; indefensibly; inexcusably.

DEFECTION

adjectives

contemplated; temporary; momentary; growing; relative; moral; impulsive.

DEFENDANT

adjectives

heroic; private; scared; frightened; worried; perjured.

verbs

accuse—; acquit—; aid—; attack—; bail—; befuddle—; bind—; challenge—; charge—; cross-examine—; discharge—; enjoin—; guard—; question—; represent—; restrain —; vindicate—; —answers; —attests; —counters; —declares; —defies; —denies; —maintains; —perjures; —pleads; —resists; —swears; —vouches; —vows.

(See defender, champion, advocate.)

DEFEND (*v*)

adverbs

elaborately; vigorously; gallantly; warmly; strenuously; stoutly; formidably; spiritedly; desperately; principally; subtly; ardently; philosophically; valorously; sturdily; passively; staunchly; brilliantly; obstinately; eloquently; competently; courageously; vigorously; determinedly; impassionedly; sensationally; unexpectedly; heroically; spiritlessly; aggressively; effectually; mutually; instinctively; unfailingly; injudiciously; unapproachably.

(See guard, protect.)

DEFENDER

adjectives

ardent; lawful; impenitent; philosophical; bold; brave; valorous; uncompromising; stout; sturdy; staunch; unconquerable; clever; gallant; passive; sincere; brilliant; steadfast; obstinate; habitual; eloquent.

verbs

acclaim—; banish—; challenge—; charge —; deploy—s; drive out—; hail—; honor —; reward—; —assails; —averts; —counters; —forsakes; —guards; —protects; —repels; —restrains; —upholds; —wards off.

(See defendant, advocate, champion.)

DEFENSE

adjectives

spirited; competent; noble; brilliant; courageous; strong; formidable; valiant; vigorous; long; determined; unassailable; involuntary; bungling; impassioned; halfhearted; weak; sensational; awkward; compelling; half-amused; adequate; national; manufactured; critical; inartificial; organized; offensive; frenzied; conceivable; unexpected; steadfast; natural; dignified; rare; spiritless; obstinate; pretty; armed; heroic; plausible; aggressive; uncompromising; honest; sorry; effectual; questionable; uncouth; eloquent; moral; capital; elaborate; gallant; adamantine; projected; womanly; leisurely; prompt; powerful; compensatory; mutual; instinctive; self; unfailing; minute; anomalous; injudicious; unapproachable.

verbs
abandon—; achieve—; argue in—; arise in—; batter—; bolster—; build—; bungle —; buttress—; demolish—; employ—; imperil—; map out—; prepare—; propound —; rally—; reenforce—; rehabilitate—; rush to—; sharpen—; smash—; spring to—; stand in—; stiffen under—; survey—; throw up—; vow—; —breaks; —crumbles; —crumples; —interposes.
(See protection, plan.)

DEFENSELESS

adverbs
tragically; unhappily; pathetically; silently; horribly; suddenly; surprisingly; utterly; bitterly; sadly; unexpectedly; scandalously; shockingly; calamitously; fatally; ignominiously; ominously; mysteriously; inexplicably.

DEFENSIVE

adverbs
eagerly; humbly; hastily; skilfully; reluctantly; angrily; confusedly; openly; awkwardly; nervously; instantly; preposterously; unnecessarily; sufficiently; profoundly; tearfully; pathetically; incoherently; sheepishly; embarrassingly; miserably; slavishly; disgustingly; deeply; half-heartedly; honestly.

DEFER (v)

adverbs
suavely; unfeignedly; condescendingly; pleasantly; scrupulously; particularly; servilely; resentfully; punctiliously; ungrudgingly; habitually; admiringly; carelessly; sympathetically.
(See delay.)

DEFERENCE

adjectives
unfeigned; suave; condescending; pleasant; exceeding; scrupulous; blissful; unfailing; chivalrous; particular; bullying; servile; secret; resentful; respectful; awesome; self-restraining; punctilious; exquisite; due; apparent; ungrudging; utmost; habitual; admiring; careless; sympathetic.

verbs
acknowledge—; allow—; bestow—; bow in—; choose out of—; claim—; conduct with—; entitle to—; grant—; nod in—; pay—; proceed with—; render—; respect —; respond to—; tender—; transact with —; treat with—; yield—.
(See respect, regard.)

DEFERENTIAL

adverbs
charmingly; pleasantly; properly; respectfully; scrupulously; exceedingly; unfailingly; chivalrously; punctiliously; exquisitely; duly; apparently; habitually; carefully; courteously; delightfully; devotedly; loyally; modestly; affably; amiably; gallantly; ceremoniously; ingratiatingly; tactfully; dutifully; decorously; sweetly; cordially.

DEFIANCE

adjectives
calm; silent; rare; quiet; fine; daring; resolute; firm; gay; mirthful; drawling; roaring; fierce; raucous; shrill; blatant; willful; ruffian; snarling; monstrous; shamefaced; reckless; desperate; murderous; mock; sneering; indignant; open; curious; passionate; exhilarating; quivering; quotable; shrinking; cringing; thundering; puny; irritating; perceptible; sudden; nomadic; scornful; admirable; maledictory; frank; potential; nonchalant; hurt; robust; half-frightened; schoolgirlish; unrighteous; mute; bristling; mortal; contemptuous; solitary; mutual; bold; actual; successful; patient; implied; indomitable; still; suppressed; savage.

verbs
attempt—; breathe—; fling—at; foster—; glare—; greet with—; hurl—; quell—; scorn—; shout—; snort—; sponsor—; stand firm in—; throw—at; uphold—.
(See challenge, opposition, provocation, contempt, rebellion.)

DEFIANT

adverbs
calmly; rarely; silently; quietly; boldly; resolutely; firmly; blithely; fiercely; blatantly; shrilly; monstrously; desperately; mockingly; indignantly; openly; sullenly; curiously; strangely; irritably; frankly; mutely; moodily; indomitably; stubbornly; obstinately; inexplicably; justly; defensibly.

DEFICIENCY

adjectives
unavoidable; fatal; evident; mental; technical; previous; glaring; psychological; marked; organic; suprarenal; noticeable.

verbs
accentuate—; allow—; balance—; compensate for—; condone—; correct—; counter-

act—; detect—; manifest—; mend—; observe—; presage—; reveal—; supply—; weep for—; —glares; —occurs.
(See defect, imperfection, shortcoming, inadequacy.)

DEFICIENT

adverbs
fatally; evidently; mentally; technically; markedly; glaringly; noticeably; crudely; lamentably; unfortunately; sadly; miserably; pitifully; woefully.

DEFICIT

adjectives
genuine; increasing; successive; alleged; alarming; startling; unaccountable.

verbs
accumulate—; arrest for—; bear—; calculate—; estimate—; expose—; falsify—; finance—; force—; halt—; mend—; pile up—; protect against—; reveal—; stagger through—; suspect—; uncover—; wipe out —; —arises; —deprives; —dwindles; —occurs.
(See deficiency.)

DEFILE

adjectives
dark; tangled; lofty; wild; rugged; rocky; towering; mountain; dangerous.

DEFILEMENT

adjectives
solemn; majestic; zonal; constructive; compact; straggling.

DEFINE (*v*)

adverbs
boldly; closely; sharply; sufficiently; particularly; bluntly; precisely; explicitly; accurately; crudely; arbitrarily; exactly; interestingly; subjectively; objectionably; essentially; technically; vigorously; invidiously; imperfectly; objectively; brilliantly; informally; vaguely; scientifically.
(See interpret, limit.)

DEFINITE

adverbs
crisply; bluntly; accurately; arbitrarily; interestingly; sharply; oddly; objectionably; thoroughly; brilliantly; pleasingly; acceptably; comfortingly; intelligibly; conspicuously; reliably; dogmatically; officially; authoritatively; authentically; vividly; graphically; comprehensibly.)

DEFINITION

adjectives
accurate; crude; representative; arbitrary; abstract; exclusive; exact; precise; interesting; perfervid; subjective; sharp; clear-cut; objectionable; famous; preliminary; unchallenged; healthy; thoroughgoing; essential; positive; vigorous; technical; analogous; invidious; objective; brilliant; informal; vague; scientific; elastic; reasonable; serviceable; imperfect.

verbs
apply—; arrive at—; construct—; determine—; establish—; restrict—; search for —; stretch—; supply—; understand—; weaken—; —defines; —describes; —determines; —enlightens; —explains; —expresses; —fixes; —limits; —satisfies; —specifies; —unfolds.
(See explanation, description, comment, exposition, interpretation.)

DEFLATION

adjectives
sweeping; monetary; postwar; credit; vicious; severe; sharp; salient; encroaching.

verbs
guard against—; master—; prepare for—; produce—; prophesy—; protect against—; release—; remedy—; repair—; sink into—; —affects; —injures; —looms; —menaces; —occurs; —produces; —reduces; —remedies; —repairs; —ruins.
(See collapse.)

DEFORMED

adverbs
woefully; physically; hideously; sadly; monstrously; congenitally; pitiably; lamentably; mysteriously; inexpressibly; horribly; deplorably; wretchedly; distressingly; incurably; irremediably; sorrily; crookedly; grossly; gruesomely; repulsively; terribly.

DEFORMITY

adjectives
apoplectic; unexpressed; pockmarked; physical; mocking; hideous; monstrous; foul; passing; hereditary.

verbs
accentuate—; avert—; brace—; correct—; enhance—; fake—; guard against—; iron out—; minimize—; overcome—; prevent—; produce—; result in—; torture into—; twist into—; —disfigures; —distorts; —impairs; —recurs.
(See blemish, abnormality.)

DEFRAUD (v)

adverbs
deliberately; coolly; villainously; cleverly; knavishly; deceitfully; unsuspectingly; deftly; sagaciously; financially.
(See cheat.)

DEFRAY (v)

adverbs
individually; regularly; belatedly; tardily; unhesitatingly; handsomely; regally; completely.
(See pay.)

DEFT

adverbs
unusually; admirably; wondrously; enviably; nimbly; marvellously; amazingly; remarkably; consistently; harmoniously; socially; conversationally; felicitously; appropriately; intelligently; shrewdly.

DEFTNESS

adjectives
marvelous; amazing; remarkable; skillful; marked; noteworthy.

DEFY (v)

adverbs
haughtily; sullenly; recklessly; arrogantly; undauntedly; menacingly; calmly; resolutely; fiercely; raucously; blatantly; snarlingly; desperately; murderously; mockingly; passionately; frankly; nonchalantly; righteously; mutely; bristlingly; mortally; contemptuously; savagely.
(See challenge, dare.)

DEGENERACY

adjectives
deplorable; nervous; physical; dissolute; irreparable; abject.

DEGENERATE

adjectives
unmoral; lazy; pathological; hopeless; irretrievable.

adverbs
grossly; outrageously; poisonously; corruptly; viciously; brutally; shabbily; effetely; decrepitly; dangerously; hopelessly; helplessly; woefully; abjectly; disgracefully; infamously; contemptibly; shamefully.

DEGENERATION

adjectives
infectious; eventual; apparent; inflammatory; progressive.

DEGRADATION

adjectives
moral; physical; unmerited; hideous; absolute; habitual; excessive; concomitant; stunting; deep; present.

DEGRADE (v)

adverbs
hopelessly; materially; ruinously; morally; unmeritedly; hideously; absolutely; deeply; shamefully; disgracefully; humiliatingly.
(See debase, disgrace.)

DEGREE

adjectives
large; high; fullest; surpassing; extreme; maximal; marked; slightest; infinitesimal; limited; imperceptible; tiny; small; astonishing; extraordinary; remarkable; amazing; startling; unusual; singular; diverse; vulgar; moderate; disgraceful; unsatisfactory; disconcerting; appalling; pre-eminent; uncanny; rare; greatest; practicable; fair; irreparable; increasing; sufficient; corresponding; artificial; intolerable; advanced; superlative; requisite; microscopic; moderate; alarming; considerable; high; unprecedented; varying; feverish; lavish; passable; measurable; adroit; incalculable; slow; adequate; improbable; surpassing; admirable; pronounced; fine; incredible; unabated; evergrowing; remote; minute; awe-inspiring; comparative; diminished; unwonted; gentle; significant; valuable; modified; paramount; unparalleled; sublime; imposing; traditional; extravagant; shameless; certain; cunning; excessive; reasonable; notable; unusual; uncommon; successive; illuminating; unsolicited; impudent; ancient; striking; valued; least; coveted; honorary; impressive; academic; doctorate; transcendent; subordinate; multiform.

verbs
ascend by—s; attain by—s; award—; change by—s; coax by—s; confer—; elevate—; exalt—; honor—; improve by—s; intensify—; lead by—s; limit—; mark—s; match—; overrate—; raise—; respect—; sharpen by—s; suffice to—; turn by—s.
See extent, rank, amount, station, position, title.)

DEITY

adjectives
tutelar; heathen; sylvan; ubiquitous; innumerable (pl); patron; anthropomorphic; beneficent; temperamental; pagan; presid-

ing; vestal; glorious; gloomy; tremendous; graceful; accursed; vital; protecting; incarnate; ascended; impotent; inferior; patronymic; numerous (pl); disowned; injured; dangling; benevolent; oracular; contemporary; iron; dishonorable; solemn.

verbs
absorb in—; adore—; appease—; befit—; believe in—; break away from—; complain to—; conceive of—; create—; defy—; deny—; despise—; dethrone—; enthrone—; incense—; offend—; please—; pray to—; renounce—; signify—; worship—; —creates; —interposes.
(See God, divinity.)

DEJECTED

adverbs
inconceivably; hopelessly; mournfully; pitiably; incurably; incredibly; piteously; horribly; tragically; alarmingly; unbelievably; singularly; oddly; strangely; miserably; comically; unreasonably; ridiculously; youthfully; ostensibly; openly; glumly; disconsolately; moodily; heavily; ludicrously.

DEJECTION

adjectives
vague; querulous; profound; complete; utter; intense; bewildered; utmost; deep; miserable; spiritless; passionate; weary.

verbs
bow in—; bury in—; cast into—; forsake—; humiliate into—; imply—; lower into—; manifest—; register—; shroud into—; sink into—; succumb to—; sustain—; throw into—; —deepens; —envelops; —fells; —weakens; —provokes.
(See depression, melancholy, discouragement.)

DELAY

adjectives
considerable; majestic; lingering; enforced; useless; injurious; unaccountable; inexplicable; petty; incomprehensible; anterior; proverbial; infamous; extended; dull; dangerous; corresponding; avoidable; needless; tedious; prolonged; slight; long; hazardous; endless; disappointing; fatal; strange; enforced; irksome; heartbreaking; exasperating; unconscionable; grievous; amorous; vexatious; sweet; parliamentary; characteristic; innumerable (pl).

verbs
advise—; brook—; counsel—; effect—; eliminate—; entail—; importune—; necessitate—; obtain—; occasion—; produce—; promise—; rebel against—; subject to—; trace—; work—; —endangers; —hinders.
(See procrastination, obstruction.)

DELAY (v)

adverbs
immeasurably; unaccountably; injuriously; temporarily; unfortunately; unreasonably; painfully; enforcedly; uselessly; incomprehensibly; infamously; tediously; fatally; disappointingly; irksomely; heartbreakingly; exasperatingly; unconscionably; grievously; vexatiously; characteristically; amorously.
(See dally. postpone.)

DELECTABLE

adverbs
refreshingly; invitingly; appetizingly; delicately; excitingly; charmingly; alluringly; altogether; consistently; irresistibly; unusually; remarkably.

DELEGATE

adjectives
messenger; rural; assembled (pl); interested; legal; ardent; recusant; lone; autochthonous.

verbs
act as—; appoint—; commission—; depute—; employ—; engage—; entrust to—; instruct—; send—; —s assemble; —attends; —s confer; —s convene; —s determine; —exercises; —manages; —performs; —represents; —wearies; —yells.
(See deputy, substitute. representative.)

DELEGATE (v)

adverbs
expressly; successfully; impressively; formally; nominally; authoritatively.
(See order.)

DELEGATION

adjectives
hilarious; impressive; express; representative; pathetic; dependable; authorized; random; select.

verbs
address—; appoint—; assemble—; entrust to—; instruct—; sway—; —attends; —chants; —cheers; —confers; —convenes;

—journeys; —represents; —subscribes to; —supports; —switches to; —votes; —wearies.
(See committee.)

DELETERIOUS

adverbs
malignly; abominably; painfully; grievously; oppressively; noxiously; perniciously; dreadfully; horribly; exceptionably lamentably; woefully; extremely; incredibly.

DELIBERATE

adverbs
evidently; sagaciously; good-humoredly; coolly; duly; sagely; wisely; gravely; ominously; vexatiously; calmly; terribly; impressively; solemnly; consciously; exaggeratedly; cleverly; curiously; pleasantly; prudently; anxiously; courteously; quietly; intently; thoughtfully; particularly; attentively; observantly; carefully; craftily; smartly; skilfully; shrewdly; cautiously; warily; discreetly.

DELIBERATE (v)

adverbs
earnestly; sagaciously; coolly; good-humoredly; sagely; gravely; calmly; solemnly; skillfully; prudently; protractedly; slowly.
(See debate, consider.)

DELIBERATION

adjectives
evident; sagacious; mature; good-humored; cool; sage; equable; grave; terrible; immense; studied; calm; solemn; joint; unexampled; impressive; congressional; knowing; conscious; curious; pleasant; skillful; prudent; public; anxious; due; maddening; courteous; protracted; considerable; massive; cutting; slow; disdainful; anguished.

DELICACY

adjectives
proper; conceivable; lineal; respectable; penetrating; covert; autumnal; fastidious; unexpected; pastel; epicurean; unbounded; ephemeral; substantial; native; exquisite; subtle; spiritual; fine; false; piercing; esteemed; great; extreme; innate; special; instinctive; charming; graceful; imaginable; fine; artistic; manly; morbid; feminine; queenly; dreamlike; complicated; bashful; dangling; exquisite; tempting; infinite; international; raw; pompous; toothsome.

DELICATE

adverbs
exquisitely; incredibly; beautifully; airily; frailly; crisply; freshly; harmoniously; pleasingly; agreeably; sweetly; bewitchingly; daintily; delightfully; ravishingly; gracefully; artistically; richly; properly; fastidiously; ephemerally; subtly.

DELICIOUS

adverbs
altogether; inexpressibly; exquisitely; pleasantly; daintily; felicitiously; palatably; appetizingly; ambrosially; utterly; unexpectedly; pungently; spicily; fragrantly; richly; stimulatingly; lusciously; sweetly.

DELIGHT

adjectives
pure; chastened; true; sincere sacred; home-felt; ecstatic; rapturous; whimsical; jubilant; tittering; utter; sheer; keen; complete; subtle; bizarre; unexpected; unnatural; strange; surprised; awed; supreme; incredulous; wondering; noisy; clamorous; wild; unrestrained; frantic; perfervid; frenzied; ungovernable; unqualified; unending; immeasurable; inexhaustible; tremendous; inexpressible; ineffable; unspeakable; unholy; dumb; fiendish; scornful; malevolent; perverted; painful; fierce; infectious; malicious; vain; frustrated; untrammeled; unalloyed; unfailing; sensuous; passionate; Epicurean; sadistic; childish; gastronomic; boyish; businesslike; chief; generous; intimate; inborn; naive; paroxysmal; extravagant; exalted; rare; drooling; varied; abiding; ardent; insatiate; frank; impossible; anticipatory; redoubled; secret; incommunicable; emulous; riotous; perfumed; idiotic; comforting; flitting; continual; awed; perpetual; sensational; occult; barren; subsequent; deep; dull; mournful; wild; swift; infinite; solicitous; rarefied; siren; lasting; inward; calm; buoyant; sentimental; unfelt; bitter; false; seasonable; hurricane; inexplicable; perpetual; hourly; hysterical; stunned; malignant; surprised; unquiet; trenchant; callous; celestial; rude; intense; ever enduring; laughing; unequalled; gay; unutterable; exquisite; flagging; soft; inebriating; subsiding; delicate; royal; bubbling; vivid; undefined; delicious; taste-tempting; mingled; languorous; unconcealed; nebulous; vigorous; rapturous; wild-beast; fresh; immortal; inestimable; divine; true; savage; anticipatory; astonished; cordial; pretended; rich; impish; tremulous; spite-

ful; obvious; special; young; unmanaged; vicious; dreamy; innocent; unchecked; preposterous; genuine; rare; giggling; measureless; peculiar; silly; breathless; sweet; placid; unmixed; fair; warm; lingering; singular; musical; mutual; fragmentary; serious; composed; dissembled; temporal; wanton; whimsical; eager; animated; vague; sustained; audible; subdued; capricious; seductive; consummated; manifold (pl).

verbs
afford—; bathe in—; behold with—; derive —; drink in—; enjoy—; exalt—; express—; extol—s of; fall into with—; feed with—; feel—; fill with—; find—in; gaze with—; hail with—; hide—; inspire—; listen with —; mar—; mount in—; offer—; pour—; recall with—; redden in—; shiver with—; smile in—; snuff out—; spread—; submerge in—; taste—; teem with—; turn to—; turn—into; weep with—; win—; yield—; —comes; —flees; —fleets; —pierces; —shines; —tempers.

(See happiness, rapture, joy, entertainment, pleasure, satisfaction.)

DELIGHTFUL

adverbs
charmingly; whimsically; utterly; strangely; unexpectedly; supremely; immeasurably; ineffably; delicately; freshly; cordially; innocently; peculiarly; particularly; youthfully; sweetly; glamorously; enchantingly; pleasantly; gracefully; entertainingly.

DELINEATE (v)

adverbs
graphically; minutely; humorously; familiarly; truthfully; recognizably; unsurpassedly; impartially; satirically.

(See depict, describe.)

DELINEATION

adjectives
humorous; familiar; truthful; recognizable; subtle; unsurpassed; impartial.

DELINQUENCY

adjectives
seeming; imaginary; juvenile; egregious; blameworthy.

DELINQUENT

adverbs
criminally; woefully; viciously; indiscreetly; enormously; outrageously; censurably; reprehensibly; objectionably; villainously; wretchedly; monstrously; loosely; unpardonably; inexcusably; carelessly; deliberately; indifferently; purposely; wantonly; wickedly; accidentally; shamefully; scandalously; disreputably; heedlessly; rashly; foolishly.

DELIRIOUS

adverbs
wildly; woefully; dangerously; alarmingly; crazily; violently; frantically; madly; feverishly; helplessly; critically; terribly; incoherently; oddly; strangely; hysterically; startlingly; uncontrollably; turbulently; distractedly; restlessly.

DELIRIUM

adjectives
mad; tossing; restless; extreme; raving; emotional; critical; blissful; confused; terrible; dreamy; prolonged; fierce; maniacal; insane.

verbs
break out into—; characterize—; dance in —; excite to—; haunt—; indicate—; induce—; murmur in—; produce—; quake with—; rave in—; seize with—; stimulate to—; suffer—; tremble with—; wander in—; —attacks; —exhausts; —impairs; —occurs.

(See insanity, hallucination, excitement, enthusiasm, rapture.)

DELIVER (v)

adverbs
simultaneously; conveniently; eloquently; solemnly; habitually; coldly; duly; consequently; sullenly; resolutely; impassionedly; volubly; hazardously; inarticulately; daily; promptly; tardily; reproachfully.

(See give, transfer.)

DELIVERANCE

adjectives
immediate; abrupt; miraculous; timely; tardy; gracious; hazardous.

verbs
achieve—; aid in—; arrange—; commemorate—; complete—; desire—; effect—; hope for—; offer—; order—; pray for—; rejoice in—; seek—; work for—; yearn for—; —liberates; —rescues; —sets free; —yields.

(See rescue, release, salvation.)

DELIVERER

adjectives
would-be; commanding; deliberate; graceful; intrepid; chance.

verbs
acclaim—; hope for—; pray for—; send—; thank—; welcome—; yearn for—; yield to—; —dispatches; —disburdens; —disposes of; —liberates; —orders; —rescues; —rids; —saves; —sets forth; —sets free; —surrenders; —releases.

DELIVERY

adjectives
resolute; voluble; impassioned; happy; complex; hazardous; inarticulate; measured; certified.

DELL

adjectives
bosky; mysterious; darksome; shaded; dreamy; labyrinthine; pathless; pastoral; narrow; hollow; diminutive; desolate; untrodden; resounding; budded; healthy; briery.

verbs
abandon—; bloom in—; frolic in—; grow in—; haunt—; hide in—; inhabit—; leap in—; perform in—; retire to—; retreat into—; ring through—; seek—; shelter in —; wander in—; —invites; —protects; —soothes; —winds.
(See valley, dale.)

DELUGE

adjectives
dawn-tinted; fiery; overflowing; binding; veritable; fearful; eternal; lawless; smothering; silvery; perfect; delectable; swashing; drowning; vapory.

verbs
bury under—; drown in—; escape—; fall before—; perish in—; pour—; release—; shower—; suffer from—; swell into—; vent—; —abates; —breaks loose; —confronts; —demolishes; —descends; —destroys; —floods; —harms; —occurs; —proceeds; —submerges; —sweeps away.
(See flood.)

DELUSION

adjectives
nightmare; cherished; fixed; superstitious; generous; grandiose; ignorant; insane; partial; monstrous; mental; shattered; anthropocentric; hollow; false; phantasmic; treasured; crazy; tenderhearted; unconquerable; pleasant; systematized; salutary; popular; miserable; long-detached; equal; mere; uncomfortable; plausible; stage; optical; pernicious; fond; empty; financial; neat; mocking; tragic; psychotic; somnolent.

verbs
cast out—; cure of—; destroy—; develop—; dismiss—; dissipate—; foster—; give up to—; guard against—; labor under—; share—; slip into—; suffer—; —exists; —misleads; —pursues.
(See illusion, deception, error, fallacy, hallucination.)

DELUSIVE

adverbs
cunningly; smoothly; insidiously; fallaciously; unfairly; starkly; inevitably; slyly; fraudulently; mendaciously; untruthfully; mistily; deceptively; ironically; strategically; incredibly; artfully; erroneously; dishonestly; perfidiously; unsoundly; trickily; treacherously; groundlessly; heretically; disingenuously; evasively; grimly.

DELVING

adjectives
curious; industrious; bibliographical; mental; scientific; relentless.

DEMAGOGUE

adjectives
consummate; selfish; irresponsible; fluent; political; inveterate; notorious; captious.

verbs
abandon to—; become the prey of—s; cultivate—; descend from—; despise—; play—; prove—; rule as—; stoop to—; —agitates; —appeals; —defends; —esponses; —fires; —influences; —leads; —obtains; —opposes; —orates; —panders; —suits; —sways; —undertakes.
(See politician, orator, leader.)

DEMAND

adjectives
ceaseless; incessant; insistent; constant; ever-increasing; rapid; mounting; growing; overwhelming; unabated; uncompromising; intransigent; persistent; obstinate; stern; strong; extreme; shouted; clamorous; roaring; exorbitant; modern; intermittent; inevitable; inescapable; irresistible; general; consistent; fluctuating; exigent; imperious; peremptory; vehement; exacting; outrag-

eous; blustering; unfortunate; unjust; unfair; relentless; surly; impossible; arrogant; abnormal; excessive; enlarged; unlimited; important; normal; human; social; industrial; consumer; decorative; popular; peculiar; multitudinous (pl); ever-changing; diminishing; emotional; unique; concrete; embarrassing; sufficient; immediate; preparatory; half-resentful; half-appealing; urgent; brusque; imaginative; craving; immense; inadmissable; definite; worthy; unprecedented; voiced; authoritative; effectual; fanatical; earnest; unsatisfied; insidious; widespread; essential; renewed; complex; paternal; insulting; nervous; remorseless; uproarious; intense; importunate; voluntary; unreasonable; necessary; explicit; widening; infrequent (pl); temporary; never-ending; feverish; unheeded; logical; sternest; tremendous; live; nationwide; huge; terrific; steady; gigantic; additional; ridiculous; temporal; emphatic; exaggerated; transient; continuing; unconditional; audacious; progressive; monstrous; arbitrary.

verbs
accede to—; accomplish—; acquiesce in—; agree to—; attend—; besiege with—s; browbeat with—s; clarify—; comply with —; confront with—; create—; deny—; divine—; dwarf—; echo—; evoke—; fulfill —; grant—; ignore—; indulge—; meet—; obey—; parry—; press—; reiterate—; reject—; respond to—; satisfy—; stabilize —; supply—; thunder—; unite in—; utter —; voice—; wake to—; yield to—; —astounds; —diminishes; —grows.

(See requirement.)

DEMAND (v)

adverbs
vibrantly; savagely; gutturally; greedily; persistently; relentlessly; frantically; unreasonably; brusquely; exorbitantly; rapaciously; sternly; bluntly; ruthlessly; briskly; scornfully; triumphantly; indignantly; truculently; riotously; clamorously; impetuously; obviously; despairingly; exactingly; unanimously; staunchly; imperatively; ultimately; stridently; cruelly; arrogantly; unconscionably; assuredly; gruffly; hungrily; curtly; incessantly; uncompromisingly; definitely; arbitrarily; formally; imperiously; sharply; furiously; virulently.

(See order, request.)

DEMEANOR

adjectives
smiling; calm; dignified; unassuming; staid; modest; composed; sweet; gentlemanly; unruffled; gentle; majestic; lordly; torpid; hangdog; wild; cold; impassive; commonplace; surly; savage; ferocious; fickle; inscrutable; accustomed; somber; unflinching; immoral; peculiar; interested; punctilious; solemn; courtly; popular; menacing; comical; contemptuous; sober; widespread; coy; laughing; obtuse; offensive; quiet; proud; sanctified; subdued; violent; pompous; puritanical; tacit; sage; haughty; meditative; cheerful; courageous; undaunted; resolute; private; unbending; unusual; unostentatious; reserved; stately; confident; cringing; dispassionate; aggressive; turbulent.

verbs
adopt—; alter—; disdain—; disguise—; exhibit—; judge by—; maintain—; mask—; soften—; trust—; —changes; —expresses; —irritates; —registers; —shames; —signifies.

(See behavior, mien.)

DEMENTED

adverbs
idiotically; sadly; inexplicably; foolishly; witlessly; frenziedly; incoherently; oddly; strangely; wildly; distractedly; dangerously; alarmingly; peculiarly; woefully; hopelessly; deplorably; pitiably; startlingly; uncontrollably; ungovernably; pathetically; tragically; unaccountably; mysteriously; stupidly; feebly; confusedly; noticeably; palpably; obviously; unmistakably; perceptibly; plainly.

DEMISE

adjectives
speedy; approaching; early; inevitable; heroic; premature; sad; lamented; long-awaited.

DEMOCRACY

adjectives
forward-looking; sham; industrial; passion-ridden; unlimited; enraged; semieducated; true; shrewd; humorous; multitudinous; kindly; economic; formidable; representative; pure; inclusive; rampant; qualified; experienced; financial; primitive; fierce.

verbs
attack—; betray—; contribute toward—; destroy—; foster—; imperil—; instill—;

jeopardize—; ordain—; preserve—; retain —; satirize—; supplant—; sustain—; threaten—; tread down—; —advances; —degenerates; —elevates; —flourishes; —functions; —levels; —marches ahead; —prevails; —survives; —asserts itself.
(See government, people, republic.)

DEMOCRATIC

adverbs
marvellously; tolerantly; broadly; unusually; magnanimously; foolishly; admirably; remarkably; embarrassingly; rampantly; amusingly; extremely; eminently; notoriously; openly; liberally; impartially; high-mindedly; violently; vociferously; unselfishly; charitably.

DEMOLISH (*v*)

adverbs
utterly; ruinously; brutally; cruelly; savagely; thoughtlessly; bestially; bloodthirstily; uncompromisingly; fiercely.
(See destroy.)

DEMON

adjectives
heroic; insatiable; unabashed; devastating; wrestling; fiery; angry; fragile; screaming; monstrous; cruel; heartless; horrible; demoralizing; protecting; trap-door; satellite; seeming; malignant; treacherous; avenging; restraining.

verbs
attribute to—; call forth—; dismiss—; drive out—; endow with—; exorcise—; introduce—; possess—; rout—; sacrifice to —; worship—; —controls; —destroys; —disturbs; —dominates; —dwells in; —enters; —frightens; —haunts; —infests; —inflicts; —inhabits; —leads; —prevails; —rules; —surrounds; —wails.
(See devil, spirit.)

DEMONIAC

adverbs
screamingly; insatiably; fierily; angrily; cruelly; monstrously; heartlessly; horribly; malignantly; maliciously; treacherously; revengefully; venomously; excitably; feverishly; hysterically; wildly; frantically; frenziedly; sensationally; dramatically; bitterly; invidiously; ruthlessly; brutally; atrociously; infamously; flagrantly; nefariously; viciously; grossly; infernally.

DEMONSTRATE (*v*)

adverbs
lucidly; tastefully; repeatedly; strictly; abundantly; practically; phenomenally; experimentally; fully; conceitedly; conclusively; convincingly; substantially; triumphantly; abstractedly; forcefully; abstrusely; approximately; ocularly; precisely; visually; cordially.
(See show, indicate.)

DEMONSTRATION

adjectives
patriotic; subtle; triumphant; abstract; abstruse; forceful; approximate; corrupt; dramatized; familiar; ocular; charitable; grandiose; active; enthusiastic; attention-compelling; simple; interesting; convincing; dynamic; startling; spot; irresistible; sales-producing; breath-taking; quick; inspiring; emphatic; salivary; quadrennial; amazing; rigorous; precise; rigid; noisy; striking; visual; grand; superb; flattering; riotous; dramatic; bitter; hostile; unfriendly; armed; elaborate; outward; cordial.

verbs
answer by—; apprehend—; crown—; defy —; establish by—; harangue—; mar—; offer—; stage—; subject to—; support—; thwart—; understand—; —exposes; —proves.
(See celebration.)

DEMONSTRATIVE

adverbs
readily; easily; triumphantly; forcefully; dramatically; spectacularly; actively; enthusiastically; interestingly; convincingly; startlingly; irresistibly; amazingly; noisily; strikingly; flatteringly; elaborately; outwardly; cordially; heartily; offensively; delightfully; charmingly; amiably; vexatiously; provokingly; foolishly; unbecomingly; unnecessarily; frankly; brazenly; boldly; ominously; markedly; conspicuously; disagreeably.

DEMORALIZE (*v*)

adverbs
profoundly; partially; utterly; speedily; swiftly; incredibly; socially; morally.
(See corrupt.)

DEMORALIZATION

adjectives
incredible; widespread; social; linguistic; nervous.

verbs
aid in—; check—; guard against—; influence—; prevent—; produce—; protect from —; yield to—; —corrupts; —deprives; —destroys; —envelops; —lowers; —reduces; —seeps in; —unnerves; —weakens.
(See corruption.)

DEMURE

adverbs
affectedly; prudishly; coyly; timidly; shyly; delightfully; gravely; quietly; unaffectedly; conspicuously; deliberately; discreetly; tranquilly; placidly; soberly; submissively; harmoniously; meekly; cleverly; purposely; ostentatiously; unnaturally; stiffly; primly; puritanically; priggishly; bashfully; skittishly; admirably; attractively; alluringly; blushingly.

DEMURENESS

adjectives
stately; slumberous; timid; lofty; aloof; deceptive; becoming.

DEN

adjectives
careless; stifling; stuffy; dark; trackless; moldy; unsanitary; loathsome; steamy; horrible; hidden; dreary; turreted; fresh-dug.

verbs
abide in—; cast into—; confine to—; convert into—; crouch in—; drive from—; dwell in—; escape to—; habitate—; hibernate in—; hide in—; immure in—; lodge in—; lurk in—; nestle in—; pace—; retire to—; retreat to—; smoke out of—; stow in—; visit—; stray about—; —conceals; —hides; —reeks.
(See lair, cave, hut, retreat.)

DENIAL

adjectives
incredulous; amused; bold; vehement; armed; cynical; indignant; visual; arrogant; gracious; telegraphic; rigid; furious; steadfast; vigorous; smiling; disarming; chivalrous; utter; peremptory; quibbling; naive; positive; emphatic.

verbs
accept—; brook—; color—; conceal with —; counter—; evoke—; ignore—; lash out—; prepare—; rebut—; request—; resign to—; spurn—; storm—; —contradicts; —discourages; —irks; —peeves (colloq.); —refuses; —refutes; —repulses; —wearies.
(See contradiction, refusal, restraint.)

DENIZEN

adjectives
long-eared; finny; astute; stately; furred; feathered; forgotten; permanent.

verbs
accept—; acquaint—; admit—; allow—; fill with—s; furnish with—s; grant to—; make—of; offer—; people with—s; populate with—s; privilege—; —dwells; —enjoys; —obtains; —occupies; —prospers; —settles.
(See inhabitant, citizen, native.)

DENOUEMENT

adjectives
curious; interesting; melodramatic; iridescent; tragic; crowning; premature.

DENOUNCE (v)

adverbs
vehemently; furiously; sternly; unsparingly; scoffingly; insultingly; bitterly; scathingly; obstreperously; violently; vociferously; witheringly; astoundingly; dramatically; vitriolically; mercilessly; roundly.
(See accuse.)

DENSITY

adjectives
sufficient; mean; different; tangled; repellent; depthless; frightful.

DENT

adjectives
sizable; slightest; permanent; cruel; hideous.

DENTIST

adjectives
ruthless; unfeeling; ultra-schooled; late-edition; glorified; hit-or-miss.

verbs
consult—; visit—; —anaesthetizes; —applies; —assembles; —caps; —closes; —drills; —examines; —extracts; —fastens; —files; —fills; —furnishes; —grinds; —inserts; —operates; —practises; —prepares; —preserves; —restores; —shapes; —treats.

DENUNCIATION

adjectives
withering; mystic; astounding; fiery; glib; unmerited; furious; spiteful; playful;

severest; loud; intemperate; sweeping; grand; impartial; effective; thorough; resounding; impassioned; dramatic; vitriolic; ominous; unsupported; combative; rabid; angry; utter; preliminary; filthy; violent; merciless.

verbs
announce—; authorize—; blast—; characterize by—; defy—; indulge in—; reiterate —; thunder—; tolerate—; —accuses; —affects; —alarms; —condemns; —deluges; —frightens; —humbles; —informs; —inveighs against; —punishes; —ruins; —scathes; —sears; —threatens; —warns; —weakens.
(See condemnation, accusation.)

DENUNCIATORY

adverbs
scarcely; dogmatically; scandalously; needlessly; strongly; bitterly; acrimoniously; jealously; enviously; inexcusably; scurrilously; abusively; profanely; execrably; thunderously; cruelly; caustically; harshly; ungraciously; ferociously; ruthlessly; sarcastically; dryly; severely; unsparingly; exceptionably; indefensibly; viciously; terribly.

DENY (v)

adverbs
hotly; unequivocally; promptly; absolutely; bitterly; indignantly; effectively; peremptorily; stoutly; inhospitably; crossly; cravenly; unselfishly; strenuously; passionately; categorically; justly; vehemently; flatly; shamelessly; arrogantly; disarmingly; positively; naively.
(See contradict, renounce.)

DEPART (v)

adverbs
voluntarily; peacefully; mysteriously; seriously; cheerfully; clandestinely; noiselessly; radically; precipitately; momentously; daringly; agitatedly; unprecedentedly; abruptly.
(See leave, quit.)

DEPARTMENT

adjectives
subsidiary; vast; systematized; countless (pl); elementary; remote; significant; drabbest; immense; irrational; beautiful; capable; experienced; vocational; public; vulgar; administrative; insular.

verbs
allot to—; assign to—; bestow upon—; boss—; branch into—s; break into—; close —; control—; convert—; create—; divide into—s; establish—; organize—; portion into—s; preside over—; regulate—; supervise—; —administers; —caters to; —handles; —practises.
(See part, division, section, branch.)

DEPARTURE

adjectives
clandestine; abrupt; refreshing; noiseless; instant; radical; precipitate; revolutionary; momentous; impending; mysterious; unannounced; impetuous; calm; imminent; immediate; rollicking; sudden; hurried; frank; frequent (pl); speedy; hasty; considerate; approaching; contemplated; daring; dinnerless; agitated; noticeable; exceptionable; controlled; compelled; maiden; expected; awaited.

verbs
arrive at—; assure of—; await—; enjoy—; facilitate—; fear—; laugh at—; notice—; occasion—; plan—; prepare—; regret—; speed—; spur to—; take—; —divides; —frees; —nears; —partitions; —saddens; —separates; —severs; —sunders; prevent—.
(See deviation, withdrawal, separation, death.)

DEPEND (v)

adverbs
utterly; unfailingly; exclusively; materially; completely; mathematically; virtually; ultimately; directly; perpetually; apparently; irksomely; fatuously; absolutely; haplessly.
(See lean, trust.)

DEPENDABILITY

adjectives
superb; absolute; steady; impeccably; invariable; inflexible.

DEPENDENCE

adjectives
utter; lifetime; helpless; indirect; apparent; perpetual; disgraceful; irksome; increasing; sure; fatuous; absolute; harmless; magnified; ultimate; humble.

DEPENDENT

adjectives
servile; wise; beggarly; penniless; mutual; weaker; helpless; hapless.

DEPENDENT

adverbs
pitifully; completely; partially; sadly; helplessly; unhappily; grievously; sullenly; subserviently; servilely; fawningly; obsequiously; hopelessly; desperately; wholly; meekly; touchingly; pathetically.

DEPICT (*v*)

adverbs
symbolically; aesthetically; dramatically; graphically; powerfully; deftly; starkly; episodically; vividly; mercilessly; shrewdly; realistically; fearlessly.
(See delineate, describe.)

DEPICTION

adjectives
episodic; merciless; stark; shrewd; realistic; fearless; vivid.

DEPLETE (*v*)

adverbs
entirely; largely; physically; utterly; definitely; swiftly; suddenly; fatally; woefully; financially.
(See exhaust.)

DEPLETION

adjectives
corresponding; physical; excessive; utter; definite; sudden; swift.

DEPLORABLE

adverbs
piteously; unwontedly; terribly; seriously; gravely; direly; especially; signally; distressingly; wretchedly; exceptionably; bitterly; dismally; woefully.

DEPLORE (*v*)

adverbs
sincerely; satirically; prophetically; loudly; tearfully; pitifully.
(See lament, regret.)

DEPORTMENT

adjectives
habitual; exigent; correct; laudable; exceeding; proper; maidenly; fashionable; graceful; amiable; blameless; fine; unexpected; inexplicable; grave; incredible.

DEPOSIT
(*general*)

adjectives
superficial; alluvial; extensive; stratified; evanescent; coralline; affected; fertile; untouched; inexhaustible; graphite; modest; fossiliferous; sacred; required; fabulous: immense; nominal; sedimentary; buttery; driftwood; precious; phosphate; turquoise; bank; large; unexpected.

DEPOSIT
(*money or property*)

adjectives
nominal; actual; legal; stipulated; optional; binding; good faith.

verbs
accumulate for—; bank—; collect—s; commit—to; deliver—; demand—; entrust with —; guard—; invest—; place—; pledge—; receive—; require—; restore—; return—; squander—; withdraw—; —benefits; —increases; —settles.

DEPOSIT (*v*)

adverbs
deliberately; daintily; noiselessly; hastily; superficially; extensively; inexhaustibly; evanescently; fabulously; immensely; unexpectedly.
(See place.)

DEPOSITOR

adjectives
luckless; frightened; hypothetical; poor; illiterate; ingenuous; middle class; unlocated; unfortunate; ultimate; robust.

DEPOT

adjectives
cavalry; temporary; commissary; indispensable; prearranged; stationary.

DEPRAVED

adverbs
wickedly; shamelessly; grossly; outrageously; corruptly; brutally; dangerously; awfully; hopelessly; woefully; abjectly; disgracefully; infamously; contemptibly; notoriously; shamefully; arrantly; dissolutely; indecently; perfidiously.

DEPRAVITY

adjectives
precocious; moral; joint; vicarious; total; horrible; rude; contented; professional; humorous.

DEPRECATE (*v*)

adverbs
forcibly; timidly; periodically; modestly; markedly; increasingly; hurriedly; mildly; vigorously; pleadingly.
(See disapprove.)

DEPRECATION

adjectives
timid; hurt; pleading; periodic; modest; hurried; abysmal.

DEPRECATORY

adverbs
timidly; pleadingly; modestly; elaborately; unnecessarily; urgently; importunately; clamorously; solicitously; compassionately; sympathetically; tenderly; critically; abusively; accusingly; sarcastically; sharply; trenchantly; censoriously.

DEPRECIATION

adjectives
marginal; disastrous; marked; ever-increasing; substantial; radical; elaborate.

DEPRESS (v)

adverbs
particularly; fearfully; dreadfully; vaguely; obviously; acutely; drastically; economically; financially; industrially; spiritually; nationally; mentally; nervously.
(See lower.)

DEPRESSED

adverbs
alarmingly; dangerously; gloomily; incurably; inconceivably; incredibly; horribly; woefully; dismally; gravely; seriously; inconsolably; sadly; unreasonably; desperately; piteously; pitifully; tragically; wanly; unduly; unnecessarily; moodily; lamentably; darkly; wearily.

DEPRESSING

adverbs
sadly; alarmingly; needlessly; terribly; unreasonably; unaccountably; inexplicably; dreadfully; acutely; grimly; painfully; cursedly; grievously; unfortunately; sorely; unluckily; intolerably; tremendously; cruelly.

DEPRESSION
(*business*)

adjectives
prolonged; agricultural; successive (pl); mild; general; current; exaggerated; dreadful; evil; aching; acute; drastic; major; vast; long; business; economic; financial; industrial; national; world; price; severe.

DEPRESSION
(*general*)

adjectives
paralyzing; epidemic; enveloping; growing; inflation.

verbs
aggravate—; alleviate—; banish—; emerge from—; intensify—; mitigate—; offset—; plunge into—; prolong—; relapse into—; survive—; tackle—; thaw out—; weather—; —annihilates; —blights; —grips; —hits; —slashes.
(See dejection, melancholy, discouragement, despondency.)

DEPRESSION
(*spirits*)

adjectives
low; nervous; sundry (pl); sympathetic; frequent; spiritual; constant; mental.

DEPRESSION
(*surface*)

adjectives
sheltered; circumscribed; shallow; cup-like; deep; noticeable; amphitheatrical; saucer-like; extreme.

DEPRIVATION

adjectives
haphazard; stringent; total; ruinous; violent; vicious; indigent.

DEPTH

adjectives
generous; unguessed; shielding; protective; underlying; deceptive.

verbs
advance from—s; attain—; bear through—s; descend to—s; discover in—s; explore—s; foul in—s; gauge—; harbor in—; judge—; launch into—s; measure—; penetrate to—of; pitch to—s; preserve from—s; probe—s; raise from—s; reach—; reflect in—; repose in—; rise from—; scour—; search—; thrust into—; venture beyond—; —closes round; —covers; —embraces; —exceeds.
(See extent, measure.)

DEPTHS

adjectives
dizzy; profound; unfathomable; considerable; perpendicular; homely; crystalline; fertile; remorseless; tremendous; melancholy; nethermost; giddiest; slumberous; remote; hollow; blank; soundless; somber; seeming; distant; inmost; glassy; shadowed; abysmal; lost; awesome; limpid; unknown; cavernous; hideous; liquid; secret; aesthetic; hidden; wondrous; unexplored; lowest; unserviceable; passionless; sleeping; adverse; warm; darkest; pearly; evil;

unimagined; ghostly; annulling; prodigious; shapeless; voiceless; forest; folded; calm; reflective; slimy; cold; frozen; agitated; yawning; luminous; inaccessible; superhuman; insatiable; pathless; dewy; vast; music-haunted; wakening; clear; shameful; gloomy; abhorrent; nightmare; sylvan; subterranean; apparent; Stygian; secure.

DEPUTY

adjectives
dishonest; hateful; gun-toting; indolent; tense; amiable; strict; presumptive; pernicious; corrupt; radiant.

verbs
appoint—; authorize—; bribe—; corrupt —; depose—; elect—; employ as—; evade —; oust—; rebuke—; swear in—; —aids; —arrests; —assists; —enforces; —fines.
(See representative, agent, delegate.)

DERANGE (v)

adverbs
irreparably; seriously; mentally; functionally; extensively; sexually; mechanically.
(See confuse.)

DERANGED

adverbs
eccentrically; incoherently; madly; strangely; unaccountably; inexplicably; queerly; foolishly; dangerously; peculiarly; woefully; hopelessly; helplessly; deplorably; pitiably; lamentably; shockingly; uncontrollably; mysteriously; noticeably; obviously; unmistakably; perceptibly; terribly.

DERANGEMENT

adjectives
mental; extensive; functional; obstinate; obsessional; intermittent.

DERBY

adjectives
battered; cherished; perforated; shabby; broken; battle-scarred; aggressively-tilted; ancient; salvaged.

DERELICT

adjectives
human; moral; physical; sleeping; floating; wretched; barnacle-incrusted.

verbs
abandon—; defend—; desert—; discover —; lift—; observe—; pity—; reduce to—; relinquish—; seize—; —s assemble; —s congregate; —drifts; —flounders; —s infest; —limps in; —s overrun; —suffers; —s swarm.

DERIDE (v)

adverbs
steadily; correspondingly; opprobriously; sourly; scornfully; lightly; ribaldly; coarsely; brutally; mercilessly; bitterly; loudly; boisterously; unsparingly; contemptuously; sharply; stingingly.
(See ridicule, jeer.)

DERISION

adjectives
mysterious; sour; scornful; light; ribald; unconquerable; coarse; brutal; merciless; filthy; bitterest; loud; boisterous; approving; pressed; uneasy; foul; unsparing.

verbs
bait with—; be in—; cackle in—; call forth —; chuckle in—; expose to—; express—; give vent to—; laugh in—; mock in—; open to—; ridicule in—; scorn—; sting by—.
(See ridicule, mockery, scorn, sarcasm.)

DERISIVE

adverbs
sharply; arrogantly; pompously; mockingly; sarcastically; cynically; offensively; officiously; disagreeably; unbearably; insufferably; mysteriously; sourly; lightly; blithely; airily; ribaldly; disrespectfully; coarsely; grossly; brutally; ignorantly; crudely; mercilessly; clumsily; bitterly; loudly; boisterously; enviously; foully.

DERIVATION

adjectives
remote; theoretical; unanswerable; grotesque; indirect; authentic.

DERIVATIVE

adjectives
direct; traceable; flattering; acknowledged; questionable.

verbs
accept—; confuse—; develop—; discover —; employ—; form—; gain—; generate—; market—; obtain—; process—; produce—; recognize—; reduce—; substitute—; use—; utilize—; —emanates from; —originates; —supplants.
(See product, word.)

DERIVE (*v*)

adverbs

recently; evidently; shamelessly; primarily; corruptly; ultimately; essentially; remotely; theoretically; grotesquely; endlessly.

(See obtain.)

DEROGATORY

adverbs

shamefully; enviously; bitterly; venomously; vengefully; maliciously; scandalously; disagreeably; peevishly; petulantly; falsely; slanderously; abusively; injuriously; shockingly; unreasonably; unwarrantably; indefensibly; vindictively; dreadfully; mercilessly; ruthlessly; openly; shamelessly; deliberately; viciously.

DERVISH

adjectives

demented; dancing; filthy; whirling; frenzied.

DESCEND (*v*)

adverbs

quickly; unexpectedly; noiselessly; sharply; gradually; hastily; giddily; benignly; impartially; laboriously; gracefully; fearsomely; pompously.

(See fall.)

DESCENDANT

adjectives

lineal; direct; eager; legitimate; homeward-flown; pure-blooded; glorious; degenerate; remote; immediate; impoverished; ill-starred; hybrid; presumed; winsome; indolent; guilty; genuine; unmixed.

verbs

acquire—; advertise for—; characterize—; extract—; leave—; nourish—; transmit to—; —s assemble; —belongs to; —carries; on; —s congregate; —s convene; —s gather; —s honor; —s inherit; —s respect; —s settle; —s spring from; —s wrangle over.

(See posterity, offspring, issue.)

DESCENT

adjectives

rapid; direct; steep; aristocratic; hasty; gradual; rocky; pitiless; precipitous; stately; deep; smooth; laborious; graceful; harsh; unblemished; ladderlike; armed; sheer; illustrious; dateless; artistic; pompous; actual; noble; maternal; barbarous; flashing; uninterrupted; royal; divine; fearsome; slow.

verbs

attempt—; balk at—; ease—; dread—; flow upon—; halt—; hazard—; hinder—; manage—; menace—; observe—; plan—; point for—; prepare—; prevent—; resume —; venture—; —dizzies; —frightens; —sharpens; —slopes.

(See fall, deterioration, slope, attack, raid.)

DESCRIBE (*v*)

adverbs

ludicrously; graphically; adequately; admiringly; pathetically; trippingly; accurately; derisively; justly; feelingly; expansively; compactly; comprehensively; elegantly; elaborately; felicitously; minutely; traditionally; eloquently; illuminatingly; succinctly; superlatively; subsequently; erroneously; fittingly; imperfectly; contemptuously; facetiously; impressionistically; boisterously; radiantly; glowingly; sentimentally; humorously; animatedly; verbally; uncensoredly; tersely; intimately; satirically; suggestively; enticingly; distortedly; imaginatively; realistically; vaguely; colorfully; briefly; essentially.

(See delineate, depict.)

DESCRIPTION

adjectives

facetious; minute; impressionistic; boisterous; admirable; exquisite; graphic; detailed; contemporary; radiant; entangled; magnificent; luminous; eloquent; adjectival; distinctive; impassioned; felicitous; faithful; elaborate; extended; racy; preceding; picturesque; punctual; lengthy; frivolous; leisurely; sublime; tolerable; restrained; appropriate; enthusiastic; illustrated; ludicrous; harrowing; truthful; accurate; glowing; sentimental; vivid; hopeless; humorous; animated; unpleasant; lucid; primitive; verbal; censored; admirable; unexcelled; pompous; threadbare; negative; terse; rhapsodical; intimate; pathetic; satiric; suggestive; enticing; distorted; savage; imaginative; authoritative; realistic; adequate; abridged; silent; magnificent; robust; vague; damning; flashing; colorful; complicated; recondite; brief; modest.

verbs

amend—; base—; baffle—; beggar—; color—; defy—; detail—; enter into—; fit—; limit—; paragon—; quote—; suit—; verify—; —centers; —clarifies; —colors; —combines; —delineates; —depicts; —

equals; —excels; —explains; —furnishes; —illuminates; —illustrates; —implies; —impresses; —introduces; —motivates; —paints; —pictures; —portrays; —presents; —provides; —suggests; —surpasses; —tires; —vivifies; —wearies.
(See portrayal, representation, definition.)

DESCRIPTIVE

adverbs
graphically; vividly; effectively; unusually; remarkably; facetiously; minutely; admirably; splendidly; magnificently; eloquently; faithfully; elaborately; extensively; racily; tolerably; appropriately; enthusiastically; ludicrously; accurately; humorously; intimately; savagely; authoritatively; adequately; vaguely; briefly; modestly; realistically.

DESECRATION

adjectives
impudent; attempted; wanton; impious; daring; inconoclastic.

verbs
accuse of—; admit—; confess—; criticize for—; enjoy—; ignore—; indulge in—; preserve from—; rear in—; sentence for—; spit—; suffer—; threaten—; —injures; —involves; —pains; —nauseates; —undermines.
(See violation.)

DESERT

adjectives
dreary; irreclaimable; flat; melancholy; rude; mountainous; rocky; burning; lifeless; alkaline; pathless; encompassing; arid; forbidding; reactionary; scorching; unspeakable; mysterious; dreadful; measureless; voiceless; bare; palpable; comfortless; vast; withered; desolated; uninhabitable; barren; waterless; open; grim; dangerous; cactus; sandy; silent; illimitable.

verbs
advance through—; border—; chart—; conceal in—; dwell in—; frequent—; gain—; inhabit—; lead into—; lose in—; patrol—; redeem—; retire to—; retreat to—; roam—; span—; swallow up by—; track—; wander in—; —envelops; —howls; —menaces; —parches; —threatens.
(See merit, reward, solitude, waste.)

DESERT (v)

adverbs
woefully; heartlessly; easily; virtually; basely; cruelly; impulsively; treasonably; wilfully; criminally; wantonly; finally.
(See forsake, abandon.)

DESERTED

adverbs
cruelly; criminally; hastily; shamefully; ingloriously; humiliatingly; mercilessly; ruthlessly; inhumanly; brutally; wickedly; iniquitously; scandalously; ignominiously; wantonly; inconsiderately; groundlessly; wilfully; deliberately; unhappily; ungratefully; wretchedly.

DESERTION

adjectives
contemplated; cruel; impulsive; treasonable; willful; proverbial; wholesale; criminal; wanton.

DESERVE (v)

adverbs
equally; notoriously; perpetually; fittingly; unreservedly; distinctly; eminently; wholeheartedly; undeniably.
(See merit.)

DESIGN
(*intention*)

adjectives
ultimate; honorable; base; fell; ill-conceived; rash; deadly; deep; evil; deliberate; stern; wicked; ostensible; malicious; oppressive; serious; importunate; hostile; ambitious; joyous; true-meant; immoral; misguided; criminal; evident; vile; matrimonial; disgusting; mischievous; far-reaching; avowed; traitorous; aggressive; lawful; villainous; perfidious; nefarious.

verbs
admit—; adopt—; approve—; arrange—; carry out—; conceive—; concur on—; declare—; discover—; disguise—; execute—; form—; frustrate—; harbor—; plan—; pursue—; relinquish—; settle on—; undertake—; —aims; —fails; —requires.
(See scheme, plan, purpose, project, intention.)

DESIGN
(*pattern*)

adjectives
authentic; immense; elaborate; inscrutable; constructive; fierce; beautiful; arabesque; border; intricate; sporting; famous; artist-

ic; ethical; fanciful; matchless; polychromatic; structural; well-known; conventional; monstrous; impractical; flowing; simple; graceful; anatomical; chevron; deliberate; heavy-duty; tentative; distinctive; exclusive; transitional; interior; conservative; unfathomable; palpable; engineering; harmonious; attractive; central; classical; crude; quaint; scientific; unintelligent; grotesque; aliform; vast; gorgeous; geometrical; efficacious; secular; smart; original; unusual; nautical; advanced; stitched; modern; staggering; unjust; superior; functional; systematic; wise; dramatic; compass; thoughtful; ingenious; feathery; engraved; mosaic; curious; huge; exotic; general; novel; tangled; cut; dried; gay; rational; brilliant; stunning; annulose.

verbs
arrange—; carve—; conceive—; contrive—; develop—; draw—; elaborate—; embellish; —embroider; —employ—; engrave—; execute—; hammer—; mark—; model—; paint —; plan—; prescribe—; sketch—; strike—; submit—; teach—; trace—; work—; —decorates; —denotes; —depicts; —improves; —ornaments; —represents; —signifies; —stresses.

(See pattern, ornament, sketch, model, representation.)

DESIGN (v)

adverbs
scientifically; properly; solely; exquisitely; seriously; admirably; specially; primarily; harmoniously; expressly; artfully; elaborately; charmingly; masterfully; skillfully; intricately.

(See intend.)

DESIGNATE (v)

adverbs
incriminatingly; innocently; erroneously; euphoniously; strictly; specifically; appropriately; felicitously; aptly; fittingly; properly; correctly.

(See identify.)

DESIGNATION

adjectives
appropriate; playful; substitutive; territorial; felicitous; apt; proudest; patrician; fitting; proper; correct.

verbs
appoint—; arrange—; arrive at—; decide —; denote—; describe—; determine—; indicate—; justify—; name—; point out—; prepare for—; refuse—; search for—; —appeals; —serves.

(See mark, name, title, epithet, arrangement.)

DESIGNER

adjectives
experienced; noted; scenic; landscape; master; skilled; leading; functional.

DESIRABLE

adverbs
utterly; enchantingly; irresistibly; temptingly; alluringly; seductively; pleasantly; quietly; intensely; vaguely; darkly; acutely; inordinately; infinitely; genuinely; specially; absurdly; practically; conveniently.

DESIRE

adjectives
intense; longing; laudable; childish; sweet; gallant; brutal; extravagant; haughty; unextinct; fair; express; elevated; deferred; sensuous; corrupt; sentimental; customary; ardent; imperious; vague; earnest; devoted; prayerful; crushing; passionate; overpowering; innocent; noble; hearty; morbid; quaint; amiable; imperative; commendable; lifelong; insatiable; irresistible; confused; dark; furious; comfortable; cold; mistaken; automatic; lost; cordial; acute; unjust; scant; feeble; magnanimous; instinctive; slightest; warm; fond; faintest; inordinate; subtle; burning; infinite; sincere; countless (pl); selfish; conscientious; petty; frenzied; anxious; mad; implacable; consuming; inhibited; troublesome; deliberate; illimitable; excessive; benevolent; impatient; keen; pure; gnawing; restless; parching; unsatisfied; prevailing; quick; impetuous; known; longing; genuine; unlawful; subdued; strong; unacknowledged; high; insane; hot; dangerous; dominant; vehement; ungratified; dimmest; vain; proud; fiery; carnal; special; evident; unholy; torturing; inflamed; scattering; anxious; nervous; appeased; individual; egotistical; wolfish; bloody; ravenous; amorous; defrauded; emotional; covetous; honest; untamable; aimless; chaste; practical; feverish; mistaken; dwarfed; perceptible; wild; increasing; repressed; sacred; soft; delicate; wistful; sordid; ungenerous; laudable; lascivious; false; philanthropic; quenchless; unbaffled; phlegmatic; personal; boundless; loving; touching; lurking; popular; absurd; reasonable; senile; universal; apparent.

verbs

accomplish—; aggravate—; appease—; arouse—; attain—; awake—; balk—; beat with—; breed—; burn with—; cater to—; chasten—; cherish—; communicate—; conquer—; curtail—; eat up with—; entertain —; equal—; exercise—; experience—; exploit—; express—; feed—; flash—; gratify —; humble—; humor—; inflame—; inhibit—; instil—; intensify—; kindle—; lack —; languish in—; loose—; master—; melt into—; nourish—; obscure—; obsess with —; overbalance—; prompt—; provoke—; quell—; quench—; quicken—; quiet—; raise—; realize—; refine—; relinquish—; repress—; reward—; satisfy—; seethe with —; seize with—; sharpen—; smother—; subjugate—; sublimate—; submit to—; tangle—s; temper—; throttle—; thwart—; undermine—; yield to—; —consumes; —disquiets; —embodies; —endures; —fires; —hounds; —hungers; —impels; —motivates; —rules; —tortures; —urges on.

(See longing, craving. learning, wish, appetite, passion, impulse, request, aspiration.)

DESIRE (*v*)

adverbs

passionately; earnestly; ardently; eminently; obviously; insistently; presumably; unquestionably; particularly; intensely; consistently; unanimously; gallantly; extravagantly; brutally; sensually; customarily; imperiously; overpoweringly; nobly; heartily; morbidly; quaintly; insatiably; automatically; cordially; acutely; inordinately; burningly; infinitely; implacably; consumingly; benevolently; impatiently; gnawingly; genuinely; unlawfully; vainly; vehemently; carnally; torturingly; egotistically; ravenously; amorously; emotionally; chastely; delicately; wistfully; sordidly; ungenerously; lasciviously; boundlessly; touchingly; personally; absurdly.

(See want, wish.)

DESIROUS

adverbs

intensely; longingly; childishly; extravagantly; expressly; sentimentally; ardently; imperiously; earnestly; prayerfully; passionately; heartily; morbidly; insatiably; darkly; furiously; inordinately; sincerely; selfishly; madly; consumingly; troublesomely; impetuously; insanely; hotly; vehemently; proudly; anxiously; perceptibly; covetously; enviously; wistfully.

DESIST (*v*)

adverbs

abruptly; entirely; partially; completely; willingly; mutually; wisely; lazily; temporarily; subsequently; eventually; deliberately; totally.

(See stop, cease.)

DESK

adjectives

broad; secluded; ancient; battered; mahogany; flat; smooth; rickety; large; carved; Renaissance; polished; oak; dull; grimy; matutinal; reading; writing; spindle-legged; ransacked; roll-top.

verbs

anchor to—; beat—; clutter up—; cover—; dust—; dawdle at—; erect—; flank—; litter —; lock—; pad—; plop at—; rummage in—; seal—; smite—; stack on—.

(See table, stand, pulpit.)

DESOLATE

adverbs

grimly; utterly; profoundly; desperately; dreadfully; indescribably; singularly; supremely; bleakly; unutterably; tragically; bitterly; unbearably; intolerably; oppressively; appallingly; drearily; emptily; dismally; wildly; fearfully; perceptibly.

DESOLATION

adjectives

blazing; harsh; lifeless; utmost; dusty; grim; willful; utter; profound; dreadful; whispering; universal; wintry; careless; degraded; rightful; indescribable; chaotic; haunted; blank; unrevenged; fancied; barren; rapid; fresh; burlesque; weird; withered; mighty; icy; rocky; striking; heartsick; singular; immense; rugged; bleak.

verbs

behold—; blast—; bury in—; clothe with—; curse with—; decry—; doom to—; dwell in—; emerge from—; face—; fade into—; fall to—; inhabit—; lift from—; mourn—; repair—; —encroaches; —entombs; —overcomes; —overwhelms; —sets in.

(See loneliness, waste, region.)

DESPAIR

adjectives

absolute; pessimistic; calm; tragic; mute; mild; stolid; endless; unending; savage; dim; sick; grim; appalling; sudden; dismal; irremediable; human; dumb; crushed; whimsical; comfortless; comical; sham;

smothered; secure; beautiful; reluctant; inward; rash; deep; perplexed; spiritual; cold; keen; suppressed; rigid; abysmal; proud; solitary; rayless; sad; abhorred; sheer; errorless; black; reckless; pleased; utmost; mad; wild; lonely; scientific; blank; patient; speechless; passionate; pitiful; comfortless.

verbs
comfort in—; crush with—; doom to—; drive to—; end in—; engender—; fan into —; gasp with—; lift from—; lighten—; listen to—; plague with—; rack with—; rescue from—; save from—; seize with—; shake with—; sink in—; slump into—; spring from—; sweep away—; swoon in—; turn to—; unveil—; wring with—; yield to—; —chills; —grips; —grows; —hovers over; —poisons; —sets in; —settles in; —wells up; —withers; —wracks.

(See hopelessness, discouragement, despondency.)

DESPERADO

adjectives
slinking; sleepless; unarmed; bloodthirsty; ferocious; brutal; murderous; bestial.

DESPERATE

adverbs
tragically; wildly; mutely; savagely; helplessly; grimly; appallingly; suddenly; dismally; dumbly; comically; inwardly; proudly; madly; pitifully; fatally; frantically; cruelly; curiously; awfully; miserably; shockingly; fearfully; obstreperously; ungovernably; excitedly; hysterically; rashly; recklessly.

DESPERATION

adjectives
sheer; blind; melancholy; suicidal; frantic; sullen; utter; ruthless; momentary; stubborn; light-hearted.

DESPICABLE

adverbs
utterly; contemptibly; inexpressibly; shamefully; basely; terribly; outrageously; scandalously; notoriously; meanly; generally; incredibly.

DESPOND (*v*)

adverbs
daily; morbidly; deeply; profoundly; suicidally; utterly; sullenly; mournfully; tearfully; abnormally; unduly; unreasonably.

(See worry.)

DESPONDENCY

adjectives
temporary; morbid; deep; dire; frank; profound; suicidal; despairing; utter; pronounced; stifling; sullen; mournful.

verbs
beset with—; burden with—; chase—; create—; encourage—; envelop in—; express—; forbid—; indulge in—; labor under —; lament—; sink in—; throw into—; wallow in—; —darkens; —deforms; —depresses; —drowns; —envelops; —oppresses; —overcomes; —seeps in; —torments; —triumphs.

(See despair, depression, dejection.)

DESPONDENT

adverbs
temporarily; morbidly; deeply; direly; ominously; significantly; frankly; openly; admittedly; incurably; profoundly; suicidally; dangerously; alarmingly; desperately; sullenly; inexplicably; palpably; mournfully; habitually; ordinarily; inordinately; irremediably; pathologically; temperamentally.

DESPOT

adjectives
merciful; outraged; insulted; fierce; angered; petty; absolute; egotistic; monstrous; municipal; dangerous; predatory; benevolent; arrogant; small-souled; stern; hot-tempered; cruel; rank; vicious; iron-willed.

DESPOTIC

adverbs
relentlessly; ruthlessly; overbearingly; overwhelmingly; intolerably; imperiously; presumptuously; harshly; severely; oppressively; cruelly; obdurately; haughtily; insufferably; unreasonably; terribly; fearfully; dreadfully; incredibly; unwarrantably; dangerously; foolishly; barbarously; heartlessly; recklessly; outrageously; monstrously; viciously; benignly.

DESPOTISM

adjectives
unlimited; mild; barbarous; native; military; benign; agelong; ceremonious; astonished; combined (pl); absolute; irresistible; insupportable; irresponsible; capitalistic; reckless; heartless; rapacious; subsequent; iron.

verbs
adopt—; allay—; apply—; crush under—; establish—; exercise—; expose to—; form

—; free from—; guard against—; launch —; organize—; preserve from—; protect from—; relax—; submit to—; support—; surrender to—; throw off—; tolerate—; —compels; —controls; —enslaves; —governs; —limits; —restrains; —survives; —wills.

(See tyranny.)

DESSERT

adjectives

abbreviated; frugal; colorful; frozen; tempting; cold; delicious; nourishing; gay-looking; tiny.

DESTINATION

adjectives

mutual; secret; final; natural; appointed; moral; different; inevitable; deeper; suitable; proposed; outlandish; religious.

DESTINY

adjectives

false; manifest; impossible; loftiest; wondrous; unaccomplished; unhappy; auspicious; blighted; terrible; myriad (pl); precarious; transcendent; magnificent; deathless; resolute; outwitting; uncertain; circumvolving; inevitable; natural; moral; human; changing; common; momentous; eternal; desolate; future; sunless; noble; solemn; bright; inexorable; tragic; divine; high; evil; inherited; strange; evident; kindest; ultimate; proud; ill-starred.

verbs

abide by—; accept—; bless—; carve—; chart—; command—; condemn by—; evade —; expand—; fight out—; fulfill—; guide —; master—; mold—; pursue—; seal—; shape—; solve—; steer—; struggle with—; succumb to—; supervise—; ward off—; waylay—; work out—; —appoints; —awaits; —beats; —bewails; —carries out; —conspires; —decrees; —dogs; —dooms.

(See fortune, doom, fate, lot.)

DESTITUTE

adverbs

absolutely; sadly; utterly; helplessly; hopelessly; pennilessly; unquestionably; miserably; wretchedly; appallingly; comparatively; abjectly; astonishingly; peculiarly; distressingly; embarrassingly; horribly.

DESTITUTION

adjectives

absolute; utter; penniless; hopeless; abandoned; indigent.

verbs

abandon to—; avoid—; engulf by—; escape —; forsake to—; imply—; lift from—; leave in—; reduce to—; throw into—; verge on—; —approaches; —deprives; —increases; —menaces; —stalks.

(See poverty, want.)

DESTROY (*v*)

adverbs

deliberately; wantonly; ruthlessly; partially; foolishly; irreparably; frequently; simultaneously; eternally; ultimately; unwittingly; rigorously; utterly; effectually; thoughtlessly; universally; mutually; eventually; indiscriminately; consequently; lawlessly; practically; remorselessly; deliberately; inevitably; mercilessly; incalculably.

(See ruin, demolish.)

DESTROYER

adjectives

fierce; parasitic; brutal; plowing; ruthless; courteous; soulless.

DESTRUCTION

adjectives

sudden; instant; universal; wanton; daily; self; total; wild; brilliant; mutual; eventual; willful; indiscriminate; probable; consequent; miserable; practical; comprehensive; threatening; remorseless; deliberate; useless; apparent; utter; flashing; inconceivable; inevitable; ominous; merciless; incalculable; ultimate; sheer; wasting; lawless; necessary; subsequent.

verbs

attempt—; await—; behold—; bring on—; contemplate—; crumble into—; dash to—; deliver from—; ensure—; foredoom to—; incline to—; invite—; involve in—; lead to—; leap to—; lure to—; redeem—; rejoice in—; rescue from—; revel in—; revenge—; rush to—; seek—; send to—; shower—; smite with—; sweep with—; suffer—; thirst for—; woo—; work—.

(See ruin.)

DESTRUCTIVE

adverbs

appallingly; unnecessarily; drunkenly; hysterically; angrily; riotously; deliberately; designedly; wantonly; universally; widely; horribly; unbelievably; lethally; instantly; eventually; indiscriminately; probably; infallibly; remorselessly; inconceivably; ominously; mercilessly; incalculably; ultimately; wastefully; carelessly; thoughtlessly; needlessly; meanly; hatefully; systematically.

DESULTORY

adverbs

merely; irregularly; disconnectedly; lazily; quaintly; exasperatingly; fatally; carelessly; unsystematically; heedlessly; negligently; nonchalantly; indifferently; blithely; smilingly; wantonly; intolerably; imperturbably; vexatiously; unluckily; placidly; serenely; plaguedly.

DETACHMENT

adjectives

alert; hard; fierce; philosophic; lofty; cool; aloof; displayed; detailed; reserved; various (pl); ever-proceeding; beautiful; hastily-gathered; successive; indolent; numerous (pl).

DETAIL

adjectives

rich; decorative; sickening; harmonious; intimate; perturbing; enduring; incredible; visual; elaborate; irrelevant; minute; ornate; amusing; personal; trivial; luscious; troublesome; unpoetical; fictitious; superficial; architectural; repugnant; alarming; impeccable; sensuous; outstanding; conventional; authentic; characteristic; confusing; ingenious; harrowing; technical; tedious; cumbersome; painful; disgusting; exquisite; complete; distinctive; profound; vivid; profuse; charming; unimportant; commonplace; agonizing; remaining; ornamental; profligate; petty; admirable; picturesque; remarkable; significant; sharp; graphic; fervid; reliable; voluminous; appropriate; devastating; realistic; revolting; hateful; trifling; little; worrisome; vexatious; delicate; subtle; gossiping; brief; merest; dull; complicated; tiniest; circumstantial; grim; sordid; collateral; sufficient; loveliest; essential; unusual; perplexing; mean; unrevealed; cleverest; homely; domestic; biographical; scenic; endless; methodical; exact; statistical; clear; restless; hampering; subordinate; heterogeneous; vulgar; needless; topographical; pedantic; faultless; historical; meager; concise; irksome; dreary; myriad (pl).

verbs

array—s; authenticate—s; avoid—; chronicle—s; contribute to—; correlate—s; describe—s; dig out—s; dispense with—; divulge—; dwell upon—; enumerate in—; furnish with—s; grapple with—; grasp—; intersperse—s; marshal—s; master—s; memorize—s; note—s; observe—s; offer in—; parade —s; rehearse—s; relate—s; repeat—s; reveal—s; set forth—s; spare—s; study—s; suppress—s; thrash out—s; treat in—; underestimate—; unearth—; waive —; wrestle with —s; —s bewilder; —s bore; —s elude; —s enrich; —s leak out; —s weary.

(See particular, item, part.)

DETAIL (v)

adverbs

minutely; intimately; visually; elaborately; irrelevantly; amusingly; trivially; lusciously; poetically; superficially; significantly; conventionally; authentically; characteristically; tediously; completely; profusely; vividly; picturesquely; fervidly; voluminously; realistically; vexatiously; briefly; sordidly; endlessly; exactly; methodically; statistically; vulgarly; meagerly; irksomely; drearily.

(See narrate.)

DETAILED

adverbs

accurately; explicitly; clearly; meticulously; punctiliously; richly; horribly; intimately; incredibly; elaborately; minutely; amusingly; alarmingly; ingeniously; tediously; painfully; disgustingly; exquisitely; completely; vividly; graphically; admirably; remarkably; sharply; reliably; appropriately; realistically; hatefully; delicately; briefly; circumstantially; sordidly; unusually; cleverly; statistically; endlessly; exactly; clearly; needlessly; faultlessly; drearily; irksomely.

DETAIN (v)

adverbs

forcibly; unavoidably; successfully; honorably; ingloriously; vexatiously; outrageously; accidentally; unhappily.

(See keep, arrest.)

DETECT (v)

adverbs

easily; cleverly; shrewdly; casually; astutely; logically; artfully; slyly; brilliantly; scientifically; accidentally.

(See discover, uncover.)

DETECTION

adjectives

casual; successful; skillful; logical; artful.

verbs

avoid—; baffle—; elude—; escape—; evade —; fear—; flee—; frustrate—; hide from

—; stumble upon—; suffer—; —alarms; —discloses; —exposes; —informs; —reveals.
(See discovery, disclosure.)

DETECTIVE

adjectives
private; geological; dental; shrewd; competent; hard; luckless; district; burly; typical; tireless; great; heroic; unsympathetic.

verbs
baffle—; commission—; dispatch—; elude—; employ—; escape—; evade—; hire—; inform—; reward—; —accuses; —corners; —discloses; —discovers; —disguises; —dogs; —executes; —exposes; —guards; —hounds; —hunts; —inquires; —inspects; —investigates; —masks; —nabs; —observes; —protects; —pursues; —raids; —reveals; —runs down; —searches; —spies; —studies; —suspects; —tracks; —tracks down; —trails; —uncovers; —unearths; —watches.
(See officer, police.)

DETENTION

adjectives
prolonged; honorable; inglorious; compulsory; vexatious; outrageous; accidental; unhappy.

DETERIORATE (*v*)

adverbs
sadly; horribly; physically; mentally; morally; bodily; inevitably; steadily; intellectually; lamentably; seriously; markedly.
(See impair.)

DETERIORATION

adjectives
physical; bodily; inevitable; mental; nervous; steady; intellectual; lamentable; serious; marked.

verbs
defend from—; detect—; employ in—; exaggerate—; preserve from—; pretend—; produce—; save from—; undergo—; —abates; —arises; —continues; —degenerates; —depresses; —destroys; —impairs; —injures; —seeps in.
(See corruption.)

DETERMINATION

adjectives
obvious; inflexible; intrinsic; great; zealous; steadfast; tireless; grim; deathly; feverish; personal; supernatural; insistent; passionate; sudden; abrupt; settled; bounding; equal; fixed; prescient; mighty; harsh; forceful; intelligent; calm; accurate; cool; early; tangible; selfish; chronological; unwilling; stubborn; dogged; warm; uniform; indefatigable; judicial; desperate; controlling; unanimous; persistent; obstinate; invincible; unflinching; resolute; cold; immutable; precise; whole-souled; ruthless; iron; inexorable; pudgy; manifest; drunken; earnest; indomitable.

verbs
change—; equip with—; flash—; forge—; inspire—; hail—; obsess with—; plod along in—; quench—; reiterate—; reward—; sharpen—; strengthen—; struggle in—; —achieves; —triumphs; —wanes.
(See decision, resolution.)

DETERMINE (*v*)

adverbs
absolutely; happily; objectively; unanimously; shrewdly; passionately; accurately; precisely; resolutely; sternly; conclusively; immediately; unceremoniously; inflexibly; zealously; grimly; stubbornly; doggedly; invincibly; unflinchingly; ruthlessly; inexorably; manifestly; indomitably; largely.
(See decide.)

DETERMINED

adverbs
firmly; inordinately; immovably; irrationally; illogically; childishly; irrevocably; stubbornly; officially; mightily; finally; courageously; quietly; inexorably; harshly; feverishly; passionately; intelligently; calmly; coolly; selfishly; desperately; ruthlessly; drunkenly; crazily; earnestly; curiously; fatally.

DETEST (*v*)

adverbs
fundamentally; thoroughly; positively; unreasonably; infinitely; exaggeratedly; definitely; markedly; obviously; noticeably; unhallowedly; violently.
(See hate.)

DETESTABLE

adverbs
utterly; incredibly; unbelievably; hatefully; abominably; completely; flagrantly; viciously; deplorably; lamentably; diabolically; noxiously; terribly; generally; woefully; odiously; repulsively; despicably; intolerably; insufferably; horridly.

DETESTATION

adjectives
infinite; prolonged; exaggerated; definite; marked; noticeable.

DETHRONE (*v*)

adverbs
ignominiously; completely; shamefully; dishonorably; pusillanimously; courageously; cowardly; brutally; violently; forcefully.
(See usurp.)

DETONATION

adjectives
remote; mystic; continuous (pl); muffled; tremendous; furious; sharp; spasmodic.

verbs
accompany by—; attribute—to; enkindle—; fire—; muffle—; produce—; result in—; —echoes; —erupts; —expels; —occurs; —reports; —rips; —shocks; —stuns; —thunders; —uproots; —violates.
(See explosion.)

DETOUR

adjectives
weary; lightning; quick; disconcerting; unexpected; wrong; bumpy; long; roundabout; wretched.

DETRACTION

adjectives
timid; rude; subtle; uninitiated; aggravated.

DETRIMENT

adjectives
clogging; acute; raw; unbiased; grave; serious.

verbs
accept—; acquire—; admit—; burden with—; cause—; free from—; harbor—; incur—; load with—; repair—; replace—; suffer—; sustain—; —accrues; —affects; —harms; —impairs; —injures; —weakens.
(See injury, loss, damage, harm.)

DETRIMENTAL

adverbs
undeniably; economically; financially; physically; terribly; unluckily; intentionally; maliciously; designedly; substantially; enormously; incalculably; irreparably; irremediably; seriously; personally; disgracefully; unintentionally; incidentally; palpably; essentially; disastrously; woefully.

DEVASTATE (*v*)

adverbs
virtually; generally; appallingly; spiritually; systematically; aimlessly; heartlessly; fiendishly; tyrannically; viciously; ferociously; brutally.
(See ruin.)

DEVASTATING

adverbs
unimaginably; horribly; incredibly; ruinously; inhumanly; savagely; vastly; universally; viciously; sinfully; iniquitously; extensively; irremediably; irrevocably; irrecoverably; heinously; dismally; calamitously.

DEVASTATION

adjectives
cyclonic; general; appalling; forest; spiritual; systematic; aimless.

DEVELOP (*v*)

adverbs
precociously; enormously; advantageously; harmoniously; indirectly; majestically; copiously; riotously; subsequently; perfectly; logically; habitually; unexpectedly; definitely; independently; inordinately; exclusively; rationally; invariably; extraordinarily; tediously; arduously; irrationally; intricately; belatedly; artistically; culturally; muscularly; socially; economically; mentally; physically; deftly; imposingly; continuously; poetically; subsequently; coherently; vindictively; scientifically; progressively; morally; spectacularly; aesthetically; uniquely; deviously; legitimately.
(See complete, unfold.)

DEVELOPMENT

adjectives
extraordinary; astonishing; startling; amazing; rapid; meteoric; long; tedious; arduous; extravagant; irrational; intricate; vast; extensive; slow; evolutionary; gradual; belated; deliberate; hirsute; artistic; cultural; muscular; social; economic; modern; mental; physical; noble; high; deft; majestic; effective; logical; imposing; egregious; intellectual; secluded; surface; inferred; diversified; further; general; continuous; eventual; recent; poetic; subsequent; surprising; coherent; architectural; vindictive; enriching; compensatory; scientific; progressive; basic; disproportionate; laudable; harmonic; individual; impartial; strained; wholesome; previous; promising; technical; organic; moral; multifarious;

psychosexual; magnificent; glorious; institutional; consequent; thematic; peculiar; spectacular; recent; liturgical; safety; empiric; aesthetic; intensive; industrial; defective; external; remoter; unique; devious; expansive; legitimate; profligate; multiple (pl); arrested.

verbs
arrest—; attain—; await—; check—; contribute to—; encourage—; enfeeble—; evaluate—; foresee—; forestall—; foster—; hail—; hamper—; hasten—; hinder—; impair—; keep abreast of—; paralyze—; retard—; 'review—; revolutionize—; rush—; speed—; spur—; stimulate—; stunt—; trace—; undergo—; visualize—; witness—; —germinates from; —proceeds; —surges forward.
(See evolution, growth, expansion, enlargement.)

DEVIATE (v)

adverbs
unconventionally; grossly; materially; peculiarly; slightly; frequently; momentarily; anomalously; occasionally; abnormally; unaccountably; oddly; exceptionally; strangely; weirdly.
(See stray, wander.)

DEVIATION

adjectives
peculiar; slight; gross; material; frequent (pl); anomalous; momentary; occasional.

verbs
accept—; allow—; ascertain—; cause—; determine—; doubt—; eliminate—; govern —; measure—; observe—; recognize—; render—; suspect—; tend toward—; —destroys; —shocks; —strays; —varies.
(See variation, divergence, error.)

DEVICE

adjectives
ingenious; grotesque; elaborate; great; fertile; clockwork; amazing; safety; unworkable; wicked; stale; petty; crude; devious; clumsy; happy; shallow; rhetorical; patriotic; labor-saving; convenient; frugal; improved; successful; hard; simple; shrewd; cunning; artful; clever; magical; sundry (pl); sufficient; heraldic; alignment; desperate; quaint; local; singular; comfortable; playful; artificial; supreme; effective; ancient; symbolic; noble; ceremonial; makeshift; curious; economic; excellent; scholastic; rotary; timesaving; automatic; protective; hazardous; discredited; suitable; chosen; favorite; optical; childish; treacherous.

verbs
abandon—; adopt—; affect—; contrive—; employ—; equip with—; finance—; hit upon —; invent—; launch—; manufacture—; patent—; resort to—; scorn—; utilize.
(See invention, scheme, strategem, symbol.)

DEVIL

adjectives
excellent; incarnate; unsympathetic; deceitful; poor; red; charming; imaginary; flaming; fever-scourged; cruel; stubborn; attractive; little; frisky; obstinate; greedy; latent; merry; destroying; exorcised; surly; eternal; good-looking; chained-up; burning; interior; tempting; mocking; malicious; foreign; raging; daring; conjuring.

verbs
bargain with—; cast out—; conquer—; conspire with—; contend with—; curb—; defy—; deny—; destroy—; drive out—; emancipate from—; exorcise—; expel—; flee from—; follow—; grapple with—; league with—; offend—; personify—; possess by—; preserve from—; "raise"—; rebuke—; resist—; sacrifice to—; scorn—; steer toward—; subject to—; take up with —; worship—; —betrays; —conjures; —deceives; —deludes; —ensnares; —enters; —entices; —harries; —mocks; —oppresses; —rules; —spurs; —tempts.
(See demon, spirit, evil.)

DEVILISH

adverbs
hatefully; inconceivably; iniquitously; irretrievably; incredibly; incorrigibly; atrociously; infernally; shockingly; manifestly; openly; exceptionably; horribly; outrageously; incurably; obdurately; stubbornly; nefariously.

DEVILTRY

adjectives
good-humored; inexhaustible; stock; petty; ineradicable.

DEVIOUS

adverbs
obscurely; circumbendibusly; sinuously; unfortunately; astutely; adroitly; unnecessarily; strangely; oddly; ominously; cur-

iously; provokingly; vexatiously; suspiciously; cleverly; cruelly; intricately; amazingly; confusingly; deliberately; craftily; sharply; fatally; obviously; inscrutably; perplexingly.

DEVISE (v)

adverbs
ingeniously; carefully; cunningly; peculiarly; subtly; specially; grotesquely; elaborately; crudely; deviously; clumsily; conveniently; frugally; shrewdly; sufficiently; comfortably; artificially; effectively; symbolically; economically; curiously; automatically; scholastically; hazardously; suitably; amazingly.
(See contrive, invent.)

DEVOLVE (v)

adverbs
wholly; unexpectedly; absurdly; startlingly; weightily; heavily; normally; politically; traditionally.
(See transmit.)

DEVOTE (v)

adverbs
exclusively; properly; faithfully; unstintingly; passionately; intensely; unreservedly; exclusively; civilly; fearlessly; zealously; earnestly; tenderly; uniquely; expressly; profoundly; religiously; patriotically; personally; mutually; humbly; doggedly; dumbly; blindly; obviously; absurdly; heroically; submissively; unselfishly; sentimentally; conscientiously; unswervingly; untiringly; recklessly; fervidly; deathlessly; assiduously; conjugally; unimpeachably; unobtrusively; agelessly; sublimely; patiently.
(See dedicate, consecrate.)

DEVOTED

adverbs
piously; profoundly; childishly; earnestly; personally; ardently; completely; humbly; mutually; doggedly; blindly; foolishly; queerly; absurdly; heroically; deeply; extremely; submissively; unselfishly; tenderly; sentimentally; exclusively; dangerously; conscientiously; genuinely; passionately; unswervingly; exquisitely; ostentatiously; conspicuously; reverently; staunchly; assiduously; fondly; unobtrusively; sublimely; patiently; openly.

DEVOTEE

adjectives
impious; reverent; average; enthusiastic; ardent; fresh; rabid; distinguished; meek; worshiping; religious; theosophic; high-minded; indigent; true; congenial; servile.

verbs
attract—; gain—; interest—; victimize—; —s assemble; —clamors; —s congregate; —consecrates; —s convene; —dedicates; —denounces; —disparages; —esteems; —exhibits; —indulges in; —introduces; —offers; —practices; —pursues; —worships.
(See follower.)

DEVOTION

adjectives
profound; wearied; religious; patriotic; infantile; earnest; lifetime; studied; personal; detached; complete; humble; mutual; dogged; real; dumb; blind; open; queer; absurd; increased; heroic; whole-hearted; obvious; deep; impious; discouraged; endless; extreme; continued; distant; submissive; unselfish; outdated; painful; tender; sentimental; spiritless; exclusive; dangerous; unceasing; conscientious; genuine; passionate; pure; unparalleled; unswerving; evening; exuberant; capable; angry; faithful; untiring; constant; unconditional; exquisite; ardent; disinterested; unostentatious; conspicuous; undiminished; reverent; speculative; reckless; consecrated; fervid; wifely; deathless; absolute; dog-like; unfaltering; respectful; mystic; desperate; obsequious; chivalric; staunch; inextinguishable; cheerful; manly; bigoted; costliest; austere; solitary; unalterable; ceremonious; idyllic; efficient; assiduous; extemporary; conjugal; outstanding; abiding; unimpeachable; incessant; fondest; invisible; protective; unobtrusive; passing; nunlike; reunited; ageless; sublime; patient.

verbs
accept—; bestow—; cease—; command—; excite—; exploit—; extend—; favor with —; glorify—; interrupt—; lavish—upon; pay—; show—; tender—; —abates; —wanes; —warms.
(See zeal, allegiance, attachment, love, worship, adoration, fidelity, religion.)

DEVOUR (v)

adverbs
ravenously; omnivorously; voraciously; greedily; rapidly; utterly; brutally; fiendishly; hoggishly; bestially; rudely.
(See eat, consume.)

DEVOUT

adverbs
profoundly; earnestly; completely; humbly; queerly; whole-heartedly; piously; submissively; unselfishly; unceasingly; reverently; conscientiously; faithfully; ardently; loyally; assiduously; unobtrusively; admirably; sincerely; solemnly; fervently; meekly.

DEW

adjectives
drenching; fragrant; cleansing; damp; dripping; murky; lethal; sparkling; heavy; melodious; filmy; glittering; glistening; warm; moonlit; starry; starlight; hoary; scented; gracious; moistening; quivering; spangled; prodigal; fiery; melancholy; ambrosial; new-dropped; fattening; ghastly; pestilent; gleaming; undried; cold; blinding; richer; unconcealing; sunlit; gathering; bitter; innocent; softest; melting; nocturnal; lingering; mellifluous; healing; falling; sickly; silvery.

verbs
bathe in—; bedabble with—; brush away—; deck with—; dip in—; dissolve in—; distill—; flower in—; sip—; spray with—; steep in—; sweep away—; wash with—; wet with—; —chills; —dabbles; —drenches; —drops; —falls; —freshens; —glistens; —moistens; —pearls; —refreshes; —revives; —spangles; —strengthens; —thickens; —twinkles.
(See moisture, tears, drop.)

DEXTERITY

adjectives
reasonable; digital; polite; amazing; bland; graceful; manual; unusual; marvelous; incredible; rapid; superior; wonderful; admirable; cool; indescribable; automatic; fatal.

DEXTEROUS

adverbs
reasonably; unusually; politically; blandly; amazingly; wonderfully; admirably; automatically; incredibly; dangerously; skilfully; particularly; consciously; proudly; ostentatiously; dramatically; expertly; felicitiously; discreetly; advantageously; acutely; shrewdly; scientifically; quickly; consummately; spectacularly; opportunely; astutely.

DIABOLIC

adverbs
inconceivably; iniquitously; incredibly; incorrigibly; atrociously; infernally; shockingly; manifestly; openly; flagrantly; exceptionably; horribly; outrageously; incurably; obdurately; stubbornly; nefariously; villainously; execrably; accursedly; inhumanly; ruthlessly.

DIABOLISM

adjectives
everlasting; widespread; apparent; marked; noticeable; flagrant.

DIADEM

adjectives
priceless; imperial; starry; kingless; stellated; royal; regal; ducal.

DIAGNOSE (*v*)

adverbs
precisely; accurately; exactly; correctly; medically; solemnly; bacteriologically; logically; scientifically; casually; conscientiously; astutely.
(See study.)

DIAGNOSIS

adjectives
exact; definite; bitter; unpromising; correct; medical; solemn; bacteriological.

verbs
conduct—; confirm—; embrace in—; form—; reach—; record—; study—; value—; weigh—; —assures; —determines; —discovers; —distinguishes; —errs; —identifies; —reveals; —warrants.
(See conclusion, judgment.)

DIAGRAM

adjectives
legible; clear; confused; graphic; explanatory; key; brief.

verbs
compose—; constitute—; draw—; examine—; exhibit—; experiment with—; improve—; mark—; measure—; outline—; produce—; —charts; —demonstrates; —directs; —illustrates; —points out; —represents; —symbolizes.
(See plan, outline, map, drawing, illustration.)

DIAL

adjectives
wavering; luminous; recessed; spacious; graduated; moss-grown; sun.

verbs
adjust—; affect—; center—; check—; discover by—; employ—; furnish with—; pro-

vide—; refer to—; set—; spin—; watch—; —aids; —counts; —describes; —directs; —indicates; —measures; —points to; —regulates; —revolves; —substantiates; —times.
(See compass, watch.)

DIALECT

adjectives
drawling; guttural; hinterland; crude; broad; garrulous; vulgar; handed-down; ancestral; forcible; unintelligible; strange; multiplying (pl); unpleasant; peculiar; nasal; native; authentic; queer; rural; overaccented; delicious; amorous; gibbering; purest; expressive; barbarous; quaint; untutored; hissing; unmusical.

verbs
adopt—; affect—; converse in—; drop—; influence—; interpret—; lay aside—; missound—; modify—; overcome—; recognize —; study—; understand—; —amuses; —confuses; —corrupts; —missounds; —retains; —vanishes.
(See language, speech.)

DIALOGUE

adjectives
fabulous; witty; short; solemn; natural; spontaneous; earnest; happy; hurried; vivid; delightful; tender; adequate; poetic; urbane; sparkling; final; mysterious; amusing; fast-paced; wooden; frothy; delicious; rapier-like; brilliant; imaginary; merry; wasted; feeble; dramatic; realistic; sustained.

verbs
carry on—; compile—; compose—; confine —to; contrive—; enter into—; entertain with—; inject into—; introduce in—; involve in—; launch into—; transcribe—; —animates; —concerns; —engrosses; —enlivens; —passes; —praises; —vivifies; interests in—.
(See conversation, talk.)

DIAMOND

adjectives
paste; oblong; spurious; illicit; sparkling; enormous; square-cut; pendent; blazing; icy; fair-sized; uncut; monstrous; starry; flashing; unlimited (pl); countless (pl); elemental; flaming; smuggled.

verbs
admire—; adorn with—; deck with—s; imbed—; mine—s; polish—; prize—; quarry —s; set—; win—; yield—s; —crowns; —flames; —flashes; —gleams; —glimmers; —glistens; —glitters; —glows; —reflects; —scintillates; —sparkles.
(See gem, stone, jewel.)

DIAPHRAGM

adjectives
crude; concave; heaving; parchment; tough; bisecting.

DIARY

adjectives
careful; meteorological; intimate; manuscript; joyous; cryptic; copious; vigorous; authoritative; conscientious; well-kept; informal; informative; gossipy; risque; bold; revealing.

verbs
cherish—; enter in—; expose—; hide—; inscribe in—; jot in—; peep into—; prepare—; publish—; recollect by—; record in—; refer to—; repose in—; scan—; —collects; —contains; —covers; —notes; —observes; —relates; —reveals.
(See record, account, book, literature.)

DIATRIBE

adjectives
notorious; violent; revengeful; brutal; incessant.

verbs
break out in—; conclude—; direct—; erupt —; fire—; fulminate—; indulge in—; regret—; set off—; thunder—; utter—; vent —; —abuses; —arouses; —contributes; —exaggerates; —offends; —provokes; —shocks.
(See invective, tirade, discourse, discussion.)

DICE

adjectives
lucky; loaded; rattling; false; unfailing; irresistible; seductive.

verbs
bet on—; box—; cast—; cheat at—; gamble with—; jostle—; load—; lose by—; play with—; scatter—; shake—; shoot—; throw —; toss—; win at—; —clack; —clink; —decide; —fall; —rattle; —reveal; —settle; —topple; —turn.

DICTATE

adjectives
definite; unheeded; vicious; infernal; soundest; passionate; fascist.

DICTATE (*v*)

adverbs
amiably; simultaneously; personally; definitely; viciously; infernally; passionately; bestially; heartlessly; fiendishly; reasonably.
(See command.)

DICTATION

adjectives
aimless; laborious; imperious; rapid; accurate; careless.

DICTATOR

adjectives
military; musical; cruel; unseen; benevolent; philosophic; willful; occult; imperious; ranking; domestic.

verbs
appeal to—; develop into—; entrust—with; fall before—; follow—; name—; prate about—s; serve under—; succumb to—; —authorizes; —bans; —checks; —coerces; —crushes; —decrees; —exercises; —forbids; —forces; —fulminates; —governs; —orders; —prescribes; —rules; —tyrannizes; —violates; —wields.
(See tyrant, monarch, ruler.)

DICTATORIAL

adverbs
absolutely; politically; offensively; unashamedly; officiously; ostentatiously; imperially; regally; imperiously; cruelly; unwarrantably; disagreeably; needlessly; arrogantly; haughtily; superciliously; hatefully; carefully; obstinately; dogmatically; fanatically; fantastically; deliberately; insolently; saucily; impertinently; bumptiously; brazenly; shamelessly; presumptuously.

DICTATORSHIP

adjectives
absolute; military; political; proletarian; economic; stultifying; unashamed; irregular; temporary; household; bloody; mighty; inefficient; imperial; popular; literary; fruitless.

verbs
accept—; assume—; attempt—; create—; cultivate—; curtail—; elect to—; entrust—to; establish—; exercise—; install—; lust for—; repulse—; revolt against—; set up—; serve under—; shake—; succumb to—; yield to—; —coerces; —compels; —crushes; —holds sway.
(See despotism, control, rule.)

DICTION

adjectives
stilted; meticulous; parietal; exquisite; tragic; dignified; metaphorical; illogical; artless; terse; elaborate; glowing; extravagant; loitering; poetic; racy; fashionable; classical; unadorned; overwhelming; peculiar; crabbed; bold.

DICTIONARY

adjectives
comprehensive; dusty; voluminous; exhaustive; unabridged; unusable; historical; universal; excellent; rhyming; biographical; scholarly; pronouncing; scriptural; phonetic; synonymic; grammatical; weighty; authoritative.

verbs
abridge—; compile—; consult—; edit—; enlarge—; have recourse to—; provide—; publish—; resort to—; revise—; —aids; —arranges; —classifies; —confirms; —contains; —decides; —defines; —determines; —informs; —interprets; —pictures; —verifies.
(See book.)

DICTUM

adjectives
energetic; famous; harsh; bold; brisk; final.

DIDACTIC

adverbs
tiresomely; tediously; wearisomely; monotonously; conceitedly; learnedly; instructively; endlessly; absurdly; egotistically; indefatigably; disagreeably; unpleasantly; ostentatiously; diffusely; preachily; sharply; academically; eruditely; expertly; bumptiously.

DIDACTICISM

adjectives
solemn; sugar-coated; obvious; patent; marked; unintelligent.

DIE (*v*)

adverbs
ultimately; unaccountably; wholly; utterly; valiantly; peacefully; sullenly; violently; gloriously; proudly; recently; providentially; stoically; pennilessly; invariably; hap-

lessly; blissfully; huskily; respectively; honorably; mysteriously; quiveringly; holily; abruptly; shamefully; accidentally; religiously; rebelliously; precipitately.
(See perish.)

DIET

adjectives
abstemious; starvation; daily; piscatory; ample; proper; modern; scant; mixed; varied; balanced; ordinary; exclusive; monotonous; nut; fastidious; invented; staple; nourishing; enriched; astringent; vitaminized; spurious; vegetarian; optimum; adequate; coniferous; correct; predominant; meat; peculiar; skimpy; rigid; sensible; intellectual; carnivorous; dangerous; strict; liquid; heavy.

verbs
adhere to—; adopt—; alter—; change—; commend—; complete—; compound—; discuss—; employ—; exclude from—; increase —; mix—; modify—; place on—; prescribe—; recover on—of; reduce—; regulate—; restrict—; spare in—; subsist on—; supplement—; vary—; yield to—; —cures; —influences; —nourishes; —reduces; —
(See fare, victuals. ration, food.)
stimulates; —supplies; —sustains.

DIETETICS

adjectives
compulsory; insipid; accessory; elementary; fundamental.

verbs
engross in—; instruct in—; interest in—; study—; —adapts; —cautions; —comprises; —cures; —defines; —extends to; —inquires; —observes; —prevents; —reforms; —regulates; —solves; —systematizes; —aids.
(See hygiene.)

DIFFER (v)

adverbs
radically; racially; decidedly; essentially; widely; profoundly; chemically; entirely; acutely; sharply; markedly; noticeably; perceptibly; infinitesimally; psychologically; mentally; religiously; gravely; appreciably; strikingly; palpably; vitally; significantly; fundamentally; philosophically; prodigiously; intrinsically; structurally.
(See disagree.)

DIFFERENCE

adjectives
sharp; marked; acute; honest; conscientious; noticeable; perceptible; decided; evident; inconsequent; infinitesimal; scant; slight; petty; racial; psychological; mental; religious; matrimonial; grave; insuperable; subtle; bitter; radical; simulated; conceded; actual; essential; utmost; striking; outstanding; profound; vast; appreciable; noteworthy; tremendous; palpable; calm; assignable; important; fresh; material; vital; sad; qualitative; pathetic; supreme; happy; minute; amazing; factional; original; significant; indefinable; supposed; superficial; magical; tribal; fundamental; irrepressible; deep-seated; philosophical; irreconcilable; prodigious; intrinsic; temporary; structural.

verbs
acquaint with—; appreciate—; bury—s; cancel—; compensate for—; correlate with —s; debate—; define—; determine—; discern—; discuss—; dread—; expose—; illustrate—; master—; notice—; obliterate—; observe—; reconcile—s; rest—s; settle—; smooth out—; —appears; —s arise; —s estrange; —s flare up; —prevents.
(See disagreement, discrimination, variation, inequality.)

DIFFERENT

adverbs
multifariously; incidentally; impertinently; harmlessly; objectionably; inadmissibly; unconformably; strangely; remotely; outlandishly; undeniably; palpably; essentially; grotesquely; disagreeably; pleasantly; obviously; inconceivably; discordantly; fantastically; exotically.

DIFFERENTIATE (v)

adverbs
legitimately; generously; elaborately; acutely; bluntly; properly; distinctly.
(See distinguish.)

DIFFERENTIATION

adjectives
subtle; elaborate; proper; acute; blunt.

DIFFICULT

adverbs
relatively; tremendously; overwhelmingly; formidably; unbelievably; supremely; seriously; administratively; physically; obviously; naturally; peculiarly; particularly;

strangely; curiously; conspicuously; alarmingly; patently; evidently; dishearteningly; impossibly; intricately; perplexingly; desperately.

DIFFICULTY

adjectives
immense; great; huge; tremendous; enormous; overwhelming; formidable; redoubtable; unbelievable; amazing; supreme; innumerable (pl); grave; serious; agrarian; domestic; emotional; administrative; technical; diplomatic; physical; economic; religious; appalling; financial; fiscal; evident; obvious; inherent; identical; underlying; insurmountable; vital; peculiar; practical; necessary; problematic; familiar; initial; insuperable; unpleasant; lamentable; invincible; conspicuous; unforeseen; functional; alarming; recurrent; endless; disheartening; relative; principal; censorship; bargaining; visual; baffling; impending; incredible; considerable; unprecedented.

verbs
adjust—; attend with—; belittle—; beset by—; breathe with—; clear up—; comprehend—; conclude—; confront with—; conquer—; contend with—; demonstrate—; double—; eliminate—; encounter—; escape —; estimate—; evade—; experience—; go to the root of—; grapple with—; grasp—; impose—; impress with—; iron out—; labor in—; minimize—; obliterate—; obviate—; pass—; perceive—; raise—; remedy—; rouse with—; shirk—; smooth away—; stir up—; strew with—; surmount—; weigh —; wrestle with; —ies accumulate; —ies arise; —grows out of; —intervenes; —looms; —persists.
(See obstacle, hindrance, quarrel, trouble.)

DIFFIDENCE

aajectives
delicate; rustic; becoming; excessive; amused; half-boyish; proper.

verbs
attack—; disperse—; enter into with—; indulge in—; lay aside—; manifest—; practise—; proceed from—; speak with—; teach —; —afflicts; —assails; —creeps over; —prevents; —shames; —submits to; —terrifies; —wounds.
(See bashfulness.)

DIFFIDENT

adverbs
delicately; provincially; becomingly; excessively; amusingly; laughably; ridiculously; needlessly; properly; nervously; anxiously; dreadfully; painfully; bashfully; blushingly; demurely; quietly; shyly.

DIFFUSE

adverbs
tiresomely; tediously; monotonously; vexatiously; endlessly; verbosely; copiously; circuitously; disagreeably; provokingly; pedantically; stupidly; dully; indirectly; interminably; prosily; maddeningly; notoriously.

DIFFUSE (v)

adverbs
naturally; delicately; excessively; wastefully; widely; copiously; freely; liberally; perplexingly.
(See scatter, disseminate.)

DIFFUSENESS

adjectives
rhythmical; excessive; expansive; limited; unshadowed; beaming; theoretical.

DIFFUSION

adjectives
wide; cultural; original; soft; vast; inexpressible; universal.

DIG

adjectives
sly; intentional; vicious; sarcastic; witty; humorous; retaliative.

DIG (v)

adverbs
laboriously; perseveringly; viciously; intentionally; purposively; industriously; indefatigably.
(See work, labor.)

DIGEST

adjectives
interesting; careful; considered; chronological; fact.

DIGEST (v)

adverbs
complacently; rapidly; internally; interestingly; carefully; chronologically; intelligently; mentally; cleverly; briefly.
(See absorb, classify.)

DIGESTION

adjectives
torpid; agreeable; disturbed; superb; sound; pure.

verbs
activate—; affect—; allay—; disturb—; govern—; impair—; improve—; interrupt —; promote—; regulate—; reinvigorate—; retard—; sour—; stimulate—; upset—.
(See health.)

DIGIT

adjectives
lone; disassociated; menacing; insignificant; discounted.

verbs
calculate—; count—; dismember—; divide into—s; decorate—; employ—; exercise—; express in—s; flex—; indicate—; memorize—; number—; ornament—; run into—s; sever—; spoil—s.
(See toe, finger, figure, number.)

DIGNIFIED

adverbs
properly; proudly; informally; graciously; simply; pleasantly; nobly; serenely; calmly; quietly; gravely; faultlessly; elaborately; coldly; indescribably; ridiculously; superbly; naturally; magisterially; matchlessly; sternly; impressively; incongruously; austerely; professionally; pompously; senselessly; gently; disagreeably; repellently; notoriously; augustly; fashionably; solemnly.

DIGNITARY

adjectives
honorable; famous; professional; local; robot; titular; learned.

DIGNITY

adjectives
proper; proud; upright; informal; happy; delicate; external; lofty; lauded; gracious; supreme; simple; majestic; pleasant; complacent; noble; robust; brave; serene; calm; quiet; grave; unwinking; studied; measured; faultless; immaculate; elaborate; sure; stilted; cold; severe; savage; impaired; faded; obedient; mysterious; social; impassive; indescribable; forensic; dashing; waddling; ridiculous; outraged; poised; trembling; spacious; potential; outward; stoical; superb; forced; unbroken; ageless; natural; silent; sententious; sad; irresistible; magisterial; distant; matchless, undeserved; ill-timed; spiritual; patriarchal; wonted; smug; scholastic; gruesome; military; threatened; short-lived; stern; pious; panoplied; leisure-class; frowning; impressive; spectral; incongruous; white; celestial; mutilated; austere; professional; youthful; additional; senseless; mournful; sedate; pompous; mock; epic; inherent; insulted; gentle; careless; unprecedented; Wagnerian.

verbs
achieve—; cast off—; detract from—; develop—; discard—; dispose of—; enhance —; grope for—; halo in—; inject—; impair—; impart—; invest with—; lend—; maintain—; outrage—; preserve—; retain —; rob of—; shed—; shrug aside—; stress —; surpass—; sustain—; treat with—; vindicate—; win—.
(See eminence, honor, distinction.)

DIGRESS (*v*)

adverbs
irrelevantly; deviously; slightly; politically; fascinatingly; descriptively; boringly; dryly; interminably; illogically.
(See wander, deviate.)

DIGRESSION

adjectives
pleasing; slight; bitter; political; fascinating; irrelevant; unintegrated; wise; agreeable; descriptive; periodic (pl).

DIGRESSIVE

adverbs
vexatiously; endlessly; wordily; verbosely; diffusely; copiously; circuitously; disagreeably; provokingly; tiresomely; unintelligibly; pedantically; vaguely; stupidly; dully; ramblingly; indirectly; interminably.

DILAPIDATED

adverbs
terribly; wretchedly; miserably; sorely; pathetically; dreadfully; ruinously; hideously; outrageously; fantastically; shabbily; shockingly; inconceivably; greatly; inexpressibly; worthlessly.

DILAPIDATION

adjectives
general; wholesale; pathetic; ragged; tumble-down; remnantal.

DILATE (v)

adverbs

endlessly; visibly; abnormally; intolerably; unprecedentedly; continuously; unreasonably.

(See swell.)

DILATORY

adverbs

injuriously; uselessly; needlessly; vexatiously; irritatingly; senselessly; unaccountably; obstinately; stubbornly; dangerously; exasperatingly; unconscionably; characteristically; habitually; gravely; terribly; impertinently; indolently; stupidly; languidly; listlessly; inertly; slothfully; drowsily; dreamily; inexcusably; unpleasantly; gallingly.

DILEMMA

adjectives

economic; awkward; annoying; ancient; veritable; insoluble; cruel; moral; pitiful; agonizing; dire; frightful; doubtful; sentimental; unpleasant; terrible; desperate; inescapable; hopeless.

verbs

balk at—; drift into—; elude—; escape from—; extricate from—; face—; founder on—; grasp—; rescue from—; seize—; solve—; take—by the horns; —baffles; —confronts.

(See choice, predicament.)

DILIGENCE

adjectives

characteristic; sullen; unwearied; savage; conscientious; guilty; true; extraordinary; exceeding; utmost; duteous; scrupulous; tenderest; dire; indefatigable; persevering; dusty; yellow; unsparing; tireless; unwonted.

verbs

admire—; apply—; dispatch with—; display—; exercise—; exert—; note—; nourish—; repay—; report—; require—; reward—; rule with—; show—; summon—; —accomplishes; —persists; —pleases.

(See industry, care, application.)

DILIGENT

adverbs

extraordinarily; carefully; innately; studiously; assiduously; industriously; busily; constantly; doggedly; faithfully; loyally; indefatigably; conscientiously; exceedingly; duteously; scrupulously; tirelessly; habitually; trustworthily; energetically; pleasantly; surprisingly; zealously; devotedly; officiously; briskly; ostentatiously; conspicuously; diplomatically; astutely; shrewdly.

DIM

adverbs

mysteriously; obscurely; strangely; curiously; oddly; nebulously; dully; faintly; cloudily; confusingly; perplexingly; disturbingly; wretchedly; miserably; pallidly; imperceptibly; unaccountably; plaguedly; infernally; dreadfully.

DIM (v)

adverbs

perceptibly; scarcely; mystically; prematurely; dramatically; awesomely; effectively; abruptly; perceptibly.

(See darken, obscure.)

DIMENSION

adjectives

important; narrow; reduced; dominating; prodigious; mere; colossal; ideal; mathematical; basic; toylike; supernatural; hugest; portentous; relative; corporal; gigantic; stupendous; miniature; scanty; horizontal; volcanic; enormous; manageable; palatial; moderate; ambitious; noble; desired; imperial; spacious; confined; incompatible.

verbs

compute—; describe—; discover—; draw—; expand—; explore—; find—; furnish—; measure—; mistake—; reach—; reduce—; require—; speculate on—; supply—; take—; —bounds; —confuses; —exceeds; —represents; —shrinks.

(See magnitude, size, extent.)

DIMINISH (v)

adverbs

perceptibly; partially; proportionally; steadily; materially; insignificantly; sensibly; seriously; vastly; appreciably; intolerably; sensibly; continuously.

(See reduce, lessen.)

DIMINUTION

adjectives

appreciable; sensible; continuous; perceptible; subtle; covert; gradual.

DIMNESS

adjectives
mystic; lovely; gracious; unreal; chequered; shadowy; dreamlike; holy; religious; premature; vast; lonely; cobwebby; misty.

DIMPLE

adjectives
reluctant; fugitive; elusive; tantalizing; fleeting; impertinent; wanton; roguish; neighboring.

verbs
bait with—; break into—; depress into—; expose—; flash—; form—; hollow into—; laugh—; mark with—; part in—; practise —; repay in—; reveal—; smile—; —captivates; —dances; —delights; —lures; —smiles; —twinkles.

DIN

adjectives
terrible; infernal; sudden; outrageous; jocund; clanging; alarming; competing; wheezing; awful; chaotic; terrific; rude; discordant; horrible; chattering; general; ominous; exclamatory; ear-splitting; merry; lively; plaintive; deafening; ever-waxing; furious; vexatious; wild; humming; resounding; reverberating; echoing; shattering; intermittent; frightful.

verbs
diminish—; drown—; endure—; muffle—; penetrate—; raise—; silence—; tremble at —; —awakens; —blasts; —breaks; —dies away; —ensues; —fades; —hisses; —reverberates; —roars; —streams forth; —waxes louder.

(See noise, clamor, uproar, rattle.)

DINE (*v*)

adverbs
prodigally; sumptuously; ostentatiously; regally; piggishly; opulently; delectably; luxuriously; gaily; talkatively; impressively; miserably; simply; abundantly; belatedly; modestly; ceremoniously; diplomatically; formally.

DINER

adjectives
agitated; gay; talkative; Epicurean; gluttonous.

verbs
cook for—; entertain—; greet—; satiate—; suit—; welcome—; —indulges; —overeats; —relishes; —samples; —stuffs; —tastes; —tips.

DINGY

adverbs
bleakly; terribly; obscurely; gloomily; faintly; disagreeably; repulsively; hatefully; disgustingly; unpleasantly; monotonously; incredibly; pitiably; surprisingly; unexpectedly; discouragingly; hopelessly; inexcusably; dishearteningly; depressingly.

DINING-ROOM

adjectives
oak-paneled; charming; huge; typical; sweltering; cheerless; tapestried; dim; quiet; empty; resplendent.

DINNER

adjectives
impressive; princely; charming; old-fashioned; pleasant; elaborate; sumptuous; delicious; gala; respectable; cheerful; good; decent; tolerable; stupid; miserable; oppressive; masculine; state; simple; abundant; belated; expensive; modest; incredible; endless; savory; magnificent; wretched; melancholy; solitary; periodical; ceremonious; diplomatic; woman-cooked; desolate; doubtful; formal; midnight.

verbs
accompany at—; address at—; attend—; dance at—; dispatch—; drop in for—; enliven—; hobnob at—; invite to—; prepare—; relish—; revel at—; ring for—; sample—; savor—; serve—; spread for—; tear at—; —cools; —nourishes; —satisfies; —steams.

(See meal.)

DIP

adjectives
invigorating; exhilarating; morning; tallow; convulsive; curious.

DIP (*v*)

adverbs
heavily; abnormally; invigoratingly; exhilaratingly; convulsively; curiously; continuously.

(See lower.)

DIPHTHERIA

adjectives
malignant; mild; tentative; membranous; controlled; dread.

verbs
afflict with—; carry—; contract—; describe —; diagnose as—; doctor for—; immunize to—; infect with—; inoculate against—; isolate—; quarantine for—; recognize—; seize with—; succumb to—; suffer from—; treat for—; —attacks; —inflames; —rages; —ravages; —takes its toll.
(See disease.)

DIPLOMACY

adjectives
tortuous; wasted; secret; minute; private; unskilled; shrewd; consummate; formal; proper; misty; tricky.

verbs
acquire—; adjust with—; adopt—; boast —; conduct with—; control by—; cultivate —; destroy—; detect—; dole out—; employ—; encourage—; exert—; favor—; fit for—; found in—; gain by—; infiltrate—; instruct in—; introduce—; manage with—; necessitate—; negotiate—; propose—; school in—; suggest—; —achieves; —attains; —conceals; —reconciles; —smooths out; —wins.
(See tact, shrewdness, craft.)

DIPLOMAT

adjectives
clever; astute; seasoned; distinguished; veteran; wary; consummate; Oriental; skillful; traditional; old-style; career; formal; suave; scholarly; incredulous; eminent; deft; accomplished; practiced.

verbs
appoint—; employ—; entrust to—; introduce—; invest—with; privilege—; prove —; receive—; select—; —arranges; —conciliates; —conducts; —humors; —"joshes"; —manages; —proposes; —smooths; —suggests; —tricks.
(See ambassador.)

DIPLOMATIC

adverbs
subtly; cunningly; shrewdly; artfully; gravely; wisely; craftily; smoothly; suavely; cleverly; astutely; instinctively; habitually; skilfully; formally; deftly; adroitly; tactfully; profoundly; courteously; cannily; discerningly; nimbly; sagaciously; sagely; blandly; wisely; affably; calculatingly; strategically.

DIPLOMATIST

adjectives
career; cunning; unscrupulous; acute; supple; wary; tenacious; dexterous; decorated.

DIRECT

adverbs
delightfully; pleasantly; helpfully; comfortingly; charmingly; gratifyingly; satisfactorily; pleasingly; ingenuously; frankly; candidly; honestly; courageously; boldly; unequivocally; agreeably; surprisingly; conveniently; childishly; bluntly; sincerely; unaffectedly; unflatteringly; crudely; curiously; strangely.

DIRECT (*v*)

adverbs
vaguely; intelligently; generally; competently; practically; brilliantly; magnificently; disastrously; dangerously; legislatively; habitually; relentlessly; ultimately; academically; arbitrarily; ignobly; intellectually; intricately; eccentrically; hurriedly; curtly; calmly; frivolously; vigorously; automatically; vainly; verbally; uniformly; perseveringly; astutely; dramatically; independently; victoriously.
(See control, guide.)

DIRECTION

adjectives
unlooked-for; vague; intelligent; competent; general; steady; practical; brilliant; magnificent; indicated; careful; unified; cohesive; disastrous; dangerous; legislative; opposite; forbidden; habitual; desirable; inhibited; oblique; relentless; distinguished; succinct; ultimate; academic; retrograde; homeward; arbitrary; ignoble; businesslike; complicated; intellectual; intricate; low-toned; eccentric; crisp; voluble; concise; hurried; curt; calm; explicit (pl); contradictory; transversal; dazzling; frivolous; minute.

verbs
comply with—; determine—; divert from —; drift in—; err in—; face in—of; gaze in—; give—to; heed—; incline—; lack—;

observe—s; respond to—; reverse—; tend in—of; train in—; transmit—s; turn in—; —swerves; —wavers.
(See instruction, course. position.)

DIRECTNESS

adjectives
commendable; uncanny; bull-headed; downright; pleasing; brisk; characteristic; engaging; arrowlike; uncompromising; simple; unstudied; brutal; revealing; clipped; unabashed; manly; military; impulsive; naive; brusque.

DIRECTOR

adjectives
capable; painstaking; regional; financial; shadowy; honorable.

DIRGE

adjectives
mournful; wailing; beautiful; prophetic; wrathful; death; funeral; undifferentiated; weird.

verbs
chant—; compose—; intone—; introduce—; moan—; occasion—; perform—; renew—; sing—; soothe with—; sound—; utter—; wail—; —commemorates; —laments; —mourns; —saddens.
(See song, poem, music.)

DIRT

adjectives
stubborn; encrusted; soft; excess; sweaty; grayish; imbedded; accumulated; unspeakable.

verbs
acquaint with—; breed in—; cast out—; defile with—; fleck with—; fling to—; frolic in—; grind into—; ingrain with—; originate from—; plant in—; pluck from—; pollute with—; scrape away—; search in—; throw—; tread in—; wade in—; wallow in—; wash away—; —accumulates; —adheres; —befouls; —clings; —soils.
(See earth, soil, filth, squalor.)

DISABILITY

adjectives
total; grim; physical; permanent; financial; partial; inescapable.

verbs
attend with—; bring on—; complain of—; cope with—; create—; cripple by—; emancipate from—; gloat over—; increase—; labor under—; lessen—; remove—; stress—; —paralyzes; —prevents; —restricts; —tortures.
(See inability, incompetence, impotence, weakness.)

DISABLE (*v*)

adverbs
totally; physically; permanently; financially; partially; inescapably; tragically; woefully; completely; entirely.
(See handicap.)

DISABLED

adverbs
tragically; oddly; sadly; utterly; strangely; dangerously; grimly; totally; partially; physically; mentally; irremediably; irrecoverably; lamentably; pitiably; deplorably; pitifully; unnecessarily; helplessly; hopelessly; recently.

DISADVANTAGE

adjectives
distinct; physical; immense; tactical; serious; obvious; ungenerous; initial; economic; particular; individual; undue; painful; tremendous.

verbs
balance—; conceal—; confront with—; deprecate—; endure—; fight at—; hurdle—; labor under—; place at—; overcome—; regret—; sell at—; surmount—; tug at—; uproot—; weight with—; —hinders; —injures; —obstructs.
(See injury, loss, inconvenience, detriment, drawback, hindrance.)

DISADVANTAGEOUS

adverbs
financially; socially; decidedly; distinctly; physically; immensely; strategically; seriously; obviously; manifestly; unfortunately; economically; particularly; unduly; painfully; tremendously; perniciously; disastrously; horribly; exceptionally; infernally; irremediably.

DISAGREE (*v*)

adverbs
spiritedly; violently; emphatically; excessively; unwittingly; vehemently; internally; utterly; bitterly; acridly; reasonably; emotionally; rationally; spitefully; venomously.
(See differ, contradict.)

DISAGREEABLE

adverbs
pathetically; utterly; atrociously; outrageously; obviously; senselessly; unreasonably; unnecessarily; horribly; disgustingly; bitterly; deliberately; unintentionally; habitually; gravely; rankly; indecently; disrespectfully; odiously; painfully; unfortunately; unbearably; plaguedly; obnoxiously; dismally; shockingly; harshly; cruelly.

DISAGREEMENT

adjectives
vehement; internal; utter; bitter; acrid.

verbs
abandon—; attribute—to; avoid—; cancel—; cause—; engross in—; evade—; expose to—; feign—; indulge in—; live in—; overcome—; pacify—; remove—; settle—; —disgusts; —displeases; —offends; —vexes.
(See difference, contention, quarrel, dispute.)

DISAPPEAR (*v*)

adverbs
mysteriously; unaccountably; abruptly; miraculously; evanescently; unquestionably; gradually; totally; effectually; unexpectedly; irretrievably; virtually.
(See vanish, recede.)

DISAPPEARANCE

adjectives
unexpected; unexplained; irretrievable; inexplicable; sudden; gradual; virtual.

verbs
achieve—; credit—to; discover—; effect—; fear—; feign—; investigate—; solve—; witness—; —astounds; —baffles; —mystifies.
(See escape.)

DISAPPOINT (*v*)

adverbs
acutely; obviously; grievously; wretchedly; woefully; bitterly; continually; visibly; childishly; distinctly; overwhelmingly; inevitably; vaguely; deeply; poignantly; remorsefully; horridly; mutually; perpetually; cruelly; repeatedly.
(See frustrate, baffle.)

DISAPPOINTED

adverbs
sadly; hopelessly; bitterly; heartbreakingly; irrecoverably; obscurely; grievously; distinctly; overwhelmingly; obviously; manifestly; inexpressibly; vaguely; definitely; deeply; poignantly; horribly; woefully; repeatedly; disconcertingly; tragically; bleakly; senselessly; foolishly; pitiably; terribly; inconsolably; forlornly; miserably; wrtechedly; cruelly.

DISAPPOINTING

adverbs
cruelly; bitterly; harshly; sharply; overwhelmingly; unbearably; sadly; grievously; distinctly; inexpressibly; vaguely; woefully; searingly; pitiably; wretchedly; terribly; tragically; fearfully; definitely; deeply.

DISAPPOINTMENT

adjectives
minor; obscure; scathing; bitter; grievous; distinct; overwhelming; obvious; hurt; expressive; inevitable; resultant; burning; vague; outward; unhappy; deep; poignant; remorseful; unrepressed; horrid; woeful; classic; mutual; perpetual; cruel; melancholy; repeated; callous; demoniac.

verbs
adjust—; conceal—; deserve—; dole out—; entail—; feign—; oppress with—; preclude—; pretend—; produce—; shoulder—; sob—; soothe—; suppress—; taste—; —dampens; —ensues; —irks; —rankles; —saddens; —teaches; —wounds.
(See frustration, dissatisfaction, chagrin, misfortune, defeat.)

DISAPPROBATION

adjectives
express; strong; bitter; haughty; hesitant; ready; spontaneous.

DISAPPROVAL

adjectives
envious; ponderous; unmistakable; cold; emphatic; mounting; marked; absent-minded; prim; shocked; icy; unanimous; stern; distinct; tragic; wordless; consistent; harsh; lofty; undisguised; united; violent; ungracious; frigid.

verbs
anticipate—; earn—; indicate—; mask—; prompt—; quench with—; register—; relax—; signify—; snort—; storm—; vent—; —abates; —dampens; —descends; —oppresses; —silences; —vexes.
(See condemnation, censure.)

DISAPPROVE (*v*)

adverbs
distinctly; heartily; obviously; strongly; unmistakably; coldly; emphatically; primly; icily; unanimously; consistently; sternly; wordlessly; harshly; violently; ungraciously; frigidly.
(See criticize, grumble.)

DISARMAMENT

adjectives
effective; universal; unilateral; world-wide; wide-spread.

verbs
affect—; agree to—; approve of—; confer on—; demand—; disagree upon—; introduce—; join in—; propose—; secure—; urge—; —deprives; —divests; —promises; —reduces; —secures; —strips; —terrifies; —weakens.

DISASTER

adjectives
black; dreadful; messy; hideous; terrible; unmitigated; unbearable; cataclysmic; overwhelming; serious; stupendous; titanic; ultimate; irreparable; irretrievable; marital; economic; melodramatic; planetary; cosmic; social; family; metaphysical; political; commercial; matrimonial; personal; unforeseen; unaccountable; unprecedented; indefinable; dim; imaginary; merited; dire; instant; sheer; sad; fresh; grievous; increasing; appalling; sweet; financial; subsequent; irremediable; awful; ominous; ignominious; illimitable; apparent; wide-spread; impending; unmerciful.

verbs
circumvent—; court—; force into—; foredoom to—; head for—; investigate—; invite—; meet with—; obviate—; presage—; prophesy—; provoke—; rush into—; salvage from—; shield from—; sow the seeds of—; spell—; suffer—; threaten—; —befalls; —dogs; —impends; —jars; —overtakes; —overwhelms; —sweeps.
(See calamity, catastrophe, mishap, misfortune, accident.)

DISASTROUS

adverbs
overwhelmingly; wholly; irremediably; inexpressibly; horribly; politically; strategically; ruinously; dreadfully; hideously; cataclysmically; seriously; stupendously; ultimately; irreparably; economically; socially; unaccountably; direly; appallingly; financially; apparently; unmercifully; exceptionally; shockingly.

DISAVOW (*v*)

adverbs
explicitly; deservedly; modestly; completely; distinctly; partially; honestly; earnestly; heatedly; excitedly; repeatedly.
(See disclaim.)

DISAVOWAL

adjectives
distinct; modest; complete; craven; rash; deliberate.

DISBELIEF

adjectives
scornful; cynical; heartsick; raucous; stuttering; total.

verbs
acquire—; adjust—; alter—; assert—; attack—; conceal—; drift into—; express—; form—; hint—; mantle—; pretend—; strip of—; —angers; —annoys; —persists; —refuses; —vexes; —rejects.
(See doubt, distrust, incredulity, skepticism.)

DISC
(*See disk*)

adjectives
flat; brilliant; polished; keen; turned; crude.

DISCARD (*v*)

adverbs
ruthlessly; consequently; permanently; gradually; partially; entirely; carelessly; uncaringly; selfishly; obliviously; cruelly.
(See throw, reject.)

DISCERN (*v*)

adverbs
dimly; faintly; clearly; scornfully; acutely; truthfully; shrewdly; enlightenedly; keenly; jealously; raptly; suspiciously.
(See distinguish, see.)

DISCERNIBLE

adverbs
easily; scarcely; quickly; obscurely; dimly; clearly; plainly; eventually; humanly; amazingly; startlingly; fatally; distinctly; intuitively; dangerously; definitely; positively; momentarily; hardly.

DISCERNING

adverbs
notoriously; profoundly; deeply; sagaciously; judicially; philosophically; expertly; adroitly; cleverly; keenly; astutely; shrewdly; solidly; quickly; brilliantly; acutely; intelligently; ingeniously; discriminatingly; wisely.

DISCERNMENT

adjectives
shrewd; human; enlightened; acute; rapt; keen; jealous.

DISCHARGE

adjectives
watchful; judicious; successful; assiduous; instant; thunderous; conscientious; ignominious; offensive; immediate; luminous; electrical; profuse; vigilant; faithful; occasional; copious.

verbs
absorb—; arrest—; check—; emit—; mop out—; purify—; stop—; suck out—; —burns; —drips; —gushes; —inflames; —irritates; —itches; —renews; —varies; —wanes.
(See firing, blast.)

DISCHARGE (*v*)

adverbs
instantaneously; intelligently; conscientiously; ingeniously; adequately; capably; briskly; faithfully; fully; punctually; judiciously; watchfully; assiduously; ignominiously; offensively; vigilantly.
(See remove, stop.)

DISCIPLE

adjectives
ardent; doubting; youthful; ignorant; inquiring; leading; prolific; uncritical; blunt; renowned; wholehearted; faithful; fervent; humble; patient; temporary; tractable; immediate; civil; primitive; hopeful; trusted.

verbs
accept—; address—; baptize—; cast out—; choose—; command—; distinguish—; instruct—; lead—; rebuke—; teach—; win—; —advances; —apprehends; —believes; —deserts; —establishes; —expounds; —fasts; —follows; —forsakes; —ministers; —prays; —propagates; —records; —understands.
(See convert, follower.)

DISCIPLINARIAN

adjectives
harsh; ferocious; stern; incompetent; ineffectual; strong-minded.

DISCIPLINE

adjectives
mental; hard; strict; unsympathizing; monastic; religious; stern; patient; firm; virtuous; gentle; effective; military; grim; iron; inflexible; rigorous; compulsory; irksome; inexorable; cellular; unfeeling; imaginative; infracted; systematic; painful; affectionate; heroic; moral; speculative; conventual; unrelenting; secret; peculiar; spasmodic; needful; unflagging; questioned; sound; absolute; perfect; modern; prudent; monastic; iron.

verbs
abate—; chafe under—; dread—; enforce —; fuse with—; impose—; maintain—; neglect—; preserve—; relax—; subject to —; wreck—; —deteriorates; —exacts; —falters; —loosens; —wavers; —weakens.
(See training, subjection, punishment, correction.)

DISCIPLINE (*v*)

adverbs
conscientiously; admirably; ardently; faithfully; patiently; strictly; morally; physically; rigorously; daily; harshly; severely; mentally; unsympathizingly; monastically; religiously; virtuously; gently; effectively; grimly; inflexibly; irksomely; inexorably; unfeelingly; conventionally; unflaggingly; soundly; prudently.
(See train, correct, punish.)

DISCLAIM (*v*)

adverbs
privately; modestly; excitedly; vehemently; repeatedly; violently; noisily; vigorously; grumblingly; eloquently; fluently; loudly; definitely; weakly; spiritedly; competently; aggressively; promptly; compellingly.
(See deny, renounce.)

DISCLOSE (*v*)

adverbs
immodestly; irreverently; recently; immediately; fully; shamelessly; modestly; staggeringly; gradually; startlingly; sensationally; diplomatically; dramatically; formally; monstrously; unflatteringly; ruthlessly.
(See reveal, expose.)

DISCLOSURE

adjectives
important; staggering; startling; gradual; cumulating; sensational; diplomatic; dramatic; undeniable; flattering; wide; formal; monstrous.

verbs
anticipate—; guard against—; prepare for —; prevent—; publish—; view—; —accuses; —liberates; —menaces; —precipitates; —reveals; —shocks; —threatens; —unfolds; —yields; —shames.
(See revelation, exhibition, display, discovery.)

DISCOLORATION

adjectives
repulsive; mottled; superficial; unsightly; dark; obtrusive.

DISCOMFIT (*v*)

adverbs
completely; embarrassingly; humiliatingly; momentarily; comically; immediately; spitefully; playfully; calculatedly.
(See humiliate, defeat.)

DISCOMFITURE

adjectives
momentary; comical; old-fashioned; humiliating; nettled; barbed.

DISCOMFORT

adjectives
conscious; visible; emotional; acute; general; agitated; human; prudent; personal; slight; apparent; uncommon; steaming; petty; postprandial; myriad (pl); picturesque; indefinite; sordid; eerie; social; mental; heavy; unendurable; heated; hospitable.

verbs
allay—; alleviate—; chafe in—; chuckle at—; endure—; inflict—; remove—; return with—; share—; suffer—; —disheartens; —dismays; —forces; —grows; —leads; —pains.
(See uneasiness, distress, pain.)

DISCONCERTED

adverbs
embarrassingly; awkwardly; deeply; profoundly; visibly; obviously; painfully; amazingly; terribly; significantly; palpably; vaguely; momentarily; considerably; violently; unmistakably; inexplicably; inadvertently; hopelessly; desperately; irreparably; vexatiously; grievously; glumly; strangely; slightly; mysteriously; oddly.

DISCONSOLATE

adverbs
visibly; apparently; sadly; heavily; pathetically; pitiably; unreasonably; irrationally; appallingly; drearily; grimly; sullenly; resentfully; oddly; ostentatiously; gloomily; biliously; pitifully; profoundly; hopelessly; wearily; desperately; unbearably; unutterably; bitterly; touchingly; genuinely; pensiveiy; mopishly; moodily; dully.

DISCONTENT

adjectives
heavy; economic; real; inevitable; chronic; moderate; prevalent; dreadful; weary; divine; habitual; sullen; desperate; patent; renewed; thoughtful; querulous; perpetual; brawling; thralled; epidemic; popular; vain; moody; gloomy; unruly; smoldering; muttered; latent; futile; growing; impious; sublime; audible; ancient; widespread; aggravating.

verbs
articulate—; awake—; calm—; curse in—; excite—; foment—; murmur—; mutter—; revolt in—; rumble—; seethe with—; sow —; spread—; —afflicts; —flames; —flares; —gathers; —impairs; —sours.
(See dissatisfaction, uneasiness.)

DISCONTINUE (*v*)

adverbs
peremptorily; permanently; temporarily; abruptly; gradually; suddenly; surprisingly; spectacularly.
(See cease, stop.)

DISCORD

adjectives
exquisite; gay; jarring; hidden; ludicrous; mournful; factional; international; jangling; grating; quavering; unmusical; melodious; bitter; unappeasable; striking; distressing; intestinal; inevitable; civic; fluctuant; causeless; lingering; fearful; multitoned.

verbs
accept—; breed—; clash in—; conquer—; correct—; fall to—; ferment—; foment—; hush—; intensify—; master—; overcome—; produce—; silence—; sow—; subject to—;

suffer—; swallow up in—; terminate in—; wipe out—; yield to—; —confounds; —destroys; —follows; —jars; —reigns; —strains.

(See dissension, disagreement, contention, strife, antagonism.)

DISCORDANCE

adjectives

bewildering; complicated; noisy; deafening; incipient; harsh; covert.

DISCORDANT

adverbs

bewilderingly; surprisingly; unexpectedly; unendurably; roughly; harshly; disagreeably; impossibly; intolerably; ludicrously; bitterly; ridiculously; oddly; strangely; exceptionally; shockingly; queerly; strikingly; distressingly; inevitably; racially; essentially; fundamentally; ideologically; unreasonably; distinctly; incongruously; incompatibly; terribly; irreconcilably.

DISCOURAGE (v)

adverbs

sepulchrally; entirely; distinctly; churlishly; wisely; heartbreakingly; pathetically; habitually; profoundly; deeply; unreasonably; ruthlessly; permanently.

(See depress, dishearten.)

DISCOURAGEMENT

adjectives

combined; heartbreaking; pathetic; habitual; profound; countless (pl).

verbs

conceal—; mask—; pretend—; produce—; register—; succumb to—; turn in—; yield to—; —abates; —chills; —dampens; —ensues; —hinders; —obstructs; —oppresses; —suppresses; —depresses.

(See despair, depression, dejection, obstacle.)

DISCOURSE

adjectives

admirable; amiable; gay; pleasant; amusing; instructive; didactic; short; humorous; ingenuous; stirring; amazing; connected; rambling; flagging; rhymed; romantic; eloquent; serious; excellent; pointed; identical; separate; vehement; fallible; intended; doctrinal; harmonic; correct; sweet; voluble; sharp; remarkable; fair; bold; moral; witty; common; erratic; profound; unsympathizing; venial.

verbs

admit in—; change—; comprehend—; control—; delight in—; deliver—; devour—; draw out—; enter into—; fill with—; interchange—; invite—; leave off—; open—; peruse—; publish—; render—; spice—; venture on—; waste—; —differs; —enchants; —ensues; —matures.

(See address, speech, dissertation, oration, conversation.)

DISCOURSE (v)

adverbs

pleasantly; accurately; prophetically; eloquently; abstrusely; incredibly; delightfully; confusingly; impressively; admirably; amiably; gaily; authoritatively; amusingly; instructively; didactically; ingenuously; humorously; stirringly; romantically; ramblingly; volubly; morally; unsympathetically.

(See speak, converse, lecture.)

DISCOURTEOUS

adverbs

churlishly; sullenly; bluntly; snarlingly; angrily; deliberately; offensively; truculently; hotly; ignorantly; intentionally; unwittingly; brutally; harshly; captiously; sulkily; pertly; saucily; repulsively; venomously; perversely; contemptibly; purposely; impudently; shamefully; crudely; roughly; impertinently; disgracefully; inherently; grossly; tactlessly; morosely; arrogantly; boldly; insolently; trenchantly; maliciously; contemptuously.

DISCOURTESY

adjectives

seeming; gross; prevalent; personal; rough; contemptuous.

DISCOVER (v)

adverbs

finally; subsequently; readily; traitorously; astoundingly; amazingly; spectacularly; startlingly; thrillingly; remarkably; stupendously; trivially; miraculously; scientifically; painfully; revolutionizingly; astonishingly; momentously.

(See disclose, ascertain.)

DISCOVERY

adjectives

cheery; delightful; heartening; pleasant; beautiful; astounding; amazing; startling; spectacular; interesting; thrilling; far-reaching; marvelous; remarkable; important; stupendous; paleontological; radical; grievous; awkward; trivial; disconnected; public; godlike; decorative; miraculous;

scientific; striking; painful; epoch-making; bold; notable; pristine; archaeological; grand; useful; initiatory; pictorial; revolutionary; glorious; mineral; laboratory; outward; astonishing; momentous; fatal; salutary; uncomfortable.

verbs
announce—; anticipate—; bring forth—; communicate—; conjure up—; corroborate —; culminate in—; discredit—; examine —; finance—; follow up—; hail—; honor —; lead to—; obtain—; pursue—; report —; stumble on—; verify—; —benefits; —discloses; —reflects; —sheds light on; —underlies.
(See detection, disclosure, revelation, exposure.)

DISCREDITABLE

adverbs
hideously; secretly; subtly; palpably; manifestly; evidently; sadly; terribly; calamitously; foully; abjectly; basely; shamefully; disgracefully; notoriously; scandalously; opprobriously; outrageously; shockingly; appallingly; pitifully.

DISCREET

adverbs
astutely; reasonably; habitually; safely; loyally; admirably; cautiously; warily; wisely; sagaciously; carefully; tremendously; invariably; rarely; absolutely; dependably; naturally; thoughtfully; considerately; oddly; superbly; shrewdly; craftily; marvelously; unerringly; consummately; prudently; vigilantly; cannily; scrupulously; sharply.

DISCREPANCY

adjectives
ironical; peculiar; irreconcilable; slight; curious; minute; embarrassing; minor; frightful; strange.

verbs
admit—; attribute—to; avoid—; clarify—; conceal—; detect—; exhibit—; expose—; harass by—; observe—; overlook—; produce—; remove—; reveal—; search for—; —displeases; —offends; —surprises; —worries.
(See variation, difference, disagreemcnt.)

DISCRETION

adjectives
over-wide; limited; safe; heroic; admirable; tremendous; official; sufficient; arbitrary; peaceable; victorious; unshaken; expert; invariable; rare; absolute; wiser; unrestrained; undefined.

verbs
act with—; answer with—; defer in—; doubt—; employ—; exercise—; guide with —; lack—; leave to—; necessitate—; practise—; preserve with—; school in—; yield to—; —befits; —distinguishes; —separates.
(See prudence, wisdom, judgment.)

DISCRIMINATE (*v*)

adverbs
sharply; nicely; emotionally; mentally; infallibly; racially; carefully; rationally; fastidiously; intelligently; scrupulously; aesthetically; artistically; dramatically; unjustly; sagaciously.
(See distinguish, contrast.)

DISCRIMINATING

adverbs
keenly; carefully; cautiously; expertly; unusually; oddly; shrewdly; nicely; fastidiously; scrupulously; naturally; infallibly; habitually; critically; duly; wisely; sagaciously; impeccably; deeply; sharply; cleverly; thoughtfully; prudently; meticulously; delicately.

DISCRIMINATION

adjectives
nice; emotional; mental; infallible; racial; preconceived; careful; rational; fastidious; intelligent; scrupulous; due; innate; geographical; open; aesthetic; ineffable; unfair; impeccable; artistic; dramatic; unjust; laborious; sensory; sagacious; rare.

verbs
apply—; approve—; attempt—; avoid—; credit—; develop—; employ—; exercise—; imply—; lack—; note—; nourish—; pretend—; tolerate—; touch with—; —bites; —earns; —rewards; —separates; —succeeds; —vexes.
(See difference, distinction.)

DISCURSIVE

adverbs
tediously; garrulously; ramblingly; fascinatingly; interestingly; tiresomely; vexatiously; provokingly; illogically; irrelevantly; disputatiously; prosily; maunderingly; verbosely; digressively; effusively; frothily; palaveringly; chattily; tattlingly; senselessly; loquaciously; pratingly; preachily.

DISCUSS (v)

adverbs

animatedly; calmly; intellectually; glibly; heatedly; unreservedly; widely; exhaustively; seriously; despondently; enigmatically; gravely; academically; audibly; robustly; noisily; eagerly; languidly; critically; lucidly; penetratingly; brilliantly; masterfully; amiably; passionately; argumentatively; violently; vitriolically; challengingly; acutely; ethically; fruitfully; colorfully; extensively; elegantly; frankly; inconclusively; philosophically; protractedly; trivially; pertinently; acridly; reasonably; sympathetically; satisfyingly.

(See argue, debate.)

DISCUSSION

adjectives

lucid; penetrating; brilliant; popular; masterful; amiable; lively; doubtful; friendly; agreeable; noisy; heated; passionate; animated; spirited; brisk; keen; argumentative; violent; vitriolic; challenging; enthusiastic; acute; radical; voluble; calm; dignified; intelligent; serious; thoughtful; embittered; acrimonious; academic; nationwide; unofficial; earnest; curtailed; spicy; lusty; ethical; fruitful; cultural; colorful; intensive; critical; concise; detailed; prearranged; extensive; fiery; unexpected; current; everlasting; elegant; miserable; frank; preliminary; fair; complicated; inconclusive; philosophic; protracted; intolerable; scientific; squalid; productive; unprofitable; perpetual; trivial; free; speculative; excited; political; domestic; salutory; group; metaphysical; stormy; pertinent; theological; wearisome; idle; grave; acrid.

verbs

advocate—; avoid—; balk at—of; block—; break into—; center—upon; characterize —; cut short—; deserve—; dominate—; drag into—; enter—; evoke—; exclude from—; influence—; launch into—; merit—; open—; plunge into—; promote—; provoke —; refrain from—; sidetrack—; —enlightens; —informs; —follows; —opens up; —takes place.

(See debate, argument.)

DISDAIN

adjectives

condescending; supercilious; pardonable; chill; withering; pathetic; haughty; high-toned; quick; icy; cynical; aggressive; bitter; well-bred; invincible; lofty; aristocratic; ineffable; proud; profound; incredulous; unutterable; constructive; uncharitable; scornful; vile; utmost; listless; cold; monotonous; immovable; unquenchable; contemptuous.

verbs

call in—; conceive—; confer—upon; convert to—; cool—; deserve—; disregard—; entertain—for; jeer in—; regard with—; reject with—; reply in—; reproach with—; retire in—; scan with—; sting with—; suffer —; taunt in—; treat with—; turn up one's nose in—; upbraid with—; view with—; wrinkle one's nose in—; —displeases; —embitters; —grows; —infuriates; —melts; —offends; —pierces; —swells; —vexes.

(See contempt, scorn, arrogance.)

DISDAIN (v)

adverbs

sneeringly; churlishly; superciliously; condescendingly; witheringly; icily; haughtily; cynically; bitterly; aristocratically; proudly; uncharitably; scornfully; coldly; contemptuously.

(See shame, scorn.)

DISDAINFUL

adverbs

arrogantly; foolishly; senselessly; fantastically; scornfully; youthfully; superciliously; pathetically; absurdly; ridiculously; ludicrously; laughably; haughtily; icily; loftily; aristocratically; proudly; profoundly; unutterably; uncharitably; humiliatingly; nonchalantly; coolly; bumptiously; blusteringly; brazenly; imperiously; insolently; flippantly; boldly.

DISEASE

adjectives

mental; malignant; lurking; prevalent; hideous; pestilential; casual; vague; infectious; incurable; mystifying; loathsome; obscure; virulent; contagious; incipient; insidious; organic; curious; communicable; subtle; fatal; childish; indigenous; inherent; devastating; corrupting; frightful; tropical; inexorable; dread; devilish; pulmonary; inveterate; epidemic; tumorous; lingering; unconquerable; chronic; bewildering; horrible; secondary; intercurrent; febrile; fungus; advanced; inflammatory; foul; sporadic; moral; constitutional; wasting; unique; well-feigned; long-extinct; progressive; unripe; nutritional; resultant; purulent.

verbs
accelerate—; afflict with—; aggravate—; alleviate—; arrest—; attribute—to; awaken —; battle—; beget—; bow down with—; breed—; carry—; characterize—; check—; combat—; communicate—; complicate—; contract—; control—; convey—; deal with —; detect—; diagnose—; disseminate—; efface—; eliminate—; engender—; eradicate —; exempt from—; expose to—; exterminate—; forestall—; fortify against—; foster —; harden to—; heal—; immunize against —; implant—; import—; induce—; infest with—; inherit—; intensify—; introduce—; isolate—; languish with—; master—; overcome—; predispose to—; recognize—; recover from—; rekindle—; relieve—; resist —; smite with—; stamp out—; succumb to—; suffer from—; transmit—; usher in —; ward off—; wrestle with—; —advances; —breaks out; —consumes; —declines; —destroys; —emaciates; —fastens itself upon; —flourishes; —gains a foothold; —hangs on; —lingers; —lurks; —manifests itself; —menaces; —plagues; —prevails; —progresses; —rages; —ravages; —runs rampant; —spreads; —springs up; —stalks; —strikes; —subsides; —threatens.

(See ailment, disorder, malady, pestilence, plague, epidemic.)

DISEASED

adverbs
horribly; unfortunately; appallingly; pitiably; cankerously; pitifully; pathetically; awfully; disgustingly; alarmingly; dangerously; mentally; hideously; incurably; irremediably; irrecoverably; infectiously; virulently; insidiously; organically; curiously; fatally; inherently; congenitally; frightfully; chronically; morally.

DISFAVOR

adjectives
absolute; mingled; high; stern; increasing; lasting; bitter.

verbs
bring into—; deserve—; dispense—; draw —of; earn—; experience—; fall into—; familiarize with—; incur—; mar with—; pour—; pretend—; regard with—; roar—; shower—; spread—; taste—; —affects; —attends; —handicaps; —hinders.

(See disapproval, dislike.)

DISFIGURED

adverbs
grotesquely; queerly; crookedly; horribly; strangely; fantastically; grossly; grimly; hopelessly; terribly; shamefully; tragically; slightly; odiously; repulsively; pitifully; pathetically; comically; bitterly; deliberately.

DISGRACE

adjectives
hideous; concealed; unmitigable; bewailed; final; crying; sad; eternal; calamitous; nominal; intolerable; foul; invisible; pardonless; indelible; manifold; infinite; glorified; personal; continual; inescapable.

verbs
acknowledge—; augment—; betray—; bewail—; derive—; dishonor with—; dread —; experience—; fall into—; heap—upon; incur—; join in—; lay—upon; lie in—; reflect—; revenge—; rise from—; shrink from—; subject to—; suffer—; sustain—; —blemishes; —deprives; —mars; —shames; —undoes.

(See reproach, infamy, ignominy, disrepute, dishonor.)

DISGRACE (v)

adverbs
publicly; wrongfully; hideously; finally; eternally; calamitously; intolerably; infinitely; personally; wantonly; spitefully; intentionally; revengefully.

(See humiliate, shame.)

DISGRACED

adverbs
permanently; shamefully; terribly; odiously; horribly; sadly; calamitously; disastrously; eternally; momentarily; inexplicably; inescapably; palpably; personally; deeply; darkly; disreputably; notoriously; publicly; outrageously; pathetically; deservedly.

DISGRACEFUL

adverbs
outrageously; wickedly; infamously; scandalously; brutally; flagrantly; atrociously; criminally; dissolutely; foully; hideously; unmitigably; intolerably; indelibly; unforgettably; grossly; shamelessly; patently; palpably; unmistakably; utterly; inexpressibly.

DISGRUNTLED

adverbs
obscurely; bitterly; distinctly; obviously; visibly; openly; inevitably; vaguely; nat-

urally; understandably; sorely; frankly; seriously; fiercely; silently; evidently; sullenly; quietly; wretchedly; miserably; fretfully; peevishly.

DISGUISE

adjectives
neutral; clever; absurd; thin; mystical; inanimate; terror-striking; strange; modest; filthy; effective; reverend; deceptive; extraordinary; impenetrable; customary; smiling; logical; credulous; troublesome; opaque; desperate.

verbs
assume—; attempt—; cloak with—; contrive—; counterfeit by—; deck in—; detect —; don—; invent—; lurk beneath—; penetrate—; pierce—; recognize—; see through —; strip off—; take refuge in—; throw off—; —alters; —conceals; —deceives; —disfigures; —masks; —misleads; —succeeds; —transforms.
(See pretense, mask, cloak, dress, costume.)

DISGUISE (*v*)

adverbs
perfectly; handsomely; cleverly; absurdly; thinly; mystically; strangely; effectively; deceptively; extraordinarily; slyly; logically; subtly.
(See mask, cloak.)

DISGUISED

adverbs
cleverly; absurdly; thinly; strangely; modestly; effectively; deceptively; extraordinarily; impenetrably; mysteriously; exactly; ridiculously; cryptically; furtively; stealthily; darkly; inviolately; secretly; palpably; harmlessly; falsely; fraudulently; unfairly; maliciously; artfully; perfidiously; mischievously; skilfully; comically; trickily; successfully; completely.

DISGUST

adjectives
implacable; sharp; vast; exasperated; angry; outraged; inherent; profound; creeping; shuddering; secret; icy; silent; honest; personal; evident; furious; intense; sheer; indignant; intolerable; weary; mingled; infinite; considerable; mutual; supreme; deep; sullen; philosophical; sickened; cruel; loathing; bewildered; excessive; previous; violent.

verbs
arouse—; assert—; attend with—; awake —; conquer—; control—; depict—; drown —; excite—; raise—; retreat in—; sicken in—; shun in—; shrug—; —deters; —dissuades; —nauseates; —offends; —wounds.
(See aversion, abhorrence, repugnance, distaste.)

DISGUST (*v*)

adverbs
presumably; thoroughly; implacably; profoundly; secretly; personally; evidently; intensely; intolerably; considerably; mutually; supremely; cruelly; loathingly; excessively; violently.
(See revolt, offend.)

DISGUSTED

adverbs
immeasurably; terribly; utterly; bitterly; painfully; intolerably; dreadfully; tremendously; exceedingly; morally; heartily; secretly; obviously; openly; sharply; profoundly; intensely; deeply; violently.

DISH

adjectives
humble; distinguished; glorious; different; tempting; delicious; time-honored; warmed-over; exotic; appetizing; delicate; fattening; sumptuous; velvet; lordly; rattling; tempting; priceless; savory; attractive; fascinating; toothsome; succulent; elaborate; unwholesome; economical; earthen; kingly; chafing; tasty; pewter; substantial; rich; sparkling; unornamental; fatal; fragile; glittering; nutritious; strange; clean; dirty; anomalous; conventional.

verbs
cover—; devour—; dip into—; eschew—; garnish—; hurl—; pile—; relish—; sauce —; scour—; serve—; smash—; sprinkle—; wipe—; —clatters; —nourishes; —rattles.
(See plate, platter, cup, food.)

DISHEARTEN (*v*)

adverbs
dismally; inwardly; decidedly; partially; purposely; unintentionally; completely; tragically; finally.
(See discourage, depress.)

DISHEARTENED

adverbs
profoundly; exceedingly; pathetically; deeply; remarkably; extremely; mysteriously; significantly; vaguely; completely; intense-

ly; utterly; miserably; wretchedly; wearily; finally; increasingly; signally; inexplicably; unaccountably; strangely; oddly; queerly.

DISHEVELED

adverbs
carelessly; negligently; wildly; merrily; laughably; shamefully; thoughtlessly; terribly; exceedingly; blithely; indifferently; untidily; recklessly; lazily; rudely; heedlessly; lumpishly.

DISHONEST

adverbs
instinctively; inherently; innately; naturally; characteristically; traditionally; slyly; racially; insidiously; invidiously; shrewdly; fiendishly; maliciously; astoundingly; trickily; surreptitiously; habitually; speciously; manifestly; essentially; abominably; detestably.

DISHONESTY

adjectives
rank; mercantile; unself-conscious; childlike; acquired.

verbs
accuse of—; conceal—; convict of—; cover —; deny—; dispose to—; expose—; renounce—; reveal—; tempt to—; uncover —; —colors; —defiles; —disgraces; —scars; —shames; —stains; —violates; —wanes.

(See fraud, cheating.)

DISHONOR

adjectives
whispered; partial; foul; ultimate; deathless; base.

verbs
bear—; bring into—; clothe in—; defile with—; die in—; meet with—; plague by—; pronounce—; root in—; sow—; stain with —; suffer—; tempt with—; tread down in—; undergo—; —blemishes; —blurs; —hounds; —lies.

(See insult, reproach, disgrace, disrepute.)

DISHONORED

adverbs
scandalously; distinctly; notoriously; infamously; publicly; permanently; unutterably; indelibly; irremediably; unforgettably; desperately; ignominiously; basely; shamefully; unjustly; unfairly; opprobriously; foully; reportedly; allegedly; immeasurably; immensely.

DISILLUSION

adjectives
stupendous; postwar; chill; bitter; heartbreaking.

DISILLUSION (*v*)

adverbs
precipitately; cruelly; completely; politely; immodestly; frankly; unthinkingly; abruptly; fiendishly; shrewdly; wisely; foolishly.

(See free, liberate.)

DISILLUSIONED

adverbs
pitiably; miserably; wretchedly; sadly; suddenly; early; unhappily; unexpectedly; cruelly; bitterly; dismally; grimly; appallingly; tremendously; inconsolably; despairingly; hopelessly; heartbreakingly.

DISILLUSIONMENT

adjectives
cruel; unembittered; complete; furious; devastating; haughty; polite.

verbs
increase—; incur—; move to—; protect against—; reject—; suffer—; —ages; —banishes; —begets; —depresses; —descends; —disappoints; —displaces; —frees from; —rocks; —sets in; —settles over; —shatters; revenge—; —arouses.

DISINCLINATION

adjectives
intolerable; deep-rooted; definite; stubborn; unreasoning.

DISINFECTANT

adverbs
effectively; infallibly; powerfully; extremely; heroically; mildly; perfectly; soothingly; correctively; specifically; simply; safely; beneficially; advantageously; commendably; highly; essentially; intrinsically.

DISINFECTION

adjectives
efficient; rigorous; unstinted; disciplinary; punitive.

verbs
practise—; subject to—; —destroys; —guards against; —nauseates; —offends; —ousts; —overcomes; —prevents; —purifies; —rejects; —routs; —safeguards.

DISINHERITED

adverbs

unfairly; unfortunately; properly; unjustly; deservedly; unluckily; miserably; wretchedly; crushingly; summarily; audaciously; cruelly; deliberately; curtly; wrongfully; unwarrantably; inexcusably; unreasonably; inauspiciously; logically.

DISINTEGRATE (*v*)

adverbs

deliberately; steadily; relentlessly; rapidly; financially; slowly; hopelessly; mentally; socially; progressively; internally; abruptly; completely; locally.

(See crumble, decay.)

DISINTEGRATION

adjectives

rapid; financial; slow; relentless; hopeless; mental; social.

verbs

blast into—; break into—; control—; demand—; detach by—; effect—; expose to—; hasten—; influence—; produce—; tend toward—; undergo—; —blurs; —destroys; —modifies; —multiplies; —proceeds from; —reduces; —separates; —sets in.

(See decay, decomposition.)

DISINTERESTED

adverbs

personally; truly; neutrally; sufficiently; obviously; manifestly; satisfactorily; demonstrably; sternly; judiciously; honestly; undeniably; avowedly; acceptably.

DISK

(*see disc*)

adjectives

scintillating; whirling; rotating; advancing; menacing.

verbs

affix—; emerge from—; grind—; hollow—; hurl—; mount—; roll—; send—; shape—; shoot—; strike—; whirl—; —careens; —loops; —protects; —revolves; — rises; —rotates.

(See plate.)

DISLIKE

adjectives

profound; inordinate; violent; instinctive; active; malicious; deep; intense; maddening; involuntary; abnormal; innate; virulent; entire; fundamental; colonial; mutual; haughty; peculiar; ardent; reasoned; expressed; incurable; foolish; irrational; everlasting; contemptuous; personal.

verbs

betray—; conceal—; consider with—; feed—; feign—; fume—; grow into—; harbor—for; impel by—; incur—; kindle—; mask—; regard with—; shudder with—; subject to—; warrant—.

(See distaste, repugnance, aversion, antipathy, hatred.)

DISLIKE (*v*)

adverbs

strongly; inherently; notoriously; heartily; profoundly; inordinately; violently; instinctively; maliciously; deeply; intensely; maddeningly; involuntarily; virulently; fundamentally; mutually; incurably; irrationally; personally; contemptuously; cordially.

(See disapprove, hate.)

DISLOCATE (*v*)

adverbs

dreadfully; fatally; tragically; calamitously; critically; severely; cruelly; devastatingly.

(See separate, dislodge.)

DISLOCATION

adjectives

serious; complex; cursory; temporary; tentative; remediable.

verbs

adjust—; bind—; cure—; exercise—; force—; impede—; involve—; place in—; prevent—; produce—; suffer—; submit to—; treat for—; —alarms; —pains; —swells.

(See displacement, disorder.)

DISLODGE (*v*)

adverbs

successfully; viciously; brutally; triumphantly; vigorously; severely; expeditiously; resolutely.

(See remove, eject.)

DISLOYAL

adverbs

shamefully; treacherously; perfidiously; disgracefully; extremely; secretly; publicly; boldly; cruelly; basely; subtly; bitterly; openly; unpardonably; incredibly; surprisingly; unexpectedly; eventually; shabbily;

tremendously; abjectly; unutterably; unscrupulously; **infamously**; **contemptibly**; **ingloriously.**

DISMAL

adverbs
drearily; drably; lonesomely; abjectly; disconsolately; irremediably; soddenly; sadly; wretchedly; excessively; irrecoverably; deeply; horribly; profoundly; incorrigibly; incurably; darkly; solemnly; anxiously; sombrely; despondently; fixedly; sullenly; heavily; dangerously; ominously; cheerlessly; intensely; terribly.

DISMAY

adjectives
incredulous; unutterable; direct; pale; goggle-eyed; stark; nameless; evident; vague; abject; dumb; genuine; dawning; dark; terrified; alarmed; extreme; mad; immeasurable; utter; indescribable; ineffable; panic-stricken.

verbs
contemplate—; cope with—; discover—; heap—; mitigate—; paralyze with—; read —; recoil in—; rout—; shake with—; spread—; swoon with—; view with—; —daunts; —defeats; —discourages; —engulfs; —threatens.
(See consternation, terror, alarm, fear.)

DISMAY (v)

adverbs
thoroughly; abjectly; dumbly; genuinely; extremely; immeasurably; utterly; indescribably; bullyingly.
(See alarm, frighten.)

DISMAYED

adverbs
unaccountably; deeply; profoundly; unreasonably; illogically; dreadfully; alarmingly; fearfully; incredibly; starkly; evidently; vaguely; abjectly; genuinely; terribly; extremely; immeasurably; significantly; utterly; indescribably; remarkably; notably visibly; wildly; bewilderingly.

DISMISS (v)

adverbs
reluctantly; summarily; finally; courteously; instantly; contemptuously; flatly; lightly; curtly; abruptly; harshly; ignominiously; impudently; brusquely; uncouthly.
(See discharge, banish.)

DISMISSAL

adjectives
contemptuous; harsh; ignominious; brusque; impudent; abrupt; summary; instant; immediate.

verbs
annul—; bow—; counsel—; demand—; denounce—; indicate—; justify—; order—; punish by—; request—; seek—; suffer—; threaten with—; urge—; wave—; —discourages; —liberates; —rectifies; —releases; —sets free.
(See discharge, removal.)

DISOBEDIENCE

adjectives
continued; alleged; filial; repeated; defiant; wilful; persistent.

verbs
construe as—; correct—; express—; fall into—; foster—; instigate—; nourish—; punish for—; reprimand for—; revenge—; rue—; subscribe to—; —annoys; —begets; —develops; —erupts; —irks.
(See defiance.)

DISOBEDIENT

adverbs
stubbornly; obstinately; impudently; impertinently; insolently; arrogantly; constantly; continually; haughtily; obdurately; peevishly; boldly; openly; flagrantly; invidiously; sullenly; morosely; carelessly; wildly; inexcusably; unduly; deliberately; consciously; flauntingly; laughingly; brazenly; allegedly; provokingly; extremely; dreadfully; rebelliously; resentfully; defiantly; restively; impatiently; resolutely.

DISORDER

adjectives
allergic; emotional; turbulent; careless; forlorn; homelike; miry; tousled; musty; unparalleled; wild; lawless; riotous; diffuse; frightful; inconsistent; tumultuous; frenzied; virulent; violent; considerable; moving; curing; gay; infectious; mental; prevailing; direst; accumulated; seeming; spasmodic; strange; degenerate; nutritional; infantile; grave; spiritual; underlying; momentary; current; shameful; neurotic; statistic; extreme; deep-seated; admired; contagious; curious; chaotic; physical; picturesque; complete; pleasant; inconceivable; ensuing; chronic; half-mended; infernal; indescribable; harlequinesque; nervous; radical; immaculate; moral.

verbs
accompany—; ascribe to—; benefit—; caution against—; fall into—; foment—; indicate—; introduce—; plague with—; produce —; relieve—; remedy—; remove—; rout—; spring from—; succumb to—; vanquish—; —surges ahead; —threatens.
(See confusion, chaos, disturbance.)

DISORDERLY

adverbs
remarkably; notoriously; turbulently; truculently; outrageously; noisily; flagrantly; violently; wildly; riotously; lawlessly; frightfully; gayly; uproariously; convivially; genially; laughingly; daringly; inconsiderately; indescribably; inconceivably; ungovernably; uncontrollably; curiously; contagiously; momentarily; mutinously; gravely; alarmingly; ominously; significantly; terrifyingly; tumultuously; tempestuously; viciously; extravagantly; excitedly.

DISPARAGEMENT

adjectives
caustic; cynical; systematic; ruthless; unsparing; merciless.

verbs
bring into—; commit—; deserve—; express —; hurl—; impose—; intend—; involve in—; justify—; lose by—; reproach for—; speak—; vilify with—; —annoys; —belittles; —degrades; —disgraces.

DISPASSIONATE

adverbs
imperturbably; provokingly; vexatiously; serenely; calmly; deeply; immovably; apparently; dreadfully; coldly; completely; carelessly; nonchalantly; discouragingly; utterly; singularly; stolidly; stonily; coolly; soberly; judicially; sagely; wisely; securely; tranquilly; placidly; philosophically; tolerantly.

DISPATCH

adjectives
calamitous; hostile; amazing; quick; marvelous; summary; rapid; convenient; diplomatic; hourly; insolent; elaborate; amended; swift; equal; vivid; detailed; telegraphic; simultaneous; importunate; important; explanatory; outspoken; uncensored; satisfactory; frequent (pl).

verbs
announce—; arrive with—; attend to—; cable—; carry—; convey—; deliver—; depart with—; hasten—; leave on—; obey—; order—; receive—; relay—; report—; rush —; seal—; send—; smuggle in—; speed—; transfer.
(See message, telegram.)

DISPATCH (*v*)

adverbs
mercifully; secretly; summarily; rapidly; diplomatically; insolently; telegraphically; swiftly; simultaneously; satisfactorily; frequently; conveniently; hastily.
(See send, forward.)

DISPEL (*v*)

adverbs
effectually; instantly; immediately; entirely; frankly; innocently; humanely; charmingly; testily.
(See withdraw, dissipate.)

DISPENSATION

adjectives
benign; critical; merciful; mysterious; special; divine; providential; heavenly; frugal; afflicting; artistic; favorable.

verbs
administer—; allow—; arrange—; claim—; conduct—; deliver—; deserve—; grant—; manage—; obtain—; order—; provide—; receive—; require—; reward with—; seek —; sue for—; undertake—; urge—; warrant—; —distributes; —pardons; —releases.
(See distribution, pardon, exemption.)

DISPENSE (*v*)

adverbs
vicariously; bountifully; gracefully; liberally; naturally; mercifully; divinely; providentially; frugally.
(See distribute, administer.)

DISPLACEMENT

adjectives
sympathetic; successive (pl); unmerited; slight; hazardous; careless; capacious.

verbs
indicate—; occasion—; order—; request—; seek—; set—; threaten with—; —disposes of; —embarrasses; —liberates; —occurs; —rectifies; —releases; —remedies; —shifts.
(See removal, discharge, dismissal.)

DISPLAY

adjectives
alluring; ceremonial; enviable; ostentatious; tawdry; unrivaled; garish; blatant;

enchanting; gorgeous; grisly; creditable; pitiful; emotional; lurid; audacious; glaring; splendid; obtrusive; amazing; magnificent; appropriate; lavish; legitimate; ludicrous; frequent (pl); color; thaumaturgic; remarkable; aggravating; autumnal; fabulous; breath-taking; triumphant; fanatical; heroic; pedantic; attractive; modern; gaudy; mass; beautiful; official; merciless; singular; wild; arresting; material; prominent; extraordinary; romantic; single-handed; elaborate; vast; brilliant; haunting; many-colored; prodigal; boasted; vulgar; maladroit; provocative; vivid; mere; admirable; barbarous; temporary; tasteful; profuse; superfluous; quixotic; childish; unfortunate; dazzling; fan-shaped.

verbs
abhor—; adorn—; arrange—; feed on—; furnish—; gape at—; nose among—s; prepare—; unfurl—; view—; wonder at—; —advertises; —appeals; —attracts; —describes; —exhibits; —explains; —expresses; —glitters; —represents; —unfolds.
(See exhibition, show.)

DISPLAY (*v*)

adverbs
pompously; flamboyantly; tastefully; magnificently; realistically; conspicuously; charmingly; habitually; refreshingly; equally; palpably; ostentatiously; vaingloriously; smartly; temptingly; vulgarly; eminently; lavishly; dazzlingly; entrancingly; alluringly; ceremonially; garishly; blatantly; pitifully; audaciously; legitimately; mercilessly; ludicrously; singularly; prodigally; temporarily; superfluously.
(See exhibit, expose.)

DISPLEASE (*v*)

adverbs
stupidly; purposely; markedly; unsophisticatedly; rudely; frankly; seriously; pettishly; ungenerously; lastingly; coldly; boorishly; carelessly; inadvertently.
(See anger, offend.)

DISPLEASED

adverbs
remarkably; extravagantly; extremely; uneasily; wearily; anxiously; miserably; unreasonably; unaccountably; sorely; heavily; horribly; vexedly; painfully; grievously; bitterly; cheerlessly; fiercely; savagely; markedly; visibly; openly; frankly; seriously; permanently; implacably; coldly; alarmingly; dangerously; unspeakably; profoundly; deeply; inordinately; justly; rightly.

DISPLEASURE

adjectives
smothered; surprised; fierce; marked; sore; sovereign; unsophisticated; frank; everlasting; serious; noble; petty; ungenerous; lasting; cold; divine.

verbs
avoid—; conceal—; display—; dread—; heighten—; incur—; indicate—; languish in—; meet with—; occasion—; provoke—; risk—; shoulder—; signify—; snort—; —annoys; —irks; —mounts; —overwhelms.
(See dissatisfaction, vexation, dislike, resentment, disapproval.)

DISPOSE (*v*)

adverbs
carelessly; antagonistically; religiously; briefly; favorably; symmetrically; ornamentally; effectually; graciously; immediately; variously; gracefully; peaceably; coolly; effectively.
(See settle, adjust.)

DISPOSITION

adjectives
pacific; amenable; amiable; covetous; docile; morose; winsome; credulous; mercurial; bromidic; penurious; depraved; petulant; avaricious; peevish; jovial; bad; sweet; equable; contentious; balky; impetuous; fiery; angelic; vivacious; unyielding; confiding; cheery; vacillating; sunny; sullen; bitter; eager; cordial; raving; delicate; characteristic; generous; noble; litigious; rough; envious; well-oiled; jealous; vicious; masterful; dreamy; increasing; testamentary; passionate; princely; violent; chilly; humane; puerile; stubborn; contemplative; unconquerable; melancholy; inquisitive; affectionate; bloodthirsty; resolute; tractable; pious; dogged; ungodly; virtuous; commiserating; natural; excellent; romantic; kind; similar; charming; pliant; stupid; tame; grateful; tranquil; speculative; favorable; skillful; alert; neurotic; suitable; innate; ingenuous; friendly; adventurous; traitorous; faithful; indolent; eager; shirking; sociable; prevailing; incomprehensible; unpredictable; classic; combative; tunable; phlegmatic; peremptory; dangerous; buoyant; secret; magnificent; thoughtful; brooding; aesthetic; primitive; humane; amicable; irregular;

submissive; methodical; venomous; fantastical; timid; hereditary; restless; roving; retiring; imperious; absolute; noxious; further; hysterical.

verbs
abuse—; admire—; alter—; change—; complete—; consider—; contrive—; derange—; disguise—; evince—; excuse—; indulge—; inherit—; judge—; punish—; soften—; sour—; specify—; submit to—; touch—; view—; —comprehends; —inclines; —precipitates; —restores; —secures.
(See mood, will, propensity, inclination, tendency, temperament.)

DISPOSSESS (*v*)

adverbs
forcibly; legally; harshly; irregularly; doggedly; calmly; cruelly; selfishly.
(See eject, remove.)

DISPUTANT

adjectives
scientific; forensic; obstinate; moral; voiceless; excited.

DISPUTATION

adjectives
public; scholastic; private; learned; religious; doubtful; prodigious; wrangling.

DISPUTATIOUS

adverbs
troublesomely; immensely; tremendously; egregiously; elaborately; intricately; eccentrically; egotistically; loftily; superciliously; tyrannically; dogmatically; extremely; learnedly; academically; provokingly; disagreeably; unpleasantly; obtrusively; officiously; conceitedly; astutely; pugnaciously; hotly; captiously; churlishly; remarkably; marvellously.

DISPUTE

adjectives
doctrinal; theological; inevitable; learned; angry; bitter; dull; vain; laughing; demoralizing; serious; uncontrollable; pending; cold; international; academic; free; conceivable; long-standing; violent; notable; fierce; perpetual; territorial; fruitless; factional; leisurely.

verbs
adjudicate—; adjust—; arbitrate—; beguile into—; conciliate—; meditate—; quash—; quell—; solve—; suppress—; take part in—; —arises; —bubbles; —evaporates; —flares up; —foreshadows; —overshadows; —rages.
(See discussion, contest, controversy, quarrel.)

DISPUTE (*v*)

adverbs
skillfully; acrimoniously; consciously; angrily; subsequently; inhumanly; successfully; publicly; privately; religiously; prodigiously; fiercely.
(See argue, wrangle.)

DISQUIET

adjectives
vague; emotional; constant; restless; growing.

DISQUIET (*v*)

adverbs
chiefly; solely; thoroughly; abruptly; subtly.
(See alarm, disturb.)

DISQUIETUDE

adjectives
serious; vague; mental; extreme.

verbs
arouse—; fear—; fill with—; infest with—; occasion—; pass with—; relay—; sow—; subject to—; trouble with—; view with—; wait with—; —alarms; —disturbs; —envelops; —spreads.
(See alarm, anxiety, fear, agitation.)

DISQUISITION

adjectives
political; clever; popular; lengthy; wordy; learned.

DISREGARD

adjectives
insane; cynical; reckless; defiant; persistent; total; unabashed; bland; pagan; brutal; generous; utter; blithe; calm; benevolent; selfish; cruel; jaunty; entire; drunken; astonishing; habitual; strange; superb; apparent; contemptuous; sublime; peremptory.

DISREGARD (*v*)

adverbs
incessantly; chronically; totally; utterly; contemptuously; insanely; cynically; recklessly; defiantly; persistently; totally; unabashedly; blandly; brutally; generously;

utterly; blithely; calmly; benevolently; recklessly; entirely; habitually; sublimely; peremptorily; selfishly.

(See ignore, overlook.)

DISREPUTABLE

adverbs

notoriously; infamously; exceedingly; generally; utterly; scandalously; opprobriously; fearfully; dissolutely; admittedly; villainously; grossly; drunkenly; coarsely; shamefully; horribly; remarkably; incredibly; unbelievably; abjectly; pitifully; ingloriously; shockingly; atrociously; viciously.

DISREPUTE

adjectives

(See disgrace.)

verbs

beget—; bring into—; clothe in—; cure of —; depart in—; disguise—; fall into—; ignore—; incur—; indicate—; instigate—; leave in—; return in—; vow—; —dampens; —excludes; —showers; —underlies.

(See disgrace, dishonor.)

DISRESPECT

adjectives

(See rudeness.)

verbs

augment—; bear—; disguise—; display—; free from—; manifest—; mention with—; nourish—; proceed from—; reprimand for —; smother—; stoop to—; suffer—; tolerate—; —indicates; —profanes; —troubles.

(See dishonor, rudeness.)

DISRESPECTFUL

adverbs

irreverently; boundlessly; utterly; blandly; recklessly; persistently; defiantly; totally; brutally; cruelly; entirely; impiously; jauntily; rashly; boldly; astonishingly; elaborately; ostentatiously; openly; habitually; chronically; strangely; particularly; peculiarly; contemptuously; disparagingly; derisively; ironically; rudely; bumptiously.

DISSATISFACTION

adjectives

unending; personal; prevailing; universal; seeming; increasing; evident; undifferentiated; rebellious; widespread.

verbs

anticipate—; be subject to—; beget—; conduct with—; confine—; exhibit—; experience—; express—; occasion—; overcome —; pretend—; smother—; veil—; —disquiets; —irks; —perplexes.

(See discontent, disapproval, displeasure.)

DISSATISFIED

adverbs

slightly; vaguely; wholly; strangely; entirely; increasingly; palpably; evidently; visibly; openly; sullenly; morosely; secretly; obviously; deeply; desperately; horribly; querulously; glumly; gloomily; austerely; sternly; implacably; crabbedly; perversely; continually.

DISSECT (*v*)

adverbs

mercilessly; tranquilly; scientifically; studiously; thoroughly; painstakingly; absorbedly.

(See cut, criticize.)

DISSEMBLE (*v*)

adverbs

politely; slyly; deeply; artfully; skillfully; ingeniously.

(See hide, conceal.)

DISSEMINATE (*v*)

adverbs

widely; unsparingly; insidiously; nationally; universally.

(See spread, circulate.)

DISSENSION

adjectives

considerable; frightful; irreconcilable; humiliating; internal; bitter; sharp; disastrous; factional; growing; intestinal; grave; turbulent; angry; perpetual.

verbs

brew—; crush—; excite—; halt—; incite —; instigate—; investigate—; review—; stir with—; —arises; —breaks out; —flares; —grows; —menaces; —tears; —threatens.

(See discord, strife, quarrel, contention, feud.)

DISSENT

adjectives

metaphysical; profound; internal; grave; effective; ignorant; ill-natured.

verbs
accept—; apprehend—; arouse—; constitute—; enter—; explain—; free of—; ignore—; interpose—; overlook—; question —; tolerate—; trace—; voice—; —prevails; —sunders.
(See disagreement, difference.)

DISSERTATION

adjectives
moral; illuminating; exhaustive; stilted; learned; rhapsodic; elaborate; pedantic; physiological; scholarly.

verbs
absorb in—; censor—; compose—; criticize—; dedicate—to; engage in—; launch upon—; level—at; pause in—; prepare—; study—; —carries; —concerns; —discusses; —treats.
(See discourse, speech, lecture.)

DISSIMULATION

adjectives
polite; deft; practiced; splendid; skilled.

DISSIPATE (v)

adverbs
abruptly; partially; voluptuously; senselessly; reprehensibly; carelessly; excessively; incessantly; disgustingly; jovially; recklessly; fashionably; tragically; thoughtlessly.
(See dispel.)

DISSIPATION

adjectives
voluptuous; senseless; reprehensible; careless; excessive; mild; incessant; besetting; solitary; minor; disgusting; jovial; reckless; polished; recreative; fashionable.

verbs
consume by—; defy—; denounce—; engage in—; imbibe in—; investigate—; lose in—; practise—; relinquish—; squander in—; warn against—; —corrupts; —endangers; —enslaves; —grinds; —penalizes; —wears.
(See diversion, crime.)

DISSOLUTE

adverbs
frightfully; utterly; irretrievably; gracelessly; irremediably; boundlessly; wantonly; recklessly; grossly; wildly; shamelessly; outrageously; perversely; irreclaimably; senselessly; remarkably; grotesquely; manifestly; abysmally; lawlessly; disgracefully; criminally; obdurately; heinously; gravely; sensually; intemperately; rakishly.

DISSOLUTENESS

adjectives
frightful; reckless; ferocious.

DISSOLUTION

adjectives
impending; natural; continual; ultimate.

DISSOLVE (v)

adverbs
partly; mutually; mysteriously; harmlessly; entirely; thoroughly; perfectly; experimentally.
(See melt.)

DISSONANCE

adjectives
excruciating; wild; unpleasant; barbarous; weird; raucous; harsh.

DISTANCE

adjectives
hazy; mean; weary; legendary; celestial; deepest; drowsy; magnificent; shooting; dusty; tantalizing; spacious; untold; extreme; impossible; obscure; safe; unattainable; perihelion; zenith; infinite; considerable; entire; visible; cautious; respectful; widening; exquisite; excessive; proportionate; inaccessible; twinkling; vast; unvarying; surlier; inscrutable; musket-shot; hailing; limited; unknown; inadequate; supporting; remote; short; surprising; observing; terrible; uncertain; linear; measured; delicate; mellow; dimmer; indefinite; required; insurmountable; discreet; sufficient; pathless; beautiful; unapproachable; ever-increasing; misty; retrospective; walking; previous; assaulting; unbridgeable; riding; running; dangerous; mean; enormous; indeterminate; broadening.

verbs
annihilate—; estimate—; fade in—; fall at—; indicate—; mark—; measure—; proportion—; rise in—; span—; stand in—; traverse—; —alienates; —enchants; —lends; hold at—.
(See space.)

DISTASTE

adjectives
profound; sordid; intellectual; furious; extreme; scornful; cynical; patient; passionate; startling; evident.

verbs
banish—; bring into—; conceive—for; cultivate—for; develop—; dismiss—; excite—; express—; heal—; imply—; inherit—; nourish—; pamper—; possess—for; produce—; regard with—; relinquish—; rescue from —; view with—; —develops; —implies; —menaces.
(See aversion, dislike, antipathy.)

DISTASTEFUL

adverbs
horribly; deeply; profoundly; sordidly; intellectually; furiously; extremely; exaggeratedly; startlingly; shockingly; inordinately; extraordinarily; remarkably; immensely; dreadfully; evidently; manifestly; palpably; fundamentally; essentially; sickeningly; nauseatingly; sorrily; plaguedly; bitterly; grimly; frightfully.

DISTENSION

adjectives
pale; chronic; acute; pestilential; fatal; feminine.

DISTENTION

verbs
attend with—; blow into—; conceal—; fill to—; force into—; guard against—; imbibe to—; inflate to—; labor under—; prevent—; produce—; protect from—; —follows; —harms; —injures; —pains; —sunders.
(See expansion, inflation.)

DISTILL (v)

adverbs
imperceptibly; specially; powerfully; elaborately; delicately; experimentally; expertly; painstakingly.

DISTILLATION

adjectives
elaborate; strong; renewed; delicate; powerful.

DISTINCT

adverbs
particularly; cruelly; meticulously; precisely; exactly; easily; accurately; wonderfully; especially; clearly; emphatically; separately; effectively; powerfully.

DISTINCTION

adjectives
striking; pedantic; arresting; moral; sweeping; manifest; artificial; crude; material; considerable; supreme; theoretical; grave; philosophic; fundamental; military; superfluous; arbitrary; ethical; social; exclusive; unreal; cruel; topographical; solid; trade; unusual; ancient; perceptible; unhappy; obvious; immediate; dubious; essential; man-made; additional; unique; sage; minor; threefold; nervous; racial; deep; literary; ephemeral; financial; singular; subtle; natural; sole; invidious; repugnant; family; color; worldly; coveted; grand; preeminent; unenviable; individual; popular; groundless; slender; fleeting; fanciful; frivolous; honorable; constitutional; sensible; moral; race; artistic; broad; innate; particular; careless; visible; inglorious.

verbs
achieve—; attain—; blur—; carry—; convey—; discern—; draw—; earn—; enhance —; grant—; hunger for—; level—; maintain—; obliterate—; obtain—; perceive—; perpetuate—; recognize—; reduce—; sense —; serve with—; trace—; uphold—; warrant—; yearn for—; yield—.
(See eminence, prominence, renown.)

DISTINCTNESS

adjectives
surprising; exquisite; sufficient; arbitrary; tragic; unmistakable; vivid; considerable; growing; luminous.

DISTINGUISH (v)

adverbs
curiously; logically; justly; pedantically; crudely; theoretically; philosophically; fundamentally; arbitrarily; obviously; uniquely; sagely; singularly; subtly; invidiously; unenviably; groundlessly; fancifully; frivolously; sensibly; morally; artistically; broadly; scientifically.
(See discriminate, discern.)

DISTINGUISHABLE

adverbs
easily; readily; generally; entirely; particularly; diversely; divergently; differentially; broadly; carefully; instantly; conveniently; immediately; altogether; separately; unmistakably; plainly; decidedly; satisfactorily; positively; definitely; absolutely; clearly.

DISTINGUISHED

adverbs
brilliantly; extraordinarily; internationally; academically; illustriously; notably; remarkably; admirably; matchlessly; profes-

sionally; prominently; nationally; supremely; impressively; splendidly; augustly; imperishably; ecclesiastically; heroically; immortally; honorably; enviably; eminently; strikingly; manifestly; singularly.

DISTORT (v)

adverbs
momentarily; painfully; fatally; obviously; ludicrously; hideously; fantastically; insanely; madly; jokingly; fiendishly
(See twist, misrepresent.)

DISTORTED

adverbs
wilfully; perniciously; purposely; deliberately; deceptively; visibly; obviously; clearly; palpably; frightfully; excessively; dreadfully; intentionally; falsely; adroitly; craftily; wickedly; academically; disputatiously; remarkably; fatally; elaborately; completely; partially; loosely; fantastically; grotesquely; grossly; harmfully; utterly; maliciously; astutely; cleverly.

DISTORTION

adjectives
pale; fatal; obvious; imbedded; elaborated; ludicrous; intentional; fantastic.

DISTRACTION

adjectives
infinite; compelling; manifold; powerful; sweet; skillful; extreme; artificial; material; innocent; bewildered; beneficial; endless; blind; great; cautious.

verbs
attend with—; avoid—; blind to—; condemn—; drive to—; fear—; justify—; labor under—; lock out—; occasion—; result in—; shut out—; view with—; —arises; —confuses; —diverts; —intercepts; —interrupts; —perturbs.
(See confusion, disorder.)

DISTRESS

adjectives
simulated; palpable; widespread; pecuniary; horrible; mental; mortal; violent; keenest; intellectual; obvious; sore; obstinate; poignant; genuine; fearful; hideous; fancied; sentimental; dark; blind; generalized; terrified; needless; supreme; spiritual; bitter; fatherless; sensitive; financial; painted; severe; extreme; pathetic; heart-searching; recurrent; sharp; sublime; deep; chronic; painful; insupportable; bare; wide-eyed; cowering; dire; evident; unrelieved; supposed; public.

verbs
afflict with—; aggravate—; answer—; bawl—; behold in—; consume with—; counsel in—; deliver from—; embolden by—; expose to—; give rise to—; pity—; relieve—; soothe—; submit in—; suffer—; wait in—; wring with—; —afflicts; —crazes; —gnaws.
(See suffering, pain, misery, agony.)

DISTRESS (v)

adverbs
deeply; shockingly; mentally; triumphantly; dreadfully; palpably; pecuniarily; horribly; mortally; violently; obviously; sorely; poignantly; genuinely; fearfully; hideously; sentimentally; needlessly; recurrently; supremely; spiritually; chronically; painfully; insupportably; direly; publicly.
(See grieve, wound.)

DISTRESSING

adverbs
extremely; remarkably; awfully; painfully; sorely; profoundly; deeply; appallingly; horribly; gravely; shockingly; incredibly; unspeakably; unmentionably; mentally; violently; keenly; poignantly; genuinely; hideously; supremely; bitterly; insupportably; evidently; unutterably; intensely; seriously; starkly; uncommonly; acutely; fundamentally; unduly; immoderately; unusually.

DISTRIBUTE (v)

adverbs
genially; exclusively; uniformly; indecisively; judiciously; equally; geographically; geometrically; irregularly; indefinitely; equitably; plentifully; scientifically; socially; ultimately; unlimitedly; symmetrically; lavishly; visibly; wastefully.
(See allot, apportion.)

DISTRIBUTION

adjectives
wide; general; equitable; liberal; wasteful; scientific; social; impracticable; ultimate; uniform; respective; symmetrical; rude; democratic; extensive; unlimited; lavish; indiscriminate; geographical; high; low; visible.

verbs
arrange—; bless with—; comprehend—; control—; effect—; enjoy—; increase—;

influence—; mention—; prepare for—; prevent—; reject—; sanction—; urge—; —abates; —aids; —disposes; —enriches; —involves; —reduces.
(See arrangement, disposition.)

DISTRICT

adjectives
outlying; thinly-populated; fashionable; simple; rural; residential; industrial; swankiest; congested; pastoral; remote; congressional; newly-gained; urban; scenic; sanitary; fertile; squalid; arid; extensive; coterminous; financial; genial-hearted; native; affected; accessible; dispatching; productive; adjacent; tenement; various (pl); charming; malodorous; populous.

verbs
appoint to—; assign to—; comprise—; constitute—; control—; divide into—s; dwell in—; elect to—; hedge in—; inhabit—; manage—; occupy—; separate into—s; supervise—; vest in—; —affords; —embraces; —envelops; —includes; —takes in; —thrives.
(See region, tract, locality, territory, circuit.)

DISTRUST

adjectives
cynical; grim; profound; paternal; morbid; reserved; instinctive; lurking; painful; lessening; vigilant; vulgar; palpable; mutual; abiding; inward; deep; prejudicial; unreasonable; vague; dawning; marked; foul.

verbs
accuse of—; acquire—; approach with—; augment—; awaken—; breed—; earn—; entertain—; eye with—; foster—; incur—; intensify—; mark with—; regard with—; silence—; view with—; warrant—; —appears; —enters; —grows; —sprouts.
(See doubt, suspicion.)

DISTRUST (v)

adverbs
instinctively; heartily; constantly; unavoidably; cynically; profoundly; morbidly; painfully; vigilantly; palpably; mutually; abidingly; deeply; unreasonably; vaguely; markedly.
(See suspect, doubt.)

DISTRUSTFUL

adverbs
gravely; alertly; watchfully; constantly; grimly; altogether; positively; profoundly; chronically; habitually; temperamentally; morbidly; painfully; instinctively; intuitively; inwardly; secretly; openly; unreasonably; vaguely; suspiciously; obnoxiously; disagreeably; wisely; warily; quietly; prudently; faintly; uneasily; seriously; momentarily; anxiously; sagaciously; nervously; timidly; horridly; skeptically.

DISTURB (v)

adverbs
inwardly; particularly; wantonly; perceptibly; profoundly; permanently; materially; deeply; grievously; emotionally; functionally; mentally; mutually; exceptionally; powerfully; pathologically; intellectually; violently; electrically; psychically; internally; glandularly; rudely; unnecessarily; unpleasantly.
(See annoy, perturb.)

DISTURBANCE

adjectives
civil; spasmodic; organic; emotional; terrific; mutual; atmospheric; insurrectionary; functional; mental; exceptional; powerful; gastric; strange; pathological; magnetic; widespread; intellectual; violent; electrical; psychic; visual; emotional; internal; agitated; glandular; serious; rude; unnecessary.

verbs
accompany by—; aggravate—; allay—; attend with—; continue—; engender—; foment—; free from—; generate—; relieve—; suffer from—; —arises; —fizzles out (colloq.); —subsides.
(See tumult, confusion, commotion, uproar, clamor.)

DISTURBING

adverbs
faintly; vaguely; definitely; seriously; gravely; alarmingly; significantly; evidently; manifestly; irrationally; palpably; visibly; noticeably; unreasonably; needlessly; maliciously; meddlesomely; shockingly; turbulently; fussily; restlessly; excitably; hysterically; tantalizingly; bitterly; miserably; intolerably; horribly; unpleasantly; disagreeably; obnoxiously; exceptionally.

DISUSE

adjectives
(See neglect.)

verbs
cast into—; come into—; drop into—; excuse—; fall into—; lapse into—; lose by—; overcome—; parch by—; proceed from—; regret—; rot away in—; rouse out of—; rust from—; stifle by—; weaken by—; —affects; —deteriorates; —prevents; grows into—.
(See neglect.)

DITCH

adjectives
briny; oozy; impassable; rain-soaked; muddy; filthy; deep.

verbs
bog in—; fall into—; level—; mire in—; plunge in—; turn in—; —ensnares; —forms; —furnishes; —serves.
(See trench, channel.)

DITTY

adjectives
sea-going; hiccup; time-honored; popular; strident; amorous; doleful; woeful; sentimental; irrelevant.

verbs
carol—; compose—; dash off—; entertain with—; hum—; mourn—; mute—; pipe—; warble—; welcome with—; —amuses; —celebrates; —cheers; —flows; —lulls; —praises; —resounds.
(See air, poem, song, tune.)

DIVAN

adjectives
perfumed; pillowed; rickety; commodious; luxurious; resplendent; inviting; comfortable.

DIVE (*v*)

adverbs
spectacularly; gracefully; unerringly; precipitately; abruptly; harrowingly; thrillingly; bravely; courageously.
(See plunge, drop.)

DIVERGENCE

adjectives
(See deviation.)

verbs
allow for—; bridge—; check—; correct—; flow in—; follow—; generate—; illustrate—; increase—; intersect—; occasion—; produce—; question—; relate with—; test—; —affects; —arises; —diminishes; —occurs; —proceeds from; —separates; —widens.
(See deviation, disagreement, difference.)

DIVERGENT

adverbs
extraordinarily; resolutely; definitely; sharply; interestingly; disputatiously; positively; harshly; discordantly; disagreeably; uncongenially; incompatibly; inaptly; terribly; endlessly; pitiably; painfully; exceptionally; deliberately.

DIVERSE

adverbs
utterly; harmlessly; momentarily; intellectually; economically; mysteriously; inexplicably; sharply; markedly; remarkably; notably; acutely; perceptibly; gravely; insuperably; racially; subtly; essentially; strikingly; fundamentally; radically; appreciably; materially; amazingly; significantly; superficially; extremely; irreconcilably; prodigiously; temperamentally; intrinsically; completely.

DIVERSION

adjectives
social; congenial; harmless; pleasurable; staple; childish; constant; unending; favorite; momentary; contemporary; popular; infantile; intellectual; sturdy; innocent; outdoor; decorous; unique; languid; incidental; seasonable; healthful; economical; agreeable; mysterious; attacking; exquisite; exhilarating.

verbs
advocate—; allow—; amuse with—; conceive—; consider—; contrive—; employ—; engage in—; forget in—; invent—; look for—; need—; occupy with—; search for—; sprout—; suggest—; —attracts; —benefits; —entertains; —excites; —fatigues; —gratifies; —withholds.
(See amusement, recreation, entertainment, sport, relaxation, pastime.)

DIVERSITY

adjectives
delightful; continental; extraordinary; infinite; outward; merry; magnificent; grave; picturesque.

DIVERT (v)

adverbs
frequently; immensely; delightfully; extraordinarily; infinitely; outwardly; merrily; magnificently; pleasurably; childishly; constantly; intellectually; uniquely; healthfully; economically; agreeably; exquisitely; exhilaratingly.
(See turn, withdraw.)

DIVERTING

adverbs
deviously; erratically; circuitously; endlessly; delusively; sharply; cleverly; artfully; adroitly; skilfully; mysteriously; cunningly; deceptively; insidiously; trickily; meretriciously; wickedly; amusingly; entertainingly; playfully; sportively; clumsily; merrily; joyously; wittily; pleasantly; cheerily; roguishly.

DIVIDE (v)

adverbs
customarily; transversely; horizontally; conveniently; finely; subtly; wisely; evenly; longitudinally; miraculously; hopelessly; equally; formally; critically; scientifically; fatally; geographically; appropriately; arbitrarily; factionally; racially; unexpectedly; originally.
(See separate, sever.)

DIVIDEND

adjectives
illegitimate; substantial; reasonable; regular; generous.

verbs
advise of—; allot—; announce—; bear—; declare—; distribute—; draw—; invest—; mail—; obtain—; pay—; present—; promise—; report—; yield—; —s accrue; —s suffice; —s support; share in—.
(See portion, amount, money.)

DIVINITY

adjectives
anthropomorphic; ancient; omnipresent; scholastic; sylvan; jealous; false; actual; utter; strange; winged; favorite; sarcastic; dying; tutelar; polemical.

verbs
attain—; claim—; conceive—; concern—; embrace—; encounter—; express—; invoke —; manifest—; preach—; reflect—; reject —; unite in—; verse in—; —governs; —inspires; —rules; —stirs.
(See deity, God.)

DIVISION

adjectives
venereal; contending; formal; minutest; critical; various (pl); proposed; scientific; astonishing; equitable; isolated; distinct; fatal; assaulting; heroic; antecedent; primary; geographical; arbitrary; appropriate; factional; racial; unexpected; original.

verbs
arrange in—s; attempt—; avoid—; cement —; control—; distinguish—; draw from—; enforce—; establish—; form—; include in —; lead—; mark—; note—; number—; observe—; place in—; separate into—s; struggle for—; supervise—; zone—; —comprises; —consists of; —distributes; —widens.
(See distribution, part, section.)

DIVORCE

adjectives
salubrious; irregular; hateful; unwholesome; deadly; collusive; welcome; long-sought; publicized; worth-while; surprise; framed.

verbs
abuse—; agree to—; apply for—; approve of—; consent to—; contemplate—; declaim against—; favor—; grant—; involve in—; lament—; pronounce—; recognize—; resort to—; sanction—; stay—; sue for—; terminate in—; warrant—; —cleaves; —corrupts; —dissolves; —frees; —privileges; —separates; authorize—; prevent—; tolerate—.
(See separation, marriage.)

DIVORCED

adverbs
irrevocably; unhappily; unfortunately; frequently; regularly; unjustly; unluckily; grievously; rightfully; properly; legally; loosely; distinctly; justifiably; judicially; profitably; recently; correctly; felicitously; irreconcilably.

DIZZINESS

adjectives
swift; paralyzing.

verbs
attend with—; diagnose—; feign—; induce —; occasion—; overcome—; produce—; strike with—; sway in—; take with—; treat for—; —diminishes; —ensues; —envelops; —forewarns; —perplexes; —relaxes; —suggests.
(See giddiness, confusion.)

DIZZY

adverbs
hopelessly; suddenly; helplessly; dangerously; alarmingly; slightly; completely; blindly; dimly; confusedly; mistily; obscurely; glaringly; sickeningly; frightfully; fearfully; inadvertently; muzzily; abnormally; deliriously; incoherently; crazily; light-headedly; uncontrollably; oddly; curiously; strangely; queerly.

DOCILITY

adjectives
noiseless; submissive.

DOCK

adjectives
shipping; humming; dingy; ancient; wet; neat.

DOCKET

adjectives
(See calendar.)

verbs
appear on—; arrange—; cancel—; file—; inclose in—; mention in—; prepare—; produce—; rearrange—; run through—; seal—; search—; strike—; survey—; —authorizes; —contains; —dispenses with; —indicates; —revolves; preserve—.
(See calendar, list.)

DOCTOR

adjectives
young; learned; vivacious; resourceful; inscrutable; lauded; illustrious; indefatigable; old-fashioned; provincial; would-be; mellifluous; tall; capable; country; handpicked; easy-going; fashionable; distracted; badgered; reverend; worthy; murderous; talented; mystic; eminent; discreet; budding; regimental.

verbs
(See physician.)

DOCTRINAL

adverbs
rigidly; austerely; augustly; sternly; undeviatingly; absurdly; devoutly; strictly; tenaciously; persistently; insistently; consistently; wholly; conscientiously; meticulously; punctiliously; ceremoniously; ritualistically; dogmatically; obstinately; stubbornly; stiffly; dismally; fundamentally; zealously; abstractly; comfortably; placidly; primarily; horribly.

DOCTRINE

adjectives
dismal; dangerous; fundamental; heretical; pernicious; incestuous; outworn; decided; zealous; positive; blessed; conflicting; revolutionary; mystical; audacious; subversive; traditional; exoteric; recondite; cold; abstract; sound; pleasant; sensational; elevated; valid; accursed; denominational; living; recurring; enlarging; rigid; evil; deliberate; vulgar; licentious; nefarious; blighting; barbarous; opposite; cherished; characteristic; unflinching; republican; unedifying; undefiled; devilish; dubious; hermeneutical; time-honored; orthodox; comfortable; vague; pregnant; imported; erroneous; traditive; evolutionary; heterodox; wildest; primary; essential; tantalizing; evangelical; shallow; bold; religious; horrible; sentimental; deistical; contrary; practical.

verbs
accept—; adhere to—; adopt—; advocate—; apply—; attack—; believe—; blaspheme—; bolster—; challenge—; commit to—; concur in—; define—; demolish—; derive—from; echo—; enunciate—; epitomize—; espouse—; expound—; illustrate—; immerse in—; impart—; inculcate—; invoke—; nullify—; obey—; pledge to—; practise—; preach—; promulgate—; propound—; put forth—; refer to—; reject—; sin against—; spread—; teach—; understand—; unite in—; —astounds; —confounds; —embraces; —governs.
(See teaching, belief, dogma, principle, precept.)

DOCUMENT

adjectives
genuine; routine; epic; intimate; tremendous; human; effective; dull; trustworthy; ethnological; authoritative; vivid; revealing; precious; obnoxious; colorless; official; controversial; immortal; fundamental; notable; living; ecclesiastical; diplomatic; temperate; extraordinary; unique; amazing; public; formidable; illuminating; brief; decorous; forceful; momentous; dangerous; pathetic; significant; rambling; equivocal; flimsy; finicky; noteworthy; singular; irreproachable; trenchant; unpublished; fatal; different-looking; authentic; ponderous; uncommon; insidious; iconographic; respective (pl); edifying.

verbs
arrange—; crowd with—s; cull from—;

draw up—; entrust with—; explore through —s; file—; inscribe in—; preserve—; produce—; refer to—; release—; scan—; seal —; search—; sign—; survey—; term—; value—; witness—; —asserts; —authorizes; —enlightens; —entitles; —informs; —points out; —proves; —records; —serves; —verifies.

(See paper, evidence, proof, record.)

DOCUMENTARY

adverbs

inescapably; genuinely; trustworthily; ecclesiastically; legally; amazingly; formidably; briefly; momentously; dangerously; significantly; irreproachably; fatally; ponderously; trenchantly; uncommonly; unexpectedly; surprisingly.

DODDERING

adverbs

tremulously; quaveringly; helplessly; feebly; pleasantly; uncertainly; hopelessly; desperately; decrepitly; wanderingly; erratically; confusedly; bewilderedly; pathetically; bravely; prematurely; nervously; besottedly; drunkenly; slowly; wearily.

DOG

adjectives

wistful; spineless; mauled; loutish; shambling; squat; well-shaped; mongrel; tubby; stray; wolf-like; well-bred; barking; marauding; placid; slinking; whipped; cringing; huge; lion-like; cross-grained; savage; vicious; sedate; beaten; avid; yelping; raging; inestimable; alien; clean; rabid; murderous; angry; hungry; handsome; stately; jubilant; worthless; gigantic; lean; gallant; happy; famished; miserable; reliable; frail; little; woolly; deep-chested; disgraceful-looking; couchant; myopic; demented; tawny; treacherous; panting; half-wolf; stripe-tailed; surly; brutal; stranger; accursed; unconscionable; patient; fierce; snapping; chivalrous; jovial; vagrant; atheistical; thievish-looking; voiceless; lame; sneaking; sad; craven; traitorous; thirsty; bipedal; gentlemanly; elderly; mangy; hellish; lounging.

verbs

cast to—s; coax—; crop—; cudgel—; lash —; soothe—; stone—; unleash—; whip—; —barks; —bays; —clambers; —crouches; —darts by; —dashes by; —depredates; —frisks; —gnaws; —growls; —herds; —howls; —invades; —laps; —licks; —limps; —lurks; —menaces; —performs; —points; —preys; —pursues; —retrieves; —skulks; —slinks off; —snaps; —snarls; —strays; —tears; —trots away; —whimpers; —whines; —wrangles; —yelps; —yowls.

(See animal, puppy.)

DOGGED

adverbs

stubbornly; obstinately; boundlessly; excessively; resolutely; sullenly; morosely; pertinaciously; glumly; silently; irresistibly; obdurately; implacably; inveterately; bravely; heroically; endlessly; surprisingly; unexpectedly; mulishly; perversely; blindly; intractably; fanatically; wilfully; intrepidly; enterprisingly; fiercely; churlishly; grouchily; moodily; crustily; grumpishly.

DOGMA

adjectives

wide-rooted; delicate; dangerous; religious; deflating; dour; theological; pungent; narrow; entrenched; intolerant; pure; sheer; rash; inscrutable; fundamental; negative; sweeping.

verbs

abandon—; assert—; defend—; expound—; follow—; formulate—; impose—; inherit—; justify—; preach—; proclaim—; propound —; put forward—; question—; sanction—; save—; state—; teach—; —convinces; —denounces; —flourishes; —satisfies; —vanishes.

(See doctrine, principle.)

DOGMATIC

adverbs

unwarrantably; disagreeably; confidently; marvelously; unaccountably; egotistically; cruelly; harshly; severely; conceitedly; bumptiously; ecclesiastically; tyrannically; officially; inexorably; stiffly; dangerously; dourly; narrowly; fundamentally; purely; utterly; singularly; austerely; arrogantly; proudly; unyieldingly; solidly; absolutely; definitely; positively; fanatically; superficially; intolerantly; provincially; remarkably; fussily; peremptorily; emphatically; solemnly.

DOINGS

adjectives

hot-headed; habitual; subsequent; infinite; valiant; ill; sinister; factual.

DOLE

verbs

apply for—; apportion—; approve of—; deprive of—; dispense—; distribute—; di-

vide—; drop from—; entitle to—; impart —; issue—; reduce to—; reward—; relinquish—; subsist on—; —eases; —supports.
(See alms, charity.)

DOLEFUL

adverbs
habitually; temperamentally; utterly; ceaselessly; deeply; darkly; foolishly; unreasonably; vexatiously; needlessly; remarkably; singularly; oddly; oppressively; inarticulately; silently; immoderately; unutterably; fundamentally; extravagantly; dismally; abjectly; glumly; gloomily; lugubriously; dreadfully; biliously; horribly.

DOLL

adjectives
mature; gorgeous; absurd; rag; exquisite; mutilated; adorable; cherished; brainless; dancing; dressed-up; dilapidated; moon-faced; battered.

verbs
collect—s; display—; dress—; entertain with—; name—; present with—; repair—; sleep with—; tire of—; wind—; yearn for —; —attracts; —cheers; —dangles; —pleases; —satisfies; —simpers; —sleeps; —surprises; —walks.
(See toy.)

DOLLAR

adjectives
precious; shrunken; tangible; advertising; paltry; appreciating; solitary; minted; countless (pl); depreciating; inflated; purchasing.

verbs
adopt—; beg—; coin—s; count—s; counterfeit—; deflate—; devaluate—; earn—; fill with—; flash—; furnish with—; inflate—; issue—; lose—; mint—s; present with—; print—s; proffer—; rate—; reduce to—; reject—; relinquish—; soil—; tear—; value —; worship—; —s accrue; —adorns; —attracts.
(See money, coin.)

DOLTISH

adverbs
unutterably; strangely; dully; apathetically; singularly; oddly; curiously; unaccountably; inscrutably; abysmally; grotesquely; palpably; essentially; incurably; irremediably; callously; shockingly; soddenly; sullenly; vacuously; ridiculously; lumpishly; grossly; coarsely; direly; blandly; stupidly; stolidly.

DOMAIN

adjectives
temporal; spiritual; allied (pl); speckless; ancestral; rough-hewn; extended; unexploited; bleak; ecclesiastical; obscure; shifting; elastic; scanty; shattered; melancholy; eminent; imperial; unassailable; forbidden; flourishing; impenetrable; outlying; all-pervading; vast.

DOME

adjectives
golden; majestic; great; granite; shallow; saucer-like; gilded; blue-tiled; truncated; bell-shaped; silent; glorious; velvety; vaulted; star-fretted; tremulous; inevitable; isolated; monastic; gaping; observatory; firmamental; clustered; shadowy; ribbed; Moorish; towering; heaven-pointing; illuminated; porphyroid.

verbs
adorn—; ascend to—; cradle in—; decorate —; dwell in—; enlarge—; gild—; illuminate—; poise on—; round off in—; stud—; survey—; swell—; —arches; —attracts; —resounds; —revolves; —shields; —sparkles; —spreads; —totters.
(See roof, building.)

DOMESTIC

adverbs
incurably; delightfully; cozily; comfortably; exaggeratedly; elaborately; ostentatiously; blatantly; offensively; conspicuously; hopelessly; charmingly; narrowly; insistently; flamboyantly; proudly; absurdly; impressively; vexatiously; boundlessly; entirely; pretentiously.

DOMESTICITY

adjectives
smug; safe; dull; suburban; hard-won.

verbs
acquaint with—; avoid—; balk at—; dabble in—; eliminate—; escape—; feign—; glance into—; incur—; indulge in—; pretend—; school in—; swallow by—; trap by—; wallow in—; weary of—; wrap in—; —annoys; —appeals; —bores; —involves; —restrains; —shelters.
(See affair.)

DOMICILE

adjectives
luxurious; semi-detached; sumptuous; self-contained; sanctified; historic; commodious; tempting.

DOMINANT

adverbs
disturbingly; arrogantly; prominently; interestingly; strangely; substantially; emphatically; markedly; primarily; remarkably; vitally; virtually; dangerously; luckily; alarmingly; fortunately; unluckily; strongly; invincibly; inescapably; supremely; disagreeably; unpleasantly; officiously; selfishly; ruthlessly; inconsiderately; politically; unfortunately; insistently; manifestly; obviously; terribly; loftily; sternly; extraordinarily.

DOMINATE (*v*)

adverbs
atavistically; powerfully; effectively; tyrannically; overwhelmingly; sternly; inevitably; insistently; solely; persistently.
(See govern, control.)

DOMINATION

adjectives
lofty; overwhelming; hard; stern; cortical; banded; extraordinary; inevitable; insistent; sole; extended.

verbs
break away from—; condemn—; curse by—; dwell in—; enlarge—; enrich—; establish—; foster—; join—; subject to—; submit to—; suffer under—; trace—to; —compels; —inflicts; —reaps; —rules; —thrives.
(See control, dominion, rule, government, tyranny.)

DOMINEERING

adverbs
disagreeably; ridiculously; amusingly; tyrannically; unreasonably; characteristically; arrogantly; clownishly; persistently; airily; shockingly; politely; officiously; ludicrously; despotically; pompously; inherently; superciliously; loftily; insistently; sharply; detestably; offensively; naturally.

DOMINION

adjectives
sole; hereditary; dim; voracious; hard; unlimited; uncurbed; supreme; gross; drear.

verbs
control—; exercise—over; explore—; form—; gain—; grant to—; grasp—; inhabit—; integrate—s; procure—over; recognize—; rule—; rule with—; sever—from; sway—; yield to—; —comprises; —extends to; —obeys; —serves; govern—.
(See sovereignty, authority, nation, empire, kingdom.)

DONATE (*v*)

adverbs
munificently; generously; charitably; anonymously; amply; lavishly; splendidly; meagerly; grudgingly; complainingly.
(See give, contribute.)

DONATION

adjectives
generous; ample; munificent.

DONKEY

adjectives
laden; tiny; gray; straggling; diminutive; plodding; modest; gentle; omnipresent; neat-stepping; patient.

verbs
burden—; fetter—; lash—; lasso—; pasture—; tether—; water—; —ambles; —balks; —draws; —grazes; —hauls; —kicks; —pulls; —shies; —snorts.
(See animal, ass.)

DOOM

adjectives
impending; ultimate; irrevocable; ignominious; inescapable; dreadful; tragic; distant; thankful; inevitable; eternal; mysterious; dark; self-wrought; everlasting; inscrutable; stormy; graceless; fatal; approaching; imminent; perpetual; dubious; ultimate.

verbs
announce—; assign—; avoid—; bear—; bide—; consign to—; curse—; draw to—; dread—; fix—; fly to—; foresee—; foreshadow—; foretell—; hasten to—; move to—; near—; precipitate—; pronounce—; read—; revoke—; seal—; sound—; spell—; threaten—; —closes in; —impends.
(See judgment, fate, destiny.)

DOOM (*v*)

adverbs
irrecoverably; irrevocably; apparently; everlastingly; prophetically; ultimately; ig-

nominiously; inescapably; dreadfully; tragically; inevitably; eternally; mysteriously; inscrutably; fatally; cruelly.
(See condemn, ruin.)

DOOMED

adverbs
irretrievably; finally; mortally; endlessly; terribly; ultimately; irrevocably; ignominiously; inescapably; dreadfully; tragically; inevitably; eternally; mysteriously; darkly; everlastingly; inscrutably; perpetually; unhappily; utterly; evidently; manifestly; fatefully.

DOOR

adjectives
massive; battered; paneled; reluctant; clamped; iron-bound; barricaded; heavy; monumental; lovely; sun-blistered; baffling; carved; solid; grilled; unyielding; bolted; humble; weather-beaten; cathedral; unlatched; ponderous; stout; studded; opening; squeaking; communicating; yawning; cringing; ancient; worm-eaten; hacked; clanging; front; fateful; mystic; perpetual; unfrequented; love-crowned; substantial; impervious; moldering; revolving; portcullis; lodge; postern; sloping; sliding; hospitable; intermediate; veiled; padded; unguarded; infernal; impalpable; paternal; mossy; adamantine; unhinged; arched; mountain; shattered; curtained; guilty; shrunken; dilapidated; feeble.

verbs
appear at—; arch—; attain—; bar—; barricade—; batter down—; beat down—; bolt—; clamor at—; command—; commune at—; darken—; defend—; encamp at—; escort to—; exclude from—; fling open—; force—; gather at—; glimmer through—; guard—; guide to—; hammer on—; hinge —; hover about—; jam—; peep through—; pry at—; repulse from—; slam—; steal through—; stream through—; tap on—; tarry at—; tend—; venture through—; —admits; —creaks; —groans; —squeaks; —yawns.
(See entrance, portal, gate, opening, doorway.)

DOOR-BELL

adjectives
(See bell.)

verbs
adjust—; answer—; attach—; connect—; hang—; press—; quiet—; ring—; sound—; —announces; —chimes; —disturbs; —interjects; —interrupts; —jingles; —pierces; —warns.
(See bell.)

DOOR-KNOB

adjectives
(See knob.)

verbs
adjust—; attach—; fasten to—; force—; grasp—; handle—; hug—; jiggle—; manipulate—; mark—; move—; ornament—; palm—; release—; toy with—; try—; tug at—; turn—; soil—; —gives way; —turns.
(See handle, knob.)

DOOR-MAN

adjectives
hulking; hard-faced; resplendent; staring; ruthless; gigantic.

DOORWAY

adjectives
sheltered; stately; doorless; curtained; unpretentious; pilastered; time-stained; flamboyant; enticing; impressive; unsavory; sculptured.

verbs
admit through—; adorn—; darken—; embellish—; enter—; file through—; flutter past—; huddle in—; jostle into—; loom in—; observe from—; occupy—; open into —; ornament—; pursue through—; scamper through—; shadow—; —beckons; —divides; —exhibits; —invites; —separates.
(See door.)

DORMANT

adverbs
temporarily; transiently; healthily; momentarily; latently; passively; inertly; heavily; lethargically; inactively; mysteriously; importantly; smoulderingly; symbolically; impenetrably; inferentially; fortunately; naturally; quiescently.

DOSE

adjectives
minimum; enormous; nauseous; attenuated; curative; large; graduated (pl); tremendous; unpalatable; minute; occasional; non-toxic; potable; protective; moderate; monstrous; therapeutic; homeopathic.

verbs
adjust—; administer—; advocate—; apply —; calm with—; concoct—; decrease—;

increase—; inject—; ladle out—; measure —; portion out—; prepare—; prescribe—; reduce—; refuse—; regulate—; repeat—; suggest—; swallow—; —alleviates; —relieves; —suffices.

(See portion, draught, amount, medicine.)

DOTING

adverbs

foolishly; absurdly; inordinately; childishly; tenderly; ludicrously; tempestuously; frankly; proudly; significantly; ridiculously; openly; ostentatiously; fatuously; fervently; idolatrously; ardently; inarticulately; inexpressibly; madly; fervidly.

DOUBLE-FACED

adverbs

subtly; cunningly; insidiously; notoriously; infamously; surreptitiously; artfully; craftily; deceitfully; remarkably; dangerously; cleverly; alarmingly; distressingly; maneuveringly; plaguedly; adroitly; successfully; underhandedly; shrewdly; proverbially; manifestly; suavely; sanctimoniously.

DOUBT

adjectives

premonitory; wondering; casual; growing; reasonable; prudent; impending; recurring; faint; presumptuous; insinuating; audacious; uneasy; horrid; black; wistful; serious; disturbing; grisly; consuming; bitter; sickening; momentary; angry; torturing; cynical; passionate; formless; unmerited; nagging; insidious; mean; conflicting; anxious; painful; pecuniary; timid; sarcastic; considerable; solitary; lingering; inseparable; floating; paralyzing; melancholy; remorseful; hideous; sorrowing; thronging; rational; hopeless; jealous; tragic; unwelcome; injurious; dark; coquettish; blasphemous; unclaimed; childish; oft-repeated; religious; unanswerable; good-humored; constitutional; grave; fiendish; sagacious; cloudy; broken; desperate; earthly.

verbs

assail with—; attend with—; banish—; breed—; brush away—; burden with—; cast into—; chill with—; circulate—; clear up—; cloud with—; conceive—; convey—; crush—; defy—; dissipate—; dissolve—; eliminate—; entertain—; erase—; express —; falter in—; fight—; interpose—; occasion—; oppress with—; raise—; remove—; rend with—; resolve—; strike with—; sustain—; sweep away—; torture with—; trouble by—; voice—; wrap in—; wring with—; —creeps in; —encompasses; —incenses; —lingers; —lurks; —overshadows; —prevails; —pursues; —springs up; —stabs; —taints.

(See uncertainty, distrust, disbelief, incredulity, skepticism.)

DOUBT (*v*)

adverbs

casually; growingly; reasonably; recurringly; seriously; disturbingly; consumingly; sickeningly; momentarily; formlessly; painfully; jealously; childishly; gravely; sagaciously; paralyzingly.

(See distrust, suspect.)

DOUBTER

adjectives

fastidious; sneering; puny.

DOUBTFUL

adverbs

altogether; reasonably; seriously; gravely; vexatiously; still; wholly; timidly; vaguely; hazily; bewilderingly; mysteriously; enigmatically; ignorantly; distractedly; nervously; uncertainly; embarrassingly; elusively; remarkably; singularly; inexplicably; oddly.

DOUGH

adjectives

tasteless; crisp.

verbs

cake—; knead—; leaven—; mix—; mould —; moisten—; prepare—; punch—; set—; shape—; sprinkle—; sweeten—; transform —into; work—; —ferments; —puffs; —rises.

(See mass.)

DOUGHNUT

adjectives

lunch-counter; sugary; forbidden.

DOVE

adjectives

crooning; staid; strengthless; mellow-mourning; lonely; sucking; milk-white; cooing; brooding; silver; snowy.

verbs

tame—; toy with—; —bills; —broods; —coos; —crouches; —grieves; —haunts; —moans; —mourns; —murmurs; —plains; —sails; —trembles; —trumpets; —tumbles; —walks.

(See bird.)

DOWAGER

adjectives
ugly; old; decorous; ill-tempered; amiable.

DOWDY

adverbs
indescribably; dismally; untidily; vaguely; shamefully; embarrassingly; pitiably; incredibly; unfashionably; inexcusably; indifferently; nonchalantly; blithely; carelessly; gloriously; laughingly; placidly; self-consciously; unconscionably; inordinately; unpardonably; vexatiously; downright; smudgily; grimily; lazily; obstinately; slouchily; gaily; negligently.

DOWER

adjectives
unconscious; fragrant; generous; sufficient; convenient.

DOWN

adjectives
solitary; dewy-glooming; callow; loaning; soft; undulating (pl); hushless (pl); beautiful; swelling (pl).

DOWNCAST

adverbs
terribly; unreasonably; needlessly; gloomily; glumly; inordinately; emphatically; dourly; sorely; irrationally; inexplicably; moodily; alarmingly; dangerously; incurably; inconceivably; incredibly; horribly; woefully; gravely; seriously; inconsolably; desperately; tragically; unduly; wearily.

DOWNFALL

verbs
anticipate—; approach—; bring about—; drag into—; escape—; expect—; experience—; fear—; guard against—; heed—; meet—; pitch to—; promise—; protect from —; recover from—; tumble to—; warn of—; —destroys; —engulfs; —teaches.
(See disgrace, ruin, destruction.)

DOWNPOUR

adjectives
torrential; thinning; increasing; steady; drenching; tropical.

DOWRY

adjectives
(See gift.)

verbs
agree upon—; amass—; assign—; assure of—; bestow—; demand—; endue with—; furnish—; grant—; guarantee—; increase —; marry for—; pay—; present with—; provide—; return—; seek—; —compensates; —impoverishes; —satisfies; —shrinks.
(See endowment, gift, property, portion, reward.)

DOZE

adjectives
noontide; surreptitious; sudden; heavy; fitful; nightmare-ridden; comfortable; wakeful; uncomfortable.

DOZE (*v*)

adverbs
peacefully; slumberously; surreptitiously; fitfully; comfortably; wakefully; interminably; lazily.
(See sleep, drowse.)

DRABNESS

adjectives
colorless; external; bleak; blank.

verbs
clothe in—; compensate for—; conceal—; envelop by—; expel—; exude—; observe—; relieve—; shroud in—; throw off—; —depresses; —displeases; —drowns; —offends; —oppresses; —overwhelms; —seeps in; —suits.
(See dullness, monotony.)

DRAFT
(*air*)

adjectives
icy; adventurous; sparkling; severe; swift.

verbs
admit—; avoid—; breathe—; create—; draw—; expose to—; force—; guard against—; inhale—; place in—; prevent—; produce—; protect against—; shiver in—; sit in—; —effects; —enters; —escapes; —harms; —passes through.
(See current, air, breeze.)

DRAFT
(*money*)

verbs
address—; approve—; cash—; date—; defer—; draw—; honor—; pay with—; produce—; send—; tender—; wire—; write—; —enables; —orders; —suffices.
(See money.)

DRAG (*v*)

adverbs
painfully; listlessly; dejectedly; bodily;

heavily; tenderly; stubbornly; forcibly; despondently; unwillingly; sternly.

(See haul, trail, pull.)

DRAGON

adjectives

undulant; cave-hid; gilded; fabulous; swift; full-gorged; transfixed; ugly; hideous; murderous; Hydra-headed; green; monstrous; bloodthirsty.

verbs

beset by—; cast out—; confront by—; crush—; pacify—; prevail against—; rout—; slay—; strike at—; vanquish—; —claws; —destroys; —fumes; —guards; —hisses; —licks; —menaces; —ravages; —snorts; —spouts forth; —swallows up; —symbolizes; —tramples; —vanishes; —wails; —writhes.

(See monster, serpent.)

DRAIN

adjectives

(See ditch, pipe, trench.)

verbs

clog—; connect to—; consign to—; dig—; discharge in—; drop into—; employ—; enter—; flush—; furnish—; insert—; pour down—; —carries off; —clears; —preserves; —prevents; —serves; washdown—.

(See gutter, channel. trench, ditch, pipe.)

DRAIN (v)

adverbs

steadily; thoroughly; partially; unscrupulously; unsparingly; entirely; completely; painfully.

(See empty, exhaust, deplete.)

DRAMA

adjectives

spiritual; modern; languid; excessive; loquacious; moving; honest; courageous; stirring; sturdy; classic; dazzling; intense; irrepressible; successful; trivial; stark; high; spectacular; unpretentious; lyric; terrific; painful; crucial; ineffective; unsettled; sensational; hidden; sinister; comic; touching; grim; vivid; gloomy; tragic; dynamic; many-sided; homely; homespun; heartrending; agonizing; absorbing; daily; rousing; weird; romantic; enthralling; raw; elemental; episodic; moon-lit; grisly; moribund; terrestrial; breathless; turgid; far-flung; unrelenting; throbbing; intensified; psychological; adulterous; quiet; piquant; stupendous; thrilling; philosophical; judicial; realistic; naturalistic; poetic; merciless; pitiless; constructive; decadent; fierce; historical; mimic; powerful; religious; impending; oft-rehearsed; voiceless; equestrian; potential; tragic; social; great; well-ordered; transpired; blustering; nefarious; well-arranged; celebrated; revolutionary; sublime; epic; passionate; vast; heroic; propaganda; depressing; exhilarating.

verbs

cast—; enact—; fashion—; foreshadow—; ground in—; intensify—; pervade—; portray—; recreate—; reform—; revive—; sense—; sketch—; spell—; take part in—; temper—; unfold—; —depicts; —electrifies; —stirs; —teeters; —unrolls.

(See play, composition, performance, tragedy, literature.)

DRAMATIC

adverbs

spectacularly; absurdly; impressively; extravagantly; emphatically; foolishly; ridiculously; laughably; profitably; undoubtedly; evidently; palpably; grotesquely; fantastically; unusually; admittedly; excessively; movingly; highly; lyrically; sensationally; weirdly; romantically; breathlessly; enthrallingly; quietly; psychologically; stupendously; marvellously; abundantly; thrillingly; mercilessly; historically; undeniably; powerfully; potentially; sublimely; epically; vastly; heroically; passionately; exhilaratingly; touchingly; immensely; intensely; boundlessly.

DRAMATIST

adjectives

celebrated; contemporary; deft; practiced; renowned; distinguished.

verbs

acclaim—; applaud—; condemn—; criticize—; inspire—; praise—; reward—; support—; sympathize with—; —composes; —conceives;— concocts; —entertains; —excels; —foreshadows; —implies; —motivates; —moves; —plans; —presents; —prevails; —relates; —stirs; —yields.

(See writer, playwright, author.)

DRAPE

adjectives

extreme; modified; easy; natural; smart; athletic; careless; fashionable; poised; proper; graceful.

DRAPE (v)

adverbs

artistically; sparingly; carelessly; archly; smartly; fashionably; properly; gracefully; gloomily; vividly; voluminously; richly; flutteringly; monotonously; fantastically; gorgeously; judiciously; dustily.

(See hang, adorn, cover.)

DRAPERY

adjectives

sweeping; gloomy; gleaming; damask; smoke-grey; vivid; chiffon; voluminous; sad; silvery; rich; orchid; taffeta; window; glistening; festooned; stifling; floating; filmy; sable; well-managed; snowy; fluttering; verdant; monotonous; undulant; translucent; sonorous; graceful; gorgeous; golden; diaphonous; flying; silken; judicious; soft; streaming; sooty; gauzy; fantastic; witching; ambulant; chintz; voile; dusty.

verbs

admire—; arrange—; clothe in—; cover with—; decorate with—; dress in—; festoon in—; fold—; furnish with—; hang—; model—; place—; select—; strip of—; suspend—; weave—; —adds —dresses; —enhances; —graces; —offsets; —ies part.

(See curtain, cloth, material.)

DRASTIC

adverbs

cruelly; intensely; inhumanly; emphatically; unscrupulously; pitifully; powerfully; intensely; virulently; poignantly; harshly; resolutely; immensely; strenuously; incisively; violently; desperately; brutally; trenchantly; strikingly.

DRAUGHT

adjectives

copious; literary; roaring; shallow; mellow; crystal; daring; refreshing; beneficial; delirious; frequent (pl); nectared; unpalatable; portentous; long; hearty; ample; fresh; considerable; acid; grateful; magic; liquorish; fiery; nut-brown; immortal; mingled (pl); fatal; assisted.

verbs

concoct—; down—; drain—; draw off—; empty—; finish in one—; imbibe—; mix—; order—; partake of—; rejoice in—; tap—; —effervesces; —foams; —quenches; —revives; —sates; —soothes; —suffices.

(See drink.)

DRAW (v)

adverbs

fiercely; reluctantly; passionately; mournfully; caressingly; silently; swiftly; contentedly; lazily; demurely; passively; haughtily; apprehensively; irresistibly; reproachfully; inevitably; hastily; affectionately; tenderly; symbolically; exquisitely; sophisticatedly; sketchily; grotesquely; impeccably; hideously; apologetically.

(See depict, sketch, pull.)

DRAWBACK

adjectives

tremendous; undeniable; numerous (pl); practical; definite.

verbs

accept—; anticipate—; control—; expect—; involve—; lack—; necessitate—; overcome —; produce—; pronounce—; refuse—; relax—; reveal—; weigh—; —diminishes; —hinders.

(See disadvantage, hindrance, defect.)

DRAWER

adjectives

secret; gilt-labelled; locked; hidden; stuffed; filled.

verbs

arrange in—; conceal in—; decorate—; discover in—; draw out—; examine—; explore —; fit in—; lock—; muss—; obtain from—; ornament—; rummage in—; search in—; wade through—s; —contains; —exposes; —reveals; —sticks; —swallows.

(See case, box.)

DRAWING

adjectives

water-color; modernistic; free-hand; magnificent; clever; amazing; delectable; symbolical; beautiful; holy; exquisite; sophisticated; sketchy; charcoal; crude; sturdy; grotesque; impeccable; bewildering; distinguished; detailed; icicle-like; naturalistic; hideous.

verbs

collect—s; embellish—; exhibit—; interest in—; model for—; pen—; pencil—; pose for—; praise—; produce—; scratch out—; sit for—; sketch—; study—; translate—; —attracts; —depicts; —imparts; —represents; —reveals; —symbolizes.

(See sketch, picture.)

DRAWING-ROOM

adjectives

frescoed; honest; staid; spacious; marble-floored.

DRAWL

adjectives

tantalizing; unexcited; calm; level; lazy; musical; indistinct; mountain; innocent; maddening; affected; enchanting; slow; steady; masculine; comforting; pleasant; ingenious; listless; haughty; sardonic; husky; amusing; amiable; quiet; soft; confidential; high; emphatic.

verbs

acquire—; adopt—; affect—; catch—; copy —; correct—; employ—; inject—; mimic—; mumble—; recognize—; retain—; translate —; understand—; utter—; —fascinates; —intrigues; —irritates; —loiters; —pleases.

(See speech, utterance, accent.)

DRAWL (*v*)

adverbs

slowly; wearily; tantalizingly; lazily; musically; indistinctly; maddeningly; affectedly; enchantingly; steadily; comfortingly; pleasantly; listlessly; sardonically; huskily; amusingly; amiably; softly; calmly.

(See speak, sound.)

DRAWLING

adverbs

lazily; sleepily; indifferently; carelessly; drowsily; yawningly; insolently; arrogantly; stupidly; impudently; slowly; indistinctly; affectedly; listlessly; languidly; huskily; interminably; endlessly; tiresomely; slackly; slouchily; leisurely; deliberately; apathetically; dully; maunderingly; inarticulately; singularly; faintly; idly; inertly; dreamily; inexcusably.

DREAD

adjectives

despising; wondrous; superstitious; half-conscious; silent; mysterious; contagious; ignorant; sickening; apprehensive; maddening; unreasonable; secret; speechless; mysterious; lurking; shrinking; shadowy; slavish; inexplicable; haunting; unimaginable; nameless; inexpressible; morbid; somber; fresh; blank; irrational; racking; stark; mutual; constant; unnamed; obscene; unnatural; foolish; abnormal; salutary; oppressive; decorous; ill-defined; vague; shuddering; subconscious; feminine; incomprehensible; grinding; popular; nervous; pious; unformulated; poignant; supernatural; recurrent; indefinable; unfathomable; overwhelming; inspiring.

verbs

attend with—; awaken—; cause—; cure of—; diagnose—; disguise—; dwell in—; hide in—of; induce—; nourish—; obsess with—; oppress by—; overcome—; produce —; provoke—; put away—; regard with—; relinquish—; ripen into—; shake with—; wrap in—; —causes; —dogs; —inspires; —overcomes.

(See fright, horror, terror, awe.)

DREAD (*v*)

adverbs

righteously; vaguely; habitually; superstitiously; ignorantly; apprehensively; unreasonably; secretly; speechlessly; shrinkingly; inexplicably; hauntingly; unimaginably; inexpressibly; morbidly; somberly; irrationally; starkly; mutually; constantly; unnaturally; foolishly; oppressively; vaguely; nervously; piously; poignantly; supernaturally; recurrently; indefinably; unfathomably; overwhelmingly.

(See fear, anticipate.)

DREADFUL

adverbs

unutterably; unspeakably; horridly; abominably; tragically; gloomily; incredibly; indescribably; absolutely; starkly; uncommonly; amazingly; astonishingly; cruelly; shockingly; startlingly; perniciously; damnably; disastrously; ruinously; arrantly; reprehensibly; execrably; irremediably; insupportably; appallingly; repulsively; abhorrently; sickeningly; calamitously; cataclysmally.

DREAM

adjectives

aerial; aching; amazing; ambitious; amusing; amethystine; angelic; antenatal; appalling; astonishing; attenuated; bad; baleful; balmy; beastly; beatific; beauteous; besetting; bewildering; bitter; blessed; blighting; blissful; botched; boyish; bucolic; captured; changing; chaste; cherished; childhood; clear; clouded; colored; confused; consecrating; constant; conversational; daring; crazy; dark; day-appearing; dazzling; dead; dearest; deep; delicate; delicious; delirious; delusive; depressed; disconnected; discordant; disjointed; disordered; distorted; distressing; disturbed; divine; dotard; doubtful; dreadful; ecstatic; drowsy; embodied; empty; enthralled; external; evil; exacerbated; exquisite; extraordinary; extravagant; exuberant; fabulous; faded; fairy tale; false; fanatical; fanciful; fancy; fantastic; favorite; fearful; feverish; fitful; flashing; flattering; fleeting; floating; fond; foolish; fragile; friendly; frightful; futile; ghastly; girlish; glorious; gloomy; golden; gorgeous; grandiose; grotesque; half-forgotten; half-remembered; hashish; hateful; haunting; hazy; hideous; horrible; horrid; horrifying; hovering; idle; idyllic; illusory; immortal; impossible; impressive; incommunicable; industrial; ineffaceable; ingenuous; insistent; inspiring; interlunar; interminable; intransitive; invisible; iridescent; jeweled; jostling; journeying; jocund; languorous; lasting; lethargic; liquored; lifelong; liberal-minded; living; loftiest; lotus-eating; lowly; luxurious; mad; maddening; magical; magnificent; melancholy; materialized; millennial; misty; mournful; mooning; morbid; nightly; nightmare; obliging; particular; pensive; perfectible; perishing; odorous; oppressive; ominous; painful; perpetual; persistent; picturesque; pipe; poetic; pompous; poor; preposterous; prophetic; quarrelsome; protracted; pure; quaint; quaking; qualm-filled; quarrelsome; quavering; queenly; quenchable; quick; quieting; querimonious; querulous; questionable; quirky; quizzical; remarkable; restless; resurrected; ridiculous; rocking-chair; romantic; rosy; senseless; sensual; significant; shameful; shattered; shivering; short-lived; sin-chastising; sprinkling; singular; sleepless; slow; smiling; solid; stern; strange; summer; sweet; symbolic; telepathic; tender; terrific; terrifying; thoughtless; topsy-turvy; torturing; transitory; trivial; troubled; tumultuous; unborn; uneasy; unmeaning; unpleasant; unquiet; unremembered; unshakable; unsubstantial; untold; vague; veritable; vernal; vicious; visionary; vivid; waking; wandering; waning; wavering; whirling; whiskey; whispered; wicked; winged; wildering; wildest; wistful; wretched; youthful; zestful.

verbs
awake from—; babble in—; blend in—; break—; calm—s; cast into—; conceive in—; create in—; delight in—; destroy—; dissipate—; exist in—; explain—; fade to —; fly away in—; foresee in—; forget—; fulfill—; glimpse in—; haunt—; hearken to—; indulge in—; interpret—; lose in—; nurse—; pass from—; perpetuate in—; produce—; realize—; rule—s; shake off—; shatter—; sink into—; slumber in—; spin —; suffer in—; transform—; understand—; wander in—; —betokens; —crumbles; —disturbs; —flees; —flowers; —foretells; —haunts; —overpowers; —overshadows; —presages; —prophesies; —puzzles; —reveals; —signifies; —startles; —terrifies; —torments; —troubles; —warns.

(See illusion, reverie, fancy, fantasy, hallucination, vision.)

DREAM (v)

adverbs
unchastely; delectably; romantically; splendidly; confusedly; fondly; contentedly; ambitiously; amusingly; astonishingly; blissfully; dazzlingly; deliciously; deliriously; disconnectedly; drowsily; distressingly; dreadfully; ecstatically; emptily; evilly; exquisitely; extravagantly; exuberantly; fabulously; fanatically; fancifully; fleetingly; gloomily; gorgeously; grotesquely; horribly; inspiringly; interminably; maddeningly; magnificently; oppressively; pensively; perpetually; persistently; picturesquely; poetically; prophetically; ridiculously; romantically; senselessly; sensually; significantly; vividly; waveringly; zestfully; deliriously.

(See fancy, imagine.)

DREAMER

adjectives
egotistic; inefficient; preposterous; imaginative; languishing; impractical; hair-splitting; drowsy; pathetic; soppy; deep; blissful; solitary; delirious; superstitious; utopian; stony.

DREAMY

adverbs
languidly; somnolently; lazily; delightfully; terribly; wonderfully; slightly; deliciously; comfortably; cosily; amazingly; amusingly; inattentively; carelessly; abstractedly; beatifically; boyishly; constantly; irritatingly; naturally; habitually; inherently; provokingly; wistfully; wickedly; vaguely; yearningly; longingly; sweetly; strangely; tenderly; uneasily; thoughtlessly; sleepily; quaintly; remarkably; restlessly; perpetually; crazily; deeply; divinely; ecstatically; extraordinarily; fancifully; fantastically; foolishly; girlishly; gloriously; hatefully; idly; interminably; pensively.

DREARINESS

adjectives
mute; funereal; cacophonous; soporific; appalling; blank.

DREGS

adjectives
wretched; bitterest; painful; basest; final; bottom; last.

DRENCH (*v*)

adverbs
instantaneously; entirely; thoroughly; fully; fatally; refreshingly; repeatedly.
(See flood, overflow.)

DRESS

adjectives
fetching; charming; daring; motley; gay; luxurious; trim; exquisite; gorgeous; delicious; evening; sky-blue; conventional; simple; starched; stiff; immaculate; adorable; homely; conspicuous; sophisticated; gauzy; filmy; gleaming; dishevelled; faded; dirty; frumpy; torn; crumpled; rumpled; flecked; queer; shabby; tattered; muslin; voile; serge; bridal; ostentatious; proper; irreproachable; azure; alpaca; holiday; low-necked; traveling; brocade; silk; hand-embroidered; ceremonial; wedding; picturesque; metal; native; turquoise; satin; fringed; beaded; buckskin; fluttering; flowing; insufficient; favorite; voluminous; old-style; detailed; antediluvian; unpretending; flaunting; shaggy; scant; plain; sumptuous; tight-fitting; sober; decorous; splendid; fantastical; ecclesiastical; airy; clean; yellow; fresh; somber; different; good-looking; extraordinary; school-girlish; flowered; varicolored; trailing; made-over; soft; sheer; identical; suitable; frivolous; flame; nondescript; gaudy; dazzling; cute; vivid; wearable; outlandish; martial; orchestral; distinctive; well-made; exceptional; fashionable; tinted; gala; lively; rich; basic; bloody; negligent; obsolete; impeccable; tailored; elegant; romantic; loose; glittering; quaint; rainy day; ragged; olive-green; outdoor; red; tulle; ballerina; becoming; masculine; fitted; boyish; convenient; hideous; fleshly; enchanting; rustic; indecent; shiny; wretched; flattering; versatile; foppish; manly; similar; alluring; gingham; incomparable.

verbs
adorn—; ban—; complete—; delight in—; don—; fancy—; fray—; gather—es; hem—; iron—; long for—; pleat—; shorten—; stitch—; straighten—; —befits; —clings; —rustles.
(See apparel, attire, gown, frock, clothing.)

DRESS (*v*)

adverbs
sparsely; impecuniously; exquisitely; ravishingly; punctiliously; fastidiously; extravagantly; flamboyantly; garishly; gaudily; flashily; uninvitingly; smartly; opulently; alluringly; superfluously; tastefully; picturesquely; gorgeously; expensively; impeccably; conservatively; fashionably; resplendently; somberly; foppishly; fantastically; drably; identically; ostentatiously; modestly; primitively; brilliantly; scrupulously; fetchingly; daringly; trimly; immaculately; dishevelledly; ceremonially; ecclesiastically; nondescriptly; distinctively; martially; obsoletely; negligently; rustically; shabbily; gallantly.
(See garb, attire, array.)

DRESSER

adjectives
consummate; flashy; top-notch.

DRESSING

adjectives
elaborate; court; surgical; decongestive; somber; passionate; undisciplined; artificial.

verbs
admire—; apply—; bedeck in—; change—; compliment—; complete—; concoct—; eat with—; occupy with—; prepare—; scrutinize—; serve with—; signal for—; soak through—; soil—; tear off—; wear—; —appeals; —eases; —preserves.

DRESSMAKER

adjectives
domestic; fashionable.

DRIFT

adjectives
pearly; scudding; glacial; pallid; irresistible; wind-swept; fallacious; wordy; imaginative; social; passing; intended; amoral; steaming; feathery; powdery; blinding; treacherous.

DRIFT (*v*)

adverbs
delightfully; quietly; naturally; casually; waywardly; lazily; smoothly; unconscious-

ly; hopelessly; tranquilly; alternately; irresistibly; indecisively; purposelessly; scuddingly; glacially; fallaciously; blindly.
(See wander, deviate.)

DRIFTER

adjectives
shiftless; disgruntled; utter.

DRIFTWOOD

adjectives
dancing; scattered.

DRILL

adjectives
arduous; painful; sword; emergency; stiff; dusty; grammatical.

DRILL (*instrument*)

verbs
attach—; man—; power—; sharpen—; sink —; yield to—; —beats out; —bores; —forces; —grinds; —plunges into; —strikes; —uncovers.
(See tool, machine.)

DRINK

adjectives
refreshing; useful; stimulating; seductive; sleepy; sparkling; zestful; hearty; robust; mellow; keen-tasting; acidulous; exhilarating; cooling; thirst-quenching; superb; delicate; delicious; appetizing; nutritious; soothing; innocuous; long-deferred; effervescent; frosty; fermented; hot; heady; tinkling; fiery; stiff; repulsive; steaming; choice; soft; wholesome; excellent; restorative; limpid.

verbs
abandon—; adulterate—; cool—; derive— from; err through—; ferment—; gulp—; ice—; indulge in—; offer—; rage with—; reek of—; regale with—; serve—; sour—; stagger with—; swallow—; thirst for—; —affects; —appeals; —assuages; —debauches; —depraves; —enslaves; —exhilarates; —intoxicates; —nourishes; —quenches; —refreshes; —satiates; —stimulates; —transforms; reel with—.
(See liquid, beverage, liquor, draught.)

DRINK (*v*)

adverbs
abstemiously; excessively; ravenously; plentifully; vilely; greedily; intemperately; copiously; thirstily; systematically; deeply; convivially; bestially; insatiably; inconsolably; loyally; deliberately; injudiciously.
(See sip, imbibe.)

DRINKER

adjectives
lusty; confirmed; chronic; mean; deadly; fat; unforgivable; suspicious; intemperate; unhealthy; inured; obstinate; problem.

DRINKING

adjectives
conspicuous; hard; excessive; copious; free; easy; constant; injudicious.

DRIP (*v*)

adverbs
monotonously; drearily; steadily; ceaselessly; intermittently; maddeningly; torturingly.
(See drop, fall.)

DRIVE (*campaign*)

adjectives
(See campaign.)

verbs
abandon—; abate—; captain—; conduct—; deadlock—; forsake—; hail—; inaugurate —; join—; lash into—; launch—; map out —; organize—; stage—; wage.
(See campaign, effort.)

DRIVE (*general*)

adjectives
fashionable; beautiful; urban; weed-grown; gravel; jolting; scenic; cliff-skirting; magnificent; wood; curving; public; leaf-strewn; coquina; steep; winding; fatal; monster; determined; concentrated; concerted; organizational; solitary; conclusive; oppressive; phenomenal.

DRIVE (*road*)

adjectives
(See road.)

verbs
amble along—; approach—; bar—; choke —; circle—; clear—; conceal—; crowd—; direct to—; emerge from—; enter—; follow —; gallop along—; hedge—; meet in—; park in—; patrol—; ramble along—; roll

along—; shout from—; skirt—; widen—; zoom into—; —beckons; —circles; —flanks; —winds; —zigzags.
(See road, avenue.)

DRIVE (v)

adverbs
ridiculously; irresponsibly; oppressively; tirelessly; tensely; erratically; heedlessly; blithely; electrically; masterfully; involuntarily; cautiously; leisurely; steadily; briskly; simultaneously; helplessly; tumultuously; precipitately; grimly; drunkenly; ineptly; furiously; irresistibly; contemptuously.
(See impel, propel.)

DRIVEL

adjectives
maudlin; meaningless; puerile; sentimental.

DRIVER

adjectives
addlebrained; grim; recumbent; cruel-visaged; skilled; trusted; insolent; sweating; wretched; reckless; superb; acrobatic; benumbed; drunken; inept; unlicensed.

verbs
apprehend—; blame—; convict—; direct—; employ—; fine—; hire—; jail—; license—; pay—; request—; summon—; tip—; trust —; —charges; —compels; —complies; —hails; —halts; —signals; —urges; arrest—.
(See engineer, operator.)

DRIZZLE

adverbs
driving; steaming; slow; spiritless; early-morning; fine; thick; cold; chill; falling.

DROLL

adverbs
entertainingly; laughably; naturally; racially; endlessly; remarkably; quaintly; oddly; deliciously; marvellously; piquantly; robustly; whimsically; fancifully; fantastically; grotesquely; genially; jeeringly; good-naturedly; spontaneously; chattily; sardonically; delightfully; coarsely; quietly; irrepressibly; irresistibly; playfully; unaccountably; inexhaustibly; effervescently; waggishly; facetiously; outlandishly.

DROLLERY

adjectives
broad; absurd.

DROMEDARY

adjectives
helmless; patient.

DRONE

adjectives
sonorous; teasing; supine; liturgic; stingless; luxurious.

DRONE (v)

adverbs
mechanically; somnolently; sonorously; monotonously; teasingly; maddeningly; dully; stupidly.
(See sound, idle.)

DRONING

adverbs
wearily; endlessly; prosaically; academically; pretentiously; incessantly; languidly; indifferently; leisurely; tiresomely; monotonously; intolerably; insufferably; unbearably; maddeningly; eternally.

DROOP

adjectives
discouraged; affectionate; pensive; pathetic; childish; weary; dissatisfied.

DROOP (v)

adverbs
gloomily; mournfully; cheerlessly; pathetically; languidly; dejectedly; alarmingly; tenderly; visibly; sleepily; pensively; wearily; tremulously.
(See fade, faint.)

DROP (fall)

adjectives
sickening; sheer.

DROP (liquid)

adjectives
minute; needle-like; pearly; crystal; myriad (pl); ambrosial; beady; glittering; blistering; infinitesimal; foolish; fresh; morning; congealed; twinkling; priceless; falling; tearful; insolent; bitterest; contiguous; bitter; ruddy; mournful; burning.

verbs
absorb—; add—; administer—; dispense —s; distil in—s; draw off—; drink—; dry —s; exude—; fall in—s; form—; give off —s; instill—s; mix with—s; moisten with —s; prepare—; save—; shed—; shower—; spill—; squeeze—; sweat—; wipe away—s;

—s appear; —s dampen; —s descend; —evaporates; —glitters; —issues from; —s stream from; —wets.
(See moisture.)

DROP (v)

adverbs
miraculously; swiftly; quietly; carelessly; listlessly; gently; significantly; tearfully; alarmingly; methodically; mournfully; lazily; heavily.
(See fall.)

DROPSY

adjectives
(See disease.)

verbs
affect with—; afflict with—; aggravate—; cure—; fall into—; incur—; relieve—; suffer from—; swell with—; treat for—; —appears; —arises; —destroys; —enlarges; —inflates; —overcharges; —pains.
(See disease.)

DROSS

adjectives
(See scum.)

verbs
allow for—; bloat with—; convert from—; dissolve into—; give off—; heap—; leave —; mass—; mix with—; mound—; purge of—; refine—; separate—; scum—; skim off—; —detracts; —floats; —remains.
(See impurity, waste, scum.)

DROUGHT

adjectives
devilish; burning; severe; prolonged; unparalleled; unprecedented; insatiate; scorching; extensive; continued; stagnant; extreme.

verbs
endure—; expose to—; flee—; prepare for —; prevent—; relieve—; subject to—; succumb to—; suffer from—; —burns; —continues; —descends; —destroys; —dries; —grips; —parches; —ravages; —ruins; —scorches; —sears.
(See heat.)

DROVE

adjectives
immense; countless.

DROWNING

verbs
avoid—; bewail—; escape—; guard against —; mark—; rescue from—; —bereaves; —takes its toll.

DROWSE (v)

adverbs
sorrowfully; deliciously; lazily; wearily; carelessly; comfortably; continually.
(See sleep.)

DROWSINESS

adjectives
overwhelming; overpowering; delicious; petulant; slight; bored; morbid.

DROWSY

adverbs
irresistibly; pleasantly; dully; deliciously; overwhelmingly; heavily; comfortably; cosily; warmly; fortunately; suddenly; fitfully; uncomfortably; inconveniently; overpoweringly; fatally; quietly; tranquilly; quietly; restfully; peacefully; drunkenly; pleasingly; mysteriously; startlingly; alarmingly; feverishly; hypnotically; dangerously; constantly; languorously; gradually; imperceptibly; idly; inertly; torpidly; lumpishly; dreamily; wearily.

DRUBBING

adjectives
(See beating.)

verbs
administer—; deserve—; earn—; expect—; impose—; inflict—; merit—; protect from—; punish with—; render—; scream under—; suffer—; threaten with—; undergo—; yield to—; —benefits; —cures.
(See beating.)

DRUDGE

adjectives
weary; household; casual; incessant; faithful; cautious; miserable; sickly; ordinary; domestic.

DRUDGE (v)

adverbs
monotonously; wearily; casually; incessantly; faithfully; miserably; domestically; deadeningly; depressingly; ceaselessly; degradingly; tediously; mechanically; unremittingly; grievously; unendingly; commercially.
(See work, labor.)

DRUDGERY

adjectives
tiresome; deadening; depressing; ceaseless; degrading; low; tedious; mechanical; grievous; unremitting; severest; formal; old-time; unending; initial; youthful; mercenary; pretty.

verbs
charge—to; condemn—; decline—; detail to—; earn by—; employ for—; expose to—; fade under—; fall into—; flee—; heap—upon; impose—upon; perform—; punish with—; put to—; release from—; relieve—; require—; subject to—; toil in—; —chokes; —wearies; —wears.
(See toil, work, labor.)

DRUG

adjectives
opiate; antisyphilitic; spicy; ancient; various (pl); somniferous; impotent; fatal; injurious; valuable; convenient; officinal; nerve-exciting; deleterious; evil-smelling; subtle; incompatible; nauseous; diluted; obnoxious; illicit; habit-forming; powerful; futile; sleep-inducing; insidious; pernicious; deadly.

verbs
addict to—; administer—; apply—; diminish—; distribute—; employ—; inhale—; label—; peddle—; prescribe—; purvey—; recommend—; rely on—; saturate with—; smuggle in—; swallow—; traffic in—; treat with—; turn to—; —affects; —aids; —allays; —alleviates; —antidotes; —controls; —heals; —induces; —poisons; —purges; —scours; inject—.
(See narcotic, poison, potion.)

DRUGGED

adverbs
disgustingly; hopelessly; pleasantly; overwhelmingly; heavily; comfortably; overpoweringly; fatally; mysteriously; startlingly; shockingly; alarmingly; dangerously; languorously; gradually; imperceptibly; inertly; dreamily; injuriously; subtly; insidiously; wickedly; inhumanly; habitually; incidentally; accidentally; deliberately; cruelly.

DRUM

adjectives
deafening; rolling; cask-like; sullen; insistent; furious; sardonic; deep-throated; bellowing; exploding; jarring; perpetual; droning; boisterous; revolving; muffled; recruiting; thumping; unbraced; churlish; distant; weird; rattling; repeating; monotonous.

verbs
belabor—; hearken to—; muffle—; rattle—; sound—; strike up—; thump—; —beats; —booms; —murmurs; —rolls; —stirs; —thunders; —warns; —welcomes.

DRUM (*v*)

adverbs
fretfully; vigorously; deafeningly; sullenly; insistently; furiously; jarringly; perpetually; droningly; muffledly; thumpingly; weirdly; monotonously.
(See beat, pound.)

DRUMBEAT

adjectives
furious; rapid; swift; staccato; far-off.

DRUMSTICK

verbs
accept—; approve of—; beat with—; bless with—; covet—; dress—; examine—; eye—; favor—; pick at—; regard—; reject—; relish—; request—; select—; squabble for—; —appeals; —appeases; —attracts.
(See meat, food.)

DRUNK

adverbs
comically; gloriously; jovially; convivially; pleasantly; beastly; soddenly; happily; deliciously; unconsciously; heartily; vacuously; fatuously; ribaldly; funnily; smartly; deeply; sleepily; drowsily; tragically; helplessly; hopelessly; terribly; utterly; desperately; dangerously; fantastically; grotesquely; palpably; morosely; glumly; woefully; mournfully; lovingly; ridiculously; ludicrously; lamentably; deplorably; pitifully; truculently; quarrelsomely; amiably; magnificently; obnoxiously; furiously; boisterously; outrageously; noisily; chattily; dizzily.

DRUNKARD

adjectives
heavy; cursing; quarrelsome; hopeless; confirmed; amiable; uncouth; magnificent; congenital; half-stupefied; reformed; infatuated; habitual; unproductive; swinish; incorrigible; abandoned.

verbs
abhor—; apprehend—; commit—to; confine—; cure—; direct—; humor—; incense

—; lock up—; perplex—; punish—; steady —; stupefy—; treat—; —assails; —disturbs; —partakes; —raves; —reels; —revels; —shocks; —staggers; —teeters; —totters; —wavers.

DRUNKENNESS

adjectives
habitual; seasonal; babbling; intemperate; usual; perpetual; rash.

verbs
abuse in—; addict to—; chain in—; cure—; denounce—; extirpate—; feign—; frown on—; imbibe to—; overcome by—; prevent —; saturate into—; seize by—; simulate—; soak into—; treat for—; yield to—; —appalls; —destroys; —envelops; —harms.

DRY

adverbs
terribly; painfully; horribly; intolerably; unbearably; unprofitably; unproductively; treelessly; dustily; torridly; hopelessly; desperately; heartbreakingly; destructively; insupportably; feverishly; parchedly.

DRYNESS

adjectives
unhealthful; satirical; extreme; intolerable.

DUALITY

adjectives
antagonistic; apparent; incredulous; baffling; unbelievable; inescapable.

DUBIOUS

adverbs
momentarily; strangely; horribly; anxiously; painfully; oddly; ominously; curiously; embarrassingly; remarkably; terribly; openly; dreadfully; frightfully; vaguely; frankly; obscurely.

DUCK

adjectives
iridescent; gabbling.

verbs
—beats water; —dives; —quacks; —rests on the water; —wings; —whirls past; —whirs.

(See fowl, bird.)

DUCT

adjectives
non-functional; necessary; essential; much-used.

verbs
discover—; draw through—; follow—; form—; introduce—; mark—; meet—; observe—; pass through—; perfect—; retreat through—; tap—; —communicates; —contains; —conveys; —directs; —dispatches; —guides; —runs; —secretes; —transmits; —turns.

(See passage, canal, conduit, pipe, channel.)

DUE

adverbs
legally; officially; naturally; recently; inescapably; conveniently; properly; justly; fairly; rightfully; reasonably; warrantably; legitimately; indefeasibly; allowably; equitably; substantially; imperatively; morally; immediately; opportunely; unexpectedly.

DUEL

adjectives
single-handed; mortal; formidable; celebrated; straight-out; valiant; political; judicial; desperate; inevitable; fatal; violent; informal; impromptu; bloody; spectacular; protracted; farcical; grudging; grim; solemn; honor-prompted.

verbs
arrange—; challenge to—; demand—; enter —; excuse from—; fight—; practise for—; stab in—; succumb in—; vanquish in—; witness—; —acquits; —decides; —discharges; —ensues; —entrances; —scars; —settles; —tests.

(See combat, encounter.)

DUES

adjectives
ecclesiastical; ample; usual.

DUET

adjectives
lively; little; long; thrilling; sentimental.

DUGOUT

adjectives
primitive; shallow; damp; foul-smelling; wartime; protective.

DUKE

adjectives
gracious; mighty; renowned; comical; fierce; noble; worthless; compassionate; virtuous; fantastical; banished; necessitous; covetous.

DULL

adverbs
abysmally; indifferently; insensitively; stupidly; strangely; stolidly; apathetically; vacantly; vacuously; ridiculously; unnaturally; singularly; oddly; peculiarly; curiously; unaccountably; inscrutably; irritatingly; vexatiously; shockingly; callously; coldly; carelessly; hopelessly; unpardonably; inexplicably; intolerably; heavily.

DULLNESS

adjectives
mysterious; pardonable; intolerable; tired; heavy; lonely; narrow; legitimate; ungenial; unbelievable; desperate; utter; everyday; kindly; incipient; vacant.

verbs
bar—; consign to—; contemplate—; correct —; curse—; dread—; mark by—; possess —; ridicule—; shroud in—; stagnate in—; tolerate—; —bores; —castigates; —distresses; —endangers; —irks; —maddens; —overwhelms; —pervades; —provokes; —surrounds.
(See apathy.)

DUMB

adverbs
pathetically; tragically; completely; suddenly; abysmally; wondrously; amazingly; stupidly; breathlessly; surprisingly; mysteriously; unutterably; wordlessly; silently; reticently; inarticulately; voicelessly; inexplicably.

DUMPY

adverbs
ridiculously; sturdily; robustly; clumsily; ludicrously; grotesquely; strangely; oddly; peculiarly; dwarfishly; elfishly; compactly; stubbily; stockily; outlandishly; comically; tragically; curiously; unfortunately; brawnily; stalwartly; stoutly.

DUNES

adjectives
darkened; shifting; lonely; sea-cast; high; tufted; transverse; desolate; shadowy; sandy; blistering; roasting; waterless; uninhabitable.

DUNGEON

adjectives
airless; subterranean; underground; miserable; bleak; awful; villainous; pagan; priestly; gloomy.

verbs
air—; bind in—; burst—; cast into—; clap into—; commit to—; conceal in—; confine to—; doom to—; dwell in—; escape from —; fling to—; gather in—; guard—; hide in—; imprison in—; incarcerate in—; lock in—; mold in—; rescue from—; rot in—; solace in—; storm—; —harbors; —incarcerates; —reeks.
(See cell, prison, hole.)

DUPE

adjectives
confiding; fair; penitent; innocent; credulous; intended; egregious.

DUPLICATE

adjectives
original; reversed.

verbs
appear in—; deliver—; encounter—; enter —; file—; furnish—; grant—; order—; part with—; provide—; purchase—; reserve—; retain—; save—; send—; sign—; supply—; take in—; transfer—; transmit—; void—; —copies; —repeats.
(See copy, replica.)

DUPLICITY

adjectives
infinite; twofold; unconscious; unworthy; patent; obvious.

DURABILITY

adjectives
utmost; increasing.

DURATION

adjectives
blooming; indefinite; customary; variable; perpetual; uncertain; momentary; endless; irregular; probable; limitless; comprehensible.

verbs
allow for—; calculate—; depend on—; fade in—; forbid—; grant—; limit—; mark—; pass—; portion—; prepare for—; propose —; time—; —continues; —lasts; —restricts; —suffices; —terminates.
(See period, time, era.)

DUSK

adjectives
growing; premature; eternal; grateful; gathering; friendly; mournful; dolorous; rainy; wet; winter; moonlit; thickening; deepening; early; glittering; clear; whis-

pering; soft; sweet; mellow; warm; humid; cool; softening; glimmering; green; deep; blue; moon-silvered; breathing.

verbs

diminish in—; dip in—; grope through—; haunt—; retire at—; wait for—; —clouds; —descends; —drifts in; —dulls; —gives away; —harbors; —hovers; —obscures; —reveals; —shades; —shadows; —swallows; —thickens; —treads.

(See twilight, evening, darkness.)

DUSKY

adverbs

prematurely; eternally; mournfully; thickly; softly; sweetly; deeply; dimly; inkily; sombrely; dingily; murkily; obscurely; nebulously; gloomily; glimmeringly; fragrantly; weirdly; fearfully; frightfully; pleasantly; restfully; peacefully; shadily; coolly; drearily; forlornly; desolately.

DUST

adjectives

cosmic; yellow; shining; fainting; dying; trifling; impalpable; valiant; undisturbed; shapeless; dreadful; sodden; titillating; red; desert; thick; blue; gray; heavy; blinding; oppressive; choking; stagnant; siliceous; shameful; trodden; dedicated; honored; long-committed; animate; fine; staining; unlovely; lonely; garnered; historical; rolling; scentless; murderous; material; injurious; sleeping; brown-colored; leveled; sunny; sunlit; suffering; kindred; burning; dim; scanty; feathery; illumined; senseless; slumbering; delicate; sacred; tawny; crumbling; vile; powdered; invisible; atomic; whirling; torturing; atmospheric; spiraling; hatred; stirred; gritty; smelly; filthy; parched; wayside; pervading; dissipating; mounting; precious; learned; flaming; uncontrolled; floating; undivided.

verbs

beat—; cake with—; carpet with—; clot with—; clothe in—; crumble to—; decompose into—; drag down to—; fall into—; filter—; form into—; go down in—; grovel in—; impregnate with—; issue from—; kick up—; lift from—; mar with—; mix with—; moulder in—; parch with—; reduce to—; remand to—; repose in—; return to—; roll in—; scatter—; scrape off—; scuff through—; shake off—; shower—; smite—; soil with—; spring from—; stamp —; stir up—; trail in—; tread in—; turn to—; write in—; —beclouds; —chokes; —clings to; —creeps in; —gathers; —permeates; —settles; —shrouds; —thickens.

(See ashes, powder, rubbish, earth.)

DUST (v)

adverbs

furiously; animatedly; industriously; vigorously; listlessly.

(See clean, polish.)

DUSTY

adverbs

disagreeably; intolerably; parchedly; painfully; uncomfortably; impalpably; dreadfully; terribly; abominably; unbearably; heavily; blindingly; oppressively; chokingly; shamefully; vilely; grittily; hatefully; filthily; pervasively; untidily; grossly; carelessly.

DUTIFUL

adverbs

carefully; beautifully; painfully; meticulously; punctiliously; assiduously; ostentatiously; passionately; pretentiously; obviously; scrupulously; devotedly; affectionately; primly; precisely; constantly; marvellously; sternly; officiously; efficiently; terribly; actively; energetically; publicly; submissively; competently; anxiously; solicitously; respectfully; politely; courteously; austerely; diplomatically; mechanically; grimly; piously; dully; rigorously; odiously; fondly; constantly; unfailingly.

DUTY

adjectives

irksome; self-assumed; unpleasant; imperative; simple; stern; domestic; humanest; arduous; boring; differential; obnoxious; official; expedient; obvious; religious; paternal; stooping; manifold (pl); bounden; inescapable; unending; inefficient; inviolable; particular; useful; terrible; serious; wide-reaching; unloved; indispensable; colorless; ever-esteemed; active; humbler; costuming; civic; social; pedagogic; creative; vexatious; nerve-racking; constitutional; public; appropriate; disagreeable; sad; monotonous; weary; dangerous; exhausting; exacting; uncongenial; painful; respective; definite; foolish; routine; submissive; competent; obstructionary; forcible; hardest; responsible; laborious; barbarous; conjugal; onerous; anxious; sickening; perilous; special; competent; childlike;

charitable; additional; ministerial; necessary; paramount; rental; far-off; pleasurable; professorial; momentous; military; eternal; vile; devotional; peremptory; respectful; easy; polite; generous; melancholy; intimate; principal; filial; unforgotten; imperious; eventual; matutinal; major; discriminating; blockading; wifely; incumbent; austere; consular; immediate; habitual; noble; irresistible; sworn; diplomatic; protective; distasteful; lowliest; fearful; unfamiliar; mechanical; tyrannous; slothful; solemn; earthly; grim; cursed; dull; high; pious; repugnant; homely; harsh; unhappy; rigorous; derelict; multifarious (pl); stern-voiced; nebulous; odious; manifest; tripartite.

verbs
assign—; assume—; attend to—; charge with—; comply with—; consign—to; define —; discharge—; disengage from—; encroach on—; engross in—; fail in—; fulfill—; impose—on; inculcate—; infringe on—; lessen—; meet—; neglect—; obey—; perform—; perish in—; pledge to—; pursue—; relieve of—; repudiate—; restrain by—; scrap—; shirk—; shoulder—; slacken in—; stand firm on—; stress—; surrender —; swerve from—; teach—; transgress—; —allows; —binds; —embraces; —enjoins; —impels; —inspires; —permits; —presses; —pricks on; —slackens; —weighs.
(See responsibility, business, work, obligation. function.)

DWARF

adjectives
deformed; rickety; stirring.

verbs
employ—; engage—; harbor—; gift—with; jeer at—; ridicule—; —antics; —busies; —carries off; —chuckles; —climbs; —covers; —dances; —hobbles; —hops; —mimics; —performs; —prances; —struts.
(See animal, manikin, clown.)

DWARFED

adverbs
hopelessly; mysteriously; grotesquely; fantastically; irremediably; unhappily; unfortunately; unluckily; singularly; oddly; strangely; queerly; sturdily; clumsily; elfishly; compactly; stockily; outlandishly; tragically; curiously; stalwartly; stoutly; pathetically; pitifully.

DWELL (v)

adverbs
luxuriously; languidly; pleasurably; laughingly; principally; impatiently; spaciously; lingeringly; occasionally; affectionately; impecuniously; inharmoniously; eternally; gloomily; artfully; gratefully; royally; unostentatiously; sedately; uncouthly; dismally; humbly; indefinitely.
(See live, abide.)

DWELLER

adjectives
dullest; admirable; planned; distinguished.

DWELLING

adjectives
planned; steadfast; isolated; ancestral; royal; prolonged; primitive; pretentious; ancient; snow-enveloped; forgetful; undisturbed; clustered; rustic; unostentatious; habitable; rapturous; odorous; sedate; time-stained; ambitious; tranquil; dismantled; rambling; uncouth; dismal; neglected; blank; underground; graceful; comfortable; humblest; stately; lovely; impressive; obscure; fabulous; patriarchal; communal; quaint; red-tiled; lacustrine; frail; abandoned.

verbs
assign to—; choose—; confine to—; decorate—; destroy—; enter—; erect—; fire—; flood—; grace—; lay waste—; move into—; occupy—; preserve—; purchase—; raze—; renovate—; restore—; retire to—; return to—; surround—; ventilate—; —appeals; —crumbles; —harbors; —invites; —shelters.
(See house, residence, abode.)

DWINDLE (v)

adverbs
amazingly; alarmingly; partially; insensibly; rapidly; markedly; obviously; scarcely; abruptly; logically; tragically; fatally.
(See decrease, diminish.)

DYE

adjectives
angry; synthetic; crimson; vegetable; progressive; autumnal.

DYNAMIC

adverbs
admirably; energetically; responsibly; socially; fortunately; acceptably; helpfully; usefully; stimulatingly; interestingly; actively; progressively; commercially; powerfully; effectively; efficiently; mightily.

DYNAMITE

adjectives
potential; swift; powerful.

verbs
arm with—; attack with—; blast with—; charge with—; contain—; convert into—; employ—; experiment with—; fire—; ignite—; mine with—; prepare—; shell—; test—; touch off—; —blasts; —blows up; —damages; —destroys; —disrupts; —explodes; —rends; —shakes; —shatters; —threatens; —uproots; —wrecks.

(See explosive, powder.)

DYNAMO

adjectives
(See motor.)

verbs
acquaint with—; employ—; examine—; exhibit—; operate—; provide—; ruin—; study—; —aids; —converts; —deposits; —excites; —generates; —induces; —purrs; —revolves; —rotates; —supplies; —transforms.

(See machine, generator, motor.)

DYNASTY

adjectives
reigning; unoffending; remote; trembling; continuous; unbroken; imperial; semi-feudal.

verbs
begin—; carry on—; cut short—; denounce—; found—; inaugurate—; maintain—; overthrow—; perpetuate—; rear—; —declines; —rules; —stems.

(See race, government, sovereignty.)

E

EAGER

adverbs
extremely; youthfully; girlishly; boyishly; childishly; unspeakably; inordinately; suspiciously; significantly; admirably; wonderfully; industriously; energetically; actively; alarmingly; adorably; ardently; fervidly.

EAGERNESS

adjectives
apologetic; utmost; excessive; passionate; extraordinary; manifest; restrained; childish; youthful; intelligent; dashing; sheer; liberal; hasty; hawk-eyed; feverish; fatal; diffident; fresh.

verbs
burn with—; conceal—; cure of—; display —; impart—; incite—; instil—; intensify —; moderate—; possess—; pursue with—; resist—; satiate—; stimulate—; temper—; —irritates; —devours; —exasperates; —maddens; —vexes.

(See impatience, fervor, intensity, zeal, ardor, impetuosity.)

EAGLE

adjectives
ravening; screaming; conquering; stuffed; rampant; princely; soaring; immense; gilded; empty; famished; symbolical; home-building.

verbs
cage—; exalt—; shelter—; —attacks; —braves; —captures; —circles; —clasps; —cleaves sky; —climbs; —destroys; —drives home; —drops; —eyes; —falls; —floats; —hawks; —hooks; —inspires; —moults; —preys on; —robs; —sails; —screams; —sights; —signifies; —soars; —surveys; —sweeps; —swoops; —symbolizes; —terrorizes; —thieves; —watches; —wheels; —zooms.

(See bird.)

EAR

adjectives
sensual; perked; dull; deaf; dozing; treacherous; attentive; unconscious; reasonable; good; licentious; thrifty; unheeding; helpless; eager; attending; sickly; pregnant; vouchsafed; kindest; external; deafened; listless; acute; greedy; reluctant; quick; sympathetic; large; cultivated; sensitive; passionate; gentler; foreboding; practiced; tesselated; apprehensive; furry; blushing; thievish; instinctive; loathing; listening; flapping; velvet; pleased; willing; public; sweet; enthusiastic; charmed; pendulous; living; dreaming; gorgeous; lobe-shaped; bewitched; trembling; ravished; waiting; dying; married; sickly; savage; aged; favorable; idle; insensible; untutored; modest; patient; inner; general; outwearied; kissed; fortified; fancy; inquisitive; royal; expectant; shuddering; reeling; mortal; unaccustomed; thoughtful; startled; proper; uninitiated; astonished; raptured; erect; impaired; innumerable (pl); flat; ill-developed; silken; uncultivated; ample; honest; grateful; aching; middle; cupped; drooping; constant; wakeful; sealed; vexed; burning; haughty; world; unwearied; uneducated; pointed; fainting; lewd; startled; straining; close-lying; public; couchant; senseless; inaudible; sylvan; favorable; leaning; hooded; untaught; silky; delicate; close-set; dainty; fine; gracious; velvety; well-set; quick; exact; sharp; critical; appreciative; alert; keen; cocked; intent; vigilant; cabbage; flabby; cauliflower; prominent; angular; preposterous; bruised; ungladdened; thick; long-lobed; enormous; stiff; droll; outstanding; uncomprehending; unattuned; unresponsive; cynical; inhospitable; unfailing; musical; irritated; entranced; thrilled; welcoming; delighted; shell-like; modern; royal; jeweled; ringing; jaunty; aloof; gullible; frisky; unjaded; well-trained; wiggly; tweaked; pert; questioning; hopeful.

verbs
abuse—; attune—to; beat against—; bend —; block—; box—; charm—; cleanse—; cock—; crop off—; deceive—; delight—; depend on—; din into—; drain—; dull—; gain—; impart to—; incline—; insert in—; irrigate—; lend—; lodge in—; meet—; muffle—; mutilate—; prick—forward; rend —; resound in—; strike—; twitch—; weary —; whisper in—; wiggle—; —s betray; —s buzz; —s devour; —discharges; —rings; —throbs; —tingles; stuff—.

(See head, ear-drum.)

EAR-DRUM

verbs

affect—; attack—; burst—; fall upon—; incise—; infect—; inflame—; injure—; meet—; perforate—; pierce—; rupture—; shatter—; split—; strike—; stun—; treat—; wound—; —admits; —pains; —protects; —vibrates.

(See membrane, ear.)

EARLY

adverbs

unusually; exceptionally; conveniently; amply; unnecessarily; remarkably; uncomfortably; unpleasantly; gloriously; appropriately; sufficiently; ridiculously; needlessly; opportunely; comfortably.

EARN (*v*)

adverbs

professionally; determinedly; lawfully; honestly; criminally; astoundingly; rapidly; drudgingly.

(See gain, procure.)

EARNEST

adverbs

enthusiastically; seriously; unusually; truly; zealously; fervently; ridiculously; habitually; eagerly; graciously; cordially; resolutely; desperately; tenaciously; inflexibly; unusually; extremely; gravely; solemnly; remarkably; indubitably; incredibly; emphatically; heartily; passionately; deeply.

EARNESTNESS

adjectives

simple; fixed; grave; intense; eager; conscientious; impressive; tragic; passionate; beseeching; aggressive; perpetual; burning; profound; characteristic; devout; somber; cold; honest; forgetful; dogged; taciturn; habitual; mighty; sanctified; mournful; solemn; downright; visible.

verbs

adopt—; allege—; begin with—; conduct with—; declare in—; endeavor with—; enter in—; express—; feign—; inculcate—; indicate—; instil—; pledge—; supplicate with—; touch by—; watch with—; —recommends; —secures.

(See ardor, sincerity, seriousness.)

EARNINGS

adjectives

scanty; exiguous; individual; fabulous; present; undistributed; sky-rocketed; hard-won; slender; stabilized.

verbs

attach—; bag—; bank—; collect—; curtail —; demand—; distribute—; enhance—; increase—; invest—; merit—; mortgage—; pledge—; save—; withdraw—; withhold—; —accrue; —decline; —recompense; —top.

(See wage, salary, pay.)

EAR-PHONE

verbs

adjust—; clamp on—; display—; furnish —; mislay—; pick up with—; require—; seek—; speak into—; —aids; —amplifies; —assists; —benefits; —clarifies; —communicates; —relieves; —rescues.

EARTH

adjectives

social; fructifying; plashy; stony; melancholy; calcareous; sunburned; verdant; daedal; thirsty; kindly; unviolated; groaning; fragrant; porous; frozen; transformed; sullen; gloomy; arching; molten; voluble; gaping; laboring; green-girt; hostile; distraught; disembowelled; chapped; unconsidered; spherical; moist; gaunt; wounded; awakening; bare; native; spongy; gladdened; powdered; delightful; frost-bound; renovated; shocked; shackled; perennial; messy; reconciling; nursing; synthetic; dull; prosaic; barren; despised; hungry; sanguine; encumbering; clodded; faithless; unawakened; arid; pendulous; easeful; wearied; sun-spangled; unyielding; virgin; mangled; filial; consecrated; turfless; frost-crisped; horrible; ancient; parched; sordid; absorbent; unmoistened; alluvial; stagnant; troubled; patient; various-mingled (pl); sinful; profiting; beleaguered; teeming; life-giving; habitable; darkened; spacious; healthy; odorous; unsinning; narrowing; menaced; lawful; burying; beauteous; faded; deep; peopled; trembling; desolate; indubitable; sleepy; bright; red; ashy; black; devastated; ordinary; shaken; fresh-turned; primeval; tenacious; widened; savage; fainting; fresh-plowed; chafed; harsh; central; pleasant; reluctant; silvery; waiting; finished; substantial; ridgy; imminent.

verbs

beautify—; blast—; bless—; bore into—; cling to—; command—; crawl upon—; create—; creep upon—; deface—; depart from —; explore—; fertilize—; gain—; grovel on—; inhabit—; inherit—; landscape—; mantle—; paw—; perish from—; plant—; plow—; pluck from—; rake—; reign on—;

replenish—; return to—; scatter over—; scorch—; scour—; sink into—; swoop to—; till—; tramp over—; trample—; veil—; wrestle with—; —abounds with; —blooms; —flowers; —heaves; —moulders; —nourishes; —quakes; —revolves; —sustains; —swallows up; —teems; —throbs; —trembles; —whirls; —renews.

(See world, globe, ground, soil, land.)

EARTHLY

adverbs

sordidly; selfishly; meanly; mercenarily; ungenerously; temperamentally; habitually; gracelessly; incredibly; basely; grossly; inconceivably.

EARTHQUAKE

adjectives

unusual; slumbering; murderous; all-devouring; disastrous; tremendous; submarine.

verbs

behold—; flee from—; record—; warn of—; —blights; —blots out; —crumbles; —destroys; —devastates; —jars; —razes; —reduces; —rends; —ruins; —rumbles; —shakes; —shatters; —subsides; —takes toll; —thunders; —topples; —wrecks.

(See tremor, shock, vibration.)

EASE

adjectives

amateur; blessed; ignoble; rakish; natural; light-hearted; tolerable; considerable; somnolent; charming; comparative; consequent; luxurious; extraordinary; miraculous; frivolous; insidious; rhythmic; dreamy; muscular; dignified; stately; material; solid; democratic; loose; astonishing; affluent; slothful; masterly; bloodless; constant; reckless; beauteous; cross-legged; disasterous; inglorious; cool; chivalric; deceptive; apparent; corrective; extreme; graceful; tranquil.

verbs

couch at—; court—; dwell in—; enhance—; enjoy—; envy—; interpose—; lack—; leap with—; live at—; loll in—; perform with—; procure with—; recline in—; rest at—; sacrifice—; seek—; spend in—; vault with—.

(See comfort, luxury.)

EASE (*v*)

adverbs

appreciably; greatly; partially; materially; markedly; miraculously; apparently; ostensibly; gracefully.

(See alleviate, soothe.)

EAST

adjectives

blustering; incandescent; lucid; purpling; blushing; blank; mummied; eyeless; fervid; mournful; bloodless.

EASY

adverbs

unusually; incredibly; remarkably; ridiculously; perfectly; comfortably; fairly; distinctly; definitely; naturally; conveniently; absolutely; suspiciously; unquestionably.

EAT (*v*)

adverbs

inordinately; leisurely; fastidiously; barbarously; enormously; bestially; heartily; regularly; hurriedly; swiftly; wolfishly; insufficiently; ravenously; incontinently; excessively; sparingly; plentifully; noisily; irrevocably; surreptitiously; swinishly; gluttonously.

(See consume, devour.)

EATABLE

adverbs

safely; deliciously; lusciously; definitely; perfectly; conveniently; unquestionably; wholesomely; avowedly; warrantably; assuredly; properly.

EATING

adjectives

mass; impudent.

verbs

abstain from—; coax into—; consider—; consume in—; exhaust by—; forbid—; reduce—; refrain from—; stimulate—; —appeases; —benefits; —bolsters; —encourages; —exhilarates; —fattens; —nourishes; —produces; —reassures; —revives; —satiates.

(See food, feeding.)

EAVES

adjectives

overhanging; lofty; dripping; gargoyled; sheltering.

EBB

adjectives
reduced; constant; alternate.

EBB (*v*)

adverbs
constantly; alternately; markedly; noticeably; scarcely; partially; wholly; entirely; slowly; tragically; fatally; rapidly.
(See flow, move.)

EBONY

adjectives
grizzled; flowing.

EBULLIENT

adverbs
effervescently; gushingly; violently; hysterically; outrageously; turbulently; riotously; obstreperously; naturally; excitedly; stormily; ungovernably; uncontrollably; terribly; highly.

EBULLITION

adjectives
youthful; sulphurous; trifling; present.

ECCENTRIC

adjectives
genial; amazing.

adverbs
highly; outlandishly; ostentatiously; fantastically; oddly; offensively; incurably; proudly; flagrantly; peculiarly; inexplicably; inscrutably; temperamentally; egotistically; exasperatingly; comically; pitiably; unfortunately; abnormally; wantonly; singularly; unaccountably; extravagantly; insanely; capriciously; whimsically; uncomfortably; unusually.

ECCENTRICITY

adjectives
gentle; hopeless; individual; amiable; violent; drunken; troublesome; benevolent; ghastly; moderate; asinine.

verbs
acquire—; adopt—; affect—; allow—; attribute to—; betray—; blame on—; condemn—; develop—; feign—; govern—; laugh at—; mimic—; overlook—; palliate—; pardon—; produce—; ridicule—; sense—; stray into—; tolerate—; —amuses; —offends; —perplexes.
(See oddity, idiosyncrasy.)

ECCLESIASTIC

adverbs
highly; completely; sacredly; judicially; lawfully; legally; reverently; strictly; soundly; literally; evangelically; faithfully; positively; infallibly; irrefutably; dogmatically; authoritatively; doctrinally; authentically; officiously; reverently; fanatically; deeply; devoutly.

ECHO

adjectives
death-groan; congenial; sonorous; eternal; faint; stunning; distorted; awaking; heartbreaking; softened; jovial; dreary; drumming; startling; sullen; melodious; unimpressive; woodland; respectable; evasive; sparse; prophetic; sharp; metallic; trashy; reverberating; resonant; hovering; wearisome; laughing; ringing; deep-resounding; high; multiplied; somnolent; battling; vibrant; obedient; mad; bellowing; wheezing; wild; tragic; mocking; haunting; silvery; reminiscent; trembling; slumbering.

verbs
evoke—; listen for—; prolong—; silence—; stir—; voice—; —answers; —breaks; —dies away; —fades; —hurls back; —repeats; —resounds; —returns; —reverberates; —rings; —roars; —shrills; —sings out.
(See sound, voice.)

ECHO (*v*)

adverbs
buoyantly; contemptuously; piously; responsively; cheerily; ominously; dubiously; joyously; anxiously; heartily; falteringly; stupidly; congenially; sonorously; faintly; heartbreakingly; jovially; drearily; sullenly; melodiously; evasively; prophetically; metallically; reverberatingly; wearisomely; ringingly; vibrantly; obediently; hauntingly; mockingly; reminiscently; tremblingly.
(See reverberate, resound.)

ECLIPSE

adjectives
mysterious; swift; dismal; temporary; absolute; ominous.

verbs
identify—; observe—; predict—; record—; study—; suffer—; throw into—; —blinds; —cloaks; —clouds; —darkens; —deprives; —dims; —extinguishes; —hides; —intercepts; —intervenes; —obscures; —occurs; —overcasts; —screens; —shadows.
(See darkness.)

ECLIPSE (*v*)

adverbs
exultantly; mysteriously; swiftly; dismally; temporarily; absolutely; ominously; skillfully; treacherously; eventually; partially; entirely; scarcely; finally; triumphantly.
(See surpass, excel.)

ECONOMICAL

adverbs
properly; methodically; systematically; carefully; frugally; stingingly; successfully; highly; overly; habitually; admirably; utterly; wonderfully; remarkably; pitifully; practically; shrewdly; thriftily; parsimoniously; selfishly; unnecessarily; shabbily; ungenerously; sordidly; miserably; necessarily; wisely; cheerfully; churlishly.

ECONOMICS

verbs
affect—; alter—; apply—; attack—; control—; deal with—; determine—; devote to—; employ—; experiment with—; govern —; improve—; manage by—; observe—; regulate—; school in—; specialize in—; understand—; —assumes; —discerns; —flourishes; —regards; —serves.
(See science.)

ECONOMIST

adjectives
professional; orthodox; political; academic.

ECONOMY

adjectives
vulnerable; rugged; centralized; reasonable; regimental; actual; domestic; scrupulous; excessive; benign; solitary; desperate; smooth-running; careful; ultimate; numerous (pl); political; drastic; niggardly; expensive; operating; utmost; satisfying; random; ready; careful; capitalistic; animal; internal; democratic; rigid; spiritual; unequalled; household; strictest; outstanding; supernatural; gasoline; false; agricultural; physical.

verbs
betray—; decree—; denounce—; disparage —; effect—; encourage—; favor—; hail—; ignore—; instil—; maintain—; necessitate —; observe—; plan—; practise—; promote—; require—; sacrifice—; systemize—; tighten—; undertake—s; —assures; —preserves; —saves.
(See management, frugality, thrift.)

ECSTASY

adjectives
sheer; delicate; mounting; artistic; tingling; silent; trembling; insane; voluble; bedazzled; boundless; untaught; brainless; anguished; mingled; delicious; spiritual; quiet; simulated; inexpressible; wonderful; unquestioned; consuming; momentary; wonderful; gentle; heaven-breathed; stolen; spontaneous; restless; modern; awed; undivided.

verbs
blast—; blunt—; burst into—; emerge from —; enthrall in—; experience—; flow in—; flutter in—; glow with—; increase—; indulge in—; inspire—; quiver with—; recall in—; respond to—; swoon in—; throw into —; tingle in—; transport into—; tremble with—; wake to—; —dissolves; —excites; —flushes; —pervades; —pulsates; —rules; —stirs.
(See bliss, happiness, delight, rapture, joy, enthusiasm.)

ECSTATIC

adverbs
rapturously; happily; unrestrainedly; blissfully; youthfully; blessedly; delightfully; extravagantly; preposterously; romantically; enthusiastically; fervently; eagerly; passionately; deeply; thrillingly; breathlessly; glowingly; hysterically; significantly; obviously; charmingly; ravishingly.

ECZEMA

verbs
exude from—; pick at—; rub—; salve—; suffer from—; treat—; x-ray—; —burns; —cracks; —discharges; —excretes; —inflames; —irritates; —itches; —pains; —smarts; —spreads; —stings; —tingles; —torments.
(See disease.)

EDDY

adjectives
whirling; murmuring; brilliant; wild; twisting; nervous; blue; boiling; curled; dimpling.

EDDY (*v*)

adverbs
irresistibly; whirlingly; murmuringly; wildly; twistingly; boilingly; dimplingly; ceaselessly; monotonously; dangerously; rapidly; sickeningly.
(See whirl, swirl.)

EDGE

adjectives
shadowed; sharpened; upturned; natural; outermost; foaming; thin; extremest; trembling; distinctive; cord; jutting; keen; cruel; marshy; raveled; cutting; frayed; frowsy; smooth-quarried; relentless; perilous.

verbs
bevel—; blunt—; crimp—; double—; drive to—; dull—; escape—; file—; flounder on—; heave over—; round—; set on—; sharpen—; slip from—; smite with—; smooth—.
(See border, verge, boundary.)

EDIBLE

adverbs
safely; undeniably; deliciously; lusciously; wholesomely; healthfully; delightfully; warrantably; refreshingly; daintily; agreeably; palatably; pleasantly; acceptably; appetizingly; definitely; highly.

EDICT

adjectives
late; strict; fearful; imperial; royal.

verbs
decry—; denounce—; enforce—; frame—; fulfill—; impose—; infringe on—; introduce —; invalidate—; issue—; legalize—; nullify—; proclaim—; revoke—; spurn—; support—; —bans; —corrects; —declares; —reforms; —stands; —subjugates.
(See decree, mandate, proclamation, ordinance.)

EDIFICATION

verbs
break down—; contribute to—; contrive—; demolish—; destroy—; dismantle—; dispense—; inspire—; justify—; profane—; promote—; prompt—; provide—; ravage—; ruin—; scoff at—; deserve—.
(See enlightenment, education, instruction, improvement.)

EDIFICE

adjectives
gaunt; holy; ramshackle; massive; time-worn; solid; sumptuous; humble; sacred; ghostly; enchanted; shattered; spiritual; historic; august; vast; splendid; stately; public; imposing; spacious; social; heathen; elaborate; ecclesiastical.

verbs
convert—; demolish—; destroy—; dismantle —; erect—; modernize—; profane—; raise —; ravage—; raze—; renovate—; ruin—; —collapses; —crumbles; —moulders; —topples.
(See building, structure, house.)

EDIT (*v*)

adverbs
skillfully; artfully; exquisitely; originally; hastily; voluminously; sympathetically; crudely.
(See prepare, check.)

EDITION

adjectives
revised; voluminous; choice; camouflaged; pirated; limited; reprint; enormous; successive (pl); telescoped; exquisite; lavish; rare; illustrated; muggier; original; ornamented; annotated; abridged; cherished; privately-printed.

verbs
amend—; annotate—; arrange into—; change—; collect—s; conceive—; copyright —; correct—; criticize—; examine—; exhaust—; favor—; furnish—; illustrate—; issue—; mend—; order—; prepare—; print —; publish—; quote from—; revise—; —abounds with; —corrects; —informs; —surpasses.
(See issue, work, book, publication, copy.)

EDITOR

adjectives
vituperative; country; important; cable-desk; guileless; pugnacious.

verbs
consult—; employ—; —arranges; —conceives; —condemns; —conducts; —criticizes; —describes; —details; —exposes; —expunges; —inserts; —manages; —pens; —plans; —prepares; —publishes; —refuses; —relates; —revises; —scorns; —selects; —suggests; —supervises.
(See journalist, publisher.)

EDITORIAL

adjectives
conspicuous; calumnious; rousing; occasional; learned; rattling; fearless.

verbs
censor—; commend—; compose—; contribute—; criticize—; grind out—; popularize —; prepare—; revise—; set up—; venture

—; word—; —embarrasses; —exonerates; —exposes; —insinuates; —intimates; —recounts; —relates; —shocks; —suggests; —unloads.
(See article, writing.)

adverbs
reliably; officially; responsibly; ridiculously; sagely; egotistically; unquestionably; notoriously; flatteringly; astutely; adroitly; obviously.

EDITORIALIZE (v)

adverbs
elatedly; pompously; calumniously; learnedly; fearlessly; ponderously; fanatically; oracularly; languidly; pathetically.
(See write, talk.)

EDUCATE (v)

adverbs
simultaneously; properly; insensibly; imperfectly; adequately; superficially; genteelly; rigorously; bookishly; progressively; classically; technically; intensively; practically; liberally; musically; undisciplinedly; systematically; formally; artistically; legitimately; aesthetically; religiously; snobbishly; methodically; scholastically; primitively; physically; idealistically; vocationally; competently.
(See instruct, teach.)

EDUCATION

adjectives
bookish; purposive; self-acquired; intellectual; progressive; priggish; aimless; technical; elementary; spiritual; mass; classical; advanced; intensive; practical; inevitable; meager; imperfect; precarious; previous; liberal; musical; systematic; military; evolutionary; formal; invigorating; confused; undisciplined; barren; wasteful; superficial; artistic; legitimate; adequate; aesthetic; wider; practicable; far-reaching; preparatory; humane; specific; religious; methodical; labored; compulsory; scholastic; primitive; interior; physical; positive; idealistic; vocational; regular; rudimentary; competent.

verbs
achieve—; broaden—; deny—; dominate—; enforce—; foster—; furnish—; glean—; influence—; laud—; liberalize—; neglect—; promote—; retard—; —biases; —broadens; —cultivates; —develops; —enlightens; —forms; —spreads.
(See culture, enlightenment, development, training.)

EDUCATIONAL

adverbs
highly; unusually; inconceivably; uncommonly; delightfully; alarmingly; formidably; distressingly; monotonously; agreeably; helpfully; tiresomely; necessarily; advantageously; acceptably; slightly.

EERIE

adverbs
uncommonly; uncannily; supernaturally; dreadfully; terribly; unusually; singularly; oddly; curiously; queerly; unnaturally; inexplicably; remarkably; frightfully; appallingly; gruesomely; grotesquely; undeniably.

EFFACE (v)

adverbs
rapidly; gradually; partially; entirely; totally.
(See obliterate, cancel.)

EFFECT

adjectives
similar; profound; influential; immediate; harmonious; beneficent; picturesque; pernicious; reactionary; ventriloquial; verbal; visible; fleeting; nutritive; continuous; external; displeasing; fearful; biologic; adverse; soothing; equal; singular; enormous; contractile; tragic; radiant; emotional; designed; salutary; useful; sinking; palpable; excellent; demoralizing; perceptible; social; festive; elegant; stimulating; smooth; modern; ultimate; tonic; fatal; harmful; cumulative; spacious; stunning; disastrous; probable; deterrent; dying-duck; powerful; atmospheric; characteristic; putrefactive; indirect; heavenly; grotto; depressing; electrical; sustained; pronounced; hypnotic; particular; recreational; prejudicial; recurrent; stabbing; continuous; important; enervating; naturalistic; exhilarating; varied; striking; outdoor; lamplight; remote; psychological; honest; combined; dreadful; decisive; charming; fair; gabardine; rejuvenating; theatrical; plaster; gravitating; dramatic; wondrous; devastating; incredible; summary; injurious; impressive; permanent; secondary; enchanting; artistic; malevolent; pathetic; accumulating; sedative; rare; extrinsic; detrimental; contrary; harmonic; metrical; rhythmical; astringent; prismatic; incomparable; startling; hardening; deleterious; decorative; supreme; paralyzing; bewildering; debasing; tranquillizing; luminous; strange; uncanny; stiffening; mechanical; striped; harsh; moral; architectural; broadening;

finished; unfailing; entrancing; orchestral; inspired; instantaneous; vivid; stormy; considerable; alkalizing; deteriorating; similar; preternatural; appreciable; marvellous; outrageous; racial; metrical; subversive; chromatic; maleficent; invigorating; ordinary; pyramidical; noble; depressing; thrilling; noticeable; rude; sinister; intended; massed; bracing; detectable; geophysical; brilliant; persuasive; enduring; distinguished; terrestrial; healthful; reciprocal; dampening; unfortunate; oratorical; regulating; tremendous; solemn; awful; polyphonic; unreal; unifying; distinctive; exotic; practical; flowered; composite; desired; invigorating; lasting; pompous; preservative; curative; magical; peculiar; unusual; textural; gratifying; subsequent; smartest; manifested; propitious; astounding; touching; suave; inevitable; twilight; dynamical; preponderant; secular; baneful; momentary; prized; destructive; dignified; perishing; thermometric; tragic; marked; binding; bizarre; half-veiled; required; scanty; baleful; exquisite; minute; kaleidoscopic; resultant; disintegrating; powerful; rhetorical; possible; absurd; mere; healing; imposing; tingling; fructifying; crushing; organ; luxurious; correspondent; errant; surprising; subtle; delicate; legitimate; acoustical; ill; variegated (pl); narcotic; nugatory; elevating; comic; deadly; sculptural; outward; happy; calamitous.

verbs
accentuate—; achieve—; analyze—; attain —; banish—; comprehend—; conceive—; counteract—; curse—; demonstrate—; destroy—; disturb—; elicit—; escape—; evaluate—; exercise—; exert—; gauge—; heighten—; ignore—; lessen—; mar—; mark—; match—; minimize—; mitigate—; neutralize—; notice—; observe—; obviate —; occasion—; offset—; predict—; prevent—; recapture—; record—; rehearse—; remove—; rob of—; speculate on—; strive for—; suffer from—; time—; trace—; visualize—; weaken—; witness—; —endures; —persists; —wears off.
(See result, realization, end, aim.)

EFFECT (v)

adverbs
speedily; insidiously; skillfully; advantageously; simultaneously; satisfactorily; unconsciously; tremendously; promptly; periodically; profoundly; perniciously; beneficently; externally; fearfully; adversely; soothingly; singularly; emotionally; perceptibly; demoralizingly; ultimately; fatally; harmfully; powerfully; characteristically; recurrently; continuously; remotely; decisively; theatrically; devastatingly; incredibly; injuriously; permanently; malevolently; pathetically; supremely; bewilderingly; debasingly; mechanically; unfailingly; racially; depressingly; curatively; gratifyingly; propitiously; dynamically; subtly; comically; calamitously.
(See accomplish, achieve.)

EFFECTIVE

adverbs
satisfactorily; highly; pleasantly; undeniably; profoundly; remarkably; sufficiently; powerfully; extremely; adequately; serviceably; practically; unusually; tremendously; admittedly.

EFFECTIVENESS

adjectives
theatric; amazing; histrionic; architectural; outstanding; dramatic; general; pictorial; decorative; haphazard; marvelous; maximum.

verbs
attain—; attend with—; augment—; direct with—; dispose with—; employ—; execute with—; follow with—; function with—; impair—; increase—; mar—; operate with —; prevent—; produce—; pursue with—; treat with—; weaken—; —accomplishes; —comforts; —decides; —produces; —rectifies; —renders.
(See efficiency, power.)

EFFECTUAL

adverbs
thoroughly; consummately; elaborately; perfectly; finally; immediately; felicitously; fortunately; highly; completely; absolutely; altogether; utterly; surprisingly.

EFFEMINATE

adverbs
disgustingly; unfortunately; unpleasantly; disagreeably; pitiably; fearfully; weakly; nervously; softly; languidly; horribly; extremely; timidly; infirmly; remarkably; vexatiously.

EFFERVESCENT

adverbs
highly; unusually; delightfully; amusingly; sparklingly; frothily; ebulliently; energetic-

ally; enthusiastically; excitedly; irrepressibly; restlessly; violently; mercurially; tempestuously; impulsively; curiously; remarkably; excessively; foolishly.

EFFETE

adverbs
horribly; lamentably; pitiably; tragically; unfortunately; deplorably; undeniably; remarkably; significantly; unsubstantially; uselessly; emptily; hopelessly; obviously.

EFFICACIOUS

adverbs
(See efficient.)

EFFICACY

adjectives
untamable; proved; constitutional; feeble.

EFFICIENCY

adjectives
calm; bustling; normal; productive; awkward; chaotic; devastating; vaunted; pedagogical; modest; maximum; extreme; technical; superior; industrial; impaired; top; outstanding; administrative; dreadful; physical; individual; creative; working; up-to-date; antiseptic; defensive; stolid; executive; incredible; added; increased; slender; swift; cleansing; expanding.

verbs
achieve—; admit—; assimilate—; demand —; destroy—; discharge with—; display—; effect—; enforce—; exhibit—; impair—; increase—; lack—; prove—; rate—; weaken—; —produces; —promotes; —saves.
(See ability, power.)

EFFICIENT

adverbs
remarkably; unusually; obviously; busily; incredibly; completely; sensibly; wisely; officiously; pleasantly; gracefully; politely; irritatingly; ostentatiously; horribly; satisfactorily; skilfully; expertly; cleverly; adroitly; ingeniously; shrewdly; ably; invaluably; surprisingly; unbelievably; uncommonly.

EFFIGY

adjectives
silent; grotesque; gilded; insensible; clumsy; crowned; sceptered; pompous; full-length; sad; recumbent; ghastly; transfixed; rueful; granite.

verbs
bear—; burn—; carry—; damn in—; display—; draw in—; dress up—; execute in—; hang in—; mount—; prepare—; —copies; —depicts; —destroys; —dramatizes; —illustrates; —portrays; —represents; —ridicules.
(See image, figure.)

EFFORT

adjectives
sheer; obvious; ceaseless; insane; sporadic; powerful; convulsive; belated; manful; stringent; fanatical; bitter; renewed; daring; conciliatory; overt; pitiful; thwarted; ponderous; childish; rash; humble; feeble; emotional; culminating; futile; creditable; clumsy; persistent; crowning; strained; zealous; individual; abortive; desperate; unscrupulous; constrained; infantile; frantic; untiring; slightest; reasonable; laborious; fragmentary; prolonged; wasted; proud; unsuccessful; painful; indomitable; stupendous; superior; strenuous; sustained; conscious; concentrated; active; stern; Herculean; visible; pictorial; vigorous; charitable; automatic; dynamic; heroic; mightiest; literary; concerted; willful; strong; intermittent; bounding; mental; feverish; immense; utmost; tentative; paramount; extra; oracular; extant; superhuman; conversational; languid; consecutive; tireless; unionized; wearisome; insufferable; historical; fruitless; human; best; spasmodic; persevering; editorial; effectual; baffled; irrelevant; determined; vague; misdirected; rash; sincere; spontaneous; notable; crude; violent; vain; inadequate; collective; immense; energetic; perilous; organized; powerful; undue; conceivable; formidable; periodic; praiseworthy; pioneering; never-ceasing; continued; self-denying; willing; exhausting; arduous; constructive; moral; fitful; creative; initial; expiratory; bizarre; rain-making; remedial; serious; apparent; sober; sympathetic; painstaking; offensive; special; colloquial; ridiculous; everlasting; sedulous; anxious; united; patient; plastic; maiden; pathetic; dutiful; generous; repetitive; financial; belated; poetic; obstinate; volunteer; co-operative; communal; religious; appropriate; published; unremitting; diligent; supreme; avowed; expired; earnest; enforcement; passionate; future; pretentious; evident; bluffing; murderous; barren; sublimest; kindly; sincere; vexed; ambitious; operatic; courageous; unwise; individual; unflinching; restraining.

verbs
belittle—; bend—; berate—; cheer—; compensate for—; concentrate—; coordinate —s; counter—; crown—; decry—; dwarf—; endorse—; enlist—s; entail—; exert—; expend—; fail in—; focus—s on; galvanize—; garble—; glorify—; hamper—; impede—; intensify—; justify—; key up for—; lend—; mock—; nullify—; quicken—; redouble—; repay—; repel—; reward—; scotch—; spare—; squander—; slacken—; stir to—; succumb to—; suppress—; suspend—; thwart—; —attains; —bears fruit; —exhausts.
(See attempt, endeavor, exertion.)

EFFRONTERY

adjectives
calculated; humorous; brazen; incredible; unabashed; hardy; vulgar; matchless.

EFFULGENT

adverbs
radiantly; glaringly; sparklingly; scintillantly; shimmeringly; dazzlingly; luminously; lustrously; unbelievably; remarkably; brilliantly; garishly; splendidly; brightly; incredibly; unexpectedly; showily; gaudily; flashily; tremendously.

EFFUSION

adjectives
amatory; tender; pathetic; vocal; gymnastic; osculatory; lyrical; rich; boisterous; copious; labored; characteristic; reducing; irrepressible; unnecessary; vaporing; hypocritical; merry; hypercritical.

EFFUSIVE

adverbs
garrulously; lavishly; chattily; enthusiastically; explosively; excessively; needlessly; ridiculously; foolishly; inappropriately; unpleasantly; comically; endlessly; noticeably; amusingly; overly; absurdly.

EGG

adjectives
pendent; ostrich; whipped; fried; poached; scrambled; hot.

verbs
addle—; beat—; burst from—; coddle—; crate—s; deposit—; emerge from—; gather —s; germinate in—; guard—s; hatch from —; hunt—; impregnate—; incubate—; market—; nest—; originate in—; poach—; puncture—; scramble—; sit on—; snatch—; spring from—; start from—; whip—; —brings forth; —curdles; —produces.

EGO

adjectives
exaggerated; inflated; restless; exalted; hard; poised; fretted; bubbling; monarchical; suppressed; assertive.

verbs
bolster up—; commiserate—; excite—; express—; foster—; gratify—; inflate—; pervert—; reflect—; satiate—; satisfy—; soothe —; submerge—; understand—.
(See personality, individuality.)

EGOISM

adjectives
sullen; puppyish; dramatic; tyrannical; justifiable; elemental; narrowing; unlimited; psychopathic; holy; sublime; sentimental; comfortable; collective; passionate; colossal; animal; narcissistic.

EGOTISM

adjectives
outrageous; instinctive; explicable; monstrous; intense; superb; stultifying; passionate; blustering; savage; solid; immense; baseless; absurd; ruthless; unselfish; indecent; vivacious; supreme; undisguised; magnanimous; friendly; dreary; compound; naive; absolute; slightest; importunate; young; cultivated; placid.

verbs
allow—; annihilate—; apologize for—; avoid—; banish—; brand—; criticize—; excuse—; justify—; pardon—; pierce—; produce—; recommend—; resist—; —absorbs; —bores; —dominates; —irks; —occupies; —offends.
(See conceit, vanity, self-esteem.)

EGOTIST

adjectives
diseased; sentimental; offensive; supreme; turbulent; hateful; fantastic; sheer; unmalleable; harmless; power-hungry.

EGOTISTICAL

verbs
shamefully; arrogantly; absurdly; outlandishly; palpably; obviously; highly; profoundly; inexcusably; ponderously; blatantly; boastfully; vaingloriously; ridiculously;

noisily; curiously; unashamedly; disagreeably; offensively; foolishly; extremely; habitually; incredibly; blindly.

EJACULATE (v)

adverbs
sarcastically; faintly; incredulously; blankly; feelingly; sententiously; forcefully; vigorously; caustically; admiringly; joyfully; fiercely; piously; angrily; indelicately; hollowly; muffledly.
(See exclaim, call.)

EJACULATION

adjectives
customary; heartfelt; fervent; profane; pious; startled; angry; indelicate; religious; barbarous; hushed; hollow; muffled.

EJACULATORY

adverbs
violently; ridiculously; needlessly; noisily; importantly; egregiously; highly; arrogantly; blatantly; suddenly; startlingly; shockingly; ludicrously; stertorously; vociferously; monstrously; immensely; outlandishly.

EJECT (v)

adverbs
forcibly; copiously; abruptly; vigorously; determinedly; suddenly.
(See discharge, expel.)

ELABORATE (v)

adverbs
minutely; successfully; eloquently; ingeniously; ridiculously; pompously; ramblingly; fully.
(See develop, perfect.)

ELABORATE

adverbs
extremely; excessively; unnecessarily; arduously; egregiously; incredibly; ostentatiously; ingeniously; skilfully; intolerably; preposterously; fearfully; unduly; inappropriately; suitably; ceremoniously; oddly; singularly; significantly; pompously; laboriously; marvellously; beautifully.

ELABORATION

adjectives
ingenious; quaintest; ridiculous; polychronic; productive.

ELASTIC

adverbs
conveniently; expediently; comfortably; immensely; extremely; marvelously; resiliently; sturdily; wonderfully; powerfully; effectively; adequately; diplomatically; buoyantly; springily; notably.

ELASTICITY

adjectives
molecular; virtual; joyous; dangerous.

verbs
acquire—; calculate—; depend on—; deprive of—; lessen—; limit—; lose—; recover—; remove—; require—; return by—; strain—; stress—; test—; —overcomes; —resists; —restores; —varies.

ELATED

adverbs
unduly; hysterically; strangely; oddly; curiously; highly; naturally; ecstatically; rapturously; proudly; quietly; properly; unusually; brightly; enthusiastically; triumphantly; merrily; exultantly; confidently; pertly; priggishly; smugly; dramatically; boastfully; indescribably; irrepressibly.

ELATION

adjectives
short-lived; undue; cruel; hysterical; strange.

ELBOW

adjectives
bony; touching; angular; fat; massive; crooked; dimpled; immaculate; hard; inert.

verbs
brace—; cap—; extend—; fit on—; fracture—; jab with—; join—; jostle with—; move—; nudge with—; pad—; prop on—; raise—; rest on—; skin—; strain—.
(See joint, arm.)

ELDER

adjectives
disillusioned; itinerant; unsuspecting; ruling; grumpy.

verbs
appeal to—; assemble—s; burlesque—; consult—; entreat—; exhort—; gather—s; grieve—; heed—; honor—; ordain—; persuade—; respect—; revere—; succeed—; worry—; —advises; —counsels; —decrees; —heads; —interposes; —judges; —officiates; —pardons; —presides over; —punishes; —rebukes; —warns.
(See deacon, minister, ruler.)

ELDERLY

adverbs

respectably; unquestionably; soberly; reliably; safely; pleasantly; comfortably; graciously; sourly; augustly; gravely; admittedly; frightfully; depressingly; incurably.

ELECT (v)

adverbs

unanimously; tacitly; spontaneously; subsequently; optionally; popularly; municipally; decisively; willingly; virtually.

(See choose, select.)

ELECTION

adjectives

farcical; obligatory; ensuing; local; optional; subsequent; degrading; frank; popular; financial; municipal.

verbs

announce—; campaign for—; climax—; conduct—; doom—; gain—; inveigh against—; merit—; nullify—; officiate at—; postpone—; propose—; revoke—; riot at—; stay—; swing—; —installs; —results in.

(See vote.)

ELECTIONEER (v)

adverbs

blatantly; flatteringly; obviously; humorously; pompously; volubly; wheedlingly; politically; masterfully; passionately; journalistically.

(See plan, campaign.)

ELECTIVE

adverbs

freely; unconditionally; fortunately; highly; frankly; wisely; generously; broadly; extensively; liberally; tolerantly; widely.

ELECTRICITY

adjectives

dynamical; spiritual; galvanic; wondrous; helpful; servant-like; static.

verbs

activate—; apply—; charge with—; communicate by—; conduct—; connect—; conserve—; consume—; develop—; direct—; discharge—; employ—; generate—; harness —; induce—; measure—; resist—; supply —; transmit—; utilize—; wire for—; —circulates; —emanates from; —flows; —magnetizes; —radiates from; —shocks; —vitalizes.

ELEGANCE

adjectives

tasteful; sartorial; unusual; impaired; gracious; extreme; solid; stately; sculptured; cheerless; superficial; concise; unfailing; luxurious; voluptuous; sovereign; chill; refining; quiet; palatial; simple; futile; dainty; urban; indescribable; modish; restrained; decorous; envied; dark; classic; restless; certain; bright; supercilious; inborn; airy; rustic; rich; cautious; inherent; chaste; subdued; austere; correct; lazy; shabby; social; verbal; defiant; peculiar; pristine.

verbs

abandon—; arrange with—; behave with —; breed in—; demonstrate—; destroy—; detest—; display—; dress with—; effect—; indulge in—; instruct in—; polish with—; surrender to—; treasure—; tutor in—; yield to—; —charms; —graces; —impresses; —prevails; —wins.

(See refinement.)

ELEGANT

adverbs

tastefully; graciously; quietly; indescribably; modishly; richly; chastely; naturally; unerringly; exquisitely; quaintly; discriminatingly; correctly; superbly.

ELEGY

adjectives

Sapphic; biblical; funeral; lamenting; somber; pastoral.

ELEMENT

adjectives

instinctive; structural; romantic; automatic; subtle; personal; opposing; radical; mutable; flavoring; incongruous; rare; hereditary; picturesque; lawless; thinkable; lymphatic; volitional; aesthetic; disproportionate; jarring; conservative; fragmentary; chemical; undefined; necessary; nationalistic; ominous; simple; discordant; valuable; discrepant; professional; poetic; complex; unalloyed; salient; airy; fighting; unlikely; limpid; primal; negligible; essential; various (pl); devouring; lurking; perverse; dramatic; exhilarated; commonest; dissolving; dreadful; unchained; recessive; liberal; unimaginative; diviner; mercantile; physic; criminalistic; regressive; nutritional; denominative; ambient; basic; ancient; uncanny; lesser; heterogeneous; individual; maltreated; unobstructed; conflicting; sensual; insignificant; cultivated;

honest; inflammable; primordial; cheerful; chalky; fantastic; simplest; positive; dominant; pitiless; divergent; pagan; lawless; inextinguishable; repeated; elliptic; seasonal; melancholy; ungenial; desirable; erotic; distinct; furious; vitamin; mineral; dissatisfied; prim; grim; sufficient; sensitive; minority; moral; decisive; sedate; opaque; disturbing; contradictory; connate; supernatural; determining; sound; hostile; visible; ultimate; fundamental; irreconcilable; bodily; contending; ideal; artistic; divers (pl); permanent; diversifying; natural; serenest; primary; untamed; eternal; incompatible; principal; unloosed; glorious; subtle; insane; comic; burning; lazy; humorous; slow; speculative; vital; harmless; food; important; valuable; mysterious; emotional; backsliding; infelicitous; restful; venal; subjective; neutralizing; metaphysical; dimorphous; cultured; celestial; alien.

verbs
coalesce—s; constitute—; disintegrate—; fathom—; inject—; introduce—; master—; mix—; nourish—; play to—; rouse—; stress—; submerge—; surrender—; symbolize—; unearth—; unite—s; —disturbs; —pervades; —predominates.
(See ingredient, constituent.)

ELEMENTAL

adverbs
distinctly; obviously; simply; powerfully; irresistibly; purely; absolutely; solely; manifestly.

ELEMENTARY

adverbs
clearly; purely; sheerly; singularly; simply; exclusively; woefully; amazingly; lamentably; unfortunately; significantly; gravely; momentously; seriously.

ELEMENTS (*weather*)

verbs
bar—; barricade against—; combat—; conquer—; contend with—; struggle with—; yield to—; —destroy; —deteriorate; —determine; —disintegrate; —flash; —fret; —govern; —rust; —wreck.
(See earth, air, fire, water.)

ELEPHANT

verbs
anger—; arouse—; climb on—; domesticate—; mount—; spear—; train—; travel upon—; —bathes; —batters; —charges; —draws; —flings; —hisses; —lumbers; —performs; —rages; —rams; —remembers; —roars; —runs amuck; —spears; —tosses; —trumpets.
(See animal.)

ELEVATE (*v*)

adverbs
morally; perceptibly; proudly; correspondingly; scarcely; partially.
(See raise, lift.)

ELAVATED

adverbs
reputably; highly; estimably; honorably; majestically; eminently; unusually; consciously; nobly; gloriously; immensely; remarkably; uncommonly; notably; famously; conspicuously; illustriously; splendidly; brilliantly; prominently; sacredly.

ELEVATION

adjectives
corresponding; proud; displeased; moral.

ELEVATOR

adjectives
special; arch; fast; slow; decorated; express.

verbs
accelerate—; block—; burden—; control—; crowd—; disable—; employ—; enter—; file out of—; install—; jam—; jostle in—; level—; man—; manipulate—; operate—; overload—; pour from—; retard—; ring for—; signal—; station at—; stream from—; —ascends; —descends; —drops; —facilitates; —hoists; —hums upward; —plunges; —transfers; —zooms.
(See platform, aeroplane.)

ELF

adjectives
happy; semi-respectable; sportive; cunning; troublesome; perverse; bad; imperturbable; vagrant; scribbling.

ELFISH

adverbs
delicately; mischievously; sportively; cunningly; perversely; vagrantly; uncannily; weirdly; impishly; undeniably; laughably; amusingly; naturally.

ELIGIBLE

adverbs
legally; capably; competently; wholly; unusually; highly; undeniably; exceptionally;

socially; becomingly; conveniently; obviously; evidently; admirably; financially.

ELIMINATE (v)

adverbs

completely; utterly; entirely; abruptly; virtually; outrageously; tyrannically; courageously; completely.

(See separate, remove.)

ELIXIR

adjectives

wondrous; imperious; youth-giving; immortal; nectarous; divine.

ELLIPSE

verbs

bound by—; circle in—; course—; cut into—; define; —describe—; disfigure—; draw—; execute—; fashion—; form—; shape into—; sketch—; wheel in—; —belts; —entertains; —frames.

(See circle.)

ELM

adjectives

hedgerow; overshadowing; lofty; spindling; immemorial; vaulted; ancient; graceful; sighing.

verbs

entwine—; rock—; trim—; —branches; —flowers; —groans; —nods; —protects; —quivers; —shades; —sheds; —shelters; —stirs; —tapers; —towers; —waves.

(See tree.)

ELOPE (v)

adverbs

blithely; lovingly; spiritedly; clandestinely; surreptitiously; furtively; secretly; slyly; stealthily; impetuously.

(See run, flee.)

ELOQUENCE

adjectives

manly; grand; bold; persuasive; gloomy; transcending; bitter; melodic; florid; voluble; wheedling; candid; political; impressive; native; seductive; caustic; hardy; stately; indignant; impersonal; sonorous; patriotic; solemn; resistless; cold; clear; pathetic; silent; denunciative; masterful; masculine; insidious; solid; flatulent; astonishing; awful; touching; imperishable; impetuous; religious; native; saucy; audacious; attractive; brilliant; passionate; luminous; clarion-like; convincing; additional; parliamentary; journalistic; fiery; rich; insinuating; supreme; consummate; rude; unstudied; lofty; picturesque; simple; fervent; abusive; prompt; gorgeous; sublime; worthy; copious; popular; ecclesiastical.

verbs

breathe out—; burst out in—; disregard—; drown in—; endow with—; prompt—; resist—; utter—; woo with—; —acquits; —colors; —flowers; —flows from—; —glitters; —induces; —moves; —pierces; —strikes; —sways.

(See speech, fluency, elegance, utterance.)

ELOQUENT

adverbs

powerfully; marvelously; incisively; impressively; dramatically; vigorously; sensationally; brilliantly; pleadingly; pithily; loftily; sublimely; touchingly; vehemently; passionately; exceptionally; astonishingly; attractively; highly; uncommonly; simply; consummately; irresistibly; persuasively.

ELUCIDATE (v)

adverbs

graphically; clearly; extensively; thoroughly; patiently.

(See describe, explain.)

ELUDE (v)

adverbs

exasperatingly; continually; slyly; ingeniously; cleverly; repeatedly; irritatingly.

(See evade, avoid.)

ELUSIVE

adverbs

cunningly; deceptively; insidiously; trickily; meretriciously; fraudulently; cleverly; artfully; abominably; evasively; adroitly; subtly; treacherously; archly; unbelievably; highly; alarmingly; singularly; terribly.

ELYSIAN

adverbs

delectably; beatifically; ecstatically; divinely; rapturously; ravishingly; seraphically; sweetly; celestially.

EMACIATED

adverbs

pitiably; outrageously; scandalously; miserably; shakily; wirily; sparely; gauntly; haggardly; tenuously; shockingly; terribly; unusually; wretchedly; unwarrantably; shamefully.

EMANATION

adjectives
divine; miasmal; primitive.

EMANCIPATION

adjectives
bourgeois; unconditional; prospective.

EMBALM (v)

adverbs
carefully; elaborately; skillfully; marvelously; artfully; professionally.
(See preserve.)

EMBALMING

adjectives
elaborate; marvelous; skilled.

EMBARGO

adjectives
silly; alternative; virtual.

verbs
adopt—; apply—; assail—; authorize—; clap on—; condemn—; counter—; declare —; effect—; employ—; enforce—; impose —; instigate—; justify—; lift—; patronize —; proclaim—; propose—; support—; threaten—; urge—; —checks; —hinders; —restrains; —starves.
(See hindrance, impediment, injunction, restraint.)

EMBARK (v)

adverbs
gleefully; sadly; joyfully; formally; unmolestedly; freely; tardily; eventually; hastily.
(See begin, venture.)

EMBARKATION

adjectives
businesslike; unmolested.

EMBARRASS (v)

adverbs
disconcertingly; satirically; startlingly; perceptibly; sadly; slyly; perplexingly; visibly; painfully; pecuniarily; secretly; acutely; considerably; strangely.
(See harass, shame.)

EMBARRASSED

adverbs
singularly; curiously; oddly; strangely; profoundly; awkwardly; deeply; shamefully; shyly; financially; socially; distressingly; painfully; publicly; secretly; timidly; occasionally; vaguely; slightly; greatly; horribly; visibly; angrily; acutely; considerably; helplessly; hotly.

EMBARRASSMENT

adjectives
visible; flattering; painful; evident; pecuniary; nervous; tingling; angry; secret; acute; considerable; strange.

verbs
betray—; blush in—; conceal—; contribute to—; ease—; flush in—; guard against—; lead to—; manifest—; pardon—; relieve—; —hinders; —prevents; —silences.
(See chagrin, perplexity.)

EMBASSY

adjectives
overburdened; heaven-like; loving.

EMBELLISH (v)

adverbs
peculiarly; handsomely; profusely; tastefully; poetically; artistically; architecturally; rhetorically; flamboyantly; gaudily; beautifully; lavishly.
(See adorn, ornament.)

EMBELLISHED

adverbs
ornately; tastefully; gaudily; crudely; garishly; beautifully; artistically; gorgeously; smartly; showily; unnecessarily; highly; extravagantly; excessively; richly; gayly; daintily; elegantly; chastely; simply.

EMBELLISHMENT

adjectives
poetical; artistic; architectural; rhetorical.

EMBER

verbs
blanket—s; conceal beneath—; fan—; feed —s; heap on—s; heat on—s; poke—s; quench—s; rake—s; roast in—s; stir—s; strew over—s; toast on—s; —blazes; —burns; —s comfort; —dies; —expires; —flames; —glows; —heats; —s sleep; —smoulders; —s warm; —chars.
(See coal, ashes, cinders.)

EMBERS

adjectives
rose-red; burnt-out; glowing; smoldering; latent; dying; dangerous; pale; dim; fading; glimmering; throbbing; slumbering; raked; inextinguishable; feeble; ruddy; ashen-gray; blue; crumbling; smoky.

EMBITTERED

adverbs
deeply; permanently; irremediably; unfortunately; justifiably; hopelessly; irrecoverably; secretly; profoundly; morbidly; sullenly; unhappily; strangely; naturally; pathetically; violently; savagely; dejectedly; desperately.

EMBLAZON (*v*)

adverbs
vividly; richly; weirdly; brilliantly; astonishingly; colorfully.
(See adorn, shine.)

EMBLAZONED

adverbs
gorgeously; colorfully; artistically; brilliantly; wonderfully; marvelously; ceremonially; magnificently; splendidly; sumptuously; dramatically; richly; glitteringly; brightly; highly.

EMBLAZONING

adjectives
dim; fiery; weird; astonishing.

EMBLEM

adjectives
talismanic; portentous; ecclesiastical; gorgeous; hieroglyphical; conventional; mortuary; graven-lined; masonic; sepulchered.

verbs
bear—; bedeck with—s; distinguish with —s; engrave—; enrich with—s; insert—; reward with—; select—; scrutinize—; vie for—; —attests; —denotes; —expresses; —flutters; —indicates; —represents; —suggests; —symbolizes; —testifies.
(See representation, symbol, sign, badge.)

EMBLEMATIC

adverbs
characteristically; truly; ecclesiastically; gorgeously; splendidly; highly; remarkably; particularly; obscurely; appropriately; suitably; graphically; felicitously; extraordinarily; uncommonly; manifestly.

EMBODIMENT

adjectives
stirring; organic; adequate; striking; rough.

EMBODY (*v*)

adverbs
satisfactorily; stirringly; organically; strikingly; adequately; roughly; successfully; convincingly.
(See combine, form.)

EMBRACE

adjectives
clinging; maddening; bearlike; straining; wordless; rapturous; mute; passionate; quiet; transparent; pure; warm; turbulent; meek; fervid; hard; stimulating; emotional; sorrowing; soothing; fierce; strict; firm; chill; rugged; silent; romantic; locked; welcoming; timid; tight; tepid; kind; lank; stormy; stiff; clumsy.

verbs
avert—; avoid—; blush at—; break—; check—; clasp in—; delight in—; enclose in—; force—; gather in—; lock in—; resist—; seek—; shelter in—.
(See clasp.)

EMBRACE (*v*)

adverbs
tenderly; blithely; lasciviously; licentiously; cheerfully; responsively; affectionately; warmly; fitfully; passionately; voluntarily; devoutly; boldly; clingingly; maddeningly; wordlessly; rapturously; emotionally; mutely; turbulently; sorrowfully; soothingly; fiercely; firmly; ruggedly; romantically; timidly; tepidly; clumsily; stormily.
(See caress, clasp.)

EMBRASURE

adjectives
gloomy; mighty.

EMBROIDER (*v*)

adverbs
dexterously; delicately; ecclesiastically; strangely; brilliantly; artfully; skillfully; fantastically.
(See sew, ornament.)

EMBROIDERY

adjectives
brilliant; sad; glittering; ecclesiastical; fancy; eyelet; cross-stitch; lace; delicate.

EMBROILMENT

adjectives
bloody; wearisome; needless; furious.

EMBRYO

verbs

abort—; disengage—; enclose—; examine —; form—; hatch—; kill—; nourish—; shape—; stifle—; stimulate—; surround—; —develops; —dwells in; —enfolds; —impresses; —matures; —occupies; —originates; —ripens.

(See germ, beginning.)

EMERALD

adjectives

living; veined; encrusted; sparkling; striking; great; square; exquisite.

verbs

adorn with—; cover with—s; delight in—; favor—; guard—; lure with—; purchase —; secrete—; value—; —crowns; —dazzles; —gleams; —glimmers; —glitters; —scintillates; —shines.

(See jewel, gem, diamond.)

EMERGE (*v*)

adverbs

dramatically; noiselessly; coolly; gradually; luminously; transcendingly; reluctantly; mystically; shyly; abruptly; unmistakably.

(See rise, come.)

EMERGENCY

adjectives

fearful; prolonged; sudden; fiscal; threatening; temporal; frequent;. peculiar; unexpected; popular; pressing; unusual; serious; desperate; international.

verbs

anticipate—; bow to—; challenge—; confront with—; cope with—; ease—; face—; guard against—; handle—; iron out—; lessen—; meet—; resign to—; rise to—; —arises; —exists.

(See crisis, exigency, necessity.)

EMETIC

verbs

act as—; administer—; does with—; employ —; prescribe—; suggest—; swallow—; —aids; —corrects; —counteracts; —cures; —empties; —excites; —induces; —produces; —prostrates; —remedies; —stimulates.

(See medicine, laxative, enema.)

EMIGRANT

adjectives

unfortunate; greenhorn; bewildered; aggressive.

EMIGRATION

verbs

admit—; advocate—; assist—; campaign for—; dodge—; embark on—; halt—; occasion—; prevent—; record—; shift—; stir —; undertake—; —drifts; —flows; —lapses; —relieves; —streams; —trickles.

(See exodus, departure, immigration.)

EMINENCE

adjectives

lofty; intellectual; grassy; bright; conspicuous; crested; humble; narrowed; specific; abrupt; sudden; immediate; gentle; incontestable; commanding; inland; archaeological; practicable; affected; sacred; cliffy; deserted; professional; unblemished; gigantic; noble.

verbs

ascend to—; assume—; attain—; command —; deserve—; elevate to—; enjoy—; enthrone in—; hope for—; merit—; perch in—; rise to—; shoot to—; surpass in—; tower in—; worship—.

(See distinction, fame.)

EMINENT

adverbs

notably; internationally; ecclesiastically; politically; socially; distinctly; illustriously; splendidly; proudly; conspicuously; honorably; deservedly; brilliantly; famously.

EMISSARY

adjectives

paid; secret; trustworthy; discreet.

verbs

assign—to; dispatch—; employ—; entrust with—; interview—; send—; —announces; —carries; —communicates; —conveys; —corresponds; —furnishes; —imparts; —implies; —informs; —performs; —pries; —promotes; —relays; —reports; —represents; —scouts; —spies.

(See agent, messenger, ambassador.)

EMISSION

adjectives

non-luminous; watery.

EMOLUMENT

adjectives

stipendiary; unearned; colossal; untaxable.

verbs

calculate—; consider—; deny—; deprive of—; derive—; earn—; enjoy—; forfeit—;

obtain—; pocket—; produce—; reap—; receive—; return—; seek—; —amends; —atones for; —comforts; —compensates; —improves; —rewards; —satisfies.

(See advantage, gain, profit.)

EMOTION

adjectives

poignant; intellectual; enthusiastic; touched; pent-up; gentle; repressed; inscrutable; barbaric; profound; blushing; conflicting; fierce; dark; complex; vague; vindictive; turbulent; painful; dominant; disturbing; desirable; private; desperate; kindled; human; extraordinary; petty; ardent; suitable; exulting; tremulous; generous; primitive; perfect; sudden; passionate; unquiet; joyful; parental; unmaidenly; chivalric; opposite; irrevocable; decadent; violent; indescribable; timid; charitable; passive; transient; repentant; trembling; contending; diverse; tumultuous; untried; sensitive; irrepressible; scornful; rapid; lively; mingled; suppressed; distinct; contradictory; intricate; dead; keen; sincere; adult; unstable; overwhelming; evident; patriotic; quivering; natural; intense; irreproachable; educated; anguished; elusive; corresponding; religious; tender; similar; singular; gushing; innocent; inner; spontaneous; aesthetic; genuine; hot-headed; silent; excited; immature; shallow; cheap; neat; compelling; inelastic; visible; awe-inspiring; incomprehensible; strong; sham; momentary; adulterated; sociable; inward; intimate; surcharged; acute; sustained; sympathetic; wandering; rebellious; compassionate; catholic; outward; tragic; burning; awakened; volcanic; uncontrollable; ineffable; synthetic; perverted; antagonistic; distressful; frozen; deepest; inmost; swelling; ill-concealed; pleasing; vehement; undisciplined; unfathomable; dumb; subdued; passion-hued; haggard; inexpressible; encompassing; unrestrained; facile; full-fledged; causeless; primal; deadened; inwrought; honest; confused; incomparable; personable; incongruous; incredible; indefinable; devastating; vivid; depressive; overpowering; simultaneous; old-fashioned; mysterious; unearthly; ultimate.

verbs

appeal to—; arouse—; awaken—; batter down—; betray—; blunt—; cherish—; choke—; conquer—; control—; cover—; curb—; disentangle—s; experience—; express—; falsify—; feign—; hide—; kindle—; lavish—on; move with—; overflow with—; palpitate with—; play with—; prompt by—; pulsate with—; quake with—; quiver with—; register—; respond to—; restrain—; still—; suppress—; sway with—; toy with—s; tremble with—; vanquish—; vent—; whip up—; wrench by—; wring with—; —s clash; —s conflict; —governs; —recurs; —s riot; —seizes; —surges; —vacillates.

(See feeling, sensation, passion, perturbation, agitation.)

EMOTIONAL

adverbs

peculiarly; deeply; ardently; unstably; eagerly; warmly; quickly; strongly; obviously; fervently; uncontrollably; ungovernably; impetuously; impulsively; hysterically; unsteadily; remarkably; inherently; naturally; expressively; violently; highly; unusually.

EMOTIONALISM

adjectives

crude; seething; accursed; florid.

EMPEROR

adjectives

illustrious; reigning; ambitious; ardent; haughty; tyrannical.

verbs

admire—; assassinate—; attend—; bow to—; cringe before—; crown—; fete—; guard—; hail—; huzza—; pledge to—; present to—; succeed—; wait upon—; —addresses; —conquers; —decrees; —dismisses; —pardons; —receives; —rules; —subdues.

(See king, monarch.)

EMPHASIS

adjectives

lingering; menacing; stubborn; marked; terrific; daring; allowable; improper; extravagant; dreadful; indignant; prodigious; fretful; passionate; prevailing; serious; trivial; joyous; sufficient; ethical; victorious; appealing; artistic; attenuated; sarcastic; flattering; languid; tantalizing.

verbs

bear—; convey—; express with—; focus upon—; lay—upon; lose—; mark—; note—; observe—; require—; shift—; voice—; —accentuates; —affirms; —delivers; —forces; —imbeds; —implies; —impresses; —inculcates; —insists; —instils; —points; —sharpens; —stresses.

(See stress, force.)

EMPHASIZE (*v*)

adverbs
significantly; repeatedly; effectively; victoriously; graciously; boastfully; adequately; menacingly; stubbornly; markedly; daringly; improperly; extravagantly; indignantly; fretfully; passionately; seriously; trivially; sufficiently; appealingly; artistically; tantalizingly.
(See stress, impress.)

EMPHATIC

adverbs
stubbornly; terribly; fretfully; joyously; aggressively; boldly; loftily; truculently; extravagantly; impudently; insolently; audaciously; arrogantly; blandly; confidently; sweepingly; dogmatically; astoundingly; autocratically; despotically; imperiously; monstrously; presumptuously; preposterously; rashly; blatantly; sarcastically.

EMPIRE

adjectives
calm; powerful; mighty; disintegrating; formidable; distracted; extensive; audacious; vain; populous; consolidated; celestial; peerless; permanent; veritable; effeminate; far-reaching; full-fledged; supernatural; gentle; colonial; barbaric; mercantile; spiritual.

verbs
bind—; bound—; build—; carve—; cement —; command—; conquer—; consolidate—; create—; destroy—; dictate—; disentangle —; divide—; forsake—; found—; govern —; invade—; overthrow—; police—; rock —; rule—; seek—; shake—; spread through —; unite—; wreck—; yoke—; —dwindles; —extends; —falls; —perishes; —ranges; —sickens; —staggers.
(See state, nation, dominion, sovereignty, kingdom.)

EMPLOY (*v*)

adverbs
habitually; conspicuously; vigilantly; anxiously; faithfully; uselessly; frequently; thriftily; steadily; methodically; profitably; gainfully; vigorously; skillfully; magically; unceasingly; temporarily; advantageously; peacefully; sparingly; incessantly; hazardously; individually; occasionally; domestically; legitimately; remuneratively; suitably; figuratively; ingloriously; systematically; actively.
(See use, work.)

EMPLOYEE

adjectives
conscientious; rank-and-file; valued; prudent; salaried; unionized.

verbs
agitate—s; assign—to; coerce—; command —; discard—; dismiss—; dock—; engage —; engross—; enroll—; intimidate—; manage—s; misuse—; regulate—s; supervise —s; —s demand; —exerts; —obeys; —s organize; —s recess; —s strike.
(See worker, workman, laborer, clerk.)

EMPLOYER

adjectives
philosophic; recusant; apprehensive; prospective; banded (pl).

verbs
demand of—; persuade—; picket—; plead with—; seek—; —acquires; —advertises; —assigns; —controls; —disposes; —economizes; —engages; —fires; —hires; —locks out; —pities; —procures; —provides; —refuses; —regulates; —supervises; —sympathizes; —tyrannizes; —understands.
(See master, owner, manager.)

EMPLOYMENT

adjectives
unconscious; hazardous; individual; occasional; domestic; legitimate; remunerative; regressive; useful; suitable; skillful; congenial; responsible; continuous; money-making; figurative; seasonable; inglorious; obvious; temporary; lucrative; profitable; regular; diverse; military; justifiable; creative; systematic; gainful; mercantile; initial.

verbs
acquire—; apply for—; assign—; avoid—; carry on—; devote to—; evade—; fit for—; insure—; necessitate—; offer—; procure—; pursue—; receive—; regulate—; reject—; seek—; stabilize—; stimulate—; throw out of—; —fluctuates; —maintains; —occupies; —preserves; —satisfies.
(See occupation, vocation, calling, business, profession, trade, job.)

EMPRESS

adjectives
chimerical; power-drunk; haughty.

EMPTINESS

adjectives
divine; ultimate; horrid; echoing; civilized; gnawing; spiritual; wide; desolate; bleak; blank; black; void; gaping; yawning.

EMPTY (v)

adverbs
surreptitiously; completely; partially; automatically.
(See deplete, exhaust.)

EMPTY

adverbs
hopelessly; deplorably; lamentably; desperately; completely; almost; obviously; visibly; dreadfully; desolately; bleakly; startlingly; awfully; dismally; unbelievably; palpably; contemptibly; unhappily; unfortunately; wretchedly.

EMULATION

adjectives
literary; perpetual; generous; envious.

EMULSION

adjectives
light; sensitive; suspended; cloudy.

ENACT (v)

adverbs
comparatively; gravely; legally; prohibitively; legislatively; socially; illegitimately; dictatorially; forcefully; dogmatically.
(See perform, accomplish.)

ENACTMENT

adjectives
statutory; prohibitive; legislative; social; revolutionary; legal.

ENAMEL

adjectives
tinted; lucid; brittle; brilliant.

ENAMOURED

adverbs
crazily; besottedly; wholly; rapturously; blindly; immensely; ecstatically; ardently; passionately; idolatrously; fervidly; deeply; inordinately; absorbingly; perilously; dangerously; absurdly; hopelessly; helplessly.

ENCHANT (v)

adverbs
magically; ravishingly; sweetly; uniquely; mysteriously; powerfully; fantastically; mystically; passionately.
(See charm, fascinate.)

ENCHANTED

adverbs
utterly; delightfully; marvellously; oddly; perfectly; curiously; unquestionably; irresistibly; openly; avowedly; completely.

ENCHANTING

adverbs
delightfully; charmingly; seductively; bewitchingly; girlishly; youthfully; marvellously; radiantly; daintily; exquisitely; courteously; divinely; gracefully; brightly; chivalrously; politely; attentively; urbanely; ingratiatingly; genially; extremely; curiously; oddly; uncommonly.

ENCHANTMENT

adjectives
grave; sweet; rapt; unique; age-old; powerful; mysterious; perpetual; varied; divine; social; heightened; drear; cool; true; aristocratic; gloomy; mystic.

verbs
brew—; cast—; drink in—; endow with—; exercise—; gaze with—; invest with—; lend—; respond to—; steep in—; succumb to—; touch with—; view with—; —allures; —assails; —beguiles; —bewitches; —captivates; —charms; —cloaks; —delights; —enraptures; —enslaves; —expires; —fascinates; —fetters; —influences; —overpowers; employ—.
(See charm, fascination.)

ENCOMIUM

adjectives
unjust; warm; eulogistic; heaped-up (pl).

ENCOUNTER

adjectives
loose; strange; accidental; constant; fierce; ordinary; bloody; murderous; romantic; amiable; strong; awkward; fatal; vile; pugilistic; sharp; chivalrous; previous; bitter.

verbs
anticipate—; avoid—; calculate—; clash in—; confess to—; contemplate—; dare—; engage in—; experience—; expose to—; fear —; flush from—; intend—; join—; launch —; match in—; plan—; relate—; risk—; shrink from—; shun—; venture—; welcome—; —follows; —unsteadies.
(See meeting, collision, contest, conflict, battle.)

ENCOUNTER (*v*)

adverbs
repeatedly; proudly; frequently; occasionally; obliquely; cheerfully; unexpectedly; fearlessly; accidentally; murderously; romantically; amiably; awkwardly; fatally; chivalrously; bitterly.
(See meet, confront.)

ENCOURAGE (*v*)

adverbs
smoothly; openly; jovially; tremendously; sympathetically; willingly; specially; genially; unduly; adroitly; enormously; affectionately; consistently; wordlessly; unceasingly; remotely; cordially; professionally.
(See aid, assist.)

ENCOURAGEMENT

adjectives
enormous; lifelong; affectionate; consistent; wordless; unceasing; remote; slender; managerial; cheerful; cordial; melancholy; fresh; misplaced.

verbs
afford—; impart—; lend—; rally to—; thrive on—; —animates; —cheers; —comforts; —enlivens; —exhilarates; —heartens; —impels; —incites; —induces; —inspires; —kindles; —promotes; —prompts; —reassures; —restores; —stimulates.
(See help.)

ENCOURAGING

adverbs
cheerily; genially; gravely; enormously; affectionately; immensely; highly; silently; cordially; sincerely; resolutely; decisively; impulsively; discreetly; deliberately; helpfully; amicably; confidently; enthusiastically; reassuringly; sympathetically; actively; genuinely; exceptionally; prudently; thoughtfully; reliably.

ENCROACH (*v*)

adverbs
steadily; progressively; unconsciously; brazenly; perpetually; aggressively; belligerently; martially; pugnaciously.
(See trespass, intrude.)

ENCROACHMENT

adjectives
noteworthy; perpetual.

verbs
justify—; observe—; prevent—; rant against—; recognize—; resent—; resist—; revenge—; seize by—; tolerate—; wrest by—; —arouses; —deprives; —disables; —irritates; —offends; —outrages; —perils; —robs; —violates.
(See intrusion, invasion.)

ENCUMBER (*v*)

adverbs
perilously; hopelessly; monstrously; tragically; fatally; tyrannically; viciously; pathologically.
(See hinder, impede.)

ENCUMBRANCE

adjectives
vast; hopeless; monstrous.

verbs
accept—; attach—; discharge—; dispel—; divest of—; free from—; load with—; master—; struggle with—; suffer—; —annoys; —burdens; —clogs; —complicates; —embarrasses; —hampers; —harasses; —hinders; —impedes; —obstructs; —oppresses; —presses; —restrains.
(See load, burden, hindrance, impediment.)

ENCYCLOPEDIA

adjectives
skeptical; exhaustive; character; walking; biographical; all-inclusive.

verbs
appear in—; compile—; comprehend—; consult—; discover in—; edit—; employ—; refer to—; require—; scan—; —comprises; —educates; —enlightens; —explains; —illustrates; —informs; —instructs; —specifies; —teaches.
(See book.)

END

adjectives
dreary; practical; extreme; definite; private; lofty; selfish; ambitious; sordid; common; remote; swanlike; unsavory; equivocal; inexorable; surprising; personal; muchcoveted; teleological; adequate; ornamental; technical; ulterior; contingent; unpitied; desirable; special; worthier; appointed; hideous; latter; petty; sad; professed; untimely; abhorred; economical; wretched; radiant; conscious; tapering; immortal; futile; spiritual; individual; chief; shameful; ephemeral; extravagant; lifeless; blunt; preconceived; ultimate; gracious; disastrous.

verbs
accomplish—; achieve—; attain—; bend to —; catch—; constitute—; continue until—; contrive—; discern—; draw to—; endure to—; fear—; fulfill—; further—; hasten—; indicate—; justify—; maintain till—; obtain—; pause at—; pray for—; progress toward—; pursue—; push to—; put to—; scorn—; serve—; sever—; sleep till—; stave off—; subserve—; waste—; welcome —; work out—.
(See purpose, intention, aim, object, goal.)

END (v)
adverbs
invariably; eloquently; feebly; amicably; mournfully; abruptly; fatally; badly; tragically; comically; sorrowfully; dramatically; coldly; virtually; intelligibly; disastrously; breathlessly; inevitably; miserably; ultimately; insignificantly; ominously; appropriately; abruptly; gradually; poetically; swiftly.
(See finish, stop.)

ENDANGER (v)
adverbs
seriously; frequently; foolishly; absurdly; carelessly; jauntily; bravely; ridiculously.
(See imperil, risk.)

ENDEARMENT
verbs
address—to; cajole with—s; caress in—; coax with—s; court with—s; exhibit—; feast on—; flatter with—s; fondle in—; pat with —; refrain from—s; secure—of; serenade with—s; utter—; wheedle with—s; whisper —s; woo with—s; —annoys; —s charm; —flatters; —pleases.
(See caress, affection, love.)

ENDEAVOR
adjectives
enthusiastic; painstaking; deformed; vain; apparent; infinite; earnest; tenacious; mournful; incessant; rash; awful; patient; desperate; passionate; humane; utmost; high; speedy; organized; fruitless; fair; stern; honest, unsuccessful; ceaseless; beneficent; personal; therapeutic; urgent; self-protective; strenuous; fierce; psychoanalytic; sanctified; junior; charitable; dead; suicidal; dull; strong; philanthropic; continuous; decorative; intellectual; foolish.

verbs
bless—; conceal—; direct—; dwarf—; emulate—; encourage—; exert in—; extend—; forestall—; forsake—; frustrate—; inspire —; lessen—; oppose—; plan—; put forth—; renew—; smile on—; struggle in—; —contributes; —ennobles; —helps; —sweeps away.
(See attempt, effort, struggle.)

ENDEAVOR (v)
adverbs
scrupulously; vainly; forcefully; energetically; constantly; primarily; inadequately; feebly; conscientiously; fruitlessly; unconsciously; gravely; heroically; ineffectually; eternally; enthusiastically; painstakingly; apparently; earnestly; tenaciously; mournfully; incessantly; patiently; desperately; passionately; humanely; strenuously; charitably; intellectually; foolishly.
(See try, strive.)

ENDING
adjectives
insignificant; ominous; tragic; gigantic; physical; abrupt; fittest; appropriate; gradual; beautiful; soft; poetic; swift.

ENDLESS
adverbs
horribly; apparently; almost; irritatingly; hopelessly; vexatiously; terrifyingly; incalculably; maddeningly; fabulously; unendurably; fearfully; frightfully.

ENDORSE (v)
adverbs
enthusiastically; tentatively; legally; legitimately; criminally; dishonestly; optimistically.
(See approve, agree.)

ENDORSEMENT
adjectives
enthusiastic; tentative.

verbs
(See indorsement.)

ENDOW (v)
adverbs
richly; invariably; exceptionally; wisely; lavishly; liberally; speedily; suitably; splendidly; mentally; spiritually; hypocritically; naturally; intellectually; physically; rarely; uncommonly.
(See give, donate.)

ENDOWMENT

adjectives
mental; spiritual; intrinsic; hypothetical; natural; decorative; intellectual; physical; rare; literary; uncommon.

verbs
assure of—; bequeath—to; bestow—upon; confer—upon; deserve—; furnish—; grant —; inherit—; lavish—on; leave—to; obtain —; present—; provide—; secure—; settle —on; solicit—; stipulate—; vest—; wheedle —; will—; —eases; —enriches; —provides for; —rescues; —supports.
(See bounty, gift, money.)

ENDURABLE

adverbs
scarcely; grimly; barely; hardly; philosophically; stoically; tolerably; heroically; reasonably.

ENDURANCE

adjectives
dignified; calm; physical; marvelous; pained; resolute; unparalleled; silent; heroic; unlimited; patient; passive; superhuman; moral; stout; brave.

verbs
attain—; bear with—; discipline to—; enhance—; harden—; impose on—; limit—; prolong beyond—; replenish—; tax—; torment beyond—; —conquers; —ebbs; —fades; —fails; —surpasses; —sustains; —terminates; —wanes.
(See persistence, fortitude, patience, forbearance.)

ENDURE (v)

adverbs
placidly; firmly; coldly; irksomely; everlastingly; impatiently; consciously; simply; daily; permanently; dignifiedly; heroically; naturally; intellectually; physically; passively; morally; stoutly; bravely.
(See suffer, bear.)

ENEMA

verbs
employ—; endure—; inject—; introduce—; order—; prepare—; prescribe—; recommend—; resort to—; urge—; —aggravates; —aids; —appeases; —comforts; —eases; —enervates; —exasperates; —infuriates; —purges; —quickens; —relieves; —soothes; —weakens.
(See medicine, laxative, emetic.)

ENEMY

adjectives
approaching; spiteful; transalpine; routed; hereditary; partisan; scrupulous; fearful; generous; retreating; domestic, vanquished; damaging; embittered; pernicious; confiding; political; patient; sagacious; faithful; malarial; sworn; potential; stern; cruel; legendary; mysterious; invisible; avowed; discomfited; malicious; vigilant; treacherous; intrenched; formidable; destructive; prejudiced; pleasant; bigoted; subtle; legionary; inveterate; aggressive; contemptuous; external; visionary; fanatical; unfair; bitter; self-reliant; resolute; common; skulking; service; ferocious; pregnant; imaginary; alien; courageous; loathed; penniless; rival; devouring; butchering; lurking; malignant; exposed; deadly; cunning; unrelenting; panic-stricken; implacable; erstwhile; exasperated; indefatigable; insidious; ruthless; vehement; vindictive.

verbs
acquiesce to—; ambush—; annihilate—; approach—; baffle—; beleaguer—; betray to —; charge—; chase—; confront—; crush—; cultivate—; curse—; deliver—; demoralize—; destroy—; disarm—; eliminate—; elude—; engage—; enslave—; entrap—; erase—; excoriate—; exterminate—; face—; fall into the hands of—; foil—; forgive—; harass—; hold—at bay; hurl back—; intercept—; inveigh against—; judge—; massacre—; mislead—; mollify—; negotiate with—; outstrip—; overpower—; overwhelm—; prey upon—; provoke—; persecute—; pursue—; rage at—; reproach—; reveal—; rid of—; scatter—; slay—; smite —; subdue—; survey—; trap—; vanquish —; yield to—; —clamors; —conspires; —falls; —invades; —launches; —lures; —lurks; —plots; —retires; —retreats; —slanders; —withdraws; overthrow—.
(See adversary, antagonist, foe, opponent, rival, competitor.)

ENERGETIC

adverbs
spasmodically; courageously; consistently; actually; indefatigably; gloriously; conspicuously; monumentally; phenomenally; creatively; colossally; stupendously; patiently; strikingly; laboriously; magnificently; spectacularly; breath-takingly; supremely; impressively; valorously; indomitably; nervously; joyously; formidably; prodigiously;

fitfully; restlessly; tremendously; appallingly; suspiciously; excitedly; disturbingly; normally; abnormally.

ENERGETICS

adjectives
metaphysical; speculative; philosophic.

ENERGY

adjectives
active; indomitable; wonted; untiring; feverish; progressive; torrential; resistless; undiminished; imperfect; newborn; constructive; cheering; felicitous; nervous; twofold; contortionary; difficult; joyous; murderous; characteristic; wondrous; abundant; lagging; formidable; surpassing; stern; resolute; boundless; uncommon; impressive; superhuman; vigorous; untamable; repressed; cumulative; imparted; latent; prevailing; overmastering; enormous; sustained; rebellious; dynamic; mysterious; creative; deceptive; tireless; youthful; fervid; patient; inexhaustible; biological; triumphant; collective; relentless; inherent; passionate; vital; vehement; available; unfaltering; invincible; exhaustless; multiform; tameless; undivided; flagging; due; never-ceasing; dampened; stormy; hopeful; tidal; liquid; administrative; striking; unabated; incalculable; intellectual; volcanic; intrepid; convulsive; destructive; sleepless; tremendous; expansive; prodigious; long-discordant; presidential; unmeasured; enlightened; hollow; despairing; impetuous; spiritual; terrible; native; productive; indefatigable; mastering; excited; reposing; diligent; discursive; overflowing; manly; radiant; well-directed; unparalleled; potential; pathetic; mechanical; unaided; concentrated; rapid; fitful; industrious; subtle; compulsive; throbbing; unwearying; distorting; hypothetical; dulled; intensive; dauntless; dashing; hopeful; ridiculous; biting; fiery; reckless; grim; capacious; rank; incomparable; magnetic; useful; unimpeded; subatomic; desperate; ruthless; vivid; searching; reserve; marked; superfluous; wasteful; dogged; restless; impartial; restricted; ultimate; scientific; electric; kinetic; mental; singular; superabundant; structural; moral.

verbs
absorb—; bend—toward; build up—; center—; conserve—; consume—; control—; convert into—; dedicate—to; demand—; derive—from; develop—; devote—to; discharge—; dissipate—; display—; drain—; endow with—; exhibit—; expend—; fill with—; flood with—; focus—upon; fritter away—; gather—; increase—; liberate—; organize—; provide—; relax—; renew—; release—; resuscitate—; retard—; reward—; smother—; spend—; squander—; store up—; tax—; transform—; transmit—; unleash—; unlock—; utilize—; waste—; —deteriorates; —flags.
(See force, power, vigor, strength, zeal.)

ENERVATING

adverbs
undeniably; terribly; unfortunately; dangerously; unbelievably; alarmingly; deplorably; definitely; horribly; strangely; oddly; visibly; hopelessly; deeply.

ENFEEBLED

adverbs
pitiably; miserably; wretchedly; hopelessly; irremediably; visibly; apparently; manifestly; outrageously; cruelly; extraordinarily; curiously; nervously; languidly; unquestionably; ominously; mysteriously; horribly; inexplicably.

ENFEEBLEMENT

verbs
brace—; fortify—; give way to—; guard against—; incur—; invigorate—; languish in—; produce—; relax in—; resist—; sustain—; totter in—; —cramps; —deprives; —drains; —impoverishes; —prevents; —reduces; —saps; —unhinges.

ENFORCE (*v*)

adverbs
rigorously; arrogantly; rigidly; stringently; steadily; strictly; promptly; obstinately; sufficiently; aggressively; roughly; nominally; doggedly; painstakingly.
(See force, compel.)

ENFORCEMENT

adjectives
vigorous; sufficient; rough; rigid; aggressive.

ENGAGE (*v*)

adverbs
professionally; professedly; obviously; industrially; industriously; controversially; earnestly; actively; pitifully; extensively; variously; picturesquely; successfully; continuously; seriously; actively; willingly; exclusively; amicably; hotly; demurely;

jointly; bindingly; allegedly; partially; obstinately; bloodily; pecuniarly; indecisively; intensively.

(See pledge, indulge.)

ENGAGEMENT

adjectives
binding; alleged; partial; bloody; obstinate; quasi-voluntary; pecuniary; long-standing; memorable; indecisive; pressing; wordy; professional.

verbs
agree upon—; announce—; anticipate—; arrange for—; attend—; break—; cancel—; celebrate—; contract—; defer—; desire—; enroll—; free from—; fulfill—; liberate from—; obtain—; prolong—; release from —; terminate—; —affiances; —betroths; —binds; —pairs; —pledges; —surprises.

(See betrothal, promise.)

ENGAGING

adverbs
irresistibly; charmingly; captivatingly; youthfully; delightfully; pleasantly; adorably; sweetly; gracefully; winningly; interestingly, fascinatingly; amiably; quietly; modestly; pertly; saucily; lovingly; attractively; enchantingly; unusually; artlessly; innocently; indefinably; extraordinarily; singularly.

ENGINE

adjectives
locomotive; palpitating; lifeless; mutilated; cruel; deadlier; mysterious; inanimate; atmospheric; fettered; awesome; devilish; asthmatic; rotary; monstrous; phenomenal; ubiquitous.

verbs
coal—; cool—; develop—; devise—; fuel—; lubricate—; muffle—; oil—; pilot—; repair—; —backfires; —batters; —buzzes; —chugs; —clatters; —coughs; —dies; —drives; —drones; —racks; —recoils; —roars; —snarls; —sputters; —throbs; —transforms; —utilizes; —wavers.

(See machine, mechanism.)

ENGINEER

adjectives
painstaking; consulting; self-styled; distinguished; research; topographical.

verbs
consult—; employ—; require—; —alters; —arranges; —bridges; —computes; —constructs; —contrives; —designs; —devises; —invents; —manages; —measures; —plans; —performs; —schemes; —suggests; —supervises; —undertakes.

(See driver, operator, manager.)

ENGINEERING

adjectives
automotive; unrivaled; chemical; civil; electrical; mechanical.

ENGLAND

verbs
ally with—; defame—; defend—; govern —; honor—; integrate—; invade—; journey to—; maim—; reign over—; represent—; revere—; rule—; —acclaims; —bleeds; —endures; —honors; —laments; —triumphs; —vanquishes.

(See country, democracy, republic, monarchy.)

ENGLISH

adjectives
clipped; civilized; thoughtful; simple; fatuous; rhythmic; plain; rough.

verbs
accent—; analyze—; comprehend—; converse in—; correct—; corrupt—; criticize—; falter in—; improve—; interpret—; polish —; purify—; render in—; rhyme—; speak —; study—; translate—; —changes; —derives from; —develops; —evolves.

(See language, literature.)

ENGRAVE (v)

adverbs
delicately; handsomely; daintily; indelibly; exquisite; curious; extraordinary; reproduced; vivid; delicate; deft; skillful.

(See carve, imprint.)

ENGRAVING

adjectives
exquisite; curious; extraordinary; reproduced; vivid; delicate; deft; skillful.

ENGROSS (v)

adverbs
constantly; deeply; chiefly; earnestly; wholly; entirely; sympathetically; entirely; passionately; successfully.

(See absorb, occupy.)

ENHANCE (v)

adverbs
enormously; vastly; radically; inexpressibly; fascinatingly; consequently; attractively.
(See increase, magnify.)

ENIGMA

adjectives
inexplicable; incomprehensible.

verbs
deal in—s; disclose—; dissect—; dissolve—; explain—; express in—; investigate—; question—; ransack—; screen in—; scrutinize—; shroud in—; solve—; —baffles; —conceals; —mystifies; —perplexes; —puzzles; —seals.
(See riddle, mystery, puzzle.)

ENIGMATIC

adverbs
bewilderingly; vexatiously; obscurely; inscrutably; oddly; curiously; peculiarly; singularly; precariously; bafflingly; unaccountably; infernally; unreasonably; inexplicably; unnecessarily.

ENJOIN (v)

adverbs
peremptorily; rudely; dictatorially; harshly; sternly; firmly; casually.
(See command, forbid.)

ENJOY (v)

adverbs
intensely; habitually; unconsciously; sagaciously; contemplatively; languidly; poignantly; acutely; hugely; profoundly; keenly; wholesomely; amazingly; vastly; tranquilly; tremendously; passively; evanescently; maliciously; mentally; meditatively; feverishly; indolently; mischievously; voluptuously; trivially; domestically; serenely; aesthetically; innocently; personally; wholeheartedly; imaginatively; idly; unpretentiously; heartily; reasonably; consciously; contemplatively.
(See gratify, like.)

ENJOYABLE

adverbs
thoroughly; utterly; occasionally; always; keenly; profoundly; heartily; immensely; altogether; delightfully; luxuriously.

ENJOYMENT

adjectives
republican; evanescent; passive; malicious; mental; meditative; different; full; feverish; stately; immediate; indolent; rapt; healthy; affected; frequent; novel; separate; mischievous; voluptuous; perfect; unwonted; trivial; unmolested; prosperous; domestic; serene; sublunary; aesthetic; surfeited; lazy; suppressed; joint; innocent; personal; whole-hearted; imaginative; idle; aimless; gluttonous; amused; refined; open; mystical; tranquil; solid; solitary; statutory; unpretentious; keen; hearty; animal; civil; wholesome; evident; reasonable; frank; conscious; exclusive; contemplative.

verbs
afford—; bless with—; charge with—; covet—; crave—; derive—; desire—; detract from—; forestall—; grasp—; indulge in—; interrupt—; lead to—; limit—; manifest—; prove—; pursue—; quench—; savor with—; scatter—; seize—; share—; spoil—; subdue—; temper—; —engrosses; —monopolizes; —occupies; —palls; —refreshes.
(See pleasure, entertainment, delight, satisfaction, happiness.)

ENLARGE (v)

adverbs
unboundedly; quickly; dangerously; abnormally; unduly; gradually; continuously; threateningly.
(See expand, broaden.)

ENLARGEMENT

adjectives
remarkable; gradual; ignorant; undue; continuous.

verbs
advocate—; attempt—; check—; curb—; curtail—; demand—; influence—; justify—; limit—; necessitate—; plan—; prepare—; prevent—; procure—; promote—; regulate—; require—; restrain—; restrict—; strangle—; strive for—; survey—; warrant—; —absorbs; —enhances; —exalts; —improves.
(See increase, extension, development, expansion, growth.)

ENLIGHTENMENT

verbs
communicate—; direct—; express—; furnish—; impart—; need—; occasion—; plan—; plead for—; present—; prompt—; seek—; shed—; signify—; strive for—; supply—; support—; suppress—; taste—; —acquaints;

—assists; —awakens; —edifies; —exhilarates; —progresses; —revives.
(See wisdom, advancement.)

ENMITY

adjectives
secret; everlasting; oblivious; lifelong; passionate; irreconcilable; unwarrantable; stolid; intense; dark.

verbs
abolish—; allay—; disarm—; drown—; earn—; enact through—; express—; frown upon—; ground on—; harbor—; incite—; incur—; nurse—; overcome—; perceive—; place—between; ponder—; set—between; sow—; vanquish—; —abates; —breaks; —separates; —severs; —splits.
(See hostility, ill-will, opposition, antagonism, hatred, animosity.)

ENNUI

adjectives
listless; eternal; mortal.

verbs
affect with—; bore with—; curse with—; die of—; divert—; feel—; overcome—; produce—; resent—; save from—; signify—; subdue—; suffer from—; taste—; weary with—; wrap in—; —abates; —attacks; —bereaves; —despairs; —dethrones; —grows; —is born; —palls; —vexes; —victimizes; —weights.
(See weariness, languor.)

ENORMOUS

adverbs
incredibly; preposterously; inordinately; tremendously; fabulously; astonishingly; absolutely; extraordinarily; indescribably; positively; frightfully; alarmingly.

ENQUIRE (*v*)

adverbs
innocently; hopefully; continually; persistently; annoyingly; repeatedly; fervently.
(See ask, question.)

ENRAPTURED

adverbs
obviously; utterly; inordinately; particularly; strangely; surprisingly; completely; deeply; indubitably; wonderfully; mysteriously; highly; avowedly.

ENRICH (*v*)

adverbs
prodigiously; delectably; abundantly; magnificently; elaborately; immensely; ultimately; considerably; ornately.
(See adorn, embellish.)

ENRICHMENT

adjectives
resultant; minor; ornate.

ENROLLMENT

verbs
check—; dismiss from—; enter in—; erase from—; inscribe in—; list—; mark—; merit —; place on—; qualify for—; record in—; refer to—; register in—; seek—; view—; —acknowledges; —approximates; —certifies; —embodies; —increases; —notes.
(See record.)

ENSCONCE (*v*)

adverbs
snugly; firmly; comfortably; safely; cozily; warmly; domestically.
(See sit, repose.)

ENSEMBLE

adjectives
impressive; rustic; harmonious; neighborhood.

ENSIGN

adjectives
national; armorial; fluttering.

verbs
cheer—; guard—; humble—; lift up—; march under—; plant—; protect—; raise—; rally round—; salute—; scatter—; shred—; spread—; tatter—; unfurl—; —advances; —blazes; —flutters; —signifies; —symbolizes; hang up—.
(See standard, flag.)

ENSLAVEMENT

verbs
cast into—; decry—; deliver from—; denounce—; drive into—; free from—; hamper by—; liberate from—; prevent—; quit —; reduce to—; release from—; repel—; return to—; submit to—; throw into—; —deprives; —disgusts; —hinders; —restrains; —stifles; —subjugates.
(See bondage, subjugation, subjection, slavery.)

ENTANGLE (*v*)

adverbs
inextricably; equally; unnecessarily; thoroughly; fatally; tragically; unfortunately; matrimonially; domestically; ceaselessly; rashly.
(See tangle, involve.)

ENTANGLEMENT

adjectives
inextricable; unnecessary.

verbs
avoid—; charm into—; extricate from—; inveigh into—; knit—; lure into—; prevent—; remove—; risk—; snare in—; unfold—; unravel—; trap in—; weave—; —complicates; —confuses; —distresses; —embarrasses; —embraces; —impedes; —implicates; —involves; —pains; —perplexes; escape—.
(See intricacy, complication, tangle.)

ENTER (*v*)

adverbs
gradually; inconspicuously; presumptuously; peremptorily; calmly; belligerently; triumphantly; obtrusively; intimately; minutely; hurriedly; intelligently; gratefully; optimistically; promptly; controversially; casually; ceremoniously; boldly; unlawfully; pompously; abruptly; simultaneously.
(See penetrate, insert.)

ENTERPRISE

adjectives
profitable; amazing; legitimate; individual; heterogeneous; successful; commercial; regional; dignified; lofty; voluntary; economic; vulgar; protracted; inadequate; stupid; philanthropic; characteristic; romantic; fresh; monumental; desperate; year-round; unscrupulous; blameless; ill-starred; magnanimous; daring; equal; vivid; manly; costly; co-operative; active; chimerical; honorable; venturesome; formidable; uncertain; serviceable; perilous; glorious; prodigious; productive; fabulous; nautical; mundane; infernal; gigantic; prominent; dangerous; hazardous; brilliant; illegal; crusading; charitable; appalling; audacious; inviting; indomitable; laudable; imaginative; delicate.

verbs
abandon—; arm for—; consider—; display—; embark on—; endanger—; enlist in—; enroll in—; exploit—; finance—; hazard—; imperil—; initiate—; manage—; partake in—; persist in—; risk—; stimulate—; struggle in—; swear to—; undertake—; venture on—; —fails; —flourishes; —prospers; —requires; —succeeds; —thrives.
(See project, task, work, undertaking.)

ENTERPRISING

adverbs
unusually; amazingly; daringly; laudably; brilliantly; prodigiously; cleverly; skilfully; alertly; smartly; energetically; marvelously; wonderfully; astutely; zealously; strenuously; earnestly; oddly; briskly; vigorously; indefatigably; industriously; diligently; intrepidly; confidently; uncommonly; competently.

ENTERTAIN (*v*)

adverbs
momentarily; seriously; pretentiously; fabulously; jovially; charmingly; extensively; lavishly; sumptuously; gravely; royally; tolerably; gaily; steadily; hospitably; vaguely; ponderously; uniformly; erroneously; rudely; incessantly; boisterously; casually; cleverly; musically; laboriously; incidentally; sparklingly; fitfully.
(See amuse, divert.)

ENTERTAINER

adjectives
talented; professional; terrified; master.

verbs
acclaim—; announce—; applaud—; boo—; deride—; encore—; encourage—; engage—; heckle—; hire—; hiss—; order—s; produce—; provide—; seek—s; supply—s; —amuses; —bores; —delights; —diverts; —enlivens; —exhibits; —performs; —pleases; —practises; —wearies.
(See hostess, actor.)

ENTERTAINING

adverbs
brilliantly; pleasantly; highly; agreeably; racily; undoubtedly; unusually; charmingly; elaborately; distinctly; delightfully; cleverly; gallantly; amusingly; wittily; sportively; hilariously; roguishly; noisily; admirably; impressively; merrily; comically; ridiculously.

ENTERTAINMENT

adjectives
charming; rude; hospitable; society; elaborate; endless; incessant; boisterous; casual; youthful; distinguished; amateur; critical; mutual; princely; diversified;

clever; friendly; dramatic; musical; honorable; momentary; laborious; sumptuous; guest; evening; varied; sparkling; incidental.

verbs
accord—; afford—; announce—; applaud—; approve of—; buy—; desire—; furnish—; guarantee—; lack—; perceive with—; prepare—; produce—; provide—; seek—; stage —; supply—; surprise with—; —annoys; —bores; —delights; —diverts; —enlivens; —interests; —pleases; —tires; —wearies.
(See performance, amusement, delight, diversion, enjoyment, recreation, hospitality.)

ENTHRALLED

adverbs
irresistibly; utterly; completely; wondrously; mysteriously; rapidly; rapturously; ecstatically; blissfully; strangely; deeply.

ENTHRONE (v)

adverbs
solemnly; grandly; ceremoniously; magnificently; pompously; regally; spectacularly.
(See raise, elevate.)

ENTHUSIASM

adjectives
rash; increasing; unbounded; fanatical; heartiest; warm; passionate; noisy; generous; ill-judged; romantic; voluble; girlish; glowing; exaggerated; weakening; boundless; fervent; ubiquitous; academic; rapt; unrestrained; passing; patriotic; polemical; rousing; gushing; uncontrolled; uncommon; positive; lyric; religious; intense; irrepressible; beautiful; delirious; vapid; proud; popular; impetuous; smoldering; healthy; altruistic; fierce; contagious; usual; greedy; human; available; misguided; rapturous; solemn; latent; unreflecting; honest; dwindled; instant; wild; frantic; temporary; buoyant; fervid; virginal; virtuous; genuine; inexhaustible; boyish; sweet; joyous; earnest; hearty; lofty; flamboyant; divine; common; contagious; actual; infectious.

verbs
admire—; arouse—; awaken—; beam with —; beget—; chill—; dampen—; dim—; display—; evoke—; express—; feed—; fire with—; halt—; imbue with—; impart—; inspire with—; muster—; pour forth—; rationalize—; respond to—; rouse—; share —; spend—; suppress—; sustain—; tolerate —; vibrate with—; —blazes; —blinds; —bubbles; —flags; —flows; —melts away; —pales; —penetrates; —perishes; —rises; —spreads; —subsides; —wanes; —waxes.
(See zeal, ecstasy, eagerness, earnestness, ardor, fervor, passion.)

ENTHUSIAST

adjectives
prominent; dreaming; zealous; culpable; martial; religious; inconsiderate; baffled; harebrained; romantic.

ENTHUSIASTIC

adverbs
unusually; sincerely; delightfully; keenly; profoundly; actively; immediately; zealously; glowingly; passionately; fanatically; warmly; generously; girlishly; fervently; childishly; loudly; boundlessly; raptly; intensely; irrepressibly; beautifully; impulsively; impetuously; fiercely; instantly; wildly; sweetly; joyously; infectiously; extravagantly; strikingly; ardently; exceptionally.

ENTITLE (v)

adverbs
unquestionably; incorrectly; legally; fully; completely; thoroughly; clearly.
(See justify.)

ENTITY

adjectives
abstract; operative; self-acting.

ENTRAILS

adjectives
massy; palpitating; intolerable.

ENTRANCE

adjectives
clairvoyant; auspicious; reputed; complicated; triumphant; unperturbed; hospitable; bricked-up; ceremonious; stormy; sudden; ragged; dirty; fitting; changeful; bursting; unobserved; sheltered; adjacent; brilliant; noisy; swaggering.

verbs
bar—; block—; camouflage—; circle—; clog —; command—; conceal—; convey to—; direct to—; disdain—; effect—; fight for—; flank—; forbid—; forsake—; gain—; guard —; lead to—; obtain—; penetrate—; procure—; reject—; win—; force—.
(See access, door, entry, gate, introduction, opening.)

ENTRANCED

adverbs
perfectly; enthusiastically; utterly; irresistibly; naturally; obviously; noticeably; visibly; delightfully; ecstatically; happily; rapturously; wholly; irrecoverably.

ENTRANT

verbs
admit—; assign—; award to—; file—; herd —s; insert—; introduce—; judge—; limit —s; privilege—; receive—; register—; require—; reward—; select—; welcome—; —s compete; —s flow past; —influences; —participates; —subscribes to.
(See beginner, applicant, competitor.)

ENTREAT (v)

adverbs
civilly; brokenly; pathetically; frankly; patronizingly; earnestly; tenderly; sighingly; fondly; urgently; reproachfully; persistently; humbly; noisily.
(See plead, urge.)

ENTREATY

adjectives
earnest; fond; urgent; boisterous; reproachful; persistent; hospitable; humble; previous; repeated (pl).

verbs
allow—; answer—; comply with—; consent to—; grant—; harass with—ies; hawk—ies; heed—; protest—; rebuff—; recite—; repulse—; resist—; tender—; tolerate—; vex with—; yield to—; —irritates; —persuades; —requests.
(See request, petition, appeal.)

ENTREE

verbs
anticipate—; arrive at—; await—; ban—; choose—; demand—; give—to; gulp—; limit—; prepare—; prevent—; procure—; provide—; refuse—; relish—; select—; serve—; value—; —tempts.
(See dish, food.)

ENTRENCH (v)

adverbs
firmly; safely; protectively; defensively; deeply; securely.
(See intensify, fortify.)

ENTRY

adjectives
forcible; partial; abrupt; official; illegal; discursive; triumphant; burglarious; grandiloquent; mere; magnificent.

verbs
cancel—; certify—; duplicate—; file—; inscribe—; insert—; jot down—; limit—s; note—; post—; record—; register—; reject—; solicit—ies; strike out—; tabulate ies—; welcome—; wipe out—; —s flood.
(See entrance, access, hall.)

ENVELOP (v)

adverbs
thickly; gaseously; materially; impenetrably; nebulously; obscurely.
(See surround, inclose.)

ENVELOPE

adjectives
gaseous; rigid; material; impenetrable.

verbs
address—; assign to—; enclose in—; fold —; gum—; knife—; pen—; seal—; stamp —; tear—; wrap in—; —bears; —confines; —contains; —covers; —encases; —protects; —surrounds.
(See wrapper, case, sheath.)

ENVELOPMENT

adjectives
nebulous; curious; obscure; ungrateful.

ENVIABLE

adverbs
utterly; eminently; vaguely; intensely; apparently; obviously; highly; undeniably; uncommonly; invidiously.

ENVIRONMENT

adjectives
unnatural; accidental; fictitious; cultural; gay; friendly; refined; smart; spiritual; stately; refreshing; restricted; unambitious; ideal; hostile; economic; early; playhouse; suitable; specific; luxurious; pseudo-social; moral; fitting; cooling; healthful; unsuited; niggardly; native; unfavorable; frontier; unusual; human; felicitous; musical; nationalistic; physical; fertile; limited.

verbs
adjust to—; alter—; control—; create—; dominate—; endure—; escape from—; fit—; harmonize with—; lift from—; modify—; shape—; share—; —corrupts; —exerts; —influences; —moulds; —shapes; —strengthens; —weakens.
(See surroundings, circumstances, conditions.)

ENVIRONS

adjectives
immediate; sheltered; picturesque; straggling.

ENVY

adjectives
petty; daggered; jealous; vile; powerless; ghoulish; malignant; poignant; pardonable; bitter; secret; gnawing; public; private; strenuous; illiberal; mixed; unnatural; sharp; sick-bed.

verbs
arouse—; awaken—; conceal—; discipline —; evoke—; excite—; exempt from—; express—; fill with—; incite—; incur—of; infect with—; move by—; murmur—; occasion—; provoke—; raise—; regard with—; sicken with—; stab with—; —blazes up; —convulses; —envelops; —inflames; —narrows; —prejudices; —swells; —threatens.
(See malice, desire, jealousy.)

ENVY (v)

adverbs
secretly; sincerely; pettishly; jealously; vilely; powerlessly; ghoulishly; malignantly; bitterly; gnawingly; privately; unnaturally; painfully.
(See suspect, desire.)

EPHEMERAL

adverbs
fleetingly; wondrously; transiently; shiftily; sadly; precariously; tantalizingly; vexatiously; transitorily; evanescently; mortally; perishably; briefly; heartbreakingly.

EPIC

adjectives
peopled; magnificent; grand; unscrupulous; extant; future; literary; counterfeiting; ponderous; medieval; pietistic; eternal; heroic; familiar; lengthy.

adverbs
traditionally; fabulously; nationally; racially; universally; nobly; significantly; majestically; splendidly; dramatically; tragically; brilliantly; deathlessly; imperishably; timelessly; sweepingly; consummately; amazingly; highly; magnificently; staggeringly; incomparably; grandly.

EPICURE

adjectives
jovial; classical; facetious; cultured; suave; fastidious; precise.

EPICUREAN

adverbs
fastidiously; delicately; luxuriously; sensuously; indulgently; daintily; discriminatingly; greedily; highly; openly; manifestly; intemperately; voluptuously; rakishly; wildly; inordinately; lamentably; extremely; deliberately; avowedly.

EPIDEMIC

adjectives
veritable; dangerous; disastrous; prevailing; periodical; acute; terrible; infectious.

verbs
approach—; constitute—; curtail—; eradicate—; fend against—; inoculate against—; succumb to—; —appears; —breaks out; —consumes; —devastates; —lingers; —prostrates; —rages; —ravages; —sweeps; —swells; —wanes.
(See disease, plague, cholera, smallpox.)

adverbs
locally; universally; currently; recently; sweepingly; commonly; prevalently; generally; infectiously; contagiously; noxiously; pestilentially; virulently; unfortunately; diffusively; dangerously; disastrously; periodically; acutely; terribly; curiously; obscurely; inexplicably; mysteriously.

EPIDERMIS

verbs
affect—; apply to—; blemish—; dab—; damage—; daub—; flay—; form—; impair —; infect—; injure—; mar—; repair—; restore—; salve—; scratch—; shed—; smear on—; —coats; —covers; —defends; —encases; —peels; —tans; —regenerates.
(See skin.)

EPIGRAM

adjectives
sparkling; feeble; biting.

verbs
abound in—s; compose—; enjoy—; indulge in—; inscribe—; master—; recite—; resent —; translate—; vent—; —charms; —condenses; —debases; —expresses; —irks; —points out; —provokes; —puzzles; —revenges; —satirizes; —stings; —consists of.
(See saying, poem, writing.)

EPIGRAMMATIC

adverbs
facetiously; waggishly; sententiously; laconically; crisply; curtly; neatly; quaintly;

pithily; concisely; summarily; wittily; cruelly; harshly; sarcastically; clownishly; drolly; jocosely; playfully; smartly; consciously; vexatiously; endlessly.

EPISODE

adjectives
impressive; dramatic; colorful; ludicrous; tragical; unsavory; extraordinary; pungent; exciting; wearing; pathetic; undignified; magnificent; ugly; continental; momentous; stirring; detached; mystical; peaceful; quixotic; picturesque; unforeseen; human; moving; trivial; soul-stirring; unfinished.

verbs
arrange—s; brood upon—; continue—; dramatize—; finish—; interject—; interpose—; introduce—; involve in—; number —s; recount—; refer to—; relate—; repeat —; resume—; —climaxes; —concerns; —crops up; —embraces; —entertains; —implicates; —intervenes.
(See incident, event, occurrence, action, story.)

EPISTLE

adjectives
famous; closely-written; absurd; tearful; heartfelt; imperial; business; monotonous; gracious; elegant; maternal; perplexing.

verbs
address—; compose—; delay—; deliver—; dispatch—; inspire—; laud—; pen—; prepare—; seal—; —aims at; —communicates; —consoles; —conveys; —declares; —explains; —indites; —instructs; —links; —relates; —reunites; —reveals; —strays; —wanders; —waxes.
(See letter, communication, writing.)

EPITAPH

adjectives
lying; mournful; pompous; uxorious; chiseled; inordinate; pitiable; simple; celebrated; original; dusty; sly; faithful; ancestral; wise; fitting; appropriate; irreverent.

verbs
bestow—on; compose—; conceive—; define —; deliver—; deserve—; hang—on; incorporate in—; inscribe—; interpret—; judge —; merit—; render in—; —adorns; —describes; —familiarizes; —glitters; —glorifies; —honors; —records; —reflects; —slanders; —vulgarizes.
(See inscription.)

EPITHET

adjectives
deranged; obnoxious; profane; insulting; deprecatory; opprobrious; polite; repeated; contumelious; endearing; courteous; balanced; fatal; significant.

verbs
answer—; apply—; bandy—s; bestow—upon; christen with—; comprehend—; convey—; design—; employ—; fix—; glory in—; indulge in—; justify—; originate—; pelt with—s; rain—s; represent with—; scatter—s; stuff with—s; —belongs; —designates; —disgraces; —justifies; —qualifies; —signifies; —terms.
(See phrase, expression, adjective, designation.)

EPITOMIZE (*v*)

adverbs
successfully; wittily; artfully; completely; shrewdly.
(See summarize, discuss.)

EPOCH

adjectives
geological; brilliant; colonial; misguided; glacial; legendary; memorable; impersonal; agitated; eventful; warfaring; climacteric; barbarous; revolutionary; haunted; chronological; antique; pagan.

verbs
begin—; commemorate—; create—; divide into—s; enhance—; form—; indicate—; inherit from—; mark—; open—; outlive—; refer to—; remember—; venerate—; —declines; —embraces; —glides on; —impresses; —produces; —provides; —survives.
(See period, era, time.)

EPOCHAL

adverbs
distinctly; significantly; markedly; notably; unforgettably; shamefully; brilliantly; memorably; legendarily; fabulously; imperishably; matchlessly; startlingly; stupendously; incalculably.

EQUABLE

adverbs
comfortably; pleasantly; dependably; naturally; happily; habitually; inherently; se-

renely; faultlessly; monotonously; reliably; drearily; methodically; agreeably; fairly; vexatiously; always; enviably.

EQUAL

adverbs
fairly; satisfactorily; agreeably; monotonously; symmetrically; broadly; practically; reasonably; legitimately; lawfully; admittedly; avowedly; synonymously; sufficiently; apparently; obviously; manifestly; evidently; incontestably.

EQUALITY

adjectives
rude; cozy; perfect; social; moral; legitimate; large; unrestricted; eternal; condescending.

verbs
abuse—; acquire—; admit—; approach—; assert—; assume—; attain—; demand—; denounce—; deny—; destroy—; disturb—; endow with—; maintain—; plead—; practice—; prate about—; prevent—; proclaim —; refuse—; require—; —breeds.

(See equilibrium, right, fairness, justice.)

EQUANIMITY

adjectives
astonishing; cool; unruffled; suave.

verbs
admire—; accept with—; approve—; bear with—; command—; concede with—; demonstrate—; digest with—; disregard with —; dwell in—; endure with—; justify—; keep in—; maintain—; possess—; recommend—; recover—; require—; restore—; suffer with—; swallow with—; wonder at —; —continues; —impresses; —persists; —surprises.

(See composure, serenity.)

EQUATION

adjectives
quadratic; personal; explanatory.

EQUILIBRIUM

adjectives
natural; balanced; unstable; happy; atmospheric.

verbs
attain—; check—; correct—; display—; exhibit—; gain—; guard—; illustrate—; maintain—; preserve—; restore—; threaten—.

(See balance, proportion.)

EQUIPAGE

adjectives
lumbering; huge; gilded; sumptuous; sufficient; somber.

EQUIPMENT

adjectives
technical; complete; optional; brilliant; recreational; obsolete; extensive; standard; defective; scanty; scientific; physical; inadequate; vocal; motorized; primitive; superior; ample; necessary; mental; intellectual.

verbs
acquire—; allot—to; complete—; contrive —; devise—; guard—; install—; modernize—; provide—; repair—; shield—; transport—; utilize—.

(See outfit, apparatus.)

EQUIPOISE

adjectives
boasted; unusual; vaunted.

EQUITABLE

adverbs
wisely; reasonably; duly; plainly; profoundly; prudently; rationally; sensibly; providently; expediently; justly; impartially; honorably; fairly; squarely; lawfully; legally; allowably; absolutely; legitimately; properly; scrupulously; punctiliously.

EQUIVALENT

adjectives
thermal; fair; modern; universal; financial; precise.

adverbs
meticulously; convertibly; tantamountly; avowedly; broadly; currently; customarily; regularly; naturally; wontedly; mathematically; genuinely; officially; strictly; basically; precisely; materially.

EQUIVOCAL

adverbs
vexatiously; irritatingly; purposely; intentionally; ambiguously; craftily; subtly; adroitly; cleverly; dubiously; debatably; insecurely; vaguely; mysteriously; ticklishly; obscurely; untrustworthily; unreliably; provokingly; cunningly; unfairly; artfully; fraudulently; perfidiously; insincerely; highly.

ERA

adjectives
crude; garish; showy; industrial; uninspired; commercialized; brief; comparative; colonial; illuminated; vamp; cultural.

verbs
acclaim—; announce—; enhance—; gild—; glorify—; hallow—; mark—; open—; symbolize—; typify—; usher in—; vulgarize—; —advances; —dawns; —emerges; —passes.
(See period, epoch, time.)

ERASURE

adjectives
lineal; untidy; unsightly; careless; blotchy; neat; nearly-invisible.

ERECT

adverbs
sturdily; staunchly; bravely; gallantly; loftily; firmly; grandly; rigidly; boldly; admirably; conspicuously; consciously; stiffly; proudly; imperiously; arrogantly.

ERECT (*v*)

adverbs
loftily; firmly; grandly; staunchly; toweringly; eloquently; triumphantly.
(See build, raise.)

ERECTNESS

adjectives
firm; conscious; natural; easy; military.

EROSION

verbs
activate—; check—; occasion—; overcome—; prevent—; produce—; protect from—; risk—; subject to—; —damages; —disintegrates; —endangers; —occurs; —strains; —weakens.
(See destruction, decay, acid.)

EROSIVE

adverbs
dangerously; wastefully; distressingly; disturbingly; unprofitably; harmfully; disastrously; detrimentally; deplorably; irremediably; inexpediently; increasingly; unfortunately; unnecessarily; grossly; outrageously; appallingly.

EROTIC

adverbs
amorously; tenderly; seductively; ardently; captivatingly; unduly; notably; particularly; interestingly; rapturously.

ERRAND

adjectives
mysterious; arrogant; uncouth; discouraging; slightest; reluctant; urgent; mournful; stumbling; futile; various (pl); wondrous.

verbs
accept—; administer—; bear—; commission for—; consent to—; discharge—; dispatch on—; execute—: fail in—; fake— (colloq); feign—; journey on—; send on—; speed on—.
(See mission, commission, communication.)

ERRANT

adverbs
incurably; nonchalantly; carelessly; incorrigibly; irresponsibly; gaily; happily; rapturously.

ERRATIC

adverbs
irregularly; habitually; characteristically; provokingly; unreliably; strangely; curiously; inscrutably; irresponsibly; inconsiderately; naturally; restlessly; mercurially; vagrantly; incurably; inveterately; fitfully; whimsically; capriciously; contrarily; uncomfortably; foolishly; inconsistently; marvelously; terribly.

ERRONEOUS

adverbs
tragically; purposely; carelessly; fallaciously; materially; foolishly; illogically; deceptively; intentionally; blunderingly; misleadingly; slightly; altogether; dreadfully; unpardonably.

ERROR

adjectives
manifest; inextricable; fatal; capital; successful; intellectual; deep-seated; common; vulgar; sweet; silly; trivial; apparent; gross; earthly; popular; strange; destructive; outstanding; biting; feeble; shallow; weak; mountainous; egregious; universal; ignoble; bare; venial; tactical; childish; unavoidable; curious; annoying; unguessed; statistical; innumerable (pl); scientific; serviceable; crumbling; pernicious; wild; warm; fantastic; glaring; opposite; chronic; dietetic; pleasing; previous; petty; profound; matrimonial; irretrievable; infinite; fundamental; unwelcome; counter; haughty; serious; damned; tempest-winged; typographical; monstrous; unfortunate; irremediable.

verbs
abound in—s; acknowledge—; adhere to—; aggravate—; atone for—; befog—; betray into—; build on—; cast out—; chafe at—; claim—; combat—; conquer—; correct—; counteract—; debate—; detect—; dispel—; escape—; expiate—; expose—; fall into—; forsake—; involve in—; lead into—; learn from—; lift above—; minimize—; neutralize—; overrule—; produce—; rebuke—; rectify—; reduce—; regret—; reject—; relinquish—; remove—; retrieve—; root in—; rue—; sense—; uncover—; unveil—; utter —; vanquish—; war against—; ward off—; wrestle with—; —contaminates; —deludes; —destroys; —impedes; —misleads.
(See fault, blunder, mistake, inaccuracy.)

ERUDITION

adjectives
mock; scholarly; extraordinary; specious.

verbs
abuse—; admire—; demand—; demonstrate —; denote—; digest—; employ—; exhibit —; feign—; freight with—; indicate—; judge—; justify—; oppress—; regard—; represent—; require—; —gratifies; —impresses.
(See knowledge, learning, wisdom.)

ERUPT (v)

adverbs
prematurely; terrifically; violently; prodigiously; volcanically; thunderously; crashingly; blindingly.
(See burst, explode.)

ERUPTION

adjectives
ruddy; cutaneous; memorable; terrific; copious; violent; prodigious; simultaneous; volcanic.

verbs
break forth in—; fear—; force—; hinder—; occasion—; prevent—; subject to—; —appears; —bursts; —discharges; —ejects; —emits; —harms; —issues forth; —occurs; —overwhelms; —shatters; —showers; —spreads.
(See outbreak, outburst.)

ESCAPADE

adjectives
suspicious; political; rash; youthful; drunken.

ESCAPE

adjectives
miraculous; precious; destitute; momentary; trivial; ignoble; impossible; marvelous; perilous; ultimate; hairbreadth; extraordinary; hair-raising; strong.

verbs
aid—; allow—; assist in—; attribute—to; conceal—; conspire—; cut off—; desire—; despair of—; effect—; enable—; guard against—; hinder—; insure—; investigate —; permit—; prevent—; scorn—; shun—.
(See flight, excuse, evasion.)

ESCAPE (v)

adverbs
exultantly; miraculously; temporarily; narrowly; easily; resolutely; audaciously; incessantly; barely; momentarily; ignobly; marvelously; perilously; ultimately; extraordinarily; hair-raisingly.
(See flee, elude.)

ESCORT

adjectives
military; proper; honorary; lounging; insufficient; barbaric.

verbs
accept—; attend in—; choose—; command —; desire—; employ—; form—; invite—; require—; serve as—; —abandons; —accommodates; —accompanies; —conducts; —conveys; —deserts; —guides; —lectures; —manages; —nurses; —protects; —serves; —supervises.
(See guard.)

ESCORT (v)

adverbs
tumultuously; barbarically; formally; ceremoniously; grandly; magnificently; regally; royally; gaily.
(See attend, follow.)

ESPIONAGE

adjectives
ostentatious; stealthy; cleverly-concealed; sympathetic.

ESPOUSE (v)

adverbs
obstinately; warmly; passionately; rabidly; ardently; rashly; impatiently; sincerely; treacherously.
(See undertake, assume.)

ESPOUSER

adjectives
ardent; rabid; rash; impatient.

ESSAY

adjectives
satirical; controversial; historical; critical; introductory; moral; discursive; provocative; delightful; notable; apathetical; celebrated; detached; literary; elaborated; sublime; fragmentary; informative; admirable; kindred; penetrating; classical; enlightening; presumptuous; remarkable.

verbs
abandon—; accept—; agree with—; attack —; caption—; compose—; criticize—; discuss—; elaborate—; judge—; laud—; offer —; praise—; prepare—; preserve—; propound—; —attempts; —encourages; —expresses; —implies; —meditates on.
(See composition, endeavor, attempt, effort, exposition.)

ESSAYIST

adjectives
critical; classical; aggressive.

ESSENCE

adjectives
seductive; intentional; tenfold; concrete; lasting; solitary; everlasting; spiritual; subtle; carnal; divine; congenial; electric; enduring; singular; ethereal; poetic; meager; heavenly; invisible; articulate; omnipresent; distinct; penetrative; volatile; rubylike; thin; fiery; winged; glassy; sensuous; impalatable; immutable.

verbs
apply—; convey—; counterfeit—; cover with—; distil—; exhale—; extract—; flavor with—; instil—; perfume with—; prepare —; preserve—; procure—; resign—; rub in—; sprinkle—; steep in—; —nauseates; —penetrates; —pervades; —refreshes; —sickens; —sinks in.
(See substance, perfume, odor, scent.)

ESSENTIAL

adjectives
salient; vital; food; absolute; minimum; basic.

verbs
ascertain—; cloud—; constitute—; deprive of—; destroy—; discern—; dispense with —; establish—; lack—; master—; obstruct —; overlook—; prove—; require—; restore —; strain—; suppress—; understand—; withhold—; —necessitates; —represents; —vanishes.
(See element, principle, quality.)

ESSENTIAL

adverbs
highly; absolutely; cardinally; emphatically; gravely; momentously; vitally; fundamentally; primarily; signally; significantly; urgently; extraordinarily; inordinately; seriously; utterly; peculiarly; unusually.

ESTABLISH (v)

adverbs
infallibly; conclusively; firmly; pompously; ultimately; solidly; definitely; indispensably; officially; permanently; triumphantly; incontestably; sufficiently; extensively; formally; rudely; splendidly; ancestrally; palatially; administratively.
(See show, prove.)

ESTABLISHED

adverbs
permanently; enduringly; stably; inviolately; thoroughly; immemorially; traditionally; generally; commonly; familiarly; conventionally; socially; regularly; officially; long; recently; firmly; easily; legally; emphatically; inescapably.

ESTABLISHMENT

adjectives
monastic; modest-looking; productive; immense; rude; conventional; splendid; primitive; odorous; penal; permanent; consular; separate; extensive; palatial; domestic; immediate; select; ancestral; manufacturing; ultimate; princely; meat-curing; administrative; costly; respectable-looking.

verbs
attack—; bar from—; conduct—; dictate —; enlarge—; evict from—; found—; guard—; hallow—; join—; legalize—; maintain—; nurture—; offend—; patronize—; set up—; superintend—; underwrite —; —crumbles; —fails; —flourishes; —prospers.
(See organization, institution.)

ESTATE

adjectives
manorial; residuary; intestate; unencumbered; landed; ancestral; precarious; competent; distressed; dark; scanty; fabulous;

feudal; impoverished; ecclesiastical; paltry; low; poor; outlying; hushed; sublunary; pretentious; unspeakable; meager; strange; uncorrupted; seignorial.

verbs
administer—; auction off—; charge to—; confiscate—; disable—; dissipate—; doom —; fall from—; fritter away—; lease—; maintain—; mortgage—; reapportion—; rent—; scorn—; settle—; shift—; tax—; —declines; —prospers; —shrinks.
(See property, possessions.)

ESTEEM

adjectives
great; rising; profound; exalted; proudest; racial; envious; impious; general; bright; favorable; sincerest.

verbs
command—; conceal—; deserve—; drop from—; enjoy—; entertain—; forfeit—; gain—; grow in—; hide—; hold in—; increase—; lose—; regard with—; value—; win—; —cools; —fades; —grows.
(See regard, respect, honor, favor, worth, opinion, value.)

ESTEEM (*v*)

adverbs
particularly; profoundly; racially; generally; sincerely; logically; enviously.
(See respect, honor.)

ESTIMABLE

adverbs
entirely; generally; highly; profoundly; undeniably; creditably; unimpeachably; obviously; worthily; dreadfully; respectably; dully; extremely; priggishly.

ESTIMATE

adjectives
impartial; production; exact; sanguine; contemptuous; accurate; accepted; modest; conservative; rough; truer; provisional; respectful; private; critical; utmost; exaggerated; judicious; reasonable; professional; slighting; undue; exaggerated; fallacious; moderate; current; contradictory; erroneous; inadequate; fantastic; theoretical; lightning.

verbs
accept—; arrive at—; attempt—; beggar—; calculate—; compute—; correct—; denounce —; entertain—; exaggerate—; extend—; forward—; govern—; harbor—; offer—; reach—; reel off—s; sway—s; —agrees; —coincides; —differs; —errs; —falls short; —indicates.
(See computation, calculation, value.)

ESTIMATE (*v*)

adverbs
conservatively; variously; accurately; critically; approximately; authoritatively; unhesitatingly; wildly; unerringly; calculatingly; fallaciously; erroneously; inadequately; fantastically; theoretically; professionally; provisionally; worthily.
(See value, appraise.)

ESTIMATION

adjectives
worthy; reverend; excessive; ludicrous; ungalled; avowed; exalted; aristocratic.

ESTRANGED

adverbs
pitiably; altogether; tragically; pathetically; curiously; inexplicably; mysteriously; oddly; silently; obviously; evidently; coldly; hatefully; temporarily; deeply; permanently; stubbornly; relentlessly; visibly; idiotically; astonishingly; lamentably.

ESTRANGEMENT

adjectives
transient; political.

verbs
bear—; brood over—; complete—; incur—; mourn—; pine in—; prevent—; rebel against—; sink in—; submit to—; suffer—; —agonizes; —burns; —dejects; —depresses; —desolates; —disheartens; —isolates; —oppresses; —pains; —wearies.

ETCH (*v*)

adverbs
vividly; powerfully; movingly; delicately; skillfully; artfully; dexterously; strikingly.
(See draw, sketch.)

ETCHING

adjectives
powerful; delicate; moving.

ETERNITY

adjectives
self-enshrined; dead; endless; shoreless; present; measureless; indivisible; dreadful; tiny.

verbs
accept—; believe in—; dwell in—; endure for—; foretaste—; glimpse—; leave to—; pass through—; probe—; prolong to—; reach—; reveal—; seems—; sing of—; spend in—; wander through—; —effaces; —exists.
(See immortality.)

ETHER

adjectives
luminiferous; finer; limpid; luminous; elastic; celestial; boundless; subtle.

verbs
administer—; apply—; float in—; put under —; sleep under—; spray—; —anaesthetizes; —affects; —deadens; —diminishes; —dims; —dissolves; —drowns; —dulls; —moderates; —numbs; —palls; —reduces; —stupefies.
(See anaesthetic.)

ETHEREAL

adverbs
daintily; airily; insubstantially; lightly; buoyantly; incredibly; delicately; vivaciously; whimsically; blithely; gracefully; sportively; inexpressibly.

ETHICAL

adverbs
punctiliously; meticulously; highly; systematically; unfailingly; ostentatiously; laboriously; carefully; naturally; habitually; professionally; strictly; rigidly; happily; gracefully; politely; diplomatically; marvellously; conscientiously; dutifully; amenably; absolutely.

ETHICS

adjectives
professional; inflexible; strict; dreary; government; ministerial; legal; cheerless; bad; heightened.

verbs
adopt—; consider—; control by—; digest—; discourse on—; embrace—; exhort—; impose by—; improve—; instruct in—; involve—; judge—; live up to—; obligate by—; observe—; rebel against—; rely on—; test—; versed in—; —directs; —guides; —provides; —raises.
(See science, rules, philosophy.)

ETIQUETTE

adjectives
fixed; punctilious; stiff; established; courtly; exclusive; rigid.

verbs
apply—; conduct with—; educate in—; impose by—; inform on—; judge by—; loosen —; observe—; polish—; practise—; prescribe—; require—; study—; transact with —; transgress—; —bans; —demands; —forbids; —improves; —obliges; —prohibits; —tames; —ties.
(See code, rules, decorum.)

EULOGISTIC

adverbs
sententiously; sincerely; properly; suitably; regularly; duly; smugly; sanctimoniously; hypocritically; highly; impressively; dramatically; immeasurably; unnecessarily; sonorously; artfully; brilliantly; magnificently; admirably; splendidly; unctuously; sycophantically; speciously; fulsomely.

EULOGIZE (*v*)

adverbs
unctuously; flamboyantly; effusively; lavishly; flatteringly; deceptively; slyly; treacherously; deceivingly.
(See laud, praise.)

EULOGY

adjectives
barren; unmeasured; artful; embarrassed; swallowing; lengthened; brilliant; indiscriminating; sorry; glowing; sounding.

EUPHEMISTIC

adverbs
cleverly; artfully; adroitly; ironically; sarcastically; wittily; smoothly; humorously; plausibly; pompously; rhetorically; merrily; teasingly; neatly; felicitously; pleasantly; inoffensively.

EUPHONY

adjectives
gushing; sheer.

EUROPE

verbs
communicate with—; denounce—; embattle —; embroil—; introduce in—; invade—; ring through—; rock—; rule—; sail for—; seize—; shock—; tour—; unite—; —allies with; —arms; —copies; —envies; —ex-

ports; —imitates; —imports; —quakes; —repudiates; —seethes; —simmers; —stands; —voices; —wars.
(See continent.)

EVACUATION

adjectives
copious; sanguinolent; alvine.

verbs
advocate—; authorize—; command—; compel—; deplore—; direct—; facilitate—; force—; impose—; insist on—; prepare—; prescribe—; promote—; resist—; submit to —; suggest—; withdraw in—; —relinquishes; order—.
(See withdrawal, discharge.)

EVADE (v)

adverbs
gracefully; studiously; partially; slyly; treacherously; cleverly; dexterously.
(See avoid, shun.)

EVALUATION

adjectives
clinical; clear.

EVANESCENT

adverbs
flittingly; impermanently; briefly; ephemerally; precariously; transiently; transitorily; perishably; mortally; sadly.

EVANGELISTIC

adverbs
ardently; zealously; sincerely; earnestly; successfully; eagerly; persistently; fervently; devotedly; fervidly; passionately; assiduously; solemnly; happily; joyously; enthusiastically; rapturously; superbly; intensely; unwearyingly; devoutly.

EVASION

adjectives
elaborate; endless; dexterous; pitiful; terror-stricken; treasonable; sly .

verbs
addict to—; criticize—; decry—; detect—; employ—; endure—; forbid—; force—; frustrate—; practice—; require—; shift in —; shuffle in—; stammer in—; suspect—; trouble with—; wrap in—; —assists; —shelters.
(See subterfuge.)

EVASIVE

adverbs
unfortunately; disturbingly; deliberately; undesirably; ambiguously; equivocally; distressingly; offensively; insultingly; suspiciously; undeniably; quibblingly; perplexingly; bewilderingly; obscurely; mysteriously; seriously; irritatingly; stolidly; vaguely; disagreeably; insidiously; significantly; stupidly; unwisely; objectionably; cunningly; cleverly; adroitly.

EVE

adjectives
autumn; dew-glistening; sealing; keener; momentous; thoughtful; dewy; ghostly; deepening.

EVENING

adjectives
lingering; tranquil; happy; occasional; curious; long; fatal; autumnal; cold; frosty; red; triumphant; sad-colored; ravishing; chilly; awkward; bacchanal; bridal; calm; swift-falling; unfortunate; deepening; sorrowful; unillumined; bronzed; sleepy; balmy; eventful; golden; peaceful; imperial; ensuing; purple; gusty; premature; sober; dewy; ghostlike; dull; shadowy; memorable; grateful; languorous; bygone; dusky; hectic; delirious; warm; muggy; uncomfortable; cheerful; amazing; preceding; quiet; starry; harmonic; roseate.

verbs
approach—; await—; chill—; cloud—; crown——; draw toward—; gild—; hush—; last till—; occupy—; overcast—; ramble through—; return at—; rift—; rise at—; solemnize—; still—; sup at—; toil till—; usher in—; —approaches; —closes; —cools; —declines; —dies; —dims; —fades; —falls; —flies; —reposes; —shades; —sobers; —steals on.
(See twilight, dusk.)

EVENNESS

adjectives
velvet; insipid; boring; smooth; pleasant.

EVENT

adjectives
solemn; unbeatable; important; comprehensive; festival; outward; outstanding; sensational; trivial; huge; memorable; extraordinary; tragic; thrilling; embarrassing; disgusting; headline; contemporary; gigantic; strange; sweet; perturbing; crowning; subsequent; tremendous; strik-

ing; confused; fortunate; true; fierce; natural; unlooked-for; obscene; preposterous; dignified; sublime; momentous; inescapable; ultimate; startling; dramatic; pivotal; exciting; deplorable; celestial; mysterious; fateful; propitious; supreme; remarkable; future; sinful; minutest; detectable; stormy; dark; hurried; bizarre; unforeseen; stirring; fortuitous; unexpected; tempestuous; miraculous; boding; melancholy; overshadowing; succeeding; naked; recurrent; domestic; insignificant; humiliating; hastened; intermediate; calamitous; historical; previous; disastrous; happy; current; impolite; pin-point; dire; dreadful; preventable; antecedent.

verbs
acclaim—; applaud—; ascribe—to; attend —; beget—; commend—; detail—; dramatize—; explain—; fashion—; forecast—; foresee—; govern—; interpret—; mark—; narrate—; ponder—; predict—; presage—; rehash—; resume—; rue—; scan—; seize upon—; shape—; stamp—; view—; witness —; —commemorates; —confuses; —evolves; —portends; —represents; —results in; —underlies.

(See occurrence, incident, episode, consequence, issue, fortune.)

EVICT (v)

adverbs
raucously; sternly; heartlessly; coldly; cruelly; dictatorially; vigorously; harshly; peremptorily; abruptly; legally; forcefully; formally.

(See expel, dispossess.)

EVICTION

adjectives
harrowing; tragic; pitiful; heartless.

EVIDENCE

adjectives
silent; fearful; happiest; overwhelming; corroborative; further; official; tangible; repeated; spectroscopic; additional; damnatory; damaging; multiplied; irrefutable; confirmatory; circumstantial; diagnostic; documentary; substantial; signal; stronger; moral; noisy; convincing; incontrovertible; concrete; inadmissible; marked; apocryphal; explicit; abundant; bibliographical; contemporaneous; irrelevant; customary; secondhand; definite; palpable; visual; unmistakable; authentic; touching; effectual; white-spotted; legendary; sufficient; internal; contemporary; speechless; striking; extraordinary; certain; conspicuous; gratifying; remarkable; scientific; faintest; absolute; unassailable; revealing; external; pragmatic; ungarbled; trustworthy; material; corrected; hearsay; impressive; factual; ample; cumulative; manifest; undoubted; lawful; modest; conclusive; positive; indubitable; unanswerable; unexceptionable; incontestable; breathing; experimental; reasonable; truthful; overt; concentrated; supporting; decisive; hopeful; notable; unconscious; considerable; undeniable; direct; usual; unerring; outward; archaeological; satisfactory; unequivocal; presumptive.

verbs
accept—; accumulate—; adduce—; alter—; amass—; base on—; confirm—; confront with—; contradict—; corroborate—; credit —; deduce—; deny—; destroy—; digest—; emphasize—; examine—; falsify—; ferret out—; gaze on—; interpret—; invoke—; offer—; overrate—; overrule—; parade—; perjure—; produce—; proffer—; recite—; regard—; reject—; review—; ruin—; search for—; seek—; sift—; submit—; substantiate—; sum up—; team with—; transcend—; unearth—; verify—; weigh—; yield to—; —collates; —damns; —discloses; —piles up; —supports; —sustains; —warrants.

(See fact, testimony, proof, demonstration.)

EVIDENT

adverbs
fearfully; overwhelmingly; irrefutably; convincingly; substantially; explicitly; unmistakably; sufficiently; strikingly; materially; conclusively; undeniably; flagrantly; easily; plainly; clearly; glaringly; reasonably; shamefully; outrageously; pitifully; dangerously; plaguedly; perilously; fortunately.

EVIL

adjectives
once-abounding; attendant; besetting; multiplied (pl); alleged; cave-keeping; substantial; dreadful; terrible; secret; manifest; necessary; infinite; inevitable; heaviest; familiar; scandalous; restless; trifling; unseen; remediable; impending; incalculable; desperate; unsubduable; imminent; weak-headed; manifold (pl); partial; temporary;

crying; accursed; ominous; future; thirsty; iniquitous; imaginary; approaching; unavoidable; abstract; moral; fixed; ruthless; necessary; human; accumulated; insidious; immeasurable.

verbs
abhor—; abolish—; abstain from—; aggravate—; alleviate—; ameliorate—; atone for—; avoid—; banish—; beset by—; besmirch with—; blind to—; breed—; cast out —; combat—; compensate for—; cope with —; counteract—; counterbalance—; cure—; deliver from—; denounce—; deplore—; dispose to—; dwell in—; effect—; eradicate—; evince—; exempt from—; fortify against —; imply—; insinuate—; intend—; intensify—; lapse into—; loathe—; master—; mitigate—; overcome—; persist in—; personify—; promote—; punish—; repent—; stir up—; strike at—; submit to—; suffer—; symbolize—; tackle—; tempt with—; uncover—; unite against—; uproot—; —befalls; —degrades; —menaces; expose to—; resist—.

(See wickedness, sin, iniquity, disaster, misfortune, reverse, injustice, wrong, affliction.)

adverbs
cruelly; flagrantly; hatefully; dangerously; mischievously; violently; irretrievably; inconceivably; poisonously; viciously; iniquitously; shamefully; incredibly; brutally; incorrigibly; atrociously; infernally; shockingly; woefully; sadly; villainously; irremediably; scandalously; manifestly; openly; avowedly; exceptionally; obnoxiously; disastrously; detestably; diabolically; perniciously; basely; irrevocably; horribly.

EVINCE (v)

adverbs
noticeably; markedly; unmistakably; obviously; sickeningly; partially; undoubtedly.

(See show, indicate.)

EVOLUTION

adjectives
regressive; rapid; uninterrupted; accelerated; lingual; mental; inevitable; intricate; uncertain; social; orderly; pious; masterly; creative; deliberate; mystic; eternal; cosmic; daring; terrestrial.

verbs
climb in—; complete—; confirm—; effect—; examine—; influence—; manifest—; observe—; produce by—; represent—; resolve by—; roll in—; speed up—; support —; verify—; —lifts; —progresses; —ripens; —spreads; —transmits; —unfolds.

(See development, growth.)

EVOLVE (v)

adverbs
scientifically; illogically; rapidly; perpetually; acceleratedly; mentally; intricately; uncertainly; splendidly; creatively; mystically; socially; daringly.

(See develop, complete.)

EWE

adjectives
mild-faced; fulsome.

EXACT

adverbs
infallibly; unimpeachably; strictly; literally; rigorously; scrupulously; painstakingly; punctiliously; mathematically; scientifically; unerringly; meticulously; authentically; absolutely; dependably; terrifyingly; uncannily; monotonously; essentiallly; astonishingly; impartially; ostentatiously; manifestly; graphically; astonishingly.

EXACT (v)

adverbs
rigidly; inexorably; harshly; cruelly; legally; painfully; strictly; formally.

(See demand, extort.)

EXACTION

adjectives
dictatorial; tyrannous.

EXACTITUDE

adjectives
graphic; conscientious; mathematical; clear-cut; scrupulous.

EXACTNESS

adjectives
scrupulous; close; ironical; crystalline; literal; elaborate; legal; unfailing; painful; technical; historical; mathematical.

EXAGGERATE (v)

adverbs
monstrously; sensationally; absurdly; vaingloriously; recklessly; grossly; amusingly;

crudely; grotesquely; rhetorically; journalistically; palpably; virulently; turbulently.
(See lie, magnify.)

EXAGGERATION

adjectives
sensational; cruel; striking; reckless; pardonable; gross; reactionary; amusing; crude; grotesque; rhetorical; passionate; journalistic; delicious; intense; palpable; rowdy; virulent; turbulent.

verbs
addict to—; anticipate—; blame—; confess —; decry—; guard against—; mark by—; reduce—; relate with—; represent—; ridicule—; sneer at—; tolerate—; warn of—; —adds; —amuses; —entertains; —harms; —misleads; —offends; —overwhelms.
(See overstatement.)

EXALT (*v*)

adverbs
boundlessly; loftily; indefinitely; religiously; mystically; sentimentally; blissfully; joyfully; spiritually; vividly; feverishly; impassionedly; hysterically.
(See magnify, elevate.)

EXALTATION

adjectives
religious; mystic; essential; sentimental; blissful; joyful; spiritual; high; nervous; vivid; dreamy; curious; feverish; impassioned; personal; unimaginable; mesmeric; perfect; harmonic.

EXALTED

adverbs
eminently; highly; conspicuously; notably; distinctly; gloriously; illustriously; splendidly; proudly; honorably; imposingly; majestically; wonderfully; remarkably.

EXAMINATION

adjectives
blind; impromptu; oral; minute; dispassionate; separate; unprejudiced; astute; unimpassioned; thoughtful; perfunctory; microscopic; critical; accurate; detailed; severe; competitive; censorial; elaborate; premarital; unsparing; stiff; fruitless; preventative; periodic; careful; searching; verbal; expert; posthumous; simultaneous; hasty; anatomical; exacting; unbiased; cooler; tedious; cursory; hostile; placid; frequent (pl); monotonous; brusque; caustic; judicial; meticulous; subsequent; systematic.

verbs
compete in—; conduct—; cram for—; crib in—; fail in—; flunk—; merit—; pass—; perform—; prepare for—; resort to—; select by—; subject to—; submit to—; summon for—; tackle—; undergo—; urge—; waive—; —discloses; —proves; —reveals.
(See scrutiny, investigation, search, review, autopsy, inquiry, test.)

EXAMINE (*v*)

adverbs
minutely; curiously; critically; superficially; studiously; gravely; closely; attentively; expertly; subsequently; ostensibly; hastily; rigorously; briefly; blindly; dispassionately; separately; astutely; perfunctorily; thoughtfully; microscopically; severely; competitively; premaritally; unsparingly; fruitlessly; preventatively; periodically; verbally; expertly; posthumously; simultaneously; anatomically; unbiasedly; tediously; cursorily; hostilely; placidly; monotonously; brusquely; caustically; judicially; meticulously; systematically; subsequently.
(See scrutinize, inspect.)

EXAMPLE

adjectives
pernicious; glaring; magnificent; picturesque; genuine; colorful; notorious; admirable; subsequent; fond; familiar; notable; remote; fatal; stirring; savage; disastrous; illustrious; shining; encouraging; extreme; servile; debasing; effective; melancholy; comparative; innumerable (pl); legible; elaborate; excellent; cruelest; supreme; imitated; striking; foremost; tardy; ultimate; enlightening; noble; unique; analogous; uncommon; impressive; attainable; painful; recorded; vicious; vindictive; concrete; classic; splendid; pathetic; judicious; morbid; eloquent; conspicuous; astounding; contagious; flagrant; haphazard; executive; pregnant; high-poised; rare; instructive; formidable; heroic; valuable; patriotic.

verbs
afford—; cite—; cull—; display as—; emulate—; encourage—; enumerate—s; exhibit —; follow—; glorify—; imitate—; interpret—; make—of; pattern on—; unearth—; view—; —defiles; —illustrates; —incites; —proves; —verifies.
(See instance, sample, specimen, model, illustration, precedent.)

EXASPERATING

adverbs
dreadfully; unbearably; intolerably; oddly; vexatiously; intentionally; unwittingly; innocently; terribly; tormentingly; naughtily; raspingly; bitterly; savagely; relentlessly; ungovernably; unusually; occasionally.

EXASPERATION

adjectives
religious; renewed; increased; inner; sardonic; frequent; intense; sudden; continual; increasing; incessant.

verbs
account for—; bear—; dispose to—; enrage with—; forbear—; incense with—; increase —; incur—; inflict—; irritate to—; load with—; occasion—; plot to—; remedy—; shiver with—; subject to—; torment to—; vent—; —disposes; —explodes; —harms; —wells up.
(See anger, irritation, provocation.)

EXCAVATION

adjectives
abandoned; lone; gaping; desolate.

verbs
direct—; discover during—; employ in—; engage in—; examine—; forbid—; place—; plan—; prevent—; require—; tunnel—; unearth in—; watch—; —divulges; —exposes; —impairs; —lays bare; —progresses; —reveals; —ruins.
(See cavity, hole.)

EXCEED (*v*)

adverbs
frequently; illegally; surprisingly; splendidly; astonishingly; notably; memorably; wildly.
(See transcend, surpass.)

EXCEL (*v*)

adverbs
unexpectedly; conspicuously; immeasurably; peculiarly; intrinsically; individually; comparatively; marvelously; surpassingly; materially; unusually; trivially; matchlessly; supremely; dramatically; genuinely; consistently; exceedingly.
(See surpass, transcend.)

EXCELLENCE

adjectives
highest; intrinsic; exceeding; compensatory; artistic; rare; individual; comparative; marvelous; unobtrusive; eternal; surpassing; minor; architectural; material; unapproached; unusual; trivial; matchless; supreme; dramatic; acoustic; professional; peerless; genuine; unrivaled; unvarying; known; consistent; unsurpassed; dateless; superior; self-made; brand-new.

EXCELLENCY

adjectives
reverend; moral.

EXCELLENT

adverbs
dependably; consistently; consciously; reliably; obviously; evidently; palpably; incomparably; matchlessly; surprisingly; brilliantly; artistically; genuinely.

EXCEPTION

adjectives
notable; memorable; violent; trifling; marked; conspicuous; solitary; occasional; delightful; important; innumerable (pl); rare; possible; inexcusable; honorable.

verbs
answer—; appeal for—; ban—; bar—; declare—; defend—; demand—; examine —; expose to—; justify—; lodge—; produce—; protect—; provide—; rule—; state —; take—to; —appears.
(See objection, omission.)

EXCEPTIONAL

adverbs
undoubtedly; highly; indubitably; conspicuously; delightfully; notably; famously; memorably; inimitably; peculiarly; eccentrically; fantastically; exotically; outlandishly; grotesquely; unconventionally.

EXCESS

verbs
accumulate—of; addict to—; burn—; eliminate—; gather—; protest—; rebuke—; refrain from—; remove—; reject—; regret —; reprove—; scatter—; spread—; waste —; —disgraces; —intoxicates.
(See extravagance, surplus, residue, intemperance.)

EXCESSES

adjectives
poor; mad; factional; deplorable; utmost; sanguinary; hideous; extravagant; intolerable; morbid; dangerous; clumsy; mischievous; wildest; witty; persistent; loathsome; personal; dreadful; careless; strained.

EXCHANGE

adjectives
typical; significant; inevitable; dexterous; mute; mutual; unauthorized; solemn; sympathetic; friendly; intimate; immediate; whispered.

verbs
agree on—; allow—; authorize—; counteract—; demand—; dote on—; give in—; grant—; lose through—; operate—; permit —; plan—; procure—; profit by—; promote —; reject—; return in—; solicit—; win—.
(See trade, traffic.)

EXCHANGE (v)

adverbs
mutely; significantly; dexterously; solemnly; sympathetically; intimately; immediately.
(See accept.)

EXCHANGEABLE

adverbs
readily; easily; conveniently; equitably; allowably; obviously; scarcely; legally; hardly; adaptably; commercially; negotiably; reciprocally; properly; warrantably; necessarily; assuredly.

EXCITABILITY

adjectives
morbid; rabid; easy; choleric.

EXCITABLE

adverbs
terribly; abnormally; easily; highly; uncommonly; unusually; temperamentally; naturally; habitually; unfortunately; absurdly; childishly; ridiculously; oddly; curiously; strangely; mysteriously; slightly; disturbingly; painfully; dangerously; significantly; extremely; excessively; outlandishly; uncontrollably; ungovernably; wildly; fussily; inexplicably; deplorably.

EXCITATION

adjectives
unnatural; noticeable; spiritual; frenzied; marked.

EXCITE (v)

adverbs
strongly; mutinously; painfully; sedulously; intensely; fiercely; supernaturally; wildly; vivaciously; pleasurably; contagiously; artificially; tremulously; exhaustingly; boundlessly; terrifically; preternaturally; sensuously; coarsely; riotously; scandalously; hilariously; hectically; intellectually.
(See arouse, stimulate.)

EXCITEMENT

adjectives
intense; fierce; vast; fascinated; fevered; constant; glowing; supernatural; wild; vivacious; pleasurable; abated; contagious; considerable; gradual; turbulent; aggressive; remorseful; stirring; flushed; perpetual; overpowering; artificial; tremulous; insolent; solemn; strong; hasty; feeble; exhausting; innocent; bubbling; dangerous; pale; adventurous; subdued; joyous; composed; avid; pleasant; tense; probable; peculiar; delicious; momentary; nervous; deep; delirious; emotional; gross; diseased; uncontrollable; sheer; cerebral; contemporary; unprovoked; healthful; frantic; involuntary; frenzied; boundless; high; extraordinary; smothered; terrific; preternatural; sensuous; coarse; perpetual; inconceivable; drawled; riotous; scandalous; hilarious; correspondent; suppressed; mental; hectic; painful; veritable; previous; neutral; intellectual; revolutionary.

verbs
arouse—; avoid—; buzz with—; calm—; conceal—; contain—; crave—; eliminate—; flash—; flush with—; guard against—; induce—; respond to—; rock with—; seethe with—; sense—; stir to—; suppress—; thirst for—; thrive on—; wheeze with—; —blazes; —dies away; —fades; —leaps high; —shines in one's eyes; —smolders; —subsides; —surges.
(See perturbation, commotion, agitation, stimulation.)

EXCLAIM (v)

adverbs
wildly; curiously; breathlessly; softly; thoughtfully; boisterously; fiercely; delightfully; acidly; admiringly; jovially; facetiously; angrily; incredulously; distressfully; bitterly; enthusiastically; solemnly; blankly; saucily; triumphantly; impulsively; testily; gleefully; savagely; boastfully; regretfully; profanely; tragically; piteously; sharply; reproachfully; anxiously; ostentatiously; disappointedly; unadvisedly; fervently; joyously; rapturously; faintly; audibly; stifledly; abruptly; ardently; helplessly; enthusiastically; frantically; shockedly; gutturally.
(See ejaculate, shout.)

EXCLAMATION

adjectives
joyous; rapturous; passionate; angry; fiery; furious; half-suppressed; faint; nervous; incoherent; mourning; audible; half-articulated; impatient; stifled; abrupt; homely; ardent; helpless; enthusiastic; sharp; frantic; indistinct; vivid; pleased; assenting; guttural; shocked.

verbs
burst out in—; drown—; elicit—; emit—; heed—; mark with—; mouth—; pour forth —; pronounce—; protest with—; startle by—; suppress—; utter—; —delights; —expresses; —pains; —resounds; —surprises.
(See outcry, utterance, cry.)

EXCLAMATORY

adverbs
dramatically; absurdly; ludicrously; needlessly; unnecessarily; noisily; violently; offensively; vexatiously; loudly; cholerically; angrily; enthusiastically; blatantly; conspicuously; boldly; urgently; impressively; ridiculously; gustily; coarsely; grossly; sympathetically; terribly; frightfully.

EXCLUDE (*v*)

adverbs
strictly; vigorously; expressly; deliberately; entirely; cautiously; jealously; utterly; rigorously; persistently.
(See omit, prevent.)

EXCLUSION

adjectives
stereotyped; utter; impolitic; studied; strictest; rigorous; perpetual; persistent.

EXCLUSIVE

adverbs
socially; discriminatingly; absurdly; wisely; necessarily; snobbishly; proudly; haughtily; carefully; significantly; purposely; designedly; unreasonably; offensively; formally; officially; safely; rigidly; ridiculously.

EXCLUSIVENESS

adjectives
scornful; fastidious.

EXCOMMUNICATION

verbs
banish to—; brood over—; delay—; demand—; denounce—; deplore—; deserve—; fulminate—; incur—; prevent—; prohibit —; pronounce—; rebel against—; repent—; restrain—; sentence to—; submit to—; suffer—; threaten with—; —ejects; —excludes; —exiles; —expels; —interdicts; —separates; —shuts out.
(See separation, expulsion.)

EXCRESCENCE

adjectives
preternatural; hideous; annoying; ugly.

EXCRETION

adjectives
wasteful; useless; diminished.

verbs
encourage—; expel during—; facilitate—; halt—; necessitate—; observe—; occasion —; prevent—; produce—; promote—; provoke—; reduce—; require—; stimulate—; suppress—; throw out in—; —cleanses; —exhausts; —occurs; —pains; —purges.
(See discharge.)

EXCRUCIATING

adverbs
terribly; unbearably; visibly; obviously; piteously; unnecessarily; inexpressibly; dreadfully; appallingly; insufferably; insupportably.

EXCURSION

adjectives
amatory; vague; opportune; equestrian; pedestrian; novel; episodical; periodical; rural; provincial; preliminary; piratical; involuntary; compulsory; sporting; restless; predatory; hunting; sketching; torch-light.

verbs
anticipate—; arrange—; delight in—; depart on—; embark on—; escape on—; join —; organize—; plan—; prevent—; start on —; take—; undertake—; venture on—; enjoy—.
(See journey, trip, expedition.)

EXCUSABLE

adverbs
easily; readily; scarcely; hardly; apparently; plausibly; fairly; barely; legitimately; defensibly; reasonably.

EXCUSE

adjectives
apparent; plausible; sheepish; sufficient; audible; penitent; ominous; coy; lawful; puerile; crazy; fair; generous; bare; specious; voluble; cleanly-coined; deft; bashful;

dingy; unblushing; flimsy; useful; reasonable; truthful; ready; legitimate; good; slightest; time-honored; inept; fabricated; unspeakable.

verbs
accept—; beg for—; condone—; defend with—; demand—; denounce—; furnish—; hatch—; invent—; judge—; offer—; plead —; pray for—; present—; produce—; propose as—; request—; require—; seek—; seize on—; shape—; —absolves; —acquits; —amends; —exonerates; —explains; —infuriates; —justifies; —patches up; —releases; —suffices; —vindicates.

(See plea, reason, apology.)

EXCUSE (v)

adverbs
ostensibly; pleasantly; apparently; plausibly; sheepishly; audibly; penitently; ominously; coyly; speciously; volubly; deftly; reasonably; ineptly.

(See forgive, pardon.)

EXECRATION

adjectives
terrible; half-smothered; frantic.

EXECUTE (v)

adverbs
imperfectly; faithfully; unquestionably; intensively; beautifully; simultaneously; brilliantly; stoutly; momentously; bureaucratically; thoroughly; successfully; duly; splendidly; unremittingly; vigorously; summarily; gracefully; practically; skillfully; admirably; knowingly; linguistically; economically; rudely; justifiably; secretly; intrepidly; imposingly; crudely; magnificently.

(See administer, perform.)

EXECUTION

adjectives
linguistic; efficient; imperfect; economic; justifiable; rude; supreme; secret; immediate; intrepid; unrivaled; imposing; brilliant; hopeful; bloody; crude; magnificent; vigorous; facile.

verbs
await—; cite—; condemn to—; delay—; deliver over to—; demand—; enforce—; entrust—to; escape—; obstruct—; postpone —; reprieve from—; risk—; stay—; warrant—; witness—; —expiates.

(See performance, accomplishment, death.)

EXECUTIVE

adjectives
able; industrial; admirable; signal; energetic; insignificant; high-powered; tyrannical; overbearing; pompous.

adverbs
responsibly; highly; legally; carefully; cautiously; supremely; imperiously; authoritatively; royally; municipally; arbitrarily; masterfully; imposingly; efficiently; brilliantly; magnificently; splendidly; vigorously; intrepidly; unquestionably; proudly; effectively.

EXECUTOR

adjectives
literary; financial; grasping; efficient.

EXEMPLARY

adverbs
admirably; famously; notably; conspicuously; illustriously; effectively; elaborately; supremely; strikingly; nobly; impressively; uncommonly; uniquely; splendidly; eloquently; heroically; valuably; dramatically.

EXEMPLIFICATION

adjectives
historic; unostentatious; significant.

EXEMPLIFY (v)

adverbs
richly; strikingly; effectively; vaingloriously; historically; significantly; unostentatiously; perfectly.

(See illustrate, prove.)

EXEMPT

adverbs
legally; officially; notably; explicitly; expressly; wisely; craftily; fortunately; adroitly; cleverly; politically; absolutely; automatically; unaccountably; mysteriously; happily; luckily; inexplicably; radiantly.

EXEMPTION

verbs
acquire—; beg—; command—; demand—; enjoy—; grant—; merit—; plead—; procure—; protest—; purchase—; renounce—; select for—; —debars; —excludes; —frees; —removes; —unburdens.

(See immunity. freedom, privilege.)

EXERCISE

adjectives
unwearied; bodily; vigorous; appropriate; pedestrian; social; sinister; manly; vacation; habitual; arbitrary; daily; princely; exhilarating; useless; ruthless; mechanical; conscientious; active; simple; unlawful; righteous; well-planned; equitable; monotonous; generous; virtuous; intelligent; fatiguing; effortless; unbiased; perpetual; delectable; injudicious; joyous; constant; conscious; graceful; unwonted; painful; divine; continued; utmost; preposterous; efficient; courtly; mental; gymnastic; unremitting; insufficient; unquestionable; enlightened; nocturnal; ecstatic; memorial; devilish; gentle; graduated; strenuous; mere; internal; plentiful; violent; muscular; recreative; intellectual; anteprandial.

verbs
adapt—to; apply—; assign—to; carry out —; delight in—; deprive of—; diminish—; forego—; graduate—; indulge in—; neglect —; perform—; practise—; recommend—; refrain from—; repeat—; restrict—; resume; —develops; —enlivens; —exhilarates; —tires.

(See act, action, activity, exertion, practise, drill, use.)

EXERCISE (*v*)

adverbs
diversely; exclusively; violently; ruthlessly; bodily; unweariedly; vigorously; appropriately; socially; habitually; uselessly; mechanically; delectably; joyously; painfully; gymnastically; unremittingly; insufficiently; mentally; nocturnally; muscularly; strenuously; recreatively.

(See exert, apply.)

EXERT (*v*)

adverbs
strenuously; vocally; undoubtedly; vigorously; unscrupulously; prodigiously; assiduously; incredibly; desperately; extraordinarily; laudably; incessantly; courageously; productively; vainly; unusually; seriously.

(See exercise, apply.)

EXERTION

adjectives
unaccustomed; equivalent; utmost; strenuous; prodigious; assiduous; redoubled; incredible; vigorous; individual; useless; unremitted; desperate; extraordinary; violent; fresh; intrepid; laudable; incessant; supernatural; polite; diurnal; courageous; fortunate; physical; mental; ceaseless; laborious; unusual; productive; ungracious; vain; joint.

verbs
abhor—; break under—; carry—of; delay —; hinder—; increase—; kindle—; manifest—; produce by—; render—; resist—; reveal—; rouse to—; stimulate to—; waste —; —agitates; —aggravates; —fags; —fatigues; —restores; —taxes.

(See effort, struggle, endeavor.)

EXHALATION

adjectives
ammoniacal; mephitic; ceaseless; foggy; loathsome; unwholesome; noxious.

EXHAUST (*v*)

adverbs
stertorously; utterly; finally; financially; totally; seemingly; mutually; racially; ruthlessly; practically; physically; spiritually.

(See deplete, prostrate.)

EXHAUSTED

adverbs
utterly; well-nigh; pitiably; shockingly; alarmingly; pathetically; portentously; ludicrously; laughingly; feebly; wheezily; grievously; faintly; perceptibly; visibly; unusually; naturally; obviously.

EXHAUSTION

adjectives
worn; mutual; racial; nervous; sheer; ruthless; practical; physical; spiritual.

verbs
approach—; carry on to—; collapse in—; cure—; diminish—; discuss to—; drain to—; drop in—; induce—; occasion—; produce—; reach—; recuperate from—; reduce to—; succumb to—; tax to—; —destroys; —enervates; —ensues; —incapacitates; —perils; —prostrates.

(See fatigue, weariness.)

EXHIBIT

adjectives
studious; mercantile; bulky; archaeological; educational; pitiable; admirable; startling; doleful; representative.

EXHIBIT (v)

adverbs
immodestly; markedly; unexpectedly; pretentiously; shamelessly; obscenely; gratuitously; glaringly; curiously; muscularly; conspicuously; educationally; persuasively; studiously; representatively.
(See show, display.)

EXHIBITION

adjectives
retrospective; permanent; positive; invidious; wholesale; detailed; spectacular; amazing; spontaneous; portentous; barefaced; frequent (pl); incomparable; theatrical; fanciful; competitive; foremost; remarkable; pitiable; noticeable; notable; comic; degrading; disgusting; enormous; colonial; spirited; creditable; outstanding; florid; symbolical.

verbs
acclaim—; applaud—; appreciate—; bill—; boycott—; display—; inspect—; participate in—; sponsor—; throng—; witness—; —amazes; —amuses; —astounds; —commemorates; —draws; —entertains; —fascinates; —instructs; —opens; —profits.
(See display, spectacle, show.)

EXHILARATE (v)

adverbs
vivaciously; briskly; momentarily; strangely; voluptuously; joyouslv.
(See excite, cheer.)

EXHILARATING

adverbs
tremendously; immensely; vigorously; wonderfully; boundlessly; highly; buoyantly; briskly; hilariously; vivaciously; sparklingly; radiantly; splendidly; superbly; surprisingly; astoundingly.

EXHILARATION

adjectives
brisk; inexplicable; momentary; elated; strange; voluptuous; joyous.

verbs
burst into—; dampen—; defer—; discourage—; enliven by—; flush in—; impart—; inspire—; kindle—; leap in—; move to—; produce—; refrain from—; repress—; skip in—; stimulate—; subdue—; suppress—; —animates; —frisks; —rollicks; —sparkles.
(See stimulation, gladness, cheer.)

EXIGENCY

adjectives
unexpected; various (pl); present.

verbs
adapt to—; contribute to—; create—; ease —; escape—; judge—; labor under—; meet —; relieve—; rise to—; satisfy—; stress—; subject to—; tolerate—; —claims; —demands; —necessitates; —pinches; —presses; —requires; —threatens.
(See necessity, demand, need, emergency.)

EXILE

adjectives
needy; administrative; imperious; melancholy; lifelong; scarred; cynical; penniless; wandering; impudent; multitudinous (pl); outlandish; prejudiced; lasting; pensive; political; communal; venturous; vagabond; involuntary; indiscriminate.

verbs
abandon to—; authorize—; banish into—; cast into—; condemn to—; die in—; doom to—; dwell in—; endure—; enter—; escape —; flee from—; follow into—; force into—; imprison in—; languish in—; liberate from —; recall from—; release from—; relegate to—; retire to—; shut in—; waste in—; —depresses; —saddens; —veils.
(See banishment, expulsion.)

EXILED

adverbs
miserably; pitiably; wretchedly; desolately; unjustifiably; deservedly; homelessly; forlornly; ignominiously; shamefully; savagely; lamentably; unhappily; shockingly; mercilessly; permanently.

EXIST (v)

adverbs
beggarly; parasitically; uninterruptedly; contemporaneously; naturally; impecuniously; cheerlessly; amicably; smoothly; gracefully; individually; primitively; socially; bodily; irregularly; animally; grossly; amiably; miserably; thoughtlessly; meagerly; spiritually; imperiously; carelessly; contemplatively; exaltedly; desolately; torpidly; lifelessly; narrowly; rudely; tranquilly; virtuously; drably; romantically; separately.
(See live, continue.)

EXISTENCE

adjectives
smooth; carefree; graceful; refined; individual; primitive; savage; reasoned; ordered; social; bodily; irregular; well-regulated; illusive; animal; dreamlike; feeble; gross; amiable; theoretical; political; obscure; intrinsic; objective; miserable; universal; thoughtless; meager; spiritual; waking; eternal; harmonious; future; contained; independent; imperious; dominating; substantial; fractional; careless; contemplative; complicated; sad; precarious; imaginary; distracted; poetical; whole; peaceful; horrible; tangible; exalted; desolate; schizophrenic; divided; wretched; spectral; general; common; artistic; warped; torpid; lifeless; unostentatious; destructive; ephemeral; secluded; charmed; congenial; tormented; dissipated; petty; restless; humdrum; semi-monastic; infantile; determined; untarnished; secular; actual; intra-uterine; mere; restrained; narrow; genuine; inevitable; stormy; moribund; inscrutable; superficial; dubious; perennial; rude; adolescent; unreal; unending; wasted; self-fixed; country; tranquil; bright; virtuous; pampered; unsympathizing; vulgar; drab; long-forgotten; material; beneficent; treacherous; triumphant; undisciplined; tropical; pleasurable; honorable; romantic; unnecessary; indolent; diversified; untroubled; separate; beauteous.

verbs
admit—of; animate—; annihilate—; contemplate—; dedicate—to; demonstrate—of; deny—of; determine—; disbelieve—; dispute—; drag out—; eke out—; grant—; guide—; heighten—; ignore—; imperil—; invigorate—; justify—; loathe—; obliterate—; pop into—; preserve—; recognize—; rule—; shape—; shatter—; struggle for—; suspect—of; sustain—; threaten—; uproot—; verify—; —bores; —continues; —wearies.
(See reality, fact, life.)

EXIT

adjectives
eccentric; clear; funnel-shaped; joyful; mysterious; hurried.

verbs
bar—; barricade—; burst from—; chain—; dramatize—; emanate from—; excrete through—; file from—; give—; issue from—; padlock—; perceive—; scorn—; search for—; sigh for—; trickle through—; witness—; —discharges; —effuses; —ejects; —erupts; —expels.
(See passage, doorway.)

EXODUS

adjectives
dramatic; wholesale; gradual.

verbs
consent to—; encounter—; force—; plan—; overtake—; speed—; start—; trace—; —abates; —attains; —commences.
(See departure, emigration.)

EXONERATE (*v*)

adverbs
completely; partially; fully; satisfactorily; entirely; unconditionally; impartially.
(See pardon, acquit.)

EXONERATED

adverbs
completely; honorably; recently; wholly; justly; happily; luckily; fortunately; easily; glibly; smoothly; craftily; publicly; properly; rightfully; legally; entirely; unquestionably; unconditionally.

EXORBITANT

adverbs
insanely; intolerably; terribly; extremely; frightfully; criminally; illegally; preposterously; inordinately; egregiously; fantastically; outrageously; outlandishly; crazily; flagrantly; grossly; incredibly; enormously; prodigiously; amazingly; glaringly; appallingly.

EXOTIC

adjectives
illustrious; tiny; rare.

EXPAND (*v*)

adverbs
progressively; rapidly; limitlessly; sufficiently; continually; sanely; monstrously; ingeniously; lustily; adroitly; tremendously; marvelously; subsequently; intellectually; ephemerally; explosively; economically; industrially; muscularly; noisily; inevitably; imperially; poisonously; chaotically.
(See dilate, enlarge.)

EXPANSE

adjectives
treeless; sealike; dreary; tranquil; sunny; shadowless; still; boundless; undulating; great; prodigious; shining; broad; vast;

trackless; bare; uncharted; endless; prairie-like; glassy; barren; pale; serene; berg-filled; measureless; limitless; windless.

EXPANSION

adjectives
transcendent; fanlike; marvelous; tremendous; subsequent; intellectual; cruel; ephemeral; vital; free; explosive; economic; prodigious; temperamental; industrial; reflex; muscular; important; noisy; amazing; ill-directed; inevitable; major; rapid; imperial; conceivable; healthful; chaotic; enormous.

verbs
advocate—; check—; confine—to; cover—; curtail—; demand—; evince—; force—; influence—; justify—; limit—; nip—; plan —; prevent—; regulate—; speed up—; strangle—; suppress—; terminate—; —continues; —ends; —follows.

(See enlargement, increase, extension, development.)

EXPANSIVE

adverbs
conveniently; adaptably; broadly; signally; remarkably; wonderfully; incredibly; exceptionally; naturally; amply; roomily; spaciously; capaciously; comfortably; amazingly.

EXPATRIATION

adjectives
instant; delayed; enforced; prolonged.

EXPECT (*v*)

adverbs
confidently; unreasonably; half-heartedly; gloomily; romantically; anxiously; vaguely; plainly; apparently; breathlessly; presumptuously; blissfully; sanguinely; ardently; benevolently; vainly; mystically; fondly; rationally; erroneously; impossibly; evidently; extravagantly; tremulously; hourly.

(See anticipate, hope.)

EXPECTANCY

adjectives
reasonable; shuddering; dread; eager; lounging; tranquil; wistful; vigilant; anxious; homeless.

EXPECTANT

adverbs
happily; joyously; mysteriously; excitedly; hysterically; passionately; thrillingly; unreasonably; impatiently; ardently; keenly; eagerly; charmingly; joyfully; fervently; anxiously; crazily; madly; nervously; confidently; vainly; hopefully.

EXPECTATION

adjectives
blissful; confident; sanguine; harrowing; exorbitant; pecuniary; ardent; benevolent; florid; vain; reasonable; appreciative; mystic; fondest; remote; rational; continual; erroneous; future; protracted; exaggerated; impossible; evident; sure; tremulous; delightful; brilliant; ulterior; anxious; hopeful; hourly; indefinite; visionary; commensurate; extravagant; distant.

verbs
await with—; blast—; confirm—; darken —; encourage—; excite—s; fall short of—; fulfill—; gamble in—; glow with—; prolong —; quiver with—; shine in—; thwart—; torment with—; warrant—; whirl in—; —becomes; —fails; —grows; —perishes; —shrinks.

(See anticipation, prospect, hope.)

EXPECTORATE (*v*)

adverbs
nauseously; excessively; disgustingly; continually; foully; filthily.

(See spit, expel.)

EXPECTORATION

adjectives
excessive; sustained.

verbs
diminish—; discharge in—; effect—; eject in—; eliminate in—; emit in—; encourage —; evict in—; excrete in—; expel in—; forbid—; hack with—; increase—; interrupt—; promote—; retch in—; warn against—; —clears; —disgorges; —dislodges.

(See sputum, spit, saliva.)

EXPEDIENCE

verbs
balance—; base on—; befit—; charge with —; conform to—; consider—; consult—; doubt—; employ—; necessitate—; require —; resort to—; sacrifice to—; suit—; —controls; —embarrasses; —guides; —perplexes; —rules; —silences; —violates.

(See utility, propriety.)

EXPEDIENT

adjectives
seducing; astute; unlawful; financial; dangerous; temporary; favorite; happy; simple; unworthy; desperate; fertile; splendid; shifty; sensible; customary; physical; various (pl); effective; readiest.

adverbs
politically; immediately; wisely; necessarily; strategically; properly; undoubtedly; opportunely; luckily; eminently; ingeniously; indisputably; astutely; dangerously; temporarily; boldly; roughly; cleverly; subserviently; usefully; adaptably.

EXPEDITION

adjectives
implemented; conquering; disastrous; maritime; elaborate; dangerous; Odyssean; hostile; filibustering; nervous; suicidal; successful; predatory; brazen; particular; nefarious; exploring; favorite; notable; rescue; zoological; costly; memorable; punitive; much-vaunted; perilous; sanguine; swiftest; abortive.

verbs
command—; defer—; endanger—; fit out—; guard—; hasten on—; head—; organize—; overwhelm—; prepare—; set forth on—; sponsor—; spur—; support—; undertake—; venture on—; —claims; —cruises; —discloses; —discovers; —sights; —uncovers; —winters.

(See journey, excursion, enterprise.)

EXPEDITIOUS

adverbs
earnestly; smartly; briskly; alertly; eagerly; intently; resolutely; vigorously; actively; energetically; uncommonly; highly; miraculously.

EXPEL (*v*)

adverbs
brutally; unceremoniously; painfully; peremptorily; summarily; abruptly; heartlessly; formally.

(See banish, eject.)

EXPEND (*v*)

adverbs
usefully; lavishly; prodigally; unwisely; honestly; modestly; extravagantly; frugally; annually; prudently; unreasonably; unfortunately; judiciously.

(See employ, consume.)

EXPENDITURE

adjectives
increasing; modest; lavish; unstinted; extravagant; frugal; loose; annual; prudent; unreasonable; prodigal; corresponding; large; undue; unfortunate; speediest; nervous; judicious; equivalent.

verbs
afford—; approve—; check—; deplore—; furnish—; grudge—; incur—; invest in—; involve—; pare down—; provide for—; purvey—; recruit—; require—; restrict—; return—; —acquires; —amounts; —crushes; —drains; —exhausts; —impoverishes; —purchases.

(See outlay, expense, payment.)

EXPENSE

adjectives
useless; prodigal; major; extreme; ruinous; extraordinary; minimum; profitless; miscellaneous; crushing; enormous; improper; maintenance; inescapable; considerable; financial; operating; imperial; advertising; personal; monstrous; trifling.

verbs
advance—; appropriate for—; defray—; dread—; entail—; increase—; incur—; involve—; necessitate—; pay—; pool—; rate —; save—; slice—; spare—; survey—; trim—; —arises; —galls; —increases; —rises; —weighs.

(See cost, expenditure, outlay.)

EXPENSIVE

adverbs
tremendously; absurdly; unreasonably; ridiculously; excessively; dreadfully; cruelly; inordinately; extremely; enormously; inevitably; inconceivably; naturally; inexpressibly; impossibly; uselessly; ruinously; foolishly; exorbitantly; extortionately; illegally; criminally; extravagantly; wastefully; abominably; amazingly; immoderately; outrageously.

EXPERIENCE

adjectives
early; expensive; novel; dreamy; profound; tragic; deadly; purifying; diversified; trying; literate; mystical; unpleasant; salient; glorious; colorful; jarring; transitory; throbbing; absolute; tedious; major; bitter; inductive; unique; considerable; personal; vigilant; spiritual; preparatory; ripe; universal; uniform; various (pl); unguessable; deplorable; practical; exceptional;

accumulated; anticipatory; horrid; disgraceful; blind; dangerous; invariable; salutary; deep-reaching; thrilling; unfavorable; memorable; financial; satisfying; professional; manifest; initial; exhaustive; confident; vulgar; perplexing; architectural; distressing; worldly; gradual; vast; crushing; fatal; intellectual; enormous; deceptive; sensory; funny; ludicrous; private; evolutionary; rich; unfortunate; sacred; extensive; infallible; disillusioning; unalterable; costly; waking; deep; versatile; amorous; augmented; collegiate; exhilarating; bitter; reportorial; traumatic; unmatched; fascinating; pioneering; imperfect; agonizing; preliminary; aesthetic; direful; dismal; analytic; hereditary; veridical; fateful; rough; pathogenic; droll; public; bitter-sweet.

verbs
accumulate—; achieve—; analyze—; attain —; cite—; continue—; deduce from—; derive—; discolor—; diversify—; enjoy—; exaggerate—; furnish—; gain—; grow out of—; marshal—; narrate—; prepare—; reject—; relate—; relive—; review—; seek —; survive—; tax—; understand—; undertake—; unfold—s; unify—s; utilize—; —delights; —discloses; —embitters; —enriches; —fathers; —guides; —harrows; —teaches; —unnerves; —verifies; —warns.
(See experiment, proof, practice, knowledge.)

EXPERIENCE (*v*)

adverbs
alternately; tediously; profoundly; tragically; mystically; gloriously; colorfully; uniquely; spiritually; variously; uniformly; practically; deplorably; horridly; financially; professionally; manifestly; fatally; intellectually; ludicrously; privately; unalterably; exhilaratingly; dismally; fatefully; drolly; accidentally.
(See endure, suffer.)

EXPERIENCED

adverbs
amazingly; smartly; cunningly; adeptly; adroitly; carefully; skilfully; unusually; competently; proficiently; ingeniously; masterfully; eminently; impressively; scarcely; broadly; profoundly.

EXPERIMENT

adjectives
lengthy; innumerable (pl); vagrant; happily-conceived; foregoing; weak; partial; cheap-money; exploded; extensive; hypnotic; ethical; unpleasant; rigid; awkward; transoceanic; trifling; memorable; vulgar; instructive; promising; crude; telepathic; gainful; unsought; hazardous; opposite; rash; inductive; vaunted; soon-abandoned; leading; momentous; complicated; supplementary; socialistic; definite; social; important; dangerous; innocent; philosophical; graceful; good-natured; analytical; disastrous; ingenious; interesting; costly; trustworthy; exhaustive; agricultural; continuous; lateral; doubtful; unfailing; amusing; preliminary; practical; revolutionary; wild; pedagogical; endless; tremendous; colossal; meticulous; interminable; absurd; mad; conclusive; cautious; daring; radical; crucial; ignoble; tentative; atrocious; laboratory; epochal; gigantic; novel; singular; misguided; deplorable; ignorant; clumsy; ill-advised.

verbs
benefit by—; conduct—; contrive—; design —; doom—; embark on—; engage in—; indulge in—; interpret—; perform—; prove by—; submit to—; tolerate—; —fails; —fares; —saddens; —suggests; —yields.
(See trial, attempt, test.)

EXPERIMENT (*v*)

adverbs
indefatigably; extensively; hypnotically; awkwardly; memorably; vulgarly; instructively; crudely; gainfully; hazardously; rashly; inductively; complicatedly; definitely; dangerously; philosophically; exhaustively; agriculturally; continuously; amusingly; practically; interminably; absurdly; cautiously; daringly; radically; crucially; ignobly; tentatively; ignorantly; ill-advisedly; clumsily.
(See try, test.)

EXPERIMENTAL

adverbs
definitely; avowedly; fantastically; openly; extensively; crudely; boldly; dangerously; exhaustively; wildly; amusingly; absurdly; madly; cautiously; clumsily; awkwardly; courageously; adventurously; expensively; heroically; tentatively.

EXPERIMENTATION

adjectives
zealous; clinical; persistent; rigid; controlled.

EXPERT

adjectives
distinguished; eminent; authentic; technical; nautical; transplanted; moral; monetary; illumination; industrious; irrigation; undisputed; tight-mouthed; acknowledged; accomplished; high-salaried; acoustical; competent; independent; manufacturing; efficiency; decoding; practical; able; two-fisted; qualified; outstanding; self-appointed.

verbs
acclaim as—; affront—; applaud—; cope with—; demand—; develop into—; employ —; flatter—; judge by—; nominate—; regard as—; require—; trust—; try—; —conquers; —criticizes; —excels in; —judges; —manages; —masters; —practises; —scowls.
(See specialist, master.)

adverbs
skilfully; obviously; reasonably; unusually; ably; adroitly; capably; competently; technically; mechanically; deftly; efficiently; handily; ingeniously; inventively; smartly; masterfully; proficiently; readily; oddly; curiously; professionally; admirably; prodigiously; uncommonly; miraculously; surprisingly.

EXPIATION

adjectives
tragic; particular; penitential; complete.

EXPLAIN (v)

adverbs
proudly; patiently; quaintly; amply; candidly; plausibly; speciously; prefatorily; redundantly; superfluously; passionately; comprehensively; adequately; essentially; partially; definitely; solemnly; carefully; sulkily; presently; sufficiently; hesitatingly; casually; paradoxically; tenderly; technically; voluntarily; minutely; undauntedly; elaborately; effectively; inaudibly; lengthily; immaterially; confusedly; ingeniously; laboredly; immediately; incongruously; philosophically; sympathetically; volubly; competently; psychologically; invaluably; tardily; apologetically; illogically; concisely; facetiously; fundamentally; comically; prosaically; disarmingly; lamely; casually; haltingly.
(See interrupt, elucidate.)

EXPLANATION

adjectives
plausible; inaudible; immaterial; lucid; hesitating; dreaded; comprehensive; confused; ingenious; satisfactory; labored; immediate; mechanistic; unreserved; fantastic; dynamic; vivid; philosophical; disjointed; incongruous; sympathetic; voluble; abbreviated; competent; adequate; scientific; rational; palliative; indiscreet; pathological; glib; specious; consequent; blind; various (pl); psychological; paralyzing; muddled; invaluable; tardy; groundless; half-true; apologetic; supreme; parenthetical; useless; attempted; flimsy; illogical; overwhelming; blithe; clarifying; concise; simplifying; aesthetic; petulant; facetious; fundamental; reasonable; common-sense; comic; struggling; tedious; elaborate; prosaic; matter-of-fact; air-tight; fictional; disarming; diluted; casual; lame; halting.

verbs
amplify—; bear—; clarify—; clear—; comprehend—; condemn—; confirm—; defy—; devise—; drown out—; elaborate—; emerge with—; frame—; fumble for—; grasp—; muddle—; offer—; stammer—; swallow—; tender—; wind up—; yield—; —clarifies; —involves; —rests on; —simplifies.
(See exposition, solution, interpretation, key.)

EXPLANATORY

adverbs
satisfactorily; aptly; effectively; sufficiently; definitely; clearly; lucidly; acceptably; liberally; roughly; carefully; crudely; artfully; skilfully; adroitly; sagely; wisely; craftily; sincerely; genuinely; plausibly; ingeniously; vividly; graphically; competently; glibly; discreetly; tardily; flimsily; fundamentally; intelligently; elaborately; casually; lamely.

EXPLETIVE

adjectives
muttered; raucous; exasperated; choice; foul-mouthed; energetic; unmeaning.

EXPLICIT

adverbs
elaborately; clearly; fully; succinctly; tersely; curtly; definitely; undeniably; unusually; highly; oddly; unnecessarily; needlessly; carefully; meticulously; strangely; curiously; noticeably; graphically; broadly; dogmatically; officially; imperiously; decisively; formally; solemnly; ominously.

EXPLODE (v)

adverbs
indignantly; successfully; prematurely; squarely; sharply; terrifically; volcanically; frightfully; violently; tremendously; initially; deafeningly; horribly; titanically; dreadfully; disastrously; catastrophically.
(See burst, erupt.)

EXPLOIT

adjectives
boldest; illustrious; quick-witted; antique; ludicrous; memorable; heroic; jocular; gigantic; engineering; dread; phenomenal; daring; dashing; transcendent; brilliant; decisive; hazardous; exuberant; unmatched; imagined; valorous; news; psychic; hair-raising; atrocious; spectacular.

verbs
achieve—; boast of—; close—; conceive —; design—; dream of—; perform—; plot —; recount—; resent—; set forth—s of; share in—; succeed in—; witness—; view —; —reverberates.
(See deed, act, feat, achievement.)

EXPLOIT (v)

adverbs
unethically; arrogantly; fully; indefensibly; ruthlessly; profitably; assiduously; cleverly; industrially; competitively; agriculturally; capitalistically; unreasonably; hideously; nationally; unscrupulously.
(See persecute, oppress.)

EXPLOITATION

adjectives
competitive; pagan; agricultural; middleman; capitalistic; reasonable; hideous; coastwise; national.

verbs
accomplish by—; achieve through—; carry on—; conduct—; consider—; curtail—; decry—; denounce—; delve into—; expose to —; frown on—; instigate—; investigate—; prohibit—; prosper through—; renounce—; resist—; reveal—; view—; —agitates; —enriches; —impoverishes; —ransacks; —reigns.
(See employment, utility, profit.)

EXPLORATION

adjectives
titanic; celebrated; linguistic; nocturnal; unproductive; extensive; arctic; authentic; geographical; daring; world-girdling; fervid; perilous; exhaustive; exotic.

verbs
absorb in—; conduct—; deserve—; discover by—; discuss—; frustrate—; instigate—; plan—; prepare for—; relate—; resume—; subscribe to—; tire of—; undertake—; —ascertains; —determines; —discloses; —inquires; —investigates; —proves; —reveals.
(See search, examination, investigation.)

EXPLORE (v)

adverbs
intelligently; carefully; completely; morbidly; zealously; undauntedly; adventurously; intrepidly; untiringly; scientifically; methodically.
(See examine, search.)

EXPLORER

adjectives
enterprising; zealous; undaunted; adventurous; literary; fortunate; intrepid; untiring; hardy; scientific.

EXPLOSION

adjectives
premature; sharp; terrific; volcanic; frightful; violent; intermittent; numbing; tremendous; deplorable; initial; deafening; magnificent; strange; horrible; dreadful; rending; staccato; titanic; disastrous; gigantic; soul-shattering; catastrophic.

verbs
augment—; forestall—; investigate—; produce—; threaten—; —alarms; —casts out; —damages; —discharges; —drives out; —ejects; —emits; —erupts; —jars; —reports; —rocks; —scars; —shatters; —shocks; —showers; —sunders; —thunders; —violates.
(See outburst, discharge, detonation.)

EXPLOSIVE

verbs
employ—; play with—; toy with—; threaten with—; touch off—; warn of—; —alarms; —blows off; —bursts; —damages; —detonates; —discharges; —drives out; —ejects; —erupts; —jars; —rocks; —shatters; —shocks; —showers; —thunders; —violates.
(See gunpowder, dynamite.)

adverbs
dangerously; reportedly; ominously; alarmingly; highly; unusually; allegedly; undeniably; notoriously; abominably; hazardously; perilously; precariously; ticklishly; terrifically; frightfully; tremendously; horribly; disastrously; easily; readily.

EXPLOSIVENESS

adjectives
volatile; choleric; ready.

EXPONENT

adjectives
able; distinguished; outstanding; scholarly; preeminent; quasi-authoritative; skilled; sole; impressive; faithful; philosophical.

EXPORT

verbs
allow—s; ban—; boycott—s; confiscate—s; deal in—s; demand—s; dispose of—s; dump—s; exchange—s; halt—s; levy against—s; license—s; minimize—s; permit—s; produce for—; reduce—s; restrain—; ship—s; speculate in—s; stimulate—; suspend—; tax—s; underwrite—s; value—s; —s decline; —s rise.

EXPORTER

verbs
bargain with—; communicate with—; consult—; exchange with—; impose on—; license—; order from—; purchase from—; remit to—; restrain—; subsidize—; tax—; —deals in; —demands; —disposes of; —dumps; —invests; —produces; —speculates; —values.

EXPOSE (*v*)

adverbs
shamelessly; unequivocally; unblushingly; reputedly; blasphemously; fearlessly; dangerously; conspicuously; piteously; improperly; sufficiently; ultimately; virtually; subsequently; unwisely; shrewdly; partially; lucidly; subtly; thrillingly; incautiously; graphically; relentlessly; ruthlessly; definitely; imprudently; inevitably.
(See denounce, accuse.)

EXPOSITION

adjectives
comprehensive; simply written; progressive; ever-varying; precise; lucid; striking; suitable; masterly; contemporaneous; courteous; erroneous; chronological; classic; sound; scientific; clear; serious; accurate; amusing; brilliant; pretentious; concise; skillful; enthusiastic; daring; illuminating; consummate; distinguished; subtle; straightforward; ethnographical; thrilling; well-reasoned; graphic; sane; forcible; passionate; lucid; fresh.

verbs
arrange—; attend—; conduct—; display at—; enter into—; finance—; hearken to—; interpret—; launch into—; present at—; prohibit—; publish—; recount—; render—; report—; show at—; view—; —advocates; —awes; —confuses; —explains; —expounds; —interests.
(See display, exhibition, essay, composition, explanation.)

EXPOSITORY

adverbs
clearly; drearily; dully; endlessly; dismally; wearily; droningly; lucidly; intelligibly; unusually; definitely; admirably; agreeably; needfully; suitably; skilfully; soundly; accurately; acceptably; artlessly; realistically; critically; wonderfully.

EXPOSTULATE (*v*)

adverbs
softly; fiercely; petulantly; madly; mildly; wrathfully; amicably; frantically; frankly.
(See protest, remonstrate.)

EXPOSTULATION

adjectives
mad; mild; wrathful; lingering; amicable; frantic; frank.

EXPOSURE

adjectives
horrible; projected; undue; serviceable; fatal; bleak; inevitable; imprudent; fearless; initial; earnest; intelligent; courageous; sociological; wanton; definite; ominous; startling; sensational; ruthless; unremitted; incautious; cruel; relentless; blatant.

verbs
anticipate—; deserve—; entail—; escape—; guard from—; lay open to—; prohibit—; protect from—; sentence to—; subject to—; suffer from—; view—; —deprives; —discloses; —displays; —divulges; —endangers; —expels; —reveals; —shames.
(See disclosure, revelation.)

EXPOUND (*v*)

adverbs
repeatedly; grimly; clearly; gravely; quaintly; mystifyingly; incomprehensibly; patiently.
(See explain.)

EXPRESS

adjectives
roaring; aerial; limited; endless.

EXPRESS (*v*)

adverbs

audibly; cordially; admirably; resignedly; lightly; precisely; visually; optimistically; poetically; pointedly; metaphorically; significantly; inelegantly; openly; peevishly; wittily; independently; frivolously; accurately; obviously; submissively; vaguely; delicately; urgently; exquisitely; eloquently; privately; succinctly; indignantly; mildly; figuratively; adequately; bluntly; repeatedly; inadequately; gratefully; forcibly; voluntarily; lucidly; ingenuously; courteously; pithily; whimsically; graphically; stupidly; placidly; felicitously; affably; affectedly; angelically; animatedly; arrogantly; appropriately; arbitrarily; benevolently; blandly; buoyantly; capriciously; caressingly; characteristically; calculatingly; contemptuously; creatively; deceptively; delicately; demurely; diabolically; dubiously; ecstatically; equivocally; ferociously; formidably; genially; grammatically; gravely; grimly; grotesquely; humorously; forbiddingly; impassionedly; indescribably; indignantly; instinctively; introspectively; journalistically; jovially; knowingly; legitimately; loftily; lugubriously; luminously; majestically; martially; meekly; melodiously; memorably; metaphysically; charmingly; mirthlessly; mutinously; momentarily; nobly; nonsensically; nostalgically; owlishly; patriotically; peculiarly; pedantically; pensively; pessimistically; petulantly; pitifully; plaintively; portentiously; radiantly; recklessly; sardonically; saturninely; savagely; secretively; sheepishly; shrewdly; sinisterly; smugly; solemnly; soothingly; sourly; superbly; spiritedly; spontaneously; sternly; strainedly; submissively; sullenly; synonymously; technically; transparently; treasonably; tritely; truculently; ultimately; uniformly; vicariously; viciously; vindictively; vivaciously; vividly; volubly; warily; wistfully; wryly; yearningly.

(See say, utter.)

EXPRESSION

adjectives

adequate; affable; affected; agonized; airy; alchemistical; all-conquering; altered; amazed; ambiguous; angelic; animated; anxious; apologetic; appalled; appealing; appraising; appropriate; arbitrary; arrogant; artistic; assertive; astonished; austere; banal; beatific; belligerent; benevolent; bewildered; bitter; blameless; bland; bleak; broken; brutish; buoyant; cabalistical; calm; capricious; careless; caressing; ceremonious; characteristic; charming; chastened; chivalric; calculating; comical; commanding; conciliatory; confidential; consecrated; conspicuous; consummate; contemplative; contemptuous; contended; contrite; countless (pl); courteous; creative; criminal; crystalline; cunning; curious; dazed; deceptive; deliberate; delicate; demoniac; demonstrative; demure; depressed; despairing; diabolic; disagreeable; disdainful; distasteful; dolorous; dithyrambic; dogged; dominant; dramatic; dreamy; dubious; dumb; ear-pleasing; eager; earnest; ecstatic; elegant; embossed; emotionless; emphatic; encouraging; equivocal; etherealized; exalted; evanescent; expectant; exterior; facial; faintest; fanglike; faraway; far-off; felicitous; feline; ferocious; fervent; fiendish; fierce; figurative; fine; fixed; fleeting; forbidding; forced; forlorn; formidable; freezing; frequent; frightened; frowning; frustrated; fundamental; furtive; genial; gentle; gladsome; glazed; gloomy; glorified; graceful; grammatical; grave; grim; habitual; grotesque; grouchy; haggard; half-absorbed; half-articulate; half-humorous; half-downright; half-pathetic; half-hearted; half-indulgent; half-suspicious; hangdog; happy; hard; hard-set; haunting; heartbroken; hearty; hereditary; homely; honest; hopeless; horrible; horrid; hospitable; humorous; ideal; idiotic; idyllic; ill-natured; imaginative; imbecilic; immobile; impassioned; imploring; implied; impressive; incidental; incredulous; indescribable; indignant; indirect; infinite; injured; inquiring; inscrutable; instinctive; intense; intent; introspective; jolly; journalistic; jovial; joyous; kindly; knowing; lackluster; legitimate; listening; listless; literary; lofty; lovable; lucid; lugubrious; luminous; majestic; malign; martial; martyrlike; maudlin; meaningful; meek; melancholy; melodious; memorable; menacing; merry; metaphysical; mirthless; moody; momentary; moral; mutinous; mysterious; mystic; noble; noncommittal; nonsensical; nostalgic; noteworthy; odd; ominous; open; outward; owlish; plain; pleasing; pantomimic; particular; passionate; patriotic; peculiar; pedantic; peevish; pensive; perfect; periphrastic; perplexed; pessimistic; petulant; physiognomic; pithy; pitiful; placid; plaintive; plastic; pleasant; poetic; poignant; popular; portentous; predatory; preoccupied; prim; professional; proper; provoking; prose; puzzled; quaint; quarrelsome; queer; questioning; quiet; quizzical; radiant; rapt; rare; rebuked; reckless; relaxed; remarkable; repelling; resentful; resolute; respective; rueful; sagacious; sad; sarcastic; sardonic; saturnine; saucy; savage; secretive; self-concentrated; seraphic; serio-comic; serious; set; severe; sharp; sheepish; shocked; shrewd; sicklied; significant; sincere; singular; sinister; slight; slow; sly; smileless; smug; soft; softened; solemn; soothing; sorrowful; sour; spacious; superb; spirited; spontaneous; sprightliest; stealthy; stern; stony; strained; structural; submissive; subtle; sulky; sullen; surprised; sweet; synonymous; taut; technical; tender; tense; theoretical; thoughtful; thought-saving; thwarted; tragic; transparent; treasonable; trite; triumphal; triumphant; troubled; truculent; ultimate; unanimous; unbelieving; unbounded; uncompromising; unelaborated; unconscious; uneasy; unfit; unforgettable; unguarded; uniform; unmoved; unstudied; unusual; upright; vacant; vague; various (pl); vehement; venomous; vibratory; vicarious; vicious; victorious; vindictive; violent; virtuous; visual; vivacious; vivid; voluble; warlike; warm; wary; wavering; well-bred; whimsical; wild; wily; wistful; woebegone; wondering; wordless; worn; worried; wry; yearning.

verbs
achieve —; assume —; crave —; cry out for —; cultivate —; distort —; divest of —; efface —; fathom —; fix —; limit —; recollect —; stifle —; strive toward —; struggle for —; translate —; understand —; wear —; — congeals; — plays; — settles.
(See utterance, statement, assertion.)

EXPRESSIVE

adverbs
clearly; particularly; distinctly; emphatically; beautifully; especially; wonderfully; accurately; powerfully; effectively; cruelly; remarkably; sympathetically.

EXPRESSIVENESS

adjectives
mobile; pregnant.

EXPULSION

adjectives
pathetic; forcible; virtual.

verbs
accept—; anticipate—; criticize—; demand —; employ —; face —; favor —; inflict —; influence —; order —; promote —; punish with —; resign to —; secure —; suffer —; threaten with —; welcome —; — benefits; — corrects; — shames.
(See discharge, dismissal.)

EXPURGATED

adverbs
mercilessly; unnecessarily; relentlessly; priggishly; carefully; zealously; absurdly; needlessly; hopelessly; inanely; ridiculously; primly; spinsterishly; puritanically; mawkishly; properly.

EXQUISITE

adverbs
daintily; charmingly; enchantingly; delicately; matchlessly; remarkably; beautifully; utterly; delicately; airily; incredibly; wonderfully; gracefully; harmoniously; richly; melodiously.

EXTEMPORANEOUS

adverbs
genuinely; sincerely; honestly; obviously; rigidly; strictly; avowedly; artlessly; spontaneously; crudely; thoughtlessly; carelessly; delightfully; impulsively; manifestly.

EXTEMPORIZE (v)

adverbs
jocosely; freely; humorously; artfully; skillfully; clumsily; cleverly; shrewdly.
(See improvise.)

EXTEND (v)

adverbs
spaciously; understandingly; beseechingly; widely; liberally; skillfully; infinitely; beneficently; enormously; generously; gradually; laterally; additionally; internationally; invitingly.
(See lengthen, project.)

EXTENSION

adjectives
infinite; enormous; generous; ideal; dangerous; gradual; further; lateral; additional; international; widest.

verbs
advocate —; check —; confine —; curtail —; grant —; justify —; influence —; limit

—; nip —; open —; permit —; plan —; plead for —; prevent —; regulate —; strangle —; terminate —; — accommodates; — eases.

(See increase, addition, expansion, enlargement.)

EXTENT

adjectives
dangerous; uncivil; unjust; perceptible; amazing; probable; unprecedented; monstrous; considerable; far-reaching; reasonable; enormous; vast; unusual; boundless; solemn; important; limitless; sufficient; immense; greater; fearful; astonishing; satisfying; bewildering; disproportionate.

verbs
ascertain —; carry to —; consider —; define —; estimate —; exercise to —; limit —; occupy to —; reach —; recognize —; rule — of; serve —; understand —; — alarms; — allures; — consists; — forces; — reduces.

(See amount, size, magnitude, degree.)

EXTERIOR

adjectives
impenetrable; rustic; indifferent; fearless; attractive; commonplace; grave; showy; valorous; calm; amphibious; passive; listless; visible; expansive; impassible; quiet; soft; cold; stolid.

EXTERMINATE (v)

adverbs
ruthlessly; gradually; certainly; speedily; inevitably; totally; subsequently; entirely; cruelly; blindly; finally.

(See destroy, remove.)

EXTERMINATION

verbs
attempt —; banish to —; demand —; drive into —; end in —; engage in —; guard against —; plan —; prevent —; prophesy —; protect against —; pursue to —; repel —; war on —; warn against —; — destroys; — drives out; — eliminates; — extirpates; — forces out; — reduces; — rids.

EXTINCTION

adjectives
final; certain; hurried; speedy; inevitable; total; subsequent.

verbs
blot into —; decay into —; demand — of; deplore —; doom to —; flicker into —; guard against —; meet —; mourn —; plan —; prevent —; suffocate into —; surrender to —; threaten with —; warn against —; witness —; yield to —.

(See destruction, extermination.)

EXTINGUISH (v)

adverbs
instantly; temporarily; instantaneously; abruptly; promptly; rudely; hastily; swiftly.

(See destroy, remove.)

EXTOL (v)

adverbs
frequently; highly; loudly; continually; flatteringly; lavishly; shrewdly; purposely; ostensibly; sincerely.

(See exalt, praise.)

EXTORT (v)

adverbs
soullessly; miserly; graspingly; meanly; exorbitantly; usuriously; heartlessly.

(See wring, force.)

EXTORTION

adjectives
oppressive; multiplied (pl); baffled; criminal.

EXTORTIONATE

adverbs
criminally; highly; illegally; terribly; absolutely; positively; unbelievably; cruelly; harshly; tyrannically; greedily; rapaciously; sordidly; meanly; ravenously; insatiably.

EXTRACT

adjectives
liquid; liberal; embryonic; subsequent; garbled; glandular; misquoted.

verbs
administer —; copy —; deduce —; derive —; discharge —; distil —; draw forth —; elicit —; employ —; evolve —; issue —; obtain —; prepare —; quote —; view —; — finishes; — flavors; — represents.

(See essence, selection.)

EXTRACT (v)

adverbs
freshly; imperfectly; wilfully; liberally; subsequently; glandularly; erroneously; illegally.

(See draw, select.)

EXTRACTION

adjectives
oral; foreign; noble.

EXTRANEOUS

adverbs
unessentially; relatively; definitely; obviously; naturally; discordantly; exotically; curiously; strangely; mysteriously.

EXTRAVAGANCE

adjectives
fine; reckless; ostentatious; unusual; tasteless; absurd; oratorical; rough; gorgeous; favorite; complete; unwarrantable; incipient; lavish; wasteful; senseless; frightful; old-time; wicked; imaginable; utmost; elegant; profligate; forensic; bromidic; unjustified; flagrant.

verbs
check —; cloak in —; consort with —; court —; criticize —; guard against —; indulge in —; involve in —; regret —; rue —; sacrifice to —; smack of —; stimulate —; supply —; warn against —; — corrupts; — destroys; — drains; — fetters; — impoverishes; — inflames; — reigns; — shocks.
(See waste, excess.)

EXTRAVAGANT

adverbs
wantonly; foolishly; madly; rapturously; lavishly; happily; drunkenly; wildly; blithely; wickedly; improvidently; fantastically; outrageously; vulgarly; proudly; ostentatiously; extremely; absurdly; ridiculously; pompously; outrageously; gayly; inordinately; exceedingly; incredibly; magnificently; splendidly; gorgeously; recklessly; fully; senselessly; flagrantly; immensely.

EXTREME

adjectives
absurd; delirious; fantastic; spiritualistic; unhealthy; uttermost; strenuous; blunt; precise; calculable; dangerous; glorious; exhaustive.

verbs
avoid—; delight in—; dress in—; drive to —; employ—; endure—; leap to—; moderate—; proceed to—; reach—; run to—; shun —; temper—; twist to—; warn against—; —begets; —blinds; —confuses; —destroys; —disturbs; —endangers; —maddens.
(See excess.)

EXTREMITY

adjectives
dire; sensuous; dread; ultimate; desperate; furthest; remotest.

EXUBERANCE

adjectives
glorious; effervescent; fantastic; brash; floral; prodigal; fitful; incondite; brisk.

verbs
attest by—; avoid—; burst into—; correct —; drain of—; exhaust—; hide—; indulge in—; inject—; lessen—; play with—; repress—; spoil—; steep in—; suppress—; teem with—; —astonishes; —overflows.
(See abundance, luxuriance, excess.)

EXUBERANT

adverbs
gloriously; fantastically; profusely; prodigally; excessively; inordinately; uncommonly; oddly; immensely.

EXUDE (*v*)

adverbs
aromatically; disgustingly; vilely; sickeningly; freely; abnormally gradually.
(See discharge, flow.)

EXULT (*v*)

adverbs
vauntingly; openly; enthusiastically; triumphantly; boastfully; happily; gloatingly; drunkenly.
(See rejoice, triumph.)

EXULTANT

adverbs
loudly; noisily; proudly; pompously; splendidly; magnificently; quietly; deeply; childishly; triumphantly; happily; incredulously; boastfully; humbly; rapturously; ecstatically; incoherently; profoundly; joyously; jubilantly; elatedly; delightedly; immensely; exceedingly; remarkably.

EXULTATION

adjectives
vaporous; justifiable; fierce; savage; childish; honest; incoherent; facetious; wonted; sublimest; raptured; menacing; splendid.

EYE

verbs
affix to—; avert—; bat—; bathe—; blear—; blink—; cast —s upon; catch—; cloud—; cock—; darken—; dazzle—; delude—; di-

late—; dim—; divert—; examine—; extract from—; feast —s upon; glue —s upon; goggle—s; inflame—; intrigue—; irrigate —; irritate—; moisten—; narrow—s; offend —; paste—s on; pin—s on; pucker up—s; rivet—s on; roll—s; screw up—s; shadow —s; shield—s; snag—; soften—s; soothe—s; stagger—; strain—s; suffuse—; tear—s away; test—; tire—s; veil—s; —s acquiesce; —s beam; —s blaze; —s brood; —s bulge; —s challenge; —s climb; —s dance; —s devour; —discerns; —s drift; —s drink in; —embraces; —s fall; —s flash; —s flicker; —s flinch; —s glare; —s gleam; —s glint; —s glitter; —s glow; —s kindle; —penetrates; —s plead; —probes; —s protrude; —s redden; —rests upon; —roams; —roves; —scans; —scorns; —scrutinizes; —shines; —smarts; —s smoulder; —s snap; —s sparkle; —s squint; —s study; —s swell; —s swim; —s twinkle; —s twitch; —s water; —s waver; —s widen; —s beseech.

(See sight.)

EYE (v)

adverbs

wistfully; piercingly; candidly; keenly; curiously; suspiciously; boldly; challengingly; squarely; critically; sternly; pathetically; attentively; thoughtfully; timidly; painfully; hungrily; contemptuously; unwaveringly; inquisitively; significantly; frigidly; derisively; moodily; covetously; soulfully; bleakly; dispassionately; fastidiously; stonily; sullenly; darkly; insatiably; beseechingly; alertly; mischievously; inquiringly; absently; abstractedly; amazedly; ardently; arrogantly; benignly; bestially; bewilderedly; bewitchingly; earnestly; enviously; intently; lovingly; piteously; intelligently; pleadingly; heavily; humorously; formidably; gaily; glassily; glintingly; glitteringly; maudlinly; joyously; mysteriously; professionally; raptly; sheepishly; steadfastly; studiously; superficially; uncritically; vacantly; watchfully; wisely; wolfishly; wonderingly; wordlessly; venomously.

(See watch, observe.)

EYEBALLS

adjectives

fierce; searing; burning; gorgeous; dead; bugle; rolling; protruding; swimming; staring; dilated; half-eaten.

EYEBROW

verbs

arch—s; cock—; corrugate—s; darken—s; jet—s; knit—s; pluck—s; quirk—; raise—; slant—s; thin out—s; tidy up—s; —s beetle; —s curve; —s shag.

EYEBROWS

adjectives

bushy; shaggy; fierce-looking; supercilious; calm; haughty; broad-arched; peaked; high; pencil-line; sandy; mastic-darkened; solemn; prominent; raised; tangled; thick; curved; heavy; bristly; stiff; silky; delicate; wispy; perfect; bent; drawn; uneven; surprised; sardonic; elevated; uplifted; bold; gloomy; mismated; boyish; languid; ginger; thin; proud; twitching; pepper-and-salt; disapproving.

EYELASHES

adjectives

sooty; dusky; mascaraed; artificial; tear-drenched; dense; dark-fringed; thick; long; sopping; dark; uplifted; beaded; blinking; sandy; absurd; beautiful; long-lashed; heavily-fringed.

verbs

bat—; clip—; lift—; —brush; —droop; —flash; —flatter; —flicker; —flutter; —fringe; —glisten; —guard; —quiver; —repose; —shade; —shimmer; —sleep; —sweep; —veil.

EYELIDS

adjectives

quivering; quiet; swollen; shaken; withered; heavy; drooping; long-fringed; broad; worn-off; fluttering; wrinkled; straight-cut; languid; trembling; waxen; bronze; bluish; opaque; leaden; tired; limp; hanging; half-closed; narrowed; closed; shriveled; lazy; tremulous; thin; pain-wrenched.

verbs

drop—; fringe—; kiss—; lift—; raise—; squeeze—; wag—; weigh—down; —ache; —droop; —fall; —flutter; —quiver: —sleep; —slumber; —twitch.

EYES

adjectives

able; abnormal; absent; accusing; abstracted; aching; actual; admirable; adorable; adoring; adulterated; adventure-seeking; aesthetic; affrighted; affronted; agate; age-dimmed; agonized; age-blue; alien; all-seeing; alluring; almond; altered; amazed; amber-colored; ambitious; amiable; amorous; amused; angered; anguished; animated; anxious; apathetic; appealing; appraising; appreciative; apprehending; approving; archeological; ardent; arrogant; ash-rimmed; assailing; assenting; astonished; astounded; attentive; attractive; august; austere; authoritative; autumn-leaf; avaricious; averted; avid; awakened; awe-inspiring; azure-tinted; baby-blue; bad; baffling; bagged; baleful; bashful; battered; battle-aged; battle-lighted; beadlike; beady; beady-bright; beaming; beautiful; beauty-loving; beetling; bemused; benignant; bent; beseeching; bestial; bewildered; bewitching; bilberry; big; bilious; bland; blazing; blue; bleak; bleared; blissful; blood-injected; bloodshot; bodeful; bold; bonny; boring; boundless; bovine; bright; brightened; brimming; brooding; brown; bruised; brown-flecked; bulbous; bulging; burrowing; bursting; button; calculating; calm; candid; canny; capricious; careless; cat-like; cautious; cavernous; celestial; challenging; chance-met; changeable; charmed; chaste; chastening; childish; cheerful; chilly; chocolate-brown; civic; clear; clever; clinging; close-set; closing; clouded; coal-black; cold; colorless; color-loving; commanding; commemorative; commiserating; compassionate; compelling; concealed; concerned; condemnatory; confused; congested; contemplative; contemptuous; contracted; contumelious; conventional; convivial; convulsed; cool; countless; courageous; covert; covetous; craving; created; critical; crumpling; crystal-clear; cunning; curious; cynical; dancing; dangerous; dark-fringed; dark-lashed; death-darting; darkness-dazed; darting; dazzled; deadly; deceiving; decorous; deep; deep-circled; deep-curtained; deep-set; deep-socketed; deep-sunk; defenseless; defiant; dejected; deliberating; delighted; delightful; demanding; demon; demure; deprecating; derisive; descriptive; desolate; despair-glazed; despairing; devastating; devilish; devouring; dewy; dilated; directing; discerning; discolored; discomfited; discontented; discovering; disdainful; disillusioned; dispassionate; dissatisfied; displeased; disquieting; dissecting; dissipated; distasteful; distempered; distended; distracting; distressed; disturbed; divining; dizzy; dog-true; doubtful; dovelike; downcast; dramatic; down-dropped; dreadful; dream-shrouded; dream-swept; dreamy; dreary; drink-filmed; drooping; drowsy; dry; dull; dusky; dying; eager; eagle; eagle-gray; eagle-keen; earnest; educated; effective; effeminate; eloquent; eluded; embittered; emerald-green; empty; enameled; enamored; enchanted; energetic; enigmatic; enlarged; enlivening; enormous; enthralled; entranced; envious; epiphyseal; evasive; ever-lusterless; ever-moving; ever-questing; evil; examining; excited; expanding; expectant; expiring; expert; expressionable; expressive; extraordinary; exulting; faded; failing; fainting; fairer; faithful; falcon; familiar; far-gazing; far-off; farseeing; far-sighted; fascinated; fastened; fastidious; fatal; fatherly; fathomless; fatigue-dimmed; favoring; fear-filled; feminine; fear-glazed; fear-laden; fearful; fearless; feeble; ferocious; ferret; feverish; fidgety; fierce; fiery; filmed; finding; fine-wrought; fishlike; fishy; fixed; flashing; flat-blue; fleshy-looking; flickering; flinty; flowerlike; flustered; fluttering; foolish; forbidden; foreboding; foreign; forgiving; formidable; formless; foul; frank; freezing; fresh; fretful; fright-filled; frightened; frosty; frowning; frozen; furious; furtive; galled; gamesome; gay; gazelle; gemlike; gentle; ghastly; gifted; gimlet; gin-cleared; girlish; glad; glaring; glassy; gleaming; glimmering; glinting; glittering; gloating; globular; glorious; glossy; glowering; glowing; glutton; goggling; golden; golden-brown; good; grave; gray; gray-steel; great; greedy; gross; grotesque; groveling; guarded; guiding; guileless; guilty; gypsy; habituated; haggard; hale; half-closed; half-defiant; half-repentant; half-shut; half-veiled; happy; harassed; hardened; haughty; haunting; hawk-brown; hazel; healthy; heart-broken; heart-reaching; heartless; heart-sick; heated; heavenly; heavy; heavy-lidded; heedless; hollow; honest; hooded; horny; horrified; hostile; housewifely; hovering; human; humble; humid; humorous; hyacinth-blue; hungry; hunted; hurt; hypnotic; hypnotized; ice-blue; icy; idealistic; ill-omened; immobile; immortal; impartial; imperious; implacable; imploring; impudent; incandescent; incredulous; incensed; incurious; indifferent; indignant; indolent; indomitable; indulgent; inebriate; inexorable; inexperienced; inferior; inflamed; innocent; innumerable; insolent; inquiring; inquisitive; insane; inscrutable; insipid; insistent; intelligent; intent; interrogating; intricate; intriguing; introspective; intrusive; intuitional; inventive; inward; inward-turning; iris-blue; jade; jaded; irradiant;

jaundiced; jewel; jolly; joy-filled; joyous; joy-pronouncing; keen; keen-puckered; kind; kindled; knowing; kohl-rimmed; laboring; lackluster; lackadaisical; lambent; landlubber; languid; languorous; large; lascivious; lashless; laughing; leaden; lecherous; leering; lenient; level; lidless; life-darting; lifted; light; limpid; lingering; liquid; listless; livid; living; loathing; lodestar; lofty; longing; lovable; love-deep; love-laden; love-lit; love-weary; loving; lucent; lurid; lumpy; lurking; lusterless; lustrous; lynx; madonna; magisterial; magnificent; mahogany; malevolent; malicious; malignant; mangling; martial; masculine; maternal; mature; maudlin; mean; medicinable; meditating; melancholy; melting; memory-ridden; menacing; microscopic; merciless; merry; meteor; mild; military; milky; miraculous; miscast; mischievous; miserable; mismatched; mistaking; misty; mocking; modest; moist; moistened; Mongolian; monstrous; moody; mortal; mortified; motionless; mottled; mournful; murderous; muddy-brown; musing; musty; mutinous; myopic; myriad; mysterious; mystical; mystifying; naked-bladed; narrow; national; neighboring; normal; observant; observing; obsidian; offering; ogling; onyx; opal; opaque; opening; oriental; outraged; outstanding; outward; overflowing; overhanging; overstrained; oxlike; owlish; pain-dimmed; pain-filled; pain-lashed; painful; pale; pale-blue; pallid; pansy-blue; pansy-dark; passing; passionate; paternal; patient; peacock; peeping; peering; peevish; pellucid; penetrating; pensive; perceiving; peremptory; perspicuous; persuasive; perverse; philosophical; phoenix; piercing; piglike; pious; piteous; pitying; placid; plaintive; pleading; pleasant; poetic; polished-looking; pondering; preoccupied; ponderous; popping; porcine; possessive; pouchy; powerful; practiced; pragmatic; predatory; probing; prodigious; profane; professional; prominent; prompting; prophetic; protecting; protuberant; proud; provocative; public; puffed; punished; purblind; pure; purged; purple; prying; puzzled; querulous; questioning; quick; quick-lifted; quick-shifting; quiet; quizzical; radiant; raccoonlike; raging; random; rapt; ratlike; ratty; ravenous; ravished; realmless; rebel; rebelling; rebuking; red-rimmed; reddened; reflecting; reflective; reluctant; remarkable; remote; reproachful; resplendent; retrospective; reverent; reverted; revengeful; rheumy; richest; rival; riveting; roaming; roguish; rolling; romantic; rose-colored; round; roving; ruddy; ruddy-brown; rueful; rust-colored; sad; saddened; sagacious; sanguine; sarcastic; sardonic; satiated; saturnine; saucy; savage; scandalized; skeptic; scornful; scowling; screwed-up; scrutinizing; sea-blue; sea-gray; sea-green; sea-spent; searching; searchlight; seductive; seeing; selfsame; sensible; seraphic; sere; serene; serious; serpent; shaded; shadow-nurtured; shadowed; shadowy; shifting; sharp; sheepish; shifty; shimmering; shining; shrewd; shrinking; shrouded; shy; sibylline; sidelong; sightless; silent; silly; single; sinister; skeptical; sky-blue; skyey; slant; slate-colored; slaty; sleep-sodden; sleepless; sleepy; slight; slitty; sly; small; smart; smarting; smiling; smoke-blue; smoldering; snake; snapping; sober; sodden; soft-winged; solemn; solicitous; solitary; sorrowing; soul-telling; soulful; soulless; sour; sparkling; speaking; spectacular; speculating; speculative; spell-set; spirit-beaming; sphered; splendid; sprightly; sprouting; stainless; starlike; staring; spirit-thrilling; stark; starry; starting; steady; steadfast; stealthy; steaming; steel; steel-bright; steel-cold; stinging; steely; stern; stony; stormy; strained; strange; straying; streaming; striking; strong; studious; stupefied; subtle; subdued; sud-filled; suffering; suffused; sullen; sulky; sulphurous; sultry; sunken; sun-clear; sun-dazzled; sunshiny; superb; superficial; surprised; surveying; suspicious; sweeping; swimming; swollen; sympathetic; Tarquin; taunting; tawny; tear-blurred; tearful; tear-marred; tear-ridden; tear-wet; telescopic; telltale; tempestuous; tender; terrible; terrifying; terror-glazed; threatening; terrorized; terror-stricken; thankful; tiger; thirsty; thoughtful; tigerish; time-dimmed; timorous; tiny; tip-tilted; tired; tired out; tolerant; tormented; tormenting; tortured; topaz; touching; town-bred; trained; traitorous; tranquil; tremendous; transcendent; transparent; zinc-colored; tremulous; triumphal; triumphant; trouble-strained; truant; truculent; true; trustful; trustless; twinkling; unabashed; unaccountable; unaccustomed; unaided; unaltering; unbelieving; unannointed; unavoided; unblended; unblinded; unblinking; uncanny; uncaptious; uncertain; unclouded; uncomprehending; unconscious; uncritical; uncultivated; uncurious; undaunted; uneasy; unencumbered; unemotional; unenlightened; unenvious; unfathomable; unflickering; unflinching; unfriendly; uninitiate; unkind; unlearned; unnatural; unoperated; unpitying; unpredictable; unpleasant; unpracticed; unprejudiced; unprepossessing; unpresumptuous; unresponsive; unrevealing; unrewarded; unscrupulous; unseeing; unshackled; unshaded; unsmiling; unsophisticated; unspeakable; unsullied; unsuspecting; untamed; unterrified; untrained; untutored; untroubled; unusual; unwearied; unworldly; upbraiding; upraised; upturned; ugly; urgent; vacant; vacuous; velvet-soft; vague; veering; veiled; veilless; veiny; velvety; vengeful; venomous; vigilant; violet-blue; virgin; visionary; visionless; vivid; vulgar; wailing; waiting; wandering; wanton; war-wearied; waxen; warning; wary; washed; wasted; watchful; watery; weak; weary; weasel; weather; weeping; welkin; whimsical; well-known; well-spaced; wicked; wide; wide-open; wild; willful; wincing; winking; wintry; wise; wistful; wolfish; wonderful; wondering; wondrous; wood-nymph; wordless; worldly-wise; worn; worried; worshipped; wrathful; wretched; yellow; yielding; youthful; zestful.

EYESIGHT

adjectives

partial; unsealed; failing; precious; weakening; impaired; inefficient; palsied; neglected.

F

FABLES

adjectives
comic; antique; contextual; wretched; trivial; impious; vivid; gorgeous; romantic; traditional; prehistoric; fantastic.

FABRIC

adjectives
political; attractive; sturdy; fine-wearing; ultra-smart; notable; practical; choicest; worsted; ideal; pure; wool; superb; tropical; rich; wearable; soft; exclusive; easy-draping; hard-finished; select; popular; excellent; mellowed; non-shrinkable; favored; summer; luxurious; wonderful; wear-packed; good-looking; sparkling; cool; expensive; original; sensational; iridescent; shivered; delicate; tinted; lustrous; gaudy; spangled; colorful; lightweight; soft-textured; quality; comfortable; easy-fitting; long-living; neutral color; rugged; famous; firm; extraordinary; lovely; apparent; hairy-surfaced; casual; unsubstantial; imported; cobweb; resilient; massive; durable; stately; identical; novelty; sheer; gossamer; distinctive; social; impregnated; misty; symmetrical; textile; clinging; accentuated; husky; brawnier; loomed; patterned.

verbs
construct—; fashion—; frame—; plan—; rebuild—; renovate—; spin—; supply—; threaten—; weave—; —awes; —endures; —inspires; —tatters.

(See cloth.)

FABRICATE (v)

adverbs
ingeniously; cleverly; hypocritically; plausibly; affectedly; falsely; maliciously; slyly; traitorously; convincingly.

(See devise, construct.)

FABRICATION

adjectives
wholesale; feeble; delicious; clumsy.

FABULOUS

adverbs
foolishly; extravagantly; egregiously; terribly; abominably; absurdly; laughably; outlandishly; whimsically; maliciously; fantastically; outrageously; mythically; ironically; perversely; romantically; utterly; manifestly; openly.

FACADE

adjectives
exquisite; unlovely; venerable; florid.

FACE

adjectives
absorbed; accusing; aggrieved; adored; aged; aghast; aging; agitated; agonized; alert; alluring; amazed; amiable; amused; flabby; angelical; angry; anguished; angular; animated; anxious; apathetic; apprehensive; approving; arresting; aquiline; arch-female; aristocratic; arrogant; artificial; ascending; ascetic; ashen; assiduous; astonished; astounding; attentive; attractive; audacious; auroral; austere; automaton; averted; awe-swept; awful; babyish; begrimed; baleful; barren; battered; beaming; beardless; beauteous; beefy; beloved; benevolent; benign; benignant; beseeching; besmeared; bestial; bewildered; bewitching; biddable; big; big-boned; big-featured; black; blackened; black-eyed; blanching; bland; blank; blear-eyed; blind; blissful; blistered; blithe; bloated; blood-faint; bloodless; bloodstained; bloodthirsty; bloody; blossomy; blubbering; blue-white; blurred; blushing; bold; bony; boulder-colored; boyish; bright; broad; broad-cheeked; brooding; brown; bruised; brutal; brutish; bucolic; burning; businesslike; cadaverous; calloused; calm; cameo; candid; capable; carbonadoed; careless; cavernous; careworn; carved-bone; cast-iron; celestial; chagrined; chalklike; changing; charitable; charming; charred; chastened; cheated; cheerful; cherubic; childlike; choleric; chubby; clammy; clawed; clean-cut; clean-shaven; clear-cut; clever; close; clouded; coarse; cold; cold-creamed; collapsed; colorless; combative; comely; comfortable; comical; commanding; complaining; complicated; composed; condemning; confident; congealed; congested; consumptive; contorted; contracted; convulsed; copper-bronzed; coppery; cordial; corpselike; corrugated; country-looking; cowardly; crafty; craggy; creamy-white; crude; cruel; crystal; cun-

ning; curious; cynical; cynically-lined; dainty; daring; dark; darkened; dark-huddled; dazed; deadly; deadly-white; dead-white; death-like; deathly-pale; death-marked; debauched; deceptive; deep-lined; deeply-marred; dejected; delicate; delicately-formed; delicately-modeled; delighted; demure; delightful; denunciatory; despairing; despotic; determined; devilish; dewy; diffident; dignified; dimpled; dirty; disagreeable; disapproving; discolored; discontented; disdainful; disfigured; disillusioned; dismal; disordered; dissipated; distinct; distinguished; distorted; distracted; disturbed; doleful; dour; downcast; dowdy; drained; dreadful; dreary; dripping; droll; drooped; drowsy; dryad; dubious; dull; dusky; dust-colored; eager; earnest; easy-mannered; effeminate; elfin; eloquent; elusive; emaciated; embarrassed; eminent; enchanting; encrimsoned; energetic; enigmatic; enormous; enraptured; erstwhile; ethereal; ever-changing; everlasting; ever-welcome; evil; exceeding; expectant; exposed; expressionless; expressive; exquisite; eyeless; familiar; faded; fainting; fair; faithful; fallen; famine-stricken; famous; fanatical; fascinating; fat; fatigued; fatuous; fawning; fear-contorted; fearless; ferret-like; fervent; fiery; fighting; filled; fine; fixed; flabby; flamboyant; flat; flattened; flattered; fleshless; fleshy; flinty; flowerlike; flower-tinted; fond; foolish; forbidding; forced; foreign; formed; forsaken; forward; frail; frank; fraternal; freckled; fresh; friendly; frightened; frightful; froglike; frosted; furious; frosty; frozen; full; full-charged; furrowed; furtive; fuzzy; gamin; gaping; gaunt; gay; genial; ghastly; ghastly-pale; gigantic; girlish; gleaming; glistening; glittering; gloating; glory-beaming; glowing; glum; gnarled; gnomish; godlike; golden; good-humored; grotesque; good-natured; grained; granite; granite-gaunt; granite-hewn; grateful; grave; great; greenish-hued; grim; grinning; groping; gross-bloated; gruesome; guileless; gypsy; haggard; hair-fringed; hairless; half-averted; half-shrinking; half-haunted; handsome; hapless; happy; harassed; hard; hard-boiled; hard-muscled; harsh-featured; haughty; hate-clouded; hawklike; hearty; healthy-looking; heart-shaped; heated; heavenly; heat-flushed; heavy; helpless; heroic; hideous; hideously-scarred; well-bred; high-cheekboned; high-spirited; hirsute; hollow; holy; homely; honest; horrible; horror-stricken; hostile; huddled; humble; humorous; hungered; hungry; hunted; husklike; hypocritic; icy; idiotic; ignominious; illuminated; immemorial; immortal; immovable; impassive; imperial; imperious; imperturbable; impish; implacable; imploring; impudent; incredulous; indifferent; indignant; indomitable; ineffable; ineffectual; inelegant; inexorable; inexpressible; inexpressive; infant; infantine; inflamed; infuriated; ingenious; innocent; innumerable (pl); inoffensive; inscrutable; intellectual; intelligent; interesting; intrepid; irregular; irritable; isolated; ivory; jolly; jovial; keen-featured; kill-joy; kind; kindling; kindly; lampblack; large; lantern-jawed; laughing; lean-cheeked; leathery; leering; lemon-yellow; lifeless; little; lined; lineless; line-old; listening; listless; lively; livid; loathsome; locked; long; long-chinned; lordly; lovable; lovely; loving; gay; lowering; luminous; lustrous; majestic; malarial; malicious; malignant; maniacal; manly; mantling; marble; marred; martial; martyr; masklike; masked; massive; meager; meek; melancholy; memorable; merciless; merrier; mild; mirth-lit; miserable; mistrustful; mobile; mocking; modeled; motionless; monstrous; moon-colored; moonlike; moon-shaped; motherly; mottled; mottled-red; mournful; mud-besmeared; much-desired; muddy; mummied; murderous; muscular; mutilated; mutinous; mysterious; naked; nervous; neurotic; noble; noncommittal; noseless; objective; nutcracked; observant; obtuse; oil-smeared; oil-streaked; oily; olive; ominous; open; oval; overcast; pain-chiseled; pain-distorted; painted; pale; pansy-shaped; pallid; parchment; passionate; passionless; pasty; pasty-white; patient; patrician; peaceful; peaked; peerless; peaked; pearly; peasant; peevish; pensive; perfect; perfectly-formed; perished; perpendicular; perspiring; pert; pictured; phantom-like; piggish; pimply; pinched; piquant; piteous; pitiable; pitying; pitted; placid; plain; plaintive; pleasant; pleasing; plump; pock-marked; poetic; pointed; poker; porcelain-tinted; potent; powdered; powerful; precipitous; predestinate; premature; prematurely-aged; prevaricating; pretty; prison-pale; proud; puckered; pudding; pudgy; puffed; puffy; pugnacious; puny; purple-colored; putty-colored; puzzled; quaint; queenly; quiet; quivering; rabbity; radiant; rage-torn;

rage-twisted; rain-drenched; rapt; ratlike; ravaged; rebellious; reckless; red; refined; reflective; relentless; reproachful; resigned; resolute; respectable; responsive; restless; reticent; retributive; retrospective; reverent; reversed; ridged; rigid; roguish; rose-petal; rose-tinted; rosebud; rosy; roughly-hewn; round; rubicund; ruddier; rueful; rustic; ruthful; sad; sagacious; saintly; sallow; salt-stung; sanguine; sardonic; satanic; saturnine; saucy; scandalized; scapegrace; scared; scarlet; scarred; scheming; scholarly; scornful; scowling; scraggly; scratched; scrawny; screech-owl; seamed; scrutinizing; searching; seared; sedate; self-assured; selfless; sensitive; sensual; sentimental; serene; serious; serpent; serpentine; set; shaded; shamed; shameful; sharp-featured; sharply-angled; shaven; shining; shocked; shockingly disfigured; shrewd; shrouded; sick-looking; sickly; sightless; silent; silly; simpering; simple; sin-scarred; sinister; slant-eyed; sleek; sly; small; smashed; smiling; smile-lit; smirking; smoke-begrimed; smooth; smooth-coated; smooth-pale; smudged; smutted; snarling; sneering; sober; soft; soldierly; sorrow; somber; sorrowful; sorrowing; sorry; spare; sparkling; speaking; spectral; spirited; spiritual; splotched; staring; spongy; square; stark; square-jawed; square-jowled; startled; startling; steadfast; steady; steaming; stern; still; stolid; stone; stony; storm-beaten; stout; straight; straight-featured; strenuous; straightforward; strained; stubbly; streaming; stricken; striking; subdued; strong; strong-featured; stupid; sublime; sulky; sullen; sunbitten; sun-browned; sunburned; sun-darkened; sun-scorched; sunken; sunny; surly; suspicious; swarthy; sweat-marked; sweat-streaked; sweating; sweet; tabid; tallow; swollen; tanned; tawny; tear-dabbled; tearful; tear-stained; tear-streaked; tear-wet; teary; tender; tense; terrible; thin; thoughtful; threatening; tight; tightening; tight-lipped; tight-skinned; tilted; time-stained; time-worn; timid; tired; toothless; tortured; tough; towering; tragic; tranquil; transfigured; transformed; transparent; triumphant; treacherous; troubled; trunkless; twisted; twittering; ugly; unabashed; unbelieving; unconscious; uncouth; uncovered; underhung; uneasy; unforgetful; unfriendly; unhealthy; unintellectual; unkempt; unlighted; unlined; unmoved; unpenciled; unreadable; unrejoicing; unremembering; unshaven; unscathed; unsmiling; unspoiled; unsunny; unsympathetic; untroubled; unwashed; unwithered; unworldly; unworried; unwrinkled; uplifted; uptilted; upturned; upward; vacant; vacuous; varnished; vanished; vapid; varying; veiled; vellum-colored; vicious; villainous; vindictive; virginal; vivacious; vulturish; waning; wan; washed; wayward; waxen; weak; weather-beaten; weather-stained; weather-worn; wedge-shaped; wee; weird; well-cut; well-featured; well-groomed; well-known; well-remembered; whimsical; whiskered; white; wicked; whitewashed; wide-eyed; wine-flushed; winsome; winter-blighted; wiry; wistful; withered; wizened; woebegone; woeful; wolfish; womanly; wonder; wrinkled; wooden; working; worn; worried; wrathful; wry; yearning; young; youthful; yeoman-built; arch; delicately-cut; frolic; lean; sleeping; slender.

verbs

animate—; blanch—; contort—; distort—; draw—; flush—; furrow—; illumine—; mop —; obscure—; pinch—; pucker up—; puff up—; read in—; scrutinize—; stamp—with; submerge—; suffuse—with; tense—; wrinkle—; —beams;— bleaches; —blooms; —brightens; —charms; —clouds; —creases; —darkens; —fascinates; —flames; —gleams; —glows; —lights up; —pales; —purples; —relaxes; —resembles; —smarts; —whitens.

(See countenance, features.)

FACE (*v*)

adverbs

haughtily; resolutely; squarely; undauntedly; challengingly; listlessly; courageously; indomitably; unflinchingly; immovably; accusingly; agitatedly; alluringly; animatedly; amiably; apathetically; apprehensively; arrogantly; ashenly; audaciously; bewitchingly; austerely; callously; chastenedly; cherubically; comically; composedly; cordially; cynically; despotically; determinedly; diffidently; disdainfully; disillusionedly; distractedly; dolefully; dourly; drearily; dubiously; eloquently; energetically; enigmatically; fanatically; fatuously; fawningly; guilelessly; humbly; hypocritically; idiotically; impassively; imperiously; imperturbably; impishly; implacably; imploringly; incredulously; indifferently; intrepidly; majestically; maniacally; martially; meekly; miserably; mutinously; neurotically; obtusely; ominously; passionately; passionlessly; pertly; priggishly; piquantly; piteously; potently; precipitously; prematurely; radiantly; rebelliously; raptly; recklessly; relentlessly; reticently; reverently; roguishly; ruefully; schemingly; selflessly; sensually; sentimentally; serenely; smirkingly; sneeringly; stubbornly; tenderly; tensely; tragically; treacherously; uncouthly; unintellectually; unsmilingly; unsympathetically; wistfully; woefully; wrathfully.

(See meet, confront.)

FACETIOUS

adverbs

comically; waggishly; entertainingly; inappropriately; unseasonably; happily; merrily; youthfully; smartly; unfortunately; fantastically; quick-wittedly; nimbly; clownishly; jovially; convivially; whimsically; amusingly; pleasantly; foolishly; banteringly; teasingly; drolly; fatuously; remarkably.

FACETIOUSNESS

adjectives

grave; sparkling; cheery; dull; unwitty.

FACETS

adjectives

sparkling; gleaming; well-cut.

FACIAL

adjectives

refreshing; hasty; stimulating; cleansing.

FACILE

adverbs

skilfully; dexterously; extremely; unusually; cleverly; adroitly; artfully; neatly; ingeniously; felicitously; deftly; smartly; expertly; capably; competently; intelligently; enthusiastically; eagerly; earnestly; amenably; heartily; glibly; conveniently; pliantly; smoothly.

FACILITATE (v)

adverbs

readily; necessarily; skillfully; automatically; unsurpassingly; commercially; mechanically; briskly; unfailingly; completely.

(See advance, hasten.)

FACILITIES

adjectives

housekeeping; intermediate; clinical; educational; characteristic; technical; limitless; equal; extra; modern; recreational; convenient; marvelous; unmatched; complete; astonishing; culinary; superior; abundant; inadequate; merger; available; unsurpassed; banking; admirable; improved; mechanical; surprising; fatal; elaborate; telegraphic; musical; subsequent; terminal; rapid-transit; existing; sanitary; commercial.

FACILITY

verbs

abuse —; accomplish with —; afford —; break down —; compose with —; contribute to —; hinder —; impede —; increase —; learn with —; manage with —; perform with —; permit of —; prove —; provide —; utilize —; wipe out —; — accelerates; — lightens; — lubricates.

(See ease.)

FACSIMILE

adjectives

diminished; alleged.

FACT

adjectives

mere; ugly; unassorted (pl); stark; unvarnished; statistical; unpalatable; vital; ultimate; iron; serious; gratifying; timely; curious; salient; undoubted; indisputable; astonishing; surprising; marvelous; miraculous; magnificent; confounding; unheard-of; singular; extraordinary; incredible; unforeseen; rarest; private; enviable; subtle; outstanding; isolated; well-established; simple; unfortunate; significant; smallest; natural; cosmic; accomplished; psychological; grim; historic; lamentable; practical; dominant; sordid; illuminating; governing; eternal; insuppressible; inexplicable; remarkable; systematizing; ineluctable; conceded; multifarious (pl); straight-from-the-shoulder; scientific; interesting; striking; noteworthy; accepted; inexorable; cruel; prosaic; hard; sprightly; inescapable; persistent; settled; essential; contradictory; embellished; deniable; stubborn; fundamental; revolting; unanswerable; disgraceful; unrelated; concomitant; intriguing; optical; naked; undeviating; instructive; damaging; changing; fluid; amazing; full; free; cold; startling; elemental; important; demonstrated; unconventional; permanent; visible; notorious; well-ascertained; brutal; preliminary; relevant; bitter; admitted; melancholy; deplorable; embodying; memorable; bare; palpable; unquestionable; authenticated; cardinal; incontrovertible; worthy; final; ultimate; absolute; graphical; quiet; special; patent; unsuspected; unguessed; reasonable; architectural; dark; mysterious; concrete; palpitating; delightful; irresistible; delicious; unimpugnable; analogous; sinful; well-known; conspicuous; clear; distinct; firm; passionless; impartial; noticed; meticulous; illuminating; scanty; inert; vivid; tremendous; previous; exact; formidable; unconnected; first; empirical; acoustical; external; perpetual; bald, encouraging; physical; plain; ascertained; convincing; horrific; central; negative; basic; tangible; indubitable; geological; suggestive; trivial; rudimentary; clenching; acquired; outward; adduced; inconvenient; major; self-evident; commonplace; verifiable; supreme; actual; positive; sheer; apparent; acknowledged; ethical; diverting; sober; unpleasant; disturbing; unpoetic; tragic; queer; fantastic; colorful; fabulous; notable; stirring; buried; laborious; discovered; overwhelming; exhaustive; multitudinous (pl); detailed; hazy; confusing; experimental; paradoxical; observed; challenging; superficial; immaterial

verbs
accept —; account for —; accumulate —s; allude to —; amplify —; apprise of —; array —s; ascertain —; ascribe — to; assail —; assemble —s; attest to —; awake to —; bear out by —; belittle —; bemoan —; blind to —; blur —; bring — to light; bring home —; certify —; cite —; collate —; color —; confirm —; conform to —; confront with —; construe —; cram with —s; credit —; debate —; deduce —; demonstrate —; deny —; deplore —; digest —; disclose —; disentangle —s; disguise —; distort —; divulge —; dodge —; embrace —; emphasize —; establish —; evidence by —; exhaust —s; exploit —; expound —; face —; found on —; garble —s; generalize —s; glean —s; grant —; grapple with —; grasp —; harp on —; ignore —; impress with —; interpret —; juggle —s; master —; misconstrue —; misrepresent —; mull over —s; obscure —; oppose —; outweigh —; overlook —; override —; ponder —; question —; recapitulate —s; reconcile —s; refute —; regale with —s; rehash —s; represent as —; rest upon —; run counter to —; sift —s; stress —; stud with —s substantiate —; suppress —; trace — to; transform —s; unearth —; verify —; weigh —; wrestle with —; —s cohere; — dawns; — depresses; — disquiets; — illustrates; — looms; — sinks in; —startles; — supports; — verifies.

(See truth, act, incident, statement.)

FACTION

verbs
attach to —; avoid —; combine —s; criticize —; defend —; disturb —; divide into —s; extinguish —; join —; maintain —; rend into —s; run into —s; sort into —s; split in —s; spread —; support —; suppress —; unite —s; — abandons; — declines; — dictates; — disperses; — springs from.

(See party, opposition.)

FACTIONS

adjectives
fluctuating; petty; discordant; embittered; wretched; defeated; turbulent; atrocious; execrable; fierce; mischievous; warring; hostile; rival; musical; exasperated; oligarchical; various; aristocratic; contending; internal; respective; opposing; imprisoned; reconciling.

FACTOR

adjectives
selective; dietary; prominent; etiological; potent; growth; various (pl); significant; vital; psychological; unfortunate; inestimable; additional; causative; determining; indispensable; compensating; prime; intellectual; dependable; encouraging; underlying; distinct; astounding; contributory; fundamental; outside; limiting; legendary; inherited; unquestioned; environmental; important; practical; dominant; industrial; external; material; essential; responsible; decisive; narcissistic; ecclesiastical; obvious; negligible; despised; dangerous; racial; geographical; constitutional; constant; motivating; all-pervasive; avoidable; incalculable.

verbs
belittle —; consider —; coordinate —s; embrace —; establish —; influence by —; limit —s; ponder —; reckon —; reveal —; unravel —; weigh —; —s converge; — determines; — emerges; —looms; —s militate against; — predisposes; — dominates.

(See element, constituent, influence, cause.)

FACTORY

adjectives
besieged; enormous; noisy; irrepressible.

verbs
boycott —; conduct —; control —; convert —; destroy —; dispose of —; equip —; erect —; establish —; examine —; improve —; inspect —; maintain —; man —; manage —; observe —; picket —; promote from —; strip —; supervise —; — employs; — idles; — produces; — specializes in.
(See plant, mill, shop, building.)

FACULTY

adjectives
contemplative; divine; unworn; ruling; bounded; healthful; bigoted; domestic; artful; visualizing; ready; rational; corporeal; biased; imaginative; perceptive; distinct; trained; reasoning; intellectual; remarkable; scientific; benumbed; integral; honorable; unimpaired; sterner; reciprocal; courageous; practised; departmentalized; balancing; glorious; winged; natural; rare; unique; primary; worldly; efficient; sublimest; wondrous; higher; dormant; aesthetic; elaborative; human; visual; imitative; cardinal; potential; awakened; penetrating; governing; administrative; spiritual; critical; cogitative; analytical; abnormal; treacherous; moral; finite; antipodal; comparative; common; creative; inventive; uncanny; obstinate; acute.

verbs
arouse —; assist —; collect —s; concentrate —ies; cultivate —ies; dazzle —; develop —ies; dull —ies; endow with —; exercise —; exhibit —; hamper —; impair —; manifest —; rally —ies; reclaim —; recruit —ies; retain —; strain —; strengthen —; stupefy —; waste—ies; — decays; — enables.
(See power, capacity, ability, skill, talent.)

FAD

adjectives
commendable; expensive; dietary; crazy; innocent; passing.

verbs
addict to —; adopt —; advocate —; annihilate —; attribute — to; conceive —; condemn —; criticize —; cultivate —; deter —; dispose to —; frown on —; gibe at —; indulge in —; nourish —; produce —; pursue —; ridicule —; start —; warn against —; — exaggerates; — passes; — seizes; — spreads; — sprouts.
(See fancy, fashion, hobby, whim.)

FADE (*v*)

adverbs
partially; gracefully; strangely; autumnally; hauntingly; dismally; inevitably; corporeally; depressingly; tragically; lingeringly.
(See droop, decay.)

FAGGED

(fagged-out)

adverbs
utterly; inexpressibly; dangerously; alarmingly; haggardly; gauntly; hopelessly; irrecoverably; lamentably; pitiably; wretchedly; miserably.

FAGGOT

adjectives
wintry; blazing; ashy; glazing.

FAIL (*v*)

adverbs
miserably; tragically; unquestionably; ridiculously; deplorably; essentially; deservedly; constantly; conspicuously; unwittingly; signally; lamentably; ignominiously; eventually; despicably; grievously; partially; scholastically; abjectly; habitually; inexplicably; indefensibly.
(See decline, deteriorate.)

FAILING

verbs
aggravate —; alter —; anticipate —; apprehend —; breed —; brood over —; compensate for —; deserve —; detect —; discover —; establish —; excuse —; exploit —; forgive —; incur —; mention —; pardon —; produce —; promote —; supply —; — enfeebles; — overtakes.
(See fault, foible, shortcoming, failure, deficiency, infirmity, defect.)

adverbs
indubitably; visibly; hopelessly; shockingly; feebly; weakly; languidly; decrepitly; desolately; shakily; perceptibly; manifestly; patently; conspicuously; noticeably; rapidly; inevitably; finally; slowly; obviously; avowedly; brokenly; wretchedly; pitifully; undoubtedly; languishingly; hopelessly; fatally; incurably; infirmly; strangely.

FAILINGS

adjectives
radical; common; inherited; proudest.

FAILURE

adjectives
impending; eventual; despicable; grievous; pathetic; distressed; architectural; expensive; wasteful; baking; partial; corresponding; miserable; irritating; repeated; dismal; celebrated; melancholy; appalling; foredoomed; regretted; vacillatory; consecutive (pl); preliminary; scholastic; abject; pitiable; sensible; ignominious; hideous; frantic; predestined; lamentable; mental; conspicuous; habitual; heroic; inexplicable; unhappy; indefensible; depressing; sudden; gigantic; pioneering.

verbs
ameliorate —; avert —; brood over —; court —; face —; foredoom to —; foretell —; grapple with —; indemnify against —; insure against —; offset —; overcome —; precipitate —; predict —; punish —; view as —; — disheartens; — dismays; — impends; — invalidates; — looms.

(See bankruptcy, neglect, short-coming, failing.)

FAINT

verbs
anticipate —; avert —; fall into a —; feign —; fight off —; produce —; recover from —; revive from —; rouse from —; simulate —; sink in —; stay —; treat for —; — confuses; — depresses; — enfeebles; — ensues; — weakens.

(See fit, paroxysm, convulsion.)

adverbs
woefully; terribly; incredibly; illegibly; powerlessly; visibly; noticeably; conspicuously; obviously; wretchedly; helplessly; dangerously; alarmingly; dreadfully; mysteriously; strangely; oddly; curiously; wearily; breathlessly; drowsily.

FAINT (*v*)

adverbs
ostensibly; charmingly; abruptly; unexpectedly; calculatingly; intermittently; designingly.

(See despond, fade.)

FAINTNESS

adjectives
present; humiliating.

FAIR

adjectives
fashionable; cruel; slumbering.

adverbs
invariably; honestly; beautifully; equitably; always; indubitably; incontestably; legally; scrupulously; meticulously; carefully; dutifully; cautiously; discreetly; reasonably; surprisingly; astutely; logically; sensibly; expediently; providently; admirably; pleasantly; grudgingly; primarily; tolerably; exceptionally; satisfactorily; remarkably; generously; strictly; rigidly; impartially.

FAIR-GROUNDS

adjectives
populous; spacious; frequented.

FAIRNESS

adjectives
supposed; scrupulous; pretended.

verbs
assail —; bestow with —; dispute —; doubt —; exhibit —; judge —; necessitate —; repay —; reward —; seek —; violate —; yield to —; — pleases.

(See justice, impartiality, honesty.)

FAIRY

adjectives
adventurous; pitiless; rough; omnipotent; venturous; good; fiendish.

verbs
transform into —; —ies array; — assumes; — charms; — circles; — dances; — darts; — enchants; — flits; — frisks; — frolics; — gambols; — hies away; — inhabits; — leaps; — meddles; —revels; — scampers; — sings; — tricks; — trips; — warbles.

(See angel, spirit.)

FAIRYLAND

adjectives
vague; misty.

FAITH

adjectives
abiding; indestructible; consolatory; sublime; gladder; scrupulous; passionate; mutual; ripening; childlike; obliterated; obliged; nobler; inflexible; implicit; efficient; pure-eyed; grim; unbounded; whimsical; plighted; sturdy; radiant; joyful; religious; rising; unbroken; rational; potential; blind;

unquestioning; manly; lesser; unfeigned; humble; trusting; unfailing; utter; undying; secure; absolute; conflicting (pl); fervid; melancholy; sincere; optimistic; earnest; all-absorbing; heartier; devouring; habitual; immaculate; lofty; unwavering; sacramental; supreme; dumb; helpless; good; willing; generous; unalterable; unshaken; true; fugitive; orthodox; public; exulting; purblind; quickened; implied; heart-enrooted; inviolate; stalwart; tardy; obedient; blighting; impious; feeble; down-sunken; deathless; customary; active; shattered; sinless; material; profound; infirm; honorable; transcendent; barren; simple; steadfast; plural (pl).

verbs
apostatize from —; break — with; cling to —; confirm —; dampen —; endure with —; exhibit —; found upon —; forsake —; fortify —; inculcate —; inspire —; invalidate —; justify —; maintain —; manifest —; mould —; persecute for —; pervert —; pin — in; preach —; proclaim —; profess —; purge —; reawaken —; reiterate —; retain —; rivet — in; shake —; share —; sway by —; voice —; — melts away; — perishes; — quickens; — stands; — survives; — wavers.

(See assurance, belief, conviction, confidence, trust.)

FAITHFUL

adverbs
affectionately; loyally; duly; honorably; scrupulously; rigidly; deeply; grimly; resolutely; sturdily; undeviatingly; joyously; blindly; humbly; utterly; absolutely; optimistically; earnestly; heartily; unwaveringly; unalterably; inviolately; steadfastly; actively; flatteringly; abjectly; punctiliously; meticulously; actively; simply; unaffectedly; candidly; openly; incorruptibly; uncommonly.

FAITHFULNESS

adjectives
utter; assertive.

verbs
believe in —; build —; cherish —; create —; demand —; display —; encourage —; justify —; necessitate —; overshadow —; praise —; prove —; rely on —; require —; reward —; suspect —; try —; — falls; — shines; — supports; — trusts.

(See loyalty, fidelity, constancy, allegiance, devotion.)

FAITHLESS

adverbs
shamelessly; terribly; abominably; timorously; basely; faint-heartedly; brazenly; coolly; openly; obdurately; detestably; execrably; audaciously; perversely; hypocritically; evasively; artfully; perfidiously; cunningly; insidiously; surreptitiously; dreadfully; unbelievably; unexpectedly; direly; disastrously; shamefully.

FAKE

verbs
conceive—; contrive—; denounce—; detect—; divine—; expose—; father—; inspire—; invent—; palm off—; perform—; plan—; plunder with—; practice—; regard as—; reveal—; shape—; taboo—; uncover—; work—; —deceives; —entrances; —fascinates; —fools; —perturbs.

(See swindle, sham, deceit.)

FALL

adjectives
tremendous; jade-green; weary; graceful; repeated (pl); preceding; virtuous; sloping; gleaming; deadliest; intertangled; bubbly; clattering; answering; melodious; dying; instantaneous; uncropt; thundering.

verbs
(See autumn.)

FALL (v)

adverbs
ultimately; noiselessly; subsequently; perpendicularly; insensibly; involuntarily; supinely; disdainfully; melodiously; resistlessly; unceasingly; inertly; precisely; incoherently; unwittingly; leisurely; dreamily; violently; intermittently; disconcertingly; fitfully; ponderously; thunderingly.

(See drop, descend.)

FALLACIOUS

adverbs
deeply; grossly; utterly; obviously; sorrily; patently; manifestly; wretchedly; clumsily; grotesquely; fantastically; absurdly; oddly; scientifically; deliberately; speciously;

egregiously; horribly; laughably; flimsily; nonsensically; evasively; blunderingly; deceptively; intentionally; perversely; shamefully.

FALLACY

adjectives
glittering; discarded; deepest; gross; sophistical; pathetic; discovered.

verbs
accept—; admit—; challenge—; correct—; demonstrate—; denounce—; discover—; disperse—ies; disprove—; explode—; rationalize—; reveal—; ridicule—.

(See delusion, error, deception, misconception.)

FALLIBILITY

adjectives
extreme; obvious; apparent.

FALLIBLE

adverbs
precariously; embarrassingly; obscurely; timidly; indecisively; vaguely; occasionally; foolishly; weakly; inconclusively; deceptively; speciously; carelessly; casually; remarkably; frequently; bewilderingly; blithely; thoughtlessly; inconsequentially; impulsively; untenably.

FALLING

adjectives
unconscious; swift; desperate.

FALLOW

adverbs
aridly; unfruitfully; unprofitably; naturally; carelessly; shiftlessly; passively; inactively; unproductively; purposely; improvidently; rudimentally; roughly; calmly; tentatively; temporarily; deliberately; advisedly; provisionally; wisely.

FALSE

adverbs
subtly; stiffly; crudely; inelegantly; crassly; grotesquely; laughably; ridiculously; awkwardly; outlandishly; stagily; cleverly; ingeniously; obviously.

FALSEHOOD

adjectives
practised; flattering; incredible; base; clumsy; downright; palpable; grotesque; blushing; deliberate; infamous; pardonable; ingenious; cheerful; illusive; hidden; hypocritical; conventional; fawning; tortured; twisted.

verbs
accept—; admit—; avoid—; challenge—; confess—; demonstrate—; denounce—; disprove—; explode—; refrain from—; utter —; —dishonors; —pervades; —reeks; —sours; —taints.

(See lie, counterfeit, mistake, error.)

FALSENESS

adjectives
glittering.

FALSETTO

adjectives
tender; querulous; mincing; anxious; senile.

FALSIFIER

adjectives
wretched; conscienceless; insidious; adept.

FALSIFY (*v*)

adverbs
mystifyingly; abundantly; basely; prodigiously; incredibly; clumsily; palpably; grotesquely; deliberately; infamously; ingeniously; hypocritically; fawningly.

(See misrepresent, distort.)

FALTER (*v*)

adverbs
technically; abruptly; quaveringly; meekly; habitually; agedly; feebly; unattractively; repeatedly; recurrently; absurdly; ridiculously.

(See tremble, hesitate, waver.)

FAME

adjectives
fabulous; dying; boundless; imperishable; philosophic; volatile; hallowed; bastard; genuine; partial; lawful; glorious; prophetic; academic; inferior; abstract; soaring; shouting; patrimonial; monumental; artistic; tremendous; spotless; matchless; immense; unqualified; illustrious; extensive; prodigious; horrible; imaginary; eternal; posthumous; spurious; stainless; spreading; vague; inordinate; legal; faultless; immortal; nascent; worthy; untainted; sinister; international; equal; envious; additional; dead; serial; unpolluted; lifelong; enduring; deadly-purchased; dingy; long.

verbs
achieve—; acquire—; amass—; covet—; dazzle with—; destine to—; establish—; exalt to—; recapture—; renounce—; secure —; snatch at—; vault to—; —expands; —glows; —reaches; —rests on; —waxes.
(See renown, reputation, eminence, glory, notoriety.)

FAMILIAR

adverbs
thoroughly; intimately; wholly; cordially; affably; unceremoniously; informally; heartily; conversantly; entirely; highly; accessibly; courteously; perfectly; completely; habitually; wontedly; long; companionably; chattily; sociably; suavely; blandly; graciously; tactfully; genially; openly; publicly; avowedly; remarkably; undoubtedly; somewhat.

FAMILIARITY

adjectives
growing; sentimental; impertinent; legitimate; insolent; becoming; affectionate; misdirected; easy; sheer; hourly; dear; curious; intimate; democratic; personal; sweet; profane.

FAMILY

adjectives
sorrowing; aristocratic; human; peaceable; imperial; citrus; helpless; defenseless; hereditary; unnurtured; well-governed; ancient; illustrious; immediate; distinguished; ever-growing; affluent; respectable; numerous; aristocratic; discriminating; exaggerating; impecunious; influential; well-ordered; harmonious; attractive; pious; august; aghast; impoverished; meritorious; indigent; regal; talented; jarring; proud; national; wrangling; mignonette; well-regulated; homeless; powerful; intimate; decayed; short-lived; close-mouthed; stiff-necked; divided; frugal; brawny; destitute; increasing; lively; handsome; chivalrous; patrician.

verbs
contribute to—; dominate—; evict—; head —; hold—together; inspire—; join—; maintain—; respect—; reunite—; rule—; stir—; warp—; —flourishes; —overflows; —quarrels; —unites; —wrangles.
(See clan, tribe.)

FAMINE

adjectives
impending; desperate; pining; consuming; fearful; feverish.

verbs
bring—; die in—; expose to—; incur—; keep—at bay; lament—; perish in—; recover from—; suffer—; threaten with—; —attacks; —besieges; —blights; —clings; —devastates; —distresses; —ensues; —frustrates; —punishes; —prevails; —ravages; —reduces; —subdues.
(See destitution.)

FAMISHED

adverbs
incredibly; dreadfully; shamefully; abominably; unbelievably; utterly; starvingly; actually; haggardly; gauntly; horribly; shockingly; startlingly; heartbreakingly; emaciatedly; hungrily; insatiably; breathlessly; pitiably; awfully; murderously; terribly.

FAMOUS

adverbs
illustriously; brilliantly; notoriously; terribly; internationally; prodigiously; tremendously; distinctly; gloriously; honorably; deservedly; ingloriously; ignobly; horribly; imperishably; splendidly; politically; proudly; nobly; undeniably; remarkably; reputably; signally; amazingly.

"FAN" (*devotee*)

verbs
breed—s; collect—s; produce—s; supply—s; —acclaims; —applauds; —attends; —cheers; —s congregate; —s flock to; —indulges in; —is addicted to; —praises; —pursues; —s rally; —responds; —"roots" for; —s turn out.
(See fanatic, devotee.)

FAN (*implement*)

adjectives
cooling; breezy; whirling; flirting; feather; winnowing.

verbs
employ—; install—; regulate—; —agitates; —airs; —blasts; —blows; —buzzes; —cools; —churns; —creates a draft; —drives; —eases; —refreshes; —relieves; —revol-

ves; —rotates; —supplies; —urges; —ventilates; —whizzes.
(See propeller.)

FAN (v)

adverbs
coolingly; breezily; whirlingly; refreshingly; pleasingly; irritatingly; maddeningly; furiously; feverishly.
(See cool, ventilate, rouse.)

FANATIC

adjectives
revolutionary; religious; unflinching; murderous; vegetarian; sour; crazed; recognized; unbalanced; miserable; vicious; passionate.

verbs
combat—; control—; enlist—; inflame—; intoxicate—; oppose—; ridicule—; scorn—; transform into—; —accomplishes; —s band; —charms; —explodes; —fevers; —imagines; —infects; —inveighs against; —kindles; —prates; —prattles; —rants; —stirs; —undermines; —uproots.

FANATICAL

adverbs
intolerantly; illiberally; narrowly; provincially; wildly; madly; insanely; terribly; unfortunately; fantastically; outrageously; outlandishly; unreasonably; stupidly; crazily; ribaldly; eccentrically; sharply; deeply; earnestly; fervently; fervidly; zealously; feverishly; hysterically; ungovernably; excitably; deliriously; moodily; dangerously; dreadfully.

FANATICISM

adjectives
ignorant; remorseless; arrogant; insupportable; growing; unbridled; harsh; contemptible; lamented; religious.

verbs
control—; delude by—; display—; evince—; express—; fire with—; heat with—; incline to—; incur—; inflame with—; manifest—; overwhelm by—; persecute for—; plant the seed of—; tolerate—; —disqualifies; —drains; —exaggerates; —ferments; —governs; —impresses; —inhibits; —intoxicates; —overdoes; —prejudices; —prohibits; —rends; —stimulates; —sunders; —terrifies.
(See intolerance, superstition.)

FANCIER

adjectives
sensitive, professional.

FANCIFUL

adverbs
gloriously; illusively; abstractly; fantastically; notionally; delusively; chimerically; phantasmagorically; romantically; fugitively; whimsically; momentarily; imperishably; extravagantly; deceptively; insubstantially; fabulously; inventively; voluptuously; comfortingly; ecstatically; ardently; playfully; wildly; grotesquely; absurdly; ludicrously; laughably; ridiculously; beautifully.

FANCY

adjectives
passing; distorted; subjective; sportive; delicate; religious; bubbling; enthusiastic; deluding; school-girl; ingenious; boundless; superstitious; starry; virgin; quainter; tenderer; changeful; fond; disturbed; poetical; stray; youthful; difficult; ungrateful; irritable; popular; flesh-imprisoned; wild; prodigal; subtle; shadowy; groundless; ridiculous; childish; morbid; curious; vagrant; wayward; thick-coming (pl); fluttering; riotous; trustworthy; fermenting; exquisite; languid; incipient; airiest; feeble; preposterous; lingering; sudden; busy; extravagant; fickle; romantic; correlated; luxuriant; restless; quaint; hopeless; hypochondriacal; cruel; angry; later; odd; gushing; fecund; timorous; sweet; strange; voluptuous; gentle; mystical; insistent; long-faded; quick-springing; torpid; ardent; credulous; rambling; captious; wheeling; playful; giddy; unfirm; crude; disordered; unreciprocated; fastidious; irregular; excited; distempered; ever-veering; pardonable; unearthly; waking; fragrant; flying; footless; viewless; fugitive; worthless; delicious; violent; gloomy; wild-looking; mere; weak-hinged; scheming; frivolous; hideous; thoughtful; unsettled; whimsical; diseased; quavering; extraordinary; idolatrous.

verbs
breed—; build with—; catch—; chime with —; cure of—; crystallize—; dally with in —ies; draw upon—; excite—; fit—; free from—; indulge in—; lead by—; press upon —; reject—; restrain—; —conceives; —

flees; —flickers; —ies gather; —pursues; — —reigns; —roams; —rushes; —travels; — —wakes; —wanders.

(See fantasy, conceit, whim, caprice.)

FANCY (v)

adverbs
chimerically; erroneously; subjectively; enthusiastically; boundlessly; superstitiously; tenderly; poetically; ridiculously; childishly; morbidly; waywardly; romantically; voluptuously; frivolously; whimsically; idolatrously.

See imagine, dream.)

FANDANGO

adjectives
shuffling; mad; whirling; wild.

FANFARE

adjectives
dying; sounding; glorious; wild; raucous.

FANGS

adjectives
sharpened; bloody; poisoned; harpy; particular; mimic; dripping; unseen; enormous; knotted; viewless.

verbs
bury—in; display—; escape—; expose—; imbed—; insert—; shed—; strike with—; —drive at; —fold back; —gnaw; —pass into; —penetrate; —perforate; —pierce; —poison; —puncture; —spike.

(See claw, talon, nail.)

FANTASTIC

adverbs
illusively; deliciously; wildly; queerly; sadly; vainly; strangely; oddly; curiously; mysteriously; romantically; whimsically; extravagantly; fabulously; divertingly; playfully; grotesquely; absurdly; ludicrously; laughably; horribly; ridiculously; unreasonably; irrationally.

FANTASY

adjectives
satirical; utopian; errant; delirious; babbling; wild; causeless; bewildering; vivid; sinful; incestuous; conjectural; winged; shadowy; scant; hideous; blasphemous; guiltless; sinuous; shaping; aboriginal; gracious; hateful; cherished; ingenious; cosmic; unconscious.

verbs
delight in—; devise—; express in—; frame in—; flutter in—; imagine in—; live in—; project—; retreat into—; scatter—; soar in —; stray in—; travel in—; view—; wander in—; —attracts; —beckons; —gallops; —hovers; —melts away; —roams; indulge in—.

(See image, illusion, fancy, dream, phantasy, caprice.)

FAR

adverbs
incredibly; fabulously; outlandishly; outrageously; remotely; inaccessibly; impossibly; immeasurably; fantastically; wearily; extremely; surprisingly; dangerously; disturbingly; discouragingly; heartbreakingly; terribly; lamentably; pitifully; incalculably.

FARCE

adjectives
coarse; physical; ghastly; gayest; moral; boisterous; solemn; gigantic; social; bawdy; glorious; brisk.

FARCICAL

adverbs
comically; laughably; ridiculously; ludicrously; fantastically; outlandishly; noisily; boisterously; uproariously; racily; ribaldly; coarsely; satirically; genially; socially; brilliantly; crudely; gayly; solemnly; gloriously; hilariously; spectacularly; luminously; nonsensically; extravagantly; preposterously; senselessly; ironically; cleverly; waggishly; facetiously; merrily; jocosely; whimsically; drolly; bombastically; irresistibly; tremendously.

FARE

adjectives
monotonous; dainty; palatable; delicious; sumptuous; heavenly; primitive; meager; frugal; unwholesome; humble; ambrosial; acceptable; penitential; bounteous; monastic; substantial.

FARE
(passage money)

verbs
calculate—; call for—; demand—; deposit —; extend—; forfeit—; furnish—; mislay —; necessitate—; produce—; reduce—; reject—; remit—; request—; require—; supply—; take up—.

(See money, amount, price.)

FARE (v)

adverbs

sumptuously; disastrously; monotonously; deliciously; primitively; penitently; bounteously; substantially; monastically.

(See live, suffer.)

FAREWELL

adjectives

stern; ceremonious; affectionate; cheerful; fervent; edifying; wifely; remaining; inimitable; sublime; reluctant; mock; secret; fantastical; dilated; hasty; tender; thundering; summary; courteous; sobbing; heart-breathed; horrible; silent; mute; long; touching; mechanical.

verbs

anticipate—; bid—; bless at—; deter—; express—; mourn—; pour out—; prolong—; regret—; remember—; shorten—; take—; wave—; weep—; —depresses; —distresses; —ensues; —pains; —saddens; —terminates.

FAR-FETCHED

adverbs

laboriously; ridiculously; ineptly; irrelevantly; absurdly; ludicrously; unfortunately; clumsily; outlandishly; discordantly; inappropriately; pointlessly; senselessly; foolishly; studiously; sedulously; speciously; vapidly; inanely; stupidly; doltishly; remarkably; vacuously; childishly.

FARM

adjectives

stud; hospitable; deserted; scattered; exhausted; allodial; collective; extensive; productive; diversified; isolated; fruitful; well-cultivated.

verbs

abandon—; cultivate—; dwell on—; equip —; establish—; forsake—; grow on—; inhabit—; labor on—; leave—; maintain—; overrun—; raise on—; settle on—; till—; transform—; vacation on—; —deteriorates; —employs; —furnishes; —nestles; —produces; —provides; —supplies.

(See land, tract, district.)

FARMER

adjectives

incautious; florid; peasant-like; hard-handed; embattled; prosperous; stricken; indifferent; sheep; border-line; enlightened; sinewy; gentleman; close-fisted; liberal-hearted; disingenuous; venturesome; stout; industrious; plodding.

verbs

grubstake—; subsidize—; tax—; —cultivates; —fertilizes; —flourishes; —furrows; —garners; —gathers; —harvests; —hoes; —labors; —markets; —ploughs; —prunes; —reaps; —slaves; —sows; —spades; —thrives; —tills; —plucks.

(See countryman, peasant.)

FARM-HOUSE

adjectives

pleasant; smiling; comfortable-looking; stout.

verbs

abandon—; care for—; conceal—; describe —; dwell in—; erect—; gather in—; locate —; long for—; renovate—; restore—; search for—; surround—; threaten—; welcome—; yearn for—; —deteriorates; —nestles; —stands; retire to—.

(See dwelling, building, house.)

FARMING

adjectives

speculative; diversified; intensive; fertile; scientific.

FASCINATE (v)

adverbs

bewitchingly; enchantingly; inexplicably; infinitely; absurdly; irresistibly; singularly; carnally; voluptuously; dangerously.

(See charm, enchant.)

FASCINATED

adverbs

inexpressibly; inordinately; incomprehensibly; radiantly; innocently; incredibly; marvellously; artlessly; unconsciously; utterly; thoroughly; completely.

FASCINATING

adverbs

adorably; attractively; bewitchingly; charmingly; inexpressibly; dazzlingly; radiantly; innocently; designedly; intentionally; cleverly; incredibly; undeniably; marvellously; inordinately; dangerously; winningly; artlessly; unconsciously; utterly; highly; thoroughly; teasingly; smartly; consciously; craftily; seductively; completely.

FASCINATION

adjectives

painful; potent; enchanting; dread; charming; horrible; occult; absorbing; inexplicable; perilous; acute; infinite; tremulous; inexhaustible; ominous; youthful; absurd; irresistible; singular; divine; wild; carnal; indefinable; wonderful; dangerous; shuddery; personal.

verbs

apply—; cast—; employ—; lie under—; overcome—; prevent—; resist—; succumb to—; surrender to—; sweep on by—; tantalize with—; withstand—; yield to—; —attracts; —binds; —compels; —draws; —freezes; —haunts; —impels; —masters; —overpowers; —perils; —prevails.

(See enchantment, charm, influence, attraction.)

FASCISM

adjectives

distinct; aggressive; insidious; power-drunk; efficient; masterful; stultifying.

verbs

admit to—; establish—; infect with—; inspire—; join—; oppose—; smack of—; succumb to—; support—; yield to—; —advocates; —aims at; —attacks; —campaigns; —controls; —crushes; —deprives; —embodies; —enforces; —girds its loins; —organizes; —ousts; —prohibits; —regulates; —revolts; —riots; —violates; —welds.

(See movement.)

FASHION

adjectives

convincing; casual; improving; scimitar; belated; futile; paternal; masterly; promising; authentic; sumptuous; peculiar; sinister; bourgeois; summery; changing; refreshing; military; charming; comical; vigorous; cold-blooded; casual; coat; outstanding; debonair; dress; sensational; gay; important; hurried; righteous; tawdry; wicked; pernicious; bygone; graceful; latest; effeminate; aesthetic; school-boy; regal; exclusive; foolish; beastly; fickle; mythical; tragic; fine; quaint; excellent; picturesque; debased; florid; symbolic; polluted; seemly; obedient; faultless; orderly; jovial; delicate; hearty; squalid; metropolitan; expensive; liberal; excited; impulsive; infantine; unstudied; unostentatious; accepted; surly; taciturn; shifting; smart; early; appealing; distinctive; formless; hellish; malignant; piquant; self-respecting; desultory; unbecoming; perfect; coordinating; candid; straightforward; corduroy; fantastic; rare; oriental; prevailing; serious; high-and-mighty; outlandish; simple; superficial; identical; classic; perpendicular; intrusive; orthodox; rude; bungling; haphazard; obvious; offensive; primitive; phlegmatic; soldierly; dramatic; feminine; fanciful; diverting; characteristic; feeble; brilliant; stimulating; fastidious; clownish; enervating; window-shutter; democratic; brutal; halting; obsolete; fugitive; literary; noble; obstinate; materialistic; unceremonious; ornate; reckless; romantic; humblest; patriarchal; gossipy; chatty; forced; upstart; plain; childish; united; inconvenient; awkward; listless; vague; antique; bovine; lavish; merciless; beneficent; contradictory; womanly.

verbs

accommodate—; anticipate—; appraise by—; attune to—; balk at—; create—; decree—; follow—; influence—; purvey—; rule—; set—; style—; —derives from; —dies out; —endures; —fades; —flickers out; —prevails; —roots in.

(See mode, method, usage, style.)

FASHION (*v*)

adverbs

primitively; crudely; superbly; flawlessly; deftly; tenderly; meticulously; delicately; comically; sensationally; gaily; perniciously; aesthetically; quaintly; picturesquely; symbolically; unostentatiously; fantastically; rudely; haphazardly; offensively; dramatically; characteristically; fastidiously; democratically; ornately; awkwardly.

(See style, make.)

FASHIONABLE

adverbs

completely; occasionally; enthusiastically; seriously; carefully; entirely; thoroughly; uncommonly; extraordinarily; habitually; conventionally; decorously; highly; modishly; socially; conformably; stylishly; jauntily; conspicuously; resolutely; determinedly; exquisitely; foppishly; flirtatiously; pretentiously; famously; notoriously; splendidly; reputably; eminently; imposingly; impressively; inveterately.

FAST

adverbs
incredibly; expeditiously; smartly; actively; mercurially; nimbly; remarkably; amazingly; marvellously; miraculously; unaccountably; intolerably; breathlessly; dangerously; alarmingly; hazardously; bewilderingly; terrifically; insanely; inordinately; immoderately; immeasurably; incalculably.

FAST (v)

adverbs
stubbornly; continually; frequently; tediously; determinedly; fatally; fanatically; rigorously; monastically; severely.
(See starve, abstain.)

FASTEN (v)

adverbs
securely; attractively; firmly; gaily; fastidiously; competently; snugly; closely; permanently; temporarily.
(See fix, secure.)

FASTIDIOUS

adverbs
inordinately; extravagantly; daintily; precisely; primly; exquisitely; neatly; habitually; punctiliously; rigidly; strictly; rigorously; arbitrarily; admirably; marvellously; meticulously; priggishly; delicately; captiously; censoriously; scrupulously.

FASTIDIOUSNESS

adjectives
aristocratic; complete; extreme; studied.

FASTNESS

adjectives
forest; wild; remote; unillumined; mountain; inaccessible; rugged; desolate; solitary.

FASTS

adjectives
frequent; bitter; tedious; hunger-strike.

FAT

adjectives
twofold; juicy; rancid; waxy; resinous; insoluble; additional; indigestible.

verbs
accrue—; accumulate—; acquire—; compose of—; devour—; digest—; emulsify—; fight against—; grow—; guard against—; live on—of; overcharge with—; prevent—; produce—; provide—; provoke—; put on —; reduce—; ridicule—; store up—; supply —; —blossoms; —forms; —nourishes; —sizzles.
(See flesh.)

adverbs
inexpressibly; unhappily; incredibly; incurably; laughably; lamentably; comfortably; contentedly; distressingly; absurdly; ridiculously; ludicrously; sadly; joyously; dangerously; heavily; gracefully; admittedly; funnily; unreasonably; incorrigibly; complacently; complainingly; mournfully; dramatically; pathetically; gracelessly; shapelessly; waddlingly.

FATAL

adverbs
unhappily; unfortunately; lamentably; deplorably; grievously; inevitably; presumably; usually; heartbreakingly; obscurely; darkly; strangely; oddly; curiously; mysteriously; unaccountably; irresistibly; inexorably; violently; mercifully; inescapably.

FATALISM

adjectives
vulgar; stubborn; reckless; hysterical; inevitable.

FATALISTIC

adverbs
inveterately; unshakably; implicitly; soberly; staunchly; confidently; incorrigibly; positively; gloomily; delusively; dispassionately; stubbornly; fantastically; calmly; unreasonably; irrationally; unfathomably; vaguely; actually; absurdly; destructively; insanely; credulously; securely; doctrinally.

FATALITY

adjectives
irresistible; all-powerful; inexorable; stark; strange; ironical.

FATE

adjectives
indulgent; tempted; solemn; inexorable; ultimate; special; pure; untoward; unchallenged; relentless; kindly; subsequent; uncommon; cruel; bitter; ignominious; blind; baffling; cramping; tragic; hostile; fixed; adverse; obedient; precious; unenviable; inevitable; awful; varied (pl); incumbent; obdurate; dismal; probable; narrower; tear-compelling; fairest; obliging; uncer-

tain; evil; chequered; vanquished; whimsical; dedicated; happy; pursuing; favoring; deplorable; melancholy; endangered; ungentle; oracular; fabled; vulgar; worldly; harsh; indifferent; ruthless; unconscious; impending; proper; insensate; hapless; thwarting; sundering; monarchial; horrible; undoubted; ample; leafless; ungracious.

verbs
accept—; challenge—; cloud—; confront by —; dodge—; fulfill—; hinge on—; impose by—; mould—; outwit—; preside over—; prophesy—; resign to—; scoff at—; seal—; share—; work out—; —crushes; —deals; —destines; —engulfs; —fashions; —hangs; —moulds; —orders; —pushes; —singles out; —tortures.

(See destiny, necessity, doom, death.)

FATED

adverbs
blindly; adversely; inexorably; inevitably; imperiously; relentlessly; inauspiciously; ominously; portentously; luckily; auspiciously; resistlessly; direly; blessedly; obscurely; propitiously; unluckily; unpropitiously.

FATHER

adjectives
doting; implacable; prosaic; crusading; reverend; illustrious; active; improvident; bustling; electioneering; mitered; groveling; virtuous; joyful; ill-tempered; fond; dreadful; peevish; noble; ghostly; banished; honored; earthly; obdurate; hilarious; strenuous; formidable; vain; hollow; heartless; persecuted; imperial; uncowled; stricken; avaricious; spendthrift; unsuspecting; benignant; narrow-praying; blustering; indulgent; worthy; irate; grimy; jaunty; tender; scholarly; venerable; adoptive; remorseful; impecunious; avaricious; dissolute; judicious; temporal; deceiving; autocratic.

verbs
adopt —; adore —; ape —; idolize —; obtain —; owe to —; respect —; revere —; — advises; — aids; — allows; — assents; — corrects; — declares; — guards; — guides; — maintains; — moulds; — neglects; — nourishes; — pampers; — permits; — pets; — presents; — prevents; — protects; — punishes; — restrains; — scolds; — spoils; — supports; — thrashes.

(See parent, ancestor, author, mother.)

FATHERLAND

adjectives
icebound; heavenly; pleasant; memorable.

FATHERLESS

adverbs
unhappily; forlornly; unluckily; unfortunately; helplessly; drearily; desolately; miserably; wretchedly; pitiably; disconsolately; haplessly; deplorably; cheerlessly; dismally; obviously.

FATHERLY

adverbs
dutifully; indulgently; severely; gently; unnecessarily; quietly; wisely; proudly; providently; lovingly; generously; warmly; humanely; benevolently; sympathetically; comfortingly; amiably; lovingly; graciously; complaisantly; bounteously; benignly; mercifully; magnanimously; tenderly; warmly; softly; accommodatingly; usefully; considerately.

FATHOMLESS

adverbs
abysmally; profoundly; mysteriously; vastly; quietly; shudderingly; drearily; tranquilly; dangerously; immeasurably; incalculably; voicelessly; terrifyingly; inscrutably.

FATIGUE

adjectives
industrial; wild; insidious; extreme; expressed; decreased; unexplainable; excessive; pure; dangerous; painful; mental; undue; alcoholic; sheer; deep; unparalleled; harsh; dreamy; curing; resultant; intolerable; unwonted.

verbs
allay —; alleviate —; avoid —; correct —; dispel —; droop in —; eliminate —; endure —; induce —; inure to —; lessen —; measure —; produce —; recover from —; recuperate from —; — daunts; — dulls; — ensues.

(See exhaustion, weariness.)

FATIGUED

adverbs
inexpressibly; alarmingly; desperately; extremely; excessively; immeasurably; remarkably; inexplicably; painfully; mentally; physically; inordinately; deeply; intolerably; utterly; terribly; seriously; haggardly; gauntly; frightfully; mysteriously; unreasonably; quickly.

FATUITY

adjectives
parental; unspeakable; apparent.

FATUOUS

adverbs
unspeakably; tiresomely; foolishly; vacuously; inanely; idiotically; senselessly; absurdly; waggishly; terribly; preposterously; egregiously; intolerably; emptily; nonsensically; bombastically; pompously; absurdly; vaguely; insignificantly; ordinarily; habitually; frivolously; inconsequentially; endlessly; wearily; plaguedly.

FAUCET

adjectives
defective; rushing; singing; whistling; mixing; shining; dripping.

FAULT

adjectives
inherited; earthly; unforgivable; social; existing; distinctive; unbelievable; beastly; serious; cold; rankest; vile; outfacing; innumerable (pl); grave; glaring; inherent; headstrong; potent; grossest; unpardonable; undeserved; evident; grievous; universal; punishable; irremediable; apparent; brilliant; contrasted; unexpiable; venial; gracious; unwilling; prime; rash; technical; shunning; pernicious; excusable; tragic; ill-favored.

verbs
accept —; atone for —; beset by —; burden with —; compensate for —; confess —; conquer —; denounce —; disclose —; evince —; excuse —; find —; flay —; guard against —; iron out —s; lapse into —; lay — on; overlook —; spare —; subdue —; — blemishes; — glares; — mars.

(See error, mistake, offense.)

FAULTLESS

adverbs
perfectly; incredibly; utterly; marvellously; inexpressibly; obviously; manifestly; immaculately; superbly; splendidly; absolutely; fashionably; rarely; technically; ineffably; remarkably; completely; theoretically; comparatively; exquisitely; overwhelmingly; matchlessly; morally; mechanically; artistically; unapproachably; unbelievably.

FAULTY

adverbs
technically; mechanically; obviously; provokingly; undeniably; intentionally; designedly; purposely; unfortunately; reprehensibly; grievously; inexcusably; unpardonably; irremediably; curiously; strangely; grossly; frightfully; slightly; unfortunately; strategically; absurdly; stupidly; cruelly; ludicrously; horribly.

FAVOR

adjectives
distinguished; heavenly; fairy; generous; sweet; fashionable; unmistakable; dissembled; supreme; gracious; royal; political; special; childish; imperial; ephemeral; trifling; scientific; singular; flattering; divine; equivalent; princely; preferential; ecclesiastical; gastronomical; private.

verbs
bask in —; bestow —; beg —; bid —; compete for —; confer — on; court —; curry — with; deny —; design —; dispense —s; efface —s; entertain — of; fall out of —; flow in — of; meet with —; seek —; win —; yield —s; — fattens.

(See kindness, benefit, advantage.)

FAVOR (v)

adverbs
patently; particularly; manifestly; fruitlessly; universally; unduly; corruptly; incidentally; uncannily; generously; sweetly; politically; childishly; ephemerally; scientifically; singularly; gastronomically; ecclesiastically; privately.

(See support, encourage.)

FAVORABLE

adverbs
highly; profoundly; obviously; certainly; sweetly; cordially; sincerely; undoubtedly; unqualifiedly; unconditionally; heartily; enthusiastically; immediately; graciously; singularly; flatteringly; publicly; unmistakably; considerately; openly; remarkably; marvelously; auspiciously; zealously; actively; altogether.

FAVORITE

adjectives
universal; overwhelming; particular; exclusive; profligate; prime; especial; eternal; general; reigning; indulged; current; perennial; summer; envious; unquestioned.

verbs
acclaim—; admire—; bestow on—; cheer—; choose—; cultivate—; deny—; grant—; gratify—; mark as—; receive—; regard as —; respect—; reveal—; shine on—; —effaces; —requests; —tumbles; —wins.

(See companion, associate, friend, etc.)

adverbs
undeniably; obviously; universally; currently; apparently; enviably; curiously; strangely; unreasonably; openly; offensively; flauntingly; pleasantly; attractively; socially; companionably.

FAVORITISM

adjectives
personal; opposing; apparent; political; annoying.

FAWN

adjectives
sportive; tender; new-roused; nursling; startled; leaping; gamboling; gentle.

FAWN (*v*)

adverbs
obsequiously; servilely; tenderly; sportively; gently; calculatingly; schemingly; slyly; traitorously; impiously.

(See flatter, cringe.)

FAWNING

adverbs
unctuously; fulsomely; servilely; humbly; slavishly; flatteringly; cringingly; abjectly; basely; meanly; obsequiously; pliantly; subtly; sycophantically; shamelessly; artfully; craftily; shrewdly; pretentiously; knavishly; deceitfully; unscrupulously; openly; unashamedly; deferentially; submissively.

FEALTY

adjectives
unswerving; lifelong; forsworn.

FEAR

adjectives
jealous; stark; harrowing; palpitating; phantasmal; mutual; sneaking; conjectural; prodigious; womanly; unaccustomed; indefinable; hideous; chilling; mingled; wonted; ghoulish; political; sweeping; degrading; irrational; surging; sharp; chasmed; mortal; deadly; supernatural; troubling; unnerving; predominant; anguished; superstitious; unspoken; ghastly; servile; abysmal; lingering; clutching; lurking; fretful; foolish; bashful; childlike; oppressive; nagging; maiden; rising; exaggerated; pet; selfish; trembling; horrible; incredible; reverential; unreasonable; haunting; depressive; pathological; scrupulous; spiritual; morbid; ghostly; prudent; dreadful; lessening; natural; vague; numbing; perpetual; general; feminine; hurtful; impatient; premonitory; growing; momentary; various (pl); nameless; slight; pious; never-buried; secret; recanting; specific; universal; strange; excessive; holy; bloodless; slavish; inextinguishable; age-old; terrible; physical; conflicting; faint-footed; prophetic; grim; pale-hearted; pleasing; devouring; tormenting; pitiable; distressing; tender; gloomy; distracted; idiotic; incomprehensible; continual; groundless; petrified; nervous; helpless; anxious; savage; primitive; uneasy; unutterable; remorseless; unaccountable; respectful; inexpressible; unnamed; shuddering; startling; trivial; shivering; yearning; dark; paltry; mysterious; dominant; crushing; scarce-hidden.

verbs
allay—; banish—; beset by—; bespeak—; brush aside—; counteract—; curtail—; dismiss—; dispel—; dissipate—; drown—; eliminate—; entertain—; eradicate—; evoke —; express—; foster—; ground—upon; harbor—; harness—; impregnate—; ingrain—; inspire—; intensify—; justify—; modify—; nourish—; obliterate—; petrify with—; play on—; quake with—; quell—; quiet—; rule by—; rout—; scoff at—; share—; shiver with—; soothe—; subdue—; surmount—; vanquish—; —blights; —chills; —clutches; —coerces; —dominates; —drives; —evaporates; —fetters; —hounds; —insinuates itself; —lurks; —materializes; —melts; —motivates; —numbs; —obsesses; —overshadows; —prevails; —preys upon; —racks; —subsides; —takes possession.

(See dread, terror, apprehension, dismay, consternation, fright, anxiety.)

FEAR (v)

adverbs

unjustifiably; instinctively; inexpressibly; grossly; unreasoningly; jealously; harrowingly; irrationally; superstitiously; abysmally; oppressively; exaggeratedly; unreasonably; hauntingly; pathologically; morbidly; momentarily; secretly; excessively; pitiably; distressingly; incomprehensibly; groundlessly; inexpressibly; mysteriously.

(See dread, apprehend.)

FEARFUL

adverbs

indefinably; childishly; unusually; unwontedly; nervously; superstitiously; fretfully; foolishly; bashfully; incredibly; unreasonably; morbidly; prudently; dreadfully; naturally; vaguely; perpetually; momentarily; constantly; namelessly; secretly; slightly; excessively; strangely; terribly; prophetically; grimly; tormentingly; pitiably; distressingly; tenderly; gloomily; idiotically; incomprehensibly; groundlessly; helplessly; anxiously; uneasily; unutterably; unaccountably; inexpressibly; shudderingly; shiveringly; darkly; coldly; mysteriously; timidly; queerly; curiously; starkly; timorously; genuinely; suspiciously; significantly.

FEARLESS

adverbs

unquestionably; utterly; curiously; oddly; unnaturally; habitually; temperamentally; always; bombastically; boastfully; pretentiously; ostentatiously; apparently; avowedly; allegedly; amazingly; incredibly; confidently; boldly; valiantly; intrepidly; calmly; serenely; quietly; courageously; firmly; doggedly; resolutely; determinedly.

FEASIBLE

adverbs

easily; smoothly; clearly; undeniably; practically; apparently; oddly; entirely; completely; unbelievably; patently; palpably; manifestly; possibly; scarcely; hardly; conceivably; perhaps; uncertainly; doubtfully.

FEAST

adjectives

solemn; artistic; annual; sinful; memorable; sumptuous; continuous; constant; horrible; royal; ample; joyful; Lucullan; endless; sacrificial; accustomed; pagan; popish; marshaled; rural; movable; fashionable; bountiful; convent; princely; wondrous; funeral; impious; nobler; inimitable; superfluous; triumphal; Saturnalian; sunborn; purveying; vernal; reasonable.

verbs

anticipate—; bless—; cater at—; celebrate with—; crown—with; destine for—; enjoy —; enter—; entertain at—; gather for—; gorge at—; hold—; honor at—; invite to—; join in—; partake of—; plan—; prepare—; rejoice at—; —cheers; —commemorates; —gratifies; —refreshes.

(See entertainment, repast, anniversary.)

FEAST (v)

adverbs

convivially; recklessly; annually; triumphantly; bountifully; gluttonously; unstintedly; sumptuously; memorably; idolatrously; lavishly.

(See dine, eat, gratify.)

FEASTING

adjectives

mutual; swinish.

FEAT

adjectives

notable; merchandising; piteous; prodigious; additional; superhuman; inconsiderable; extraordinary; curious; noble; herculean; elaborate; pugilistic; haughty; brilliant; spectacular; dashing; marvelous; warlike; magic; miraculous; incomparable.

verbs

acclaim—; accomplish—; advertise—; applaud—; duplicate—; emulate—; enact—; enjoy—; equal—; exploit—; gasp at—; perfect—; perform—; practise—; praise—; recount—; regale with—; watch—; work—; —awes; —dazzles; —delights; —displays; —enthralls; —pleases; —punctures.

(See act, performance, deed, exploit, achievement.)

FEATHER

adjectives

flying; rumpled; motionless; courteous; superincumbent; molted; decorative; draggled; animated; varicolored (pl); lofty; silky; mottled; drooping; variegated (pl).

verbs

adorn with—; attach—; bristle with—s; clothe with—s; cover with—s; crop—s; de-

corate with—s; deck with—s; display—s; exhibit—s; fledge with—s; furnish—s; molt —s; ornament with—s; pick—s; pluck—; plume with—s; preen—s; provide—s; ruffle —s; rumple—s; rustle—s; shake—s; smooth —s; strip of—s; wave—; wear—s; —floats; —tickles.
(See ornaments.)

FEATURE (of the face)

verbs
age—s; blur—s; characterize—s; cheat of —; cloak—s; cloud—s; contort—s; define —s; discern—s; distinguish—s; inherit—; mark—; obliterate—s; scar—; sketch—; weary—; —s beam; —s express; —s glare; —s glisten; —s gloom; —indicates; —s pucker up; —s shine.
(See shape, form, face.)

FEATURE (part)

verbs
acclaim—; applaud—; appraise—; bar—; conceal—; detect—; eliminate—; embody—; evince—; execute—; incorporate—; negate —; plan—; present—; preserve—; recognize—; schedule—; strike at—.
(See item, characteristic, point.)

FEATURE (v)

adverbs
exclusively; faultlessly; consistently; animatedly; monotonously; characteristically; classically; conspicuously; disastrously; decorously; distinctively; distortedly; dominatingly; eloquently; graphically; harmoniously; irrationally; legitimately; offensively; picturesquely; piquantly; perennially; specifically; dominantly.
(See portray, delineate.)

FEATURES

adjectives
active; added; additional; advanced; agitated; agreeable; air-cooling; alabaster; altered; amazing; angular; angelic; animated; anxious; aristocratic; aquiline; arrogant; ascetic; attractive; astonishing; automatic; awkward; battered; bearded; bearish; bold; beauteous; benevolent; benignant; bewitching; bizarre; bloated; brightest; blurred; bronzed; Caesarean; calm; characteristic; charming; chiseled; clean-cut; classical; clear-cut; clearly-chiseled; coarse; comely; comfortable; commonplace; composed; concealed; conforming; conspicuous; constructive; contorted; convenient; convulsed; corpselike; correct; craggy; crowning; daring; dark; decorated; decorous; delicate; delightful; desirable; desperate; determined; detestable; difficult; disastrous; distinctive; distinguishing; distorted; distressing; divers; diversified; dominant; dripping; dominating; dusky; eager; ebon; eloquent; effective; elongated; embarrassing; embrowned; engrossing; entrancing; essential; epic; evil; exasperating; exceptional; exclusive; expansive; exploitational; expressive; exquisite; extraneous; extraordinary; fabric; fair; familiar; fascinating; ferocious; fervent; fierce; fine; finely-cut; firm; flawless; flexible; flower-like; forbidding; fundamental; gaunt; gay; genial; gentle; geologic; glorious; graphic; grave; haggard; handsome; hand-tailored; harmonious; hawk-like; haughty; healthful; heavy; high; high-priced; homely; hueless; humorous; immovable; important; impassive; impressive; indelible; indistinguishable; ineffable; inherited; innocent; insensible; insipid; intellectual; interesting; iron; intriguing; irrational; kindly; lamentable; large; leading; lean; legitimate; light; long; lovely; majestic; malignant; marked; massive; medieval; melancholy; mild; minor; mobile; mocking; modern; molded; monstrous; natural; neat; new; noble; notable; noteworthy; noticeable; objectionable; offensive; operating; occult; oppressive; original; ornamental; outstanding; pain-drawn; pain-seamed; pallid; passionless; particular; passionate; patented; patrician; peaked; perplexing; peculiar; perennial; persisting; personal; physical; picturesque; piquant; pivot-turning; placid; plastic; positive; pock-marked; poignant; practical; predominant; prevailing; prominent; protective; proscriptive; quality; questionable; quivering; quizzical; rare; recognized; recreational; recurring; redeeming; refined; regular; remarkable; restful; revolting; rigid; rough; rugged; sad; safety; saggy; salient; saturnine; scapegrace; scenic; scowling; sculptured; sensational; Semitic; semi-constructional; sensitive; serious; severe; shrunken; significant; sharp; singular; sinister; slumbering; small; smiling; socialistic; softened; sophisticated; sordid; sorry; sport; special; specific; splendid; square; stain-preventing; stellar; sterile; stern; striking; strategic; strong; structural; style; suffering; sunken; superior; swarthy;

swollen; symmetrical; tanned; thoughtful; tightly-drawn; ugly; unaffected; uncertain; ineloquent; unique; unmistakable; unrevealed; unshaven; unsightly; unusual; upraised; useful; valuable; visible; varied; vital; vivid; wasted; weazened; welcome; well-balanced; well-cared-for; well-cut; well-marked; well-proportioned; worn-out.

FECUNDITY

adjectives
incredible; mental; artificial.

FEDERAL

adverbs
impressively; inescapably; finally; predominantly; imperiously; authoritatively; officially; imperatively; compulsively; autocratically; decisively; conclusively; grandly.

FEDERATION

adjectives
loose; irksome; compact.

verbs
accomplish—; ally with—; condense into—; contract—; dismember—; establish—; form —; join—; organize—; propose—; readjust —; unite—; —advocates; —authorizes; —campaigns; —controls; —delegates; —despairs; —develops; —manages; —performs; —supports.
(See league, alliance, association, union.)

FEE

adjectives
ceremonious; unpredictable; hateful; wandering; prodigious; undeserved.

verbs
accept—; augment—; beg for—; bill—; calculate—; command—; demand—; entitle to —; execute—; expect—; fatten on—; fix—; grant—; hold in—; incur—; limit—; merit —; perform for—; procure—; promise—; refuse—; require—; rob of—.
(See payment, reward, wage.)

FEEBLE

adverbs
pitiably; lamely; hunchedly; forlornly; lugubriously; pleasantly; comfortably; placidly; admittedly; distressingly; passively; plaintively; touchingly; helplessly; utterly; frequently.

FEEBLENESS

adjectives
infantine; boyish; inherent; gathering; negligent; accustomed.

verbs
commit to—; conceal—; convince of—; cure —; degenerate into—; delight in—; fall in —; feign—; guard against—; imply—; indicate—; inflict—; loathe—; minimize—; mourn—; pity—; produce—; resist—; ridicule—; —afflicts; —deters; —prevents.
(See debility, weakness, infirmity.)

FEED (v)

adverbs
serenely; omnivorously; sumptuously; gluttonously; continually; artfully; carefully; delicately; dietetically; scientifically; consistently; regularly; beneficially; sparingly.
(See nourish, subsist.)

FEEDING

adjectives
careful; destructive; faithful; delicate; worthy; fast.

verbs
abstain from—; administer—; anticipate—; attempt—; call for—; crown—with; encourage—; force—; gorge in—; invite to—; join in—; manage—; partake of—; plan—; prepare—; provide—; regulate—; rely upon —; serve—; surfeit—; supervise—; —chokes; —nourishes; —refreshes; —satiates; govern—.
(See food, eating.)

FEEL (v)

adverbs
instinctively; genuinely; sweetly; exquisitely; amiably; turbulently; reverently; maternally; triumphantly; graciously; exuberantly; vindictively; poetically; spontaneously; tyrannically; morbidly; mutually; congenially; compassionately; philanthropically; vehemently; profoundly; spiritually.
(See touch, grope, handle.)

FEELING

adjectives
grateful; peculiar; deep-souled; instinctive; undiminished; sensitive; partisan; genuine; suppressed; subdued; pragmatic; sweet; exaggerated; repressed; empty; artistic; exquisite; amiable; ardent; selfish; con-

gealed; sad; vague; solemn; painful; exasperated; intuitive; strange; sickening; horrible; ineffable; bitter; ancient; feudal; passionate; regenerated; turbulent; dreadful; reciprocal; lofty; high-wrought; bewildered; unmistakable; soapy; reverent; excited; cognate; sacred; anti-clerical; preponderant; triumphant; imaginative; sublime; gracious; expansive; tender; profound; humble; vindictive; apparent; inward; unshared; poetic; spontaneous; remorseful; strangled; exuberant; tight; revolted; morbid; hostile; tyrannical; pent-up; shamed; kindly; grosser; evident; aesthetic; enthusiastic; unfounded; overcharged; mutual; subconscious; rancorous; remorseful; diminished; absurd; universal; annoying; intense; haughty; strange; telltale; fantastic; congenial; burning; dim; compassionate; appreciative; philanthropic; suspicious; ruffled; discordant; queer; ripened; awesome; uneasy; sick; half-ironical; half-superstitious; affectionate; dysphoric; nervous; innermost; mingled; maternal; erroneous; poignant; acute; stilted; upleasant; differentiated; unfilial; immoral; rarest; uncanny; overburdened; potent; unworthy; felicitous; vehement; complicated; dormant; fortified; taut; strained; dissimilar; mercenary; jealous; devotional; democratic; unhappy; wounded; pious; fancied; resultant; superior; uncomfortable; profound; mightiest; domestic; warm; hangdog; worn-out; ill; benevolent; indescribable; restless; blissful; liberal; selfish; holiest; lingering; contrary; half-defined; resentful; noble; national; subtler; ungovernable; amicable; subordinate; individual; refreshing; genial; embarrassed; lethargic; unspeakable; sincere; kindred; tight-throated; breathless; repressed; energetic; martial; honest; playing; heady; oldish; forlorn; uncertain; spiritual.

verbs

abate—; analyze—; awaken—; capture—; cherish—; deaden—; disturb—; divulge—; engender—; evince—; evoke—; excite—; experience—; express—; foster—; gratify —; guard—; harbor—; hide—; impart—; inflame—; inhibit—; injure—; instill—; manifest—; mask—; modify—; outrage—; pen up—; petrify—; probe—; provoke—; quicken—; regard with—; reveal—; rouse —; soothe—; stir up—; strain—; strengthen —; subdue—; suffuse with—; tamper with —; tinge—; vent—; voice—; wound—; —blossoms; —dominates; —envelops; —explodes; —impends; —impresses; —overpowers; —overwhelms; —persists; —pervades; —pours from; —rests upon; —runs high; —subsides.

(See sensation, emotion, sentiment, consciousness, conviction.)

FEET

adjectives

tender; multitudinous; dancing; delicate; pattering; marshy; scuffing; indolent; industrious; accursed; reluctant; whispering; undelaying; dainty; wicked; wanton; unwearied; aimless; overlarge; charming; rugged; untrammelled; twinkling; trampling; faltering; restless; uncertain; racing; dimpled; fear-sped; clammy; golden; errant; daring; blistered; webbed; tripping; willing; strolling; straddling; small; silvery; marshalled; angel; dangling; swift; flying; aristocratic; slender; tortured; erring; distorted; impious; unshod; wary; bare; romping; glorious; shuffling; noiseless; stumbling; wandering; shod; trembling; claw; moccasined; scurrying; cautious; hurried; shoe-encased; churlished; infinitesimal; desultory; approaching; substantial; windy; hastening; airy; grappling; morning-winged; mournful; running; consecrated; staggering; myriad; veined; spreading; peace-abiding; wayward; bleeding; rushing; careless; adroit; feathery; bruised; radiant; big; muddy; charging; dirty; countless; silent; aching; echoing; shrivelled; calloused; sagging; desperate; lagging; leaden; wild; timorous; ivory-channeled; skipping; eager; jumping; cursed; stealthy; faultless; tiny; swirling; swift; frenzied; nimble; ample; heroic; huge; tottering; none-too-steady; unsure; immovable; obstinate; halting; dragging; indifferent; sweaty; ragged; graceless; slipshod; deformed; crippled; swollen; faltering; arched; slim; elongated; narrow; cloven; squared; padded; innumerable; slippered; heavily-shod; sandaled; velvet; clay; piggish; clattering; thudding; hobbled; stockinged; satined; rubbered; thumping; pounding; wandering; scampering; stamping; marching; little; shuffling; naked; parched; outraged; uncivilized; trusting; tireless; wary; bound; tangled; unseen; departing; protruding; unguided; educated; prodding; frantic; creeping; booted; thick; mad; clawing; immortal; fetter-incumbered; plundering.

FEIGN (v)

adverbs

calculatingly; slyly; cleverly; expressly; treacherously; artfully; skillfully; deftly; fawningly; dissolutely; roguishly; knavishly.

(See pretend, simulate, assume.)

FEINT

adjectives

preliminary; solitary; diplomatic.

FELICITATION

verbs

accept—; acknowledge—; anticipate—; bestow—; compliment with—; delight in—; enjoy—; exchange—; express—; extend—; greet with—; incur—; inspire—; offer—; present—; produce—; promote—; pronounce—; receive—; return—; thank for—; —pleases.

(See congratulation.)

FELICITOUS

adverbs

auspiciously; opportunely; happily; supremely; superbly; grandly; splendidly; inexpressibly; undeniably; altogether; consummately; utterly; singularly; unexpectedly; harmoniously; delightfully; rapturously; extremely; unusually; uncommonly.

FELICITY

adjectives

earthly; engaging; exalted; supreme; expressional; uninterrupted; singular; eternal; true; pastoral; curious; domestic; Arcadian.

FELLOW

adjectives

chuckle-headed; absurd; lovable; tainted; jolly; sturdy; brash; lusty; amiable; scurvy; woodland; underbred; fine-spoken; clever; clean-living; intelligent; tractable; generous; light-hearted; industrious; bustling; common-looking; gaunt; ill-visaged; jovial-looking; loathsome; riotous; unrefined; honorary; guileless; robustious; muffled; massive; great-shouldered; muscled; lewd; merry; manly; sharp; amiable-looking; impudent; feeble; noble; pestilent; funniest; good-natured; hearty; broad-faced; dapper; fierce; valiant; cunning; admirable; wiry; sallow; enviable; heartless; worthless; indignant; craggy-faced; gnomish; odd; unaccountable; fluctuating; irresolute; voluble; slender; prattling; hilding; captious; hale; hard-bitten; big; handsome; back-slapping; rollicking; villainous; good-hearted; easy-going; devil-may-care; kindly; lawless; open-hearted; brilliant; gentle-mannered; plausible; unthoughtful; innocent; sneaking; talkative; enthusiastic; unstudious; vulgar-looking; officious; engaging; swarthy; smock-faced; coal-blackened; florid; prettier; magnificent-looking; gallant; hulking; meager; verdant; brawny; stale; licentious; white-bearded; hatchet-faced; sheepish; awkward; respected; desperate; foppish; bluff; blunt; indiscreet; self-assured; conceited; celestial; melancholy; abominable; beetle-browed; powerful; marvelous; witty; eloquent; prodigious; fine; staring; inexorable; ghostly; disgruntled; capricious; insignificant; simpering; intelligent; courageous; good-humored; roguish; ignorant; noisy; unweighing; notable; good; dull; vicious; dissolute.

FELLOWSHIP

adjectives

sweet; pleasant; superficial; close-linked; accursed; generous.

verbs

admit—; build up—; enjoy—; enter into—; entitle to—; honor—; instil—; obtain—; necessitate—; participate in—; receive in—; refuse—; reject—; renounce—; separate from—; share in—; shatter—; unite in—; —honors; —predominates.

(See companionship, association.)

FELON

adjectives

acquitted; larcenous

FELONIOUS

adverbs

dastardly; outrageously; contemptibly; obviously; openly; heinously; infamously; basely; grossly; shamelessly; scandalously; brutally; atrociously; scurvily; diabolically; terribly; frightfully; horridly; insanely; venomously; fiendishly.

FELT

adjectives

faded; clean.

FEMALE

adjectives

buxom; irresponsible; elderly; frivolous; elegant; delicate; sour-faced; anemic; hysteric; shivering; tattered; bewildered; unimpeachable; upholstered; parthenogenetic; large; desirable; muscular; unattached; angular; firm-faced; formidable; grim.

FEMININE

adverbs
daintily; sweetly; delightfully; ravishingly; ineffably; seductively; bewitchingly; charmingly; lovably; utterly; provokingly; wantonly; weakly; dependently; irritatingly; clingingly; comfortingly; gracefully; graciously; altogether.

FEMININITY

adjectives
stigmatized; collective; rampant; disquieting; flagrant; desirable.

FENCE

adjectives
woven-wire; straggling; distorted; elaborate; bushy; pitiless; verbal; locust; split-rail; hurdle; whitewashed; spiritual; weather-beaten.

verbs
break through—; construct—; erect—; fortify with—; hurdle—; jump—; leap—; level —; provide—; repair—; skirt—; straddle —; surround with—; —bars; —defends; —deters; —encloses; —guards; —hinders; —limits; —partitions; —protects; —repels; —restricts; —screens; —shields; —wards off; —yields.

(See defence, wall.)

FENCE (v)

adverbs
deftly; skillfully; artfully; vigorously; expertly; professionally; fascinatingly; mentally; courageously; intelligently; arrogantly.

(See evade, shift.)

FENDER

verbs
attach—; bump—; clod—; crack—; damage —; dent—; run into—; rust—; secure—; splash—; split—; spray—; streamline—; strike—; —s collide; —guards; —prevents; —protects; —rattles; —shimmies; —squeaks; —vibrates.

FERMENT

adjectives
putrid; foreign; alcoholic; microscopic; anarchistic; violent; subtle; tumultuous; active; political; irresistible.

FERMENT (v)

adverbs
putridly; alcoholically; microscopically; violently; subtly; tumultuously; politically; irresistibly; actively.

(See decay, excite.)

FERMENTATION

adjectives
vinous; offensive; natural.

verbs
agitate to —; control —; employ —; excite to —; give rise to —; hinder —; incur —; occasion —; produce —; subject to —; suffer —; undergo —; work —; — aids; — results; — sours; — subsides.

(See decomposition, transformation.)

FERN

adjectives
discolored; luxuriant; water-loving; minute; exquisite; metallic; lacelike; sprouting.

FEROCIOUS

adverbs
savagely; inexpressibly; cruelly; diabolically; unspeakably; atrociously; brutally; pretentiously; comically; dutifully; unduly; mercilessly; ruthlessly; inhumanly; malevolently; coldly; unnaturally; unbelievably; stonily; barbarously; heinously; utterly; uncommonly; unutterably.

FEROCITY

adjectives
gloomy; deft; reckless; uncommon; brutal; diabolic; dull; pitiless; cruel; vigilant; admirable; frightful; unmitigated; martial; senseless; terrific; moist; clammy; mad; hair-raising; ill-concealed; blazing; incredible; unlimited; ungovernable; lurid; smoldering.

verbs
abate —; display —; escape —; fire with —; generate —; incur —; inflame to —; occasion —; ponder —; provoke to —; recover from —; salve —; shake with —; subdue —; — alarms; — blights; — destroys; — frightens; — overwhelms; — terrifies.

(See cruelty, fury.)

FERRY

adjectives
improvised; antiquated; electric.

FERTILE

adverbs
creatively; productively; luxuriantly; abundantly; fruitfully; teemingly; richly; plenteously; inexhaustibly; incredibly; remarkably; superbly; amazingly; incomparably; matchlessly; satisfactorily; surprisingly; naturally; highly; completely.

FERTILITY

adjectives
triumphant; personal; exuberant; teeming; superior; incredible; inexhaustible; dauntless; absolute; amazing; singular; improved; intellectual; unrivaled; incomparable.

FERTILIZER

verbs
advocate —; apply —; broadcast —; employ —; enrich with —; gorge with —; introduce —; purchase —; stock with —; supply —; — enhances; — enriches; — generates; — replenishes.

FERVENT

adverbs
warmly; sincerely; ardently; zealously; eagerly; significantly; earnestly; actively; utterly; heartily; fanatically; uncommonly; remarkably; contagiously; piously; magnetically; eloquently; feverishly; passionately; youthfully; dynamically; intensely; tremendously; solemnly; amazingly.

FERVID

adverbs
intensely; emotionally; contagiously; infectiously; feverishly; nervously; peculiarly; oddly; curiously; abnormally; strangely; glowingly; hotly; impressively; rapturously; breathlessly; zealously; absorbingly; fanatically; impetuously; magnificently.

FERVOR

adjectives
contagious; inward; renewed; religious; superficial; unprecedented; magnetic; disinterested; eloquent; undiminished; poetic; feverish; lurid; intolerable; passionate; revolutionary; equinoctial; meridian; devotional; exalted; involuntary; racy; youthful; vain; primitive; nationalistic; dynamic; patriotic; blazing; fascinating; emotional; intense; defensive; animated; tremendous; artificial; lyric; solemn; romantic; prophetic; loving; simple; noontide.

verbs
arouse —; bridle —; cool —; execute with —; fill with —; flush with —; inflame with —; instil —; join with —; pitch to —; quench —; replace —; shape with —; starve —; sweat with —; waste —; — animates; — boils; — blazes; — glows; — rages; — torments.

(See ardor, intensity, zeal, enthusiasm.)

FESTAL

adverbs
delightfully; joyously; charmingly; companiably; chattily; convivially; noisily; happily; jovially; gregariously; magnificently; splendidly; brilliantly; sparklingly; sumptuously; highly; elaborately; extravagantly; uproariously; unexpectedly; ineffably; tumultuously; excitedly; inexpressibly; innocently; spontaneously; exultantly; radiantly; supremely; highly.

FESTER (*v*)

adverbs
malignantly; hideously; horridly; disgustingly; fatally; repeatedly; continually; agonizingly; hatefully; devastatingly.

(See pain, suffer.)

FESTIVAL

adjectives
solemn; religious; torchlight; domestic; magnificent; sumptuous; nocturnal; carousing; democratic; annual; circling; memorial; high; brilliant; recurring; community; notorious; extravagant; licentious; elaborate; holiday; clamoring; grandiose.

FESTIVE

adverbs
hilariously; boisterously; uproariously; informally; happily; gaily; gloriously; utterly; absurdly; ineffably; blithely; irrepressibly; merrily; unaccountably; unexpectedly; noisily; magnificently; intimately; spontaneously; radiantly; tumultuously; inexpressibly.

FESTIVITY

adjectives
brilliant; boisterous; final; compelled; holiday; maudlin.

FESTOONS

adjectives
scalloped; looping; flung; graceful; ethereal.

FETE (v)

adverbs
ceremonially; blithesomely; handsomely; joyfully; magnificently;. sumptuously; annually; memorially; brilliantly; notoriously; extravagantly; elaborately; grandiosely.
(See celebrate, feast.)

FETID

adverbs
offensively; rankly; horridly; unbearably; mustily; suffocatingly; impossibly; unspeakably; abominably; noisomely; terribly; disagreeably; frightfully; malodorously; foully; strongly; grossly; pestilentially; unwholesomely; perniciously; poisonously; extremely; inconceivably.

FETISH

adjectives
popular; patriotic; exploded; carved; wooden; much-loved.

FETTER

verbs
chain with —s; clap into —s; commit to —s; escape —s; fasten —s; free from —s; hobble in —s; impose —s; load with —s; loose —s; release from —s; relieve of —s; relinquish —s; secure —s; shackle with —s; shake off —s; — binds; — checks; — confines; — constrains; — guards; — hinders; — prevents; — restrains; — restricts; — tortures; — vexes.
(See bond, shackle, chain.)

FETTERS

adjectives
gratuitous; triple; brazen; rose-blossom; adamantine; galling; unmeasured; creed-imposed; riven; fleshly.

FEUD

adjectives
fatal; fresh; bitter; fruitful; private; lasting; internal; dismal; revamped; primeval; mutual; tribal; relentless; grim; long-standing; age-long; nasty; murderous; deadly; domestic; personal; ancient; futile; hereditary.

verbs
activate —; arouse —; beget —; carry on —; clash in —; convert into —; declare —; enjoy —; entangle in —; inflame into —; instigate —; interrupt —; justify —; prevent —; rankle into —; renew —; root out —; — agitates; —continues; — disturbs; — flares up; — originates; compete in —.
(See strife, hostility, enmity, animosity, bitterness, quarrel.)

FEUDALISM

verbs
abhor —; bring under —; check —; convert into —; incline to —; influence —; overthrow —; practise —; recognize —; reject —; subject to —; support —; — bridles; — clutches; — deprives; — originates; — persists; — reduces; — stultifies; — survives; — treads on; — tyrannizes.
(See system.)

FEUDATORY

adjectives
mutinous; disaffected; tyrannical.

FEVER

adjectives
contagious; eruptive; ravenous; rheumatic; cruel; irregular; low; violent; fitful; prevalent; swamp; intermittent; bilious; high; malignant; unhallowed; infectious; splenic; rapid; raging; morbid; gnawing; malarial; typhus; envious; puerperal; riotous; obvious; tortured; lurking; deadly; perpetual; acute; childbed; hunting; burning; inflammatory; slow.

verbs
accompany by —; allay —; attend with —; characterize by —; come down with —; contract —; control —; develop —; heighten —; induce —; predispose to —; reduce —; retard —; transmit —; — burns; — consumes; — continues; — devours; — grips; — heats; — infects; — persists; — rages; — smoulders; — subdues.
(See excitement, disease.)

FEVERISH

adverbs
cruelly; violently; terribly; highly; extremely; obviously; dangerously; alarmingly; uncomfortably; fearfully; deliriously; acutely; dreadfully; hysterically; deplorably; burningly; restlessly; wildly; unusually; uncommonly; curiously; peculiarly.

FEW

adjectives
unscornful; far-visioned; desperate; favored; comparative; privileged; hateful; chosen.

FEW

adverbs
remarkably; extremely; strangely; lamentably; significantly; deplorably; miserably; wretchedly; fortunately; happily; curiously; mercifully; presumably.

FIASCO

adjectives
mountainous; official.

FIBER

adjectives
fleecy; pusillanimous; secret; ancestral; civic; resonant; ligneous; crude; tough; tenacious; delicate; flaccid; genuine; spiritual; moral; quivering; unexperienced; twisting; intellectual; sensitive; coarser; maguey.

FIBRE

verbs
bind with —; compose of —; connect —s; consist of —; develop —; draw into —; exhibit —; furnish with —; join —; knot —; produce —; rig with —; shred —; stretch —; swathe in —; twist —; weave —; — connects; — girdles; — hangs; — links.

FIBRIN

adjectives
coagulated; increased; exudative.

FICKLE

adverbs
disgustingly; uncertainly; unstably; mercurially; changeably; irresolutely; capriciously; whimsically; unfortunately; remarkably; exceedingly; sensationally; undependably; unhappily; deplorably; habitually; temperamentally; irresolutely; erratically; waywardly; terribly.

FICTION

adjectives
luxuriant; native; sensational; convenient; evasive; romantic; serious; bold; mythological; improbable; extravagant; picturesque; conventional; monstrous; short-lived; distinguished; unmitigated; frothy; introspective; current; sentimental; contemporary.

verbs
cast away —; compose —; condemn —; consume —; criticize —; desire —; devise —; distinguish from —; embroider —; prefer —; produce —; reject —; relate —; select —; steep in —; turn into —; — charms; — confuses; — copies; —delights; — diverts; — enchants; — informs; — influences; — instructs; — interests; — pleases; — poisons; — transports; — unwinds.

(See story, novel, narrative, myth.)

FICTITIOUS

adverbs
harmlessly; allegedly; avowedly; undoubtedly; whimsically; nonsensically; suppositiously; extravagantly; probably; grotesquely; fantastically; ironically; obviously; manifestly; ingeniously; romantically; preposterously; utterly; surprisingly; completely; hypothetically; dreamily; innocently; wildly.

FIDDLE

adjectives
nocturnal; uncivilized.

FIDDLER

adjectives
diligent; rascal; rollicking; peripatetic.

FIDELITY

adjectives
conjugal; eye-taking; doglike; unswerving; undying; utmost; undeviating; eternal; scrupulous; minute; marvelous; assured; realistic; rigid; inviolable; subtle; flawless; dull; unwavering; long-tried; intense; reverent; sober; unblemished; sorrowful; lifelike; profound; historic; pastoral; diving; true-hearted; noteworthy; everlasting.

verbs
abuse —; appreciate —; arouse —; bestow —; buy —; depend on —; endow with —; entwine with —; exact —; incûr —; instil —; nourish —; rivet —; shake —; strengthen —; support with —; swear —; threaten —; violate —; — endears; — endures; — palls; — perishes.

(See faithfulness, loyalty.)

FIDGET (*v*)

adverbs
uneasily; unceasingly; impatiently; painfully; embarrassedly; unpleasantly; secretly; fruitlessly; suppressedly.

(See move, stir, jump.)

FIDGETY

adverbs
suspiciously; terribly; unnecessarily; annoyingly; vexatiously; uneasily; uncomfortably; fussily; officiously; clamorously; excitably; hysterically; foolishly; impatiently; irrepressibly; curiously; peculiarly; oddly; odiously; strangely; significantly; atrociously; unpleasantly; extremely; needlessly.

FIELD

verbs
capture —; clothe —; crop —; deplete —; dominate —; double —; encumber —; entrench —; fence —; invade —; litter —; lord over —; pioneer —; plod across —; preempt —; replenish —; sow —; tap —; tramp across —; usurp —; wall —; — extends; — lies; — slumbers; — stretches.
(See meadow, land.)

FIELDER
(*baseball or cricket*)

verbs
contract for —; fire —; hire —; release —; trade —; — catches; — chases; — covers; — drops; — fields; — holds out; — juggles; — misjudges; — muffs; — races; — runs; — slides; — slips; — snares; — spears; — sprints; — steals; — stops; — returns; — traps; — whips.
(See player, athlete.)

FIELDS

adjectives
gray-green; emerald; frost-bitten; whitened; glistening; ripened; sun-parched; windswept; sparse; billowing; fertile; soft; wet; untrodden; picturesque; stubble; rolling; tremendous; uncrowded; virgin; untouched; fruitless; crimsoned; bloody; drowned; molding; barren; swamped; useful; conquered; disturbed; tented; grazing; plowed; fragrant; archaeological; fenceless; weedy; spring; amaranth; aesthetic; desolate; raingullied; swelling; smoky; blossoming; wanton; hunting; encompassing; uncarved; welldressed; twilight; fallow; unchartered; productive; silken; wintry; remnant; subterranean; feathered; extensive; beautiful; economic; poisonous; illimitable; tobaccojetted; hard-fought; coal; industrial; deserted; joyless; sedgy; abandoned; untried; magnetic; interpretative; somber; azure; languishing; stricken; teeming; sequestered; electrostatic.

FIEND

adjectives
despiteful; foul; stout; incarnate; shivering; father; consummate; possessing; kindred; infernal; abandoned; impetuous; cursed; lubber; human; delicate; malignant; viewless; glaring; sneering.

FIENDISH

adverbs
unspeakably; inexpressibly; uncommonly; brutally; incomprehensibly; unthinkably; odiously; atrociously; heinously; flagrantly; outrageously; outlandishly; grotesquely; inscrutably; barbarously; coldly; stonily; diabolically; inhumanly; unnaturally; defiantly; ominously; ungovernably; uncontrollably; insatiably.

FIERCE

adverbs
implacably; incredibly; intentionally; barbarously; cruelly; ungovernably; impetuously; vehemently; uproariously; brutally; outrageously; fantastically; abruptly; uncontrollably; savagely; irrepressibly; sarcastically; dreadfully; bitterly; explosively; irately; blusteringly; relentlessly; pitilessly; remarkably; amazingly.

FIERCENESS

adjectives
unscrupulous; brutal; suppressed; dramatic; intense.

FIG

adjectives
luscious; large; tasty; over-ripe.

FIGHT

adjectives
inextricable; unflinching; miscellaneous (pl); portentous; isolated; murderous; desultory; bloody; furious; sublimated; ensuing; serious; trench; unavailing; arduous; heavy; futile; ever-losing; factional; running; desperate; winning; memorable; successful; strenuous; tumultuous; showdown; sea-convulsing; manful; vulturous; incessant; dreadful; unequal; dubious; mortal; bitter.

verbs
accept —; augur —; conduct —; evade —; gird for —; lack —; participate in —; reopen —; rouse to —; schedule —; show —;

stage —; wage —; witness —; —embitters; — grows; — rages; — wanes; — waxes; pledge to —; precipitate —.

(See strife, struggle, battle, conflict, combat.)

FIGHT (v)

adverbs

murderously; desultorily; furiously; unavailingly; memorably; strenuously; manfully; dubiously; mortally; viciously; vaingloriously; stolidly; simultaneously; rebelliously; gallantly; doggedly; magnificently; sanguinarily; ostentatiously; vindictively.

(See combat, battle, struggle.)

FIGHTER

adjectives

infuriated; stubborn; considerable; effective; unimaginable; undisciplined; malicious; fearless; reputed; aggressive; ruthless.

verbs

cheer —; condition —; cow —; cuff —; goad —; hack —; incite —; sponge —; spur —; urge —; — bangs; — beats; — bruises; — clinches; — cuts; — dances; — dodges; — drops; — ducks; — feints; — flinches; — jumps; — practises; — punches; — reels; — retreats; — sags; — skips; — slams; — slips; — tallies; — taps; — whacks; — winces.

FIGMENT

adjectives

seductive; idle; imaginative.

FIGURE

verbs

accept —s; bandy —s; cite —s; compile —s; delineate —s; deluge with —s; juggle —s; publish —s; quote —s; scribble —s; splotch —s; —s claim; —s pour in; — soars.

(See digit, number, amount.)

FIGURE (general)

adjectives

able; absurd; advancing; allegorical; aged; alluring; ample; appealing; ardent; arrestive; athletic; august; battered; belligerent; beloved; benignant; bent; bestial; blue-clad; blurred; bony; bouncing; bulky; buoyant; buxom; cherubic; clever; cloyed; colorful; colossal; comfortable; comical; comparative; compelling; conspicuous; contorted; cool; cosmopolitan; courtly; cowering; crabbed; credible; crouched; crumpled; curious; dainty; dark; dashing; defenseless; defiant; dejected; demure; departing; desolate; dignified; dim; diminutive; discreet; dismal; distinguished; distorted; dominant; domineering; dramatic; draped; drawn; dressed; dwarfed; eager; elegant; emaciated; emblematical; enameled; enchanting; energetic; enigmatic; enormous; epauletted; erect; eternal; excited; exquisite; exuberant; famous; fatigued; fashionable; fawning; flat; flexible; foregoing; forlorn; formless; frail; fragmentary; full-grown; furtive; gagged; gallant; gaunt; geometric; ghastly; girlish; glowing; gorilla-like; grandiose; grappling; grave; grotesque; heroic; growing; haloed; heavy; horrid; huddled; hurrying; ideal; imperious; incalculable; independent; indifferent; indistinguishable; inert; influential; innocent; inscrutable; insignificant; interesting; international; irridescent; irrelevant; jaunty; kneeling; lagging; lawless; lax; leading; lean; legendary; limping; literary; lithe; little; lost; lumbering; lurid; lurking; magnetic; majestic; marvelous; masculine; massive; mean; melancholy; memorable; menacing; minor; mocking; miserable; misshapen; monosyllabic; motionless; mountainous; mournful; muffled; mummy-like; mythic; naive; national; nautical; neglected; negligible; nervous; noble; notable; nude; odious; ominous; ornamental; osseous; outlandish; outstanding; pale; panting; pathetic; perfect; petite; pinched; picturesque; pitiful; plastic; pliant; podgy; poetic; poignant; portentous; powerful; preserved; principal; prominent; prone; prostrate; puny; quadrilateral; quaint; quivering; quixotic; rapid; rare; reclining; recumbent; reeling; related; respected; resplendent; retreating; ridiculous; rigid; romantic; rounded; rustic; salient; sardonic; sauntering; semi-legendary; shaking; shameless; shapeless; shrewd; silent; shrinking; shriveled; shuddering; shrouded; silhouetted; sinister; sluggish; skinny; sleek; smart; sob-shaken; solitary; somber; spiritless; sprawled; spry; stalwart; stiff; stocky; stolid; stooping; straight; stricken; strong; stunted; stupendous; sunburned; superb; supple; svelte; swaying; sylphlike; symbolical; tabulated (pl); talented; tatterdemalion; tense; thickset; tottering; unattractive; tragic; tremendous; trim; truculent; turbulent; typical; uncouth; uniformed; unique; unkempt; unobtrusive; veiled; venerable; vigorous;

vestlike; wasted; weak; well-loved; well-molded; whirling; white-clad; wild; winsome; wiry; wizened; wooden; worthy; tall; wretched; writhing; young; radiant; quaking; queenly; quiet.

FIGURE
(*physique*)

verbs
blur—; conceal—; corset—; develop—; enhance—; forge—; guard—; illuminate—; jeopardize—; nurture—; silhouette—; uncoil—; visualize—; —looms; —s mill; —symbolizes; —writhes.
(See shape, form.)

FIGURE (*v*)

adverbs
conspicuously; deliberately; absurdly; prominently; allegorically; appealingly; belligerently; benignantly; colorfully; comically; domineeringly; dramatically; irrelevantly; fashionably; grandiosely; lawlessly; luridly; mythically; negligibly; picturesquely; portentously; ornamentally; saliently; typically; unobtrusively.
(See calculate, contrive.)

FILE
(*catalogue or cabinet*)

verbs
arrange in—; assemble in—; catalogue—; clean—; destroy—; dig into—; feed—; go through—; lodge in—; prepare—; preserve in—; pull from—; rank in—; refer to—; search—; store in—; wade through—; —aids; —arranges; —facilitates; —separates.
(See list, catalogue, collection, cabinet.)

FILE
(*general*)

adjectives
endless; extensive; newspaper; glittering; moldering; lengthening; four-ranked; successive (pl); straggling; droning.

FILE
(*tool*)

verbs
employ—; slide—; yield to—; —abrades; —evens; —finishes; —glazes; —gnaws; —grates; —grinds; —nicks; —polishes; —reduces; —removes; —restores; —scratches; —sharpens; —smooths; —wears down.

FILE (*v*)

adverbs
sedately; painstakingly; noiselessly; endlessly; monotonously; stragglingly; patiently; ceaselessly; solemnly; incessantly.
(See smooth, cut, walk.)

FILIBUSTER (*v*)

adverbs
bombastically; wordily; vigorously; exasperatingly; venomously; repeatedly; uncontrollably.
(See hinder, prevent, argue.)

FILL (*v*)

adverbs
adequately; creditably; efficiently; generously; amply; faultlessly; cleverly; partially; greedily; graciously; constantly; skillfully; exclusively; scantily; systematically.
(See satisfy, occupy.)

FILLING

adjectives
continuous; systematic; adequate.

FILM
(*camera*)

adjectives
color; sooty; celluloid; supersensitive; exposed; iridescent.

FILM
(*covering*)

adjectives
transitory; glossy; sanguine; adherent; shadowy; permanent; half-drawn; base; clogging.

verbs
break—; cover with—; emerge from—; penetrate—; remove—; —dims; —envelops; —floats; —forms; —grows; —hides; —hinders; —obscures; —prevents.
(See membrane, cover.)

FILM
(*picture*)

verbs
acclaim—; applaud—; ban—; bar—; censor—; criticize—; cut—; develop—; enjoy—; expose—; feature—; guard—; legalize—; manipulate—; preview—; rave about—; —burlesques; —satirizes; —portrays.

FILTH

adjectives
squalid; undiluted.

verbs
abhor—; collect—; detest—; drag through —; expose—; fling—; forbid—; gather—; live in—; loathe—; purge of—; reek with —; remove—; revolt at—; shun—; suffer —; swarm with—; wallow in—.
(See dirt.)

FILTHY

adverbs
grossly; coarsely; unspeakably; incredibly; grotesquely; horribly; abominably; grimily; foully; beastly; offensively; slovenly; squalidly; unpardonably; inexcusably; unreasonably; needlessly; hideously; unwarrantably; piteously; pitiably; deplorably; outlandishly; wretchedly; singularly; exceptionally; extraordinarily.

FIN

verbs
cut off—s; course with—s; cruise with—s; employ—s; injure—; insert—s; paddle with —s; support with—s; swim with—s; —s flap; —s flip; —s lash; —s navigate; —s project; —s propel; —s steer.

FINAL

adverbs
tragically; conclusively; heartbreakingly; egotistically; pompously; acrimoniously; officially; irrevocably; ultimately; catastrophically; elaborately; hopelessly; decisively; absolutely; definitely; unmistakably; inevitably; unchangeably; unimpeachably; dogmatically; authoritatively; authentically; clearly.

FINALE

adjectives
ludicrous; wonderful.

verbs
approach—; compose—; encore—; enjoy—; perfect—; play—; rehearse—; render—; —completes; —concludes; —delights; —disposes of; —ends; —pleases; —terminates; —winds up.
(See end, conclusion.)

FINALITY

adjectives
unmistakable; consecrated; unshakable; helpless; brutal.

FINANCE (*v*)

adverbs
niggardly; soundly; scientifically; ceremoniously; pragmatically; ingenuously; professionally; unscrupulously; unethically; ingeniously.
(See provide, manage.)

FINANCES

adjectives
declining; pitiful; low; unsound; prospective.

verbs
accumulate—; amass—; clear up—; conceal—; deplete—; destroy—; drain—; imperil—; manipulate—; patch up—; pervert —; provide—; rally—; shake—; strain—; —accrue; —accumulate; —dwindle.
(See income, revenue, funds.)

FINANCIAL

adverbs
inescapably; naturally.

FINANCIER

adjectives
unscrupulous; accurate.

verbs
beseech—; curb—; employ—; provide—; ruin—; —accomodates; —accumulates; —amasses; —collects; —conducts; —controls; —demands; —deposits; —invests; —judges; —levies; —manages; —operates; —persuades; —recruits; —secures; —supports; —swindles.
(See manager.)

FIND

adjectives
consequent; definite; important; right; ghastly.

FIND (*v*)

adverbs
inevitably; eventually; invariably; conclusively; ultimately; locally; intuitively; distinctly; frequently; officially; promptly; consequer /; definitely.
(Se acquire, attain, discover.)

FINDING

adjectives
malicious; specific; pertinent; scientific.

verbs
chance on—; consider—; determine—; elucidate—; endorse—; examine—; expose—; furnish—; inquire about—; inspect—; labor for—; observe—; owe—to; pay for—; pick up—; preserve—; procure—; produce—; provide—; reveal—; supply—; view—; —aids; —clarifies; —reveals.
(See discovery.)

FINE

verbs
anticipate—; agree upon—; condemn to—; evade—; exact—; execute—; exempt from —; impose—; incur—; lament—; levy—; obtain—; pass—on; pronounce—; remit—; settle—; subject to—; suffer—; —compensates; —punishes; —reduces; —releases; —restrains.
(See penalty, money, sum, payment.)

FINE (v)

adverbs
heavily; unscrupulously; punitively; legally; unethically; maliciously; cruelly; sternly.
(See dispossess, punish, attack.)

FINERY

adjectives
metropolitan; priceless; grotesque; worthless; gaudy; tawdry; verdant; shimmering; bright; thin; elaborate; ruinous; scarlet; barbaric; natural.

verbs
addict to—; adorn in—; appreciate—; bedeck in—; clothe in—; crave—; deck in—; decorate in—; degenerate into—; display—; dress in—; envy—; exhibit—; indulge in—; observe—; prefer—; sport (colloq.)—; view —; —amazes; —attracts; —impresses; —consoles.
(See ornament, splendor.)

FINES

adjectives
enormous; aggregate; unfair; wholesale.

FINGER

verbs
beckon with—; bend—; cramp—; cut—; distend—; drum with—; extend—; level—at; prick—; snap—s; —s clutch; —s fly; —s fumble with; —s hover near; —s twist; —s twitch.
(See digit, thumb, hand.)

FINGER (v)

adverbs
significantly; nervously; delicately; tremulously; feverishly; tremblingly; intimately; lingeringly; caressingly; fumblingly; rheumatically; lustfully; authoritatively; cannily; agilely.
(See handle, touch.)

FINGERNAIL

verbs
bite—; break—; chew—; claw with—; clean —; clip—; cream—; dig with—; employ—; excavate with—; file—; jag—; manicure—; polish—; round—; shape—; split—; trim—; —s attract; —s scratch; —s shine.

FINGERNAILS

adjectives
rose-tinted; pointed; unimpeachable; untidy; long; sharp; shiny-rouged; talon-like; crooked; yellow; polished.

FINGERS

adjectives
guiding; tapering; prisoned; tremulous; uncut; slim; deft; searching; exquisite; listless; merciless; dimpled; slender; artistic; patient; careless; knotted; dewy; numbed; icy; outstretched; fevered; imitative; sharp; clumsy; nimble; skilled; ferocious; plastic; hushing; bloody; trembling; unresisting; needle-marked; guiding; interlacing; chubby; jeweled; pointed; weary; marble; radiant; horny; gloved; ineffectual; groping; invisible; ghostly; pensive; accusing; sensitive; solicitous; shaking; reverent; lily; grubby; bruised; flitting; dextrous; lingering; fairy; waxen; talented; intimate; tense; rosy; unseen; cruel; pale; bony; moistened; lean; nervous; quick; grimy; courageous; forced; benumbed; dirty; benign; rapid; transparent; shriveled; brown; coral-tipped; rosy-nailed; soft; rose-tinted; vigorous; premonitory; amethyst; skeleton; effacing; pinching; clutching; tenacious; solemn; iron; glowing; choppy; mortal; beckoning; swathed; royal; pilfering; sudden; microscopic; wasted; barky; unraised; nicotine-stained; false; hungry; catechising; heavily-ringed; uncontrolled; gentle; caressing; limp; lax; hesitating; idle; pitying;

beguiling; chilled; awkward; ready; cautious; scorched; imperative; feeble; fluttering; disengaged; itching; indignant; warning; denunciatory; admonitory; busy; exploring; cold; prying; covetous; searching; blundering; greedy; mischievous; playful; meddling; offensive; slight; thieving; usurious; exploratory; tapping; snatching; gripping; fumbling; grasping; emphasizing; stiff; rheumatic; tendril-like; skinny; fleshy; blunt-tipped; thick; ruthless; plump; lustful; felonious; deadly; predatory; sinewy; powerful; rough; agile; smudgy; soiled; dingy; square; flat; stubby; freckled; curled; strong; spatulate; arched; huge; crooked; firm; authoritative; steady; experienced; well-groomed; manicured; quick; canny; excited.

FINGER-TIPS

adjectives

reverent; slim; caressing; calloused; semiconscious; warm; sensitive; chill; gentle.

FINICKY

adverbs

frivolously; idly; inanely; uncommonly; absurdly; unreasonably; ludicrously; primly; priggishly; vexatiously; bumptiously; loudly; unnecessarily; intolerably; tiresomely; inordinately; extravagantly; elaborately; pitifully; ridiculously; shabbily; amazingly.

FINISH

adjectives

elaborate; high; literary; permanent; pictorial; sleek; glace; gleaming; harmonious; artistic; lustrous; meticulous; smooth; ill-conceived; warm; mellow; oratorical; scholarly; surface; admirable; exquisite; attractive; interior; rare; delicate; subtle.

verbs

acquire—; adorn with—; anticipate—; await—; design—; destroy—; exhibit—; lay—; mar—; obtain—; plan—; polish to—; prepare—; produce—; provide—; restore—; select—; —perfects.

(See perfection.)

FINISH (*v*)

adverbs

uniformly; leisurely; deliberately; neatly; minutely; solemnly; abstractedly; hurriedly; elaborately; lustrously; meticulously; exquisitely; delicately; subtly.

(See complete, end.)

FINISHED

adverbs

perfectly; unquestionably; irrevocably; recently; satisfactorily; smoothly; politely; irremediably; finally; consummately; highly; definitely; unfortunately; beautifully; fundamentally; exquisitely; wonderfully; amazingly; faultlessly; cleverly; ingeniously; expertly; artistically; elaborately; splendidly.

FINITE

adverbs

materially; inevitably; essentially; mortally; lamentably; fitly; tragically; appropriately; evanescently; merely; transitorily; passingly; humanly.

FIRE

adjectives

scattering; withering; blasting; raging; scorching; penal; scared; continuous; purging; oracular; crimson; cheerful; incessant; smoldering; suicidal; contagious; dormant; enfilading; unquenchable; horrid; eternal; dullest; answering; celestial; heavenly; constant; heavy; ethereal; gnawing; latent; cozy; untoward; baleful; closest; starry; aromatic; blinding; plumed; combined (pl); elemental; fearful; liquid; inextinguishable; rolling; long-suffering; barbed; singular; permeating; blinking; fruitless; accustomed; lambent; all-consuming; volcanic; ardent; innumerable (pl); central; lively; unfathomed; insatiate; mirrored; living; destructive; well-directed; unwonted; pulsating; cordial; sweet; slumbering; murderous; impetuous; undermining; swift; mystic; golden; unapparent; unavailing; mocking; molten; soul-scorching; subtile; ruddy; capricious; cleansing; solar; blazing; terrific; plucky; feeble; strange; electric; corrosive; tempestuous; powerless; conflicting; thrifty; deadly; flaming; beamless; dusky; twilight; overwhelming; tremulous; soft; unspotted; grim; roaring; intolerable; lurid; well-directed; effective; flickering; baser; raking; devastating; tempering; azure; deep; spiritual; restless; steady; opalescent; remorseless; avenging; divine; nightly; slow; pale; fresh-lit; instantaneous; animating; vestal; monumental; branding; hallowed; turf; boisterous; pernicious; ancestral; incipient; unhallowed; galling; solitary; musketry; unhealthful; ravenous; wild; disastrous; immortal; wandering; smokeless; ceaseless; considerable; impassioned; appalling; magic; incense; illuminating; sea-coal; immeasurable; unearthly; velvet; dead; drowsy; desultory; extraordinary; insignificant; languid; freezing; diverging; chaster; commingling; subterranean; parental; mortal; specifical; waning; unslackened; merry; fanatical; respective; elfin; spiral; conquering; theologic; everlasting; fluttering; hoarded; dreadful; open; hot-burning; council; actual; covered; hectic; kindly; combined; prophetic; shafted; impatient; inward; sleeping; mad; suppressed; bright; flashing; purifying; undivided; amber; sheathing; lightless; fierce; sprightly; vaporous; telling; crackling.

verbs
assail with—; concentrate—; douse (colloq.) —; extinguish—; feed—; intensify—; lower—; quench—; rake—; replenish—; revive—; smother—; stoke—; torture with—; vent—; witness—; yield to—; —breaks out; —consumes; —crackles; —devastates; —devours; —flashes; —gnaws; —leaps; —menaces; —rages; —ravages; —razes; —reaches out; —roars; —scorches; —shrivels; —slakes down; —smolders; —snaps; —sputters; —whips through.

(See blaze, flame, conflagration.)

FIRE (*v*)

adverbs
electrically; witheringly; blastingly; scorchingly; incessantly; fearfully; destructively; lethally; murderously; perniciously; mortally; fiercely; shatteringly; devastatingly.

(See explode, burn, blaze.)

FIREFLY

verbs
capture—; welcome—; —blinks; —cheers; —emits; —flames; —flashes; —flickers; —glimmers; —glitters; —glows; —illuminates; —lights; —scintillates; —shimmers; —spangles; —sparkles; —twinkles; —winks.

(See insect.)

FIRELIGHT

adjectives
flickering; wan; lifeless; bright; glaring; warm; drab; dull.

verbs
behold—; emit—; neglect—; observe—; provide—; quench—; —blinks; —casts; —cheers; —flames; —flashes; —flickers; —gleams; —glimmers; —glows; —illuminates; —rages; —sparkles; —transmits; —twinkles; —warms; —warns.

(See light.)

FIREPLACE

adjectives
rustic; capacious; radiant; immense; stone; clean-swept; spacious; desolate; high; cheery; white-tiled.

verbs
congregate around—; crackle in—; delight in—; gather 'round—; lounge around—; nestle near—; pave—; provide—; rejoice 'round—; toast at—; —blinks; —cheers; —furnishes; —glimmers; —heats; —illuminates; —welcomes.

FIREWORKS

verbs
arrange—; attack with—; cast—; celebrate with—; charge with—; dedicate with—; design—; display—; execute—; exhibit—; honor with—; prepare—; present—; start —; —appear; —burn; —conclude; —cover; —disturb; —excite; —explode; —harm; —represent; —spark; —splutter.

FIRING

verbs
attend to—; commence—; halt—; inspire—; instigate—; lead to—; minimize—; perceive —; prepare for—; prevent—; prohibit—; require—; restrain—; slacken—; start—; subject to—; warn against—; —ceases; —destroys; —ruins; —wanes.

(See attack.)

FIRM

adjectives
salvaging; futile; magnanimous; munificent; enterprising; business; successful; mercantile; bankrupt.

verbs
alter—; associate with—; bankrupt—; designate—; establish—; head—; indict—; join —; manage—; supervise—; —advises; —agrees; —delivers; —dissolves; —engages; —perishes; —promotes; —sells; —solicits; —trades; —transacts.

(See partnership, corporation, company.)

adverbs
stably; dependably; securely; safely; sufficiently; satisfactorily; immovably; obdu-

rately; stubbornly; severely; wisely; carefully; affectionately; paternally; desperately; sullenly; relentlessly; pitilessly; curiously; remorselessly; primly; priggishly; officially; professionally; vexatiously; unnecessarily; resolutely; decisively; emphatically; remarkably; singularly; particularly; uncommonly.

FIRMAMENT

adjectives
beautiful; boundless; darkling; airy; star-spangled; full-arched; starry; azure; cloudless; aerial; spacious; frosty; all-encircling; unquestionable; rolling; economic; overcast; pellucid; twinkling; terrestrial; expectant.

FIRMNESS

adjectives
desperate; gloomy; relentless; curious; remorseless; fatal; necessary; exemplary; practical; miscalled; fresh; equal; temperate; unexampled; futile.

FISH

adjectives
fin-twinkling; fiery; armored; magnificent; surface; fatted; voracious; darting; glistening; golden; artificially-grown; live; game; broiled; diminutive; silly; slim; silvery; tawny; iridescent; sodden; much-comforted; playful; meddlesome; mystical; speckled; bony; lacelike; cartilaginous; salmonoid; shining; putrid; floating; edible; brain-giving.

verbs
abound in—; catch—; cure—; drag for—; feed—; harbor—; limit—; plant—; prepare—; raise—; shred—; steam—; yield—; —darts off; —deposits eggs; —flashes past; —flops about; —hovers near; —inhabits; —schools; —spawns; —squirms; —swoops past.

FISH (v)

adverbs
intently; contentedly; placidly; somnolently; abstractedly; ruminatively; enthusiastically; skillfully; professionally; devotedly.
(See search, seek.)

FISHERMAN

verbs
ban—; enthrall—; license—; permit—; tantalize—; tempt—; —anchors; —angles; —attempts; —baits; —casts; —catches; —collects; —courts; —displays; —disturbs; —elicits; —enthuses (colloq.); —hauls in; —hooks; —nets; —occupies; —pulls; —snaps; —strives; —struggles with; —supplies; —trawls.

FISHERMEN

adjectives
energetic; skillful; stalwart; unsuccessful; professional; lowly; ideal; shabby; devoted; rude.

FISHING

verbs
acclaim—; ban—; bar—; contemplate—; control—; employ in—; offer—; permit—; popularize—; prevent—; rely on—; supervise—; thrive on—; tutor in—; —bores; —disturbs; —diverts; —entertains; —lags; —pleases; —supplies; —supports; —tests; —tires; —yields.
(See sport.)

FIST

adjectives
clenched; rocklike; parental; fat; helping; husky; tense; skillful; clumsy; practised; dimpled; huge; solid; hamlike; giant; heavy; ample; pudgy; iron; hard-knuckled; useful-looking; great; raw; calloused; knotted; gnarled; vengeful; angry; furious; shaking; defiant; rage-driven; smashing; whirling; swinging; pounding; thudding; closed; hairy; doubled; impotent; knuckle-torn; rock-laden; mailed; choking; eager; oxlike.

verbs
bandage—; box with—; clasp in—; clench—; close into—; conceal in—; dodge—; double into—; drive with—; feint with—; fight with—; flourish—; fold into—; grasp with—; injure—; lay on with—; shake—; strike with—; swing—; wield—; —clutches; —crushes; —descends; —grips; —shoots out; —staggers.
(See hand (colloq. for fist.)

FISTICUFFS

adjectives
childish; brutal; scientific.

FIT

adjectives
fainting; plethoric; smooth; trim; excellent; slenderizing; violent; immoderate; jealous; snug; periodical; poetic; painful; dreadful; melancholy; sullen; apoplectic; hysterical;

natural; morose; economical; perfect; permanent; wild; suave; comfortable; superior; proper; lasting; soft; custom; superb; correct; assured.

verbs
ail with—; anticipate—; attack with—; burst into—; check—; convulse in—; cure of—; fall into—; fear—; master—; scream in—; seize with—; shake with—; sweat in —; take with—; throw into—; treat for—; —exhausts; —possesses; —seizes; —wracks.
(See spasm, convulsion, paroxysm.)

adverbs
remarkably; splendidly; magnificently; capably; competently; expertly; skillfully; amazingly; opportunely; conveniently; appropriately; brilliantly; robustly; sturdily; gratifyingly; pleasantly; unusually; marvelously.

FIT (*v*)

adverbs
snugly; exquisitely; adorably; peculiarly; permanently; specifically; curiously; delicately; smoothly; periodically; economically; superbly.
(See adorn, wear.)

FITFUL

adverbs
erratically; irregularly; capriciously; vexatiously; undependably; unsystematically; haltingly; changeably; inconstantly; terribly; oddly; restlessly; waywardly; fantastically; whimsically; captiously; inconsistently; surprisingly; unpleasantly; disturbingly.

FITNESS

adjectives
practical; vital; exquisite; highest; personal; harmonious; absolute; visible.

FIX

adjectives
awkward; monetary; erroneous; frightful; dreadful.

FIX (*v*)

adverbs
hypnotically; firmly; arbitrarily; unalterably; inherently; accurately; steadily; steadfastly; ingeniously; rigidly; awkwardly; momentarily.
(See fasten, secure, arrange.)

FIXED

adverbs
irrevocably; firmly; irresistibly; finally; resolutely; permanently; unalterably; inevitably; immovably; persistently; immutably; steadfastly; obstinately; ineradicably; irretrievably; indelibly; traditionally; officially; absolutely; inviolately.

FLABBERGASTED

adverbs
wondrously; breathlessly; mysteriously; unutterably; unspeakably; utterly; completely; helplessly; confusingly; confoundedly; obviously; embarrassingly; peculiarly; entirely; ludicrously; comically; pitiably.

FLABBY

adverbs
uselessly; pliably; flexibly; limply; malleably; inadequately; slackly; helplessly; hopelessly; wretchedly; miserably; terribly; disgustingly; vexatiously; dreadfully.

FLAG

adjectives
rippling; hoisted; wind-swayed; tattered; crimson; insulted; back-blown; radiant; saucy; faltering; drooping; enchanted; movable; fluttering; enormous; quadrangular; constabulary; tricolored; shameful; lozenge-shaped; scoured; ominous; hearth; withered; common; many-colored; gaudy; simplest; easiest; veranda; garish; unfurled; hostile; invincible; draped; precious; historic.

verbs
accept—of; bear—; crowd 'round—; display—; elevate—; extend—; flaunt—; guard—; half-mast—; haul down—; hoist —; jeopardize—; level—; moor—; nail—; pay homage to—; rally 'round—; unfurl—; wave—; —ascends; —cheers; —descends; —flutters; —symbolizes; —unfurls; —whips in the breeze.
(See banner, ensign.)

FLAGRANT

adverbs
arrantly; notoriously; patently; strikingly; incredibly; unconcealably; scandalously; publicly; grossly; atrociously; indecorously; indiscreetly; iniquitously; nefariously; reprehensibly; shamelessly; unconscionably; exceptionally; emphatically; indefensibly; wickedly.

FLAIR

adjectives
vicious; promotional; remarkable; definite; noticeable.

FLAKES

adjectives
lazy; starry; quivering; fervent; wandering; hoariest; ash; thick-descending; jetty; crackling; crunchy; flavor-packed; discolored; sun-ripened; delicately-browned; whole-wheat; tender; luscious; flying; snow; wavering; radiant; whirling; white; mated; blinding; elfish.

verbs
blow—; break into—; chip off—; cover with—; cut into—; dress in—; fall in—; peel in—; powder with—; scale—; scrape into—; separate into—; silver with—; spread with—; strip into—; —descend; —fly; —pave.
(See fragment, chip.)

FLAMBOYANT

adverbs
conspicuously; openly; ostentatiously; brazenly; daringly; audaciously; floridly; sonorously; pompously; egotistically; rhetorically; bombastically; flashily; noisily; terribly; marvelously; uproariously.

FLAME

adjectives
vivid; dancing; flapping; unshapely; lean; bursting; unresting; pitiless; candle; hungry; fever; solar; sunny; fragrant; cheerful; inward; pointed; dying; lambent; livelier; spiritual; devouring; sacrificial; quickening; unconsuming; conscious; immediate; celestial; dull; low-lit; pure; changeless; ruddy; sulphurous; polluted; generous; inferior; floating; rival; innocent; sacred; showering; mutual; enormous; heavenly; self-divided; restless; pale; earnest; pallid; elusive; ethereal; many-colored; irregular; guiding; quick; darting; stiller; variegated; white; ardent; tired; leaping; noiseless; flickering; lawless; wasting; writhing; hurrying; subtle; penetrating; torturing; amorous; evangelic; lurid; vital; feeble; blue; scarlet; greenish; luminous; dreadful; incandescent; vengeful; empyreal; midnight; heavenward; sudden; irregular; joyful; inexorable; springing; clearest; delusive; intermittent; chastening; accustomed; outrageous; withering; purer; livid; authentic; spiral; cold; radiant; captive; flashing; baleful; inextinguishable; mumuring; rapid; quenchable; serpent; seraphic; furious; ill-dissembled; all-absorbing; sullen; wrathful; prismatic; loyal; purple; liquid; bickering; deep-red; mounting; embracing; peaceful; creeping; unshelterable; blessed; vestal; transported; avenging; breathing; oxyhydrogen; tossing; productive; lustral; coral; powerful; imagined; internal; ceaseless; roaring; unchanging; unimprisoned; silver; gigantic; lustrous.

verbs
burst into—; deliver up to—; dim—; extinguish—; feed—; kindle—; spout—; spray with—; —blisters; —breathes; —chars; —consumes; —crackles; —curls; —devours; —flickers; —hovers over; —leaps; —licks; —overcomes; —plays; —rages; —ravages; —roars; —spreads; —spurts; —subdues; —subsides; —trembles; —wanes; —wavers.
(See fire, blaze.)

FLAME (*v*)

adverbs
gorgeously; vividly; lambently; spiritually; sacrificially; ruddily; dartingly; writhingly; amorously; inextinguishably; unquenchably; sullenly; wrathfully; furiously; mountingly; ceaselessly; lustrously.
(See blaze, burn.)

FLANK

adjectives
bleeding; belathered; vertical; universal; monstrous; cavernous; bulging; heaving; towered.

FLANNEL

adjectives
spotless; tawdry; immaculate; easily-cleaned; rough.

FLAP (*v*)

adverbs
aimlessly; incessantly; irritatingly; monotonously; lustily; carelessly; impotently; characteristically.
(See beat, flutter, quiver.)

FLARE (*v*)

adverbs
vividly; repeatedly; luminously; torridly; heatedly; destructively; celestially; ethereally; balefully; blindingly; luridly.
(See flicker, dazzle, blaze.)

FLASH

adjectives
incessant; vicious; simultaneous (pl); continual (pl); temporary; vivid; rapid; illuminating; serpentine; forked; lurid; brilliant; sardonic; momentary; fiery; intellectual; blinding; deafening; free; intolerable; luminous; long-lingering; quick; eager; impetuous; sulphurous; flambeaux; electric; astonishing; meteoric; rhythmic; quivering; kaleidoscopic; sublime; downward; opalescent; white; clean-cut; fitful.

verbs
create—; criticize—; develop into—; disclose—; display—; fire—; produce—; rebound in—; repeat—; ridicule—; shoot—; strike with—; wait for—; —appears; —arouses; —astounds; —attracts; —blazes; —bursts; —directs; —displays; —disturbs; —exposes; —flares; —flaunts; —flouts; —gleams; —ignites; —illumines; —indicates; —occurs; —passes over; —relinquishes; —reveals; —signals; —spurts; —vanishes; —violates.
(See blaze, gleam.)

FLASH (*v*)

adverbs
briefly; brilliantly; gloriously; vindictively; instantaneously; irresistibly; fiercely; restlessly; intermittently; radiantly; lambently; simultaneously; serpentinely; luridly; electrically; meteorically; kaleidoscopically; opalescently; fitfully.
(See sparkle, gleam.)

FLASH-LIGHT

verbs
douse (colloq.)—; employ—; necessitate—; replenish—; resort to—; supply—; —beams; —blinks; —brightens; —dazzles; —exposes; —flickers; —floods; —glares; —glimmers; —guides; —illuminates; —reflects; —reveals; —shines; —spots; —uncovers.
(See light.)

FLASH-LIGHT (*photography*)

verbs
anticipate—; ban—s; bar—s; blink at—; conceal—; employ—; guard against—; jump at—; permit—; pose for—; protect from—; refuse—; —enrages; —explodes; —illumines; —interrupts; —irritates; —pops; —reveals; —scares; —startles; —surprises.
(See flash.)

FLASHY

adverbs
pretentiously; gaudily; garishly; flauntingly; daringly; highly; wonderfully; cheaply; grossly; coarsely; attractively; ornately; smartly; pompously; gorgeously; indecorously; unbecomingly; rudely; provincially; outlandishly; fantastically; grotesquely; dreadfully; horribly.

FLASK

adjectives
supernal; primitive; tapering; liquor; pocket-size.

FLAT

adverbs
monotonously; tiresomely; vapidly; disagreeably; invariably; intolerably; uninterestingly; wearily; tediously; endlessly.

FLATS

adjectives
dangerous; vile; sumptuous; inhospitable; cluttered; crowded; sewage-polluted; fertile; streaming; occidental; windowed; various; tenement; lurid.

FLATTER (*v*)

adverbs
obsequiously; fondly; grossly; hugely; slavishly; unduly; artfully; immeasurably; prettily; cunningly; adeptly; adroitly; deftly; coyly; treacherously; deceptively; coarsely; egregiously; sleekly; fatuously; expertly.
(See compliment, praise.)

FLATTERED

adverbs
happily; blushingly; pleasantly; rosily; smilingly; highly; pleasingly; delightfully; convivially; excitedly; jubilantly; artlessly; inordinately; uncommonly.

FLATTERER

adjectives
impudent; cunning; defective; adept; adroit.

FLATTERY

adjectives
coarse; temporizing; sordid; graceful; innumerable (pl); gross; egregious; judicious; servile; friendly; unconscious; grateful; sleek; supple; dulcet; cautious; fatal; infinite; verbal; blazoned; expert; delicate; commonplace.

verbs
abhor—; accept—; addict to—; conceal with —; court—; detest—; endure—; expand under—; fall for—; feed with—; fool by—; savor of—; steel to—; succumb to—; thicken with—; withstand—; yield to—; —deceives; —soothes; —tricks.
(See adulation.)

FLAUNT (v)

adverbs
arrogantly; insultingly; saucily; pertly; exasperatingly; tantalizingly; maliciously; subtly; coyly; mortifyingly.
(See parade, show.)

FLAVOR

verbs
acclaim—; adulterate—; affect—; create—; detect—; dislike—; extract—; marvel at—; mask—; protect—; retain—; scent—; smell —; —appetizes; —burns out; —delights; —dies; —rivals; —stales.
(See taste, savor.)

FLAVOR (v)

adverbs
delectably; delicately; exotically; appetizingly; pungently; inimitably; matchlessly; characteristically; originally; temptingly; palatably; exhilaratingly; toothsomely; incomparably.
(See season, taste.)

FLAVORING

verbs
add—; dislike—; employ—; impart—; inject—; lack—; mix with—; necessitate—; savor—; season with—; select—; spice with —; taste—; try—; —enhances; —flatters; —pleases; —stings; —teases.
(See extract, spice, etc.)

FLAVORS

adjectives
marvelous; exotic; luscious; appetizing; oleaginous; pleasant; juicy; spirited; unapproachable; delicate; aristocratic; pungent; inimitable; distinctive; exclusive; minty; matchless; characteristic; delicious; intellectual; imaginative; full-bodied; treacherous; international; original; satisfying; grand; extra-fresh; odorous; acrid; individual; abominable; faint; infused; sublime; palatable; tender; supreme; exhilarating; delicious; native; tempting; subtle; apparent; mellow; reminiscent; unique; mild; tangy; toothsome; peculiar; balanced; smoky; dry; hearty; popular; unusual; fine; criminal; appetizing; old-time; incomparable; clinging.

FLAW

adjectives
foul; inherent; blemishing; inscrutable; apparent; age-old; inherited.

verbs
accept—; conceal—; consider—; constitute —; detect—; develop—; discern—; discover —; eradicate—; exempt from—; free from —; guard against—; hide—; jade with—s; overcome—; —blemishes; —mars; irons out —.
(See defect, blemish, imperfection, fault, crack.)

FLAWLESS

adverbs
perfectly; incredibly; marvelously; utterly; unbelievably; delicately; simply; tastefully; chastely; obviously; superbly; splendidly; absolutely; technically; ineffably; completely; comparatively; exquisitely; matchlessly; artistically.

FLEE (v)

adverbs
incontinently; instinctively; peremptorily; precipitately; timorously; tremulously; impetuously.
(See run, abandon.)

FLEECE

adjectives
delicate; silky; plenteous; warm.

FLEECY

adverbs
warmly; softly; comfortingly; comfortably; incredibly; genuinely; agreeably; pleasantly; tenderly; sleekly; smoothly; shaggily; delightfully; snugly; delicately.

FLEET

verbs
antiquate—; assemble—; assign to—; command—; dispatch—; expand—; increase—; mobilize—; observe—; order—; recondition —; —anchors; —blockades; —celebrates; —cruises; —exhibits; —files in; —journeys;

—migrates; —navigates; —passes; —performs; —plies; —sails; —shifts; —ships; —speeds; —travels.
(See squadron, navy.)

adverbs
incredibly; nimbly; gracefully; marvelously; splendidly; remarkably; expeditiously; smartly; actively; lightly; mercurially; inordinately; unwontedly; naturally; unusually; surprisingly; amazingly; trippingly.

FLEETING

adverbs
impermanently; evanescently; mortally; transiently; transitorily; perishably; quickly; temporally; illusively; elusively; sadly; unhappily; ephemerally; pitifully; terribly.

FLEETNESS

adjectives
sleek; eager; easy; unapproachable; swift.

FLEETS

adjectives
allied; provisional; myriad; trade; mimic; royal; confederate; formidable; cumbrous; grim; multitudinous; death-dealing.

FLESH

adjectives
mortifying; famished; fever-stricken; palatable; cumbrous; festering; quivering; lank; unsavory; overroasted; flower-tinted; soft; pink; sun-bronzed; ivory; pale; waxen; bruised; shuddering; swollen; dusty; exhausted; putrefying; carrion; miserable; half-cooked; pierced; mad; attractive; common; living; sweet; tender; transfigured; dead; redundant; yielding; warm; lumpy; scalded; mangled; tainted; wrinkled; ample; muscular; decrepit; quaky; firm; human; crawling; swooping; swelling; slippery; sensitive; blooming; decaying; rebellious; seraphic; gangrenous; overwearied; quick; aching; adhering; mutinous; torn; elaborate; dressed; sinful; avaricious.

verbs
accumulate—; chafe—; char—; crucify—; denounce—; derive from—; flavor—; gain —; gather—; grind—; inject into—; market —; mutilate—; produce—; reduce—; waste —.
(See meat, fat.)

FLESHY

adverbs
mortifyingly; cumbrously; comfortably; burdensomely; embarrassingly; dreadfully; inordinately; dangerously; amiably; miserably; wretchedly; clumsily; awkwardly; strangely; warmly; stockily; alarmingly; heavily; hideously; shockingly; wholesomely; merrily; nonchalantly; cheerfully.

FLEXIBLE

adverbs
conveniently; adaptably; suitably; appropriately; diplomatically; agreeably; pliantly; tractably; complaisantly; affably; pleasantly; indulgently; easily; manageably; smoothly; fortunately; properly.

FLICKER

adjectives
curious; small; tiny; rapid; abrupt; unseen.

verbs
emit—; observe—; reduce to—; repeat—; shake with—; vibrate in—; —annoys; —dies out; —disturbs; —flames; —mottles; —remains; —warms; —warns; —wavers.
(See light.)

FLICKER (v)

adverbs
inscrutably; involuntarily; fitfully; rapidly; incessantly; repeatedly; mysteriously; interminably.
(See flutter, waver.)

FLIER

verbs
employ—; examine—; exhaust—; inform—; license—; overtake—; strain—; test—; —achieves; —accomplishes; —ascends; —attempts; —charts; —circles; —controls; —descends; —dips; —endures; —lands; —loops; —manipulates; —navigates; —operates; —perceives; —pilots; —somersaults; —speeds; —takes off; —transports; —zooms.
(See aviator, aeroplane.)

FLIES

adjectives
lazy; insolent; gilded; unfortunate; shrivelled; swarming; glittering; incautious; stinging; vicious; bothersome.

FLIGHT

adjectives
pattering; comely; droning; fagging; impetuous; wheeling; gay; labored-looking; ceaseless; joyous; temporary; cankerous; vehement; tireless; unreturning; bold; poetic; rhythmic; self-same; erratic; hysterical; epochal; prolonged; intertwined; nuptial; mocking; impeded; principal; common; angry; unjust; disguising; pretended; ignominious; airy; troublesome; perceptible; humanitarian; risky; mediocre; freshening; industrious; frolic; promiscuous; illuminated; tremendous; precipitate; untried; aery; lagging; filmy; fleeting; rapturous; fearful; perilous; howling; ambitious; imperial; interminable; ponderous; winding; higher; unwearied; intrepid; hurried; undulating; unbounded; upward-hovering; never-ending; impudent; swift; rickety; tremulous; transitory; wide; worn; persistent; cloistered; cowardly; voluptuous; orderly; annual; unsustained; measureless; distant.

verbs
accomplish—; accustom to—; attempt—; depart in—; drop in—; hasten in—; impede —; lose in—; mount in—; move to—; observe—; plan—; pursue in—; record—; resume—; retreat in—; sally forth in—; scatter—; soar in—; witness—; —exhausts; —fails.

(See journey, trip.)

FLIGHTY

adverbs
comically; wantonly; cheerfully; happily; merrily; charmingly; vexatiously; curiously; deliriously; strangely; oddly; queerly; alarmingly; dangerously; insanely; whimsically; wildly; capriciously; fantastically; lightly; drunkenly; heedlessly; thoughtlessly; carelessly; inadvertently; remarkably; utterly.

FLIMSY

adverbs
absurdly; airily; vaguely; tenuously; unreasonably; nonsensically; foolishly; slightly; ridiculously; miserably; wretchedly; contemptibly; pitifully; unmanageably; unserviceably; objectionably.

FLING

adjectives
overhand; disdainful; senseless; disjointed; surreptitious; ill-natured.

FLING (*v*)

adverbs
mechanically; dramatically; fiercely; jauntily; simultaneously; impetuously; violently; harshly; carelessly; savagely; tauntingly; disdainfully; ill-naturedly; contemptuously; extravagantly.

(See hurl, cast.)

FLINTS

adjectives
stubborn; clattering; brittle; steely.

FLIPPANCY

adjectives
extravagant; friendly; verbal; studied; marked; open; definite; disgusting.

FLIPPANT

adverbs
impertinently; carelessly; insouciantly; audaciously; daringly; brazenly; charmingly; attractively; giddily; heedlessly; jauntily; saucily; unblushingly; shamelessly; wantonly; unduly; disrespectfully; comically; inappropriately; unbecomingly; inopportunely; youthfully; glibly; smartly; inconsiderately; sacrilegiously; terribly.

FLIRT

adjectives
saucy; harmless; wild.

FLIRT (*v*)

adverbs
blatantly; shamelessly; saucily; wildly; outrageously; unconscionably; boldly; coyly; shyly; immodestly; voluptuously; arduously; impassionedly; trivially; desultorily.

(See coquette, love.)

FLIRTATION

adjectives
sly; anonymous; literary; unworthy; miserable; pleasant; hit-and-run; trivial; desultory; detached; discreet; swift; arduous; meaningful; mere; summer; unimpassioned.

verbs
arouse—; arrest—; cease—; coach—; commit—; continue—; delight in—; express in —; interrupt—; overlook—; recount—; regard as—; renew—; school in—; tease in —; —deceives; —excites; —grows; —inspires; —invites; —involves; —stimulates.

FLIRTATIOUS

adverbs
innocently; harmlessly; amusingly; designedly; resolutely; definitely; systematically; assiduously; sedulously; charmingly; noticeably; curiously; oddly; habitually; seductively; irresistibly; coquettishly; philanderingly; merrily; openly; obviously; palpably; whimsically; engagingly.

FLIT (*v*)

adverbs
errantly; feverishly; vaguely; joyously; tantalizingly; momentarily; casually; ephemerally; temporarily.
(See flutter, fly.)

FLOAT (*v*)

adverbs
nebulously; airily; buoyantly; lazily; gracefully; listlessly; majestically; drowsily; delicately; miraculously; gorgeously; lumberingly; glitteringly.
(See move, billow, creep, drift, hover.)

FLOATS

adjectives
gossamer; lumbering; horse-drawn; glittering; beautiful; papier-mache; river; gorgeous; glorious.

FLOCK

adjectives
close-pinned; golden; crowding; divided; trembling; scattered; endless; fleecy; blood-bought; patriarchal; afflicted; nibbling; snowy; browsing; timorous; homeward; clustering; healthful; pictorial; benighted.

verbs
appeal to—; call on—; care for—; guide—; journey in—; manage—; muster—; preach to—; supervise—; travel in—; —assembles; —congregates; —flees; —gathers; —journeys; —occupies; —supports; —swarms.
(See pack, group, herd, congregation.)

FLOCK (*v*)

adverbs
protectively; reposefully; timorously; clusteringly; pictorially; benightedly; habitually; characteristically; seasonally.
(See assemble, crowd.)

FLOOD

adjectives
intoxicating; impetuous; sluggish; vitreous; soaking; mighty; torrential; creeping; short-lived; devastating; human; babbling; untamable; spring; savory; copious; shoreless; seething; passing; brackish; fearful; crystal; maddened; foaming; phenomenal; raging; steaming; shining; redundant; weltering; unfathomable; shaded; disastrous; shallow; uncurling; surging; horned; isle-fretted; moon-lit; breaking; all-destroying; advancing; overflowing; post-glacial; drenching; shedding; glowing; turbid; sparkling; storied; wondrous; full; eternal; main; wasteful; lashing; fiery; glassy; urgent; tranquil; azure; furious; unbroken; frigid; ice-imprisoned; tropical; roaring; all-engulfing; gathering; clearest; fretful; unwelcome; poured-out; eddying; vaporous; theoretic; wandering; widespread.

verbs
abate—; ameliorate—; check—; dam—; guard against—s; halt—; mitigate—; recoil from—; stem—; swirl with—; unloose—; —cripples; —devastates; —inundates; —overwhelms; —recedes; —submerges; —sweeps away.
(See deluge.)

FLOOD (*v*)

adverbs
fatally; partially; impetuously; torrentially; devastatingly; untamably; copiously; seethingly; foamingly; phenomenally; ragingly; disastrously; drenchingly; sparklingly; furiously; roaringly; eddyingly.
(See overflow, submerge, drench.)

FLOOR

adjectives
watery; dark-stained; polished; topmost; unpretentious; sanded; desolate; glassy; olive; opalescent; light; stained; glittering; gleaming; seedy; oaken; translucent; sinking; mosaic; drafty; musty; gritted; amethystine; spotless; desert-yellow; charred; cloudy; slimy; draughty; well-swept; untrodden; mirrored; clammy; brazen; tremulous; expansive; diamond-paved; planet-powered; dilapidated; brick; herbless; carpetless; conscious; vaster; threshing; blazing; shining; scholastic; marble; iron-bound; tessellated; tiled.

verbs
board—; cement—; crowd—; inlay—; joist —; lay—; litter—; nail to—; polish—; rest on—; root to—; scrape—; shellac—; slip on—; splinter—; strew—; swab—; tread on —; varnish—; warp—; wax—; —collapses; —creaks; —rots; —sags; —supports.
(See surface, platform.)

FLORID

adverbs
ruddily; uncommonly; dangerously; alarmingly; healthily; intensely; freshly; blowzily; warmly; wholesomely; unusually; remarkably; oddly; habitually; unwontedly; naturally.

FLOUNDER (v)

adverbs
bewilderingly; haphazardly; awkwardly; comically; clumsily; helplessly; wretchedly.
(See stumble, struggle.)

FLOUNDERING

adjectives
haphazard; ignoble; awkward; laughable.

FLOUR

adjectives
ill-mixed; unadulterated; unbolted; bleached.

verbs
bag—; barrel—; bin—; bleach—; brush off —; cover with—; employ—; grade—; grind into—; manufacture—; mill—; mix with—; obtain—; pulverize into—; reduce to—; select—; sift—; sprinkle—; triturate into—; —dusts; —whitens.
(See cereal, powder.)

FLOURISH

adjectives
ornamental; periodic; sudden; joyous; eloquent; graceful; festive; indignant; brazen.

FLOURISH (v)

adverbs
chiefly; luxuriously; gloriously; vigorously; periodically; gracefully; festively; brazenly; heartily; boisterously.
(See thrive.)

FLOURISHING

adverbs
highly; uncommonly; remarkably; prosperously; successfully; sturdily; steadily; indubitably; certainly; materially; apparently; evidently; manifestly; splendidly; magnificently; obviously; fortunately; luckily; deservedly; extremely.

FLOUT

adjectives
wounding; brash; resounding.

FLOW

adjectives
inward; sonorous; cheerful; increasing; intermitting; eternal; long-accustomed; dual; lurid; spontaneous; irrepressible; beneficent; sluggish; restless; maladjusted; seething; social; dolorous; endless; lateral; never-ending; excessive; constant; boisterous; agreeable; continuous; metrical; wavy; taintless; melodious; uneventful; quiescent; exuberant; imaginative; babbling; enclasping; incessant; gracious; balanced; rhetorical; unceasing; rippling; perpetual; lyrical; literary; everlasting.

verbs
accelerate—; bar—; check—; control—; dam—; diminish—; direct—; increase—; induce—; lessen—; prevent—; produce—; re-establish—; reiterate—; restrain—; still —; stimulate—; —advances; —ceases; —progresses.
(See stream, current, outpouring, fluency, abundance.)

FLOW (v)

adverbs
diffusely; noiselessly; divergently; tortuously; incessantly; lazily; mutely; sluggishly; inevitably; serenely; spontaneously; vehemently; placidly; seethingly; melodiously; quiescently; babblingly; rhetorically; perpetually; lyrically.
(See move, pass, float.)

FLOWER

verbs
arrange—s; array—s; awaken—s; bear—s; blanket with—s; crush—; cultivate—s; cull —s; fertilize—s; gather—s; landscape with —s; pluck—; press—; putter among—s; strew with—s; surround with—s; trample —; —s beckon; —s bob; —s cascade; —s cluster; —droops; —s drink in; —emerges; —fades; —nods; —ravishes; —shrivels; —springs up; —sways in the breeze; —unfolds; —withers; —waves.
(See blossom, plant, rose, lily, etc.)

FLOWER (v)

adverbs

resplendently; fragrantly; consummately; opulently; transiently; garishly; pendulously; wantonly; fugitively; vernally; deathlessly; luxuriantly; autumnally; vernally.

(See blossom, bloom.)

FLOWERS

adjectives

fragrant; spicy; graven; inwrought; constellated; starry; drooping; withering; consummate; tender; venturesome; wasted; amassing; wave-reflected; hybrid; thirsting; flamelike; wilting; carven; modest; spangled; variable; tissued; varicolored; opulent; delicate; pearling; transient; venomous; exotic; shy; climbing; homely; balmy; bewailing; garish; budding; laughing; uncropped; prim; thriving; fresh; expanded; dewy; perishable; sculptured; sweet; maiden; transitory; unfolding; unpretentious; satisfactory; pendulous; mystic-passion; wanton; fugitive; brilliant; rootless; storm-marred; busy; wilted; unthroned; immeasurable; infinite; scattering; manifold; sweet-tipped; festal; precious; thorny; summer-swelling; gazing; fair-named; visionary; indomitable; sanguine; waxen; multicolored; richly-colored; brightly-hued; frost-white; gorgeous; faded; fragile; printless; clustering; choicest; curious; crocus; wayside; artificial; unfolded; beauteous; tinted; tributary; achromatous; welcome; air-sown; mysterious; glowing; helpless; sweet-smelling; vernal; fullest; big; gallant; splashy; shaded; deathless; moisture-loving; classic; new-bloomed; unblown; heaven-plated; soft-breathing; incense-mingling; snow-white; changing; scented; meanest; fairest; pressed; foolproof; heartier; hand-planted; unperishing; promiscuous; luxuriant; earthly; autumnal; votive; ligulate; new-sprung; fantastic; torn; dissimilar; saffron; silvery; languishing; thread-hung; barren; uncourted; flourishing; enameled; discriminating; cleft-born; belated; sculptured; innocent; unconscious; prolific; resting; crimson-petalled; woodland; departed; chief; goodly; angel-missioned; breathing; stately; golden-hearted; overflowing; wordlike.

FLOWERY

adverbs

absurdly; ridiculously; bombastically; pompously; egotistically; importantly; blatantly; ornately; elaborately; ludicrously; bumptiously; sonorously; sententiously; egregiously; outlandishly; fantastically; inordinately; senselessly; preposterously; extravagantly.

FLUCTUATE (v)

adverbs

feverishly; violently; transiently; perceptibly; normally; cyclically; seasonally; economically.

(See waver, vary.)

FLUCTUATION

adjectives

violent; silken; alternate; transient; considerable.

FLUENCY

adjectives

extreme; rare; deplorable; inexhaustible; sweet; inimitable; impressive; illimitable.

verbs

acquire—; administer with—; declaim with—; deliver with—; discharge with—; dispatch with—; emit—; exhibit—; express with—; flow with—; increase—; orate with—; pen with—; proceed with—; promote—; recite with—.

(See ease.)

FLUENT

adverbs

amazingly; surprisingly; admirably; consistently; enviably; gracefully; readily; naturally; habitually; easily; felicitously; rhythmically; delightfully; wonderfully; strikingly; splendidly; eloquently; impressively.

FLUFFY

adverbs

delightfully; delicately; deliciously; warmly; softly; smoothly; remarkably; surprisingly; correctly; comfortably; comfortingly; deeply; amazingly; genuinely; uncommonly; extremely; distinctly; completely; lightly.

FLUID

adjectives

innumerable (pl); life-giving; gummy; intoxicating; subtle; vapid; sizy; scarce; lacteal; germinating; dark-hued; amber-colored; opaque; overabundant; turbid; electric; illusive; bleaching; unwholesome; precious; drinkable; vital; inky; incompressible; ethereal.

verbs
absorb—; consume—; discharge—; drain—; draw off—; effuse—; employ—; expel—; exude—; generate—; inject—; introduce—; secrete—; spill—; tap—; —circulates; —stains.
(See liquid, liquor, gas.)

FLUIDITY

adjectives
noticeable; linguistic; remarkable.

FLURRY

adjectives
undeniable; smiling; spiteful; abortive; pinwheel; angry.

FLUSH

adjectives
hectic; bloomy; unwonted; happy; momentary; blackish; brick-red; dull-red; fiery; gentle; helpless; fading; rosy; mahogany; perceptible; embarrassed; uneasy; novel; irritated; delicate; angry.

verbs
arouse—; cover with—; emit—; glow with —; overcome—; produce—; provoke—; redden into—; robe with—; subdue—; suffuse with—; —allures; —animates; —ebbs; —exasperates; —mantles; —overspreads; —throbs; —veils.
(See glow, blush, excitement, bloom.)

FLUSH (*v*)

adverbs
painfully; faintly; violently; delicately; miserably; singularly; passionately; transparently; hectically; unwontedly; rosily; perceptibly; embarrassingly; angrily.
(See blush, glow, thrill.)

FLUSHED

adverbs
extremely; drunkenly; feverishly; excitedly; apoplectically; alarmingly; dangerously; significantly; shyly; embarrassingly; ruddily; rosily; violently; angrily; furiously; madly; insanely; terribly; dreadfully; inordinately; frightfully; unnaturally; unusually.

FLUSTERED

adverbs
nervously; awkwardly; clumsily; significantly; helplessly; pitifully; weakly; terribly; agitatedly; hopelessly; ineptly; distractedly; distressingly; comically; absurdly; unreasonably; distinctly; undoubtedly; unwontedly; merrily; gloriously; drunkenly; tipsily.

FLUTE

adjectives
meditative; pastoral; oaten; perpendicular; enchanted; breathing.

verbs
dance to—; employ—; finger—; ornament —; pipe—; pitch—; practise on—; render on—; scale—; sound—; tootle on—; transpose on—; —blends; —cheers; —complains; —enraptures; —harmonizes; —shrills; —utters; —whines; —whistles.

FLUTTER

adjectives
unconscious; faint; indescribable; continual; perpetual; gay; sleek.

FLUTTER (*v*)

adverbs
recurrently; lightly; tremulously; gently; wantonly; ominously; convulsively; persistently; gaily; indescribably
(See tremble, fluctuate.)

FLY

adjectives
aggressive; officious; untrapped; pestering; stuttering; intolerable.

verbs
abandon to—ies; bar—ies; guard from—ies; harbor—ies; protect from—ies; screen off —ies; torture with—ies; —ies breed; —buzzes; —ies crawl; —drones; —glitters; —ies infest; —lays eggs; —lights on; —plagues; —settles; —torments; —ies swarm.
(See insect.)

FLY (*v*)

adverbs
professionally; gracefully; undauntedly; breath-takingly; basely; fantastically; cheerily; intrepidly; instinctively; precipitately; characteristically; swiftly; unerringly.
(See soar, flee.)

FLYER

adjectives
feathered; unsuccessful; dare-devil; intrepid; courageous; fearless; inimitable; daring; great; world-wide; seasoned; professional; careful; negligent; lawless; nerveless.

FOAM

adjectives
tainted; snow-soft; circumambient; ocean; fantastic; dashing; driven; creamy; panting; loose; wasteful; pale; fleet; lacteal; rainbow-colored; sea; rolling; fragile; salt; sweet; flamelike; delicious; wind-tossed; yeasty; fleecy; border; crested; carded; moonlit; seething; springtide; surging; uneasy; luminous; enchanted; twinkling; cruel; crawling; constellated; barren; sparkling; wild.

verbs
aggregate—; beat to—; boil to—; break into—; cover with—; crest with—; emit—; ferment—; fill with—; fleck with—; toss off—; —bubbles; —drips off; —effervesces; —floats; —froths; —gurgles; —issues from; —reams; —scuds; —smothers; —streaks; —washes.
(See froth.)

FOCUS

adjectives
constant; sharp; blurred; careful; precise; accurate.

FOCUS (v)

adverbs
sharply; precisely; accurately; deftly; skillfully; blurredly; scientifically; exactly.
(See concentrate, adjust.)

FOE

adjectives
prostrate; headless; murderous; mortal; prejudiced; vanquished; imaginary; spectral; intestinal; foreign; malicious; private; prevailing; ruthless; fierce; inveterate; exhausted; ghastly; remorseless; embodied; overweening; fallen; formidable; mailed; bigoted; blushing; contemptible; sensuous; inferior; daring; wily; ribald; wicked; sternest; unseen; countless (pl); implacable; victorious; ferocious; bitter; monstrous; invading; immortal; inexorable; mental; invisible; effective; heartless; treacherous; insolent; despicable; ubiquitous; stubborn; blaspheming; deadliest; cunning; contending; faint; blood-seeking; hereditary; lurking; bitterest; over-confident; one-time; hellish; persistent; dark; encircled; external; mocking; unexpected; savage; alert; hostile; ironclad; captured; defeated; cowering; principal; dastardly.

verbs
curse—; defy—; denounce—; disarm—; discover—; dislodge—; embolden—; grapple with—; halt—; inflame—; inflict on—; inveigh against—; overwhelm—; persecute—; puzzle—; reconcile—; subdue—; vanquish—; —advances; —approaches; —assaults; —attacks; —falls; —looms up; —strikes.
(See enemy, adversary, opponent, antagonist.)

FOG

adjectives
transparent; antarctic; autumnal; dank; treacherous; opalescent; thick; black; rolling; gray; heavy; white; pea-soup; dense; chill; contagious; low-lying; relentless; increasing; germ-laden; midsummer; silent; drooping; blinding; impenetrable; miasmal; curling; dismal; decided; wall-like; opaque; blanketing; heartless.

verbs
cut—; dispel—; disperse—; dissipate—; emerge from—; fathom—; grope in—; penetrate—; —abates; —blankets; —clears; —creeps up; —devours; —fades; —lifts; —settles on; —swallows up; —wraps around.
(See mist, haze, darkness.)

FOGGY

adverbs
mysteriously; unluckily; unfortunately; thickly; slightly; lightly; strangely; alarmingly; fearfully; dangerously; frightfully; impossibly; darkly; impenetrably; muddily; hazily; vaporously; wetly; mistily; nebulously; murkily; uncommonly; opaquely.

FOIBLE

adjectives
harmless; amiable; pitiable; laughable; pleasant; cheery; understandable.

verbs
acknowledge—; correct—; cure of—; detect—; disclose—; discover—; entail—; expose—; inherit—; observe—; overcome—; perceive—; produce—; resent—; reveal—; ridicule—; screen—; tempt—; —appears; —arises; —hinders; —irritates; —results.
(See fault, failing, weakness, defect, frailty.)

FOIL

adjectives
glistening; glittering; gleaming; sharp; glinting; swift.

FOLD

adjectives

enchanting; mazy; misty; snapping; secret; drowsy; brazen; caressing; snowy; floating; dimpled; thick; amorous; effeminate; ample; vaporous; voluminous; wind-flowing; loosened; deep-shadowed; clammy; becoming; sweeping; glistening; filmy; radiant; horizontal; fatal; strangling; gold-fringed; overhanging; graceful; meaningless; pinching; shivering; unapproachable.

FOLD (*v*)

adverbs

tensely; neatly; unconsciously; ostentatiously; quaintly; placidly; threateningly; wearily; voluminously; tenderly.

(See embrace, clasp.)

FOLDER

adjectives

descriptive; illustrated; well-printed; lucid; advertising.

verbs

arrange in—; assemble in—; attach to—; collect in—; destroy—; distribute—s; go through—; lodge in—; pass out—s; place in—; pore over—; prepare—; preserve in —; pull from—; refer to—; search in—; store in—; —advertises; —contains; —discloses.

(See catalogue, record.)

FOLIAGE

adjectives

cloudy; profuse; scattering; sapless; admirable; gracious; feathered; fresh; brilliant; luxuriant; delicate; evanescent; tropical; polished; gorgeous; golden; bright; tinted; silvery; bluish-gray; tender; scarlet; autumnal; shining; clustering; wasted; observable; sunny; dense; colored; fiery; blunt; curly; knotted; entangled; massive; dropping; ruddy; fresh; rustling; scant; softened; umbrageous; dying; intervening; voluminous; graceful; ornamental; protecting; overhanging; disease-resistant; impenetrable; screening; glossy.

verbs

admire—; bear—; behold—; decorate with —; don—; drench—; refresh—; shed—; shower—; sprout—; welcome—; yield—; —abounds; —adorns; —appears; —bathes; —blooms; —dies; —rustles; —shadows; —surrounds; —trembles.

(See leaves.)

FOLIO

adjectives

illuminated; ponderous; rare; inestimable; unhandy.

FOLK

adjectives

quick-witted; trivial; cross-tempered; quarrelsome; finical; guileful; guarded; suspicious; anxious; furtive; purposeful; true-hearted; famished; complacent; eavesdropping; ordinary; old-fashioned; showy; shadowy; placid; unexcitable; wee; shepherd; pert; novelty-loving; scribbling; fashionable; timorous; humble; hard-working; religious; peaceful; indigenous; unwieldy; slow; heavy; pale; prosperous; happy; furtive; cunning; hysterical; well-mannered; reaping; invincible; marooned; congenial; worthy; bourgeois; plain.

FOLKS

verbs

amuse—; enjoy—; please—; study—; visit —; —abide by; —adhere to; —admit; —cherish; —cleave to; —cling to; —congregate; —flourish; —follow; —frolic; —gambol; —gather; —inherit; —instil; —persevere; —resent; —revel.

(See people, nation, family, relatives.)

FOLLOW (*v*)

adverbs

instinctively; abjectly; trustfully; inevitably; irresistibly; reverently; wistfully; obsequiously; relentlessly; heedlessly; slavishly; reluctantly; unswervingly; gallantly; mechanically; traditionally; dutifully; dumbly; placidly; mutely; logically; religiously; grudgingly; undeviatingly; automatically; implicitly; doggedly; devoutly; diligently; sedulously.

(See chase, pursue.)

FOLLOWER

verbs

attract—s; beget—s; beguile—; conduct—; dictate to—; direct—; exhort—; fascinate —; gather—s; goad—; instruct—; retain—; secure—s; spurn—s; woo—s; —accepts; —accompanies; —admires; —assists; —imitates; —obeys; —practises; —s preserve; —serves.

(See disciple.)

FOLLOWERS

adjectives

heterogeneous; heretical; despairing; immediate; unruly; conservative; obsequious; faithful; diffident; egregious; wayworn; insuperable; sincerest; discontented; favorite; influential; scattered; stout-hearted; deluded.

FOLLOWING

adjectives

prodigious; tremendous; overbearing; unnatural; popular; huge; national; inspired.

verbs

guide—; instruct—; retain—; secure—; spurn—; whip up—; —adheres; —attends; —disbands; —pursues.

(See follower.)

FOLLY

adjectives

sheer; ludicrous; violent; prostrate; wilful; gratuitous; vain; shouting; stupendous; industrious; crowning; derogatory; egregious; serious; rash; present; deplorable; superfluous; sordid; idiotical; capricious; incurable; human; sentimental; disastrous; daring; amiable; pernicious; extreme; enormous; impious; obvious; ingrained; youthful (pl); amorous; harmless; pretty; wild; glaring; covert; pretentious; incredible; ridiculous; countless (pl); flagrant; repudiated; irritating; repented; repeated; absurd; intermittent (pl).

verbs

accuse of—; balk at—of; commit to—; decry—; deplore—; discern—; emancipate from—; fall into—; flatter into—; guard against—; lure into—; mitigate—; regret—; ridicule—; rue—; run after—ies; scorn—; uncover—; vex with—; work—.

(See foolishness, indiscretion, absurdity, infatuation.)

FOMENTATIONS

adjectives

copious; generous; applied; restful; unexpected.

FOND

adverbs

foolishly; unutterably; inordinately; infatuatedly; undyingly; obsequiously; genuinely; unwontedly; particularly; remarkably; childishly; extremely; tenderly; mawkishly; warmly; filially; dutifully; enthusiastically; intensely; spasmodically; ludicrously; demonstratively; temperately; tempestuously; gratefully; impulsively; respectfully; passionately; sincerely; beautifully; frankly; proudly; violently; sentimentally; deeply; heart-warmingly; gratifyingly; temperately; innately; essentially; confessedly; ridiculously; ostentatiously; understandably; justly; devotedly; incongruously; professedly; obviously; palpably.

FONDNESS

adjectives

thoughtful; foolish; maternal; exaggerated; inordinate; unutterable; inbred; infatuated; undying; obsequious; undiscriminating; genuine; unwonted; particular; remarkable; regal; evident; childish; solicitous; usual; extreme; gruesome; hoarded; faithful; unusual; tender; mawkish; precocious.

FOOD

adjectives

unwholesome; essential; wholesome; synthetic; spiritual; health; celestial; unsating; best; marvelous; intellectual; digestible; exceptional; repulsive; abundant; nutritious; natural; precious; unscrupulous; untasted; leathery; toothsome; heedful; unusual; attractive; delicious; inferior; unsavory; highly-spiced; concentrated; smoking; inedible; nectar; canned; adulterated; medicinal; palatable; enjoyable; protective; satisfying; superb; substantial; desirable; piscatorial; frosted; frozen; tonic; out-of-season; obnoxious; packaged; non-fattening; tempting; accustomed; rejuvenating; cheapest; sharp-tasting; execrable; inadequate; concentrated; well-cooked; raw; fundamental; automatic; elaborate; ambrosial; plenteous; delectable; scanty; superb; assimilated; vitalizing; luscious; world-famous; choice; dainty; tasty; good; fine; appetizing; excellent; splendid; inspired; insufficient.

verbs

absorb—; accumulate—; anoint—; assimilate—; bolt—; brown—; consume—; contaminate—; convey—; crave—; deprive of—; devitalize—; dilute—; dispense—; dole out—; expel—; flavor—; forage for—; freight—; masticate—; munch—; order—; partake of—; peptonize—; predigest—; prescribe—; puke—; purvey—; ration—; refine—; requisition—; restrict—; season—; shovel down—; snatch at—; sniff—; subsist on—; vomit—; withdraw—; wolf—; —agrees with; —decreases; —ferments; —irritates; —putrefies; —sustains; —upsets.

(See nourishment, nutriment, meat, bread, rations, victuals, viands, refreshments.)

FOOL

verbs

appear like—; play the—; prove oneself a —; put the—upon; remain—; ridicule—; suspect oneself—; think one a—; turn—; —apes; —beckons; —capers; —complains; —counterfeits; —disregards; —diverts; —dotes; —gambols; —ignores; —jests; —lets slip; —mistakes; —possesses; —prates; —preaches; —sidles; —mocks.

(See idiot, clown.)

FOOL (*v*)

adverbs

amiably; ignorantly; wantonly; pitifully; blindly; hatefully; vulgarly; tediously; clumsily; unfeelingly; ungratefully; venomously; deliberately; sportively; shallowly.

(See deceive, trick.)

FOOLERIES

adjectives

bygone; humorous; insouciant.

FOOLHARDY

adverbs

ignorantly; youthfully; boldly; ridiculously; absurdly; sadly; recklessly; fecklessly; carelessly; daringly; desperately; rashly; idiotically; preposterously; indiscreetly; extravagantly; imprudently; childishly; dangerously; terribly; senselessly.

FOOLING

adjectives

gracious; admirable; airy; flippant.

FOOLISH

adverbs

ridiculously; absurdly; ludicrously; unreasonably; insanely; extravagantly; idiotically; ineptly; inanely; irrationally; childishly; stupidly; blatantly; brainlessly; fatuously; injudiciously; rashly; simply; weakly; altogether; supremely; senselessly; fantastically; manifestly; grossly; pathetically.

FOOLISHNESS

adjectives

potent; drunken; colossal; unspeakable.

verbs

awaken—; cast aside—; confess—; convert into—; criticize—; forsake—; govern by—; grieve over—; ignore—; indicate—; persuade to—; practise—; pretend—; provide —; reprimand—; resent—; ridicule—; rue —; shape—; sneer at—; suffer for—; —amuses; —befits; —persists; —smarts; —tempts; prevent—.

(See folly, absurdity; imprudence, indiscretion.)

FOOLS

adjectives

calf-like; luckless; flatulent; simple-minded; amiable; bleating; superstitious; superannuated; ignorant; weak-minded; poor; dappled; wanton; blind; pitiful; blasted; badgering; family; dull; impractical; incapable; honest; besotted; blundering; hateful; crack-brained; veritable; tuneful; precious; misguided; puling; pale; scrawny; wretched; vulgar; allowed; frantic; proud; tedious; witty; clumsy; gullible; strait-laced; soft; dull-eyed; shallow; learned; sweeter; unfeeling; inconstant; damnable; ungrateful; hairy; accursed; motley; officious; positive; brazen; venomous; yawning; consummate; obstinate; conspicuous; fond; deliberate; contemplative; rash; patient; scoundrelly.

FOOT

adjectives

wandering; blistered; emphatic; itching; fiery; stealthy; mutilated; inaudible; noiseless; crushing; punctilious; spurning; feathered; ponderous; restless; fearful; godlike; diminutive; forgetful; cautious; unresisting; swelled; slight; slender; bounding; maladjusted; individual; tentative; struggling; cloven; careless; investigating; nimble; fairy; exquisite; shapely; tiniest; beautiful; small; bare; dangling; naked; extended; sensitive; sandaled; exploring; large-booted; gout-ridden.

verbs

ail—; bandage—; bare—; brace—; chafe —; control—; drum—; elevate—; expose—; injure—; journey on—; lame—; lay—on; massage—; plant—; plunk (colloq.)—; scramble to feet; shod—; shuffle feet; spring to feet; stagger to feet; stamp—; trample under—; wander on—; —aches; —drags;

—pounds; —presses; feet scurry; —sinks in; —soils; feet slacken their pace; —treads on; —trips; —lags; —marks; feet patter.

FOOTFALL

adjectives
lightest; stealthy; pattering (pl).

FOOT-HILLS

adjectives
desolate; barren; uninhabitable.

FOOTHOLD

adjectives
meager; scant; precarious; tentative.

verbs
acquire—; apply—; climb by—; contrive—; devise—; effect—; employ—; gain—; grab —; lose—; manage—; necessitate—; recover—; relax—; release—; warrant—; —agonizes; —enables; —saves.
(See support, hold.)

FOOTING

adjectives
insecure; surer; friendly; uncertain; indispensable; equal; solid; unsteadfast; treacherous; unsteady.

FOOTLIGHTS

verbs
crave—; diminish—; employ—; hover at —; reach—; require—; —attract; —color; —deceive; —divert; —emblazon; —enhance; —flash; —flatter; —flood; —glare; —illumine; —shine; —soften; —suffuse.
(See light, stage, theater.)

FOOTMAN

adjectives
servile; stiff-necked; powder-headed; select.

FOOT-NOTE

adjectives
humble; elusive; helpful; necessary.

FOOTPRINTS

adjectives
fading; fiery; veritable; dim; blurred; blood-stained; halting.

FOOTSTEP

verbs
anticipate—; characterize—; dim—; identify—; listen for—; muffle—; obliterate—; pad—; recognize—; trace—; tread in—; —destroys; —exposes; —lags; —mars; —marks; —patters; —presses; —resounds; —reveals; —sinks in; —soils; —surprises; —warns; anticipate—.
(See step.)

FOOTSTEPS

adjectives
ringing; impartial; martial; harmless; pattering; plainer; faltering; retreating; ethereal; cautious; shuffling; early; tranquil; hastening; hurried; tottering; hallowed; errant; unwary; coming; paternal; trembling; visiting; rapid; parting; softened; rustling; foul; light; bounding.

FOOTSTOOL

adjectives
radiant; battered; comfortable.

FOOTWAY

adjectives
grass-grown; discernible; winding.

FOOTWEAR

adjectives
superior; expensive; exclusive; comfortable.

FOP

adjectives
priggish; suave; conceited; bold; overdressed; rash; silk-stockinged.

FOPPERIES

adjectives
exaggerated; indescribable; undesirable; unthinkable.

FOPPISH

adverbs
effeminately; fashionably; gallantly; preposterously; foolishly; ludicrously; absurdly; senselessly; conceitedly; ostentatiously; showily; flauntingly; jauntily; blithely; habitually; outlandishly; outrageously; disgustingly; pretentiously; proudly; pridefully; detestably; offensively; abominably.

FORAGING

adjectives
criminal; adept; clumsy; exploratory.

FORAYS

adjectives
occasional; frequent; sudden; ill-starred; remorseless; endless.

FORBEARANCE

adjectives

friendly; generous; unusual; wonderful; abounding; systematic; passive; unexpected; affectionate; good-natured; gentle.

verbs

admire—; commend—; conduct with—; end—; endure with—; excel in—; extort—; feign—; indulge in—; justify—; laud—; learn—; occasion—; practise—; praise—; pretend—; submit with—; suffer—; treat with—; —surprises.

(See patience, mercy, indulgence, tolerance.)

FORBID (v)

adverbs

specifically; ostentatiously; positively; dogmatically; rudely; pugnaciously; reluctantly; vehemently.

(See restrain, hinder, prevent.)

FORBIDDING

adverbs

sternly; disagreeably; unreasonably; unpleasantly; wryly; frightfully; gracelessly; grossly; grimly; shockingly; roughly; repulsively; monstrously; horridly; haggardly; dreadfully; odiously; appallingly.

FORCE

adjectives

tangential; orthogonal; material; automatic; selling; striving; provisional; elastic; diminished; perturbative; brainless; all-compelling; intensified; organizing; victorious; quickening; despoiling; radial; disturbing; insurgent; expeditionary; ethical; considerable; available; dramatic; hoplite; campaigning; resistless; influential; chemical; odious; cumulative; inadequate; powerful; imperious; sufficient; tremendous; superior; crushing; irresistible; apogee; vital; antagonistic; extraordinary; deadly; imperial; sullen; enduring; overwhelming; thwarting; civilizing; working; financial; deterring; conflicting; enormous; deterrent; molecular; static; latent; incomprehensible; invading; opposing; mechanical; insuperable; inorganic; vast; mental; formidable; unvarying; headlong; superior; intense; artistic; demoralized; meditative; self-formed; scattered; unguided; blind; striking; social; constant; besieging; threatening; protective; centrifugal; centripetal; objective; spiritual; ignoble; unwieldy; retarding; natural; frictional; universal; concentrated; entire; spontaneous; operant; devitalizing; permanent; virile; efficient; blasphemous; exuberant; attacking; unrestrained; creative; excessive; electro-motive; well-disciplined; human; reverberating; impelling; synthetic; injurious; swelling; explosive; negative; indivisible; malevolent; instrumental; reactionary; fivefold; overpowering; subterranean; repellent; auxiliary; comparative; insignificant; genuine; meager; potent; fearful; harnessed; terrible; unknown; frontier; outnumbered; selective; cohesive; divided; frightful; calculable; fluid; disturbing; controlling; muscular; superhuman; physical; ameliorative; unaided; brute; tragic; moral; missionary; numerical; defending; living; nervous; passionate; innovating; armed; all-pervading; compulsory; disheartened; elemental; original; lacking; famished; available; hostile; demoniac; peculiar; bodily; uncommon; magnetic; mere; undiminished; pneumatic; lifting; terrifying; supplementary; persuasive; domestic; ascensional; revolting; overmastering; equivalent; driving; deep; remedial; vegetative; sheer; dubious; competent; incisive; generative; unrelenting; sacred; quiet; unmerciful; educational; dynamic; almighty; omnipresent; effectual; wavering; plastic; dumb-gazing; supernatural; unrestricted; destructive; reliable; tractive; emotional; multiple; caressing; illustrative; ethereal; subversive; masterful; philosophical; colonial; unseen; international; furious; economic; wave-whirled; gravitating; sustaining; mercenary; much-needed; propulsive; undeniable; motley; subtle; ceaseless; bull-like; sales; uniformed; unpitying; elevatory; inherent; royal; obstructive; dominant; great; contending; innate; imperious; constructive; psychological; exigent; exhausted; prevalent; warring; primal.

verbs

absorb—; accelerate—; acquire—; assail by —; combat—; concentrate—s; defy—; diminish—; discipline—s; dislodge by—; divert —; employ—; focus—upon; join—s; gather —s; generate—; hamper—; harmonize—s; harness—; impede—; intensify—; let loose —s; marshal—s; mass—s; muster—s; neutralize—; nullify—; rally—s; react upon with—; recruit—s; resist—; resort to—; stymie—; suspend—; suppress by—; transmit—; triumph over—; utilize—; weaken—; —s battle; —s engulf; —impels; —s motivate; —subdues; —subsides; —s underlie; —s war.

(See energy, power, strength.)

FORCE (v)

adverbs

deliberately; instinctively; ruthlessly; offensively; gradually; automatically; dramatically; antagonistically; financially; ignobly; spontaneously; blasphemously; malevolently; potently; demoniacally; incisively; dynamically; psychologically; odiously.

(See oblige, compel.)

FORCEFUL

adverbs

impressively; immensely; unwontedly; admirably; intensely; ably; dynamically; potentially; persuasively; vigorously; invincibly; sublimely; eloquently; influentially; strikingly; effectively; effectually; energetically; intentionally; deliberately; trenchantly; vehemently; violently; sensationally; boldly; passionately; vividly.

FORD

adjectives

practicable; convenient.

FOREARMS

adjectives

wiry; sinewy; hairy.

FOREBEARS

verbs

admire—; claim—; commemorate—; extol —; honor—; inherit from—; invent—; judge—; receive from—; uphold—; venerate—; wean away from—; —achieve; —accomplish; —found; —inspire; —instil; —lead; —migrate; —produce; —settle; —suffer.

(See ancestors.)

FOREBODING

verbs

arouse—; assail by—; cast aside—; disperse—; fly from—; heed—; realize—; relate—; ridicule—; —advises; —betokens; —divines; —foretells; —oppresses; —overhangs; —prophesies; —signifies; —warns.

(See apprehension, anticipation, prognostication.)

FOREBODINGS

adjectives

vague; gloomy; dismal; unfavorable; cynical; sorrowful; dim; retroactive; chilling; undefinable; wretched; sinister; grim; inexplicable; incorrect.

FORECAST

adjectives

judicious; vivid; conservative; surprising; accurate; exultant; enlightened; broad; prophetic; provident.

verbs

abide by—; arise from—; believe—; commend—; flout—; heed—; inquire of—; provide—; read—; rectify—; ridicule—; study —; trust—; —advises; —anticipates; —dejects; —indicates; —predicts; —promises; —warns.

(See prophecy, estimate.)

FOREFATHERS

adjectives

crusading; physical; pioneering.

FOREFINGER

adjectives

absolute; gnarled; coercive; swarthy; grimy; argumentative; slim; beckoning; pointed; long; flapping; thick; blunt; admonitory; crooked; mocking.

FOREHEAD

adjectives

flaming; tattooed; unfretful; expanded; marble; smooth; swarthy; luminous; tanned; pale; pallid; mantling; frowning; mountainous; square; fretted; bulging; lofty; spacious; jutting; powerful; branded; fabled; dusky; livid; ample; dirty; well-developed; unsustained; knobby; somber; tranquil; exquisite; disfigured; shaped; wide; massive; cloudless; wrinkled; deep-grooved; damp; moist; perspiring; mean; calm; burning; towering; bold; throbbing; princely; well-shaped; fine; narrow; aristocratic; intelligent; brainy; anxious; receding; unbashful.

verbs

cloud—; distinguish by—; furrow—; knot —; mop—; raise—; scar—; —wrinkles; —puckers; —pulsates; —throbs.

(See face, head.)

FOREIGN

adverbs
harmlessly; objectionably; inadmissably; unconformably; strangely; remotely; irrelevantly; outlandishly; undeniably; ostentatiously; palpably; essentially; obviously; disagreeably; inconceivably; relatively; discordantly; impertinently; fantastically; exotically; intrusively; inimically; disinterestedly; extraneously.

FOREIGNER

adjectives
high-born; cursed; invading; enlightened; hated; distinguished.

verbs
accept—; admit—; allow—; Americanize—; beguile—; deport—; enhance—; entertain —; examine—; limit—s; lodge—; naturalize—; reject—; school—in; smuggle in—s; welcome—; —s colonize; —s crowd; —s intrude; —s settle in.
(See alien.)

FORERUNNER

adjectives
elegant; early; indigenous.

FORESEE (*v*)

adverbs
dimly; timorously; morbidly; clairvoyantly; vividly; mysteriously; supernaturally; unerringly.
(See anticipate, prepare, foretell.)

FORESIGHT

adjectives
shrinking; patriotic; economic; fiery; sagacious; divine; prudent; keen.

FOREST

adjectives
dull; motionless; intricate; illimitable; isolated; teak; aboriginal; virgin; lonely; primeval; ilex; adjacent; unawakened; green-haired; trackless; preservable; cathedral-vaulted; thick-studded; favoring; natural; solemn; tropical; impenetrable; solitary; mildew; uncleared; enchanted; rank; moon-illumined; great; silent; desolate; interminable; incense-bearing; magnificent; fragrant; murmuring; umbrageous; blackened; sun-filled; flaming; black; golden; tinted; unspoiled; moaning; boundless; thicketed; still; thick; rude; untrodden; dripping; shadowed; unwilling; melancholy; somber; tangled; pine-carpeted; infinite; tantalizing; hazy; unbroken; coniferous; panther-peopled; odorous; stretching; hoary; intervening; matted; immense; majestic; fast-darkening; surrounding; dreary; leafless; silver-powdered; limitless; disenchanted; unsurveyed; thrifty; unwholesome; girdling; trackless; frowning; consuming; scathed; ancient; encircling; mighty; massy; monotonous; luxuriant; sleeping; uncouth; miniature; black-bearded; encroaching; slumberous.

verbs
conserve—s; denude—s; deplete—; dot with —s; entangle in—; fell—; guard—; harbor in—; infest—; invade—; jeopardize—s; level—; patrol—; poach in—; preserve—; raze—; skirt—; thin out—; wipe out—; —abounds in; —encircles; —extends; —flourishes; —ranges; —whispers.
(See jungle.)

FORETELL (*v*)

adverbs
portentously; sensationally; uncannily; clairvoyantly; accurately; unerringly.
(See predict, portend, foresee.)

FORETHOUGHT

adjectives
divine; anxious; endless; deliberate.

verbs
commend—; decide with—; discipline to—; employ—; exercise—; exhibit—; indulge in —; mark by—; necessitate—; note for—; praise—; provide—; save by—; submit to —; urge—; —assures; —determines; —enables; —impedes; —influences; —obviates; —overcomes; —prepares; —reaps.
(See consideration, prudence, precaution.)

FORFEIT

adjectives
unredeemable; profitless; vain.

verbs
call—; demand—; exact—; impose—; incur—; lose—; offer—; pay—; penalize with —; punish with—; redeem—; remit—; subject to—; take—; —clears; —deprives; —redeems; —releases; —ruins.
(See fine, penalty.)

FORFEIT (v)

adverbs
automatically; legally; irrevocably; inevitably; provisionally; nominally.
(See fine, pay.)

FORGE

adjectives
gleaming; sounding; flashing.

FORGE (v)

adverbs
laboriously; dexterously; artfully; audaciously; deliberately; daringly; subtly.
(See force, push.)

FORGERY

adjectives
literary; flimsy; deliberate; audacious.

FORGET (v)

adverbs
mercifully; promptly; speedily; momentarily; eternally; wantonly; deliberately; conveniently; prudently; flagrantly.
(See ignore, neglect, overlook.)

FORGETFUL

adverbs
lamentably; carelessly; idly; inattentively; senilely; agedly; hopelessly; deplorably; unfortunately; conveniently; tactfully; forgivingly; gracefully; irritatingly; provokingly; vexatiously; incurably; helplessly; nervously; weakly; treacherously; sadly; terribly; inexcusably; criminally; tragically.

FORGETFULNESS

adjectives
conceivable; dull; momentary; frank; heavenly; atrocious; slumberous; unkind; eternal.

FORGIVE (v)

adverbs
graciously; magnanimously; indulgently; meekly; heartily; mutually; patiently; solemnly; cordially; spiritually.
(See excuse, acquit.)

FORGIVENESS

adjectives
infinite; mutual; implored.

FORGIVING

adverbs
gracefully; indulgently; wisely; discreetly; wholly; tolerantly; tactfully; generously; graciously; infinitely; nobly; magnanimously; charitably; benignly; unexpectedly; surprisingly; chivalrously; gallantly; affably; extremely.

FORGOTTEN

adverbs
sadly; altogether; unhappily; conveniently; cold-heartedly; unfeelingly; wretchedly; unpardonably; inexcusably; carelessly; brutally; thoughtlessly; mercilessly; selfishly; ungratefully; thanklessly; friendlessly; desolately; forlornly; miserably; disconsolately; appallingly; shockingly.

FORK

adjectives
gesticulating; triple; excoriated; soft; tender; furrowy; vibrating; tuning.

verbs
barb with—; brandish—; cast with—; convey on—; draw with—; hook with—; impale on—; jab with—; lift—; pursue with—; stab with—; —pierces; —prongs; —spears; —transfers.
(See knife.)

FORLORN

adverbs
lonesomely; terribly; pitiably; pathetically; uncommonly; utterly; listlessly; silently; glumly; resignedly; profoundly; weirdly; singularly; immensely; blankly; unutterably.

FORM

adjectives
absurd; active; acute; admirable; adorable; aesthetic; aggravated; airy; ample; analogic; angular; antique; apparent; archaic; archangelic; architectural; artistic; athletic; attenuated; barbarous; barest; beastlike; beautiful; bent; bestial; bewildering; bewitching; birdlike; blanketed; blasting; bleeding; bliss-inspiring; bloated; bounding; boyish; briefest; brigand-like; broken; buckskin-clad; burly; changing; charming; chaste; childish; chronic; circular; clamorous; classic; clothed; codified (pl); collectible; colloidal; comely; commanding; compact; complicated; concentrated; conciliatory; concrete; condensed; constitutional; contrary; convenient; conventional; corrupt-

ed; countless (pl); creeping; crowded; crumpled; cultivated; cumulative; curvilinear; debasing; cylindrical; dainty; decrepit; desired; definite; democratic; detailed; determinate; diabolic; diluted; disguised; disrobed; dissolving; distressing; distribution; durable; earliest; ecstatic; elastic; elegant; elliptic; emasculated; erect; ephemeral; epistolary; equitable; established; erroneous; eventual; exaggerated; express; expurgated; exquisite; faded; fair; faltering; famished; fan-shaped; fantasmalike; fantastic; faultless; feigned; feminine; fiery; flawless; flitting; floral; fluid; fragile; fruitful; gallant; fundamental; garbled; gaseous; gigantic; gasping; gaunt; geometrical; ghostly; glancing; gleaming; gloomy; glorious; glowing; gnarled; graceful; goodly; graceless; grandiose; granular; graphic; greyhound-like; groaning; guileless; handsome; harmless; harmonic; heavenly; herculean; heroic; historic; horrible; huddled; hulking; human; hungry; hurrying; ill-clad; imposing; improvisational; incoherent; inconvenient; indirect; individual; indurate; inert; inexorable; infantile; ingenious; intimate; instrumental; intricate; irritated; jovial; jostling; kicking; languid; lanky; lifeless; long; low; magnified; majestic; malignant; mainfold; manly; mantled; maritime; metrical; microscopic; milder; mitigated; moderate; modified; moldering; monophonic; monumental; motionless; motley (pl); moving; mundane; myriad; mythologic; native; never-shifting; needleshaped; obese; offensive; oligarchic; operatic; organic; outward; palpable; palatable; particular; pathetic; permanent; plastic; pliant; poetic; pompous; portly; prescribed; pretentious; printed; pristine; prone; proper; prostrate; protesting; proverbial; provincial; puerile; puerperal; pure; quantitative; quivering; rebellious; recitative; recumbent; regular; related; reluctant; repugnant; respectful; retiring; rhythmic; robust; rigid; sardonic; scholastic; semicircular; semi-elliptical; senseless; serpentine; shadowy; shaky; shapely; simple; shivering; shriveled; shrouded; sinking; shrunken; singular; skeleton; slender; slim; smug; slouching; slumping; spare; spectral; spheroidal; spiritualized; squalid; staggering; standard; startling; stately; stiff; strange; strong; structural; struggling; stunted; subsumed; suffering; suitable; superb; swallow-tailed; symmetrical; tall; tapering; technical; tedious; theistic; thickening; thin; tiny; titanic; tortuous; tottering; towering; traditional; transient; typical; unadulterated; unblemished; undulating; undying; unhealthy; unimaginable; unintelligible; united; unmatched; unnatural; unphonetic; unremembered; unsubstantial; unusual; vacant; valuable; vaporous; varied; vast; veiled; venerable; vicarious; villanelle; virulent; visible; visionary; warlike; wasted; wedge-shaped; weird; well-balanced; willowy; feeble; coherent; wolflike; wooden; writhing; conversational; peculiar; pedagogic; peerless; phantom.

verbs

accept—; adhere to—; assume—; conventionalize—; develop—; distort—; enhance —; evince—; gain—; insist on—; jeopardize—; lend—to; model on—; pattern—; retain—; scoff at—; standardize—; —embraces; —sways.

(See method, ritual, style, model.)

FORM (*v*)

adverbs

voluntarily; theoretically; successively; gracefully; dexterously; expeditiously; inadvertently; prematurely; originally; insensibly; ultimately; delicately; collectively; ingeniously; durably; aesthetically; constitutionally; cumulatively; democratically; diabolically; ephemerally; erroneously; fantastically; geometrically; grandiosely; majestically; organically; symmetrically; tortuously.

(See shape, mould.)

FORMAL

adverbs

extremely; unusually; officially; strictly; conventionally; dogmatically; ritualistically; legally; ecclesiastically; absolutely; undeviatingly; explicitly; solemnly; ceremoniously; curiously; gracefully; splendidly; brilliantly; terribly; awesomely; punctiliously; meticulously; particularly; needlessly; coldly; unnecessarily; foolishly.

FORMALITY

adjectives

concluding; statuesque; affected; stiff; precise; professional; imposing; architectural; stately; icy; tired; tiring; degrading; rigid; joyless.

verbs

adopt—; break—; conduct with—; conform to—; discard—; dress in—; don—; ease—;

encase in—; end—ies; endure—; engage in —; execute with—; exercise—; insist on—; observe—ies; perform—ies; peach—ies; preserve—ies; relax—; require—; school in —; shed—; shun—; —corsets; —exasperates; —retards; —stifles; —preserves.

(See conventionality, ceremony.)

FORMATION

adjectives

geological; humanistic; proper; peculiar; meteoric; tertiary; harmonic; crude; various (pl); fantastic; shaft-like; remarkable; delusional; delicate; inanimate; slow.

verbs

abet —; aid —; bar —; check —; conceal — of; discover —; divest of —; emerge from —; precede —; prevent —; shake —; sponsor —; suppress —; whip into —; — breaks; — divides; — splits; — takes place.

(See arrangement, development.)

FORMULA

adjectives

mathematical; moral; abstract; original; magical; aphoristic; invariable; devotional; bristling; perfected; barren; creative; dead; noble; majestic; definite.

verbs

accept—; apply—; apprise of—; bungle—; change—; coin—; compound—; compute—; devise—; employ—; evolve—; express in—; falsify—; fetter by—; fulfill—; reduce to—; simplify—; utilize—; work from—; —clarifies; —curbs; —states.

(See rule, form, prescription, principle, ritual.)

FORMULATE (v)

adverbs

peculiarly; scientifically; enterprisingly; academically; skillfully; dexterously; crudely; professionally.

(See plan, prepare.)

FORMULATION

adjectives

academic; scientific; definite; crude.

FORSAKE (v)

adverbs

reluctantly; unnaturally; disastrously; faithlessly; shamefully; churlishly; unfeelingly.

(See abandon, quit, leave.)

FORSAKEN

adverbs

desolately; lamentably; desperately; helplessly; shockingly; utterly; unhappily; coldheartedly; unfeelingly; wretchedly; miserably; appallingly; friendlessly; mercilessly; unpardonably; thoughtlessly; cruelly; brutally; disconsolately; dreadfully; pitifully.

FORT

adjectives

outlying; improvised; grim; silent; impregnable; well-garrisoned; deserted; strategic; hidden; camouflaged.

FORTIFICATION

adjectives

wasted; noble; remarkable; permanent; extensive; grim; stupendous; medieval; tremendous; useless; antiquated.

verbs

arm —; assail —; charge —; erect —; fire on —; maintain —; march to —; necessitate —; plan —; provide —; require —; shatter —; — defends; — guards; — overlooks; — preserves; — protects; — repels; — shields; — surrounds; — yields.

(See castle, stronghold.)

FORTIFY (v)

adverbs

unwaveringly; speedily; stalwartly; mysteriously; testily; crudely; powerfully; permanently; grimly; medievally; antiquatedly; extensively.

(See defend, guard, protect, resist.)

FORTITUDE

adjectives

Christian; matchless; admirable; uncomplaining; unpretentious; placid; remarkable; surprising; stoic; unshakable; intestinal; sustained; physical; iron; enduring; calm; extraordinary; sufficient; stolid.

verbs

admire —; arm with —; bear with —; commend —; conduct with —; consider —; endure with —; excel in —; exhibit —; laud —; mark by —; occasion —; practice —; praise —; require —; summon —; tolerate with —; treat with —; — amazes; — surprises.

(See courage, endurance, strength.)

FORTRESS

adjectives
level; mighty; permanent; improvised; baronial; gloomy; island; feminine; garrisoned; inaccessible; dismantled; frowning; seductive; insulated; frost-locked; grim; walled; magnificent; medieval; ragged; beleaguered; rock-bound; impregnable; isolated.

FORTUITOUS

adverbs
curiously; obviously; luckily; presumably; casually; wholly; comically; inexplicably; mysteriously; admittedly; ludicrously; certainly; providentially; frequently; purportedly; evidently; luckily; awkwardly; pleasantly; tragically; undependably; uneasily; uncertainly; opportunely; ironically; favorably; conveniently.

FORTUNATE

adverbs
blessedly; splendidly; politically; incidentally; moderately; luckily; unwontedly; propitiously; systematically; regularly; uniformly; brilliantly; inherently; triumphantly; inexpressibly; inscrutably; signally; notoriously; unaccountably; unwarrantably; significantly; mysteriously; immensely; marvellously; ultimately; enviably; conveniently; ingeniously; accidentally; reasonably; highly; extremely; happily; fairly; auspiciously; luckily; providentially; remarkably; unusually; consistently; gratifyingly; pleasantly; agreeably; fittingly; delightfully; appropriately.

FORTUNE

adjectives
fairer; munificent; fallen; rude; adverse; cursed; blessed; varying; colossal; competent; considerate; gracious; splendid; political; forlorn; individual; shattered; ample; stupendous; unparalleled; equal; favorable; blind; moderate; stormy; good; fitful; frowning; drooping; public; invulnerable; tottering; wretched; rare; fluctuating; enormous; crooked; humbled; squandered; dire; subsequent; brilliant; indulgent; inconstant; princely; changing; gloomy; wild; patrimonial; narrow; fierce; keen; adventurous; sunny; superior; promising; dissipated; extraordinary; desperate; fouler; spiritual; broken; prodigious; relenting; signal; hostile; unconfirmed; fretted; sure; disastrous; dependent; ultimate; doubtful; waning.

verbs
accumulate —; amass —; bemoan —; bewail —; dissipate —; establish —; fall into —; garner —; hazard —; mend —; net —; prophesy —; reap —; recoup —; replenish —; restore —; retrieve —; stake — on; struggle for —; tempt —; wipe away —; wreck —; —s ascend; —s crash; — ebbs; — fails; — favors; — flows; — melts away.

(See chance, fate, destiny, estate, possessions, success, wealth.)

FORWARD (*v*)

adverbs
conscientiously; progressively; unselfishly; magnanimously; munificently; disastrously; ultimately.

(See advance, send.)

FORWARDNESS

adjectives
intrusive; brusque; brash.

FOSSIL

adjectives
Paleozoic; contained; stone-pervaded; mammalian; minute; significant.

FOSTER (*v*)

adverbs
cunningly; gradually; effectually; deliberately; diligently; cordially; subtly; diabolically; treacherously; philosophically.

(See support, promote.)

FOULNESS

adjectives
horrid; Stygian; dank; miasmic.

FOUNDATION

adjectives
massive; explanatory; moral; splendid; well-laid; unorthodox; rational; permanent; slender; substantial; antiquated; shifting; virtual; respectable; monstrous; dangerous; durable; treacherous; solid; floating; everlasting; enviable; philosophic; sufficient; economical; lasting; broad; crumbling; reciprocal; thrilling; slenderizing.

verbs
build —; correct —; deprive of —; dig at —; erect —; founder at —; ground on —; jeopardize —; lay —; protect —; ruffle —; sap —; shake —; strike at —; undermine —; — crumbles; — remains; — shudders; — stands; — supports.

(See base, basis, principles.)

FOUNDER

adjectives
traditional; energetic; patient; spiritual.

FOUNDLING

adjectives
helpless; undernourished; scantily-clad.

FOUNT

adjectives
sapphire; never-failing; continual; perennial; babbling; sacred; consecrated; youth-giving.

FOUNTAIN

adjectives
paved; wide-spreading; inexhaustible; burning; searchless; trickling; foul; ancient; perennial; bitter; many-voiced; spouting; celestial; ever-filling; welling; untainted; fresh; life-sealed; gurgling; weedy; pleasant; fire-laden; reedy; living; perpetual; hillside; fiery; soulless; bubbling; distant; sporting; earthly; fresh; ceaseless; gushing; unlocked; unfailing; lightning; cool; ablutionary; flashing; geyserlike.

verbs
admire —; choke —; illuminate —; — bubbles; — dances; — flings; — floods; — gleams; — gurgles; — gushes; — plays; — sallies; — scintillates; — sings; — sparkles; — splashes; — spouts; — sprinkles; — spurts; — twinkles; — weeps.

(See spring, brook, spray.)

FOUNTAIN-PEN

verbs
feed —; fill —; illustrate with —; pocket —; press on —; regulate —; reserve in —; store in —; transcribe with —; uncap —; — blotches; — drips; — leaks; — scratches; — spills; — stains.

(See pen.)

FOWL

adjectives
domestic; plump; glossy; long-billed; gluttonous; winged; screaming; sea; poor; miserable; ravenous; fearful; wild; skinny; sapless; lagging; ungainly; succulent; lean.

verbs
behead —; boil —; breed —s; call —; catch —; devour —; feed —s; house —s; roast —; serve —; shoo —; snare —; steal —; — cackles; — crows; —s flock; —s gather; — pecks; — scratches.

(See hen, rooster, bird, chicken, turkey, duck, etc.)

FOX

adjectives
stealthy; caverned; cunning; loping; sly; sleek; slinking.

verbs
chase —; ensnare —; farm —; pursue —; raise —es; skin —; trap —; — burrows; — claws; — darts; — digs; — displays; — excavates; — fools; — leaps; — outwits; — preys on; — roams; — tricks.

(See animal.)

FOXY

adverbs
naturally; cautiously; shrewdly; artfully; abominably; treacherously; trickily; subtly; sharply; evasively; skilfully; adroitly; astutely; deceptively; cunningly; unexpectedly; profoundly; unusually; diplomatically; insidiously; deplorably; unfortunately; strategically; commercially; financially; cannily.

FOYER

adjectives
bare; grotesque; sumptuous.

FRACAS

verbs
bridle —; curb —; describe —; enjoy —; enter —; indulge in —; inflame to —; inquire into —; instigate —; interrupt —; invite —; involve in —; occasion —; prevent —; produce —; quell —; raise —; referee —; — annoys; — irritates; — subsides; — unnerves.

(See fight, brawl, uproar, disturbance.)

FRACTION

adjectives
insignificant; minute; undue; slender; mixed.

verbs
break into —s; denote —; diminish to —; dispense with —; dispute —; divide into —s; dwindle to —; express —; include —;

indicate —; instruct in —s; measure by —; observe —; piece into —s; reduce to —; — irks; — puzzles.
(See fragment.)

FRACTIOUS

adverbs
unmanageably; irritatingly; distressingly; undeniably; notoriously; uncontrollably; ungovernably; abominably; detestably; petulantly; highly; utterly; terribly; peculiarly; singularly; oddly; queerly; churlishly; excitably; snappily; captiously; cantankerously; restively; intolerably; utterly.

FRACTURE

verbs
cast —; compound —; depress —; examine —; expose —; fasten —; incur —; inflict —; prevent —; produce —; recognize —; reconcile —; reduce —; splice —; splint —; support —; x-ray —; — divides; — heals; — mends; — shocks; — splits; — splinters; — unites.
(See rupture, breach.)

FRAGILE

adverbs
delicately; infirmly; weakly; languidly; increasingly; terribly; totteringly; tremulously; decrepitly; defensely; flimsily; nervously; frightfully; shakily; hopelessly; irremediably; uncommonly.

FRAGMENT

adjectives
unrelated; expurgated; enormous; intelligible; welcome; warlike; sparkling; numberless (pl); cumbrous; colossal; tattered; insignificant; scattered (pl); hissing; weary; whirling; clattering; chaotic; shattered; quarried; incoherent; isolated; misty; artless; halting; detached; ill-smelling; connected; cometary; heterogeneous; massive; indubitable; massy; rough; curious; countless (pl); weary; fancy; important; disjointed; grand; beauteous; sculptured; pitiful; brilliant; restless; exquisite.

verbs
break into—s; cast into—s; cherish—s; conceal—s; discard—s; excise—s; extract—s; gather up—s; hack into—s; preserve—s; reduce to—s; retain—s; rip into—s; scatter —s; splinter into—s; strew—s; tear into—s; —embarrasses; —s fill; —projects; —s scatter.
(See part, portion, piece, remnant, chip.)

FRAGRANCE

adjectives
fruity; heady; worldly; delicious; favorite; faint; clinging; delightful; ardor-awakening; sweet; visible; strong; tea; delicate; full-blown; nocturnal; powerful; cloverlike; midsummer; ambrosial; breathing; wholesome; odorous; salty; diffusing; fog; subtle; autumnal; exotic; worldly; unmatched; feverish; ineffable; homelike; dewy; aromatic; spicy; manifold; healthful; nutlike; honied; evanescent; blended; provocative; woody; sense-dissolving; embodied; balmy.

verbs
admire—; anoint with—; delight in—; diffuse—; emit—; exude—; fill with—; gather —; inhale—; savor—; share—; veil in—; yield—; —assaults; —clouds; —edifies; — floats; —outlasts; —permeates; —pleases; —scents; —stirs.
(See sweetness, cdor, perfume, scent, smell.)

FRAGRANT

adverbs
pleasantly; spicily; redolently; sweetly; pungently; arrestingly; refreshingly; seductively; pleasingly; alluringly; strongly; delicately; faintly; exquisitely; enchantingly; charmingly; overpoweringly; overwhelmingly; delectably; intoxicatingly; lingeringly; exotically; romantically; evanescently.

FRAIL

adverbs
terribly; pitifully; unusually; increasingly; nervously; feebly; decrepitly; languidly; defenselessly; helplessly; hopelessly; appallingly; shockingly; miserably; wretchedly.

FRAILTY

adjectives
human; decorous; female; universal; patent; obvious; apparent; inexcusable.

verbs
admit—; condemn—; confess—; crush—; cure—; disguise—; draw—; fall into—; hide—; inherit—; overcome—; play on—; remove—; reveal—; seek—; surrender to —; tempt—; tolerate—; treat—; —s cheat; —shames.
(See weakness.)

FRAME

adjectives

consistent; wasted; mortal; lordly; narrow; thrilling; graceful; universal; spreading; comfortable; lean; becoming; ebonite; tottering; decrepit; unhelpful; nerveless; ponderous; imposing; corporal; unbreathing; stalwart; elastic; weary; lank; long-limbed; grateful; smitten; impassioned; growing; iron; sinful; kindred; anxious; well-knit; wretched; ultimate; chilled; feeble; inexplicable; racked; bent; gilded; blanket-covered; spiritless; huge; husky; faltering; tortured; powerful; pain-worn; portly; delightful; luminous; gaunt; slender; fine; massive; reluctant; dying; arabesque; unlovely; large; meager; hardy; well-proportioned; trembling; oddest; tuneful; irksome; emaciated; attentuated; vigorous; buxom; vital; mystic; uneasy; moldering; unpleasant; perforated; unresisting; shriveled; goodly; measured; spare; matchless; hardy; ethereal; unearthly; daring; vandal; delicate; physical; shrunken; magnificent; seductivê; vast; rugged; muscular; vigorous; sky-scraper; flexible; gigantic; stocky; osseous; thick-set; hard; light; wiry; loose; stolid; weak.

verbs

adjust—; brace—; construct—; dissolve—; enclose in—; enter into—; fashion—; fence with—; fix to—; lodge in—; move—; overthrow—; place in—; regulate—; set in—; set up—; shape on—; weave on—; —arises; —collapses; —s differ; —shuts out; —stretches.

(See structure, case.)

FRAME (*v*)

adverbs

brilliantly; picturesquely; substantially; inexplicably; vaguely; gracefully; imposingly; luminously; seductively.

(See devise, contrive, plan.)

FRAMEWORK

adjectives

rigid; skeletal; essential.

FRANCHISE

adjectives

elective; tangible; legal; limited.

verbs

acquire—; admit to—; advocate—; bequeath —to; deprive of—; enjoy—; establish—; exercise—; forbid—; grant—; invest with —; limit—; possess—; purchase—; renew —; restore—; seek—; sell—; violate—; —benefits; —empowers; —exempts; —privileges; —protects.

(See right, exemption, freedom.)

FRANK

adverbs

delightfully; charmingly; bitterly; cruelly; attractively; distressingly; unusually; characteristically; sarcastically; crudely; appallingly; refreshingly; inordinately; artlessly; innocently; ingenuously; plainly; guilelessly; unaffectedly; apparently; strikingly; naively.

FRANKNESS

adjectives

manly; irrevocable; perfect; natural; cordial; timid; placid; virtuous; medical; absolute; inestimable; unsophisticated; superfluous; careless; unprepossessing; engaging; simple; uncomplimentary; brotherly; military; hearty; beautiful; intimate; indolent; imperious; brisk; medieval; sardonic; straightforward; youthful; uninhibited; repellent; naive; savage; genial; painful.

verbs

admit—; confess with—; declare with—; experience—; inflict—; meet with—; occasion—; permeate with—; relish—; require —; return—; reveal—; —annoys; —cuts; —disquiets; —hurts; —mortifies; —nettles; —offends; —pains; —pricks; —ruffles; —stings; —wounds.

(See candor, fairness, liberalism.)

FRANTIC

adverbs

irritably; passionately; distractedly; feverishly; hysterically; nervously; wildly; eccentrically; crazily; fanatically; incoherently; insensately; rabidly; starkly; acutely; desperately; uncontrollably; irrepressibly; unappeasably; ungovernably; terribly; pitifully; frightfully.

FRATERNAL

adverbs

genially; convivially; generously; warmly; indulgently; closely; remotely; intimately; congenially; harmoniously; tranquilly; dependably; quietly; remarkably; securely; comfortably.

FRAUD

adjectives
unremitting; shameful; presumable; wretched; economic; mercenary; pious; gigantic; petty; manifest; glaring; meditated; flagrant; barefaced.

verbs
beguile with—; commit—; cover—; declaim against—; design—; detect—; discern—; draw into—; engage in—; execute—; impose—upon; indulge in—; glory in—; lament—; perceive—; perpetrate—; practise —; prevent—; punish—; rectify—; reveal —; suspect—; taint with—; uncover—; unearth—; —amuses; —deceives; —dejects; —enables; —provokes; —ruins; —succeeds.
(See deception, deceit, trick, dishonesty, cheat, swindle.)

FRAUDULENT

adverbs
criminally; obviously; manifestly; apparently; openly; flagrantly; subtly; artfully; shrewdly; cleverly; adroitly; sharply; smartly; miserably; indefensibly; basely; grossly; knavishly; villainously; disgracefully; ignominiously; meanly; shabbily; unscrupulously; extremely; infamously; notoriously; surreptitiously.

FRAY

adjectives
deadly; fair; bloody; lawless; late; obstinate; youthful; horrid; clamorous; devilish; holy; mimic; thundering; insidious; nefarious.

verbs
charge into—; clash in—; commence—; crush in—; curb—; describe—; indulge in —; inquire into—; instigate—; interrupt—; involve in—; occasion—; plunge into—; raise—; referee—; —boils; —disperses; —frightens; —irritates; —unnerves; —disturbs.
(See fracas, combat, fight, commotion.)

FREAK

adjectives
grotesque; sudden; disgraceful; wanton; fashionable; unaccountable; fierce; impossible; peculiar.

FREAKISH

adverbs
outlandishly; ostentatiously; manifestly; absurdly; shamelessly; intentionally; disgustingly; inexcusably; laughably; idiotically; teasingly; tormentingly; erratically; eccentrically; fantastically; whimsically; particularly; wantonly; waywardly; uncomfortably; frivolously; terribly; unexpectedly.

FRECKLES

verbs
bleach—; conceal—; discern—; encourage —; mark with—; produce—; remove—; spangle with—; sprinkle with—; —cover; —dapple; —discolor; —dot; —embarrass; —mar; —spot; —stain; —variegate.

FREE

adverbs
gloriously; joyously; happily; independently; finally; utterly; completely; absolutely; unconditionally; irrepressibly; irresponsibly; gaily; blithely; merrily; unaccountably; gladly; jubilantly; incredibly; fortunately; luckily; unbelievably; unexpectedly.

FREE (v)

adverbs
ultimately; eventually; legally; economically; filially; unrestrainedly; magnanimously; unquestionably.
(See liberate, release.)

FREEDOM

adjectives
incomparable; bold; unbounded; perfect; unquestioned; unnoticed; personal; newly-regained; unchecked; untrammeled; licentious; perpetual; untamed; unbridled; annihilating; determined; brave; practical; deserving; airy; courtly; subjective; reverent; half-bashful; half-saucy; hopeless; complete; comparative; dignified; economic; accustomed; refined; filial; spotless; exceptional; intellectual; unbroken; unrestrained; priceless; dearly-bought; bloody; unwonted.

verbs
achieve—; advocate—; alienate—; announce—; assert—; break for—; confer—on; curb—; curtail—; deprive of—; encroach on—; expand with—; exult in—; flutter to—; guarantee—; hamper—; heighten—; impair—; imperil—; infringe on—;

menace—; relinquish—; resign—; retain—; strive for—; suppress—; surrender—; thrill in—; trample—; wed to—.
(See liberty, independence, ease, frankness.)

FREEZE (v)

adverbs
nightly; seasonally; spectrally; glacially; dangerously; tragically; formidably; permanently.
(See congeal, chill.)

FREEZING

adjectives
unexpected; bulk; seasonal; costly; artificial.

FREIGHT

adjectives
human; perishable; superannuated; additional; weary; animate; precious.

verbs
bear—; charge for—; convey by—; deduct for—; deposit—; despatch by—; export—; handle—; hold up—; load—; pay—; protect —; store—; transport by—; —s collide; —costs; —weighs.
(See cargo, load, transportation.)

FRENZIED

adverbs
deliriously; joyously; madly; wildly; excitedly; feverishly; insanely; fanatically; violently; completely; pathetically; jealously; inexpressibly; appallingly; alarmingly; dangerously; abnormally; incurably; deplorably.

FRENZY

adjectives
astonishing; fanatical; violent; selfish; poetic; complete; pathetic; maddening; full; jealous; dread; untimely; dreadful; inexpressible.

verbs
anticipate—; attack in—; dart with—; drive to—; fall into—; fight with—; imbue with —; incur—of; indulge in—; inflame to—; infuriate to—; inspire—; lash into—; plunge into—; provoke—; roll in—; salve —; seize with—; shake with—; shriek in—; strike with—; subject to—; throw into—; unloose—; —alarms; —descends; —disturbs; —seizes.
(See agitation, fury, madness, enthusiasm, fanaticism.)

FREQUENCY

adjectives
determinate; disheartening; distasteful; persistent; increasing; nervous.

verbs
commit with—; condemn—; diminish—; displease with—; encourage—; endure—; enjoy—; impose with—; increase—; justify—; occur with—; necessitate—; reduce—; relax—; repeat with—; return with—; vary—.
(See speed.)

FREQUENT

adverbs
annoyingly; disturbingly; unnecessarily; unusually; recurrently; monotonously; tiresomely.

FREQUENT (v)

adverbs
intermittently; habitually; persistently; carelessly; rashly; daringly; unconventionally; customarily.
(See visit.)

FRESH

adverbs
delightfully; unquestionably; genuinely; lusciously; deliciously; lately; exquisitely; excellently; capitally; superlatively; inimitably; admirably; pleasantly; agreeably; wonderfully; marvelously; emphatically; perfectly.

FRESHNESS

adjectives
original; enviable; dewy; lyrical; immortal; permeating; morning; faded; dreadful; youthful; infinite; cool; guaranteed; astonishing; clean; abounding; genial; delicate; sweet; unsunned; soothing; bracing; glorious; frosty; gay; perennial; breezy; elastic; vernal; odorous; wholesome.

FRET (v)

adverbs
pettishly; childishly; morbidly; irritatingly; unreasoningly; unintelligently; abnormally; pathologically.
(See vex, irritate, tease, annoy.)

FRETFUL

adverbs
whiningly; peevishly; complainingly; nervously; spitefully; feverishly; pathetically; unfortunately; unbearably; intolerably; sullenly; restlessly; capriciously; jealously; ap-

pallingly; shockingly; surprisingly; unreasonably; foolishly; needlessly; groundlessly; sadly; unwisely; shrewishly; querulously; cantankerously; restively; perversely; terribly; captiously.

FRIABLE

adverbs

desirably; admirably; sufficiently; satisfactorily; duly; frangibly; impalpably; wonderfully; astonishingly; surprisingly; superbly; splendidly; adequately; amply.

FRIAR

adjectives

coarse; unreverend; unhallowed; bungling; mendicant; saucy; true; meddling; frantic; humble; pious.

FRICTION

adjectives

constant; incessant; insufficient; sectional; cheerful; spiritual; unnecessary; destructive; laborious; tidal; continual; unpleasant.

verbs

expose to—; ignite by—; prophesy—; suffer —; sustain—; transmit—; undergo—; —agitates; —blisters; —chafes; —corrodes; —develops; —endangers; —grates; —polishes; —resists; —rubs; —scrubs; —smooths; —stings; —tingles; —torments; —wears away.

(See resistance.)

FRIEND

adjectives

indefatigable; well-meaning; circumspect; valued; discriminating; influential; wonderful; feathered; familiar; perfidious; neglecting; faithless; thankless; all-seeing; political; social; frank; loyal; impressionable; impetuous; fiery; sworn; intimate; gracious; genial; impartial; democratic; discouraging; unprofitable; disinguished; disinterested; ardent; benignant; charitable; obliging; light-hearted; disapproving; enthusiastic; serviceable; congenial; dexterous; hollow; affectionate; distressful; devoted; indiscreet; candid; bubbling; esteemed; immediate; marvelous; illustrious; indisposed; courtly; unfortunate; lasting; solid; lifelong; profligate; distant; utmost; roistering; tyrannous; ancient; medieval; timid; loving; acquainted; unflinching; high-toned; imaginary; lawless; ecclesiastical; sable; caressing; inconstant; confidential; honorable; quondam; bleating; censorious; departed; much-lamented; scrutinizing; numerous (pl); timorous; magnanimous; mute; amiable; philanthropic; treacherous; absent; traitorous; consumptive; blushing; hospitable; lazy; valuable; firm; velvet; festive; veteran; sweet; judicious; coolest; biteless; inebriated; unselfish; inestimable; gentle; spirited; puissant; officious; powerful; epicurean; banished; bosom; inseparable; obliging; staunch; long-sustaining; beloved; worthy; trusty; conservative; liberal; secret; nameless; common; late-embarked; warmest; true; literary; importunate; merry; dissipated; vindictive; benevolent; strong; creditable; rival; family; steadfast; unswerving; unrepentant; provoking; pock-marked; middle-aged; satirical; reasonable; particular; virtuous; modest; long-tried; long-known; gossiping; courageous; unwavering; sympathizing; questioning; suspicious; unconditional; choice; well-tried; false; sad; well-advised; irritable; gifted; prying.

verbs

accept as—; accost—; affront—; alienate —; berate—; betray—; cast away—; concede to—; exasperate—; exempt—s; favor —; forsake—; harbor—; idolize—; join—; lack—; let down—; muster—s; part with—; protect—; sacrifice—; succor—; sustain—; take leave of—s; value—; vex—s; wish—; yield to—; —consoles; —s drift away; —lends a hand; —prevails; —stands by; —supports.

(See associate, ally, companion, favorite.)

FRIENDLINESS

adjectives

patronizing; beaming; familiar; ignoble; truest; genuine; curious; paternal; effusive; heavenly.

FRIENDLY

adverbs

disarmingly; consistently; unquestionably; essentially; extremely; gratifyingly; courteously; placidly; gravely; smilingly; cordially; helpfully; quietly; remarkably; palpably; ostentatiously; condescendingly; singularly; charmingly; genuinely; sincerely; unaffectedly; naturally; delightfully; politely; openly; heartily; scrupulously; loyally; enchantingly; engagingly; altogether.

FRIENDSHIP

adjectives
platonic; distinguished; diplomatic; remarkable; acknowledged; disinterested; traditional; proffered; supercilious; partisan; equal; hereditary; warmest; informal; subsidiary; steadfast; deathless; ardent; resistless; lasting; ancient; problematical; practical; confidential; ill-assorted; heaping; tranquil; precious; intimate; true; poetic; intellectual; pure; lifelong; three-cornered; expedient; serviceable; loyal; commercial; estranged; deep; benevolent; unreturned; familiar; generous; dignified; cordial; warm; patronizing; profound; casual; adoring; unusual; strict; fragile; ominous; well-known; inseparable; unquenchable; passionate; restful; sober; youthful; energetic; bosom; offered; exquisite; literary; ancient; protracted; expansive.

verbs
accept—of; attain—of; bask in—; cultivate—; destroy—; disrupt—; encourage—; endanger—; enhance—; foster—; gain—of; hold out the hand of—; jeopardize—; kill—; manifest—; taint—; voice—; —blossoms; —cools; —fades; —flowers; —ripens.

(See affection, attachment, amity, intimacy, devotion.)

FRIEZE

adjectives
professional; magnificent; dignified.

FRIGHT

adjectives
perfect; whispered; sudden; supernatural; helpless; violent; overwhelming; quivering; collective; intolerable; morbid.

verbs
blanch with—; conceal—; convulse in—; cower in—; crouch in—; die of—; exhaust with—; harrow with—; hesitate in—; impel by—; quake with—; quiver with—; recoil in—; shake with—; start in—; subject to—; sweat with—; take—; thrill with—; throw into—; tremble with—; —abates; —freezes; —paralyzes; —petrifies; —slackens; —shocks; shiver with—.

(See alarm, fear, dismay, terror, consternation.)

FRIGHTEN (*v*)

adverbs
genuinely; horribly; supernaturally; violently; morbidly; collectively; intolerably; overwhelmingly; instinctively; devilishly; nefariously; insidiously.

(See alarm, terrify.)

FRIGHTFUL

adverbs
hideously; awfully; shockingly; appallingly; grimly; unspeakably; inexpressibly; incalculably; indescribably; peculiarly; particularly; utterly; insupportably; cruelly; brutally; grimly; uncommonly.

FRIGID

adverbs
obnoxiously; calmly; arrogantly; bitterly; languidly; impassively; phlegmatically; unemotionally; indifferently; callously; imperturbably; unconcernedly; maddeningly; discourteously; abominably; insufferably.

FRINGE

verbs
adorn with—; bear—; border with—; deck with—; drape—; edge with—; finish with—; hang by—; knot—; ravel—; rip—; suspend—; swing—; toy with—; —beautifies; —dances; —dangles; —fascinates; —quivers.

(See border.)

FRINGES

adjectives
fleecy; raveling; icy; angry-looking; luxuriant; amber; penumbral; straggling; outermost; solid; mysterious; cotton; ball; scalloped; hand-knotted; luminous; sleek; tattered; tasseled; delicate.

FRIPPERY

adjectives
feminine; tawdry; meretricious.

FRISK (*v*)

adverbs
joyously; gaily; laughably; unconventionally; youthfully; wantonly; scandalously; thoughtlessly; dissipatedly.

(See leap, skip, frolic.)

FRISKING

adjectives
joyous; carefree; unconventional; animal.

FRISKY

adverbs
youthfully; childishly; vivaciously; nimbly; happily; blithely; smartly; eagerly; delightfully; charmingly; interestingly; buoyantly;

jauntily; airily; lightsomely; brightly; joyously; sportively; gleefully; trickily; jocosely; exultantly; jubilantly; irrepressibly; exhilaratingly; indescribably; playfully.

FRIVOLITY

adjectives
scholastic; Gallic; irresponsible; scandalous.

verbs
attack—; beckon in—; celebrate with—; condemn—; denounce—; discard—; display—; exhibit—; pretend—; prevent—; repudiate—; ridicule—; —amuses; —attracts; —excites; —flourishes; —irks; —vexes.
(See frolic, fun.)

FRIVOLOUS

adverbs
wildly; foolishly; entertainingly; absurdly; gaily; blithely; idly; childishly; utterly; senselessly; lightly; ridiculously; ludicrously; capriciously; fantastically; giddily; wantonly; freakishly; blatantly; extravagantly; nonsensically; vacantly; hilariously.

FROCK

adjectives
smartest; charming; sheerer; gleaming; silver; filmy; close-fitting; icy; twice-turned; chic; dowdy.; spangled; gayest; refreshing; fashionable.

verbs
adore—; alter—; arrange—; compliment on—; design—; discard—; dislike—; display—; don—; envy—; fit—; injure—; purchase—; renovate—; select—; slip into—; yearn for—; —attracts; —becomes; —befits; —exposes; —flatters; —reveals; —slenderizes.
(See garment, gown, dress, robe.)

FROG

verbs
can—s; farm—s; persecute—s; —blinks; —burrows; —croaks; —damages; —dips; —s disperse; —dives; —evolves; —excavates; —jumps; —leaps; —snatches; —swims; —trills.
(See animal.)

FROGS

adjectives
croaking; reasonable; vulgar.

FROLIC

adjectives
carnal; lively; midnight.

verbs
bridle—; curb—; enter into—; gambol at—; gather for—; indulge in—; interrupt—; invite to—; observe—; provide—; reprimand—; revel at—; savor—; subdue—; suffer for—; —amuses; —delights; —tempts.
(See merriment, sport, prank, fun.)

FROLIC (v)

adverbs
boyishly; gleefully; jocundly; winsomely; exuberantly; sportively; blithesomely; drunkenly.
(See leap, skip, play.)

FROLICSOME

adverbs
genially; gaily; gleefully; vivaciously; irrepressibly; mirthfully; hilariously; noisily; boisterously; laughingly; merrily; jovially; joyously; brightly; lightly; delightedly; happily; jauntily; immensely; immeasurably; infectiously; pleasantly; playfully; waggishly; amazingly.

FRONDS

adjectives
dark; sempiternal; pinnate; magnificent; beauteous; waving; hoving.

FRONT

adjectives
formidable; starry; atheist; willing; bastionlike; undaunted; proud; defying; bold; blazoned; blushless; time-stained; ivory; immediate; pompous; ardent; honorable; confident; veneered; gallant.

verbs
bound—; direct to—; display—; edge—; erect—; enter—; face—; forge to—; form at—; furnish—; limit—; move to—; pertain to—; place at—; provide—; scale—; situate at—; skirmish on—; station at—; unite—; —crumbles; —extends; —shields.
(See rear.)

FRONTIER

verbs
charge—; command—; defend—; dispatch to—; extend—; guard—; inhabit—; invade—; repel at—; scale—; settle on—; shun—; situate on—; station at—; thrust to—; unite

—; —advances; —bounds; —limits; —presses forward; —recedes; —resists; —shifts; —surrounds.
(See border, boundary.)

FRONTIERS

adjectives
narrow; indefensible; remotest; flexible; dangerous; maritime; rude; guarded; expanding; constraining.

FROST

adjectives
flowery; white; radiant; pondering; wondrous; make-believe; ceaseless; wintry; dazzling; crackling; sharp; keen; relentless; singeing; killing; envious; autumn; audacious; piercing; blighting; withering; fettering; bitter; heavy; gray; iridescent; chilly; hard; snapping; untimely; hoar.

verbs
form—; hang with—; lace with—; trace with—; —bites; —chills; —covers; —damages; —decorates; —descends; —designs; —draws; —etches; —falls; —glimmers; —glistens; —glorifies; —injures; —lingers; —nips; —projects; —settles on; —sharpens; —silvers; —sprays; —transforms.
(See snow.)

FROSTY

adverbs
sharply; refreshingly; bitterly; appetizingly; freshly; bleakly; bitingly; nippingly; terribly; cruelly; destructively; slightly; invigoratingly; delightfully.

FROTH

adjectives
sudden; flowery; flying; idlest.

verbs
agitate to—; beat to—; boil to—; break into—; churn up—; cover with—; crest with—; emit—; ferment to—; fleck with—; shake into—; toss off—; —bubbles; —creams; —effervesces; —floats; —foams; —gurgles; —issues from; —reams.
(See foam.)

FROTHY

adverbs
lightly; airily; volatilely; thickly; effervescently; sparklingly; lusciously; fizzily; deliciously; genuinely; attractively; invitingly.

FROWN

adjectives
ominous; ireful; discontented; blackening; mournful; rumorous; bitter; puzzled; chilling; feudal; gloomy; sternest; habitual; steady; churlish; crusty; fastidious; gathering; old-fashioned; restrained; drunken; petulant; searching; angry; pedantic; unfeeling; charming; fleeting; deep-furrowed.

verbs
assume—; blemish with—; contract in—; cringe before—; disclose—; display—; form—; incur—; observe—; overcome—; perceive—; rebuke with—; relax—; suppress—; wrinkle into—; —belies; —commands; —corrugates; —creases; —deters; —expresses; —intimidates; —punishes; —reprimands; —terrorizes.
(See scowl.)

FROWN (v)

adverbs
sullenly; belligerently; blackly; wrathfully; inauspiciously; reprovingly; dismally; majestically; ferociously; austerely; ominously; mournfully; bitterly; sternly; habitually; churlishly; petulantly; uncongenially.
(See scowl.)

FROWZY

adverbs
carelessly; roughly; inexcusably; neglectfully; dreadfully; miserably; nonchalantly; wretchedly; merrily; cheerfully; indifferently; unconcernedly; inordinately; terribly; excitedly.

FRUGAL

adverbs
carefully; necessarily; thriftily; cautiously; warily; watchfully; ostentatiously; habitually; naturally; amazingly; cooperatively; inherently; meanly; sensibly; providently; moderately; parsimoniously; admirably; intelligently; judiciously.

FRUGALITY

adjectives
ostentatious; necessary; apologetic; helpful; customary; habitual; native.

verbs
bare—; commend—; conceal—; conduct with—; display—; endure—; expose to—; found—; justify—; mark—; occasion—;

practise—; praise—; reduce to—; relieve—; require—; resent—; resign to—; reveal—.
(See economy, thrift.)

FRUIT

adjectives
forbidden; copious; unavailing; immediate; fairy; delicious; grateful; acid; just; divine; mellow; pulpy; ambrosial; monthly; teeming; autumnal; fuller; beatific; wholesome; fragrant; delightful; deciduous; luscious; bitter; discordant; blessed; apparent; bleeding; sacred; proper; gushing; clustering; golden; compensating; disastrous; ruddy; detested; glorious; exotic; immortal; alluring; natural; noble; fresh; cordial; panting; wandering; fairest; legitimate; sun-ripened; vigorous; personal; pouting; celestial; cherished; ripe; fallacious; unknown; blushing; sole; mellow; seasonal; proper; wind-tossed; choicest; dazzling; tolerable; ornamental; sprouting; ripe-cheeked; remarkable; nectarine; oversized; divinest; flesh-colored; rotten; wormy.

verbs
attack—; bear —; blight—; blossom into—; consume—; damage—; develop into—; diet on—; gather—; load with—; partake of—; produce—; reap—; relish—; replenish with —; savor—; serve—; spray—; store—; yield—; —abounds; —delights; —rots; —satiates.
(See crop, harvest.)

FRUITFUL

adverbs
profitably; satisfactorily; unusually; prolifically; luxuriantly; admirably; genuinely; copiously; abundantly; teemingly; sparsely; apparently; ordinarily; remarkably; sufficiently; surprisingly; plentifully; richly; uberously.

FRUITFULNESS

adjectives
mellow; uncommon; tropical.

FRUITION

adjectives
instant; tantalizing; unalloyed; ceaseless.

FRUITLESS

adverbs
grievously; disappointingly; inconsequentially; terribly; disconcertingly; ruinously; unfortunately; unluckily; wretchedly; miserably; pitiably; pathetically; naturally; inevitably; irremediably; sadly; dreadfully.

FRUMPISH

adverbs
crabbedly; morosely; perversely; moodily; sulkily; intolerably; utterly; doggedly; grumpily; peevishly; crustily; inscrutably; vaguely; sourly; unreasonably; habitually; usually; disagreeably

FRUSTRATE (*v*)

adverbs
effectually; treacherously; legitimately; vindictively; jealously; subtly; basely; temporarily.
(See prevent, defeat, disappoint.)

FRUSTRATION

verbs
avoid—; balk at—; condemn—; curb—; denounce—; endure—; hurdle—; overcome—; resent—; subdue—; suffer—; —baffles; —circumvents; —defeats; —deters; —harms; —hinders; —injures; —interrupts.
(See failure, defeat, disappointment.)

FRYING-PAN

verbs
adhere to—; blacken—; brandish—; cleanse —; dent—; employ—; escape—; grease—; mix in—; necessitate—; place in—; polish —; scour—; —clatters; —jangles; —rattles; —shines; —sizzles.
(See pan.)

FUEL

adjectives
premium; inflammable; volatile; self-sustaining; exhausted; available; solid; fresh.

verbs
acquire—; burn—; employ as—; fill with—; furnish—; ignite—; necessitate—; obtain—; produce—; replenish—; require—; select—; supply—; —explodes; —flames; —heats; —illumines; —inflames; —sustains.
(See wood, coal, etc.)

FUGITIVE

adjectives
gallant; young; suppliant; mangled; royal; solitary; panting; sole; wretched; stricken; returning; frenzied.

verbs
conceal—; deter—; endanger—; espy—; harbor—; nab—; prevent—; protect—; pur-

sue—; search for—; shelter—; track down —; —absconds; —deserts; —escapes; —flees; —hides; —journeys; —wanders.
(See prisoner.)

adverbs
elusively; shyly; evasively; remotely; evanescently; transiently; ephemerally; etherally; nebulously; perishably; mortally; temporally; transitorily; unhappily; sadly; unfortunately; tormentingly.

FULFILL (v)

adverbs
magnificently; admirably; conscientiously; abundantly; moderately; approximately; swiftly; blindly; ultimately; immutably; adequately; partially.
(See accomplish, complete.)

FULFILLMENT

adjectives
adequate; abundant; mere; rigid; speedy; partial.

verbs
accomplish—; allow—; anticipate—; attain —; attempt—; concede—; defeat—; effect —; execute—; express—; grant—; perform —; pray for—; predict—; promote—; reach —; supply to—; yearn for—; —completes; —disappoints; —satiates; —satisfies.
(See accomplishment, realization.)

FULL

adverbs
moderately; satisfactorily; sufficiently; completely; fortunately; gloriously; abundantly; measurably; adequately; liberally; generously; pleasantly; agreeably.

FULLNESS

adjectives
quiet; flaring; swelling; grim; apparent; arduous; generous; lavish; flaccid; abounding; messy; eloquent; all-excluding; immeasurable; molded.

FUMBLE (v)

adverbs
casually; nervously; drunkenly; clumsily; fruitlessly; tremulously; ineffectually; absurdly; pedantically.
(See blunder, flounder, miss, stumble.)

FUME (v)

adverbs
indignantly; sulphurously; poisonously; unendurably; odoriferously; exasperatedly; angrily; wrathfully; blatantly; prodigiously.
(See rage, bluster.)

FUMES

adjectives
noxious; greasy; odoriferous; resinous; unendurable; earthly; unkindly; poisonous; fishy; devilish; disagreeable; sulphurous.

verbs
bear—; blow—; disperse—; discharge—; emit—; exhale—; fill with—; flood with—; give off—; inhale—; scent—; send forth—; spray with—; —creep out of; —mantle; —overcome; —pass off; —perfume; —please; —preserve; —rise; —smother; —stifle; —vanish.
(See vapor, smoke.)

FUN

adjectives
spirited; capital; innocent; fairy; hilarious; practical; legitimate; gentle; monstrous; genuine; nonsensical; boisterous; monotonous; tremendous; bitter; nasty; ill-timed; painful.

verbs
carouse in—; create—; drown—; entertain with—; exclude—; indulge in—; play for—; poke—at; pretend in—; spare—; —amuses; —ceases; —cheers; —diverts; —enlivens; —grows; —relaxes; —wearies.
(See frolic, joke, mirth, gayety, merriment, amusement.)

FUNCTION

adjectives
ministerial; vital; legitimate; valuable; useful; manifold (pl); ritualistic; perverted; nerve; judicial; impaired; aesthetic; beneficent; natural; economic; animal; normal; consular; religious; executive; cherished; intellectual; pitiable; hospitable; cognitive; imitative; precise; sacerdotal; essential; basest; appropriate; principal; civilian; impaired; numerous (pl); social; obsolete; inescapable; diminished; proper; primary; indispensable; frightful; spiritual; gracious; ecclesiastical; sociological; diversified (pl); imperfect; varied (pl); episcopal.

verbs
abuse—; arrest—; associate with—; block —; centralize—; check—; delegate—to; discharge—; embarrass—; energize—; exercise —; fulfill—; impair—; improve—; invest with—; magnify—; perform—; preserve—; promote—; regulate—; resume—; restore—; subserve—; vest—in; —s overlap one another.

(See duty.)

FUNCTION (v)

adverbs
automatically; efficiently; biologically; splendidly; sluggishly; elaborately; ministerially; beneficently; economically; indispensably; spiritually.

(See perform, discharge.)

FUND

verbs
abscond with —s; abuse—; administer—; advance —s; allocate —s; allot —s; appropriate —s; audit—; bolster—; campaign for —s; deplete—; divert from—; draw from —; embezzle —s; endow with—; juggle —s; misappropriate —s; muster —s; pool —s; seek —s; solicit —s; stretch —s; struggle for —s; supplant—; swell—; utilize—; —benefits; —dwindles; —increases; —s roll in.

(See money, capital.)

FUNDAMENTAL

adverbs
definitely; indispensably; radically; significantly; essentially; ineradically; inherently; intrinsically; virtually; substantially; absolutely; fairly; basically; undeniably.

FUNDAMENTALS

verbs
cleave to—; cling to—; deviate from—; doubt—; exhaust—; implant—; inculcate—; inform in—; instruct in—; interfere with—; involve—; necessitate—; preserve—; recognize—; regard—; reiterate—; rely on—; require—; revere—; subject to—; submit to—; sway from—.

(See essential, rule, principle, law.)

FUNDS

adjectives
stabilization; exhaustless; contingent; accumulated; unlimited; reserve; insurance; pegging; special; slush; inexhaustible; charitable; needed; unlimited; unequalled; tremendous; misused; supplemented; baffling; available; endowment; meager; misappropriated.

FUNERAL

adjectives
leafy; lugubrious; genteel.

verbs
announce—; arrange—; ease—; eulogize at —; expend on—; follow—; reign at—; mourn at—; observe—; officiate at—; preside at—; proceed at—; toll at—.

(See death.)

FUNEREAL

adverbs
solemnly; lugubriously; quietly; reverently; murmurously; depressingly; gloomily; disconsolately; dismally; gravely; heavily; horribly; oppressively; sadly; dully; mournfully; cheerlessly; frightfully; lamentably; dolefully; incredibly; unnecessarily; absurdly; extremely; inordinately.

FUNGUS

adjectives
decayed, dismal.

verbs
cover with—; divest of—; neglect—; nourish—; —chokes; —corrupts; —damages; —encrusts; —enervates; —flourishes; —gathers; —harms; —injures; —invades; —kills; —overruns; —penetrates; —poisons; —ripens; —spreads; —rots.

(See plant.)

FUNNY

adverbs
hilariously; laughably; excruciatingly; uproariously; comically; wholesomely; divertingly; delightfully; drolly; drily; quaintly; entertainingly; merrily; facetiously; smartly; extravagantly; ridiculously; fantastically; whimsically; outlandishly; extremely; exceedingly.

FUR

adjectives
shimmering; sleek; rich; warm; glossy; jet; ruffled; luxurious; silk-soft; semiprecious; camouflaged; prickly; ice-covered; tawny; sumptuous; imitation; expensive; woolly; fuzzy.

verbs
adjust—; clothe in—; deck with—; display —; dress in—; encase in—; face with—; fluff—; hunt for —s; line with—; muffle in —; ornament with—; sheathe in—; strip of —; stroke—; trade in —s; trim with—; value—; wrap in—; —encircles; —envelopes; —flies; —protects.
(See coat, skin, hair.)

FURIOUS

adverbs
senselessly; sullenly; suddenly; intolerably; hotly; justly; obviously; foolishly; ridiculously; dangerously; alarmingly; terribly; dreadfully; coldly; genuinely; uncontrollably; passionately; violently; sternly; implacably; unjustly; inordinately; insanely; naturally; ludicrously; unnaturally; curiously; oddly; strangely; unappeasably; recklessly; inconsiderately; blindly; savagely; jealously; indescribably; tragically; absurdly; hysterically; inanely; idiotically; groundlessly; boisterously; desperately; murderously; fearfully; frightfully; fiercely; truculently; diabolically; brutally; needlessly; horribly.

FURLOUGH

adjectives
delightful; precious; desired; short; happy.

verbs
absent on—; authorize—; beg—; concede—; defer—; demand—; earn—; favor with—; forbid—; grant—; leave on—; license—; obtain—; order—; overstay—; permit—; refuse—; request—; restrict—; return from —; take—; warrant—.
(See vacation.)

FURNACE

adjectives
fiery; sacred; untiring; molten; smelting.

verbs
bake in—; cast into—; dry in—; feed—; fire —; fuel—; install—; issue from—; operate —; rake—; start—; supply—; tap—; tend —; —burns; —converts; —emits; —exhales; —heats; —sighs.
(See stove.)

FURNISH (v)

adverbs
abundantly; defectively; meanly; gaudily; bizarrely; adequately; scantily; sumptuously; tastefully; exquisitely; luxuriously; rudely; drably; modernistically.
(See provide, supply.)

FURNITURE

adjectives
scanty; enduring; somber; haircloth; simple; meager; hand-made; custom-made; time-worn; elegant; unfriendly; commodious; ecclesiastical-looking; space-saving; antique; luxurious; rude; best-styled; massive; costly; dim; drab; incidental; hideous; rickety; bulky; modernistic; streamlined.

verbs
appoint—; arrange—; clutter with—; cover —; damage—; decorate—; design—; equip with—; fill with—; inherit—; nick—; outfit with—; overcrowd with—; place—; polish —; possess—; scratch—; select—; stock with —; store—; van—; —fits; —harmonizes; —matches; —suffices.
(See equipment, outfit, chair, table, etc.)

FUROR

adjectives
bacchic; devilish; raucous; riotous; frenzied.

FURROW

adjectives
sounding; foul; fat; unmeaning; roaring; mucky; silvery; sonorous; fruitless; shining; rectangular; dry-drawn; unthrifty; vertical.

FURTIVE

adverbs
craftily; adroitly; cleverly; uncommonly; habitually; suspiciously; strangely; oddly; curiously; warily; evasively; mysteriously; cryptically; whisperingly; needlessly; significantly; unduly; cautiously; extremely; remarkably; particularly.

FURY

adjectives
domestic; utmost; irresistible; civil; unappeasable; suppressed; violent; tempestuous; warlike; unabated; reckless; undiminished; exasperated; empty; whirling; drink-engendered; satiate; direful; fierce; concentrated; snake-locked; everlasting; fighting; manifest; indiscriminate; inconsiderate; uncontrolled; steelhearted; perfect; hellish; exterminating; blistering; blindfold; mineral; revolutionary; mad; governable; bestial; increasing; unreasoning; sparkling; un-

bridled; coming; sudden; implacable; chaotic; overpowering; disappointed; savage; unchained; vindictive; obvious; concentrated; pretty; jealous; unrelenting; indescribable; blind; incarnate; tragic.

verbs
blast with—; conceal—; dignify—; drive to —; encounter—; engender—; fan—; fly into —; gaze in — at; mutter in—; rage in—; roar in—; seethe with—; simmer with—; vent—; whip into—; work into—; —abates; —increases; —lets down; —subsides.
(See anger, rage, passion, frenzy, excitement.)

FUSE

adjectives
unreliable; burning; hissing; short; time.

FUSILLADE

adjectives
murderous; fierce; random; furious; brutal; bloody; merciless.

verbs
discharge—; emit—; keep up—; pour—; protect from—; rain—; run from—; shower —; spout—; swear—; warn of—; withstand —; —assaults; —butchers; —ceases; —executes; —levels; —massacres; —mows down; —shatters; —terrorizes.
(See volley, barrage.)

FUSION

adjectives
fiery; graceful; necessary; remarkable.

FUSS

adjectives
indignant; noisy; quarrelsome; sudden; nasty; unspeakable.

FUSSY

adverbs
needlessly; tiresomely; irritatingly; restlessly; excitedly; foolishly; ineptly; unduly; eternally; noisily; annoyingly; feverishly; briskly; officiously; uneasily; twitteringly; naggingly; abominably; detestably; unbearably; remarkably; intolerably; hatefully.

FUTILE

adverbs
lamentably; invariably; unfortunately; deplorably; helplessly; unluckily; unhappily; feebly; weakly.

FUTILITY

adjectives
clumsy; apparent; sweet; fantastic; magnificent; obvious; patent; accepted.

verbs
battle with—; bemoan — of; break in—; contend with—; curse—; dispose of—; evade—; fritter into—; lapse into—; lose in —; manifest—; object to—; recognize—; reduce to—; result in—; screen—; strike at —; while away in—; —appears; —confronts; —conquers; —dies.
(See uselessness, worthlessness.)

FUTURE

adjectives
ever-better; magnetic; blest; naturalistic; impending; imminent; immediate; luminous; physical; immortal; distant; impossible; eternal; financial; promising; boundless; uncertain; commercial; brilliant; infinite; interesting; cruel; ruthless; secure; dubious; dim; black; significant; controlling; happy; measureless; hopeless; cheerful; supramundane; heterogeneous; somber; altered; terrestrial; fantastic; invisible; far-stretching; friendless; permanent; real; gloomy; glorious; unlimited; profitable; assured; lurid; long-time; cosmopolitan.

verbs
anticipate—; blast—; chart—; cloud—; despair of—; endanger—; entrust to—; explore —; fear for—; figure out—; forecast—; foretell—; gamble away—; gaze into—; glance into—; guide—; hope for—; jeopardize—; lay — open; menace—; mortgage —; overshadow—; peer into—; project into —; prophesy—; read—; risk—; save for—; secure—; stake — on; view—.
(See outlook.)

G

GABLE

adjectives
sculptured; towering; fantastic; peaked.

GADGET

adjectives
life-saving; lethal; noise-making; education-al.

GAIETY

adjectives
fictitious; unfeigned; served; wild; airy; fortunate; exuberant; uncanny; bounding; fatigued; inward; forced; brilliant; charming; facile; heedless; social; jaded; seeming; careless; prevalent; nimble; leaden; affectionate; bewitching; sparkling; teasing; surface; delirious; animating; exhausting; false; spurious; customary; ironical; childlike; mock; embarrassed; tempered; alternate; enticing; unearthly; wholehearted.

verbs
(See gayety.)

GAIN

adjectives
glorious; immense; sure; intellectual; eternal; substantial; capital; selfish; adequate; personal; speculative; happy; immediate; indubitable; obvious; fruitful; fallacious; indicated; unhallowed; qualitative; scanty; treacherous; pecuniary; proper; equivalent; territorial; untold; mystic; appreciable; unjust; corporate; hopeless.

verbs
accomplish—; acquire—; begrudge—; claim —; content with—; count—; derive—; dissipate —s; forego—; promise—; register—; seek—; serve for—; spurn—; struggle for —; yield—; —astonishes; —benefits; —decreases; —increases; —mounts; —outweighs.
(See profit, advantage.)

GAIN (v)

adverbs
vastly; legally; lawfully; ethically; deservedly; definitely; unquestionably; incredibly; consistently; incessantly; singularly; substantially; gloriously; immensely; speculatively; indubitably; unhallowedly; pecuniarily; territorially; subtly.
(See profit, win.)

GAINFUL

adverbs
amazingly; securely; certainly; magically; mysteriously; unexpectedly; productively; surprisingly; admirably; luckily; fortunately; happily; providentially; adequately; curiously; valuably; oddly; legally; definitely; unquestionably; incredibly; gloriously; immensely; subtly; pecuniarily; financially; singularly.

GAIT

adjectives
staid; swinging; rolling; stooping; shuffling; awkward; majestical; unremitted; aerie; true; haggard; lofty; shambling; weary; gentle; traveling; unnatural; pacing; common; ponderous; rapid; stately; princely; habitual; heavy; feeble; swaggering; musing; measured; lumbering.

verbs
change—; fix—; go at—; hobble in—; limp in—; lumber in—; mimic—; mock—; practise—; quicken—; recognize—; settle down to—; shift—; slacken—; slow up—; solemnize—; stagger in—; steady—; stumble in—.
(See walk, step.)

GALAXY

adjectives
splendid; cooperative; successive (pl).

GALE

adjectives
treacherous; spicy; approaching; lurid; angry; shrieking; tearing; frantic; passing; sunrise; dreadful; furious; boisterous; merry; heavy; southern; viewless; favoring; odor-scented; cold; wet; carping; keel-compelling; sinking; coming; mocking; pleasant; heroic; terrific; strenuous; destroying; freshening; gracious; shadowy; rising; balmy; sighing; reveling.

verbs
buck—; combat—; encounter—; —abates; —accelerates; —arises; —blusters; —carries away; —damages; —disperses; —fans; —fumes; —lashes; —rages; —rampages; —

riots; —screams; —shrieks; —stiffens; —sweeps away; —violates; —whips up; —wreaks.

(See breeze, current, wind, tempest.)

GALL

adjectives

burning; soul-tormenting; hypercritical.

GALLANT

adjectives

open-handed; trim; gay; pleasant-spoken; boisterous; high-spirited; faultless; chivalric.

adverbs

splendidly; valorously; heroically; courteously; unwontedly; unusually; consistently; habitually; inherently; intrepidly; fearlessly; boldly; courageously; resolutely; adventurously; bravely; audaciously; firmly; confidently; daringly; dangerously; pluckily; fiercely; doughtily; urbanely; suavely; dutifully; blandly; graciously; obsequiously; ingratiatingly; immeasurably.

GALLANTRY

adjectives

generous; uncouth; delicate; desperate; sheepish; wonted; conspicuous; boyish; distinguished; rare; calm; consistent; premature; excessive; imputed; timeless; self-conscious; overdone; elaborate; natural; practical; noticeable.

verbs

accost with—; applaud—; attend with—; bear with—; behave with—; breathe—; conduct with—; court with—; deck in—; defend with—; display—; escort with—; exaggerate—; exchange —s; exhibit—; lay aside—; mock—; premeditate—; rejoice in —; —captures; —steals away; —wins.

(See bravery, courage, heroism, chivalry, prowess.)

GALLERY

adjectives

elliptical; gilded; elaborate; dirty; immense; encircling; frequented; extensive; whispering; formal; gracious; classical; ignorant; subterranean; loaded; starlit; vaulted.

verbs

assemble in—; exhibit in—; guide through —; hang in—; lounge in—; occupy—; parade through—; play to—; proclaim from—; rail—; set up in—; speak from—; subdue —; support—; visit—; —edifies; —heckles; —hushes; —surrounds.

(See corridor, balcony, audience.)

GALLOP

adjectives

thunderous; false; perilous; rapid; soundless; clattering; morning; daily; historic; breathless.

GALLOP (*v*)

adverbs

furiously; picturesquely; gallantly; stiffly; thunderously; swiftly; perilously; clatteringly; breathlessly.

(See run, trot.)

GALLOWS

verbs

bring to—; cheat—; condemn to—; conduct to—; correct on—; deliver from—; deserve —; erect—; escape—; execute on—; hang on —; inflict—; punish on—; reprieve from—; save from—; sentence to—; threaten with —; —cures; —tames; —terrifies; —terrorizes.

(See gibbet.)

GAMBLE (*v*)

adverbs

habitually; inveterately; suavely; besottedly; professionally; foolhardily; passionately; improvidently.

(See risk.)

GAMBLER

adjectives

passionate; ready; riverboat; incarnate; prodigious; professed; besotted; adept; inveterate; skilled; sleek; suave.

GAMBLING

verbs

abhor—; bewail—; campaign against—; cheat at—; defraud at—; degenerate into—; denounce—; hedge in—; play at—; rail at —; resist—; resort to—; risk in—; shackle to—; share in—; speculate in—; stake for —; thrive on—; trap in—; wager on—; —destroys; —disgraces; —dismembers; —harms; —preys on; —relaxes; —ruins; —wrecks.

(See game.)

GAMBOLS

adjectives
wanton; noisy; joyous; insufferable; dainty; uncouth; frolicsome; pleasant; childish.

GAME

adjectives
mocking; dangerous; toilsome; impious; heroic; risky; thrilling; open; intricate; formidable; tedious; shut; attractive; daily; mimic; impassioned; unmeaning; poetic; lawful; Olympic; card; disappearing; contested; skillful; endless; arrayed; high-powered; intellectual; bickering; strenuous; political; national; cordial; nobler; entrancing; tight; overtime; professional; heated.

verbs
announce—; cheat in—; dabble at—; emerge from—; enjoy—; enliven—; enthuse (colloq.) over—; feature—; follow—; improve —; indulge in—; invent—; join in—; judge —; master—; practise—; referee—; quarrel at—; score—; share—; strive in—; view—; witness—; —amuses; —contents; —cripples; —delights; —diverts; —entertains; —enthralls; —excites; —stales; —tires; —wanes; —wearies.
(See contest, recreation, sport.)

GAME
(*animals*)

verbs
bag—; cherish—; destroy—; ensnare—; enthrall by—; exterminate—; follow—; preserve—; prey upon—; relish—; rouse—; search for—; stalk—; trap—; view—; —abounds; —flees; —flourishes; —thrives; pursue—.
(See animal.)

GAMESOME

adverbs
amusingly; enliveningly; briskly; smartly; energetically; divertingly; happily; entertainingly; unusually; marvellously; enthusiastically; airily; blithely; buoyantly; exhilaratingly; hilariously; delightfully; jauntily; jovially; merrily; playfully; rollickingly; roisteringly; waggishly.

GAMESTER

adjectives
vehement; embryo; experienced; common; desperate; lukewarm.

GANG

verbs
associate with—; attract—; break up—; control—; disperse—; form—; head—; hire —; join—; lead—; manage—; regulate—; reprimand—; supervise—; —dissipates; —gathers; —meets; —operates; —separates; —troops in.
(See group, band, company, crew, crowd, squad.)

GANG-PLANK

verbs
(See gangway.)

GANGRENE

verbs
affect with—; cure—; decompose with—; defile with—; heal—; infect with—; lop off —; occasion—; result in—; seize with—; treat for—; —begins; —corrupts; —endangers; —pains; —oozes; —sets in; —spreads.

GANGSTER

verbs
accuses—; apprehend—; battle—; consort with—; employ—; round up—; rub out—; track down—; —bribes; —foments; —"hides out"; —intimidates; —maltreats; —murders; —s operate; —s organize; —revenges; —smuggles; —snuffs out; —terrifies; —terrorizes; —wounds.
(See thief.)

GANGWAY

verbs
ascend—; assemble at—; climb—; confine to—; crowd—; enter by—; file down—; hoist—; leave by—; lower—; pass down—; raise—; rush up—; stream down—; stride up—; take up—; —accommodates; —extends; —bridges.
(See platform.)

GAP

adjectives
wide; appalling; unbridgeable; tremendous; invisible; innumerable (pl); perceptible; ghastly; apparent; long; conversational; glaring.

verbs
break into—; bridge—; cut—; discover—; enter—; escape through—; form—; mend —; notch into—; open into—; pass through

—; patch—; span—; stop—; wear into—; —diminishes; —heals; —interrupts; —separates; —unites; —widens.
(See passage, breach.)

GARAGE

verbs
direct to—; equip—; grease at—; inspect at—; maintain—; operate—; paint at—; polish—; repair in—; stock—; store in—; wash at—; —distributes; —furnishes; —harbors; —itemizes; —services; —supplies; manage—; weld at—.

GARB

adjectives
fantastic; offensive; splendid; angelic; penitential; puritanical; sacred; dazzling; holiday; traditional; eccentric; shaggy; fleshy; severe; brighter; half-clerical; ecclesiastical; curious; symbolic; rustic; pompous; mourning; disordered; humble; shapeless; picturesque; antique; chronic; somber.

GARB (*v*)

adverbs
immaculately; spectacularly; fantastically; puritanically; eccentrically; ecclesiastically; symbolically; rustically; drably; somberly; modestly.
(See clothe, array, dress.)

GARBAGE

verbs
accumulate—; complain of—; destroy—; discard as—; disintegrate—; dispose of—; dump—; heap—; incinerate—; litter with—; object to—; separate—; sterilize—; strew with—; utilize—; —contaminates; —decomposes; —fertilizes; —menaces.
(See waste.)

GARBLED

adverbs
hopelessly; senselessly; sadly; ridiculously; vexatiously; incoherently; wildly; deliberately; carelessly; ignorantly; disastrously; indescribably; intentionally; maliciously; dishonestly; unfairly; cunningly; adroitly; mischievously; terribly; inexcusably; indefensibly; horribly.

GARDEN

adjectives
colonization; mellowing; exotic; luxuriant; bowery; celebrated; fateful; private; curious; aquatic; countless (pl); tranquil; radiant; delicious; odorous; fabled; spacious; desolate; ample; rustic; walled; extensive; seedy; orchard; ravaged; shady; tiny; broken; terraced; revived; alluring; vigorous; suburban; enchanted; sequestered; neglected; stately; weedless; beautiful; untidy; hanging; sunny; formal; productive; magnificent; illuminated; rock; delightful; dainty.

verbs
cultivate—; delve in—; fence—; fringe—; girdle—; hedge in—; plan—; plot—; preserve—; putter in—; rejoice in—; sow—; sprinkle—; stroll through—; till—; tour—; transplant to—; wall in—; water—; —delights; —flourishes; —thrives.
(See yard.)

GARGLE

verbs
advise—; advocate—; apply—; bathe with—; dilute—; employ—; prepare—; require—; treat with—; wash with—; —cools; —eases; —heals; —relieves.
(See liquid, preparation.)

GARISH

adverbs
cheaply; glitteringly; unpleasantly; surprisingly; unexpectedly; intensely; crudely; discordantly; inharmoniously; rudely; monstrously; obtrusively; pretentiously; pompously; spectacularly; dramatically; unbecomingly; ridiculously; intensely; preposterously.

GARLAND

adjectives
funereal; live; jeweled; lovely; immortal; leafy; beauteous; victorious.

verbs
bear—; compete for—; crown with—; deck with—; display—; festoon with—s; lay—; mantle with—; reward with—; set—upon; swathe in—; wind—; —adorns; —decorates.

GARMENT

adjectives
drenched; banqueting; tattered; ordinary; sacerdotal; wretched; voluminous; trailing; coarse; operating; dignified; delicate; fragile; sober; mortal; perennial; discarded; stage; bridal; transparent; necessary; glittering; rustic; vaporous; shabby; shapeless; magic; exquisite; clean; flimsy; seductive; upper; radiant; charity; appropriate; superb; snowy; sweeping; fluttering; flat-

tering; luxurious; handsome; custom; cool; elegant; exclusive; poisoned; untimely; imperial; dusty; modest; everlasting.

verbs
admire—; damage—; design—; dishevel—; display—; dye—; envy—; exhibit—; fashion—; fumigate—; injure—; model—; repair—; sew—; shroud in—; strip off—; sweat in—; weave—; yearn for—; —attracts; —befits; —clings to; —flatters; —reveals.
(See dress, coat, gown.)

GARNISHED

adverbs
tastefully; beautifully; generously; gayly; colorfully; invitingly; attractively; pleasingly; decoratively; becomingly; gorgeously; showily; simply; lusciously; deliciously; elaborately; cleverly; laboriously; ingeniously; unbelievably.

GARRET

verbs
accumulate in—; ascend to—; betake to—; conceal in—; deposit in—; evict from—; furnish—; heap in—; hoard in—; inhabit —; lodge in—; mount to—; preserve in—; remove to—; renovate—; reserve in—; search in—; stock in—; store in—; stow away in—; —garners; —projects; —totters.
(See attic, room.)

GARRISON

adjectives
intrusive; ample; large; floating; stalwart; retreating; slender; beleaguered; sturdy; strong; well-manned.

verbs
assault—; beset—; besiege—; bombard—; build—; charge—; erect—; fire upon—; invade—; maintain—; march upon—; quarter in—; reinforce—; station at—; threaten—; —defends; —guards; —shields; —surrenders; —withdraws.
(See fortification.)

GARRISON (*v*)

adverbs
sturdily; feebly; inadequately; stalwartly; smartly; prodigiously; effectually; adeptly.
(See supply, furnish.)

GARRULITY

adjectives
senile; unflagging; increased; nauseous; feminine; usual; boring; customary.

GARRULOUS

adverbs
endlessly; tediously; happily; chattily; genially; illuminatingly; knowledgeably; tiresomely; toothlessly; cacklingly; ribaldly; merrily; nauseatingly; unusually; habitually; highly; inescapably; incorrigibly; ponderously; monotonously; feverishly; excitedly; mumblingly.

GAS

adjectives
illuminating; foul; lethal; vivifying; incandescent; subtle; insidious; continuous; nebulous; congealed; fermenting; beneficent; transmuted; superseded; liquefied; mystery; deadly; noxious; injurious; rarefied; offensive; healthful.

verbs
accumulate—; battle—; bottle—; burn—; develop—; exhale—; guard against—; inhale—; isolate—; overcome by—; saturate with—; —asphyxiates; —emerges; —escapes; —expands; —flows; —fouls; —lifts; —poisons; —rises; —seeps in; —fuels.
(See oxygen.)

GASH

adjectives
deep; ghastly; fearful; fatal; abominable; hideous; deadly; murderous; bloody.

GASH (*v*)

adverbs
mortally; deeply; fatally; abominably; hideously; murderously; fearfully; savagely; fiendishly; diabolically.
(See slash, cut, tear.)

GASP

adjectives
convulsive; painful; long; grieving; struggling; broken; terrific; fitful; gurgling; last.

GASP (*v*)

adverbs
incredulously; breathlessly; unintelligibly; audibly; convulsively; fitfully; dramatically; brokenly; startlingly.
(See pant, breathe.)

GATE

adjectives
rusty; unclosed; churlish; inexorable; curtained; yawning; swinging; wooden; steel; decorated; awful; moon-lit; spectral; monumental; thronged; fast-locked; characteristic; facile; infernal; adamantine; massive; mosque; million-dollar; forbidden; figured; eastern; widest; celestial; huge; planched; applauding; painted; hospitable; silent; folding; sculptured; gorgeous; occidental; shadowy; postern; seaward; enchanted; grim; guarded; wicket; latched.

verbs
admit at—; bar—; beat against—; besiege —; fling open—; furnish—; guard—; knock on—; latch—; mend—; pass through —; repair—; storm—; swing on—; —bars; —hangs; —prevents.
(See opening, entrance, door.)

GATEWAY

adjectives
dilapidated; massive; secluded; crumbling; decorated; illumined.

GATHER (*v*)

adverbs
methodically; unpretentiously; seditiously; amiably; posthumously; tenderly; laboriously; noiselessly; cautiously; comprehensively; assiduously; formally; gaily; annually; riotously; raucously; exclusively.
(See assemble, congregate, accumulate.)

GATHERING

adjectives
informal; gay; insufficient; considerable; quiet; blind; assiduous; fashionable; indignant; annual; uncultured; democratic; eclectic; prompt; distinguished; noisy; unruly; riotous; unusual; raucous; notable; select; exclusive.

verbs
address—; arrange—; call—; collect into—; compose—; disperse—; dissipate—; enrage —; govern—; guide—; lead—; prevent—; provoke—; pull—; sway—; swell—; threaten—; —buzzes; —clamors; —contributes; —crowds; —impresses; —murmurs; —packs; —proposes; —views.
(See assembly, crowd.)

GAUDY

adverbs
unusually; unutterably; terribly; shockingly; extravagantly; oddly; gracelessly; unexpectedly; ridiculously; childishly; preposterously; horribly; offensively; disgustingly; unpleasantly.

GAUGE

verbs
adjust—; affect—; apply—; attach—; devise—; employ—; examine—; refer to—; test—; —advances; —ascertains; —determines; —fluctuates; —limits; —marks; —measures; —mounts; —notes; —records; —registers; —safeguards; —warns.
(See measure, standard.)

GAUGE (*v*)

adverbs
accurately; scientifically; correctly; skillfully; professionally; logically; mentally.
(See measure, estimate.)

GAUNT

adverbs
forbiddingly; haggardly; crookedly; unbelievably; terribly; awfully; unpleasantly; disagreeably; touchingly; miserably; portentously; wretchedly; ominously; alarmingly; horribly; uncommonly; meagerly; wanly; pallidly.

GAUZE

adjectives
theatrical; motionless; artful; vague; dappled; filmy.

verbs
apply—; bandage with—; brace with—; clean—; disinfect—; guard with—; join with—; sterilize—; strain through—; support with—.
(See fabric, silk.)

GAVEL

verbs
administer—; bang—; beat with—; drum —; employ—; hammer with—; heave—; inflict with—; knock—; rap with—; sound —; strike with—; —entreats; —hushes; —interferes; —interrupts.
(See hammer.)

GAWKY

adverbs
incredibly; pitiably; ludicrously; absurdly; inexcusably; sadly; utterly; remarkably;

clownishly; deliberately; pretentiously; comically; grotesquely; outlandishly; sensationally; theatrically; stupidly; heavily; youthfully.

GAY

adverbs
gracefully; boyishly; lightly; cheerfully; inexpressibly; racily; blithely; airily; saucily; proudly; carelessly; joyously; confidently; buoyantly; mystically; fantastically; devilishly; dashingly; artlessly; disarmingly; refreshingly; fashionably; racially; playfully; wantonly; roguishly; bewitchingly; engagingly; radiantly.

GAYETY

verbs
beget—; blush with—; commend—; displace—; eclipse—; feign—; flush in—; imbue with—; indulge in—; release—; revive —; rollick in—; thirst for—; unloose—; wreathe in—; yield to—; —blazes; —bubbles up; —cheers; —refreshes; —reigns; —ripples; —wearies.

(See merriment, fun, frolic, sport, liveliness, vivacity.)

GAZE

adjectives
uncertain; tributary; penetrating; mute; orphaned; relentless; quiet; kindred; probing; inquiring; abstracted; presumptuous; loving; searching; uncomplaining; earnest; averted; steady; enraptured; somber; maternal; inspiring; animated; shrewd; level; answering; admiring; bright; intent; compelling; concentrated; modest; steadfast; unwinking; calm; large; curious; living; dark; keen; vulgar; shrinking; piercing; hostile; disembodied; fervid; trained; appalling; complacent; unrestricted; astonished; lecherous; universal; dimmed; commanding; patient; long; prying; magic; painful; strained; imploring; ardent; melancholy; motionless; malevolent; questioning; different; tender; impartial; rapt; sullen; passionate; disdainful; reverent; magisterial; drowsy; mild; fixed; undeviating; yearning; enamored; ferret-like.

verbs
avoid—of; fix—on; quail beneath—; screen from—; shun—; stand at—; strain—toward; turn—upon; wilt beneath—; wince beneath—; writhe under—; —chills; —falls; —falters; —pierces; —searches; —wanders.

(See look, stare, glare.)

GAZE (*v*)

adverbs
vacantly; indifferently; inquiringly; deliberately; mournfully; impassionedly; trustfully; steadfastly; searchingly; furtively; blankly; defiantly; wistfully; dreamily; intently; sympathetically; impertinently; apprehensively; menacingly; disconsolately; reflectively; piercingly; keenly; obtrusively; insinuatingly; mockingly; beseechingly; profanely; piteously; perplexedly; meditatingly; yearningly; shrewdly; lecherously; ardently; malevolently.

(See look, stare.)

GEAR

adjectives
new-fashioned; dainty; dangerous; diminishing; adamantine; shapeless; bloody; military.

verbs
change—; connect—s; damage—s; drive in —; equip with—; fit with—; grease—; lock—; provide—; put into—; repair—; reverse—; rip—; strip—s; throw into—; —grinds; —s mesh.

(See equipment, mechanism.)

GEAR (*v*)

adverbs
adequately; delicately; mechanically; intricately; complicatedly; highly; scientifically.

(See prepare.)

GELATINE

verbs
abhor—; box—; coat with—; contain—; convert into—; contaminate—; dissolve—; garnish—; mold—; prepare—; relish—; serve—; shape—; utilize—; —preserves; —shakes; —shimmies; —trembles; —wobbles.

GEM

verbs
adorn with—s; collect—s; cut—; discover —; display—; engrave—; fashion—; girdle with—s; mine for—s; polish—; prize—; unearth—; value—; weigh—; —delights; —glistens; —glitters; —illuminates; —scintillates; —spangles.

(See stone, jewel, emerald, diamond, ruby, etc.)

GEMS

adjectives
sparkling; infusorial; twinkling; expensive; superb; flashing; shining; glittering; oracular; priceless; dainty; sunborn; reflecting; radiant; costly; animated; burnished; brilliant; carven.

GENEALOGY

verbs
admit—; commend—; dig up—; insert in—; interest in—; investigate—; mark—; note in—; praise—; reckon—; record—; register—; trace—; view—; —enumerates; —exhibits; —proves; —verifies.
(See record.)

GENERAL

adverbs
admittedly; broadly; surprisingly; necessarily; astonishingly; mysteriously; inexplicably; naturally; unaccountably; unwarrantably; fortunately; illimitably; sweepingly; inclusively; significantly; evidently; amazingly; dreadfully.

GENERAL (*army*)

adjectives
politic; intrepid; merciful; permanent; commanding; grim; skilled; knowing; trained; clever; bungling; immortal; cruel; brash; stubborn; brutish; worsted; incipient; respective (pl); sagacious; shelved.

verbs
commission as—; decorate—; promote to—; respect—; salute—; —accuses; —administrates; —authorizes; —castigates; —commands; —conducts; —controls; —disposes of; —entrusts; —exercises; —leads; —maltreats; —orders; —plans; —posts; —quarters; —supervises; —terrorizes.
(See officer, commander, leader, chief.)

GENERALITIES

adjectives
polite; vague; inane; solemn; inept; illogical; meaningless.

GENERALITY

verbs
agree on—; arrive at—; avoid—; comment on—; comprehend—; confine to—s; deal in —s; descend from—s; evade—; guide—s; judge—; limit to—s; propound—; question —s; relegate to—s; resort to—s; restrain —s; skip—s; sound—s; stress—s; test—.
(See statement.)

GENERALIZATION

adjectives
easy; mystic; embracing; fantastical; scientific; hazardous; metaphysical; unsupported.

GENERATE (*v*)

adverbs
spontaneously; swiftly; sturdily; corruptly; endlessly; ceaselessly; intemperately; prolifically.
(See produce, reproduce, propagate.)

GENERATION

verbs
activate—; beget—; compute—; expose to —; glorify—; introduce—; laud—; praise —; reckon—s; remove from—; urge—; —arises; —s cherish; —s gather; —s heap; —s inherit; —involves; —s issue from.
(See period, time, age.)

GENERATIONS

adjectives
modest; innumerable; spontaneous; remote; sturdy; pompous; extremest; corrupt; countless; endless; coming; rising; future; spirited; existing; depraved; succeeding; frustrated; spurious; perished; analytical; tongueless; false; illiterate; whole; experimental; aesthetic; ceaseless; previous; intemperate; traveling.

GENERATOR

verbs
drive—; employ—; operate—; simplify—; —alternates; —converts; —draws; —heats up; —produces; —revolves; —rotates; —whines; —whirs; —winds.
(See machine, apparatus, dynamo.)

GENEROSITY

adjectives
impetuous; impulsive; unwonted; eager; judicious; amazing; consummate; pious; trustful; unparalleled; scornful; fond; divine; hearty; bitter; lavish; hospitable; celestial; careless; unquestioning; understandable; widespread; designing; dastardly.

verbs
admit—; bestow with—; commend—; credit —; distrust—; endow with—; exceed in—; expose—; flatter—; indulge—; owe to—; practise—; praise—; reveal—; rival—; shower with—; subscribe with—; temper with—; —bribes; —delights; —deprives; —drains.
(See benevolence.)

GENEROUS

adverbs
sincerely; quixotically; fantastically; ostentatiously; publicly; extremely; altruistically; charitably; benevolently; instinctively; distinctly; spontaneously; lavishly; extravagantly; habitually; truly; genuinely; amazingly; notably; essentially; magnificently; splendidly; essentially; unselfishly.

GENIAL

adverbs
pleasantly; courteously; affably; amiably; heartily; merrily; jovially; altogether; consistently; resolutely; fraternally; comfortingly; charmingly; cordially; delightfully; engagingly; marvelously; extraordinarily; unusually; habitually; conspicuously.

GENIALITY

adjectives
frank; shrewd; artificial; suave; hearty; boyish; artistic; feigned; real; soothing; effervescent; everlasting; annoying.

verbs
accustom to—; bask in—; diffuse—; flush with—; light up with—; practise—; receive with—; smile with—; welcome with —; —animates; —cheers; —delights; —endears; —exhilarates; —inspires; —warms.
(See cordiality, cheerfulness, warmth.)

GENIUS

adjectives
consummate; presiding; intellectual; inherent; interpretative; evil; unique; sublimest; engineering; sheer; ardent; sceptered; acute; fanciful; eloquent; bounding; sartorial; extraordinary; executive; untutored; unfettered; renovated; amiable; universal; persistent; various (pl); rare; decorative; sardonic; prodigious; military; solemn; solitary; gloomy; dramatic; inventive; erratic; hereditary; singular; fresh; organizing; malignant; incredible; financial; disciplined; obscure; recessive; rich; evident; peculiar; diabolical; culinary; assured; stupendous; poetical; veritable; commanding; mathematical; autocratic; superior; musical; misdirected; unclarified; intrepid; dormant; harsher; precocious; strange; brightest; gigantic; statesmanlike; vigorous; feminine; inventive; meditative; political; desultory; unique; pining; irritated; artificial; middling; majestic; maiden; innate; contriving; sullen; capricious; saturnine; fertile; legislative; bountiful; puissant; tutelary; individual; creative; special; ethnic; massive; fiery; lofty; true; masterly; evil; mature; adroit; tragic; predominant; mundane; characterized.

verbs
acclaim—; attain—; befriend—; endow with—; exhibit—; inspire—; marvel at—; nourish—; nurture—; produce—; recognize —; starve—; tincture—with; trifle with—; waste—; worship—; —aspires to; —creates; —enlightens; —produces; —fructifies; —glows; —ripens; —triumphs.
(See talent, power, creator, artist.)

GENTEEL

adverbs
proudly; nobly; aristocratically; inherently; genuinely; truly; admittedly; tenaciously; handsomely; elegantly; impressively.

GENTILITY

adjectives
brave; stripped; plated; faded; shabby; penniless; sham; decayed; decadent; worn; worked; noticeable .

verbs
bear with—; borrow—; claim—; confute—; convey—; counterfeit—; cultivate—; degrade from—; diffuse—; exhibit—; expel—; patronize—; pursue—; recognize—; reveal —; stand on—; vanquish—; —decays; —enhances; —fades; —graces.
(See dignity, politeness, elegance, refinement.)

GENTLE

adverbs
considerately; sympathetically; indulgently; remarkably; particularly; affably; curiously; compassionately; mercifully; understandingly; softly; tolerantly; calmly; forbearingly; patiently; gravely; quietly; serenely; complaisantly; politely; ingratiatingly; amazingly.

GENTLEMAN

adjectives
worthy; dignified; conservative; old-fashioned; prosy; antique; majestic; country; whiskered; eligible; aristocratic; credulous; digressive; gallant; decorous; opulent; polished; decrepit; unusual; chivalrous; superannuated; curious; studious; lovely; legal-looking; vacuous-looking; benevolent; eccentric; elderly; ceremonious; fastidious;

venerable; scholarly; valiant; flippant; loyal; downright; reverend; inane; decayed; clerical; suave; heedless; sober; fat; landed; frayed; frail; silk-stockinged.

verbs
admire—; bear like—; be born—; behave like—; conduct like—; define—; denote—; disguise as—; educate as—; grace—; mellow into—; pass for a—; perfect—; produce—; respect—; transform into—; welcome—; —considers; —forbears; —honors; —reproaches; —respects; —submits; —sympathizes; —understands.

GENTLENESS

adjectives
stately; infinite; intelligent; supreme; caressing; surface; unassuming; deprecating; wonted; unbelievable; tender; heartfelt.

GENTLEWOMAN

adjectives
shrewd; virtuous; fresher; dainty; elegant.

GENTRY

adjectives
landed; minor; cocked-hat; light-fingered.

GENUINE

adverbs
unquestionably; veritably; obviously; manifestly; unimpeachably; indubitably; essentially; authentically; incontestably; substantially; inimitably; invaluably.

GEOGRAPHY

verbs
add to—; confuse—; familiarize with—; perfect—; refer to—; resort to—; subdue—; verse in—; —defines; —describes; —explains; —informs; —reveals; —treats of.

(See science.)

GERM

verbs
check—s; combat—; crawl with—s; destroy —; detect—; disseminate—s; eliminate—s; fall prey to—; filter—s; harbor—; identify —; infect with—; infest with—; isolate—; resist—; sow—s; track down—; transmit—; —inhabits; —invades; —lodges in; —migrates; —multiplies; —strikes; —thrives.

(See disease.)

GERMICIDE

verbs
advocate—; disinfect with—; employ—; flush with—; fumigate with—; wash with —; —allays; —arrests; —cleans; —cures; —destroys; —evaporates; —exterminates; —heals; —overpowers; —prevents; —purifies; —rids; —routs; —sterilizes.

(See disinfection.)

GERMS

adjectives
natural; fruitful; virulent; organic; pernicious; fundamental; floating; delicate; vegetable; infant; marauding; infectious; prolific; insidious.

GESTICULATE (v)

adverbs
violently; ludicrously; dramatically; expressively; suavely; gleefully; impatiently; sweepingly; airily; affectedly; ecstatically; significantly; authoritatively.

(See gesture.)

GESTURE

adjectives
wild; authoritative; mental; ponderous; conciliatory; magnificent; ungoverned; convulsive; dreadful; despairing; angry; spontaneous; imploring; eloquent; generous; affectionate; threatening; pitying; ferocious; airy; truculent; dignified; dramatic; expressive; vulgar; romping; abrupt; symbolic; fine; impetuous; helpless; parting; joyous; excited; gentle; sweeping; negative; impatient; uncouth; insolent; respectful; tentative; violent; spasmodic; careless; grateful; absurd; polite; gleeful; animated; significant; vehement; arbitrary; regal; emphatic; heroic; deprecatory; faint; pretty; chivalrous; spectacular; interrogatory; emotional; superstitious; childish; renunciatory; magnanimous; effective; imperceptible; furious; inexplicable; disparaging; frivolous; courtly; menacing; frail; analyzing; pioneering; possessive; benignant; scarce; wide; graceful; invincible; masterful; quick; noble; imperious.

verbs
accompany with—s; ape—; emphasize with —; employ—; execute—; express by—; indulge in—; imitate—; mix with—; moderate —s; motion with—; note—; perform—; record—; refuse—; restrict—s; ridicule—; speak with—s; signify by—; —s express; —s harmonize.

(See motion, posture.)

GESTURE (v)

adverbs
wildly; ponderously; magnificently; convulsively; despairingly; spontaneously; generously; ferociously; truculently; vulgarly; symbolically; uncouthly; animatedly; vehemently; regally; emphatically; spectacularly; menacingly; benignantly; imperiously; masterfully.
(See gesticulate.)

GEYSER

verbs
—blows off; —boils; —bubbles; —darts; —ejects; —emits; —erupts; —explodes; —gurgles; —gushes; —jets; —plays; —pours; —relaxes; —ruins; —shoots; —snorts; —spouts; —spurts; —swells; —throws off.
(See spring, fountain.)

GHASTLY

adverbs
incredibly; unbelievably; inexpressibly; horribly; awfully; fearfully; shockingly; portentously; appallingly; monstrously; formidably; weirdly; terribly; utterly.

GHOST

adjectives
sheeted; gigantic; livid; lofty; gliding; glowing; drab; pale; frighted; silvery; collaborating; sweet; songless; pathetic; slender; reflected; mad; aimless; restless; peaceful; infernal; beckoning; disturbed; pensive; pious; haunting; handsome; graphical; headless; shrouded; honest.

verbs
give up—; harbor—; perceive—; raise—; shape—; speak to—; —beckons; —cries; —flits; —follows; —glares; —haunts; —howls; —points; —prowls; —pursues; —returns; —scares; —shadows; —stalks; —torments; —vanishes; —visits.
(See apparition, phantom, spirit, shade, soul.)

GHOSTLY

adverbs
weirdly; alarmingly; immaterially; spectrally; uncannily; appallingly; mysteriously; inscrutably; horribly; terribly; inexplicably; comically; strangely; curiously; oddly; unbelievably; remarkably; singularly.

GIANT

adjectives
mental; financial; rich; juicy; shock-headed; glorious; massy; mysterious; petrified; supernormal; stupendous; genial; peaceable; useless; pastoral; deformed; hideous; monstrous.

verbs
conquer—; crush—; dread—; flee from—; grapple with—; mount—; overthrow—; quell—; wrestle with—; —heaves; —inhabits; —menaces; —overpowers; —overwhelms; —roars; —shoulders; —terrifies; —threatens; —tramples.
(See monster.)

GIBBER (v)

adverbs
ghoulishly; drunkenly; disgustingly; idiotically; aimlessly; inanely; unintelligibly; insanely.
(See chatter, jabber.)

GIBBET

adjectives
shameful; gloomy; intellectual; menacing; ancient; unused; life-snatching.

verbs
chain to—; condemn to—; conduct to—; deserve—; erect—; escape—; execute on—; gaze at—; punish on—; save from—; send to—; sentence to—; suffer—; tie to—; —frightens; —glooms.
(See gallows.)

GIBE

adjectives
rude; insolent; stinging; jocose; exultant; nasty; bitter; raucous; friendly.

GIDDINESS

verbs
anticipate—; bring on—; condemn—; cure—; delight in—; faint with—; fall in—; incur—; occasion—; repent—; stagger with—; swim with—; tolerate—; whirl with—; —bewilders; —confuses; —creeps over; —envelops; —infuriates; —maddens; —ruins; —vexes.
(See dizziness.)

GIDDY

adverbs
wildly; heedlessly; distractedly; carelessly; dreamily; happily; rapturously; blithely;

capriciously; wantonly; deliriously; incoherently; foolishly; irresolutely; irresponsibly; amazingly; reprehensibly; erratically; fitfully; fantastically; unstably; freakishly; waywardly; captiously; frivolously.

GIFT

adjectives
charming; lasting; valuable; expensive; mental; worthless; poetic; lovely; heavenly; worth-while; exceptional; inalienable; practical; satirical; equal; especial; divine; conversational; ample; promised; fragile; higher; festive; peaceful; myriad (pl); fair; genuine; lyrical; hospitable; innate; pious; glozing; distinctive; versatile; gracious; sacramental; brilliant; healing; compensating; acceptable; wonderful; appropriate; sweet; random; suitable; melancholy; unavailing; entrusted; transcendent; golden; youthful; fecund; rare; graceful; clever; placating; superlative; godlike; lyrical; trifling; sponsorial; unique; prophetic; precious; pure; cankering; free; mysterious; ineffable; cherished; imitative; peerless; wondrous; oratorical; clever; dangerous; matchless; propitiatory; social; costly; formidable; different; spicy.

verbs
apologize with—; bestow — upon; cherish—; cultivate—; endow with—; enhance —; exercise—; favor with—; grant—; honor with—; lavish —s upon; offer—; proffer—; scorn—; surprise with—; value—; —delights; —elates; —enriches; —impresses; —obligates; —persuades; —s pour in.
(See present, endowment, talent, benefaction, contribution.)

GIFTED

adverbs
brilliantly; unusually; wonderfully; magnificently; notably; consummately; peculiarly; expertly; intellectually; eminently; admirably; illustriously; aptly; conspicuously; extraordinarily; supremely; uncommonly; highly.

GIGANTIC

adverbs
incredibly; stupendously; tremendously; unbelievably; inexpressibly; colossally; prodigiously; overwhelmingly; terrifyingly; appallingly; marvellously; terribly; astonishingly; astoundingly.

GIGGLE

adjectives
rich; girlish; antiquated; sudden; nervous; loud.

verbs
burst into—; convulse in —s; cure of —s; degenerate into —s; laugh in —s; set into —s; suppress—; throw into —s; utter—; —annoys; —bores; —disgusts; —disturbs; —interrupts; —sickens; —sparkles; —tickles; —wearies.
(See laugh.)

GIGGLE (*v*)

adverbs
nervously; hysterically; self-consciously; intermittently; abruptly; explosively; coquettishly; alluringly.
(See snicker, titter.)

GILD (*v*)

adverbs
radiantly; lavishly; artfully; tastefully; professionally; superfluously; richly; ornamentally.
(See cover, color.)

GILL

verbs
breathe with—; close—; cuff—; draw into —; expand—; furnish with—; stroke—; inhale through—; strain—; —absorbs; —admits; —flaps; —inhales; —quivers; —receives; —sucks; —swells.

GIN
(liquor)

adjectives
meditative; sullen; accursed.

verbs
abstain from—; denature—; distill—; imbibe—; legalize—; loathe—; reek of—; resist—; —destroys; —dulls; —grogs; —inebriates; —influences; —intoxicates; —overcomes; —regales; —seduces.
(See liquor.)

GIRAFFE

verbs
anger—; arouse—; cage—; exhibit—; lasso —; pet—; train—; —ambles; —batters; —browses; —forages; —gallops; —s herd; —kicks; —plucks; —roams; —straddles.
(See animal.)

GIRL

adjectives
sylvan; docile; unaffected; much-courted; cuddlesome; dear; delightful; stricken; robust; athletic; country; serving; frowzy; wishy-washy; tawdry; expensive; clumsy; urgent; watchful; passionate; anserine; adolescent; elegant; slim; confiding; artful; sensible; true; scrawny; giddy; sweet; gentle; beautiful; ornamental; casual; suitable; frail; sympathetic; light; colored; timbrel; ambitious; radiant; exotic; truthful; semi-wild; utilitarian; blushing; alluring; unregulated; debilitated; loitering; singsong; impecunious; trembling; dependent; sullen; charming; pluckiest; dainty; sober; uneducated; freckle-faced; worthless; industrious; ridiculous; swarthy; sophisticated; vigorous; decent; virtuous; enthusiastic; patrician; perverse; unruly; willful; flippant; comely; awkward; sad; shiftless; peevish; commonplace; emotional; suicidal; coquettish.

verbs
betroth—; bud into—; consort with —s; —beguiles; —blushes; —charms; —dances; —giggles; —loves; —lures; —mystifies; —pouts; —prates; —smiles; —sulks.

(See infant, child, youth, damsel.)

GIRTH

adjectives
generous; broad; immense; cumbersome; muscular; spanless; bountiful.

GIST

verbs
convey—; define—; deviate from—; explain—; follow—; glimpse—; overlook—; phrase—; sum up—; translate—; understand—; wade through—; —deals with; —denotes; —lies in; —necessitates.

(See substance, core. essence.)

GIVE (*v*)

adverbs
exclusively; grudgingly; charitably; benevolently; abundantly; grumblingly; discriminately; spontaneously; magnificently; methodically; unsparingly; discreetly; conscientiously; periodically; impartially; infallibly; subsequently; wantonly; invariably; ultimately; intentionally; substantially; prodigally; legitimately.

(See bestow, accord, grant.)

GIVER

adjectives
undiscerning; venerable; judicious; Indian.

GLACIER

adjectives
grinding; upended; extinct; immense; unnamed; glistening.

verbs
climb—; consolidate into—; cross—; form—; melt—; press into—; slide into—; warn of—; —chokes; —confronts; —creeps; —derives from; —drifts; —glistens; —glitters; —glows; —lodges; —sparkles.

(See stream, ice, snow.)

GLAD

adverbs
genially; laughingly; wholly; definitely; heartily; truly; genuinely; wholeheartedly; amazingly; pathetically; childishly; sincerely; radiantly; delightedly; enthusiastically; profoundly; quietly; visibly; boundlessly; solemnly; exceedingly; gloriously; rapturously; hysterically; excitedly; serenely.

GLADE

adjectives
rustling; steep; hopeful; enchanted; shaded; woodland; mossy; purple; shadowy; umbrageous; sheltered; tropic.

GLADNESS

adjectives
tender; whimsical; quiet; visionary; subdued; visible; sunny; hidden; bursting; boundless; solemn; ignorant; maniacal; exceeding; glorious; unfeigned; abrupt; tranquil; immortal; effervescent; sober; ebullient.

verbs
bring on—; cloak in—; comprehend—; couch in—; crush—; derive — from; deserve—; dispense—; emit—; enliven with—; exude—; flush with—; occasion—; overwhelm—; quell—; radiate—; send out—; trample—; —confuses; —enhances; —speaks.

(See delight, exhilaration, joy, pleasure.)

GLAMOROUS

adverbs
seductively; delightfully; undeniably; beautifully; gloriously; irresistibly; peculiarly; utterly; adorably; charmingly; exotically;

wantonly; girlishly; deliberately; carefully; calculatingly; immeasurably; inconceivably; incomparably; naturally; purposely; cleverly; bewitchingly; unconsciously; darkly; **brilliantly; entrancingly.**

GLAMOUR

adjectives
harmless; romantic; laughing; longing; sophisticated; midnight; theatrical; lingering; pictorial; extraneous; fortuitous.

verbs
capture—; create—; deck in—; dim—; invest with—; recapture—; sacrifice—; savor —; surround with—; win with—; yield to —; —allures; —attracts; —awes; —bewitches; —charms; —dazzles; —deceives; —deludes; —enchants; —entrances; —fades; —fascinates; —magnetizes; —stirs; —wears off.

(See charm, enchantment, fascination, glory, spell.)

GLANCE

adjectives
tender; sidelong; mirthful; dreamy; wistful; mechanical; furtive; fierce; maternal; reproachful; hasty; keen; languid; quick; pitying; uneasy; mingled; oblique; timid; mischievous; departed; pure; half-inviting; flaming; penetrating; vindictive; imploring; comprehensive; passing; interrogatory; approving; satisfying; chastened; sinister; deep; hostile; malevolent; tranquil; curious; apologetic; crawling; mortal; wild; expressive; mournful; fantastical; unseeing; fiery; covert; careless; bridling; suspicious; clear; significant; inquiring; admiring; rapid; errant; frightened; unintercepted; single; heartfelt; nervous; wandering; absorbing; baleful; annihilating; superficial; farewell; dull; bird; momentary; vertical; frank; casual; contemptuous; supplicating; conciliatory; fleeting; expectant; indolent; genuine; sudden; sharp; malign; critical; heavy; meteor; furious; meaning; steady; hurried; meager; backward; irresistible; exquisite; surprised; evil; dubious; compassionate; venomous; irresolute; proud; soulful; swift; pleading; expiring; confused; cold; mild; satanical; luminous; ripened; abstracted; frowning; murderous; incidental; saucy; ominous; wondering; beseeching; appealing.

verbs
bestow — upon; cast — upon; detect at a—; flash—; intercept—; quail beneath—; rivet —upon; shift—; shoot — at; steal — at; survey at—; —chills; —falters; —pricks; — rests on; —strays.

(See look, gleam, glimpse, flash.)

GLANCE (v)

adverbs
curiously; complacently; suspiciously; furtively; rebelliously; piercingly; cursorily; indifferently; disconsolately; disdainfully; involuntarily; contemptuously; critically; reproachfully; apprehensively; surreptitiously; wistfully; inquisitively; significantly; tenderly; malignantly; covertly; casually; instinctively; passionately; imperiously; intuitively; dubiously; deferentially; maliciously.

(See beam, gleam, glitter.)

GLAND

adjectives
lymphatic; dormant; secretive; master; lively; sex; ineffective; swollen; abnormal.

verbs
affect—; block—; graft—; inflame—; reduce—; reinvigorate—; transplant—; —controls; —enlarges; —functions; —indurates; —opens into; —pours forth; —produces; —responds; —secretes; —suppurates; —swells.

(See organ.)

GLARE

adjectives
savage; bright; burning; furious; warning; ghastly; gaudy; blinding; blistering; sun; dull; interested; meteoric; dancing; kingly; fearful; fiery; pale; lurid; ruddy; rifted; wild; frozen; desert; awful; brazen; blank; merciless; yellow; chill.

verbs
bask in—; bate—; cast—; destroy with—; fix—; incur—; ignore—; mark—; observe —; relieve—; remove—; shade—; shine with—; —angers; —blinds; —dazzles; —exposes; —lights; —reveals.

(See light, look, gaze, splendor.)

GLARE (v)

adverbs
ferociously; comically; fiercely; scowlingly; balefully; resentfully; vindictively; hostilely; stonily; remorselessly; oddly; blazingly.

(See frown, stare.)

GLASS

adjectives
undersized; sapphire; frosted; gleaming; spilled; parenthetical; arid; iridescent; bifocal; misted; delicate; preparatory; smoky; sumptuous; watery; tarnished; steaming; shattered; spattering; neglected; molten; poor; distorted; stained; cobwebbed; superstitious; irregular; untasted; social; translucent; medieval; brimming; swirled; rimmed; uncolored; inverted; dimpling; opaque.

verbs
brandish—; blow—; cast—; chip—; clink —s; color—; cover with—; crack—; drain —; engrave—; etch on—; file—; fondle—; frame with—; glaze with—; grind—; mold —; nick—; pulverize—; shape—; shatter—; split—; stain—; —s clash; —s clatter; —s clink.

(See crystal, mirror.)

GLAZE

adjectives
dreamy; monotonous; sincere; defiant; granite; iridescent; thin; death.

GLEAM

adjectives
rare; momentary; occasional; varied (pl); silvery; dazzling; diabolic; sorrowful; cool; phosphorescent; portentous; troubled; lurid; livid; fiery; brilliant; distant; convex; dull; new; hateful; crafty; starry; subdued; unpleasant; sulphurous; metallic; stray; elusive; polar; waning; pallid; summer; flickering; bountiful; bright; ruddy; spasmodic; pale; alluring; determined; ineffectual; faint; vagrant; tearlike; broken; wilder; solitary; opaline; visionary; formless; evanescent; greasy; angry; illusive; moon-lit; splendid.

verbs
behold—; cast—; diffuse—; emit—; flare into—; flash—; light up with—; obscure—; reflect—; send—; shoot—; spread—; —blazes; —dazes; —dazzles; —flickers; —glitters; —illuminates; —pales; —shimmers; —shudders; —sparkles; —twinkles.

(See light, flash, beam, ray.)

GLEAM (*v*)

adverbs
weirdly; unnaturally; ominously; tigerishly; obscurely; fitfully; dangerously; momentarily; dazzlingly; diabolically; phosphorescently; portentously; sulphurously; pallidly; spasmodically; flickeringly; evanescently; illusively.

(See shine, glow.)

GLEE

adjectives
rapturous; malicious; unconscious; strange; noisy; defying; childish; uncouth; unbidden; counterfeited; fiendish; sparkling; tumultuous; pelting; innocent; laughing; intemperate; venturous; chortling.

verbs
advance with—; bubble with—; condemn—; dance in—; display—; exhibit—; exude—; feign—; flaunt—; grin with—; increase—; jump in—; laugh with—; leap in—; occasion—; plunge into with—; rub the hands in—; sport with—; titter in—; turn into—; —envelops; —infects; —spreads.

(See mirth, gayety, merriment, joy.)

GLEEFUL

adverbs
blithely; enthusiastically; infectiously; innocently; happily; irresistibly; completely; naturally; elatedly; triumphantly; joyously; light-heartedly; merrily; hilariously; sportively; utterly; openly; laughingly; noisily; effervescently; ecstatically; wholesomely; habitually.

GLEN

adjectives
peaceful; shadowy; shrubby; narrow; unfrequented; mountain; leafy; woody; silent; obscurest; darkened; solitary; shaded; sunless.

GLIB

adverbs
blandly; smoothly; cleverly; adroitly; deceptively; astutely; suspiciously; blatantly; suavely; socially; professionally; unctuously; fluently; nimbly; easily; felicitously; dexterously; affably; complaisantly; urbanely; civilly; politely; ingratiatingly; entertainingly; persuasively; resourcefully; amazingly; extraordinarily; strikingly.

GLIBNESS

verbs
admire—; beget—; criticize with—; deliver with—; impede—; judge by—; mistrust—; perform with—; practise—; praise—; proceed with—; speak with—; unfold with—;

utter with—; —charms; —deceives; —delights; —impresses; —misleads; —oils.

(See fluency.)

GLIDE (v)

adverbs

smoothly; gracefully; unobtrusively; serenely; majestically; sinuously; noiselessly; dreamily.

(See slide, slip.)

GLIMMER

adjectives

misty; fading; uncertain; ghostly; pale; gleaming; dying; quivering; ignorant; confused; faint; quiet; pallid.

GLIMMER (v)

adverbs

dimly; phosphorescently; spasmodically; intermittently; evanescently; uncertainly; pallidly; gaily; mistily.

(See gleam, shine.)

GLIMPSE

adjectives

intriguing; touching; vivid; interesting; incidental; electric; vague; marvelous; amusing; faint; transient; picturesque; tempting; comforting; occasional; tantalizing; leafy; fleeting; delicious; shadowy; shimmering; cautious; prophetic; furtive; chilly; flashing; unveiled; mysterious; passing; murky; desired.

verbs

afford—; catch—; deny—; detect at—; drink in—; flash—; hope for—; obtain—; prevent—; procure—; win—; yearn for—; yield—; —dazzles; —delights; —glimmers; —glitters; —perforates; —reveals; —shimmers; —shines.

(See flash, glance.)

GLINT

adjectives

moiled; rigid; ravishing; fiery; murderous; nasty; wicked.

GLINT (v)

adverbs

suspiciously; antagonistically; brutally; angrily; murderously; wickedly; fiendishly; viciously; vindictively.

(See gleam, flash, glitter.)

GLISTER

adjectives

faint; ruddy; scornful; spotless.

GLITTER

adjectives

prismatic; gilded; steely; intense; jeweled; scaly; fiery; mercurial; dangerous; sinister; streaked; sarcastic; dull; wandering; pristine; weary; effeminate; blinding; ghastly; opulent; gaudy.

GLITTER (v)

adverbs

lustrously; prismatically; intensely; mercurially; sinisterly; coldly; devilishly; blindingly; opulently; gaudily.

(See sparkle, gleam, flash.)

GLOAT (v)

adverbs

spitefully; hilariously; selfishly; pettishly; triumphantly; hatefully; jealously; vindictively; morbidly; victoriously.

(See covet, lust, ogle.)

GLOBE

adjectives

terrestrial; habitable; ponderous; gorgeous; spotty; gluey; heavenly; stupendous; terraqueous; bewildering; celestial; native; many-mortaled; whirling; spinning; careening.

verbs

circle—; circumnavigate—; consult—; discern on—; employ—; fill—; form into—; girdle—; perfect—; refer to—; revolve—; rotate—; suspend—; —defines; —describes; —explains; —points; —represents; —rolls; —rotates; —spins; —whirls.

(See ball, sphere, earth, world.)

GLOBULAR

adverbs

amazingly; overwhelmingly; stupendously; astonishingly; astoundingly; totally; inconceivably; boundlessly; extraordinarily; unprecedentedly; strangely; unwontedly; surprisingly; singularly.

GLOBULES

adjectives

teeming; swarming; insignificant; minute; porous.

GLOOM

adjectives
congregated; dark; ascetic; deepening; shady; solemn; hopeless; malodorous; partial; anxious; lingering; additional; thick; funereal; desponding; murkier; dishwater; moving; gathering; chilly; fixed; slumbrous; melancholy; impenetrable; somber; sacred; grateful; ceaseless; minister; surrounding; forest; eternal; atmospheric; unromantic; perpetual; sepulchral; profound; pregnant; damp; warm; divine; convent; azure; woven; settled; sullen; dungeon; foreboding; sympathetic; twilight; wintry; intensified; lurid; coiled; starving; unavailing; heavy; persistent; dreary; pervasive; darkling; glowing; unobtrusive; dangerous; conventional; glorious; coppery; verdurous; gorgeous; adamantine; arched; natal; cheerless; silent; sable; oppressive; dank; languid; prairie; utter; ethereal; delicate; sheer; blighting; roseate; abnormal; rich; curtained; sibylline; haunting; stained; shadowed; Stygian.

verbs
assimilate—; cast upon—; detach from—; dispel—; envelop in—; exude—; harbor—; overcome—; overhang with—; overwhelm with—; pierce—; wrap in—; —assails; —deepens; —dwells on; —oppresses; —pervades; —settles on; —thickens.

(See darkness, obscurity, melancholy, sorrow, misfortune, despondency, dejection.)

GLOOMY

adverbs
abjectly; helplessly; depressingly; incurably; inconceivably; hopelessly; incredibly; piteously; horribly; tragically; unbelievably; singularly; unreasonably; miserably; needlessly; comically; ridiculously; ostensibly; obviously; desperately; heavily; sadly; mournfully; moodily; pensively; sulkily; inconsolably; desolately; disconsolately; dismally; gravely; woefully; glumly; wanly; unnecessarily; irritatingly.

GLORIFY (*v*)

adverbs
insanely; enthusiastically; boisterously; lovingly; martially; sumptuously; posthumously; eternally; physically; radiantly; ancestrally; feudally; imperially; romantically; regally; matchlessly; barbarically.

(See praise, adore.)

GLORIOUS

adverbs
effulgently; brilliantly; splendidly; superbly; unexpectedly; martially; inestimably; radiantly; proudly; regally; ecstatically; peculiarly; matchlessly; supremely; barbarically; distinctly; solemnly; sublimely; remarkably; eminently; imperishably; transcendently.

GLORY

adjectives
ghastly; martial; gaping; reflected; sumptuary; posthumous; fainter; semblance; coeternal; inevitable; liquid; elemental; sudden; butchered; native; physical; inner; athletic; shining; paternal; short-lived; earthly; radiant; proud; ancestral; gentle; false; golden; pristine; endless; evolving; hirsute; mild; celestial; eclipsed; incipient; abandoned; lustrous; living; feudal; spectacular; insubstantial; universal; passive; imperial; romantic; artistic; transient; setting; crimson; western; lineal; lasting; regal; undulating; naked; meridian; peerless; ebbed; imperishable; meteoric; shadowy; flaming; ecstatic; boasted; crowning; supernal; floral; lambent; heroic; scenic; promised; unclouded; unknown; peculiar; unclasped; matchless; lesser; barbaric; original; untasted; quiet; everlasting; pinnacled; bloody; departing; concentrated; sole; inestimable; imaginary.

verbs
accentuate—; bask in—; blaze in—; blind to—; crown with—; debilitate—; dissipate—; elect to—; encircle with—; elevate to—; extol—; flaunt—; mark for—; participate in—; reflect—; revel in—; reward with—; raise to—; shed—; —passes; —shines; —suffuses; revivify—.

(See honor, fame, renown, pomp, splendor, grandeur, praise.)

GLOSS

adjectives
opaque; ultimate; faultless; brilliant; shining; raven; stimulating; firm.

GLOVE

adjectives
frosted; leathern; long; slim; cloth; fringed; greasy; primrose; easy; cheveril; snug-fitting; warm; worn.

GLOW

adjectives

lurid; phosphorescent; rainbow; pallid; vinous; rich; fitful; silvery; ruby; vague; starry; full; strong; suffusing; warm; chastened; dim; joyous; transparent; luminous; dreamy; brilliant; soft; scorching; fiery; mystical; pectoral; molten; original; reflected; white; youthful; inward; comfortable; feverish; unaccustomed; sunset; faint; summer; somber; evening; latent; wavering; conscious; clustering; earthly; fearful; hectic; tropic; genial; emotional; refracted; refulgent; ethereal; blessed; hideous; sorrowing; tremulous; seraphic.

verbs

agitate to—; burn to—; clothe in—; emit—; feel—; heat to—; kindle—; pale—; quench —; quicken to—; shade—; suffuse with—; —brightens; —captivates; —cheers; —declines; —deepens; —flushes; —guides; —illuminates; —irradiates; —lights up; —radiates; —scorches; —shines; —subsides; —warms.

(See flush, animation, ardor, warmth.)

GLOW (v)

adverbs

morosely; intensely; luminously; nebulously; sardonically; auspiciously; mellowly; perceptibly; luridly; phosphorescently; mystically; vaguely; ruddily; feverishly; genially; hectically; ethereally; tremulously; seraphically.

(See shine, beam.)

GLOWING

adverbs

radiantly; softly; dimly; perceptibly; brilliantly; splendidly; gorgeously; endlessly; magnificently; sumptuously; constantly; ineffably; lustrously; phosphorescently; vividly; brightly; intensely; resplendently; marvellously; luridly; richly; fitfully; joyously; transparently; whitely; faintly.

GLUM

adverbs

dismally; incurably; stupidly; cheerlessly; immovably; terribly; hopelessly; lugubriously; darkly; anxiously; despondently; curiously; profoundly; heavily; drearily; dangerously; dreadfully; abnormally; significantly; silently; unreasonably; sulkily; mopishly; strangely; disconsolately; exasperatingly.

GLUT (v)

adverbs

swinishly; brutishly; disgustingly; inordinately; madly; unrestrainedly; ravenously.

(See gorge, eat.)

GLUTTONOUS

adverbs

unbelievably; insanely; disgustingly; repulsively; strangely; crudely; grossly; hungrily; greedily; voraciously; extremely; excessively; wolfishly; inordinately; recklessly; dangerously; extravagantly; horribly; horridly; ravenously; insatiably; offensively; revoltingly; abominably; incredibly.

GNARLED

adverbs

roughly; ruggedly; scraggily; crookedly; sturdily; agedly; stumpily; robustly; massively; tenuously; thickly; rheumatically; gauntly; wirily.

GNASH (v)

adverbs

incessantly; frenziedly; horribly; furiously; fiercely; hungrily; fiendishly; dreadfully; insanely.

(See rage, fume, storm.)

GNAW (v)

adverbs

hungrily; ravenously; furiously; madly; brutishly; bestially; vigorously; ferociously; famishedly.

(See chew, bite.)

GOAD

adjectives

insistent; galling; sharp; inexorable.

GOAL

adjectives

veiled; ultimate; luminous; common; glittering; incentive; stimulating; selfsame; receding; unreachable; refined; successive (pl); utmost; mortal; illusory; desired; tertiary; inevitable; traditional; amaranthine; mysterious; hard-gained; fictitious.

verbs

achieve—; attain—; bar—; cherish—; defeat—; effect—; forge forward—; gain—; guard—; hamper—; move toward—; propel toward—; realize—; strive for—; surmount to—; sway from—; swerve from—; swing from—; touch—; push toward—.

(See end, aim, destiny, mark.)

GOAT

adjectives
romantic; silky; browsing; sure-footed; metamorphosed; mutinous; sacrificial.

verbs
domesticate—; clip—; exercise—; fleece—; herd—s; pasture—; shear—; stall—; tether —; —attacks; —butts; —forages; —grazes; —leaps; —pastures; —supplies; —yields.
(See animal.)

GOBLET

adjectives
knobbed; embossed; smoke-colored.

GOD
(*divine being*)

adjectives
faultless; unalterable; sacred; immortal; stern; everlasting; deathless; compassionate; ever-living; serene; inspiring.

god
(*idol*)

adjectives
monstrous; extemporal; bestial; goat-nursed; stalwart; unappeasable; bleating; victim-nourished; appeasable; defiant; contending; drunken; fire-robed; distant; tinseled; winged; capricious; exasperated; petty; crumbled; artificial; blinded; associate; banished; inexorable; unsolicited; false; materialized; frivolous; deposed; auxiliary.

verbs
banish—; beseech—; blaspheme—; defy—; deify—; discover—; exalt—; herald—; implore—; invoke—; placate—; propitiate—; recognize—; reveal—; revere—; revile—; vow before—; worship—; wrestle with—; —commands; —grants; —guides; —illumines; —judges; —ordains; —prevails.
(See deity, divinity, idol, ruler, creator, Jesus Chirst.)

GODDESS

adjectives
libidinous; voluptuous; impending; fickle; glorious; loving; beauteous.

GODLESS

adverbs
horribly; impiously; perversely; fanatically; recklessly; avowedly; sacrilegiously; blasphemously; profanely; heartbreakingly; graciously; obstinately; obdurately; unhappily; irrationally; unreasonably; immovably; openly; skeptically; materially; agnostically; faithlessly; indifferently.

GODLIKE

adverbs
wondrously; peerlessly; angelically; seraphically; undeniably; charitably; sweetly; piously; virtuously; humbly; beatifically; consecratedly; spiritually; reverently; purely; incredibly; utterly.

GODLY

adverbs
beautifully; devotedly; humbly; piously; reverently; consistently; devoutly; actively; justly; remarkably; eminently; notably; transcendently; earnestly; zealously; illustriously; wondrously; consecratedly; faithfully.

GOLD

adjectives
fraud-accumulated; burnished; sculptured; transparent; crystal; molten; wrought; mealy; fretted; refined; virgin; bright; hard-earned; rusted; intense; gleaming; mossy; dominant; vaporous; tested; gravel; supple; gaudy; damning; barbaric; powdered; sterilized; coronation; beaten; clearest; drowned; countless; vile; richest; hoarded; stamped; fluid; fairy; blowing; musty; shimmering; iridescent; cloudy; streaked; shining; fragrant; faint; floral; glittering; ruined; banked; clean; coarse; ruddy.

verbs
alloy—; amass—; beat out—; bless with—; bribe with—; delve for—; desire—; dig for —; discover—; emboss with—; hammer—; harden—; heap—; hide—; hoard—; load with—; melt—; mine—; pan—; plot for—; roll—; salvage—; search for—; separate—; spurn—; squander—; thirst for—; treasure —; —blinds; —chains; —charms; —clinks; —corrupts; —curses; —degenerates; —glitters; —glistens; —occurs; —sparkles.
(See metal, element, treasure.)

GOLF

verbs
compete in—; concentrate on—; contend at —; enjoy—; gamble at—; improve—; pair off in—; practise—; tie in—; score in—;

—beguiles; —diverts; —engrosses; —entertains; —excites; —exerts; —interests; —wearies.
(See sport, game.)

GOLF COURSE

verbs
compete on—; construct—; cover—; design—; develop—; extend—; form—; idle on—; open—; operate—; visit—; wander over—; —attracts; —beckons; —stretches.

GONG

adjectives
clangorous; dreadful; sounded; resonant; echoing.

verbs
clash—; drum on—; hammer—; hearken to—; strike—; —alarms; —assembles; —calls; —clanks; —clatters; —deafens; —resounds; —reverberates; —signals; —sounds; —summons; —surprises; —thunders; —vibrates.
(See bell.)

GOOD

adjectives
indifferent; supreme; possible; garnered; public; tender; unimagined; infinite; irreconcilable; celestial; chief; ultimate; timely; final; permanent; common; spiritual; sovereign; unmitigated; worldly; satiating; everlasting; unchanging; weak; universal.

verbs
accept—; admire—; approve of—; ascertain—; augur—; commend—; devote to—; distinguish by—; endorse—; expound—; favor—; invite—; laud—; nullify—; offer—; relish—; repay—; reward—; welcome—; —benefits; —merits; —pleases; —profits; —prospers.
(See advantage, benefit, virtue, welfare.)

adverbs
exceptionally; wonderfully; incontrovertibly; undeniably; absolutely; faultlessly; commercially; spiritually; materially; supremely; innately; naturally; inherently; essentially; unusually; uncommonly; consistently; fairly; completely; unquestionably; intrinsically; genuinely; pricelessly; unutterably.

GOOD-HUMORED

adverbs
delightfully; pleasantly; genially; merrily; jovially; immensely; unfailingly; invariably; wholesomely; amazingly; marvelously; patiently; visibly; notably; remarkably; indulgently; considerately; graciously; generously.

GOODNESS

adjectives
mantled; wholesome; innate; inherent; natural; hearty; infinite; adorable; undeserved; essential; true; full; awful; delicious; breathing; invisible; unusual; universal; tasty; obedient; hypocritical.

GOODS

adjectives
glittering; worldly; perishable; unwanted; transitory; worthless; non-durable; treasured.

GOOD-WILL

verbs
abuse—; cultivate—; dispense—; earn—; enjoy—; evoke—; favor with—; foster—; further—; gain—; grant—; inculcate—; inherit—; merit—; obtain—; pay with—; permit—; procure—; promote—; regard with—; seek—; sell—; solicit—; speak with—; spread—; win—; work for—; —privileges; —wanes.
(See reputation, favor.)

GOOSE

verbs
—attacks; —braves; —cackles; —captures; —circles; —clasps; —cleaves sky; —climbs; —destroys; —dives; —drives; —drops; —eyes; —floats through; —hawks; —hooks; —moults; —perches; —preys on; —robs; —sails; —screams; geese sever themselves; —sights; —soars; —sweeps.
(See bird.)

GOPHER

verbs
—burrows; —devastates; —digs; —honeycombs; —scuds.
(See animal.)

GORE

adjectives
stiffened; gladiatorial; sacred; dusky; quivering; unheeded; stagnant; hideous.

GORGE

verbs
cut—; descend into—; dig—; enter—; furrow—; hollow—; scoop out—; scour—; skirt—; traverse—; wear—; —bends; —confronts; —deepens; —extends; —frightens; —slopes.
(See canyon.)

GORGE (v)

adverbs
unrestrainedly; hungrily; ravenously; brutishly; swinishly; nauseously; habitually; insatiably; immoderately.
(See glut, eat.)

GORGEOUS

adverbs
brilliantly; splendidly; magnificently; uncommonly; unusually; dazzlingly; resplendently; superbly; supremely; glitteringly; vividly; richly; harmoniously; imposingly; impressively; extravagantly; inordinately; strikingly.

GORGES

adjectives
twisting; shadowy; picturesque; sunlit; wondrous; narrow; deep; unscaled; roaring; windy; desolated; immediate; mountainous; intricate; melting; protected; tremendous; rock-fanged.

GORILLA

verbs
—challenges; —chews; —cries; —crushes; —drums; —entertains; —nurses; —rages; —raids; —roars; —rushes; —shies; —tears; —terrifies; —wanders.
(See animal.)

GORY

adverbs
unspeakably; horribly; murderously; distressingly; wretchedly; hideously; abominably; beastly; grossly; awfully.

GOSPEL

adjectives
political; radiant; fiery; bitter; gradual; everlasting; healing; long-repeated; timeworn; helpful.

verbs
carry—; crusade—; decry—; denounce—; explode—; herald—; narrate—; preach—; propagate—; propound—; spread—; transmit—.
(See truth, story, narrative, tale, teachings, Bible, Scriptures.)

GOSSIP

adjectives
habitual; savory; baseless; interested; slanderous; mighty; idle; laggard; good-natured; dashing; careless; ubiquitous; censorious; drowsy; cheerful; impertinent; agreeable; withering; contemporaneous; neighborhood; useful; whispered; undercover; vulgar; insignificant; malicious; scandalous; social; ugly.

verbs
cackle—; center—on; circulate—; deal out —; exchange—; feed on—; indulge in—; interchange—; interest in—; ladle out—; savor—; sputter—; whisper—; —buzzes; —floats about; —libels; —maligns; —slanders.
(See rumor.)

GOSSIP (v)

adverbs
gregariously; inanely; incautiously; inimically; indiscreetly; loquaciously; baselessly; habitually; slanderously; censoriously; impertinently; witheringly; vulgarly; maliciously; jealously; enviously; treacherously.
(See talk, rumor, tattle.)

GOVERN (v)

adverbs
inharmoniously; dictatorially; paternally; intricately; nobly; tyrannically; bureaucratically; autocratically; democratically; plutocratically; ruthlessly; despotically; aristocratically; ephemerally; legitimately; perfidiously; constitutionally; prudently.
(See rule, control.)

GOVERNMENT

adjectives
hard up; executive; tyrannical; municipal; patriarchal; long-lived; authoritarian; radical; shameful; jealous; odious; provincial; paternal; stable; supernatural; ruthless; despotic; representative; aristocratic; free; unprosperous; ephemeral; puppet; vacillating; irresponsible; legitimate; mushroom; acknowledged; ill; deceased; consular; perfidious; industrious; consolidated; constitutional; orderly; imperial; dangerous; re-

spective; monarchial; central; moral; provisional; prudent; autonomistic; conservative; totalitarian; bankrupt.

verbs
abuse—; balance—; castigate—; centralize—; control—; corrupt—; criticize—; defraud—; hoodwink—; jeopardize—; lose faith in—; maintain—; obliterate—; plot against—; preserve—; reverence—; revolt against—; surrender—to; undermine—; upbraid—; usurp—; —capitulates; —cooperates with; —crumbles; —functions; —launches; —regulates; —subsidizes; —succors; —teeters; —thrives.

(See administration, authority, management.)

GOVERNOR

adjectives
sturdy; testy; saucy; assiduous; unerring.

verbs
appoint—; criticize—; draft for—; honor—; impeach—; nettle—; nominate for—; override—; remove—; welcome—; —abuses; —administers; —admonishes; —allows; —authorizes; —s confer; —consents; —controls; —s convene; —executes; —heads; —oppresses; —pilots; —represents; —reprieves; —resides at; —rules; —steers; —vetoes; —visits.

(See master, ruler, guardian.)

GOWN

adjectives
fragile; star-sprinkled; long; flowing; tattered; curtailed; goodly; fluttering; sleeveless; sophisticated; rusty; glamorous; enticing; dull; flapping; saffron; flounced; ruffed; rustling; conventional; silk; close-fitting; sacred; furred; soiled; waxen; low-cut.

verbs
admire—; damage—; design—; don—; exhibit—; fashion—; fit—; model—; repair—; sew—; shed—; tread on—; yearn for—; —becomes; —exposes; —flatters; —flows; —flutters; —reveals; —ripples; —s vary.

(See dress, robe, garment.)

GOWN (v)

adverbs
exquisitely; tastefully; dully; ecclesiastically; spectacularly; gaily; strikingly; vividly; richly; ornately.

(See dress, garb.)

GRAB (v)

adverbs
ruthlessly; despotically; fanatically; autocratically; selfishly; brutishly; vulgarly; nefariously; offensively.

(See seize, clutch, grasp.)

GRACE

adjectives
exquisite; petitionary; tempting; homicidal; impartial; luxuriant; aerial; fruitless; reviving; crowning; singular; refined; supple; literary; lasting; gleaming; natural; apt; gloomy; nameless; strengthening; ineffable; quiet; soft; fluent; tranquil; tolerable; precise; wild; resolute; majestic; lazy; vigorous; inward; flexuous; nobler; sovereign; supreme; jocund; infant; caressing; redeeming; animating; gentle; negligent; perceptible; restoring; extreme; fugitive; melancholy; manly; extenuating; demure; bewildering; boundless; matchless; youthful; inexplicable; happy; evolvent; lingering; saving; ideal; summer; irresistible; extraordinary; antique; old-fashioned; loathsome; condescending; insinuating; chivalrous; swaying; sufficient; outward; pardoning; habitual; infinite; feminine; musical; living; rude; lascivious; languished; fugitive; jaunty; superb; careless; celestial; needful; easy; sinuous; divine; touching; subtle; good; peculiar; maiden; classical; awkward; virginlike; golden; regal; languid; invigorating; charming; courtly; ravishing; unconscious; casual; heavenly; winsome; winning; poetic; tactful; fraternal; sweetest; mundane; tragic; abounding; fastidious; heroic; hopeless; girlish; perfect; cordial; righteous; pastoral; serious; calm; stately; lordly; truer; lurid; celestial; slow; modern; airy; eloquent; simple; sportive; hidden; stupendous; breezy; beauteous; social; pitying; fleeting; coy; capricious; inimitable; facile; undulating; human; inferior.

verbs
admire—; approach—; attain—; commend—; conduct with—; divest of—; endow with—; exhibit—; express with—; form with—; imitate—; invoke—; lend—; move with—; possess—; serve with—; —attracts; —distinguishes; —charms.

(See favor, kindness, mercy, prayer, beauty, love.)

GRACEFUL

adverbs
amiably; pleasantly; unusually; definitely; slenderly; skillfully; wonderfully; delightfully; uncommonly; naturally; habitually; instinctively; exquisitely; singularly; aptly; ineffably; quietly; softly; lazily; supremely; extremely; superbly; matchlessly; youthfully; irresistibly; extraordinarily; ineffably; carelessly; charmingly; unconsciously; felicitously; unaffectedly; attractively; quaintly.

GRACELESS

adverbs
harshly; stiffly; awkwardly; crudely; offensively; grotesquely; bluntly; carelessly; appallingly; rudely; clumsily; shockingly; inexcusably; viciously; lawlessly; indecorously; incorrigibly; indiscreetly; obdurately; stubbornly; indefensibly; shamefully; obstinately; frightfully; terribly.

GRACIOUS

adverbs
charmingly; delightfully; indulgently; cordially; courteously; unusually; consistently; habitually; exceedingly; sincerely; warmly; hospitably; eagerly; amenably; heartily; suavely; ceremoniously; obsequiously; deferentially; attentively; unctuously; ingratiatingly; benevolently; kindly; considerately; unusually.

GRADATION

adjectives
subtle; organic; beautiful; cold; fractional; manifest; intermediate; ravishing; insensible; rapid; minute; infinitesimal.

GRADE

adjectives
laborious; convenient; intermediate; successive (pl); correct; seasonal; lower.

verbs
approve—; branch into —s; classify —s; compare —s; criticize—; delineate —s; enter—; examine—; organize—; promote—; recognize—; skip—; withdraw—; —guarantees; —indicates; —promises; —satisfies.

(See degree, step, rank, division.)

GRADE (*v*)

adverbs
legitimately; fairly; delicately; skillfully; laboriously; scholastically; provisionally; academically; nominally.

(See calculate, estimate.)

GRADUAL

adverbs
progressively; comparatively; intentionally; purposely; significantly; wisely; designedly; necessarily; inevitably; imperceptibly; slowly; inexpressibly; extremely; sensibly; intelligently; subtly; insidiously; cleverly; deliberately; shrewdly.

GRADUATE

verbs
assemble —s; confer on—; congratulate —s; employ—; enlist—; examine—; fete—; gift —; honor—; laud—; pose as—; praise—; present to—; privilege—; train—; —completes; —excels in; —harks back; —qualifies; —understands.

(See student.)

GRADUATE (*v*)

adverbs
creditably; subsequently; formally; ultimately; eventually; respectfully.

(See win, finish.)

GRAFT

adjectives
foreign; niggling; vigorous; huge; amazing; regular; stupendous; successful.

verbs
devise—; employ—; induce—; introduce—; support—; yield to—; —accomplishes; —attracts; —begets; —flourishes; —instils; —interests; —intrigues.

(See fraud.)

GRAIN

adjectives
burdening; natural; waving; distinct; fine; springing; gathered; sprouting; garnered; hardy; scanty; coarse; vintage; pungent; generous; well-ripened; rustling; indigenous.

verbs
bag—; cast — to; char—; collect—; distill from—; feed on—; ferment—; gather—; glean—; harvest—; injure—; plant—; prepare—; prize—; reap—; sow—; stack—; yield—; —fattens; —flourishes; —invites; —nourishes; —ripens.

(See seed, crop.)

GRAMMAR

verbs
abide by—; abuse—; conform to—; criticize —; disregard—; fumble with—; heed—; judge—; master—; obey—; observe—; rel-

ish—; violate—; —concerns; —confuses; —demands; —explains; —informs; —ordains; —rules.

(See rhetoric.)

GRAND

adverbs

impressively; imposingly; magnificently; infinitely; sublimely; majestically; augustly; eminently; superbly; illustriously; ineffably; essentially; fundamentally; resplendently; remarkably; transcendently.

GRANDEUR

adjectives

wild; political; religious; weird; imposing; solemn; primitive; tantalizing; gloomy; inherent; contemplative; tumultuous; superior; ancient; superlative; labored; monotonous; human; venerable; sustained; shadowy; rough; solitary; husbanded; superficial; desolate; poetic; magnificent; severe; false; massive; hideous; infinite; melodious; pristine; architectural; sarcastic; deceitful; dilapidated; original; savage; civic; sublime; dreary.

verbs

abate—; acquaint with—; borrow — from; contemplate—; debase—; discipline—; emulate—; equal—; exhibit—; intimate—; love —; parade—; perceive—; reduce—; ridicule—; rise in—; sacrifice—; stagger by—; touch with—; witness—; —diminishes; —expands; —impresses; —impels; —soars.

(See display, splendor, elegance.)

GRANITE

adjectives

unhewn; barren; straited; enduring; everlasting; defiant; cumbersome.

verbs

build on—; carve from—; chip—; crack—; demolish—; hammer—; hew from—; lay—; mix—; pave with—; pierce—; quarry—; shatter—; smooth—; spike—; split—.

(See rock, stone.)

GRANT

adjectives

authentic; fairest; legislative; definite.

GRANT (*v*)

adverbs

liberally; tacitly; exclusively; subsequently; courteously; grudgingly; graciously; originally; readily; fairly; legislatively; definitely.

(See allow, permit.)

GRAPE

adjectives

shrivelled; luscious; choicest; ripened; celestial; rare; intoxicating; blossoming; autumn; noble; sweet; rich; sour.

GRAPES

verbs

abound with—; bag—; bear—; crate—; gather—; glean—; harvest—; mash—; seed —; skin—; squash—; suck—; —hang; —ripen; —ferment.

(See fruit.)

GRAPPLE

adjectives

iron; death; watchful; painful; damaging; bruising.

GRAPPLE (*v*)

adverbs

frantically; painfully; bruisingly; fiercely; vigorously; methodically; firmly.

(See clutch, seize.)

GRASP

adjectives

relaxing; iron; monstrous; bitter; prosperous; slender; weak; oblique; unrelaxing; stiffening; consumptive; immature; godlike; unaccommodating; intuitive; conscious; fearful; warm; tenacious; hot; masculine; cordial; prophetic; mental; timorous; vigorous; incisive; childish; octopus-like; passionate; dying; despotic; encyclic; double; fevered.

verbs

beguile into—; carry off in—; crush in—; elude—; entice into—; evade—; gain—; loosen—; relax—; release—; shake from—; wrest from—; yank (colloq.) from—; —bruises; —pains.

(See grip, embrace.)

GRASP (*v*)

adverbs

frantically; avariciously; selfishly; rudely; firmly; convulsively; cordially; impetuously; tightly; loosely; greedily; unrelaxingly; tenaciously; passionately; despotically.

(See seize, clutch.)

GRASS

adjectives
tangling; waving; succulent; full-grown; pure; lush; new; long; gentle; fruitful; comfortable; pleasant; dull; starved; trampled; straggling; luxuriant; cut; dry; reedy; dripping; wiry; gaunt; shaven; parched; associated; pinched; nutritious; tedded; flowering; scented; aromatic; delicate; wilted; mossy; rank; russet; aquatic; ornamental; bladed; inland; silent; tumbled; hindering; peopled.

verbs
clip—; crop—; fence off—; mow—; pasture on—; plow through—; sow—; sprinkle—; tread on—; —beautifies; —blankets; —carpets; —cloaks; —covers; —creeps up; —dots; —flows; —pushes up; —spreads; —springs up; —trembles.
(See herb, plant, hay, pasture.)

GRASSHOPPER

verbs
exterminate—; plague with—s; swarm with —s; —alights; —chews; —chirrups; —s damage; —leaps; —limps; —races; —reposes on; —secretes; —sings; —sips; —skips; —s strip; —vaults; —wings.
(See insect.)

GRATE

adjectives
gaping; glowing; abhorred; ponderous; old-fashioned.

GRATE (v)

adverbs
harshly; unendurably; roughly; irritatingly; exasperatingly; monotonously; continually; ceaselessly; repeatedly.
(See rub, irritate.)

GRATEFUL

adverbs
utterly; heartily; thankfully; sincerely; pathetically; significantly; inexpressibly; curiously; oddly; volubly; openly; obviously; extremely; inordinately; delightedly; embarrassingly; overwhelmingly; speechlessly; extravagantly; genuinely.

GRATIFICATION

adjectives
refined; instant; external; personal; aesthetic; innocent; pretty; natural; sensual; speechless; solitary; idle; perfect; vilest; profound; correspondent; intellectual; emotional.

verbs
afford—; anticipate—; bestow—; consider with—; crave—; derive—; experience—; express—; incur—; indulge in—; observe with—; obtain—; offer—; receive—; —attends; —recompenses; —satisfies.
(See satisfaction, pleasure, reward.)

GRATIFIED

adverbs
extremely; highly; uncommonly; happily; proudly; pleasantly; inordinately; ineffably; visibly; noticeably; naturally; marvellously; wonderfully; overwhelmingly; volubly; shyly; utterly; inexpressibly.

GRATIFY (v)

adverbs
lustfully; sexually; aesthetically; profoundly; adequately; personally; sensually; intellectually; emotionally; innocently.
(See please, indulge.)

GRATITUDE

adjectives
admiring; endless; intense; natural; virtuous; innocent; deep; passionate; permanent; respectful; noble; erring; bewildered; elementary; pathetic; tender; meek; universal; heartfelt; devout; profound; earnest; fervent; reverent; patriotic; humble; genuine; characteristic; everlasting; sincere; simple.

verbs
acknowledge with—; earn—of; exact—; expect—; express—; feel—; reject—; return in—; reward with—; thrive on—; touch with—; —embarrasses; —humiliates; —justifies; —overflows; —pains.
(See appreciation, adoration, affection.)

GRATUITOUS

adverbs
unexpectedly; surprisingly; acceptably; generously; pleasantly; unnecessarily; cordially; genially; graciously; tactfully; helpfully; impulsively; incredibly.

GRAVE

adjectives
prehistoric; volcanic; nameless; humble; grassy; putrid; innocent; artless; shallow;

desolate; nobler; trodden; sullen; yawning; unmarked; liquid; triumphant; ecstatic; dishonored; burning; solitary; watery; tenantless; sacred; ocean; unblessed; pauper; heaving; insatiate; curtained; scented; bloody; untimely; populous; dusky; mimic; new-made; gloomy; hastily-dug; forgotten; gaping; unmade; dismal; destitute; obscure; dreary; mattress; close-set; stone; inglorious.

verbs
bequeath to—; confine to—; couch in—; hound to—; lie in—; loot—; lower into—; mourn over—; pillage—; pray at—; rest in—; shudder in—; sleep in—; slumber in—; snatch from—; tear open—; turn in —; unearth—; weep at—; wrest from—; —reconciliates; —silences; —snatches; —swallows.
(See tomb, death.)

adverbs
habitually; critically; alarmingly; preternaturally; profoundly; intensely; extremely; frightfully; indescribably; essentially; incalculably; downright; emphatically; cruelly; shockingly; inconceivably; momentously; signally; eventfully; pregnantly; impressively; urgently; solemnly; saliently; portentously; grievously; deplorably; insupportably; disastrously; exceptionably.

GRAVEYARD

adjectives
various (pl); silent; ancestral; country; populous.

GRAVITATE (v)

adverbs
naturally; habitually; paradoxically; customarily; ominously; affectionately; supernaturally; awfully; specifically.
(See attract, sink.)

GRAVITATION

adjectives
irresistible; mutual; pervading; touching; constant.

GRAVITY

adjectives
mock; fantastic; portentous; comic; habitual; sustained; becoming; superb; accustomed; unusual; ominous; dreamless; amused; paradoxical; affectionate; sudden; heavy; elaborate; melancholy; supernatural; dark; colder; awful; attentive; abundant; specific; technical; pompous; frowning; affected.

verbs
challenge—; mitigate—; preserve—; recover—; repel—; robe in—; —alters; —attracts; —directs; —draws; —exercises; —forces; —increases; —influences; —produces; —restricts; —tends.
(See seriousness, solemnity, importance.)

GRAY

adjectives
smiling; salt; mottled; austere; soft; ashen; joyless; fallow; bluish; uncertain; subtle; dark; pearly; dappled; warm; smart; dim; gleaming.

GRAYNESS

adjectives
spring; arrested; dense; spectral; grim; premature; recurring; whitish.

GRAZE (v)

adverbs
peacefully; contentedly; ruminatively; habitually; ceaselessly; monotonously; beneficially.
(See feed.)

GREAT

adverbs
supposedly; naturally; unaffectedly; apparently; fairly; substantially; essentially; fundamentally; downright; immeasurably; incalculably; pleasantly; surprisingly; incredibly; marvellously; wonderfully; amazingly; unusually; singularly; admittedly; undeniably; distinctly; illustriously; reputably; conspicuously; eminently; brilliantly; famously; locally; nationally; internationally; splendidly; sublimely; deservedly; transcendently; memorably; remarkably; unassumingly.

GREATNESS

adjectives
false; intellectual; enduring; moral; natural; ingenuous; true; simple; affected; immeasurable; veiled; esteemed; imperial; patent; corresponding; undiminishable; deserved; apparent; recognized.

verbs
achieve—; advertise—; attain—; bestow—upon; contemplate—of; envy—; expatiate on—; gain—; inspire—; perceive—; pursue—; reach—; seize—; sweep into—; thrust—upon; —affects; —appeals; —elevates; —fetters; —serves; —torments.
(See magnitude, eminence, distinction, importance, seriousness.)

GREED

adjectives
pulpit; inordinate; disappointed; reckless; instinctive; intrenched; insatiable; rapturous; internecine; misapplied; misdirected; methodical; physical; miserly.

verbs
clog with—; curse with—; devour with—; indulge—; loathe—; occasion—; overcome with—; prey upon—of; quench—; resent—; satiate—; torment with—; vanquish—; —annoys; —chokes; —deforms; —drags; —drains; —repels; —shames; —sickens; —stints; —tempts.
(See avarice.)

GREEDY

adverbs
inordinately; covetously; avidly; ravenously; insatiably; voraciously; incurably; incorrigibly; strangely; instinctively; painfully; embarrassingly; irreclaimably; hopelessly; shamelessly; perpetually; appallingly; shamefully; scandalously; indecently; brazenly; palpably; unmistakably; obviously; openly; manifestly.

GREEK

verbs
accent—; decipher—; interpret—; laud—; smatter—; translate—; utter—.
(See language, literature.)

GREEN

adjectives
shimmering; woodsy; opaque; dense; diversified; aqueous; resonant; luxuriant; dull; quiet; waving; pale; varied; feathery; delicate; wanton; pistache; exquisite; emerald; dim; faint; mossy; luminous; malachite; leaping; neutral; festive; luscious; slimy; lesser; consecutive; tender; tainted; translucent; glossy; arbute; rusty; delicious; willow; fresher; serpent; turquoise.

GREENERY

adjectives
tangled; moist; varying; well-kept.

GREET (*v*)

adverbs
affably; jovially; charmingly; affectionately; cordially; effusively; ardently; sympathetically; benignly; blandly; genially; brusquely; civilly; fraternally; perfunctorily; hilariously; boisterously.
(See hail, accost, address.)

GREETING

verbs
accost with—; address—to; approach with—; embrace in—; evoke—; exchange—s; express—; ignore—; meet with—; nod—; return—; salute with—; shun—; —arouses; —surprises; —welcomes.
(See salutation, salute, welcome, compliment.)

GREETINGS

adjectives
cordial; civil; playful; absent; kindly; usual; respectful; undemonstrative; paschal; fraternal; joyous; spasmodic; innumerable; sad; perfunctory; affable; effusive; hospitable; hilarious; daily; neighborly; flustered; boisterous; inaudible; affectionate; holiday; warm; mutual; unspoken.

GREGARIOUS

adverbs
jovially; socially; politically; companionably; incurably; heartily; naturally; instinctively; inherently; pleasantly; hospitably; freely; sociably; healthily; wholesomely; briskly; unusually; normally.

GRENADE

verbs
charge with—; catapult—; employ—; fire—; flee from—; fling—; hurl—; roll—; —assaults; —bursts; —dispenses; —explodes; —s harass; —injures; —maims; —levels; —s terrorize; —wounds.
(See bomb, shell.)

GRENADIER

adjectives
gallant; grim; warlike; various (pl); pleasant; gaudy; eye-pleasing.

GRIDIRON
(colloq. for football field)

verbs
battle on—; clash on—; compete on—; condition—; construct—; cover—; design—; excel on—; injure on—; meet on—; pack —; subsidize—; swarm—; witness on—; —attracts; —extends; —beckons; —lies.

(See field, battlefield.)

GRIEF

adjectives
reproachful; national; silent; burning; irremediable; hysterical; immoderate; hopeless; purposeless; needless; passionate; private; strong; sincere; idle; truer; beauteous; half-smothered; poignant; chastening; successive (pl); domestic; lasting; overwhelming; elegiac; endless; casual; unutterable; remorseful; hateful; proud; sudden; mortal; inconsolable; innocent; conjectured; barren; sacred; sentimental; angry; deeper; selfish; lighter; paroxysmal; unmanly; stark; arbitrary; single; withered; fettered; ancient; vanished; callous; uncontrollable; compensated; inward; perished; cloudy; unavailing; fundamental; relentless; utmost; fòrecasted; wayward; bitter; eternal; touching; present; household; greatest; genuine; pure; young; excessive; second; extravagant.

verbs
assail with—; assuage—; bring to—; confide—in; disguise—; drown—; emerge from —; fight—; overcome by—; overwhelm with —; rush into—; smite with—; stifle—; submerge—; —abates; —lessens; —overwhelms; —spends itself.

(See sorrow, sadness, anguish, distress, tears.)

GRIEVANCE

adjectives
intense; industrial; undoubted; lofty; maritime; maudlin; intolerable; eternal; permanent; serious; heartfelt; deep; deadly.

verbs
adjust—; air—; allege—; arbitrate—; bound with—; conceal—; detail—; exploit —; iron out—; outline—s; recount—; voice —; yield to—; —justifies; —warrants.

(See wrong, injustice, resentment, complaint.)

GRIEVE (v)

adverbs
perpetually; obstinately; silently; unfeignedly; hysterically; immoderately; hopelessly; passionately; poignantly; endlessly; remorsefully; uncontrollably; bitterly; touchingly; genuinely; excessively; extravagantly.

(See lament, mourn.)

GRIEVOUS

adverbs
deplorably; lamentably; sadly; piteously; distressingly; intolerably; appallingly; horribly; unaccountably; unwarrantably; irremediably; unutterably; uncontrollably; bitterly; touchingly; genuinely; grimly; sorely; cruelly; inexpressibly; inordinately; terribly.

GRILLING

verbs
conduct—; cringe from—; criticize—; denounce—; dread—; escape—; overdo—; resent—; suffer—; tense for—; withstand—; wrestle with—; yield to—; —exposes; —irritates; —reveals; —threatens.

(See questioning, examination, inquiry, inquisition.)

GRIM

adverbs
horribly; terribly; cruelly; bitterly; unutterably; unaccountably; unwarrantably; acutely; austerely; brutally; cynically; morosely; perversely; discourteously; sullenly; unceremoniously; impolitely; horridly; sternly; severely; depressingly; oppressively; heavily; forlornly; frightfully; irredeemably.

GRIMACE

adjectives
admiring; mocking; mental; fantastic; convulsive; furious; comical; passing; sour; droll; cold; dissatisfied; idiotic; wry; harrowing.

GRIMACE (v)

adverbs
facetiously; fiercely; humorously; dourly; mockingly; fantastically; convulsively; furiously; drolly; idiotically; wryly.

(See leer, sneer, smirk, scowl.)

GRIMY

adverbs

inexcusably; unspeakably; merrily; laughably; nonchalantly; carelessly; offensively; hopelessly; inevitably; momentarily; repulsively; irretrievably; laughingly; smudgily; dustily; darkly; grotesquely; fantastically; outlandishly; shamelessly; unconcernedly; coolly; indifferently; unashamedly.

GRIN

adjectives

tigerish; noble; wooden; homely; amused; cast-iron; broad; triumphant; insolent; sardonic; lewd; specious; jubilant; ingenuous; incredible; mocking; leering; sympathetic; understanding; unmitigated; lopsided; sheepish; saucy; fiendish; doubtful; relieved; affable; sly; horrible; courageous; infectious; whimsical; saturnine.

verbs

attempt—; break into—; broaden into—; conceal under—; expand in—; force—; manage—; master—; muster—; provoke—; restrain—; salute with—; smother—; stab with—; wear—; wrinkle into—; —creases; —delights; —embarrasses; —fades; —lurks; —recurs; —widens; —wreathes.

(See smile, smirk.)

GRIN (v)

adverbs

genially; wistfully; bashfully; flatteringly; sheepishly; affably; stupidly; skeptically; amiably; sympathetically; complacently; impudently; derisively; ironically; toothlessly; ruefully; fulsomely; tantalizingly; wryly; broadly; engagingly; craftily; lewdly; jubilantly; ingenuously; saturninely.

(See smirk, laugh, smile.)

GRIND
(colloq. for drudgery)

verbs

abhor—; avoid—; coach—; detest—; enforce—; labor on—; necessitate—; perform at—; plod at—; reduce to—; toil away at —; —crushes; —exacts; —harasses; —prepares; —oppresses; —sharpens; —torments; —wearies; —wears down.

(See drudgery, labor, work.)

GRINNING

adverbs

foolishly; facetiously; fatuously; vacuously; vacantly; cheerfully; happily; mischievously; teasingly; pertly; tormentingly; suavely; blandly; indulgently; slyly; broadly; triumphantly; jubilantly; sheepishly; joyously; sympathetically; mockingly; elaborately; openly.

GRIP
(grasp)

adjectives

tight; paralyzing; momentary; firm; muscular; nervous; burning; remorseless; herculean; frantic; throttling; fiendish; intellectual.

verbs

loosen—; relax—; release—; —pains; —reassures; —slips; —strains; —wearies.

(See clutch, grasp.)

GRIP
(colloq. for valise)

verbs

clasp—; clutch—; fit into—; grab—; insure —; load in—; seize—; stow—; —wearies.

(See satchel, bag.)

GRIP (v)

adverbs

fervently; licentiously; momentarily; nervously; remorselessly; frantically; fiendishly; vigorously; selfishly; figuratively.

(See seize, grasp.)

GRIPE

adjectives

convulsive; mincing; communicated.

GRIT
(sand)

adjectives

blinding; parching; grinding; unpleasant; rough.

verbs

brush away—; conceal—; dissolve—; fill with—; free of—; gather—; scour with—; sieve—; sift—; slip on—; sprinkle with—; strain off—; sweep away—; wash away—; —chokes; —impairs; —injures; —irritates; —scratches.

(See sand.)

GRITTY
(plucky)

adverbs

pluckily; sturdily; stoutly; resolutely; indomitably; firmly; courageously; spunkily.

GRITTY
(*sandy*)

adverbs
roughly; harshly; coarsely; crudely; grossly; impossibly; uselessly; desirably; friably; suitably; properly; unduly; terribly; remarkably; extremely; uncommonly; excessively.

GRIZZLED

adverbs
wintrily; crabbedly; hoarily; dingily; sadly; gently; gloriously; patriarchally; fabulously; honorably; proudly; mellowly; vainly.

GROAN

adjectives
rheumatic; tortured; deep; indignant; expiring; solemn; ghastly; frequent (pl); fierce; thrilling; smothered; unutterable; subdued; loud; bubbling; agonizing; dying; heartrending; deadly; dismal; passionate; unsolaced; convulsive; self-accusing; mirthful; gurgling; heavy; mortifying; unwilling; bitter; penitential.

verbs
blanket—; convulse with—; drown—; emit—; murmur—; restrain—; stifle—; utter—; —distresses; —disturbs; —haunts; —rends; —resounds; —subsides.
(See moan, sigh, sound.)

GROAN (*v*)

adverbs
audibly; painfully; agonizingly; dreadfully; inwardly; bitterly; involuntarily; unutterably; heartrendingly.
(See moan, complain, scream.)

GROOM

adjectives
diminutive; natty; surly; envious; unpolished; sturdy; surfeited; industrious; bashful; nervous; worried.

GROOM (*v*)

adverbs
foppishly; tastefully; immaculately; nattily; handsomely; fittingly; appropriately; decoratively; impressively.
(See dress, brush.)

GROOMED

adverbs
perfectly; carefully; immaculately; recently; lately; meticulously; punctiliously; primly; starchily; fastidiously; fashionably; especially; obviously; manifestly; freshly; radiantly; sophisticatedly; remarkably; elaborately.

GROOVE

adjectives
habitual; prosaic; uncongenial.

verbs
excavate—; fall into—; flow in—; force along—; furrow—; hollow out—; lapse into—; lie in—; mark with—; obstruct—; provide—; rust in—; sink into—; slide in—; throw out of—; travel in—.
(See channel, rut, routine, course.)

GROPE (*v*)

adverbs
futilely; blindly; vaguely; wildly; ineffectually; dazedly; mentally; uncertainly.
(See feel, search.)

GROSSNESS

adjectives
intermingled; material; mortal; swinelike.

GROTESQUE

adverbs
outlandishly; fantastically; clownishly; elaborately; ornately; abnormally; eccentrically; monstrously; singularly; oddly; curiously; exceptionally; egregiously; unusually; extraordinarily; queerly; unconscionably; capriciously; whimsically; extravagantly; barbarically; horribly; uncommonly; immeasurably; unnaturally; absurdly; ridiculously; ludicrously; highly.

GROTTO

verbs
adorn—; construct—; excavate—; exhibit—; ornament—; nestle in—; retreat to—; —beautifies; —delights; —displays; —echoes; —pleases; —shades; —solaces.
(See cave, recess, cavity.)

GROUCH

verbs
irritate—; nurse—; serve—; tolerate—; —complains; —deplores; —frets; —frowns;

—growls; —grumbles; —laments; —moans; —roars; —scowls; —wails; —whines.

(See anger, bitterness, ferocity.)

GROUND
(earth)

adjectives

analogical; habitual; ticklish; enchanted; avowed; crinkled; soggy; slightest; shaky; tedious; rugged; fragrant; difficult; sanctified; vantage; unexpressed; sterile; dry; azure; emotional; vulgar; tainted; solid; interesting; attractive; plausible; pastel; teeming; scientific; spacious; moaning; moral; delicate; callous; bordering; hallowed; innate; wounded; cultivated; fissured; commanding; incontrovertible; common; terraced; happy; conceded; illogical; dangerous; practical; rough; insufficient; good; bloody; reasonable; haunted; holy; treacherous; proper; thirsting; technical; theological; sluttish; slippery; burning; vivid; eudaemonistic; trampled; adequate; sanctified; superior; extensive; shuddering; filthy; familiar; untouched; unmarked; spawning; various (pl); debatable; heartless; quaking; reigning; cleared; obscure; ridgy; aesthetic; desolate; plain; ornamented; intuitive; neutral; remoter; grassy; subjective; dwelling; dewy; irregular; consecrated; excellent; tenable; dubious; sole; base; sectional; tufty; objective; highest; waste; alien; precise; casting.

verbs

assign—to; carpet—s; cast to—; congest—s; cultivate—; encamp on—s; gain—; parch —; plod over—; plow—; shift—; spade—; stand—; strew—; trample—; tread—; work —; writhe on—.

(See earth, soil, land, clay, dirt.)

GROUNDLESS

adverbs

nonsensically; flimsily; foolishly; absurdly; undeniably; palpably; obviously; patently; manifestly; maliciously; inconclusively; inconsistently; irrationally; unreasonably; inexcusably; unscientifically; unwarrantably; delusively; fallaciously; illogically; untrustworthily; unsubstantially; intentionally; deliberately; deceitfully; malignly; perversely; disastrously; ruinously; ridiculously.

GROUNDS
(reasons)

verbs

afford—for; attack on—; maintain—; object on—.

(See reason, consideration, premise, motive, inducement.)

GROUNDWORK

verbs

accomplish—; add to—; depend on—; enhance—; exhibit—; expand—; finish—; form—; hurry—; lay—; manage—; perform —; plan—; spurn—; supervise—; undermine—; —benefits; —precedes.

(See basis, foundation.)

GROUP

adjectives

ancillary; afflicted; exclusive; oncoming; limited; select; co-ordinated; ethnic; personified; heterogeneous; non-listening; cultural; pedimental; garrulous; chattery; valid; specialized; waning; geographical; parental; enthusiastic; civic; statuesque; spurious; flitting; sparse; straggling; considerable; loitering; vocational; remarkable; federated; unscrupulous; racial; efficient; distinct; sympathetic; lethargic; careless; weird; complete; dominant; diversified; overlapping; huddled; gesticulating; noisiest; lazy; divers (pl); representative; congenial; curious; listless; clustering; odious; humiliated; stalwart; grotesque; irregular; silent; lounging; intramural; brilliant; singular; denominational; allegorical; fearful; impressive; loquacious; detached; emblematic; spectacular; hedgehog; jovial; executive; jeering; sullen; craning; militant; prolific; controlling; anarchical; indispensable; producing; tractable; mournful; isolated; sobbing; pressure; elaborate; hostile; molecular; negligible; decorative.

verbs

assemble in—; belong to—; break with—; cluster in—; collect in—; compose—; divide into—s; disperse—; draft—; form—; gather —; huddle in—; lead—; scatter in—; segregate—s; split into—s; stand in—; work in —; —congregates; —co-operates; —gathers; —roves; —s spring up; —survives; —thins; —visions; —wanes; —yields.

(See crowd.)

GROUP (v)

adverbs
systematically; logically; categorically; picturesquely; vocationally; carelessly; representatively; congenially; elaborately; decoratively.
(See cluster, crowd.)

GROUPINGS

adjectives
picturesque; molecular; effective; attractive; fundamental; confused; huddled; fragmentary; photographic.

GROUSE

verbs
bag—; pelt—; retrieve—; roast—; —alights; —bellows; —booms; —cackles; —clucks; —dodges; —drums; —flutters; —glides; —grumbles; —haunts; —hides; —hoots; —roves; —ruffles; —rustles; —scratches; —scurries; —squats; —struts; —thumps; —thunders.
(See bird.)

GROVE

adjectives
shadowy; inviolate; sacred; melancholy; Elysian; lofty; haunted; celestial; primeval; pathless; fringed; boundless; musical; hoary; warbling; thriving.

GROVEL (v)

adverbs
obsequiously; humbly; servilely; slavishly; flatteringly; abjectly; debasingly; shamelessly.
(See cringe, fawn.)

GROW (v)

adverbs
tremendously; luxuriously; abundantly; proportionately; sensibly; vigorously; culturally; inevitably; formidably; abnormally; densely; miraculously; infinitely; ulcerously; wantonly; pendulously; phenomenally; intellectually; malignantly; tropically; vernally; spiritually.
(See increase, develop.)

GROWL

adjectives
meaning; significant; warning; low; audible; indignant; guttural; angry; friendly; fierce.

verbs
break into—; charge with—; emit—; enrage to—; incur—; mutter—; reiterate—; restrain—; stifle—; utter—; —arouses; —s drown; —eclipses; —reverberates; —rises from; —terrifies; —terrorizes; —thunders; —vibrates.
(See rumble, complaint, roar, grunt.)

GROWL (v)

adverbs
ominously; pugnaciously; disapprovingly; menacingly; furiously; warningly; audibly; ferociously; formidably; irascibly; surlily; gutturally.
(See grumble, snarl.)

GROWTH

adjectives
coarse; sturdy; vigorous; rock-loving; spontaneous; miraculous; arborescent; continuous; ulcerous; wanton; rooted; pendulous; phenomenal; inoperable; luxuriant; ghostly; stunted; monstrous; perpetual; stupendous; morbid; cancerous; unpleasant; intellectual; remarkable; tropical; unconscious; parasitic; healthy; native; scanty; incessant; record; evolutionary; puny; unexampled; developmental; unequal; hasty; mushroom; successive (pl); intervening; unbroken; astounding; endless; vital; rapid; sterile; outward; nutritious; proper; innate; funguslike; differenial; continuous; enormous; plant; malignant; sudden; psychic; unabated; contorted; wayside; vernal; marked; knotty; tremendous; arrested; constant; fateful; lush; spiritual; secular; unkept; strong; millennial; bushy; dense.

verbs
augment—; check—; control—; foster—; govern—; hinder—; induce—; promote—; stunt—; suppress—; thwart—; retard—; strengthen—; witness—; —commences; —develops; —swallows up.
(See development, increase, extension, enlargement.)

GRUDGE

adjectives
private; personal; economic; ancient; bitter.

verbs
annul—; avenge—; bear—; brush aside—; bury—; cherish—; engender—; harbor—;

incur—; lay aside—; nurse—; owe—; pursue—; relinquish—; resent—; warrant—; —troubles; —vexes.

(See malice, hatred, antipathy, rancor, enmity, resentment.)

GRUESOME

adverbs

horribly; cadaverously; horridly; unbearably; forbiddingly; squalidly; frightfully; grimly; grossly; monstrously; odiously; repulsively; shockingly; appallingly; intolerably; dreadfully; impossibly; inconceivably; unspeakably; inexpressibly; indescribably; preposterously; exceedingly.

GRUFF

adverbs

unnecessarily; intolerably; uncivilly; discourteously; needlessly; naturally; habitually; unfortunately; deliberately; unconsciously; rudely; grossly; sullenly; churlishly; intentionally; discouragingly; reluctantly; professionally; bluntly; curtly; captiously; moodily; abusively; boorishly; sarcastically; crudely; clumsily; snarlingly; venomously; significantly; surprisingly; particularly; remarkably.

GRUMBLE (v)

adverbs

captiously; discontentedly; pessimistically; forebodingly; cantankerously; vindictively; monotonously; gloomily.

(See growl, snarl.)

GRUNT

adjectives

complacent; mingling (pl); peculiar; roaring; occasional; satisfied; whining; disdainful; rebellious; startled; long; swinish.

verbs

acquiesce with—; answer with—; concede with—; manage—; resent—; snort—; suffer—; understand—; tolerate—; —annoys; —disturbs; —irritates; —s subside.

(See growl.)

GRUNT (v)

adverbs

audibly; complacently; peevishly; contemptuously; swinishly; disdainfully; rebelliously; appreciatively; approvingly.

(See croak, mumble, bray, stammer.)

GUARANTEE

adjectives

sufficient; money-back; sensational; satisfaction; iron-clad; official; further; serious; perpetual; limited; broken; vague; unfulfilled.

verbs

accompany with—; afford—; apply for—; base—on; break—; chain to—; consider—; demand—; enforce—; enter into—; forfeit—; fulfill—; propose—; test—; utilize—; witness—; —assures; —secures; —suffices.

(See security, reparation, insurance, protection, safeguard, safety.)

GUARANTEE (v)

adverbs

solemnly; unconditionally; unethically; unequivocally; scrupulously; fully; reliably.

(See promise, pledge.)

GUARD

verbs

arouse—; assign—to; bait—; conceal—; decoy—; deride—; double—; eject—; escape—; evade—; flank with—s; hail—; limit—; mount to—; muster—; post—; rile—; stand on—; station—; —manhandles; —patrols; —seizes; —s swarm; —s swarm round.

(See sentry, patrol.)

GUARD (v)

adverbs

closely; jealously; adequately; warily; zealously; rigidly; exclusively; circumspectly; sedulously; dependably.

(See defend, watch.)

GUARDED

adverbs

cautiously; carefully; watchfully; constantly; warily; discreetly; prudently; vigilantly; respectfully; affectionately; tenderly; devotedly; reverently; piously; punitively; sternly; skillfully; successfully; effectively; adroitly; cleverly; subtly; heavily; inefficiently; carelessly; insufficiently; perfectly; scrupulously; pitilessly; faithfully; temporarily; currently; elaborately; invincibly.

GUARDIAN

adjectives

ghostlike; gloomy-winged; particular; faithful; wary; fearless; dissembling; glistering; zealous; legal; appointed; temporary; greedy.

verbs
appoint—; choose—; commit to—; employ—; entrust—; necessitate—; respect—; —administers; —defends; —executes; —governs; —guides; —manages; —performs; —preserves; —protects; —supervises; —watches.
(See guard, defender, keeper.)

GUARDS

adjectives
pitiless; dependable; provost; vigilant; dust-choked; abdominal; imperturbable; scrupulous; inexorable; affrighted; angelic; advanced; obsequious; fearful.

GUESS

adjectives
admirable; happy; accepted; shrewd; instinctive; various (pl); ridiculous; worst; elaborate; wild.

verbs
attempt—; base—on; calculate—; chance—; estimate—; form—; hazard—; measure—; necessitate—; vary—; venture—; weigh—; withdraw—; —amazes; —coincides; —deceives; —rescues.
(See conjecture, surmise, supposition, speculation.)

GUESS (v)

adverbs
shrewdly; instinctively; profoundly; cleverly; skillfully; miraculously; intuitively; luckily; unerringly.
(See imagine, suppose.)

GUEST

adjectives
illustrious; forward; flirting; solitary; plebeian; gathering (pl); sparing; ungreeted; adoring; applauding; agreeable; telltale; long-awaited; welcome; neglected; lovelorn; parting; delightful; fastidious; distinguished; elegant; congenial; kingly; tedious; unexpected; taciturn; believing; late; surreptitious; terrible; unloved; continual; invited; straggling; boisterous; sour; involuntary; princely; glorious; entranced; sundry (pl); favorite; dreaded; shipwrecked; tolerated; frivolous; sybaritic; celestial; crowding; transient; honored; monster; mortal.

verbs
arrange—s; circulate among—s; delight—s; escort—; fete—; honor—; lodge—; prepare for—; regale—; speed—; —s assemble; —departs; —s mill about; —returns; present—.
(See visitor, friend.)

GUFFAW (v)

adverbs
coarsely; boisterously; crudely; obstreperously; sardonically; ribaldly; vulgarly; rudely; unrestrainedly; frivolously; drunkenly.
(See laugh.)

GUIDANCE

adjectives
tactful; energetic; vocational; celestial; continuous; psychiatric; genial; economic; perverse; fresh; cheering; altruistic.

verbs
bring under—of; commit to—; direct—of; entrust to—of; manage—; necessitate—; observe—; operate under—; relinquish—; remove—; resist—; respect—; supervise—; teach by—; —controls; —influences; —preserves; —protects; —trains.
(See protection, patronage, direction.)

GUIDE

verbs
commit to—; employ—; exhort—; provide—; —climbs; —conducts; —controls; —courses; —directs; —explains; —indicates; —influences; —leads; —lectures; —manages; —pilots; —plans; —points out; —rambles; —supervises; —tests; —trains.
(See conductor, pilot.)

GUIDE (v)

adverbs
fearlessly; intelligently; insensibly; tactfully; genially; altruistically; competently; intrepidly.
(See steer, conduct.)

GUIDES

adjectives
magnetic; careless; portly; trustworthy; baldpated; impassive; unerring; competent; powerful; greasy; spiritual; trusty; loving; infallible; intrepid; mysterious; sun-swart; foolhardy.

GUILD

verbs
admit to—; elect to—; impede—; organize—; regulate—; supervise—; support—; —aids; —benefits; —controls; —dispenses; —educates; —exhibits; —honors; —offers; —pursues.

(See association, fraternity, society, corporation, brotherhood.)

GUILE

adjectives
political; baleful; false; innocent; spiritual; fatal; venerable; smooth; sweet.

GUILELESS

adverbs
unaffectedly; apparently; delightfully; incredibly; refreshingly; touchingly; childishly; wonderfully; manifestly; charmingly; ravishingly; surprisingly; unbelievably; ingenuously; youthfully; unquestionably; candidly.

GUILT

adjectives
mutual; accessorial; exultant; hideous; apparent; open; inexpiable; stubborn; frustrate; tyrannic; supposed; bounteous; admitted; dread; enormous; ineffable; occulted; imputed; traitorous; murderous; uneasy; multiplied; heinous; miserable.

verbs
accept—; adduce—; ascertain—; betray—; blush with—; conceal—; exhibit—; experience a sense of—; expose—; hide—; incur—; induce—; measure—; prove—; repudiate—; reveal—; shoulder—; take—; uncover—; —attends; —dishonors; —shames.

(See sin, offense, wrong, crime.)

GUINEA-PIG

verbs
breed —s; dissect—; experiment with—; inject into —s; propagate —s; test —s.

(See animal.)

GUISE

adjectives
altered; secret; abstracted; fitting; festal; mortal; novel; startling; attractive; celestial; compellent; lowly; truthful; human; opalescent; reputable; gentler; murky; artful; silken; modern; winning.

GUITAR

adjectives
accustomed; tinkling; roaring; vigilant; humming; strumming; vibrant.

verbs
accompany with—; brush—; employ—; finger—; feet—; handle—; peck—; pick on—; pluck—; provide—; serenade with—; string—; strum—; tune—; twang—; —delights; —harmonizes; —moans; —throbs; —tinkles.

(See banjo.)

GULF

adjectives
voracious; winding; foaming; starlit; yawning; impassable; remoter; deep; tragic; unfathomable; roaring; pebbly; fiery; envious; breaking; starry; mystic; mediate; azure.

verbs
bridge—; deepen into—; dip into—; span—; —absorbs; —confronts; —hides; —opens; —roars; —separates; —sweeps.

(See chasm, separation, whirlpool, bay, vortex.)

GULL

adjectives
curving; circle; flannel; flapping; laughing; fading; strenuous; notorious; gleaming.

verbs
—barks; —bullies; —chatters; —s colonize; —darts; —fishes; —floats; —s flock; —s fraternize; —s prey on; —rends the air; —robs; —roves; —sails; —screams; —shrills; —skims; —soars; —squalls; —swoops; —wails; —wheels; —wings out to sea.

(See bird.)

GULLIBLE

adverbs
credulously; foolishly; weak-mindedly; dully; inanely; weakly; thoughtlessly; blindly; unthinkingly; easily; disastrously; unfortunately; fatuously; vacuously; childishly; superstitiously; confidently; exceptionally; obviously; manifestly; absurdly; ridiculously; idiotically; imprudently; indiscreetly; witlessly; brainlessly; amazingly; unexpectedly.

GULLY

verbs
excavate—; force along—; form—; furrow —; hollow into—; rise from—; scramble up —; straddle—; —deepens; —extends; —graduates; —opens.

(See gorge, channel, hollow, gutter, ditch, gulf.)

GULP (*v*)

adverbs
noisily; disgustingly; hungrily; vulgarly; eagerly; nauseously; rapaciously; ravenously.

(See swallow, eat.)

GUM

verbs
barrel—; consume—; dissolve—; glue with —; harden into—; secrete—; spread—; utilize—; twist—; yield—; —issues from; —preserves; —prevents; —stiffens.

GUMS

adjectives
enormous; toothless; odorous; lucid; precious; aromatic.

GUN

adjectives
honeycombed; squirrel; strong; pneumatic; murdering; resounding; hungry; rapid-fire; threatening; crackling; truculent; booming; resonant.

verbs
brave —s; cover with—; deflect—; jab—at; level—at; loose—at; man —s; mount—; muster —s; notch—; sheathe—; sight—; train—on; whip out—; —barks; —belches fire; —blazes away; —bombards; —booms; —s clatter; —demolishes; —enfilades; —glints; —grumbles; —jams; —pours; —roars; —rumbles; —spits; —spurts; —thunders; —volleys; —whines.

(See rifle, cannon, musket, pistol.)

GUN-FIRE

verbs
attack with—; break into—; charge with—; dodge—; flee from—; order—; rake with —; retreat from—; spatter with—; —assaults; —breaks loose; —crackles; —damages; —destroys; —disperses; —explodes; —reverberates; —tears up; —terrorizes.

(See firing, bombardment, fusillade, shots, volley.)

GUNPOWDER

verbs
agitate—; blast with—; charge with—; compound—; discharge—; inflame—; kindle—; reek with—; store—; —detonates; —explodes; —flashes; —smokes.

(See ammunition, dynamite, explosive.)

GURGLE

adjectives
slobbery; liquid; rich; childish; thick; horrible; oozing.

GURGLE (*v*)

adverbs
drearily; monotonously; pleasantly; musically; melodiously; ceaselessly; perpetually; spasmodically.

(See hiss, ripple, whisper.)

GUSH (*v*)

adverbs
copiously; spontaneously; terrifically; roaringly; richly; impetuously; foamingly; unrestrainedly; loquaciously.

(See rush, flow.)

GUSHING

adverbs
elaborately; volubly; fluently; foolishly; effusively; sentimentally; ecstatically; rapturously; joyously; inanely; absurdly; ridiculously; inconsequently; excitedly; nervously; warmly; racily; breathlessly; hysterically; impressively; pretentiously; ostentatiously; showily; unpleasantly; offensively; uncommonly; habitually; constantly; impetuously; vivaciously; tiresomely; endlessly; interminably.

GUST

adjectives
chill; fitful; hot; unusual; violent; fierce; stormy; buffeting; extreme; passionate; sudden; scented; eddying; angry.

GUSTO

adjectives
culinary; geyserish; racy; joyous; wholesome; great; inartistic; rare; sardonic; hearty; solemn.

verbs
discharge in—; drag in—; drift down—; furrow—; jostle into—; lodge in—; recline in—; slope to—; stream down—; sweep into —; wear away—; —carries away; —irrigates; —drains;.

(See channel, ditch, groove.)

adverbs

deeply; brokenly; inarticulately; pleasantly; heavily; outlandishly; exotically; grotesquely; absurdly; mockingly; thickly; hesistantly; distinctly; extremely; undisguisedly; surprisingly.

H

HABIT

adjectives

moral; ferocious; mental; celestial; tranquil; quasi-religious; barbarian; sedentary; unclean; desultory; unrestrained; invariable; systematic; social; separate; idle; economical; sober; contrary; old-fashioned; disconcerting; lifelong; healthful; steady; taciturn; lifetime; precious; established; estranged; unsettled; long-existing; philosophical; popular; spendthrift; cleanly; incurable; religious; offensive; courteous; innate; sidewalk; ill; parti-colored; vulgar; devilish; aquatic; fixed; personal; priceless; dissolute; important; peculiar; cherished; sociable; outdoor; baneful; migratory; industrious; indelicate; retrospective; steady; gregarious; exasperating; tutored; psychological; fastidious; immoral; virtuous; asthmatic; intense; wandering; acquired; uncanny; vicious; comparative; harmless; injurious; prevalent; confirmed; spending; abominable; feminine; deadly; expensive; drinking; mating; unsightly; bloodcurdling; unhygienic; pernicious; voracious; proper; degrading; unproductive; intemperate; honorable; natural; unfortunate; orderly; watchful; flabby; dainty; epicurean; cherished; virile; judicious; ineradicable; purgative; disputatious; busy; convivial; frugal; industrious; temperate; ascetic; studious; nascent; leisurely; hurtful; depraved; mean; intoxicating; careless; fatal; constant; inexcusable; incompatible; physical; silly; dreadful; disgusting; beguiling; autocratic; sluggish; roving; debauched; evil; remorseless; ingrained; domestic; active; awkward; licentious; luxurious; extravagant; artificial; dishonest; mourning; filthy; untoward; piscatory; unmanageable; corrupt; slovenly; indolent; humble; simple; unfixed; dietetic; stylish; unassuming; sordid; demure; synthetic; deliberate; daring; terrible; worse; improvident; intellectual; watchful; unconscious; detestable; dangerous.

verbs

acquire—; adopt—; assume—; break up—; breed—; check—; contract—; cultivate—; deplore—; develop—; discard—; dissolve —; diverge from—; eradicate—; establish —; fall into—; gain—; inculcate—; induce —; indulge in—; instill—; protest against —; pursue—; regulate—; relinquish—; renounce—; set up—; teach—; unlearn—; upset—; —accustoms; —binds; —compels; —loses its hold; —persists; —roots; —takes possession.

(See custom, practice, inclination.)

HABITATION

adjectives

devoted; personal; moving; crude; squalid; humble; peaceful; dismal; commodious; isolated.

HABITUAL

adverbs

idly; disconcertingly; incurably; deliberately; carefully; peculiarly; traditionally; inherently; harmlessly; unfortunately; automatically; ineradicably; studiously; dreadfully; awkwardly; dangerously; methodically; prosaically; conveniently; unconsciously.

HACKNEYED

adverbs

tiresomely; boresomely; ineffectively; tritely; prosaically; typically; bookishly; learnedly; academically; pedantically; professionally; banally; conventionally; pedagogically; unctuously; sententiously; wearisomely; stupidly; monotonously; flatly; terribly; dully.

HAEMOGLOBIN

verbs

break down—; combine with—; count—; destroy—; enrich—; gain in—; lessen—; measure—; study—; —circulates; —conveys; —crystallizes; —dispenses; —oxidizes; —provides.

HAG

adjectives

unseemly; edentate; withered; repulsive; blear-eyed; hideous; ferocious; wretched; wicked; secret; black; midnight.

HAGGARD

adverbs

terribly; alarmingly; surprisingly; pitiably; pathetically; fearfully; unwontedly; extremely; frightfully; mysteriously; significantly; distressingly; disturbingly; gauntly; shockingly; appallingly; wearily; uncommonly; singularly; strangely; cruelly.

HAIL

adjectives

continuous; lashing; sonorous; pearly; sulphurous; incessant; cursing; dreadful.

verbs

deluge with—; escape—; pour—; send down —; shower with—; volley—; —assails; —chills; —descends; —desolates; —falls; —pierces; —ravages; —shatters; —spatters; —stones; —tattoos; —whistles round.

(See rain, snow.)

HAIL (v)

adverbs

exultingly; rapturously; imperatively; enthusiastically; resoundingly; boisterously; thunderously; obstreperously; vigorously.

(See salute, accost.)

HAIR

adjectives

abnormal; abominable; abounding; abundant; agglutinated; alluring; amber; amorous; ash-blonde; ash-colored; asthetic; auburn; back-blown; backward-streaming; bad; battling; beautiful; bleached; blowing; blond; blue-black; bobbed; boyish; braided; brick-colored; bright; bristling; brittle; bronzed; brunette; brushed; bushy; carefully-brushed; careless; carroty; chestnut; close-curling; close-cut; close-trimmed; clustering; coal-black; coiled; colored; copious; coppery; corn-colored; correct; cottony; crinkly; crisp; crownless; cumbersome; curled; dabbled; dark; dazzling; dewy; disarranged; dirty; discolored; disheveled; disordered; drab; dressed; dripping; drowning; dull; dusky; dusty; dyed; ebon; effulgent; elaborately-dressed; electrified; erect; entangled; excessive; faded; fair; falling; fiery; filthy; fine; finespun; flamelike; flattened; flaxen; flecked; floating; flowing; fluffy; fluttering; flying; forlorn; frizzed; frowzy; fussy; fuzzy; garlanded; glamorous; gleaming; glinting; glittering; glorious; glossy; golden; gorgeous; gray; graying; greasy; grimy; grizzled; haggard; hard; harsh; hay-colored; hazel; heavy; helmeted; hempy; henna; hoary; honey-colored; horrent; horrible; horrid; impeccable; impetúous; incredible; iron-gray; jet; jet-black; jeweled; kinky; knotted; lambent; lank; lifeless; light; limp; long; loosening; loose-waved; lovely; luminous; lustrous; luxuriant; mahogany; marcelled; marvelous; massive; matted; metallic; mis-dressed; misty; mortal; mouse-colored; muddy; mussed; mustard-colored; neat; neglected; nut-brown; objectionable; oily; odorous; over-bleached; overgrown; overlong; pale; palled; pallid; palsied; parted; pendulous; perfumed; plaited; plentiful; plastered; pomaded; poppied; portentous; powdered; precious; prematurely-gray; prim; princely; problematical; prodigious; profuse; puffed; queenly; quiet; radiant; ragged; raven; ravishing; rebellious; reddish; reddled; refractory; reverend; ribboned; rich; riotous; rippling; romantic; rough; ruffled; rumpled; russet; rusty; sandy; satiny; scant; scattered; scented; scorched; scraggly; sculptured; shadowy; shaggy; sheeny; shining; shingled; short; short-cropped; silken; silver-gilt; silvery; sleek; slender; slicked; sluttish; smoky; smoothed; smothering; snowy; soft; soggy; spiky; spilling; sprouting; starchy; steel-gray; stiff; stiff-looking; straggly; straight; straw-colored; streaked; subtle; streaming; strength-giving; stringy; strong; stubbly; stubby; sun-blanched; sunny; sun-bleached; sustaining; swart; sylvan; swarthy; sweaty; taffy; tangled; tawny; thick; tidy; time-hallowed; tiny; tousled; tow-colored; tumbled; turbulent; twining; twisted; two-toned; unbound; uncompromising; unconquered; uncurled; undone; undulating; unhealthy; unkempt; unkinked; unmanageable; unruly; untidy; unwashed; usurping; vegetable; velvety; venerable; vibrant; vivid; voluminous; waved; wavy; waxed; well-brushed; well-known; weltering; wet; wild; wind-blown; wind-rumpled; wind-whipped; wiry; wondrous; wreathless; youthful; zephyr-blown; burnished.

verbs

arrange—; beribbon—; braid—; curl—; deck—; discipline—; dishevel—; fluff out—; glue down—; groom—; ruffle—; rumple—; train—; whisk back—; —bristles; —frames; —gleams; —glistens; —glows; —luxuriates; —projects; —ripples; —shimmers; —shines; —straggles; —waves.

(See beard, whiskers, curls.)

HALCYON

adverbs

gently; calmly; peacefully; gratefully; delightfully; gloriously; enviably; agreeably; providentially; happily; sunnily; smoothly; charmingly; blissfully; comfortably; beatifically; cloudlessly; unbelievably; refreshingly; felicitously; miraculously; incomparably.

HALE

adverbs
delightfully; sturdily; stoutly; vigorously; vivaciously; cheerily; healthily; soundly; hardily; robustly; ordinarily; vibrantly; exuberantly; remarkably; incredibly; exceptionally; unwontedly; enthusiastically; unbelievably; cheerfully.

HALF-HEARTED

adverbs
obviously; unconcealedly; openly; frankly; manifestly; curiously; indifferently; timidly; indecisively; lazily; indolently; insolently; capriciously; indeterminately; irresolutely; phlegmatically; languidly; nonchalantly; carelessly; inattentively; imperturbably; extraordinarily; inexplicably; unaccountably; irresponsibly; insouciantly; vexatiously; lackadaisically; noticeably; conspicuously.

HALL

adjectives
moody; boundless; cerulean; pillared; gilded; naked; windy; dimly-lighted; spacious; brilliant; low-browed; gaslit; upper; festal; voiceless; lofty; hospitable; marble-paved; ancestral; ancient; unillumined; dusky; enormous; capacious; shallow; subterranean; barrel-vaulted; main; oak-lined; paternal; palatial; roofless; lonely; ample; gloomy; ethereal.

verbs
appropriate—for; assemble in—; convert—into; gather in—; grace—; jam—; loiter in—; occupy—; receive in—; transact in—; preside over—.

(See building, room, auditorium, passage, entry.)

HALLOW (v)

adverbs
traditionally; solemnly; formally; religiously; pompously; perfunctorily.

(See reverence, bless.)

HALLUCINATION

adjectives
visionary; engendering.

verbs
abolish—; dispose to—s; entertain—s; expel—; molest with—; produce—; suffer—s; wander into—; welter in—; wrap in—; —annoys; —arises; —envisions; —harasses; —hounds; —preys upon; —suggests; —sweeps away; —worries.

(See delusion, illusion.)

HALLWAY

adjectives
frigid; austere; narrow.

HALO

adjectives
majestic; radiant; glistening; hollow.

verbs
award—; crown with—; display—; fashion—; form—; garland with—; invest with—; spread—around; suspend—; weave—; —appears; —blinks; —encircles; —encompasses; —girdles; —glorifies; —hovers over; —radiates; —surrounds; —wreathes.

(See glory, circle, light.)

HALT

adjectives
panting; dead.

verbs
bring to—; call—; come to—; command—; earn—; fall to—; induce—; merit—; necessitate—; plead for—; sound—; stumble to—; urge—; —refreshes; strengthens; —vivifies.

(See truce.)

HALT (v)

adverbs
abruptly; irresolutely; awkwardly; instantaneously; jarringly; completely; permanently.

(See stop, cease.)

HAMLET

adjectives
scattered (pl); rude; nameless; obscure; favored; humble; huddled; disheveled; insignificant.

HAMMER

adjectives
ponderous; polished; deafening.

verbs
beat with—; clasp—; crush with—; drive with—; employ—; flourish—; guide—;

labor with—; rap with—; shape with—; smite with—; strike with—; swing—; tap with—; wield—; —injures; —menaces; —suffices.
(See gavel, club, hatchet.)

HAMMER (v)

adverbs
untiringly; repetitiously; energetically; deafeningly; maddeningly; industriously; monotonously; vigorously; thunderously.
(See beat, pound.)

HAMMOCK

adjectives
concealing; leafy; creaking.

verbs
bear in—; cradle in—; ensconce in—; hang in—; hide in—; loll in—; nest in—; relax in—; rest in—; shroud in—; sling—across; slip into—; suspend—; turn into—; —holds; —swings; —upsets.
(See bed, couch.)

HAMPER (v)

adverbs
disastrously; tragically; purposely; fatefully; seriously; painfully; cruelly; superfluously.
(See impede, restrain.)

HAND

verbs
aspire to—of; beckon with—; callous—; clap—s; clasp in—; clench—; denote with—; employ—; extend—; flex—; flick—; flourish—; gain—of; indicate with—; join—s; paralyze—; proffer—; pump—; spread—; splint—; tender—; wring—; —quivers; —trembles; —twitches.
(See palm, claw, fingers, marriage.)

HANDCLASP

adjectives
latticed; fluid; fervent.

HANDFUL

adjectives
paltry; unshackled; comparative; thorny; scanty; scattered; promiscuous.

HANDICAP

adjectives
difficult; generous; cruel; troublesome; personal.

verbs
burden with—; compensate for—; gain—; impose—; insist on—; load with—; offset—; overcome—; require—; resent—; suffer under—; survive—; —alters; —equalizes; —evens; —hampers; —penalizes; —reduces.
(See disadvantage.)

HANDICAP (v)

adverbs
hopelessly; heavily; physically; psychically; spiritually; economically; maritally.
(See hinder.)

HANDKERCHIEF

adjectives
glaring; necktie; napkin; shabby; scandalous; unclean; tear-stained; immaculate; wadded.

verbs
adorn—; border—; display—; embroider—; expose—; fringe—; monogram—; perfume—; pocket—.
(See cloth, silk, linen.)

HANDLE

adjectives
knob; lever; hollow; detachable; composition; substantial.

verbs
clasp—; clutch—; deprive of—; fly off—; grab—; grasp—; grip—; hold by—; manage—; manipulate—; nab—; operate—; snatch—; twist—; —controls; —protrudes; —regulates.
(See knob.)

HANDLE (v)

adverbs
effectively; dexterously; summarily; severely; rudely; technically; awkwardly; individually; arbitrarily; competently; urgently; suavely; adroitly; skillfully.
(See manipulate, touch.)

HANDLING

adjectives
masterly; ill; indecisive; adroit; clever; rough; technical; dexterous; unexceptionable; guileful; skillful.

adjectives

able; accursed; accomplished; achieving; active; admonishing; aged; affectionate; agile; agitated; aggressive; airy; almighty; ambitious; angelic; applauding; aristocratic; armed; arresting; artistic; atrocious; audacious; automatic; avaricious; awkward; balmy; barbarous; bare; beautiful; beckoning; begrimed; bejeweled; beneficent; benumbed; beseeching; bewildered; black; branded; black-gloved; blanched; bleeding; blistered; blithe; bloodless; bloody; blundering; bony; botanic; bounteous; bountiful; brawny; broad; bronzed; brown; bruised; brutal; bungling; burning; callous; capable; careless; caressing; casual; cautious; cemented; chafed; chamois-gloved; chapped; charitable; cheap; cheery; chill; chilly; childish; chopped; chubby; clammy; clapping; clasping; clawing; clawlike; clean; clenched; clever; cold; clinched; clumsy; clutching; coarse; comforting; colossal; confident; conscious; considerate; consoling; cordial; craven; cringing; crooked; cunning; curative; cushionlike; dainty; damaging; darting; deadly; deeply-tanned; defiling; deft; deformed; delegated; delicate; deprecating; despairing; despoiling; detaining; dexterous; diamond-ringed; disguised; dirty; dimpled; discolored; disdainful; disengaged; disrobing; divine; dogmatic; doll-like; dominating; dreadful; drooping; drink-shaken; dubious; dying; eager; eclipsing; eloquent; emaciated; emphatic; enameled; enchanting; energetic; envious; erudite; ever-open; ever-awakening; excellent; execrable; expensive; experienced; expert; explanatory; exploring; exquisite; extended; eye-instructed; fair; facile; failing; fairy; faithful; false; faltering; fanless; fastidious; fatigued; favoring; fearless; feeble; ferocious; fevered; fidgety; fiery; filthy; fine; firm; flabby; flaccid; flattering; flawless; fleshless; fleshy; flexible; floury; fluttering; foam-white; folded; foraged; frank; frantic; fratricidal; freckled; free; frenzied; friendly; fumbling; furtive; fussy; gaunt; gauntleted; generous; gentle; gesticulating; girlish; gloating; glorified; gloved; glowing; gnarled; gorilla; gracious; grasping; graspless; greasy; green; grimy; groomed; groping; grubby; guiding; hairy; hallowed; hamlike; hammer-hard; handsome; hanging; hard; hard-palmed; hasty; hateful; healthful; hearty; heavy; heavy-veined; heedless; helpful; helping; high; hollowed; holy; honest; honored; horny; hospitable; hovering; huge; human; humble; hurried; icy; idle; ignoble; immaculate; immediate; immense; immortal; impatient; imperious; impious; imploring; impulsive; incarnadined; inconsequent; indignant; indiscriminate; indolent; indomitable; ineffective; inexperienced; infant; innocent; innocuous; inquisitive; insistent; instinctive; instrumental; intelligent; interpretative; intractable; intruding; invisible; iron; irresolute; irresponsible; irreverent; ivory; jerking; jeweled; kindly; knotted; knuckled; labor-calloused; lacerated; lacerating; lame; languid; lavish; lax; lean; leathery; legible; lemon-scented; lenient; dishpan; wise; liberal; limp; listless; lithe; little; locked; lone; long; long-fingered; long-stretched; long-taloned; loose-hanging; lordly; loving; lustful; mailed; magnetic; malicious; malignant; manacled; manicured; manipulating; martial; massive; masterly; maternal; meager; menacing; merciful; mere; mighty; ministering; miscalculating; mittened; moist; molded; motionless; mottled; mournful; much-ringed; murderous; munificent; nameless; narrow; neighborly; nerveless; nervous; nestling; niggardly; nimble; noiseless; numbed; offending; old-looking; olive; outdoor; outflung; outstretched; pale; pallid; palsied; pampering; parched; parricidal; passive; patrician; peaceful; persistent; persuasive; pierced; pious; pitiless; placid; plastic; plenty-dropping; plump; poised; portraying; powder-blackened; powerful; practiced; pragmatic; praying; presumptuous; priestly; prim; primitive; prodigal; profane; proffered; prompt; proper; protective; providential; providing; pudgy; puffy; pulpy; pure; quavering; quizzical; rash; rapacious; raw; reassuring; reaching; reckless; relaxed; remorseless; relentless; reluctant; resolute; respectful; responsive; restless; restraining; reverent; rheumatic; rigid; rigorous; ringed; ringless; robust; rose-leaf; rose-petal; rosy; rough; royal; rude; ruinous; ruthless; sacred; sacrilegious; sallow; satiny; saving; sceptered; scheming; scholarly; scornful; sculptured; searching; seared; severe; sinless; shadowy; shaking; shapely; shattered; shiny; shriveled; shuddering; signaling; sin-avenging; sinew-swelled; sinewy; skeleton; skillful; slack; slender; slim; slimy; slippery; slow; sly; small; smooth; smudgy; snowy; soaked; soft; soiled; solid; soot-grimed;

staying; steady; stealthy; stiffened; stodgy; stout; straggling; straining; strange; strengthening; strong; stubby; subtle; sudden; suing; sunburned; supine; supple; supplicating; supporting; sure; surreptitious; sustaining; swarthy; swollen; sympathetic; tactful; tainted; tampering; tanned; tapering; tear-dampened; tempestuous; tender; thick; thievish; thin; threatening; throttling; tied; tight-clasped; timid; tiny; tiring; titanic; toil-hardened; toilworn; toiling; torn; trained; translucent; transparent; treacherous; trembling; tremendous; tremulous; trusting; tugging; twitching; tyrannous; unaided; uncertain; unclasped; unconscious; uncovered; unequal; unerring; unfamiliar; unfettered; ungainly; ungloved; ungrudging; uninhibited; unlineal; unresisting; unresponsive; unseen; unskilled; unsparing; unsteady; unswerving; untrained; untrembling; unvenerable; unwilling; uplifted; upstretched; useful; useless-looking; usurious; valorous; victorious; viewless; vigorous; violent; vital; vulgar; wan; wandering; wanton; warm; warning; warring; wasted; water-shriveled; wavering; waxlike; weather-browned; welcoming; well-bred; well-cared-for; well-formed; well-shaped; willing; withered; work-hardened; lifeless; working; work-marked; wounded; work-soiled; wrapped; wrinkled; wretched; clear; soothing; upraised; spider; sprawling; sprightly; vandalous; vast; veined; venerated.

HANDSOME

adverbs
dazzlingly; gloriously; intangibly; matchlessly; fiercely; surprisingly; sullenly; compellingly; richly; darkly; duskily; cruelly; stormily; vitally; singularly; imposingly; impressively; proudly; sternly; triumphantly; resplendently; glowingly; startlingly; regally; glamorously.

HANDWORK

adjectives
painstaking; plodding; patient; deft.

HANDWRITING

adjectives
sprawling; attested; unmistakable; feeble; quavering; distinctive; intelligent; inelegant; bold; clear; poor; scrawly; uncultivated; crabbed.

verbs
admire—; alter—; counterfeit—; decipher—; develop—; forge—; judge—; recognize—; —fascinates; —flourishes; —reveals; —wavers.

(See writing.)

HANDY

adverbs
extremely; providently; conveniently; exceptionally; remarkably; carefully; delightfully; cleverly; unusually; perfectly; uncommonly; thoughtfully; noticeably; incomparably; serviceably; advantageously; practically; appropriately; readily; ingeniously; miraculously.

HANG (v)

adverbs
fatefully; debatably; imminently; dolefully; fondly; precariously; waveringly; indecisively; tenderly; listlessly; stubbornly; conspicuously; breathlessly; lankly; disconsolately; doggedly; flaccidly.

(See lynch, execute.)

HANGINGS

adjectives
leafy; wholesale; sumptuous; inflammable.

HAPHAZARD

adverbs
casually; carelessly; indolently; informally; adventitiously; incidentally; nonchalantly; indifferently; fortuitously; delightfully; abominably; terribly; atrociously; reprehensibly; joyously; merrily; irresponsibly; gloriously; dreadfully; inconveniently.

HAPPEN (v)

adverbs
opportunely; propitiously; auspiciously; allegedly; subsequently; historically; spontaneously; mysteriously; logically; promptly.

(See occur, befall.)

HAPPENINGS

adjectives
alleged; accidental; subsequent; historical; ordinary; spontaneous; vital; invented; unbelievable; strenuous; mysterious.

HAPPINESS

adjectives
boundless; excited; fireside; tranquil; resultant; connubial; crowning; legitimate; incomparable; wild; overwhelming; keen;

grave; peaceful; celestial; passive; humble; supreme; human; cheap; vulgar; true; romantic; buoyant; puerile; subsequent; unproductive; unclouded; scant; pure; golden; glowing; earthly; mutual; secret; rapturous; eternal; visionary; unexpected; highest; solid; unexcelled; redundant; unutterable; radiant; sublunary; sublime; unappreciated; dizzy; surface; delusive; temporal; exquisite; soft; personal; dear; strange; domestic; virulent; poor; neighborly; pastoral; exalted; joyous; healthy; close-woven; superhuman.

verbs
achieve—; assail—of; bar from—; betoken —; breathe—; conceal—; convert to—; derive—from; destroy—; extract—from; hamper—; inhale—; jeopardize—; overrate—; predestine to—; promote—; recapture—; rescue—; salvage—; shut out—; stake everything on—; strive for—; struggle for —; tend toward—; voice—; void—; yield —; —endures; —evades; —fades; —lingers; —reposes in; —touches; —visits; —wanes.

(See prosperity, gladness, delight, pleasure, bliss, joy, comfort, enjoyment, satisfaction.)

HAPPY

adverbs
radiantly; beamingly; beautifully; bonnily; curiously; rosily; smilingly; ridiculously; openly; innocently; childishly; shyly; modestly; frankly; brightly; rapturously; excitedly; tranquilly; quietly; incomparably; wildly; keenly; overwhelmingly; supremely; secretly; unutterably; joyously; ecstatically; ineffably; profoundly; tenderly; deliriously; breathlessly.

HARANGUE

adjectives
mere; soporific; seditious; inflammatory; tempestuous; conciliatory; soldierly; unintelligible; coherent; explanatory; fiery; belligerent.

HARANGUE (v)

adverbs
bombastically; vehemently; seditiously; tempestuously; unintelligibly; coherently; fiercely; belligerently; vigorously.

(See orate, address.)

HARASS (v)

adverbs
consistently; grievously; ceaselessly; perpetually; maddeningly; irksomely; irritatingly; exasperatingly; incessantly.

(See distress, persecute, trouble.)

HARASSMENT

adjectives
ceaseless; perpetual.

HARBOR

adjectives
immense; sun-splashed; sunlit; little; green-bordered; earthly; exposed; secret; miniature; landlocked; fortified; blue; restless; mountain-bound; all-creating; bustling; glassy; neutral; matchless; noble; placid; sheltered; fair; unrivaled.

verbs
admit to—; afford—; anchor in—; assign to—; blockade—; drift to—; lie in—; lodge at—; obtain—; put into—; seek—; set out of—; slip into—; —accommodates; —conceals; —protects; —quarters; —shelters.

(See refuge, haven, shelter, retreat.)

HARD

adverbs
stonily; wilfully; unyieldingly; pitilessly; obdurately; unrelentingly; unrepentantly; inexorably; stubbornly; obstinately; mulishly; doggedly; perversely; fanatically; resolutely; determinedly; unmercifully; cruelly; maliciously; vengefully; implacably; bitterly; sternly; unreasonably; manifestly; palpably; undeniably.

HARDEN (v)

adverbs
glacially; excessively; immoderately; perpetually; scientifically; methodically; mechanically.

(See season, invigorate.)

HARDIHOOD

adjectives
slipshod; reckless; barbaric; desperate.

HARDNESS

adjectives
iron; steely.

verbs
allay—; arm with—; crust with—; deliver from—; dissemble—; inure to—; incur—;

loathe—; overcome—; penetrate—; produce —; rub off—; shed—; suffer—; —defends; —endures; —protects; —resists.
(See difficulty, harshness, cruelty, severity.)

HARDSHIP

adjectives
continued; increasing; inevitable; nameless; physical; appreciable; incredible; tremendous; unnecessary; unexpected; early; unrepining.

verbs
allay—; alleviate—; ameliorate—; bear—; bow under—; condemn to—; ease—; endure —; entail—; evade—; groan under—; impose—; inflict—; learn through—; oppress with—; share—; suffer—; taste—; tolerate —; torment with—; —anguishes; —destroys; —discourages; —presses.
(See privation, injury, affliction, adversity, trouble, pain.)

HARDY

adverbs
resolutely; intrepidly; courageously; stoutly; sturdily; robustly; boldly; fortunately; indubitably; obviously; indefatigably; dependably; strongly; staunchly; vigorously; stalwartly; inexhaustibly; courageously; audaciously; pluckily; wonderfully; irresistibly; astonishingly; prodigiously.

HARE

adjectives
purblind; timorous; fluffy; flying.

HARLEQUIN

adverbs
erratically; capriciously; changeably; mercurially; kaleidoscopically; vagrantly; waywardly; fleetingly; nimbly; swiftly; fleetly; trippingly; stagily; dramatically; spectacularly; comically; trickily; lightly; clownishly; jocosely; waggishly; fabulously; entertainingly; laughingly; mockingly.

HARM

adjectives
sullen; bodily; enormous; substantial; tremendous; imminent; delicious; irreparable; incalculable; chief; outward; serious; personal.

verbs
anticipate—; avert—; commit—; correct—; counterbalance—; forgive—; heed—; inflict —; lament—; offset—; prevent—; protect against—; rectify—; remedy—; render—; resent—; ruminate upon—; save from—; suffer—; sustain—; weigh—; —afflicts; —angers; —distresses; —pains; —threatens.
(See injury, damage, evil, wrong.)

HARMFUL

adverbs
terribly; immediately; ultimately; distinctly; admittedly; obviously; maliciously; venomously; deliberately; innocently; unconsciously; ignorantly; intentionally; purposely; irrevocably; irremediably; calamitously; disastrously; dreadfully; outrageously; atrociously; perniciously; exceptionably; deplorably; uncommonly; frightfully; immeasurably; incalculably.

HARMLESS

adverbs
innocently; distinctly; assuredly; avowedly; obviously; manifestly; definitely; altogether; utterly; comparatively; allegedly; perfectly; impeccably; virtually; substantially; practically; negligibly; essentially; presumably; reasonably; assuredly.

HARMONIOUS

adverbs
agreeably; fortunately; sweetly; luckily; unquestionably; happily; felicitously; unbelievably; unexpectedly; sociably; ineffably; cordially; heartily; obviously; manifestly; sincerely; highly; entirely; uncommonly; remarkably; particularly; delightfully; serenely; exquisitely; seraphically; gloriously; inexpressibly.

HARMONY

adjectives
ingenious; distinguished; plaintive; serene; subtle; thrilling; ringing; sublime; unutterable; amiable; developed; divine; ravishing; inner; absolute; complete; whirlwind; primal; undisturbed; entire; methodical; perfect; ethereal; general; incomparable; celestial; angelic; pre-established; exquisite; multitudinous (pl); many-sounding; unbroken; heavenly; household; deceiving; liquid; delightful; peculiar; inarticulate; eternal; discordant; canarylike; complicated; blatant; enchanting; weird; insured; glorious; limitless; soft; subdued; inexpress-

ible; aerial; unconjectured; color; intoxicating; far-linked; elemental; impromptu; autumnal; wonderful; rugged; lugubrious; consonant; palatable; chiseled.

verbs
admire—; beget—; bind into—; cement—; compose into—; destroy—; dispose toward —; insure—; maintain—; melt into—; stress —; strike—; weave in—; work in—; —charms; —delights; —emanates from; —enchants; —grows; —pervades; —prevails; —smooths.
(See friendship, agreement, peace, consistency.)

HARP

adjectives
murmuring; piano; neglected; cunning; mysterious; sullen; reproofless; impaled; aeolian; smitten; solemn; sounding; sweet; tuneful.

verbs
flow from—; marry to—; pitch—; string—; strum—; touch—; tune—; waken—; welcome—; —chimes; —disarms; —enervates; —entrances; —pleases; —reverberates; —rings out; —sings; —sleeps; —soothes; —thrills; —trembles; —whispers.
(See guitar, banjo.)

HARP (*v*)

adverbs
exclusively; repetitiously; irksomely; naggingly; inexorably; bitterly; moodily; venomously; groundlessly; sullenly.
(See persist, repeat.)

HARPING

adjectives
constant; mysterious; celestial.

HARROW (*v*)

adverbs
mercilessly; cruelly; superfluously; gratuitously; sadistically; grimly.
(See wound, distress, torture.)

HARSH

adverbs
dreadfully; needlessly; unnecessarily; bitterly; inexplicably; austerely; irritably; discourteously; forbiddingly; irritatingly; inexcusably; deliberately; maliciously; incredibly; unreasonably; vengefully; disconcertingly; tyrannically; despotically; dogmatically; imperiously; authoritatively; terribly; uncompromisingly; stubbornly; cruelly; unmitigatedly; mercilessly.

HARSHNESS

adjectives
terrible; stubborn; momentary; sinister; mellowed.

verbs
apply—; assail with—; avoid—; clash with —; correct—; creak with—; pardon—; resent—; resist—; rub with—; shed—; subdue—; taste—; temper—; thunder—; —arises from; —displeases; —grates; —sours.
(See severity, cruelty, hardness.)

HARVEST

adjectives
terrible; reaped; pecuniary; costly; easy; sorrowful; rich; bounteous; promising; uncertain; preposterous; golden; ripened; abundant; heavenly; full; fair; millennial; hidden; glorious; unshared; full-sheaved.

verbs
bear—; celebrate—; enrich—; gather—; glean—; heap—; house—; invite to—; mar —; promise—; reap—; rear—; ruin—; sickle—; toil in—; treasure—; —cheers; —contents; —glows; —graces; —repays; —rewards; —satisfies; —wearies.
(See crop, yield, product, reward, fruit, proceeds, result, return.)

HASTE

adjectives
heedless; breathless; duteous; delirious; phantom; disciplined; desperate; unseemly; wrathful; fiery; undue; hot; wild; indecent; purblind; unscrupulous; lamentable; eager; irreverent; barbarous; clumsy; nervous; noiseless; mad; frantic; reckless; uncivil; feverish; deadly; frenzied; disgraceful; rash; ruthless; moderate; dread; incredible; unusual; straining; over-credulous; tremulous; generous; noticeable.

HASTEN (*v*)

adverbs
instinctively; obsequiously; anxiously; vastly; materially; dutifully; nervously; unscrupulously; irreverently; frantically; uncivilly; feverishly; incredibly; tremulously.
(See urge, hurry.)

HASTY

adverbs

disgracefully; inexcusably; rudely; unforgivably; shamefully; hysterically; impetuously; impulsively; ridiculously; unnecessarily; unfortunately; madly; insanely.

HAT

adjectives

drab; shiny; tomato-colored; glazed; straw; rusty; soiled; silk; glossy; discolored; sleek; napless; chocolate; absurd; shabby; ordinary; archaic; hereditary; beaver; crownless; conical; jaunty; battered; distinguished; befeathered; beribboned; broad-brimmed; sugar-loaf; hard; high; cocked; cavernous; flattish; stunning; featherweight; felt; rush; high-crowned; flopping; dilapidated; fantastic; misshapen; much-worn; coquettish; beguiling; casual; slouched; formless; distinctive; fashionable; devastating; smart; shovel; horrible; becoming; plumed; infinitesimal; shapeless; dun-colored; soft; fetching; flowered; slouch; dishpan-shaped; delicate; battered; cunning.

verbs

clap on—; cock—; deck—; design—; discard—; display—; doff—; don—; fancy—; fashion—; plume—; scorn—; shed—; sport (colloq)—; tide—; tip—; trim—; wave—; —awes; —flatters; —s fly; —perches; —protects; —reposes on; —shocks; —teeters.

(See cap, helmet.)

HATCHET

verbs

brandish—; crush with—; drive—into; employ—; flourish—; hew with—; knock down with—; sharpen—; smite with—; split with—; strip with—; strike with—; threaten with—; wield—; yield to—; —cuts; —destroys; —lacerates; —menaces; —severs; —splits; —subdues; —wounds.

(See axe, hammer, club, bat, gavel.)

HATE

adjectives

high-strung; prejudiced; vigorous; counterfeiting; morbid; malevolent; racking; vanquished; constant; hideous; sectional; murderous; savage; steadfast; individual; groveling; immortal; deadly; inflexible; unfilial; grudging; envious; despotic; lodged; impious; heavy; ancestral; sullen; ill-dissembled; consuming; unrelenting; strong; bitter; mutual; irrevocable; quenchless; shameful; successful; unspoken; misbegotten; unmistakable; supernatural; vehement.

HATE (v)

adverbs

perniciously; implacably; cordially; insatiably; invariably; vindictively; jealously; instinctively; mutually; passionately; inflammably; politically; irrepressibly; unconquerably; groundlessly.

(See detest, dislike.)

HATED

adverbs

utterly; abominably; repugnantly; mortally; intolerably; impossibly; incredibly; completely; shockingly; detestably; disgustingly; insufferably; horribly; terribly; odiously.

HATEFUL

adverbs

bitterly; utterly; unspeakably; odiously; offensively; completely; abominably; disgustingly; insufferably; intolerably; horribly; terribly; shockingly; profoundly; uncommonly; intensely; unnaturally; curiously; passionately; venomously; infernally; furiously; consummately.

HATER

adjectives

reputed; persistent.

HATRED

adjectives

native; innate; instinctive; internal; caustic; patient; deadly; profound; intense; bitter; rancorous; mutual; unaffected; unnatural; unsleeping; hidden; curious; lifelong; strong; ineradicable; passionate; moody; fierce; obscure; inextinguishable; revolutionary; inflammable; virtuous; vigorous; apparent; venomous; smiling; inexorable; immodest; antique; ancient; fanatical; unleavened; hearty; national; raw; implacable; political; irrepressible; partisan; nauseous; jealous; racial; infernal; base; active; indurated; color; perfidious; relentless; furious; vindictive; violent; unconquerable; baffled; undying; consuming; groundless.

verbs

allay—; appease—; breed—; cherish—; conceal—; deepen—; depict—; deplore—; endure—; excite—; focus—upon; incite to—; justify—; kindle—; manifest—; nourish—; nurse—; placate—; regard with—; quicken—; scatter—; shower with—; stir up—; summon—; sustain—; turn to—; voice—; —blazes; —bubbles; —convulses; —embitters; —festers; —impels; —lingers; —maligns; —stings; —subsides; —ravages; —rends; —sunders; —wanes; —waxes.

(See abomination, animosity, antagonism, contempt, enmity, hostility, indignation, jealousy.)

HAUGHTINESS

adjectives
staring; unconscious; self-approving.

HAUGHTY

adverbs
arrogantly; deliberately; pompously; absurdly; unreasonably; unnecessarily; offensively; ridiculously; egotistically; insolently; bumptiously; imperiously; superciliously; impertinently; shamefully; laughably; swaggeringly; presumptuously; contemptuously; .contemptibly; justifiably; atrociously; extremely; unusually.

HAUL (v)

adverbs
economically; daily; professionally; customarily; speedily; laboriously; vigorously; painfully; lumberingly.

(See pull, draw, drag.)

HAUNCHES

adjectives
powerful; cold.

HAUNT

adjectives
genteel; childhood; authenticated; private; familiar; hideous; reptile; undergraduate; classical; cheerful; frequent; gay; frightful; native; brightened; strange; indigenous; delightful; swampy; deserted; weary; unaccustomed; popular; picturesque; mysterious; public; garden; melodious; shaded; inaccessible.

HAUNT (v)

adverbs
bewitchingly; lecherously; dejectedly; privately; hideously; frightfully; indigenously; mysteriously; bewilderingly.

(See persecute.)

HAVEN

adjectives
windless; beauteous; spacious; commodious; sheltered; wished.

verbs
admit to—; afford—;. bar from—; conceal in—; enter—; establish—; flee to—; lodge —; retreat to—; seek—; —accommodates; —consoles; —protects; —quarters; —shelters; —solaces; —supports; —welcomes.

(See harbor, shelter, refuge, retreat, asylum.)

HAVOC

verbs
anticipate—; come to—; create—; cry—; decry—; fortify against—; pass into—; play —; practise—; repair—; resist—; survey—; witness—; work—; wreak—; —confounds; —distresses.

(See destruction, waste, ruin.)

HAWK

verbs
—alights; —attacks; —dashes; —destroys; —dodges; —floats; —glides; —gyrates; —pounces on; —preys on; —prowls about; —sails; —scans; —screams; —screeches; —seizes; —severs; —skims; —soars; —somersaults; —squeals; —sweeps down; —twists; —swerves; —swoops; —wheels around; —whistles.

(See bird.)

HAWKER

verbs
license—; patronize—; —advertises; —attracts; —babbles; —barks; —barters; —bears; —bellows; —carries; —disposes of; —cries; —expatiates on; —jabbers; —plies; —prates about; —rants about; —rattles off; —spiels; —travels; —vends; —wanders.

(See merchant, salesman.)

HAY

adjectives
nutritious; crisping; new-mown; fragrant; sun-scorched; fresh; half-tanned.

verbs
basket—; bundle—; cart—; cock—; conceal —; consume—; fork—; hook—; load—; market—; mow—; pitch—; preserve—; rake —; press—; spade—; stack—; store—; toss —.

(See grass.)

HAYSTACK

adjectives
high-shouldered; proverbial.

HAZARD

adjectives
structural; lessened; unreasonable; reduced; glorious; industrial; temporary; human; intrinsic; specified; extreme; blind; skidding; physical; tremendous; awful; extraordinary; perilous; dust.

verbs
avoid—; dally with—; dare—; doubt—; eliminate—; expose to—; face—; incur—; obviate—; overcome—; preserve from—; risk—; run—; stand—; stake on—; venture —; view—; —allures; —endangers; —obstructs; —perils; —threatens.

(See chance, risk, danger, peril, stake.)

HAZARDOUS

adverbs
extremely; recklessly; perilously; presumably; obviously; manifestly; unreasonably; gloriously; tremendously; awfully; extraordinarily; mysteriously; ominously; alarmingly; terribly; attractively; alluringly; notoriously; undeniably; adventurously; exceedingly; strangely.

HAZE

adjectives
blossomy; luminous; suspended; soft; emotional; hueless; silver; blue; purple; smoke; gauzy; transparent; waterish; golden; mellowing; murky; burning; yellow; soft; faint; autumnal; amber; glittering; diaphanous; fictitious; Indian Summer; nebulous; iridescent; mournful; dim; gray; damp; misty; penumbral; somnolent; fluid; shimmering; reddish; sumptuous; moonlit; drowsy; vanishing; undefinable; deepening; shining; tremulous; glimmering; noontide; languorous.

verbs
clear—; disappear in—; falter in—; grope in—; lose in—; mingle with—; penetrate—; —develops; —dims; —encompasses; —lifts; —frosts; —hangs; —hovers over; —melts; —mists; —obscures; —rests on.

(See vapor, smoke, mist, fog, obscurity, clouds.)

HAZY

adverbs
dangerously; obscurely; dimly; incredibly; curiously; oddly; strangely; queerly; peculiarly; particularly; unpleasantly; unintelligibly; incomprehensibly; intentionally; deliberately; perilously; vexatiously; darkly; nebulously; uncertainly; foggily.

HEAD

adjectives
abominable; aching; acknowledged; addled; administrative; aggressive; ambitious; ample; antique; apprehensive; ashen; aspiring; asymmetrical; attentive; auburn; auspicious; averted; bald; bandaged; banished; battered; bedraggled; beautiful; beloved; bent; bewildering; blameless; blighted; blunt; bobbed; bowed; boyish; braided; brainless; bright; bristling; bruised; bullet; burnished; bursting; bushy; cavernous; classic; clean; clean-swept; clear; close-clipped; clumsy; coiffed; collective; comely; common; confused; copper; country; cowering; craven; cropped; crowned; crumpled; crushed; curious; curling; cursed; dark; dastardly; deathless; defending; deathlike; defenseless; defiant; delicate; delightful; desperate; devoted; diminished; disordered; dispirited; distant; dizzy; doll-like; downcast; downy; drooping; drowsy; drunken; dusky; early-silvering; elegant; elegantly-wigged; elfin; elongated; enticing; erect; executive; extravagant; fanciful; fascinating; fast-whitening; feathered; feeble; fine; finely-molded; firm; flame-red; flattened; flaunted; flaxen; fleshy; flowerless; forked; forlorn; frizzled; frowzy; gasping; ghastly; gleaming; glossy; golden; golden-mouthed; good-natured; gossipy; graceful; graduated; grizzled; grotesque; hairless; hairy; handsome; happy; haughty; heaven-saluting; heavy; heavy-jawed; heavy-jeweled; helmeted; helpless; henna; hideous; high-held; hoary; hooded; hopeless; horny; horrible; horrid; huge; hunted; ignorant; immortal; impassioned; imperial; imperious; impotent; impressive; impudent; impulsive; inclined; incongruous; inert; inexperienced; inquisitive; intellectual; intelligent; intermediate; intervening; iron-gray; irregular; irrevocable; joyful; keen; kingly; kinky; knavish; languid; large; learned; leonine; limp; lingering; little; living; logical; lofty; lolling; long; long-haired; lowered; low-lying; magnificent; mangled; massive; meek; melancholy; menacing; mighty; military; mob-

capped; molded; mossy; mottled; mountainous; muddy; mummylike; nightcapped; nodding; obsequious; obtuse; old; oval; ovate; overhanging; overheated; packed; palsied; pantomime; patchily-bald; patchy; patriarchal; patrician; pendent; pensive; periwigged; pictured; picturesque; plebeian; plumy; poetic; powdered; practical; presumptive; pretty; prostrate; proud; remarkable; queenly; racking; regal; responsible; restless; retracted; reverend; ridiculous; rolling; romantic; round; rude; saintly; satiny; saucy; sculptured; seemingly-devoted; sensible; shaggy; shaken; shamed; shapely; shameless; shaven; shiny; shrunken; sickly; silken; simple; sleek; sleeping; sleepless; slender; slightly-bald; small; smooth; snowy; sorrow-bowed; sovereign; spaniel; specular; spiritual; splendid; sprouting; square; stained; stately; steady; steaming; steel-hard; stupid; sturdy; suave; subtle; sufficient; sumptuous; sun-baked; sun-bleached; sunburned; tangled; thorny; thick-curled; thorn-crowned; throbbing; tilted; titled; titular; tombless; tonsured; tormenting; tossing; tousled; tremendous; troublesome; turbaned; twisted; ugly; uncovered; uncrowned; undishonored; unhonored; unkempt; unmellowed; unprotected; unshaven; unsuspecting; upheld; uptilted; upturned; veiled; venerated; virile; virtual; vivacious; vulgar; wabbling; wagging; weak; weary; weird; well-balanced; well-bleached; well-constructed; well-formed; well-poised; well-proportioned; well-shaped; whimsical; white-wigged; wigged; wobbly; woolly; yoke-encumbered; youthful.

verbs
adorn—; balance on—; bare—; bob—; bow—; cock—; crown—; erect—; hang—; incline—; involve—; pillow—; pound—; raise—; split—; surge to—; tilt—; wag—; waggle—; —buzzes; —protrudes; —reels; —sings; —spins; —swims; —throbs.

(See skull, mind, crown.)

HEADACHE

adjectives
frightful; agonizing; excruciating; satisfactory; attendant; racking; incessant; violent; splitting; insidious.

verbs
aggravate—; allay—; alleviate—; assail with—; attack with—; banish—; confine with—; cure—; dispose of—; ease—; groan with—; incur—; mitigate—; relieve—; remedy—; soothe—; subdue—; subject to—; temper—; throb with—; treat for—; —ensues; —indisposes; —prostrates; —returns; —weakens; —yields to.

(See pain.)

HEADDRESS

adjectives
gleaming; horned; immense.

HEADING

adjectives
cabalistic; comprehensive; general; definite.

HEADLAND

adjectives
graceful; misty; picturesque.

HEADLIGHT

adjectives
dazzling; blinding; blinking.

verbs
adjust—; dim—; extinguish—; focus—; regulate—; shun—; turn on—; —beams; —blinds; —dazzles; —flares; —flickers; —glares; —gleams; —illuminates; —penetrates; —reflects; —reveals; —shimmers; —shines.

(See light.)

HEADLINE

verbs
consult—; garner —s; hush down —s; pop into —s; scan —s; —alarms; —amazes; —announces; —asserts; —attracts; —awakens; —blares; —blazes; —blazons forth; —discloses; —disquiets; —hints; —misleads; —proclaims; —reports; —s protest; —suggests; —screams (colloq.); —shrieks; (colloq.).

(See title, advertisement, announcement, proclamation.)

HEADQUARTERS

adjectives
harried; military; ecclesiastical.

verbs
assume — at; convey to—; direct from—; dispatch to—; inhabit—; move into—; operate from—; order from—; repair to—; report to—; respect—; transact at—; —an-

nounces; —bars; —conceals; —decrees; —harbors; —issues; —reinstates; —shelters.

(See quarters, center, residence, house.)

HEADSTRONG

adverbs

stubbornly; wilfully; indomitably; doggedly; obdurately; obstinately; absurdly; ridiculously; unreasonably; violently; untractably; cantankerously; unmanageably; ungovernably; uncontrollably; persistently; inveterately; habitually; dreadfully; frightfully; inherently; incorrigibly; hopelessly; invincibly; sturdily; extremely.

HEAL (v)

adverbs

marvelously; miraculously; permanently; temporarily; superficially; medically; scientifically.

(See cure, repair.)

HEALING

adjectives

divine; sovereign; transient; miraculous.

HEALTH

adjectives

accustomed; decayed; comely; hardy; declining; failing; rude; tolerable; inexhaustible; robust; rustic; shattered; delicate; fundamental; glowing; particular; ever-uncertain; buxom; departing; saving; comparative; sweet; virile; ruddy; rose-tinted; vibrant; summer; absolute; universal; buoyant; positive; vigorous; precarious; glorious; moral; trying; blasted; flagrant; lonely; redundant; informing; frail; invigorating; dynamic; impaired; feeble; infirm; inexhaustible; exuberant; reacquired; required; physical; drunken; mental.

verbs

bankrupt—; battle for—; brace—; bubble with—; confer — upon; cultivate—; deprive of—; deteriorate in—; drain upon—; drink —; enjoy—; entrust—; foster—; hazard—; impair—; imperil—; improve—; influence —; injure—; insure—; lower—; maintain —; promote—; preoccupy with—; recapture —; restore to—; sacrifice—; sap—; shatter —; strive for—; sustain—; undermine—; —breaks; —continues; —fails; —improves; —suffers.

(See welfare, prosperity, strength.)

HEALTHFUL

adverbs

presumably; allegedly; bracingly; invigoratingly; restoratively; curatively; notoriously; reputably; famously; distinctly; remarkably; wonderfully; demonstrably; manifestly; evidently; undeniably; marvellously; unquestionably; extremely.

HEALTHY

adverbs

robustly; normally; unusually; admirably; wonderfully; fortunately; tolerably; fundamentally; comparatively; altogether; completely; buoyantly; vigorously; radiantly; gloriously; exuberantly; sturdily; happily; constitutionally; remarkably; excellently; magnificently; splendidly.

HEAP

adjectives

moldering; promiscuous; mountainous; tumbled; contorted; dismaying; enormous; undistinguishable; solemn; compost; wretched; writhing; convulsed; bony; wind-driven; sprawled; silvery; shapeless; lifeless; apparent; hoarded; inextricable; despicable.

verbs

accumulate into—; amass—; cast into—; collect in—; cone—; form—; gather into—; level—; lie in—; load into—; pile up—; relegate to—; rise in—; stand in—; store up—; throw into—; —grows; —overwhelms; —rises.

(See pile, mass.)

HEAP (v)

adverbs

massively; promiscuously; impartially; confusedly; profusely; indiscriminately; contortedly; convulsively; shapelessly; inextricably.

(See pile, accumulate.)

HEAR (v)

adverbs

accidentally; distinctly; occasionally; keenly; inevitably; audibly; dumbly; unconsciously; subconsciously; perpetually.

(See listen, perceive.)

HEARER

adjectives

eloquent; complacent; indefatigable; critical; attentive.

verbs

attract—s; bore —s; convince —s; crave—; enchant—; impress—; inflame—; inform—; instruct—; interest—; move—; obtain—; preach to—; tire—; weary—; —assents; —complies; —heeds; —judges; —learns; —listens; —perceives.

(See audience, listener, spectator.)

HEARING

adjectives

respectful; impaired; defective; harsh; distinct; impartial; favorable; younger.

verbs

accede to—; bar from—; block—; crave—; defer—; dull—; favor with—; grant—; judge—; prejudice—; preside at—; question —; rant at—; sustain—; weaken—.

(See meeting, investigation.)

HEARKEN (*v*)

adverbs

wistfully; respectfully; expectantly; eagerly; nervously; excitedly; cautiously; instinctively.

(See hear, perceive, listen.)

HEART

adjectives

abysmal; aching; adulterate; affectionate; affection-starved; agitated; alien; alienated; anguished; animated; anxious; ardent; arid; attentive; barren; bursting; base; beating; beauty-broken; beauty-loving; beclouded; beefy; befuddled; besotted; bewildering; black; bland; blank; blazoned; bleeding; blighted; boding; bounding; brave; breaking; breathless; broken; brute; bucklered; burdened; burning; bursting; busy; callous; careless; cheerful; cheering; cheery; childlike; clamorous; cold; compassionate; conscious; conservative; constant; constricted; contented; contrite; coreless; corrupted; courtly; covetous; cowardly; critical; crushed; dark; darkened; dauntless; dazzling; dead; deceitful; dedicated; defying; delicate; delighted; desolate; despairing; disappointed; discontented; diseased; divided; dormant; double; doubting; drained; dreary; drowsy; dull; duteous; eager; echoing; ecstatic; editorial; effeminate; emptied; enchanted; encouraged; energetic; entranced; erring; ever-beating; everlasting; exacting; excited; fainting; faithful; false; famished; famous; farseeing; fascinated; faultless; fearful; fecund; feeble; feminine; fevered; fiendish; fierce; fiery; firm; fleshy; flinty; wrung; fluttering; foolish; forestalled; forever-shattered; fragrance-laden; frail; frank; freer; fretted; frightened; frost-bound; frosted; frowning; frozen; gallant; general; generous; gentle; genuine; girlish; gleeful; graceless; grateful; gravel; grieved; guileless; half-snared; hammering; happy; haughty; heavenly; heavy; heedless; hereditary; heroic; hidden; humanitarian; humble; hungering; hurrying; hushed; idolatrous; impassioned; impious; impressionable; improvident; impulsive; inconstant; indecent; individual; indolent; indurated; inmost; inner; innocent; intense; irritable; joyous; kind; kindling; kindred; laboring; lacerated; laggard; languid; laughing; lavish; leaden; life-giving; light; lively; living; lofty; lonely; long; long-enduring; long-pent; long-wandering; longing; loudly-beating; love-pampered; loving; low; low-hushed; maddening; manful; manly; marble; mean; meditative; merry; mighty; moist; mourning; mountain; moved; mysterious; mystic; naked; noble; obdurate; open; oppressed; orphaned; outraged; overburdened; overflowing; overfull; overladen; overworked; pained; palpitating; passionate; paternal; pearly; penitent; pent; perfect; perplexed; perturbed; perverse; pinched; pious; pitiless; pitying; plighted; poisoned; poor; popish; popular; poverty-stricken; private; profane; profound; propelled; prophetic; proud; pulsating; puny; pure; pusillanimous; quaking; queenly; queer; quenched; quick-beating; quick-breathed; quickened; rapt; rapture-filled; ravaged; rebellious; reckless; relenting; repressed; responsive; restless; returning; reverent; riotous; rising; rocky; rough; royal; rude; rugged; rusting; saddened; satisfied; scented; scheming; scorching; seated; self-accusing; sensitive; shadowy; shallow; sheer; shuddering; sickly; sincere; sinewy; singing; single; sinking; slight; slow; smitten; smothered; softened; solitary; somber; sore; sorrowful; spotless; stagnant; stainless; stalwart; starry; steadfast; sterner; still-renewed; stirring; stony; stout; straitened; stricken; strong; struggling; stubborn; sturdy; suffocating; sullen; sunny; superstitious; susceptible; swelling; sweltering; sympathetic; tavern-like; tempest-tossed; tender; terrified;

thankful; thoughtless; thought-propelled; throbbing; thumping; tortured; tossed; towering; trembling; tremulous; troubled; trusting; tumultuous; turbulent; tyrannous; unassisted; uncaged; unconjectured; undivided; uneasy; unfettered; unfortified; unfrozen; unguarded; universal; unmoved; unpurchasable; unquickened; unquiet; unselfish; unsophisticated; unsuspecting; untutored; unwavering; unworn; unyielding; upright; vacant; veritable; virgin; wakening; wandering; warm; wasting; waxing; wayward; weak; weary; well-contented; well-disposed; wicked; widowed; wild; wintry; withering; womanly; wooing; wordless; worldly; worried; worshipping; wounded; wretched; yearning; zealous.

verbs
appeal to—; beguile—; chill—; depress—; dilate—; ease—; engage—; enshrine in—; furrow—; gather—; gladden—; harden—; hug to—; lay open—; melt—; mend—; pluck at—; pour out—; smite—; stab to—; stimulate—; take to—; warm—; wring—; —awakens; —betrays; —bleeds; —blinds; —contracts; —craves; —expands; —fails; —hungers; —jumps; —misgives; —overflows; —palpitates; —pines; —pounds; —prompts; —quakes; —races; —responds; —sinks; —softens; —swells; —throbs; —ticks; —yearns.

(See essence, core, pulse, organ, affection, passion, courage, strength.)

HEARTBEAT

adjectives
tumultuous; vexing.

HEARTBREAK

adjectives
terrible; human.

HEART DISEASE

verbs
convalesce from— —; correct— —; cure of — —; examine for— —; incur— —; indicate— —; recover from— —; resist— —; suffer from— —; treat— —; — —degenerates; — —dilates; — —menaces; — —pains; — —ravages; — —subsides.

(See disease, sickness, malady.)

HEARTH

adjectives
blazing; domestic; lonely; imperial; glittering; familiar; heavenly; glowing; inmost; desolated; tiled; hospitable; altar; ancestral; dreary; lowly; sordid.

HEARTLESSNESS

adjectives
cruel; perfect; undisguised; criminal.

verbs
bare—; brook—; conceal—; deny—; excuse—; steep in—; wither into—; —bites; —contrives; —crushes; —dejects; —despairs; —embitters; —lurks; —murders; —pains; —strikes; —wounds.

(See cruelty.)

HEARTY

adverbs
sincerely; enthusiastically; graciously; spontaneously; warily; impressively; rapturously; eagerly; cordially; impetuously; impulsively; openly; splendidly; sympathetically; devotedly; cheerily; jovially; entirely; exceptionably; extremely; unusually; noticeably; conspicuously; especially.

HEAT

adjectives
primitive; intense; intercepted; parching; hardening; dulling; destructive; resisting; sulphurous; automatic; self-regulating; unifying; genial; ordinary; subterranean; excessive; steaming; shimmering; white; fervent; gray; heartburning; yellow; incandescent; dancing; breathless; blood-red; imminent; midday; prickly; internal; sweltering; fierce; subtle; central; controlled; oppressive; tempered; incarnate; scalding; blistering; ferocious; feverish; heroic; fortunate; visceral; vague; withering; imperial; scorching; restless; blinding; tremulous; torturous; masculine; radiant; deadly; incremental; defying; infernal; furious; palpable; saturating; wet; devoted; overpowering; polished; rash; false; aching; clean; efficient; dependable; effortless; healthful; boisterous; instant; steady; terrestrial; boiling; unspeakable; tropical; love-devouring; uniform; intolerable; bristling; generous; luminous; beneficial; glowing; perpendicular; savage; unendurable; suffocating; kindly; animal; brooding; fantastic; sickening; fierce; quivering; stifling; freezing; stimulating; intolerable; exceptional; fluent, temperate; extreme; concentrated; continuous; expensively-produced; transmuted; burning,

verbs
apply—; bask in—; control—; foment—; generate—; maintain—; measure—; raise —; regulate—; relieve—; sustain—; swelter in—; swoon from—; transform into—; treat with—; utilize—; —blights; —blisters; —encompasses; —escapes; —evolves; —parches; —scorches; —stifles; —subsides.
(See fire, flame.)

HEAT (v)

adverbs
fiercely; intensely; destructively; sulphurously; automatically; excessively; subtly; oppressively; witheringly; scorchingly; palpably; blisteringly; tropically; intolerably; beneficially; suffocatingly; concentratedly.
(See warm.)

HEATH

adjectives
flowery; vast; uncultivated; blasted; magnificent; pastoral; bleak; tottering; menacing; stultifying; ugly; murky; dismal.

verbs
clip—; crop—; cut—; grow—; plant—; roof with—; tend—; thatch with—; utilize —; —abounds; —banks; —blazes; —flourishes; —flowers; —perfumes; —stretches.
(See land, area, plant, flower.)

HEATHEN

adjectives
benighted; tiresome.

HEATHENISH

adverbs
shamelessly; cruelly; deliberately; grossly; ignorantly; savagely; brutally; barbarously; unconscionably; inordinately; terribly; dreadfully; unbelievably; inexpressibly; atrociously; shamefully; brazenly; ostentatiously; openly; crudely; blindly; darkly; coarsely; rudely; brutishly; shockingly; appallingly.

HEAVE (v)

adverbs
bodily; fulsomely; breathlessly; spasmodically; tumultuously; intermittently; laboriously; oppressively.
(See throw, lift.)

HEAVEN

adjectives
frosty; righteous; luminous; cloudless; precipitating; overhanging; bounteous; transfigured; untrod; starry; sublunar; clear; subjugated; high; bending; miniature; smiling; avenging; tranquil; angry; broad; firmamental; unfolding; swelling; bending; unrelenting; gladsome; spangled; insulted; unpavilioned; troubled; merciful; unimagined; clear-eyed; naked; unclouded; pitying; crystal; hollow; influent; frowning; slumberless; impenetrable; jealous; deepening; unimaginable; sweet; vaulty; cloudless; piteous; encompassing; unpitying; remote; glorious; star-deserted; crystalline; unobstructed; immeasurable; middle; material; warm-colored; pinky-purple; bland; placid; stainless; sick; scoffing; propitious; flaming; deaf.

verbs
abide in—; ascend to—; bless in—; conduct to—; contemplate—; deny—; depart for—; depict—; descend from—; dwell in—; enthrone in—; gain—; long for—; look up to —; offend—; prepare for—; prevail in—; rail at—; reign in—; reside in—; rest in—; rise to—; seek—; steal into—; transport to—; trust in—; visit in—; win—; —s dazzle; —s look down; —s open; —promises; —radiates.

(See paradise, sky, Providence, .God.)

HEAVENLY

adverbs
delectably; ecstatically; divinely; utterly; altogether; consummately; ineffably.

HEAVINESS

adjectives
unaccustomed; palpable; dreamy; lifeless; curious; embraced; languid; singular; deceptive; moody.

verbs
augment—; burden with—; cast—over; counterbalance—; discard—; drowse under —; dump—; enter with a sense of—; lament —; seize with—; shed—; —angers; —dejects; —displeases; —enrages; —manifests; —oppresses; —saddens; counterpoise—.

(See weight, gravity, sadness, despondency, dejection.)

HEAVINGS

adjectives

tumultuous; needless; intermittent.

HEAVY

adverbs

grievously; financially; painfully; economically; unwarrantably; dreadfully; pitifully; gravely; unendurably; increasingly; unnecessarily; inescapably; seriously; insufferably; dangerously; unusually; strangely; unfortunately; cumbrously; monstrously; oppressively; aggravatingly; vexatiously; unjustly; tragically; embarrassingly.

HECKLER

verbs

"bounce" out—; court—; encounter—; oust —; remove—; subdue—; —annoys; —bests; —bothers; —catechizes; —chastises; —contends; —derides; —examines; —irks; —irritates; —plagues; —questions; —scolds; —teases; —wrangles.

(See pest, audience.)

HECTIC

adverbs

feverishly; terribly; tensely; excitably; emotionally; crucially; breathlessly; hysterically; impetuously; poignantly; thrillingly; violently; hotly; angrily; decidedly; bitterly; intensely; peculiarly; curiously; strangely; queerly; extremely; inexplicably; unaccountably; unwarrantably; unusually.

HEDGE

adjectives

lofty; wayside; impenetrable; rustic; decorative; thorny; prickly; flowery.

HEED

adjectives

prudent; accurate; immediate; absent.

HEED (v)

adverbs

carefully; scrupulously; painstakingly; anxiously; prudently; cautiously; instinctively; characteristically; habitually.

(See attend, notice, regard.)

HEEDLESS

adverbs

provokingly; intolerably; inherently; habitually; thoughtlessly; incorrigibly; stupidly; nonchalantly; indifferently; wilfully; obstinately; stubbornly; sadly; grievously; cruelly; pathetically; unwisely; foolishly; frivolously; inexcusably; recklessly; rashly; dangerously; deplorably; lamentably; incurably; shockingly; frightfully.

HEEL

adjectives

hindermost; unmesmerized; official; wavering; hoofed; despotic; miry; flying; cloven; heavy.

verbs

blister—; click—s; clutch at—s; cool—s; crush with—; drive—into; hang up by—s; squat on—s; trample beneath—; —s clatter; —s kick up dust.

(See foot, end, bottom.)

HEIFER

adjectives

illustrious; languid; breathing.

HEIGHT

adjectives

level; pinnacle; considerable; winged; excessive; unsuspected; glimmering; definite; prayerful; azure; wooded; extreme; odorous; pernicious; opposite; embattled; sequestered; serene; gigantic; hoary; mountain; empty; dizzy; commanding; tiptoeing; entrenched; glittering; extravagant; windworn; crystal; preposterous; towering; dark; craggy; moon-bewildering; garden; considerable; grand; sunlit; yonder; streamriven; fixed; heavenly; immortal; fantastic; mounting; reachless; impressive; matchless; panoramic; helpless; immeasurable; divine; daring; obvious; empyreal; utmost; heroic; lofty; bristling; perilous; superb; dusky; eloquent; slippery; desolate; gleaming; barren; sovereign; immense; barometric; melancholy; distant; emerald; rocky; stately; adverse; unscalable; noble; massy; sunscorched; bleak; appointed; waxen; grassy; historic; fortified; starry-headed; inordinate; difficult; full; gray; grave; rugged; precipitous; supernal; financial.

verbs

ascend to—; attain—; attempt—; average —; depend on—; descend—; discover—; fall from—; gain—; mount—s; raise to—; reach—s; rise to—; scale—; set on—; situate on—; soar to—; view from—; —amazes; —slopes down.

(See altitude, stature, eminence, zenith, summit.)

HEINOUS

adverbs
atrociously; abominably; diabolically; criminally; brutally; shamefully; basely; feloniously; flagitiously; flagrantly; deliberately; foully; villainously; viciously; wickedly; incalculably; iniquitously; immeasurably; inexpressibly; grossly; shamelessly; indecently.

HEIR

adjectives
spiritual; immediate; unexpected; lineal; natural; indolent; unwitting; blissful; legitimate; recognized; lavish; contentious; beauteous; joyous; adopted; prodigal; illustrious; peasant-born; true; spendthrift; gilded; impatient.

verbs
apportion to—s; bear—; bequeath to—; curse—; endow—; enrich—; extort from—; guard—; impose on—; nominate—; present with—; prey on—s; tax—s; will to—; yearn for—; —acquires; —is entitled to; —overjoys; —succeeds.

(See offspring, child.)

HELL

adjectives
pitiless; multitudinous; impious; dismal; high-vaulted; yawning; gratuitous; incipient; tangible; monster-teeming; ever-burning; social; inevitable; fabled; jealous; fearsome; inextricable; earth-consuming.

verbs
boil in—; burn in—; chain in—; condemn to—; damn to—; deliver from—; descend to—; doom to—; dwell in—; embark for—; escape—; lead to—; parch in—; plunge into—; punish in—; purify in—; sink in—; torment in—; torture in—; —breaks loose; —devours; —flames; —gapes; —scorches; —shadows; —threatens.

(See torment, torture, flame.)

HELLISH

adverbs
barbarously; fiendishly; inhumanly; inexpressibly; unutterably; indecently; abysmally; accursedly; basely; flagitiously; nefariously; enormously; monstrously; outrageously; obscenely.

HELM

adjectives
thronging; prosperous; passive; obedient.

verbs
abandon—; control—; course—; ease—; govern—; handle—; lash to—; menace—; manipulate—; meddle with—; mind—; operate—; order to—; post at—; slander—; steer at—; wrestle with—; —cares; —directs; —guides.

(See wheel, guidance, helmet, pilot, guide, command; control, administration.)

HELMET

adjectives
pith; vicious-looking; fire; leather; superb; spiked; conical; flat-topped; glittering.

verbs
arm with—; attire in—; balance—; bear—; break through—; furnish—; open—; pad—; penetrate—; pierce—; polish—; provide—; supply—; top with—; —clanks; —crowns; —defends; —prevents; —protects; —reflects; —resists; —rests on.

(See hat.)

HELP

adjectives
indispensable; senseless; agreeable; distinct; explanatory; simple; invaluable; adventitious; slender; ever-present; effective; sympathetic; availing; unbiased; beneficial; relative; mutual; timely; injurious.

verbs
afford—; clamor for—; consent to—; furnish—; invoke—; obtain—; present—; procure—; profit by—; promise—; provide—; purchase—; refuse—; render—; seek—; —ameliorates; —amends; —augments; —benefits; —delivers; —extricates; —relieves; —remedies.

(See aid, assistance, remedy, relief, succor, co-operation, support.)

HELP (*v*)

adverbs
chivalrously; effectually; materially; cheerfully; perversely; personally; generously; precipitately; leisurely; adventitiously; sympathetically; beneficially; mutually.

(See aid, assist, alleviate.)

HELPFUL

adverbs

ingratiatingly; amiably; delightfully; obsequiously; ostentatiously; pompously; unspeakably; amazingly; providentially; accommodatingly; cordially; willingly; eagerly; courteously; habitually; unusually; significantly; heartily; resolutely; dutifully; civilly; servilely; loftily; exceedingly; extremely; gravely; graciously; charmingly; freely; gruffly; roughly; awkwardly; childishly; lovingly; affectionately; skillfully; politely; bluntly; generously; splendidly; surprisingly.

HELPFULNESS

adjectives

patient; cordial; mutual; unassuming.

HELPLESS

adverbs

pitiably; weakly; incurably; intentionally; gloomily; abjectly; depressingly; desolately; inconceivably; ludicrously; comically; horribly; woefully; dismally; gravely; seriously; inconsolably; sadly; desperately; obviously; unreasonably; piteously; tragically; actually; absolutely.

HELPLESSNESS

adjectives

silent; ignominious; sudden; revealed; unconscious; utter; galling; bitter.

verbs

accuse of—; alleviate—; attack—; conceal —; degenerate into—; discover—; grieve over—; increase—; lament—; relieve—; remedy—; retire into—; ridicule—; scorn —; sink into—; —amazes; —angers; —crushes; —despairs; —distresses; —oppresses.

(See weakness.)

HELPMATE

adjectives

devoted; feeble; imperious.

HELTER-SKELTER

adverbs

horribly; laughingly; hilariously; precipitately; confusedly; boisterously; joyously; triumphantly; hastily; breathlessly; impetuously; riotously; tumultuously; uproariously; madly; wildly; inordinately; extraordinarily; tempestuously; happily.

HEMISPHERIC

adverbs

broadly; surprisingly; expansively; extensively; liberally; hospitably; comprehensively; increasingly; generously; magnanimously; necessarily; commonly; strangely; designedly; intentionally; significantly; preferably.

HEMORRHAGE

verbs

arrest—; check—; control—; delay—; diminish—; excite—; induce—; prevent—; produce—; repress—; risk—; stem—; succumb to—; suffer—; treat—; —ceases; —diminishes; —endangers; —ensues; —gushes; —pours; —recurs; —spouts.

(See discharge, bleeding, blood.)

HEN

adjectives

scrawny; rained-on; cackling; maternal; speckled; teeming (pl); unsung; matronly-minded.

verbs

(See chicken, bird.)

HERALD

adjectives

pale; perfect; tempestuous; flame-tongued; sad-faced.

HERB

adjectives

winged; aromatic; tender; fragrant; artificial; vivid; bespangling; poisonous; tufted; enchanted; beneficial; culinary; trodden; baneful; pungent; grassy.

verbs

administer—; collect—s; crop—s; cultivate —s; devour—; feast on—s; feed on—s; flavor with—s; garnish with—s; gather—s; market—s; overgrow with—s; prescribe—s; yield to—; —abounds; —cures; —flowers; —stimulates; —withers.

(See plant, grass.)

HERBAGE

adjectives

sprouting; autumnal.

HERCULEAN

adverbs

distressingly; arduously; obscurely; obviously; evidently; notably; desperately; formidably; toilsomely; laboriously; operosely; stoutly; gigantically; hardily; overwhelmingly; robustly; irresistibly; inexhaustibly; wirily; unconquerably; invincibly; astonishingly; remarkably; inexpressibly; admirably; wondrously; enormously; onerously; extraordinarily; tremendously.

HERD

adjectives
bellowing; stolid; fear-crazed; vulgar; weanling; scaly; meager; wild; wanton; maddening; weaponless; turbulent; servile; careless; drooping; wandering; innumerable (pl); untamable; countless (pl); incomparable; quiet; gentle; sarcastic; nightmare; diminishing; woolly; profane; galloping; tempting.

verbs
abandon—; assemble in—; associate with—; break—; breed in—; cluster in—; congregate in—; control—; destroy—; drive—; gather in—; guard—; join—; lead—; mingle among—; prey on—; rule—; single out of—; slaughter—; stall—; stampede—; —lows; —grazes; —perishes; —ranges; —treks.

(See rabble, crowd, flock.)

HEREDITARY

adverbs
supposedly; probably; definitely; questionably; sadly; unfortunately; allegedly; highly; occasionally; decidedly; basically; intrinsically; invariably; naturally; ineradicably; lamentably; possibly; undoubtedly.

HEREDITY

adjectives
contaminated; established; epileptic; definite; patent.

verbs
boast of—; claim—; degenerate from—; disparage—; doubt—; envy—; interest in —; praise—; renounce—; revere—; revile —; scorn—; stain—; trace—; transmit by —; —burdens; —constrains; —decays; —governs; —heightens; —influences; —instills; —polishes; —weakens.

(See ancestors, birth, father.)

HERESY

adjectives
literary; passing; downright.

verbs
abhor—; accuse of—; confess—; create—; curb—; dare—; defeat—; denounce—; destroy—; excommunicate for—; incur—; interpret as—; protest—; renounce—; revenge —; ridicule—; scan—; shake off—; work—; —denies; —enrages; —mocks; —offends; —scoffs; —taints; —tolerates.

HERETIC

verbs
approve—; burn—; consider—; curb—; denounce—; deprive—; disapprove of—; disperse—s; ignore—; lament—; punish—; regard—; reject—; ridicule—; scoff at—; tolerate—; weed out—s; —denies; —disbelieves; —disobeys; —disregards; —enrages; —mocks; —offends; —preaches; —professes.

HERETICS

adjectives
obstinate; upstart; vile; gruff; brash.

HERITAGE

adjectives
national; rich; common; splendid; precious; deathless; destined; princely; classic; inalienable; unexpected; useless; noble; sempiternal; dramatic.

verbs
acquire—; administer—; allot—; bequeath —; bestow—; bless—; cherish—; claim—; curse—; devolve—; endow—; entitle to—; envy—; execute—; extort—; govern—; present—; preserve—; provide—; reserve—; shear of—; stipulate—; transmit—; —devolves; —overjoys; —provides.

(See inheritance, birthright, estate.)

HERMIT

adjectives
stalwart; genial; lesser; lone; withered; solitary.

HERO

adjectives
unambitious; grotesque; noble; ghostly; beauteous; self-made; admirable; laureled; wonder-working; overbearing; martyred; spiritual; chivalrous; scatterbrained; ornithological; fettered; picturesque; classic; omnipresent; unassuming; stalwart; fabulous; incompetent; energetic; honored; renowned; contemporary; mythic; legendary; vulgar; gentle; immaculate; doughty; stout;

worthy; transcendental; portentous; immortal; barbarous; discomfited; erring; illustrious; incomparable; splendid.

verbs
acclaim—; admire—; cheer—; decorate—; distinguish—; emulate—; enhance—; esteem —; glorify—; hail as—; honor—; identify oneself with—; indebt to—; pity—; respect —; reverence—; shoulder—; supplant—; sympathize with—; venerate—; worship—; —achieves; —braves; —conquers; —courts; —deserves; —excels in; —fades; —regales; —rescues; —rises; —suffers; —withers.
(See champion, character, actor, God.)

HEROIN

verbs
addict to—; analyze—; confiscate—; crave —; derive—from; dissolve—; dose with—; drug with—; forbid—; import—; ingest—; inject—; insufflate—; smuggle—; subject to —; —allays; —anaesthetizes; —depresses; —enslaves; —numbs; —relieves; —victimizes.
(See narcotic, drug.)

HEROINE

adjectives
persecuted; peerless; sentimental; fallen; durable; revengeful.

verbs
acclaim—; identify oneself with—; worship —; —beguiles; —bewitches; —blushes; —captivates; —charms; —enchants; —enraptures; —entrances; —fascinates; —gladdens; —ravishes; —shrinks; —suffers; —transports; —wins.
(See character, hero.)

HEROISM

adjectives
volcanic; unmatched; reckless; romantic; foredoomed; cowering; potential; fierce; intolerant; dauntless; latent; melodramatic; ostentatious; vulgar; showy.

verbs
abate—; aim at—; commend—; conduct with—; contemplate—; crown with—; display—; emulate—; extol—; frown upon—; illustrate—; imitate—; laud—; perform—; reflect—; reward—; sacrifice to—; —dazzles; —glorifies; —merits; —sparkles.
(See valor, courage, bravery, fortitude.)

HERON

verbs
—calls; —circles; —colonizes; —croaks; —fishes; —flaps; —gossips; —impales; —roosts; —shies away; —snaps up; —soars; —squawks; —wades; —wings.
(See bird.)

HERONS

adjectives
long-necked; crested; great; night; long-beaked; stately; graceful.

HESITANCY

adjectives
strange; grave; characteristic; reserved; courteous; apparent; awkward; blushing.

HESITANT

adverbs
capriciously; captiously; uncertainly; reluctantly; doubtfully; stammeringly; changeably; indecisively; timidly; weakly; irresolutely; deliberately; falteringly; waveringly; feebly; tormentingly; infirmly; unsteadily; tremulously; significantly; fearfully.

HESITATE (*v*)

adverbs
fatally; ominously; dubiously; thoughtfully; inexplicably; imperceptibly; timorously; characteristically; coquettishly; momentarily.
(See vacillate, falter.)

HESITATION

adjectives
sensitive; obvious; imitative; painful; surprised; charming; inexplicable; imperceptible; timorous; controlled; characteristic; awkward; coquettish; momentary; ineloquent.

verbs
banish—; conceal—; decry—; deny—; grieve over—; lament—; pretend—; reproach—; shrink in—; stagger in—; stammer in—; tear with—; —confounds; —endangers; —frustrates; —haunts; —loses; —perplexes; —prevents; —shames; —tortures; —embarrasses.
(See doubt, uncertainty.)

HEW (*v*)

adverbs
roughly; bravely; ambitiously; vigorously; industriously; stalwartly; robustly; untiringly.
(See cut, sever.)

HIDE

adjectives
tawny; spotted; shaggy; strange-colored; swarthy; horny; silken; callous; precious; crafty; withered; tanned.

HIDE (v)

adverbs
effectually; obscurely; modestly; instinctively; completely; craftily; skillfully; subtly; avariciously.
(See conceal, mask, cloak.)

HIDEBOUND

adverbs
inordinately; deplorably; unfortunately; stubbornly; obstinately; oddly; curiously; provincially; narrowly; dogmatically; intolerantly; fanatically; immovably; inflexibly; perversely; tenaciously; doggedly; mulishly; ungenerously; terribly; notably; notoriously.

HIDEOUS

adverbs
outrageously; inordinately; extraordinarily; unbearably; grossly; terribly; indescribably; starkly; grotesquely; immoderately; monstrously; piteously; cruelly; shockingly; dreadfully; pathetically; horribly; repulsively; inexpressibly; appallingly.

HIDEOUSNESS

adjectives
naked; unshaped; outward; grim; gross.

HIDING-PLACE

adjectives
primeval; undisturbed; criminal; undiscovered; discreet.

HIERARCHY

adjectives
lofty; definite; centralized; disciplined; administrative; apostolical.

HIGH

adverbs
eminently; prominently; gigantically; monstrously; terrifyingly; incredibly; inordinately; supremely; toweringly; enormously; immensely; infinitely; astonishingly; essentially; extraordinarily; fabulously; preposterously; prodigiously; unsuitably; impossibly; confoundedly; frightfully; horribly; immeasurably; incalculably; delightfully; gloriously; marvellously; particularly; peculiarly; dangerously; perilously; hazardously; singularly; strikingly; woefully; cruelly; awfully; wonderfully; miraculously.

HIGHBORN

adverbs
aristocratically; nobly; notably; gently; undeniably; obviously; evidently; unmistakably; unquestionably; proudly; consciously; illustriously; eminently; admittedly; palpably; undeniably; avowedly; allegedly; probably.

HIGHNESS

adjectives
imperial; incredible; unspeakable; breathless.

HIGH-SPIRITED

adverbs
unusually; delightfully; infectiously; ineffably; happily; radiantly; irrepressibly; hilariously; boisterously; blithely; merrily; mirthfully; teasingly; mockingly; contagiously; charmingly; immeasurably; ardently.

HIGHWAY

adjectives
crooked; invisible; leaf-hung; imperial; dusty; dubious; traffic-crowded; smooth; sleek; arterial; tree-lined; panoramic.

verbs
block—; cruise on—; drive along—; follow —; frequent—; keep to—; laud—; motor along—; patrol—; perceive—; protect—; roll along—; stream down—; traverse—; tread—; —connects; —divides; —endures; —gleams; —leads to; —winds.
(See road, thoroughfare, way.)

HIGHWAYMAN

verbs
apprehend—; defend against—; execute—; hang—; overtake—; protect from—; pursue—; resist—; —appropriates; —deprives of; —escapes; —frequents; —frightens; —gorges on; —plagues; —preys upon; —terrorizes; —victimizes.
(See robber, thief.)

HILARIOUS

adverbs
uproariously; merrily; heartily; noisily; infectiously; contagiously; enthusiastically; effervescently; audaciously; mischievously; intensely; uncommonly; deliriously; unbe-

comingly; convulsively; irrepressibly; unmanageably; irresponsibly; joyously; blithely; enviably; delightfully; sociably; foolishly; nonsensically; senselessly; consummately; utterly; unrestrainedly; uncontrollably; youthfully; magnificently; jubilantly; inexplicably; warrantably; gleefully.

HILARITY

adjectives
audacious; mischievous; intense; reckless; increasing; delirious; unbecoming; misdirected.

verbs
attempt—; conceal—; conduce to—; enliven to—; excite to—; feign—; flush with—; inspire—; overcome with—; provoke—; reduce—; season with—; spend in—; temper —; —brightens; —diverts; —fades; —flows; —palls; —pours from; —seizes; —solaces; —tires; —wanes; —wearies.
(See mirth, glee, gayety, jollity.)

HILL

adjectives
gleaming; moon-tortured; green-clad; emerald; autumn-tinted; moon-swept; dense; verdured; moonlit; silver; verdant; radiant; silent; shimmering; bright; stony; tawny; soft; rolling; gentle; peak; shadowed; scarred; rock-ribbed; primeval; neighboring; dripping; innocent; reverberating; ferny; naked; forest-cinctured; long-contested; alluring; picturesque; arid; delicious; slanting; soilless; heathery; dry; parched; savage; desolate; ghastly; treeless; volcanic; lower; square-topped; uprooted; eternal; full-grassed; lavish; granite; terraced; breezy; heaped; ever-changing; windy; environing; many-faced; vine-covered; overhanging; massive; bare; steep; incomparable; squalid; encompassing; disturbed; sequestered; pastoral; haughty; bald; bleak; commanding; breezy; ancient; folded; pulpy; conical; cup-shaped; quaking; parched; steadfast; skirting; everlasting; undulating; opprobrious; huge; inferior; barren; disconsolate; invisible; chalk; low-lying; alluvial; rolling; smooth; dawning; wooded; remote; defiant; eternal; silent; dominating; romantic; pestilent; rhododendron; distant; thicketed; sunny; dusty; windy; colored; precipitous; echo-giving; sun-baked; classical; retiring; cindery; pine-clad; spotless; milken; swelling; carven; monumental; forked; savage; timbered; rocky; rock-ribbed; answering; ice-clad; templed; leaping; heathery; pastoral; reeking; distorted; detached; high; utmost; flowery; populous; bustling; fertile; bedimmed; dreary; dark; cloud-capped; sun-kissed; umbrageous; misty; lowering; superb; billowy; consecrated; sterile; craglike; dewy; trembling.

verbs
ascend—; cap—; clear away—; coast down —; crown—; descend—; dwell in —s; heap into —s; observe from—; peep over—; retreat to —s; scale—; settle in —s; stray to —s; survey from—; toil up—; tumble down —; —arises; —charms; —s dot; —s encroach; —s entrance; —flanks; —s greet; —interposes; —shades; —shadows; mount —.
(See heap, mountain.)

HILLOCK

adjectives
scattered (pl); mortal; isolated; palmy; snowy.

HILLSIDE

adjectives
exposed; rounded; blackened; placid; flower-starred; pine-plumed; swelling; sunburned; slippery; sloping; stony; rocky; steep.

verbs
belt—; conceal in—; conduct to—; devastate —; frequent—; inhabit—; mount—; outline —; ravage—; roam—; rove—; settle on—; stream down—; survey—; —blooms; —charms; —flowers; —slopes.
(See hill, bank.)

HILLTOP

adjectives
arduous; breezy; grassy; sun-begoldened.

HIND

adjectives
loitering; heartless.

HINDER (v)

adverbs
unendurably; insurmountably; irritatingly; tremendously; irksomely; painfully; burdensomely.
(See retard, obstruct.)

HINDRANCE

adjectives
outward; tremendous; insurmountable.

verbs
condemn—; contribute—; decry—; endure —; erect—; grieve over—; lament—; object to—; overcome—; present—; provide—; remove—; —embarrasses; —frustrates; —objects; —perplexes; —perturbs; —prevents; —threatens.

(See obstruction, obstacle, interruption, delay, restraint, disadvantage.)

HINGE

verbs
attach with—; bind with—; hang on—; join with—; lift off—; lubricate—; manipulate on—; nail—; pin—; pivot on—; prop on—; rest on—; revolve on—; swing on—; turn on—; —groans; —supports; —unites; —yields.

(See joint.)

HINGES

adjectives
rusty; rusted; pregnant; musical.

HINT

adjectives
significant; practical; private; curious; advantageous; prompt; dark; rude; lavish; sundry (pl); ineffectual; equivocal; grotesque; doubtful; oblique; vague; suggestive; friendly; occult; elusive; unintelligible; insinuated; intimated.

verbs
afford—; catch—; comprehend—; contemplate—; convey—; derive — from; heed—; ignore—; infer—; interpret—; perceive—; proffer—; provide—; respond to—; seek—; seize on—; suggest—; weigh—; —distresses; —implies; —indicates; —insinuates; —promises.

(See intimation, insinuation, suggestion.)

HINT (*v*)

adverbs
barely; delicately; obscurely; wickedly; privately; bashfully; significantly; curiously; vaguely; suggestively; unintelligibly.

(See intimate, imply.)

HIPPOPOTAMUS

verbs
—ambles; —bathes; —charges; —crushes; —damages; —dives; —floats; —s herd; —puffs; —scoops; —sinks; —snorts; —submerges; —splashes; —swims; —tramples.

(See animal.)

HIPS

adjectives
supple; spacious; smooth; rounded; flabby; powerful; streamlined; swaying; bolstered; slim; sinewy; snake-like.

HIRELING

adjectives
sanguinary; base.

HISS

verbs
deride with—; disapprove with —s; dread —; drive away with —s; emit—; express in —; greet with—; ignore—; inject—; overhear—; revile with—; scorn with—; utter —; voice in—; whisper—; —drowns; —disparages; —disturbs; —heckles.

(See sound, noise.)

HISS (*v*)

adverbs
menacingly; vehemently; venomously; sibilantly; spitefully; viciously.

(See whisper, sound, sing.)

HISTORIAN

adjectives
eloquent; contemporary; romancing; hostile; elegant; fact-grubbing; ecclesiastical; celebrated; apt.

HISTORIC

adverbs
minutely; authoritatively; authentically; accurately; specifically; allegedly; avowedly; evidently; obviously; verifiably; graphically; scarcely; valuably; splendidly; eminently; significantly; serviceably; admirably; indubitably; undeniably.

HISTORICAL

adverbs
slightly; suggestively; traditionally; pleasantly; entertainingly; reminiscently; extravagantly; crudely; accurately; extraordinarily; dully; monotonously; tiresomely; artistically; thrillingly; graphically; entirely; instructively; nostalgically; broadly; generally; altogether; closely.

HISTORY

adjectives
administrative; thrilling; painful; fashion; family; significant; ecclesiastical; contemporary; much-revised; educational; diplo-

matic; stormy; dazzling; tragic; informal; revolutionary; fateful; detailed; typographical; limited; subsequent; pertinent; simple; painstaking; scathing; episodical; future; institutional; human; lamentable; uneventful; monumental; inglorious; noble; pathetic; spiritual; artistic; chronological; natural; eminent; curious; remote; consecutive; authentic; sacred; profane; feigned; forgotten; informative; terrible; impartial; tumultuous; confused; picturesque; incontrovertible; financial; commercial; secret; ancestral; copious; accurate; narrative; inductive; impartial; venerable; social; governmental; international; aesthetic; piteous; wondrous; separate; tender; eventful; glorious; wretched; wisdom-woven; tribal; invaluable; naval; religious; prejudiced; conjectural; school; unrecorded; benevolent; problematical; winged; eventful; gradual; fragrant; subsequent; early; economic; anecdote; magnificent; musical; political; dignified; literary; exhaustive; fantastic; subsequent; authoritative.

verbs
burrow into—; "debunk"—; delve into—; derive from—; dig through—; exhibit in—; expatiate on—; falsify—; garnish—; glean from—; informalize—; modify—; record—; recount—; review — of; shape—; suppress —of; telescope—; trace—; unfold—of; —dates back to; —enchants; —enshrines; —extends to; —recurs; —reflects; —throws light upon.

(See narrative, tale, story, book, account.)

HISTRIONIC

adverbs
attractively; technically; alluringly; seductively; extravagantly; spectacularly; ludicrously; dramatically; absurdly; brilliantly; splendidly; inexpressibly; unexpectedly; illustriously; magnificently; competently; melodramatically; ably; tragically; operatically; stagily; stupendously; sensationally; incurably; immensely; pleasantly; exaggeratedly; uncommonly; remarkably; fantastically.

HIT

verbs
acclaim as—; anticipate—; applaud—; chance—; effect—; gain—; obtain—; pray for—; pronounce—; provide—; score—; strike—; —astonishes; —delights; —enriches; —reveals; —surprises.

(See blow, success, stroke, victory, triumph.)

HIT (*v*)

adverbs
severely; viciously; repeatedly; injuriously; cruelly; brutally; vigorously.

(See strike, beat, pound.)

HITCH (*v*)

adverbs
unconsciously; impatiently; unexpectedly; clumsily; mechanically; automatically.

(See fasten, attach.)

"HITCH-HIKER"

verbs
accommodate—; arrest—; bar —s; convey —; dispose of—; forbid—; maroon—; outlaw—; pick up—; prohibit—; —attacks; —begs; —"bums"; —bunks (colloq.); —"chisels"; —clambers aboard; —dodges; —s dot; —freights; —legs; —signals; —tramps; —thumbs.

HIVE

adjectives
scandalous; prolific; considerable; overloaded; nest.

verbs
board in—; crowd—; destroy—; forsake—; gather in—; inhabit—; issue from—; locate in—; lodge in—; occupy—; store in—; swarm to—; watch over—; —busies; —buzzes; —houses; —shelters; —teems; —worships.

(See swarm, crowd, bees, box, home.)

HOARD (*v*)

adverbs
avariciously; jealously; niggardly; meanly; fanatically; selfishly; desperately.

(See store, accumulate.)

HOARSE

adverbs
curiously; strangely; alarmingly; dangerously; fearfully; inexplicably; speechlessly; stridently; harshly; coarsely; raucously; unpleasantly; gruffly; angrily; sepulchrally; deeply; gratingly; terrifyingly; suddenly; uncommonly; extraordinarily; remarkably; discordantly; terribly; horribly; excruciatingly.

HOARY

adverbs
venerably; patriarchally; ripely; perfectly; snowily; gracefully; distinctly; majestically; gloriously; honorably; splendidly; conspicuously; grandly; nobly.

HOAX

verbs
accept—; conceive—; contrive—; denounce —; espy—; frame—; impose — upon; manufacture—; perpetrate—; plan—; practise —; reveal—; spring—; vend—; —amuses; —deceives; —mystifies; —ridicules; —succeeds; —scares; —victimizes.
(See deception, joke, trick.)

HOBBLE (v)

adverbs
painfully; feebly; laboriously; miserably; slowly; waveringly; falteringly.
(See limp, falter, walk.)

HOBBLING

adverbs
ineffectually; lamely; quietly; forlornly; wretchedly; limply; stumblingly; brokenly; distressingly; grievously; woefully; slowly; painfully; awkwardly; cumbrously; dreadfully; pathetically; sadly; uncomfortably; sturdily; crookedly; gayly; mournfully.

HOBBY

adjectives
dominant; fascinating.

verbs
advocate—; allow—; dabble in—; devote to —; excel at—; favor—; indulge in—; permit—; pursue—; ride—; school in—; suggest—; sympathize with—; tinker with—; trifle with—; —amuses; —delights; —diverts; —enthralls; —occupies; —relieves.
(See occupation, interest, vocation, topic, plan, pursuit.)

HOBNOB (v)

adverbs
jovially; fraternally; loquaciously; extravagantly; boisterously; democratically.
(See associate, mingle.)

HOG

adjectives
goaded; ill-bred.

verbs
auction —s; breed —s; exhibit—; fatten—; market—; pen—; roast—; slaughter—; stable—; stick—; —devours; —farrows; —grunts; —hobbles; —snorts; —squeaks; —squeals; —wallows; —yields.
(See animal, pig.)

HOLD (grip)

adjectives
spiritual; demoniac; tenacious; vise-like; passionate; careless; fragile; imploring; pocket.

verbs
bar—; break—; catch—; correct—; divert —; emerge from—; escape—; evade—; force—; gain — on; knit—; loose—; maintain—; mend—; obtain—; seize—; take—; —slips; —supports; —yields.
(See grasp, grip, authority, power, stronghold, refuge.)

HOLD (ship)

verbs
assemble in—; ballast—; cache in—; chain in—; conceal in—; condemn to—; confine to —; couch in—; hide in—; lock in—; provide—; replenish—; stock in—; store in—; stow in—; stuff—.
(See interior, prison.)

HOLD (v)

adverbs
stubbornly; desperately; proudly; tenaciously; securely; frenziedly; obstinately; inviolably; jealously; staunchly; tenderly; tremulously; deferentially; permanently; stoutly; hungrily; tentatively; gingerly; dexterously; automatically; diplomatically.
(See grasp, clutch.)

HOLDING

adjectives
large; theoretical; allotted.

"HOLDUP"

verbs
abet—; appropriate in—; curb—; deprive in —; escape—; execute—; frustrate—; plague with —s; protect from—; reduce —s; resist —; surprise in—; —appalls; —terrorizes.
(See assault, robbery.)

HOLE

adjectives
huge; nest; shallow; halfway; effective; deep; ragged; obvious; death-spitting; oc-

casional; furtive; treacherous; dull; ghastly; obscure; ominous; vast; circular; expansive; inmost; gaping.

verbs
bore—; burrow—; conceal—; drill—; drive —; escape—; excavate—; hollow—; lurk in —; perforate—; pick —s; pierce—; plant in —; plug—; rot in—; sink into—; smother in —; thrust into—.
(See opening, cavity, pit, flaw, defect, hollow.)

HOLIDAY

adjectives
enforced; universal; conventional; invigorating; golden; pastoral; piecemeal; summer; sunshine; sparkling.

HOLINESS

adjectives
pharisaical; penitential; assumed; outward.

verbs
brighten with—; cherish in—; commend—; dedicate to—; diffuse—; dispose to—; dwell in—; glow with—; manifest—; possess—; seek—; share—; shroud in—; touch with—; violate—; —beautifies; —charms; —glorifies; —inspires; —purifies.
(See sanctity, piety, sacredness, purity.)

HOLLOW

verbs
bellow through—; blow through—; bore—; depress—; enclose—; excavate—; fashion—; occupy—; rest in—; shape—; shelter in—; sink into—; thrust into—; —interposes.
(See cavity, depression, channel, basin, valley, hole.)

HOLLOWNESS

adjectives
dreadful; echoing.

HOLLOWS

adjectives
fleshless; intricate; unsuspected; desolate; windless; curving; curdled; starved; fearful; marshy; dreadful; dampish; arid; delicate; wide; cloudy; gaping; grassy.

HOLY

adverbs
reverently; sacredly; divinely; altogether; consummately; perfectly; utterly; eternally; gloriously; infinitely; celestially; spiritually; ineffably; majestically; triumphantly; solemnly; consecratedly.

HOMAGE

adjectives
poor; devoted; disinterested; glorious; reluctant; decorous; regal; unpurchasable; lowly; dreadful; wild; respectful; spontaneous; corporate; due; assiduous; grateful; humble; instinctive; loyal.

verbs
acknowledge—; bow in—; demand—; do—; kneel in—; offer—; owe—; present—; profess—; render—; renounce—; submit to—; swear—; yield — to.
(See respect, deference, obeisance, loyalty.)

HOME

adjectives
kitchen; inn; lodge; nest; suitable; well-ordered; contemporary; devout; rustic; frugal; veritable; industrial; blazing; discriminating; earthly; deep-thatched; undiscovered; devastated; deep-sea; kindred; humble; hereditary; antiquated; exclusive; delegated; desolate; charming; handsome; eternal; secluded; cheerful; terrestrial; stately; gay; cool; inviting; vast; ancestral; unfathomable; peaceful; tainted; remote; simple; material; fond; sheaf-gathered; commodious; sumptuous; unpretentious; reeking; love-guarded; sordid; trim-built; stainless; convenient; historic; palatial; sullen; cloudy; sylvan; silent; distinguished; year-round; fine; perfect; holiday; ideal; primeval; airy; wanton; antenatal; sheltered; chaotic; glory; flooded; peasant; spacious; uninhabitable; artistic; eternal; comfortable; resplendent; imperiled; tiny; congenial; dismantled; annihilated; defenseless; orthodox; dainty.

verbs
abide at—; admire—; banish from—; bless —; cleave to—; cut loose from—; dream of —; escort—; evict from—; flee from—; frequent — of; install in—; lodge at—; long for—; lounge at—; master—; nurse in—; prefer—; preserve—; prize—; provide—; repair to—; sequester in—; survey—; tie to —; troop—; uproot from—; wander from —; welcome—; —beckons; —charms; —cheers; —comforts; —delights; —eases; —protects; —shelters.
(See abode, house, residence, dwelling.)

HOMELESS

adverbs

miserably; wretchedly; desolately; pitiably; cruelly; bitterly; unhappily; incredibly; unfortunately; unluckily; forlornly; pitifully; deservedly; naturally; oddly; curiously; particularly; outrageously; desperately; dreadfully; hopelessly; helplessly; lonesomely; friendlessly; inconceivably; unbelievably; definitely; ironically; disconsolately; dismally; drearily.

HOMELY

adverbs

forbiddingly; awkwardly; clumsily; frightfully; gracelessly; gauntly; haggardly; horribly; monstrously; shockingly; undeniably; simply; plainly; manifestly; curiously; unaffectedly; strangely; dully; avowedly; undisguisedly; outlandishly; indifferently; uncommonly; oddly; cheerfully; sturdily; imperturbably; wholesomely; pleasantly; unconcernedly.

HOMESICK

adverbs

actually; seriously; evidently; manifestly; signally; dangerously; alarmingly; fearfully; frightfully; truly; irrecoverably; desperately; extraordinarily; naturally; slightly; extremely; comprehensibly; bitterly; ruefully; sorely; insatiably; woefully; miserably; sadly; wretchedly; appallingly; shockingly; critically; unaffectedly; irremediably; unaccountably; terribly.

HOMESICKNESS

adjectives

drear; desperate; dread; supportable; nostalgic; prolonged; pronounced.

verbs

affect with—; conceal—; control—; doom to —; intensify—; moan in—; waste in—; yield to—; —afflicts; —arises; —depresses; —eats; —fatigues; —mars; —recurs; —saddens; —steals over; —troubles; —wracks.

(See nostalgia, sadness.)

HOMILY

verbs

address—; ascribe — to; attribute—; compose—; cultivate—; deliver—; excel in—; issue—; preach—; pronounce—; —awes; —bores; —edifies; —explains; —impresses; —moralizes; —pursues; —tires; —wearies.

(See sermon, discourse.)

HONEST

adverbs

absolutely; naturally; sincerely; honorably; morally; downright; altogether; completely; ingenuously; innately; inherently; unreservedly; habitually; constitutionally; virtuously; courageously; bravely; fearlessly; candidly; impartially; fairly; faithfully; sometimes; usually; spasmodically; incorruptibly; loyally; punctiliously; meticulously; respectably; reputably; scrupulously; trustworthily; conscientiously; frankly; inviolably; stainlessly; staunchly; uprightly; utterly; strictly; basically; unimpeachably; fundamentally; essentially; unshakably; apparently.

HONESTY

adjectives

basic; unimpeachable; unquestioned; belated; savage; strict; intrinsic; childlike; shakable; tribal; crystal; rigid; sham; confirmed; intellectual; surface; apparent.

verbs

approve—; assert—; boast of—; conduct with—; consider—; corrupt—; depend on—; desire—; inspect—; instill—; praise—; proclaim—; require—; respect—; test—; trust —; try—; undermine—; violate—; —repays; —rewards; —shines.

(See integrity, sincerity, fairness.)

HONEY

adjectives

pure; limpid; thick; flavored; fine; fermented; amber; sweet; nectareous.

HONEYSUCKLE

verbs

attire in—; bear—; cultivate—; naturalize —; ripen—; shower—; suck—; —attracts; —beautifies; —blooms; —clings; —clutches; —crawls; —creeps; —entwines; —exudes; —flowers; —garlands; —glorifies; —scents; —wreathes.

(See flower, plant, shrub, vine.)

HONOR

adjectives

dropsied; chivalrous; grave; cleansed; distinguished; well-earned; disinterested; enduring; foolish; royal; material; artistic; literary; scientific; sensitive; unprecedented; worldly; assaulted; blushing; academic; unviolated; unending; proffered; divine; proclaiming; professional; questionable; murdered; high; hereditary; especial; bridal; double; unsullied; primitive; imposing; petty; immortal; moral; worthy; blushing; liberal; empty; posthumous; fading; false; unblemished; sunny; perpetual; troublesome; maiden; special; unwonted; proud; dangerous; unsolicited; unexpected; long-transmitted; diplomatic; low-declined; conspicuous; haughty; civic; reverent; jealous; innumerable (pl); scrupulous; dangerous; platonic; strict; dimmed; unpretending; doubtful; sacred; slight; actual; mother-city.

verbs
accord—; assail—; attest to—; avenge—; bestow—; clothe with—; confer—upon; covet—; heap—; invoke—; lavish—; outrage —; pay—; preserve—; reflect upon—; sacrifice—; satisfy—; sell—; solicit—; stain—; steal—; sully—; vie for—; walk away with —; —overjoys.

(See esteem, respect, chastity, virtue, glory, reverence, reputation, dignity.)

HONOR (v)

adverbs
chastely; scrupulously; undeviatingly; academically; uniquely; faithfully; royally; materially; artistically; scientifically; scholastically; professionally; perpetually; posthumously; diplomatically; formally.

(See revere, esteem, respect.)

HONORABLE

adverbs
reputably; supposedly; allegedly; unshakably; irreproachably; sincerely; strictly; fundamentally; naturally; basically; dependably; reliably; altogether; innately; virtuously; fearlessly; intrepidly; courageously; impartially; incorruptibly; loyally; carefully; apparently; utterly; staunchly; scrupulously; meticulously; remarkably; notably; notoriously; illustriously; eminently; utterly.

HOOD

adjectives
riven; purpled; drooping.

HOODLUM (colloq.)

breed—s; chastise—; denounce—; disperse —s; punish—; shelter—; warn—; —annoys; —absconds; —baffles; —damages; —drifts; —dodges; —escapes; —evades; —s gang; —s gather; —harms; —snatches; —threatens.

(See gangster, robber, thief, criminal.)

HOOF

verbs
caulk—s; file—s; muffle—s; paw with—s; protect—s; shoe—s; stamp—s; trim—s; —s clang; —s clank; —s clatter; —s clink; —s drum; —s furrow the ground; —s pound; —s roar; —strikes; —thuds.

(See foot.)

HOOFS

adjectives
stamping; cloven; devilish; edged; delicate; ironshod; flying; plunging; unshod; clattering; clumsy; galloping; clanging; rattling; death-dealing; heavy; awkward.

HOOK

adjectives
nail; peg; rusty; anchoring.

verbs
arm with—; angle with—; bait with—; bend with—; capture with—; cast—; drag with—s; draw—; grapple with—; grasp with—; hang on—; raise with—s; seize with—; snare with—; suspend from—; —catches; —cuts; —links; —penetrates; —secures; —snags.

(See clasp, snare, trap, pin.)

HOOT

adjectives
terrified; clanging.

HOOT (v)

adverbs
disconsolately; dismally; dolefully; scoffingly; monotonously; eerily; mockingly; jeeringly.

(See deride, denounce, shout.)

HOP (v)

adverbs
nimbly; agilely; gaily; swiftly; lightly; sportively; merrily.

(See jump, frisk, bound.)

HOPE

adjectives
ardent; debarred; lingering; honest; deathless; best; sustaining; tremendous; awakened; buried; presumptuous; unearthly; fond;

sole; latent; fiery; buoyant; visionary; absurd; unacknowledged; dead; darkened; false; trusting; unbounded; flowering; roseate; strained; sanguine; groveling; unraveled; indefatigable; twin-born; beautiful; inexperienced; baffled; extravagant; winged; frustrated; high-hearted; generous; departing; dauntless; quenchless; ripening; pale-cheeked; blighted; reverent; perfect; deceptive; patient; half-revealed; smallest; wildest; renewed; gray-haired; inspiriting; troublous; faltering; bursting; dazzling; holy; glorious; wandering; reactionary; lingering; flickering; dying; ardent; heartfelt; improbable; ruined; faded; freshening; blasted; fair; reasonable; trembling; increasing; slender; toppling; absolute; indefinite; dull; atrocious; vague; half-rallied; fruitless; parched; fervent; unchristian; untransmitted; histrionic; definite; decaying; broken; submissive; withered; forlorn; confident; earthly; full; fluttering; savage; pure; budding; tranquil; ultimate; shattered; vague; dreamy; inhaling; celestial; boundless; barren; thrilling; stubborn; ambitious; tortured; dear; flattering; sweet; delusive; feeble; troubled; hovering; unworthy; impossible; natural; blessed; disappointed; prophetic; bright; raised; vain; realized; fallacious; dawning; gaudy; vulgar; future; delicious; exultant; brilliant; odious; perpetuating; latent; polite; desperate; famished; appointed; rekindled; reckless; improbable; countless (pl); yearning; feverish; joyous; sleeping; pathetic; obedient; spacious; intenser; perpetual; confiding; remote; innocent; grim; philosophic; cheerful; unheeded; supreme; trusting; undying; abandoned; inconsistent; earnest; greedy; blossoming.

verbs
afford—; attain—; base—on; blast—; blight—; center—s in; cherish—; cling to—; console with—; crush—s; culminate in—; dash—s; defer—; delude with—; discourage—; divest of—; entertain—; exaggerate—; fall from—; falsify—; flush with—; frustrate—; fulfill—; hatch—; hold out—; impart—; infuse—; inspire—; justify—; kindle—; pin—s on; prompt—; relinquish—; restore—; rouse—; splinter—; stimulate—; substantiate—; undermine—; voice—; —blossoms; —collapses; —deserts; —exalts; —flickers; —glimmers; —is born; —leaps high; —lingers; —looms; —mounts; —perks up; —sinks; —springs; —stirs; —vanishes; —wanes; realize—.

(See trust, reliance, expectation, optimism, anticipation.)

HOPE (v)

adverbs
vainly; fervidly; philosophically; optimistically; piously; fondly; desperately; fervently; devoutly; irresistibly; ardently; deathlessly; presumptuously; reverently; fallaciously; fruitlessly.

(See pray, desire, wish.)

HOPEFUL

adverbs
joyously; mysteriously; unaccountably; pleasurably; excitedly; hysterically; passionately; thrillingly; unreasonably; impatiently; ardently; keenly; eagerly; charmingly; joyfully; fervently; patiently; gloriously; fairly; increasingly; stubbornly; naturally; exultantly; pathetically; philosophically; earnestly; crazily; presumptuously; fondly; absurdly; reverently; extraordinarily.)

HOPEFULNESS

adjectives
desperate; perennial; gentle; indulgent.

HOPELESS

adverbs
probably; apparently; unfortunately; pitiably; wretchedly; miserably; forlornly; utterly; desperately; disconcertingly; insuperably; absolutely; calmly; tragically; bitterly; stolidly; grimly; appallingly; secretly; blankly; speechlessly; frantically; utterly; extremely; undeniably; obviously; manifestly; finally; frightfully.

HOPELESSNESS

adjectives
utter; cruel; black; dark; despairing.

verbs
bow down by—; complain of—; confront with—; doom to—; fret over—; groan with—; incline to—; lose in—; overcome—; paralyze with—; recognize—; reflect—; shroud in—; weight with—; —afflicts; —agonizes; —anguishes; —burdens; —clouds; —deadens; —desolates; —deters; —discourages; —saddens; —submerges; —weakens.

(See despair, despondency, pessimism, sadness.)

HORDE

adjectives
miserable; motley; implacable; maddened; antlike; gray; conquering; impious; existing; vandal; rabble; elfish; veteran; rebellious; bleeding; barbarian; retreating; moving; turbulent; infuriated; undisciplined; roving.

verbs
accumulate—; congregate—; gather in—; spring from—; —bands; —concentrates; —congests; —crowds; —crushes; —disbands; —disperses; —dwells; —flocks; —floods; —howls; —migrates; —mills about; —packs; —roams; —scatters; —stampedes; —strays; —swarms; —throngs; —thunders; —wanders.

(See crowd, swarm, pack, throng, multitude.)

HORIZON

adjectives
heavy; landscape; flushed; solar; soft; endless; ruddy; glowing; magnificent; dim; open; historical; sunny; misty; tinted; dull; dusky; hazy; mother-of-pearl; contracted; lost; dreadful; vaporous; moral; circling; wide; intellectual; mental; imperial; boundless; ever-receding; expanding; far-off.

verbs
blacken—; broaden—; emerge from—; enlarge—; expand—; hesitate on—; loom on —; obscure—; open—; survey—; widen—; —beckons; —broadens; —embraces; —lightens; —recedes.

(See line, range, border, boundary.)

HORN

adjectives
toppling; dolorous; signaling; heavenly; masked; crescent; pellucid; sultry; impatient; lusty; sullen; formidable; barbarous; monstrous; cruel; long; twanging; curving; gilded; distinct; insistent; audacious; clangorous.

verbs
bear—; defend with—; develop—; drive—s into; impale on—s; loose—s; pierce with—; pinion down with—; —butts; —drills; —s endanger; —s frighten; —s gore; —s lance; —s prick; —s punch; —s puncture; —s rip; —s spike; —s threaten; —s wound.

(See antler, pin, point.)

HORNET

verbs
arouse—s; provoke—s; —attacks; —basks in; —bites; —hums; —s infest; —inflicts; —s nest; —perforates; —pierces; —pricks; —regurgitates; —riots; —s swarm.

(See wasp, bee, insect.)

HORRIBLE

adverbs
grimly; unexpectedly; surprisingly; naturally; inevitably; dismally; alarmingly; awfully; frightfully; tremendously; unforgettably; unspeakably; inexpressibly; abhorrently; sickeningly; nauseatingly; unbearably; intolerably; incredibly; wildly; gruesomely; dreadfully.

HORRID

adverbs
disgustingly; repulsively; shockingly; appallingly; offensively; abominably; atrociously; intolerably; unbearably; hideously; frightfully; unbelievably; incredibly; peculiarly; outrageously; unaccountably; positively; unendurably; insufferably; uncommonly; unduly.

HORRIFIED

adverbs
utterly; amazingly; dreadfully; astoundingly; blankly; startlingly; breathlessly; wordlessly; appallingly; indescribably; fearfully; inexpressibly.

HORROR

adjectives
profound; damp; amused; attendant; alien; gentle; bragging; ignorant; scaly; untold; speechless; weary; blank; cloudy; congenial; superstitious; instinctive; unmitigated; invariable; distant; pious; ridiculous; accumulated; gloomy; hovering; incredulous; indescribable; quaint; formless; dismal; pursuing; sleepy; blank; misbegotten; fantastic; grisly; inseparable; supernumerary; unspeakable; stunned; anxious; nameless; ghastly; large-eyed; inconvenient; silent; inconceivable; insuperable; peculiar; infinite; tragic; cold; pungent; unimaginable; affected; incredible; dreary; unaccountable; shadowy; grim; journalistic; stunned; burlesque; incumbent; inactive; uncouth; utter; imaginary; positive; irrational; piercing; unfeigned; frightful; inexorable; intolerable; bloody; distant; mingled (pl); pale; unburied; childlike.

verbs
banish—; chill with—; conceal—; depict—; enhance—; expose—; freeze with—; ponder over—; recoil in—; reconstruct—; rise to the height of—; strike—; survey—; transfix with—; view with—; witness—; —grows; —strikes.
(See fear, dread, consternation.)

HORSE

adjectives
mustang; livestock; startled; dozing; hot; unbroken; riderless; steaming; petrified; winged; prancing; enchanted; massive; heavy; plodding; unwilling; spurred; vicious; docile; broken-down; unweaned; ghostly; pack; chubby; unmanageable; mettlesome; reluctant; well-broken; spirited; redoubtable; outspent; sorry; maniacal; generous; light-limbed; restive; bang-tailed; great-limbed; true; beautiful; foam-flecked; mottled; moth-eaten; dilapidated; straining; stalking; solemn; ramping; slender; rawboned; sweating; plow; blazed-faced; well-breathed; arrogant; unafraid; fiery; exhausted; weary; bony; dispirited; disemboweled; jibbing; drooping; jaded; foam-lipped; indifferent; admirable; harrowed; blooded; plunging; corn-stuffed.

verbs
bed down—; corral—; breed—s; currycomb—; guide—; harbor—; hobble—; jockey—; lash—; leap from—; mount—; pace—; rein in—; round up—s; saddle—; spur—; stable—; straddle—; tether—; tumble off—; —balks at; —bolts; —bucks; —canters; —capers; —caracoles; —champs at the bit; —dances; —falls to feeding; —founders; —hurdles; —neighs; —paws; —plods; —prances; —quivers; —races; —rears; —shies; —shivers; —snorts; —tramples; —trots; —vaults; —veers; —wheels; —whickers; —whinnies.
(See colt, animal, mare.)

HORSEBACK

verbs
canter on—; charge on—; convey by—; excel on—; exhibit on—; gallop in on—; journey on—; joust on—; mount—; race on—; sport on—; traverse on—; trot on—; vault on—.
(See horse.)

HORSEMAN

adjectives
brave; coated; mystic; unwary; gallant; solitary; admirable; steel-clad; headless; unhorsed.

verbs
—men assemble; —bestrides; —breeds; —charges; —coaches; —controls; —exhibits; —fancies; —flogs; —halts; —lashes; —manages; —mounts; —performs; —pets; —plods; —rears; —reins in; —spurs; —strokes.
(See rider, cowboy, soldier.)

HORSEMANSHIP

adjectives
consummate; daring; showy; superb.

HOSE

adjectives
stout; dusty; russet; silken; gossamer; diaphanous; cotton; worsted; shrunken.

HOSE
(*conduit*)

verbs
burst—; couple—; drench with—; pump through—; sprinkle with—; water with—; —bursts; —conducts; —conveys; —showers.
(See pipe.)

HOSIERY

adjectives
unsatisfactory; beautiful; sheer; cobwebby.

verbs
don—; draw on—; mend—; rip—; roll—; shed—; snag—; snap—; —fades; —glistens; —runs.

HOSPITABLE

adverbs
graciously; warmly; delightfully; cordially; generously; bounteously; liberally; munificently; splendidly; magnificently; freely; handsomely; pleasantly; sociably; happily; merrily; heartily; jovially; genially; urbanely; companionably; informally; gregariously; remarkably; immensely; courteously; enthusiastically; exuberantly; inordinately; good-naturedly; unobtrusively; lavishly; quietly; genuinely; charmingly; wholeheartedly.

HOSPITAL

adjectives
contemporary; improvised; convalescent; dingy; special; cheerless; contagious.

HOSPITALITY

adjectives

courteous; sailorlike; effusive; uncommon; exuberant; mellowed; proverbial; rival; discreet; lasting; stinted; princely; elegant; undiscriminate; thankful; rural; good-natured; dignified; generous; professional; profuse; reluctant; wonted; hearty; cordial; unobtrusive; cheerful; genial; unwearying; lavish; quiet; warm; surpassing; genuine; old-time; luxurious; hearty; charming; homelike; famous; unique; cordial; warm-hearted; incredible; gracious; reluctant; extempore; southern; wholehearted.

verbs

dispense—; enjoy—; maintain—; offer—; practise—; provide—; repay—; reward—; ruffle—; share—; warm with—; —blossoms; —charms; —cheers; —dwindles; —eases; —flourishes; —flows; —relieves.

(See entertainment, generosity, friendship.)

HOST

adjectives

dejected; ungracious; disagreeable; heavenly; secondary; routed; subtle; benignant; tragic; starry; affable; reluctant; straggling; new-found; genial; angelic; crusading; illimitable; shadowy; numerous; overweening; inseparable; chafing; kind; legionary; indignant; embattled; celestial; spangled; assaulting; heathen; conquering; amiable; heavenly; pensive; battle-broken; visionary; countless; smiling; ranting; ill-fated; motley; square; swarthy; ethereal; tombless; venerable; frugal; innumerable; hurrying; mustering; frank; miserable; prospective; glorified; radiant; niggardly; weary; generous; bewildered.

verbs

besiege—; honor—; praise—; —amuses; —appears; —approves; —befriends; —bids; —charms; —comforts; —delights; —enlivens; —flatters; —greets; —plans; —presides; —provides; —relieves; —welcomes.

(See entertainer, actor, friend.)

HOSTESS

adjectives

temporary; noble; popular; impromptu; attentive; exuberant; lavish; ambitious; small; fat; good-natured; fair; charming; gracious; air; amiable; tidy; buxom.

HOSTILE

adverbs

coldly; politely; secretly; surreptitiously; inscrutably; openly; candidly; absurdly; hatefully; malevolently; venomously; maliciously; viciously; ominously; portentously; villainously; inscrutably; inexplicably; irreconcilably; antagonistically; dangerously; alarmingly; curiously; strangely; oddly; queerly; unreasonably; irrationally; exceptionally; tragically; inconveniently; irrevocably; horribly.

HOSTILITY

adjectives

determined; quiet; small; quenched; implacable; slumbering; languid; perpetual; unexpressed; sudden; smiling; unnecessary; undiluted; expensive; alert; expectant; uncompromising; indecent; provoking; bitter; unintermitting; implacable; innate; jealous; frequent (pl); wily; deadly; concealed; smoldering; methodical; intuitive; evident; legislative; defensive; interfering; neighborly; unprofitable; fanatical.

verbs

arouse—; break—s; cease—; encourage—; engage in—s; enter—s; evince—; excite—; fan—; incur—of; loose—s; renew—s; suspend—s; temper—; view with—; —frightens; —grows.

(See enmity, animosity, opposition, warfare, anger.)

HOT

adverbs

devilishly; horribly; unbearably; unusually; remarkably; abnormally; feverishly; unnaturally; angrily; dangerously; apparently; unseasonably; strangely; intolerably; sufficiently; scarcely; inordinately; queerly; peculiarly; curiously; unfortunately; oppressively; swelteringly; stiflingly; bakingly; blazingly; suffocatingly; intensely.

HOTEL

adjectives

superb; smart; first-class; fine; famous; quiet; dignified; luxurious; distinguished; friendly; notable; favored; complete; beachfront; residential; delightful; attractive; skyscraper; seaside; centrally-located; modern; perfect; cheerful; warm; inviting; traditional; unique; outstanding; swanky; distinguished; exclusive; apartment; ambitious; wooden; cozy; commercial; resort;

small; provincial; rambling; frame; vermin-infested; temperance; convenient; grand; comfortable; charming; nice; hospitable; cosmopolitan; well-kept; well-organized; innumerable (pl); glamorous.

verbs
convene at—; dwell at—; inhabit—; loll in—; patronize—; retain at—; stow away in—; —accommodates; —caters to; —comforts; —delights; —employs; —flourishes; —offers; —provides; —serves; —welcomes; —furnishes.

(See inn, house, building, tavern.)

HOUND

adjectives
overrash; cadaverous; lean; ugly; couchant; degenerate; long-eared; deepmouthed; patient; fox; aged; hot; scent-snuffing; baffled; phenomenal; howling; licking; fawn-colored; thirsty-looking; cunning; toothless; graceful.

verbs
pat—; quiet—; unleash—; whip—; —bays; —dashes by; —growls; —s harry; —howls; —points; —pursues; —snarls; —tears; —whines; —yelps; —yips.

(See dog, animal.)

HOUR

adjectives
accustomed; additional; agonizing; all-glorious; amazing; appointed; arid; atoning; awful; baleful; bitter; black; bleak; blessed; blighted; blue-eyed; bounteous; brawling; breakfast; breathless; brief; bright; calm; captive; careful; cheerless; closing; cloudless; comfortless; coming; conditioned; confident; consecrated; countless (pl); cramped; critical; crucial; customary; darkened; darkling; dawning; definite; delicious; designated; desirable; disastrous; discouraged; dolorous; dread; dreadful; dream-haunted; dreaming; dreary; drinking; dull; dusky; early; eerie; elected; ensuing; enthusiastic; eventful; evil; exciting; fair; famished; fatiguing; favored; fearful; fervent; feverous; flaming; forbidden; forgetful; forlorn; forsaken; fragrant; fruitful; generous; gentle; giddy; gleeful; gloom-clad; glutted; gory; gradual; hallowed; happy; hateful; hazy; heavenly; heavy; heinous; heterogeneous; hushed; hustling; hypnotic; idle; illuminating; imperious; impossible; impressionable; impressive; inauspicious; incessant; industrious; inevitable; instant; interminable; jocund; jovial; joyful; jubilant; laborious; languorous; lasting; lazy; leisure; lingering; lonely; long; luckless; lyric; meet; melancholy; memorable; merciless; meridian; merry; midnight; moonlit; mortal; mourning; murderous; natal; new-fledged; niggard; noteless; nuptial; old; optional; pallid; particular; parting; passing; peaceful; perilous; placid; pleasant; precious; precise; prefixed; prescribed; promised; rare; regretful; regulated; retributive; rosy-fingered; sacred; sauntering; secret; serene; serious; shadowed; shiny; short; sleepless; slow-paced; social; soft; solemn; somber; sorrowful; spent; splenetic; starless; stormy; strange; suffering; sunny; sunset; superincumbent; supreme; surviving; swift; tedious; thorny; thoughtful; thrilling; torturing; tranquil; transient; treacherous; trembling; tremulous; troublous; trysting; twilight; unbearable; unborn; unconscionable; unfortunate; unlucky; unnatural; unreturning; unseasonable; unsuspecting; untroubled; usual; valuable; vast; vehement; vesper; voluptuous; wakeful; wasted; weary; wedlock; weird; weeping; white-robed; wholesome; wild; wonted; working; wretched.

verbs
appoint—; budget—s; consume—s; count—s; crowd—; devote—s to; employ—; fix—; fritter away—s; kill—s; laze away—s; note—; postpone—; read—of day; reckon—; regulate—s; set—; —approaches; —s crawl by; —s drag; —elapses; —s fly; —s lag; —s ripen; —strikes; —s wear on.

(See time, occasion.)

HOUSE

adjectives
mansion; miserable; enchanting; cat-encumbered; solitary; scattered (pl); gloomy; dilapidated; true; pretentious; archetypal; echoing; painted; battlemented; imperial; ambitious; dignified; quaint; religious; gaunt; comfortable; straggling; disreputable; showy; imaginative; practical; reminiscent; adjacent; shiftless; austere; aristocratic; poultry; gliding; modest; tile-roofed; haunted; burnished; conspicuous; illustrious; farm; gnarled; jolly; deserted; squatty; lonely; first-run; widespreading; rayless; darksome; crafty; magnificent; ancestral; lofty; supply; substantial; idyllic; shamble; economical; town; continental;

shell-pitted; giddy; shabby; pillaged; ladylike; shameful; dower; blithe; ugly; hallowed; powerful; low-browed; inviting; tenement; triangular; terraced; humble; wretched; wattled; dull; lucrative; untenantable; paltry; inconvenient; dreamy; ruined; ducal; ill; country; dismantled; useless; gay; gambling; naughty; celestial; neat; treasure; festive; warm; jovial; sunny; luxurious; embellished; pharmaceutical; comfortable-looking; log; dwelling; tremendous; unpeeled; well-insulated; mobile; trembling; gay-roofed; little; popular; swarming; stuccoed; irregularly-scattered (pl); handsome; respectable; bleak; hospitable; ill-furnished; filthy; dirty; isolated; thatch-roofed; cane; respected; faltering; unobtrusive; ancient; narrow; flimsy; reigning; royal; desolate; fair; vast; treasure; identical; tumble-down; boxlike; unquiet; crowded; parental; eery; model; lodging; commodious; stately; unreal; excellent; pretentious; swell-front; shutterless; old-fashioned; once-fashionable; clattering; adobe; ranch; sheltering.

verbs
adorn—; bedizen—; billet in—; demolish—; design—; ensconce in—; inhabit—; model —; pattern—; refurbish—; renovate—; sanctify—; shatter—; tenant—; undermine —; waddle into—; —hushes; —looms; —nestles; —springs up.
(See building, abode, home.)

HOUSE (v)
adverbs
luxuriously; warmly; faithfully; imperially; quaintly; disreputably; practically; shiftlessly; austerely; aristocratically; hospitably; magnificently; economically; shabbily; commodiously; pretentiously.
(See shelter, protect.)

HOUSEHOLD
adjectives
ducal; decorous; quiet; turbulent; tyrannical; literary; minute.

HOUSEKEEPER
adjectives
active; manifest; procrastinating.

HOUSEKEEPING
adjectives
modern; efficient.

HOUSEWIFE
adjectives
fastidious; primitive; chaste; querulous; busy; lazy.

HOUSING
adjectives
better; overcrowded; low-cost; planned; government-supported.

HOVEL
adjectives
poverty-stricken; ruinous; lowly; wretched

HOVER (v)
adverbs
perpetually; perilously; caressingly; ceaselessly; expectantly; eagerly; protectingly; lovingly.
(See flutter, linger.)

HOWL
adjectives
long; loud; piteous; increasing; reverberate; unearthly; occasional; barbaric; tumultuous; deep; wild; ghastly; triumphant; angry; prolonged; fearful; dismal; lugubrious.

verbs
break into—; muffle—; prolong—; subdue —; unleash—; utter—; —arises; —astonishes; —breaks out; —distresses; —frightens; —penetrates; —pierces; —rends; —rips through; —terrifies; —confuses.
(See cry, wail, noise.)

HOWL (v)
adverbs
dismally; incessantly; bleakly; victoriously; gruesomely; sickeningly; heart-rendingly; ironically; blatantly; eerily.
(See roar, wail.)

HOWLING
adjectives
melancholy; weird; ear-rending.

HOYDENISH
adverbs
gaudily; boisterously; coarsely; noisily; conspicuously; flauntingly; blatantly; publicly; shamelessly; barbarously; boorishly; remarkably; lamentably; extravagantly; queerly; unfortunately; horribly; indecorously; monstrously; indecently; terribly; outlandishly; outrageously; wantonly; ri-

baldly; particularly; shabbily; provincially; shockingly; uncivilly; extremely; horribly; inexcusably.

HUBBUB

adjectives
chaotic; universal; confused; inarticulate.

HUDDLE

adjectives
low; confused.

verbs
band in—; concentrate in—; congregate in —; crowd in—; crush in—; emerge from—; flock in—; gather in—; lie in—; mingle in —; move in—; throng in—; tumble into—; spring from—; swarm in—; —confuses; —disperses; —writhes.
(See group, crowd.)

HUDDLE (v)

adverbs
pathetically; sluggishly; comfortably; protectingly; snugly; patiently; instinctively; dolorously.
(See crouch, pack, crowd.)

HUE

adjectives
intense; stone; tender; undecided; vivid; varied (pl); native; prismatic; exuberant; deathly; roseate; unalterable; ashy; glorious; brimstone; golden; somber; autumn; ghastly; celestial; pallid; pronounced; rainbow; healthy; firm; unshimmering; kindred; slaughterous; predominating; faint; myriad (pl); intense; unwithering; sad; blended; heavenly; tawny; universal; melodious; tempting; chameleon; damask; sulphurous; manifold (pl); livid; pallid; pure; lovely; somber; curious (pl); virgin; sublimer; azure; florid; ghastly; voluptuous; enchanting; homely; lurid; brassy; sightly; rich; fair; unwashed; fading; sunburned; evanescent; normal; unnatural; brilliant; predominant; wild; unpropitious; delicate; unfading; charming; different; changing; sanguine; decided; dazzling; doubtful; generous; washed-out; nondescript; aerial; shifting; burnished; iridescent; gorgeous; undying; kaleidoscopic; twilight; various (pl).

verbs
blend—s; dab—; daub with—; dim—; dip into—; enhance—; flush—; mix—; paint—; smear—; stroke—; teem with—; —brightens; —delights; —enchants; —fades; —glows; —melts; —merges.
(See color, shade.)

HUG

adjectives
affectionate; exemplary; ecstatic.

HUG (v)

adverbs
brazenly; amorously; affectionately; ecstatically; lustily; brutishly; stalwartly; tenderly; voluptuously; lasciviously.
(See clasp, grip, embrace.)

HUGE

adverbs
remarkably; bulkily; monstrously; awkwardly; stupendously; grossly; grotesquely; queerly; impossibly; overwhelmingly; ponderously; prodigiously; sensationally; unusually; formidably; unduly.

HULK

adjectives
lumbering; shallow; unprizable; lifeless.

HULL

adjectives
polished; rough; swift; graceful.

verbs
confine to—; discard—; divest of—; enrobe in—; equip with—; fashion—; shed—; shell —; swathe in—; wrap in—; —armors; —covers; —encases; —encompasses; —encrusts; —envelops; —hides; —protects; —reverberates.
(See frame, blanket.)

HUM

adjectives
busy; murmurous; beelike; soft; bubbling; hideous; endless; peaceful; lily-muffled; dolorous; distant; discordant; hoarse; pleasant; sonorous; faint; musical; drowsy.

verbs
endure—; heed—; ignore—; join in—; muffle—; perceive—; raise—; subdue—; —attracts; —bothers; —charms; —delights; —disturbs; —plagues; —waxes.
(See murmur.)

HUM (v)

adverbs
tremulously; blithely; discordantly; hoarsely; sonorously; drowsily; musically; melodiously; monotonously.
(See drone, buzz, croon.)

HUMAN

adjectives
frail; feeble; fallible.

adverbs
charitably; generously; sympathetically; compassionately; kindly; tenderly; lovingly; mercifully; graciously; understandingly; intelligently; gently; uncommonly; remarkably.

HUMANE

adverbs
benevolently; tenderly; intelligently; consistently; dependably; charitably; comfortingly; considerately; graciously; warmly; mercifully; philanthropically; altruistically; patriotically; generously; leniently; admirably; wonderfully; actively; naturally; habitually.

HUMANITARIAN

adverbs
constructively; altruistically; benevolently; beneficently; public-spiritedly; generously; sincerely; actively; compassionately; effectively; admirably; superbly; magnificently; nobly; worthily; eminently; immensely; intensely; definitely; broadly.

HUMANITY

adjectives
enslaved; misshapen; outraged; frail; struggling; downtrodden; common; kindred; communal; exalted; suffering; unexpected; active; frank; sturdy; armed; heated; rugged; semi-tropical; multiform; profound; natural; polluted; redeemed; despairing; glorious; rekindled; warm; adorned; consistent; chained.

verbs
claim for—; contemplate—; contribute to—; educate—; enrich—; exhibit—; found on —; imitate—; regard—; observe—; pity—; portray—; prompt by—; relieve—; rely on —; rule—; stir—; uplift—; —inclines; —mitigates; —restrains.
(See mankind, human nature, compassion, tenderness, kindness, benevolence, civilization, world.)

HUMAN NATURE

verbs
appeal to—; attribute to—; benefit—; bewail—; characterize—; contemplate—; lament—; observe—; regard—; rely on—; scrutinize—; subjugate—; —balks at; —behaves; —evolves; —pursues; —responds; —revolves.
(See character, disposition, temperament, constitution, mankind, humanity.)

HUMBLE

adverbs
quietly; unusually; sincerely; modestly; shyly; timidly; obsequiously; submissively; abjectly; astoundingly; timorously; unassumingly; guiltily; demurely; devoutly; reverently; solemnly; gravely; consecratedly; penitently; contritely; sadly; unexpectedly; unnecessarily; extremely.

HUMBLE (v)

adverbs
abjectly; painfully; utterly; profoundly; unmeritedly; shamefully; sadistically; vindictively.
(See debase, humiliate.)

HUMBLENESS

adjectives
whispering; profound.

HUMBUG

adjectives
solemn; intolerable; sleek; hypocritical; dishonest.

HUMDRUM

adverbs
flatly; dully; stupidly; uninterestingly; monotonously; intolerably; usually; habitually; conspicuously; laboriously; tediously; prosily; dismally; wearisomely; tiresomely; prosaically; endlessly; interminably; baldly; disgustingly; ponderously; heavily; impossibly; curiously; unbearably.

HUMID

adverbs
suffocatingly; sultrily; horribly; dreadfully; frightfully; unusually; uncommonly; highly; extremely; excessively; damply; muddily; soggily; reekingly; drippingly; oppressively; uncomfortably; relatively; remarkably; surprisingly.

HUMIDITY

adjectives
oppressive; rotten; dense; unusual; relative; extreme; unwholesome; uncomfortable.

HUMILIATE (*v*)

adverbs
bitterly; horribly; ineffably; profoundly; spitefully; hatefully; jealously; enviously; treacherously.

(See humble, debase, shame.)

HUMILIATED

adverbs
extremely; deeply; profoundly; intolerably; shamefully; unnecessarily; needlessly; intentionally; deliberately; cruelly; bitterly; painfully; brutally; publicly; utterly; direly; sorely; deplorably; scandalously; outrageously; inexcusably; unforgivably; criminally; shockingly; basely; terribly; dreadfully.

HUMILIATION

adjectives
painful; jovial; utter; imagined; frequent; just; ineffable; anticipated; profound; deep; unmerited; subsequent.

verbs
bow in—; break in—; deserve—; end in—; expose to—; incur—; inure to—; invite—; go down in—; kneel in—; overcome with—; pretend—; purchase by—; resign to—; sink in—; submit to—; suffer—; walk in—; —humbles; —shames; —tortures.

(See mortification, dishonor, ignominy.)

HUMILITY

adjectives
proud; abrupt; deep; profound; singular; matchless; laughable; egotistic; mock; vast; mild; utmost; true; provoking; apparent; shamed; cringing; honest; servile; false; respectable; marked; passionate.

verbs
accept with—; affect—; breathe—; commend—; feign—; fill with—; gown in—; practice—; relish—; submit with—; walk with—; —contents; —satisfies; —tempers.

(See modesty, humiliation.)

HUMMING

adjectives
gentle; intermittent; audible; drowsy.

HUMMINGBIRD

verbs
—beaks; —chirps; —flits; —hops; —hums; —skims about.

(See bird.)

HUMOR

adjectives
gay; ironic; wonted; savage; drawling; malicious; lively; cantankerous; dismal; sportive; piquant; homely; arrogant; mingled; delighted; good; robust; devastating; oppressive; mixed; clumsy; puppy; whimsical; tender; resistless; genial; boisterous; bubbling; caustic; pestilent; parched; jeering; grave; playful; unhappy; gentle; satirical; headstrong; frank; companionable; unaccountable; secondhand; good-natured; capricious; obliging; black; little; melancholy; arresting; pleasant; ponderous; audacious; grim; true; spleeny; splenetic; cynical; acrid; biting; fertile; irresistible; lordly; proper; sarcastic; racy; inexhaustible; overwhelming; excellent; charming; fiery; delightful; vile; morbid; insolent; grotesque; fantastical; broad; quizzical; seditious; grave; holiday; unruffled; sly; subtle; bawdy; effervescent; ironic; fickle; reigning; buoyant; ebullient; ill-concealed; quaint; impatient; serious; flattering; irrepressible; admirable; sneering; ready; quiet; wholesome; fireside; mocking; reckless; testy; bitter; coarse; choice; sectional; ill; unconfined; sanguine; unfailing; trading; gossiplike; querulous; careless; salty; unquarrelsome; sardonic; irregular; universal; exquisite; farcical; Rabelaisian; aqueous; comparative; limited; pitiless; painful; acute; sullen; toplofty; spontaneous; sulphurous; meditative; burlesque; irreverent; unhappy; bizarre; corresponding.

verbs
appreciate—; attempt—; bar—; color with—; conceive—; delight in—; disdain—; execute—; indulge in—; milk dry of—; regale with—; sense—in; subdue—; subtilize—; tame—; —abates; —bores; —eases; —effervesces; —enlivens; —flashes; —flows; —palls; —pales; —penetrates; —ruffles; —scintillates; —shines through; —wanes; —wears thin.

(See disposition, mood, caprice, whim, fancy, fun, mirth, merriment, play.)

HUMOR (v)

adverbs

patronizingly; slyly; indulgently; consciously; ironically; maliciously; whimsically; grotesquely; fantastically; subtly; mockingly; coarsely; sardonically; irreverently.

(See laugh, giggle.)

HUMOROUS

adverbs

smartly; sharply; habitually; temperamentally; wittily; unusually; uncommonly; delightfully; pleasantly; keenly; charmingly; entertainingly; divertingly; waggishly; robustly; lustily; gustily; noisily; boisterously; outrageously; irrepressibly; spontaneously; naturally; broadly; cleverly; brilliantly; whimsically; merrily; comically; wonderfully; endlessly; uncommonly; highly; amazingly; unfailingly.

HUNCH

verbs

believe in—; consider—; contemplate—; deal in —s; follow—; heed—; indulge in—; inspire with—; mark—; observe—; pursue —; stake on—; submit to—; trust—; —implies; —hints; —proves; —suggests.

(See impression, belief.)

HUNCHBACKED

adverbs

unfortunately; pitiably; incurably; slightly; crookedly; grotesquely; terribly; dreadfully; nonchalantly; gallantly; bravely; extremely; possibly.

HUNGER

adjectives

coarse; alleviated; gaunt; gluttonous; deep; ravening; healthful; vulturous.

verbs

abate—; abolish—; appease—; excite—; expire from—; faint in—; press by—; quiet—; risk—; satiate—; satisfy—; spur on by—; stave off—; suffer—; weaken by—; —irritates; —predisposes; —threatens; —vexes.

(See craving, desire, appetite, famine.)

HUNGRY

adverbs

insatiably; terribly; slightly; greedily; pitiably; incessantly; habitually; extremely; unspeakably; alarmingly; ravenously; eagerly; seriously; gauntly; cadaverously; gluttonously; healthily; wolfishly; impatiently; avidly; wistfully; curiously; strangely; irritably; awfully; restlessly; fretfully.

HUNK

adjectives

substantial; seditious; luscious; juicy; flavorful.

HUNT

adjectives

fruitless; scavenger; vengeful; man.

HUNT (v)

adverbs

mercilessly; patiently; anxiously; fruitlessly; enthusiastically; intrepidly; passionately; wantonly; humanely; daringly.

(See seek, search, pursue.)

HUNTER

adjectives

venerable; winged; passionate; unsuccessful; novice; persistent; pugnacious; gold; lifelong; unthinking; wanton; humanity; outstanding; fair-weather; daring; intrepid.

HUNTING

adjectives

purposed; realistic.

HURDLE

verbs

balk at—; brace—; break—; construct—; erect—; fence with—; fly over—; fortify with—; gain—; jump—; leap over—; spring over—; stride—; take—; vault—; —bars; —encloses; —obstructs; —topples.

(See barrier, frame, fence.)

HURL (v)

adverbs

viciously; heedlessly; relentlessly; vigorously; boisterously; stalwartly; prodigiously; thunderously; flagrantly; tempestuously.

(See fling, cast.)

HURRICANE

adjectives

untamed; furious; aimless; tempestuous; lightning.

verbs

cast away by—; dread—; encounter—; perish in—; report—; wallow in—; —bedevils; —breaks; —bursts; —ceases; —confuses; —destroys; —devastates; —falls upon; —

overthrows; —persecutes; —rages; —ravages; —rends; —riots; —shrieks; —sweeps; —takes toll; —violates; —whirls.

(See storm, tempest, typhoon, snow, blizzard.)

HURRIED

adverbs
unfortunately; carelessly; inefficiently; urgently; nervously; harassingly; terribly; intensely; monstrously; foolishly; ineptly; excitedly; feverishly; hysterically; restlessly; violently; wildly; irrepressibly; impolitely; uncivilly; discourteously; boorishly; ungraciously; furiously; breathlessly; desperately; unduly; indecently; unscrupulously; clumsily; madly; noticeably; visibly; obviously.

HURRY

adjectives
monstrous; national; raging; frivolous; hot.

HURRY (*v*)

adverbs
nervously; merrily; conservatively; gallantly; furtively; tremulously; precipitately; anxiously; madly; feverishly; mechanically; blindly; confusedly.

(See hasten, dispatch.)

HURT

adjectives
unbandaged; real; painful; dull; deep; permanent; growing; bodily; mortal; nagging; aroused.

HURT (*v*)

adverbs
grievously; hideously; deeply; permanently; acutely; bodily; fatally; superficially; incurably.

(See injure, damage, wound.)

HURTFUL

adverbs
mischievously; intentionally; deliberately; innocently; unconsciously; dreadfully; perniciously; maliciously; obnoxiously; legally; disastrously; venomously; villainously; exceptionably; deplorably; pitiably; lamentably; wretchedly; sadly; reprehensibly; confoundedly; hopelessly; purposely; irremediably; dangerously; alarmingly; seriously; hopelessly; desperately; unusually; incredibly.

HURTLE (*v*)

adverbs
recklessly; swiftly; spectacularly; gloriously; furiously; blazingly; daringly; fiercely.

(See throw, hurl.)

HUSBAND

adjectives
frigid; itinerant; shiftless; distraught; loveselfish; unworthy; allowing; truant; worthless; war-blinded; unfaithful; affianced; attached; exacting; impecunious; obstinate; unhopeful; disgruntled; cynical; captive; coarse; instructive; ill; indolent; divorced; heavy; uxorious; precise; devoted; appreciative; scandalous; imaginary; bereaved; cruel; cantankerous; wild; noble; generous; dissipated; irascible; maddening; distracted; ingenious; indignant; fiery; stolid; jealous.

verbs
abide with—; attend—; chide—; divorce—; nag—; obtain—; rebuke—; respect—; serve—; submit to—; —abandons; —chastises; —defends; —deserts; —domineers; —heads; —lords over; —philanders; —rebukes; —represses; —reprimands; —reproves; —rules; —supports.

(See master.)

HUSBANDRY

adjectives
prolific; animal; skilled; economical.

HUSH

adjectives
sudden; expectant; breathless; dread; timeless; primeval; windless; unbreathing; evening; instinctive; religious; all-pervasive; awed; deadly; starlight; deep; peculiar; grim; instant.

verbs
command—; demand—; enforce—; expect—; impose—; pierce—; procure—; reduce to—; restore—; seek—; split—; spread—; welcome—; —calms; —charms; —deepens; —delights; —disturbs; —ensues; —hangs heavy; —invades; —pervades; —rules.

(See stillness, silence, quiet.)

HUSH (*v*)

adverbs
significantly; breathlessly; instinctively; peculiarly; cautiously; temporarily; abruptly.

(See silence, repress, suppress.)

HUSHED

adverbs
solemnly; reverently; quietly; quickly; unusually; wonderfully; swiftly; inordinately; uncommonly; gloomily; irritably; suddenly; breathlessly; instinctively; deeply; profoundly; grimly; instantly; particularly; peculiarly; curiously; queerly; horribly; oddly; infinitely; strangely; temporarily; momentarily; eternally.

HUSK

adjectives
scholastic; fruitless; bearded; wrinkled.

HUSKY
(*strong*)

adverbs
vigorously; robustly; mightily; powerfully; sturdily; stoutly; irresistibly; incontestably; inexhaustibly; stubbornly; soundly; magnificently; splendidly; remarkably; brutally; immensely; prodigiously; evidently; incredibly; obviously; manifestly; palpably; surprisingly; matchlessly.

HUSKY
(*voice*)

adverbs
faintly; deeply; murmurously; languorously; hoarsely; softly; audibly; throatily; seductively; seriously; dreadfully; terribly; deliberately; stagily; whisperingly; melodiously; musically; raucously; brutally; sepulchrally; hollowly; permanently; temporarily; purposely; alarmingly; amazingly; fearfully; slightly.

HUSSY

adjectives
cantankerous; brazen; brash; loud-mouthed.

HUSTLE (*v*)

adverbs
unceremoniously; precipitately; abruptly; undignifiedly; characteristically; breathlessly; enthusiastically.
(See hurry, hasten.)

HUSTLING

adverbs
restlessly; constantly; fitfully; zealously; noisily; happily; everlastingly; ceaselessly; cheerily; actively; energetically; assiduously; diligently; earnestly; eagerly; excitedly.

HUT

adjectives
unaired; mud-walled; abandoned.

HYBRID

adverbs
undeniably; obviously; cheaply; miserably; indiscriminately; palpably; manifestly; peculiarly; singularly; unaccountably; noteworthily; fantastically; unfashionably; professedly; quaintly; promiscuously; heterogeneously; openly.

HYDROGEN

adjectives
nascent; carbureted.

HYENA

verbs
—attacks; —battles; —barks; —carries away; —crushes; —devours; —feeds on; —inhabits; —laughs; —overpowers; —preys on; —scavenges; —stalks.
(See animal.)

HYGIENE

verbs
deride—; heed—; improve—; instruct in—; obey—; practise—; preach—; prescribe—; promote—; scorn—; verse in—; violate—; —defends; —extends to; —guards against; —preserves; —prevents; —resists; —sustains.
(See science, health, cleanliness.)

HYGIENIC

adverbs
wonderfully; satisfactorily; unusually; unquestionably; commendably; appreciably; safely; warrantably; authoritatively; properly; duly; appropriately; securely; perfectly; completely; agreeably; prophylactically; sanitatively; sanitarily; usefully; remarkably; wholesomely; avowedly; allegedly; matchlessly; superbly; supremely; acceptably; splendidly.

HYMN

adjectives
celestial; anguished; tuneful; joyful; measured; ceaseless; wrathful; pious; solemn; undying; ancient; impassioned; nuptial; appropriate; choral; swelling; pretty; dreadful; metaphorical; edifying; impious; vernal; sentimental; angelic; warbled; exulting.

verbs
adore with—; arrange—; carol—; chant—; compose—; express in—; honor with—; hum —; quote—; rehearse—; whistle—; worship with—; —bursts forth; —delights; —extols; —glorifies; —honors; —praises; —resounds; —thanks.

(See song, composition, poem, music.)

HYPERBOLE

adjectives
eloquent; extravagant; original.

HYPNOTIC

adverbs
mysteriously; scientifically; strangely; professionally; amateurishly; allegedly; curiously; oddly; inscrutably; questionably; incredibly; supposedly; probably; possibly; slightly; incontrovertibly; dreadfully; fearfully; alarmingly; frightfully; highly; uncommonly; curatively; helpfully; experimentally; dangerously; terrifyingly; marvellously; ominously.

HYPNOTISM

verbs
advocate—; approve of—; consent to—; deride—; induce—; inject—; interest in—; fall into—; place under—; practise—; resist —; submit to—; succumb to—; treat by—; utilize—; witness—; —amends; —cures; —influences; —intrigues; —relieves.

(See sleep, spell.)

HYPOCHONDRIAC

adverbs
gloomily; dismally; incurably; unfortunately; miserably; sadly; distressingly; alarmingly; disturbingly; fanatically; insensately; unreasonably; irrationally; pitiably; blankly; abjectly; despondently; heavily; biliously; dreadfully; grimly; lamentably; lugubriously; inordinately; senselessly; helplessly; hopelessly; desperately; surprisingly.

HYPOCRISY

adjectives
smooth; habitual; adjusted; smug; unsleeping; transparent; coarse; blustering.

verbs
accuse of—; befog with—; blanket in—; clothe in—; couch in—; denounce—; despise —; detest—; discern—; explode—; feed—; oil with—; protest—; prove—; purge of—; repent—; steep in—; trick by—; —beguiles; —deceives; —disgusts; —frames; —veils.

(See insincerity, pretence, sham, affectation, trickery.)

HYPOCRITE

adjectives
honest; mealy-mouthed; vamped-up; cruising; canting; consummate; sharp; pompous; oily; lowborn.

verbs
denounce—; despise—; detect—; detest—; discern—; expose—; purge—; —affects; —beguiles; —binds; —blinds; —deceives; —disgusts; —feeds; —feigns; —oils; —poisons; —pretends; —tricks; —veils.

(See liar, snob.)

HYPOCRITICAL

adverbs
shamefully; obviously; palpably; evidently; scandalously; notoriously; infamously; outrageously; atrociously; undependably; faithlessly; disloyally; sanctimoniously; openly; falsely; contemptibly; atrociously; abominably; detestably; flagrantly; artfully; insincerely; evasively; flatteringly; ingeniously; perfidiously; craftily; shrewdly; basely; dangerously; terribly.

HYPOTHESIS

adjectives
problematical; unreal; rationalistic; unverified; monstrous; creative; metaphysical; untenable; tentative; scientific; cherished; inaccurate; superficial; unlikely.

verbs
accept—; advance—; apply—; argue on—; build up—; condemn—; consider—; deduce —; demonstrate—; depend on—; deride—; dispute—; draw—; evolve—; frame—; put forth—; reason by—; rest on—; state—; work on—; wreck—; —assumes; —embraces.

(See theory, supposition, assumption, information, fact.)

HYPOTHETICAL

adverbs
thinly; disguisedly; obviously; manifestly; usually; cleverly; shyly; serviceably; usefully; dubiously; vaguely; obscurely; precariously; supposably; academically; presumptively; stimulatingly; probably.

adjectives
military; imminent; continual; giggling.

verbs
augment—; blaze into—; convulse with—; excite to—; goad to—; indicate—; indulge in—; laugh in—; overcome—; prevent—; produce—; remedy—; restrain—; soothe—; struggle in—; subject to—; —attacks; —bubbles; —disturbs; —hovers near; —occurs; —presses; —wrecks.

(See nervousness, excitement, anger.)

adverbs
wildly; foolishly; remarkably; unreasonably; rabidly; loudly; nervously; intentionally; habitually; conveniently; profitably; contemptibly; provokingly; pitiably; unduly; insufferably; deliberately; miserably; helplessly; incoherently; capriciously; erratically; uncontrollably; ungovernably; incurably; incorrigibly; disconcertingly; distressingly; dreadfully; deliriously; furiously; passionately; angrily; fanatically; violently; uncommonly; highly.

I

ICE

adjectives
enchanted; tinkling; never-melting; thick-ribbed; confounded; congealed; treacherous; translucent; cerulean; gathered; perennial; anchor; polished; liquefied; crevassed; cushioned; crashing; everlasting; grinding; blue-white; glittering; phosphorescent; pellucid; transparent; overwhelming; drifted.

verbs
chip—; congeal to—; crush—; engulf in—; scar—; scrape—; shave—; sheet with—; smooth—; thaw—; tong—; —barricades; —blocks; —clinks; —drifts; —gleams; —glistens; —jams; —shimmers; —shines.

(See diamond, light, snow.)

ICEBERG

adjectives
glittering; sharp; jagged; ghostly; colossal; murderous; silent; ominous.

ICE-BOAT

adjectives
dainty; swift; wind-swept; dashing; gliding.

ICE-DRIFT

adjectives
heavy; ruinous.

ICICLE

adjectives
pendent; petrified; callous; living.

verbs
chip—; flow from—; —crashes; —s decorate; —drips; —endangers; —gleams; —glistens; —glitters; —shimmers; —shines; —suspends from; —thaws; —s weight.

ICINESS

adjectives
calm; bitter; calculated.

ICING

adjectives
rich; creamy; sparkling; sugar.

ICONOCLASTIC

adverbs
terribly; habitually; temperamentally; brutally; critically; harshly; inconsiderately; impiously; evilly; cruelly; dreadfully; unreasonably; wantonly; deliberately; irreverently; atheistically; disrespectfully; blasphemously; profanely; idiotically; egotistically; unintelligently; pretentiously.

ICY

adverbs
terribly; unbearably; significantly; horribly; unexpectedly; perilously; dangerously; hazardously; fearfully; impossibly; remarkably; peculiarly; curiously; hideously.

IDEA

adjectives
abiding; absorbing; abstract; adequate; admirable; aggressive; amazing; antiquated; approximated; artistic; ascetic; associated; attractive; bare; baseless; basic; beautiful; blasphemous; bold; brilliant; casual; charming; clashing; cherished; chimerical; classical; clear; cognate; cold; commanding; complete; confused; concrete; confined; conflicting; concluding; congealed; contemporary; contemptible; contrasting; conventional; crafty; critical; crude; cryptic; delicious; delirious; democratic; despicable; destructive; determinate; devouring; dim; disastrous; distinct; divergent; divine; dominant; dynamic; economical; educational; elementary; elevating; embryo; empty; endearing; entangled; entire; erroneous; essential; evolutionary; exaggerated; excellent; explicit; explosive; extraordinary; faintest; false; fantastic; fashionable; fastidious; fixed; flattering; fleeting; forward-moving; fundamental; funny; geographical; graceful; grandiose; grotesque; habitual; hazy; heathen; heroic; immature; impalpable; impolitic; impure; inane; inconceivable; inconvenient; industrial; ingenious; innate; insane; irruptive; jolly; literary; lofty; ludicrous; malicious; manifest; meditative; melodic; miscalled; mistaken; momentary; monarchic; musical; moral; money-making; nascent; nebulous; new; noble; notorious; novel; obvious; oft-repeated; opulent; original; pastoral; patentable; perfect; philosophical; picturesque; platitudinous; plebeian; poetical; ponderous; popular; preconceived; preposterous; prevailing; previous; primitivistic; private; profit-making; progressive; puzzling; quaint; radical; rational; realized; remote; repressed; retrogressive;

revolutionary; romantic; selling; sensational; sentimental; singular; sketchy; slightest; snob; sound; speculative; spiritual; spontaneous; spurious; stable; startling; sterling; stern; stimulating; striking; structural; sufficient; suggested; synthetic; systematic; tasteful; tempting; terrible; theologic; theoretical; traditional; tranquilizing; tutelary; twisted; ugly; unhappy; underlying; undesired; unexpected; unfulfilled; uninteresting; universal; unjust; unsound; vagrant; vague; vaporous; varied (pl); vile; well-grounded; whimsical; widespread; womanish; wonderful.

verbs
absorb—; amplify—; apprehend—; assemble—s; assimilate—s; balk at—; boil down —; brood upon—; cherish—; clarify—; color—; communicate—to; conceive—; concentrate on—; conform to—; contribute—; convey—; crystallize—; cultivate—; curb —; deride—; devote to—; disclose—; discredit—; dispel—; dissociate—from; divest of—; divulge—; elaborate on—; embed—in; endorse—; entertain—; entrench—; envisage—; evolve—; explode—; exploit—; expound—; favor—; fertilize—; formulate —; foster—; grasp—; grope for—; guard —; hail—; harbor—; hatch—; hit upon—; illuminate—; illustrate—; imbue with—; implant—; impose—; impregnate with—; incubate—; inculcate—; inspire—; interchange—s; invest with—; jot down—; launch—; modify—; mold—; mull over—; nourish—; obliterate—; obsess with—; overflow with—; patent—; pervert—; pioneer with—; play with—; ponder—; pounce upon —; promote—; promulgate—; pursue—; rally to—; recoil from—; refute—; reject —; relish—; repudiate—; retain—; reverse —; revive—; root—in; scoff at—; scorn—; set forth—; spike—; sprout—; stifle—; sum up—; superimpose—; suppress—; surrender to—; sustain—; symbolize—; toy with—; unfold—; visualize—; —clings; —s crowd; —dominates; —emanates from; —emerges; —endures; —flashes upon; —germinates; —haunts; —incorporates; —is born; —lurks; —matures; —permeates; —persists; —pops up; —predominates; —prevails; —progresses; —seeps in; —springs from; —takes shape; —wells up; embody in—; instil—; master—.

(See thought, opinion, design, plan, project, conception, impression, apprehension, ideal, belief, theory.)

IDEAL

verbs
assimilate—; betray—; cherish—; cling to —; consecrate to—; cultivate—; defend—; depart from—; elevate—s; embody—; exemplify—; extol—; forsake—; foster—; further—; imbue with—; inculcate—; ingrain—; inspire—; instill—; maintain—; mutilate—; nourish—; nurse—; owe to—; personify—; play havoc with—; preserve—; sacrifice to—; satisfy—; shatter—; shape—; symbolize—; weld to—; worship—; —aims at; —binds; —inspires; —permeates; —rests upon; realize—.

(See model, pattern, standard.)

adverbs
chimerically; dreamily; fantastically; perfectly; impossibly; extravagantly; romantically; preposterously; notionally; unsubstantially; whimsically; vaporously; entertainingly; emphatically; beautifully; charmingly; emptily; nebulously; speculatively; ridiculously; vaguely.

IDEALISM

adjectives
crystallized; poetical; romantic; moral; altruistic; impulsive; abstract; soaring; poignant.

verbs
breathe—; clothe in—; decry—; dwell in—; encourage—; found on—; inculcate—; marvel at—; nurse—; prate about—; sacrifice to—; temper with—; value—; voice—; tinge with—; —affirms; —compensates; —denies; —hampers; —melts; —reigns; —teaches; —transcends.

(See honesty, confidence, faith, trust.)

IDEALIST

adjectives
unconscious; rash; fatuous.

verbs
chain—; criticize—; delude—; disenchant —; disillusion—; enthrall—; frustrate—; hamper—; —cherishes; —contemplates; —despises; —dreams; —envisions; —regards; —sacrifices; —speculates on; —values.

(See poet, writer, philosopher, artist, author.)

IDEALITY

adjectives
refined; poetic; muzzy; confused; muddled.

IDEALS

adjectives

chivalrous; romantic; fatal; perfect; undigested; adequate; false; poetic; elevating; sublime; temperate; vague; educational; cherishing; retrograde; fanciful; picturesque; exalted; abstract; empty; ultimate; spiritual; collective; theoretical; factitious; racial; intangible; entrancing; complete; visionary; industrial; literary; ascetic; divine; unfulfilled; tutelary; cherished; degrading; distant; bric-a-brac; noble; affecting; unavowed; unclean; ethical; secret; antiquated; stern; unattainable.

IDENTIFICATION

adjectives

imputed; obliterated; spurious.

IDENTIFY (*v*)

adverbs

unconsciously; mystically; irrevocably; peculiarly; . mechanically; ecclesiastically; prominently; nominally.

(See recognize, ascertain.)

IDENTITY

adjectives

concealed; conscious; obliterated; substantial; separate; sweet; veritable; undiscovered; revealed; fictitious.

verbs

assure of—; conceal—; convince of—; demand—; determine—; discourage—; doubt —; establish—; forfeit—; grope for—; lose —; merge—with; preserve—; recognize—; reveal—; seek—; substantiate—; suggest—; suspect—; —leaks out; —perplexes; prove—.

(See similarity, individuality, accuracy.)

IDIOCY

adjectives

sublimest; teeth-chattering; morbid; impertinent.

IDIOM

adjectives

delicate; racial; succinct; racy; vulgar; national; quaint; absurd.

verbs

approve of—; cherish—; excel in—s; express in—; familiarize with—; interpret—; maintain—; repeat—; speak in—; translate —; transmit in—s; —amuses; —confuses; —differs; —glows; —perplexes.

(See expression, phrase, speech, dialect, jargon, word, thought.)

DIOSYNCRASY

adjectives

personal; morbid; sickly; separate.

verbs

ban—; dispense with—; foster—; humor—; imitate—; indulge in—; inherit—; parade —s; permit—; protest—; question—; restrain—; ridicule—; tolerate—; transmit—; understand—; warrant—; wonder at—; —embarrasses; —perplexes; —puzzles.

(See eccentricity, characteristic, habit.)

IDIOT

adjectives

mad; contemplative; congenial; insolent; blinking; sloppy; sentimental; monumental; stargazing; optimistic; notorious.

verbs

bar—; behave like—; conceal—; content—; control—; guard—; incarcerate—; lament —; manage—; mistrust—; play—; please —; shelter—; tolerate—; treat—; witness —; —amuses; —blinks; —dotes on; —giggles; —mistakes; —misunderstands; —ogles; —stares.

(See fool, imbecile, dunce, lunatic.)

IDIOTIC

adverbs

pathetically; hopelessly; incurably; congenitally; insolently; monumentally; crazily; purposely; maddeningly; utterly; foolishly; infatuatedly; rashly; recklessly; simply; childishly; nonsensically; blatantly; dully; extravagantly; grossly; idly; inappropriately; injudiciously; obtusely; ridiculously; senselessly; unwisely; stolidly; stupidly; spoonily.

IDLE

adverbs

vexatiously; languidly; lazily; slothfully; constitutionally; preferably; naturally; habitually; obesely; contemptibly; selfishly; sleepily; delightfully; continually; obstinately; stupidly; deliberately; torpidly; stubbornly; irresponsibly; reprehensibly; inexcusably; unduly; remarkably; strangely; unusually; dreadfully.

IDLE (v)

adverbs
frivolously; disreputably; intellectually; listlessly; aimlessly; wantonly; blissfully; degenerately; disgracefully; talkatively.
(See trifle, loaf.)

IDLENESS

adjectives
disgraceful; good-night; busy; unwilling; chatty; disreputable; intellectual; enforced; compulsory; conscientious; ancient; shapeless; elegant; rapturous; summer; absent; fatal; listless; sheer; aimless; settled; inert.

verbs
avoid—; banish—; denounce—; dread—; excuse—; hatch in—; maintain in—; pillow in—; repose in—; reproach—; revel in—; shake off—; stagnate in—; thrive in—; wallow in—; waste in—; —beguiles; —breeds; —demoralizes; —destroys; —harms; —poisons; —rusts; —shames; —tempts; —wearies.
(See indolence, futility.)

IDLER

adjectives
luxurious; busy; dependent; shiftless; studied; practiced.

IDOL

adjectives
burning; particular; subterraneous; lifeless; baser; grim; brass; vile; well-painted; matinee; youthful; gross; shapeless; gilded; bewitching; celebrated.

verbs
bless—; bow before—; cast down—; chant to—; clasp—; found—; mock—; offer to—; profane—; prostrate before—; renounce—; sacrifice to—; serve—; worship—; —embodies; —represents.
(See image, representation, effigy, notion, fallacy, hero, altar.)

IDOLATROUS

adverbs
fanatically; foolishly; infatuatedly; fatuously; inordinately; fantastically; extravagantly; irrationally; fervently; ridiculously; absurdly; oddly; passionately; superstitiously; credulously; bigotedly; wildly; enthusiastically; rabidly; grossly; inconceivably; blindly.

IDOLATRY

adjectives
social; long-upheld; popular; passionate; bloody; religious; foolish; enthusiastic.

IDOLIZE (v)

adverbs
inordinately; foolishly; lovingly; adoringly; passionately; madly; religiously; fervently; faithfully; fanatically.
(See adore, worship.)

IDYLLIC

adverbs
blissfully; romantically; sentimentally; rapturously; ecstatically; fancifully; extravagantly; inexpressibly; indescribably; beautifully; marvelously; utterly.

IGNITE (v)

adverbs
spontaneously; abruptly; dangerously; spectacularly; swiftly; furiously; startlingly; brilliantly; mechanically.
(See kindle, excite, rouse, burn.)

IGNOBLE

adverbs
basely; undeniably; surprisingly; despicably; unbelievably; horribly; contemptibly; grossly; consciously; deliberately; innately; naturally; inexpressibly; hopelessly; notoriously.

IGNOMINIOUS

adverbs
shamefully; contemptibly; ingloriously; scandalously; abjectly; arrantly; shockingly; dreadfully; terribly; unmentionably; outrageously; obscurely; inexpressibly; unbelievably; humbly; vaguely.

IGNOMINY

adjectives
imputed; complete; undesired.

verbs
arise from—; base on—; bear—; bow in—; confess to—; cover with—; crumble into—; endure—; eradicate—; fall into—; hide in —; reveal—; rise above—; spring from—; subject to—; suffer—; veil—; —chains; —degrades; —dishonors; —pursues.
(See disgrace, dishonor, infamy, defeat.)

IGNORAMUS

adjectives
splendid; hopeless; obvious; posturing.

IGNORANCE

adjectives
presumptuous; simple; personal; intelligent; self-loved; brutal; complete; deplorable; widespread; absolute; prevailing; singular; guilty; primitive; genteel; amazing; gross; fatuous; pure; universal; mingled; sheer; miraculous; timid; sanctified; blissful; faithless; desperate; profound; admirable; modest; entire; woeful; unpained; learned; crass; barbaric; swirling; helpless; disconcerting; honest; deep; extreme; violent; popular; general; culpable; intense; daring; dense; blind; humble; spotless; impertinent; naked; glooming; united; intellectual; polished; manifold; feigned; maidenly; perpetual; childish.

verbs
alienate through—; bare—; betray—; brand —; breed—; conceal—; condemn—; confess —of; deplore—; emancipate from—; expose —; forgive—; foster—; lapse into—; mock —; nurture—; remain in—; remedy—; scoff at—; shroud in—; tolerate—; yield to—; —blinds; —darkens; —deforms; —prejudices; —shames.
(See stupidity, foolishness, illiteracy.)

IGNORANT

adverbs
hopelessly; blissfully; dully; abjectly; absurdly; shamefully; utterly; merrily; stupidly; crassly; stolidly; contentedly; obviously; terribly; criminally; inexcusably; unfortunately; deplorably; curiously; strangely; grossly; woefully; painfully; helplessly; deeply; culpably; amazingly; uncommonly.

IGNORE (*v*)

adverbs
snobbishly; blandly; blatantly; antagonistically; scornfully; contemptuously; sneeringly; uncivilly; impudently.
(See snub, disregard.)

ILL

adjectives
oppressive; infinite; unmitigated; cruel; invisible; obscure; vindictive; false; malign; financial; cureless; sundry (pl); swooning; foulest; specific; dreadful; violent; approaching; virulent; knowing; earthly; willing; matchless; economic; hastening; invented.

verbs
banish—; better—; correct—; decry—; defend from—; destroy—; endure—; expatiate on—; feign—s; foreshadow—s; grieve over —; incur—; number—s; occasion—; remedy —; suffer—; unravel—; work—s; —s befall; —s beset; —s confront; —s disappear; —s distress; —s imperil; —shadows.
(See evil, misfortune, disease, pain.)

ILL

adverbs
seriously; desperately; slightly; temporarily; violently; honestly; strangely; fatally; mortally; naturally; extremely; cruelly; incurably; terribly; irrecoverably; unhappily; unfortunately; woefully; recently.

ILL-BRED

adverbs
boorishly; crassly; grossly; downright; unbelievably; notoriously; shamelessly; terribly; unbearably; offensively; barbarously; cruelly; intolerably; shamefully; deplorably; lamentably; woefully; obnoxiously; extremely; dreadfully; curiously; obviously.

ILLEGAL

adverbs
notoriously; admittedly; obviously; dangerously; trickily; shamelessly; vaguely; obscurely; flagrantly; perilously; riskily; openly; daringly; audaciously; villainously; viciously; flagitiously; shamefully.

ILLEGALITY

adjectives
obvious; apparent; declared; widespread.

verbs
censor—; charge—; conceal—; condemn—; criticize—; cure of—; deal with—; espy—; foster—; oppose—; permit—; protest—; punish—; rectify—; taint with—; tolerate —; war on—.
(See crime, dishonesty.)

ILLEGIBLE

adverbs
utterly; quasi; entirely; hopelessly; shamefully; vexatiously; carelessly; childishly; purposely; intentionally; deliberately; aged-

ly; scrawlingly; indecipherably; pompously; unfortunately; unluckily; crampedly; deplorably; woefully; strangely; unusually; habitually; uncommonly; feebly.

ILLEGITIMATE

adverbs
nefariously; criminally; obviously; admittedly; horribly; cruelly; woefully; deliberately; dangerously; riskily; hazardously; audaciously; daringly; heinously; extremely; curiously; flauntingly; flagrantly; shamelessly; hopelessly; notoriously.

ILLIBERAL

adverbs
fanatically; narrowly; bigotedly; stingily; meanly; basely; selfishly; cruelly; parsimoniously; sordidly; uncharitably; necessarily; temperamentally; innately; naturally; habitually; prejudicially; provincially; dogmatically; stupidly; unreasonably; penuriously; shabbily; exceedingly; remarkably; notoriously.

ILLICIT

adverbs
criminally; obviously; shamefully; furtively; stealthily; perilously; ignominiously; strangely; desperately; contemptibly; horribly; cruelly; dangerously; fearfully; unaccountably; terribly.

ILLITERACY

adjectives
pitiful; undesirable; brutish; inert.

verbs
campaign against—; conceal—; condemn—; curse with—; excuse—; hide—; induce—; judge—; nourish—; plead—; rectify—; reform—; remedy—; ridicule—; shroud in—; test—; tolerate—.

(See ignorance, blunder, error, stupidity.)

ILLITERATE

adverbs
boorishly; shamefully; provincially; hopelessly; helplessly; innocently; unduly; lazily; slothfully; shamelessly; surprisingly; unexpectedly; woefully; deplorably; amazingly; utterly; remarkably; unreasonably; inexplicably; pitiably; sadly; completely; barbarously; terribly.

ILL-MANNERED

adverbs
unpardonably; unforgivably; crudely; sensationally; boorishly; exceptionally; woefully; pitifully; ignorantly; hopelessly; offensively; curiously; strangely; inexplicably; oddly; surprisingly; terribly; amazingly; inordinately; inexcusably; utterly; positively; unbearably; unendurably; ungraciously; flagrantly; boisterously.

ILL-NATURED

adverbs
peevishly; fretfully; meanly; unbearably; innately; naturally; constitutionally; curiously; strangely; inexplicably; oddly; querulously; viciously; brutally; maliciously; slanderously; obviously; dreadfully; implacably; harshly; sternly; unutterably; completely; irremediably.

ILLNESS

adjectives
deadly; wearisome; passing; desperate; pernicious; chronic; prolonged; unsuspected; fatal; exhausting; disabling; frequent (pl); trifling; acute; separate; particular; severe; protracted; slow; gradual; wearing; dangerous; absolute; serious; violent; hopeless; lingering.

verbs
attend with—; combat—; contract—; convalesce from—; cure—; diagnose—; exempt from—; guard against—; hinder by—; induce—; recuperate from—; report—; succumb to—; suffer—; —abates; —debilitates; —enfeebles; —prostrates; —seizes; —weakens.

(See disease, malady, sickness, ailment, complaint, indisposition.)

ILLOGICAL

adverbs
strangely; absurdly; vexatiously; alarmingly; dangerously; ridiculously; ominously; perilously; irrationally; terribly; deliberately; ignorantly; shortsightedly; unstably; trickily; speciously; inordinately; irritatingly; wildly; viciously; particularly; dreadfully; uncommonly; impulsively; evasively; foolishly.

ILLUMINATE (*v*)

adverbs
singularly; brilliantly; gloriously; vividly; feebly; sparklingly; indirectly; partially.

(See brighten, adorn.)

ILLUMINATION

adjectives

full; softened; glorious; public; burning; phosphoric; faintest; brilliant; secondary; partial; competent; rude; veritable; indirect.

ILLUMINE (*v*)

adverbs

clearly; vividly; brilliantly; fully; faintly; publicly.

(See adorn, brighten.)

ILLUSION

adjectives

self-imposed; transparent; phantasmagorical; egregious; optical; innocent; grave; desired; ambrosial; childlike; brief; gorgeous; fantastic; strange; dramatic; auditory; kindred (pl); terrifying; momentary; sacred; brilliant; vague; exquisite; romantic; beloved; concrete; shattered; spectral; charming; dazzling; sweet; pleasing; multiplied (pl).

verbs

awaken from—; beguile with—; cherish—; complete—; create—; cultivate—; destroy—; dispel—; dispose of—; dissolve—; entertain—; extirpate—; harbor—; illustrate—; maintain—; mask—; prolong—; shatter—; strip of—; suffer—; sweep away—; triumph over—; uncover—; wander in—; —blinds; —crumbles; —haunts; —lulls; —persists; —prevails; —robs; —stupefies.

(See misconception, delusion, hallucination, idea, fallacy.)

ILLUSIVE

adverbs

fancifully; imaginarily; romantically; ideally; whimsically; extravagantly; fabulously; notionally; insubstantially; visionarily; fantastically; phantasmally; spectrally; imaginatively; chimerically; wildly; singularly; preposterously; absurdly; unreasonably; ridiculously; irrationally.

ILLUSTRATE (*v*)

adverbs

profusely; copiously; adequately; abundantly; humorously; liberally; vividly; lavishly; dramatically; admirably; splendidly; graphically; superbly; instructively; vivaciously; curiously; decoratively.

(See draw, engrave, describe.)

ILLUSTRATION

adjectives

suppositious; striking; sublime; graphic; prophetic; amusing; practical; accompanying; superb; helpful; gorgeous; excellent; plentiful; delightful; crude; sufficient; fearful; extreme; lithographic; sketchy; notable; instructive; apt; vivacious; curious; profuse; inimitable; elaborate; occasional; decorative; interesting; irrelevant; concrete; dreamy; brilliant; cogent; vivid; dramatic; fair; typical; forcible; modest; touching; well-known; supreme; elusive; descriptive; pleasant; puerile; exotic; magnificent.

verbs

afford—; commend—; criticize—; design—; display—; draw—; embellish—; exhibit—; lend to—; popularize—; pour forth—s; —adorns; —attracts; —caricatures; —depicts; —emphasizes; —exemplifies; —explains; —glorifies; —indicates; —interests; —proves.

(See comparison, example, picture, sketch, photograph.)

ILLUSTRIOUS

adverbs

splendidly; brilliantly; distinctly; broadly; orably; famously; proudly; unimpeachably; generally; conspicuously; imperishably; hon-deservedly; enviably; nobly.

ILL-WILL

verbs

bear—; derive—; display—; haunt by—; incite—; incur—; infect with—; level—at; mock with—; moderate—; nourish—; poison with—; regard with—; repent—; resent—; scorn—; —barks; —bites; —blinds; —chills; —curdles; —disturbs; —lashes.

(See malice, hatred, antipathy, resentment, rancor, grudge.)

IMAGE

adjectives

dead; latest; fixed; dull; mimic; remembered; faint; delusive; watery; sacred; mental; faithful; concise; imperial; wavering; colossal; familiar; pathetic; discreet; wandering; visionary; helpless; fallen; blurred; falsest; contrasted; imperfect; radiant; licentious; agreeable; vague; tissued; thronging (pl); sweetest; tremulous; reduced; indistinct; sainted; idolatrous; teasing; rude; carved; graven; serene; sublime; heavenly; impassive; bronze; waxen;

scattered (pl); flying; livid; exact; unsculptured; spitting; distorted; monstrous; confused; hampered; lovely; mysterious; visible; newborn; ludicrous; perceptible; royal; peace-bearing; magnified; graceful; wonder-working; wrinkled; heroic; constant; effective; fallen; luminous; palpitating; deathlike; fantastic; delicate; pleasant; vivid; poetical; horrible; foul; votive; reflex; compendious; dreamlike; artificial; subordinate; molten.

verbs
bow before—; call up—; carve—; confront with—; conjure up—; convey—; distort—; efface—; etch—; evoke—; evolve—; exalt —; focus—; perpetuate—; picture—; preserve—; project—; reflect—; reject—; retain—; scorn—; stamp—; summon—; transform—; transmit—; —blooms; —gleams; —glimmers; —represents; —terrifies.

(See imitation, representation, conception, idea, figure, statue, hallucination, picture.)

IMAGERY

adjectives
mental; external; woven; obscene; metaphorical; definite; amorphous; oriental; passionate; childish; vivid; pensive; carven; sculptured; learned; wondrous; colorful; glowing; inapplicable.

IMAGINABLE

adverbs
scarcely; easily; readily; horribly; illusively; barely; possibly; hardly; dimly; vaguely.

IMAGINARY

adverbs
undoubtedly; probably; highly; possibly; unquestionably; assuredly; vexatiously; pitiably; hypothetically; supposedly; illusively; definitely.

IMAGINATION

adjectives
luxuriant; emotional; proud; copious; splendid; morbid; ardent; vivid; exacting; realizing; kindling; atavistic; inquisitive; teeming; creative; youthful; pure; retired; somber; poetic; sympathetic; rustic; capricious; irreverent; kindly; lively; indolent; veracious; astounding; exuberant; glorious; fertile; constructive; powerful; sanest; diseased; dim; contemporaneous; heated; restless; headlong; respective; fond; sluggish; cultivated; warm; historic; disorderly; ardent; ribald; popular; foul; cumulative; daring; tensest; fruitful; disordered; morbid; pure; solitary; retired; limitless; salty; fever-driven; agile; plastic; epic; hyperbolical; inventive; apt; quick; gifted; robust; defective; delicate; irrepressible; unconfinable; dire; dark; mortal; heated; distempered; boyish; idealizing; burning; jaded; penetrating; scientific; riotous; melancholic.

verbs
ballast—; capture—; check—; confine—; confound—; curb—; develop—; distort—; drift in—; dull—; enslave—; exercise—; fire—; flow from—; inflame—; infuse into —; kindle—; nurture—; parade before—; pursue in—; revel in—; seize—; spur—; stagger—; stain—; stimulate—; stretch—; tax—; transcend—; breaks loose—; —elucidates; —envisages; —pictures; —recoils; —runs away; —soars; —vaults.

(See conception, image, fancy, fantasy, vision, mind, brain, power.)

IMAGINATIVE

adverbs
highly; wildly; violently; unstably; obviously; creatively; inventively; usefully; inconsistently; untrustworthily; romantically; admirably; wonderfully; remarkably; brilliantly; artistically; extremely; deeply; beautifully; inordinately; fearfully; dangerously.

IMAGINE (v)

adverbs
optimistically; poetically; nobly; vainly; fondly; swiftly; vividly; vaguely; naively; emotionally; morbidly; ardently; capriciously; irreverently; indolently; exuberantly; heatedly; sluggishly; daringly; irrepressibly; scientifically; riotously.

(See dream, suppose, fancy.)

IMAGININGS

adjectives
vain; bilious; untutored; profound; fervid; horrible; chimerical; fertile; mystic; audacious.

IMBECILE

adjectives
financial; inept; vacuous; egregious.

IMBECILITY

adjectives
vehement; congenital; wonted; cheerful; incurable.

verbs
confirm—; contemplate—; contend against —; cure—; curse with—; foster—; lament —; punish—; reduce to—; shelter—; sustain—; verge on—; —confounds; —damages; —endangers; —irks; —itches; —maddens; —provokes.
(See foolishness, feebleness, stupidity.)

IMBED (*v*)

adverbs
deeply; firmly; permanently; snugly; concretely; securely.
(See bury.)

IMBIBE (*v*)

adverbs
copiously; sympathetically; insensibly; generously; freely; liberally; unstintingly.
(See drink, absorb, assimilate.)

IMBIBING

adjectives
generous; profuse; ravenous insatiate.

IMBUE (*v*)

adverbs
thoroughly; deeply; wholesomely; morally; naturally; insidiously; tacitly; psychologically.
(See impress, tinge.)

IMITATE (*v*)

adverbs
ludicrously; successfully; fearlessly; superfluously; inimitably; consciously; effectively; exquisitely; preposterously; authentically; creditably; slavishly; palpably; obviously.
(See impersonate, simulate, copy.)

IMITATION

adjectives
literal; unintentional; corrupt; preposterous; considerable; cunning; sorry; dead; wretched; lifeless; authentic; cheap; mortifying; makeshift; exaggerated; showy; flattering; excellent; creditable; sickly; curious; slavish; miserable; laughable; clumsy; accurate; effective; vociferous; direct; narrative; palpable; elaborate; obvious; apish.

verbs
alter—; condemn—; disguise—; praise—; recognize—; reduce to—; savor of—; —borrows; —defaces; —falters; —feeds on; —injures; —mimics; —models; —ransacks; —resembles; —steals.
(See copy, counterfeit, parody.)

IMITATIVE

adverbs
cleverly; skillfully; brilliantly; adroitly; expertly; unconsciously; deliberately; preposterously; fantastically; cheaply; admiringly; derisively; laughably; accurately; effectively; devotedly; affectionately; extraordinarily; perfectly; apishly; absurdly.

IMITATIVENESS

adjectives
selective; sycophantic; vigilant; wary.

IMITATOR

adjectives
literal; servile; accidental; circumspect.

IMMACULATE

adverbs
usually; perfectly; extraordinarily; completely; admirably; wonderfully; amazingly; utterly; faultlessly; consummately; sprucely; neatly; tidily; daintily; delicately; nattily; beautifully; pleasantly; attractively; wondrously; indescribably; entrancingly.

IMMATERIAL

adverbs
vaguely; definitely; admittedly; palpably; ephemerally; transiently; momentarily; temporarily; wholly.

IMMATURE

adverbs
ridiculously; disgustingly; rosily; appealingly; helplessly; delicately; shyly; absurdly; hopelessly; sweetly; wretchedly; crudely; surprisingly; coarsely; roughly; thoughtlessly; shiftlessly; terribly; unsuitably; unfortunately; preposterously; unbelievably; miserably; painfully; awkwardly; adorably; gawkily; feverishly; obviously; noisily; blithely; inexpressibly; markedly; dully; ingeniously; garrulously; incredibly.

IMMENSITY

adjectives
vast; involved; sublime; actual; unfriendly; unknowable; roofless; increate.

IMMERGE (v)

adverbs
partially; abruptly; wholly; suffocatingly; fatally; protectively; instinctively.
(See plunge, dip.)

IMMERSION

adjectives
continuous; partial; total.

IMMIGRANT

verbs
assimilate—s; awe—; bar—s; check—s; confuse—; distress—; finance—s; limit—s; perplex—; puzzle—; reduce—s; refuse—; shelter—; succor—; —Americanizes; —s crowd to; —lands; —settles.
(See alien, foreigner, stranger.)

adverbs
indiscriminately; transiently; recently; outlandishly; awkwardly; bewilderingly; conspicuously.

IMMIGRATION

adjectives
indiscriminate; limited.

verbs
assimilate—; ban—; check—; control—; curtail—; discourage—; finance—; govern —; harbor—; influence—; limit—; permit —; reduce—; restrict—; stimulate—; —distresses; —fluctuates; —shifts; —slackens.
(See invasion, penetration.)

IMMINENT

adverbs
immediately; terribly; ominously; perilously; dangerously; significantly; portentously; dreadfully; woefully; alarmingly; suddenly; fatally; gloomily; dismally; actually; inevitably; inescapably.

IMMOBILE

adverbs
stiffly; rigidly; curiously; absolutely; oddly; strangely; inexplicably; sternly; severely; altogether; stolidly; implacably; inimically; harshly; stubbornly; stupidly; phlegmatically; skeptically; uncomprehendingly; silently; statically.

IMMOBILITY

adjectives
intelligent; skeptical; perfect; awe-inspiring; deathly; masklike.

IMMODERATE

adverbs
foolishly; fantastically; palpably; wildly; inexcusably; hysterically; woefully; notoriously; inanely; distressingly; grievously; miserably; grossly; astoundingly; singularly; outlandishly; glaringly; fundamentally; naturally; innately; habitually; unfortunately.

IMMODEST

adverbs
dreadfully; inordinately; reprehensibly; wantonly; seductively; alluringly; shamefully; terribly; inexcusably; unpardonably; naturally; always; spitefully; unconsciously; deliberately; thoughtlessly; alarmingly; coarsely; grossly; crassly; brazenly; flagrantly; notoriously; offensively; horribly.

IMMODESTY

verbs
accuse of—; array in—; chasten—; decry—; denounce—.
(See coarseness, obscenity.)

IMMOLATE (v)

adverbs
religiously; selflessly; traditionally; customarily; perfunctorily; cruelly; barbarically.
(See sacrifice.)

IMMOLATION

adjectives
determined; enforced.

IMMORAL

adverbs
grossly; openly; audaciously; daringly; obstinately; insufferably; crassly; flagrantly; heinously; terribly; obviously; extraordinarily; blithely; carelessly; incurably; unwarrantably; iniquitously; criminally; viciously; brazenly; scandalously; infamously; notoriously; sadly; atrociously; brutally; despicably; incorrigibly; malevolently; obdurately.

IMMORALITY

adjectives
coarse; cruel; wanton; flagrant; ugly; blatant; obvious; evident; daring; reprehensible; impenitent; hardened; hopeless; notorious; gross; boundless.

IMMORTAL

adverbs
divinely; gloriously; ineffably; immemorially; sublimely; sacredly; illustriously.

IMMORTALITY

verbs
achieve—; admit—; allege—; assure of—; commune with—; crown with—; deny—; destine to—; dwell in—; earn—; escape to —; flourish in—; rejoice in—; seek—; win —; —degrades; —endures; —exempts.
(See infinity, permanence, stability, sanctity, holiness.)

IMMOVABLE

adverbs
obstinately; stubbornly; altogether; completely; stiffly; firmly; stably; permanently; fixedly; inveterately; indestructibly; quietly; tenaciously; mulishly; inexorably; doggedly; wilfully; inertly; dogmatically; horribly; sternly; harshly; obdurately.

IMMUNE

adverbs
naturally; happily; fortunately; luckily; freely; properly; warrantably; authoritatively; legally; exceptionably; constitutionally; presumptively; duly; legitimately.

IMMUNITY

adjectives
national; glorious; happy; tolerable; various (pl); just; precarious; comparative.

verbs
acquire—; break—; confer—upon; enjoy—; favor with—; grant—; guarantee—; hope for—; induce—; observe—; preserve—; prove—; purchase—; test—; —exempts; —frees; —lasts.
(See exemption, freedom.)

IMMUTABLE

adverbs
divinely; sacredly; naturally; celestially; spiritually; permanently; securely; timelessly; marvelously.

IMP

adjectives
impudent; squabbling; mercurial; sturdy; unmerciful.

IMPACT

adjectives
modulated; joyous; sharp; abrupt; physical.

verbs
calculate—; prepare for—; prevent—; resist —; —communicates; —destroys; —drives; —impresses; —jams; —pinions; —presses; —rends; —resounds; —shatters; —splits; —stamps; —vibrates; —violates; —wedges.
(See collision, force, contact, blow.)

IMPAIR (*v*)

adverbs
palpably; seriously; disastrously; permanently; superficially; fatally; dangerously; cruelly.
(See ruin, injure, weaken.)

IMPALPABLE

adverbs
evanescently; transitorily; ephemerally; vaporously; nebulously; vexatiously; tormentingly; evasively; intangibly; teasingly; curiously; oddly; alluringly; altogether.

IMPART (*v*)

adverbs
concisely; confidentially; abundantly; secretly; trustingly; tacitly; freely; uninhibitedly.
(See communicate, give, grant, disclose.)

IMPARTIAL

adverbs
thoroughly; carefully; judicially; meticulously; particularly; admirably; properly; scarcely; cautiously; punctiliously; affectionately; paternally; grudgingly; cleverly; astutely; craftily; sagaciously; wisely; reasonably; prudently; keenly; sharply; shrewdly; perfectly; discreetly; considerately; politically; moderately; faithfully; scrupulously; conscientiously.

IMPARTIALITY

adjectives
editorial; historic; deliberate; absolute; pretended; imperial; known; magnanimous; perfect.

verbs
approve of—; commend—; conduct with—; depart from—; encourage—; favor with—; feign—; judge with—; maintain—; observe —; perform with—; practice—; praise—;

prescribe—; preserve—; profess—; seek—; stamp with—; submit to—; veer from—; witness with—; —assures.

(See fairness, justice, equity.)

IMPASSABLE

adverbs
utterly; completely; undeniably; obviously; clearly; obstinately; desperately; hopelessly; incontrovertibly; admittedly; evidently; manifestly.

IMPASSIONED

adverbs
rapturously; ecstatically; ardently; fervently; feverishly; utterly; sublimely; eloquently; fervidly; amorously; gloriously; vehemently; wildly; fiercely; enthusiastically; fanatically; eagerly; impulsively; impetuously; irrepressibly; excitedly; utterly; violently; foolishly; vainly.

IMPASSIVE

adverbs
stoutly; phlegmatically; stupidly; dully; stolidly; apathetically; neutrally; quietly; serenely; provokingly; resolutely; deliberately; frightfully; alarmingly; dreadfully; ominously; portentously; deafly; blindly; obtusely; obdurately; languidly; indifferently; uncommonly; deeply; carelessly; callously; imperturbably; maddeningly.

IMPATIENCE

adjectives
intolerable; nervous; polyglot; vehement; thwarted; balked; obvious; angry; insolent; feverish; languishing; demonstrative; rash; surprised; ungovernable; helpless; ill-concealed; unreasonable; singular; restless; filial; enraged; domineering; passionate; ferocious; repressed; uncalculating; rude; burning; subdued; bored; irritating; fidgety.

verbs
betray—; burn with—; calm—; chastise—; crack with—; detect—; dispose toward—; enrage with—; fever with—; prance with —; rage in—; remedy—; sheathe—; spur on by—; struggle with—; warn against—; —amazes; —angers; —grasps; —irritates; —stings; control—.

(See restiveness, restlessness, uneasiness, nervousness.)

IMPATIENT

adverbs
peevishly; fretfully; wildly; violently; vehemently; nervously; unduly; peckishly; vexatiously; surprisingly; inexcusably; incorrigibly; irritatingly; provokingly; feverishly; habitually; always; unpardonably; eagerly; happily; rapturously; childishly; inordinately; extremely; oddly; curiously; strangely; remarkably; unaccountably; inexplicably; unreasonably; disagreeably; unnecessarily.

IMPEACHMENT

adjectives
unfair; soft; withering; amusing.

verbs
acquit of—; anticipate—; carry—; clamor for—; conduct—; demand—; expose to—; justify—; lament—; prevent—; proceed to —; remove by—; suggest—; —disqualifies; —shames; —suspends.

(See accusation, arraignment, trial, arrest.)

IMPECCABLE

adverbs
admittedly; wholly; notoriously; altogether; clearly; exceptionally; consciously; unquestionably; utterly; notoriously; virtuously; incomparably.

IMPECUNIOUS

adverbs
wretchedly; pitiably; admittedly; obviously; terribly; woefully; uneasily; desperately; evidently; manifestly; strangely; curiously; destitutely; distressingly; embarrassingly; alarmingly; hopelessly.

IMPEDE (*v*)

adverbs
unaccountably; tragically; purposely; premeditatedly; totally; partially; mechanically.

(See hinder, obstruct.)

IMPEDIMENT

adjectives
sundry (pl); formidable; sluggish; occasional; visible; unaccountable.

verbs
admit—; bear—; breed —s; brush aside—; correct—; cure—; curse—; hurl aside—; pass—; remove—; resist—; —chains; —con-

strains; —delays; —disconcerts; —hinders; —irritates; —obstructs; —petrifies; —restrains; —restricts; —strangles; —vexes.

(See obstruction, hindrance, obstacle, difficulty, bar, barrier, encumbrance.)

IMPEL (v)

adverbs

blindly; steadily; simultaneously; instinctively; naturally; normally; sexually; emotionally; subconsciously.

(See drive, urge, incite.)

IMPENETRABLE

adverbs

dimly; darkly; densely; thickly; massively; absolutely; utterly; strangely; mysteriously; altogether; terribly; fearfully; blindly; unaccountably; solidly; pathlessly; inscrutably; hopelessly; defiantly; stubbornly; definitely; manifestly.

IMPERATIVE

adverbs

vitally; essentially; fundamentally; urgently; pressingly; harshly; severely; austerely; arbitrarily; absolutely; legally; tyrannically; strictly; rigidly; uncompromisingly; inexorably; dreadfully; highly.

IMPERCEPTIBLE

adverbs

altogether; definitely; materially; infinitesimally; miserably; comparatively; almost; unaccountably; impalpably; evanescently; nebulously; vaporously; obscurely; fuzzily; curiously; symbolically; inferentially; covertly.

IMPERFECT

adverbs

crassly; grossly; carelessly; obviously; manifestly; inexplicably; disastrously; wretchedly; unsatisfactorily; defectively; sketchily; crudely; disgustingly; annoyingly; inexcusably; hopelessly; unbelievably.

IMPERFECTION

adjectives

hateful; technical; degrading; moral.

verbs

alter—; complain of—; conceal—; criticize —; detect—; expose—; gloat over—; manifest—; note—; observe—; perceive—; remove—; reveal—; view—; x-ray for —s; —blemishes; —mars.

(See deficiency, fault, blemish, defect, flaw, shortcoming.)

IMPERIAL

adverbs

arrogantly; dogmatically; haughtily; regally; magisterially; domineeringly; royally; grandly; splendidly; pompously; proudly; beneficently; dictatorially; generously; cruelly; authoritatively; tyrannically; bossily; fussily; absolutely; supremely; magnificently; boldly.

IMPERIL (v)

adverbs

outrageously; recklessly; foolhardily; gallantly; thoughtlessly; intrepidly; daringly.

(See endanger, risk.)

IMPERIOUS

adverbs

disagreeably; regally; ridiculously; amusingly; tyrannically; arbitrarily; unreasonably; arrogantly; clownishly; airily; shockingly; unwarrantedly; officiously; ludicrously; despotically; hatefully; pompously; inherently; superciliously; loftily; haughtily; proudly; sharply; offensively; naturally; rudely; grossly.

IMPERIOUSNESS

adjectives

mighty; apparent.

IMPERISHABLE

adverbs

gloriously; lustrously; solemnly; splendidly; sublimely; eminently; magnificently; memorably; brilliantly; immutably; unchangeably; forever; grandly; astonishingly; incomparably.

IMPERSONAL

adverbs

coldly; vaguely; ineptly; indifferently; politely; disagreeably; evasively; nonchalantly; casually; frigidly; disinterestedly; vexatiously; unpardonably; horribly; detestably; broadly; sweepingly; generally; arrogantly.

IMPERSONATE (v)

adverbs
inimitably; jocosely; vulgarly; lewdly; dexterously; shrewdly; artfully; histrionically; adequately; fancifully; phlegmatically.
(See represent, assume.)

IMPERSONATION

adjectives
heroic; scattered (pl); inadequate; succeeding; fanciful; phlegmatic.

IMPERTINENCE

adjectives
light; stunning; intrusive; damned; chirping; superb; delicate; female; fond; idiotic; preposterous.

IMPERTINENT

adverbs
grossly; ignorantly; foolishly; senselessly; inanely; unreasonably; disrespectfully; deliberately; crudely; purposely; intentionally; subtly; furtively; openly; flagrantly; defiantly; stupidly; unfortunately; idiotically; preposterously; astoundingly; blithely; outlandishly; crassly; brazenly; blatantly; ostentatiously; rudely; superciliously; saucily; pertly; bumptiously; shamelessly; boisterously; swaggeringly; terribly.

IMPERVIOUS

adverbs
tightly; snugly; callously; securely; satisfactorily; scientifically; hermetically; hopelessly; entirely; utterly; manifestly; reportedly; allegedly; actually; genuinely.

IMPETUOSITY

adjectives
characteristic; jocose; vehement; sinewy; flamboyant; irresistible.

verbs
attack with—; bear—; bridle—; check—; curb—; flame with—; mistrust—; obey—; overcome—; reply with—; repress—; rush into with—; subdue—; suppress—; —blunders; —endangers; —forces; —spurs; —tempts.
(See eagerness, passion, enthusiasm, exuberance, violence.)

IMPETUOUS

adverbs
foolishly; wildly; childishly; rashly; recklessly; thoughtlessly; inconsiderately; uncontrollably; violently; blithely; merrily; happily; precipitately; dangerously; generously; delightfully; enchantingly; engagingly; astonishingly; uncommonly; highly; roughly; boisterously; explosively; stormily; noisily; vivaciously; restlessly; indiscreetly; wantonly; adventurously; dreadfully.

IMPETUS

adjectives
accumulated; momentous; logical; considerable; enormous; great; fresh; intellectual; moral; united; desired.

verbs
acquire—; add—; bridle—; curb—; gather—; mistrust—; receive—; repress—; rush with—; struggle for—; —carries; —destroys; —directs; —forces; —overcomes.
(See momentum, impulse, incentive, stimulus.)

IMPIETY

adjectives
pure; natural; heinous; filial; negative; sacrilegious.

IMPIOUS

adverbs
dreadfully; disrespectfully; reprehensibly; irreverently; scornfully; terribly; scoffingly; deliberately; purposely; insultingly; inordinately; extraordinarily; ostentatiously; unforgivably; offensively; audaciously; frowardly; waywardly; blasphemously; profanely; unspeakably; infamously; astoundingly.

IMPLACABLE

adverbs
hopelessly; terribly; appallingly; shockingly; horribly; inexorably; harshly; sternly; severely; amazingly; suddenly; temperamentally; pitilessly; remorselessly; ruthlessly; cruelly; stolidly; immovably; uncommonly; remarkably; notoriousiy.

IMPLANT (v)

adverbs
deeply; vigorously; insidiously; skillfully; artfully; scientifically; artificially; subconsciously.
(See instill, plant.)

IMPLEMENTS

adjectives
martial; agricultural; trashy; crude; homemade; medicinal; fantastic; facile; ungainly; gainly.

IMPLICATE (v)

adverbs

rashly; vaguely; tacitly; socially; treacherously; shamefully; premeditatively; thoughtlessly; spitefully.

(See involve, entangle.)

IMPLICATION

adjectives

materialistic; covert; historical; moral; practical; far-reaching; small; tacit; social.

verbs

convey—; deny—; detect—; detest—; dodge —; fathom—; involve—; judge—; justify —; lament—; leave to—; pale at—; prove —; —confuses; —disturbs; —entangles; —entwines; —hints; —infers; —irritates; —shocks.

(See suggestion, entanglement, deduction, inference.)

IMPLICIT

adverbs

allusively; inferentially; expressly; subtly; secretly; doctrinally; indirectly; covertly; understandably; carefully; profoundly; cunningly; diplomatically; artfully.

IMPLORE (v)

adverbs

piteously; heartrendingly; beseechingly; plaintively; fruitlessly; ceaselessly; noisily; blatantly; repetitiously.

(See beg, entreat.)

IMPLY (v)

adverbs

obviously; virtually; suggestively; meaningfully; vaguely; slanderously; slyly.

(See signify, infer.)

IMPOLITE

adverbs

unbelievably; subtly; deliberately; ignorantly; crudely; awkwardly; unintentionally; purposely; inexcusably; habitually; always; cruelly; appallingly; shockingly; uncivilly; imprudently; indiscreetly; unfortunately; offensively; distastefully; openly; intentionally; superciliously; arrogantly; boisterously; roughly; noisily; grossly; brazenly; flagrantly.

IMPORT (*meaning*)

adjectives

sinister; serious; mystic; peaceful; physiological; enormous; direful; violent; spiritual; immediate; ominous; mysterious; weighty; reliable; hideous.

verbs

bear—; contemplate—; convey—; discern—; doubt—; overlook—; question—; value—; weigh—; —amazes; —baffles; —betokens; —disconcerts; —implies; —indicates; —interests; —involves; —perplexes; —states.

(See meaning, purport, signification, importance, significance.)

IMPORT (*trade*)

adjectives

vast; domestic; agricultural; mineral; excisable; dutiable.

IMPORT (v)

adverbs

exclusively; professionally; domestically; agriculturally; annually; legally.

IMPORTANCE

adjectives

paramount; distressing; incalculable; portentous; relative; pressing; subordinate; considerable; direct; practical; outstanding; primary; unworthy; vital; supreme; unspeakable; signal; slight; moral; overwhelming; valetudinarian; genuine; artistic; fictitious; decisive; intrinsic; comparable; rising; overstrained; anticipatory; preeminent; consequent; infinite; tremendous; historic; utmost; overshadowing; trifling; negligible; lingering; transcendent; commercial; strategic; proportionate; significant; requisite; enormous; commanding; vast; honorable; commercial; secondary; endless; profound; glowing; fundamental; grave; vanishing; conspicuous; apparent; absolute; mighty; plenary; immense; major; increasing; exaggerated; sufficient; exceptional; constitutional; far-reaching; perpetual; startling; cultural; infinitesimal; true; evident; ultimate; radical.

verbs

accentuate—; amplify—; assume—; attach —to; belittle—; bolster up—; convey—; detract from—; diminish—; dwarf—; enhance —; exaggerate—; feign—; imbue with—;

manifest—; minimize—; overemphasize—; overestimate—; overrate—; overwhelm with —; puff out with—; rob of—; signify—; stress—; swell with—; underestimate—; underrate—; weigh—of.
(See value, consequence, worth.)

IMPORTANT

adverbs
highly; urgently; gravely; seriously; materially; scarcely; terribly; extraordinarily; mysteriously; secretly; implicitly; unusually; personally; internationally; immeasurably; incalculably; ominously; vitally; genuinely; infinitely; tremendously; historically; commercially; exceptionally; peculiarly; particularly; oddly; astonishingly; profoundly.

IMPORTS (*merchandise*)

verbs
blockade—; curtail—; affect—; gain in—; increase—; levy on—; restrict—; stimulate —; tax—; —dwindle; —recede; —wane.
(See merchandise, wares.)

IMPORTUNATE

adverbs
persistently; endlessly; teasingly; provokingly; annoyingly; vexatiously; harrassingly; bothersomely; indiscreetly; incredibly; inappropriately; inconsiderately; inveterately; clamorously; unpleasantly; disagreeably; obnoxiously; piteously; pathetically; dreadfully; uncommonly; highly.

IMPORTUNE (*v*)

adverbs
shamelessly; rapturously; irritatingly; persistently; pressingly; incessantly; ceaselessly.
(See implore, beg.)

IMPORTUNITIES

adjectives
precluded; trivial; renewed.

IMPORTUNITY

verbs
ease—; endure—; experience—; indulge in —; labor under—; relax—; restrain—; sacrifice to—; satisfy—; suffer—; yield to—; —annoys; —chafes; —clamors; —goads; —irks; —irritates; —pains; —torments; —troubles.
(See insistence, urge, demand.)

IMPOSE (*v*)

adverbs
inordinately; wilfully; deliberately; tyrannically; disgracefully; legally; tactlessly; selfishly; thoughtlessly.
(See command, enjoin.)

IMPOSING

adverbs
splendidly; brilliantly; tremendously; magnificently; sublimely; incomparably; undeniably; satisfactorily; carefully; sensationally; dramatically; solemnly; remarkably; grandly; nobly; significantly; eminently; signally; immensely; enormously.

IMPOSITION

adjectives
tyrannical; disgraceful; illegal; tearful.

verbs
agree to—; avert—; avoid—; bar—; burden with—; enforce—; escape—; inflict—; levy—; necessitate—; overcome—; pay—; punish with—; refuse—; subject to—; suffer—; suspect—; —irks; —irritates.
(See abuse, tax, oppression, burden.)

IMPOSSIBILITIES

adjectives
wild; apparent; utter; undesired.

IMPOSSIBILITY

verbs
accomplish—; achieve—; admit—; argue—; attempt—; consider—; contemplate—; fret over—; hurdle—; lessen—; master—; overcome with—; remove—; render—; stress—; strip of—; wander in—; —chafes; —torments.

IMPOSSIBLE

adverbs
highly; probably; practically; altogether; presumably; allegedly; obviously; manifestly; evidently; naturally; hopelessly; desperately; wildly; utterly; absurdly.

IMPOSTOR

adjectives
privileged; crafty; latent; artistic; ignorant; vile; wretched.

IMPOTENCE

adjectives
peevish; terrorized; pitiful; glaring; languishing; unstable.

verbs
afflict with—; betray—; bewail—; denounce —; expose—; feel—; feign—; grieve over —; incur—; jibe at—; reduce to—; —agonizes; —displeases; —limits; —provokes; —restrains; —shames; —torments.

(See weakness, deficiency, fatigue, inefficiency.)

IMPOVERISHED

adverbs
somewhat; pitiably; ruinously; slightly; altogether; utterly; considerably; hopelessly; helplessly; incredibly; grievously; embarrassingly; distressingly; indigently; terribly; wretchedly; unfortunately; unbelievably; immeasurably.

IMPOVERISHMENT

verbs
conceal—; descend to—; discover—; dread —; endure—; further—; grind to—; inflict —; reduce to—; relieve—; steep in—; suffer —; tax to—; wallow in—; —attends; —distresses; —embitters; —scorches.

(See poverty, distress, need, privation.)

IMPRACTICABLE

adverbs
absurdly; terribly; notionally; absolutely; utterly; foolishly; manifestly; obviously; desperately; hopelessly; formidably; awkwardly; perplexingly; completely.

IMPRECATION

adjectives
dreadful; articulated; profane; elaborate; good-natured; loud; tumultuous; petulant; solemn; unprecedented.

verbs
abuse with—s; blacken with—; blast with —; crush with—; curse with—; fling—at; hurl—at; lash out—; mutter—; perish under —; pour out—; scorn—; shower—; whip with—; wilt under—; —frightens; —outrages; —pains; —stings.

(See oath, curse, denunciation.)

IMPREGNABILITY

verbs
attack—; beat at—; condemn—; defy—; deny—; derive—from; lessen—; overcome —; prove—; threaten—; —assures; —counteracts; —deteriorates; —discourages; —obstructs; —perishes; —represses; —repulses; —resists; —withstands.

(See strength, toughness, tenacity, security.)

IMPRESS (*v*)

adverbs
deeply; immensely; tremendously; vividly; profoundly; indelibly; forcibly; pitilessly; unduly; disagreeably; strikingly; palpably; vehemently; painfully; emotionally; humorously; solemnly; mysteriously; charmingly; austerely; superficially; fraudulently; spiritually; permanently.

(See affect.)

IMPRESSION

adjectives
vivid; mysterious; external; erroneous; weak; correct; tremendous; optimistic; exchanged (pl); charming; curious; chilling; half-preternatural; hoarse; dual; instantaneous; ineffaceable; misleading; ludicrous; sprawling; artistic; pleasant; immediate; violent; indelible; favorable; austere; cultural; false; lasting; explicable; earliest; subtle; majestic; feeble; deep; imperfect; unanalyzed; current; superficial; dissimilar; severest; half-farcical; painful; ungainly; prominent; suitable; profound; undiscernible; confused; intelligible; surface; repellent; powerful; momentary; unwelcome; mistaken; uneasy; desolate; penetrating; firm; childhood; sensual; journalistic; consequent; perceptible; private; acoustic; lively; dominant; outward; nameless; needful; orderly; illusory; delightful; divine; vague; amusing; ill-founded; fraudulent; faint; obscure; distinct; sincere; irresistible; all-pervading; antecedent; awful; reverent; indefinable; absolute; personal; grotesque; unmistakable; dangerous; maximum; chief; cheerful; undiscernible; spiritual; superstitious; comparative; prevalent; permanent; credulous; scarlike.

verbs
absorb—; analyze—; communicate—; confirm—; convey—; correct—; create—; crystallize—; deepen—; discount—; dissipate—; dull—; efface—; evoke—; formulate—; gain—; give rise to—s; interpret—; jumble —; justify—; record—; reproduce—; sharpen—; soften—; stamp—; strengthen—; sum-

marize—s; sum up—; sustain—; translate —; verify—; weaken—; —fades; —flickers out; —persists; —prevails; —seeps in.
(See effect, result, picture, action, achievement.)

IMPRESSIVE

adverbs
tremendously; splendidly; touchingly; deeply; uncommonly; oddly; incredibly; surprisingly; majestically; royally; powerfully; profoundly; unmistakably; sincerely; affectingly; overwhelmingly; mysteriously; inexplicably; strangely; subtly; vaguely; immensely.

IMPRINT (v)

adverbs
deeply; indelibly; permanently; artistically; strongly; professionally; skillfully.
(See print, stamp, mark.)

IMPRISON (v)

adverbs
temporarily; unjustly; legally; permanently; tyrannically; harshly; perpetually.
(See confine, restrain.)

IMPRISONMENT

adjectives
ignorant; severe; subsequent; prolonged; dreary; unjust; tyrannical; perpetual.

verbs
cast into—; condemn to—; confine to—; doom to—; frown upon—; inflict—; justify —; lament—; release from—; resort to—; sentence to—; suffer—; —bridles; —deprives; —deters; —divests; —gags; —scandalizes.
(See restriction, prison.)

IMPROBABLE

adverbs
altogether; entirely; curiously; palpably; highly; wholly; naturally; presumptively.

IMPROMPTU

adverbs
awkwardly; obviously; delightfully; enchantingly; diffidently; undisguisedly; spontaneously; gracefully; altogether; evidently; warmly; cordially; sincerely; wholly; charmingly.

IMPROPER

adverbs
shockingly; altogether; terribly; wantonly; carelessly; insolently; impudently; highly; inappropriately; offensively; flagrantly; defiantly; obstinately; ignorantly; bumptiously; recklessly; rashly; indiscreetly; imprudently; vexatiously; disagreeably; unpleasantly; wildly; incorrigibly; dreadfully; subtly; vaguely.

IMPROVE (v)

adverbs
markedly; rapidly; tremendously; suitably; infinitely; unquestionably; artificially; verbally; gradually; admirably; progressively; intellectually; definitely.
(See enhance, gain.)

IMPROVEMENT

adjectives
artificial; needed; pronounced; astonishing; invariable; substantial; admirable; ecclesiastical; religious; theoretical; decorative; laudable; salutary; effective; urban; progressive; noteworthy; sensible; revolutionary; eternal; intellectual; sensational; definite; industrious; profitable; corresponding; outstanding; internal; general; countless; continual; objective; perceptible; beneficial; concrete; perpetual; proposed; acoustic; mutual.

verbs
acclaim—; adopt—; applaud—; campaign for—; depart for—; evince—; experience—; institute—; manifest—; mark—; note—; observe—; pioneer—; promote—; push—; register—; restrict—; retard—; subject to —; undertake—; venture—; win—; yield—.
(See reform, recovery.)

IMPROVIDENT

adverbs
lamentably; unfortunately; culpably; hopelessly; incorrigibly; vexatiously; tragically; unbearably; impossibly; heedlessly; recklessly; rashly; thoughtlessly; inattentively; negligently; arrantly; flagrantly; cruelly; brutally; shiftlessly; injudiciously; wildly; impulsively; senselessly; culpably.

IMPROVISE (v)

adverbs
freely; dexterously; artistically; roughly; crudely; professionally; brilliantly.
(See extemporize, perform.)

IMPROVISED

adverbs
hastily; visibly; obviously; cleverly; skillfully; experimentally; oddly; instantly; adroitly; comically; adequately; successfully; impulsively; brilliantly; splendidly; marvellously; crudely; dexterously.

IMPRUDENT

adverbs
incorrigibly; hopelessly; altogether; carelessly; heedlessly; wantonly; strangely; wastefully; defiantly; disagreeably; rashly; recklessly; desperately; wildly; flagrantly; curiously; obstinately; utterly; precariously; indiscreetly; adventurously; dreadfully; astonishingly; uncommonly; highly.

IMPUDENCE

adjectives
overbearing; shameless; brazen; amazing; useless; passable; increasing; unbounded; bland; stupefying; happy; uncommon; magniloquent; interrupting.

IMPUDENT

adverbs
disgustingly; obstinately; stubbornly; stolidly; incurably; incorrigibly; oddly; strangely; curiously; noticeably; visibly; openly; flagrantly; noisily; boisterously; ostentatiously; recklessly; rashly; insolently; snobbishly; arrogantly; hopelessly; offensively; disagreeably; insufferably; heedlessly; wantonly; ignorantly; deliberately; purposely; terribly; astoundingly; surprisingly; habitually; occasionally; always.

IMPULSE

adjectives
peculiar; sudden; abrupt; unconscious; bibulous; burning; mad; perverse; speculative; visionary; violent; admirable; kindly; generous; irresistible; poetical; unintelligent; mutual; wandering; malignant; choice; successive (pl); lively; kinesthetic; changing; mighty; repressed; spontaneous; august; inward; dreadful; confiding; grateful; rash; strong; suspended; dramatic; subtle; pleasurable; lyrical; natural; deepest; simpler; animating; maddening; national; mysterious; creative; popular; simultaneous; senseless; unanimous; intensified; headlong; sonorous; inexplicable; selfsame; involuntary; overmastering; fierce; missionary; repressed; deep-reaching; celestial; morbid; immortal; disturbing; frustrated; blind; vital; governing; patriotic; analytic; upward; primary; chivalrous; wondrous; initial; common; romantic; instinctive; primitive; powerful; lightning; consecutive; intensifying; restless; motivating; piquant; unreasoning; singular; cordial; original; separate; drunken; obscure; latent; aristocratic; unguarded; indescribable; isochronous; unequaled; unprecedented; boisterous; warm; regular; excitable; westward; varying (pl); recurrent; uncontrollable; mastering; transcendent; catlike; electric; artistic; praiseworthy.

verbs
arouse—; block—; blunt—; choke—; control—; cultivate—; curb—; deaden—; destroy—; direct—; eradicate—; exercise—; exhaust—; follow—; impart—; manifest—; obey—; perform on—; respond to—; restrain—; sense—; sidetrack (colloq.)—; stifle—; subordinate—; suppress—; yield to—; —departs; —overwhelms; —persists; —rends; —sweeps over; —travels.

(See motive, incentive, impetus, ambition, desire.)

IMPULSIVE

adverbs
charmingly; utterly; habitually; temperamentally; innately; obviously; incorrigibly; wildly; enchantingly; alarmingly; extraordinarily; unstably; undependably; unreliably; indescribably; interestingly; dangerously; flightily; lamentably; deplorably; terribly; incredibly; imprudently; indiscreetly; bewitchingly; enthusiastically; irresistibly; heedlessly; adventurously; fanatically.

IMPURE

adverbs
definitely; positively; terribly; unfortunately; lewdly; indelicately; grossly; crassly; brazenly; indecently; foully; immodestly; obscenely; coarsely; lamentably; deplorably; meretriciously.

IMPURITY

verbs
cleanse of—; contaminate with—; defile by—; expel—; fling forth—; free from—; guard against—; inhale—; pollute with—; prevent—; purge of—; rid of—; swarm with—; tempt to—; —corrupts; —s deluge; —detracts from; —enters; —offends; —spreads.

(See dirt, filth, pollution, infection, squalor.)

IMPUTATIONS

adjectives
unworthy; injurious; scandalous.

IMPUTE (v)

adverbs
generally; erroneously; fallaciously; lavishly; speciously; injuriously; scandalously; unworthily; slanderously; viciously; vindictively.

(See charge, attribute.)

INABILITY

adjectives
sheer; restless; obvious; consequent; patent.

verbs
accept—; afflict with—; certify as to—; conceal—; dwell on—; judge—; observe—; overcome—; recognize—; regard—; remove —; respect—; —disqualifies; —distresses; —disturbs; —limits; —pains; —restrains; —restricts; —shames.

(See inefficiency, incompetence, helplessness, weakness, impotence, stupidity.)

INACCESSIBLE

adverbs
hopelessly; almost; desperately; altogether; presumably; allegedly; reportedly; remotely; utterly; incredibly; maddeningly; lamentably; preposterously; deplorably; positively; definitely; terribly; incredibly; tragically.

INACCURACY

adjectives
demoniac; unintentional; slight; gross.

verbs
calculate—; conceal—; condemn—; contain —s; correct—; couch in—; criticize—; curse —; deal in—; detect—; observe—; overlook—; plague with—s; prove—; rectify—; suffer—; —astonishes; —overwhelms.

(See error, blunder, mistake, misconception.)

INACCURATE

adverbs
lamentably; unacceptably; definitely; scientifically; mathematically; hopelessly; culpably; criminally; deliberately; slyly; utterly; slightly; fallaciously; mendaciously; purposely; carelessly; incautiously; calculably; positively; craftily; subtly; vaguely; bewilderingly; unbelievably; erroneously; accidentally; blunderingly; deceitfully; illusively; nefariously; egregiously.

INACTION

adjectives
unaccustomed; dreadful; silent; fruitless; enforced; inevitable; prolonged.

INACTIVE

adverbs
necessarily; helplessly; tragically; unfortunately; preferably; habitually; naturally; temperamentally; lamentably; unhealthfully; unluckily; lazily; languidly; torpidly; idly; indolently; sleepily; indifferently; lumpishly; passively; unintelligently; terribly; incredibly; hopelessly; undependably; unreliably; unhelpfully; sluggishly; vexatiously; disagreeably; cruelly; selfishly.

INACTIVITY

adjectives
sluggish; hopeless; enforced; protracted.

INADEQUACY

verbs
compensate for—; cure—; curse—; demonstrate—; denounce—; inveigh against—; observe—; overcome—; refer to—; regard—s; suffer from—; —chafes; —distresses; —hampers; —hinders; —limits; —overwhelms; —pains; —plagues; —restrains; —restricts; —tortures; —undermines; —vexes.

(See lack, deficiency, need, deficit.)

INADEQUATE

adverbs
hopelessly; entirely; lamentably; deplorably; miserably; wretchedly; cruelly; bitterly; wholly; utterly; disproportionately; deliberately; incredibly; stingily; criminally; iniquitously; mercilessly; ruthlessly; grievously; pitifully; altogether.

INADMISSABLE

adverbs
legally; socially; conventionally; altogether; definitely; positively; usually; highly; objectionably; inconveniently; unfortunately; unluckily; exceptionally.

INADVERTENT

adverbs
unfortunately; negligently; forgetfully; carelessly; inexcusably; unintentionally; la-

mentably; gracelessly; dreamily; reprehensibly; thoughtlessly; absently; disconcertingly; altogether.

INADVISABLE

adverbs
highly; altogether; utterly; wholly; completely; prudently; commercially; financially; personally; socially; locally; expediently; positively.

INANE

adverbs
fatuously; foolishly; witlessly; utterly; unconscionably; senselessly; hopelessly; vexatiously; curiously; irritatingly; disagreeably; impossibly; tenuously; vaguely; vacuously; thoughtlessly; absently; irrationally; flimsily; contemptibly; uselessly; futilely; oppressively; ridiculously.

INANITY

adjectives
oppressive; mythological; expressional.

INAPPLICABLE

adverbs
hopelessly; entirely; unserviceably; distressingly; ridiculously; wretchedly; outlandishly; discordantly; incongruously; inappropriately; unseasonably; definitely; utterly; disappointingly; vexatiously; ineptly; unfortunately; unluckily.

INAPPROPRIATE

adverbs
distinctly; deplorably; unfortunately; reprehensibly; subtly; dimly; sadly; definitely; indecorously; irreverently; wantonly; terribly; deliberately; unconsciously; tragically; comically; unbecomingly; inaptly; offensively; vexatiously; awkwardly; embarrassingly; highly; exceptionably; objectionably; inconveniently; immeasurably; remarkably; flagrantly; absurdly; ridiculously; wildly; altogether; senselessly; ludicrously; entirely; completely; discordantly; oddly; curiously; hilariously; incongruously; exceptionally; extremely; distressingly; dreadfully.

INARTICULATE

adverbs
unfortunately; diffidently; shyly; awkwardly; timidly; gruffly; ridiculously; ludicrously; extremely; taciturnly; heavily; stammeringly; tremulously; stiffly; gawkishly; silently; laconically; curtly; reticently; reservedly; gravely; bewilderingly; strangely; unwisely.

INARTISTIC

adverbs
grossly; crudely; childishly; amazingly; remarkably; strangely; unbelievably; painfully; cruelly; loudly; garishly; tawdrily; cheaply; blatantly; forbiddingly; shapelessly; crookedly; gracelessly; stiffly; awkwardly; clumsily; hideously; frightfully; horribly; shockingly; gaudily.

INATTENTION

adjectives
sheer; consequent; impolite; trivial.

INATTENTIVE

adverbs
rudely; disagreeably; visibly; obviously; significantly; dreamily; drowsily; remarkably; heedlessly; mindlessly; impolitely; insolently; arrogantly; superciliously; scornfully; learnedly; impertinently; openly; distractedly; vacantly; absently; vacuously; negligently; vexatiously; defiantly; provokingly; extremely.

INAUDIBLE

adverbs
almost; unfortunately; miraculously; pleasantly; intentionally; deliberately; painfully; distressingly; irritatingly; provokingly; disappointingly; unnecessarily; carelessly, mumblingly; confusedly; faintly.

INAUGURATE (*v*)

adverbs
ceremoniously; jubilantly; ostentatiously; enthusiastically; triumphantly; festively.
(See install, begin.)

INAUSPICIOUS

adverbs
deplorably; direly; dreadfully; grievously; ominously; portentously; lamentably; pitifully; signally; woefully; wretchedly; miserably; oppressively; sadly; curiously; definitely; desperately; extremely.

INCANTATION

verbs
bewitch with—; chant—; charm with—; defy—; moan—; mouth—; mutter—; mumble—; pour forth—; practise—; ridicule—;

whisper—; —amuses; —beseeches; —cures; —enchants; —exorcises; —summons; recite —.

(See song, magic, sound, melody, tune, air, harmony, ballad, poem.)

INCAPABLE

adverbs

helplessly; desperately; pitiably; languidly; ineptly; stupidly; grossly; arrantly; carelessly; terribly; provokingly; woefully; utterly; extremely; obviously; embarrassingly; miserably; wretchedly; unserviceably; hopelessly; clumsily; doltishly; vapidly; obtusely; deliberately; feignedly; undisguisedly; frankly.

INCAPACITY

adjectives

permanent; social; innate; ruinous; witless; confessed.

INCARNATION

adjectives

blameless; critical; astonishing; previous; distributive.

INCAUTIOUS

adverbs

definitely; undoubtedly; wildly; vexatiously; alarmingly; perilously; tragically; dangerously; terribly; recklessly; rashly; absurdly; unreasoningly; irresponsibly; unwittingly; doltishly; stupidly; foolishly; senselessly; amazingly; witlessly; youthfully; unpardonably.

INCENSE

adjectives

grateful; lavish; mystic; rare; impatient; delicate; hoarded; perpetual; dreadful; hallowed; stale.

verbs

bear—; breathe—; offer—; pray with—; scatter—; scent with—; suffuse with—; —ascends; —clouds; —curbs; —fumigates; —mists; —perfumes; —permeates; —pervades; —rises; —rolls; —smokes; —sweetens.

(See perfume, breath, fragrance, odor, aroma, spice, flowers.)

INCENTIVE

adjectives

noblest; renewed; conceivable; external; powerful; perpetual; high; especial.

verbs

arouse—; crush—; design as—; restore—; smother—; —beckons; —encourages; —excites; —induces; —inflames; —influences; —inspires; —prevails; —provokes; —springs from; —spurs; —stirs; —sways.

(See ambition, motive, inducement, provocation, influence, inspiration.)

INCESSANT

adverbs

intolerably; unbearably; mysteriously; garrulously; needlessly; maddeningly; vexatiously; curiously; oddly; incredibly; torturously; tormentingly; painfully; agonizingly; plaguedly; infernally; peculiarly; crazily.

INCH

adjectives

furthest; shuddering; single; available; proverbial; last.

INCIDENT

adjectives

tragic; astonishing; romantic; fictitious; cheery; comic; marvelous; simultaneous; moving; thrilling; well-connected; pleasing; dramatic; principal; ludicrous; trifling; amusing; terrifying; noteworthy; curious; related; significant; humorous; minutest; absurd; disturbing; long-forgotten; developing; ignoble; cruel; well-invented; chief; burlesque; dreadful; historic; picturesque; maddening; outstanding; shameful; illustrative; fruitful; illuminating; creditable; affecting; noticeable; distorted; unimportant; stirring; weird; dramatic; unrelated; spectacular; poetic; expected; traumatic; petty; noble; innocent; nonsensical; absurd; frightful; monotonous.

verbs

ascribe—to; climax—; compile—s; devise—; found on—; illustrate—; lead up to—; misinterpret—; narrate—; record—; relate—; shudder at—; vivify—; —demonstrates; —exasperates; —exposes; —occurs; —reveals.

(See event, circumstance, occurrence, episode.)

INCIPIENT

adverbs

mildly; indeterminately; fortunately; apparently; obviously; definitely; luckily; manifestly.

INCISION

adjectives
deep; unauthorized; curving; external.

INCISIVE

adverbs
clearly; sharply; acrimoniously; maliciously; sarcastically; cruelly; bitterly; scornfully; inquisitively; strangely; remarkably; quickly; painfully; terribly; needlessly; harshly; severely; sternly; questioningly; gruffly; intensely; acutely; caustically; vigorously; impressively; autocratically; magisterially; piercingly; poignantly; fanatically.

INCITE (v)

adverbs
deliberately; treacherously; spitefully; vindictively; artfully; slyly; dangerously; perversely; intentionally; maddeningly; passionately; violently; overwhelmingly; excessively.
(See stimulate, arouse.)

INCLEMENT

adverbs
stormily; disastrously; severely; harshly; roughly; forbiddingly; incredibly; remarkably; surprisingly; unexpectedly; unnecessarily; unreasonably; injudiciously; needlessly; frigidly; bitterly; keenly; coldly; austerely; relentlessly; arbitrarily; tyrannically; cruelly; mercilessly.

INCLINATION

adjectives
undue; irresistible; religious; conspicuous; matrimonial; sensual; jaunty; treacherous; particular; respectful; haughty; profound; courteous; natural; mutual.

verbs
acquire—; beget—; endow with—; evince—; follow—; gratify—; obviate—; oppose—; repress—; restrain—; sharpen—; smother—; stifle—; stimulate—; suppress—.
(See desire, tendency, propensity, aim.)

INCLINE

adjectives
wicked; slow; stony; flinty.

INCLINE (v)

adverbs
significantly; beneficently; unconsciously; tolerantly; favorably; seriously; piously; respectfully; benevolently; philosophically; naturally; diversely; subconsciously; affectionately; viciously; peaceably; wickedly.
(See slope, lean.)

INCLOSE (v)

adverbs
completely; darkly; securely; snugly; safely; oppressively; mechanically; thoroughly; lovingly.
(See surround, circumscribe.)

INCLOSURE

adjectives
delicious; little; dark; circular; large; grassy; mosque; square; walled; utilitarian.

INCLUDE (v)

adverbs
ultimately; parenthetically; implicitly; fundamentally; specifically.
(See comprehend, inclose.)

INCLUSIVE

adverbs
broadly; generally; promiscuously; indiscriminately; democratically; comprehensively; pleasantly; agreeably; satisfactorily; sufficiently; astonishingly; diplomatically; courteously.

INCOHERENCE

adjectives
colossal; maddening; affectionate; intentional.

INCOHERENT

adverbs
stammeringly; inarticulately; timidly; nervously; hysterically; wildly; feverishly; tragically; chokingly; sobbingly; sorrowfully; sadly; eagerly; enthusiastically; excitedly; frantically; frenziedly; fanatically; insanely; screamingly; bewilderingly; hopelessly; perplexingly; extremely; helplessly; strangely.

INCOME

adjectives
slender; living; taxable; ample; modest; lowered; comfortable; net; retirement; moderate; steady; gratifying; definite; diminished; precarious; subsequent; substantial; national; slim; meager; inadequate; unimpaired; dependable; prosperity; nice; splendid; profitable; cash; good; daily.

verbs
aid—; augment—; budget—; control—; curb—; curtail—; derive — from; devastate—; diminish—; divert from—; expand —; fritter away—; glean—; invest—; reduce—; stabilize—; tax—; —fluctuates; —oscillates; —rises; —wanes.

(See profits, revenue, proceeds, salary, wages.)

INCOMPATIBLE

adverbs
frankly; hopelessly; admittedly; evidently; manifestly; innately; temperamentally; unusually; admittedly; unfortunately; unluckily; violently; sadly; bitterly; acutely; stupidly; signally; remarkably; irreconcilably; openly; strangely; dreadfully; irremediably; highly.

INCOMPETENCE

verbs
cure—; decry—; denounce—; diminish—; display—; eliminate—; exclude—; maim with—; object to—; overcome—; remedy—; remove—; —arises; —corrupts; —cramps; —cripples; —hampers; —hinders; —pre vails; —unnerves; —weakens.

(See inefficiency, inability, stupidity, dullness, carelessness.)

INCOMPETENT

adverbs
incredibly; hopelessly; irremediably; idly; lazily; stupidly; doltishly; immeasurably; unfortunately; ignorantly; frankly; surprisingly; unexpectedly; unmitigably; maddeningly; provokingly; presumably; allegedly; possibly; utterly; amazingly; terribly; uncommonly.

INCOMPREHENSIBLE

adverbs
incoherently; unreasonably; unnecessarily; unusually; highly; evasively; delusively; deliberately; utterly; vexatiously; perplexingly; inscrutably; mysteriously; symbolically; provokingly; unaccountably; curiously; uncomfortably; cryptically; embarrassingly.

INCONGRUITIES

adjectives
careless; apparent; pitiful; inexplicable; curious.

INCONGRUITY

verbs
abolish—; commit—; detect—; perceive—; rectify—; sense—; smile at—; utter—; —arises; —denotes; —fouls; —glares; —inconveniences; —interferes; —intrudes.

(See discord, sin, wrong, discrepancy, error, mistake.)

INCONGRUOUS

adverbs
ridiculously; fantastically; utterly; grotesquely; painfully; awkwardly; embarrassingly; completely; strangely; oddly; curiously; crudely; pitifully; inexplicably; mysteriously; unpleasantly; unhappily; unreasonably; flimsily; discordantly; inharmoniously; inartistically; noticeably; terribly; highly.

INCONSEQUENTIAL

adverbs
foolishly; utterly; senselessly; inanely; manifestly; legally; quite; evasively; trivially; absurdly; ridiculously; wretchedly; quibblingly; illusively; speciously; inordinately; unusually; obviously.

INCONSIDERABLE

adverbs
altogether; modestly; miserably; comparatively; practically; pitiably.

INCONSIDERATE

adverbs
thoughtlessly; selfishly; cruelly; crassly; constantly; harshly; surprisingly; terribly; pitiably; wretchedly; miserably; ignorantly; carelessly; hideously; bitterly; inexcusably; unpardonably; grossly; flagrantly; noticeably; notoriously; naturally; characteristically; utterly; uncharitably; inadvertently; heedlessly; rashly; recklessly; ruthlessly; impulsively; impetuously.

INCONSISTENCY

adjectives
curious; astounding; allowable; charming; political; apparent; innocent; uncommon; feminine.

verbs
accuse of—; argue—; charge—; despise—; display—; exhibit—; frown on—; imply—; observe—; practise—; prove—; unfold—; wonder at—; —confounds; —contradicts; —distresses; —irks; —perplexes; —vexes.

(See discord, stupidity.)

INCONSISTENT

adverbs
unfortunately; manifestly; carelessly; heedlessly; illogically; indiscreetly; dangerously; embarrassingly; politically; expediently; habitually; strangely; ridiculously; annoyingly; provokingly; perilously; horribly; fantastically; utterly; highly; uncommonly; provokingly; unreliably; unstably; impulsively; vaguely; preposterously; egregiously; stupidly; blatantly; injudiciously; astoundingly.

INCONSOLABLE

adverbs
bitterly; miserably; utterly; sadly; mournfully; desolately; uncommonly; manifestly; evidently; unhappily; hopelessly; dismally; lamentably; dreadfully; drearily; ruefully; disconsolately; forlornly; desperately; pitiably; pathetically; hysterically; tragically.

INCONSPICUOUS

adverbs
timidly; diffidently; shyly; busily; usually; habitually; preferably; naturally; deliberately; vaguely; quietly; obscurely; discreetly; wisely; modestly; unassumingly; unaffectedly; meekly; sweetly; gracefully; serenely; contentedly.

INCONSTANT

adverbs
notoriously; flagrantly; blithely; recklessly; ruthlessly; pitilessly; carelessly; reprehensibly; obviously; curiously; habitually; temperamentally; highly; egregiously; inordinately; unfortunately; unstably; unreliably; dreadfully; gaily; restlessly; erratically; capriciously; waywardly; incorrigibly.

INCONVENIENCE

adjectives
least; possible; accidental; immediate: unnecessary; mutual; supposed.

verbs
abuse with—; avert—; bemoan—; hurdle—; ignore—; lead to—; observe—; rectify—; remedy—; spare—; submit to—; suffer—; —arises; —interferes; —torments.

(See disadvantage, drawback, handicap, trouble, misfortune.)

INCONVENIENT

adverbs
highly; seriously; embarrassingly; provokingly; irritatingly; utterly; troublesomely; awkwardly; unseasonably; financially; expensively; inconsiderately; extremely; unmanageably; terribly; curiously; hideously.

INCORRECT

adverbs
shamefully; carelessly; unfortunately; incautiously; idly; viciously; deliberately; intentionally; evasively; mendaciously; criminally; unaccountably; inexcusably; foolishly; inconsistently; speciously; troublesomely; hopelessly; wretchedly; intentionally; erroneously; fallaciously; obviously; manifestly; deceitfully; infamously; cruelly; indefensibly.

INCORRIGIBLE

adverbs
presumably; altogether; utterly; deplorably; manifestly; evidently; allegedly; notoriously; tragically; wretchedly; stubbornly; obdurately; mulishly; perversely; waywardly; obstinately; hopelessly; terribly; viciously; impenitently; gracelessly; heartbreakingly; unspeakably; portentously.

INCREASE

adjectives
corresponding; apparent; abnormal; ultimate; prodigious; anticipated; rational; periodical; sporadic; inevitable; goodly; relative; imperceptible; unprecedented; unexampled; happy; subsequent; sharp; considerable; marked; progressive; definite; commensurate; concomitant; enormous.

verbs
anticipate—; calculate—; check—; cite—; compute—; decree—; derive — from; entitle to—; estimate—; occasion—; order—; promote—; rejoice in—; reward with—; stimulate—; urge—; welcome—; yield—; —cheers; —enthuses (colloq.).

(See addition, expansion, growth, reward.)

INCREASE (v)

adverbs
materially; alarmingly; acutely; enormously; perseveringly; notably; perceptibly; grotesquely; grossly; enormously; noticeably; infinitely; relentlessly; boundlessly; perpetually; proportionably; stupendously; manifestly; abnormally; rationally; sporadically; commensurately; concomitantly.

(See multiply, enlarge, extend.)

INCREDULITY

adjectives

concealed; total; impertinent; angry; pathetic; complete; petulant; polite.

verbs

arouse—; convert to—; display—; dispose to —; expose to—; ignore—; incur —; indicate —; prompt—; receive with—; remove—; study with—; —distresses; —irks; —robs; —vexes.

(See amazement, disbelief, distrust, confusion, surprise, perplexity, wonder.)

INCREDULOUS

adverbs

blindly; youthfully; suspiciously; openly; distrustfully; skeptically; doubtfully; frankly; laughingly; amusedly; teasingly; blasphemously; scoffingly; gracelessly; impolitely; rudely; ignorantly; totally; impertinently; angrily; pathetically; comically; politely; petulantly.

INCREMENT

adjectives

unearned; substantial; annual.

INCRIMINATING

adverbs

definitely; positively; manifestly; unquestionably; incontrovertibly; unfortunately; unexpectedly; unanswerably; tragically; implicitly; gravely; seriously; dangerously; alarmingly; ominously; dreadfully; inescapably; profoundly; momentously.

INCULCATE (v)

adverbs

weightily; firmly; vigorously; forcefully; unforgettably; vividly; skilfully; academically.

(See implant, impress.)

INCUR (v)

adverbs

legitimately; thoughtlessly; indulgently; lamentably; excessively; superfluously.

(See assume, accept.)

INCURABLE

adverbs

definitely; positively; grievously; altogether; presumably; supposedly; allegedly; hitherto; lamentably; deplorably; tragically; purportedly; wretchedly; unhappily; unfortunately; hopelessly; essentially; normally; usually; fundamentally; unluckily.

INCURSIONS

adjectives

dangerous; nocturnal; savage; hostile.

INDEBTED

adverbs

deeply; insolvently; embarrassingly; seriously; hopelessly; helplessly; gravely; heavily; slightly; pleasantly; increasingly; everlastingly; enormously; tremendously; unbelievably; gratefully; thankfully; personally; profoundly; inextricably.

INDECENT

adverbs

horribly; slightly; tremendously; altogether; somewhat; utterly; flagrantly; boisterously; carelessly; recklessly; viciously; offensively; shamelessly; broadly; grossly; publicly; unbelievably; inexcusably; inexpressibly; culpably; vilely; villainously; grossly; outrageously; basely; insufferably; criminally; perniciously; nefariously; heinously.

INDECIPHERABLE

adverbs

strangely; exotically; mysteriously; altogether; almost; evidently; deliberately; purposely; unfortunately; horribly; oddly; outlandishly; hopelessly; dimly; faintly; presumably; supposedly; sadly; provokingly; bewilderingly; perplexingly; disconcertingly; maddeningly; vexatiously; disappointingly; unaccountably; inscrutably; enigmatically; fantastically.

INDECISION

adjectives

ludicrous; chronic; momentary; fatal; gentlemanlike; habitual; costly; temporary; customary.

INDECISIVE

adverbs

evasively; waveringly; hesitantly; timorously; feebly; weakly; timidly; provokingly; maddeningly; abjectly; habitually; always; uncertainly; perplexingly; bewilderedly; irresolutely; variably; capriciously; unstably; mercurially; fitfully; unreliably; strangely; curiously; unaccountably; inexplicably; unpleasantly; disagreeably; indolently.

INDECOROUS

adverbs
unintentionally; flagrantly; rashly; impudently; irreverently; outlandishly; outrageously; deliberately; fantastically; disagreeably; unpleasantly; unacceptably; boorishly; crassly; grossly; rudely; stupidly; coarsely; impolitely; discourteously; habitually; intentionally; gracelessly; awkwardly; terribly; oddly; strangely.

INDEFATIGABLE

adverbs
sturdily; stoutly; robustly; apparently; evidently; manifestly; inordinately; surprisingly; astoundingly; astonishingly; unexpectedly; marvellously; almost; pluckily; indomitably; manfully; actively; zealously; nimbly; strenuously; resolutely; busily; restlessly; amazingly; marvellously; miraculously; unbelievably.

INDEFINITE

adverbs
exasperatingly; politically; sagaciously; evasively; delusively; craftily; maddeningly; bewilderingly; perplexingly; preposterously; crudely; cruelly; bitterly; weakly; timorously; viciously; vaguely; deliberately; vexatiously; embarrassingly; foggily; casually; mysteriously; obscurely; enigmatically; distressingly; inordinately; inscrutably; terribly; highly.

INDELICATE

adverbs
conspicuously; gracelessly; shamefully; immodestly; grossly; rudely; wantonly; improperly; openly; defiantly; boorishly; intrusively; coarsely; indecorously; unsympathetically; obtusely; impertinently; unbecomingly; loudly; boisterously; obscenely; foully; viciously; villainously; flauntingly; flagrantly; terribly; inexcusably; incorrigibly; unbelievably.

INDEPENDENCE

adjectives
sturdy; industrial; patrimonial; constitutional; proud; aggressive; inexorable; supreme; cherished; characteristic; fearless; modest; virtual; personal; mental; extraordinary; immediate; daring; lofty; rough; uncouth; insolent; wrathful; virtual; unsurpassed; leisurely; saucy; harmonic; masterful; inflexible.

verbs
afford—; assert—; assume—; boast—; breed—; cherish—; defend—; encroach on —; enjoy—; favor—; inspire—; maintain —; preserve—; prize—; quell—; relish—; respect—; restore—; revel in—; safeguard —; share—; strive for—; suppress—; taste —; undermine—; —increases; —irritates.

(See strength, freedom, liberty, privilege, power, security, individuality.)

INDEPENDENT

adverbs
immeasurably; delightfully; selfishly; resolutely; manfully; openly; arrogantly; rightfully; freely; happily; boldly; courageously; tenaciously; fortunately; luckily; nationally; fearlessly; intrepidly; extraordinarily; inordinately; miraculously; unbelievably; marvellously; affluently; comfortably; absolutely; entirely.

INDEX

adjectives
refractive; flattering; classified; elaborate; cephalic; prosaic; analytical; unusable; helpful.

INDIAN

adjectives
bronze-skinned; wily; athletic; dark-looking; garrulous; stealthy; keen-sighted; cigar-store.

verbs
govern —s; overcome —s; tutor —s; —dances; —fishes; —s flourish; —hunts; —s maraud; —s pillage; —s plunder; —s roam; —scalps; —shrieks; —slays; —squats; —trails; —vanishes; —s war; —whoops.

(See savage, native, barbarian.)

INDICATE (v)

adverbs
fairly; specifically; definitely; broadly; irresistibly; unmistakably; forcibly; conclusively; accurately; vaguely; tersely; vividly.

(See designate, signify.)

INDICATION

adjectives
suspicious; surface; perceptible; powerful; vouchsafed; definite; convincing; genuine; obvious; smiling; picturesque; cold; peculiar; sufficient; unmistakable; syntactic; conjectural.

verbs
afford—; await—; derive — from; exaggerate—; follow—; forsake—; heed—; measure —; neglect—; note—; observe—; reduce—; respect—; —denotes; —enlightens; —hints; —implies; —misleads; —promises; —signifies.

(See evidence, symptom, sign, manifestation.)

INDICTMENT

adjectives
extraordinary; blistering; quashed.

verbs
advocate—; demand—; dismiss—; draw up —; endorse—; ignore—; justify—; launch into—; oppose—; plead—; present—; propose—; protest—; quash—; suffer—; suspend—; upset—; witness—; —engrosses; —shames.

(See accusation, charge.)

INDIFFERENCE

adjectives
polished; apparent; entire; lordly; chilling; nodding; forced; Olympian; dreadful; blind-walled; perfect; suicidal; semi-barbarized; luxurious; exquisite; moral; complete; purposeless; immense; lofty; offhand; careless; calm; public; artless; gallant; simulated; nonchalant; discouraging; utter; singular; profound; stolid; drunken; lethargic; negligent; gloomy; cold-blooded; passive; hardened; stony; supreme; evident; listless; curious; delightful; disdainful; callous; unteachable; reckless; criminal; affected; studied; proud; political; wandering; cynical; mere; uncomfortable; affable; heartbreaking.

verbs
attain—; bare to—; buttress with—; case in —; commend—; cultivate—; cure of—; ice with—; feign—; lure by—; maintain—; mourn—; profess—; regard with—; shed—; signify—; slight by—; —chills; —depresses; —dulls; —torments.

(See apathy, carelessness, impartiality.)

INDIFFERENT

adverbs
dully; stupidly; strangely; stolidly; apathetically; vacantly; ridiculously; singularly; oddly; peculiarly; curiously; unaccountably; irritatingly; vexatiously; shockingly; callously; coldly; carelessly; hopelessly; unpardonably; inexplicably.

INDIGENT

adverbs
pitiably; constantly; seriously; tragically; pathetically; needlessly; shiftlessly; lazily; idly; impecuniously; miserably; wretchedly; helplessly; hopelessly; strangely; mysteriously; unaccountably; unwarrantably; incomprehensibly.

INDIGESTION

verbs
anticipate—; develop—; dose for—; fume with—; induce—; palliate—; reap—; seize with—; sow—; suffer from—; —agonizes; —attacks; —crucifies; —indisposes; —tortures; —vanishes; —wracks.

(See sickness, disease, pain.)

INDIGNANT

adverbs
horribly; wildly; violently; mildly; justly; righteously; deeply; loudly; boisterously; drunkenly; foolishly; profoundly; justifiably; dangerously; properly; silently; alarmingly; furiously; resentfully; inordinately; absurdly; foolishly; needlessly; unaccountably; unusually; unwarrantably; unappeasably; implacably; sternly; harshly; stonily; irrecoverably; vengefully; bitterly; sorely; sadly; grievously.

INDIGNATION

adjectives
virtuous; unrelaxed; unmitigable; righteous; mollified; noble; repressed; rising; natural; speechless; furious; pent-up; tempered; sincere; loyal; moral; capacious; overwhelming; expressive; popular; utmost; hearty; tumultuous; superb; becoming; impotent; uncommon; foaming; dignified; satirical; passionate; warm; astonished; violent; cruel; fiery.

verbs
blow up in—; burn with—; curb—; dread —; embitter by—; experience—; heap—upon; incense with—; move to—; mantle—; overflow with—; pour out—; quench—; restrain—; rock with—; rouse—; scorn—;

shock into—; shriek—; snort with—; swell with—; vent—; —blinds; —effervesces; —glows; —mounts; —waxes.

(See anger, violence, contempt, fury, rage, wrath, resentment, passion.)

INDIGNITY

adjectives

excessive; various (pl); supposed; glaring; sensible; amusing; intolerable; harsh; fresh; egregious.

verbs

ignore—; nurse—; persecute with—s; prompt—; punish—; restrain—; revenge—; subject to—; submit to—; suffer—; —aggravates; —heats; —inflames; —kindles; —riles (colloq.); —stings; —vexes; —nettles.

(See insult, injury, offense, outrage, contempt.)

INDIRECT

adverbs

perplexingly; disturbingly; distressingly; intricately; needlessly; absurdly; circumbendibusly; deliberately; evasively; irritatingly; atrociously; maliciously; unhappily; unnecessarily; circuitously; craftily; nefariously; artfully; adroitly; astutely; outrageously; outlandishly; insidiously; shiftily; ingeniously.

INDISCREET

adverbs

amazingly; gravely; dreadfully; dangerously; compromisingly; thoughtlessly; heedlessly; carelessly; youthfully; awkwardly; unsophisticatedly; unconsciously; rashly; recklessly; imprudently; innocently; harmlessly; impulsively; stupidly; incomprehensibly; surprisingly; egregiously; idiotically; senselessly; ridiculously; madly; unbelievably; strangely; curiously; inexpressibly.

INDISCRETION

adjectives

manifest; culpable; racy; childish; abominable; lamentable.

verbs

abandon—; absolve from—; assail—; commit—; conceal—; conduct with—; curb—; curtail—; mar by—; mute—; rationalize—; repent—; soil with—; suffer for—; —reflects; —scandalizes; —shames; —tempts.

(See error, mistake, recklessness, foolishness, act.)

INDISPENSABLE

adverbs

vitally; fundamentally; essentially; presumably; supposedly; allegedly; purportedly; curiously; oddly; strangely; utterly; emphatically; imperatively; unquestionably; absolutely.

INDISPOSITION

adjectives

casual; slight; physical.

verbs

aggravate—; correct—; detain by—; evince—; increase—; induce—; irritate—; recover from—; rectify—; sweeten—; —confines; —deters; —hampers; —hinders; —interrupts; —repels; —restricts; —tantalizes; —vexes.

(See reluctance, unwillingness, aversion, illness.)

INDISPUTABLE

adverbs

curiously; altogether; legally; officially; authoritatively; evidently; palpably; manifestly; oddly; mysteriously; professedly; scientifically; mathematically; technically; strangely; incomprehensibly; positively; absolutely; truly.

INDISTINCT

adverbs

curiously; unfortunately; deliberately; intentionally; inaudibly; purposely; bewilderingly; confusedly; chaotically; dimly; faintly; remotely; vexatiously; unsatisfactorily; unacceptably; fantastically; miserably; wretchedly; lamentably; grievously; deplorably; disagreeably; unexpectedly; mysteriously; carelessly; obscurely; vaguely; sadly.

INDIVIDUAL

adjectives

happy-looking; erratic; numerable; jocular; distinguished; determinate; obscure; coatless; dismal; intelligent; unchanged; transfigured; progressive; independent; self-centered; disciplined; tattered; troublesome; reasonable; bellicose; enfeebled; conservative; irresponsible; thinking; noxious; adventurous; acquisitive; privileged; enthusiastic; laborious; intoxicated; gifted; uncommon; dignified; arrogant; vanishing; unworthy; ill-conducted; beef-faced; unlucky; scant-haired; hardy; amoral; fearless; quiet-spoken; remarkable; enterprising; under-slung; myriad (pl); peculiar; famed; delightful; relaxed, maladjusted; hesitant; harmonious; unprepared; unhappy; perverse.

verbs
bequeath to—; characterize—; depend on—; direct to—; dwarf—; ignore—; incense—; insulate—; intrude on—; isolate—; mold—; shape—; support—; —achieves; —strives.
(See person, being.)

INDIVIDUALISM

adjectives
rugged; blind; intense; excessive; pioneering; exaggerated; ruinous; obtrusive.

INDIVIDUALITY

adjectives
separate; abstract; persistent; piquant; genuine; characteristic; pronounced; intense; well-equipped; powerful; indolent; decided; magnetic; distinct.

verbs
assert—; cherish—; contrive—; crush—; desert—; distinguish by—; divest of—; efface—; enlarge—; impart—; inspire—; justify—; lose—; maintain—; mold—; preserve—; reflect—; respect—; retain—; sacrifice—; season with—; shield—; submerge —; sustain—; throttle—.
(See personality, independence, strength, freedom, liberty, power, security.)

INDOLENCE

adjectives
lifeless; alternate; listless; habitual; regal; dreamy; inert; bland; easy; lackadaisical.

verbs
avoid—; banish—; bask in—; breed—; deplore—; dispose to—; overcome—; pillow in —; reproach—; revel in—; shake off—; stagnate in—; stretch in—; strangle by—; wallow in—; waste in—; —demoralizes; —destroys; —ensnares; —rusts.
(See idleness, apathy, lethargy, procrastination.)

INDOLENT

adverbs
lackadaisically; delightfully; abominably; atrociously; comfortably; drowsily; lazily; deplorably; meretriciously; inexcusably; inherently; constitutionally; obstinately; gaily; blithely; contentedly; immovably; slothfully; feebly; wisely; vexatiously; maddeningly; restfully; peaceably; peevishly; quietly; serenely; brilliantly; mentally; unpardonably; unforgivably; selfishly; heavily; torpidly; stubbornly; inconsiderately; amazingly; thoughtlessly.

INDOMITABLE

adverbs
sturdily; resolutely; determinedly; surprisingly; unexpectedly; marvelously; invincibly; vigorously; staunchly; stubbornly; heroically; gallantly; bravely; boldly; courageously; habitually; hardily; irresistibly.

INDORSE (*v*)

adverbs
enthusiastically; unwittingly; unsuspectingly; legitimately; laconically.
(See attest, approve, confirm.)

INDORSEMENT

adjectives
peremptory; terse; enthusiastic; ill-natured; laconic; premature.

verbs
authorize—; carry—; examine—; necessitate—; note—; pen—; question—; refuse—; require—; respect—; seek—; sign—; transfer by—; witness—; —confirms; —sanctions.
(See approval, sanction, ratification.)

INDUCE (*v*)

adverbs
automatically; involuntarily; effectively; strongly; fawningly; cleverly; slyly; immorally; patiently.
(See influence, persuade, urge.)

INDUCEMENTS

adjectives
soul-sustaining; flattering; principal.

adverbs
coin—; contrive—; decline—; frame—; hold out—; ignore—; offer—; repeat—; —

determines; —influences; —motivates; —persuades; —procures; —sways; —urges.
(See incentive, motive, stimulus, provocation.)

INDUCTIONS

adjectives
absolute; reflective; subsequent; logical; dangerous.

INDULGE (*v*)

adverbs
excessively; fallaciously: incontinently; unscrupulously; moderately; incessantly; passionately; heartily; luxuriantly; habitually; viciously; sensually; immorally.
(See gratify, satisfy, allow.)

INDULGENCE

adjectives
idle; habitual; passing; social; partial; expensive; pampered; rare; caustic; plenary; legal; vicious; indeterminable; unseasonable; vile; unrestrained; sensual; excessive; prolonged; maternal; classic; immoral; pitying; polite; complaint; further; unaesthetic.

verbs
abstain from—; beg—; check—; curb—; curse—; feast on—; grant—; humor with—; live in—; permit—; practise—; reproach for—; share in—; temper—; tempt to—; treat with—; wallow in—; yield to—; —fattens; —gratifies; —shackles; —weakens.
(See gratification, luxury, sin, crime, wickedness, violence.)

INDULGENT

adverbs
unfortunately; over; unhappily; lazily; carelessly; spasmodically; intermittently; tenderly; lovingly; unwisely; sympathetically; sadly; idly; thoughtlessly; unluckily; short-sightedly; foolishly; vacuously; affectionately; graciously; complacently; serenely; good-naturedly; tolerantly; torpidly; benevolently; warmly; humanely; ridiculously; excessively; uncommonly.

INDUSTRIALIST

verbs
enrich—; organize—; protect—; rouse—; satisfy—; spur—; support—; urge—; —achieves; —derives; —directs; —governs; —labors; —plies; —plods; —pushes; —submerges; —supplies; —yields to.
(See boss, executive, banker, farmer, manager.)

INDUSTRIOUS

adverbs
painfully; perseveringly; dependably; unremittingly; energetically; actively; carefully; constantly; temperamentally; characteristically; busily; reliably; amazingly; unusually; uncomplainingly; happily; cheerfully; unwaveringly; invariably; uniformly; persistently; insistently.

INDUSTRY

adjectives
domestic; ignorant; large; indefatigable; honest; urban; diversified; pious; prodigious; persistent; purposeless; scheduled; languid; necessitous; productive; peaceable; incomparable; much-vexed; myriad-shaped; indigenous; extraordinary; untiring; vast; growing; refining; charming; laudable; seasonal; unwearied; promising; middling; patient; technical; all-absorbing; mingled; damnable; unflagging; depression-born; unfaltering; modest; native; skilful; adoring; subsidized; persistent; unaided; predominating; dark-armed.

verbs
blossom into—; bulwark—; chastise—; cow—; cripple—; dislocate—; dominate—; evolve into—; father—; fortify—; foster—; gag—; merge—s; modernize—; organize—; paralyze—; prod—; reconstruct—; regulate—; rejuvenate—; resurrect—; retard—; revitalize—; revive—; sovietize—; speed up—; stimulate—; subsidize—; threaten—; tie up—; —booms; —buzzes; —collapses; —flourishes; —languishes; —perks up; —rallies; —squirms.
(See business, company, manufacture, trade, profession, enterprise, pursuit, vocation.)

INEFFECTIVE

adverbs
tragically; pitifully; surprisingly; disappointingly; utterly; wholly; strangely; suddenly; finally; painfully; curiously; singularly; unluckily; occasionally; feebly; weakly; tiresomely; languidly; stodgily; pitiably.

INEFFICIENCY

verbs
affirm—; characterize by—; condemn—; couch in—; degenerate to—; execute with—; observe—; plague with—; rectify—; relapse

into—; remove—; suffer from—; —accounts for; —bankrupts; —impoverishes; —scandalizes; —ruins; overlook—.

(See carelessness, stupidity, indifference.)

INEFFICIENT

adverbs

tragically; hopelessly; pitiably; miserably; wretchedly; helplessly; feebly; provincially; ignorantly; ineptly; clumsily; awkwardly; nervously; bashfully; shyly; self-consciously; inexpertly; crudely; grossly; flagrantly; crassly; surprisingly; harmlessly; dreadfully.

INELEGANT

adverbs

crudely; slightly; uncommonly; highly; gracelessly; awkwardly; boorishly; garishly; stiffly; rudely; inartistically; roughly; gaudily; grotesquely; artificially; vulgarly; coarsely; remarkably; unbelievably; incredibly.

INEPT

adverbs

stupidly; frightfully; foolishly; vacuously; terribly; comically; unfortunately; incompetently; miserably; wretchedly; senselessly; painfully; embarrassingly; unserviceably; lamentably; deplorably; pitiably; dreadfully.

INEQUALITIES

adjectives

inevitable; seeming; shameless; mountainous; irritating; supplementary; patent; sensible; glaring; gross; parallactic; slight; planetary.

INEQUALITY

verbs

complain of—; conduce to—; consider—; detect—; dispute—; frown on—; grieve over—; lament—; observe—; occasion—; owe to—; reconcile—; rectify—; treat with —; —glares; —shocks· —unbalances.

(See injustice, inferiority.)

INERT

adverbs

passively; dully; drowsily; heavily; indolently; lethargically; noddingly; quietly; sluggishly; stupidly; torpidly; dreamily; idly; lazily; lumpishly; sleepily; motionlessly; somnolently; apathetically; callously; habitually; unusually; uncommonly; phlegmatically; unconcernedly; imperturbably.

INERTIA

adjectives

gross; somber; amiable; ordinary; insurmountable.

verbs

display—; fall into—; force—; lull into—; overcome—; reform—; shed—; stimulate—; subject to—; suspend—; weary of—; while away in—; —consumes; —dulls; —prevents; —resists; —weakens.

(See indolence, idleness.)

INEVITABLE

verbs

accept—; bow to—; buck—; condone—; defer—; foresee—; foretell—; ignore—; predict—; prophesy—; resign to—; resist—; submit to—; yield to—.

(See fate.)

adverbs

tragically; embarrassingly; naturally; terribly; certainly; fatally; lamentably; fortunately; happily; awfully.

INEXCUSABLE

adverbs

wholly; altogether; entirely; manifestly; naturally; shamefully; hopelessly; flagrantly; scandalously; unfortunately; unluckily; irremediably; absolutely; admittedly; gravely; seriously.

INEXHAUSTIBLE

adverbs

boundlessly; generously; abundantly; luxuriantly; gorgeously; happily; naturally; apparently; miraculously; fortunately; surprisingly; evidently; marvelously; inexplicably; mysteriously; curiously; oddly; utterly; strangely; copiously; exuberantly; lavishly; gratefully; pleasantly.

INEXORABLE

adverbs

terribly; unfeelingly; unsympathetically; brutally; stiffly; severely; hard-heartedly; stonily; coldly; utterly; unreasonably; unaccountably; inexplicably; pitilessly; mercilessly; scornfully; pitiably; miserably; craftily; rigidly; uncompromisingly; austerely; haughtily; cruelly; tyrannically; imperiously; unsparingly; puritanically; authoritatively.

INEXPEDIENT

adverbs

palpably; obviously; awkwardly; inconveniently; embarrassingly; perplexingly; intricately; vexatiously; disconcertingly; bewilderingly; obstructively; objectionably; viciously; manifestly; utterly; clearly; painfully; glaringly; grossly; senselessly; terribly; grotesquely.

INEXPENSIVE

adverbs

surprisingly; amazingly; curiously; naturally; gratifyingly; delightfully; fortunately; conveniently; attractively; prudently; unexpectedly; cleverly; luckily; agreeably; pleasingly; remarkably; quite; comparatively.

INEXPLICABLE

adverbs

altogether; fantastically; utterly; strangely; inscrutably; mysteriously; peculiarly; mystifyingly; obscurely; darkly; capriciously; captiously; wantonly; impulsively; curiously.

INFALLIBILITY

verbs

acquire—; admit—; assure of—; boast of—; confirm—; confute—; deride—; doubt—; judge—; overrate—; praise—; promise—; prove—; puff up with—; reveal—; strain —; tempt—; test—; witness—.

(See skill, judgment, ability, ingenuity.)

INFALLIBLE

adverbs

unctuously; smugly; pompously; arrogantly; sapiently; sagaciously; practically; usually; consciously; reputably; notoriously; admittedly; apparently; supposedly; avowedly; bumptiously; maddeningly; gallingly; offensively; ostentatiously; proudly; blusteringly; swaggeringly; curiously.

INFAMOUS

adverbs

scandalously; vilely; notoriously; unjustly; unutterably; inexpressibly; grossly; crassly; brazenly; wickedly; odiously; atrociously; unbelievably; incredibly; ingloriously; unmentionably; shamefully; arrantly; shockingly; outrageously; pitifully; atrociously; shabbily; fantastically; uncommonly; deplorably.

INFAMY

adjectives

unutterable; callous; clumsy; vilest; perpetual; crushing; immortal.

verbs

bear—; blot out—; brand—; challenge—; consign to—; deface with—; denounce—; doom to—; endure—; hold up to—; incur—; infer—; inflict—; mire with—; scar with —; suffer—; work—; —disgraces; —pains; —shames; stain with—.

(See disgrace, dishonor, shame, scandal.)

INFANCY

adjectives

smiling; philologic; unlearned; fretting; cherub; innocent; dauntless; endless; careless; slumbering; unpracticed; mewling.

verbs

cloud—; develop in—; emerge from—; extend—; form in—; foster from—; guide through—; impress in—; mould in—; nourish in—; nurse in—; plead—; regress to—; soothe in—; terrorize in—; train in—; utter in—; —precedes; —unfolds.

(See childhood.)

INFANT

adjectives

well-educated; squalling; bewildered; undipped; unvaccinated; sucking; clay-faced; blue-lipped; baptized; conventional; miraculous; swaddling; ragged; hungry; mute; speechless; suffering; sentient; premature; trustful; vigorous.

verbs

christen—; cradle—; cuddle—; govern—; guard—; guide—; pamper—; quell—; soothe—; suckle—; swaddle—; swathe—; wean—; —bawls; —chatters; —howls; —mewls; —prattles; —pukes; —scampers about; —squalls.

(See child, baby.)

INFANTRY

adjectives

redoubtable; intrenched; disciplined; unsupported; trampling; well-armed; spiritless.

verbs
collect—; distress—; snipe at—; —advances; —assails; —besieges; —charges; —defends; —guards; —harries; —invades; —maneuvers; —marches; —mops up; —parries; —peppers; —presses; —reconnoiters; —retreats; —shields; —storms; —strikes; —wars on.
(See army, regiment, soldier.)

INFATUATION

adjectives
judicial; sad; incomprehensible; girlish.

verbs
besot with—; blame—; blind with—; deride—; fire by—; free from—; infect with—; overcome by—; provoke—; resist—; suffer—; stun by—; —dazzles; —dopes; —overwhelms; —perturbs; —ruffles; —ruins; —sharpens; —thrills.
(See love, charm, passion, tenderness.)

INFECTION

adjectives
diphtheritic; acute; common; respiratory; wide-spread; bacterial; innocent; recurrent; severe.

verbs
breathe—; combat—; cope with—; contract—; convey—; diagnose—; eradicate—; escape—; expose to—; exterminate—; immunize against—; incise—; introduce—; localize—; predispose to—; purge of—; risk—; scatter—; transmit—; —derives from; —enters; —lingers; —ravages; —spreads.
(See disease, malady, plague.)

INFECTIOUS

adverbs
highly; dangerously; easily; alarmingly; uncommonly; definitely; positively; portentously; slightly; supposedly; allegedly; probably; surprisingly; remarkably; particularly; acutely; seriously; gravely; fearfully.

INFER (*v*)

adverbs
hastily; carelessly; vaguely; unfoundedly; unreasonably; absurdly; rationally; irresistibly; confidently.
(See imply, gather, deduce.)

INFERENCE

adjectives
decisive; ruinous; vague; astounding; pathological; unfounded; unreasonable; bare; typographical; absurd; rational; charitable; irresistible; justifiable; sharp.

verbs
accept—; argue—; condemn—; conclude—; consider—; deduce—; derive—from; dispute—; draw—from; indulge in—s; justify—; pour out—s; resent—; respect—; scoff at—; scorn—; —implies; —indicates; —insinuates; —troubles.
(See opinion, thought, conclusion, consequence.)

INFERENTIAL

adverbs
probably; carelessly; naturally; logically; ruinously; vaguely; obscurely; incontrovertibly; soundly; unreasonably; absurdly; fallaciously; shrewdly; undeniably; covertly; obviously.

INFERIOR

adverbs
hopelessly; comparatively; pitifully; manifestly; palpably; shockingly; appallingly; terribly; unmistakably; oddly; curiously; patently; apparently; greatly; dreadfully; mentally; physically; essentially; materially; utterly; inexplicably; unaccountably; unacceptably.

INFERIORITY

adjectives
decent; mental; intellectual; alleged; admitted.

verbs
burden with—; conceal—; consider—; curse—; detect—; experience—; fret over—; lament—; prove—; overcome—; suffer—; —anguishes; —cramps; —gnaws; —shames; —stings; —vexes.
(See complex, inequality, injustice, mediocrity.)

INFERNO

adjectives
gasoline; raging; lurid; hot; white.

INFEST (*v*)

adverbs
horribly; pestiferously; peculiarly; grossly; luxuriantly; unpleasantly; extraordinarily; perniciously; fatally.
(See overrun, haunt, annoy.)

INFIDEL

adjectives
perilous; professed; stalwart.

INFIDELITY

adjectives
foolish; matrimonial; religious.

verbs
admit—; blot with—; commit—; confess—; flaunt—; inspire—; motivate—; repent—; reproach for—; sully with—; —dejects; —desolates; —destroys; —disgraces; —dishonors; —poisons; —stains; —taints; —threatens.
(See unfaithfulness, treachery, sin.)

INFILTRATION

verbs
advocate—; consider—; curb—; fill by—; halt—; introduce by—; lead to—; observe—; permeate through—; receive—; travel by—; —alarms; —breeds; —endangers; —preserves.
(See penetration.)

INFINITE

adverbs
gloriously; spiritually; divinely; ineffably; vastly; mysteriously; impenetrably; boundlessly; immensely; incomprehensibly; fearfully; occultly; unknowably; inexpressibly; incalculably; unapproachably; unfathomably; immeasurably.

INFINITY

verbs
ascend into—; dwell in—; infringe on—; lead to—; measure—; pattern—; range in—; represent—; understand—; yield to—.
(See eternity.)

INFIRM

adverbs
decrepitly; weakly; languidly; brokenly; defenselessly; helplessly; pitiably; unbelievably; horribly; lamentably; pathetically; nervously; powerlessly; shakily.

INFIRMITIES

adjectives
physical; hideous; besetting; divine; mortal; unique; growing; venial; deplorable; quotidian; speedy.

INFIRMITY

verbs
bare—; bear—; brace—; discover—; escape—; lament—; linger in—; master—; pretend—; relieve—; suffer—; trample on—; —blights; —constrains; —desolates; —despairs; —enfeebles; —gnaws; —relents; —restrains.
(See weakness, feebleness, illness, disease.)

INFLAME (*v*)

adverbs
superficially; fatally; excessively; chronically; temporarily; painfully; treasonably.
(See provoke, excite.)

INFLAMMABLE

adverbs
highly; criminally; uncommonly; easily; dangerously; seriously; illegally; hazardously; perilously; probably; indubitably; instantly; terribly; extremely.

INFLAMMATION

adjectives
excessive; fatal; chronic.

verbs
allay—; avert—; check—; clear up—; confine—; diminish—; excite—; indicate—; palliate—; reduce—; relieve—; subdue—; undergo—; —abates; —accompanies; —extends to; —proceeds; —ravages; —sustains.
(See infection, sore, ulcer, pain.)

INFLATION

verbs
advocate—; authorize—; block—; border on—; condemn—; criticize—; distrust—; head for—; predict—; propose—; puff by—; resort to—; spike—; suffer—; threaten—; veer from—; —benefits; —devaluates; —dilates; —distends; —enhances; —swells.
(See expansion, prosperity, depression, success.)

INFLEXIBLE

adverbs
rigidly; obdurately; stiffly; arrogantly; austerely; autocratically; brutally; strictly; imperiously; domineeringly; tyrannically; sharply; rigorously; hardly; haughtily; inexorably; peremptorily; severely; uncompromisingly; unsparingly; sternly; hatefully; notoriously; intolerably; heartbreakingly; obstinately; tenaciously; resolutely; de-

terminedly; stubbornly; unreasonably; consistently; immovably; indomitably; unflinchingly.

INFLICT (*v*)

adverbs
thoughtlessly; painfully; cruelly; heavily; superfluously; unpleasantly; perniciously.
(See impose, strike.)

INFLUENCE

adjectives
prevailing; inspirational; disintegrating; brutalizing; powerful; benignant; incalculable; tidal; starry; tyrannical; fructifying; sinister; corrosive; parental; controlling; good; withering; gentler; similar; malevolent; baneful; potent; intimate; political; soft; corrupt; personal; iron; sullen; defiant; hypnotic; restless; formative; considerable; disorganizing; maleficent; variable; appealing; cogent; malign; permanent; mephitic; evil; favorable; insidious; pathetic; depressing; scathing; consequent; important; solemn; educational; disastrous; restraining; controlling; enormous; gentle; diminishing; inhibiting; compelling; helpful; mesmeric; mysterious; deadly; healing; persuasive; warping; demoniac; sober; useful; fair; stabilizing; decisive; overgrown; beauteous; internal; unquestioned; uncanny; court; mellow; moonlight; human; morbid; fierce; undue; wide; partisan; precious; magical; reviving; environmental; divine; hypnotic; genial; disciplinary; evangelical; adverse; favorable; prodigious; conservative; calamitous; censorial; baleful; demoralizing; ultimate; subtle; revolutionary; wholesome; destined; dispiriting; sobering; extensive; marked; destructive; foreign; soothing; vague; reassuring; mitigated; pernicious; gracious; jangling; exhilarating; sympathetic; refining; prenatal; stupefying; quickening; heinous; softening; enlightening; literary; guiding; imponderable; predisposing; invigorating; moral; repressing; ethnographical; incalculable; territorial; desolating; broadening; omnipotent; overgrown; weakening; irritating; lasting; liberal; credible; spreading; tremendous; single; sinister; poetical; disquieting; profound; invariable; witching; dominating; unconscious; balmiest; hasty; compensating; ultimate; environing; secret; disturbing; proportional; steadying; damping; unperceived; dwarfing; ennobling; corrupting; subtle; secondary; political; immense; beneficent; various (pl); salutary; vast; transcendent; despotic; commanding; trivial; sovereign; civilizing; protective; nerve-depleting; subjective; potential; blighting; wide-spread; many-mingled; reflex; problematical; sacred; sweet; transitory; misleading; ethical; marvelous; awful; antecedent; beneficial; unmindful; pernicious; jealous; vivifying; magical; subsequent; unexampled; infinite; invasive; emotional; soothing; tranquilizing; blasting; benumbing; propitious; aesthetic; toughening; gladdening; immediate; suggestive; carnicular; lost; predominating; underhand; materializing; mollifying; all-embracing; unconditional; mitigating; restraining; icy; moderating; celestial; superlative; narrowing; inaugurating; perceptible.

verbs
arrest—; bow to—; broaden—; come under —of; cramp—; curb—; diffuse—; exercise —; exert—; fall under—; impose—; infuse —; labor under—; lend—; manifest—over; measure—; multiply—; paralyze—; preserve from—; press—; promote—; reflect—; resist—; spread—; stem—; subject to—; survive—; wield—; yield to—; —bends; —corrupts; —declines; —extends to; —prevails; —reigns; —sways; —undermines; —wanes.
(See control, sway, prestige, persuasion, authority, strength, power.)

INFLUENCE (*v*)

adverbs
profoundly; powerfully; significantly; phenomenally; subsequently; adversely; unduly; vitally; strikingly; insensibly; unwillingly; remotely; benignantly; brutalizingly; parentally; malevolently; banefully; hypnotically; depressingly; exhilaratingly; despotically; jealously; morbidly; restrainingly.
(See induce, compel.)

INFLUENTIAL

adverbs
highly; remarkably; mysteriously; darkly; extremely; generally; peculiarly; politically; financially; notoriously; ominously; dangerously; alarmingly; helpfully; socially; nationally; sagaciously; powerfully; disastrously; enormously; quietly; calmly; tremendously; profoundly; artfully; immensely; persuasively; craftily; openly; obviously; palpably; manifestly; inexplicably; unaccountably; marvelously; wisely; secretly.

INFLUX

adjectives
vast; miraculous; steady.

INFORM (*v*)

adverbs
tremulously; blandly; personally; authoritatively; gruffly; unequivocally; officially; credibly; curtly; superficially; confidentially; comprehensively; fallaciously; dogmatically.

(See instruct, notify.)

INFORMAL

adverbs
graciously; intimately; delightfully; carelessly; charmingly; elaborately; deliberately; artfully; intentionally; happily; sweetly; pleasantly; amiably; agreeably; enchantingly; surprisingly; naively; remarkably; attractively; naturally; oddly; unexpectedly; heartily; cordially; diplomatically; exceedingly; habitually.

INFORMALITY

adjectives
pleasant; admirable; well-bred; delightful; charming.

INFORMATION

adjectives
instructional; imparted; common; broiling; miscellaneous; superficial; authentic; precise; vague; coordinating; scanty; solid; criminal; practical; household; substantial; summarized; trustworthy; factual; accurate; elusive; genuine; scientific; encouraging; inviting; astounding; exact; useful; further; detailed; comprehensive; false; up-to-the-minute; startling; practical; reliable; usable; behind-the-scenes; understandable; fallacious; gloomy; invaluable; superfluous; curious; anterior; accumulated; tabulated; profit-building; current; comparative; restricted; dogmatic; fascinating; unpleasant.

verbs
abound in—; absorb—; accumulate—; acquire—; authenticize—; bear—; buttress—; clamor for—; compile—; contribute—; convey—; coordinate—; correlate—; derive—; dig out—; digest—; dispense—; disseminate—; distort—; divulge—; elicit—; falsify —; garner—; glean—; impart—; misinterpret—; plead for—; prod for—; pump for —; relay—; rely on—; retail—; solicit—; summon—; suppress—; tabulate—; thirst for—; unburden oneself of—; utilize—; verify—; volunteer—; vouchsafe—; wheedle—; withhold—; worm—; yield—; —embodies; —leaks out.

(See knowledge, intelligence, data, facts, understanding, wisdom, science, statistics.)

INFRACTION

verbs
accuse of—; chastise for—; condemn—; detect—; fine—; harass by—; lament—; overlook—; penalize—; plague with—s; suffer —.

(See breach, error, violation, infringement.)

INFREQUENT

adverbs
painfully; frigidly; usually; remarkably; vexatiously; probably; luckily; fortunately; gratifyingly; uncertainly; erratically; undeniably; mysteriously; inscrutably; happily; negligibly.

INFRINGEMENT

verbs
abet—; allege—; curb—; enjoin—; observe —; protest—; punish—; resent—; restrain —; rue—.

(See violation, breach, infraction.)

INFUSION

adjectives
organic; putrescible; imperceptible; sterilized; steeped; imaginable; dormant.

INGENIOUS

adverbs
cleverly; artfully; skilfully; unusually; notably; famously; remarkably; adroitly; particularly; artistically; diplomatically; admirably; amazingly; marvelously; helpfully; extremely; capably; intelligently; unbelievably; exceedingly; dexterously; expertly; deftly; resourcefully; smartly; shrewdly; incredibly.

INGENUE

adjectives
raw; artless; guileless.

INGENUITY

adjectives
considerable; mechanical; inventive; misguided; speculative; wonderful; naive;

fiendish; subtle; puerile; interwoven; productive; devilish; unbetrayed; calumnious; extraordinary; conjectural.

verbs
acknowledge—; conceive by—; defy—; demand—; display—; employ—; excel in—; encourage—; endow with—; exercise—; feign—; invent by—; observe—; profit by —; strain—; swathe in—; tax—; witness—; —conquers; —triumphs.
(See infallibility, skill, ability, genius.)

INGENUOUS

adverbs
youthfully; openly; childishly; pleasantly; unsuspectingly; candidly; naturally; sincerely; innocently; honestly; frankly; bluntly; marvellously; unusually; unexpectedly; utterly; exceedingly; extraordinarily; surprisingly; amazingly; strikingly; astonishingly; miraculously; unaffectedly.

INGRATIATING

adverbs
deliberately; skilfully; artfully; politically; purposely; pleasantly; craftily; disgustingly; abjectly; insidiously; invidiously; diplomatically; amiably; curiously; elaborately; obsequiously; ceremoniously; suavely; gently; courteously; urbanely; gallantly; unctuously; blandly; cordially; affably; civilly; extremely.

INGRATITUDE

adjectives
occasional; habitual; horrible; foul; base.

verbs
brood over—; complain of—; denounce—; expose to—; suffer—; taint with—; treat with—; wipe out—; —barbs; —bites; —bruises; —oppresses; —pains; —pierces; —provokes; —shames; —thrives; —undermines.
(See oppression, infidelity, treachery, selfishness.)

INGREDIENTS

adjectives
healing; costly; dry; delicious; sifted; accidental; sweetening; unintelligible; prominent; basic; malicious; principal; choicest; modern; balanced; seething; pernicious; commonplace; poisonous; necessary; muddy; nutritive; nourishing.

verbs
adjust—; analyze—; calculate—; concoct of —; denounce—; discover—; gather—; measure—; memorize—; mix—; note—; prepare —; produce—; reduce—; separate—; skimp on—; test—.
(See parts, elements, materials.)

INHABIT (*v*)

adverbs
thinly; comfortably; successively; wretchedly; swarmingly; solely; misguidedly; placidly; domestically; humbly.
(See abide, dwell, live.)

INHABITANTS

adjectives
strange; glorious; unmolested; unobtrusive; aboriginal; intimate; permanent; larger; wretched; respective; awe-struck; diverse; fortunate; cordial; respectable; unambitious; rustic; brawny; feathered; defenceless; plague-stricken; tender; placid; amazed; pious; ancient; wretched; swarming.

verbs
confer on—; consider—; entitle — to; grant to—; privilege—; regulate—; rule—; urge —; —attend; —benefit; —complain; —congregate; —dwell; —enjoy; —frequent; —organize; —rejoice; —revolt; —rise; —tenant; —welcome.
(See individual, native.)

INHALE (*v*)

adverbs
audibly; deeply; luxuriously; spasmodically; gaspingly; sharply; agonizingly; laboriously.
(See breathe.)

INHARMONIOUS

adverbs
unpleasantly; inexplicably; annoyingly; disastrously; inexcusably; unreasonably; utterly; freqeuntly; mysteriously; obscurely; unnecessarily; strangely; disgustingly; fearfully; ominously; significantly; unbelievably; oddly; curiously; extremely.

INHERENT

adverbs
disturbingly; ineradicably; indubitably; obviously; manifestly; fortunately; happily; palpably; deeply; essentially; fundamentally.

INHERIT (v)

adverbs
legally; unexpectedly; spectacularly; dramatically; nominally; traditionally; customarily; fortunately.
(See receive, possess, derive.)

INHERITANCE

adjectives
dismal; fairest; fallen; ill-starred; astounding; storied; entailed; occasional; moderate; racial.

verbs
administer—; bequeath—; bless with—; come into—; confirm—; derive—from; divide—; enjoy—; entitle to—; forfeit—; forsake—; grant—; lay claim to—; portion—; preserve—; profit by—; relinquish—; restore to—; scatter—; squander—; succeed to —; tax—; —enriches; —falls to.
(See legacy, estate, money, property, profits.)

INHIBITION

verbs
detect—; express—; harass by—; incur—; persecute with—; proceed from—; remove —; suffer—; sympathize with—; veil—; vent—; —arrests; —disappears; —haunts; —plagues; —restrains; —restricts; —torments; —tortures.
(See restraint, fear, complex, restriction.)

INHOSPITABLE

adverbs
strangely; rudely; uncivilly; inexcusably; curiously; coldly; unpardonably; deliberately; openly; ostentatiously; purposely; discourteously; oddly; inexplicably; unaccountably; miserably; wretchedly; terribly; gruffly; brusquely; roughly; distinctly; unsociably; churlishly; ungraciously; forbiddingly; extremely; unforgettably; peculiarly; remarkably; significantly.

INHUMAN

adverbs
brutally; brutishly; curiously; incredibly; savagely; unbelievably; strangely; deliberately; barbarously; cruelly; ferociously; atrociously; ruthlessly; relentlessly; fiendishly; fantastically; viciously; diabolically.

INIMICAL

adverbs
essentially; radically; fundamentally; altogether; naturally; antagonistically; malevolently; maliciously; secretly; mysteriously; inexplicably; unaccountably; strangely; unreasonably; obviously; oddly; unexpectedly; palpably; manifestly; significantly; sadly; violently; spitefully; constitutionally; ominously; dangerously.

INIMITABLE

adverbs
altogether; remarkably; utterly; incomparably; peerlessly; brilliantly; perfectly; artistically; preciously; peculiarly; delightfully; faultlessly; avowedly; reputedly; presumably.

INIQUITIES

adjectives
conjugal; juvenile; aged; crowning; manifest.

INIQUITOUS

adverbs
atrociously; unbelievably; inexpressibly; unspeakably; obscenely; heinously; invidiously; egregiously; inordinately; exceptionally; unmentionably; diabolically; grievously; irremediably; banefully; criminally; unwarrantably; immorally; unimaginably; viciously; nefariously; malevolently; impiously; unconscionably; basely; vilely; savagely.

INIQUITY

verbs
acquit of—; bring forth—; cleanse of—; cling to—; conceive of—; confess—; defile with—; delight in—; disclose—; drown in —; forgive—; foul with—; perish in—; punish for—; purge of—; rebuke—; redeem from—; reveal—; steep in—; taint with—; turn from—; work—; —flourishes.
(See sin, wickedness, abomination, crime.)

INITIATE (v)

adverbs
festively; ceremoniously; dramatically; annually; imaginatively; originally; forcefully; beneficently.
(See begin, instruct, introduce.)

INITIATION

adjectives
practical; exceptional; unwilling; elementary; baptismal.

INITIATIVE

adjectives
unusual; private; unfettered; individual; untrammeled; unparalleled; aggressive; independent; popular.

verbs
cripple—; crush—; curb—; demonstrate—; develop—; display—; encourage—; exhibit —; imbue with—; kill—; manifest—; observe—; praise—; provoke—; reward—; —activates; —yields.

(See originality, ability, skill, genius, proficiency.)

INJECT (v)

adverbs
hypodermically; intravenously; insidiously; spitefully; slyly; salaciously; maliciously; medically; scientifically; methodically.

(See put, introduce, insert, interject.)

INJUDICIOUS

adverbs
thoughtlessly; senselessly; foolishly; indiscreetly; imprudently; childishly; heedlessly; vengefully; ignorantly; unintentionally; unfortunately; sadly; disastrously; blindly; rashly; impulsively; impetuously; adventurously; heedlessly; inexpediently; recklessly; wantonly; stupidly; ridiculously; absurdly.

INJUNCTION

adjectives
solemn; serious; conflicting; sternest; strict; vehement; permanent; pretty; curt; tacit; restraining; temporary.

verbs
apply for—; consecrate—; deny—; enforce —; grant—; hand down—; justify—; obey —; refuse—; suspend—; sustain—; —bans; —bars; —blocks; —restrains; —restricts; — ties up.

(See action, order, instructions, command, requirement.)

INJURE (v)

adverbs
severely; dangerously; wilfully; critically; incurably; shockingly; permanently; unwittingly; atrociously; wantonly; gravely; internally; materially; irreparably.

(See damage, hurt, wound.)

INJURIES

adjectives
atrocious; potent; wanton; conscious; protracted; sinister; dreaded; serious; widespread; multiplied; repeated; grave; previous; internal; incredible; permanent; material; mental; disabling; irreparable; incalculable.

INJURIOUS

adverbs
distinctly; presumably; definitely; positively; irremediably; slightly; surprisingly; distressingly; unintentionally; indiscreetly; mysteriously; maliciously; deliberately; desperately; highly; perniciously; seriously; destructively; tragically; outrageously.

INJURY

verbs
avenge—; bewail—; compensate for—; entail—; expose to—; inflict — upon; insure against—; occasion—; preserve from—; proclaim—; receive—; recover from—; recuperate from—; resist—; suffer—; sustain—; work—; —cripples; —outrages; —restricts; —unnerves.

(See wound, damage, wrong, outrage, mischief, pain, injustice.)

INJUSTICE

adjectives
murderous; temporary; wanton; cruel; tyrannic; abominable; cruelest; flagrant; social; crowning; peculiar; horrible; artistic; shocking; unspoken; treacherous; inherent; unintentional; immemorial; atrocious; gross.

verbs
accept—; attack—; belabor—; bewail—; brood over—; cite—; crush with—; decry —; denounce—; detect—; eliminate—; extirpate—; impose—; inflict—; lament—; inveigh against—; persist in—; reek of—; remedy—; sense—; shrink from—; swallow —; wallow in—; work—.

(See inequality, injury, unfairness, grievance, wrong.)

INK

adjectives
corroding; potent; sympathetic; invisible.

verbs
battle with—; blacken with—; blot with—; cloud with—; color with—; dilute—; dip into—; drip—; eject—; expel—; reservoir

—; smear—; smirch with—; —blurs; —spatters; —spots; —stains.
(See paint.)

INMATES

adjectives
temporary; cowering; exasperating; feeble-minded; querulous; miserable-looking; destitute; licentious; unhappy; mad.

INN

adverbs
dwell in—; establish—; frequent—; keep—; lodge in—; maintain—; put up at—; repair to—; reside in—; sojourn at—; stop at—; —accommodates; —houses; —invites; —provides; —quarters; —warms; —welcomes.
(See hotel, home, apartment, tavern.)

INNOCENCE

adjectives
harmless; loveliest; virgin; extreme; spotless; intrinsic; recognized; inviolable; unsuspecting; helpless; strange; fulsome; unabashed; childish; deliberate; despairing; injured; elaborate; pretended; starry; lofty; conscious; departed; primitive; heavenly; gentle; hapless.

verbs
assert—; betray—; commend—; despoil—; feign—; guard—; hallow—; immortalize—; jeopardize—; maintain—; plead—; prey on —; protest—; prove—; seduce—; smile in —; vindicate—.
(See purity, simplicity, sincerity.)

INNOCENT

adverbs
delightfully; childishly; naturally; legally; sweetly; presumably; girlishly; charmingly; playfully; beautifully; helplessly; apparently; manifestly; palpably; irresistibly; gently; essentially; virtuously; positively; artlessly; sincerely; unaffectedly; ingenuously; frankly; admirably; unbelievably; happily; refreshingly; naively; touchingly; wonderfully; alluringly; graciously; ravishingly; exquisitely; alluringly; adorably.

INNOCUOUS

adverbs
utterly; advantageously; valuably; unobjectionably; vacuously; inoffensively; negligibly; presumably; probably; wholesomely; safely; undoubtedly; definitely.

INNOVATION

adjectives
striking; political; unquiet; distasteful; ghastly; outward; unauthorized; startling; tyrannical; interesting; radical; endless; inexpedient; recent; countless (pl).

verbs
champion—; clamor for—; curb—; demand —; disapprove of—; discourage—; favor—; plan—; protest against—; resist—; sprout —; stay—; suspect—; welcome—; —attracts; —improves; —revolutionizes; encourage—.
(See change, improvement, style, fashion, movement.)

INNUENDO

adjectives
unspoken; malicious; biting; salacious.

verbs
convey by—; employ—; indulge in—; insinuate by—; interpret—; utter—; —annoys; —hints; —implies; —intimates; —libels; —peeves (colloq.); —puzzles; —slanders; —suggests.
(See insinuation, suggestion.)

INOCULATE (v)

adverbs
successfully; scientifically; experimentally; automatically; prudentially.
(See protect, insert, introduce, inject.)

INOFFENSIVE

adverbs
utterly; safely; negligibly; warrantably; assuredly; surely; completely; wholly; avowedly; indubitably; satisfactorily; fairly; probably; quietly; amiably; diplomatically; wisely; sagaciously; discreetly.

INOPERATIVE

adverbs
provokingly; vapidly; vexatiously; hopelessly; idly; lately; legally; harmlessly; untenably; wholly; utterly.

INOPPORTUNE

adverbs
awkwardly; embarrassingly; vexatiously; wholly; singularly; peculiarly; financially; politically; commercially; disastrously; unfortunately; presumably; socially; signally;

seriously; unfortunately; unluckily; inexpediently; inaptly; clumsily; stupidly; foolishly; terribly; sadly; miserably; wretchedly.

INQUIRE (v)

adverbs
solicitously; perfunctorily; boldly; mischievously; curiously; sarcastically; diligently; concernedly; incredulously; laconically; superficially; placidly; ominously; bluntly; officially; passionately; skeptically; apprehensively; dolorously; innocently; curtly.

(See ask, seek, question.)

INQUIRER

adjectives
individual; diligent; curious; historical; philosophical; profane.

INQUIRY

adjectives
investigational; liberal; audacious; vindictive; studious; calm; dispassionate; laconic; rigorous; extensive; horrified; breathless; minute; confidential; particular; skeptical; recent; diligent; patient; successful; urgent; sarcastic; apprehensive; exacting; troubled; cold; sanctioned; sleepy; dolorous; fruitless; competent; respectful; troublesome; subsequent; eager; physical; point-blank; thorough; sincere; innocent; direct; discreet; pertinent; scientific; suave; vain; solid; indefinite; tentative; strict; sad; accurate; unthinking; suspicious; sarcastic; mild; hospitable; formal; curt; brisk; brash.

verbs
bombard with—s; conduct—; deter—; institute—; meet—; occasion—; overwhelm with—s; press—; provoke—; pursue—; push—; renew—; repeat—; reply to—; resume—; subject to—; waive—; —discloses.

(See question, investigation, research, examination.)

INQUISITION

adjectives
tyrannous; ceaseless; imperious; bootless; comfortable; solemn; merciless; cruel.

verbs
demand—; escape—; fall foul of—; justify—; launch—; occasion—; propose—; search by—; suggest—; sweep by—; —explores; —irks; —proves; —reviews; —trespasses.

(See investigation, inquiry, research.)

INQUISITIVE

adverbs
inordinately; offensively; curiously; oddly; persistently; maliciously; meddlesomely; tiresomely; offensively; venomously; innocently; harmlessly; miserably; distressingly; unpardonably; inexcusably; discourteously; unforgivably; dangerously; significantly; alarmingly; intellectually; scientifically; intrusively; pryingly; mysteriously; egregiously; openly; expertly; officiously; relentlessly; impolitely; boundlessly; insatiably.

INQUISITORS

adjectives
delegated; persecuting; mealy-mouthed; death-dealing.

INROADS

adjectives
destructive; perpetual; frequent; constant; serious; casual; blighting.

INSANE

adjectives
wildly; slightly; probably; mildly; presumably; avowedly; violently; slightly; permanently; periodically; pathetically; tragically; recently; allegedly; notoriously; dangerously; pitiably; miserably; hopelessly; irremediably; irrecoverably; dreadfully; incurably; utterly; deliriously; fanatically; eccentrically; hysterically; incoherently; distressingly.

INSANITY

adjectives
true; warlike; intellectual; temporary; dire; pious; incipient; incurable; speculative; hysterical; harmless; systematic; delusional; hereditary.

verbs
anticipate—; banish—; border on—; condemn to—; correct—; detect—; discern—; drive to—; hush—; lament—; lead to—; observe—; plead—; produce—; sense—; simulate—; subdue—; suffer—; thrust into—; treat—; —desolates; —imprisons; —seizes; overcome—.

(See mania, madness, frenzy, delirium.)

INSATIABLE

adverbs
greedily; voraciously; miserably; shamelessly; hungrily; terribly; pitiably; rapacious-

ly; unbelievably; curiously; strangely; grossly; avidly; covetously; cravingly; sordidly; openly; manifestly.

INSCRIBE (*v*)

adverbs
lightly; erroneously; appropriately; decoratively; legibly; hieroglyphically; tenderly; officially; historically.
(See imprint, write.)

INSCRIPTION

adjectives
analogous; trilingual; sham; inappropriate; monumental; absorbing; cuneiform; simple; lofty; horizontal; decorative; legible; duplicate; flattering; mural; libelous; hieroglyphical; ominous; effaced.

verbs
bear—; carve—; chisel—; decipher—; engrave—; furnish—; mark—; pen—; place —; study—; survey—; trace—; word—; —adorns; —commemorates; —dedicates; —denotes; —heads; —indicates; —records; —reminds.
(See record, handwriting, monument, document.)

INSCRUTABLE

adverbs
mysteriously; oddly; hopelessly; curiously; impenetrably; altogether; strangely; utterly; unaccountably; wholly.

INSECT

adjectives
individual; venomous; luminous; aculeate; industrious; blundering; coral; silken-winged; bloated; noisome; dormant; swarming; glittering; populous; all-devouring; melodious; gorgeous; countless (pl); injurious; ubiquitous; energetic; acquisitive; sweet; throbbing; mottled; destructive; painless; annoying; voracious; multitudinous (pl).

INSECTS

verbs
allure—; breed—; combat—; exterminate—; feed on—; hunt—; lure—; net—; overrun with—; trap—; —annoy; —buzz; —demolish; —devour; —dismantle; —distress; —fertilize; —hum; —nest; —pest; —plague; —pupate; —ravage; —sap; —settle on; —swarm; —swirl; —undergo a metamorphosis; —creeps.
(See individual insects.)

INSECURE

adverbs
pitiably; alarmingly; distressingly; fearfully; hopelessly; flimsily; embarrassingly; awkwardly; vaguely; bewilderingly; precariously; dangerously; carelessly; inexcusably; critically; ominously; perilously; curiously; dreadfully; horribly; undeniably; fatally; continuallly; wearily; professionally; pathetically; apprehensively; uncomfortably; anxiously; tormentingly; grievously; financially.

INSENSIBLE

adverbs
curiously; stolidly; dully; apathetically; sluggishly; languidly; torpidly; utterly; callously; indifferently; phlegmatically; drowsily; somnolently; sleepily; stupidly; dazedly; obtusely; lethargically; imperturbably; inattentively; unconcernedly; unbelievably; incredibly.

INSEPARABLE

adverbs
affectionately; insistently; physically; scientifically; technically; financially; politically; logically; commercially; naturally; cohesively; firmly; solidly; tenaciously; securely; legally; authoritatively; officially; warrantably.

INSERT (*v*)

adverbs
parenthetically; expressly; daily; meticulously; formally; officially; logically; derogatorily.
(See inject, interject.)

INSIDIOUS

adverbs
peculiarly; subtly; dangerously; alarmingly; appallingly; cunningly; shrewdly; terrifyingly; particularly; shockingly; ominously; uncomfortably; deceptively; surreptitiously; elusively; fraudulently; slyly; profoundly; cleverly; artfully; astutely; shabbily; wickedly; perfidiously; shamefully; trickily.

INSIGHT

adjectives
clearer; intuitive; vivid; profound; spiritual; rare; true; mythic; penetrating; partial; uncanny; sympathetic; psychological;

pathetic; keen; intellectual; comprehensive; steady; sagacious; curious; imaginative; prophetic; dramatic; clearest; scientific; objective; valid; mature; mystic.

verbs
acquire—; endow with—; flash—; follow with—; furnish with—; gain—; give—; lack—; obtain—; possess—; ripen into—; understand through—; —comprehends; —discerns; —fathoms; —penetrates; —perceives; —rewards; —searches.
(See understanding, wisdom.)

INSIGNIA

adjectives
distinguishing; military; graceful.

INSIGNIFICANCE

adjectives
paltry; essential; sallow; miserable; puny.

verbs
bury in—; crouch in—; dwindle into—; fade into—; pale into—; plunge into—; reduce to—; ridicule—; scorn—; sink into—; spring from—; suffer—; —engulfs; —prostrates; —swallows.
(See obscurity, seclusion, trifle, oblivion.)

INSIGNIFICANT

adverbs
altogether; negligibly; admittedly; avowedly; inconsequentially; weakly; pitifully; contemptibly; ridiculously; vaguely; absurdly; fatuously; inanely; pathetically; terribly; ultimately.

INSINCERE

adverbs
woefully; curiously; obviously; strangely; indubitably; palpably; hopelessly; arrantly; evidently; shamefully; transparently; absurdly; slyly; evasively; pretentiously; flatteringly; cruelly; insidiously; bitterly; clearly; unmistakably; grossly; dreadfully.

INSINCERITY

verbs
abhor—; charge with—; clog with—; condemn—; detect—; embroider with—; engage in—; falsify with—; incline toward—; witness—; —adulterates; —deceives; —disgraces; —disguises; —distorts; —forfeits; —shames.
(See unfaithfulness, treachery, deception, hypocrisy.)

INSINUATE (v)

adverbs
brazenly; slanderously; coyly; pointedly; delicately; calumniously; offensively; adroitly; covertly; reticently; outrageously.
(See imply, hint, suggest.)

INSINUATION

adjectives
calumnious; conscientious; adroit; slanderous; covert; nasty; reticent; evil; unguarded; offensive; outrageous; terrible; unfortunate; slow.

verbs
contemplate—; dare—; defeat—; deliver—; dispose of—; omit—; perceive—; weigh—; wince at—; —alludes; —creeps in; —hints; —implies; —informs; —instills; —shocks; —suggests.
(See accusation, innuendo, intimation, suggestion, hint.)

INSIPID

adverbs
stupidly; feebly; unusually; habitually; naturally; hopelessly; tiresomely; vacuously; fatuously; colorlessly; vexatiously; tediously; prosaically; dully; doltishly; inertly; passively; phlegmatically; listlessly; lackadaisically; recklessly; uninterestingly; monotonously; depressingly; unbearably.

INSIPIDITY

adjectives
conventional; slumbrous; stereotyped.

INSIST (v)

adverbs
hotly; glowingly; indignantly; belligerently; stolidly; perversely; deliberately; pedantically; resolutely; pointedly; pertinaciously; disobligingly; uniformly; emphatically; vehemently; strenuously; obstinately; blandly; sternly; eloquently.
(See urge, persist, press.)

INSISTENCE

adjectives
stern; steadfast; deliberate; important; melancholy; eloquent; perpetual; pathetic; stereotyped.

verbs
assert with—; increase—; relax—; require—; silence—; steel against—; stick with—;

—annoys; —conquers; —determines; —irks; —relents.

(See persistence, determination, intensity, perseverance.)

INSISTENT

adverbs

vexatiously; tiresomely; intolerably; annoyingly; captiously; peevishly; cruelly; tyrannically; discourteously; violently; disagreeably; unpleasantly; hospitably; generously; aggressively; inescapably; urgently; embarrassingly; pestiferously; cantankerously; distressingly; dictatorially; resolutely; firmly; tenaciously; obstinately.

INSOLENCE

adjectives

haughty; increasing; disobedient; smiling; beefy; studied; ferocious; displeasing; gigantic; personal; insane; wanton; flat-faced; mutinous; puffed.

INSOLENT

adverbs

unbearably; atrociously; arrogantly; proudly; haughtily; arrantly; inordinately; egregiously; intolerably; ridiculously; unpardonably; disrespectfully; terribly; flippantly; pertly; saucily; crudely; grossly; abusively; outrageously; outlandishly; scandalously; loudly; brazenly; crassly; bumptiously; imperiously; highly; audaciously; inexcusably.

INSOLVENT

adverbs

pitiably; suddenly; finally; pathetically; unfortunately; admittedly; hopelessly; sorrowfully; desperately; deeply; unluckily; unhappily; impecuniously; embarrassingly; ruinously; unaccountably; inexplicably; mysteriously; curiously; incredibly; needlessly.

INSOMNIA

verbs

afflict with—; conquer—; correct—; ease—; grapple with—; labor under—; release—; subject to—; suffer—; —hinders; —interferes; —provokes; —stupefies; —unnerves; —weakens.

(See disease, pain.)

INSOUCIANT

adverbs

inconsiderately; blithely; giddily; dizzily; heedlessly; dreamily; gaily; cheerily; carelessly; unconcernedly; imperturbably; recklessly; rashly; serenely; calmly; heartily.

INSPECT (v)

adverbs

intently; circumspectly; fastidiously; judiciously; rigidly; periodically; personally; cursorily; cautiously; painstakingly.

(See examine, investigate.)

INSPECTION

adjectives

immediate; rigid; bare; painstaking; periodic; cursory; cautious; personal.

INSPIRATION

adjectives

passionate; fatal; unmistakable; fresh; happy; healthier; subtle; verbal; sudden; heroic; divine; adequate; overpowering; mystic; elevated; dramatic; inward; maternal; incarnate; mighty; unbiased; natural; irrepressible; sustaining; struggling; feeblest; laborious; ennobling.

verbs

conflict with—; derive—from; exhaust—; foster—; gain—; kill—; presage—; pray for—; preserve—; restore—; suppress—; whisper—; —cheers; —flags; —rallies; —seizes; —visits; —wells from.

(See enthusiasm, fervor, influence, genius.)

INSPIRE (v)

adverbs

religiously; divinely; nocturnally; unceasingly; invariably; passionately; fatally; happily; subtly; verbally; heroically; mystically; dramatically; maternally; irrepressibly; feebly; laboriously; tenderly.

(See kindle, arouse, rouse, animate.)

INSTABILITY

adjectives

emotional; molecular; psychic; permanent; mental.

verbs

aggravate—; betray—; buttress—; condemn—; convey—; deplore—; detect—; judge—; lament—; lead to—; observe—; reflect on—; reform—; support—; survey—; —irks; —threatens.

(See weakness, impotence.)

INSTALL (v)

adverbs
magnificently; ceremoniously; regularly; comfortably; formally; scientifically; modernistically; charitably; governmentally; legislatively; dictatorially.
(See establish, place.)

INSTALLMENT

verbs
administer—; commend—; consent to—; direct—; glorify—; herald—; honor by—; influence—; inspire—; invite to—; observe—; occasion—; perform—; plan—; preside at —; seek—; view—; —climaxes; witness—.
(See payment.)

INSTANCE

adjectives
contradictory; isolated; individual; noteworthy; wonderful; abundant; well-authenticated; striking; inconsiderable; parallel; continued; dramatic; precise; memorable; far-famed; admirable; melancholy; conspicuous; arresting; notable; forcible; unfortunate; characteristic; splendid; abortive; comparable; notorious; tragic; recorded; solitary; unrelated; typical; worthy; particular; extreme; delightful; present; illustrious; rare; undeniable; remarkable.

verbs
afford—; cite—; contradict—; demand—; dispute—; experience—; furnish—; multiply —s; offer—; point out—; provide—; quote —; ridicule—; solicit—; study—; —exemplifies; —illustrates; —indicates; —proves; —reminds.
(See example, illustration, precedent.)

INSTANT

adjectives
unseasonable; luminous; approaching; flashing; terrible; fleeting; single; breathless; fatal; swift.

verbs
accomplish in an—; convey in—; depart for —; emerge in—; flicker out in—; pause for —; separate for—; —passes; —presses.
(See moment, hour, time.)

INSTIL (v)

adverbs
ridiculously; subtly; insidiously; cleverly; slyly; perfidiously; covertly; mystically; paternally; scholastically.
(See introduce, impress, implant.)

INSTINCT

adjectives
poetic; indefinable; impulsive; hereditary; faithful; natural; holy; warm; brutal; prophetic; profoundest; subtle; dramatic; vague; combative; protective; military; proper; religious; beneficent; noble; aesthetic; conservative; inherited; artistic; self-preserving; denied; invisible; maternal; unerring; refined; gentle; deepest; semi-barbaric; perverted; animal; sterile; amorphous; conservative; universal; deep-rooted; formal; ennobled; delicate; driving; human; heroic; grosser; native; transcendental; tameless; sympathetic; long-dormant; disorderly; journalistic; monastic; social; irresistible; fine; quality; predominating; provident; spiritual; tender; wonderful; mechanical; prudential; fiery; grateful; innate; sudden; scientific; imperative; sure; trained; superhuman; speculative; irrrelevant; snob; groping; gregarious; terrible; herd; independent; fortunate; selective; kindly; unconscious; purest; common; iconoclastic; logical; racial; brutal; derogatory.

verbs
cloud—; control—; curb—; develop—; endow with—; follow—; gratify—; numb—; obey—; offend—; pander to—; rely on—; repress—; rouse—; stir—; succumb to—; suppress—; thwart—; violate—; —deceives; —guides; —impels; —motivates; —persists; —s war within.
(See impulse, desire, skill, nature.)

INSTITUTION

adjectives
frail; cherished; extraordinary; charitable; religious; popular; temporary; essential; instrumental; professional; venerable; august; notable; existing; ecclesiastical; sacerdotal; preparatory; necessary; time-honored; infant; remarkable; major; peculiar; sundry (pl); aristocratic; feudal; fiduciary; diverse (pl); flourishing; ancient; dignified; free; popular; bestial; inevitable; liberal; respective; lauded; social; distinctive; dominant; economic; benevolent; perfidious; bureaucratic; long-established; various (pl); abhorrent; moneyed; powerful; notorious; parochial; superb; monstrous.

verbs
abolish—; acclaim—; bar from—; charter —; commit to—; confirm—; discard—; endow—; grant to—; herd in—s; lampoon—;

maintain—; patronize—; support—; undermine—; —crumbles; —flourishes.

(See establishment, club, society, school.)

INSTRUCT (v)

adverbs

peremptorily; urgently; artistically; solemnly; forcefully; adequately; laconically; ethically; clinically; parochially; tediously; theoretically; intellectually; facetiously; vaguely; academically; formally; inspirationally; diligently.

(See teach, command, direct.)

INSTRUCTION

adjectives

adequate; hurried; scattered; bloody; laconic; inevitable; careful; explicit; brave; ethical; botanical; clinical; stimulative; parochial; official; minute; thoughtful; elementary; theoretical; intellectual; facetious; pleasurable; cabled; hazy; vague; religious; tedious; classroom; parliamentary.

verbs

abide by—; attend to—; authorize—; comply with—; conform to—; contravene—; counsel—; deluge with—; desire—; disqualify for—; follow—; hearken to—; impart—; lack—; overwhelm with—s; prescribe—; profit by—; radio—; refuse—; —corrects; —guides.

(See teaching, information, education.)

INSTRUCTOR

adjectives

clerical; capable; competent; sober; sordid; reticent.

INSTRUMENT

adjectives

physical; master; keyboard; gracious; godlike; negotiable; outstanding; dictating; grand; musical; ingenious; expensive; unfit; precision; potent; rude; glorious; philosophical; penitent; facile; perfect; rough; extraordinary; noble; exceptional; component; heavenly; murderous; incomprehensible; spellbound; blunt; passive; unconscious; compact; scorned; supple; astronomical; serviceable; quaking; dental; cunning; greedy; sacred; tolerable; immediate; graceful.

verbs

contaminate—; contrive—; devise—; employ—; encase—; fashion—; forge—; guard—; hamper—; hinder—; introduce—; lubricate—; manipulate—; obstruct—; perform with—; project—; resist—; utilize—; yield to—.

(See tool, utensil, method, document, machine.)

INSTRUMENTAL

adverbs

definitely; helpfully; necessarily; admittedly; covertly; secretly; furtively; openly; proudly; ostentatiously; usefully; diabolically; benevolently; obscurely; inscrutably; valuably; serviceably; fortunately; capably; competently.

INSUBORDINATE

adverbs

insufferably; unbearably; intolerably; recklessly; rashly; brazenly; sullenly; subtly; openly; unaccountably; deliberately; arrantly; accidentally; purposely; unconsciously; unpardonably; hopelessly; grossly; crassly; flagrantly; slyly; audaciously; mutinously; seditiously; treacherously; incredibly; restively; impatiently; egregiously; amazingly; dangerously; childishly; senselessly.

INSUBORDINATION

adjectives

sharp; colonial; criminal; flagrant; rank.

INSUBSTANTIAL

adverbs

terribly; hopelessly; tragically; nebulously; imaginatively; dreamily; pitifully; wretchedly; airily; tenuously; vaguely; dimly; altogether; blankly; obviously; utterly.

INSUFFERABLE

adverbs

utterly; disagreeably; incredibly; altogether; haughtily; boisterously; rudely; arrantly; grossly; crassly; crudely; boorishly; arrogantly; swaggeringly; scornfully; loudly; maliciously; slanderously; invidiously; importunately; abhorrently; odiously; generally.

INSUFFICIENT

adverbs

pitiably; tragically; wretchedly; altogether; stingily; parsimoniously; unbelievably; evidently; palpably; ungenerously; thoughtlessly; piteously; miserably; criminally; incredibly; shockingly; appallingly; awfully.

INSULAR

adverb

incredibly; happily; safely; securely; narrowly; narrow-mindedly; bigotedly; fanatically; contentedly; smugly; dogmatically; stupidly; surprisingly; naturally; peacefully; complacently; inordinately; rustically; provincially.

INSULT

adjectives

harsh; unfeeling; endurable; rash; crowning; biting; personal; cruel; grossest; veiled; monstrous; fresh; mortal; stinging; deadly; persistent; dire; supposed; petty.

verbs

avenge—; barb with—; bawl—; brook—; condone—; decry—; endure—; exchange —s; fling—at; hurl—at; ignore—; shout—; suffer—; take affront at—; —grieves; —infuriates; —libels; —rebuffs; —slanders; pardon—.

(See outrage, offense, wrong.)

INSULT (v)

adverbs

scurrilously; desperately; vilely; impudently; grossly; brazenly; outrageously; sullenly; wantonly; unendurably; monstrously.

(See affront, abuse, offend.)

INSULTING

adverbs

horribly; unpardonably; intolerably; unbearably; insufferably; boorishly; cruelly; subtly; covertly; sneeringly; cynically; ironically; openly; deliberately; intentionally; inexcusably; coarsely; grossly; publicly; superciliously; impudently; flagrantly.

INSUPPORTABLE

adverbs

altogether; evidently; manifestly; fantastically; obviously; heavily; tragically; pitiably; wretchedly; lamentably; indubitably; visibly; shockingly; pitifully; physically; painfully; grievously; finally; oppressively; tormentingly.

INSURANCE

verbs

collect—; consider—; examine for—; obtain —; pay—; prefer—; refuse—; regulate—; transfer—; value—; undertake—; underwrite—; —guarantees; —indemnifies; —invests; —lapses; —provides; —reassures; —safeguards.

(See security, guarantee.)

INSURE (v)

adverbs

prudentially; customarily; rashly; paradoxically; conventionally; conservatively; liberally.

(See protect, assure.)

INSURGENTS

verbs

accede to—; beat down—; check—; disperse —; inflame—; kindle—; quell—; repel—; repulse—; rout—; stir—; subdue—; —arise; —conspire; —demand; —dictate; —intrigue; —occupy; —oppose; —overthrow; —plot; —revolt; —spring up; —tyrannize.

(See enemy, rebel, foe, rival, competitor.)

INSURMOUNTABLE

adverbs

heavily; oppressively; appallingly; manifestly; admittedly; apparently; perplexingly; bafflingly; absurdly; desperately; seriously; gravely; unfortunately; curiously; altogether; legally; disconcertingly; embarrassingly; awkwardly; cruelly.

INSURRECTION

adjectives

muting; wide-spread; hopeless; subsequent; servile; absurd; serious; laughable; domestic.

verbs

check—; conspire—; crush—; encourage—; engage in—; excite—; finance—; foment—; head—; inflame—; instigate—; kindle—; plot—; quell—; resist—; restrain—; support—; suppress—; —alarms; —breaks out; —bursts forth; —dismays; —endangers; —menaces; —sweeps away; —threatens.

(See revolution, rebellion, fight.)

INTACT

adverbs

blessedly; luckily; fortunately; incredibly; happily; visibly; safely; securely.

INTANGIBLE

adverbs

evanescently; undeniably; practically; dimly; vaguely; obscurely; fleetingly; provokingly; legally; foggily; indeterminately; temporally; darkly; unintelligibly; naturally; mysteriously; faintly.

INTEGRITY

adjectives
territorial; constitutional; innate; unimpeachable; sturdy; delicate; unassailable; sterling; unbending; unquestioned; determined; administrative; incorruptible; moral; transparent; intellectual; perfect; stubborn; stern; indisputable.

verbs
blemish—; breed—; commend—; doubt—; esteem—; impair—; laud—; maintain—; note—; preserve—; question—; require—; reserve—; retain—; reward—; root in—; taint—; test—; trust—; sacrifice—; vow—.
(See honesty, virtue, truth, sincerity.)

INTELLECT

adjectives
cultured; keen; expanded; happy; considerable; godlike; high; stern; jaded; powerful; sluggard; prostrated; ruthless; unclouded; benighted; noble; restless; unguided; comprehending; austere; elevated; sluggish; brilliant; ordinary; lofty; inferior; articulate; frightened; active; provincial; haggard; fertile; ripening; profound; undying; imperial; superior; aroused; cultivated; crudest; discerning; prepared; meddling; humble; cold; resourceful; human; shadowy; penetrating; colossal; wavering; uninformed; grasping; singular; mightiest; reasoning; many-sided; stagnant; refined; stirring; seraphic; all-subtilizing; amazing; constructive; massive; eternal.

verbs
balance—; cobweb—; cultivate—; destroy—; dissipate—; distort—; educate—; enlarge—; enthrone—; excel in—; expand—; impair—; judge—; perfect—; reflect—; shake—; sharpen—; stunt—; train—; weigh—; —comprehends; —deteriorates; —discerns; —enslaves; —revolts; —speculates.
(See brain, mind, understanding, intelligence.)

INTELLECTUAL

adverbs
proudly; blatantly; swaggeringly; consciously; brilliantly; immensely; keenly; sharply; shrewdly; astutely; highly; profoundly; seriously; soberly; cleverly; solidly; alarmingly; incredibly; gravely; heavily.

INTELLIGENCE

adjectives
earliest; remorseless; keen; patient; banded; reassuring; native; alarming; sluggish; subtlest; extreme; swift; alert; shrewd; melancholy; luminous; elusive; mysterious; afflicting; morbid; restless; human; vulgar; musing; diagnostic; presiding; matrimonial; conscious; coherent; welcome; obvious; informed; supreme; unwonted; infinite; unexpected; hideous; magnified; detached; unfailing; lofty; meanest; mediocre; wide; untutored; vivid; concentrated; prophetic; polished; quick; weakened; precocious; unclouded; creative; clear; rapid; rarefied; omniscient; cheering; passive; divine; sympathetic; disagreeable; crushing; cold; hard; penetrating; astounding; musical; sharp; sad; singular; diseased; supreme; bizarre; energetic; pure; sagacious.

verbs
approach with—; assert—; bow to—; brim with—; dim—; dull—; endow with—; exercise—; gamble on—; impart—; mock—; radiate—; register—; reveal—; sharpen—; subjugate—; —controls; —dominates; —governs.
(See ability, intellect, insight, mind, wisdom, talent.)

INTELLIGENT

adverbs
unwontedly; keenly; patiently; naturally; alarmingly; subtly; extremely; swiftly; alertly; shrewdly; mysteriously; vigilantly; restlessly; consciously; obviously; supremely; unexpectedly; unfailingly; infinitely; broadly; loftily; vividly; prophetically; creatively; precociously; clearly; omnisciently; cheeringly; sympathetically; divinely; disagreeably; coldly; penetratingly; warmly; astoundingly; singularly; sagaciously; apparently; cleverly; profoundly; fairly; thoughtfully; politically; discriminatingly; manifestly; exceedingly; significantly.

INTELLIGIBLE

adverbs
wholly; fairly; hardly; easily; surprisingly; scarcely; explicitly; instantly; graphically; unmistakably; strikingly; barely; clearly.

INTEMPERANCE

verbs
abstain from—; addict to—; atone for—; avoid—; betray—; burst with—; cure—; drown in—; err through—; fall into—; forego—; indulge in—; outlaw—; rack by —; sink into—; slide into—; —burns; —clouds; —defaces; —degenerates; —dissipates; —reigns; —sickens.
(See drunkenness, excess, debauchery, wickedness.)

INTEMPERATE

adverbs
foolishly; fatally; recklessly; dangerously; rashly; unaccountably; senselessly; extravagantly; voluptuously; luxuriously; wildly; rakishly; drunkenly; dreadfully; occasionally; habitually; notoriously; absurdly; preposterously; dissolutely; indiscreetly.

INTEND (*v*)

adverbs
characteristically; primarily; virtually; incalculably; originally; complimentarily; ostensibly; wantonly; subtly; unquestionably; maliciously; tyrannically; amiably; cruelly; dictatorially; loyally; jocularly; irreverently.
(See design, propose.)

INTENSIFY (*v*)

adverbs
vividly; inordinately; furiously; dramatically; emotionally; subjectively; morbidly; infinitely; fiercely; tragically; gloriously.
(See aggravate, emphasize, magnify.)

INTENSITY

adjectives
intermediate; decreasing; dreadful; lyrical; savage; scorching; barbarous; varying; unsurpassable; dramatic; clear; severe; low; unequal; mystical; emotional; subjective; white-faced; waning; morbid; infinite; desired; fierce; bare; dramatized; tragic; peculiar; heightened; glorified.

verbs
denote—; exhibit—; glow with—; increase —; live with—; measure—; note—; observe —; register—; relax—; revive—; slacken —; —grows; —overcomes; —strains; —taxes; —tires; —trebles; —wanes.
(See energy, force, strength, power, zeal.)

INTENT

adjectives
deliberate; wicked; mad; late; charitable; swift; amorous; bad; fierce; conscious; absurd; unlawful; evil; original; sublime; obvious; malicious.

adverbs
curiously; strangely; absently; wholly; abstractedly; oddly; deeply; eagerly; deliberately; carefully; wisely; impressively; earnestly; seriously; closely; resolutely; diplomatically; considerately; thoughtfully; critically; studiously; markedly; vigilantly; flatteringly; raptly; breathlessly; zealously; uncommonly.

INTENTION

adjectives
serious; deliberate; immoral; especial; tyrannous; docile; murderous; honorable; ulterior; honest; supposable; amiable; emotional; benignant; cordial; cruel; benevolent; wicked; wise; avowed; hospitable; definite; travelling; alleged; evil; dictatorial; loyal; earthly; original; industrial; festive; greedy; hostile; fixed; charitable; unconscious; evident; speculative; objective; cold; calculated; liberal; apparent; pacific; testamentary; treacherous; profound; matrimonial; suicidal; warlike; irreverant; jocular; private.

verbs
burst with—; cancel—; communicate—; conceal—; declare—; deny—; disavow—; disclaim—; err in—; impede—; miscarry—; misconstrue—; mistake—; proclaim—; purify—; reaffirm—; reiterate—; relinquish—; stick to—.
(See plan, aim, desire, purpose.)

INTERACTION

adjectives
ethical; unsuspected; incessant; harmonious.

INTERCEPT (*v*)

adverbs
subtly; dexterously; slyly; treacherously; inimically; jealously; hatefully; selfishly; zealously; perfidiously.
(See seize, take, prevent.)

INTERCHANGE

adjectives
healthful; interesting; provident; sweet; so-

cial; savage; constant; wearisome; pleasant; mutual; rapid; unfettered.

INTERCOURSE

adjectives
sexual; amicable; continual; free; frigid; convivial; pleasant; innocent; mutual; beautiful; intimate; unrestrained; sweet; genial; delightful; formal; beneficial; unhappy; courteous; social; personal; vile; intimate; habitual; commercial; unreserved; constant; diplomatic; friendly; frequent; intellectual.

verbs
abstain from—; avoid—; bind by—; carry on—; discontinue—; employ—; encourage —; engage in—; limit—; open—; overindulge in—; prevent—; prohibit—; refrain from—; relax—; stimulate—; survey—; —balances; —debilitates; —declines; —increases.

(See communication, commerce, conversation, traffic, transaction.)

INTERDICT (*v*)

adverbs
solemnly; formally; legally; tyrannically; dictatorially; officially; religiously.

(See restrain, repress.)

INTEREST

verbs (attention or concern)
absorb—of; accentuate—; alienate—; attach — to; awaken—; betoken—; catch—; cultivate—; dim—; display—; distract—; eclipse —; elicit—; engage—; enlist—; evoke—; excite—; exude—; feed—; feign—; focus—; inspire—; intensify—; kill—; kindle—; lend —; manifest—; muster—; note with—; pique—; quicken—; recapture—; regain—; revive—; rivet — upon; share—; smother—; stimulate—; sustain—; switch—; whip up —; —abates; —s bind; —centers on; —deepens; —ebbs; —endures; —fades; —flags; —mounts; —palls; —picks up; —wanes; engross—.

(See concentration, attention, vigilance.)

INTEREST

adjectives (general)
far-flung; special; national; religious; commercial; personal; passing; indulgent; individual; detached; momentous; property; selfish; minority; friendly; complicated; irresistible; affected; benevolent; primary; historic; philanthropic; superstitious; restrained; exorbitant; busy; final; jarring; well-meant; equal; presbyterian; literary; pecuniary; mercantile; great; attentive; missionary; extreme; evident; general; popular; genuine; lively; mournful; careful; bosom; paradoxical; private; growing; central; probable; pathetic; worldly; fraternal; universal; renewed; confessed; touching; paramount; amused; sudden; indifferent; satirical; feverish; certain; philosophic; intelligent; lasting; considerable; painful; respective; appalling; intense; thoughtful; overrated; immense; absorbing; surpassing; ultimate; connected; warm; widespread; national; stealthy; furtive; insistent; proprietary; vital; languid; energetic; diverse; bibliographical; thrilling; ennobling; peculiar; intellectual; overmastering; economic; vital; theoretical; active; gloomy; bankrupt; principal; endless; suave; urgent; sustained; human; racial; keenest; direct; jealous; discriminating; tepid; shadowy; languid; overmastering; contemporaneous; extraordinary; exclusive; philosophical; characteristic; surpassing; aesthetic; childish; anthropological; particular; enduring; extraneous; antiquarian; truant; exaggerated; crowning; inimical; lofty; revived; enormous; satisfying; undisturbed; parochial; medieval; ancient; awesome; neverceasing; student; sectional; humanitarian; public-spirited; diminished; real; sincere; insatiable; courteous; pathological; unutterable; coincidental; deepest; involved; expressional; inexhaustible; controlling; active; exceptional; long-nursed; wistful; faintest; unconquered; vaguest; passionate; grim; chauvinistic; lukewarm; vested; ethical; interwoven; compounded; dark; conflicting; perfunctory; elusive; persistent; particular; academic; world-wide; critical; heightened; potential; imperialist; affectionate; ignorant; domestic; alarmed; burning; solicitous; stirring; sordid; discriminating; perplexing; antipodal; lingering; dissimilar (pl).

INTEREST (*financial*)

verbs
affect—; amass—; cater to—; cherish—; control—; defend—; enlarge—; enumerate —; fortify—; foster—; merge—; promote —; regulate—; represent—; safeguard—; strengthen—; subverse—; unite—s of; weld —s of; —s flourish; —s overlap; —s prosper.

(See business, advantage, good, benefit.)

INTEREST
(money)

verbs
bear—; borrow on—; calculate—; charge —; claim—; compound—; entitle to—; fix —; figure—; forfeit—; obtain—; reckon—; request—; return—; subtract—; —accrues; —compensates; —taxes.
(See amount, sum, money, profit.)

INTEREST (v)

adverbs
proportionately; consistently; particularly; profoundly; excessively; keenly; genuinely; ingeniously; intensely; moderately; religiously; commercially; selfishly; affectionately; benevolently; philanthropically; paradoxically; jealously; philosophically; passionately; perfunctorily; academically; potentially; solicitously.
(See concern, excite.)

INTERESTING

adverbs
thrillingly; absorbingly; breathlessly; specially; historically; extremely; generally; genuinely; intensely; vitally; economically; extraordinarily; particularly; pathologically; vaguely; curiously; keenly; charmingly; strangely; attractively; pleasantly; engrossingly; marvelously; especially.

INTERFERE (v)

adverbs
boisterously; materially; consciously; energetically; unreasonably; irrationally; officiously; arrogantly; providentially; destructively; judicially; jealously; enviously; vindictively.
(See conflict, intermeddle, intervene.)

INTERFERENCE

adjectives
slightest; untimely; impertinent; feeble; ill-judged; arrogant; avoidable; unwarranted; providential; destructive; judicial; intolerant; mutual; optical; hostile; unexpected; unauthorized; supernatural; jealous; imperative; humane; watchful; hot; outside; needless; powerful.

verbs
brook—; counteract—; encounter—; inveigh against—; justify—; oppose—; overcome—; provoke—; refrain from—; resent—; restrict—; tolerate—; withdraw—; —agitates; —blocks; —chokes; —clogs; —disheartens; —distresses; —hinders; —impedes; —meddles; —retards.
(See opposition, collision, intervention, resistance, hostility, obstacle.)

INTERIOR

adjectives
distinctive; ambitious; distinguished; sumptuous; superb; opaque; domestic; webby; capacious; unmodified; colonial; costly; austere; musty; dusty; wretched; pierced.

verbs
acquaint with—; advance into—; creep into —; display—; enter—; harmonize—; invade —; line—; lose in—; penetrate—; press into —; pry into—; push into—; situate in—; withdraw into—; worm into—; —awes; —impresses; —unfolds.
(See jungle, recess, middle, center.)

INTERJECT (v)

adverbs
bitingly; devoutly; unexpectedly; harshly; abruptly; piercingly; rudely; coarsely; fiercely; wittily; indignantly; unreasonably; nervously; ferociously; instructively; irritatingly.
(See inject, insert.)

INTERLINE (v)

adverbs
warmly; richly; comfortably; luxuriously; expensively; matchlessly; ornamentally.

INTERLOCUTOR

verbs
employ—; —acquaints; —amuses; —announces; —asserts; —communicates; —corrects; —explains; —expresses; —informs; —instructs; —interferes; —interposes; —introduces; —intrudes; —leads; —prompts; —opens; —outlines.
(See speaker, debater, actor, clown.)

INTERLUDE

adjectives
strange; musical; brief; charming; circling; underworld; calm.

INTERMENT

adjectives
pious; showy; honorable.

INTERMINGLE (v)

adverbs
gregariously; grotesquely; democratically; unrestrictedly; swarmingly; offensively; perpetually; extraordinarily.
(See mingle, mix.)

INTERMISSION

adjectives
seasonable; lucid; irregular (pl); much-needed.

INTERMIXTURE

adjectives
occasional; subtle; helpful.

INTERPOSE (v)

adverbs
unwillingly; deftly; providentially; mercifully; mysteriously; deliberately; fortunately; designedly; vainly; aggressively; zealously; blankly.
(See intervene, interrupt.)

INTERPOSITION

adjectives
deft; timely; providential; renewed; merciful; divine.

INTERPRET (v)

adverbs
literally; objectively; narrowly; allegorically; sympathetically; intelligently; boldly; unfavorably; adequately; superficially; metaphysically; speculatively; offensively; poetically; charitably; mythologically.
(See translate, construe, render.)

INTERPRETATION

adjectives
superficial; corresponding; metaphysical; polyphonic; diverse (pl); legal; rabbinical; speculative; conflicting; mental; probable; ingenious; thoughtful; offensive; fascinating; authoritative; understandable; subtle; mystic; poetic; mythological; imperfect; lyric; base; musical; scriptural; allegorical; inexperienced; uncharitable.

verbs
abuse—; accept—; advance—; broaden—; contemplate—; correct—; deduce—; evolve—; hand down—; infer—; lend—; misconstrue—; misquote—; offer—; reiterate—; reject—; question—; scorn—; —mutilates; —signifies.
(See conception, explanation, idea.)

INTERPRETER

adjectives
urbane; euphuistical; noble; zealous; penetrating; coarse; apt; false; picturesque.

INTERROGATE (v)

adverbs
sumptuously; rudely; impudently; roughly; impishly; boldly; formally; characteristically; frankly; pompously; fraternally; authoritatively.
(See question, examine.)

INTERROGATION

adjectives
incredible; fresh; impish; wondering.

INTERRUPT (v)

adverbs
rudely; joyously; hastily; frequently; blatantly; judiciously; indignantly; earnestly; conveniently; peremptorily; momentarily; irrelevantly; abruptly; vaguely; temporarily; prematurely; spasmodically; repetitiously.
(See interpose, obstruct, retard.)

INTERRUPTION

adjectives
frequent; serious; spasmodic; jarring; abrupt; stern; absolute; continual; palpable; reasonable; momentary; temporary; unseemly; extraordinary; external.

verbs
attempt—; beg—; forgive—; hinder with—; tolerate—; welcome—; wince at—; witness—; —angers; —disturbs; —infringes; —provokes; —severs; —thwarts.
(See pause, rudeness, impudence, delay.)

INTERSPERSE (v)

adverbs
widely; thoroughly; comfortably; regularly; conveniently; occasionally; methodically.
(See mix, scatter, distribute.)

INTERTWINE (v)

adverbs
inextricably; elaborately; amorously; delicately; endlessly; complexly; haphazardly; artfully; skilfully; curiously.
(See entangle, twine, wind.)

INTERVAL

adjectives
slender; irregular; fitting; considerable;

feeding; torpid; measured; painful; equidistant; suitable; stated; frequent (pl); wide; fathomless; varying (pl); tranquil; rapid; indeterminate; endless; rare; twilight; reasonable; precious; dreadful; starless; recurring; lucid; mystical; harmonic; immeasurable; brief; stipulated; enormous; ensuing; conceivable; stolen; lesser; unflattering; spasmodic; long.

verbs
administer at—s; bridge—; consider in—; designate at—s; doze at—s; fill—; fritter away—; grant—; increase—s; pause for—; regulate—s; review—; sleep at—s; span—; —annoys; —delays; —separates; —vanishes.

(See space, pause, distance.)

INTERVENE (v)

adverbs
actively; impetuously; diabolically; miraculously; demoniacally; indiscreetly; venomously; slyly; paternally; hatefully; habitually; jealously.

(See interpose, interrupt.)

INTERVENTION

adjectives
armed; miraculous; indiscreet; diabolical; perpetual; untoward; demoniacal.

verbs
appeal for—; approve of—; consider—; decry—; denounce—; deplore—; employ—; exercise—; frame—; grant—; necessitate—; plead for—; seek—; terminate—; —aids; —annoys; —impedes; —interrupts; —irks; —relieves; —wanes.

(See opposition, interference, resistance.)

INTERVIEW

adjectives
satisfactory; valuable; confiding; affecting; complicated; unauthorized; interesting; clandestine; frequent; stormy; remarkable; painful; expressive; tussling; unchaperoned; vesper; transient; short-sighted; frank; preliminary; childish; protracted; brief; unexpected; psychoanalytic; parting; unsatisfactory; disastrous.

verbs
allow—; chronicle—; conclude—; confine—to; demand—; draw into—; elicit in—; endure—; evade—; grant—; obtain—; promise—; publish—; report—; request—; seek—; shirk—; terminate—; transpire at—; —degrades; —reveals; —tires; —wearies.

(See discussion, talk, conversation, conference.)

INTERVIEW (v)

adverbs
genially; professionally; confidentially; journalistically; daily; secretly; clandestinely; politically.

(See question.)

INTERWEAVE (v)

adverbs
artfully; intimately; mysteriously; dexterously; laboredly; elaborately; delicately; ornamentally; richly; intricately.

(See weave, intermingle.)

INTERWEAVING

adjectives
labored; dexterous; endless; elaborate; delicate.

INTESTINE

verbs
afflict—; attach to—; attack—; block—; clog—; constrict—; distend—; ferment in—; penetrate—; poison—; puncture—; obstruct—; putrefy in—; strangle—; twist—; —absorbs; —adheres; —coils; —discharges; —functions; —kinks; —mats; —provides.

INTIMACY

adjectives
annoying; agreeable; increasing; pleasant; peculiar; apparent; unfriendly; amorous; unseemly; lifelong; affectionate; curious; surprised; seeming; daily; closest; sudden; true; delicious; clandestine; immemorial; homely; rare; patronizing; embarrassed; mutual.

verbs
attempt—; brook—; court—; crush—; desire—; display—; draw back from—; enjoy—; enter with—; establish—; forbid—; question—; poison—; press into—; relax—; resist—; ripen into—; solicit—; strike up—; —arises; —mitigates; —reveals; —springs up.

(See friendship, fellowship, companionship, love, tenderness.)

INTIMATE

adverbs
exceptionally; reprehensibly; curiously; inordinately; strangely; charmingly; closely; unusually; uncommonly; pleasantly; affectionately; embarrassingly; oddly; sweetly; confidentially; particularly; peculiarly; singularly; artlessly; cordially; devotedly; companionably; agreeably; gently; graciously; unbecomingly.

INTIMATE (v)

adverbs
bitterly; silently; darkly; distinctly; simultaneously; tacitly; mystically; officially; unpleasantly; slyly; diabolically; delicately; plausibly.
(See hint, indicate.)

INTIMATION

adjectives
slightest; evident; injurious; mystical; official; silent; scattered; delicate; subjective; free; previous; unpleasant.

verbs
acknowledge—; advance—; contemplate—; dare—; furnish—; heed—; perceive—; ridicule—; seek—; weigh—; —creeps in; —denotes; —hints; —indicates; —informs; —interests; —leaks out; —notifies; —suggests.
(See accusation, innuendo, hint, suggestion, implication.)

INTIMIDATE (v)

adverbs
illegally; jealously; forcefully; unfairly; fiercely; ferociously; ruthlessly; formidably; economically; physically; deliberately; rudely.
(See frighten, scare, threaten.)

INTIMIDATED

adverbs
brutally; constantly; illegally; criminally; unquestionably; evidently; horribly; cruelly; tyrannically; daily; perceptibly; ignorantly; ridiculously; spinelessly; terribly.

INTOLERABLE

adverbs
absolutely; painfully; finally; naturally; odiously; grievously; oppressively; grimly; abhorrently.

INTOLERANCE

adjectives
fierce; unchecked; ecclesiastical; fiery; narrow; marked; wicked.

verbs
accuse of—; attend with—; campaign against—; deplore—; indicate—; observe—; overcome—; provoke to—; show—; suffer from—; —scorns; —shames; —treads on; —vitiates.
(See fanaticism, wickedness.)

INTOLERANT

adverbs
harshly; sternly; austerely; fretfully; rigidly; dogmatically; professionally; narrowly; ignorantly; generally; inexcusably; unduly; unpleasantly; disagreeably; terribly; inconsistently; strangely; extremely; conspicuously; arrogantly; superciliously; emphatically; stubbornly; obdurately; unyieldingly; cruelly; bitterly; provincially; fanatically; doctrinally; mulishly; doggedly; impatiently; fiercely; officially.

INTONATION

adjectives
pitying; different; soft; searching; ascending; calm; genuine; limpid; liquid; sweet; steadfast; wilful; contemptuous; languorous; asthmatic; nasal; characteristic; bellowing; lazy; nervous; guttural; perceptible; muffled.

INTONE (v)

adverbs
sanctimoniously; languorously; sepulchrally; melodiously; sweetly; gutturally; monotonously; characteristically.
(See speak, recite, sing.)

INTOXICATION

adjectives
subduing; complete; serene; habitual; partial; sweet; giddy; prolonged; utter; helpless.

INTRACTABLE

adverbs
perversely; incorrigibly; provokingly; vexatiously; unbearably; intolerably; stubbornly; wilfully; offensively; defiantly; utterly; doggedly; stolidly; wildly; capriciously; uncontrollably; cantankerously; mulishly; pitifully; violently; obstinately; scandalously;

sullenly; waywardly; formidably; hopelessly; restively; peevishly; churlishly; inveterately; narrow-mindedly.

INTRENCH (*v*)

adverbs
strongly; safely; securely; inviolably; firmly; strategically; protectively.
(See encroach, invade, entrench.)

INTREPID

adverbs
valorously; gallantly; chivalrously; boldly; feignedly; conversationally; swaggeringly; boastfully; audaciously; spunkily; resolutely; determinedly; heroically; valiantly; pluckily; marvellously; remarkably; uncommonly; adventurously; firmly; apparently; stoutly.

INTRICACY

verbs
comprehend—s; conceal in—s; conduct through—s; cut off—s; ease—; enmesh in—s; entangle in—s; involve—s; lessen—; map out—s; overcome—; probe—s; understand—; unravel—s; —bewilders; —complicates; —perplexes; —puzzles.
(See complication, complexity, tangle, confusion, obstruction.)

INTRICATE

adverbs
perplexingly; obscurely; obstructively; hopelessly; strangely; unduly; embarrassingly; objectionably; needlessly; terribly; deliberately; tortuously; subtly; awkwardly; formidably; provokingly; unnecessarily; clumsily.

INTRIGUE

adjectives
romantic; genuine; peaceful; violent; perpetual; criminal; sinuous; revolutionary; paltry; scandalous; sordid; ambitious; political; continental; double; indefatigable; dynastic; sacrilegious; abortive; tortuous; poor; clever; private.

verbs
bristle with—; conspire—; detect—; enjoy—; expose—; fall into—; infuse—; involve in—; meddle with—; plot—; plunge into—; share in—; stimulate—; uncover—; unearth—; —accomplishes; —deceives; —embarrasses; —mystifies.
(See adventure, plot, scheme, mystery.)

INTRODUCE (*v*)

adverbs
deliberately; simultaneously; ceremoniously; advantageously; casually; decorously; mischievously; commercially; conventionally; perfunctorily; unblushingly; orchestrally; formally.
(See present, insert, commence.)

INTRODUCTION

adjectives
preliminary; basic; promiscuous; impressive; appreciative; conventional; appropriate; perfunctory; coveted; improbable; wearisome; illicit; unblushing; depressing; orchestral; embarrassing; formal; labored.

verbs
contribute to—; crave—; demand—; manoeuvre—; plan—; prefix—; refuse—; survey—; wangle—; —agitates; —comments on; —communicates; —delights; —eulogizes; —explains; —makes known; —prepares; —presents.

INTRODUCTORY

adverbs
pleasantly; favorably; agreeably; courteously; smoothly; graciously; cordially; eulogistically; approvingly.

INTROSPECTION

adjectives
cold; morbid; pitiless.

INTROSPECTIVE

adverbs
curiously; unwontedly; unfortunately; unduly; overly; oddly; habitually; naturally; highly; sorrily; ominously; dangerously; morbidly; sensitively; pitifully; moodily; incurably; deplorably; lamentably; absurdly; miserably; incorrigibly; inveterately.

INTRUDE (*v*)

adverbs
presumptuously; bumptiously; rashly; irksomely; startlingly; irritatingly; exasperatingly; selfishly; jealously; obnoxiously; perpetually; pompously; impertinently; forcibly; abruptly; unwontedly.
(See obtrude, invade, encroach, intrench.)

INTRUDER

adjectives
base; peaceful; queenly; friendly; troublesome; miserable; solitary; murderous; burglarous.

verbs
dislodge—; dispose of—; eject—; evict—; ignore—; object to—; punish—; warn—; —disrupts; —encroaches; —forces; —infringes; —invades; —oversteps; —transgresses; —trespasses; —usurps.
(See robber, thief, villain, intrusion, invader, enemy.)

INTRUSION

adjectives
pompous; foul; resented; impertinent; forcible; involuntary; pale; swift; abrupt; noisy; hated; unwonted; rude.

verbs
deplore—; embitter by—; enter by—; excuse —; inform of—; loathe—; observe—; prevent—; protect from—; refuse—; threaten —; —disturbs; —pains; —violates; resent—.
(See intruder.)

INTRUSIVE

adverbs
obnoxiously; provokingly; annoyingly; uncommonly; meddlesomely; inexcusably; discourteously; inquisitively; amazingly; pertly; insolently; rudely; miserably; insidiously; abominably; maliciously; crudely; ignorantly; disgustingly; tiresomely; terribly; grossly; brazenly; persistently; unpardonably; troublesomely.

INTRUST (v)

adverbs
particularly; subsequently; willingly; tacitly; faithfully; confidently; authoritatively; cautiously; legislatively; medically; economically; pecuniarily; financially.
(See confide, commit.)

INTUITION

adjectives
divinest; deepest; pure; unerring; special; sensible; extraordinary; mysterious; half-desolate; womanly; instinctive; judicious.

INTUITIVE

adverbs
amazingly; marvellously; miraculously; naturally; uncommonly; highly; unusually; impulsively; vaguely; unscientifically; absurdly; inconsequently; notoriously; psychically; distinctly; infallibly; strangely; oddly; curiously; fantastically; unbelievably; astonishingly; incredibly; inconsequentially.

INVADE (v)

adverbs
ruthlessly; perilously; outrageously; ferociously; heartlessly; monstrously; totally; unnaturally; belligerently; bellicosely; illegally.
(See encroach, intrench, trespass.)

INVADER

adjectives
ruthless; ferocious; upstart; heathen; petty; expelled; filthy; ragged.

verbs
battle—; beat back—; drive off—; expose to —; harass—; repel—; resist—; vanquish—; withstand—; —assaults; —eludes; —encroaches; —entrenches; —infringes; —intrudes; —penetrates; —ravages; —violates.
(See enemy, intruder, army, troops, soldiers, multitude, robber.)

INVALID

adjectives
habitual; brave; gallant; bedridden; incurable; reeling; bawling; hopeless; feverish; nervous; marked; secluded; chronic; weak; despairing; comfortable; eager.

verbs
comfort—; delight—; discharge—; encourage—; entertain—; exhaust—; pension—; raise—; render—; report—; shelter—; treat —; visit—; —despairs; —recovers; —struggles.

adverbs
untenably; undeniably; groundlessly; absurdly; fallaciously; evasively; deceptively; cunningly; deplorably; legally; unluckily; unfortunately; inoperatively; spuriously; meretriciously.

INVALIDISM

adjectives
temporary; cruel; continual; increasing; nervous; chronic.

INVALIDITY

adjectives
established; judicial; utter; obvious.

INVALUABLE

adverbs
inestimably; extremely; marvellously; pricelessly; unusually; incredibly; astoundingly; wonderfully; indubitably; notoriously; distinctly; manifestly; prodigiously; extraordinarily; inexpressibly; unconscionably; unbelievably.

INVARIABLE

adverbs
incredibly; wonderfully; surprisingly; comfortingly; steadily; consistently; amazingly; warrantably; essentially; fundamentally; intrinsically; monotonously; habitually; drearily; tiresomely; hatefully; conventionally; agreeably; prosaically; typically; doctrinally; deliberately; wisely; purposely; designedly.

INVASION

adjectives
meditated; atrocious; premature; rebel; fratricidal; pioneer; advancing; contaminating; unauthorized; hostile; apparent; lawless; threatened; long-continued; air.

verbs
avert—; curb—; defend against—; deplore —; fight—; inform of—; plan—; persist in —; protect from—; repel—; resist—; stage —; stem—; suffer—; threaten—; yield to—; —destroys; —embitters; —succeeds.

(See raid, aggression, infringement, encroachment, violation.)

INVECTIVE

adjectives
indignant; opprobrious; unreasonable; furious; insulting; bitter; indiscriminate; coarsest; classical; fierce; witty; heated.

verbs
burst into—; deluge with—s; discharge—; drench with—; express in—; flay with—; fling—at; hurl—at; pour forth—; provoke —; rail—; rain—s; roar—; shoot at—; suffer—; shower—s; volley—s at; —angers; —denounces; —embitters.

(See sarcasm, abuse, oath.)

INVEIGH (v)

adverbs
censoriously; violently; bitterly; spitefully; vindictively; cantankerously; treacherously; acrimoniously; acidly; blasphemously; insidiously; sternly; roughly; ruthlessly; ferociously.

(See censure, reproach, rail.)

INVENT (v)

adverbs
deftly; creatively; infernally; matchlessly; diabolically; inexhaustibly; sensationally; dangerously; maliciously; technically; fantastically; poetically; prodigally; marvelously; spectacularly; singularly.

(See devise, contrive, discover, originate.)

INVENTION

adjectives
matchless; sad; infernal; stupendous; neoteric; diabolical; dangerous; exorbitant; gymnastic; multitudinous (pl); fervid; inexhaustible; florid; sensational; proposed; dangerous; numerous (pl); distributive; sheer; malicious; divine; technical; melodic; considerable; labor-saving; arbitrary; modern; fantastic; admirable; plausive; poetic; harassing; breath-taking; greatest; perfected; prodigal; modistic; topical; feeble; honest; marvelous; remarkable; sensational; patented; amazing.

verbs
accelerate—; beget—; commemorate—; contrive—; devise—; exploit—; introduce—; laud—; paralyze—; perfect—; seek—; stumble on—; submit—; suppress—; —eases; —enlightens; —improves.

(See discovery, patent, device, stratagem, improvement.)

INVENTIVE

adverbs
cleverly; amazingly; ingeniously; skilfully; wonderfully; expertly; surprisingly; profitably; scientifically; extraordinarily; conveniently; handily; crudely; curiously; shrewdly; broadly; expediently; fortunately; necessarily; unusually; uncommonly; highly; resourcefully; magnificently; dexterously; unbelievably; deftly; competently; capably; delightfully; fortunately; luckily; inexhaustibly; admirably.

INVERSION

adjectives
unnatural; monstrous; total.

INVERT (v)

adverbs

confusingly; perplexingly; complicatedly; abnormally; eccentrically; characteristically; humorously; habitually.

(See reverse, turn, overthrow.)

INVEST (v)

adverbs

fraudulently; annually; temporarily; forcibly; financially; shrewdly; austerely; astutely; strategically; judiciously; modestly; initially.

(See clothe, dress, surround.)

INVESTIGATE (v)

adverbs

promptly; personally; intensively; duly; vigorously; anatomically; tediously; assiduously; tranquilly; legislatively; analytically; diligently; intellectually; comprehensively; judicially; conclusively; abstractly; inquisitively; physiologically; methodically; aimlessly.

(See examine, inquire, probe.)

INVESTIGATION

adjectives

vast; anatomical; tedious; empiric; unprejudiced; eager; assiduous; futile; patient; tranquil; personal; cautious; legislative; analytical; literary; diligent; shouldered; racial; intellectual; careful; clinical; elaborate; journalistic; contemporary; comprehensive; judicial; hostile; rigorous; subsequent; conclusive; minuter; abstract; introspective; inquisitive; empirical; embarrassing; physiological; methodical; aimless.

verbs

carry on—; conduct—; contribute to—; dismiss—; exhaust—; facilitate—; institute—; ponder—; promise—; submit to—; summarize—; throttle—; yield to—; —brings to light; —concentrates; —convinces; —discloses; —drags; —indicates; —reveals; —wearies.

(See inquiry, examination, research, inquisition.)

INVESTMENT

adjectives

sound; gilt-edged; attractive; healthy; strategic; permanent; lifetime; elaborate; comparative; conservative; judicious; defenceless; economical; individual; modest; initial; desirable; careful; extraordinary; substantial; definite.

verbs

convert—; derive from—; discourage—; gain by—; impair—; necessitate—; preserve —; profit by—; pyramid—; represent—; sacrifice—; safeguard—; sell out—; subscribe to—; —accumulates; —crashes; —diminishes; —skyrockets (colloq.).

(See stocks, shares, bonds, property, interest, money.)

INVESTORS

adjectives

institutional; individual; hypothetical; multitudinous; thoughtful; painstaking.

INVIGORATE (v)

adverbs

artificially; scientifically; medically; alcoholically; mentally; physically; emotionally; beneficially; hurtfully; detrimentally.

(See animate, encourage.)

INVIGORATING

adverbs

pleasantly; highly; refreshingly; definitely; notoriously; conspicuously; unquestionably; wholesomely; fortunately; infallibly; gratefully; unexpectedly; surprisingly; strangely; marvellously; curiously; wonderfully; permanently; gloriously; progressively; restoratively; incredibly; miraculously; splendidly; remarkably; magnificently.

INVINCIBLE

adverbs

sturdily; stoutly; amazingly; unexpectedly; proudly; notoriously; conspicuously; surprisingly; preposterously; incredibly; genuinely; apparently; evidently; manifestly; curiously; strangely; oddly; fantastically; indomitably; insuperably; doggedly; stubbornly; obstinately; mightily; powerfully; splendidly; magnificently; irresistibly; mysteriously; unbelievably.

INVISIBLE

adverbs

mysteriously; curiously; strangely; incredibly; oddly; fantastically; designedly; provokingly; disappointingly; vexatiously; minutely; mistily; foggily; mystically; significantly.

INVITATION

adjectives
colorful; specific; long-standing; cordial; smart; flattering; outright; friendly; cheerful; implied; indefinite; actual; unanswered; clamorous; open; unexpected; sinister; original; unauthorized; pressing; liberal; hearty; perpetual; vague; inescapable.

verbs
answer—; besiege by —s; decline—; dine by —; draft—; ignore—; issue—; limit—; long for—; prepare—s; present—; prize—; procure—; —allures; —amuses; —delights; —flatters; —gladdens.
(See summons, call, question.)

INVITE (*v*)

adverbs
cordially; formally; frequently; graciously; peculiarly; forcibly; daintily; vociferously; specifically; flatteringly; originally; nominally; suavely; fatally; ostensibly.
(See ask, induce, summon, call.)

INVITING

adverbs
charmingly; delightfully; pleasantly; coolly; refreshingly; warmly; cordially; hospitably; marvellously; unexpectedly; attractively; bewitchingly; cordially; cheerfully; heartily; politely; comfortably; lusciously; delectably; alluringly; temptingly; irresistibly; wonderfully; surprisingly.

INVOCATION

adjectives
brief; unknown; sweet; solemn.

INVOKE (*v*)

adverbs
eloquently; ardently; solemnly; incessantly; reverently; briefly; earnestly; verbally; monotonously.
(See pray, beseech, beg.)

INVOLVE (*v*)

adverbs
markedly; shockingly; tragically; unfathomably; inextricably; hopelessly; abstrusely; problematically; ultimately; tremendously; scandalously.
(See implicate, include, entangle, embarrass.)

INVULNERABILITY

verbs
acclaim—; appreciate—; boast—; charge—; demand—; doubt—; estimate—; mistrust—; relax—; respect—; shake—; strain—; test —; threaten—; —defends; —sustains; —irks.
(See strength.)

INVULNERABLE

adverbs
proudly; ominously; happily; fortunately; consciously; remarkably; strongly; obviously; manifestly; completely; supposedly; presumably; apparently; allegedly; securely; safely; tenably; snugly; confidently.

IODINE

verbs
apply—; antidote—; disinfect with—; inject —; impregnate with—; paint with—; smear —; tint with—; treat with—; —poisons; —relieves; —safeguards; —sterilizes.
(See chemical, antiseptic, medicine.)

IRASCIBLE

adverbs
insufferably; highly; hotly; moodily; cholerically; capriciously; inexplicably; temperamentally; habitually; naturally; inexcusably; unreasonably; illogically; snappishly; querulously; contentiously; excitably; restively; uncommonly; rudely; captiously.

IRATE

adverbs
dangerously; alarmingly; highly; unusually; terribly; inexplicably; extremely; fearfully; sullenly; silently; noisily; tempestuously; unreasonably; savagely; senselessly; moodily.

IRE

adjectives
political; vengeful; patriot; noble; raging; avenging.

verbs
appease—; arouse—; assuage—; avert—; awake—; draw—of; dread—; ferment—; flush with—; fume with—; glow with—; moderate—; pale with—; provoke to—; shake with—; sharpen—; shelter from—; slake—; subdue—; —effervesces; —erupts; —riots.
(See anger, rage, wrath, passion, vexation, temper.)

IRIDESCENT

adverbs

shimmeringly; beautifully; amazingly; uncommonly; gloriously; splendidly; magnificently; delicately; daintily; flashily; curiously; oddly; marvellously; inexplicably; unexpectedly; attractively; highly; uncommonly.

IRKSOME

adverbs

tediously; wearily; heavily; distastefully; monotonously; dully; stupidly; vaguely; unpleasantly; dismally; drearily; oppressively; onerously; laboriously; vexatiously; provokingly; formidably; grievously; bitterly.

IRON

adjectives

adamantine; crushing; hot; assimilated; magnetized; tempered; redcoated; stubborn; rusted.

verbs

alloy with—; cast—; employ—; forge—; gird with—; hammer—; lathe—; magnetize —; mold—; plate with—; polish—; puddle —; roll—; shackle in—; shod with—; smelt —; utilize—; weld—; —clangs; —corrodes; —grates; —masters; —rusts.

(See metal, steel.)

IRONICAL

adverbs

bitterly; suddenly; justifiably; calmly; sarcastically; shrewdly; terribly; insolently; acidly; keenly; scoffingly; sneeringly; mockingly; tauntingly; teasingly; cleverly; perspicaciously; astutely; inscrutably; unduly; rudely; disagreeably; offensively; openly.

IRONY

adjectives

discordant; malignant; secret; terrible; masterly; characteristic; calm; strange; fearless; melancholy; subtle; laughing; delicate; enchanting; quaint; unconscious; wanton; unpleasing; fine; gentle; trivial; dramatic; civilized; somber; delicious; amiable; tragic.

verbs

afford—; aim at—; convey—; exhibit—; imply—; pierce with—; prick with—; recognize—; relish—; stress—; suggest—; suspect —; tinge with—; wince at—; —amuses; —barbs; —cuts; —nips; —penetrates; —rebukes.

(See sarcasm, satire, ridicule, mockery.)

IRRADIATION

adjectives

intense; imponderable; hidden; compulsory.

IRRATIONAL

adverbs

pathetically; portentously; absurdly; ridiculously; senselessly; stupidly; irascibly; fallaciously; crazily; preposterously; extravagantly; alarmingly; strangely; oddly; unwontedly; impulsively; evasively; nonsensically; obstinately; foolishly; incredibly.

IRRECLAIMABLE

adverbs

hopelessly; tragically; legally; virtually; lamentably; deplorably; altogether; presumably; allegedly; shamefully; viciously; impenitently; defiantly; recklessly; unfortunately; unluckily; lucklessly; wickedly; unconscionably; conclusively; apparently; manifestly.

IRRECOVERABLE

adverbs

desperately; hopelessly; lamentably; unfortunately; sadly; unhappily; utterly; presumably; probably; allegedly.

IRREDEEMABLE

adverbs

hopelessly; strangely; cruelly; officially; unluckily; legally; authoritatively; curiously; mysteriously; probably; definitely; unquestionably; incontrovertibly; absolutely.

IRREGULAR

adverbs

shamefully; disgracefully; furtively; openly; strangely; deplorably; cruelly; dangerously; secretly; unfortunately; terribly; slightly; gravely; seriously; suspiciously; egregiously; highly; utterly; wildly; lamentably; unpardonably; inexcusably; unsatisfactorily; unacceptably; disagreeably; disgustingly; indiscreetly; imprudently; unhappily.

IRREGULARITIES

adjectives

technical; faint; odd; quaint; exasperating; clumsy; rugged; fatal; ruddy.

IRREGULARITY

verbs
acknowledge—; adjust—; admit—; commit—; condone—; detect—; disperse—; file down—; generalize—s; lament—; magnify—; note—; penalize—; perform—; relent—; rue—; —debars; —disqualifies; —impedes.
(See abnormality, error, mistake, wrong, oversight.)

IRRELEVANCE

adjectives
boring; inextricable; apparent; complete; established.

IRRELEVANT

adverbs
disturbingly; vexatiously; insolently; suddenly; shrewdly; sadly; purposely; deliberately; hopelessly; uselessly; unserviceably; impracticably; impertinently; nonchalantly; casually; coolly; outlandishly; inappropriately; incongruously; exceptionally; oddly; unreasonably; foolishly; inanely; ridiculously; absurdly; unbelievably.

IRRELIGIOUS

adverbs
outlandishly; irreverently; curiously; terribly; unpardonably; conspicuously; flagrantly; inconceivably; sadly; flauntingly; inveterately; offensively; quietly; stolidly; stubbornly; immovably; impiously; grievously; irremediably; atheistically; indifferently; ostentatiously; dreadfully; strangely.

IRREMEDIABLE

adverbs
evidently; unluckily; grievously; sadly; unfortunately; presumably; possibly; apparently; hopelessly; forlornly; curiously; singularly; extraordinarily; peculiarly; particularly; avowedly; significantly; heartbreakingly; queerly; incomprehensibly.

IRREPARABLE

adverbs
curiously; hopelessly; oddly; strangely; unfortunately; unluckily; bitterly; cruelly; dismally; absolutely; apparently; obviously; manifestly; indubitably; palpably; haplessly; unhappily; distressingly; disturbingly; grievously.

IRREPRESSIBLE

adverbs
obstreperously; riotously; uproariously; curiously; vexatiously; alarmingly; obviously; wantonly; mischievously; garrulously; independently; absolutely; offensively; restlessly; boisterously; noisily; feverishly; hysterically; violently; hot-headedly; fanatically; impulsively; disagreeably; unbecomingly; strangely; blatantly.

IRREPROACHABLE

adverbs
notoriously; consistently; conspicuously; generally; altogether; unquestionably; wholly; presumably; emphatically; positively; incontrovertibly; ineffably; assuredly; warrantably; securely; acceptably; implicitly; impressively; probably.

IRRESISTIBLE

adverbs
charmingly; delightfully; utterly; absolutely; wholly; fascinatingly; inexhaustibly; altogether; persuasively; indomitably; argumentatively; logically; consciously; personally; oddly; singularly; powerfully; attractively; strangely; evidently.

IRRESOLUTE

adverbs
feebly; timidly; indecisively; weakly; singularly; senselessly; strangely; particularly; incredibly; foolishly; pliantly; hesitantly; infirmly; capriciously; whimsically; lamentably; oddly; captiously; nervously; restively; stupidly; unwisely; noticeably; dreadfully; timorously; tremulously; warily.

IRRESPONSIBLE

adverbs
gaily; blithely; insouciantly; nonchalantly; wantonly; hopelessly; singularly; deplorably; curiously; outlandishly; fantastically; oddly; strangely; vexatiously; unpleasantly; maddeningly; wildly; heedlessly; utterly; painfully; incorrigibly; alarmingly; dangerously; intolerably; palpably; sadly; incredibly; inveterately; temperamentally; incurably; obviously.

IRREVERENT

adverbs
impiously; flagrantly; offensively; unforgivably; rudely; grossly; crudely; thoughtlessly; unbecomingly; painfully; unutterably; unspeakably; arrantly; invidiously; insolently; terribly; crassly; brazenly; senselessly; utterly; blasphemously; sacrilegiously; deliberately; singularly; peculiarly; carelessly;

unpardonably; ignorantly; boorishly; insultingly; outrageously; scandalously; shamefully; egregiously; irremediably.

IRREVOCABLE

adverbs

lamentably; terribly; disastrously; ruinously; calamitously; hopelessly; desperately; sadly; lamentably; horribly; tragically; seriously; gravely; legally; pitiably; validly; indelibly; unintentionally; patently; inexorably; fortunately; happily.

IRRIGATION

adjectives

minute; plenteous; land-saving; colonic.

IRRITABILITY

verbs

control—; exaggerate—; fan—; lament—; manifest—; observe—; plague to—; rouse to —; salve—; stimulate—; —annoys; —lessens; —pains; —vexes.

(See irritation.)

IRRITABLE

adverbs

silently; resentfully; extremely; evidently; horridly; fiercely; violently; bitterly; absurdly; senselessly; foolishly; unreasonably; increasingly; slightly; definitely; hotly; furiously; mightily; unbearably; intolerably; grievously; sorely; ludicrously; plaguedly; annoyingly; wretchedly; miserably; distinctly; unfairly; deeply; easily; unhappily; comically; unjustly; ill-temperedly.

IRRITATE (v)

adverbs

unduly; nervously; perpetually; exasperatingly; sharply; temporarily; psychologically; physically; childishly; needlessly; excessively; superfluously.

(See provoke, vex, annoy, offend.)

IRRITATION

adjectives

stifled; puerile; deep-seated; concealed; nervous; perpetual; passing; burning; infinite; teasing; increasing; private; lulling; sharp; temporary; psychological; childish; consequent; needless; excessive.

verbs

allay—; alleviate—; arouse—; augment—; bear—; check—; convey—; endure—; excite —; expose to—; express—; fume with—; master—; relieve—; respond to—; seethe with—; stimulate—; stir up—; subject to—; thunder—; —bursts forth; —ferments; —lashes; —subsides.

(See pain, anger, impatience, vexation, temper, irritability.)

ISLAND

adjectives

extensive; weedy; barren; fragrant; glacier-polished; sea-girt; adjacent; desolate; smiling; marshy; imaginary; rugged; low; swampy; ill-fated; oozy; barricaded; secluded; moraine; river-girt; bare; cozy; floating; uninhabited; beautiful; verdant; glittering; serene; wretched; industrial; volcanic; antique; irregular; classical; sterile; rocky; roaming; substantial; dismal; sun-drenched; southern; romantic; veritable; uttermost; jeweled; remote; late-sacked.

verbs

banish to—; batter—; bombard—; desolate —; encompass—; infest—; isolate—; maroon on—; overrun—; populate—; plunder —; rule—; settle on—; sight—; strand on —; strew with —s; stud with —s; surround —; survey—; take root on—; winter on—; —blooms; —chains; —s dot; —enchants; —flowers; —overlooks; —shelters; —swarms with; —veers off; —yields.

(See land, shore.)

ISLE

adjectives

oozy; lofty; desolate; peaceful; flat; bloomy; mystic; shady; weeping; volcanic; low; wooded; hateful; pumice; bee-pasturing; tributary; foamless; outlying; execrable; high-favored; storm-encompassed.

ISOLATE (v)

adverbs

pathetically; voluntarily; effectively; dismally; advisedly; temporarily; virtually; morally; politically; physically; formidably; geographically; financially; economically; legally.

(See segregate, separate.)

ISOLATED

adverbs

somewhat; lamentably; fortunately; happily; necessarily; cruelly; bitterly; preferably; remotely; terribly; relatively; comparatively; desolately; drearily; singularly;

oddly; curiously; particularly; strangely; deliberately; unwillingly; inconveniently; inhospitably; snugly; safely; securely; unsociably.

ISOLATION

adjectives
moral; lonely; luxurious; infinite; blank; self-centered; studied; prompt; sectional; moribund; lofty; exposed; sheltered; physical; stupendous; selfish; desolate; deliberate; absolute; anguished; formidable; self-perceived; geographical; awful; magnificent; economic; financial; terrible.

verbs
advocate—; bear—; condemn to—; contemplate in—; delight in—; dread—; dwell in —; expel into—; meditate in—; penetrate —; procure—; punish by—; resign to—; retire into—; risk—; shake from—; suffer —; wrap in—.
(See privacy, solitude, loneliness, seclusion, retirement.)

ISSUE (v)

adverbs
spuriously; portentously; anonymously; particularly; publicly; officially; politically; controversially; triumphantly; victoriously; colorfully; significantly.
(See result, terminate, proceed.)

ISSUE

adjectives
sequent; political; momentous; controversial; great; fruitful; genuine; fundamental; ethical; indirect; unlimited; clear; dearest; profuse; precarious; degenerate; precise; vital; moral; abundant; tragic; confused; doubtful; remarkable; fascinating; colorful; basic; supreme; stupendous; irrelevant; insignificant; luckier; proposed; proud; concrete; adverse; felicitous; unlucky; immeasurable; tremendous; happy; disinherited; discussable; uncertain; dreadful; coming; involved; wartime; particular; recent; national; unforeseen.

verbs
analyze—; ban—; clarify—; confuse—; crystallize—; debate—; decline—; determine —; dismiss—; dodge—; dramatize—; duck —; dwarf—; elaborate on—; entangle—; evade—; force—; forego—; gloss over—; inject—; judge—; obliterate—; outlaw—; prejudice—; scrutinize—; set forth—; sharpen—; side-step—; speed—; split on—; state—; subordinate—; swamp—; tackle—; terminate—; —burns; —s conflict; —emerges; —involves.
(See outcome, result, consequence, question, point.)

ITCHING

adjectives
considerable; intense; profuse; excessive; unbearable.

verbs
affect with—; aggravate—; allay—; cure —; ease—; increase—; relieve—; remedy —; renew—; soothe—; wash—; —annoys; —attends; —indicates; —maddens; —tickles; —torments; —vexes.
(See disease, pain, torment, torture.)

ITEM

adjectives
important; inconspicuous; imperative; various (pl); replacement; indispensable; popular; rarest; fascinating; seasonable; considerable; middling; crucial; drab; related; restricted; associated; central; profit; essential; outstanding; lively; unpretentious; derogatory.

verbs
calculate—s; charge—; check—; classify—; compute—s; enter—; enumerate—s; exempt —; muster—s; note—; plow through—s; register—; specify—; total—s; —tempts.
(See amount, details.)

ITERATION

adjectives
monotonous; caressing; deliberate.

ITINERANT

adverbs
irresponsibly; necessarily; compulsively; happily; willingly; recklessly; pleasantly; profitably; adventurously; extravagantly; vagrantly; politically; lazily; vapidly; inanely; foolishly; vigilantly; nomadically; erratically; restlessly; vexatiously; peculiarly; outlandishly; whimsically; expensively; grievously; piteously; interestingly; fascinatingly; thrillingly; attractively; amazingly; unaccountably; idly.

ITINERARY

verbs

approve—; arrange—; contemplate—; describe—; draw up—; follow—; measure—; plan—; prepare—; refer to—; study—; —delights; —informs; —mentions; —proposes.

(See program, plan, project, scheme.)

IVORY

adjectives

waxen; tinted; delicate; rose-ensanguined; carved.

IVY

adjectives

clinging; poison; variegated; linked; wandering; climbing; embowering.

verbs

crown with—; direct—; train—; —bowers; —canopies; —clasps; —climbs; —clings; —creeps; —curls; —decorates; —feeds on; —hangs; —hides; —jackets; —leaps; —nods; —twines; —twists; —wanders; —wreathes.

(See plant, flower, vine.)

J

JAB (v)

adverbs
viciously; repeatedly; verbally; savagely; bitterly; ferociously; brutally; vindictively; malignantly.
(See thrust, poke, dig.)

JABBER (v

adverbs
bestially; perpetually; enthusiastically; excitedly; cheerfully; effusively; idiotically; loquaciously.
(See talk, babble, chatter.)

JACKDAW

verbs
tame—; —babbles; —cackles; —caws; —chatters; —clacks; —flits; —frequents; —gabbles; —gossips; —hops; —imitates; —jabbers; —steals; —thieves.
(See bird.)

JACKET

adjectives
undress; soft; bright; embroidered; wadded; silk; familiar; long; reversible; ill-fitted; clumsy.

verbs
adorn—; box in—; conceal under—; divest of—; don—; emerge from—; fortify with —; fray—; stain—; tatter—; utilize—; —preserves; —protects.
(See coat, overcoat, cloak.)

JADE

adjectives
veriest; outworn; brazen-faced; veined; unruly; tired.

JADED

adverbs
wearily; exhaustedly; gaspingly; tiredly; haggardly; uncommonly; gauntly; entirely; finally.

JAGGED

adverbs
angularly; dangerously; roughly; ruggedly; sharply; crookedly; obliquely; curiously; fearfully; perilously; strangely; hazardously; terribly; ominously; frightfully; unpleasantly; painfully; disagreeably; horridly; hideously; distressingly.

JAIL

adjectives
fantastic; infernal; distasteful; pleasant; comfortable.

verbs
break—; clamp in—; clap into—; commit to—; confine to—; deliver from—; deposit in—; detain in—; dwell in—; free from—; guard—; imprison in—; incarcerate in—; languish in—; parole from—; patrol—; release from—; secure in—; slap into—; —confines; —corrects; —penalizes; —rehabilitates.
(See prison.)

JAM

adjectives
absolute; fearful; traffic; inextricable.

JANGLE (v)

adverbs
crudely; dissonantly; inharmoniously; irritatingly; blatantly; exasperatingly; ceaselessly; hideously.
(See clang, clash.)

JAR

adjectives
dripping; giddy; subsequent; intestinal; mortal; endless; importunate; tempestuous; family-sized; inharmonious; treble.

JAR (v)

adverbs
rudely; terrifically; tempestuously; roughly; disastrously; mysteriously; awkwardly; economically.
(See jolt, shock, grate.)

JARGON

adjectives
wretched; broken; unscientific; courtly; meaningless; commonplace; unintelligible; barbarous; infernal; pitiful; busy.

verbs
babble—; chatter—; despise—; interpret—; master—; prate—; ring with—; translate

—; —confounds; —confuses; —delights; —grates; —perplexes; —prevails.
(See language, dialect, slang, speech.)

JAUNDICE

verbs
afflict with—; induce—; occasion—; tincture with—; treat for—; —appears; —deranges; —discolors; —disquiets; —distresses; —torments; —worries; —attacks.
(See disease.)

JAUNDICED

adverbs
biliously; querulously; regrettably; unhappily; incurably; slightly; jealously; evidently; visibly; clearly; unmistakably; highly; fulvously; inferentially; prejudicially; blindly; provincially; narrowly; fanatically; dogmatically; stupidly; illiberally; terribly.

JAUNT

adjectives
pleasure; summer; daring; mental.

JAUNTY

adverbs
blithely; carelessly; buoyantly; fashionably; delightfully; smilingly; nonchalantly; wholesomely; charmingly; lightly; brightly; insouciantly; laughingly; swaggeringly; heedlessly; wantonly; happily; rollickingly; saucily; comically; ludicrously; whimsically; cheerfully; gaily; gleefully; airily; heartily; joyously; playfully; sportively; marvelously; effervescently; jubilantly; remarkably.

JAW

adjectives
set; prominent; stern-set; grinning; outstanding; poisonous; delicate; mastic; bloody; protruding; resolute; aristocratic; firm; square-cut; pugilistic; marble; powerful; massive; protuberant; horrible; ponderous; unshaven; hollow; underhanging; infernal; poor; weasel; monstrous; champing; brutal; malevolent; grim; ravening; snarling; mighty; square-set; strong; clamped; industrious; determined; dogged; hard; iron; formidable; heavy; immense; bulging; clean-cut; elastic; inflexible; locked; lean; recessive; foaming; loose; distended; uplifted; pikelike; scarred; flaring; gaping; yawning; snapping; triangular; pierlike; haggard; beefy; flabby; jutting; projecting; lower; prognathous; combative; fighting; sagged; drooping; hanging; fallen; sharp; tense.

verbs
brace—; click—s; crack—; fracture—; tear with—s; wire—; work—s; —s clasp; —s close; —s crunch; —s crush; —drops; —s embrace; —s foam; —gapes; —juts out; —sags; —s snap; —s tighten.
(See teeth.)

JAY

verbs
—destroys; —hops; —mimics; —s mob; —pipes; —preys on; —scolds; —screams; —shies; —tears; —teases.
(See bird.)

JAZZ

verbs
beat out—; blare—; bridle—; entertain with—; inspire—; mute—; record—; repress—; revolt against—; seethe with—; sprinkle with—; trumpet—; welcome—; —agitates; —arouses; —batters; —cradles; —evolves from; —predominates; —reigns; —rushes.
(See music, melody, song, noise.)

JEALOUS

adverbs
inordinately; insanely; madly; wildly; furiously; violently; slightly; somewhat; justly; reasonably; naturally; intensely; venomously; pitiably; pathetically; unutterably; vengefully; supposedly; allegedly; probably; suspiciously; miserably; wretchedly; groundlessly; unbearably; insufferably; wonderfully; basely; disgracefully; contemptibly; foolishly; dangerously; deplorably; unbearably.

JEALOUSY

adjectives
insensate; fond; green-eyed; intense; self-harming; dangerous; popular; continual; savage; lively; maternal; mutual; inventive; instinctive; furious; narrow; mad; excessive; exaggerated; needless; lurking; smoldering; petty; miserable; frantic; unreasonable; improvident; habitual; acute; sensitive; active; selfish; fiercest; exalted; self-betraying; watchful; rare; retrospective; sentimental; malignant; factional; alternating; blinding; naive; overwrought; commercial; rancorous; undefined.

verbs
abhor—; arouse—; beget—; conceal—; cure —; curse with—; dread—; extinguish—; fire—; incur—; nourish—; occasion—; overcome—; squirm in—; strangle—; —blasts; —corrodes; —dictates; —disturbs; —frustrates; —grips; —harms; —magnifies; —pains; —perverts; —poisons; —subsides; —torments; —tortures; —wanes.
(See suspicion, distrust, curiosity, selfishness.)

JEER

verbs
cripple with—; deride with—; flog with—; flout with—; incur—s of; inflict—; heat with—s; pelt with—s; punish with—s; scorn —s; silence—s; stone with—s; —bruises; —disconcerts; —mocks; —perturbs; —taunts; —unnerves; —upsets.
(See taunt, ridicule, derision, sneer, laughter.)

JEER (*v*)

adverbs
scornfully; sardonically; vindictively; sarcastically; enviously; bitterly; spitefully; acrimoniously; acidulously.
(See mock, ridicule.)

JEERING

adverbs
scornfully; irreverently; disrespectfully; contemptuously; derisively; cruelly; bitterly; savagely; mockingly; insultingly; outrageously; superciliously; sarcastically; basely; tauntingly; dreadfully; tormentingly.

JEOPARDIZE (*v*)

adverbs
recklessly; rashly; foolhardily; absurdly; superfluously; idiotically; madly; passionately; deliriously.
(See risk, imperil, endanger.)

JERK (*v*)

adverbs
spitefully; instinctively; desperately; ludicrously; furiously; intermittently; ignominiously; frantically; mechanically; repetitiously; violently.
(See twitch, snatch.)

JERKY

adverbs
unnaturally; abnormally; lamentably; miserably; deplorably; pitiably; incurably; regularly; strangely; spasmodically; convulsively; suddenly; inexplicably; curiously; fitfully; recurrently; restlessly; singularly; peculiarly; surprisingly; woefully; frightfully.

JEST

verbs
beware of—s; enjoy—; fashion—; flash—s; glean—s; harass with—; interpret—s; refine—; repeat—; season with—; share—; speak in—; suppress—; time—; —affronts; —amuses; —cures; —delights; —pains; —ridicules; —slings; —taunts.
(See joke, witticism, parody, satire.)

JEST (*v*)

adverbs
indelicately; indecently; subtly; amiably; recklessly; satirically; slanderously; scurrilously; wittily; boisterously; unrestrainedly; foolishly.
(See joke, clown, fool.)

JESTER

verbs
appreciate—; encourage—; humor—; maintain—; retain—; —aims; —attempts; —directs; —diverts; —entertains; —excites; —indulges; —jokes; —makes game of; —makes merry; —makes sport of; —provokes; —treats.
(See clown, actor.)

JESTING

adverbs
roguishly; mischievously; broadly; teasingly; tormentingly; merrily; banteringly; waggishly; facetiously; playfully; comically; frivolously; whimsically; airily; idly.

JESUS

verbs
accept—; behold—; betray—; blaspheme—; crown—; crucify—; follow—; forsake—; glorify—; hallow—; invest—with; proclaim —; reject—; —bleeds; —comforts; —cures; —forgives; —heals; —reigns; —rises; —saves; —suffers; —weeps.
(See Christ, God.)

JETS

adjectives
silvery; sparkling; glittering; branching; augmenting.

JEWEL

adjectives
dull; cloudy; glistening; glittering; sparkling; sullied; dumb; barbaric; treasured; molten; rich; costly; heavenly; gleaming; glowing; burnished; eternal; graceful; propitious; best; fluid.

verbs
begem with—; box—; collect—s; display—; exhibit—; insure—; mount—; offer—; pawn —; retrieve—; set with—s; stud with—s; swathe in—s; value—; —adorns; —awes; —s bedeck; —dazzles; —flashes; —gleams; —glistens; —glitters; —ornaments; —sparkles.

(See gem, diamond, gold, pearl, ruby.)

JEWELER

verbs
—adorns; —deals in; —decorates; —determines; —estimates; —furnishes; —imports; —inscribes; —mounts; —prices; —prizes; —purveys; —sets; —values; —vouches for; —insures.

(See merchant.)

JEWELRY

adjectives
abundant; delicate; ponderous; glimmering; subtlest; starry; resplendent.

JILT (v)

adverbs
senselessly; brazenly; cruelly; heartlessly; capriciously; frivolously; selfishly; disgracefully.

(See flirt, coquette.)

JINGLE

adjectives
petulant; spasmodic; clear; discordant; pleasant; foolish.

JINGLE (v)

adverbs
melodiously; musically; petulantly; spasmodically; discordantly; gaily; genially; pleasantly; propitiously.

(See ring, resound.)

JOB

adjectives
rapid; life-toning; craftsmanlike; daily; tedious; practical; identical (pl); thankless; nefarious; constricting; definitive; dirty; difficult; bungling; advertising; hack-writing; unpleasant; needless; remodeling; political; surrealistic; executive; assured; thorough; faultless; royal.

verbs
abandon—; abolish—; apply for—; attack —; buckle down to—; bungle—; chuck—; contemplate—; cut out for—; decry—; despatch to—; equip for—; fumble at—; harness to—; jeopardize—; land (colloq.)—; nail—; quail at—; register for—; swing into—; tackle—; threaten—; undertake—; usurp—; wangle—; —fazes (colloq.); —materializes.

(See position, work, situation, employment, engagement.)

JOCOSE

adverbs
facetiously; waggishly; convivially; playfully; whimsically; foolishly; fatuously; pleasantly; drolly; clownishly; banteringly; quick-wittedly; humorously; fantastically; teasingly; whimsically; quibblingly; entertainingly; happily; naturally; cheeringly.

JOCULAR

adverbs
immensely; always; habitually; entertainingly; genially; amiably; charmingly; divertingly; dependably; heartily; wholesomely; good-naturedly; characteristically; amusingly; agreeably; waggishly; broadly; banteringly; comically; drolly; dryly; whimsically; facetiously; merrily; pleasantly.

JOCULARITY

adjectives
nervous; perplexed; forced; mock.

JOCUND

adverbs
pleasantly; wittily; archly; cheerfully; amusingly; heartily; irrepressibly; blithely; admirably; imperturbably; consistently; naturally; charmingly; lustily; noisily; boisterously; incomparably.

JOG (v)

adverbs
monotonously; ceaselessly; cheerfully; automatically; conventionally; dismally; uneventfully; tediously; arduously; toilsomely.

(See shake, push, jar, jolt.)

JOIN

adverbs
enthusiastically; obsequiously; slavishly; matrimonially; lustily; indissolubly; devoutly; mechanically; temporarily; snugly.
(See add, annex, knit.)

JOINT

adjectives
diminishing; stiffened; distorted; affected; enlarged; stubborn; firm-knit.

verbs
bandage—; cement—; connect at—; dislocate—; displace—; fit—; form—; hinge—; lay—; limber up—; lubricate—; mend—; nodulate—; shake out of—; strengthen—; support—; sustain—; turn on—; —creaks; —squeaks.
(See bone.)

JOKE

adjectives
rude; matter-of-fact; practical; outrageous; affectionate; oft-repeated; grave; crowning; pathetic; sly; obscene; indelicate; cynical; mocking; foolish; fermented; repressed; bibliomaniacal; deplorable; mutual; uncountable (pl); endless; inopportune; wonderful; delicious; off-color; miserable; particular; impish; questionable; horrible; priceless.

verbs
censor—; exchange—s; flash—; guffaw at —; interpret—; laugh at—; perpetrate—; refine—; report—; retail—s; season with —; share—; swap (colloq.)—s; time—; understand—; —affronts; —amuses; —caps; —climaxes; —delights; —offends; —pains; —stings; —wears thin.
(See jest, witticism, parody, satire.)

JOKER

adjectives
absolute; loud-tongued; misused.

JOLLITY

adjectives
innocent; unrestrained; frenzied; youthful.

verbs
arrest—; dampen—; dip in—; enjoy—; feed —; immerse in—; occasion—; overcome with—; prolong—; relent—; repent—; share —; split in—; steep in—; yield to—; —exhausts; —inebriates; —palls; —prevails; —wanes.
(See fun, mirth, merriment, relaxation, recreation, laughter.)

JOLLY

adverbs
immensely; invariably; consistently; heartily; wholesomely; delightfully; tremendously; inveterately; indomitably; constitutionally; naturally; habitually; unusually; uncommonly; extravagantly; exceedingly; unsuitably; blithely; merrily; sportively; teasingly; tormentingly; mockingly; inopportunely; roguishly; unquenchably; whimsically; exuberantly; mischievously; impishly; marvelously.

JOLT

adjectives
staggering; nasty; gigantic; painful.

JOLT (*v*)

adverbs
heavily; crunchingly; staggeringly; terrifically; thunderously; rudely; destructively; disastrously.
(See shock, grate, jar.)

JOLTING

adjectives
unendurable; incessant.

JOURNAL

adjectives
musical; vivacious; naked; satirical; enterprising; independent; distinguished; inflated; pompous; veracious.

JOURNALIST

adjectives
well-informed; eminent; cultured; conscientious; flamboyant; inspired; death-defying; disreputable; able; irresponsible; brilliant; prolific.

verbs
bribe—; condemn—; congratulate—; criticize—; fear—; hire—; —awes; —composes; —corrupts; —describes; —edits; —expounds; —humanizes; —itemizes; —publishes; —reports; —serves; —sums; —vulgarizes.
(See writer, reporter, publisher, editor.)

JOURNEY

adjectives

frightful; tedious; dreaded; proposed; fruitless; interesting; expeditious; fatiguing; fatal; costly; weary; innumerable (pl); arduous; self-appointed; unspeakable; dismal; unsteady; stately; longing; measureless; long; foggy; subsequent; daily; harrowing; troubled; wearisome; leisurely; evangelizing; extended; unexpected; uneventful; triumphant; adventurous; shorter; rumored; aimless; perilous; sentimental; celebrated; plodding; memorable; romantic; toilsome; infinite; mysterious; accursed; triumphal; pleasant; homeward.

verbs

accompany on—; break—; contemplate—; embark on—; enjoy—; plan—; proceed on —; quicken—; set out on—; shape—; undertake—; —benefits; —fatigues; —interests; —pleases; —tires; —wearies.

(See trip, tour, voyage.)

JOURNEY (*v*)

adverbs

tediously; fruitlessly; fatiguingly; fatally; arduously; dismally; daily; harrowingly; leisurely; uneventfully; triumphantly; aimlessly; perilously; memorably; romantically; triumphally.

(See travel, tour.)

JOURNEYINGS

adjectives

tiresome; constant; endless; costly.

JOVIAL

adverbs

immensely; extremely; heartily; wholesomely; amusingly; cordially; warmly; teasingly; companionably; sociably; convivially; happily; pleasantly; comfortably; familiarly; amiably; freely.

JOY

adjectives

earth-born; malignant; fiendish; serene; spirit-piercing; unreasoning; intense; sounding; ineffable; tumultuous; material; inexpressible; deceitful; exultant; domestic; vernal; secret; insecure; temporary; concentrated; inward; unbelieving; early; awkward; cradle; pretty; profound; unchecked; immortal; innumerable (pl); hearty; guilty; furious; deluding; fierce; thankful; transient; palpable; rapturous; strange; frank; unsubstantial; unbidden; grateful; youthful; deep; innocent; parental; deluding; lasting; spontaneous; superabundant; benevolent; eloquent; insidious; savage; unsuppressed; strained; increasing; mutual; triumphant; corroding; shivering; brief; embodied; overborne; sheer; wonderful; passionate; voluptuous; chastised; sober; unchecked; passionless; indistinct; heavenly; reviving; lively; presented; common; unappreciated; gentle; truant; boisterous; exulting; wild; celestial; overwhelming; plenteous; aching; general; quiet; unimaginable; ghastly; restrained; expectant; lustful; holy; exquisite; submissive; monumental; lovely; worldly; universal; passing; attainable; petty; dangerous; doubtful; unprecedented; incommunicable; tender; true; withered; acute; fleeting; artistic; beguiled; sharp; natural; wretched; thronged; unutterable; solemn; diversified; infant; curious; unmingled; abiding; murmuring; inconceivable; unmitigated; gushing; homely; unbodied; tranquil; flawless; majestic; equable; sedate; taintless; blustering; boundless; Lethean; amazed; delirious; incredulous; life-giving; purest; wordless; ill-natured; costlier; bridal; keen-witted; mild; suffused; refined; barbaric; human; overmastering; deepest; religious; radiant; breathless; narrow; thrilling; mixed; constant; vivid; explosive; animal; comforting; never-fading; lofty; stolen; unmingled; heartfelt; supreme; palpitating; eager; disguised; unbounded; hideous; abstract; perennial; eternal; prolonged; beatific; social; hackneyed; intoxicating; equal; filial; stern; fretful.

verbs

anticipate—; awaken—; blight—; conceal —; dampen—; derive—; experience—; extinguish—; forego—; impart—; intoxicate with—; leap for—; revel in—; snatch—; swoon with—; throw into a paroxysm of—; veil—; —floods the soul; —mounts; —riots in his eyes; —rises.

(See fun, mirth, merriment, happiness, pleasure, rapture.)

JOYFUL

adverbs

triumphantly; victoriously; magnificently; splendidly; brilliantly; naturally; exceedingly; marvelously; wonderfully; elatedly; exuberantly; overwhelmingly; quietly; secretly; proudly; humbly; gratefully; thankfully; utterly; speechlessly; unspeakably; inexpressibly; ineffably; rapturously; ecstatically; obviously; visibly; openly; professedly; apparently; downright; decidedly; infinitely; immeasurably; properly.

JOYOUSNESS

adjectives
symbolic; trustful; subdued.

JUBILANT

adverbs
naturally; marvellously; duly; triumphantly; happily; unspeakably; loudly; deeply; noisily; exultantly; boisterously; clamorously; immoderately; hilariously; vivaciously; spiritedly; tremendously; emphatically; riotously; turbulently; tumultuously; appropriately; hearteningly; utterly; unusually; noticeably; visibly; unconcealedly; secretly.

JUBILEE

adjectives
fierce; careless; wildly-celebrated.

JUDGE

adjectives
existing; rash; self-appointed; sagacious; equitable; discriminating; sympathetic; competent; imaginary; sole; honorable; terrible; ruthless; fitting; elective; dyspeptic; supreme; eminent; worthy; rightful; ecclesiastical; upright; learned; fastidious; capable; brutal; wicked; finicky; frowning; dispassionate; wanton; constitutional; capital; shrewd; disinterested; favorable.

verbs
appeal to—; appear before—; appoint—; elect—; impeach—; oust—; —administers; —admonishes; —assigns; —authorizes; —awards; —condemns; —deliberates; —determines; —grants; —hears; —holds; —investigates; —outlaws; —pardons; —penalizes; —presides; —pronounces; —sentences; —weighs.

(See president, umpire, congressman, senator.)

JUDGE (v)

adverbs
summarily; harshly; rigidly; rashly; righteously; wrathfully; hastily; cursorily; superficially; sentimentally; sagaciously; discriminatingly; equitably; competently; ruthlessly; ecclesiastically; learnedly; fastidiously; brutally; wickedly; wantonly; constitutionally; disinterestedly; impartially; inflexibly; objectively; adversely; shallowly.

(See decide, discern, discriminate, consider.)

JUDGMENT

adjectives
solid; impartial; casual; profound; unerring; veritable; astonishing; declamatory; primitive; clearest; unfavorable; unimpeachable; scornful; verdant; aesthetic; historical; stern; intellectual; inappropriate; solemn; melodious; capricious; moral; subtle; snap; considered; artistic; sound; healthy; noble; fundamental; manifest; perverted; educated; critical; righteous; biased; discriminating; unflattering; jealous; ripe; tolerant; affectionate; cold; inflexible; popular; calm; awful; invaluable; depraved; unbiased; sober; silent; ready-made; disciplined; erroneous; imitative; military; discretionary; irritating; full-grown; burning; superior; qualitative; withering; adverse; objective; masculine; exulting; poetic; shallow; strict; true; interested; brawling; temperate; kindly; false; settled; unstable; dispassionate; rash; presentative; tautological; individual; unmerciful; reformed; lame; tried; admirable; enlightened; harsh; synthetic; advanced; maturer; ablest; retributive; cooler; strong; simple.

verbs
confirm—; derange—; distort—; endorse—; enfeeble—; exercise—; formulate—; impair—; impose—; impugn—; influence—; interfere with—; modify—; obtain—against; pass—; pervert—; pronounce—; render—; reverse—; ripen—; stimulate—; suspend—; temper—; venture—; voice—; waive—; warp—; withhold—; —affirms; —coerces; —impels.

(See decision, decree, sentence, verdict, opinion.)

JUDICIAL

adverbs
gravely; seriously; discreetly; officially; scarcely; pompously; magisterially; sagaciously; competently; capably; honorably; equitably; calmly; ruthlessly; cruelly; serenely; discriminatingly; supremely; eminently; fastidiously; coldly; deliberately; brutally; dispassionately; shrewdly; disinterestedly; impartially; splendidly; wonderfully.

JUDICIARY

adjectives
elective; appointive; corrupt; effective; independent.

JUDICIOUS

adverbs
remarkably; admirably; unusually; surprisingly; carefully; thoughtfully; soberly; sensibly; discreetly; keenly; acutely; astutely; discerningly; profoundly; considerately; uncommonly; wisely; habitually; temperamentally; dependably; reliably; comfortingly.

JUG

verbs
crack—; drain—; mold—; replenish—; seal —; shape—; shatter—; sterilize—; stew in —; store in—; —preserves; —protects; —tapers.
(See glass.)

JUGGLE (v)

adverbs
dexterously; skillfully; marvelously; professionally; verbally; grotesquely; spectacularly.
(See manipulate, handle.)

JUGGLING

adjectives
grotesque; verbal; remarkable.

JUICE

adjectives
concocted; helleboric; resinous; vegetable; rich; natural; savory; precious; rare-flavored; cooling; sweetened; vilesome; gastric; autumnal; acrid; necessary; fermented; joyful; bilious; ruddier; inspissated; gelatinuous; pungent; viscous; aerial; nectarian.

verbs
derive—from; dilute—; draw off—; drink —; express—; extract—; flavor with—; moisten with—; relish—; save—; secrete—; squeeze out—; strain—; suck—; suffuse—; tap—; wring out—; —dries; —drips—; exudes; —flows; —intoxicates; —oozes.
(See liquid, water, fluid, solution.)

JUICY

adverbs
lusciously; deliciously; palatably; sufficiently; scarcely; slightly; satisfactorily; sufficiently; delightfully; wonderfully; remarkably; surprisingly; unexpectedly; drippingly; soppingly; terribly; delectably; extremely.

JUMBLE

adjectives
absurd; sad; wearisome; confused; incoherent.

JUMBLED

adverbs
hopelessly; terribly; intricately; miscellaneously; heterogeneously; miserably; unsystematically; promiscuously; chaotically; carelessly; confusedly; inexcusably; indefensibly; hastily; perplexingly; distressingly; disconcertingly; indiscriminately; indistinguishably; erratically; wantonly; dreadfully; impossibly; unimaginably; desperately; inextricably; frightfully; messily.

JUMP

adjectives
daring; awkward; high; corkscrew; vehement.

JUMP (v)

adverbs
nimbly; lightly; lumberingly; daringly; threateningly; smartly; gingerly; awkwardly; precipitately; rashly; gallantly; gracefully; thoughtlessly; agilely.
(See hop, spring, bound.)

JUMPY

adverbs
strangely; curiously; nervously; hysterically; foolishly; inanely; ostentatiously; painfully; shockingly; incurably; appallingly; helplessly; hopelessly; desperately; pitifully; stupidly; childishly; fearfully; unreasoningly; irremediably; pathetically; tragically.

JUNCTURE

adjectives
present; alarming; dangerous.

JUNGLE

adjectives
encroaching; hobo; steaming; unhealthy; uninhabited; vibrant; familiar; artificial; impenetrable; misty.

verbs
abandon in—; beat—; clear—; conceal in—; creep through—; cultivate—; desert—; explore—; guide through—; hack through—;

infest—; inhabit—; invade—; lose in—; overhang with—; penetrate—; tangle in—; thread through—; trudge through—; —enmeshes; —hems in; —looms; —swamps; —terrifies.

(See woods, thicket, forest.)

JUNK

adjectives

toy; majestic; gaudy; bright.

verbs

cart—; collect—; consume—; convert—; deal in—; discard—; dispose of—; eject—; employ—; enlist—; exhume—; fill with—; peddle—; refuse—; sack—; salvage—; sweep away—; utilize—.

(See rubbish, mess, sewage, waste.)

JURISDICTION

adjectives

reciprocal; exclusive; consular; provisional; military; constitutional; doubtful; competent; ecclesiastical; conflicting (pl).

verbs

abolish—; arrive within—; assume—; demand—; exempt from—; exercise—; extend—; free from—; include in—; infringe on—; invade—; limit—; relax—; resent—; subject to—; submit to—; vest—in; —embodies; —empowers; —extends.

(See authority, power.)

JURIST

adjectives

ermined; impartial; eminent; able; robed.

JURY

adjectives

absurd; impartial; swayed; emotional; prejudiced.

verbs

address—; appoint—; bribe—; challenge—; charge—; intimidate—; lay before—; panel—; plead with—; submit to—; summon—; swear in—; —acquits; —ballots; —conducts; —considers; —decides; —deliberates; —discharges; —haggles; —indicts; —meditates; —judges; —recommends; —retires; —takes oath; —withdraws.

(See tribunal, committee, hearers, court, judge.)

JUST

adverbs

undeniably; absolutely; impartially; admittedly; admirably; profoundly; unerringly; veritably; astonishingly; clearly; unimpeachably; uncommonly; unusually; appropriately; sternly; solemnly; soundly; nobly; fundamentally; righteously; coldly; tolerantly; strictly; temperately; dispassionately; entirely; manifestly; substantiallv; roughly; terribly; frightfully; remarkably.

JUSTICE

adjectives

distributive; poetical; passionless; ridiculous; temperate; biased; manifest; remarkable; substantial; inordinate; exemplary; swordless; armed; dreadful; summary; strictest; reasoned; eternal; stern; ultimate; resolute; unfailing; knavish; irascible; poetic; distorted; impartial; criminal; universal; rough-handed; wild; even-handed; scanty; presiding; sparing; perfect; divine; social; retributive; conservative; inflexible; vindictive; moral; common; private; ample; striking; strict; tardy; conceded; recompensive; bare; drowsy; immovable; equal; exact; slow; cruel; tied-up.

verbs

achieve—; administer—; advance—; defeat—; deny—; despair of—; dispense—; do—to; elude—; execute—; hamper—; imperil—; insure—; mete out—; obstruct—; paralyze—; preserve—; render—; taint—; thirst for—; trample—; —evolves; —grows; —hinges on; —rests.

(See righteousness, right, virtue, purity, truth.)

JUSTIFIABLE

adverbs

eminently; splendidly; scarcely; expediently; entirely; legally; morally; unquestionably; substantially; fundamentally; essentially; possibly; supposedly; presumably; apparently; sufficiently; reasonably; plausibly; barely; advantageously.

JUSTIFICATION

adjectives

substantial; abundant; gradual; creative; theoretical.

JUSTIFY (v)

adverbs

completely; amply; definitely; sufficiently; reasonably; righteously; unmistakably; manifestly; undoubtedly; substantially; abundantly; theoretically.

(See excuse, absolve, warrant.)

JUT (v)

adverbs

prodigiously; precipitately; sharply; abnormally; prominently; frightfully; dangerously.

(See protect, protrude.)

K

KALEIDOSCOPIC

adverbs
variably; restlessly; changefully; colorfully; shiftily; perilously; unstably; waveringly; interestingly; dizzily; artfully; terribly; surprisingly; amazingly; incredibly; perplexingly; mysteriously; queerly; inconveniently; oddly; dreadfully; uncertainly.

KANGAROO

verbs
—balances; —carries; —expels; —fights; —gnashes; —hops; —jumps; —pouches; —races; —nibbles.
(See animal.)

KEEN

adverbs
intelligently; unwontedly; sharply; acutely; naturally; subtly; extremely; shrewdly; sensibly; mysteriously; obviously; supremely; unfailingly; infallibly; prophetically; precociously; penetratingly; astoundingly; singularly; uncannily; sagaciously; wisely; apparently; obviously; profoundly; thoughtfully; exceedingly.

KEENNESS

adjectives
hereditary; uncanny; catlike.

KEEP (*v*)

adverbs
perniciously; charitably; surreptitiously; deliberately; shamelessly; tenderly; sedulously; discreetly; stubbornly; courteously; religiously; undeviatingly; ceaselessly; perpetually; inevitably; ostentatiously; jealously.
(See preserve, celebrate, observe, maintain.)

KEEPER

adjectives
pernicious; charitable; inquisitive.

verbs
appoint—; dodge—; elude—; escape—; install—; evade—; —abandons; —administers; —attends; —chastises; —controls; —governs; —guards; —inspects; —preserves; —prosecutes; —pursues; —retains; —scans; —snatches.
(See manager, guardian.)

KEEPING

adjectives
watchful; devoted; perfect.

KEN

adjectives
inscrutable; human; widest.

KENNEL

adjectives
loathsome; dubious; extensive; ghostly.

KERCHIEF

adjectives
bleached; pale; square-drooping.

KETTLE

adjectives
prophetic; simmering; melting; steaming.

verbs
beat—; brew in—; brush—; drain—; polish —; replenish—; scour—; scrub—; stew in —; strike—; strum on—; —chirps; —gleams; —hisses; —hums; —simmers; —sings; —trills; —whistles.
(See caldron, pot, tub, vat.)

KEY

adjectives
crystal; romantic; feeble; excellent; foreboding; tentative; strategic; interrogative; ponderous; unwieldy; tingling; massy.

verbs
belt —s; fit—; force—; fumble with—; inject—; grope for—; insert—; jangle—; mislay—; pocket—; ram — into; respond to—; —s clank; —s jingle; —s rattle.

KEY
(music)

adjectives
rigid; plaintive; tender; sad; minor; cracking.

KEYBOARD

adjectives
console-like; magic; complicated; master.

verbs
belabor—; caress—; dance on—; finger—; journey over—; perform on—; pounce upon

—; recite on—; render on—; run along—; skip over—; trip along—; work—; —gleams.

(See instrument, banjo, piano.)

KEYNOTE

verbs

elaborate on—; fire—; hit—; introduce—; reach—; recognize—; reveal—; seek—; sound—; strike—; touch—; —arouses; —attracts; —excites; —impresses; —interests; —stirs.

(See point, policy, idea.)

KEYSTONE

adjectives

indispensable; all-supporting.

KICK

adjectives

mighty; harmless; ceremonious.

KICK (v)

adverbs

affectionately; profanely; unmercifully; brutally; furiously; spasmodically; carelessly; frantically; simultaneously; unceremoniously; savagely; clumsily; murderously; madly; viciously; vindictively; ferociously.

(See oppose, resist, recoil.)

KID

adjectives

healthy; irresponsible; squalling.

KIDNAPPER

verbs

apprehend—; contact—; negotiate with—; prosecute—; pursue—; —abducts; —decoys; —delivers; —demands; —directs; —entices; —frightens; —lures; —operates; —snatches; —spirits away; —surveys; —threatens.

(See thief, robber, murderer.)

KIDNEY

adjectives

hard-worked; distressing; paining.

verbs

belt—; block—; congest—; dilate—; engorge—; impair—; inflame—; obstruct—; pad—; support—; —enlarges; —excretes; —filters; —floats; —fuses; —moves; —swells.

(See bladder, liver, organ, intestines.)

KILL (v)

adverbs

incessantly; simultaneously; accidentally; designedly; uselessly; intentionally; instantly; wantonly; ferociously; brutally; pitilessly; insanely; savagely; basely; sportively.

(See murder, slay, assassinate.)

KILLER

adjectives

tyrannical; pitiless; brutal; mad.

KILLING

adjectives

merciless; unrestricted; unsolved.

verbs

atone for—; avenge—; conceal—; confess—; contrive—; indulge in an orgy of—s; lament—; observe—; perform—; plan—; resent—; revenge—; stifle—; uncover—; unearth—; warrant—; witness—; —awes; —incenses; —infuriates; —offends; —puzzles; —shocks.

(See murder, slaughter, massacre, assassination.)

KIN

adjectives

blood; nearest; surviving.

KIND

adjectives

refractory; voracious; abstracted; unexpected; corresponding; literal; positive; unworthy; fraternal; direst; various (pl); wondrous; honey-gathering; tingling; haphazard; curious; mortal; fascinating; heavier; weakest; baser; unlike; particular; noblest; sprightliest; restless; elaborate; expensive; barbarous; branching; peculiar; indifferent; unsatisfied; awful; lonesome; effectual; defensive; increasing; adventurous; equivocal.

adverbs

graciously; generously; hospitably; helpfully; unexpectedly; extremely; exceedingly; habitually; naturally; indulgently; gently; mistakenly; thoughtfully; lovingly; unaffectedly; effusively; officiously; sincerely; cordially; unspeakably; unusually; uncommonly; openly; apparently; noticeably; unselfishly; sympathetically; amiably; affably; unwontedly; considerately; humanely; complaisantly.

KINDLE (v)

adverbs
patiently; skillfully; daily; purposely; premeditatively; punctually; swiftly; spectacularly; vividly.
(See ignite, burn, inflame, rouse.)

KINDLINESS

adjectives
tranquil; clear; close-fisted; proverbial; eager; unaffected; sincere; comfortable.

KINDNESS

adjectives
gracious; ostentatious; undiminished; manifest; systematic; sickening; honey; paternal; sneaking; fraternal; mysterious; selfsame; indulgent; mistaken; loving; thoughtful; false; mellow; anxious; maddening; touching; like; present; patient; generous; fair; subtle; covetous; usurious; impersonal; marked; quizzical; proffered; grave; considerable; lukewarm; cruel; extreme; homely; exceeding; benevolent; natural; indolent; remorseful; hospitable; commended; native; cordial; unbought; forbearing; apparent; untaught.

verbs
bestow—upon; bless with—; confer—; enslave by—; extend—; overflow with—; render—; scatter—; trust—; —charms; —comforts; —conquers; —converts; —enriches; —gladdens; —melts; —shines; —soothes.
(See tenderness, tolerance, charity.)

KING

adjectives
maleficent; deposed; uncrowned; shameful; tributary; wily; grisly; besieging; cautious; guarded; crafty; lofty; apostate; bereaved; loving; nominal; bonanza; well-intentioned; penitent; harlot; veritable; anointed; uxorious; lawful; captive; prostrate; rightful; boastful; mythological; guileless; pious; colorless; blameless; lottery; faithless; untamed; sanguine; unwholesome; resplendent; fangless; landless; provincial; incredulous; fratricidal; licentious; dissimulating.

verbs
acknowledge—; anoint—; consort with—s; crown—; dethrone—; exile—; forsake—; guard—; honor—; praise—; respect—; serve—; —abdicates; —administers; —awes; —commands; —governs; —reigns; —rules; —surveys.
(See monarch, queen, god, ruler.)

KINGDOM

adjectives
infernal; peasant; teeming; animal; mineral; island; watery; moss-hung; hereditary; unconquerable; petty; stout; little; enchanting; enduring; dull; vassal.

verbs
banish from—; conquer—; divide—; forsake—; govern—; grant—; infect—; inhabit—; invade—; overthrow—; partition—; reign over—; renounce—; resign—; rule—; serve—; skirt—; split—; subdue—; —embraces; —extends; —ranges.
(See kingship, realm, monarchy, jurisdiction, dominion, empire.)

KINGLY

adverbs
undeniably; admittedly; consciously; notably; admirably; strikingly; astonishingly; superbly; estimably; magnificently; splendidly; consummately; expertly; aristocratically; nobly; unimpeachably; judiciously; benevolently; resplendently; absolutely; authoritatively; influentially; supremely; autocratically.

KINGSHIP

verbs
abdicate—; abolish—; accept—; bestow—upon; forsake—; honor—; invest—with; ordain to—; propose—; respect—; survey—.
(See kingdom.)

KINSHIP

adjectives
emotional; spiritual.

KINSMEN

adjectives
distinguished; lamented; honorable; moldering.

KISS

adjectives
salt; sterile; spiritlike; melancholy; squandered; multiplied (pl); successive (pl); bought; barren; piteous; breathless; rapturous; wafted; indulgent; passionate; energetic; perfunctory; burning; glowing; inplacable; ungiven; farewell; hot; silent;

fleeting; mute; deep-drawn; fruitful; horizontal; cancerous; treacherous; lovely; sisterhood; famished; tempting; punctuating; loving; holy; sovereign; furious; honeyed; guileless; humbled; fervent; furtive; impassioned; ardent; rarely-tempered; admiring; compassionate; serio-comic; reverent; vigorous; abstracted; random; sincere; airy; moist; reassuring; iron; eager; hasty; laughing; latter; timorous; broken; delicious.

verbs
bestow—upon; blow—; blush at—; brush—; cement with—; cling in—; dab—; dot with —; pluck—; press—; print—upon; promise with—; resist—; sever—; smother with—s; snatch—; steal—; taste—; tempt with—; wed in—; yield—; —disturbs; —enraptures; —entrances; —pecks; —quenches; —subdues; —thrills.
(See caress, embrace.)

KISS (v)

adverbs
passionately; resoundingly; reverently; clumsily; violently; tenderly; airily; ravenously; earnestly; brazenly; soberly; intimately; exultantly; crudely; tantalizingly; fondly; perfunctorily; devoutly; dutifully; vivaciously; mutely; timorously.
(See caress, salute, embrace.)

KISSING

adjectives
voluptuous; continual; heated; promiscuous; ignominious; passioned.

KITCHEN

adjectives
commodious; fragrant; detached; reeking; itinerant; greasy; pretty; well-designed.

verbs
avoid—; consign to—; convey from—; drudge in—; equip—; inspect—; loiter in —; preside over—; retire to—; rule—; scrub—; slave in—; survey—; sweat in—; toil in—; work in—; —enslaves; —gleams; —shines; —smells of.
(See home, room, shop, factory, laboratory.)

KITES

adjectives
carrion; marauding; ravenous.

KITTEN

adjectives
imaginary; striped; playful; impish.

verbs
pet—; stroke—; —amuses; —antics; —basks; —capers; —diverts; —frisks; —frolics; —gambols; —laps; —meows; —plays; —romps; —toys with.
(See cat, puppy, lamb, baby, calf.)

KNACK

adjectives
mechanical; instinctive.

KNAVE

adjectives
cowardly; luckless; unthrifty; lunatic; base; poor; gallant; false; arrant; jealous; decayed; shrewd; ingenious; foolish; rascally; whoreson; beetle-headed; flap-ear; misshapen; pestilent; foul-mouthed; calumnious; scurvy; railing; wrangling; thin-faced; fantastical; doting; sooty; veritable; sinful.

KNAVERY

verbs
brew—; check—; condemn—; confess—; curb—; despise—; escape—; frustrate—; observe—; resist—; shun—; suffer—; suspect—; unfold—; witness—; yield to—; —jars; —shocks; —tempts.
(See wickedness, villainy, vice, crime.)

KNAVISH

adverbs
arrantly; downright; notoriously; grossly; consummately; egregiously; abominably; atrociously; villainously; viciously; infamously; daringly; wickedly; brazenly; extraordinarily; outrageously; monstrously; unbelievably; sinfully; terribly; insufferably; unscrupulously; insidiously; ingloriously; lawlessly; disreputably; scandalously; incorrigibly; shamelessly; astoundingly .

KNEAD (v)

adverbs
savagely; industriously; vigorously; laboriously; mechanically; experimentally; patiently; wholesomely; furiously.
(See fashion, massage, mould, mix.)

KNEE

adjectives
guiding; shaking; shaken; bended; knotted; twinging; naked; rocky; suppliant; feeble;

mailed; pliant; trembling; faltering; up-gathered; relentless; silken; immaculate; sagged; well-molded; sagging; bony; flaccid; tottering; wobbly; weak; exposed; bare; numb; stalwart; buckling; jutting; drawn-up; clasped; scratched; dimpled; enticing.

verbs
bend—; beseech on—s; bow—; brace—; bruise—; climb on—; drop on—; entreat on —s; fall upon—; flex—; implore on—; sink to—; smite—; supplicate on—; —s buckle; —s fold; —s sag; —s weaken.

KNEEL (v)

adverbs
heavily; laboriously; devoutly; submissively; reverently; blindly; prayerfully; imploringly; meekly; religiously; adoringly .
(See surrender, bend.)

KNELL

adjectives
doleful; perpetual; inevitable.

KNIFE

adjectives
ill-directed; harmful; murderous; crooked; keen; burning; long; two-edged; broad; sharp-pointed; naked; big; tempered; curved; brass-handled; blunt; hatchetlike; pointless; whetted; blood-stained.

verbs
brandish—; carve with—; clasp with—; fling—; flourish—; hack with—; heave—; hone—; hurl—; pare with—; pocket—; sheathe—; slash with—; slay with—; stab with—; thrust—; whirl—about.
(See sword, stiletto.)

KNIGHT

adjectives
moralizing; valiant; dauntless; adventurous; tender-smelling; solitary; gallant; cheerful; virgin; sinful; dissembling; blended; belted; irreverent; greasy; assailing; tight-lipped; stalwart; particular; fabled; dubbed; brave.

KNIGHTLY

adverbs
dauntlessly; intrepidly; courteously; gallantly; invariably; habitually; splendidly; superbly; magnificently; generously; chivalrously; distinctly; eminently; nobly; benevolently; delightfully; charmingly; pleasantly; affably; uncommonly; unusually; exceptionally.

KNIT (v)

adverbs
indefatigably; industriously; vigorously; busily; exquisitely; laboriously; patiently; domestically; artistically; beneficially; healthfully; swiftly; monotonously.
(See tie, unite, join, weave.)

KNITTING

verbs
abandon—; admire—; busy with—; commend—; concentrate on—; display—; enjoy —; exhibit—; instruct in—; interrupt—; observe—; occupy with—; survey—; teach —; unravel—; —annoys; —bores; —contents; —delights; —fascinates; —satisfies; —takes form.
(See work.)

KNOB

adjectives
battered; rusty; bent; twisted; turning.

verbs
adjust—; affix—; force—; furnish—; grasp —; grope for—; handle—; jiggle—; locate —; manipulate—; move—; raise—; shake —; turn—; —juts out; —opens; —resists; —submits.
(See handle.)

KNOCK

adjectives
welcome; jarring; thundering; timid; hesitating; parlous; cheerful; imperative; timorous; hard; unwonted; resounding.

KNOCK (v)

adverbs
sharply; clamorously; deliberately; accidentally; respectfully; irritably; resoundingly; unwontedly; thunderously; echoingly; startlingly.
(See rap, clash, beat, strike.)

KNOLL

adjectives
neighboring; sandy; moon-lit; wooded; treeless; timber-covered; rising; verdant.

KNOT

adjectives
inextricable; mystic; intricate; unsuccess-

ful; curious; murderous; true-love; shaggy; salient; writhing; snaky; sagest; feathered.

verbs
curl into—; disentangle—; do up in—; draw into—; form—; knit into—; loop into—; loose—; secure with—; unravel—; untwine —; weave into—; —assures; —mystifies; —perplexes; —puzzles.

KNOTTED

adverbs
dreadfully; tightly; nervously; angrily; inextricably; roughly; strangely; queerly; loosely; carelessly; deliberately; unevenly; jaggedly; hopelessly; terribly; untidily; indiscriminately; mischievously; maliciously; incurably; irreparably; perniciously; vexatiously; inexcusably.

KNOW (v)

adverbs
precisely; intimately; distinctly; intuitively; authoritatively; affectionately; grimly; casually; graciously; jocularly; abstractly; instantaneously; superficially; alliteratively; imperfectly; officially; familiarly; presumably; academically; traditionally; personally; fallaciously.

(See apprehend, realize, understand, ascertain, recognize.)

KNOWLEDGE

adjectives
technical; subtle; painful; pleasurable; experimental; distinct; tinctured; hearsay; extensive; intuitive; slight; detailed; repugnant; profound; dark; uncanny; sudden; acquired; human; systematic; psycho-analytic; copious; elementary; unique; well-known; definite; fuller; academic; intimate; precise; rudimentary; prodigious; barren; bookish; extemporary; unimparted; uncertain; critical; boundless; accurate; specialized; exhilarating; unwelcome; superior; guilty; dangerous; swift; unrelated; superficial; miraculous; worldly; unutterable; imperfect; substantial; immense; preliminary; fluent; growing; untimely; proficient; inestimable; complete; improved; practical; symbolic; consummate; masterful; extraordinary; previous; satisfying; medieval; organized; theoretical; advanced; wearisome; crafty; instinctive; varied; seeming; increased; thorough; lawful; inexhaustible; phenomenal; accumulated; comprehensive; preternatural; gradual; learned; unerring; scientific; definite; clearer; objective; special; lesser; naturalistic; adequate; hard-won; competent; masculine; shrewd; natural; deeper; desecrated; inherited; cynical; rapidly-acquired; delivering; deep-fetched; limited; dread; defective; positive; indisputable; fallacious; educational; gossipy; colloquial; all-embracing; traditional; questionable; acquired; laborious; working; premature; verified; superfluous; meager; personal; astronomic; contemptuous; inward; actual; earthly; secure; rooted; fiendish; fascinating; up-to-the-minute; priceless; happiest; nobler; inferior; well-founded; momentary; unrivaled.

verbs
absorb—; accumulate—; acquire—; apply —; arm with—; assimilate—; attain—; augment—; broadcast—; confront with—; contribute to—; convey—; cultivate—; derive —; digest—; disavow—; disseminate—; draw upon—; employ—; enlarge—; enrich with—; equip with—; evince—; evolve—; exhibit—; expand—; extend—; feed with—; flash—; flaunt—; grope for—; illuminate with—; impart—; imply—; obscure—; pool —; prize—; promulgate—; purchase—; record—; retain—; retard—; safeguard—; soak up—; spread—; thirst for—; treasure —; utilize—; yearn for—; —enlightens; —boils down to.

(See learning, facts, information, understanding, wisdom.)

KNUCKLE

adjectives
bleeding; white; pudgy; bruised; skinned; swarthy; abraded; brass.

L

LABEL

adjectives
progressive; registered; bothersome.

verbs
affix—; destroy—; investigate—; note—; require—; scan—; seal with—; slap on—; stamp—; —attests; —clings; —describes; —designates; —indicates; —represents.
(See mark, stamp, notice, badge, trademark.)

LABEL (v)

adverbs
legally; sarcastically; laconically; carelessly; perfunctorily; cursorily; painstakingly; methodically; decoratively; attractively; concisely; symbolically; fantastically; characteristically.
(See classify, mark.)

LABOR

adjectives
enormous; arduous; sedentary; colossal; persevering; unskilled; lofty; conscientious; praiseworthy; enlightened; earnest; patient; painful; fastidious; graver; uplifting; exhausting; toilsome; unceasing; intellectual; self-imposed; initiatory; faithful; incredible; useless; indefatigable; ceaseless; reproachful; assiduous; unsparing; manual; wonderful; immense; manifold; ill-paid; unimaginable; attendant; unremitting; nocturnal; incessant; endless; grievous; journalistic; intermittent; wearisome; strenuous; unrequited; exploited; loving; sleepless; sweated; diligent; untiring; confining; unceasing; steadfast; imperative; degraded; superfluous; insurgent; inconceivable; fantastic; bucolic; herculean; honorable; skilled; mighty; guiltless; daring; infinite; moderate; effective; congenial; smoke-grimed; gratuitous; united; earnest; unbroken; painstaking; influential; powerful; culinary; unselfish; historical; interrupted; successive (pl); backbreaking; previous; subordinate; organized; active; unwearying; vilified; productive; tremendous; exacting; harsh; aspiring; patient; painful; tedious; ideal; untasked; convict; dreadful; rural; additional; sylvan; pleasant; astrological; oppressed; wonted; tutorial; symbolical; evasive; menial; ever-successful; short-lived; literary; coarse; ferocious; professional; ministerial; heartbreaking.

verbs
absorb in—; bleed (colloq.)—; discipline—; enslave—; free from—; mar—; necessitate —; organize—; placate—; prohibit—; recompense—; recuperate from—; regulate—; reward—; stimulate—; supplement—; surmount—; thrive upon—; undertake—; —profits; —reaps; —supports; —sustains.
(See work, workers, task, industry, toil, production.)

LABOR (v)

adverbs
systematically; incessantly; indefatigably; assiduously; unmercifully; industriously; vigorously; tirelessly; prodigiously; diligently; tumultuously; arduously; fastidiously; unsparingly; gratuitously; congenially; productively; exactingly; unwontedly; tutorially; symbolically; menially; ferociously; professionally.
(See work, toil, drudge.)

LABORATORY

adjectives
destructive; stupendous; metallurgical.

verbs
dissect in—; emit from—; employ in—; establish—; experiment in—; inspect—; investigate in—; lecture in—; manufacture in—; prepare in—; rig out—; stock—; test in—; tinker in—; turn out of—; verify in —; work in—; —discloses; —nauseates; —reeks of; —discovers.
(See kitchen, shop, factory.)

LABORER

adjectives
diverting; solitary; bucolic; devoted; potential; agricultural; diligent; luckless.

LABORIOUS

adverbs
extremely; oppressively; intricately; objectionably; unexpectedly; surprisingly; unremittingly; sedulously; overwhelmingly; enormously; immensely; painfully; incred-

ibly; grievously; strenuously; fantastically; moderately; dreadfully; pleasantly; wholesomely; backbreakingly; elaborately; wearisomely; terribly; undeniably; unbelievably.

LABYRINTH

adjectives
slimy; close; mighty; vast; trackless; burning; weary; watery; aboreal; inextricable.

LABYRINTHINE

adverbs
intricately; hopelessly; perplexingly; curiously; queerly; alarmingly; amazingly; dreadfully; surprisingly; mysteriously; dangerously; perilously; complexly; sinuously; tortuously; troublesomely; circuitously; vexatiously; terrifyingly; ominously.

LACE

adjectives
tawdry; exquisite; cream; supernumerary (pl); billowing; meandering; delicate; passementerie; erring; fluttering; elaborate; tarnished; creamy; tinted.

LACE (v)

adverbs
tightly; suffocatingly; fashionably; injuriously; oppressively.
(See fasten, tie, bind.)

LACERATION

verbs
incur—; inflict—; occasion—; soothe—; sterilize—; stitch—; suture—; tourniquet—; —appals; —bares the bone; —distresses; —heals; —horrifies; —inflames; —pains; —scars; —shocks; —throbs; —tortures.
(See wound, injury, pain, cut.)

LACK

adjectives
pretended; noticeable; all-round; deplorable; disorderly; overwhelming; impressive; plentiful; definite; obvious.

verbs
atone for—; bare—; bemoan—; compensate for—; confess—; decry—; disclose—; imply —; perceive—; recognize—; recompense for —; remedy—; sense—; suffer—; supply—; suspect—; —crushes; —disgraces; —handicaps; —humbles; —irks; —offends; —ostracizes; —saddens.
(See inadequacy, need, want.)

LACK (v)

adverbs
lamentably; puzzlingly; vainly; essentially; wretchedly; sorely; utterly; sadly; deplorably; definitely; obviously; tragically; dramatically.
(See need, want.)

LACKADAISICAL

adverbs
nonchalantly; ostentatiously; obviously; foolishly; sentimentally; romantically; languidly; dreamily; inanely; provokingly; drunkenly; stupidly; crazily; pretentiously; foppishly; vainly; unnaturally; artificially; languishingly; heavily; terribly; gravely; thoughtfully.

LACKEY

adjectives
saucy; liveried; silk-stockinged.

LACONIC

adverbs
meagerly; unsatisfactorily; emphatically; disappointingly; vexatiously; habitually; tersely; drily; drolly; crisply; curtly; comprehensively; summarily; trenchantly; curiously; oddly; officially; arrogantly; cynically; laudably; neatly; compactly; sententiously; professionally; provokingly; remarkably; wonderfully; notably; famously; uncommonly; highly; amazingly; incredibly; effectively.

LACONISM

adjectives
formal; concise; annoying; notable.

LACQUERS

adjectives
decorative; shiny; protective; gaudy; bright.

LAD

adjectives
malicious; lethargic; raw; daring; sober; gallant; joyous; vigorous; singular; loutish; fine; gentlemanly; valiant; painstaking; capable; ambitious; blithe; sensitive; sweet; rosy; mad; delirious; promising; struggling.

LADDER

adjectives
petal-woven; corded; rude; commodious; symbolical; palpable; golden; heavenly.

verbs
ascend—; clamber up—; drop from—; employ—; extend—; hoist—; leap up—; mount —; rung—; scale—; scramble up—; shake —; shift—; support—; teeter on—; —aids; —bridges; —conveys; —dizzies; —totters; travel up—.
(See steps, stairs.)

LADY

adjectives
demure; spare; grave; worthy; estimable; double-dealing; venerable; generous; gallant; out-sized; perennial; gracious; blushing; haughty; pitiful; excellent; accomplished; wretched; audacious; quick-fingered; quick-witted; quick-eyed; sacred; horny-handed; virtuous; sweet; innocent; good-natured; courageous; beauteous; incredulous; celestial; disloyal; hopeful; miserable; conventional; decorous; well-mannered; dejected; soft-spoken; square-faced; starched; profound; interested; autocratic; languid; well-brought-up; masterful; delicate; high-bred; pink-cheeked; reverend; vixenish; colossal; dignified; elderly; flustered; skeptical; diminutive; blameless; giddy; charming; gentle; fortunate; little; chubby; prudent; pleasant-spoken; exotic; sentimental; thrice-fair; pleasant-spirited; desolate; poor; wrong; chic; acidulated; chaste; agreeable; prepossessing; illustrious; elegant; glittering; ingenuous; favorite; metallic; solicitous; pearly-robed.

LADYLIKE

adverbs
oppressively; exquisitely; absurdly; delightfully; overwhelmingly; fastidiously; foolishly; agreeably; pleasantly; graciously; comically; modestly; demurely; coyly; decorously; genteelly; formally; properly; fashionably; appropriately; conventionally; aristocratically; politely; courteously; ostentatiously; stylishly; elegantly; ceremoniously; stiffly; awkwardly; pretentiously; affably; complaisantly; charmingly; enchantingly.

LAG

adjectives
cultural; common; noticeable.

LAGOON

verbs
approach—; cover—; cross—; describe—; enclose—; enter—; form—; observe—; open into—; row in—; sail in—; separate—; skirt—; swim in—; —appears; —beckons; —extends; —invites.
(See lake, bay, pond.)

LAIR

adjectives
frigid; equatorial; shaggy; rosy; dreadful; jungle; deathless.

verbs
conceal in—; corner in—; discover—; dwell in—; ensconce in—; enter—; expose—; harbor in—; lodge in—; nestle in—; recline in—; repose in—; retreat to—; reveal—; track to—; uncover—; venture upon—; —comforts; —reeks; —shelters.
(See den, refuge, retreat.)

LAKE

adjectives
shimmering; tranquil; climbing; lily-mantled; darkling; grassy; azure; misty; stagnant; placid; bitter; weedy; far-reaching; encircling; shattered; picturesque; forest-bosomed; crystal; encompassing; starry; lovely; seething; translucent; calm-flowing; rumored; universal; parent; sleeping; lucid; contrasted; burning; smiling; argent; glittering; airy; lonely; ruffled; liquid; mirrored; fringed; dazzling; noble; dusky.

verbs
angle in—; cast into—; encompass—; fish in—; navigate—; ramble by—; row on—; sail—; shade—; sight—; skim over—; skirt —; slip into—; surround—; waft across—; —affords; —dazzles; —gleams; —glimmers; —laps; —mirrors; —reflects; —ripples; —shimmers; —spangles; —winks; —yawns.
(See lagoon, river, stream, bay, pond, sea.)

LAMB

adjectives
bleating; parti-colored; sinful; sacrificial; silly; twinned; heaven-sent.

verbs
brand—s; cuddle—; fatten—s; market—; roast—; sacrifice—; slaughter—; —baas; —bleats; —capers; —frisks; —frolics; —gambols; —grazes; —nuzzles; —prances; —symbolizes.
(See kitten, calf, sheep, animal, baby, puppy, cat.)

LAMBENT

adverbs
delicately; gently; flickeringly; effulgently; flashingly; gloriously; steadily; luminously; phosphorescently; shimmeringly; softly; recurrently; lustrously; scintillatingly; unusually; peculiarly; strangely.

LAMENT

adjectives
constant; loud; inevitable; lugubrious; passionate.

LAMENT (*v*)

adverbs
dolorously; pitifully; pathetically; eternally; morbidly; passionately; lugubriously; quaveringly; tearfully; abnormally; hysterically; affectionately.

(See weep, wail, grieve.)

LAMENTABLE

adverbs
altogether; downright; pitiably; bitterly; sorely; direly; utterly; exceptionally; shockingly; appallingly; horribly; unusually; extremely; fearfully; frightfully; tragically; wretchedly; indescribably; sadly; absolutely; unspeakably; inexpressibly; singularly.

LAMENTATION

adjectives
piteous; moderate; importunate; frantic; grand; purposeless; loud; diabolical; silent; sublime; quavering; burlesque.

verbs
censure—; deplore—; fill with—; forego—; forestall—; regret—; restrain—; staunch—; stifle—; utter—; wail in—; —arises; —ceases; —encompasses; —haunts; —increases; —rends the air; —resounds; —weakens.

(See tears, sadness, grief, sorrow.)

LAMP

adjectives
flickering; wharf; quenchless; fragrant; incandescent; glimmering; respectable; acetyline; blear; trembling; mirrored; tawdry; frail; light-giving; intoxicating; ill-trimmed; wasting; pendulous; failing; rain-splashed; glow-worm; festooned; slow-sliding; meteoric; impudent; innumerable (pl); classic; sleepy; street; eternal; oil-dried; fluorescent; midnight; smoky; outburnt; shaded; reading; bronze; copper; shining; winking; flashing; soft; colored; tiny; sputtering; gas; oil; luminous; twinkling; vital; studious; flaring; kindled; dewy.

verbs
blast—; deck with—s; extinguish—; grope for—; quench—; restore—; strangle—; suspend—; switch on—; —beautifies; —blinds; —brightens; —cheers; —comforts; —directs; —enhances; —fails; —flickers; —glimmers; —glows; —mellows; —reveals; —shines; —silhouettes.

(See light, candle, flame, fireworks, match, sunshine, twilight, spark.)

LANCE

adjectives
ill-headed; gleaming; thirsty; leafy; quivering; strong; shivered; rusted; splintered; unused.

verbs
cast—; charge with—s; harpoon with—; shatter—; slay with—; spear with—; splinter—; stab with—; thrust—; wield—; —cripples; —defends; —disfigures; —injures; —maims; —pierces; —scratches; —shivers; —splinters; —splits; —threatens; —wounds.

(See spear, sword, stiletto.)

LAND

adjectives
brawny-breasted; weather-beaten; tempting; wide; uninhabited; fruitful; radiant; rolling; toiling; devastated; depreciated; desolate; swampy; bleeding; cultivated; uncharted; intolerant; sylvan; eloquent; unshorn; exhausted; delightful; twilight; favored; death-polluted; dying; delectable; woeful; venerable; alluvial; granitic; barren; arable; heavenly; sickly; dewy; contiguous; pastoral; sun-soaked; virgin; enchanted; ceded; broad; monotonous; flat; factious; romantic; quaggy; guilty; boggy; habitable; sterile; forbidden; allodial; lifeless; gasping; sheltering; delicious; forsaken; debatable; enlightened; guileless; dirty; mortgaged; dawning; smiling; genial; sullen; scorched; superior; unhappy; untraveled; chivalric; gracious; inspirational; wretched; time-stricken; foreign; extreme; sprightly; listening; neighboring; untilled; goodly-growing; fertile; fallen; long-promised; hostile; springtime; sinless; disburdened; dipping; defenceless; unappropriated; wilderness; unoccupied; well-contented; watered; dependent; curtained; ruined; gentler;

sorrow-stricken; shadowy; hazy; ice-prisoned; white; useless; beautiful; vacation; placid; tight; upheaved; sculptured; aesthetic; undulous; dim; vast; tranquil; irrigable; rich; blatant; fabled; misty; scrubby; furrowed; shadowless; antique; divers (pl); unseated; high-cost; touch-and-go; sluggish; marshy; fettered; hollow; bustling; native; derelict; waste; heath; many-tinted; boundless; prosperous; bountiful; invisible; timeless; sodden; unexplored; unconcerned; financial; fairy; luxuriant; exhaustless; desirable; agricultural; surrounding; night-enfolded; spiritual; unknown; gullied; middling; hereditary; distant; alien; dismembered; stubble; blossoming.

verbs
apportion—; bargain for—; cede—; claim —; cleanse—; corrupt—; cultivate—; darken—; defile—; denude—; despoil—; dower —; engulf—; enrich—; exploit—; fertilize —; inhabit—; inherit—; lease—; link—; nurse—; plow—; portion—; purge—; rule —; scour—; sow—; squat on—; sweep—; till—; vest—s in; —abuts; —adjoins; —yields.
(See earth, soil, ground, farm.)

LANDHOLDER

adjectives
wealthy; pampered; heavily-taxed; frugal.

LANDING

adjectives
rude; haphazard; prosaic; steamboat; three-point; perfect; fatal; forced.

verbs
anticipate—; bar—; contemplate—; effect—; forestall—; hinder—; hope for—; impede —; limit—; meet at—; prepare for—; prohibit—; salute—; superintend—; survey—; swoop to—; view—.
(See platform, finish.)

LANDLADY

adjectives
callous; slipshod; overpositive; shrieking; untrained; half-distracted; miserly.

LANDLORD

adjectives
absentee; lonely; liberal; grasping.

LANDMARK

adjectives
ghostly; tall; treasured; celebrated; obliterated; ancient; historical; well-kept; awe-inspiring.

LANDSCAPE

adjectives
ideal; imaginative; volcanic; broad; wet; dreary; reposeful; shadowy; manifold (pl); glorious; delicate; gliding; desolate; dismal; rolling; inspiring; autumnal; harmonious; limited; extravagant; bewildered; poetical; suggestive; naked; receding; twilight; motionless; mystic; glimmering; colored; austere; stupendous; delicious; ungenial; ravaged; forbidding; bitter; peaceful; perfect; winter; untrodden; melancholy; impressive; serious; shivering; imposing; large; dreamy; terrestrial; hoary; lunar; hazy; sunlit; glowing; variegated; pastoral; scarred; vernal; withered; dim; embrowned; distant.

verbs
clutter—; contemplate—; denude—; desecrate—; design—; dot—; enhance—; exhibit—; gaze on—; gild—; glorify—; integrate—; intersperse—; perfect—; photograph—; regard—; scrutinize—; shade—; tinge—; view—; —charms; —delights; —educates; —gratifies; —spreads; —stretches.
(See country, countryside, view, scene, picture, scenery.)

LAND-SLIDE

adjectives
fashion; fatal; crushing; spectacular.

LANE

adjectives
dark; solitary; hedgerowed; grassy; seaward; rambling; turfy; cattle-haunted; leafy; pleached; neighboring; winding; miry; isolated; infrequent; sandy; rectory; bowery; dirty; rutty; hollow; shaded; forest; high-walled; quiet; deep-shaded.

verbs
adhere to—; bolt down—; clear—; follow —; labor up—; lurk in—; mantle—; pause in—; rest in—; scamper down—; shade—; shadow—; shun—; skirt—; tarry in—; veer from—; —diverges; —flanks; —meanders; —spirals; —swerves; —twists; —wanders; —winds.
(See road, alley, passage, path, street, thoroughfare, walk.)

LANGUAGE

adjectives

various (pl); symbolical; evasive; abusive; well-known; clear; understandable; simple; clarified; easy; peculiar; profane; psychoanalytic; lovely; figurative; neighboring; luminous; ungracious; graceless; energetic; ominous; satirical; adopted; subservient; impassioned; rhythmical; strenuous; lucid; emphatic; precise; noble; judicious; conversational; similar; amicable; forcible; violent; unseemly; flexible; musical; refined; primitive; wide-spread; copious; metrical; native; expressive; unmistakable; worthy; passionate; maternal; extinct; warming; dead; universal; reviling; elegant; opprobrious; inoffensive; biblical; scrupulous; classical; provincial; concise; sublime; appropriate; nervous; unintelligible; official; elaborate; stilted; bombastic; temperate; winning; cordial; sensible; semibarbarous; mystic; glowing; tart; strong; persuasive; inadequate; provocative; hearty; lustful; animated; rude; decorous; uncensored; remarkable; felicitous; colloquial; declarative; emotional; melodious; informal; striking; paradoxical; imaginative; contemptuous; coarse; embellished; pleasurable; impossible; vehement; rugged; vigorous; idiomatic; austere; traditional; high-flown; hidden; spiritual; characteristic; artificial; lifeless; sacred; colorless; symbolic; euphonious; literary; immoderate; festive; impious.

verbs

abuse—; bolt—; broaden—; clothe in—; command—; corrupt—; decipher—; decode —; defile—; interpret—; manipulate—; master—; mold—; mutilate—; purify—; restrict—; revive—; strangle—; vitalize—; vulgarize—; —abounds in; —bears witness; —bristles with; —flows; —lilts; —survives.

(See speech, dialect, slang, jargon.)

LANGUID

adverbs

listlessly; dreamily; lazily; idly; deliberately; deliciously; softly; blissfully; unwontedly; delightfully; pensively; thoughtfully; wearily; mildly; strangely; unusually; peculiarly; alarmingly; ominously; oddly; dispiritedly; dejectedly; indifferently; indolently; inertly; uncommonly; woefully; significantly; particularly; constitutionally; objectionably; exasperatingly; provokingly; inveterately.

LANGUISH (*v*)

adverbs

piteously; idly; gradually; pathetically; sickly; wanly; pensively; wearily; dreamily; amorously; listlessly; unwontedly; blissfully; lazily; agonizingly; passionately; ceaselessly; lovingly.

(See pine, droop, faint, weaken.)

LANGUOR

adjectives

increasing; ladylike; apparent; wearisome; delicious; gentle; delightful; pensive; passionless; restive; melancholy; sensuous; dreamy; amorous; unwonted; listless; gracious; soft; blissful; divine; mortal; exceeding; lazy.

verbs

complain of—; depress into—; diffuse—; droop in—; exhibit—; exude—; fall into—; perceive—; relieve—; shake off—; sink into —; sway with—; —arrests; —floats over; —oppresses; —pervades; —spreads.

(See lassitude, exhaustion, weariness.)

LANKY

adverbs

unbelievably; comically; ludicrously; increasingly; awkwardly; clumsily; bashfully; haggardly; hungrily; terribly; pathetically; woefully; weedily; gauntly; slenderly; extremely; preposterously; fantastically; impressively; dreadfully; inexpressibly; curiously; laughably; particularly; peculiarly; strangely.

LANTERN

adjectives

port-colored; multicolored; treacherous; exquisite; smoky; ill-smelling.

LAP

adjectives

flowery; mossy; verdant; commodious; soft; inviting.

LAP (*v*)

adverbs

greedily; thirstily; affectionately; hungrily; fawningly; cringingly; ingratiatingly.

(See lick, eat.)

LAPSE

adjectives

careless; temporary; momentary; single; liquid; deplorable; smooth; strong; venial;

occasional; incredible; atrocious; enormous; soothing; sad; moral; melancholy; abrupt.

verbs
attribute—to; dispel—; emerge from—; expose to—; fall into—; glide into—; recover from—; sink in—; slip into—; spend—; suffer—; vacate—; —avails; —decays; flow into—.
(See mistake, error, indiscretion.)

LAPWING

adjectives
wanton; swift.

LARCENY

adjectives
petit; grand; mammoth.

LARDER

verbs
deposit in—; drain—; exhaust—; hang in —; invade—; load—; purge—; raid—; replenish—; resort to—; sack—; stock—; store in—; tap—; —abounds in; —conserves; —gratifies; —overflows; —preserves.
(See stock, supply, store.)

LARGE

adverbs
extremely; incalculably; incredibly; immeasurably; preposterously; exceedingly; particularly; overwhelmingly; infinitely; enormously; monstrously; prodigiously; astoundingly; marvelously; remarkably; notoriously; uncommonly; immoderately; inordinately; signally; strikingly; amazingly; tremendously; immensely; comparatively; incomparably; imposingly; formidably; sensationally; unusually; amply; satisfactorily; sufficiently.

LARK

adjectives
veritable; merry; late; full-throated; mounting; morning; winging.

verbs
—carols; —chants; —chimes; —chirrups; —circles; —composes; —s congregate; —s flock; —heralds the dawn; —improvises; —instills; —molts; —ravishes; —sharps; —showers melody; —shrills; —slurs; —sprinkles notes; —squats; —startles; —strains; —trills; —whistles.
(See bird.)

LASH

adjectives
drooping; burning; sweeping; sooty; dark; arrowy; invisible; sleepy; scattered (pl); fluttering; glistening; torturing; flickering; stinging; inky; silky; languid; bristly; downcast; molten; delicate; pale; long; flaxen; biting; verbal.

LASH (v)

adverbs
viciously; furiously; frenziedly; maniacally; vilely; brutally; sadistically; murderously; madly.
(See whip, scold, beat, punish.)

LASHING

adjectives
ominous; merciless; cruel; interrupted; crippling; bloody; bitter; mad; furious; fierce; frenzied; maniacal.

verbs
bemoan—; bestow—upon; cringe under—; crucify with—; denounce—; experience—; gloat over—; inflict—; suffer—; wince at —; writhe under—; yield to—; —angers; —convulses; —cows; —infuriates; —maddens; —subdues; —tortures.
(See scolding, punishment, beating.)

LASS

adjectives
prettiest; lowborn; morbid; enticing; dark-eyed; bouncing; tidy-looking; flat-faced; modest; buxom; bewitching; pleasant; vivacious; smiling.

LASSITUDE

adjectives
despairing; general; poppied; speechless; languorous; drowsy; dreamy; hopeless.

verbs
combat—; depress into—; diffuse—; droop into—; exhibit—; induce—; perceive—; remedy—; shake off—; sink into—; tie with —; yield to—; —arrests; —envelops; —floats over; —flows over; —oppresses; —pervades; —spreads; —takes hold.
(See languor, exhaustion, weariness, fatigue.)

LAST (v)

adverbs
interminably; unendurably; unreasonably; briefly; unconsciously.
(See endure, continue, remain.)

LATCH

adjectives
clinking; welcoming.

LATE

adverbs
extremely; horribly; preposterously; hideously; terrifyingly; alarmingly; significantly; dreadfully; intentionally; deliberately; carelessly; unfortunately; disastrously; calamitously; nonchalantly; lazily; inconsiderately; strangely; curiously; understandably; habitually; inexcusably; unpardonably; inexplicably; ungraciously; excusably; justifiably; unavoidably; apologetically; incredibly; vexatiously; unluckily; inordinately; terribly; uncommonly.

LATENESS

adjectives
preposterous; repeated; excusable.

LATENT

adverbs
imperceptibly; mysteriously; inferentially; implicitly; unsuspectedly; darkly; confusingly; mistily; indistinguishably; astoundingly; unhappily; impenetrably; unfortunately.

LATHER

adjectives
sudsy; brushless; shaving; foamy; plentiful; softening.

verbs
agitate to—; beat up—; burst into—; confect—; enjoy—; exercise into—; form—; give—; mix into—; sponge with—; swathe in—; thrash up—; wash in—; whip into—; work up—; —agrees with; —bubbles; —cleanses; —foams; —fortifies; —froths; —gushes; —overflows; —penetrates; —purifies; —refreshes; —sinks deep; —sputters; —stimulates; —tingles.
(See cream, soap, foam, froth.)

LATIN

verbs
acquaint with—; deliver in—; discourse in —; express in—; honor—; interpret—; mumble—; recite—; spout—; translate—; vent—; —bewilders; —confuses; —conveys; —dismays; —distracts; —flourishes; —revives; —stumps (colloq.).
(See dialect, language, literature.)

LATITUDES

adjectives
utmost; boundless; beloved; heliographical; medieval.

LATTICES

adjectives
stormy; antique; caged.

LATTICEWORK

adjectives
quaint; artistic; delicate.

LAUD (v)

adverbs
flatteringly; fawningly; foolishly; extravagantly; sincerely; fervently; enthusiastically; passionately; exaggeratedly.
(See sing, praise, celebrate.)

LAUDATORY

adverbs
fawningly; flatteringly; admiringly; politically; unctuously; officially; ostentatiously; fulsomely; subtly; appreciatively; blatantly; lavishly; sincerely; moderately; humbly; unnecessarily; reluctantly; eloquently; heartily; solemnly; warmly; profusely; effusively; highly; excessively.

LAUGH

adjectives
scornful; cackling; incredulous; wild; abrupt; gruesome; childish; simple; gay; subdued; hoarse; low; relieved; inaudible; approving; forced; rippling; mild; familiar; horrid; distracted; funny; hard; little; tremulous; unpleasant; wheezy; triumphant; irritating; crackling; gentle; noisy; spiteful; uneasy; jeering; sarcastic; mocking; eerie; sinister; terrible; unmelodious; hearty; arch; frightful; constrained; blunt; malicious; sweet; vain; ringing; young; enchanting; trifling; suppressed; loud; evil; coarse; chuckling; fierce; jovial; silent; slight; cheery; rapturous; polite; merry; choked; melodious; careless; clumsy; gibing; cold; gurgling; startling; humorous; tinkling; boisterous; wild; impish; fearsome; bitter; drunken; sweet; mirthless; meaningful; fiendish; bubbling; wicked; harsh; ironical; taunting; tuneful; carnivorous; hysterical; delicious; silver; horse; self-conscious; childlike; joyous; grating; gasping; throaty; deep; hearty; good-humored; half-desperate; discordant; brit-

tle; characteristic; woeful; roguish; irritable; rattling; complacent; derisive; convulsive; hospitable; mingled (pl); sardonic; sonorous; supercilious; astonished; penitent; rueful; angry; sobbing; weak; musical; tittering; bursting; ghostly.

LAUGH (v)

adverbs
incredulously; gruesomely; tremulously; triumphantly; irritatingly; spitefully; jeering ly; sarcastically; triflingly; jovially; boisterously; humorously; impishly; drunkenly; mirthlessly; fiendishly; gratingly; discordantly; complacently; convulsively; sardonically; sonorously; superciliously; musically; croakingly; gleefully; mordantly; uproariously; jauntily; ruefully; derisively; significantly; ironically; constrainedly; sheepishly; unquenchably; grimly; idiotically; dramatically; jubilantly; exultantly; reassuringly; gustily; insolently; immoderately.

(See roar, giggle, snicker, titter.)

LAUGHABLE

adverbs
ludicrously; comically; monstrously; ironically; absurdly; quaintly; delightfully; uncommonly; moderately; scarcely; heartily; frankly; amusingly; prankishly; pleasantly; rousingly; stimulatingly; cleverly; admissibly; outlandishly.

LAUGHTER

adjectives
silent; delighted; thistle-down; immoderate; boisterous; mingled; shrill; subdued; uncontrolled; resonant; restrained; refreshing; rude; discordant; ill-natured; smothered; derisive; inward; mocking; deluded; resolute; hearty; artificial; soft; wild; hysteric; cackling; lifeless; zealous; delicious; high-pitched; murmurous; joyous; careless; frank; wholesome; meaningless; lovely; honest; unbelted; babbling; intellectual; faltering; Homeric; irreverent; rapid; irresistible; internal; confident; everlasting; hysterical; rippling; childish; unholy; sincerest; rollicking; bitter; mortal; intermingling; wilder; beery; innocent; immortal; foolish; free; bubbling; silvery; sudden; scary; throaty; excessive; gushing; hoarser; treble; shallow; fairy; savage; riotous; inheld.

verbs
break into—; burst into—; check—; constrain—; convulse in—; dimple in—; draw —; elicit—; enjoy—; evoke—; excite—; explode in—; flood with—; forgive—; join in —; occasion—; provoke—; raise—; reel in—; refrain from—; repress—; roar with —; rock with—; roll in—; scorn—; split with—; stifle—; stab with—; suppress—; swallow—; tumble into—; turn to—; wrinkle into—; —dances; —delights; —distorts; —ebbs; —explodes; —fizzles out (colloq.); —flows; —jars; —jets; —punctures; —quivers; —resounds; —rings out; —spills from; —warms; —wins.

(See mirth, grin, smile, merriment, snicker.)

LAUNCH

verbs
anchor—; appoint—; buffet—; endanger—; navigate—; propel—; repair—; slap—; view from—; —capsizes; —chugs; —circles; —courses; —cruises; —dances in; —drifts; —glides; —noses past; —ploughs; —rocks; —steams; —transports.

(See boat, tugboat, motor-boat, ship, steamer, schooner, yacht, vessel.)

LAUNCH (v)

adverbs
simultaneously; ceremoniously; auspiciously; vigorously; politically; enthusiastically; formally; diplomatically.

(See start, begin.)

LAURELS

adjectives
congregated; unsunned; untwined; bright; barren; fadeless; windless; unplucked; mingling.

verbs
acquire—; bestow—; blast—; crown with —; display—; envy—; garnish with—; look to—; merit—; reap—; regain—; repose on —; rest on—; retire on—; reward with—; seek—; snatch—; —delight; —enhance.

(See medal, prize, reward, trophy, crown.)

LAVA

adjectives
disintegrated; fluid; naked; incandescent; basaltic; massed; molten; smoking.

verbs
discharge—; disgorge—; drool—; emit—; pour—; puke—; spew—; —boils; —bubbles; —bursts; —courses down; —crushes; —deluges; —devastates; —envelops; —erupts; —expands; —flows; —gurgles; —inundates; —issues from; —oozes; —overflows; —percolates; —ravishes; —solidifies; —streams from; —swoops down.

(See water, mortar, liquid, plaster, bullet.)

LAVISH

adverbs
astoundingly; extravagantly; exceedingly; overwhelmingly; regally; royally; ridiculously; exorbitantly; profusely; disgustingly; inordinately; needlessly; unnecessarily; ostentatiously; proudly; pompously; wastefully; improvidently; thriftlessly; foolishly; inanely; witlessly; idiotically; generously; charitably; benevolently; benignly; amiably; graciously.

LAVISH (*v*)

adverbs
impulsively; vainly; extravagantly; regally; royally; affectionately; tenderly; passionately; adoringly; liberally; immoderately; recklessly.

(See spend, bestow.)

LAVISHNESS

adjective
glittering; sparse; regal.

LAW

adjectives
immutable; sacred; penal; violated; stringent; fundamental; impartial; salutary; comprehensive; valid; international; eternal; sumptuary; important; traditional; inexorable; remedial; flagitious; changeless; singular; angry; constricting; physical; standing; secular; unwritten; common; mild; conciliatory; criminal; invariable; certain; efficacious; unfailing; adequate; inoperative; severest; bloody; existing; conscription; never-to-be-formulated; geometric; organic; unspectacular; non-corporation; bogus; supreme; primitive; scientific; radiant; antiquated; prohibitory; uniform; rigorous; hideous; undiscriminating; drastic; continuous; all-building; recorded; subjective; severe; inescapable; biting; benignant; unconstitutional; sharp; evident; economic; oppressive; empirical; righteous; anatomic; deathless; conservation; mundane; beneficent; harsh; sumptuary; ceremonial; querulous; sanguine; chancery; rigid; outraged; unequal; civil; social; hidden; substantive; obnoxious; mortal; stern; slavery-fashioned; ungracious; admirable; dramatic; academic; irreversible; active; indwelling; immovable; murderous; primal; unwieldy; tyrannical; blind; furious; unreasoning; crude; complex; clumsy; fiery; brutal; underlying; strictest; sordid; indiscreet; fantastical; expiring; ridiculous; restraining; proposed; express; protective; ultimate; martial; fallible; human; intolerant; preadjusted; physiological; clocklike.

verbs
amend—; administer—; apply—; array against—; bow to—; challenge—; circumvent—; clarify—; codify—; comply with—; comprehend—; conform to—; defy—; denounce—; dispute—; disregard—; dodge—; draft—; elude—; enact—; enforce—; expound—; flout—; forge—; forsake—; frame —; grind out—s; heed—; impose by—; infringe—; instigate—; interpret—; invoke—; mock—; modify—; nullify—; promulgate—; rail against—; ratify—; repeal—; repudiate —; resist—; run afoul of—; stiffen—; subject to—; supersede—; supplant—; suspend —; sustain—; systematize—; tamper with —; tighten—; transgress—; uphold—; —broadens; —clamps down; —curbs; —decrees; —defines; —differentiates; —empowers; —isolates; —prescribes; —relaxes; —restricts; —sanctions; —stipulates.

(See bill, statute, ordinance, regulation, edict, decree, mandate, rule, legislation.)

LAW-ABIDING

adverbs
carefully; duly; cautiously; respectfully; reputably; generally; habitually; usually; remarkably; always; scarcely; voluntarily; conscientiously; ordinarily; publicly; obviously; uniformly; invariably; obediently; willingly; passively; actively; faithfully; loyally; devotedly; superbly; consistently; customarily; exceptionally; notably.

LAWFUL

adverbs
definitely; expressly; explicitly; officially; ordinarily; prescriptively; properly; duly; acceptably; admissibly; equitably; constitutionally; downright; completely; funda-

mentally; authentically; singularly; emphatically; unquestionably; unimpeachably; currently; altogether.

LAWLESS

adverbs
dangerously; alarmingly; youthfully; heedlessly; daringly; audaciously; lamentably; deplorably; openly; actively; defiantly; insurgently; seditiously; restively; insubordinately; mutinously; rebelliously; tumultuously; treasonably; incorrigibly; persistently; obstinately; incredibly.

LAWLESSNESS

adjectives
rash; irresponsible.

verbs
assail—; condemn—; condone—; countenance—; crush—; decry—; denounce—; infest with—; reform—; suffer—; survive—; subscribe to—; yield to—; —breaks out; —fascinates; —grinds; —offends; —oppresses; —reigns; —spreads; —sullies.

(See crime, vice, anarchy, communism, wickedness, sin.)

LAWN

adjectives
dewy; grassy; upland; smooth; squared; summery; sunny; carpetlike; sun-baked; unkempt; dew-besprinkled; russet; spacious; sleek; sun-bathed; well-kept; flowered; shadow-chequered; wintry; sun-soaked; moon-lit; thick; velvety.

verbs
adorn—with; besprinkle—; border—; design—; fence in—; gird—; hedge in—; injure—; mow—; pluck from—; romp on—; shadow—; sprinkle—; tread—; —beautifies; —carpets; —clothes; —creeps; —extends; —flowers; —slopes.

(See grass, field, garden.)

LAWSUIT

adjectives
vexatious; improper; ugly; ruinous; prolonged; endless; trumped-up; expensive.

verbs
avoid—; bear—; condemn—; contest—; drop—; elude—; encounter—; incur—; institute—; judge—; propose—; saddle with—; subpoena for—; support—; wrangle over—; —confounds; —drags; —harasses; —perplexes; —tires; —wearies.

(See litigation, suit, case, prosecution.)

LAWYER

adjectives
crooked; gray-haired; briefless; solemn-faced; shyster; contemporary; constitutional; struggling; well-trained; prominent; competent; sharp; cunning; tricky; conceited; supercilious; dignified; profound; learned; callow; bullying; quick-witted; capable; unconventional; eccentric; eminent; good; skinflint; rascally; kindly.

verbs
employ—; retain—; —addresses; —advocates; —appeals; —battles; —blusters; —cavils; —charges; —confounds; —cross-examines; —defends; —expounds; —interprets; —litigates; —objects; —outwits; —pleads; —pounds; —practises; —queries; —questions; —quibbles; —shifts; —solicits; —strives; —wrangles.

(See orator, congressman, senator, attorney.)

LAX

adverbs
surprisingly; inscrutably; mysteriously; deliberately; criminally; negligently; leniently; indulgently; lamentably; incomprehensibly; regrettably; terribly; disastrously; calamitously; scandalously; outrageously; atrociously; dangerously; ominously; carelessly; languidly; lazily; indifferently; unusually; unwontedly; habitually; inexcusably; noticeably; obviously; apparently; dreadfully.

LAXATIVE

verbs
addict to—s; advocate—; dose with—; employ—; necessitate—; order—; require—; resist—; resort to—; suggest—; —abuses; —cleanses; —cures; —dispels; —eases; —loosens; —purges; —relieves; —unloads.

(See medicine, enema, remedy.)

LAXITY

adjectives
social; moral; parental.

LAYERS

adjectives
peripheral; thin; successive; innumerable;

reflecting; stratified; conglomerate; favorable; superficial; aerial; saline; serrated.

LAYMEN

adjectives
impertinent; unhallowed; incompetent; unpracticed.

LAYS

adjectives
embroidered; melodious; deathless; mirthful; mystic.

LAZINESS

adjectives
intense; mental; incorrigible; lifelong; noticeable.

LAZY

adverbs
unbelievably; deliciously; delightfully; utterly; incurably; inexcusably; openly; flauntingly; nonchalantly; blithely; carelessly; admittedly; vauntingly; intensely; mentally; incorrigibly; horribly; selfishly; inconsiderately; ungraciously; curiously; unpardonably; impudently; blatantly; flagrantly; insufferably; unbearably; lethargically; languidly; heavily; lumpishly; inertly; dreamily; sleepily; drowsily; terribly; provokingly.

LEA

adjectives
windy; russet; flowery; darkening; emerald; shadowed; rich; calm.

LEAD

adjectives
hissing; murderous; dull; unencumbered; smoke-blackened; merciless; proper.

verbs
cast—; expose—; fuse—; melt—; mine—; refine—; sheet—; smelt—; solder—; treat with—; unearth—; weight with—; —corrodes; —poisons; —softens; —tarnishes.

(See metal, iron, steel.)

LEAD (v)

adverbs
deceitfully; gallantly; boldly; intrepidly; triumphantly; victoriously; mercilessly; ceremonially; dexterously; ultimately; fatefully; enterprisingly; illustriously; imaginatively; reluctantly; gallantly; despotically; fanatically; energetically; intelligently; unscrupulously; nominally; ecclesiastically; incomparably; supremely.

(See command, direct, guide.)

LEADER

adjectives
enterprising; illustrious; reluctant; doubtful; foremost; cavalry; political-minded; creative; imaginative; naive; eminent; come-by-chance; spiritual; fanatical; party; befeathered; distinguished; despotic; conspicuous; prudent; prominent; submissive; insurgent; acknowledged; subjugated; ascetic; inspiring; quality; moderate; unquestioned; energetic; intelligent; self-constituted; unscrupulous; popular; typical; halting; patriot; nominal; revolutionary; adored; ecclesiastical; incomparable; brilliant; knightly; liberal; natural; recognized; crestfallen; typical; supreme.

verbs
adhere to—; distinguish—; emulate—; engage—; flock to—; gather 'round—; pattern on—; rally 'round—; support—; trust—; —arises; —commands; —conducts; —controls; —directs; —fires; —guides; —harangues; —influences; —marshals; —pilots; —presides; —unites; —voices.

(See minister, clergyman, boss, manager, official.)

LEADERSHIP

adjectives
lamentable; vital; accepted; inspired; vigorous; skillful; unchallenged; fashion; undisputed; intelligent; consummate; compensating; careful; aggressive; heroic; daring; recognized; judicious; palsied.

verbs
anticipate—; assume—; commend—; compete for—; crave—; favor—of; follow—; flourish under—; grant—to; offer—; overthrow—; prosper under—of; recognize—; rely on—; require—; settle—; stress—; strive for—; succeed to—; sustain—; trust to—; yield to—.

(See command, direction, guidance, protection, patronage.)

LEAF

adjectives
dancing; folded; garrulous; delicate; weary; laurel; latest; rueful; retuse;

voluminous; withered; minutest; rustling; medicinal; sleeping; braided; tender; plaited; glossy; primordial; peopled; drifted; vibrant; blushing; flattering; needlelike; drooping; notched; lanceolate; stirring; succulent; heedless.

LEAFAGE

adjectives
rustling; spreading; luxuriant.

LEAGUE

adjectives
united; endless; weary; hostile; moribund; nuptial; immeasurable; remarkable; unconscious; stormy.

verbs
ally with—; appeal to—; associate with—; band into—; crack—; criticize—; enter—; excite—; join—; renounce—; resuscitate—; —assists; —confers on; —defends; —safeguards; —sanctions; —shelters; —threatens; —unites.
(See society, club, organization, union, association.)

LEAGUE (v)

adverbs
inseparably; nuptially; protectively; firmly; perpetually.
(See combine, unite, associate.)

LEAK

verbs
block—; bare—; choke—; dam—; detect—; drill—; indicate—; master—; plug—; repair—; riddle with—s; seal—; spring—; —drains; —frightens; —gapes; —sinks; —weakens; —yawns.
(See hole, gap, flow.)

LEAKY

adverbs
dangerously; intentionally; slightly; unconscionably; uselessly; inconsequentially; suspiciously; mysteriously; ominously; treacherously; apparently; wastefully; terribly; unfortunately; miserably; extremely; fearfully; increasingly; wretchedly.

LEAN (v)

adverbs
slumberously; placidly; mechanically; gracefully; slantingly; wearily; impulsively; perilously; listlessly; indolently; dizzily; confidentially.
(See incline, recline, slope, tend, depend.)

LEAP

adjectives
imperious; breezy; astonishing; demoniacal; sudden; flying; rash; concealed; vigorous; mortal; quick; tremendous; horrid; queer; bold; gathered.

verbs
admire—; attempt—; calculate—; complete—; dare—; endeavor—; observe—; perfect—; practice—; rebound from—; record—; venture—; —amazes; —awes; —impresses.
(See feat.)

LEAP (v)

adverbs
lissomely; simultaneously; blithely; surefootedly; frolicsomely; nimbly; spryly; boisterously; perilously; demoniacally; boldly; vigorously; swiftly; agilely.
(See jump, spring, bound.)

LEARN (v)

adverbs
aptly; brilliantly; instinctively; normally; precociously; scientifically; pedagogically.
(See acquire, attain, master, obtain.)

LEARNER

adjectives
incipient; reputed; polite; awkward; brilliant.

LEARNING

adjectives
typical; harsh; crabbed; abstruse; unorganized; worldly; barren; superficial; serviceable; detrimental; optimistic; polite; philosophic; higher; extensive; carnal; varied; introvertive; inconsiderable; subtle; radiant; classical; supposed.

verbs
consume—; digest—; drink in—; feed on—; foster—; impart—; lack—; overestimate—; revive—; shun—; stamp out—; swallow—; test—; underestimate—; value—; wonder at—; —crowns; —discerns; —enlightens; —flourishes; —intoxicates; —penetrates; —polishes; —serves; —shines; —sobers; —speeds; —upbraids.
(See knowledge, wisdom, facts, information, understanding.)

LEASE

verbs
approve—; cancel—; comply with—; de-

mand—; enjoy—; gain—; grant—; ignore —; nullify—; obtain—; renew—; study—; terminate—; violate—; —expires; —guarantees; —protects; —runs out; —satisfies; extend—.

(See contract, pact, treaty, promise, agreement.)

LEASH

verbs

attach—; drag on—; exert—; hunt on—; lug on—; ply—; pull at—; secure with—; slip—; strain—; tow on—; tug at—; —confines; —controls; —restrains; —restricts; —yields; draw in—.

(See chain, strap, cord, string.)

LEATHER

adjectives

superlative; bronzed; well-oiled; sumptuous; dusty.

verbs

bind in—; bleach—; buff—; coat—; convert into—; damage—; dip—; drum—; paddle —; pickle—; roll—; shave—; soak—; spray —; stretch—; tan—; treat—; trim—; —creaks; —discolors; —preserves.

(See cotton, cloth, wool.)

LEATHERY

adverbs

darkly; stubbily; sturdily; sallowly; grubbily; robustly; pleasantly; vigorously; unbelievably; dilapidatedly; increasingly; oddly; quaintly; fantastically; grotesquely; uncommonly; remarkably; noticeably; conspicuously.

LEAVE

adjectives

tedious; gracious; affectionate; ceremonious; sick; instant.

LEAVE (v)

adverbs

unceremoniously; inadvertently; incautiously; judiciously; unwittingly; politely; diplomatically; reluctantly; prudently; voluntarily; affectionately; ultimately; irrevocably.

(See depart, retire, start.)

LEAVES

adjectives

tender; dank; trembling; unstirring; murmuring; myriad; aromatic; cordial; soggy; shifting; shivering; shimmering; frosted; glittering; withered; dewy; arching; glossy; listening; rustling; crumpled; brilliant; interlaced; ripened; dentated; glistering; crystal; frost-crisped; close-shut; pounded; suspended; motionless; pendant; lusty; sere; implicated; delicate; clustering; scented; amorous; soft; silken; summer; verdant; healing; fading; painted; falling; crowded; velvet; rejected; sweet; barren; yellowing; crimson; brazen; lapping; shining; russet; serrated; fingery; languid; twinkling; silent; retuse; dying; drifted; mantling; blanched; steaming; sweeping; wind-tossed; flaming; tiny; soiled; age-worn; vellum; tremulous; hardy; gay; autumn; burning; polished; dark; copious; mottled; sweet-fern; wintry; fanlike; agitated; coarse; grasslike; lucent; twining; fair; false; bruised; remembered; swarth; sodden; porcelain; unwritten; many-tinted; beauteous; drooping; wild; somber; parti-colored; joyous.

verbs

bedew—; decorate with—; flush—; gather —; scatter—; shed—; sprout—; thatch with —; tinge—; —blazon; —blend; —drift down; —droop; —float down; —flutter; —mat; —overspread; —quiver; —redden; —rustle; —shade; —shower down; —swirl; —tremble; —unfold; —wave; —whisper; —wilt; —wither.

(See foliage, plant.)

LECTURE

adjectives

edifying; inaugural; compulsory; scientific; interminable; wide-spread; celebrated; didactic; boring; ill-attended.

verbs

assimilate—; attend—; concoct—; deliver —; instruct by—; preach—; profit by—; temper—; —admonishes; —asserts; —assists; —attracts; —confounds; —interests; —perplexes; —rebukes; —reprimands; —reproaches; —stirs; —uplifts.

(See lesson, speech, address, narration, narrative; oration.)

LECTURE (v)

adverbs

tediously; graphically; eruditely; vividly; edifyingly; scientifically; interminably; didactically; boringly; inspiringly; inspirationally; eloquently.

(See address, discourse, speak.)

LEDGE

adjectives
shaven; dangerous-looking; slippery; narrow; pine-clad; overhanging; rocky; dirty-backed; solid; basalt; shaded; craggy; projecting; bare; inaccessible; shelving.

verbs
clamber up—; cleave to—; cling from—; hover on—; hug—; lean from—; peer over —; pitch from—; scale—; teeter on—; totter on—; tumble from—; —gives way; —juts; —projects; —protrudes.
(See edge, ridge, shelf, reef.)

LEECH

verbs
apply—; breed—es; employ—; fatten—; —absorbs; —adheres; —bleeds; —clings; —cures; —draws; —evacuates; —extracts; —heals; —relieves; —remedies; —sticks; —sucks.
(See parasite, physician, doctor.)

LEER

adjectives
impudent; jealous; complacent; silly; half-triumphant; roguish; fawning; malignant.

LEER (*v*)

adverbs
obscenely; idiotically; spitefully; impudently; murderously; despicably; sardonically; jealously; complacently; malignantly; fawningly; roguishly.
(See look, sneer, glance, stare.)

LEERY

adverbs
slightly; altogether; artfully; cunningly; trickily; warily; guardedly; cleverly; suspiciously; diplomatically; strategically; cautiously; prudently; deliberately; discreetly; coolly; habitually; cannily; charily; politically; vigilantly; dependably; uncommonly; carefully.

LEG

adjectives
excellent; bowed; rickety; timber; gouty; graceful; sturdy; bandy; lower; convulsed; stockinged; shapely; long; fluted; sinewy; brawny; spindle; incased; thin; shivering; toothsome; amputated; thread-like; leaden; muscular; bony; pitiful; tiny; slender; knotted; hacked; jagged; hairy; gaitered; lovely; graceful; bulging; slim.

verbs
admire—; bow—s; brace—; condition—s; elevate—; expose—; fetter—s; fracture—; massage—; peer at—s; reel on—s; reveal —; straddle with—s; strengthen—; trust —s; —s entwine; —s fly; —protrudes; —s sag; —supports; —s taper; —s twitch; —s weary.
(See foot, knee.)

LEGACY

adjectives
supplemented; limited; personal; precious; unexpected; hereditary.

verbs
administer—; allocate—; anticipate—; bequeath—; contemplate—; court—; deprive of—; direct—; envy—; fritter away—; grant—; inherit—; parcel—; partition—; provide—; reckon—; —dwindles; —enriches.
(See estate, property, money, wealth, inheritance, resources.)

LEGAL

adverbs
entirely; incontrovertibly; admittedly; unquestionably; allowably; authoritatively; duly; prescriptively; warrantably; presumptively; absolutely; unimpeachably; equitably; constitutionally; properly; securely.

LEGEND

adjectives
fearful; golden; traditionary; fanciful; facile; splenetic; heroic; marvelous; primeval; shadowy; serviceable; diffused; epic; fading; picturesque; contemporary; medieval; confusing; profane; puissant; fictitious; interminable; conventional.

verbs
blast—; carry on—; confute—; demolish—; destroy—; detach from—; discard—; dispel —; dispose of—; embroider—; emerge from —; exploit—; extenuate—; interpolate—; lampoon—; perpetuate—; peruse—; —attests to; —grows from; —persists; —portrays.
(See story, tale, myth, lie, narrative.)

LEGENDARY

adverbs
wholly; vestigially; acceptably; admittedly; daringly; inventively; romantically; fanci-

fully; ingeniously; purportedly; theoretically; notionally; fairly; authentically; presumably; doubtfully; probably; highly; vaporously; heroically; picturesquely; pleasantly.

LEGIBILITY

verbs
admire—; appreciate—; approve—; commend—; demand—; desire—; emblazon—; esteem—; extol—; heighten—; increase—; praise—; prize—; regard—; recommend—; value—.

LEGIBLE

adverbs
clearly; perfectly; gratifyingly; pleasantly; crudely; altogether; neatly; plainly; easily; distinctly; definitely; precisely; graphically; unmistakenly; scrawlingly; hieroglyphically; eventually; pleasingly; extremely; immediately; satisfactorily.

LEGION

adjectives
gallant; ragged; puissant; well-disciplined; iron-breasted; scouring; locust; swarthy; victorious; invincible.

verbs
array in—; assemble—; decimate—; direct —; fill with—s; follow—; gather—; overthrow—; secure—; sustain—; unite in—; —congregates; —defends; —drifts; —engages; —flocks; —participates; —serves; —strives.

(See army, crowd, association, enemy.)

LEGISLATE (*v*)

adverbs
precipitately; shrewdly; beneficently; malignantly; oppressively; economically; socially; constitutionally; perniciously; ecclesiastically; appropriately; arbitrarily; unscrupulously.

(See effect, enact.)

LEGISLATION

adjectives
oppressive; economic; sumptuary; social; preferential; intemperate; critical; unconstitutional; pernicious; injurious; ecclesiastical; educational; dangerous; absolute; remedial; appropriate; defunct; amendatory; arbitrary; refined; adverse; unscrupulous; undesirable; vindictive; class.

verbs
acclaim—; admire—; broaden—; enact—; enforce—; influence—; invalidate—; jam—through; lobby for—; motion for—; pile up —; propose—; sanction—; schedule—; sponsor—; stifle—; strangle—; sustain—; urge —; veto—.

(See law, bill, statute, ordinance, regulation.)

LEGISLATIVE

adverbs
augustly; imposingly; strictly; exclusively; oppressively; coolly; impersonally; absolutely; scrupulously; impartially; finally; irrevocably; wisely; providentially.

LEGISLATOR

verbs
criticize—; elect—; invest—with; nominate —; —attempts; —authorizes; —s convene; —deliberates; —devises; —interprets; —judges; —moves; —proposes; —propounds; —serves.

(See congressman, senator, politician, statesman.)

LEGISLATURE

verbs
appoint to—; nominate for—; recommend to—; —affirms; —appropriates; —confirms; —defeats; —deliberates; —dismisses; —enacts; —frames; —overrules; —passes; —propounds; —reveals; —revokes; —suspends; —congregates; —convenes.

(See congress, parliament, legislator, government.)

LEGITIMATE

adverbs
wholly; unquestionably; substantially; plainly; unqualifiedly; unimpeachably; authoritatively; authentically; genuinely; verily; allowably; unconditionally; justly; absolutely; duly; properly; completely; rightly.

LEISURE

adjectives
scant; elegant; extreme; endowed; practicable; sour; patient; graceful; multitudinous; everlasting; abundant; fallow; infinite; precious; tranquil; unbroken; spiritual; ample; dignified; literary; sufficient; unholy; superfluous; holiday; dilettante; calm; machine-created; wasted.

verbs
bankrupt of—; beautify—; burden with—; court—; devote—to; discipline—; dispense with—; employ—; enjoy—; fill—; indulge at —; occupy—; pursue at—; rejoice in—; retire into—; revel in—; reward with—; steal —; wallow in—; weary of—; —civilizes; —delights; —enriches; —entombs; —polishes.
(See time.)

LEMON

verbs
bear—s; box—s; crate—s; cultivate—; express from—; extract from—; flavor with —; gather—s; harvest—s; pack—s; peel—; pickle in—; pierce—; scent with—; ship—s; sort—s; squeeze—; wrap—; —clings; —puckers; —ripens.
(See fruit.)

LEND (*v*)

adverbs
grudgingly; conveniently; conditionally; gracefully; innocently; legitimately; unscrupulously; willingly; gratuitously.
(See accommodate, assist, furnish.)

LENDER

adjectives
legitimate; money; licensed; unscrupulous.

LENGTH

adjectives
learned; barbarous; apparent; extortionate; manlier; abbreviated; intolerable; variable; irregular; average; ludicrous; unaltered; extreme; considerable; unconscionable; enormous; interminable; majestic; pellucid; lamentable; shameful; immoderate; standard; ancient; unwieldy; startling; weary; apportioned; slender; infinite; wondrous; measured; treacherous; vine-clad.

LENGTHEN (*v*)

adverbs
indefinitely; ludicrously; unconscionably; interminably; immoderately; infinitely; disproportionately.
(See extend, stretch.)

LENGTHY

adverbs
interminably; intolerably; tiresomely; monotonously; unbelievably; endlessly; ramblingly; reminiscently; diffusely; effusively; wretchedly; miserably; wearisomely; unconscionably; ludicrously; sadly; terribly; shamefully; incredibly; inexcusably.

LENIENT

adverbs
habitually; conveniently; indulgently; affectionately; spasmodically; considerately; mercifully; courteously; hospitably; graciously; weakly; supinely; deliberately; gently; calmly; absent-mindedly; nervously; pacifically; reasonably; blandly; purposely; lamentably; unduly; wisely; helpfully; disgustingly; feebly; temperately; tolerantly; complaisantly; compassionately; humanely; exceedingly.

LENITY

adjectives
half-contemptuous; half-calculated; sufficient; vaunted; customary; assumed; apparent.

LENS

adjectives
immense; photographic; concave; shadowy; convex; powerful.

LEOPARD

verbs
bag—; creep up on—; ensnare—; infest with—s; skin—; trap—; —attacks; —barks; —charges; —claws; —climbs; —depredates; —devours; —drags off; —lies in ambush; —pounces; —preys on; —pulls down; —rages; —roars; —screams; —seizes; —slaughters; —slinks; —springs; —stalks; —steals upon; —wails; —infests.
(See animal, lion, tiger.)

LEPER

verbs
ban—; bar—; cleanse—; cure—; heal—; incarcerate—; isolate—; purge—; quarantine—; restore—; segregate—; shelter—; —befouls; —begs; —contaminates; —defiles; —infects; —stigmatizes; —suffers; —taints,
(See beggar, invalid, parasite.)

LEPROUS

adverbs
fatally; tragically; horribly; unfortunately; miserably; wretchedly; infirmly; incurably; pitiably; morally; mortally; indubitably; dreadfully.

LESION

adjectives
local; organic; mechanical; healed.

LESSEN (*v*)

adverbs
abnormally; scientifically; beneficially; mechanically; gradually; agreeably; appreciably.
(See diminish, reduce, decrease.)

LESSON

adjectives
crowning; salutary; rude; strategical; humiliating; valuable; distasteful; sacred; deathless; wholesome; exemplary; object; copious; pioneer; curious; striking; stern; impressive; instructive; ethical; important; nobler; outstanding; painful; baneful; tremendous; fruitful; needful; hard; silent.

verbs
assign—; deliver—; experience—; expound —; imply—; inculcate—; instill—; memorize—; preach—; project—; rebel at—; recite—; spice—; yield—; —penetrates; —rebukes; —reprimands; —sinks in.
(See lecture, talk, speech, moral.)

LETHARGY

adjectives
intellectual; torpid; icy; blind; pleasant; patriarchal; complete; apparent; inglorious; passive; utter.

verbs
arouse from—; breed—; descend into—; fade into—; fall into—; fix in—; lie in—; lift from—; mumble in—; overcome—; —attacks; —blinds; —chokes; —envelops; —hinders; —paralyzes; —restrains; —seduces; —seizes; —stupefies.
(See languor, weariness, fatigue, exhaustion, lassitude.)

LETTER

adjectives
rare; deprecatory; terrible; much-discussed; anonymous; unfeeling; complimentary; entertaining; amusing; exhaustive; innumerable; confidential; charming; loathsome; vitriolic; insolent; threatening; overbearing; pensive; seditious; amiable; commendatory; pitiful; subjoined; promised; obliging; impassioned; strange; incoherent; obscure; incomprehensible; bulky; pattern; civil; simple-minded; subsequent; obnoxious; elementary; discursive; nonsensical; dead; unfriendly; repentant; passionate; adulatory; indiscreet; ill-spelled; runic; affectionate; shameful; orderly; menacing; luminous; feigned; curt; immediate; interminable; pithy; gilt; full; convincing; esteemed; accusing; interesting; specific; deep-cut; reprehensive; pastoral; brief; terse; condensed; emphatic; exculpatory; beautiful; eloquent; touching; conspicuous; good; unjust; delicious; sweet; patient; wise; tender; painful; abusive; round-robin; often-recurring; chance-preserved; introductory; burning; generous; handsome; mystical; explanatory; racy; exquisite; slanderous; ill-written; libelous; crafty; brusque; unsound; stilted; pleading; naive; denunciatory; easy-flowing; inevitable; long; reproachful; sparkling; enigmatical; depressing; assisting; condemnatory; faded; fatal; clandestine; ridiculous; agreeable; hasty; impudent; enthusiastic; unauthenticated; taunting; dedicatory; chatty; kindhearted; cheery; journalistic; happy; timely; conclusive; effective; admonitory; indignant; spiteful; pathetic; dainty; memorable; sad; begging; witty; misguiding; resounding; fascinating; inquisitive; occasional; compromising; laconic; needless; unfinished; genuine; obedient.

verbs
append to—; bear—; besiege with—s; bombard with—s; censor—; communicate by—; convey—; deluge with—s; devise—; devour —; dictate—; frame—; peruse—; post—; scribble—; seal—; skim through—; speed—; suppress—; welcome—; —acquaints; —assures; —breathes; —cheers; —commends; —commissions; —consoles; —conveys; —expatiates; —gushes; —imparts; —links; —s pour in; —reveals; —unites.
(See communication, note, correspondence, message, telegram.)

LEVEL

adjectives
portentous; maintenance; conversational; unlovely; vulgar; conciliating; preeminent; remunerative; childish; artistic; unending; windy; desirable; reflecting; usual; varying; harmless; unmeaning; humdrum; common; ordinary.

verbs
attain—; defile—; degrade to—; destroy—; discover—; drain—; elevate to—; find—;

gain—; hold—; jump to—; lie within—; maintain—; mark—; preserve—; raise above—; reduce to—; regress to—; sink to —.

(See height, depth, altitude, summit, mark.)

adverbs
meticulously; exactly; monotonously; conveniently; smoothly; endlessly; uniformly; tiresomely; changelessly; drearily; continuously; symmetrically; roughly; unevenly; ruggedly; fairly.

LEVER

verbs
adjust—; apply—; brace—; heave out with —; jack with—; manipulate—; yank (colloq.)—; —disembowels; —dislodges; —elevates; —expels; —lifts; —overthrows; —pries open; —raises.

(See handle, bar.)

LEVITY

adjectives
incorrigible; enervate; uncanonical; responsive; unpardonable; superficial; dreadful; careless; shameful; bitter; exquisite; undesirable; foolish; unnecessary; unbecoming; surface.

LEVY

adjectives
forced; undisciplined; successive (pl).

LEWD

adverbs
ribaldly; boisterously; inexcusably; gustily; evilly; immodestly; shamelessly; wantonly; habitually; inexplicably; unaccountably; unwarrantably; hilariously; terribly; ostentatiously; unscrupulously; crudely.

LIABILITY

verbs
account for—; admit—; burden with—; clog with—; confess—; display—; exempt from —; free from—; impose—; limit—; load with—; meet—; relieve of—; saddle with —; shoulder—s; —cramps; —deters; —disheartens; —hampers; —impedes; —imposes; —obligates; —oppresses; —shackles; —weighs.

(See trouble, responsibility, misfortune, reverse, debt, obligation.)

LIABLE

adverbs
criminally; undeniably; unfortunately; financially; morally; legally; unhappily; fatally; inescapably; inevitably; embarrassingly; deeply; inconveniently; properly; ethically; prescriptively.

LIAR

adjectives
congenial; false-hearted; designing; monstrous; virtuous; probable; political; prophesying; beneficent; notorious; endless; generous.

verbs
accuse—; avoid—; condemn—; criticize—; despise—; judge—; punish—; reprimand—; reproach—; shame—; spurn—; support—; —beguiles; —blinds; —contrives; —convinces; —deceives; —devises; —forges; —fumbles; —invents; —libels; —raves; —relates; —slanders; —stabs; —violates.

(See criminal robber, thief, hypocrite, quack.)

LIBATION

adjectives
wonted; copious; devout.

LIBEL

adjectives
infamous; poisonous; criminal; seditious; scandalous; outrageous; intentional; anonymous; atrocious.

verbs
accuse of—; contradict—; convict of—; denounce—; disprove—; forge—; incur—; institute—; introduce—; oppose—; publish—; rebut—; serve—; sue for—; —accuses; —alleges; —assails; —charges; —declares; —defames; —discredits; —implies; —slanders.

(See slander, rumor.)

LIBERAL

adverbs
naturally; habitually; generally; always; extremely; charitably; considerately; lavishly; thoughtfully; ostentatiously; grudgingly; calculatingly; carelessly; unwarrantably; improvidently; moderately; bountifully; generously; munificently; handsomely; unwisely; unselfishly; thoroughly; unfailingly; dependably.

LIBERALISM

adjectives
militant; enlightened; extreme; journalistic.

verbs
absorb—; adopt—; advocate—; convert to —; criticize—; crusade for—; cultivate—; endanger—; exercise—; inculcate—; interpret—; plant—; plead for—; restrain—; scorn—; stifle—; stimulate—; unite in—; weaken—; —affords; —aims at; —emerges from; —involves; —prevails; —thrives.

(See democracy, freedom, socialism, communism, movement.)

LIBERALITY

adjectives
unstinted; decent; unbounded; mutual; enlarged; patriotic.

LIBERATE (v)

adverbs
promptly; magnanimously; industrially; philosophically; politically; temporarily; economically; nobly; rationally; partially; subversively.

(See free, release, deliver.)

LIBERTY

adjectives
elemental; unwarrantable; glorious; philosophical; wild; popular; hard; political; natural; temporary; unrestrained; sanctioned; economic; industrial; religious; ignoble; pagan; secure; atheistic; unequalled; unbridled; headstrong; false; stormy; intermittent; universal; rational; partial; subversive; adored; masculine; excessive; perfect; lyric; dearly-bought.

verbs
abdicate—; champion—; concede—; confiscate—; conspire against—; defend—; deprive of—; encroach upon—; enjoy—; forsake—; grant—; imperil—; infringe upon —; invade—; jeopardize—; maintain—; prate of—; purchase—; sacrifice—; scorn —; sequester—; shackle—; spurn—; suppress—; suspend—; taint—; threaten—; violate—; —crumbles; —perishes; —vanishes.

(See rights, freedom, privilege, independence.)

LIBRARY

adjectives
provincial; extensive; circulating; immense; somber; reference; astronomical; valuable; comprehensive; well-balanced; technical.

verbs
bequeath to—; browse in—; bury in—; cherish—; confine to—; drink from—; endow—; enrich—; establish—; labor in—; refer to—; repose in—; resort to—; revel in—; shelve in—; subscribe to—; —circulates; —collects; —entombs; —feeds; —fines; —lends; —nourishes; —preserves; —records; —safeguards; —stores.

(See book, literature.)

LIBRETTOS

adjectives
innocuous; unappealing; poetical; complete.

LICENSE

adjectives
passionate; poetic; uncontrolled; mocking; wanton; warrantable; unpunished; unchecked; transport; boldest; amplest; unbridled; graceful; roving; ignoble; extraordinary; democratic; driving; vending.

verbs
abuse—; acknowledge—; concede—; deny —; display—; draw—; enjoy—; forge—; grant—; inspect—; obtain—; observe—; practise under—; require—; revoke—; withdraw—; —authorizes; —permits; —protects; —vouches.

(See right, privilege.)

LICENSE (v)

adverbs
legally; medically; authoritatively; officially; nominally; wantonly; properly.

(See permit, authorize.)

LICENTIOUS

adverbs
unwarrantably; riotously; ungovernably; dissolutely; wickedly; despicably; contemptibly; terribly; disgustingly; viciously; unimaginably; dreadfully; unexpectedly; villainously; wildly; rakishly; deplorably; lamentably; unforgivably.

LICENTIOUSNESS

adjectives
unbridled; evil; uncurbed; repeated.

verbs
campaign against—; check—; curb—; defend—; denounce—; explode—; harbor—;

impute to—; inflict—upon; regret—; taste —; tolerate—; tumble into—; witness—; —irks; —occurs; —offends; —prevails; —reigns; —vexes.

(See wickedness, vice, sin.)

LID

adjectives

just-raised; placid; translucent; drooping; long; sly; flaming; veinous; opaque; blue-veined; drowsy; flower-soft; fringed; unsullied; squinted; lower; eternal; coarse; triangular-shaped; low; wrinkled; conscious; timorous; heavy.

verbs

clamp—on; clap—on; fit—; force—; overlay—; plant—on; pry—off; seal—; tap—; tighten—; —conceals; —preserves; —prevents; —protects; —resists; —restrains; —screens; —yields to.

(See cover, canopy.)

LIE

adjectives

glittering; vicious; monkey-faced; vivid; spectral; glib; painted; plausible; sin-born; wanton; endless; improbable; consoling; intolerable; libelous; deadliest; drowsing; diplomatic; ungentlemanly; organized; conventional; filthy; original; convincing; blaspheming; preposterous; gracious; sustained; surpliced; costly; pious; calm; quaint; shameless; damnable; dumb; helpless; glorious; puny; rotten; absurd; magnificent; unnumbered; iniquitous; measured; poisonous; deliberate; purchased.

verbs

acknowledge—; censure—; condemn—; condone—; confess to—; decry—; detect—; evolve—; promulgate—; propagate—; reject—; rend—; reveal—; spill—s; uncover —; utter—; —blackens; —cheats; —cloaks; —defrauds; —dishonors; —falsifies; —fetters; —frees; —perplexes; —swindles.

(See crime, statement, falsehood, misrepresentation.)

LIE (v)

adverbs

nervelessly; slothfully; smoothly; perversely; atrociously; malignly; glibly; supinely; profusely; portentously; outrageously; mutely; composedly; plausibly; wantonly; libelously; preposterously; shamelessly; iniquitously.

(See fabricate, misrepresent.)

LIEUTENANT

adjectives

lion-hearted; self-important; selected.

LIFE

adjectives

abhorred; abject; abnormal; abstract; aboriginal; abundant; academic; active; action-craving; affluent; agonized; agreeable; agricultural; all-embracing; altruistic; amazing; ambrosial; angelic; antecedent; antenatal; artificial; ascetic; astonished; austere; bad; beneficent; benevolent; blameless; blithe; blooming; boulevard; bountiful; bright-eyed; broad; broken; brute; bubbling; buoyant; busy; bygone; bird-cage; cankerous; carefree; careful; changing; charmed; civic; civilized; cloistral; cold-blooded; collective; college; colorful; commercial; commonplace; communal; concentrated; consistent; constant; contemplative; contemporary; contemptuous; convenient; convulsive; cordial; corporate; cosmic; country; crescent; cruel; crystal; cultivated; cultured; darkened; darkling; darting; deadening; decorous; deep-bosomed; defaced; delightful; democratic; demonstrable; deplorable; desultory; devouring; diffusive; diminished; diplomatic; disastrous; discontented; disfigured; dishonored; disjointed; disposed; dissipated; dissolute; distasteful; distracted; dividing; double; domestic; doubtful; dull; dusky; dutiful; easy-going; eccentric; economic; effete; effective; effeminate; elemental; emancipated; embittered; emotional; enlarging; ennobling; ephemeral; equal; erotic; equivocal; essential; eternal; eventful; existing; exotic; expanding; external; extinguished; exuberant; exultant; factitious; familiar; farcical; farmyard; fascinating; fashionable; fast-fleeing; fast-withering; fettered; feudal; feverish; fictionized; flabby; flickering; floating; flourishing; foreign; fragrant; free; friendless; frisking; frivolous; frugal; fruitful; fugitive; fullest; genuine; gushing; grimy; groovelike; gypsy; half-revealed; hapless; hard-working; harmless; healthful; helpful; hideous; hoary; high-pressure; homely; honest; human; humdrum; hygienic; ideal; idyllic; imagined; imaginative; immortal; impatient; impeccable; imperfect; imperiled; imperishable; impish; incarnate; increasing; independent; individual; indulgent; industrious; infantile; informal; inglorious; inherent; inner; innermost; insect; unsociable; integrated; intellectual; intense; interior; intimate; irresponsible; irregular; joyless; kindly; knowable; laborious; large; licentious; lifeless; liquid; listless; literary; livable; loathed; long; low; lush; lusterless; luxurious; magnanimous; many-sided; married; material; maximum; meditative; melancholy; mental; meteoric; middle-married; milder; millennial; mingled; mirthful; miserable; modest; monastic; monotonous; moral; mortal; moving; multitudinous (pl); mythological; namby-pamby; nervous; nobler; nomadic; objectless; obscure; old-maidish; ordinary; orgiastic; outer; out-of-town; outside; paltry; palpitating; pampered; parasitic; parental; peaceful; perilous; permeating; perverted; phenomenal; pioneer; plausible; pleasant; plenteous; practical; precarious; prevailing; priceless; private; progressive; prosperous; prosaic; provincial; prudent; pseudo-social; psychical; public; pulsating; pulseless; pure; quickening; radical; rampant; realistic; redundant; regular; rejuvenated; reproductive; renovated; restive; restless; retired; revolutionary; rhythmical; rollicking; rough; roving; ruddy; rural; sacred; sacrificial; scandalous; scanty; secluded; secret; secular; sedentary; sensuous; sequestered; serene; sheltered; shifting; shudderable; simpering; simple; singing; single; skilful; sky-wedded; sleeping; slow-moving; sluggish; smiling; smug; snug; sobered; social; solitary; sophisticated; spiritual; spontaneous; sportive; starved; steady; sterile; stimulating; straggling; strenuous; studious; subsequent; sunless; sunlit; supersensual; sustaining; sweet; swinish; tangled; temperate; tempestuous; tender; terrestrial; thin-spun; thoughtless; thwarted; toilsome; torpid; tortured; tragic; tramping; tree; trite; troubled; tumultuous; turbulent; tyrant; unambitious; unassuming; unbearable; unceasing; unchanging; unconventional; uncircumscribed; undeniable; unendurable; undistinguished; uneventful; unjaded; unprofitable; unprosperous; unrealized; unresisting; unsatisfactory; unseen; unseparable; unsettled; unsightly; unsophisticated; unstable; upright; useful; urban; various (pl); vagrant; vicious; veritable; vigorous; vile; virtuous; wagering; wandering; warm; wasted; wayside; wayward; well-lost; wholesome; wild; winged; wistful; womanly; wonted; workless; worldly; worthless; worthy; wretched; youthful; action-filled; adequate; adventurous.

verbs

abbreviate—; alter—; bare—of; beautify —; blight—; blot out—; burst into—; carve —; challenge—; cling to—; commence—; comprehend—; conceive—; consecrate—to; cope with—; dedicate—to; degrade—; delve into—; depict—; deplete—; detach from—; devote—to; devour—; disorganize—; dissipate—; diversify—; drag out—; drain of—; embitter—; endanger—; endow with —; enhance—; ennoble—; equip for—; erase—; exemplify—; face—; flash into—; flinch from—; foreshorten—; foster—; fritter—away; galvanize into—; gamble—on; immerse in—; insulate against—; intercede for—; interpret—; intrude upon—; invade—; isolate—; jeopardize—; maim—; maintain—; manifest—; mar—; mend—; mock—; mold—; muddle through—; nourish—; oppress by—; pay with—; permeate —; plunge into—; portray—; probe—; prolong—; race through—; radiate—; rebuild —; reconstruct—; rekindle—; resuscitate —; retire from—; revel in—; routinize—; shock into—; skim through—; snuff out—; squander—; stake—on; submerge—; sum up —; sustain—; taste—; terminate—; thirst for—; tranquilize—; trifle away—; uplift —; vitiate—; warp—; weigh—; —blossoms; —buzzes by; —disintegrates; —ebbs; —evolves; —flowers; —flows; —hangs; ——s intertwine; —persists; —pulsates; —quickens; —rallies; —surges; —trudges on; —unfolds; —withers.

(See career, existence.)

LIFELESS

adverbs

dully; inactively; languidly; inertly; lazily; idly; torpidly; quiescently; silently; actually; heavily; passively; sluggishly; unusually.

LIFETIME

verbs

concentrate in—; curtain—; devote—to; endure—; fill—; guide through—; pledge—; pour into—; record—; seek—; spend—; spin —; strive—; stumble through—; terminate —; withstand—; wrap in—; —grinds; —slides by; —wearies.

(See time, age, century.)

LIFT (*v*)

adverbs
momentarily; stalwartly; vigorously; feebly; reverently; instinctively; responsively; daintily; involuntarily; alertly; simultaneously; perceptibly; stealthily.
(See elevate, raise, support.)

LIGAMENT

verbs
rupture—; sever—; strain—; strengthen—; stretch—; suture—; tear—; tie—; treat—; —attaches; —binds; —connects; —couples; —extends; —fastens; —joins; —reinforces; —supports; —unites.
(See muscle, cord, tie, bond.)

LIGATURE

verbs
apply—; —arrests; —binds; —checks; —clamps; —collapses; —compresses; —constricts; —contracts; —curbs; —heals; —remedies; —restrains; —squeezes; —stems; —strangulates.
(See bandage, tape.)

LIGHT

adjectives
accusing; adequate; advancing; all-beholden; all-surprising; altering; amber; ample; amusing; angelic; angry; approaching; arrowy; artificial; ashy; attractive; auroral; austral; available; baleful; beacon; becoming; bewildering; blinding; blinking; blissful; blithe; burning; borrowed; bright; broken; brutal; calm; celestial; center; chalky; changeless; chastening; chatoyant; cheering; clear; cloudless; collateral; comforting; confused; congealed; contrasting; cool; coppery; coruscating; crystal; curious; dancing; danger-dissipating; dark; dawning; dazzling; day; deadly; deceitful; deceptive; deep; defiant; delusive; departing; despairing; despondent; dewy; dim; diaphanous; diffused; dirty; discernible; disheveled; distant; distressing; divine; doubtful; dreadful; dreamy; dry; dusky; dying; earliest; effulgent; elfin; enlivening; enkindling; emerging; emitting; erroneous; emotional; eternal; evening; everlasting; evermoving; factitious; fading; faint; fair; falling; fanning; feeble; featureless; filtered; fitful; flaming; flaring; flash; flashing; flighty; fluctuating; fluttering; fuller; garish; gas; gentle; ghastlier; ghostly; gladsome; glancing; glaring; glazed; gleaming; gleamy; glimmering; glorious; glowing; gradual; hallowed; hard; harnessed; harsh; hateful; hazy; heavenly; holy; hovering; illimitable; immortal; imperfect; inaudible; incandescent; indefinite; indistinct; ineffable; inexorable; influential; inner; innumerable (pl); inquisitive; insolent; intellectual; interfused; internal; intrinsic; inward; irreligious; joyous; laborious; leaning; legendary; lessening; lesser; liquid; literary; livid; lofty; lonelier; lovely; luminous; lunar; lurid; malicious; marquee; melancholy; mellow; melting; meridian; meteor; midday; mingling; ministering; minute; mobile; momentary; morning; mourning; murderous; murky; myriad (pl); mysterious; naked; native; nebulous; nocturnal; northern; obscured; odor-giving; opalescent; opposing; patient; pecuniary; peerless; perpetual; petulant; phantasmal; phantom; phosphorescent; piercing; pitiless; planetary; poisoned; political; primogenital; prismatic; propitious; pure; purging; quivering; rackless; rational; ravishing; reflected; remoter; restored; returning; revealing; rising; roseate; rough; ruddy; rush; rushing; sanctioned; sanguine; satisfactory; sacred; scattered (pl); serious; sectarian; serene; sevenfold; shaping; shadowing; shifting; shimmering; shining; shrouded; sickly; slanting; smoky; smothered; soft; solar; solitary; sparkling; stagnant; starry; steady; steely; straggling; streaming; strengthened; subtle; sudden; suffering; sullen; sulphurous; summer; sunset; swimming; tempered; tender; terrific; time-wasting; timid; transmitted; transparent; tremulous; trembling; uncanny; unaccustomed; unapproached; twinkling; uncertain; unclouded; uncreated; undivided; undoubted; undulating; undying; unenvied; unfading; unfavorable; unnatural; unpitying; unsettled; unshadowed; unshaken; unsifted; unspeakable; untainted; unwavering; unwelcome; unwilling; upspringing; vacillating; valiant; varied; vehement; victorious; wandering; waning; warming; wave-divided; wavering; weak; weeping; weird; welcoming; well-diffused; well-loved; wishing; wistful; wondrous; worldly; zigzag.

verbs
adjust—; bathe in—; blot out—; centralize—; douse (colloq.)—; extinguish—; flood with—; focus—upon; glory in—; grope for—; kindle—; muffle—; obscure—; radiate—; refract—; rejoice in—; shed—upon; shield from—; soften—; wreathe in—; —

blazes; —blinds; —blinks; —creeps in; —dances; —dazzles; —diffuses; —dwindles; —exposes; —fades; —filters in; —flares; —flickers; —gleams; —glitters; —glows; —illumines; —penetrates; —pierces; —seeps in; —stabs; —streams in; —streaks; —twinkles; —wanes; —wavers; —wells from; —winks.

(See lamp, candle, flame, fireworks, match, sunshine, spark.)

adverbs
insignificantly; extremely; exceedingly; unusually; uncommonly; unbelievably; airily; buoyantly; brilliantly; garishly; pallidly; faintly; indifferently; passably; tolerably; ordinarily; scarcely; manageably; conveniently; happily; jauntily; briskly; brightly; cheerfully; surprisingly; bewilderingly; comfortably; gloriously; mysteriously; unaccountably.

LIGHT (v)

adverbs
brilliantly; spectacularly; visibly; adequately; scantily; partially; gracefully; blindingly; cheerfully; exquisitely; vividly.

(See illumine, illuminate, ignite.)

LIGHTEN (v)

adverbs
blazingly; blindingly; dreadfully; terrifyingly; vividly; explosively; spectacularly.

(See flash, illuminate.)

LIGHT-HEARTED

adverbs
cheerfully; exhilaratingly; genially; good-humoredly; naturally; temperamentally; laughingly; optimistically; roguishly; briskly; blithely; brightly; buoyantly; bonnily; hilariously; youthfully; hopefully; jauntily; jubilantly; winsomely.

LIGHTNESS

adjectives
imaginative; graceful; innumerable (pl); dry; extreme; cheerful; exquisite; boyish; sheer; buoyant; inexpressible.

LIGHTNING

adjectives
blind; parching; internal; wicked; uncommunicated; consuming; volcanic; unleashed; lovelier; poisonous; irreversible; silent; mercy-winged; congregated; artificial; naked; sheet; baleful; arrowy; reverberating; restless; glaring; keener; livid; harmless; nimble; diffused; yoked; indirect; vivid; deadly.

verbs
—bolts; —chars; —cleaves; —dances; —darts; —demolishes; —destroys; —flames; —flashes; —flickers; —glows; —ignites; —illumines; —illuminates; —plays; —rends; —reveals; —streaks; —terrifies; —wreaks; —zigzags.

(See light, lamp, storm, thunder, spark, tornado, typhoon, wind, hurricane.)

LIKE (v)

adverbs
scarcely; extremely; metaphorically; universally; faithfully; persistently; constantly; mutually; momentarily; superficially.

(See fancy, approve, choose.)

LIKELY

adverbs
fairly; somewhat; plausibly; reasonably; speciously; hardly; perhaps; questionably; undoubtedly; dependably; positively.

LIKENESS

adjectives
striking; unaltered; unsubstantial; intrinsic; rude; tangible; graphic; distorted; hideous; speaking; inaccurate; mysterious; generic; grotesque; immortal; mutual; faithful; famous; executed; momentary; consistent; family; rudimental; mute; persistent; phantasmal.

LILIES

adjectives
lazy; sculptured; unsullied; lolling; slumbrous; gleaming; water; waxen; vast; ineffable; fair; pure; languid; pale; sere; mystic; robust; careworn; wind-sown.

LILY

verbs
attire in—; bear—; blight—; crown with —ies; cultivate—ies; stain—; sully—; tint —; —blushes; —ies clothe; —droops; —fades; —ies fester; —flourishes; —glistens; —heaves; —nods; —symbolizes; —unfolds; —withers.

(See flower, plant.)

LIMB

adjectives
vast; swollen; rigid; unshapely; weary;

wan; trembling; unnatural; withered; unbroken; willing; fervid; coarse-featured; uncouth; unfettered; mangled; gouty; childish; sturdy; knotted; writhing; arching; leafless; half-frozen; scabby; severe; tossing; leprous; shivering; pulsed; oily; corded; stiffened; languid; immovable; unhewn; shrunken; painful; degraded; gangling; puny; little; putrefying; chafed; feeble; naked; denuded; burning; helpless; drooping; sinewy; long-laboring; jaded; massive; thin; weather-beaten; charred; loving; queenly; bare; crippled; paralytic; distorted; wreathing; gentle; tawny; tender; wondrous; supplemental; mutilated; delicate; bending; shuddering; exquisite; lithe; agile; artificial; palsied; aged.

verbs
amputate—; bare—; brace—; char—; cramp—; deform—; develop—; drag—; employ—; exercise—; fracture—; inject into —; paralyze—; strain—; torture—; —shrinks; —supports; —withers.
(See leg, foot, body, elbow.)

LIME-LIGHT

verbs
avoid—; bask in—; crave—; earn—; emerge from—; extinguish—; fade from—; gain—; glory in—; quench—; seek—; steal —; throw into—; —dazzles; —glows; —notorizes; —publicizes; —smoulders; —wanes.
(See fame, publicity, notoriety, renown, reputation.)

LIMES

adjectives
arching; quiet-leaved; bitter; ripened.

LIMIT

adjectives
narrow; rigid; geographic; predetermined; municipal; severe; definite; maximum; uttermost; extended; lazy; ultimate; treaty; broad; hallowed; corporate; judicious; narrowest; practicable; confined; ancient; utmost; wiser; extreme; true; insurmountable; fenceless; transcending; glimmering; constitutional; remotest; legitimate; sanctified; certain; whimsical; original; modest; sensible; reasonable; appointed.

LIMIT (v)

adverbs
grammatically; rigidly; definitely; constitutionally; narrowly; infinitely; scientifically; inescapably; practically; mathematically; morally; fastidiously.
(See confine, restrict, circumscribe.)

LIMITATIONS

adjectives
spheric; rigid; constitutional; reasonable; proper; narrow; hereditary; infinite; inner; scientific; inevitable; immediate; self-imposed; mortal; finite; inescapable; practical.

verbs
abandon—; acknowledge—; amend—; circumscribe—; circumvent—; discern—; dispel—; dispute—; enforce—; escape—; establish—; extricate from—; impose—; prescribe—; subject to—; transcend—; —bar; —bridle; —check; —confine; —constrain; —curb; —expire; —fetter; —incarcerate; —repress; —restrain; —restrict; —yoke.
(See restriction, restraint, limit.)

LIMITED

adverbs
indescribably; legally; unfortunately; strictly; viciously; exclusively; unchangeably; necessarily; conveniently; rigidly; ridiculously; wickedly; inexcusably; traditionally; conventionally; legislatively; excessively; absurdly; wisely; imperiously; irrevocably.

LIMITLESS

adverbs
incredibly; expansively; awesomely; terribly; broadly; generously; inexpressibly; unutterably; incomprehensibly; fearfully.

LIMITS

verbs
act with—; authorize—; bind by—; compress—; define—; exceed—; extend—; fall within—; indicate—; lift—; measure —; narrow—; order—; overstep—; sanctify—; slip over—; sound—; transgress—; urge to—; —bar; —constrain.
(See bounds, restraint, restriction, scope, limitations.)

LIMP

adverbs
languidly; wearily; lankly; soggily; wetly; sadly; hopelessly; helplessly; absurdly;

laughably; feebly; powerlessly; flabbily; pliantly; flimsily; ludicrously; drunkenly; breathlessly; utterly; ridiculously.

LIMP (v)

adverbs

laboriously; painfully; sorely; hideously; piteously; pathetically; feebly; jadedly; wanly; uncouthly; repulsively.

(See hobble, walk, falter.)

LIMPID

adverbs

beautifully; transparently; coolly; serenely; clearly; pellucidly; innocently; trustingly (eyes); ripplingly; translucently.

LINE

adjectives

fine; skirmish; untutored; soft; flowing; harmonious; never-ceasing; demolished; graceful; melodic; undulating; depending; transparent; rippling; continuous; scientific; collateral; advancing; extended; capricious; oblique; sounding; intertwisted; impromptu; important; imaginary; beautiful; impregnable; policy; gleaming; opposing; exiled; converging; occasional; legitimate; feeling; half-illegible; pencil-traced; tighter; sensuous; emphatic; inspiring; minute; fleeting; never-varying; fringing; sharpened; youthful; subtle; insuperable; agitated; endless; divergent; special; curving; dainty; never-relaxing; flexible; roaring; sensitive; equinoctial; curling; flimsy; absolute; straight; feudal; suave; dignified; body-traced; crisp; wide; well-proportioned; smart; smart-draping; distinguished; tapering; easy; exclusive; distinctive; vulnerable; ravaged; sonorous; unbroken; monastery; bread; uneven; ragged; cramped; parallel (pl); eccentric; sleepless; irregular; pathetic; wabbling; quivering; ensuing; paternal; wavering; decided; eastward; fringing; fortified; etched; shapely; style; constricting; exterior; remotest; rent; successive (pl); slim; stirring; insolent; decisive; mystic; long; urbane; broad; tedious; swagger; classic; apostolic; complete; swinging; transcontinental; surging; stunning; weight-bearing; traditional; characteristic; honied; poetic; circumvallating; radial; moral; interconnecting; natural; jeweled; slender; wanton; rambling; trim; immortal; smart-tailored; ever-lengthening; stubborn; sleek; sun-tempting; back; dauntless; luxuriant; unreturning; fantastic; momentous; placid; solemn; noiseless; intertangled; infinitesimal; oblique; shoddy; eloquent; narrative; witty; preparatory; hypothetical; impassioned; unpunctuated; inimitable; telegraphic; harsh; effective; circling; competing; bristling; faint; intrenched; brilliant; vanquished; horizontal; cabalistic; sinuous; preconcerted; completed; well-defined; stateliest; unfading; glittering; never-ending; allied; quaint; experimental; nodal; prosaic; radiating (pl); trimmer; industrial; intellectual; heroic; improvised; illustrious; admirable; hard; grim; humble; imitative; ghostly; foul; swelling; touching; foolish; connecting; imperiled; unpolished; bobbing; unrelated; brief; plumb; slimmer; compact; simple; unconquered; vocal; holy; therapeutic; theoretic; charging; ferocious; thought-tracked; genealogical; sublime; fleshly; surging; dividing.

verbs

alternate—s; blur—; delineate—; derive—from; eradicate—; extend—; foul—; fracture—; intersect—; overrun—; scale—; thread—; trace—; warp—; wipe out—s; —bounds; —s coincide; —deviates; —digresses; —dips; —grades; —graduates; —limits; —parallels; —progresses; —s radiate from; —refracts; —represents; —straggles; —swerves; —veers; —verges; —wobbles.

(See mark, boundary, outline, route, road.)

LINEAGE

adjectives

ancient; imperial; injured; honorable.

LINEAMENTS

adjectives

haughtiest; stricken; pallid; striking; noble; dead; hideous; mental; exaggerated; warworn; strong; sculptured; impertinent; personal; shifting.

LINED
(wrinkled)

adverbs

deeply; humorously; scowlingly; ripely; puckeringly; agedly; patriarchally; terribly; significantly.

LINEN

adjectives

blood-clotted; snowy; dubious; age-yellowed; spotless; filthy; foul; stout; dainty; immaculate; embroidered; outward-surging; convent.

verbs
array in—; attire in—; bleach—; brocade —; carbonize—; card—; comb—; disentangle—; drape—; dress—; embroider—; fringe with—; garb in—; gird in—; grade —; hackle—; hank—; ret—; soak—; spin —; vest in—; warp—.
(See cloth, silk, velvet.)

LINGER (v)

adverbs
tenderly; affectionately; vaguely; monotonously; boringly; obtrusively; wearily; confusedly; regretfully; perilously; idly; irresolutely; indecisively.
(See loiter, saunter.)

LINGUIST

adjectives
skilled; ready; manifold; comparative; accomplished; brilliant; celebrated.

LINIMENT

verbs
administer—; apply—; drench with—; yield to—; —cools; —limbers; —mollifies; —palliates; —relaxes; —relieves; —restores; —soothes.
(See medicine, iodine, tonic, remedy, ointment, salve.)

LINING

verbs
strip of—; stud with—; —chafes; —coats; —crusts; —inflames; —jackets; —pads; —preserves; —sheathes; —wads.
(See cloth, silk, velvet, wrapper.)

LINK

verbs
cement—; dissolve—; fuse—; partition into —s; pivot on—; rend—; sever—; solder—; sunder—; terminate—; —affiliates; —allies; —bridges; —cleaves; —coincides; —communicates; —correlates; —facilitates; —fetters; —hinges; —leagues; —shackles; —spans; —unites; —leashes.
(See chain, bond, tie, ring, union, part, ligament, ligature.)

LINK (v)

adverbs
indissolubly; inextricably; rhythmically; inevitably; inseparably; perpetually; incessantly; slanderously; humorously; incongruously; incompatibly.
(See join, connect, unite.)

LINKS

adjectives
intervening; thought; special; connecting; accustomed; mystic; clay-cold; adamantine; successive; breezy.

LINNET

verbs
—collects; —s flock; —mimics; —pipes; —warbles.
(See bird.)

LINOTYPE

verbs
dump—; ink—; melt—; print from—; set—; trim—; —assembles; —casts; —clanks; —composes; —distributes; —facilitates; —stereotypes; —transcribes.
(See type, metal.)

LION

adjectives
tameless; tawny-bearded; prisoned; rampant; jagged-jawed; wondrous.

verbs
encounter—; rouse—; slay—; —attacks; —carries off; —claws; —creeps upon; —devours; —drags off; —forages; —glares; —growls; —menaces; —paws; —preys on; —purrs; —rages; —rampages; —roams; —roars; —rolls over; —slaughters; —springs; —stalks; —stretches; —tears; —yawns.
(See animal, tiger, leopard.)

LIONIZE (v)

adverbs
bizarrely; enthusiastically; customarily; fraternally; hospitably; jovially; congenially; sportively; agreeably.
(See glorify, adore, exhibit, display.)

LIPS

adjectives
kissing; bridled; bearded; ripe; marble; burning; dimpled; fervent; rosy; trembling; quivering; seldom-parted; seductive; pendulous; curdled; ruddy; seeking; tender; sensitive; clear-cut; blistering; coward; carmine; glowing; loving; gaping; languid; wet; rosy; pallid; sinful; placid; downdrawn; brazen; dewy; blanched; swollen; bold; parching; flaccid; pursed; tightened; generous; thin; gummed-up; villainous; straight; pale; discolored; unpainted; roughed; pinched; dry; rosebud; ruby; whitening; crystal; shiny; coral; wide;

over-red; livid; bloodless; velvet; blanched; cerise; lead-colored; flower-petal; sardonic; projecting; compressed; unbreathing; protruding; heavy; half-open; full; purpled; flower-soft; traitorous; dainty; milk-fed; loose; eloquent; scornful; curse-laden; icy; mute; opened; stern; set; fevered; fettered; fleshless; babbling; mortal; ample; living; warm; sealed; eased; tired; willing; gifted; insatiable; sinuous; unseen; mobile; contorted; angel; squandering; innocent; imperial; firm; uncaressing; love-enkindled; luscious; appreciative; hueless; perjured; voluptuous; lifeless; dying; republican; wax-red; grim; nectared; bristled; mocking; unfettered; gnarled; miserable; careless; winning; girlish; sallow; frothing; lax; slight; haughty; proud; retracted; sad; voiceless; severed; curled-up; flashing; skinny; full; incense-breathing; sensuous; intertwisted; carved; calm; pure; thirsty; grosser; guarded; writhing; drooping; obsequious; shrunken; puckered; slanderous; relaxing; half-pouting; crooked; pendulous; mellow; prehensile; meager; tortured; honeyed; unclosed; averted; starved; covetous; convivial; unclean; well-cut; ineffectual; scorched; passionate; leopard; lily; stammering; infant; panting; cracked; stifling; rapid; chiseled; milkless; wrinkled; long-silent; devout.

verbs
compress—; depress—; excoriate—; glue—; gnaw—; lock—; parch—; pucker—; purse —; seal—; smack—; sully—; thin—; tumble from—; wring from—; —beguile; —curl; —falter; —pout; —proclaim; —profane; —protrude; —quiver; —scorn; —snarl; —stir; —thin; —tremble; —writhe; —yield.
(See mouth.)

LIQUID

adjectives
malodorous; viscous; foul; limpid; combustible; sparkling; denser; anesthetizing; lifeless; ecstatic; rosy; plain; noxious; queer-looking; seminal; unliquidating; colorless; swarming; consecrated; putrid; opaque.

verbs
charge—; chill—; dabble in—; deluge with —; dilute—; discharge—; drain—; draw off —; exude—; gargle—; gulp—; imbibe—; immerse in—; infiltrate—; inject—; precipitate—; spout—; squirt—; steep in—; strain —; submerge—; tap—; —babbles; —gurgles; —ripples; —saturates.
(See water, fluid, liquor, beverage, drink.)

LIQUOR

adjectives
amber; muddy; intoxicating; crimson; fuming; pleasant; drowsy; rebellious; sparkling; grand; spiritual; hateful; nectarial; exquisite; stimulating.

verbs
abstain from—; age—; carouse with—; compound —; dilute—; distill—; ferment—; grade—; imbibe—; overindulge in—; perfume—; reek of—; reel with—; restrict—; stamp—; sublimate—; sweeten—; tax—; traffic in—; —inebriates; —stupefies.
(See whiskey, brandy, beer, ale, wine.)

LISP (v)

adverbs
affectedly; mincingly; insipidly; captivatingly; emulously; irritatingly; annoyingly; sibilantly.
(See utter, talk, speak.)

LISSOME

adverbs
slenderly; daintily; youthfully; girlishly; beautifully; attractively; unusually; uncommonly; delightfully; softly; yieldingly; tenderly; gracefully; charmingly.

LIST

adjectives
inexhaustible; extensive; provisional; authoritative; stupendous; representative; eligible; pompous; voting; growing; metrical; interminable; fatal; appalling; shining; gratifying; alarming; casualty; diversified; abbreviated; annotated; prescribed; protesting; mere; certain; inexorable; illegitimate.

verbs
approve—; audit—; check—; circularize—; compile—; delete—; enroll in—; extend—; investigate—; muster—; rattle off—; recapitulate—; review—; supplement—; swell—; —accounts; —calendars; —catalogues; —computes; —declines; —dwindles; —enumerates; —indexes; —measures; —polls; —recedes; —registers; —schedules; —scores; —sums up; —wanes.
(See schedule, sum, amount, account, record, statistics, statement, program.)

LISTEN (v)

adverbs
apprehensively; indulgently; intently; attentively; dreamily; compassionately; piously; obediently; intelligently; impassively; reflectively; languidly; aimlessly; sympathetically; interminably; gratifyingly; raptly.
(See attend, heed, hearken, obey.)

LISTENER

adjectives
attentive; sympathetic; untutored; intelligent; chance; anxious; uninitiated; puzzled; radiant; discriminating; unprejudiced; admiring; individual; laconic; impassive; wondering; mute; rapt; unobtrusive; defiant; close; trembling.

verbs
admonish—; bar—; bore—; enchant—; entrance—; inform—; reproach—; rouse—; spellbind—; —absorbs; —bends an ear; —s chorus; —considers; —eavesdrops; —grasps; —hearkens; —heeds; —pricks up his ears; —regards; —senses; —wearies.
(See audience, congregation, hearer, visitor, guest, crowd.)

LISTLESS

adverbs
provokingly; languidly; inertly; lazily; dully; carelessly; heedlessly; indifferently; irritatingly; vexatiously; arrogantly; obviously; visibly; unaccountably; inexplicably; insufferably; impolitely; discourteously; insolently; inconsiderately; helplessly; drowsily; distractedly; dreamily; terribly; amazingly; surprisingly; dreadfully.

LITERAL

adverbs
painfully; punctiliously; insufferably; legally; meticulously; intolerably; ostentatiously; professionally; officiously; unctuously; learnedly; academically; boresomely; unduly; unnecessarily; mercilessly; ruthlessly; unimaginatively; prosaically; mathematically; correctly; severely; uncompromisingly; curiously; exaggeratedly; awfully; uncommonly.

LITERATURE

adjectives
vigorous; national; contemporary; classical; related; city-bred; romantic; descriptive; illustrated; tinted; creative; imperishable; vernacular; inventive; satirical; critical; superficial; current; periodical; obscene; extensive; mainstream; complete; forensic; personal; ancient; primitive; social; significant; majestic; disciplined; prolific; imaginative; vitalized.

verbs
acclaim—; appreciate—; assail—; bar—; censor—; create—; criticize—; dabble in—; delve into—; evaluate—; execute—; foster —; haunt—; interpret—; nurse—; patronize —; relish—; revaluate—; sanctify—; stabilize—; unify—; —charms; —communicates; —conveys; —enlightens; —delights; —enraptures; —eternizes; —expresses; —immortalizes; —incites; —informs; —inspires; —portrays; —provides; —redeems; —reveals; —stimulates; —transfuses; —transports.
(See art, story, biography, newspaper, press, essay, fiction, poetry, writing, book, magazine.)

LITIGATION

adjectives
expensive; sufficient; recent; weary; furious; prolonged; bitter.

verbs
appeal—; clinch—; discharge—; dispose of —; dispute—; evidence—; execute—; judge —; speed—; support—; —apprehends; —arraigns; —clashes; —distrains; —drags; —embroils; —impeaches; —indicts; —jars; —prosecutes; —squabbles.
(See lawsuit, case, suit (law), argument, verdict, results, decision, settlement.)

LITTER

adjectives
sable; terrible; intellectual; huge.

LITTER (v)

adverbs
confusedly; untidily; sloppily; haphazardly; disheveledly; obtrusively.
(See scatter, separate, intersperse.)

LITTLE

adverbs
precious; confoundedly; pitiably; inconsequentially; remarkably; miserably; cruelly; incredibly; inadequately; infinitesimally; wretchedly; blessedly.

LIVE (*alive*)

adverbs
actively; mentally; amazingly; animatedly; perilously; briskly; eagerly; mysteriously; sensitively; energetically; spiritually; fiercely; unmistakably; joyously; secretly; keenly; spiritedly; emotionally; intellectually; persistently; tragically; enterprisingly; exuberantly; vigorously; undeniably; restlessly; substantially; strongly; warmly; wretchedly; vivaciously; vitally; acutely; flourishingly; impatiently; tenaciously; exultantly; resolutely; happily.

LIVE (*v*)

adverbs
lavishly; dangerously; originally; expansively; improvidently; actively; profligately; opulently; ostentatiously; excessively; inconsequentially; affluently; gloriously; immortally; significantly; luxuriously; fantastically; penuriously; pretentiously; sumptuously; dissolutely; harmoniously; religiously; precariously; blithely; exclusively; spiritually; economically; abstemiously; scandalously; barbarously; monotonously; strenuously.

(See exist, abide, dwell.)

LIVELIHOOD

adjectives
meager; humble; bare; reputable; honest.

verbs
acquire—; afford—; bereave of—; command —; derive—from; draw—from; earn—; furnish—; gain—; grub—; insure—; maintain—; offer—; procure—; reap—; scrape together—; strip of—; yield—.

(See living, support, sustenance, income, wages, salary.)

LIVELINESS

verbs
animate with—; frolic in—; manifest—; radiate—; sparkle in—; stimulate—; —cheers; —effervesces; —elates; —enlivens; —exhilarates; —gladdens; —inspirits; —perks up.

(See animation, action, activity, vivacity, life.)

LIVELY

adverbs
immensely; joyously; noisily; naturally; unwontedly; unbelievably; briskly; gloriously; conspicuously; strikingly; fitfully; abnormally; dramatically; ostentatiously; ridiculously; singularly; habitually; disturbingly; pleasantly; refreshingly; enchantingly.

LIVER

adjectives
unchaste; torpid; spotted.

verbs
afflict—; attack—; congest—; damage—; derange—; disorganize—; impair—; infect —; —deteriorates; —discharges; —ejects; —excretes; —expels; —functions; —lodges; —purifies; —secretes; —shrivels.

(See bladder, organs, heart, kidney.)

LIVERY

adjectives
silver; reclusive; religious; gorgeous; cunning; destined; sober; bare; showy; beauteous; humble; drab-colored; gilded; royal; special.

LIVES

adjectives
best-regulated; scandalous; infinite; sedentary; weary; frivolous; deplorable; millennial; constricted; barbarous; valueless; luxurious; fateful; uncultivated; eventful; precious; regimented; craven; misplaced; strenuous; acceptable; fashionable; worthy; stunted; solitary; unnumbered; pale; virgin; disordered; imaginative; carnivorous; intermittent; lawless; divided; brutish; monotonous.

LIVESTOCK

verbs
auction off—; brand—; confine—; corral—; deal in—; free—; insure—; obliterate—; pasture—; shelter—; stable—; tend—; tether—; water—; —grazes; —sickens; —stampedes; —tramples; —wanders.

(See cow, horse, cattle, oxen, mule, sheep, lamb.)

LIVID

adverbs
terribly; hideously; terrifyingly; painfully; awfully; gruesomely; darkly; dreadfully; ashenly; coldly.

LIVING

adjectives
riotous; monotonous; concentrated; fruitful; flourishing; luxurious; scandalous; enjoy-

able; precarious; lucrative; gracious; contemporary; successful; happy; reckless; useful; dissipated; sufficient; vicarious; fat; independent; complicated; healthier; clean; ascetic; cheap; moderate; contented; strenuous; satisfactory; pleasurable; honorable; generous; primitive; scanty; quiet; fine; inexpensive; congenial; restful; wasteful.

verbs
acquire—; afford—; derive—from; earn—; eke—; fend for—; furnish—; gain—; garner—; glean—; offer—; simplify—; wrest —from.
(See livelihood, support, sustenance, income, wages, salary.)

LIZARD

verbs
—burrows; —claws; —crawls; —dives; —erects; —flies; —frequents; —invades; —paddles; —poisons; —preys upon; —reproduces; —sheds; —slithers; —suns itself; —swims; —whips its tail; —wounds; —wriggles.
(See reptile, animal, snake.)

LOAD

adjectives
bounteous; dark; weary; precious; concentrated; work; moaning; dead-weight; groaning; grievous; cumbrous; harsh; life-compelling; monstrous; tremendous.

verbs
ameliorate—; augment—; bear—; bend under—; bow by—; collect—; discharge—; droop under—; strap—on; support—; weigh —; —burdens; —clogs; —encumbers; —hampers; —impedes; —oppresses; —overwhelms; —restrains; —weakens.
(See burden, weight, pressure.)

LOAF (v)

adverbs
contentedly; idly; improvidently; dreamily; disgracefully; drunkenly; corruptly; enjoyably; congenially; wastefully.
(See dawdle, lounge, loiter, loll.)

LOAM

adjectives
fresh; woodland; tenacious; yielding; smeared.

LOAN

adjectives
brief; willing; stagnant; inadequate; exorbitant.

verbs
acknowledge—; advance—; amortize—; confer—upon; contract—; contribute—; extend—; facilitate—; float—; force—; grant —; inveigle—; launch—; obtain—; pledge —; press—; procure—; raise—; solicit—; subscribe—; —gratifies; —indebts.
(See debt, money, funds, payment.)

LOATHSOME

adverbs
unspeakably; abominably; disgustingly; mortally; sickeningly; insufferably; intolerably; uncommonly; impossibly; utterly; completely; horribly; repulsively; detestably; shockingly; hatefully.

LOATHING

adjectives
indignant; deepest; instinctive; enormous.

LOBBY

adjectives
commodious; magnificent; new; busy; quiet; economical; impressive; appointed; cheerful; furnished; luxurious.

verbs
appropriate—; decorate—; frequent—; lounge in—; pace—; page in—; retire to —; retreat to—; throng—; wait in—; —connects; —echoes with; —resounds; —swarms.
(See hall, corridor, passage, room.)

LOCAL

adverbs
apparently; allegedly; merely; luckily; strongly; unquestionably; evidently; emphatically.

LOCALITY

adjectives
affected; attractive; residential; memorable; isolated; miserable.

verbs
acclimate to—; annihilate—; assign to—; canvass—; examine—; explore—; fix—; in-

habit—; investigate—; mold to—; scan—; scour—; search—; seek—; select—; sever from—; shift—; view—; —militates.

(See territory, region, neighborhood, vicinity, district.)

LOCATE (v)

adverbs

systematically; centrally; conveniently; precisely; picturesquely; distinctly; matchlessly; conveniently; strategically; geographically.

(See place, establish.)

LOCATION

adjectives

pleasant; choice; favored; unexcelled; preferred; ideal; unique; matchless; convenient; superb; beautiful; quiet; splendid; particular; strategic; changing; available; interesting; hazardous; advantageous; geographical; outstanding; efficient; mythical; industrial; peculiar; unrivaled.

LOCK (hair)

adjectives

unkempt; curling; raven; clustering; flowing; luxuriant; thin; dangling; straggling; whitened; crisped; snaky; golden; recalcitrant; massy; obstinate; bushy; truant; glossy; sunny; intertwining; straying; shining; tumbled; dense; shaggy; well-groomed; shorn; stiff; flat; dripping; hoary; clustering; sparse; unruly; fearful; floating; silken; careless; scanty; disheveled; plaited.

LOCK (mechanical)

adjectives

shattering; languid; crude; mitered; profuse; keyhole; intricate; burglar-proof.

verbs

adjust—; design—; force—; jimmy—; pick —; set—; tamper with—; test—; unbar—; withdraw—; —clasps; —clicks; —embraces; —repulses; —resists; —responds; —seals; —secures.

(See bolt, bar.)

LOCK (v)

adverbs

discreetly; cautiously; prudently; mechanically; automatically; modestly; suspiciously; covetously; staunchly.

(See fasten, fix, secure.)

LOCOMOTIVE

verbs

board—; derail—; dismount from—; fuel —; propel—; —chugs; —halts; —hammers; —overtakes; —pants; —puffs; —screeches; —shrieks; —shuffles; —speeds; —sputters; —stammers; —steams; —traverses; —wails; —wheezes; —whizzes.

(See train, engine.)

LOCUST

verbs

crush—; exterminate—s; —bores; —burrows; —s cloud; —cymbals; —destroys; —drones; —drums; —s migrate; —molts; —s plague; —rasps; —rattles; —sings; —sucks; —s swarm; —s symphonize; —undergoes; —s descend.

(See insect, grasshopper.)

LODGE

adjectives

ivy-covered; rude; supreme; nightly; country; hunting.

verbs

abandon—; charter—; confine to—; enjoy —; invite to—; luxuriate in—; occupy—; organize—; repose in—; reside at—; retire to—; retreat to—; vacate—; —accommodates; —comforts; —harbors; —shelters; —solaces.

(See club, home, residence, society, room.)

LODGE (v)

adverbs

snugly; firmly; fatally; temporarily; miserably; congenially; uniquely; conveniently; strategically; advantageously; industrially; permanently.

(See stay, remain, abide.)

LODGING

adjectives

inferior; hard; primitive; comfortable; barren.

verbs

afford—; assure of—; demand—; engage—; enjoy—; find—; furnish—; grant—; guarantee—; inquire into—; lease—; offer—; procure—; scorn—; secure—; seek—; warrant—; —delights; —refreshes; —shames.

(See shelter, refuge, room, rest, repose, sanctuary.)

LOFTY

adverbs
arrogantly; notoriously; incalculably; ridiculously; eminently; majestically; exaltedly; impressively; imposingly; proudly; toweringly; incredibly; tremendously; imperiously; strangely; ludicrously.

LOG

adjectives
smoldering; inanimate; unhewn; hollowed; flaming; back; blazing; hickory; yule; drunken; senseless; floating; ostensible; patent; moldered.

verbs
batter with—; bear—; char—; fire—; hew—; ignite—; kindle—; poke—; stir—; toast over—; vault—; —chills; —flames; —fuels; —glows; —seethes; —smokes; —smoulders.
(See club, wood, flame, fire, board, timber.)

LOGIC

adjectives
unerring; remorseless; persistent; energetic; soundest; dangerous; delightful; rigorous; symbolic; feminine; erstwhile; convincing; uncharitable; unanswerable; aesthetic; dispassionate; vast; cruel; hasty; imperfect; triumphant; inexorable; simple; compelling; pitiless; easy; strict; subtle; inevitable; unyielding; blundering; naked; suicidal.

verbs
condemn—; defy—; demonstrate—; endorse—; govern by—; indicate—; judge—; lame—; practise—; question—; reduce to—; refute—; require—; review—; warp—; ween from—; —analyzes; —annihilates; —convinces; —deduces; —determines; —dictates; —evolves; —prevails; —solves; —speculates.
(See reason, theory, accuracy.)

LOGICAL

adverbs
entirely; historically; skilfully; unfailingly; admirably; justly; remarkably; inevitably; unerringly; alarmingly; inexorably; fearfully; inescapably; undeniably; amazingly; uncommonly; wholly.

LOINS

adjectives
unknown; frozen; supple; girt; proper.

LOITER (*v*)

adverbs
undecidedly; jauntily; lackadaisically; tantalizingly; idly; luxuriously; persistently; excessively.
(See loaf, dawdle, lounge, loll.)

LOLL (*v*)

adverbs
luxuriantly; idly; listlessly; carelessly; wearily; impassively; frivolously; wantonly.
(See lounge, loaf, dawdle.)

LONE

adverbs
desolately; noticeably; distinctly; prominently; tragically; cheerlessly; remotely; intensely; solitarily; terribly; remarkably; uniquely; dreadfully.

LONELINESS

adjectives
supreme; visionary; abstracted; infinite; mossy; tragic; bowery; unutterable; oppressive; indescribable; multitudinous; infinitesimal; appalling; palatial; dreary; empty; bitter; unbearable; intolerable.

verbs
abate—; assuage—; conceal—; decry—; dissipate—; drive away—; evince—; fear—; guard against—; heighten—; overcome—; ravage by—; shroud in—; stress—; succumb to—; —accompanies; —assails; —engulfs; —envelops; —penetrates.
(See seclusion, solitude, isolation, dullness.)

LONELY

adverbs
strangely; unbelievably; unaccountably; naturally; oddly; forlornly; unbearably; unendurably; unnecessarily; distressingly; portentously; infinitely; tragically; unutterably; bitterly; intolerably; drearily; appallingly; indescribably; inexpressibly; pitiably; irremediably; pathetically; cruelly.

LONESOME

adverbs
dismally; reminiscently; gloomily; serenely; lazily; jealously; unhappily; terribly; intensely; peevishly; fretfully; drearily; supremely; absurdly; inexpressibly; grievously; hopelessly; pathetically; deservedly; unexpectedly; remarkably; curiously; dimly; vaguely; startlingly; extremely.

LONG

adverbs

extraordinarily; endlessly; interminably; monotonously; unbearably; ridiculously; excessively; remarkably; singularly; extremely; unbelievably; unnecessarily; sufficiently; tediously; inexcusably; unserviceably; unconscionably; incredibly; diffusely; tiresomely; wearily; terribly; curiously; unaccountably; unwarrantably.

LONG (v)

adverbs

nostalgically; impassionedly; wildly; sentimentally; fondly; inexplicably; fruitlessly; morbidly; restlessly; irresistibly; insatiably; singularly; inexpressibly; lingeringly; buoyantly; irrationally.

(See yearn, crave.)

LONGEVITY

verbs

contribute to—; derive—; endure—; enjoy —; entail—; evoke—; forestall—; hinder—; increase—; induce—; invest with—; procure—; produce—; provoke—; secure—; shatter—; —enfeebles; —results.

(See health.)

LONGING

adjectives

wild; nostalgic; vain; impassioned; sympathetic; premature; indefinite; wholesome; satisfied; strange; unpenetrated; mad; hopeless; immortal; musical; fond; earnest; unconscious; unchaste; new-born; inexplicable; vague; anxious; unceasing; indefinable; passionate; animal; earliest; patent; potent; half-deadly; half-voluptuous; persistent; bitter; fruitless; diseased; morbid; innermost; undefined; restless; ungratified; irresistible; painful; cruel; insatiate; ceaseless; upward; uncontrollable; faded; singular; doglike.

verbs

abate—; conceive—; devour by—; fulfill—; gratify—; hatch—; live in—; quench—; respect—; sate—; satisfy—; suffer—; uproot—; —burns; —destroys; —gnaws; —palls; —tantalizes; —tears at.

(See desire, yearning, craving, nostalgia.)

LOOK

adjectives

absent; agonized; alabaster; appealing; alert; amorous; animated; approving; arch; ardent; artless; attenuated; backward; bantering; beaming; beguiling; beseeching; bewildered; bitter; black; brazen; bleached; brown; bullying; burning; careworn; colorless; comic; compassionate; complacent; comprehensive; conjunctive; contemptuous; contented; counterfeit; critical; cross; crystal; cunning; curious; cursory; damp; dazed; deadly; deep; defiant; dejected; delicate; delirious; demure; deserted; despairing; desperate; despondent; dim; discontented; disdainful; dismal; dissipated; dissembling; distasteful; disturbed; doubting; downcast; drawn; dreamy; droopy; dubious; dying; elusive; enthralling; envious; expectant; exultant; fair; faraway; far-off; fearful; fear-stunned; flashing; frequent (pl); frightened; furtive; gentle; gloomy; glowering; glum; good; gracious; grateful; grave; grieved; guileless; haggard; half-laughing; hanging; haunting; heartbroken; helpless; honest; hopeless; hostile; hunted; hurried; hurt; icy; impertinent; imploring; indignant; innocent; inquiring; inscrutable; intelligent; intent; intimidating; irreverent; jaunty; keen; kind; knowing; languid; latent; lean; lingering; loftiest; longing; lowering; luminous; melancholy; melodramatic; merry; mild; mischievous; momentary; moody; mute; mysterious; naughty; obdurate; oblique; occasional; ogling; ominous; open; outdoor; pale; pathetic; penetrating; perplexed; phantasmal; piercing; pitiful; plaintive; pleading; predatory; preoccupied; prepossessing; prolonged; provocative; puzzled; queenly; queer; questioning; quick; quizzical; rakish; reluctant; resigned; reverend; riveted; robust; rueful; roguish; rowdy; rugged; sad; saucy; scared; scornful; scowling; searching; seeking; seraphic; serene; serious; shy; shamed; sidelong; significant; silky; silly; smart; soft; somnambulistic; sorrowful; sour; spectral; speculative; speechless; spiteful; sprightly; startled; steady; staunch; stealthy; stereotyped; stiff-necked; strained; stricken; stunned; sulky; sullen; surprised; suspicious; swift; swarthy; sweetest; tearful; thick; timely; threatening; timid; tired; tranquil; truculent; unfathomable; unflinching; ungentle; unguarded; united; unrestful; unseeing; unusual; vacant; valiant; vexed; vindictive; vivid; waiting; wan; weak; weather-beaten; welcoming; wild; whimsical; wistful; wise; withering; woebegone; wonderful; wondering; worn; worshipful; yearning.

verbs
acclaim with—; belie—; conceal—; confuse —; evade—; flash—; manufacture—; quail before—; shoot—; snatch—; sneak—; sour —; —challenges; —cows; —probes; —rebukes; —scorches; —shines; —wanes; —wavers; —withers.
(See glance, gaze, scrutiny, glimpse.)

LOOK (v)

adverbs
amorously; beseechingly; cursorily; compassionately; demurely; disdainfully; impertinently; dubiously; haggardly; reverently; ominously; pathetically; provocatively; intimidatingly; roguishly; seraphically; speculatively; vacantly; vindictively; witheringly; uncomprehendingly; covertly; sagaciously; stonily; meditatively; disconsolately; ferociously; ponderingly; wistfully; raptly; keenly; frivolously; mockingly; sheepishly; woefully; querulously; significantly; incredulously.
(See gaze, glance, stare.)

LOOM

adjectives
rustling; webless; creaking; interwoven; ages-old; wooden; handicraft; triumphant; primitive; magic; precious.

LOOM (v)

adverbs
ominously; thunderously; portentously; threateningly; impressively; belligerently; direly; stupendously; awesomely.
(See shine, rise, appear.)

LOOSE

adverbs
dangerously; fearfully; oddly; inexplicably; perilously; hazardously; distinctly; insecurely; inexcusably; terribly; accidentally; mysteriously; undeniably; unstably; carelessly; incautiously.

LOOSEN (v)

adverbs
radically; sufficiently; comfortably; medically; beneficially; healthfully; scientifically; partially.
(See free, separate, unfasten.)

LOOT

verbs
appropriate—; bag—; bicker over—; con ceal—; divide—; embrace—; feed on—; forage for—; gather—; nab—; parcel—; plunder for—; pocket—; ransack for—; sack for—; scramble for—; smuggle—; snap up —; snatch—; strip of—; suckle on—; vie for—; wean on—.
(See spoils, plunder, graft.)

LOQUACIOUS

adverbs
interminably; wildly; garrulously; chattily; maliciously; undeniably; highly; endlessly; inanely; glibly; clackily; flippantly; tiresomely; insufferably; amusingly; vexatiously; incredibly; hysterically; verbosely; repetitiously; dreadfully; amazingly; strangely; nonsensically.

LOQUACITY

adjectives
irrepressible; nervous; unlimited; noticeable.

LORD
(gentleman)

adjectives
stalwart; pampered; truant; absolute; predestined; rapacious; dread; native; gracious; illustrious; dethroned; worthy; courteous; brindled; merry; distressed; mocking; sovereign; faithless; new-trothed; filthy; scurvy; unworthy; unnatural; self-complacent; honored.

LORD
(divine being)

verbs
accept—; beseech—; bow to—; cherish—; exalt—; invoke—; offer unto—; praise—; pray to—; supplicate—; worship—; —anoints; —bestows; —controls; —heals; —judges; —masters.
(See God, Christ, Jesus.)

LORDLY

adverbs
arrogantly; insufferably; naturally; imposingly; impressively; absurdly; ridiculously; ludicrously; magnificently; splendidly; magnanimously; majestically; distinctly; notoriously; eminently; conspicuously; superciliously; imperiously; incredibly; proudly; laughably; curiously.

LORE

adjectives
slothful; poetic; listless; childlike; astrologic; legendary; idle; mythical; sublimest; exhaustless; technical; nauseous; immortal;

deceptive; inmost; shining; civilizing; gentlest; lascivious; mystic; legal; golden; preternatural; eternal; divinest.

verbs
acquire—; arm with—; banish—; comprehend—; delve into—; exaggerate—; gather —; ignore—; initiate into—; instruct in—; master—; perpetuate—; preserve—; steep in—; strip of—; substantiate—; unearth—; —deludes; —impresses; —misleads; —survives.

(See legend, tale, story, wisdom, learning.)

LOSER

verbs
condole—; declare—; deprive—; deride—; dispossess—; draw—; jeer—; renounce—; ridicule—; spot—; sympathize with—; —beseeches; —blunders; —complains; —deplores; —discards; —fails; —falls; —grumbles; —laments; —pledges; —prates; —protests; —sacrifices.

(See failure.)

LOSS

adjectives
consequent; wasteful; proportional; total; threatened; mournful; irreparable; considerable; excessive; disastrous; serious; unendurable; continual; awakened; prospective; infinite; intolerable; vague; frightful; heavy; trifling; financial; tragic; fearful; trivial; melancholy; sickening; crushing; shocking; inconsiderable; dear; moisture; perceptible; slight; petty; gainful; immeasurable; ultimate; imminent; undetectable; aggregate; lamentable; moneyed; irretrievable; tremendous; frightful; complete; appalling; preventable; numerical; maiden; partial; positive; anticipated; grievous.

verbs
absorb—; attribute—to; bemoan—; brood over—; cloak—; compensate for—; concede —; counterbalance—; curtail—; deplore—; grieve over—; incur—; lament—; lighten—; mourn—; occasion—; offset—; outweigh—; recoup—s; redress—; regard—; reimburse —; repent—; report—; retrieve—; smart under—; suffer—; sustain—; swallow—; —anguishes; —maddens; —s mount; —shames; —s soar.

(See bankruptcy, defeat, failure, misfortune.)

LOST

adverbs
irrecoverably; irretrievably; recently; altogether; forever; temporarily; lamentably; deplorably; utterly; strangely; curiously; terribly; unfortunately; incredibly; miserably.

LOT

adjectives
adjacent; adventurous; vacant; disreputable; enviable; dreary; toilsome; cheerless; loose-living; human; picturesque; unfortunate; homely; future; worthless; scrubby; uncomfortable; cloudless.

verbs
administer—; apportion—; assign—; bequeath—to; cast—s; deplore—; detail—; dispense—; distribute—s; draw—s; elect by —; embrace—; parcel—; partition—; remedy—; sacrifice—; share—; throw—in with.

LOTION

adjectives
creamy; soothing; cool; pleasant; unguent.

verbs
bathe with—; dilute—; dissolve in—; gargle —; immerse in—; saturate with—; steep in —; vend—; —beautifies; —heals; —perfumes; —purges; —purifies; —refreshes; —repairs; —repels; —soothes.

(See ointment, salve, soap.)

LOUD

adverbs
boisterously; terribly; crashingly; fearfully; impressively; unbelievably; clamorously; deafeningly; tumultuously; infernally; uncommonly; strangely; unnecessarily; unduly; appallingly; shockingly; thunderously; tempestuously; shrilly; objectionably; explosively; unmistakably; insufferably; unbearably.

LOUD-SPEAKER

verbs
boom through—; muffle—; suppress—; thunder through—; —amplifies; —bellows; —blares; —blasts; —deafens; —discharges; —grates; —produces; —shrieks; —startles; muzzle—.

(See bugle, bagpipe, trumpet.)

LOUNGE

verbs

assemble in—; dawdle in—; decorate—; dillydally in—; gather in—; idle in—; loaf in—; loiter in—; loll in—; relax in—; retire to—; saunter into—; skulk in—; slouch in—; —soothes; —swarms.

(See bedroom, room, chair, apartment.)

LOUNGE (v)

adverbs

idly; disconsolately; unambitiously; lasciviously; slothfully; trivially; comfortably; shamelessly; sensually.

(See recline, rest.)

LOUNGERS

adjectives

cultivated; suave; beach; dingy-looking.

LOUT

adjectives

foolish; gross; clumsy; lazy.

LOVABLE

adverbs

entirely; charmingly; delightfully; bewilderingly; bewitchingly; fascinatingly; indescribably; inexpressibly; unusually; uncommonly; tenderly; graciously; sweetly; attractively; engagingly; amiably; enchantingly; captivatingly; irresistibly; genially; heartily; ingratiatingly; adorably.

LOVE

adjectives

abiding; absorbing; abstract; adulterous; all-absorbing; all-discerning; ambitious; animal; animated; approving; ardent; arduous; artless; baffled; barbaric; barefaced; beholding; betrayed; bleeding; blissful; boundless; bounteous; brave; brittle; brotherly; burning; calculating; casual; celestial; changeful; changeless; changing; chasing; childlike; chastising; chivalrous; clandestine; condemned; coerced; comely; common; comprehensive; condescending; confessed; confiding; connubial; consanguine; consenting; consoling; condemned; conventional; corrupt; costly; courtly; cunning; cutting; dear; deathless; debasing; debatable; deep-buried; deepening; deep-rooted; deep-seeing; depraved; descending; despised; despiteful; dire; disgusting; distilling; divine; domestic; duteous; earnest; earthly; eloquent, embittered; emblematic; endearing; enduring; enlightened; ennobling; enthusiastic; equal; entrancing; erring; everlasting; exacting; exceeding; faddist; faithful; faithless; false; fantastical; fastidious; fathomless; faultless; feigning; fervent; festering; filial; florid; flustered; foolish; forgiving; forgotten; fostering; fraternal; frustrated; genuine; glorified; great; hapless; hard-believing; heavenly; heavy; hereditary; holy; highest; hoarded; hollow; heroic; honest; honor-loving; hopeless; humble; humiliated; hungry; illicit; imagined; immoderate; immortal; immune; impetuous; inborn; inbred; incalculable; inestimable; inexpressible; inextinguishable; inextricable; infinite; instinctive; intense; intellectual; intimate; invincible; irradiating; jealous; languid; lavish; lessening; lifelong; lively; light; limitless; living; long-suffering; lordliest; loveless; loveliest; luminous; manly; masterful; matchless; maternal; meek; melancholy; meritorious; militant; misguided; mother; mutual; mystical; nameless; nascent; newborn; never-wearying; new-found; noble; noiseless; obdurate; obscure; obsequious; one-sided; overmastering; painful; palsied; paltry; pardonable; parental; passionate; pathetic; perennial; persistent; philosophic; physical; pigeon; platonic; potential; pounding; predominating; proffered; primal; profound; prosperous; protecting; provident; public; puerile; pure; purifying; rational; real; reasonable; reassuring; recovering; redeeming; redoubtable; relenting; remorseful; rending; renouncing; repentant; repudiated; responsive; resurgent; reunited; reverent; romantic; sacrificial; satiated; selfish; self-renouncing; sensual; sensuous; sentimental; sham; shamed; shameless; shining; shy; silent; sin-destroying; sinful; sleepless; spiritual; spontaneous; steadfast; stilled; stimulated; stirring; strong; stupendous; sustaining; sweet; sweet-suggesting; tamed; tender; thankful; thoughtful; thwarted; tragic; tranquil; transient; transparent; true; true-confirmed; trusting; truthful; unalterable; unavailing; unbecoming; unbounded; unchanging; unconquerable; undying; unconscious; unexaggerated; unfashionable; unfathomable; unfocused; unfortunate; universal; unlawful; unmanly; unpropitious; unqualified; unquestioned; unreasonable; unregarded; unrelenting; unrequited; unrestful; unreturned; unruly; unsatisfactory; unselfish; unspoken; untaught; unutterable; unvowed; unwed; valiant; vigorous; violent; virtue; virtuous; visionary;

vivacious; vivid; wandering; wanton; warped; wasted; wasteful; weakening; welcoming; well-deserved; well-earned; well-known; well-quitted; willing; wilting; wonder-filling; wondrous; wonted; worst; worthiest; wrenching; wronged; yearning; youthful; zealous.

verbs
abide in—; arm with—; awaken—; cultivate—; enthrone in—; excite—; feign—; fire with—; forsake—; fulfill—; idealize—; inculcate—; instill—; insure—; lavish—upon; overflow with—; overshadow—; pine for—; proffer—; profess—; recapture—; reject—; revive—; ripen into—; scorn—; shatter—; smite with—; strangle—; sublimate—; —anguishes; —burns; —chastens; —dawns upon; —enchains; —endures; —ennobles; —illumines; —inspires; —reigns; —seizes; —smites; —tortures; —vanishes; —wells up; —wounds.
(See passion, tenderness, friendship, affection, devotion, infatuation.)

LOVE (v)

adverbs
irretrievably; immortally; fondly; passionately; instinctively; engrossingly; disinterestedly; possessively; ardently; inordinately; uniquely; jealously; profoundly; devotedly; virtuously; violently; exquisitely; heroically; exclusively; utterly; unrequitedly; illicitly; carnally; steadfastly; mawkishly; abstractly; adulterously; arduously; artlessly; boundlessly; blissfully; celestially; casually; clandestinely; connubially; corruptly; deathlessly; debasingly; fantastically; fastidiously; fathomlessly; feigningly; fervently; festeringly; inexpressibly; languidly; masterfully; parentally; philosophically; physically; zealously; platonically; rationally; romantically; sensually; sensuously; spiritually; spontaneously; sustainingly; transiently; unfathomably; vigilantly.
(See like, admire, adore.)

LOVELINESS

adjectives
solitary; perennial; attractive; boasted; female; soft; budding; informing; surpassing; vernal; uncommon; evanescent; shamed; enchanting; exquisite; ineffable; radiant; virgin; pensive; fragile; lustrous; unnoticed; luminous; chaste; uncultivated; exceeding; passing; twofold; sheer; pristine; inner; genuine; ethereal; breath-taking; moral; unaccountable; unthrifty; winning; supernal; superb; imperious; sensuous; placid; scattered; petite; tempestuous; modest; incomparable; stately; mild; exalted; opulent; conventional.

verbs
admire—; adorn with—; appreciate—; bloom in—; cultivate—; deface—; devour—; flaunt—; garment in—; glow with—; mar—; praise—; preserve—; sully—; taint—; —charms; —dazzles; —enchants; —endures; —glitters; —haunts; —hypnotizes; —shines; —surpasses.
(See beauty, grace, charm, splendor.)

LOVELY

adverbs
charmingly; adorably; indescribably; utterly; delicately; gracefully; delightfully; absorbingly; artlessly; exquisitely; gently; softly; ineffably; enchantingly; radiantly; breath-takingly; unutterably; sweetly; genuinely; superbly; incomparably; incredibly; completely.

LOVER

adjectives
tender; considerate; laggard; betrothed; melancholy; disconsolate; romantic; passionate; despairing; hot; beseeching; universal; entwined (pl); advanced; weary; ardent; triumphant; meek; changing; newly-plighted; lifelong; patriarchal; listening; whispering; greatest; fond; ethereal; accepted; estranged; impassioned; tragic; redeeming; remorseful; starved; hesitating; loathsome; lowly; memorable; enthusiastic; forsaken; notable; subtle; clinging; faithful; monastic; unhappy; distracted; true; flaming-breasted; truant; sleepless; sempiternal; pattern; fearful; credulous; youthful.

verbs
anger—; deceive—; exact from—; excite—; inflame—; renounce—; reward—; ridicule—; sting—; —beams; —blesses; —capers; —caresses; —desires; —devotes; —dotes upon; —dreams; —frets; —muses; —reflects upon; —repents; —reveres; —s rift; —sacrifices; —sighs; —thirsts; —treasures; —woos; —yearns; —yields.
(See suitor, sweetheart, admirer, friend.)

LOVING

adverbs
ardently; tenderly; exceedingly; excessive-

ly; ostentatiously; proudly; fervently; adoringly; idolatrously; infatuatedly; passionately; rapturously; yearningly; wistfully; coquettishly; flirtatiously; excitedly; sweetly; seductively; devotedly.

LOW

adverbs
inconceivably; extremely; abysmally; exceedingly; uncomfortably; peculiarly; mysteriously; alarmingly; curiously; inconveniently; unnecessarily; unduly; impossibly; terribly; disagreeably; unpleasantly.

LOWER (v)

adverbs
mechanically; cautiously; appreciably; materially; economically; charmingly; coyly; tremulously; bestially.
(See reduce, drop, depress, diminish, fall.)

LOWLY

adverbs
childishly; inconceivably; sweetly; humbly; surprisingly; modestly; plainly; humbly; unpretentiously; unaffectedly; marvellously; admirably; wondrously.

LOYAL

adverbs
unaffectedly; genuinely; unquestionably; unimpeachably; sincerely; utterly; undeviatingly; sturdily; stoutly; faithfully; constantly; devotedly; unswervingly; negatively; positively; incredibly; reliably; dependably; steadily; militantly; patriotically; obediently; eagerly; ardently; meticulously; tremendously; utterly; uncommonly; steadfastly.

LOYALTY

adjectives
unswerving; instinctive; recovered; fastidious; stanch; inflexible; unconditional; fresh; religious; willing; unflinching; enthusiastic; savage; indestructible; mistaken; human; habitual; obstinate; fervent; filial; tenacious; intense; racial; quixotic; passionate; clan; true; ardent; alternate; unwavering; devoted; unchanging; affectionate; vaunted; basic; stubborn.

verbs
acknowledge—; attend with—; awaken—; chain by—; command—; discharge with—; exact—; fix—; follow with—; inspire—; overcome—; owe—; pledge—; profess—; protest—; prove—; retain—; reward—; shift—; stress—; submit with—; sustain—; —ennobles; —flames; —prevails.
(See faithfulness, devotion, love, faith, zeal.)

LUBBERLY

adverbs
heavily; awkwardly; ridiculously; laughably; absurdly; good-naturedly; unmanageably; inconveniently; unfortunately; terribly; lazily; massively; lumpishly.

LUBRICANT

verbs
enlist—; feed—; inject—; react to—; —benefits; —clears; —eases; —facilitates; —frees; —lightens; —nourishes; —promotes; —quickens; —relieves; —smooths; —speeds; —unclogs; —waxes.
(See oil, soap, lather.)

LUBRICATE (v)

adverbs
thoroughly; seasonally; periodically; mechanically; systematically; annually.
(See facilitate.)

LUCID

adverbs
unusually; beautifully; satisfactorily; transparently; clearly; vividly; brilliantly; splendidly; especially; peculiarly; oddly; brightly; curiously; particularly; distinctly; luminously; delightfully; amazingly; astonishingly.

LUCK

adjectives
imaginable; ragged; blundering; unmerited; hard; monumental; good; ill; incredible; unearned; foolish.

verbs
ascribe to—; bemoan—; beset by—; bewail—; deplore—; earn—; encounter—; face—; fall into—; stake on—; trust to—; —attends; —befalls; —chases; —deals; —deserts; —disheartens; —ebbs; —favors; —mocks; —pursues; —singles out; —soars.
(See chance, fortune, risk, misfortune, reverse.)

LUCKLESS

adverbs
wretchedly; miserably; always; consistently; unfortunately; habitually; markedly; notoriously; distinctly; positively; unhap-

pily; conspicuously; disastrously; calamitously; deplorably; lamentably; constantly; altogether; pitiably; dreadfully; uncommonly.

LUCKY

adverbs
always; inexplicably; auspiciously; fortunately; inherently; blessedly; shrewdly; deservedly; adroitly; triumphantly; advantageously; inexpressibly; deucedly; remarkably; surprisingly; inscrutably; notoriously; unaccountably; unwarrantably; mysteriously; strangely; oddly; curiously; immensely; cleverly; admirably; wonderfully; miraculously; marvellously; ingeniously; conveniently; boastfully; surpassingly; accidentally; reasonably; assuredly; casually; incidentally; unexpectedly; blessedly.

LUCRATIVE

adverbs
commendably; admirably; enviably; commercially; happily; duly; naturally; distinctly; definitely; astonishingly; surprisingly; mysteriously; measurably; incalculably; moderately; immensely; tremendously; exceedingly; pleasantly; immoderately; unexpectedly; satisfactorily; profitably; advantageously; curiously; unbelievably.

LUDICROUS

adverbs
immoderately; grotesquely; fantastically; curiously; uproariously; extravagantly; monstrously; whimsically; quaintly; outlandishly; eccentrically; preposterously; drolly; contemptibly; decisively; strangely; irresistibly; inconceivably; amazingly; intensely; unexpectedly; marvellously; inordinately.

LUGUBRIOUS

adverbs
miserably; wretchedly; inconsolably; determinedly; ostentatiously; funereally; gloomily; ridiculously; inordinately; uncommonly; terribly; unbearably; absurdly; unreasonably; pompously; showily; dreadfully; solemnly; demurely; grimly; disconsolately.

LULL (*v*)

adverbs
deliciously; magically; miraculously; momentarily; intermittently; sweetly; melodiously; maternally; affectionately.

(See hush, subside.)

LULLS

adjectives
reverberate; hopeless; magic; intermittent.

LUMBER (*v*)

adverbs
ponderously; heavily; monotonously; peacefully; stupidly; phlegmatically; lifelessly; solidly; soddenly; stolidly; passionlessly.

(See move, walk, stagger.)

LUMINARY

adjectives
legal; heavenly; glorious; kindliest.

LUMINOUS

adverbs
brilliantly; gloriously; effulgently; radiantly; splendidly; magnificently; phosphorescently; resplendently; scintillantly; shimmeringly; intermittently; steadily; beautifully; remarkably; intensely; extremely; unusually.

LUMPISH

adverbs
stupidly; dully; awkwardly; stolidly; boorishly; ignorantly; incredibly; remarkably; fantastically; terribly; inertly; drowsily; heavily; listlessly; languidly; lazily.

LUMPS

adjectives
rude; painful; lifeless; restive; solid; phlegmatic; deformed; soft; persistent; translucent; sympathetic; painless; obstinate; helpless; sodden; monstrous.

LUNATIC

adjectives
criminal; privileged; harmless; wild; rough.

adverbs
wildly; unmanageably; ungovernably; violently; absurdly; uproariously; ravingly; frenziedly; drunkenly; deliriously; daftly; fanatically; fantastically; strangely; curiously; unaccountably; irresponsibly; suddenly; frantically; dreadfully.

LUNCH

adjectives
well-balanced; belated; frugal; costly; convivial; substantial; suitable; abundant; half-wrapped; cold.

LUNCH (v)

adverbs

frugally; convivially; substantially; abundantly; swiftly; fraternally; hospitably; gaily; appetizingly; insatiably.

(See eat, dine.)

LUNCHEON

adjectives

grim; enormous; hilarious; sacrilegious; scant; well-attended.

verbs

conclude—; cram in—; design—; digest—; honor at—; indulge in—; savor—; scorn—; tender—; welcome to—; —appeals; —beguiles; —cheers; —contents; —inaugurates; —lubricates; —nourishes; —satisfies; —tempts.

(See supper, dinner, breakfast, meal, food, repast.)

LUNG

adjectives

prodigious; spongy; bursting; choked; skeleton; delicate; iron.

verbs

collapse—; compress—; congest—; deflate—; enter—; envelop—; examine—; infect—; inflate—; perforate—; scar—; solidify—; spot—; traverse—; waste—; —decays; —expands; —heaves; —labors; —retracts; —rots; —shrivels.

(See balloon, chest.)

LURCH (v)

adverbs

drunkenly; crazily; perilously; dizzily; rashly; abruptly; sensually; fatally; comically.

(See stagger, sway, roll.)

LURE

adjectives

constant; obvious; velvet.

verbs

bait—; betray into—; expose to—; follow—; inveigle into—; manoeuvre—; risk—; spread—; succumb to—s; swindle by—; —attracts; —beguiles; —deceives; —deludes; —enchants; —ensnares; —entices; —tempts; —tricks; —victimizes.

(See bait, temptation.)

LURE (v)

adverbs

delusively; obscenely; lustfully; coyly; lasciviously; sexually; sensually; joyously; suavely; wantonly.

(See tempt, attract.)

LURID

adverbs

sensationally; disgracefully; terribly; remarkably; reprehensibly; inordinately; comically; ridiculously; gloomily; dismally; awfully; repulsively; obscurely; deeply; dingily; faintly; ruddily; oddly; strangely; peculiarly.

LURK (v)

adverbs

slyly; obscurely; insidiously; deceptively; treacherously; diabolically; instinctively; viciously; grimly.

(See prowl, steal, stalk.)

LUSCIOUS

adverbs

remarkably; admirably; particularly; delectably; deliciously; pleasantly; attractively; invitingly; agreeably; acceptably; gratefully; daintily; delicately; appetizingly; sweetly; richly; peculiarly; uncommonly; unusually.

LUSH

adverbs

abundantly; luxuriantly; amazingly; unusually; particularly; freshly; refreshingly; remarkably; juicily; marvellously; admirably; attractively.

LUST

adjectives

short-sighted; careless; burning; monstrous; ruffian; healthy; mad; hurtful; amber-scented; mute; melancholy; sordid; ignoble; worldly; hellish; alien; decrepit; devilish; unnatural; exceeding; inbred; vile; ever-craving; coarse; concupiscible; greedy; fleshy; intemperate; tyrannous; ominous; drunken.

verbs

abhor—; cater to—; cool—· conquer—; couch in—; extinguish—; intoxicate with—; loathe—; melt in—; quench—; resist—; satiate—; sink in—, —blemishes; —burns; —

consumes; —corrupts; —decays; —defiles; —frenzies; —maddens; —massacres; —overthrows; —ruins; —scandalizes.
(See wickedness, sin, abomination, iniquity.)

LUST (v)

adverbs
obscenely; insatiably; devilishly; ceaselessly; monstrously; madly; mutely; sordidly; ignobly; unnaturally; vilely; pervertedly; concupiscibly; intemperately; intoxicatedly; ominously.
(See desire, long.)

LUSTER

adjectives
joyless; exceeding; collective; dazzling; sparkling; added; undiminished; feeble; refreshing; smooth; vitreous; glossy; dull; intolerable; classic; freshening; full; subdued; feverish; transient; ethereal; brilliant; iridescent; penetrating; timid; ancient; soft; purer; growing; spectral; hoary; starry; nebulous; pearly; antique; welcome; sulphurous; natural; hungry; original.

LUSTY

adverbs
remarkably; robustly; vigorously; unusually; enviably; sturdily; exceptionally; extraordinarily; amazingly; notoriously; dependably; luckily; fortunately; incredibly; surprisingly.

LUTE

adjectives
short-stringed; warbling; enfeebling; fragile; long-neglected; ravishing.

LUXURIANCE

adjectives
tropical; unchanged; prodigal; rank; wild.

verbs
abate—; attire in—; burst forth in—; cushion in—; display in—; feed on—; indulge in—; prune—; ransack—; soak in—; surrender to—; taste—; wallow in—; —diffuses; —enslaves; —entices; —flourishes; —inebriates; —overwhelms.
(See wealth, luxury.)

LUXURIANT

adverbs
abundantly; unusually: tropically; amazingly; uncommonly; exceptionally; unbelievably; naturally; surprisingly; profitably; amply; satisfactorily; richly; incalculably; advantageously; opportunely.

LUXURIATE (v)

adverbs
blissfully; joyously; exaggeratedly; carnally; sentimentally; drunkenly; wantonly; profanely; riotously; boastfully.
(See lavish, bestow.)

LUXURIOUS

adverbs
delightfully; pleasantly; agreeably; actually; unexpectedly; amazingly; indescribably; unconscionably; inordinately; extravagantly; gratifyingly; comfortably; refreshingly; enjoyably; enchantingly; cheerfully; blissfully; extraordinarily; incredibly; elaborately; expensively; gorgeously; happily.

LUXURY

adjectives
refined; lapping; useless; unfailing; sublime; elaborate; costly; leafy; swinish; expensive; voluptuous; hateful; sordid; manly; easy; light; innocent; prejudicial; incommunicable; colossal; subtle; multiform; unusual; gorgeous; invalid; higher-priced; rare; harmless; accustomed; profuse; wanton; superfluous; unequaled; almost-forgotten; cramping; attendant; sleek; pagan; indecent; unnecessary; sensual; idle; unobtrusive; quiet; secluded; modern.

verbs
afford—; bless with—; contemplate—; couch in—; crave—; diffuse—; dispense with—; intoxicate with—; lack—; loll in—; nurse in —; pamper with—; revel in—; steal—; swathe in—; thirst for—; —cushions; —hinders.
(See luxuriance, wealth.)

LYMPH

adjectives
pellucid; transparent; lava.

verbs
absorb by—; discharge—; dissolve in—; extract—; exude—; inject in—; secrete—; —

assimilates; —attenuates; —coagulates; —deteriorates; —dilutes; —escapes; —flows; —percolates; —streams.

LYNCH (v)

adverbs

madly; ferociously; bestially; insanely; swiftly; horrifyingly; sadistically; heartlessly; cruelly; tigerishly.

(See kill, murder, hang, punish.)

LYRE

adjectives

slumberous; sparkling; sweet-toned; tuneful; darling; lascivious.

LYRICAL

adverbs

sweetly; smoothly; tunefully; fluently; unusually; completely; utterly; curiously; softly; gently; clearly; enchantingly; fascinatingly; euphoniously; pleasantly; agreeably; roughly; perfectly; crudely; correctly; harmoniously; remarkably; magnificently; splendidly.

LYRICS

adjectives

poignant; rural; conventional; occasional; studied; dramatic; satirical; infrequent; sentimental.

M

MACHIAVELLIAN

adverbs
shrewdly; craftily; unbelievably; astutely; wickedly; colossally; designingly; subtly; arrantly; dreadfully; archly; crookedly; evasively; viciously; dangerously; alarmingly; curiously; fearfully; insidiously; nefariously; invidiously; profoundly; cleverly; notoriously; deceptively; heinously.

MACHINATE (v)

adverbs
diabolically; politically; unscrupulously; subtly; insidiously; perfidiously; treacherously; ambitiously.

(See plot, scheme.)

MACHINATIONS

adjectives
sublime; subtlest; insidious; political; perfidious.

MACHINE

adjectives
unmoral; cosmic; efficient; propaganda; specialized; vending; merciless; infernal; admirable; memorial; vast; fantastic; protected; ponderous; domestic; cranky; undependable; ill-omened; senseless; electrical; slow; expensive; leased; extraordinary; radical; omnipresent; colossal.

verbs
abolish—; clog—; construct—; control—; demonstrate—; exalt—; fuel—; humanize —; install—; lubricate—; master—; meter —; putter with—; sublimate—; subordinate —; tamper with—; tinker with—; transmute —; worship—; —accommodates; —clicks; —enslaves; —functions; —roars; —rumbles; —stamps.

(See engine, apparatus, instrument, drill, elevator, generator, dynamo, mechanism.)

MACHINE-GUN

verbs
nest—; place—; set up—; —bellows; —blasts; —chatters; —deafens; —drums; —fulminates; —mows down; —mutters; —rakes; —raps; —rat-tat-tats; —rends; —retaliates; —reverberates; —rolls; —spatters; —tattoos; —yammers (colloq.); —crackles.

(See gun, cannon, pistol, revolver, rifle.)

MACHINERY

adjectives
physical; warlike; experimental; elaborate; agricultural; complicated; economical; tireless; arbitration; internal; domestic; suspended; educational; cumbrous; subtle; stupendous; disinterested; specialized; budgetary; commonplace; dread; multiplied; comprehensive; unified; irrigating; newfangled.

MAD

adverbs
incoherently; fanatically; hopelessly; incurably; pathetically; violently; distractedly; bewilderedly; frantically; insanely; suddenly; periodically; hysterically; wildly; tragically; irrecoverably; irremediably.

MADMAN

verbs
arouse—; chain—; coddle—; confine—; cudgel—; enchain—; enkindle—; fetter—; harness—; immure—; imprison—; incarcerate —; infuriate—; isolate—; liberate—; manacle—; overpower—; perturb—; pinion—; pique—; restrain—; shackle—; subdue—; yoke—; —dotes; —drivels; —flames; —foams; —fumes; —gibbers; —leers; —rages; —rambles; —raves; —scowls.

(See fool, idiot.)

MADNESS

adjectives
feigned; apparent; inexplicable; amorous; sweet; mingled; incipient; mysterious; strange; mob; tender; autumnal; supernatural; solemn; studied; sacred; solitary; cruel; voluntary; midsummer; centrifugal; harmonious; moody; utter; suicidal; decided; sad; merry; drunken.

verbs
cloud with—; feign—; ramble in—; rave in —; —aberrates; —afflicts; —deranges; —diseases; —disorders; —embroils; —infects;

—invalidates; —possesses; —ravages; —seizes; —shatters; —taints; —unbalances; —undermines; —warps.
(See frenzy, insanity, stupidity, delirium, hysteria, mania.)

MAELSTROM

verbs
circumvent—; sweep into—; —agitates; —boils; —buffets —churns; —circulates; —drenches; —flings; —foams; —gyrates; —jets; —revolves; —rolls; —spouts; —threatens; —trundles; —whirls.
(See whirlpool, rain, river, turmoil, torrent, waves.)

MAGAZINE

adjectives
short-lived; humorous; independent; reputable; liberal; entertaining; lively; all-around; popular; foremost; smart; fast-growing; up-to-date; progressive; incipient; sectarian; well-storied; short-story.

verbs
censor—; contribute to—; dip into—; disseminate—s; extol—; glean from—; hawk —s; launch—; linotype—; peruse—; rack —s; sanction—; scan—; set up—; —accounts; —blazes; —chronicles; —circulates; —condenses; —delineates; —depicts; —digests; —polls; —promulgates; —records; —reports; —reviews; —summarizes; —supports.
(See literature, newspaper, press, publication, book, story, volume.)

MAGIC

adjectives
supernatural; practised; foul; peculiar; curative; traditional; subtle; powerful; sheer; wild; all-subduing; aimless; lush.

verbs
conjure up by—; contrive—; exercise—; influence by—; practise—; reek of—; skill in —; —bedevils; —bewitches; —casts spells; —divines; —enchants; —exorcises; —fascinates; —forecasts; —foretells.
(See incantation, trick, miracle, manipulation.)

MAGIC

adverbs
bewilderingly; occultly; cleverly; subtly; amazingly; undeniably; wondrously; miraculously; curiously; strangely; unbelievably; wickedly; ascendan ly; weirdly; cabalistically; mystically; mysteriously; slyly; obviously; presumably.

MAGISTERIAL

adverbs
officiously; ostentatiously; authoritatively; arrogantly; superciliously; offensively; vexatiously; sternly; severely; harshly; cruelly; tyrannically; rigidly; unnecessarily; ridiculously; absurdly; gravely; solemnly; droningly; coldly; strictly; intolerably; overbearingly; imperiously; pretentiously; stiffly; magnificently; ceremoniously; arbitrarily.

MAGISTRATE

adjectives
unmeriting; proud; violent; teasing; lawful; principal; inferior; directing; venal; elective; civil; presiding; stipendiary.

verbs
commit to—; impeach—; plead with—; vest in—; —acquits; —administers; —arbitrates; —arraigns; —assigns; —authorizes; —commands; —concedes; —deprives; —determines; —dispenses; —empowers; —exempts; —exonerates; —grants; —judges; —pronounces; —prosecutes; —restrains; —reviews; —sanctions; —sentences; —summons.
(See judge, consul, legislator, governor, president.)

MAGNANIMITY

adjectives
delicate; unbounded; peaceable; critical; rough; splendid; unlimited.

MAGNANIMOUS

adverbs
unusually; dependably; conspicuously; wonderfully; remarkably; unexpectedly; surprisingly; delightfully; beneficently; magnificently; utterly; habitually; unwontedly; unselfishly; generally; loftily; chivalrously; admirably; generously.

MAGNETIC

adverbs
highly; strongly; amazingly; surprisingly; delightfully; attractively; charmingly; unusually; powerfully; potently; preponderantly; influentially; persuasively; temptingly; irresistibly; unaccountably; immensely; extremely; remarkably.

MAGNETISM

adjectives
permanent; terrestrial; animal; proudest; universal.

MAGNIFICENCE

adjectives
mournful; profuse; calculated; theatrical; oriental; solid; fancied; barbaric; gorgeous; stern; multiplied; tawdry; ephemeral; pristine; unquestionable; snowy; lavish; incredible; wide-spread; somber.

MAGNIFICENT

adverbs
splendidly; gorgeously; grandly; sumptuously; brilliantly; gaudily; regally; extraordinarily; remarkably; marvelously; ceremonially; majestically; pompously; formally; highly; unspeakably; beautifully; elegantly; overwhelmingly; stupendously; colossally; resplendently; richly; imposingly; sublimely; matchlessly; impressively.

MAGNIFY (v)

adverbs
stereoptically; enormously; stupendously; gloriously; theatrically; barbarically; audaciously; scientifically; mechanically; prodigiously.

(See enlarge, exaggerate, augment.)

MAGNITUDE

adjectives
enhanced; prodigious; audacious; infinite; imposing; sensible; intermediate; considerable; swelling.

verbs
amplify—; comprehend—; extend—; heighten—; limit—; reduce—; restrict—; swell to —; —abates; —diminishes; —soars.

(See dimension, extent, greatness, measurements.)

MAGPIE

verbs
molest—; persecute—; tame—; —amuses; —chatters; —cheeps; —scolds; —shies; —steals; —talks; —thieves.

(See bird.)

MAHOGANY

adjectives
massive; rich; heavy; clumsy.

MAID

adjectives
unwilling; thoughtless; imprudent; poor; lowly; sentimental; lovelorn; wronged; meek; graceful; chariest; expiring; cleaner; sun-swart; deflowered; wretched; deceitful; sprightly, dark-tressed; loud-screaming; ungrateful; uncommon; guileless; kind; virtuous; fasting; blooming; lurking; milking; volatile; butterfly; kittenish; old; heavenly; stainless; recreant; pretty; chaste; simple; buskined; confiding; serving; stately; pale; impassioned; virginal; orphaned; fair; cruel; careless.

MAIDEN

adjectives
modest; guileless; simple; barefoot; dimpled; timid; white-veiled; sainted; home-keeping; cherry-cheeked; rosy-lipped; burlesque; gleeful; toddling; pastoral; dejected; snow; movie-mad; timid; willful; loose-girdled; affectionate; hapless; orbed; pale; avaricious; virtuous; rigid; decked; broad-backed; unfortunate; bright-eyed; enamored.

MAIDENHOOD

adjectives
delectable; stainless; frank; lean; profaned; blooming.

MAIDENLY

adverbs
demurely; coyly; sedately; shyly; decorously; becomingly; modestly; blushingly; rosily; suitably; properly; sweetly; graciously; conventionally; attractively; quietly; serenely; bashfully; appropriately.

MAIL

adjectives
glittering; ubiquitous; outgoing; departed; brisk.

verbs
assemble—; bag—; bear—; certify—; classify—; collect—; communicate by—; consign to—; convey—; defraud by—; distribute—; flood—; fly—; insure—; loot—; plunder—; register—; rifle—; transmit by—.

(See message.)

MAIN

adjectives
troubled; unfathomable; whitening; infinite; boundless; molten; azure; pulseless; tideless; billowed; murmuring; immeasurable; moaning.

MAINTAIN (*v*)

adverbs
stubbornly; willfully; inexorably; unreservedly; automatically; gallantly; scrupulously; peremptorily; diabolically; resolutely; unblushingly; stoutly; intensely; ignorantly; vigorously; inflexibly; normally; agreeably; perpetually; progressively; jealously; adequately.

(See claim, sustain, support, affirm.)

MAINTENANCE

adjectives
continued; scanty; perpetual; fitting; progressive; standing; adequate; jealous.

MAIZE

adjectives
tall; spiky; twinkling; sun-loving; ripening; towering; tasseled.

MAJESTIC

adverbs
splendidly; gloriously; brilliantly; imposingly; solemnly; ceremonially; augustly; sublimely; impressively; grandly; formally; pompously; superbly; imperially; loftily; sumptuously; gorgeously.

MAJESTY

adjectives
essential; ghostlike; wonted; collective; impressive; angered; sluggard; unfamiliar; sheer; serene; characteristic; conscious; outraged; awful; singular; tranquil; dreadful; comparable; gentle; vigorous; tropical; sweet; rare; commanding; overshadowing; apparent; unspeakable; glittering; unascended; inaccessible; colossal; shadowy; mutilated; certain; dispelled; clouded; unshakable; rayless; ineffable; grotesque; ethereal; swarthy; dramatic; imperious; pastoral; sublime; somber.

MAJORITY

adjectives
overwhelming; popular; hostile; legislative; phenomenal; vast; handsome; compact; emphatic; bare; preponderant; ignorant; enlarged.

verbs
attain—; bow to—; endow with—; gain—; increase—; pile up—; poll—; purchase—; reach—; render—; sway—; swell—; —balances; —carries; —determines; —exceeds; —overtops; —overwhelms; —predominates, —prevails; —surpasses.

(See generality, age, minority, multitude, throng, crowd.)

MAKE (*v*)

adverbs
powerfully; eventually; inevitably; ultimately; unquestionably; crudely; obviously; inadvertently; advisedly; persistently; unwittingly; unhesitatingly; temporarily; subsequently; superbly; indiscriminately; laboriously; lawfully; delicately; scientifically.

(See create, compose, invent, manufacture.)

MAKESHIFT

adverbs
cleverly; ingeniously; obviously; carelessly; shiftlessly; adroitly; permanently; clumsily; awkwardly; evidently; dexterously; smartly; handily; pitifully; crudely; presumably; miserably; wretchedly; comically; suitably.

MAKE-UP

verbs
apply—; blanch under—; disguise with—; renew—; represent by—; strip of—; —ages; —alters; —clogs; —colors; —embellishes; —ornaments; —smudges; —tones.

(See paint, color, disguise, mask, pose, pretense, sham.)

MALADIES

adjectives
putrid; incurable; terrible; relievable; organic; infinite; still-clinging; kindred; mortal; deadly; grievous; past-cure; corporeal; painful; expensive; pestiferous; reparable.

MALADJUSTMENT

adjectives
serious; temperamental; deep-seated.

MALADROIT

adverbs
absurdly; unexpectedly; ridiculously; laughably; comically; ludicrously; surprisingly; inexpertly; clumsily; awkwardly; shyly; bashfully; deliberately; purposely; intention-

ally; helplessly; pitiably; miserably; wretchedly; hopelessly; oddly; stupidly; obtusely; gawkily; embarrassingly; shockingly; uselessly.

MALADY

verbs
afflict with—; aggravate—; allay—; arrest —; communicate—; contract—; control—; diagnose—; eradicate—; expose to—; immunize against—; infest with—; inherit—; isolate—; recognize—; succumb to—; withstand—; —consumes; —lingers; —menaces; —prostrates; —reasserts itself.
(See ailment, disease, infection, illness, sickness.)

MALE

adjectives
monstrous; inexhaustible; art-shy; dominant; rival; smug.

verbs
attract—; lure—; —begets; —fertilizes; —fructifies; —fuses; —generates; —husbands; —implants; —impregnates; —incorporates; —infuses; —preserves; —procreates; —propagates; —sires; —unifies.
(See parent, father.)

MALEDICTION

adjectives
profane; parting; bitter; hearty; muffled.

verbs
address with—s; bluster—; call down—; fulminate—; invoke—; thunder—; utter—; —abuses; —anathematizes; —clamors; —curses; —denounces; —execrates; —scolds; —threatens.
(See curse, slander, denunciation.)

MALEVOLENT

adverbs
viciously; vengefully; savagely; terribly; brutally; sternly; harshly; incredibly; mercilessly; relentlessly; ruthlessly; unspeakably; desperately; villainously; alarmingly; dangerously; notoriously; infamously; criminally; actively; nefariously; inordinately; utterly; incurably; inescapably; heinously; dreadfully; rancorously; spitefully; barbarously; bitterly.

MALICE

adjectives
burning; insane; fairy; devilish; venomous; ancient; fiendish; sportful; serpent; deepest; diabolical; ingenious; crafty; partisan; womanly; warm; dancing; genial; cold-blooded; ferocious.

verbs
bear—; betray—; breed—; excite—; express —; harbor—; impel to—; impute to—; incite—; intend—; provoke—; recoil from—; regard with—; rile to—; sense—; shudder at—; sow—; tinge with—; view with—; wreak—upon; —embitters; —harasses; —hardens; —harries; —molests; —ripens.
(See bitterness, grudge, ill will, envy, anger, rage, violence, wrath.)

MALICIOUS

adverbs
flagrantly; dangerously; violently; irretrievably; inconceivably; poisonously; abominably; accursedly; perniciously; viciously; basely; deplorably; diabolically; disastrously; dreadfully; exceptionally; grievously; hatefully; venomously; violently; manifestly; subtly; irremediably; irrevocably; immeasurably; villainously; sadly; woefully; shockingly; cruelly; infernally; atrociously; incredibly; shamefully; iniquitously.

MALIGN

adverbs
ominously; portentously; dangerously; undeniably; disastrously; calamitously; ruinously; venomously; poisonously; treacherously; ruthlessly; relentlessly; slanderously; incredibly.

MALIGNANT

adverbs
openly; deliberately; studiously; hatefully; curiously; incorrigibly; evilly; desperately; outrageously; cruelly; bitterly; harshly; venomously; truculently; atrociously; dangerously; poisonously; abominably; perniciously; disastrously; exceptionally; grievously; subtly; sadly; woefully; shockingly; infernally.

MALIGNITY

adjectives
impure; incredible; factious; fiendish; drunken; elaborate; devilish.

MAMMALS

adjectives
branch-building; aquatic; ungulate.

MAMMOTH

adverbs

colossally; gigantically; incredibly; unbelievably; inconceivably; immeasurably; monstrously; incalculably; mythically; stupendously; toweringly; overwhelmingly.

MAN

adjectives

able; acclaimed; alert; ambitious; amiable; anile; arbitrary; armed; austere; available; avaricious; bad; bald; bearded; beetle-browed; bemused; benevolent; benighted; bibulous; big-waisted; bizarre; blind; bloody; boastful; bony; boorish; boyish-looking; brawny; brilliant; broken; broken-hearted; burly; business; cadaverous; cannon-voiced; carefree; careful; carnal; celebrated; charming; chipper; coming; commercial; compassionate; completed; condemned; conscientious; contemplative; corpulent; corruptible; cultivated; cumbersome; cunning; cynical; dapper; dauntless; deathless; decorous; defeated; deep-dimpled; difficult; dilatory; disappointed; disengaged; disinterested; dissipated; double-chinned; dull; dumb; dusky; dynamic; easy-going; eccentric; effeminate; egotistic; elemental; eloquent; emancipated; embarrassed; energetic; enterprising; entertaining; envious; envisaging; estimable; exact; excellent; exceptional; exemplary; experienced; fair-haired; family; famous; fat; fierce; fine-looking; fine-shaped; firm; fit; flaunting; florid; formidable; fractious; frail; frivolous; frustrated; full; full-rigged; function-free; fussy; gallant; general; genial; godless; gossiping; graceless; great-hearted; gregarious; half-naked; handicraft; hard-fisted; hard-working; hawk-headed; headless; heavy-built; heroic; highbred; hoary; homely; honest; hooked-nose; hospitable; hot-tempered; huge; human; humorous; hungry; husky; idle; ill-instructed; ill-natured; illustrious; imperious; impertinent; impious; incomparable; incredible; incurious; indefatigable; indispensable; industrious; influential; informed; ingrateful; inner; inscrutable; intemperate; intrepid; irate; isolated; jolly; jovial; key; kind; knowing; lank; large; lawless; lean; lettered; literary; little; lonely; lovable; magnificent; magnified; married; masterless; mediocre; meditative; meek; merciful; merry; middle-aged; mild-appearing; mild-mannered; mincing; moaning; modest; much-experienced; mustached; myopic; myriad-wrinkled; mysterious; narrow-minded; new-married; niggardly; noble; obstinate; olive-skinned; omnivorous; overconfident; over-sexed; pallid; pampered; patriarchal; petrified; phenomenal; plain-spoken; phlegmatic; plighted; politic; poorly-dressed; pragmatical; premature; primitive; prominent; proper; propertied; prospering; prudent; pushing; puzzled; quiet; rapid-fire; rational; ready; red-eyed; reflective; repentant; reticent; rich; riddled; rising; rough-looking; round; ruthless; sad; sane; saturnine; savage; seafaring; selfish; self-helping; self-isolated; self-made; self-poised; sensitive; sensual; sharp-eyed; sharp-witted; shock-headed; silent; silly; simple-minded; sinful; sleek; sleight-of-hand; smoking; sober; society; soft-voiced; sound; spoiled; spotted; square-set; squat-figured; staunch; steel-sinewed; stocky; strange; strange-voiced; stray; studious; successful; sullen; sunburned; superior; supple; sure-poised; sweaty; taciturn; talented; tempestuous; tender-hearted; toothless; tormented; ugly; unabashed; unabsolved; unadaptable; unbookish; unbreakable; unburied; uncompanionable; unfortunate; ungrateful; universal; unlettered; unquestioning; unrepentant; unrevolving; untidy; untutored; upright; useless; wayfaring; well-conditioned; wealthy; well-informed; well-proportioned; whimsical; witless; wind-swept; wiry; wise; worthy; vague; wretched; vain; vigorous; virtuous; yellow-visaged; voluptuous; youthful.

MANACLE

adjectives

mortal; menacing; hampering.

verbs

bind with—; clamp on—; don—; fetter with —; forge—; —bridles; —checks; —confines; —constrains; —controls; —curbs; —handcuffs; —prohibits; —restrains; —restricts; —secures; —shackles; —tethers.

(See fetter, restraint.)

MANAGE (v)

adverbs

economically; dexterously; effectively; humanely; judiciously; exclusively; bunglingly; artistically; ingeniously; peremptorily; governmentally; politically; systematically; conservatively; prudently; profitably; incompetently; adroitly; admirably.

(See conduct, supervise, administer, handle.)

MANAGEABLE

adverbs

easily; smoothly; carefully; thriftily; commercially; financially; scarcely; altogether; strategically; subtly; strangely; readily; diplomatically; unexpectedly; quietly; tractably; tactfully.

MANAGEMENT

adjectives

municipal; marvelous; topsy-turvy; duped; frightened; conservative; generous; consolidated; wise; dietary; bungling; systematic; operative; prudent; profitable; admirable; good; adroit; clumsy; wasteful; incompetent; group; capable; vigorous.

verbs

acquire—; administer—; charge with—; conduct—; contrive—; control—; decry—; demean—; denounce—; direct—; enact—; guide—; manipulate—; master—; qualify for—; shift—; skill in—; superintend—; —negotiates; —transacts.

(See direction, government, economy, conduct, charge, legislature, owner, manager.)

MANAGER

adjectives

dexterous; peremptory; unyielding; operatic.

verbs

install—; —directs; —governs; —heads; —helms; —inspects; —orders; —oversees; —pilots; —regulates; —steers; —superintends; —supervises; —surveys; —threatens.

(See boss, industrialist, employer, superintendent, leader, management, owner.)

MANDATE

adjectives

constitutional; official; illegal; tragic; scholastic; royal; titular.

verbs

cite—; comply with—; enact—; issue—; lay down—; prescribe—; remand—; seal—; yield to—; —appoints; —bids; —commands; —controls; —decrees; —deposes; —directs; —dictates; —enjoins; —imposes; —ordains; —proclaims; —summons; —orders.

(See law, measure, decree, edict, command, warrant, regulation, ordinance, order, summons.)

MANE

adjectives

flowing; tossing; dripping; luxuriant; braided; hanging; illimitable; plaited; leonine; sudden; flaring.

verbs

brush—; corrugate—; crumple—; gnarl—; knot—; roughen—; ruffle—; rumple—; seize by—; stroke—; toss back—; —adorns; —crests; —droops; —erects; —flows; —fringes; —ripples; —shags.

(See hair, mustache, whiskers, plumage, beard.)

MANEUVER

adjectives

adroit; loving; little; ingenious; thrilling; sordid; political; important; inexplicable; pernicious; odious; shabby; perfunctory; legal; sensational; innocent; dishonest; decisive; skillful; polished; ticklish; ladylike; bold; engineering; intricate.

verbs

achieve—; circumvent—; commit—; contrive—; design—; detail—; enact—; evolve—; execute—; expedite—; organize—; outline—; participate in—; perform—; perpetrate—; practise—; project—; propose—; sanction—; systematize—; transact—; —conceals; —juggles; —temporizes.

(See method, strategy, tactics, subterfuge, trick, move.)

MANEUVER (*v*)

adverbs

skillfully; adroitly; ingeniously; thrillingly; dexterously; perfunctorily; legally; sensationally; decisively; diplomatically; boldly; rashly; daringly; intricately.

(See plan, scheme.)

MANFUL

adverbs

boldly; bravely; confidently; courageously; firmly; gallantly; hardily; intrepidly; sturdily; pluckily; resolutely; spunkily; valorously; nobly; honorably; virtuously; dauntlessly; splendidly; indomitably; stoutly; venturesomely; venturously; admirably.

MANGLE (*v*)

adverbs

hideously; shamefully; murderously; ruthlessly; savagely; bestially; brutishly; insanely; stupidly; outrageously; sordidly; perniciously.

(See torture, tear.)

MANHOOD

adjectives

generous; neglected; ripe; moral; sober; prosperous; blasted; pitiless; riper; stormy; toilworn; debonair; relentless; martial; remorseless; civilized; sturdy; vigorous; returning.

MANIA

adjectives

sad; dreadful; melancholy; fantastic; undoubted; infernal.

verbs

amount to—; control—; obsess with—; —abates; —attacks; —crazes; —deludes; —deranges; —enthuses (colloq.); —excites; —fades; —impassions; —rages; —wanes.

(See madness, insanity, frenzy, hysteria, delirium.)

MANIAC

adjectives

religious; raving; fettered; gesticulating; fugitive.

verbs

arouse—; chain—; confine—; enchain—; fetter—; harness—; imprison—; incarcerate —; isolate—; liberate—; overpower—; restrain—; shackle—; subdue—; —flames; —foams; —fumes; —howls; —leers; —rages; —rambles; —raves; —scowls.

(See madman.)

MANIFEST

adverbs

unwisely; conspicuously; demonstrably; distinctly; explicitly; boldly; strikingly; publicly; fortunately; unluckily; brazenly; shamefully; pitifully; alarmingly; fearfully; clearly; glaringly; plainly.

MANIFEST (v)

adverbs

obscurely; plainly; vividly; predominantly; broadly; speciously; exclusively; strenuously; universally; frankly; ingenuously; externally; exaggeratedly; conspicuously; whimsically; outwardly; directly; morbidly; physically.

(See reveal, show.)

MANIFESTATION

adjectives

incipient; exaggerated; contemporaneous; external; remarkable; terrestrial; temporary; visible; startling; conspicuous; moderate; astounding; fiery; impolitic; practical; imperial; special; whimsical; extraordinary; outward; historical; tawdry; distinct; decrepit; amplified; direct; recorded; morbid; external; troublesome; extravagant; physical.

verbs

discourage—; overshadow—; ponder—; render—; suppress—; —alludes to; —attests; —bears out; —conveys; —discloses; —evidences; —expresses; —implies; —indicates; —proves; —purports; —reveals; —signifies; —suggests; —symbolizes.

(See indication, evidence, display, disclosure, demonstration.)

MANIKIN

verbs

drape on—; photograph—; view—; —demonstrates; —depicts; —displays; —exhibits; —illustrates; —imitates; —impersonates; —mimics; —models; —parades; —personifies; —projects; —represents.

(Seee model.)

MANIPULATE (v)

adverbs

delicately; deceptively; dexterously; mysteriously; tactfully; secretly; adroitly; technically; surgically; automatically; mechanically; conservatively; deftly.

(See operate, handle.)

MANIPULATION

adjectives

secret; delicate; adroit; technical; surgical; mechanical; automatic; localized; conservative; deft.

verbs

absorb in—; admire—; circumvent—; contrive—; disparage—; employ—; execute—; necessitate—; observe—; practise—; refrain from—; resort to—; skill in—; transact—; —exercises; —stimulates.

(See magic, strategy, trick, mischief, management, treatment.)

MANKIND

adjectives
menaced; married; miserable; unregenerate; redeemed; beauteous.

verbs
admonish—; apprize—; beguile—; benefit —; confer on—; edify—; enlighten—; humanize—; immortalize—; judge—; liberate —; present to—; raise—; trace—; —achieves; —deifies; —evolves; —progresses; —wars on; —worships.

(See civilization, world, family, population, race, society.)

MANLINESS

adjectives
ancient; rugged; ripening; native; barbarous.

MANLY

adverbs
boldly; sturdily; admirably; wonderfully; stoutly; robustly; courageously; valiantly; gallantly; pluckily; resolutely; confidently; adventurously; heroically; fiercely; staunchly; candidly; splendidly.

MANNA

adjectives
animal; celestial; hidden; unexpected; heavenly.

MANNER

adjectives
absorbing; abstracted; acceptable; accessible; accustomed; acquiesced; affable; affectionate; aggressive; agitated; aimless; alarming; altered; ambiguous; amicable; amplest; apologetic; appropriate; approved; argumentative; aristocratic; arrogant; artificial; artist-like; assuming; astonishing; attitudinizing; authoritative; awkward; bantering; barbarous; base; bizarre; blackguardly; bland; bookish; boyish; brotherly; brusque; brutal; buoyant; burlesque; businesslike; calm; candid; casual; caustic; cautious; charming; chatty; cheap; chilling; circuitous; classical; clerkly; cogitating; collected; commodious; compendious; complacent; comprehended; confidential; connected; consummate; continuous; conventional; coquettish; cordial; corporate; correct; correctional; courteous; courtly; cowardly; creditable; crushing; cunning; customary; dainty; dazzling; debonair; deceptive; deferential; defying; delicate; delightful; depraved; deranged; derisive; derivative; despiteful; desultory; detached; dictatorial; different; diffident; dignified; discovered; discreditable; disdainful; disillusioned; disagreeable; derogatory; disquieting; distinctive; distressful; dreadful; earnest; elegant; embarrassed; enchained; enchanted; endearing; engaging; engrossed; entertaining; enviable; erratic; exasperating; exceptional; exhaustive; expressive; extraordinary; fantastic; fawning; festive; filial; finished; formal; forthright; frank; friendly; frugal; gallant; gentle; glaring; gleeful; greedy; guilty; guileless; gross; haphazard; harmonious; haughty; hearty; heavy; heedless; heroic; hideous; hospitable; hurried; identical; illiberal; imitating; immortal; impatient; impeccable; imperfect; imperturbable; imploring; incomparable; incomprehensive; incongruous; independent; indescribable; indispensable; indolent; inexplicable; ingenious; ingratiating; inimitable; insinuating; insolent; insulting; interesting; intimate; intolerant; intricate; invidious; invincible; irreproachable; irreverent; irritated; joyless; kind; kingly; lamblike; languid; laughing; law-abiding; legitimate; lethargic; lifelike; loathed; longing; ludicrous; maidenly; majestic; manufactured; masonic; masterful; meek; meditative; metaphorical; methodic; modern; modest; monotonous; muffled; musing; native; negligent; obsessive; obstinate; odd; offensive; orderly; ordinary; orthodox; outrageous; particular; overbearing; patronizing; peerless; peculiar; perfunctory; persuasive; pert; pettish; picaresque; piquant; piteous; plausible; poetic; polished; polite; pompous; positive; pragmatic; precise; premature; prepossessing; priestlike; profitless; promiscuous; proper; propitiatory; prosy; protesting; provoking; punctilious; quiet; rational; rattling; realistic; reasonable; reckless; refreshing; reluctant; repulsive; respectable; rough; roundabout; rustic; ruthless; satisfactory; saucy; savage; self-reliant; selfsame; sensational; sententious; sentimental; serene; shoddy; signal; silken; similar; simplified; simulated; sketchy; soft; slovenly; social; solemn; spectacular; spurious; stainless; suave; sublime; substantial; suitable; summary; sumptuous; supercilious; superficial; superlative; systematic; tactful; tender; terrifying; theoretical; thoughtful; touching; two-fold; triumphant; tumultuous; typical; unaccountable; unaffected; unassuming; uncompromis-

ing; undemonstrative; undiscriminating; undisguised; unemotional; unenthusiastic; uneven; uneventful; unforgettable; ungracious; unique; unmistakable; unobtrusive; unofficial; unostentatious; unprecedented; unpremeditated; unprincipled; unprofitable; unreserved; unsightly; unswerving; unusual; unwavering; uproarious; urbane; warning; warring; wholesome; winning; vivacious; youthful; laughable.

verbs
affect—; acquire—; adopt—; ape—; corrupt—s; embolden—; evolve—; flaunt—s; inculcate—s; modify—; recover—; revitalize—; revolt against—s; tolerate—; transform—; —bullies; —cools; —enrages; —s root in; —shocks; adapt—.

(See behavior, air, method, style, mannerism, vogue, mode, mien, means.)

MANNERISM

adjectives
inscrutable; developing; humiliating; musical; romantic; severe; compulsive; obstreperous.

verbs
abandon—; accentuate—; addict to—; affect—; caricaturize—; conventionalize—; endow with—; fall into—; inherit—; jeer at—; mimic—; mock—; ridicule—; satirize—; sustain—; —dandifies; —exemplifies; —individualizes; —simpers.

(See manner, eccentricity, style, method.)

MANNERLY

adverbs
inherently; naturally; carefully; beautifully; pleasantly; agreeably; studiously; unaffectedly; ostentatiously; always; scarcely; barely; urbanely; suavely; smoothly; affably; gallantly; chivalrously; obsequiously; respectfully; humbly; unctuously; blandly; graciously; genially; heartily; modestly; quietly; unfailingly; ceremoniously.

MANNIKIN

adjectives
flesh-hinged; mortal; god-driven; mechanic.

MANSION

adjectives
cheerless; mossy; determinate; ostentatious; commodious; moldered; noble; desolate; executive; hospitable; dim; fatigued; reticent; old; feudal; happy; elegant; studious; solitary; heavenly; blissful; rich-chambered; eternal; sun-mellowed; stout; substantial; white-pillared; gloomy; dolorous; marble; noisy; aristocratic; baronial; shut-up; palatial; intricate; stately; extensive; stormy; steady; temple like; beautiful; decorated; colonnaded; antiquated; fragile.

verbs
convert—; dwell in—; haunt—; inhabit—; modernize—; occupy—; permeate—; redecorate—; remodel—; renovate—; reside in—; restore—; —awes; —houses; —inspires; —quarters.

(See castle, structure, palace, residence, house, apartment.)

MANTLE

adjectives
judicial; imperial; furred; motley; verdant; somber; russet; silver; curious; sable; invisible; ermine; many-colored; grassy; flowery; stained; autumn.

MANUAL

adjectives
comprehensive; illustrated; constructive; informative; training; exquisite; helpful; complete.

MANUFACTURE (v)

adverbs
exclusively; prosperously; rudely; synthetically; coarsely; reputably; legally; successfully; preeminently.

(See make, create, invent, compose.)

MANUFACTURER

adjectives
coarsest; recalcitrant; obdurate; prominent; exclusive; reputable; preeminent; alert; successful.

MANUSCRIPT

adjectives
maltreated; moldered; crabbed; blazoned; lost; delusive; illuminated; scrawly; cuneiform; original; religious; written; quaint; typed; rare; valuable; long-penned.

verbs
acknowledge—; approve—; attest—; compile—; cull—; decipher—; decline—; edit—; engross in—; polish—; publish—; reject—; rewrite—; scratch out—; scrawl—; scribble—; transcribe—; witness—.

(See story, novel, message, romance, theme, thesis, volume.)

MAP

adjectives
density; topographical; previous; rude; accurate; road; aerial; changing.

verbs
design—; draft—; scale—; sketch—; —acquaints; —apprizes; —charts; —communicates; —conveys; —delineates; —describes; —details; —directs; —enlightens; —estimates; —guides; —imparts; —informs; —pilots; —portrays; —represents; —specifies.
(See chart, diagram, outline, plan.)

MARAUDER

adjectives
sanguine; terrible; ferocious; licentious; burglarious; deadly; stealthy.

MARBLE

adjectives
mottled; blended; breathing; variegated; wrought; remarkable; chill; polished; synthetic; lusterless; ponderous; snowy; chiseled; cold; imitation.

MARCH

adjectives
torturing; severe; fruitless; tedious; silent; famous; dreary; rapid; forced; cautious; circuitous; toilsome; dreadful; disorderly; victorious; bloody; irresistible; hobbling; retrograde; triumphant; arduous; dramatic; confused; slow; glorious; stealthy; measureless; marvelous; magnificent; unprecedented; stately; prolonged; endless; ordered; steady; stormy; victorious; general; monotonous.

verbs
command—; direct—; extend—; force—; renew—; resort to—; retard—; review—; steal—on; —advances; —circuits; —deviates; —parades; —precedes; —rambles; —shuffles; —straggles; —veers; —wends; —zigzags.
(See charge, advance, action, move, attack.)

MARCH (v)

adverbs
pompously; triumphantly; steadily; tirelessly; leisurely; endlessly; menacingly; circuitously; stalwartly; uninterruptedly; briskly; morosely; intrepidly; aimlessly; ignominiously; fruitlessly; cautiously; irresistibly; arduously; dramatically; magnificently; monotonously.
(See advance, walk.)

MARCHER

verbs
—advances; —jogs; —journeys; —normalizes; —patrols; —plods; —proceeds; —promenades; —rambles; —roves; —salutes; —saunters; —shuffles on; —strolls; —struts; —threads his way; —tramps; —treads; —trudges.
(See traveler, tourist, passenger.)

MARE

adjectives
striking-looking; nervous; high; infuriated; whinnying; placid; brood; riderless; sleek; calico; thoroughbred.

verbs
break—; bridle—; check—; curb—; curry—; groom—; mount—; rein in—; —bares; —balks; —canters; —conveys; —foals; —gallops; —hurdles; —neighs; —prances; —shies; —trots; —whinnies.
(See horse, colt, mule, donkey. ass, pony.)

MARGIN

adjectives
invisible; flowery; satisfactory; embarrassing; narrowing; refreshing; substantial; distinct; sedgy; slight; regular.

MARGINAL

adverbs
broadly; safely; dangerously; insecurely; permissibly; perilously; riskily; hazardously.

MARINER

adjectives
shipwrecked; ancient; sunswart; chartless; faint-hearted; cowering; cautious; ingenious; homesick; deft; seaworthy.

MARK

adjectives
destructive; decisive; gracious; distinguished; well-founded; separate; dreadful; wedge-shaped; venerable; evident; conspicuous; special; privy; unobtrusive; peculiar; visible; imperceptible; external; transient; deepened; brilliant; delicate; guiding; aimless; unchanging; indelible; tiny.

verbs
bear—; better—; detect—; hold—; overshoot—; recognize—; regard—; scale—; scrutinize—; surpass—; toe—; —attests to; —betokens; —brands; —characterizes; —denotes; —directs; —guides; —identifies; —indicates; —periods; —ranks; —relates to; —signalizes; —signifies; —symbolizes; —symptomizes.
(See goal.)

MARK (v)

adverbs
distinctly; gratefully; delicately; unalterably; conspicuously; dismally; boldly; indelibly; obviously; destructively; venerably; privately; peculiarly; imperceptibly; externally; aimlessly; brilliantly.
(See brand, stamp, indicate.)

MARKET

adjectives
immediate; limited; glutted; rising; alternative; volume; extensive; matrimonial; prominent; inchoate; essential; public; prosperous; domestic; non-competitive; bristle; eager; growing; wide; open; huge; blooming.

verbs
barter in—; bear—; bottle up—; bull—; congest—; deflate—; dominate—; dump on—; flood—; glut—; invest in—; job in—; kill—; negotiate in—; overload—; procure—for; purvey at—; quote—; ravage—; speculate in—; stabilize—; survey—; swamp—; tax—; trade in—; traffic in—; transact at—; underbid—; vend in—; —booms; —fluctuates; —oscillates; —sags; —slumps.
(See exchange, trade, business, speculation, store, merchandise.)

MARKETABLE

adverbs
permanently; highly; seasonably; readily; easily; scarcely; always; occasionally; faddishly; uncertainly; remarkably; positively; currently; advantageously; profitably; opportunely; extremely; unusually; stably; durably; steadily; invariably; conveniently; fortunately.

MARRIAGE

adjectives
mercenary; reckless; indissoluble; heterodox; cradle; wealthy; international; immediate; advantageous; previous; unhappy; crude; dubious; ungentle; placid; conjectural; unworthy; bogged; subsequent; ill-starred; spiteful; wondrous; fat; ceremonious; intelligent; dubious; possible; ideal; continual; intended; somber; imprudent; hasty; impending; private; ensuing; repented; plural; honorable; brilliant; acceptable; sudden; monstrous; morganatic; uncertain; consanguineous; impecunious; impromptu; loveless; convenient; derogatory; ill-matched; idiotic; imprudent; impetuous; necessary.

verbs
absolve—; annul—; attend—; bless—; cement—; consummate—; contract—; dissolve—; ensure—; give in—; indicate—; precipitate—; romanticize—; sancitfy—; sanction—; terminate—; undermine—; —materializes; —sanctifies; —unites; plunge into—.
(See hand, wedding, nuptial, union, matrimony.)

MARROW

verbs
chill to—; convey through—; freeze—; inculcate in—; infect—; ingrain in—; moisten with—; suppurate—.
(See blood, being, bone, soul.)

MARRY (v)

adverbs
inadvertently; subsequently; advantageously; eventually; hastily; shamefully; recklessly; indissolubly; dubiously; congenially; spitefully; ceremoniously; imprudently; honorably; morganatically; lovelessly; impecuniously; conveniently; imprudently; impetuously.
(See espouse, wed.)

MARSH

verbs
bog down in—; drain—; dwell in—; flourish in—; infest—; inhabit—; mire in—; rehabilitate—; sink in—; slough in—; thrive in—; —breeds; —contaminates; —inundates; —menaces; —reeks; —stagnates; —submerges.
(See island, peninsula, swamp, valley, jungle, forest.)

MARSHAL

adjectives
provost; undaunted; fiery; daunted.

MARSHAL (v)

adverbs
sternly; vigorously; militaristically; undauntedly; patriotically; dutifully; gallantly.
(See arrange, adjust, settle.)

MARSHES

adjectives
malarial; pestiferous; inhospitable; dreary; fever-haunted; deadly; venomous; unmarshlike; treacherous; desolate; steaming.

MART

adjectives
humming; considerable; desperate; imperceptible; prosperous.

MARTIAL

adverbs
splendidly; brilliantly; gorgeously; portentously; ominously; dominantly; belligerently; contentiously; predominantly; magnificently; noisily; grimly; subtly; ostentatiously; deliberately; offensively; fearfully; daringly.

MARTIN

verbs
—aids; —arrays; —attacks; —banks; —s colonize; —s journey; —migrates; —pierces; —preys on; —rounds; —scratches; —skims; —smooths; —spreads.
(See bird, swallow.)

MARTYR

adjectives
ancient; unheralded; exulting; patient; resolute; selfish; grave; unpractical; fiery; sainted; magnanimous; crucified.

MARTYRDOM

adjectives
heroic; disdainful; uplifting; voluntary; long-sought.

MARVEL

adjectives
admiring; fantastic; infinite; accomplished; dreamlike.

verbs
accomplish—; admire—; behold—; gape at—; paint—; stand aghast at—; —amazes; —astonishes; —astounds; —awes; —baffles; —bewilders; —dazes; —dazzles; —dumbfounds; —electrifies; —fascinates; —flabbergasts (colloq); —overwhelms; —strikes dumb; —stuns; —stupefies; —staggers.
(See wonder, beauty, radiance, splendor, mystery, success.)

MARVEL (v)

adverbs
secretly; fantastically; infinitely; mutely; impassively; joyously; candidly.
(See wonder, amaze.)

MASK

adjectives
servile crescentlike; grisly; laughing; smiling; newest; impenetrable; lifeless; impassive; theatrical; acquired; hideous; wanton; deceitful; well-trained; sun-expelling; dainty; waxen; placid; tragic; changing; child-faced; stately.

verbs
adjust—; cloak with—; doff—; emerge from—; fashion—; —beguiles; —blinds; —conceals; —deceives; —deludes; —depicts; —disguises; —eclipses; —lures; —portrays; —veils; don—.
(See cloak, disguise, make-up, masquerade.)

MASK (v)

adverbs
partially; cunningly; demurely; servilely; impassively; wantonly; deceitfully; daintily; tragically; deceptively; treacherously; hideously; ironically; slyly.
(See disguise, hide, veil, masquerade.)

MASON

verbs
employ—; hire—; —achieves; —blocks; —carves; —chips; —chisels; —constructs; —drills; —erects; —fabricates; —forges; —frames; —heaves; —hews; —lugs; —models; —molds; —rears; —shoulders; —sunders.
(See worker, workman.)

MASONRY

adjectives
roofless; arched; delicate; beautiful.

MASQUERADE

adjectives
brilliant; glittering; ghastly; savage; phantom; speaking; ironic; ghostly.

verbs
attend—; organize—; plan—; reveal—; —bamboozles (colloq.); —beguiles; —blinds; —cloaks; —conceals; —counterfeits; —curtains; —decoys; —deludes; —diverts; —eclipses; —enlivens; —hoodwinks; —lures; —masks; —muffles; —mystifies; —relaxes; —screens; —secretes; —shades; —shrouds; —stifles; —suppresses; —veils.

(See mask, disguise, misrepresentaion, dance, sham.)

MASQUERADE (v)

adverbs
bizarrely; brilliantly; savagely; ironically; enthusiastically; spectacularly; joyously; ceremonially; formally; perfunctorily.

(See mask, hide, veil, disguise.)

MASS
(general)

adjectives
heterogeneous; midnight; bucking; regimented; gloomy; immense; agitated; promiscuous; frowning; withered; helpless; physical; mighty; confused; prosaic; frantic; vulgar; ever-moving; phalanxed; unmanaged; specious; aggregate; straggling; celebrated; clinking; homogeneous; inert; buttressed; tangled; wrestling; ungrateful; disloyal; neutral; spheroidal; somber; animated; woolly; ponderous; oscillating; floating; bloated; crashing; continuous; seething; chaotic; heaving; solid; desiccated; melancholy; pulplike; discouraging; whirling; remarkable; gigantic; fermenting; tumultuous; imposing; gummy; ill-defined; nebulous; rushing; roaring; irresistible; flickering; whale-like; luminous; continuous; immeasurable; indiscriminate; glowing; gross; steely; leaping; sinking; cutting; amorphous; bristling; repugnant; insensible; dark; impending; unbroken; burnished; entangled; pinnacled; conglomerate; gigantic; agitated; restless; incoherent; inarticulate; quivering; resplendent; rough; packed; incandescent; unyielding; accumulating; inanimate; successive (pl); tough; leathery; somber; indistinct; charred; gelatine.

MASS
(lump, assemblage, heap, etc.)

verbs
accumulate—; aggregate—; bulk—; cement in—; cluster in—; compile—; constitute—; crush—; disintegrate—; dissolve—; embody —; focus in—; heap in—; integrate—; lump in—; measure—; muster—; scrape—; verge in—; —expands; —ferments; —rises; —soars; —swells; —thickens; —towers; —transcends.

(See dough, generality, crowd, amount, heap.)

MASS
(religion)

verbs
administer—; anthem—; attend—; bow at —; chant—; chorus—; devote to—; give praise at—; kneel at—; mumble—; perform —; worship at—; —glorifies; —invokes; —offers; —salvages; —uplifts.

(See church, rite, ceremony, sacrament.)

MASSACRE

adjectives
atrocious; brutal; indiscriminate; cruel; fierce; horrid; dreadful; treacherous; wholesale; judicial; bloody .

verbs
decry—; denounce—; execute—; expire in —; frown on—; lust for—; perpetrate—; plot—; rebuke for—; reproach for—; resign to—; succumb in—; yield to—; —despatches; —enrages; —ensanguines; —incenses; —rages; —scandalizes; —scars; —stains; —threatens.

(See bloodshed, killing, murder, assassination, slaughter, violence.)

MASSAGE

adjectives
invigorating; stimulating; scientific; frictional; healing.

verbs
—enlivens; —exhilarates; —invigorates; —limbers; —quickens; —refreshes; —regenerates; —relaxes; —relieves; —soothes; —smooths; —ungnarls.

(See remedy, medicine, liniment, masseur.)

MASSAGE (v)

adverbs
industriously; actively; invigoratingly; stimulatingly; scientifically; healingly; beneficially.

(See rub, knead.)

MASSES (general)

adjectives
singular; vapory; quadrangular; comet-shaped; thunderous; dusky; cosmic; exultant; dense; congested; multitudinous; surging; accumulated; struggling; huddled; flame-shaped; crushing; impenetrable; enormous; enthusiastic; metallic; hurrying; disorderly; grateful; cross; incensed; vast; bold; fleeing; irregular; illiterate; listening; glittering; shadowy; dusky; dull; huge; menacing; obedient; luminous.

MASSES (people)

verbs
benefit—; cajole—; deride—; educate—; enkindle—; enslave—; exhort—; exploit—; ferment—; inflame—; indoctrinate—; lift —; move—; rally—round; subjugate—; submerge—; sway—; tread on—; weld—; —erupt; —revolt; —seethe.

(See public, population, multitude, mob, society, throng, crowd.)

MASSEUR

verbs
train—; —comforts; —eases; —kneads; —manipulates; —massages; —pats; —pounds; —quiets; —rectifies; —rubs; —spanks.

(See massage.)

MASSIVE

adverbs
enormously; awkwardly; stupendously; impossibly; overwhelmingly; grotesquely; strangely; ponderously; grossly; monstrously.

MAST

adjectives
staggering; derrick-like; ripened; tapering; straining; naked; raking; towering; broken; snapped.

verbs
clamber up—; erect—; lash to—; lower—; nail to—; raise—; rig—; sail before—; spring—; step—; strain—; —creaks; —extends; —rises; —splinters; —supports; —sustains; —sways.

(See post, beam.)

MASTER

adjectives
imperious; profound; lurid; disloyal; captious; contemporary; testy; intriguing; sweet; urban; provincial; absolute; clouted; majestic; unrighteous; supreme; former; money; dish-faced; prayer; inglorious; independent; exasperating; unsuccessful; tyrannical; foremost; inward; school; mystic; industrial; noble; undisputed; accepted; perturbed; indignant; formidable; marvelous; proficient; blithe; shrewd; unworthy; injudicious; intractable; manful; jovial.

verbs
acknowledge—; appeal to—; attend—; betray—; bow to—; conspire against—; emulate—; enjoin—; follow—; salute—; serve —; supersede—; —authorizes; —censures; —controls; —directs; —disciplines; —enslaves; —governs; —guides; —judges; —lashes; —oversees; —rewards; —rules; —supervises.

(See expert, husband, commander, employer.)

MASTER (v)

adverbs
skillfully; imperiously; profoundly; absolutely; majestically; tyrannically; undisputedly; formidably; marvelously; proficiently; shrewdly; jovially; injudiciously; dictatorially.

(See handle, rule, command.)

MASTERPIECE

adjectives
ambitious; fair; exquisite; crisp; vivid; brief; restrained; unequaled; unsurpassed; literary; involuntary; eminent; symphonic; heroic.

verbs
acclaim—; accomplish—; achieve—; applaud—; appreciate—; cast—; chance upon —; contemplate—; emulate—; esteem—; examine—; extol—; hail as—; interpret—; laud—; match—; pay tribute to—; praise —; reproduce—; rival—; study—; transcribe—; value—; work—; —excels; —depicts; —portrays; —reposes in; —surpasses; —survives; —transcends.

(See picture, photograph, portrait, painting, model, plan, statue.)

MASTERY

adjectives
unrivaled; intelligent; barbarous; seductive; technical: imperfect; physical; complete.

verbs
aim at—; assay—; assert—; assume—; attain—; command—of; crown with—; dispute—; distinguish by—; exercise—; gain —; maintain—; match—; perform with—; prove—; regain—; relinquish—; spur to—; strive for—; struggle for—; surpass—; wield—; —awes; —dominates; —prevails; —sways.

(See perfection, proficiency, skill.)

MATCH (*fire*)

verbs
apply—; dip—; extinguish—; ignite—; impregnate—; quench—; scratch—; smother —; tip—; touch off—; —chars; —devours; —dies; —enkindles; —flickers; —fuses; —glows; —incinerates; —simmers; —singes; —smoulders; —sputters.

(See lamp, light, flame, fire.)

MATCH (*general*)

adjectives
brilliant; unwise; brief; ordinary; shameful; suitable; mad; rich; honorable; championship; unholy; inappropriate; love.

MATCH (*parallel, mate, boot, etc.*)

verbs
arrange—; challenge to—; compete i –; contest—; enter—; judge—; negotiate—; officiate at—; promote—; prove—for; regulate—; scorn—; spurn—; view—; witness —; —corresponds; —duplicates; —mirrors; —parallels; —pairs; —resembles.

(See bout, fight, race (sport), contest.)

MATCH (*v*)

adverbs
equally; boldly; madly; rashly; foolhardily; brilliantly; unwisely; honorably; shamefully; improvidently.

(See oppose, challenge, defy, dare.)

MATE

adjectives
trembling; truant; incongruous; all-beautiful; nested; afflicted; vile; sincere; sweet; shivering; unloved; lovely; unkind; brooding; equal; imprudent; inharmonious; beauteous.

verbs
abandon—; choose—; compete for—; desert —; discard—; divorce—; espouse—; estrange from—; forsake—; guard—; join —; protect—; quit—; relinquish—; renounce —; vie for—; —matches; —parallels; —resembles.

(See comrade, husband, wife, friend.)

MATERIAL (*general*)

adjectives
biographical; suggestive; front-page; illustrative; corrosive; supplementary; ennobling; inexhaustible; complex; delicate; gauzy; acoustical; intellectual; suitable; biblical; health; preserved; objectionable; documentary; infinite; mournful; hilarious; extensive; tangible; concentrated; factual; authoritative; vast; repressed; anthropological; exquisite; impressionable; ample; outside; moraine; underworld; heterogeneous; mailable; muscle-building; copious; rustable; combustible; superfine; prepared; quality; misleading; rubberlike; tenacious; unpromising; noble; rugged; infantile; washable; special; volatile; polished; positive; elastic; unformed; nutritive; discordant; packaging; cool; raw; molten; protective; illustrative; septic; superlative; conglomerating; basic; rude; superfluous; durable; versatile; abrasive; miraculous; abundant; unimpeachable; picturesque; inorganic; fragmentary; coarse; scanty; shining; intractable; disjointed; choicest; insulating; mulch; thematic.

MATERIAL (*information*)

verbs
absorb—; accumulate—; amass—; arrange —; array—; assemble—; assort—; catalogue—; collect—; compile—; concentrate on —; delve into—; digest—; disseminate—; gather—; glean—; group—; jot down—; marshal—; muster—; rake up—; reduce—; sift—; simplify—; treat—; unify—.

(See knowledge, facts, science, copy, information, wisdom.)

MATERIAL
(*matter*)

verbs
allot—; amass—; apportion—; assemble—; consume—; derive—from; drain—; exhaust —; expend—; garner—; heap—; lay in—; load—; manipulate—; measure—; order—; reserve—; sift—; squander—; stock with—; store—; waste—; —fritters away.

(See cloth, drapery, ingredients, supply, food, merchandise.)

adverbs
grossly; flagrantly; selfishly; highly; essentially; vitally; fundamentally; gravely; eminently; indispensably; crassly; seriously; urgently.

MATERIALISM

adjectives
ruthless; dialectical; advanced; practical; lifeless; brutal; unreligious; coarse; scientific; crass.

verbs
absorb by—; accentuate—; cloak—; degenerate into—; disparage—; infest with—; lapse into—; shrink from—; sink into—; tend to—; transmute—; —blasphemes; —desecrates; —doubts; —hardens; —perverts; —profanes; —questions; —scorns; —wanes.

(See modernism, paganism, atheism, realism.)

MATERNAL

adverbs
fondly; fiercely; tenderly; solicitously; possessively; obsessively; jealously; proudly; comfortingly; unduly; naturally; habitually; admirably; charmingly; sweetly; placidly; serenely; imperturbably; dominantly; indulgently; good-humoredly; warmly; softly; bounteously; generously; providently; curiously; thoughtfully.

MATERNITY

verbs
anticipate—; arouse—; balk at—; delight in —; endear to—; exalt—; guard—; impair —; overwhelm by—; prepare for—; prevent —; pride in—; recognize—; train for—; —bores; —nauseates; —secures.

MATHEMATICS

verbs
advance by—; apply—; base on—; compile by—; demonstrate—; depend on—; dispute —; fathom by—; ferret out by—; formulate —; introduce—; —computes; —disciplines; —educes; —enthralls; —sharpens; —solves; —systematizes; —trains; —verifies; —weighs.

(See science, logic, solution, problem.)

MATING

adjectives
auspicious; seasonal; beneficial; integral.

MATRIARCHAL

adverbs
venerably; insistently; tyrannically; gently; tenaciously; uncommonly; highly; imperiously; oddly; naturally; unyieldingly; obviously; irrevocably; proudly; haughtily.

MATRIMONY

verbs
abhor—; blast—; cloud—; commit to—; consent to—; dissolve—; embark on—; entice into—; evade—; reconcile to—; sacrifice to —; scorn—; spurn—; surrender to—; —circles; —exacts; —knits; —mars; —preserves; —shackles; —survives; —torments; —unites.

(See marriage, wedding, nuptials, union.)

MATRON

adjectives
substantial; sober; ancient; stately; ailing; bulky; sharp-faced; fluttering; dignified; sober-suited; modest; pedantic; gracious; haughty.

verbs
appoint—; tip—; train—; vest in—; —administers; —assists; —cradles; —furnishes; —inspects; —manages; —obliges; —presides —reinforces; —resides; —serves; —superintends; —supervises; —supplies.

(See servant, housekeeper, wife.)

MATRONLY

adverbs
pleasantly; proudly; unexpectedly; charmingly; admirably; sedately; demurely; comfortably; serenely; imperturbably; undeniably; sweetly; graciously; happily; gently; tranquilly; placidly; remarkably.

MATTER

adjectives

subject; specific; triturated; perfunctory; doleful; heterogeneous; inconsequential; unimportant; spiritual; combustible; urgent; prudential; luminous; worldly; esoteric; indigent; trivial; imminent; spiritual; superficial; heavy; calcareous; internal; fixed; fluid; humid; dry; unctuous; crude; hard; soft; simple; veiny; compound; similar; organical; imponderable; extraneous; controversial; inevitable; critical; unpalatable; speculative; jesting; granular; erupted; exterior; analogous; ample; essential; brute; country; mineral; weighty; pertinent; waste; baser; suspended; countless (pl); theoretical; pecuniary; impending; critical; putrid; encrusted; tarry; bare; nitrogenous; stony; regrettable; indolent; protuberant; empty; forgotten; ecclesiastical; inert; testamentary; suspended; mighty; graver; inexhaustible; commonplace; relevant; remote; subtle; indifferent; inflammable; financial; earnest; hideous; abstruse; fascinating; temporal; coloring; worthy; woody; perishable; money; unattainable; carbonaceous; artistic; grave; morbid; cognate.

verbs

adjust—; aggravate—; brood over—; clinch —; deal with—; debate—; deliberate—; discuss—; dispute—; elucidate—; expedite—; forsake—; go to the root of—; inquire into —; judge—; mince—s; ponder—; press—; report—; shape—; simplify—; smooth—; visualize—; weigh—; —drifts; —engages; —engrosses; —lingers; —pertains to.

(See business, affair, event, question, problem.)

MATTRESS

verbs

construct—; fluff—; handle—; hollow—; hump—; launder—; lug—; pad—; quilt—; stitch—; strain—; stuff—; tuck under—; tuft—; —comforts; —cushions; —eases; —molds; —pits; —refreshes; —supports.

(See bed, pillow.)

MATURE

adverbs

suddenly; undeniably; admirably; sensibly; sagaciously; sturdily; responsibly; unexpectedly; remarkably; curiously; strangely; surprisingly; reasonably; sufficiently; presumably; scarcely; thoroughly; progressively; strikingly; completely; fully; obviously; fairly; terribly; precociously; indescribably; gratifyingly; wisely; emotionally; physically; appallingly; supposedly; intellectually; unquestionably.

MATURITY

adjectives

fairest; complete; precocious; ripened; mysterious; surprising; hypothetical; indescribable; emotional; warm; rapid; cold; respectable; serene; luxuriant; sumptuous; buxom.

verbs

abide till—; approach—; attain—; grow in —; impede—; merge into—; settle into—; tarry—; undergo—; —charms; —limits; —mellows; —ripens; —subdues; —sweetens; —teaches; —transforms.

(See development.)

MAUDLIN

adverbs

drunkenly; foolishly; senselessly; incoherently; intoxicatedly; joyously; merrily; crazily; utterly; stupidly; oddly; disgustingly; hopelessly; helplessly; egregiously; heavily; tipsily; gloriously; comically; shamefully; happily; irresponsibly; excitedly; hysterically.

MAUVE

adjectives

soft; pale; brilliant.

MAXIM

adjectives

horrible; favorite; terse; common; sublime; wholesome; elevated; political; shrewd; sagacious; execrable; salutary; ethical; moral; polite; profane; semibarbarous.

verbs

apply—; coin—; comprehend—; condense into—; consider—; defend—; draw from—; interpret—; invoke—; mold—; observe—; propose—; retain—; speculate on—; weigh —; —concludes; —directs; —embodies; —guides; —philosophizes; —relates to.

(See adage, proverb.)

MAXIMUM

verbs

assign—; attain—; calculate—; conduct to —; distend to—; establish—; reach—; record—; test—; strain—; strike—; weigh—; —bears; —corresponds; —limits.

(See amount, average, degree, position, status, limit.)

MAZE

adjectives

quaint; murmuring; surging; tangled; institutional; flitting; uncouth; moon-loved; flowery; backward; vague; hopeless; musky-circled; mirthful; tortuous; statistical; mystic; intriguing; shadowy; winding; insane; bewitching; laborious; shifting; curious; intoxicating.

verbs

crack—; dissolve—; entangle in—; extricate from—; grope through—; guide through—; immure in—; retrace—; struggle through —; submerge in—; wander in—; weave—; —bewilders; —confounds; —confuses; —entwines; —perplexes; —puzzles; —twists; —winds; —wreathes.

(See mystery, perplexity, problem.)

MEADOW

adjectives

romantic; grassy; intervening; frost-flowered; luxuriant; bloody; fruitful; slushy; starry; outlying; tender; enameled; smooth; saturated; dewy; serene; mountain; sheltered; bright; undulating; extensive; quaint; parched; dim-seen; damp; open; homely; scorching; laughing; swelling; rolling; billowy; unmown; emerald.

verbs

amble through—; crop—; cultivate—; drench—; dress—; luxuriate in—; mow—; paint—; parch—; pasture in—; plough—; prance in—; romp in—; stain—; —blooms; —extends; —invites; —scents; —slopes.

(See field, grass, flowers, plant, country, lawn.)

MEAGRE

adverbs

pitifully; scantily; miserably; wretchedly; pitiably; deplorably; lamentably; pathetically; unnecessarily; unaccountably; unreasonably; criminally; stingily; meanly; cruelly; bitterly; hopelessly; desperately; incredibly; unbelievably; meretriciously; skimpily; contemptibly.

MEAL

adjectives

supplementary; sunset; ominous; scanty; small; floating; satisfying; well-balanced; belated; abominable; miserable; vegetable; frugal; hearty; hasty; elaborate; slender; indigested; sumptuous; savory; lavish; hot; jovial; quick; homelike; sailor-cooked; quiet; infantile; dismal; miraculous; assured; plenteous; solitary; luxurious; economical; accustomed; superb; delectable; tempting; perfect; appetizing; famous; marvelous; generous; tasty; home-cooked; thrilling; abundant.

verbs

beg—; consume—; despatch—; dispose of —; enhance—; lubricate—; relish—; savor —; snatch—; terminate—; —nourishes; —proceeds; —sustains; —tempts.

(See dinner, luncheon, food, breakfast, supper.)

MEALY-MOUTHED

adverbs

insufferably; perversely; pretentiously; humbly; deceitfully; mendaciously; perfidiously; hypocritically; cunningly; insidiously; treacherously; invidiously; trickily; meretriciously; atrociously; abominably; satirically; inconceivably.

MEAN

adverbs

abominably; terribly; stingily; viciously; maliciously; horribly; incredibly; inordinately; unbelievably; brutally; cruelly; bitterly; greedily; shamefully; despicably; outrageously; disgracefully; treacherously; selfishly; jealously; enviously.

MEANING

adjectives

mysterious; common; inexpressible; pathetic; doubtful; mythical; majestic; secondary; imploring; earnest; ominous; ambiguous; solemn; veiled; gentle; odious; candid; double; true; remote; ultimate; uncertain; specific; significant; obvious; generous; wicked; eucharistic; fearful; undecipherable; patriotic; platonic; heavenly; universal; philosophical; shrunken; painful; lawful; mean; historic; symbolic; irresolute; serious; deadly; unmistakable; plain; dark; intelligible; cloudy; abstruse; legitimate; moral; profound; folded; hideous; concrete; precise; borrowed; infinite; intellectual; spiritual; unaffected; unattractive; huge; hybrid; cryptic; secular; sexual; incredible; second; elusive; considerable; instant; involved; vague; express; accumulated; vital.

verbs
absorb—; adulterate—; apprehend—; ascribe—to; bestow—upon; clarify—; comprehend—; discover—; elaborate on—; elucidate—; embody—; extricate—from; grasp —; illustrate—; imply—; impregnate with —; pervert—; ponder—; reflect upon—; seek—; sum up—; translate—; weigh with —; wresle with—; attach—to.
(See reason, significance.)

MEANS

adjectives
iniquitous; effective; downright; legitimate; solid; extraordinary; vociferous; plunging; continuous; ample; systematic; peaceful; prying; drastic; efficient; radical; clumsy; hygienic; scantiest; slender; superficial; rapid; showy; artificial; honorable; comfortable; undue; subtle; unlawful; effectual; vast; superior; remote; mysterious; unexplained; considerable; subservient; further; highhanded; useful; indispensable; occult; earthly; inarticulate; mechanical; pecuniary; approved; devious; gigantic; accidental; instrumental; faint; conflicting; realistic; blessed; inadequate; extremest; practicable; readiest; apparent; double; abundant; unrestrained; speediest; lavish; quick; individual; moderate; miraculous; flagitious; potent; valuable; creditable; instinctive.

verbs
adopt—; attain—; contrive—; desire—; devise—; employ—; find—; invent—; meditate on—; outline—; resort to—; secure—; supplant—; suggest—.
(See agency, method, way, manner, policy.)

MEASLES

verbs
afflict with—; attack with—; convey—; develop—; dispose to—; immunize to—; isolate—; stud with—; usher in—; —abates; —blotches; —endangers; —erupts; —fades; —infects; —invades; —patches; —spreads; —stains; —weakens.
(See sickness, malady, disease, smallpox.)

MEASURE (*general*)

adjectives
effectual; dictatorial; decisive; mystic; unconstitutional; delightful; harsher; faltering; aesthetic; star; buskined; domestic; extreme; classical; diminished; good; considerate; large; hostile; rustic; merriest; precautionary; equal; discriminatory; infinite; quaint; drastic; pending; intemperate; judicious; repressive; defiant; puretoned; irregular; solemn; unattainable; compulsory; undeserved; hygienic; conservative; corrective; preventive; radical; contemptuous; potent; energetic; conciliatory; violent; pernicious; tempestuous; sinister; undaunted; scant; retaliatory; large; fluctuating; rhythmical; brimming; galloping; tuneful; vigorous; airy; stringent; generous; just; final; unexpected; accurate; weightiest; flowing; unrhymed; stately; financial; sweeping; inevitable; hostile; ample; aggressive; individual; tyrannical; dusty; highhanded; swelling; smallest; compromise; dulcet; preliminary; prompt; satisfactory; boundless; sterilizing; sufficient; proposed; doubtful; desperate; tedious; irregular; considerate; quantitative; rude; severe; vulgar; hasty; lavish; strained; pacific; debated; stark; concentrated; burning; central; centuried; organic; diverse (pl); eugenic; suitable; disciplinary; ruinous; emergency; corresponding; undreamed; contestable; gracious; bold; oppressive.

MEASURE (*legislation, course.*)

verbs
adopt—; advance—; advocate—; block—; combat—; defy—; effect—; enact—; enforce—; execute—; exert—s; force—through; install—; institute—; introduce—; outlaw—; pilot—; promote—; promulgate —; reject—; repass—; resort to—; subscribe to—; suggest—; threaten with—s; —affords relief; —clamps down on; —corrects; —embodies; —embraces; —evolves from.
(See bill, law, rule, ordinance, statute, mandate.)

MEASURE (*v*)

adverbs
scientifically; mechanically; accurately; consciously; effectually; constitutionally; aesthetically; mystically; classically; equally; intemperately; judiciously; financially; individually; tediously; quantitatively; lavishly; radically.
(See gauge, rule, estimate.)

MEASUREMENTS

adjectives
micrometrical; accurate; geodetic; refined.

verbs
adopt—; appraise for—; ascertain—; calculate—; cling to—; collect—; confirm—; deduce—; derive—; determine—; estimate—; probe—; reckon—; report—; review—; sound—; stipulate—; —allow; —coincide with.

(See magnitude, size, dimension.)

MEAT

adjectives
lean; sizzling; homely; substantial; immortal; choleric; wretched; corrupted; unctuous; miserable; wholesome; manufactured; perishable; fatty; generous; preserved; tainted.

verbs
abstain from—; broil—; brown—; carve—; consume—; crave—; dispatch—; dive into—; dress—; dry—; extract from—; grill—; grind—; inspect—; market—; parch—; pickle—; prepare—; refrigerate—; roll—; salt—; savor—; shred—; store—; tenderize—; tub—; weigh—; —ages; —deteriorates; —putrefies.

(See flesh, game, food, stew.)

MECHANIC

adjectives
shrewd; roused; expert; trained; competent; skilled.

MECHANICAL

adverbs
cleverly; ingeniously; dexterously; marvelously; dully; automatically; altogether; accurately; conveniently; advantageously; profitably; precisely; unerringly.

MECHANISM

adjectives
literal; extremely delicate; intricate; lifeless; wondrous; dexterous; primary; gorgeous; elaborate; inanimate; greasy; interior; insensate; unconscious; instrumental.

verbs
acquaint with—; analyze—; approve—; construct—; design—; develop—; explain—; improve—; inspect—; install—; invent—; operate—; substitute—; tamper with—; tinker with—; understand—; —eases; —performs; —specializes; —speeds.

(See gear, engine, machine, dynamo, apparatus.)

MEDAL

verbs
accord—; award—; bestow—; cast—; confer—; decorate with—; engrave—; favor with—; grant—; honor with—; inscribe on—; jingle—s; mold—; present with—; prize—; strike—; —commemorates; —distinguishes; —encourages; —records; —represents; —signifies; —symbolizes.

(See laurels, trophy, badge, memorial, reward.)

MEDDLESOME

adverbs
vexatiously; irritatingly; maliciously; incredibly; unaccountably; maddeningly; incurably; offensively; unpleasantly; disagreeably; unbelievably; busily; officiously; unpardonably; intrusively; invidiously; atrociously; inexcusably; curiously; inquisitively; inveterately; unscrupulously; incorrigibly; grievously.

MEDIA

adjectives
sympathetic; turbid; diffracting; fluctuating.

MEDICATION

adjectives
pre-anesthetic; proper; penetrating; soothing.

MEDICINAL

adverbs
warrantably; highly; splendidly; advantageously; incidentally; profitably; strangely; oddly; beneficially; opportunely; properly; admirably; wonderfully; extraordinarily; amazingly; surprisingly; unaccountably; extremely; acceptably; uncommonly; usefully.

MEDICINE

adjectives
loathed; cooling; sudorific; preventive; multiplying; domestic; reform; heavenly; native; proprietary; astringent.

verbs
administer—; anoint with—; dispense—; endorse—; gulp down—; instil—; measure—; overdose with—; prescribe—; reject—;

specialize in—; swallow—; verse in—; —allays; —alleviates; —palliates; —purges.
(See iodine, emetic, enema, laxative, liniment.)

MEDIOCRE

adverbs
hopelessly; indefensibly; undeniably; stupidly; dully; stodgily; uninterestingly; boresomely; tediously; monotonously; crudely; crassly; inexcusably; unaccountably; surprisingly; amazingly; terribly; unexpectedly; unwarrantably; awkwardly; provincially; tiresomely; dreadfully; pitiably; miserably; wretchedly.

MEDIOCRITY

adjectives
solemn; witless; practiced; superlative.

verbs
allow—; approve—; attain—; avoid—; condemn—; cringe in—; criticize—; disparage—; lift from—; respect—; —begets; —endures; —eclipses; —perseveres; —starves; —subjugates; —succeeds.
(See inferiority.)

MEDITATE (*v*)

adverbs
pensively; gloomily; seriously; morbidly; sedately; dispassionately; bitterly; wilfully; restlessly; whimsically; religiously; serenely; monotonously; characteristically; habitually.
(See muse, ponder, reflect, think.)

MEDITATION

adjectives
profound; portentous; heavenly; important; threadbare; silent; devout; thoughtless; restless; solemn; pensive; starred; whimsical; crude; fearful; plotting; holy; rapid; sullen; lofty; numerous (pl); serene; reconstructive; continual.

verbs
abide in—; absorb in—; bathe in—; build in—; discern through—; draw from—; fall into—; fix in—; immerse in—; neglect—; recall in—; recess in—; recline in—; shroud in—; spend in—; steep in—; wander in—; weave in—; wrap in—; —ensures; —nurses; —solaces; —strengthens.
(See contemplation, thought, philosophy, reflection, reverie.)

MEDITATIVE

adverbs
gravely; quietly; habitually; temperamentally; strangely; naturally; seriously; soberly; deeply; profoundly; studiously; reminiscently; remarkably; unduly; thoughtfully; inscrutably; solemnly; earnestly; dangerously; pensively; wistfully; philosophically; pointedly.

MEDIUM

adjectives
congenial; diaphanous; sympathetic; fleeting; meteoric; tangible; appropriate; accurate; ethereal; desirable; suitable; pictorial; cooling; proselytizing; surrounding; reliable; graphic; inaccurate; just; ridiculous; interpreting; ambient; pulsing; circulating; supporting; favored; laborious.

MEEK

adverbs
gently; quietly; submissively; modestly; humbly; supplicatingly; serenely; disgustingly; obsequiously; unnecessarily; provokingly; stupidly; miserably; wretchedly; tragically; passively; tranquilly; patiently; placidly; philosophically; gracefully; sedately; demurely; contentedly.

MEEKNESS

adjectives
proud; subdued; female; reverent; swaggering.

MEET (*v*)

adverbs
coincidentally; accidentally; nocturnally; surreptitiously; forcibly; casually; unwaveringly; tacitly; traditionally; solemnly; memorably; convivially; temperately; fraternally.
(See confront, encounter.)

MEETING

adjectives
turbulent; commonplace; accidental; pleasant; pietistic; traditional; conducive; friendly; solemn; merry; accidental; fortunate; momentous; revival; immediate; memorable; fictitious; soul-trying; convivial; midweek; agitated; temperance; memorial; factious; revolutionary.

verbs
address—; anticipate—; arrange—; ban—; convoke—; devise—; dwell on—; enjoy—; forecast—; foster—; plan—; plot—; promote—; shun—; —brightens; —charms; —delights; —excites; —pains; —quickens; —rekindles; —revives; —sharpens; —thrills; —unites.

(See convention, conference, hearing, assembly, appointment, encounter.)

MELANCHOLY

adjectives
gentle; tranquil; appropriate; natural; funereal; vague; delicious; dull-eyed; hungry; deep; tired; congenital; silent; soft; waning; quiet; gloomy; faithful; inviting; mild-eyed; sweetest; moral; vague; forbidding; bovine; resolute; rude; touching; moody; lovely; customary; profound; savage; constitutional; young; sentimental; somber; depressing.

verbs
charge with—; chase away—; conceal—; discern—; dissipate—; merge into—; sink into—; succumb to—; suffer—; —oppresses; —perks up; —shadows; —touches.

(See gloom, depression, dejection, mood, sadness.)

adverbs
alarmingly; unduly; incurably; stupidly; moodily; churlishly; sullenly; strangely; naturally; inherently; temperamentally; dangerously; doggedly; extraordinarily; inordinately; gloomily; heavily; cheerlessly; unhappily; lugubriously; mournfully; solemnly; dismally; lamentably; glumly; pensively; grimly; desolately.

MELLOW

adverbs
lusciously; delectably; pleasantly; agreeably; softly; richly; naturally; ripely; charmingly; benevolently; harmoniously; melodiously; sweetly; gorgeously; delicately; progressively; groggily; perfectly; adequately; sufficiently; amazingly; surprisingly; astonishingly; unexpectedly.

MELODIOUS

adverbs
delicately; exquisitely; triumphantly; enchantingly; thrillingly; convivially; boomingly; companionably; agreeably; plaintively; ecstatically; sweetly; liltingly; gracefully; meltingly; unutterably; strangely; soothingly; blissfully; lightly; lingeringly; saucily; hauntingly; catchingly; rollickingly; romantically; softly.

MELODRAMA

adjectives
virtuous; cheap; sentimental; exciting; underdone; celebrated; morbid; bloodcurdling.

verbs
applaud—; climax—; compose—; descend to—; dress in—; engage in—; formulize—; hiss—; impassion—; introduce—; lean toward—; overrate—; pattern—on; rehearse —; revive—; ridicule—; sink into—; —appeals; —bores; —exaggerates; —inspires; —intrigues; —lags; —thrives; —thrills; —touches.

(See play, opera, magic, pantomine, performance, tragedy, trick, act, comedy.)

MELODY

adjectives
celestial; untutored; strenuous; cloying; minstrel; delightsome; uplifted; faint-toned; venomed; wild; joyous; wondrous; beguiling; triumphant; exquisite; delicate; ravishing; stirring; vagrant; organic; harmonic; enchanting; sweetest; heavenly; thrilling; booming; siren; high; sky-born; congenial; conjuring; ancient; plaintive; unfailing; untaught; agreeable; liquid; chastened; efflorescent; breaking; consoling; unintelligible; symmetrical; ecstatic; oblivious; unearthly; hireling; nerve-dissolving; elegant; fresh; enchanted; delicious; pathetic; characteristic; rhythmic; facile; inspired; sustained; superabundant; acquired; original; sweet; lilting; exalted; stately; terrible; distinct; enervating; immortal.

verbs
air—; chant—; chorus—; compose—; drench in—; drown—; hum—; imprison—; improvise—; join in—; lilt to—; modulate —; wheedle—out of; —gratifies; —haunts; —heralds; —lingers; —rings out; —soars; —wanes.

(See chant, air, jazz, incantation, song, refrain.)

MELT (*v*)

adverbs
indistinctly; indefinably; silently; exquisite-

ly; scientifically; methodically; deliciously; sweetly; appetizingly.

(See dissolve.)

MEMBER

verbs

admit—; coerce—; collaborate with—s; defend—; elect—; entertain—; honor—; invite —; limit—s; register—; —attends; —s band; —benefits; —charters; —contributes; —s convene; —heeds; —s incorporate; —organizes; —s rally; —undertakes; —votes.

(See faculty, classmate, congressman.)

MEMBERS

adjectives

prominent; mutinous; respectable; superfluous; consistent; confidential; eligible; eminent; numerous; obscure; vivacious; distinguished; myriad; mateless; influential; sundry; impecunious; self-respecting; illustrious; discordant; efficient; able; honorable; daring; exemplary; acceptable; conspicuous; representative; worthy; significant; right-thinking; learned; excitable; geometric; noxious; surviving; discredited; objectionable; disjointed; privileged; fat; sturdy; self-respecting; honest; erratic; devout; subsidiary; law-abiding; amiable; nicely educated; infatuated; disaffected; insubordinate; sundry (pl); corporeal; oracular; useless; unruly; violent; arbitrary; pronounced; cherished.

MEMBERSHIP

adjectives

distinguished; enormous; compulsory; unstable.

verbs

admit to—; desire—; discontinue—; elect to—; forfeit—; increase—; invite to—; limit —; register—; renew—; seek—; tabulate —; usher in—; vote on—; —concentrates; —expires; —includes; —requires; —terminates.

MEMBRANE

adjectives

previous; feather-covered; thin; gauzelike.

verbs

affect—; incise—; irritate—; perforate—; puncture—; shed—; soothe—; stretch—; swell—; thicken—; ulcerate—; —atrophies; —bulges; —erodes; —lines; —ruptures; —vibrates; —wastes.

(See film, eardrum.)

MEMENTO

adjectives

painful; ever-changing; grave; appropriate; melancholy; lovely; sacred.

MEMORIAL

adjectives

cypress; suitable; tender; dubious; frail; worthy; peevish; poetic; sculptured; faded; dogmatic; energetic; living.

verbs

address—; bestow in—; carve—; contribute to—; dedicate—; draw up—; endow—; engrave—; erect—; inscribe—; merit—; petition for—; raise—; —commemorates; —credits; —describes; —glorifies; —honors; —perpetuates; —portrays; —preserves; —recounts.

(See medal, trophy, monument.)

MEMORIES

adjectives

comfortless; tragic; ungracious; hurting; multicolored; muscular; grateful; faithful; hateful; pious; projected; rustling; suggestive; prompt; retentive; feeble; thronging; lamentable; long-to-be-cherished; conscious; color; unshaken; magnificent; unwelcome; artificial; white-lipped; sightless; puissant; vivid; surprising; ineffable; distinct; jarring; royal; incomparable; healthiest; disastrous; seductive; encyclopedia; disordered; glistening; usurious; aching; retributive; vindictive; solemn; ludicrous; blessed; confused; melodious; agreeable; natural; delightful; uncanny; bellicose; dark; animated; passionate; primeval; delicious; immortal; gay; infamous; ballad; dear; capacious; personal; living; impressive; vital; sacred; withered; sorrowful; pleasant; trifling; haunting; drowsy; fragrant; cherished; gossipy; atrocious; submerged; vapid; remorseful; tenacious; prodigious; amused; lingering; bright; stirred; sluggish; human; personified; resplendent; biographical; vague; fleeting; half-forgotten; endearing; dusty; eventful; fragmentary; weary; exhausted; deadly; deficient; precious; unbreathed; overwhelming; ghostlike; distorted; honored; detailed; time-fraught; everlasting; mutual; unfading; hereditary; intimate; lofty; public; blurred; rueful; embarrassed; unaccountable; imperfect;

bitter; accurate; emergent; grisly; musical; phenomenal; inevitable; priceless; unconscious; amazing; lurid; dormant; warming; enticing.

MEMORY (*faculty of remembering*)

verbs

blur—; bury in—; cloud—; commit to—; drug—; dull—; engrave upon—; escape—; explore—; impair—; imprint on—; quote from—; strike—; coruscates; —paints; —pictures; —retains; —wanders.

(See mind, brain, consciousness, intellect.)

MEMORY (*reminiscence*)

verbs

awaken—ies; blot out—; brood over—ies; cherish—; cling to—; dim—; dispel—; elucidate—; erase—; evoke—ies; freshen—; hallow—; honor—; haunt—; live in—; nurse—; nurture—; obliterate—; refresh—; revive—; shun—; suppress—; swap—ies; toy with—; treasure—; venerate—; —fades; —gnaws; —lingers; —pains; —surges; —survives.

(See remembrance, recollection.)

MEN

adjectives

vainglorious; succeeding; smooth-shaven; trampled; deft; glowing-eyed; up-and-doing; fashion-minded; fallible; able-bodied; orthodox; cringing; soft-conscienced; clear-witted; pusillanimous; decayed; banished; laconic; traitorous; hackneyed; sated; childless; huge-limbed; best-informed; best-tempered; insensate; ruling.

MENACE

adjectives

triple; significant; constant; mingled; dismal; ever-fearful; ominous; positive; deadly; feeble; dangerous; international; wrathful; crushing; serious; perpetual; fierce; terrible; transparent; owl-eyed; enticing; subdued; black.

verbs

avert—; banish—; conceal—; constitute—; denounce—; eradicate—; fear—; guard against—; harbor—; inveigh against—; invoke—; level—; share—; stamp out—; uncover—; ward off—; —endangers; —jeopardizes.

(See threat, peril, danger.

MENACE (*v*)

adverbs

seriously; portentously; ominously; dismally; dangerously; perpetually; fiercely; blackly; morally; seductively.

(See threaten, portend.)

MENAGE

verbs

adopt—; attach to—; bully—; conduct—; govern—; head—; install in—; involve—; join—; manage—; occupy—; recommend—; regulate—; superintend—; supervise—; support—; visit—; —bickers; —delights; —disperses.

(See home.)

MEND (*v*)

adverbs

appreciably; exquisitely; deftly; dexterously; cleverly; artfully; radically; expertly; artistically.

(See repair, patch, improve.)

MENDACIOUS

adverbs

wickedly; venomously; spitefully; vengefully; maliciously; hatefully; viciously; notoriously; infamously; openly; shamelessly; treacherously; dangerously; trickily; craftily; arrantly; undeniably; brazenly; slyly; surreptitiously; atrociously; deplorably; lamentably; oddly; unaccountably; terribly; deliberately; shrewdly; meretriciously.

MENDACITY

adjectives

conscienceless; bugbear; deliberate; habitual; disreputable.

MENIAL

adverbs

odiously; basely; meanly; humbly; obsequiously; cringingly; pliantly; terribly; unaccountably; obediently; subserviently; obscurely; boorishly; pitiably; miserably; wretchedly; churlishly; incredibly.

MENSTRUATION

verbs

arrest—; delay—; disorder—; endure—; establish—; force—; induce—; perform—; retard—; stimulate—; suffer during—; suppress—; —ceases; —commences; —distresses; —exhausts; —fatigues; —impoverishes; —pains; —pauses; —strains.

MENTALITY

adjectives
subconscious; practical; assumed; criminal; twisted; careless; subnormal; unbalanced.

verbs
burden—; check—; clog—; contemplate—; contribute to—; develop—; endow with—; exhaust—; furnish with—; impede—; limit —; nourish—; perfect—; relax—; repair—; strain—; tax—; tug at—; undermine—; —evolves from; —flags; —slackens.

(See brain, faculty, cleverness, brilliance, talent.)

MENTION

adjectives
special; passing; honorable; casual; fleeting; complimentary; occasional; copious; nonchalant.

verbs
deserve—; earn—; forbid—; merit—; peeve at (colloq.)—; report—; —alludes to; —describes; —disgusts; —excites; —inflames; —offends.

(See repetition, notice, remark, statement, utterance.)

MENTION (*v*)

adverbs
secretly; umbrageously; incidentally; mincingly; modestly; casually; nonchalantly; ominously; slanderously; slyly; inadvertently.

(See tell, reveal, relate, advise, expose.)

MENU

adjectives
proper; prescribed; balanced; convalescent; varied; nourishing.

verbs
alter—; approve—; arrange—; check—; compose—; consult—; dispatch—; glean from—; plan—; relish—; serve—; vary—; —appeals; —catalogues; —details; —lists; —nourishes; —offers; —prices; —suggests; —sustains; —tempts.

(See program, list.)

MERCANTILE

adverbs
highly; profitably; successfully; propitiously; negotiably; speculatively; stably; regularly; admirably; advantageously; prosperously; usefully; preeminently; obviously.

MERCENARY

adverbs
stingily; sordidly; basely; penuriously; greedily; deliberately; openly; obviously; manifestly; amazingly; surprisingly; selfishly; shamelessly; avowedly; miserably; wretchedly; blandly; frankly; ungenerously; rapaciously; avariciously; palpably; outrageously; inconsiderately; harshly; extortionately; churlishly; unbelievably; uncommonly.

MERCHANDISE

adjectives
timely; fashionable; quality; heterogeneous; exclusive; styled-right; jointed; seasonable.

verbs
assess—; bargain for—; catalogue—; claim —; close out—; convey—; dispense—; endow with—; evaluate—; hawk—; invest in —; liquidate—; overstock with—; peddle —; purchase—; purvey—; retail—; sacrifice—; salvage—; surrender—; turn over —; underwrite—; wholesale—.

(See imports, material, supply.)

MERCHANT

adjectives
respected; shaggy; successful; affluent; prudent; timorous; independent; prominent; sagacious; enterprising; prosperous; staid; sensible; clear-eyed; retired.

verbs
bargain with—; patronize—; —auctions; —deals in; —dispenses; —disposes of; —hawks; —jobs; —markets; —negotiates; —profits; —purveys; —puts under the hammer; —realizes a profit; —retails; —speculates; —traffics in; —transacts; —vends; —wholesales; —undersells.

(See hawker, jeweler, banker.)

MERCIFUL

adverbs
abundantly; benevolently; benignly; suddenly; habitually; kindly; generously; surprisingly; unaccountably; gravely; happily; fortunately; moderately; remarkably; exceedingly; compassionately; wondrously; uncommonly; infinitely; tenderly.

MERCILESS

adverbs
cruelly; bitterly; terribly; ruthlessly; pitilessly; relentlessly; stonily; sanctimonious-

ly; rigidly; unfeelingly; hard-heartedly; maliciously; basely; incredibly; immovably; unspeakably; coldly; vengefully; unsparingly; tyrannically; sternly; abominably; barbarously; brutally; savagely; uncommonly; habitually.

MERCURIAL

adverbs

blithely; capriciously; delightfully; captivatingly; nimbly; actively; captiously; wantonly; cheerfully; changefully; inconstantly; craftily; unpredictably; problematically; perplexingly; irrationally; unreasonably; vivaciously; fascinatingly; temperamentally; unstably; merrily; erratically; waywardly; vagrantly; restlessly; nomadically; lightly; interestingly; casually.

MERCURY

verbs

administer—; anoint with—; drain—; inject —; scale—; —ascends; —contracts; —corrodes; —descends; —estimates; —expands; —gauges; —graduates; —impends; —measures; —poisons; —sublimates; —threatens; —warns.

(See chemical, medicine, thermometer, barometer.)

MERCY

adjectives

intellectual; wondrous; holy; tender; weak-eyed; ill-judged; noble; infinite; crowning; marvelous; common; eternal; devilish; saving; scant; lawful; hopeless; imperial; wonted; mutual; single; pardoning; gentle.

verbs

beg—; crown with—; dispose toward—; excite—; exercise—; extend—; favor with —; forbear out of—; grace with—; grant —; howl for—; implore—; invoke—; judge with—; lack—; lend—; plead for—; recommend—; rejoice in—; soften in—; sue for —; supplicate—; temper with—; tender—; throw upon—of; vouchsafe—; win—; —relents; —restrains; —spares; —thaws; —yields.

(See forbearance, grace, clemency, compassion, pity.)

MERETRICIOUS

adverbs

abominably; atrociously; unmentionably; dreadfully; unspeakably; pretentiously; shamelessly; bawdily; spuriously; indecorously; coarsely; grossly; barbarously; outlandishly; monstrously; horridly; painfully; shockingly; particularly.

MERGE (*v*)

aaverbs

gradually; perpetually; conveniently; artfully; artistically; unconsciously; completely; superficially.

(See absorb, swallow.)

MERIT

adjectives

unusual; intrinsic; eminent; neglected; spectacular; unpopular; respective; artistic; patient; peculiar; multifarious; remarkable; comparative; indignant; solid; bashful; starving; toilworn; injured; mute; relative; ostensible; supereminent; accumulated; palpable; scientific; telling; strongest; transcendent; distinctive; technical; all-sufficient; literary; aesthetic; striking; humbled; uneven; prime; essential; rare; tangible; productive; singular; doubtful; weaker; lap-dog; cardinal; noticeable; satisfying; conspicuous.

verbs

attain—; authorize—; award—; claim—; command—; confer—upon; detract from—; discuss—s; disclaim—; disclose—; dispute —; emulate—; entitle to—; esteem—; exhibit—; impute—to; judge—s; mark with —; overrate—s; rate—; reward with—; rival—; sanction—; test—; value—; vie for—; vindicate—; warrant—.

(See reward, advantage.)

MERIT (*v*)

adverbs

modestly; genuinely; justly; unquestionably; substantially; incalculably; ostensibly; justifiably; intrinsically; eminently; aesthetically; essentially; conspicuously.

(See deserve, earn.)

MERITORIOUS

adverbs

highly; uncommonly; manifestly; admirably; marvelously; unusually; laudably; exceptionally; splendidly; magnificently; indubitably; satisfactorily; estimably; appreciably; commendably; extremely.

MERRIMENT

adjectives
spasmodic; boisterous; continual; misplaced; hollow; apparent; considerable; tricksy; inward; thoughtless; sympathetic; ill-timed; quavering; rustic; mocking; chilling; joyous; merciless; excited; openhearted; adventurous; disproportional; infinite.

verbs
contribute to—; disport with—; feign—; frolic in—; frown on—; occasion—; regale with—; rejoice in—; reproach for—; revel in—; romp in—; —amuses; —brightens; —cheers; —convulses; —dies; —drives away care; —eases; —enlivens; —entertains; —flows; —palls; —perks up; —relaxes; —solaces; —titillates.

(See frolic, humor, glee, gayety, laughter, jollity, joy, fun.)

MERRY

adverbs
blithely; happily; mischievously; childishly; excitedly; madly; bewitchingly; ecstatically; joyously; naturally; habitually; inherently; mysteriously; noisily; boisterously; apparently; infinitely; hilariously; facetiously; jovially; genially; convivially; sportively; extremely; delightfully; fascinatingly; comically; drolly; briskly; exceedingly.

MESH

adjectives
mysterious; golden; tangled; guilty; glittering; shattered; legal; airy.

verbs
avert—; construct—; dangle in—; drain through—; elude—; entangle in—; extricate from—; interlace—; thread through—; weave—; —cages; —deceives; —ensnares; —fences off; —nets; —nonpluses; —perplexes; —puzzles; —sifts; —traps.

(See chain, complication.)

MESS

adjectives
nasty; dreadful; horrible; entire; filthy; viscid; savory; unholy; utmost; jovial; hoggish.

verbs
adulterate—; blend—; brew—; concoct—; entangle in—; ferment—; hash—; jumble into—; knead—; pound to—; reduce to—; shuffle into—; unravel—; —complicates; —confuses; —disarrays; —disorders; —embarrasses; —litters; —muddles; —perplexes; —ruffles; —rumples.

(See junk, rubbish, waste.)

MESSAGE

adjectives
effective; divine; heartfelt; urgent; eternal; lucid; affectionate; turbulent; diabolical; true; expressive; unheeded; heated; spurred; dusty; private; precious; loving; telegraphic; sociological; farewell; verbal; pertinent; leaden; conciliatory; unanswered; assuring; rebukeful; laconic; distinct; luminous; terse; cryptic; hurried; alarming; instant; pitying; mysterious; speechless; heavenly; jubilee; anticipated; thrilling; crumpled; civil; rock-hewn; flattering; peevish; horrid; universal; vaunting; insurgent; faltering; ringing.

verbs
authenticate—; bear—; cable—; charge with—; communicate—; confirm—; convey—; decipher—; despatch—; dictate—; entrust—to; flash—; impart—; interpret—; issue—; narrate—; relay—; report—; signal—; telegraph—; transmit—; —informs; —rings; —stirs; deliver—.

(See errand, dispatch, letter, mail, manuscript.)

MESSENGER

adjectives
celestial; gracious; convenient; pure; winged; mindful; bonded; dusky; mourning; surly; arbitrating; angelic; trustworthy; distempered; shining; impatient; giddy; mystical; special; courageous; strong; churlish; guiltless; awe-stricken; wing-footed; breathless; welcome; better.

verbs
appoint—; assign—; consign to—; delegate—; dispatch—; —apprizes of; —bears; —communicates with; —confirms; —conveys; —declares; —delivers; —embarks; —forwards; —heralds; —imparts; —informs; —races; —reports; —reveals; —speeds; —transfers; —wings.

(See apostle, angel, emissary, delegate.)

MESSY

adverbs
abominably; dreadfully; hopelessly; unnecessarily; unduly; needlessly; confusedly; chaotically; intricately; confoundedly; un-

tidily; shapelessly; irreducibly; inexcusably; unpardonably; unusually; inexplicably; unwarrantably; unspeakably; carelessly; filthily; crazily; surprisingly; extremely; indescribably.

METAL

adjectives
barren; engraving; sonorous; basic; combustible; glittering; mystical; precious; serviceable; non-tarnishable; best-tempered; burnished; invaluable; well-wrought; twisted; gleaming.

verbs
alloy—; assay—; cast—; congeal—; decarbonize—; engrave—; excavate—; hammer out—; model in—; mold—; prospect for—; refine—; render—; sheathe in—; smelt—; stamp—; strike—; value—; weld—; —corrodes; —expands; —oxidizes; —preserves.
(See lead, copper, coin, gold, iron, mineral.)

METAPHOR

adjectives
far-fetched; abundant; developed; suggestive; consistent; bucolic; striking.

verbs
abound with—s; apply—; employ—; —allegorizes; —alludes to; —collates; —colors; —compares; —contrasts; —depicts; —identifies; —illuminates; —illustrates; —likens; —parallels; —personifies; —portrays.
(See figure, word, phrase, paragraph, simile.)

METEOR

adjectives
disastrous; new-forged; unexpected; lurid; ominous; alarming; sudden; wandering; large; mighty; scarlet; cloud-encircled; descending; unctuous; deceitful.

METEORIC

adverbs
luridly; alarmingly; startlingly; swiftly; gloriously; incredibly; glowingly; splendidly; brilliantly; unbelievably; inconceivably; curiously; abruptly; miraculously; strangely; amazingly; astonishingly.

METER
(*instrument*)

adjectives
mystic; unconventional; inaccurate; dainty.

verbs
check—; feed—; flood—; —allots; —appoints; —apportions; —appraises; —assesses; —assizes; —compounds; —dispenses; —estimates; —graduates; —measures; —portions; —plumbs; —probes; —proportions; —records; —scales; —values.
(See barometer, thermometer, mercury.)

METHOD

adjectives
opposite; economical; selfsame; ingenious; inductive; haphazard; peaceful; laborious; scrupulous; numberless; hustling; indirect; exalting; novel; honorable; elaborate; summary; unostentatious; artistic; deductive; radio; unnatural; advantageous; clumsy; gruesome; commercialized; painless; convenient; statistical; authoritarian; getting; instinctive; conservative; picturesque; substantial; unique; dangerous; antiseptic; photographic; modern; up-to-the-minute; unsurpassed; therapeutic; orthodox; old-fashioned; lucid; prudent; time-honored; patented; scientific; sweet; objective; tentative; wholesome; plating; monstrous; philosophical; primitive; factory; despotic; imperturbable; feasible; transient; advertising; suitable; vociferous; unceremonious; naturalistic; lawful; evasive; subjective; preposterous; superstitious; accepted; surreptitious; particular; thoughtful; subversive; dilatory; peculiar; realistic; comely; inferior; outworn; analytic; amazing; humane; unpretending; histrionic; mystical; foolish; political; exclusive; dogmatic; equitable; ever-changing; descriptive; revolting; slack; peaceable; costly; doctrinal; appropriate; shrewd; false; ideal; autographic; financing; simplified; parliamentary; reproductive; pedantic; dictatorial; administrative; mild; barbarous; ignominious; collaborative; time-tried; indistinguishable; desultory; efficacious; inconsequent; injudicious; obsolescent; intuitive; glamorous; subtle; prosodic; avowed; current; fixation; enlarged; straightforward.

verbs
abandon—; abuse—; adopt—; advocate—; antedate—; ape—; apply—; conceive—; condemn—; design—; develop—; devise—; discard—; discover—; employ—; evolve—; exploit—; formulate—; introduce—; justify —; modify—; probe—; propose—; pursue

—; reform—; repudiate—; resort to—; revolutionize—; supplant—; supplement—.
(See procedure, process, fashion, manner.)

METHODICAL

adverbs
carefully; habitually; inherently; dependably; reliably; warrantably; overly; punctiliously; meticulously; outlandishly; comically; absurdly; rigidly; painfully; vexatiously; admirably; laudably; naturally; systematically; pleasantly; disagreeably; incredibly; unduly; uncomfortably; terribly.

METICULOUS

adverbs
carefully; painfully; disagreeably; uncomfortably; unduly; curiously; extremely; admirably; laudably; unfailingly; systematically; outlandishly.

METRICAL

adverbs
cleverly; pleasantly; melodiously; carefully; smartly; cunningly; ingeniously; delightfully; tunefully; skillfully; harmoniously; enchantingly; mellifluously; artfully.

METROPOLIS

adjectives
exciting; throbbing; expectant; dazzling; holiday; commercial; perfume; mystical; huge; monstrous.

METTLE

adjectives
invincible; unimproved; scientific.

METTLESOME

adverbs
highly; vivaciously; animatedly; boldly; undauntedly; dauntlessly; cheerfully; sturdily; actively; pluckily; courageously; spiritedly; gayly; uncommonly; remarkably; notoriously; commendably; obviously; unusually; energetically; strenuously; vigorously; intensely; restlessly; ungovernably; uncontrollably; audaciously; valiantly; adventurously.

MEW (*v*)

adverbs
plaintively; sympathetically; maternally; shrilly; vociferously.
(See cry, wail.)

MICROPHONE

verbs
adjust—; announce through—; broadcast through—; confront—; perform before—; —amplifies; —clarifies; —communicates with; —conveys; —enables; —intensifies; —magnifies; —transmits.
(See loudspeaker.)

MICROSCOPE

verbs
adjust—; contemplate through—; discern through—; employ—; examine under—; focus—; glance into—; incline—; observe under—; peep through—; peer into—; rivet upon—; scrutinize through—; squint through —; view through—; —augments; —detects; —distinguishes; —enables; —enlarges; —exaggerates; —magnifies; —reveals.
(See telescope.)

MICROSCOPIC

adverbs
minutely; infinitesimally; incredibly; curiously; ingeniously; unbelievably; amazingly; imperceptibly.

MIDDLE

verbs
ascertain—; assemble in—; balance in—; cast in—; cleave in—; cling to—; concentrate in—; contract in—; converge on—; designate—; focus on—; intersect in—; narrow toward—; proceed from—; situate in —; split in—; taper toward—; —averages; —centralizes; veer toward—.
(See interior, surface, center, bottom.)

MIDDLE-AGED

adverbs
hopelessly; permanently; persistently; miserably; wretchedly; doggedly; pertinaciously; arthritically; rheumatically; pleasantly; hoarily; venerably; patriarchally; wirily; delightfully; obviously; youthfully.

MIDNIGHT

adjectives
impenetrable; fierce; profoundest; sedentary; sleek; beautiful; drear; blackest.

MIDSHIPMAN

verbs
amuse—; appoint—; consign—to; convey—; delegate—; furlough—; promote—; school

—; train—; —crams; —embarks; —hoists; —marches; —plies; —promenades; —rooms; —sails; —tours.
(See sailor, officer, soldier.)

MIEN

adjectives
stately; gallant; placid; sullen; distant; spirited; haughty; conciliating; graceful; awe-inspiring; impressive; dejected; warlike; thoughtful; majestic; haggard; awkward; portentous; joyless; free; daring; noble; solemn; lofty; bold; withering; somber; undaunted; royal.

verbs
alter—; amend—; assume—; contemplate—; convert—; devise—; disguise—; eye—; influence—; modify—; present—; repose—; —awes; —conveys; —distresses; —disturbs; —enhances; —glares; —glows; —inspires; —menaces; —sours; —threatens.
(See demeanor, air, aspect, manner.)

MIGHT

adjectives
eternal; transparent; royal; truehearted; imposing; congregated; individual; withered; conquering; irresistible; apparent; fancied; divine; austere; intimate; unimaginable; ravenous; spacious; towering; resistless; delicious; outworn; borrowed; restless; wholesome; human; overmastering; brutal.

MIGRATION

adjectives
voluntary; forcible; autumnal; barbaric; instinctive.

MILD

adverbs
harmlessly; pleasantly; serenely; compassionately; reasonably; urbanely; blandly; suavely; affably; genially; tolerantly; complaisantly; leniently; judiciously; discreetly; diplomatically; carefully; placidly; imperturbably; philosophically; sedately; demurely; patiently; unctuously; graciously; ingratiatingly; winningly; tactfully.

MILDNESS

adjectives
resigned; mellow; incomparable; delicate.

MILE

verbs
advance—; clear—; detour—; estimate—; extend—; lag—; march—; progress—; pursue—; race—; recede—; total—s; trail for—s; trek—; withdraw—; —s drag; —s separate; —s weary.
(See distance.)

MILEAGE

adjectives
railroad; tire; maximum; gasoline; trip.

MILES

adjectives
dusky; tortuous; uncheered; weary; glistening; merry; laborious; geographical; delectable; glittering; appalling; snow-covered.

MILITARIST

adjectives
battering; greedy; professional; grasping; bloodthirsty; heartless.

MILITIA

adjectives
uniformed; hurrying; insubordinate.

verbs
arm—; arouse—; call out—; drill—; encounter—; enlist in—; discipline—; maintain—; muster—; qualify for—; recall—; regulate—; round up—; train—; —combats; —defends; —guards; —interferes; —mobilizes; —patrols; —pickets; —repels.
(See army, navy, regiment, soldier, troops.)

MILK

adjectives
tepid; acidophilus; skimmed; innocent; pulpy; metabolized; putrid; sour.

verbs
absorb—; administer—; churn—; concentrate—; condense—; contaminate—; curdle—; deprive of—; dilute—; draw—; extract from—; flavor—; pasteurize—; predigest—; rear on—; sip—; skim—; sour—; subsist on—; substitute—; taint—; thicken—; wean on—; —nourishes; —sustains.
(See food, cream.)

MILL

adjectives
neighboring; clanking; slander; mortgaged; social; busy; penetrating; muffled.

verbs
design—; establish—; guard—; manage—; operate—; picket—; report to—; set up—; speed up—; stock—; supervise—; —composes; —constructs; —frames; —manufactures; —organizes; —produces; —shuts down; —unionizes.
(See factory, shop, business, company, laboratory.)

MILL (*v*)

adverbs
eddyingly; riotously; alarmingly; tumultuously; disorderly; boisterously; actively.
(See reduce, crush.)

MILLION

adjectives
hardy; countless; shatterproof; mildewed; dark.

MILLIONAIRE

adjectives
senatorial; practical; decrepit; radical; amiable; myopic; eccentric; dirty-handed.

MIME

adjectives
mechanic; deft.

MIMIC (*v*)

adverbs
skillfully; audaciously; sardonically; sedulously; aptly; deftly; professionally; irritatingly; exasperatingly; roguishly.
(See mock, imitate.)

MINARETS

adjectives
slender; delicate; candle-extinguisher.

MINCE (*v*)

adverbs
primly; exaggeratedly; fastidiously; fashionably; wantonly; affectedly; delicately.
(See walk, step.)

MIND

adjectives
agitated; iron; conclusive; grosser; trained; thrifty; astute; observing; unbalanced; liberal; logical; far-seeing; poetic; subtle; self-assured; conniving; contented; invisible; taintless; zealous; capricious; towering; feminine; swift; virtuous; shallow; untutored; courageous; languid; downcast; discriminating; controlling; well-trained; creative; philosophical; illustrious; pulverized; wavering; versatile; earthly; uncomplex; illuminated; earnest; weak; effeminate; careless; mortal; anxious; troubled; unthinking; terrestrial; dispassionate; exalted; elegant; reluctant; sympathetic; backward-looking; vigorous; romancing; ingenuous; tranquil; thoughtful; vulgar; twisted; imaginative; expanding; longing; pensive; unclean; virgin; sublimest; youthful; unconventional; flexible; restless; lethargic; conservative; apprehensive; erring; educated; enlightened; impressible; golden; distracted; lofty; inventive; disordered; undebauched; meditative; invoking; irritated; silly; fractional; preoccupied; giant; pure; soaring; gifted; exploring; ill-trained; independent; active; disburdened; ingenious; colossal; turbulent; callous; affrighted; cultivated; inattentive; exasperated; infinite; writhing; queasy; well-purged; honest; charming; quivering; unconquerable; wooing; ennobling; supersensitive; glowing; speculative; disciplined; scientific; slick; freckled; unfolding; infected; patriarchal; resourceful; unfettered; uninitiated; rude; mute; healthy; determined; mighty; realistic; abject; selfish; learned; far-reaching; devious; discriminating; plastic; brilliant; medieval; flurried; upright; respective; managerial; critical; priggish; sanguine; deferential; mercantile; superstitious; gullible; twofold; finite; percipient; grasping; mournful; wayless; reproductive; docile; theorizing; deliberating; unregenerate; reverential; unhinged; wounded; drunken; unaffected; fatuous; retentive; savage; inhospitable; self-formed; unrebellious; desecrated; diseased; sensitized; keen; serious; frivolous; infinite; robust; dissipated; intuitive; medical; canny; narrow; tabloid; deft; solitary; ductile; undergraduate; scholarly; unclouded; cheerful; nature-loving; idle; devotional; prying; high-sailing; immortal; eternal; petulant.

verbs
addle—; agitate—; assail—; attune—to; baffle—; banish—; bend—; bewilder—; broaden—; burden—; condition—; corrode—; corrupt—; convey to—; cultivate—; debauch—; delude—; depress—; detach—; de-

throne—; disabuse—; disorient—; dispel from—; distort—; divert—; drug—; ease —; emancipate—; enfeeble—; engrave on —; enslave—; explore—; fertilize—; fetter —; filter into—; focus—on; harass—; haunt —; inflame—; impress on—; lodge in—; muddle—; plant in—; penetrate—; permeate —; pervade—; pop into—; rankle in—; reproach—; seep into—; shackle—; sharpen —; stamp on—; steel—; stimulate—; torture —; unbalance—; unbare—; unburden—; unhinge—; unsettle—; warp—; weigh in—; wrench—; —conceives; —dallies; —darts back; —deteriorates; —dictates; —disturbs; —dwells upon; —dwindles; —evolves; —envisages; —masters; —pictures; —probes; —reels; —roams; —seethes; —succumbs; —wanders; —wars.

(See consciousness, brain, imagination, head, intellect, memory.)

MINDFUL

adverbs
considerately; graciously; observantly; attentively; thoughtfully; affectionately; solicitously; tenderly; compassionately; carefully; discreetly; warily; prudently; providently; courteously; admirably; remarkably; sweetly; delightfully.

MINE

adjectives
gnomed; torched; fathomless; well-developed; abandoned; vast; rich; enwombed; exhaustless; hydraulic; inexhaustible.

verbs
abandon—; bore into—; burrow into—; cede —s to; confine in—; descend into—; emerge from—; excavate—; exhaust—; extract from —; gouge—; lower into—; operate—; ravage—; scoop from—; seal—; spring—; survey—; tunnel—; work—; —extends; —yields.

(See vein, earth, ground.)

MINER

verbs
asphyxiate—; confine—; disinter—; lower —; trap—; —bores; —burrows; —descends; —digs; —emerges; —excavates; —extracts; —gropes; —saps; —scoops; —shafts; —strikes; —tunnels; —uncovers; —unearths.

(See mole.)

MINERAL

adjectives
mortal; rare; vitreous; insignificant; tooth-building; essential.

verbs
abound in—s; alloy—; assay—; drill for —s; examine—; excavate—; extract—; prospect for —s; refine—; reveal—; scoop out —; uncover—; unearth—; utilize—; value —; —nourishes.

(See lead, metal, copper, gold, iron.)

MINGLE (*v*)

adverbs
democratically; promiscuously; inextricably; discreetly; affectionately; conspicuously; bizarrely; ostensibly; curiously; blasphemously; curiously; heterogeneously; profanely.

(See associate, mix.)

MINGLING

adjectives
rough; melancholy; charming; strange; promiscuous.

MINIATURE

adverbs
delicately; curiously; fragilely; incredibly; valuably; exceptionally; uncommonly; exotically; quaintly; fantastically; fashionably; modishly; pricelessly; expensively; exquisitely; matchlessly; incomparably.

MINIMUM

adjectives
irreducible; unimportant; smallest.

MINION

adjectives
pliant; sleek; dainty; luxurious; saucy; mindless.

MINISTER

adjectives
weak; debile; empyreal; nonconformist; accredited; formidable; efficient; gracious; sullen; shortsighted; puppet; irritated; gentle; misty; mournful; thoughtful; merciful; respective; refractory; shifty; retired; influential; unprincipled; powerful; grave; obstinate; right-hand.

verbs
appoint—; charge—with; invest—with; ordain—; —chastens; —cheers; —conducts; —converts; —consoles; —corrects; —dissents;

—executes; —imparts; —influences; —meditates; —offers; —officiates; —prays; —performs; —preaches; —rebukes; —reflects; —serves; —tames; —worships.
(See elder, deacon, leader, clergy, rabbi.)

MINISTERIAL
adverbs
gravely; authoritatively; officially; urbanely; suavely; blandly; unctuously; officiously; judicially; solemnly; pompously; professionally; considerately; subserviently; affably; genially; sympathetically; formidably; graciously; gently; influentially; courteously; ostentatiously; pleasantly; agreeably; sternly; cautiously; warily; wisely; admirably; wonderfully; acceptably; curiously.

MINISTRATION
adjectives
unfaltering; kindly; feminine; servile; pulpit; sleuthing; merciful.

MINISTRY
adjectives
maternal; pestilential; virgin; corrupt; tyrannical; radiant; hopeless; arduous; gracious; angelic; stated; bright-winged; incompetent; dictatorial.

verbs
acquaint with—; appoint to—; execute—; forsake—; fulfill—; invest—; obey—; ordain by—; plunge into—; retire from—; suspend from—; train for—; —assents; —chastens; —corrects; —meditates; —officiates; —performs; —rebukes.
(See cabinet, congress, management, government, church, legislature.)

MINK
verbs
dress in—; exhibit—; farm—; market—; prize—; skin—; value—; —burrows; —digs; —dives; —excavates; —inhabits; —shies; —swims.
(See animal, fur.)

MINOR
verbs
advise—; counsel—; cradle—; dictate to—; direct—; govern—; guard—; guide—; instruct—; manage—; model—; mold—; nourish—; prompt—; shape—; sustain—; —anticipates; —assumes; —attains; —matures; —ripens into.
(See child, boy, girl, youth.)

MINORITY
adjectives
enlightened; considerable; miserable; optimistic; aggressive; loud; troublesome; excitable; strong; substantial; intelligent; zealous; fanatic; hopeless; sulky; cultured.

verbs
bind—; defeat—; deprive—; dispense with—; eliminate—; emerge from—; oppress—; organize—; overrun—; overthrow—; tyrannize—; weed out—; —bows to; —engages; —fights; —opposes; —sacrifices; —struggles; —suffers; —thins.
(See childhood, majority, alien, foreigner.)

MINSTRELSY
adjectives
college; crude; barbaric.

MINUET
verbs
compose—; create—; excel at—; fancy—; form—; hum—; lead—; popularize—; step—; walk—; —amuses; —bewitches; —charms; —delights; —dignifies; —fascinates; —flourishes; —graces.
(See dance, waltz.)

MINUTE
verbs
(See moment.)

MINUTE
adverbs
infinitesimally; incredibly; embryonically; microscopically; unbelievably; imperceptibly; extremely; invisibly; undiscoverably; unimaginably; immeasurably; incalculably; inconceivably.

MINUTES
adjectives
joy-absorbing; leaden; immortal; thievish; exquisite; marvelous; soft; miserable; hopeless; breathless; tumultuous; golden; long-cold; precious; weary; interminable; searching; copious; unoccupied; fleeting.

MINUTES
*(**notes**)*
verbs
depict in—; elaborate on—; enter into—; examine—; extract from—; jot down—; present—; record—; refer to—; report—;

submit—; —describe; —enlighten; —preserve; —recall; —refresh; —retain; —retrace; —specify; —sum up.
(See entry, notes, description, record, item.)

MIRACLE

adjectives
culinary; celestial; numerous (pl); unfathomable; perpetual; incomprehensible; financial; inscrutable; established; blessed; midnight; infinite; recorded; tenderest; gracious; medieval; year-born.

verbs
accept—; accomplish—; achieve—; ascribe —to; behold—; confirm—; contradict—; credit—; deny—; display—; divine—; foretell—; gape at—; hail as—; marvel at—; prophesy—; render—; work—; —astounds; —baffles; —bewilders; —convinces; —inspires; —mystifies; —dumbfounds; —unfolds; —violates.
(See magic, wonder, surprise, mystery.)

MIRACULOUS

adverbs
unbelievably; incredibly; remarkably; wonderfully; solemnly; breath-takingly; divinely; indubitably; warrantably; manifestly; assuredly; unfathomably; inscrutably; extraordinarily; strangely; marvelously; mysteriously; ineffably; stupendously; astoundingly; unquestionably.

MIRAGE

adjectives
holy; distorted; sound; floating; vapory; exquisite.

verbs
blink at—; chase—; contemplate—; paint—; reveal—; speculate on—; view—; —confuses; —dazzles; —deludes; —disperses; —dissolves; —fades; —flickers; —hoodwinks; —lifts; —looms; —melts away; —resembles; —shifts; —tantalizes; —vanishes.
(See maze, sight, view, vision, ghost.)

MIRE

adjectives
tenacious; puddled; lamp-reflecting; sensual; foul; sucking.

verbs
cast into—; drag through—; plunge in—; sink in—; spatter in—; splash in—; stumble in—; struggle through—; trample in—; tread in—; wallow in—; —absorbs; —contaminates; —engulfs; —reeks; —sullies; —swallows.
(See mud, swamp, marsh, dirt.)

MIRROR

adjectives
lie-consuming; spacious; distorting; wavering; retroscope; disposed; silver; gleaming; magic; crystal; glorious; tarnished; liquid; blurred; level; innumerable (pl); convex; concave; enchanted; fleckless; frameless; unflattering; detachable.

verbs
address—; behold in—; consult—; discern in —; espy in—; flash in—; inspect in—; observe in—; panel—; polish—; peep in—; perceive in—; spangle with —s; stare in—; view in—; —exposes; —flickers; —glimmers; —magnifies; —reflects; —reveals; —shimmers.
(See glass, reflection, water.)

MIRROR (v)

adverbs
skillfully; distortedly; waveringly; magically; liquidly; flatteringly; realistically; unfalteringly.
(See reflect, revert.)

MIRTH

adjectives
heart-easing; profane; painful; affected; musing; careless; prolific; uproarious; sunburnt; roguish; petulant; buck-shrieked; innocent; sacred; simple; festal; unquenchable; saturnine; sympathetic; immeasurable; violent; tragical; resounding; boisterous; heathenish; uncouth; harmless; whimsical; fictitious; twinkling; Olympian; pagan; melodious; guiltless; desperate; undissembled; hollow; ill-timed; suppressed; Philistinic; dynamic; quaint; impish; ungrateful; cryptic; exuberant; frolic; rural; hysterical; meditative; unconfined; dignified; pretended; marvelous.

verbs
bar—; bathe in—; choke with—; convulse with—; disguise in—; elicit—; feign—; flood with—; glide into—; light up with—; provoke—; repent—; repress—; reprove—; shake with—; sparkle with—; wreathe in —; —bubbles; —eases; —ripples; —solaces; —swells; —trespasses; —vexes.

(See joy, glee, fun, laughter, hilarity, humor.)

MIRTHFUL

adverbs
irrepressibly; hilariously; boisterously; noisily; scintillatingly; entertainingly; uproariously; blithely; gaily; merrily; playfully; comically; mischievously; roguishly; effervescently; indescribably; youthfully; happily; significantly.

MISANTHROPIC

adverbs
dreadfully; hatefully; cynically; unhappily; miserably; wretchedly; strangely; unaccountably; painfully; stupidly; obdurately; obstinately; fanatically; bitterly; morosely; moodily; cruelly; unreasonably; queerly; incorrigibly; vexatiously; lugubriously; curiously; oddly; anti-socially; unbearably; insufferably; intolerably; unfortunately.

MISAPPREHENSION

verbs
flounder in—; incur—; labor under—; lament—; sense—; —addles; —agitates; —bewilders; —confounds; —confuses; —deludes; —distorts; —embarrasses; —muddles; —perplexes; —tortures; —twists.

(See misunderstanding, uncertainty, shame, suspense, misconception.)

MISBEHAVE (*v*)

adverbs
notoriously; ceaselessly; profanely; impishly; unregenerately; drunkenly; fatuously; intolerably; maliciously; wantonly; mortifyingly; wilfully.

(See act, conduct.)

MISCARRIAGE

verbs
agitate to—; avert—; brood over—; convalesce from—; deplore—; incite—; provoke—; succumb to—; ward off—; —bereaves; —disappoints; —disconcerts; —disheartens; —frustrates; —robs; —undermines; —weakens.

(See abortion, failure, mistake, indiscretion, blunder, unhappiness.)

MISCELLANEOUS

adverbs
discouragingly; confusingly; perplexingly; promiscuously; carelessly; hopelessly; delightfully; strangely; unsystematically; unmethodically; curiously; oddly; deliberately; untidily; indiscriminately; typically; characteristically.

MISCHIEF

adjectives
desperate; secret; direst; enormous; desultory; intolerable; tormenting; malicious; wanton; mortifying; anticipated; supernatural; irreparable; impish; private; willful; stomachic.

verbs
actuate—; conceive—; confess—; contrive—; devise—; dog with—; instigate—; molest with—; plague with—; rectify—; share in—; work—; —agitates; —befalls; —besets; —disorganizes; —distresses; —enrages; —grates; —harasses; —hatches; —incenses; —piques; —provokes; —rankles; —ruffles; —torments; —trails.

(See injury, harm, damage, offense, oppression, trouble.)

MISCHIEVOUS

adverbs
incorrigibly; innocently; delightfully; teasingly; harmlessly; viciously; deliberately; childishly; merrily; thoughtlessly; maliciously; vengefully; terribly; intolerably; vexatiously; maddeningly; deliberately; studiously; craftily; shamefully; desperately; secretly; furtively; wantonly; irreparably; impishly; elfishly; purposely; wilfully; openly; defiantly; obstinately; persistently; perniciously; noxiously; naughtily; unbearably; poisonously.

MISCONCEPTION

adjectives
dangerous; huge; unworthy; singular; complete; dreadful; harmful; definite; deliberate; studied.

verbs
dissipate—; expose to—; flounder in—; scent—; twist in—; —addles; —agitates; —bewilders; —confounds; —confuses; —deludes; —distorts; —embarrasses; —endangers; —muddles; —perplexes; —torments; —tortures.

(See error, inaccuracy, fallacy, illusion, misapprehension.)

MISCONDUCT

adjectives

intentional; prankish; private; flagrant; alleged; violent; open.

MISCONSTRUE (v)

adverbs

persistently; chronically; inevitably; recurringly; intentionally; profoundly; wilfully; tragically; cavalierly.

(See distort, twist, change.)

MISCREANT

adjectives

loathsome; meaner; apprehended; vile.

MISDEED

verbs

actuate—; boast—; confess—; confine—to; harass with —s; hatch—; lament—; molest with —s; repent—; rue—; share in—; —annoys; —distresses; —dogs; —enrages; —grates; —incenses; —piques; —rankles; —ruffles.

(See crime, deed, offense, conduct.)

MISDEMEANOR

adjectives

trifling; unlawful; ingenious.

MISER

verbs

abhor—; detest—; hiss—; scoff at—; scorn—; torment—; —accumulates; —acquires; —begrudges; —broods; —covets; —endures; —fears; —grasps; —hoards; —pinches; —sacrifices; —scants; —skins; —starves; —stints; —wrests.

MISERABLE

adverbs

wretchedly; unutterably; poignantly; visibly; helplessly; desolately; uncommonly; dismally; lonesomely; heavily; gloomily; drearily; hopelessly; disconsolately; forlornly; abjectly; dejectedly; downright; singularly; peculiarly; bitterly; cruelly; unwontedly; fretfully; sorely; oddly; incurably; intensely.

MISERLY

adverbs

inherently; incurably; basely; selfishly; crazily; stupidly; horribly; avariciously; penuriously; unaccountably; perniciously; mendaciously; sordidly; unspeakably; churlishly; greedily; rapaciously.

MISERY

adjectives

untried; unrelieved; sticky; disintegrating; life-deserting; unutterable; gnawing; shadow-vested; motionless; piercing; dim; beauteous; poignant; past; selfish; eternal; uncounted; quiet; consequent; human; tyrannical; vicious; frightful; splendid; lonely; far-off; helpless; slow; unspeakable; seething; extremest; intolerable; parasitical; petty; fictitious; attendant; remediless; lessening; dumb; appalling; deserved.

verbs

allay—; alleviate—; assuage—; augment—; deplore—; escape—; heighten—; lighten—; moan in—; moderate—; mollify—; reduce—; relieve—; repent in—; rid of—; shelter—; spare—; steep in—; waste away in—; —diminishes; —disheartens; —eases.

(See anguish, distress, ache, pain.)

MISFORTUNE

adjectives

unwonted; impending; domestic; terrible; irreparable; vital; serious; human; constant; private; possible; grave; crushing; prevailing; dire; especial; cursed; signal; admitted; unparalleled; lone.

verbs

bear—; beset by—; bow beneath—; endure—; lament—; plunge into—; remedy—; rise above—; shake off—; sob—; suffer—; triumph over—; —afflicts; —assails; —befalls; —blasts; —burdens; —distresses; —gnaws; —harrows; —heckles; —nips; —outstrips; —overtakes; —sleeps; —sours.

(See ill, evil, loss, disappointment, calamity, catastrophe, adversity, affliction, disaster.)

MISGIVINGS

adjectives

serious; shamed; dim; conscientious; restless; nervous; grave; strange; profound; sceptical; ominous.

verbs

admit—; entertain—; excite—; fence with—; flinch beneath—; harbor—; hesitate from—; inspire—; overwhelm by—; shrink in—; wrap in—; wince beneath—; —alarm; —awe; —cloud; —creep over; —disquiet; —haunt; —overwhelm; —prey on; —strike; —torment; —weigh.

(See anxiety, solicitude, worry, apprehension.)

MISGUIDED

adverbs
utterly; unfortunately; wilfully; deliberately; perniciously; unutterably; unhappily; perversely; inconsiderately; foolishly; tragically; lamentably; deplorably; woefully; sadly.

MISHAP

adjectives
untoward; dire; industrial; unavoidable; preventable; serious.

verbs
allay—; avert—; avoid—; bridge—; culminate in—; curtail —s; dodge—; guard from—; labor under—; minimize —s; mourn —; secure from—; share—; succumb to—; —botches; —swallows; —swamps.
(See disaster, accident, misfortune, catastrophe, adversity.)

MISINFORMED

adverbs
lamentably; perfidiously; sadly; bitterly; cruelly; wilfully; deliberately; treacherously; unhappily; unfortunately; maliciously; purposely; peculiarly; unwittingly; erroneously; blindly; stupidly; unwittingly; deceitfully; craftily.

MISJUDGE (*v*)

adverbs
utterly; artlessly; pathetically; perniciously; grossly; deplorably; irritatingly; ludicrously; awkwardly.
(See decide, judge.)

MISLAY (*v*)

adverbs
inadvertently; accidentally; artlessly; senselessly; singularly; absently; disastrously; deliberately; carelessly; obtusely.
(See misplace.)

MISLEAD (*v*)

adverbs
deliberately; treacherously; intentionally; evilly; murderously; unwontedly; perniciously; cruelly; irrationally.
(See decline, cheat.)

MISPLACE (*v*)

adverbs
thoughtlessly; carelessly; absently; casually; unconsciously; unfortunately.
(See mislay.)

MISREPRESENT (*v*)

adverbs
grossly; vindictively; unjustly; scandalously; intentionally; artfully; hatefully; villainously; falsely; hypocritically.
(See distort, falsify.)

MISREPRESENTATION

adjectives
gross; willful; flagrant; specious; singular; monstrous; calculated.

verbs
deceive with—; decry—; denounce—; detect—; disclose—; fall victim to—; fathom —; interpret—; refute—; sense—; suffer from—; —aggravates; —amplifies; —deludes; —distorts; —dupes; —exaggerates; —falsifies; —magnifies.
(See lie, fallacy, deception.)

MISS (*v*)

adverbs
accidentally; coincidentally; seriously; narrowly; dreadfully; tragically; unavoidably; preventably.
(See omit, overlook.)

MISSHAPEN

adverbs
cruelly; bitterly; miserably; pitiably; horribly; unspeakably; pitifully; lamentably; woefully; pathetically; accidentally; congenitally; permanently; unfortunately; unluckily; awkwardly; clumsily; helplessly; hopelessly; irremediably; grotesquely; fantastically; outlandishly; peculiarly; sadly; tragically; crookedly; gauntly; forbiddingly; grossly; frightfully.

MISSILE

adjectives
divine; deadly; terrifying; ineffectual; innocent; squashy; living; unremitting; rebounding; speedy; well-directed.

verbs
arm with—s; assail with—s; direct—; discharge—; fire—; fling—; hurl—; pelt with —s; scatter—s; shoot—s; —shakes; —stabs; —stings; —stuns; —s torment.
(See dart, weapon, arrow, bullet, stone, shot, spear.)

MISSING

adverbs
tragically; hopelessly; irrecoverably; sadly;

blankly; starkly; undeniably; presumably; supposedly; avowedly; unmistakably; mysteriously; strangely; suspiciously; curiously; altogether; allegedly; shockingly; startlingly; disconcertingly; perplexingly.

MISSION

adjectives
intuitive; blushing; world-wide; fruitless; terrestrial; proposed; divine; unearthly; honorable; great; arduous; delicate; merciful; avowed; vicarious; perilous; momentous; indefinite; sublime; apostolic; secret; diplomatic; peaceful; dubious; memorable; celestial; loftiest; subsequent; novel; cultural; consequential; hardy; noble.

verbs
accept—; authorize—; charge with—; confide—to; deter—; entrust with—; equip for—; fulfill—; gain—; hamper—; hasten—; hinder—; impose—upon; journey on—; perform—; proceed on—; reveal—; select for—; speed—; undertake—.

(See errand, commission, purpose, object, view, trust.)

MISSIONARY

adjectives
itinerant; devoted; intelligent; adroit; shabby; gentle; eloquent; conscientious.

MISSPELL (*v*)

adverbs
habitually; intentionally; grossly; carelessly; absently; humorously; stupidly; inanely.

(See spell.)

MISSTATE (*v*)

adverbs
unblushingly; ungenerously; intentionally; artfully; shrewdly; legally; solemnly; cynically; characteristically; humorously; monstrously; eccentrically.

(See distort, falsify, misrepresent.)

MISSTATEMENT

adjectives
willful; unconsidered; ungenerous; planned; leading.

MIST

adjectives
azure; horrid; genial; shimmering; jealous; thin; fragrant; friendly; shrouding; sulphurous; sickening; contaminating; matutinal; morning; undistinguishable; sea-green; starry; dark; whirling; damp; parting; chronic; impenetrable; chilly; indistinct; blinding; luminous; feudal; jeweled; coral; semilucent; opaline; silvery; golden; happy; drenching; rolling; tenuous; square; unwholesome; gleamy; amber; malarial; driving; winged; amorous; earth-born; overhanging; radiant; flaky; descending; opal; heavy; glamorous; impalpable; drifting; odorous; murky; lowering; shifting; stultifying; hoary; rising; northern; ghastly; tremulous; midnight; visionary; feeble.

verbs
emerge from—; falter in—; flounder in—; swathe in—; —befogs; —blinds; —blurs; —clears; —clings about; —darkens; —deepens; —disperses; —encircles; —enfolds; —enshrouds; —envelops; —hangs over; —hides; —lifts; —obscures; —rises; —surrounds; —veils; —wraps.

(See fog, haze, clouds, smoke, spray, steam, vapor.)

MISTAKE

adjectives
grievous; pernicious; curious; strange; dreadful; frightful; pitiful; gross; slight; desperate; fatal; unfortunate; administrative; doltish; tactical; cardinal; traffic; capital; absurd; stupid; deplorable; irritating; felicitous; unavoidable; ludicrous; contradictory; horrible; awkward; petty; tragic; initial; natural; miraculous; cruel; pathetic; military.

verbs
account for—; avoid—; bare—; blush at—; commit—; convince of—; eradicate—; minimize—s; obscure—; observe—; obviate—; overlook—; pardon—; plunge into—; rectify—; regard—.

(See lapse, inaccuracy, fault, falsehood, error, incongruity, indiscretion, blunder.)

MISTAKE (*v*)

adverbs
grievously; grossly; perniciously; curiously; desperately; doltishly; absurdly; felicitously; ludicrously; tragically; pathetically.

(See misunderstand.)

MISTAKEN

adverbs
grossly; curiously; stupidly; senselessly; perversely; stubbornly; awfully; frightfully; blindly; tragically; emphatically; griev-

ously; pitiably; desperately; absurdly; ridiculously; pathetically; horribly; outrageously; manifestly; doggedly; preposterously.

MISTREAT (v)

adverbs
brutally; cruelly; sadistically; evilly; heartlessly; callously; pervertedly.
(See abuse, misuse.)

MISTREATMENT

verbs
bear—; beset by—; bow beneath—; bridle —; brood on—; burden by—; confess to—; endure—; fear—; harass with—; harrow by—; heap—upon; lament—; resent—; revenge—; subdue by—; subject to—; suffer —; —distresses; —embitters; —enrages; —frustrates; —incenses; —numbs; —wrecks.
(See abuse, pain, torture.)

MISTRESS

adjectives
gentle; mature; worthless; doting; fair; merry; accomplished; rare; gracious; white-handed; fine; queenly; slowly-fading; exacting; sovereign; indulgent; flaming; deserted; dread; petty; proud; dainty; virtuous; mischievous; brilliant; coquettish.

verbs
attend—; chain to—; desert—; devote to—; discard—; escort—; harbor—; maintain—; restrain—; serve—; squire—; stray to—; support—; —enslaves; —escapes; —submits.
(See lover, sweetheart, master, matron, friend.)

MISTRUSTFUL

adverbs
prudently; discreetly; habitually; temperamentally; chronically; insolently; anxiously; cautiously; intolerantly; insufferably; uncomfortably; darkly; subtly; sharply; absurdly; jealously; apprehensively; nastily; instinctively; suddenly; vaguely; inwardly.

MISTY

adverbs
strangely; terribly; obscurely; dimly; nebulously; cloudily; smokily; oddly; curiously; extremely; mysteriously; deliberately; dangerously; surprisingly; astonishingly; perplexingly; frightfully; ominously; intensely; alarmingly; abominably; fragrantly; impenetrably; heavily; gloomily; dismally; drearily; vaporously; frostily; foggily.

MISUNDERSTAND (v)

adverbs
deliberately; obtusely; idiotically; illogically; doltishly; pathetically; characteristically; normally.
(See mistake, disagree.)

MISUNDERSTANDING

adjectives
mutual; future; ever-recurring; chronic; inevitable; costly.

verbs
apologize for—; avert—; avoid—; bridge —; conquer—; cope with—; decry—; eradicate—; expose to—; fear—; grapple with —; guard from—; iron out—; risk—; smooth over—; —alarms; —endangers; —excites; —incites.
(See misapprehension, misconception, controversy, disagreement.)

MISUSE (v)

adverbs
brutally; crudely; ruinously; ungenerously; pitilessly; insensately; irrationally; grievously.
(See mistreat, abuse.)

MITE

adjectives
wee; musical; round-bellied; microscopic.

MIX (v)

adverbs
experimentally; inextricably; confusingly; intimately; determinedly; marvelously; discreetly; curiously; ludicrously.
(See associate, mingle.)

MIXED

adverbs
hopelessly; indiscriminately; perplexingly; delightfully; frightfully; incongruously; artfully; cleverly; beautifully; unbelievably; exasperatingly; vexatiously; curiously; mysteriously; grotesquely; disastrously; advantageously.

MIXTURE

adjectives
singular; strange-looking; flecked; hybrid; curious; whimsical; miscellaneous; bright; prodigious; ineffable; fascinating; effervescent; elemental; incongruous; racemic; unbalanced; incoherent; aromatic; piquant; heavy; paradoxical; greasy; sticky; complicated; engaging; fiery; impotent; confused; irrational; ragged; conglomerate; messy.

verbs
administer—; apply—; boil—; compound—; dilute—; drain—; emerge from—; garnish —; saturate—; stir—; swallow—; —coagulates; —hardens; —simmers; —thickens.
(See compound, medicine, chemical, solution.)

MOAN

adjectives
tender; sullen; insidious; enchanted; solemn; untimely; dying; peevish; stifled; weird; faint; alternate; pathetic; broken; everlasting; repentant; languid; lovely; wailing; low; perpetual; sobbing; desolate; shivering; harmonious; angry; doleful; occasional; harsh; short; mortal.

verbs
emit—; endure—s; muffle—; silence—s; stifle—; swell—s; throttle—; tolerate—; —chills; —disquiets; —escapes the lips; —gnaws; —pierces; —rends; —stirs; —weighs; —wrenches.
(See groan, sigh, whine, sob, cry.)

MOAN (v)

adverbs
dolefully; spasmodically; lugubriously; disconsolately; heartrendingly; fitfully; tremulously; grievously; pathetically; tragically; agonizingly; appallingly; distractedly; desolately; weirdly; inarticulately.
(See groan, mourn, lament, complain.)

MOANING

adjectives
dismal; thunderous; weird; desolate; inarticulate; faint.

MOB

adjectives
pitiless; patriotic; reactionary; lawless; furious; heartless; hostile; bewildering; bawling; swaying; union; emotion-charged; insensate; grinning; unruly; irrationalized; numerous; surging; distracted; great; mere; clumsy; hot-headed; fickle; ignorant; sadistic; immense; savage; supreme; angry; disorganized; noisy; mingled; infuriated; inflammable; riotous.

verbs
attract—; confront—; frustrate—; harangue —; inflame—; restrain—; sway—; —clamors; —disperses; —heckles; —huzzas; —jeers; —lynches; —pelts; —riots; —swarms; —storms; —withdraws.
(See crowd, masses, multitude, public, throng.)

MOBILE

adverbs
advantageously; curiously; skilfully; ingeniously; suddenly; sadly; variably; inconstantly; curiously; beautifully; handily; splendidly; conveniently; unstably; capriciously; erratically; unsteadily; waywardly; actively; vagrantly; captiously; nomadically.

MOCK (v)

adverbs
sneeringly; heartlessly; derisively; vindictively; sardonically; blandly; hollowly; jeeringly; cynically; impotently; despicably; maliciously.
(See mimic, imitate.)

MOCKERY

adjectives
hollow; unreal; solemn; unsubstantial; empty; cynical; standing; ghastly; forced; impotent; hideous; sardonic; bland.

verbs
bear—; endure—; expose to—; ignore—; persecute with—; provoke—; regret—; roast in—; —agonizes; —discomposes; —disconcerts; —disheartens; —humiliates; —mortifies; —rankles; —ruffles; —saddens; —wearies; —weighs upon; —wounds.
(See irony, derision, banter, sarcasm, ridicule.)

MOCKING

adverbs
hideously; hatefully; laughingly; teasingly; disrespectfully; tauntingly; sarcastically; skilfully; artfully; dramatically; scornfully; entertainingly; rudely; ironically; chaffing-

ly; derisively; insufferably; vexatiously; unbearably; intolerably; disagreeably; unpleasantly; offensively; contemptuously; cruelly; unpardonably; sardonically.

MOCKINGBIRD

verbs

admire—; prize—; —copies; —grieves; —defends; —cackles; —imitates; —jests; —jibes; —mews; —mimics; —pours forth; —scoffs; —shakes music; —shrieks; —utters; —wails; —whistles.

(See bird.)

MODE

adjectives

compact; varying; simpler; desultory; perfected; sagacious; happy-go-lucky; sentimental; singular; adequate; proscribed; equivocal; subconscious; prevailing; pompous; uncivilized; feudal; indispensable; scenical; disagreeable; equitable; progressive; frizzling; questionable; hospitable; artless; peculiar; fleeting; ostentatious; ruinous; expeditious; mercenary; hygienic; languid; cheap; irregular; capricious; enjoyable; ultra-modern; ingenuous; ingenious.

verbs

accept—; approve—; burlesque—; conform to—; consent to—; deride—; endorse—; fix—; govern by—; observe—; overdo—; pattern—; prefer—; protest—; revive—; subscribe to—; —disfigures; —enslaves; —succumbs.

(See fashion, manner, mannerism, vogue, standard, trend.)

MODEL

adjectives

exclusive; stunning; venerable; hallucinatory; dressy; hanging; rustic; unique; classical; mechanical; mangled; conservative; casual; inspired; swagger; straight-line; jigger; uniform; unthrifty; worldly; fancy; lacy; stylish; slim.

verbs

borrow from—; construct—; copy—; depart from—; design—; devise—; draw up—; erect—; emulate—; evolve—; explain from—; follow—; imitate—; improve—; mould—; pattern on—; perfect—; refer to—; reproduce—; serve as—; shape—; —embodies; —represents.

(See example, ideal, design, classics, manikin, masterpiece.)

MODEL (v)

adverbs

deliberately; artistically; sedulously; mechanically; imitatively; conservatively; uniformly; uniquely; fashionably.

(See mould, fashion, shape.)

MODERATE

adverbs

sensibly; admirably; judiciously; sagaciously; wisely; acceptably; reasonably; altogether; frugally; prudently; discreetly; thriftily; modestly; singularly; astonishingly; cautiously; notoriously.

MODERATION

adjectives

false; illogical; genial; equal; due; classical; sworn; practiced; remarkable; notable.

verbs

advise—; caution—; confine to—; counsel—; cultivate—; inure by—; prefer—; prescribe—; prize—; recline in—; seat in—; taper to—; treasure—; treat in—; —calms; —combats; —contents; —sobers; —subdues; —suffices; —tempers.

(See conservatism, caution, temperance, restraint.)

MODERN

adverbs

fashionably; stylishly; acceptably; satisfactorily; sufficiently; delightfully; progressively; refreshingly; presumably; warrantably; conveniently; screamingly; attractively; noticeably; incongruously.

MODERNISM

verbs

accent—; bind in—; cater to—; challenge—; combat—; define—; defy—; diffuse—; dispense with—; evolve—; fashion in—; favor—; immerse in—; temper—; touch with—; welcome—; resist—; —amazes; —attracts; —enhances; —excites; —impresses; —prevails; —refreshes; —transforms.

(See materialism, religion, philosophy, socialism.)

MODEST

adverbs

extremely; girlishly; engagingly: charmingly; peculiarly; becomingly; naturally; foolishly; ridiculously; touchingly; adorably; absurdly; comically; demurely; delicately; decently; decorously; admirably; attractively; pleasingly.

MODESTY

adjectives
shaking; womanly; delicate; singular; maidenly; pleasing; extreme; daring; beauteous; virgin; innate; incredible; hypocritical; unassuming; characteristic; austere; bashful; becoming; habitual; marital; ill-placed; boastful; cold; false; indignant; artful.

verbs
bait with—; counterfeit—; deport with—; discern—; extinguish—; feign—; inculcate —; personify—; recommend—; respect—; veil in—; violate—; wrap in—; —charms; —compels; —enjoins; —guards; —heightens; —hides; —padlocks; —restrains; —shuns; —survives.

(See decency, constraint, bashfulness, humility, purity, reserve.)

MODIFICATION

adjectives
slow; serious; substantive; profound; tiny; prescribed.

verbs
publish with—s; require—s; smooth into—; sober into—; undergo—; vary by—; —appeases; —deviates; —diverges; —hushes; —mollifies; —satisfies; —smothers; —softens; —subdues; —tempers; —tones down.

(See alteration, change, transition, variation.)

MODIFY (v)

adverbs
deferentially; partially; essentially; substantially; subsequently; drastically; profoundly; intrinsically; dogmatically.

(See adjust, limit.)

MODISH

adverbs
fashionably; extremely; remarkably; amazingly; oddly; delightfully; attractively; alluringly; temptingly; expensively; extravagantly; absurdly; unexpectedly; stylishly; unusually; uncommonly; astoundingly; daintily; tastefully; elegantly; conventionally; presentably; punctiliously; meticulously; showily; gaudily; quietly; acceptably.

MODULATE (v)

adverbs
exquisitely; mellifluously; coherently; harmoniously; musically;

(See adapt, adjust.)

MODULATION

adjectives
indiscriminate; learned; incoherent; inharmonic; mellifluous; surprising.

verbs
accord—; effect—; introduce—; perceive—; resign to—; value—; —delights; —enchants; —finishes; —flatters; —harmonizes; —pleases; —represses; —shades; —soothes; —subdues.

(See accent, adjustment, music, quiet.)

MOILS

adjectives
dynastic; imperial; far-flung; terrestrial.

MOIST

adverbs
excessively; extremely; unpleasantly; disagreeably; dangerously; unfortunately; satisfactorily; sufficiently; disastrously; continually; humidly; oppressively; soggily; swampily; conveniently; productively.

MOISTURE

adjectives
perpetual; heavenly; oppressive; suspicious; refreshing; needed; precipitated; genial; bounteous; dark; filthy; fated; destructive; pleasant; over-much; scant.

verbs
absorb—; boil away—; charge with—; condense into—; dabble in—; deprive of—; diffuse—; dim with—; emit—; exude—; inject —; precipitate—; restrain—; saturate with —; sponge with—; sprinkle with—; suck—; vaporize—; wring from—; —dampens; —irrigates; —refreshes; —seeps in.

(See dew, liquid, water, spray, vapor.)

MOLASSES

adjectives
dark; sorghum; fermented; tasty; rubber-like.

MOLD

adjectives
inflexible; heroic; delicate; vulgar; primitive; ethereal; determined; giant; virtuous;

rude; splendid; human; precision; wintry; gentle; beauteous; hollowed; arbitrary; muscular; different; dark; fresh; mossy; earthly; decaying; mortal; massive.

verbs
(See mould.)

MOLE

verbs
run down—; skin—; —burrows; —devastates; —destroys; —digs; —emerges; —excavates; —menaces; —preys on; —scoops; —shovels; —tunnels; —vacates.
(See animal, miner.)

MOLECULE

adjectives
blundering; organic; asymmetric; infinitesimal.

verbs
blast—; break down—; detect—; dissociate into—s; ionize—s; split—; store in—; weigh —; —attracts; —bombards; —charges; —clings; —collides; —composes; —fascinates; —s group; —s pair off; —puzzles; —retains; —s unite.
(See corpuscle, element.)

MOLLIFIED

adverbs
considerably; mercifully; reasonably; quietly; finally; ultimately; gradually; wholly; gently; visibly; eventually; happily; luckily; fortunately; presumably; somewhat; slowly; greatly; perceptibly; admittedly.

MOMENT

adjectives
decisive; spiteful; uncertain; voluptuous; critical; silent; lyrical; ludicrous; tragic; disagreeable; pictorial; appalling; musing; inspired; leisure; awful; microscopical; infinite; extraordinary; propitious; enlightened; proud; willful; little; heavier; immortal; delightful; high-tide; opportune; prolonged; gravest; radiant; usurped; bitter; highest; prearranged; charming; sulky; brisk; solemn; intuitive; giddy; whirling; supreme; omnipotent; inauspicious; unguarded; precise; culminating; single; blemished; gayest; rare; cantabile; shining; psychological; undecided; spellbound; earliest; vital; dreamy; affected; briefest; dramatic; heartrending; occasional; embittering; cooler; appointed; pleasant; illuminated; waking; breathless; hungry; ardent; lessened; important; flashing; crucial; theoretical; fading; poignant; fleeting; fateful; exalted; miraculous; pregnant; hostile; erotic; affectionate; necessary; sunny; impressive; reconciling; precise; tense; leisure; staggering; lofty; intimate; startled; inspirational; futile; practical; careless; sardonic; skinned; intent; delightful; lonely; golden; memoried; particular; few (pl); confused; swift; bold; brief; natal; troubled; deplorable; awful; sickening; inexpressible; tingling; cheerless; unnecessary; sunny.

verbs
acclaim—; anticipate—; consume in—; endure—; pause for—; relish—; seize—; snatch—; squeeze—dry; —flits by; —thrills; —troubles.
(See flash, instant, time.)

MOMENTOUS

adverbs
gravely; seriously; importantly; signally; unutterably; immensely; relatively; overwhelmingly; singularly; peculiarly; particularly; impressively; imposingly; strangely; mysteriously; secretly; inscrutably; exceptionally; infinitely; decisively; historically; tremendously; transcendently; insuperably; incomparably.

MOMENTUM

verbs
accumulate—; acquire—; defy—; gain—; lend—to; repel—; resist—; submit to—; withstand—; —batters; —butts; —drives; —impels; —increases; —prods; —shoves; —thrusts.
(See impetus, speed, force, velocity.)

MONARCH

adjectives
constitutional; magnanimous; affable; determined; degenerate; incompetent; conquering; pretentious; maddening; riotous; insolent; absolute; presumptuous; generous; rash; romantic; throned; deposed; new-crowned; ambitious; irrepsonsible; disheveled; unwilling; potent; forest; progressive; luxurious; unengaging; crumpled; affable; sensual; effeminate; puissant; opulent; sagacious; ill-starred; mighty; legendary; capricious; barbarous; factious; turbulent.

verbs
ape—; attack—; attend—; behead—; crown —; depose—; enthrone—; laud—; overthrow—; rebel against—; rule—; submit to—; —abdicates; —compels; —domineers; —imposes; —liberates; —misrules; —oppresses; —ordains; —reigns; —succeeds to; —surveys; —tramples; —yields.

(See emperor, dictator, king, monarchy, nobility, royalty.)

MONARCHY

adjectives
limited; restored; feudal; hereditary; absolute; constitutional; restricted; centralizing; flourishing; undisputed; despotic; serviceable; liberal; free; kingless.

verbs
attack—; destroy—; discontinue—; dispute —; establish—; head—; overthrow—; restore—; revive—; revolt against—; rout—; submit to—; survey—; tolerate—; —compels; —crumbles; —crushes; —falls; —imposes; —oppresses; —taxes; —treads on; —tyrannizes.

(See kingdom, monarch.)

MONASTERY

adjectives
vast; deserted, ruinous; secluded; flourishing.

verbs
cloister in—; conceal in—; desert—; enter —; exile in—; explore in—; foster in—; ramble through—; resort to—; retire to—; retreat to—; seclude in—; sequester in—; shut up in—; supervise—; —charms; —cowls; —disciplines; —embraces; —grants sanctuary; —harbors; —shelters; —soothes; —taboos.

(See prison, seclusion, religion.)

MONEY

adjectives
funded; depreciated; considerable; precious; reluctant; scattering; hoarded; dirty; cheaper; irredeemable; fraudulent; limp; grimy; paper; pin; parental; cold; hard; well-meant; flat; speculator; embezzled; continental; forfeited; worthless; counterfeit; inflated.

verbs
amass—; apportion—; bestow—upon; bilk of—; cling to—; coin—; counterfeit—; covet —; devalue—; divert—from; divest of—; exact—; expend—; extort—; fritter away —; hoard—; importune for—; lavish—upon; mulct of—; pile up—; pilfer—; plunk down—; pocket—; raise—; rake in—; restore—; revaluate—; risk—; salt away (colloq.)—; scrape together—; squander—; utilize—; wheedle—from; wring—from; —dribbles away; —dwindles; —flows in; —melts away.

(See investment, currency, fund, dollar, legacy, coin, cash, capital, inheritance.)

MONGREL

adverbs
despicably; basely; indubitably; indiscriminately; confoundedly; nondescriptly; peculiarly; anomalously; funnily; quaintly; fantastically; undeniably; contemptibly; ridiculously; remarkably.

MONGRELS

adjectives
sycophantic; engaging; brindled; dirty; swinelike.

MONK

adjectives
fanatical; ascetic; tonsured; preaching; cloistered; patient; persecuting; indifferent; excommunicated; abominable; lecherous.

MONKEY

adjectives
horrible-looking; meddling; misanthropic; withered-up; howling; cautious; monocled; grinning; manlike.

verbs
—antics; —s band together; —bounds; —capers; —climbs; —clings; —collects; —cuffs; —entertains; —fascinates; —fights; —frets; —grieves; —grimaces; —grins; —hangs; —howls; —imitates; —laughs; —leaps; —quarrels; —resembles; —scratches; —screams; —squeals; —swings; —tears; —warns; —wheels; —whines.

(See animal, ape.)

MONOCLE

verbs
adjust—; affix—; blink through—; discern through—; dislodge—; employ—; examine through—; fasten—; finger—; flip—; lurk behind—; peer through—; squint through—; tack—to; —dangles; —falls; —hangs from; —magnifies; —screws into.

(See spectacles, telescope, microscope.)

MONOLOGUE

adjectives
indignant; drowsy; inimitable.

MONOPOLIZE (*v*)

adverbs
selfishly; greedily; pretentiously; dictatorially; craftily; vigorously; legally.

MONOPOLY

adjectives
unlimited; sectional; unified; virtual; national; natural; insidious; wicked; wasteful; wretched; proposed.

verbs
bag—; break down—; confer—upon; denounce—; enjoy—; foster—; free from—; infringe on—; possess—; promote—; protest—; resent—; secure—; —controls; —enriches; —fetters; —gags; —masters; —prices; —reaps; —smothers.

(See power, authority.)

MONOTONE

adjectives
solemn; enchanting; dolorous; maddening; chanting; soothing; weirdly-spoken; mumbling; eternal; indistinguishable.

MONOTONOUS

adverbs
drearily; tediously; dreadfully; boresomely; endlessly; dismally; cheerfully; dully; intolerably; wearily; unbearably; unendurably; garrulously; ponderously; uninterestingly; repetitiously; unvaryingly; vapidly; irksomely; flatly; drowsily; droningly; prosily.

MONOTONY

adjectives
apparent; routine; unused; extreme; inescapable; desolate; endless; gray; maddening; studious; unvarying; fatiguing; deadening; dull; machine-like; unnatural; exasperating; inevitable; tedious; slumberous; loathsome; lazy; painful; hideous; dreary; dreadful; tiresome; wearisome; smooth; objectless.

verbs
allay—; beguile—; bewail—; curse—; deplore—; distract—; emerge from—; endure—; extinguish—; inflict with—; intensify—; object to—; overcome with—; relieve—; repose in—; sink into—; usher in—; while away—; yawn through—; —abates; —bores; —depresses; —drags; —threatens; —tires; —wearies.

(See drabness, oppression, pain, tedium, boredom.)

MONSTER

adjectives
patient; carniverous; insatiable; sprawling; strong-limbed; grim; hardhearted; unfeeling; cruel; devouring; insatiate; uncouth; slimy; fabled; wallowing; colossal; steaming; papyral; formidable; Briarean; slumbering; vile; modern; entangled; furry; hydra-headed; diabolical; pestilent; grotesque; accursed; eerie; quaint; pediculous.

verbs
abound with—s; beget—; condemn to—; dread—; fear—; overcome—; quell—; satiate—; subdue—; tame—; —coils; —devours; —frightens; —horrifies; —howls; —looms; —offends; —roams; —spouts; —terrifies; —terrorizes.

(See giant, beast, dragon, barbarian, animal; savage; villain; brute.)

MONTH

adjectives
healing; memorable; sweet; dreary; anxious; withered; story-book; ensuing; tedious; corresponding; brief; silent; wintry; tempestuous; treacherous; stretched; gentle; much-abused; crabbed; meager.

verbs
attain in—; endure—; enjoy—; estimate—s; extend—; finish—; indicate—; mark—; pass—; remain—; spend—; survive—; tide over—; waste—; —elapses; —fades; —separates.

(See time, week, year.)

MONUMENT

adjectives
imperishable; wondrous; vast; sarcophagus-like; wasting; lasting; worthy; enduring; extant; venerable; deathless; tawny; stately; strange; gigantic; divine; living; everlasting; endless; colossal; marble; notorious; mysterious; charred; sepulchral; immemorial; pompous; majestic; equestrian; mighty; impressive; lofty; surviving; splendid; kindred; obvious; conspicuous; public.

verbs
boast—; dedicate—; deface—; earn—; elevate—; engrave—; erect—; gild—; inscribe on—; restore—; —adorns; —commemorates; —endures; —glorifies; —immortalizes; —perpetuates; —preserves; —records; —represents; —signifies; —symbolizes; —towers.

(See inscription, trophy, memorial, statue, tomb.)

MONUMENTAL

adverbs
overwhelmingly; stupendously; massively; unbelievably; colossally; gigantically; incomparably; vastly; matchlessly; prodigiously; tremendously; inexpressibly.

MOOD

adjectives
similar; changing; characteristic; grateful; unwavering; rarest; ungentle; furtive; discontented; beguiling; half-dreaming; selfless; mysterious; exquisite; guileful; musing; uncertain; affectionable; wrathful; fantastic; willful; dominant; intemperate; adventurous; morbid; exuberant; genial; articulate; irregular; parleying; silent; ironic; lifelong; rebellious; imperious; bewildered; genial; chaffing; comfortable; freakish; reminiscent; impassioned; subjective; absonant; pensive; unimagined; enchanted; sprightly; sullen; impetuous; rebel; extinguished; mirthful; penitential; disagreeable; wrought-up; thoughtful; receptive; habitual; depressed; philosophic; merry; sentimental; misprized; fear-stricken; romantic; sanguine; pliant; dreamy; exacting; concurrent; raging; beneficial; rapid; garrulous; favorable; variable; placid; wayward; respectful; contemplative; stern; sarcastic; working; expectant; flippant; steadfast; affable; mournful; despondent; indifferent; submissive; idea-less; senseless; frantic; shallow; evanescent; presageful; central; morbid; gruesome; demagogic; indispensable; humane; hysterical; inquisitorial; capricious; alien; jealous; melancholy; habitual; impious; reflective; facetious; chastened; philosophic; anti-radical; religious; docile; hasty; loitering; artificial; successive (pl); dreaded; ascetic; intense; uneven; kindly; changeful; icy; mandatory; shuddering; springtime; berserk; conciliatory; permissive; shifting; minor; angelic; unfavorable.

verbs
combat—; communicate—; crystallize—; defer to—; depict—; dispel—; fathom—; fix —; govern by—; induce—; interpret—; jolt out of—; kindle—; lighten—; overstrain—; rage in—; recall—; reflect—; shock out of —; soothe—; submit to—; succumb to—; sustain—; temper—; voice—; wrap in—; yield to—; —presages; —prevails; —strikes; —vanishes.

(See disposition, melancholy, feeling, emotion.)

MOODY

adverbs
captiously; ominously; sullenly; bitterly; cynically; alarmingly; seriously; unaccountably; occasionally; unreasonably; perplexingly; morbidly; fearfully; portentously; significantly; dangerously; unusually; capriciously; irascibly; fretfully; perversely; glumly; grimly; frequently; rarely; seldom; doggedly; intractably; intolerably; insufferably; unendurably.

MOON

adjectives
envious; filmy; brilliant; full-orbed; Orient; airless; queenly; angry; infantine; misty; fleeting; morning; gibbous; sphered; wintry; melancholy; inconstant; smiling; carven; curved; semi-tropic; lifeless; crescent; triumphant; flying; tranquil; stormy; softer; waxing; prying; dying; mourning; bloody; setting; languorous; red; distorted; pale; cold; waning; mellow; sleepless; listening; harvest; laboring; dying; solitary; shining; hollowed; blazing; marvelous; climbing; broad; sickle; gracious; jealous; watery; fruitless; coined; fair; overcast; wandering; shrouded; slow; haunting; desolate; naked; belated; lingering; sacred; horned; large-lighted; tranquil; smiling; withered; changeless; overwhelming; beauty-seeking; temperamental; winter; unassuming; peeping; summer; round; intense; luminous; full; cruel; yellow; green; harvest; marigold; honey-colored; arctic; hazy; lucent; slow; silvery; frosted; apple-shaped; purple; sad; climbing.

verbs
behold—; encircle—; fringe—; gaze at—; obscure—; veil—; view—; —barges (colloq.); —beams; —blushes; —brightens; —climbs; —dances; —dies; —dips into; —drifts beyond; —emerges; —enamors; —en-

chants; —gleams; —glimmers; —glows; —impassions; —mellows; —peeps out; —reigns; —sails over; —scowls; —shimmers; —silvers; —sinks; —voyages; —wanes; —waxes.
(See sun, stars, clouds, sky.)

MOONBEAM

adjectives
opalescent; dim; blended; sluiced; cold; quivering; misty; mellow.

verbs
shed—; wash by—; —brightens; —dances; —dazzles; —drips; —enchants; —floods; —glimmers; —hallows; —kisses; —illumines; —mantles; —shrouds; —silvers; —sparkles; —sweeps; —swells; —trembles; —whitens.
(See ray, light, radiance, spark, sunshine, sunlight, twilight, moonlight.)

MOONLIGHT

adjectives
glinting; gentle; sickly; bleached; mellow; liquid; rich; down-slanting; mystical; cold; dewy; molten; golden; pleasant; pale; bubbling; magnificent; generous; weird; streaming; faint; white; muffled; fitful; ribboned; sacred; harvest; painted; vivid; glistening; tropic; autumn; sallow; milky; tremulous; slanting.

verbs
bathe in—; drip—; shroud in—; wash by—; —casts spell; —checkers; —enchants; —illuminates; —kindles; —streaks; —streams in; —swathes; —sweeps; —unveils; —wanes.
(See moonbeam.)

MOONSHINE

adjectives
white; sweet; silvery.

MOONSTRUCK

adverbs
crazily; outlandishly; queerly; fantastically; giddily; foolishly; bewilderingly; ridiculously; undoubtedly; hazily; foggily; daftly; incoherently; deliriously; unstably; heedlessly; witlessly.

MOOR (v)

adverbs
primitively; safely; permanently; seasonally; cautiously; habitually; prudently.
(See fasten, fix.)

MOORING

adjectives
sheltered; primitive; diplomatic.

verbs
anchor to—; attach to—; break—; cable to —; command—; direct—; drag from—; drive from—; drop from—; hinder—; quit —; secure—; shackle to—; slacken—; slip —; swing at—; wreck in—.
(See post.)

MOOSE

verbs
bait—; breed—; exhibit—; experiment with —; lure—; pet—; plague with—; stalk—; stuff—; trap—; —climbs; —frightens; —haunts; —hurries; —infects; —infest; —munches; —nibbles; —runs; —scurries; —shies; —squeals; —shuns; —digs.
(See animal, deer.)

MOPE (v)

adverbs
glumly; dismally; gloomily; morbidly; despondently; romantically; drearily; pallidly; sadly; abnormally.
(See sulk, brood.)

MORAL

adjectives
fearful; strictest; obtrusive; intellectual; pretty; austerest; admirable; latent; righteous; public; fallible; obvious; creditable; immovable; political; abstract; philosophical.

adverbs
chastely; sternly; strictly; rigidly; uncompromisingly; intolerantly; righteously; self-consciously; proudly; apparently; self-righteously; preachily; ostentatiously; blatantly; presumably; avowedly; virtuously; remarkably; astonishingly; tiresomely; unbelievably; sanctimoniously; unctuously; blandly.

MORALE

verbs
acclaim—; assail—; break down—; destroy —; fortify—; impair—; instill—; lower—; shatter—; stimulate—; strengthen—; —ascends; —descends; —sinks; —wanes.
(See nerve, courage, strength, valor, spirit, virtue.)

MORALIST

adjectives
rigid; fashionable; futile; shallow; pretending; dissembling; confirmed.

MORALITY

adjectives
provincial; austere; puritanical; strait; trite; wholesome; creditable; restrictive; hereditary; flabby; intolerant; rigorous; fastidious; semi-religious; predominant; collar-and-wrist-band; Christian; political; true; scrupulous; marital; speculative.

verbs
abandon—; cant—; contemplate—; develop —; discard—; elevate—; guard—; inspire —; instruct—; observe—; regulate—; revive —; stimulate—; sustain—; uphold—; whitewash (colloq.) —; —crumbles; —decays; —elevates; —enlightens; —improves; —protects; —raises.

(See virtue, purity, integrity, righteousness, honor, truth.)

MORALIZE (*v*)

adverbs
jocosely; piously; monotonously; religiously; paternally; irritatingly; indefatigably.

(See preach, teach.)

MORALS

verbs
annihilate—; communicate—to; compromise —; corrupt—; destroy—; disapprove of—; disregard—; draw—from; emancipate—; improve—; influence—; outrage—; point to —; —degenerate; —deteriorate.

(See lesson, ethics, habit, ideals.)

MORASS

adjectives
drear; dismal; frightful.

verbs
deluge—; dip in—; drain—; emerge from —; immerse in—; penetrate—; plunge into —; soak in—; steep in—; swamp in—; swash through—; wallow in—; wander into —; —bogs; —engulfs; —mires.

(See mire. swamp, marsh.)

MORBID

adverbs
profoundly; abnormally; distressingly; forlornly; dangerously; inordinately; preposterously; crankily; incurably; miserably; pathetically; pitiably; vexatiously; unreasonably; outlandishly; outrageously; disagreeably; intolerably; terribly; irrationally; ominously; horribly.

MORN

adjectives
cloudy; radiant; rosy; returning; balmy; fateful; lily-wristed; incense-breathing; hallowed; double-pillowed; unsullied; gaudy; summer; delusive; valorous; propitious; immortal; breaking; weeping; spring; lagging; misty; struggling; smiling; dismal; endless; gusty; silent; vernal; new-made; awful; refluent; radiant; silver-flecked; blooming; apocalyptic.

MORNING

adjectives
cold; sunless; identical; dreary; propitious; yellow-robed; amber; splendid; dazzling; breezeless; vapory; absorbing; historic; invigorating; precious; faultless; memorable; uneventful; cruel; glorious; listless; dun-colored; bridal; dull; delicious; quiet; sullen; dreadful; raw; lurid; misty; clear; shining; perpetual; fresh; auspicious; soft; sharp; frosty; hoary; merry; pallid; portentous; drear; foggy.

verbs
herald—; usher in—; wash—; —ascends; —awakens; —beckons; —blooms; —breaks through; —checkers; —crowns; —dawns; —drones along; —glimmers; —is born; —rises; —shrouds; —smiles; —tints; —uncurtains; —unfolds.

(See dawn, day, afternoon, evening, time.)

MOROSE

adverbs
dismally; incorrigibly; unreasonably; unaccountably; pathetically; unbearably; horribly; crabbedly; cantankerously; churlishly; boorishly; ominously; inordinately; uncommonly; outrageously; inexcusably; rudely; uncivilly; impolitely; ungraciously; inexplicably; inscrutably; silently; suddenly; irascibly; perversely; restively; intractably; implacably; sourly; immovably.

MORPHEUS

verbs
court—; invoke—; resist—; yield to—; —approaches; —caresses; —conquers; —cradles; —delights; —deludes; —enfolds;

—develops; —harasses; —lulls; —purifies; —rejuvenates; —shades; —smooths; —soothes; —strokes; —treads; —weaves.
(See sleep, rest, slumber, lethargy.)

MORSELS

adjectives
tantalizing; epicurean; picturesque; luscious; piquant; nauseous; locutionary; exquisite; petty; piteous; succulent; lawn-wrapped; hungry; delicious; tempting; inviting-looking.

MORTAL

adjectives
contemporary; melancholy; great; rough; rapid; reason-boasting; wretched; sacred; scarcest; meekest; ordinary; venturesome; wee; worn.

MORTALITY

adjectives
indued; miserable; international; enormous; human; waning; dull; recreant; allotted; normal; sad; massed (pl); heaven-oppressed.

verbs
abate—; account for—; constitute—; control —; lower—; rate—; —alarms; —ascends; —decimates; —descends; —effaces; —increases; —piles up; —staggers; —varies; —wanes.
(See death, murder, plague, slaughter, suicide.)

MORTAR

verbs (vessel)
abrade—; beat in—; comminute in—; crumble in—; crunch in—; crush in—; granulate in—; grind in—; pound in—; powder in—; pulverize in—; rasp in—; reduce in—; stamp in—; triturate in—.

MORTGAGE

verbs
assign—; borrow on—; cancel—; confirm—; contract—; convey—; discharge—; foreclose —; fulfill—; grant—; lift—; melt into—; pay off—; undertake—; —assures; —burdens; —devours; —guarantees; —insures; —saps; —warrants.
(See loan, payment, bond, obligation, debt.)

MORTGAGE (v)

adverbs
hopelessly; rashly; improvidently; optimistically; lucklessly.
(See loan.)

MORTIFICATION

verbs
bear—; blush in—; cast into—; color in—; flush in—; hang in—; spare—; stoop in—; submit to—; swallow—; —confuses; —destroys; —crushes; —frustrates; —pains; —sobers; —treads on; —vexes.
(See chagrin, shame.)

MORTIFIED

adverbs
needlessly; horribly; shamefully; cruelly; unreasonably; extremely; humiliatingly; pitifully; naturally; exceedingly; terribly; unnecessarily; unaccountably; inexplicably; modestly; searingly; shockingly; bitterly; sorely.

MOSAICS

adjectives
golden; elaborate; curious; rare; radiant; glorious.

MOSQUITOES

verbs
devour by—; exterminate—; infest with—; spray—; —annoy; —buzz; —disquiet; —draw; —extract; —feast on; —infest; —pester; —plague; —poison; —puncture; —serenade; —suck; —swarm.
(See insects, fly.)

MOSS

adjectives
downy; fragrant; bright; idle; quaggy; silvered; creeping; branched; tender; sea-colored; hanging; velvetlike; bannered; spongy; furred; moldering.

MOTH

adjectives
soft; startled; resurrected; damage-wreaking.

verbs
singe—; snatch at—; —blights; —contaminates; —destroys; —deteriorates; —devours; —flutters; —gnaws; —harasses; —hovers about; —impairs; —s infest; —injures; —s plague; —preys on; —ravages.
(See insects, butterfly.)

MOTHER

adjectives

provident; prudent; glorious; peasant; impatient; frail; beautiful; admirable; pious; doting; mahogany-colored; tedious-working; bereaved; commonplace; potential; infuriated; jealous; indulgent; frowzy; venerable; melancholy; famishing; earthly; vigorous; aggressive; elemental; insatiate; spirited; celestial; prolific; strong-armed; authentic; incestuous; delicate; bountiful; over-fatigued; querulous; imaginary; virgin; green-girdled; sorrowing; devoted; foolish; widowed; subtle; deft; spiteful; adopting; altruistic; unnatural.

verbs

anchor—; cherish—; cling to—; deliver of —; devote to—; hound—; obey—; —bears; —cradles; —conceives; —embraces; —fondles; —forsakes; —nourishes; —nurses; —protects; —punishes; —rears; —rocks; —sacrifices; —suckles; —weans.

(See father, nurse, parent, woman.)

MOTHERLY

adverbs

affectionately; graciously; affably; comfortably; indulgently; gently; sympathetically; understandingly; intelligently; charmingly; unfailingly; tenderly; lovingly; wisely; altogether; admirably; wondrously; marvellously; incomparably; eagerly; happily; joyously; pleasantly; agreeably; good-naturedly; tolerantly; warmly; amiably; complacently; imperturbably; serenely; calmly; quietly; wholesomely.

MOTION

adjectives

ceaseless; visible; measured; dignified; airy; quivering; legal; alternative; perpetual; hesitating; subtle; delighted; stable; inconstant; measureless; appealing; chopping; lulling; spiral; captivating; slow; irregular; sickening; uncertain; nautical; natural; wavy; rapid; mighty; apparent; musical; mincing; proximate; dreamlike; hingelike; graceful; flickering; undulous; mechanic; arresting; awkward; lifelike; ceaseless; obvious; orbitual; well-ordered; elliptic; parabolic; intended; revolving; sensible; relative; gyratory; convulsive; gentle; vibratory; dreary; slow; lateral; giddy; planetary; faltering; diurnal; reciprocating; retrograde; scythelike; liquid; horizontal; parallactic; warm; constant; gliding; lightning; heavy; rhythmic; astonished; comparative; metallic; erratic; primitive; increasing; habitual; rapturous; universal; admired; inward; feeble; delicious; extravagant; insectlike; unnumbered (pl); tiring; abrupt; veritable; molecular; atomic; nimble; many-valued.

verbs

arrest—; constrain—; express—; ferment into—; guide—; impel—; lose—; practise —; quell—; regulate—; restrain from—; restrict—; retard—; set into—; slide into—; sustain—; whirl into—; —agitates; —expresses; —saps.

(See gesture, flicker, action, movement.)

MOTIONLESS

adverbs

suddenly; silently; warily; breathlessly; strangely; curiously; oddly; watchfully; noiselessly; frightfully; incredibly; absolutely; utterly; statuesquely; unbelievably; miraculously; stealthily; scrupulously; cautiously; prudently; discreetly; secretly.

MOTION PICTURE

verbs

(See "movie.")

MOTIVE

adjectives

chivalrous; tragic; corrupt; predominant; incidental; ambitious; attributed; selfish; altruistic; kind; underlying; commercial; corrupt; worthy; interested; ignoble; greedy; intrusive; conscientious; plausible; priceless; principal; lofty; invented; ostensible; colonial; unmixed; misleading; professional; perplexing; secondary; high; generous; explanatory; interesting; complicated; auxiliary; disinterested; evil; urgent; improper; hedonistic; differing; compelling; imputed; ulterior; patriotic; melodic; inferior; mercenary; fatal; upright; pure; commanding; sufficient; keen; guiding; impugning; impelling; dominant; identical; basilar; ruling; potent; laudable; understandable; cryptic; bread-and-butter; segmented; sculptured; hidden; scarce-known.

verbs

abolish—; acknowledge—; appreciate—; assign—for; attribute—to; destroy—; impute —to; mock—; obscure—; ponder—; probe into—; recognize—; review —s; reward—;

weigh—; —actuates; —governs; —impels; —induces; —inspires; —prompts; —stimulates; —sways.
(See cause, grounds, incentive, impulse, inducement.)

MOTOR

adjectives
creaking; coughing; inactive; compression; oil-driven; whirring; undependable; wheezing.

verbs
accelerate—; choke—; fuel—; recondition —; stall—; —balks; —coughs; —drones; —fails; —fouls; —gasps; —hums; —purrs; —roars; —rasps; —rattles; —splutters; —steams; —whines.
(See generator, machine, engine, propeller.)

MOTORBOAT

verbs
anchor—; buffet—; moor—; test—; throttle —; —bobs; —capsizes; —chugs; —churns; —coughs; —drifts; —heads; —noses for; —splutters; —spurts; —sputters; —whisks; —whizzes; —zooms.
(See launch, ship, tugboat, yacht, vessel, steamer.)

MOTORCYCLE

verbs
straddle—; throttle—; —blasts; —breezes by; —chokes; —chugs; —coughs; —leans; —roars; —shoots by; —splutters; —sputters; —whisks away; —whizzes by; —wriggles; —zigzags.
(See automobile, taxi, motor.)

MOTTO

verbs
adopt—; apply—; coin—; condense into—; design—; devise—; digest—; heed—; inscribe—; misstate—; phrase—; quote—; recite—; recognize—; relish—; sing forth—; —emphasizes; —exalts; —glorifies; —provides; —signifies; —stresses; —symbolizes.
(See poetry, epigram, proverb, parable, saying.)

MOULD

verbs
adjust—; bake in—; cast—; cleave to—; conform to—; design—; drain into—; oil—; pattern—; pour into—; press—; set in—; shape—; —cools; —fashions; —frames; —hardens; —imitates.
(See form.)

MOULD (v)

adverbs
exquisitely; trimly; faultlessly; subtly; realistically; professionally; deftly; skillfully; artistically; symmetrically; sensuously; voluptuously; meretriciously.
(See model, fashion, shape.)

MOULDY

adverbs
dangerously; deeply; poisonously; infectiously; rottenly; putridly; rankly; rancidly; offensively; grossly; noxiously; injuriously; terribly; riskily; presumably; apparently; extremely; obviously; manifestly.

MOUND

adjectives
pious; countless; rural; hideous; grass-grown; craggy; conical; sorrow-laden; shapeless; pyramidal; solitary; moldering.

MOUNT

adjectives
lofty; sloping; tireless; mimic; apocalyptic; flame-fringed; spectacular.

MOUNT (v)

adverbs
reluctantly; magnificently; awkwardly; perpetually; gradually; rigidly; reluctantly; mechanically; reticently; stealthily; spectacularly.
(See ascend, rise.)

MOUNTAIN

adjectives
shimmering; bare; cold; eroded; rugged; dizzy; faraway; wintry; forested; beacon-lighted; multitudinous; glacier-laden; pine-encircled; adamantine; dominating; spirit-haunted; cultivated; plain; melancholy; moonlit; steep; uncouthly-cut; beholding; inaccessible; lifeless; precipitous; gloomy; lifeless; variegated; flaring; relentless; soft-looking; enchanted; heaven-reaching; timberless; worshipful; huge; new; craggy; misty; fractured; snowy; moody; severed; tremendous; intervening; prickly; glittering; ruddy; delectable; remote; offensive; jagged; rude; slumbering; overhanging; pensive; eagle-baffling; ice-crowned; terraced;

round-topped; sharp-peaked; redoubtable; messy-looking; environing; tumbling; scarlet; morning; disintegrated; barren; symmetrical; volcanic; vast; everlasting; verdant; fabled; naked; sentinel; scarped;unscaled; windless; towering; colorless; ancient; timbered; gloomy; ponderous; prodigious; unique; weltering; steepy; circumjacent.

verbs
abandon—; ascend—; carve—; circumvent—; fortify—; furrow—; level—; plow through—; reconnoitre—; scale—; straddle—; trudge up—; —awes; —hinders; —looms up; —obscures; —obstructs; —overawes; —shadows; —stands sentinel; —towers.

(See hill, bank, peak, precipice, tower.)

MOUNTAINEERS

adjectives
mythic; benighted; hardy; intractable; redoubtable; wary.

MOUNTAINOUS

adverbs
gloriously; hazardously; terribly; magnificently; splendidly; gorgeously; gloomily; disastrously; impenetrably; densely; impassably; scenically; steeply; bleakly; tremendously; perilously; dangerously; attractively; invitingly; alluringly; adventurously; notoriously; presumably.

MOURN (v)

adverbs
pathetically; sincerely; touchingly; nationally; primitively; tragically; barbarically; oppressively; jealously; querulously; unnaturally; piously.

(See grieve, regret, lament.)

MOURNER

adjectives
flap-mouthed; pensive; desolate; sorrowful; heartbroken.

condole—; console—; sympathize with—; —s attend; —despairs; —s file out; —laments; —grieves; —rends; —s respect; —screams; —sheds; —sobs; —suffers; —wails; —weeps; —groans.

MOURNFUL

adverbs
desolately; forlornly; dismally; drearily; hopelessly; helplessly; bitterly; sadly; tragically; pitiably; unutterably; unspeakably; unbearably; grievously; profoundly; irremediably; disagreeably; uncomfortably; shockingly; cruelly; gloomily; grimly; disconsolately; inconsolably; plaintively; querulously; resentfully; rebelliously.

MOUSE

adjectives
smallest; monstrous; realistic; scampering.

verbs
attract—; bait—; corner—; panic—; pursue—; snare—; stir—; trap—; —burrows; —cowers; —disturbs; —dodges; —gnaws; —nibbles; —ransacks; —rifles; —rummages; —scampers; —scurries; —scuttles; —whisks.

(See animal.)

MOUSTACHE

verbs
adorn with—; coil—; cultivate—; curl—; dye—; finger—; nourish—; pluck at—; roll—; ruffle—; smooth—; stroke—; trim—; twirl—; twist—; wax—; wipe—; —bristles; —charms; —curls; —droops; —gleams; —trembles; —wilts.

(See mane, beard, whiskers, curls.)

MOUTH

adjectives
smiling; deep; innocent; loud-ringing; mobile; enraged; foamy; sweet; rosy; impressive; good-humored; loving; alkaline; irritable; deathful-grinning; funnel-shaped; compressed; fine; sensuous; musty; winsome; cooing; dimpled; tender; relaxed; generous; unpampered; prudent; extraordinary; wide; wry; foul; brazen; cavernous; resolute; lascivious; delicate; frothy; churning; handsome; full; firm; querulous; ascetic; yawning; coral; ravishing; facile; perilous; puckered; toothless; rabbit; baby; branching; sulky; acid; gaping; arch; eloquent; unmelodious; bloodless; voluble; glad; expressive; economical; breathless; slobbering; serious; savage; insistent; sardonic; purposeful; shapeless; hungry; furnace; munching; painted; heavy; vermilion; distended; luscious; wrinkled; cruel; modeled.

verbs
convey to—; froth at—; honey—; introduce into—; irritate—; padlock—; paint—; pout

—; proceed from—; pucker up—; seal—; screw up—; sponge—; smite on—; swab—; —droops; —hardens; —lures; —quirks; —quivers; —relaxes; —tightens; —twitches; —utters.

(See lips, face, opening.)

MOVABLE

adverbs

conveniently; easily; handily; adjustably; cleverly; comfortably; appropriately; serviceably; usefully; freely; readily; lightly; adaptably; conformably; curiously.

MOVE

adjectives

ill-planned; latest; strategic; opening; vulnerable; subordinate; rusty; eccentric; hostile; brilliant; ambitious; fancy; stultifying.

verbs

abet—; alternate —s; attempt—; calculate —; concede—; determine—; devise—; encourage—; guard—; limit —s; speculate on —; study—; undertake—; —captures; —deceives; —misleads; —tricks.

(See march, maneuver, movement.)

MOVE (*v*)

adverbs

gracefully; automatically; perceptibly; sinuously; precariously; simultaneously; involuntarily; caressingly; violently; rashly; spasmodically; cautiously; deftly; impatiently; rhythmically; profoundly; visibly; sedately; invisibly; fearsomely; serenely; unintelligibly; blithesomely; drearily; stealthily; dubiously; erratically; sluggishly; obliviously; agilely; phelegmatically; passively; invincibly; warily; strategically; abortively; brusquely; tremulously; timorously; martially.

(See step, walk.)

MOVEMENT (*action, change of* position, etc.)

verbs

accentuate—; accomplish—; attempt—; avoid—; cease—; control—; diminish—; effect—; enliven—; facilitate—; hamper—; impede—; induce—; minimize—; necessitate—; practise—; repeat—; restrain from —; restrict—; reverse—; —agonizes.

(See current, motion, move.)

MOVEMENT (campaign)

verbs

actuate—; annihilate—; applaud—; ban—; block—; combat—; cripple—; criticize—; defeat—; dominate—; endorse—; engage in —; engineer—; facilitate—; father—; fling into—; found—; frustrate—; govern—; inaugurate—; initiate—; involve in—; launch —; mask—; promote—; quell—; rally to—; sponsor—; support—; —coagulates; —collapses; —commences; —culminates in; —dies; —flourishes; —originates in; —penetrates to; —springs from; —suffers; —symbolizes; —wanes.

(See crusade, fascism, innovation, cause.)

MOVEMENT (*general*)

adjectives

anxious; contemplated; spasmodic; commendable; romantic; recent; involuntary; strategical; deliberate; planetary; wild; busy; complicated; passionate; graceful; revolutionary; impulsive; metallic; rude; unobtrusive; important; erratic; impatient; abortive; alternative; careless; rhythmic; bustling; wandering; uncapturable; delicate; pending; retrograde; offensive; flank; convulsive; scooping; life-sustaining; contemplated; self possessed; messianic; living; hostile; rebellious; particular; painful; cooperative; bridling; incessant; aesthetic; willowy; celestial; intentional; philanthropic; turbulent; fitting; silent; wasteful; insurrectionary; muscular; imperceptible; dexterous; soothing; foregoing; extensive; composite; clicking; nautical; masterly; terrorist; kneading; responsive; flexible; religious; insensible; tremulous; brusque; grandiose; silly; subsequent; slinking; crushing; fantastic; unconvulsive; guillotine-like; discerning; serpentine; energetic; circumspect; vigorous; recreation; zigzag; interdependent; lyrical; supple; agonized; timorous; hazardous; calm; cabalistic; springy; free; desultory; syncopated; enveloping; unanticipated; blithe; glacial; martial; present; cyclic; toss-over.

MOVER

adjectives

prime; mortal; fairest; unseen.

"MOVIE"

verbs

censor—; construct—; cram—with; direct —; film—; howl at—; inspire—; prevent—;

produce—; repress—; review—; romp through—; —amuses; —appeals; —attracts; —conveys; —depicts; —entertains; —excites; —refreshes; —surges; —thrills.

(See film, play, story.)

MUCOUS

verbs

cast out—; discharge—; eject—; emit—; excrete—; expel—; exude—; secrete—; —drains from; —emanates from; —issues; —lubricates; —moistens; —oozes.

(See secretion, discharge.)

MUD

adjectives

gurgling; oozing; sticky; flung; black; tenacious; dragging; poisonous; treacherous; viscous; sluggish; slimy; clinging; great; ancient; sloshing; hopeless; frozen; fertilizing; dense; respectable; spattered; caked; dried; jellylike.

verbs

bake—; bathe in—; bespatter with—; bog in—; cake—; dabble in—; daub with—; emerge from—; flounder in—; lodge in—; mire in—; plod through—; roll in—; sling—; spatter with—; steep in—; swash through—; wade through—; wallow in—; —cakes; —gurgles; —spatters; —sucks.

(See mire, dirt, filth, swamp, marsh.)

MUDDLE

adjectives

appalling; miserable; vicious; intricate; indescribable.

MUDDLED

adverbs

hopelessly; strangely; unfortunately; helplessly; mysteriously; vaguely; comically; tragically; disastrously; completely; horribly; indescribably; obviously; unmistakably; visibly; manifestly; dazedly; brokenly; pathetically; inexpertly; laughably; foolishly; greatly.

MUDDY

adverbs

untidily; deeply; impassably; horribly; distressingly; grimily; thickly; turbidly; foully; disagreeably; unpleasantly; inconceivably; unexpectedly; astonishingly; impossibly; dangerously; obstructively; swampily; quaggily.

MUFFLED

adverbs

dimly; obscurely; deliberately; unpleasantly; closely; furtively; stealthily; carefully; warily; softly; inaudibly; sepulchrally; confidentially; evasively; tremulously; curiously; peculiarly; faintly; cautiously.

MUGGY

adverbs

unpleasantly; disagreeably; humidly; damply; soggily; suffocatingly; smotheringly; breathlessly; unhealthily; duskily; dimly; obscurely; strangely; remarkably; extremely; peculiarly; confusingly; foggily; mistily; warmly; intolerably; distressingly.

MULE

adjectives

burdened; unshod; bare-backed; toil-enduring; snail-paced; flea-bitten; fruit-laden; sure-footed; lagging; jaded; opinionative; jingling; patient.

verbs

burden—; fetter—; guide—; manage—; rein—; tether—; water—; —balks; —s caracole; —carries; —endures; —groans; —hauls; —haunches; —kicks; —pulls; —shies; —snorts; —strains; —wearies.

(See mare, livestock, animal, donkey.)

MULISH

adverbs

doggedly; intractably; intolerably; disagreeably; unpleasantly; obstinately; sullenly; stubbornly; defiantly; dogmatically; immovably; inflexibly; obdurately; perversely; sulkily; stiffly; tenaciously; waywardly; wilfully; determinedly; obstreperously; remarkably; notoriously; inveterately; confoundedly; terribly.

MULLIONED

adverbs

artistically; elegantly; richly; elaborately; gorgeously; splendidly; magnificently; beautifully.

MULTIPLY (v)

adverbs

ceaselessly; prodigiously; exceedingly; miraculously; alarmingly; lustily; mathematically; beneficially; wantonly; deliberately; disconcertingly.

(See increase, enlarge.)

MULTITUDE

adjectives

vast; breathless; productive; feathered; rude; assembled; furious; buzzing; pleased; barbarous; flocking; lessening; tawny; infuriated; anarchic; immense; applauding; dripping; straggling; carven; hushed; pestilence-stricken; considerable; interminable; prostrate; polluting; thronging; picturesque; kindred; shadowy; overawed; blissful; soaring; promiscuous; babbling; dauntless; heavenly; superfluous; inextinguishable; captive; blind; panting; white-robed; distracted; unthoughtful; dizzy; potent; joyous; clamorous; trampled; groaning; adoring.

verbs

assail—; condemn—; convert—; convey to —; despise—; enthrall—; govern—; harangue—; inspire—; move—; rouse—; rule —; scorn—; —blasphemes; —congregates; —flees; —gathers; —masses; —swarms; —throngs; —worships.

(See crowd, invader, horde, legion, masses, mob.)

MUM

adverbs

discreetly; prudently; wisely; carefully; decently; reliably; securely; sagely; sagaciously; taciturnly; laconically; reticently; quietly; calmly; resolutely; determinedly; uncommunicatively; cautiously; warily; loyally; judiciously; considerately; courteously; shrewdly; judiciously; sensibly; discerningly; remarkably; deliberately; significantly.

MUMBLE (*v*)

adverbs

inarticulately; vaguely; bashfully; gruffly; querulously; idiotically; roughly; monotonously; irreverently; formidably; outlandishly; grotesquely; gruesomely.

(See mutter, utter.)

MUMMERY

adjectives

ghostly; profane; present; unmeaning.

MUNCH (*v*)

adverbs

placidly; cozily; contentedly; dreamily; greedily; famishedly; toothlessly; insatiably.

(See chew, nibble, eat.)

MUNICIPALITY

adjectives

obsequious; sham; ring-ridden; patriotic.

MUNIFICENT

adverbs

lavishly; surprisingly; astonishingly; bountifully; extravagantly; incredibly; wastefully; abundantly; bounteously; unimaginably; excessively; preposterously; ostentatiously; exorbitantly; inordinately; magnificently; philanthropically; pompously; notably; charitably.

MURDER

adjectives

cold-blooded; wanton; complicated; anarchic; mightiest; mortal; contested; high-handed; potential; unparalleled; unprovoked; foul; direful; nihilistic; sacrilegious; treacherous; willful; judicial; deliberate; various (pl); ruthless; gruesome.

verbs

atone for—; avenge—; contrive—; cover—; exalt—; execute—; expiate—; perform—; perpetrate—; plan—; plot—; punish—; redeem—; relish—; repent—; reveal—; revenge—; —awes; —confuses; —scandalizes; —terrifies.

(See killing, assassination, massacre, mortality.)

MURDER (*v*)

adverbs

pitilessly; deliberately; foully; treacherously; inhumanly; wantonly; unprovokedly; direfully; sacrilegiously; gruesomely; ruthlessly; irrationally; sadistically.

(See kill, butcher.)

MURDERER

adjectives

cowardly; viperous; notorious; guilty; cursed; egregious; bloody.

verbs

apprehend—; curse—; execute—; glorify—; hunt—; incarcerate—; inspire—; net—; overtake—; overwhelm—; pardon—; penalize—; reproach—; reveal—; sate—; sentence—; spot—; stain—; terrify—; —contrives; —flees; —stifles.

(See assassin, kidnapper, robber, thief.)

MURDEROUS

adverbs

savagely; cruelly; vengefully; brutally; insanely; fiercely; strangely; alarmingly; dangerously; ominously; dreadfully; portentously; unmistakably; presumably; stealthily; fearfully; enormously; undeniably; incontestably.

MURKY

adverbs

strangely; unaccountably; curiously; dimly; smokily; faintly; obscurely; darkly; duskily; thickly; dangerously; alarmingly; ominously; frighteningly; unseasonably; gloomily; dismally; drearily; dankly; somberly; mistily; muggily; dingily; awfully.

MURMUR

adjectives

awed; sad; long-pent; softer; prolonged; exacting; rapid; prophetic; perpetual; crunching; splashing; faint; applauding; tender; portentous; thrilling; pervading; mimic; sullen; startling; depreciating; powerless; homely; monotonous; rustic; singing; inarticulate; gurgling; hasty; pleasing; shallow; wailing; drowsy; self-contemptuous; hurtful; satisfying; ominous; inarticulate; deepening; mournful; foreboding; whispering; lulling; popular; confused; gentle; kindling; querulous; broken; hushed; perturbed; irrepressible; plaintive; dissentient; cheerful; reverent; hollow; melodious; sympathetic; elusive; low; formidable.

verbs

break—; breathe—; buzz with—s; emit—; melt into—; restrain—; smother—; soften into—; stifle—; still—; subdue—; —floats; —flows; —perturbs; —pervades; —ripples in; —trickles through.

(See hum, sigh, sob.)

MURMUR (v)

adverbs

demurely; complacently; involuntarily; dreamily; drowsily; ceaselessly; whimsically; despondently; moodily; plaintively; apologetically; ruefully; ecstatically; dolefully; hoarsely; deprecatingly; languorously.

(See whisper, mutter.)

MUSCLES

adjectives

well-strung; saddle; noble; flaccid; facial; intestinal; sagging; important; massive; fatigued; aching; expressive; quivering; strengthened; painful; wild; bulging; sturdy; smashing; sledge-hammer; important; strained; swelling; gnarled; swollen; weary; prominent.

verbs

bring—into play; contract—; control—; distort—; embed in—; employ—; enlarge—; exercise—; exert—; expand—; flex—; govern—; incise—; inflame—; invigorate—; limber—; lodge in—; massage—; reeducate —; rejuvenate—; relax—; stiffen—; swell —; tense—; tone up—; weaken—; —atrophy; —bulge; —degenerate; —knot; —quiver; —ripple; —support; —twitch.

(See ligament, body, tendon.)

MUSCULAR

adverbs

amazingly; incredibly; robustly; sturdily; brawnily; athletically; wonderfully; unusually; uncommonly; remarkably; vigorously; powerfully; wirily; admirably; wondrously; soundly; tremendously; invincibly; unbelievably; unconquerably.

MUSE (v)

adverbs

pensively; dolefully; romantically; affectionately; nostalgically; irrelevantly; disconsolately; regretfully.

(See meditate, ponder, reflect.)

MUSES

adjectives

mournful; worst-humored; inspiring; gentle; dreamy; dauntless; humanizing.

MUSEUM

adjectives

local; desolate; veritable; admirable; provincial; miniature.

verbs

assemble in—; bequeath to—; congregate in —; dedicate—to; donate—; endow—; exhibit in—; flock to—; guide through—; muster in—; pack—; ransack—; refer to—; store in—; stream through—; —accumulates; —aggregates; —amasses; —collects; —compiles; —displays; —inspires; —preserves; —sponsors.

MUSIC

adjectives

unregarded; undying; orchestral; barbaric;

instrumental; contemporary; pianoforte; virginal; classical; charming; polyphonic; effective; sparkling; picturesque; elegiac; tragic; sonorous; higher; symphonic; concerted; random; intellectual; homophonic; starry; potential; excellent; secular; voluptuous; low; molten; bold; incidental; mechanized; martial; negroid; jocund; sweet; sinewy; brilliant; torrential; melancholy; mournful; heady; graceful; exquisite; grotesque; vocal; echoing; surging; nationalistic; dumb; ethereal; prismatic; deep-sweet; transporting; melting; evening; tinkling; shrill; steady; enchanted; worthy; unearthly; lively; reeling; dancing; ecclesiastical; liturgical; discordant; seraphic; sensuous; sacred; repining; contrapuntal; roaring; unutterable; half-delirious; pensive; chamber; gay; lilting; mere; persuasive; complex; outlandish; glad; contemporary; preluding; tawdry; delicious; hushed; sparkling; tantalizing; deathless; cadent; sobbing; measureless; brassy; meretricious; triumphant; soul-awakening; grinding; mewling.

verbs
mingle with—; ring with—; set to—; silence —; soften—; strum out—; sway to—; —awakens; —beats; —blares; —charms; —clashes; —electrifies; —elevates; —ensnares; —enthralls; —fascinates; —floats from; —humanizes; —kindles; —lessens; —moans; —mourns; —pauses; —rolls; —sobs; —soothes; —subsides; —swells; —throbs; —tingles; adapt—; drink in—.
(See hymn, modulation, jazz, song, melody.)

MUSICIAN

adjectives
erudite; excellent; graceful; temperamental; foreign-bred; self-taught; skilled; indignant; impertinent; capable; endowed; contemporary; airy; authoritative; eminent; talented; influential.

verbs
acclaim—; accord—; applaud—; encourage —; entreat—; inspire—; welcome—; —bows; —charms; —delights; —dreams; —enchants; —expresses; —interprets; —loosens; —moves; —pours; —renders; —soothes; —speaks; —strays; —thrills.
(See artist.)

MUSKET

adjectives
old-fashioned; smoky; percussion; ancient; unused.

verbs
arm with—; bear—; combat with—; discharge—; employ—; enlist—; force from—; provide—; repel with—; retaliate with—; salute with—; shoulder—; storm with—; wield—; —crackles; —flashes; —glitters; —rattles.
(See gun, pistol, machine gun, rifle.)

MUSLIN

adjectives
saffron; superior; unbleached; spotless; cream-tinted.

MUSSY

adverbs
inexcusably; unpleasantly; untidily; inexplicably; unnecessarily; unaccountably; senselessly; carelessly; shiftlessly; confusedly; chaotically; troublesomely; vexatiously; irritatingly; intolerably; disagreeably; inchoately; incidentally; casually; improvidently; wastefully; inconsiderately.

MUSTACHE

adjectives
cream-colored; tobacco-stained; thick; immature; stiff; iron-gray; jaunty; white; budding; sprouting; sandy; swooping; dashing; curling; tawny; twirled; waxed; indomitable; walrus; sleek; slight; silken; well-trimmed; disdainful; grizzled; blond; silver-streaked; fierce; pepper-and-salt; weedy.

MUSTANG

verbs
retreat before—; break—; breed—s; bridle —; captivate—; check—; confine—to; consign—to; corral—; domesticate—; entrap —; restrain—; round up—s; spur—; stable —; tame—; tether—; —roves; —shies; —wanders.
(See horse.)

MUSTARD

verbs
anoint with—; cultivate—; flavor with—; grind—; mix—; plaster—on; prepare—; relish—; savor—; season with—; smear—;

spice with—; spoon—; spread—; —bites; —flatters; —heightens; —sharpens; —stings.
(See salt, spice.)

MUTES

adjectives
obedient; congenital; deaf; wistful.

MUTILATION

verbs
conceal—; fear—; lament—; mend—; punish by—; recover from—; resort to—; sentence to—; suffer—; —attends; —blemishes; —blights; —defaces; —deforms; —deprives; —disfigures; —disables; —handicaps; —pains; —shocks; subject to—.
(See laceration, sabotage, injury, violence.)

MUTINOUS

adverbs
uncontrollably; ungovernably; tumultuously; rebelliously; turbulently; uproariously; unmanageably; riotously; chaotically; dangerously; ominously; portentously; intensely; terribly; alarmingly; doggedly; sullenly; brutally; sternly; murderously; seditiously; truculently; wildly; restlessly; disturbingly; oddly; uneasily; secretly.

MUTINY

adjectives
abortive; famous; practical; incited; exciting; long-planned.

verbs
attempt—; commit—; conspire—; draw into —; encounter—; inspire—; instigate—; invite—; overcome—; quash—; quell—; quench—; rise in—; rouse to—; seethe with —; snuff out—; suppress—; —roars; —smashes; —strikes; —threatens; —unfolds.
(See revolution, rebellion, insurrection.)

MUTTER

adjectives
incessant; drowsy; articulate; growling; low.

MUTTER (v)

adverbs
threateningly; despairingly; incoherently; mournfully; huskily; inaudibly; fitfully; defiantly; savagely; grimly; indistinctly; incessantly; drunkenly; thickly; bestially.
(See murmur, utter.)

MUTTERING

adjectives
internal; magic; bewildered; instant; habitual; unpleasant; inane; drear; visceral.

MUZZLE

adjectives
outstretched; creamy; glittering; shiny; gleaming.

verbs
burst—; clap on—; disengage—; emerge from—; impose—; jam on—; link—; require—; secure—; —checks; —controls; —curbs; —gags; —masks; —prevents; —represses; —restrains; —restricts.
(See brake, collar.)

MYRIADS

adjectives
phantom; propagated; humbler; countless; breathing; swarming; misty.

MYSTERIOUS

adverbs
altogether; strangely; perplexingly; uncomfortably; distressingly; unutterably; occultly; inscrutably; mystically; preposterously; pretentiously; unreasonably; foolishly; unnecessarily; vaguely; cryptically; inordinately; unfathomably; impenetrably; indefinitely; darkly; inviolately; evasively; queerly.

MYSTERY

adjectives
sweet; solemn; unsolved; bewildering; mighty; durable; inscrutable; profound; dread; artistic; baffling; overpowering; woodland; unaccountable; venerable; incarnate; hateful; fashionable; ridiculous; inevitable; unfolded; delicate; gray; unanswerable; ecstatic; unborn; worshipful; embarrassing; unexplored; mild; bearded; abstruse; labyrinthine; sacred; solemn; prime; sublime; peculiar; subtle; unfathomable; hungering; occult; sensational; painful; brooding; wingy; domestic; indescribable; deluding; juggling; physical; shrouding; selfsame.

verbs
absorb in—; cloak in—; comprehend—; concoct—; confront with—; deepen—; delve into—; dispel—; dissipate—; elucidate—; encompass by—; envelop in—; explore—ies of; fathom—; ferret out—; heighten—; init-

iate into—; penetrate—; plumb—; ponder —; reveal—; shroud in—; solve—; unlock —; unravel—; unveil—; wrap in—; —baffles; —prevails; —surrounds.

(See marvel, miracle, enigma, secret, maze.)

MYSTIC

adverbs

casually; vaguely; mysteriously; obscurely; precariously; unintelligibly; unfathomably; inscrutably; curiously; strangely; oddly; queerly; nebulously; symbolically; darkly; inferentially; impenetrably; covertly; magically; incomprehensibly.

MYSTICISM

adjectives

mellow; spiritual; sensuous; dramatic; philosophical.

verbs

achieve—; capitulate to—; chatter—; cloud by—; contemplate—; dabble in—; derive—from; devour—; entertain with—; immerse in—; involve—; poison by—; rationalize—; ridicule—; speculate on—; steep in—; wallow in—; —deludes; —pervades; —perverts; —poses as.

(See magic, doctrine, belief.)

MYTH

adjectives

nature; heroic; solar; ancient; aboriginal; domestic.

verbs

blast—; conceive—; dispel—; dissipate—; eradicate—; explode—; give rise to—; narrate—; preserve—; shatter—; strangle—; trace—; —antedates; —deals with; —develops; —evolves from; —explains; —grows; —portrays; —reflects; —relates; —reverberates; —survives; —wanes.

(See legend, fiction, story.)

MYTHOLOGICAL

adverbs

fabulously; fantastically; fancifully; presumably; probably; supposedly; speculatively; presumptively; preposterously; presumably; remotely; fantastically; groundlessly; purely; authentically; authoritatively; altogether; wholly.

N

NAG (v)

adverbs

shrewishly; maddeningly; unceasingly; monotonously; repetitiously; bitterly; acrimoniously; offensively; vehemently; viciously; diabolically.

(See tease, torment.)

NAIL

adjectives

tapering; cruel; brass-headed; sulphurous; diamond; slim; sturdy; bent; rusty.

verbs

cast—; clip off—; drive—; fabricate—s; fasten with—; hammer—; impale on—; mend with—; pound in—; secure with—; strike—; stud with—s; suspend from—; thump—; whack—; —impinges; —pierces; —rivets; —splinters.

(See fang, claw, pin, rivet, point, hook.)

NAIVE

adverbs

charmingly; unexpectedly; ingenuously; quaintly; childishly; incredibly; pitifully; pathetically; absurdly; ridiculously; laughably; ludicrously; unaccountably; inexplicably; surprisingly; sweetly; obviously; overwhelmingly; plainly; disarmingly; delightfully; refreshingly; cheerfully; unsuspiciously; utterly.

NAKED

adverbs

shamelessly; distressingly; pitiably; pathetically; grievously; scandalously; miserably; utterly; painfully; shockingly; horribly; wretchedly; deplorably.

NAKEDNESS

adjectives

primitive; sad; uncomely; cherubic; utter.

NAMBY-PAMBY

adverbs

hopelessly; feebly; pathetically; vexatiously; irritatingly; absurdly; unutterably; disgustingly; reprehensibly; ridiculously; deplorably; incurably; naturally; inherently; detestably; nervously; incomprehensibly; surprisingly; spinelessly; submissively; pliantly.

NAME

adjectives

republican; specious; altered; immortal; ambitious; fictitious; high-sounding; low; humble; feigned; aristocratic; charming; potent; endearing; opprobrious; musical; spotless; sacred; unworthy; blighted; generic; prosaic; gentle; uncommon; lasting; mystic; glorious; uncomfortable; interchangeable (pl); fashionable; bucolic; revolting; disreputable; creditable; naked; baptismal; beloved; honored; untarnished; hapless; worthless; ill; fair; mellifluous; doubtful; sonorous; imperial; servant; ancient; deathless; charitable; all-adored; stainless; ragged; abominable; deferential; saucy; everlasting; meaningless; ungentlemanly; hateful; illustrious; dreadful; flattering; inappropriate; grotesque; sheltering; hieroglyphic; long-living; distinguished; imposing; significant; unforgettable; deep-cut; humorous; childish; almighty; noble; unpronounceable; imperishable; respected; contemptuous; complaining; beauteous; musical; impious; wonted; graceless; inconspicuous; revered; phantom; soft; foremost; idolized; lustrous; poisonous; unblemished; influential; important; excellent; famous; good; euphonious; exact; renowned; night-begotten; authoritative; lofty; florid; vaunting; cherished; latinized; assumed; characteristic; family; poetic; suggestive; incongruous; wounded; borrowed; unsoiled; botanical; eminent; alluring; international; classical; inviolable; inoffensive; impressed; heroic; patrician; objectionable; half-mocking; haughtier; shining; fashionable.

verbs

adopt—; append—to; apply—to; assume—; attach interest to—; bear—; besmirch—; bestow—upon; blaspheme—; brand—; coin —; conjure with—; couple—s of; deprecate —; dignify—; dismiss—; divulge—; glorify —; identify with—; inscribe—; link—with; perpetuate—; preserve—; reveal—; scrawl —; stain—; thunder—; usurp—; venerate —; —blazes; —bobs up; —conveys; —derives; —embodies; —implies; —recurs; —shines; —strikes terror; —suggests.

(See title, character, reputation.)

NAME (v)

adverbs

speciously; ambitiously; fictitiously; humbly; aristocratically; musically; generically; prosaically; mystically; mellifluously; sonorously; deferentially; significantly; contemptuously; characteristically; offensively; heroically; haughtily; originally; appropriately; promptly.

(See entitle, designate.)

NAMELESS

adverbs

obscurely; curiously; remotely; ingloriously; unhappily; humbly; meekly; strangely; unfortunately; ignominiously; purposely; sadly; significantly; necessarily; abjectly; opprobriously; pathetically; diplomatically; strategically.

NAPKIN

verbs

edge—; fold—; fringe—; gather—; hold —; monogram—; mop with—; ring—; soil —; sponge with—; tuck—; utilize—; whip open—; wrinkle—; —assures; —catches; —protects; —safeguards.

(See handkerchief, cloth, towel.)

NARCOTICS

verbs

abstain from—; addict to—; control—; distribute—; drowse under—; inhale—; inject —; load with—; peddle—; purvey—; smuggle—; specialize in—; swallow—; trade in —; traffic in—; warn against—; —corrupt; —defile; —degenerate; —deteriorate; —ease; —induce; —menace; —poison; —ravage; —stultify; —wreck.

(See drug, heroin, medicine.)

NARRATE (v)

adverbs

bizarrely; absorbingly; vividly; romantically; grippingly; dramatically; movingly; deftly; tensely; vigorously; artfully; prosaically.

(See tell, recite, relate.)

NARRATION

adjectives

dramatic; bare; vivid; gripping; moving; swift; sure; deft; skilled; breathless.

verbs

blend into—; color—; commend—; discuss —; embellish—; enter into—; introduce into —; publish—; recite—; recount—; rehearse —; resume—; set forth in—; state in—; —delights; —depicts; —enchants; —enthralls; —portrays; —reveals; —unfolds.

(See lecture, story, tale.)

NARRATIVE

adjectives

dry; boasting; comprehensive; epical; enticing; shocking; contemporary; lugubrious; disjointed; digested; romantic; autobiographical; superficial; sober; poetical; imaginative; touching; dramatic; tragic; vivid; melodramatic; sacred; graphic; connected; superb; splendid; fictitious; thrilling; faithful; concise; mirthful; chequered; trustworthy; serious; earnest; authentic; metrical; truthful; personal; descriptive; persuasive; fantastic; voluminous; incredible; celebrated; present; masterly; supernatural; painful; pathetic.

verbs

acclaim—; blend into—; commend—; complicate—; condense—; embellish—; enliven —; impair—; interlard—; introduce in—; peruse—; recount—; set forth in—; spice —; strew throughout—; sum up—; —delights; —enchants; —flows; —portrays; —strikes; —unfolds.

(See fiction, lecture, legend, anecdote, story, tale.)

NARROW (v)

adverbs

appreciably; markedly; abruptly; perilously; impracticably; strikingly.

(See reduce, contract.)

NARROW

adverbs

impossibly; terribly; unbelievably; remarkably; painfully; inconveniently; inexplicably; outlandishly; stingily; frugally; parsimoniously; absurdly; ridiculously; perilously; hazardously; dangerously; inexcusably; outrageously; shockingly; terrifyingly; uselessly; unserviceably; curiously; undesirably; vexatiously; perplexingly; uncommonly.

NARROW-MINDED

adverbs

stubbornly; intolerably; intractably; obdurately; wilfully; incurably; incorrigibly; persistently; fanatically; perniciously; obstinately; hopelessly; mulishly; incomprehensibly; inveterately.

NARROWNESS

adjectives
ignoble; puritanic; old-fashioned; mental; moral; unexpected.

NASTY

adverbs
squalidly; obscenely; indelicately; disgustingly; offensively; repulsively; odiously; disagreeably; unnecessarily; unpardonably; indecently; loathsomely; nauseatingly; diabolically; terribly; sickeningly; unhealthfully; pestilentially; dangerously; unsanitarily.

NATION

adjectives
powerful; puissant; guarded; shopkeeping; delivered; advanced; expectant; friendly; regenerated; dusky; surrounding (pl); liberated; disenchanted; grateful; altruistic; respective; warring; neighboring; restless; energetic; impressionable; civilized; happy; peaceable; wretched; impoverished; delusive; motley; swarming; greedy; aggressive; magnificent; resolute; impudent; unpolished; conquered; diverse; unsubdued; maritime; capitalist; woeful; eminent; scientific; long-suffering; declining; raw; mercantile; gentle; moral; uncivilized; stunned; helpless; leaderless; loyal; barbarous; brave; vigorous; ignorant; incredulous; benighted; sacred; homogeneous; burdened; stricken; unfriended; ambitious; progressive; wild; corrupted; exceptional; callous; courageous; brave; enslaved; eager; fickle; ill-assorted; ancient.

verbs
awaken—; blanket—; compensate—; convulse—; envelop—; filch from—; further—; incite—; inflame—; jolt—; liberate—; menace—; realign—; seduce—; terrorize—; trample—; —decays; —embarks on; —quakes; —retaliates; —rises; —s vie for.
(See folk, country, empire, public.)

NATIONAL

adverbs
strongly; ardently; narrowly; broadly; strictly; eagerly; fervently; intensely; devotedly; fiercely; zealously; indifferently; enthusiastically; sharply; selfishly; actively; admirably.

NATIONALISM

adjectives
intense; spiritual; ardent; growing; evident; forced; powerful.

verbs
advocate—; base on—; breed—; cultivate—; defend—; encourage—; favor—; foster—; institute—; justify—; maintain—; prate of—; prescribe—; respect—; seethe with—; steep in—; threaten—; value—; —characterizes; —comforts; —shields; —smooths.
(See democracy, atheism, socialism, independence.)

NATIONALITIES

adjectives
dominant; jarring; divers; healthy; autonomous.

NATIONALITY

verbs
annihilate—; cast off—; characterize—; color—; denote—; deny—; describe—; distinguish—; efface—; extinguish—; ferret out—; protest—; renounce—; threaten—; —pains; —vanishes.
(See heritage, nation.)

NATIVE

adverbs
unquestionably; genuinely; happily; indigenously; unaffectedly; frankly; plainly; obviously; advantageously; contentedly; indubitably; conveniently; warrantably.

NATIVES

adjectives
frightened; superstitious; credulous; bedizened; grinning; influential; energetic; polygamous; well-connected; indifferent; effeminate; nondescript; bronzed; free-born; wretched; exiled; unprejudiced; guileless; predatory; genuine; belated.

verbs
astonish—; commend—; dispute with—; encounter—; fraternize with—; interrogate—; scuffle with—; —adhere; —adopt; —fashion; —inhabit; —merit; —populate; —praise; —rear.
(See inhabitant, Indian, negro, peasant.)

NATURAL

adverbs
essentially; inherently; artlessly; honestly; ingenuously; openly; unaffectedly; spontane-

ously; simply; frankly; naively; cordially; delightfully; suddenly; altogether; refreshingly; touchingly; wondrously; charmingly; ravishingly; unbelievably; graciously; innocently; alluringly; childishly; guilelessly; youthfully; pleasantly.

NATURALIST

adjectives

well-known; inoffensive; abstracted; wise.

verbs

appeal to—; unfold to—; —breeds; —classifies; —collects; —conserves; —examines; —exhausts; —fathoms; —gazes on; —invades; —investigates; —marvels at; —observes; —preserves; —reflects; —studies; —tabulates; —treasures; —treks; —verifies; —worships.

(See scientist, philosopher.)

NATURALIZATION

verbs

approve—; await—; consider—; deny—; desire—; dispute—; encourage—; gain—; merit—; prepare for—; protest—; qualify for—; question—; seek—; undergo—; —commends; —ensues; —insures; —privileges.

(See citizenship.)

NATURE

verbs

attune to—; conform to—; defy—; endow by—; master—; mirror—; observe—; portray—; reflect—; rely on—; return to—; struggle with—; subdue—; supplant—; take refuge in—; wring from—; —allures; —arrays; —bestows; —decrees; —exacts; —imposes; —molds; —paints; —plays; —rejoices; —sanctions; —shapes; —stages; —thwarts; —unfolds; supplement—.

(See instinct, God, life, convention, conventionality.)

NATURE (*character*)

adjectives

abject; able; adventurous; affectionate; agitating; angelic; animate; arduous; arrogant; artistic; awakening; awed; belated; beneficent; binding; boisterous; blind; blithesome; bloody; blunt; brooding; brute; bubbling; buoyant; calculating; calm; cantankerous; cautious; capricious; celestial; chivalrous; clinging; cold; combative; communicable; complicated; composite; conceited; concentrated; confiding; conscientious; conservative; contracted; contradictory; contrary; controversial; corporeal; craven; creating; cruel; crumbling; cursed; cynical; daring; darkening; dazzled; definite; delicate; delightful; desperate; determined; diabolical; dictatorial; difficult; diligent, dismal; disordered; distasteful; diversified; domineering; dual; dynamic; easygoing; ecclesiastical; elemental; elevated; emotional; enduring; encouraging; engrossing; erratic; essential; everlasting; evil; exacting; exaggerating; exclusive; exhilarating; expansive; exquisite; external; extraordinary; false; fastidious; fearless; fiendish; fiery; finite; forbearing; forbidding; formidable; frank; friable; frivolous; functional; generous; gloomy; gracious; half-savage; great; gross; hardy; harmonious; harsh; hateful; haughty; hazardous; heaven-born; hereditary; heretical; hidden; hideous; high-strung; honest; honorable; horrible; hostile; human; illustrious; hysterical; immaterial; immutable; imperfect; imperious; impetuous; imperturbable; impracticable; inanimate; incomprehensible; incongruous; indigenous; infectious; infinite; inherent; inmost; inorganic; inscrutable; inspired; intellectual; intense; internal; interpretative; intimate; intrinsic; introspective; intuitive; invertebrate; kind; irritable; latent; lavish; leonine; light; living; lofty; lovable; luxuriant; maimed; magnetic; marked; martial; mean; material; mechanical; melancholy; mid-summer; mercurial; merry; mild; mischievous; miraculous; mismade; moral; murky; mute; mysterious; neutral; niggard; noble; obscure; observant; omnipotent; onerous; operative; opposed; opulent; oracular; ostentatious; outward; painful; paradoxical; parallel; parsimonious; passionate; patriotic; peculiar; pecuniary; personal; phantasmagorical; planetary; playful; pliant; poetic; polished; popular; populous; precise; praiseworthy; prime; primitive; private; probable; prodigal; profaning; prophetic; protracted; proud; quarrelsome; quick; radiant; rash; rational; reasonable; recalcitrant; receptive; recondite; religious; reluctant; restless; retiring; revengeful; rude; sanguine; sardonic; savage; seasonal; self-effacing; self-sacrificing; sensitive; sensuous; sentient; sentimental; severe; shallow; shrinking; silent; sluggish; social; sordid; soldierly; sorry; sound; specific; spiritual; spiteful; spoiled; spontaneous; sterling; stifled; strong; struggling; subordinate; sturdy; subtle; sunny; sympathizing;

swampy; tangible; teaching; temperate; tenacious; thoroughgoing; timid; transitional; transitory; trite; trivial; truthful; ultimate; unadvanced; unblemished; uncompromising; uncultivated; undisciplined; unending; unfatherly; ungentlemanly; ungracious; unique; universal; unoffending; unpoetic; unpredictable; unprofessional; unrepentant; unselfish; unsociable; unstable; untaught; untractable; untrained; upright; vacant; vague, vain; vehement; vengeful; virile; vital; vivacious; voiceless; volatile; volcanic; voluntary; voracious; vulgar; wary; weak; weighty; well-derived; wild; willful; winged; wiry; wistful.

verbs
alter—; ascertain—; bewail—; crush—; determine—; disfigure—; dwarf—; elevate—; flaunt—; indicate—; manifest—; mold—; offend—; recognize—; sate—; temper—; —prompts.
(See character, quality.)

NAUGHTY

adverbs
roguishly; mischievously; childishly; disagreeably; thoughtlessly; embarrassingly; slyly; furtively; innocently; unbearably; maliciously; surprisingly; unwontedly; unusually; vexatiously; remarkably; perversely; incorrigibly; curiously; uncommonly; extremely; scampishly; prankishly; gracelessly.

NAUSEA

verbs
escape—; excite—; induce—; loathe—; relieve—; overcome with—; remedy—; sate to —; seize with—; shock into—; stifle—; suffer—; —agonizes; —disgusts; —dispirits; —grieves; —wearies.
(See vomiting, disgust, resentment, hatred.)

NAUSEOUS

adverbs
terribly; uncommonly; disagreeably; offensively; unnecessarily; unpardonably; unbearably; grievously; painfully; bitterly; obnoxiously; mortifyingly; intolerably; appallingly; hatefully; hideously; insufferably.

NAUTICAL

adverbs
correctly; properly; appropriately; unquestionably; completely; admirably; wildly; charmingly; brightly; nattily.

NAVAL

adverbs
strictly; gloriously; strongly; invincibly.

NAVIGATE (v)

adverbs
precariously; professionally; deftly; skillfully; seasonally; intrepidly; daringly; fearlessly; disastrously.
(See sail, guide, steer.)

NAVIGATION

adjectives
celestial; uninterrupted; protracted; widespread; ocean.

NAVY

adjectives
auxiliary; unexploring; dauntless; protective; strong; fearless; well-manned; undersized; great.

verbs
enlist in—; equip—; maintain—; modernize —; volunteer for—; —defends; —manoeuvres; —patrols; —practises; —recruits; —safeguards; —schools; —trains; —transports; —yields.
(See militia, fleet, army.)

NEAR

adverbs
intimately; advantageously; conveniently; pleasantly; agreeably; handily; surprisingly; remarkably; unexpectedly; ominously; unfortunately; happily; luckily; opportunely; profitably.

NEARNESS

adjectives
immediate; familiar; unknown; breathless.

NEAT

adverbs
painfully; pleasantly; incorrigibly; particularly; remarkably; incomparably; curiously; intolerably; placidly; extremely; admirably; perfectly; habitually; incurably; uniformly; immaculately; daintily; exquisitely; jauntily; attractively; spotlessly; miraculously.

NEATNESS

adjectives
expectant; chilly; unusual; indescribable; extreme; miraculous; meticulous; incomparable.

NEBULAE

verbs

cluster into—; cover with—; —beautify; —charm; —decorate; —embellish; —enchant; —enhance; —fascinate; —illuminate; —mantle; —mass; —mist; —patch; —powder; —thicken; —whirl.

(See stars, clouds.)

NEBULOUS

adverbs

vaguely; dimly; obscurely; umbrageously; foggily; mistily; faintly; confusingly; bewilderingly; vaporously; unfathomably; dangerously; hazardously; alarmingly; perplexingly; unpleasantly; extremely.

NECESSARY

adverbs

strictly; hardly; scarcely; entirely; absolutely; completely; undeniably; obviously; definitely; manifestly; unquestionably; financially; economically; apparently; cruelly; unfortunately; unluckily; bitterly; imperatively; unavoidably; tragically; embarrassingly; terribly.

NECESSITY

adjectives

prime; humiliating; absolute; economic; empowered; stern; imperative; sheer; pecuniary; obvious; irresistible; physical; crying; urgent; relative; material; highborn; deplored; indispensable; mathemetical; righteous; pressing; time-honored; everyday; unalterable; inexorable; immutable; dire; expressive; practical; military; objective; cruel; dread; inevitable; invincible; belittling; strict; immediate; vicious; temporary; factitious; mortifying; fatal; unavoidable; logical; desperate; burning; fancied; superfluous; metaphysical; domestic; implacable; unyielding; marvelous; physiological; hypothetical; tragic; bitter; apparent; startling; household; amazing; fast-selling; feminine; clever; business; daily; money-saving.

verbs

argue—; feel—; fortify by—; illustrate—; impel by—; inspire by—; minister to—; obviate—; ponder—; preclude—; relieve of—; skimp on —s; urge—; yield to—; —abates; —arises; —cements; —compels; —forces; —pinches; —s pop up; —presses.

(See fate, emergency, exigency, compulsion, requirement, want, need.)

NECK

adjectives

beguiling; withered; distended; ivory; stiffening; corrigible; mottled; humbled; misshapen; glossy; feminine-looking; naked; graceful; gaunt; sinewy; glowing; gleaming; chic; square; distressful; shimmering; stately; snowy; athletic; scalloped; dry-skinned; nervous; wrinkled; thin; flattered; arching; queenly; silly; well-turned; sleek; jeweled; enameled.

verbs

adorn—; arch—; bow—; button at—; clutch by—; crane—; decorate—; dislocate—; exercise—; furbish—; jerk—; massage—; powder—; sever at—; wreathe—; yoke by—.

NECKTIE

verbs

adjust—; criticize—; examine—; knit—; knot—; loosen—; pattern—; print—; spot—; stripe—; weave—; yank (colloq.)—; —blazes; —exaggerates; —flames; —impresses; —infuriates; —matches; —overwhelms; —shocks.

(See cravat, handkerchief.)

NECTAR

verbs

bathe in—; draw — from; drown in—; nourish with—; relish—; secrete—; seek—; sink in—; spout—; suck—; tongue—; —cools; —delights; —intoxicates; —oozes; —gratifies; —steams.

(See sweetness, liquid, beverage, drink.)

NEED

adjectives

individual; imperative; critical; profound; fundamental; airy; spiritual; specialized; self-existing; genuine; unnumbered (pl); warranted; changing; pressing; burning; dubious; desperate; emergency; tragic; primitive; dreadful; urgent; future; spiritual; action-shaping; absolute; obvious; perpetual; definite; private; increasing; artless; shameful; dearest; psychic; extravagant; sorest; inexorable; diverse; economic; home; preliminary; intellectual; emotional; distinct; supreme; pervading; particular; deepest; practical; cruel; bitter; degrading; corporate; quiet.

verbs
anticipate—; ascertain—; awaken to—; beget—; bend to—; conceal—; define—; eliminate—; enunciate—; evince—; emphasize —; express—; meet—; minimize—; minister to—; portray—; reveal—; satisfy—; serve —; smother—; study—; supplant—; supply —; suppress—; survey—; torture by—; voice—; —arises; —dictates; —presses.

(See lack, impoverishment, inadequacy, exigency, necessity, want, poverty.)

NEED (v)

adverbs
direly; imperatively; horribly; desperately; sorely; urgently; critically; fundamentally; spiritually; genuinely; tragically; inexorably; economically; degradingly.

(See lack, require, want.)

NEEDLE

adjectives
magnetic; shining; cambric; trembling; glancing.

verbs
case—; direct—; dodge—; draw—through; grope for—; magnetize—; mend with—; ply —; polish—; prick with—; stick with—; thread—; tug at—; work with—; —designs; —flies; —penetrates; —perforates; —punctures.

(See pin, point.)

NEEDLESS

adverbs
utterly; apparently; altogether; absurdly; obviously; wholly; ridiculously; manifestly; inconsequentially.

NEEDY

adverbs
desperately; undoubtedly; warrantably; tragically; pitiably; pathetically; pitifully; hopelessly; helplessly; surprisingly; avowedly; lamentably; extremely; distressingly; unfortunately; sadly; strangely; unaccountably; obscurely; unquestionably; wretchedly; miserably; inexpressibly.

NEFARIOUS

adverbs
incomparably; abominably; diabolically; extremely; incredibly; unfathomably; wildly; deplorably; dangerously; unconscionably; grossly; scandalously; malevolently; reprehensibly; gracelessly; shamelessly; monstrously.

NEGATIVE

adjectives
strange; audacious; emphatic; startled; definite; clear.

adverbs
feebly; hopelessly; fortunately; luckily; unquestionably; emphatically; flatly; peremptorily; blankly; virtually; completely; incontrovertibly; discouragingly; distressingly; unhappily; unexpectedly; avowedly; allegedly; presumably; probably.

NEGLECT

adjectives
habitual; ostentatious; unintentional; willful; deplorable; hideous; high-spirited; comparative; loving; disdainful; intended; culpable; apathetic; predestined; monstrous; infamous; total.

verbs
atone for—; breed—; charge with—; complain of—; convict of—; die of—; goad by —; pardon—; rescue from—; suffer—; throw into—; wither in—; —corrodes; —damages; —endangers; —harms; —injures; —insults; —rusts; —saps.

(See failure, default, carelessness.)

NEGLECT (v)

adverbs
habitually; ostentatiously; deplorably; hideously; wilfully; disdainfully; apathetically; monstrously; infamously; totally; shamefully; slovenly; impudently; improvidently.

(See ignore, disregard.)

NEGLIGENCE

adjectives
studied; sluggard; tonsorial; official; unwonted; thoughtless; military; criminal; occasional; gross; repeated; lazy; intermittent.

NEGLIGIBLE

adverbs
comparably; comparatively; altogether; somewhat; scarcely; shamefully; ignominiously; infamously; insignificantly; ridiculously; contemptibly; politically; socially; financially.

NEGOTIATE (v)

adverbs

craftily; astutely; ingeniously; zealously; diplomatically; solemnly; tactfully; separately; commercially; internationally.

(See treat.)

NEGOTIATIONS

adjectives

premature; pending; platonic; commercial; proposed; concurrent; abortive; temporal; complex; long-drawn-out; matrimonial; solemn; friendly; mercantile; secret; peace.

verbs

advocate—; assemble for—; bolt—; carry on—; commence—; depart from—; enter into—; favor—; open—; reopen—; renew —; suspend—; terminate—; —bore; —fail; —falter; —flounder; —succeed; —tire; —weary.

(See collective bargaining, meeting, conference.)

NEGRO

adjectives

tattered; superb; shiftless; accused; harassed; free; diligent; music-loving; melodious.

verbs

auction—es; deal in—es; educate—; emancipate—; lynch—; sympathize with—; tolerate—; understand—; uplift—; whip—; —chants; —coaxes; —es congregate; —contorts; —stomps; —"trucks"; —worships.

(See native, denizen, inhabitant.)

NEIGHBOR

adjectives

uncharitable; formidable; reticent; congenial; toxophilitic; pretentious; anarchist; near; marvelous; influential; good; overbearing; backbiting; stout-shouldered; barbarian; amiable; peaceable; civilized; weaker; territorial; inquisitive; frivolous; infidel; gaping; charitable; calculating; dangerous; wingless; good-natured; barbarous; parallel; singular; perfidious; miserly; pleasant; companionable; afflicted; gossipy; enisled.

verbs

acknowledge—; associate with—; bicker with—; consort with—s; denounce—; drive out—; hedge—; respect—; rouse—s; sanctify—; scandalize—s; wrangle with—; —s band; —befriends; —complains; —contends; —gossips; —imposes; —quarrels; —rivals; —visits.

(See friend, woman, enemy.)

NEIGHBORHOOD

adjectives

audacious; fashionable; moneyed; residential; frequented; immediate; disreputable; malodorous; adjoining; noisome; deteriorating; gruff.

verbs

arouse—; attract to—; avoid—; crowd—; denounce—; drive from—; explore—; huddle in—; inflame—; master—; preserve—; rule—; scandalize—; shun—; visit—; —appeals to; —bands together; —befriends; —congregates; —petitions.

(See locality, section, city, village, town, district.)

NEIGHBORLY

adverbs

actively; heartily; generously; wonderfully; agreeably; delightfully; helpfully; sincerely; sociably; extremely; unwontedly; incredibly; amicably; chattily; hospitably; gregariously; companionably; remarkably; heart-warmingly.

NEPHEW

adjectives

warming; prodigal; chubby; scapegrace; celebrated; spurious; disinherited.

NERVE

adjectives

firm; strained; tingling; marble; gustatory; languid; irritable; underlying; shaky; delicate; tremulous; sensitive; ragged; gentle; taut; excellent; iron; curious; auditory; miraculous; invisible; sciatic; wailing; harassed; shattered; vibrating; overstrained; optic; inconceivable; adamantine; shrinking; uncertain; tender; overstrung; revolutionary; high-strung; pneumogastric; exhausted; jangled; shuddering; silent; excitable; sympathetic; physical; oversusceptible; overwrought.

NERVELESS

adverbs

pitiably; helplessly; ineffectually; incompetently; curiously; pathetically; distressingly; miserably; wretchedly; ineptly; pitifully; limply; strangely.

NERVES

verbs
addle—; calm—; constrict—; deaden—; desensitize—; dilate—; disturb—; drag at—; exhaust—; fray—; impinge upon—; irritate —; involve—; jangle—; jolt—; jar—; numb —; pad—; relax—; sever—; shatter—; shock—; soothe—; steady—; stimulate—; strain—; tranquilize—; unstring—; —bristle; —jump; —respond; —snap.

NERVOUS

adverbs
highly; uncommonly; extremely; significantly; pitifully; hysterically; feverishly; unnecessarily; strangely; absurdly; ridiculously; guiltily; curiously; physically; secretly; apparently; timidly; bashfully; childishly; exceedingly; pitiably; pathetically; ludicrously; sadly; touchingly; laughably; miserably; alarmingly; ominously; unfortunately.

NERVOUSNESS

adjectives
concealed; excessive; mere; feverish; subtle.

verbs
allay—; decline into—; enhance—; manifest —; overcome—; overpower—; remedy—; scoff at—; spring from—; suffer from—; —confuses; —debilitates; —deprives; —distresses; —disturbs; —enervates; —enfeebles; —shakes; —strains; —weakens.
(See hysteria, impatience, sickness.)

NERVOUS SYSTEM

verbs
derange— —; ease— —; excite— —; flow through— —; govern— —; guard— — from; impair— —; nourish— —; overwork — —; stimulate— —; strain— —; support — —; tax— —; — —collapses; — —cramps; — —links; — —recovers; — —responds.

NEST

adjectives
drowsy; clamorous; broodless; deserted; eternal; central; quiet; mossy; watery; northern; unmaternal; hungry; enlightened; pensile; well-built; shattered; windless; distant; balmy; spicy; sheltered; warm; cozy.

verbs
camouflage—; construct—; deposit in—; discover—; disturb—; expose—; hollow out —; huddle in—; incubate in—; isolate—; lodge in—; perch in—; pillage—; protect —; pry into—; quit—; retire to—; rob—; scoop out—; swing—; tree—; —comforts; —cradles; —shelters.
(See home, shelter, hole, hive. lair, refuge.)

NESTLE (v)

adverbs
snugly; cozily; domestically; tenderly; drowsily; warmly; affectionately.
(See cuddle.)

NET

adjectives
fishing; anchored; elastic; weblike; impassable; inescapable; closely-woven.

verbs
bag with—; capture in—; cast—; confine in—; construct—; dip—; dredge with—; dry—; fish with—; knit—; lower—; pay out —; repair—; secure with—; slip through—; spin—; spread—; stretch—; sweep into—; swim into—; trap in—; trawl with—; —drifts; —ensnares; —entangles.
(See trap, snare, mesh, network.)

NETTLE (v)

adverbs
intolerably; exasperatingly; maddeningly; spitefully; vengefully; cruelly; formidably; bitterly.
(See provoke, irritate.)

NETWORK

adjectives
gigantic; ramified; endless; ingenious; complicated; broadcasting; national; social.

verbs
bind into—; chain into—; construct—; control—; convey over—; extend—; hook up on —; incorporate—; interfere with—; join—; localize—; present over—; tie up with—; unravel—; weave—.
(See system, net.)

NEUROSIS

verbs
accentuate—; classify—; despise—; dispel —; explain—; group—es; ignore—; pronounce—; resist—; shake—; stem—; suffer from—; usher in—; —attacks; —cripples; —exists; —irritates; —nags; —obsesses; —persists; —upsets.
(See complex, disease, sickness.)

NEUROTIC

adjectives
advanced; compulsive; unfortunate; lifelong; hapless.

adverbs
undeniably; vexatiously; hopelessly; pathetically; absurdly; helplessly; incurably; intolerably; miserably; wretchedly; lamentably; needlessly; unfortunately; exceedingly; curiously; deplorably; incomparably; cursedly; deucedly; conveniently; disgustingly.

NEUTRAL

adverbs
resolutely; dependably; altogether; strictly; rigidly; infallibly; sagaciously; wisely; carefully; cautiously; unimpeachably; sincerely; honorably; respectfully; deliberately; determinedly; indifferently; alertly; judiciously; intelligently; interestedly; evasively; necessarily; pluckily; stoutly; conveniently; steadily; unwaveringly; irreproachably.

NEUTRALITY

adjectives
stern; hostile; selfish; benevolent; malevolent; political; blameless; precarious; armed; maintained; difficult.

verbs
advocate—; break—; commend—; disrupt—; enjoy—; express—; favor—; foreswear—; infract—; maintain—; observe—; pledge—; preserve—; profess—; propose—; renounce—; respect—; uphold—; violate—; —balances; —continues; —endangers; —gratifies.
(See attitude, position.)

NEWCOMERS

verbs
befriend—; criticize—; denounce—; fend off—; judge—; limit—; mold—; pity—; quarrel with—; repel—; snub—; suspect—; train—; wrangle with—; —band; —impress; —invade; hedge—.
(See foreigner, alien, stranger.)

NEWLYWEDS
(*colloq.*)

verbs
davise—; bless—; caution—; endow—; fete—; fetter—; mock—; serenade—; sever—; —beam; —blush; —cherish; —clasp; —coo; —dream; —flush; —honeymoon (colloq.); —nest; —rejoice; —repent.
(See lover, sweetheart, husband, wife, suitor.)

NEWS

adjectives
lamentable; alarming; distasteful; inevitable; ill; current; pleasant; inestimable; cheerful; especial; unwelcome; electrifying; disastrous; positive; serious; fresh; irrelevant; dire; long-expected; glorious; interpretative; astonishing; dreadful; vengeful; amazing; definite; startling; fashionable; comparative; distressing; encouraging; exciting; reassuring; deplorable; stupefying; blackest; domestic; panic; inside; sharp; ominous; hopeful; unacceptable; uncertain; unsatisfactory; major; vital; ghastly; significant; condensed; below-the-surface; latest; accurate; fevered; world; heartbreaking.

verbs
bear—; bound into—; broadcast—; bruit about—; comb for—; crop into—; disseminate—; dominate—; edit—; falsify—; flash into—; glean—; greet—; hail—; impart—; overshadow—; purvey—; relay—; scan—; scream—; sift—; spot—; suppress—; verify—; —blazes; —breaks; —fades; —filters through; —stuns; —trickles in.
(See report, word, rumor, message, telegram.)

NEWSPAPER

adjectives
enterprising; disloyal; daily; influential; sensational; leading; matrimonial; conservative; weekly; contemporaneous.

verbs
blazon on—; clip from—; comb—; creep into—; crumple—; deliver—; hawk—s; peddle—s; peruse—; pore over—; purvey—s; scan—; scoop—; skim through—; supplement—; syndicate—; —campaigns; —circulates; —devotes to; —functions; —suppresses.
(See literature, magazine, periodical, publication, press.)

NEWSPAPERMAN

adjectives
astute; hateful; well-respected; enterprising; bold.

NEW YORK

verbs
crowd— —; dash to— —; drift to— —; enjoy— —; mill through— —; pack— —; plunge into— —; stream through— —; taxi 'round— —; tour— —; — —astonishes; — —bewilders; — —clutches; — —enchants; — —excels; — —excites; — —irritates; — —pains; — —sparkles; — —thrills; — —towers; — —unfurls.
(See city.)

NIBBLE (*v*)

adverbs
tantalizingly; daintily; teasingly; cautiously; intermittently; shyly; coyly.
(See munch, bite.)

NICE

adverbs
extraordinarily; particularly; wonderfully; scrupulously; punctiliously; meticulously; invariably; incomparably; unsurpassably; unquestionably; apparently; obviously; manifestly; admirably; unusually; inherently; exquisitely; marvellously; altogether; remarkably.

NICETY

adjectives
peculiar; critical; professional; scrupulous; utmost; painful.

verbs
accomplish with—; acknowledge—ies; appreciate—; delight in—ies; demonstrate —ies; educate in—ies; express with—; frame in—; manage with—; question—; require—; stand upon—; verse in—ies; — prevails; —ies serve for; offend—ies; operate with—.
(See precision, efficiency, skill, tact.)

NICHE

adjectives
comfortable; murky; opposite; appropriate; temporary.

verbs
assign—; attain—; carve out—; claim—; contrive—; crack—; decorate—; dig—; examine—; fill—; find—; gain—; hew—; hollow out—; molest—; occupy—; place in—; select—; sink into—; —protects.
(See corner, place.)

NICKNAME

verbs
adopt—; assume—; bear—; bedevil with—; bestow—upon; brand with—; coin—; contrive—; define—; dub with—; earn—; incur—; —adheres; —annoys; —clings; —labels; —mocks; —sticks; —survives; —vexes.
(See name, title.)

NICKNAME (*v*)

adverbs
aptly; sneeringly; vindictively; viciously; scoffingly; slurringly; hatefully; fraternally; jovially; humiliatingly; facetiously.
(See entitle, designate.)

NIGGARDLY

adverbs
grossly; unreasonably; meanly; basely; unutterably; inconsiderately; greedily; unnecessarily; disgustingly; penuriously; sordidly; crassly; unbelievably; terribly; shabbily; despicably; contemptibly; wretchedly; overwhelmingly; unutterably; absurdly.

NIGHT

adjectives
mantling; naked; hopeless; perpetual; long; tedious; dull; brooding; frosty; waxing; restless; feverish; deepening; cloudless; moonlight; stark; unspeakable; cloud-hung; sleepless; hideous; sweating; dim; darksome; sultry; fatal; unfathomable; eternal; earth-shaking; wretched; lyric; carved; impelling; precarious; bespangled; congenial; weary; anxious; noiseless; cheerless; tempestuous; brilliant; magic; tortuous; fearsome; gusty; wakeful; wassail; tolerable; large-eyed; silvery; desolate; romantic; watchful; deep-winding; utter; stifling; memorable; broad-winged; difficult; previous; star-studded; lingering; bridal; stagnant; extended; revolving; abysmal; peerless; summer; capped; subtle; serene; somber; cooling lustrous; light; bottomless; fragrant; dewy; profound; departing; shining; dreamless; drizzly; unalienable; heaviest; glimmering; soft; agate; tourmaline; glass-clear; overcast; milky; ghastly; black; impenetrable; perfumed; smiling; pale; live; black-frost; sable; lurid; moonless; slowly-gathering; eyeless; raving; blessed; eventful; prolonged; irksome; unlanterned; unsocial; stormy; gradual; unseeing; ugly; laboring; fashionable; clear; pallid; bright; golden; sweet-smelling; obscure; dumb;

lingering; limitless; inky; star-silent; earthly; moon-mad; hushed; crimeful; enchanting; divine; shadowy; moonshiny; comfortless; merciless; feeding; pitchy; vaporous; interlunar; supperless; identical; ecstatic; fateful; careful; dreaming; dreary; ill-starred; sweltering; gathering; festival; breathless; humorous; black-faced; azure; auspicious; polar; grim; notable; voluptuous; sightless; lonely.

verbs
contemplate—; fritter away—; lapse into—; lurk in—; pierce—; repose at—; sink into —; —blankets; —calms; —clouds over; —creeps up; —curtains; —depresses; —descends; —drags; —engulfs; —enshrouds; —envelops; —inspires; —mantles; —oppresses; —reigns; —robs; —shades; —tiptoes; —veils; —wanes; —waxes; —yawns.
(See evening, twilight, darkness, dusk.)

NIGHTINGALE

adjectives
wakeful; unenvying; tempestuous; triumphant; full-throated; voluptuous; importunate; undying; beauteous.

verbs
—anthems; —bewails; —bursts out; —chants; —charms; —cheers; —complains; —courts; —crowds; —delights; —enchants; —hurries; —lullabies; —mourns; —pierces; —precipitates notes; —pours forth; —ravishes; —shies; —sings out woe; —sobers; —thrills; —transports; —trills; —utters; —vocalizes; —wails; —warbles.
(See bird.)

NIGHTMARE

adjectives
horrifying; preposterous; fiendish; racking; catapulting; portentous; indistinguishable; intolerable; weird; half-vanishing; hideous; weary; eyeless; horrible; financial; veritable.

verbs
beset with—; conceive in—; convulse in—; fancy in—; free from—; imagine in—; picture in—; plunge into—; sink into—; toss in —; unloose—; —alarms; —chokes; —distresses; —settles on; —strains; —strangles; —suffocates; —terrifies; —tortures; —weighs.
(See menace, dream, vision, delusion.)

NIMBLE

adverbs
actively; alertly; unbelievably; surprisingly; remarkably; miraculously; noticeably; obviously; amazingly; unusually; lightly; deftly; adroitly; cleverly; smartly; expertly; peculiarly; incredibly; dexterously; wondrously; briskly; vigilantly.

NIPS

adjectives
fatal; surreptitious; powerful; piercing.

NITROGEN

verbs
combine with—; derive—from; expel—; extract—; furnish with—; manufacture—; market—; mix with—; obtain—; reveal—; store—; temper with—; unite—with; —dilutes; —evaporates; —extinguishes.
(See chemical, acid, mixture, solution.)

NOBLE

adverbs
naturally; quietly; innately; aristocratically; genuinely; truly; admittedly; tenaciously; inherently; actually; elegantly; splendidly; unaffectedly; avowedly; unquestionably; essentially; eminently; grandly; imposingly.

NOBILITY

adjectives
rapacious; transcendent; conspicuous; dubious; mental; latent; impoverished; inherent; austere; powerless; factious; outraged; certain; pervading.

verbs
acknowledge—; attract—; conceal—; crown with—; display—; enhance—; forfeit—; glory in—; honor—; meet—; rouse—; seat among—; smack of—; steep in—; —characterizes; —distinguishes; —enriches; —graces; —outlives; —pedigrees; —shines.
(See aristocracy, gallantry, monarch, splendor, supremacy.)

NOBLEMAN

adjectives
needy; veritable; self-respecting; impoverished; fiery; dissolute; sporting; eminent.

NOBLENESS

adjectives
natural; native; quiet; free; inborn; innate.

NOBLES

adjectives
violent; hereditary; thoughtful; dissolute; dense; emigrant; malevolent; indolent; faithful; prudent; high-taught; philosophic; dastard; rapacious; cushioned; factious; arrogant; haughty; speculative.

NOD

adjectives
jolly; little; swaggering; impertinent; approving; placid; gracious; wrenlike; imperceptible; insinuating; impatient; laconic; emphatic.

NOD (*v*)

adverbs
sagely; comprehendingly; vehemently; incisively; crisply; dreamily; benignly; solemnly; drowsily; assuringly; significantly; pensively; urbanely; affably; energetically; complacently; sagaciously; affirmatively; rhythmically; positively; assentingly; jovially; philosophically; speculatively.
(See bow, bend.)

NOISE

verbs
ban—; contribute to—; eliminate—; emit—; endure—; exclude—; guard against—; intensify—; reproduce—; resound with—of; saturate with—; simulate—s of; suppress —; —abates; —s blend; —confuses; —hampers; —hinders; —shuffles; —stuns; —subsides.
(See crash, howl, hiss, din, clash, roar.)

NOISELESS

adverbs
completely; warrantably; avowedly; allegedly; reasonably; absolutely; reputably; incredibly; remarkably; mysteriously; magically; unbelievably; peculiarly; furtively; stealthily; solemnly; awfully; alarmingly.

NOISES

adjectives
sharp; pattering; unfamiliar; rustling; shuffling; sniffling; appalling; sundry; booming; audible; ejaculatory; creaking; thunderous; cowing; ruder; sympathetic; tempestuous; rattling; increasing; frightful; pitiful; snivelling; humming; sinister; melancholy; shattering; prodigious; discordant; stringed; croaking; meaningless; buzzing; roaring; barbarous; sullen; sufficient; continuous; humming; guttural; distant; singular; dangling; whirring; clumping; ripping; rumbling; loud; damnable; whining; impetuous; swishing; confused; unique; unexplained; confounded; midnight; murmuring; shrill; distinct; sudden; subtler; unexpected; startling; unbelievable; objectionable; doubtful; rushing; softest; ill-resounding; slightest; diabolical; unmeaning; vulgar; outside; explosive; deafening; violent; grating; cool; chirping; jocund; fiendish; spiteful; terrifying; dull; unseemly; vague; harsh; unearthly; everlasting; ceaseless.

NOISY

adverbs
clamorously; vociferously; restlessly; uproariously; happily; childishly; screamingly; thunderously; stentoriously; lustily; ribaldly; naturally; boisterously; oddly; unwontedly; curiously; hoydenishly; audaciously; excitedly; hysterically; wildly; intolerably; provokingly; habitually; uncontrollably; ungovernably.

NOMADIC

adverbs
naturally; inherently; nonchalantly; happily; blithely; habitually; voluntarily; periodically; erratically; aimlessly; restlessly; adventurously; profitably; stubbornly; incurably; incorrigibly; remarkably; curiously; strangely; elusively; extraordinarily; recklessly; indefatigably; merrily.

NOMINAL

adverbs
considerately; altogether; merely; absurdly; obviously; curiously; usually; conventionally; conveniently; generously; deliberately; purposely; prudently; intentionally; deceptively; circumspectly; discreetly; simply.

NOMINATE (*v*)

adverbs
unanimously; jubilantly; independently; modestly; spontaneously; aptly; democratically; thunderously.
(See name, designate.)

NOMINATION

adjectives
spontaneous; caucus; predetermined; independent; unanimous.

verbs
acquiesce in—; aim at—; arrange—; authorize—; confer—upon; control—; court—; decline—; favor—; limit—s; offer for—; propose—; refuse—; reject—; rejoice in—; second—; seek—; —gratifies; —honors.

(See vote, selection, suggestion.)

NONCHALANCE

adjectives
trenchant; enticing; exasperating; debonair; knavish; affected; exquisite; suave; easy; practiced; deft.

verbs
affect—; assume an air of—; feign—; harden into—; listen with—; penetrate—; prefer—; pretend—; prick—; subdue—; tire of—; —crusts; —impresses; —interests; —irks; —nauseates; —pervades; —provokes; —tantalizes.

(See indifference, carelessness, silence.)

NONCHALANT

adverbs
habitually; blithely; indifferently; arrogantly; superciliously; inherently; naturally; usually; remarkably; studiously; deliberately; ominously; cleverly; intentionally; resolutely; charmingly; attractively; apparently; apathetically; coolly; disinterestedly; carelessly; significantly; decidedly; peculiarly; strangely; wonderfully; uncommonly; unwontedly.

NONDESCRIPT

adverbs
inexplicably; noticeably; conspicuously; curiously; strangely; oddly; hopelessly; unaccountably; unutterably; carelessly; defiantly; needlessly; fantastically; grotesquely; eccentrically; exceptionally; monstrously; singularly; peculiarly.

NONSENSE

adjectives
unmitigated; victorious; fatuous; continued; puerile; idiotic; nimble; incomprehensible; tawdry; driveling; nostalgic; undiluted; inexcusable; intelligible; licentious; good-natured; delicious; unadulterated; abject; frothy; palpable; amusing; blasted; airy; ridiculous; pleasant; absolute; blatant; extravagant; aristocratic.

verbs
dare—; denounce—; disapprove of—; disfavor—; emit—; frown on—; quibble in—; relish—; reproach for—; scoff at—; spare—; swallow—; tolerate—; wrap in—; —clouds; —confuses; —eases; —perplexes; —prevails; —revolts; —romps; —shames; —stigmatizes.

(See absurdity, folly, stupidity.)

NONSENSICAL

adverbs
fantastically; whimsically; utterly; delightfully; completely; charmingly; pleasantly; freakishly; fancifully; quaintly; oddly; wildly; drolly; frivolously; foolishly; absurdly; preposterously; inordinately; wholly.

NOOK

adjectives
sunny; lovely; shadow-haunted; sunnier; shady; obscurest; sequestered; narrow; fleshly; winding; advantageous; cobwebby; sheltered; trysting; secluded; unfrequented; leafy; studious.

NOON

adjectives
drowsy; stainless; calm; summer; joyous; burning; breezy; celestial; ardent; melting; languid; shadeless; sultry; glorious; blue-skied; liquid; sweet; clean; fiery.

NORMAL

adverbs
fairly; wholly; scarcely; altogether; comfortably; admirably; wholesomely; comfortingly; practically; finally; happily; fortunately; luckily; allegedly; avowedly; delightfully; apparently; manifestly.

NOSE

adjectives
aquiline; simple; aggressive; inquisitive; waggling; genial; flexible; innocent; arrogant; astute; weird; rueful; ferret; unerring; pudgy; rubicund; pink; blushing; cherry; streaming; crimson; sunburned; reddened; lavendar-tinted; handsome; diabolic; pug; microscopic; Grecian; fiat; saddle; endless; protruding; intrepid; hooked; well-cut; pointed; arched; showy; little; sensitive; depressed; impertinent; thin; delicate; sharp; meager; twitching; peeled; ruby; exceptional; scornful; typical; flabby; pendulous; enormous.

verbs
cock up—; crinkle—; flatten—; impact in—; sniff up—; spray—; squinch—; thumb—; tweak—; wrinkle—; —bleeds; —curls; —quivers; —streams; —twitches.
(See nostrils, nozzle.)

NOSEY

adverbs
intolerably; despicably; obnoxiously; incurably; incorrigibly; inquisitively; childishly; harmlessly; maliciously; unbearably; dangerously; ominously; alarmingly; odiously; hatefully; poisonously; invidiously; insatiably; intrusively; inordinately; mischievously; impertinently; rudely; officially; singularly; unbelievably; unwarrantably; horribly; inescapably.

NOSTALGIA

verbs
aggravate—; bewail—; crush—; cure of—; deplore—; dread—; ease—; endure—; expect—; foster—; hamper by—; induce—; infect with—; lament—; satisfy—; suffer from—; —discontents; —harrows; —impels; —preys upon; —weighs.
(See homesickness, loneliness, seclusion, sadness.)

NOSTRILS

adjectives
overdelicate; slight; distended; dilated; quivering; tremulous; dullest; creased; straining; sensitive; wide; huge.

verbs
affront—; assail—; clog—; dilate—; discharge from—; irrigate—; lift—; obstruct—; paint—; protect—; spray—; titillate—; —quiver; —tremble.
(See nose.)

NOTABLE

adverbs
universally; nationally; internationally; splendidly; extraordinarily; distinctly; conspicuously; unusually; extremely; illustriously.

NOTE
(*music*)

adjectives
low; full-chested; cool; musical; gracious; flutelike; recognizable; hopeful; pensive; imitative; piping; hoarser; varied (pl); discordant; penetrative; cultural; eternal; mocking; tender; accenting; plaintive; triumphant; vibrant; resounding; rambling; piercing; profound; deepest; sentimental; brooding; mingled (pl); rich; husky; shrill; screech-owl; tingling; simpering; soft; shaken; complaining; dominant; long-drawn; wretched; whimpering; sweeter; prelusive; grieving; mournful; pleasing; soaring; tuneful; teasing; despairing; cocked-hat; golden; tinkling; tentative; air-feeding; fundamental; voluminous; confused; rapturous; wondrous; echoing; pealing; gentle; blending; herald; dirgelike; grandest; warbling; wailing; full; liquid; subduing; resulting; momentary; rasping; trembling; rising; sustained; melodious; untunable; drowsy; rare; faltering; metallic.

verbs
chant—; emit—; hit—; inject—; peal—; pitch—; scale—s; soften—; sound—; stress—; strike—; thump—; utter—; wail—; warble—; —dies away; —reverberates; —shrills; —trembles; —weakens.
(See tone.)

NOTE
(*writing*)

adjectives
fundamental; melting; kindly; mirthful; occasional; ironical; dangerous; congratulatory; courteous; cordial; little; ardent; personal; copious (pl); piercing; crisp; crackling; joyous; subdued; pathetic; loud; tragic; triumphant; brief; hasty; quaint; wild; livelier; sweet; authoritative; changed; satirical; despairing; menacing; endless; pervading; disjointed; expiring; impulsive; warning; insistent; vexed; additional; indefinable; lesser; curious; unexpressive; noble; contemporary; special; optimistic; jubilant; blithest; spry; rebellious; improvised; erudite; admirable; incontrovertible; curt; potent; definite; pleasing; precious; sweet; agreeable; nimble; mental; queer; tense; confidential; illegible; wild; proper; mighty; jeering; choked; depreciated; animated; timid; funeral; authentic; illustrative; tonic; national; short; perfunctory; hieroglyphic; tender; scholarly; warning; flourishing; elaborate; significant; alternate; purer; premonitory; dissentient; impulsive; unmeasured; ironical; bubbling; exquisite; neat; culminating; voluble; flattering; merry; heedful; perjured; marginal; wary; centrifugal; wandering; liked; recurrent; penciled; promissory; inspiring; soiled; de-

scriptive; disconnected; exultant; greatest; impassioned; salutary; prefatory; desultory; fragmentary; hurried; jocund; coaxing; brief; official; kindly; confusing; infallible; unsealed; prophetic; consecutive (pl); simultaneous; dominant; brisk; monotonous; twisted; cursory.

verbs
append—; attest to—; blunt—; deliver—; direct—; dispatch—; interpret—; peruse—; point—at; scrawl—; tender—; veil—in; —elucidates; —engrosses; —explains.
(See message, letter, comment, explanation.)

NOTE (v)
adverbs
consciously; faithfully; vaguely; mirthfully; personally; triumphantly; authoritatively; satirically; curiously; eruditely; perfunctorily; impulsively; ironically; marginally; impassionedly; fragmentarily; officially; prophetically; simultaneously.
(See record, comment.)

NOTED
adverbs
nationally; unusually; brilliantly; splendidly; conspicuously; universally; nationally; locally; happily; curiously; remarkably; famously; singularly; prominently; eminently; fabulously; tremendously; reputably.

NOTEWORTHY
adverbs
distinctly; remarkably; illustriously; undoubtedly; singularly; extremely; unusually; gratifyingly; conspicuously; altogether; admittedly; emphatically; predictably.

NOTHINGS
adjectives
pronounced; airy; empty; pointless; merciful; seeming; sublime; invulnerable; poetical.

NOTICE
adjectives
hypercritical; appreciative; timely; repeated; forbidding; incidental; threatening; attentive; sympathetic; numerous (pl); disparaging; palpable; advance; favorable; sweet; obituary; previous; smiling; appropriate; perceptible; casual; parting; scanty; scrawled; commonplace; hasty.

verbs
bill—; court—; draw—; escape—; observe —; peer at—; review—; scrutinize—; —advises; —attracts; —beckons; —discloses; —enlightens; —imparts; —informs; —instructs; —interests; —intimates; —mentions; —points out; —prescribes; —specifies; —warns.
(See mention, announcement, advertisement, label.)

NOTICE (v)
adverbs
curiously; pityingly; dispassionately; pathetically; graphically; emphatically.
(See observe, see, recognize.)

NOTICEABLE
adverbs
glaringly; shamefully; brazenly; decidedly; singularly; curiously; uncommonly; strikingly; surprisingly; painfully; miserably; shockingly; pitiably; blatantly; distressingly; eminently; prominently; inescapably.

NOTIFY (v)
adverbs
portentously; officially; formally; nominally; sympathetically; appropriately; customarily.
(See tell, inform.)

NOTION
verbs
adopt—; cling to—; convey—; disprove—; distort—; embrace—; entertain—; entrench —; explode—; express—; gather —s; inculcate—; inherit—; justify—; retain—; ridicule—; scoff at—; tolerate—; —misleads; —persists.
(See caprice, conception, idea, opinion, view.)

NOTIONAL
adverbs
strangely; eccentrically; quaintly; fantastically; oddly; grotesquely; capriciously; captiously; remarkably; vexatiously; intolerably; unpredictably; undependably; unreliably; erratically; freakishly; egregiously; inordinately; provokingly; painfully; restlessly; nervously; feverishly; fussily; troublesomely; extremely.

NOTIONS
adjectives
moral; preposterous; inadequate; craziest;

pretty; settled; current; disparaging; odious; patriotic; tolerable; vaguest; baby; sudden; dangerous; modern; eerie; fictitious; illusory; elaborate; predestinarian; vergent; contradictory; diametric; opposed; basic; sensual; distinct; nonsensical; amiable; hateful; obscure; silly; chivalrous; inapplicable; fallacious; mistaken; blind; fabulous; confused; cheerful; half-blown; superstitious; rationalistic; idolatrous; glimmering; exaggerated; rudimentary; faint; vehement; pious; preconceived; feeble; pregnant; previous; monstrous; persistent; economical; dreamy; elementary; idealistic; false; excusable; frugal; civilized; ridiculous; cranky; definite; eccentric; strange; fantastic; crude; conceivable; erroneous; imperfect; ghoulish; half-assimilated; strained; conventional; imbecile; dictator; vitiated; childish; unformed.

NOTORIETY

adjectives
newspaper; despised; unpleasant; criminal; unenviable; public; scandalous; romantic; infamous; melancholy.

verbs
achieve—; acquire—; avoid—; burden with —; delight in—; devote to—; exult in—; flaunt—; heap—on; hunt—; labor under—; outshine—; raise to—; seek—; wallow in—; —attracts; —bridles; —decomposes; —enthrones; —glorifies; —overshadows; —palls; —shames.

(See limelight, fame, publicity, renown, reputation.)

NOTORIOUS

adverbs
nationally; generally; locally; unhappily; illustriously; shamefully; brilliantly; eminently; disgracefully; egregiously; splendidly; magnificently; universally; politically; infamously.

NOURISH (v)

adverbs
beneficially; healthfully; maternally; affectionately; sympathetically; substantially; spiritually.

(See nurture, feed, foster.)

NOURISHING

adverbs
incredibly; notably; admittedly; curiously; altogether; wholesomely; pleasantly; invigoratingly; healthfully; highly; uncommonly; exceptionally; extremely; strangely; admirably; notably; noticeably; strikingly; remarkably; substantially.

NOURISHMENT

adjectives
delicious; tasty; concentrated; virtual; sympathetic; necessary; proper; spiritual; healthy; substantial; daily.

verbs
administer—; beg—; decline—; deny—; deprive of—; draw—from; furnish—; gulp down—; impart—; inject—; lack—; offer —; provide—; refuse—; request—; resist—; supply—; volunteer—; —builds up; —comforts; —restores; —satiates.

(See food, nutrition, meal.)

NOVEL

adjectives
powerful; cherished; gifted; historical; pretty; lurid; liberal; daring; surging; trifling; psychological; well-contrived; mysterious; admirable; humorous; meritorious; successful; crude; indecent; imitative; masterly; engrossing; melancholy; improbable; sensational; popular; ambitious; episode; brilliant; ingenious; well-made; subtle; profound; contemporary; fast-moving; dramatic; frank; sympathetic; conventional; distinguished; social; florid; sentimental; slipshod; inflated; proletarian; romantic; biographical; jejune; fine; light; sex-free; sentimental; absorbing; exotic; diverting; comprehensive; vivid; accurate; late; experimental; original; convincing; readable; excellent; magnificent; moving; interesting; pleasant; glowing; enjoyable; grand; fascinating; early; stirring; famous.

verbs
acclaim—; applaud—; clamor for—; climax —; construct—; contemplate—; copyright—; create—; denounce—; devour—; embark on —; engross in—; interpret—; introduce—; peruse—; plan—; portray in—; scribble—; weave into—; —appears; —centers about; —deals with; —depicts; —enthralls; —evolves; —portrays; —reveals; —treats of; —unfolds.

(See fiction, book, manuscript, story, tale.)

NOVELIST

verbs
applaud—; berate—; criticize—; laud—; —

alters; —characterizes; —compares; —composes; —complains of; —copies; —creates; —dedicates; —depicts; —describes; —details; —dictates; —imagines; —indites; —insinuates; —narrates; —pens; —portrays; —rearranges; —relates; —retires; —rewrites; —satirizes; —scribbles; —sets forth; —unfolds.

(See poet, author, journalist, writer, artist.)

NOVELTY

adjectives

solemn; realistic; perfect; myriad (pl); startling; latest; dazzling; ever-changing; puzzling; divine; semi-tropical; constant.

verbs

clamor for—; create—; discard—; exhaust —; indulge in—; invent—; laud—; marvel at—; praise—; quicken with—; seek—; spur on by—; wonder at—; —amuses; —captures; —charms; —dazzles; —delights; —disquiets; —diverts; —entrances; —impresses; —palls.

(See change, innovation, originality, oddity.)

NOVICE

adjectives

anxious; musing; humble; beautiful; bashful.

verbs

advise—; befriend—; discipline—; discourage—; enlighten—; impress—; improve—; instruct—; order—; prime—; train—; —botches; —bungles; —conquers; —drills; —familiarizes; —fumbles; —imitates; —labors; —masters; —practises; —profits; —qualifies.

(See beginner, amateur, apprentice.)

NOXIOUS

adverbs

disastrously; calamitously; terribly; shockingly; appallingly; admittedly; notoriously; irremediably; pestillentially; virulently; inevitably; notably.

NOZZLE

verbs

adjust—; affix—; block—; clog—; dam—; direct—; flow from—; grease—; insert—; introduce—; manipulate—; obstruct—; ooze from—; regulate—; screw on—; service—; —emits; —projects; —protrudes; —spouts; —spurts.

(See nose, pipe, tube.)

NUCLEUS

adjectives

unyielding; convenient; unrivaled; solid.

NUDE

verbs

admire—; adorn—; dismiss—; divest to—; enfold—in; examine in—; expose—; glance at—; model in—; parade in—; pose in—; sanction—; scorn—; strip to—; study—; survey—; undrape to—; —astonishes; —defames; —disgusts; —horrifies; —revolts; —shocks.

(See body, figure, painting, sculpture, statue, drawing.)

adverbs

chastely; innocently; artistically; embarrassingly; shamelessly; distressingly; pitiably; pathetically; grievously; scandalously; sadly; miserably; utterly; painfully; completely; shockingly; wretchedly; horribly; seductively; alluringly; unconsciously; beautifully; deplorably; entirely.

NUISANCE

adjectives

prodigious; insufferable; unmitigated; civic; intolerable; rejected; everlasting; universal.

verbs

abate—; bear—; beset by —s; eliminate—; endure—; exterminate—; harass with —s; harrow with —s; inflict with —s; inveigh against—; overcome—; rectify—; upbraid —; —chafes; —distresses; —encumbers; —irks; —irritates; —offends; —pains; —plagues; —smarts; —weighs on.

(See annoyance, pest, plague, condition.)

NULL

adverbs

abeyantly; absently; baselessly; fabulously; unreally; unsubstantially; inanely; groundlessly; ethereally; airily; visionarily; actually; ridiculously.

NUMB

adverbs

alarmingly; completely; fortunately; blessedly; mercifully; unaccountably; suddenly; occasionally; apathetically; appallingly; surprisingly; pathetically; pitiably; strangely; curiously; oddly; remarkably; inertly; unconcernedly; callously; portentously; ominously; heartlessly.

NUMBER

verbs
affix — to; allot—; ascertain—; check—; conjecture—; decimate —s; demonstrate with —s; deplete —s; dwarf in—; inscribe with —; limit—; memorize—; recall—; recite —s; repeat—; run over —s; select—; —dwindles; —shrivels; —wanes.
(See figure, quantity, amount.)

NUMBER (v)

adverbs
correspondingly; overwhelmingly; countlessly; adequately; prodigiously; extravagantly; increasingly; definitely; interminably; mystically; proportionally; lavishly.
(See count, figure.)

NUMBERS

adjectives
countless; reasonable; considerable; sufficient; requisite; undiminished; fluctuating; unmitigated; incalculable; overwhelming; adequate; infinite; unequal; quantum; subsequent; superior; indeterminate; prodigious; extravagant; stipulated; certain; gentle; qualified; useless; singular; overpowering; gratifying; depleted; unwieldy; immense; actual; unknown; incredible; increasing; harmonious; laggard; jocund; definite; preponderating; fuller; respectable; rhythmic; untold; lofty; superfluous; goodly; augmented; possible; greatest; previous; uncountable; conceivable; scanty; unending; interminable; unvanquishable; diminutive; mystic; comparative; small; mournful; unavoidable; substantial; unrecorded; fiery; choral; fearful; proportional; lavish (pl).

NUMBNESS

adjectives
mental; fortunate; complete; vibrant; deadly; stealthy.

verbs
affect with—; create—; incur—; massage—; overcome with—; receive—; remedy—; —creeps over; —deadens; —dulls; —enfeebles; —hardens; —hibernates; —impairs; —ossifies; —paralyzes; —stupefies.
(See paralysis.)

NUNS

adjectives
undedicate; uncloistered; self-loving; chanting; holy; sincere.

NUPTIALS

verbs
assemble for—; attend—; bless—; celebrate —; consummate—; defer—; discharge—; gather for—; mar—; officiate at—; perform —; plan—; rehearse—; simplify—; solemnize—; —climax; —impress; —join; —symbolize; —unite.
(See marriage, matrimony, wedding.)

NURSE

adjectives
devoted; sedulous; mercenary; sole; hireling; avid; sapient; foul; exemplary; heroic; smart; bustling.

verbs
employ—; notify—; recruit —s; register—; train—; —administers; —allays; —alleviates; —assuages; —attends; —bathes; —cajoles; —cheers; —comforts; —consoles; —dresses; —eases; —massages; —refreshes; —reports; —salves; —smooths; —soothes.
(See mother, doctor, physician.)

NURSE (v)

adverbs
assiduously; devotedly; sedulously; avidly; heroically; maternally; gratuitously; affectionately; sympathetically.
(See attend, tend.)

NURSERY

adjectives
potent; airy; exquisite; huge; profitable.

NURTURE (v)

adverbs
delicately; exquisitely; tenderly; solicitously; appropriately; intellectually; spiritually; lovingly; selflessly.
(See nourish, foster, feed.)

NUTRIMENT

adjectives
appropriate; slight; elemental; intellectual.

verbs
administer—; advise—; digest—; double—; furnish—; infuse with—; lack—; necessitate—; offer—; order—; refuse—; resist—;

rob of—; savor—; spurn—; —aids; —amends; —appeals; —brightens; —improves; —promotes; —refreshes; —renews.

(See nourishment, nutrition.)

NUTRITION

verbs

deprive of—; draw—from; furnish—; improve—; lack—; limit—; maintain—; necessitate—; obtain—; offer—; pervert—; promote—; provide—; refuse—; regulate—; retard—; scorn—; spurn—; supply—; —absorbs; —comforts; —utilizes.

(See nourishment, food, nutriment.)

NUTRITIOUS

adverbs

unusually; wonderfully; remarkably; exceptionally; pleasantly; agreeably; singularly; curiously; scientifically; admittedly; warrantably; delightfully; usefully; extraordinarily; properly; substantially; usefully; valuably; inexpensively; wholesomely; healthfully; conveniently; extremely.

NYMPH

adjectives

slim; skilful; inebriated; ambrosial; attending; woodland; gaudy; jeweled.

verbs

—s array; —awes; —cheers; —charms; —dances; —delights; —frolics; —gambols; —gladdens; —graces; —inspires; —meanders; —rejoices; —roams.

(See fairy, angel, saint.)

O

OAK

adjectives
stunted; branched; gnarled; ancestral; enormous; hoary; gouty; rugged; knotted; heaven-delighting; deciduous; mossy; well-worn; monumental; perforated; stern; leafless; doting; twisted; sturdiest; massive; polychromed; stiff.

verbs
beam with—; cleave to—; fell—; moss—; timber with—; —braves; —commands; —crowns; —defies; —droops; —endures; —flourishes; —outlasts; —protects; —reigns; —roofs; —rules; —spreads; —stretches; —towers.
(See tree.)

OAR

adjectives
gliding; cautious; skimming; stalwart; busy; groaning; flashing; ponderous; muffled; paddling; suspended; lingering; laborious; golden; dipping; lazy; languid; rhythmic.

verbs
arm with—; drag—; heave—; manipulate—; paddle with—; ply with—; propel with—; splinter—; steer with—; stroke—; tug on—; —brushes; —cuts; —dips; —furrows; —impels; —splashes; —stirs; —sweeps.
(See paddle.)

OASIS

verbs
come upon—; dwell on—; encounter—; guide to—; refresh at—; seek—; sight—; welcome—; —attracts; —cheers; —delights; —invigorates; —nourishes; —relieves; —renews; —restores; —soothes; —strengthens.
(See fountain, safety, security.)

OATH

adjectives
grating; simultaneous; strange; furious; blood-curdling; infringed; binding; imperial; solemn; dreadful; round; sacred; pretty; horrible; slippery; sailor; continental; protesting; frantic; furious; new-found; consecrating; mouth-filling; royal; fearsome; rude; knightly; deadly; dismal; blistering; raucous; bold-beating; favorite; meaningless; soul-confirming; tremendous; angry; ingenious; inviolable; bombastic; ancient; solemn; confounding; unfeigned; innocent; brave; deep; little; bellowing; muttered; iron-clad; sacramental.

verbs
administer—; break—; cast—; flay with—; hiss—; launch—at; hurl—; repudiate—; spit out—; subscribe to—; utter—; —breaks from; —consummates; —solemnizes; —s stream from; —symbolizes; —vows; falsify under—.
(See curse, invective, ban, imprecation.)

OBDURATE

adverbs
sternly; stubbornly; incorrigibly; implacably; terribly; harshly; roughly; callously; mulishly; cantankerously; grossly; tenaciously; sullenly; perversely; dreadfully; shockingly; dogmatically; austerely; stiffly; uncompromisingly; tyrannically; puritanically; cruelly; bitterly; unaccountably; unbearably; intolerably.

OBEDIENCE

adjectives
military; implicit; hallowed; mechanical; true; fractional; infallible; divine; prompt; strict; characteristic; punctilious; scrupulous; instinctive; faithful; universal; rigid; unquestioning; weary; filial; instant; compliant; blind; passive; voluntary; plausible; slavish; transitory; hideous; docile; reverential.

verbs
abjure—; approve—; coerce into—; demand—; dispute—; enforce—; enslave by—; exact—; feign—; owe—to; profess—; reduce to—; submit in—; suffer—; train to—; yield—; —binds.
(See submission, obeisance.)

OBEDIENT

adverbs
highly; altogether; unfailingly; meekly; submissively; devotedly; affectionately; absurdly; promptly; always; scarcely; deferentially; respectfully; reverently; piously; ridiculously; readily; compliantly; obsequiously;

unctuously; ostentatiously; diplomatically; obviously; stupidly; doltishly; grudgingly; implicitly; meticulously; surprisingly; painstakingly; strictly; passively; grudgingly.

OBEISANCE

adjectives
graceful; surly; humble; profound; ironical; flattering.

verbs
approve—; bow in—; feign—; owe—; pay —; sacrifice to—.
(See homage, obedience, reverence, allegiance, devotion.)

OBESE

adverbs
alarmingly; uncomfortably; comically; tragically; unnecessarily; ridiculously; indescribably; clumsily; dangerously; ominously; significantly; grossly; awkwardly; embarrassingly; lumpishly; unhappily; unfortunately; unbelievably; peculiarly; strangely; dropsically; unaccountably; inherently.

OBESITY

verbs
brood over—; dread—; eat into—; fear—; lament—; overcome—; reduce—; remedy—; repress—; resist—; threaten with—; —alarms; —astounds; —dejects; —depresses; —encumbers; —endangers; —hinders; —irks; —restrains; —restricts.
(See stoutness.)

OBEY (v)

adverbs
dully; unquestioningly; hypnotically; reluctantly; mechanically; implicitly; systematically; involuntarily; infallibly; filially; punctiliously; scrupulously; rigidly; passively; voluntarily; slavishly; docilely; reverentially.
(See comply, heed.)

OBJECT

adjectives
salient; varied (pl); beloved; conspicuous; well-defined; practicable; spiritual; compassionable; irrelevant; tender; unworthy; contrary; opaque; warlike; foreign; venerable; slipping; benevolent; charitable; repressed; commanding; dark; uncouth; pear-shaped; dreadful; immediate; humanitarian; isolated; chimerical; hideous; accidental; ulterior; characteristic; manifest; fruitful; darling; concealed; staple; primary; animated; imperfect; half-seen; principal; determinate; sensuous; loathsome; nobler; far-distant; beneficent; desired; frequent (pl); inanimate; forlorn; ornamental; definite; closest; supernatural; impersonal; gruesome; express; homely; prominent; unoffending; acceptable; exclusive; specific; interesting; commonplace; innumerable (pl); solitary; innocent; cardinal; celestial; terrific; natural; secondary; enigmatical; unappetizing; sausage-like; engrossing; incompatible; shining; rugged; sensible; objectionable; visible; baser; sufficient; noteworthy; ostensible; memorable; avowed; sublime; absorbing; pure; visual; alluring; baleful; infamous; remarkable; transparent; repulsive; dusky; legitimate; tangible; dispassionate; praiseworthy; respective; incommunicable; worthy; sole; indifferent; outward; distinct; obtrusive; demagogical; personified; requisite; laudable; engaging; supreme; important; honorable; distinguishing; death-dealing; central; vital; striking; shapeless; petty; sparse; impressive; unreasoning; particular; ludicrous; external; conceivable.

verbs
achieve—; acquaint with—; aim at—; attain —; consecrate to—; contemplate—; embrace —; endorse—; expose—; frustrate—; glorify—; labor for—; oppose—; perceive—; pursue—; represent—; reveal—; serve—; —hinders; —interposes; —interrupts; —obstructs.
(See aim, end, view, goal, objective, mission, purpose.)

OBJECT (v)

adverbs
strenuously; gruffly; pointedly; perversely; incompatibly; legitimately; passionately; dogmatically; unreasonably; graciously; ludicrously; fruitlessly; snobbishly; ultimately; sturdily; singularly.
(See oppose, disapprove.)

OBJECTION

adjectives
fatal; forcible; futile; insuperable; overt; plausible; critical; insurmountable; principal; gracious; embarrassing; feeble; strenuous; snobbish; ultimate; trivial; various (pl); rooted; violent; further; sturdy; depressing; ingenious; incompetent; singular.

verbs
anticipate—; brush aside—; cease—; disparage—; entertain—; justify—; meet—; outbalance—; overcome—; provoke—; put forward—; reply to—; surmount—; temper —; voice—; —arises; —enlarges; —impedes; —wilts.
(See challenge, exception, opposition, interference.)

OBJECTIONABLE

adverbs
positively; highly; uncommonly; remarkably; unutterably; altogether; definitely; violently; singularly; particularly; personally; professionally; exceptionally; socially.

OBJECTIVE

adjectives
definite; ostensible; constructive; vicious; avowed; economic; clear; precise.

verbs
acclaim—; achieve—; advance upon—; applaud—; back—; complete—; conceal—; deny—; honor—; menace—; surrender—; threaten—; conquer—.
(See object, purpose, goal, mission.)

OBLIGATION

adjectives
financial; solemn; filial; reciprocal; cruel; divine; irksome; contractual; sacred; eternal; inexpressible; mystic; mutual; superadded; maturing; unlucky; pecuniary; deep; universal; external; tacit; parental; religious; corresponding; solemn; effectual.

verbs
accept—; acknowledge—; balk at—; bind by—s; discharge—; disregard—; evade—s; free from—s; fulfill—; impose—; incur—; perform—; place under—; release from—; repudiate—; satisfy—; shirk—; stud with —s; transfer—.
(See bond, debt, mortgage, payment, loan.)

OBLIGATORY

adverbs
dreadfully; rigorously; inescapably; legally; morally; financially; sadly; stringently; rigidly; unfortunately; sternly; inflexibly; appallingly; strictly.

OBLIGE (*v*)

adverbs
flatteringly; gushingly; reluctantly; infinitely; financially; mutually; morally.
(See please, accommodate.)

OBLIGING

adverbs
pleasantly; amiably; generously; graciously; infallibly; unfailingly; willingly; immediately; gladly; helpfully; expertly; considerately; politely; courteously; tactfully; cordially; heartily; genially; cheerfully; happily; instantly.

OBLITERATE (*v*)

adverbs
instantaneously; completely; abruptly; wholly; cruelly; dictatorially.
(See efface, blot, remove.)

OBLIVION

adjectives
dusty; complete; mute; utter; dark; sweet; keen; blank.

verbs
accept—; bask in—; bury in—; cast into—; consign to—; doom to—; drag from—; emerge from—; fade into—; flounder in—; gain—; join in—; merit—; overtake—; seek —; sink into—; speed to—; threaten with—; yield to—.
(See insignificance, failure, obscurity.)

OBLIVIOUS

adverbs
vexatiously; carelessly; indifferently; ungratefully; thanklessly; abstractedly; dreamily; drowsily; selfishly; inconsiderately; egotistically; stupidly; apathetically; completely; unfeelingly; utterly; inexcusably; unpardonably; grossly; heartlessly; blindly; coolly; curiously; rudely.

OBNOXIOUS

adverbs
entirely; highly; uncommonly; extremely; deeply; odiously; reprehensibly; unnecessarily; manifestly; curiously; disastrously; exceptionably; detestably; abominably; deliberately; bitterly; shockingly; appallingly; frightfully; unbearably.

OBOE

verbs
finger—; pitch—; render on—; scale—; solo

on—; sound—; tune—; —beseeches; —buzzes; —chants; —confounds; —hums; —mourns; —penetrates; —pleads; —wails; —whispers.
(See bagpipe.)

OBSCENE

adverbs
frightfully; illegally; unimaginably; filthily; terribly; ribaldly; grossly; coarsely; offensively; disgustingly; hatefully; shamefully; lewdly; suggestively; intolerably; broadly; wantonly; meretriciously; abominably; particularly; unexpectedly; unwarrantably.

OBSCENITY

verbs
besmirch by—; censure—; decry—; denounce—; deplore—; devour—; disapprove of—; escape—; foul by—; gorge on—; indulge in—; loathe—; pardon—; repent—; revel in—; wallow in—; —defiles; —nauseates; —offends; —perishes; —revolts; —shocks; —stains; —violates.
(See immodesty, sin, perversion, abomination, corruption.)

OBSCURE

adverbs
lamentably; altogether; curiously; inconveniently; darkly; murkily; cloudily; foggily; mistily; dimly; confusingly; bewilderingly; unintelligibly; unfortunately; unluckily; unaccountably; unnecessarily; unsatisfactorily; vaguely; mysteriously; remarkably; vexatiously; disappointingly.

OBSCURE (v)

adverbs
mysteriously; gloomily; puzzlingly; artfully; purposely; cunningly; hopelessly; patently; diplomatically; politically.
(See darken, eclipse.)

OBSCURITY

adjectives
patient; habitual; deep; obscene; comparative; elusive; humble; ever-deepening; impenetrable; dark; polite; hopeless; smooth; dense; unmerited.

verbs
bury in—; doom to—; drag from—; drive into—; drown in—; exile to—; face—; fade into—; languish in—; perplex with—; plunge into—; retire into—; return to—; sink into—; slip into—; —shields; —veils.
(See darkness, gloom, insignificance, oblivion.)

OBSEQUIOUS

adverbs
blandly; suavely; unctuously; professionally; exceptionally; deferentially; humbly; ingratiatingly; submissively; cringingly; tactfully; curiously; oddly; strangely; unaccountably; slavishly; servilely; abjectly; significantly; mysteriously; pliantly; inexplicably; pitiably; lamentably; sadly; eagerly; reverentially; ceremoniously; unnecessarily.

OBSERVANCE

adjectives
sacred; rigorous; over-curious; strict; puritanical; ceremonious; mute; ritual; superstitious; cordial; religious; cheerful; meticulous; faithful; devout.

verbs
advise—of; advocate—of; celebrate in—; comply with—; demand—; direct—; exact—; extend—; fulfill—; inspire—; join in—; necessitate—; preclude—; relish—; sponsor—; —aids; —obligates; —satisfies.
(See celebration, anniversary, fulfillment)

OBSERVANT

adverbs
keenly; aptly; expertly; skilfully; intelligently; acutely; sharply; critically; terribly; dreadfully; alarmingly; officiously; impertinently; impudently; offensively; vexatiously; carefully; watchfully; cautiously; attentively; remarkably; noticeably; alertly; prudently; thoughtfully; meticulously; amusingly; unusually; punctiliously.

OBSERVATION

adjectives
necessary; specific; dispassionate; punctilious; silent; unaided; personal; quiet; continued; searching; accurate; direct; common; shrewd; watchful; pertinent; judicious; questioning; satirical; surface; natural; homely; penetrating; insignificant; detached; outward; celestial; phrenological; objective; tentative; cursory; august; trifling; encouraging; friendly; consistent; curious; delicate; loving; sufficient; extensive; facetious; astronomical; glib; unlimited; minute; childish; conflicting (pl); discrim-

inating; detailed; mere; abstract; meridional; restless; wondrous; quiet; sundry (pl); original; loose; vague; keen; assiduous; controlled; humorous; insufficient; subsequent; faulty; practiced; meteorological; disconcerted.

verbs
bias—; bolster—; confirm—; elude—; enlarge—s; escape—; exchange—s; guide—s; offer—; record—s; report—; resume—; shun—; voice—; —authenticates; —confirms; —discloses; —reveals; —shocks; —stuns.
(See view, remark, conversation, opinion.)

OBSERVE (v)

adverbs
alertly; philosophically; astutely; slyly; profoundly; significantly; oracularly; sagaciously; parenthetically; studiously; complacently; autobiographically; wistfully; bluntly; impartially; religiously; skeptically; scrupulously; cordially; composedly; spontaneously; infallibly; sentimentally; primly; systematically; punctiliously; shrewdly; pertinently; judiciously; tentatively; facetiously; meteorologically.
(See notice, see.)

OBSERVER

adjectives
stupefied; hasty; wise; phlegmatic; casual; expert; superficial; extraterrestrial; philosophic; silent; attentive; vigilant; practiced; sympathetic; distinguished; rocking-chair; dispassionate; devoted; unprejudiced; uninitiated; scientific; inattentive; careful; careless; numerous; keen-eyed; sagacious; disinterested; unconscious; constant; slight; ignorant; sharp; experienced; political; deliberate; energetic; sarcastic; inexpert; impartial; hasty; indignant.

verbs
admit—s; allow—s; attract—s; confine—s to; deceive—; delude—; limit—s; mislead —; permit—s; present to—s; surprise—s; —beholds; —comprehends; —concentrates; —concludes; —contemplates; —s crowd; —detects; —meddles; —notes; —relishes; —surveys; —views; —witnesses.
(See witness, individual, public.)

OBSESSION

verbs
actuate—; assail by—; beset by—; fret over—; molest with—; plague by—; —annoys; —bedevils; —discomposes; —disquiets; —distresses; —disturbs; —grasps; —grates; —haunts; —hovers over; —inhabits; —inspires; —persecutes; —plagues; —ruffles; —seizes; —tortures; —vexes; —weighs.
(See prejudice, delusion, daydream, idea, hallucination, illusion, nightmare.)

OBSTACLE

adjectives
insuperable; unforeseen; hideous; apparent; tremendous; insurmountable; appalling; usual; effectual; recognized; hopeless; formidable; technical; trifling; prodigious; imaginary; unseen; serious; fatal; stubborn; frightful; infrequent (pl); specific; unexpected; artificial; successful; puny; impending; considerable; practical; impassable; solid-looking; stupendous; petty.

verbs
anticipate—; brush aside—; circumvent—; cut through—; encounter—; gauge—; interpose—; level—; meet with—; overcome—; remove—; surmount—; vanquish—; —arises; —hinders; —restrains; —restricts; —thwarts.
(See bar, impediment, hindrance, difficulty, interference, trouble.)

OBSTINACY

adjectives
senile; dogged; brutal; sheer; wrong-headed; inveterate; hellish; lawless; sufficient; desperate; gentle; suicidal; natural; surprising; misdirected; inflexible; unyielding; invincible; somber.

verbs
adhere with—; attack by—; break—; fatigue—; fight with—; harden into—; induce —; maintain—; narrow into—; rebuke—; relent—; repent—; steel with—; stiffen in —; —conquers; —disconcerts; —endures; —inflames; —perseveres; —persists; —petrifies; —resists; —smothers; —sulks.
(See stubbornness, opposition, antagonism, hostility.)

OBSTINATE

adverbs
doggedly; wilfully; inflexibly; stubbornly; astonishingly; disagreeably; dangerously; incorrigibly; surprisingly; naturally; wonderfully; unexpectedly; implacably; stern-

ly; brutally; inveterately; desperately; habitually; obnoxiously; obdurately; viciously; dreadfully.

OBSTREPEROUS

adverbs

unmanageably; ungovernably; uncontrollably vexatiously; intolerably; habitually; always; altogether; annoyingly; shamefully; mischievously; roguishly; teasingly; tormentingly; violently; wildly; boisterously; viciously; desperately; outrageously; stormily; strangely; unaccountably; unwarrantably; unbelievably; indescribably.

OBSTRUCT (v)

adverbs

deliberately; premeditatedly; doggedly; desperately; unyieldingly; pettishly; formidably; stupidly; forcibly; strenuously; economically; viciously.

(See oppose, retard.)

OBSTRUCTION

adjectives

artificial; mere; insurmountable; blank; formidable; cold; frequent; acute.

verbs

accumulate into—; attempt—; clear away —; complain of—; devise—; localize—; mourn—; offer—; pierce—; purge of—; suffer—; treat—; —arrests; —bars; —clogs; —hinders; —interposes; —resists; —restrains; —shuts out; —stems; —thaws; —delays.

(See impediment, bar, barrier, hazard, hindrance.)

OBTAIN (v)

adverbs

legally; effectually; unethically; surreptitiously; rapaciously; honorably; selfishly; uncharitably; legitimately; singularly; disgracefully; unceremoniously.

(See gain, procure.)

OBTAINABLE

adverbs

recently; currently; conveniently; easily; readily; inexpensively; probably; certainly; assuredly; warrantably; possibly; scarcely; hardly; barely; measurably; later.

OBTRUDE (v)

adverbs

inconsiderately; impudently; irrelevantly, voluntarily; forcefully; vigorously; selfishly; bluntly; formidably.

(See intrude, encroach.)

OBTRUSIVE

adverbs

inconveniently; irritatingly; pestiferously; inquisitively; impertinently; rudely; inexcusably; boorishly; innocently; mischievously; constantly; miserably; vexatiously; unpardonably; bluntly; meddlingly; meddlesomely; grossly; indecorously; unbecomingly; shockingly; surprisingly; oddly; impolitely; pertly; rudely; inconsiderately; ignorantly; discourteously.

OBTUSE

adverbs

pitiably; terribly; unbelievably; unimaginably; incurably; boorishly; rudely; incomprehensibly; inordinately; shockingly; inexpressibly; callously; stupidly; heavily; stolidly; doltishly; dully; unusually; uncommonly.

OBTUSENESS

adjectives

mental; moral; monumental; colossal; apparent.

OCCASION

adjectives

innocent; ceremonial; last-mentioned; rare; various (pl); utmost; ample; dire; approaching; long-expected; abundant; subsequent; memorable; numerous (pl); lugubrious; insignificant; gala; separate; auspicious; festal; appropriate; trivial; extraordinary; momentous; impressive; everyday; obvious; picturesque; solemn; world-famous; little-known; grand; festival; ordinary; virtuous; sacred; proudest; notable; exceptional; peculiar; unprecedented; joyful; speedy; multiple; fateful; celebrated; infrequent; mellow; critical.

verbs

afford—; commemorate—; contrive—; feast on—; hunger for—; observe—; offer—; present—; rise to—; seduce by—; seek—; seize —; snatch—; spurn—; —demands; —merits; —prompts; —slips by; —warrants.

(See hour, opportunity, occurrence.)

OCCULT

adverbs
mysteriously; annoyingly; confusingly; bewilderingly; unmistakably; marvellously; undeniably; indubitably; abstrusely; darkly; impenetrably; incomprehensibly; inscrutably; obscurely; vaguely; unfathomably; perplexingly; puzzlingly; disturbingly; peculiarly; strangely.

OCCUPANT

adjectives
voiceless; sheeted; tossing; imaginary; solitary; primitive; sparse.

verbs
confine—; cradle—; discharge—; eject—; evict—; expel—; intrude on—; oust—; remove—; retain—; —s abandon; —admits; —appropriates; —departs; —establishes; —s gather; —nestles; —s pack; —roosts; —s stream from; —tenants; —withdraws.
(See inhabitant.)

OCCUPATION

adjectives
final; praiseworthy; trivial; illegal; congenial; intellectual; agreeable; youthful; earnest; disastrous; hellish; intense; unquiet; beloved; indispensable; triumphant; enviable; sedentary; remunerative; arduous; hazardous; breadwinning; productive; monotonous; strenuous; absorbing; profitable; dignified; various; useful; restful; savory; untidy; joint; undesirable; favorite; degrading; menial; brutalizing; solitary; prosaic; doubtful; unimportant; nightly; chief; ignoble.

verbs
absorb in—; chain to—; cherish—; choose —; comprehend—; despise—; employ in—; engage in—; escape—; follow—; lack—; postpone—; practise—; profit by—; pursue —; qualify for—; seek—; shun—; train for —; —contents; —enthralls; —interests; —rusts; —wearies.
(See business, calling, course, hobby, employment, work.)

OCCUPY (*v*)

adverbs
extensively; variously; solely; incessantly; densely; assiduously; intermittently; profoundly; temporarily; arduously; triumphantly; congenially; intellectually; hazardously; monotonously; strenuously; profitably; menially; prosaically; ignobly.
(See keep, hold, possess.)

OCCUR (*v*)

adverbs
perpetually; sporadically; coincidentally; propitiously; phenomenally; historically; contemporaneously; miraculously; incredibly; circumstantially; preternaturally; distressingly; fortuitously; deplorably; marvelously.
(See happen, befall.)

OCCURRENCE

adjectives
striking; unusual; shadowy; historical; contemporaneous; miraculous; incredible; biennial; similar; inexplicable; menstrual; determined; alleged; trifling; circumstantial; preternatural; untoward; distressing; supernatural; disgraceful; fortuitous; frequent; shocking; deplorable; unnoticed; joyful; marvelous; unforeseen.

verbs
advertise—; anticipate—; compile—s; count —s; edit—; endure—; experience—; impute —to; meet with—; narrate—; note—; record—; report—; —brings to light; —interrupts; —supervenes; —surprises.
(See course, affair, event, episode, adventure, incident.)

OCEAN

adjectives
treacherous; salt-waved; wild; wreck-strewn; gushing; measureless; distant; dancing; purpling; leaden; madfoam; mighty; voluminous; darkling; momentary; moaning; sanguine; neglected; freshening; circumfluous; turbulent; wasteful; blue; winter; hungry; gleaming; tempestuous; shoreless; wine-dark; surging; charmed; lifeless; bursting; unresting; tossing; illimitable; tumultuous; homeless; boundless; unconfined; ethereal; wasteful; unruffled; infinite; close-lying; yearning; cheerless; boiling; chafed; small-sized; bottomless; mimic; glaucous; vast; calm; unfruitful; resistless.

verbs
brave—; cradle in—; girdle—; harness—; launch on—; —booms; —bubbles; —buffets; —flashes; —foams; —grumbles; —hammers at; —heaves; —lashes; —leaps; —lulls; —

moans; —murmurs; —pitches; —plays; —ravages; —resounds; —rolls; —shoulders; —sighs; —smiles; —spumes; —surges; —swells; —tosses; —washes; —whispers.

(See sea, waves, breakers.)

ODD

adverbs

decidedly; inexplicably; grotesquely; fantastically; unfortunately; positively; extraordinarily; uncommonly; disagreeably; offensively; unpleasantly; awkwardly; comically; boorishly; outlandishly; barbarously; shamefully.

ODDITY

adjectives

individual; numerous (pl); definite.

verbs

appreciate—; deride—; display—; exhibit —; marvel at—; reveal—; ridicule—; scoff at—; scorn—; stare at—; tolerate—; value for—; —amuses; —astounds; —awes; —bewilders; —decorates; —dumbfounds; —flabbergasts (colloq.); —startles; —strikes.

(See eccentricity, novelty.)

ODDS

adjectives

overwhelming; rushing; confounding; fearful; moderate; tremendous; worthless; conceivable; formidable; reckless; highest.

verbs

acquire—; approve—; calculate—; demand —; discourage—; enjoy—; justify—; play —; reckon—; reduce—; refuse—; request —; submit to—; —despair; —increase; —prevail; —protect.

(See disadvantage, advantage.)

ODE

adjectives

imperishable; turgid; lofty; mortal; patriotic; celebrated.

ODIOUS

adverbs

extremely; uncommonly; extraordinarily; detestably; abominably; atrociously; unusually; flagrantly; egregiously; intolerably; incredibly; shockingly; disgustingly; particularly; singularly; peculiarly; monstrously.

ODOR

adjectives

sickening; objectionable; universal; savory; mingled; musty; offensive; reconciling; mysterious; undefinable; charnel; thick; mephitic; delicious; exquisite; peculiar; indescribable; characteristic; prison; vague; influent; delicate; undesirable; dreamy; sweet-scented; succulent; fragrant; keen-edged; greasy; sweetish; spicy; strange; pervading; fugitive; single-flower; dry; arrowy; autumn; champac; rich; vigorous; nightly; butyric; body; mystical; dewy; faint; cloying; perspiration; sweaty; sulphurous; suffocating; poisonous; disagreeable; unsanitary; national; underarm; subtlest; sour; soft; pungent; balsam; charming; dainty; languishing; heavy; grateful; soul-dissolving; aromatic; fecund; breezy; chafed; durable; evil; intoxicating; ambrosial; insufferable; subtle; noxious; distinctive; embarrassing; pleasant.

verbs

combat—; detect—; diffuse—; efface—; emit —; exhale—; impregnate with—; inhale—; retain—; snuff up—; waft in—; —assails; —s commingle; —emanates; —floats from; —greets; —invigorates; —mingles; —pervades; —sickens.

(See aroma, incense, essence, fragrance, smell, stench.)

OFFEND (*v*)

adverbs

mortally; inevitably; desperately; deeply; morally; spiritually; socially; personally.

(See wound, affront, hurt.)

OFFENDED

adverbs

mortally; heinously; grievously; continually; slightly; deeply; irreparably; gravely; definitely; unreasonably; senselessly; bitterly; sorely; grievously; frightfully; distressingly; mightily; dangerously; hotly; obviously; openly; ludicrously; extremely; absurdly; foolishly; unfortunately; throughout.

OFFENDER

adjectives

inveterate; hardened; banished; desperate; misguided; repeating.

verbs

apprehend—; chastise—; detain—; fine—; forgive—; pardon—; penalize—; punish—;

reform—; resent—; restrict—; reveal—; subject—to; try—; —commits; —displeases; —infringes; —transgresses.

(See loser, criminal, thief, robber.)

OFFENSE

adjectives

criminal; indecent; mortal; dire; flagrant; heinous; aggravated; imputed; trivial; penitentiary; deliberate; actual; supreme; vile; grievous; giddy; voluntary; heavy; continual; superficial; dismissed; similar; odious; impeachable; primitive; slightest; unpardonable; vicious; enormous; grave; excruciating; rank.

verbs

bewail—; commit—; condone—; countenance—; decry—; denounce—; excuse—; fear —; indict for—; lash for—; palliate—; penalize—; punish—; rue—; uncover—; —besmirches; —debases; —defaces; —disgraces; —involves; —libels; —slanders.

(See crime, insult, guilt, misdeed.)

OFFENSIVE

verbs

act on—; assume—; choose—; detail—; dispose to—; launch—; occupy—; plan—; rely on—; take up—; —aggravates; —batters; —drives; —grapples; —harries; —instigates; —invades; —presses; —storms; —strikes.

(See aggression.)

adverbs

distinctly; strikingly; conspicuously; highly; terribly; unexpectedly; boorishly; impertinently; cruelly; bitterly; amazingly; monstrously; daringly; deliberately; purposely; intentionally; unpardonably; inexcusably; execrably; abominably; disagreeably; unnecessarily; unwarrantably; disgracefully; shamefully; aggressively.

OFFER

adjectives

repeated; palliative; munificent; magnificent; friendly; coherent; intelligent; special; introductory; liberal; amazing; low-priced; unusual; dubious; engaging; particular; disinterested; magnanimous; outstanding; singular; remarkable; unique; combination; inexpensive; generous; hospitable; private; testimonial; unprecedented; polite; irresponsible; spectacular; ridiculous; positive; greatest; free; no-risk; demonstrator; smashing; money-making; quick-starting; astounding; trial; startling; genuine.

verbs

accept—; advance—; avail oneself of—; bombard with—s; consider—; decline—; disdain—; entertain—; hawk about for—s; invite—s; jump at—; present—; press—; propose—; propound—; refuse—; reject—; renew—; resent—; solicit—s; spurn—; tender—; waive—; withhold—; —entices; —satisfies.

(See bid, bribe, gift, opportunity, proposition.)

OFFER (*v*)

adverbs

generously; exclusively; zealously; gratuitously; voluntarily; tentatively; stolidly; temptingly; facetiously; magnanimously; obtrusively; munificently; liberally; dubiously; disinterestedly; uniquely; unprecedentedly; demonstratively; genuinely.

(See bid, propose.)

OFFERING

adjectives

bounteous; princely; freewill; mortuary; exceptional; votive; propitiatory; imposing; annual; rustic; odious; magnificent; appropriate; polluted; sensational; great; strange; intelligent; purest; definite; acceptable; feeble; faithful; worthy; never-fading; extraordinary; remarkable.

OFFICE (*general*)

adjectives

imperial; holy; ill; drafty; administrative; magnificent; paneled; imposing; nobler; elective; unpretentious; kind; breviary; basest; oldest; established; beneficent; executive; menial; subordinate; domestic; melancholy; appointed; choked; modest; distinct; turbaned; charitable; required; lofty; invidious; courteous; truer; permanent; pious; sceptered.

OFFICE (*place of business*)

verbs

abandon—; assign to—; clerk in—; collect at—; conduct at—; establish—; glower around—; head—; inquire at—; lodge in—; pour into—; supervise—; transact at—;

transfer—to; usher into—; —buzzes; —dispenses; —drones; —employs; —functions; —hums; —operates.

(See room, building, place.)

OFFICE
(position, duty, etc.)

verbs

abolish—; abuse—; assume—; catapult into —; chain to—; dawdle in—; elevate to—; entitle to—; fill—; hoist into—; hound out of—; induct into—; oust from—; perform —; qualify for—; railroad out of (colloq.) —; resign—; retire from—; slide into—; soar to—; undertake—.

(See capacity, position, job, duty, service.)

OFFICER

adjectives

estimable; rebellious; ranking; administrative; courageous; handsome; gallant; high-minded; energetic; health; faithful; adroit; unscrupulous; sagacious; ragged; efficient; straggling; presiding; preventive; regimental; prefectual; cautious; conservative; consular; arrogant; slothful; executive; subordinate; treacherous; astute; sensitive; embarrassing; resisting; staff; audacious; senior; liberal; peevish; pelting; petty; accomplished; downhearted; hard-working; harassed; mortal; vigilant; competent; superior; liaison; newly-fledged; glaring; unblushing; confidential; native; eminent; forceful; high-spirited; subaltern; disobedient.

verbs

appoint—; consult—; court-martial—; elect —; empower—; refer to—; resist—; —administers; —admonishes; —assembles; —attends; —authorizes; —chastises; —commands; —conducts; —directs; —disbands; —inspects; —records; —serves.

(See constable, deacon, midshipman, detective, commander, general.)

OFFICIAL

adjectives

cruel; incompetent; distinguished; bureaucratic; incorruptible; fearless; intelligent; mere; salaried; corrupt; negligent; faithless; amiable; dignified; foreign; blustering; unappreciative; overdriven; energetic; aesthetic; suspicious; obstinate.

verbs

appoint—; consult—; direct—; elect—; huddle with—s; invest—with; rebuke—; refer to—; serve as—; staff with—s; —administers; —advocates; —s assemble; —attends; —authorizes; —blusters; —chastises; —conducts; —directs; —inspects; —judges; —orders; —presides; —summons.

(See leader, ambassador, legislator, congressman, governor, magistrate, president.)

adverbs

undeniably; admittedly; avowedly; assuredly; obviously; evidently; manifestly; authentically; authoritatively; absolutely; reliably; dependably; solemnly; actually; indubitably; unmistakably; odiously; irresistibly; cruelly; sternly; responsibly; imposingly; shockingly; studiously; weightily.

OFFICIOUS

adverbs

pompously; disagreeably; offensively; foolishly; absurdly; ridiculously; unwarrantably; unnecessarily; proudly; meddlesomely; impertinently; unbecomingly; ceremoniously; ingratiatingly; magisterially; unpleasantly; strangely; egotistically; busily; actively; zealously; smartly; expertly; persistently; ardently; restlessly; alertly.

OFFSPRING

adjectives

precocious; illegitimate; turbulent; new-fledged; frightened; hideous; speckled; spotted; numerous; unfilial; valiant; inferior; diminutive; sole; resulting; fatherless; groveling; motherless.

verbs

bestow—upon; bless with—; enjoy—; idolize—; issue—; mother—; present with—; produce—; promise—; rear—; transmit to —; yearn for—; —blossom; —burden; —comfort; —delight; —gather; —inherit; —torment.

(See fruit, child, heir, brood, generation, descendant.)

OGLE *(v)*

adverbs

flirtatiously; affectedly; amorously; lasciviously; voluptuously; lustfully; unblushingly; immodestly; brazenly; coyly.

(See look, stare.)

OIL

adjectives
volatile; subtle; raw; golden; unbleached; soothing; midnight; rich; rugged; chemic.

verbs
adulterate—; anoint with—; disseminate—; distil—; distribute—; drill for—; drive by —; extract—; feed—; force—; flush—; fuel with—; lubricate with—; market—; power with—; press—from; prospect for—; pump —; refine—; saturate with—; spout—; —accumulates; —drips; —flows; —seeps through; —smooths.
(See lubricant, fuel.)

OILY

adverbs
unpleasantly; dangerously; surprisingly; admirably; satisfactorily; sufficiently; extremely; uncommonly; significantly; wonderfully; unfortunately; treacherously; hazardously; evenly; mildly; pleasantly; soothingly.

OINTMENT

verbs
absorb—; advocate—; apply—; assimilate —; dose with—; dress with—; plaster—on; prepare—; smear—on; —assuages; —cleanses; —corrects; —draws; —eases; —palliates; —relieves; —remedies; —restores; —salves; —soothes.
(See balm, liniment, lotion, salve.)

OLD

adverbs
genuinely; unquestionably; decrepitly; incredibly; truly; apparently; evidently; obviously; deceptively; smartly; graciously; genteelly; absurdly; beautifully; proudly; valuably; unbelievably.

OLD-FASHIONED

adverbs
ridiculously; charmingly; sedately; sweetly; laughably; eccentrically; obstinately; consistently; serenely; placidly; hopelessly; carelessly; indifferently; pricelessly; whimsically; fantastically; grotesquely; shabbily; innocently; deliberately; intentionally; absurdly; barbarously; unpleasantly; embarrassingly; unconcernedly; nonchalantly; unashamedly; pleasantly; unpretentiously.

OMEN

adjectives
ill; auspicious; prophetic; fearful; unfavorable; parlous; favorable; happy; pleasant; cheery.

OMINOUS

adverbs
unmistakably; significantly; disturbingly; distressingly; sadly; prophetically; alarmingly; unpleasantly; dismally; markedly; noticeably; drearily; fearfully; terribly; heartbreakingly.

OMISSION

adjectives
voluntary; merciful; insidious.

verbs
check—; frown on—; discover—; incur—; lament—; object to—; observe—; overcome —; protest—; rectify—; scoff at—; supply —; —detracts; —irks; —magnifies; —resounds; —scandalizes; —shocks.
(See default, error, mistake.)

OMIT (*v*)

adverbs
premeditatedly; accidentally; tragically; pointedly; voluntarily; mercifully; insidiously; hazardously; rashly; cavalierly.
(See ignore, disregard.)

ONE

adjectives
unsubstantial; eclectic; lisping; heterogeneous; irresistible; delicate; reluctant; silent; memorable; uncivil; awe-inspiring.

ONEROUS

adverbs
unusually; remarkably; uncommonly; formidably; embarrassingly; objectionably; tremendously; grievously; cruelly; unexpectedly; perplexingly; bewilderingly; desperately; irksomely; unaccountably; surprisingly; singularly.

ONLOOKERS

adjectives
uncomprehending; unsophisticated; silent; innocent; conspiring.

ONRUSH

verbs
check—; elude—; instigate—; master—; stem—; —breaks; —deluges; —issues from;

—stampedes; —swamps; —sweeps by; —tramples.
(See onslaught.)

ONSET

adjectives
spiteful; insidious; thunderous; brilliant; impetuous; unyielding; intellectual.

ONSLAUGHT

adjectives
ubiquitous; furious; unscrupulous; merciless; ludicrous; savage; direct; hasty; rapid; murderous.

verbs
anticipate—; check—; curb—; dread—; escape—; fear—; flee from—; fortify against —; prompt—; stem—; subdue—; succumb to—; surrender to—; weather—; witness—; —destroys; —horrifies; —overpowers; —terrorizes.
(See assault, attack, onrush.)

OPALESCENT

adverbs
brilliantly; wonderfully; unusually; colorfully; marvelously; beautifully; uncommonly; splendidly; magnificently; barbarically; remarkably; singularly; peculiarly; particularly; oddly; attractively; gorgeously; wondrously; amazingly.

OPAQUE

adverbs
inconveniently; absolutely; satisfactorily; necessarily; completely; hazily; muddily; cloudily; vaporously; mysteriously; strangely; admirably; disappointingly; smokily; bafflingly; perplexingly; bewilderingly.

OPEN

adverbs
invitingly; mysteriously; conveniently; comfortably; advantageously; yawningly; widely; constantly; continually; evidently; palpably; apparently; indulgently; allowably; legally; officially; hospitably; unconditionally; currently; generously; broadly; liberally; helpfully.

OPEN (v)

adverbs
rarely; partially; tempestuously; listlessly; conveniently; drowsily; automatically; haphazardly; incautiously; beneficently; cautiously; unwarily; modestly; invitingly; portentously; prematurely; symmetrically.
(See reveal, unfold.)

OPEN-HANDED

adverbs
lavishly; extravagantly; liberally; indulgently; foolishly; senselessly; considerately; graciously; benevolently; wastefully; munificently; thoughtfully; freely; hospitably; incomparably; particularly; generously; indiscriminately; diplomatically; strategically; kindly; amazingly; affluently; eminently.

OPEN-HEARTED

adverbs
generously; liberally; charitably; magnanimously; always; dependably; reliably; consistently; indulgently; cordially; candidly; sincerely; frankly; artlessly; unaffectedly; notably; conspicuously; remarkably; splendidly; magnificently; lavishly.

OPENING

adjectives
portentous; moderate; auspicious; friendly; arched; chiseled; ambitious; proffered; numerous (pl); advantageous; premature; crescent; smaller; high-placed; symmetrical.

verbs
await—; desire—; enter—; intersperse with —s; miss—; neglect—; observe—; present —; scuttle through—; seize—; seek—; spurn —; widen into—; —affords; —discloses; —narrows; —offers; —promises; —reveals.
(See chasm, gate, door, opportunity, chance.)

OPERA

verbs
applaud—; aspire to—; attend—; compose —; conceive—; enjoy—; fancy—; patronize —; perform—; produce—; subscribe to—; —allures; —attracts; —captivates; —delights; —diverts; —enamors; —enchants; —enraptures; —enthralls; —fascinates; —flourishes; —thrills.
(See melodrama, theatre, play, music, drama.)

OPERATE (v)

adverbs
onerously; insidiously; mechanically; scientifically;injuriously; skillfully; deftly; effectually; primarily; economically; mystically;

legitimately; viciously; defensively; legally; rhythmically; laboriously; logically; mentally; physiologically; physically; psychologically; disastrously; maligantly; surgically; hygienically.

(See manipulate, manage, handle.)

OPERATION (*general*)

adjectives
gradual; primary; difficult; economical; subsequent; celestial; offensive; excessive; gas-wasting; low-gear; efficient; costly; wasteful; expensive; powerful; military; mythic; decisive; ultimate; justifiable; hazardous; expeditious; elaborate; legitimate; vicious; fiscal; industrial; diversified; important; active; gigantic; divine; successful; ceaseless; defensive; relentless; fiery; smooth; business; authentic; undisturbed; unlimited; hygienic; rhythmic; immediate; distinct; vandalic; intermediate; sequential; imperceptible; proposed; tremendous; preliminary; laborious; logical; mental; mining; primitive; brilliant; unprecedented; disastrous; delicate; malignant; surgical; exploratory.

verbs
absorb in—; assimilate in—; coordinate—s; curtail—; demonstrate—; employ—; execute—; expand—; expedite—; facilitate—; frustrate—; mask—; paralyze—; promote—; repeat—; subject to—; suspend—; transact—; —renews.

(See action, activity, process.)

OPERATION (*surgical*)

verbs
advocate—; contraindicate—; convalesce from—; entail—; perform—; recover from—; recuperate from—; repeat—; submit to—; undergo—; witness—; —allays; —alleviates; —restores; —revitalizes; —scars.

(See abortion, procedure, surgery.)

OPERATIVE

adverbs
skilfully; profitably; actively; serviceably; wonderfully; successfully; eminently; conspicuously; amazingly; expertly; deftly; smoothly; dexterously; adroitly; cleverly; usefully; advantageously; currently; locally; incessantly; apparently; evidently.

OPERATOR

verbs
hinder—; recommend—; —controls; —despatches; —effects; —engages in; —executes; —handles; —investigates; —manipulates; —observes; —performs; —plies; —undertakes; —wields.

(See agent, engineer.)

OPIATE

verbs
addict to—s; administer—; inject—; —allays; —alleviates; —anaesthetizes; —balms; —eases; —lulls; —narcotizes; —numbs; —paralyzes; —restrains; —soothes; —tranquillizes.

(See narcotic, drug.)

OPINION

adjectives
conflicting; erroneous; well-founded; preconceived; weightier; fallacious; dispassionate; vulgar; triumphant; optimistic; imperfect; admitted; inconsistent; weening; lagging; mistaken; unequivocal; dissenting; unanimous; immediate; liberal; hard; essential; vain; decorous; ill; misguided; diverse (pl); presumed; clashing; effeminate; half-fabulous; intolerant; hideous; confirmed; candid; desponding; contrary; universal; progressive; plausible; singular; golden; hasty; conciliating; humble; discretional; true; temperate; speculative; undisguised; transient; present-day; contradictory; avowed; realistic; political; extravagant; dwarfed; emancipated; conservative; non-evolutionary; valueless; damning; exaggerated; expert; imperious; religious; public; unbiased; high; antagonistic; unsought; prevailing; adverse; atheistical; critical; reprehensible; authoritative; sincere; unasked; well-informed; monstrous; forceful; swollen; individual; inmost; revolutionary; false; editorial; dissenting; confidential; exalted; adulterated; awed; eccentric; contemptuous; mighty; expressed; implied; prevalent; rash; established; light.

verbs
abandon—; adhere to—; air—; alter—; assert—; base—on; bow to—of; cling to—; coincide with—; concur in—; condemn—; confirm—; controvert—; convert from—; convey—; crystallize—; defend—; dispute—; echo—; embody—; enforce—; formulate—; further—; justify—; modify—; muzzle—; offer—; moderate—; modify—; prepare

—; proclaim—; qualify—; reconcile —s; reflect—; rescind—; reserve—; retain—; shade—; shape—; submit—; subscribe to—; utter—; venture—; voice—; —carries weight; —s clash; —s conflict; —crystallizes; —s differ; —s diverge; —fluctuates; —hinges upon; —prevails.

(See idea, belief, inference, judgment.)

OPINIONATED

adverbs

insufferably; conceitedly; selfishly; egotistically; pompously; arrogantly; domineeringly; dogmatically; bigotedly; narrowly; ridiculously; senselessly; absurdly; foolishly; stubbornly; doggedly; doltishly; intolerably; decidedly; unbearably; unreasonably; offensively; blatantly; brazenly; rudely; grossly; crassly.

OPIUM

verbs

drowse under—; smoke—; smuggle—in; steep in—; trade in—; traffic in—; —allays; —assuages; —benumbs; —blunts; —deadens; —dulls; —enslaves; —mitigates; —palliates; —poisons; —stimulates; —stuns; —stupefies; —subdues.

(See opiate, narcotic, drug.)

OPOSSUM

verbs

—adheres to; —anchors to; —claws; —clings; —feigns; —grips; —licks; —mounts; —pouches; —preys on; —rolls; —seizes.

(See animal.)

OPPONENT

adjectives

formidable; political; honorable; strenuous; extreme; partizan; imaginary; worthy; determined; agile; masterful; malignant; foremost; fervent; energetic; prominent; unsympathetic.

verbs

capitulate to—; conquer—; discredit—; elude—; oust—; overwhelm—; rebuff—; —antagonizes; —condemns; —contends; —contests; —defends; —disputes; —maintains; —objects; —proposes; —resists; —struggles; —yields to.

(See foe, enemy, competitor, antagonist, adversary.)

OPPORTUNE

adverbs

delightfully; seasonably; fortunately; luckily; happily; conveniently; surprisingly; unexpectedly; felicitously; amazingly; particularly; providentially; extraordinarily; splendidly; unusually.

OPPORTUNITY

adjectives

plausible; perennial; exhaustible; golden; favorable; meager; extraordinary; superior; rare; magnificent; abundant; scanty; splendid; spacious; speedy; momentary; favorable; precarious; innumerable (pl); awaited; vast; long-coveted; ample; wasted; tempting; social; characteristic; natural; pleasing; crude; infinite; unusual; propitious; selling; notable; trial; sensational; golden; astounding; money-making; amazing; wonderful; big; superlative; masculine; heaven-sent; ill-annexed; limitless; glorious; boundless; final; well-used; early; convenient; adequate; enervating; indulgent; unequalled; decisive; generous; sorrowful; promising; indefinite; admirable; shrewd; unscrupulous; neglected; educational; irresistible; unsurpassed; growing; attractive; favorable; genuine; lifetime; astonishing; unparalleled; matchless; extra-money; new; profit; surprising; enviable; business; exceptional; non-competitive; grand; greatest.

verbs

afford—; anticipate—; avail oneself of—; awake to—; curtail—for; drain of —s; enlarge —s for; extend—; grasp—; heed—; ignore—; impoverish—for; jump at—; offer —; respond to—; seize—; sense—; snatch —; —beckons; —blooms; —fades; —flees; —knocks; —presents itself; —recurs.

(See occasion, opening, chance, possibility.)

OPPOSE (*v*)

adverbs

conscientiously; violently; stubbornly; diametrically; stoutly; virulently; fiercely; gallantly; obstinately; vigorously; ardently; clamorously; persistently; militantly; zealously; strenuously; cantankerously; radically; determinedly; avowedly; prematurely; fatally; maliciously; seditiously; redoubtably; vainly.

(See resist, combat.)

OPPOSED

adverbs
violently; bitterly; subtly; fundamentally; persistently; racially; openly; politically; outspokenly; frankly; candidly; vindictively; fanatically; traditionally; formidably; irreconcilably; relentlessly; utterly; strangely; oddly; ironically; inexplicably; patently; palpably; significantly; basically; alarmingly; unaccountably; unwarrantably; immoderately; unflaggingly; powerfully; unmistakably.

OPPOSITE

adverbs
diametrically; directly; almost; exactly; incompatibly; antagonistically; hostilely; inimically; strangely; mysteriously; contrastingly; oddly; emphatically; curiously.

OPPOSITION

adjectives
cantankerous; uncompromising; radical; persistent; violent; reasonable; serious; determined; slow; powerful; considerable; downright; vigorous; astounding; avowed; rousing; direct; positive; liberal; open; strenuous; peevish; fictitious; bitter; stiffer; virulent; diametric; premature; filibustering; striking; skillful; bloody; fatal; malicious; ticklish; seditious; scholarly; vindictive; parliamentary; frightful; continual; redoubtable; brawling; vain; fierce.

verbs
align with—; antagonize—; anticipate—; batter down—; brook—; browbeat—; confront—; deter—; dispel—; encounter—; incite to—; manifest—; mow down—; mystify—; overcome—; persevere against—; provoke to—; pummel—; raise—; revive—; stimulate—; stir—; vanquish—; —clamors; —melts away; —stiffens.

(See objection, hostility, antagonism, defiance, interference.)

OPPRESS (*v*)

adverbs
sorely; sternly; vigorously; viciously; ruthlessly; odiously; dictatorially; unremittingly; cruelly; spiritually; rigidly; hideously.

(See persecute, aggrieve.)

OPPRESSION

adjectives
military; ruthless; discomfited; proud; ungrateful; ungracious; needless; odious; iron; long; indefinable; dismal; heavy; unbounded; subordinate; systematic; unremitting; super-inhuman.

verbs
bear—; chain to—; crumble under—; decry—; resist—; sacrifice to—; shake off—; slay by—; struggle with—; tyrannize wtih—; —chafes; —controls; —crushes; —destroys; —frustrates; —hushes; —masters; —ravages; —reigns; —silences.

(See burden, cruelty, tyranny, depression, imposition.)

OPPRESSIVE

adverbs
heavily; unbearably; intolerably; insufferably; dismally; cruelly; barbarously; bitterly; tyrannically; heartbreakingly; gallingly; domineeringly; savagely; brutally; inhumanly; drearily; ruthlessly; needlessly; systematically; incredibly; incomparably; grievously; obnoxiously; shockingly; appallingly; frightfully; odiously; tragically.

OPPRESSOR

verbs
boycott—; chastise—; crumble under—; defy—; denounce—; despise—; fear—; inveigh against—; loathe—; master—; resist—; —chains; —confiscates; —crushes; —despoils; —destroys; —dominates; —enforces; —enslaves; —exterminates; —fetters; —gags; —horrifies; —hushes; —inflicts; —intimidates; —misrules; —oppresses; —outrages; —persecutes; —reigns; —restricts; —rules; —silences; —spies; —suppresses; —terrorizes; —tramples; —tyrannizes; —victimizes.

(See tyrant, dictator.)

OPTIMISM

adjectives
slothful; radiant; placid; sober; incurable; misguided; bourgeois; innate; superb; baseless; unfailing; shallow; feeble; horrible; extravagant; militant; strident; undue; hollow; pretended.

verbs
bolster by—; crown with—; dispel—; feign—; pretend—; voice—; yield to—; —blinds; —cheers; —comforts; —cools; —encourages; —glows; —impresses; —penetrates; —pierces; —prevails; —stimulates; —warms.

(See hope, cheerfulness.)

OPTIMISTIC

adverbs
joyously; mysteriously; unaccountably; unreasonably; pleasurably; thrillingly; impatiently; ardently; charmingly; crazily; radiantly; superbly; unduly.

OPTION

verbs
abandon—; acquire—; assign—to; execute —; exercise—; purchase—; reject—; share —; specify in—; utilize—; vote on—; —expires; —guarantees; —insures; —provides; —relinquishes; —reserves; —seduces; —tempts.

(See choice, alternative, preference.)

OPULENCE

adjectives
lazy; undemocratic; approaching; unearned; sinful.

OPULENT

adverbs
amazingly; incredibly; fantastically; fabulously; magnificently; splendidly; monstrously; unbelievably; superbly; unsurpassably; incomparably; marvellously; miraculously; curiously; inexplicably; enviably; admirably; gloriously; contentedly; complacently.

ORACLE

adjectives
godlike; riddling; received; heathen; sublime; prescient; stalking; ambiguous; literary; ancient; mendacious; burning; commanding.

ORACULAR

adverbs
shrewdly; sapiently; wisely; alarmingly; frequently; confidently; dogmatically; blusteringly; solemnly; piously; mystically; seriously; gravely; soberly; reverentially; portentously; suddenly; remarkably; reputably; allegedly; avowedly.

ORATE (*v*)

adverbs
vaingloriously; verbosely; melodramatically; sonorously; pontifically; seditiously; facetiously; traitorously; thunderously; inspiringly; monotonously; ornately.

(See speak, talk.)

ORATION

adjectives
powerful; sham; eloquent; passionate; infantile; panegyrical.

verbs
blurt out—; comprehend—; criticize—; deliver—; dispute—; frame—; garnish—with; plan—; pour forth—; recite—; render—; spout—; —declaims; —decries; —exhorts; —expounds; —harangues; —incites; —inflames; —informs; —impassions; —sways.

(See declamation, address, discourse, lecture, speech, sermon.)

ORATOR

adjectives
natural; sand-lot; soapbox; idiosyncratic; stay-at-home; brilliant; political; revolutionary; loud-voiced; distinguished; classical; impassioned; effective; discerning; patriotic; genuine.

verbs
distinguish—; introduce—; —addresses; —arouses; —berates; —bombards; —charms; —declaims; —defends; —delivers; —disquiets; —enchants; —enthralls; —fulminates; —gesticulates; —hurls; —incites; —inflames; —mouths; —pleads; —rants; —raves; —spellbinds; —wields.

(See lawyer, demagogue, attorney, congressman, legislator, minister.)

ORATORICAL

adverbs
splendidly; magnificently; emphatically; eloquently; pompously; bombastically; dramatically; comically; absurdly; vainly; egotistically; ridiculously; unctuously; laughably; needlessly; unreasonably; ludicrously; effectively; impressively; imposingly; brilliantly; ardently; passionately; patriotically; grandiloquently.

ORATORY

verbs
amplify—; burst into—; delight in—; excel in—; judge—; pour—; thunder—; —burns; —enchants; —flows from; —floods; —glitters; —glorifies; —hypnotizes; —impassions; —impresses; —persuades; —streams from; —sways; —thaws; —touches.

(See declamation, orator, talk, speech.)

ORB

adjectives
huge; brilliant; radiant; glaring; shining; freezing; cold; lifeless; sightless; multitudinous (pl); ruined; piercing; prominent; numerous (pl); intelligent; sickly; serene; mounting; fatal; flaming; parent; unfathomable; wan; planetary; mysterious; small; arch; restless; ruddy; whirling.

ORBIT

adjectives
implicated; moral; common; planetary; definite; independent; lurid; respective; mathematical; elliptic.

ORCHARD

adjectives
abounding; blooming; sappy; starry; fantastic; ravaged; new-planted; wind-swept; dripping; festive; beauteous; aromatic.

verbs
blight—; cultivate—; enclose—; fertilize—; frost—; harvest—; irrigate—; plan—; protect—; prune—; rob—; stock from—; tour —; —blooms; —blossoms; —supplies; —yields.

(See crops, farm, tree, fruit.)

ORCHESTRA

adjectives
errant; magnificent; revamped; mammoth; itinerant; nationally-known; broadcasting; favorite; popular; unrivaled; recording.

verbs
direct—; follow—; guide—; lead—; strike up—; uniform—; —accompanies; —attunes to; —beats time; —blares; —charms; —delights; —enchants; —expresses; —greets; —improvises; —pipes; —performs; —sweeps a chord; —tweedles.

(See band, music, musician.)

ORCHESTRAL

adverbs
splendidly; magnificently; tunefully; harmoniously; delightfully; gorgeously; impressively; sonorously; resoundingly; grandly; superbly; brilliantly; dazzlingly; richly; triumphantly.

ORDEAL

adjectives
painful; dreadful; crucial; tremendous; numbing; perilous; premature; coming; fiery.

verbs
bear—; doom to—; endure—; flinch from —; fortify for—; resign to—; submit to—; suffer—; tolerate—; undergo—; wince at—; —agitates; —chastens; —ensues; —proves; —shatters; —sobers; —tests; —verifies.

(See suffering, pain, torture.)

ORDER

(command)

adjectives
peremptory; positive; executive; advance; admirable; divers (pl); liberal; rigid; rarest; extortionate; patriarchal; frantic; vast; abstract; existing; suspicious; preliminary; hostile; spiritual; convulsive; promised; imperative; social; secondary; inferior; sweeping; subsequent; additional; imminent; allied; urgent; superior; makeshift; established; showy; actual; thundering; relenting; conflicting; visible; alphabetical; preposterous; determinate; successive (pl); obstructing; provident; retaliatory; metropolitan; explicit; sinister; treasonable; logical; half-conscious; handsome; privileged; elegant; restricted; marching; spacious; chronological; switchback; notorious; noiseless; unfilled; agrarian; positive; retrograde; tesselated; fraternal; strategic; ill-conceived; sealed; beneficent; contrary; preconcerted; opposite; pretty; gallant; supplementary; internal; welcome; probable; injunction; excellent; shocking; meek; florid; melting; previous; intellectual; gracious; malignant; complacent; lucid; auspicious.

verbs
accept—; comply with—; disregard—; establish—; execute—; flash—; issue—; maintain—; modify—; obey—; preserve—; receive—; record—; rescind—; restore—; violate—; whip into—; —bans; —bars; —compels; —decrees; —hampers; —manifests itself; —reigns.

(See command, commandment, injunction, mandate, discipline.)

ORDER

(organization, system, arrangement)

adjectives
requisite; subsequent; existing; cloistered; festive; favored; valiant; venerable; celest-

ial; vexatious; congenial; imperative; eternal; slender; ethereal; chronological; outward; symmetrical; mystic; eerie; rude; admirable; lower; reiterated; petty; social; solemn; beneficial; dubious; private; revised; economic; different; financial; lofty; honorable; privileged; patrician.

verbs
adhere to—; annihilate—; ape—; bury—; challenge—; establish—; fit into—; institute —; perpetuate—; rage against—; undermine —; —passes; —pervades.
(See arrangement, class, system, government.)

ORDER
verbs (*sales*)
book —s; boost (colloq.)—; confirm—; consign—to; fill—; lose—; overwhelm with —s; procure—; realize—; reject—; ship—; solicit—s; swamp with—s; —s filter in; —grosses; —s mount; —nets; —s pour in; —s slacken.
(See purchase, sales.)

ORDER (v)
adverbs
peremptorily; explicitly; indiscriminately; treacherously; bluffly; reluctantly; insolently; sternly; quaintly; imperiously; congenially; pettishly; dubiously; economically; malignantly.
(See command, dictate.)

ORDERLY
adverbs
satisfactorily; unusually; wonderfully; remarkably; particularly; always; altogether; admirably; regularly; uniformly; scrupulously; meticulously; habitually; unwontedly; uncommonly.

ORDINANCE
adjectives
oppressive; divine; surrendered; solemn; secession; ill-starred; detested.

verbs
administer—; cite—; codify—; confirm—; enact—; enforce—; formulate—; frame—; promulgate—; remand—; transgress—; violate—; —commands; —decrees; —directs; —enjoins; —imposes; —legalizes; —ordains; —prescribes.
(See edict, decree, law, legislation, mandate.)

ORE
adjectives
useful; good-looking; metallic; massy; pavonine; vermilion-colored; rich; precious; manganese; iridescent; rough.

ORGAN
adjectives (*general*)
full-toned; deep-throated; vital; bodily; singular; discordant; lovely; mysterious; visual; sensual; improper; charming; delicate; deep-laboring; digestive; unique; damaged; sentient; rudimentary; reproductive; respiratory: administrative; generative; ardent; delegated; virile; olfactory.

ORGAN
verbs (*of the body*)
affect—; attack—; cleanse—; congest—; derange—; enliven—; impair—; inflame—; invade—; irrigate—; irritate—; nourish—; tone up—; tune—to; vitalize—; —atrophies; —decays; —functions; —recuperates.
(See heart, kidney, etc.)

ORGANISM
adjectives
finished; vital; political; alert; courageous; aggressive; social; diverse (pl); vegetable; precious; terrific; mysterious; living; active; sensuous; enfeebled; specific; composite; elaborate; molded; unicellular.

verbs
constitute—; culture—; examine—; stain—; study—; —attacks; —excretes; —flourishes; —functions; —invades; —poisons; —reproduces.
(See bacteria, embryo, germ.)

ORGANIZATION
adjectives
inadequate; active; magnificent; complete; accurate; hierarchical; ecclesiastical; far-flung; rudimentary; resounding; various (pl); producing; worthy; efficient; sweetly-functioning; secret; farsighted; vital; underlying; scientific; unified; matchless; constitutional; laborious; elaborate; competitive; well-drilled; distributing; independent; eleemosynary; internal; quasi-benevolent; quasi-military; odious; gigantic; monolithic; associational; nervous; abstinence; chartered; well-formed; stupendous; marvelous; militant; mammoth.

verbs
disband—; dominate—; effect—; encourage —; endow—; envision—; evolve—; foster —; initiate—; penetrate—; perfect—; preside over—; revive—; sponsor—; subsidize —; suppress—; weaken—; —expands; —functions; —s merge.
(See club, league, establishment.)

ORGANIZE (v)

adverbs
admirably; politically; seditiously; treacherously; radically; delicately; efficiently; constitutionally; independently; militantly.
(See arrange, form.)

ORGANIZED

adverbs
highly; carefully; secretly; skilfully; recently; elaborately; simply; surreptitiously; admirably; independently; complexly; regularly; methodically; systematically; strategically; cleverly; intelligently; masterfully; fully; efficiently; marvellously; incomparably.

ORGY

adjectives
bloodiest; speculative; disgusting; emotional; verbal; loathed; sex; lustful; pagan; midnight; disgraceful; nocturnal; drunken; sinful; degrading.

verbs
carouse in—; feast in—; indulge in—; plunge into—; recoil from—; revel in—; submerge in—; wallow in—; welter in—; —debauches; —gratifies; —intoxicates; —nauseates; —palls; —revolts; —wearies.
(See merriment, sin, drunkenness.)

ORIGIN

adjectives
volcanic; unpolished; humble; supernatural; psychogenic; variant; remote; doubtful; genial; miraculous; accidental; bourgeois; genetic; overseas; subjective; celestial; moral; racial; contractual; recent; classical; obscure; communal; antique; ultimate; legendary; fiery; modern; ignoble; common; recent; soulless; synthetic; childish; germinal; historical; illegitimate; plebeian; proximate; abnormal; evolutionary; medieval.

verbs
ascribe—to; derive—from; mist—; outline —; owe—to; question—; reveal—; shroud—in; trace—; uncover—; —explains; —revolves about.
(See birth, beginning, cause, source.)

ORIGINAL

adjectives
select; authenticated; uncertain; vivid.

verbs
alter—; conceive—; copy—; counterfeit—; create—; design—; deviate from—; diverge from—; duplicate—; exhibit—; fabricate—; imitate—; modify—; outdo—; overshadow —; parallel—; prize—; reproduce—; treasure—.
(See model, duplicate, copy.)

ORIGINALITY

adjectives
everyday; characteristic; fixed; refreshing; unconscious; ignorant; reckless; intellectual; prophetic; notable; illiterate; absolute; contra-distinguished; transcendent; inspired.

verbs
dispense with—; encourage—; exercise—; foster—; gain—; induce—; inspire—; lack —; require—; reward—; stifle—; stimulate —; stress—; urge—; value—; want—; —attracts; —flourishes; —merits.
(See initiative, novelty, ability, talent.)

ORIGINATE (v)

adverbs
artificially; primevally; mysteriously; exclusively; authenticatedly; germinally; volcanically; celestially; legitimately; normally; mythically.
(See begin, start.)

ORNAMENT

adjectives
foliated; literary; lovely; sweet; insipid; conspicuous; enviable; heraldic; wealthy; feather-inlaid; glittering; distinguished; appropriate; elaborate; characteristic; beseeming; wonted; vacant; simple; trifling; sculptured; complicated; meretricious; showy; fatal; bedecking; gold-embossed; historic; desirable; delightful; barbaric.

verbs
convert into—; discard—; fashion—; flourish—; strip off —s; —beautifies; —s bedeck; —bedizens; —decorates; —embellishes; —

emblazons; —enriches; —furbishes; —garnishes; —gilds; —glitters; —spangles; —trims.

(See finery, feather, design, button, bead, braid.)

ORNAMENT (v)

adverbs

grotesquely; gaudily; tastefully; decoratively; profusely; insipidly; conspicuously; appropriately; elaborately; simply; meretriciously; barbarically.

(See decorate, embellish.)

ORNAMENTAL

adverbs

gracefully; pleasantly; delightfully; artistically; unusually; highly; remarkably; tastefully; unbelievably; delicately; structurally; gaudily; floridly; cheaply; richly; scarcely; beautifully; clumsily; daintily; conspicuously; appropriately; barbarically; exotically; impressively; smartly; gorgeously; particularly; noticeably; expensively.

ORNAMENTATION

adjectives

whimsical; graceful; bristling; riotous; hideous; rich; floral.

ORNATE

adverbs

absurdly; unusually; surprisingly; remarkably; highly; uncommonly; peculiarly; curiously; unexpectedly; unwontedly; gaudily; smartly; flashily; richly; gorgeously; splendidly; colorfully; magnificently; brilliantly; architecturally; conspicuously; strangely; attractively; gracefully.

ORPHAN

adjectives

frail; exotic; white-faced; helpless; lonely; homeless.

ORTHODOX

adverbs

regularly; highly; unusually; rigidly; strictly; sternly; severely; uncompromisingly; intolerantly; dogmatically; bigotedly; narrowly; admirably; reverently; consistently; conventionally; conformably; invariably; conspicuously; unyieldingly; soundly; faithfully; truly.

OSCILLATION

adjectives

electric; gorgeous; vibrating; rushing.

OSTENTATION

adjectives

inelegant; mourning; isolated; minor; vain; ironical; brusque.

OSTENTATIOUS

adverbs

deliberately; significantly; purposely; sagaciously; impressively; absurdly; foolishly; egotistically; pompously; blatantly; noisily; arrogantly; dramatically; spectacularly; ridiculously; showily; ludicrously; cheaply; disgustingly; habitually.

OSTRACISM

verbs

deserve—; endure—; live down—; merit—; result in—; —banishes; —castigates; —crushes; —deprecates; —disparages; —excludes; —estranges; —exiles; —outlaws; —reprimands; —secludes; —sequesters; —shuts out.

(See banishment, obscurity.)

OUTBREAK

adjectives

incipient; sporadic; curious; periodical; rebellious; dusky; unexpected; vehement; audible; occasional.

verbs

aggravate—; alleviate—; down—; excite—; foment—; fulminate in—; incite—; instigate—; irritate to—; launch—; mitigate—; provoke—; quell—; quench—; suppress—; —disunites; —embroils; —foams; —fumes; —gushes; —razes; —scorches; —shocks; —thunders; —vents.

(See rebellion, revolution, eruption.)

OUTBURST

adjectives

sudden; restrained; warrantable; wild; spontaneous; mutinous; emotional; overwhelming; eloquent; rash; sacred; passionate; jolly; lyrical; unprecedented; thunderous; tempestuous; national; petulant; swift; sincere; hysterical; thoughtless.

verbs

excite—; plague to—; quell—; quiet—; staunch—; —boils; —discharges; —drains; —distracts; —effervesces; —emanates; —

evacuates; —fevers; —flushes; —gushes; —heats; —issues; —oozes; —perturbs; —rages; —storms; —strains; —wears away.

(See explosion, eruption, attack, onslaught.)

OUTCAST

adjectives

nameless; wretched; houseless; miserable; scathed; diseased; destitute; blighted; reprobated; shamefaced; wronged; ragged.

OUTCAST

adverbs

pitiably; reprehensibly; deservedly; viciously; wretchedly; miserably; wrongfully; pathetically; pitifully; shamefully; disgracefully; ingloriously; disreputably; scandalously; unfortunately; forlornly; desolately; obscurely; humiliatingly; cruelly.

OUTCOME

adjectives

eventual; useless; sublime; strangest; felicitous; unlucky; fatal.

verbs

announce—; anticipate—; blight—; contemplate—; declare—; determine—; doom—; effect—; endanger—; foresee—; predestine—; predict—; preordain—; prophesy—; temporize—; threaten—; —disappoints; —hinges on; —staggers; forestall—.

(See issue, consequence, result, effect.)

OUTCRY

adjectives

passionate; hysterical; absurd; violent; indignant; pitiful; diabolical.

verbs

bawl—; bellow—; mingle with—ies; minimize—; muffle—; restrain—; squeal—; still—; suppress—; whoop—; —bewails; —bursts forth; —clamors; —deafens; —deplores; —dies; —fades; —laments; —scandalizes; —wrings at; raise—; stifle—.

(See cry, exclamation, howl, noise)

OUTFIT

adjectives

colorful; spring; luxurious; pert; demure; effective; queer.

verbs

accoutre in—; array in—; attire in—; divest of—; don—; drape—; equip with—; gear in—; invest in—; prepare—; refurbish—; renew—; rig in—; slip on—; strip off—; trap in—; —enrobes; —envelops; —mantles.

(See coat, overcoat, jacket.)

OUTFLOW

verbs

breast—; check—; contend with—; control—; cope with—; curb—; dam—; filter—; gauge—; oppose—; resist—; restrain—; restrict—; stem—; —drains; —effuses; —endangers; —exudes; —gushes; —spouts; —sweeps away.

(See flow, outpouring.)

OUTGROW (*v*)

adverbs

manifestly; prolifically; unrestrictedly; prodigiously; abundantly; abnormally.

(See surpass, grow.)

OUTLANDISH

adverbs

extraordinarily; surprisingly; strikingly; ridiculously; boorishly; doltishly; heathenishly; meretriciously; oddly; monstrously; indecorously; particularly; shockingly; uncivilly; absurdly; egregiously; unaccountably; singularly; unpleasantly.

OUTLAW

adjectives

excommunicated; renegade; tattered; dauntless.

OUTLAW (*v*)

adverbs

legitimately; legally; socially; morally; spiritually; economically; timorously; passionately; traditionally.

(See interdict, renounce.)

OUTLAY

verbs

absorb—; account for—; allow for—; appropriate for—; atone for—; audit—; exhaust—; expend—; fleece of—; garble—; invest—; recoup—; recover—; redeem—; rehabilitate for—; reimburse for—; remit—; restore—; retain—; reward—; subsidize—; —bleeds (colloq.); —drains; —indebts.

(See expenditure, expense, money, payment, profit.)

OUTLET

adjectives
manipulative; convenient; retail; common; satisfactory; obscure; constructive; agreeable; sufficient; emotional; noblest; stupendous.

verbs
bore—; bare—; clog—; crave—; drain—; drill—; effuse from—; emanate from—; exude from—; furnish—; gain—; leak from —; perforate—; plug—; provide—; puncture—; seek—; stem—; strive for—; —gapes; —yawns.
(See hole, chasm, opening.)

OUTLINE

adjectives
vague; sublime; cathedral-like; stubbly; shadowy; rude; circular; precise; fine; picturesque; distinct; rolling; faint; graceful; flowing; delicate; charming; crude; undefined; rugged; misty; harsh; unmistakable; broad; melodic; geographical; analytical; tentative; ghastly; soft; rounded; noble; majestic; irregular; angular; spirited; intellectual; arrowlike; imperfect; depressed; monotonous; lambent.

verbs
analyze—; blot out—; conceive—; diagram —; discern—; draft—; draw—; fashion—; launch into—; organize—; plan—; prepare —; scrutinize—; sketch—; stencil in—; trace —; —abstracts; —abbreviates; —condenses; —contracts; —digests; —guides; —represents; —reviews; —shortens; —skims over; —summarizes.
(See figure, line, map, diagram, sketch.)

OUTLINE (v)

adverbs
scholarly; studiously; purposefully; precisely; vaguely; delicately; rudely; crudely; unmistakably; geographically; intellectually; monotonously.
(See sketch, draw.)

OUTLOOK

adjectives
cosmopolitan; confident; savage; philosophic; passionate; desolate; tolerant; humorous; sectional; unwarped; disheartening; superb; model; fundamental.

verbs
alter—; blacken—; broaden—; convert—; darken—; dim—; foster—; modify—; narrow—; overcast—; reverse—; shade—; transform—; widen—; —brightens; —cheers; —disheartens.
(See future, hope.)

OUTPOURING

adjectives
unstudied; passionate; spontaneous; fervent; morbid; unsearchable.

verbs
erupt in—; escape—; evade—; quell—; restrain—; restrict—; stem—; —cools; —diminishes; —eases; —endangers; —immerses; —quenches; —ravages; —relieves; —roars; —swells; —weakens.
(See flow, outflow.)

OUTPUT

adjectives
prolific; excessive; profitable; mechanical; steady.

verbs
amplify—; augment—; decrease—; develop —; diminish—; dwarf—; enlarge—; expand —; govern—; halt—; market—; restrict—; stem—; treble—; utilize—; —climbs; —declines; —depreciates; —dwindles; —ebbs; —overloads; —shrinks; —subsides; —wanes; swell—.
(See production, crops, proceeds, product.)

OUTRAGE

adjectives
intolerant; unparalleled; dreadful; treacherous; uncivil; flagrant; atrocious; hideous; living; frantic; vile; miserable; brutal; cowardly; highhanded; ungentlemanly; rancorous; incredible.

verbs
absolve of—; acquit of—; avenge—; brand as—; commit—; condone—; countenance—; decry—; denounce—; disparage—; fulminate against—; incite—; inflict—; perpetrate —; punish—; —aggrieves; —blights; —debases; —despoils; —fans; —infuriates; —perverts; —stigmatizes.
(See injury, indignity, insult, atrocity.)

OUTRAGE (v)

adverbs
grossly; foully; treacherously; flagrantly;

atrociously; hideously; brutally; sexually; rancorously; incredibly.
(See offend, encroach.)

OUTRAGEOUS

adverbs
barbarously; despicably; incredibly; atrociously; intolerably; insufferably; appallingly; shockingly; execrably; dreadfully; unimaginably.

OUTSKIRTS

verbs
avoid—; circumvent—; direct to—; flank—; fortify—; hover on—; stretch to—; swerve to—; —border; —edge; —encompass; —extend; —parallel; —range; —surround.
(See boundary, border, barrier, edge, line.)

OUTSPOKEN

adverbs
unfortunately; unhappily; unwisely; foolishly; unpleasantly; displeasingly; absurdly; injudiciously; impolitically; indiscreetly; recklessly; pertly; impertinently; disrespectfully; rudely; boorishly; uncivilly; ignorantly; carelessly; brusquely; bluntly; disagreeably; roughly.

OUTSTRIP (v)

adverbs
masterfully; physically; mentally; economically; legally; vigorously; swiftly; overwhelmingly.
(See surpass, outgrow.)

OUTWEIGH (v)

adverbs
enormously; tremendously; markedly; indubitably; characteristically; personally.
(See exceed, surpass.)

OUTWIT (v)

adverbs
cunningly; subtly; deftly; slyly; dexterously; treacherously; nimbly.
(See defeat, surpass, cheat.)

OVARY

verbs
dislocate—; displace—; fertilize—; fructify—; impregnate—; inflame—; operate on—; remove—; sterilize—; —atrophies; —discharges; —distends; —enlarges; —functions; —generates; —germinates; —reproduces; —secretes; —shrivels; —swells.
(See organ.)

OVATION

adjectives
perfect; tremendous; significant; thunderous; enthusiastic.

verbs
rejoice in—; render—; shout—; tender—; voice—; —acclaims; —cheers; —clamors; —gratifies; —honors; —rewards; —rings; —thunders.
(See cheering, celebration, triumph.)

OVERBEARING

adverbs
insufferably; pompously; arrogantly; egotistically; selfishly; tyrannically; importantly; domineeringly; intolerably; disagreeably; imperiously; superciliously; shockingly; appallingly; despicably; contemptibly; impertinently; extremely; presumptuously; terribly.

OVERCOAT

adjectives
heavy; worn; woolly.

verbs
array in—; divest of—; don—; fray—; huddle in—; model—; patch—; peel off—; penetrate—; shed—; tailor—; —assures; —fends off; —guarantees; —insulates; —insures against; —protects; —shelters; —wards off.
(See coat, jacket, outfit, clothing.)

OVERCOME (v)

adverbs
physically; militantly; vigorously; passionately; stoutly; defiantly; mentally; legally; energetically.
(See conquer, master.)

OVERFLOW

adjectives
natural; periodic; kind; spontaneous; simple.

OVERFLOW (v)

adverbs
naturally; prodigiously; periodically; seasonally; spontaneously.
(See flood, fill, pervade.)

OVERGROWN

adverbs

hopelessly; sadly; luxuriantly; weedily; irremediably; irrecoverably; shiftlessly; carelessly; neglectfully; terribly; desperately; irreparably; curiously; inexplicably; unfortunately; unrecognizably.

OVERHEAD

verbs

augment—; charge to—; cover—; cut—; lighten—; meet—; —ascends; —descends; —mounts; —staggers; —swamps.

(See expense, sum, amount, profits.)

OVERHEAR (*v*)

adverbs

inadvertently; innocently; accidentally; coincidentally; unflatteringly; tragically; fatally; thoughtlessly

(See hear.)

OVERLAP (*v*)

adverbs

richly; amply; largely; statistically; unavoidably; repeatedly; harmoniously.

(See encroach.)

OVERLOADED

adverbs

tremendously; shamefully; terribly; pathetically; pitiably; dangerously; alarmingly; disastrously; ruinously; dreadfully; unwisely; foolishly; absurdly; wretchedly; unfortunately; imprudently; awfully; bitterly; intolerably; unbearably; cruelly.

OVERLOOK (*v*)

adverbs

obligingly; tacitly; magnanimously; sullenly; naturally; selfishly; unfeelingly; delicately.

(See neglect, disregard, ignore.)

OVERPOWER (*v*)

adverbs

vigorously; physically; brutally; lustfully; cruelly; dictatorially; bestially.

(See conquer, overcome.)

OVERRATE (*v*)

adverbs

grossly; carelessly; confidently; egoistically; mistakenly; fatally; intellectually; morbidly.

(See exaggerate.)

OVERRUN (*v*)

adverbs

destructively; overwhelmingly; prodigiously; atrociously; brutally; victoriously; pugnaciously; seasonally; periodically.

(See invade, trespass.)

OVERSIGHT

adjectives

unparalleled; unwary; imprudent.

OVERSTATEMENT

verbs

avoid—; concoct—; foist—upon; purvey—; resort to—; —amplifies; —beguiles; —cheats; —colors; —decoys; —deludes; —embroiders; —exaggerates; —heightens; —libels; —lures; —magnifies; —meshes; —misleads; —strains; —stretches; —swindles.

(See exaggeration.)

OVERTHROW (*v*)

adverbs

decisively; victoriously; illegally; brutally; vindictively; petulantly; mutinously; unrestrainedly; tempestuously; seditiously; passionately; diabolically.

(See overpower, defeat.)

OVERTONE

adjectives

attendant; objectionable; pathetic; brisk.

OVERTURE

adjectives

diplomatic; unfeeling; ineffectual; delicate; joint; friendly.

OVUM

verbs

develop—; discharge—; exude—; fertilize—; impregnate—; secrete—; —enlarges; —generates; —germinates; —reproduces; —unites with; —yields.

(See egg, cell.)

OWE (*v*)

adverbs

fatally; hopelessly; tragically; fatefully; morally; spiritually; stupendously.

(See obligate.)

OWL

adjectives

moping; staring; melodious; vile; great; horned; nocturnal; clamorous; uncouth.

verbs
—attacks; —bodes; —bolts; —circles; —clamors; —claws; —devours; —flutters; —glides off; —grasps; —hisses; —hoots; —mocks; —perches; —pounces on; —protests; —prowls; —reigns; —sails; —sallies forth; —scans; —screams; —screeches; —shrieks; —skims along; —stares; —wails; —whistles; —explores.
(See bird.)

OWN (v)

adverbs
privately; rightfully; legally; legitimately; originally; enthusiastically; gratefully; luxuriously; selfishly.
(See have.)

OWNER

adjectives
rightful; truculent; same; enthusiastic; untutored; original; favored; dishonest; unfortunate; legitimate.

verbs
divulge—; fine—; indemnify—; levy against —; tax—; —assents; —auctions; —bans; —bars; —disputes; —enlarges; —evicts; —leases; —lodges; —mortgages; —occupies; —prohibits; —renovates; —rents.
(See manager, management, employer.)

OWNERSHIP

adjectives
enthusiastic; beneficial; undisputed; municipal; implied; multiple.

OX

adjectives
stately; primitive; well-fed; fattened.

verbs
burden—; employ—; fetter—; harness—; load—; tether—; water—; yoke—; —balks; —carries; —charges; —gores; —halts; —hauls; —pulls; —rages.
(See buffalo, livestock, animal, bull, cow.)

OXEN

adjectives
patient; meek-eyed; broad-foreheaded; long-suffering.

OXYGEN

verbs
absorb—; administer—; combine with—; curtail—; dissolve—; employ—; extract— from; lack—; liberate—; prepare—; require —; supply—; unite with—; —invigorates; —restores; —resuscitates; —saves; —sustains; —sterilizes.
(See gas, chemical, medicine, tonic.)

OYSTERS

verbs
can—; consume—; crush—; cull—; cultivate—; dislodge—; dry—; farm—; fatten —; grade—; harvest—; irritate—; market —; prey upon—; rake for—; replant—; scallop—; scrape for—; shuck—; stew—; transplant—; —anchor to; —bob around; —imbed; —spawn.

P

PACE

adjectives
tranquil; unperturbed; swift; stealthy; measured; rapid; restless; incredible; stately; heedless; moderate; breakneck; jaunty; sluggish; hopping; sauntering; furious; precipitate; brisk; dashing; lively; deliberate; even; slow; sentry-like; inoffensive; ragged; eager; divers (pl); tremendous; quick; petty; trembling; evenly-geared; jubilant; killing; portly; quickened; moderate; feverish; terrific.

verbs
allay—; ease—; hold—; maintain—; quicken—; regulate—; set—; slacken—; smooth —; sustain—; —devours; —tires; —wearies.

(See step, gait, speed, stride.)

PACE (v)

adverbs
stormily; excitedly; moodily; meditatively; restlessly; furiously; tranquilly; heedlessly; sluggishly; deliberately; jubilantly; feverishly.

(See walk, amble, step.)

PACIFIC

adverbs
resolutely; calmly; serenely; assiduously; consistently; diplomatically; earnestly; definitely; urgently; quietly; inherently; naturally; insistently; harmoniously; amicably; reassuringly; marvellously

PACIFIST

verbs
defend—; denounce—; oppress—; persecute—; support—; —abstains; —advocates; —arbitrates; —argues; —decries; —hinders; —minimizes; —preserves; —proclaims; —refuses; —resists; —shrinks from.

(See coward.)

PACIFY (v)

adverbs
seductively; profoundly; artfully; domestically; prudently; diplomatically; politically; nationally.

(See calm, appease.)

PACING

adjectives
restless; mechanic; captive; nervous.

PACK

adjectives
damned; crumpled; lathered; baying; clamorous; weighty.

verbs
hunt with—; loose—; muster—; whistle for —; —attacks; —congregates; —defends; —deluges; —disbands; —disburses; —flocks; —gathers; —pursues; —roams; —rushes; —scatters; —storms; —strays; —surges; —throngs; —troops; —unites; —wanders.

(See crowd, flock, herd, hive, horde.)

PACK (v)

adverbs
suffocatingly; densely; scientifically; compactly; tastefully; professionally; deftly; artfully; medically.

(See bundle, wrap.)

PACKAGE

adjectives
convenient; cumbersome; deceptive; enormous; economical; nifty; seductive; bridal; sundry; airtight.

verbs
bear—; bow under—; burden with—; cart —; clutch—; dispatch—; haul—; heap—s on; load with—s; lug—; relieve of—; stoop under—; —weighs; —weights.

(See bundle, parcel.)

PACT

adjectives
futile; defensive; warning; unenforceable; joint; worthless.

verbs
abide by—; acclaim—; bind by—; challenge —; conclude—; confine—to; disregard—; fear—; guard—; implement—; inveigh against—; join—; negotiate—; regard—; scrap—; sustain—; violate—; —allies; —insures; —strengthens; —unites; —weakens.

(See treaty, accord, agreement, bargain, compact, covenant, lease.)

PAD

adjectives
shielding; smooth; thick; soothing.

PADDLE

verbs
chastise with—; dip—; drag—; guide with —; ply—; propel—; strain at—; thwack with—; whack with—; —brushes; —dabbles; —flays; —ploughs; —slides; —smacks; —spanks; —steers; —strikes; —sweeps.
(See oar.)

PADDLE (*v*)

adverbs
noiselessly; desperately; skillfully; deftly; indefatigably; arduously; unerringly; intrepidly.
(See row, propel.)

PADLOCK

adjectives
stout; jingling; burglar-proof; trusty.

PAGANISM

adjectives
aesthetic; poetic; devoted; honest; extreme.

verbs
convert from—; degenerate to—; denounce —; exterminate—; meddle in—; oppose—; practise—; relinquish—; revert to—; sink to—; succumb to—; —blends; —blinds; —destroys; —fancies; —fetters; —outrages; —sacrifices; —worships.
(See atheism, materialism.)

PAGE

adjectives
barren; blistered; storied; long-faded; rattling; historic; fervid; idle; dog-eared; glorious; written; interesting; voluminous; intricate; pregnant; sparkling; colorful; fascinating; provocative; illuminated; labored; naughty; saucy; discolored; classic; poetic; stone; vivacious; succeeding; remote; various (pl); precise; glowing; loitering; impish; vivid; blank; sleepy; luminous; scornful; pretty; knavish; ingenious; unopened; title; lying; wondrous; bare-kneed; boy scout; well-reputed; wormy; crumbling; long; emblazoned; ample; penciled; large-margined.

verbs
bind—s; charge—with; flick—; flip—; fray —; peruse—s; ponder—; reel off—s; skim over—s; sprinkle—s with; stream across—s; —cumbers; —sparkles; splash across—s.
(See sheet, paper, book, copy, advertisement, picture, text.)

PAGEANT

adjectives
idle; dismal; unsubstantial; extensive; imposing; woeful; inspiring; melodious; martial; ostentatious; magnificent; doleful; colorful; insubstantial; crumbling; fond; warlike; motley; gleamy; proud.

verbs
acclaim—; applaud—; solemnize—; stage —; view—; witness—; —colors; —commemorates; —delineates; —depicts; —glitters; —impresses; —portrays; —predicts; —signifies; —symbolizes; —traces; —wends.
(See celebration, demonstration, parade, spectacle.)

PAGEANTRY

adjectives
adventurous; colorful; antique; ostentatious.

PAGODAS

adjectives
delicate; gilded; slender.

PAIL

adjectives
clicking; brimming; immense.

PAIN

adjectives
racking; sharp; gnawing; tolerable; sympathetic; straining; sleepless; hard-featured; rankling; long-stifled; terrible; labor; passing; dull; keen; lonely; stinging; sacrificial; momentary; unbearable; excruciating; impotent; subtle; passionate; scrupulous; yearning; convulsive; intense; severe; lifelong; wise; palpitating; accusing; secret; willing; ceaseless; ecstatic; unrepentant; divine; sublime; wriggling; fearful; utmost; molten; mortal; pure, exquisite; poisonous; poignant; aromatic; vile; violent; pleasurable; hopeless; soothing; extraordinary; infinite; unendurable; burning; rheumatic; helpless; perpetual; quivering; full-blown; unmitigated; mutual; interrupting; incestuous; fierce; numbing; doggish; peculiar; gratuitous; distorted; mingled (pl); penitential; morbid; licensed; tingling; throbbing; unlanguaged; deteriorated; enduring; cancerous; jealous; ex-

treme; long-drawn; travail; immediate; sweet; aching; transforming; courteous; accepted; recreant; acute; soul-racking; perceivable; hidden; needless; conquering; retributive; anticipated; bodily; afflicting; frightful; remorseful; tender; despairing; positive; stabbing; uncommon; voluntary; eternal; agonizing; heartfelt; longing; unsuccessful; grammatical; stifled; vague; cruel; melancholy; tortuous; frenzied.

verbs
accompany by—; aggravate—; allay—; alleviate—; assuage—; attend by—; combat —; deaden—; deprave with—; experience —; give rise to—; inflict—; intensify—; mark by—; mitigate—; occasion—; pant from—; relieve—; report—; seize with—; soothe—; stifle—; still—; subdue—; throb with—; writhe in—; —abates; —agonizes; —departs; —distracts; —extends to; —flashes up; —gnaws; —gripes; —hammers; —lancinates; —persists; —racks; —radiates from; —shoots; —stabs; —subsides.
(See headache, ill, ache, agony, injury, torture, pang, irritation.)

PAIN (v)

adverbs
acutely; intolerably; excruciatingly; poignantly; unendurably; gratuitously; stabbingly; cruelly; agonizingly.
(See hurt, torture.)

PAINFUL

adverbs
distressingly; terribly; intolerably; slightly; dreadfully; noticeably; apparently; excruciatingly; pitiably; unexpectedly; rackingly; intensely; acutely; extraordinarily; extremely; inordinately; unavoidably; moderately; bitterly; grievously; uncomfortably; unaccountably; pathetically; tremendously; deucedly.

PAINLESS

adverbs
happily; marvellously; miraculously; ostensibly; avowedly; allegedly; unbelievably; blessedly; comfortably; wonderfully; amazingly; incredibly; veritably; unaccountably; gratifyingly.

PAINSTAKING

adverbs
carefully; cautiously; meticulously; strikingly; surprisingly; unexpectedly; deftly; expertly; unusually; habitually; inordinately; unnecessarily; patiently; conscientiously; diligently; remarkably; admirably; consistently; unfailingly; courteously.

PAINT

adjectives
plastic; formidable; war; congealed; melodious; filmy; gaudy; lasting.

verbs
blend—; daub—on; scrape—; smear—; —brightens; —covers; —crusts; —emblazons; —enamels; —enriches; —faces; —fades; —gilds; —glosses; —peels; —preserves; —protects; —sheathes; —sheens; —smudges; —tinges; —tints; —veneers; —waterproofs.
(See complexion, hue, shade, color, ink, make-up.)

PAINT (v)

adverbs
gaudily; sensuously; exquisitely; realistically; artistically; consummately; garishly; formidably; atrociously; professionally; eminently; decoratively.
(See sketch, picture.)

PAINTER

adjectives
impressionist; squalid; supreme; ragged; decorative; itinerant; celebrated; eminent; perpetual; methodical; inexhaustible; extreme; distinguished; peripatetic; atheist; embattled; contemporary; continuous; sanguinary; experienced.

verbs
acclaim—; honor—; model for—; —blocks in; —caricaturizes; —chalks out; —dashes off; —delineates; —depicts; —designs; —enamels; —illustrates; —portrays; —scratches out; —shades; —silhouettes; —sketches; —squares out; —symbolizes; —traces.
(See sculptor, poet, artist, writer, painting.)

PAINTING

adjectives
gracious; barbaric; portrait; ornamental; gaudy; noteworthy; contemporary; immort-

al; elaborate; effective; labial; delicate; graceful; freakish; unpurchasable; priceless.

verbs
acclaim—; applaud—; authenticate—; copy —; dash off—; embellish—; exhibit—; illuminate—; illustrate—; prize—; value—; —depicts; —personifies; —portrays; —represents; —symbolizes.
(See picture, pattern, sketch, photograph, masterpiece, canvas.)

PAIR

adjectives
pensive; incestuous; assorted; canniest; trusting; happy; inseparable; immense; innocent; elegant; gorgeous; excitable; newly-married; epic; spindle; bereaved; newly-hatched; illustrious; imprudent; wedded; paltry; particular; ill-sorted; lively.

PALACE

adjectives
bridal; magnificent; enchanted; primeval; high-roofed; rural; floating; pleasure; gorgeous; spacious; fantastic; crystal; celestial; colonnaded; sumptuous; ducal; proud; shingle; pretentious; medieval; diminutive; golden-bright; imperial; domed; ethereal.

verbs
assemble in—; barricade—; besiege—; fortify—; guard—; inhabit—; lease—; lodge in—; loot—; plunder—; quarter in—; ransack—; renovate—; retreat to—; sojourn at —; tenant—; —dazzles; —looms; —towers; —yields.
(See house, castle, abode, dwelling, home, mansion.)

PALATABLE

adverbs
extremely; unusually; unexpectedly; delightfully; delectably; lusciously; surprisingly; remarkably; altogether; deliciously; daintily; tastily; toothsomely; pleasantly; definitely.

PALATE

adjectives
effeminate; unperverted; vitiated; crude; gratified; spoiled; censorious.

verbs
cleave to—; harden—; jade—; malform—; reeducate—; refine—; soften—; tempt—; tickle—; —acclaims; —revolts; —savors; —tempts.
(See taste, appetite.)

PALATIAL

adverbs
gorgeously; splendidly; surprisingly; dazzlingly; brilliantly; luxuriously; overwhelmingly; impressively; imposingly; proudly; magnificently; richly; sumptuously; extraordinarily; magically; superbly; pretentiously; unexpectedly.

PALAVER

adjectives
shameless; windy.

PALE

adverbs
ghastly; horribly; inexplicably; ominously; distressingly; alarmingly; significantly; dangerously; suddenly; strangely; curiously; oddly; sadly; disturbingly; naturally; unnaturally; significantly; unaccountably; noticeably; timidly; nervously; fearfully; apprehensively; remarkably; uncommonly.

PALENESS

adjectives
marble; pastry; deadly; natural; livid; pained; unnatural; grisly.

PALETTE

adjectives
crowded; radiant; glowing.

PALFREY

adjectives
superb; good; small; dainty.

PALISADE

adjectives
gothic; nature-hewn; impregnable.

PALL

adjectives
leaden; fearful; lurid; fleecy; universal; velvet; dark; motionless.

verbs
cast—over; —cloaks; —descends; —disgusts; —enshrouds; —mantles; —nauseates; —subdues; —veils.
(See gloom, darkness, dusk, haze, night.)

PALLET

adjectives
curtainless; wretched; hard.

PALLOR

adjectives
lovely; pasty; chalky; bloodless; petal; luminous; deepening; wan; translucent; ashen; shadowy; ivory; dusky; swarthy; ghastly; moon-lighted; deadly; first-communion.

PALM

adjectives
sweating; ennobling; blistered; labor-hardened; calloused; sentry-like; occasional; branded; virginal; delicate; satin; sudden-moistured; sheltering; upreared; sympathetic; grimy; horny; feathery; white-gloved; slanted; scooped; paddling; moon-lit; verdant; solitary; ashen-colored; graceful; itching; lifeless; gorgeous; supplicating; thrilling; gauntleted; extended; meaningful; open.

verbs
clench—; clinch in—; clutch in—; cover—; cross—with; cup—; grasp in—; read—; retain in—; transfer to—; —itches; —unfolds.
(See hand.)

PALMY

adverbs
altogether; wondrously; happily; desirably; marvellously; miraculously; affluently; luckily; prosperously; agreeably; buoyantly; providentially; unexpectedly; strikingly; unbelievably; exhilaratingly; hopefully.

PALPITATION

adjectives
violent; horrible; blissful; skyey.

PALSIED

adverbs
tragically; venerably; hopelessly; miserably; pitiably; obviously; manifestly; irremediably; shakily; wretchedly; crookedly; infirmly; ingloriously; resentfully; helplessly; pathetically; completely.

PAMPHLET

adjectives
successive; controversial; truth-telling; ironical; little; allegorical; belligerent; scurrilous; libellous; seditious; descriptive.

verbs
circulate—; comment on—; criticize—; digest—; disseminate—s; edit—; issue—; peruse—; publish—; scatter—s; spread—s; —advertises; —discusses; —proclaims.
(See book, catalogue, magazine, publication, periodical.)

PAN

adjectives
greased; brimming; heated.

verbs
blacken—; brandish—; churn in—; grease—; liquefy in—; melt in—; rinse—; roast in—; scar—; scour—; scrape—; —seethes; —simmers; —steams; —whistles.
(See dish, kettle, pot, frying-pan.)

PANACEA

verbs
ascribe to—; brand as—; denounce—; deprecate—; disparage—; introduce—; offer—; proffer—; propose—; scoff at—; scorn—; seek—; sneer at—; spring—; suggest—; —corrects; —cures; —heals.
(See plan, remedy.)

PANE

adjectives
dingy; rain-streaked; twinkling; small; sparkling; quaint; clouded; dim-streaming; greenish; half-translucent; unbreakable.

PANEL

adjectives
worm-fence; complete; horizontal; brick-like.

PANG

adjectives
sweet; jealous; brutal; death; irresistible; abiding; bitter; maddening; acute; morbid; unceasing; still-varying; sharp; fierce; personal; short; impossible; throbbing; deep; joyful; vivid; intolerable; faint; vacant; wasting; icy.

verbs
endure—; —convulses; —cramps; —cuts; —deceives; —deludes; —excruciates; —misleads; —pierces; —shoots through; —tortures; —twinges.
(See pain, ache, affliction, agony, anguish, torture.)

PANIC

adjectives
terror-stricken; evident; commercial; guilty; precocious; long-feared; uncontrollable; intense; motionless; bewildered; sudden; memorable; subterranean; prevailing; widespread; needless.

verbs
fall into—; flinch in—; flutter in—; halt—; hesitate in—; overcome with—; overwhelm by—; provoke—; quiver in—; result in—; shudder in—; sink into—; stampede in—; survive—; throb in—; throw into—; tremble in—; —deepens; —descends upon; —ensues; —hangs over; —overpowers; —seizes; —spreads.
(See alarm, fright, terror, fear, horror, consternation.)

PANICKY

adverbs
extremely; intensely; absurdly; reasonably; naturally; significantly; astonishingly; suddenly; terribly; nervously; timidly; bashfully; shyly; unaccountably; inexplicably; amazingly; strangely; curiously; unreasoningly; unnecessarily; unfortunately; avowedly; ominously; unluckily.

PANIC-STRICKEN

adverbs
unfortunately; nervously; groundlessly; hysterically; needlessly; terribly; helplessly; utterly; suddenly; horribly; disastrously; appallingly; unaccountably.

PANORAMA

adjectives
surprising; miserable; long-anticipated; characteristic; misty; brilliant; magnificent; limitless; beautiful; moving; specious; glamorous; colorful.

verbs
luxuriate in—; mar—; perceive—; revel in —; shade—; survey—; view—; —awes; —bewitches; —blends; —delights; —enchants; —flows; —gratifies; —impresses; —spreads; —unfolds; —unrolls.
(See landscape, view, picture.)

PANT (*v*)

adverbs
breathlessly; voluptuously; hoarsely; excitedly; eagerly; exhaustedly; prodigiously.
(See gasp, puff.)

PANTHER

verbs
lasso—; trap—; —attacks; —charges; —claws; —dodges; —glides; —hisses; —leaps; —paws; —rolls over; —scratches; —skulks; —slinks; —snarls; —springs; —tears; —yowls.
(See leopard, animal.)

PANTING

adjectives
voluptuous; hoarse; grievous.

PANTOMIME

adjectives
tongueless; ambiguous; careless; indifferent; shadowy; expressive.

verbs
convey in—; dash off—; denote by—; emphasize—; entertain with—; excel at—; exhibit—; represent in—; signify by—; —amuses; —diverts; —dramatizes; —expresses; —mimics; —outrages; —suggests.
(See drama, magic, comedy, opera, actions, melodrama.)

PANTOMIME (*v*)

adverbs
animatedly; vigorously; expressively; artistically; suggestively; professionally; obscenely.
(See gesture, gesticulate.)

PANTS (*colloq.*)

adjectives
striped; invisible; distinct; tight-fitting.

verbs
alter—; cuff—; divest of—; don—; drape —; hitch up—; patch—; refurbish—; repair—; tailor—; —bag; —flare; —fray; —shriek; —tatter.
(See trousers, coat, suit.)

PAPER

adjectives
pulpy; fluttering; patient; infamous; sensitized; provincial; evening; coppery; impecunious; scented; note; diplomatic; several (pl); fragile; influential; country; old-fashioned; fancy; state; special; descriptive; dreadful; illustrated; inconvertible; white; conventional; respectable; moist; marginal; fly-specked; critical; captured; astounding; humorous; thick; ministerial; mammoth;

precious; chancery; incriminating; exclusive; crumpled; unauthenticated; suspicious; anti-regicide; lithographic; admirable; melancholy; short-lived; neatly-folded; scribbled; motley; snowy; stained; discolored; metropolitan; rag; nice; charred; sundry (pl); notable; transmitted; unsafe; precarious; lined; obnoxious; printed; velvet; brittle; clean; dusty; depreciated; mold-rotten; bond.

verbs
crumple—; deliver—; fiddle with—; glance at—; glaze—; pelt with—; plunge into—; rustle—; score—; search through—; strew with—; —bristles; —circulates; —editorializes; —flutters.

(See sheet, newspaper, article, book.)

PARABLE

verbs
construct—; couch in—; familiarize with—; inculcate by—; interpret—; narrate—; recite—; sum up—; unfold—; value—; —convinces; —describes; —edifies; —moralizes; —teaches.

(See proverb, adage, story, saying, moral, motto.)

PARACHUTE

verbs
bale out with—; dangle on—; float on—; fold—; foul—; inspect—; knot—; leap with—; pack—; patch—; provide with—; repair—; rig—; tug at—; twist—; —checks; —entwines; —expands; —protects; —resists; —safeguards; —settles; —tangles; —unfolds.

PARADE

adjectives
empty; imposing; dusty; unlicensed; halted; spectacular; bizarre; noisy; drunken.

verbs
climax—; display in—; exhibit in—; flock to—; inspect—; marshal—; muster—; organize—; prink for—; review—; stage—; witness—; —blazes; —files; —glitters; —protests; —surges; —winds.

(See celebration, pageant, demonstration, spectacle.)

PARADE (v)

adverbs
spectacularly; ostentatiously; rebelliously; aimlessly; imposingly; drunkenly; obstreperously; clamorously; militantly; imposingly.

(See display, show, flaunt.)

PARADISE

adjectives
flower-enameled; painted; pagan; undefiled; terrestrial; youthful; undreamed-of; lively.

verbs
anticipate—; bask in—; breathe—; deny—; deprive of—; drive from—; envision—; glory in—; loll in—; promise—; relish—; surpass—; taste—; transform into—; wallow in—; —enchants; —enraptures; —enthralls; —harbors.

(See heaven, utopia.)

PARADOX

adjectives
cruel; painful; dampening; apparent; permissible; curious; audacious; perpetual; distressing; frivolous; subtle; hideous.

verbs
admit—; afford—; conceive—; confront with—; contemplate—; induce—; involve—; maintain—; propound—; prove—; savor of—; scorn—; skirt—; speculate on—; utter—; —conflicts; —contradicts; —mystifies; —perplexes; —puzzles.

(See statement, lie, truth, contradiction.)

PARADOXICAL

adverbs
strangely; inexplicably; obscurely; ironically; slightly; curiously; particularly; uncommonly; perplexingly; problematically; inscrutably; oddly; preposterously; fantastically; enigmatically; extremely.

PARAGON

adjectives
seeming; earthly; vertical; princely.

PARAGRAPH

adjectives
scandalous; scurrilous; inky; injurious; editorial; priceless; linking; pregnant; pathetic; illuminating; offensive; striking; long; trenchant; involved; complicated; overlong; transitional; brisk.

verbs
aggregate —s; amass —s; arrange in —; confine to—; connect—s; constitute—; couch

in—; divide into —s; indent—; partition into —s; phrase—; quote—; recast—; recount—; stumble upon—; —communicates; —deals with; —embodies; —expresses.
(See sentence, words, thought, statement.)

PARALLEL

adjectives
fitting; astonishing; close; fanciful; fortunate; striking.

verbs
approximate—; attempt—; collate—; contribute—; destroy—; draw—; extend in—; fix —; furnish—; identify—; model—; observe —; render—; tilt—; —balances; —conspires; —copies; —emulates; —reflects.
(See line, comparison.)

PARALLEL (*v*)

adverbs
precisely; strikingly; coincidentally; astonishingly; fancifully.
(See compare.)

PARALYSIS

adjectives
hysterical; creeping; intellectual; definite; magical; virtual; infantile; numbing.

verbs
affect with—; detect—; feign—; labor under —; languish in—; stun into—; suffer—; —benumbs; —blunts; —creeps upon; —cripples; —deadens; —deprives; —disables; —disqualifies; —halts; —incapacitates; —palls; —sears; —shatters; —silences.
(See disease, lethargy, laziness, stagnation, numbness.)

PARALYZE (*v*)

adverbs
intellectually; momentarily; permanently; magically; hypnotically.
(See stun, shock.)

PARALYZED

adverbs
completely; partially; unhappily; pitiably; hopelessly; lamentably; curiously; strangely; unaccountably; tragically; helplessly; decrepitly; incurably; irremediably; irrecoverably; pathetically; miserably; wretchedly; apparently; obviously.

PARAPET

adjectives
substantial; rugged; gilded; glistening; silvery; military; gun-studded; ominous; warlike; bloody.

PARAPHRASE

adjectives
harmonic; unique; ingenious; stilted; silly; worthless.

PARAPHRASE (*v*)

adverbs
skillfully; satirically; ingeniously; uniquely; harmoniously; smoothly; studiously.
(See quote, say.)

PARASITE

adjectives
harmless; business; tiny; formidable; smiling; smooth; detested; destructive; plant; social.

verbs
breed—; detest—; infest with —s; maintain —; nourish—; plague by —s; serve—; tend —; —absorbs; —attaches; —burrows into; —draws; —exacts; —fattens on; —flatters; —frequents; —lodges in; —penetrates; —robs; —sucks; —depends on.
(See cockroach, fly, mosquito, tramp, bugs, leper, leech.)

PARASITIC

adverbs
miserably; submissively; slavishly; helplessly; sycophantically; dependably; subserviently; obsequiously; inexplicably; obscurely; inscrutably; strangely; pitiably; contemptibly; amazingly; singularly; needlessly; pusillanimously; feebly; disgustingly; distressingly; hatefully; odiously; incomprehensibly.

PARASOL

verbs
extend—; hide behind—; poke—; spread—; tilt—; twirl—; —bobs; —caps; —conceals; —defends; —guards; —protects; —screens; —shades; —shields; —shelters; —veils.
(See umbrella, shade, cane.)

PARCEL

adjectives
youthful; bulky; untied; mysterious; clumsy; heavy.

verbs
accumulate —s; agglomerate —s; assort —s; deal out—s; deliver—; dispense—s; distribute—s; dole out—s; fumble—; group—s; heap—s; jumble—s; mislay—; mete out—s; rake up—s; share—s; —s litter; —s scatter; —tumbles.

(See bundle, package.)

PARCHED

adverbs
miserably; hopelessly; pitifully; cruelly; unprofitably; wretchedly; feverishly; bitterly; aridly; hotly; terribly; strangely; dreadfully; uncommonly; dangerously; alarmingly; distressingly; ruinously; disastrously; awfully.

PARCHMENT

adjectives
worthy; yellowed; valuable.

PARDON

adjectives
remorseful; free; present; unconditional; long-sought; welcome; humble.

verbs
accept—; beg—; buy—; crave—; expect—; grant—; implore—; invoke—; purchase—; refuse—; seek—; —absolves; —conciliates; —condones; —heals; —placates; —propitiates; —purges; —ransoms; —repairs; —reprieves; —whitewashes (colloq.).

(See forgiveness, mercy, relief, dispensation.)

PARDON (v)

adverbs
magnanimously; benignly; unconditionally; freely; indulgently; leniently.

(See acquit, forgive, excuse.)

PARDONABLE

adverbs
reasonably; justly; expediently; fairly; altogether; innocently; scarcely; wholly; understandably; somewhat; hardly; obviously; palpably; clearly; undoubtedly; undeniably; definitely.

PARENTAGE

adjectives
illegitimate; worshipful; angelic; obscure; unknown; verified.

PARENTHETICAL

adverbs
significantly; curiously; importantly; carelessly; noticeably; insignificantly; strangely; inexplicably; unaccountably; deliberately; intentionally; cleverly; deftly; informatively; illuminatingly; casually; pointedly; contemptuously; markedly.

PARENTS

adjectives
unnoticed; natural; evolutionary; dissenting; heroic; stubborn; obdurate; conscientious; frantic; imaginary; stern; careworn; reluctant; distressed; doting; honored; forward; narrow-minded; divine; harsh; vaporing; royal; jolly; lovable; perfect; splendid; health-minded; astonished; indignant; unloving; unscrupulous; grasping; ignorant.

verbs
forsake—; honor—; obey—; reassure—; respect—; revere—; revolt against—; —advise; —bless; —comfort; —discipline; —enlighten; —instruct; —judge; —provide; —punish; —restrain; —train; —tutor; —warn.

(See father, mother, husband, wife.)

PARISH

adjectives
humble; quiet; tiny; beautiful.

PARK

adjectives
permanent; pavilion; urban; extensive; spacious; odious; well-kept; dismantled; wooded; adjacent; artificial; moon-lit; umbrageous; city; cool.

verbs
caper in—; carouse in—; dally in—; disport in—; enclose—; frequent—; frisk in—; frolic in—; gambol in—; holiday in—; inhabit—; rake—; romp in—; tend—; weed—; —amuses; —beguiles; —bores; —diverts; —tires; —wearies.

(See country, field, grass, lawn, garden, meadow.)

PARLANCE

adjectives
theatrical; dramatic.

PARLIAMENT

adjectives
insular; empiric.

verbs
attend—; call—; conduct—; consult—; dissolve—; invest in—; petition—; represent in —; request—; summon—; sway—; —advises; —appropriates; —assembles; —convenes; —debates; —discusses; —frames; —imposes; —levies.
(See congress, senate, meeting, board, legislature, commission.)

PARLIAMENTARY

adverbs
highly; strictly; rigidly; regularly; curiously; pointedly; uncommonly; noticeably; rigorously; formally; unquestionably; impressively; overwhelmingly; magnificently; undeviatingly; splendidly; ceremoniously; gorgeously; scrupulously; meticulously; carefully.

PARLOR

adjectives
wainscoted; fire-lit; ample; long; darkened.

verbs
arrange—; chat in—; confer in—; convene in—; converse in—; deck—; entertain in—; frame—; furnish—; invade—; prepare—; receive in—; retire to—; shoo from—; squire into—; stuff—.
(See room, apartment.)

PARODY

adjectives
mocking; excellent; clever; discerning.

verbs
comment on—; decipher—; elucidate—; lend to—; snigger at—; translate—; —amuses; —caricatures; —distorts; —enrages; —exposes; —mimics; —mocks; —perverts; —ridicules; —roasts; —scoffs; —strains; —twits.
(See ridicule, writing, comedy, joke, jest.)

PAROLE

verbs
acquire—; advise—; advocate—; authorize —; dismiss on—; earn—; forfeit—; foster —; frame—; free on—; grant—; liberate on—; petition for—; plead for—; request—; sanction—; seek—; violate—.
(See pledge, promise, vow, agreement.)

PAROXYSM

verbs
cast into—; choke back—; curb—; discharge in—; fear—; kindle—; mitigate—; provoke to—; quiver with —s; restrain—; suffer—; throw into—; vent in—; —bursts; —disturbs; —explodes; —flares; —frightens; —froths; —incapacitates; —recurs; —rushes; —weakens.
(See convulsion, explosion, recklessness, violence.)

PARROT

adjectives
intrepid; spoiled; well-trained; confounded; petted; loud; mocking.

verbs
cage—; capture—; pamper—; pelt—; teach —; train—; —amuses; —attacks; —claws; —copies; —entertains; —imitates; —mimics; —mocks; —pecks; —perches; —senses; —squawks; —strokes; —whistles.
(See bird.)

PARRY (v)

adverbs
adroitly; deftly; skillfully; professionally; agilely; lithely; invincibly.
(See avert, evade, prevent.)

PARSLEY

verbs
chop—; cultivate—; deck with—; dot with —; dry—; grind—; sprig with—; sprinkle with—; —adorns; —crowns; —decorates; —dresses; —flavors; —garnishes; —seasons; —tones; —tops.
(See vegetable, herb, plant.)

PARSON

adjectives
bibulous; licentious; sociable; agreeable; careless; half-starved; unlucky; serious; sedate; lovable; diligent.

PARSONAGE

adjectives
country; unconventional; pure; generous; commodious; comfortable.

PART

adjectives
tragic; constituent; pompous; closely-fitted; moving; disconsolate; balancing; affected; integral; drossy; prime; splendid; significant; remote; authoritative; confused; convivial; eastern; pendulous; dissimilar; initial; sensitive; intimate; symbolical; animate; imaginative; tender; essential; dis-

tinguished; energetic; conspicuous; swaggering; moneyed; plump; outer; considerable; leading; prominent; decisive; manful; susceptible; formative; timely; striking; negative; tropical; immense; stubborn; uncourteous; oratorical; sequestered; active; subordinate; barbarous; relevant; invaluable; coloristic; abiding; incalculable; prudent; injurious; airy; speculative; theoretical; arid; generous; working; corresponding; aspiring; appropriate; reflex; innermost; understandable; related; declining; conventional; substantial; cumbrous; active; respectable; uttermost; metaphysical; slavish; various (pl); prefatory; effective; creditable; corresponding; over-stately; brilliant; evanescent; hindmost; worshipful; legitimate; retrenched; low; discreet; comedy; wondrous; fundamental; subsequent; external; virtuous; inherent; precipitous; inseparable; singular; choice; dominating; arduous; painful; brute; honorable; amiable; generous; sovereign; obnoxious; worthy; component; outward; membranous; mirthful; serious; vulgar; contiguous; incombustible; unsettled; vulnerable; pleasant; unprofitable; important; pathetic; virtuous; analogous; impertinent; midland; outlying; dissipated; vital; structural; treacherous; adjacent; retired; uninteresting; personal; formal; shady; loud-sounding; individual; restricted; inglorious; ghostly; romantic; impressive; desolate; sudden; prodigious; disjointed; inaccessible; disheartening; intrepid; lamentable.

verbs
accept—; acclaim—; balk at—; convey—; enact—; exaggerate—; live—; master—; perform—; render—; reproduce—; scorn—; sink into—; slip into—; treat—; wangle—; —affords; —allows.

(See lines, detail, character, scene.)

PART (v)

adverbs
despairingly; amicably; haughtily; meekly; convivially; pathetically; formally; romantically; lamentably.

(See divide, separate.)

PARTAKE (v)

adverbs
enthusiastically; joyously; convivially; cheerfully; gratefully; hungrily; ceremoniously; festively; fraternally.

(See share, participate.)

PARTIAL

adverbs
disgracefully; shamefully; illegally; unconstitutionally; openly; palpably; unfortunately; cruelly; bitterly; inexplicably; unjustifiably; unaccountably; miserably; wretchedly; prejudicially; unfairly; unjustly; obviously; openly; defiantly; perversely; curiously; strangely; amazingly.

PARTIALITY

adjectives
parental; sectarian; excessive; overweening; laudable; patent; noticeable.

verbs
avoid—; criticize—; entertain—; gain—; investigate—; lavish—; repel—; report—; shrink from—; —alienates; —distorts; —dotes; —forejudges; —incenses; —irritates; —provokes; —riles (colloq.); —shocks; —warps; —woos.

(See conviction, bias, prejudice.)

PARTICIPANTS

adjectives
interesting; prime; actual; leading.

verbs
cheer—; desire—; goad—; identify—; limit—; reckon as—; register—; seek—; test—; —assemble; —contest; —demonstrate; —enter; —labor; —share; —train; —vie for.

(See contestant, athlete.)

PARTICIPATE (v)

adverbs
willingly; jovially; energetically; heartily; enthusiastically; prominently; futilely; vigorously.

(See share, partake.)

PARTICIPATION

adjectives
undivided; active; human; futile; amateur.

verbs
anticipate—; incapacitate for—; join in—; prepare for—; revel in—; share in—; train for—; vie for—in; welcome—.

(See indulgence, enjoyment, association.)

PARTICLES

adjectives
granulated; seething; invisible; divine; irritating; scattering; constituent; colliding;

shining; impalpable; ultimate; invading; material; distinguishing; great; fruitful; harmful; discoloring; ignoble; gelatine.

PARTICULAR

adverbs
painfully; terribly; absurdly; meticulously; ridiculously; gruffly; scrupulously; conscientiously; extremely; considerately; dependably; reliably; vigilantly; unimpeachably; rigorously; scientifically; curiously; punctiliously; fastidiously; exactingly; inordinately; vexatiously; assiduously; unpleasantly; disagreeably; dreadfully; curiously; unnecessarily; distressingly; nervously; fussily; obnoxiously.

PARTICULARITY

adjectives
circumstantial; undue; over-luxurious.

PARTICULARS

adjectives
unexperienced; remarkable; multiplex; obvious; unnoticed.

verbs
adhere to—; afford—; contemplate—; disregard—; embody—; ignore—; inspect—; omit —; overlook—; mark—; record—; revise—; scan—; slight—; skim—; skip over—; slur —; —absorb; —explain.

(See details, information, facts.)

PARTING

adjectives
gracious; various (pl); undemonstrative; dreadful; present; frivolous; solemn; sweet; sorrowful.

PARTISAN

adjectives
zealous; extreme; undue; conscientious; conspicuous; immovable; long-dreaded; hated; factious.

adverbs
absurdly; rigidly; bigotedly; narrow-mindedly; dogmatically; oddly; strenuously; industriously; actively; thoughtlessly; witlessly; senselessly; unwaveringly; strongly; steadily; stubbornly; obstinately; zealously; confidently; inflexibly; mulishly; resolutely; incomparably.

PARTISANSHIP

adjectives
virulent; verified; insincere; fervid; honest; preposterous.

PARTITION

adjectives
saucer-shaped; unwarranted.

PARTNER

adjectives
semirecumbent; full; dignified; equal; junior; thick-skinned; rock-ribbed; dreadless; erudite; criminal; desperate.

verbs
admit—; couple with—; desire—; forsake —; heed—; require—; silence—; trust—; —agrees; —consults; —contemplates; —debates; —dissolves; —divides; —haggles; —joins in; —profits; —severs; —shares; —squabbles; —s unite.

(See ally, associate, brother, colleague, companion.)

PARTNERSHIP

adjectives
everlasting; effective; lifelong; endless.

verbs
annul—; cement—; combine in—; compose —; dissolve—; inaugurate—; pry apart—; seek—; sever—; undo—; —concurs; —conduces to; —confederates; —cooperates; —conspires; —requires; —seconds; —unites; —withstands.

(See friendship, alliance, company, corporation, society, firm.)

PARTRIDGE

verbs
domesticate—; flush—; startle—; —airs; —amuses; —beats; —bellows; —bills; —captivates; —challenges; —darts; —explores; —feigns; —s flush; —flutters; —glides; —jerks; —nods; —ranges; —roves; —rumbles; —scratches; —squeals; —steals.

(See grouse, bird, bob-white.)

PARTY

adjectives (*general*)
assorted; hostile; revolutionary; serenading; tomahawk; staged; raiding; scalping; jovial; retiring; ill-starred; surprise; house; united; scattered; corrupt; fanatical; sectional; wild; antagonistic; dominant; quilting; lively; merry; traveling; singular;

constituted; detached; visionary; invisible; unbiased; exclusive; pleasure; desperate; contracting; foraging; conversation; lawless; luckless; straggling; skulking; disaffected; obtruding; reconnoitering; augmenting; rustic; storming; contending; shipwrecked; skirmishing; covering; excursion; dominant; fatigue; contending; misguided; marching; victorious; select; harmonious; ecclesiastical; scouting; reactionary; inimitable; litigating; all-day; paralyzing; imperial; informal; assaulting; fashionable; defenseless; radiant; bounding; invincible; discontented; amused; aggrieved; torchlight; zealous; ridiculous; joyous; especial; tramping.

PARTY (*political*)

verbs

appraise—; bolt—; cleave to—; consolidate —; dominate—; override—; purge—; rejuvenate—; scatter—; serve—; split—; supplant—; support—; wreck—; —advocates; —cleans house; —collapses; —declines; —flounders.

(See group, gang, following, faction.)

PARTY (*social*)

verbs

attend—; augment—; enliven—; fancy—; flock to—; invite to—; regale—; —amuses; —beguiles; —bores; —cheers; —disgusts; —diverts; —entertains; —palls; —solaces; —wearies.

(See meeting, theatre, ball, entertainment.)

PASS

adjectives

dolorous; desolate; silly; inaccessible; mountain; ragged; permissive; stupendous; perpendicular; gleaming.

PASS (*v*)

adverbs

translucently; invariably; harmoniously; deliberately; meekly; obliquely; placatingly; economically; wistfully; triumphantly; consciously; tediously; successively; victoriously; irresolutely; sedately; serenely; jauntily; leisurely; dolorously.

(See move, advance.)

PASSAGE (*general*)

adjectives

easy; pathetic; painful; palatial; sparred; tortuous; favorable; rickety; half-remembered; dimly-lighted; hazardous; objectionable; latticed; random; secret; perilous; octave; well-concealed; impassable; wading; sloping; striking; arched; dark; particular; prosperous; speedy; matted; neglected; furious; poetical; disputed; exquisite; descriptive; remarkable; sensational; slippery; precarious; vaulted; circuitous; unedifying; abrupt; narrow-paneled; tedious; practicable; romantic; vivid; characteristic; sumptuous; ill-quoted; brilliant; gloomy; subterranean; stormy; despised; hackneyed; purple; redundant; rhetorical; brief; narrow; thorough; roomy; stirring; significant; secret; political; swift; honey; winding; awful; laudatory; adulatory; untrammeled; disjointed; perihelion; certain; frequent; glowing; oratorical; walled-up; impossible; scorching; alternate; lyric; musical; amorphous; melodious; rumbling; dramatic; instantaneous; treacherous; imaginative; arduous; elevated; lofty; impressive; sublime.

PASSAGE (*literary*)

verbs

acclaim—; applaud—; analyze—; blend —s; cite—; delete—; erase—; interpret—; paraphrase—; quote—; —castigates; —expunges; —glows; —reveals, —stings.

(See paragraph, thought, sentence, portion, section, quotation, selection.)

PASSAGE (*way, avenue*)

verbs

accomplish—; bar—; block—; clog—; constrict—; emerge from—; fence in—; gain—; guard—; impede—; jeopardize—; offer—; protect—; quicken—; restrict—; safeguard —.

(See way, access, approach, lobby, exit, corridor, hall.)

PASSENGERS

adjectives

hurrying; unhappy; protesting; hooded; unsuspecting; stealthy; horror-struck; bustling; belated; frivolous; churlish; distinguished; fastidious; half-rate.

verbs

accommodate—; amuse—; assign—to; assure—; bore—; comfort—; enchant—; entertain—; enthrall—; escort—; excite—; guide—; reassure—; reveal to—; tire—; transport—; —fret; —fume; —idle; —tour; —thread; —weary.

(See marcher, audience, gathering.)

PASSION

adjectives

absorbing; acrimonious; afflicting; aimless; angry; ardent; autobiographical; awakened; black; blazing; bestial; base; bad; bitter; bittersweet; blended; boisterous; bottomless; boyish; brutal; burning; bursting; busy; capital; certain; chivalrous; choleric; coarse; comfortable; concentrated; conflicting; contending; contrary; corrosive; damnable; dark; deadly; deathly; deceased; deep; deforming; degrading; delicious; deluding; democratic; departed; determinate; devastating; diabolical; dimmed; distempered; disturbing; divine; earthly; electric; elemental; enduring; energetic; engendered; engrossing; enthusiastic; envied; errant; erratic; eternal; everlasting; evil; exacerbated; exceeding; exciting; exquisite; extraordinary; exultant; fantastical; favorite; fervent; fierce; fitful; flaming; foaming; foul; frantic; frivolous; frozen; frustrated; fugitive; fundamental; futile; gambling; generous; gnawing; gross; guilty; half-accomplished; headlong; hidden; heavenly; high; hurtful; hopeless; human; humble; honest; idealistic; idealized; idiotic; ignoble; illicit; imprudent; inborn; incestuous; indignant; infernal; inflammable; insatiable; instinctive; intellectual; intense; intermediate; invisible; involuntary; ireful; irregular; irrepressible; irresistible; jealous; kindred; lasting; lawless; licentious; loving; lurid; lustful; master; masterful; merry; mischievous; morbid; mortal; mutinous; mutual; newfound; noble; obtuse; original; outrageous; overmastering; overt; overwhelming; pale-mouthed; pallid; partisan; patriotic; pent-up; personate; petty; philanthropic; pitying; preceding; present; prevailing; primal; primitive; private; prosperous; pseudo; radical; raging; rare; rash; religious; repressed; requisite; romantic; rude; ruling; selfish; secondary; silent; sophisticated; sordid; sore; sorry; southern; spectral; speechless; stifled; stirred; stormy; strange; subdued; strong; struggling; sudden; superior; suppressed; swelling; swift; tender; tempestuous; towering; thoughtful; thronging (pl); thwarted; torrid; tragic; tranquil; transient; transitory; triumphant; troubling; true; turbid; tyrannous; unaccustomed; unbridled; unchecked; undying; ungovernable; unhallowed; universal; unnoted; unprofitable; unregulated; unrequited; unsoothed; unsuspected; untainted; untamed; untrained; untried; unwise; unwomanly; unworthy; variable; vehement; vengeful; veritable; vindictive; violent; virile; wanton; warning; wayward; wild; worried; worst; youthful; zealous; exaggerated.

verbs

animate with—; arouse—; boil with—; bridle—; cherish—; declare—; distort with—; enchain by—; evoke—; extinguish—; fly into—; gratify—; impel by—; intensify—; nourish—; pledge to—; quicken with—; reciprocate—; redden with—; respond to—; restrain—; revive—; share—; unleash—; vanquish—; vent—; —consumes; —cools; —inflames; —rules; —seethes; —simmers; —tortures.

(See impetuosity, craving, appetite, ire, enthusiasm, emotion, infatuation, love, indignation.)

PASSIONATE

adverbs

amorously; angrily; cholerically; lovingly; uncontrollably; ungovernably; inordinately; uncommonly; innately; inherently; naturally; notoriously; warmly; ardently; enthusiastically; zealously; earnestly; violently; excitably; captiously; querulously; moodily; mercurially; violently; furiously; impulsively; irrepressibly; strangely.

PASSIVE

adverbs

strangely; apathetically; curiously; disgustingly; provokingly; incomprehensibly; dully; inertly; sluggishly; bluntly; inertly; doltishly; lazily; vexatiously; indolently; obediently; subserviently; hopelessly; servilely; submissively; pliantly; imperturbably; stoically; placidly; meekly; stupidly; stolidly; carelessly.

PASSIVITY

adjectives

despondent; disposed; dejected; dreamy; lazy; inert; stolid; unwavering; slumbrous; dull; dead.

PAST

adjectives

romantic; sorrowful; vanished; voiceless; foolish; monstrous; accumulated; remote; wintry; complacent; immemorial; stormy; immeasurable; gracious; artificial; dim; scarred; remorseless; dark; sinful; mischievous; precious; turbulent; receding; spectral; mysterious; irrevocable; blighted;

ducal; unfathomed; inexorable; changeless; bitter; rough; emotional; ungentle; ambiguous; unrelenting; long-distant; disputable; restored; embalmed; irreproachable; hideous; well-filled; boundless; unrelenting; unhallowed; glorious; ungracious; pathetic; picturesque; melancholy.

verbs
clarify—; decipher—; dip into—; discern—; enrich—; evoke—; grope in—; penetrate—; plumb—; recapture—; recreate—; reflect on —; regret—; relive—; resurrect—; shake off —; —fades; —haunts; —survives; —vanishes.
(See memories, future, life.)

PASTE

adjectives
milk-white; slippery-looking; lackluster; sticky; gelatinous.

PASTEL

adjectives
luscious; summer; gleaming; white.

PASTIME

adjectives
favorite; youthful; kindred; risky; innumerable (pl); gentlemanlike; delightful; brawling; gracious; light; refreshing; uncanonical.

verbs
absorb in—; advocate—; enjoy—; indulge in—; lack—; seek—; —amuses; —cheers; —diverts; —eases; —enlivens; —entertains; —recreates; —solaces; —soothes.
(See game, amusement, diversion.)

PASTOR

adjectives
ungracious; scholarly; zealously; flabby.

verbs
appoint—; ordain—; serve as—; submit to —; venerate—; —administers; —attends to; —consoles; —converts; —guides; —ministers; —negotiates; —pleads; —prays; —preaches; —protects; —rebukes; —reconciles; —rules; —sways; —sympathizes with; —teaches; —visits.
(See minister.)

PASTORAL

adverbs
sweetly; pleasantly; refreshingly; admirably; gently; firmly; mildly; agreeably; pleasingly; acceptably; comfortingly; helpfully; delightfully.

PASTRY

verbs
bolt—; crunch—; despatch—; do honor to —; feast on—; garnish—; gormandize—; knead—; leaven—; munch—; nibble—; roll —; top off with—; —appeals; —attracts; —fattens.
(See food, etc.)

PASTURE

adjectives
recumbent; poisonous; perpetual; sodden; naked; bleak; browsed; boulder-strewn; flowery; pleasant; neighboring; undulous; reeky; stony; verdant; coarse; scant; silver-shrouded.

verbs
abound in—; browse in—; conserve—; devour—; feast on—; feed on—; gnaw—; graze on—; patch—with; plow—; roam—; scrape—; survey—; wander on—; —extends; —fattens; —spreads.
(See grass, field, meadow.)

PAT (v)

adverbs
reassuringly; benignly; affectionately; comfortingly; approvingly; awkwardly; mechanically; caressingly; paternally.
(See tap, caress.)

PATCH

adjectives
vivid; broken; ugly; thrifty; phosphorescent; superficial; numerous (pl); insignificant; single.

PATCH (v)

adverbs
laboriously; awkwardly; deftly; eccentrically; thriftily; superficially; geometrically; pathetically.
(See repair, mend.)

PATE

adjectives
lean; understanding; ponderous; learned; bald; shiny.

PATENT

adjectives
valuable; formal; longed-for; secret.

verbs
grant—; infringe—; limit—; permit—; request—; restrict—; secure—; seek—; —authorizes; —blocks; —clinches; —empowers; —excludes; —expires; —favors; —guards; —pends; —protects; —seals; —vouchsafes.
(See invention, license, right, privilege.)

adverbs
glaringly; openly; plainly; unmistakably; conspicuously; undisguisedly; lawfully; notoriously; freely; safely; securely.

PATERNAL

adverbs
kindly; generously; indulgently; fondly; graciously; proudly; awkwardly; considerately; liberally; clumsily; benevolently; amiably; genially; complacently; complaisantly; tenderly; humanely; benignantly; ad monishingly; warningly; pompously; noisily; actively; virtuously; hilariously; autoeratically; domineeringly; absurdly; amusingly; happily.

PATERNALISM

adjectives
beneficient; beauteous; true.

verbs
advocate—; assume—; attempt—; contemplate—; induce—; propose—; wield—; —administers; —cements; —dominates; —governs; —preserves; —protects; —regulates; —reigns; —supplies.
(See power, action, care, control, government.)

PATERNITY

verbs
anticipate—; consider—; doubt—of; establish—of; forfeit—; hail—; impose—; respect—; revere—; spare—; venerate—; welcome—; —awes; —burdens; —comforts; —honors; —inspires; —salutes.
(See right, descent.)

PATH

adjectives
hollow-worn; pragmatic; steep; hillocky; obliterated; slippery; murmuring; gleaming; damp; luring; zigzag; fringed; twilight; winding; bushy; slender; straitened; adventuresome; hidden; trodden; dissimilar (pl); pleasant; unknown; upward; tempting; circumterrestrial; wild; lone; joyous; numerous (pl); rustling; sinuous; mountain; impracticable; bridle; predetermined; readier; pebbly; tortuous; desolated; endless; outgoing; dusk-shrouded; perilous; silvery; sacred; golden; green-bordered; hazardous; thorny; rough; pleasant; destructive; intricate; unstable; primrose; haughty; delicate; fairylike; factious; grave; beaten; fatal; enticing; pretty; gloomy; overgrown; dreary; chequered; dubious; flashing; conventional; inaccessible; solitary; untried; arduous; blustering; eccentric; homeward; radiating; frequented; lowly; shadowy; perpendicular; stone-flagged; artistic; tiny; intersecting; graveled; destined; somber; labyrinthine; acclivous; giddy; narrow; paved; devious; peaceful; lonesome; pilgrim; darkling; firm; desolate; downward; gravel; doctrinaire; difficult; insecure; shelving; intermediate; climbing; uncharted; converging; unconscious; enchanted; weary; precarious; shady; thankless; triumphal; right; dark; curved; comfortless; coincident; parabolic.

verbs
bury—; choose—; cut—; deck—; depart from—; discern—; establish—; inveigle into—; map out—; reflect—; smooth—; strew—; —allures; —beckons; —diverges; —entices; —invites; —swerves; —veers; —winds.
(See lane, road.)

PATHETIC

adverbs
touchingly; unusually; uncommonly; pitiably; infinitely; altogether; poignantly; deeply; grievously; appallingly; shockingly; oddly; immeasurably; heartbreakingly; extraordinarily; dreadfully.

PATHLESS

adverbs
terrifyingly; alarmingly; appallingly; shockingly; perplexingly; bewilderingly; confusingly; dangerously; perilously; hazardously; unaccountably; hopelessly; boundlessly; distressingly; calamitously; disastrously; formidably; forbiddingly; ruggedly; impassably; impermeably; impenetrably.

PATHOS

adjectives
infinite; poignant; anxious; half-baked; puerile; sharp; exquisite; melodious; thin; instant; ever-present; intense; sobbing; despairing; expressible; grim; deep; extraordinary; celestial; stern; unfathomable.

verbs
bear—; catch—; endure—; experience—; harbor—; taste—; —affects; —agitates; —dwells; —impresses; —infects; —mantles; —moves; —palpitates; —pierces; —produces; —responds; —shakes; —warms.

(See sadness, unhappiness, suffering, affliction, sorrow, pity, sympathy, passion.)

PATHWAY

adjectives
murmurous; flinty; aerial; swaying; perilous; persistent; segmental; historic; radiant; shadowy; lightning; immemorial; predestined; rocky; lush; overhung; blind; corkscrew; crooked.

PATIENCE

adjectives
human; placid; simple; courteous; uncomplaining; untiring; gracious; pathetic; musing; chaotic; mild; commendable; inexhaustible; heavenly; self-restrained; melancholy; characteristic; strict; infinite; well-established; boundless; admirable; resigned; creditable; unwearying; haggard; struggling; unconscious; genial; elastic; deliberate; long-suffering; tender; saintly; helpless; mock; dogged; counseled; unwearied; bitter; cruel; unexampled; sad; heroic; serene; gentle; endless; trustful; precious; laboring.

verbs
cultivate—; employ—; entail—; exercise—; exhaust—; manifest—; necessitate—; require—; strain—; try—; —dwindles; —fails; —frays; —wears thin.

(See forbearance, perseverance, endurance, fortitude.)

PATIENT

adjectives
bedridden; unruly; noble; satisfied; reluctant; lucrative; passionate; individual; indignant; docile; fever; diabetic; ill; psychopathic; rheumatic; recalcitrant; susceptible; paranoiac; resolved.

verbs
caution—; discharge—; examine—; exhaust—; guard—; hospitalize—; incapacitate—; inspire—; irritate—; nauseate—; refresh—; relieve—; restore—; resurrect—; sponge—; tide—over; —expectorates; —rallies; —recovers; —relapses; —responds to.

adverbs
unbelievably; incredibly; sweetly; gently; imperturbably; uncomplainingly; quietly; serenely; wisely; sagaciously; indulgently; genially; tenderly; affectionately; expertly; persistently; indefatigably; placidly; courteously; charmingly; habitually; infinitely; unwearyingly; doggedly; resolutely; amazingly; uncommonly.

PATRIARCH

adjectives
hoary; dusky; aged; seafaring; aboriginal; venerable.

PATRIARCHAL

adverbs
properly; appropriately; proudly; arrogantly; domineeringly; imperiously; undeniably; uncommonly; incurably; haughtily; tyrannically; immensely; delightfully; amiably; indulgently; unforgettably; venerably; unyieldingly; obviously; obstinately; tenaciously; insistently; jealously; stubbornly.

PATRICIAN

adverbs
undeniably; innately; inherently; naturally; unmistakably; truly; genuinely; dominantly; proudly; palpably; obviously; evidently; manifestly; undeniably; nobly; conspicuously; eminently; exaltedly; renownedly; splendidly.

PATRIOT

adjectives
ardent; virtuous; sterling; devoted; zealous; epistolary; venerable; misguided; sturdy; prejudiced; worthy.

PATRIOTIC

adverbs
splendidly; curiously; ostentatiously; undeniably; nobly; unselfishly; genuinely; magnificently; grandly; unusually; inherently; truly; unquestionably; quietly; naturally; devotedly; conventionally; ardently; actively; assiduously; intelligibly; thoughtful-

ly; discriminatingly; wisely; sagaciously; alertly; vigilantly; altruistically; uncommonly; highly; extraordinarily.

PATRIOTISM

adjectives
fainting; flamboyant; haughty; devoted; pious; religious; uncompromising; engendering; impulsive; vigorous; irrepressible; serious; ardent; epidemic; sincere; jealous; disinterested; fearless; heroic; individual; fervent; sublime.

verbs
acclaim—; advocate—; applaud—; breed—; burst with—; choke—; develop—; exploit—; extinguish—; feign—; guard with—; harbor out of—; inflame with—; inspire—; justify—; kindle—; lampoon—; tear between—.
(See Americanism, love, devotion, loyalty.)

PATROL

verbs
elude—; evade—; maintain—; push through—; —guarantees; —guards; —insures; —paces; —protects; —safeguards; —scours; —traverses.
(See guard, sentry.)

PATROL (v)

adverbs
systematically; vigilantly; ceaselessly; cautiously; periodically; hourly; perpetually.
(See watch, march, protect.)

PATRON

adjectives
gentle; influential; munificent; august; fostering; unbidden; imperial; contemptuous; mighty; passing; perpetual.

PATRONAGE

adjectives
condescending; titled; continued; liberal; constant; increasing; political; admiring; generous; extensive; lucrative; obsequious; advised; loyal; proprietary; aldermanic.

verbs
cherish—; dispense—; enjoy—; extend—; foster—; gain—; seek—; solicit—; swell—; withdraw—; —abets; —advances; —aids; —benefits; —bolsters; —cheers; —feeds; —influences; —nourishes; —overrides; —succors.
(See guidance, support, encouragement, aid, leadership, protection.)

PATRONIZE (v)

adverbs
deferentially; liberally; advisedly; lucratively; loyally; extensively; habitually.
(See encourage, favor, promote.)

PATRONIZING

adverbs
arrogantly; unduly; insufferably; intolerably; unbearably; intolerantly; pompously; haughtily; overbearingly; absurdly; comically; ludicrously; laughably; foolishly; ridiculously; inanely; terribly; fatuously; loudly; noisily; objectionably; provokingly; disagreeably; unpleasantly; obnoxiously; unreasonably; strangely; incredibly.

PATTERN

adjectives
curious; significant; exclusive; intricate; delicate; existing; original; distinctive; ornamental; complex; decorative; pronounced; wondrous; ageless; accurate; complicated; tasteful; metrical; tremulous; frigid; animal; primitive; blotchy; mental; shadow; effective; whimsical; comprehensive; unknown; arbitrary; geometrical; experimental; mosaic; balanced; agricultural; unpretentious; running; ever-present; schizoid; wanted; rich; vivid; starched; perfect; unconventional; operatic; rudimentary; tawdry; aesthetic; ideal; inconspicuous; characterful; scroll; serene; architectural; everlasting; colorful; new; striped; neat; smart; diversified; selective; beautiful; unusual; quiet; spring; stimulating; popular; plaid; plumage; subdued; dark; striking; artificial; attractive; exclusive; fabric; sprightly; authentic; young-blooded; lacy.

verbs
cling to—; comply with—; conform to—; copy—; devise—; follow—; improve upon—; infringe on—; knit—; mark—; observe—; surpass—; trace—; transcend—; violate—; weave—; —baffles; —exemplifies; —guides; —illustrates; —indicates; —regulates; —represents; —simplifies.
(See copy, ideal, design.)

PATTERN (v)

adverbs

exquisitely; exclusively; intricately; delicately; accurately; whimsically; geometrically; vividly; unconventionally; authentically.

(See copy, model, imitate.)

PATTY

adjectives

solid-looking; overdone; tiny.

PAUNCH

verbs

cram—; develop—; distend—; fill—; gorge —; heave—; load—; pamper—; reduce—; simulate—; stuff—; wad—; —craves; —encumbers; —expands; —gnaws; —protrudes.

(See belly, abdomen, stomach, intestines.)

PAUSE

adjectives

slow; awkward; haunting; appreciable; unconscious; normal; week-end; effect-collecting; thoughtful; cogitative; awful; terrible; pensive; ominous; brief; perceptible; discontented; reminiscent; deep; melancholy; decided; musing; appalling; stifling; suitable; inexplicable; humming; solemn; reticent; doubtful; grateful; considerable; frequent (pl); rapturous; transitory; uncomfortable; eternal; determined; respectful; transient; convenient; ensuing; natural; thrilling; present; discreet; wild-swan; habitual; rhetorical; painful; eloquent.

verbs

abstain from—s; destroy—; incur—; observe—; supply—; waste in—; —arrests; —emphasizes; —ensues; —falls; —halts; —hovers; —hushes; —impresses; —interposes; —interrupts; —intervenes; —persists; —suspends.

(See interruption, interval, lapse.)

PAUSE (v)

adverbs

reflectively; dramatically; reminiscently; instinctively; irresolutely; briefly; delicately; meaningfully; diffidently; lingeringly; ominously; deliberately; pensively; solemnly; discreetly.

(See waver, stop.)

PAVEMENT

adjectives

solitary; unsafe; brick; untrodden; ragstrewn; billowy; shady; deserted; dappled; grass-grown; firmamental; circular; insufficient; damp; marble; noiseless; dimly-lighted.

PAVILION

adjectives

vast; silk; glimmering; sumptuous; luminous; arabesque; gay.

verbs

decorate—; flock to—; garnish—; gather in—; ornament—; throng—; —accommodates; —encloses; —harbors; —protects; —rings; —rises; —shades; —shelters; —spreads; —swarms; —swelters.

(See canopy, tent, building.)

PAW

adjectives

tremendous; searching; tactile; bony; moist; unhallowed; horny; bloody.

PAW (v)

adverbs

fitfully; ineptly; vaguely; savagely; brutishly; clumsily; roughly; searchingly; lustfully.

(See stroke, strike.)

PAY

adjectives

sour; retirement; exorbitant; retroactive; scanty; meager; back; advance.

verbs

acquire—; attach—; claim—; crave—; cut —; derive—; deserve—; draw—; entitle to—; exact—; insist on—; merit—; raise—; restore—; solicit—; yield—; —accrues; —compensates; —defrays; —rewards; —squares (colloq.).

(See earnings, payment, profits, wages, money.)

PAY (v)

adverbs

moderately; handsomely; grudgingly; bounteously; heavily; cheerfully; annually; punctually; roundly; scantily; meagerly; exorbitantly.

(See compensate, reward.)

PAYMENT

adjectives

iniquitous; vicarious; substantial; convenient; easy; permanent; equivalent; coming; political; stipulated; benefit; preliminary; monthly; annual.

verbs
acknowledge—; afford—; await—; cease—; collect—; default—; deserve—; disburse—; evade—; reap—; recover—; refund—; resume—; suspend—; —discharges; —effaces; —pains.

(See pay, profits, wages.)

PAYROLL

verbs
add to—; anticipate—; calculate—; disburse—; distribute—; draw—; guard—; hold up (colloq.)—; insure—; pare down—; prepare—; protect—; reduce—; rob—; survey—; trim—; —increases; —mounts; —surpasses.

(See funds, profits, earnings.)

PEACE

adjectives
intellectual; bitter; profound; durable; dishonorable; unbroken; joyous; healthy; tolerable; enduring; industrial; internal; lovely; lasting; honorable; long-lost; heavenly; mellow-eyed; ineffable; dictated; passionate; meek-eyed; unresting; domestic; rapturous; neighborhood; absolute; unaccustomed; ignominious; settled; endless; everlasting; fruitful; speedy; temporary; ripening; universal; permanent; humiliating; eternal; deep; constant; indescribable; taunting; supplicated; unruffled; uneven; unsuspecting; treacherous; sweet; pale; ultimate; sinless; patched-up; barbaric; prudent; shameful; blissful; perpetual; honeyed; unbroken; inner; wealthy; silken; advantageous; luxurious; infinite; unspeakable; happy; ancient; sacred; poetic; unfluctuating; especial; external; repugnant; intimated; serene; balmy; profound; technical; ignoble; endurable; spiritual; windless; exquisite; riteless; incomparable; shining; fraternal; utter; immemorial; well-earned; pastoral.

verbs
achieve—; agitate for—; assure of—; botch—; breed—; compel—; crusade for—; destroy—; disrupt—; endanger—; enthrone—; further—; herald—; impose—; maintain—; menace—; negotiate—; prate about—; promote—; restore—; risk—; serve—; spurn—; sue for—; symbolize—; threaten—; unsettle—; upset—; vouchsafe—; —pervades; —prevails; —reigns.

(See harmony, amity, friendship, quiet, tranquillity.)

PEACEABLE

adverbs
inherently; naturally; continuously; resolutely; placidly; mildly; tranquilly; habitually; determinedly; inoffensively; serenely; calmly; imperturbably; unimaginably; curiously; racially; soberly; blandly; unbelievably; uncommonly; reasonably.

PEACEFUL

adverbs
beatifically; serenely; happily; blessedly; rapturously; amiably; pleasantly; contentedly; unbelievably; delightfully; entrancingly; remarkably; gloriously; perfectly.

PEACOCK

verbs
—preens; —prides himself; —stalks; —strides; —strolls; —struts.

(See bird.)

PEAK

adjectives
pinnacled; singular; volcanic; dazzling; furrowed; rounded; perilous; lambent; herbless; snowy; rugged; airy; fierce; savage; glistening; bristling; glittering; isolated; barren; angular; mountain; celestial; gigantic; lofty; successive (pl); precipitous; single; steeple-like; sunlighted; abrupt; ermine-clad; pathless; frowning; craggy; unique; brumal; jagged; environing (pl); rock; multitudinous (pl); scalped; snow-patched; fantastic; snow-covered; solstitial.

verbs
ascend—; cap—; climb—; cuff—; culminate in—; push to—; rise to—; scale—; sharpen—; —commands; —crowns; —heightens; —hovers; —juts; —points; —projects; —rears; —soars; —tapers; —tops; —towers.

(See mountain, tower, hill, top, point, summit.)

PEAL

adjectives
silvery; yawning; merry; angry; repeated; strange; fearful; terrific; dismal; tuneful;

full-hearted; paschal; joyous; hideous; solemn; spasmodic; tremendous; thrilling; dreadful.

PEAL (v)

adverbs
melodiously; softly; gently; gaily; joyously; festively; merrily; angrily; terrifically; solemnly; spasmodically.
(See echo, resound, reverberate.)

PEANUTS

verbs
blanch—; chop—; clean—; consume—; crush—; cultivate—; dig up—; dry—; express from—; extract from—; hawk—; hurl —at; munch—; package—; ripen—; roast —; salt—; shell—; steam—.

PEAR

adjectives
yellow; waxen; withered; mellowing; hoary; blushing; frozen.

PEARLS

adjectives
oriental; ungathered; lustral; barbaric; shimmering; pink; glistening; creamy; iridescent; liquid; imitation; intermingled; sleepy; enormous; carven; inlaid; snowy; pellucid; perfect; melting; glittering.

verbs
collect—; covet—; cultivate—; deposit—in; dissolve—; dive for—; drill—; embellish with—; fish for—; imitate—; polish—; prize —; string—; value—; yield—; —adorn; —decorate; —enhance; —glitter; —ornament.
(See jewel, gem, diamond.)

PEARLY

adverbs
iridescently; beautifully; incredibly; exquisitely; sumptuously; opalescently; frostily; intensely; richly; gorgeously; sweetly; delicately; daintily; incredibly; marvelously; miraculously; creamily; consummately; indescribably; ineffably.

PEARS

verbs
bear—; blight—; box—; bruise—; can—; cook—; crate—; gather—; grade—; infect —; market—; pare—; pluck—; preserve—; select—; serve—; spray—; stew—; wrap—; —cluster; —decay; —exude; —ripen; —rot; —thrive.
(See fruit, apple.)

PEAS

adjectives
dwarf; delicate; wild.

verbs
box—; can—; crate—; cultivate—; gather —; grade—; harvest—; injure—; plant—; process—; refrigerate—; row—; scoop up —; separate—; shell—; ship—; wash—; —germinate; —mature.
(See vegetables.)

PEASANTS

adjectives
unspoiled; passionate; raw; rude; jubilant; squalid; white-bearded; wretched; shelter-seeking; hopeless; gentle; naked; vindictive; insurgent; healthy-looking; well-dressed; trilingual; downtrodden; distrustful; hard-faced; unforgiving; self-assertive; universal; swarthy; enterprising; bewildered; unlettered; grimy; prating; honest-hearted; ruddy-cheeked; uncultivated.

verbs
agitate—; aid—; appease—; banish—; dominate—; enslave—; exile—; tyrannize over—; —assemble; —clamor; —herd; —economize; —immigrate; —rebel; —revolt; —toil; —uprise; —weary.
(See natives, countryman, farmer, worker, alien, foreigner.)

PEBBLES

adjectives
dewy; rounded; polished; sun-kissed; hard-flung; clean; colored.

PECCABLE

adverbs
unfortunately; unhappily; admittedly; unwontedly; naturally; unquestionably; pitifully; helplessly; probably; alarmingly; outrageously; undeniably; exceptionably; miserably; wretchedly; recklessly; irremediably.

PECULIAR

adverbs
racially; highly; distinctly; definitely; quaintly; strikingly; remarkably; curiously; oddly; highly; outlandishly; exotically; unaccountably.

PECULIARITY

adjectives
petty; salient; social; seasonal; manifold; awful; definite; well-known; humorous; quaint; minute; arbitrary; marked; intellectual; striking; mental; sectional.

PECUNIARY

adverbs
distinctly; exclusively; wholly; avariciously; fortunately; undeniably; definitely; conveniently; opportunely; luckily.

PEDAGOGICAL

adverbs
unmitigatedly; absolutely; definitely; pedantically; wholeheartedly; monotonously; tediously; loudly; blatantly; opinionatedly; patiently; studiously; meticulously; wisely; tiresomely; intelligently; boresomely; mildly; resolutely; ostentatiously; vainly; egotistically; priggishly; pompously; humbly; modestly; pretentiously; self-consciously; self-righteously; emphatically; insistently; dogmatically; proudly; impossibly.

PEDAGOGUE

adjectives
groveling; admirable; gross; stupid; harassed.

PEDANT

adjectives
sand-blind; miserable; fiery; academic; forward; wrangling.

PEDANTIC

adverbs
unmistakably; unshakably; tiresomely; insufferably; proudly; intolerably; ostentatiously; self-righteously; insistently; vexatiously; primly; assertively; confidently; solemnly; sharply; monotonously; incurably; absurdly; unwarrantably; scrupulously; consciously; punctiliously; unbearably; meticulously.

PEDANTRY

adjectives
display—; encrust with—; engender—; ridicule—; savor of—; scorn—; shake off—; —affects; —concludes; —disgusts; —dogmatizes; —obtrudes; —overestimates; —overacts; —poses; —prejudices; —presumes; —proceeds from; —repels.
(See learning, vanity.)

PEDDLER

adjectives
itinerant; flesh; pavement; unscrupulous; stentorian.

PEDESTAL

adjectives
elevated; formal; equal.

verbs
adorn—; bestride—; construct—; erect upon—; mount on—; ornament—; prop on—; repose on—; rest on—; topple from—; totter on—; —affords; —bases; —bolsters; —maintains; —supports; —sustains.
(See base, support, foundation.)

PEDESTRIAN

adjectives
belated; faulty; dust-covered; tall; muscular; travel-stained; raw-boned; successful; ardent; jay-walking.

verbs
accord to—; assist—; block off—s; educate—; endanger—; hamper—; injure—; signal—; warn—; —co-operates; —crosses; —disobeys; —dodges; —evades; —observes; —tires; —tours; —travels; —wearies.

PEDIGREE

adjectives
unbroken; feudal; proud.

PEEP

adjectives
fair; momentary; hasty.

PEEP (*v*)

adverbs
shyly; slyly; shrinkingly; daringly; audaciously; modestly; coyly; flirtatiously.
(See peer, look.)

PEER

adjectives
painstaking; puissant; contemporary; penniless; wrong-incensed; gentle; lustrous; witty; notorious; impecunious; favorite.

PEER (*v*)

adverbs
earnestly; intently; timidly; curiously; cautiously; anxiously; fearfully; furtively; surreptitiously; slyly.
(See peep, look.)

PEERAGE

verbs

bestow—upon; congratulate—; convoke—; create—; entitle—to; forfeit—; influence—; limit—; privilege—; represent—; —adheres; —controls; —convenes; —honors; —serves.

(See aristocracy, nobility.)

PEEVISH

adverbs

unspeakably; unreasonably; unwarrantably; terribly; disagreeably; unfortunately; unpleasantly; horribly; uncommonly; habitually; naturally; querulously; feverishly; childishly; fretfully; captiously; obstinately; incurably; acrimoniously; vexatiously; intolerably; insufferably; unaccountably; inexplicably; curiously; strangely; oddly; significantly; brusquely; snappishly; embarrassingly; humiliatingly.

PEG

adjectives

rustic; wooden; unfitted.

verbs

bind to—; dangle from—; drive—; hammer —; hang on—; hitch to—; insert—; pin with—; pound—; repose on—; tie to—; whittle—; —catches; —fastens; —holds; —projects; —protrudes; —supports; —sustains.

(See nail, hook.)

PELICAN

adjectives

rangy; large-billed; awkward.

verbs

—fishes; —gorges; —plunges; —secretes; —seizes.

(See bird.)

PELLUCID

adverbs

beautifully; admirably; unusually; wonderfully; marvellously; delightfully; incomparably; unsurpassably; limpidly; surprisingly; pricelessly; extraordinarily; inimitably; exquisitely; incomparably; peculiarly.

PEN

adjectives

educated; guided; gifted; severe; unbiased; inexhaustible; spiteful; brilliant; shy; inexpressive; horrible; abler; plaguy; ill-natured; ready; fascinating; vile; enigmatic; substantial; facile; untrained; sprightly; blithesome; humorous; truant; burning; barbarous; dreadful; lucid; inadequate; young; passion-guided; trenchant.

verbs

dip—; exercise—; grasp—; poise—; pour from—; probe—into; scrawl with—; whisk —across; wield—; —assails; —comes to life; —exposes; —falters; —libels; —sears; —unfolds; —voices.

(See fountain-pen, writer, author, pencil.)

PEN (v)

adverbs

obscurely; trenchantly; spitefully; inexhaustibly; brilliantly; expressively; fascinatingly; enigmatically; facilely; passionately.

(See record, compose, write.)

PENAL

adverbs

unnecessarily; cruelly; bitterly; justly; correctively; exceptionably; acidulously; inordinately; egregiously; excessively; mildly; ineffectively; formally; terribly.

PENALIZE (v)

adverbs

ironically; severely; rigorously; painfully; barbarously; harshly; stringently.

(See punish, discipline.)

PENALTY

adjectives

tremendous; painful; mad; inescapable; grievous; similar; severe; proportionate; efficient; enrolled; suitable; spiritual; barbarous; fearful; easy.

verbs

accept—; assert—; assess—; balk at—; condemn to—; decry—; escape—; entail—; evade—; exact—; impose—; inflict—; levy —; pay—; —atones; —recompenses; —rehabilitates.

(See forfeit, fine, punishment, indictment.)

PENANCE

adjectives

fearful; secret; atrocious; purgatorial; easy; spiritual; barbarous; suitable; amorous; cruel; harsh; solemn; hearty; superstitious; severe; lingering; true-hearted; honest.

PENCHANT

verbs
admit—; avoid—; cling to—; eschew—; excite—; exhibit—; incur—; indulge—; —burns; —devours; —disgusts; —irritates; —horrifies; —lusts; —riles (colloq.).
(See desire, inclination, attraction.)

PENCIL

adjectives
stubby; artistic; energetic; mechanical; unsharpened; blunt; coarse.

verbs
clasp—; depict with—; draw with—; drum with—; poise—; scribble with—; sharpen—; tip—; —copies; —dashes off; —delineates; —inscribes; —jots; —marks; —outlines; —scrawls; —scurries; —sketches; —tattoos; —tints.
(See pen.)

PENDANT

adjectives
quaint; inflamed; haughty.

verbs
display—; fashion—; flourish—; hook—; strip off—s; suspend—; —attracts; —bobs; —dazzles; —dangles; —decks; —enhances; —flaps; —fringes; —hangs; —impresses; —ornaments; —swings; —weights.
(See drop, jewel, gem.)

PENDENT

adverbs
terribly; perilously; hazardously; dangerously; decoratively; attractively; delicately; daintily; lustrously; dazzlingly; brilliantly; curiously; strangely; grotesquely; fantastically; quaintly; strikingly.

PENDULOUS

adverbs
heavily; clumsily; awkwardly; corpulently; uncertainly; flabbily; dangerously; indeterminately; wabblingly; loosely; unbecomingly; curiously; strangely.

PENDULUM

adjectives
ponderous; large; rhythmic.

verbs
adjust—; hook—; —controls; —dances; —maintains; —oscillates; —pulsates; —regulates; —rocks; —suspends; —swaggers; —swings; —tick-tocks; —vibrates; —wags; —waves.

PENETRATE (*v*)

adverbs
accurately; accidentally; decisively; freely; scientifically; discerningly; gradually.
(See pierce, bore, affect.)

PENETRATING

adverbs
curiously; deeply; warrantably; peculiarly; particularly; remedially; soothingly; alleviatingly; surprisingly; remarkably; strikingly; incredibly; unusually; uncommonly; acutely; shrewdly; intelligently; keenly; sharply; discerningly; cleverly; sagaciously; profoundly; incisively; impressively; unfailingly; highly.

PENETRATION

adjectives
profound; calm; accurate; usual; subtle; intuitive; bland; noiseless; perfect; uncanny; characteristic; instinctive; partial; infallible; tender; masterly; sympathetic.

verbs
attempt—; block—; escape—; evade—; force—; induce—; pretend—; resist—; unite by—; wonder at—; —awes; —discerns; —discriminates; —gores; —shoots; —uncovers; —yawns.
(See infiltration.)

PENINSULA

verbs
approach—; fortify—; guard—; inhabit—; near—; overrun—; surround—; view—; watch—; —adjoins; —beckons; —extends; —lengthens; —projects; —protrudes; —reaches; —ranges; —stretches.
(See marsh, island, land.)

PENITENCE

adjectives
haggard; pale; celestial; pathetic; anxious; prescribed.

PENITENT

adverbs
deeply; sincerely; sorrowfully; painfully; naturally; contritely; meekly; humbly; embarrassingly; truly; unduly; ruefully; obviously; evidently; manifestly; pitiably; confessedly; terribly.

PENNILESS

adverbs
pitiably; undeniably; finally; terribly; sadly; frightfully; dreadfully; ruefully; laughably; merrily; blithely; carelessly; nonchalantly; miserably; wretchedly; helplessly; hopelessly; vexatiously; embarrassingly; obviously; humiliatingly; manifestly; actually; evidently; strangely; inexplicably; unaccountably; purposely; intentionally; adroitly; cleverly; resolutely.

PENNY-WISE

adverbs
cleverly; carefully; penuriously; thriftily; cannily; shrewdly; capriciously; extravagantly; wastefully; absurdly; unreasonably; ridiculously; improvidently; lavishly; inconsistently; recklessly; ludicrously; incongruously.

PENSION

adjectives
contributory; liberal; retiring; literary; subsidiary; old-age.

verbs
assign—; authorize—; bestow—upon; derive —from; establish—; exact—; fix—; forfeit —; grant—; merit—; proffer—; provide—; request—; reserve for—; retire on—; welcome—; yield—; —assists; —enables; —encourages; —supports; —sustains.

(See pay, payment, allowance, subsidy.)

PENSIVE

adverbs
abstractedly; incongruously; strangely; silently; absent-mindedly; sweetly; quietly; soberly; anxiously; remotely; dreamily; ruefully; mournfully; dully; deeply; gravely; solemnly; happily; contentedly.

PENTHOUSE

verbs
decorate—; enjoy—; establish in—; furnish —; inhabit—; occupy—; offer—; philander on—; provide—; renovate—; view from—; —allures; —appeals; —attracts; —caps; —crowns; —delights; —enchants; —overlooks; —tops.

(See tower, apartment, roof.)

PENURIOUS

adverbs
intolerably; terribly; necessarily; pitiably; meanly; basely; incomprehensibly; inexplicably; unreasonably; unpardonably; suspiciously; suddenly; inherently; naturally; inconveniently; conspicuously; strangely; incorrigibly; greedily; irremediably; unreasonably; disagreeably; unnecessarily; needlessly; unaccountably; niggardly; miserly; inexcusably; stingily; crustily; gruffly; wretchedly; avariciously; uncommonly; extremely; absurdly; miserably; sordidly.

PENURY

adjectives
cold; hard; frosty; tedious; unvanquishable; sordid; forgetful; utter; gripping; miserable.

verbs
burden by—; conceal—; fear—; feign—; reduce to—; resist—; survive—; —afflicts; —aggrieves; —deprives; —distresses; —embarrasses; —harasses; —irks; —narrows; —necessitates; —pains; —weighs upon.

(See poverty, want, destitution.)

PEOPLE

adjectives
aboriginal; abused; accursed; adventurous; affectionate; agile; alert; amiable; amused; aristocratic; aspiring; astounding; austere; aware; barbaric; benevolent; benighted; bent; border; brave; brusque; bustling; celebrated; charitable; chivalrous; civilized; cold; common; commonplace; communicative; congenial; congregated; conquering; constructive; contemplative; conventional; credulous; cruel; cultivated; debonair; decadent; decent; defenseless; degraded; deluded; democratic; desperate; devoted; diminutive; discontented; distinguished; discriminating; dissipated; distinct; doglike; distressed; egotistical; elbowing; eminent; energetic; enervated; enslaved; enfranchised; engrossing; enlightened; enterprising; erect; estimable; excited; everlasting; expatriated; extravagant; factious; fanciful; fashionable; fertile; fastidious; fickle; filthy; frenzied; fun-loving; friendless; friendly; frivolous; gaily-dressed; gay; generous; gloomy; grateful; great; growing; high-minded; homogeneous; humble; humdrum; hurrying; idolatrous; illiterate; impoverished; impulsive; inarticulate; indestructible; indignant; industrious; infatuated; inflamed; infuriated; insane; intense; kind-hearted; interesting; jealous; law-loving; kindly-faced; laboring; learned; liberty-loving; light; lighter; litigious; lively; malicious;

martial; materialistic; mediocre; merry; milling; miserable; modest; missionary-minded; money-making; nice; much-praying; mysterious; neighboring; niggardly; noble; nomadic; notable; noteworthy; obscure; oppressed; outrageous; overfed; packed; panic-stricken; peace-loving; panting; paradoxical; pastoral; peculiar; pediatric; perfect; persistent; persuadable; pessimistic; picturesque; pious; polished; polite; poor; poorly-dressed; practical; precise; prehistoric; preposterous; primitive; progressive; prominent; proud; provoking; quarrelsome; refined; reflective; restless; rich; rigid; rude; rugged; rushing; sagacious; sanguine; seafaring; selfish; sensible; self-seeking; semi-literate; sensitive; sentimental; servile; shabby; shade-loving; sightless; sleek; snobbish; smart; sober; social-minded; solitary; sore; sovereign; special; started; startled; stiff; strange; strong; stupid; sturdy; stylish; supine; substantial; suffering; sufficient; superior; superstitious; swollen; terror-stricken; thoughtful; tempted; thinking; tiresome; thoughtless; timid; tranquil; turbulent; ulcerous; unambitious; unclassical; uncouth; uncultivated; uncultured; unfortunate; unnatural; unobtrusive; unpoetic; unpolished; unreasonable; unreasoning; verbose; vigilant; vigorous; virile; virtuous; visiting; volatile; weak; well-dressed; well-informed; wholesale; wise; wonderful; wondering; worthless; young.

verbs
chide—; color—; conciliate—; corral—; denounce to—; depict—; fraternize with—; instigate—; jolt—; liberate—; outsmart (colloq.)—; portray—; regiment—; tyrannize over—; —arise; —flock to; —gather 'round; —rally to; —revolt; —sanction.

(See English, folk, race, tribe, nation, persons, community.)

"PEP"

verbs
gain—; inject—; lack—; —gains; —brightens; —buoys; —cheers; —emboldens; —endures; —enthuses (colloq.); —glows; —fosters; —impresses; —infects; —inspires; —palls; —reassures; —tingles; —wanes; —warms.

(See energy, power, zeal, vigor.)

PERAMBULATION

adjectives
glad; stealthy.

PERCEIVABLE

adverbs
easily; readily; completely; manifestly; instantly; openly; immediately; perfectly; remarkably; strikingly.

PERCEIVE (v)

adverbs
vividly; tangibly; dimly; sagely; tremulously; instinctively; vaguely; distinctly; superficially.

(See discern, observe.)

PERCENTAGE

adjectives
unknown; doubtful; high.

verbs
calculate—; check—; compute—; cut—; deduct—; demand—; derive—; draw—; exact—; extract—; fix—; reduce—; stabilize—; yield—; —abates; —ascends; —exceeds; —mounts; —staggers.

(See amount, sum, proportion, part, rate, quantity.)

PERCEPTIBLE

adverbs
dimly; readily; scarcely; easily; cruelly; bitterly; instantly; immediately; finally; distinctly; conspicuously; plainly; clearly; mistily; hardly.

PERCEPTION

adjectives
triumphant; keen; dimmest; acute; quick; startling; single; ominous; honest; innate; intuitive; vivid; sharp; intellectual; mental; artistic; sudden; passive; dreamlike; accurate; exquisite; prodigious; vague; confused; sentimental; simultaneous; mystic; infallible; subtle; extra-sensory; spiritual; cloud; sure; steadfast; moral; awful; luminous; interior; penetrating; practical; human.

verbs
attain—; blind—; blunt—; clarify—; display—; dull—; heighten—; stimulate—; warp—; —adjusts; —aids; —appreciates; —apprehends; —fathoms; —matures; —scans; —warns.

(See eye, feeling, sensation.)

PERCH

adjectives
convenient; incongruous; precarious; lofty.

PERCH (*v*)

adverbs

conveniently; precariously; loftily; importantly; securely; gracefully; daringly.

(See sit, place.)

PERDITION

adjectives

everlasting; bottomless; eternal.

verbs

condemn to—; consume to—; —annuls; —batters; —blasts; —blots out; —confounds; —crashes; —crumbles; —demolishes; —desolates; —devastates; —devours; —engulfs; —eradicates; —overwhelms; —perplexes; —prostrates; —swamps.

(See hell, ruin, destruction.)

PEREMPTORY

adverbs

disagreeably; proudly; dictatorially; extremely; unnecessarily; arrogantly; emphatically; bumptiously; incisively; cuttingly; unwarrantedly; officially; formally; coldly; sharply; sternly; severely; trenchantly; unfortunately; offensively; unwisely; deliberately; habitually; unconsciously.

PERENNIAL

adverbs

conveniently; dependably; delightfully; satisfactorily; reliably; imperishably; comfortably; durably; happily; fortunately.

PERFECTION

adjectives

absolute; delicate; abnormal; classic; spontaneous; aesthetic; time-softened; infinite; divine; optical; fashionable; rare; strained; technical; ineffable; trim; studied; flattering; pure; balanced; complete; supreme; ravishing; final; theoretical; comparative; prosperous; exquisite; unlimited; overwhelming; matchless; constant; minute; moral; true; mechanical; imaginable; artistic; pure; tailored; unapproachable.

verbs

achieve—; acquire—; admire—; approximate—; attain—; disclaim—; emulate—; gain—; invest with—; lack—; mature to—; realize—; ripen to—; sacrifice—to; seek—; strive for—; transcend—; vie for—; —clinches; —crowns; —eludes; —saturates; —seals.

(See beauty, mastery, precision, accuracy.)

PERFIDIOUS

adverbs

dreadfully; treacherously; habitually; racially; inherently; terribly; seditiously; personally; highly; uncommonly; unforgivably; manifestly; cruelly; barbarously; savagely; dangerously; sadly; undeniably; disloyally; untrustworthily; dastardly; basically; horribly; wickedly; deliberately.

PERFIDY

adjectives

armed; household; unspeakable; calculated.

PERFORM (*v*)

adverbs

unwittingly; gallantly; energetically; creditably; pleasantly; dramatically; conscientiously; theatrically; gratuitously; brilliantly; capably; faithfully; methodically; scrupulously; publicly; effectively; zealously; punctually; rigorously; harmoniously; superlatively; exceptionally; consummately.

(See accomplish, execute, play, act.)

PERFORMANCE

adjectives

relative; theoretical; undignified; smooth; eager; zealous; arduous; singular; dependable; punctual; proved; pirated; exhibition; indubitable; silent; rigorous; maximum; choice; splendid; shoddy; slipshod; pantomimed; effective; harmonious; superficial; sensational; spectacular; laudable; charity; magnanimous; humdrum; incisive; top; charitable; superlative; decennial; periodic; scrupulous; sparkling; exceptional; ill-considered; splendid; faithful; vigorous; painstaking; proper; careless; innocuous; astonishing; fearless; brazen; discreditable; irresponsible; graceful; improper; superb; middling; subsequent; persuasive; impressive; remarkable; brilliant; magnificent; consummate.

verbs

acclaim—; affect—of; applaud—; broadcast—; direct—; engage in—; infuse into—; inject into—; key—; laud—; render—; reward for—; sponsor—; stage—; suspend—; witness—; —involves; —thrills.

(See feat, deed, entertainment, melodrama, play.)

PERFORMER

adjectives

accomplished; creditable; gratuitous; exact.

PERFUME

adjectives
delicate; sweet; enchanted; native; well-remembered; swooning; drowsy; overpowering; excellent; faint; melodic; exquisite; powerful; delectable; floating; rhetorical; soft; pungent; intoxicating; haunting; filthy; lingering; rich; poisoned; attractive; dead; exotic.

verbs
anoint with—; dab—; distill—; douse with —; drench with—; emit—; exude—; haunt by—; inhale—; recognize—; reek with—; saturate in—; spray with—; steep in—; waft—; —clings; —delights; —exudes; —floods; —nauseates; —offends; —oppresses; —overcomes; —overwhelms; —pervades; —pleases; —scents; —tints.

(See aroma, essence, incense, fragrance.)

PERFUME (*v*)

adverbs
exquisitely; exotically; sweetly; delectably; intoxicatingly; hauntingly; richly; lingeringly; voluptuously.

(See scent.)

PERFUNCTORY

adverbs
arrogantly; smugly; carelessly; disagreeably; unpleasantly; unpardonably; indifferently; apathetically; heedlessly; incautiously; mechanically; thoughtlessly; coolly; unconcernedly; coldly; hastily; inexcusably; inexplicably; unaccountably; horribly; cruelly; unfeelingly.

PERIL

adjectives
approaching; utmost; manifold; sundry (pl); imminent; extreme; extraordinary; real; vague; instant; personal; probable; attendant; vegetable; serious; formidable; growing; imaginary; nimble; incredible; besetting; innumerable (pl); unavoidable; deadly; slight; weird; ever-recurring; encompassing; great; unexpected.

verbs
anticipate—; brave—; chance—; dare—; defy—; encounter—; expose to—; face—; hazard—; incur—; rescue from—; risk—; steel against—; survive—; terrify by—; venture—; warn of—; —endangers; —jeopardizes; —menaces; —oppresses; —threatens.

(See hazard, danger, menace, risk.)

PERILOUS

adverbs
notoriously; notably; undeniably; obviously; terribly; ghastly; miserably; peculiarly; infernally; undisguisedly; unutterably; mortally; bitterly; dreadfully; extremely; inordinately; ominously; mercilessly; prodigiously.

PERIOD

adjectives (*time*)
secluded; adequate; successive (pl); tortured; immediate; postwar; remote; unlimited; towering; prehistoric; immature; dismal; prolonged; engine-creating; brief; chronological; pivotal; corresponding; severe; dangerous; characteristic; distinct; critical; definite; mental; extended; smiling; frivolous; traditional; respective; well-defined; pretentious; momentous; dark; potential; bubble; rude; vigorous; stirring; long; glamorous; creative; controversial; dead; spiritual; modern; specified; variable; brilliant; devastating; limited; fruitful; disturbed; predetermined; unquiet; unmoral; corrupt; medieval; immense; pagan; formative; melancholy; calamity; measurable; pretty; reasonable; considerable; conversational; sidereal; productive; eventful; glorious; previous; lurid; palmy; contagious; glacial; noteworthy; tickling; indefinite; nebulous; typical; anomalistic; sluggish; provincial; impressionable; chaotic; comfortable; proscribed; transition; flourishing; definite; pioneering; congested; amusing; long-forgotten; genial; happy; tranquil; expired; stated; moot; shameful; fecund; wondrous; discreditable; creative; probationary; trying.

verbs
characterize—; conclude—; inaugurate—; launch—; perpetuate—; personify—; plunge into—; shorten—; usher in—; —achieves; —advances; —consumes; —dawns; —dies; —elapses; —embarks; —embraces; —expires; —flows; —glides; —intervenes; —terminates.

(See era, epoch, age, cycle, decade, generation.)

PERIODIC

adverbs
regularly; fortunately; reliably; dependably; wisely; ordinarily; invariably; infallibly; officially; necessarily; duly.

PERIODICAL

adjectives
fledgling; exoteric; esoteric; short-lived; spectacular; fireside; sarcastic; unread.

verbs
dispense—; disseminate—; distribute—; edit —; found—; hawk—; heap —s; hoard —s; launch—; publish—; preserve—; refer to—; scan—; subscribe to—; treasure—; —advertises; —amuses; —delights; —diverts; —illustrates; —informs.

(See newspaper, magazine, publication.)

PERISH (v)

adverbs
desolately; miserably; simultaneously; ignominiously; inevitably; agonizingly.

(See die, decay.)

PERISHABLE

adverbs
highly; uncommonly; unfortunately; remarkably; unluckily; extravagantly; unhappily; particularly; peculiarly; terribly; dreadfully; wastefully; undesirably; inordinately.

PERJURY

adjectives
false; flat; atrocious; cunning; extraordinary.

PERKY

adverbs
roguishly; smartly; saucily; stylishly; fashionably; irresistibly; tomboyishly; quaintly; fascinatingly; interestingly; piquantly; pleasantly; modishly; charmingly; ingeniously.

PERMANENCE

adjectives
historic; unnatural.

verbs
ascertain—; confirm—; establish—; guarantee—; intensify—; retain—of; sense—; threaten—; —drags; —endures; —evaporates; —fades; —flickers; —perseveres; —persists; —protracts; —totters; —weathers.

(See immortality, stability.)

PERMANENT

adverbs
comfortably; securely; admirably; assuredly; warrantably; unquestionably; fortunately; safely; reasonably; steadfastly; unchangeably; durably; inescapably; legally.

PERMISSIBLE

adverbs
expressly; generously; always; scarcely; socially; officially; intimately; obviously; evidently; patently; unconditionally; reportedly; reputedly; apparently; unquestionably; manifestly; definitely; explicitly; palpably; luckily; fortunately.

PERMISSION

adjectives
abstracted; unsolicited; verbal; express; requisite; reluctant; willing.

PERMIT (v)

adverbs
unsolicitedly; verbally; expressly; reluctantly; graciously; lazily; incidentally; promiscuously; readily; gratuitously; stolidly; magnanimously.

(See allow, consent.)

PERORATION

adjectives
justly-admired; noble; sprawling.

PERPETRATE (v)

adverbs
cruelly; fiendishly; illegally; vilely; wickedly; lustfully; crudely; murderously.

(See commit, accomplish.)

PERPLEX (v)

adverbs
facetiously; amazingly; sorely; painfully; cunningly; slyly; verbally; mentally.

(See bewilder, confuse.)

PERPLEXING

adverbs
unaccountably; disturbingly; genuinely; indescribably; strangely; fearfully; insuperably; dishearteningly; depressingly; terribly; vexatiously; alarmingly; unreasonably; uncomfortably; vaguely; subtly; awkwardly; stubbornly; extremely; secretly; annoyingly; exasperatingly; inexplicably.

PERPLEXITY

adjectives
inevitable; great; dim; insoluble; unexplained; sad; natural; painful; unrighteous; mingled; hopeless; dangerous; broken-hearted.

verbs
conceal—; flounder in—; grapple with—;

grope in—; hesitate in—; relieve—; tremble in—; unravel—; view with—; —bewilders; —bothers; —burdens; —confuses; —darkens; —embarrasses; —enmeshes; —entangles; —hounds; —muddles; —nets; —overwhelms; —weaves.

(See amazement, incredulity, bewilderment, uncertainty, complication.)

PERSECUTE (v)

adverbs

mercilessly; relentlessly; odiously; pettishly; determinedly; whimsically; remorselessly; senselessly; bitterly; unjustly; repeatedly; unflaggingly; doggedly; incredibly; unfalteringly.

(See oppress, torment.)

PERSECUTION

verbs

bewail—; criticize—; fear—; inflict—; intensify—; intimidate by—; resist—; single out for—; subject to—; suffer—; temper—; —aggrieves; —dispirits; —grinds; —harasses; —haunts; —pains; —offends; —oppresses; —outrages; —tramples; —weighs.

(See oppression, tyranny.)

PERSECUTOR

adjectives

odious; petty; subtle; religious; domestic; determined; unjust; whimsical; cold-hearted; systematic; unmerited; remorseless; senseless; merciless; relentless; languid; fiery; bitter; imperial; miserable; actual; repeated.

PERSEVERANCE

adjectives

unflagging; relentless; tugging; resolute; dogged; steady; indefinite; incredible; majestic; patient; indomitable; scheming; unfaltering; mechanical.

verbs

acclaim—; acquire by—; instil—; reward —; tax—; wed to—; yield to—; —buckles down; —clings; —devotes; —drives; —falters; —fights; —persists; —plods; —plunges.

(See insistence, patience, persistence.)

PERSEVERE (v)

adverbs

steadily; pluckily; characteristically; unflaggingly; relentlessly; resolutely; doggedly; incredibly; indomitably; unfalteringly; mechanically.

(See continue, persist.)

PERSEVERING

adverbs

resolutely; tenaciously; stubbornly; patiently; gently; mildly; irritatingly; vexatiously; tiresomély; monotonously; wildly; obstinately; mulishly; endlessly; unremittingly; singularly; oddly; peculiarly; awfully; commendably; admirably; terribly; conspicuously; doggedly.

PERSIFLAGE

adjectives

insolent; witty; swift; bantering.

PERSIST (v)

adverbs

archly; insubordinately; doggedly; undauntedly; audaciously; vigorously; stubbornly; enthusiastically; logically; relentlessly; ardently; faithfully; inextinguishably; triumphantly; morbidly; unreasonably.

(See persevere, continue.)

PERSISTENCE

adjectives

marked; ardent; unabated; culpable; faithful; indomitable; cruel; inextinguishable; wonderful; tiresome; patient; triumphant; appalling; morbid; further; uncomplaining; wearisome; adequate; unreasonable.

verbs

dog with—; instil—; tax—; —achieves; —attacks; —continues; —drags; —endures; —fades; —gains; —palls; —survives; —wanes.

(See application, insistence, perseverance.)

PERSISTENT

adverbs

vexatiously; disagreeably; inescapably; unpleasantly; obnoxiously; admirably; remarkably; uncommonly; highly; tiresomely; ardently; passionately; amazingly; incredibly; unreasonably; doggedly; determinedly; obstinately; stubbornly; maddeningly; insufferably; terribly.

PERSON

adjectives

acidulated; acrid; affected; apprehensive; arbitrary; argumentative; arrogant; attractive; bald-headed; bandy-legged; benevolent; blind; blunt; bold; brazen; brokenhearted; captious; capricious; captivating; charming; chivalrous; clear-headed; comely; commanding; compassionate; conceivable; consoling; consumptive; contemplative; conventional; corpulent; courteous; critical; crotchety; cunning; cute; deformed; delicate; democratic; designing; devout; diabolic; diminutive; disagreeable; discontented; discriminating; domestic; distinguished; divine; double; dubious; easygoing; effeminate; eloquent; erect; eminent; entertaining; estimable; firm; excessive; exotic; fastidious; florid; flourishing; fortunate; freckle-faced; frivolous; garrulous; gentle; ghastly; ghostly; gracious; great; grotesque; grizzily; handicapped; hearty; hard-looking; heavenly; heavy; hook-nosed; humorous; hump-shouldered; ignoble; ignominious; illustrious; imaginary; immense; impeccable; impertinent; impious; inconsiderate; indecorous; indolent; industrious; inelegant; influential; informed; ingenious; inimitable; inquisitive; insignificant; insolvent; just; instructed; intelligent; joking; little; knowledged; laughing; legendary; loquacious; malevolent; malicious; massive; masterly; matching; matter-of-fact; meaner; meek; menacing; mild; milk-livered; mocking; modern; moody; morbid; morose; mortified; namby-pamby; nervous; neurotic; never-smiling; nondescript; normal; obedient; obnoxious; obstinate; obstreperous; obvious; occult; odious; officious; ogreish; ordinary; original; outlandish; outrageous; outwitted; zeal-filled; overbearing; overmastering; overt; overweening; pale; pampered; passable; perfect; perfidious; perjured; persevering; phantasmal; phenomenal; phlegmatic; prejudiced; presumptuous; private; prime; profane; proper; prosperous; pugnacious; punctilious; reckless; reflecting; regular; reputable; respectable; reticent; rude; sacred; scientific; sedate; self-effacing; self-indulging; selfish; selfless; sensitive; sentimental; skilled; slim; slippery; small; smiling; solid; sophisticated; stricken; striking; stuffy; stupid; sublime; substantial; superior; susceptible; talkative; sympathetic; thinking; tiresome; traitorous; unaccountable; unapproachable; unauthorized; uncongenial; uncouth; undesirable; unenterprising; unobtrusive; unpeaceable; unruly; useless; unskilled; unvalued; unwieldy; vindictive; unworthy; venerable; veracious; versatile; virtuous; volatile; wall-eyed; well-disposed; well-dressed; well-informed; well-intentioned; willful; wild; wily; witty; wordy; worldly; worthy; outstanding; young; assertive; fictitious.

PERSONABLE

adverbs
altogether; charmingly; unusually; uncommonly; highly; remarkably; obviously; undeniably; delightfully; pleasantly; definitely; emphatically; fortunately; admirably; irresistibly; singularly; particularly; completely.

PERSONAGE

adjectives
trusty; eminent; silent; respectable; shabby; grimy; despondent; bitter; pallid; muse-like; prominent; venerable; radiant; expansive; leading; all-compelling; allegorical; luminous; historical; leathery; filmy; showy; complex; singular; tutelary; fictitious; arrogant; noble; pompous; exalted; illustrious; subsidiary; favorite; powerful; gnarled; cynical; romantic; miraculous; tragic; nude; stalwart; whimsical; honorable; formidable; poetical; important; tremendous; fine; comely; worthy; ruddy; royal; unimportant; distinguished; sordid; strange-looking; shadowy; august; sympathetic.

verbs
conceal—; esteem—; honor—; introduce—; uncover—; —attracts; —awes; —enhances; —fosters; —graces; —impresses; —inspires; —overwhelms; —thrills.

(See individual, person, character.)

PERSONAL

adverbs
intimately; pleasantly; graciously; undeniably; particularly; unusually; remarkably; highly; uncommonly; specifically; significantly; unpleasantly; definitely; emphatically; obviously; curiously; manifestly; evidently; cruelly; flatteringly; bitterly.

PERSONALITY

adjectives
vivid; perfect; tenuous; fascinating; self-determining; judicial; calumnious; melancholy; unreasonable; erratic; projected; winning; fictitious; operatic; strong; abounding; poetic; vital; charming; intuitive; forceful; robust; integrated; recognizable; eminent; endowed; imaginative; meditative; potent; intense; aggressive; unimpaired;

distinct; agreeable; austere; vigorous; delightful; sinister; conscious; dignified; courteous; general; amiable; unfettered; exciting; dual; sure-fire; predominating; dramatic; arresting; exquisite; variegated; inward; unlicensed; curious; intense; embarrassed; aloof; conspicuous; dominant; big; vibrant; dynamic; powerful; attractive; winning; glowing; composite; serene; underlying; ostensible; unique; thorough; childlike; miserable; wholesome; firm; definite; recurrent.

verbs
absorb in—; build—; destroy—; develop—; disintegrate—; distort—; divest of—; electrify—; enhance—; enrich—; evolve—; lack —; radiate—; relapse into—; shed—; stamp —; stimulate—; submerge—; veil—; vitalize—; warp—; —matures; —s merge; —splits.
(See character, individuality, ego.)

PERSONIFICATION

adjectives
restful; dumpy; shadowy; tremendous.

PERSONNEL

verbs
alter—; charge—with; criticize—; enhance —; increase—; limit—; reduce—; retain—; superintend—; supervise—; train—; —assists; —inspects; —manages; —merits; —strikes; —votes.
(See staff, employees.)

PERSPECTIVE

adjectives
theatrical; artificial; monotonous; accurate; wide; historical; brilliant; scornful; infinite; dim; calm; true; enchanting; celestial; vast; soft; permanent; clear; interminable; deep; remarkable; boundless; artistic.

verbs
adjust—; broaden—; check—; clarify—; contemplate—; depend on—; develop—; gain—; influence—; lack—; maintain—; narrow—; reduce—; —assumes; —astonishes; —clears; —differs; —matures; —warps.
(See outlook, view, position.)

PERSPICACIOUS

adverbs
unusually; keenly; shrewdly; uncommonly; highly; brilliantly; astutely; penetratingly; subtly; craftily; warily; cleverly; undeniably; uncommonly; sharply; sagaciously; wisely; quietly; observantly; gravely; signally; amazingly; marvellously.

PERSPIRATION

adjectives
violent; perpetual; clammy; profuse; excessive; flabby; cold; healthy; copious; odorous.

verbs
bathe in—; check—; drench with—; effuse —; excrete—; exude—; induce—; promote —; —annoys; —beads; —breaks from; —dampens; —drains; —escapes; —filters; —flows; —glistens; —gushes; —oozes; —purges; —reeks; —saturates; —streams from; —trickles.
(See sweat.)

PERSPIRE (v)

adverbs
profusely; perpetually; clammily; excessively; copiously; odorously; disgustingly; nauseatingly.
(See sweat, discharge.)

PERSUADE (v)

adverbs
readily; ultimately; tactfully; forcibly; vigorously; firmly; unobstructively; eloquently; argumentatively; soothingly.
(See convince, induce, urge.)

PERSUASION

adjectives
different; forcible; vigorous; firm; fanciful; deep; kind; parental; instinctive; womanly; melancholy; powerful; unobstructive; eloquent; persistent; argumentative; intimate; undoubting; kindly; soothing; demagogic.

verbs
advocate—; exercise—; possess—; rely upon —; resort to—; yield to—; —baits; —bewitches; —convinces; —entices; —forces; —impresses; —influences; —overcomes; —overwhelms; —seduces; —tames; strive for —.
(See belief, influence.

PERSUASIVE

adverbs
smoothly; irresistibly; graciously; cordially; sternly; suavely; politely; overpoweringly; passionately; enthusiastically; ardently;

overwhelmingly; subtly; insinuatingly; ingratiatingly; imperceptibly; forcibly; violently; loudly; crassly; disagreeably; pleasantly; completely.

PERT

adverbs
saucily; prettily; roguishly; mischievously; brazenly; impudently; insufferably; suddenly; trickily; archly; wantonly; insolently; rudely; flippantly; frivolously; idly; boldly; amazingly; daringly; naughtily; glibly; smartly.

PERTINACITY

adjectives
savage; playful; relentless; unprecedented; unwavering.

PERTINENT

adverbs
opportunely; advantageously; gravely; curiously; significantly; admirably; commendably; undeniably; profitably; happily; remarkably; unexpectedly; strikingly; helpfully; serviceably; usefully; fortunately; harmoniously; critically.

PERTURB (*v*)

adverbs
irritably; mentally; habitually; mutually; emotionally; superficially; impatiently; pathetically.
(See excite, disturb, agitate.)

PERTURBATION

adjectives
irritable; curious; mental; observed; habitual; internal; planetary; mutual; past; lunar; evident.

verbs
bear—; cool—; endure—; experience—; ferment—; inflict—; provoke—; shake with —; smart under—; wince in—; writhe in —; —chafes; —chokes; —enrages; —infects; —inflames; —jolts; —shakes.
(See excitement, emotion, disturbance.)

PERTURBED

adverbs
naturally; slightly; deeply; inwardly; secretly; obviously; visibly; incomprehensibly; shockingly; inordinately; extremely; curiously; strangely; painfully; pathetically; gravely; seriously; helplessly; subtly; absurdly; momentarily; terribly.

PERUSAL

adjectives
candid; careful; calm; submissive; cool; studied.

PERUSE (*v*)

adverbs
studiously; exhaustively; intensely; candidly; calmly; coolly; professionally; determinedly; imaginatively; sympathetically.
(See read, scan.)

PERVADE (*v*)

adverbs
intimately; intensely; foully; insidiously; curiously; morbidly.
(See penetrate, pierce, affect.)

PERVASIVE

adverbs
strangely; utterly; offensively; unpleasantly; disagreeably; delightfully; agreeably; fragrantly; pleasantly; pungently; aromatically; alarmingly; dangerously; deliberately; ominously; suddenly; terribly; sweetly; nauseatingly; acridly.

PERVERSE

adverbs
obstinately; wilfully; stubbornly; intractably; ungovernably; sadly; dreadfully; doggedly; waywardly; wantonly; purposely; deliberately; captiously; capriciously; inexplicably; inscrutably; unexpectedly; uncommonly; malignantly; hatefully; spitefully; fearfully; irritatingly; vexatiously; viciously; mischievously; incorrigibly.

PERVERSION

adjectives
horrible; abominable; monstrous; palpable; sexual; wilful.

verbs
practise—; resort to—; uncover—; unravel —; —abuses; —blemishes; —corrupts; —decimates; —defiles; —distorts; —impairs; —infects; —misdirects; —misleads; —poisons; —warps; —weakens; —misinterprets.
(See abuse, obscenity, corruption.)

PERVERSITY

adjectives
elaborate; hidden; curious.

verbs
brave—; condemn—; endure—; inflict—upon; temper—; treat with—; yield to—; —aggrieves; —angers; —astonishes; —chafes; —checks; —inflames; —insults; —irks; —jars; —provokes; —resists.
(See obstinacy, stubbornness.)

PERVERT (v)

adverbs
odiously; horribly; abominably; monstrously; palpably; wilfully; sexually.
(See debase, falsify.)

PESSIMISM

adjectives
sour; melancholy; polite; morbid; counterbalancing.

verbs
balance—; droop in—; infuse—; propagate—; remedy—; ridicule—; shake off—; warrant—; wilt under—; yield to—; —crushes; —dampens; —dashes; —dejects; —depresses; —despairs; —disconcerts; —disheartens; —preys upon; —prostrates; —reigns; —represses; —saddens; —shadows; —shrouds; —weighs upon; —withers.
(See hopelessness, cynicism.)

PESSIMIST

adjectives
confirmed; polite; genial; deliberate.

verbs
desolate—; doom—; paralyze—; —clouds; —doubts; —complains; —condemns; —cowers; —disconcerts; —disheartens; —flinches; —funks; —grumbles; —laments; —poisons; —quails; —shies; —suspects.

PESSIMISTIC

adverbs
incorrigibly; incurably; deliberately; apparently; stubbornly; obstinately; horribly; unaccountably; gloomily; moodily; mournfully; miserably; wretchedly; intolerably; disgustingly; woefully; pitiably; unreasonably; morbidly; superstitiously; absurdly; foolishly; ridiculously.

PEST

adjectives
domestic; vicious; uninvited; injurious; destructive; lifelong.

verbs
chastise—; eradicate—; extirpate—; —annoys; —inflicts; —molests; —nettles; —offends; —piques; —plagues; —preys upon; —racks; —rankles; —riles (colloq.); —ruffles; —scourges; —torments; —tries; —vexes.
(See nuisance, disease, plague, insect, parasite.)

PESTIFEROUS

adverbs
intentionally; purposely; cantankerously; deliberately; wantonly; persistently; continually; unbearably; meanly; maliciously; venomously; woefully; wretchedly; miserably; curiously; strangely; intolerably; disgustingly; capriciously; naggingly; mischievously; trickily; annoyingly; oddly; wilfully.

PESTILENCE

adjectives
buoyant; great; hateful; occasional; infidel; life-poisoning; spreading; instinctive; infectious; tropical; air-borne.

verbs
breed—; confine—to; ease—; free from—; remedy—; succumb to—; suffer—; survive—; —abuses; —affects; —aggrieves; —breaks out; —devastates; —endures; —oppresses; —outrages; —pains; —prostrates; rages; —ravages; —swamps; —tramples; —victimizes.
(See contagion, disease, plague.)

PET

verbs
caress—; cater to—; cherish—; court—; cradle—; cuddle—; embrace—; favor—; fondle—; hug—; indulge—; maul—; pamper—; patronize—; praise—; serve—; spoil—.
(See child, baby, kitten, puppy.)

PETALS

adjectives
beauteous; flaming; plumy; richly-tinted; smoldering; faded; rich; plucked-out; dusky; yielding; nipped; rained; gauzy; scriptured; drenched; drifting.

verbs
bag—; dry—; gather—; lacerate—; pluck —; press—; tear—; tint—; —adorn; —blanket; —cup; —drop; —open; —shower; —spread; —strew; —unfold; —wilt.
(See flower, plant, leaf.)

PETITION

adjectives
suitable; begging; respectful; vain; bare; urgent; signed; lengthy; eloquent; specific; unanswered; discarded.

verbs
address—; deny—; enter—; evoke—; file —; press—; repeat—; resort to—; seek in —; solicit—; —appeals to; —s beset; —demands; —pleads; —protests; —supplicates.
(See appeal, application, entreaty.)

PETITION (v)

adverbs
fruitlessly; legally; urgently; lengthily; eloquently; specifically; vainly; slavishly; humbly.
(See entreat, pray.)

PETTICOAT

adjectives
balloon; kilted; elegant; lace-trimmed; braided; ankle-length; old-fashioned; billowy.

PETTINESS

adjectives
ironical; quaint; usual; needless.

PETTISH

adverbs
fretfully; peevishly; annoyingly; nervously; feverishly; childishly; jealously; impossibly; unbearably; intolerably; persistently; miserably; curiously; unwontedly; uncommonly; extremely; dreadfully; absurdly; impishly; wretchedly; forlornly.

PETTY

adverbs
frivolously; meanly; insignificantly; ridiculously; contemptibly; miserably; absurdly; childishly; pitiably; curiously; singularly; particularly; extraordinarily; extremely; terribly.

,PETULANCE

adjectives
charming; impatient; cowardly; pathetic; habitual; lasting; proud; angry; pouting; becoming.

PETULANT

adverbs
unusually; abnormally; feverishly; nervously; hysterically; fretfully; wantonly; mischievously; crossly; captiously; habitually; naturally; strangely; oddly; intolerably; inexcusably; curiously; incorrigibly; disagreeably; unpleasantly; obnoxiously; hatefully; wistfully; whiningly.

PEW

adjectives
high-backed; respectable; dusty; uncomfortable; crowded; unused.

verbs
allocate—s; array in—s; commit to—; cram —; cushion—; direct to—; enter—; fill—; kneel in—; occupy—; perch in—; rent—; reserve—; scan from—.
(See place, seat, bench, compartment.)

PHALANX

adjectives
martial; invincible; cunning.

PHANTASIES

adjectives
guilty; childish; unconscious; elaborate; horrid; weird; distempered.

PHANTASY

verbs
coin—; concede—; conjure up—; devise—; dream—; efface—; excogitate—; fabricate —; improvise—; invent—; picture—; strike —; suggest—; —crumbles; —delights; —deludes; —dissolves; —fades; —floats; —passes.
(See picture, vision, image, illusion, delusion.)

PHANTOM

adjectives
sceptered; lurid; ghostly; formless; dismal; ugly; transparent; horrible; ignoble; glorious; charming; terrible; impudent; holy; melancholy; faithless; summer; granite;

pale; fair; cloudy; colossal; secular; recurring; august; prodigious; pleasurable; deceitful; monstrous; solemn; benignant; dark; simulated; majestic; midnight.

verbs
banish—; devise—; ogle at—; observe—; picture—; spy—; stare at—; —appears; —departs; —dissolves; —evaporates; —fades; —glares; —leers; —looms; —melts away; —passes; —retires; —vanishes.
(See apparition, ghost, vision.)

PHASE

adjectives
various (pl); intimate; personal; extreme; pioneering; ethical; sectional; curious; transitional; manifold (pl); subtle; intermediate; dramatic; conciliating; increasing; unavoidable; varying; unknown; disinterested; ever-changing; important; precise; enthusiastic; nascent; indispensable; interesting; vehement; exceptional; strenuous; submerged; characteristic; delicate; dreadful; periodic; gibbous; special; renewed; pathetic; romantic; significant; peculiar; diversified (pl).

verbs
alter—; assume—; discover—; enjoy—; explore—; exhibit—; form—; interpret—; investigate—; labor through—; master—; pry into—; recognize—; restore—; shape—; undo—; view—; —determines; —melts; —passes; —shifts.
(See condition, state, aspect.)

PHEASANT

verbs
domesticate—; flush—; hunt—; —beats; —bellows; —bills; —challenges; —crows; —feigns; —flutters; —glides; —haunts; —jerks; —pants; —roves; —rumbles; —rustles; —scratches; —steals; —struts; —thumps; —thunders; —whirs.
(See fowl, bird.)

PHENOMENA

adjectives
singular; neutral; visible; manifold; historical; sensible; mental; moral; capricious; multitudinous; brilliant; hypnotic; naked; ordinary; sundry; chromatic; scientific; degrading; spiritualistic; subjective; perplexing; interesting; bowling; entrancing; phonetic; characteristic; absurd; hopeful; remote; impressive; extraordinary; sublime; universal; curious; ambiguous; social; linguistic; transitory; remarkable; unprecedented; striking; continuing; nervous; natural; capital; disturbing; electrical; kindred; unrelated; sporadic; physical; rare; volcanic; analogous; ingenious; mysterious; poetical; psychic; ghastly; monstrous; psychasthenic; expressional.

PHENOMENAL

adverbs
amazingly; incredibly; strangely; oddly; unbelievably; curiously; particularly; extremely; extraordinarily; abnormally; inexplicably; surprisingly; indubitably; matchlessly; superhumanly; superbly; extravagantly; fantastically; grotesquely; magnificently; splendidly; brilliantly; unutterably; indescribably; mysteriously; strikingly.

PHENOMENON

verbs
account for—; adduce—; aggravate—; belittle—; clarify—; elucidate—; exhibit—; explain—; exploit—; marvel at—; observe—; study—; stumble upon—; uncover—; view—; witness—; —amazes; —deludes; —excites; —indicates; —interests; —proves.
(See sight, miracle, fact, event.)

PHILANTHROPIC

adverbs
nobly; ostentatiously; sincerely; generously; admirably; commendably; unusually; notably; admittedly; consistently; dependably; lavishly; cordially; graciously; benignantly; magnanimously; broadmindedly; charitably; amiably; considerately; bounteously; altruistically; naturally; genuinely.

PHILANTHROPIST

adjectives
pretended; distinguished; irresponsible; long-headed; misguided; sundry (pl); disinterested; paralytic; generous; sanguine; supposed.

PHILOSOPHER

adjectives
pragmatic; classical; political; contemporary; quietistic; talkative; pompous; mystic; awe-stricken; physical; amiable; sour-grape; constitutional; disputative; logical; advanced; grave· weary; deistic; famous; dramatic.

verbs
comprehend—; dispute—; —applies; —asserts; —assists; —concludes; —contemplates; —dreams; —guides; —idealizes; —instructs; —observes; —perceives; —perfects; —proves; —records; —regulates; —restores; —searches; —speculates; —studies; —transcends.
(See idealist, naturalist, scientist.)

PHILOSOPHICAL

adverbs
distinctly; notably; comfortably; consistently; brilliantly; wisely; soundly; serenely; imperturbably; calmly; quietly; sagaciously; comfortingly; gravely; temperately; coolly; thoughtfully; placidly; composedly; tranquilly; deeply; profoundly; intelligently; conspicuously; extraordinarily; consummately.

PHILOSOPHIZE (*v*)

adverbs
sardonically; eloquently; sagely; politically; pompously; mystically; amiably; logically; gravely; ironically; fatalistically.
(See reason, predict.)

PHILOSOPHY

adjectives
inadequate; high; unruffled; healthful; stoical; occult; organized; clammy; comfortable; false; satisfactory; prudential; flippant; half-sportive; shameless; characteristic; educational; primitive; economic; synthetic; seductive; active; natural; fashionable; mental; terrible; positive; classical; calm; fruitful; natural; unoriginal; eclectic; speculative; fatalistic; cruel; worldly; mature; rude; democratic; sustaining; close-webbed; subtle; unprincipled; ruthless; flexible; pessimistic; reminiscent; archaic; seeming; mystical; stern; cynical; droll; lenient; enlightened; ancient; ultra-radical; social; growing; scholastic; coherent; ethnic; haughty; specious; obtrusive; self-centered; intellectual; authentic.

verbs
air—; bespeak—; condemn—; cultivate—; dismiss—; dispense—; dress out—; elaborate—; embody—; emit—; enshrine—; epitomize—; evolve—; execute—; exemplify—; expound—; formulate—; frame—; imbue with—; indulge in—; oppose—; outline—; postulate—; quote—; rear on—; set forth—; shape—; share—; sift—; sum up—; voice —; —consoles; —edifies; —pervades.
(See ethics, modernism, psychology, knowledge, wisdom, thought.)

PHLEGMATIC

adverbs
apathetically; dully; temperamentally; naturally; habitually; constantly; irritatingly; impossibly; vexatiously; incredibly; strangely; curiously; racially; maddeningly; oddly; imperturbably; indifferently; stoically; impassively; heavily; coldly; callously; hopelessly; incurably; dreadfully; inexplicably; stolidly; stupidly.

PHOSPHORESCENT

adverbs
mysteriously; brilliantly; strangely; curiously; frightfully; unexpectedly; terrifyingly; iridescently; magically; conveniently; advantageously; alarmingly; weirdly; fantastically; grotesquely; evanescently; serviceably; magnificently; splendidly; luridly; glowingly; amazingly.

PHOTOGRAPH

adjectives
existing; cherished; superb; appropriate; candid; telescopic; luxurious; insouciant; instantaneous; mammoth; irrelevant; dramatic; large; clear; intimate; vivid; gripping; rare; distinctive; beautiful; portrait; brilliant; enlarged.

verbs
blur—; enlarge—; exhibit—; expose—; frame—; illustrate with—; pose for—; request—; shade—; shadow—; snap—; superimpose on—; tint—; —adorns; —catches; —depicts; —fades; —flatters; —lies; —pleases; —reflects.
(See illustration, masterpiece, picture, sketch, portrait.)

PHOTOGRAPHER

adjectives
straggling; traveling; famous.

verbs
patronize—; shield from—; train—; —arranges; —s cluster about; —decorates; —drapes; —endeavors; —exposes; —focuses; —operates; —practises; —rejects; —selects; —shades; —shadows; —snaps; —solicits; —tints; —views.
(See artist.)

PHOTOGRAPHY

adjectives
professional; instantaneous; distinguished.

verbs
apply—; dabble in—; practise—; study—; utilize in—; —advances; —aids; —attracts; —awes; —captures; —impresses; —improves; —prints; —progresses.
(See science, art.)

PHOTOPLAY

adjectives
swift-moving; hilarious; serious.

PHRASE

adjectives
witty; explicit; ill; fantastic; tragic; poisonous; pompous; exclamatory; characteristic; vivid; musical; impressive; commanding; scriptural; glib; expressive; striking; occult; holiday; pedantic; appropriate; subtle; historic; cold; ringing; invariable; redoubled; banal; polished; recondite; learned; idiomatic; canting; studied; varying (pl); euphemistic; penetrative; useful; circuitous; handled; labored; judicial; modern; specific; introductory; depressed; hackneyed; catchy; authority-bearing; indispensable; superfluous; euphonious; overworked; courtly; sharp; isolated; sonorous; ingenious; allusive; convenient; homely; stereotyped; adulating; incoherent; perfect; sarcastic; technical; detached; silvery; obnoxious; ecstatic; metaphysical; vivid; familiar; poetic; poignant; grandiloquent; rabbinical; audacious; honeyed; theological; trivial; celebrated; sacred; pensive; plaintive; prolegomenous; empty; well-worn; suspicious; fanciful; eloquent; vibrant; comfortable; pungent; parliamentary; painful; vague; choice; polite; editorial; vile; swinish; ejaculatory; charming; dark; terrible; painted; inapplicable; high-sounding.

verbs
cling to—; create—; cull—; echo—; employ—; enunciate—; mouth—; omit—; pelt with —s; quibble over—; stumble over—; toss —s at; —enchants; —escapes; —falls upon; —haunts; —intrigues; —illustrates; —originates in; —scalds; —signifies; —springs from.
(See epithet, idiom, metaphor, idea, thought.)

PHRASE (*v*)

adverbs
subtly; concretely; colloquially; tersely; poetically; redundantly; explicitly; fantastically; vividly; scripturally; glibly; appropriately; euphemistically; ingeniously; obnoxiously; technically; fancifully; pungently; editorially.
(See style, express.)

PHRASEOLOGY

adjectives
accustomed; unhappy; diabolical; realistic; ordinary; commonplace.

PHRASING

adjectives
odd; Ciceronian; intelligent.

PHYSICIAN

adjectives
reluctant; renowned; departing; conscientious; competent; helpful; sagacious; incredulous; understanding; distinguished; eminent; respectable; tolerable; observant; overzealous; consecrated; conservative.

verbs
assist—; communicate with—; confer with—; confound—; consult—; inform—; —administers; —counsels; —decrees; —devotes to; —diagnoses; —examines; —guards; —prescribes; —pronounces; —recommends; —rules; —serves; —warns.
(See teacher, nurse, doctor.)

PHYSIOGNOMY

adjectives
unequivocal; faded; capacious.

PHYSIQUE

adjectives
infinitesimal; ungraceful; delicate; insignificant.

verbs
admire—; approve—; cramp—; endanger—; enfeeble—; esteem—; harden—; improve—; mold—; praise—; reduce—; strain—; strengthen—; vivify—; —deteriorates; —sustains; —toughens.
(See constitution, body.)

PIANIST

adjectives
phenomenal; admirable; fascinating; sleepy.

PIANO

adjectives
grimy; little; tinkling; mechanical; grand; untuned; hideous.

verbs
attune to—; bang on—; beat—; caress—; finger—; instruct on—; perform on—; pound—; practice on—; scale—; strike—; strum on—; —deafens; —distracts; —enchants; —expresses; —peals; —rends; —resounds; —tinkles
(See keyboard, harp, music, banjo.)

PIAZZA

verbs
commit to—; enjoy—; festoon—; meet on —; overhang—; paint—; repose on—; rest on—; retire to—; screen—; shade—; —attracts; —cools; —delights; —refreshes; —spreads.
(See pavilion, porch, courtyard.)

PICK

verbs
brandish—; drive—; dull—; implant—; inject—; plunge—; ram in—; twist—; wield —; —chips; —chops; —cleaves; —cracks; —disperses; —eliminates; —gashes; —hacks; —loosens; —minces; —pierces; —rips; —severs; —shatters; —splinters; —slits; —strikes; —sunders; —uproots; —wrenches.
(See hatchet, axe, knife, tool.)

PICK (*v*)

adverbs
hastily; painfully; captiously; contentiously; aimlessly; obediently; precariously; laboriously; cautiously; mercifully; argumentatively; democratically; shrewdly.
(See select, choose.)

PICNIC

adjectives
perpetual; prolonged; never-ending; impromptu.

PICTORIAL

adverbs
conveniently; serviceably; highly; beautifully; advantageously; profitably; usefully; altogether; intelligibly; graphically; effectively; entertainingly; amusingly; accurately; appropriately; suitably.

PICTURE

adjectives
naturalistic; consistent; coordinated; exaggerated; kaleidoscopic; flaming; ineloquent; amorous; portrait; furry; spectacular; muscular; alert; surreptitious; delicate; dazzling; smiling; luminescent; casual; gay; authentic; elucidating; heavenly; amusing; handsome; paltry; striking; charming; improbable; tender; colored; ineffectual; vivid; conventional; scandalous; arresting; constant; wide; unchanged; forbidding; fascinating; living; veracious; touching; poetic; idyllic; affecting; ensemble; monotonous; pathetic; sacred; classical; religious; unrelated; tragic; philanthropic; dramatic; imaginary; lifeless; vitalized; tone; far-spreading; intimate; varied; dreary; unattractive; entrancing; ludicrous; truthful; well-painted; jumbled; provocative; lurid; moderate; radiant; dumb; black; horrible; finished; idealized; breathing; accurate; lively; grim; etched; mental; deplorable; incomparable; fresh; gilt; moving; notable; comprehensive; imposing; ghastly; emblematic; melancholy; crimson; degrading; allegorical; verbal; coherent; lovely; world-famous; unusual; illuminating; creamy; colorful; outstanding; nature; marvelous; remarkable; alluring; suggestive; candid; contemporaneous; immortal; gloomy; delightful; fleeting; cloud; inimitable; priceless; resplendent; bright; stark; impressive; retinal; choice; instantaneous; incredible; unique; interesting; distinct; decorative; imaginary; blurred; depressing; rhetorical; crude; symmetrical; bewitching; hideous; commercial; glowing; realistic; ghostly; unforgettable; fantastic; penitentiary; composite; dreamy.

verbs
animate—; ban—; blur—; cherish—; clarify —; complicate—; conjure up—; convey—to; delineate—; digest—; distort—; dominate —; embellish—; evoke—; execute—; exhibit—; fade from—; fashion—; harmonize with—; intersperse with—s; mar—; obliterate—; relish—; reproduce—; shade—; shadow—; transmute—; —contrasts with; —depicts; —materializes; —reveals; —revolves around; —unfolds; focus upon—.
(See image, impression, film, canvas, illustration, masterpiece, drawing.)

PICTURE (v)

adverbs

vividly; authentically; artistically; brilliantly; faithfully; eloquently; effectually; scandalously; speculatively; fatalistically; ruthlessly; mystically; cynically; speciously; intellectually.

(See draw, sketch.)

PICTURESQUE

adverbs

highly; uncommonly; magnificently; splendidly; undeniably; wildly; unusually; brilliantly; delightfully; grotesquely; fancifully; fantastically; stupendously; immensely; graphically; singularly; uniquely; oddly; gorgeously; superbly; imposingly; resplendently; sublimely; incomparably; unsurpassably; indescribably; unutterably.

PICTURESQUENESS

adjectives

elaborate; undeniable; vivid; superficial; startling; professional; sublime.

PICTURING

adjectives

dreamy; historical; sumptuous.

PIDDLING

adverbs

absurdly; trivially; vexatiously; idly; foolishly; insignificantly; inconsequentially; horribly; senselessly; stupidly; childishly; preposterously; nonsensically; wastefully; inexcusably; witlessly; ineptly.

PIE

adjectives

silken; leathery-looking; delicious; half-demolished; chattering; browned; fresh; tasty; luscious; steaming.

PIECES

adjectives

inanimate; charming; accessory; exhibitionistic; historical; isolated; perilous; truncated; distinctive; lush; suitable; fugitive; exquisite; impressive; singular; eloquent; dangerous; pendent; crooked; inferior; nimble; complicated; bizarre; honest; vivid; unexpected; ponderous; majestic; solemn; sordid; three-piled; imposing; curious; scientific; adventurous; shaped; bold; atrocious; complex; florid; pathetic; obvious; priceless; detached; merited; miscellaneous; miscreant; neglected; striking; conspicuous; abject; ignoble; deplorable; dilated; volatile; visionary; popular; choral; fruitful; prodigious; gorgeous; wanton; instrumental; floral; character; infernal; sour; heavy-looking; grease-enveloped; first-rate; mere; abominable; delicate; dominating.

verbs

aggregate—; amass—; batter to—; cement—; clutch—; crack into—; crumble into—; crush to—; disintegrate into—; gather—; integrate—; mold—; portion—; smash to—; split into—; unite—; —constitute; —crash; —scatter.

(See chip, fragment.)

PIER

adjectives

elaborate; compound; tropical; much-used.

verbs

anchor at—; buffet—; construct at—; dock at—; destroy—; enclose—; land at—; lash to—; miss—; moor to—; nuzzle into—; offer—; pound—; reserve—; spray—; wash away—; —extends; —projects; —protects; —stretches.

(See landing.)

PIERCE (v)

adverbs

effectually; fatally; mortally; accurately; deeply; ruthlessly; ferociously.

(See stab, bore.)

PIERCING

adverbs

sharply; keenly; acutely; discerningly; accusingly; unpleasantly; disagreeably; unwontedly; incomparably; significantly; suddenly; painfully; uncomfortably; deliberately; astutely; craftily; cunningly; sagaciously; subtly; inescapably.

PIETY

adjectives

deadened; intense; ingrained; filial; quaint; strait; fervent; practical; scrupulous; unaffected; idiotic; humble; punctual; consistent; tempered; intentional; parenthetical; systematic; individual; infant; celestial; instructed.

verbs

commend—; display—; exhibit—; favor—; feign—; influence—; instil—; laud—; practise—; prefer—; pretend—; protest—; re-

semble—; respect—; revere—; —cheers; —converts; —excels; —inspires; —shields.
(See holiness, patriotism, sanctity, kindness, virtue.)

PIG

adjectives
gaping; fastidious; enormous; impious; cadaverous; good-natured; kicking.

verbs
auction—; exhibit—; fatten—; graze—; market—; pen—; slaughter—; stable—; tend—; trough—; —gobbles up; —grunts; —hobbles out; —snorts; —squeals; —stumbles; —swarms; —wallows.
(See hog, cattle, cow, ox.)

PIGEON

adjectives
nimble; plumaged; monogamous; carrier; useful; homing; well-trained.

verbs
drive—s; capture—; market—s; net—s; tame—s; —broods; —consumes; —coos; —s darken; —darts; —s flock; —flushes; —flutters; —gluts; —incubates; —nestles; —strays.
(See bird.)

PIGGISH

adverbs
horribly; brazenly; crassly; grossly; openly; sadly; unashamedly; greedily; rapaciously; voraciously; noisily; terribly; unbelievably; boldly; hoydenishly; brutally; gluttonously; insatiably; selfishly; naturally; inherently; incorrigibly; inexpressibly; definitely.

PIG-HEADED

adverbs
immovably; stupidly; resolutely; implacably; obdurately; stolidly; incurably; inherently; naturally; temperamentally; obstinately; steadily; inexorably; senselessly; unreasonably; distinctly; unmistakably; cruelly; foolishly; absurdly; inanely; pertinaciously; contumaciously; truculently; offensively.

PIGMENT

adjectives
brilliant; bright; waterproof.

verbs
apply—; approve—; combine—; deposit—; employ—; infuse—; insert—; mix—with; secrete—; —blends; —colors; —constitutes; —enhances; —harmonizes; —imbues; —tinges; —tints.
(See paint, color.)

PILE

adjectives
smoldering; vast; honest; unaffected; scholarly; dignified; heterogeneous; monumental; towering; amorphous; sumptuous; colossal; rambling; immense; enormous; unintelligent; gigantic; blazing; aspiring; proud; gothic; voluptuous; chaotic; sunny; frothy; venerable; gloomy; wretched.

verbs
accumulate—; amass—; disperse—; erect—; heap—; knock down—; level—; mow down—; squash—; rummage through—; scatter—; spread—; strew—; upset—; —topples; —totters; —towers; —tumbles; —wanes.
(See heap, fortune, money.)

PILE (*v*)

adverbs
methodically; indiscriminately; commercially; toweringly; heterogeneously; monumentally.
(See heap, accumulate.)

PILGRIM

adjectives
travel-weary; true-devoted; humble; adoring; devout; earnest; forlorn; fanatical; passionate; disconsolate; white-robed; ambulant.

PILGRIMAGE

adjectives
perilous; nightly; sentimental; mocking; annual; holy; poetical; earthly; reverential; earned; pious; connubial; stormy; unwilling; long-promised; useless; macabre; angry; weary; zealous; previous; peaceful; inspiring; maiden; amorous; enforced.

PILL

adjectives
gilded; bitter; curative; magic.

PILLAR

adjectives
lasting; well-deserving; fiery; shrinking; fluted; rocky; cloudy; towering; immovable;

crossed; crowded; decapitated; beauteous; fantastic; shining; vine-clad; unconscious; tottering; petrified; glistening; massive; lone; huge; gigantic; lofty.

PILLORY

verbs
condemn—; deserve—; expose on—; sentence to—; undergo—; whip on—; writhe on—; —agonizes; —disciplines; —enrages; —frightens; —inflicts; —pains; —rebukes; —threatens; —tortures.
(See punishment, torture.)

PILLOW

adjectives
pretty; fringed; skimpy; seaweed; hard; deaf; feverous; unsolaced; dream-haunted; coal; nut-brown; sleepless; downy; humble; tossed; lacy; comforting; nightmared.

verbs
bury in—; grovel in—; heave—; knead—; mash—; prop up with—s; raise on—s; rearrange—; recline on—; relax on—; repose on—; sink into—; support on—; tarry on—; —comforts; —embeds; —envelops; —hushes; —lulls; —supports; —yields.
(See mattress, bed, cushion.)

PILOT

adjectives
desperate; sagacious; visiting; sublime; competent; wartime; licensed; lightning; skilled.

verbs
—communicates with; —conducts; —governs; —guides; —manages; —navigates; —occupies; —prescribes; —regulates; —sounds; —steers; —weathers.
(See guide, helm.)

PILOT (v)

adverbs
daringly; courageously; intrepidly; gallantly; desperately; sagaciously; competently.
(See direct, guide, steer.)

PIMPLES

verbs
break into—; dot with—; eradicate—; pinch —; salve—; squeeze—; treat—; —blotch; —bunch; —deface; —disfigure; —embarrass; —emboss; —mar; —speckle; —spread; —sprout; —swell; —undermine.
(See blemish.)

PIN

verbs
affix with—; attach with—; bristle with—s; jab with—; join with—; load with—s; locate—; mark with—; plant—; secure with —; tuck in with—; —barbs; —connects; —encloses; —fastens; —lodges; —penetrates; —pricks; —scratches; —stabs; —unites.
(See bolt, hook, horn, needle, nail.)

PIN (v)

adverbs
securely; tidily; firmly; mercilessly; relentlessly.
(See fasten, fix.)

PINCH

adjectives
emphatic; warning; relishing; gentlemanly; record; consecutive (pl); imperial; hurting.

PINCH (v)

adverbs
approvingly; emphatically; warningly; playfully; facetiously; cruelly; spitefully; coyly.
(See squeeze, oppress.)

PINCHED

adverbs
miserably; wretchedly; shamefully; woefully; pitiably; pitifully; sadly; haggardly; gauntly; embarrassingly; terribly; helplessly; unusually; unbelievably.

PINE

adjectives
tossing; pillared; mountain; unpolished; longing; runty; serried; lofty; scrubby; gnarled; wind-swept; odorous; immortal; venerable; swaying; gloomy; scattered; palpitating; vocal; dark; unwavering; parasol; scathed; legendary; rocking; storm-battered; pitchy; quick-growing; fragrant; passionless; blackening; glimmering; glutinous.

verbs
hew—; house under—s; —arches; —exudes; —fans; —graces; —moans; —overspreads; —purrs; —rises; —shadows; —shelters; —sighs; —sings; —tips; —tosses; —towers; —waves; —nods.
(See tree.)

PINE (v)

adverbs
miserably; secretly; homelessly; incessantly;

ceaselessly; tragically; woefully; morbidly.
(See long, yearn.)

PINING

adjectives
endless; homeless; heartfelt; secret; lonely.

PINION

adjectives
regal; outworn; borrowed; stooping; joyful; daring; downy; soft-tinted; lightning-braided; fearless; delighted; dusky; trembling; celestial; unimpeded; swanlike; silver; timorous; exultant.

PINK

adjectives
pearl; silver; sparkling; shell; salmon; rose; orchid; delicate; frothy; arresting; translucent; soft; raspberry; light; chalk; lavender; childish; gaudy; pathetic.

PINNACLE

adjectives
far-shadowing; massive; queer; eccentric; silent; lofty; lonely; snow-girt; mountainous; skyey.

verbs
achieve—; adorn—; ascend to—; attain—; descend from—; reach—; set on—; —caps; —crowns; —culminates; —juts; —ornaments; —projects; —rises; —supports; —terminates; —tops; —towers
(See tower, height, zenith, summit, peak, spire.)

PIONEER

adjectives
laboring; primal; rugged; celebrated; veritable; hardy; courageous; daring; undaunted; adventurous; venturous.

verbs
accoutre—; arm—; hark back to—; immortalize—; inure—; ridicule—; —blazes; —braves; —confronts; —conquers; —dares; —endures; —envisions; —equips; —faces; —foresees; —plods; —primes; —rigs.
(See colonist, explorer.)

PIONEER (v)

adverbs
daringly; loyally; laboriously; courageously; undauntedly; intrepidly; vainly; ruggedly; boisterously.
(See brave, defy, dare.)

PIOUS

adverbs
painfully; primly; sedately; priggishly; disgustingly; hypocritically; sincerely; truly; reverently; pharisaically; self-righteously; ostentatiously; suddenly; conveniently; judiciously; astutely; honestly; pretentiously; apparently; manifestly; evidently; strangely; unwontedly; habitually; temperamentally; keenly; remarkably; notably; distinctly; meekly; ardently; fervently; humbly; intensely.

PIPE
(conduit, etc.)

verbs
attach—; block—; clog—; couple—; explore—; flow through—; insert—; join—; lay—; pass through—; pour into—; stream through—; weld—; —bursts; —carries off; —connects; —conveys; —discharges; —emits; —expands; —freezes.
(See hose, conduit, nozzle, duct, drain.)

PIPE
(general)

adjectives
light; short-stemmed; precious; fragrant; rustic; peace; malodorous; masculine-looking; amber; mellow; rich; ripe; giant; fluted; accursed; golden; affluent; seductive; earthen; pastoral; generous; lascivious; faithful; gleeful; smoke-blackened; organ; wide-stopped; foul.

PIPE
(smoking)

verbs
addicted to—; clean—; crust—; draw on—; enjoy—; mislay—; mouth—; pack—; pocket—; scrape—; stuff—; suck on—; —cakes; —cheers; —eases; —fumes; —glows; —mellows; —solaces; —soothes.
(See tobacco, cigar, cigarette.)

PIPING

adjectives
mellow; sad; loud; mild; harmonious; sweet.

PIQUANCY

adjectives
peculiar; quaint; subtle; original; charming; becoming.

PIQUANT

adverbs
saucily; tartly; racily; gaily; charmingly; delightfully; amazingly; highly; entertainingly; interestingly; sharply; pointedly; amusingly; uncommonly; fascinatingly; vigorously; incisively; impressively; pithily; curiously; smartly; distinctly; arrestingly; catchily.

PIQUE

adjectives
momentary; private; definite; petty; pouting.

verbs
—abashes; —aggravates; —crushes; —disgraces; —enrages; —humbles; —humiliates; —irks; —irritates; —mortifies; —provokes; —rankles; —riles (colloq.); —ruffles; —stirs; —strikes; —treads; —vexes; —wounds.
(See anger.)

PIRACY

adjectives
governmental; undiscovered; intellectual; organized.

PIRATE (*v*)

adverbs
ruthlessly; mercilessly; ferociously; dangerously; notoriously; openly.
(See rob, steal, plunder.)

PIRATES

adjectives
ruthless; smiling; merciless; benevolent; ferocious; uncouth; notable; sanctimonious; wrangling; gallant; notorious; bloody; modern.

verbs
execute—; punish—; resist—; —capture; —chase; —conceal; —confiscate; —cruise; —dare; —despoil; —hang; —murder; —pillage; —ply; —plunder; —rove; ——scour; —scuttle; —smuggle; —torture; —venture; —violate.
(See robber, criminal, highwayman.)

PISTOL

verbs
arm with—; brandish—; click—; fear—; flourish—; impound—; load—; snatch—; —cracks; —discharges; —frightens; —kills; —pops; —reports; —rings out; —scares; —sounds; —spits fire; —threatens; —volleys; —wounds.
(See gun, machine-gun, musket.)

PIT

adjectives
fiery; bottomless; infernal; ghastly; fathomless; charnel; abysmal; enchanting; round; stupendous; blazing; murky; sepulchral.

verbs
bore—; burrow—; delve into—; drill—; excavate—; explore—; hollow out—; mine from—; pitch into—; plug—; plunge into—; scoop—; seal—; sound—; —gapes; —traps; —undermines; —yields.
(See hole, opening.)

PITCH

adjectives
extreme; creative; alarming; sharp; overstrained; heightened; uncommon; dolorous; breezy; seething; extraordinary; ruinous; varied; nervous.

PITCH (*v*)

adverbs
drunkenly; plaintively; alarmingly; seethingly; nervously; craftily; professionally; unruffledly; prodigiously; rashly.
(See hurl, toss, throw.)

PITCHER (*baseball*)

adjectives
all-time; great; clever; smooth; easy-working; jerky; wary; unruffled; valuable; undependable; wild; nerveless; crafty.

verbs
bench—; relieve—; —balks; —blazes; —hurls; —nips; —retires; —strikes; —tightens; —toes the slab; —whips; —winds up; —zips; —burns; —controls; —delivers; —fans.
(See player, athlete, fielder.)

PITCHER (*crockery*)

adjectives
emptied; handleless; capacious.

PITEOUS

adverbs
unhappily; distressingly; woefully; grievously; remarkably; uncommonly; disturbingly; undeniably; unusually; indescribably; singularly; extraordinarily; exceedingly.

PITFALL

verbs
avoid—; beset with—; chase into—; conceal—; encounter—; inveigle into—; lure into—; perceive—; perish in—; rescue from—; save from—; suspect—; tumble into—; warn of—; —captures; —ensnares; —overpowers; —surprises; —traps; cover —.

(See ambush, trap, pit.)

PITHY

adverbs
pungently; drily; drolly; remarkably; smartly; absurdly; amusingly; cleverly; wonderfully; amusingly; trenchantly; paradoxically; scintillatingly; brilliantly; wittily; facetiously; curtly; quaintly; humorously; expressively; inimitably; incomparably; succintly.

PITIABLE

adverbs
shockingly; terribly; definitely; deplorably; grievously; miserably; deservingly; truly; intensely; unspeakably; immeasurably; singularly; especially; particularly; peculiarly; unusually.

PITIFUL

adverbs
gently; comfortingly; mildly; wisely; intelligently; sympathetically; helpfully; compassionately; sweetly; indulgently; tolerantly; mercifully; leniently; immensely; unusually; humanely.

PITILESS

adverbs
coldly; cruelly; sternly; implacably; unappeasably; stoically; bitterly; immovably; terribly; horribly; unbelievably; callously; stubbornly; apathetically; mercilessly; inexorably; woefully; ruthlessly; inexcusably; incalculably; incredibly; inexplicably; unaccountably; dreadfully.

PITTANCE

adjectives
slender; remaining; contemptible; meager; trifling; bare; worthless; welcome.

verbs
acquire—; allot—; allow—; beg—; derive—; dole out—; donate—; drain—; draw—; exist on—; live on—; provide—; solicit—; yield—; —contents; —suffices.

(See wages, earnings, money, dole.)

PITY

adjectives
anxious; wondering; contemptuous; melancholy; inexpressible; faded; divine; fluttering; sacred; supplicating; confident; thrilling; scornful; indulgent; misapplied; self-forgiving; infant; ineffable; inner; painful; grave; double; treble; strenuous; unsuspected; tender; infinite; shocked; subtle; languid; affectionate; unutterable; pathetic; immense; foolish; solemn; unfortunate; respectful; anguished; unspeakable; reverent; vanquished; little; careless; continued; skinless; natural; human; divine; profound; angelic; malignant; amazed; indignant; spurious; unrighteous.

verbs
betray—; claim—; eye with—; feign—; implore—of; persecute without—; regard with —; shadow with—; stir to—; submerge in —; waste—on; wrap in—; yield to—; —dries up; —expires; —grips; —moves; —smites; —touches; —tortures.

(See compassion, mercy.)

PLACABLE

adverbs
genially; politely; urbanely; genteely; unexpectedly; impressively; fortunately; luckily; pleasantly; surprisingly; tolerantly; mercifully; blandly; indulgently; reasonably; moderately; thoughtfully.

PLACARD

adjectives
vile; scurrilous; screaming.

verbs
affix—; circulate —s; diffuse —s; disperse —s; display on—; disseminate —s; emblazon with—s; post—; publish—s; set up—; —advertises; —announces; —attracts; —broach-

es; —heralds; —propagates; —screams; —tempts.

(See announcement, advertisement, notice.)

PLACE

adjectives

friendly; delightful; homelike; ideal; comfortable; mournful; war-torn; shrineless; prosperous; logical; halting; unsanctified; tenable; rough; important; joyous; pathless; contrary; prominent; incompatible; rival; lonely; bearable; distinctive; important; dormant; well-chosen; unwholesome; strange; lofty; perilous; objectionable; vulnerable; conspicuous; exalted; native; dwelling; outraged; burial; odd; gloomy; strategic; alleged; ruinous; nestling; shocking; enviable; supreme; sheltered; estimable; noisome; jubilant; wonted; blithe; permanent; wonderful; armed; mossy; foremost; straggling; appointed; seething; knotty; extensive; ancestral; ultimate; floral; popular; accustomed; nocturnal; resting; glorious; unexpected; breeding; venerable; ill-ventilated; foul-smelling; principal; flame-lit; despicable; craggy; prominent; amusing; waste; monastic; undisputed; unbelieving; desert; cozy; distinguished; suitable; subordinate; ill-omened; desolate; legitimate; unsearchable; important; dilapidated; beautiful; historic; pleasant; precarious; ineffable; slippery; well-ordered; tender; garish; big; ghostly; horrible; authentic; undisturbed; colonized; assigned; appropriate; unexpected; forsaken; special; free; easy; ostentatious; genial; fascinating; necessary; distinct; secondary; private; desecrated; hideous; flowery; cherished; noble; holy; definite; rightful; shallow; honorable; inaccessible; hackneyed; provisioned; customary; cheerless; dainty; humble; respective; sacred; shady; sequestered; wretched; parasitic; urbanized; calculated; prominent; languorous; tenement; wondrous; commodious; enormous; typical; predicted; gorgeous; exclusive; considerable; leafy; dreadful; separated; churlish; melancholy; ticklish; impudent; worthy; doleful; far-off; possible; impassible; evident; fearsome; especial; accessible; depressing; horrid; out-of-the-way; green-watered; abiding; enchanted; well-assured; cheerless; retired; window-barred; unique; rude; benighted; equal; convenient; homely; adequate; sacred; remote; proper; tumble-down; miserable; strange; beautiful; subordinate; desired; envied; decided.

verbs

depart from—; disclose—; dislodge from—; empty—; enjoy—in; fall into—; hold—; occupy—; relegate to—of; retain—; seek—; situate in—; snoop about—; transfer from —; usurp—; vacate—.

(See spot, room, locality, space, position, building, town, city.)

PLACE (*v*)

adverbs

voluntarily; precisely; unwittingly; obligingly; publicly; unreservedly; poetically; honorably; superficially; temporarily; conspicuously; recklessly; judiciously; impulsively; impersonally; tenderly; logically; objectionably; vulnerably; exaltedly; depressingly; accessibly; uniquely; rudely; subordinately.

(See establish, locate.)

PLACID

adverbs

immovably; sweetly; generously; vexatiously; serenely; terribly; imperturbably; fortunately; singularly; particularly; habitually; temperamentally; coolly; resolutely; stoically; philosophically; demurely; submissively; sedately; icily; patiently; remarkably; unexpectedly; surprisingly.

PLACIDITY

adjectives

spiritual; austere; frozen; eternal.

PLAGIARISM

adjectives

phenomenal; criminal; audacious; discovered; unintentional; obvious; deliberate; barefaced; bald.

verbs

accuse of—; resort to—; —apes; —borrows; —emulates; —mirrors; —models; —parallels; —patterns; —poaches; —purloins; —simulates; —sponges; —steals.

(See theft, dishonesty.)

PLAGUE

adjectives

destroying; wasting; ordaining; abhorrent; prevalent; devastating; immedicable; grasshopper; noxious; virulent; noisome; vile; deadly; dreaded; remorseless; incurable.

verbs

conquer—; control—; disperse—; guard against—; inoculate against—; —breaks out; —creeps through; —decimates; —descends upon; —rages; —ravages; —slays; —swoops upon; —traverses; —wanes.

(See curse, contagion, disease, infection.)

PLAIN

adjectives

alluvial; dewy; pool-studded; olive-plumed; alluring; torrid; fluctuating; capacious; friendless; brown; sunburnt; smiling; vast; barren; central; abounding; twilight; pensive; mournful; sterile; murderous; ravaged; sunny; harvest-shining; upland; high; delightful; skirting; rugged; rocky; celestial; sandy; trackless; melancholy; comforting; circumfluous; featureless; wan; infernal; illimitable; stubborn; ravished; wide-stretching; idol-burdened; rainy; billowy; fertile; cultivated; extensive; terraced; pastoral; variegated; desolate; prostrate; half-dreary; semibarren; extensive; ethereal; tilted; elevated; semibarbaric; sun-dried; dusky; grassy; placid; cactus; happy; watered; ivory; verdurous; unsheltered; empty; tawny; shimmering; ringing; joyous; delicious; immitigable; flower-paved; smiling; sultry; horrible; boundless; grassless; treeless; long; deep; sandy; wide; deluged; native; chequered; somber; iridescent; sun-blistered; moonlit; pensive; windswept; dazzling; fruitful; burning; ringing (pl); shadowed; immortal; horizon-bounded; stubble; dust-beclouded; undulating; extensive; cattle; classic; redolent; broad; dreary; narrow; soaring; temperate.

verbs

cultivate—; dwell in—; follow—; frequent —; inhabit—; level into—; overlook—; people—; roam—; scan—; till—; travel—; wander over—; —extends; —rolls; —stretches; —unfolds; —unrolls.

(See battlefield, valley, country, land, prairie.)

PLAIN (*unadorned*)

adverbs

emphatically; undeniably; pleasantly; hopelessly; significantly; severely; inartistically; monotonously; invariably; chastely; rigorously; unaffectedly; gracelessly; awkwardly; unfortunately; frightfully; hideously; curiously; singularly; horribly; forbiddingly.

PLAIN (*clear*)

adverbs

delightfully; distinctly; graphically; singularly; curiously; brilliantly; obviously; admirably; conveniently; vividly; unmistakably; extraordinarily; commendably; unusually; extremely; ingeniously.

PLAINNESS

adjectives

rigorous; emphatic; dignified; studious; elaborate; becoming; neat.

PLAIN-SPOKEN

adverbs

fearlessly; bluntly; gruffly; courageously; embarrassingly; irritatingly; dangerously; unwisely; foolishly; senselessly; imprudently; indiscreetly; impoliticly; injudiciously; inexpediently; harshly; offensively; absurdly; ineptly; exasperatingly; awkwardly; harshly; ungraciously; extremely; uncommonly; amazingly; outrageously.

PLAINT

adjectives

pathetic; doleful; somber; noisy.

verbs

breathe—; cease—; detect—; endure—; heave—; reiterate—; renew—; sob—; suppress—; throat—; utter—; whine—; —bursts; —distresses; —fades; —greets; —melts; —moves; —wearies.

(See cry, complaint.)

PLAINTIFF

verbs

allot—; award to—; vest in—; —accuses; —alleges; —appeals; —asserts; —blames; —brands; —challenges; —charges; —contends; —claims; —demands; —denounces; —exacts; —implicates; —imputes; —lodges; —prevails; —reproaches; —waives.

(See defendant, lawyer.)

PLAINTIVE

adverbs

deeply; querulously; tearfully; whiningly; mutteringly; sorrowfully; exasperatingly; sadly; pitifully; endlessly; exceedingly; lamentably; superfluously; unduly; monotonously; obscurely.

PLAN

adjectives

architectural; hazy; delectable; comprehensive; ill-contrived; parricidal; revolutionary; extempore; logical; homely; deferred; startling; intricate; makeshift; deliberate; concerted; showy; ambitious; feasible; cherished; immediate; tentative; denominational; trivial; careful; elaborate; insecure; sundry (pl); inscrutable; execrable; frugal; mercenary; eternal; complicated; primitive; frantic; oft-advanced; definite; extended; weird; detailed; welfare; harmonious; enthusiastic; proved; insurrectionary; simple; daring; grandiose; unproductive; long-concealed; tyrannical; far-trumpeted; solid; subtle; clean-cut; different; merchandising; unbelievable; profit-sharing; odd; cooperative; sensational; thrilling; guaranteed; confidential; startling; unusual; powerful; business; stimulating; certified; mail-order; exclusive; helpful; money-making; sales; new; easy; amazing; premium; business-building; selling; unique; coupon; original; complete; astounding; trade; starting; consistent; uttered; foolish; futile; extensive; complex; ultra-modern; vacation; treacherous; rational; intimate; exclusive; pensive; equitable; sagacious; low; time; payment; quixotic; indivisible; cohesive; philanthropic; meritorious; respective; apparent; eternal; widespread; treadmill; miscarried; nefarious; strict; consecutive; first-mentioned; coercive; expensive; melodramatic; best-laid; far-seeing; earnest; educational; strategic; standard; maternal; passioned.

verbs
abandon—; adopt—; advance—; analyze—; bolster—; broach—; buttress—; clarify—; concoct—; contemplate—; crystallize—; defeat—; design—; detail—; devise—; discard —; disclose—; divulge—; draft—; embark upon—; enact—; endorse—; engross in—; evolve—; expound—; foil—; formulate—; frame—; hatch out—; improvise—; inaugurate—; junk—; launch—; map out—; mull over—; obstruct—; pattern—on; promulgate —; propound—; ratify—; revamp—; reveal —; revise—; rout—; sidetrack—; snag—; sponsor—; submit—; terminate—; thwart —; upset—; veto—; withdraw—; —advocates; —s coincide; —crumbles; —embraces; —fizzles; —matures.

(See idea, itinerary, intention.)

PLAN (v)

adverbs
fantastically; subtly; magnificently; purposefully; zealously; methodically; tentatively; divinely; deliberately; meticulously; competently; cunningly; daintily; systematically; gloriously; architecturally; comprehensively; intricately; primitively; harmoniously; tyrannically; sensationally; confidentially; sagaciously; philanthropically; meritoriously; nefariously; strategically.

(See scheme, contrive.)

PLANE

adjectives
realistic; conversational; convex; experimental; inclined; reconnoitering; fast; luxurious; powerful; ascending; vertical; emerald; transport; swift; passenger; streamlined; metal; mail; tri-motored.

verbs
bail out of—; bank—; contact—; fuel—; hop (colloq.)—; license—; maroon—; navigate —; pilot—; throttle—; —bores up; —drones; —flashes over; —gleams; —gyrates; —swoops; —takes off; —taxies out; —twists; —whirs; —wings; —zooms.

(See aeroplane.)

PLANET

adjectives
leaden; populous; wheeling; sin-ridden; vexatious; bawdy; glorious; household; ill; sleepy; turbulent; beautious; virginal; glittering; bruised; influential; perturbed; riming; dead; many-mortalled; spinning; sunless; careering.

PLANK

adjectives
grimy; raw; rotting; sturdy; proposed; political; fastened.

PLANNING

adjectives
adroit; unassuming; constructive; thoughtful; tedious; haphazard.

PLANT

adjectives
experimental; sapient; showy; microscopic; companionless; indigenous; remote; thorny; umbelliferous; greedy; naturalized; obstinate; efficient; marsh; vigorous; leguminous; set; aquatic; insectivorous; luxuriant; aromatic; hardy; celebrated; frost-nipped; reduction; wrinkled; branched; parasitic; intruding; stemless; yielding; ill-assorted (pl); infusorial; characteristic; ornamental; enchanting; liliaceous; baccate; happy; esculent; fragrant; nutritious; ignoble; in-

harmonious; succulent; rank; potted; sun-scorched; dwarf; gaudy; umbrageous; established; trailing; rubbed; redolent; long; water; drooping; wind-fertilized; herbaceous; exotic; native; neglected; curious; conventionalized; ballast; submerged; flowering; unsuccessful; ramshackle; precious.

verbs
cultivate—; develop—; hedge—; nurse—; perpetuate—; pollenize—; propagate—; prune—; scatter —s; strangle—; tend—; trim—; uproot—; vitalize—; —bears; —branches; —droops; —emerges; —flourishes; —flowers; —goes dormant; —puts forth; —roots in; —shoots up; —sprouts; —thrives.
(See bulb, herb, ivy, flower, bud, vine, grass.)

PLANT (v)
adverbs
triumphantly; solidly; immovably; advantageously; indigenously; vigorously; aquatically; luxuriantly; characteristically; ornamentally; nutritiously; succulently; conventionally.
(See establish, set.)

PLANTATION
adjectives
flourishing; tidewater; well-managed; substantial-looking; communal; artistic; superabundant; rich.

PLANTER
adjectives
eccentric; remote; poverty-stricken; brusque; affluent; large-scale.

PLANTING
adjectives
permanent; spring; high-growing; experimental.

PLAQUE
verbs
border—; decorate—; exhibit—; figure—; hang—; inscribe on—; insert—; polish—; preserve—; reburnish—; reveal—; study—; unveil—; —acclaims; —commemorates; —honors; —inspires; —ornaments; —shines.
(See metal, ornament.)

PLASH
adjectives
appalling; muffled; startled; noisy.

PLASTER
adjectives
pale-hued; sovereign; peeling; moldering.

verbs
apply—; bedaub with—; cast—; dab—; daub—; mix—; repair—; smear—; spread—; stir—; surface—; —adheres; —cements; —cracks; —crumbles; —crusts; —cures; —encases; —faces; —hardens; —overlays; —surfaces; —survives.
(See paste, paint, cement.)

PLATE
adjectives
special; deep; piping-hot; untouched; burdensome; leaden; circular; photographic; burnished; rimless; elastic; lustrous.

verbs
arrange —s; chip—; cram—; lick—; load—; mar—; retrieve—; scour—; shatter—; stack —s; —crashes; —gleams; —s harmonize; —rotates; —shatters; —shines.
(See dish, disk, platter.)

PLATEAU
adjectives
inhospitable; remote; rock-strewn; undulating; extensive; endless; bare; high.

verbs
ascend to—; cover—; culminate in—; form—; traverse—; view from—; —awes; —extends; —fascinates; —inspires; —rises; —skirts; —stretches.
(See mountain, land, plain.)

PLATFORM
adjectives
movable; desolate; aggressive; rampart; terraced; portico; splintered; mosque; skeletonized; party.

verbs
ascend to—; construct—; crowd—; declaim from—; design—; entertain from—; erect—; flit across—; gather 'round—; jam—; help up—; leap upon—; pace—; perform on—; reveal—; squat on—; straggle over—; —extends; —harbors; —projects; —protects; —rises; —shelters.
(See deck, stage, floor.)

PLATITUDE

adjectives
pompous; sugared; old; theoretic; stale; worthless.

verbs
avoid —s; condemn—; excuse—; fall into —; hide under—; indulge in—; prate —s; take refuge in—; twaddle in—; —bores; —depresses; —dulls; —exasperates; —irks; —lulls; —tires; —vexes; —wearies.
(See proverb, maxim.)

PLATONIC

adverbs
coolly; strictly; altogether; supposedly; perhaps; utterly; amiably; studiously; sedately; thoughtfully; contemplatively; philosophically; calmly; tranquilly; stoically; soberly; demurely; presumably; dispassionately; disinterestedly; decorously; decently; honestly; virtuously; ridiculously; chastely.

PLATONISM

adjectives
delicate; refined; desirable; unsatisfactory.

PLATTER

adjectives
hideous; huge; well-filled; curious.

verbs
arrange —s; garnish—; glean from—; load —; replenish—; stack —s; support—; —crashes; —gleams; —shatters; —sizzles.
(See dish, plate.)

PLAUDITS

adjectives
anticipated; derogatory; noisy; sincere; deserved.

PLAUSIBILITY

adjectives
solemn; delusive; remote; scant; minute.

verbs
admit—; allow—; bear out—; commend—; convince of—; demonstrate—; doubt—; gloss over—; harbor—; lend—; maintain—; mince—; overestimate—; plead—; warrant —; —defends; —enables; —reconciles.
(See sincerity, integrity.)

PLAUSIBLE

adverbs
scarcely; altogether; extremely; manifestly; reasonably; highly; glibly; apparently; craftily; adroitly; pretentiously; remotely; deceptively; evasively; subtly; cleverly; remarkably; indisputably.

PLAY

adjectives (*general*)
amorous; much-performed; immortal; informal; infant; unfair; melodramatic; morality; careless; idle; fitful; miracle; steady; dignified; devilish; painful; boisterous; prismatic; swift; touching; tempestuous; superficial; fantastic; foul; hampered; harmless; firing; delightful; blithe; imaginative; heedless; stately; heroic; illimitable; desperate; unmatched; prophetic; varying; vivid; frivolous; stodgy; unusual; freak; ceaseless; deft; interminable; tragic; somber; witless; ambitious; wretched; immoral; mutual; brawling; rousing; petty; thin; diplomatic; meaningless; jocund; contemporary; clever; dubious; radical; cut-and-thrust; clumsy; uncontrollable; well-arranged; rapid; supernatural.

PLAY

verbs (*theatrical*)
acclaim—; attend—; commend—; criticize —; revive—; sponsor—; stage—; —bores; —charms; —diverts; —endears; —grips; —holds forth at; —impresses; —intrigues.
(See comedy, humor, opera, movie, melodrama, performance, game, sport, recreation, exercise, fun, amusement.)

PLAY (*v*)

adverbs
fervidly; cleverly; amorously; informally; boisterously; tempestuously; witlessly; blithely; frivolously; immorally; idly; brawlingly; jocundly; clumsily; angelically; capriciously; fantastically; seductively; incomparably; demurely; caressingly; adroitly; recklessly; melodiously; diligently; exquisitely.
(See frolic, romp.)

PLAYED-OUT

adverbs
altogether; finally; pitiably; entirely; miserably; helplessly; pathetically; needlessly; strangely; curiously; wretchedly; alarmingly; completely; undoubtedly; sincerely; utterly.

PLAYER

adjectives
sturdy; accurate; wandering; steely-finger-

ed; ardent; comprising; incompetent; impecunious; phenomenal; orchestral; strolling; professional; inspired; skilled; shrewd; nonchalant.

verbs
cast —s; cheer —s; encore—; "razz"—; recruit —s; spur —s on; star—; subsidize —s; —amuses; —charms; —delights; —dramatizes; —emotes; —enacts; —endears; —entertains; —impresses; —magnetizes; —overacts; —portrays; —redeems; —rehearses; —supports.
(See athlete, actor, musician, etc.)

PLAYFUL

adverbs
rapturously; delightfully; teasingly; ecstatically; happily; amiably; annoyingly; sportively; friskily; amusingly; brightly; vivaciously; archly; coltishly; childishly; amazingly; frolicsomely; merrily.

PLAYFULNESS

adjectives
dignified; reverent; impetuous; elephantine; overburdened; half-serious; quizzical; ferocious; satirical; buoyant; effervescent.

PLAYGROUND

adjectives
endless; city; needed; crowded; well-equipped.

PLAYING

adjectives
unwitting; coloratura; brilliant; ingenious.

PLAYMATE

adjectives
sweet; desirable; agreeable; well-matched (pl); boisterous.

PLAYTHING

adjectives
broken; coarse; colored.

PLAYWRIGHT

verbs
acclaim—; award to—; criticize—; honor —; laud—; recognize—; —caters to; —composes; —contributes; —creates; —designs; —dramatizes; —impresses; —formulates; —offers; —thrives.
(See dramatist, artist, writer, author.)

PLEA

adjectives
suggestive; eloquent; dastard; masterly; eternal; half-stifled; unmoral; impassioned; specious; irrational; pettifogging; ingenious; common; special; confederate.

verbs
address—; anticipate—; endorse—; file—; heed—; impair—; justify—; necessitate—; oppose—; press—; protest—; put aside—; respond to—; satisfy—; support—; witness —; —penetrates; —softens; —touches; —urges.
(See apology, allegation, excuse, prayer.)

PLEAD (*v*)

adverbs
eloquently; persuasively; convincingly; vehemently; indignantly; ostensibly; earnestly; brokenly; meekly; despairingly; touchingly.
(See beg, entreat.)

PLEADING

adjectives
patient; fervent; humble; vain; disinterested; impassioned; guilty; incessant.

PLEASANT

adverbs
consistently; extremely; essentially; sweetly; gratifyingly; courteously; placidly; gravely; unfailingly; graciously; smilingly; cordially; quietly; remarkably; ostentatiously; singularly; charmingly; genuinely; sincerely; unaffectedly; jocosely; whimsically; playfully; facetiously; delightfully; maturely; politely; waggishly; openly; heartily; humorously; scrupulously; enchantingly; engagingly; altogether; urbanely; obligingly; good-humoredly; fearlessly; furtively.

PLEASANTRIES

verbs
banter—; dally with—; enjoy—; exchange —; feast on—; perpetuate—; school in—; sport—; —cheer; —delight; —divert; —ease; —engage; —entertain; —impart: —solace; —titillate.
(See banter, jest.)

PLEASANTRY

adjectives
indigestible; familiar; humoristic; formal; uncouth; ill-timed; fluent; bland; coarse; colloquial.

PLEASE (v)

adverbs

graciously; exceedingly; bewitchingly; inwardly; graciously; instinctively; aesthetically; fleetingly; sensuously; momentarily; blithely; grossly; legitimately; voluptuously; frankly; thrillingly; salaciously.

(See cheer, satisfy.)

PLEASED

adverbs

highly; graciously; exceedingly; momentarily; inordinately; frankly; openly; obviously; extremely; uncommonly; happily; proudly; ineffably; naturally; visibly; noticeably; marvellously; overwhelmingly; utterly; inexpressibly.

PLEASURABLE

adverbs

entirely; delightfully; hilariously; refreshingly; utterly; extremely; surprisingly; unexpectedly; strikingly; acceptably; measurably; moderately; actually; charmingly; splendidly; distinctly.

PLEASURE

adjectives

childish; fleeting; wanton; fearful; personal; supreme; playful; sensual; distinct; extraordinary; faithless; uninterrupted; gross; noisy; birdlike; frank; exalted; sweet; uninstructive; cordial; wild; pensive; agonizing; domestic; private; glorious; cruel; profligate; darling; innocent; unnecessary; tranquillizing; worthy; quiet; infinite; dizzy; sportsmanlike; fantastic; firm; rife; stern; fashionable; youthful; illicit; deceiving; tasteless; sheer; wingless; palling; malicious; guilty; multitudinous (pl); forbidden; grievous; untold; earth-born; selfish; peculiar; girlish; dangerous; melancholy; divine; delicate; ferocious; malignant; headlong; unrevealed; solid; unspeakable; tickling; strange; inoffensive; sensible; quickening; prodigious; infantile; warm; refined; gentle; glittering; curious; sweet; wincing; honest; personal; toiling; unmixed; eternal; giddy; voluptuous; indescribable; puerile; gracious; sensitive; unalloyed; unfeigned; mean; proud; exquisite; idle; profound; monotonous; joint; visible; vivid; scanty; unglorious; sincere; smoking; legitimate; pulsing; mischievous; frank; unabating; questionable; thrilling; frequent (pl); inexpressible; false; compensating; tenfold; primary; royal; grim; mysterious; proper; simple; hollow; luxurious; profound; petty; monotonous; growing; delicious; dreadful; heartfelt; wholesome; unmeasured; persisting; perishing; agitating; secret; alluring; attendant; calm; celestial; varied; blithe; queer; perpetual; singular; base; harmless; avid; unearned; unreproved; infinite; intellectual; sunny; momentary; solemn; fiendish; mournful; unblinking; costless; kind; evident; prickling; bygone; faint; positive; piquant; sensuous; secondary; melancholy; ecstatic; vicious; malicious; macabre; unremembered; perverse; pure; alien; mere; silent; admirable; unadulterated; fermenting; unsubstantial; dissolute; intense; undisguised; natural.

verbs

addicted to—; afford—; bask in—; dampen —; derive—from; deprive of—; drink up—; enhance—; experience—; forego—; heighten —; indulge in—; partake of—; prolong—; pursue—; rejoice in—; relish—; resign—; sacrifice—; smile in—; squirm in—; taste —; weary of—.

(See gratification, happiness, gladness, delight, enjoyment.)

PLEBEIAN

adverbs

altogether; distinctly; unexpectedly; surprisingly; naturally; inevitably; terribly; pathetically; loudly; roughly; meanly; vexatiously; indecorously; unendurably; singularly; strangely; oddly; overwhelmingly; hopelessly.

PLEDGE

adjectives

sacred; temperance; tender; written; decided; solemn; terse; uncompromising; positive; eternal; uttered; indefinite; uncertain; reliable; unredeemed; noble.

verbs

accept—; administer—; contract—; enter into—; exact—; forfeit—; honor—; offer—; pawn—; redeem—; repudiate—; respect—; subscribe to—; undertake—; violate—; —assures; —binds; —commits; —guarantees; —secures; —ties; —warrants.

(See covenant, agreement, promise.)

PLEDGE (v)

adverbs

solemnly; mutually; enthusiastically; sacredly; tenderly; uncompromisingly; eternally;

definitely; reliably; nobly; nominally; gallantly.
(See promise, assure.)

PLENTIFUL

adverbs
reasonably; unexpectedly; presumably; luxuriantly; scarcely; lavishly; abundantly; adequately; exuberantly; profusely; sufficiently; immeasurably; incalculably; providentially; mercifully; fortunately; luckily; opportunely; auspiciously; happily.

PLENTY

adjectives
admired; wanton; boarded; wasted; unused.

verbs
bless with—; bristle with—; desire—; obtain —; produce—; reign in—; scatter—; shower —; swim in—; wallow in—; wish for—; —abounds; —flows; —teems.
(See abundance, affluence.)

PLIABLE

adverbs
conveniently; opportunely; reasonably; extremely; scarcely; fortunately; luckily; hardly; somewhat; adaptably; suitably; easily; advantageously; comfortably; readily; usefully; measurably; moderately; adequately; remarkably; marvellously; uncommonly.

PLIGHT

adjectives
lamentable; forsaken; sorry; ill; admirable; evil; pathetic; patient; chronic; grievous; shameful; pitiable; dolorous; sad; doleful; sorrowful; unfortunate.

verbs
betray—; exploit—; favor—; foster—; muse on—; reduce to—; swear to—; vow to—; —alarms; —assures; —binds; —contracts; —depresses; —guarantees; —puzzles; —secures; —shocks.
(See condition, predicament, state.)

PLOD

adjectives
painful; prosaic; barefoot.

PLOD (*v*)

adverbs
contentedly; monotonously; wearily; tirelessly; mechanically; ceaselessly; prosaically; steadily; dejectedly; stupidly.
(See tramp, trudge.)

PLODDING

adverbs
patiently; insistently; steadily; doggedly; stubbornly; stolidly; uncomplainingly; laboriously; resolutely; determinedly; admirably; commendably; hopefully; resignedly; firmly; staunchly; unwaveringly; tenaciously; perseveringly; undauntedly; unswervingly; courageously

PLOT

adjectives
exaggerated; formidable; comprehensive; dramatic; sandy; insidious; tyrannical; thin; thickening; naughty; grassy; murderous; lurid; audacious; inhuman; marshy; detestable; ill-omened; unfrequented; complicated; daisied; infernal; precious; horrible; pretty; fertile; neglected.

verbs
abet—; concoct—; construct—; cook up (colloq.)—; crush—; disclose—; entangle—; fancy—; found—on; frill—; garnish—; get wind of—; harmonize—; hatch—; implicate —; invent—; nip—; plunge into—; resolve —; spring—; summarize—; unmask—; weave—; —derives from; —generates; —smacks of.
(See argument, intrigue, conspiracy.)

PLOT (*v*)

adverbs
devilishly; maliciously; grimly; infernally; diabolically; formidably; insidiously; tyrannically; audaciously; inhumanly; detestably; perniciously; traitorously; seditiously.
(See scheme, machinate.)

PLOTTER

verbs
exile—; uncover—; —circumvents; —concocts; —contrives; —designs; —devises; —frames; —hatches; —intrigues; —manoeuvres; —overreaches; —schemes; —stoops; —undermines; —snatches
(See conspirator.)

PLOUGH (*v*)

adverbs
extensively; seasonally; laboriously; deeply; annually.
(See dig, labor.)

PLOVER

adjectives
graceful; scudding; snowy-winged.

PLOW

adjectives
flying; sulky; useful; ancient; improved.

verbs
employ—; equip with—; —bites; —breaks; —cuts; —delves; —digs; —furrows; —grooves; —intrudes; —loosens; —prepares; —uncovers; —wedges; —weeds.

PLUCK

adjectives
invincible; gallant; amazing; redoubtable; unusual; gigantic; great; noticeable.

PLUCK (*v*)

adverbs
petulantly; surreptitiously; courageously; agitatedly; idiotically; industriously; thievishly; haphazardly.
(See pick, pull.)

PLUCKY

adverbs
unbelievably; unusually; resolutely; naturally; inherently; habitually; remarkably; marvellously; uncommonly; amazingly; courageously; recklessly; determinedly; gallantly; valiantly; intrepidly; undauntedly; stoutly; manfully; tenaciously; indomitably.

PLUG

verbs
cram—into; drive—into; insert—; remove—; tap—; —bars; —blocks; —chokes; —dams; —obstructs; —prevents; —resists; —seals; —stuffs; —traps.
(See stopper.)

PLUG (*v*)

adverbs
tightly; effectually; firmly; completely; wholly; satisfactorily; efficiently.
(See plod, work.)

PLUMAGE

adjectives
splendid; fantastic; rich-colored; peculiar; rustling; lacy; glossy; entrancing; iridescent; black; glistening; glittering; ribboned; rosy; light; fluttersome; brilliant; demure; unmatchable.

verbs
adjust—; admire—; bear—; bunch—; display—; preen—; prime—; ruffle—; rumple—; smooth—; —adorns; —bedecks; —decorates; —embellishes; —glitters; —nods; —ornaments; —tufts.
(See mane, feather.)

PLUMBING

verbs
approve—; condemn—; criticize—; demolish—; display—; examine—; improve—; install—; lack—; modernize—; renovate—; repair—; sanction—; tear—down; wrench—apart; —sanitizes.
(See pipe.)

PLUME

adjectives
idle; stooping; dancing; waving; funeral; fantastic; sunny; bronze; striped; straining; advanced; rustling; sable; fancy; shining; magnificent; gay; dripping; resinous; fiery; snowy; graceful; shaken; tossing.

PLUMP

adverbs
delightfully; desirably; commendably; terribly; pleasantly; admirably; childishly; overly; unhappily; chubbily; stalwartly; strappingly; thumpingly; extraordinarily; remarkably; charmingly; daintily; rosily; exquisitely; pleasingly.

PLUMPNESS

adjectives
appreciable; unwanted; stodgy; awkward; pleasant.

PLUNDER

adjectives
nefarious; hideous; indiscriminate; winged; licentious; accumulated; plentiful; barbarous; piratical.

verbs
abstain from—; abhor—; acquire—; bag—; commit—; conceal—; convey—; locate—; seize—; share—; smuggle—; submit to—; transfer—; uncover—; —despoils; —ravages; —strips.
(See bribery, loot.)

PLUNDER (*v*)

adverbs
rapaciously; flagrantly; nefariously; hide-

ously; indiscriminately; barbarously; piratically; lustfully; dictatorially.
(See rob, steal.)

PLUNGE

adjectives
occasional; desperate; constant (pl); useless; despised; sounding.

PLUNGE (v)

adverbs
rashly; daringly; heavily; wildly; impetuously; determinedly; fiercely; violently; desperately.
(See dive, fall, drop.)

PLURALIST

adjectives
splendid; blatant; unblushing.

PLURALITY

verbs
abandon—; amass—; attract—; attribute—to; elect by—; pile up—; question—; require—; secure—; seek—; solicit—; stem—; —chooses; —decides; —determines; —expresses; —follows; —judges; —patronizes.
(See vote, majority, multitude.)

PLUSH

adjectives
moth-eaten; restful.

PLY (v)

adverbs
industriously; constantly; intermittently; diligently; vigorously; ambitiously; unweariedly; indefatigably.
(See work, apply.)

POCKET

adjectives
greedy; sagging; redundant; ragged; attenuated; hidebound; closed; warm; well-filled.

verbs
accumulate in—; button—; charge—with; conceal in—; deposit in—; dig in—; dislodge from—; draw from—; extract from—; fumble in—; grope in—; joggle in—; line—s; quarter in—; tuck in—; —bulges; —jingles; —swells.
(See basket, reservoir, hold.)

POD

verbs
bruise—; crack—; empty—; split—; —binds; —conceals; —defends; —discloses; —encases; —encloses; —enfolds; —faces; —guards; —preserves; —protects.
(See cover.)

POEM

adjectives
poisonous; excellent; patriotic; fantastic; tiny; ancient; typical; conventional; dramatic; simple; mystical; admirable; sentimental; immortal; negligible; genealogical; centenary; lyrical; remarkable; non-dramatic; epic; licentious; heroic; narrative; noble; painful; artificial; humorous; divine; devotional; unified; pastoral; deeply-felt; rare; imperishable; elegiac; Homeric; abiding; commemorative; mere; quizzical; contemplative; puerile; didactic; striking; elegant; personal; impressive; brief; historical; unequal; elevated; preposterous; faulty; primitive; laudatory; symphonic; curious; insipid; amatory; soulless; philosophical; dainty; unpopular; psychological.

verbs
acclaim—; appreciate—; chorus—; create—; evolve—; peruse—; rewrite—; work into—; —amuses; —appeals; —commemorates; —conveys; —depicts; —diverts; —echoes; —expresses; —flows; —inspires; —invokes; —rings; —romances; —sings; —transfuses; —voices.
(See poetry, hymn, ballad, incantation, ditty, epigram, romance, sonnet, dirge, ballad.)

POESY

adjectives
perennial; heaven-bred; inspired.

POET

verbs
acclaim—; appreciate—; award to—; chide—; criticize—; immortalize—; interpret—; laud—; quote—; recognize—; —beautifies; —builds; —chants; —commemorates; —composes; —contributes; —designs; —eternizes; —experiences; —expresses; —impresses; —laments; —offers; —redeems; —rimes; —scans; —sings; —teaches; —thrives; —versifies.
(See author, artist, creator, idealist, novelist.)

POETIC

adverbs
distinctly; delightfully; musically; rhythmically; deeply; melodiously; abstrusely; notably; sublimely; pleasantly; exquisitely; ingeniously; unexpectedly; truly; eloquently; vigorously; passionately; glowingly; impressively; fancifully.

POETRY

adjectives
pastoral; clear; academic; allegorical; visionary; smooth; respectable; lyrical; essential; faulty; satirical; joyful; dramatic; descriptive; subservient; romantic; charlatan; tragic; epic; devotional; delicate; meditative; riotous; spiritual; imaginative; impassioned; bewildering; elder; tender; high-mannered; dreamy; austere; barbarous; glorious; mournful; vague; original.

verbs
conceive—; cultivate—; deliver—; like—; interpret—; mold—; resort to—; toy with —; —charms; —conveys; —delights; —eases; —elevates; —enchants; —endures; —flourishes; —humanizes; —inspires; —narrates; —reflects; —reveals; —softens; —soothes; —springs from.
(See literature, poem, story, sonnet, etc.)

POETS

adjectives
derivative; lofty; erotic; impecunious; contemporary; Ionian; notable; capricious; romantic; quick-conceiving; prominent; sublime; spontaneous; true; subtle; worthy; distinguished; satirical; celebrated; philosophical; tragic; well-known; spasmodic; scurrilous; ecclesiastical; saturnine; laurelled; descriptive; sensitive; earnest; prattling; exquisite; synthetic; budding; specific; denominated; authentic; secular; pining; humorous; amorous; lyrical; peasant; ingenious; heathen; isolated; playful; religious; illustrious; mature; esteemed; vernacular; psychic; classical.

POIGNANT

adverbs
intensely; sharply; singularly; curiously; strangely; inscrutably; unexpectedly; apparently; manifestly; painfully; smartly; remarkably; strikingly; unbearably; trenchantly; vividly; suddenly.

POINT
(feature, issue, question, etc.)

verbs
admit—; allow—; attend to—; carry—; concede—; debate—; dispose of—; dodge—; drive home—; dwell on—; emphasize—; grant—; illustrate—; interrogate—; labor —; miss—; pursue—; reinforce—; rule on —; settle—; stress—; sympathize on—; —illustrates; —s interlock.
(See angle, feature, issue.)

POINT
(general)

adjectives
standard; essential; peevish; standing; transitional; original; sore; favorable; vulnerable; geographical; objective; delicate; varying; vindictive; fundamental; advantageous; knotty; statistical; luminous; trivial; weighty; crucial; rallying; superficial; physical; culminating; controverted; dazzling; desired; fiery; inconsiderable; sentimental; thorny; unsavory; noteworthy; narrow; mooted; burning; converging; unguarded; significant; well-selected; worldly; practical; inhuman; chivalric; principal; systematic; pivotal; assailable; prominent; equinoctial; strategic; contrary; suggestive; radiant; favorable; slippery; salient; aesthetic; artistic; remote; material; corrective; designated; matrimonial; elevated; indecomposable; critical; exposed; statistical; disputed; changeless; home-coming; pathetic; conceded; preconceived; minute; projecting; crowning; bitter; unimportant; knotty; decisive; sandy; epigrammatic; rallying; preliminary; characteristic; supreme; saturation; absurd; terminal; contentious; dubious; heterodox; unendurable; stagnant; impressive; dangerous; intangible; inappreciable; restricted; cardinal; determinable; ludicrous; speculative; ample; technical; yawning.

POINT (*v*)

adverbs
triumphantly; mysteriously; significantly; timidly; conclusively; mournfully; excitedly; scornfully; directly; peevishly; ludicrously.
(See indicate, designate.)

POINTED

adverbs
cruelly; barbarously; hatefully; bitterly; caustically; sarcastically; unmistakably; personally; meanly; maliciously; venomously;

impolitely; viciously; intentionally; deliberately; rudely; roughly; ungraciously; bluntly; brusquely; dogmatically; significantly; curtly; crisply; sententiously; bitingly; incisively; impressively.

POINTLESS

adverbs
pitifully; feebly; inanely; fatuously; inconsequentially; insignificantly; monotonously; ponderously; banally; trivially; vaguely; flatly; insipidly; endlessly; foolishly; vacuously; ridiculously; intolerably; tiresomely; absurdly.

POISE

adjectives
calm; serene; contemplative; aristocratic; swerveless; exquisite; intellectual; aloof; physical; domineering; admirable; culminating; coquettish; calculating; mental; dangerous; sturdy; equal.

verbs
acquire—; admire—; affect—; attain—; envy—; exhibit—; lack—; maintain—; practise—; recover—; regard with—; restore—; school in—; shatter—; value—; —assures; —conquers; —controls; —impresses; —polishes; —tones

(See equilibrium, ease, balance, stability.)

POISE (v)

adverbs
serenely; delicately; calmly; daringly; exquisitely; coquettishly; rashly; courageously; undauntedly.

(See balance, pose.)

POISON

adjectives
bottom; virulent; simmering; consuming; offensive; infusing; unseasonable; vanquished; occidental; insidious; intoxicating; infidel; rank; putrefactive; deadly; corrosive; inorganic; delicious; innocuous; slow-working.

verbs
absorb—; antidote—; assimilate—; control—; counteract—; distil—; eliminate—; excrete—; exude—; impregnate with—; infect with—; inject—; neutralize—; reek with—; —accumulates; —circulates; —ravages.

(See germicide, venom, drug.)

POISON (v)

adverbs
insidiously; murderously; premeditatively; maliciously; organically; corrosively; intoxicatingly; basely; diabolically.

(See kill, murder.)

POISONOUS

adverbs
mildly; slightly; fatally; dangerously; mortally; alarmingly; seriously; dreadfully; noxiously; maliciously; venomously; viciously; pestilentially; curiously; unexpectedly; singularly; miserably; manifestly; obviously; invariably.

POKE (v)

adverbs
coyly; tantalizingly; brutally; warningly; cautiously; teasingly; facetiously; delicately; humorously; amorously.

(See thrust, excite.)

POLE

adjectives
boreal; slender; curtained; terrestrial; resonant; telephone; splintered; austral.

POLEMIC

adjectives
staunch; commonplace; bitter; ruthless.

POLICE

adjectives
adequate; lynx-eyed; executive; ubiquitous; ornamental; interested; ineffective; rustic; ingenious; indignant.

verbs
commend—; detail—to; evade—; tangle with—; —accost; —apprehend; —clash; —corner; —escort; —espy; —intimidate; —patrol; —protect; —raid; —regulate; —scout; —trace; —track down; —trail; —trap; —warn.

(See detective, constable.)

POLICY

adjectives
obvious; parsimonious; aggressive; tyrannous; questionable; conservative; enlightened; peace; paltry; time-honored; ecclesiastical; dilatory; prudent; insidious; comprehensive; inconsistent; foreign; cherished; let-alone; well-defined; vacillating; broad; immediate; reasonable; ruinous; cruel; attractive; shameful; honorable; intricate;

liberal; magnanimous; intriguing; devious; public; vicious; dissimulating; beneficent; straightforward; emancipation; subsequent; hostile; medium; prevailing; handsome; odious; maritime; ostensible; shortsighted; Fabian; relentless; habitual; abhorrent; all-important; oppressive; unsound; studied; sound; earnest; logical; determined; rigid; dominant; alternate; consistent; strategic; uniform; alterant; unwavering; reactionary; evasive; effective; crafty; exclusive; kindred; taxing; fiscal; unadulterated; national; increasing; effective; committal; economic; constant.

verbs
abandon—; adhere to—; adjust—; adopt—; advance—; alter—; amend—; chart—; cling to—; defend—; define—; denounce—; dictate—; dominate—; draft—; effectuate—; embark on—; endorse—; enforce—; excoriate—; execute—; expound—; fashion—; forge—; formulate—; frame—; frown upon—; inaugurate—; initiate—; institute—; justify—; modify—; orient—; overhaul—ies; propound—; pursue—; reflect—; resolve—; reverse—; shape—; sponsor—; —embitters; —hinges on; —prevails; —wobbles.

(See principle, theory, course, prudence, procedure.)

POLISH

adjectives
patrician; massive; gleaming; sleek; high.

POLISH (*v*)

adverbs
painstakingly; superficially; vigorously; industriously; gleamingly; glitteringly; highly; splendidly.

(See rub, smooth.)

POLISHED

adverbs
fashionably; smoothly; suavely; urbanely; socially; smugly; aristocratically; expertly; adroitly; graciously; extraordinarily; admirably; remarkably; incomparably; unsurpassably; matchlessly; splendidly; gorgeously; magnificently; brilliantly; conspicuously; arrogantly; delightfully; charmingly; commendably; elegantly; unctuously; blandly; gravely; affably; gallantly; ingratiatingly.

POLITE

adverbs
dutifully; punctiliously; meticulously; particularly; excessively; deliberately; resolutely; determinedly; naturally; graciously; amiably; delightfully; properly; carefully; cautiously; nervously; awkwardly; clumsily; reluctantly; chivalrously; gallantly; ingratiatingly; suavely; smoothly; urbanely; unctuously; adroitly; formidably; scrupulously; ridiculously; absurdly; remarkably; courteously; obsequiously; affably.

POLITENESS

adjectives
exaggerated; veneered; formidable; pretty; unwavering; hollow; unwearying; determined; freezing; cold; ironical; oriental; indefatigable; grave; affected; insolent; oily; strained; scrupulous; refined; icy.

verbs
applaud—; breach—; conform to—; commend—; enjoy—; exhibit—; laud—; practise—; praise—; struggle with—; —appeals; —conciliates; —pleases; —polishes; —refines.

(See civility, courtesy, gallantry.)

POLITICAL

adverbs
artfully; shrewdly; strategically; craftily; subtly; obviously; manifestly; naturally; keenly; cleverly; necessarily; cunningly; deeply; profoundly; intriguingly; slyly; insidiously; astutely; adroitly; sensibly; judiciously; prudently; soberly; warily; watchfully; expediently; inveterately; wisely; cannily.

POLITICIAN

adjectives
practical; artful; budding; shrewd; designing; unguided; unfledged; malevolent; noisy; timorous; kid-gloved; cunning; ordinary; mechanical; vulgar; hoary; practical; cynical; peanut; conservative; corrupt; cheap; astute; impecunious; unprincipled; redoubtable; superficial; radical.

verbs
corrupt—; oust—; pay tribute to—; support—; —addresses; —administers; —conducts; —contrives; —controls; —directs; —governs; —manages; —orates; —orders; —panders to; —presides; —solicits; —steers.

(See boss, demagogue, legislator.)

POLITICS

adjectives
contemporary; inculcating; domestic; fundamental; partisan; sentimental; crooked; fading; corrupt; practical; economic; financial; moral; befuddled; stormy; puzzled.

verbs
bury in—; dabble in—; delve in—; immerse in—; inveigh against—; meddle with—; muddle in—; participate in—; plunge into —; prostitute—; retire from—; shun—; steer clear of—; tangle with—; verse in—.
(See government, management, affairs, business.)

POLITY

adjectives
primitive; well-ordered.

POLL

adjectives
taxable; voting; straw; nation-wide.

POLLEN

adjectives
wind-blown; insect-borne; widespread.

verbs
carry—; diffuse—; disperse—; disseminate —; dust with—; gather—; issue—; sensitize to—; shed—; sprinkle—; strew—; —drifts; —fertilizes; —germinates; —scatters; —seeds; —sows.

POLLS

verbs
bribe at—; crowd—; entice to—; flock to—; guard—; herd to—; preside at—; rally to —; regulate—; station at—; swamp—; visit —; —protect; —register.

POLLUTED

adverbs
foully; utterly; slightly; poisonously; unnecessarily; infamously; noticeably; visibly; obviously; manifestly; evidently; mysteriously; criminally; dangerously; alarmingly; seriously; pestilentially; odiously; distressingly; illegally; horribly; abominably.

POLLUTION

adjectives
horrible; fat; moral; abhorrent; waterside.

verbs
befoul with—; complain of—; expose to—; labor under—; reproach for—; —brands; —corrupts; —defaces; —defiles; —degrades; —disgraces; —harms; —impairs; —infects; —mars; —offends; —overshadows; —pillages; —saps; —scathes; —shames; —stains; —sullies; —taints.
(See impurity, corruption.)

POLYGAMY

adjectives
praiseworthy; desirable; indiscriminate; outlawed.

POMP

adjectives
painted; regal; mournful; cumbrous; long; worthless; warlike; stately; disposed; solitary; disproportionate; unprecedented; episcopal; vain; bloody; apparent; vulgar; embarrassing; infinite; dazzling; decorative; moving; papistical; liturgical; inimitable; long-drawn; despotic; bloodless; visionary; wonted; wind-blown; solemn; superfluous; contented.

verbs
affect—; display—; exhibit—; relax—; relish—; sacrifice to—; —attracts; —awes; —blazons; —dazzles; —flaunts; —glitters; —sparkles; —splashes; —wearies.
(See display, splendor, magnificence.)

POMPOSITY

adjectives
affable; rollicking; attenuated; affected; bloated; unspeakable.

POMPOUS

adverbs
insufferably; ludicrously; self-righteously; absurdly; gorgeously; officiously; ridiculously; noisily; swaggeringly; affectedly; ostentatiously; blatantly; grandiloquently; splendidly; boastfully; showily; superbly; pettily; dramatically; spectacularly; remarkably; amazingly; drolly; comically; preposterously; crassly.

POND

adjectives
steel-bright; misty; mill; midsummer; fowl; clear; circular; tranquil; darksome; shining; bottomless.

verbs
dabble in—; deposit in—; dive in—; fish in —; immerse in—; merge into—; plunge into—; wade in—; —accumulates; —beautifies; —graces; —laps; —ripples; —sparkles; —washes.
(See lake, water, lagoon.)

PONDER (*v*)

adverbs
silently; meditatively; sagely; monotonously; seriously; patiently; perplexedly; morbidly; moodily; closely; reverently; meekly; darkly; philosophically.
(See think, reflect, muse.)

PONDEROUS

adverbs
seriously.; weightily; gravely; momentously; heavily; mightily; clumsily; awkwardly; impressively; crudely; formally; stiffly; stupidly; dully; flatly; tiresomely; monotonously; prosaically; intolerably; strangely; insipidly; pointlessly; singularly; incomparably; inexpressibly.

PONTOON

verbs
attach—; employ—; equip with—; lower —; moor to—; travel on—; —buoys; —carries; —enables; —floats; —guards against; —holds; —indicates; —insures; —saves; —supports; —sustains.
(See bridge, boat.)

PONY

adjectives
restless; thin; woebegone.

verbs
breed—ies; corral—ies; curry—; guide—; lash—; mount—; saddle—; tether—; tumble off—; —balks; —bolts; —canters; —capers; —paws; —prances; —shies; —trots; —whinnies.
(See horse, colt, mare.)

POODLE

adjectives
wretched; shaved; frolicsome.

POOL

adjectives
rank; glistening; gloomy; palm-edged; stagnant; seething; sullen; slumbrous; slimy; motionless; mirrorlike; broad; willowy; glassy; tepid; rippling; little; whirling; pebbled; dreaming; malarial; shadowed; mottled; shining; iridescent; scintillating; deep; amber; limpid; quiet; flowing; silent; brimming; oblivious; placid; swirling; loathsome; polished; spacious; outdoor; wholesome; dimpled; indicated; narrow; foaming; transparent; reedy; fish; frog; frozen; smooth.

verbs
chlorinate—; construct—; crowd—; dip into —; drain—; house—; plunge into—; splash in—; wade in—; —delights; —glistens; —invites; —laps; —ripples; —shimmers; —simmers; —sparkles; —tempts; dive into—.
(See river, lake, pond.)

POOR

adjectives
fancy; solitary; wily; nameless; neighboring; grateful; undeserving; unattended; shamefaced; neglected; sickly.

adverbs
miserably; wretchedly; deplorably; lamentably; pitiably; pitifully; helplessly; hopelessly; strangely; amazingly; remarkably; terribly; incredibly; unfortunately; unhappily; uncommonly; unusually; embarrassingly; uncomfortably; horribly; desperately; awfully.

POPE

verbs
bow before—; consult—; defy—; support—; visit—; —addresses; —administers; —appeals to; —beads; —blesses; —controls; —governs; —interviews; —officiates; —orates; —prays; —reprimands; —sanctions; —secludes; —supplicates.
(See minister, king.)

POPLAR

adjectives
attendant; showery; huge; shuddering; feathery; towering.

POPPY

adjectives
foolish; scarlet; bloody; flaming; crumpled; memorial.

POPULACE

adjectives
murmurous; giddy; barbarous; infuriated; squalid; malcontent; insolent; virtuous; excited; noisy; irritable.

POPULAR

adverbs

amazingly; incredibly; deservedly; surprisingly; strikingly; particularly; incomparably; unexpectedly; undeniably; manifestly; obviously; definitely; distinctly; evidently; widely; personally; politically; professionally; unmistakably; uncommonly; highly; socially; locally.

POPULARITY

adjectives

contemporary; formidable; respectful; facile; ageless; world-wide; unbounded; amazing; tremendous; zooming; prewar; illogical; apparent; corresponding; increasing; glaring; undeniable; universal; widespread; fickle; assured; fading; undetermined.

verbs

achieve—; attain—; begrudge—; bolster—; hinder—; jeopardize—; reduce—; reinstate —; ride to—; risk—; soar to—; spring into—; suffer—; sweep into—; —declines; —recedes; —tumbles; —wanes.

(See fame, glory, greatness.)

POPULATE (v)

adverbs

thickly; densely; teemingly; sparsely; turbulently; squalidly; swarmingly; homogeneously; animatedly; urbanly.

(See inhabit.)

POPULATION

adjectives

scattered; floating; indolent; communicative; teeming; wage-earning; bucolic; industrious; curious; inflammable; resident; indigenous; migratory; proper; crowded; ancient; coming; stunted; haggard; lifeless; varied; predatory; sparse; strenuous; adventurous; squalid; turbulent; rebellious; surplus; predominant; intractable; hostile; miserable; swarming; aboriginal; motley; much-slaughtered; abstemious; shifting; enormous; nomadic; supplicating; homogeneous; submissive; sufficient; voting; dense; warlike; sluggish; energetic; active; workless; rustic; animated; agricultural; urban.

verbs

control—; decimate—; harbor—; immunize —to; increase—; oppress—; scourge—; teem with—; —ascends; —decreases; —dwindles; —expands; —mounts.

(See masses, mankind.)

POPULOUS

adverbs

uncommonly; definitely; distinctly; overly; congestedly; thickly; problematically; inconveniently; perplexingly; particularly; unpleasantly; unmanageably.

PORCELAIN

adjectives

unglazed; transparent; rare; imported.

verbs

bake—; cast—; decorate—; dip—; finish—; form—; glaze—; mold—; paint—; polish—; prize—; scour—; shape—; shatter—; smooth—; value—; —gleams; —graces; —shines.

(See china, crockery.)

PORCH

adjectives

vine-clad; spacious; sculptured; flowery; dripping; dingy; shrouded; glass-enclosed; jutting; rude; classic; shaded.

PORCUPINE

verbs

anger—; frighten—; —arches; —baffles; —bristles; —climbs; —clings; —defends; —erects; —inflicts; —preys on; —rattles; —rolls into a ball; —rushes; —scares off; —sticks; —wounds.

(See animal.)

PORE (v)

adverbs

painfully; industriously; studiously; bookishly; academically; scholastically; ambitiously.

(See study, ponder.)

PORES

adjectives

subtile; serried; drained-out; minute; clotted; stopped; non-functioning; enlarged; ugly; fine.

verbs

block—; choke—; cleanse—; clog—; contract—; enlarge—; escape from—; filter through—; flow from—; issue from—; obstruct—; penetrate—; plug—; purge—; —discharge; —effuse; —exude; —ooze; —open.

(See skin, hole, opening.)

PORK

verbs
barbecue—; condemn—; cure—; devour—; dine on—; examine—; freeze—; garnish—; gobble up—; gnaw—; infect—; inspect—; nibble—; prepare—; putrefy—; relish—; roast—; salt—; sandwich—; serve—.
(See meat.)

POROUS

adverbs
unfortunately; unsalably; inconveniently; unluckily; objectionably; unserviceably; advantageously; intentionally; purposely; curiously; singularly; manifestly; minutely; scientifically; plainly.

PORT

adjectives
alluring; tropical; princely; delectable; centuried; heavenly; intervening; broad-brimmed; broad-armed; tranquil; convenient; favorite; neighboring; unfrequented; swaggering; blockaded; difficult; hostile; much-used.

PORTABLE

adverbs
easily; readily; luckily; conveniently; completely; inexpensively; compactly; invisibly; inconspicuously; particularly; comfortably; lightly; handily; appropriately; serviceably; suitably; instantly.

PORTALS

adjectives
flashing; forbidden; frowning; mysterious; ancient; time-beaten; ruby-colored; massy; gorgeous; somber; subterranean; welcoming; subtle; outer-most; sparkling; gloomy; shadowy; oaken; statue-crowned; ogival; wrought; open; swinging; creaking.

verbs
block—; choke—; crash—; cross—; crowd —; enter—; file from—; filter through—; gain—; invite through—; issue from—; obstruct—; secure—; swarm about—; throw open—; —gape; —welcome; —yawn.
(See door, entrance.)

PORTEND (*v*)

adverbs
gloomily; darkly; unfavorably; banefully; dolefully; evilly; stormily; symbolically; ominously; prophetically; direly.
(See foretell, predict.)

PORTENT

adjectives
unmistakable; vast; fiery; baneful; worse; doleful; evil.

verbs
disregard—; fear—; realize—; recognize—; —depresses; —disconcerts; —disturbs; —frightens; —indicates; —looms; —oppresses; —promises; —perplexes; —puzzles; —shadows; —shrouds; —warns.
(See warning, meaning.)

PORTENTOUS

adverbs
heavily; grievously; sadly; ominously; gravely; seriously; critically; imminently; unmistakably; direly; solemnly; oddly; significantly; particularly; oddly; dangerously; immensely; sorely; manifestly; frightfully; tremendously; alarmingly; dreadfully; momentously; deeply; profoundly; calamitously.

PORTER

adjectives
suppliant; dark; drowsing; fat; oily; station; slovenly; obsequious; neat; industrious; heavily-laden.

PORTICO

adjectives
antique; classic; gaunt; unfinished; huge.

PORTION

adjectives
dense; important; ascending; priceless; descending; prodigal; hearty; healthful; considerable; flourishing; prescribed; plenteous; energetic; edible; introductory; cascading; dim; minute; mobile; speculative; residual; petty; various (pl); regenerative; generous; chasm-like; valuable; untouched; inviting; vast; integral; tolerable; lofty; broad; compensated; dangerous; uncovered; equitable; unexplored; submerged; astonishing; large; continued; remote; silvery; disinterested; alloted; soluble; superficial; protruding; substantial; picturesque; fleshy.

verbs
allot—to; allow—; break into—s; carve into—s; deal—s; distribute—s; divide

into—s; dole out—s; integrate—s; mete out—s; sample—; share—; stint—; —appeases; —protrudes; —satiates.
(See **share**, inheritance, quota.)

PORTION (v)

adverbs
fairly; equitably; substantially; prodigally; magnanimously; arbitrarily.
(See share, divide.)

PORTLY

adverbs
inexpressibly; unhappily; incredibly; incurably; laughably; lamentably; comfortably; contentedly; distressingly; absurdly; ridiculously; ludicrously; sadly; joyously; dangerously; heavily; funnily; complacently; complainingly; mournfully; dramatically; pathetically; shapelessly; waddlingly.

PORTRAIT

adjectives
undisputed; ancestral; unfavorable; satirical; penned; unequaled; poetical; gallery; posthumous; deathlike; faded; dark; coarse; staring; notable; vivid; authentic; mezzotint; sharp; vulgar; inimitable; somber-toned; characteristic; spirited; initial; pathetic; unlifelike; gloomy; brilliant; vigorous; distinct; demure; alluring; late; realistic; whole-length; somber; painstaking; delectable; carnationed; rubicund; hard-favored; accurate; sympathetic; untouched.

verbs
admire—; adumbrate—; delineate—; detail—; display—; dress up—; embellish—; hang—; obscure—; pose for—; prepare—; shade—; shadow—; sit for—; sketch—; unveil—; —adheres to; —copies; —depicts; illustrates.
(See masterpiece, painting, picture.)

PORTRAITURE

adjectives
idealized; truthful; moral; rigid.

PORTRAY (v)

adverbs
magnificently; graphically; vigorously; ironically; accurately; vividly; objectively; nebulously; sharply; pathetically; alluringly; realistically; somberly; sympathetically; poetically.
(See picture, paint.)

PORTRAYAL

adjectives
truthful; sympathetic; single-scene; heart-warming; objective; realistic; ethical; ever-fresh.

verbs
achieve—; applaud—; commend—; criticize—; detail—; draw—; enjoy—; practise—; rehearse—; render—; review—; —characterizes; —delights; —depicts; —describes; —relates; —recounts; —unfolds.
(See description, portrait.)

POSE

adjectives
quiet; easy; dignified; habitual; theatrical; traditional; professional; unmistakable; ridiculous; deliberate; conventional; individual; classic; charming; hieratic; autocratic; swan-like; lordly; stiff; heroic; ultimate; hereditary; effective; obsequious; countless (pl).

verbs
affect—; animate—; assume—; carve—; cast—; fashion—; hold—; imitate—; maintain—; overdo—; regard—; ridicule—; shape—; strike—; —appeals; —attitudinizes; —caricaturizes; —characterizes; —copies; —impresses.
(See attitude, posture.)

POSE (v)

adverbs
professionally; importantly; strikingly; statuesquely; dignifiedly; ridiculously; deliberately; classically; autocratically; heroically; obsequiously.
(See balance, poise.)

POSITION

adjectives
absurd; admirable; advantageous; alphabetical; altered; ambiguous; amiable; angular; anomalous; arduous; anonymous; argumentative; artistic; aristocratic; asinine; attributive; awkward; belligerent; brilliant; broad; choice; commanding; compensating; conducive; competitive; conspicuous; consular; contrasting; coveted; creditable; defensive; cramped; crouching; dangerous; definite; degraded; delicate; deplorable; dependent; desirable; desperate; despondent; desultory; detestable; dignified; different; disagreeable; dreadful; dominant; ecclesiastical; elevated; embarrassing; eminent; enviable; envious; erroneous; essen-

tial; exalted; exasperating; executive; exposed; extraordinary; fatiguing; fiscal; formidable; fortified; genial; geographical; grand; gratifying; grotesque; handy; hardy; hated; homeless; honorable; idiotic; ignominious; illustrious; imperial; important; impoverished; impregnable; inartistic; insignificant; indefensible; insular; intact; intellectual; interesting; intermediate; irksome; irretrievable; isolated; legal; lucrative; literary; lofty; long-continued; lower; luxurious; masked; mercurial; military; modest; natural-minded; obscure; oceanic; odious; official; opposite; painful; peculiar; perilous; permanent; perplexing; picturesque; pivotal; poised; precarious; precise; premier; prominent; reclining; recognized; reconnoitered; recumbent; relative; relaxed; remarkable; resolute; respectable; responsible; risky; retired; secluded; semi-reclining; serious; shifting; social; solid; stationary; sophisticated; static; strained; strong; strategic; subordinate; subservient; substantial; superfluous; supreme; tedious; technical; tenable; theological; theoretical; thoughtful; threatening; transitional; unambitious; unassailable; uncivil; uncomfortable; unconscious; unendurable; undistinguishable; unequivocal; unfashionable; unfavorable; unique; unlovely; unquestioned; unrivaled; unsupported; unstable; untenable; unworthy; virulent; weak; wicked; worldly; worth-while; wretched.

verbs
acquire—; alter—; aspire to—; challenge—; check—; clarify—; complicate—; compromise—; consolidate—; damage—; defend—; demote—; dignify—; elevate to—; indicate—; jeopardize—; jockey for—; justify—; maintain—; maneuvre for—; regain —; reiterate—; restore—; resume—; retain—; shift—; solidify—; struggle for—; surrender—; survey—; usurp—; wrest — from; —attracts; —reimburses
(See job, situation, rank, status.)

POSITIVE

adverbs
disagreeably; aggressively; boldly; emphatically; truculently; extravagantly; insolently; audaciously; arrogantly; offensively; blandly; calmly; confidently; astoundingly; monstrously; preposterously; rashly; blatantly.

POSSESS (v)

adverbs
legally; intellectually; incontestably; legitimately; intrinsically; originally; potentially; proudly; territorially; undisputedly; conclusively; hereditarily; tranquilly; hazardously; uniquely; enduringly; formally; nominally.
(See own, occupy.)

POSSESSIONS

adjectives
forcible; territorial; illegal; undisturbed; valuable; new; substantial; colonial; uncontrolled; priceless; exclusive; peaceful; dear; steady; imperishable; complete; undisputed; insolent; miserable; calm; vast; limited; overbearing; humble; prized; conclusive; hereditary; earthly; distant; cool; unassisted; narrow; tranquil; cherished; profitable; unquestioned; rightful; kindred; hazardous; naive; small; unique; scenic; remarkable; defiling; precious; enduring; formal; comparative; demoniacal; masterly; favored.

verbs
accrue—; auction off—; command—; cull—; enjoy—; entangle—; estimate—; expand—; forfeit—; gain—; gather—; harbor—; inherit—; liquidate—; mislay—; procure—; reap—; recover—; redeem—; restore—; savor—; value—.
(See estate, assets, fortune, property.)

POSSESSIVE

adverbs
rapturously; ardently; devoutly; jealously; selfishly; fanatically; abnormally; strangely; curiously; maternally; uncommonly; peculiarly; singularly; incorrigibly; foolishly; senselessly; unfortunately; overly; desperately; ridiculously; comically; unpleasantly; embarrassingly; highly; devotedly.

POSSESSOR

adjectives
original; potential; successive (pl); privileged; peaceful; boastful; proud.

POSSIBILITY

adjectives
limping; limitless; remote; easy; dramatic; profit; abstract; contingent; dismal; money-saving; opulent; honest; transcendent; tremendous; horrid; far-reaching; awful; flexible; domestic-social; undiminished;

mental; generous; evolutional; fearful; charming; plausible; iridescent; future; subsequent; divine; envisioned; improbable; extravagant; rhythmic; unfathomable; serene.

verbs
afford—; appreciate—; bolster—; broach—; comprehend—; deny—; determine—; diminish—; disclose—; dissipate—; embroider—; entertain—; envisage—; exhaust—; exploit —; explore—; face—; jump at—; open—; preclude—; raise—; realize—; reject—; ridicule—; rule out—; —appeals to; —dawns upon; —looms; —lurks in; —pales.
(See chance, contingency, potentiality.)

POST

adjectives (*place*)
strategic; arduous; worthless; perilous; impregnable; respective; important; significant; established; permanent; fortified; newly-created; farthest; diplomatic; faint; unbodied; lucrative; sedulous.

verbs
abandon—; assign to—; banish to—; confine to—; establish—; join—; locate—; occupy —; relinquish—; settle at—; station at—; strengthen—; vacate—; —discharges; —lodges; —mobilizes; —quarters.
(See position, situation, job, place, support.)

POST (v)

adverbs
ostentatiously; publicly; secretly; strategically; perilously; intermittently; permanently; periodically; diplomatically.
(See mail, send.)

POSTER

adjectives
frigid; salacious; safety.

verbs
circulate —s; diffuse —s; disseminate —s; plaster with —s; publish —s; —advertises; —advocates; —announces; —blazons; —broaches; —flourishes; —hawks; —heralds; —noises about; —proclaims; —promulgates; —trumpets.
(See placard, advertisement, announcement, notice.)

POSTERITY

adjectives
grateful; unloving; forgetful; unworried.

verbs
bequeath to—; hand down to—; record for —; —commemorates; —condemns; —defaces; —disgraces; —emulates; —exhumes; —glorifies; —honors; —inherits; —outshines; —pales; —perpetuates; —reflects; —reproaches; —reveres; —shames; —sullies; —surpasses; —traces.
(See descendants, family, offspring.)

POSTHUMOUS

adverbs
ironically; unfortunately; tardily.

POSTPONE (v)

adverbs
indefinitely; vaguely; arbitrarily; discreetly; regularly; permanently; temporarily; ultimately; disappointingly; formally.
(See delay, defer.)

POSTPONEMENT

adjectives
indefinite; unwelcome; regular; long-awaited.

POSTSCRIPT

adjectives
lengthy; apologetic.

POSTURE

adjectives
lifeless; bending; studious; stooping; unusual; healthful; spiritual; reclining; graceful; squatting; thoughtful; ungainly; abject; limp; suggestive; impressive; absurd; inelegant; sitting; unmalicious; faulty; easy; painful; incorrect; recumbent; unmanly; supplicating; favorable; poor.

verbs
acquire—; affect—; alter—; assume—; correct—; derange—; fix—; improve—; maintain—; remedy—; ridicule—; shift—; study —; —apes; —characterizes; —impresses; —mars; —tires.
(See gesture, attitude, pose.)

POSTURING

adjectives
dramatic; virile.

POSY

adjectives
fragrant; pretty.

POT

adjectives
earthenware; tea; unusual; molded; glazed; oddly-shaped.

verbs
blacken—; hook—; immerse in—; label—; load—; preserve in—; replenish—; scour—; scrape—; scrub—; —adorns; —boils; —dangles; —glistens; —seethes; —simmers.
(See caldron, kettle.)

POTATION

adjectives
sparkling; nightly; plentiful; spirituous; bubbling; joyous.

POTATO

adjectives
underdone; mashed; baked; frozen; scalloped; sweet; fried; eyeless.

POTENCY

adjectives
tragic; changeful; extraordinary; supernatural; changeful; outstanding; intense; remarkable; long-lived.

POTENT

adverbs
unexpectedly; surprisingly; fatally; peculiarly; singularly; incredibly; amazingly; moderately; scarcely; unusually; commendably; influentially; politically; personally; admittedly; officially; effectively; sufficiently; uncommonly; adequately; overwhelmingly; satisfactorily.

POTENTATE

adjectives
prodigal; rebel; pitiless; powerful; crowned; wealthy; temporal; illustrious; peerless; dread; prudent; wicked.

POTENTIALITY

adjectives
scattered (pl); lasting; remarkable; latent.

verbs
choke—; confer—; cripple—; develop—; discover—; double—; exhaust—; exploit—; force—; lame—; maim—; muzzle—; realize—; recognize—; shatter—; silence—; strangle—; strengthen—; suppress—; utilize—; weaken—.
(See power, possibility.)

POTION

adjectives
bittersweet; direful; deadly; narcotic; soporific.

verbs
concoct—; dose with—; drain—; gulp down—; lap up—; mix—; quaff—; sip—; swallow—; swig—; swill—; toss off—; wash down—; —nauseates; —palliates; —relieves; —remedies; —restores.
(See dose, medicine, poison, liquid.)

POTTERY

adjectives
shattered; valuable; unusual; native; handmade.

POUCH

adjectives
capacious; gorgeous; bulging.

POULTICE

verbs
apply—; pat on—; smear—; surround with—s; treat with—; —allays; —alleviates; —balms; —comforts; —cures; —eases; —foments; —mitigates; —palliates; —refreshes; —relieves; —remedies; —soaks; —soothes.
(See salve, ointment.)

POUNCE (*v*)

adverbs
viciously; vindictively; furiously; instantaneously; murderously; diabolically; formidably; belligerently.
(See jump, dash.)

POUND

adjectives
scant; full; generous.

POUND (*v*)

adverbs
obstreperously; tirelessly; vigorously; lustily; bestially; vociferously; thunderously.
(See beat, strike.)

POUR (*v*)

adverbs
unceasingly; incessantly; liberally; hospit-

ably; effusively; unstintingly; hysterically; liquidly; melodiously; insatiably.

(See flow, stream.)

POUT (v)

adverbs

pettishly; sulkily; prettily; coyly; petulantly; tearfully; despondently.

(See sulk, scowl.)

POVERTY

adjectives

pinching; appalling; relative; hated; imaginary; benumbing; absolute; comparative; inevitable; abject; astonishing; squalid; wretched; genteel; peculiar; hard-working; deepening; irremediable; everlasting; low; continual; lifelong; haughty; distressful; speedy; extreme; general; worthless; utter; honorable; contorted; consequent; disgraceful.

verbs

abhor—; abolish—; accept—; banish—; boast of—; drive off—; outwit—; plead—; prolong—; suffer—; —callouses; —degrades; —dogs; —fetters; —oppresses; —overtakes; —pursues; —ravages; —stalks; —stigmatizes.

(See destitution, impoverishment, need, penury.)

POWDER (general)

adjectives

smokeless; bronze; ordered; resultant; odorless; moistened; deadly; notorious; fetid; capsulated; dictatorial; heavy; inferior; murderous.

verbs

apply—; dab in—; dip in—; dust with—; prink with—; reduce to—; smear—; spread—; touch up with—; —beautifies; —conceals; —embellishes; —glorifies; —harmonizes; —improves; —mellows; —perfects; —pretties; —primes; —soothes; —tricks; —whitens.

(See make-up, dust, gunpowder.)

POWDER (v)

adverbs

fashionably; flirtatiously; glamorously; exaggeratedly; fascinatingly; bewitchingly; enchantingly.

(See perfume, scent.)

POWER

adjectives

abiding; abrogating; abrupt; absent; absolute; absorbing; abundant; active; advancing; adverse; afflicted; all-consuming; allegorizing; all-embracing; allied; all-inhering; amazing; ample; alternative; amorous; analytic; ancestral; ancient; antipathetic; apostolic; appalling; appointing; arbitrary; arch-angelic; architectural; argumentative; assertive; assumed; autocratic; belligerent; autonomous; balanced; beneficent; bestial; blessed; blighted; boasted; braking; boundless; brilliant; budding; buying; capricious; catapulting; celestial; centralizing; chameleon-like; coercive; chemic; civil; clairvoyant; cloven; coming; clerical; colossal; colonizing; comic; commanding; communicative; complete; compelling; composing; compulsive; concentrated; concocted; confederated; confident; confirming; conscious; considerable; consequent; consistent; constitutional; constructive; contending; contingent; contracting; corporate; cosmic; conversational; cosmetic; creative; critical; crowned; curative; curious; deepening; dangerous; defensive; delegated; deliberative; delicate; delightful; denuding; departed; desolate; despotic; destructive; developed; dictatorial; discretional; discerning; disorderly; disturbing; divine; dominant; dormant; driving; dramatic; dulled; dynamic; earning; earth-prisoned; ecclesiastical; educational; effulgent; elastic; elemental; emotional; enchanted; enhanced; energizing; enlarged; enormous; exceeding; erosive; ever-dreaded; evident; exalted; exceptional; excessive; exchangeable; executive; exhaustive; existing; expansive; exorbitant; explosive; extemporaneous; extraordinary; facile; fangless; fatal; far-reaching; fatherly; feeble; feudal; fertilizing; fierce; filial; financial; first-rate; flawless; flexible; formative; full; formidable; fraudulent; frightful; fundamental; generative; generous; genial; genuine; gigantic; godlike; heartfelt; granted; graphic; grasping; growing, guiding; hateful; healing; heavy; high; heavenly; heroic; hidden; hypnotic; imaginative; immature; immeasurable; immediate; immense; immortal; imperial; impossible; imperialist; implied; inborn; incomprehensible; indefinite; individual; indomitable; industrial; inexplicable; inevitable; infective; infernal; infinite; influential; ingrained; inherent; insensate; inimitable; inner; insensible; insubordinate; intellectual; intelligent; intermittent; interposing; intoxicating; intrinsic; intuitive; inutile; invalid; inventive; inveterate; invincible; invisible; irresistible; irresponsible; jealous; judicial; just; keen; kindly; kingly; lasting; latent; lawless; learning; legal; legislative; lifting; limited; linguistic; living; lordly; lubricating; luminous; luxurious; magical; magnetic; magnifying; maiming; malevolent; malign; marvelous; massive; mastering; mature; mental; mesmeric; microscopic; mighty; miraculous; monarchical; moneyed; moral; motive; mortal; murderous; muscular; narcotic; musical; myriad (pl); mysterious; necessary; necromantic; nefarious; obnoxious; nominal; nutritive; objurgatory; occult; omnipotent; omnipresent; ominous; omniscient; oratorical; oracular; organizing; original; overmastering; oxidizing; overwhelming; paramount; parliamentary; particular; passive; patient; patriarchal; peaceable; peculiar; penetrating; perceptive; pernicious; personal; perilous; periodical; persuasive; plastic; poetic; poisonous; political; potential; practical; preponderant; prevailing; primal; primordial; productive; profit; projectile; prolific; proper; prophetic; protecting; psychologic; public; purchasing; purging; quickening; rare; rational; reasoning; reckless; recumbent; recognized; recuperative; regal; relentless; remarkable; remorseless; renewed; reparative; reportorial; reserve; repulsive; requisite; resisting; restless; restrained; resultant; ripening; rival; revolutionary; rounded; royal; ruling; ruthless; sardonic; satanic; scant; secular; scathing; secret; seductive; seer-like; seething; self-dependent; selfish; self-realizing; self-restraining; sinister; selfsame; self-succeeding; silky; singular; sinless; siren; slow-moving; sole; speculative; sophisticated; spiritual; spontaneous; sprightly; springing; stagnant; startling; stimulating; sufficient; subtle; substantial; sullen; superior; superhuman; supernal; supernatural; supreme; surcharged; surging; surpassing; surprising; sustained; sweet; technical; temporal; terrible; thunderous; tranquil; transcendental; transforming; transporting; tremendous; tumultuous; twofold; tyrannous; ultimate; unappealable; unappeased; unborn; unbounded; uncanny; unconscious; undoubted; unexpected; unearthly; unequaled; unfettered; unfamiliar; unhallowed; uninviting; united; universal; unjust; unlimited; unmeasured; unprecedented; unrivaled; unqualified; unrestricted; unseen; unsightly; unspent; unsuspected; untried; unusual; unwearied; unwomanly; uplifting; urgent; utmost; vague; versatile; various (pl); vested; vibrant; victorious; violent; vital; vitalizing; waning; warlike; wearied; wondrous; worsted; worn; smooth; sufficient; self-sustaining.

verbs
abuse—; achieve—; animate with—; ascertain—; bask in—; bid for—; bolster—; bulwark by—; centralize—; check—; climb to —; clip—; clothe in—; confer—upon; consolidate—; crave—; curb—; curtail—; delegate—to; deprive of—; derive—from; dilute —; diminish—; disseminate—; dissipate—; dwarf—; elect to—; endow with—; enhance —; entrust with—; evince—; exercise—; exhaust—; fathom—; fatten on—; forfeit —; generate—; grant—; harness—; impair —; impart—to; impute—to; intensify—; intoxicate with—; lodge—in; lust for—; manifest—; nullify—; offset—; paralyze—; radiate—; regain—; resent—; restrict—; sap —; seize—; sense—; shake—; shear of—; stem—; strip of—; strive for—; surrender —; thirst for—; transmit—; unleash—; undermine—; usurp—; vest—in; vote into —; wield—; worship—; —decays; —declines; —resides in; —wanes; —waxes; —withers.

(See authority, influence, predominance, faculty, force, energy.)

POWERFUL

adverbs
inscrutably; amazingly; omnisciently; dangerously; dreadfully; unbelievably; vigorously; spiritually; influentially; irresistibly; indomitably; intensely; resolutely; acutely; cruelly; brutally; trenchantly; materially; commercially; socially; politically; universally; incredibly; terribly.

POWERLESS

adverbs
pitiably; desperately; hopelessly; inefficiently; altogether; remarkably; deplorably; unhappily; ineptly; awkwardly; clumsily; timorously; terribly; lamentably; miserably; wretchedly; incredibly; curiously; oddly; singularly; pathetically; stupidly; astoundingly; utterly.

PRACTICABILITY

adjectives
concrete; definite; inherent.

PRACTICABLE

adverbs
immediately; usefully; serviceably; opportunely; overwhelmingly; completely; happily; fortunately; conveniently; scientifically; easily; definitely; distinctly; particularly; unexpectedly; strikingly; remarkably; amazingly; luckily; sensibly; profitably; valuably; absolutely; reliably; dependably; positively.

PRACTICAL

adverbs
thoroughly; sensibly; wisely; usefully; commendably; particularly; admirably; fortunately; altogether; sagaciously; splendidly; happily.

PRACTICE

adjectives
ascetic; bayonet; cynical; lucrative; objectionable; lewd; diversified; tedious; competitive; time-honored; arduous; adulterous; traditional; wanton; long; vile; base; private; constant; nefarious; enthusiastic; ancient; shameless; magical; pernicious; assiduous; pagan; treasonable; normal; engineering; recognized; cunning; dangerous; corrupt; horrible; forensic; prevalent; monopolistic; augmented; ungentleman-like; consulting; unvarying; sedulous; ruined; extensive; actual; unique; psychoanalytic; questionable; contrary; licentious; deliberating; consequent; insidious; eminent; degrading; active; flourishing; present; superstitious; robust; irregular; choir; hateful; religious; fascinating; attendant; idolatrous; polygamous; unnatural; universal; prejudiced; comprehensive; revolutionized.

verbs
abandon—; acquire by—; addict to—; adhere to—; adopt—; neglect—; observe—; oppose—; perpetuate—; repress—; resort to—; restrict—; revive—; sanction—; —involves; —survives.
(See habit, conventionality, custom, exercise, performance.)

PRACTICE (*v*)

adverbs
spontaneously; discordantly; surreptitiously; diligently; vigorously; ambitiously; industriously; assiduously; professionally; sedulously; competitively; privately; forensically; periodically.
(See exercise, train, apply.)

PRACTITIONER

adjectives
successful; unqualified; ardent; ignorant; medical; mercenary.

PRAIRIE

adjectives
bleak; naked; blessed; spacious; teeming; carpeted; flowery; unbroken; corn-bladed; stubble-lined; wild; beautiful; short-turfed; great; undulating; sun-browned; verdant; rolling; broken; shaking.

verbs
course—; dwell on—; inhabit—; retire to—; ride—; roam—; traverse—; trek across—; view—; wander over—; wend across—; —blazes; —bores; —confronts; —extends.
(See plain, valley.)

PRAISE

adjectives
voluble; artless; sincere; partial; vain; moderate; humble; lavish; benignant; ignoble; love-pervaded; perfect; unstinted; aggressive; thriftless; expiatory; copious; unnecessary; untimely; reluctant; cynical; muted; awful; unmerited; unspoken; lofty; eloquent; elicited; unstinted; dolesome; passive; hearty; ill-considered; unworthy; unacceptable; deserved; solemn; ceaseless; partial; enthusiastic; unsought; warm; profane; silent; everlasting; unceasing; flattering; grudging; immortal; endless; virtuous; mingled; profuse; judicious; hollow; unqualified; melodious; implied; veiled; eternal; effusive; great; absent; fair; unbroken; lavish; excessive; exaggerated; intemperate; high; undeserving; compulsory.

verbs
administer—; apportion—; aspire to—; bestow—upon; bloom under—; capture—; deny—; desist from—; earn—; entitle to—; excite—; exhaust—; heap—upon; inspire—; justify—; pour out—; proclaim—; shower—upon; sing—; sum up—; swamp with—; —diminishes; —warms.
(See glory, approbation, compliment, adulation, commendation, applause.)

PRAISE (v)

adverbs

extravagantly; effusively; voluntarily; universally; judiciously; fulsomely; sincerely; flatteringly; rhapsodically; volubly; goldenly; immoderately; lavishly; benignantly; unstintedly; copiously; eloquently; intemperately.

(See extol, laud.)

PRAISEWORTHY

adverbs

deservedly; meritoriously; unusually; admirably; admittedly; conspicuously; modestly; highly; uncommonly; remarkably; exceptionally; undoubtedly; genuinely; highly; singularly; immensely; extremely; impressively; signally; unimpeachably; matchlessly; incomparably.

PRANCE (v)

adverbs

spiritedly; mincingly; vigorously; picturesquely; madly; freakishly; sportively.

(See cavort, spring.)

PRANK

adjectives

hoyden; mad; fruitless; common; wily; extravagant; gamesome; humorous; idle; freakish; youthful.

verbs

anticipate—; beguile with—s; concoct—; dodge—; indulge in—; relish—; smother—; —amuses; —disgusts; —diverts; —irks; —seduces; —tires; —traps; —tricks; —vexes.

(See frolic, joke, jest.)

PRANKISH

adverbs

mischievously; roguishly; teasingly; persistently; unexpectedly; incorrigibly; playfully; innocently; foolishly; absurdly; merrily; persistently; ludicrously; idly; frivolously; remarkably; cleverly; ingeniously.

PRANKSTER

verbs

chastize—; dodge—; evade—; forestall—; rebuke—; reprimand—; reproach—; —beguiles; —concocts; —contrives; —disports; —entertains; —wearies.

(See clown, fool, jester.)

PRATE (v)

adverbs

idiotically; foolishly; maliciously; vindictively; spitefully; boastfully; sacreligiously.

(See talk, chatter.)

PRATING

adjectives

solemn; continuous; noisy; bothersome.

PRATTLE

adjectives

winsome; foolish; intermittent.

PRATTLE (v)

adverbs

vapidly; artlessly; childishly; inanely; coyly; winsomely; foolishly; jejunely; insipidly.

(See talk, chatter, babble.)

PRAY (v)

adverbs

fervently; earnestly; distractedly; conspicuously; solemnly; humbly; devoutly; audibly; passionately; effusively; dumbly; supplicatingly; tremulously; blasphemously; inarticulately; wordlessly; virtuously; fruitlessly; sepulchrally.

(See entreat, beg.)

PRAYER

adjectives

idle; fervent; audible; professional; passionate; effectual; effusive; little; soft; prattled; sobbing; boding; priestly; dumb; nightly; chanted; humble; unuttered; dying; melting; weak; pious; supplicating; creditable; stated; conscious; bootless; earnest; perpetual; weekly; specious; poor; hearty; masticated; wistful; sublime; tremulous; common; granted; sunrise; contemptible; insane; trembling; blasphemous; pattered; morning; awed; inarticulate; wordless; fair; consecrating; virtuous; sepulchral; long-groaned; puling; reluctant; grateful; voluble; thankful; vociferated; wrestling; high-blooded; unlawful; true; pagan; fruitless; pleading; hallowing.

verbs

address—; avert by—; attend—; blend in—; bless in—; bow in—; chant—; console by—; fall down in—; fulfill—; grant—; intone—; kneel in—; offer up—; rattle off—s; unite in—; utter—; —beseeches; —

deifies; —entreats; —glorifies; —importunes; —petitions; —reconciles; —supplicates.

(See benediction, mass, entreaty, confession.)

PREACH (v)

adverbs

unctuously; eloquently; rabidly; narrowly; militantly; independently; sonorously; sanctimoniously; sublimely; vociferously; tiresomely; zealously; austerely; itinerantly.

(See speak, advise, teach.)

PREACHER

adjectives

dissenting; eloquent; judicious; tiresome; poor; dark-lantern; moonlight; fiery; zealous; austere; ordinary; misguided; eminent; opposition; devoted; itinerant; traveling; understanding.

PRECARIOUS

adverbs

obviously; naturally; unduly; admittedly; necessarily; terribly; painfully; gravely; awfully; fearfully; alarmingly; grievously; frequently; peculiarly.

PRECAUTION

adjectives

commendable; polite; absolute; sure; obvious; ordinary; oratorical; futile; former; due; extraordinary; well-known; sensible; businesslike; lifesaving; vigilant; utmost; absurd; remarkably; sanitary; superfluous; vital; undue; attentive.

verbs

advocate—; disregard—; employ—; enforce —; exercise—; heed—; necessitate—; neglect—; observe—; omit—; snelve—; suggest —; urge—; view with—; —assures; —arms; —guards; —preestablishes.

(See caution, care.)

PRECAUTIONARY

adverbs

carefully; punctiliously; meticulously; laudably; strangely; unfailingly; vigilantly; warily; significantly; oddly; ominously; portentously; momentously; unusually; surreptitiously; secretly; furtively; quietly; thoroughly; strikingly.

PRECEDENT

adjectives

laudable; rigorous; historical; auspicious; social; romantic; inappropriate; mighty; semi-barbaric.

verbs

afford—; bolster by—; break—; concede to —; defeat—; establish—; follow—; govern by—; invoke—; quote—; refer to—; shatter —; shun—; suffer from—; —controls; —determines; —enslaves; —justifies; —regulates; —rules.

(See custom, authority.)

PRECEPT

adjectives

repeated; benevolent; mild; excellent; civil; sage; strange; abstruse; divine; averaged; dull; moral; traditional; innumerable (pl); sublime.

verbs

advocate—; authorize—; compile—s; disobey—; dispense—; entrust—; formulate—; fulfill—; issue—; promulgate—; sanction—; submit to—; violate—; —decrees; —dictates; —forbids; —imposes; —instructs; —limits; —ordains; —orders; —prohibits; —requests; —requires; —restrains; —restricts.

(See order, principle, teaching, commandment, instruction.)

PRECINCT

adjectives

attractive; holy; warm; hallowed; consecrated; awful; sordid; local.

PRECIOUS

adverbs

unusually; adorably; remarkably; pricelessly; unreasonably; incredibly; singularly; curiously; altogether; unbelievably; understandably; uncommonly; amazingly; fantastically; immensely; immeasurably; incalculably.

PRECIPICE

adjectives

frowning; dizzy; granite; vertical; dread; superb; hanging; wooded; tremendous; beetling; cloven; rimmed; slippery; ivy-covered; stupendous.

verbs

careen down—; clamber up—; cling to—; hang on—; hazard—; risk—; scan—; slide

down—; survey—; teeter on—; venture on —; —blocks; —cuts off; —endangers; —engulfs; —jeopardizes; —imperils; —swallows.
(See cliff, mountain.)

PRECIPITATION

adjectives
complete; extraordinary; daily.

PRECIPITOUS

adverbs
steeply; impossibly; dangerously; riskily; alarmingly; terribly; terrifyingly; incredibly; unreasonably; unspeakably; deucedly; murderously; roughly; icily; tremendously; impressively; imposingly; magnificently; superbly; splendidly; grandly; incalculably; immeasurably; dizzily; stupendously.

PRECISE

adverbs
overwhelmingly; absolutely; dependably; scrupulously; ridiculously; infallibly; remarkably; uncannily; meticulously; mechanically; monotonously; invariably; deliberately; unimpeachably; rigidly; mathematically; scientifically; carefully; particularly; painstakingly; rigorously; insatiably; avidly; necessarily; punctiliously; compellingly; impartially; uniformly.

PRECISION

adjectives
academic; calm; classical; scientific; unerring; rigorous; exquisite; passionate; inflexible; finical; rapid; utmost; careless; nauseating; antique; mechanical; geometrical; marvelous; rhythmic; remarkable; military; delighted; mathematical; melancholy; masterly; convincing; grammatical; admirable; meticulous; faithful; deadly; tolerable; delicate; sufficient; faultless; austere; overwhelming.

verbs
achieve—; applaud—; commend—; demonstrate—; denote—; disclose—; display—; evince—; exhibit—; lack—; manifest—; reveal—; urge—; —assures; —clarifies.
(See accuracy.)

PRECOCIOUS

adverbs
amazingly; remarkably; smartly; keenly; unusually; unpleasantly; disagreeably; impertinently; imprudently; knowingly; pertly; offensively; saucily; boldly; flippantly; bumptiously; obtrusively; oddly; incredibly; uncommonly; surprisingly.

PRECONCEPTION

adjectives
profound; definite; sentimental; unusual.

PREDATORY

adverbs
cruelly; rapaciously; voraciously; uncommonly; naturally; savagely; maliciously; wantonly; ravenously; barbarously; incorrigibly; piratically; cleverly; ungovernably; reprehensibly.

PREDECESSORS

adjectives
resourceful; superstitious; illustrious; ghostly.

verbs
commemorate—; emulate—; excel—; inherit from—; outshine—; succeed—; surpass—; trace—; —advise; —bequeath; —construct; —design; —floor; —found; —frame; —record; —will to.
(See ancestor.)

PREDICAMENT

adjectives
distressing; piteous; unhappy; mechanical; desperate; awkward; terrible.

verbs
alleviate—; avoid—; disentangle—; enjoy —; evade—; labor through—; manage—; risk—; sentimentalize—; shroud—; tackle —; unravel—; view—; —confronts; —distresses; —embarrasses; —flusters; —restrains; —shames.
(See dilemma, embarrassment, position, problem, situation.)

PREDICT (*v*)

adverbs
prophetically; confidently; correctly; lugubriously; mournfully; dismally; darkly; complacently; boldly; astrologically; miraculously.
(See foretell, portend.)

PREDICTION

adjectives
sure-fire; warlike; aristocratic; past; off-

hand; dominant; scientific; dismal; astrological; thunderous; poetical; overconfident; remarkable.

verbs
base—on; cast—; challenge—; divine—; justify—; upset—; venture—; verify—; —augurs; —betokens; —bids; —bodes; —excites; —foreshadows; —foretells; —forewarns; —heralds; —indicates; —portends; —precurses; —presages; —prognosticates; —promises; —prophesies.
(See prognostication, prophesy.)

PREDILECTION

adjectives
perverse; striking; traditional; broad-headed; ancient; well-understood.

PREDISPOSITION

adjectives
eternal; obvious; hereditary.

PREDOMINANCE

adjectives
oppressive; hoar; acknowledged; humorous; imperious; definite.

verbs
acquire—; assert—over; attain—; challenge—; gain—; garner—; spread—; —assures; —influences; —leads; —overbears; —overpowers; —overrides; —outweighs; —pervades; —prevails; —rages; —roots in; —succeeds.
(See power.)

PREDOMINANT

adverbs
rightfully; authoritatively; eminently; officially; regularly; imperiously; proudly; offensively; regally; electively; admittedly.

PREEMINENCE

adjectives
distinguished; dignified; established; unquestionable; intellectual.

verbs
acquire—; attain—; crave—; crown with—; culminate in—; demand—; reach—; shadow—; —eclipses; —glorifies; —inflates; —outbalances; —outstrips; —outweighs; —precedes; —prevails; —transcends; —whips.
(See fame, prominence, eminence, excellence.)

PREFACE

adjectives
hilarious; forcible; well-composed; epigrammatic.

PREFER (v)

adverbs
vastly; personally; infinitely; particularly; politically; individually; overwhelmingly; unaccountably; emotionally.
(See choose, pick.)

PREFERABLE

adverbs
decidedly; altogether; slightly; definitely; unquestionably; commercially; sensibly; practically; artistically; indubitably; genuinely; popularly; politically.

PREFERENCE

adjectives
personal; particular; exaggerated; political; individual; calculated; affectional; premature; overwhelming; unaccountable; definite.

verbs
acquire—; allow—; determine—; express—; exercise—; fix—; harbor—; indulge in—; list—; mark—; muse over—; offer—; permit—; poll—; select—; shout—; single out—; —culls; —decides; —elects; —espouses; —fancies.
(See choice, alternative.)

PREGNANCY

verbs
detect—; determine—; evade—; examine for—; fear—; generate in—; incur—; induce—; prevent—; procreate in—; produce—; suggest—; yield in—; —alters; —ensues; —increases; —irritates; —multiplies; —nauseates.

PREJUDICE

adjectives
antique; arrogant; feudal; vile; personal; violent; popular; abandoned; tender; ingrained; sectional; unworthy; virulent; vulgar; unflinching; established; unreflective; aristocratical; tainted; logical; conservative; superficial; pious; unconscious; tribal; present; frivolous; patrician; ignorant; senile; unreasonable; miserable; political; tenacious; sexual; bitter; undue; absorbing; intense; inveterate; imperial; unfounded; entrenched; fierce; social; furious; insular; religious; economic; invincible; superstitious.

verbs
arouse—; awaken—; beget—; beset with—; break down—; combat—; defy—; dictate by—; emancipate from—; erase—; exploit —; lampoon—; nourish—; oust—; pander to—; preach—; purge of—; shed—; subserve—; survive—; —distorts; —flourishes; —influences; —persists; —poisons; —shades; —vanishes; —undermines; —weakens.

(See bias, obsession, hate, judgment, opinion.)

PREJUDICE (*v*)

adverbs
hopelessly; personally; violently; sectionally; vulgarly; aristocratically; logically; unconsciously; ignorantly; irrationally; sexually; socially; inveterately; religiously; economically; superstitiously; politically.

(See injure, hurt.)

PREJUDICED

adverbs
unreasonably; unfavorably; affectionately; indulgently; viciously; maliciously; unfortunately; happily; absurdly; jealously; enviously; unfairly; narrowly; senselessly; terribly; doctrinally; politically; mischievously; indelibly; wrongfully; provincially; fanatically; outrageously; dreadfully; hopelessly.

PREJUDICIAL

adverbs
strongly; unfavorably; criminally; highly; incontrovertibly; definitely; fanatically; outrageously; scandalously; obviously; manifestly; evidently; wrongly; secretly; perniciously; disastrously; exceptionably; grievously; horribly; reprehensibly; inadvisably; unpardonably.

PRELATE

adjectives
haughty; fatuous; foreign; pampered; reverend; gallant; distinguished; princely; shrewd.

PRELIMINARY

adjectives
mysterious; invariable; essential; valuable; inevitable; indispensable.

verbs
anticipate—; arrange—; engage in—; miss —; observe—; settle—; stage—; view—; —allays; —appeals; —entertains; —heads; —introduces; —leads; —precedes; —prefixes; —ushers in; —bridges; —prepares.

(See introduction, opening, ceremony, preface, prelude.)

PRELUDE

adjectives
fatal; mellow; formal; unpretentious; necessary.

PREMATURE

adverbs
unfortunately; unwisely; thoughtlessly; senselessly; recklessly; ineptly; clumsily; maladroitly; unskilfully; foolishly; imprudently; indiscreetly; disastrously; undiplomatically; inexpediently; calamitously; ill-advisedly; treacherously; sadly.

PREMEDITATED

adverbs
criminally; admittedly; wickedly; brutally; savagely; mischievously; outrageously; scandalously; maliciously; carefully; furtively; conclusively; unanswerably; inferentially; manifestly; cruelly; obviously; nefariously.

PREMISE

adjectives
false; petty; inconceivable; assumed; fundamental; unsound; unexamined; insufficient; academic; specific; cardinal.

verbs
assume—; bank on—; contradict—; depend on—; discuss—; endorse—; establish—; examine—; follow—; guard—; impair—; oppose—; question—; ratify—; rebut—; rely on—; stand upon—; support—; uphold —; verify—.

(See proposition, assumption, supposition, hypothesis.)

PREMONITORY

adverbs
distinctly; formidably; terribly; inferentially; fearfully; thoughtfully; surreptitiously; obviously; manifestly; unmistakably; woefully; horribly; coldly; cruelly; fortunately; subtly; significantly; gravely; deliberately; generously; fraternally; helpfully; suggestively; threateningly.

PREOCCUPATION

adjectives
smiling; intellectual; harassed; religious.

verbs
arouse from—; bury in—; cloud in—; distract from—; erase—; examine in—; immerse in—; interrupt—; necessitate—; notice—; observe—; scan in—; seal in—; view with—; —entertains; —reflects; —revises; —shrouds.
(See reverie, lethargy.)

PREOCCUPY (*v*)

adverbs
incessantly; intellectually; religiously; studiously; ambitiously; vigorously; clerically; mentally.
(See absorb, occupy.)

PREPARATION

adjectives
ineffectual; anatomical; excellent; nervous; proprietary; essential; initial; frantic; skillful; painstaking; elaborate; manifold; active; warlike; energetic; constant; secret; formidable; impartial; adequate; virtuous; mercurial; vigorous; imperfect; extensive; pain-killing; mighty; scientific; healthful; food; scant; minute; needful; intellectual; effectual; incessant.

verbs
advocate—; demand—; drill in—; justify—; lack—; plunge into—s; —aids; —arms; —arrays; —edifies; —enlightens; —expounds; —familiarizes; —grounds; —implants; —introduces; —organizes; —tunes.
(See qualification, training.)

PREPARATORY

adverbs
gravely; soberly; sadly; woefully; horribly; carefully; cautiously; completely; happily; rapturously; ecstatically; excitedly; frenziedly; heartbrokenly; hastily; deliberately; unwillingly; reluctantly; wildly; eagerly; anxiously; surreptitiously; resolutely; gallantly; thoughtfully; quietly; noisily; serenely; calmly; generously; ardently; piously; reverently; prayerfully.

PREPARE (*v*)

adverbs
amicably; gallantly; delectably; professionally; tastefully; manifestly; gravely; gratuitously; previously; independently; vigorously; sedulously; duly; amply; privately; cautiously; ceremoniously; wilfully; effectually; elaborately; energetically; formidably; minutely.
(See fit, provide, adapt.)

PREPARED

adverbs
well; badly; completely; scarcely; hardly; wonderfully; remarkably; eminently; fully; admirably; competently; fairly; barely; fortunately; skilfully; carefully; generously; altogether; unusually.

PREPONDERANCE

adjectives
undue; tremendous; noticeable; unquestioned.

PREPONDERANT

adverbs
heavily; unfairly; beneficially; influentially; dangerously; increasingly; politically; socially; dreadfully; unfortunately; imperiously; currently; tellingly; authoritatively; curiously; outrageously; naturally.

PREPOSSESSION

adjectives
personal; sudden; unfortunate; religious; unfavorable.

PREROGATIVE

adjectives
entrenched; personal; enviable.

verbs
allow—; assert—; authorize—; challenge—; demand—; disqualify—; entitle to—; exact—; extend—; grant—; insist on—; merit—; relax—; usurp—; violate—; wield—; —arrogates; —encroaches; —infringes.
(See privilege, right.)

PRESCIENCE

adjectives
slumberous; indistinct; passionate; hollow; unresisted; mystic.

PRESCRIBE (*v*)

adverbs
punctiliously; wisely; sagely; variously; preposterously; exclusively; legally; specifically; medically; medicinally; methodically.
(See order, advise.)

PRESCRIPTION

adjectives
favorite; exclusive; specific; deep-rooted; legal; unfailing; definite; mystic; age-old.

verbs
acquire—; addict to—; adhere to—; concoct —; dispense—s; fill—; follow—; formulate —; issue—; mix—; order—; recommend—; require—; write—; —alleviates; —eases; —instructs; —palliates; —relieves; —remedies; —soothes.
(See formula, medicine, direction.)

PRESENCE

adjectives
portly; reassuring; immediate; comely; inconspicuous; instant; palpitating; hateful; pale; glorious; visible; posthumous; gracious; protecting; unfamiliar; distinct; august; imposing; resplendent; singular; semiluminous; important; haunting; noiseless; royal; wondrous; palpable; ruddy; tranquil; effulgent; eternal; masked; universal; intolerant; abhorred; grim; imperial; impressive; ignoble; threatened; culprit; enchanting; maternal; detected; solemn; chastening; visionary; transforming; protecting; admirable; close; tender; celestial; gaunt; ramshackle; habitual; blighted; stately; passionate; continual; dreadful; perpetual; animate; pervading; abrupt; excellent; unrecognized; mortal; declared; commanding; dignified; unauthorized; unwelcome; striking; majestic; private; blessed; divine; invisible; engaging; stately; handsome; shadowy; cheering; unconjectured; gentle; combined.

verbs
acknowledge—; advertise—; announce—; ascertain—; conduct into—; detect—; enjoy—; mark—; reveal—; tolerate—; usher into—; —disturbs; —evokes; —impresses; —irritates.

PRESENT

adjectives
immediate; solid; magnificent; spontaneous; elegant; appropriate; ever-fleeting; eternal; realistic; substantial; grief-shadowed; reluctant; alien; visionary; stormy; placid.

verbs
accept—; acknowledge—; bedeck—; beribbon—s; bestow—s upon; conceal—; decline —; guard—s; lavish with—s; offer—; present with—; solicit—; tender—; view—s; —dazzles; —excites; —flatters; —pleases; reconciles; —s shower upon; —stems; dispense—s.
(See gift.)

adverbs
inappropriately; unsuitably; inconveniently; fortunately; happily; conveniently; opportunely; always; seldom; occasionally; objectionably; embarrassingly; unwarrantably; unfortunately; ever; constantly; unexpectedly; auspiciously; generously; considerately; graciously.

PRESENT (v)

adverbs
modestly; formally; humbly; appropriately; reluctantly; satirically; adequately; realistically; brazenly; providentially; ethically; imploringly; casually; repeatedly; materially.
(See give, offer, introduce.)

PRESENTATION

adjectives
technical; diligent; elaborate; artistic; condensed; demon; superb; graphic; ruddy; attractive; dispassionate; illustrative; terse; farewell.

verbs
acknowledge—; administer—; anticipate—; beg for—; favor with—; ignore—; postpone —; propose—; refuse—; reject—; seek—; welcome—; withhold—; —accords; —bestows; —conciliates; —introduces; —reveals.
(See introduction.)

PRESENTIMENT

adjectives
fearful; cold; apt; uneasy; vague; unquiet; undefinable; decisive; guilty.

verbs
argue—; harbor—; heed—; laugh down—; ridicule—; —aggravates; —augurs; —betokens; —bids; —bodes; —disturbs; —excites; —foreshadows; —foretells; —forewarns; —grows; —precurses; —troubles; —visits; —presages.
(See anticipation, apprehension, fear.)

PRESENTMENT

adjectives
counterfeit; vague; forceful; definite.

PRESERVATION

adjectives
perfect; inflexible; miraculous; exquisite; unbelievable.

PRESERVE (v)

adverbs
miraculously; mercifully; unbelievably; marvelously; sagaciously; permanently; painfully; laboriously; durably; prudently; immortally; perpetually.
(See keep, save.)

PRESERVED

adverbs
carefully; reverently; thriftily; skilfully; duly; richly; fortunately; luckily; meticulously; punctiliously; cautiously; perfectly; miraculously; exquisitely; incredibly; well; permanently; inviolately; safely; secretly; doggedly; sacredly; divinely; mysteriously; inexplicably; magnificently; splendidly.

PRESIDENT

adjectives
honorable; unqualified; wearied.

verbs
consult—; impeach—; inaugurate—; induct as—; —addresses; —adjourns; —administers; —advises; —appoints ; —berates; —conducts; —controls; —directs; —drives; —governs; —orates; —orders; —pilots; —presides; —rules; —sanctions.
(See official, chairman, judge, magistrate, executive, legislator.)

PRESS

adjectives
fluctuating; sensational; hostile; radical; daily; periodical; increasing; indefatigable; groaning; gagged; obnoxious; printing; vigilant; militant; bourgeois; respective; converted; brick; clashing; illustrated.

verbs
affiliate with—; divulge to—; gag—; meddle in—; regale—; ruffle—; tumble from—; —alludes to; —argues; —denounces; —discusses; —howls; —screams; —shouts; —spits out; —whirls.
(See literature, magazine, newspaper.)

PRESS (v)

adjectives
sorely; tenderly; vigorously; convulsively; affectionately; emotionally; hotly; forcibly; desperately; courteously; cautiously; vigilantly; militantly.
(See compress, crowd.)

PRESSING

adverbs
strangely; curiously; immediately; insistently; persistently; inconveniently; instantly; inescapably; direly; embarrassingly; unduly; imperatively; absorbingly; desperately; gravely; critically; significantly; inordinately; portentously; momentously; ominously; peculiarly.

PRESSURE

adjectives
systolic; lingering; diplomatic; lateral; injurious; fierce; unreasoning; excessive; fluid; common; great; stupendous; aggressive; warm; angry; burning; teasing; atmospheric; irresistible; inevitable; convulsive; mechanical; extreme; sympathetic; cordial; normal; persistent; social; tremendous; superincumbent; opposing; diminished; insupportable; delicate; immense; inconstant; uniform; organized; undue; pecuniary; artificial.

verbs
alleviate—; apply—; counteract—; ease off—; employ—; exert—; expose to—; halt—; obliterate—; submit to—; succumb to—; subject to—; wobble under—; work under—; yield to—; —diminishes; —increases; —welds.
(See load, stress, force, power.)

PRESTIGE

adjectives
mysterious; personal; intellectual; frantic; national; original; unprecedented; considerable; glorious; battered; military; relative; enormous; extended; weighty; external.

verbs
acquire—; aspire to—; augment—; capitalize—; crack—; enhance—; enjoy—; extend —to; gain—; guarantee—; impair—; lessen —; lower—; preserve—; revive—; rival—; solidify—; threaten—; weaken—; —declines; —jumps.
(See influence.)

PRESUMABLE

adverbs
readily; reasonably; altogether; sensibly;

credibly; scarcely; hardly; barely; naturally; legally; easily; appropriately; particularly; circumstantially; wholly.

PRESUME (*v*)

adverbs
unblushingly; boldly; conceitedly; petulantly; insolently; arrogantly; insistently; pettishly.
(See assume, dare.)

PRESUMPTION

adjectives
subsequent; general; arrogant; insistent; petulant; insolent; fundamental; unwarranted; scientific.

PRESUMPTUOUS

adverbs
impertinently; ungraciously; offensively; conspicuously; boldly; audaciously; self-importantly; inexcusably; boorishly; uncivilly; disrespectfully; irreverently; brazenly; ignorantly; flippantly; obnoxiously; atrociously; unpardonably; egregiously; surprisingly; crassly; strikingly; arrogantly; recklessly; indiscreetly; imprudently; unbelievably; daringly; youthfully; obstinately; challengingly; obstreperously; foolishly; senselessly.

PRESUPPOSE (*v*)

adverbs
arrogantly; confidently; selfishly; carelessly; egotistically; independently.
(See assume, presume.)

PRETEND (*v*)

adverbs
satirically; childishly; deliberately; extravagantly; chimerically; groundlessly; idiotically; irrationally; sportively.
(See simulate, feign.)

PRETENDER

adjectives
sole; cowled; contemptible; royal.

PRETENSE

adjectives
specious; elaborate; cunning; slight; vile; selfish; theatrical; plausible; vain; boyish; transparent; empty; offensive; innocent; weary; unfounded; scorned; boastful; mere; false; insincere; melancholy; listless; emotional.

verbs
abandon—; accuse of—; afford—; assume —; avoid—; breed—; concoct—; criticize —; don—; eradicate—; fabricate—; garb in—; inveigh against—; justify—; offer—; penetrate—; pierce—; possess—; relax—; ridicule—; simulate—; strip of—; wallow in—; —awes; —deceives; —disguises;—distorts; —encroaches; —masks; —minces; —misbecomes; —misrepresents; —ornaments; —overacts; —overcharges; —perverts; —poses; —strains; —transgresses.
(See disguise, hyprocisy, sham, affectation, subterfuge, deception.)

PRETENSION

adjectives
groundless; ladylike; extravagant; capital; chimerical; present; unreasonable; aesthetic; arrogant; modish; aristocratic; lofty; faint; supernatural; obnoxious; serious; military; specific; rational; foolish; intellectual; genealogical; medieval; additional.

verbs
(See pretense.)

PRETENTIOUS

adverbs
foppishly; stiltedly; mincingly; simperingly; stagily; abominably; absurdly; ridiculously; ludicrously; laughably; disgustingly; pathetically; pompously; arrogantly; noisily; elaborately; cunningly; cleverly; theatrically; transparently; offensively; boastfully; harmlessly; unreasonably; loftily; unnecessarily; fantastically; artlessly; amusingly; prodigiously; colossally; tediously; stiffly.

PRETEXT

adjectives
specious; trifling; vulgar; plausible; worthy; reasonable; friendly; convenient; insignificant.

PRETTINESS

adjectives
bewildering; unearthly; verbal; slim; youthful; stiff; fantastic; painted.

PRETTY

adverbs
innocently; delightfully; rosily; childishly; seductively; alluringly; unbelievably; charmingly; undeniably; naturally; artlessly; unaffectedly; sweetly; unusually; bewitchingly; altogether; remarkably; strik-

ingly; unexpectedly; fascinatingly; wholesomely; radiantly; glowingly; unconsciously; pertly; smartly; artfully; particularly; uncommonly; matchlessly.

PREVAIL (v)

adverbs
ultimately; universally; unanimously; dominantly; uniformly; normally; imperiously; appallingly; annoyingly; turbulently.
(See rule, dominate.)

PREVALENCE

adjectives
marked; imperious; overwhelming; appalling; strong; everlasting; annoying.

PREVALENT

adverbs
widely; generally; currently; recently; naturally; disastrously; unfortunately; inexplicably; significantly; unhappily; unaccountably; ideologically; deucedly; blightingly; destructively; oddly; fashionably; transiently; momentarily; temporarily; insignificantly; briefly; formidably.

PREVENT (v)

adverbs
permanently; effectually; effectively; forcibly; admirably; cautiously; methodically; automatically; mechanically; scientifically; medically.
(See avert, hinder, thwart.)

PREVENTION

verbs
effect—; employ—; investigate—; —averts; —baffles; —blankets; —chokes; —cramps; —disconcerts; —disheartens; —dooms; —encounters; —hampers; —impedes; —nips; —stifles; —thwarts.
(See obstruction, hindrance, impediment.)

PREVENTIVE

adjectives
continual; effectual; admirable; extraordinary.

adverbs
highly; successfully; presumably; helpfully; usefully; actively; moderately; prudently; remarkably; uncommonly; usually; supposedly; credibly; possibly; unquestionably; sometimes.

PREY

adjectives
miserable; finny; helpless; predestined; unexhausted; lawful; accustomed; fair; universal; shattered; specious; legitimate; unambitious; stern; silent; yielding; righteous; reluctant.

verbs
attack—; corner—; descend on—; ensnare —; evade—; fall—to; grasp—; lurk for—; mangle—; pursue—; reconnoiter—; strike—; wrestle with—.
(See victim.)

PRICE

adjectives
unbelievable; prohibitive; exorbitant; heavy; minute; prevailing; comparative; minimum; sacrifice; advancing; rising; prehistoric; dirt-cheap; bottom; wholesale; sensational; competitive; amazing; fabric; specific; cash; low; proportionate; remarkable; sale; moderate; original; ridiculous; extreme; countless (pl); fractional; irresistible; bewildering; unheard-of; insufficient; trivial; possible; popular; basic; fantastic; reasonable; modest; imposing; absurd; attractive; bargain; reduced; exceptional; stiff; outrageous; unjustifiable; frightful; diurnal; internal; history-making; reserve; proportionate; remunerative; fabulous; interesting; impressive; modest; astonishing; anniversary; advertised; democratic; thrifty; wholesale; onerous; money-saving; pleasant; consistent; unusual; national; phenomenal; singular; characteristic; factory-to-you; impressive; astounding; concrete; idle; introductory; retail; disproportionate; losing.

verbs
bolster—; command—; demur at—; depress —; enhance—; fix—; haggle over—; hoist —; inflate—; reduce—; slash—; threaten—; —falls; —fluctuates; —flurries; —shoots up; —soars; —tumbles.
(See cost, amount, fee, tax, expense, value, charge, worth.)

PRICE (v)

adverbs
sensationally; attractively; reasonably; exorbitantly; modestly; economically; prohibitively; ridiculously; outrageously; fabulously; competitively; sensationally; disproportionately.
(See value.)

PRICELESS

adverbs

curiously; absolutely; sacredly; definitely; presumably; almost; altogether; sensationally; fantastically; immeasurably; incalculably; naturally; inimitably; superbly; magnificently; indescribably.

PRIDE

adjectives

absurd; adoring; amorous; arrogant; angry; aristocratic; barbarous; bounded; boyish; bubbling; calm; careful; bulldog; carnal; childish; civic; coeval; cold; commendable; competitive; conscious; considerable; contiguous; considerate; contemptible; craggy; daring; counterfeit; dark; defiant; delicious; demon; despairing; determined; disappointed; dormant; drooping; emulated; evident; excessive; exultant; fair; false; fantastical; fatuous; fiendish; fiery; firm; flattered; flowery; foamy; foolish; full-blown; garish; gay; generous; gentle; golden; gracious; grim; guiltless; hasty; haughty; heroic; hidden; high-blown; high-bred; holy; honest; housewifely; hurt; hypocritic; ignorant; imperial; inconsistent; indescribable; indomitable; inordinate; insolent; intellectual; interminable; intolerable; laudable; just; justifiable; legitimate; lingering; local; lofty; lovely; loyal; maiden; martial; masculine; matchless; maternal; melancholy; mingled; moderate; modest; monarchal; moral; morning; mortal; mortified; motley; much-vaunted; narrow; national; noble; obdurate; obstinate; offended; overweening; overwhelming; pardonable; particular; patrician; patriotic; personal; pertinacious; philosophic; piqued; piscatorial; pleasing; plunging; positive; pouting; prim; provincial; proper; purple; rapturous; reassuring; reflected; regal; ruthless; restless; reprehensible; retrospective; sad; sanctimonious; satisfactory; saucy; serpent; school-taught; secret; self-torturing; self-complacent; self-conscious; sensitive; shallow; sheltered; short-lived; signal; silent; single; snobbish; sober; special; spirited; splendid; spotless; stoic; stainless; stranded; stubborn; subdued; stupid; subtle; summer; sweet; tampering; tender; thankless; theatric; touchy; tyrannic; unendurable; ungenerous; unmixed; unsuspected; unvanquished; unwonted; vainglorious; vicarious; voluptuous; well-ing; wicked; worldly; womanly; wounded; wretched.

verbs

awaken—; beam with—; bloat with—; conceal—; flush with—; fortify—; glow with —; gratify—; humble—; injure—; lacerate —; pocket—; preserve—; reflect—; repress —; restrain—; rouse—; ruffle—; salve—; sting—; stir—; swallow—; swell with—; —animates; —armors; —bloats; —revolts; —supports.

(See conceit, vanity, arrogance, self-esteem.)

PRIEST

adjectives

solemn; white-robed; ministering; venerable; full; dull; frocked; persecuting; attendant; ash-smeared; long-haired; eagle-taloned; half-mad; wandering; native; pretended; sandaled; renegade; officiating; treacherous; unyielding; shameful; stout; rustic; rich; homey; luxurious; solitary; adorned; incensed; idolatrous; little; high; chanting; smooth-tongued; easy-living.

verbs

cloister—; confess to—; ordain—; —admonishes; —addresses; —attends; —baptizes; —blesses; —chants; —confirms; —consecrates; —converts; —fines; —genuflects; —hallows; —imposes; —instructs; —intercedes; —ministers to; —orders; —sanctifies; —serves; —supplicates.

(See minister, clergyman, clergy.)

PRIESTHOOD

adjectives

royal; idolatrous; self-constituted.

PRIESTLY

adverbs

reverently; devoutly; gently; sternly; helpfully; carefully; tolerantly; dutifully; fervently; admirably; estimably; zealously; ardently; diligently; earnestly; unfailingly; consistently; irreproachably.

PRIG

adjectives

sapless; offensive; hopeless; unsocial; obnoxious; well-meaning.

PRIGGISH

adverbs

intolerably; disagreeably; self-righteously; ostentatiously; uncomfortably; deucedly; unbearably; hatefully; immeasurably; unbelievably; miserably; unpleasantly; atrociously; inflexibly; pretentiously; awfully; suddenly; inveterately; incurably; offensively.

PRIM

adverbs
demurely; sedately; coyly; naturally; disagreeably; incurably; shyly; unsophisticatedly; pleasantly; uncomfortably; innocently; attractively; suddenly; unexpectedly; unaccountably; singularly; remarkably; amazingly; inscrutably; distinctly; self-consciously; bashfully; unnecessarily; needlessly; unfortunately; crudely; virtuously; prettily.

PRIMACY

adjectives
hierarchal; archangelic; established.

PRIME

adjectives
dancing; dominant; golden; autumnal; refulgent; blooming; young; luxuriant; lusty; early; unvalued.

PRIMITIVE

adverbs
unexpectedly; impossibly; intolerably; beautifully; unfashionably; stylishly; restfully; strikingly; pathetically; incredibly; curiously; grotesquely; fantastically; dramatically; spectacularly; uncomfortably; entertainingly; interestingly; singularly; hopelessly; undesirably; quaintly; sweetly; fearfully; miserably; comfortably; happily.

PRIMROSE

adjectives
full-faced; colored; fragrant; meaningful.

PRINCE

adjectives
sovereign; ambitious; praiseworthy; covetous; sagacious; pious; illustrious; merciful; faithful; humane; religious; upright; worthy; trained; petty; imperious; ecclesiastical; independent; chivalrous; tyrannical; scrupulous; economical; democratic; dethroned; barbarian; reigning; renowned; pusillanimous; arbitrary; sweet; auspicious; confiscating.

PRINCELY

adverbs
gorgeously; magnificently; lavishly; splendidly; brilliantly; regally; superbly; nobly; incredibly; indescribably; unutterably; unimaginably; immeasurably; imperiously; absolutely; graciously; gallantly; distinctly; imposingly; impressively; genuinely.

PRINCESS

adjectives
sanctimonious; enchanted; long-despoiled; extravagant; disinherited; meddlesome; overfrivolous.

PRINCIPAL

adjectives
skilled; deft; practiced; renowned; respected.

PRINCIPALITY

adjectives
ecclesiastical; autonomous; tributary; scanty.

PRINCIPLE

adjectives
political; fundamental; moral; poetical; infallible; unsuspected; applicable; acknowledged; essential; immortal; revolutionary; rigid; guiding; ultimate; wholesome; just; competitive; cantilever; inductive; mistaken; common; immutable; particular; thoughtful; sexual; strict; eternal; underlying; false; animating; incorporating; vital; involved; party; maleficent; despotic; sacred; religious; uniform; methodological; architectural; patriotic; latent; antagonistic; vigorous; virtuous; odious; death-bringing; pervading; evolutionary; anti-centralizing; active; chemical; unimpeachable; humanitarian; first; vicious; internal; untrue; inductive; mischievous; settled; rational; human; leading; exhausted; distorted; one-term; critical; intuitive; basic; ruling; durable; adverse; honorable; beautifying; abandoned; intelligible; simple; commonsense; fixed; cooperative; rudimental; scientific; irreconcilable; immaterial; preposterous; philosophical; artistic; cardinal; warlike; favorite; sound; unquestionable; established; high; proper; enlightened; better; novel; demonstrative; sound; self-exploding; moving; dynamic; ethical; phonetic; elementary; unjust; spirited; uniform; dazzling; racial; germinal.

verbs
abhor—; accept—; adhere to—; apply—; base on—; commit to—; comprehend—; compromise—; concur on—; contravene—; deduce—; dispute—; dissect—; embody; —embrace—; endorse—; enunciate—; espouse—; establish—; exemplify—; expound—;

extend—; formulate—; grasp—; illustrate —;inculcate—; infract—; infuse—; instill —; invest with—; invoke—; obscure—; oppose—; pledge to—; proclaim—; promulgate —; refute—; reiterate—; safeguard—; steep in—; trample—; unfold—; utilize—; vaunt —; vindicate—; violate—; —decays; —justifies; —triumphs; —underlies.

(See dogma, doctrine, fundamental, formula, essential, law, rule, policy.)

PRINT

adjectives (*ink*)

vivid; monotone; riotous; conspicuous; well-penetrated; impartial.

PRINT

verbs (*news*)

break into—; compose—; creep into—; dash off—; decipher—; draw up—; impress—; scan—; summarize—; type—; —arouses; —blazons; —broaches; —circulates; —diffuses; —engrosses; —enlightens; —exposes; —heralds; —proclaims; —reports; —reveals; —rumors.

(See press, newspaper, news.)

PRINT

adjectives (*picture*)

unframed; bright; false; colored; sticking; beauteous.

verbs

appreciate—; auction —s; brighten—; collect —s; color—; design—; frame—; imitate —; prize—; select—; study—; value—; —adorns; —attracts; —depicts; —embellishes; —harmonizes; —portrays; —suspends.

(See photograph, picture, painting.)

PRINT (*v*)

adverbs

slanderously; anonymously; indelibly; elegantly; professionally; impartially; irritatingly; sensationally; boldly; seditiously; scandalously; flatteringly.

(See publish.)

PRINTER

adjectives

enterprising; active; energetic; skilled; deft.

verbs

engage—; prepare for—; —arranges; —bundles; —composes; —copies; —effaces; —errs; —inscribes; —issues; —measures; —presses; —publishes; —rushes; —sets up; —stains; —transcribes; —types.

(See publisher.)

PRISM

adjectives

refracting; colorful; revolving; perfect.

PRISMATIC

adverbs

gorgeously; iridescently; colorfully; beautifully; magnificently; magically; mysteriously; unbelievably; splendidly; phenomenally; gloriously; awesomely; unexpectedly; strikingly; matchlessly; brilliantly; dazzlingly; bewilderingly; fascinatingly; stunningly; astoundingly.

PRISON

adjectives

expensive; nonsensical; windowless; verbal; polluted; model; various (pl); wiry; medieval; repulsive; gloomy; twilight; squalid; voluntary; glittering; millennial; gilded; unsanitary.

verbs

cast into—; commit to—; languish in—; pine in—; rot in—; scuttle into—; throw into—; —bars; —cloisters; —confines; —encages; —gags; —harbors; —immures; —incarcerates; —paroles; —rehabilitates; —releases; —restrains; —yokes.

(See jail, dungeon, imprisonment, monastery, pillory.)

PRISONER

adjectives

panting; pardoned; life; sullen; self-made; incestuous; affable; emaciated; affable; defiant; careless; high-hearted; unfortunate; well-dressed; distinguished; disheartened; virtual; unprincipled; pale; wounded; linked; sorrowful; feathered; miserable; desperate.

verbs

arraign—; brand—; charge with—; denounce—; exonerate—; guard—; herd —s; incriminate—; indict—; liberate—; lodge—; prosecute—; release—; reproach—; restrain —; saddle—; slur—; stigmatize—; taunt—; twit—; vindicate—; —confesses; —implicates.

(See convict, captive, criminal.)

PRIVACY

adjectives
modified; necessary; outraged; perfect; absolute; tumultuous; defended; domestic; actual; comparative; boudoir; long-enjoyed; pleasing; desirable.

verbs
bottle up in—; couch in—; creep into—; demand—; deny—; destroy—; draw into—; embrace—; enjoy—; ensconce in—; infringe on—; impinge upon—; retire to—; rob of—; ruffle—; seclude in—; sink into—; yearn for —; —buries; —curtains; —fences; —mystifies; —puzzles; —repels; —shrouds.
(See concealment, isolation, seclusion, secrecy.)

PRIVATE

adverbs
strictly; necessarily; diplomatically; securely; safely; supposedly; sacredly; presumably; delightfully; furtively; secretly; particularly; confidentially; officially; intimately; appropriately; mysteriously; inviolably; surreptitiously; reticently; stealthily; pleasantly; happily; fortunately.

PRIVATION

adjectives
rigorous; material; signal; melancholy; revolting; ascetic; inevitable; personal; utmost; bitter; cruel; severe.

verbs
bear—; beget—; conceal—; endure—; experience—; expose to—; incur—; inflict—; meet with—; steel against—; suffer—; undergo—; —agitates; —agonizes; —chafes; —gnaws; —grates; —hinders; —pinches; —purifies; —racks; —smothers; —tortures.
(See hardship, impoverishment, poverty.)

PRIVILEGE

adjectives
royal; peculiar; ancient; valuable; additional; sublime; honorable; desolating; unrestricted; glorious; inestimable; immemorial; treasured; admirable; feudal; obsolete; cut-and-dried; antique; abused; fleeting; exclusive; exceptional; distinguishing; retirement; further; social; franking; chartered; undoubted; ancient; sovereign; accepted; cherished; irresistible.

verbs
abuse—; accord—to; assert—; bestow—upon; claim—; confer—upon; deprive of—; destroy—; encroach on—; extend—to; forego—; grant—; jeopardize—; overstep—; seek—; share—; strip of—; surrender—; wangle—; —enables; —expires.
(See independence, exemption, liberty, right.)

PRIVILEGED

adverbs
highly; especially; unfairly; fortunately; unaccountably; mysteriously; peculiarly; particularly; uniquely; inexplicably; financially; curiously; politically; socially; unusually; deservedly; indulgently; graciously; affectionately; freely; aristocratically; unconditionally; legally; duly; constitutionally; prescriptively; absolutely; properly.

PRIZE

adjectives
priceless; glittering; scarlet-bound; choice; coveted; easy; useless; savory; hard-earned.

verbs
acquire—; award—to; bestow—upon; capture—; collect —s; derive—; draw—; earn —; forfeit—; gain—; glean —s; merit—; obtain—; offer—; reap —s; reward with—; value—; win—; —allures; —enriches; —tempts.
(See laurels, medal.)

adverbs
inordinately; exceptionally; morbidly; casually; affectionately; ardently; exaggeratedly; memorably.
(See value, esteem.)

PRIZE-FIGHTER

verbs
—blocks; —bounds; —clinches; —counters; —dances; —ducks; —feints; —fouls; —groans; —hooks; —jabs; —launches; —levels; —pile-drives; —puffs; —skips; —smashes; —spars; —stabs; —stalls; —shadow-boxes; —trains; —unleashes; —uppercuts; —weakens; —whirls; —winds.
(See fighter, boxer.)

PROBABILITY

adjectives
inconceivable; golden; human; inherent; precarious; imminent.

verbs
consider—; contemplate—; erase—; evaluate —; ground on—; ignore—; invest with—; point to—; seek—; snort at—; speculate on —; study—; trace—; —diminishes; —implies; —fathers; —justifies; —tempts.

(See chance, opportunity, possibility.)

PROBABLE

adverbs
highly; circumstantially; scarcely; hardly; barely; naturally; extremely; confidently; apparently; reasonably.

PROBATION

adjectives
healthful; troubled; temporary.

PROBATIONARY

adverbs
wisely; prescriptively; experimentally; naturally; sensibly; venturesomely; fortunately; virtually; luckily; distinctly; undoubtedly.

PROBE (v)

adverbs
secretly; deeply; curiously; morbidly; surgically; deftly; searchingly.

(See examine, investigate.)

PROBLEM

adjectives
sufficient; invincible; insolvable; residue; important; age-old; perplexing; harassing; abstruse; complicated; puzzling; criminal; psychological; lifelong; farming; everyday; pretty; metaphysical; decorative; vital; serious; ultimate; speculative; surgical; menacing; technical; arduous; executive; ethical; comparative; easy; confusing; vast; terrifying; moral; unsolved; dramatic; tremendous; duplex; profound; acute; specific; changing; individual; challenging; intricate; mathematical; deep; basic; striking; personal; contemporary; social; workable; troublesome; transportation; intellectual; urgent; practical; vexatious; conflicting; integral; defined; passionless; terrible; graphic; discouraging; weighty; insoluble; delicate; great; rising-hour; unanswerable; rapid; accumulating; mooted; childish; evolutionary; economic; doleful; original; stupendous; pressing; uncontrollable; abstract; orientation; individual; connected; vexing; philosophic; veiled; shopping.

verbs
absorb in—; aggravate—; analyze—; approach—; attack—; boil down—; circumvent—; come to grips with—; complicate—; confront with—; constitute—; contemplate —; cope with—; deal with—; detour—; dismiss—; dispose of—; dissect—; dodge—; engross in—; envisage—; expound—; face with—; focus on—; formulate—; grapple with—; high-light—; illuminate—; labor over—; master—; meditate on—; misconceive—; outline—; ponder—; pose—; precipitate—; propound—; restate—; shed light on—; smooth out—; solve—; struggle with —; survey—; tackle—; wrestle with—; —s baffle; —bedevils; —s beset; —embraces; —looms; —narrows down to; —plagues; —ruffles; —vexes.

(See riddle, matter, mathematics, predicament.)

PROBLEMATICAL

adverbs
ticklishly; delicately; altogether; precariously; distinctly; fearfully; critically; definitely; painfully; disturbingly; unusually; nicely; obscurely; intricately; perplexingly; curiously; singularly; disconcertingly; vexatiously; plaguedly; extremely.

PROCEDURE

adjectives
characteristic; momentous; amiable; peaceful; unprovoking; abstract; simple; obstinate; intellectual; mystical; well-established; critical; specific; analytic; scandalous; energetic; wonted; tiresome; practical; routine; educational; emergency; complicated.

verbs
adopt—; alter—; bear—; condemn—; conduct—; devise—; discharge—; disrupt—; enact—; execute—; handle—; justify—; manage—; open—; participate in—; practise—; shape—; study—; suggest—; terminate—; transact—; wind up—; —awes; —bores; —"clicks".

(See transaction, process, routine, usage.)

PROCEED (v)

adverbs
softly; moderately; nonchalantly; systematically; circuitously; divergently; solemnly; resolutely; vigorously; majestically; awk-

wardly; monotonously; cautiously; methodically; inquisitorially; suspiciously; summarily; critically; amiably; characteristically.

(See advance, progress.)

PROCEEDING

adjectives

rash; solemn; revolutionary; factious; ominous; hot; comely; furious; cumbrous; inquisitorial; cautious; ungrateful; odious; perfect; characteristic; momentous; customary; tumultuous; suspicious; mean; false; summary; manifest; violent; mere; negligent; offensive.

PROCEEDINGS

verbs

annul—; avoid—; conclude—; conduct—; denounce—; disturb—; institute—; legalize—; threaten—; —betray; —bore; —commence; —drag; —tire; —undo; —weary.

(See investigation, action.)

PROCEEDS

adjectives

pecuniary; astounding; unexpected; small.

verbs

deliver—; derive—; devote—to; draw—; inherit—; net—; pay—; procure—; raise—; realize—; reap—; secure—; swell—; treasure—; yield—; —accrue; —accumulate; produce—.

(See income, profit.)

PROCESS

adjectives

administrative; beautifying; combustion; tedious; abrasion; continuing; lucrative; doubtful; elaborate; same; dreary; exclusive; refining; expert; improved; unequivocal; cognitive; delicate; wrapping; ingenious; carving; artificial; evident; fundamental; cultural; glaucomatous; quick-freezing; digestive; tentative; clarifying; fertilizing; subjective; summary; manufacturing; simple; unconscious; intertwined; elementary; pleasant; logical; inductive; volitive; culinary; exacting; continuous; just; cream-choking; regular; inflammatory; obscure; complicated; mental; ricocheting; wasteful; technical; careful; expressive; circumrotary; punitive; reproductive; pressure; patented; sluggish; merciless; inflationary; remedial; primitive; monotypic; dynamic; fascinating; predictable; complex; artful; essential; physical; aquatint; haphazard; physiological; secret; scientific; expensive; oriental; concentrated; painful; embarrassing; minor; bleaching; ordinary; coercive; democratic; purifying; informal; improved; incubating; involuntary; curbing; evolutionary; learning; laborious; uncertain; orderly; rational; inevitable; chemical; diabetic; synthetic; unique; extensive; blood-atonement; new-discovered; searching; creative; psychological; cyanide; deleterious; beneficient; educational; actual; organic; ineradicable; stultifying; variegated; miraculous; deliberate; artistic; torturing; gradual-reduction; persuasive; developed; exasperating; needless; natural; familiar; enlightened; subsequent; chastening; enormous; suitable; morbid.

verbs

accelerate—; advocate—; clarify—; develop—; disclose—; engross in—; facilitate—; hinder—; perfect—; prolong—; push—; regulate—; reject—; retard—; revamp—; reverse—; simplify—; subject to—; terminate—; undergo—; —evolves through; —fabricates; —refines.

(See operation, method, procedure.)

PROCESSION

adjectives

melancholy; pompous; bright; proud; solemn; dim; spangle-clad; funeral; timely; triumphal; torch-light; dull; spontaneous; gaudy; unnoticed; monkish; phantom; festal; unending; ant-like; stately; impressive; historic; parading; demure; triumphant; endless; dripping; religious; sacrificial; white-robed; imposing; mournful; motley; pensive; uniformed; sad; priestly; continuous; rustling; pale; picturesque; straggling; slow; lamentable; penitential; votive.

verbs

arrange—; disconcert—; interpose—; interrupt—; review—; —ambles; —attracts; —blazons; —bowls along; —courses; —displays; —files by; —glides by; —jogs; —paces; —plods; —shuffles; —struts; —trots; —wends.

(See parade, expedition, excursion, marchers, pageant.)

PROCESSIONAL

adverbs

gorgeously; ceremoniously; ceremonially; reverently; harmoniously; magnificently; splendidly; brilliantly; pretentiously; decoratively; decorously; joyously; triumphantly; conventionally; patriotically; mournfully; quietly; majestically; gravely; properly; appropriately.

PROCLAIM (v)

adverbs
formally; proudly; publicly; triumphantly; ostentatiously; loquaciously; boisterously; exuberantly; boldly; enthusiastically; seditiously; exultantly; solemnly.
(See announce, publish.)

PROCLAMATION

adjectives
celebrated; artful; supplementary; seditious; atrocious; insidious; magniloquent; flowery; preliminary; stirring; exultant; solemn; defiant; brilliant; plain-speaking; feeble.

verbs
authorize—; emit—; issue—; post—; prepare—; promulgate—; publish—; recite—; —announces; —blazons; —broaches; —circulates; —diffuses; —disseminates; —heralds; —spreads; —surprises.
(See ban, edict, headline, announcement, notice.)

PROCLIVITY

adjectives
hopeless; sentimental; dangerous; insidious.

verbs
denounce—; endow with—; limit—; promote—; redound to—; temper—; warp—; —affects; —bends; —bids; —conduces; —disposes; —enables; —gravitates; —inclines; —predisposes; —tends; —verges.
(See tendency, inclination, propensity.)

PROCRASTINATION

verbs
addict to—; remedy—; —cools; —defers; —delays; —endangers; —irks; —irritates; —postpones; —prorogues; —protracts; —retards; —stalls; —staves off; —suspends; —waives; —wearies.
(See delay, indolence.)

PROCURE (v)

adverbs
legally; lustfully; lasciviously; salaciously; seasonally; carnally; periodically; sentimentally.
(See acquire, obtain, achieve.)

PRODIGAL

adjectives
good-natured; niggardly; rehabilitated; unconscionable; returning; prodigious; guilty; sinful; wicked; selfish.

adverbs
wastefully; reprehensibly; foolishly; wantonly; dissolutely; sadly; unthriftily; blithely; recklessly; rashly; lavishly; senselessly; thoughtlessly; selfishly; extravagantly; needlessly; immensely; witlessly; absurdly; ridiculously; wickedly; inordinately; unhappily.

PRODIGALITY

adjectives
boundless; reckless.

PRODIGIOUS

adverbs
incredibly; inordinately; amazingly; unbelievably; unaccountably; immeasurably; incalculably; strikingly; miraculously; uncommonly.

PRODIGY

adjectives
flashing; unique; infant; valorous; accompanying; juvenile; extraordinary; necromantic.

PRODUCE

adjectives
scanty; rude; dark; peaceful.

PRODUCE (v)

adverbs
prolifically; lavishly; magically; legitimately; enthusiastically; artificially; characteristically; infallibly; generously; systematically; wantonly; dramatically; luxuriantly; agriculturally; indigenously.
(See generate, yield.)

PRODUCER

adjectives
potential; multitudinous (pl); independent; rich.

PRODUCT

adjectives
national; advertised; fundamental; better; uncrystallizable; commercial; vegetable; salable; sole; glandular; seasonable; staple; meager; pharmaceutic; morphine; accepted; appetizing; attractive; abundant; delicious; wholesome; poisonous; natural; lusty; re-

sultant; non-perishable; noble; choice; dubious; abundant (pl); pristine; spontaneous; admired; extant; filthy; humble; phantastic; extraordinary; good; sensational; amazing; fast-selling; quality; rare; useful; guaranteed; liked; wanted; diversified (pl); allied (pl); abrasive; amphibious; definite; super-standard; multiform (pl); delectable; menacing; insidious; basic; efficient; amalgamated; recent; superior; barbarous; unforced; representative; marvelous; luxurious; dutiable; unpalatable; uniform; miraculous.

verbs
acclaim—; clamor for—; consume—; contribute to—; convert—; degrade—; deposit —; evolve—; finish—; handle—; market—; purvey—; retail—; transform—; transport —; utilize—; waste—.
(See fruit, crop, harvest, output.)

PRODUCTION

adjectives
attractive; quantity; continuous; figure; indigenous; abortive; rhythmical; luxuriant; deep; earned; increased; labored; earnest; aggregate; mechanical; dramatic; chief; finished; varied; conventional; prolific; industrial; assembly-line; plastic; digestible; commercial; poetical; intensive; economic; spontaneous; carnal; appropriate; estimated; curtailed; dramatic; celebrated; aboriginal; vegetable; interrupted; momentary; capacity; crude; intelligent; monstrous; multifarious; maximum; agricultural; dewless; artificial; elaborate; faultless; isolated; immortal; composite; stimulated.

verbs
absorb—; accelerate—; ascribe—to; augment—; bolster—; boom—; cancel—; control—; curtail—; delay—; determine—; disrupt—; doom—; expand—; guide—; hamper—; measure—; quadruple—; rehearse —; scuttle—; simplify—; sponsor—; stimulate—; suspend—.
(See output, product.)

PRODUCTIVE

adverbs
unusually; amazingly; strikingly; miraculously; conveniently; opportunely; profitably; commercially; surprisingly; sensationally; spectacularly; satisfactorily; adequately; highly; fortunately; experimentally; scientifically; naturally; famously; eminently; remarkably; uncommonly.

PROFANATION

adjectives
proposed; foul; ruinous; picturesque; menaced; lingering; definite; calculated; monstrous.

PROFANE

adverbs
irreverently; brazenly; openly; blasphemously; perversely; sacrilegiously; scoffingly; intolerably; terribly; godlessly; indefensibly; inexcusably; scandalously; wickedly; offensively; indecorously; scurrilously; luridly; startlingly; horribly; unspeakably; abominably; hideously; unbecomingly; shrilly; noisily; mutteringly; unutterably; impossibly; impiously; shamelessly.

PROFANE (v)

adverbs
obscenely; blasphemously; raucously; vulgarly; uncouthly; villainously; barbarously; diabolically.
(See violate, debase.)

PROFANITY

adjectives
inarticulate; smothered; delicate; picturesque; time-honored; extraordinary; unbelievable; purposeless; shocking; disgusting; unmanly; stubborn; raucous; unnecessary; deliberate.

PROFESS (v)

adverbs
ignorantly; ostentatiously; impulsively; boldly; gaily; carelessly; obstreperously; vainly; vigorously; shamelessly; enthusiastically.
(See admit, claim, avow.)

PROFESSION

adjectives
peaceful; rich; dissimilar (pl); dramatic; sacred; lettered; universal; knavish; solemn; kind; respectable; lucrative; clerical; shining; hard-working; shady; pacific; stupid; grave; educated; destined; medical; fraternal; chivalrous; preserved; inherited; honorable; paternal; private; noble; remunerative; knowing; earnest; obvious; elaborate.

verbs
commit to—; contract—; devote oneself to —; engage in—; enter—; fill—; follow—; honor—; overcrowd—; ply—; practise—; prosecute—; prosper in—; pursue—; struggle in—; undertake—; —adjures; —binds; —employs; —engages; —exacts; —obligates; —occupies.

(See calling, employment, industry, law, teaching.)

PROFESSIONAL

adverbs
strictly; scarcely; hardly; highly; expertly; self-consciously; ridiculously; absurdly; suddenly; incredibly; pretentiously; obscurely; insistently; consistently; supposedly; emphatically; assertively; dogmatically; formally; solemnly; conspicuously; unmistakably; prodigiously; ostentatiously.

PROFESSIONALISM

verbs
acquire—; commit to—; denounce—; discontinue—; display—; don—; drop—; exhibit —; practise—; shroud in—; study—; —annoys; —attends; —exacts; —irks; —irritates; —proselytes; —ties; —wearies.

PROFESSOR

adjectives
renowned; theorizing; mournful; dogmatizing; world-famed; controlling; volunteer; unsympathetic; eminent; assiduous; miserable; braintrust; unemployed; unlearned; grave; wizened; wise; absent-minded; kindly; knowing; eccentric; research; modest; masterful.

PROFICIENCY

adjectives
speedy; practical; established; technical; similar; obvious; palpable; notable; demonstrated.

verbs
acquire—; commend—; demand—; gain—; maintain—; misapply—; perceive—; possess —; praise—; profess—; realize—; recognize—; —accomplishes; —conquers; —defeats; —lags; —masters; —outflanks; —overcomes; —prevails; —succeeds; —triumphs; —weathers.

(See mastery, skill, ability, power.)

PROFICIENT

adverbs
obviously; unmistakably; marvelously; amazingly; emphatically; unfailingly; miraculously; singularly; curiously; indubitably; skilfully; expertly; remarkably; unsurpassably; matchlessly; profoundly; dexterously; deftly; felicitously; confidently; cunningly; admirably; commendably; consummately.

PROFILE

adjectives
sloping; inquisitive; clean-cut; architectural; Roman; sable; coin-clear; melancholy; aquiline; energetic; bold; flawless; regular; delicate; fine; vapid; athletic; Grecian; Nordic; gaunt; grisly; smooth; fetching; sagging; gripping; romantic; grim; noble; criminal.

PROFIT

adjectives
generous; quick; sensational; large; cash; clear; general; liberal; tremendous; amazing; steady; spot-cash; repeated; enormous; real; old-fashioned; staggering; unlimited; startling; additional; volume; big; daily; handsome; easy; distributed; potential; competitive; personal; substantial; immense; mutual; divided; moderate; reinvested; small; healthy; material; extortionate; sharp; singular; prospective; present; estimated; inconceivable; colossal; immediate; slender; honest; regular; individual; speculative; utmost; increasing; absolute; illicit; pecuniary; monetary; usurious; abnormal.

verbs
account for—; amass—; ascertain—; assure of—; consume—; create—; derive—from; eat—; educe—; eliminate—; evolve—; net —; pocket—; preclude—; reap—; retain—; spell—; squeeze—; swell—; —accrues; —booms; —evaporates; —lures; —materializes; —piles up; —s rise; —shoots from.

(See income, gain, emolument, pay, money.)

PROFIT (v)

adverbs
sensationally; liberally; enormously; potentially; competitively; personally; moderately; materially; colossally; pecuniarily; usuriously; abnormally.

(See gain, benefit.)

PROFITABLE

adverbs
highly; unusually; commercially; financially; professionally; remarkably; surprisingly; amazingly; inordinately; extraordinarily; extremely; unexpectedly; scarcely; hardly; altogether; socially; secretly; mysteriously; shadily; peculiarly; strangely.

PROFLIGATE

adjectives
despairing; lecherous; hopeless; debauched; drunken; unsocial.

verbs
admonish—; chastise—; condemn—; convert from—; punish—; rebuke—; reform—; reproach—; scald—; —brutalizes; —corrupts; —demoralizes; —deviates; —errs; —lapses; —offends; —sins; —slips; —strays; —transgresses; —trespasses; —sinks.
(See scoundrel, villain, criminal.)

PROFOUND

adverbs
mystically; abstrusely; obscurely; pedantically; eruditely; theologically; provokingly; prosaically; gravely; admittedly; politically; sagaciously; distinctly; shrewdly; keenly; astutely; rationally; impartially; thoughtfully; perspicaciously; oracularly; impressively; amazingly; inscrutably; doctrinally.

PROFUSE

adverbs
wonderfully; uncommonly; delightfully; unexpectedly; surprisingly; amazingly; curiously; strangely; exuberantly; luxuriantly; profitably; overly; wastefully; extravagantly; foolishly; senselessly; abundantly; amply; unsparingly; wickedly.

PROFUSION

adjectives
utmost; sheer; lavish; tempting; sumptuous; vernal; incalculable; happy; thick; ostentatious; glossy; luxuriant; extraordinary; disorderly; gothic.

PROGENY

adjectives
little; ungracious; twin-born; vigorous; numerous; enslaved; multiplied.

PROGNOSTICATION

adjectives
gloomy; financial; anguished; supernatural.

verbs
cast—; contemplate—; ignore—; justify—; —augurs; —betokens; —bids; —calculates; —discerns; —excites; —foreshadows; —foretells; —forewarns; —heralds; —points to; —precurses; —predicts; —presages; —promises; —senses; —signifies; —worries.
(See foreboding, prediction, forecast, prophecy.)

PROGRAM

adjectives
rigorous; coherent; laborious; inviting; commercial; aggressive; sponsored; balanced; serious; comprehensive; reading; great; fiction; economical; diagnosed; voluntary; relief; constructive; abstergent; seductive; varied; modernization; entertaining; aesthetic; exhaustive; ultra-professional; systematic; selfsame; sustaining; peace; nationwide; educational; social.

verbs
adhere to—; adopt—; attack—; bowl over —; carry out—; defer—; design—; devote to—; elaborate on—; embark on—; endorse —; evaluate—; evolve—; expand—; familiarize with—; formulate—; initiate—; institute—; integrate—; launch—; map out—; modify—; oppose—; outline—; participate in—; pound away at—; sketch—; submit—; supervise—; swamp—; thread through—; vary—; view—; —embraces; —languishes.
(See itinerary, list, menu.)

PROGRESS

adjectives
educational; marvelous; amazing; unbroken; moral; physical; successful; beneficent; actual; material; phenomenal; torturing; excellent; painful; joyous; eventful; social; obvious; mechanical; sufficient; luxurious; artistic; enormous.

verbs
abate—; achieve—; arrest—; blight—; block—; check—; control—; curb—; curtail —; expedite—; extend—; facilitate—; halt —; herald—; hinder—; impede—; imperil —; indicate—; insure—; keep abreast of—; mark by—; measure—; promote—; record —; retard—; survey—; trace—; yield to—.
(See advance, advancement, civilization, development, growth.)

PROGRESS (v)

adverbs
exultantly; boldly; methodically; spectacularly; enormously; swiftly; tardily; phenomenally; socially; mechanically; artistically; markedly.
(See advance, proceed.)

PROGRESSION

adjectives
audacious; endless; constant; harmonic; chromatic; upward.

PROGRESSIVE

adverbs
naturally; unusually; exceptionally; satisfactorily; ambitiously; pseudously; slowly; dependably; reliably; steadily; amazingly; happily; remarkably; startlingly; incredibly; unbelievably; unexpectedly; highly; gratifyingly; solidly; substantially; brilliantly; undeniably.

PROHIBITION

adjectives
virtual; positive; perpetual; reiterated.

verbs
annul—; defy—; denounce—; deplore—; dispute—; enforce—; ignore—; laud—; support—; undermine—; uphold—; urge—; —debars; —forbids; —restrains; —restricts; —revokes; —smothers; —suppresses; —taboos.
(See taboo, embargo, ban, edict.)

PROHIBITIVE

adverbs
meanly; unhappily; unwisely; sordidly; racially; inordinately; senselessly; foolishly; viciously; strictly; sternly; legally; officially; authoritatively; narrowly; dogmatically; imperiously; unwarrantably; unfairly; narrow-mindedly; ineptly; antagonistically; disagreeably; unconscionably; unnecessarily; groundlessly; wisely; necessarily; warily; vigilantly; shrewdly; carefully; financially; prescriptively.

PROJECT

adjectives
ambitious; titanic; resettlement; juvenile; cherished; philosophical; cunning; sublime; modified; unrealized; reclamation; cumbersome; wild; murderous; audacious; brilliant; stupendous; immense; rehabilitation; relief; works; national.

verbs
abandon—; broach—; dedicate—; develop—; discard—; discourage—; expand—; formulate—; horn in on—; incubate—; launch—; lose in—; plan—; quash—; turn down—; —centers upon; —collapses; —goes awry; —marches to completion; —takes shape.
(See idea, design, enterprise.)

PROJECT (v)

adverbs
stereoscopically; distinctly; obtrusively; naively; infinitesimally; sharply; fantastically; ruggedly.
(See extend, jut, protrude.)

PROJECTILE

verbs
bolt—; cast—; discharge—; drive—; emit—; expel—; fire—; heave—; hurl—; pitch—; propel—; shoot—; sling—; toss—; —darts; —forces; —impels; —screams by; —whistles.
(See bomb, bullet.)

PROJECTION

adjectives
rugged; blunted; infinitesimal; gnomonic; jutting; far-reaching; sharp.

PROLETARIAT

verbs
assail—; debar—; denounce—; grind—; incite—; restrain—; restrict—; smother—; stir—; support—; suppress—; trammel—; tyrannize over—; —defies; —degrades; —inflames; —labors; —rises; —revolts; —strikes.
(See bourgeoisie, foreigner, alien, peasant, worker, employer.)

PROLIFIC

adverbs
unusually; highly; distinctly; healthily; sadly; happily; fortunately; amazingly; normally; uncommonly; surprisingly; remarkably; undeniably.

PROLOGUE

adjectives
symphonic; learned; explanatory; necessary; useless; space-filling.

PROLONG (v)

adverbs
indefinitely; unduly; agonizingly; perpet-

ually; embarrassingly; tantalizingly; excessively.
(See lengthen, extend.)

PROMENADE

adjectives
mental; solitary; public; sociable; daily; amorous; fashionable.

PROMINENCE

adjectives
political; literary; excessive; high; rocky; dominating; naked; especial; extraordinary; historical; disturbing; modest.

verbs
attain—; bounce into—; burst into—; deplore—; drag up to—; elevate to—; expose to—; hoist to—; jump into—; lift to—; merit—; mount to—; soar to—; —awes; —commands; —crowns; —exalts; —heightens; —mantles; —perches; —weighs.
(See distinction, fame, eminence.)

PROMINENT

adverbs
unusually; questionably; brilliantly; impressively; wickedly; boldly; audaciously; officially; officiously; curiously; strangely; inexplicably; noticeably; conspicuously; brazenly; eminently; gorgeously; gloriously; radiantly; rightfully; majestically; splendidly; memorably; illustriously.

PROMISCUITY

verbs
condemn—; denounce—; drift into—; refrain from—; shrink from—; suffer—; —agitates; —brews; —corrupts; —deranges; —diffuses; —disorders; —entangles; —reduces; —ruffles; —rumples.
(See indifference, mixture.)

PROMISCUOUS

adverbs
strangely; inexplicably; unaccountably; naturally; inevitably; democratically; significantly; necessarily; shamefully; reprehensibly; embarrassingly; unmanageably; unexpectedly; obviously; complexly; indiscriminately; casually; fortuitously; accidentally.

PROMISE

adjectives
optimistic; heartfelt; significant; solemn; dormant; fertile; considerable; whispered; liberal; maudlin; tremendous; firm; indefinite; conservative; drunken; rash; cheerful; exceptional; remorseful; valiant; unbreakable; vernal; flattering; cheering; gracious; false; definite; scant; pathetic; tacit; doubtful; unredeemed; brilliant; deceiving; high; express; faithful; unfulfilled; light; haughty; scorching; stout-limbed; implied; nugatory; imperial.

verbs
avail oneself of—; carry out—; clutch—; dangle—; dispense—s; elicit—; enforce—; extort—; extract—; fulfill—; gain—; ignore—; issue—; nullify—; puncture—; redeem—; violate—; void—; —binds; —s clash; —electrifies; —implies; —materializes; —pledges; —sanctifies.
(See bond, contract, covenant, compromise, pledge.)

PROMISE (*v*)

adverbs
blithely; solemnly; vehemently; punctually; devoutly; cheerfully; blandly; speciously; optimistically; liberally; maudlinly; graciously; flatteringly; tacitly; lightly.
(See pledge, assure.)

PROMISING

adverbs
brilliantly; altogether; hopefully; unquestionably; remarkably; uncommonly; highly; splendidly; indubitably; auspiciously; distinctly; definitely.

PROMONTORY

adjectives
beaked; eminent; sea-beaten; keen-faced; salubrious; hoary; rock-girt; remote; mountainous; rugged; wooded; high; moon-bathed; venerable.

PROMOTE (*v*)

adverbs
infrequently; essentially; subsequently; wisely; swiftly; promptly; tardily; gratuitously; insidiously; seditiously; skillfully; ambitiously.
(See advance, encourage.)

PROMOTER

adjectives
zealous; doughty; enterprising; high-pressure; genial; sports; deft; skilled.

PROMOTION

adjectives
picturesque; swift; deserved; lineal; gratuitous; prompt.

verbs
award—; deserve—; favor—; foster—; gain—; merit—; reward by—; secure—; seek—; —ameliorates; —betters; —bolsters; —brightens; —cheers; —elevates; —encourages; —enhances; —enriches; —invigorates; —smooths.
(See progress, advancement.)

PROMPT

adverbs
dependably; reliably; punctiliously; surprisingly; meticulously; carefully; always; curiously; significantly; suspiciously; courteously; considerately; graciously; cheerfully; politely; ingratiatingly; wisely; usually; unfailingly; pleasantly; gratifyingly.

PROMPTING

adjectives
imperious; deep-seated; inner; physiological; base; quiet; serious; definite.

PROMPTNESS

adjectives
absolute; self-satisfied; incredible; well-meant; characteristic; soldierly; utmost; unexampled; noncommittal; deliberate; practiced; remarkable.

PRONOUNCE (*v*)

adverbs
whimsically; unanimously; syllabically; solemnly; unhesitatingly; emphatically; impressively; weightily; definitely; academically.
(See speak, utter.)

PRONOUNCEMENT

adjectives
weighty; impressive; scientific; definite; startling.

verbs
authorize—; await—; circulate—; issue—; post—; prepare—; promulgate—; publish —; relay—; spread—; —blazons; —broaches; —diffuses; —disseminates; —heralds; —proclaims; —rings out.
(See proclamation, announcement.)

PRONUNCIATION

adjectives
careful; defective; smooth; facile; slipshod; hasty; inaccurate; local; improper; incorrect; antiquated; slovenly; lip-lazy; faulty; outlandish; uncouth; arbitrary; accepted.

verbs
accentuate—; alter—; aspirate—; bark—; clarify—; correct—; criticize—; detect—; drawl—; drown—; improve—; lament—; mangle—; mutter—; practise—; ridicule—; swallow—; —confuses; —perplexes.
(See accent, utterance.)

PROOF

adjectives
absolute; remarkable; experimental; confirming; ample; undeniable; refined; positive; indisputable; incontestable; irrefragable; actual; traditional; palpable; vulgar; abundant; similar; conclusive; distinct; documentary; lucid; secondary; innate; strenuous; tangible; irresistible; gratifying; strict; historical; convincing; incompatable; forcible; presumptive; convenient; melancholy; corroborative; perpetual; decisive; indubitable; gallery; ocular; bedrock; added; definite; practical; sufficient; triumphant; divine; dingy; authentic; shadowy; exemplary; formal; continuing; quick; legal; hourly; insidious; cruel; doubtful; dramatic; concrete; phenomenal; childhood.

verbs
advance—; cite—; demand—; demonstrate —; devise—; dig—; digest—; draw—; establish—; evince—; prepare—; question—; reflect upon—; seek—; strike at—; —checks; —leaks; —s multiply; —settles; —substantiates;.—verifies.
(See argument, evidence, confirmation.)

PROPAGANDA

adjectives
sedulous; sentimental; insidious; insistent; commercial; primitive; blatant; suicidal; incessant; educational; systematic; subversive; sinister; treacherous; political.

verbs
assail—; bedevil with—; denounce—; deny —; direct—at; dispute—; disseminate—; distrust—; doubt—; found on—; grind out —; impregnate with—; ignore—; mask—; pump—into; question—; release—; swallow —; weave—; —bewilders; —convinces; —

deceives; —edifies; —enlightens; —exploits; —familiarizes; —ignites; —implants; —impresses; —inculcates; —inflames; —misinforms; —misrepresents; —pervades; —perverts; —staggers; —startles; —threatens; —undermines.

(See message, doctrine, lie.)

PROPAGATE (v)

adverbs

peacefully; seditiously; agriculturally; radically; cunningly; audaciously; seasonally.

(See increase, reproduce.)

PROPEL (v)

adverbs

vigorously; swiftly; deftly; skillfully; leisurely; brilliantly; valiantly; daringly; rashly.

(See drive, force, impel.)

PROPELLOR

verbs

jerk—; rake—; start—; tug—; yank (colloq.)—; —arouses; —actuates; —calms; —drives; —forces; —halts; —hushes; —impels; —lashes; —revolves; —rotates; —spins; —urges; —whirs; —whizzes; —wrenches.

(See motor, fan.)

PROPENSITY

adjectives

martial; bad; edifying; cruel; feline; gregarious; bucaneering; degraded; mischievous; piscatorial; unsuspected; social; vulgar; erratic; indignant; unconscious; amorous; remarkable; noteworthy; unusual.

verbs

denounce—; gratify—; promote—; temper—; tempt—; —affects; —bends; —bids; —conduces; —disposes; —fancies; —gravitates; —inclines; —tends; —thirsts; —verges.

(See inclination, disposition, proclivity.)

PROPER

adverbs

conventionally; socially; altogether; acceptably; legally; punctiliously; carefully; cautiously; anxiously; graciously; courteously; politely; deferentially; respectfully; reverently; quietly; serenely; laboriously; easily; becomingly; demurely; correctly; unfailingly.

PROPERTY

adjectives

toxic; consular; medicinal; sonorous; outcropped; curative; beneficial; stimulating; private; extensive; desired; elaborate; inalienable; injurious; historical; magnetic; virgin; intellectual; inherent; structural; mechanical; business; essential; surplus; immense; profitable; defunct; physical; admirable; tonic; virtuous; airy; violent; ultimate; poisonous; permanent; living; distinctive; landed; deliquescent; exclusive; health-giving; contested; luminous; papal; adjacent; unpredictable; ice-melting; acid-resisting; agreeable; specific; absolute; phonetic; substantial; acoustic; immutable; unentailed; nutritious; clinging; ancestral; existing; emollient.

verbs

acquire—; allocate—; assess—; confiscate—; deplete—; deprive of—; destine to—; destroy—; exalt—; expropriate—; fence—; guard—; inherit—; insure—; levy on—; liquidate—; retain—; saddle—; squander—; transfer—; —abuts; —includes.

(See estate, legacy, asset, inheritance, possessions.)

PROPHECY

adjectives

unpleasing; vaunting; bitter; humbler; gloomy; drunken; backward-glancing; optimistic; retrospective; impassionate; mad; imposing; painful; fanciful; ominous; dogmatic; numerous (pl); enkindling; maiden; pessimistic; apocalyptic; omnipresent; sanguine; fulfilled; inspired; prospective.

verbs

divine—; fulfill—; ignore—; mock—; scoff at—; sustain—; —augurs; —betokens; —bodes; —excites; —forecasts; —foreshadows; —foretells; —heralds; —points to; —precurses; —predicts; —presages; —promises; —warns.

(See forecast, prediction, foreboding, prognostication.)

PROPHET

adjectives

maddening; dumb; twice-tongued; fiery; courageous; master; disbelieved.

PROPHETIC

adverbs

wildly; hysterically; gravely; seriously;

oracularly; crazily; soberly; gloomily; cynically; sagely; reflectively; thoughtfully; alarmingly; ominously; gloriously; optimistically; groundlessly; profoundly; deeply; boldly; reasonably; sanely; sadly; pessimistically; wishfully; hopefully; sagaciously; intelligently; far-seeingly; perspicaciously; curiously; strangely; startlingly; highly; audaciously.

PROPITIATE (*v*)

adverbs
flatteringly; servilely; artfully; fawningly; cunningly; shrewdly; timidly; earnestly; studiously.

(See pacify, calm, soothe.)

PROPITIOUS

adverbs
pleasantly; agreeably; seriously; altogether; happily; delightfully; fortunately; opportunely; appropriately; graciously; pleasingly; advantageously; unusually; uncommonly; providentially; entirely; encouragingly; supposedly; singularly; particularly; especially.

PROPORTION

adjectives
cyclonic; impressive; modelled; splendid; respectable; portentous; heavy; exact; cavernous; tremendous; symmetrical; incredible; extensive; luxurious; heroic; sublime; ignoble; overwhelming; exaggerating; classic; inverse; geometrical; colossal; impudent; sizable; gigantic; enormous; proper; monstrous; rotund; sturdy; massive; divine; direct; balanced; faultless; increasing; staggering; unbelievable; inconsiderable; excessive; diminishing; relative; regal; varying; huge; ethical; progressive; majestic; large; meager; just; prodigious; consistent; constituent; pyramid; distinct; major; aldermanic; artistic; slender; clumsy; rude; due; far-reaching; equal; robust; national; vibrating; horrible.

verbs
allot—; allow—; amass—; assign—; assume —s; attain—s; consign—s; contort—; deal —s; deform—s; dispense—s; divide into—s; dole out—s; evaluate—s; indicate—s; misshape—s; preserve—s; retain—s; twist—s; warp—.

(See equilibrium, percentage, size, extent, degree, dimensions, share.)

PROPORTION (*v*)

adverbs
delicately; exquisitely; admirably; femininely; correctly; superbly; symmetrically; luxuriously; geometrically; massively; regally; meagerly; clumsily; rudely; equally; prodigiously.

(See divide, adjust, apportion.)

PROPORTIONATE

adverbs
fairly; justly; carefully; correspondingly; diplomatically; agreeably; satisfactorily; respectively; congruously; consistently; admissibly; felicitously; acceptably; quantatively; relatively; distinctly; impartially; equitably; laudably; legally; regularly.

PROPOSAL

adjectives
friendly; romantic; infamous; unique; alternative; oral; impracticable; ridiculous; lame; flattering; foolhardy; audacious; ambitious; crackpot; definite.

verbs
accept—; adopt—; argue—; back—; block —; carry out—; commend—; condemn—; denounce—; deride—; dismiss—; entertain —; explode—; heed—; inspire—; oppose—; pooh-pooh—; raise—; reject—; sanction—; submit—; support—; turn down—; vitiate —; withdraw—; —emanates from; —excites; —falls through.

(See bid, proposition, offer, deal, transaction, plan, suggestion, scheme.)

PROPOSE (*v*)

adverbs
spontaneously; seriously; dogmatically; originally; deliberately; impiously; insidiously; theoretically; philosophically; untenably; ominously; flatteringly; conditionally; passionately.

(See offer, discourse.)

PROPOSITION

adjectives
equitable; due; plausible; theoretical; unintelligible; tough; preposterous; brutal; solemn; definite; businesslike; philosophical; attractive; abstract; meaningless; untenable; ominous; mannerly; distasteful; marvelous; undeniable; dynamical; moneymaking; fundamental; flattering; conditional; general; novel; true; palpitating; astounding.

verbs
acclaim—; applaud—; balk at—; convey—; dedicate—; deliver—; demonstrate—; engage in—; entertain—; fancy—; immerse in—; jeopardize—; lay down—; misconstrue—; reject—; relate—; support—; —allures; —invites; —tempts.
(See offer, proposal, bid, deal.)

PROPOUND (v)

adverbs
academically; philosophically; theoretically; argumentatively; dispassionately; conditionally.
(See offer, propose.)

PROPRIETARY

adverbs
proudly; legitimately; comically; possessively; justly; graciously; absurdly; properly; pompously; ostentatiously; conspicuously; blatantly; ridiculously; modestly; anxiously; watchfully; responsibly; vigilantly; disagreeably; unctuously; suavely; smoothly; blandly; rapturously.

PROPRIETOR

adjectives
affluent; genial; antiquarian; ecclesiastic.

PROPRIETY

adjectives
unconscious; editorial; peculiar; established; equal; perfect; complacent; eminent; dramatic; rigid; obvious; sacred; dreamy.

verbs
adhere to—; admire—; befit—s; conform to—; contravene—s; fulfill—s; impose—; incur—; justify—s; observe—; respect—; satisfy—; suit—; undermine—; —becomes; —binds; —exacts; —obliges; —prescribes; —requires; —saddles.
(See decorum, convenience, decency.)

PROSAIC

adverbs
hopelessly; consciously; dully; flatly; tediously; unimaginatively; monotonously; stupidly; tiresomely; endlessly; unconsciously; pretentiously; pitiably; miserably; vacuously; inanely; diffusely; heavily; drearily; impossibly; terribly.

PROSE

adjectives
rhythmical; impassioned; polyphonic; newspaper; idealistic; strenuous; poetical; rhyming; lucid; glittering; immortal; artistic; famous; dull; heroic; harmonious; sinewy; uncerebral; hard-hitting; straight-from-the-shoulder; extensive; physical; humorous; conventional; flashing; elaborate; measured; conversational; dreamy; grand; mingled; salable; vigorous; poetic; puissant; supple; mellifluous; swift; masculine.

verbs
acclaim—; analyze—; compose—; contemplate—; dwell on—; enjoy—; —abounds in; —amplifies; —bores; —describes; —dilates; —discusses; —protracts; —rambles; —repeats; —swells; —thrills; —wearies.
(See poetry, writing, story, style.)

PROSECUTE (v)

adverbs
actively; recklessly; fearlessly; relentlessly; vindictively; diabolically; legally; spitefully; energetically; impassionedly; repulsively.
(See sue.)

PROSECUTION

adjectives
vigorous; persistent; inevitable; victorious; unceasing.

verbs
avert—; avoid—; demand—; endure—; escape—; evade—; file—; lodge—; order—; prefer—; risk—; suffer—; —brands; —implicates; —saddles; —slanders; —slurs; —stigmatizes; —weighs against.
(See lawsuit, suit (legal), arrest.)

PROSPECT

adjectives
dusky; melancholy; near; gloomy; smiling; brilliant; immediate; favorable; calm; peaceful; hideous; extreme; prosperous; tempting; flattering; consolatory; dazzling; brightening; adjacent; flaming; delightful; honorable; turbulent; bare; feeble; glorious; coveted; varying; bright; scanty; better; dismal; inexpressible; unobstructed; dim; gleaming; domestic; shadowy; repulsive; tempting; spacious; ineffable; glittering; blighted; bleak; dreary; embarrassing; glorious; cheering; depressing; grim; substantial; gay; happy; pleasing.

verbs
bait—; blanch at—; cripple—; dash—;

deter by—; eliminate—; entertain—; gaze at—; guard—; harbor—; insure—s; jeopardize—; open—; relinquish—; relish—; sustain—; tremble at—; —lures; —ponders; —speculates; —tempts; —s wane; —yields. See future, expectation, view, outlook, chance.)

PROSPER (v)

adverbs

materially; privately; personally; abundantly; excessively; illusively; financially; economically; miraculously; spectacularly.

(See thrive, gain, benefit.)

PROSPERITY

adjectives

material; public; infectious; rapid; nourishing; crass; common; supposititious; deserved; private; ever-increasing; riotous; exemplified; apparent; unexampled; abundant; excessive; fair illusive; sensual; worldly.

verbs

annihilate—; attain—; attribute—to; boom into—; boost—; build—; climb to—; contribute to—; enhance—; enjoy—; experience—; foster—; guarantee—; hamper—; induce—; promote—; re-establish—; retard—; revive—; share in—; —continues; —intoxicates; —permeates; —stems from; —vanishes.

(See boom, happiness, health, inflation.)

PROSPEROUS

adverbs

happily; comfortably; fortunately; extremely; pleasantly; gratifyingly; agreeably; surprisingly; serenely; enviably; snugly; sufficiently; fabulously; independently; tremendously; conspicuously.

PROSTITUTION

verbs

attack—; censor—; drift into—; eradicate—; extirpate—; lapse into—; suffer—; suppress—; wipe out—; —contaminates; —corrupts; —debauches; —defiles; —degrades; —depraves; —discolors; —embitters; —impairs; —mangles; —pollutes; —vitiates; —warps.

(See crime, sin, corruption.)

PROSTRATE (v)

adverbs

reverently; humbly; weakly; fawningly; cringingly; servilely; nervously; speechlessly; utterly.

(See overthrow, overpower, defeat.)

PROSTRATION

adjectives

nervous; servile; indolent; extreme; inanimate; utter.

PROTECT (v)

adverbs

adequately; legally; permanently; chivalrously; amply; unequivocally; honorably; sedulously; sacredly; nominally; automatically; scientifically; parentally; financially; dubiously.

(See defend, guard.)

PROTECTED

adverbs

tenderly; completely; unusually; remarkably; warmly; heavily; affectionately; ardently; carefully; cautiously; vigilantly; constantly; officially; unnecessarily; distinctly; deliberately; strangely; covertly; secretly; openly; successfully; always; legally.

PROTECTION

adjectives

positive; permanent; extra; especial; effectual; benign; immediate; invaluable; inadequate; satisfactory; maximum; parental; sublime; atrocious; mutual; lubricant; efficient; all-around; adequate; momentary; blow-out; generous; fancied; financial; sad-visaged; scanty; extended; gracious; indifferent; humiliating; warm; dubious; inexpensive; weatherproof.

verbs

afford—; bestow—upon; deny—; furnish—; gain—; grant—; insure—; legalize—; maintain—; seek—; sustain—; —assures; —eases; —preserves; —safeguards.

(See guidance, leadership, patronage.)

PROTECTOR

adjectives

guilty; desirable; sole; staunch; potent; courageous.

PROTEIN

adjectives
concentrated; coagulating; necessary.

verbs
absorb—; advocate—; assimilate—; burn—; class as—; consume—; digest—; disintegrate—; inject—; lack—; necessitate—; utilize—; —builds; —corrects; —regulates; —strengthens.
(See food, carbohydrates, starch, sugar, calorie.)

PROTEST

adjectives
indignant; feeble; ineffective; vigorous; humble; passionate; persistent; comic; vociferous; courageous; somber; ancient; incautious; startled; religious; earnest; emphatic; living; masculine; voluble; vehement; inarticulate; shouted; shocked; hurt; stubborn; half-scornful; howled; feigned; energetic; unavailing; timid; manly; undersigned; respectful; harassing; passionate; fiery; undignified; noisy; unwelcome.

verbs
anticipate—; arouse—; awaken—; brush aside—; dismiss—; echo—; elicit—; explode in—; file—; give rise to—; growl in—; grumble—; howl in—; ignore—; issue—; laugh away—; lodge—; maintain—; override—; provoke—; register—; rise in—; scowl—; storm in—; summarize—s; voice —; waive—; —emanates from; —infuriates; —s pour in; —flames forth.
(See complaint, grievance, objection, answer.)

PROTEST (*v*)

adverbs
drawlingly; vehemently; rebelliously; solemnly; sullenly; violently; keenly; earnestly; lustily; fiercely; indignantly; suavely; energetically; passionately; feebly; extravagantly; ungraciously; formally; persistently.
(See remonstrate, expostulate.)

PROTESTANT

verbs
oppress—; persecute—; —accedes; —acknowledges; —approves; —attends; —contradicts; —criticizes; —demurs; —flays; —opposes; —persecutes; —practices; —preaches; —protests; —questions; repudiates; —worships; —endorses.
(See church-goers.)

PROTESTANTISM

verbs
approve—; confirm—; convert to—; endorse —; practice—; preach—; promise—; —accedes to; —acknowledges; —contradicts; —demurs; —denies; —differs; —envelops; —flays; —involves; —protests; —questions; —repudiates.
(See religion, Christianity, protest.)

PROTESTATION

adjectives
passionate; jittery; grateful; shrieking; roaring; injurious; characteristic; solemn; extravagant; earnest; amorous.

PROTESTING

adjectives
pure; earnest; vigorous.

PROTRACTED

adverbs
unendurably; endlessly; foolishly; tragically; unhappily; purposely; wickedly; painfully; tiresomely; drearily; unbearably; miserably; wearily; hopelessly; inexplicably; unaccountably; deliberately; purposely; intentionally; distressingly; viciously; lengthily; interminably; unendurably.

PROTRUDE (*v*)

adverbs
puffily; abnormally; flabbily; unusually; hideously; disgustingly; prominently; exaggeratedly.
(See jut, project, extend.)

PROTUBERANCE

adjectives
horny; auricular; bulging; dimpled; elliptical; flabby; unusual; unsightly.

PROTUBERANT

adverbs
extremely; crookedly; pitiably; seriously; gravely; noticeably; conspicuously; prominently; bulbously; tumorously; alarmingly; dreadfully.

PROUD

adverbs
absurdly; arrogantly; boyishly; coldly; contemptibly; defiantly; excessively; fatuously;

foolishly; haughtily; honestly; rightfully; indescribably; inordinately; justly; moderately; pardonably; rapturously; regally; saucily; secretly; snobbishly; splendidly; stubbornly; stupidly; subtly; tenderly; unendurably; ungovernably; wretchedly; essentially.

PROVE (v)

adverbs

lucidly; axiomatically; irrefutably; conclusively; incontrovertibly; incontestably; ultimately; indubitably; abundantly; substantially; experimentally; undeniably.

(See verify, corroborate.)

PROVERB

adjectives

enigmatical; prudential; silly; ungracious; bold; quaint; untruthful; well-worn. notable.

verbs

apply—; comprehend—; condense into—; contract into—; formulate—; frame—; jewel with—s; memorize—; recall—; refute—; value—; —directs; —embodies; —impresses; —instructs; —moralizes; —prescribes; —sparkles; —teaches; —warns.

(See adage, maxim, motto, epigram.)

PROVIDE (v)

adverbs

graciously; hospitably; duly; suitably; abundantly; sparely; properly; liberally; adequately; specifically; copiously; expressly; indulgently.

(See furnish, supply.)

PROVIDENCE

adjectives

beneficent; special; divine; shocking; indulgent; inscrutable; innocent; adverse; overruling.

verbs

beseech—; depend on—; meditate on—; ponder—; rely on—; —blesses; —creates; —decrees; —elects; —glorifies; —governs; —interposes; —intervenes; —justifies; —ordains; —predestines; —sanctifies; —smiles upon; —upholds.

(See Heaven, God.)

PROVIDENT

adverbs

carefully; cautiously; habitually; generously; thriftily; cannily; scarcely; adequately; satisfactorily; lavishly; extravagantly; proudly; ostentatiously; noticeably; famously; notoriously; wisely; sagaciously; intelligently; admirably; commendably; unfailingly; prudently; considerately; thoughtfully; sensibly; elaborately.

PROVIDENTIAL

adverbs

divinely; fortunately; blessedly; highly; undoubtedly; unmistakably; curiously; mysteriously; strangely; happily; opportunely: auspiciously; gloriously; beneficently.

PROVINCE

adjectives

neighboring; fruitful; extensive; specific; outcrying; petitioning; ostensible; archiepiscopal; opulent; diverse; singular; discordant; subjugated; baffling; petty; dreaded; remote; invaded; turbulent; outlying; detailed; slender; idle; nugatory; qualificatory; stupendous; contradictory; tinned; illiberal; constitutional; suitable; severe; manipulated; complex; uncertain; antimanipulation; miraculous; adequate; obnoxious; ample; sweeping; stringent; institutionalized; standard; highly-important; scanty; illogical.

verbs

banish to—; border—; divide into—; dwell in—; edge—; encroach on—; extend—; inhabit—; lay waste—; occupy—; retire to—; rule—; settle in—; skirt—; tax—; tyrannize over—; visit—; —extends; —harbors; —trades.

(See jurisdiction, kingdom, territory.)

PROVINCIAL

adjectives

uncouth; remote; daring; simple; single-minded; hopeless; ignorant; narrow.

adverbs

narrowly; utterly; hopelessly; boorishly; coarsely; bluntly; brusquely; remarkably; naturally; undisguisedly; illiberally; stupidly; credulously; awkardly; outlandishly; bashfully; self-consciously; strikingly; noticeably; unexpectedly; obviously; markedly.

PROVISION

verbs
adhere to—s of; annul—; balk at—; contemplate—; decry—; disregard—; enforce —; evade—; exempt from—; heed—; ignore—; incorporate—; infract—; insert—; inveigh against—; nullify—; sanction—; violate—; —amends; —augments; —compels; —eases; —elaborates on; —embodies; —wobbles.
(See clause, amendment, preparation, law.)

PROVOCATION

adjectives
abundant; severe; inscriptional; random; slight; mild.

verbs
agitate—; arouse to—; avoid—; electrify—; enkindle—; evoke—; fan—; foment—; impassion—; inflame—; irritate—; sharpen—; —boils; —disturbs; —fumes; —rages; —seethes; —simmers.
(See defiance, exasperation, hatred, stimulus, incitement.)

PROVOKE (*v*)

adverbs
wrathfully; unwittingly; deliberately; libelously; despicably; needlessly; unduly; abundantly; calculatingly; tremendously; maddeningly; irritatingly.
(See displease, incite, offend.)

PROVOKING

adverbs
particularly; intolerably; naughtily; mischievously; intentionally; deliberately; teasingly; disagreeably; foolishly; seriously; constantly; unbearably; uncommonly.

PROW

adjectives
beaked; glistening; pitch-black; pushing; unremembering; steadfast; reinforced; sharp; shining; gleaming.

PROWESS

adjectives
confirmed; mortal; martial; exploitative; memorable; amatory; mental; bodily; spiritual.

verbs
admire—; diminish—; display—; expose—; necessitate—; obscure—; reveal—; "tout"—; —beards; —braves; —dares; —defies; —emboldens; —encourages; —defies; —overcomes; —overwhelms; —reassures; —shocks; —ventures.
(See gallantry, power, strength, bravery, valor.)

PROWL (*v*)

adverbs
nefariously; nocturnally; satanically; thievishly; viciously; slyly; characteristically; hellishly; perniciously; rapaciously; fiendishly; mutely.
(See wander, search, sneak.)

PROWLER

adjectives
vicious; thieving.

PROXIMITY

adjectives
welcome; perilous; tantalizing; suspicious.

PRUDE

adjectives
grave; waning; strict.

verbs
avoid—; condemn—; deride—; detest—; ostracize—; ridicule—; scandalize—; —affects; —attitudinizes; —bores; —irritates; —overacts; —patronizes; —poses; —simpers; —sneers; —vexes.

PRUDENCE

adjectives
habitual; rational; tottering; honorable; premeditated; calm; worldly; diplomatic; wise; uniform; traditional; mutual; slow.

verbs
acclaim—; applaud—; bolster with—; cherish—; employ—; endorse—; exercise—; extol—; ignore—; practise—; preach—; violate—; —assures; —cautions; —dictates; —forestalls; —gains; —guards; —prepares; —warns.
(See caution, forethought, consideration.)

PRUDISH

adverbs
ridiculously; comically; awkwardly; provincially; inherently; narrowly; fanatically; provokingly; vexatiously; annoyingly; affectedly; senselessly; ostentatiously; formally; stiffly; obdurately; puritanically; absurdly; ludicrously.

PSYCHOLOGY

verbs
apply—; approve—; delve into—; digest—; dominate—of; employ—; endorse—; illustrate—; involve—; lack—; practise—; —aids; —appreciates; —comprehends; —conceives; —copes with; —evolves; —fathoms; —meditates; —realizes; —studies; —understands.
(See philosophy, science.)

PUBERTY

verbs
anticipate—; attain—; confirm—; digest—; embrace—; reach—; recognize—; reveal—; —arms; —creeps upon; —despairs; —encourages; —envelops; —generates.
(See age, maturity, period.)

PUBLIC

adjectives
receptive; intellectual; alienated; fun-loving; disinterested; aroused; palpitating; surfeited; reverent; morbid; sentimental; trusting; enlightened; gullible; motoring; enduring; theatergoing; authentic; multifarious; indignant; mad; fighting; promiscuous; unorganized; indifferent; jaded; yearning; heartless; blameless; ungrateful; cynical; avid; acquiring; enlightened; attentive; fickle; exacting; ignorant; modern; credulous; importunate; consuming; investing; uneducated.

verbs
appeal to—; beguile—; captivate—; cater to —; deceive—; defraud—; divert—; enlighten—; foist on—; impress—; incite—; scan —; shrink from—; shun—; slip over on—; snare—; swindle—; —applauds; —flocks to; mystify—; present to—.
(See individual, community, masses, mob, nation, observer.)

PUBLICATION

adjectives
illegitimate; ultimate; laborious; conspicuous; wretched; facile; disreputable; posthumous; popular; unrivaled; vigorous; art; fastest-growing; unusual; interesting; outstanding; illustrated.

verbs
achieve—; advertise—; censor—; edit—; emit—; forge—; hatch—; prepare for—; reach—; restrain—; sanction—; suspend—; translate—; —blazons; —broaches; —circulates; —edifies; —relates.
(See edition, magazine, newspaper, periodical.)

PUBLICITY

adjectives
unwanted; unfavorable; undesirable; immediate; wholesome; unsparing; unpleasant; humiliating; vague; unsavory; national; wide-spread; long-sought.

verbs
achieve—; attain—; avoid—; balk at—; court—; decry—; elude—; favor with—; gain—; leash—; maneuver for—; release—; screen from—; shower with—; shrink from —; shun—; submit to—; suffer—; sustain—; yearn for—; —celebrates; —engulfs; —fames; —glares.
(See limelight, notoriety, fame.)

PUBLIC OPINION

verbs
arouse—; consolidate—; count on—; crystallize—; excite—; formulate—; inspire—; mobilize—; muster—; prize—; rely on—; seek —; suppress—; sway—; value—; —alters; —approves; —condemns; —decides; —denounces; —sanctions; —scorns; —selects; —speculates; —tempers; —vetoes.
(See opinion, belief, sentiment.)

PUBLISH (v)

adverbs
posthumously; exclusively; surreptitiously; libelously; fraudulently; extensively; anonymously; boldly; advantageously; voluminously; compulsorily; seditiously.
(See print, announce, circulate.)

PUBLISHER

adjectives
unscrupulous; ungenerous; august; influential; heroic.

verbs
consult—; entreat—; —advertises; —edits; —emits; —heralds; —proclaims; —rejects; —rushes; —sanctions; —weans.
(See journalist, editor, printer.)

PUCKER (v)

adverbs
resentfully; coyly; teasingly; attractively; quaintly; sweetly; amorously.
(See crease, purse, wrinkle.)

PUDDING

verbs
bake—; cool—; dish—; flavor—; garnish —; mix—; mold—; relish—; serve—; spoon —; steam—; stir—; sweeten—; —curdles; —delights; —graces; —hardens; —tempts; —thickens.
(See cake, food, dessert.)

PUDDLE

adjectives
dirtiest; muddy; slopping; ugly.

PUERILE

adverbs
pitiably; inexplicably; frivolously; ridiculously; unfortunately; fatuously; inanely; trivially; surprisingly; hopelessly; vacuously; ineptly.

PUFF (v)

adverbs
prodigiously; violently; meditatively; reminiscently; pensively; breathlessly; laboredly.
(See blow, pant.)

PUGILISTIC

adverbs
skilfully; notoriously; famously; truculently; quarrelsomely; insistently; contentiously; argumentatively; expertly; eagerly; enthusiastically; zealously; unwarrantably; sturdily; stoutly.

PULL

adjectives
dreadful; energetic; vigorous; hearty; vicious; necessary.

PULL (v)

adverbs
rapidly; laboriously; vigorously; violently; unconscionably; irresistibly; energetically; frantically; tremulously; viciously; forcibly; heartily.
(See draw, haul.)

PULP

verbs
assay—; beat to—; compose of—; convert —; crush to—; derive from—; obtain—; pound to—; reduce to—; strain through—; test—; tread to—; —adheres; —fattens; —fills; —lines; —stuffs.
(See powder, mass.)

PULPIT

verbs
adorn—; ascend to—; climb to—; encrust— with; erect—; face—; orate from—; preach from—; support—; thunder from—; —attracts; —condemns; —decries; —denounces.
(See desk, platform, rostrum.)

PULSATE (v)

adverbs
rhythmically; markedly; regularly; periodically; throbbingly; violently; flutteringly; feverishly; turbulently; passionately; tremulously; hectically.
(See beat, throb.)

PULSE

adjectives
choral; throbbing; violent; new; bounding; fluttering; burning; ineradicable; languid; feverish; accelerated; rapid; quickened; chaster; pounding; arrested; fleshy; heightened; possible; turbulent; passionate; purple; haggard; energetic; hurried; leaping; firm; wearied; generous; tremulous; immortal; dormant; thrilling; hectic; emotional; inward; audible.

verbs
accelerate—; flag—; quicken—; record—; slow—; stir—; whip up—; —beats; —bounds; —drums; —flows; —flutters; —leaps; —responds; —slackens; —surges; —throbs.
(See stream, flow, vibration.)

PUMP

verbs
elevate—; handle—; labor with—; man—; manipulate—; operate—; require—; work —; —compels; —draws; —eases; —empowers; —enables; —fathoms; —forces; —presses; —pulls; —raises; —rectifies; —squirts; —sucks.

PUN

adjectives
arrant; copious; irresistible; unnecessary; stringing; weak; stupid; childish.

PUNCH (blow)

adjectives
essential; crisp; sinewy.

PUNCH (drink)

verbs
drain—; flavor—; ladle—; relish—; replenish—; savor—; serve—; sip—; soak in—; spike—; steep in—; swill—; thirst for—; —befuddles; —flows; —inebriates; —lushes; —quenches; —refreshes.
(See liquor, beverage, wine.)

PUNCTILIOUS

adverbs
overly; carefully; deferentially; ceremoniously; formally; conventionally; officially; meticulously; especially; peculiarly; infallibly; unbendingly; remarkably; particularly; uncommonly; highly; terribly.

PUNCTUAL

adverbs
usually; seldom; scarcely; infallibly; unfailingly; resolutely; painfully; ostentatiously; disagreeably; satisfactorily; notoriously; noticeably; quietly; serenely; pleasantly; unusually; coolly; habitually; pompously; deferentially; ceremoniously; respectfully; ingratiatingly; singularly.

PUNGENT

adverbs
spicily; pleasantly; arrestingly; refreshingly; strongly; faintly; overpoweringly; richly; attractively; aromatically; sharply; penetratingly; bitterly; hotly.

PUNISH (v)

adverbs
indiscriminately; summarily; barbarously; cruelly; justly; nominally; sparingly; vindictively; officially; exemplarily; ignominiously; ingeniously; atrociously.
(See discipline, penalize.)

PUNISHMENT

adjectives
dreadful; supplementary; inhuman; penitentiary; helpless; corporal; vindictive; servile; severe; direful; ignorant; eternal; adequate; express; impending; barbarous; everlasting; official; fitting; permanent; frightful; exemplary; summary; ignominious; brave; insufferable; ingenious; pleasing; dreadful.

verbs
administer—; condemn to—; enforce—; evade—; inflict—upon; mete out—; prohibit—; rain—upon; rebel against—; reserve—for; risk—; subject to—; suffer—; undergo—; —abates; —atones; —frightens.
(See lashing, discipline, torture, torment, penalty.)

PUNY

adverbs
feebly; miserably; whiningly; undoubtedly; obviously; manifestly; evidently; admittedly; unfortunately; wretchedly; pitifully; deplorably; incomparably; lamentably; shamefully; incurably; incredibly; strangely; unaccountably; hopelessly; discouragingly.

PUPIL (eye)

verbs
damage—; enlarge—; examine—; exercise—; expose—; film—; harm—; impair—; injure—; mar—; mist—; pierce—; strain—; —contracts; —dilates; —responds.
(See eye.)

PUPIL (general)

adjectives
apt; docile; individual; dilated; illustrious; ill-omened; interesting; ungifted; alert; unpromising; expressionless; unwilling; incapable; progressive; precocious; impressionable; desired; bewildered; diligent; apathetic; steely.

PUPIL (student)

verbs
chastise—; encourage—; entertain —s; examine —s; grade —s; graduate—; impart to—; inculcate in—; instil in—; instruct—; limit —s; prepare—; question—; reprimand—; —competes; —comprehends; —crams (colloq.); —demonstrates; —flunks (colloq); —grasps; —passes; —responds; —surpasses; —understands.
(See student.)

PUPPET

adjectives
gyrating; mere; painted; exceeding; skilled; gesticulating.

verbs
carve—; dress up—; employ—; enjoy—; manipulate—; represent by—; —amuses; —

capers; —delights; —depicts; —diverts; —enacts; —entertains; —frisks; —impersonates; —mimics; —mocks.
(See clown, doll.)

PUPPY

adjectives
contumacious; playful; hydrophobic; pleasant; tiny; helpless.

verbs
abandon —s; coax—; cuddle—; cudgel—; drown—; leash—; lose—; pet—; play with —; soothe—; train—; whelp —s; whip—; —annoys; —barks; —capers; —darts by; —frolics; —licks; —performs; —pursues; —whimpers; —whines; —yelps.
(See dog, animal, pet.)

PURCHASE

adjectives
remarkable; ill-considered; enforced; judicious; special; important; systematic; infinitesimal; fortunate; careless; opportune.

verbs
cart —s; charge—; check —s; collect —s; deliver—; dispose of—; gather —s; glean —s; inveigle into—; limit —s; mislay—; pile up —s; procure—; redeem—; ship—; weigh—; —s accrue; —loads.
(See merchandise, bundle, parcel, package.)

PURCHASE (*v*)

adverbs
substantially; advantageously; hypothetically; unwittingly; judiciously; systematically; shrewdly; astutely.
(See buy, acquire, secure.)

PURCHASER

adjectives
careless; persistent; potential.

verbs
advertise for—; allure —s; assure—; deceive—; net—; please—; satisfy—; tempt —; —charges; —complains; —demands; —dispenses; —markets; —patronizes; —procures; —selects; —shops.
(See buyer, customer.)

PURE

adverbs
perfectly; 100%; 99%; chastely; incredibly; warrantably; singularly; incredibly; unsurpassably; incomparably; consummately; immaculately; spotlessly; absolutely; unadulteratedly; innocently; childishly; devoutly; virtuously; artlessly; genuinely; utterly.

PURGATIVE

adjectives
powerful; stimulating; violent; bitter.

verbs
addict to—s; avoid—s; employ—; —clarifies; —defecates; —expurgates; —filters; —flushes; —frees; —purges; —purifies; —racks; —refines; —removes; —scours; —sifts; —strains; —washes; —weeds.
(See sedative, medicine, remedy, enema.)

PURGATIVE

adverbs
thoroughly; warrantably; successfully; safely; remedially; necessarily; scientifically; naturally; ʹunfailingly; genuinely; receptably.

PURITANICAL

adverbs
painfully; primly; sternly; unyieldingly; inflexibly; unbendingly; rigidly; priggishly; sedately; quietly; stoically; gravely; severely; strictly; austerely; obviously; silently; rigorously; harshly; seriously; learnedly; justly; fairly; ascetically; precisely; forbiddingly; dourly; inexorably; uncompromisingly; stiffly; dreadfully.

PURITANISM

verbs
advocate—; crusade against—; enshrine in —; inflict—; inspire—; practise—; suffer—; tolerate—; —condemns; —consecrates; —narrows; —oppresses; —reveres; —rules; —sanctifies; —simplifies; —smiles; —stints; —tramples.
(See protestantism, christianity.)

PURITY

adjectives
ethical; intellectual; womanly; classical; spotless; rare; pristine; absolute; racial; inexpressible; moral; unconscious; seraphic; touching; delicate; original; infinite; exalted; crystal; coldest; celestial; quiet; immaculate; perfect; impious; comparative; scholastic; sinless; earnest; extreme; displayed; conscious; personal; cherished; political; naked; sufficient; singular; snow-white.

verbs
achieve—; admire—; advocate—; attain—; defile—of; incur—; procure—; recommend —; revere—; select—; stain—; taint—; violate—; —awes; —eliminates; —pervades; —satisfies.

(See justice, holiness, innocence, chastity; modesty, morality.)

PURPLE

adjectives
imperial; intense; darkling; dun; regal; pansy; visual; tenderest; livid; rich; ruddy; soft; pale.

PURPORT

adjectives
dramatic; mystical; true; dim.

PURPOSE

adjectives
hellish; undefined; cosmic; syndicating; ambitious; fell; sinister; experimental; better; dire; sworn; pious; excellent; sacramental; critical; reference; avowed; moral; studied; persistent; communal; speculative; lofty; dramatic; practical; underlying; beneficent; voiceless; contrary; serious; artistic; specific; resolute; definite; high; honorable; constant; malignant; reasoned; deliberate; sufficient; laudable; primary; productive; exalted; menial; avowed; large; grim; unchanging; resurging; unswerving; ungenerous; broken; multitudinous (pl); keener; sternest; breeding; sugar-coated; ephemeral; rational; boundless; unaccomplished; restrained; unfathomed; dark; consuming; patient; altruistic; decorative; finite; defensive; distinct; hostile; aggressive; genuine; benevolent; energetic; earnest; common; essential; disinterested; ultimate; sole; poetical; finical; forlorn; flighty; infallible; willful; orbed; insurrectionary; notable; rugged; robust; tragic; humane; philosophical; unheeded; didactic; patriotic; double; extraneous; aesthetic; unchaste; intramural; visual; tolerable; ruthless; noble; corrupt; ulterior; salutary; public; histrionic; educational; patent; malicious; life; manifest; introductory; express; pernicious; heroic; inhospitable; visible; awkward; deadly; theoretical; unvarying; weighty; fraudulent; prudent; propagandist; temporary; deceptive; immediate; precautionary; domestic; abandoned; unsettled; luxurious; salubrious; iron; negative; unlawful; proper; fixed; diabolical; eternal; obstinate; pure; commercial; industrial; therapeutic; pacific; enduring; divine; microscopic; apposite; doubtful; especial; colloquial; admirable; dumb; insuperable; ineradicable; ostensible; selfsame; infirm; half-formed; prime; economic.

verbs
achieve—; adhere to—; attain—; contrive for—; convey—; crystallize—; defeat—; disclose—; divert from—; divine—; extract —from; fulfill—; galvanize into—; inspire by—; intend for—; interpret—; overcloud —; pursue—; serve—; stiffen—; subserve —; swerve from—; thwart—.

(See end, aim, effect, intention, mission, object, objective.)

PURR (v)

adverbs
amiably; demurely; cozily; domestically; comfortably; contentedly; drowsily.

(See murmur, whisper.)

PURSE

adjectives
well-filled; borrowed; evading; slow; slender; humble; yawning; long; cunning; shut; over-gorged; privy.

verbs
clasp—; cling to—; conceal—; consign to —; decorate—; dent—; draw from—; fatten —; fumble in—; lose—; mislay—; pocket—; relinquish—; replenish—; snap—; snatch—; stuff—; suit—; swell—; —accrues; —amasses; —bulges; —flashes.

(See wallet, bag, pocket.)

PURSE (v)

adverbs
coyly; squeamishly; fastidiously; cunningly; aristocratically.

(See pucker, wrinkle, crease.)

PURSUE (v)

adverbs
adventurously; remorselessly; indefatigably; warily; energetically; lustfully; relentlessly; lasciviously; invariably; resolutely; diligently; doggedly; ardently; stolidly; blandly; sedulously; mechanically; strenuously; zealously; imprudently.

(See chase, follow, seek.)

PURSUIT

adjectives
peaceful; immediate; hot; relentless; systematic; agricultural; innocent; intellectual; vigorous; dissipated; artistic; serious; exciting; studious; active; business; industrial; intimate; profitable; unjust; scuffling; professional; energetic; strenuous; relentless; sedentary; brilliant; weird; furious; peaceful; laboratory; vulgar; cultural; dangerous; unique; zealous; eager; imprudent; mercantile; athletic; worthy; hardy; wearisome; military; sluggish; sordid; sylvan; amphibious; lawful; honorable; compulsory; happy; invigorating; dogged; humble; lucrative; ardent; serious; irreparable; useless; rabid; favorite; scientific; ultimate; unavailing; instant; severer; evident; swift; illegitimate; blind; delusive; scholarly; idealistic; sedulous; disordered; engrossing; elevating; uninterrupted; vile; prompt; fascinating; passionate.

verbs
abandon—; avert—; avoid—; contemplate —; devote to—; distract from—; dog in—; engage in—; engross in—; enter—; follow in—; hinder—; hound in—; obstruct—; press—; prevent—; rush in—; spurn—; —annoys; —irks; —threatens.

(See hobby, industry, profession, quest, occupation, business, chase.)

PUS

verbs
cough up—; discharge—; drain—; eject—; emit—; expel—; fester—; localize—; produce—; —befouls; —contaminates; —defiles; —escapes; —exudes from; —fills; —forms; —offends; —oozes from; —pollutes; —reeks; —smears; —spatters; —sullies.

(See saliva.)

PUSH

adjectives
warning; vigorous; desperate; significant; determined; zealous.

verbs
climax—; necessitate—; require—; resist—; —boots (colloq.); —casts; —discharges; —drives; —expels; —favors; —forces; —heaves; —hurls; —impels; —jerks; —launches; —pitches; —startles.

(See charge, attack.)

PUSH (*v*)

adverbs
cautiously; sententiously; uncompromisingly; unceremoniously; adroitly; instinctively; vigorously; presumptuously; superciliously; unfalteringly; rudely; laboriously; mechanically.

(See shove, impel.)

PUSILLANIMOUS

adverbs
pitiably; insufferably; unhappily; miserably; wretchedly; shamefully; timorously; pitifully; contemptibly; atrociously; meanly; inexplicably; strangely; remarkably; disgracefully; basely; incredibly; hopelessly; disgustingly; pathetically.

PUTTY

verbs
apply—; case with—; coat with—; dab on —; lay—; mold—; plaster—; press—; reduce to—; smear—; spread—; squeeze—; —cements; —conceals; —covers; —faces; —holds; —pastes; —sticks.

(See mortar, plaster, cement.)

PUZZLE

adjectives
inexplicable; provocative; insolvable; fascinating; frightening; baffling.

verbs
disclose—; disentangle—; dissolve—; explain—; extricate—; popularize—; present —; reveal—; scramble—; solve—; study—; unfold—; unravel—; untie—; —baffles; —entertains; —involves; —irks; —irritates; —mystifies; —perplexes.

(See trick, riddle, problem, perplexity.)

PUZZLED

adverbs
strangely; terribly; bewilderingly; bafflingly; bitterly; cruelly; utterly; embarrassingly; painfully; obscurely; profoundly; seriously; completely; admittedly; confusingly.

PUZZLING

adverbs
sadly; naturally; hopelessly; dangerously; seriously; unreasonably; alarmingly; depressingly; unaccountably; disturbingly; genuinely; strangely; indescribably; fearfully; dishearteningly; maddeningly; unusually; terribly; vexatiously; vaguely; definitely; uncomfortably; subtly; awkwardly; extremely; annoyingly; exasperatingly; inexplicably.

Q

QUACK

verbs

betray—; detect—; father—; patronize—; warn of—; —bamboozles (colloq.); —bilks; —cajoles; —deceives; —dupes; —ensnares; —fakes (colloq.); —gammons; —gulls; —hoaxes; —lures; —outwits; —traps.

(See liar, hypocrite, quackery.)

QUACKERY

verbs

denounce—; expose—; practice—; prevent—; support—; worship—; —cheats; —circumvents; —contaminates; —corrupts; —debases; —deludes; —pretends; —swindles; —tricks.

(See quack.)

QUAFF (*v*)

adverbs

deeply; unhesitatingly; thirstily; eagerly; fraternally; jubilantly.

(See drink, sip.)

QUAGGY

adverbs

hopelessly; impassably; undesirably; soggily; dangerously; uselessly; abominably; strangely; irremediably; unsalably; unfortunately; squashily; swampily; occasionally; seasonally.

QUAIL

verbs

domesticate—; flush—; —barks; —bills; —cruises; —feigns; —flushes; —flutters; —glides; —haunts; —jerks; —nods; —roves; —rumbles; —rustles; —scratches; —squeals; —struts; —tattoos; —trills; —thumps; —thunders; —yelps.

(See bird, bob-white, partridge.)

QUAINT

adverbs

delightfully; demurely; altogether; deliciously; exceptionally; extraordinarily; uncommonly; exotically; unfashionably; enchantingly; attractively; whimsically; bewitchingly; charmingly; pleasantly; alluringly; unusually.

QUAINTNESS

verbs

cultivate—; enjoy—; instil—; notice—; overdo—; practise—; reveal—; ridicule—; —appeals; —attracts; —becomes; —blooms; —deceives; —delights; —intrigues.

(See strangeness, beauty.)

QUALIFICATION

adjectives

inner; original; sterilizing; eminent; remotest; conventional; special; indispensable; scientific.

verbs

arm with—; contemplate—; disclaim—; discount—; dispute—; endow with—; ignore—; impugn—; increase—; seek—; tax—; vouch for—; weigh—; —adapts; —empowers; —enables; —fits; —strengthens; —warrants.

(See power, endowment, essential.)

QUALIFIED

adverbs

competently; capably; entirely; unusually; exceptionally; singularly; well; wonderfully; acceptably; suitably; especially; particularly; incomparably; proficiently; technically; felicitously; obviously; evidently; manifestly; peculiarly; marvelously.

QUALIFY (*v*)

adverbs

patently; eminently; severely; admirably; splendidly; nominally; scientifically; medically; conventionally.

(See limit, modify, restrict.)

QUALITY

adjectives

absorptive; abstract; adaptive; academic; acoustical; adhering; administrative; aesthetic; affectionate; affrontive; allotted; analytical; anecdotal; antipyretic; appealing; ardent; aristocratic; artistic; atmospheric; authoritative; available; average; blended; blooming; blossom-like; brilliant; cardinal; characteristic; charming; childlike; companionable; chivalric; considerable; contradictory; cooking; correspondent; dependable; daredevil; decorative; deep-reaching; deep-rooted; demonstrable; desirable; despised; determining; developmental; diagnostic; disciplinary; disinfectant; distinctive; divine; dogged; distinguished; dramatic; driving; dubious; educational; effective; electric; elusive; embracing; emollient; emotional; empty; enduring; energetic; entrancing; essential; ethical; evident; exasperating; exceptional; fabric; faithless; famous; fertilizing; fatal; feminine; filtering; fine; first; flawless; fleshy; floating; flowery; food; free-lathering; friendly; generous; genial; gentlemanly; genuine; good; gracious; guaranteed; handmade; haunting; health-giving; high; honest; imaginary; imperturbable; indubitable; inefficient; inestimable; infectious; inferior; inherent; inherited; innate; inoperative; insulative; intellectual; integral; intrinsic; introspective; invigorating; lasting; laughable; literary; luxurious; lyrical; machine-like; magnificent; masculine; maternal; maximum; mellow; melodic; mental; militant; minimum; mixing; moral; mordant; musty; mysterious; narcotic; national; nightmare; noble; noticeable; nutritious; objectionable; occult; opiate; outstanding; outward; overlooked; pagan; passive; pedigreed; peculiar; personal; pervasive; physical; pictorial; picturesque; practical; predominant; preemient; preternatural; prime; primest; profuse; protective; provoeative; pulsating; pregnant; pungent; real; realistic; redeeming; relaxing; reliable; remarkable; representative; restraining; robust; romantic; saccharine; ruder; rugged; sachet; sensational; sedative; serious; shameless; sheer; shimmering; showy; singular; slurred; smooth; social; spiritual; sterling; statuesque; sterner; steely; subtle; strengthening; studious; stylistic; subordinate; superior; superlative; syllogistic; tangible; temperamental; tempered; top; toxic; unbeatable; uncertain; unexpected; unfailing; unfitting; unfostered; uniform; united; universal; unreasoning; unquestioned; unsatisfactory; unsought; unsuitable; unsurpassed; untiring; unusual; varied (pl); venomous; vibrating; vital; warlike; wearing; whimsical; windy; womanly; wondrous; zestful; workmanlike; worthy; wretched.

verbs

appraise—; appreciate—; ascribe—to; define—; determine—; discern—; display—; divest of—; endow with—; evaluate—; extol—; impair—; impart—; improve—; inherit—; intensify—; maintain—; recognize —; refine—; revere—; sacrifice—; share—; temper—; underrate—; —eludes; —predominates.

(See essence, attribute, characteristic, nature.)

QUALM

adjectives

conscience; sudden; bitter; unwonted.

verbs

arouse—; challenge—; incur—; justify—; raise—; register—; satisfy—; suffer—; —abashes; —alarms; —deprives; —frightens; —harrows; —hinders; —impedes; —lingers; —obstructs; —swerves; —unnerves.

(See scruple, fear, misgiving.)

QUANTITY

adjectives

exhaustless; immense; insufficient; unprecedented; unknown; indefinite; changeable; limited; astonishing; enormous; normal; unlimited; illustrative; dumb; untold; abstract; excessive; staggering; substantial; greater; surface; commercial; vast; goodly; monstrous; arbitrary; sufficient; minus; measurable; negligible; distorted; useless; unmanageable; surprising; considerable; incredible; generous; equivalant; adequate.

verbs

accumulate—; amass—; ascertain—; collect —; distribute—; estimate—; gather—; issue —; lessen—; limit—; measure—; muster—of; rake up—; reduce—; regulate—; —dwindles; —masses; —mounts; —soars; —transcends.

(See dose, amount, total, sum.)

QUARANTINE

verbs

demand—; enforce—; escape——; necessitate—; require—; repulse—; resist—; warrant—; —assures; —elapses; —excludes; —fences; —forbids; —houses; —isolates; —protects; —restrains; —restricts.

(See isolation, taboo, ban, boycott.)

QUARREL

adjectives

frequent (pl); monkish; unjust; petty; equivalent; theological; incipient; warranted; dignified; violent; private; intestine;

jealous; holy; comic; ancient; sudden; sharp; false; splendid; empty; continual; wretched; pretty; ecclesiastical; inconsequential; wrongful.

verbs
arouse—; deplore—; evoke—; lament—; patch up—; pick—; provoke—; regret—; repent—; sow—; stir up—; —breaches; —disconcerts; —embitters; —ensues; —gratifies; —rages; —sours.
(See brawl, dissension, disagreement, dispute.)

QUARREL (v)

adverbs
shamelessly; heatedly; pettishly; impertinently; theologically; jealously; acrimoniously; bitterly; squalidly; hatefully; vindictively.
(See dispute, disagree, wrangle.)

QUARRELSOME

adverbs
disagreeably; hotly; offensively; obstinately; abusively; stubbornly; irritatingly; violently; needlessly; nervously; excitably; unnecessarily; bitterly; foolishly; truculently; brutally; intolerably; unsufferably; disputatiously.

QUARRY

verbs
bait—; beguile—; contemplate—; corner—; draw—; gain on—; hole up—; investigate—; offer—; play for—; pursue—; risk—; speculate on—; tree—; vie for—; —delights; —lures; —tempts.
(See prey, victim.)

QUARTERS

adjectives
commodious; limited; exalted; charming; squalid; pleasant; deficient; distant; unsavory; fair; dingy; desolate; fashionable; moderate; heated; precise; comfortable; light-housekeeping; desponding; authoritative; ruined; cramped; ransacked; sumptuous; immigrant; bourgeois; treacherous; humble; unknown; cheerless.

verbs
assign to—; defile—; establish—; invade—; investigate—; locate—; lodge in—; picket—; pitch—; plant—; post—; remove—; report to—; retire to—; set up—; situate—; station at—; take up—; vacate.
(See barracks, place, position, headquarters.)

QUAVER (v)

adverbs
tremulously; weakly; sickeningly; peculiarly; characteristically.
(See shake, tremble, quiver.)

QUAVERING

adverbs
anxiously; diffidently; despairingly; apprehensively; despondently; dismally; dreadfully; nervously; restlessly; solicitously; terribly; tremulously; agedly; eagerly; stammeringly; wearily; abjectly; timidly.

QUEEN

adjectives
refulgent; haughty; fairy; pale; papist; fiend-like; gracious; love-sick; mob-led; stately; legitimate; buxom; helmeted; amorous; crownless; well-intentioned; dark; peerless; uncrowned; crafty; potent.

verbs
attend—; crown—; escort—; guard—; honor—; pamper—; revere—; salaam before—; serve—; squire—; —abdicates; —appeals to; —ascends; —assigns; —commends; —dazzles; —orders; —punishes; —reigns; —rewards; —rules; —symbolizes.
(See king, monarch, ruler.)

QUEER

adverbs
outlandishly; terribly; exotically; egregiously; alarmingly; singularly; abominably; mysteriously; unaccountably; suddenly; dreadfully; ominously; fantastically; uncommonly; extraordinarily; comically; grotesquely; exceptionally; unwontedly; hopelessly; incurably; incorrigibly.

QUEERNESS

verbs
deride—; develop—; incur—; overlook—; permit—; pose—; relieve—; remedy—; ridicule—; study—; tolerate—; —baffles; —creeps into; —infringes; —perplexes; —surprises; —violates.
(See oddity.)

QUELL (v)

adverbs

effectually; forcefully; momentarily; outwardly; effectively; vigorously; legitimately; officiously; legally; demonstrably; brutally.

(See suppress, subdue, crush.)

QUERIES

adjectives

valued; amusing; superstitious; unfortunate; idiotic; sceptical; excellent; everlasting; clattering; desperate; fantastic.

QUERULOUS

adverbs

hatefully; uneasily; restlessly; exceptionally; habitually; extremely; insufferably; disagreeably; pitiably; pitifully; endlessly; crabbedly; morosely; moodily; lonesomely; unhappily; perversely; crossly; sulkily; understandably; helplessly.

QUERY (v)

adverbs

sharply; deprecatingly; deliberately; romantically; significantly; stubbornly; breathlessly; anxiously; curtly; scornfully; perplexedly.

(See question, ask, inquire.)

QUEST

adjectives

chivalrous; eternal; unsuccessful; lawful; terrible; hopeless; contrarious; eager; uncertain; original; evangelical; adventurous; furious; vain; winged; doubtful; childish; selfsame.

verbs

abandon—; aim—at; engage in—; follow—; join in—; justify—; tire of—; value—; —allures; —beguiles; —demands; —eludes; —escapes; —evades; —leads; —requires; —tempts; —wearies.

(See pursuit, journey, trip, adventure.)

QUESTION

adjectives

compound; innocent; prying; rhetorical; debatable; embarrassing; unvoiced; historic; ultimate; comprehensive; unthinkable; controversial; probing; tentative; point-blank; covert; perfidious; insidious; awkward; searching; identification; artless; incisive; unconscious; sad; vermicular; brute; philosophical; theological; touching; vexed; burning; tabooed; academic; angry; contemptuous; essential; clamorous; suspicious; physical; irrational; prompt; diverse; fundamental; trying; improper; gloomy; immodest; muttered; delicate; difficult; mooted; incessant; pertinent; hideous; intelligent; abstract; stale; celebrated; troublesome; long-pending; dreadful; social; unsettled; idle; constant; bald; agonized; piercing; present; impertinent; deciding; prominent; insolent; disputed; pressing; affable; ambiguous; germane; stern; unanswerable; dormant; sensible; sorrowful; inconvenient; serious; brusque; vital; disencumbered; horrible; frenzied; large; unsuitable; transit; profound; intricate; irritating; imminent; teasing; explosive; argumentative; innumerable (pl); reasonable; concrete; cheerless; ill-bred; cogent; momentous; political; financial; humanitarian; national; absurd; relevant; foregoing; technical; barbed; perennial; multiplying; combustive; tantalizing; beggarly; tremendous; peculiar; perfect; natural; broader; ironical; much-discussed; steep; pending; motherly; untiring; numberless (pl); pregnant; eternal; banal; lustier; dynastic; constitutional; abstruse; unsettled; ever-burning; confidential; ethical; austere; vexatious; economic; insolvable; rude; insatiate; complex; perplexing; basic; uneasy; frivolous; speculative; customary; blunt; trick; similar; exhaustive; civil; religious.

verbs

adjudicate—; bar—; bear upon—; bombard with—s; brood over—; complicate—; comprehend—; confront with—; constitute—; cope with—; darken—; debate—; deluge with—s; dispute—; elucidate—; evade—; face—; fire—at; fling—at; focus on—; formulate—; frame—; go to the heart of—; grapple with—; hammer with—s; hurl—at; open to—; parry—; ply with—s; ponder—; propound—; raise—; revive—; shelve—; shy away from—; solve—; split on—; submit—to; throw light upon—; touch upon—; voice—; wrestle with—; —agitates; —arises; —elicits; —embarrasses; —hangs fire; —involves; —looms; —obtrudes upon; —plagues; —pops up; —poses itself; —relates to; —revolves itself; —rings out; —simmers; —vexes.

(See issue, matter, problem, inquiry, questioning.)

QUESTION (*v*)

adverbs
importunately; cryptically; audaciously; curiously; vaguely; incredulously; blankly; ruefully; sarcastically; sophistically; prefatorily; minutely; impudently; reluctantly; tactfully; innocently; clamorously; delicately; improperly; sternly; brusquely; momentously; technically; ironically; banally; abstrusely; confidentially; speculatively; bluntly; exhaustively.
(See query, inquire.)

QUESTIONABLE

adverbs
highly; morally; controversially; argumentatively; distinctly; darkly; uncomfortably; naturally; particularly; legally; ticklishly; undeniably; mysteriously; inferentially; conventionally.

QUESTIONAIRE

verbs
circulate—; compile—; conduct—; contemplate—; distribute—; grapple with—; induce from—; infer from—; issue—; mark —; propound—; reply to—; return—; score —; —aids; —decides; —enables; —forecasts; —inquires; —interrogates; —investigates; —irks; —puzzles; —requests; —reveals; —settles.
(See application, petition, appeal.)

QUESTIONING

adjectives
continual; suicidal; interminable; inward; prudent; over-curious.

verbs
avert—; arraign for—; conduct—; dodge —; investigate—; pursue—; refuse—; review—; —agitates ; —analyzes; —canvasses; —delves into; —demands; —elicits; —ferrets out; —overhauls; —probes; —pumps; —ransacks.
(See grilling.)

QUEUE

verbs
arrange—; braid—; clip—; dress—; tug at—; twist—; weave—; wind—; wrap—; —attracts; —hangs; —jiggles; —trails; —suspends; —sways; —swings.
(See braid, hair, tail.)

QUIBBLING

verbs
avoid—; brush aside—; check—; detest—; endure—; ignore—; incur—; suffer—; —annoys; —betrays; —deceives; —eludes; —evades; —glosses over; —hampers; —hinders; —irks; —provokes; —shuffles; —taxes; —vexes.
(See evasion, excuse.)

QUICK

adverbs
devilishly; surprisingly; alarmingly; incredibly; wonderfully; efficiently; normally; abnormally; extremely; cruelly; mentally; maliciously; diabolically; remarkably; duteously; feverishly; ordinarily; expertly; impulsively; mercifully; comically; uncomfortably; breathlessly; perilously; marvelously; unaccountably; luckily; astonishingly; dangerously; unbelievably.

QUICKNESS

adjectives
surprising; dizzy; devilish; irresolute.

QUICK-WITTED

adverbs
remarkably; astonishingly; nimbly; commercially; socially; disturbingly; incredibly; simply; admirably; sparklingly; scintillatingly; wonderfully; enviably; scintillantly; naturally; habitually; unsurpassably.

QUIESCENCE

verbs
arouse from—; endure—; lull to—; maintain—; quell to—; snub into—; —abides; —charms; —envelops; —flows; —hushes; —persists; —pleases; —stagnates.
(See lethargy, quiet, repose.)

QUIESCENT

adverbs
temporarily; luckily; fortunately; significantly; customarily; peculiarly; seasonally; remarkably; ominously; naturally; silently; immovably; usually.

QUIET

adjectives
dimmed; remarkable; restful; absolute; undisturbed; restoring; rural; subduing; penitential; endless; dull; luxurious; reverent; lifeless; ominous; domestic; graceful; aimless; formidable; passive; idealic; pastoral; peaceful; enforced.

verbs
brook—; envelop in—; insure—; reduce to —; stir from—; wrap in—; —allays; —appeals; —appeases; —calms; —cools; —governs; —lulls; —maddens; —pervades; —quells; —reigns; —smooths; —soothes.
(See hush, silence, rest, repose, quiescence, peace.)

adverbs
utterly; particularly; carefully; absurdly; cautiously; furtively; stealthily; considerately; attentively; courteously; graciously; pensively; anxiously; deliberately; dreamily; satisfactorily; temporarily; significantly; miraculously; calmly; astonishingly; sullenly; moodily; gloomily; awesomely; terrifyingly; alarmingly; suspiciously; significantly; mysteriously; appallingly; uncommonly.

QUIETNESS

adjectives
inviolable; unobtrusive; external; extreme; pensive; subdued.

QUIETUDE

adjectives
surprising; comforting; unusual; extraordinary; sartorial.

QUILL

adjectives
tuneful; enchanted; porcupine; many-colored; tinkling; venal.

QUIT (*v*)

adverbs
reluctantly; sadly; dejectedly; eventually; hastily; abruptly; impetuously; significantly; gloomily; mysteriously; consequently.
(See cease, stop.)

QUIVER

adjectives
solemn; convulsive; subtle.

QUIVER (*v*)

adverbs
nervously; exasperatedly; wantonly; abnormally; violently; sluggishly; markedly; excitedly; passionately.
(See shake, tremble, quaver.)

QUIVERING

adjectives
mysterious; gentle; anxious.

adverbs
nervously; tremulously; helplessly; feverishly; pathetically; pitiably; miserably; visibly; angrily; grievously; timidly; affrightedly; curiously.

QUIZ (*v*)

adverbs
narrowly; closely; methodically; thoroughly; perfunctorily austerely; vexatiously; rudely; speculatively; civilly; sternly; abstrusely.
(See question, banter.)

QUOTA

adjectives
assigned; respective; insignificant.

verbs
acquire—; allot—; apportion—; attain—; cede—; deal—; derive—; divide—; endow —; fulfill—; furnish—; impose—; pledge —; portion out—; present—; raise—; receive—; subscribe—; supply—; yield—.
(See portion, share, part.)

QUOTATION

verbs
apply—to; bejewel with—s; comprehend—; condense into—; contract into—; eschew—; fling—at; frame—; memorize—; ooze—s; pepper with—s; recall—; refer to—; value —; —directs; —embodies; —exemplifies; —illustrates; —impresses; —instructs; —prescribes; —sparkles; —teaches; —warns.
(See saying, maxim, proverb, passage.)

....*QUOTATIONS*

adjectives
biblical; poetical; irreverent; copious; innumerable; modest; half-remembered; seasonable; habitual; felicitious; capital; garbled; illustrative; multifarious.

QUOTE (*v*)

adverbs
copiously; philosophically; widely; extensively; oracularly; preeminently; plaintively; magnanimously; ardently; biblically; poetically; habitually; felicitously; illustratively; multifariously; aptly; erroneously.
(See repeat, extract.)

R

RABBI

verbs
induct—; ordain—; —authorizes; —blesses; —communes; —confirms; —consecrates; —officiates; —performs; —preaches;—ritualizes.
(See minister, priest, teacher.)

RABBIT

adjectives
juicy; misplaced; tasty.

verbs
domesticate—; dress—; experiment with —s; fence out—; pen—; pet—; shoot—; skin—; —bounds off; —burrows; —crouches; —devastates; —digs; —flashes by; —hops; —jumps; —leaps; —nibbles; —plagues; —scampers away; —scurries; —subsists on.
(See animal, pet.)

RABBLE

verbs
arouse—; class with—; concentrate—; court—; dispel—; disperse—; exclude—; harangue—; mingle with—; pander to—; restrain—; rout—; silence—; sway—; —assembles; —congregates; —masses; —mobs; —rules; —rushes; —storms; —surges; —throngs.
(See mob, crowd, proletarian.)

RABID

adverbs
insensately; wildly; unaccountably; dangerously; appallingly; fanatically; eccentrically; terribly; hysterically; downright; curiously; insatiably; violently; bitterly; absurdly; crazily; relentlessly; unbelievably; appallingly; shockingly; incredibly.

RACE (*competition*)

verbs
accelerate—; approve—; clinch—; compete in—; contend in—; enter—; judge—; observe—; oppose in—; outdistance in—; postpone—; promote—; protest—; wager on—; —enlivens; —enraptures; —excites; —fascinates; —petrifies; —revives; —thrills.
(See match, game, contest.)

RACE (*general*)

adjectives
severed; vengeful; sacerdotal; antipathetic; bloody-minded; fading; earth-born; alien; idle; girdled; amphibious; literary; infinite; indestructible; civilized; chequered; wasted; kindred; blissful; canine; impromptu; solid; tenacious; energetic; fecund; teeming; hectic; fallen; separate; radiant; golden; high-born; beauteous; touchy; savage; warlike; blind; blundering; knightly; proverbial; brave; despicable; barbarous; desperate; well-marked; swarming; obstinate; lascivious; titanic; lawless; hardy; thrifty; ethereal; jocund; elimination; inscrutable; uncultivated; wild; human; contemptible; singing; indigenous; glorious; sturdy; godly; best; fierce; studious; invincible; ill-fated; breathless; oppressed; melodious; long-lived; valiant; sullen; ancient; reprobated; intractable; dominant; unfortunate; subjugated; dwarfish; noble; incapable; aggressive; miserable; bounding; degraded; volatile; well-known; perished; magnificent; frolicsome; dusky; inveterate; unreturning; interesting; ghostly; short-distance; primitive; purblind; domestic; polished; courageous; stoical; decorative; semi-civilized; headlong; gentle; aboriginal; high-hearted; timid; proud; shining; inoffensive; illustrious; pitiless; invalid; unconverted; cultural; hostile; fickle; ruling; backward; impious; antediluvian; rudest; obstacle; delicate; nurtured; greedy; contested; untrustworthy; hard; beastly; vagrant; malignant; feverish; wise; shadowy; interloping; buxom; cognate; active; consequent; awkward; depraved; self-opinionated.

RACE (*nationality*)

verbs
characterize—; conquer—; detest—; distinguish—; exterminate—; limit—; mark—; perpetuate—; purify—; sow—; strengthen —; study—; uplift—; —ebbs; —evolves; —perishes; —prospers; —subsists; —vanishes; —wanes.
(See breed, mankind, strain, nationality.)

RACE (v)

adverbs
tirelessly; vengefully; lawlessly; awkwardly; gloriously; invincibly; boundingly; frolicsomely; courageously; greedily; feverishly; spectacularly.
(See run, scamper, flee.)

RACIAL

adverbs
inherently; strongly; naturally; inseparably; peculiarly; inescapably; indestructibly; tenaciously; proverbially; gloriously; distinctly; significantly; fiercely; dominantly; proudly.

RACK

adjectives
fierce; low-trailing; cruel; commercialized; money-lending; corporeal.

RACKET

adjectives
noisy; gloomy; theatrical; vicious; favorite; flourishing; terrible; resounding.

verbs
—breaks; —clacks; —clashes; —crashes; —deafens; —dins; —drowns; —drums; —penetrates; —pierces; —resounds; —roars; —rumbles; —shakes; —snaps; —splits; —stuns; —thunders.
(See clamor, noise.)

RACY

adverbs
breezily; pungently; pithily; smartly; curiously; brilliantly; pleasantly; boldly; eloquently; piquantly; trenchantly; vigorously; unusually; amazingly; interestingly; arrestingly.

RADIANCE

adjectives
serene; glaring; rapturous; full; ruddy; variegated; clear; reflected; pale; milder; celestial; fathomless; indistinct; farewell; calm; soft; uniform; transitory; subdued; blinding; seraphic; secret; growing; orange; indescribable; mailed; tenderest; warm; flooding; sickly; prismatic; marvelous; bewildering; downcast; fantastic.

verbs
beam with—; blemish—; cloud—; dim—; dull—; eclipse—; extinguish—; glow with—; obscure—; overshadow—; shed—; —blazes; —enchants; —enhances; —flames; —gilds; —gleams; —glistens; —graces; —illuminates; —overspreads; —sparkles; —sublimates; —surrounds; —enlightens.
(See moonbeam, happiness, brilliance.)

RADIANT

adverbs
gloriously; splendidly; conspicuously; noticeably; visibly; happily; joyously; triumphantly; rapturously; ecstatically; jubilantly; exultantly; blissfully; contentedly; serenely.

RADIATOR

verbs
adjust—; bask near—; polish—; throttle—; —affords; —assures; —comforts; —diffuses; —glows; —parches; —scorches; —singes; —simmers; —warms.

RADICAL

adjectives
avowed; univalent; unreasonable; ill-balanced.

verbs
—contaminates; —corrupts; —demoralizes; —disparages; —fulminates; —harangues; —heckles; —ignites; —impairs; —pillories; —poisons; —pollutes; —raves; —taints; —undermines; —vituperates; —anathematizes; —cankers; —condemns.
(See anarchist, socialist, communist.)

adverbs
boldly; daringly; definitely; distinctly; deeply; thoroughly; uncompromisingly; sweepingly; appallingly; necessarily; downright.

RADIO

verbs
broadcast over—; communicate by—; filter into—; toy with—; tune down—; —amplifies; —bears; —blares forth; —bleats; —booms; —clarifies; —contacts; —conveys; —deafens; —disconcerts; —facilitates; —hums; —proclaims; —receives; —transmits; —unites.
(See loud-speaker.)

RAFT

adjectives
well-banded; fatal; formidable; ruined; prodigious; timber.

verbs
climb to—; crowd—; hoist on—; lap—; lash to—; punt—; rig—; slap—; smack—; support on—; sway—; threaten—; —bobs; —dips; —floats; —guides; —rocks; —transports; —troughs.

(See boat.)

RAFTER

adjectives
smoke-stained; gloomy; slender; resonant; skeleton.

verbs
bear on—; bestride—; hang from—; recline on—; repose on—; rest on—; straddle—; —abuts; —affords; —aids; —bolsters; —maintains; —s ring; —snaps; —supports; —sustains; —underprops; —upholds.

(See beam, timber, board.)

RAGE

adjectives
withering; impetuous; towering; foaming; tacit; guilty; fresh; grievous; righteous; inarticulate; impotent; extreme; cold; merciless; appeasing; disappointed; breathless; gloomy; punic; outflung; murderous; sudden; affectionate; haughty; divine; fierce; animal-like; mightier; furious; resolute; violent; pernicious; appertaining; indescribable; white-hot; unwonted; quick; hostile; unmitigated; sparkling; baffled; generous; unintelligible; silken; tremendous; ceaseless; prophetic; elemental; kindling; stormy; relentless; recurrent; concentrated; mental; pitiful; explosive; instantaneous; trembling; hard-favored; heathen; noble; female; overmastering.

verbs
blind with—; bluster in—; enkindle—; explode in—; fan—; fire with—; flush with—; fly into—; foment—; fume with—; glower with—; inflame with—; justify—; lash into—; pour out—; quiver with—; rouse—; shriek in—; snort with—; sputter with—; storm in—; thunder in—; tremble with—; vent—; work into—; —boils over; —effervesces; —ferments; —seethes; —smolders; —spends itself; —surges; —transports; —vanishes.

(See fury, indignation, anger, impatience, ire.)

RAGE (v)

adverbs
inwardly; magnificently; incessantly; momentarily; tremendously; fearfully; furiously; dangerously; fiercely; impetuously; foamingly; inarticulately; impotently; murderously; perniciously; unintelligibly; elementally; explosively; mentally.

(See storm, fume.)

RAGGED

adverbs
terribly; carelessly; pitiably; negligently: pathetically; impossibly; irregularly; disgracefully; contemptibly; shabbily; appallingly; shamefully; shockingly; unnecessarily; heedlessly; blithely; gleefully; hoydenishly; tomboyishly; nonchalantly; pitifully; deliberately; mischievously.

RAGING

adverbs
furiously; violently; tempestuously; angrily; resentfully; virulently; helplessly; stormily; hysterically; needlessly; deliriously; fanatically; feverishly; brutally; fiercely; tyrannically; madly; uncontrollably; bitterly; savagely; rabidly; uselessly; terribly; shockingly.

RAGS

adjectives
smelly; picturesque; grotesque; flattened; clean; slanting; riddled.

verbs
apparel in—; array in—; deck in—; discard —; divest of—; don—; envelop in—; sheathe in—; shun—; swaddle in—; swathe in—; vest in—; —humble; —humiliate.

(See clothing, raiment, apparel.)

RAID

adjectives
intrepid; mutual; memorable; bridge-burning; cavalry; unjustifiable; dreadful; marauding; foraging; rebel; murderous; copious (pl); conducted; similar; swift.

verbs
anticipate—; check—; engineer—; launch—; parry—; plan—; repel—; repulse—; resist —; retaliate for—; shield from—; stem—; —aims at; —assails; —attacks; —beleaguers; —besieges; —harries; —provokes; —saps; —storms; —thrusts at; —violates; —whips.

(See invasion, attack.)

RAID (v)

adverbs

lawlessly; intrepidly; memorably; unjustifiably; maraudingly; treacherously; rebelliously; murderously; cunningly; devastatingly; swiftly; belligerently.

(See attack, seize.)

RAIL

adjectives

shattered; sanded; twisted; continuous; purgatorial.

verbs

erect—; grasp—; —barricades; —bars; —checks; —circumscribes; —confines; —encloses; —fences; —fringes; —girdles; —protects; —restrains; —safeguards; —skirts; —terminates; —withstands; —restricts.

(See fence, barrier, barricade.)

RAIL (v)

adverbs

fretfully; bitterly; acrimoniously; acidly; sarcastically; devastatingly; witheringly; relentlessly; pitifully; plaintively; monotonously; copiously.

(See censure, reproach, upbraid.)

RAILROAD

adjectives

infant; pioneered; subtransatlantic; state-owned; opulent; efficient; necessary; well-run.

verbs

plan—; route—; sanction—; tear up—; utilize—; —advertizes; —covers; —enables; —extends; —facilitates; —guarantees; —insures; —invades; —opens; —prospers; —solicits.

RAIMENT

adjectives

snowy; gallant; gay; flying; shining; sumptuous; predestined; scanty.

verbs

admire—; cast off—; divest of—; don—; perk—; remove—; strip of—; swaddle in—; —clothes; —covers; —drapes; —enrobes; —flatters; —laps; —mantles; —muffles; —sheathes.

(See apparel, clothing.)

RAIN

adjectives

drizzling; drenching; summer; impalpable; fiery; mizzling; misty; melting; crushing; silent; blistering; inconceivable; frozen; lukewarm; quiet; dismal; frequent (pl); generous; gusty; recent; fertilizing; sudden; prodigious; hearty; long; continued; cold; abundant; driving; rapid; soft; violent; vernal; invisible; falling; pattering; roaring; passionate; autumn; pouring; swirling; incessant; heavy; pelting; pitiless; quickening; singing; sterile; substantial; windy; mellowing; plenteous; thick; sooty; gusty; healing; love-cast; irised; refreshing; unabated; sheeted; continual; dim; lashing; undecided; sweetest; snow-soft; emerald; chilling; immortal; biting; silver; frozen; constant; superannuated; reluctant; veritable; unprecedented; fitful; uninterrupted; dreary; heaven-sent; swishing.

verbs

brave—; dodge—; —blights; —crescendos; —dashes against; —deluges; —drenches; —drums; —gurgles; —gushes; —inundates; —jets; —lashes; —moistens; —patters; —pelts; —rattles; —relents; —roars; —slithers off; —spatters; —spurts; —teems; —threatens; —thuds; —wanes; —ripples; —trickles.

(See hail, shower, sleet, storm.)

RAIN (v)

adverbs

dismally; heavily; monotonously; desultorily; drizzlingly; prodigiously; abundantly; violently; vernally; patteringly; roaringly; pitilessly; unabatedly; fitfully; unprecedentedly.

(See shower, pour.)

RAINBOW

adjectives

momentary; live; wonderful; myriad (pl); glorified; ephemeral; wondrous; emerald.

RAINY

adverbs

unusually; uncommonly; extraordinarily; terribly; torrentially; softly; dreamily; drowsily; thunderously; drizzlingly; windily; gustily; unfortunately; unluckily; disappointingly; opportunely; seasonally; fortunately; providentially; strangely; gloomily; dismally; drearily; pleasantly; agreeably; lightly; suddenly.

RAISE (v)

adverbs
corruptly; insolently; deferentially; instinctively; eloquently; unscrupulously; defiantly; delicately; significantly; impressively; mechanically; expressively; daintily; warningly; majestically; deliberately; quizzically.
(See lift, elevate.)

RAKE

verbs
drag—; draw—; employ—; tug at—; —dredges; —eliminates; —extricates; —gathers; —grubs; —refines; —scratches; —smoothes; —unearths; —uproots.

RAKE (v)

adverbs
thoroughly; searchingly; painstakingly; questioningly; inquiringly.
(See gather, search.)

RAKISH

adverbs
wildly; recklessly; dissolutely; madly: blithely; gaily; hilariously; idly; merrily; boisterously.

RALLY (v)

adverbs
faithfully; gallantly; ardently; instinctively; fiercely; courageously; heartily.
(See collect, recover.)

RAMBLE (v)

adverbs
garrulously; blindly; monotonously; ceaselessly; maddeningly; purposelessly; pointlessly.
(See stroll, stray.)

RAMBLING

adverbs
pleasantly; quaintly; comfortably; leisurely; irregularly; idly; wantonly; happily; freely; interestingly; endlessly; aimlessly; capriciously; erratically; casually; artlessly; quietly; effortlessly; errantly; desultorily; vagrantly; blissfully.

RAMPANT

adverbs
roughly; obstreperously; uncontrollably; ungovernably; predominantly; buoyantly; noticeably; expansively; singularly; remarkably; naturally; spontaneously; insuppressibly; unmanageably; merrily.

RAMPART

verbs
array on—; batter—; communicate with—; erect—; fret—; pass along—; patrol—; penetrate—; storm—; strengthen—; surmount—; —bulwarks; —defends; —protects; —resists; —surrounds; —unites.
(See defense, fortification, barricade.)

RAMSHACKLE

adverbs
deplorably; hopelessly; discouragingly; challengingly; dingily; dismally; interestingly; inexpensively; terribly; comically; brightly; charmingly; fascinatingly; merrily; curiously; scandalously; completely; rattily; incredibly; manifestly.

RANCID

adverbs
sourly; bitterly; acridly; odoriferously; obviously; outrageously; impossibly; disgustingly; hopelessly; shamefully; mustily; nauseatingly; uselessly; terribly; disagreeably; noticeably; evidently; vexatiously; miserably; undisguisably; visibly.

RANCOR

adjectives
unmitigated; violent; unrelenting; smothered.

verbs
arouse—; betray—; burst with—; defy—; harbor—; inflict—; protest—; repress—; unloose—; wreak—upon; —abuses; —blasts; —embitters; —irritates; —pierces; —shakes; —snarls; —sours; —stabs.
(See grudge, animosity, ill-will, bitterness.)

RANCOROUS

adverbs
unreasonably; senselessly; maliciously; venomously; relentlessly; incorrigibly; outrageously; shamefully; atrociously; dangerously; naturally; alarmingly; fearfully; singularly; insufferably; extraordinarily; violently; fanatically; uncontrollably.

RANGE

adjectives
considerable; extensive; narrow; point-blank; cruising; indicated; effective; enor-

mous; massy; limited; encyclopedic; far-stretching; irregular; cloud-capped; snowy; interminable; billowy; unbounded; easy; flanking; infinite; widened; teeming; formidable; fluid; inexhaustible; vaster; ancient; longitudinal; wonted; unactive; colossal; icy.

verbs
amplify—; ascertain—; broaden—; encompass—; enlarge—; expand—; extend—; localize—; magnify—; narrow—; restrict—; scan—; spread—; sweep—; widen—; —fluctuates; —oscillates; —soars; develop—.
(See horizon.)

RANK

adjectives
high; foremost; crowding; honorable; illustrious; scholarly; serried (pl); unbroken; dense; poetical; bending; unwearied (pl); superior; wasting; preeminent; hostile (pl); distinguished; swaying (pl); teeming (pl); glittering (pl); myriad (pl); titled; depleted (pl); innumerable (pl); obscurest; riddled (pl); stalwart (pl); regular; inferior; extinguished; culinary; extrinsic; intermediate; exhausted (pl); shattered (pl); disordered (pl); relative; jeweled; stately; immortal; intellectual; melancholy; interminable; mournful; rightful; respective; enveloping (pl); princely; gathering (pl); delicate; swelling (pl); fastfalling (pl); equal; riven (pl); reeling (pl).

verbs
accredit—; achieve—; acquire—; ascend to —; aspire to—; assign to—; break—s; denote—; desert—s; divest of—; earn—; eject from—s; elevate to—; forfeit—; honor—; praise—s; promote to—; reduce to—s; respect—; scatter—; shatter—s; signal—s; solidify—s; split—s; swell—s; win—; —dignifies; —eclipses; —glorifies; —outshines; —surpasses; —transcends.
(See degree, grade, caste, class, position.)

RANK (v)

adverbs
deservedly; poetically; obscurely; relatively; intellectually; rightfully; aristocratically; humbly.
(See classify, group.)

RAP (v)

adverbs
smartly; vigorously; authoritatively; vivaciously; persistently; furiously; tempestuously.
(See knock, thump.)

RAPACIOUS

adverbs
furtively; terribly; wickedly; scandalously; outrageously; shamefully; greedily; ravenously; insatiably; rabidly; ungovernably; uncontrollably; madly; monstrously; abominably; detestably; peculiarly; astonishingly; unbelievably; uncommonly.

RAPID

adverbs
unbelievably; effortlessly; invisibly; increasingly; mercifully; crazily; expertly; distressingly; painfully; breathlessly; impetuously; perilously; unaccountably; surprisingly; astonishingly; moderately; dangerously; lightly.

RAPIDITY

adjectives
incredible; fair; sufficient; inconceivable; fearful; marvelous; feverish; facial; dexterous; appalling; lightning; extraordinary; extreme; disconcerting; amazing; racial.

RAPIER

verbs
brandish—; evade—; fence with—s; flourish—; parry—; sheathe—; thrust with—; wield—; —lacerates; —penetrates; —pierces; —sheds.
(See sword, lance.)

RAPTURE

adjectives
ultimate; transient; holy; lasting; random; wounding; blissful; pure; speechless; dizzy; boundless; exquisite; heartfelt; divine; mute; radiant; heavenly; guilty; honest; fervid; careless; secret; rhetorical; mysterious; imaginative; maniacal; enveloping; unreasoning; serene; romantic; fading; suppressed; ecstatic; tumultuous.

verbs
breathe in—; cherish—; dilate with—; evoke—; exalt in—; excite—; exclaim in—; express—; feast on—; move to—; muse in —; regard with—; smite with—; speak in —; touch with—; tremble in—; —bewitches; —entrances.
(See ecstasy, delight, delirium, bliss, joy.)

RAPTUROUS

adverbs
supremely; blessedly; truly; idiotically; ineffably; charmingly; unforgettably; enormously; dreamily; innocently; mysteriously; ecstatically; tumultuously; curiously; openly; childishly; rosily; ridiculously; shyly; frankly; excitedly; tranquilly; wildly; unutterably; joyously; tenderly; deliriously.

RARE

adverbs
unusually; valuably; singularly; inimitably; remarkably; pricelessly; incalculably; immeasurably; fantastically; amazingly; unbelievably; momentously; signally; marvelously; incredibly.

RASCAL

adjectives
merry; glaring; bald-pated; meddlesome; lying; barren; mean; consummate; muddy-mettled; mercenary; stretch-mouthed; designing; tawny; lovable; scheming; vile; unmitigated; dishonest; cony-catching; villainous; worthless.

RASCALLY

adverbs
mischievously; outrageously; outlandishly; incorrigibly; unmanageably; fearfully; maliciously; boyishly; trickily; craftily; shamefully; smoothly; atrociously; detestably; insidiously; contemptibly; singularly; appallingly; reprehensibly; treacherously; dishonestly; unregenerately; inveterately; bitterly; hatefully.

RASH

verbs
afflict with—; attribute—to; break into—; daub on—; produce—; solve—; swab—; treat—; —confines; —disappears; —effloresces; —erupts; —fades; —indicates; —irritates; —patches; —plagues; —speckles; —spreads; —subsides.
(See sore, boil.)

adverbs
adventurously; indiscreetly; imprudently; audaciously; unfortunately; wilfully; inconsiderately; foolishly; thoughtlessly; inadvertently; ignorantly; heedlessly; intrepidly; wantonly; desperately; misguidedly; flippantly; absurdly; preposterously; alarmingly; unaccountably; fearlessly.

RASHNESS

adjectives
noble; unguided; weakest; stretched; general.

verbs
prevent—; protest—; repent—; rue—; warn against—; —breaks; —chances; —destroys; —endangers; —ignores; —irks; —provokes; —risks; —suffers; —ventures; —vexes; —wrecks.
(See recklessness, audacity.)

RASP (*v*)

adverbs
harshly; unmelodiously; atrociously; discordantly; gratingly; exasperatingly.
(See grate, file, offend.)

RAT

verbs
experiment on—s; exterminate—s; infest with—s; plague with—s; poison—s; rid of —s; trap—; —burrows; —digs; —excavates; —s frequent; —gnaws; —haunts; —infects; —nibbles; —penetrates; —pillages; —preys on; —ravages; —roves; —scampers; —scurries; —thrives.
(See animal.)

RATE

adjectives
prevailing; reasonable; high; proud; annual; special; low; surprising; respectable; comparable; amazing; expense; balancing; unusual; moderate; stipulated; incredible; differential; fluctuating; minimum; unconscionable; interest; usurious; legal; astounding; tremendous; alarming; reckless; standard; present; noble; rapid; overwhelming; attractive; fearful; death; furious; marvelous; trifling; enormous; modest; prodigious; nominal; unvarying; right; sensible; economical; remarkable; daily; weekly; monthly; thrifty; considerate; extreme; agreeable.

verbs
apply—; assess—; assign—; calculate—; command—; compute—; demand—; deprecate—; determine—; estimate—; fix—; impose—; proportion—; reduce—; slash—; stabilize—; standardize—; subject to—; tax —; —appraises; —corresponds to; —evaluates; —fluctuates; —prevails; —skyrockets; —varies.
(See tax, amount.)

RATE (v)

adverbs
soundly; harshly; disagreeably; furiously; wrathfully; discordantly; scorchingly.
(See appraise, estimate, value.)

RATIFICATION

verbs
fight for—; hinder—; submit for—; —admits; —alters; —attests; —authenticates; —certifies; —concerns; —corroborates; —endorses; —evinces; —indicates; —involves; —recognizes; —seals; —subverts; —upholds; —verifies.
(See approval, confirmation, indorsement.)

RATIFY (v)

adverbs
wisely; amicably; agreeably; ostentatiously; solemnly; internationally.
(See confirm, sanction.)

RATIONAL

adverbs
intelligently; philosophically; soundly; academically; intuitively; sensibly; perfectly; psychologically; coldly; irresistibly; fairly; cosmically; inferentially; elementally; profoundly; fundamentally; presumptively; penetratingly; discernibly; contemplatively; doctrinally; spiritually; innately; ideologically; speculatively; consciously; soberly; speciously; logically; persuasively; convincingly; conclusively.

RATIONS

adjectives
insufficient; deficient; regulation; delicious; balanced; emergency; abundant; scant; half; magic; particular; starvation; wartime.

verbs
allot—; carve—; cast—; consume—; crave—; cut—; deal—; distribute—; divide—; mete out—; parcel—; portion out—; reduce—; replenish—; share—; supply—; —appease; —relieve; —sate; —satisfy; —strengthen.
(See food, diet, supplies.)

RATTLE (general)

adjectives
remote; sudden; tempestuous; globular; unheeded; peremptory; pulsing.

RATTLE (toy)

verbs
chew—; employ—; —amuses; —appeases; —attracts; —clashes; —crashes; —delights; —diverts; —entertains; —fascinates; —interests; —pleases; —subsides; —tinkles.
(See toy, noise, racket.)

RATTLE (v)

adverbs
cacophonously; crisply; peremptorily; tempestuously; rudely; abruptly; irritatingly.
(See clatter, prattle.)

RAUCOUS

adverbs
noisily; curiously; hoarsely; blatantly; boisterously; disagreeably; uncommonly; unusually; unpleasantly; sepulchrally; rudely; raspingly; stertoriously; distinctly; horribly; obnoxiously; unnaturally; offensively; piercingly; peculiarly; curiously; strangely; intolerably; indescribably.

RAVAGES

adjectives
fearful; excessive; increased.

verbs
curb—; preserve from—; stay—; succumb to—; suffer—; —blemish; —blight; —cripple; —damage; —debase; —decimate; —deface; —defile; —desecrate; —disfigure; —embitter; —mutilate; —overwhelm; —prostrate; —ruin; —swamp.
(See damage, injury.)

RAVE (v)

adverbs
senselessly; rapturously; idiotically; drunkenly; fearfully; ominously; furiously; insanely; feverishly; pathetically; passionately; romantically; ecstatically; tumultuously.
(See rage, storm.)

RAVEN

adjectives
presaging; colored; somber; croaking; ominous.

verbs
—attacks; —beaks; —bellows; —bodes; —carries off; —croaks; —destroys; —flits; —kills; —pesters; —plagues; —prates; —preys on; —thieves.
(See bird, crow.)

RAVINE

adjectives
sandy; wooded; picturesque; stained; impenetrable; gaunt; difficult; luminous; inaccessible; bushy; rough; burning; steep; rocky; numerous (pl); precipitous.

RAVISH (v)

adverbs
violently; brutally; lustfully; lasciviously; fearfully; viciously; criminally; grossly; sordidly; passionately; bestially; sickeningly.
(See enchant, transport.)

RAVISHING

adverbs
incomparably; delectably; enchantingly; unbelievably; happily; inexpressibly; transportingly; rapturously; ecstatically; divinely; matchlessly; radiantly.

RAW

adverbs
awkwardly; grotesquely; repulsively; unbelievably; angularly; oddly; ludicrously; deplorably; strangely; fantastically; amusingly; pathetically; distressingly; terribly; horribly; grievously; ridiculously; singularly; queerly; drolly; curiously; painfully; crudely; coarsely; thoughtlessly; ignorantly.

RAY

adjectives
solar; deathless; fresh; glaring; dewy; ripening; cheering; evening; gilded; funeral; cosmic; oblique; pounding; visual; scattered (pl); darting; medullary; primary; blushing; early; unrefracted; discomforting; potent; castrated; glowing; lingering; celestial; penetrating; redoubled; luminous; mystic; changing; level; converging; chance; fiery; actinic; tender; unclouded; purest; lurid; overflowing; dimmer; sunny; reviving; dull; fervent; blood-red; transverse; propitious; genial; occasional; beauteous; rising; gladdening; enlivening; killing; hospitable; eternal; controlled; dauntless; diverging; slanting; everlasting; angry; piercing; sportive; parent; heavenly; splendid; dismembered; bewildering; indifferent; curative; reflected; glimmering; dissolving; vertical; illusive; liquid; angelic; streaming; orient; misty; silver; frozen; pensive; radiating; derived; sickly; unwelcome; jubilant; rapid; scorching; dim.

verbs
bend—; diffuse—; dim—; emit—; expose to—; focus—upon; obscure—; shed—; shield from—; shoot—; throw—; —dances; —dazzles; —s diverge; —illuminates; —penetrates; —pierces; —plays upon; —reveals; —shimmers; —streams from.
(See beam, gleam, moonbeam, light.)

RAZOR

verbs
blunt—; brandish—; dull—; employ—; grind—; hone—; nick—; sheathe—; stroke —; strop—; whet—; wield—; —denudes; —incises; —smooths.
(See knife, blade.)

REACH

adjectives
desolating; endless; sighing; automatic; utmost; extended; boundless; upper; illimitable; giddiest; naughty; sandy; vast; arid; easy; keen; timid; wistful; trackless.

REACH (v)

adverbs
promptly; simultaneously; automatically; impulsively; conveniently; timidly; ultimately; rapturously; greedily; vainly; wistfully.
(See touch, strike.)

REACT (v)

adverbs
discreditably; instantaneously; adversely; strangely; abnormally; divergently; feverishly; violently; passionately; intuitively; romantically; physically; logically; blindly.
(See resist, recoil, oppose.)

REACTION

adjectives
energetic; painful; emotional; necessary; feverish; varied; premature; strong; disastrous; consumer; unequivocal; fatigued; violent; protective; inevitable; deep-seated; vigorous; unexpected; natural; photochemical; uncomfortable; passionate; intuitive; impulsive; instantaneous; chemical; antagonistic; romantic; infantile; chronic; physical; barbarous; pleasant; artificial; individual; astounding; logical; sympathetic; dramatic; blind; unromantic; sanguinary.

verbs
awaken—; control—; defeat—; determine —; emphasize—; evaluate—; excite—; experience—; foresee—; forestall—; induce—;

observe—; produce—; promote—; provoke —; repute—; reverse—; study—; suffer—; test—; —astounds; —ensues; —sets in; —warns.

(See answer, reply, response.)

REACTIONARY

adverbs

commendably; dangerously; manifestly; defiantly; openly; curiously; inexplicably; unaccountably; unreasonably; lamentably; stimulatingly; progressively; energetically; ominously; favorably; admirably; politically; irresolutely; unreliably; antagonistically; painfully; astonishingly; reprehensibly; undependably.

READ (v)

adverbs

omnivorously; perpetually; insipidly; profoundly; nonchalantly; listlessly; attentively; extensively; drowsily; assiduously; advisedly; monotonously; genially; voraciously; habitually; casually; industriously; stimulatingly; desultorily; promiscuously; surreptitiously; haltingly; sporadically; judiciously.

(See peruse, scan, study.)

READABLE

adverbs

instantly; easily; readily; pleasantly; fascinatingly; entertainingly; delightfully; interestingly; scarcely; barely; instructively; highly; uncommonly; remarkably; singularly; definitely; distinctly; plainly; unusually.

READER

adjectives

eager; intelligent; constant; everyday; enthusiastic; serious; gentle; phenomenal; browsing; sagacious; assiduous; casual; insatiable; captious; extensive; persistent; dilettante; confused; unsuspecting; continental; absorbed; negligent; omnivorous; copy; discriminating; stumbling; uncomprehending; fastidious; indefatigable; industrious; prudish; voracious; ponderous; innocent; voluminous; ardent; attentive; arid; rapid; faulty; lifelong.

verbs

absorb—; acquaint—; amuse—; divert—; edify—; enlighten—; entertain—; guide—; inform—; instruct—; lay before—; outrage —; persuade—; tickle—; train—; —appreciates; —browses; —comprehends; —cons; —consumes; —criticizes; —delights; —delves into; —dips into; —discerns; —enjoys; —gleans; —imbibes; —masters; —peruses; —plunges into; —pores over; —refers to; —scans; —thumbs; —wades through; —apprehends.

(See student, scholar, pupil.)

READINESS

adjectives

dreary; extreme; stubborn; belligerent; astonishing; sulky; useful; disconcerting.

READING

adjectives

essential; constructive; fascinating; stimulating; available; up-to-date; quick; intelligent; delightful; laborious; choral; extensive; assiduous; coarse; prodigious; random; absorbing; hurried; entertaining; tedious; monotonous; desultory; required; attentive; surreptitious; promiscuous; flighty; diverting; irregular; dreary; dull; omnivorous.

verbs

assign—; coach in—; comment on—; define —; enjoy—; expound—; improve—; interpret—; recite—; render—; study—; translate—; unfold—; unravel—; wade through —; —acquaints; —delights; —edifies; —entertains; —serves; —yields.

(See story, lesson, interpretation, book.)

READJUSTMENT

adjectives

heroic; fundamental; sharp; comprehensive; difficult.

verbs

advocate—; demand—; effect—; intensify —; measure—; necessitate—; undergo—; —accommodates; —adapts; —balances; —copes with; —countervails; —equalizes; —evens; —levels; —matches; —poises; —restores; —satisfies; —trims.

(See change, adjustment.)

READY

adverbs

resolutely; instantly; finally; recently; altogether; promptly; eagerly; intrepidly; warily; vigilantly; alertly; evidently; providently; prudently; painfully; carefully; scrupulously; always; unfailingly; heroically; gallantly; formidably; fortunately; luckily; opportunely; reasonably; sensibly; practically; almost.

REAL

adverbs
intensely; fantastically; oppressively; tangibly; vividly; mercilessly; horribly; dangerously; vitally; painfully; starkly; solidly; hideously; grossly; crudely; temporally; mundanely; appallingly; hauntingly; monotonously; ponderously; eternally; sordidly; inexorably; basically; sternly; terribly; gloriously; glamorously; crassly; crudely; humanly; demonstrably; substantially; graphically; stubbornly.

REALISM

adjectives
wounding; decadent; gripping; graphic; unflinching; pure; gross; unshrinking; unpitying; surprising; lifelike; nauseating; inartistic; crude; bare.

verbs
advocate—; compromise—; conform to—; delve into—; dip into—; establish—; examine—; imbibe—; practise—; touch—; transcend—; composes—; —divests; —enthrones itself; —portrays.
(See science, philosophy, psychology, reality, art.)

REALIST

adjectives
destitute; uncompromising; sumptuous; selective; skilled.

REALISTIC

adverbs
dramatically; spectacularly; utterly; unusually; undeniably; distinctly; admirably; notoriously; commendably; surprisingly; unexpectedly; astonishingly; intensely; vividly; mysteriously; incredibly; mercilessly; dangerously; beautifully; delightfully; happily; entertainingly; interestingly; unsurpassably; incomparably; faithfully; startlingly; appallingly.

REALITY

adjectives
grim; sordid; intense; fantastic; naked; oppressive; tangible; passionate; beneficient; clamant; vivid; living; ideal; typical; blunt; mysterious; infinite; waking; existing; sober; practical; elusive; commonplace; accidental; fearful; unfathomable; clear; conceived; spiritual; concrete; exacting; vulgar; fictitious; specific; merciless; peremptory; subtle; nautical; glassy; horrid; stern; dangerous; vital; painful; stark; solid; gloomy; beneficent.

verbs
bear—; convey—; deal with—; descend to —; divorce from—; endure—; enslave to —; escape—; evade—; face—; flee from—; gain—; gloss over—; grasp for—; ground on—; obscure—; pursue—; question—; return to—; spare—; varnish—; wrap in—.
(See realism.)

REALIZATION

adjectives
hideous; evident; uninterrupted; vivid; devotional; bitter; dawning; living; piteous; stabbing; poseful; shocking; exact; eternal; dark.

verbs
achieve—; anticipate—; attain—; demand —; effect—; fancy—; jar into—; jolt into —; labor under—; register—; strive for—; struggle for—; —completes; —crowns; —dawns; —dazes; —discharges; —fulfills; —grows upon; —perfects; —strikes; —stuns.
(See effect, fulfillment.)

REALIZE (*v*)

adverbs
sickeningly; nervously; instinctively; emphatically; dimly; speedily; vividly; vaguely; faintly; gloriously; partially; feebly; happily; piteously; stabbingly; shockingly.
(See achieve, complete.)

REALM

adjectives
sterile; populous; empty; untrodden; mysterious; free; rival; sleepy; blissful; boundless; wealthy; sunnier; historic; airy; glorious; unsubstantial; masculine; interminable; intellectual; famous; impenetrable; ancient; loftier; starry; flowery; shuddering; conquered; unproductive; capricious; captivating.

verbs
conquer—; command—; control—; dominate —; dwell in—; explore—; govern—; inhabit

—; invade—; locate—; master—; misrule —; occupy—; overrun—; preside over—; seize—; sway—; visit—.
(See kingdom, region, province.)

REAP (v)

adverbs
meritoriously; vigorously; seasonally; happily; gratefully; handsomely; rightfully.
(See gather, collect.)

REAR

verbs
bring up—; construct—; dog—; guard—; join—; lay—; —closes; —concludes; —determines; —ends; —finishes; —follows; —lags; —nullifies; —shadows; —skirts; —terminates; —trails; —treads.
(See front, back.)

REAR (v)

adverbs
viciously; dangerously; skittishly; wildly; blindly; capriciously; materially; domestically; shelteredly; innocently.
(See raise, elevate.)

REARMAMENT

verbs
advocate—; condemn—; demand—; forbid —; hinder—; limit—; permit—; plan—; question—; reduce—; refuse—; repress—; request—; restrain—; restrict—; sanction —; —abuses; —agitates; —brews; —despairs; —endangers; —incenses; —protects.
(See armament.)

REASON (general)

adjectives
sensible; valid; potent; indignant; individual; sufficient; sentimental; unshackled; imperceptible; legal; intelligent; physical; holy; sound; artistic; abundant; mere; naked; alleged; supposed; cogent; religious; punitive; exquisite; abstract; shattered; intangible; weighty; passive; mournful; root; indisputable; ostensible; aesthetic; public; human; satirical; unknown; contradicting; inclusive; cold; improbable; crying; philosophic; prosaic; irresistible; calm; special; prudential; earthly; sovereign; obscure; honest; sharp; convincing; sententious; fundamental; liberal; impossible; precise; obvious; justifying; mysterious; firm; foremost; dawning; immense; powerful; natural; plain; unconscious; manly; hampering; insufficient; overwhelming; carnal; indefinable; inexplicable; righteous; cool; immortal; definite; odious; respectable; trivial; weightiest; evident; hollow; inscrutable; sober; apparent; occult; willful; eternal; bright; pure; practical; benevolent; painful; plausible; logical; absurd; conceivable; organic; pompous; ethnological; inexperienced; unselfish; patent; specious; ultimate; pressing; simple; palpable.

REASON (grounds, argument, etc.)

verbs
adduce—; advance—; analyze—; assign—for; bolster—; cite—s; conceal—; convey—; cook up—; debate—; discern—; draw—from; elicit—; evidence—; feign—; omit—; outline—s; overstep—; summarize—; —explains; —looms; —motivates; —underlies.
(See excuse, grounds, cause.)

REASON (intellectual, faculty, common-sense, logic)

verbs
appeal to—; base on—; derange—; employ —; evince—; impregnate with—; invoke—; supplant—; —crumbles; —determines; —dictates; —impels; —ordains; —prevails; —totters; —wanders; —yields to.
(See logic, intellect, sense, sanity.)

REASON (v)

adverbs
coherently; inconsistently; persuasively; solemnly; dialectically; deductively; logically; ridiculously; deviously; ineffectually; intelligently; circuitously; validly; sentimentally; cogently; prosaically; sententiously; plausibly; speciously.
(See argue, debate.)

REASONABLE

adverbs
intelligently; philosophically; soundly; academically; intuitively; sensibly; perfectly; psychologically; coldly; fairly; cosmically; inferentially; elementally; essentially; profoundly; fundamentally; presumptively; penetratingly; discernibly; contemplatively; doctrinally; spiritually; theologically; ideologically; speculatively; consciously; soberly; spaciously; logically; persuasively; convincingly; conclusively.

REASONER

adjectives
accurate; habitual; profound; lawless; admirable; acute; careful; painstaking; deft; clever.

REASONING

adjectives
seductive; sober; secular; immethodized; speculative; unstable; judicial; vicious; hypothetical; inductive; erroneous; stern; calm; infantile; physiological; precocious; scientific; deliberate; sustained; fallacious; syllogistic; abstract; explicit; conclusive; logical.

REASSURANCE

adjectives
peaceful; hopeful; tremendous; slender.

REASSURING

adverbs
completely; comfortingly; genially; judicially; gravely; amiably; wisely; pleasantly; indulgently; graciously;. smpathetically; understandingly; encouragingly; helpfully; hopefully; optimistically; considerately; affectionately; warmly; hospitably; pleasantly; mildly; earnestly; enthusiastically; confidently; definitely; distinctly.

REBEL (*v*)

adverbs
vindictively; heartily; hatefully; intellectually; patriotically; desperately; blindly; abortively; mutely; hopelessly; technically.
(See revolt, defy, resist.)

REBELLION

adjectives
technical; appeasing; incipient; perpetual; gigantic; extensive; righteous; seething; violent; open; unqualified; hurt; blind; abortive; memorable; vain; mute; persistent; universal; manifest; hopeless; futile.

verbs
abet—; confine—; finance—; fire—; foment —; incite to—; intensify—; liquidate—; plan—; plot—; plunge into—; quash—; quell—; repress—; restrain—; set down—; threaten with—; uncover—; verge on—; —breaks out; —perishes; —seethes; —stirs; —undermines.
(See insurrection, mutiny, revolution.)

REBELLIOUS

adverbs
sullenly; doggedly; drearily; unhappily; bitterly; incorrigibly; incurably; unmanageably; sadly; justly; rightfully; intelligently; sensibly; wildly; cruelly; insensately; furiously; violently; uncontrollably; cantankerously; atrociously; detestably; unreasonably; justifiably; naturally; woefully; stubbornly; obstinately; desperately; dangerously; ominously; unfortunately; unluckily; unwisely; finally; instantly; resentfully; angrily; secretly; quietly.

REBELS

adjectives
intellectual; patriotic; incorrigible; vile; contending; repentant; desperate.

verbs
exile—; punish—; restrict—; silence—; —arise; —arm; —betray; —conspire; —corrupt; —defy; —infringe upon; —intrigue; —mutiny; —plot; —resist; —strike; —violate; —withdraw.
(See insurgents, opponent.)

REBUFF

adjectives
unforeseen; stupid; rude; unsympathetic; studied; complete; deserved.

verbs
cower before—; impel—; incur—; render —; resist—; sense—; smart under—; undergo—; withhold—; —chills; —crushes; —cuts; —insults; —jostles; —raps; —reviles; —revolts; —scandalizes; —shocks; —slaps; —smarts; —snubs.
(See insult, defeat, rebuke, refusal.)

REBUFF (*v*)

adverbs
superciliously; sneeringly; rudely; aristocratically; impertinently; proudly; vindictively.
(See resist, repulse, repel.)

REBUFFED

adverbs
definitely; unreasonably; distinctly; neatly; saucily; arrogantly; needlessly; unwarrantably; insolently; impudently; impertinently; unnecessarily; undeservedly; unaccountably; startlingly; surprisingly; properly; deservedly; properly; politely; adroitly; in-

geniously; subtly; disconcertingly; promptly; urbanely; suavely; uncivilly; unceremoniously; sharply; definitely; officially; blandly.

REBUILD (*v*)

adverbs
patiently; vigorously; hopefully; courageously; repeatedly; gloriously; imitatively.
(See build, repair.)

REBUKE

adjectives
pertinent; merited; grave; whispered; sour; stinging; artless; delicate; savage; frightened; stern; uncompromising; paternal; dignified; proud; smart; standing; sulphurous; scornful; sad; promptest.

verbs
administer—; endure—; imply—; offset—; submit to—; suffer—; thrust—at; —abashes; —corrects; —disconcerts; —hurts; —maddens; —silences.
(See rebuff, reprimand, ridicule.)

REBUKE (*v*)

adverbs
indignantly; priggishly; sternly; pertinently; gravely; stingingly; paternally; sulphurously; scornfully; briskly; curtly; cuttingly; incisively.
(See admonish, censure, reprove.)

REBUKED

adverbs
sternly; harshly; unreasonably; unaccountably; undeservedly; constantly; recently; saucily; officially; seriously; gravely; ominously; publicly; openly; quietly; deservedly; properly; naturally; necessarily; woefully; rudely; ungraciously; unwarrantably; unjustly; cruelly; wantonly; subtly; loudly; furiously; brusquely; bluntly; rudely; unforgivably; unforgettably.

RECALCITRANT

adverbs
cantankerously; habitually; always; disagreeably; unpleasantly; offensively; politically; obnoxiously; detestably; despicably; unfailingly; obstinately; stubbornly; unreasonably; unaccountably; naturally; stupidly; boorishly; doggedly; singularly; peculiarly; presumptiously; bumptiously.

RECALL (*v*)

adverbs
vividly; affectionately; palpably; momentarily; distinctively; perpetually; bitterly; vaguely; greedily; idly; passionately.
(See annul, retract.)

RECEIVE (*v*)

adverbs
courteously; precisely; graciously; affably; reluctantly; hospitably; opportunely; glowingly; morosely; willingly; scornfully; consciously; mournfully; credulously; gratuitously; supinely; indiscriminately; haughtily; cordially; royally; ceremoniously; frostily.
(See accept, take.)

RECEIVERSHIP

verbs
accept—; anticipate—; avoid—; demand—; enter into—; fall into—; grant—; lapse into—; repel—; resist—; save from—; succor from—; verge on—; —embarrasses; —safeguards; —satisfies; —terminates.
(See bankruptcy.)

RECEPTACLE

adjectives
sacred; unsightly; unworthy; hideous; secret; hidden.

RECEPTION

adjectives
unfriendly; sumptuous; canine; flattering; popular; suitable; favorable; enthusiastic; affectionate; honorable; courteous; critical; problematical; ceremonious; unprejudiced; instant; general; cordial; wonderful; traditional; frosty; grand; stormy; official; magnificent; bloody; court; extraordinary; welcome; royal; friendly; sympathetic; hospitable; tame; sullen.

RECEPTIVE

adverbs
intelligently; astonishingly; brilliantly; attentively; eagerly; ardently; gratefully; thankfully; utterly; actively; pleasantly; helpfully; sharply; keenly; particularly.

RECESS

adjectives
fathomless; remotest; dark; dim; glowing; tangled; innermost; profound; various (pl); mystic; grassy; appalling; cool; capacious; intimate; little-known; soul-haunting; shy; shady.

verbs
deny—; enjoy—; grant—; lull in—; prescribe—; suggest—; welcome—; —affords; —allays; —disburdens; —dispels; —eases; —refreshes; —relaxes; —relieves; —revivifies; —vents.
(See rest, vacation, pause.)

RECESSION

adjectives
financial; business; widespread; nationwide; gripping.

RECIPE

verbs
adhere to—; attempt—; clip—; commend—; devise—; follow—; interpret—; necessitate —; refer to—; scan—; seek—; study—; —acquaints; —eases; —edifies; —enlightens; —guides; —informs; —prevents; —satisfies; —suggests.
(See formula, method.)

RECIPROCAL

adverbs
agreeably; pleasantly; accommodatingly; publicly; readily; systematically; contractually; interchangeably; helpfully; sympathetically; openly; reluctantly; eagerly; proportionally; satisfactorily; conveniently; advantageously; profitably.

RECITAL

adjectives
bolting; warm; light; summary; amusing; quaint; dejected; tedious; dispassionate; instructive.

verbs
narrate—; rehearse—; render—; sum up—; unfold—; —edifies; —enchants; —enlightens; —enthralls; —entrances; —inspires; —pictures; —portrays; —recounts; —relates; —unravels.
(See performance, concert, speech, poem.)

RECITATIVE

adverbs
crooningly; endlessly; effectively; monotonously; raucously; huskily; dully; unmelodiously; comically; hilariously; clownishly; curiously; dramatically; melodiously; rhythmically; qauintly; dramatically; incomparably; strangely; pleasantly.

RECITE (*v*)

adverbs
drolly; faithfully; feelingly; passionately; ardently; quaintly; instructively; repetitiously; monotonously; drearily.
(See relate, repeat.)

RECKLESS

adverbs
desperately; daringly; audaciously; blithely; merrily; hilariously; bitterly; cruelly; inconsiderately; thoughtlessly; heedlessly; deliberately; optimistically; wickedly; disconcertingly; improvidently; extravagantly; exceedingly; fantastically; outlandishly; outrageously; grotesquely; ostentatiously; spectacularly; dramatically; wildly; indiscreetly; financially; commercially; politically; personally; inexcusably; insensately; angrily; furiously; jealously; pitiably.

RECKLESSNESS

adjectives
wanton; stubborn; unfelt; lavish; uncalculating; staid; fastidious; daring; fatal; gallant.

verbs
admonish—; protest—; repent—; rue—; tempt—; tolerate—; warn against—; —destroys; —endangers; —exposes to; —ignores; —irritates; —provokes; —risks; —suffers; —ventures; —wrecks.
(See audacity, indiscretion.)

RECKONING

adjectives
annual; lunar; dreadful; final; false; dead; swift.

verbs
confuse—; demand—; discharge—; discount—; estimate—; ignore—; probe—; value—; weed out of—; —accounts for; —acquits; —balances; —clarifies; —dishonors; —fathoms; —nullifies; —repays.
(See account, computation, calculation, consideration.)

RECLINE (*v*)

adverbs
lazily; somnolently; cozily; comfortably; swinishly; calmly; artlessly; unambitiously.
(See rest, relax.)

RECLUSE

adjectives
literary; curious; poetical; sanctified; churlish; venerable; staid.

RECOGNITION

adjectives
abbreviated; instant; reverent; warmest; rigid; deserved; continuous; momentary; enforced; long-awaited; critical; unbroken; increasing; welcome; cold; unmistakable; faint; intelligent; courteous; legislative; mutual; dismayed; admiring; tacit; grateful; orderly; affectionate; public; sole; formal; emphatic; full; familiar; premature; clouded; flattering; hard-won.

verbs
accord—; alter beyond—; arouse—; concede—; confer—; demand—; evade—; escape—; extend—; gain—; lose—; merit—; permit—; prompt—; receive—; refuse—; struggle for—; suggest—; win—; —confirms; —corroborates; —recalls.
(See fame, greatness, position.)

RECOGNIZABLE

adverbs
easily; readily; distinctly; unfailingly; instantly; unmistakably; singularly; manifestly; memorably; unforgettably; peculiarly; particularly; positively; transparently; conspicuously; glaringly; unconcealably; strikingly; remarkably.

RECOGNIZE (v)

adverbs
distinctly; instinctively; definitely; universally; formally; frankly; deservedly; coldly; courteously; mutually; affectionately; tacitly; formally; publicly; prematurely.
(See distinguish, acknowledge.)

RECOIL

adjectives
vicious; impetuous; silent; tardy; nervous.

RECOIL (v)

adverbs
instinctively; involuntarily; modestly; impatiently; impetuously; nervously; abruptly; abnormally; tremblingly.
(See react, shrink.)

RECOLLECT (v)

adverbs
agreeably; humiliatingly; delightfully; hatefully; gratefully; remorsefully; vaguely; uneasily; romantically; painfully; affectionately.
(See remember, recall.)

RECOLLECTION

adjectives
nightmare; agreeable; humiliating; delightful; grateful; hateful; glorious; contemptuous; dark; stern; remorseful; vanished; importunate; dim; vague; sweet; eternal; uneasy; romantic; sudden; simultaneous; humbling; distinct; melancholy; painful; accurate; faithful; perfect; tangled; livelier; pleasant; dormant; vivid; hazy; blissful; ungracious; cloudy; affectionate.

verbs
attempt—; betray—; crowd—s; drown—; escape—; evade—; hallow—; hinder—; obliterate—; prompt—; seek—; shudder at —; sink into—; stimulate—; stir—; suggest —; urge—; verify—; —dawns; —dims; —fades; —refreshes.
(See memory, remembrance, reminiscence.)

RECOMMEND (v)

adverbs
conscientiously; respectfully; unreservedly; cordially; urgently; expressly; unanimously; confidently; unhesitatingly; vigorously; earnestly; aptly; eloquently; subtly; emphatically; consistently.
(See suggest, commend, praise.)

RECOMMENDATION

adjectives
definite; additional; nimble; sweet; subtle; novel; emphatic; hesitating; sound; impolitic; consistent.

verbs
carry out—; confer—; consult—; demand—; gain—; glean—s; incorporate—s; offer—; sketch—s; —advises; —advocates; —favors; —flatters; —glows; —impresses; —informs; —refers to; —reports; —suggests.
(See commendation, approval, approbation, reference.)

RECOMMENDED

adverbs
highly; enthusiastically; favorably; well; exceptionally; unconditionally; earnestly;

justly; readily; acceptably; thoughtfully; unreservedly; strongly; eminently; explicitly; expressly.

RECOMPENSE

adjectives

godlike; solid; immortal; earnest; noblest; friendly; generous; exciting; abundant; insufficient; scant.

RECONCILABLE

adverbs

easily; readily; scarcely; hardly; wholly; partially; entirely; logically; reasonably; sensibly; naturally; fortunately; pleasantly; amiably; generously; amicably; fortunately; consistently.

RECONCILE (*v*)

adverbs

peremptorily; briefly; conveniently; permanently; forgivingly; touchingly; dramatically; logically; philosophically.

(See adjust, settle.)

RECONCILIATION

adjectives

perfect; convenient; short-lived; sweet; lasting; generous; forgiving.

verbs

arrange—; declare—; draw—; effect—; exact—; gain—; refuse—; seek—; —allays; —appeases; —heals; —hushes; —pacifies; —placates; —renews; —restores; —settles; —smooths; —squares.

(See conciliation, peace, reunion.)

RECONDITION (*v*)

adverbs

efficiently; professionally; thoroughly; permanently; periodically.

(See renew, repair.)

RECONNOITRE (*v*)

adverbs

audaciously; slyly; dutifully; courageously; cautiously; brazenly.

(See examine, inspect.)

RECONSIDER (*v*)

adverbs

hastily; subsequently; consequentially; meditatively; contemplatively; reflectively; serenely.

(See review, contemplate.)

RECONSTRUCTION

adjectives

orderly; benign; inartistic; voluntary.

verbs

advise— facilitate—; necessitate—; retard—; —converts; —corrects; —cures; —heals; —recoups; —rectifies; —redresses; —refreshes; —reinforces; —rights.

(See repairs, improvement, change.)

RECORD

adjectives

attainable; successful; enviable; reliable; long; indispensable; unsavory; scriptural; manifold (pl); authenticated; mystical; honorable; engrossed; splendid; imperfect; woeful; forlorn; formless; faithful; creditable; distinguished; chronological; continuous; vivid; subtlest; illustrious; unapproachable; earliest; historic; stenographic; boasted; bristling; erroneous; lingering; shameful; surprising; trivial; fond; illustrated; contemporary; parliamentary; voluminous; damning; priceless; definite; terse; cold; literal; comparable; accurate; individual; progressive; glorious; formal; lasting; tabulated; valuable; supernatural; available; confessed; trustworthy; indelible; notarial; pathetic; dumb; accumulated; aggregated; official; flawless; unpretending; artistic; clinical; imperishable; enthralling; factual; romantic; commendable; tragic; exemplary; phenomenal; heraldic.

verbs

achieve—; afford—; assemble—s; best—; blast—; bolster—; catalogue—s; compare—s; compile—s; delve into—s; divulge—; establish—; filch from—s; hang up—; illuminate—; inscribe—; live up to—; obliterate—; pound out—; pore over—s; probe—s; produce—; top—s; —s set forth; —s vary.

(See chronicle, archives, list, reputation.)

RECORD (*v*)

adverbs

faithfully; accurately; precisely; amusingly; regularly; minutely; authentically; industriously; impassively; uninterruptedly; scripturally; mystically; creditably; chronologically; vividly; subtly; historically; graphically; trivially; voluminously; literally; formally; flawlessly; clinically; factually; commendably; phenomenally.

(See note, reserve.)

RECORDED

adverbs

duly; accurately; carefully; meticulously; indelibly; graphically; intricately; officially; memorably; secretly; punctiliously; promptly; instantly; immediately; beautifully; realistically; photostatically; precisely; faithfully; legally; methodically; systematically; lovingly; vividly; completely.

RECOVER (*v*)

adverbs

mechanically; sufficiently; extraordinarily; miraculously; swiftly; speedily; tardily; moderately; fortunately; gradually; spectacularly; normally.

(See repair, restore.)

RECOVERY

adjectives

slow; gradual; rapid; ultimate; languid; spontaneous; happy; noble; spectacular; permanent; extraordinary; receding.

verbs

anticipate—; attribute—to; effect—; envisage—; expedite—; facilitate—; fumble with—; hasten—; hinder—; impede—; insure—; jeopardize—; promote—; retard—; speed—; stimulate—; —cheers; —ensues; —follows.

(See improvement, convalescence, restoration.)

RECREANT

adverbs

detestably; incredibly; shamefully; grossly; meanly; stubbornly; disgracefully; blasphemously; fearfully; infirmly; infamously; tortuously; insidiously; ignominiously; knavishly; unworthily; gracelessly; irreclaimably; unconscionably; basely.

RECREATION

adjectives

stimulating; intellectual; sweet; healthful; inexpensive; joyous; subsidiary; luxurious; innocent; solitary; wholesome; mutual; constructive.

verbs

arrange—; enjoy—; indulge in—; plan—; provide for—; seek—; —amuses; —beguiles; —bores; —cheers; —diverts; —drags; —enlivens; —entertains; —palls; —relaxes; —revivifies; —tires; —wearies.

(See game, entertainment, jollity, diversion, amusement.)

RECRIMINATION

adjectives

mutual; bitter; incessant; cruel; repeated (pl).

RECRUDESCENT

adverbs

fortunately; surprisingly; advantageously; profitably; startlingly; strangely; luckily; opportunely; periodically; conveniently; fortuitously; resurgently; providentially; blessedly.

RECRUIT (*v*)

adverbs

intelligently; forcefully; faithfully; mainly; militaristically; martially; haphazardly.

(See furnish, raise.)

RECRUITS

adjectives

clownish; manifold; raw; unwilling; well-drilled; flustered; trustworthy; intelligent; unarmed; discouraged.

verbs

attract—; contribute—; furnish—; initiate—; lure—; tempt—; —advance; —assist; —attend; —brace; —cheer; —expedite; —fortify; —prop; —protect; —reenforce; —rescue; —steel; —sustain; —vivify.

(See volunteers, soldier.)

RECTITUDE

adjectives

extreme; utter; absolute; conscious; primeval; aesthetic; strict; self-styled.

RECTOR

adjectives

lisping; stern; devout; earnest; pious.

verbs

consult—; support—; unfrock—; —administers; —admonishes; —announces; —conducts; —crusades; —directs; —governs; —guides; —ministers; —orates; —preaches; —prepares; —prescribes; —presides; —supervises.

(See minister.)

RECTUM

verbs
abscess—; act on—; cleanse—; dilate—; distend—; flush—; inflame—; inject into—; irritate—; plug—; purge—; support—; terminate in—; trouble—; —extends.
(See bowels.)

RECUPERATE (*v*)

adverbs
expectedly; normally; beneficently; placidly; markedly; tardily; extendedly; passively; entirely.
(See rally, improve.)

RECUPERATIVE

adverbs
highly; strongly; vigorously; happily; fortunately; wholesomely; healthfully; sturdily; slowly; steadily; quietly; incredibly; luckily; carefully; successfully; patiently; resolutely; calmly; undeniably.

RECUR (*v*)

adverbs
successively; intermittently; constantly; insanely; sporadically; unexpectedly; infrequently; abruptly; irritatingly; explosively.
(See return, restore.)

RECURRENCE

adjectives
infrequent; delicate; sweet; constant; emphatic; intermittent; noisy; angry.

verbs
anticipate—; endure—; insure against—; prepare for—; suffer—; survive—; —bores; —drums; —redoubles; —refreshes; —renews; —resumes; —revolves; —rings; —shocks; —surprises; —wearies.
(See frequency, occurrence, repetition.)

RED

adjectives
deep; bloody; hectic; ruby; flamingo; latest; blazing; shimmering; livid; angry; tuneful; vivid; cochineal; unnatural; bright; orange; gleaming; rich; velvety; rosy; lifeless; brightish; monochromatic; fiery; gaudy; eye-closing; garish.

REDDEN (*v*)

adverbs
hotly; coyly; blushingly; shyly; modestly; timidly; enthusiastically; visibly; furiously; feverishly; indignantly.
(See flush, blush.)

REDEEM (*v*)

adverbs
ultimately; promptly; spiritually; subsequently; everlastingly; honorably; faithfully.
(See recover, rescue.)

REDEEMABLE

adverbs
currently; locally; immediately; fortunately; conveniently; profitably; undoubtedly; warrantably; fairly; easily; proportionally; lucratively; admissibly; unquestionably; legally; definitely; contractually; readily.

REDEMPTION

adjectives
ultimate; everlasting; foul; prompt; subsequent; spiritual; complete.

REDNESS

adjectives
shimmering; dewy; startling; rheumy.

REDOLENT

adverbs
pungently; spicily; sweetly; fragrantly; deliciously; delightfully; pleasantly; aromatically; refreshingly; suggestively; woodsily; surprisingly; lingeringly; strongly; highly; uncommonly.

REDRESS

adjectives
adequate; instant; warlike; immediate.

REDS
(communists)

verbs
support—; suppress—; —advocate; —agitate; —aggravate; —band; —forfeit; —idealize; —inflame; —instigate; —invade; —pillage; —plot; —promise; —resist; —revolt; —riot; —strike; —undermine.
(See communist, anarchist.)

REDUCE (*v*)

adverbs
materially; sharply; correspondingly; emphatically; deliberately; necessarily; rigorously; substantially; markedly; radically; drastically.
(See diminish, lower.)

REDUCTION

adjectives
substantial; successive (pl); inexplicable; tremendous; marked; enormous; proper; radical; honest; ample; drastic; smashing; equitable; perpetual; scant.

REED

adjectives
jungle; pastoral; balmy; stiff; solacing; bruised; swampy; bending; unsustaining; plaited; vocal; whispering; silvery.

REEF

adjectives
submerged; hidden; sunken; encircling; subterranean; lisping; bluff; leering; scowling; frowning; darkling; dangerous; black-browed.

verbs
avoid—; cast upon—; drift to—; drive upon—; doom to—; founder on—; lash—; pound—; shatter on—s; thunder on—; —descends; —extends; —menaces; —ranges; —stretches; —threatens.
(See beach, rocks, shore.)

REEK (*v*)

adverbs
foully; alcoholically; vilely; powerfully; nauseatingly; disgustingly.
(See smoke, smell.)

REEL (*v*)

adverbs
visibly; weakly; drunkenly; dizzily; abruptly; sickeningly; swayingly.
(See stagger, sway.)

REFER (*v*)

adverbs
sarcastically; ironically; indelicately; pointedly; caustically; vaguely; satirically; unequivocally; sneeringly; sagaciously; affectionately; cursorily; contemptuously; pertinently; hilariously; obscurely; vaguely.
(See allude, hint, intimate.)

REFERENCE

adjectives
contemptuous; satisfying; constant; complimentary; barren; innumerable (pl); pathetic; pertinent; bibliographical; polite; solitary; never-ending; unmistakable; figurative; hilarious; documentary; mutual; offhand; obscure; touching; specific; sudden; sly; gratifying; vague; slighting.

verbs
avoid—to; demand—s; furnish—s; heed—; request—s; seek—s; vouchsafe—s; weigh—s; —compliments: —concerns; —counsels; —flatters; —instructs; —justifies; —mentions; —pertains to; —prescribes; —relates to; —satisfies; —suggests; —warns.
(See allusion, recommendation, mention, hint, record.)

REFINEMENT

adjectives
vital; technical; conscious; artistic; subtle; structural; utmost; high; intellectual; fresh; inventive; studied; nameless; classic; elaborate; sophistical; characteristic; delicate; accentuated; expert; exquisite; distilled; soft; false; incidental.

verbs
cultivate—; discern—; infuse—; profit by—; touch with—; weigh—; —ameliorates; —discriminates; —distinguishes; —enhances; —enriches; —graces; —improves; —mellows; —mitigates; —polishes; —promotes; —sifts.
(See elegance, civilization, refinement, culture.)

REFLECT (*v*)

adverbs
calmly; meditatively; sparklingly; contemplatively; cannily; piously; pensively; moodily: morbidly; somberly; grimly; opportunely; serenely; ingenuously; cynically; bitterly; miserably; delicately; philosophically; coherently; candidly; logically.
(See mirror, revert.)

REFLECTION

adjectives
delicate; vivid; surface; opposite; dreadful; somber; sagacious; gloomy; grave; unpleasant; sobering; impersonal; colorless; mature; injurious; sage; passionate; solemn; admirable; unbroken; wicked; judicious; interesting; cheering; dazzling; rusty; satirical; rich; best; philosophic; melancholy; bitter; careful; subtle; calm; unconscious; dim; perturbed; mortifying; unquiet; dancing; rosy; perplexing; drowsy; powerful; spectral; shortest; profound; brooding; dis-

tracting; nostalgic; silvery; recurring; homely; disagreeable; agitating; adequate; philosophical; coherent; assuring; heart-shaking; candid; prosaic; continuous; harrowing; disturbing; splendid; logical.

verbs
absorb in—; air—; bolster by—; bury in—; console with—; emerge from—; feign—; immerse in—; sustain by—; veil in—; wrap in—; —calms; —convinces; —flatters; —mirrors.
(See consideration, contemplation, image, study, meditation.)

REFLECTIVE

adverbs
philosophically; lazily; idly; pensively; wistfully; actively; alertly; keenly; gravely; seriously; earnestly; studiously; deeply; profoundly; aimlessly; restfully; quietly; calmly; serenely; gloomily; pessimistically; sadly; happily; pleasantly; peacefully; unwontedly; habitually.

REFORM

adjectives
obstinate; headlong; subsequent; constitutional; valuable; great; liberal; beneficent; mimetic; effectual; important; educational; ideological; dietary; phonetic; baronial; simultaneous; rigid; radical; feverish; temperance; energetic; imposed; rational.

verbs
adapt to—; adopt—; advocate—; approve—; deal with—; dramatize—; effect—; enforce—; facilitate—; formulate—; initiate—; institute—; labor for—; overemphasize—; proffer—; propose—; stalemate—; —overtakes; —slogs along; —surges over.
(See improvement, change, amendment.)

REFORM (*v*)

adverbs
speedily; constitutionally; beneficently; educationally; ideologically; radically; temperately; energetically; rationally.
(See convert, change.)

REFORMER

adjectives
hardy; prison; ardent; pugnacious; theoretical; phonetic; joy-killing; meretricious; disorderly; impetuous; respectable; temperance.

verbs
—advocates; —ameliorates; —betters; —corrects; —cultivates; —directs; —doctors; —eases; —foists upon; —fosters; —mends; —prates; —promotes; —purifies; —rants; —relieves; —remedies; —reorganizes; —repairs.
(See apostle, minister.)

REFRACTORY

adverbs
hopelessly; uncommonly; highly; remarkably; incredibly; incomparably; unmanageably; stubbornly; doggedly; mulishly; obstinately; obdurately; contumaciously; naturally; incorrigibly; desperately; uncontrollably; stiffly; perversely; disobediently; impertinently; mischievously; vexatiously; intolerably; inscrutably; inexplicably; unreasonably; embarrassingly; atrociously.

REFRAIN

adjectives
everlasting; drear; wild; unmeaning; recurring; plaintive; irreverent; sadder; wearisome; constant; weird.

verbs
chant—; chorus—; drum—; endure—; join in on—; paraphrase—; renew—; resume—; shout—; sing—; —bores; —refreshes; —revolves; —hinges; —rings; —shocks; —surprises; —survives; —tires; —wearies.
(See chorus, melody, verse, song.)

REFRAIN (*v*)

adverbs
prudently; deliberately; purposely; pointedly; sagely; resolutely; cautiously; wisely.
(See restrain, check, curb.)

REFRESH (*v*)

adverbs
deliciously; delectably; periodically; deliberately; potently; seasonally; hospitably.
(See renew, restore, revive.)

REFRESHED

adverbs
delightfully; wholly; unbelievably; completely; permanently; momentarily; temporarily; pleasantly; helpfully; heartily; incredibly; surprisingly; unexpectedly; visibly; noticeably; evidently; marvelously; miraculously; curiously; mysteriously; highly; amazingly; deeply; profoundly; unmistakably.

REFRESHING

adverbs
healthfully; wholesomely; thoughtfully; delightfully; pleasantly; interestingly; surprisingly; strikingly; gloriously; vigorously; restfully; peacefully; quietly; extremely; deliciously; coolly; comfortably; graciously; keenly; hospitably; invigoratingly; sharply; simply; wholly.

REFRESHMENTS

adjectives
delicate; potent; invigorating; apparent; elaborate; suitable; cool; nightcap; delicious; edible; smoky; surprising; delectable.

verbs
afford—; gorge on—; relish—; —appeal; —appease; —cheer; —comfort; —console; —delight; —invigorate; —quench; —repair; —restore; —revive; —sate; —stimulate.
(See food, luncheon.)

REFUGE

adjectives
hunted; walled; sheltered; flimsy; comforting; grateful; soothing; time-honored; secret; unavailing; temporary; modest; blessed; permanent.

verbs
abandon—; afford—; erect—; establish—; find—; grant—; hide in—; offer—; provide—; seek—; threaten—; uncover—; yield—; —assures; —comforts; —conceals; —defends; —preserves; —protects; —secures; —shelters; —shrouds.
(See shelter, protection, lodging, haven, nest, home.)

REFUGEE

adjectives
repatriating; testy; penniless; favorite; sick; unwelcome.

verbs
aid—; harbor—; overtake—; prosecute—; pursue—; search for—; shelter—; succor—; —s abandon; —absconds; —departs; —eludes; —endeavors; —escapes; —evades; —flees; —migrates; —s pour into; —s retreat; —trudges.
(See prisoner, criminal, fugitive.)

REFUSAL

adjectives
frightened; explicit; peremptory; persistent; periodic; positive; obstinate; varied; resolute; decided; energetic; melodramatic; kind; courteous; flat; gracious; contemptuous.

verbs
confront with—; consider—; ignore—; incur—; issue—; rehearse—; —contravenes; —declines; —denies; —depresses; —irks; —nullifies; —oppresses; —rebuffs; —revokes; —saddens; —squelches; —stays; —suppresses.
(See denial, dissent, rebuff, repulse.)

REFUSE (v)

adverbs
curtly; tacitly; mutinously; courteously; obdurately; scornfully; sternly; doggedly; positively; arbitrarily; inexorably; austerely; snobbishly; flatly; emphatically; sullenly; steadfastly; scrupulously; peremptorily; indignantly; spitefully; prudently; persistently; contumaciously; vehemently; delicately; unequivocally; haughtily; honorably; characteristically; invariably; habitually; graciously.
(See deny, repulse.)

REFUTATION

adjectives
serious; violent; sincere; practical; labored; complete; adequate.

REFUTE (v)

adverbs
undeniably; indisputably; violently; completely; adequately; laboredly; spectacularly; rudely.
(See question.)

REGAL

adverbs
gloriously; grandly; majestically; brilliantly; gorgeously; splendidly; magnificently; sumptuously; ceremonially; ceremoniously; processionally; incredibly; pompously; proudly; superbly; appropriately; suitably; marvelously; incomparably; unsurpassably; uncommonly; resplendently; eminently; consummately; mightily; imposingly; impressively; richly.

REGALE (v)

adverbs
pleasingly; boisterously; affluently; conviv-

ially; ostentatiously; hospitably; sumptuously; joyously; fraternally.
(See entertain, feast, gratify.)

REGARD

adjectives
cordial; affectionate; cold; platonic; reverential; eloquent; glorious; general; rueful; intense; delicate; mutual; prudential; due; profound; deepening; repulsive; wearisome; scrupulous; conscientious; sagacious; unalterable; popular; infantine; undue; deep; heartiest; faint; austere; pure; candid; tender; habitual; indispensable; religious; charitable; critical; decorous; slightest; deliberate.

verbs
acquire—; bear—; command—; entertain—; feign—; gain—; inspire—; observe with—; recognize—; relax—; signalize—; solicit—; win—; —arises from; —distinguishes; —flatters; —glorifies; —honors; —outshadows; —shines.
(See favor, esteem, deference, attention.)

REGARD (v)

adverbs
contemptuously; patiently; affectionately; passionately; ruthlessly; lewdly; practically; fondly; narrowly; enviously; attentively; pensively; appraisingly; solemnly; severely; pugnaciously; skeptically; vindictively; curiously; hopelessly; maliciously; ruefully; cordially; platonically; reverentially; sagaciously; austerely; candidly; tenderly; religiously; decorously.
(See observe, consider, heed.)

REGARDFUL

adverbs
deferentially; carefully; considerately; graciously; ingratiatingly; respectfully; punctiliously; meticulously; diplomatically; cautiously; vigilantly; warily; shrewdly; keenly; watchfully; mindfully; attentively; highly; profoundly; alertly; courteously; unfailingly.

REGENERATION

adjectives
political; physical; successful; spiritual; remarkable.

REGIME

adjectives
fascist; competitive; acid-neutralizing; sanguinary; scandalous; despotic; complete; dominant; established; totalitarian; royalistic; democratic; memorable; tyrannical.

verbs
abolish—; control—; denounce—; discredit —; enjoy—; encroach on—; establish—; influence—; introduce—; labor under—; overthrow—; relax—; shape—; support—; sway —; tolerate—; —alters; —dictates; —exercises; —overawes; —usurps.
(See reign, rule, government, power.)

REGIMEN

adjectives
better; strict; unruly; careful; systematic.

REGIMENT

adjectives
ragged; red-coated; magnificent; opinionated; various (pl); redoubtable; crack; splendid.

verbs
distribute—; locate—; lodge—; quarter—; —advances; —assembles; —attacks; —concentrates; —disbands; —flocks; —focuses on; —gathers; —overspreads; —pitches; —retreats; —separates; —throngs .
(See brigade, infantry, militia, soldier.)

REGIMENTED

adverbs
overly; bureaucratically; dangerously; hopelessly; strictly; helplessly; terribly; ominously; unconsciously; frankly; unwillingly; insidiously; alarmingly; unsuspectingly; portentously; deliberately; significantly; disastrously; tyrannically; despotically; calamitously.

REGION

adjectives
devastated; tenuous; remote; spiritual; considerable; untraversed; indiscriminate; saturnine; shadowy; equatorial; ugly; raw; dreaded; airy; desolate; dreary; caudal; mountainous; fertile; wild; antique; inland; nobler; ionized; humid; lonely; unfooted; icy; enchanting; dense; inspiring; equinoctial; interesting; grazing; sequestered; burning; afflicted; constellated; empyreal; disputed; mystical; sterile; ravaged; subterranean; celestial; frontal; arid; unknown; reflecting; barbarous; purer; inferior; boundless; embryonic; hospitable; romantic; idyllic; prolific; unexplored; neigh-

boring; condensed; immense; atmospheric; forest; extensive; infernal; crooked; habitable; healthy; industrial; untrod; low; lumbar; cardiac; gloomy; wooded; enchanted; picturesque; blooming; tropical; imperiled; agricultural; rarefied; adjacent; hypogastric; limited; uncultivated; fruitful; exhausted; semibarbarous; lacustrine; insulated; bleak; ill-defined; thrilling.

verbs
bound—; divide—; dominate—; dwell in —; endow—with; evacuate—; fortify—; infest—; inhabit—; invade—; locate in—; mark—; migrate to—; occupy—; rule—; settle in—; skirt—; visit—.
(See field, country, district, locality, valley, plain.)

REGRET

adjectives
pious; undersigned; relentful; idle; unspeakable; fond; tender; contrite; indignant; mingled (pl); continued; passionate; bitter; serious; unmeaning; dead; keenest; constant; deep; hopeless; meek; vain; frantic; proud; repentant; immeasurable; formal; torturing; sweet; sensible; vague; wistful; inextinguishable; immense; sincere; unfeigned; momentary; endless; unhappy; fierce; subsequent; inexpressible; restless; fundamental; maudlin; unequivocal; unavailing.

verbs
accept—s; betoken—; bewail in—; cherish —; convey—s; croak—s; express—; lament —s; offer—s; plague with—s; send—s; —s chafe; —s confuse; —s disappoint; —s disconcert; —s dishearten; —s humiliate; —oppresses; —saddens; —s vex.
(See sorrow, grief, misery.)

REGRET (v)

adverbs
audibly; pitifully; officially; deeply; bitterly; exceedingly; mournfully; piously; fondly; passionately; keenly; vainly; inexpressibly; vaguely; wistfully; maudlinly; unequivocally; unavailingly.
(See deprecate, deplore.)

REGULAR

adverbs
strictly; sternly; horribly; chastely; systematically; methodically; altogether; painfully; strangely; artificially; stiffly; formidably; unnaturally; formally; legally; detestably; beautifully; curiously; perfectly; unnecessarily; conveniently; surprisingly; marvelously.

REGULARITY

adjectives
chronological; vulgar; mechanical; absolute; commonplace; surprising; comparative; rhythmic; accustomed; unfailing; faultless; bashful; monotonous; clock-like.

verbs
acquire—; adjust to—; chime in—; drum with—; fall in—; form with—; level to—; maintain—; perform with—; range in—; sustain—; —conforms to; —offsets; —wearies.
(See consistency, harmony, persistence.)

REGULATE (v)

adverbs
stringently; socially; solely; mechanically; scientifically; bureaucratically; autonomously; dictatorially; tyrannically; austerely.
(See direct, control.)

REGULATIONS

adjectives
existing; labeling; influential; arbitrary; stupid; special; conflicting; cast-iron; elaborate; stringent; complicated; administrative; admirable; sanitary; military; martial; hostile; celebrated; barbarous; inviolable; local; wide-spread; federal; civic.

verbs
adopt—; approve—; bar by—; block—; comply with—; conform to—; control by—; decry—; defy—; denounce—; enforce—; govern by—; legislate—; impose—upon; improve—; promulgate—; provide—; revise —; submit—; sustain—; violate—.
(See legislation, bill, arrangement, law, mandate, rule.)

REHABILITATE (v)

adverbs
completely; entirely; refreshingly; spectacularly; miraculously; superficially.
(See restore, renew, revive.)

REHEARSE (v)

adverbs
incessantly; harmoniously; perfunctorily; dutifully; painstakingly; faithfully.
(See practice, say.)

REIGN

adjectives
transient; dismal; passionate; present; illustrious; imperial; unbreathing; subsequent; reasoning; secure; inexorable; abdicated; horrid; preceding; unsurpassed; liberal; unmolested; remotest; prosperous; gaudy; troublous; happy.

verbs
force—; limit—; overthrow—; submit to—; suffer under—; terminate—; undermine—; tolerate—; usurp—; —chafes; —contents; —dictates; —symbolizes; —trammels; —tramples on; —treads upon; —tyrannizes.
(See regime, government, dominion.)

REIGN (*v*)

adverbs
imperially; inexorably; liberally; prosperously; tyrannically; lustfully; beneficently; imperiously; supremely; austerely; contemporaneously; gloriously; rovallv.
(See govern, rule.)

REIMBURSE (*v*)

adverbs
appreciatively; satisfactorily; fully; generously; financially; liberally; unstintingly.
(See repay, avenge.)

REINDEER

verbs
bag—; domesticate—; exhibit—; mount—; preserve—; stalk—; team—; —draws; —herds; —inhabits; —migrates; —retreats; —scrapes; —sheds; —shies; —traverses.
(See animal, deer.)

REINFORCE (*v*)

adverbs
substantially; materially; firmly; enormously; strategically.
(See aid, assist.)

REINFORCED

adverbs
strongly; firmly; unbreakably; suddenly; necessarily; conveniently; advantageously; completely; appropriately; suitably; substantially; enormously; materially; providentially; immensely; opportunely; duly.

REINFORCEMENT

adjectives
enormous; seasonable; material; welcome; momentary; unexpected.

REINS

adjectives
commanding; jingling; loosened; leathern; dangling.

verbs
check with—; control—; discard—; dress—; grasp—; grease—; hand over—; jerk on—; knot—; loop—; master—; pluck at—; relax—; release—; respond to—; rustle—; saw with—; slap with—; spank—; take over—; tangle—; yank (colloq.)—; —check; —control; —dangle; —direct.
(See bit.)

REITERATE (*v*)

adverbs
incessantly; substantially; emphatically; characteristically; monotonously; maddeningly; intermittently.
(See repeat.)

REJECT (*v*)

adverbs
summarily; scornfully; disdainfully; scoffingly; unconditionally; overwhelmingly; airily; petulantly; incontinently; contemptuously; utterly; haughtily; stubbornly; indignantly; peremptorily; flatly; unanimously; sullenly; brusquely; bluntly; pointedly.
(See refuse, repulse.)

REJECTION

adjectives
sullen; intellectual; subsequent; pointed; blunt; brusque.

REJOICE (*v*)

adverbs
convivially; immoderately; festively; hilariously; exultantly; openly; gleefully; enthusiastically; spontaneously; impulsively; fraternally.
(See cheer, exult.)

REJOICED

adverbs
greatly; highly; uncommonly; radiantly; gloriously; proudly; triumphantly; splendidly; exultantly; elatedly; naturally; genuinely.

REJOICING

adjectives
endless; enthusiastic; excited; ravenous; spontaneous; surface; incessant; half-hearted.

adverbs
reverently; hilariously; uproariously; riotously; loudly; quietly; calmly; deeply; profoundly; thoughtfully; boisterously; triumphantly; gayly; merrily; happily; rapturously; wildly; enthusiastically; hysterically; excitedly; exuberantly; madly; tumultuously; heartily.

REJOIN (v)

adverbs
ultimately; laughingly; daringly; stingingly; passionately; flippantly; curtly; pointedly; tartly; quaintly; tardily; shrewdly; bitterly; sympathetically; reluctantly; icily; haughtily; calmly; musingly.
(See reply, answer.)

REJOINDER

adjectives
laughing; daring; stinging; passionate; flippant; curt; pointed; tart; clever; quaint; sad; usual; nasty; tardy.

REJUVENATION

verbs
buy—; draw—from; induce—; quaff—; retard—; seek—; —aids; —cures; —eludes; —rallies; —reanimates; —rectifies; —redresses; —repairs; —stimulates; —thrills.
(See youth, health, cure, remedy.)

RELAPSE

adjectives
subsequent; moral; fatal; momentary; swift; sure; unavoidable; inevitable.

verbs
anticipate—; deplore—; fall into—; incur—; lament—; preclude—; sink into—; slide into—; undergo—; verge on—; warn against—; —occurs; —recoils; —retrogrades; —reverts to.
(See recurrence.)

RELATE (v)

adverbs
mirthfully; speciously; variously; tediously; succulently; incredibly; intimately; gravely; confidently; graphically; sympathetically; monotonously.
(See tell, narrate.)

RELATED

adverbs
closely; remotely; intimately; personally; officially; scarcely; materially; inescapably; obviously; naturally; circumstantially; conditionally; accidentally; casually; incomprehensibly; practically; obviously; manifestly; conveniently.

RELATIONS

adjectives
brotherly; hostile; uninterrupted; definite; long-dreaded; exacting; intimate; selfish; delicate; ecclesiastical; wretched; harmonious; pedagogic; causative; domestic; truthful; evident; sublimest; unbroken; genial; agreeable; confiding; pacific; veiled; peculiar; paternal; filial; diplomatic; untried; blessed; typical; mysterious; unobtrusive; sympathetic; conjugal; occult; amicable; prejudiced; nominal; friendly; necessary; supernatural; uncaressing; unsympathizing; dynamical; independent; complex; current; healthful; antagonistic; marital; coetaneous; incestuous; distinct; parallel; causal; scandalous; far-reaching; frank; simultaneous; cordial; piquant; amiable; perverse; confidential; innumerable; organic; mutual; fixed; uniform; established; determinate; passional; external; feudal; conflicting; unnatural; sex; altruistic; mathematical; antenuptial; consistent; symbolic; industrial; decorative; subsequent; clerical; strained.

verbs
achieve—; bear—with; break off—; cement—; cloud—; cripple—; deny—with; disturb—; entertain—with; establish—; facilitate—; govern—; harmonize—; ignore—; maintain—; mar—; preserve—; reestablish—; sever—; sharpen—; shun—; smooth—; strain—; suppress—; sustain—; —bind; —cool; —prevail; —tie.
(See relationship, affairs, connection.)

RELATIONSHIP

adjectives
intimate; unconventional; confidential; harmonious; hierarchical; personal; simple; monotonous; illicit; family; intelligible; intellectual; domestic; healthful; closer; sympathetic; marked; economic.

RELATIVES
(kin)

adjectives
distant; harmless; elderly; endangered; illustrious; erring; reluctant; interfering; interested; portly; unsympathetic; departing; circumspect; disagreeable; unpleasant.

verbs
characterize—; claim—; endure—; link—; plague with—; reconcile—; support—; —assemble; —bicker; —commemorate; —congregate; —convene; —criticize; —drift; —honor; —implore; —intrude; —pester; —quarrel; —recount; —report; —sanction; —trace.
(See friend, family.)

RELATIONSHIP

verbs
affect—; claim—; comprehend—; criticize—; discern—; draw from—; endure—; enter into—; expose—; form—; intrude on—; mar—; probe—; prove—; report—; sanction—; sever—; split—; terminate—; warp—; —associates; —binds; —comforts; —involves; —links.
(See alliance, connection, affiliation, relation.)

RELAX (*v*)

adverbs
momentarily; restfully; contentedly; totally; completely; beneficially; healthfully; blissfully; drowsily; refreshingly.
(See slacken, rest.)

RELAXATION

adjectives
acquiescent; complete; attendant; humanizing; universal; momentary; amused; necessary.

verbs
attain—; conduce toward—; loll in—; lounge in—; participate in—; practice—; seek—; —alleviates; —arouses; —calms; —composes; —modifies; —pacifies; —palliates; —quiets; —refreshes; —rests; —smoothes; —stills; —subdues; —tempers; —tranquilizes; —wastes.
(See diversion, jollity, recreation.)

RELAXED

adverbs
pleasantly; mentally; idly; momentarily; suddenly; wholly; delightfully; restfully; rarely; serenely; lazily; irresponsibly; unwontedly; surprisingly; comfortably; fortunately; beautifully; finally; drowsily; dreamily; satisfactorily; refreshingly; unbelievably; miraculously; curiously.

RELEASE

adjectives
impassioned; speedy; merciful; ultimate; eventual; anticipated; unaccountable; long-sought.

verbs
attempt—; beg for—; grant—; hinder—; permit—; procure—; sanction—; schedule for—; secure—; withhold—; —absolves; —acquits; —clears; —exonerates; —frees; —unbars; —unclogs; —unlooses.
(See bail, deliverance, discharge.)

RELEASE (*v*)

adverbs
unconditionally; instantaneously; blamelessly; consequently; subsequently; deftly; ultimately; unaccountably.
(See free, acquit)

RELENT (*v*)

adverbs
graciously; grudgingly; tardily; beneficently; remorsefully; partially; smilingly.
(See yield, repent.)

RELIANCE

adjectives
affectionate; rugged; implicit; noble; sober; loving; just; calm; pretended; reciprocal; manly; centering; imbecilic; humble.

verbs
cherish—; consider—; doubt—; foster—; place—in; presume—; produce—; prove—; rest on—; shake—; trust—; —buoys; —encourages; —impresses; —inspires; —persuades; —satisfies.
(See hope, confidence, assurance, trust.)

RELIC

adjectives
antediluvian; hoary; visible; lacustrine; precious; melancholy; holy; fascinating; pathetic; prehistoric; sartorial; exquisite; venerable; sacred; unmistakable; quaint; supposed; amusing; incensing; celebrated; curious; archaeological; unseemly; tender; quivering; cherished; moldering.

RELIEF

verbs
administer—; afford—; derive—from; experience—; extend—; gain—; gasp with—;

grant—; hail—; heave a sigh of—; indulge —; mark by—; seek—; speed—; voice—.
(See help, aid, assistance, consolation.)

RELIEF
(charity, dole.)

verbs
apply for—; infringe upon—; promote—; slash—; —allays; —assuages; —cheers; —comforts; —disburdens; —eases; —encourages; —insures; —mitigates; —remedies; —solves; —smooths; —sustains.
(See payment, dole, charity.)

RELIEF
(general)

adjectives
consequent; speedy; hysterical; parochial; intense; joyous; beautiful; inevitable; delighted; complete; permanent; temporary; marked; distinct; regular; pronounced; infinite; immediate; effective; actual; spiritual; pretended; considerable; delicious; partial; decided; mean; instant; scant; sheer; welcome; urgent; national; decorative; reliable.

RELIEVE (*v*)

adverbs
tactfully; effectually; painlessly; ultimately; intensely; temporarily; spiritually; partially; economically; nationally.
(See alleviate, lessen.)

RELIGION

adjectives
scurvy; ritual; rudimentary; concentrated; positive; fierce; absurd; austere; profane; constructive; inaccessible; sanguinary; powerful; fervent; blessed; unalterable; irrevocable; distinct; revealed; peaceful; maudlin; professed; easy-minded; blatant; doctrinal; gripping; saving.

verbs
adopt—; attack—; cast aside—; cherish—; corrupt—; defile—; define—; devote to—; discredit—; embrace—; formulate—; inculcate—; interpret—; profess—; renounce —; ridicule—; side-track—; stamp out—; traduce—; venerate—; —comforts; —consoles; —elevates; —fetters; —influences; —moulds; —nourishes; —paralyzes; —perishes; —prevails; —purges; —purifies; —sanctifies; —sways; —unifies; —wanes.
(See devotion, faith, worship, Christianity, modernism.)

RELINQUISH (*v*)

adverbs
silently; nobly; gallantly; magnanimously; voluntarily; completely; reluctantly; philosophically; gloomily; unselfishly; logically.
(See surrender, waive, cede.)

RELISH

adjectives
savory; exciting; peculiar; anticipatory; derisive; insatiable; unwonted; evident; higher; callous; complacent; keen; savage; added; natural; acquired.

RELISH (*v*)

adverbs
heartily; appreciatively; intellectually; spicily; pungently; enjoyably.
(See enjoy, taste.)

RELUCTANCE

adjectives
resentful; sullen; unfeigned; fierce; reverent; unaffected; infinite; pretty; lingering; natural; insurmountable; shuddering; evident; double; general; untamed; curious; studied.

verbs
assume—; complain of—; dispel—; employ with—; feign—; harbor—; imply—; incite —; incur—; invite—; overcome—; prompt —; stifle—; —baits; —provokes; —resists; —restrains; —sharpens; —tantalizes; —whets.
(See distaste, aversion, unwillingness, repugnance, dislike.)

RELUCTANT

adverbs
inexplicably; terribly; visibly; evidently; sternly; inflexibly; unyieldingly; palpably; manifestly; strangely; harshly; morosely; undeniably; resentfully; unpleasantly; discourteously; impolitely; sullenly; uncivilly; roughly; unaffectedly; naturally; curiously; superstitiously; timidly; shyly; bashfully; fearfully; timorously; senselessly; sensibly; wisely; thoughtfully; profoundly; secretly; oddly; peculiarly; significantly; particularly; uncommonly.

RELY (*v*)

adverbs
implicitly; exclusively; chiefly; trustfully;

faithfully; tacitly; affectionately; reciprocally; soberly; humbly; calmly.
(See depend, trust.)

REMAIN (v)

adverbs
constantly; hopefully; tensely; determinedly; indefinitely; courageously; voluntarily; impassively; motionlessly; tranquilly; inflexibly; wilfully; permanently; peacefully.
(See stay, linger.)

REMAINS

adjectives
mangled; undemolished; mutilated; honored; numerous; jagged; august; fossilized; dreary; lifeless; insensible; imperishable; charred; mortal; architectural; heterogeneous; comic; disinterred; dingy; scattered; petrified; colorless; archaeological.

verbs
cart away—; conceal—; consign—to; cremate—; disinter—; dispose of—; dissect—; embalm—; entomb—; exhume—; expose—; honor—; inter—; mummify—; rescue—; ship—; trace—.
(See ashes, debris, dust, corpse, remnants.)

REMARK

adjectives
laughing; bantering; automatic; delighted; editorial; pregnant; noncommittal; ill-bred; futile; felicitous; stinging; harsh; preliminary; taunting; fertile; disparaging; commonplace; inaccurate; terse; hasty; vicious; candid; malicious; concluding; immortal; cryptic; appreciative; unpremeditated; enigmatical; unexpected; profound; brittle; opprobrious; deprecatory; chance; sententious; derogatory; outspoken; complimentary; incidental; tomfool; satiric; material; boorish; insubordinate; sage; insolent; coarse; cheerful; desultory; treasonable; merry; philosophic; withering; sarcastic; drunken; significant; casual; illuminating; laconic; feeble; caustic; pat; obscure; verbal; simultaneous (pl); surly; skeptical; mischievous; philosophical; egotistical; independent; special; characteristic; graceful; frolicsome; priceless; careless; indiscreet; prelusory; slurring; ejaculatory; animated; scintillating; epithetical; facetious; deathless; calescent; disputed; trivial; acrimonious; disgusting; critical; allusive; appropriate; judicious.

verbs
ban—; bar—; comprehend—; couch—; deliver—; digest—; drop—; emit—; exchange —s; insert—; occasion—; open—s; poise—; preface—; propose—; punctuate—; repress —; —deprecates; —disparages; —embitters; —falls; —indicates; —issues from; —interrupts.
(See mention, comment, observation, statement.)

REMARK (v)

adverbs
gratuitously; banteringly; ambiguously; anxiously; dryly; wittily; significantly; dispassionately; disparingly; illogically; mendaciously; casually; emphatically; judicially; modestly; complacently; affably; ruefully; vigorously; inquisitively; confidently; whimsically; indifferently; exuberantly; pathetically; sympathetically; sententiously; contemptuously; cynically; deftly; laconically; demurely; pointedly; wistfully; tenatively; caustically; editorially; pregnantly; noncommittally; felicitously; disparagingly; viciously; candidly; appreciatively; boorishly; obscurely; acrimoniously; allusively; appropriately; judiciously; skeptically; egotistically.
(See comment, assert.)

REMEDIABLE

adverbs
easily; fortunately; luckily; quickly; immediately; supposedly; probably; expensively; distinctly; definitely; manifestly; now; altogether; undoubtedly.

REMEDY

adjectives
worthless; potent; favorite; time-tested; present; similar; valuable; misbranded; fraudulent; mythical; accepted; manifold (pl); rational; insidious; infallible; palliative; celebrated; universal; unavailing; irrational; precious; radical; ancient; drug; original; effective; fruitless; costly; extreme; innocent; heroic; futile; makeshift.

verbs
advocate—; apply—; concoct—; denounce —; employ—; furnish—; grope for—; hail —; persevere with—; prescribe—; propose —; provide—; recommend—; rely upon—;

seek—; —alleviates; —eases; —palliates; —purges; —relieves; —soothes.

(See cure, liniment, laxative, purgative, medicine.)

REMEDY (*v*)

adverbs

concurrently; similarly; rationally; fraudulently; traditionally; heroically; medically; beneficially; miraculously.

(See cure, heal.)

REMEMBER (*v*)

adverbs

vividly; mechanically; graphically; sorrowfully; remorsefully; irrelevantly; dimly; subconsciously; vaguely; passionately; generously; superstitiously; gratefully; fondly; affectionately; morbidly; eternally; mournfully; involuntarily.

(See recollect, recall.)

REMEMBRANCE

adjectives

pleasant; affectionate; clear; lasting; loving; proud; grateful; fond; dull; discourteous; intuitive; melancholy; morbid; gray; desolate; yielding; burning; fevered; ennobling; ineffaceable; lively; personal; deep; triumphant; tender; ancestral; undimmed; foul; mournful; eternal; faithful; ignominious; listening; evil; gracious; involuntary; stern; worthiest; slow; honorable; sufficient; unwelcome; fading; delighted; constant; kindly; grateful; vivid; lifelong.

verbs

con—; bear in—; honor—; incite—; indulge in—; prompt—; retain—; rivet in—; suggest—; —commemorates; —diverts; —fades; —flatters; —impresses; —renews; —stings; —wanes.

(See memory, compliment, recollection, reminiscence.)

REMIND (*v*)

adverbs

relentlessly; grimly; persistently; poignantly; irksomely; demurely; accusingly; irrationally; determinedly; vigorously; vividly; pleasantly; personally; tenderly; painfully; laughingly; spitefully.

(See recall.)

REMINDER

adjectives

grim; curious; visible; painful; neat; tangible; pitiful; laughing; continual.

REMINISCENCE

adjectives

agreeable; uncomfortable; indistinct; haunting; glorified; vulgarized; distinguishable; tender; historical; pleasing; vague; barren; commonplace; crisp; humorous; incoherent; divine; fascinating.

verbs

awaken—; delight in—; dispel—; embarrass by—; enjoy—; indulge in—; interpose—; prolong—; revel in—; review in—; steep in—; veil—; —cheers; —colors; —consoles; —delights; —s flood; —warms; interrupt—.

(See remembrance, recollection, memory.)

REMINISCENT

adverbs

delightfully; happily; tiresomely; unendingly; crisply; humorously; divinely; fascinatingly; vaguely; pleasingly; tenderly; gloriously; teasingly; incoherently; uproariously; convivially; genially; embarrassingly; surprisingly; foolishly; deliriously; garrulously; unsteadily; wistfully; feebly; constantly.

REMISS

adverbs

apologetically; confessedly; admittedly; terribly; unpardonably; gravely; seriously; heedlessly; nonchalantly; criminally; tragically; inexplicably; unaccountably; strangely; curiously; unconsciously; unintentionally; carelessly; hopelessly; sorely; unacceptably; frequently; negligently; indifferently; atrociously.

REMNANTS

adjectives

sufficing; laggard; straggling; placable; salvaged; shrunken; scorched; enduring; shattered; discarded; miserable; pathetic; quaint; wretched; fugitive; lingering; greater; saving.

verbs

bag—; cherish—; collect—; conceal—; consume—; gather—; heap—; leave—; market—; offer—; piece—; proffer—; salvage—;

scatter—; store—; utilize—; value; —disappear; —survive.
(See fragment, residue, piece, remains.)

REMONSTRANCE

adjectives
passionate; energetic; rash; urgent; mutinous; bitter; temperate; tender; lukewarm; childish; indignant; peaceful; final; earnest; useless; obvious; eloquent; angry; rational; resentful.

REMONSTRATE (*v*)

adverbs
waggishly; vainly; rudely; incessantly; earnestly; calmly; passionately; energetically; mutinously; bitterly; tenderly; childishly; eloquently; rationally; resentfully.
(See protest, expostulate.)

REMORSE

adjectives
useless; sisterly; gnawing; fictitious; bitter; unconfessed; light; violent; vile; abrupt; unceasing; dull; poignant.

verbs
burden with—; confess—; depress by—; experience—; incite—; overcome with—; overwhelm with—; palliate—; relieve—; shake with—; shroud in—; smite with—; sober by—; suffer—; tinge with—; wrap in—; —colors; —devours; —humbles; —maddens; —overwhelms; —racks; —shatters; —subdues; —stirs; —surges within; —undermines.
(See contrition, regret, qualm, repentance.)

REMORSEFUL

adverbs
naturally; admittedly; openly; manifestly; miserably; tardily; wretchedly; pitiably; pitifully; pathetically; tragically; immeasurably; terribly; sorely; significantly; sincerely; sobbingly; weakly; duly; penitently; contritely; deeply; profoundly.

REMOTE

adverbs
coldly; distantly; proudly; shyly; timidly; arrogantly; superciliously; intellectually; absent-mindedly; abstractedly; philosophically; naturally; dreamily; discourteously; deliberately; resolutely; gravely; unsocially; inscrutably; mysteriously; vexatiously; gruffly; gravely; judiciously; absurdly.

REMOTENESS

adjectives
romantic; apparent; comparative; patent.

REMOVAL

adjectives
successful; prompt; repeated; forcible; swift.

verbs
advocate—; allow—; balk at—; compel—; delay—; demand—; ease by—; entail—; hamper—; hinder—; impede—; instigate—; order—; recommend—; rejoice in—; resist—; upset by—; —alters; —annoys; —confuses; —disturbs.
(See dismissal, displacement, withdrawal, change.)

REMOVE (*v*)

adverbs
dexterously; clumsily; skillfully; cautiously; surreptitiously; slyly; permanently; temporarily; forcefully; promptly; swiftly.
(See transfer, withdraw.)

REMUNERATIVE

adverbs
providentially; extravagantly; sufficiently; fairly; justly; adequately; highly; satisfactorily; surprisingly; astoundingly; remarkably; gratifyingly; incredibly; opportunely; finally; profitably; scarcely; duly; advantageously; usefully; fantastically; richly; uncommonly.

RENAISSANCE

verbs
anticipate—; characterize—; contribute to—; create—; foster—; hail—; instigate—; pertain to—; promote—; prompt—; terminate—; voice—; —alters; —flourishes; —produces; —reforms; —renews; —restores; —reveals; —revivifies; —stimulates; —unfolds.
(See birth, revival, restoration.)

RENDER (*v*)

adverbs
passively; powerfully; exquisitely; peculiarly; necessarily; infallibly; barely; charmingly; admirably; poetically; realistically; artistically.
(See repay, restore.)

RENDERING

adjectives
realistic; photographic; elusive; exquisite; independent; artistic.

RENDEZVOUS

adjectives
picturesque; favorite; charming; famous; appointed; storied; legendary; modern.

RENEW (*v*)

adverbs
modernistically; periodically; auspiciously; mysteriously; generously; harmoniously; incessantly; wholly; reverently; seasonally.
(See repair, restore.)

RENOUNCE (*v*)

adverbs
dogmatically; courageously; boldly; rashly; lawfully; faithlessly; virtually; eternally; voluntarily; passionately; shamelessly; explicitly; frankly.
(See reject, disclaim.)

RENOVATED

adverbs
perfectly; pleasingly; usefully; delightfully; acceptably; inexpensively; skilfully; marvelously; astoundingly; amazingly; opportunely; duly; attractively; newly; recently; properly; appropriately; lately; cleverly; artistically; substantially; admirably; satisfactorily; beautifully.

RENOWN

adjectives
splendid; posthumous; unfulfilled; ancient; chaste; temporary; contemporary; godlike; provincial; unspeakable; wide-spread; notorious.

verbs
accept—; accredit—; achieve—; acquire—; cherish—; feign—; gain—; glean—; radiate—; reflect—; respect—; rise to—; sing—; win—; —glorifies; —overshadows; —overwhelms; —shines; —spoils.
(See glory, fame, limelight, distinction, notoriety.)

RENT

adjectives
great; ragged; artificial; ghastly; economic; reconciling; preposterous; numerous (pl); outrageous.

RENUNCIATION

adjectives
passionate; shameless; sublime; frank; perfect; explicit.

REORGANIZATION

adjectives
intensive; careful; economic; periodical; necessary.

REPAIR (*v*)

adverbs
temporarily; hastily; haphazardly; amply; ceaselessly; extensively; technically; judiciously; medically.
(See restore, mend.)

REPAIRED

adverbs
obviously; recently; badly; handsomely; adroitly; secretly; visibly; skilfully; beautifully; marvelously; completely; aptly; expensively; reasonably; extensively; shoddily; ably; expertly; ingeniously; wonderfully; unnoticeably; perfectly; patently; imperceptibly; exquisitely; awkwardly; clumsily; sufficiently; satisfactorily

REPAIRS

adjectives
extensive; judicious; necessary; expensive; technical; obvious; happy.

verbs
effect—; resume—; undergo—; view—; —ameliorate; —bolster; —compensate; —convert; —enhance; —purge; —rectify—; redeem; —refresh; —relieve; —remedy; —restore; —strengthen.
(See reconstruction, improvement.)

REPARATIONS

verbs
cancel—; demand—; forego—; liquidate—; offer—; refuse—; repudiate—; review—; —acknowledge; —appease; —atone; —correct; —indemnify; —pacify; —recompense; —redeem; —redress; —requite; —restore; —reward; —satisfy.
(See insurance, atonement, restoration.)

REPARTEE

adjectives
insulting; clever; humorous; colloquial; icy; restless; victorious; spicy; sparkling; witty.

verbs
banter—; engage in—; excel in—; furnish —; prolong—; quicken—; school in—; stimulate—; suffer—; surpass in—; —amuses; —arouses; —beguiles; —cheers; —delights; —diverts; —entertains; —excels; —frisks; —romps; —scintillates; —sparkles; —wanes.
(See answer, banter, reply.)

REPAST

adjectives
unsavory; sumptuous; cannibal; nocturnal; precious; disgusting; substantial; satisfying; ridiculous; extravagant; delicious; tumultuous.

verbs
crave—; devour—; donate—; gorge—; invite to—; partake of—; prepare—; relish—; spread—; wash down—; yield to—; —allays; —appeases; —attracts; —nourishes; —quells; —sates.
(See eating, luncheon, feast, meal, food.)

REPAY (v)

adverbs
promptly; severely; cheerfully; lavishly; amply; faithfully; conscientiously; legally; graciously.
(See reimburse, avenge.)

REPEAL

verbs
abolish—; advocate—; agitate for—; authorize—; celebrate—; demand—; desire—; discard—; favor—; fight—; induce—; overrule—; permit—; promote—; recommend—; reverse—; sanction—; seek—; welcome—; —ameliorates; —cheers; —dissolves; —gladdens; —improves; —nullifies; —relieves.
(See dismissal, displacement.)

REPEAL (v)

adverbs
expressly; totally; legally; harshly; dogmatically; unanimously; promptly.
(See retract, recall.)

REPEAT (v)

adverbs
idiotically; tediously; foolishly; maliciously; vindictively; icily; incredulously; insistently; vaguely; fatuously; insultingly; emphatically; peevishly; multitudinously; stubbornly; mechanically; simultaneously; musingly; fluently; deprecatingly; monotonously; interrogatively; authoritatively; aimlessly; tenderly; musically.
(See reiterate.)

REPEATED

adverbs
endlessly; monotonously; emphatically; frequently; necessarily; tediously; whiningly; sullenly; unbearably; tiresomely; foolishly; maliciously; garrulously; senselessly; accurately; erroneously; imprudently; indiscreetly; secretly; confidentially; cruelly; derisively; unfortunately; unluckily; malevolently; scoffingly; deliberately; treacherously; surreptitiously; slyly; intelligibly; audibly; authoritatively; ominously; significantly.

REPEL (v)

adverbs
obstinately; stubbornly; vigorously; forcefully; courageously; staunchly; determinedly; gallantly.
(See oppose, repulse.)

REPENT (v)

adverbs
religiously; remorsefully; bitterly; genuinely; submissively; sincerely.
(See regret, grieve.)

REPENTANCE

adjectives
genuine; unavailing; bitter; submissive; generous; deep; sad; shamefaced; deathbed; sincere; sullen.

verbs
burden with—; confess—; experience—; feign—; incite—; overcome with—; wrap in—; —appeases; —condones; —humbles; —oppresses; —overwhelms; —pacifies; —palliates; —relieves; —shrouds; —sobers; —subdues; —tinges.
(See remorse, contrition, regret.)

REPERTOIRE

verbs
acclaim—; acquire—; announce—; applaud —; arrange—; balance—; choose—; enact —; enlarge—; exhaust—; expand—; include in—; increase—; list—; plan—; practice—; rehearse—; round out—; —covers; —delights; —embraces; —engages; —includes; —unfolds.
(See program, plan, list.)

REPETITION

adjectives

insane; mannered; verbal; constant; monotonous; wholesale; frequent; musical; maddening; fine; unmeaning; steady; endless; broken; emphatic; undulating; useless; decorative; injudicious; vague; tragic; idiotic; deadly; suasive; meaningless; diverting; explanatory; forceful.

verbs

clamor for—; demand—; endure—; influence—; justify—; permit—; request—; stifle —; suffer—; survive—; threaten—; —bores; —emphasizes; —impresses; —irritates; —prolongs; —recalls; —refreshes; —teaches; —tires; —wearies.

(See mention, recurrence.)

REPLACE (v)

adverbs

surreptitiously; effectively; effectually; faithfully; graciously; promptly; intelligently; skillfully.

(See repay, restore.)

REPLICA

verbs

commend—; compare—; criticize—; prepare —; produce—; —adheres to; —appears; —attracts; —condenses; —copies; —deceives; —duplicates; —follows; —recalls; —reproduces.

(See duplicate, copy.)

REPLY

adjectives

suitable; lackadaisical; unexpected; frank; modest; judicial; unembarrassed; shameless; monosyllabic; disrespectful; short; temperate; haughty; elaborate; silly; immediate; ungracious; good-humored; noncommittal; guarded; discouraging; cold; pettish; memorable; gracious; categorical; contemptuous; impatient; ready; biting; caustic; tart; scornful; unmoved; intelligent; inarticulate; incoherent; tactful; tremulous; humble; proper; audible; chaffing; austere; obvious; correct; negative; preoccupied; conclusive; stumbling; impromptu; sound; impertinent; garbled; distorted; satisfactory; politic; magnanimous; chilling; languid; impressive; idiotic; chary; pungent; consolatory; evasive; angry; emphatic; unanimous.

verbs

calculate—; contemplate—; demand—; deign—; elicit—; evoke—; mutter—; overhaul—; probe—; propose—; provoke—; rejoin—; —acknowledges; —affirms; —alleviates; —answers; —clarifies; —clears; —determines; —explains; —informs; —interrogates; —rebuts; —refutes; —satisfies; —solves.

(See answer, response, retort, repartee.)

REPLY (v)

adverbs

evasively; solemnly; tonelessly; affirmatively; crisply; bitingly; equivocally; impertinently; promptly; auspiciously; grimly; dolefully; defiantly; wistfully; mechanically; elusively; falteringly; gravely; archly; laboriously; hilariously; dubiously; incoherently; inexorably; tremulously; petulantly; casually; tensely; modestly; placidly; jocosely; listlessly; cautiously; musingly; dejectedly; reflectively; mordantly; haughtily; serenely; maliciously; decisively; acrimoniously; pensively; meekly; dryly; sententiously; laconically; pettishly; ambiguously; indulgently; monosyllabically; temperately; noncommittally; magnanimously; pungently; emphatically.

(See answer, respond.)

REPORT

adjectives

verbatim; exact; unbiased; unanimous; distant; illustrated; first-hand; stimulating; clear; understandable; supplementary; complete; unconfined; successive (pl); dependable; inflammatory; untruthful; precise; flattering; plausible; gratifying; preliminary; press; energetic; sly; insidious; formal; official; partial; detailed; inaccurate; dazzling; hearsay; critical; archeological; suppressed; statistical; disheartening; neat; reassuring; ardent; vague; alarming; typical; regular; aggregated; voluble; orderly; condensed; annual; authentic; snobbish; veracious; written; admirable; pestiferous; outspoken; hopeless; voluminous; sensational; elaborate; shocking; frightened; thundering; commercial; reverberating; varying; random; astounding; enthusiastic; exaggerated; published; confused; pretentious; stenographic; unwelcome; explicit.

verbs

allay—s; append to—; bungle—; challenge —; chronicle—s; circulate—; confirm—;

corroborate—; counteract—; deluge with —s; draw up—; echo—; evaluate—; fudge —; indorse—; pigeon-hole—; prepare—; qualify—; render—; scoff at—; shelve—; summarize—; transmit—; verify—; wind up —; —bears out; —bolsters; —discloses; —emanates from; —embodies; —persists; —recommends; —spreads.

(See fame, account, news, rumor, record.)

REPORT (v)

adverbs
faithfully; precisely; currently; alarmingly; capably; officially; adversely; duly; glumly; graciously; verbally; insidiously; formally; partially; critically; archeologically; statistically; reassuringly; vaguely; volubly; annually; authentically; veraciously; sensationally; reverberatingly; exaggeratedly; pretentiously; stenographically.

(See announce, describe.)

REPORTER

adjectives
rushing; mere; prying; realistic; inquisitive; disreputable; disgruntled; clever; skilled.

verbs
besiege by—s; hush up—s; loathe—s; muffle —s; stifle—s; —alludes to; —announces; —s beleaguer; —s descend upon; —disguises; —eavesdrops; —expresses; —fences; —hints; —imparts; —imposes; —interviews; —intimates; —libels; —mentions; —mobs; —prowls; —reserves; —reviews; —"scoops"; —slanders; —specifies; —tips off; —withholds.

(See journalist, detective, writer.)

REPORTING

adjectives
franker; alert; candid.

REPOSE

adjectives
soothing; calm; innocent; serene; undisturbed; sullen; delicious; charmed; noble; blissful; final; comforting; grave; irksome; profitless; chronic; supreme; mental; stolid; permanent; scornful; effeminate; statuesque; long-coveted; profound; peaceful; solemn; comparative; orbed; unreached; vile; languorous; dreamy; passionless; weak; healthful; everlasting; fathomless; equivocal; intellectual; infamous; exquisite; last; rheumatic; particular; spacious; exasperating; deep; echoless; fitful; indolent; placid; dull; sweet; dignified; complete; stupid; prolonged; cultivated; studied; momentary; outward; grave-like; grim; stern; thoughtful; reason-wrought; voluptuous.

verbs
advocate—; disturb—; dwell in—; indulge in—; seek—; while away in—; —energizes; —frees; —lulls; —preserves; —refreshes; —relaxes; —relieves; —rests; —soothes; —stagnates; —stems; —vivifies.

(See composure, rest, sleep, quiet, peace.)

REPOSE (v)

adverbs
lazily; soothingly; calmly; serenely; sullenly; deliciously; effeminately; profoundly; passionlessly; rheumatically; placidly; momentarily; voluptuously.

(See rest, relax.)

REPOSEFUL

adverbs
pleasantly; sweetly; oddly; calmly; serenely; unusually; gratefully; duly; dully; prosaically; quietly; lazily; blissfully; deliciously; soothingly; somnolently; drowsily; dreamily; idly; languidly; listlessly; deliberately; heavily; silently; immovably; incredibly; unexpectedly; utterly; happily.

REPREHENSIBLE

adverbs
lamentably; undeniably; openly; flagrantly; particularly; unpardonably; admittedly; miserably; shamefully; wretchedly; curiously; unwarrantably; uncommonly; highly; utterly; exceptionably; gravely; indiscreetly; unconscionably; inordinately; terribly.

REPRESENT (v)

adverbs
copiously; faithfully; magnificently; initially; beneficently; allegorically; fantastically; diagrammatically; materially; adequately; speciously; personally; orally; substantially; symbolically; conventionally; fictitiously; ludicrously; realistically.

(See portray, depict.)

REPRESENTATION

adjectives
oral; adequate; easily-understood; hallucinatory; pasteboard; hearty; disproportionate; concrete; animated; distinct; substantial; graphic; definite; direct; diplomatic; count-

less (pl); urgent; decennial; striking; vigorous; symbolic; democratic; renewed; just; faithful; pictorial; mental; material; fraudulent; proportioned; august; mere; earnest; specious; tolerable; abstract; wild; conventional; mimic; dramatic; one-sided; untruthful; harmonious; factual; fictitious; softened; sensuous; ludicrous; natural; unfair; realistic; archaic.

verbs
carve—; comprehend—; deprive of—; dress up—; mold—; rehearse—; yield to—s; —alludes to; —betokens; —depicts; —describes; —designates; —enlightens; —illustrates; —indicates; —informs; —points out; —portrays; —signifies; —symbolizes; —typifies.
(See description, comedy, design, reproduction, art, portrayal, drama.)

REPRESENTATIVE

adjectives
dwarfed; local-minded; fitting; dazzling; mentionable; assembled (pl); accredited: prominent; cold; correct; tremulous; striking; exemplary; placement; shy; awkward; authorized; diplomatic; surviving; lineal; avowed; arrogant; cold-brained; brilliant; fraudulent; traveling.

verbs
accredit—; apportion—s; antagonize—; delegate—; interchange—s; obligate—; replace —; —bandies; —calls; —commutes; —introduces; —offers; —reciprocates; —redeems; —retaliates; —serves; —solicits; —supersedes; —supplants.
(See consul, delegate, agent, deputy.)

adverbs
typically; truly; fairly; justly; altogether; officially; authoritatively; adequately; satisfactorily; substantially; diplomatically; tolerably; unfairly; scarcely; hardly; entirely; accurately; concisely; legally; uncommonly; warrantably; specifically; appropriately; singularly; functionally; appointively.

REPRESS (v)

adverbs
sternly; tyrannically; stoically; impatiently; amiably; severely; dictatorially; dogmatically; rudely; ruthlessly; systematically.
(See restrain, suppress.)

REPRESSED

adverbs
cruelly; naturally; morbidly; sternly; severely; harshly; unduly; pitiably; successfully; immediately; barbarously; opportunely; promptly; effectively; pitiably.

REPRESSION

adjectives
prompt; impartial; intense; sublime; self; particular; sexual; severe; definite.

REPRIMAND

verbs
expose to—; inflict—; load with—s; protest —; resist—; submit to—; subject to—; taunt with—s; —accuses; —anathematizes; —annoys; —cavils; —condemns; —corrects; —deprecates; —disparages; —execrates; —lashes; —rebukes; —reproaches.
(See rebuke, blame, censure, reproach.)

REPRIMAND (v)

adverbs
rigorously; sternly; publicly; officially; severely; sharply; violently; paternally; judicially.
(See reproach, scold.)

REPRINT (v)

adverbs
popularly; widely; multitudinously; perpetually; extensively; accurately; legally; faithfully.
(See print, reproduce.)

REPRISAL

adjectives
prompt; legitimate; indiscriminate; fearful; legal; swift; deadly; unerring.

verbs
anticipate—; breast—; check—; deserve—; draw—; elicit—; face—; fear—; grapple with—; offer—; provoke—; return—; stifle —; suppress—; visit—upon; —caps; —climaxes; —confronts; —dismays; —exchanges; —strikes; —subdues.
(See retaliation, punishment, penalty.)

REPROACH

adjectives
sorrowful; violent; constant; continual; disgustful; subtle; unutterable; thick-tongued; serious; bitter; ingenuous; mute; passion-

ate; galling; unjust; mild; smiling; dumb; tacit; mystic; selfish; fierce; self; mingled; undeserved; angry; generous.

verbs
attach—to; cast—upon; disfavor—; expose to—; fling—at; imply—; justify—; overwhelm with—; resist—; support—; warrant —; —blots; —corrects; —cuts; —disgraces; —implicates; —reflects; —slurs; —sullies; —upsets.
(See blame, dishonor, disgrace, censure, disapproval.)

REPROACH (v)

adverbs
passionately; bitterly; abusively; violently; sorrowfully; subtly; mutely; gallingly; tacitly; fiercely; undeservedly; ungenerously; selfishly.
(See reprimand, scold.)

REPROACHFUL

adverbs
mildly; gently; softly; harshly; cruelly; moderately; sternly; severely; unforgivingly; hatefully; atrociously; intolerably; openly; publicly; secretly; abusively; immoderately; unnecessarily; needlessly; violently; vehemently; loudly; vociferously; vengefully; vituperously; unfairly; brutally; offensively; terribly; inflexibly; outrageously; arrantly; unwarrantably; pitilessly; viciously; gravely.

REPROBATE

adjectives
thorough; degenerate; notorious; malicious; energetic; self-styled.

REPRODUCE (v)

adverbs
superbly; scrupulously; perfectly; voluntarily; plastically; authentically; quaintly; historically; adequately; slavishly; mechanically; painstakingly; accurately; elaborately.
(See imitate, portray.)

REPRODUCTION

adjectives
plastic; authentic; quaint; historic; incessant; adequate; slavish; mechanical; subsequent; painstaking; accurate; elaborate.

REPROOF

adjectives
tacit; stinging; distinct; sour.

REPROVE (v)

adverbs
acridly; smartly; harshly; sternly; vigorously; bitterly; stingingly; tacitly; mutely; violently; verbally; expressly; explicitly; furiously; spiritedly.
(See reprimand, reproach.)

REPTILE

adjectives
venomous; hideous; characteristic; scaly; croaking; fishy; abhorrent; snakish; ugly; useful; groveling.

verbs
—coils; —consists; —contorts; —crushes; —encircles; —entwines; —glides; —lashes; —lies in wait; —meanders; —poisons; —slithers; —springs; —squeezes; —squirms; —strains; —strikes; —swirls; —swishes; —tightens; —twists; —undulates; —warns; —wounds; —writhes.
(See crocodile, alligator, lizard, snake.)

REPUBLIC

adjectives
model; visionary; peaceful; progressive; long-lived; rebellious; well-ordered; popular.

verbs
administer—; approve—; betray—; control —; disrupt—; dominate—; establish—; form—; govern—; organize—; override—; preserve—; preside over—; revolt against —; rule—; sway—; tolerate—; undermine —; wreck—; —relaxes; —triumphs.
(See country, democracy, government, state.)

REPUDIATE (v)

adverbs
instinctively; utterly; wholly; violently; faithlessly; unreservedly; flatly; ultimately.
(See reject, renounce.)

REPUGNANCE

adjectives
unforeseen; loathing; secret; invincible; sentimental; horrible; undefinable; strong; real; deep-seated.

verbs
allay—; arouse—; assuage—; avoid—; bear —; conceive—; dispel—; entertain—; excite —; feign—; incur—; mitigate—; mollify—;

overwhelm—; recoil from—; withdraw in —; —estranges; —intrudes; —palls; —riles (colloq.); —shocks.

(See disgust, dislike, opposition, antipathy, inconsistency, aversion.)

REPULSE

adjectives
virtual; bloody; severe; brisk; complete.

verbs
encounter—; —abduces; —chases; —dashes; —dispels; —hurtles; —impedes; —impinges; —jerks; —jogs; —prods; —pushes; —resounds; —slaps; —spurs on.

(See defeat, refusal, rebuff, denial.)

REPULSE (v)

adverbs
briskly; stoutly; stalwartly; successfully; sharply; readily; unceremoniously; severely; violently.

(See repel, reject.)

REPULSION

adjectives
reciprocal; lively; utter; mutual; instinctive; deadly; bitter; indescribable; singular; remarkable.

REPUTATION

adjectives
freshest; popular; rising; senseless; local; unassailable; well-earned; murdered; magnificent; swollen; formidable; subverted; enviable; commonplace; civic; evanescent; posthumous; untarnished; immature; artistic; unblemished; literary; mushroom; exceptional; wounded; established; merited; spotless; exaggerated; reverend; enduring; undue; skittish; slender; bubble; unquestioned; professional; priceless; outstanding; terrible; pious; vile; tender; savory; damaged; fabulous; poetic; lamentable.

verbs
achieve—; acquire—; belie—; blacken—; build—; carve—; destroy—; enhance—; enjoy—; establish—; injure—; jeopardize—; justify—; mar—; mature—; merit—; outlive—; prostitute—; protect—; rival—; sacrifice—; save—; stake—on; —blooms; —languishes; —precedes; —precludes; —spreads; —swells; —withers.

(See fame, name, character, distinction, honor, notoriety, glory.)

REPUTE

adjectives
grave; ill; considerable; honorable; doubtful; prominent; local; scientific; charitable; provincial; high.

REQUEST

adjectives
conflicting; unusual; continual; commonplace; inopportune; dying; special; urgent; humble; whispered; emphatic; unreasonable; unconsidered; universal; pointed.

verbs
accede to—; acquiesce in—; assail with—s; bombard with—s; comply with—; convey—; dodge—; grant—; gratify—; heed—; justify—; meet—; pester with—s; repeat—; swamp with—s; urge—.

(See desire, entreaty, application, appeal, demand.)

REQUEST (v)

adverbs
urgently; haughtily; earnestly; fawningly; emphatically; reluctantly; graciously; ultimately; insistently; particularly; reasonably; humbly; importunately.

(See ask, beg, entreat.)

REQUIRE (v)

adverbs
passionately; urgently; perpetually; vitally; imperatively; strictly; reasonably; ethically; personally; physically; medically; aesthetically.

(See exact, want, demand.)

REQUIRED

adverbs
legally; inescapably; naturally; technically; inexorably; peremptorily; recently; authoritatively; officially; arbitrarily; tyrannically; dogmatically; reasonably; rigorously; rigidly; absolutely; socially; conventionally; prescriptively; lawfully; openly; duly; constitutionally; decently; traditionally.

REQUIREMENTS

adjectives
postnatal; eminent; classic; reasonable; relative; ethical; basic; collective; exacting; hygienic; traditional; rigorous; technical; strictest; human; personnel; specific; professional; complex; certain; maximum; minimum; residential; absolute; physical; rhythmic; aesthetic; sanitary; imperative.

verbs
check—; comply with—; condemn—; dispense with—; draw up—; fulfill—; furnish —; justify—; lack—; meet—; necessitate—; occasion—; offer—; overlook—; point out —; produce—; raise—; remove—; respect —; supply—; tabulate—; violate—; —apply to; —call for; —demand; —impede.
(See demand, injunction, necessity.)

REQUISITE

adjectives
regular; prime; definite; essential; indispensable.

REQUITAL

adjectives
humble; ungenerous; unworthy; poor; scant; fair; satisfactory.

RESCUE

verbs
aid in—; dash to—; deplore—; clog—; cumber—; expedite—; hamper—; hasten—; hinder—; impede—; interrupt—; obstruct—; perform—; pray for—; retard—; speed—; —delivers; —discommodes; —embarrasses; —preserves; —relieves; —saves.
(See deliverance, release.)

RESCUE (v)

adverbs
nobly; heroically; triumphantly; gallantly; stalwartly; rashly; boldly; courageously.
(See save, release.)

RESEARCH

adjectives
vigilant; philosophical; indefatigable; antiquarian; abstract; hydrological; subsequent; perpetual; relentless; celestial; original; brilliant; infinite; useless; enthusiastic; conscientious; scientific; extensive; microscopical; commercial; philological; bold; ingenious; effective; exhaustive; photographic; valuable; painstaking; patient; profound; deliberate; sociological; mysterious; laborious; masterly; comprehensive; stellar; ceaseless; critical; historical; malignant; archaeological; tireless; multitudinous (pl); psychoanalytic; obscure; profitable.

verbs
commence—; conduct—; direct—; engage in —; enter upon—; instigate—; launch—; maintain—; promote—; publish—; stimulate —; —analyzes; —awakens; —contributes; —culminates in; —determines; —discloses; —enlightens; —enriches; —exposes; —explores; —fathoms; —ferrets out; —imparts; —peers; —reveals.
(See inquiry, investigation, inquisition, study.)

RESEMBLANCE

adjectives
intricate; mimetic; enchanted; successful; extraordinary; fancied; natural; striking; faraway; vague; distant; self-evident; divine; partial; mysterious; close; protective; inaccurate; defensive; aggressive; capital; inexplicable; recognizable; unexpected; startling.

verbs
accentuate—; approximate—; assimilate—; bear—; detect—; discern—; evoke—; kindle —; savor of—; sharpen—; —amazes; —astounds; —disturbs; —moves; —shocks; —smites; —stirs; —strikes.
(See similarity, identity.)

RESEMBLE (v)

adverbs
strikingly; curiously; precisely; particularly; spectacularly; adequately; protectively; recognizably; startlingly; mysteriously; markedly; superficially.
(See favor.)

RESENT (v)

adverbs
forcibly; morbidly; vehemently; bitterly; subconsciously; indignantly; sternly; passionately; humorously; secretly; mutely; violently; keenly; fiercely; murderously; disdainfully; sullenly.
(See disapprove, begrudge.)

RESENTFUL

adverbs
angrily; dangerously; bitterly; passionately; sullenly; bluntly; sadly; cruelly; venomously; maliciously; vengefully; acrimoniously; violently; vociferously; strangely; unaccountably; unreasonably; insatiably; stubbornly; implacably; unappeasably; openly; secretly; fantastically; obviously; manifestly; evidently; furiously; irascibly; truculently; uncommonly; ominously; disastrously; permanently.

RESENTMENT

adjectives

terrible; increasing; admiring; individual; implacable; obstinate; dull; furious; keen; angry; impulsive; blind; half-sore; animal; fierce; intense; murderous; incipient; vigorous; sturdy; hot; disdainful; momentary; jealous; brooding; bitter; impotent; sagged; hasty; spirited; sullen; hard; viperish; astonished; impatient; additional; passionate; protecting; personal; desperate; general; generous; just; fancied.

verbs

arouse—; call forth—; cherish—; display—; engender—; evoke—; excite—; exhibit—; fill with—; flood with—; kindle—; reflect with—; shake off—; smother—; stir up—; —flares; —is born; —melts; —mounts; —wells; —yields to.

(See grudge, ill-will, anger, grievance.)

RESERVATION

adjectives

mental; explicit; express; common-sense; forest; experimental; heedful; definite; specific.

RESERVE

adjectives

scholarly; cash; considerable; substantial; emotional; chaste; appreciable; haughty; preliminary; habitual; dignified; sullen; mistrustful; maidenly; stately; sorrowful; stern; cold; unsympathizing; timberland; stubborn; approaching; singular; natural; compulsory; lawful; precious; womanly; ungenerous; freezing; naive; analytical; mysterious; alkaline; impenetrable; defective; delicate; mutual; watchful; critical.

verbs

break down—; deplete—; discard—; emerge from—; ignore—; inspire—; intensify—; penetrate—; pierce—; prick—; retain—; —cloaks; —conceals; —covers; —masks; —melts; —mystifies; —piques; —protects; —secludes.

(See aloofness, modesty, reticence, restraint, shyness, diffidence, fund.)

RESERVE (*v*)

adverbs

expressly; shrewdly; delicately; covetously; exclusively; faithfully.

(See retain, restrain.)

RESERVED

adverbs

quietly; demurely; sedately; characteristically; habitually; naturally; inherently; discreetly; strategically; prudently; wisely; gravely; judicially; arrogantly; proudly; shyly; bashfully; unduly; unfortunately; extremely; strangely; curiously; oddly; placidly; serenely; coyly; timidly; mysteriously; extraordinarily; sensibly; vexatiously.

RESERVOIR

adjectives

tapering; immense; ducal; copious; sheltered; inexhaustible.

verbs

construct—; dam—; exhaust—; flow from—; form—; inspect—; replenish—; tax—; —accumulates; —collects; —preserves; —reserves; —stores; —yields.

(See supply, tank.)

RESIDENCE

adjectives

episcopal; commodious; costly; palatial; comfortable; handsome; peculiar; official; ungarnished; stately; enlarged; wretched; permanent; seasonal; picturesque; temporary; monastic; ambitious; baronial; paternal; suitable; prolonged; sumptuous; modest.

verbs

establish—; frequent—; guard—; lack—; maintain—; neglect—; occupy—; regulate—; secure—; take up—; view—; invite to—.

(See home, establishment, mansion, dwelling.)

RESIDENT

adjectives

influential; distinguished; valued; temporary; permanent.

RESIDENTIAL

adverbs

pleasantly; strictly; expensively; exclusively; desirably; aristocratically; swankily; modestly; primarily; wholly; assuredly; delightfully; scrupulously; unmistakably; quietly; peacefully; agreeably.

RESIDUE

adjectives

harmful; visible; sweetest; solid; miserable; final; greasy; gummy; soapy; mournful.

verbs
bag—; consume—; cherish—; conceal—; discard—; gather—; heap—; "junk"—; leave—; offer—; proffer—; retain—; salvage—; scatter—; scrap—; store—; utilize —; value—; —disperses; —survives.
(See ashes, excess, cinders, remnant.)

RESIGN (v)

adverbs
reluctantly; voluntarily; nominally; officially; cheerfully; piously; fatalistically; irrevocably; philosophically; wearily.
(See abdicate, withdraw.)

RESIGNATION

adjectives
fatalistic; grim; virtual; dreamy; melancholy; serene; unsurprised; meek; patient; irrevocable; perverted; conscious; apparent; unwilling; quiet; infinite; philosophical; appalling; angelical; unhappy; spiritless; youthful; sorrowful; perfect; pathetic; tacit; passive; somber; gentle; mournful; despondent; voluntary; wearied; gloomy.

verbs
announce—; anticipate—; bewail—; compel —; decline—; deplore—; grant—; lament —; offer—; order—; present—; regret—; tender—; weigh—; —alters; —confuses; —disappoints; —disconcerts; —humbles; —mortifies.
(See surrender, retirement.)

RESIGNED

adverbs
philosophically; passively; quietly; scarcely; hardly; apathetically; resolutely; grimly; meekly; apparently; perfectly; shamelessly; appallingly; incredibly; eventually; obviously; strangely; humbly; pathetically; obediently; submissively; pliantly; weakly; calmly; imperturbably; stolidly; stupidly.

RESILIENT

adverbs
satisfactorily; unusually; highly; extraordinarily; smoothly; appreciably; pleasantly; desirably; adequately; extremely; conveniently; surprisingly; suitably; buoyantly; advantageously; uncommonly.

RESIST (v)

adverbs
stubbornly; vigorously; skillfully; dexterously; passively; blusteringly; modestly; sternly; heroically; effectively; violently; stoutly; physically; insurmountably; feebly; resolutely.
(See oppose, withstand.)

RESISTANCE

adjectives
rust; permanent; unexpected; forcible; popular; stern; unyielding; strenuous; heroic; prompt; amazing; pretended; successful; prolonged; stubborn; indignant; glorious; increased; warlike; crushed; desperate; enfeebled; stout; substantial; sad; perceiving; vague; militant; fierce; faint; humble; bold; incredulous; keener; tenacious; ineffectual; organized; gladiatorial; countervailing; rationalized; unlawful; unconscious; determined; patriotic; creditable; passive; severest; awed; earnest; coy; physical; meditating; stagnated; obstinate; rugged; hopeless; insurmountable; armed; feeble; resolute; vain; appreciable; angry.

verbs
acquire—; batter down—; break down—; build—; compensate for—; crush—; deplete —; determine—; encounter—; exercise—; harden for—; increase—; lower—; meet with—; prolong—; rationalize—; reduce—; stiffen—; weaken—; —collapses; —cracks; —lessens; —melts away.
(See antagonism, strength, opposition, hostility.)

RESOLUTE

adverbs
courageously; doggedly; stubbornly; intrepidly; gallantly; staunchly; persistently; immovably; steadily; unwaveringly; stoutly; dauntlessly; obstinately; cruelly; bitterly; determinedly; tragically; pluckily; tenaciously; indomitably; sadly; fanatically; dogmatically; ungenerously; inexorably; relentlessly; admirably; commendably; earnestly; zealously; enthusiastically; confidently; heroically; amazingly; remarkably; terribly.

RESOLUTION

adjectives
constitutional; settled; defiant; dogged; sensible; inflexible; virtuous; submissive; deliberate; jaunty; unanimous; daring; restless; generous; thoughtful; robust; gloomy; stern; tremendous; determined; austere; firm; immense; rash; obituary; indomitable; undaunted; desperate; philosophical; bold; early; stubborn; energetic; impulsive;

concurrent; invincible; passionate; dangerous; joint; vigorous; loyal; essential; satisfactory; freighted; fierce; unalterable; chivalrous; sacred; evanescent; memorable; momentous; gathering; congressional; pious; irrevocable; wise; courageous; godly; determined; heroic; imprudent; epic; unchangeable; queer; decisive.

verbs
abandon—; acclaim—; adhere to—; adopt —; applaud—; bolster—; convey—; crystalize into—; draft—; formulate—; fortify—; introduce—; prime with—s; shake—; stiffen —; uphold—; weaken—; —s pour in; —s strengthen.
(See decision, determination, bill, law.)

RESOLVE

adjectives
absolute; strained; secret; deliberate; fearless; rash; added; stern; desperate; virtuous; firm; deeper; mental; pertinacious; iron; concluding; excellent; courageous; calm; dominant; high; wise; terrible; unswerving; dauntless; mortified; inflexible; feeble-framed.

RESOLVE (v)

adverbs
ultimately; prudently; mentally; rationally; solemnly; privately; unanimously; stubbornly; inflexibly; deliberately; impulsively; fiercely; chivalrously; momentously; imprudently.
(See determine, dissolve.)

RESONANT

adverbs
pleasantly; deeply; unusually; harmoniously; surprisingly; marvellously; admirably; distinctly; hollowly; agreeably; strikingly; peculiarly; curiously; remarkably.

RESORT

adjectives
strict; brilliant; cold; lowest; fair; pleasure; attractive; little; embryonic; mountain; seasonal; favorite; fashionable; expanding; imposing; dissolute; habitual; desperate; summer; mundane; complete; seashore; family; self-contained; beach; delightful; best-loved; premier; world-famous; wonderful.

verbs
crowd—; fill—; frequent—; infest—; retire to—; repair to—; swamp—s; —advertises; —appeals; —attracts; —consoles; —delights; —eases; —offers; —refreshes; —strengthens.
(See hotel, refuge.)

RESOUND (v)

adverbs
thunderingly; discordantly; tremendously; dreadfully; awesomely; thunderously; reverberatingly.
(See peal, reverberate.)

RESOURCEFUL

adverbs
ingeniously; amazingly; skilfully; conveniently; fortunately; luckily; unusually; miraculously; incredibly; inventively; cleverly; adroitly; expediently; expertly; handily; adaptably; deftly; intelligently; felicitously; happily; particularly; manifestly; unfailingly; naturally; inimitably.

RESOURCES

adjectives
natural; decorative; perpetual; ever-present; fertile; meager; spiritual; financial; utmost; therapeutic; magnificent; manifold; productive; unfailing; mineral; artistic; boundless; reasonable; enormous; gigantic; technical; infallible; visual; limited; despairing; legitimate; exhausted; immense; physical; cyclopedic; immeasurable; temporal; material; healing; military; diplomatic; delightful; sole; insignificant; colossal; extensive; vast; tremendous; dramatic; strategic; privileged; unfailing; endless; slender; pecuniary; ready; adequate; scanty; prodigious.

verbs
assemble—; augment—; cast upon—; concentrate—; cultivate—; deplete—; develop —; employ—; encourage—; exhaust—; expend—; fortify—; impair—; liquidate—; mobilize—; paralyze—; squander—; strain —; tap—; tax—.
(See finances, assets, property, means.)

RESPECT

adjectives
exalted; regretful; greatest; idolatrous; reverential; utmost; impassive; continued; affectionate; proper; astonished; wholesome; compassionate; graceful; self; dignified; profound; temporal; haughty; deferential; pitying; punctilious; merited; apologetic;

indignant; unfeigned; listening; mutual; essential; delicate; tender; unqualified; grudging; devout; reluctant; important; high; lasting; credulous; weak; infinite; indescribable; extorted; extreme; considerate; habitual; corresponding; scant; diminished; genuine; remarkable; enormous; undefinable; unbounded; ambiguous; regretful; increased; expensive; constant; dutiful; particular; astonishing; popular; thoughtful; pusillanimous; diffident; marked.

verbs
broaden into—; command—; compel—; deepen—; deserve—; draw—; earn—; engender—; entitle to—; forfeit—; heighten —; impair—; inspire—; insure—; merit—; pay—s; preserve—; reflect—; retain—; train in—; violate—; win—.
(See esteem, deference, honor, homage, admiration, respectability.)

RESPECT (v)

adverbs
scrupulously; sympathetically; intuitively; universally; deferentially; punctiliously; unfeignedly; mutually; reluctantly; genuinely; unboundedly; dutifully; wholesomely; markedly; affectionately.
(See revere, esteem.)

RESPECTABILITY

adjectives
decent; indisputable; bourgeois; unshadowed; worldly; irreproachable; unimpeachable; unblemished; private; undeniable; obvious; dignified; spotless; triumphant; suburban; utilitarian.

verbs
acquire—; assume—; claim—; cleave to—; confer—; crown with—; don—; emulate—; feign—; gain—; preserve—; reflect—; renounce—; sacrifice—; shed—; wear—; —dignifies; —distinguishes; —elevates; —flourishes; —narrows; —restricts; —stifles.
(See respect.)

RESPECTABLE

adverbs
highly; eminently; decently; notably; unimpeachably; undeniably; obviously; admirably; extremely; admittedly; uncommonly; estimably; oppressively; painfully; ostentatiously; self-righteously; flauntingly; indisputably; scarcely; supposedly; pleasantly; harmlessly.

RESPECTFUL

adverbs
deferentially; ingratiatingly; servilely; slavishly; enthusiastically; affectionately; genuinely; sincerely; devotedly; devoutly; piously; reverently; graciously; gravely; flatteringly; amiably; courteously; politely; attentively; earnestly; ardently; nonchalantly; casually; significantly; solemnly; filially; dutifully; ardently; officiously; diplomatically; subserviently; gracefully; pleasantly; agreeably; hospitably; exceedingly; chivalrously; significantly; overwhelmingly; habitually.

RESPIRATION

adjectives
momentary; diminished; violent; labored; artificial.

verbs
clog—; disorder—; embarrass—; force—; govern—; heighten—; impede—; increase —; involve—; labor—; persevere with—; record—; stimulate—; sustain—.
(See breath, breathing.)

RESPITE

verbs
appeal for—; consume—; cut short—; demand—; enjoy—; grant—; seek—; spend —; —arrests; —delays; —elapses; —interrupts; —intervenes; —overjoys; —refreshes; —rescues; —stems; —tides over.
(See delay, rest, suspension, pause.)

RESPOND (v)

adverbs
royally; affably; felicitously; brilliantly; generously; curtly; brusquely; pertly; acridly; sarcastically; reluctantly; enigmatically; passionately; imperturbably; grimly; nervously; enthusiastically; patriotically; gallantly; genially; humorously; suitably; affectionately; ambiguously; felicitously; crabbedly; boisterously; sententiously; tardily.
(See reply, answer.)

RESPONSE

adjectives
unpalatable; affectionate; eager; astounding; loving; blessed; unfavorable; ready; gloomy; generous; cordial; patriotic; emotional; appropriate; feminine; immediate; popular; copious; instinctive; evident; oracular; verbal; ambiguous; sympathetic;

characteristic; hearty; felicitous; instantaneous; beauteous; tremendous; typical; accurate; crabbed; calm; quick; liquid; untimely; boisterous; remote; passive; enthusiastic; shallow; brutal; joint; sententious; rough.

verbs
avert—; awaken—; bark—; bolster—; call forth—; convey—; correlate—s; determine —; elicit—; evoke—; force—; gain—; guard—; hail—; invite—; level—at; mumble—; mutter—; provoke—; question—; quicken—; restrain—; welcome—; —dismays; —encourages; —gladdens; —heightens; —lessens.
(See answer, echo.)

RESPONSIBILITY

adjectives
executive; unending; fearful; pecuniary; colossal; immense; sacred; dubious; painful; divided; individual; incidental; administrative; gravest; moral; serious; dreadful; direct; frightful; tremendous; numerous (pl); weighty; corresponding.

verbs
absolve from—; awaken to—; assume—; bear—; cast off—; charge with—; confer—; deviate from—; delegate—; discard—; disregard—; dodge—; dread—; entail—; evade—; expand—; face—; impose—; incur—; inherit—; involve—; lighten—; meet—; obviate—; overburden with—; realize—; relieve of—; saddle with—; shield from—; shift—; shirk—; shoulder —; shrink from—; shy away from—; tackle—; undertake—; —devolves upon; —exacts; —presses; —reposes in; —rests on.
(See duty, charge.)

RESPONSIBLE

adverbs
admittedly; personally; individually; fearfully; unfortunately; entirely; directly; criminally; legally; accidently; voluntarily; peculiarly; indisputably; terribly; undoubtedly; officially; allegedly; indirectly; certainly; partially; reliably; sincerely; heavily; altogether; perfectly; safely; gravely; seriously; unhappily; completely; tragically; frightly; tremendously; naturally; incidentally; temporarily; permanently; momentarily; duly; morally; financially; deeply; carefully; wholly.

REST

adjectives
ecstatic; listless; ignoble; needful; saintly; unutterable; heavy-laden; comfortable; peaceful; common; prolonged; life-preserving; spacious; everlasting; fitting; unadulterated; grave; wholesome; predestined; eternal; tumultuous; sullen; gracious; mental; refreshing; frequent; happy; placid; noontide; recumbent; interminable; absolute; perpetual; balmy; breathless; comparative; saintly.

verbs
abstain from—; advocate—; afford—; deserve—; desist from—; enjoin—; enjoy—; fold in—; refrain from—; terminate—; —comforts; —delays; —eases; —invigorates; —refreshes; —rejuvenates; —relaxes; —relieves; —renews; —slackens; —soothes; —stagnates; —unburdens.
(See delay, pause, respite, sleep.)

REST (v)

adverbs
ultimately; unsoundly; implicitly; perpetually; philosophically; impassively; ostentatiously; placidly; serenely; firmly; securely; listlessly; eternally; interminably.
(See relax, stop, repose.)

RESTAURANT

adjectives
celebrated; exclusive; world-famous; exotic; modest; open-air; low-ceilinged; clattering; bustling; unpretentious; dingy; little; lighted; gay; bright; modern; excellent; glamorous; diverting; exciting; fine; distinctive; air-cooled; moderate; colorful; fashionable; renowned.

verbs
inspect—; license—; rig up—; —advertises; —appeals; —attracts; —caters to; —delights; —employs; —patronizes; —plans; —pleases; —prepares; —offers; —solicits; —specializes.
(See hotel, tavern, inn.)

RESTFUL

adverbs
quietly; pleasantly; agreeably; beautifully; unusually; lazily; moderately; comparatively; entirely; wholly; extremely; singularly; curiously; peculiarly; incomparably; unspeakably; gratefully; strangely; simply; irresponsibly; unutterably; refreshingly; in-

effably; inexpressibly; unbelievably; easily; invitingly; irresistibly; dreamily; drowsily; safely; miraculously; marvelously; soporiferously.

RESTITUTION

adjectives
quantitative; hopeless; spiritual; complete.

RESTIVE

adverbs
strangely; oddly; unmanageably; naturally; hopelessly; incurably; pathetically; obstinately; constantly; pitiably; understandably; helplessly; painfully; impatiently; nervously; feverishly; fractiously; reluctantly; openly; visibly; unconcealably; undisguisedly; unhappily; wretchedly; extraordinarily.

RESTLESS

adverbs
noticeably; visibly; hopelessly; actively; energetically; painfully; undisguisedly; ostentatiously; impolitely; inattentively; feverishly; nervously; heedlessly; strangely; curiously; significantly; oddly; unpleasantly; disagreeably; sullenly; unhappily; impatiently; physically; inordinately; extraordinarily; inexplicably; unaccountably; unreasonably; seriously; alarmingly; dangerously; irritably; vexatiously; anxiously; uncomfortably; disquietingly; distressingly; disturbingly.

RESTLESSNESS

adjectives
morbid; incessant; fevered; undulating; covert; pallid; inexplicable; repining; abrupt; unsteady; mercurial; infinite; ragged.

verbs
allay—; appease—; breed—; brook—; calm—; endure—; foment—; master—; overcome—; repress—; suffer—; toss in—; undergo—; yield to—; —chafes; —distresses; —fumes; —grips; —pains; —rages; —tears; —torments.

(See impatience, agitation, excitement, delirium, uneasiness, discontent.)

RESTORATION

adjectives
joyful; tranquil; refreshing; prompt; speedy; cleansing.

verbs
authorize—; direct—; discuss—; inspire—; lament—; order—; plead for—; repel—; resist—; sanction—; —appeases; —converts; —corrects; —enhances; —humbles; —improves; —pacifies; —repairs.

(See revival, reconstruction.)

RESTORATIVE

adverbs
pleasantly; effectively; successfully; usually; safely; definitely; distinctly; notably; prescriptively; supposedly; agreeably; dependably; reliably; actively; powerfully; adequately; satisfactorily; remarkably; highly.

RESTORE (*v*)

adverbs
accurately; unquestionably; ultimately; genuinely; miraculously; subsequently; skillfully; dexterously; faithfully; medically; speedily; promptly.

(See repair, renew.)

RESTRAIN (*v*)

adverbs
vigorously; voluntarily; gently; firmly; forcibly; narrowly; unreasonably; judiciously; legally; lawfully; tyrannically; artificially; irksomely; rigidly; vexatiously; oppressively; benevolently; commercially.

(See repress, suppress.)

RESTRAINED

adverbs
cautiously; discreetly; prudently; warily; austerely; patiently; judicially; wisely; carefully; politely; courteously; absurdly; unduly; stiffly; cruelly; determinedly; deliberately; resolutely; significantly; unusually; habitually; ominously; portentously; extraordinarily; strangely; singularly; oddly; unaccountably.

RESTRAINT

adjectives
parental; irksome; conventional; apparent; moral; strange; needful; artistic; uncommon; dignified; perceptible; strict; noble; outrageous; necessary; comparative; intense; rigid; practiced; wearisome; dry; grim; compelled; severe; professional; heroic; determined; habitual.

verbs
burst—; compel—; deplore—; dispel—; enforce—; exercise—; forge—; impose—; insist upon—; loosen—; necessitate—; relax

—; require—; resist—; throw off—; —binds; —burdens; —checks; —controls; —curbs; —despairs; —gags; —intensifies; —melts.

(See constraint, embargo, denial, inhibition, limitation.)

RESTRICT (v)

adverbs

parentally; irksomely; grimly; rigidly; severely; selfishly; ascetically; maddeningly; pettishly.

(See restrain, limit.)

RESTRICTIONS

adjectives

commercial; narrow; arbitrary; quantitative; impassable; oppressive; benevolent; diet; unreasonable; sharp; judicious; enforced; vexatious; regulatory; rigid; irksome; artificial; tyrannical.

verbs

abolish—; advocate—; disregard—; establish—; impose—; lift—; maintain—; subject to—; surmount—; throw off—; tighten —; yield to—; —ban; —chafe; —check; —destroy; —doom; —embrace; —forbid; —hedge in; —inhibit; —limit; —prohibit; —restrain; —stifle.

(See limits, inhibition, restraint, limitations.)

RESULT

adjectives

historical; admirable; indecisive; promising; exquisite; barren; declared; discouraging; magnificent; half-starving; pernicious; tangible; observed; ripe; immediate; ultimate; substantial; gratifying; disastrous; outstanding; intractable; astounding; brilliant; amazing; dazzling; astonishing; consistent; momentous; pertinent; involuntary; deducible; decorative; splendid; detrimental; creditable; bewildering; positive; triumphant; natural; unfailing; pecuniary; moral; estimated; salubrious; winning; direct; beneficial; effective; calculated; appreciable; proportional; invariable; tangible; vociferated; hilarious; multitudinous (pl); casual; primary; encouraging; unobserved; crowning; fatal; necessary; naked; tardy; advantageous; lasting; honest; ambrosian; excellent; revealing; satisfactory; successful; inevitable; unanticipated; quantitative; accomplishing; speculative; unbelievable; pitiful; conclusive; startling; remarkable; wonderful; abundant; extraordinary; profitable; therapeutic; agreeable; notable; satisfactory; desirable; intelligible; practical; confusing; fine; disappointing; outward; sifted; unquestionable; scientific; identical; valuable; accurate; infallible; marvelous; capital; auspicious; typical; startling; memorable; obvious; competent; educative; sweeping; surprising; rapid; partial; ethereal; expectable; living; prosperous; extreme; salutary; established; fruitful; equivocal; riotous; happy; comic; deferred; important; verified; feverish; exhausting; logical; gradual; factitious; disheartening; contradictory; traceable; ludicrous; demoralizing; delightful; damaging; chastening; beneficent; valid; sentimental; required; secondary; unreliable; compromising; unified; legitimate; stupendous; deplorable; fearful; net.

verbs

accept—; accomplish—; achieve—; anticipate—; assay—; attain—; cap—; challenge —; claim—; confirm—; decry—; discredit —; embody—; envisage—; evaluate—; falsify—; forecast—; garner—s; predict—; sum up—s; tally—s; trace—s; visualize—; yield—s; —s accrue; —s attend; —s justify.

(See consequence, effect, issue, outcome.)

RESULT (v)

adverbs

fatally; invariably; inevitably; appreciably; ludicrously; damagingly; demoralizingly; legitimately; deplorably; astonishingly; proportionally; infallibly.

(See terminate, end.)

RESUME (v)

adverbs

reluctantly; haughtily; diligently; placidly; traditionally; complacently; cheerily; voluntarily; uncomplainingly; blandly; customarily.

(See begin, start.)

RESURRECTION

adjectives

artificial; joyful; queer; summer; spiritual.

verbs

anticipate—; arrange for—; escape—; evade—; inspire—; mold—; plan—; promise—; seek—; shape—; stay—; suggest—; support—; warn of—; —restores; —threatens.

(See renaissance, restoration, revival.),

RETAIN (v)

adverbs

invariably; indefinitely; selfishly; voluptuously; basely; gloriously; righteously.

(See hold, keep, reserve.)

RETAINER

adjectives

taciturn; gorgeous; confidential; faithful; marshaled.

verbs

beckon—; chastise—; despatch—; discharge —; flout—; order—; recommend—; reprove —; suffer—; —accompanies; —aids; —arranges; —attends; —betrays; —confronts; —eases; —endures; —refers; —serves.

(See following, servant, matron.)

RETALIATE (v)

adverbs

revengefully; viciously; vindictively; pitilessly; treacherously; poisonously; hatefully; despicably; violently; insidiously; traitorously.

(See repay, avenge.)

RETALIATION

adjectives

pitiless; provoking; youthful; treacherous; angry.

verbs

avert—; draw—; grapple with—; ignore —; incur—; invite—; offer—; overlook—; smother—; threaten with—; withstand—; —avenges; —harms; —inflames; —kicks; —pierces; —rankles; —repulses; —revenges; —stems; —stings.

(See punishment, revenge, discipline, penalty.)

RETARD (v)

adverbs

mechanically; deliberately; inevitably; cautiously; expediently; automatically.

(See hinder, obstruct.)

RETENTION

adjectives

undue; stubborn; corresponding; enforced.

RETENTIVE

adverbs

highly; unusually; phenomenally; miraculously; extraordinarily; marvelously; astonishingly; amazingly; unbelievably; incredibly; conveniently; curiously; peculiarly; singularly; particularly; incomparably.

RETICENCE

adjectives

noble; diplomatic; exaggerated; introspective; masterly; strict; womanly; haughty; dignified; excessive; dogged; cautious; judicious.

verbs

couch in—; discard—; lapse into—; penetrate—; pierce—; shroud in—; sink into—; —blinds; —cloaks; —conceals; —curtains; —envelops; —masks; —mystifies; —perplexes; —puzzles; —screens; —veils; —withholds.

(See modesty, reserve, aloofness.)

RETICENT

adverbs

austerely; needlessly; absurdly; naturally; habitually; unnecessarily; highly; curiously; unreasonably; sensibly; singularly; oddly; peculiarly; unduly; taciturnly; foolishly; disagreeably; noticeably; unfortunately.

RETINUE

adjectives

glittering; brilliant; imperial; numerous (pl); copious; radiant; perilous.

RETIRE (v)

adverbs

timidly; cautiously; snobbishly; unwillingly; meekly; modestly; deferentially; shamefacedly; noiselessly; discreetly; decently; voluntarily; precipitately.

(See retreat, withdraw.)

RETIREMENT

adjectives

voluntary; imminent; short; quiet; suspicious; comparative; peaceful; secular; close; unobtrusive; romantic; precipitate; sweet; monastic; ostentatious; beloved; temporary.

verbs

creep into—; draw into—; drive into—; emerge from—; forego—; hasten—; hold in —; loathe—; remain in—; resist—; shame

into—; shut into—; sink into—; slate for —; surrender to—; —abjures; —bores; —cuts off; —deprives; —stagnates.
(See isolation, resignation, retreat, seclusion.)

RETIRING

adverbs
unusually; shyly; timidly; studiously; habitually; naturally; diffidently; unsocially; inhospitably; reticently; taciturnly; forbiddingly.

RETORT

adjectives
gruff; famous; skillful; impulsive; scornful; spirited; readiest; instant; severest; stinging.

verbs
draw—; fire—; parry—; provoke—; —acknowledges; —appeases; —clinches; —confutes; —crushes; —defeats; —determines; —explains; —irks; —leaps to one's lips; —parries; —rebuts; —solves; —shatters; —silences; —verifies.
(See answer, reply, response, repartee.)

RETORT (*v*)

adverbs
sharply; curtly; absurdly; shrewdly; effectively; acrimoniously; comically; resentfully; spiritedly; caustically; facetiously; scurrilously; waspishly; petulantly; gruffly; stingingly.
(See respond, reply.)

RETRACT (*v*)

adverbs
pusillanimously; timidly; ultimately; cautiously; fearfully; ignominiously; hastily; dishonorably; despairingly.
(See recall, disavow.)

RETREAT

adjectives
tardy; ignominious; hasty; immediate; subterranean; verdant; hospitable; bloody; sacred; timely; final; hurried; sunless; precipitate; reckless; swift; panic-stricken; dignified; grateful; epic; flurried; chosen; beloved; circuitous; masterly; lonely; secluded; orderly; crippled; hasty; base; ultimate; snug; double-quick; disastrous; cavernous; rural; gracious; foul; ruinous; secure; serene; secret; favorite; despairing; soft; honorable; glorious.

verbs
advocate—; beat—; censure—; chase into —; drive into—; fall back in—; flee in—; force into—; hasten—; move in—; occasion —; order—; shrink in—; sound—; withdraw in—; —averts; —defeats; —saves.
(See retirement, isolation.)

RETREAT (*v*)

adverbs
cringingly; ignominiously; precipitately; irrationally; coquettishly; cravenly; disastrously; ruinously; serenely; honorably; despairingly; pusillanimously.
(See retire, withdraw.)

RETRENCH (*v*)

adverbs
financially; cautiously; conservatively; sensibly; enforcedly; periodically; disastrously; shrewdly.
(See lessen, limit.)

RETRIBUTION

adjectives
trenchant; severest; utmost; tardy; righteous; bloody; just; speedy.

verbs
anticipate—; award—; defy—; deserve—; fear—; ignore—; measure—; reap—; resist —; reveal—; sow—; —amends; —atones; —harries; —evens; —retaliates; —revenges; —upbraids.
(See justice, compensation, punishment, penalty.)

RETROACTIVE

adverbs
fortunately; disastrously; luckily; happily; opportunely; expediently; legally; wisely; unconditionally; unexpectedly; acceptably.

RETROSPECT

adjectives
widening; melancholy; drowsy; foregoing; deep; briefest; gratifying; entertaining

RETROSPECTIVE

adverbs
lamentably; curiously; tiresomely; unprofitably; unfortunately; dismally; stagnantly; stubbornly; sorrowfully; obstinately; fearfully; incorrigibly; incurably; inveterately.

RETURN

adjectives
ordinary; periodical; honorable; tedious; successive (pl); infallible; pecuniary; physical; exuberant; inevitable; speedy; visible; reassuring; adequate; alleged; impending; bountiful; unprofited; scant; monetary; diminishing; abundant; circling; material; peaceful; tangible; swift; beggarly; immediate; imperfect; fortuitous.

verbs
anticipate—; deter—; foresee—; forestall—; foretell—; hamper—; hinder—; narrate—; observe—s; predict—; presage—; recount —s; relate—; resume on—; —s echo; —overjoys; —pleases; —s pour in; —redoubles; —renews.
(See harvest, report, profit, reply.)

RETURN (*v*)

adverbs
periodically; seasonally; sardonically; traditionally; habitually; customarily; testily; dubiously; deliberately; unceremoniously; subsequently; expeditiously; reluctantly; incessantly; triumphantly; fortuitously; infallibly; tediously; honorably.
(See recur, repay.)

REUNION

adjectives
chaotic; select; plotting; prominent; formal; ultimate; happy.

verbs
arrange—; attend—; band in—; bring about—; clasp in—; delay—; effect—; embrace in—; entwine in—; gather in—; invite to—; participate in—; plan—; —embodies; —interests; —overjoys; —recalls; —renews; —unites.
(See meeting, gathering, union.)

REVEAL (*v*)

adverbs
penetratingly; candidly; vividly; graphically; immodestly; daringly; traitorously; partially; concisely; deplorably; spaciously; strikingly; unmistakably; fluently; injudiciously; dismally; painfully; courageously; supernaturally.
(See disclose, expose.)

REVEL

adjectives
lurid; nightly; bestial; heavy-headed; profligate.

REVELATION

adjectives
astonishing; unexpected; lightning; sickening; fluent; divine; deathlike; injudicious; ultimate; startling; veritable; awful; curious; vivid; unsuspected; successive (pl); celestial; appalling; dismal; unforeseen; cool; judicial; painful; incessant; intimate; supernatural; guarded; frightful; amazing; courageous.

verbs
color—; deplore—; fear—; inspire—; interpret—; prod to—; resist—; —admits; —awes; —bares; —concedes; —corrects; —disburdens; —discloses; —divulges; —embarrasses; —enlightens; —exposes.
(See disclosure, exposure, discovery.)

REVELER

adjectives
joyous; lusty; bright; profane; unconventional.

REVELRY

adjectives
wild; gay; wanton; drunken; rustic; wildest; ardent.

REVENGE

adjectives
dire; luscious-toothed; unlearned; sworn; desperate; frightful; implacable; passionate; undisturbing; stinging; delicate; meaningless; bloody; fierce; prophesied; timid; meditated; swift; secret; spiteful; just; wild; refined; doubtful; sweet.

verbs
aggravate to—; avert—; contrive—; evoke—; incur—; itch for—; provoke to—; restrain—; suppress—; vow—; wreak—; —angers; —confuses; —enrages; —evens; —exasperates; —flares; —foams; —grinds; —infuriates; —stings.
(See retaliation, vengeance, hatred, hate.)

REVENGE (*v*)

adverbs
diabolically; ingeniously; logically; direly;

frightfully; implacably; passionately; swiftly; secretly; spitefully; deliberately.
(See avenge, retaliate.)

REVENUE

adjectives
confiscated; royal; overflowing; advertising; surplus; princely; accruing; requisite; gross; expected; present.

verbs
acquire—; apportion—; bear—; boost (colloq.)—; claim—; derive—; dissipate—; draw—; expend—; forfeit—; gain—; increase—; invest—; possess—; produce—; promise—; seek—; spend—; untie—; yield —; —accrues; —dribbles in.
(See income, money, profit, wages.)

REVERBERATE (v)

adverbs
raucously; thunderously; overwhelmingly; threateningly; portentously; musically; crashingly; clangingly; deafeningly.
(See resound, peal.)

REVERBERATING

adverbs
dimly; loudly; thunderously; resonantly; faintly; distantly; strangely; hollowly; sepulchrally; frightfully; fearfully; dully; rumblingly; mournfully; dolefully; madly; jubilantly; triumphantly; wildly.

REVERBERATION

adjectives
rocking; surly; crashing; clanging; thunderous; deafening.

REVERE (v)

adverbs
religiously; blindly; adoringly; idolatrously; spiritually; physically; fanatically.
(See honor, respect.)

REVERENCE

adjectives
professed; increasing; unquestioning; profound; easy; infinite; worshipful; mystical; devotional; meek; habitual; involuntary; superstitious; apprehensive; pious; subdued; peculiar; grateful; serious; high; honest; dutiful; awed; defensive; unaffected; instinctive; forward; personal; wanting; servile; special; religious; nominal; implicit; instant; better-proportioned; overgreat; inexpressible; filial.

verbs
arouse—; bear—; bestow—; cherish—; command—; dedicate in—; deserve—; entertain —; evince—; feign—; inculcate—; ingrain —; inspire—; kneel in—; observe with—; pay—; present—; produce—; question—; win—; —edifies; —elevates; —enshrines; —overawes.
(See awe, honor, adoration, respect, obeisance.)

REVERENCE (v)

adverbs
devoutly; unquestionably; profoundly; infinitely; mystically; superstitiously; piously; dutifully; religiously; servilely; filially; inexpressibly.
(See venerate, revere.)

REVERENT

adverbs
respectfully; devoutly; piously; quietly; silently; duly; becomingly; fittingly; sincerely; deeply; profoundly; noticeably; commendably; visibly; carefully; habitually; inherently; truly; unusually; worshipfully; unaffectedly; unobtrusively; implicitly.

REVERIE

adjectives
dreamful; embowered; abstracted; absorbed; voluptuous; pensive; sublime; scornful; perplexed; anxious; gloomy; celestial; silent; uneasy; brief; delicious; motionless; pleasant; indignant; indefinable; blissful; intoxicating; unconscious; fantastic; enamored.

verbs
absorb in—; awake from—; base on—; bask in—; compose—; crack—; drift into—; engage in—; envelop in—; fall into—; fashion—; float into—; imbibe in—; indulge in —; intoxicate with—; lapse into—; lose in —; pursue in—; recall in—; rouse from—; shroud in—; sink into—; start from—; steep in—; —attains; —dances; —exalts; —promises; —reflects; —revolves; —sustains.
(See dream, meditation.)

REVERSE

adjectives
occasional; ominous; appalling; disastrous; catastrophic.

verbs
allay—; bear—; compare—s; contend with —s; encounter—s; lament—; mitigate—; shoulder—; suffer—; teach—; —annuls; —cancels; —damages; —deposes; —depresses; —dissolves; —overrides; —saddles.
(See misfortune, calamity, defeat, adversity.)

REVERSE (v)

adverbs
dramatically; automatically; mechanically; strategically; desperately; strikingly; appreciably.
(See invert, overthrow.)

REVERSIBLE

adverbs
conveniently; adaptably; fittingly; appropriately; easily; readily; comfortably; advantageously; usefully; serviceably; quickly; instantly; smartly; handsomely.

REVERSION

adjectives
far-off; natural; certain; inevitable.

REVERT (v)

adverbs
normally; customarily; traditionally; historically; instinctively; naturally; inevitably.
(See return, recur.)

REVIEW

adjectives
balanced; impartial; crisp; accurate; honest; unbiased; news; up-to-the-minute; annual; embracing; enthusiastic; competent; prejudiced; financial; artistic; dispassionate; critical; sweeping; elaborate; exhaustive; strict; dignified; prodigal; learned; lumbering; involuntary; copious; philosophical; adulatory; brief; flippant.

verbs
march in—; pass in—; —blasts; —censures; —commends; —criticizes; —discusses; —exposes; —fatigues; —honors; —lauds; —scorches; —suggests; —surveys; —treats of; —unfolds.
(See analysis, study, parade, survey, examination.)

REVIEW (v)

adverbs
appreciatively; courteously; briefly; cursorily; formally; perfunctorily; critically; impartially; accurately; unbiasedly; annually; competently; dispassionately; elaborately; exhaustively; philosophically; acrimoniously.
(See reconsider, contemplate.)

REVISED

adverbs
recently; cleverly; handsomely; advantageously; profitably; wisely; ably; considerably; skilfully; satisfactorily; appropriately; acceptably; broadly; somewhat; ingeniously; capably; completely; substantially; carefully; admirably.

REVISION

adjectives
substantial; patient; endless; downward; quarrelsome; slight; careful; desperate.

verbs
advise—; advocate—; balk at—; complete —; consider—; guide—; meditate on—; note —; pass—; prepare—; publish—; survive —; —astonishes; —condenses; —corrects; —improves; —seasons; —suppresses .
(See censorship, change, correction, alteration.)

REVIVAL

adjectives
neo-classic; poetic; impetuous; incidental; literary; religious; romantic; wide-spread.

verbs
assume—; attempt—; costume—; deserve—; display—; hiss—; justify—; merit—; necessitate—; rejoice over—; retard—; wish for —; —commences; —exhausts; —confuses; —reawakens; —refreshes; —regains.
(See resurrection, renaissance.)

REVIVE (v)

adverbs
popularly; neo-classically; seasonally; poetically; religiously; spectacularly; dramatically; athletically; spiritually; physically.
(See restore, rally.)

REVOLT

adjectives
successful; meditated; wide-spread; minor; projected; healthy; tentative; mental; incoherent; energetic; personal; inconsistent.

REVOLT (v)

adverbs
traitorously; viciously; vigorously; vindic-

tively; successfully; tentatively; abortively; unanimously; bloodlessly; violently; periodically; socially; ineffectively; inevitably.
(See rebel, shock.)

REVOLTING

adverbs
hideously; grossly; inordinately; extraordinarily; extremely; abominably; atrociously; nauseatingly; incredibly; unspeakably; detestably; unutterably; inexpressibly; particularly; strangely; painfully; appallingly; shockingly; grimly; unbearably.

REVOLUTION

adjectives
anomalistic; bloodless; veritable; successive (pl); interior; public; complete; impending; synodic; radical; dynastic; incarnate; social; industrial; sidereal; inevitable; ineffective; orbital; hideous; violent; solemn; proletarian; periodic; fickle; salutary.

verbs
betray—; consummate—; chronicle—; crush —; drive to—; engineer—; foment—; forestall—; hail—; hatch—; instigate—; justify —; launch—; map—; plunge into—; promote—; resist—; shatter—; sponsor—; spur —; stamp out—; stave off—; subdue—.
(See anarchy, insurrection, mutiny, outbreak, rebellion.)

REVOLUTIONARY

adverbs
ominously; completely; moderately; incredibly; genuinely; dangerously; alarmingly; fearfully; dreadfully; significantly; pointedly; appallingly; shockingly; grimly; restively; ungovernably; uncontrollably; riotously; mutinously; unsubmissively; insurgently; sullenly.

REVOLVE (v)

adverbs
incessantly; mechanically; automatically; perpetually; periodically; sidereally; synodically.
(See roll, spin.)

REVOLVER

verbs
conceal—; confiscate—; discharge—; display —; draw—; juggle—; oil—; pack—; pocket —; prohibit—; snatch—; —barks; —frightens; —peppers; —protects; —reassures; —spatters; —spits fire.
(See machine-gun, gun, weapon, pistol.)

REVULSION

adjectives
bitter; rapid; extraordinary; violent; desperate.

verbs
develop—; direct—; encounter—; fall into —; incur—; meet with—; recover from—; shake off—; suffer—; —dizzies; —evolves; —overturns; —shocks; —spins; —uncoils; —whirls.
(See disgust, aversion, repugnance, dislike, sickness.)

REWARD

adjectives
comprehensive; particular; swift; dazzling; palpable; sufficient; material; slender; momentary; temporal; flat; ample; adequate; rich; destined; utmost; arbitrary; tangible; sure; due; coveted; political; just; crowning; pecuniary; monetary.

verbs
assign—; assure of—; confer—; contend for —; gather—; increase—; merit—; offer—; post—; promise—; reap—; scorn—; strive for—; woo—; —blesses; —decorates; —inspires; —recompenses.
(See merit, laurel, fee, dowry, medal, prize.)

REWARD (v)

adverbs
munificently; lavishly; graciously; handsomely; fitly; amply; abundantly; dazzlingly; monetarily; financially; tangibly; politically; pecuniarily.
(See offer, compensate.)

RHAPSODIZE (v)

adverbs
furiously; bombastically; vigorously; oratorically; maddeningly; eloquently; superfluously.
(See improvise, recite, play.)

RHAPSODY

adjectives
extravagant; romantic; incoherent; mystical.

RHETORIC

adjectives
subtle; empty; heavenly; florid; full-voiced; ambitious; glowing; exuberant; judicial.

verbs
adhere to—; condemn—; consider—; exhibit —; frame—; hammer—into; heed—; indulge in—; inspect—; unmask—; lecture in —; obey—; observe—; polish—; refurbish —; school in—; steep in—; —confuses; —convinces; —expresses; —impresses; —influences; —languishes; —persuades.
(See style, prose, art, eloquence, elegance, oratory.)

RHEUMATIC

adverbs
painfully; gallantly; laughingly; embarrassingly; helplessly; hopelessly; desperately; permanently; incurably; extremely; obviously; manifestly; irremediably; crookedly; unfortunately; terribly; slightly; somewhat; distressingly; undoubtedly; noticeably; woefully.

RHEUMATISM

verbs
afflict with—; endure—; inflict with—; mitigate—; salve—; suffer from—; —attacks; —confines; —irks; —irritates; —lames; —locates; —pains; —racks; —ravages.
(See disease, pain.)

RHINOCEROS

verbs
cage—; capture—; —batters; —charges; —defends; —drowses; —feeds; —gores; —inflicts; —inhabits; —preys on; —puffs; —rams; —roams; —snorts; —waters.
(See animal.)

RHYME

adjectives
pairing (pl); lofty; feverish; uncouth; ruder; golden; bootless; tender; efficacious; ringing; visionary; facile; feminine; careless; nondescript; ever-varying; nobler; meaningless; accepted; refluent; scornful; fettered; unbaptized; brawling; rollicking; emblazoned; unmoving; frozen; nursery; euphonious; mournful; initiative; silvery; innocent; dangerous.

RHYTHM

adjectives
blithe; tantalizing; tenderest; doggerel; accelerated; settled; trotting; vibrating; visual; seductive; intriguing; wailing; sensuous; fluctuating; mighty; rowdy; dull; monotonous; incisive; abrupt; regulated; insinuating; characteristic; maddening; graceful; perfect; rustic; vehement; whirring; exquisite; maudlin; tragic; jarring; primal; natural; pulsating; throbbing; harmonious.

verbs
abuse—; accelerate—; accent—; attune to —; break—; dash into—; depend on—; derive—; determine—; lose—; measure—; regulate—; sing in—; set to—; stress—; sway to—; "swing" to—; synchronize—; —charms; —descends; —flows; —harmonizes; —persists; —reigns.
(See swing, flow.)

RIBALD

adverbs
coarsely; comically; hilariously; disgustingly; grossly; indecently; uproariously; boisterously; shockingly; appallingly; crassly; brazenly; blatantly; flagrantly; openly; notoriously; infamously; inexcusably; unpardonably; villainously; deliberately; impudently; shamelessly; shamefully; daringly.

RIBALDRY

adjectives
public; raucous.

RIBS

adjectives
overweathered; internal; irregular; glistening.

verbs
adhere to—; cling to—; crack—; crush—; develop—; divide into—; grate—; injure—; knuckle—; poke—; rend—; smash—; stick to—; stuff—; —brace; —compose; —extend; —frame; —protect; —snap; —support.

RICH

adverbs
moderately; affluently; opulently; comfortably; unbelievably; incredibly; immeasurably; incalculably; magnificently; mysteriously; suddenly; unquestionably; extremely; secretly; unimaginably; surreptitiously; exceedingly; sumptuously; abundantly marvelously.

RICHES

adjectives
boundless; inherent; ineffectual; unsearchable; manifold; exceeding; intellectual; generous; singular; countless; heavy; unbelievable; fabulous; inordinate; enormous; undreamed-of; superfluous.

verbs
accumulate—; acquire—; administer—; amass—; bestow—; command—; covet—; desire—; despise—; draw—; enjoy—; estimate—; gather—; overwhelm with—; pile up—; possess—; spurn—; store—; treasure—; trust—; worship—; wring—; —abound; —content; —corrupt; —endanger; —enslave; —flow; —govern; —hinder; —serve.
(See affluence, wealth, money, income.)

RICHNESS

adjectives
inexhaustible; vivid; mellow; smooth; changing; vibrant; gilded; decorative; amazing; singular; exceeding; medieval.

RICKETY

adverbs
absurdly; comically; dangerously; fearfully; amusingly; extremely; hazardously; impossibly; alarmingly; curiously; noisily; perilously; laughably.

RID (*v*)

adverbs
effectually; permanently; ultimately; completely; logically; thoroughly; scientifically.
(See dispose.)

RIDDLE

adjectives
fustian; psychological; diplomatic; puzzling; insoluble; unread; inscrutable; miserable; torturing.

verbs
compose—; construct—; contrive—; couch in—s; desire—; dissolve—; evolve—; guess—; interpret—; propose—; propound—; record—; resolve—; solve—; speak in—s; weave—; —amuses; —diverts; —perplexes; —puzzles; —torments; —vexes; —yields.
(See enigma, puzzle, problem, mystery.)

RIDE

adjectives
dusty; daring; subsequent; starry; desperate; tedious; delightful; tireless; midnight; fabled.

verbs
accept—; enjoy—; extend—; gain—; hasten—; invite for—; promise—; solicit—; terminate—; "thumb"—; —bores; —delights; —refreshes; —thrills; —tires; —wearies; —diverts.
(See trip, journey, tour.)

RIDE (*v*)

adverbs
thunderously; swiftly; triumphantly; furiously; victoriously; gallantly; blindly; leisurely; wildly; proudly; blithely; ruthlessly; roughly; desperately; dashingly; daringly; gracefully; decisively; superbly.
(See move, travel.)

RIDER

adjectives
consummate; heavy; gallant; superb; unmovable; dashing; expert; audacious; warlike; daring; decisive; groomless; graceful.

verbs
bear—; carry—; equal—; obey—; throw—; train—; unnerve—; —charges; —dismounts; —drags; —drives; —joggles; —lashes; —mounts; —pats; —reigns; —soothes; —spurs; —tires; —travels; —vaults; —wearies; —whips.
(See horseman.)

RIDGE

adjectives
cruciform; melancholy; woody; parallel; hummocky; hog-backed; wind-swept; barren; perpendicular; tremendous; mountain; formidable; lofty; precipitous; loosened; ice; craggy; gentle; encircling; shaggy; commanding; uncultivated; sunken; extended; crowned; hillocky.

verbs
climb to—; dance on—; discern—; dread—; drive to—; dwarf—; form—; fortify—; quit—; —beams; —caps; —chains; —crests; —elevates; —rises; —runs; —stretches; —tempts.
(See bank, range, mountain, hill.)

RIDICULE

adjectives
stinging; comic; raucous; merciless; person-

al; angry; bitter; traditional; abusive; sarcastic; scathing; biting.

verbs
bear—; defy—; expose to—; fear—; heap —; indulge in—; move to—; overcome—; resort to—; share—; subject to—; sustain—; taste—; turn to—; —bites; —checks; —cuts; —disgraces; —embarrasses; —embitters; —enrages; —pains; —smothers; —storms; —strips.

(See **banter, jeer,** irony, mockery, derision.)

RIDICULE (*v*)

adverbs
ruthlessly; sarcastically; cruelly; tenderly; spitefully; stingingly; raucously; mercilessly; angrily; bitterly; abusively; bitingly; scathingly.

(See mock, jeer.)

RIDICULOUS

adverbs
foolishly; absurdly; unreasonably; laughably; palpably; crazily; extravagantly; irrationally; childishly; stupidly; grotesquely; blatantly; whimsically; gaily; airily; intentionally; injudiciously; recklessly; weakly; senselessly; nonsensically; grossly; manifestly; rashly; unwisely; pathetically.

RIFLE

adjectives
leather-cased; handled; speckless; omnipresent; unwieldy; pneumatic; handsome; new; grimy; deathdealing; express; crackling; dreaded.

verbs
arm with—; brandish—; bristle with—s; conceal—; discharge—; examine—; fear—; inspect—; point—; provide with—s; shoulder— ;—crackles; —frightens; —gleams; —mows down; —speaks.

(See gun, machine-gun, musket.)

RIFT

adjectives
horrid; savage; gusty; keen; little; widening; convenient.

verbs
fill—; lament—; span—; —appears; —breaches; —brews; —disjoins; —disunites; —gapes; —heals; —overhangs; —rends; —rips; —ruptures; —separates; —splits; —widens.

(See breach, gap.)

RIGHT

adjectives
outward; authoritative; individual; inalienable; hereditary; unrestricted; colonial; prescriptive; litigious; indefeasible; peculiar; legal; belligerent; relative; legitimate; marital; sacred; inviolable; unquestionable; undisputed; natural; respective; concrete; undoubted; exclusive; purchased; immemorial; substantial; inestimable; municipal; injured; prime; invaded; inborn; constitutional; derivative; inherent; obedient; vanquished; common; riparian (pl); conceded; poetical; autonomic; conjugal; functional; vested; unquestioned; beautiful; proprietary; antique; terrible; illimitable; civil; perfected; manorial; executive; formal; sable-vested; shameful; feudal; covenanted; immutable; invulnerable; unalterable; abstract; ecclesiastical; unclaimed; statutable; possessory; proprietary; lucrative; impugned; questionable; absolute; vital; senescent; uncontested; divine; irrevocable; provincial; vindicated.

verbs
abolish—; accord—; acknowledge—; arrogate—; assert—; assume—; cherish—; clamor for—; concede—; confer—; confiscate—; curtail—; defend—; deprive of—; derive—; dispose of—; dispute—; disregard —; earn—; embody—; encroach on—; establish—; exercise—; forfeit—; grant—; impair—; infringe upon—; insure—; invade —; invest with—; prate of—s; preserve—; protest—; relinquish—; remand—; respect —; restore—; retain—; revoke—; safeguard—; surrender—; suspend—; suppress —; terminate—; transgress—; undermine —; uphold—; urge—; vindicate—; violate —; vouchsafe—; waive—; win—; wrest—; — resides with; —triumphs.

(See liberty, license, franchise, **justice, privilege, authority, prerogative.**)

RIGHTEOUS

adverbs
rigidly; sincerely; consciously; utterly; completely; uprightly; inherently; carefully; ostentatiously; austerely; undeviatingly; strictly; painfully; ostensibly; incredibly; apparently; overly; dutifully; duly; unduly;

pretentiously; manifestly; pharisaically; uncompromisingly; stiffly.

RIGHTEOUSNESS

adjectives
divine; inherent; ungodly; final; spotless; haughty; imputed.

verbs
forsake—; found on—; garb in—; hunger for—; judge in—; maintain—; observe with —; proclaim—; thirst for—; uphold—; —advances; —exalts; —falters; —flourishes; —rewards; —withstands; —yields; impute —.

(See justice, good, virtue, purity.)

RIGID

adverbs
stiffly; painfully; terribly; dreadfully; stonily; bleakly; uncompromisingly; intolerably; woefully; coldly; harshly; austerely; cruelly; bitterly; sternly; severely; brutally; ungenerously; narrow-mindedly; dogmatically; tyrannically; puritanically; doctrinally; intolerantly.

RIGOR

adjectives
utmost; merciless; logical; decisive; religious; protracted; grizzly; coveted; unsparing; remorseless; pedantic.

RIGORS

verbs
allay—; alleviate—; ease—; endure—; enforce—; fear—; feel—; ferment—; guard against—; preserve from—; relax—; resist —; shelter from—; smart under—; survive —; temper—; —affect; —distress; —harden; —reduce.

(See difficulty, trouble, obstacle, severity, harshness.)

RILL

adjectives
narrow; wandering; babbling; dancing; tinkling; solitary; winding; sylvan; clear; fuming; glancing; gushing; waking; frosted; limpid; rebounding; singing; summer; flowing; purling; classic.

RING

adjectives
metallic; ducal; marriage; granite; tinkling; jubilant; carved; babyish; magnificent; diamond; diurnal; dry; subtle; typic; glittering; rhythmic; betrothal; determined; watery; wondrous; closing; luminous; superb; old; scaly; mournful; insistent; diverting; contorted; stifling; clustering; lubricous; tense; monumental; familiar; sinister; dancing; flat; oval; solid; great; massive; dingy; continuous; concentric (pl).

verbs
admire—; appraise—; bedeck with—s; finger—; mislay—; restore—to; return—; tinkle—s; value—; —adorns; —binds; —dazzles; —encircles; —espouses; —imitates; —gleams; —glimmers; —glitters; —recalls; —seals; —sparkles; —weds.

(See diamond, jewel, gem.)

RING (v)

adverbs
incessantly; musically; harshly; dolefully; drowsily; monotonously; feebly; impatiently; blithely; resonantly; piercingly; metallically; vigorously; jubilantly; tinklingly.

(See resound, chime.)

RIOT

adjectives
prodigal; noiseless; bloody; subsequent; prison; licentious; golden; wild; senseless; springtide; transient.

verbs
deplore—; describe—; expose to—; incite to—; instigate—; pitch into—; provoke—; quash—; quell—; subdue—; suppress—; —bursts forth; —disorders; —ensues; —jeopardizes; —protests; —strikes; —upsets; —violates.

(See commotion, revolution, strike, disturbance, turmoil, violence.)

RIOTERS

verbs
calm—; condemn—; disperse—; incite—; pardon—; punish—; quell—; restrain—; suppress—; —agitate; —aggravate; —attack; —clamor; —demand; —harry; —pillage; —plunder; —ravage; —storm; —transgress.

(See striker, anarchist, terrorist, communist, scab.)

RIOTOUS

adverbs
dangerously; alarmingly; boisterously; seditiously; mutinously; disgracefully; inordinately; extraordinarily; strangely; uncon-

trollably; ungovernably; murderously; insensately; wildly; violently; vociferously; grimly; daringly; defiantly; tumultuously; seditiously; uproariously; terribly; sullenly.

RIPE

adverbs
finally; quite; entirely; altogether; lusciously; deliciously; completely; satisfactorily; perfectly; unexpectedly; pleasantly; sufficiently; extremely; unduly; evidently.

RIPEN (v)

adverbs
seasonally; wholesomely; deliciously; normally; luxuriantly; goldenly; succulently.
(See develop, complete.)

RIPPLE (v)

adverbs
idly; sleekly; liquidly; bubblingly; luminously; gildedly.
(See wave, sway.)

RIPPLES

adjectives
glad; silvery; purled; innumerable; foamy; moon-lit; timid; minute; bubbling; passing; luminous; breeze-ridden; transparent; sungilt; liquid.

verbs
agitate—; blow—; flow in—; form—; mark by—; observe—; smooth—; —fascinate; —glisten; —ruffle; —shimmer; —subside; —undulate; —wash.
(See wave, billow, breaker.)

RIPPLING

adverbs
merrily; cheerfully; pleasantly; clearly; smoothly; pleasantly; sparklingly; flashily; plashily; happily; blithely; brightly; brilliantly; laughingly; quietly; audibly; noisily.

RISE

adjectives
meteoric; successful; sufficient; miraculous; unprecedented; phenomenal; important; thermometric; nocturnal; gradual; corresponding; extraordinary; unpredictable; speedy.

verbs
anticipate—; check—; deplore—; forestall —; gauge—; heighten—; mount—; predict —; produce—; stem—; stimulate—; tremble on—; —advances; —ceases; —continues; —frightens; —indicates; —profits; —thrills.
(See beginning, advance, progress, increase.)

RISE (v)

adverbs
dizzily; abruptly; majestically; airily; militantly; reluctantly; unanimously; gradually; mysteriously; solemnly; impulsively; leisurely; ceremoniously; conspicuously; deliberately; involuntarily; lingeringly; reverently; obediently; perpendicularly; instinctively; amiably; meteorically; phenomenally; unpredictably.
(See arise, ascend.)

RISK

adjectives
imminent; tremendous; operative; alarming; infinite; serious; continual; unaccustomed; canine; known; desirable; considerable; unjustifiable; extraordinary.

verbs
accept—; assume—; avoid—; balk at—; court—; decry—; diminish—; entail—; exclude—; expose to—; free from—; guard against—; harbor—; increase—; incur—; involve—; justify—; lessen—; obviate—; preclude—; preserve from—; question—; undergo—; underwrite—.
(See danger, chance, hazard, speculation.)

RISK (v)

adverbs
alarmingly; unjustifiably; rashly; heroically; needlessly; considerably; superfluously.
(See endanger, imperil.)

RISKY

adverbs
dangerously; ominously; perilously; alarmingly; hazardously; definitely; peculiarly; particularly; immensely; incalculably; admittedly; unwarrantably; unfortunately; always; manifestly; extremely; uncommonly; commercially; altogether; notoriously; obviously; gravely; seriously; inescapably; unavoidably; undeniably; inordinately; unaccountably; immeasurably; incalculably; desperately; appallingly; hideously; pitiably; fearfully; tragically; adventurously; distinctly.

RITE

adjectives

superstitious; purifying; pleasing; funeral; sanguinary; sensual; true; sacramental; courtly; bloody; pagan; nuptial; connubial; ecclesiastical; abominable; sacred; gorgeous; dismal; mysterious; wanton; barbaric; religious; gloomy; hideous; ceremonial; blessed; ancient; obnoxious; various (pl); horrid; preparatory; repulsive; propitiatory; gentle; solemn.

verbs

adhere to—; celebrate—; follow—; ignore —; institute—; observe—; perform—; prolong—; refrain from—; relinquish—; retain—; stage—; value—; —consists of; —honors; —impresses; —symbolizes.

(See ceremony, function, ritual.)

RITUAL

adjectives

social; captivating; visible; complicated; artistic; elaborate; burdensome.

verbs

adhere to—; adopt—; attempt—; attend—; elaborate—; evolve—; instruct in—; mumble—; observe—; offend by—; perform—; prepare for—; recite—; supply—; suspend —; —animates; —beautifies; —celebrates; —colors; —dignifies; —sanctifies; —symbolizes.

(See form, formula, rite, ceremony, function.)

RITUALISTIC

adverbs

elaborately; ceremonially; reverently; extravagantly; unusually; highly; profoundly; peculiarly; particularly; exotically; mysteriously; strangely.

RIVAL

adjectives

insolent; mutinous; unworthy; formidable; ribald; potent; irresistable; disagreeable; intolerable; vexatious; insolent; celebrated; successful; gallant; richer; traditional; guiltless; powerful; fallen; testy; scheming; hostile; confiding; incredible; favorable; importunate; circumstanced; angry; covetous; dangerous; strenuous; worthy; patriotic; distinguished; hopeless; domestic; rising; hated.

verbs

appraise—; defy—; emulate—; encounter —; excel—; oust—; outlast—; restrain—; shoulder aside—; surpass—; tolerate—; trail—; —aspires; —bewails; —s clash; —competes; —contends; —disputes; —equals; —excels; —glares; —opposes; —pursues; —s scramble; —spars; —squares off; —strives; —vies.

(See enemy, competitor, contestant, antagonist, insurgent.)

RIVALRY

adjectives

female; impious; dawning; fierce; ruthless; malignant; generous; unwitting; amiable; professional; ambitious; jealous; passionate; keen; sectional; kindly; municipal; bloody; inherent; dangerous; eager; bitter.

verbs

confess—; create—; eliminate—; endure—; engage in—; forbid—; forsake—; intensify —; promote—; subordinate—; —confronts; —continues; —divides; —intervenes; —separates; —subsides; —wanes; —threatens.

(See competition, enmity, opposition, antagonism.)

RIVER

adjectives

channeled; raucous; solemn; foaming; noble; unfranked; chafing; brimming; crystal; narrowed; exulting; far-off; pelting; babbling; ringing; racing; saturnine; rapid; fruitful; leaping; clear; deep-banked; booming; limpid; swollen; abominable; rushing; rife; turbid; ruinous; slow; noiseless; flowing; remarkable; ironical; encroaching; torrential; murmuring; roaring; peculiar; majestic; spectral; winding; mighty; darkening; unfordable; full-grown; peaceful; sunlit; meandering; cheerful; pebble-paved; immense; wandering; turbulent; incorrigible; glassy; brattling; capricious; hurrying; sparkling; resplendent; sobbing; weariest; useless; failing; reflecting; royal; quiet; doubling; hesitating; white-robed; subterranean; trickling; golden; unbridged; whirling; solitary; speeding; sluggish; mystic; subsiding; salmon-thronged; soft-flowing; ever-deepening; imaginary; freshening; frozen; long; gray; swanlike; impassable; hissing; swift; silent; sweet-voiced; hard-working; historic; mocking.

verbs
breast—; bridge—; divert—; emerge from —; ford—; ply—; plunge into—; stock—; —abounds in; —babbles; —batters; —bawls; —chatters; —churns; —eddies; —flows; —foams; —frets; —glides; —glitters; —growls; —gurgles; —laps; —laughs; —leaps; —loiters; —meanders; —murmurs; —races; —rises; —roars; —sallies; —stirs; —subsides; —swells; —threads.
(See liquid, stream, brook.)

RIVET

verbs
beat—; bind with—; bucket—; force—; hammer—; heat—; insert—; join with—; loose—; secure with—; set—; strain—; —braces; —s clatter; —clinches; —fastens; —projects; —secures; —tightens; —unites; —welds.
(See nail, link, bond, fetter, band.)

RIVULET

adjectives
merry; shady; woodland; shrunken; clear; babbling; noisy; tinkling; cheerful; glittering; ever-joyous; melancholy; widely-wandering.

ROAD

adjectives
endless; beaten; unfrequented; homeward; arduous; gliding; country; grass-grown; monotonous; impassable; lifeless; miry; shady; sunny; winding; smiling; serpentine; misty; worthless; conventional; parched; dusty; corduroy; superb; dilapidated; wood; rutty; rugged; vicinal; circuitous; white; sand; sun-splashed; tortuous; steep; hilly; silver; swarming; mended; half-defined; romantic; turfy; unguarded; lakeside; starless; forsaken; military; thorny; fated; unknown; coral-bordered; red; rutted; surest; moon-lit; wrong; disused; miraculous; chocolate-colored; holy; intricate; dreary; elevated; bumpy; glaring; subtler; dubious; frozen; shaded; heavenly; indistinguishable; interminable; various (pl); treacherous; miserable; smoother; level; macadamized; translucent; narrow; sinuous; weary; unfamiliar; dappled; scenic; uneven; undulating; zigzagging; ready; unbroken.

verbs
bank—; bounce over—; clock—; clog—; deviate from—; diverge from—; infest—; jog along—; jounce over—; level—; patrol —; plod along—; skim along—; slog over —; skirt—; surface—; trudge along—; —ambles; —s converge; —meanders; —s radiate from; —rambles; —swarms; —sweeps along; —wanders; —wearies; —winds.
(See avenue, highway, lane, drive.)

ROADSIDE

verbs
bank—; beautify—; border—; carpet—; defile—; dot—; fall to—; follow—; grace —; lie along—; lodge on—; plant—; sprawl over—; strew—; tramp—; tread—; view from—; —appeals; —borders; —charms.
(See countryside, field, land.)

ROADSTER

adjectives
asthmatic; resplendent; low-slung; sport; sleek; swift; streamlined; battered; shiny.

verbs
sport (colloq.)—; —bounces along; —careens; —chugs; —gleams; —glitters; —hurtles; —performs; —rattles; —rolls along; —slows up; —speeds; —sputters; —spurts; —thrills; —whirs; —whizzes.
(See car, automobile.)

ROAM (*v*)

adverbs
casually; freely; leisurely; carelessly; buoyantly; lightly; circuitously; extensively.
(See wander, stray.)

ROAR

adjectives
deep; incessant; snarling; perpetual; majestic; indistinguishable; ebbing; shutter-like; swelling; quavering; continuous; dreadful; cannon-like; living; sullen; endless; incredible; hoarse; subdued; solemn; baffled; hideous; unremitting; drumming; deepening; heavy; monotonous; gusty; painful; distressed; awful; massive; sealike; enormous; universal; stifled; muffled; deafening; dull; suppressed; confused; moaning; intermittent; tremendous; gesturing; wildest; mingled; simultaneous; prolonged; suggestive; vague; wavering; unceasing; full-throated; dry; wild; triumphant; angry; steady; tumultuous; high-keyed; crackling; appalling.

verbs
deafen by—; imitate—; muffle—; restrain —; suppress—; swell into—; utter—; —blasts; —deafens; —disembowels; —drowns out; —echoes; —enrages; —excites; —frightens; —horrifies; —interrupts; —pains; —rends; —splits the air.
(See noise, sound, uproar, thunder, rumble.)

ROAR (v)

adverbs
thunderously; awesomely; terrifically; brutally; imperiously; vigorously; unremittingly; incessantly; incredibly; hoarsely; hideously; deafeningly; triumphantly; tumultuously; appallingly; full-throatedly.
(See bellow, boom.)

ROB (v)

adverbs
systematically; professionally; slyly; insidiously; successfully; nocturnally; brazenly; boldly; impudently.
(See plunder, steal.)

ROBBER

adjectives
nocturnal; bloody; prowling; brutalized; successful.

verbs
apprehend—; deliver from—; incarcerate —; —s congregate; —s conspire; —depredates; —despoils; —divests; —dodges; —evades; —filches; —guts; —s infest; —s invade; —loots; —marauds; —pilfers —pillages; —plucks; —plunders; —purloins; —ranges; —ransacks; —rifles; —sacks; —strips; —tricks.
(See burglar, bandit, hoodlum, intruder, liar, offender.)

ROBBERY

verbs
addict to—; commit—; conceal—; contrive —; discover—; escape—; fear—; implicate in—; interrupt—; mourn—; perform—; perpetrate—; plot—; punish—; report—; reveal—; uncover—; —impoverishes; —occurs; —strips.
(See "holdup", plagiarism, theft, plunder.)

ROBE

adjectives
canonical; luxuriant; tattered; tinsel; foot-catching; flowing; flaunting; gossamer; trailing; glistening; magnificent; operatic; fantastic; painted; outspread; snowy; unconfined; sable; virgin; brocaded; spotless; ceremonial; gorgeous; shimmering; conventional; somber; glittering; unreverent; sacerdotal; festive; priestly; woven; sweeping; brilliant; dripping; cerulean; incomplete; freckled; princely; transitory; ducal; officious; ruddy; royal; close-fitting; blood-stained; transparent; vestal; musty; ample; saffron; mortal; festal; gold-trimmed; shroudlike; delicate; bridal; pompous; little.

verbs
array in—; bestow—upon; cast off—; clothe in—; disguise in—; doff—; don—; embroider—; fold—; huddle in—; gather—; invest —; line—; strip of—; —beautifies; —enfolds; —envelops; —flows; —glorifies; —heightens; —streams; —trails.
(See frock, blanket, gown, clothing.)

ROBE (v)

adverbs
magnificently; luxuriantly; fantastically; spectacularly; ceremonially; conventionally; sacerdotally; ecclesiastically.
(See shroud, cloak.)

ROBIN

verbs
befriend—; welcome—; —announces Spring; —booms; —braves; —busies; —cheers; —chirrups; —cocks; —darts; —defies; —digs; —flutters; —hops; —moults; —pokes; —snaps up; —swoops; —soars.
(See bird.)

ROBUST

adverbs
sturdily; splendidly; stoutly; healthily; vigorously; wholesomely; magnificently; enviably; admirably; stockily; brawnily; physically; amazingly; heartily.

ROCK (v)

adverbs
paternally; maternally; desolately; disconsolately; dizzily; patiently; tenderly.
(See sway, vacillate.)

ROCKET

verbs
bombard with—s; discharge—; display—; eject—; fire—; fuse—; ignite—; project—; propel—; set off—; signal with—; spark—;

touch off—; —bursts; —darts; —endangers; —hurtles; —illumines; —s scatter; —showers; —sizzles; —terrifies; —vanishes; —zooms.

(See bullet, shot, projectile.)

ROCKS

adjectives

bare; torpid; porphyritic; hospitable; darker; native; volcanic; craggy; glistening; fantastic; dazzling; picturesque; chalky; friable; jagged; sheltering; single; naked; ragged; spiritual; adamant; shelving; ancient; steep; sun-heated; rough-hewn; lichen-covered; fissured; cloven; miraculous; calcareous; low-browed; irresistable; living; igneous; perilous; precipitous; enwombed; sharp; splintered; riven; gaunt; flinty; stubborn; dun-colored; wave-encircled; disintegrated; inhospitable; sheer; tempest-beaten; submissive; sublime; traitorous; shadowing; jutting; steadfast; tidal; silver-fretted; impregnable; vine-clad; imperishable; hanging; unmistakable; merchant-marring; tall; cruel; burly-shouldered; shapeless; mantel-like; sea-beaten; shivering; wave-lapped; noticeable; senseless; sacrificial; gloomy; ice-bound; grass-covered; fearful; storied; incumbent; shining; rooted; cavernous; gneissic; sedimentary; genial; humid; monumental; ashy; mossy; projecting; massive; sparkling; sliding; peaked; curved; hoary; smitten; vaulted; churning; multitudinous; rigid; cream-colored; conspicuous; onlooking; echoing; unhewn; frowning; sullen; high-ascending; field; galled; kelp-covered; storm-drenched; cliffy; rugged; overhanging; wrinkled; glaciated; highest; insensible; basaltic; raging; serrated; time-stained; underlying; dangerous; dreary; weed-hung.

verbs

avoid—; bivouac on—; blast—; carve from —; crack—; crush—; dash against—; direct—; dislodge—; fear—; heap—; hew—; hurl—; quarry—; run upon—; shatter on —; split—; strike—; surmount—; —batter; —bound; —crest; —disintegrate; —erode; —fortify; —girdle; —hurtle; —jut; —project; —stud; —tower.

(See crag, reef, stone, granite, cliff.)

ROCKY

adverbs

painfully; arduously; extremely; impassably; roughly; dangerously; exceedingly; incredibly; unexpectedly; surprizingly; amazingly; terribly; perilously.

ROD

adjectives

chastening; pastoral; bayonet; mystic; avenging; radiant; metallic; sharpest; transparent; sin-avenging; uplifted; gubernatorial; merciless.

ROGUE

adjectives

unconscionable; poor; drunken; damnable; false-hearted; cunning; dissentious; wenching; cowardly; fair-haired; little; consummate; unmitigated; tedious; pestilent; loitering; complete; overweening.

verbs

accuse—; apprehend—; deal with—s; denounce—; discomfit—; distrust—; punish —; quell—; rebuke—; reproach—; —baits; —beguiles; —deceives; —designs; —deviates; —devises; —entices; —fools; —"foxes"; —lures; —shirks; —swindles; —tricks.

(See robber, scoundrel, profligate.)

ROGUISH

adverbs

mischievously; comically; lovably; rascally; innocently; merrily; teasingly; tormentingly; actively; ingeniously; inveterately; incurably; incorrigibly; naturally; wantonly; secretly; trickily; craftily; knavishly; particularly; villainously; peculiarly; singularly; notoriously.

ROISTERING

adverbs

noisily; playfully; mirthfully; boisterously; capriciously; boldly; waggishly; wantonly; uproariously; sportively; prankishly; absurdly; inordinately; swaggeringly; boastfully; fantastically; outlandishly; blusteringly; tumultuously; turbulently; bombastically; merrily.

ROLE

adjectives

inquisitorial; crucial; subordinate; inglorious; dominating; important; restricted; decisive; benevolent; influential; essential; pessimistic; responsible; unsavory; villainous; significant; prominent; destined; tremendous; suitable; self-imposed.

verbs
acclaim—; adopt—; animate—; bolster—; color—; convey—; denounce—; enact—; ennoble—; exploit—; extol—; fill—; fire—; illuminate—; immortalize—; jade—; overact—; portray—; renounce—; romp through —; spice—.
(See part, character.)

ROLL

adjectives
luscious; harsh; delicate; lumbering; bloody; uncanny; condescending; mystic; mathematic; rhythmic.

ROLL (v)

adverbs
heavily; furiously; enchantingly; impetuously; luxuriously; dangerously; exultantly; fiercely; smoothly; sluggishly; lumberingly; rhythmically.
(See whirl, revolve.)

ROLLICKING

adverbs
blithely; gaily; happily; frivolously; hilariously; boisterously; laughingly; divertingly; entertainingly; loudly; comically; clownishly; cheerfully; buoyantly; recklessly; jauntily; vivaciously; noisily; gleefully; sportively; joyously; mirthfully; jubilantly.

ROMANCE

adjectives
picaresque; somber; fictitious; touching; rooted; veritable; synthetic; bottled; budding; unknown; boyish; chivalrous; brilliant; spirited; pure; ennobling; pastoral; degenerate; headlong; elegant; passionate; singular; stormy; tempestuous; tawdry; interminable; enthralling; nautical; mawkish; comic; tragic; prose; prodigal; charming; audacious; fiery; insipid; colorless; cosmopolitan; fantastic; habitual; metrical; blighted; discursive; wild; bloody; hazy; sentimental.

verbs
color with—; crave—; culminate in—; delve into—; denude of—; divest of—; dull—; embalm—; enact—; guard—; nurture—; permeate with—; repudiate—; taste—; tinge with—; wreck—; —blinds; —blooms; —blossoms; —conceives; —dissolves; —fades; —flourishes; —flowers; —glows; —illuminates; —soars; —transports; —uplifts.
(See love, passion.)

ROMANTIC

adverbs
incurably; naturally; venturously; adventurously; unusually; absurdly; incorrigibly; extravagantly; wildly; fantastically; sentimentally; imaginatively; picturesquely; incredibly; singularly; oddly; boldly; recklessly; whimsically; capriciously; magnificently; brilliantly; daringly; splendidly.

ROMP (v)

adverbs
sportively; boisterously; gaily; enthusiastically; irresistibly; intoxicatedly; pastorally; amorously; rustically.
(See play, frolic.)

ROOF

adjectives
matted; distant; pyramidal; multitudinous; (pl); consecrated; crumbling; picturesque; gabled; timbered; weather-toned; unpretentious; terraced; milky; huddling; leafy; sloping; brook-eaved; irregular; gambrel; fantastic; embowered; purple-peaked; projected; moonwashed; slanting; majestical; radiant; high-pitched; verdant; branching; fretted; permanent; blackening; wavy; crystal; graceful; arched; high-peaked; mansard; lowly; vaulted; flowery; sagging; ragged; thatched; dusky; mountainous; atrocious; long; movable; waving; collapsing; great; massive.

verbs
examine—; ornament—; paint—; patch—; pierce—; provide—; repair—; ruin—; shatter—; test—; thatch—; vault—; —affords; —crests; —extends; —leaks; —projects; —shades; —sheds; —shelters; —slants.
(See cover, ledge, dome.)

ROOK

verbs
—builds; —caws; —clamors; —flocks; —s jangle; —mounts; —plunders; —pours forth; —s quarrel; —s swarm; —torments; —s wrangle.
(See bird.)

ROOM

adjectives
vaulted; modest; furnished; peaceful; shadowy; secluded; bleak; spacious; well-swept; neighboring; immaculate; reading; sunny; abutting; luxurious; desolate; well-proportioned; charming; livable; warmed; fire-

proof; light; slashing; ink-smelling; paper-littered; commodious; crowded; midnight; frescoed; tobacco-scented; emergency; colorless; haunted; utmost; wide; spiritual; dismal; disordered; habitable; cheerless; sunlit; saddening; sundry (pl); comfortable; wretched; gracious; octagonal; beam-roofed; rectangular; barny; squalid; scanty; generous; pleasant; drafty; poverty-stricken; plaster-dropping; adjoining; shabby; large; clean; dim; sick; dingy; dreary; dimly-lit; fencing; tranquil; guest; tolerable; stiff; moon-lit; immense; solitary; low-ceilinged; dark; uncarpeted; low; smoke-filled; banqueting; unattractive; remote; awesome; foul; polluted; elegant; slant-roofed; earthly; dull; musty; handsome; sunny; raftered; airy; upper; quaint; mirror; projection; squalid; air-conditioned; uncomfortable; sordid; stuffy; charming; dormer-windowed; gloomy; darkening; lonely; eerie; cozy; smart; impressive; intimate; restful; remarkable; delightful; ultra-modern; homelike; perfect; unusual; beautiful; exquisite; appointed; outside; tasteful; attractive; livable; modern; sleeping; well-planned; inexpensive; appealing; excellent; faultless; amazing; fine; great; decorated; becoming; sound-proof; bright; oversize.

verbs
air—; bar—; barge into (colloq.)—; bundle out of—; bunk in—; burst into—; bustle out of—; confine to—; clutter—; darken—; direct to—; flank—; fresco—; furnish—; jam—; mass in—; pace—; pop into—; repair to—; saunter into—; scuttle from—; seclude in—; slip from—; stalk out of—; stump out of—; sweep from—; ventilate—; —buzzes; —invites.

(See classroom, lounge, lobby, cell, hall, chamber, apartment, bedroom, kitchen, office.)

ROOMY

adverbs
delightfully; charmingly; pleasantly; comfortably; satisfactorily; acceptably; unnecessarily; spaciously; magnificently; adequately; amply; pleasantly; luxuriously; agreeably; conveniently.

ROOSTER

verbs
behead—; exhibit—; fatten—; pen up—; wire in—; —flutters about; —gobbles up; —invades the hennery; —molts; —pecks; —perches; —scratches; —squawks; —struts; —waxes indignant.

(See fowl, hen.)

ROOTS

adjectives
nocturnal; grasping; aerial; ulcerating; lurid; mucilaginous; insipid; antique; vigorous; nutritious; fibrous; giant; unsearchable; musty; inconsiderable; extraneous; spreading; wasting; parched; bulbous; sexless; powdered; moss-cushioned; orbed; goodly; gnarled; deep-lying; aromatic; venerable; cooling; fantastic; palatable; homeliest; vile; corrugated; babbling; wiry; old; uptorn; clasping; social; severed.

verbs
affix to—; choke—; dig to—; enrich—; feed—; fertilize—; ground—; grub among—; involve—; kill—; manure—; nourish—; stimulate—; uncover—; unearth—; —absorb; —bury in; —canker; —function; —go deep; —insinuate themselves into; —moor to; —project above; —supply; —thrust.

(See stem, cause, source, plant.)

ROPE

adjectives
graceful; greasy; hempen; rag; dangling; fatal; dragging; efficacious; innumerable (pl); rescuing; improvised; rain-bleached.

verbs
attach—; bind with—; braid—; cast—; haul on—; knife—; lay—; plait—; secure with—; snag—; strain—; tighten—; tug—; twist—; wind—; —binds; —chafes; —entwines; —fastens; —girdles; —secures.

(See cable, cord, string, chain.)

ROSE

adjectives
transient; fading; refreshing; quaint; distinctive; colorful; full-blown; fresh-blown; belated; wild; damask; dusty; shaken; panting; white-petaled; golden-centered; imperial; bubbled; winter; transcendent; amorous; fossil; glimmering; glowing; flowerless; newborn; burning; snowy; branching; delicate; blooming; embroidered; autumnal; countless (pl); fragrant; blushing; deeper; victorious; heavenly; living; immeasurable; wide-hearted; queenliest; virgin; magic; late.

verbs
bear—; crown with—s; gather—s; hawk—s; infect—s; pluck—; prize—; strew with—s; strip—; —adorns; —blooms; —blossoms; —blushes; —buds; —charms; —fades; —flames; —glows; —lingers; —perfumes; —perishes; —strews; —survives; —trembles; —withers; prune—.
(See flower, plant.)

ROSTRUM

verbs
adorn—; advance toward—; appeal from—; ascend—; assemble on—; erect—; exhort from—; glide into—; harangue from—; mount—; orate from—; pace—; speak from—; —quakes; —tremors.
(See pulpit, platform, stage.)

ROSY

adverbs
beautifully; charmingly; bewitchingly; blushingly; bloomingly; buxomly; happily; shyly; bashfully; modestly; hopefully; artlessly; naturally; sweetly; innocently; childishly; laughingly; healthfully; wholesomely; pleasantly; prettily.

ROTE

adjectives
rapt; aesthetic; rhythmal.

ROTTEN

adverbs
utterly; uselessly; ruinously; abominably; unfortunately; disgustingly; unserviceably; unusably; disastrously; disgustingly; dangerously; hopelessly; indescribably.

ROTUND

adverbs
amusingly; prosperously; becomingly; perfectly; healthily; laughably; ludicrously; slightly; somewhat.

ROUGH

adverbs
unpleasantly; extremely; uncommonly; disagreeably; unevenly; jaggedly; unusually; peculiarly; strangely; curiously; stiffly; harshly; rockily; unexpectedly; surprisingly; distressingly; uncomfortably; dreadfully; intolerably.

ROUND

adjectives
diurnal; dutiful; mazy; ambitious; tedious; unheroic; lucent; subsequent; monotonous; merciful; heathen; airy; weary; terrible; unfailing; luminous; solemn; frequent; periodical; ceaseless; dizzy; mortal; daily.

ROUSE (v)

adverbs
abruptly; violently; startlingly; dutifully; daily; faithfully; harshly; habitually; instinctively.
(See arouse, excite.)

ROUTE

adjectives
circuitous; rigorous; diversified; branching; baffled; river; caravan; slow; laborious; disused; shorter; sylvan; convenient; quaint; ignominious; extensive; unobstructed; unusual; principal; roundabout; dangerous; pilgrim; time-honored; rebellious; wanton; practicable; meandering; direct; devious; passable; regular; profitable; common; traditional; elusive; untried.

verbs
assure of—; chart—; choose—; clog—; conceive—; course—; cover—; deviate from—; direct to—; enter by—; follow—; invade—; memorize—; reconnoiter—; seek—; signify—; survey—; travel—; traverse—; —diverges; —entrances.
(See line, channel, road, course.)

ROUTE (v)

adverbs
completely; devastatingly; ignominiously; wholly; rebelliously; ruthlessly.
(See direct, plan.)

ROUTINE

adjectives
irksome; obscure; home; pleasure-seeking; foul; mechanized; ostentatious; systematic; hack; ordinary; laborious; slavish; dull; dreary; pleasant; wearisome; habituated; professional; indolent; systematized; monotonously; hated; soul-degrading; regular.

verbs
acquaint with—; adhere to—; adopt—; chafe under—; discharge—; eliminate—; endure—; establish—; fix—; identify with—; lift from—; mire in—; perform—; quit

—; reduce to—; relax—; settle into—; sink into—; —bores; —dulls; —encases; —rusts; —stagnates; —wears.
(See rule, conventionality, habit, custom.)

ROW

adjectives
parallel; endless; bowing; everlasting; courtesying; straggling; interminable; legioned; branchy; pale; tranquil; burnished; flaring; monotonous; serried; formal; answering; tenement; impenetrable; lusty; tremendous; dreadful; numberless (pl); venerable.

verbs
arrange in—s; break—; disrupt—; draw from—; emerge from—; file in—; fix—; mark in—; mow down—; rank in—; realign —; reinforce—; station in—; string in—s; verge from—; —dazzles; —impresses; interrupt—.
(See line, series.)

ROW (v)

adverbs
strenuously; energetically; industriously; heroically; monotonously; tirelessly; vigorously; victoriously.
(See paddle, propel.)

ROWDY

adverbs
uncommonly; indecorously; uncivilly; intolerably; disagreeably; coarsely; boorishly; outlandishly; disreputably; shamefully; opprobriously; arrantly; shockingly; appallingly; disturbingly; outrageously; scandalously; boisterously; audaciously; uncontrollably; inherently; deliberately; daringly; naturally; incorrigibly; insufferably; blusteringly; defiantly.

ROYAL

adverbs
magnificently; splendidly; brilliantly; gorgeously; gloriously; imperiously; dominantly; imperially; arrogantly; proudly; authoritatively; absolutely; superbly; grandly; augustly; magnanimously; justly; majestically; sumptuously; munificently; lavishly; extravagantly.

ROYALISTS

adjectives
triumphant; ardent; passionate; staunch; erratic; economic; loyal.

verbs
exterminate—; favor—; inspire—; oust—; overthrow—; repel—; resist—; restore—; —adhere; —advance; —deplore; —flee; —progress; —support; —yield.
(See nobility, aristocracy, peerage.)

ROYALTY (v)

verbs
ascribe to—; assume—; desert—: fear—; imitate—; inherit—; mingle with—; pretend —; profane—; regain—; regard—; relinquish—; support—; suspect—; treat as—; usurp—; worship—; —departs; —functions; —oppresses; —privileges.
(See royalists, monarch, aristocracy, peerage.)

RUB (v)

adverbs
briskly; frantically; industriously; vigorously; mechanically; incessantly; injuriously; maddeningly; furiously; skillfully.
(See polish, massage.)

RUBBISH

adjectives
worthless; dripping; fragmentary; inconceivable; unutterable; intelligent-sounding; hypocritical; delightful; sea-drifted; noxious; mental.

verbs
cart—; cast—; clutter with—; consign to—; dig in—; dispose of—; haul—; heap—; mingle with—; object to—; reject as—; relegate to—; remove—; sweep away—; trample on—; —offends; —reeks; —stains
(See junk, dust, debris, filth, dirt.)

RUBY

verbs
adorn with—ies; appraise—; blemish—; crust with—ies; cut—; deck with—ies; distinguish—; imitate—; polish—; prize—; set —; tinge—; value—; —blazes; —flushes; —gleams; —glitters; —glows; —sparkles; —ies stud.
(See gem, jewel, ornament, stone.)

RUDDERLESS

adverbs
hopelessly; helplessly; flounderingly; pathetically; desolately; forlornly; woefully; unfortunately; aimlessly; sadly; powerlessly; unhappily.

RUDE

adverbs
coarsely; ignorantly; bitterly; boorishly; naturally; characteristically; inexcusably; unnecessarily; vulgarly; unintentionally; indefensibly; awkwardly; particularly; contemptibly; inordinately; unwittingly; colossally; shockingly; drunkenly; churlishly; disrespectfully; impudently; mischievously; moodily; morosely; coolly; unpardonably; unpleasantly; disagreeably; deliberately; boisterously; offensively; unconsciously; artlessly; insufferably; innately; unceremoniously.

RUDENESS

adjectives
downright; ineffaceable; apparent; equal; barbarous.

verbs
betray into—; encounter—; forgive—; loathe—; palliate—; pardon—; soften—; subject to—; tolerate—; —appears; —irks; —offends; —provokes; —shames; —springs from; —unveils; —vexes.
(See barbarism, coarseness, disrespect.)

RUDIMENTS

verbs
acquire—; convey—; detect—; drill in—; embellish—; furnish—; inculcate—; ingrain —; instruct in—; master—; pick up—; nourish—; receive—; reduce to—; teach—; tutor in—.
(See knowledge, elements, idea, principles, essentials.)

RUEFUL

adverbs
forlornly; terribly; pathetically; sorrowfully; dismally; desolately; hopelessly; pitiably; drearily; darkly; helplessly; miserably; wretchedly; unspeakably; strangely; distressingly.

RUFFIAN

adjectives
burly; black-looking; solitary; sordid; staring; shy; young; true; malignant-looking; miserable; swaggering; madcap; cowardly; unprincipled.

RUFFLE (v)

adverbs
truculently; frivolously; jocosely; boisterously; placidly; violently; deliberately.
(See pucker, wrinkle.)

RUFFLES

adjectives
triple; full; frivolous; atheistic; shirred; hemmed; double-picot.

verbs
arrange in—; draw into—; gather—; iron out—; press into—; smooth—; —adorn; —decorate; —droop; —enhance; —frill; —ornament; —sag; —trim; —wilt.
(See wrinkle, braids, lace, fringe.)

RUG

adjectives
thick; sumptuous; brilliant; luxurious; shaggy; lustrous; reversible; valuable.

verbs
beat—; cushion—; dye—; fold—; pattern—; place—; roll—; shampoo—; tack—; trip over—; weave—; —covers; —protects; —shields.
(See carpet.)

RUIN

adjectives
rambling; picturesque; dustless; temporary; irremediable; financial; dismantled; mossy; calamitous; magnificent; silent; remarkable; undistinguished; smoldering; mental; glorious; partial; treasured; weed-covered; irretrievable; blood-stained; accumulated; wild; reeking; moldering; twisted; hungry; venerable; ivy-wreathed; hideous; final; complete; crumbling; barricaded; fragmentary; unsightly; blazing; dirty; scattered; undecipherable; frowning; majestic; pathetic; chaotic; promiscuous; deathless; piteous; impending; smoking; sudden; graceful; sprawling; private; melancholy; sandswept; stark; gloomy; mournful; hopeless; discreditable; black.

verbs
avert—; batter to—; behold—; brood over —; bury in—; drag to—; drift to—; escape —; expire in—; fall to—; foresee—; hide —; mourn—; prophesy—; reduce to—; reflect—; repair—; rescue from—; restore—;

secure from—; shield from—; speed—; verge on—; —impends; —threatens.
(See defeat, downfall, destruction.)

RUIN, (v)

adverbs
irreparably; miserably; utterly; ruthlessly; ingeniously; traitorously; vindictively; vengefully; irretrievably; irremediably; hideously; calamitously; financially; economically; politically.
(See overthrow, destroy.)

RULE

adjectives
artificial; bayonet; dynastic; brutal; declaratory; invariable; fixed; prescribed; odalisque; stipulated; mistaken; cut-and-dried; military; benign; uncivil; arbitrary; elaborate; melodic; beneficent; ethical; absurd; dictatorial; disciplinary; rigid; capricious; chivalrous; parliamentary; vexatious; drastic; paternal; classical; meticulous; strict; unavoidable; eligibility; violent; aristocratic; supposititious; abstemious; cardinal; orthodox; accepted; general; long; brutal; fundamental; special; red-tape; stern; authentic; mob; maiden; enlightened; inflexible; convenient; infallible; profitable; respected; eventful; municipal; sceptral; awful; definite; adequate; unfailing; clogging; ancient; austere; common; operose; vigorous; iron-clad; equitable; inviolable; contradictory; inexorable; conventional.

verbs
abandon—; abide by—s; adhere to—; apply—; ascertain—; chafe under—; challenge—; cleave to—; conform to—; devise—; disregard—; enforce—; establish—; fix—; formulate—; ignore—; impose—; lay down—; liberalize—; memorize—; observe—; prescribe—s; reiterate—; revise—; subject to—; submit to—; sum up—; violate—; yield to—; —decrees; —fetters; —hampers; —prevails; —regulates; —stipulates.
(See ethics, routine, law, decree, formula, fundamental, method.)

RULE (v)

adverbs
imperiously; indomitably; despotically; munificently; cunningly; democratically; implicitly; arbitrarily; capriciously; brutally; conventionally; inexorably.
(See dominate, govern, influence.)

RULER

adjectives
predominant; ruthless; beneficient; incapable; effete; venerated; constitutional; influential; absolute; distant; despotic; discredited; ecclesiastical; sagacious; moneyed; dynastic; unscrupulous; successive (pl).

verbs
acclaim—; advise—; bless—; bow to—; crown—; dethrone—; dictate to—; exile—; ordain—; praise—; trust—; yield to—; —abdicates; —administers; —authorizes; —commands; —controls; —defends; —divines; —heads; —judges; —manages; —respects.
(See king, God, sovereign, dictator.)

RULING

verbs
abide by—; adhere to—; amend—; anticipate—; authorize—; comprehend—; correct—; decry—; ignore—; justify—; manufacture—; post—; presage—; question—; refer to—; sustain—; threaten—; uphold—; warrant—; —decrees; —forbids; —menaces; —prohibits.
(See regulation, announcement, decision, proclamation, amendment.)

RUMBLE

adjectives
confused; formidable; endless; throbbing; subterranean; dull; low; incessant; terrifying; mysterious.

verbs
dull—; emit—; muffle—; prolong—; scorn—; utter—; —arouses; —breaks; —bursts; —clashes; —cracks; —dins; —disturbs; —drowns out; —issues from; —rends; —resounds; —rolls; —travels.
(See growl, roar, echo, noise, thunder.)

RUMBLE (v)

adverbs
portentously; ominously; threateningly; resoundingly; reechoingly; formidably; mysteriously; terrifyingly; incessantly; intermittently.
(See reverberate, resound.)

RUMOR

adjectives
absurd; perennial; malicious; persistent; untimely; hideous; vague; traditionary; convincing; pitiful; faint; insane; wild;

universal; exciting; contradictory; apparent; wildest; dreadful; false; ghastly; painful; splintered; sinister; fake; baseless; scandalous.

verbs
brand as—; bruit about—; buzz with—; confirm—; deny—; discount—; disprove—; explode—; foster—; further—; give rise to—; lend color to—; manufacture—; overshadow—; promulgate—; ridicule—; scotch —; seethe with—; set afloat—; set to rest —; suppress—; track down—; —blossoms; —buds; —carries weight; —circulates; —flies; —gains ground; —grows; —hints at; —menaces; —persists; —seeps out; —spreads; —startles; —suggests.

(See libel, gossip, news, secret, report, lie.)

RUMOR (v)

adverbs
ridiculously; absurdly; perennially; maliciously; persistently; falsely; baselessly; slyly; scandalously; vindictively.

(See circulate, spread.)

RUMPUS (colloq)

verbs
denounce—; design—; devise—; endure—; loathe—; muffle—; plan—; quell—; restrain —; stir up—; suffer—; suppress—; —disconcerts; —distracts; —diverts; —enrages; —horrifies; —terminates in; —vexes.

(See fight, brawl, quarrel, wrangle, disturbance, fracas.)

RUN (v)

adverbs
refractorily; blindly; obediently; efficiently; deliberately; capriciously; noiselessly; infallibly; smoothly; greedily; spontaneously; tortuously; frantically; riotously; violently.

(See hasten, scamper.)

RUPTURE

adjectives
final; violent; irreducible; sudden; inexplicable; public.

verbs
acquire—; avert—; brace—; complete—; cure—; develop—; excite—; hint at—; incur—; induce—; suffer—; —breaches; —discloses; —ensues; —severs; —strangulates; —weakens.

(See fracture, discord, dissension, breach.)

RURAL

adverbs
delightfully; charmingly; pleasantly; refreshingly; expensively; invitingly; attractively; advantageously; desirably; gratifyingly; appropriately; conveniently; spaciously; invigoratingly; healthfully; wholesomely; admirably; commendably; enviably; enjoyably; dismally; drearily; inconveniently; undesirably; shabbily.

RUSE

adjectives
innocent; favorite; desperate; ready-witted; clever.

verbs
contrive—; detect—; design—; devise—; elude—; evade—; plan—; plant—; suggest —; —ambushes; —baits; —beguiles; —distracts; —diverts; —ensnares; —lures; —succeeds; —tempts; —traps; —tricks; —waylays.

(See trick, hoax, subterfuge, stratagem.)

RUSH

adjectives
headlong; swift; hectic; precipitate; despairing; violent; blowing; flying; impulsive; engulfing; shrieking; blossomy; trampling; sickening; steady; titanic; madder; furious; pounding; rioting; never-ending; nodding; tumultuous; veritable; memorable; impetuous; recurrent; mighty; soft; chilly; onward; slimy.

verbs
attempt—; avert—; check—; control—; curb—; discharge—; foresee—; halt—; predict—; prophesy—; stem—; —abates; —carries along; —drives; —forces; —impels; —overcomes; —overwhelms; —severs; —strains; —surges; —swells; —sweeps; —traps.

(See attack, charge.)

RUSH (v)

adverbs
tumultuously; deliberately; powerfully; incoherently; blindly; irrepressibly; unceremoniously; impetuously; violently; recklessly; madly; sickeningly; precipitately.

(See press, hurry.)

RUST

adjectives
devouring; killing; protective.

RUSTIC

adjectives
boorish; austere; impudent; honest; patient; egregious; simple.

adverbs
artlessly; shabbily; quaintly; boorishly; bluntly; rudely; clownishly; cheaply; remotely; inconveniently; uncomfortably; undesirably; intolerably; roughly; clumsily; outlandishly; unattractively.

RUSTLE

adjectives
silken; delicate; indefinable; slow; occasional; sad; uncertain; attractive.

verbs
emit—; muffle—; produce—; restrain—; suppress—; —arouses; —attracts; —bestirs; —discloses; —distracts; —disturbs; —falls; —issues; —perturbs; —reveals.

(See sound, hum, murmur, whisper.)

RUSTY

adverbs
ruinously; unserviceably; unusably; horribly; impossibly; dangerously; unfortunately; terribly; singularly; extremely; hopelessly; uselessly; worthlessly; disagreeably.

RUT

verbs
approach—; avoid—; bounce over—; cut—; deplore—; drift into—; erode—; excavate—; groove—; heed—; hollow out—; lumber along—s; pursue—; settle into—; sink into—; wear—; —deepens; —disgraces; —envelops.

(See groove, hole, channel, track, habit.)

RUTHLESS

adverbs
atrociously; viciously; maliciously; vengefully; bitterly; cruelly; barbarously; brutally; ferociously; malevolently; venomously; outrageously; unbelievably; unimaginably; nefariously; wickedly; unutterably; strangely; unaccountably; inherently; terribly; shockingly; appallingly; astonishingly; horribly.

S

SABER

adjectives
hilted; gilded; cruel; clashing; gleaming.

SABOTAGE

verbs
accomplish—; advocate—; charge with—; convict of—; disclose—; frustrate—; resort to—; thwart—; uncover—; unveil—; —cripples; —delays; —destroys; —disorganizes; —hinders; —impedes; —injures; —obstructs; —violates.
(See mutilation, destruction, delay.)

SAC

verbs
clog—; dilate—; distend—; impair—; incise—; irritate—; lodge in—; obliterate—; penetrate—; pierce—; rupture—; tap— ;—contracts; —discharges; —encloses.

SACK

verbs
bear—; convey in—; dip into—; emerge from—; forage with—; hoist—; mend—; plunge into—; transport in—; twill—; weave—; —yields.
(See basket, box, case.)

SACRAMENT

verbs
administer—; deny—; observe—; partake of—; receive—; take—; —baptizes; —betokens; —binds; —canonizes; —christens; —confirms; —consecrates; —dedicates; —imposes; —impresses; —obligates; —ordains; —pledges; —promises; —ritualizes; —sanctifies; —seals; —signifies; —symbolizes.
(See ceremony, rite, benediction, matrimony.)

SACRED

adverbs
unutterably; inviolably; personally; universally; traditionally; locally; racially; curiously; inexplicably; affectionately; solemnly; carefully; augustly; impressively; genuinely; nationally; peculiarly; inordinately; unaccountably; inscrutably; mysteriously.

SACREDNESS

verbs
attach—to; blaspheme—; blemish—; despoil—; encroach on—; enshrine in—; esteem—; infringe upon—; mar—; preserve—; revere—; sense—; taint—; tamper with—; venerate—; violate—; —consecrates; —hallows; —glorifies; —secludes; —sets apart.
(See holiness, religion, benevolence, justice, integrity, sanctity, piety.)

SACRIFICE

adjectives
useless; prodigious; vicarious; living; idle; bloodless; fatal; patriotic; willing; personal; ruinous; superstitious; supreme; approaching; fearful; easy; tremendous; enormous; severe; ghastly; dreadful; exposed; inevitable; virtuous; appropriate; unimaginable; necessary; saving; sweeping; deliberate; unprofitable; mock; undue; eucharistic; economic; gratifying; numberless (pl); heroic; searching.

verbs
bemoan—; decry—; dramatize—; entail—; impose—; involve—; modify—; occasion—; offer—; ritualize—; submit to—; suffer—; undergo—; —absolves; —atones for; —compensates; —deifies; —deprives; —exemplifies; —expiates; —hallows; —purges; —purifies; —sanctifies; —sheds; —shrives; —symbolizes.
(See atonement, loss.)

SACRIFICE (*v*)

adverbs
repentantly; deliberately; economically; heartlessly; wantonly; shamefully; bloodlessly; patriotically; superstitiously; heroically; personally; supremely; fatally.
(See surrender.)

SACRILEGE

verbs
brand with—; commit—; deplore—; —blasphemes; —curses; —defiles; —desecrates; —injures; —insults; —offends; —outrages; —profanes; —reviles; —scandalizes; —violates.
(See sin, crime, vice.)

SAD

adverbs
habitually; naturally; inherently; incurably; lonesomely; curiously; unaccountably; heedlessly; inconsolably; inexplicably; awfully; profoundly; anxiously; deplorably; grievously; piteously; pathetically; pensively; ostentatiously; plaintively; dreamily; uncommonly; ominously; strangely.

SADDLE

verbs
break to—; cling to—; cushion—; ease from —; grip—; hop into—; ornament—; pad—; perch on—; polish—; rub—; slip from—; stir in—; straddle—; stud—; sway in—; sweep from—; swing into—; tear from—; vault into—.
(See seat ,chair.)

SADNESS

adjectives
settled; deadly; unmannered; uncultivated; treasured; great; real; simple; lyrical; pensive; inexpressible; wintry; shady; mild; sober; pleasing; unfathomable; unrecumbent; sudden; unbidden; clinging; preposterous; penetrating; thrilling; primeval; tender; good; prophetic; breathed; silent; mortal; humorous; painful; moody; haunting; profound; grateful; quaintest; utter; galling; compassionate; exquisite.

verbs
afflict with—; bow in—; brood in—; dispel —; exude—; incline toward—; induce—; mope in—; occasion—; —dampens; —deepens; —dejects; —depresses; —disheartens; —downcasts; —envelops; —hangs over; —pains; —pervades; —prevails; —racks; —rends; —seizes; —sheathes; —shrouds; —sobers; —touches; —weighs upon; —wrings.
(See grief, melancholy, homesickness, nostalgia, pathos.)

SAFARI

verbs
equip—; fit out—; gear—; guide—; organize—; outfit—; rig up—; —beats a path; —breaks camp; —explores; —fatigues; —films; —halts; —hunts; —records; —takes the trail; —thrills; —trails; —traverses; —treks; —uncovers.
(See expedition.)

SAFE

adverbs
fortunately; luckily; happily; thankfully; comparatively; fairly; altogether; reasonably; supposedly; presumably; probably; forever; finally; ultimately; gratefully; relatively; permanently.

SAFEGUARD

verbs
adopt—; dispense with—; employ—; inspect —; offer—; prescribe—; preserve—; promote—; sweep away—; —affords; —bridles; —exempts; —flanks; —insures; —protects; —reassures; —screens; —shelters; —shields; —shrouds; —wards off.
(See guard, protection.)

SAFETY

adjectives
precious; maximum; greatest; inglorious; comparative.

verbs
advance with—; advocate—; afford—; campaign for—; contrive for—; dwell in—; endanger—; engender—; enhance—; foster—; further—; hazard—; heighten—; insure—; jeopardize—; menace—; preach—; pro mote—; reduce—; risk—; scurry to—: threaten—.
(See security, protection, stability.)

SAG (v)

adverbs
concavely; dilapidatedly; hideously; mournfully; partially; weakly; abruptly; markedly; weakly.
(See sink, yield.)

SAGA

verbs
compose—; edit—; narrate—; publish—; relate—; treasure—; unfold—; —depicts; —entertains; —fascinates; —glories in; —honors; —interweaves; —intrigues; —perishes; —portrays; —recites; —recounts; —sings of; —stirs; —grips.
(See adventure, book, story, narrative.)

SAGACIOUS

adverbs
shrewdly; drolly; drily; eminently; dependably; notably; reputably; maturely; unusually; unexpectedly; strangely; coolly; marvelously; admirably; surprisingly; sharply; astutely; keenly; uncommonly; unfailingly.

SAGACITY

adjectives

superior; strange; clear-sighted; undimmed; shrewd; political; commercial; cool; crafty; mortal; unerring; marvelous; equal; practical; consummate; characteristic.

SAGE

verbs

acclaim—; consult—; venerate—; —counsels; —decrees; —foresees; —foretells; —predicts; —prescribes; —proclaims; —pronounces; —prophesies; —visions.

(See philosopher, scientist, master, counselor.)

adverbs

perceptibly; discerningly; profoundly; shrewdly; reputedly; notably; remarkably; unusually; uncommonly; extraordinarily; estimably; learnedly.

SAGES

adjectives

literary; rapt; puissant; honored; ancient; pungent; blundering; venerable; martyred; dusty; august; life-taught; hoary; erudite; analytical; cautious.

SAIL

verbs

cross—s; distend—; draw—; expand—; hoist—; lash—; lower—; puff out—; reef —; reenforce—; rig—; shorten—; slack—; stain—; strain—; stretch—; strike—; unfurl—; whip—; —billows; —booms; —dips; —droops; —flaps; —flutters; —propels; —shudders.

(See canvas, cloth.)

SAIL (v)

adverbs

peacefully; pensively; majestically; adventurously; prosperously; invincibly; gracefully; longitudinally; deftly; serenely.

(See embark, navigate.)

SAIL-BOAT

verbs

(See ship.)

SAILING

adjectives

emotional; gossiping; deft; smooth; superior; skilled; adept; seaworthy; landlubberly; graceful; accomplished; notable; crowded; intermittent; regular; spasmodic; announced; final; expected.

SAILOR

adjectives

shanghaied; storm-driven; outlandish-looking; swarthy; stray; apparent; sufficient; roistering; unwary; gesticulating; skillful; slow; homesick; roving; practical; drenched; mahogany-faced; stalwart; practised; trained; experienced; dissolute; debauched.

verbs

drill—s; elevate—; maroon—; quarter—s; —charts; —departs; —embarks; —fares; —guides; —mutinies; —navigates; —provisions; —voyages; command—; court-martial—; decorate—.

(See midshipman, soldier.)

SAILS

adjectives

bellying; cunning; swelling; gliding; roaring; snowy; vapory; drifting; flashing; slanting; rising; whitening; winglike; tattered; dead-leaf; slippery; riddled; flapping; torn; noisy; useless; sere.

SAINT

adjectives

criticizing; mounting; imaged; elder; loveliest; sublimest; particular; honored; toiling; felicitous; heavenly; apostolic; propitious; invisible; canonized; shoddy; glorious; beatified; latest; espoused; guardian; mortal; pastoral; mild-eyed; earthly; sentimental; pagan; reviling; lost; martyred; impolluted.

verbs

acclaim—; address—s; canonize—; esteem —; exalt—; glorify—; hail as—; hallow—; honor—; importune—; invoke—s; martyr —; persecute—; placate—s; prostrate before—; reverence—; supplicate—s; venerate—; worship—.

(See God, hero, angel, idol.)

SAINTED

adverbs

recently; devoutly; ceremoniously; ritualistically; deservedly; happily; piously; solemnly; formally; ceremonially; publicly; magnificently; officially; ecclesiastically.

SAINTLY

adverbs
downright; incredibly; drolly; sincerely; punctiliously; piously; ostentatiously; absurdly; unnecessarily; incongruously; excessively; stiffly; genuinely; extraordinarily; comically.

SALACIOUS

adverbs
unnecessarily; disagreeably; unreadably; abominably; detestably; loosely; disgustingly; coarsely; grossly; indecently; dreadfully; inordinately; highly.

SALADS

adjectives
excellent; tempting; crisp; cold; floating; bitter; green.

SALARY

adjectives
picayune; admirable; weekly; meager; terrific; substantial; moderate; tiny; exceptional; scanty; stated; adequate; unearned.

verbs
attach—; deprive of—; draw—; fix—; invest—; reap—; restore—; shear—; slash —; withhold—; —compensates; —fluctuates; —recompenses; —redresses; —remunerates; —rewards.

(See income, livelihood, earnings, wages.)

SALES

adjectives
thrilling; spectacular; periodic; miscellaneous; insignificant; summer; sensational; sluggish; private; dynamic; previous; widespread; current.

verbs
advertise—; advise—; advocate—; balk at —; bolster—; climax—; close—; contrive—; disclose—; double—; facilitate—; force—; interfere with—; jeopardize—; kill—; prohibit—; promote—; push—; restrict—; stimulate—; unearth—; —accelerate; —decline; —diminish; —drop; —dwindle; —ebb; —jump; —rise; —soar; —spurt; —toboggan.

(See trade, traffic, purchase.)

SALESMAN

adjectives
traveling; live; direct; aggressive; real; well-paid; slick; super-annuated; **invaluable**; able; unusual; persuasive; **well-dressed**; suave; sleek; pleasant.

verbs
commission—; drill—; employ—; engage—; organize—; stall—; teach—; train—; —arouses interest; —beguiles; —colors; —convinces; —creates; —demonstrates; —enables; —exhibits; —explains; —interviews; —lures; —markets; —paints; —points out; —pushes; —tempts.

(See employee, clerk, worker.)

SALIVA

verbs
absorb—; convey—; drivel—; drool—; emit—; excrete—; issue—; ooze—; pour out—; remove—; secrete—; slaver—; slobber—; swallow—; —aids; —defiles; —flows; —mixes; —moistens; —sterilizes.

SALLIES

adjectives
erratic; piquant; impotent; brilliant; massed; liveliest; occasional; sudden; futile; hot; outrageous; bitter.

SALONS

adjectives
glittering; philosophical; illegal; artistic; gaudy; gilded.

SALOON

adjectives
gorgeous; gilded; shadowy; luxurious; spacious; decorous; old-time; mirrored.

verbs
abolish—; assemble in—; crowd—; denounce—; frequent—; furnish—; hie to—; license—; line—; maintain—; permit—; renounce—; tax—; wreck—; —clamors; —reeks of; —resounds.

(See tavern, restaurant, inn, hotel.)

SALT

adjectives
insinuating; resultant; solid; valuable; **mineral**; specific; complex; relaxing; systematic; desolating; insoluble; deliquescent; shrill; atmospheric; iodized; celery.

verbs
add—; apply—; conserve—; dab in—; **dash** —; dissolve—; export—; imbue with—; **immerse in—**; impregnate with—; **iodize—**;

lack—; powder—; prepare—; preserve in —; refine—; require—; season with—; spice with—; sprinkle—; —destroys; —influences.

(See mustard, sugar, spice.)

SALTY

adverbs

impossibly; extremely; dangerously; satisfactorily; unnecessarily; bitterly; stingingly; sharply; unexpectedly; unsavorily; brackishly; disagreeably; impossibly; unpleasantly; unpalatably; rankly; unappetizingly; inexcusably.

SALUBRIOUS

adverbs

invigoratingly; stimulatingly; measurably; unquestionably; bracingly; usefully; definitely; obviously; manifestly; famously; notably; reputably; undeniably; advantageously.

SALUTATION

adjectives

rude; elaborate; original; friendly; courteous; cordial; mock; boisterous; impressive; noisy; grateful; murmured; expressive; pleasant; grim; crude;. hearty.

verbs

acknowledge—; condense—; discharge—; dispense with—; exchange—s; express—; gain—; greet with—; ignore—; rehearse—; return—; shout—; word—; —befits; —compliments; —favors; —honors.

(See greeting, kiss, embrace.)

SALUTE

adjectives

obedient; reverential; characteristic; rattling; roistering; royal; noisy; parting; graceful; sketched; customary; silent; presidential.

verbs

acknowledge—; bestow—; bow to—; conceive—; fire—; give—; greet with—; master —; perform—; present—; return—; —announces; —compliments; —expresses; —favors; —honors; —troubles.

(See greeting, kiss.)

SALUTE (v)

adverbs

courteously; formally; cordially; thunderously; respectfully; civilly; vehemently; gravely; obediently; fraternally; affectionately; obsequiously.

(See hail, greet.)

SALVATION

adjectives

lovely; eternal; certain; promised; rosy; imaged.

verbs

achieve—; desire—; despair of—; exhort—; find—; gain—; interfere with—; offer—; plead—; preach—; prove—; relish—; secure—; seek—; suffer—; venture—; win—; work out—; —depends on; —opens to.

(See atonement, deliverance.)

SALVE

verbs

apply—; anoint with—; concoct—; daub—; mix—; smear—; spread—; —comforts; —consoles; —cures; —eases; —heals; —mitigates; —palliates; —soothes.

(See lotion, balm, liniment, poultice, ointment.)

SAMENESS

adjectives

deadly; long; illusive; very; dull; boring; repetitious.

SAMPLE

adjectives

original; fair; random; disheartening; odd; pretty; splendid; generous.

verbs

apply for—; collect—s; examine—; furnish —; judge by—; match—; obtain—; present with—; secure—; show—; survey—s; view —; witness—; —confirms; —illustrates; —represents; —serves.

(See merchandise, goods, example, specimen.)

SANATIVE

adverbs

commendably; approvedly; acceptably; reputably; exceptionally; assuredly; securely; conclusively; decisively; demonstrably; conspicuously; successfully; unusually; miraculously; marvelously; unexpectedly; unfailingly.

SANCTIFIED

adverbs
sincerely; piously; devoutly; strangely; suddenly; rapturously; contentedly; serenely; recently; naturally; ecclesiastically; ceremonially; actually; reverently; fervently; solemnly; radiantly; zealously.

SANCTIMONIOUS

adverbs
absurdly; ridiculously; affectedly; ostentatiously; laughably; insincerely; disagreeably; pretentiously; smoothly; blandly; suavely; unctuously; prudishly; pharasaically; hollowly; intolerably.

SANCTION

adjectives
philosophical; express; tacit; highest; pragmatic; legislative; rational; theologic; divine; unequivocal; venerable.

verbs
abolish—s; announce—; invoke—s; lend—; offer—; receive—; regard—; require—; seek—; —allows; —assures; —authorizes; —benefits; —confirms; —encourages; —establishes; —permits; —pleases; —supports.

(See approval, indorsement, confirmation, approbation.)

SANCTION (*v*)

adverbs
unequivocally; solemnly; expressly; philosophically; tacitly; ecclesiastically; legislatively; beneficently; paternally.

(See approve, conform.)

SANCTITY

adjectives
marital; purest; superior; profound; angelic; quiet; magical; supposed; humorless.

verbs
abrogate—; approach—; assume—; cloak in—; conceive in—; defile—; exhibit—; fame for—; hallow—; honor—; intrude upon—; possess—; question—; retain—; simulate—; tamper with—; translate—; vindicate—; violate—; —decays; —invades.

(See holiness, piety, sacredness.)

SANCTUARY

adjectives
startled; heavenly; ancient; tapering; desecrated; vast; veiled; lifelong.

verbs
admit to—; afford—; crowd—; dedicate—; defile—; dwell in—; embrace—; enshrine in—; expel from—; frequent—; gain—; hallow—; inhabit—; raze—; seek—; unveil —; —consoles; —invites; —protects; —shelters.

(See refuge, immunity, cathedral, church, temple, retreat.)

SAND

adjectives
ribbed; spangling; tinted; unending; milky; drooping; sea-deserted; shifting; pathless; torrid; angry; damp; quick; perpetual; swampy; conniving; silver; sounding; slippery; sun-bleached; restless; drifting; slushy; bituminous; dissolving; auriferous; wrinkled; ruby; dreary; worthless; clinging; treeless; sweltering; coralline; wan; volatile; shallower; parched; sinking; sighing; endless; penurious; tropic; stinging; swishing.

verbs
bury in—; crush into—; elevate—; finger—; heap—; intermix with—; lose in—; overlay with—; plod through—; plough through—; polish with—; precipitate—; shovel—; sift —; trace in—; tread—; wade through—; wrinkle—; —hems; —shifts; —smooths.

(See grit, powder, dust.)

SANDALS

adjectives
placid; ambrosial; winged; tropic; worn.

SANDPIPER

verbs
bog—; decoy—; gun for—; —arrays; —bobs; —booms; —bows; —darts; —defies; —flits; —flutes; —glides; —honks; —patters about; —probes; —sails; —settles down; —soars; —squats; —whirs; —zigzags.

(See bird.)

SANDWICH

verbs
broil—; consume—; devour—; fill—; garnish—; gobble—; lunch on—es; munch—; pack—es; relish—; savor—; serve—; spread —; sup on—es; toast—; —appeals; —refreshes.

(See food.)

SANDY

adverbs
admirably; usefully; satisfactorily; advantageously; fortunately; grittily; disagreeably; unluckily; ordinarily; unpleasantly; unpalatably; terribly; dreadfully.

SANGUINE

adverbs
groundlessly; unreasonably; overly; cheerfully; absurdly; brightly; optimistically; buoyantly; happily; enthusiastically; unwarrantably; foolishly; confidently; ardently; warmly; earnestly; excitedly; characteristically; naturally; inherently.

SANITARY

adverbs
wholly; satisfactorily; surprisingly; completely; safely; meticulously; carefully; inelligently; adequately; extremely; sufficiently; uncommonly; highly; scrupulously.

SANITY

verbs
approach—; attest to—; derange—; display —; doubt—; enjoy—; forsake—; gain—; guard—; jeopardize—; question—; recover —; restore to—; retain—; return to—; test —; —flags; —languishes; —wanes.
(See reason, knowledge, sense.)

SAP

adjectives
torpid; impregnate; sciential; tasty.

SAPIENT

adverbs
acutely; cunningly; discerningly; perceptibly; sensibly; intelligently; profoundly; reasonably; subtly; pompously; proudly; garrulously; chattily; brightly; jocosely; astutely; slyly; cannily; cleverly; piercingly; sharply; shrewdly; soundly; nimbly; wittily.

SAPLINGS

adjectives
flimsy; round; silvered; spiny; sturdy; bent; twisted; hardy.

SARCASM

adjectives
coarse; chilling; taunting; evident; good-natured; needless; irritating; sweeping; quiet; elaborate; cutting; sneering; juster; mocking; withering; hurtling; keener; premeditated; deadly; biting; mild; veiled; obvious; bludgeoning; savage; shivering; painful.

verbs
employ—; flout—; gird in—; indulge in—; pour forth—; vary—; vent—; temper—; —affronts; —bites; —cuts; —detracts; —embitters; —flays; —insults; —piques; —scars; squelches; —strikes; —taunts; —scathes; —smarts.
(See cynicism, invective, mockery, derision, irony.)

SASH

adjectives
tarnished; silken; flaunting; voluminous.

SATCHEL

verbs
check—; clasp—; cram—; dig into—; explore—; guard—; hug—; mislay—; probe —; replenish—; stuff—; tuck in—; —bulges; —contains; —discloses; —swings.
(See bag, baggage, grip, brief-case.)

SATIN

adjectives
lustrous; glossy; shimmering; creamy; gleaming; sheeny; wrinkled; warm.

SATIRE

adjectives
delicate; sharp-pointed; effective; harmless; humorous; scorching; coarse; sober; cosmic; irresistible; shy; genial; deadly; nobler; modest; mild; personal; implied; biting; social; unsparing; scathing; keen; critical; ribald; savage; political.

verbs
aim—at; direct—; employ—; fear—; flash —; interpret—; introduce—; partake in—; resent—; sharpen—; soften—; subject in—; wield—; —amuses; —cuts; —declaims; —denounces; —derides; —exaggerates; —exposes; —jeers; —lashes at; —reproves; —ridicules; —runs riot.
(See irony, jest, joke, mockery.)

SATIRICAL

adverbs
bitterly; cruelly; stingingly; curiously; cleverly; unexpectedly; unnecessarily; scathingly; savagely; derisively; ironically; caustic-

ally; contemptibly; boorishly; disagreeably; meanly; unpleasantly; gracelessly; grossly; keenly; brilliantly; effectively.

SATIRIZE (v)

adverbs
spitefully; pungently; ruthlessly; delicately; effectively; comically; bitterly; scorchingly; passionately; politically; socially; diabolically; astutely; acrimoniously.
(See ridicule, lash.)

SATISFACTION

adjectives
relaxing; inexpressible; tolerable; aesthetic; obtrusive; obscure; proud; mutual; partial; subjective; excessive; complete; unspeakable; unbounded; suitable; comfortable; outward; disguised; evident; anxious; fine; phonetic; nostalgic; mirthful; immense; mournful; peculiar; compensating; lasting; enduring; all-around; absolute; elegant; unctuous; sweet; unique; lively; ferocious; melancholy; subtle; smug; inward; grim; cold; unhappy; hearty; elevated; mental; mundane; unconcealed; pecuniary; hauling; unfeigned; rash; physical; wholesome; pleasurable; unmarried; meager; indwelling; paltry; complacent; sinister; deep; lasting; inner; fleeting; unnatural; universal; obvious; drunken; full; solemn; secret; ample; heartfelt; vicarious; internal; permanent; extreme; reasonable; ultimate; keenest; lofty; honest.

verbs
achieve—; afford—; beam in—; conceal—; consume with—; crave—; derive—; demand —; desire—; experience—; express—; feign —; gain—; heighten—; indulge in—; lessen —; offer—; procure—; scorn—; yield—; —results; —soothes; seek—.
(See delight, contentment, gratification, happiness, enjoyment.)

SATISFACTORY

adverbs
highly; charmingly; wholly; genuinely; providentially; luckily; gratifyingly; acceptably; reasonably; vastly; unexpectedly; profoundly; particularly; absolutely; unusually; socially; financially; universally; generally; officially; utterly; entirely; seldom; rarely; scarcely; happily.

SATISFIED

adverbs
completely; perfectly; adequately; sufficiently; utterly; wholly; pleasantly; happily; contentedly; luckily; altogether; comfortably; complacently; easily; serenely; cheerfully.

SATISFY (v)

adverbs
temporarily; amply; abundantly; aesthetically; uniquely; pecuniarily; vicariously; sexually; reasonably; ultimately; keenly; rationally; intellectually; philosophically; lustfully; lasciviously; sensually.
(See appease, gratify.)

SATYRIC

adverbs
horribly; leeringly; foully; evilly; frightfully; hideously; monstrously; repulsively; grinningly.

SAUCE

adjectives
luscious; delicate; unstudied; well-seasoned; inimitable; tasty; sizzling.

SAUCY

adverbs
impertinently; incredibly; incurably; impudently; boldly; prettily; insolently; pertly; grossly; unpleasantly; disrespectfully; oddly; singularly; inexplicably; brazenly; smartly; cheaply; audaciously; flippantly; presumptuously; unpardonably; inexcusably; brashly; discourteously; amazingly; singularly; dreadfully; foolishly; dangerously.

SAUNTER (v)

adverbs
lazily; leisurely; unconcernedly; carelessly; brazenly; boldly; nonchalantly.
(See loiter, linger.)

SAVAGE

adverbs
cruelly; bestially; unbelievably; inhumanly; brutally; ferociously; fiercely; furiously; barbarously; pitilessly; ruthlessly; unmercifully; grossly; relentlessly; wildly; singularly; lawlessly.

SAVAGERY

adjectives
asserted; untamed; absolute; idiotic; genial; degraded; outlying; eternal; methodized; abject.

SAVAGES

adjectives

incurable; hostile; primitive; squalid; shiftless; sensitive; naked; brown; superstitious; unchristian; innocent; guileless; malicious; carnivorous; dreadful; livid; rudimentary; untutored; howling; sentimental; splendid; malignant.

verbs

appease—; civilize—; condemn—; encourage—; fear—; incite—; quell—; quiet—; soothe—; tame—; —attack; —beset; —charm; —distress; —guide; —inhabit; —murder; —overtake; —rage; —spare; —stampede; —worship.

(See monster, barbarian, Indian, ferocity, native.)

SAVE (v)

adverbs

prudently; judiciously; scrupulously; substantially; phenomenally; spectacularly; privately; unprecedentedly; miraculously; penuriously; rashly; courageously; heroically.

(See rescue, deliver.)

SAVING

adjectives

considerable; great; guaranteed; substantial; systematic; conventional; miraculous; phenomenal; bankable; epigrammatic; unbelievable; additional; important; exciting; tremendous; aggregate; definite; private; valuable; unprecedented; supreme; sensational; extraordinary; spectacular.

SAVINGS

verbs

acquire—; afford—; amass—; apply—to; bequeath—; deplete—; deposit—; effect—; entrust with—; exhaust—; heap—; hoard—; preserve—; put by—; rake together—; retire on—; store—; treasure up—; —accrue; —accumulate; —dwindle; —pension.

(See money, profits, income, earnings.)

SAVOR

adjectives

luscious; sharp; immortal; odious; putrid; lovely; appetizing.

verbs

blend—; destroy—; dispel—; lack—; lose—; perfect—; relinquish—; retain—; —allures; —baits; —beguiles; —departs; —differs; —excites; —relishes; —tempts; —varies.

(See flavor, taste, fragrance, perfume, odor.)

SAY (v)

adverbs

plaintively; fiercely; cryptically; artlessly; graciously; tremulously; compassionately; complacently; impatiently; brokenly; casually; hoarsely; ruefully; reflectively; insistently; decisively; unsteadily; consolingly; acutely; deprecatingly; reflectively; roisterously; resignedly; emotionally; passionately; soothingly; involuntarily; wistfully; craftily; sententiously; reassuringly; searchingly; tentatively; doggedly; dogmatically; derisively; exultingly; sardonically; impetuously; musingly; coaxingly; wrathfully; authoritatively; emphatically; triumphantly; candidly; blandly; demurely; naively; impetuously; brusquely; magnanimously; philosophically; bluntly; dubiously; tremulously; sensitively; ostentatiously; insinuatingly; decisively.

(See speak, utter.)

SAYING

adjectives

humorous; skin-deep; magnanimous; faithful; blunt; apt; prudent; sententious; bold; quaint; pregnant; mirthful; well-known; pithy; indiscreet; needle-pointed; witty; dim; deft; true; wise.

verbs

accept—; advance—; amend—; attribute—to; compose—; contradict—; heed—; quote—; recall—; refer to—; —amplifies; —angers; —attests; —emphasizes; —epitomizes; —summarizes; —voices.

(See adage, epigram, quotation, motto.)

SCAB (industry)

verbs

disband—s; lynch—; manhandle—; oust—; prohibit—s; protect—; threaten—; —s offend; —s organize; —rebels; —resists; —troubles; —s unite.

(See striker, rioter.)

SCALES

adjectives

grander; chromatic; glistening; diatonic; extensive; colossal; sordid; stupendous; generous; artistic; lavish; prodigal; elaborate; manifest; glittering; gigantic; diminutive; realistic; defective; adequate; ambitious; industrial; burnished; respectable; miniature.

verbs
collect—; detach—; form—; peel off—; penetrate—; separate—; shed—; strip of—; —armor; —cover; —defend; —enhance; —fall; —overlap; —overlay; —protect; —radiate.
(See flake, film.)

SCALP

adjectives
bare; fearful; transformed; clean; sickly; dry; itching; diseased; scaly.

verbs
adorn—; affect—; apply to—; cover—; crust—; cut—; distend—; heal—; imbed in—; irritate—; lacerate—; massage—; move—; pierce—; rip—; strip—; tear—; wound—; —erodes; —reddens; —tenses; —tingles.
(See head, skin.)

SCAMP

adjectives
slick; premature; pitiful; conscienceless; frolicsome; potential; worthless; wicked; unsocial.

SCAMPER (*v*)

adverbs
hurriedly; swiftly; playfully; boisterously; friskily; joyously; blithely.
(See run, hasten.)

SCAN (*v*)

adverbs
earnestly; anxiously; minutely; industriously; wearily; studiously; critically; eagerly; casually; superficially; desultorily; intently; pedantically.
(See look, distinguish.)

SCANDAL

adjectives
darker; latest; typical; inconspicuous; frightful; amazing; frequent (pl); fantastic; judicial; family; appalling; tea-table; foul; vulgar; flagrant; grave.

verbs
air—; bear—; blaze into—; breathe—; curb—; degenerate into—; despise—; dig up—; diffuse—; disclose—; discredit—; dissect—; enjoy—; face—; free from—; garnish with—; involve in—; monger—; shroud in—; spread—; wipe away—; —allures; —arises; —damages; —defaces; —defames; —disgraces; —excommunicates; —harms; —injures; —offends; —persecutes; —shames; —shocks; —trickles in.
(See infamy, aspersion, slander, gossip.)

SCANDALOUS

adverbs
unfortunately; openly; uncommonly; arrantly; terribly; shamefully; undeniably; flagrantly; admittedly; highly; regrettably; sadly; deplorably; grossly; notably.

SCANT

adverbs
dangerously; alarmingly; indecently; pitiably; inexplicably; unmercifully; shamefully; curiously; significantly; fearfully.

SCAR

adjectives
honorable; raised; deep; mental; private; frightful; hideous; dreadful; unsightly; fratricidal.

verbs
bear—; expose—; inflict—; jest at—; plaster—; retain—; reveal—; seam with—s; —attests to; —blemishes; —disfigures; —mars; —marks; —proves; —remains; —results from; —sustains; —traces.
(See blemish, defect, flaw, sore.)

SCARCE

adverbs
alarmingly; seriously; critically; locally; universally; lamentably; fearfully; uncommonly; unusually; curiously; unaccountably; inexplicably; inconveniently; miserably; unexpectedly; evidently; deplorably; remarkably; singularly; suddenly.

SCARCITY

adjectives
restful; increasing; definite; chronic; noticeable; dangerous; fearful.

SCARE

adjectives
baseless; wild; sorry; hopeless.

verbs
exaggerate—; foment—; heed—; manufac-

ture—; occasion—; report—; strike with—; work—; —arouses; —fizzles out (colloq.); —overcomes; —seizes; —stimulates; —terrifies; —unnerves; —excites; —fades.

(See fright, terror, fear, dread, anxiety.)

SCARE (v)

adverbs

instinctively; baselessly; unavoidably; agitatingly; dreadfully; abominably; waggishly.

(See frighten, terrify.)

SCARED

adverbs

terribly; shockingly; awfully; irrecoverably; frightfully; unmercifully; cruelly; brutally; desperately; apparently; somewhat; wildly; foolishly; hideously; ignorantly; miserably; heartlessly; secretly; suddenly; mortally.

SCARF

adjectives

flaunting; downy; fluttering; traditional; square; fringed; flamboyant; daring; flashing.

SCATTER (v)

adverbs

profusely; liberally; generously; promiscuously; philanthropically; confusedly; haphazardly; carelessly.

(See separate, dispel.)

SCATTERED

adverbs

widely; pitifully; wastefully; erratically; lavishly; wantonly; fortunately; luckily; sparsely; extravagantly; thinly; thickly; singularly; intentionally; cleverly; diplomatically; profitably; intentionally.

SCENARIO

verbs

alter—; collaborate on—; complete—; compose—; condense—; detail—; draw up—; elaborate on—; fill in—; outline—; purchase—; reject—; rewrite—; sketch—; submit—; —calls for; —depicts; —dramatizes; —portrays; —thrills; —unfolds.

(See story, play.)

SCENE

adjectives

striking; moving; appropriate; painful; pastoral; mad; magnificent; solemn; shameless; sanguinary; sublime; grotesque; tedious; frightful; idyllic; desolate; lively; licentious; dramatic; affecting; decorous; chaotic; animating; hopeful; delicious; brilliant; semi-tragic; violent; passionate; comical; pitiable; circling; martial; distant; enchanting; lofty; remote; novel; mythological; celestial; garish; foregoing; barren; fine; enveloping; cheerless; troubled; riotous; visionary; sylvan; wondrous; convivial; mountain; sunny; powerful; trial; tropical; odious; immediate; binding; classic; picturesque; exquisite; murky; shifting; droll; torturing; grateful; flattering; varied; melodramatic; death-bed; adventurous; squalid; fateful; historic; astonishing; mournful; pirate; pathetic; turbulent; previous; terse; wild; imposing; conspicuous; animated; human; dreadful; memorable; engrossing; realistic; night; impressive; imprisoned; mimic; shocking; pungent; horrible; distressing; harrowing; preliminary; soul-searching; ennobling; fearful; dismal; stirring; rollicking; vivid; agitating; perilous; heroic; touching; awful; renovated; sequestered; strange; trying; toiling; festive; tragic; quaint; singular; universal; monotonous; precarious; verdant; pacific; tranquil; beauteous.

verbs

alter—; applaud—; behold—; cloud—; conceive—; conjure up—; contemplate—; detail—; dispatch to—; dominate—; dramatize—; eavesdrop upon—; enact—; flee—; hover over—; indulge in—; overshadow—; portray—; reconstruct—; reproduce—; retire from—; smirk at—; storm across—; stumble upon—; visualize—; weigh—; —depicts; —drifts; —motivates; —shifts; —takes momentum.

(See aspect, spectacle, view, place, scenery.)

SCENERY

adjectives

picturesque; distant; rugged; salient; impressive; glorious; noble; savage; diversified; quieting; grandiose; monstrous; fascinating; superlative; mountainous; sumptuous; gaudy; animated; admirable.

verbs

admire—; behold—; contemplate—; design—; devour—; enjoy—; feed on—; light—; present—; view—; —affects; —attracts; —awes; —changes; —delights; —enhances;

—enraptures; —enthralls; —impresses; —inspires; —magnetizes.
(See landscape, scene.)

SCENT

adjectives
foreign; pleasing; floral; alluring; spicy; faint; delicious; keen; remarkable; patriarchal; chosen; dusty; dry; sweet; delicate; exalted; lingering; hot; flower; pungent; cunning; unmemoried; impromptu; dull; peppery; balmy; pretty.

verbs
abhor—; breathe—; convey—; derive—from; detect—; discern—; employ—; eschew—; extract—; follow—; impregnate with—; inhale—; load with—; lose—; pick out—; pursue—; recognize—; recover—; seek—; sniff up—; stimulate—; visualize—; —aids; —disguises; —indicates; —overwhelms; —perceives; —permeates; —pervades; —recalls; —rises; —survives; —wanes; —yields to.
(See essence, fragrance, aroma, odor.)

SCENT (v)

adverbs
instinctively; fragrantly; deliciously; pungently; delicately; brazenly; boldly.
(See perfume.)

SCENTED

adverbs
permanently; odiously; disgustingly; fragrantly; sweetly; exotically; expensively; exquisitely; delicately; opulently; seductively; alluringly; excitingly; pleasantly; nauseatingly; sickeningly; cheaply; mysteriously; evanescently; delightfully; cleverly.

SCEPTRE

adjectives
social; pacific; golden; age-old; jeweled; beauteous; royal; magic.

verbs
bear—; confer—on; entitle to—; govern with—; invest with—; ornament—; rule with—; shake—; sway—; swear by—; touch with—; wield—; —awes; —dignifies; —empowers; —signifies; —symbolizes.
(See baton, power, staff.)

SCHEDULE

adjectives
preconcerted; rigorous; diverse (pl); fixed; timed; daily; temporary.

verbs
abolish—; adhere to—; alter—; arrange—; consult—; discard—; establish—; expand—; fall behind—; follow—; insert in—; maintain—; map out—; observe—; note—; present—; publish—; refer to—; slash—; threaten—; throw off—; —regulates; —sets forth; —specifies.
(See list, calendar, itinerary.)

SCHEME

adjectives
curious; artistic; nameless; recognized; comprehensive; suitable; subtile; beautiful; selling; ambitious; philanthropic; systematic; ingenious; illusory; unphilosophical; mature; marvelous; impractical; dualistic; seditious; educational; critical; far-reaching; imperial; iconographic; poaching; dubious; hostile; gigantic; cherished; social; multiform (pl); elaborate; improvident; decorative; extensive; despotic; rascally; visionary; promising; constructive; wild; speculative; gardening; unbodied; prearranged; entangled; abominable; interesting; tortuous; iniquitous; rational; ludicrous; extravagant; feasible; generous; well-weighed; detailed; warm; cheery; perfidious; chimerical; digesting; eternal; desolate; providential; prodigal; cowardly; particular; flying; fantastic; vast; homely; harmonious; artless; selfish; colossal; bold; notable; advantageous; flimsy; seductive; wonderful; darling; complicated; shallow; monotonous.

verbs
abandon—; administer—; adopt—; back out of—; blast—; broach—; commit to—; concoct—; contemplate—; dally with—; demonstrate—; devise—; discern—; foist—upon; formulate—; fulfill—; further—; immerse in—; launch—; mature—; mull over—s; organize—; promote—; prosecute—; puzzle out—; resurrect—; scrap—; scrutinize—; seethe with—s; spin—; stymie—; undertake—; view—; —concentrates on; —goes awry; —hatches; —intrigues; —unfolds.
(See idea, project, plan.)

SCHEME (v)

adverbs
covetously; traitorously; diabolically; vic-

iously; abominably; extravagantly; chimerically; artlessly; advantageously; systematically; politically; seditiously; tortuously; perfidiously.

(See plan, plot.)

SCHEMING

adjectives
wily; political; amiable; nefarious; wicked; skillful.

adverbs
innocently; mischievously; childishly; pleasantly; mysteriously; secretly; openly; brazenly; maliciously; meanly; cleverly; politically; astutely; adroitly; madly; viciously; criminally; heartlessly; cattily; brutally; dangerously; lovingly; hatefully; successfully; artfully; ingeniously; cunningly; craftily; sharply; slyly; warily; unscrupulously; insidiously; disloyally; treacherously; thoughtfully; prudently.

SCHOLAR

adjectives
learned; elegant; tolerable; potential; distinguished; convent; renowned; eminent; quiet; reserved; brilliant; famous; studious; ivory-towered; absent-minded; profound; reputed; classical; astonished; feeble; famishing; desperate; crude; credulous; facile; austere; advanced; professional; rude; ripe; amiable; painstaking; imaginative; pedantic; competent; able; grammatical; true; refractory.

verbs
discipline—; enlighten—; guide—; honor—; instruct—; reward—; test—; tutor—; train—; —acknowledges; —acquaints with; —attains; —attends; —comprehends; —crams; —embraces; —follows; —inquires; —investigates; —merits; —professes; —searches.

(See reader, student, pupil, disciple, follower.)

SCHOLARLY

adverbs
extremely; amazingly; brilliantly; deeply; profoundly; singularly; eminently; particularly; reasonably; broadly; assiduously; industriously; forbiddingly; abstrusely; alarmingly; splendidly; consciously.

SCHOLARSHIP

adjectives
theological; eminent; profound; deficient; unusual.

SCHOOL

adjectives
vigorous; trivial; hostile; hungering; monastic; cursory; archaeological; law; creditable; fashionable; eclectic; spasmodic; collegiate; skill-contending; elaborate; up-to-date; hard-boiled; realistic; red-brick; immemorial; illustrious; foremost; decadent; haggard; magazine; formal; parochial; consummate; evolutionary; subordinate; toilful; celebrated.

verbs
approve—; attend—; bar from—; disband—; endow—; enroll in—; enter—; exclude from—; expel from—; father—; foster—; found—; graduate from—; impair—; join—; maintain—; rank—; rate—; revisit—; —attracts; —designates; —examines; —flourishes; —prepares; —suspends; —thrives.

(See college, institution, seminary, library, university.)

SCHOOL-BOY

verbs
chastise—; discipline—; enlighten—; examine—; harass—; impress—; oppress—; rebuke—; reprimand—; reproach—; tutor—; —attends; —cheers; —comprehends; —derides; —detects; —enjoys; —s gather; —pens; —romps; —sports; —taunts; —violates.

(See student, pupil, scholar.)

SCHOOLING

verbs
afford—; confine to—; continue—; ignore—; lack—; neglect—; overlook—; profit by—; refuse—; test—; utilize—; value—; —edifies; —enlightens; —grounds; —imbues; —infuses; —instills; —overcomes; —polishes; —prepares; —trains.

(See training, preparation, education.)

SCHOONER

adjectives
splendid; helpless; respectable; dilapidated; coasting; piratical; trading.

verbs
anchor—; becalm—; con—; convert—; convey by—; design—; fit out—; handle—; launch—; navigate—; rig—; steer—; —bears off; —clears; —cruises; —gleams; —graces; —heels; —plies; —ports; —rushes; —sheers; —shoves off; —signals; —skims; —sounds; —tacks; —tosses.
(See boat, launch, ship.)

SCIENCE

adjectives
substantial; principal; adequate; universal; physical; pseudo; mysterious; experimental; practical; laborious; economic; dominant; non-remunerative; biological; kindred (pl); contiguous; astronomical; industrial; spatial; liberal; specific; miracle; profane; systematic; political; grotesque; falsified; deepest; hypnotic; abstract; speculative; occult; intricate; daring; applied; imaginary; sister; pure; auxiliary; mechanical; visionary; various (pl); direct; bloodless; collateral.

verbs
acclaim—; applaud—; apply—; bolster by —; correlate—s; elucidate—; foster—; further—; grapple with—; live for—; pertain to—; suppress—; —contributes to; —contrives; —demonstrates; —dissects; —explores; —flourishes; —investigates; —proves; —pursues; —reveals; —scoffs at; —scorns —surpasses; —sustains; —teaches; —tests; —trains; —utilizes; —voices; —wages a fight.
(See economics, anatomy, psychology.)

SCIENTIFIC

adverbs
carefully; meticulously; accurately; highly; gravely; extremely; necessarily; scarcely; distinctly; profoundly; undeniably.

SCIENTIST

adjectives
heckling; over-impulsive; distinguished; attuned; pure; dissecting; rejuvenated; equipped; enraptured; objective; skilled; famous.

verbs
enrage—; honor—; perplex—s; puzzle—s; —concludes; —considers; —converts; —cultivates; —deduces; —delves; —devotes; —discerns; —discloses; —disputes; —dissects; —envisions; —examines; —fathoms; —formulizes; —infers; —reasons; —researches; —seeks; —solves; —stresses; —studies; —verifies.
(See naturalist, philosopher.)

SCION

adjectives
dormant; remaining; fiery; illustrious; gentler; decadent; dissipated; royal.

SCISSORS

verbs
grind—; ply—; resharpen—; wield—; —clips; —crops; —dangles; —nicks; —pares; —pieces; —pierces; —removes; —shears; —smooths; —snips.
(See shears.)

SCOLD (*v*)

adverbs
harshly; pedantically; maddeningly; monotonously; irritatingly; exasperatingly; malignantly; shrewishly.
(See reprimand, lecture.)

SCOLDING

verbs
addict to—; incur—; inflict—; justify—; merit—; relent—; rue—; vent—; —abuses; —bites; —corrects; —curbs; —cuts; —descends upon; —disciplines; —disturbs; —mortifies; —rebukes; —reproaches; —shames.
(See lashing, rebuke, ridicule.)

COPE

adjectives
ample; determined; economic; confined; unlimited; gracious; intellectual; international; institutional; plentiful; utmost; unrestricted; free; comprehensive; unusual; unsuspected.

verbs
appreciate—; afford—; ascertain—; broaden —; comprehend—; confine—; desire—; dissipate—; dwarf—; enlarge—; exceed—; extend—; gain in—; limit—; measure—; muse over—; narrow—; question—; restrict—; survey—; widen—; —embraces; —extends; —ranges.
(See limit, range, extent.)

SCORCH (*v*)

adverbs
superficially; ruinously; hopelessly; carelessly; partially; markedly; obviously.
(See burn, shrivel.)

SCORE

adjectives
mortal; creditable; voluminous; operatic; trifling; one-sided; brilliant; breath-taking.

verbs
collate—s; compose—; compress—; copy—; distribute—; familiarize with—; mark—; note—; play—; practice—; recall—; rehearse—; strike off—; tabulate—.

(See music, manuscript, account, reckoning.)

SCORE (v)

adverbs
deftly; precisely; accurately; brilliantly; repeatedly; victoriously; creditably; overwhelmingly.

(See record, enter.)

SCORN

adjectives
sullen; compassionate; rising; indignant; ineffable; casual; virtuous; supercilious; helpless; hopeless; merry; revengeful; unconcealed; quiet; tameless; haughty; curious; intolerable; unaffected; languid; tender; triumphant; indescribable; infidel; shameful; profound; defiant; hard; superficial; superior; writhing; bitter; frank; casual; withering; sensitive; mingled; magnanimous; spitting; fine; chivalric; idle; constant; contemptuous; amused; foul; old-fashioned; supreme; ribald; dazzling; womanly; unutterable; unsavory; incredulous; incalculable; contemptuous.

verbs
bristle in—; cloak in—; convey—; deride in —; expose to—; express—; feign—; heap—; imply—; point in—; quiver in—; regard with—; sneer in—; snort in—; submit to—; treat with—; wither with—; —deepens; —grows; —offends.

(See disdain, derision, contempt.)

SCORN (v)

adverbs
theoretically; unutterably; sullenly; indignantly; superciliously; haughtily; intolerably; triumphantly; indescribably; casually; contemptuously; hatefully.

(See reject, disregard.)

SCORNFUL

adverbs
arrogantly; pompously; insolently; unbearably; offensively; youthfully; blithely; ridiculously; ignorantly; significantly; pityingly; unpleasantly; defiantly; learnedly; utterly; thoughtlessly; laughingly; malignantly.

SCOUNDREL

adjectives
unscrupulous; upstanding; infamous; pompous; church-going; blatant; unprincipled; hypocritical; infernal; murderous; remorseless; dissolute; swindling; insolent.

verbs
associate with—; berate—; harbor—; master—; oust—; punish—; regiment—s; rebuke—; reprimand—; shelter—; —degrades; —eludes; —evades; —shocks; —sullies; —tricks.

(See profligate, villian, rogue, criminal.)

SCOURGE

adjectives
national; appointed; dreadful; appalling; inexorable; lifted; controversial; fatal; chastening; penitential; dreaded.

verbs
afflict with—; anticipate—; bemoan—; check—; curb—; cure of—; deplore—; halt —; incur—; lift—; overcome—; prevent—; stamp out—; succumb to—; —befalls; —besets; —destroys; —exterminates; —plagues; —ravishes; —routs; —settles on; —spreads; —wipes out.

(See curse, disease, plague.)

SCOUTING

verbs
discover—; encourage—; engage in—; enjoy—; foster—; found—; instruct in—; perform—; practice—; train in—; venture into —; —conduces to; —drills; —engenders; —offers; —prepares; —teaches; —toughens.

(See athletics, exercise, activity.)

SCOWL

adjectives
envious; unbecoming; slight; swarthy; anxious; sullen; suffering; malignant; fierce; terrific; lowering.

verbs
assume—; cast—; draw into—; exhibit—; gather into—; ignore—; incur—; perpetuate—; receive—; send forth—; —darkens;

—departs; —expresses; —fouls; —glowers; —relents; —sours; —threatens; —wilts; —withers.

(See frown, glare, look, sneer.)

SCOWL (v)

adverbs

morosely; vindictively; bitterly; savagely; threateningly; pugnaciously; belligerently; enviously; sullenly; malignantly; fiercely; rudely; uncouthly.

(See frown.)

SCRAMBLE

adjectives

ethical; wild; persistent; rough; unseemly; exhilarating; nerve-destroying; fearful; noisy.

verbs

decipher—; define—; degenerate into—; interpret—; protest—; regard—; survey—; —confuses; —disorders; —disperses; —displeases; —disturbs; —hampers; —impedes; —perplexes; —upsets; —wanes.

(See rush, struggle.)

SCRAPE

adjectives

unfortunate; typhoid; frequent (pl); tight.

SCRAPS

adjectives

sundry; reminiscent; abject; babbling; infected; disdained; discreditable.

SCRATCH (v)

adverbs

industriously; eagerly; perplexedly; harassedly; composedly; complacently; reflectively; meditatively; uncouthly.

(See scribble, scrawl.)

SCRATCHING

verbs

induce—; necessitate—; weary of—; —annoys; —chafes; —eases; —endangers; —gratifies; —infects; —inflames; —irks; —irritates; —mars; —relieves; —vexes.

SCRAWL

adjecives

unhallowed; blotted; rapid; tragic; anguished; hurried; illegible.

SCRAWL (v)

adverbs

illegibly; laboriously; feebly; crudely; rudely; clumsily; hurriedly; unconventionally.

(See scribble, scratch.)

SCRAWNY

adverbs

dingily; haggardly; pitiably; terribly; inexplicably; decrepitly; horridly; scurvily; sorrily; pitifully; feebly.

SCREAM

adjectives

half-stifled; ear-splitting; feminine; frantic; faint; long; mocking; unearthly; eloquent; inarticulate; defiant; hoarse; sharp; piercing; querulous; shrill; piteous; pretty; multitudinous (pl); pulsating; ecstatic; suppressed.

verbs

emit—; issue—; muffle—; pour forth—; resound with—s; restrain—; silence—; stifle—; suppress—; —alarms; —curdles; —freezes; —lances; —penetrates; —pierces; —rends; —rocks; —shakes; —shatters; —terrorizes.

(See cry, yell, noise, howl, roar.)

SCREAM (v)

adverbs

piercingly; shrilly; madly; frantically; triumphantly; agonizedly; harshly; mockingly; eloquently; ecstatically; piteously.

(See yell, shriek, screech.)

SCREECH (v)

adverbs

dissonantly; insanely; wildly; bestially; hideously; irrationally; shamefully; ribaldly.

(See scream, shriek.)

SCREEN

adjectives

featureless; leafy; costly; omnipresent; mendacious; little; hand; impenetrable; luminous; stubble; theoretical; shadowy; fluorescent.

verbs

contrive—; employ—; fold—; frame—; hinge—; insert—; necessitate—; observe through—; project on—; remove—; view on—; —encloses; —envelops; —guards; —

obscures; —prevents; —protects; —shelters; —shields; —shrouds; —wards off.

SCREEN (v)

adverbs
protectively; effectually; leafily; faithfully; modernistically; coveniently.
(See protect, conceal.)

SCRIBBLE (v)

adverbs
carelessly; unbeautifully; furiously; illegibly; unreadably; crabbedly; grotesquely; characteristically.
(See scrawl, scratch.)

SCRIBBLED

adverbs
weakly; dimly; faintly; coarsely; grossly; childishly; illegibly; crookedly; sprawlingly; finely; clearly; feebly; desperately; hurriedly; hastily; hopefully; eagerly; carelessly; untidily; secretly.

SCRIBE

adjectives
romantic; daily; deft; professional; poison-spirited; capable.

SCRIPT

adjectives
legible; spidery; unfinished; tiny; unreadable.

verbs
abolish—; clarify—; comprehend—; decipher—; decode—; direct from—; form—; imitate—; interpret—; practise—; recognize—; reproduce—; revise—; study—; translate—; —attracts; —awes; —confuses; —differs; —puzzles; —resembles.
(See handwriting, writing, manuscript.)

SCRIPTURAL

adverbs
genuinely; authentically; authoritatively; piously; incontrovertibly; convincingly; persuasively; undeniably; provokingly; unanswerably; formidably; comfortingly; prophetically; highly.

SCRIPTURES

verbs
accept—; attack—; bolster with—; cite—; con—; embody in—; embrace—; employ—; enjoy—; limit—; mark—; memorize—; mouth—; recall—; refer to—; regard—; review—; study—; —enlighten; —guide; —illuminate; —reveal; —sanctify.
(See Bible, Gospel, writing.)

SCROLL

adjectives
scented; bible; brilliant; talismanic; unsullied; graven; awful; gentle; parchment.

SCRUB (v)

adverbs
scrupulously; diligently; spotlessly; industriously; methodically; ambitiously; tirelessly; vigorously; ceaselessly.
(See rub, polish.)

SCRUPLES

adjectives
weak; conscientious; ceremonious; utmost; immovable; commendable; spiritual; tiresome; religious; desperate; formal; wayward; ceremonial; confirmed.

verbs
avoid—; banish—; cling to—; disregard—; dull—; entertain—; express—; lack—; mold—; overcome—; override—; question—; raise—; shape—; sharpen—; shelve—; silence—; stand on—; tamper with—; —plague; —restrain; —trouble; —weigh upon.
(See qualm. doubt, skepticism, suspicion, hesitation.)

SCRUPULOUS

adverbs
habitually; carefully; dependably; unusually; remarkably; admirably; commendably; highly; vigilantly; laudably; reliably; painstakingly; genuinely; meticulously; honestly.

SCRUTINIZE (v)

adverbs
avidly; critically; intently; cannily; quizzically; keenly; minutely; circumspectly; cautiously; persistently; suspiciously; hostilely; irreverently; boldly; shrewdly.
(See examine, inspect.)

SCRUTINY

adjectives
persistent; prolonged; assiduous; suspicious; terrible; distant; calm; curious; intent; searching; accurate; hostile; critical; sullen;

deliberate; attentive; cool; irreverent; silent; keen; overclose; bold; telescopic; appalling; strictest; shrewd; ignorant; earnest; wondering.

verbs
avoid—; cringe under—; defy—; discard on—; invite—; lead to—; meet—; resent—; sharpen—; stretch—; subject to—; threaten with—; undergo—; —detects; —discloses; —disqualifies; —informs; —reveals; —rewards; endure—; expose to—.
(See look, examination, search, inquiry.)

SCUFFLE

adjectives
rough; momentary; noisy; veritable; violent.

verbs
encounter—; join in—; lament—; subdue in—; —bursts forth; —confuses; —cripples; —disturbs; —ensues; —irks; —irritates; —menaces; —rages; —results in; —roars; —threatens; —upsets; —vexes; —wearies.
(See fight, struggle.)

SCULPTOR

verbs
acclaim—; award to—; criticize—; model for—; pose for—; —adorns; —carves; —chisels; —conceives; —engraves; —executes; —expresses; —finishes; —forms; —hews; —immortalizes; —molds; —shapes.
(See artist, painter.)

SCULPTURE

adjectives
monumental; shapeless; classic; antique; symbolic; mortuary; shadowy; matchless; colossal.

SCULPTURE (v)

adverbs
curiously; quaintly; deftly; exquisitely; monumentally; modernistically; bizarrely; intricately.
(See carve, engrave.)

SCUM

adjectives
precocious; muddy; leprous; vulgar; common.

verbs
clear of—; collect—; form—; gather—; purge—; reject—; retain—; sift off—; strain—; throw off—; work up—; —covers; —films; —floats; —rises; —settles; —thickens; —veils.
(See dross, dirt, debris, filth.)

SCURRILOUS

adverbs
illegally; unpardonably; meanly; maliciously; basely; vulgarly; damagingly; hideously; intentionally; unforgivably; unforgettably; foully; indecently; unnecessarily; vilely; audaciously; boldly; challengingly; tauntingly; opprobriously.

SCURVY

verbs
afflict with—; communicate—; cure of—; ease—; heal of—; remedy—; salve—; suffer from—; —blemishes; —blights; —mars; —scourges; —spreads; —visits; —wipes out.
(See disease.)

SCUTTLED

adverbs
shamefully; ignominiously; secretly; necessarily; finally; desperately; furtively; reluctantly; completely.

SEA

adjectives
fair; boisterous; bland; sterile; sepulchral; savage; motionless; circumfluous; billowy; depraved; turbulent; choppy; coral; shoreless; crystal; glistening; varied; multitudinous (pl); unknown; shimmering; full-toned; homeless; orient; whispering; foaming; rocking; walled; moon-lit; heartless; glassy; sullen; primeval; tideless; wrinkled; insatiate; dense; flowing; undreamed; rough; complaining; unsalted; spacious; calmest; discharged; laughing; tropic; rushing; unfirm; sharp; voracious; wild; abhorred; remorseless; tranquil; treacherous; chainless; illumined; choral; uncanny; dim; leaden; tempestuous; sleeping; raging; troubled; ancient; isolating; throbbing; islanded; arctic; silken; mossy; opaline; empty; whelming; soundless; heaving; slimy; polished; gradual; agitated; murderous; summer; sparkling; plangent; democratic; wondering; lucent; unfathomed; climbing; hoary; intervening; straitened; waveless; arching; corpse-encumbered; misty; unpastured; wan; interlunar; undulating; distant; tossing; molten; full; boiling; unreluctant; peaceful; sandy; terrestrial; neglected; slumbrous; lulled; surging; inward; ugly;

extended; stainless; inviolate; violent; tumbling; careening; hindering; rainy; elongated; moral; winter; spendthrift; changeless; shoaling; rolling; enchanted; azure; delicious; phosphoric; mighty; placid; brilliant; wasting; sunny; pleasant; shivering; windy; abysmal; immemorial; trackless; barren; milky; harmonious; ordinary; narrow; rippling; tinted; incessant; southern; swollen; unresting; stern; limpid; farthest; glad; dancing; haughty; familiar; unstable; invisible; triumphant; rosy; perfumed; incarnadined.

verbs
cast up by—; challenge—; chart—; embark on—; fan—; head out for—; launch on—; plow through—; streak—; traverse—; —allures; —beats against; —bristles; —chastises; —chops; —dashes; —foams; —hems in; —murmurs; —s pile up; —pounds; —pursues; —retreats; —ripples; —rustles; —sighs; —sleeps; —sweeps; —thrashes; —thunders; —whispers; —yields up.
(See lake, ocean, wave, river, surf.)

SEAL

adjectives
dangling; sulphur; violated; experimental; sweet; wax; official; broken.

SEAL (v)

adverbs
hermetically; effectively; mechanically; scientifically; officially; automatically; nominally; legally; bindingly.
(See confirm, attest.)

SEALED

adverbs
hermetically; tightly; completely; successfully; properly; finally; officially; securely; safely; confidently; expertly; sufficiently; satisfactorily; hopelessly; firmly; legally.

SEAMAN

adjectives
distant; broken; disbanded (pl); skillful; proficient; doughty; unimaginative; conscientious; obsequious; groaning.

SEAMED

adverbs
oddly; conspicuously; remarkably; extremely; senilely; frostily; merrily; terribly; deeply.

SEAMS

adjectives
fossiliferous; chintz-welted; innumerable; whitened.

SEAPORT

adjectives
old; drowsy; conspicuous; populous; busy; modern.

SEARCH

adjectives
diligent; preliminary; keen; futile; quiet; breathless; fruitless; unreasonable; evident; deliberate; repeated; systematic; reckless; exhaustive; resolute; protracted; obnoxious; blindfolded; vain; intensive; vague; patient; relentless; superstitious; terrestrial; proposed; personal; narrow; prolonged; studious; frantic; roaming; vigorous; weary; nationwide.

verbs
baffle in—; cease—; conduct—; commence —; devote to—; discontinue—; entail—; enter into—; entrust—to; escape—; instigate —; institute—; justify—; relinquish—; renew—; undertake—; venture on—; weary of—; —ascertains; —consumes; —extends to; —pains; —reveals; —results in; —uncovers; —unearths.
(See examination, exploration, scrutiny, inquiry.)

SEARCH (v)

adverbs
deliberately; diligently; frenziedly; blindly; frantically; intently; rigorously; fruitlessly; cautiously; tirelessly; systematically; recklessly; protractedly; vainly; relentlessly; vaguely; legally; indefatigably.
(See hunt, seek.)

SEARCHING

adjectives
patient; intelligent; laborious; restless.

adverbs
unusually; rigorously; thoroughly; profoundly; uncommonly; rigidly; unpleasantly; heartlessly; inescapably.

SEARCH-LIGHT

verbs
desire—; exhibit—; fit with—; supply—; suspend—; switch on—; —beams; —dazzles; —diffuses; —enables; —exposes; —

facilitates; —flickers; —gleams; —illumines; —pierces; —penetrates; —reflects; —reveals; —signals.
(See light.)

SEASON

adjectives
singing; sickly; glorious; buried; tempestuous; heated; due; ordinary; rainy; favored; sultry; propitious; modish; virtuous; unapparent; festive; winter; holiday; gala; due; faithful; adverse; gentle; true; ominous; pestilential; youthful; beneficent; suitable; advancing; autumnal; convenient; unchanged.

verbs
adapt to—; divide into—s; fill—; inaugurate—; launch—; measure—s; —s alternate; —advances; —clothes; —creeps along; —develops; —drifts by; —fades; —flowers; —lapses; —matures; —s merge; —proceeds; —progresses; —promises; —ripens; —rolls around; —s vary; —waxes.
(See autumn, spring, summer, winter.)

SEASON (*v*)

adverbs
pungently; deftly; professionally; skillfully; richly; deliciously.
(See flavor.)

SEASONABLE

adverbs
pleasantly; safely; congruously; stylishly; fashionably; reasonably; appropriately; carefully; fastidiously; conveniently; happily; luckily; agreeably; fairly; sensibly.

SEAT

adjectives
proffered; rustic; glorious; battered; pleasant; splayed; favorite; airy; chiefest; princely; storied; regal; supreme; cheap; blissful; dismal; shady; secure; venerable; rural; capacious; luxurious; exalted; imperial; ancestral.

verbs
arrange—s; discover—; emerge from—; fill—s; group—s; mark—; number—s; occupy—; offer—; order—; pad—; proffer—; range—s; relinquish—; reserve—; slump in—; vacate—; wedge into—; —accommodates; —collapses.
(See chair, saddle.)

SEAT (*v*)

adverbs
musingly; peacefully; airily; cozily; carelessly; abruptly; wearily; drowsily; idly; calmly; rustically; regally; blissfully; exaltedly; imperially; ostentatiously; modestly; demurely; unobtrusively.
(See usher, establish.)

SEATED

adverbs
firmly; gingerly; shakily; nervously; permanently; resolutely; immovably; shyly; timidly; determinedly; finally; primly; demurely; stiffly; gravely; pompously; carefully; respectfully; slouchily; disrespectfully; lazily.

SECESSION

adjectives
successful; timely; foolish; peaceable.

SECLUDED

adverbs
carefully; happily; distantly; completely; pleasantly; comfortably; desirably; terribly; desolately; palatially; unsociably; conveniently; agreeably; inhospitably; delightfully; inexplicably; singularly; curiously; significantly.

SECLUSION

adjectives
obliterating; wearisome; elegant; mummied; dignified; studied; comforting; deep; haughty; bleak; aristocratic; motionless; strict; sweet; utter; tropical; slothful; ascetic; comparative; sullen; torpid; flowery; virtual; sunshiny; blank.

verbs
advise—; advocate—; afford—; attempt—; contemplate in—; emerge from—; enjoy—; gain—; hide in—; interrupt—; meditate in—; offer—; prize—; raise in—; rouse from—; seek—; strive for—; subject to—; —bores; —consoles; —dulls; —stagnates; —disciplines.
(See isolation, loneliness, concealment, retirement, retreat.)

SECOND

adjectives
condemned; supercharged; frozen; significant; reckless; precise; fleeting; precious; recaptured; wasted; breathless.

SECRECY

adjectives
mysterious; enjoined; half-pretended; inviolate; romantic; strictest; indispensable; profound; infinite; tremendous; necessary; sworn.

verbs
delve into—; encroach upon—; intrude upon —; obscure with—; pervade—; pierce—; —fosters; —mystifies; —solaces; —veils.

(See seclusion, privacy, retirement, retreat, solitude.)

SECRET

adjectives
unnecessary; enrapturing; golden; tender; yearning; solemn; terrible; guilty; precious; close-locked; fatal; sublime; effective; minute; open; delicious; damaging; dreadful; mysterious; unrevealed; innocent; priceless; efficient; scientific; ultimate; subtle; treasured; serious; sterile; elfish; grim; divine; curious; shameful; conventual; vital; untold; elemental; unsavory.

verbs
betray—; disclose—; discover—; divulge—; entrust—; explore—; expose—; exult in—; ferret into—; ferret out—; glean—s; guard —; harbor—; hug—; impart—; laden with —s; penetrate—; probe—; pry into—; recount—; rediscover—; rejoice in—; relieve of—; relish—; reveal—; secure—; share—; spill—; take into—; unbosom—; unearth—; unfold—; unlock—; utter—; wheedle—; wrest—from; wring—from; yield—; —breaks; —leaks out; —mystifies.

(See confidence, mystery.)

adverbs
apparently; closely; carefully; profoundly; inviolably; necessarily; dangerously; darkly; pleasantly; mysteriously; deeply; furtively; vexatiously; foolishly; wisely; inscrutably; childishly.

SECRETARY

adjectives
indefatigable; confidential; delinquent; honorary; obsequious; legation; subservient; household; flippant; suave; diplomatic.

verbs
acquaint—; confide in—; depend on—; despatch—; dispense with—; entrust—; provide with—; —attends; —records; —transacts.

(See assistant, accessory.)

SECRETION

adjectives
nauseating; acrid; animal; pungent; endocrinous; curdy; life-giving.

verbs
deposit—; discharge—; emit—; extract—; furnish—; influence—; inject—; limit—; pour—; stimulate—; suppress—; throw off —; undergo—; —covers; —flows; —emanates; —exudes; —increases; —issues; —oozes.

(See liquid, saliva, bile.)

SECRETIVE

adverbs
curiously; furtively; mysteriously; unpleasantly; unnecessarily; oddly; importantly; absurdly; ridiculously; laughably; foolishly; craftily; extraordinarily; inordinately; unreasonably; senselessly; habitually; fantastically; crazily; morbidly; comically.

SECT

adjectives
persecuted; denominational; dissenting; unresting; reigning; separated; dogmatical.

verbs
attach to—; distinguish—; divide into—s; extirpate—; honor—; found—; originate—; persecute—; profess—; scatter—; test—; —adheres; —believes; —confounds; —deviates; —distracts; —endures; —observes; —banishes; —springs up; —worships.

(See party, religion.)

SECTION

adjectives
fresh; concluding; pointed; elongated; adjunctive; remote; identical; covered; rugged; rural; insurgent; progressive; benighted; geographical; colored; peaceful; pure; omitted; subsequent; luscious; internal.

verbs
break up into—s; combine—s; curtain off—; desert—; designate—; detach—; divide into —s; enlarge—; present—; rate—; split up into—s; unite—s; —constitutes; —s join.

(See division, compartment, department, segment.)

SECURE

adverbs
entirely; remarkably; financially; reasonably; probably; unusually; extraordinarily; prosperously; fortunately; undeniably; palpably; dependably; reliably; confidently; authentically; happily.

SECURE (v)

adverbs
conditionally; expeditiously; triumphantly; blamelessly; questionably; privately; eventually; legitimately; promptly; fortunately; effectually; financially.
(See gain, obtain.)

SECURITY

adjectives
unfathomable; false; stable; specific; mundane; comparative; fancied; individual; absolute; carnal; imperfect; universal; symbolized; tolerable; proper; reasonable; effectual; foreign; financial; smiling; essential; contented.

verbs
attain—; build up—; dwell in—; enjoy—; evince—; guarantee—; imperil—; insure—; lull into—; maintain—; preserve—; receive —; ruffle—; threaten—; undermine—.
(See impregnability, independence, safety.)

SEDATE

adverbs
gravely; comically; habitually; naturally; pleasantly; priggishly; ridiculously; peculiarly; unusually; properly; modestly; serenely; thoughtfully; calmly; occasionally; forbiddingly; curiously.

SEDATIVE

adjectives
admirable; efficient; bitter; harmful.

verbs
act as—; addict to—s; administer—; employ—; prescribe—; —calms; —eases; —lulls; —mitigates; —palliates; —quells; —quiets; —relieves; —weakens; —soothes.
(See medicine, opiate.)

SEDENTARY

adverbs
disagreeably; unfortunately; monotonously; conveniently; comfortably; harmfully; injuriously; necessarily; providentially; tediously.

SEDGE

adjectives
waving; rustling; bonnet; thick.

SEDIMENT

adjectives
ignoble; dark; useless.

SEDITION

verbs
convict of—; direct—; protest against—; seethe with—; —agitates; —arouses; —disorders; —disparages; —distracts; —disturbs; —incites; —offends; —prejudices; —upsets.
(See treason, disturbance, agitation, commotion.)

SEDITIOUS

adverbs
viciously; desperately; meanly; secretly; vilely; dangerously; alarmingly; powerfully; churlishly; insidiously; furtively; loudly; resentfully; aggressively; actively; openly; audaciously; boldly; influentially.

SEDUCTION

adjectives
vulgar; didactic; deliberate; lulling; invisible.

SEDUCTIVE

adverbs
mysteriously; deliberately; utterly; delightfully; disturbingly; provokingly; intentionally; cleverly; designedly; diabolically; successfully; bewilderingly; amazingly; irresistibly; unquestionably; wondrously; marvelously; unexpectedly; remarkably; surprisingly; coolly; radiantly; joyously; quietly; consciously; tauntingly; tormentingly; overwhelmingly; provocatively; unconsciously.

SEE (v)

adverbs
vividly; graphically: objectively; subjectively; dimly; faintly; distinctly; picturesquely; nakedly; comprehensively; belatedly; previously.
(See view, observe, notice.)

SEED

adjectives
deathless; fruitful; heavenly; worthy; spurting; generous; untainted; true; blind; vigorous; healthy; sanguine; diversified; nox-

ious; alated; degenerate; extensive; foreign; winged; spiritual; germinating; shriveled.

verbs
bear—; bruise—; carry—; implant—; propagate—; scatter—; sow—; —clings; —falls; —flowers; —fructifies; —germinates; —matures; —splits; —springs open; —springs up; —yields.
(See germ, grain.)

SEEDY

adverbs
disagreeably; unpleasantly; decrepitly; sorrily; shabbily; wearily; distressingly; pitiably; miserably; lamentably; deplorably; carelessly; raggedly; wretchedly; unhappily; unusually; unnecessarily; gracelesssly; desolately.

SEEK (v)

adverbs
frivolously; sensually; patiently; idly; sedulously; contemptuously; unavailingly; desperately; habitually; persistently; instinctively; contentiously; adventurously; diligently; vainly; aimlessly; scientifically; involuntarily; tirelessly; faithfully; impiously; perseveringly; industriously; obstinately.
(See search, hunt.)

SEEKER

adjectives
frivolous; sincere; tranquil; selfless; inactive; inexperienced; vivacious; sensation.

SEERS

adjectives
profound; pretentious; discomfited; infallible; vegetarian; solitary; statistical; worldly-wise; omniscent.

SEGMENTS

adjectives
decorated; manageable; separated; equal.

verbs
arrange—; compose—; compress—; designate—; divide—; join—; rivet—; unite—; —constitute; —form.
(See section, division, department, part.)

SEGREGATE (v)

adverbs
racially; designedly; dictatorially; viciously; invidiously; seasonally; virtually; diplomatically.
(See isolate, separate.)

SEGREGATED

adverbs
carefully; inhospitably; cruelly; unnecessarily; happily; preferably; mercilessly; significantly; thoughtfully; intolerantly; arrogantly; illegally; undemocratically; uncharitably; perniciously.

SEIZE (v)

adverbs
peremptorily; selfishly; impulsively; roughly; rapaciously; greedily; lustfully; diabolically; bestially; unceremoniously; summarily; rudely; uncouthly; desperately; arbitrarily; illegally.
(See snatch, grasp.)

SEIZURE

adjectives
prolonged; epileptic; impending; arbitrary; convulsive; permanent; abrupt; peremptory; illegal; unwarranted.

SELECT (v)

adverbs
intelligently; discreetly; painstakingly; arbitrarily; tastefully; variously; fastidiously; ostentatiously; judiciously; exquisitely; infallibly; methodically; legitimately.
(See choose, pick.)

SELECTION

adjectives
marvelous; smartest; extensive; huge; enormous; perverse; customary; dazzling; unusual; noteworthy; careful; judicious; vocational; grand; current; natural; exquisite; unlimited; intelligent; methodical; representative; widest; infallible; artificial; dire; euphuistic; copious; fine; vast; occasional; rapid; conscious; singular; eager; immediate; legitimate; confident; complete; varied.

SELF

adjectives
inmost; past-created; unchanged; progressive; insignificant; whimsical; full-formed; reverend; beautiful; profane; gushing; substantial; piquant; buoyant; perfect; pretended; fancied; malignant; dead; worthless; central; bold; customary; real; gracious; wittiest; sweet; maternal; irregular; tortured; double; forgotten.

SELF-APPRECIATION

verbs
bear—; dissipate—; flush with—; inflate—; inspire—; promote—; puff up with—; resort to—; —contents; —provokes; —rewards.
(See egotism, self-esteem.)

SELF-CONFIDENCE

adjectives
sturdy; brave; youthful; sublime; brash; bright; hard-won; serene.

SELF-CONSCIOUSNESS

adjectives
sharp; perpetual; absurd; puerile; exaggerated; embarrassed; obvious.

verbs
affect—; afflict with—; attain—; blush in—; conquer—; defeat—; dispel—; divert from —; free from—; ignite—; nettle by—; overcome—; plague with—; relinquish—; rout —; simper in—; sweep away—; triumph over—; —absorbs; —affects; —annoys; —hinders; —irks; —provokes; —sensitizes.
(See awkwardness, clumsiness, embarrassment.)

SELF-CONTROL

adjectives
persistent; rigid; systematic; supreme; long-practiced; resolute; wondrous.

SELF-ESTEEM

verbs
alter—; build—; center in—; enlarge—; favor—; flatter—; impair—; lower—; modify—; pique—; polish—; raise—; smite—; value—; —assures; —grounds on; —melts; —overrates; —profits.
(See egotism, conceit, pride, vanity.)

SELFISH

adverbs
incredibly; shamelessly; lazily; incurably; inherently; habitually; naturally; unbelievably; atrociously; thoughtlessly; abominably; cruelly; unforgivably; shamefully; blithely; heedlessly; undutifully; ungrateably; remarkably; arrantly; egregiously; grossly; stingily; arrogantly; sordidly; indolently; uncommonly; unhappily; miserably; grossly; greedily; avariciously; blatantly; openly; curiously; strangely .

SELFISHNESS

adjectives
inconsiderate; blind; intense; enlightened; rigid; obstinate; sordid; willful; cold; debasing; ghastly; overweening; shallow; individual; solitary; petty; sheer; querulous; intelligent.

verbs
censure—; coddle—; conquer—; decry—; foster—; inculcate—; indulge in—; nurse—; practice—; pursue—; overcome—; oppose —; restrain—; route—; screen—; transcend —; —angers; —centers; —concentrates; —covets; —curses; —embroils; —narrows; —pains; —pampers.
(See jealousy, ingratitude, materialism, egotism, cruelty.)

SELF-RELIANCE

verbs
admire—; appreciate—; beget—; breed—; demand—; destroy—; display—; encourage —; engender—; esteem—; evince—; foster —; generate—; implant—; inculcate—; infuse—; instil—; praise—; prize—; smother —; stifle—; urge—; value—; —fortifies; —sustains.
(See confidence, faith, assurance.)

SELF-RESPECT

verbs
betray—; brace—; breed—; debase—; degrade—; destroy—; foster—; heighten—; hoist—; humble—; inculcate—; lower—; maintain—; nurture—; promote—; sustain —; reduce—; value—; weaken—; wound—.
(See pride, vanity, egotism, respect.)

SELF-RESTRAINT

verbs
discard—; esteem—; exercise—; impose—; train in—; value—; —abstains; —binds; —coerces; —checks; —curbs; —declines; —desists; —disciplines; —fetters; —forbears; —governs; —impels; —inures; —moderates; —shackles; —restricts; —tempers.
(See discipline, training, restraint, control.)

SELL (*v*)

adverbs
systematically; professionally; constructively; rationally; profitably; legitimately; irregularly; intelligently.
(See exchange, transfer.)

SELVES

adjectives
gross; glorified; restored; corruptible; deserted; petty.

SEMBLANCE

adjectives
tragic; striking; equal; princely; simple; rare; ghostly; sham; grotesque; airy; figurative; bustling; outward.

verbs
admit—; afford—; ascertain—; assume—; bear—; communicate—; discern—; expose—; furnish—; impart—; maintain—; offer—; recognize—; regard—; reveal—; ridicule—; scrutinize—; sustain—; uncover—; wear—of; —approximates; —burlesques; —caricatures; —copies; —deceives; —mirrors; —parallels; —simulates; —smacks of.
(See appearance, aspect, look, similarity.)

SEMINARY

verbs
enroll in—; father—; found—; —breeds; —cherishes; —cultivates; —disciplines; —enlightens; —equips; —expands; —expels; —flourishes; —fosters; —inculcates; —informs; —infuses; —instructs; —nurtures; —polishes; —prepares; —propagates; —qualifies; —refines; —trains.
(See college, school, institution, university.)

SENATE

adjectives
venerable; complaisant; servile; reverend; venal; strong; popular.

SENATORS

adjectives
energetic; businesslike; influential; odious; easily-influenced; brilliant; lame-duck; independent.

verbs
convoke—; embroil—; impeach—; muster—; support—; —address; —adjourn; —admit; —assemble; —campaign; —confirm; —convene; —demand; —formulate; —legislate; —orate; —propose; —sit; —stampede; —filibuster.
(See legislator, congressman, judge, lawyer.)

SEND (*v*)

adverbs
swiftly; despairingly; providentially; equitably; expressly; anonymously; simultaneously; tirelessly; incessantly; vigorously; peremptorily; promptly; precipitately.
(See forward, dispatch.)

SENILE

adverbs
terribly; tragically; pathetically; dingily; ridiculously; desolately; rosily; drunkenly; lamentably; crabbedly; feebly; disgustingly; horribly; weakly; degenerately; gracelessly; depressingly; startlingly; woefully; hopelessly; prematurely; mournfully.

SENILITY

adjectives
sheer; sham; self-indulgent

SENSATION

adjectives
enlightening; disagreeable; wonderful; delicious; sinking; buoyant; literary; tingling; satisfying; pleasing; overpowering; formless; void; spry; variable; sparkling; luxurious; burning; queer; beneficent; strong; tremendous; strange; overnight; immense; peculiar; perverted; unique; smashing; prodigious; profound; tactual; creeping; enormous; bright; funny; crazed; broken; refined; horrible; aristocratic; restful; exuberant; stinging; abrupt; curtain; passive; reigning; advertising; inner; tactile; absorbing; outstanding; atrocious; heavy; nervous; wretched; darting; pricking; extraordinary.

verbs
convey—; create—; excite—; derive—; experience—; fan—; illustrate—; impart—; interpret—; inspire—; lower—; jade with—; overshadow—; parade—; perceive—; produce—; retain—; revive—; stir—; transmit—; —agitates; —animates; —arouses; —enkindles; —enraptures; —fascinates; —flushes; —flusters; —galvanizes; —impresses; —infects; —inflames; —infuriates; —intoxicates; —penetrates; —perishes; —perturbs; —petrifies; —pierces; —piques; —overwhelms; —ravishes; —renders; —ruffles; —rushes; —staggers; —startles; —strikes; —warms; —entrances; rekindle—; report—; reproduce—.
(See perception, consciousness, mood, emotion, feeling, sensationalism.)

SENSATIONAL

adverbs

definitely; curiously; intentionally; shockingly; offensively; singularly; undeniably; garishly; wickedly; extraordinarily; downright; cleverly; tremendously; profitably; deliberately; designedly; purposely; adroitly; ingeniously; attractively; dramatically; spectacularly; surprisingly.

SENSATIONALISM

verbs

abominate—; abhor—; addict to—; avoid —; bear—; condone—; detest—; deplore—; dispose toward—; dodge—; eschew—; frown upon—; incline toward—; recoil from—; refrain from—; reject—; shun—; shy from—; —blazons; —cheapens; —corrupts; —defiles; —disgusts; —publicizes; —sullies.

(See notoriety, publicity, sensation.)

SENSE

adjectives

real; miraculous; pleading; evil; indefatigable; cowering; abounding; moral; accommodated; final; soothing; confused; instinctive; crude; vulgar; intuitive; prophetic; exaggerated; dreary; supplementary; aesthetic; helpless; wakeful; superstitious; false; disparaging; practical; deepening; different; unscientific; distinct; inward; common; crushing; artistic; vigorous; corporeal; elementary; glimmering; intellectual; penetrating; cruel; mystical; colder; sterling; surly; strictest; baffled; extravagant; sickening; normal; suffocating; human; secret; dusty; serene; shrewd; automatic; unwitting; insidious; critical; curious; divers (pl); literal; momentary; accretive; mobile; external; exhilarating; genuine; superior; just; dull; seeming; modest; jubilant; cultivated; mysterious; innate; brute; scriptural; academic; imperturbable; half-conscious; delicate; lingering; practical; devout; sobering; pedagogical; magnetic; noisome; leaping; ethnological; renewed; morbid; anguished; realizing; universal; humble; dimmer; rhetorical; subtile; eminent; sardonic; impaired; hazy; pleasant; constant; tacit; painful; stable; jealous; complimentary; puzzled; narrow; uncanny; absorbed; dewy; rigorous; caviling; kennel; boiling; precocious; jaded; blunted; perceptive; untechnical; warring; palpitating; esoteric; dismal; arithmetical; architectonic; half-dormant; degraded; irresistable; pseudo-pantheistic; nascent; sudden; immanent; plain; wretched; terrible; withering; odious; balancing; apparent; military; dim; symbolic; inborn; reputable; etymological; hypothetical; ineffaceable; eternal; sleepy; inarticulate; pedantic; acquired; implicit; benumbed; solemn; keener; reverted; exterior; lofty; magic; stored; languid; testifying; lively; finer; abstract; social; quibbling; amiable; earnest; material; mobile; offended; sound; exceeding; deficient; due; mechanical; seeing; pathological; receptive; grosser; slumbering; acute; gratified; oppressive.

SENSE (v)

adverbs

intuitively; instinctively; vaguely; uncannily; morbidly; nervously; miraculously; prophetically; secretly; automatically; mysteriously; jealously; precociously; keenly.

(See recognize, perceive.)

SENSE of HUMOR

verbs

cultivate—; derange—; develop—; display —; dull—; exhibit—; foster—; instil—; lack —; necessitate—; pervert—; prize—; require—; treasure—; value—; —eases; —lightens; —responds; —rewards.

(See wisdom, knowledge, ability.)

SENSES

verbs

annihilate—; assail—; awaken—; benumb —; bereave—; blunt—; cultivate—; conquer —; deaden—; deprave—; distort—; doubt —; dull—; educate—; enrapture—; govern —; gratify—; heighten—; inflame—; impair —; injure—; lose—; outrage—; overwhelm —; paralyze—; perceive by—; possess—; purify—; quicken—; refine—; regain—; stimulate—; stir—; titillate—; vex—; —convey; —deceive; —delude; —dictate; —disconcert; —endow; —estrange; —guide; —play; —respond; —stifle; —stray; —swim; —tingle; —conflict.

(See emotion, feeling, sensation, mood.)

SENSIBILITIES

verbs

awaken—; benumb—; blunt—; cloud—; cultivate—; deaden—; discern—; dull—; dwarf—; engender—; lose—; offend—;

paralyze—; perceive—; restore—; revive—; resuscitate—; sharpen—; stupefy—; surrender to—.
(See senses.)

SENSIBILITY

adjectives
quivering; refined; finer; glowing; elegant; profound; natural; tender; delicate; exquisite.

SENSIBLE

adverbs
undoubtedly; scarcely; financially; economically; practicably; solidly; profoundly; usually; stolidly; soundly; substantially; particularly; honestly; thoughtfully; wisely; instinctively; crudely; cruelly; serenely; shrewdly; curiously; dully; imperturbably; pleasantly; painfully; dismally; eminently; remarkably; sincerely; apparently; palpably; evidently; manifestly; highly; altogether; entirely; commendably; laudably; admirably; delightfully; refreshingly; inherently; naturally; innately; discreetly; sagely; gravely; stodgily; odiously; oppressively.

SENSITIVE

adverbs
morbidly; unusually; unreasonably; curiously; oddly; extravagantly; nervously; timidly; shyly; awkwardly; extremely; unfortunately; unnaturally; foolishly; ridiculously; absurdly; deplorably; distressingly; heartbreakingly; preposterously; terribly.

SENSITIVENESS

adjectives
astonishing; pardonable; quivering; morbid; abnormal; fantastic; artistic; overstrained; excessive; infinite; unnatural; emotional; perilous; womanly; feverish.

verbs
dull—; lack—; sharpen—; —pains; —pierces; —prompts; —shocks; —varies; —wrings.
(See feeling, emotion, pain.)

SENSUAL

adverbs
coarsely; basely; grossly; dissolutely; vilely; undeniably; unfortunately; scandalously; broadly; indecently; deplorably; flagrantly; outrageously; utterly.

SENSUOUS

adverbs
keenly; artistically; refreshingly; poetically; enthusiastically; eagerly; appreciatively; responsively; acutely; intensively; quickly; poignantly; avidly; deeply; profoundly; unusually; alertly.

SENSUOUSNESS

adjectives
inert; controlled; rarefied; captivating; rare.

SENTENCE
(*general*)

adjectives
dispossessed; suspended; extravagant; turgid; involved; hurried; merciful; animated; charming; epigrammatic; vigorous; memorable; concluding; incoherent; suggestive; characteristic; functionary; fragmentary; monotonous; lucid; obscure; final; irritable; drastic; angry; incoherent; weird; vibrant; telegraphic; haunting; jerky; dreadful; dumb; childish; swift; stimulating; discreet; scathing; mangled; whispered; favorite; frigid; oracular; appalling; too-lenient; pithy; hard; immediate; consecutive; fresh; slovenly; declarative.

SENTENCE
(*punishment*)

verbs
advocate—; annul—; commute—; deal out —; defer—; execute—; faint at—; impose —; justify—; mete out—; pass—; proclaim —; pronounce—; —binds; —expires.
(See judgment, punishment, justice.)

SENTENCES
(*words*)

verbs
balance—; build—; construct—; declaim—; disclaim—; detach—; embody—; hurl—; mutter—; paraphrase—; quote—; recast—; recollect—; reconstruct—; round—; sum up —; toss—; transcribe—; —pound; —roll; —swing.
(See thought, paragraph, idea, word.)

SENTIMENT

adjectives
affectionate; baseless; filthy; tender; favorable; contradictory; ennobling; growing; mawkish; elevated; incongruous; liberal; enduring; aristocratic; patriotic; frivolous; secret; universal; public; delicate; fresh;

fiery; emotional; poetical; mingled; vague; noble; kindly; recurring; adverse; collective; profane; grateful; delicious; natural; absorbing; vivid; congenial; generous; traditional; buried; maudlin; trivial; warm; creeping; virtuous; humanizing; chivalric; ominous; unaltered; national; pious; exotic; elusive; romantic; artistic; unexpressed; pompous; unexaggerated; altruistic; enduring; detached; silky; potent; heroic; similar; sympathetic; moral; confused; warm; affectionate; false; serious; decisive; contemptuous; fitting; noble; slighting; perpetual; lackadaisical; bombastic; opposite; wintry; endearing; uneasy; stubborn; grandiose; aroused; excessive; muddled; growing; outspoken; pretty; exalted; puerile; minority; masculine; morbid; paltry; reactionary; delectable.

verbs
arouse—; awaken—; check—; communicate —; control—; consummate—; convey—; corrupt—; crystallize—; discard—; echo—; encourage—; express—; gag—; induce—; inscribe—; moderate—; reflect—; sweep—; venerate—; voice—; —blossoms; —blurs; —chills; —defies; —expresses; —falls; —flits; —flowers; —grows; —hangs; —nurtures; —possesses; —reflects; —shifts; —shapes; —solidifies; —swings; —switches; —survives; —veers; —violates; —works.
(See feeling, emotion, tenderness, sentimentality.)

SENTIMENTAL

adverbs
pleasantly; extremely; absurdly; touchingly; incurably; secretly; openly; probably; romantically; feelingly; unusually; somewhat; deeply; profoundly; particularly; ostentatiously; mawkishly; sincerely; genuinely.

SENTIMENTALISM

adjectives
racial; unmanly; romantic; spurious; feigned; western.

SENTIMENTALIST

adjectives
gushing; slobbering; sincere.

SENTIMENTALITY

adjectives
sheer; foolish; posturing; stupid; queer; betraying; unnatural; silly; erotic; sallow.

verbs
affect—; appeal to—; avoid—; burlesque—; confess—; depreciate—; detect—; discard —; dismiss—; disparage—; display—; evince—; exclude—; exhibit—; express—; feign—; profess—; reject—; ridicule—; scoff at—; shun—; —complicates; —creeps; —exaggerates; —oozes; —riles (colloq.); —softens.
(See sentiment.)

SENTINELS

adjectives
watchful; dauntless; delinquent; vigilant; cheerful; motionless; faithful; sleeping.

SENTRIES

adjectives
successive; pacing; red-coated.

SENTRY

verbs
address—; appoint—; circumvent—; discharge—; elude—; escape—; evade—; ignore—; lure—; post—; replace—; salute—; shun—; stand—; —abandons; —accosts; —admits; —advances; —alarms; —arouses; —bars; —challenges; —dozes; —escorts; —guards; —hails; —intrenches; —paces; —patrols; —signals; —warns.
(See patrol, guard.)

SEPARATE (v)

adverbs
cruelly; symmetrically; partially; insuperably; formally; nominally; subsequently; legally; permanently; effectually; physically; fatally; inevitably; deplorably; eternally; conventionally; gradually; austerely.
(See sever, divide.)

SEPARATION

adjectives
physical; unavoidable; laborious; uncertain; prolonged; fatal; inevitable; deplorable; eternal; earthly; conventional; gradual; forcible; austere; subsequent; mysterious; compulsory.

verbs
cement—; effect—; endure—; hazard—; propose—; recommend—; —accomplishes; —bisects; —breaches; —disengages; —disjoins; —dismembers; —enforces; —isolates; —jeopardizes; —reconciles; —rends; —sad-

dens; —segregates; —severs; —splices; —sunders; —unleashes; —wrings.
(See exile, divorce, excommunication, departure, seclusion.)

SEPULCHER

adjectives
fair; uncovered; enormous; magnificent; dreamless; august; tenantless; immense.

SEPULCHRAL

adverbs
deeply; coldly; hollowly; darkly; gauntly; dreadfully; alarmingly; woefully; lugubriously; gloomily; miserably; incongruously; inexplicably; curiously; preposterously; absurdly; designedly; terrifyingly; inauspiciously; repulsively; needlessly; terribly; unwontedly; mournfully; bafflingly.

SEQUENCE

adjectives
logical; invariable; melancholy; historical; natural; dramatic; impressive; unusual; fragmentary; consecutive; chronological; true; interminable; rapid; intended; inflexible; honorable; chromatic; passionate; coherent; single; listless.

SERAPH

adjectives
burning; unseen; sinless.

SERENADE

verbs
applaud—; compose—; execute—; perform—; praise—; silence—; sing—; utter—; —arouses; —awakens; —charms; —enchants; —enraptures; —entertains; —expresses; —extols; —moves; —soothes; —stills; —stirs; —thrills; —unfolds.
(See music, song.)

SERENITY

adjectives
conceited; domestic; undisturbed; cloudless; calm; symmetrical; ineffable; celestial; wondrous; stern; sweet; unalterable; supreme; radiant.

verbs
bask in—; bathe in—; bear—; blast—; discompose—; disperse—; disturb—; menace—; recover—; repose in—; threaten—; —breaks; —dominates; —charms; —composes; —enchants; —pacifies; —radiates; —reconciles; —reigns; —ruffles.
(See calm, complacency, composure.)

SERFDOM

verbs
abolish—; deliver from—; denounce—; emancipate from—; eradicate—; liberate from—; reduce to—; release from—; sink into—; —binds; —debases; —constrains; —enchains; —fetters; —harnesses; —oppresses; —represses; —shackles; —subjugates; —suppresses; —tethers; —tramples; —enslaves.
(See slavery, bondage, servitude.)

SERIES

adjectives
attractive; interesting; stately; well-known; periodical; distinct; regressive; definite; extensive; painstaking; rhythmic; continuous; ingenious; graduated; unbroken; deliberate.

verbs
alternate—; arrange in—; blend into—; break—; chain in—; compile—; construct—; continue—; deliver—; discontinue—; edit—; endure—; engage in—; enumerate—; extend—; file in—; follow in—; grade in—; interrupt—; issue—; join in—; partition—; pen—; prolong—; protract—; publish—; record—; regulate—; relate—; sponsor—; sum up—; tabulate in—; wind in—.
(See row, set, group.)

SERIOUS

adverbs
gravely; critically; extremely; unquestionably; apparently; evidently; manifestly; curiously; secretly; palpably; ominously; portentously; mysteriously; admittedly; oddly; resolutely; decidedly; emphatically; grimly; severely.

SERIOUSNESS

adjectives
conscientious; portentous; unpleasant; nervous; unnecessary; owl-like; touching; especial; melancholy; ironic; sudden; apparent; pitiful; mock; reverential; surpassing.

verbs
abate—; acknowledge—; aggravate—; alleviate—; assuage—; compensate for—; conjecture—; decry—; detect—; determine—;

diminish—; doubt—; estimate—; exaggerate—; heighten—; intensify—; ignore—; judge—; magnify—; minimize—; mitigate—; modify—; reflect upon—; recognize—; —assures; —invades; —sobers.

(See gravity, earnestness, solemnity.)

SERMON

adjectives

extempore; controversial; funeral; soft; assize; elaborate; erudite; incomparable; splendid; stirring; sincere; brilliant.

verbs

acclaim—; borrow—; deliver—; design—; extol—; feed on—s; misinterpret—; prepare—, polish up—; revise—; —bores; —censures; —declaims; —discourses on; —edifies; —elucidates; —enlightens; —eulogizes; —exhorts; —expatiates on; —expounds; —guides; —harangues; —inspires; —moralizes; —rebukes; —reproves; —thunders; —uplifts; —wearies.

(See oration, address, homily, speech.)

SERMONIZE (*v*)

adverbs

allegorically; monotonously; paternally; morally; bombastically; mawkishly; conventionally; turgidly; irritably; animatedly; epigrammatically; characteristically; religiously; fanatically.

(See compose, preach.)

SERPENT

adjectives

poisonous; fiery; gilt; immense; treacherous; cursed; troubled; traitorous; writhing; lumbering; belligerent; venomous; monstrous; swollen.

verbs

exhibit—; slay—; —beguiles; —buzzes; —churns; —coils; —entwines; —glides; —hisses; —rustles; —sibilates; —spirals; —stings; —strikes; —struggles; —uncoils; —undulates; —writhes; —envenoms.

(See dragon, snake, reptile.)

SERUM

verbs

administer—; dilute—; derive—; devise—; discover—; drain—; employ—; impregnate with—; infuse—; inoculate—; inject—; introduce—; invent—; prepare—; rush—; —assists; —checks; —combats; —controls; —exempts; —generates; —immunizes; —insures; —moderates; —neutralizes; —overcomes; —remedies; —stagnates; —stems.

(See medicine, fluid, remedy, tonic, antitoxin.)

SERVANT

adjectives

cloistered; shining; numerous (pl); diligent; good natured; gracious; primitive; menial; indentured; authorized; private; confidential; natural; trustworthy; domestic; voluntary; respectful; solitary; stolid; disinterested; faithful; zealous; vile; gentle; assigned; laden; magnanimous; noiseless; unjust; inattentive; corrupt; public; flowered; natty; obedient; docile; superannuated; sorrowful.

verbs

bond—; command—; commend—; curse—; discharge—; dismiss—; employ—; extol—; humble—; rebuke—; reimburse—; reproach—; reprove—; retain—; reward—; sack—; station—; —announces; —attends; —beguiles; —betrays; —devotes; —details; —enlightens; —humbles; —identifies; —obeys; —pilfers; —ushers in; reprimand—.

(See matron, slave, assistant.)

SERVE (*v*)

adverbs

deftly; graciously; whole-heartedly; elegantly; gratuitously; conspicuously; unwittingly; valiantly; judiciously; indifferently; admirably; exclusively; eminently; generously; simultaneously; gloriously; faithfully; apathetically; tenderly.

(See deal, distribute.)

SERVICE

adjectives

right; courteous; efficient; thoughtful; unmatched; celebrated; gracious; willing; flawless; fine; unusual; alert; deft; helpful; extra; fast; expert; gallant; lip; financial; insurgent; domestic; unedifying; invidious; trustworthy; distinguished; meritorious; inestimable; deferred; memorial; typographic; professional; priestly; peaceful; suitable; religious; imposing; costly; gratuitous; humblest; valuable; haulage; exalted; gruelling; maximum; reluctant; economical; perfunctory; abiding; engineering; impressive; essential; thankless; desperate; dependable; perpetual; honorable; promising; brisk; consecrated; immense; unionized; superior; committal; disastrous; proffered; beneficial; table; scant; eminent; civil; diplomatic;

scientific; gloomy; garrison; reasonable; unselfish; surgical; superlative; industrial; imperative; utility; erection; unique; satisfactory; management; continuous; lasting; hazardous; charitable; meticulous; unmenaced; silver; ceremonious; arduous; glorious; solitary; strenuous; specific; secretarial; mutual; hateful; particular; duteous; advisory; supervisory; auxiliary; filial; golden; dependable; prompt; consular; diffused; manifold (pl); musical; meager.

verbs
abandon—; arise in—; attend—; attribute —; bribe—; call for—; command—; conduct —; correlate—; crave—; culminate—; dedicate—; dislocate—; dispense with—; display—; dispose of—; distinguish—; draw into—; engage in—; enlist—; experience—; force from—; induce into—; introduce into —; lay down—; maintain—; modernize—; obligate to—; paralyze—; participate in—; prepare for—; press into—; provide—; regiment into—; render—; review—; reward—; slash—; sublimate—; supplant—; suspend—; terminate—; toil in—; unify—; volunteer—.
(See work, employment, practice.)

SERVICEABLE

adverbs
extremely; undeniably; valuably; helpfully; practically; infinitely; generously; unusually; highly; conveniently; extraordinarily; obediently.

SERVILE

adverbs
obsequiously; disgustingly; pitiably; cringingly; miserably; innately; sickeningly; pitifully; abjectly; unctuously; blandly; basely; humbly; meekly; ingratiatingly; fawningly; subserviently; remarkably; significantly; oddly; inexplicably; unaccountably; openly.

SERVITOR

adjectives
faithful; swarthy; favored.

SERVITUDE

adjectives
penal; involuntary; loving; political; gilded; marital; prisoned; martial.

verbs
abolish—; bear—; betray into—; debase by —; deliver from—; drag into—; free from —; lead into—; liberate from—; reduce to —; resign to—; sentence to—; subject to—; —degrades; —chains; —enslaves; —expires; —fetters; —harnesses; —shackles; —weighs upon.
(See bondage, serfdom.)

SESSION

adjectives
executive; prolonged; nominal; secret; winter; all-night; plenary; extraordinary; lengthy; fruitless; extra; special.

verbs
adjourn—; attend—; complicate—; conclude —; convoke—; disband—; dismiss—; disperse—; emphasize—; extend—; open—; prolong—; protract—; resume—; wind up —; —administers; —achieves; —accomplishes; —appropriates; —assembles; —convenes; —deliberates; —effects; —formulates; —frames; —legislates; —recesses.
(See court, meeting, conference, assembly, council.)

SET

adjectives
unreasonable; artistic; brawling; unwelcome; gambling; hard-drinking; military; basic; uncut; prosaic; deplorable; intelligent; fair; poisonous; shiftless; social.

verbs
accumulate—; acquire—; associate in—s; arrange—s; classify in—s; collect—; compile—; complete—; compose—; compound —; conclude—; consort in—s; constitute—; create—; cut—; designate—; dispose of—; dissolve—; divide—; effect—; employ—; form—; fuse—; muster—; pair off in—s; procure—; sever—; sort into—s; supply—; weld—; —comprises; —includes.
(See series, group.)

SET (v)

adverbs
cunningly; perceptibly; resolutely; grimly; firmly; stubbornly; sternly; ingeniously; illogically; intuitively; primly; obstinately; deliberately; calmly; relentlessly; coquettishly; daintily; partially; courageously; awkwardly.
(See place, establish.)

SET-BACK

verbs
bear—; brood over—; endure—; fear—;

meet with—; suffer—; —abashes; —confuses; —crushes; —dejects; —discourages; —hinders; —humiliates; —impedes; —mortifies; —rebuffs; —relapses; —retards; —retrogrades; —reverses; —weakens.
(See disaster, calamity, mishap, misfortune.)

SETTING

adjectives
irrational; incongruous; atmospheric; half-comic; contemporary; tragic; insensitive; balanced; pastoral; superb; romantic; brilliant; gorgeous; drab; cumbrous; suggestive.

verbs
—assures; —calls for; —confuses; —depicts; —enhances; —extorts; —hinders; —impedes; —implies; —necessitates; —obstructs; —provides.
(See background, scene, environment.)

SETTLE (v)

adverbs
traditionally; cozily; sparsely; voluntarily; colonially; permanently; conclusively; mercilessly; satisfactorily; peacefully; amicably; contentedly; thinly; vaguely; prosperously; pecuniarily; arbitrarily; harmoniously.
(See adjust, fix.)

SETTLEMENT (colony)

verbs
abandon—; attack—; attempt—; defend—; desert—; endanger—; establish—; forsake—; fortify—; garrison—; guide—; imperil—; oppress—; plant—; ravage—; reinforce—; rule—; tyrannize over—; —decays; —colonizes; —dwindles; —governs; —flourishes; —languishes; —perishes; —pioneers; —progresses; —prospers; —thrives.
(See colony.)

SETTLEMENT (decision)

verbs
appeal for—; award—; arrange for—; arrive at—; balk at—; conclude—; confirm—; contract—; delay—; denounce—; dictate—; dispute—; effect—; favor—; gain—; hasten—; negotiate—; pledge—; postpone—; procure—; question—; ratify—; —determines; —disposes of; —grants; —provides for; —stipulates.
(See litigation, compromise, decision, adjustment.)

SETTLEMENT (general)

adjectives
amicable; prosperous; sparse; rapid; pecuniary; ultimate; defenseless; pretty; lasting; flourishing; equitable; arbitrary; scattered (pl); organized; peaceful; stable; separate; speedy; quiet; numerous (pl); sensible; penal; discordant; harmonious; ecclesiastical; parochial; upper; important.

SETTLER

adjectives
important; befuddled; outlying; early; staunch; brave; hardy; pious; first.

SEVER (v)

adverbs
permanently; completely; fatally; partially; hopelessly; voluntarily; legally; financially; economically; socially.
(See divide, separate.)

SEVERE

adverbs
harshly; gravely; puritanically; rigorously; rigidly; uncompromisingly; inflexibly; unsparingly; arbitrarily; domineeringly; imperiously; sternly; unmitigatedly; unrelentingly; relentlessly; odiously; atrociously; detestably; tyrannically; haughtily; brutally; needlessly; intolerably; abominably; barbarously; unwisely; senselessly; unreasonably; warrantably; properly.

SEVERITY

adjectives
unjust; uncompromising; stern; unsmiling; inexorable; unrelaxed; exemplary; unbending; extraordinary; mingled; brutal; presaging; intemperate; amused; burlesque; unnecessary; wholesome; hypocritical; righteous; relentless; formidable; calm; clear-cut; merciless; just; unusual; ill-directed.

verbs
abate—; abolish—; accentuate—; acknowledge—; aggravate—; allay—; ameliorate—; apologize for—; assuage—; determine—; ease—; extenuate—; heighten—; ignore—; impose—; increase—; intensify—; judge

with—; magnify—; mitigate—; modify—; palliate—; relax—; relieve—; scrutinize—; vary—; —exacts; —tires; —wears down.

(See cruelty, hardness, harshness.)

SEW (v)

adverbs

domestically; exquisitely; delicately; professionally; habitually; fastidiously; artistically.

(See stitch, fasten.)

SEWAGE

verbs

carry off—; convey—; discharge—; dispose of—; drain—; filter—; wallow in—; —breeds; —contaminates; —emanates from; —fouls; —hatches; —infects; —overflows; —pollutes; —precipitates; —reeks; spreads; —taints.

(See junk, garbage, filth, waste.)

SEX

adjectives

immured; gentle; fragile; inconstant; variable; bewitching; sterner; respective; dominant; grasping; enigmatical; weaker; dependent; deadlier.

verbs

arouse—; characterize—; cloak—; conceal—; debauch—; destroy—; determine—; distinguish—; equalize—s; eulogize—; honor—; pervert—; purify—; respect—; screen—; segregate—s; shroud—; unite—s; —boasts; —claims; —emphasizes; —mystifies.

(See males, women, distinction.)

SHACKLES

verbs

fuse—; liberate from—; rend—; sever—; sunder—; tear—; throw off—; unleash—; weld—; —bind; —burden; —encumber; —frustrate; —hamper; —link; —restrict; —restrain; —torture; —yoke.

(See chain, fetter.)

SHADE

adjectives

thick; cool; melancholy; symbolic; desolate; chequered; odorous; forlorn; deepest; awful; grim; heavenly; thorny; various (pl); numberless (pl); noonday; minutest; venerable; fleeting; solemn; unmoving; exact; consecrated; sullen; tender; tremulous; illustrious; brilliant; translucent; smoky; emphatic; summer; deepening; silent; bashful; evening; tangled; mottled; somber; sprouting; hideous; harmonious; complementary; finer; doleful; religious; grateful; waning; murky; fragrant; mellow; tufted; peaceful; leafy; veiled; vengeful; popular; floating; suburban; stunted; dewy; midnight; natural-looking; beautiful; quivering; reluctant; delicate; cerise; endless; partial; pulsating; pointed; blank; balmy; weltering; imperial; arching; pastel; blending; slender; new; pleasant; smart; wanted; solid; virile; lengthened; plain; popular; rich; exclusive; inviting; welcome; pendent; unexpected; endless; moonlight; implacable; steadfast; monastic; wandering; audacious; blessed; heterogeneous; powerful; disfiguring; lucid; wider; wavering.

verbs

abandon—; afford—; bury in—; gain—; illuminate—; recline in—; repose in—; retire to—; search for—; seek—; welcome—; —curtains; —deepens; —dims; —eclipses; —envelops; —obscures; —overcasts; —screens; —shelters; —shrouds; —veils.

(See darkness, gloom, shadow.)

SHADE (v)

adverbs

dismally; somberly; sullenly; invitingly; coolly; monastically; partially.

(See screen, cloud.)

SHADOW

adjectives

silvery; wandering; magnified; somber; impervious; stupendous; pale; brooding; luminous; gathering; swift; spectral; gentle; misty; lengthening; majestic; grotesque; thoughtful; sudden; protecting; eloquent; mellow; flocking; thin; transparent; tremulous; clear; portentous; monstrous; dappled; opaque; vague; lifelong; walking; gigantic; ghostly; heavy; deepest; magic-lantern; condemning; swimming; grim; gloomy; cool; noble; fantastic; horrible; mysterious; moonlight; twilight; dim; baleful; popular; softest; absurd; skulking; rustling; illuminated; distorted; flickering; haughty; intermittent; dense; violet; shapeless; evening; rosy; empty; translucent; sinister; weird; glimmering; defensive; fitful; ghastly; straight; unnatural; celestial; meager; ambrosial; apotheosized; vaporous; gusty; noisome; shining; slatted; illusive; impalpable; slanting; elongated; transparent; changing; whispering; misty; bold; dread;

veiled; solemn; encroaching; lifeless; thickening; bounding; trembling; houseless; liquid; citron; characteristic; lessening; disturbing; meaner; lank; chiseled; constitutional.

verbs
banish—; cast—; clutch at—; devise—; emerge from—; extend—; grope in—; haunt—; lurk in—; penetrate—; pierce—; repose in—; —blots; —casts; —creeps; —crouches; —dances; —dims; —disintegrates; —eclipses; —encircles; —engulfs; —falls; —flickers; —flits; —hangs; —haunts; —hovers; —hugs; —lengthens; —loiters; —looms; —melts; —plays; —radiates; —retreats; —shifts; —shrouds; —stretches; —trembles; —tosses.
(See shade, ghost, phantom, reflection.)

SHADY

adverbs
refreshingly; gratifyingly; pleasantly; excessively; beautifully; attractively; fortunately; questionably; suspiciously; darkly; invitingly; providentially.

SHAFT

adjectives
serene; granite; spotless; clustering; various (pl); rich; oblique; fluted.

verbs
ascend—; cleave—; descend—; erect—; grasp—; ground—; imbed—; loose—; mount—; sink—; shoulder—; splinter—; straddle—; suspend from—; —bears; —commemorates; —projects; —protrudes; —soars; —supports; —sustains; —towers.
(See column, post, tower, spear, arrow, lance, handle.)

SHAGGY

adverbs
roughly; softly; expensively; pleasantly; naturally; warmly; fashionably; extremely; slightly; beautifully; stylishly; untidily.

SHAKE

adjectives
impressive; impatient; melancholy; solemn; nervous; dubious; significant; respectful; weary.

SHAKE (v)

adverbs
convulsively; nervously; agitatedly; furiously; rudely; violently; negatively; skeptically; energetically; pitilessly; inwardly; pathetically; lustily; viciously; vigorously; sternly; ominously; vehemently; passionately.
(See jar, jolt.)

SHAKESPEARE

verbs
analyze—; commemorate—; criticize—; discuss—; disparage—; glorify—; honor—; idolize—; immortalize—; laud—; perform—; perpetuate—; portray—; revere—; venerate—; worship—; —depicts; —dramatizes; —eternizes; —excels; —lives.
(See literature, artist, poet, creator, dramatist.)

SHAKY

adverbs
tremulously; feebly; weakly; nervously; insecurely; helplessly; hopelessly; desperately; undeniably; obviously; hazardously; perilously; ominously; critically; precariously; forlornly; incurably; infirmly; decrepitly; embarrassingly.

SHALLOW

adverbs
extremely; pleasantly; safely; scandalously; impracticably; desperately; dangerously; obviously; particularly; sufficiently; fortunately; conveniently; unduly; disappointingly.

SHAM

verbs
cloak—; denounce—; discard—; disclose—; divulge—; expose—; fabricate—; uncover—; penetrate—; rebuke—; resort to—; reveal—; suppress—; unveil—; —deceives; —defrauds; —deludes; —disguises; —distorts; —feigns; —imposes upon; —mimics; —perverts; —pretends; —simulates.
(See fake, imitation, deception, counterfeit, hypocrisy.)

SHAME

adjectives
divulged; alluring; sweet; irreparable; maiden; perpetual; conscious; notable; eternal; stinging; sluggish; pure; innocent; passing; burning; penetrative; treble; bashful; sudden; blushing; wounding; virtuous; guilty; tender; murderous; notorious; sec-

ret; ingenious; infernal; deep; passionate; blighting; primal; engendered; earthly; naked; desolate; cherished; disgusting; defiant; tolerated; humble; utter; girlish; villainous; angry; lovely; crying; unvalued; lasting; natural.

verbs
accept—; avenge—; bequeath—; blush in—; bow in—; cloak—; condemn—; cover—; cower in—; cringe in—; deaden to—; disparage—; endure—; evoke—; expel in—; flush with—; hide in—; impute to—; put to —; rid of—; sink with—; slink away in—; suffer—; —blots; —burns; —debases; —defames; —defiles; —degrades; —dishonors; —humiliates; —mixes; —overcomes; —possesses; —scandalizes; —slurs; —stains; —stigmatizes; —sullies; —sweeps; —taints; —tarnishes; —villifies; —disgraces; bring to—.
(See humiliation, disgrace, dishonor, mortification.)

SHAME (v)

adverbs
consciously; viciously; ingeniously; jealously; disgustingly; traitorously; lustfully; vindictively.
(See humiliate, mock.)

SHAME-FACED

adverbs
embarrassingly; sheepishly; guiltily; foolishly; ridiculously; comically; absurdly; unnecessarily; instantly; curiously; significantly; amazingly; modestly; demurely; timidly; fearfully; childishly; awkwardly.

SHAPE

adjectives
vague; graceful; fundamental; sublime; stray; vampire; manifold (pl); imagined; lordly; phantom; ultimate; globular; nobler; streaming; slim; articulate; withered; invisible; various (pl); questionable; uniform; unaccustomed; goodly; delicate; monstrous; expanded; chimerical; clownish; archaic; convenient; cowled; gaudy; false; coarser; uncouth; transitory; prodigious; obscene; execrable; original; orthodox; delusive; lusty; checkered; perfect; glorious; exquisite; stalwart; airy; tangible; dim; minutest; distinctive; oblong; unimagined; quaint; imposing; stately; pillared; elliptic; gross; human; unique; pigmy; symmetrical; castled; alien; swarthy; habitable; nameless; peculiar; frightful; loathly.

verbs
alter—; caricaturize—; define—; delineate —; depict—; determine—; dim—; discern —; disguise—; distort—; draft—; hack at —; hack into—; hew into—; knead—; lick into—; modify—; mold—; obscure—; outline—; pad—; perceive—; regard—; sketch —; twist into—; —assumes; —suggests.
(See figure, feature, form, outline.)

SHAPE (v)

adverbs
adroitly; divinely; deftly; skillfully; professionally; gracefully; delicately; conveniently; conventionally; exquisitely; distinctively; quaintly; elliptically; symmetrically.
(See form, fashion, mould.)

SHAPELESS

adverbs
lumpishly; cumbrously; heavily; grotesquely; carelessly; awkwardly; fantastically; coarsely; grossly; loutishly; gawkily; consciously; hopelessly; pitiably; miserably; wretchedly; curiously; utterly; pathetically.

SHAPELY

adverbs
beautifully; alluringly; perfectly; divinely; seductively; prettily; unusually; remarkably; strikingly; noticeably; conspicuously; attractively.

SHARE

adjectives
ample; proportionate; individual; sufficient; adequate; full; fertile; fair; due; horrid; considerable; major; requisite; insignificant; proper; scanty; eccentric; usual; corresponding.

verbs
accept—; acquire—; adjust—; allocate—; allot—; apportion—; assign—; assume—; bequeath—; claim—; command—; consume —; deprive of—; disclaim—; distribute—; divert—; draw—; forfeit—; issue—; net—; partake of—; procure—; reap—; refuse—; regulate—; retain—; scorn—; usurp—; waive—; —doubles; —drops; —entitles.
(See part, investment, portion, proportion.)

SHARE (v)

adverbs
vicariously; affectionately; profitably; unsparingly; philanthropically; richly; equitably; gratuitously; faithfully; proportionately; adequately.
(See apportion, divide.)

SHARK

verbs
elude—s; repel—s; —s abound; —attacks; —bolts; —devours; —s endanger; —overturns; —plunges; —preys upon; —pursues; —s ravage; —skims; —skulks; —thrashes; —s victimize.
(See whale, fish.)

SHARP

adverbs
maliciously; unnecessarily; deliberately; bitterly; viciously; purposely; hatefully; spitefully; resentfully; venomously; designedly; cunningly; insinuatingly; incisively; antagonistically; needlessly; unwisely; mercilessly; obnoxiously; churlishly; snarlingly; rancourously; unsparingly; bitingly; adroitly; strategically; unwontedly; naturally; subtly; sensibly; schemingly; extremely; alertly; shrewdly; mysteriously; indubitably; obviously; supremely; unexpectedly; infallibly; infinitely; broadly; precociously; sympathetically; astoundingly; sagaciously; politically; cleverly; profoundly; deeply.

SHATTER (v)

adverbs
utterly; devastatingly; ruinously; spiritually; morally; physically; economically; financially; fundamentally.
(See shiver, demolish.)

SHAVE (v)

adverbs
daily; industriously; fastidiously; neatly; cleanly; closely; meticulously; customarily; habitually.
(See cut, clip.)

SHEARS

adjectives
abhorred; sounding; large; sharp.

verbs
apply—; blunt—; edge—; employ—; clip with—; file—; grind—; manipulate—; sharpen—; whet—; —bristle; —curtail; —level; —lop off; —reduce; —shave.
(See scissors.)

SHEATH

verbs
deposit in—; discard—; divest of—; draw from—; enclose in—; ensconce in—; extract from—; penetrate—; pierce—; pluck from —; repose in—; rest in—; withdraw from —; —encases; —encompasses; —enfolds; —envelops; —girds; —houses; —preserves; —protects; perforate— .
(See envelope, case.)

SHEAVES

adjectives
scattered; nodding; ripened; rusted.

SHED

adjectives
battered; nightly; tumbling; rickety.

SHED (v)

adverbs
periodically; seasonally; annually; naturally; normally; wastefully; luminously.
(See discard, cast.)

SHEEN

adjectives
starlight; spangled; dissolving; changing; original; placid; glistening; glorious; wavy; weird; alternate; superb; tremulous; variegated; metallic; dazzling; lustrous; smoky.

SHEEP

verbs
auction—; breed—; clip—; confine—; cross —; domesticate—; fleece—; herd—; market —; shear—; shelter—; slaughter—; tend —; —bleat; —browse; —climb; —graze; —huddle; —pasture; —produce; —ramble; —roam; —secrete; —straggle; —stray; —taint; —flock.
(See lamb, livestock, animal.)

SHEEPISH

adverbs
somewhat; obviously; naturally; naively; blushingly; absurdly; comically; laughably; ludicrously; awkwardly; guiltily; modestly; bashfully; uncomfortably; adorably.

SHEETS (general)

adjectives
cotton; stray; smooth; crisp; winding; bedraggled; tattered; torn; dampened; silver; unintermitting; delicious; loneliest; slumbrous; troublesome; standard; stinging; ghostlike; written.

SHEETS
(bed)

verbs
air—; befoul—; begrime—; bleach—; crease—; deodorize—; disinfect—; dispose of—; flounce—; fumigate—; gather—; hem —; launder—; pin—; plait—; reverse—; roll—; ruck—; ruffle—; rumple—; stain—; smooth—; snuggle in—; sully—; tuck in—; wrinkle—.
(See pillow, cloth, fabric.)

SHELF

adjectives
crowded; empty; pendent; continental; hanging; china.

verbs
adhere to—; bolster—; brace—; deplete—; deposit on—; dislodge from—; disorder on —; elevate—; hoist to—; incline—; lodge on—; prop—; recline on—; replenish—; repose on—; suspend from—; —facilitates; —rocks; —slopes; —sustains; —totters; —supports.
(See ledge, board.)

SHELL
(cannon)

verbs
clinch—; crack—; deflect—; rain—s; —annihilates; —blots out; —bursts; —crashes; —cripples; —demolishes; —detonates; —devastates; —discharges; —dismembers; —effaces; —erases; —obliterates; —plasters; —puffs; —rends; —screams; —sighs; —shatters; —smoulders; —uproots; —whines: —whistles; —whizzes.
(See bomb, grenade, shot, projectile.)

SHELL
(general)

adjectives
curved; fantastic; skimmed; hissing; rifled; awe-inspiring; orchestra; blazing; almond-shaped; veined; withered; crumbling; bivalve; splitting; knife-edged; screeching; chorded; spherical; tainted; sputtering; outgrown; box-like; misgrown; clinging; microscopic; single; solid; glass; bursting; soundless; woody; reflecting; sea; castaway.

SHELTER

adjectives
offered; sacred; solacing; delightful; generous; despicable; treacherous; grateful; hospitable; insufficient; rude; continual; artificial; noontide; respectable; safe; honorable.

verbs
abandon—; afford—; avail oneself of—; deny—; escort to—; expose—; extend—; gain—; grant—; imperil—; jeopardize—; maintain—; obtain—; procure—; retreat to —; scurry for—; secure—; seek—; utilize —; withdraw from—; —nurtures; —screens; —wards off.
(See haven, sanctuary, security, defense.)

SHELTER (*v*)

adverbs
paternally; faithfully; gratefully; generously; hospitably; artificially; protectively; honorably.
(See defend, protest.)

SHELTERED

adverbs
carefully; extremely; tenderly; unduly; prudishly; protectively; safely; warmly; securely; satisfactorily; duly; grudgingly; hospitably; painfully; comfortably; adequately; affectionately; permanently; insecurely; temporarily; pleasantly; barely.

SHEPHERD

adjectives
faithful; erratic; wandering; boding; homeless.

SHERIFF

adjectives
varlet; burly; brooding; mean.

verbs
authorize—; baffle—; commission—; delegate—; dodge—; elude—; empower—; evade—; frustrate—; perplex—; thwart—; vest in—; —apprehends; —compels; —confines; —deputizes; —enforces; —escorts; —grapples; —implicates; —incriminates; —repossesses; —restrains; —sanctions; —serves; —snares.
(See police, officer, constable.)

SHIELD

adjectives
mirrored; brazen; gilded; caudal; serried; ponderous; bright; protecting; worthless; clanging; dusky; siliceous; heraldic.

verbs
adorn—; batter—; bear—; emblazon—; engrave—; forge—; polish—; split—; —burdens; —protects.
(See badge, emblem, armor, screen.)

SHIFT (v)

adverbs
nervously; obligingly; uneasily; restlessly; momentarily; visibly; impatiently; inoffensively; perceptibly.
(See turn, change.)

SHIFTLESS

adverbs
incurably; habitually; constitutionally; inherently; naturally; oddly; curiously; singularly; unpardonably; crazily; offensively; provokingly; audaciously; openly; negligently; foolishly; loutishly; lazily; indolently; untidily; nonchalantly; indifferently; shamefully; grossly; unwarrantably; improvidently; stupidly; senselessly; stolidly; ineptly.

SHIFTY

adverbs
untrustworthily; shamefully; terribly; inherently; naturally; disgracefully; obviously; manifestly; miserably; wickedly; extremely; cleverly; adroitly; notably; notoriously; insidiously; treacherously; dangerously; despicably; contemptibly; artfully; warily; infamously.

SHIMMER (v)

adverbs
sparklingly; gloriously; metallically; tremulously; gildedly; brightly.
(See shine, flicker.)

SHIN

verbs
abrade—; bandage—; bare—; bark—; batter—; brace—; bruise—; buffet—; expose—; fracture—; gash—; lacerate—; pad—; rend—; scrape—; shield—; skin—; splinter—.
(See leg.)

SHINE (v)

adverbs
serenely; auspiciously; brilliantly; glaringly; perpendicularly; lucidly; radiantly; hazily; luminously; gloriously; goldenly; dazzlingly; feverishly; fitfully; tremulously; majestically; intermittently; fiercely; capriciously.
(See gleam, glitter.)

SHINY

adverbs
attractively; conspicuously; brilliantly; garishly; brightly; gloriously; momentarily; gaudily; unbearably; unpleasantly; gorgeously; proudly; glitteringly; scintillatingly; luminously; phosphorescently; unfashionably; conspicuously; intolerably; admirably; commendably; amazingly; singularly; peculiarly.

SHIP

adjectives
opposing; stratosphere; rolling; advertising; hostile; full-rigged; fearful; turbine-driven; stranded; tempest-winged; ocean-going; expected; blowing; distressed; pursuing; isolated; laboring; embryo; stately; rickety; shapely; specter; cloud; disastrous; myriad (pl); gallant; dismantled; water-logged; butchered; deep-water; whaling; leather-armored; unfortunate.

verbs
abandon—; apportion—; board—; charter—; delay—; drive—; escort—; man—; moor—; navigate—; nose—; propel—; scuttle—; —anchors; —bears; —blows; —bounds; —churns; —crawls; —flounders; —grounds; —lurches; —plies; —plows; —rears; —runs; —sails; —scuds; —shears; —shudders; —sidles; —slithers; —steams; —swings; —tosses; —turns.
(See boat, motorboat, aeroplane, launch.)

SHIP (v)

adverbs
seasonally; internationally; expressly; disastrously; promptly; customarily; faithfully.
(See transport, dismiss, send.)

SHIPMENT

verbs
allow—; admit—; authorize—; bear—; charge with—; check—; consign—; convey—; curtail—; dispose of—; exclude—; guarantee—; imperil—; insure—; limit—; obtain—; pledge—; prohibit—; release—; safeguard—; slate—; tax—; transport—; underwrite—; verify—; —burdens; —includes.
(See goods, merchandise.)

SHIRK (v)

adverbs
timidly; faithlessly; pusillanimously; basely; meanly; cowardly; ingeniously; falsely.
(See neglect, avoid, evade.)

SHIRT

adjectives
fringed; clammy; foul; higher; homespun; woven; unwearable; ruffled; spotless; sleeveless; pleated; wrinkled; irreproachable; fringed; buckskin; hair; dress; work; shrunken.

verbs
attire in—; damage—; divest of—; doff—; don—; expose—; mend—; patch—; pierce —; rend—; shred—; slit—; starch—; strip off—; stuff—; tatter—; tuck—; vend—; —frays; —shields; —swathes.
(See clothing, dress, garment.)

SHIVER

adjectives
cold; electric; simultaneous; protesting; timid; live; nervous.

verbs
allay—s; calm—s; repress—; restrain—; tremble with—; —agitates; —betrays; —convulses; —disquiets; —perturbs; —quavers; —ripples; —runs; —stirs.
(See sob, sigh, thrill, shudder.)

SHIVER (*v*)

adverbs
involuntarily; coldly; abnormally; timorously; inwardly; ceaselessly; feverishly.
(See shake, tremble.)

SHOALS

adjectives
narrow; dangerous; sable; deadly; treacherous.

verbs
circumvent—; encounter—; escape—; espy —; evade—; extricate from—; discern—; flounder on—; ground on—; risk—; snag on —; sight—; shunt—; —abound; —endanger; —force; —imperil; —jeopardize; —menace; —restrain.
(See reefs, rocks, shore, coast, island.)

SHOCK

adjectives
suggestive; surgical; psychic; paralyzing; overpowering; foaming; immediate; terrific; thundering; surging; unlooked-for; stern; moral; galvanic; dreadful; irresistible; fearful; quivering; rude; feeble; desolating; shivering; shattering; acknowledged; tremendous; harmonious; sudden; jangling; violent; visiting; stunned; physical; sublunar.

verbs
absorb—; attribute—; cushion—; displace —; outweigh—; receive—; subject to—; suffer—; survive—; withstand—; throw off —; —s ensue; —freezes; —galvanizes; —occurs; —persists; —reacts; —recurs.
(See collision, impact, agitation.)

SHOCK (*v*)

adverbs
morally; profoundly; astoundingly; unspeakably; physically; paralyzingly; terrifically; irresistibly; tremendously; violently; surgically.
(See terrify, astound.)

SHOCKED

adverbs
immeasurably; intensely; duly; indignantly; suddenly; terribly; awfully; incalculably; horribly; desperately; alarmingly; appallingly; fearfully; wildly; miserably; perilously; genuinely; manifestly; shamefully; cruelly; irrecoverably; obviously.

SHOCKING

adverbs
tragically; terribly; scandalously; outlandishly; unexpectedly; grossly; unquestionably; oddly; horribly; undeniably; miserably; wretchedly; shamefully; brutally; needlessly.

SHOD

adverbs
daintily; finely; extravagantly; expensively; stylishly; fashionably; incongruously; inharmoniously; crudely; heavily; warmly; insufficiently; coarsely; cloddishly; carelesslv; comfortably; wretchedly; miserably; poorly; ridiculously; inadequately; meanly; raggedly; outlandishly; conspicuously; tastefully; well.

SHOES

adjectives
clumsy; capacious; preposterous; patched; silken; russet; worn; well-cut; abusive; sorry-looking; little; sun-baked; spiked; tin; tattered; irksome; nail-clad; battered; flimsy.

verbs
don—; bear—; fashion—; gloss—; hurl—; manufacture—; mend—; polish—; retrieve —; revamp (colloq.)—; sheathe in—; sole —; —compress; —crunch; —nip; —pinch; —support; —squeeze; —torture.

SHOOT (v)

adverbs
accurately; obliquely; involuntarily; professionally; skillfully; fatally; tragically; maniacally; blindly; wildly.

(See fire, discharge.)

SHOP

adjectives
endless; exclusive; garish; desolate; filth-strewn; multiple (pl); inviting; showy; decent; dull; dingy; discriminating; intrepid; out-of-the-way; glittering; fashionable; specialty; matrimonial; dirty.

verbs
clutter up—; enlarge—; equip—; line—; loot—; man—; patronize—; support—; —accommodates; —adjusts; —caters to; —dispenses; —disposes of; —expands; —furnishes; —offers; —prospers; —purveys; —flourishes; —pledges; —retails; —stocks; —thrives; —undersells; —vends.

(See factory, garage, store.)

SHOP (v)

adverbs
voraciously; meticulously; tirelessly; fashionably; daily; gregariously; industriously; enthusiastically; vigorously; insensately.

(See purchase, visit.)

SHORE

adjectives
fading; pebbled; happy; fertile; beaten; swampy; receding; desolate; concave; exalted; far-off; crescent; rocky; sundered; emerald; inhospitable; waveless; dreadful; solitary; sighing; grateful; gloomy; cliff-like; scanty; delicious; shining; smiling; sterile; verdant; lily-lined; melancholy; pastoral; slimy; celestial; treeless; craggy; hoary; lonely; tumbling; accessible; pleasant; crepuscular; laughing; wasting; rival; kindred; upbraiding; sunny; bold; beautiful; chill; distant; furrowed; pitiless; sordid; porous; proximate; cressy; crumbling; friendlier; cheerless; peopled; savage; darksome; teeming; unprotected; changeless; boundless; tranquil; ghostly; mist-covered; peaceful; rugged; breezy; caressing; lonesome; radiant; spicy; stormless; bloody; imagined; weary; sandy; wintry; arid; perilous; alluvial; heterogeneous; echoic.

verbs
batter—; behold—; blockade—; buffet—; buttress—; coast to—; dash upon—; espy —; explore—; fortify—; frequent—; gain —; hail—; hasten to—; intrench on—; kiss —; maroon on—; pace—; patrol—; plant on—; ramble on—; repel from—; roam—; saunter on—; seek—; skirt—; strive for—; stroll along—; view from—; wash—; win —; —resounds; —tapers.

(See coast, island, beach, shoals, rocks.)

SHORT

adverbs
ridiculously; offensively; delightfully; agreeably; pitifully; disappointingly; relatively; tragically; scandalously; mercifully; wantonly; humanely; unreasonably; dramatically; disgustingly; smartly; inexcusably; characteristically; shamefully; curiously; extremely; remarkably; unconscionably; unpardonably; unexpectedly.

SHORTCOMING

adjectives
intellectual; obvious; spiritual; convenient; pleasant.

verbs
adjust—; atone for—; balance—; betray—; cloak—; compensate for—; condemn—; cope with—; correct—; counteract—; countervail —; denounce—; develop—; discern—; disclose—; divulge—; equalize—; expose—; indicate—; neutralize—; nullify—; overcome—; reconcile to—; redeem—; reproach —; reprove—; reveal—; perceive—.

(See defect, deficiency, failing, failure, imperfection.)

SHORT-HANDED

adverbs
obviously; manifestly; unfortunately; undeniably; lamentably; dreadfully; curiously; admittedly; helplessly; desperately; despairingly; distressingly; painfully; inconveniently; unprofitably; gloomily; sadly.

SHORT-SIGHTED

adverbs
deplorably; unintelligently; formidably; in-

auspiciously; unforgivably; politically; horribly; despicably; improvidently; foolishly; unhappily; disastrously; ruinously; calamitously; unpardonably; ineptly; hopelessly; irretrievably; lamentably; tragically; sorrily; selfishly; unwarrantably.

SHOT

adjectives
quick; succulent; tender; successive (pl); effectual; candid; chance; sprouting; calamitous; stray; deflected; pelting; native; hostile; scattering (pl); desultory; wondrous; hopeful; pendulous; argumentative; dead-sure; steady.

verbs
fill with—; hurl—; pour—; pump—; —beats; —belches; —bombards; —cracks; —fusillades; —nicks; —rains; —reverberates; —ricochets; —spatters; —sprays; —sputters; —streams; —thunders; —wails; —whistles; —whizzes.

(See bullet, shell, gun-fire, projectile, missile.)

SHOULDER

verbs
brush—; huddle—; lower—; shrug—; strengthen—; —dislocates; —droops; —flinches; —humps; —hunches; —inclines; —rubs; —sags; —stoops; —twitches; —wriggles.

SHOULDER (*v*)

adverbs
courageously; staunchly; vigorously; gallantly; bravely; patiently; reluctantly; stalwartly; promptly.

(See assume, bear.)

SHOULDERS

adjectives
naked; drawn; lofty; weary; careless; bowed; patient; shabby; unworthy; averted; decisive; slim; competent; reluctant; indolent; stooped; drooping; slender; quaking; resolute; dislocated; glorious; glimmering; disproportionate; milk-white; misshapen; ponderous; stalwart; heavy; broad; collective; strapping; submissive; hunched; shining; unresponsive; massive; slouching; willing; artful; half-nude; lurching; glossy; immortal; bony; jutting.

SHOUT

adjectives
faint; confused; unrestrained; clamorous; answering; universal; exultant; joyous; defiant; reckless; unreal; melancholy; gratified; uproarious; tumultuous; derisive; enthusiastic; untimely; windy; lusty; painful; distant; muffled; tiny; incessant; rough; cordial; deferential; blithesome; sporadic; deafening; involuntary.

verbs
muffle—; mute—; raise—; restrain—; stifle—; still—; smother—; —alarms; —arises; —breaks; —deafens; —dims; —s drown out; —entreats; —penetrates; —pierces; —rends; —rings; —resounds; —rouses; —splits; —spurs; —stabs; —startles; —terrifies; —thunders; —weaves.

(See call, cry, yell, shriek.)

SHOUT (*v*)

adverbs
profanely; turbulently; obstreperously; vociferously; jovially; dramatically; hoarsely; ecstatically; derisively; furiously; impatiently; triumphantly; stentoriously; defiantly; clamorously; recklessly; enthusiastically; roughly; cordially; fraternally; deafeningly; blithesomely.

(See yell, call.)

SHOVE (*v*)

adverbs
rudely; uncouthly; vulgarly; boisterously; playfully; bullyingly; brutally; carelessly; vigorously.

(See crowd, push.)

SHOVEL

verbs
apply—; brandish—; discard—; employ—; muster—s; scoop in—; till with—; —burrows; —clatters; —cuts; —delves; —discloses; —excavates; —exposes; —gouges; —grates against; —lays bare; —unearths.

SHOW (*colloq*)

verbs
acclaim—; applaud—; back—; censor—; conclude—; extol—; finance—; flock to—; hail—; offer—; produce—; render—; review—; revise—; stage—; —beguiles; —draws; —traduces.

(See circus, display, exhibition, play, performance.)

SHOW (v)

adverbs
distinctly; conclusively; vaguely; picturesquely; deftly; negatively; devoutly; conspicuously; adroitly; accurately; unequivocally; ingeniously; photographically; subsequently; reluctantly; ostentatiously; delusively; spectacularly; formidably; imperially.
(See display, exhibit.)

SHOWER

adjectives
genial; fiery; russet; intellectual; frizzling; passing; dewy; honeyed; arrowy; icy; myriad; soft; winking; sprinkling; sulphurous; frequent; gracious; fruitful; distilling; ambient; blinding; shimmering; pelting; rainbow-winged; sunlit; continual; whitening; accidental; dropping; scant; summer; spectacular; vernal; falling; heavy.

verbs
long for—; welcome—; —abates; —chills; —continues; —darkens; —deluges; —diminishes; —gushes; —inundates; —issues; —lets up; —plunges; —streams; —surges; —whirls.
(See rain.)

SHOWER (v)

adverbs
generously; genially; unstintedly; fruitfully; ceaselessly; intermittently; vernally.
(See rain, pour.)

SHOWMANSHIP

verbs
applaud—; proclaim—; —acclaims; —advertises; —attracts; —bandies; —dazzles; —embellishes; —emblazons; —features (colloq.); —flames; —flashes; —garnishes; —glitters; —heralds; —parades; —publicizes; —promulgates; —trumpets.
(See display, exhibition.)

SHOWS

adjectives
kingly; unrivaled; temporal; regional; grouped; ostentatious; brilliant; delightful; brave; giddy; miserable; triumphal; frightful; delusive; hideous; spectacular; venerable; outstanding; sorry; harmless; formidable; glittering; pitiful; master; extensive; tumultuous; idle; elaborate; detestable; farcical; mock; brilliant; shallow; rich; gaudy; gallant; brave; imperious; full; phantasmagoric; spangled; marionette.

SHOWY

adverbs
garishly; ornately; cheaply; miserably; unnecessarily; unduly; disgracefully; tawdrily; grossly; foolishly; stupidly; childishly; gracelessly; elaborately; deceptively; gorgeously; pompously; magnificently; inordinately; delusively; expensively; outlandishly; fantastically; excessively.

SHREDS

verbs
bind—; cement—; convert into—; lacerate into—; pare—; reduce to—; rend into—; sever—; snatch—; snip—; tatter into—; tear to—; wear to—.
(See fragment, pieces.)

SHREW

adjectives
chirping; aquatic; occasional; ferret; curst; humorous; noisy; blatant; clamant; raucous.

SHREWD

adverbs
suavely; infinitely; uncannily; adroitly; cleverly; subtly; urbanely; artfully; designingly; slyly; insidiously; dangerously; admirably; practically; commercially; alarmingly; extremely; astoundingly; singularly; thoughtfully; profoundly; precociously; obviously; amazingly; unexpectedly; socially; deliberately; politically; sagaciously; cautiously; wisely; invariably; habitually; customarily; astutely; deftly.

SHREWDNESS

adjectives
infinite; uncanny; apparent; cynical; suave.

verbs
acquire—; ascertain—; commend—; contrive with—; cultivate—; demand—; develop—; discern—; exercise—; gain—; inherit—; intensify—; lack—; mark—; parallel—; penetrate—; recognize—; respect—; reveal—; value—; —dazzles; —discriminates; —endows; —foresees; —impresses; —qualifies.
(See diplomacy, tact, skill, ingenuity.)

SHREWISH

adverbs
disagreeably; scurrilously; scandalously; unpleasantly; intolerably; unbearably; poignantly; sarcastically; unbelievably; notoriously; inexcusably; outlandishly; infamous-

ly; inordinately; despicably; contemptibly; abominably; trenchantly; particularly; brutally; scorchingly; cruelly; bitterly; mercilessly.

SHRIEK

adjectives
vehement; myriad; wailing; hilarious; faint; passionate; inquiring; shrill; piercing; loud; unrestrained; great; long; ghastly; sensational; frantic; delirious; discordant; piteous; demoniacal.

verbs
drown out—; emit—; muffle—; restrain—; stifle—; utter—; —alarms; —chills; —curdles; —echoes; —harrows; —penetrates; —petrifies; —pierces; —rends; —resounds; —rings; —rouses; —smothers; —splits; —startles; —unnerves.
(See cry, shout, call, yell.)

SHRIEK (*v*)

adverbs
agonizingly; heartrendingly; imperatively; stridently; shrewishly; vehemently; passionately; unrestrainedly; piteously; discordantly; demoniacally.
(See yell, scream.)

SHRILL

adverbs
piercingly; cuttingly; alarmingly; horribly; murderously; intolerably; fearfully; incredibly; horridly; raucously; suddenly; contemptibly; disagreeably; naturally; incurably; desperately; cruelly; undisguisedly; deliberately; designedly; purposely; meanly; penetratingly; sharply.

SHRINE

adjectives
popular; tourist; despoiled; innumerable (pl); unhallowed; mysterious; desecrated; veritable; haunted; exploited; cherished; celebrated; echoing; secret; competing; wayside; nameless; inmost; fragrant; happy; gloomy; unrivaled; miraculous.

verbs
abandon—; banish from—; bar from—; consecrate—; contaminate—; convert into —; dedicate—; deface—; defile—; desecrate —; dismantle—; enthrone in—; exalt—; hallow—; immortalize—; invade—; isolate —; mutilate—; penetrate—; pervert—; prostitute—; sanctity—; seclude in—; sequester in—; transgress—; violate—; worship in—; —symbolizes.
(See altar, tomb, sanctuary, temple.)

SHRINK (*v*)

adverbs
perceptibly; timorously; modestly; instinctively; visibly; dumbly; involuntarily; shyly.
(See recoil, wince.)

SHRINKING

adverbs
shyly; painfully; coldly; terribly; desperately; visibly; instinctively; pitiably; guiltily; pathetically; timidly; submissively; servilely; slavishly; basely; tragically; inwardly; noticeably; childishly; perceptibly; pitiably; unaccountably; significantly.

SHRIVEL (*v*)

adverbs
abnormally; prematurely; markedly; partially; ruinously; sadly; tragically.
(See shrink, dwindle.)

SHRIVELED

adverbs
slightly; meagerly; cadaverously; gauntly; emaciatedly; haggardly; scrawnily; skinnily; dreadfully; curiously.

SHROUD

adjectives
vibrant; bloody; flecked; misty; sable; spotted; leafy; clinging; rattling; streamlined; putrid; thin.

verbs
clothe in—; discard—; divest of—; invest in —; —circumscribes; —cloaks; —darkens; —dims; —disguises; —eclipses; —enfolds; —envelops; —obscures; —overcasts; —screens; —shades; —veils.
(See raiment.)

SHROUD (*v*)

adverbs
effectually; permanently; modestly; closely; protectively; partially; darkly; somberly; gloomily.
(See screen, cloak.)

SHRUB

adjectives
blossoming; aromatic; crowding (pl); luxuriant; ornamental; skirting; tranquil; unpruned; widowed; warm-tinted; stunted.

verbs
blast—; blight—; choke—; cultivate—; debilitate—; eradicate—; extirpate—; fertilize—; impoverish—; starve—; strangle—; trim—; uproot—; —beautifies; —declines; —droops; —s enhance; —fades; —flourishes; —graces; —luxuriates; —languishes; —thrives; —trembles; —wanes.
(See bush, honeysuckle, bud, plant.)

SHRUGS

adjectives
expressive; dumb; impertinent; good-natured; impatient; indifferent; significant; contemptuous.

SHUDDER

adjectives
strong; involuntary; passing; ecstatic; visible; slight; repressed; pious; elaborate; intuitive; violent.

verbs
arrest—; elicit—; excite—; feign—; impel—; induce—; inspire—; occasion—; provoke—; repress—; restrain—; —agitates; —betrays; —convulses; —disconcerts; —electrifies; —paralyzes; —perturbs; —ripples through; —ruffles.
(See shiver, sob, sigh.)

SHUDDER (*v*)

adverbs
spasmodically; physically; instinctively; figuratively; apprehensively; involuntarily; violently; feverishly; abnormally; perceptibly.
(See tremble, shake, shiver.)

SHUFFLE (*v*)

adverbs
noiselessly; slyly; wearily; uncouthly; sluggishly; clumsily; imperturbably; drearily.
(See drag, walk.)

SHUN (*v*)

adverbs
timorously; fastidiously; aristocratically; intelligently; cautiously; scrupulously; systematically; studiously.
(See elude, shift, avoid.)

SHUT (*v*)

adverbs
clamorously; obligingly; stealthily; inexorably; convulsively; sullenly; mysteriously; impatiently; drowsily; abruptly; cautiously.
(See close, exclude.)

SHUTTER

adjectives
awry; heavy-barred; supplementary; iron-cased; closed.

verbs
draw—; elevate—; unfold—; —bars; —blinds; —eclipses; —mantles; —masks; —obscures; —rattles; —restrains; —shades; —veils.
(See screen.)

SHUTTLE

verbs
propel—; swivel—; —alternates; —gyrates; —lurches; —oscillates; —pulsates; —quivers; —revolves; —rotates; —see-saws; —swerves; —swirls; —trembles; —trundles; —wabbles; —whirls; —vibrates.

SHY

adverbs
awkwardly; uneasily; childishly; self-consciously; timidly; uncomfortably; engagingly; embarrassingly; charmingly; painfully; peculiarly; strangely; unwontedly; becomingly; unnaturally; fearfully; clumsily; foolishly; ridiculously; pitiably; touchingly; adorably; comically; absurdly; exquisitely; habitually; deliciously; extremely; incredibly; oddly; curiously; unnecessarily.

SHYNESS

adjectives
delicious; provincial; confused; virgin; rural; exquisite; innate; wonted; girlish; unconquerable; maiden; blushing.

verbs
blush in—; falter in—; feign—; flinch in—; overcome with—; quail in—; —abashes; —afflicts; —arrests; —blenches; —bridles; —confuses; —constrains; —cows; —curbs; —daunts; —deters; —distorts; —distresses; —fetters; —humiliates; —leashes; —overawes; —overwhelms; —perturbs; —represses; —restrains; —smothers.
(See bashfulness, modesty.)

SIBILANT

adverbs
softly; affectedly; ridiculously; laughably; hissingly; toothlessly; lispingly; comically;

warningly; persistently; curiously; derisively; mockingly; disturbingly; pitiably; unpleasantly; strangely; disagreeably.

SICK

verbs
comfort—; heal—; palliate—; prescribe for —; rebuild—; reclaim—; regenerate—; rehabilitate—; relieve—; rescue—; restore—; revive—; soothe—.
(See patient, invalid.)

adverbs
chronically; continually; seriously; habitually; unfortunately; unusually; curiously; oddly; strangely; unaccountably; inexplicably; seriously; critically; recently; definitely; unfortunately; frequently; squeamishly; feverishly; mentally; dangerously; painfully; embarrassingly; inopportunely; inconveniently; awkwardly; desperately; slightly; unendurably.

SICKEN (v)

adverbs
visibly; swooningly; biliously; fatally; tragically; woefully; gradually; speechlessly; mutely; nauseatingly.
(See disgust, languish.)

SICKLY

adverbs
distressingly; unfortunately; bafflingly; always; strangely; inexplicably; wretchedly; unhappily; apparently; curiously.

SICKNESS

adjectives
speechless; desperate; prolonged; swooning; everlasting; pining; violent; bilious; deadly; lasting; soul.

verbs
allay—; alleviate—; banish—; check—; combat—; conquer—; convalesce from—; curse—; eradicate—; feign—; induce—; occasion—; subdue—; —abates; —afflicts; —aggravates; —besets; —cankers; —confines; —cripples; —desolates; —harasses; —heals; —incommodes; —indisposes; —induces; —invalids; —maims; —oppresses; —overcomes; —predisposes; —racks; —ravages; —sears; —seizes; —smites; —sours; —torments; —undermines; —vitiates; —wastes; —withers.
(See ailment, disease, illness, malady.)

SIDE

adjectives
ludicrous; balanced; unbaked; instrumental; paternal; humane; gruesome; seamy; rusty; perilous; luminous; unengaged; massive; verdant; windy; pierced; liberal; stretched-out; obverse; ample; sorrowful; practical; engaging; interminable; nobler; tangled; grassy; ridiculous; bank; valuable; translucent; hairy; wounded; gaping; deep; precipitous; semi-nomadic; perpendicular; distinctive; sloping; lighter; respective; intellectual; outward; emotional; shrinking; spiritual; extravagant; fathomless; pierced; showy; administrative; executive; psychological; spotted; gorgeous; brawny; craggy; neglected; aesthetic; diametrical; opposite; fanciful; starboard; maternal; ventral; exposed; protected; dreamy; winning; objective; superstitious; shuddering; woolly.

SIDE-SPLITTING

adverbs
absurdly; mirthfully; uproariously; boisterously; comically; ridiculously; laughably; farcically; drolly; tumultuously; prankishly; outlandishly; merrily; ludicrously.

SIDEWALK

adjectives
swarming; gravel; moving; unpaved; scented; innocent-looking; broken; wide; cobbled; brick; winding; slippery.

verbs
fence—; gad about—; jog along—; pace—; patrol—; promenade—; ramble along—; saunter along—; straggle along—; traverse —; trudge over—; —crumbles; —deviates; —glistens; —jams.
(See walk.)

SIEGE

adjectives
vigorous; lingering; wanton; severe; bitter; disastrous; moving; protracted; creditable; wreckful; amiable; fatal; famous; fearful; implacable; repeated; hateful; bloody.

verbs
brave—; breast—; endure—; engage in—; extend—; intrench against—; lay—; maintain—; parry—; prolong—; protract—; repel—; resist—; submit to—; survive—; yield to—; weather—; withstand—; —anni-

hilates; —beleaguers; —devastates; —grips; —impoverishes; —lags; —ravages; —starves; —undermines; —blockades.
(See attack, blockade.)

SIEVE

adjectives
meshed; trembling; captious.

verbs
—filters; —purges; —refines; —separates; —sifts; —sorts; —strains; —winnows.

SIFT (v)

adverbs
mechanically; academically; curiously; patiently; industriously; painstakingly; suspiciously; legally; automatically.
(See investigate, bolt.)

SIGH

adjectives
gasping; thriftless; gusty; impatient; aimless; fruitless; expiring; deep; burning; sharp; puzzled; plenteous (pl); perpetual; relieved; desponding; perfumed; vain; friendly; delicious; reproachful; sultry; monitorial; lingering; compassionate; mournful; sympathetic; piteous; profound; heavy; quick; slumberous; useless; contrite; false; wistful; feeble; thirsty; pensive; alien; restful; repentant; half-forlorn; audible; inauspicious; inharmonious; short; joyous; passing; impatient; interjectional; watery; philosophic; wasteful; sumptuous; sad; amorous; short; tantalizing; gasping; exasperated; mistaken; miserable; odorous; reckless; infallible; comprehensive; relaxing; desolate; feigned; inaudible; occasional; sorry; yearning; pleased; stifled; disgusted; loud; long; persuasive; gratified; moral; involuntary; relieved; thriftless; convulsive.

verbs
breathe—; burst into—; draw—; elicit—; evoke—; heave—; hush—; muffle—; murmur—; mute—; restrain—; smother—; stifle—; suppress—; utter—; whisper—; —betrays; —bursts from; —deprecates; —flutters; —laments; —racks; —rends; —stirs; —wrings.
(See groan, sob, moan, murmur.)

SIGH (v)

adverbs
dismally; profoundly; soulfully; romantically; audibly; pensively; retrospectively; sentimentally; plaintively; appealingly; woefully; tremulously; dejectedly; reminiscently; nostalgically; wistfully; involuntarily; eloquently; compassionately; contritely; forlornly; desolately; inaudibly.
(See grieve, lament.)

SIGHT

adjectives
inward; melting; wondrous; novel; weird; startling; wide; stirring; goodly; uncommon; piteous; enraptured; stimulating; irresistible; aching; holiest; impressive; dilated; refreshing; dismal; touching; remarkable; doleful; spiritual; richer; purer; fairer; heterogeneous; dubious; ravishing; amusing; cheery; instructive; wretched; portentous; clouded; exhilarating; imposing; horrifying; unusual; curtained; solemn; gorgeous; triumphant; precious; fearful; loveliest; continuous; infant; grand; thrilling; unaided; disturbing; curious; quickened; wished; ludicrous; marvelous; appalling; translatable; ghastliest; gallant; truest; bleared; distressing; horrible; swimming; majestic; fine; exceptional; welcome; powerful; sickening; glorious; purblind; joyful; inspiring; all-searching; steadfast; unacquainted; approved; gladdened; straining; extraordinary; splendid; worthless; loathsome; lucent; unveiled; absolute; deadening; glistening; bewildered; unaided; mortal; awful; sorry; genial; saltatory; nocturnal; priceless; secret; whimsical; prettiest; feebler; perfect.

verbs
abhor—; blur—; check—; cloud—; confuse—; conjure—; control—; dim—; distort—; distract—; dull—; focus—; impair—; intensify—; loathe—; lose—; obscure—; obstruct—; recover—; regain—; rely upon—; restore—; sharpen—; shun—; sink from—; stimulate—; tuck out of—; veil—; visualize—; —dazzles; —dissipates; —declines; —enriches; —fails; —invigorates; —outrages; —pollutes; —weakens.
(See vision, view, phenomenon, spectacle, mirage.)

SIGHTLY

adverbs
agreeably; pleasantly; splendidly; magnifi-

cently; unusually; delightfully; extraordinarily; unexpectedly; gloriously; gorgeously; beautifully; entrancingly; remarkably; exceptionally; impressively; thrillingly; dramatically; inexpressibly.

SIGN

adjectives
encouraging; mournful; conspicuous; deep-drawn; premonitory; ideographic; ghastly; indubitable; extreme; hopeful; mute; incomprehensible; regretful; fraternal; important; fluttering; perpetual; visible; ambitious; assured; supplementary; watery; subtle; undoubted; geometric; inauspicious; palpable; bursting; celestial; impressive; depressing; labial; creaking; ominous; frantic; peculiar; optimistic; fragrant; lying; visible; eloquent; translucent; manifold (pl); fearful; natural; symbolic; cabalistic; physical; doubtful; infallible; obscure; elaborate; mysterious; decreased; useless; evident; abject; imperial; characteristic; affecting; faintest; conclusive; sacred; discernible; lamentable; perceptible; talismanic.

verbs
betray—; discern—; drape—; evince—; experience—; interpret—; mistakes—s; question—; trace—s; visit—; watch for—; wipe out—; —appears; —characterizes; —glares; —warns.
(See emblem, indication, signal, notice, mark.)

SIGN (*v*)

adverbs
legally; formally; perfunctorily; nominally; bindingly; willingly; felicitously.
(See signify, indicate.)

SIGNAL

adjectives
emergency; customary; imperceptible; suggestive; descriptive; preconcerted; true; prompt; cautionary; warning; unheeded.

verbs
await—; beat—; blaze—; breathe—; dispatch—; disperse at—; drum—; exchange—s; flash—; flourish—s; flout—; heed—; gather at—; interpret—; issue—; predetermine—; prescribe—; respond to—; —cautions; —summons; —winks.
(See alarm, beacon, sign.)

SIGNATURE

adjectives
bold; scrawling; sundry; conscious; sprawling; scribbled; unreadable.

verbs
affix—; attest to—; counterfeit—; dash off—; duplicate—; embellish—; enter—; familiarize with—; identify—; pen—; produce—; scratch out—; scrawl—; scribble—; stereotype—; strike out—; submit—; trace—; transcribe—; verify—; vouch for—; witness—; —endorses; —flows; —ripples from; —seals; —s tally.

SIGNIFICANCE

adjectives
drear; mental; emotional; lofty; ghastly; particular; sufficient; supreme; intense; tremendous; spiritual; sad; unsuspected; historic; sound; functional; representative; special; popular; malign; symbolical; mystifying; double; profound; dramatic; ultimate; fine; enormous; vital; tragic; social; immense; contemptuous; intrinsic; lasting; artistic; cruel; prophetic; rude; poignant; gloomy; threatening; highest; arresting; larger; stinging; deep; permanent; transcendent; insolent; convincing; musical; ominous; prime; curious; minor; fatal; moral.

verbs
acquire—; assign—; assume—; attach—; attain—; awaken to—; broaden—; consider—; convey—; dwell upon—; eschew—; fathom—; feel—; forget—; grasp—; heighten—; measure—; narrow—; unfold—; —grows; —overshadows.
(See importance, consequence, import, meaning.)

SIGNIFICANT

adverbs
horribly; menacingly; portentously; pleasantly; happily; immensely; remarkably; distinctly; suddenly; curiously; ominously; deliberately; unmistakably; alarmingly; threateningly; openly; marvelously; tremendously; auspiciously; cruelly.

SIGNIFY (*v*)

adverbs
clearly; concretely; vividly; undeniably;

affirmatively; comprehensively; plainly; obviously; graphically.

(See show, indicate.)

SILENCE

adjectives

profound; obstinate; mysterious; complete; discomfited; infant; horrid; sullen; majestic; pale; sickening; indignant; melodious; deep; sarcastic; reverent; roaring; morose; heated; honorable; listening; chilling; awkward; demure; musing; stagnant; suitable; unaccountable; voluptuous; resentful; horrified; fearful; astonished; expectant; respectful; oppressive; dignified; deathly; distressful; chagrined; awed; luxurious; bashful; stern; total; snowy; religious; solemn; involuntary; warm; perfumed; defiant; apologetic; lazy; everlasting; moody; attentive; absolute; abstracted; heavy; motionless; stifling; tense; sympathetic; discreet; slumberous; limp; sunlit; momentary; industrious; embarrassed; somber; sulky; dogged; prevailing; hushed; depressing; blank; mute; fruitful; punctuated; painful; broken; ominous; mannerless; grateful; awful; funeral; universal; gathered; uninterrupted; silvery; infinite; tearless; appalling; fragile; eloquent; severe; sepulchral; thoughtful; dismal; empty; thick; sunken; mysterious; guilty; enforced; strange; magical; solvent; freezing; infuriated; bewildered; vibrant; imperative; curious; cold; complete; long; meditative; inhuman; gracious; intense; passive; spellbound; noisy; monumental; museful; brooding; perfect; breathless; lengthened; white; hostile; hideous; dignified; poetic; disciplined; sacred; smiling; forbidding; aggravating; tangible; flushing; unreproved; unsociable; stern; grim; comparative; arid; appealing; maiden; azure; deafening; rapturous; horrible; simple; welcome; bashful; mournful; enamored; despairing; pregnant; shaded; eternal.

verbs

acquiesce in—; appraise—; awaken—; bear—; break—; cajole into—; constrain—; covet—; drop into—; endure—; enjoin—; feel—; impose—; inculcate—; interpret—; lapse into—; lie in—; maintain—; penetrate —; plead for—; preserve—; press into—; put to—; quench—; reduce to—; reflect in —; relapse into—; retreat in—; rip—; sift —; sink into—; slump into—; survey in—; wrap in—; worship—; —cloaks; —descends; —enchants; —encompasses; —ensues; —explodes; —falls; —fills; —follows; —grows; —hammers; —hangs; —imposes; —pervades; —pounces; —prevails; —reigns; —rolls; —settles; —sinks; —supervenes; —swallows; —throbs; —troubles.

(See hush, quiet, stillness.)

SILENCE (v)

adverbs

effectually; completely; mysteriously; sarcastically; discreetly; awkwardly; sternly; apologetically; momentarily; grimly.

(See suppress, hush.)

SILENT

adverbs

absolutely; remarkably; unusually; pleasantly; practically; sufficiently; warrantably; reasonably; positively; significantly; usually; reticently; gravely; alarmingly; amusedly; impressively; dangerously; ominously; indulgently; haughtily; angrily; happily; magnanimously; charitably; bewilderingly; strangely; singularly; maddeningly; obstinately; stolidly; sadly; sullenly; mischievously; furtively; stealthily; warily; cautiously; carefully; naturally; guardedly; breathlessly; dreadfully; terrifyingly; gloomily.

SILHOUETTE

adjectives

dark; sliding; streamline; sleek; shadowy; grim; fitted; meager.

SILK

adjectives

watered; seeded; pompadour; domestic; heavy; fresh; delicate; faded; exquisite; glistening; pleated; scarlet; flimsy; newspun; delicate-filmed.

verbs

apparel in—; arrange—; array in—; attire in—; bale—; begrime—; braid—; cast off —; divest of—; drape—; dress in—; entwine—; export—; fabricate—; fringe with —; import—; impregnate—; invest in—; lace—; mat—; net—; plait—; shear—; shred—; skein—; spin—; tangle—; veil in —; warp—; weave—; —fades; —rustles; —tears.

(See handkerchief, cloth, gauze, lining, linen.)

SILLY

adverbs

miserably; incurably; senselessly; stupidly;

loutishly; clownishly; purposely; amusingly; entertainingly; feignedly; absurdly; laughably; imprudently; indiscreetly; hopelessly; disagreeably; intolerably; disgustingly; contemptibly; curiously; pitiably; lamentably; deplorably; wretchedly; disastrously; utterly; hopelessly.

SILVER

adjectives

sheeny; quivering; rippling; transparent; gleaming; wavering; glowing; burnished; shimmering; filigree; massive.

verbs

bedeck with—; burnish—; caparison in—; chase (emboss)—; devaluate—; fabricate—; fashion—; glorify with—; hoard—; mine—; refine—; work in—; —blazons; —coruscates; —enriches; —glints; —glitters; —glows; —tarnishes.

(See metal, steel, jewel.)

SIMILAR

adverbs

indistinguishably; bewilderingly; inconveniently; dangerously; curiously; strangely; naturally; laughably; somewhat; congenially; sufficiently; accidentally; intentionally; deliberately.

SIMILARITY

adjectives

assumed; singular; increasing; psychological.

verbs

attend with—; direct attention to—; discern—; indicate—; observe—; regard—; sense—; —bewilders; —bores; —ceases; —confuses; —echoes; —flusters; —reflects; —mirrors; —parallels; —perplexes; —reproduces; —strikes.

(See identity, resemblance.)

SIMILE

adjectives

absurd; chilling; amiable; expressive; good; swift; felicitous; sickly; oft-repeated; natural; arctic; happy; apt.

verbs

employ—; enlist—; garble—; resort to—; revel in—; —alludes; —colors; —contrasts; —conveys; —clarifies; —expresses; —implies; —paints; —parallels; —pictures; —strikes.

(See metaphor, comparison.)

SIMPER (v)

adverbs

affectedly; coyly; bashfully; embarrassedly; coquettishly; naively; childishly.

(See smile, smirk.)

SIMPERING

adverbs

coyly; demurely; deliberately; foolishly; provokingly; cleverly; designingly; senselessly; hopefully; flirtatiously; ridiculously; archly; cunningly; subtly; wittingly; girlishly; craftily; engagingly.

SIMPLE

adverbs

beautifully; expensively; unnecessarily; utterly; delightfully; artlessly; graciously; refreshingly; intelligibly; pleasantly; fortunately; needlessly; starkly; childishly; severely; chastely; elegantly; gracefully; tastefully; harmoniously; appropriately; ingenuously; naively; bluntly; foolishly; delicately; daintily; charmingly; idiotically; crazily; inanely; fatuously; mindlessly.

SIMPLICITY

adjectives

rich; extreme; precise; subtle; orthographic; sublime; gradual; impressive; chaste; touching; primitive; everlasting; striking; thoroughgoing; scanty; unostentatious; severe; studied; luminous; noble; childlike; solid; medieval; pathetic; laughable; courteous; classic; majestic; low; rude; idyllic; healthful; fundamental; patrician; stolid; limpid; naive; habitual; grave; unique; native; frank; austere; unconscious; sad; patriarchal; serious; absolute; affectionate; stunning; miraculous; antique; pastoral; poignant; inscrutable; rustic; cheerful; exquisite; polite; boyish; striking; vigorous; venerable.

verbs

abandon—; acclaim—; achieve—; advocate—; afford—; applaud—; aspire to—; commend—; desert—; feign—; forsake—; glory in—; inspire—; pretend—; relinquish—; seek—; simulate—; welcome—; —allures;

—attracts; —beguiles; —charms; —deceives; —delights; —disarms; —enchants; —entrances; —fascinates; —inveigles; —refreshes; —renounces.

(See innocence, sincerity, frankness, plainness.)

SIMPLIFY (v)

adverbs
extremely; amazingly; precisely; subtly; orthographically; impressively; fundamentally; uniquely.

(See arrange.)

SIMULATE (v)

adverbs
ingeniously; deftly; artfully; skillfully; professionally; traitorously; slyly; insidiously; venomously.

(See feign, pretend.)

SIMULATED

adverbs
carefully; cleverly; fraudulently; deceptively; adroitly; skillfully; wickedly; deliberately; viciously; artfully; secretly; successfully; mendaciously; smoothly; accurately; exactly; correctly; authentically; theatrically; dramatically; spectacularly; impressively; graphically; wonderfully.

SIN

adjectives
maddening; fundamental; unpardonable; original; dark; deadly; fleshly; grievous; cardinal; damning; regretted; heinous; familiar; unexpiated; shameful; untold; vilest; hidden; foul; mystic; implied; besetting; appalling; bygone; cunning; virtuous; intellectual; grave; venial; detested; imaginary; delightful; conscious; characteristic; precious; penitential; disorderly; superficial.

verbs
abandon—; absolve of—; abstain from—; acknowledge—; ameliorate—; atone for—; banish—; clean from—; commit—; compensate for—; conceive in—; deliver from—; do penance for—; divest of—; excoriate—s; expiate—; extenuate—; forsake—; grapple with—; inherit—; lapse into—; offer for —s; overcome—; pardon—; plunge into—; purge of—; relinquish—; repeat—; reproach—; reveal—; shrive of—; steep in—; stray into—; uncover—; unveil—; wash away—; wallow in—; whip for—; wrestle with—; —corrupts; —damns; —defiles; —depraves; —flourishes; —hardens; —pollutes; —purges; —surges; —tortures; —traduces; —transgresses; —weighs upon.

(See iniquity, licentiousness, abomination, evil, crime, lust.)

SIN (v)

adverbs
fundamentally; incorrigibly; unwittingly; grievously; egregiously; carnally; intellectually; venially; knowingly; unsuspectingly; lustfully.

(See transgress, trespass.)

SINCERE

adverbs
unaffectedly; charmingly; graciously; affably; cordially; pleasantly; utterly; delightfully ; ardently; honestly; remarkably; plainly; genuinely; dependably; scrupulously; earnestly; fervently; enthusiastically; punctiliously; particularly; reliably.

SINCERITY

adjectives
evident; transparent; artistic; flaming; perfect; despairing; well-feigned; worshiping; obvious; impetuous; unaffected; noble; deep; forlorn; sterling; grave; violent; fierce; youthful; bashful; robust; abominable; sorrowful; patent; grim.

verbs
attest to—; cherish—; declare—; doubt—; express—; feign—; impeach—; impugn—; maintain—; pledge—; pretend—; question —; ring with—; smack of—; stir—; test—; value—; verify—; vow—; —beguiles; —burns; —deludes; —falters; —impresses; —pervades; —vacillates.

(See candor, simplicity, earnestness, honesty, innocence, integrity.)

SINFUL

adverbs
deliberately; wilfully; maliciously; blasphemously; coarsely; consciously; boldly; audaciously; defiantly; impiously; brazenly; openly; flagrantly; incredibly.

SING (v)

adverbs
fervently; quaveringly; nocturnally; effortlessly; audibly; angelically; lustily; bewitchingly; blithely; responsively; derisively; impetuously; exultingly; merrily; conscientiously; extemporaneously; vigorously;

raptly; melodiously; vibrantly; hilariously; magnificently; discordantly; vociferously; throatily; congregationally; professionally; lucretively.
(See hum, croon.)

SINGER

adjectives
notable; malignant; eloquent; inimitable; flattering; pensive; cunning; skillful; splendid; renowned; trained; unseen.

verbs
acclaim—; accompany—; applaud—; belittle—; extol—; prepare—; train—; —carols; —enraptures; —enthralls; —executes; —s harmonize; —impresses; —intones; —matures; —modulates; —pitches; —renders; —stirs; —syncopates; —thrills; —trills; —uplifts.
(See choir, chorus, singing, musician, artist.)

SINGING

adjectives
magical; merry; remote; clear; concerted; congregational; delectable; interlaced; comic; vociferous; fervent; hearty; throaty.

verbs
accompany—; arrange—; coach—; direct—; dominate—; harmonize—; modulate—; rejoice in—; syncopate—; —amuses; —diverts; —echoes; —penetrates; —pervades; —precipitates; —smites; —voices.
(See singer, music.)

SINGSONG

adverbs
intolerably; monotonously; dully; droningly; tediously; unbearably; lullingly; soothingly; drowsily; deliberately; dreamily; sleepily; prosaically; persistently; interminably; endlessly; maddeningly; outlandishly; disagreeably.

SINISTER

adverbs
horribly; ominously; portentously; alarmingly; terrifyingly; deliberately; oppressively; gloomily; unhappily; disturbingly; distressingly; significantly; unmistakably; darkly; hopelessly; fearfully; dismally; deplorably; insidiously; uncommonly; actually; unquestionably; seriously; undoubtedly.

SINK (v)

adverbs
exhaustedly; despondently; swiftly; fatally; gratefully; unfathomably; dejectedly; partially; relaxedly; markedly; continuously.
(See fall, descend.)

SINLESS

adverbs
impossibly; immaculately; chastely; incredibly; sacredly; divinely; beatifically; blessedly; angelically; immortally; eternally; seraphically; innocently.

SINNER

adjectives
tortured; corrigible; wretched; vile; rebellious; ever-living; obdurate; dainty; reckless; hardened.

SINUS

verbs
cauterize—; congest—; drain—; infect—; inflame—; irrigate—; obliterate—; obstruct—; suppurate—; tap—; —clogs; —discharges; —poisons; —secretes; —tortures; —undermines; —racks.
(See sore, cavity, opening.)

SIP (v)

adverbs
demurely; sparingly; fastidiously; aristocratically; delicately; sickeningly; disgustingly; noisily; vulgarly.
(See drink, absorb, suck.)

SIRE

adjectives
sweet; sapient; heathen; illustrious; loving.

SIREN

verbs
resist—; withstand—; yield to—; —allures; —attracts; —beckons; —bewitches; —cajoles; —captivates; —charms; —enamours; —entices; —fascinates; —impels; —inveigles; —intrigues; —lures; —magnetizes; —tempts; —screams; —seduces; —shrieks; —wheedles.
(See lover, woman.)

SISTER

adjectives
impressionable; droll; diverting; desolate; fair; erring; beauteous; barren; unchaste;

weird; hard-boiled; woodland; honored; religious; sterner; younger; incredulous; innocent.

verbs
adore—; caress—; cherish—; claim—; dote on—; embosom—; embrace—; endear to—; esteem—; favor—; glorify—; idolize—; prize—; revere—; worship—.
(See mother.)

SISTERLY

adverbs
warmly; sympathetically; comfortingly; tenderly; affectionately; assiduously; persistently; adroitly; patiently; indulgently; hopefully; insistently; consistently; cleverly; impulsively; noticeably; carefully; unfailingly; pleasantly; agreeably.

SIT (*v*)

adverbs
decorously; ignominiously; mutely; moodily; calmly; inscrutably; placidly; unobtrusively; picturesquely; impassively; dejectedly; disconsolately; despondently; voicelessly; spiritlessly; dispiritedly; quiescently; majestically.
(See rest, repose.)

SITE

adjectives
admirable; impregnable; noble; suitable; magnificent; restricted; appropriate; splendid.

SITUATE (*v*)

adverbs
conveniently; centrally; fortunately; geographically; romantically; favorably; picturesquely; alarmingly; dramatically; uniquely; remotely; depressingly; dismally; secludedly; ridiculously; precariously; perilously; anomalously.
(See place, establish.)

SITUATION

adjectives
sentimental; silly; messiest; equivocal; dramatic; ticklish; cheerful; recurrent; enviable; unpleasant; extreme; alarming; horrifying; tragic; embarrassing; peculiar; speech; tense; detrimental; momentous; dangerous; farcical; desolate; unique; slippery; economic; international; effective; social; urgent; charming; analogous; painful; dependent; aggravating; remote; material; depressing; financial; defiant; unhappy; countless (pl); rational; humorous; precise; secluded; curious; relative; important; insular; hopeless; lonesome; incredible; immoral; dismal; strategical; favorable; arduous; defenseless; conspicuous; parlous; dispersed; pragmatic; dismaying; strained; unfortunate; picturesque; melancholy; appalling; commanding; accessible; ridiculous; subordinate; paradoxical; delicate; difficult; much-coveted; awkward; isolated; distressing; diplomatic; precarious; sequestered; desperate; exposed; forfeited; military; healthy; romantic; comfortable; fearful; perilous; ironic; anomalous.

verbs
alleviate—; alter—; analyze—; barge into (colloq.)—; contemplate—; control—; crash into—; define—; denounce—; dismiss—; dramatize—; clarify—; command—; conceive—; confess—; cope with—; create—; cripple—; deal with—; divulge—; evaluate —; exaggerate—; excogitate—s; gloss over —; grapple with—; grasp—; handle—; master—; plunge into—; ponder over—; relieve—; remedy—; resolve—; save—; sense —; size up—; soften—; sum up—; take stock of—; trace—; unscramble—; utilize—; view—; visualize—; —aggravates; —appeals; —s arise; —baffles; —calculates; —carries; —clears; —confronts; —demonstrates; —develops; —discloses; —disturbs; —dominates; —eases; —grows; —illuminates; —intensifies; —portrays; —recurs; —relaxes; —relinquishes; —revolves; —solves; —suffers; mull over—; neglect—; overdramatize—.
(See position, condition, predicament.)

SIZE

adjectives
enormous; remarkable; immense; cap; apparent; defined; prodigious; stunted; comparative; generous; respectable; stupendous; imposing; sensational; unusual; unwieldy; minute; inexpensive; substantial; convenient; formidable; monstrous; gargantuan; heroic; graduated; sample; small; serving; requisite; undue; tangible.

verbs
attenuate—; augment—; calibrate—s; compute—; diminish—; distend—; estimate—; exaggerate—; exceed—; expand—; fix—; gauge—; grade—s; graduate—s; inflate—; magnify—; modify—; plumb—; reduce—;

register—; restrict—; standardize—; surpass in—; swell—; tabulate—s; vary—; —dwindles; —s range from; —shrinks.
(See dimension, measurement, extent, magnitude.)

SKELETON

adjectives
decaying; sheeted; fleshless; homogeneous; rickety; moldering; colossal; human; metallic; uncouth; bleached; grinning; moldy.

verbs
build on—; cremate—; disinter—; embalm —; exhume—; expose—; inter—; preserve —; prop—; reduce to—; shrivel to—; uncover—; unearth—; —bears; —crumbles; —grins; —reveals; —supports; —sustains.

SKEPTIC

adjectives
obstinate; staunch; satisfied; complete; confirmed.

verbs
assure—; brook—; overawe—s; overwhelm —s; impress—; persuade—; quiet—; stagger—s; —cavils; —challenges; —demurs; —discredits; —disputes; —dissents; —distrusts; —entertains; —doubts; —hesitates; —queries; —vacillates; —wavers.
(See atheist, critic, heretic.)

SKEPTICAL

adverbs
openly; publicly; scoffingly; jeeringly; derisively; contemptuously; significantly; conspicuously; persistently; obstinately; stubbornly; stolidly; distrustfully; arrogantly; oddly; curiously; extremely; profoundly; secretly.

SKEPTICISM

adjectives
pretended; indulgent; cold; inveterate; painful; native; learned; extreme; happy; definite; flippant; worthwhile; safe; rationalistic.

verbs
assume—; attribute to—; betray—; break down—; collapse into—; confute—; criticize—; deny—; dispose to—; excuse—; fall into—; incline to—; incur—; involve—; justify—; lament—; minimize—; profess—; prompt—; rebuke—; regard—; taint by—; —amuses; —asserts; —overthrows; —persuades; —prevails; —sweeps; —vanishes.
(See atheism, disbelief, doubt.)

SKETCH

adjectives
pastel; charming; unfinished; occasional; faint; historical; insufficient; vigorous; impressionistic; autobiographical; loose; effective; brief; colossal; concise; panoramic; biographical; hospital; vivid; vignette; critical; characteristic; orchestral; malignant; dramatic; imaginative; good-humored; accompanying; rambling; belated; spirited; despairing; ingenious; lifelike.

verbs
dash off—; design—; disclose—; draft—; execute—; reproduce—; scrutinize—; submit—; trace—; transcribe—; —charts; —delineates; —depicts; —details; —diagrams; —enlightens; —facilitates; —guides; —illustrates; —outlines; —portrays; —prescribes; —represents; —sets forth.
(See drawing, design, illustration, plan, outline.)

SKETCH (*v*)

adverbs
realistically; vaguely; imperfectly; roughly; artistically; vividly; graphically; covertly; ridiculously; satirically; impressionistically; autobiographically; panoramically; biographically; dramatically; imaginatively; ingeniously.
(See draw, portray.)

SKETCHY

adverbs
inadequately; unsatisfactorily; carelessly; unserviceably; hopelessly; disappointingly; singularly; curiously; ineffectively; provokingly; inexcusably; unpardonably.

SKI (*v*)

adverbs
boisterously; dexterously; artfully; professionally; sportively; amateurishly; daringly.
(See slide, skim.)

SKIFF

verbs
batter—; buffet—; convoy—; embark on—; man—; navigate—; punt—; ram—; scull —; swamp—; waft—; —bears; —conveys;

—drifts; —glides; —plies; —puts to sea; —sallies forth; —scuds; —sweeps; —weighs anchor.
(See boat.)

SKILL

adjectives
experimental; inordinate; persevering; diagnostic; dangerous; tactical; moderate; ancient; profound; manual; technical; artistic; trained; superior; exceptional; subtle; acquired; dramatic; linguistic; deft; infinite; descriptive; acknowledged; inventive; competent; matchless; tattered; martial; prodigious; strict; uncanny; untaught; professional; diplomatic; considerable; consummate; daredevil; executive; shallow; exquisite; simple; barren; quaint; detached; methodic; journalistic; masterly; practical; unavailing; athletic; unusual; creative; analytical; potent; monastic; unsurpassed; fearful; unfaltering; comparative; mechanical; rare; quick; sufficient.

verbs
absorb—; acquire—; applaud—; capitalize —; challenge—; confound—; contend with —; develop—; devise—; discern—; display —; evince—; execute with—; exhaust—; exhibit—; extol—; manifest—; overestimate —; surpass—; transfer—.
(See ability, faculty, ingenuity, capability.)

SKILLED

adverbs
moderately; exceptionally; professionally; profoundly; subtly; definitely; admittedly; infinitely; matchlessly; prodigiously; uncannily; diplomatically; consummately; exquisitely; quaintly; rarely; undeniably; incontrovertibly; unusually; creatively; powerfully; fearfully; comparatively; notably; strikingly; diabolically; marvelously; incredibly; dangerously; obviously; constitutionally; naturally; innately; inherently; instinctively; capably; competently; proficiently; deftly; discreetly; conveniently.

SKILLFUL

adverbs
amazingly; remarkably; particularly; miraculously; eminently; conspicuously; unusually; genuinely; admittedly; adequately; presumably; brilliantly; famously; inexpressibly; modestly.

SKIM (v)

adverbs
cursorily; perfunctorily; carelessly; hastily; rapidly; studiously; critically.
(See scan, read.)

SKIMP (v)

adverbs
penuriously; niggardly; meanly; parsimoniously; selfishly; fanatically.
(See save.)

SKIMPY

adverbs
ridiculously; fantastically; comically; absurdly; inexcusably; outrageously; miserably; inadequately; pitifully; pitiably; pathetically; grotesquely; ingenerously; stingily; carelessly; awkwardly; unbecomingly; unfashionably; uncomfortably; unfortunately.

SKIN

adjectives
clear; ruddy; tanned; mortal; dainty; tawny; parchment; tender; dry; scratchy; shaggy; accumulated; tough; defensive; roughened; ivory; olive; ardent; incarnate; wrinkled; transparent; sensitive; sleekest; edible; sunburned; lustrous; untanned; sallow; gay; dead; painted; scaling; waxy; bronzed; superfluous; crinkled; redundant; mottled; narrow.

verbs
affect—; aggravate—; bathe—; chafe—; dust—; enervate—; expose—; harden—; inflame—; ingrain—; injure—; irritate—; macerate—; paint—; pat—; peel—; prick —; pull off—; rejuvenate—; rinse—; rub —; ruffle—; safeguard—; save one's—; scratch—; shed—; smear—; soften—; soothe —; sponge—; ulcerate—; —adapts; —blanches; —erupts; —forms; —furrows; —glows; —jaundices; —parches; —quivers; —scars; —shrinks; —splits; —stains; —thickens; —warts; —wrinkles.
(See epidermis, surface.)

SKIRT

adjectives
sable; close-clinging; silken; short; awful; antiquated; tight; divided; ample; jaunty; flared; voluminous; fleecy; cloudy; smooth; draggled; vaporous; gaudy; wide; hoop; gloomy; umbrella; rustling; gathered; pleated; slit; form-fitting; wrinkled.

verbs
accoutre in—; attire in—; bare—; baste—; cling to—; divest of—; enfold in—; garb in —; gusset—; hem—; pleat—; rig in—; rumple—; ruffle—; soil—; strip off—; swaddle in—; tack—; tuck in—; —cloaks; —s flutter; —mantles; —swathes; —s swirl; —s swish.
(See dress.)

SKITTISH

adverbs
nervously; wildly; fearfully; spiritedly; alarmingly; dangerously; absurdly; ridiculously; laughably; outlandishly; awkwardly; simperingly; fatuously; wantonly; capriciously; captiously; unreliably; unsteadily; undependably; unsteadily; erratically; unpredictably; vexatiously; remarkably.

SKULKING

adverbs
furtively; warily; cautiously; soundlessly; fearfully; constantly; unhappily; miserably; wretchedly; guiltily; frightfully; watchfully; secretly; abjectly; pitiably.

SKULL

adjectives
brainless; eyeless; cast-iron; perfect; grinning; gleaming; empty.

verbs
abrade—; batter—; compress—; contuse—; crack—; crush—; drain—; fracture—; imbed in—; lacerate—; measure—; mummify —; penetrate—; perforate—; pierce—; scrape—; split—; tap—; trepan—; trephine —; —contracts; —deflects; —protects.
(See head, brain, mind.)

SKUNK

verbs
rear—; skin—; trap—; —burrows; —controls; —defiles; —depredates; —digs; —ejects; —exudes; —grunts; —hibernates; —inhabits; —plagues; —preys on; —robs; —secretes; —squirts; —stalks; —stinks.
(See animal.)

SKY

adjectives
flooded; crystal; far; distant; radiant; moon-lit; nether; insufficient; thickening; sweltering; fair; twinkling; viewless; ancient; fantastic; lurid; starry; cloudless; turbulent; glowing; wintry; unruffled; interesting; frightening; dappled; stormy; sullen; balmy; leaden; empty; kindred; utmost; mature; beneficent; natural; elusive; upper; smiling; wonted; sunset; pathless; flaming; glorious; broad; frowning; domestic; copper; velvety; violent; nocturnal; delicious; curdled; humid; bright; narrowing; arched; burning; grinning; showery; granite; haunted; overcast; bitter; palpitating; deep; luminous; roseate; unconscious; lulling; sounding; ethereal; blinding; shrinking; softest; western; boundless; sapphire; barren; serene; enchanting; fragrant; alien; frosty; embroiling; triumphant; lowering; changing; unbarred; tidy; middle; pitiless; flawless; palpitant; fated; envious; star-studded; living; rosy; stainless; candid; gorgeous; peacock; tropic; hueless; sultry; night; summer; windless; resplendent; adverse; spacious; turquoise; sombre; placid; menacing; universal; primrose; angry; wonted; steely; vaulted; winking; saffron; nimbus.

verbs
clothe—; fleck—; flutter from—; freak—; gaze at—; gild—; lighten—; rule—; scan —; streak—; weave across—; —blackens; —blazes; —broods; —casts; —clouds; —darkens; —entrances; —glows; —marbles; —obscures; —patterns; —rifts; —curdles.
(See heaven, cloud.)

SLABS

adjectives
mortuary; thick; steaming; monolithic; shattered; boneless; original; huge; sepulchral.

SLACK

adverbs
weakly; lazily; shiftlessly; indolently; incorrigibly; habitually; naturally; inherently; innately; curiously; dreadfully; unpardonably; inexcusably; intolerably; unprofitably; thriftlessly; negligently; improvidently; uncommonly; utterly; apathetically; dangerously; languidly; carelessly; heedlessly; thoughtlessly; inconsiderately; clumsily; indifferently.

SLACKEN (v)

adverbs
materially; markedly; appreciably; gradually; abruptly; experimentally; comparatively.
(See reduce, loosen.)

SLANDER

adjectives
cursing; malicious; honest; cruel; lame; covered; cunning; abominable; impossible; libelous.

verbs
acquit of—; babble—; decry—; disprove—; inveigh against—; refute—; spread—; vindicate of—; —bespatters; —blackens; —brands; —calumniates; —defames; —deprecates; —derogates; —detracts; —disparages; —incenses; —infuriates; —libels; —maligns; —stigmatizes; —traduces; —vilifies.
(See aspersion, calumny, libel, malediction.)

SLANDER (*v*)

adverbs
libelously; scurrilously; foully; viciously; hatefully; vindictively; criminally; illegally; spitefully; maliciously; cunningly; cruelly; covertly; abominably; libelously.
(See defame, traduce.)

SLANDEROUS

adverbs
shamefully; boldly; altogether; openly; actually; admittedly; unexpectedly; shockingly; disgracefully; utterly; infamously; notoriously; uncommonly.

SLANG

adjectives
picturesque; vulgar; descriptive; polyglot; current; sporting; two-fisted; bold; understandable; local; accepted.

verbs
adopt—; ban—; colloquialize—; debar—; evolve—; express in—; frown upon—; interpret—; invent—; popularize—; taboo—; translate—; —amuses; —assumes; —colors; —corrupts; —enlivens; —invigorates; —mutilates; —revises; —spreads; —tends; —vulgarizes.
(See jargon, language.)

SLANGY

adverbs
disagreeably; unpleasantly; trenchantly; catchily; cheaply; coarsely; unnecessarily; crudely; tawdrily; boorishly; loutishly; ignorantly; gruffly; churlishly; indelicately; remarkably; gracelessly.

SLAP (*v*)

adverbs
smartly; brutally; cruelly; viciously; impatiently; indignantly.
(See box, strike.)

SLAP-DASH

adverbs
carelessly; blithely; hastily; nonchalantly; excitedly; hurriedly; untidily; thoughtlessly; inconsiderately; boyishly; inexcusably; habitually; incorrigibly; hopelessly; unsatisfactorily; unpleasantly; unluckily.

SLASH (*v*)

adverbs
ruthlessly; economically; murderously; energetically; conclusively; furiously; vindictively; bestially.
(See cut, gash.)

SLATTERNLY

adverbs
wretchedly; miserably; untidily; intolerably; incorrigibly; unattractively; unpleasantly; unfortunately; actually; carelessly; unconventionally; nonchalantly; desperately; sadly; hopelessly; habitually; unwontedly; displeasingly; offensively.

SLAUGHTER

adjectives
needless; terrific; deep; deadly; dreadful; ignoble; red; fratricidal; ruthless; sheer; persistent; brutal; indiscriminate; terrible; hopeless; unheard-of; causeless; awful; unworthy; fearful; subsequent; treacherous; incidental; wholesale.

verbs
avenge—; check—; condone—; countenance—; curb—; denounce—; exonerate of—; justify—; implicate in—; prosecute for—; regret—; restrain—; subdue—; succumb in—; stem—; —debauches; —decimates; —defiles; —deletes; —depraves; —ravages; —shames.
(See bloodshed, massacre.)

SLAUGHTER (*v*)

adverbs
professionally; blindly; ruthlessly; carelessly; bellicosely; insensately; needlessly; ignobly; indiscriminately; causelessly; treacherously; fearfully.
(See butcher, kill.)

SLAVE

adjectives

perfidious; veriest; humble; submissive; observant; delegated; fugitive; mercenary; ferocious; cringing; sceptered; myriad (pl); devilish; absconding; tawdry; supernumerary; thin; swarming (pl); pernicious; hollow-chested; runaway; factious; transgressing; crouching; drunken; absolute; faithful; purchased; fingering; past-saving; unmannerly; meanest; refractory; groveling; classified; insulting; monastic; luxurious; sanguine; base; superfluous; liberated; gigantic; loathed.

verbs

awe—; chastise—; emancipate—s; castigate—; fetter—; lash—; leash—s; liberate—s; manacle—; market—s; oversee—s; repress—; return—; shackle—s; spare—; subdue—; subjugate—s; trade in—s; tyrannize over—; yoke—s; —attends; —bows; —s colonize; —drudges; —ministers to; —reveres; —s revolt; —salaams.

(See servant, captive.)

SLAVERY

adjectives

virtual; social; voluntary; blissful; abject; merciful; mechanical.

verbs

abolish—; ban—; deliver from—; denounce—; drudge in—; efface—; enforce—; lead into—; liberate from—; outlaw—; perpetuate—; prohibit—; redeem from—; sell into—; subject to—; submit to—; suppress—; traffic in—; —binds; —crushes; —chains; —demoralizes; —fetters; —flourishes; —manacles; —restrains; —shackles; —subjugates.

(See bondage, enslavement, captivity.)

SLAVISH

adverbs

amazingly; unspeakably; meanly; servilely; pitiably; unbearably; totally; willingly; cheerfully; sullenly; temporarily; rebelliously; patently; mockingly; devotedly; ludicrously; ridiculously; apparently; pathetically; humbly; basely; manifestly; contentedly; contemptibly; openly; markedly; exaggeratedly.

SLAY (v)

adverbs

treacherously; traitorously; vindictively; revengefully; soullessly; nefariously; heartlessly; ruthlessly.

(See kill, slaughter.)

SLEEK

adverbs

smoothly; glossily; extremely; inordinately; unpleasantly; blandly; smugly; consciously; remarkably; excessively; suavely; attractively; unbelievably.

SLEEP

adjectives

flattering; noble; comfortable; common noonday; night; profound; trembling; bankrupt; heavy; eternal; pink-tinged; magnetic; fatal; transient; smiling; bestial; tranquil; scanty; deep; secret; marble; breathing; quiet; restful; sound; unbroken; refreshing; wintry; dreamless; peaceful; fitful; beloved; mystic; metamorphic; downy; lethargic; unstirring; portioned; poppied; sudden; drunken; alcoholic; short; convulsed; uninterrupted; fevered; pleasing; enchanted; mysterious; stealthy; startling; forgetful; hypnotic; frozen; troubled; filmy-eyed; speechless; violated; watchful; solacing.

verbs

arouse from—; beguile in—; call in—; desire—; disturb—; feign—; incline to—; induce—; intensify—; lack—; lull to—; mutter in—; produce—; relieve—; repose in—; require—; rock to—; rouse from—; secure—; sink into—; trail into—; —curtains; —curtails; —engulfs; —insures; —overpowers; —reigns; —renews; —soothes; —steals; —transfers.

(See repose, rest, slumber.)

SLEEP (v)

adverbs

heavily; peacefully; stertorously; profoundly; habitually; fitfully; comfortably; transiently; tranquilly; dreamlessly; alcoholically; hypnotically.

(See doze, slumber.)

SLEEPLESS

adverbs

vigilantly; alertly; nervously; deliriously; feverishly; anxiously; distressingly; painfully; unfortunately; remarkably; puzzlingly; unaccountably; incurably; alarmingly; disturbingly; unhappily; excitedly; curiously; wakefully; restlessly; restively; apprehensively; uneasily; vexatiously; ironically; inconveniently; dangerously; confoundedly; strangely.

SLEEPY

adverbs
uncontrollably; irresistibly; inordinately; strangely; oddly; curiously; particularly; significantly; extremely; alarmingly; dangerously; specially; unusually; wretchedly; miserably; naturally; abnormally; surprisingly; unaccountably; inexplicably; mysteriously; conveniently; perilously; confoundedly; strangely.

SLEET

adjectives
slapping; driving; eddying; arrowy; stimulated; shiny; dangerous.

verbs
brave—; encounter—; melt—; precipitate —; —assails; —bites; —blasts; —blights; —devastates; —endangers; —glazes; —impairs; —imperils; —nips; —pelts; —penetrates; —pierces; —pinches; —rattles on; —ravages; —thaws.

(See ice, snow, hail.)

SLEETY

adverbs
miserably; fearfully; dangerously; suddenly; wretchedly; unmanageably; dreadfully; terribly; freezingly; disagreeably; unpleasantly; frightfully; chillingly; bitterly; perilously; hazardously.

SLEEVE

adjectives
puffed; long; short; flowing; pendent; capacious; tapered; luxurious; charming; slashed; lounging; molded; draw-string.

verbs
adorn—; alter—; append—; baste—; chuckle into—; cuff—; drape—; embellish —; extend—; flounce—; fray—; frill—; fringe—; hem—; knit up—; ruffle—; rumple—; shred—; starch—; tatter—; trim —; —girds.

SLENDER

adverbs
gracefully; unusually; remarkably; delightfully; pleasantly; attractively; exceptionally; marvelously; extremely; beautifully; exquisitely; youthfully; prettily.

SLEUTH

verbs
employ—; engage—; tip off (colloq.)—; —analyzes; —apprehends; —beguiles; —cloaks—; cross-examines—; —deduces; —detects; —discloses; —disguises; —divulges; —dodges; —exposes; —fathoms; —ferrets out; —grills; —interrogates; —investigates; —mystifies; —outwits; —overhauls; —peers; —pries into; —probes; —prowls; —queries; —questions; —ransacks; —reveals; —scents; —scrutinizes; —shadows; —threshes out; —traces; —tracks down; —trails; —uncovers; —unearths; —unmasks; —veils.

(See detective.)

SLIDE (*v*)

adverbs
imperceptibly; appreciably; terrifyingly; greasily; languidly; violently; deftly; cautiously.

(See glide, slip.)

SLIM

adverbs
boyishly; girlishly; childishly; delightfully; gracefully; unusually; extremely; normally; abnormally; attractively; noticeably; youthfully; unwontedly; distressingly; admirably; pleasantly.

SLIME

adjectives
subsiding; blistering; brute; primeval; bestial.

SLIP

adjectives
artless; warped; native; costly; silken; shapely; sheeny; fitted; necessary.

SLIP (*v*)

adverbs
stealthily; elusively; artfully; treacherously; evanescently; surreptitiously; insidiously; silently.

(See slide, glide.)

SLIPPER

adjectives
mended; imaginary; high-heeled; fur-lined; flowered; sharp-pointed; comfortable; battered; pinching.

SLIPPERY

adverbs

unmanageably; always; alarmingly; perilously; dangerously; hazardously; terribly; desperately; wretchedly; miserably; disturbingly; evidently; dreadfully; frightfully; unusually; extremely.

SLOGAN

verbs

adopt—; assail—; chant—; chorus—; dramatize—; coin—; flaunt—; hail—; offer—; rally to—; reject—; shout—; shrill—; thunder—; —elaborates; —rings; —stirs; —symbolizes; —takes hold; —wafts.

(See motto, cry, phrase.)

SLOP (*v*)

adverbs

carelessly; disgustingly; violently; abruptly; clumsily.

(See soil, drink.)

SLOPE

adjectives

fruitful; inaccessible; dappled; parallel; inclined; haunted; sunny; springing; grassy; intervening; declivitous; luminous; gentler; slippery; verdant; scarred; swelling; reverse; trampled; precipitous; rapid; flattish; upland; glimmering; terraced; neglected; westering; desert; wooded; monotonous; savage.

verbs

afford—; avoid—; capsize on—; careen down—; grade—; level—; maintain—; scale—; scamper down—; skirt—; sustain—; —ascends; —banks; —distorts; —endangers; —inclines; —lurches; —recedes; —sags; —streams; —tilts.

(See bank, hill.)

SLOPE (*v*)

adverbs

gradually; markedly; steeply; gently; greenly; inaccessibly; grassily; swellingly; precipitously.

(See incline.)

SLOTH

adjectives

silken; dilatory; cowardly; cushioned; sensual; deliberate; drowsy.

SLOTHFUL

adverbs

notoriously; habitually; naturally; incorrigibly; incurably; lazily; indolently; evidently; openly; admittedly; brazenly; laughingly; unaccountably; drowsily.

SLOUCH (*v*)

adverbs

heavily; carelessly; sullenly; obnoxiously; wearily; visibly; deliberately.

(See droop, hang.)

SLOUGH

adjectives

dreadful; pestiferous; humble; deadly; dreaded.

SLOVENLY

adverbs

inexcusably; unreasonably; shamefully; sadly; embarrassingly; unpardonably; lazily; shamelessly; unpleasantly; repulsively; curiously; negligently; thoughtlessly; insouciantly; casually; nonchalantly; laughingly; unbecomingly; discourteously; crassly; boorishly; outlandishly; outrageously; scandalously; unnecessarily; offensively.

SLUGGISH

adverbs

strangely; stupidly; loutishly; dully; torpidly; indolently; inertly; supinely; negligently; carelessly; indifferently; lethargically; strangely; unwontedly; unusually; exceptionally; intolerably; provokingly; vexatiously; hopelessly; wretchedly; unprofitably.

SLUMBER

adjectives

refreshed; pleasant; profound; heavy; dreamless; weary; unnatural; troubled; breathless; rigid; riveted; shady; careless; charmed; sufficient; famous; alert; eternal; fearful; soft; noontide; tickled; enervating; tranquil; healthful; colossal; unconscious; stagnant; prostrate; silent; lighter; dusty.

verbs

blast—; burst from—; consume in—; curtail—; doze into—; induce—; shatter—; toss in—; —enfolds; —envelops; —grips; —reanimates; —regenerates; —relaxes; —renews; —revitalizes; —revives; —seizes.

(See sleep.)

SLUMBER (v)

adverbs
refreshingly; sweetly; pleasantly; profoundly; dreamlessly; enervatingly; tranquilly; healthfully.
(See doze, sleep.)

SLUMP

verbs
allay—; alleviate—; balance—; check—; counteract—; curb—; descend into—; emerge from—; halt—; mitigate—; moderate —; stem—; suffer—; survive—; —abates; —depresses; —endangers; —fizzles out (colloq.); —jeopardizes; —reduces; —relaxes; —retards; —slackens; —troubles.
(See depression, fall, melancholy.)

SLUMS

verbs
abolish—; comb—; dismantle—; efface—; eradicate—; erase—; explore—; exterminate—; infest—; level—; prowl about—; lurk in—; raze—; rise from—; roam—; root out—; scour—; skulk in—; stamp out —; wallow in—; —breed; —congest; —deface; —defile; —pollute; —reek; —screen; —sully; —teem.
(See district.)

SLUSHY

adverbs
miserably; unhealthfully; disagreeably; wretchedly; messily; unpleasantly; unusually; deucedly.

SLY

adverbs
subtly; surreptitiously; furtively; actually; insidiously; abominably; dangerously; warily; undiscoverably; undoubtedly; extrememely; successfully; miserably; hatefully; maliciously; cleverly; adroitly; astutely; politically; commercially; trickily; curiously; marvelously.

SMACK

adjectives
emphatic; hearty; clamorous; affectionate; loud; stunning.

SMALL

adverbs
gracefully; pleasantly; prettily; infinitesimally; minutely; extraordinarily; pitifully; pathetically; miserably; compactly; handily; conveniently; daintily; delicately; miraculously; unbelievably.

SMALLNESS

adjectives
compact; frivolous; suggestive; aristocratic; dainty; handy.

SMALLPOX

verbs
afflict with—; characterize—; contract—; convey—; diagnose as—; expose to—; exterminate—; extirpate—; immunize to—; infect with—; inoculate against—; isolate —; prevent—; quarantine—; succumb to—; transmit—; usher in—; —communicates; —confines; —disfigures; —incubates; —invalids; —marks; —pits; —prostrates; —ravages; —scars; —taints; —vitiates.
(See epidemic, measles, disease.)

SMART

adverbs
comically; facetiously; banteringly; foolishly; jestingly; cleverly; felicitously; uncommonly; brilliantly; unusually; thoroughly; ingeniously; amazingly; admirably; wonderfully; wittily; drolly; sparklingly; acutely; capably; cunningly; craftily; sensibly; reasonably; sagely; prudently; subtly; consciously; impressively; learnedly; notoriously; proverbially; assiduously; alertly; sedulously; earnestly; actively.

SMARTNESS

adjectives
figure; lasting; style; exceptional; distinguished; dramatic; stimulating; superficial; uncouth; fabulous; slovenly; alert; conservative; demure; forced; clumsy

SMASH (v)

adverbs
relentlessly; ruthlessly; vigorously; impulsively; violently; thunderously; terrifically; frightfully.
(See wreck, crush.)

SMELL

adjectives
offensive; pungent; rutting; rank; sharp; foul; conglomerate; musty; villainous; luscious; putrid; faint; concentrated; warning; sickish; sweet; dreadful; grateful; elegant; pervading; spicy; powerful; rebellious; hor-

rid; unholy; evil; heavy; acrid; fishy; damp; moldy; balsam; overpowering; breathless; heavenly; balmy; odious; cold; oppressive; dank.

verbs
abhor—; abominate—; banish—; deodorize—; inhale—; intensify—; loathe—; recognize—; relish—; retain—; waft—; —asphyxiates; —assails; —clings; —corrupts; —edges; —entices; —floats; —gags; —incenses; —irritates; —lures; —mingles; —nauseates; —offends; —permeates; —pervades; —ranks; —repels; —revolts; —sickens; —suggests; —taints; —tempts.
(See fragrance, stench, scent, odor.)

SMELL (v)

adverbs
repulsively; objectionably; heavenly; evilly; repugnantly; offensively; noisomely; pungently; abominably; provokingly; potently; sweetly; odiously; dankly; delectably.
(See scent, perfume.)

SMELLY

adverbs
hideously; odiously; horridly; sickeningly; nauseatingly; startlingly; definitely; disgustingly; unbearably; curiously; overpoweringly; suffocatingly.

SMILE

adjectives
rustic; uneasy; gracious; regretful; winning; surprised; radiant; broad; bitter; reminiscent; whimsical; wreathed; metallic; faint; apologetic; affectionate; sweet; amiable; solitary; pitying; ridiculous; quizzical; spicy; special; contagious; fawning; amused; icy; wistful; courteous; crafty; withering; beaming; ravished; enormous; uncontrolled; sickly; sly; maternal; eager; naked; frank; joyous; complacent; brilliant; answering; forced; angry; sympathetic; wanton; contemptuous; deadly; sad; simulated; audible; illumined; parting; approving; ironical; mocking; sudden; indulgent; welcoming; irradiating; agreeable; restrained; watery; rare; playful; superior; arch; perpetual; innocent; big; somber; polished; responding; irrepressible; religious; peculiar; convenient; everlasting; tolerant; vapid; priceless; vague; racked; complicated; smart; polite; murderous; disdainful; sunny; indomitable; sinister; diabolical; complaisant; dim; patient; haughty; endless; rapid; passing; benign; lurid; crooked; placid; hot; grave; malicious; incredulous; timid; nervous; kind; involuntary; smothered; ardent; bland; provocative; peerless; vivacious; mellow; wan; new; quiet; calm; abrupt; loving; sagacious; buoyant; greasy; sardonic; conciliatory; sidelong; nasty; dawning; grim; ironical; false; meaning; sustaining; saucy; atoning; cynical; prodigal; charming; natural; indifferent; tolerant; wry; little; visible; mournful; weary; patronizing; languid; deprecating; fitful; humorous; seductive; sarcastic; mutual; idiotic; frigid; enrapt; doleful; hospitable; doubtful; ingratiating; counterfeit; curious; mischievous; childlike; exultant; saturnine; speculative; pensive; immutable; condescending; pert; impish; roguish; ghastly; rueful; hollow; unctuous; inane; joyless; wild; satirical; reassuring; slow; hideous; flattering; listless; parting; fleeting; engaging; severe; immortal; insipid; moonshine; fascinating; facile; beatific; restless; scornful; bosomed; wondering; moony; senile; ambrosial; covert; airy; incisive; faded; shy; social; angelic; envious; debonair; bashful; artificial; waking; antiseptic; paternal; dubious; hungry; pale; ready; clear; thoughtless; gentle; infectious; conscious; timorous; haughty; frequent; backward; enamored; obnoxious; pallid; derisive; beguiling; excited.

verbs
achieve—; answer with—; bestow—; cloud—; conceal—; crinkle into—; extinguish—; extract—; flash—; grant—; illuminate with—; induce—; loosen—; manage—; mock—; permit—; provoke—; quench—; repress—; rouse—; share—; shed—; suppress—; throw—; toss—; wear—; wreathe in—; wrinkle into—; —abashes; —basks; —confronts; —contorts; —creases; —crinkles; —deludes; —departs; —disconcerts; —disparages; —fades; —flashes; —flickers; —hides; —hovers; —lightens; —lingers; —mantles; —plays; —reassures; —renders; —reveals; —twitches.
(See grin, laughter, smirk.)

SMILE (v)

adverbs
delightedly; approvingly; shrewdly; affectionately; cherubically; reluctantly; ecstatically; whimsically; tolerantly; radiantly; indulgently; benevolently; tremulously;

grimly; sympathetically; blandly; beamingly; wanly; auspiciously; impudently; disarmingly; mischievously; magnanimously; unctuously; contemptuously; lewdly; winsomely; wryly; languidly; artificially; automatically; apathetically; benignly; contagiously; ingratiatingly; facetiously; superciliously; superficially; demurely; guilelessly; angelically; affably; ambiguously; coyly; cynically; cunningly; exultantly; exaggeratedly; cryptically; ruefully; benevolently.
(See grin, laugh.)

SMIRK

adjectives
conscious; genteel; empty; confidential; nasty.

verbs
affect—; check—; curb—; force—; raise—; repress—; restrain—; wipe away—; wither with—; —dampens; —depresses; —derides; —disdains; —droops; —flushes; —indicates; —reveals; —ridicules; —scorns; —sinks; —sours.
(See grin, smile.)

SMIRK (*v*)

adverbs
unpleasantly; slyly; treacherously; cynically; sarcastically; hideously; covertly; artificially; obnoxiously; satirically; saturninely.
(See sneer, simper.)

SMITE (*v*)

adverbs
ruthlessly; resoundingly; mercilessly; cruelly; bestially; heartlessly; shatteringly.
(See strike, hit.)

SMOKE

adjectives
after-dinner; favorite; stale; filthy; suffocating; thin; ribbon; pallid; curling; sulphur; helpless; inky; lurid; eddying; leaping; bituminous; faint; dense; resinous; blinding; sour; crooked; foul; columned; acrid; venomous.

verbs
enfold with—; spurt—; —asphyxiates; —belches; —billows; —blinds; —blackens; —blights; —carries; —chokes; —clouds; —conceals; —curls; —dissolves; —drifts; —eclipses; —emits; —envelops; —floats; —gags; —grimes; —hangs; —hovers; —looms; —obscures; —overcomes; —penetrates; —pervades; —pours; —puffs; —reeks; —screens; —seeps in; —shrouds; —shuts out; —smothers; —smudges; —soars; —spirals; —stifles; —suffocates; —swirls; —uncurls; —veils; —vitiates; —whirls; —wraps; —wreathes.
(See fumes, haze, mist, soot, fog.)

SMOKE (*v*)

adverbs
complacently; jovially; fraternally; leisurely; somnolently; gravely; endlessly; atrociously; deliciously; philosophically; reflectively; meditatively; incessantly.
(See fume, reek.)

SMOKY

adverbs
densely; alarmingly; suffocatingly; terribly; dangerously; dingily; invisibly; perilously; unpleasantly; unbearably; disagreeably; odiously; acridly; blindingly; abominably; hazardously.

SMOOTH

adverbs
politely; mysteriously; significantly; amiably; civilly; genteely; courteously; craftily; obsequiously; good-temperedly; suavely; urbanely; suspiciously; sweetly; graciously; ingratiatingly; fashionably; alluringly; superficially; seductively; hypocritically.

SMOOTH (*v*)

adverbs
diplomatically; socially; mechanically; skillfully; artfully; benevolently.
(See stroke, calm.)

SMOOTHNESS

adjectives
polished; fashionable; exclusive; alluring; oily; excessive; matronly; surface.

SMOTHER (*v*)

adverbs
fatally; painfully; incontinently; politely; insidiously; socially; economically; politically; viciously.
(See repress, extinguish.)

SMOULDERING

adverbs
slowly; dangerously; luridly; fantastically; glowingly; alarmingly; actively; dully;

dimly; faintly; perilously; hazardously; hatefully; evidently; persistently; steadily; apparently.

SMUDGY

adverbs

unacceptably; carelessly; illegibly; dingily; grimily; grittily; darkly; unpleasantly; offensively; unattractively; amazingly; inexplicably; deliberately; intentionally; impossibly; contemptibly; disagreeably.

SMUG

adverbs

unbearably; disgustingly; disagreeably; irritatingly; unreasonably; ridiculously; pompously; chestily; overly; vexatiously; maddeningly; ostentatiously; complacently; pretentiously; laughably; contentedly; priggishly; imperturbably.

SMUGGLING

verbs

abandon—; abolish—; charge with—; cloak —; confess to—; convict of—; countenance —; cover—; deter—; disclose—; engage in —; expose—; frown upon—; justify—; practice—; screen—; suppress—; traffic in —; uncover—; —defrauds; —mulcts; —profits; —violates.

(See robbery, theft.)

SNAIL

verbs

cultivate—; prey on—; search for—; uncover—; —buries; —crawls; —emerges; —hides.

(See animal.)

SNAKE

adjectives

sinuous; sacred; venomous; gaping; dazzling; strong; quick; watching; hissing; gigantic; poisonous.

verbs

cage—; capture—; charm—; —coils; —constricts; —contorts; —crawls; —deposits eggs; —drapes around; —drops upon; —emerges; —encircles; —engulfs its prey; —entwines; —feigns; —frightens; —glides; —hibernates; —hisses; —lunges; —poisons; —recoils; —retreats; —scurries; —seizes; —slides; —slithers; —squirms; —stalks; —stings; —stirs; —strangles its prey; —strikes; —struggles; —suns itself; —surprises its prey; —swallows its prey; —sways; —terrorizes; —thrashes about; —threatens; —twines; —twists; —undulates; —vibrates; —whips its tail; —worms its way; —wraps around; —wriggles; —writhes; —zigzags.

(See lizard, reptile.)

SNAKY

adverbs

circuitously; sinuously; insidiously; maliciously; artfully; craftily; subtly; slanderously; insinuatingly; surreptitiously; deceitfully; despicably; treacherously; wilily; subtly; archly; crookedly.

SNAP (v)

adverbs

explosively; exultantly; joyously; irritatingly; nervously; intermittently; repeatedly.

(See snarl, growl.)

SNAPPY

adverbs

disagreeably; bracingly; stimulatingly; coldly; unpleasantly; extremely; bitterly; cruelly; stingingly; harshly; exceedingly; terribly; dreadfully.

SNARE

adjectives

silken; wavering; female; alluring; sensual; treacherous; drowsing; harmless; opal; lying; elfish; marvelous; sentimental; cursed.

verbs

bait—; decoy into—; entangle in—; escape —; lure into—; mend—; plant—; —attracts; —deludes; —entices; —intrigues; —menaces; —tempts; —victimizes.

(See cobweb, net, trap.)

SNARL (v)

adverbs

tigerishly; fiendishly; formidably; fiercely; viciously; portentously; furiously; rapaciously; terrifyingly; bestially; diabolically.

(See growl, snap.)

SNARLS

adjectives

perfect; hoarse; angry; rasping; screaming.

SNATCH (v)

adverbs

instantaneously; swiftly; thievingly; insolently; hurriedly; selfishly; callously; gluttonously.

(See grasp, grab.)

SNEAKY

adverbs
notoriously; infamously; reputedly; disagreeably; detestably; abominably; atrociously; shamefully; wickedly; viciously; maliciously; incurably; fearfully; strangely; naturally; habitually; alarmingly; suspiciously; furtively; guiltily.

SNEER

adjectives
dull; veiled; significant; copious (pl); perceptible; subtle; drifting; powdery; haughty; frozen; bitter; infernal; chronic; sinister; twisted; mocking.

verbs
check—; curb—; curl into—; force—; indulge in—; parry—; repress—; restrain—; wither with—; —affronts; —castigates; —chides; —derides; —desecrates; —disparages; —gibes; —jeers; —mocks; —outrages; —rebukes; —scorns; —taunts.
(See jeer, ridicule, contempt.)

SNEER (v)

adverbs
derisively; contemptuously; aristocratically; scornfully; hatefully; superciliously; fastidiously; priggishly.
(See jeer, smirk.)

SNEEZE (v)

adverbs
violently; explosively; abruptly; repeatedly; significantly; obstreperously; exasperatingly.
(See cough.)

SNICKER

verbs
check—; curb—; disregard—; restrain—; voice—; —admonishes; —chides; —derides; —disparages; —insults; —issues; —mimics; —scoffs; —taunts; —withers; —twits.
(See giggle, laughter, smirk, grin.)

SNICKER (v)

adverbs
contemptuously; indecently; irreverently; ribaldly; ludicrously; exasperatingly; slyly; maliciously; irresistibly; insolently.
(See titter, smirk, simper.)

SNIFF

adjectives
tremendous; sarcastic; hearty; prodigious; premonitory.

SNIFF (v)

adverbs
greedily; haughtily; warily; instinctively; audibly; suspiciously; ostentatiously.
(See scent, smell.)

SNOB

verbs
crush—; deflate—; humble—; loathe—; pique—; sober—; —affects; —apes; —assumes; —condescends; —cringes; —cuts (colloq.); —disdains; —flushes; —humiliates; —inflates; —overbears; —overweens; —preens; —pretends; —puffs up; —regards; —scoffs at; —scorns; —swaggers; —swells; —worships.
(See hypocrite.)

SNOBBISH

adverbs
unwarrantably; groundlessly; absurdly; curiously; oddly; meanly; grossly; crudely; crazily; pompously; bombastically; cheaply; laughably; arrogantly; haughtily; ridiculously; ludicrously; particularly; uncommonly; unpardonably; unbearably; disagreeably; unpleasantly.

SNORE

adjectives
simultaneous; melodious; feminine; smothered; annoying; regular; buzzing.

SNORE (v)

adverbs
intoxicatedly; sonorously; peacefully; stertorously; irritatingly; exasperatingly; melodiously; incessantly; annoyingly; perpetually.
(See sleep, slumber, breathe.)

SNORT

adjectives
impatient; angry; loud; trumpeting; audible; roaring.

SNORT (v)

adverbs
impatiently; indignantly; audibly; trumpetingly; roaringly; terrifically; disgustingly; violently; vulgarly.
(See snarl, growl.)

SNOW

adjectives
wintry; flaky; feathery; melting; downy; driven; whirling; benumbing; trackless;

eternal; summer; innocent; chilling; caressing; consecrated; glittering; shrinking; powerful; winged; rugged; drifting; crunching; scattering; untrampled; dazzling; solidified; crisp; sharp; virgin; unfathomable; shrouded; pure; homogeneous; receding; perpetual; wondrous; strange; crusted; dissolving; frozen; sculptured; flying; unsunned; sparkling; untrodden; hard; heavy; wasting; powdery; whipped; crackling; dreaded.

verbs
crunch—; scan—; scrunch (colloq.)—; sculpture in—; stamp—; thaw—; —avalanches; —blankets; —caps; —crowns; —dazzles; —deadens; —diminishes; —drifts; —envelops; —falls; —flashes; —flurries; —glistens; —hides; —hushes; —lies; —mantles; —masks; —muffles; —pelts; —penetrates; —piles; —retreats; —ribs; —sails; —scuds; —sculptures; —settles; —shrouds; —sifts; —tinges; —tints; —veils; —wraps.
(See snowflakes.)

SNOW-BLIND

adverbs
completely; momentarily; temporarily; frantically; terrifyingly; suddenly; perilously; inopportunely; curiously; merely; unluckily; tormentingly.

SNOWFLAKES

verbs
drive—; —accumulate; —adorn; —bite; —blanch; —checker; —chill; —cling; —dazzle; —deluge; —fleck; —frost; —glitter; —nip; —obscure; —shudder; —silver.
(See snow, crystal, flake.)

SNOWY

adverbs
beautifully; exquisitely; fortunately; spectacularly; brilliantly; dazzlingly; dangerously; unbelievably; deeply; persistently; incredibly; unseasonably; unexpectedly; surprisingly; perilously; blindingly; hazardously; dreadfully; fearfully; frightfully; suddenly; windily.

SNUB

adjectives
deliberate; suggestive; cold; shrewd; nasty.

verbs
construe as—; expose to—; resent—; risk—; rue—; —abashes; —bewilders; —discomposes; —disconcerts; —discredits; —humbles; —humiliates; —overwhelms; —petrifies; —reddens; —reproaches; —slurs; —staggers; —stuns; —takes down a peg.
(See insult, rebuff, rebuke.)

SNUB (v)

adverbs
deliberately; coldly; acrimoniously; invidiously; permanently; contemptuously; hatefully; conceitedly.
(See ignore, disregard.)

SNUG

adverbs
compactly; securely; safely; closely; comfortably; happily; fortunately; pleasantly; warmly; reasonably; agreeably; delightfully; luckily; sufficiently; satisfactorily; deliciously.

SOAP

verbs
adulterate—; enrich—; rinse off—; —agrees with; —deodorizes; —disinfects; —fortifies; —invigorates; —lathers; —launders; —laves; —protects; —purges; —refreshes; —restores; —saturates; —scours; —shampoos; —soothes; —stimulates; —tingles.
(See lather, lotion.)

SOAPY

adverbs
sufficiently; warmly; satisfactorily; pleasantly; reasonably; slightly; strongly; occasionally; unpleasantly; pungently; comfortably; comfortingly.

SOAR (v)

adverbs
magnificently; lazily; serenely; majestically; pretentiously; daringly; gracefully; incessantly; loftily; effortlessly; daringly; transcendingly.
(See fly, mount.)

SOB

adjectives
tearless; dying; convulsive; hysterical; heaving; tremulous; noiseless; desolate; innumerable (pl); loud; indignant; audible; hopeless; diminished; confused; gulping; choked; painful; feeble; commingled (pl); conventional; wild; stifled; gasping; panting; racking; renewed; stormy; deep.

verbs
burst into—s; check—; heave—; repress—; restrain—; smother—; stifle—; strangle—; suppress—; whimper—; —disarms; —engulfs; —gurgles; —lacerates; —laments; —melts; —moves; —overwhelms; —racks; —rends; —shakes; —softens; —touches; —wells up; —wrings.
(See moan, murmur, sigh, shiver, shudder.)

SOB (v)

adverbs
piteously; audibly; miserably; bleakly; passionately; hysterically; violently; convulsively; bitterly; monotonously; tearlessly; tremulously; rackingly; pantingly; gaspingly.
(See weep, cry.)

SOBBING

adjectives
gentle; frightened; unrestrained; monotonous.

adverbs
convulsively; heavily; desolately; lonesomely; heartbreakingly; repentantly; remorsefully; bitterly; cruelly; miserably; loudly; quietly; silently; interminably; continually; unreasonably; absurdly; ridiculously; deliberately; purposefully; profitably; suddenly; violently; unaccountably; hysterically; grievously; angrily; happily; nervously.

SOBER

adverbs
unusually; gravely; unwontedly; uncommonly; extremely; unquestionably; occasionally; usually; seldom; rarely; scarcely; reluctantly; habitually; substantially; moderately; drearily; dismally; pensively; thoughtfully; speculatively; wistfully; wishfully; reasonably; dispassionately; judicially; suddenly; earnestly; judiciously; amazingly; strangely; studiously; alarmingly.

SOBRIETY

verbs
commend—; conduce to—; dispose toward—; dwell in—; lack—; maintain—; moderate—; persist in—; preserve—; pursue—; restore—; suspend—; —represses; —restrains; —spares; —tempers.
(See temperance, moderation, gravity.)

SOCIABLE

adverbs
delightfully; sincerely; charmingly; agreeably; habitually; extremely; usually; rarely; scarcely; affably; genially; highly; cordially; familiarly; quietly; noisily; hilariously; heartily; gracefully; chattily; unusually; exceedingly; extraordinarily; clumsily; suddenly; unexpectedly; excessively; designedly; chummily; warmly; truly; uncommonly; remarkably; significantly; ostentatiously.

SOCIAL

adverbs
pleasantly; agreeably; genially; jovially; happily; festively; sportively; affably; usually; highly; companionably; remarkably; openly.

SOCIALISM

verbs
advocate—; combat—; define—; frown upon—; oppose—; prate of—; promote—; rant against—; reject—; —burrows into; —cankers; —confiscates; —controls; —disposes of; —ebbs; —equals; —flourishes; —frees; —humanizes; —levels; —liberates; —manifests; —paralyzes; —regulates; —relinquishes; —remedies; —shares; —shatters; —undermines; —wages; —wars against.
(See communism, liberalism, modernism, nationalism.)

SOCIALIST

verbs
silence—; —abolishes; —bands; —cements; —clashes; —discards; —distributes; —expatiates on; —hails; —harangues; —heckles; —indoctrinates; —organizes; —prates; —rants; —spreads; —theorizes; —undermines.
(See anarchist, communist.)

SOCIETY

adjectives
plutocratic; polished; vigorous; cultivated; fashionable; cold; open; integrated; agreeable; desolate; exotic; honorable; competitive; provincial; artistic; civilized; charitable; cheerful; distinguished; human; frivolous; shattered; unevolved; distinct; formal; martyrized; decorous; polite; heartless; inorganic; intellectual; fastidious; insensitive; brilliant; literary; aristocratic; primitive; high-toned; perpetual; congenial;

purified; benevolent; exclusive; peripatetic; reputable; sordid; monastic; immoral; notorious; respectable; wild; scientific; contemporary; industrial.

verbs
abandon—; admit to—; debar from—; denounce—; deprive—; destroy—; displease—; elevate—; expel from—; introduce into—; mingle with—; negate—; plunge—; purge—; redeem—; remodel—; shun—; step into—; usher into—; —animates; —arrays; —binds; —brands; —campaigns; —conciliates; —conforms; —controls; —copes; —disintegrates; —establishes; —expands; —expels; —frowns upon; —lauds; —obligates; —organizes; —outlaws; —plagues; —polishes; —recruits; —rends asunder; —revolutionizes; —sanctions; —serves; —shackles; —springs from; —uproots; —wars on; —withdraws.

(See brotherhood, community, companionship, state.)

SOCIETY
(*association*)

verbs
address—; conciliate—; convoke—; disband—; found—; harangue—; head—; league in—; link in—; mobilize—; muster—; preside over—; sever—; —adjourns; —assembles; —convenes; —defines; —disseminates; —elects; —flocks to; —pledges; —preys; —promulgates; —supports.

(See league, association, club, guild, lodge.)

SOD

adjectives
peace-giving; stubborn; velvet; verdant; spongy; lifeless; moldering.

SODA

verbs
bottle—s; cap—s; carbonate—; charge—; color—; dispense—; dissolve in—; down—; flavor—; manufacture—; mix—; prepare—; purvey—s; siphon—; sweeten—; —effervesces; —exhilarates; —refreshes.

(See beverage, drink, liquor.)

SODDEN

adverbs
dismally; gloomily; heavily; irretrievably; disagreeably; unpleasantly; strangely.

SOFA

adjectives
imposing; embroidered; matted; satin-damask; comfortable; battered.

verbs
bolster—; crouch behind—; curl in—; ensconce in—; loll on—; lounge on—; prop—; perch on—; recline on—; refurbish—; renovate—; repose on—; slump on—; straddle—; upholster—; —accommodates; —bears; —beckons; —graces; —sinks; —supports; —sustains.

(See couch.)

SOFT

adverbs
deliciously; adorably; pleasantly; delightfully; comfortably; admirably; conveniently; invitingly; warmly; comfortingly; curiously; particularly; commendably; pliably; delicately; tenderly; compassionately; sympathetically; gently; adaptably.

SOFT-HEARTED

adverbs
leniently; indulgently; judiciously; understandingly; occasionably; pliably; naturally; usually; unwontedly; graciously; hospitably; admirably; curiously; charitably; generously; magnanimously; notoriously; foolishly; usually.

SOFTNESS

adjectives
passionate; sapping; lovely; liquid; musical; purring; tremulous; feline; infinite; melting; bewitching; displeasing; velvet; shy; unbelievable; sudden; cat-like.

SOFT-SPOKEN

adverbs
blandly; usually; habitually; normally; pleasantly; agreeably; delightfully; deceivingly; indulgently; naturally; invariably; curiously; admirably; deliberately; purposely.

SOGGY

adverbs
unpleasantly; unserviceably; curiously; unwholesomely; heavily; irredeemably; unfortunately; unprofitably; admittedly; irremediably; unexpectedly; remarkably; dreadfully.

SOIL

adjectives
humid; volcanic; fenny; blood-stained; hallowed; luxuriant; teeming; sterile; sifted; repressed; alluvial; enchanted; thirsty; marshy; unbroken; unproductive; friendly; noxious; ill-smelling; fertile; wholesome; friable; sacred; desolate; accursed; fruitful; parched; arid; sandy; indistinguishable; ancient; smoking; niggardly; poor; rich; radiant; favored; fallow; cultivated; kind; surrounding; ungrateful; neglected; peaty; wretched; congenial; tillable; swampy; burning; mangled; barren; foreign; adjacent; drenched; crusty; virgin; exhausted; devastated; mortal; tropic; native; alien; nitrous; conquered; oozy; crumbling.

verbs
cleave—; conserve—; cultivate—; devitalize—; drain—; enrich—; fertilize—; furrow—; harrow—; irrigate—; impregnate—; preserve—; pry from—; renew—; renounce —; revitalize—; ridge up—; rob—; root in —; scratch—; set foot on—; smell—; sow—; starve—; till—; wring from—; —begrimes; —blesses; —erodes; —procreates; —satisfies; —smudges.
(See land, earth, ground, farm.)

SOIL (*v*)

adverbs
carelessly; obnoxiously; markedly; hopelessly; disgustingly; annoyingly; exasperatingly.
(See taint, spoil.)

SOJOURN

adjectives
dreary; aimless; endless; short; enforced; protracted; permanent; bloody; previous; brief; accursed; autumnal; obscure; pleasant.

SOLACE

adjectives
individual; airy; idle; melancholy; immeasurable; ecstatic; scant; repenting; little.

verbs
afford—; accord—; bestow—; decline—; derive—; extend—; grant—; offer—; proffer —; reject—; tender—; volunteer—; yield —; —allays; —appeases; —assuages; —beguiles; —cheers, —comforts; —draws; —diverts; —mitigates; —palliates; —salves; —smooths.
(See comfort, consolation.)

SOLDIERS

adjectives
fanatical; languid; wilted; faceless; gallant; brave; illiterate; true; trusty; rough; career; drunken; godless; volunteer; surviving; harassed; well-tried; distinguished; capable; maddened; struggling; brutal; sausage-legged; valiant; weary; rowdy; unrelenting; mercenary; butchered; disbanded; decorative; deluded; accomplished; improvident; straggling; disorderly; good; hardy; wandering; disaffected; lion-hearted; stout; demoralized; gaunt; intrepid; stern; fearless; hot-tempered; heroic; veteran; lice-ridden; sentimental; indomitable; obdurate; eager; doughty; steady; fortunate; condemned; besotted; chivalrous; vulgar; magnanimous; forlorn; staring; resolute; inebriated; weary; mutilated; sleepy; disillusioned.

verbs
arm—; command—; conciliate—; court-martial—; dispatch—; drill—; harry—; mobilize—; mow down—; quarter—; train—; —advance; —barricade; —beleaguer; —besiege; —brandish; —break step; —bristle; —bluster; —campaign; —charge; —coerce; —crusade; —desert; —enlist; —enroll; —engage; —flock; —garrison; —invade; —intrench; —jostle; —lay siege; —mutiny; —patrol; —parry; —plod—; rake; —repulse; —retaliate; —revive; —slog; —snipe; —squander; —storm; —surrender; —tramp; —trudge; —ward off; —wield.
(See besieger, infantry, army, invader, militia.)

SOLDIERY

adjectives
ruthless; insolent; ferocious; desperate; sanguine; brutal; well-clad; riotous; vagabond; grim-faced; licentious; architectural; fierce.

SOLEMN

adverbs
unduly; curiously; ceremoniously; sacredly; piously; religiously; devoutly; reverentially; fervently; ritualistically; judicially; sternly; austerely; ponderously; gravely; seriously; alarmingly; forbiddingly; unnecessarily; ominously; portentously; depressingly; impressively; magnificently; extraordinarily; gravely; grimly; ridiculously; absurdly; ludicrously; unreasonably; occasionally; unexpectedly; unusually; curiously; strangely; reverently; uncommonly.

SOLEMNITY

adjectives

severe; majestic; religious; rare; mysterious; quaint; guarded; significant; pretentious; accustomed; symmetrical; grievous; unutterable; impressive; formal; professional; inaccessible; profound; dismal; preternatural; sweet; shallow; mournful; livid; royal.

verbs

alleviate—; dedicate in—; ease—; enthrone in—; impress—; maintain—; mar—; perform with—; preserve—; relax—; ruffle—; sustain—; temper—; —abashes; —awes; —chastens; —dampens; —dazzles; —depresses; —deters; —glooms; —inspires; —oppresses; —pervades; —sobers; —subdues.

(See ceremony, gravity, seriousness.)

SOLICIT (*v*)

adverbs

impudently; courteously; importunately; pertinaciously; timorously; underhandedly; earnestly; pressingly; urgently; insinuatingly.

(See request, ask, seek.)

SOLICITATION

adjectives

hinted; earnest; sickening; pressing; tearful; urgent; insinuating.

verbs

brush aside—s; dismiss—; elicit—; endure —; ignore—; pursue—s; yield to—; —s carry weight; —influences; —irks; —moves; —plagues; —provokes; —riles (colloq.); —ruffles; —sways; —touches; —vexes; —wrings.

(See request, invitation, entreaty.)

SOLICITORS

adjectives

best-moving; fair; government; prominent; insistent.

SOLICITOUS

adverbs

tenderly; anxiously; eagerly; frantically; curiously; strangely; pretentiously; ostentatiously; cursorily; lovingly; affectionately; protectively; absurdly; ridiculously; responsibly; forebodingly; terribly.

SOLICITUDE

adjectives

constant; peculiar; passionate; quiet; liveliest; dismal; tenderest; loving; frozen; selfish; affectionate; profound; glorious; trembling; pitying; sincere; voluntary; paternal; friendly; deep.

verbs

allay—; assuage—; blench in—; cloak—; conceal—; deserve—; display—; distrust—; dwell in—; ease—; exhibit—; expose—; feign—; manifest—; relieve—; relish—; screen—; —besets; —deters; —harrows; —haunts; —obsesses; —perturbs; —preys on; —unnerves; —wracks; —wrings; inspire—.

(See anxiety, misgiving, care, concern, attention.)

SOLID

adverbs

unusually; satisfactorily; fortunately; securely; stably; remarkably; immovably; finally; desirably; sufficiently; safely; financially; structurally; commercially; warrantably; splendidly; undoubtedly; unbreakably.

SOLIDARITY

verbs

cement—; cleave—; compromise—; disrupt —; endanger—; fracture—; gnaw at—; hazard—; impair—; jeopardize—; link in —; maintain—; mar—; menace—; mould —; nurse—; preserve—; rend—; rupture—; sap—; shake—; split—; strain—; sustain —; threaten—; undermine—; weld—; —crumbles; —disintegrates; —prevails; —totters.

(See power, authority, leadership, union.)

SOLIDITY

adjectives

combined; moral; little; primitive; costly; imposing; mellow; false; stable.

SOLIDS

adjectives

atomic; precipitated; flaccid; geometrical; quiescent; elastic.

verbs

compress—; congeal into—; convert into—; dissolve—; excrete—; liquefy—; pierce—; precipitate—; pulverize—; vaporize—; —cohere; —contract; —disintegrate; —displace; —expand.

(See mass.)

SOLILOQUIZE (v)

adverbs

philosophically; morbidly; dejectedly; monotonously; ceaselessly; academically; sepulchrally.

(See utter, talk.)

SOLILOQUY

verbs

breathe—; deliver—; emit—; indulge in—; murmur—; mutter—; reflect in—; unfold —; utter—; voice—; —considers; —contemplates; —discourses; —expatiates on; —mediates; —moves; —ponders; —reasons; —reproaches; —reveals; —revolves; —touches.

(See speech, talk.)

SOLITARY

adverbs

restfully; delightfully; formidably; gloomily; forbiddingly; cheerlessly; pathetically; unhappily; remotely; alarmingly; disagreeably; desperately; desolately; impossibly; tragically; preferably; comfortably; selfishly; unexpectedly; undesirably; uncommonly; curiously; amazingly; insistently.

SOLITUDE

adjectives

mighty; unhallowed; dismal; heaving; tranquil; great; sylvan; proud; expectant; gladsome; splendid; social; musing; crowded; decent; dreary; sealed; oppressive; perfect; wildest; unbroken; mountain; vast; misty; populous; convenient; careless; morose; meditative; patient; arctic; fearful; rural; chilly; mystic; unweeping; delicious; utter; obscure; midnight; grave; dewy; gigantic; twilight; artificial; deep; majestic; moorland; solemn; inaccessible; sullen; serene; pastoral; restored.

verbs

abandon to—; abide in—; afford—; burden —; bear—; crave—; encompass—; endure —; evince—; incline to—; loathe—; long for—; mope in—; muse in—; ponder in—; recall in—; relegate to—; relish—; retire to—; sequester in—; shatter—; shun—; suffer—; welcome—; yearn for—; —cloaks; —deceives; —depresses; —detaches; —isolates; —penetrates; —stagnates.

(See isolation, loneliness, seclusion.)

SOLUBLE

adverbs

scarcely; highly; instantly; chemically; easily; obviously; manifestly; conveniently; handily; quickly; adaptably; commendably.

SOLUTION (explanation)

verbs

approach—; arrive at—; clarify—; comprehend—; demonstrate—; disagree with—; facilitate—; formulate—; furnish—; gain—; offer—; reach—; seek—; trace—; —coincides; —implies; —points; —racks.

(See explanation, interpretation.)

SOLUTION (general)

adjectives

dilute; saline; partial; attenuated; elusive; commonplace; classic; irritating; logical; colloidal; formless; transparent; decent; pacific; ultimate; dirt; deodorizing; obvious; antiseptic; adaptive; delightful; consequent; rational; supernatural; basic; successful; supersaturated; practical; satisfying; contemporary; sensible; equitable; ideal; peaceful; ordinary; lofty.

SOLUTION (mixture)

verbs

dilute—; dip—; gargle—; inject—; saturate with—; sponge—; —mixes; —strengthens; seek—.

(See mixture, juice, liquid, medicine.)

SOLVE (v)

adverbs

definitely; accurately; promptly; swiftly; mechanically; scientifically; ultimately; constructively; ingeniously; practically; basically; partially.

(See clear, explain.)

SOLVENT

adverbs

responsibly; reputedly; reputably; admirably; safely; financially; manifestly; acceptably; satisfactorily; fortunately; absolutely.

SOMBERNESS

verbs

alleviate—; brighten—; brood in—; droop in—; reflect—; relax—; relieve of—; ruffle —; sink into—; sulk in—; sustain—; —abashes; —awes; —dampens; —darkens; —

deepens; —dejects; —depresses; —envelops; —glooms; —illuminates; —oppresses; —permeates; —pervades; —saddens; —shadows; —weights.

(See darkness, melancholy, gravity, gloom.)

SOMBRE

adverbs

lugubriously; gloomily; dismally; unaccountably; unnecessarily; unpleasantly; richly; sumptuously; harmoniously; fashionably; conventionally; disagreeably; overwhelmingly; mournfully; gravely; gruesomely; terribly; hauntingly; horribly.

SOMERSAULT

verbs

achieve—; avert—; avoid—; culminate in —; execute—; perfect—; perform—; practise—s; reverse—; —amazes; —astounds; —climaxes; —inverts; —surprises.

(See trick, leap.)

SOMETHING

adjectives

undefinable; coquettish; intangible; infinitesimal; misty; solemn; inestimable; unnatural; ghastly; unnamable; curious.

SOMNOLENT

adverbs

overwhelmingly; unaccountably; irresistibly; strangely; dully; overpoweringly; uncontrollably; inexplicably; abnormally; embarrassingly; alarmingly; inexpressibly.

SON

adjectives

giddy; mutilated; slow-minded; intended; scapegrace; accursed; hardy; illegitimate; reckless; instinctive; lawful; patriotic; enigmatic; murdered; hapless; prodigal; equivocal; misunderstood; degenerate; virtuous; astonished; blooming; surviving; indolent; observant; unkempt; gallant; ransomed; poor; illustrious; dutiful; purblind; film-loving; admirable; accursed; docile; stalwart; valiant; obedient; accomplished; wayward; humbled; tortured; first-born; enchanting; ungracious; goodly; brisk; eldest; handsome; patriotic; elegant; amiable; free-hearted; insignificant; mercenary; unappreciated; rude; energetic; exiled.

verbs

alienate—; bear—; beget—; castigate—; chastise—; conceive—; crave—; discipline —; disinherit—; disown—; endear to—; expel—; guide—; hunger for—; inculcate in —; ingrain in—; instill in—; pamper—; renounce—; yearn for—; —assumes; —begets; —cherishes; —inherits; —relinquishes; —toddles.

(See child, offspring, daughter.)

SONG

adjectives

emotional; melodious; dramatic; characteristic; throbbing; shanty; voluntary; comic; faultless; boisterous; spiritual; mournful; scurrilous; pealing; solemn; humorous; ineffable; choral; monotonous; rapturous; tranquil; echoing; vapid; immortal; buoyant; deathless; cheerful; weird; antiquated; impassioned; speechless; perpetual; artful; amorous; affectionate; irksome; unconnected; everlasting; protracted; joyous; provoking; unmusical; indolent; savage; drawling; ringing; lifeless; ribald; generous; gusty; rich; blithe; unpremeditated; mystic; shrill; laborious; foolish; magnetic; quivering; syncopated; pastoral; dropping; wondrous; jubilant; plaintive; tragic; parting; chastening; saucy; desperate; ear-breaking; coarse; sunny; eddying; arduous; grandest; wailing; fatal; medicinal; worthless; doleful; visible; yearning; piquant; rollicking; fiery; stifling; hideous; twilight; adventurous; belligerent; noble; nuptial

verbs

accompany—; break out into—; breathe—; carol—; chant—; compose—; dash into —; diffuse—; echo—; execute—; exploit —; flood with—; hum—; improvise—; intone—; lilt—; perform—; pipe—; perpetuate—; render—; stifle—; strike up—; trill —; twitter—; warble—; whistle—; —breaks out; —descends upon; —dwindles; —expresses; —evolves; —laments; —merges; —moderates; —modulates; —pierces; —s pour; —quavers; —recaptures; —ripples; —shatters; —subsides; —swells; —uplifts; —vibrates.

(See melody, jazz, ditty, incantation, music, chant, refrain, carol, hymn.)

SONGSTER

adjectives

exquisite; plumed; lingering; feathered; lifeless; medieval; radio.

SONNET

adjectives
commendatory; true; glowing; halting; wailful; memorable; soaring; conventional; stock; beauteous; insincere.

verbs
compose—; consecrate—; dash off—; dedicate—to; indite—; peruse—s; scan—; transcribe—; weave—; —amuses; —delights; —expresses; —glorifies; —immortalizes; —impresses; —reflects; —rhymes; —sentimentalizes; —treats of; —versifies.
(See poem.)

SONOROUS

adverbs
impressively; unctuously; chantingly; deeply; profoundly; resoundingly; challengingly; richly; magnificently; splendidly; remarkably; strangely; compellingly; majestically; regally; authoritatively.

SOOT

verbs
—begrimes; —besmears; —besmirches; —blackens; —blots; —blurs; —contaminates; —defiles; —eclipses; —flocculates; —jets; —obscures; —reeks; —screens; —settles; —smears; —smirches; —smudges; —soils; —sullies; —tarnishes; —veils.
(See carbon, powder, dust, smoke, fog.)

SOOTHE (*v*)

adverbs
maternally; infinitely; benevolently; compassionately; harmoniously; effectually; pleasingly.
(See pacify, calm.)

SOOTHING

adverbs
refreshingly; comfortingly; curatively; graciously; serenely; mildly; pleasantly; softly; gratefully; quietly; coolly; gently; blandly; especially; satisfyingly; remarkably; marvelously; tenderly; maternally; mercifully.

SOPHISTICATED

adverbs
consciously; impressively; proudly; vivaciously; absurdly; ridiculously; haughtily; pretentiously; extremely; unexpectedly; bitterly; stylishly; fashionably.

SOPHISTICATION

adjectives
subtle; sly; cool; quaint; hard-boiled; studied; brittle; surface; cruel.

verbs
acquire—; breed—; cultivate—; develop—; discard—; ingrain—; jar—; mould—; pierce—; stamp with—; shock—; —attracts; —beguiles; —bores; —enhances; —glosses; —impresses; —polishes; —reeks; —varnishes; —veneers.
(See manner, style.)

SOPHISTRY

adjectives
subtle; pompous; wild; delinquent; apparent.

SOPRANO

verbs
acclaim—; applaud—; present—; train—; —carols; —cracks; —cultivates; —enthralls; —entrances; —executes; —exercises; —expresses; —flutes; —lilts; —modulates; —moves; —performs; —renders; —strains; —tours; —trills; —twitters.
(See singer, choir, chorus.)

SORCERER

adjectives
miserable; hostile; unfortunate; accused; wicked.

SORDID

adverbs
disagreeably; undoubtedly; atrociously; curiously; basely; uncommonly; unreasonably; unbelievably; incredibly; unthinkably; outrageously; outlandishly; scandalously; terribly; fearfully; detestably; barbarously; unspeakably; stingily; grossly; miserably; churlishly; greedily; foully; unaccountably; unwarrantably; strangely; utterly; undeniably.

SORE

adjectives
swollen; embossed; inward; festering; ever-fretting; raw; horrid.

verbs
aggravate—; cauterize—; diagnose—; disinfect—; dress—; extirpate—; irritate—; lance—; lick—; salve—; treat—; —atrophies; —breaks out; —cankers; —chafes; —defaces; —discharges; —disfigures; —en-

venoms; —festers; —ferments; —infects; —inflames; —occurs; —persists; —rankles; —responds; —scabs; —suppurates; —taints; —throbs.

(See rash, inflammation, canker, abscess, blister, boil.)

adverbs
painfully; curiously; extremely; miserably; infectiously; dangerously; alarmingly; unaccountably; strangely; fearfully; feverishly; unfortunately; cruelly; exceedingly; naturally.

SORROW

adjectives
dreaming; querulous; sole; profound; despondent; inextinguishable; poignant; sacred; slow; imperious; human; stormy; transient; impetuous; faithless; helpless; unfeigned; sleepless; premature; stifled; domestic; dying; eternal; bitter; silent; deep; hearty; trampling; mortal; uncheered; sentimental; dark; dumb; passionate; crushing; unmitigated; sincere; romantic; imagined; fantastic; foolish; vehement; dried; accumulated; gnarling; noisy; desperate; oppressive; peculiar; grievous; dull; present; aesthetic; inarticulate; strange; concealed.

verbs
afflict with—; appease—; assail with—; assuage—; brim with—; cast—; cloak—; console—; contain—; couch in—; crush—; depict—; derive—; fade out of—; inflict—; intensify—; lament—; multiply—s; relieve—; remedy—; restrain—; share—; swallow—; unfold—; —befalls; —blights; —burdens; —chastens; —consumes; —darkens; —deepens; —embraces; —mars; —overburdens; —overwhelms; —purges.

(See commiseration, sadness, suffering, grief.)

SORRY

adverbs
pitifully; wretchedly; sincerely; genuinely; truly; pitiably; miserably; grievously; profoundly; deeply; abjectly; remorsefully; embarrassingly; humbly; bitterly; regretfully; penitently; admittedly; extremely; immeasurably; reasonably; somewhat.

SORT

adjectives
particular; unsatisfactory; enthusiastic; whimsical; barren; vulgar; prophetical; stimulating; grossest; truest; meanest; desultory; outspoken; odd.

SOUL

adjectives
repentant; harmonic; circling; stormy; witty; genial; learned; troubled; hopeful; flaming; lost; living; amiable; kindred; sinful; erring; frank; reviving; poisonous; ardent; aesthetic; pagan; raptured; maddened; pervading; poetic; wronged; cheated; stagnant; unblemished; zealous; sensitive; loving; neat; gentle; departed; passive; tortured; malignant; impassive; noblest; helpless; starved; susceptible; silly; ravished; withered; luckless; chastened; desolate; lofty; singular; eager; radiant; wondrous; vile; daring; suspended; genial; trusting; polluted; vigorous; willing; separate; fettered; visionary; human; righteous; heroic; grateful; ingenious; deathless; rapt; naked; lifted; ecstatic; flagging; heated; dear; dawning; deluded; vitriolic; artist; full; loyal; groveling; solitary; agitated; gross; fainting; secret; silent; resolute; defeated; common; maddening; divine; brooding; incarnate; harmonious; convivial; morbid; comprehensive; speaking; priceless; wounded; craven; inmost; smitten; offending; spheric; guilty; poisonous; tender; pervading; universal; delicious; haughty; debilitated; passionate; progressive; saturate; feeble; liberal; multitudinous (pl); plastic; unripened; unstained; antique; agitated; festered; regal; truthful; trembling; kingly; emaciated; torpid; nimble; embryonic; redeemed; manly; devastated; reptile; shuddering; unwasting; frivolous; exploring; blotched; dead; scintillating; ransomed; pious; enthralling; delicate; pessimistic; tardy; virile; active; dauntless; altered; crude; eccentric; wakeful; elevated; cavalier; cantankerous; bleeding; clearest; stubborn; yearning; truant; dying; prevailing; introspective; credulous; misguided; exalted; angelic; cautious; charitable; grieved; timid; ardent; merry; spotted; callous; watchful; jealous; departed; intercurrent; countless (pl); rational; hungry; abstracted; wiser; patient; inviolable; obstinate; sordid; guileless; preserved; rich; bewildered; mean; knightly; sober; hideous; distracted; practical; simple; immortal; torn; famished; straying.

verbs
beguile—; beleaguer—; benefit—; bruise—; clothe—; clutter—; commit—; consign—; crush—; deliver—; deplore—; drain—; drown—; empty—; ennoble—; enrapture—; explore—; feast—; feed—; fire—; fortify—; gratify—; harrow—; impel—; incarnate—; incrust—; inflame—; loose—; mask—; mold —; nourish—; perjure—; pour—; purge—; purify—; rack—; raise—; release—; rend —; reveal—; salve—; satisfy—; saturate—; scourge—; sear—; search—; sell—; shadow —; smite—; soothe—; stain—; steep—; stir —; surrender—; tear— touch— transplant —; unburden—; untrim—; unveil—; wrap —; weary—; wrench—; —awakens; —bows; —breathes; —cries; —dares; —exults; —flames; —grieves; —governs; —lives; —palsies; —pants; —perishes; —quails; —quickens; —rebels; —revolts; —sees; —shudders; —struggles; —thirsts for; —wakens; —wavers; —wells up.
(See spirit.)

SOUND

adjectives
incongruous; obdurate; joyful; financial; explosive; ecstatic; numerous (pl); roaring; hissing; peculiar; quavering; plaintive; sprinkled; similar; lamentable; languid; unauthorized; elementary; crisp; muffled; unearthly; affrighting; thundering; lulling; empty; winged; perfidious; tinkling; imposing; ear-splitting; flat; petulant; scratching; powerful; human; horrid; answering; pulsating; puffing; monotonous; cropping; discordant; ominous; multitudinous (pl); articulate; distinct; terrible; mysterious; harmonious; faint; moaning; jarring; agreeable; perfect; blithe; thwacking; sad; romantic; weird; furtive; immortal; obnoxious; maddening; unresting; hideous; menacing; onomatopoeic; agglomerative; endearing; tuneful; stormy; incessant; plain; strange; dentilingual; obstructed; hoarse; chuckling; caressing; murmuring; animated; understanding; munching; increasing; howling; hollow; sullen; meaningless; cruel; heterogeneous; droning; pinging; wandering; delicious; cracking; kindred; spiritual; convulsed; clattering; perpetual; humming; evil; flattering; various (pl); murderous; consecutive; rumbling; gurgling; sensuous; rattling; joyous; dubious; rushing; monosyllabic; muttering; celestial; sweet; stealthy; whizzing; soothing; slight; throaty; suggestive; melodious; eminent; confused; melancholy; healing; whistling; vague; clashing; raving; siren; repining; soft; recurrent; lambent; portentous; carefree; grunting; mirthful; false; sighing; raspy; idle; vocal; conversational; hammering; chirping; shocking; rhythmic; blissful; scientific; droll; harsh; fundamental; continuous; appalling; ghostly.

verbs
absorb—; alter—; attune to—; carry—; communicate—; deaden—; detect—; dilute —; direct—; disguise—; echo—; elicit—; emit—; give forth—; induce—; lessen—; limit—; mellow—; muffle—; interpret—; sharpen—; smother—; transmit—; waft—; visualize—; smother—; —alarms; —babbles; —ceases; —comforts; —dins; —echoes; —emanates; —s emerge; —falls; —s gibber; —s gurgle; —lulls; —penetrates; —reawakens; —reechoes; —registers; —reverberates; —scatters; —s trouble; —vanishes.
(See noise.)

adverbs
fortunately; wholesomely; securely; luckily; admirably; commendably; satisfactorily; unusually; magnificently; splendidly; impressively; gloriously; perfectly; remarkably; excellently; sufficiently; superbly; miraculously.

SOUND (v)

adverbs
peremptorily; exasperatingly; incessantly; harshly; audibly; incredibly; importunately; celestially; mournfully; incongruously; thunderously; monotonously; discordantly; ominously; mysteriously; jarringly; thwackingly; weirdly; obnoxiously; portentously; appallingly.
(See express, hear.)

SOUNDLESS

adverbs
breathlessly; curiously; strangely; eerily; mysteriously; oddly; extraordinarily; miraculously; admirably; pleasantly; fortunately; furtively; stealthily; carefully; cautiously; warily; perfectly; remarkably; incredibly.

SOUP

adjectives
thick; substantial; hearty; savory; scalding; canned.

verbs
administer—; bolt—; brew—; concoct—; dispatch—; gulp—; guzzle—; imbibe—; ladle—; prepare—; relish—; savor—; season—; sip—; spice—; strain—; swill—; —gelatinizes; —invigorates; —nourishes; —replenishes; —scalds; —tempts; —thickens; —tickles the palate.
(See broth, food, liquid.)

SOUR

adverbs
disagreeably; acridly; yeastily; pleasantly; horribly; startlingly; unexpectedly; oddly; mustily; offensively; inedibly; overly; extremely; curiously; unpalatably; unpleasantly; rancidly.

SOURCE

adjectives
copious (pl); reliable; various (pl); authentic; abundant (pl); external; outside; delightful; usual; proximate; inexhaustible; scanty; respectable; distorted; vital; real; occult; festering; fruitful; paternal; worthwhile; known; classical; valuable; bounteous; recurrent; vulgar; artificial; full-fed; radiant; prolific; frequent; unrelated; continued; grand; editorial; important; shallow; true; inactive; miscellaneous; invisible; authoritative.

verbs
attack—; borrow from—; determine—; dry up—; flow from—; emanate from—; exhaust —; poison—; replenish from—; search for —; spring from—; stamp out—; strike at —; tap—; trace to—; track down—; utilize —; —constitutes; —feeds; —supplies.
(See origin, beginning.)

SOUTH

adjectives
aromatic; fragrant; far; soft; fiery; quiet; feudal; warm.

SOVEREIGN

adjectives
neutral; successive (pl); ruthless; ambitious; legitimate; hapless; territorial; hereditary; joint; youthful; sceptered; vigilant; squatter; spiritual; unchallenged; inscrutable; tribal; feeble; diminished; glorious; gracious; individual.

SOVEREIGNTY

verbs
ascend to—; assume—; endanger—; exercise —; exert—; extend—; gain—; impair—; invest with—; jeopardize—; limit—; maintain—; relinquish—; respect—; retain—; usurp—; weaken—; yield—; —crumbles; —spreads; —sways; —totters; —wields.
(See crown, dominion, power.)

SOW (*v*)

adverbs
mechanically; scientifically; scatteredly; widely; sparsely; thickly; luxuriantly.
(See scatter, plant.)

SPACE

adjectives
shoreless; encumbered; furlong; ample; plenteous; eternal; coming; boundless; allotted; inconsiderable; porous; astonishing; globular; unnecessary; limitless; tumultuous; immense; adequate; stabling; intervening; trackless; vast; endless; editorial; unoccupied; wide; infinite; successive (pl); watery; projecting; sufficient; weary; choking; unbounded; awful; pervading; shaded; hoary; stellar; vaulted; neutral; storage; restricted; azure; generous; interminable; imaginary; dimensional; intermediate; ethereal; tenantless; breathing; grudging; surface; mightiest; betokened; available; soundless; angry.

verbs
acquire—; augment—; confine to—; cramp for—; dash—; define—; determine—; devote—; diminish—; encamp on—; estimate —; evacuate—; extend—; grant—; insert in —; lack—; limit—; lodge in—; narrow—; nestle in—; penetrate—; permeate—; pervade—; provide—; regulate—; stare in—; tenant—; transmit through—; withdraw from—; —accommodates; —dwindles; —expands; —ranges.
(See capacity, area.)

SPACIOUS

adverbs
adequately; satisfactorily; delightfully; wonderfully; amply; unexpectedly; amazingly; uncommonly; extremely; unnecessarily; admirably; commendably; extraordinarily; magnificently; splendidly; remarkably; conveniently; charmingly; reasonably; vastly.

SPACIOUSNESS

verbs
disclose—; relax in—; reveal—; revel in—; survey—; —affords; —allows; —dazzles; —emancipates; —enables; —enthralls; —facilitates; —frees; —gives scope; —leaves; —liberates; —overawes; —overwhelms; —permits; —unfolds.
(See luxury, comfort, vastness.)

SPAN

adjectives
incredible; toil-stained; fleeting; artistic; infinitesimal; pitiful; allotted; sapphire; natural; life; useful.

verbs
abbreviate—; bridge—; elongate—; fuse—; interlink—; limit—; prolong—; protract—; reduce—; shorten—; stretch—; survive—; terminate—; unite—; —breaches; —elapses; —extends; —spreads; —stretches.
(See bridge, spread, extent.)

SPANK (*v*)

adverbs
resoundingly; heartlessly; cruelly; penally; repeatedly; viciously; explosively.
(See whip, paddle.)

SPARE (*v*)

adverbs
mercifully; generously; benevolently; willingly; voluntarily; magnanimously; nobly; benignantly.
(See save, refrain.)

SPARKLE

adjectives
fiery; exciting; phosphoric; odd; epigrammatic; conversational.

SPARKLE (*v*)

adverbs
splendidly; radiantly; frostily; keenly; luminously; phosphorically; gaily; spectacularly.
(See glitter, gleam.)

SPARKLING

adverbs
brightly; youthfully; ingenuously; happily; comically; brilliantly; wittily; facetiously; humorously; pleasantly; whimsically; nonsensically; fantastically; drolly; scintillatingly; delightfully; entrancingly; piquantly; thrillingly; stimulatingly.

SPARKS

adjectives
wandering; poor; glimmering; smoldering; enkindling; glowing; broad; bold; angry; starry; numbered; primitive; benignant; luminous; involuntary; immortal; feeble; hot; compensatory; latent; dubious; lively.

verbs
apply—; extinguish—; fan—; kindle—; quench—; smother—; snuff out—; —dazzle; —die; —dwell; —endanger; —enkindle; —flicker; —fly; —glow; —grow; —ignite; —illuminate; —inflame; —radiate; —shoot from; —smoulder; —strike; —tremble.
(See light, fire, flame, flash.)

SPARROW

verbs
—busies; —chases; —cheers; —chirps; —circles; —drifts; —flocks; —flutters; —s haunt; —perks up; —plagues; —robs; —soars; —steals; —thrives on; —tucks away; —twitters; —wanders; —warbles; —wheels; —whistles.
(See bird.)

SPARTAN

adverbs
resolutely; intrepidly; dauntlessly; determinedly; unflinchingly; marvelously; invincibly; fearlessly; heroically; valiantly; doughtily.

SPASM

adjectives
blind; unseemly; terrible; temporary; social; fierce; clonic; tonic; violent; sudden; painful.

verbs
afflict with—s; alleviate—; assuage—; burst into—; characterize by—s; check—; contract in—s; diagnose—; excite—; mitigate—; moderate—; pacify—; prevent—; prolong—; quell—; reduce—; relieve—; subdue—; —affects; —agonizes; —convulses; —denotes; —jerks; —lessens; —overcomes; —passes; —ruffles; —seizes; —strains; —s wrack.
(See convulsion, fit, contraction.)

SPASMODIC

adverbs
convulsively; curiously; strangely; inexplicably; regularly; oddly; terrifyingly; violent-

ly; bafflingly; perplexingly; heartbreakingly; unpredictably.

SPEAK (v)

adverbs

epigrammatically; euphemistically; characteristically; impressively; vaguely; pompously; grandiloquently; verbosely; melodiously; euphonically; pointedly; periodically; mournfully; rationally; derogatorily; disparagingly; judiciously; coaxingly; optimistically; respectfully; articulately; conservatively; tremulously; uncompromisingly; reassuringly; energetically; laconically; icily; mellifluously; glibly; contemptuously; indulgently; discursively; tensely; venomously; circuitously; edifyingly; directly; simply; impudently; figuratively; passionately; sublimely; scurrilously; precipitantly; solicitously; warily; emphatically; volubly; ironically; negatively; persuasively; exquisitely.

(See talk, say, express.)

SPEAKER

adjectives

distinguished; influential; conspicuous; adequate; fluent; brilliant; liberal; adroit; inspiring; dependable; impressive; boring; eloquent; timorous; scarred; hardy; flippant; principal; effective; polished; obstreperous; finished; handicapped; unintelligible; scintillating; deft.

verbs

applaud—; badger—; compliment—; confuse—; divert—; eulogize—; heckle—; introduce—; jibe—; laud—; silence—; —addresses; —admonishes; —articulates; —besmirches; —blares; —castigates; —chastises; —condemns; —conveys; —disclaims; —delivers; —digresses; —drawls; —drives home; —enunciates; —expatiates; —expostulates; —fulminates; —gesticulates; —gestures; —harangues; —insinuates; —inveighs against; —laments; —orates; —pounds; —prates; —proclaims; —rants; —raps; —rebuts; —refutes; —shocks; —slanders; —slings; —slurs; —snaps; —stammers; —stutters; —utters; —discourses.

(See debater, orator, politician, minister.)

SPEAR

adjectives

battled; glittering; enormous; broad; well-balanced; serried; splintering; stabbing; bloody; couched; barbed; beaming; shadowy; poisoned; brazen-headed.

verbs

arm with—; barb—; brandish—; cast—; edge—; extract—; fashion—; fling—; hurl—; impale on—; let fly—; level—; taper—; —s bristle; —fells; —flies; —gores; —penetrates; —perforates; —pricks; —punctures; —riddles; —spikes; —stabs; —staves in; —whirs; —whizzes.

(See dart, lance, missile.)

SPECIALIST

adjectives

celebrated; pretended; minute; cold-blooded; qualified; experienced; high-priced.

verbs

baffle—; consult—; employ—; engage—; recommend—; recruit—s; —advocates; —analyzes; —assures; —concludes; —s confer; —counsels; —diagnoses; —discerns; —exhorts; —prescribes; —relieves; —resurrects; —restores.

(See expert, physician, scholar.)

SPECIALTY

verbs

characterize—; designate—; determine—; devote to—; emphasize—; engage in—; excel in—; foster—; indicate—; master—; recognize—; restrict to—; stress—; warrant—.

(See work, science, art, knowledge.)

SPECIES

adjectives

particular; gigantic; important; superior; representative; prehistoric; foreign; tropical; new; dominant; extinct; distinct; collective; terrestrial; principal; mimetic; delightful; incipient; corresponding; subtle; unique; domesticated; nobler; nigh-perfected; rare.

verbs

breed—; classify—; corrupt—; cross—; discover—; elevate—; exalt—; exterminate—; group—; inbreed—; perpetuate—; preserve—; propagate—; refine—; reproduce—; revive—; segregate—; uplift—; vitiate—; —abounds; —congregates; —degenerates; —embraces; —evolves; —includes; —ornaments; —rehabilitates; —relates; —survives.

(See race, group, classification, variety, category.)

SPECIFIC

adverbs

highly; helpfully; particularly; accurately; singularly; intimately; markedly; appropriately; typically; usually; uncommonly; satisfactorily; duly; conveniently; pertinently; advantageously; especially; minutely; sufficiently; conclusively; ·opportunely.

SPECIFICATIONS

adjectives

factory; provisional; essential; exact; strict; broad; detailed; minute; manufacturing; stated; licensed; general; sweeping; all-inclusive.

verbs

abide by—; adhere to—; cleave to—; deviate from—; diverge from—; draw—; embody in—; follow—; require—; standardize —; —call for; —conform; —define; —demand; —describe; —designate; —detail; —determine; —embrace; —enumerate; —itemize; —particularize; —regulate.

(See regulations, definition, details, items.)

SPECIFY (*v*)

adverbs

definitely; distinctly; provisionally; essentially; strictly; broadly; minutely; generally.

(See designate, name.)

SPECIMEN

adjectives

stalwart; active; unique; marvelous; abundant (pl); splendid; favorable; knobby; sundry (pl); hard-looking; precious; complete; admirable; acknowledged; superb; handsome; genuine; huge; lingering; superior; excellent; sickly; occasional; ferocious; prolonged; pleasing; puny; given; enormous; good-looking; unfair.

verbs

attract—; bag—; collect—s; dissect—; exhibit—; guard—; hunt—; mount—; preserve—; prize—; pursue—; search for—; seek—; snare—; stalk—; stuff—; trap—; value—; —evades; —exemplifies; —illustrates.

(See animal, sample.)

SPECK

adjectives

frothy; nebulous; morbid; inconsequential; eccentric; tiniest; swimming; microscopic; isolated; brilliant; shadowy; furthest; pitted.

SPECKLED

adverbs

unpleasantly; unfortunately; unluckily; prettily; beautifully; artificially; inconveniently; unsalably; unprofitably; completely; strangely; oddly; perplexingly; unaccountably; inexplicably.

SPECTACLE (*general*)

adjectives

ghastly; pleasant; wild; impressive; weird; singular; garish; bewildering; placid; awful; imposing; depressing; appalling; revolting; remarkable; religious; owl-eyed; solemn; lordly; striking; stupendous; damp; theatrical; picturesque; hideous; finer; shameful; elaborate; fairy; odious; inspiring; unhallowed; impassioned; fearful; miserable; gorgeous; sly; beaming; savage; gala; silent; triumphant; pitiful; novel; benevolent; magnificent; direful; daring; wondrous; entrancing; ignoble; attractive; unwonted; unexpected; unique; grandmotherly; extraordinary; splendid; everlasting; mossy; monstrous; menacing; chorographic; unprecedented.

SPECTACLE (*show*)

verbs

unfold—; view—; witness—; —affords; —appeals; —caricatures; —fascinates.

(See exhibition, show, display.)

SPECTACLED

adverbs

heavily; forbiddingly; formidably; grimly; primly; unwillingly; unattractively; unbecomingly; horribly; comically; carefully; helpfully; carefully; skilfully; finally; stylishly; protectively; fashionably; demurely; deceptively.

SPECTACLES (*glasses*)

verbs

adjust—; blink through—; exhibit—; prescribe—; toy with—.

SPECTACULAR

adverbs

highly; impressively; magnificently; splendidly; brilliantly; regally; royally; colorfully; gorgeously; gloriously; imposingly; majestically; dazzlingly; processionally; dramatically; fantastically; unusually; sensationally; superbly.

SPECTATORS

adjectives
passing; broad; bold; angry; unpracticed; indifferent; festive; singular; curious; distinguished; impartial; patient; unlearned; passive; crowded; astonished; dignified; plebeian; bored; ambitious; attentive; callous.

verbs
accommodate—; affront—; amaze—; amuse —; astound—; attract—; awe—; beguile—; bore—; cheat—; dazzle—; dumbfound—; electrify—; enrage—; entrance—; impress —; petrify—; regale—; scan—; stun—; thrill—; —applaud; —behold; —clamor; —cram; —disperse; —fret; —gasp; —heckle; —irk; —jam; —lure; —marvel; —pour; —rivet; —witness.
(See hearer, crowd, bystander, audience.)

SPECTER

adjectives
ridiculous; gibbering; looming; dancing; ghastly; gloomy; ghostly; confused; grim; grisly; horrid.

verbs
cast—; fight off—; goggle at—; —dissolves; —dreads; —evaporates; —fades; —floats; —glares; —glowers; —haunts; —looms; —melts away; —penetrates; —permeates; —petrifies; —plagues; —terrifies; —vanishes.
(See apparition, phantom, ghost.)

SPECULATE (*v*)

adverbs
disastrously; rashly; divertingly; chimerically; philosophically; casually; adroitly; financially; contemplatively; ridiculously; abstractly; vaguely; theoretically; ingeniously; shrewdly.
(See meditate, guess.)

SPECULATION

adjectives
grandest; casual; discursive; sympathetic; delighted; daring; philosophic; adroit; colossal; presumptuous; abstruse; financial; humble; enthusiastic; humanitarian; idle; imaginative; contemplative; doubtful; loftier; fantastic; visionary; ridiculous; moody; gambling; delectable; awful; mercenary; disastrous; abstract; rational; improbable; favorite; empty; vague; sad; wild; unpremeditated; amused; adventurous; original; heedless; affectionate; erring; theoretical; ingenious; prejudicial; deep.

verbs
absorb in—; admonish—; arouse—; denounce—; deter from—; discourage—; dismiss—; dominate—; engage in—; hush—; indulge in—; license—; plunge into—; prohibit—; restrain—; resume—; risk in—; stake on—; torture—; —chances; —endangers; —fascinates; —gropes; —jeopardizes; —lures; —prohibits; —ventures.
(See gambling, meditation, transaction.)

SPECULATOR

adjectives
unscrupulous; dauntless; ingenious; grasping; keen; able; scientific; curbstone; shrewd; plunging; rich.

SPEECH

adjectives
thoughtless; voluble; angry; goodly; copious; long; stirring; maiden; gracious; heartless; chanting; epigrammatic; purest; wholesome; noblest; unrestrained; irrelevant; whispered; ambiguous; occasional; dual; sacred; moderate; impromptu; dedicatory; average; normal; saucy; meaningless; familiar; true; strict; after-luncheon; nebulous; laughing; decent; much-abused; impertinent; strong; vague; well-prepared; oracular; disrespectful; impressive; indignant; devoted; candid; elaborate; derogatory; characteristic; voiceless; extraordinary; eloquent; perfunctory; persuasive; masterly; articulate; demonstrative; rough; facetious; muddled; rasping; plaintive; powerful; whining; fraudulent; graceless; sibilant; complimentary; winged; taciturn; resistance; appropriate; sententious; consonantal; immemorial; intolerant; yearning; pedantic; supposititious; seditious; appreciative; villainous; patriotic; intelligible; expressive; champagne; stump; explosive; inflammatory; treasonable; high; momentous; pursuing; melted; deprecatory; flattering; lazy; composite; private; deliberating; flamboyant; explicit; flirtatious; fluent; luxuriant; royal; ghost-written; effective; reserved; rhetorical; voluble; fastidious; stifled; funeral; artistic; morning; inaudible; incharitable; wandering; dangerous; previous; strict; corrupted; free; manly;

broken; rattling; skillful; triumphant; graceful; higher; untimely; aimless; desolate; florid; fervid; common; impudent; nasal; uncensored; farewell; long-winded; memorized.

verbs
adjust—; ape—; augment—; book—; coach —; color—; compose—; confine—; cultivate —; deliver—; deprecate—; dismiss—; embellish—; endow—; extend—; flood—; incorporate in—; interlard—; intersperse—; polish—; pour forth—; prolong—; recite—; reel off—; respond to—; salt—; spout—; stumble through—; suppress—; time—; —appraises; —betrays; —declaims; —degenerates; —drones; —eulogizes; —flows; —glitters; —humors; —matures; —mingles; —thunders; —transcends; —wearies.

(See lecture, recital, declamation, discourse, oration, address.)

SPEECHLESS

adverbs
suddenly; strangely; utterly; curiously; embarrassingly; pathetically; bashfully; awkwardly; ineptly; shyly; clumsily; timidly; boorishly; loutishly; overwhelmingly; emotionally; miserably; wretchedly; unaccountably.

SPEED

adjectives
violent; dependable; superior; furious; imagined; convenient; breakneck; impressive; wonted; requisite; initial; amazing; thrilling; noiseless; specified; railway; evil; frightful; uninterrupted; incredible; utmost; high; accelerated; skyey; desired; fabulous; surprising; sufficient; diminished; careless; incredible; flashing; electric; lightning; moderate; reasonable; sustained; intoxicating; bidding.

verbs
accelerate—; arrest—; attain—; check—; curb—; diminish—; exceed—; gauge—; goad to—; maintain—; moderate—; propel at—; regale—; slacken—; spur to—; sustain —; throttle—; urge—; —alarms; —endangers; —exhilarates; —facilitates; —intoxicates; —jeopardizes; —menaces; —outstrips; —spurts.

(See momentum, velocity.)

SPEEDY

adverbs
incredibly; increasingly; effortlessly; mercifully; crazily; tragically; awkwardly; uncomfortably; distressingly; painfully; breathlessly; impetuously; perilously; unaccountably; surprisingly; astonishingly; moderately; dangerously; lightly; remarkably; precipitately; incalculably.

SPELL

adjectives
potent; unsolvable; heavenly; fascinating; mesmeric; drowsy; breathing; springtime; subtle; melancholy; hideous; maddened; baleful; appreciable; beguiling; cabalistical; funereal; wondrous; ineffable; savage; mighty; undying; wizard.

verbs
allay—; assuage—; cast—; conjure up—; exercise—; exert—; intensify—; overcome —; struggle under—; weave—; wield—; —bewitches; —charms; —enthralls; —fascinates; —hypnotizes; —lures; —magnetizes; —overwhelms; —permeates; —persists; —prevails; —ruffles; —entrances.

(See charm, enchantment, glamor, incantation.)

SPELL (v)

adverbs
accurately; promptly; involvedly; complicatedly; abbreviatedly; originally.

(See unravel, unfold.)

SPELLBOUND

adverbs
rapturously; raptly; earnestly; intently; magically; fascinatedly; eagerly; completely; utterly; curiously; strangely; marvelously; involuntarily; helplessly.

SPEND (v)

adverbs
tranquilly; recklessly; exclusively; lavishly; rashly; affluently; liberally; fabulously; idly; clandestinely; royally.

(See expend, squander.)

SPHERE

adjectives
glimmering; exalted; higher; bewildering; wheeling; murderous; mortal; youthful; native; diurnal; dusky; starriest; lucid; kingless; sublunary; luscious; ripe; great; mental; unthinking; crystal; softer; danc-

ing; stormy; pure; social; destined; heavenly; singing; unknown; calmer; mundane; alien; blazing; martial; political; far-off; willing; different; enchanted; celestial; humble; reachless; sensuous; untrodden; benighted; legitimate; whirling; poised; interstellar.

verbs
allot—; broaden—; confine to—; deepen—; dominate—; emerge from—; enlarge—; extend—; invade—; limit—; narrow—; penetrate—; permeate—; pierce—; preserve—; reject from—; restrict—; rule—; tread—; widen—; —s narrow; —s overlap; —ranges.
(See jurisdiction, region, position, province, globe.)

SPICE

adjectives
pungent; rich; strange; bartered; powerful; strong; odorous.

verbs
adulterate—; blend with—; impart—; infuse—; inject—; savor—; —bites; —embalms; —flavors; —nauseates; —pervades; —pickles; —preserves; —scents; —seasons.
(See mustard, flavoring.)

SPICY

adverbs
pleasantly; fragrantly; pungently; redolently; lingeringly; arrestingly; refreshingly; freshly; pleasingly; strongly; delicately; exquisitely; enchantingly; charmingly; delectably; intoxicatingly; richly; attractively; exotically.

SPIDER

adjectives
intrusive; bloated; putrid; weaving; hardy.

verbs
—attacks; —clambers up; —clings; —constructs; —dances; —dangles; —devours; —emerges; —entices; —envenoms; —s infest; —inhabits; —lies in wait; —loops; —paralyzes; —poisons; —s possess; —preys upon; —scrambles; —scurries; —snares; —spins; —stalks; —strikes; —suspends from; —traps; —weaves.
(See insect.)

SPIN (v)

adverbs
scientifically; assiduously; tirelessly; automatically; vigorously; industriously; dizzily; monotonously; sickeningly.
(See twirl, whirl.)

SPINE

verbs
brace—; compress—; curve—; damage—; dislocate—; expose—; fracture—; impair—; inflame—; inject into—; irritate—; lacerate—; protect—; puncture—; sheathe—; strengthen—; support—; tap—; x ray—; —bristles; —controls; —flashes; —quivers; —shudders; —transmits.
(See bone.)

SPINELESS

adverbs
utterly; despicably; contemptibly; cravenly; arrantly; palpably; obviously; notoriously; confessedly; openly; pitiably; shamefully; ingloriously; infamously; terribly; unconscionably; recreantly; distressingly; pitifully; disgustingly.

SPINSTER

adjectives
ardent; unpredictable; resigned; anemic; withered; hopeless; contented; man-shy; miserable.

SPIRE

adjectives
humble; ornate; tapering; slender; friendly; jagged; feathery; tranquil; flaming; graceful; gleaming; soaring; mountain; steadfast; diminishing; rocky; numberless (pl); octagonal; exquisite; far-off.

verbs
ascend—; clamber up—; descend—; discern—; erect—; impale on—; mount—; raze—; scale—; surmount—; suspend from—; —s bristle; —s cluster; —looms; —s shimmer; —soars; —tapers; —topples.
(See tower, stalk.)

SPIRIT

adjectives
abiding; absent; adventurous; aggravated; aggressive; airy; alleged; altruistic; animal; animating; apathetic; ardent; arrogant; artistic; aspiring; audacious; barren; beauteous; becoming; bellicose; belligerent; benevolent; bodiless; benignant; blessed;

boastful; bold; boundless; braced; braver; brazen; bubbling; buoyant; burgeoning; Byronic; burlesquing; calculating; cernuous; combative; charming; chaste; chastened; cherished; chimerical; churlish; commercial; common; compassionate; competitive; complacent; confident; congenial; contagious; contented; contrite; courageous; courtier; craving; creative; critical; damned; dangerous; darksome; dedicated; dejected; demonic; determined; devilish; disconsolate; disembodied; divine; drooping; earnest; ebbing; electric; embittered; emancipated; emulous; encumbered; enlightened; enlivened; enticing; ephemeral; equable; erect; erring; ever-soaring; ethereal; excellent; excited; evil; exclusive; exuberant; facinorous; faint; fallen; familiar; fantastic; fastidious; fervent; festive; feverish; fiery; fighting; flabby; flaming; flashy; flexible; fluttering; foreign; fractious; fraternal; free; fresh; gay; generous; genial; gentle; gloomy; glorious; goaded; grave; gray; grudging; guiding; hackneyed; happy; harassed; hardy; haughty; heedless; helpless; heroic; high; horrible; hospitable; hostile; huge; illustrious; imaged; immaterial; immortal; impatient; imperial; imperishable; impertinent; impetuous; inborn; incongruous; inconstant; indefatigable; independent; indignant; indomitable; inexorable; inexpiable; insurgent; internal; intrepid; introspective; intuitive; invincible; irascible; iron; joyous; judicial; kindly; kindred; kingly; laboring; laggard; lavish; leading; lewd; liberal; lonely; lovable; low; lustrous; magnanimous; majestic; malicious; malignant; managing; martial; masculine; meanest; mercenary; mercurial; migratory; militant; ministering; misguided; mixed; moderate; moving; mutinous; mysterious; nameless; neighboring; neutral; nimble; normal; noble; noxious; obdurate; paradoxical; parting; patronizing; perfect; persecuting; pert; perturbed; pervading; petulant; philanthropic; philosophical; poetic; practical; predominant; presumptuous; profane; prosaic; proscriptive; provincial; public; purest; purged; pythonic; quaint; queer; querulous; rabid; questioning; racial; radical; rallied; rampant; ransomed; rapacious; rare; rational; reasonable; rebellious; regenerate; released; repugnant; resolute; responsive; restless; romantic; roving; ruling; sacerdotal; sacred; scattered; scientific; searching; secret; secular; self-conscious; sensitive; serene; serious; silent; skipping; skittish; lewd; sleeping; slothful; slow; smoothed; smug; soaring; soldiering; solemn; somber; sound; sparkling; stanch; stern; stout; submissive; supercilious; sympathetic; tempered; tolerable; tolerant; tough; traditional; tragic; troubled; turbulent; tumultuous; unbridled; uncaged; undefiled; unfair; unfettered; unhaggling; unhappy; unmoved; unnatural; unquiet; unresting; valiant; valorous; valuable; vanguard; vanishing; vanquished; vital; vehement; venomous; vivid; volatile; wandering; wanton; warlike; weak; weary; weeping; wicked; wild; worthy; wounded; zealous.

verbs

allude to—; annihilate—; affront—; bolster —; bruise—; burn—; chafe—; commend—; commune with—; comprehend—; drink of —; drench—; exalt—; exorcise—; fetter—; flood—; hamper—; humble—; immortalize —; implant—; inflame—; inject—; oppose —; purge—; raise—; re-animate—; recapture—; reveal—; reverence—; stamp out—; submerge—; sustain—; symbolize—; teach—; typify—; violate—; war against—; wash—; worship—; yield to—; —abides; —actuates; —animates; —appeases; —arises; —awakens; —blights; —bolsters; —breathes; —broods; —buoys; —caters; —cheers; —climbs; —communes with; —communicates; —conjures; —connotes; —conquers; —conveys; —dampens; —daunts; —departs; —displays; —diverts; —embodies; —endows; —engages; —excites; —exhausts; —exhibits; —expands; —expresses; —extracts; —fatigues; —frets; —haunts; —imbibes; —imbues; —impoverishes; —inculcates; —indulges; —infuses; —lags; —lingers; —maintains; —molests; —narrows; —obscures; —overrules; —paralyzes; —partakes; —perceives; —permeates; —pervades; —pierces; —pours out; —preserves; —prevails; —rankles; —reflects; —reigns; —relates; —reveres; —revives; —sinks; —stalks; —stems; —stimulates; —stirs; —strengthens; —strives; —succumbs; —survives; —summons; —swells; —tempers; —tires; —touches; —unfolds; —uplifts; —wails; —wars; —washes.

(See soul, life, specter.)

SPIRITED

adverbs

ardently; briskly; unusually; uncommonly; exceedingly; alertly; busily; friskily; vivaciously; unwontedly; delightfully; splendidly; actively; intelligently.

SPIRITUAL

adverbs
naturally; personally; subjectively; devoutly; faithfully; piously; religiously; reverently; instinctively; celestially; gloriously; intuitively; beautifully; immoderately; blessedly; humbly; solemnly; consciously; innately; simply; inherently.

SPIT

verbs
eject—; emit—; excrete—; exude—; moisten with—; regurgitate—; slaver—; slobber—; squirt—; —drivels; —drools; —nauseates; —showers; —slobbers.
(See saliva, liquid, sputum, expectoration.)

SPIT (*v*)

adverbs
venomously; vulgarly; carelessly; disgustingly; nauseatingly; incessantly; obstreperously; accurately; explosively.
(See sputter.)

SPITEFUL

adverbs
naturally; habitually; always; detestably; dangerously; maliciously; viciously; abominably; incorrigibly; incurably; atrociously; hatefully; enviously; unhappily; unfortunately; strangely; absurdly; deplorably; bitterly; cruelly.

SPLASH

adjectives
gaudy; tremendous; quickening; confounded; tiny; ignominious; audible; weltering; rhythmic.

verbs
avert—; raise—; —begrimes; —besmirches; —deluges; —douses; —drenches; —fouls; —inundates; —moistens; —ruffles; —rumples; —showers; —smears; —smudges; —souses; —spatters; —swashes.
(See wave, water, liquid.)

SPLEEN

adjectives
merry; scornful; weakest; testy; heaving.

verbs
affect—; enlarge—; excise—; excite—; provoke—; remove—; rile (colloq.)—; ruffle —; vent—; vex—; —depresses; —enlarges; —execrates; —ferments; —functions; —governs; —secretes.
(See bile.)

SPLENDID

adverbs
gorgeously; luminously; brilliantly; vividly; dazzlingly; radiantly; richly; sumptuously; artistically; extraordinarily; amazingly; regally; unexpectedly; barbarically; fantastically; romantically; imposingly; impressively; majestically; imperially; royally; colorfully; imperishably; unforgettably; ornately; dramatically; ceremonially; ritualistically.

SPLENDOR

adjectives
oriental; reflected; intrinsic; glamorous; divine; temporal; lonely; dazzling; scarlet; superficial; infernal; reminiscent; dark; transitory; prodigious; immense; liquid; intellectual; hurrying; vermeil; profuse; passionless; clinging; celestial; sumptuous; lofty; spectral; barbaric; mild; queenly; magnificent; external; meaning; wasteful; crimson; faded; lurid; mellow; dewy; new; starry; chilled; sultry; ancient; modest; baleful; meridian; opulent; prismatic; radiant; scaly; level; unhealthy; monarchical; visionary; chromatic; delusive; arrogant; lustrous; vulgar.

verbs
belittle—; blur—; crown—; envy—; mar—; rejoice in—; —blazes; —blinds; —bursts forth; —crowns; —dazzles; —intoxicates.
(See brilliance, glory, grandeur.)

SPLINT

verbs
apply—; bear—; bind—; discard—; improvise—; pad—; wear—; —affords; —assures; —bolsters; —braces; —maintains; —necessitates; —props; —protects; —serves; —supports; —sustains; —trusses; —underpins.
(See brace, protection.)

SPLINTER

verbs
cleave into—s; draw—; eject—; extract—; impale on—; pluck—; remove—; rend into —s; sever into—; shiver into—s; transfix on

—; withdraw—; —barbs; —gashes; —gauges; —infects; —perforates; —pierces; —punctures.
(See fragment, piece.)

SPLIT

verbs
cement—; fuse—; intervene—; wedge in—; weld—; —bisects; —breaches; —disjoins; —disrupts; —extends; —fractures; —gapes; —halves; —leaves; —mars; —rives; —shatters; —shivers; —splinters; —widens.
(See breach, crack.)

SPLURGE (colloq.)

verbs
create—; cut—; deplore—; indulge in—; lament—; reproach—; rue—; —beguiles; —celebrates; —dazzles; —deludes; —displays; —exhibits; —flaunts; —flourishes; —glitters; —swaggers; —shows off; —splashes.
(See extravagance, waste, demonstration.)

SPOIL (v)

adverbs
ultimately; hopelessly; sadly; disastrously; effectively; partially; sickeningly.
(See plunder, damage.)

SPOILS

adjectives
envied; frequent; glittering; private; recking; sluttish; consecrated; trophied.

verbs
appropriate—; cache—; capture—; confiscate—; covet—; display—; dispose of—; exhaust—; exhibit—; filch—; hunger for—; lust for—; pilfer—; pillage for—; pounce upon—; plunder for—; prize—; purloin—; reap—; retain—; sack—; scramble for—; seize—; swoop to—; value—; win—; wrench—; —accrue; —allure; —attract.
(See loot, graft.)

SPONGE

verbs
apply—; dampen—; fish for—s; hook—; infiltrate—; market—; moisten—; mop with—; rinse—; saturate—; scour with—; swab with—; —absorbs; —soaks up; —sucks up.

SPONGY

adverbs
usefully; naturally; profitably; conveniently; adaptably; flexibly; yieldingly; absorbently; pleasantly; comfortably; hopelessly; porously; swampily; quaggily; dangerously; impassably.

SPONSER (v)

adverbs
enthusiastically; financially; annually; necessarily; faithfully.
(See indorse, finance.)

SPONSOR

verbs
acquire—; conciliate—s; gain—; inspire—s; obligate to—; redeem—; seek—; —assures; —contracts; —discharges; —encourages; —exhorts; —finances; —furthers; —guarantees; —indorses; —observes; —pioneers; —pledges; —vouches for.
(See contributor, owner, manager.)

SPONTANEOUS

adverbs
eagerly; obviously; enthusiastically; utterly; manifestly; remarkably; absolutely; palpably; unquestionably; warmly; fervently: heartily; undoubtedly; intensely; exceptionally; sympathetically; unusually.

SPOOKY

adverbs
designedly; deliberately; pleasantly; mischievously; unusually; mysteriously; disagreeably; creepily; dismally; desolately; alarmingly; weirdly; uncannily; eerily; fearfully; wretchedly; miserably; uncomfortably; startlingly; horribly; ominously.

SPORT

adjectives
false; rare; willing; noisy; spectator; cruel; merry; sanguinary; biologic; equestrian; rustic; glorious; healthy; solitary; competitive; childish; malicious; domestic.

verbs
coach—; engage in—; enthuse about (colloq.)—; excel in—s; follow—; forsake—; hurl into—; indulge in—; pursue—; revive—; take up—; —attracts; —beguiles; —diverts; —endangers; —enlivens; —fascinates; —invigorates; —strains; —takes hold; —wearies.
(See amusement, diversion, fishing, frolic, game, golf, baseball, etc.)

SPORT (v)

adverbs

ludicrously; boisterously; enthusiastically; animatedly; merrily; competitively; childishly; rustically; noisily; uncouthly.

(See frolic, play.)

SPOT

adjectives

secluded; sheltered; distinguishable; tuneful; convenient; hovering; dusky; delicious; threadbare; unpromising; chosen; hallowed; shady; retired; dreary; sunlit; selfsame; forsaken; elevated; sleek; wet; treacherous; sore; unknown; dry; beauty; mildewed; curious; desolate; seductive; devoted; perceptible; faulty; unsightly; formidable; sequestered; secure; moist; sacred; swampy; malarial; plague; trysting; vital; lovely; haunted; drearest; barren; memorable; remote; vicious; infinitesimal; secure; insidious; weak; doleful; consecrated; solitary; dreariest; neglected; limited; tender; designated; unfertile; isolated; vulnerable; silent; tranquil; burning; loathsome; ulcer; sanctified; attention-arresting; favorable; veritable; wave-walled.

verbs

bear—s; confine—; designate—; detect—; efface—; eradicate—; lurk near—; incrust —; obliterate—; patch—; scatter—s; scour —; —attracts; —s bespatter; —s besmirch; —betokens; —blemishes; —blurs; —blotches; —s checker; —connotates; —defiles; —mars; —represents; —smudges; —sullies; —transfixes.

(See freckles, mark, blemish.)

SPOTLIGHT

verbs

concentrate—; eclipse—; elude—; evade—; extinguish—; focus—; obscure—; retire from—; share—; shrink from—; shun—; shy from—; steal—; —dazzles; —diffuses; —disperses; —flickers; —glares; —glimmers; —guides; —illuminates; —penetrates; —pierces; —plays upon; —radiates; —scintillates; —shimmers.

(See light, limelight.)

SPOUSE

adjectives

indignant; tempestuous; expatriated; faithful; repulsive; pesty; skillful; plighted; exquisite; preternatural; waxen.

SPRAWL (v)

adverbs

grotesquely; drunkenly; violently; lazily; indolently; clumsily; uncouthly.

(See spread, lie.)

SPRAWLY

adverbs

inconveniently; awkwardly; inexpediently; unnecessarily; terribly; unhandily; unfortunately; undesirably; objectionably.

SPRAY

adjectives

belching; out-wafting; glistening; salt-sea; bloomy; brackish; heavy; vagrant; beechen; sleepless; bent; white-hot; trailing; radiant; dissolving; drooping; yeasty; blinding; delicate; saltless; birchen; seething; writhen; flying; lofty; tumbling; sheeted; misty; deadly.

verbs

diffuse—; distil—; expel—; —beclouds; —befogs; —disinfects; —evaporates; —fizzes; —foams; —fumigates; —gleams; —glitters; —hazes; —mists; —moistens; —obscures; —overcasts; —radiates; —saturates; —sparkles; —spatters; —spumes; —drenches.

(See fountain, mist, moisture, steam, vapor.)

SPRAY (v)

adverbs

periodically; scientifically; automatically; annually; agriculturally.

(See scatter, sprinkle.)

SPREAD

adjectives

stunning; mortal; cloudless; dainty; solemn; delicious; immeasurable; tasty; delectable; eye-filling.

verbs

augment—; confine—; diminish—; enhance —; enlarge—; exaggerate—; expand—; extend—; extenuate—; heighten—; intensify —; limit—; magnify—; prevent—; reduce —; swell—; —embraces; —ranges.

(See cover, extent.)

SPREAD (v)

adverbs

insidiously; contagiously; swiftly; malicious-

ly; spaciously; industriously; generously; parsimoniously; invidiously; internationally.
(See expand, circulate.)

SPREE

adjectives
gigantic; conquering; periodic; prolonged; measured; violent; headlong.

SPRIGHTLY

adverbs
inordinately; exceedingly; unusually; extremely; pleasantly; nimbly; delightfully; gleefully; divertingly; merrily; briskly; vivaciously; alertly; blithely; vigorously; joyously; mercurially.

SPRING

adjectives
trickling; sparkling; hasty; delightful; elegant; plashy; convulsive; fruitless; smiling; wayside; copious; muscular; bubbling; sagging; clear; perpetual; tongue-tied; secret; crystal; bitter; inexhaustible; powerful; quivering; amorous-breathing; bursting; fern-wreathed; purling; covert; young; whispering; tardy; lasting; latent; limpid; filthy; lagging; balmy; exulting; budding; portentous; endless; sinuous; babbling; unfading; living; phantom; fathomless; unsealed; humbler; unusual.

verbs
apostrophize—; bid—to; greet—; hail—; prophesy—; reveal—; salute—; taste—; welcome—; —adorns; —arrives; —boasts; —breathes; —brings; —bursts; —calls forth; —comes; —cries; —departs; —flies; —flourishes; —forsakes; —greets; —laughs; —murmurs; —questions; —returns; —rushes; —says good-bye; —smiles; —spreads; —supplies; —takes leave; —takes wing; —unbosoms; —unlocks; —visits; —wakens; —whips away; —works.
(See autumn, summer, winter.)

SPRING (*well*)

verbs
contaminate—; drain—; drill—; emanate from—; issue from—; pollute—; seep into—; tap—; trace—; vent—; —advances; —awakens; —babbles; —discharges; —dribbles; —gurgles; —gushes; —jets; —murmurs; —oozes; —opens; —originates in; —pulsates; —refreshes; —reinforces; —rises; —swashes; —swells; —trickles.
(See fountain, geyser, well, brook.)

SPRING (*v*)

adverbs
agilely; impetuously; hazardously; independently; amazingly; spontaneously; impulsively; joyously; viciously; vindictively; dexterously.
(See leap, bound.)

SPRINKLE (*v*)

adverbs
freshly; thickly; uniformly; liberally; profusely; delicately; sporadically.
(See scatter, spray.)

SPRITE

adjectives
elfin; shadowy; bright-eyed; wretched; dusky; melancholy; airy; elusive; devilish; mischievous; impish.

SPRUCE

adverbs
jauntily; nattily; unusually; habitually; attractively; smugly; carefully; designedly; unwontedly; remarkably; consciously; admirably; proudly; curiously; noticeably; conspicuously.

SPRY

adverbs
ostentatiously; absurdly; foolishly; proudly; pretentiously; resolutely; conspicuously; fatuously; deceptively; jauntily; curiously; showily; remarkably; unusually; ridiculously; crookedly; actively; naturally; habitually; pleasantly; alertly.

SPUNKY

adverbs
delightfully; sufficiently; smartly; inherently; merrily; actually; independently; absurdly; comically; ridiculously; extremely; unreasonably; uncommonly.

SPUR

adjectives
pricking; sluggish; continental; continual; clanking; dizzy; knightly; goading.

SPURIOUS

adverbs
disgracefully; obviously; evidently; manifestly; shamefully; cleverly; deceptively; in-

geniously; unquestionably; transparently; admittedly; unexpectedly; daringly; outrageously; ostensibly; visibly; ridiculously; cheaply.

SPUTTER (v)

adverbs
irately; indignantly; furiously; vindictively; violently; obnoxiously; vulgarly.
(See spit.)

SPUTTERING

adverbs
constantly; fitfully; fretfully; unreasonably; tetchily; shrewishly; irritably; ill-temperedly; futilely; uselessly; vainly; loudly; sullenly; excitedly; eternally.

SPUTUM

verbs
charge—; cough up—; discharge—; emit—; examine—; expectorate—; sterilize—; test—; —accumulates; —characterizes; —congests; —contaminates; —conveys; —dries; —disseminates; —endangers.
(See spit.)

SPY

adjectives
true; prying; universal; omnipresent; unfortunate; jealous; traveling; clumsy; frail; involuntary.

SPY (v)

adverbs
pryingly; jealously; professionally; slyly; involuntarily; insidiously; unscrupulously; traitorously; treacherously; suspiciously; omnisciently; cautiously.
(See watch, search.)

SPYING

verbs
charge with—; cloak—; convict of—; detect—; deter—; disclose—; expose—; goad into—; harry—; mask—; penalize—; perpetrate—; reveal—; uncover—; —acquaints one with; —adorns; —betrays; —brands; —divulges; —enables; —informs; —intrigues; —jeopardizes; —menaces; —reveals; —stigmatizes; —unveils.
(See curiosity, examination, search, discovery, scrutiny.)

SQUABBLE

adjectives
personal; contemptible; musty; money; petty; grudge; lulling; vulgar; miserable.

verbs
obviate—; arbitrate—; avert—; avoid—; check—; conclude—; curtail—; intervene in—; join in—; judge—; pacify—; precipitate—; preclude—; stage—; subdue—; terminate—; —breaches; —disconcerts; —embroils; —estranges; —expires; —fractures; —ill-becomes; —mars; —rages; —ruptures; —threatens; —vexes.
(See fight, quarrel, dispute.)

SQUAD

adjectives
trained; investigation; motorized; formidable; awkward; mustering; firing; death; narcotic.

verbs
augment—; bar from—; bolster—; captain—; caution—; condition—; disband—; dispatch—; enlarge—; flank—; limit—; maintain—; mobilize—; muster—; quarter—; reanimate—; regiment—; reinforce—; reinstate—; rejuvenate—; revamp (colloq.)—; —assembles; —demolishes; —disperses; —embarks; —huddles; —intrenches; —mobilizes; —patrols; —sallies forth; —s troop.
(See gang, band, group.)

SQUADRON

adjectives
outflanking; feinting; reconnoitering; rushing; prancing; blockading; retreating; magnificent; kindred; lucid; thundering; watchful; well-built: woven-winged; murderous.

SQUALID

adverbs
miserably; wretchedly; incredibly; impossibly; inexpressibly; utterly; pitiably; deplorably; lamentably; shamefully; unnecessarily; needlessly; grossly; terribly; horribly; hopelessly.

SQUALOR

verbs
abolish—; endure—; eradicate—; fester in—; purge—; thrive amidst—; —begrimes; —blots; —contaminates; —corrupts; —de-

bases; —defaces; —defiles; —emphasizes; —offends; —pollutes; —rankles; —reeks; —smothers; —sullies; —tarnishes.
(See dirt, filth, abomination.)

SQUANDER (v)

adverbs
recklessly; rashly; improvidently; liberally; royally; prodigiously; fantastically; wantonly.
(See waste, spend, expend.)

SQUARE

adjectives
quaint; open; desolate; inverse; drawling; fountained; principal; hollow; dusty; silent; diagonal; budding; conspicuous; perfect.

SQUAT (v)

adverbs
vulgarly; cozily; somnolently; pugnaciously; characteristically; habitually; complacently; threateningly.
(See corner, crouch.)

SQUATTERS

verbs
allure—; attract—; dislodge—; encourage—; evict—; invite—; tax—; tempt—; —abound; —claim; —colonize; —deprive; —domesticate; —encamp; —lease; —settle on; —tenant; —usurp.
(See denizen.)

SQUAWK (v)

adverbs
cacophonously; raucously; indignantly; hideously; persistently; plaintively; endurably.
(See squeal, yell.)

SQUEAK

adjectives
shrill; impassioned; high-pitched; serene; tiny; persistent; elusive.

SQUEAKY

adverbs
shrilly; comically; curiously; oddly; unfortunately; annoyingly; embarrassingly; vexatiously; alarmingly; ominously; unfortunately; unluckily; treacherously; dangerously; provokingly.

SQUEAL (v)

adverbs
piteously; shrilly; agonizingly; piercingly; penetratingly; desolately; wrathfully; impassionedly.
(See cry, yell.)

SQUEAMISH

adverbs
unusually; delicately; extremely; terribly; prudishly; pretentiously; ostentatiously; presumably; notoriously; fastidiously; daintily; absurdly; comically; ridiculously; helplessly; disgustingly; overly; nervously.

SQUEEZE

adjectives
brotherly; mollifying; affectionate; hard; warm; tender.

SQUEEZE (v)

adverbs
imploringly; passionately; mollifyingly; affectionately; fraternally; warmly; tenderly; oppressively; impetuously.
(See compress, crowd.)

SQUINT (v)

adverbs
drolly; sinisterly; suspiciously; knowingly; penetratingly; affectedly; comically; threateningly.
(See wince, peer.)

SQUIRE

adjectives
stupid; rustic; ponderous; parliamentary; proper; blunt.

SQUIRREL

adjectives
flippant; tawny; watchful.

verbs
protect—s; tame—s; —barks; —burrows; —cracks; —curses; —darts; —digs; —dodges; —evades; —flirts its tail; —frolics; —gathers; —harvests; —hides; —jeers; —munches; —nibbles; —quivers; —scampers; —shies; —stores; —trembles; —whisks himself off.
(See animal, chipmunk.)

STAB

adjectives
adroit; bleeding; gashed; hateful; verbal.

verbs
deflect—; inflict—; —agonizes; —convulses; —despatches; —excruciates; —impales; —

inflames; —gushes; —gnaws; —lacerates; —penetrates; —perforates; —pierces; —punctures; —slays; —throbs; —twinges; —twitches.

(See wound.)

STAB (v)

adverbs

adroitly; fatally; dangerously; hideously; vindictively; passionately; treacherously.

(See pierce, thrust.)

STABILITY

adjectives

emotional; social; razor-keen; great; civic.

verbs

afford—; ascertain—; assure of—; attain—; cherish—; commend—; confirm—; destroy—; determine—; detract from—; endanger—; forfeit—; insure—; investigate—; jeopardize—; maintain—; measure—; necessitate—; nurture—; offer—; question—; reinforce—; restore—; retain—; secure—; sustain—; value—; wreck—; —hinges on; —insures; —ruffles; —totters; —wanes.

(See permanence, constancy, firmness, strength, steadiness.)

STABILIZE (v)

adverbs

economically; effectively; politically; democratically; emotionally; governmentally; legislatively; socially.

(See fix.)

STABLE

adverbs

reliably; dependably; fortunately; securely; safely; entirely; financially; emotionally; creditably; eminently; commercially; indestructibly; delightfully; supposedly; presumably; reputably; uncommonly; solidly.

STAFF
(cane)

verbs

arm with—; bear—; brandish—; cudgel with—; discard—; flourish—; flutter on—; relinquish—; shatter—; shoulder—; splinter—; surrender—; wield—; —bludgeons; —braces; —deflects; —sags; —supports; —sustains; —sways.

(See cane, baton, stick.)

STAFF
(general)

adjectives

knotted; managerial; faithful; official; efficient; consultant; inventive; research; energetic; intelligent; glittering.

STAFF
(personal)

verbs

appoint to—; augment—; clutter—; discharge—; employ—; evacuate—; inspect—; resign from—; recruit—; suspend from—; —surrenders.

(See personnel.)

STAFF (v)

adverbs

efficiently; faithfully; officially; scientifically; periodically; annually; seasonally.

(See support, provide.)

STAGE

adjectives

verdant; primitive; well-set; mental; commencing; formative; inglorious; momentous; incipient; successive (pl); veiled; obstructed; various (pl); miraculous; analytic; realistic; developmental; trembling; uncertain; restorative; early; domestic; infantile; tentative; rudimentary; middle; well-trod; experimental; indifferent; tragic; legitimate; explosive; worthier; hypothetical; pudding; condensed; baffling; intermediate; infectious; important; imperceptible; dilapidated; milky; maturing; initial; diminutive; perilous; naked; painful; buskined; regressive; embryonic; uncontrollable; usurped.

verbs

abandon—; advance—; cherish—; conceive—; connect—s; dedicate to—s; define—; desert—; destine for—; devote to—; elevate—; exalt—; extol—; forsake—; frisk onto—; glorify—; hoot off—; install—; perform—; prostitute—; quit—; relinquish—; renounce—; retire from—; set—; strut upon—; unsettle—; vindicate—; wed to—; —allures; —attracts; —debases; —entices; —fascinates; —immortalizes; —impassions; —notorizes; —seduces; —succeeds; —s unfold.

(See board, footlights, platform, theatre.)

STAGE (v)

adverbs
stupendously; spectacularly; awesomely; grandiosely; handsomely; dramatically.
(See produce, effect.)

STAGE-FRIGHT

verbs
afflict with—; induce—; intensify—; manifest—; quell—; smite with—; subdue—; suffer—; surmount—; vanquish—; —abates; —barbs; —chills; —consumes; —curdles; —disconcerts; —distresses; —harasses; —hounds; —irks; —nauseates; —overawes; —overcomes; —overwhelms; —plagues; —racks; —ruffles; —sickens; —tenses; —terrifies.
(See fright, fear, terror, nervousness.)

STAGEY

adverbs
absurdly; pretentiously; undisguisedly; outlandishly; transparently; ridiculously; obviously; fantastically; outrageously; flimsily; cheaply; manifestly; disagreeably; unpleasantly; undeniably; bombastically; pompously; laughably; patently.

STAGGER (v)

adverbs
intoxicatedly; weakly; clumsily; stumblingly; helplessly; blindly; faintingly.
(See reel, sway.)

STAGNANT

adverbs
hopelessly; unfortunately; putridly; pestiferously; dangerously; inexplicably; palpably; uselessly; completely; dully; carelessly; indifferently; stolidly; contentedly; lazily.

STAIN

adjectives
primal; perspiration; tender; cloudy; hot; tyrant; haunting; powder; indelible; imputed; crimson; inborn; ineradicable.

STAIRCASE

adjectives
labored; pinched; twisted; steep; monumental; marble; secret; palatial; principal; quaint; little; lofty; filthy; winding; mossy; graceful.

STAIRS

adjectives
broken; skatish; lazar; mountain; wooden; singing; cramped; dingy; ill-kept; cold; cheerless; rocking; interminable; dark; winding; discolored; spacious; polished; dim; tackled; corkscrew.

verbs
ascend—; avoid—; bear up—; blockade—; bolt down—; bounce down—; bound from —; clamber up—; clatter down—; climb—; descend—; design—; grope on—; guide down—; labor up—; limp up—; mount—; pause on—; scale—; scramble up—; scurry up—; skip up—; survey from—; tear up—; thrust down—; thunder down—; topple from —; totter on—; tumble from—; vault—; —creak; —diverge; —spiral; —wind.
(See ladder, step.)

STAKE

adjectives
black; windward; sharp-pointed; metal.

verbs
affix to—; avoid—; drive—; extract—; hitch to—; impale on—; implant—; moor to—; plant—; sink—; shackle to—; suspend from—; transfix to—; withdraw—; —directs; —fences; —guides; —indicates; —marks; —penetrates; —signalizes.
(See post.)

STALACTITES

verbs
—bracket; —dazzle; —derive from; —fashion; —gleam; —glitter; —glimmer; —incrust; —line; —ornament; —radiate; —spur; —stud; —suspend; —taper.
(See icicle.)

STALE

adverbs
uselessly; terribly; obviously; unluckily; alarmingly; indubitably; mustily; unprofitably; tastelessly; inexcusably; unacceptably; disgustingly; wearily; injuriously; unhealthfully; unwholesomely; unwarrantably; objectionably; disagreeably; unpleasantly.

STALENESS

verbs
bar—; estimate—; incur—; loathe—; resent —; resist—; —alters; —flattens; —prevails; —provokes; —offsets; —shames.
(See odor, stench, smell.)

STALK

adjectives
green; juicy; martial; tall; withered.

verbs
attach to—; cast away—; crush—; dry—; gather—; pile—; shake—; sickle—; —bears; —connects; —curves; —s elevate; —juts; —protrudes; —rises; —springs; —supports; —sways; —s tangle; —tapers; —waves.
(See stem.)

STALK (v)

adverbs
dramatically; implacably; grimly; jauntily; nonchalantly; haughtily; stealthily; martially; vigorously; triumphantly; swaggeringly.
(See stride, strut.)

STALWART

adverbs
sturdily; remarkably; huskily; resolutely; valorously; intrepidly; trustworthily; amazingly; conspicuously; unusually; remarkably; marvelously; uncommonly; obviously; vigorously; doggedly; splendidly; dependably; uncommonly; naturally; reliably.

STAMENS

verbs
bear—; examine—; form—; support—; —burst; —cohere; —contain; —discharge; —shed; —split open.

STAMINA

verbs
break—; calculate—; deteriorate in—; develop—; evince—; lack—; exhaust—; increase—; lower—; possess—; preserve—; require—; restore—; supply—; test—; —ebbs; —endures; —lessens; —mounts; —resists; —succumbs; —wanes; —withstands.
(See strength, endurance.)

STAMMER (v)

adverbs
chokingly; inarticulately; laboriously; confusedly; hesitatingly; incoherently; timidly; embarrassedly.
(See stumble, falter.)

STAMP

adjectives
broken; legal; indelible; legislative; witching; occasional; intellectual; unmistakable; rubber.

verbs
affix—; attach—; bear—; collect—; design—; display—; hammer—; impress—; issue—; lick—; mark—; moisten—; pound—; provide—; sponge—; —adheres; —attests; —authorizes; —certifies; —s cover; —guarantees; —seals; —signifies; —sticks; —validates; —warrants.
(See label, mark, impression.)

STAMP (v)

adverbs
petulantly; angrily; indelibly; violently; vigorously; viciously; ruthlessly; impotently; unmistakably; permanently.
(See imprint, impress.)

STANCH

adverbs
loyally; fearlessly; unwaveringly; steadily; firmly; reliably; admirably; commendably; laudably; unusually; marvelously; courageously; gallantly; intrepidly; valiantly; valorously; unexpectedly; enthusiastically; eagerly; earnestly; immovably.

STAND

adjectives
drowsy; desperate; stubborn; unalterable; dimension; brutal; last; unflinching; lofty; unequivocal; final; roadside; definite.

verbs
advocate—; appreciate—; criticize—; depend on—; drive from—; hold—; maintain—; plan—; prepare for—; reiterate—; resist—; retain—; —annoys; —arrests; —checks; —recoups; —refreshes; —repels.
(See position, opinion.)

STAND (v)

adverbs
preeminently; militantly; stalwartly; indubitably; obediently; squarely; habitually; tremulously; haughtily; forlornly; conspicuously; precariously; courageously; picturesquely; valiantly; meekly; irresolutely; ostentatiously; sullenly; boldly; perilously; wistfully; unfalteringly; erectly.
(See endure, bear.)

STANDARD

adjectives
critical; ethical; altered; accepted; zoned; inherent; abstract; superior; dingy; infallible; artistic; accursed; unrivaled; barbarian; highest; hackneyed; crafty; persistent;

quantitative; capricious; moral; minimum; tentative; legal; well-defined; average; ordinary; tattered; acknowledged; shadowy; unconscious; secular; ponderous; proud; lofty; prospective; artificial; dietary; unhonored; exacting; rigorous; tangible; intellectual; inflexible; journalistic; accessible; rising; rigid; incontestable; single; recognized; unimpeachable; complaisant; conventional.

verbs
accept—; adopt—; advance—; apply—; attain—; conform—; desert—; deviate from —; elevate—; establish—; degrade—; formulate—; frame—; improve—; indoctrinate —; judge—; lift to—; lower—; maintain—; measure up to—; obtain—; prescribe—; preserve—; raise—; rally to—; reconcile—; record—; represent—; require—; serve—; set—; unfurl—; uplift—; violate—; —s collapse; —s conform; —s dictate; —s melt away; —prevails; —reflects.
(See flag, ideal.)

STANDARDIZATION

verbs
adopt—; advocate—; apply—; approve—; assume—; demand—; devise—; encourage —; examine—; formulate—; necessitate—; overcome—; perfect—; promise—; —insures; —progresses; —rears.
(See system.)

STANDING

adjectives
scholastic; better; scientific; legal; world-wide; logical; amateur; requisite; social.

verbs
aspire to—; better—; command—; confine —; create—; declare—; elevate—; esteem —; exceed in—; favor—; grade—; honor —; inquire as to—; judge—; reckon—; regain—; respect—; threaten—.
(See position, reputation, status.)

STANDPOINT

adjectives
elementary; artistic; favorable; psychoanalytic; outside; critical; prejudiced; academic; anagogic; decorative; practical; pagan; unbiased.

verbs
adopt—; alter—; assume—; compare—; contemplate—; criticize—; direct—; insure —; interpret—; maintain—; measure—; move—; occupy—; regard—; sanction—; select—; shake—; view from—; —affords; —contents.
(See view, position, conception.)

STANZA

adjectives
elegiac; quaint; complicated; pious; long; staccato; unrhyming; experimental; sweeping.

STAR
(*actor*)

verbs
abuse—; admire—; advertise—; celebrate —; credit—; direct—; discover—; distinguish—; glimpse—; glorify—; groom—; hail—; highlight—; interview—; laud—; mob—; present—; publicize—; uncover—; —appears; —attracts; —delights; —interprets; —performs; —portrays; —thrills; —triumphs.
(See hero, actor, artist.)

STAR
(*celestial*)

verbs
discern—; —appears; —beams; —dims; —s flee; —gleams; —glitters; —guides; —hangs; —kindles; —lingers; —s perform; —plumes; —s reign; —s revolve; —s shed radiance; —spangles; —s unfold; —s wander; —s wane.
(See sun.)

STAR
(*general*)

adjectives
celestial; sanguine; mightiest; innumerable (pl); unsetting; evening; air-dissolved; bright; unchanging; ever-burning; polar; gold; glistening; innocent; scattered (pl); literal; happy; glory-beaming; sparkling; luckiest; tenderer; blinking; wide; pink; shy; waking; charitable; blazing; soaring; scintillating; dynastic; solemn; guiding; keen; fixed; remote; fiery; consenting; swart; panting; periodical; tremulous; folding; occulted; azure; guardian; teeming (pl); fragrant; ushering; brooding; meliorating; vagabond; mighty; deathless; wizard; wild; dying; friendly; summer; equidistant; secret; dumb; twinkling; unfinished; vanished; intense; steadfast; burning; patient; watery; pendulous; sentinel; rushing; solitary; dependent; baneful; wheel-

ing; glancing; lurid; bright; downcast; tranquil; solid; winking; sliding; clear; intimate; obscure; gaudy; actual; moist; melancholy; declining; luminous; alien; beamless; prickly; pilot; budding; imperial; favorable; unanchored; cooperative; untroubled; lonely; elderly; newest; white; splendor-winged; utmost; journeying; attending; remorseless; truer; tyrant; palpitating; unstable; fortunate; sinking.

STARCH

verbs
apply—; convert—; dip into—; immerse in —; lose—; object to—; prepare—; remove —; store up—; —finishes; —galls; —hardens; —irritates; —stiffens.
(See food, constituent, carbohydrate.)

STARE

adjectives
studious; dull; stupid; algid; defiant; disfigured; glassy; fascinated; hostile; audible; vacant; grave; angry; meditative; absent-minded; sidelong; frigid; concentrated; appraising; unwinking; gloomy; fixed; dreamy; long; admiring; wondering; irreverent; stony; maniac; noncommittal; disgusted; spectral; superior; wild; bemused; questioning; hesitating; incredulous; hungry; sullen; limpid; owlish; insolent; unmitigated; oily; fascinated; solemn; wide-eyed.

verbs
blanket—; comprehend—; cast—; fix—; note —; prolong—; transfer—; —absorbs; —arouses; —astonishes; —excites; —irritates; —provokes; —startles.
(See look.)

STARE (v)

adverbs
impudently; fixedly; sullenly; persistently; solemnly; abstractedly; impassively; hypnotically; perplexedly; obtrusively; moodily; hostilely; arrogantly; apathetically; incredulously; fixedly; truculently; speculatively; insolently; fascinatedly; morbidly; rudely; vacantly.
(See look, gaze.)

STARLIGHT

adjectives
glittering; cool; boundless; glorious; pale; bright; shining; wondrous; magic; romantic.

verbs
be wrought by—; emerge from—; exhibit —; reveal—; shed—; view—; —appears; —awes; —cheers; —comforts; —creeps; —dimples; —embraces; —frames; —glitters; —guides; —scatters; —spangles; —splits; —unfolds; —works.
(See light, star.)

STARLING

verbs
introduce—; naturalize—; rid of—s; —s blot out; —s damage; —dives; —s feast on; —passes over; —quarters; —robs; —thrives.
(See bird.)

STARRY

adverbs
luminously; brilliantly; luckily; fortunately; unusually; brightly; helpfully; romantically; desirably; providentially; auspiciously; remarkably; amazingly.

START

adjectives
theatrical; undisguised; palpable; rheumatic; infinite; hopeful; reluctant; convulsive; guilty; running; involuntary; troubled; vigorous; tremulous; slight; longing; answering; painful; terrified; sudden; fitful.

START (v)

adverbs
violently; precipitately; perceptibly; distractedly; simultaneously; impetuously; reluctantly; jauntily; involuntarily; tremulously; fitfully.
(See embark, launch.)

STARTLE (v)

adverbs
inexpressibly; abruptly; playfully; ludicrously; stupidly; repeatedly.
(See scare, surprise.)

STARTLING

adverbs
unbelievably; unusually; utterly; alarmingly; extremely; unpleasantly; suddenly; strangely; curiously; disconcertingly; painfully; terribly; dreadfully; fearfully; tremendously; remarkably; singularly; oddly; appallingly; disturbingly; unexpectedly; disagreeably; peculiarly.

STARVATION

adjectives
absolute; oxygen; bitter; aesthetic; mental; cruel; slow.

verbs
alleviate—; avoid—; brave—; conceal—; endure—; face with—; hide—; influence—; perish by—; produce—; overcome—; reduce —; reveal—; stave off—; subject to—; —burdens; —devastates; —stalks; —threatens; —victimizes; —weakens.

(See hunger, suffering, need, death.)

STARVE (v)

adverbs
deliberately; cruelly; pennilessly; genteelly; parsimoniously; penuriously; niggardly; mentally; gradually; agonizingly; ceaselessly; miserably.

(See weaken.)

STATE (condition)

verbs
aggravate—; allay—; alleviate—; arrest—; assuage—; attribute—; breed—; cloak—; comprehend—; conceal—; condemn—; ease —; establish—; excite—; expose—; induce —; intensify—; palliate—; prolong—; relieve—; restore—; resuscitate—; reveal—; revive—; screen—; shroud—.

(See condition, predicament, plight.)

STATE (general)

adjectives
happy; unpropitious; deplorable; ordered; hopeful; kingly; humble; healthy; wandering; transitional; insipid; distended; totalitarian; bastard; sepulchral; disordered; throned; altered; lamentable; turbulent; dropsical; political; fossil; semi-conscious; feverish; frenzied; blissful; burdened; needful; pathetic; flourishing; honorable; excessive; deplorable; slovenly; anterior; cramped; crude; relaxed; supernal; deluded; spirited; ecstatic; variable (pl); dejected; inarticulate; primitive; impressible; autonomous; surrounding; morbid; feeble; former; dilapidated; democratic; semi-liquid; peaceful; enlightened; industrious; homogeneous; populated; tangled; emotional; authoritative; opulent; neurotic; compound; deliberate; existing; destitute; well-settled; semi-savage; impressible; comatose; depressed; corresponding; ordered; indissoluble; dreadful; bedraggled; retired; bulwarked; infant; transitional; social; primordial; slow; undetermined; scrambled; unsteadfast; neutral; passionless; dormant; exalted; perpetual; stronger; neutral; anomalous; unravaged; decapitated; unpleasant; knotted; unassailable; embryonic; conflicting; solitary; regal; stoic; vacillating; unique; frail; loose; electrical; quiescent; unwonted; melancholy; miserable; joyless; alarming; wretched; troubled; fair; outcast; forlorn; self-governing; distracted; dissolved; candid; enfeebled; pitiful; rebellious; palmy; coward; rapid; disadvantageous; natural; joyful; stable; budding; unwelcome; savage; apparent; enviable; desirable.

STATE (political)

verbs
ally with—; annex—; bow to—; carve out —; dominate—; empower—; encroach upon —; enslave—; evacuate—; exalt—; forfeit to—; found—; industrialize—; infringe upon—; invade—; partition—; quell—; reduce—; subdue—; subjugate—; unite—; vanquish—; weld—; yield to—; —administers; —appropriates; —domiciles; —exercises; —s federate; —maintains; —persecutes; —racks with; —requisitions; —tramples; —tyrannizes; —wields.

(See empire, commonwealth, republic, country, nation.)

STATE (v)

adverbs
parenthetically; succinctly; tersely; concisely; impressively; broadly; specifically; metaphorically; authoritatively; emphatically; laconically; explicitly; solemnly; officially; substantially; tranquilly.

(See say, affirm, declare.)

STATELY

adverbs
becomingly; unusually; habitually; naturally; inherently; attractively; beautifully; proudly; regally; royally; majestically; magnificently; splendidly; appropriately; pompously; ceremoniously; gravely; properly; graciously; impressively.

STATEMENT

adjectives
misleading; big; hurtful; irrefutable; preceding; explicit; souring; terse; emphatic; fallacious; sententious; itemized; facetious;

contradictory; lucid; cardinal; unproved; colorless; written; definite; ineradicable; judicious; conflicting; defamatory; comparative; quaint; admirable; humorous; adroit; confident; intelligible; inaccurate; conservative; groundless; naked; specious; plausible; previous; remarkable; uncompromising; hazardous; ridiculous; penetrating; accompanying; publicized; distorted; oracular; attributive; precise; ingenuous; comprehensive; sensible; trifle-sounding; absurd; startling; hyperbolical; vague; foregoing; elucidated; derogatory; fervid; immortal; amazing; reiterated; graphic; detailed; articulate; erroneous; periphrastic; sweeping; dogmatic; positive; direct; superfluous; candid; authoritative; substantial.

verbs
allude to—; alter—; amplify—; base—on; bolster—; buttress—; certify to—; cite—; compile—; contradict—; controvert—; convey—; correlate—; dig up—; discredit—; draft—; edit—; elaborate—; elicit—; evade —; exaggerate—; extract—; fling out—; follow up—; heed—; impugn—; infer from —; issue—; label—; misquote—; modify—; qualify—; quote—; reiterate—; rest upon—; subsidize—; transmit—; unravel—; utter—; verify—; weigh—; —challenges; —depresses; —discloses; —implies; —jars; —justifies.

(See allegation, assertion, declaration, expression, remark.)

STATESMAN

adjectives
influential; sagacious; unhackneyed; darksome; bold; eminent; contending; practised; astute; senile; distinguished; wary; brash; far-seeing; liberal; haughty; dogmatic; brilliant; deft.

verbs
acclaim—; commemorate—; honor—; laud —; —arbitrates; —confers; —contracts; —counsels; —directs; —emancipates; —elevates; —executes; —exhorts; —formulates; —forges; —furthers; —governs; —guides; —helms; —manipulates; —negotiates; —steers; —struggles; —takes over; —transacts; —uplifts.

(See diplomat, legislator, ambassador, statesmanship.)

STATESMANSHIP

adjectives
businesslike; perjured; treacherous; inadequate; clear-sighted; far-seeing; conservative; pitiful.

verbs
acclaim—; cloak in—; demonstrate—; discern—; employ—; endow with—; exercise —; —alleviates; —averts; —dodges; —eases tension; —extricates; —flounders; —lightens; —machinates; —maneuvers; —pilots; —smooths; —steers; —unravels.

(See statesman, diplomacy, management.)

STATION

adjectives
enviable; desolate; supernatural; allotted; recruiting; way; unmoving; equivocal; biological; unshrinking; elevated; responsible; dust-driven; distributing; intermediate; fragile; conspicuous; meteorological; dingy; smoky; native; low; service; future; passenger; retreading; control; prostrate; dinky.

verbs
accumulate at—; confine to—; deposit at—; maintain—; remain at—; trundle to—; wait at—; —distributes; —quarters.

(See place, post, location.)

STATION (*v*)

adverbs
ingeniously; elevatedly; conspicuously; intermittently; frequently; advantageously.

(See post, place.)

STATIONARY

adverbs
mysteriously; alarmingly; bewilderingly; apparently; deliberately; helpfully; significantly; curiously; evidently.

STATISTICS

adjectives
complex; staple; stupendous; controversial; appalling; cold; official; available; accurate; scanty; untrustworthy; glowing; devastating; remarkable; pitiless; convincing; definite.

verbs
combine—; compile—; dig into—; eschew —; marshal—; plow through—; quote—; —arm; —bury under; —demonstrate; —dis-

close; —embrace; —hammer; —substantiate; —support; —terrify; —unleash; —verify.

(See list, information, book, knowledge.)

STATUE

adjectives

gigantic; plaster; impulsive; urgent; sepulchral; sylvan; portrait; earthen; colossal; symbolic; charming; strict; grotesque; memorial; emblematic; insignificant; mutilated; grave; multi-farious (pl); magic; marble; rigorous; dominating; painted.

verbs

carve—; cast—; chisel—; disrobe—; erect —; exhibit—; hew—; inscribe on—; model —; mould—; mount—; mutilate—; perch on—; prize—; prop—; shatter—; straddle —; topple—; unveil—; value—; —adorns; —commemorates; —depicts; —embellishes; —honors; —illustrates; —portrays; —symbolizes.

(See figure, masterpiece, monument, plaque.)

STATURE

adjectives

intellectual; veritable; simulated; commanding; mental; physical; moral; unusual; frail; gigantic; diminutive; stately; proud; dilating; slender; apparent; middle; financial; intellectual; political; herculean; unusual; exceptional; colossal; tall.

verbs

achieve—; alter—; attain—; augment—; check—; determine—; exalt—; extend—; heighten—; lack—; limit—; magnify—; measure—; stunt—; surpass in—; —bulks; —dwindles; —looms; —overawes; —towers.

(See height, growth, development.)

STATUS

adjectives

recognized; financial; front-rank; primitive; honorific; present; moral; usual; definite.

verbs

abandon—; acquire—; alter—; approve—; ascertain—; assume—; attack—; attain—; confuse—; corrupt—; defend—; define—; degrade—; designate—; detect—; determine —; dignify—; discredit—; elevate—; ennoble—; exalt—; forfeit—; glorify—; grant —; humble—; improve upon—; impugn—; insure—; investigate—; maintain—; merit —; recover—; relinquish—; restore—; resurrect—; retain—; revolutionize—; suspend—; sustain—; taint—.

(See position, standing, state, condition.)

STATUTE

adjectives

penal; contravened; dead; oppressive; protective; unfair; age-old; unenforced; heartless; unjustifiable.

verbs

advocate—; abolish—; abrogate—; annul—; codify—; comply with—; countermand—; decry—; denounce—; discard—; doom—; enact—; enforce—; evade—; flout—; formulate—; frame—; ignore—; infringe—; invoke—; nullify—; observe—; ratify—; repeal—; retract—; transgress—; uphold—; veto—; violate—; void—; —annuls; —authorizes; —bans; —bars; —classifies; —decrees; —delegates; —enlightens; —empowers; —establishes; —exists; —legalizes; —limits; —prescribes; —prohibits; —provides.

(See law, legislation.)

STATUTORY

adverbs

impressively; inescapably; recently; unfortunately; luckily; inflexibly; vexatiously; curiously; wisely.

STAY

adjectives

fruitless; protracted; transient; pertinacious; subsequent: laggard; unprofitable; prolonged; tremulous; short; pleasant; amusing; lengthy.

verbs

abandon—; anticipate—; conclude—; discontinue—; enforce—; extend—; grant—; interrupt—; plead for—; press for—; prolong—; protract—; resume—; terminate—; welcome—; —defers; —elapses; —expires; —relaxes; —reprieves; —retards; —wanes.

(See stand, support.)

STAY (v)

adverbs

unobtrusively; adamantly; stubbornly; miraculously; traditionally; customarily; habitually; perpetually; temporarily; fruitlessly; protractedly; transiently; briefly; pertinaciously.

(See remain, lodge.)

STEADFAST

adverbs

loyally; dutifully; affectionately; properly; dependably; reliably; faithfully; eagerly; enthusiastically; zealously; filially; lovingly; fondly; piously; fervently; ardently; unwaveringly; curiously; remarkably; utterly.

STEAL (v)

adverbs

furtively; craftily; slyly; insidiously; basely; covertly; subtly; discreetly; mercilessly; noiselessly; jealously; suspiciously; ominously.

(See rob, plunder.)

STEALING

verbs

charge with—; convict of—; deplore—; disclose—; forsake—; indict for—; penalize—; practise—; rebuke for—; reduce to—; relinquish—; renounce—; reproach for—; resort to—; reveal—; scorn—; —defiles; —degrades; —deprives; —dishonors.

(See theft.)

STEALTHY

adverbs

guiltily; necessarily; warily; unusually; suspiciously; extraordinarily; remarkably; mischievously; furtively; carefully; naturally; uncommonly; craftily; cleverly; adroitly; mysteriously; cautiously; suspiciously; gingerly.

STEAM

adjectives

corrosive; scalding; fainting; sanguine; oppressive; exhaust; unsavory; poisonous; fragrant; spouting; hot; stinking; hissing; rich.

verbs

compress—; gauge—; generate—; harness—; inhale—; meter—; spew—; spout—; spray—; vent—; —befogs; —bursts; —clouds; —condenses; —drenches; —forces; —jets; —mists; —moistens; —obscures; —propels; —scalds; —wilts.

(See mist, spray, smoke.)

STEAMER

adjectives

charter; borrowed; prosaic; boarded; tramp; coastwise; filibustering; delinquent; lazy; dismantled; ocean; sumptuous; elegant; warping.

verbs

convoy—; launch—; —circumnavigates; —ferries; —glides; —hauls; —maneuvers; —plies; —rolls; —rots; —rusts; —speeds; —transports.

(See boat, launch, motor-boat, ship.)

STEAM-SHOVEL

verbs

—batters; —burrows; —s clank; —deepens; —devours; —discloses; —effaces; —erases; —excavates; —facilitates; —gorges; —gnaws at; —gulps; —hollows; —levels; —ravages; —swallows; —trenches; —unearths.

STEED

adjectives

bounding; angular; proud; fiery; flying; dashing; ribbed; unmanageable; mangy; fine-limbed; snowy; mercurial; heavenly; resistless; prancing; border; mottled; fire-breathing; well-proportioned; riderless; reinless; strong; livid; headstrong; frantic; smoking; noble; mighty; shadowy; aerial; stalwart; spirited; wild.

STEEL

adjectives

vengeful; ingot; thrusting; rushing; coarse; thin; nervous; well-tempered; field; jagged; massive; gleaming; shrewd; scorching; mirroring; unpolished; toughened; incomplete; brandished; lateral; carbonized; flashing; molten; crashing; fiery; roweled.

verbs

alloy—; analyze—; cast—; clash against—; compound—; convert into—; deoxidize—; desulphurize—; encase in—; forge—; frame with—; ladle—; lathe—; magnetize—; melt—; mold—; polish—; process—; purify—; roll—; smelt—; tap—; temper—; test—; weld—; —armors; —congeals; —corrodes; —decomposes; —deflects; —oxidizes; —reinforces; —resists; —transmits.

(See iron, lead, metal.)

STEEP

adverbs

precipitously; alarmingly; impossibly; startlingly; unexpectedly; perilously; hazardously; suddenly; starkly; abruptly; unreasonably; excessively; remarkably; incalculably;

inaccessibly; boldly; exorbitantly; extravagantly; unwarrantably; unreasonably; painfully; formidably; forbiddingly; curiously; particularly; immoderately.

STEEPNESS

verbs

bolt—; cap—; culminate—; elevate—; exaggerate—; mount—; surmount—; —declines; —exalts; —impresses; —inspires; —looms; —overwhelms; —soars; —towers.

(See height, altitude.)

STEER (*v*)

adverbs

erratically; unerringly; dexterously; deftly; skillfully; cautiously; accurately; conscientiously.

(See control, guide.)

STEM

adjectives

enchanted; deathless; gnarled; immovable; tapering; supple; tough; knotted; fibrous; apparent; sacred; insignificant; succulent; climbing; nourishing; straggling; fan-edged; fruitless; slender; bending.

verbs

clasp—; crop—; ground—; heighten—; hinge on—; level—; pivot on—; pluck from —; snip—; spring from—; sway on—; —curves; —extends; —forks; —rises; —supports; —sustains.

(See stalk.)

STENCH

adjectives

noisome; fetid; obscene; horrible; nasty; intolerable; nauseating.

verbs

cast—; diffuse—; emit—; inhale—; —assails; —clings; —contaminates; —corrupts; —defiles; —galls; —lingers; —nauseates; —offends; —overcomes; —overwhelms; —penetrates; —pervades; —pollutes; —reeks; —sickens; —taints; —thickens; —turns.

(See odor, smell, staleness.)

STEP

adjectives

decisive; quickened; radical; important; imperious; weary; restless; tremulous; painful; pilgrim; homeless; elastic; impudent; lascivious; desperate; fainting; toiling; firm; unfaltering; cautious; single; false; dragging; light; fleet; ungainly; rugged; swinging; uncertain; innumerable; listless; fearless; certain; tottering; rapid; mincing; echoless; zigzag; winding; incomprehensible; successive; witching; assured; gradual; vast; desirable; inadvertent; laggard; graceful; stately; devious; backward; conquering; unpracticed; uneven; timid; reeling; feeble; dictating; trembling; buoyant; practicable; pregnant; irrevocable; gigantic; grassy; drastic; vacillating; sagging; suspended; joyful; dignified; requisite; sedative; long; slow; concluding; still; instinctive; honest; resounding; slackened; furtive; ponderous; social; doubtful; disordered; inevitable; slippery; military; languid; reluctant; ample; rustic; rude; parting; shuffled; hospitable; crunching; boundless; measurable; precautionary; gentle; weak; flagging; rosy; stone; jerky; comely; confident; hasty; gradual; immense; unhurrying; beehived; springy; homeward; irreverent; hushed; decorous; constructive; haughty; threatening; stealthy; undeviating; indispensable; silken; wandering; logical; subsequent; dainty; hazardous; momentous; bold; panting; finite; erratic; deft; noiseless; palsied; tottering; impious; soldierly; intermediate; martial; disspirited; stiff.

verbs

acclaim—; advance—; advocate—; applaud —; appraise—; approve—; ascend—; avert —; comprehend—; contrive—; defend—; design—; devise—; frame—; graduate—; lay out—; loll on—; lumber up—; map out —s; mount—; ooze down—s; plan—; reconsider—; regard—; regret—; retrace—s; rue —; scale—s; slant down—; slip down—s; steal down—s; survey—; systematize—; toil up—; trip down—; urge—; weigh—; —commences; —intrudes; —retreats; —s retrograde.

(See ladder, stairs, footstep, advance.)

STEP (*v*)

adverbs

discreetly; mincingly; awkwardly; clumsily; boldly; gingerly; defiantly; noiselessly; deliberately; resolutely; reluctantly; majestically; fearlessly; shufflingly; stealthily.

(See stride, pace.)

STERILE

adverbs
safely; securely; absolutely; warrantably; completely; assuredly; protectively; supposedly; presumably; carefully.

STERILITY

adjectives
general; panting; superficial; artistic; painful; shamed.

verbs
advocate—; bewail—; decry—; determine —; induce—; produce—; —annuls; —blasts; —blights; —dashes; —deprives; —devitalizes; —disconcerts; —emasculates; —frustrates; —nullifies; —thwarts.
(See weakness, fatigue.)

STERN

adverbs
gravely; puritanically; rigorously; uncompromisingly; inflexibly; unsparingly; arbitrarily; imperiously; severely; tyrannically; brutally; odiously; atrociously; needlessly; intolerably; senselessly; unreasonably; properly; necessarily.

STERNNESS

adjectives
strange; awful; considerable; unwonted; black; meaningful; frowning.

STEW

adjectives
hot; sickly; peppered; savory-looking; terrible.

verbs
bolt—; brew—; compound—; concoct—; dispatch—; fare on—; gulp—; prepare—; relish—; savor—; season—; sniff—; swill—; —blisters; —quells; —satiates; —seethes; —simmers; —slakes; —whets.
(See meat, food.)

STICK

adjectives
dead-brown; gnarled; knobbed; thick; knotted; sturdy; twisted; pointed.

verbs
arm with—; bear—; belabor with—; brandish—; deflect with—; fling—; flog with—; flourish—; goad with—; hurl—; prop on—; repulse with—; splinter—; thrash with—; thrust—; thwack with—; twirl—; wave—; whack with—; whittle—; —coerces; —intimidates; —supports; —sustains.
(See cane, baton, club.)

STICK (v)

adverbs
tenaciously; manfully; faithfully; firmly; adhesively; sturdily; jealously.
(See jab, stab.)

STICKY

adverbs
unaccountably; perniciously; inconveniently; unpleasantly; disagreeably; terribly; unexpectedly; hatefully; inexcusably; carelessly; messily; unfortunately; handily; usefully; serviceably; properly; suitably; adaptably; amazingly; dependably; insufficiently.

STIGMA

adjectives
infernal; irredeemable; lifelong; viscid; social; scandalous.

verbs
abolish—; bear—; destroy—; efface—; endure—; eradicate—; escape—; extricate—; incur—; inveigh against—; nullify—; purge of—; shun—; suffer—; tolerate—; vindicate of—; wipe out—; —aggravates; —brands; —clings; —defames; —detracts from; —humiliates; —marks; —ostracizes; —reflects upon; —sullies; —taints; —traduces; —defiles.
(See disgrace, dishonor.)

STILETTO

verbs
bury—; edge—; extract—; fling—; hilt—; hurl—; impale on—; plunge—; sheathe—; withdraw—; —s clash; —cleaves; —gashes; —lacerates; —penetrates; —perforates; —pierces; —pricks; —punctures; —rends; —severs; —slashes; —slits; —sunders.
(See knife.)

STILL

adverbs
alarmingly; desolately; lonesomely; absolutely; strangely; peculiarly; curiously; oddly; gruesomely; pleasantly; comfortably; serenely; calmly; refreshingly; appropriately; happily; contentedly; peacefully; suddenly; unaccountably; exceptionally; unusually; remarkably; amazingly; mysteriously; significantly; appallingly.

STILLNESS

adjectives
comparative; monastic; prolonged; modest; gloomy; hideous; solemn; earnest; ominous; deathly; profound; appalling; majestic; deepest; utter; glittering; sepulchral; ghostly; unearthly; weird; succeeding; sullen; soft; rural; reverential; curtained; outdoor; sacred; abysmal; intense; fetid; prevailing; suffocating; sabbatical; willful; pensive; deep; black; obstinate; sunny; absolute; audible; dreaming; unwonted; midnight; hushed; awed.

verbs
break—; cherish—; endure—; murmur in—; penetrate—; permeate—; perpetuate—; pervade—; prolong—; rend—; resound in—; ruffle—; shatter—; shroud in—; —calms; —dejects; —depresses; —envelops; —grips; —haunts; —pervades; —reigns; —soothes; —stifles; —sulks; —unnerves.
(See calm, hush, silence.)

STILTED

adverbs
formally; uncomfortably; uneasily; stupidly; ineptly; unfortunately; curiously; crudely; awkwardly; terribly; nervously; gracelessly; pretentiously; absurdly; fantastically; outlandishly; bombastically; bashfully; inexpertly; grossly; unwontedly; unreasonably.

STIMULANT

adjectives
active; overpowering; mental; excellent; strange; intoxicating; favorite; necessary; helpful.

verbs
abstain from—; addict to—; administer—; avoid—; dilute—; impart—; indulge in—; infuse—; inject—; introduce—; prescribe—; require—; —agitates; —buoys; —compresses; —electrifies; —enkindles; —excites; —flushes; —galvanizes; —impassions; —inflames; —intoxicates; —provokes; —quickens; —reanimates; —rejuvenates; —rekindles; —revives; —shocks.
(See coffee, tonic, medicine, alcohol, whiskey.)

STIMULATE (*v*)

adverbs
lasciviously; artificially; alcoholically; electrically; simultaneously; instantaneously; erotically; refreshingly; injuriously; healthfully; beneficially; perniciously; agreeably; languidly; morbidly; sexually; psychologically.
(See incite, excite.)

STIMULATION

adjectives
sensory; self-satisfying; unnatural; psychological; sexual; useless; painful; gentle.

verbs
acquire—; afford—; convey—; derive—; furnish—; impart—; indulge in—; offer—; provide—; resist—; supply—; yield to—; —accelerates; —overexerts; —quickens; —subsides.
(See excitement, exhilaration.)

STIMULUS

adjectives
temporary; peculiar; reviving; new; sufficient; provocative; external; intellectual; immense; artificial; natural; native; unsound; keen; biting; sharp.

verbs
add—; afford—; apply—; balance—; furnish—; gain—; implant—; lessen—; react to—; reduce—; respond to—; want—; —allures; —assails; —baits; —declines; —diminishes; —incites; —induces; —produces; —recedes; —responds; —survives; —tempts; —wanes.
(See impetus, inducement, incentive.)

STING

adjectives
momentary; jealous; sudden; unworthy; painful; galling; rancorous; brutish; fiery; myriad; careless; venomous.

verbs
allay—; alleviate—; escape—; inflict—; mitigate—; palliate—; relieve—; salve—; treat—; wince at—; —envenoms; —incenses; —inflames; —irritates; —lancinates; —nettles; —perforates; —piques; —poisons; —pricks; —punctures; —rends; —tingles.
(See bite.)

STINK

verbs
(See stench.)

STINT (v)

adverbs
parsimoniously; fanatically; meanly; niggardly; selfishly; scandalously; unwontedly.
(See limit, restrain.)

STIPULATE (v)

adverbs
solemnly; financially; specifically; shrewdly; generally; minutely.
(See agree, state.)

STIR

adjectives
fluttering; quick; multitudinous; tremulous; nervous; gentle; tremendous; angry; noiseless; pleasant; enormous; ceaseless; restless; subdued; faint; considerable; unnoticed.

verbs
agitate—; brook—; create—; embroil in—; endure—; quash—; quell—; restrain—; subdue—; suppress—; tolerate—; —bustles; —convulses; —disconcerts; —disquiets; —distracts; —diverts; —ebbs; —excites; —intensifies; —persists: —perturbs; —sharpens; —subsides.
(See commotion, agitation, movement, activity.)

STIR (v)

adverbs
contentiously; frantically; emotionally; spiritually; imperceptibly; profoundly; incessantly; restively; caressingly; tremulously; ceaselessly; agitatedly.
(See move, arouse, rouse.)

STIRRUPS

verbs
adjust—; discard—; loll on—; maintain—; mount by—; polish—; post on—; reinforce—; rise in—; slip from—; stand up in—; strain—; suspend—; weaken—; —afford; —bear; —brace; —dangle; —enable; —gird; —hang; —receive; —relieve; —support; —sustain.

STITCH (v)

adverbs
patiently; diligently; dexterously; cleverly; ceaselessly; indefatigably; industriously; skillfully.
(See sew, fasten.)

STITCHES

verbs
alternate—; bias—; dissolve—; interlace—; interlink—; rend—; unravel—; —baste; —bind; —conjoin; —fuse; —hem; —insure; —knit; —reinforce; —restrain; —seal; —save; —tack; —unite.

STOCK
(finance)

verbs
bear—; bull—; burden with—; certify—; counterfeit—; dabble in—; devaluate—; dispose of—; dump—; inflate—; invest in—; issue—; juggle—; liquidate—; market—; recommend—; renew—; retain—; relinquish—; speculate with—; stabilize—; traffic in—; unload—; —ascends; —booms; —crashes; —dwindles; —fluctuates; —impoverishes; —oscillates; —skyrockets (colloq.); —soars; —toboggans; —vacillates.
(See business, investment, capital, thermometer, barometer, shares.)

STOCK
(general)

adjectives
chitinous; parent; diversified; rejuvenated; calcareous; gilt-edged; inferior; reputable; revolutionary; rolling; suspicious; peaceful; heterogeneous; degenerate; serious; enormous; linguistic; inclusive; parish; tremendous; replaceable; sapling; surplus; extensive; common; fine; venturesome; pioneer; deficient; pathetic; ranging; selected; wild.

STOCKING

adjectives
foul; prosaic; merino; silk; wool; rayon; cotton; webbed; coarse; rough; rubber; wrinkled; rolled.

STOCKY

adverbs
sturdily; huskily; stalwartly; thickly; exceptionally; remarkably; distinctly; peculiarly; unusually; noticeably; unforgettably; chubbily; brawnily.

STOICAL

adverbs
marvellously; naturally; philosophically; courageously; intrepidly; calmly; serenely; valiantly; inflexibly; patiently; coolly; imperturbably; immovably; resolutely; exceptionally.

STOLID

adverbs
strangely; **dully; apathetically**; singularly; oddly; curiously; unaccountably; inscrutably; irritatingly; vexatiously; shockingly; callously; abysmally; **hopelessly**; inexplicably; **incurably.**

STOMACH

adjectives
tripartite; grateful; excellent; heroic; distended; empty; lean; outraged; unbounded; queasy; nervous; upset; hollow; bulging; protruding.

verbs
abuse—; alkalize—; constrict—; cramp —; derange—; dilate—; displace—; distend—; drain—; empty—; flood—; incise—; irritate—; **knead—**; lodge in—; offend—; overload—; **pump from—**; purge —; reduce—; **remove from—**; scald—; sour —; strangulate—; **turn—**; upset—; wash out —; —assimilates; —converts; —distresses; —excretes; —falls; —houses; —prolapses; —protests; —reduces; —regurgitates; —retains; —revolts; **—shrinks; —turns.**

STONE

adjectives
mossy; sacrificial; senseless; heavy; ragged; jagged; votive; pallid; timeworn; graven; veritable; ribbed; crumbling; moldering; ancient; crystal; shattered; stumbling; quarried; flying; wrought; misshapen; scarlet; flawless; contumelious; cold; miry; typical; sizzling; destructive; corresponding; hollow; coarse; lithographic; sun-heated; precious; dangerous; showering; blasted; unpolished; barren; silent; greasy; monumental; enameled; uneven; rifted; breathing; bruising; solemn; rigid; massive; splintered; nameless; **smoldered; chiseled**; perfect; priceless.

verbs
carve in—; cast in—; chisel in—; dislodge —; face—; fashion of—; heave—; hew from—; hurl—; inscribe on—; perpetuate in—; project—; quarry—; rib with—; unveil—; work in—; —bruises; —crushes; —erodes; **—facets**; —s rattle; **—rumbles**; —supports; —sustains; —wedges.
(See rock, gem, jewel.)

STONY

adverbs
roughly; unpleasantly; ruggedly; disagreeably; impassably; curiously; amazingly; indescribably; terribly; unmanageably; cruelly.

STOOP (v)

adverbs
cautiously; humbly; dejectedly; wearily; miserably; subserviently; abjectly; obsequiously.
(See bend, descend.)

STOP

adjectives
sudden; tender; multiple; occasional; traffic; express; surprising.

STOP (v)

adverbs
abruptly; suddenly; instantaneously; instinctively; imperiously; constantly; effectually; timorously; virtually.
(See halt, pause.)

STOPPER

verbs
employ—; fasten—; perforate—; ram in—; stave in—; tamp—; valve—; —checks; —chokes; —corks; —dams; —gags; —insures; —obstructs; —plugs; —restrains; —seals; —stems.
(See plug.)

STORE

adjectives
hideous; wholesome; commodious; hidden; heterogeneous; priceless; strange; corner; frugal; department; fragrant; truly-beautiful; tributary; increasing; plundered; rich; chain; vegetable; bounteous; sorrowful; shoe; overflowing; swanky; smart; glistening; plentiful; wondrous; inexhaustible; gorgeous; mystic; unprotected; ordnance; milky; humble; exclusive; abundant; reliable; provident; vast; cöoperative; subsistence; gigantic; literary; undiminished; mustering; huge; immense; proud; untried; prodigious; lavish; winnowing; present; colorful; sparkling; absorbing; exciting; action; adventure; entertaining; amazing; amusing; picked; delightful; captivating; thrilling; true.

verbs
canvass—s; departmentalize—; **draw from**

—s; expand—; patronize—; —adjusts; —branches out; —caters to; —dispenses; —disposes of; —flourishes; —guarantees; —markets; —purveys; —renovates; —retails; —services; —thrives; —undersells; —unloads; —vends; —wholesales.
(See market, shop, source, supply, provision, food.)

STORE (v)

adverbs
providentially; consequently; secretly; bounteously; inexhaustibly; abundantly; immensely; lavishly; prodigiously; adequately.
(See save, hoard.)

STORK

adjectives
stilted; devouring; brisk; unwelcome; gawky; awkward.

verbs
alarm—; gun for—; stir up—; —claws; —fishes; —floats; —gyrates; —hovers; —rakes; —sails over; —skims; —soars; —strokes; —wades; —wheels.
(See bird.)

STORM

adjectives
teacup; lurid; freezing; irresistible; majestic; blinding; blustering; tumultuous; driving; maddened; harsh; adverse; murky; wintry; fearful; mocking; wrestling; gathering; factual; insatiate; devastating; cyclonic; purifying; conflicting; rising; surly; mingling; slanted; revolving; violent; forgotten; howling; bloody; persistent; rushing; clarifying; dissipated; psychologic; terrific; heavy; raging; confluent; coming; shipwrecking; vicious; beating; expiring; pelting; financial; cyclic; unkind; transitory; recurrent; coast; whistling; perfect; subsiding; blinding; appraising; commingling (pl); rollicking; savage; full-grown; slanting; driving; momentary; deluging; long-continued; tremendous; theologic; awakening; wreckful; drenching; political.

verbs
allay—; battle through—; encounter—; fly before—; foretell—; front—; ride—; scoff at—; shelter from—; stir up—; survive—; tarry in—; unleash—; weather—; —abates; —batters; —brawls; —breaks; —brews; —bursts; —calms; —develops; —flashes; —gathers; —grumbles; —lashes; —rages; —roars; —seethes; —thunders; —wears out; —whips through; —whistles.
(See blizzard, hurricane, lightning, rain.)

STORM (v)

adverbs
overpoweringly; relentlessly; furiously; irresistibly; thunderously; passionately; devastatingly.
(See fume, rage.)

STORMY

adverbs
wildly; drearily; inordinately; terribly; perilously; tempestuously; thunderously; gustily; roughly; furiously; relentlessly; alarmingly; extraordinarily; violently; fiercely; intensely; unusually; disastrously; dreadfully; fearfully; unusually; extremely; uncommonly; cyclonically; icily.

STORY

adjectives
pathetic; candid; stirring; mouthed; chivalrous; complicated; wonderful; plausible; ludicrous; priceless; naive; moving; roaring; sublime; unexpurgated; eye-opening; authentic; detailed; graphic; specious; woeful; improbable; harrowing; idyllic; rambling; poignant; outrageous; self-told; true; ill-natured; gripping; unpublished; painful; legendary; rudimentary; mystery; absorbing; stupendous; incredible; cruel; mournful; inimitable; apocryphal; unembellished; shameful; threadbare; circumstantial; speaking; typical; thrilling; perishing; revealing; hackneyed; dubious; ribald; conflicting; calumniating; unfinished; veritable; dismal; squalid; wondrous; well-known; age-worn; amusing; time-honored; unbelievable; priceless; adventure; self-effacing; blood-curdling; delectable; inspiring; pungent; fictitious; witty; racy; rapid; complete; amorous; laborious; heroic; commonplace; smooth-flowing; sea; fruitful; innocent; eloquent; darling; appropriate; absurd; perpetual; horrid; abominable; unconnected; tragic; curious; edifying; lustful; copious; spicy; readable; ridiculous; realistic; uppermost; lame; finest; romantic; monotonous; facetious; sad; thought-provoking; sordid; slanderous; eventful; melodramatic; uninterrupted; homely; accredited; grim; tender; didactic; unbiased; tribal; mess-worn; disastrous; well-told; instructive; fascinating; upper; shallow; garbled; delicious; hall-marked;

unreticent; heinous; elaborate; sensational; exquisite; accepted; harrowing; alive; complete; distinguished; deep; entertaining; horror; full-blooded; intimate; inside; light; swift-moving; top-notch; veracious; well-written; well-paced.

verbs
accumulate—s; belittle—; bolster—; cast—; circulate—; climax—; conceive—; concoct —; construct—; dash off—; criticize—; devour—; discredit—; dominate—; dramatize —; dwarf—; embroider—; enact—; fabricate—; fashion—; forge—; hail—; interpret—; invent—; issue—; load—; manufacture—s; narrate—; overload—; paint—; peg away at—; pour out—; present—; peruse—; question—; recapitulate—; reel off —; reiterate—; relate—; release—; relish —; scoff at—; scotch—; spin—; thread—; transcend—; turn out—; verify—; wade thru—; weave—; worm out—; —centers; —confirms; —consoles; —corroborates; —degenerates; —denounces; —depends; —elicits; —emanates; —embellishes; —engrosses; —enhances; —etches; —fascinates; —flows; —hurtles; —implicates; —inspires; —lacks; —links; —marches; —moves; —originates; —pictures; —pieces; —plunges; —progresses; —recounts; —regales; —reigns; —revolves; —rounds off; —shapes; —skirts; —slanders; —slants; —survives; —throws; —tingles; —touches; —travels; —unfolds.

(See legend, fiction, prose, "movie," history, narrative, myth, narration, manuscript, anecdote, book, episode, novel.)

STOUT

adverbs
brawnily; vigorously; unexpectedly; incredibly; invincibly; dependably; unusually; reliably; intrepidly; unbelievably; fortunately; remarkably; surprisingly; uncommonly.

STOUT-HEARTED

adverbs
intrepidly; fearlessly; ridiculously; uncommonly; admirably; undauntedly; immovably; cheerfully; steadfastly; wonderfully; valiantly; boldly; unfailingly; gaily; heroically; pluckily; resolutely; confidently; indomitably; uncommonly; spunkily.

STOUTNESS

verbs
accentuate—; augment—; deplore—; deride—; exaggerate—; magnify—; mitigate —; predispose to—; reduce—; ridicule—; scoff at—; snigger at—; tend toward—; —aggravates; —deforms; —discommodes; —distorts; —dwarfs; —embarrasses; —endangers; —hampers; —hinders; —inconveniences; —mars; —renders ugly; —restrains; —restricts; —stagnates; —threatens; —towers; —wanes.

(See obesity.)

STOVE

adjectives
solemn; nameless; diminutive; roaring; hot; ancient; fiery; sputtering.

verbs
bask by—; consign to—; dampen—; draft —; extinguish—; feed—; hover over—; kindle—; quench—; replenish—; tend—; —affords; —comforts; —diffuses; —dies; —fumes; —insures; —reeks; —roars; —smoulders; —thaws.

(See fire, flame.)

STRAIGHT

adverbs
invariably; perfectly; unwaveringly; commendably; undeniably; exactly; accurately; correctly; admirably; unquestionably; uncommonly; exceptionally; unerringly; authentically; officially; conveniently; comparatively.

STRAIGHTFORWARD

adverbs
commendably; admirably; eminently; unusually; manifestly; evidently; reliably; unquestionably; delightfully; helpfully; artlessly; candidly; unaffectedly; naturally; inherently; obviously; bluntly; ingenuously; childishly; remarkably; uncommonly; scrupulously.

STRAIN

adjectives
sunny; metaphysical; inspiring; harmonious; terrific; bastard; impure; celestial-ordered; subtle; indomitable; echoing; windy; wild; passionate; parting; true-breeding; jubilant; self-same; soft; andante; majestic; exalted; tidal; lofty; untaught; ceaseless; meditative; strenuous; thrilling; singular; unwonted; sublime; aesthetic; adoring; onward; seraphic; taut; minor; thrilling; virile; homiletic; heated; mystical; musical; haunting; audacious; furious;

melancholy; shrill; intellectual; magic; creeping; nameless; unending; delicious; solemn; ventriloquous; gloomy; exultant; epic; lamentable; humorous; immortal; nervous; ravishing; fluent; intense; melodious; dirgeful; noble; thrilling; severe; pompous; intolerable; arresting; serious; mournful; extraordinary; full-fraught; sententious; chaste; racial; emotional; semi-humorous; muscular; individual; violent; true; profitless; indigenous; tender; steady; existing; successive (pl); mystic; pathetic; half-forgotten; polemic; vicious; curious; iterant; somber; martial; tremendous; terrible; inspired; syncopated; subdued; evoked; local; humble; unpolished; sweet; fierce; divine; crushing; enchanting; inevitable.

verbs
avoid—; develop—; disturb—; endure—; entail—; impose—; lift—; mutate—; relieve of—; overtake—; remove—; risk—; slacken—; stand—; subject to—; withstand—; —swells.
(See tension, exertion, stress.)

STRAIN (v)

adverbs
incompatibly; prodigiously; inordinately; feebly; passionately; furiously; intellectually; lamentably; excessively.
(See force, stretch.)

STRAIT-LACED

adverbs
absurdly; extremely; priggishly; puritanically; ridiculously; immovably; austerely; arbitrarily; unreasonably; unfortunately; rigidly; unwisely; uncompromisingly; forbiddingly; peremptorily; inexorably; tyrannically; foolishly; prudishly.

STRAITS

adjectives
pecuniary; dire; interminable; imaginary; sounding; desperate; narrow; great; bitter.

STRAND

adjectives
braided; remotest; everlasting; rippling; deserted; great; deep; dark; tragic; mysterious; siren-footed; genial; intertwisted (pl); blistering; dreary; uneven; lonely.

STRANGER

adjectives
formidable; mysterious; unutterable; illustrious; witless; unfriended; well-bred; wandering; forlorn; curious; waiting; humble; unsuspecting; audacious; comparative; thorough; inferior; wayfaring; dreadful; distinguished; swarthy; total; casual; ungenial; sympathetic; neat; unsavory; strange; queer; fluttering; passing; houseless; adulated; unnaturalized; insignificant; unheralded; blooming; detested; shrewd; plain-spoken; earth-born; rough-looking; drunken; drawling-voiced.

verbs
acquaint—with; admit—; appraise—; apprehend—; beguile—; bilk—; confide in—; cultivate—; deceive—; defraud—; delude—; discuss—; distrust—; dupe—; enlighten—; entertain—; exclude—s; extend to—; greet—; guide—; hail—; harbor—; implicate—; inform—; interrogate—; investigate—; mislead—; question—; receive—; regard—; salute—; snarl at—; trail—; usher in—; victimize—; welcome—.
(See alien, immigrant, newcomers, foreigners.)

STRANGLE (v)

adverbs
cruelly; excruciatingly; demoniacally; fiendishly; deliberately; maniacally; lustfully; sordidly; horridly; sensationally; horribly; amorously.
(See choke, kill.)

STRAP

verbs
affix—; braid—; buckle—; clasp—; detach—; reinforce—; rend—; sever—; slacken—; tense—; —binds; —couples; —curbs; —fetters; —impedes; —leashes; —links; —restrains; —supports; —sustains.
(See leash, belt, band.)

STRATEGIC

adverbs
cleverly; opportunely; conveniently; expediently; diplomatically; profoundly; secretly; wisely; prudently; discreetly; brilliantly; cunningly; craftily; insidiously; cannily; successfully; splendidly; usefully; profitably; immeasurably; financially; politically; commercially.

STRATAGEM

adjectives
successful; deadlier; vicious; daring; clumsy; clever; brilliant; military.

verbs
conceive—; concoct—; devise—; employ—; frame—; hatch—; practice—; resort to—; —accomplishes; —baffles; —baits; —befools; —beguiles; —bluffs; —confounds; —decoys; —defrauds; —deludes; —distracts; —diverts; —entices; —frustrates; —hoodwinks; —lures; —rebuffs; —repulses; —routs; —snares; —succeeds; —thwarts.
(See fraud, strategy, deception.)

STRATEGY

adjectives
half-baked; adroit; military; triumphant; ancient; superlative; absurd; sound; naval; aggressive; offensive; thrill-packed.

verbs
achieve—; administer—; adopt—; advise—; approve—; beguile with—; condemn—; counsel—; direct—; effect—; employ—; execute—; fashion—; frame—; guide—; pilot —; plan—; prescribe—; proceed with—; resort to—; steer—; work out—; —defeats; —outwits; —stems from.
(See maneuver, method, stratagem.)

STRAW

adjectives
patient; plaiting; helpful; apparent; damp; frowzy; synthetic; oaten.

verbs
bale—; bed with—; bleach—; discard—; embed in—; glean—; macerate—; plait—; scatter—; shed—; stuff with—; thresh—; weave—; —insures; —litters; —pads; —protects; —thatches.
(See chaff, hair, hay.)

STRAY (v)

adverbs
ostensibly; widely; irrationally; idiotically; adventurously; lustfully; senselessly.
(See roam, wander.)

STREAK

adjectives
ruthless; momentary; rotary; blood-red; uncouth; dingy; shy; cruel; tenderer; glimmering; faithless; vivid; zigzag; dancing; evident; pale; amphibious; glittering; long

STREAKY

adverbs
dingily; unfortunately; carelessly; sorrily; strangely; unaccountably; shabbily; dimly; luminously; curiously; disagreeably; faintly; shamefully; unattractively; unpleasantly.

STREAM

adjectives
swampy; bounding; echoing; whispering; turning; turbid; crystalline; rude; sharp; rippled; torrent; crystal; playful; straining; purling; shoreless; sluggish; eddying; immemorial; rushing; muddy; murmuring; trickling; rock-encumbered; translucent; fiery; feeding; dancing; summer; gliding; eternal; forbidden; steady; reedy; milky; sullen; solitary; gentle; sourceless; augmented; intervening; surcharged; trembling; fervid; plashing; cooling; glacial; salutary; lucid; sylvan; brown; quickening; livelier; fond; silly; wizard; tributary; voiceless; slender; flashing; lurid; cleansing; impetuous; yellow; constant; placid; fertilizing; simpering; bashful; unreluctant; fascinating; chiding; precipitous; intermittent; volcanic; ever-flowing; precious; fleeting; gushing; inert; navigable; pebbly; constant; enormous; comet-like; wayward; muddied; merry; visible; mighty; rapid; irrigating; whispering; living; delicate; substantial; boundless; celestial; Stygian; picturesque; bleeding; branching; feeble; blended; innumberable (pl); accepted; running; hairy; hurrying; hidden; formidable; indolent; reverent; sinister; pale; melancholy; doubled; storied; haunted; equable; formless; continuous; languid; cascading; copious; swollen; flowing; leaping; exuberant; bone-dry; imperial; golden; attractive; rippling; mountain; icy; undulating; petty; epigrammatic; diverging; inland; shallow; joyous; electric; gracious; singing; motionless; childhood; ignoble; lyrical; venomous; traffic; subterranean; returning; limpid; salt; mighty; numerous; brackish; foaming; verbose; dwindling; desolate; flattering; adventurous; brimming.

verbs
bridge—; ford—; head—; purify—; trace —; —boils; —bubbles; —clogs; —complains; —disappears; —drifts; —dwindles; —s harass; —s languish; —s meander; —narrows; —races; —ripples; —shimmers;

—s splash; —trickles; —tumbles; —washes; —s wind.

(See brook, creek, river.)

STREAM (v)

adverbs

tortuously; monotonously; unceasingly; perpetually; giddily; incessantly; boundingly; turbulently; turbidly; torrentially; eddyingly; translucently; copiously; exuberantly; undulatingly; subterraneanly; limpidly.

(See gush, pour, run.)

STREET

adjectives

dingy; medieval; winding; disreputable; squalid; crooked; blazing; quiet; sleepy; narrow; shaded; paved; silent; filthy; attractive; monotonous; littered; still; prominent; startled; unlovely; crowded; embowered; desolate; misty; impassable; moon-lit; forbidden; greasy; populous; unwatered; prominent; darksome; glaring; gutted; deep; darkling; sloppy; racy; straggling; arcaded; dusty; fearful; surging; charted; tortuous; peopled; intersecting; waking; dazzling; slippery; sunny; irregular; frozen; principal; wandering; obscure; deserted; adjacent; respectable; starry; twilight; glittering; little; clean-washed; ill-kept; palaced; corresponding; throngful; unpaved; spacious; rugged; murmuring; roaring; crooked; sultry; marching; residential; adroit; sunburnt; arid; gray; miry; melancholy; thronged.

verbs

amble about—; bedeck—; clutter—; deface—; front—; gain—; lay out—s; litter—; maintain—; patrol—; parade—; ramble thru—; roam—; strew—; stride thru—s; thread—s; throng in—; trudge along—; wander down—; —bakes; —flanks; —joins; —s shine; —swarms; —thunders.

(See sidewalk, lane, avenue, alley, thoroughfare.)

STRENGTH

adjectives

humble; fragile; clumsy; monstrous; raw; hairy; exhaustless; repellant; numerical; vigorous; passionate; sacred; augmented; national; united; central; shining; living; immortal; undivided; superhuman; effective; untiring; elastic; needless; superior; full; remarkable; herculean; barbaric; concentrated; masterful; magnificent; unwasting; natural; alcoholic; unyielding; unimaginative; rockbound; dogged; joyous; remaining; sudden; brute; double; ultimate; lusty; victorious; fear-crazed; desperate; thoughtful; enormous; awkward; voting; unconquerable; immense; immeasurable; silent; lavish; social; impregnable; sturdy; intellectual; unaided; determined; party; sinewy; tensile; massive; artistic; irresistible; renovated; intense; dominating; prodigious; financial; drowsy; superior; revived; aggressive; firm; lasting; muscular; evident; innate; banded; unbroken; conscious; reserved; lofty; excellent; steadfast; divine; ruthless; huge; comparative; placid; relative; pungent; unabated; manlier; solid; sufficient; concentrated; incredible; residing; surprising; unerring; matchless; authorized; spiritual; moral; gigantic; inseverable; skilled; sober; nervous; ambitious; passionless; lyric; honorable; unfolding; mysterious; welded; splendid; fiery; infinite.

verbs

accumulate—; augment—; betray—; confer—upon; conserve—; deny—; derive—; diffuse—; diminish—; drain—; endow with—; equal—; exhaust—; gain—; gather—; husband—; imbibe—; indicate—; maintain—; match—; measure—; muster—; pit—; possess—; pray for—; preserve—; prune—; recover—; regain—; reserve—; restore—; restrain—; sap—; scatter—; signify—; strain—; tax—; undermine—; unite—; —declines; —endures; —falters; —flows; —manifests itself; —spends itself.

(See energy, fortitude, force, power, health, impregnability.)

STRENUOUS

adverbs

disagreeably; dangerously; zealously; eagerly; laboriously; painfully; terribly; extremely; arduously; incredibly; dreadfully; impossibly; energetically; doggedly; vigorously; intensely; indefatigably; wearisomely; formidably; remarkably; unbelievably; unspeakably; unusually; exceptionally; particularly; singularly; peculiarly; unwholesomely.

STRESS

adjectives

unavailing; emotional; special; urgent; adamantine; particular; critical; unobtrusive; unnatural; artificial; plastic; tremendous; intestinal.

verbs
allay—; alleviate—; attach—to; avoid—; demand—; ease—; emphasize—; entail—; lay—upon; mitigate—; occasion—; palliate —; pronounce—; redouble—; relax—; subject to—; —accentuates; —aggravates; —declines; —taxes; —tenses; —wanes; —weighs upon.

(See emphasis, accent, pressure, strain.)

STRESS (v)

adverbs
faintly; markedly; precisely; particularly; exclusively; repeatedly; adamantinely; artificially; obtrusively; vigorously.

(See accent, emphasize.)

STRETCH (v)

adverbs
inordinately; gruesomely; indulgently; beauteously; dismayingly; generously; moderately; tightly; abnormally; piteously; consciously; symmetrically; interminably; indolently; casually.

(See extend, spread.)

STRETCHES

adjectives
sun-scorched; haggard; symmetrical; lilac; mighty; magnificent; interminable; treeless; ample; fragrant; indolent; endless; barren; mysterious; fertile; mossy; casual; wide.

STRICT

adverbs
unreasonably; particularly; singularily; needlessly; narrowly; dogmatically; narrowmindedly; intolerantly; uncharitably; unnecessarily; foolishly; unwisely; cruelly; bitterly; moderately; severely; oddly; illogically; inconsistently; brutally; piously; conventionally; viciously; habitually; dreadfully; wisely; sensibly; moderately; uncommonly; austerely; uncompromisingly; terribly; hideously.

STRICTNESS

verbs
adhere to—; ameliorate—; conform to—; diminish—; ease—; enforce—; infringe—; mitigate—; relax—; violate—; —crushes; —demands; —disciplines; —domineers; —exacts; —hampers; —impresses; —inures; —oppresses; —overrides; —restricts; —revolts; —strains; —taxes; —tramples; —tyrannizes; —yokes.

(See severity, rules, harshness.)

STRIDE

adjectives
heavy; tumultuous; nervous; proud; rhythmical; careless; consuming; self-assuring; enormous; slouching; unprecedented; swinging; prodigious; immense; disordered; free; athletic; short; lofty; majestic; irregular; fearless; formidable; sinking; ravishing; restless; martial; manly; rapid; sober.

verbs
accelerate—; break—; burlesque—; exaggerate—; halt—; hasten—; lengthen—; mimic—; quicken—; regain—; regulate—; relax—; ridicule—; secure—; smooth—; spur to—; —covers; —devours; —outdistances; —overhauls; —shuffles; —spurts; —strains; —taxes.

(See step, walk, pace, gait.)

STRIDE (v)

adverbs
vigorously; austerely; grimly; furiously; swiftly; dramatically; fearlessly; tirelessly; sturdily; rhythmically; prodigiously; athletically; majestically; martially; rapidly; soberly.

(See strut, stalk.)

STRIDENT

adverbs
unpleasantly; raucously; disagreeably; loudly; harshly; quarrelsomely; inelegantly; naturally; insistently; hatefully; offensively; coarsely; cruelly; brutally; pugnaciously; daringly; suddenly; broadly; repulsively; shockingly; disgustingly; ridiculously.

STRIFE

adjectives
unprofitable; elemental; deadly; stern; sexual; frivolous; murderous; fragrant; patient; sacrificial; noble; ambiguous; harmonious; domestic; continued; fruitful; party; barren; unceasing; eternal; vain; inward; harmless; civil; victorious; bloody; dying; absorbing; ignoble; midnight; surging; household; languid; sordid; political; ineffectual; harsh; expiring; constant; idle; inevitable; whirlwind; turbulent; industrial; uncongenial; tortured; feverish; unselfish; victorious; convulsive; theological; varied; bitter; selfish; inhuman; classic; dawning; spiritual; perpetual; unreposing; useless; foolish.

verbs
avert—; maneuver—; perpetuate—; plague with—; renew—; stir up—; —afflicts; —breaks out; —breeds; —brings; —dissolves; —flares; —harasses; —locks; —prolongs; —racks; —seethes; —surges; —tears.
(See discord, dissension, fued, conflict, contention, competition.)

STRIKE

verbs
avert—; ban—; break—; condemn—; crush—; deal with—; direct—; engage in—; foment—; forbid—; forestall—; handle—; interfere in—; precipitate—; prolong—; resort to—; stage—; stave off—; submit without—; support—; terminate—; tolerate—; weigh—; —breaks out; —develops; —s drag on; —embroils; —grips; —intervenes; —paralyzes; —rages; —spreads; —threatens; —wanes; breed—.
(See strife, conflict, feud.)

STRIKE (*v*)

adverbs
firmly; sullenly; pronouncedly; simultaneously; forcibly; spontaneously; instinctively; energetically; significantly; thunderously; heavily; intermittently; aimlessly; accidently; swiftly; mysteriously.
(See hit, slap.)

STRIKERS

verbs
acquit—; bow to—; champion—; conciliate—; disperse—; exonerate—; harangue—; pacify—; placate—; unite—; —arbitrate; —arm; —bar; —charge; —cooperate; —deride; —evict; —heckle; —intimidate; —jeer; —organize; —picket; —pillage; —relent; —repudiate; —riot; —sit down; —taunt; —violate; —demand.
(See rioters, crowd.)

STRIKING

adverbs
conspicuously; impressively; significantly; unusually; ominously; brilliantly; gorgeously; blatantly; garishly; gaudily; unbecomingly; inelegantly; magnificently; gloriously; beautifully; satisfactorily; artistically; luminously; overwhelmingly; delicately; daringly; boldly.

STRING

adjectives
hampering; friendly; sleeping; trembling; sinless; dissonant; silken; melodious; speaking; clanging; stubborn; tinkling; twined; tremulous; consecrated; quivering; veritable; sturdy; dusty; gouty; tightening; dangling; wayward; vibrating; tuneful; slackened.

verbs
braid—; cleave—; draw—; plait—; secure with—; sever—; shred—; slash—; stretch—; sunder—; suspend from—; tense—; —couples; —girds; —sustains; —yokes.
(See cord, leash, chains.)

STRINGENT

adverbs
unwisely; disagreeably; unbearably; intolerably; unintelligently; necessarily; inescapably; terribly; irritatingly; vexatiously; dangerously; ominously; unreasonably; injudiciously; stupidly; inexpediently; ill-advisedly; absurdly.

STRINGY

adverbs
unpleasantly; inconveniently; disagreeably; necessarily; unavoidably; naturally; gummily; uselessly; sufficiently; satisfactorily.

STRIP

adjectives
tenacious; popular; marginal; shadowy; pestilential; tiny; strong.

STRIPES

adjectives
brisk; contrast; vivid; severe; oblique; polychromatic; longitudinal; bright; broad; service; tiny.

STRIVE (*v*)

adverbs
ineffectually; laboriously; ambitiously; earnestly; indomitably; energetically; incessantly; valiantly; patiently; bull-headedly; stubbornly; ineffectively; nobly; dutifully; filially; fiercely; seditiously; diligently; vainly.
(See try, struggle.)

STRIVING

adjectives
human; eternal; earnest; ineradicable; hopeful; wishful; useful; bitter; wistful; vain.

STROKE (v)

adverbs

reflectively; meditatively; caressingly; affectionately; tenderly; absently; moodily; gently.

(See calm, smooth, touch.)

STROKES (boating)

verbs

accelerate—; coach—; develop—; employ—; execute—; invigorate—; pace—; perfect—; polish—; regulate—; scull with—; synchronize—; time—; —cut; —exhaust; —lash; —outdistance; —overhaul; —propel; —strain; —tax; —tell; —tire; —weary.

(See blow.)

STROKES (general)

adjectives

fatal; parliamentary; overhand; crowning; silver; unkind; vulgar; paralytic; heavy; bloodless; careful; cautious; ignorant; vicious; prevailing; impulsive; vigorous; concussive; subtle; blessed; specious; fragrant; lusty; spasmodic; rapid; rhythmic; blind; mortal; apoplectic; disastrous; mortuary; oft-repeated; calumnious; forceful; stinted; fanciful; hostile, curious; brilliant; terrific; coarse; sturdy; despairing; measured; unprecedented.

STROLL

adjectives

aimless; meditative; memorable; undisturbed.

STROLL (v)

adverbs

leisurely; languidly; dejectedly; philosophically; reflectively; nonchalantly; idly; contemplatively; pleasantly; dreamily

(See roam, ramble.)

STRONG

adverbs

brutally; remarkably; physically; powerfully; vigorously; vitally; incontestably; pitilessly; tenaciously; toughly; unquestionably; indubitably; remarkably; exceedingly; undeniably; manifestly; evidently; unexpectedly; determinedly; resolutely; cruelly; unyieldingly; incredibly; obviously; supremely; amazingly; incalculably.

STRONGHOLD

adjectives

impregnable; unconquerable; abandoned; gloomy; ruined.

verbs

abandon—; abdicate—; bar—; barricade—; bolt—; bombard—; escort to—; fortify—; garrison—; imperil—; intrench in—; invade—; jeopardize—; maintain—; menace—; padlock—; patrol—; repel from—; retire to—; retreat to—; screen—; subject—; —preserves; —shields.

(See fortifications, castle, citadel.)

STRUCTURE

adjectives

pyramidal; interesting; domineering; intricate; cosmical; rudimentary; ill-smelling; intended; fanciful; economic; serpentine; naked; mossy; asteriated; elaborate; circular; bonelike; metropolitan; solid; classical; dignified; ephemeral; ambitious; hideous; cellular; imposing; confused; rhythmical; chemical; vernacular; inner; stereotyped; cell; restless; inorganic; sensible; spiritual; streamlined; feathery; phantasmic; substantial; worldly; choral; patchwork; ecumenical; jointed; industrial; commodious; natural; unsightly; hair-growing; administrative; flexible; complicated; institutional; airy; continuous; underlying; ill-conceived; flimsy; internal; laminated; graceful; grave; supporting; artistic; various (pl); unwieldy; rambling; uniform; fragile; stately; urbane; sensible; unambitious; synthetic; magnificent; patriarchal; barn-like.

verbs

bind—; bore into—; complete—; elevate—; erect—; house in—; obliterate—; prop up—; rebuild—; tear down—; threaten—; underlie—.

(See building, edifice, frame, mansion.)

STRUGGLE

adjectives

tragic; intestinal; convulsive; protracted; brutal; obstinate; ineffectual; actual; intense; constant; inner; impending; arduous; continuous; painful; confused; perpetual; unending; imperialist; tremendous; fearful; dying; dire; terrific; heroic; vehement; strenuous; vain; gallant; victorious; stout-hearted; prodigious; embittered; wild; unceasing; spiritual; thwarted; savage; sustained; eternal; ancient; deplorable; unequal; herculean; impotent; universal; unbrotherly; awful; bitter; foolish; lifelong; passionate; severe; inevitable; internecine; sanguine; subjective; desperate; slight; despairing; unaided; bloody; sharp; titanic; doubtful; bootless; parochial; fierce; unlettered; unremitting; brilliant; pioneer; apprehended; hidden; obscure; rough; melancholy; muscular; writhing; selfish; ardent; human; evident; moral; expressionable; creative; momentous.

verbs
desert—; engage in—; finance—; indulge in —; intercede in—; localize—; look upon—; participate in—; settle down to—; undergo —; wage—; yield in—; —culminates; —eliminates; —emaciates; —fills; —resolves; —harries; —summons; —swings in.

(See combat, contention, fight, effort, exertion, contest.)

STRUGGLE (v)

adverbs
flounderingly; terrifically; frantically; vainly; heroically; vigorously; savagely; weakly; feebly; manfully; ingeniously; obstinately; gallantly; turbulently; protractedly; vehemently; herculeanly; bootlessly; momentously.

(See labor, grapple.)

STRUT (v)

adverbs
stalwartly; vainly; proudly; conceitedly; arrogantly; pompously; complacently; jauntily; preposterously; magnificently; vulgarly; pugnaciously; valiantly.

(See swell, swagger.)

STUBBORN

adverbs
obstinately; astonishingly; surprisingly; naturally; incorrigibly; wonderfully; unexpectedly; infinitely; implacably; sternly; bull-headedly; doggedly; brutally; inveterately; desperately; inflexibly; habitually; obdurately; viciously; dreadfully.

STUBBORNNESS

adjectives
infinite; impious; implacable; stern; vainglorious; bull-headed.

verbs
allay—; conciliate—; decry—; denounce—; display—; evince—; exhibit—; moderate—; rebuke—; relax—; reproach—; reprove—; revolt at—; submit to—; —goads; —irks; —resists; —riles (colloq.); —stiffens; —withstands; —yields to.

(See obstinacy, perversity.)

STUDENT

adjectives
diligent; research; discriminating; deep; promising; earnest; fastidious; formal; impartial; docile; special; facetious; ardent; aspiring; insatiable; careless; assiduous; indefatigable; veritable; irresponsible; tireless; thorough; languid; abstract; unprejudiced; historical; noble; able; sober-minded; learned; painstaking; talented; subsequent; tireless; candid; self-helping; laboratory; divinity; apathetic; enthusiastic; agile; negligent; inquisitive; critical; philosophical; scientific; thoughtful; impassioned.

verbs
assign—; bewilder—; baffle—; delude—; discipline—; dismiss—; edify—; enlighten —; enroll—; examine—; expound to—s; grade—; guide—; herd—s; honor—; inculcate in—; indoctrinate—s; ingrain—; initiate—; propound to—s; rear—; recruit—s; reprimand—; reproach—; tutor—; vex—s; —acquires; —advances; —attains; —attunes himself to; —s carouse; —concentrates; —cows; —crams; —cuts; —dips into; —drills; —familiarizes himself with; —flunks (colloq.); —gleams; —interprets; —peruses; —prepares; —qualifies; —translates; —wades through.

(See reader, pupil, graduate, apprentice, classmate.)

STUDIO

adjectives
shabby; wonderful; separate; silk-hung; aggressive; lofty; colossal; comfortable; broadcasting.

STUDIOUS

adverbs
earnestly; curiously; keenly; avidly; eagerly; energetically; tirelessly; actively; naturally; feverishly; gravely; seriously; resolutely; delightfully; overly; alarmingly; profoundly; deeply; uncommonly; happily; ambitiously; obviously; diligently; enthusiastically; oppressively; solemnly; erratically; spasmodically; occasionally.

STUDY

adjectives

antiquarian; unsympathetic; superficial; graduate; modern; comparative; remarkable; illuminating; long-continued; scientific; painstaking; extraordinary; systematic; unfavorable; preparatory; revealing; proper; comprehensive; extensive; book-lined; judicial; concise; forthright; up-to-the-minute; provocative; expert; full-length; fundamental; flippant; exhaustive; philosophical; continuous; assiduous; daring; delightful; watchful; careful; serious; old; desperate; concentrated; patient; theological; authoritative; morbid; analytical; technical; advanced; striking; instructive; candid; crude; suggestive; academic; intensive; satirical; vigorous; compulsory; fossil; obvious; diversified; profitless; linguistic; detailed; actual; thorough; curious; measured; topographical; ornamental; valuable; practical; searching; artistic; cartographic; tempting; clever; immediate; qualitative; perpetual; useless; passionate; lifetime; whimsical; sample; persistent; slight; consecutive; historic; constant; sociological; diligent; rational; economic; indispensable; illusory; rough-hewn; brilliant-hued; convincing; long-interrupted; solitary; utmost; exalted; laborious; statistical; contrapuntal; profound; daily; conscientious; energetic; sublime; penetrating; vivid; incessant; exciting; complicated; mathematical; desultory; previous; ethnographical; probing; intimate; monumental.

verbs

carry on—s; commence—; confine—; delve into—; devote time to—; direct—; distract from—; embrace—of; engage in—; engross in—; enlarge range of—; facilitate—; focus—on; further—; guide—s; impel—; incorporate—; neglect—; plunge into—; proclaim—of; pursue—; select—; simplify—; specialize in—; stabilize—; standardize—s; thirst for—; toy with—; undertake—; —compensates; —discloses; —edifies; —enlightens; —occupies; —reveals; —rewards; —sharpens; absorb in—; apply—; buckle down to—.

(See curriculum, research, learning, application, history, English, science, etc.)

STUDY (v)

adverbs

desultorily; diligently; extensively; minutely; assiduously; scrupulously; meticulously; persistently; exhaustively; historically; systematically; conscientiously; earnestly; fervently; obstinately; theoretically; monastically; unremittingly; indefatigably; abstractly; philosophically.

(See muse, concentrate.)

STUFF

adjectives

pleasing; fiery; masquing; dismal; immortal; rich; colored; mortifying; stern; garden; embroidered; vitriolic; proud; branded; stinging; warming; luminous.

STUFFY

adverbs

intolerably; overwhelmingly; absurdly; uncommonly; odorously; aristocratically; elegantly; pedantically; snuffily; uncomfortably; distressingly; oppressively; stupidly; unbearably; clamorously; noisily; swarmingly.

STUMBLE (v)

adverbs

blindly; stupidly; awkwardly; falteringly; inadvertently; drunkenly; soddenly; vacantly.

(See trip, fall.)

STUN (v)

adverbs

momentarily; physically; emotionally; staggeringly; spiritually; utterly; partially; terrifically.

(See overcome, bewilder.)

STUNTED

adverbs

cruelly; crookedly; distressingly; criminally; pitiably; oddly; wretchedly; miserably; dwarfishly; scrawnily; elfishly; queerly; unfortunately; incredibly; hopelessly; pudgily.

STUPEFIED

adverbs

oddly; suddenly; astonishingly; bewilderingly; grievously; queerly; curiously; dopily; soddenly; utterly; strangely; helplessly; hopelessly; maliciously; hypnotically; sleepily; mysteriously; unaccountably; dazedly.

STUPID

adverbs

abysmally; strangely; unutterably; vacuously; ridiculously; oddly; peculiarly; curiously; unaccountably; irritatingly; vexatiously; shockingly; fatally; callously; carelessly; hopelessly; unpardonably; inexplicably; innately; soddenly; sullenly; grossly; direly; blankly.

STUPIDITY

adjectives
innate; sodden; impenetrable; ineffable; sullen; stultifying; blundering; pompous; designed; gross; useless; current; vacant; insuperable; dire.

verbs
bemoan—; betoken—; bewail—; contemplate —; decry—; deplore—; deride—; disclose —; display—; evince—; feign—; manifest —; marvel at—; observe—; overcome—; realize—; reveal—; ridicule—; shriek at—; stress—; —confounds; —flabbergasts colloq.); —overwhelms; —prejudices.

(See inefficiency, mediocrity, imbecility, inability, dullness, incompetence, ignorance.)

STUPOR

adjectives
dull; partial; obstructing; vacant; empty; silly; blank.

verbs
arouse from—; bring on—; collapse in—; induce—; shock into—; —benumbs; —binds; —blunts; —deadens; —dulls; —envelops; —ensues; —exhausts; —overtakes; —paralyzes; —petrifies; —prostrates; —shatters; —stuns; —suspends; —overcomes.

(See coma, lethargy, languor, unconsciousness.)

STURDY

adverbs
splendidly; admirably; remarkably; surprisingly; stoutly; healthily; vigorously; boyishly; magnificently; stockily; brawnily; enviably; physically.

STYLE

adjectives
slenderizing; tailored; frilly; florid; artificial; dashing; architectural; concise; effective; halting; figurative; extra-colloquial; episodical; anithetical; correct; pleasing; all-pervading; comprehensible; heathenish; slovenly; fantastic; grotesque; balanced; conservative; honorable; latinized; showy; literary; satirical; classic; unsurpassed; impeccable; authentic; complimentary; trim; genuine; sparkling; alert; distinctive; advance; permanent; commanding; behavioristic; friendly; clear; baronial; polished; brilliant; admirable; rushing; secular; barbaric; lucid; unacademic; dapper; legitimate; single; expensive; established; important; gigantic; swagger; magniloquent; pianoforte; loving; conventional; vigorous; monumental; captivating; pungent; simple; habitual; inherited; arrogant; offensive; flamboyant; browbeating; ceremonious; limited; piquant; epistolary; representative; soft; journalistic; swashbuckling; engaging; dramatic; unambiguous; elegant; ambitious; burial; peculiar; learned; elevated; cataloguing; quiet; incongruous; inoffensive; handsome; fitted; architectural; sleek-fitting; youthful; decent; becoming; pointed; pathetic; superior; interesting; cryptic; ostentatious; stilted; nervous; lucid; epigrammatic; forcible; inimitable; laminated; logical; bald; imperial; reprehensible; thrill-provoking; metrical; dissimilar; typical; sonorous; conceivable; didactic; historic; successive (pl); rebellious; prose; puny; damnatory; native; patriarchal; exclamatory; unequaled; poetic; fine; wrought; singular; dazzling; appropriate; favored.

verbs
acclaim—; adopt—; affect—; approve—; breed—; burlesque—; characterize—; cling to—; cloak—; coarsen—; conceive—; conform to—; couch—; cramp—; cultivate—; design—; develop—; distinguish—; distort —; elaborate—; fabricate—; fashion—; fix —; flag—; formulate—; introduce—; lack —; mar—; mature—; model—; modify—; mold—; polish—; popularize—; purify—; refine—; ridicule—; satirize—; set—; strain —; study—; —bears; —s decree; —discriminates; —embraces; —expresses; —glitters; —indicates; —lends charm; —palls; —takes your fancy; —varies.

(See form, manner, character, fashion.)

STYLE (v)

adverbs
smartly; individually; spectacularly; exquisitely; casually; correctly; euphemistically; universally.

(See fashion, create.)

STYLISH

adverbs
conventionally; extremely; elegantly; properly; unusually; curiously; engagingly; enchantingly; inordinately; consciously; not-

iceably; conspicuously; impressively; imposingly; aristocratically; undeniably; amazingly; astoundingly; skillfully; expensively; naturally; delightfully; charmingly; beautifully; agreeably.

SUAVE

adverbs
unctuously; blandly; resolutely; steadily; deliberately; ominously; politely; ceremoniously; chivalrously; conspicuously; gently; helpfully; craftily; adroitly; disarmingly; charmingly; engagingly; unwontedly; painstakingly; diplomatically; carefully; warily; cleverly.

SUBCONSCIOUSNESS

verbs
arouse from—; control—; fix in—; induce —; influence—; penetrate—; pervade—; reduce to—; —clings to; —dematerializes; —disembodies; —dwells; —ensues; —retains; —reigns; —roams; —spiritualizes; —strays; —wanders.

(See mind, intellect.)

SUBDUE (v)

adverbs
valiantly; unconditionally; absolutely; ignominiously; degradingly; compulsorily.

(See conquer, overpower.)

SUBJECT

adjectives
contemporary; congenial; cognate; bruited; unhappy; abstract; apt; truer; humble; elevated; practical; tragical; touching; imaginable; despairing; dutiful; recurring; distressed; rebellious; incongruous; turbulent; daring; controversial; unruly; absorbing; varied (pl); analogous; fruitful; painful; related; utilitarian; historical; well-determined; idealistic; copious (pl); immediate; hypnotic; impressionable; intoxicating; diversified; rich; miscellaneous (pl); delicate; responsive; base; scriptural; antiquated; facetious; non-technical; allegorical; extraneous; unpleasant; proposed; dominant; precipient; docile; kindred; thinking; suitable; abstruse; dehydrated; unwelcome; invaluable; horrified; corpulent; unwilling; traitorous; ephemeral; foolscap; stern; passive; coherent; striking; ethical; admissable; tributary; somber; decorative; obscure; vexed; isolated; leisure; least; unfortunate; tempted; philosophical; sentient; dehumanized; aggrieved; obtuse.

verbs
abuse—; allude to—; ally to—; approach—; assail—; bedevil—; branch off—; broach—; brood over—; brush upon—; circumvent—; comment on—; comprehend—; converse on —; debate on—; delve into—; depict—; dismiss—; draw upon—; edit—; evade—; exhaust—; exorcise—; expatiate on—; expound—; grasp—; hurry through—; introduce—; investigate—; master—; mention—; nourish—; obscure—; phrase—; ponder over—; pursue—; return to—; scorn—; shake—; summarize—; tackle—; wrap oneself up in—; —associates; —baffles; —s bruit; —deals; —engages; —exalts; —illuminates; —s interweave; —intrigues; —s range; —reacts; —recurs; —stimulates; —takes shape; —throws; —treats; —unfolds; —warms; harp on—.

(See matter, proposition, question, history, English, etc.)

SUBJECT (v)

adverbs
minutely; perpetually; humiliatingly; rigorously; civilly; morally; debasingly; tyrannically; dictatorially.

(See expose, uncover.)

SUBJECTION

adjectives
entire; debasing; discomfited; enforced; civil; total; absolute; moral; humble.

verbs
accomplish—; achieve—; assail—; batter to —; coerce into—; complete—; contrive—; culminate in—; curb—; exempt from—; gain—; halt—; reduce to—; repress—; resist—; restrain—; secure—; terminate—; undermine—; wrestle into—; —binds; —oppresses; control—.

(See discipline, enslavement, exposure, subjugation, subserviency.)

SUBJUGATION

verbs
endure—; escape—; lead into—; liberate from—; reduce to—; resist—; —bridles; —blights; —constrains; —curbs; —enslaves; —fetters; —leashes; —muzzles; —restricts; —shackles; —suppresses; —weighs upon; —yokes.

(See bondage, enslavement, subjection.)

SUBMARINE

verbs

batter—; charter—; command—; communicate with—; engulf—; ground—; navigate —; propel—; ram—; scuttle—; swamp—; —s blockade; —convoys; —descends; —dips; —dives; —ejects; —endangers; —escorts; —explores; —founders; —immerses; —s patrol; —plummets; —plunges; —probes; —scurries; —settles; —slides; —sounds; —squats; —submerges; —tips; —torpedoes.

SUBMERGE (v)

adverbs

forcibly; totally; completely; fatally; instinctively; involuntarily.

(See plunge, sink.)

SUBMISSION

adjectives

unconditional; absolute; calm; vile; dishonorable; willing; unexpected; hopeless; tame; humble; quiet; ignominious; coy; continued; supine; abject; prompt; slavish; degrading; piteous; gentle; formal; proud; patient; pretended; deprecating; compulsory; mute.

verbs

advise—; advocate—; bait into—; bend in —; bow in—; coerce into—; compel—; cuff into—; demand—; endure—; enforce—; enjoin—; exact—; force into—; reduce to—; resign to—; tame into—; tolerate—; yield to—; —chastens; —humbles; —humilitates; batter into—.

(See acquiescence, compliance, obedience.)

SUBMISSIVE

adverbs

obsequiously; compliantly; loyally; passively; obediently; modestly; meekly; humbly; philosophically; necessarily; quietly; apathetically; dully; grimly; apparently; perfectly; shamelessly; appallingly; incredibly; strangely; pathetically; pliantly; weakly; calmly; resolutely; imperturbably; stolidly; stupidly; curiously; mysteriously; evidently; tragically; presumably.

SUBMIT (v)

adverbs

graciously; willingly; passively; uxoriously; spinelessly; coyly; voluntarily; placidly; informally; tamely; ignominiously; unconditionally; docilely; apathetically; supinely; slavishly; mutely; deprecatingly.

(See surrender, yield.)

SUBORDINATE

adverbs

gracefully; cheerfully; respectfully; deferentially; carefully; cautiously; unfailingly; abjectly; slavishly; miserably; wretchedly; pleasantly; courteously; obediently; contentedly; admiringly; willingly; admittedly; apparently.

SUBPOENA

verbs

default—; dispatch—; evade—; issue—; request—; serve—; —apprehends; —arraigns; —bids; —calls upon; —commands; —compels; —constrains; —informs; —instructs; —orders; —requires; —specifies; —summons.

(See order, command.)

SUBSCRIBE (v)

adverbs

heartily; sincerely; earnestly; willingly; immediately; annually; cheerfully; voluntarily.

(See sign, agree.)

SUBSCRIPTION

adjectives

voluntary; annual; huge; cheerful; suggested.

verbs

advance—; afford—; bestow—; cancel—; conclude—; confer—; contribute—; donate —; entrust with—; favor with—; increase —; plead for—; pledge—; raise—; reduce —; renew—; swamp with—s; —aids; —assists; —s pour in; —reinforces; —relieves; —rescues; —succors.

(See contribution.)

SUBSERVIENCY

adverbs

assail—; bow in—; cower in—; cringe in—; decry—; emancipate from—; grovel in—; kneel in—; prostrate in—; reduce to—; stoop in—; submit to—; —abases; —defaces; —degrades; —discountenances; —humiliates; —oppresses; —yokes.

(See subjection.)

SUBSERVIENT

adverbs

willingly; unfortunately; humbly; meekly; slavishly; wretchedly; abjectly; helplessly; sullenly; agreeably; deferentially; respectfully; voluntarily; eagerly; zealously; remarkably; amazingly; oddly; strangely; unaccountably; curiously; unwontedly.

SUBSIDE (v)

adverbs

abruptly; gradually; growlingly; brokenly; ultimately; spontaneously; markedly; intermittently.

(See sink, fall.)

SUBSIDY

verbs

advance—; appropriate—; disburse—; expend—; yield—; —abets; —assists; —bolsters; —enables; —encourages; —fosters; —furthers; —protests; —rejuvenates; —relieves; —rescues; —resuscitates; —succors; —supports; —sustains; —wrests.

(See aid, gift.)

SUBSIST (v)

adverbs

frugally; intellectually; meagerly; precariously; scantily; barely; penuriously.

(See maintain, exist.)

SUBSISTENCE

adjectives

meager; precarious; degraded; scanty; bare; mere.

verbs

animate—; destroy—; ennoble—; justify—; maintain—; preserve—; prolong—; protract —; rely on for—; revive—; support—; vitalize—; vivify—; invest—; wrest—; —furnishes; —wanes; —waxes.

(See livelihood, living, employment.)

SUBSTANCE

adjectives

natural; softening; unsightly; poisonous; combustible; essential; spiritual; tremendous; obstructing; tolerated; sterner; toxic; demulcent; emotional; intellectual; earthly; noble; insulating; viscid; gelatinous; perfumed; innocuous; permeable; authenticating; inert; injurious; scanty; metallic; waste; watery; abrasive; adulterate; pulpy; deleterious; luminous; delicate; innumerable (pl); gummy; artificial; material; life-giving; synthetic; convertible; reorganized; vital; incorruptible; homogeneous; prepared; solid; bituminous; dilated; harsh; caustic; refulgent; rebellious; vitreous; glossy; tenacious; malleable; gaseous; porous; desiccated; durable; mollifying; slovenly; putrid; versatile.

verbs

absorb—; administer—; alter—; compound —; condense—; convert—; dehydrate—; desiccate—; disperse—; dissolve—; embody in—; employ—; express—; fritter away—; lack—; lose—; market—; oxidize—; pulverize—; reach—; reflect—; secrete—; value —; —activates; —congeals; —crumbles; —disintegrates; —endures; —ossifies; —petrifies; —produces; —resists; —yields; produce—.

(See chemical, essence, material, matter.)

SUBSTANTIAL

adverbs

admirably; unusually; remarkably; financially; structurally; commendably; luckily; acceptably; satisfactorily; unexpectedly; agreeably; amazingly; delightfully; providentially.

SUBSTITUTE

adjectives

improvised; sufficient; acceptable; comprehensive; facile; agreeable; ancient; temporary; satisfactory; reasonable; ingenious; occasional; wooden; bloodless; plausible; inadequate; appropriate; selective; human; solid.

verbs

accept—; accredit—; approve—; authorize —; commend—; commission—; concede to —; consent to—; consider—; create—; delegate—; deprecate—; discard—; employ—; frown upon—; grant—; hail—; indorse—; invest—with; offer—; regard—; reimburse —; reject—; sanction—; weigh—; yield to —; —conforms to; —constitutes; —replaces; —supersedes; —supplants; empower—.

(See delegate, agent, representative.)

SUBSTITUTE (v)

adverbs

successfully; definitely; deftly; slyly; insidiously; ingeniously; plausibly; adequately; appropriately; invidiously.

(See exchange.)

SUBTERFUGE

verbs

cloak in—; employ—; resort to—; screen—; veil in—; —beguiles; —conceals; —counterfeits; —deceives; —deludes; —dodges; —eludes; —evades; —falsifies; —feigns; —glosses over; —impostures; —juggles; —misleads; —misrepresents; —obscures.

(See evasion, artifice.)

SUBTLETY

adjectives

ceremonious; absurd; obvious; airy; delicate; hidden; natural; shadowy; time-woven.

verbs

bare—; comprehend—; discern—; enlighten—; interpret—; mask in—; pierce—; see through—; —beguiles; —cloaks; —curtails; —deludes; —disguises; —hints; —misleads; —obscures; —pervades; —prompts; —screens; —shrouds; —suggests; —veils.

(See cunning, deceit, distinction.)

SUBURB

adjectives

smiling; residential; initial; dingy; depressing; thriving; adjoining; flourishing; smug; convenient; fragrant; charming; obscure; foreign; immediate; picturesque; shabby; gardened; mysterious; remote.

SUBVERT (v)

adverbs

monstrously; utterly; viciously; completely; insidiously; secretly; debasingly; civilly; politically; governmentally.

(See overthrow, destroy.)

SUBWAY

verbs

construct—; dash into—; flow from—; jam—; —bears; —bores; —conveys; —courses; —extends to; —facilitates; —hums; —replaces; —roars; —screams; —traverses; —tunnels; —unloads; —unites.

(See train, railroad, tunnel.)

SUCCEED (v)

adverbs

patently; credibly; notably; inevitably; eminently; legitimately; admirably; scholastically; financially; triumphantly; precociously; superficially; materialistically; phenomenally; significantly; sensationally; ephemerally; commercially; economically.

(See attain, accomplish.)

SUCCESS

adjectives

scholastic; undoubted; international; popular; bad; social; pretentious; booming; enduring; grand; prodigious; mounting; continued; alternate; dawning; instantaneous; pecuniary; inferior; competitive; particular; tremendous; unexampled; imperial; unreached; triumphant; checkered; immense; precocious; transient; superficial; proper; political; indifferent; ill; clumsy; material; brilliant; emphatic; petty; overawed; ultimate; gratifying; enduring; lasting; unbroken; substantial; howling; phenomenal; significant; outstanding; fugitive; considerable; conspicuous; soaring; universal; overnight; amazing; sensational; artistic; perfect; superb; grandiose; ephemeral; commercial; financial; poor; youthful; extraordinary; definite; prompt; unqualified; dramatic; equal; dubious; established; signal; double; spontaneous; notable; permanent; marvelous; facile; astonishing; monetary; evanescent; sufficient; well-merited; temporary; economic; noticeable; growing; worldly; eventual; reigning.

verbs

achieve—; aspire to—; assure—; attain—; attend with—; beset—; claim—; correlate—; crown with—; earn—; enjoy—; fight to—; flush with—; glean—; hinder—; impede—; jeopardize—; predict—; reckon with—; score—; secure—; smash into—; taste—; train for—; —arises; —attests to; —blasts; —comes; —completes; —crowns; —embitters; —emboldens; —encourages; —hails; —hinges; —insures; —paves; —pays for; —pursues; —signalizes; —springs; —tempts; —wears.

(See fortune, victory, triumph, achievement, supremacy, wealth, fame.)

SUCCESSFUL

adverbs

happily; unusually; consistently; fortunately; triumphantly; extremely; unexpectedly; luckily; felicitously; buoyantly; hilariously; thrillingly; boisterously; excitedly; highly; incomparably; uncommonly; marvelously.

SUCCESSION

adjectives
uninterrupted; dreary; perpetual; observed; lashing; swift; delicious; destined; strange; rapid; continual; sweet; tragic; barbarous; fierce; hereditary; rigid; melodious; medieval; connected; fortuitous; constant.

SUCCOR

verbs
afford—; cherish—; extend—; find—; gain—; furnish—; lend—; plead for—; refuse—; reject—; render—; seek—; withdraw—; withhold—; yield—; —cheers; —nurtures; —relieves; —supports; —sustains.
(See aid, help, relief, assistance.)

SUCCULENT

adverbs
lusciously; deliciously; delightfully; palatably; nutritiously; strangely; unexpectedly; especially; unusually; incomparably; agreeably; pleasantly; delicately; commendably; healthfully.

SUCCUMB (*v*)

adverbs
fatally; feebly; unconditionally; weakly; gradually; partially; dangerously; ultimately; unresistingly; promptly
(See submit, sink, yield.)

SUCK (*v*)

adverbs
thirstily; vigorously; greedily; insatiably.
(See absorb, imbibe.)

SUDDEN

adverbs
rudely; unfortunately; startlingly; whimsically; intentionally; astonishingly; mercifully; shockingly; amusingly; disconcertingly; ridiculously; laughably; offensively; inexcusably; unforgivably; dangerously; unreasonably; lamentably; unintentionally; abruptly; breathlessly; unpardonably; precipitately; prematurely.

SUE (*v*)

adverbs
importunately; legally; litigiously; ruthlessly; vindictively; logically; irrationally.
(See prosecute, arrest.)

SUFFER (*v*)

adverbs
agonizingly; distressingly; severely; stoically; intensely; dismally; atrociously; grievously; acutely; keenly; proportionately; deservedly; heroically; mentally; extensively; mutely; monetarily; infinitely; miserably; chronically; wretchedly.
(See endure, bear.)

SUFFERER

adjectives
lifelong; innocent; glorious; distinguished; chronic; mighty; indignant; surviving; wretched; immediate.

verbs
agonize—; attend—; cheer—; comfort—; condole with—; console—; convulse—; crucify—; deliver—; depress—; disburden—; ease—; flog—; nurse—; soothe—; treat—; wrack—; wrap up—; wring—; —baffles; —endures; —groans; —laments; —moans; —rallies; —retaliates; —revives; —survives.
(See invalid, victim.)

SUFFERING

adjectives
prolong; imitative; indignant; passive; self-inflicted; awful; needless; subtle; intense; meek; angelic; vicarious; spiritual; supreme; cruel; ignominious; pecuniary; virtuous; fictitious; tempestuous; poignant; unnecessary; protracted; inevitable; patient; unmerited; terrible; acute; untold; petty; decisive; universal; mortal; everlasting.

verbs
antidote—; appease—; assuage—; augment—; avoid—; bear—; doom to—; endure—; exhibit—; experience—; fight—; impose—; indulge—; lessen—; minimize—; palliate—; perfect through—; persevere in—; probe—; prolong—; quench—; reassure—; remedy—; —aggravates; —alleviates; —burdens; —convinces; —defaces; —diminishes; —entails; —expiates; —mitigates; —obviates; —racks; protract—.
(See distress, pain.)

SUFFICIENT

adverbs
sufficient; luckily; gratifyingly; wonderfully; quite; satisfactorily; admirably; luxuriantly; abundantly; amply; copiously; inexhaustibly; amazingly; happily; fortunately.

SUFFOCATION

verbs

avert—; await—; doom to—; escape—; face with—; forestall—; hazard—; rescue from—; result in—; risk—; stave off—; verge on—; —cuts short; —ensues; —follows; —impends; —looms; —menaces; —occurs; —severs; —supervenes; —threatens; —wipes out.

(See drowning, failure.)

SUFFRAGE

adjectives

popular; unsolicited; unrestricted; universal; unappreciated.

verbs

authorize—; campaign for—; claim—; confer—on; curtail—; demand—; deny—; deprive of—; endow with—; enjoy—; entitle to—; extend—; gain—; merit—; relinquish—;restore—; restrict—; revoke—; sanction—; solicit—; throttle—; yield—; —voices.

(See right, vote.)

SUGAR

adjectives

swarthy; permissible; vital; energy-giving; tasty.

verbs

abstain from—; adulterate—; box—; consume—; convert—; crystallize—; cure with—; decompose—; dissolve—; excrete—; grade—; granulate—; market—; prepare—; pulverize—; purify—; refine—; transform into—; utilize—; —candies; —honeys; extract—.

(See nectar, sweetness.)

SUGGEST (*v*)

adverbs

promptly; slyly; insidiously; respectfully; tactfully; whimsically; sagaciously; facetiously; pacifically; deftly; mildly; casually; subtly; wistfully; significantly; poetically; gloomily; sardonically; rationally; contemptuously; craftily; irrelevantly; hypnotically; specifically.

(See intimate, hint, insinuate.)

SUGGESTION

adjectives

taunting; detailed; sinful; compelling; hypnotic; sound; sensible; inexhaustible; meritless; wild; plausible; pregnant; delicate; obvious; subtle; delusive; least; startling; perpetual; hopeful; fantastic; imaginative; timorous; sorrowful; rational; implied; ironical; pantomimic; illusory; remotest; reasonable; helpful; adverse; constructive; outside; ashamed; pained; casual; inspiring; terrifying; native; endless; mute; practical; specific; opulent; timely; cheerful; bare; solemn; hopeful.

verbs

acknowledge—; adopt—; afford—; combat—; conceive—; contribute—; convey—; dare—; enforce—; frame—; hazard—; launch—; offer—; propound—; put forth—; reject—; submit—; venture—; waive—; yield to—; —alludes to; —assumes; —counsels; —dies; —expedites; —facilitates; —hints; —misleads; —prescribes; —recommends; —speculates; —stimulates; —surmises; —theorizes.

(See intimation, hint, insinuation, implication, innuendo.)

SUICIDE

adjectives

involuntary; would-be; eventual; political; cold; brave; planned.

verbs

avert—; commit—; conceal—; contemplate—; feign—; flirt with—; goad to—; grieve over—; incite to—; resign to—; resort to—; reveal—; —allures; —betrays; —closes; —dramatizes; —exposes; —frees; —mystifies; —relinquishes.

(See death, murder.)

SUIT

adjectives

elaborate; exclusive; hopeless; washable; riding; luxury; classic; play; tardy; excellent; humble; strong; imported; new; striking; summer; choice; suave; durable; draped; wool; terraced; charming; sumptuous; business; fresh; smart; dressy; distinctive; smooth; conservative; sturdy; worsted; fine; rainy-day; losing; faded; pepper-and-salt; habitual; boldest; sober; customary; gorgeous; libel; honest; superb; neat; repeated; wrong; presumptuous.

verbs

adorn—; alter—; apparel in—; array in—; attire in—; divest of—; doff—; don—; fray—; garb in—; mend—; tatter—; vest in—;

—disguises; —mantles; —protects; —shields.

(See uniform, coat, overcoat, garment.)

SUIT (v)

adverbs

specifically; exactly; definitely; admirably; logically; rationally; precisely; peculiarly; superbly.

(See fit, adapt.)

SUITABLE

adverbs

eminently; wholly; ineffably; conveniently; opportunely; seasonably; comfortably; stylishly; highly; delightfully; unquestionably; fortunately; appropriately; becomingly; providentially; beautifully.

SUITOR

adjectives

unnumbered (pl); bashful; anxious; importunate; eligible; princely; renowned; bold; probable; accepted; slighted; scrupulous; pernicious; woeful.

verbs

attract—s; bind—; cherish—; discourage—; encourage—; gain—; secure—; slight—; —adores; —affiances; —aspires to; —bids for; —bows; —s clamor for; —idolizes; —implores; —importunes; —kneels; —offers; —pleads; —plights; —presses; —professes; —reveres; —solicits; —s throng; —vows; —woos; —troths.

(See lover, sweetheart.)

SULK (v)

adverbs

obstinately; glumly; adamantly; persistently; mutely; unreasonably; miserably; hatefully; woefully.

(See pout, brood.)

SULKY

adverbs

disagreeably; actively; poutingly; glumly; noisily; grimly; dangerously; unpleasantly; vengefully; hatefully; smoulderingly; unaccountably; unreasonably; absurdly; ridiculously; oddly; comically; strangely; gloomily; intolerably.

SULLEN

adverbs

desperately; glumly; dourly; inveterately; habitually; usually; incorrigibly; defiantly; perversely; stolidly; silently; moodily; obstinately; ungraciously; uncivilly; resentfully; angrily; shamefully; disagreeably; unpleasantly; obviously; undisguisedly.

SULTRINESS

verbs

droop in—; swelter in—; —chokes; —dampens; —depresses; —disheartens; —dispirits; —envelops; —flushes; —frets; —glooms; —oppresses; —permeates; —prostrates; —reeks; —seethes; —simmers; —smothers; —sulks; —weighs upon.

(See heat, weather.)

SULTRY

adverbs

unpleasantly; disagreeably; ominously; significantly; distressingly; wretchedly; miserably; strangely; oppressively; smotheringly; curiously; steamily; inauspiciously; intolerably; uncomfortably; alarmingly; extremely; breathlessly.

SUM

adjectives

nominal; fabulous; moderate; untold; successive (pl); meager; pitiful; gross; vast; reasonable; stupendous; trifling; substantial; lawful; formidable; exorbitant; munificent; phonetic; staggering; utmost; unprecedented; round; appalling; pretty; small; enormous; paltry; objective; aggregate; satisfying; tabled; tidy; specified; high; modest.

verbs

accrue—; accumulate—; aggregate—; allot—; amass—; arrive at—; audit—; bestow—; calculate—; check—; compute—; disburse—; discount—; distribute—; embezzle—; entail—; expend—; file—; issue—; necessitate—; realize—; reckon—; register—; represent—; subscribe—; —diminishes; —dwindles; —soars; —staggers.

(See amount, list, number, overhead, profits.)

SUMMARIZE (v)

adverbs

roughly; casually; generally; completely; concisely; statistically; luminously; logically; vividly; convincingly; intelligibly.

(See add, combine.)

SUMMARY

adjectives

statistical; running; intimate; authoritative; apt; contradictory; luminous; logical; concise; slumberous;, singular; striking; necessary; helpful.

SUMMER

adjectives

parting; bitter; relentless; broiling; costly; gorgeous; slow; humid; troubled; hot; promised; husky; trailing; northern; luxurious; strenuous; exciting; colorful; proud; economic; delicate; heavy; perished; perpetual; epitomized; immediate.

verbs

await—; bask in—; bear the stamp of—; long for—; prolong—; suspend for—; thrive in—; usher in—; welcome—; yearn for—; —begets; —blooms; —breeds; —burgeons; —colors; —conceives; —dresses; —enriches; —fades; —gilds; —kisses; —mellows; —parches; —renews; —unfolds; —vitalizes; —wanes; —waxes; —wilts; —yields.

(See autumn, spring, winter, season.)

SUMMIT

adjectives

peaked; serene; towering; jagged; snow-clad; feathery; ornamental; dreadful; topmost; snowy; wild; pathless; lone; seared; blasted; sacred; sloping; breathless; flowering; hoary; islanded; unique; subordinate; commanding; bleak; sunburned; roofless; unscaled; intangible; toppling.

verbs

achieve—; ascend to—; aspire to—; cap—; clamber to—; crown—; grope for—; link—; mount to—; plunge from—; precipitate from—; scale—; soar to—; strive for—; topple from—; view from—; —allures; —climaxes; —crests; —culminates; —erodes; —tempts.

(See crown, culmination, height, pinnacle.)

SUMMON (*v*)

adverbs

domineeringly; commandingly; dictatorially; dogmatically; harshly; sternly; peremptorily; courteously; unceremoniously; tersely; arrogantly; emphatically; petulantly; urgently; vociferously.

(See command, call.)

SUMMONS

adjectives

emphatic; collective; peremptory; gracious; petulant; authoritative; coincident; silent; final; hasty; urgent; dread; long-waited; vociferous; strange.

verbs

abrogate—; announce—; answer—; countermand—; dismiss—; dispatch—; enforce—; heed—; ignore—; nullify—; quash—; serve with—; —apprehends; —arraigns; —bids; —cites; —coerces; —commands; —demands; —directs; —informs; —notifies; —orders.

(See call, invitation, mandate, order, command.)

SUMPTUOUS

adverbs

comfortably; surprisingly; actually; luxuriously; delightfully; unexpectedly; miraculously; significantly; invitingly; unnecessarily; extravagantly; pleasantly; designedly; lavishly.

SUN

adjectives

noontide; withdrawing; scarlet; warm; pleasant; never-hurrying; soul-expanding; waning; devouring; traveling; extinguished; external; burning; keen; morning; night; meridian; invisible; declining; rising; dipping; lowering; centrifugal; dazzling; unconquered; pitiless; kindling; blazing; bronze; material; sinking; fierce; retiring; vanished; setting; cruel; earthly; ancient; climbing; ardent; glorious; outdoor; brazen; dying; cloudless; scorching; lurid; rounding; smoldering; tropic; vertical; slanting; circling; majestic; vernal; merciless; killing; radiant; mimic; autumn; descended, glaring; unveiled; temperate; retreating; warmer; conflagrant; sickly; wheeling; early; impassioned; surviving; unruly; gaudy; fair; utmost; worshipped; garish; hateful; insistent; fervent; uncurled; central; bleak; naked; universal; smiting; westering; liberal; vaporous; broiling; blushing; sleepy; fierce; ruddy; sudden; sovereign; treacherous; unshaded; alien; bloody; earth-invisible (pl).

verbs

bask in—; bathe in—; block off—; eclipse—; expose to—; obscure—; protect from—; revel in—; salute—; scorn—; shield from—;

squint at—; worship—; —anneals; —ascends; —bakes; —beats down; —blinds; —blisters; —blushes; —breaks; —burnishes; —climbs; —clouds; —clothes; —creeps; —crowns; —dazzles; —declines; —dims; —dips; —dogs; —draws; —drenches; —eclipses; —fades; —filters; —flames; —flays; —floods; —gilds; —gyrates; —haunts; —heralds; —melts; —mirrors; —nourishes; —paints; —parches; —peeps out; —penetrates; —pours; —presses down; —radiates; —renews; —retreats; —salutes; —sears; —shadows; —shines; —sinks; —smiles upon; —smites; —stimulates; —strikes; —tinges; —vanishes; —veils; —wearies; —withdraws; —withers.

(See moon, heat, sunlight.)

SUNLIGHT

adjectives

morning; flowing; bright; thinned; reflected; hazy; marvelous; ardent; roseate; windy; sweet; slanting; choicer; naked; mellow; purging; stealing; unfallen; glancing; blinding; forenoon; laughing; dancing; imprisoned; watery; joyous; quivering; pitiless; mocking; parting; dappled; shaded; healthful; spring-eyed.

verbs

bask in—; emerge into—; flash in—; —arises; —dies; —exposes; —filters; —hallows; —lingers; —penetrates; —quivers; —slides through; —streams; —touches.

(See moonbeam, light, sun.)

SUNNY

adverbs

radiantly; pleasantly; happily; wholesomely; delightfully; cheerily; vivaciously; merrily; brightly; blithely; buoyantly; helpfully; winsomely; exultantly; optimistically; sparklingly; jauntily.

SUNSET

adjectives

forlorn; crimson; sunken; hollow; brilliant; sinking; fiery; dying; silent; pompous; lingering; glorious; peaceful; polychrome; fading; refulgent; wintry; bloody.

verbs

cloud—; loiter till—; linger to—; obscure—; view—; —beams; —colors; —dazzles; —declines; —diffuses; —eclipses; —enchants; —enthralls; —entrances; —gilds; —gleams; —glimmers; —glows; —glowers; —radiates; —reflects; —scintillates; —shimmers.

(See twilight, daylight, dawn.)

SUNSHINE

adjectives

perpetual; brilliant; sudden; sparkling; searching; westering; tawny; cruel; eternal; clear; radiant; embodied; vital; glancing; dreaming; tingling; satin; sweet; mellow; vivid; open; harsh; broad; pitiless; illimitable; everlasting; imprisoned; peaceful; unclouded; beauteous; precious; continuous; genial; merciless.

verbs

drink in—; flood with—; luxuriate in—; —bleaches; —bursts forth; —caresses; —dances; —energizes; —enlivens; —filters through; —flatters; —gladdens; —glitters; —greets; —illumines; —melts; —parches; —permeates; —pervades; —renews; —shimmers; —showers.

(See light, moonbeam, sunlight, sun.)

SUNSHINY

adverbs

brilliantly; gorgeously; gloriously; delightfully; unusually; fortunately; luckily; wonderfully; marvelously; dazzlingly; faintly; scarcely; hotly; unbearably; intolerably; scorchingly; burningly; mercilessly; glaringly.

SUP (v)

adverbs

sumptuously; regally; bountifully; clandestinely; domestically; fraternally; formally; genially.

(See dine, eat.)

SUPERCILIOUS

adverbs

intolerably; uncivilly; deplorably; haughtily; stupidly; oddly; magnificently; laughably; arrogantly; proudly; offensively; ridiculously; incurably; unpardonably; smugly; irritatingly; insolently; presumptuously; coolly; insufferably; condescendingly; purposely; splendidly; brashly; brazenly; idiotically; ostentatiously; rudely; egotistically; conceitedly; pretentiously; unblushingly; impudently; saucily; swaggeringly; flippantly; shamelessly.

SUPERINTENDENT

adjectives
tutorial; strict; immediate; personal; careful; watchful.

verbs
closet with—; consult—; —admonishes; —arbitrates; —commends; —deliberates; —dickers with; —directs; —exhorts; —goads; —governs; —guides; —manages; —officiates; —pilots; —prescribes; —presides; —pulls strings; —regulates; —sacks; —steers.
(See manager, employer, boss.)

SUPERIOR

adjectives
race; intellectual; immediate.

SUPERIORITY

adjectives
feline; racial; cool; innate; muscular; spurious; numerical; overwhelming; intellectual; essential; absolute; economic; whimsical; scornful; astonishing; obvious; compassionate; ineffable; menaced; lofty; simpering; contemptuous; historical; infinite; fancied; dignified; inherent; masculine; base; adventitious; conscious; immense; extrao•inary; assumed.

verbs
acclaim—; achieve—; assert—; assume—; attest to—; belittle—; challenge—; consider—; demonstrate—; disclose—; display—; enhance—; evince—; exaggerate—; exalt—; exhibit—; manifest—; proclaim—; prove—; regard—; reveal—; verify—; vie for—; weigh—; —eclipses; —outshines; establish—.
(See supremacy, eminence.)

SUPERSEDE (*v*)

adverbs
gradually; temporarily; invidiously; ultimately; logically; expectedly.
(See replace, supplant.)

SUPERSTITION

adjectives
barbarous; colorful; idle; monstrous; exploded; fantastic; capricious; brutal; religious; ethnic; silly; deepest; contemporary; narrow; vain; enormous; popular; conflicting; pure; childish; puerile; vulgar; imaginative; pestilent; singular; degrading; illustrious; bizarre; insatiate; grossest; primitive; unbelievable; fanciful; confused; ancient; haunting; pre-existing.

verbs
abolish—; efface—; encrust with—; eradicate—; explode—; free from—; ignore—; refute—; revive—; rid of—; swallow—; —beguiles; —blinds; —chains; —deludes; —dominates; —dupes; —enslaves; —fetters; —persists; —prejudices; —prevails; —shackles; —shrouds; —subjugates; —warps.
(See fanaticism, ignorance, prejudice, myth.)

SUPERSTITIOUS

adverbs
absurdly; sincerely; ridiculously; unreasonably; foolishly; terribly; fearfully; honestly; gullibly; nervously; incredibly; fanatically; piously; exceedingly; curiously; oddly; strangely; credulously; romantically; fearsomely; inveterately; incurably; anxiously.

SUPERVISE (*v*)

adverbs
personally; intelligently; successfully; strictly; cautiously; professionally.
(See manage, direct.)

SUPERVISION

adjectives
constant; censorial; direct; rigid; jealous; provincial; voluntary; human; chilling; controlling; governmental; strict; careful.

verbs
assume—; enforce—; maintain—; prescribe—; recommend—; relax—; retain—; subject to—; —administers; —chains; —curbs; —fetters; —guides; —irks; —leashes; —pilots; —restrains; —restricts; —wanes.
(See management, control.)

SUPPER

adjectives
champagne; bountiful; scanty; hearty; solemn; sumptuous; bare; rich.

verbs
bid to—; bolt—; climax—; conclude—; cram in—; deprive of—; devour—; gobble—; gorge—; grace—; gulp—; relish—; savor—; summon to—; —nauseates; —refreshes; —reinvigorates; —renews; —satiates; —tickles the palate.
(See meal, luncheon, breakfast, dinner.)

SUPPLANT (v)

adverbs
inevitably; permanently; ultimately; temporarily; unexpectedly; ruthlessly; dictatorially.
(See supersede, replace.)

SUPPLE

adverbs
youthfully; incredibly; naturally; slenderly; sturdily; amazingly; extremely; uncommonly; admirably; particularly; delightfully; unusually; remarkably; fortunately.

SUPPLEMENT (v)

adverbs
elaborately; fully; completely; authoritatively; definitely; adequately.
(See add, complete.)

SUPPLICATION

adjectives
formal; strong; affecting; frantic; fervent; piteous; reverent; honest.

SUPPLIES

adjectives
stable; continuous; inexhaustible; plentiful; abundant; precarious; visible; regulated; virgin; providential; needed; pecuniary; liberal; considerable; limited; constant; deficient; perennial; adequate; unbounded; scant; table; ample; warlike; extensive; dependable; bountiful; countless; permanent; miserable; muddy; vast; commercial.

SUPPLY

verbs
augment—; avail oneself of—; bolster—; check—; crave—; curb—; curtail—; deplete—; dispense—; entreat—; exceed—; exhaust—; facilitate—; guarantee—; insure—; procure—; replenish—; stabilize—; stock with—; warehouse—; —dwindles; —evaporates; —flows.
(See store, merchandise, stock, surplus, product.)

SUPPLY (v)

adverbs
bounteously; liberally; indifferently; exclusively; infallibly; amply; abundantly; plentifully; faithfully; scantily; continuously; pecuniarily; adequately; permanently; commercially; liberally.
(See furnish, yield.)

SUPPORT

adjectives
substantial; powerful; generous; overwhelming; intermediate; eloquent; wholesale; warm; earnest; mere; thoughtful; zealous; uniform; effective; firm; frail; elusive; principal; hearty; abated; stalwart; urgent; ephemeral; enthusiastic; scarce; vigorous; adequate; superficial.

verbs
angle for—; barter for—; bestow—upon; command—of; consolidate—; derive—; earn—; enlist—; foster—; lend—; lessen—; line up—; maintain—; muster—; pledge—; rally to—; repel—; repudiate—; seek—; share in—; whip up—; —comforts; —consoles; —dissolves; —fails.
(See living, help, livelihood, assistance.)

SUPPORT (v)

adverbs
adequately; steadfastly; appreciatively; respectfully; structurally; plausibly; conscientiously; adamantly; abundantly; substantially; theoretically; warmly; zealously; effectively; heartily; enthusiastically; vigorously.
(See defend, back.)

SUPPORTERS

adjectives
shadowy; ardent; persistent; staunchest; faithful; devoted; fanatical; unconditional; jubilant; regular.

verbs
alienate—; assure of—; estrange—; gather—; lure—; rally—; vex—; —advance; —authenticate; —back; —bear; —bolster; —cheer; —comfort; —expedite; —foster; —found; —further; —maintain; —promote; —sustain.
(See contributor, friend, advocate.)

SUPPOSE (v)

adverbs
rationally; erroneously; falsely; fallaciously; unsuspectingly; hopefully; optimistically.
(See assume, presume.)

SUPPOSITION

adjectives
false; analogous; indolent; staggering; contrary; probable; mitigating.

verbs
argue on—; concede—; confirm—; contra-

dict—; forsake—; grant—; hazard—; maintain—; overthrow—; refute—; speculate on —; support—; unfold—; weigh—; work on —; —alludes; —assumes; —carries weight; —conjectures; —hints; —originates in; —presumes; —presupposes; —surmises; —theorizes; ridicule—.

(See assumption, guess, hypothesis, conjecture.)

SUPPRESS (v)

adverbs

silently; insidiously; traitorously; ruthlessly; undemocratically; viciously; vindictively; overtly; covertly; rigorously; generally; summarily; studiously; tyrannically.

(See repress, restrain.)

SUPREMACY

adjectives

literal; feudal; authorized; universal; maritime; scholarly; secular; naval; ecclesiastical; political; restored; righteous; long-sought; matrimonial; domestic.

verbs

achieve—; acknowledge—; admit—; assert —; battle for—; bolster—; confirm—; demonstrate—; dispute—; insure—; maintain —; preserve—; prove—; renounce—; reveal —; seek—; struggle for—; surrender—; veil —; —crumbles; —sways; —totters.

(See domination, success, achievement, victory.)

SURE-FOOTED

adverbs

amazingly; sufficiently; particularly; unfailingly; fortunately; assuredly; comfortingly; luckily; alertly; gracefully; faithfully; confidently; intrepidly; fearlessly; unquestionably; reliably; trustworthily.

SURF

adjectives

booming; roaring; boiling; raging; damaging; foamy; retreating; relentless; murderous; turmoiling.

verbs

—agitates; —babbles; —batters; —billows; —boils; —booms; —breaks; —buffets; —chops; —deluges; —drenches; —foams; —froths; —hisses; —inundates; —licks; —murmurs; —pounds; —ripples; —roars; —seethes; —sluices; —sprays; —spumes; —surges; —swashes; —swells; —washes.

(See billow, wave, breaker.)

SURFACE

adjectives

silky; simmering; inferior; temporary; highway; brushed; rough; sparkling; shaggy; heaving; mirror-like; limiting; leaden; inelastic; refracting; troubled; raised; rugged; crawling; vibratory; undulating; reasonable; polished; sensitive; smooth; gleaming; faceted; rolling; agitated; glassy; intellectual; lumpy; metallic; unbroken; radiant; vitreous; sloping; broad; burnished; sprayed; convex; prismatic; sluggish; slotted; plaited; external; tourist; warmer; exposed; muddy; bright; stony; pliant; tenacious; general; plane; driving; suede-like.

verbs

abrade—; becalm—; burnish—; corrugate —; dent—; detect upon—; dip below—; duck below—; engrave on—; explore—; face—; finish—; flash upon—; furrow—; glaze—; inflame—; level—; mar—; penetrate—; plunge beneath—; polish—; probe below—; ruffle—; rumple—; scan—; scour —; scratch—; skim—; smite—; smooth—; veneer—; venture upon—; warp—; weather —; wrinkle—.

SURGE

adjectives

eternal; furious; relentless; toiling; fiery; sulphurous; knelling; rolling; volcanic; boiling; whispering; roaring; restless; broken; imperious.

SURGE (v)

adverbs

confusedly; wildly; thunderously; turbulently; violently; relentlessly; sulphurously; volcanically; boilingly; roaringly; imperiously.

(See swell, heave.)

SURGERY

adjectives

plastic; radical; painful; bold; bloody; magic; life-saving.

verbs

advise—; baffle—; botch—; defy—; employ —; hail—; perform—; practise—; rally from—; resort to—; skill in—; survive—; weather—; —adjusts; —binds; —converts; —delivers; —endangers; —facilitates; —

reanimates; —reconstructs; —rectifies; —rehabilitates; —rejuvenates; —removes; —renovates; —repairs; —restores; —resuscitates; —staunches.

(See operation, remedy, medicine.)

SURLY

adverbs

bluntly; terrifyingly; cruelly; unnecessarily; heedlessly; inexcusably; discourteously; disrespectfully; unpardonably; unwarrantably; boorishly; angrily; roughly; intolerably; churlishly; unaccountably; strangely; curiously; alarmingly; darkly; ominously; unusually.

SURMISE

adjectives

false; intellectual; vague; anxious; wide; wild.

verbs

advance—; concede—; denounce—; form—; grant—; hazard—; offer—; refute—; resort to—; speculate on—; submit—; —alleges; —alludes to; —assumes; —coincides with; —conjectures; —hints; —postulates; —presumes; —presupposes; —suggests; —theorizes.

(See guess, conjecture.)

SURMISE (*v*)

adverbs

shrewdly; intuitively; rationally; slyly; astutely; vaguely; anxiously; pessimistically; jealously; enviously.

(See suppose, guess.)

SURMOUNT (*v*)

adverbs

exultantly; victoriously; boisterously; triumphantly; ambitiously; incredibly.

(See conquer, overcome.)

SURPASS (*v*)

adverbs

amazingly; exultantly; exceedingly; incredibly; astoundingly; spectacularly; sensationally.

(See excel, exceed.)

SURPLUS

adjectives

destructive; labor; unavoidable; re-invested; unsellable; huge; undistributed; profitable.

verbs

accrue—; accumulate—; afford—; amass—; avert—; discard—; disclose—; dispose of —; exaggerate—; invest—; market—; pile up—; reveal—; squander—; swallow—; —assures; —augments; —brims; —burdens; —congests; —deluges; —floods the market; —gorges; —gluts; —insures; —overflows; —strains; —supersaturates; —weighs upon.

(See excess, supply.)

SURPRISE

adjectives

unspeakable; dull; wistful; pleasant; perpetual; quaint; unfortunate; unfeigned; amiable; delightful; unaffected; infinite; contemptuous; calm; charming; effusive; admiring; geological; solemn; shameful; sordid; sweet; bewildered; acceptable; painful; strange; melancholy; glad; excessive; hollow; curt; pompous; horrified; agreeable; blank; puzzled; annoyed; dramatic; drab; swift; exquisite; cordial; inexcusable; continual; quick; speculative; tremendous; mingled; hurt; immense; comic.

verbs

affect—; anticipate—; conceal—; express—; feign—; gape in—; induce—; manifest—; occasion—; prepare—; reveal—; strike with —; —bewilders; —dazzles; —electrifies; —flabbergasts; —overwhelms; —petrifies; —ruffles; —rumples; —shocks; —staggers; —startles; —stuns; —throws one off guard.

(See amazement, miracle, astonishment.)

SURPRISE (*v*)

adverbs

curiously; agreeably; innocently; utterly; mildly; faintly; mutually; unspeakably; amiably; quaintly; unfeignedly; delightfully; infinitely; painfully; excessively; exquisitely; cordially; tremendously; comically.

(See astonish, amaze.)

SURRENDER

adjectives

easy; traitorous; joyous; pusillanimous; instant; unconditional; forced; forlorn; verbal; resigned; peaceable.

SURRENDER (*v*)

adverbs

utterly; impatiently; meekly; affectionately; peaceably; unconditionally; voluntarily;

graciously; traitorously; forlornly; pusillanimously.

(See yield, abandon.)

SURROUND (v)

adverbs

opulently; inextricably; enthusiastically; triumphantly; fraternally; apprehensively; artificially; uncongenially; felicitously; luxuriously; tranquilly; picturesquely; grotesquely; nobly; trivially; quaintly; rustically; pastorally; inspiringly.

(See entrench, inclose.)

SURROUNDINGS

adjectives

artificial; uncongenial; iron; appalling; felicitous; tropical; sociable; pleasant; superb; smart; cultural; refined; luxurious; tranquil; picturesque; dignified; affectionate; unique; harsh; primitive; grotesque; grander; indulgent; noble; trivial; quaint; frigid; charming; beautiful; dingy; rustic; pastoral; unwonted; inspiring; modern.

verbs

absorb in—; acclimate to—; acquaint with —; adapt to—; alter—; blind to—; condition by—; contemplate—; darken—; deduce from —; encompass—; engross in—; escape—; explore—; inspect—; orient to—; pervade —; recognize—; reconnoiter—; regard—; rise above—; scan—; scrutinize—; skirt—; survey—; transcend—; —breed; —depress; —enchant; —enthrall; —foster; —impress; —oppress; —suggest; —symbolize.

(See environment, circumstances, conditions.)

SURVEILLANT

adverbs

warily; vigilantly; suspiciously; significantly; carefully; alertly; inquisitively; constantly; watchfully; incessantly; generally; conscientiously; meticulously; punctiliously; dependably; reliably.

SURVEY

adjectives

mournful; calm; ordnance; cursory; interior; official; leisure; compiled; recent; hopeless; impassioned; casual; severe; quick; optimistic; independent; sweeping; chronological; decisive; unbiased; preliminary; perspective; impartial; exhaustive.

verbs

authenticate—; check—; cite—; condense—; conduct—; contemplate—; extend—; initiate —; regard—; scan—; —astounds; —calculates; —catalogues; —computes; —confirms; —demonstrates; —discloses; —discovers; —embraces; —enables; —enumerates; —estimates; —evaluates; —gauges; —indicates; —informs; —measures; —probes; —records; —reveals; —scales; —startles; —uncovers; —verifies.

(See study, investigation, examination.)

SURVEY (v)

adverbs

extensively; gloomily; tranquilly; critically; curiously; morbidly; maliciously; suspiciously; officially; leisurely; optimistically; unbiasedly; impartially.

(See view, examine.)

SURVIVAL

adjectives

unique; barbaric; unconscious; fortunate; race; evolutionary; bare.

SURVIVE (v)

adverbs

vigorously; miraculously; heroically; undauntedly; staunchly; courageously.

(See live, exist.)

SURVIVORS

adjectives

terrified; ill-fated; reimbursed; heroic; injured; struggling; belated.

SUSCEPTIBILITY

adjectives

morbid; exquisite; excessive; strong; foolish; obvious; observant; moral; vivid; extreme; patent.

verbs

affect—; allay—; augment—; cancel—; conceal—; compensate for—; counteract—; cultivate—; excite—; exempt from—; increase —; intensify—; neutralize—; promote—; raise—; repress—; sense—; sharpen—; stir —; —endangers; —exposes; —inclines; —jeopardizes; —predisposes; —tends toward.

(See propensity, inclination, tendency.)

SUSCEPTIBLE

adverbs

highly; unusually; easily; emotionally; extremely; quickly; alarmingly; romantically;

strangely; curiously; uncommonly; amazingly; inherently; naturally.

SUSPECT

verbs
absolve—; acquit—; bail—; challenge—; clear—; cross-examine—; defend—; detain —; discharge—; dismiss—; exculpate—; exempt—; exonerate—; free—; grill—; harbor—; hold—; jail—; liberate—; lynch—; question—; release—; retain—; round up —s; shake—; trap—; vindicate—; whitewash—; —denies; —defends; —escapes; —vindicates.

(See prisoner, criminal.)

SUSPECT (*v*)

adverbs
unjustifiably; shrewdly; secretly; previously; gravely; unfairly; generally; justly; insanely; jealously; personally; intrusively.

(See surmise, doubt.)

SUSPENSE

adjectives
absorbed; waiting; agonizing; irresolute; tremulous; sultry; lowering; painful; frighted; unrelaxed; dramatic; clever; intolerable; agitated; prolonged; awful; tedious; awakening.

verbs
allay—; alleviate—; bear—; cower in—; ease—; face—; flinch at—; heighten—; intensify—; lessen—; maintain—; mitigate—; moderate—; palliate—; preserve—; relinquish—; survive—; sustain—; swoon in—; withdraw—; —abates; —agonizes; —embarasses; —relaxes; —rends; —shatters; —strains; —subsides; —taxes; —tenses; —wanes; —weighs upon.

(See perplexity, excitement, tension, anxiety, uncertainty.)

SUSPENSION

adjectives
premature; simultaneous; mature; critical; permanent; definite.

SUSPICION

adjectives
mingled; habitual; mean; mutual; bitter; aggressive; horrible; overawing; harsh; common; inscrutable; special; deep; plentiful; lingering; unworthy; dull; aroused; lively; hard; terrible; prying; jealous; waked; chilly; furtive; infusing; perpetual; groundless; merest; faint; horrid; diminished; tormented; additional; shrewd; excited; angry; unmanly; personal; general; intrusive; sharp; sly.

verbs
absolve of—; allay—; arouse—; brand with —; breed—; cherish—; confirm—; conquer —; consolidate—s; dispel—; entertain—; evade—; excite—; ground—; heighten—; inspire—; justify—; lull—; occasion—; regard with—; resent—; sweep aside—; veil —; voice—; —crosses the mind; —dawns upon; —deepens; —grows; —pervades; —prevails; —thickens.

(See distrust, jealousy, anxiety, doubt.)

SUSPICIOUS

adverbs
unreasonably; jealously; meanly; cruelly; foolishly; dangerously; terribly; ridiculously; warily; extravagantly; inordinately; curiously; significantly; fearfully; uncertainly; vaguely; definitely; oddly; absurdly; needlessly; wildly; strangely; disagreeably; unpleasantly; odiously; perplexingly; unworthily; craftily.

SUSTAIN (*v*)

adverbs
precisely; spiritually; materially; faithfully; casually; honorably; unanimously; magnificently; heroically; vigorously; faithfully; disastrously; courageously.

(See support, uphold.)

SUSTENANCE

verbs
afford—; arrest—; avail of—; begrudge—; deprive of—; dispatch—; dispense—; exhaust—; furnish—; grant—; grope for—; grovel for—; obtain—; offer—; plead for —; proffer—; provide—; refuse—; strive for—; struggle for—; suspend—; tender—; yield—; extract—.

(See living, livelihood.)

SWAB

verbs
begrime—; besmirch—; brush with—; contaminate—; dab with—; discard—; disinfect with—; dispose of—; foul—; introduce —; precipitate on—; rinse—; saturate—; scour with—; smudge—; taint—; —absorbs; —purges; —soaks up; —sponges.

(See sponge, mop.)

SWAGGER

adjectives
lordly; indolent; imposing; consequential; new; boxy; outstanding; shallow; jaunty; loose; brusque; impudent.

SWAGGER (v)

adverbs
theatrically; boisterously; obstreperously; pretentiously; shamelessly; impudently; dramatically; indolently; jauntily; nonchalantly.
(See swell, strut.)

SWAIN

adjectives
low-spirited; responsive; bashful; rustic; lusty; laboring; ephemeral; despairing; awkward; forlorn; ashy; country; reaping; wary; mistrustful.

verbs
deride—; ground—; impassion—; —attracts; —bewitches; —captivates; —caresses; —cherishes; —courts; —declares; —enamours of; —endears; —pleads; —prates of; —proclaims; —professes; —reveres; —serenades; —woos; —yearns.
(See lover, sweetheart, peasant.)

SWALLOW

adjectives
skimming; twittering; innumerable (pl); blithe; garrulous; chaffering; beauteous.

verbs
—arranges; —banks; —busies; —chirps; —circles; —s colonize; —dares; —s flock; —flutters; —journeys; —migrates; —swims low; —smooths; —snatches; —spreads wings; —sweeps; —twitters.
(See bird, martin.)

SWALLOW (v)

adverbs
avidly; vigorously; hastily; glumly; greedily; thickly; embarrassedly; spasmodically.
(See gulp, eat.)

SWAMP

adjectives
torrid; busy; moss-hung; impassable; fetid; pestilential; tamarack; tangled; unsightly; overtowering; adjacent; brackish; tropical; unhealthy; lonely; salty; inaccessible; social.

verbs
bog in—; brave—; drain—; foul in—; frequent—; hazard—; infest—; inhabit—; meander through—; mire in—; prowl in—; restore—; roam—; skirt—; slog through—; stray into—; traverse—; vanish into—; wallow through—; —breeds; —endangers; —enfolds; —engulfs; —jeopardizes; —mars.
(See marsh, mire, morass, mud.)

SWAMPY

adverbs
muddily; quaggishly; squashily; softly; unwholesomely; malarially; pestilentially; irremediably; hopelessly; unpleasantly; impracticably; disturbingly; distressingly; dangerously; deplorably; undesirably; unfortunately; unhealthfully; unluckily.

SWAN

adjectives
mysterious; drowsy; floating; solitary; ruthless; ruffling; graceful; dying.

verbs
—arches; —chants; —dips; —floats; —idles on water; —immerses; —lies; —mantles; —murmurs; —nibbles; —probes; —sails; —shies away, —steers; —strays; —swims; —trumpets; —wanders; —whoops; —flocks.
(See bird, duck, goose.)

SWANKY

adverbs
absurdly; luxuriously; pompously; arrogantly; superbly; aggressively; ostentatiously; extraordinarily; stylishly; sumptuously; elegantly; manifestly; flauntingly; gorgeously; conspicuously; consciously; quietly; genuinely.

SWARM

adjectives
unsuspected; solar; countless (pl); snow-soft; bony; prodigious; tremendous; ignoble; invading; droning; singing; meteoric; thieving; prolific.

verbs
capture—; disperse—; herd—; restrain—; rout—; smoke—; stir up—; —bristles; —buzzes; —clamors; —clusters; —converges on; —deluges; —emigrates; —filters from;

—focuses on; —hums; —multiplies; —overwhelms; —pours out; —presses; —settles; —surges; —teems; —throngs.
(See hive, horde, crowd.)

SWARM (v)

adverbs
noisomely; prodigiously; prolifically; thunderously; multitudinously; spectacularly; rushingly; engulfingly.
(See flock, cluster.)

SWAY

adjectives
illimitable; righteous; feeble; departed; unquestioned; long-time; potent; ancient; undisputed; mightier; steadfast; insolent; kindred; arbitrary; gracious; territorial; viceregal; double; singular; patriarchal; uncomquerable; antique; despotic; sovereign; frigid; intolerable; murmurous; usurped; omnipotent; mischievous.

verbs
administer—; augment—; cripple—; deaden —; diminish—; exercise—; exert—; extend —; invalidate—; paralyze—; scotch—; undermine—; strengthen—; wield—; —controls; —dominates; —dwindles.
(See dominion, influence, power.)

SWAY (v)

adverbs
dizzily; rhythmically; musically; gently; indolently; perilously; alluringly; entrancingly; violently; restlessly; emotionally; psychologically; tremendously; dreamily; religiously.
(See lurch, swing.)

SWEAR (v)

adverbs
vigorously; fiercely; ferociously; solemnly; lustily; audibly; roundly; abominably; traitorously; earnestly.
(See curse, affirm, testify.)

SWEAT

adjectives
bitter; body; profuse; chilly; bloody; cold; tremendous; copious; continual; peasant; goblin.

verbs
check—; glisten with—; induce—; secrete —; —beads; —chills; —develops; —diffuses; —diminishes; —drenches; —drips; —droops; —glistens; —pours off; —rolls; —stains; —starts; —wilts.
(See perspiration.)

SWEAT (v)

adverbs
copiously; prodigiously; profusely; tremendously; coldly; abnormally.
(See perspire, exude.)

SWEEP

adjectives
outward; wavering; everlasting; soft; long; heaving; exulting; comprehensive; windy; majestic; gentle; irresistible; pitiless; magnificent; wild; enormous; dramatic; dread; liberal; joyous; shining; semi-circular.

verbs
condense—; deflect—; determine—; direct —; enlarge—; extend—; limit—; magnify —; realign—; restrict—; shift—; switch—; —declines; —deviates; —diverges; —embraces; —expands; —ranges; —swerves; —zigzags.
(See speed, range.)

SWEEP (v)

adverbs
capriciously; irresistibly; bitterly; majestically; resistlessly; frightfully; terrifically; silently; mutely; hoarsely; gracefully; surreptitiously; vigorously; tumultuously; relentlessly; heartlessly; confusedly; magnificently; dramatically.
(See carry, move, sway.)

SWEETHEART

verbs
adore—; betroth to—; caress—; cherish—; devote to—; dismiss—; estrange—; forsake —; gain—; idolize—; jilt—; libel—; reject —; revere—; treasure—; woo—; yearn for —; —bewitches; —captivates; —charms; —enchants; —endears; —enraptures; —infatuates.
(See lover, mistress, siren, swain.)

SWEETNESS

adjectives
liquid; mournful; seductive; subtle; womanly; voluptuous; brooding; wild; earnest; penetrating; venerable; palling; ineffable; tender; wanton; balmy; admirable; listless; enduring; deceptive; ravishing; continuous; infantile; exceeding; unbelievable; luscious; drowsy; patient; plaintive; withering;

strained; direful; earthly; penetrative; alarming; awful; saucy; summer; capricious; fragrant; cloying; singular; sacred; wayward; sunny; girlish; prattling; secret; twittering; benign; candied; profuse; simpering.

verbs
adulterate—; affect—; commend—; emit—; enjoy—; feign—; inhale—; inject—; relish—; savor—; —allures; —baits; —cloys; —deceives; —depresses; —nauseates; —permeates; —revolts; —sickens; —smothers; —tempts.
(See nectar, fragrance, sugar, candy.)

SWELL (v)

adverbs
abnormally; hideously; pretentiously; indignantly; gently; powerfully; perceptibly; proudly; enormously; voluptuously; bulbously; incredibly; spectacularly.
(See expand, dilate.)

SWELLING

adjectives
imperceptible; proudest; puffy; slight; harmless; stormy; unfathomed; alternate; hive-like; solemn; gentle; cockney; serious; enormous; voluptuous; bulbous; secret.

verbs
accentuate—; allay—; alleviate—; avert—; characterize by—; compress—; diagnose—; ease—; extend—; overcome—; reduce—; remedy—; restrain—; vent—; —abates; —dilates; —diminishes; —disfigures; —distends; —dwindles; —ebbs; —exaggerates; —indicates; —mars; —presses; —projects; —protrudes; —stiffens; —subsides; —tortures; —wanes.
(See inflammation.)

SWERVE (v)

adverbs
deviously; perilously; dangerously; fatally; erratically; drunkenly.
(See deviate, turn.)

SWIFTNESS

adjectives
incredible; electric; tireless; usual; feline; stunning; menacing; bounding; amazing; wave-like.

SWIM (v)

adverbs
desperately; heroically; vigorously; unflaggingly; lustily; courageously; boldly; staunchly; gallantly.
(See float, move.)

SWINDLE

adjectives
churlish; loving; squealing; enormous; obstinate; snorting; public; huge; monstrous; wide-spread.

verbs
disclose—; execute—; guard against—; participate in—; penalize—; perpetrate—; reveal—; uncover—; unearth—; —bilks; —deprives; —despoils; —diverts; —extorts; —fleeces; —impoverishes; —infuriates; —mulcts; —rooks; —shears; —strips.
(See fake, fraud.)

SWING

adjectives
sensuous; breathless; undulating; rhythmic; unrestricted; smooth; romantic; graceful; saber; glittering; unerring; sweet; fascinating; swaying; crazed.

SWING (v)

adverbs
gracefully; playfully; noiselessly; creakingly; recklessly; gratingly; peremptorily; grotesquely; adroitly; lazily.
(See sway, wave.)

SWIRL

adjectives
eddying; unmistakable; nasty.

SWIRL (v)

adverbs
turbulently; dizzily; incessantly; aimlessly; eddyingly; vertiginously.
(See whirl, twist.)

SWOON

adjectives
profound; interlunar; deathlike; summer; drunken; amorous; sweet; pretended; opportune.

SWORD

adjectives
deputed; drawn; shining; unsheathed; glittering; angry; bold; senseless; naked; virgin; pitiless; reeking; tapered; temporal;

victorious; handsome; self-pointed; ponderous; unsullied; theological; tyrannous; prompted; swift; leaden; two-edged; flaming; boisterous; trusty; noisy; grasping; rusty; knightly; ornamented; sated.

verbs
accoutre with—; affix—; arm with—; bear —; besmirch—; brandish—; draw—; edge —; equip with—; extract—; fall before—; fence with—; flaunt—; flourish—; govern by—; insert—; oppose with—; perish by—; plunge—; purge by—; send home—; sheathe —; slash with—; slay with—; smite with—; stain—; strike with—; swish—; temper—; thrust—; unsheathe—; wave—; wear—; wield—; win by—; woo with—; —clanks; —s clash; —s cut; —drips; —flames; —flashes down; —glitters; —hacks; —pierces; —s slash against; —stuns; —whirs; —wounds.

(See knife, rapier, lance, cutlass, stiletto.)

SYCOPHANCY

adjectives
prodigious; courtly; crude.

verbs
approve—; brand with—; detect—; favor —; forbid—; induce—; lament—; patronize —; ply—; practise—; pursue with—; reject —; resist—; ridicule—; —infests; —irks; —irritates; —nauseates; —pollutes; —wins.

(See flattery.)

SYLLABLES

adjectives
ponderous; liquid; redundant; hideous; hissing; stressed; difficult; long; staccato; unaccented.

SYLVAN

adverbs
delightfully; refreshingly; shadily; sweetly; songfully; pleasantly; charmingly; fragrantly; attractively; spaciously.

SYMBOL

adjectives
mystic; 'prefiguring; appropriated; rigid; graphic; repulsive; shining; magic; national; valiant; barren; companionable; impressive; universal; sacred; accidental; elaborate; mingled (pl); living; everlasting; hallowed; suggestive; dramatic; revolutionary; crude; archaic; sound.

verbs
compose—; comprehend—; conceive—; define—; engrave—; examine—; inquire into —; interpret—; regard—; renounce—; seek —; study—; substitute—; value—; —denotes; —overshadows; —proves; —represents; —signifies; —suggests; —typifies.

(See attribute, device, emblem, mark, sign.)

SYMBOLIC

adverbs
mystically; inscrutably; significantly; faintly; clearly; definitely; intentionally; artistically; mysteriously; curiously; abstrusely; cleverly; consistently; conspicuously; apparently.

SYMMETRY

adjectives
studied; adolescent; absolute; vertical; artificial; admirable; exquisite; broken; structural; rare; matchless; bilateral; sinewy; perfect.

SYMPATHETIC

adverbs
delightfully; warmly; lovingly; companionably; comfortingly; ardently; understandingly; intelligently; cooperatively; actively; zealously; energetically; feelingly; compassionately; indignantly; touchingly; harmoniously; pitifully; altogether; heartily; cordially; effusively; amiably; affectionately; helpfully; humanely; benevolently; generously.

SYMPATHIZE (v)

adverbs
gushingly; profoundly; effusively; complacently; keenly; warmly; earnestly; paternally; spontaneously; compassionately; frankly.

(See understand.)

SYMPATHY

adjectives
vivacious; fatherly; imperfect; awful; silent; active; understanding; filial; instinctive; unspoken; poetic; trivial; genuine; noble; mock; wholehearted; extensive; delighted; tender; vivid; rebel; secret; loving; intelligent; consoling; utter; spiritual; glorious; passionate; nameless; inexplicable; irrepressible; frightened; reverent; fervent; mysterious; intense; mystic; irresistible; inborn; jeering; natural; impotent; mental; infinite; effusive; unconscious; energetic;

fanciful; fervid; spasmodic; boundless; divided; middle; conditional; placid; ardent; morbid; painful; presumed; healing; patient; cordial; magnetic; imaginative; practical; flaunted; respective; apparent; generous; prudent; subtle; spontaneous; warm; instantaneous; tentative; majestic; sincere; emotional; elaborate; profound; fraternal; unwelcome; synthetic; affectionate; peculiar; sobbing; loving; indissoluble; young; sweet; deferential; intelligent; kindly; passionate; adaptable; demonstrative; impersonal; gentle; radical; frank; solemn; universal; fearful.

verbs
afford—; alienate—s; arouse—; attract—; bestow—; desire—; elicit—; engage—; enlist—; evince—; exercise—; extend—; exude —; feign—; flare up in—; gain—; lack—; limit—; pledge—; reject—; shut off from—; spare—; steel against—; stir—; suppress—; whip up—; win—; woo—; —binds; —consoles; —cools; —eases; —lashes together; —moves; —tempers; —touches; —twinges; —unites.

(See compassion, pity, tenderness, affection.)

SYMPHONIC

adverbs
triumphantly; gloriously; brilliantly; dazzlingly; hamoniously; blaringly; delicately; beautifully; tenderly; merrily; scarcely; thunderously; soothingly; pleasantly; ineffably; impressively; splendidly; magnificently.

SYMPHONY

adjectives
light; airy; pathetic; descriptive; majestic; massive; angelic; universal; seraphic; pert; marvelous; awe-inspiring.

verbs
attend—; compose—; constitute—; develop —; direct—; execute—; introduce—; interpret—; join in—; perform—; present—; produce—; score—; —bursts forth; —charms; —delights; —enchants; —entices; —floats; —provokes; —thrills; —uplifts.

(See music, composition, orchestra.)

SYMPTOMS

adjectives
alarming; positive; terrifying; terminal; prevailing; anomalous; marked; inward; subsequent; dangerous; ominous; warning; dramatic; serious; peculiar; premonitory; unpleasant; distressing; hysterical; troublesome; insidious; bellicose; mitigated; feverish; characteristic; aggravated; decisive; individual; constant; threatening; recurring.

verbs
aggravate—; allay—; alleviate—; attend with—; complicate—; deprecate—; describe —; detail—; develop—; discern—; distrust —; eliminate—; enumerate—; evaluate—; evince—; exhibit—; give rise to—; heed—; ignore—; interpret—; mask—; observe—; regard—; relieve—; subdue—; —abate; —accompany; —advance; —appear; —confound; —continue; —decline; —distress; —indicate; —manifest; —mark; —subside; —vanish; —vary.

(See evidence, sign, indication.)

SYNCHRONIZE (*v*)

adverbs
delicately; nicely; scientifically; automatically; exactly.

SYNCOPE

verbs
endure—; expire from—; induce—; lapse into—; produce—; suffer—; —contracts; —endangers; —strains; —unnerves.

SYNDICATE

verbs
appoint to—; combine in—; empower—; form—; head—; —adjourns; —contracts for; —controls; —directs; —disposes of; —dupes; —forces; —introduces; —manages; —meets; —promotes; —purchases; —pushes; —raises; —schemes; —transacts; —undertakes.

(See committee, board, group, association, concern.)

SYNTHESIS

verbs
arise from—; comprehend—; construct by—; delve into—; devise—; disclose—; effect—; employ—; exhibit—; facilitate—; form—; hail—; observe—; produce by—; unite in—; —compounds; —restores; —results in; —yields.

(See combination, method.)

SYPHILIS

verbs
afflict with—; campaign against—; contract

—; control—; cure—; diagnose as—; eradicate—; expose—; fear—; indicate—; inflict with—; recognize—; relieve—; reveal—; stamp out—; suspect—; test for—; treat—; —attacks; —cripples; —destroys; —devastates; —menaces; —ravages; —strikes; —yields to.
(See disease.)

SYRINGE

verbs
compress—; employ—; exhaust—; fit—; force from—; inject with—; manipulate—; squeeze—; —cleanses; —discharges; —draws in; —ejects; —emits; —pours; —spouts; —sprinkles into; —squirts.
(See pump.)

SYSTEM (*general*)

adjectives
pure; monetary; runaway; star; terrestrial; flexible; rational; corporate; constitutional; delicate; cumbrous; foul; elective; optical; pernicious; maudlin; digestive; mythic; rotting; intricate; dark; prefectorial; monarchical; nervous; overtaxed; routined; innovating; differing; bloc; reducing; judicial; enormous; expensive; utmost; proposed; gymnastic; defective; cumbersome; complicated; correlated; absolute; anatomical; preposterous; stellar; pedantic; beneficent; feudal; ecclesiastical; rigorous; harmonious; sequential; barbarous; infallible; elliptic; native; addled; metrical; prudent; tragic; voluntary; atrocious; equitable; selfish; medieval; debased; feasible; vicious; respected; effective; rapid; voluminous; defensive; conventual; diverse; elevated; closed; expiring; weak; inferior; scientific; harmful; equivalent; merit; subtle; formidable; existing; elastic; extraordinary; philosophic; sympathetic; competitive; imperial; reflective; disastrous; antiquated; subversive; respiratory; vascular; chronological; vigilant; unstable; impersonal; representative; profit; excellent; severe; fruitless; vain; infant; patronage; magnificent; distribution; experimental; ethical; full; compact; discordant; regulated; imperial; antiseptic; abstruse; drying.

SYSTEM (*plan, scheme, etc.*)

verbs
accept—; adapt to—; adhere to—; adopt—; afford—; apply—; base on—; brace—; buck—; cling to—; consolidate—; contrive—; corrupt—; curb—; demonstrate—; devise—; discard—; disrupt—; dominate—; elucidate—; entrench—; establish—; evolve—; extend—; fashion—; father—; formulate—; forsake—; found—; inaugurate—; incorporate in—; install—; institute—; "knock"—; map out—; master—; modify—; mold—; outmode—; overthrow—; promulgate—; reduce to—; reform—; restore—; shake—; shatter—; subscribe to—; supervise—; vindicate—; wed to—; —bars; —decrees; —disintegrates; —functions; —governs; —hinges on; —insures; —rears; —totters.
(See plan, program, scheme, method, order.)

SYSTEM (*human body*)

verbs
absorb into—; alkalize—; animate—; break down—; build up—; deplete—; derange—; drain—; emaciate—; fetter—; gear—; impoverish—; invade—; invigorate—; involve—; nourish—; poison—; purge—; recharge—; regulate—; relieve—; tone up—; traverse—.
(See body.)

SYSTEMATIC

adverbs
habitually; naturally; carefully; cautiously; painfully; pedantically; punctiliously; meticulously; incredibly; painstakingly; satisfactorily; commendably; admirably; tiresomely; needlessly; overly; unnecessarily; occasionally; emphatically.

T

TABERNACLE

adjectives
cloudy; mortal; earthly; quivering; fleshy; incarnate; spiritual.

verbs
abide in—; achieve—; conceive—; construct—; create—; disseminate through—; dwell in—; erect—; establish—; fill—; form—of; frequent—; inhabit—; lay foundation of—; occupy—; organize—; people—; permeate—; put together—; raise—; revere—; shun—; take up one's abode in—; —arises; —breeds; —brings forth; —fosters; —stands; —teems with.
(See church, temple, tent.)

TABLE

adjectives
shrouded; imperial; padded; tottering; wine-smeared; transparent; warped; tolerable; comely; bounteous; clean; zinc-topped; work; modest; rude; separate; abundant (pl); sphered; banqueting; polished; cluttered; immense; hospitable; gaming; sturdy; extension; reading; well-spread; cheerful; washing; rickety; weather-beaten.

verbs
adorn—with; burrow under—; carve—; compose—of; construct—; clutter—; drape—; drum upon—; emboss—; fashion—; furnish—; gild—; grace—; gorge at—; head—; inlay—; litter—; load—with; pile on—; prepare—; spread—; support—; —bears; —groans; —stands; —sustains.
(See desk, bench, furniture.)

TABLOID

verbs
decipher—; interpret—; launch—; —abuses; —adulterates; —clamors; —commits; —cries out; —defiles; —disseminates; —holds forth; —horrifies; —inculcates; —nurtures; —pictures; —prostitutes; —seduces; —teems with; —violates; —vulgarizes.
(See press, newspaper.)

TABOO

verbs
countenance—; denounce—; enforce—; ignore—; impose—; observe—; remove—; set up—; —bans; —bars; —debars; —excludes; —forbids; —hampers; —hinders; —inhibits; —interdicts; —prohibits; —restrains; —restricts; —stands in the way.
(See ban, restriction.)

adverbs
racially; conventionally; inanely; snobbishly; socially; piously; ceremonially; strictly; traditionally; ecclesiastically; irrationally; inexplicably; utterly; politically; seriously; curiously; gravely.

TABULATE (v)

adverbs
tirelessly; accurately; industriously; statistically; neatly; mathematically.
(See record, arrange.)

TACIT

adverbs
implicitly; unobtrusively; inferentially; inarticulately; usually; timorously; validly; legally.

TACITURN

adverbs
provokingly; reticently; shyly; morosely; gloomily; observantly; amazingly; deliberately; habitually; naturally; unusually; incurably; usually; inexplicably; unaccountably; interestingly; curtly; laconically; notoriously; secretively; evasively; incredibly; strangely; usually; oddly; peculiarly; inveterately; consistently; extraordinarily.

TACT

adjectives
subtle; external; sympathetic; gracious; delicate; unerring; perfect; cheerful; diplomatic; exquisite; rare; pecuniary; admirable; female; genuine; discriminating; requisite; faultless; extraordinary; critical; consummate; customary; fine.

apply—; bring—into play; cast—to the winds; discard—; dispense with—; employ—; enlist—; evince—; make away with—; practice—; require—; shelve—; throw aside—; throw—overboard; utilize—; —brings to bear; —conduces; —serves; —subserves.
(See diplomacy, shrewdness, discretion.)

TACTFUL

adverbs

easily; graciously; pleasantly; affably; urbanely; agreeably; ingratiatingly; pleasingly; inoffensively; diplomatically; prudently; discreetly; unusually; notoriously; signally; significantly; gratefully; gracefully; helpfully; serviceably; unwontedly; carefully; cautiously; warily; sympathetically; unctuously; deliberately; wisely; tenderly; acutely; delicately; shrewdly; expertly; reasonably; profoundly; cleverly; thoughtfully; subtly; courteously; chivalrously; politely

TACTICS

adjectives

piscatory; able; skillful; terrorist; astute; medieval; imperfect; preliminary; wily; militant; tough; company; defensive; cautious; amazing; successful; driving; obstructive; ingenious; original; matrimonial; similar; turncoat.

verbs

adopt—; apply—; base—on; condone—; credit—; denounce—; develop—; devise—; dispute—; employ—; engage in—; influence —; introduce—; modify—; predict—; resort to—; revamp (colloq.)—; shift—; vary—; —aim; —assist; —cause; —demand; —effect; —enable; —evolve; —produce; —protect; —result in; —revolt; —shift.

(See maneuver, strategy, plan.)

TACTLESS

adverbs

unfortunately; unwittingly; thoughtlessly; ineptly; blunderingly; awkwardly; gracelessly; cruelly; embarrassingly; unluckily; clumsily; innocently; bluntly; ungraciously; carelessly; brutally; unfeelingly; unsympathetically; coldly; strangely; unexpectedly; lamentably; deplorably; unpardonably; insufferably; unpleasantly; disagreeably; unpredictably; blindly.

TADPOLE

verbs

convert—into; evolve from—; swarm with —s; view—; —adheres to the surface; —approaches; —s attach themselves; —breathes; —breeds; —changes to; —clings; —develops into; —emerges; —glides; —hatches; —is transformed into; —metamorphoses; —nibbles; —regenerates; —rushes; —sallies; —undergoes transformation; —wiggles; —wriggles.

(See fish.)

TAIL

adjectives

real; curling; flickering; forked; prehensible; stumpy; monstrous; false; fantastic; lambent; lashing; deadly; stinging; scraggy.

verbs

agitate—; cover—; fasten—; flick—; flourish—; hitch—; infest—; swish—; toss—; wag—; whisk—; —balances; —collides with; —dangles; —dashes; —hangs; —jerks; —lashes; —quivers; —slaps; —smacks; —strikes; —sweeps; —swings; —taps; —twitches; —whacks; —whisks; —wiggles.

(See braid, hair, end, rear.)

TAILOR

adjectives

trained; efficient; master; custom; union; experienced; faultless; loquacious; careful; hand; fine; lusty; soft; skillful; artistic; elaborate; casual; provincial; meticulous.

verbs

—accoutres; —alters; —apparels; —arrays; —attires; —biases; —borders; —designs; —drapes; —fits out; —flounces; —frills; —fringes; —gears; —hems; —outfits; —refurbishes; —renovates; —rigs; —seams; —sheathes; —styles; —tacks.

TAILOR (v)

adverbs

expertly; superbly; smartly; properly; stylishly; luxuriously; expensively; handsomely; faultlessly; exquisitely; flawlessly; scientifically; meticulously; impeccably; artistically.

(See fit, clothe.)

TAINT (v)

adverbs

disgustingly; sickeningly; dangerously; poisonously; partially; subtly; odorously; vilely.

(See corrupt.)

TAINTED

adverbs

unfortunately; ineradicably; indelibly; undisguisedly; fatally; indubitably; vilely; slightly; terribly; lamentably; strangely; unexpectedly; immeasurably; infectiously; noxiously; disgracefully; dangerously; completely; curiously; thoroughly; undeniably; unpleasantly; disagreeably; inexplicably.

TAKE (v)

adverbs
selfishly; invariably; graciously; voluntarily; figuratively; consciously; voraciously; recklessly; unhesitatingly; reluctantly; forcibly; sparingly; literally; ostentatiously; affectionately; seriously; indiscriminately; ostensibly; ceremoniously; roughly.

(See seize, apprehend.)

TAKING

adverbs
marvellously; attractively; charmingly; remarkably; prettily; beautifully; unusually; especially; pleasantly; interestingly; arrestingly; irresistibly; curiously; extraordinarily; enchantingly.

TALE

adjectives
half-told; monotonous; scandalous; sentimental; apocryphal; unbelievable; ecclesiastical; ridiculous; gloomy; foam-like; specious; supernatural; wondrous; pathetic; dismal; legendary; instructive; untold; tedious; mournful; exquisite; beautiful; passionate; flattering; effective; grievous; enchanting; true; riotous; shameful; diverting; evil; extraordinary; soothing; idle; definite; harrowing; melancholy; heavy; romantic; childish; uneventful; successful; crowning; gruesome; desolating; horrible; blissful; sensible; tragic; blood-curdling; artless; ever-young; saddest; magical; incoherent; tempting; merry; wild; transmitted; improbable; family; baseless; unpainted; tavern; taking; piteous; unvarnished; facetious; incomprehensible; intoxicating; sinister; amorous; long-winded; thrilling; melodramatic; mystic; abbreviated; touching; boastful; analogous; trifling; debonair; mingled (pl); seafaring; graphic; metrical; idle; free.

verbs
bear—; beguile with —s; center—; close—; compose—; conceive—; concoct—; construct—; depict—; drink in—; embody in—; follow up—; pervade—; plunge into—; pour out—; relate—; revive—; spin—; testify to—; treat—; unfold—; vary—; weave—; —s abound; —s drift into mind; —enhances in interest; —entertains; —lengthens; —portrays; —progresses.

(See legend, narrative, narration, novel, story, "yarn," poem.)

TALENT

adjectives
genuine; distinguished; peculiar; superficial; satirical; histrionic; stifled; dramatic; marked; copious; kindred; administrative; brilliant; hidden; intuitive; inherited; native; undisciplined; vivid; social; admirable; innate; conspicuous; rare; precocious; evinced; delicate; original; sturdy; eminent; inconsiderable; gastronomic; choice; undoubted; uncommon; musical; wild; inventive; practical; interior; inborn; extraordinary; rising; latent; constructive; outside; mediocre; undoubted; comic; adoring; culinary; military; exquisite; budding.

verbs
applaud—; bring to light—; call upon—; confine—; cultivate—; demonstrate—; detect—; develop—; discover—; display—; dissipate—; enlist—; esteem—; eulogize—; expand—; exploit—; extol—; glorify—; inherit—; laud—; magnify—; misuse—; nurture—; panegyrize—; pay tribute to—; pervert—; prostitute—; smother—; stifle—; trace—; transcend—; weigh—; worship—; —buds; —decays; —germinates; —issues from; —ministers; —nourishes; —sprouts; —sustains; —transcends.

(See ability, mentality, intelligence, capacity, genius, skill.)

TALENTED

adverbs
eminently; conspicuously; extraordinarily; genuinely; peculiarly; particularly; remarkably; admirably; uncommonly; ingeniously; amazingly; signally; dazzlingly; surprisingly; splendidly; magnificently.

TALK

adjectives
buoyant; hearty; revolutionary; comprehending; fanciful; heartening; ineffable; passionate; furtive; prodigious; vainglorious; blasphemous; sneering; obscene; scandalous; heated; vigorous; unpleasant; willful; casual; yelling; loud; arduous; tedious; fragmentary; elliptical; rambling; everlasting; brilliant; indeterminate; bawdy; unmeaning; customary; spontaneous; vile; unmannerly; imperious; assuming; endless;

racy; confounded; solemn; droning; abundant; convincing; delightful; straight; impersonal; unusual; wanton; desultory; masculine; common; sprightly; buzzing; provincial; vain; loose; boyish; stimulating; inflammatory; inane; frivolous; vague; enjoyable; wicked; malignant; stammering; pious; discursive; alluring; facile; empty; silly; heart-searching; interesting; poetic; half-whispered; tumultuous; eloquent; bantering; wearisome; spasmodic; confidential.

verbs
cease—; compose—; deliver—; distinguish —; hush—; muffle—; mute—; muzzle—; silence—; stifle—; still—; substantiate—; tone down—; —allures; —annoys; —baits; —charms; —convinces; —distracts; —disturbs; —diverts; —edifies; —elucidates; —enlightens; —induces; —interests; —rumors.
(See speech, conversation, discourse, lecture.)

TALK (v)

adverbs
ramblingly; briskly; indefinitely; garrulously; animatedly; fluently; tediously; volubly; amicably; articulately; indiscreetly; blithely; shrewdly; casually; incoherently; pathetically; vivaciously; informally; interminably; mysteriously; unceasingly; eloquently; affectedly.
(See converse, speak.)

TALKATIVE

adverbs
incorrigibly; fluently; garrulously; chattily; informatively; incessantly; pleasantly; graciously; sociably; inveterately; naturally; habitually; incurably; happily; foolishly; loosely; effusively; eloquently; gushingly; prolixly; glibly; flippantly; unwisely; indiscreetly; imprudently; endlessly; tiresomely; strangely; remarkably; marvelously; incredibly; wearisomely; repetitively.

TALL

adverbs
slenderly; extraordinarily; splendidly; handsomely; lankily; absurdly; magnificently; commandingly; cadaverously; gauntly; awkwardly; laughably; gawkily; consciously; proudly; admirably; wonderfully; amazingly; unfortunately; ungainly; immeasurably; unusually; incredibly; attractively; conveniently.

TALLOW

verbs
affect—; boil—; compress—; convert into—; dissolve—; harden—; ignite—; liquefy—; melt—; mold—; purify—; refine—; separate—; solidify—; yield—; —consolidates; —confuses; —lumps; —thaws; —thickens.
(See wax.)

TALONS

verbs
bag with—; bare—; clip—; clutch in—; grasp in—; hook—; lay hold with—; pare —; pinion with—; retain in—; seize in—; sharpen—; —claw; —clench; —clinch; —detain; —gash; —gripe; —lacerate; —rend; —scar; —slash; —tear; —throttle.
(See fang, claw.)

TAME

adverbs
strangely; unexpectedly; finally; curiously; affectionately; tractably; unusually; downright; harmlessly; vexatiously; uninterestingly; dully; insipidly; submissively; lamentably; deplorably; compliantly; dutifully; apparently; obediently; surprisingly; sycophantically; tediously; insufferably.

TAME (v)

adverbs
partially; domestically; thoroughly; sufficiently; subtly; assiduously; rationally.
(See discipline, conquer.)

TAMELESS

adverbs
ardently; vehemently; enthusiastically; irrepressibly; utterly; violently; wildly; absolutely; savagely; ferociously; impatiently; stormily; inordinately; boisterously; crazily; riotously; temperamentally.

TANGIBLE

adverbs
comfortably; solidly; comfortingly; incontrovertibly; actually; finally; scarcely; ultimately; eventually; unexpectedly.

TANGLE

adjectives
dense; hopeless; confused; shining; mossy; feudal; matted; mazy; hereditary; complicated; blossoming; unexpected.

verbs
decipher—; dissolve—; elucidate—; extricate from—; fathom—; key—; liquidate—; resolve—; unravel—; unriddle—; unsnarl—; —confounds; —convulses; —deranges; —disconcerts; —dishevels; —jumbles; —meshes; —muddles; —perplexes; —perturbs; —puzzles; —ruffles; —rumples; —shuffles; —weaves; —webs.
(See intricacy, entanglement, mystery, riddle.)

TANGLE (v)

adverbs
perplexingly; desperately; hopelessly; complicatedly; designedly; confusedly; haphazardly; diplomatically; economically.
(See involve, perplex.)

TANGLED

adverbs
hopelessly; terribly; unfortunately; financially; curiously; embarrassingly; inextricably; strangely; deplorably; lamentably; oddly; darkly; odiously; laughably; ineptly; awkwardly; uncommonly; ridiculously; ludicrously; unskilfully; perplexingly; bewilderingly; guiltily; innocently; unwittingly; gullibly; helplessly; pitifully.

TANK (general)

adjectives
special; septic; large; spacious; clogged; rusty; useful.

TANK (military)

verbs
armor—; bullet-proof—; construct—; convert into—; design—; evade—; man—; manoeuvre—; mount—; propel—; surrender—; turret—; —attacks; —bombards; —caterpillars; —climbs; —crushes; —disperses; —lumbers; —negotiates; —repels; —rolls; —rumbles; —wheels.

TANTALIZING

adverbs
idly; absurdly; tormentingly; playfully; unbearably; teasingly; incalculably; terribly; oddly; merrily; continually; comically; outlandishly; uncommonly.

TAP (v)

adverbs
nervously; impatiently; rudely; gracefully; lightly; significantly; intermittently; irritatingly; incessantly; periodically.
(See rap, knock.)

TAPE

verbs
rend—; shred—; —adheres; —agglutinates; —binds; —cements; —cleaves; —clings; —coheres; —conglutinates; —couples; —glues; —gums; —seals; —shackles; —unites.
(See ligature, band, bandage.)

TAPER

adjectives
glimmering; gleaming; beaming; midnight; waxen; burning; sickly; flickering; tall; graceful; slender.

verbs
glut with—s; obscure—; quench—; snuff out—; —beams; —diffuses; —flames; —flares; —flickers; —flutters; —gleams; —glimmers; —glows; —gutters; —illuminates; —radiates; —scintillates; —shadows; —twinkles.
(See candle, wick, light.)

TAPERING

adverbs
gracefully; symmetrically; slenderly; gradually; suddenly; eventually; unfortunately; beautifully; lamentably; unexpectedly.

TAPESTRY

adjectives
star-inwoven; fluttering; desolate; suncolored; blossoming; luxuriant; low-toned; smirched; enameled.

verbs
embellish—; exhibit—; hang—; line—; mount—; mutilate—; prize—; rend—; shade—; suspend—; value—; weave—; —adorns; —beautifies; —decorates; —depicts; —landscapes; —portrays.
(See picture, painting.)

TARDY

adverbs
unfortunately; disastrously; unluckily; extremely; unaccountably; deleteriously; unreasonably; needlessly; infamously; unaccountably; indiscreetly; lamentably; deplorably; fatally; unconscionably; habitually; characteristically; exasperatingly; inexcus-

ably; unpardonably; discourteously; impolitely; grossly; indecorously; surprisingly; disappointingly; irreparably.

TARGET

adjectives
uplifted; flaming; sensible; suitable; vulnerable; conspicuous; momentary; superb; helpless; receptive; rapid; moving; human; disappearing.

verbs
align with—; batter—; buffet—; collide with—; deflect from—; deflect—; deviate from—; direct toward—; diverge from—; fall short of—; flay—; level at—; rebound from—; riddle—; smite—; speed toward—; steer toward—; swerve from—; thwack—; —eludes.

(See mark, object.)

TARIFF

verbs
abolish—; absorb in—; adopt—; bandy—; bear—; bruit about—; exact—; legislate—; levy—; modify—; nullify—; parry—; rate—; reciprocate—; reduce—; regale with—; regulate—; revise—; scrap—; set—; silence—; slash—; steer—; yield—; —bamboozles (colloq.); —discourages; —distrains; —fades; —flows; —impedes; —limits; —prohibits; —protects; —ranges; —rates; —restrains; —restricts; —schedules; —subsides; —touches upon; —veers toward.

(See taxes, amount.)

TARNISHED

adverbs
slightly; remediably; temporarily; momentarily; wholly; unfortunately; curiously; ingloriously; morally; deeply; irrecoverably; pitiably; deplorably; unluckily; irretrievably; suddenly; hopelessly; sadly; manifestly.

TART

adverbs
sharply; pleasantly; interestingly; disagreeably; unnecessarily; keenly; discriminatingly; tastefully; laughably; cleverly; piquantly; poignantly; bewilderingly; ungraciously; deliberately; unpleasantly; gracelessly; tactlessly; extremely; suddenly; overly; inexcusably.

TASK

adjectives
barren; acrid; incongruous; diabolical; humble; pensive; considerable; self-imposed; toilsome; glorious; zealous; perilous; imaginative; present-day; uninspired; unpleasing; weary; appalling; tremendous; difficult; strenuous; bleak; ungracious; painful; willing; inevitable; hazardous; dormant; amusing; staggering; cheerless; mental; pedagogical; delightful; knotty; spiritual; irksome; arduous; dreaded; hopeless; delicate; simplified; futile; endless; unfulfilled; impossible; herculean; costly; thankless; onerous; graceful; alloted; anxious; abhorrent; rough; pleasing; laborious; unnatural; noble; primary; astounding; prosaic; formidable; musical; colossal; congenial; recurring; neglected; ungrateful; vulgar; heavy; exacting; suitable; disheartening; menial; priestlike; self-appointed; troublesome; tender; distasteful; useless; easy; discordant; venturesome; intellectual; sales; basic; discouraging; joyous; docile; fatiguing; appalling; dizzy; sublime.

verbs
absorb in—; accept—; achieve—; allot—; appoint—; approach—; assign—; assume—; attempt—; buckle down to—; charge with—; complicate—; confront—; consecrate to—; dedicate to—; develop—; devote to—; discharge—; dispose of—; ease—; engage in—; engross in—; enlist in—; entrust—; essay—; expend on—; facilitate—; fit for—; fulfill—; glorify—; impose—; intrust—; inure to—; lighten—; lump—s; perform—; plunge into—; prescribe—; present—; rally to—; render—; reward—; rob—; set to—; shirk—; shoulder—; shunt—; spur on to—; toil at—; undertake—; view—; whittle down—; —bores; —confronts; —consumes; —exhausts; —fatigues; —involves; —taxes; —wearies.

(See labor, chore, work, job.)

TASTE

adjectives
worst; impeccable; distinctive; congenial; artificial; pictureque; startling; acrid; artistic; luxurious, agreeable; aesthetic; considerable; fanciful; unpleasant; barbarous; educated; nauseous; bizarre; provincial; fastidious; incongruous; desultory; native; refreshing; controlling; exquisite; intellectual; superior; bookkeeping; cultivated; unusual; costly; execrable; elevated; vulgar;

classical; horrible; magic; varying; ludicrous; lustrous; cosmopolitan; barbaric; philanthropic; tangy; good; scientific; admirable; ancestral; erroneous; musical; precious; astringent; literary; uncertain; developed; popular; brazen; massive; instinctive; diminished; enlightened; ephemeral; pronounced; elegant; mortal; clean; honorable; gross; individual; delicious; aromatic; radical; savage; odious; characteristic; surprising; questionable; critical; unperverted; inimitable; plebeian; histrionic; taffy; bitter; schoolmastery; fashionable.

verbs
accumulate—; alter—; betray—; concoct—; criticize—; cultivate—; deprave—; disguise —; dispel—; elevate—; endure—; feign—; gratify—; impair—; indulge in—; manifest —; minister to—; modify—; outgrow—; overrate—; pander to—; pervert—; possess —; polish—; purify—; refine—; reflect—; relish—; simplify—; spice—; —appeals; —bites; —blossoms; —characterizes; —clings; —collapses; —crystallizes; —discriminates; —guides; —gormandizes; —intoxicates; —lingers; —nauseates; —rasps; —reflects; —sickens; —smacks of.

(See desire, craving, impulse, inclination, flavor, appreciation.)

TASTE (v)

adverbs
sparingly; tentatively; fastidiously; perniciously; poisonously; odiously; horribly.

(See relish, eat.)

TASTEFUL

adverbs
delicately; deftly; naturally; richly; chastely; instinctively; inherently; innately; unerringly; exquisitely; fastidiously; quaintly; ingeniously; intrinsically; discriminatingly; expertly; correctly; academically; admirably.

TASTY

adverbs
pleasantly; unusually; gracefully; beautifully; delicately; delightfully; unexpectedly; surprisingly; deliberately; laboriously; invitingly; luxuriously; artistically.

TATTLE (v)

adverbs
childishly; faithlessly; traitorously; pettishly; hatefully; peevishly; vindictively.

(See babble, gossip.)

TATTLING

adverbs
maliciously; garrulously; innocently; cheerily; cheerfully; deliberately; dangerously; purposely; intentionally; childishly; meanly; mischievously; idly; diffusely; endlessly; snidely; dangerously; viciously; vindictively; malignantly; venomously; inanely; mindlessly; senselessly; thoughtlessly; witlessly; contemptibly; despicably; basely.

TAUNT

adjectives
parting; bitter; stinging; unmerited; unfeeling; good; reproachful.

verbs
bristle at—s; disregard—; fling—; hurl—; ignore—; repay—; repress—; restrain—; stifle—; tolerate—; utter—s; —affronts; —brands; —cuts; —disparages; —irks; —irritates; —jeers; —lashes; —outrages; —pervades; —ridicules; —slurs; —stings; —twits.

(See jeer, insult, reproach.)

TAUT

adverbs
curiously; nervously; dangerously; solidly; securely; sufficiently; perilously; finally; completely; lamentably; deplorably; inconveniently; rigidly; strangely; unaccountably.

TAVERN

adjectives
dusky; uninviting; well-restored; popular.

verbs
beguile in—; frequent—; frolic at—; haunt —; patronize—; regale in—; relax in—; reside at—; revel in—; stagger from—; visit —; weary of—; —accommodates; —beckons; —dispenses; —diverts; —lodges; —lures; —resounds; —rings; —welcomes.

(See hotel, inn.)

TAWDRY

adverbs
cheaply; unacceptably; reprehensibly; inexcusably; definitely; positively; inconceivably; incredibly; emphatically; admittedly; inadmissibly; disagreeably; contemptibly; insubstantially; obtrusively; dreadfully; noticeably; conspicuously; undisguisedly; blatantly; inordinately; extremely; sordidly; meanly; cheaply; offensively.

TAXATION

adjectives
confiscatory; direct; excessive; equitable; ingenious; oppressive; unequal; stealthy; extortionate; merciless; enormous; staggering; arbitrary; unpitying; burdensome.

TAXES

adjectives
hidden; local; inspection; prohibitive; punitive; social; fantastic; exclusive; grievous; external; superfluous; onerous; arbitrary; oppressive; exceptionable; inequitable; personal; incredible; odious.

verbs
abscond with—; apply—; appraise for—; appropriate from—; assess—; authorize—; default—; denounce—; derive—; discount—; divert from—; dodge—; eliminate—; enact —; evade—; exempt from—; extort—; grumble about—; impose—; inveigh against —; legislate—; levy—; outlaw—; question —; rate—; reduce—; repeal—; squeeze—; —accrue; —burden; —constitute; —crush; —defray; —design; —enable; —extend; —impoverish; —mount; —prorate; —ruin; —stifle; —support; —total; —yield; expend—.
(See tariff.)

TAXI

verbs
avail oneself of—; commandeer—; employ —; flag—; hail—; hire—; license—; man—; mobilize—s; pursue in—; recruit—s; resort to—; scramble for—; whistle for—; —careens; —conveys; —s file by; —meanders; —pick its way; —rolls away; —rumbles; —scuds; —s scurry; —skids; —swerves; —threads thru traffic; —transports; —traverses; —whizzes.
(See automobile.)

TAXPAYERS

verbs
address—; besiege—; burden—; coerce—; delude—; harass—; impoverish—; irk—; overburden—; promise—; ruffle—; soothe —; stir—; swindle—; tyrannize over—; —array against; —band; —campaign for; —declaim; —decry; —elect; —groan; —clamor; —league; —moan; —petition; —protest; —repudiate; —rise; —unite; —voice.
(See citizen, public, people.)

TEA

adjectives
numberless (pl); well-creamed; smuggled; elemental; contraband; rare; licorice; softened; melodious; perfumed; fragrant; aphrodisiac.

verbs
abstain from—; addict to—; brew—; concoct—; dispatch—; dispense—; drain—; entertain at—; flavor—; gulp—; ice—; imbibe—; import—; quaff—; sip—; spice—; strain—; sweeten—; swill down—; —appeases; —moistens; —quenches; —revives; —simmers; —stimulates; —thickens.
(See coffee, drink, beverage.)

TEACH (*v*)

adverbs
professionally; explicitly; elaborately; exclusively; extensively; laboriously; effectually; systematically; dispassionately; ethically; scrupulously; conscientiously; competently; eminently; zealously; erroneously; inspirationally.
(See instruct.)

TEACHABLE

adverbs
easily; scarcely; hardly; eagerly; responsively; clearly; manifestly; readily; ordinarily; extraordinarily; unusually; alertly; quickly; intelligently; admirably; exceptionally; surprisingly.

TEACHER

adjectives
perspicacious; competent; well-trained; mute; pious; imaginative; established; enthusiastic; delightful; admirable; discontented; notable; eminent; fledged; brilliant; illustrious; foremost; understanding; zealous; distinguished; religious; discouraged; primary; incapable; stimulating.

verbs
commend—; disqualify—; extol—; honor—; prejudice—; revere—; —adjusts; —breeds; —coaches; —cultivates; —disciplines; —discourses; —drills; —edifies; —emancipates; —enlightens; —equips; —expounds; —fledges; —fosters; —guides; —harangues; —hews; —holds forth; —illumines; —impregnates; —inculcates; —indoctrinates; —infiltrates; —infuses; —interprets; —initiates; —inspires; —instils; —instructs; —liberates; —matures; —molds; —nurtures;

—poises; —prepares; —shapes; —sheds light; —sows; —rears; —tutors; —uplifts.
(See master, orator, scholar.)

TEACHING

adjectives
assiduous; blind; austere; orthodox; political; time-honored; positive; inspired; inner; basic; rational; erroneous; stern; polytheistic; ethical; false; lofty; skeptical.

verbs
accept—; acquaint with—; adhere to—; advance—; afford—; bias—; blind to—; certify for—; contradict—; convey—; demonstrate—; enlarge—; evolve—; follow—; glean from—; heed—; introduce—; labor at —; memorize—; practise—; prejudice—; propagandize—; reiterate—; reject—; standardize—; suppress—s; treasure—; —affords; —directs; —embraces; —enlightens; —guides; —inculcates; —infuses; —instils; —matures; —qualifies; —prepares; —unveils.
(See doctrine, gospel, precept, instruction, profession.)

TEA-CUP

adjectives
rattling; tiny; dainty; china; fragile.

TEAM

adjectives
well-matched; splendid; phlegmatic; ill-mated; willing; panting; serviceable.

verbs
acclaim—; assemble—; captain—; cleave—; coach—; condition—; discipline—; dominate —; drill—; forsake—; harangue—; harness —; heckle—; inspire—; instil in—; mobilize—; oppose—; rend—; reward—; sever —; subsidize—; transport—; —bows; —concedes; —conquers; —contends; —cooperates; —drubs; —files out; —flounders; — hampers; —manoeuvers; —proselytes; — surmounts; —trains; —triumphs; —upsets; —vanquishes.
(See crew, athlete, contestant.)

TEAR (*v*)

adverbs
distractedly; viciously; hideously; extensively; impatiently; ravenously; rudely; wolfishly; literally; wantonly; ceaselessly; ruthlessly; dreadfully.
(See divide, sever.)

TEARFUL

adverbs
touchingly; maddeningly; vexatiously; deliberately; purposely; profitably; pathetically; sympathetically; pitiably; unfortunately; readily; easily; ridiculously; comically; ludicrously; hysterically; nervously; timidly; shyly; bashfully; tragically; angrily; fearfully; overwhelmingly; embarrassingly; helplessly; anxiously; happily; boisterously; noisily; piteously.

TEARS

adjectives
superabundant; solemn; unshed; melodious; sorrowful; hysterical; timid; passionate; unavailing; heartbroken; fruitless; flowing; glowing; dying; passion-ridden; soul-brought; subduing; glorious; silent; weak; unreclaiming; stealing; idiot; sharp; sweet; bitter; dewy; struggling; treacherous; crystal; impending; grateful; honest; frozen; immortal; happy; salt; undropped; scalding; maudlin; untimely; eternal; joyful; repentant; unremembered; plenteous; tributary; emotional; ungovernable; immense; kindred; continual; gathering; contending; solemn; reminiscent; unavailing; sparkling; briny; unconscious; sympathetic; noiseless; sleepless; merry; crocodile; foolish; supplicating; patriotic; obsequious; excessive; imploring; intermittent; future; celestial; smarting; spiteful; involuntary; resistless; furious; parting; softening; mingled; submissive; saccharine; foreboding; purple; stanchless; contrite; peevish; quenched; humble; feigned; brimming; noble; penitential; dreadful; transparent; vanished; impotent; silver-shedding; mighty; fertile.

verbs
agitate to—; allay—; bathe in—; blind with —; brush away—; burst into—; check—; conceal—; consecrate with—; dab at—; dim with—; dissolve into—; dry—; emit —; feign—; flood with—; give vent to—; ignore—; inspire—; melt down—; move to —; provoke—; relieve—; secrete—; shed —; snivel in—; stem—; sting to—; summon —; swallow—; tinge with—; water with —; wink back—; wipe away—; wring—; —bedew; —blind; —choke; —dissolve; — dry up; —fall; —flow; —glisten; —glitter; —gush forth; —impassion; —melt; —move; —rack; —rain down; —scald; —soften; — start; —sting; —stream down; —sway; —

touch; —tremble; —trickle; —wash away; —well up; —wet; blink back—.
(See lamentation, dew, grief.)

TEASE (v)

adverbs
wilfully; provokingly; irritatingly; exasperatingly; bullyingly; boisterously; slyly; insidiously; viciously; vindictively; subtly; blithely.
(See torment, harass.)

TEASING

adverbs
blithely; playfully; persistently; comically; merrily; wildly; noisily; tormentingly; foolishly; inordinately; pestiferously; ludicrously; nonsensically; absurdly; merrily; airily; immoderately; hilariously.

TECHNICAL

adverbs
clearly; purely; merely; probably; narrowly; strictly; wholly.

TECHNICALITIES

verbs
acquire—; avoid—; bores one with—; botch —; bungle—; denote—; detail—; discard —; dispense with—; dissolve—; enlighten —; exhibit—; explain—; ignore—; insist upon—; master—; necessitate—; plague with —; simplify—; strip—; weigh—; —bewilder; —confuse; —particularize; —perplex.
(See detail, technique.)

TECHNICALITY

adjectives
theological; ecclesiastical; selling; trivial; tiny.

TECHNIQUE

adjectives
comprehensive; scarce; specified; perfected; grooming; inborn; natural; creative; operating; educational; photographic; administrative; first-rate; incredible; piano; impressionistic; remarkable; dramatic; masterly; sterile; histological; surgical; brushing; delicate; facile; amazing; complex.

verbs
acclaim—; achieve—; acquire—; attain—; change—; commend—; contrive—; crown —; dispatch with—; display—; develop—; devise—; employ—; endow with—; evolve —; excel in—; exhibit—; forge—; formulate—; improve—; introduce—; laud—; master—; perfect—; practise—; revolutionize—; stamp with—; suggest—; —aids; —enhances; —equips.
(See skill, method, manner.)

TEDIOUS

adverbs
intolerably; monotonously; profoundly; irksomely; tiresomely; uniformly; boringly; terribly; wearisomely; inordinately; feebly; exhaustingly; dully; mortally; prosily; disgustingly; unbearably; wearily; flatly; stupidly.

TEDIUM

verbs
allay—; chafe at—; decry—; disperse—; divert from—; ease—; relieve—; revolt at —; —assails; —beguiles; —bores; —burdens; —disintegrates; —exhausts; —fags; —fatigues; —harasses; —irks; —jades; —overwhelms; —prostrates; —sours; —stagnates; —strains; —taxes; —vexes; —wearies; —weighs upon.
(See monotony, weariness.)

TEETER (v)

adverbs
precariously; dizzily; dangerously; comically; drunkenly; weakly; painfully.
(See sway, balance.)

TEETH

adjectives
feeble; mottled; dazzling; tortuous; milky; ravenous; sharpened; jagged; clenched; hooked; pearly; tartarous; compressed; ferocious; flashing; foam-laced; blunted; glittering; chattering; convulsive; horrid; neglected; decayed; black; lacquered; wolfish; short; ivory; gnashing; snowy; close-shut; dagger-like; grinding.

verbs
abscess—; brace—; clamp—on; clench in—; cut—; dislodge—; drill—; engage with—; extract—; gnash—; grate—; grit—; groove —; imbed—in; lock—; polish—; retain—; —chatter; —crunch; —cut; —disintegrate; —emerge; —erupt; —flash; —gnaw; —lacerate; —pierce; —poison; —project; —reduce.
(See fang, bone.)

TELEGRAM

adjectives
congratulatory; visual; ocular; co-working; worrying; speedy.

verbs
acknowledge by—; convey—; decipher—; decode—; dispatch—; seal—; unfold—; —advises; —alarms; —announces; —authorizes; —s bombard; —confirms; —congratulates; —discloses; —divulges; —directs; —excites; —informs; —orders; —s pour in; —protests; —reveals.
(See letter, dispatch, news, message.)

TELEGRAPH (*v*)

adverbs
swiftly; instantly; faithfully; peremptorily; authoritatively; fraternally.
(See communicate, dispatch.)

TELEGRAPHIC

adverbs
mysteriously; swiftly; emotionally; marvellously; silently; confidentially; comically; fleetly; unmistakably; mercifully; sympathetically.

TELEPATHIC

adverbs
emotionally; sympathetically; instinctively; unmistakably; mysteriously; naturally; definitely; demonstrably; presumably; distinctly; possibly; imaginably; curiously; strangely; admissibly; credibly.

TELEPHONE

adjectives
limitless; effective; clattering; mute.

verbs
acquire—; communicate by—; confirm by—; disconnect—; drone into—; inform by—; install—; necessitate—; remove—; repair—; scurry to—; sever—; —assists; —awakens; —clamors; —distracts; —diverts; —eases; —enables; —facilitates; —jangles; —lightens; —persists; —shrills.

TELESCOPE

verbs
contemplate through—; design—; direct—at; discern through—; level—at; mount—; peek through—; peer through—; perceive through—; rivet—on; scan with—; squint into—; study through—; survey with—; —aids; —clarifies; —discovers; —distinguishes; —enlarges; —enlightens; —facilitates; —magnifies; —ranges; —reveals; —sweeps the heavens.
(See microscope.)

TELESCOPIC

adverbs
amazingly; incredibly; marvellously; authentically; credibly; highly; evidently; conveniently; compactly; cleverly; handily; disconcertingly.

TELL (*v*)

adverbs
succinctly; impassively; hysterically; vehemently; conclusively; frankly; vigorously; jestingly; vividly; reluctantly; impressively; vaguely; musically; candidly; effectively; complacently; fluently; simply; circumstantially; reverently; artfully; reproachfully; accordingly; bluntly; genially; dispassionately; arrogantly; fervently; glibly; poignantly; gravely; inconsistently.
(See communicate, speak.)

TELLING

adverbs
vividly; trenchantly; brilliantly; eloquently; unusually; impressively; uniquely; significantly; graphically; dramatically; vigorously; authoritatively; positively; sensationally; remarkably; extremely; singularly; marvellously.

TELLTALE

adverbs
undisguisably; innocently; embarrassingly; indubitably; convincingly; ineradicably; inescapably; manifestly; ridiculously; undeniably; significantly; remarkably; conspicuously; noticeably; visibly; graphically.

TEMPER

adjectives
generous; reckless; subjective; suspended; creative; critical; gusty; querulous; peevish; suspicious; inflammable; gracious; charitable; terrible; ethereal; youthful; judicial; penurious; violent; dauntless; ruffled; indolent; collective (pl); frayed; bad; easy; convivial; uncertain; predominant; revengeful; skeptical; chivalrous; complacent; malignant; malleable; slumbering; imperious; independent; fixed; haughty; jarring; serene; buoyant; amiable; indifferent; chastened; earthly; ruthless; jovial; unspent; unsunned; fiery; lively; loquac-

ious; self-willed; passionate; columned; delicate; noble; docile; imperturbable; characteristic; mirthful; sweet; queer; philosophic; irritable; lethargic; meek; placid; sunny; equable; changeable; curious; polemical; cold; irreligious; merry; conciliatory; unforgiving; fretful; invincible; pedantic; heroic; unaltered; keen; despondent; ungovernable; inquisitive; impatient; admirable; combative; childish; turbulent; choleric; gunpowder; aspiring; dignified; villainous; boisterous; resentful; coddled; schizoid; benevolent; calm; ferocious; submissive; confident; crusading; eddying; iron-like; tart; feeble.

verbs
allay—; assuage—; blunt—; calm—; chasten—; compose—; curb—; dulcify—; exhibit —; fire—; ignite—; lull—; manifest—; moderate—; mollify—; pacify—; palliate—; quell—; quench—; restrain—; rule—; smooth—; sober—; subdue—; sweeten—; —blazes; —erupts; —explodes; —flames; —flares; —foams; —foments; —fumes; —seethes; —simmers; —snaps.
(See ire, anger, disposition, temperament.)

TEMPERAMENT

adjectives
adventurous; uncertain; artistic; cheerful; nervous; bilious; romantic; brooding; poetical; fierce; ardent; sanguine; morbid; observing; restless; nerveless; classic; highbred; individual; aspiring; unchangeable; philanthropic; sprightly; apathetic; emotional; mercurial; equable; grave; warlike; peculiar; heroic; inborn; fervent; oratorical; impetuous; undisciplined; genial; melancholy; mournful; indolent; pugnacious; fitful; delicate; rare; sunny; passionate; peculiar; physical; overcharged.

verbs
attune—to; bend—; characterize—; curse with—; display—; dispose toward—; exhibit—; fire—; foment—; harmonize—s; imbue with—; incline toward—; inflame—; influence—; inherit—; modulate—; mollify —; mould—; warp—; wrestle with—; —s clash; —flares; —indicates; —piques; —seethes; —simmers.
(See character, disposition.)

TEMPERAMENTAL

adverbs
highly; inconveniently; tempestuously; provokingly; bewilderingly; naturally; proverbially; characteristically; insufferably; unpredictably; allegedly; unmanageably; uncontrollably; violently; interestingly; perplexingly.

TEMPERANCE

verbs
advocate—; campaign for—; commend—; exhort—; laud—; pledge—; promote—; —abstains; —allays; —alleviates; —chastens; —composes; —denies; —forbears; —mitigates; —moderates; —refrains; —sobers; —softens; —spares; —tranquillizes.
(See moderation, sobriety, restraint.)

TEMPERATE

adverbs
definitely; mildly; judiciously; moderately; calmly; pleasantly; safely; honestly; cautiously; discreetly; prudently; reasonably; certainly; occasionally; habitually; naturally; soberly; consistently; modestly; quietly; inveterately; surprisingly; meticulously; punctiliously; scrupulously; usually.

TEMPERATURE

adjectives
accurate; congenial; equable; unexpected; high; balmy; tepid; terrestrial; physical; low; critical; ruinous; debilitating; varying; aggregate; uniform; intolerable; mean; cheap; consistent; elevated.

verbs
ascertain—; determine—; expose to—of; indicate—; maintain—; measure—; record —; regulate—; swelter in—of; —chars; —chills; —chafes; —climbs; —congeals; —descends; —fluctuates; —flushes; —fuses; —ignites; —mounts; —nips; —parches; —petrifies; —pinches; —refreshes; —sinks; —skyrockets (colloq.); —soars; —thaws; —toboggans.
(See mercury, barometer, meter, weather.)

TEMPEST

adjectives
terrible; howling; winter; renewed; spirit-brewed; shadowy; embattled; hideous; giddy; aerial; social; weltering; thundering; laboring; furious; careening; commanding; ruinous; damaging.

verbs
calm—; still—; sway in—; —abates; —agitates; —batters; —bellows; —blusters; —

buffets; —churns; —clamors; —crackles; —devastates; —drenches; —fumes; —howls; —lashes; —rages; —roars; —seethes; —shrieks; —subdues; —swells; —uproots; —whisks; —whistles; —subsides.
(See gale, hurricane, storm.)

TEMPESTUOUS

adverbs
violently; uncontrollably; passionately; stormily; dangerously; unmanageably; remarkably; unusually; insufferably; notoriously; sensationally; melodramatically; feverishly.

TEMPLE

adjectives
druidical; blushing; foreign; mystical; unworthy; versatile; abolished; graceful; wind-swept; throbbing; soniferous; burning; shattered; hairy; pagan; proud; pillared; wooden; gorgeous; projecting; ancient; holy; arching; magnificent; veined; heated; solemn; sumptuous; shattered; battered; numerous (pl); anointed; airy; glass; monumental.

verbs
attend—; banish from—; beseech in—; blaspheme—; bow in—; commune in—; convert into—; dedicate—; defile—; degrade—; desecrate—; design—; enshrine in—; erect —; expel from—; found—; ordain—; profane—; purge—; quarter in—; refuge in—; rend—; retire to—; sully—; swear by—; taint—; visit—; whip from—; —rises; —sanctifies.
(See church, tabernacle, cathedral.)

TEMPORAL

adverbs
evanescently; merely; transitorily; briefly; fleetingly; fugitively; perishably; transiently; mutably; precariously; impermanently; painfully; unhappily; frailly; ephemerally; utterly; sadly; uncertainly; insecurely.

TEMPORARY

adverbs
fortunately; merely; definitely; presumably; luckily; unfortunately; probably; presumably; definitely; supposedly; allegedly.

TEMPT (v)

adverbs
diabolically; fiendishly; insidiously; viciously; lewdly; appetizingly; intolerably; unwittingly; irresistibly; unduly; incestuously; mystically; maddeningly; goadingly.
(See induce, lead.)

TEMPTATION

adjectives
constant; incestuous; sore; stronger; fierce; irresistible; external; various (pl); succulent; inviting; urban; insidious; testy; urgent; mystical; repeated; enticing; usurped.

verbs
accede to—; avoid—; conquer—; deliver from—; fling aside—; grapple with—; heighten—; intensify—; prevail against—; resist—; shun—; steel to—; subdue—; succumb to—; surrender to—; vanquish—; withstand—; wrestle with—; subdue—; —allures; —attracts; —baits; —beckons; —beguiles; —biases; —goads; —lures; —overcomes; —overwhelms; —seduces; —spurs; —sways; —tantalizes.
(See desire, passion, appetite.)

TEMPTING

adverbs
delectably; alluringly; subtly; viciously; cleverly; slily; guilelessly; seductively; irresistibly; curiously; strangely; exotically; perilously; boldly; wickedly; deliciously; charmingly; pleasurably; insidiously.

TENABLE

adverbs
scarcely; soundly; rationally; reasonably; logically; incontrovertibly; obviously; undeniably; easily; manifestly; validly; legally; satisfactorily; basically; effectively; inferentially; sensibly; fundamentally; essentially.

TENACIOUS

adverbs
stubbornly; obstinately; piously; dogmatically; doctrinally; doggedly; toughly; persistently; obdurately; resolutely; grimly; uncompromisingly; indomitably; stiffly; fanatically; inexplicably; disagreeably; ungraciously; tactlessly; surprisingly; churlishly; grossly; vexatiously.

TENACITY

adjectives
unyielding; peculiar; pathetic; amazing; bulldog; breathless; obstinate; desperate;

extraordinary; unmatched; dogged; agonized; marvelous.

verbs
buckle with—; cling with—; display—; exhibit—; inherit—; marvel at—; value—; —droops; —fails; —flags; —flinches; —impresses; —irks; —piques; —rankles; —resists; —riles (colloq.); —stiffens; —wavers; —yields to.
(See impregnability, stubbornness, persistence, strength.)

TENANT

adjectives
delinquent; peripatetic; impoverished; previous; worshipful; shuddering; defaulting; noisome; troublesome.

TEND (v)

adverbs
progressively; auspiciously; affectionately; subversively; obliquely; sedulously; faithfully; maternally; materially; religiously; fervently.
(See contribute, incline.)

TENDENCY

adjectives
pensive; sadistic; moralizing; abnormal; consequent; contrary; general; inevitable; exhibitionistic; decadent; abortive; immoral; dominant; latent; worldly; picturesque; belated; remote; revolutionary; marked; overruling; hereditary; evil; boyish; vicious; rationalistic; opposing; neurotic; abounding; pernicious; ambivalent; diverging; apprehensive; curtailed; philosophical; unconscious; speculative; primitive; morbid; life-abridging; transitory; herding; incestuous; rising; tubercular; undevout; natural; progressive; youthful; extravagant; erratic; notable; irreligious; conflicting; realistic; cancerous; centripetal; social; chronic; growing; powerful; stubborn; pseudo-classic; gravitating; materializing; obnoxious; dispositional; constitutional; pragmatic; aggravating; prevalent; remarkable; dangerous; healthy; observable; incorrigible; curious; devotional; pernicious; dispersive; culinary; commercial; monopolistic.

verbs
augment—; bolster—; check—; combat—; counteract—; counterbalance—; cultivate—; decry—; deplore—; deprecate—; dispose of—; eliminate—; encourage—; exhibit—; foster—; inherit—; neutralize—; nurse—; nurture—; observe—; offset—; outgrow—; overcome—; perceive—; promote—; reflect—; resist—; restrain—; smother—; stifle—; temper—; warp—; —conduces toward; —endangers; —jeopardizes; —predisposes.
(See inclination, proclivity, disposition.)

TENDER

adverbs
affectionately; maternally; infinitely; mercifully; passionately; amorously; impulsively; impetuously; eagerly; amiably; gently; curiously; naturally; oddly; unexpectedly; lovingly; caressingly.

TENDERNESS

adjectives
respectful; wounded; tearful; solemn; passionate; renewed; marked; sexual; dawning; yearning; melting; latent; pardonable; quaint; compassionate; human; spontaneous; newborn; bountiful; boundless; exquisite; conjugal; maternal; growing; unutterable; secondary; paternal; natural; deep; laughing; patriarchal; credulous; brief; immense; profound; elephantine; saddened; masculine; ineffable; touching; increasing; pathetic; grateful; infinite; unaccustomed; majestic; flowery; rugged; zealous; connubial; wishful; infinite; malicious; grave; wild; ineffable; excessive; rough; unvarying; flavorsome; graceful; universal; etherealized; brooding; shy; surpassing; patronizing; ideal; searching; sufficient; eternal; heavenly; uneradicated; peculiar.

verbs
affect—; arouse—; cherish—; display—; evince—; excite—; exhibit—; infuse—; inspire—; move to—; propitiate in—; relent in—; sense—; temper with—; treasure—; —assuages; —captivates; —charms; —disarms; —engages; —floods; —melts; —mitigates; —mollifies; —pervades; —pierces; —stirs.
(See love, kindness, compassion, pity, mercy.)

TENDON

verbs
bind—; cleave—; dissect—; incise—; lacerate—; penetrate—; pull—; rend—; seg-

ment—; sever—; strain—; strip—; —couples; —jams; —knots; —pains; —supports; —unites.

(See muscle, ligament.)

TENEMENTS

adjectives

spacious; frail; tessellated; dreary; newly-painted; fire-trap; dilapidated; unsafe; nauseating; filthy; close-packed; unsightly; disgusting; squalid.

verbs

condemn—; decry—; dwell in—; eject from —; evict from—; inhabit—; inveigh against —; poke about—; raze—; reside in—; roost in—; scurry through—; —breed; —confine; —defile; —dot; —engender; —harden; —overspread; —reek; —sully.

(See building, structure, home, slums.)

TENOR

adjectives

constant; noiseless; general; loud; expressionless; diminutive; same; habitual; operatic; even.

TENSE

adverbs

nervously; utterly; anxiously; rigidly; stiffly; terribly; oddly; uneasily; apprehensively; dreadfully; curiously; visibly; noticeably; manifestly; fearfully; self-consciously; excitedly; eagerly; unusually; remarkably; feverishly; warily; watchfully; quietly.

TENSION

adjectives

diminished; surface; severe; tremendous; increased; relieved; ocular; wonted; nervous; mental; spasmodic; unendurable; vigorous; bitter; emotional; extreme; unnatural; ominous; elastic; awful; high; electric.

verbs

allay—; alleviate—; ameliorate—; blunt—; ease—; erase—; generate—; inure to—; reduce—; relax—; release—; relieve—; soothe—; stir up—; sustain—; —burdens; —exhausts; —flares; —heightens; —jades; —mounts; —prostrates; —snaps; —strains; —taxes; —unnerves; —wearies.

(See misapprehension, anxiety, fear, strain, intensity.)

TENT

adjectives

invading; striped; tall; mat-walled; little; swarthy; stationary; convenient; superfluous; abominable; gauze; solitary; prim; tight.

verbs

assemble in—; avail oneself of—; batter—; buffet—; dwell in—; encamp in—; pelt—; pitch—; stake—; whisk away—; —affords; —comforts; —conceals; —enshrouds; —envelops; —flaps; —flutters; —obscures; —preserves; —shelters.

(See canvas, home, house, pavilion.)

TENTACLES

adjectives

long; trailing; murderous; multitudinous; clutching.

verbs

clutch in—; deliver from—; disengage—; elude—; ensnare in—; escape—; evade—; expand—; extricate from—; hug in—; liberate from—; relax—; release from—; seize in—; sever—; unloose—; —cling to; —contract; —entwine; —grasp; —retain; —smother; —snatch; —suffocate.

(See grasp, grip, talons, claw, clutch.)

TENURE

adjectives

property; fixed; solitary; lifelong; permanent; indefinite.

TEPID

adverbs

sickeningly; nauseously; uninterestingly; pleasantly; harmlessly; agreeably; safely; disagreeably.

TERM
(*general*)

adjectives

stringent; mechanistic; concrete; triumphant; remunerative; inexorable; appreciative; uncompromising; precise; brilliant; purposed; mysterious; familiar; interchangeable; plain; warm; ambiguous; proffered; unexpired; dubious; unhallowed; disastrous; convincing; abusive; modest; sudden; limited; strong; vile; festival; subsequent; equivalent; respectable; growling; impending; vague; hyperbolical; personal; unqualified; successful; downright; specific; generous; explicit; glowing; wrathful; conciliatory; budget; honorable; obscure; silent; rash; affectionate; convertible; installment; speedy; anagogic; emphatic; disapproving; attractive; original; indefinite; complied; gross; measured; absolute; uncalculating; following; misapplied; extravagant; equal; silken; liberal; uncouth; synonymous; flattering; satisfactory; hyperbolical; chameleon; advantageous; immense; tedious; convenient; endurable; psychoanalytic; unreasonable; generic; relative; intimate; eloquent; terrible; tender; fashionable; amicable; equivocal; favorable; complimentary; penitentiary; recollected; degrading; much-abused; express; comprehensive; antiquated; impressive; feeble; technical; essential; respectful; fundamental; abominable; unmistakable; graphic; energetic; monetary; figurative; opprobrious; unmistakable.

TERM (*words*)

verbs
accentuate—; amplify—; analyze—; apply —; clarify—; cloak in—s; clothe in—s; coin—; condense—; confine—; corrupt—; couch in—; define—; derive—; employ—; illustrate—; interpret—; object to—; paraphrase—; stilt—; stress—; voice in—s; —bewilders; —colors; —confuses; —degenerates; —disgraces; —embraces; —emphasizes; —expresses; —implies; —insinuates; —veils.

(See phrase, expression, word.)

TERM (*v*)

adverbs
vulgarly; improperly; euphemistically; confidentially; appropriately; aptly; irrelevantly; sneeringly; jestingly; satirically; equivocally; degradingly; technically; graphically; figuratively; opprobriously; affectionately; modestly; wrathfully; ambiguously; hyperbolically.

(See call, name.)

TERMAGANT

adverbs
brazenly; uncontrollably; boisterously; savagely; rudely; incredibly; obviously; laughably; ridiculously; unreasoningly; habitually; oddly; crazily; biliously; excitably; pugnaciously; truculently; bewilderingly; cruelly; scurrilously; obscenely.

TERMINATE (*v*)

adverbs
abruptly; tediously; innocently; happily; disastrously; seedily; inevitably; effectually; fatally; legitimately; swiftly; successfully; amazingly.

(See end, conclude.)

TERMITES

verbs
control—; deter—; exterminate—; infest with—; resist—; seethe with—; shield from —; teem with—; trample—; —abound; —ally with; —attack; —blight; —bore through; —burrow; —colonize; —construct; —deface; —despoil; —destroy; —devastate; —devour; —excavate; —forage; —gnaw; —hollow out; —impair; —incubate; —injure; —invade; —menace; —moult; —mound; —mutilate; —nest; —overrun; —penetrate; —raid; —ravage; —raise; —sap foundations; —store; —swarm; —tunnel through; —undermine.

(See ant, insect.)

TERMS (*conditions*)

verbs
accede to—; acknowledge—; acquiesce to —; adopt—; allude to—; approve—; assent to—; challenge—; comply with—; concede to—; confine to—; consent to—; consider —; contract on—; corroborate—; couch in —; dictate—; disclose—; divulge—; enforce—; haggle over—; impose—; indorse —; mince—; propound—; ratify—; regard —; restrict to—; shorten—; sign—; submit —; subscribe to—; translate into—; yield to—; —apply; —conciliate; —imply; —include; —pacify; —placate; —yoke.

(See condition, demand, proposition, provision, limitation.)

TERRACE

adjectives
successive (pl); sloping; spacious; narrow; zigzag; beautiful; rounded; landscaped.

TERRESTRIAL

adverbs
manifestly; disappointingly; materially; comfortably; obviously; ridiculously.

TERRIBLE

adverbs
utterly; consummately; unbearably; appall-

ingly; fascinatingly; luridly; overwhelmingly; indescribably; astoundingly; portentously.

TERRIFIED

adverbs

utterly; basely; brutally; cruelly; mercilessly; irrationally; unusually; highly; dismally; hopelessly; desperately; distressingly; painfully; pathetically; secretly; dreadfully; inwardly; strangely; curiously; wildly; violently; hysterically.

TERRIFY (*v*)

adverbs

pusillanimously; psychically; unreasoningly; manifestly; irrationally; superstitiously; secretly; frantically; vicariously; immoderately; direly; blindly; overwhelmingly; supernaturally; abjectly.

(See frighten, scare.)

TERRITORY

adjectives

extensive; adjacent; contiguous; debatable; adjoining; valuable; disputed; immense; imperial; worthless; contracted; neutral; condemned; excellent; dangerous; virgin; ideal; productive; paltry; vast; annexed; choice; rich; unassigned; inexhaustible; restricted; best; protected.

verbs

abandon—; absorb—; administer—s; annex—; border—; cede—; claim—; commandeer—; covet—; devastate—; dispose of—; embrace—; endow with—; expropriate—; flank—; forfeit—; fortify—; gain—; impound—; invade—; lay waste—; lease—; mandate—; partition—; patrol—; ravage—; reconquer—; retain—; reward with—; rule—; seek—; skirt—; traverse—; value—; yield—; —confronts; —flourishes; —revolts; —seethes.

(See district, province, locality, jurisdiction, country.)

TERROR

adjectives

mute; avowed; blasphemous; striking; pusillanimous; loving; mutual; bodily; abject; abysmal; mysterious; coquettish; conventional; chastening; conquering; psychic; manifest; rattling; hasty; inconceivable; avenging; haunting; forest; imaginary; instinctive; vague; limitless; unreasoning; sheer; absurd; majestic; dissolving; wild; grisly; superstitious; shuddering; bouncing; roaring; rigid; secret; breathless; dispelled; vigorous; frantic; natural; undefinable; solemn; rhythmic; deadly; fantastic; vicarious; tinkling; vengeful; faltering; prudential; dreadful; groundless; panicky; moderate; anticipative; veritable; pregnant; scattered; cold; paralyzing; dire; sickly; blind; constant; soul-chilling; overwhelming; unreasonable; supernatural; suppressed; simultaneous; efficient; increasing; unconvinced; ignoble.

verbs

allay—; attest to—; beleaguer by—; bend in—; blanch with—; cower in—; dispel—; entertain—; flinch in—; hesitate in—; incite—; inspire—; live in—; pale in—; palpitate in—; paralyze—; plunge into—; prostrate with—; quake in—; quiver in—; read—; retreat in—; sense—; shrink in—; shudder in—; squirm in—; tremble in—; —aggravates; —catches; —chills; —deters; —harrows; —haunts; —looms; —nauseates; —overwhelms; —petrifies; —racks; —recoils; —reigns; —seizes; —shapes itself; —springs; —stalks; —strikes; —stuns; —weighs upon.

(See dread, dismay, fear, alarm, fright, consternation.)

TERRORISM

verbs

assail—; castigate—; check—; curb—; inflict—; have recourse to—; revolt against—; subject to—; suppress—; tolerate—; —cankers; —coerces; —crushes; —dictates; —domineers; —oppresses; —overrides; —persecutes; —ravages; —reigns; —restrains; —rides roughshod; —snuffs out; —stings; —tyrannizes; —tramples; —wreaks; —yokes.

(See tyranny, intimidation.)

TERRORIST

verbs

quail before—; root out—s; —bridles; —coerces; —desecrates; —devastates; —domineers; —intimidates; —outrages; —pillages; —plunders; —ravages; —restrains; —retaliates; —sheds; —shocks; —suppresses; —tramples; —usurps.

(See anarchist, striker, revolutionist.)

TERROR-STRICKEN

adverbs

disastrously; nervously; awfully; unaccountably; unmercifully; tragically; utterly; hopelessly; curiously; helplessly; pitiably; irrecoverably; direly; sorely; unduly; grievously; naturally; inevitably; appallingly.

TERSE

adverbs
carefully; incisively; bitterly; cuttingly; sarcastically; insolently; indifferently; coldly; officially; wearily; cautiously; discreetly; formidably; rigidly; frigidly; curiously; perplexingly; unreasonably; unnecessarily; brusquely; bluntly; ominously; significantly; oddly.

TEST

adjectives
microscopic; summit; crucial; quick; fiery; acid; practical; universal; elaborate; exhaustive; innumerable (pl); conceiving; grueling; stringent; selective; triumphant; bacteriological; preliminary; careful; rigid; convincing; dangerous; supreme; experimental; actual; great; definite; discriminative; supplementary; instrumental; theological; temporal; complicated; infallible; provocative; prescribed; routine.

verbs
apply—; broaden—; cite—; concoct—; confront with—; conceive—; conduct—; —confirm—; devise—; employ—; essay—; exercise—; fail in—; flunk (colloq.)—; grapple with—; institute—; perform—; question—; rehearse—; repeat—; subject to—; submit to—; survive—; undergo—; utilize—; work out—; wrestle with—; —analyzes; —ascertains; —appraises; —authenticates; —confirms; —determines; —discloses; —dissects; —judges; —overwhelms; —reveals; —springs; —verifies; —vindicates; —weighs.

(See experiment, examination, criterion.)

TEST (*v*)

adverbs
scientifically; experimentally; practically; thoroughly; periodically; crucially; elaborately; exhaustively; rigidly; definitely; discriminatively; theologically; infallibly; provocatively.

(See quiz, question.)

TESTIFY (*v*)

adverbs
ethically; essentially; obstreperously; traitorously; flatteringly; falteringly; abundantly; mutely; unflinchingly; solemnly; unequivocally; corroboratively; irrelevantly; negatively; consequently; unanimously; unbiasedly; personally; unimpeachably; conflictingly; sincerely; incontrovertibly; emphatically.

(See assert, tell.)

TESTIMONIAL

adverbs
vividly; reminiscently; suggestively; intimately; pleasantly; flatteringly; deservedly; significantly; unforgettably; indelibly; permanently.

TESTIMONY

adjectives
solitary; jubilant; concurrent; equivocal; miraculous; honeyed; corroborative; irrelevant; remarkable; appreciative; negative; contemporary; inward; consequential; unsupported; indubitable; unanimous; abundant; silent; sufficient; unbiased; uniform; princely; magnificent; personal; willing; ample; unimpeachable; genuine; unique; conflicting; venerable; clear; professional; precious; enthusiastic; damaging; glorious; cheerful; sincere; explicit; oral; unbroken; incontrovertible; emphatic.

verbs
adduce—; analyze—; authenticate—; bear—; blast—; cite—; conform—; contradict—; corroborate—; deduce—; deliver as—; deny—; dispute—; expose—; express—; falsify—; file—; impair—; marshal—; perjure—; punctuate—; question—; record—; refute—; repudiate—; reverse—; review—; substantiate—; sustain—; uncover—; undermine—; uphold—; verify—; —authenticates; —bears; —carries weight; —conflicts; —convinces; —deludes; —differs; —discloses; —disturbs; —divulges; —floods; —reveals; —stuns; —vindicates; —warrants.

(See evidence, proof, declaration.)

TEXT

adjectives
trivial; pregnant; trite; faultless; miraculous; holy; sanguine; adopted; descriptive; infallible; authentic; expanded; obscene; widely-used; brilliant; edited.

verbs
acquaint with—; adhere to—; allude to—; analyze—; bear upon—; contemplate—; con-

tradict—; convey—; copyright—; digress from—; engross in—; explore—; express in —; follow—; heed—; peruse—; ponder—; pore over—; ransack—; regard—; reflect on—; review—; revise—; scan—; scrutinize—; supplement—; tamper with—; transform—; —depicts; —informs; —portrays.

(See matter, composition, book, story, subject, topic, theme.)

TEXTURE

adjectives

mysterious; basic; satiny; exquisite; grainy; permanent; delicate; misty; superb; soft; fine; springy; homely; unstylish; porous; rude; harmonic; historical; slippery; exclusive; crinkled; sheer; delicious; substantial; orthodox; even; fragile; smooth; shimmering; translucent; bubbled; surface; peachlike.

THANK (v)

adverbs

adequately; inarticulately; devoutly; cordially; heartily; formally; humbly; profusely; reverently; sincerely; appreciatively; fulsomely; haughtily; cursorily; dutifully; churlishly.

(See appreciate.)

THANKFUL

adverbs

utterly; delightedly; joyously; gratefully; unusually; particularly; singularly; exceptionally; enthusiastically; devoutly; reverently; deeply; profoundly; appreciatively; inordinately; obviously; earnestly; sincerely; truly; redundantly; unquestionably; remarkably; peculiarly.

THANKLESS

adverbs

dismally; sadly; ungraciously; grimly; heartbreakingly; utterly; bitterly; tragically; distressingly; drearily; cruelly; amazingly.

THANKS

adjectives

distracted; allegiant; humble; shy; fulsome; haughty; savage; impious; cordial; lively; dutiful; public; hearty; beggarly; silent; churlish; mumbled; half-hearted.

verbs

accept—; acknowledge—; declare—; derive —; express—; extend—; feign—; gush—; inspire—; offer—; overflow with—; proclaim—; proffer—; render—; return—; reward with—; tender—; —beguile; —gratify.

(See gratitude, appreciation.)

THATCHED

adverbs

attractively; recently; picturesquely; admirably; quaintly; satisfactorily; inadequately; thickly; greenly; fragrantly; curiously; intricately; generously; sparsely; thinly; stingily.

THEATRE

adjectives

legitimate; elegant; stupendous; imaginary; sensational; outdoor; woody; vast; gigantic; sublime; air-cooled; immense; comfortable; pleasant; troublesome; costly.

verbs

acclaim—; convert—; flow from—; forsake —; frequent—; install in—; jam—; participate in—; reject—; renounce—; storm—; —affords; —allures; —beckons; —beguiles; —claims; —diverts; —emblazons; —fascinates; —glitters; —immortalizes; —inspires; —presents; —publicizes; —relaxes; —solaces; pack—.

(See opera, footlights, stage, drama.)

THEATRICAL

adverbs

absurdly; ridiculously; professionally; unexpectedly; skilfully; artistically; surprisingly; laughably; imposingly; impressively; pompously; bombastically; extravagantly; crassly; affectedly; crudely; showily; insincerely; gaudily; sensationally; consummately.

THEFT

verbs

accomplish—; acquire by—; apprehend for —; bewail—; charge with—; commit—; denounce—; disclose—; divulge—; forestall —; insure against—; penalize—; plan—; plot—; reveal—; uncover—; —baffles; —distresses; —impoverishes; —violates.

(See plagiarism, robbery.)

THEME

adjectives

lofty; abstract; everlasting; anti-social; pathetic; prolific; gracious; inspiring; majestic; unpleasant; paramount; inviting;

curious; earnest; amusing; unsympathetic; spiritual; characteristic; animating; exotic; weak; idle; imperial; debatable; supermundane; pastoral; poetic; varying; irksome; inexhaustible; realistic; extraneous; fruitful; favorite; rusty; dangerous; conversational; immediate; romantic; human; pregnant; copious (pl); prevailing.

verbs
allot—; alter—; clothe—; color—; comprehend—; criticize—; discard—; dramatize—; elucidate—; embellish—; embody—; evolve —; exhaust—; expatiate on—; expound—; found—; give rise to—; handle—; harp on —; interpret—; intertwine—; launch—; plunge into—; revert—; set forth—; tackle —; unfold—; variate—; vary—; ventilate —; voice—; weave—; —deals; —depicts; —dominates; —portrays; —stands upright; —symolizes.

(See text, subject, topic, idea, essay, composition.)

THEOLOGICAL

adverbs
strictly; narrowly; bigotedly; dogmatically; completely; soundly; devoutly; liberally; restrictively; obstinately; broadly; intolerantly.

THEOREM

verbs
admit—; analyze—; apply—; base on—; comprehend—; contrive—; expound—; fashion—; formulize—; ground on—; ponder —; refer to—; regard—; unfold—; —assumes; —derives from; —postulates; —proves; —solves.

(See problem, principle, law, formula.)

THEORETICAL

adverbs
obstinately; absurdly; impractically; unreasonably; infeasibly; stupidly; impracticably; impossibly; absolutely; merely; vaguely; presumably; fanatically; obscurely; entirely.

THEORIZE (v)

adverbs
philosophically; abstractly; optimistically; plausibly; psychoanalytically; experimentally; atomically; coherently; psychologically; nebulously; poetically; geometrically; destructively; ingeniously; extravagantly; classically; absurdly; relatively; dynamically; morally; politically; economically; vaguely.

(See philosophize, talk.)

THEORY

adjectives
favorite; plausible; vibratory; psychoanalytic; experimental; undulatory; imaginative; unsound; universal; constructive; atomic; fanciful; antediluvian; coherent; unsatisfactory; elaborate; psychological; rounded; shaky; buttressed; nebulous; physical; artistic; vague; communistic; protectionist; elliptic; geometrical; evolutionary; color; straightforward; antiquated; ethical; mistaken; collision; philosophical; aesthetic; destructive; cherished; reprehensible; underlying; ingenious; deliberate; extravagant; chemical; classical; absurd; unsupported; oft-expressed; plausible; preconceived; tremendous; fantastic; secular; fossilized; coherential; radical; original; futile; abstract; relative; dynamic; irreconcilable; musical; impracticable; utopian; moral; religious; vague; suicide; economic.

verbs
abandon—; absorb in—; accept—; adopt—; advance—; antiquate—; apply—; arrive at —; authenticate—; base on—; blast—; check—; commit to—; comprehend—; conceive—; confirm—; contradict—; corroborate—; crush—; defend—; demolish—; devise—; discard—; discredit—; dismiss—; disprove—; dispute—; elaborate—; embrace —; entertain—; evolve—; exhaust—; explode—; explain—; hail—; hazard—; illustrate—; incline to—; incorporate in—; investigate—; maintain—; nurse—; outline—; propound—; refute—; reject—; relinquish —; scorn—; set forth—; speculate on—; submit—; subscribe to—; substantiate—; support—; test—; unveil—; upset—; verify —; visualize—; —s clash; —concludes; —deludes; —holds water; —opposes; —proposes; herald—.

(See idea, interpretation, hypothesis, logic.)

THERAPY

adjectives
vaccine; occupational; analytic; radio.

verbs
apply—; baffle—; devise—; expound—

hail—; herald—; practise—; prolong—; protract—; recommend—; revolutionize—; —ameliorates; —mitigates; —palliates; —rectifies; —relieves; —restores; —resuscitates; —revives.

(See cure, treatment.)

THERMOMETER

verbs

consult—; disinfect—; grade—; immerse—in; insert—; impair—; obscure—; shake down—; shatter—; suspend—; —ascends; —deceives; —dives; —indicates; —measures; —ranges from; —records; —registers; —reveals; —rises; —skyrockets (colloq.); —soars; —testifies; —toboggans; —warns; —wavers.

(See meter, price, barometer, mercury.)

THESIS

adjectives

aesthetic; alternative; voluminous; graduate; requisite; dull; pedantic; plagiarized; useless; incompetent; startling; established; brilliant; heavily-footnoted; well-documented.

verbs

acclaim—; analyze—; applaud—; build—; compose—; criticize—; dash off—; elaborate on—; formulate—; illustrate—; peruse—; propound—; submit—; support—; sustain — ;—airs; —brings to light; —comments on; —compiles; —discusses; —dissertates; —embraces; —expatiates; —proposes; —recites; —theorizes; —treats of; —ventilates.

(See manuscript, book, composition, essay.)

THICK

adverbs

substantially; satisfactorily; acceptably; admirably; commendably; impenetrably; sufficiently; tremendously; unimaginably; distressingly; unmanageably; densely; suffocatingly; unreasonably; impassably; curiously; strangely; undesirably.

THICKET

adjectives

bowery; high; spicy; neighboring; branch; straggling; impenetrable; shady; grotesque; dripping; miniature; cool; darksome; fragrant; leafless; impervious; thorny; prickly.

verbs

conceal in—; frequent—; lop off—; nest in —; plunge into—; prune—; spring from—; stir among—s; trim—; uproot—; —affords; —s choke; —s eclipes; —hinders; —impedes; —obscures; —restrains; —rustles; —shelters.

(See bush, jungle.)

THICK-SET

adverbs

solidly; substantially; sturdily; healthily; stoutly; remarkably; noticeably; staunchly; unusually; particularly; conspicuously; singularly; curiously; uncommonly.

THIEF

adjectives

arrant; filthy; door-waylaying; contented; self-satisfied; insect; child; low; vile; sacreligious; adulterous; practised; slovenly; deformed; unimaginative; hard-headed; raw-boned; snaky-haired; dwarfish; injured; timorous; subtle; merciless; escaped; deft; honorable.

verbs

apprehend—; convict—; grapple with—; handcuff—; incarcerate—; interpret—; parole—; penalize—; pinion—; sentence—; —assaults; —bilks; —defrauds; —eludes; —evades; —extorts; —filches; —fleeces; —loots; —marauds; —mulcts; —palms; —pilfers; —plunders; —poaches; —purloins; —rifles; —rooks; —sacks; —strips.

(See highwayman, gangster, kidnapper, intruder, robber.)

THIEVISH

adverbs

impishly; naturally; habitually; watchfully; incorrigibly; viciously; incurably; wickedly; inveterately; loutishly; dangerously; remarkably; uncommonly; trickily; mischievously; smartly; furtively; stealthily; adroitly; dexterously; cunningly; artfully; ingeniously

THIN

adverbs

astonishingly; extremely; excessively; tenuously; pathetically; insecurely; alarmingly; dangerously; palpably; flimsily; unsatisfactorily; terribly; sufficiently; extraordinarily; expensively; dreadfully; incredibly; conveniently.

THING

adjectives

goodly; extravagant; travailing; heterogeneous; existing; fantastic; disproportioned; blind; sharp; single; terrestrial; unutterable; fragile; brute-hooved; insatiable; living; delightful; horrible; atrocious; subtle; elusive; unstable; contemptible; inexplicable; faraway; sublunary; terrene; inanimate; glorious; good; ignoble; treacherous; dreadful; distressful; ill-used; quixotic; ridiculous; painful; groping; plaguy; exasperating; sacred; intangible; desirable; manifold; plaintive; pitiful; semi-accidental; demented; secondary; devastating; rustling; created; willful; grotesque; logical; miserable; haunting; hazardous; interesting; essential; peculiar; prudent; traditional; dark; irrelevant; manly; trivial; infinite; unusual; feathered; kingly; horrid; castaway; venomous; pesky; flimsy; improbable; external; roguish; weird; piquant; odious; powerless; hateful; indispensable; insulting; complete; sinister; heartbreaking; inferior; incongruous; squirming; unheeded; petty; mealy-mouthed; ticklish; accepted; unpardonable; incalculable; divine; blamed; mischievous; rightful; immaterial; serious; unprecedented; salutary; omnipotent; creaking; unchained; momentous; detestable; arduous; portentous; unintelligible; interminable; devilish; needful; senseless; hidden; spectral; rotten; native; fresh; priceless; fearful; extraordinary; bohemian; combustible; vast; stupid; terrible; creepy; uncommon; melancholy; valueless; gaudy; dear; vulgar; formed; precious; pinched; subordinate; ruthless; brittle; selfsame; unkind.

THINK (*v*)

adverbs

abstractly; sensually; despairingly; humorously; frenziedly; contemplatively; habitually; desolately; conscientiously; precisely; instinctively; vaguely; incessantly; idly; poetically; deliberately; remorsefully; constructively; grimly; anxiously; candidly; erratically; scoffingly; divergently; morosely; desultorily; contemptuously; connectedly; hysterically; rapturously; shrewdly; vehemently; dispassionately; diversely; independently; grievously; dismally; creatively; wishfully; incisively; psychoanalytically; subtly; cunningly.

(See meditate, muse.)

THINKING

adjectives

independent; ill; archaic; infantile; inferior; sustained; honest; clear; differentiated; exact; thorough; inventive; original; grievous; dismal; untrammeled; conceptive; creative; wishful; accurate; incisive; psychoanalytic; spacious; subtle; cunning; symmetrical.

verbs

absorb in—; avoid—; bias—; betray—; clarify—; confuse—; discipline—; distract—; divert—; encourage—; engender—; engross in—; exercise—; foster—; give food for—; guide— ;indulge in—; influence—; lose in—; nurture—; occupy in—; pervert—; prejudice—; stimulate—; trust to—; —depresses; —digresses; —focuses on; —penetrates; —revolves about.

(See thought, contemplation, reflection, meditation.)

THIN-SKINNED

adverbs

unfortunately; delicately; inordinately; sensitively; terribly; evidently; acutely; abnormally; unusually; exceptionally; strangely; absurdly; unreasonably; noticeably; palpably; foolishly.

THIRST

adjectives

immortal; unqeunchable; insatiable; vulgar; sanctifying; hot; burning; eternal; baffled; fierce; aimless; inextinguishable; human; ardent; opulent; wholesome; reckless; inordinate; universal; pretended; exacting; unhallowed; incessant; savage; slakeless; feverish; parching; urgent; intolerable; perpetual; frantic; distressing; pallid; acquired; marked.

verbs

allay—; arouse—; assuage—; create—; experience—; extinguish—; gratify—; indulge in—; intensify—; kindle—; overcome by—; quell—; quench—; satiate—; satisfy—; sharpen—; slake—; stimulate—; subdue—; suffice—; whet—; —maddens; —plagues; —rages; —torments.

(See appetite, desire, craving, longing.)

THIRSTY

adverbs

continually; painfully; terribly; habitually; strangely; feverishly; inordinately; crazily; constitutionally; curiously; cravingly; desperately; alarmingly; inveterately; cruelly; conveniently; avidly; significantly; dreadfully; evidently; suddenly; distressingly.

THORN

adjectives

flowering; barren; fruitful; poisonous; pungent; prickly; mean; insipid; venomed; cruel; blazing; piercing; wind-warped.

verbs

bristle with—s; escape—s; impale on—; snag on—; —barbs; —s crucify; —s fence about; —s harass; —lacerates; —lancinates; —penetrates; —pierces; —plagues; —pricks; —punctures; —rends; —spikes; —s torture.

(See sting, needle, nail.)

THORNY

adverbs

painfully; extremely; dangerously; perilously; strangely; intolerably; undesirably; disagreeably; thickly; unpleasantly; unexpectedly; surprisingly; disadvantageously; inconveniently; slightly; terribly; exceptionally; unusually; unfortunately.

THOROUGHBRED

adverbs

unmistakably; conspicuously; unquestionably; warrantably; decidedly; authentically; highly; obviously; manifestly; palpably; patently; positively; absolutely; notably.

THOROUGHFARE

adjectives

dusty; celebrated; bewildering; glistening; busy; trodden; ambitious; murmurous; tumultuous.

verbs

amble down—; blockade—; clog—; clutter—; cut—; direct to—; enter—; evade—; extend—; file along—; forsake—; frequent—; intersect—; jam—; line—; litter—; obstruct—; pave—; proceed down—; promenade—; strike—; traverse—; —deviates; —swerves; —winds in and out.

(See highway, avenue, street.)

THOUGHT

adjectives

undecided; lingering; leading; angry; systematic; chiming; dream; naked; shining; horrible; flurried; importunate; lofty; numbing; forcible; effective; translucent; marvelous; golden; vagrant; fiery; poetic; habitual; self-torturing; abstract; impassioned; appalling; boundless; high; myriad; accidental; dissonant; unseasonable; restless; ripe; clever; heaven-born; speculative; divine; bitter; darting; darkling; complacent; carking; ill; longing; faithful; soft; unresisting; ennobled; metaphysical; contemplative; virtuous; inscrutable; sober; sinful; impetuous; distracting; knitted; narrow; exhilarating; trustful; teeming; pensive; empirical; moody; innermost; reproachful; contradictory; gentle; dying; odious; adventurous; holy; quiet; eclectic; invisible; wrecked; desponding; roving; hairy; engrossing; brutal; viper; dangerous; discontented; rebellious; selfsame; interesting; economic; studious; suggesting; unutterable; painful; sifted; transcending; endless; fond; thankful; satirical; sorrowful; awakened; disconnected; woundless; haunting; persistent; rash; irreverent; sorry; benighted; uncertain; wistful; morbid; anxious; oft-spurned; lifting; frail; tumultuous; incestuous; constant; laborious; treasonable; grand; pleasant; heartwarming; paramount; insupportable; presumptuous; mere; mournful; monopolized; everpresent; half-formed; collateral; associated; winged; pedantic; serene; tangible; unwelcome; soaring; pacific; shattered; clamorous; gastronomic; ungovernable; lawless; rational; misanthropic; unfathomable; licentious; flattering; chaotic; slaughterous; freezing; somber; fleeting; concentrated; morbid; luminous; far-soaring; indistinct; philosophic; intimate; compelling; celebrated; vain; unquiet; intransigent; unschooled; unpractised; swift; passing; dismal; genial; hasty; likely; formless; hateful; thornless; manlike; matchless; aidless; unstained; loving; innocent; deliberate; dreamy; harsh; confused; exhaustive; vigorous; questioning; humiliating.

verbs

absorb in—; analyze—s; appraise—; arrest—; associate with—; awaken—; banish—; bias—s; blend—s; brood over—; center—s upon; check—; cherish—; clarify—s; collect—s; color—; comprehend—; compress—; confirm—; convey—; counterbalance—; cultivate—; dally with—; disclose—; disorder—s; distort—s; divert—s; divine—; dwell upon—; echo—s; efface—; electrify—; embody in—; endure—; engage in—; engross in—; enlarge upon—; enrich—s; entertain

—; erase—; etch—; evoke—; exclude—; execute—; expand—; expel from—s; expose—s; fashion—; formulate—s; furnish food for—; further—; fuse into—s; govern —s; grasp—; groove—s; hamper—; harbor—; immerse in—; impart—; implant—; impregnate with—; induce—; indulge in—; —; interpret—; interrupt—; isolate—; jot down—; kindle the pulse of—; lose in—; impede—; mould—; nurse—; obliterate—; occupy with—; open avenues of—; parallel —; paralyze—s; perpetuate—; preserve—; prompt—; purify—s; react upon—; read—s; recoil from—; reflect—s; reject—; restate —; reveal—; round out—s; saturate—s; scramble—s; scoff at—; shape—s; shrink from—; spit out—; stimulate—; tincture —s; toy with—; transcribe—s; tremble at —; unite—s; utter—; vent—s; vitiate—; voice—; weigh—; wrap in—; —appeals; —corrodes; —creeps into; —crosses the mind; —s crowd; —dominates; —enraptures; —enthralls; —escapes; —filters into; —flashes; —germinates; —haunts; —impresses; —intrudes; —leans toward; —leaps into; —matures; —numbs; —obsesses; —oppresses; —permeates; —perturbs; —petrifies; —possesses; —presents itself; —s ramble; —recalls; —recurs; —relapses into; —s revert to; —s revolve about; —shakes; —shifts to; —sobers; —springs from; —stings; —strikes; —suggests; —swirls up; —symbolizes; —terrifies; —torments; —uplifts; —s waver.

(See idea, concept, conception, consideration, imagination, opinion, meditation.)

THOUGHTFUL

adverbs

graciously; pleasantly; courteously; considerately; agreeably; unusually; quietly; busily; naively; unfailingly; remarkably; marvellously; practically; helpfully; prudently; providently; tactfully; sensibly; thoroughly; completely; charmingly; studiously; earnestly; gravely; seriously; judicially; deliberately; significantly; wonderfully; soberly; profoundly; deeply; dreamily; wistfully.

THOUGHTLESS

adverbs

carelessly; selfishly; dreamily; blindly; innocently; youthfully; boyishly; girlishly; blithely; unwittingly; unconsciously; cruelly; bitterly; meanly; inconsiderately; ungraciously; impolitely; discourteously; terribly; dangerously; significantly; desperately; hopelessly; unpardonably; inexcusably; remarkably; strangely; incredibly; gaily.

THRASH (*v*)

adverbs

brutally; soundly; wildly; cruelly; viciously; bestially; penally; fiercely; passionately.

(See beat, whip.)

THREAD

adjectives

imaginary; aimless; scarlet; dramatic; protecting; snagged; sacred; broken; crossed; delicate; ligeneous; gossamer; basting; swift-running; darkened; fluffy; wool-like; rhyming; knotted; allotted; frayed.

verbs

baste with—; cleave—; dangle by—; draw —; entwine in—; fray—; loop—; reinforce —; rend—; sever—; shear—; stitch with—; sunder—; suspend from—; tack—; weave —; wear to—.

(See cotton, fibre, string, cord.)

THREAD (*v*)

adverbs

skillfully; dexterously; delicately; complicatedly; involvedly; intricately; unerringly.

(See wind, weave.)

THREADBARE

adverbs

shabbily; shockingly; dreadfully; dingily; carelessly; pathetically; diaphanously; pitiably; miserably; curiously; inexplicably; mustily; desperately; cruelly; unutterably; sadly; grotesquely; fantastically; unnecessarily; parsimoniously; terribly; distressingly; painfully; humiliatingly; shamefully; nonchalantly; imperturbably.

THREAT

adjectives

invincible; silent; bawling; thundering; terrible; cloudy; stifled; obscure; serious; muttered; ruffian; dark; playful; mysterious; desperate; fearful; insolent; parting; fantastic; bitter; petty; absurd; contemporaneous; drunken; implied; private; tense; whispered; violent; sullen; tyrannous; sibylline.

verbs

aim—at; bandy—s; fling—at; fulminate—; hurl—; mutter—; retract—; resort to—s;

roar—; thunder—; thwart—; unleash—; veil—; yield to—s; —alarms; —bluffs; —browbeats; —coerces; —compromises; —cows; —daunts; —deters; —disconcerts; —distresses; —hangs over; —haunts; —indicts; —intimidates; —jeopardizes; —menaces; —obsesses; —perturbs; —preys upon; —stings; —unnerves; —weighs upon; —awes.

(See menace, oath, curse, imprecation.)

THREATEN (v)

adverbs

illimitably; direfully; darkly; terrifyingly; sinisterly; seriously; adroitly; mutteringly; sullenly; violently; tyrannically; bitterly.

(See menace, portend.)

THREATENING

adverbs

undeniably; plainly; odiously; hatefully; alarmingly; significantly; seriously; gravely; desperately; clearly; definitely; absolutely; positively; graphically; sensationally; dramatically; obviously; terribly; dreadfully; ominously; curiously; darkly; mysteriously; palpably; obscurely; vaguely; dimly; feebly; violently; truculently; absurdly; ridiculously; openly; apparently; frankly; furtively; stealthily.

THRESHOLD

adjectives

unhallowed; shadowed; sacred; glimmering; dread; lucky.

verbs

achieve—; arrive at—; attain—; bar from—; bestride—; block—; cloud—; dwell on—; enter—; file through—; flank—; gain—; huddle at—; reach—; reverence—; screen—; seek—; skirt—; strand at—; stumble over—; veil—.

(See entrance, gate, door.)

THRIFT

adjectives

prudent; extreme; constant; balanced; contented; pecuniary; incomprehensible; reasonable.

verbs

demand—; emphasize—; encourage—; enforce—; extol—; foster—; imbue with—; implant—; inculcate—; ingrain—; necessitate—; practise—; preach—; stress—; —grudges; —infects; —redeems; —saves.

(See economy, frugality.)

THRIFTLESS

adverbs

inexcusably; habitually; naturally; inherently; strangely; picturesquely; presumably; possibly; odiously; hopelessly; incurably; incorrigibly; carelessly; thoughtlessly; improvidently; distressingly; shabbily; deplorably; lamentably; provokingly; intolerably; insufferably; vexatiously; terribly; blithely; gaily; insouciantly.

THRIFTY

adverbs

fortunately; carefully; providently; shrewdly; invariably; unfailingly; wisely; sagely; sensibly; happily; pleasantly; profitably; distinctly; moderately; judiciously; graspingly; overly; uncomfortably; ostentatiously; flourishingly; manifestly; enviably; admirably; commendably; laudably; unusually; habitually; naturally; intensely; inherently; innately; particularly; commercially; happily; luckily; thoughtfully.

THRILL

adjectives

double; distinguished; charmful; warming; renewed; shuddering; delicious; awed; amazed; intoxicating; continuous; restoring; silent; incredulous; horrible; tragic; metallic; original; sympathetic; supernal; biggest; involuntary; vicarious; nascent; poetic; gentle; unpleasant; amusing; exultant; compensating; electric; passionate; comforting; equestrian; eloquent.

verbs

cherish—; crave—; derive—from; excite—; experience—; furnish—; gain—; glow with—; inspire—; itch for—; respond to—; seek—; sense—; —enthuses (colloq.); —fires; —flushes; —impassions; —infects; —pierces; —prickles; —shoots through; —stabs; —tickles; —vibrates through; —warms; —warns; —tingles.

(See shiver, vibration, excitement, tremor.)

THRILL (v)

adverbs

blissfully; tenderly; involuntarily; vicariously; poetically; exultantly; passionately; eloquently.

(See excite, arouse.)

THRILLED

adverbs
enchantingly; interestingly; excitably; tremendously; emotionally; unutterably; remarkably; apparently; evidently; visibly; terribly; utterly; strangely; oddly; marvellously; inexpressibly; utterly; magnificently; splendidly; completely; unwontedly; apparently; immensely; thoroughly; indescribably; positively.

THRILLING

adverbs
utterly; indescribably; unusually; inexpressibly; marvellously; tremendously; superbly; magnificently; immensely; completely; unusually.

THRIVE (v)

adverbs
miraculously; bountifully; exceedingly; markedly; amazingly; prodigiously.
(See prosper, succeed.)

THRIVING

adverbs
steadily; gradually; remarkably; amazingly; indubitably; miraculously; incredibly; deservedly; unquestionably; suddenly; curiously; strangely; marvellously; splendidly; stupendously; salubriously; slowly; substantially; pleasantly; happily.

THROAT

adjectives
sinewy; blithest; dreadful; lucid; thundering; soft; impudent; thick; stretching; dazzling; unslaked; slender; infantile; sanded; sore; creamy; harsh; irritated; parched; shaggy; quivering; warbling; swan-like; exquisite; mellow; feminine; supple; scorched; swelling; brown; bursting; corded; careless; listless; myriad (pl); furry; incapable; snowy; slit; gushing; vulture; dividing; careless.

verbs
clear—; clutch—; congest—; disinfect—; dust—; ease—; emerge from—; clog—; infect—; inflame—; introduce into—; irritate —; lacerate—; lodge in—; massage—; medicate—; paint—; ram down—; ravage —; seize by—; sponge—; spray—; strain—; swab—; tickle—; ulcerate—; —contracts; —swells; —tightens.

THROB

adjectives
rhythmic; trembling; belated; harmonic; fondest; minutest; romantic; exulting; fleeing; steady; fluttering; heart; ecstatic; blissful.

THROB (v)

adverbs
palpitatingly; violently; rapidly; riotously; swiftly; visibly; fitfully; tumultuously; rhythmically; romantically; exultingly; ecstatically; blissfully.
(See pulsate, beat.)

THRONE

adjectives
angelic; heavenly; sanguine; everlasting; jeweled; conspicuous; tear-gemmed; ivory; maiden; towering; empyreal; usurped; sunlike; crystalline; venerable; unenvied; western; lofty; dynastic; sullen; sublime; tarnished; boundless; glorious; cambric; malignant; stately; universal; meridian; ancestral; rocky; peaceful; disputed; constellated; forsaken; tottering; sovereign; blissful; imperial; sapphire; moldy.

verbs
abandon—; abdicate—; accede to—; ascend aspire to—; attend—; bow before—; burnish—; covet—; defy—; depose from—; desert—; ensconce on—; establish on—; forsake—; gain—; lay claim to—; loll on—; occupy—; overthrow—; plant on—; relinquish—; renounce—; restore to—; retire from—; seek—; usurp—; vacate—; vest in —; win—; —authorizes; —empowers; —tyrannizes; seize—.
(See kingdom, kingship, power, sovereignty, seat, chair.)

THRONG

adjectives
trampling; demoniac; well-dressed; countless (pl); burdened; motley; shadowy; grateful; tumultuous; ragged; threadbare; accusing; ill-bred; billowy; worshipping; sinless; unreposing; innumerable (pl); riotous; fearful; eager; thoughtless; seething; lean; exultant; hungry; starving; ghostly; angelic; excited; expectant; blood-washed; terror-stricken; beauteous; bewinged; adoring; laughing; chattering; moveless; trembling; crushed-down; spectral; listening; sceptered; invisible; festal; armed; emotional; spending; foolish; shining; pros-

trate; immense; base; impish; multitudinous; bestial; pressing; teeming; shoeless; struggling; shaggy; ravenous; unhealthy; edifying; toiling; whirling; amorous; moiling.

verbs
disband—; disperse—; muster—; pacify—; plunge through—; provoke—; rejoin—; scatter—; silence—; slip through—; —assembles; —concentrates; —clamors; —converges on; —deluges; —eddies 'round; —flocks; —masses; —mills about; —mobs; —presses; —swarms; —focuses on.
(See mob, crowd, multitude.)

THRONG (v)

adverbs
tumultuously; ceaselessly; demoniacally; countlessly; innumerably; seethingly hungrily; expectantly; multitudinously; incongruously; bestially; moilingly
(See swarm, congregate.)

THROW (v)

adverbs
violently; recklessly; haughtily; deliberately; dejectedly: bodily; savagely; profligately; passionately; lavishly; systematically; significantly; defiantly; adroitly.
(See hurl, heave.)

THRUSH

verbs
—bodes; —cheers; —choruses; —gushes; —hymns; —moults; —pipes; —pours forth; —retires; —trills.
(See bird.)

THRUST

adjectives
vain; repeated (pl); vital; prompt; final; shrewd-planned; unlikely; sore; tireless; unlucky.

THRUST (v)

adverbs
impudently; impatiently; brutally; determinedly; agilely; obtrusively; conspicuously; methodically; resolutely; demurely; belligerently; rudely; wrathfully.
(See stab, stick.)

THUMB

adjectives
black; shuffling; peaked; vigorous; wadded; solitary; broken; waving; fatty.

verbs
bind—; brush with—; crush—; deform—; dislocate—; extend—; flex—; knead with —s; lacerate—; manipulate—; sever—; sprain—; twiddle—s; —gropes; —throbs.
(See finger.)

THUMP (v)

adverbs
furiously; emphatically; repetitiously; impatiently; indignantly; thunderously; powerfully; dramatically.
(See beat, hit.)

THUNDER

adjectives
howling; blasting; intermittent; interrupted; heavy; frightful; thrilling; melodious; mountain; angry; swarthy; sullen; editorial; muttering; branding; oracular; suspended; flameless; ominous; harmless; rumbling; direful; serious; muffled; wrathful; lounging; artillery; hateful; clothed; incessant; threatening; stage; earthly; sweet; rattling; brazen; volleying.

verbs
brave—; shoot forth—; —blusters; —booms; —claps; —crashes; —deafens; —detonates; —dins; —discords; —disturbs; —echoes; —fulminates; —menaces; —petrifies; —pierces; —rattles; —rends;; —reverberates; —roars; —rolls; —rumbles; —shatters; —shocks; —splits; —startles; —threatens; —volleys.
(See lightning, detonation, noise, discharge, report, explosion.)

THUNDER (v)

adverbs
appallingly; violently; ominously; tremendously; terrifically; frightfully; rumblingly; muffledly; wrathfully; threateningly; repeatedly; awesomely.
(See crash, resound.)

THUNDEROUS

adverbs
ominously; positively; portentously; triumphantly; enthusiastically; acclaimingly; mutinously; threateningly; significantly; swellingly; curiously; strangely; deafeningly; splendidly; loyally.

THWART (v)

adverbs
effectually; diligently; successfully; tempo-

rarily; discouragingly; righteously.
(See defeat, baffle.)

THWARTED

adverbs
dangerously; hopelessly; suddenly; painfully; distressingly; unfairly; meanly; odiously; hatefully; cruelly; desperately; curiously; strangely; inscrutably; adroitly; maliciously; cleverly; ingeniously; artfully; craftily; shrewdly; inexplicably; stealthily; quietly; successfully; helplessly; unaccountably; maliciously; dreadfully; discouragingly.

TICKER-TAPE

verbs
festoon with—; insert—; perforate—; read —; shower with—; stabilize—; steady—; —announces; —clutters; —communicates with; —fluctuates; —indicates; —informs; —lists; —litters; —notifies; —oscillates; —quotes; —records; —transmits; —unreels; —vacillates.

TICKET

verbs
arm with—; counterfeit—s; discard—; dispense—s; enumerate—s; grant—; hawk—s; purchase—; register—s; speculate on—s; stamp—s; tag with—s; —admits; —authorizes; —betokens; —checks; —enables; —evidences; —informs; —indicates; —labels; —permits; —testifies to; —vouchsafes.
(See ballot, coupon, label, permit, certificate.)

TICKLE (v)

adverbs
humorously; boisterously; playfully; teasingly; verbally; rudely; roughly; clownishly.
(See tease.)

TICKLED

adverbs
roguishly; mischievously; merrily; enormously; gleefully; ridiculously; obviously; visibly; prankishly; jubilantly; exceedingly; inordinately; wickedly; naughtily; amazingly.

TIDE

adjectives
undulating; brimming; ebbing; insurging; aerial; eventful; boundless (pl); multitudinous (pl); human; restless; falling; arrested; waveless; silent; terrible; mysterious; tossing; joyous; sidereal; ancient; surging; chafing; reactionary; capricious; passionate; forward-flowing; sultry; confused; overwhelming; subsiding; tumultuous; headlong; swollen; rippling; green-blue; conflicting; theologic; over-running; hastening; primal; refluent; glassy; brimful; rising; whelming; billowing; retiring; fickle; pellucid; foaming; interminable; incoming; trackless; latent; lulling; adverse; patriotic; sucking; angry; roving; golden; hurrying; flooding; perennial; contrary; westering; crystal; turbid; dusty-gray; misty; river; silvery; summer; deep-breathing; sliding; treacherous; rhythmic.

verbs
battle with—; breast—; drift with—; harness—; oppose—; stem—; swim with—; yield to—; —crawls out; —deluges; —ebbs; —fluctuates; —inundates; —invades; —moans; —overtakes; —recedes; —regresses; —retires; —retreats; —roars; —swamps; —swells; —throbs; —wanes; —washes; —withdraws.
(See flow, flood, current.)

TIDINGS

adjectives
dismal; bad; joyful; unpleasant; frightful; inarticulate; glad; blissful; unimpeded; evil; gracious; accurate; astonishing; startling; heart-stirring; swift; hopeless.

TIDY

adverbs
scrupulously; painfully; terribly; carefully; unwontedly; unusually; dreadfully; spotlessly; remarkably; unexpectedly; suddenly; attractively; invitingly; pleasantly; agreeably; sufficiently; cosily; alluringly; distressingly; starkly; oppressively; miraculously; incredibly.

TIE

adjectives
subtle; weakened; cunning; common; primary; senseless; sordid; lifelong; mysterious; tenderest; singular; indissoluble; deep; domestic; silken; conjugal; sacred; foppish; unsubstantial; frail.

TIE (v)

adverbs
securely; fantastically; heroically; intri-

cately; involvedly; complicatedly; firmly; cunningly; indissolubly.
(See fasten, bind.)

TIER

adjectives
ascending; graceful; proportioned; blazing.

TIES

verbs
acknowledge—; adhere to—; cement—; cherish—; dissolve—; forsake—; knit—; preserve—; rend—; renounce—; saddle with—; sever—; shatter—; strain—; sunder—; treasure—; —affiliate; —bind; —couple; —fetter; —link; —obligate; —pledge; —restrain; —restrict; —shackle; —weaken.
(See bond, band, obligation.)

TIFF

adjectives
domestic; daily; lifelong; hateful; unnerving.

TIGER

adjectives
tawny; brindled; enraged; pouncing; man-eating; mangled; shrinking; clawing; murderous; lightning-fast; muscled; vicious; cunning; lunging; circling; snapping; growling; leaping; skulking; furious; mighty; teeth-baring; ferocious; creeping; catapulting; royal; determined; striped; spotted; fractious; frenzied; deadly; Sumatra; sabre-toothed; swift; slinking; villainous; demoniac; coughing; treacherous; cantering.

verbs
cage—; exterminate—s; infuriate—; lash—; perform with—s; train—; —climb; —crouches; —depredates; —devours; —haunts; —s infest; —lashes out at; —maims; —marauds; —mauls; —mews; —paws; —preys; —purrs; —rages; —ravages; —rends; —roars; —romps; —seizes; —slithers along the path; —snarls; —springs; —tears.
(See animal, lion, leopard.)

TIGERISH

adverbs
vaguely; furtively; fawningly; warily; vigilantly; fearsomely; attractively; slinkingly; alluringly; seductively; alarmingly; dangerously; contemptibly; slinkily; fiercely; perceptibly; indubitably; unmistakably; fatally; indescribably; inexpressibly; inescapably; undeniably.

TIGHT

adverbs
uncomfortably; sufficiently; unfortunately; fatally; terribly; occasionally; dreadfully; happily; blithely; completely; painfully; odiously; distressingly; gloriously; blissfully; permanently; momentarily; disgracefully; shamefully; strangely; unusually; ridiculously; dangerously; injuriously; revealingly; satisfactorily.

TIGHTEN (*v*)

adverbs
gradually; partially; remorselessly; lovingly; passionately; abruptly; insidiously; subtly.
(See grip, squeeze.)

TIGHTS

verbs
accoutre in—; array in—; attire in—; bare—; cavort in—; divest of—; doff—; don—; equip with—; fray—; spangle—; strip of—; tatter—; vest in—; —display; —enable; —expose; —facilitate.
(See costume, uniform, garment.)

TILT (*v*)

adverbs
awkwardly; negligently; jauntily; nonchalantly; precariously.
(See teeter, sway.)

TIMBER

adjectives
shaky; massive; long-used; slashed; marketable; reverberating; rotten; superb; fringing; graceful; useful.

verbs
avail oneself of—; blast—; conserve—; debark—; fell—; knot—; level—; market—; preserve—; process—; provide—; raze—; reinforce—; strip of—; treat—; value—; —decays; —erodes; —jams; —rots.
(See log, beam, wood.)

TIMBERED

adverbs
heavily; profitably; densely; wisely; fortunately; well; luckily; thickly; amazingly; sparsely; thinly; neglibly; valuably; reputedly; allegedly; immensely.

TIME

adjectives

valuable; sufficient; troublous; inexpedient; curious; happy; righteous; irresponsible; unconscionable; precious; primitive; arduous; historic; auspicious; predestined; patristic; solemn; evil; official; tolerating; troubled; reasonable; unfit; glorious; fantastic; thoughtless; later; frivolous; rococo; dark; considerable; former; palmy; unsettled; priceless; injurious; appointed; bygone; substantial; fruitful; halycon; impatient; fleeting; ample; boundless; descending; civilized; recorded; intervening; trying; woeful; sorry; appreciable; casting; measurable; degenerate; fittest; unseasonable; stormy; mutual; lessened; uneasy; turbulent; indefinite; despicable; unquiet; factious; immemorial; sacred; fated; apostolic; moral; periodic; unused; record-breaking; virtuous; distracted; tuning; affirmed; chaotic; opportune; fitting; abundant; corroding; pairing; exciting; unemployed; sultry; costly; millennium; propitious; rough-and-tumble; subversive; potential; scented; calamitous; gleaning; leisure; unborn; melodious; charitable; barbarous; anxious; flowering; ridiculous; blissful; squalid; dicing; administrative; invaluable; mournful; pleasant; specified; remote; pointed; abysmal; thin-faced; terrible; discouraging; feudal; stirring; naughty; restless; statutory; perilous; altered; conquering; shadowed; accustomed; unhallowed; limited; envious; significant; awful; intermediate; various (pl); classic; inconvenient; broadening; inevitable; breathing; regenerated; prehistoric; equinoctial; scriptural; scant; dusky; ill-devouring; portentous; assigned; limited; disorderly; revolutionary; unaccustomed; hasty; balmy; prosperous; guilty; growing; distant; profitable; subsequent; enormous; rippling; amphibious; short; swift-footed; regretted; spacious; cloudless; discouraging; stormy; unfavorable; fairy; future; due; consumed; emotional.

verbs

abide—; allot—; begrudge—; beguile—; bide for—; budget—; calculate—; conserve —; consume—; devote—to; devour—; endure—; engross—; exhaust—; fritter away —; indicate—; inform of—; lack—; lavish —on; limit—; mark—; measure—; prolong —; protract—; record—; reveal in—; spare —; squander—; "stall for"—; tarry for—; terminate—; while away—; —advances; —approaches; —blots out; —discloses; —disintegrates; —dissolves; —dwindles; —elapses; —expires; —fades; —flies; —flits; —glides on; —heals; —marches on; —matures; —mellows; —nears; —outmodes; —presses; —races; —ripens; —recedes; —rolls around; —rolls back; —shadows; —tempers; —unfolds; —vanishes; —vindicates; —wanes; —withers.

(See interval, hour, leisure, month, instant, moment, day.)

TIMED

adverbs

opportunely; wisely; seasonably; wonderfully; fatally; precisely; meticulously; exactly; uncannily; viciously; brutally; heinously; tragically; carefully; scientifically; automatically; cautiously; cleverly; auspiciously; apparently; murderously; punctiliously; promptly; considerately; thoughtfully; graciously; obviously.

TIMELY

adverbs

pleasantly; fortunately; altogether; unusually; particularly; singularly; providentially; remarkably; miraculously; marvellously; curiously; felicitously; wonderfully.

TIMID

adverbs

modestly; constitutionally; shyly; bashfully; groundlessly; anxiously; deliciously; unreasonably; unwontedly; tremulously; childishly; nervously; foolishly; incredibly; naturally; vaguely; momentarily; secretly; excessively; strangely; distressingly; incomprehensibly; temperamentally; helplessly; hopelessly; unaccountably; uneasily; queerly; curiously; genuinely; unaffectedly; significantly.

TIMIDITY

adjectives

modest; early; scrupulous; constitutional; ill-grounded; shy; bashful; refined; anxious; delicious; skulking; irrational; sententious; unwonted; tremulous.

verbs

conceal—; conquer—; cower in—; despise —; feign—; flinch in—; induce—; inspire —; master—; mock—; overcome—; pretend —; prevail over—; quail in—; retire in—; reveal—; simulate—; smite with—; suffer

—; —abashes; —besets; —cows; —daunts; —deters; —dismays; —distresses; —haunts; —overwhelms; —petrifies.

(See cowardice, bashfulness, shyness, modesty, fear.)

TIMOROUS

adverbs

shyly; bashfully; self-consciously; modestly; guiltily; sheepishly; naturally; inherently; merely; habitually; usually; foolishly; sadly; pitiably; miserably; unfortunately; childishly; wretchedly; unreasonably; needlessly; strangely; oddly; curiously; inexplicably; unaccountably; ridiculously; positively; actually.

TINGE

adjectives

sunset; bright; silky-green; confidential; pantheistic; mauve; transient; sanguinary; abundant; slight.

TINGE (v)

adverbs

brilliantly; markedly; slightly; occasionally; deeply; transiently; luridly.

(See imbue, color.)

TINKER

adjectives

itinerant; mean; preaching; strong.

TINKLE

adjectives

inviting; pleasant; cheery; liquid; laughing; lilting.

TINNY

adverbs

unpleasantly; inexcusably; unacceptably; disagreeably; curiously; raucously; intolerably; strangely; unpalatably; tawdrily.

TINT

adjectives

vivid; dismal; acquainted; delicate; pearly; exquisite; unobtrusive; shifting; somber; prophetic; smoky; rainbowed; combative; bloody; delicate; gathering; changing; positive; beauteous; prismatic; prevailing; general; brilliant; mellow; harmonious; tender; original.

TINT (v)

adverbs

delicately; gracefully; richly; vividly; somberly; beauteously; prismatically; brilliantly; harmoniously; mellowly.

(See tinge, color.)

TINY

adverbs

unbelievably; incredibly; infinitesimally; microscopically; minutely; extremely; remarkably; actually; marvelously; positively; dwarfishly; insignificantly; elfishly; fantastically; unimaginably; grotesquely; terribly.

TIP

verbs

cap—; crown—; daub on—; gild—; impale on—; veneer—; whet—; —bristles; —penetrates; —pierces; —projects; —protrudes; —punctures; —stabs.

(See edge, point.)

TIPSY

adverbs

gloriously; shamefully; helplessly; comically; sadly; alarmingly; insecurely; happily; foolishly; comically; ridiculously; laughably; ludicrously; grossly; crassly; offensively; disagreeably; unpleasantly; hopelessly; inordinately; slightly; extremely; terribly; continually; occasionally; definitely; indubitably; suddenly; inexplicably; undeniably; hilariously; noisily; boisterously; uproariously; sullenly.

TIRADE

adjectives

jeering; tedious; patriotic; shrill; positive; cumulative; belated; bitter; lengthy.

verbs

declaim in—; deliver—; fulminate—; halt—; launch—; pour out—; prolong—; rant—; recite—; silence—; spout—; utter—; —anathematizes; —castigates; —censors; —chastises; —declaims; —defames; —denounces; —deprecates; —disparages; —excoriates; —execrates; —harangues; —inveighs against; —lampoons; —lashes; —reprimands; —reproaches; —reproves; —thunders.

(See diatribe, scolding, invective, speech.)

TIRE

adjectives
spare; pneumatic; first; strong; deflated; retreaded; worn; slippery; useless.

verbs
deflate—; depress—; dilate—; distend—; fray—; gauge—; imbed in—; inflate—; mount on—s; perforate—; pierce—; pump —; puncture—; retread—; scrape—; value —; vulcanize—; —erodes; —grazes; —pads; —preserves; —skids.

TIRE (*v*)

adverbs
acutely; rapidly; abnormally; sadly; noticably; patently.

(See exhaust, bore.)

TIRESOME

adverbs
pedantically; monotonously; gushingly; garrulously; dully; uninterestingly; prosaically; long-windedly; endlessly; preachily; tediously; irksomely; boresomely; intolerably; unpleasantly; harmlessly; disagreeably; undeniably; terribly; needlessly; dreadfully; unfortunately; abominably; disgustingly; desperately; droningly.

TIRING

adverbs
unexpectedly; unwittingly; uncommonly; extraordinarily; dangerously; extremely; unintentionally; terribly; dreadfully; unwontedly; sadly; unfortunately; strangely; curiously; oddly; unnecessarily; needlessly; distressingly; painfully; obviously; palpably; inconsiderately; unaccountably; terrifically; grievously; unwarrantably; pitifully; seriously; oppressively; profoundly; inordinately.

TISSUE

adjectives
superficial; rich; silver; muscular; dermatoid; vegetable; damaged; disposable; cellular; social; desensitized; adipose; glandular; fibrous; abundant; innermost; plaited; excess; transpicuous; siliceous.

verbs
abscess—; canker—; consume—; cramp—; crush—; curette away—; desiccate—; destroy—; distend—; excise—; graft—; harden—; incise—; infect—; inflame—; inject into—; invade—; involve—; knead—; massage—; mould—; nourish—; regenerate —; support—; suture—; transplant—; —degenerates; —infiltrates; —languishes; —relaxes; —shrivels; —wastes; —withers.

TITANIC

adverbs
monstrously; tremendously; unbelievably; unimaginably; superbly; magnificently; gloriously; majestically; overwhelmingly; gorgeously; stupendously; inconceivably; cumbersomely; incomparably; unsurpassably.

TITLE

adjectives
honorary; precarious; elusive; religious; fabulous; trumped-up; bombastic; imposing; soul-stirring; vague; successive (pl); preliminary; forfeited; neglected; optimistic; seductive; pompous; impressive; shrill; legitimist; grotesque; attractive; hereditary; quaint; numerous (pl); clerical; imperial; distinguishing; illogical; vainglorious; appertinent; fantastic; ingenious; significant; ironic; prescriptive; smoothing; subscriptive; whimsical; homely; honorable; resounding; worse; dubious; newly-obtained; suggestive.

verbs
assume—; award—; bear—; claim—; covet —; decorate with—; defile—; degrade—; disparage—; dub with—; earn—; inherit—; invent—; renounce—; respect—; retain—; revere—; surrender—; underline—; usurp —; —awes; —connotes; —cows; —distinguishes; —epitomizes; —implies; —impresses; —misleads; —symbolizes; —signifies; —veils.

(See name, degree, nickname, rank.)

TITLED

adverbs
nobly; grandly; gloriously; proudly; royally; imperially; austerely; ecclesiastically; divinely; piously; devoutly; legitimately; officially; absurdly; bombastically; ridiculously; ironically; truly; self-; vainly; foolishly; unreasonably; realistically; popularly; ignominously; jeeringly; affectionately; lovingly; derisively; comically; shamefully.

TITTER

adjectives
slight; shamefaced; electric; damaging; explosive.

TITTER (v)

adverbs
affectedly; irrepressibly; involuntarily; girlishly; unsophisticatedly; explosively; naively; rudely; comically; hysterically; affectedly; coyly.
(See laugh, giggle.)

TOAD

adjectives
loathed; soft; sizable; well-fed; blinking; ugly; venomous; bucolic.

verbs
infest with —s; —burrows; —s bury themselves; —creeps; —croaks; —emits a noise; —hibernates; —hops; —jumps; —leaps; —metamorphoses; —plagues; —secretes; —springs; —squats; —vaults.

TOAST

adjectives
complimentary; appropriate; enthusiastic; celebrated; tasty; scorching; crisp; burned; crackling; crunching.

verbs
cheer—; drink—; hail—; join in—; propose —; rejoice in—; suggest—; utter—; voice —; acclaims—; —commemorates; —compliments; —eulogizes; —extols; —flatters; —glorifies; —hallows; —honors; —pledges; —solemnizes.
(See tribute, praise, sentiment, bread.)

TOAST (v)

adverbs
convivially; appropriately; crisply; cracklingly; victoriously; fraternally; boisterously.
(See congratulate, celebrate.)

TOBACCO

adjectives
aromatic; heavy; suggestive; coarse.

verbs
abhor—; abstain from—; addict to—; age —; auction—; blend —s; consume—; crave —; cross —s; cultivate—; cure—; denicotinize—; ferment—; filter—; grade—; hunger for—; inhale—; market—; mellow—; mentholize—; moisten—; plug—; powder—; purvey—; ripen—; roast—; scent—; store —; toast—; yearn for—; —braces; —calms; —clouds; —deteriorates; —discolors; —dulls; —impairs; —irritates; —lifts; —matures; —ravages; —reeks; —repels; —soothes; —steadies; —stunts; —tempts; —tranquillizes; —undermines; —vitiates.

TOE

adjectives
jagged; elfin; pliant; superfluous; contemptuous; shuffling; blunt; nimble; outraged; fantastic; dance-weary; festered; infected.

verbs
amputate—; bare—; brace—; bruise—; cramp—; crush—; dance on—; deform—; dislocate—; distort—; flex—; fracture—; pad—; sever—; skip on —s; splint—; stub —; teeter on—; web—; —pinches; —projects; —protrudes.

TOIL

adjectives
precarious; unhonored; manly; unrequited; exhausting; terrible; profitable; wholesome; philanthropic; unremitting; irksome; contented; hideous; pernicious; happy; filthy; sporadic; wasting; eager; smiling; rugged; blundering; griping; unceasing; earnest; delicious; fragrant; loving; arduous; sickening; desperate; earthly; successful; anxious; double; brave; stormy; noble; honest; meridian; ferocious; sultry; humble; squalid; elaborate; unrepaid; spasmodic; wasting; sullen; drudging; captive; patient; unhallowed; benignant; productive; fatiguing; congenial; ingenious; unusual; incessant; pernicious; sportive.

verbs
abate—; achieve by—; amass by—; cease—; consume in—; delight in—; ease—; hallow —; mitigate—; necessitate—; obviate—; plunge into—; relax—; reward—; shirk—; slacken—; —exhausts; —fags; —fatigues; —jades; —strains; —taxes; —wearies.
(See labor, drudgery, work, effort.)

TOIL (v)

adverbs
patiently; laboriously; ceaselessly; uncomplainingly; manfully; bodily; stealthily; painfully; assiduously; conscientiously; vigorously; sickeningly; precariously; exhaustingly; philanthropically; irksomely; incessantly; arduously; fatiguingly; perniciously.
(See work, labor.)

TOILER

adjectives
self-sufficient; patient; possessionless; laborious.

TOILET

adjectives
elaborate; hasty; unfinished; hurried.

TOILSOME

adverbs
terribly; dreadfully; undesirably; inescapably; unavoidably; brutally; cruelly; bitterly; exhaustingly; horribly; curiously; inordinately; extremely; unexpectedly; shockingly; miserably; wretchedly; shamefully; monotonously; tediously.

TOILWORN

adverbs
terribly; pathetically; significantly; apparently; palpably; extremely; unusually; miserably; obviously; evidently; wretchedly; lamentably; unaccountably; unexpectedly; deplorably; pitiably; inexcusably; remarkably; unmistakably; utterly.

TOKEN

adjectives
unmistakable; especial; tiniest; expressive; personal; unanimous; crushing; unique; singular; mystic; sensible; glorious; visible; palpable; bounteous; beauteous; outward; tremendous; sunny; amorous; leaden; irritating; meaningful.

TOLERABLE

adverbs
scarcely; barely; fairly; apparently; easily; eventually; finally; gradually; evidently; hardly; actually.

TOLERANCE

adjectives
kindly; legal; habitual; courteous; lazy; contemptuous; scientific; moral; apathetic; easygoing; amused; mischievous; indolent; gentle.

verbs
acclaim—; achieve—; advocate—; bear with —; breed—; cherish—; commend—; exemplify—; exhort—; foster—; further—; lack—; nurture—; preach—; preserve—; regard with—; sustain—; temper with—; —ameliorates; —pervades.

(See charity, forbearance, kindness, benevolence.)

TOLERANT

adverbs
sensibly; generously; broadly; wisely; discreetly; diplomatically; tactfully; overly; indulgently; reasonably; moderately; unusually; inordinately; unwisely; charitably; foolishly; rabidly; patiently; calmly; imperturbably; quietly; serenely; easily; mildly; sagely; marvellously; magnanimously; splendidly.

TOLERATE (*v*)

adverbs
eternally; consciously; patiently; magnanimously; generously; legally; courteously; lazily; contemptuously; morally; indolently; gently.

(See endure, permit.)

TOLERATION

adjectives
universal; further; religious; generous; absolute; quiet; superficial; indifferent; continued.

TOLL

adjectives
devilish; patient; terrible; enormous; death; preposterous.

verbs
assess—; augment—; bear—; charge—; deflate—; demand—; enforce—; exact—; fix —; levy—; quote—; rate—; set—; take—; subject to—; —burdens; —enables; —mounts; —taxes; —yields.

(See price, payment, tap.)

TOLL (*v*)

adverbs
solemnly; mournfully; dismally; repetitiously; funereally; fatally; heavily; vibrantly.

(See ring, clang.)

TOMB

adjectives
rock-hewn; sumptuous; brazen; dateless; neglected; wandering; ancestral; vacant; gilded; traditional; crumbling; antenatal; interdicted; indefinable; fin-winged; flowering; melancholy; untimely; fiery; ponderous; lingering; wintry; vast; impregnable; ferocious; watery; murmurous; slender; unlamented; reverend; drear; somber; miry.

verbs
adorn—; bar—; consign to—; deface—; de-

file—; delve in—; desecrate—; disinter from —; erect—; explore—; guard—; haunt—; illuminate—; incarcerate in—; inter in—; mould in—; patrol—; register upon—; rest in—; seal—; shadow—; unearth—; wreath —; —depresses; —envelops; —muffles; —receives; —reeks; —shrouds; —yields up.

(See shrine, grave, monument.)

TOMB-LIKE

adverbs

coldly; horribly; unbearably; supernaturally; terribly; fearfully; wretchedly; intolerably; frighteningly; appallingly; gruesomely; grimly; depressingly; dispiritingly; dismally; woefully; forbiddingly; curiously; grotesquely; fantastically.

TOME

verbs

compose—; concoct—; criticize—; dash off —; deliver—; immortalize—; inscribe—; pen—; polish—; pour forth—; publish—; wade through—; —commemorates; —eulogizes; —honors; —soliloquizes; —treats.

(See book, volume.)

TONE

adjectives

faltering; contemptuous; deprecating; soothing; passive; clear; angelic; deep-strung; provocative; milder; customary; diverse (pl); rueful; answering; solitary; frightened; braggart; ethereal; saddened; dearest; varying (pl); suggestive; victory; vindictive; low; lover-like; gentlest; confidential; sweet; gracious; joyous; regretful; rich; smothered; imperative; sanctimonious; moral; elastic; agitated; startled; careless; romantic; senatorial; breathless; pleading; pitiful; conciliatory; anguished; dictatorial; pastel; dominant; ringing; wailing; dark; bright; intermediate; marine; modified; colorful; didactic; inward; free; callous; hearty; beautiful; unceremonious; unconscious; boisterous; sullen; timid; flippant; blunt; nasal; moral; beseeching; shapeless; mean; menacing; soft; stentorian; confident; savage; faltering; preoccupied; child-like; earnest; imperious; dispassionate; conversational; scorching; intimate; sarcastic; threatening; soul-stirring; exulting; solemn; yearning; vibrating; impatient; luscious; tremulous; philosophic; supercilious; enamored; altered; crimson; distressful; amicable; honeyed; cathedral; ironical; displeasing; monotonous; ordinary; listless; aggressive; ivory; melodious; melting; tranquil; caressing; intriguing; half-pensive; indescribable; transient; well-guarded; promiscuous; martial; subdued; authoritative; maniac; unctuous; contrasting; assured; measured; despairing; archaic; mournful; whining; composite; paternal; drawling; bellicose; officer-like; ruminative; piping; metallic; bantering; incongruous; well-remembered; fretful; exquisite; hollow; vigorous; vexed; animated; witching; clarion; constituent; agonized; eager; healthy; complimentary; brisk; audible; penetrating; subduing; dreamy; piqued; apologetic; fluttering; caustic; proper; courteous; argumentative; nauseated; good-humored; haunting; dulcet; wonted; general; imperious; abominable; doubtful; abrupt; terrified; wheedling; innocent; considerable; tranquil; scoffing; thin; emphatic; sepulchral; liquid; silvery; jocular; harmonious; insolent; condescending; wistful; suppressed; fundamental; reflective; blustering; reproachful; controversial; burnt; unworldly; respectful; precious; lachrymose; unemotional; hungry; revolutionary; convinced; indifferent; untrammeled; strong; expostulating; insinuating; stately; inadequate; feeble; ever-pealing; grown-up; reminiscent; determined; musing; thoughtful; unmusical; exotic; mimic; professional; lugubrious; mordant; suppressed; mollified; frosted.

verbs

accentuate—; adopt—; alter—; amplify—; chasten—; deepen—; elevate—; falsify—; govern—; impart—; inflect—; lack—; lend —; lower—; magnify—; mimic—; modulate—; muffle—; silence—; strengthen—; subdue—; utter—; —betrays; —chastises; —elevates; —expresses; —harmonizes; —indicates; —irritates; —manifests; —mocks; —nettles; —predominates; —reproaches; —reproves; —reveals; —reverberates; —vibrates.

(See note, sound.)

TONGUE

adjectives

serpent; tuneful; partial; piercing; hissing; envious; forked; golden; indignant; wagging; moistened; dead; prattling; cloven; wily; complaining; lambent; gluttonous; foamless; evil; caustic; raise; immortal; furred; feverish; quivering; rapid; dominant; slick; leaping; unbound; classic; calumnious; lolling; earnest; unintelligible; gossiping; faltering; shrewish; gentle; polished; carping; cautious; boyish; halting; biting; coated; hasty; scoffing; silent; slurring; fervent; perfidious; flattering; finedividing; ancient; glowing; base; boundless; romancing; casual; heedless; proper; multitudinous (pl); uncivilized; oily; bitter; unbridled; joyous; unwilling; iron; soul-subduing; persuasive; slanderous; malicious; double; nimble; national; candied; pleading; discreet; lamenting; droning; viperish; railing; forbidden; woe-wearied; facile; flexible; foul; censorious; unintelligible; ill; lying; pliant; learned; modern; pioneer; glib; railing; nerveless; boastful; unknowable; brazen; liquid; soothing; slippery; stammering; scorched; teasing; glowing; shallow; whispering; pleasing; immortal; cynical; masterful; captious; gentle; guileless; inestimable; woodland; mother; selfsame.

adjectives
blister—; bridle—; candy—; chafe—; clip cluck—; curb—; discipline—; envenom—; examine—; fur—; furrow—; hold—; hush —; hypnotize—; inflame—; insert—; irritate—; lap with—; loosen—; mute—; paralyze—; provoke—; roll off—; sever—; silence—; smack—; stifle—; still—; suppress —; swab—; tempt—; tickle—; tie—; train —; wag—; —charms; —cleaves to; —falters; —laps; —lashes; —licks; —moistens; —projects; —protrudes; —rasps; —relishes; —savors; —slanders; —slips; —traduces; —voices; —wounds.

TONGUE-TIED

adverbs
deplorably; congenitally; lamentably; unfortunately; pitiably; pathetically; wretchedly; miserably; clumsily; awkwardly; unluckily; embarrassingly; shockingly; uncomfortably; bashfully; shyly; timidly; self-consciously; guiltily; curiously; unwontedly; unusually; peculiarly; strangely; unaccountably; suddenly; apparently.

TONIC

adjectives
valuable; intellectual; antiseptic; exhilarating; bracing; useful; provocative; bitter; healthful; mental; excellent.

verbs
addict to—s; administer—; consume—; dose with—; prescribe—; recommend—; —bolsters; —builds up; —enriches; —nauseates; —purges; —reanimates; —rejuvenates; —renews; —renovates; —restores; —resuscitates; —revivifies; —stimulates.

(See laxative, medicine, wine.)

TONIC

adverbs
refreshingly; wholesomely; definitely; effectively; really; dependably; reliably; assuredly; strongly; splendidly; invigoratingly; desirably; noticeably; evidently; positively; indubitably; admirably; wonderfully; commendably; marvellously; miraculously; incredibly; unexpectedly; delightfully; satisfactorily; remarkably; particularly .

TONSILS

verbs
apply to—; attack—; coat—; disease—; drain—; enlarge—; enucleate—; excite—; extract—; infect—; inflame—; invade—; swab—; swell—; —envenom; —filter; —indicate; —poison; —project; —suppurate; —ulcerate; paint—; scrutinize—; sever—; shrink—.

TOOL

adjectives
unconscious; passive; obedient; legitimate; vital; tempered; shaped; dexterous; edged; brittle; trenchant; unaccustomed; ready; obsolete; congenial; subservient; exquisite; keen.

verbs
apply—; devise—; employ—; enlist—; fashion—; guide—; hew with—; manipulate—; mechanize—; operate—; skill with—; stamp —; strain—; tax—; utilize—; wield—; —bevels; —bores; —eases; —facilitates; —lightens; —smooths.

(See instrument, apparatus, machine.)

TOOLING

adjectives
vigorous; firm; dazzling.

TOOTH

adjectives
rankling; determined; raging; rotten; cavity-eaten; filled; aching; film-covered; sparkling; false; broken; jagged.

verbs
(See teeth.)

TOOTHACHE

adjectives
serious; agonizing; unrelieved; comic; painful.

TOOTHLESS

adverbs
hideously; repulsively; pitifully; incoherently; unintelligibly; powerlessly; infirmly; utterly.

TOOTHSOME

adverbs
especially; particularly; agreeably; surprisingly; definitely; actually; unexpectedly; delectably; deliciously; lusciously; temptingly; extremely; undeniably; unusually; uncommonly; invitingly; pleasantly

TOP

adjectives
slender; inviolate; grisly; hill; sterile; gloomy; sun-bleached; singed; massive; eminent; pryamided; lofty.

TOP-HEAVY

adverbs
dangerously; inartistically; unfortunately; peculiarly; unsatisfactorily; objectionably; oddly; strangely; unluckily; hazardously; clumsily; awkwardly; impractically; unreliably; riskily; obviously; manifestly; unreasonably; crazily; unacceptably; abnormally; precariously; insecurely; uncommonly.

TOPIC

adjectives
dangerous; recondite; related; aforementioned; conversational; wary; religious; hackneyed; various (pl); disagreeable; dreadful; current; absorbing; conservative; tempting; concrete; conceivable; numerous (pl); forbidden; doubtful; political; one-sided; allied; abandoned; important; tiresome; celestial; magazine; commonplace; complicated; wholesome.

verbs
absorb in—; air—; analyze—; argue—; condense—; converse on—; digress from—; disclose—; dismiss—; dissect—; dissertate on—; divert from—; do justice to—; exhaust—; expatiate on—; expound—; grapple with—; limit—; obscure—; probe—; propose—; pursue—; rant about—; resume—; revive—; seize upon—; shrink from—; unfold—; ventilate—; —fascinates; —treats of.

(See subject, theme, question.)

TOPSY-TURVY

adverbs
unpleasantly; crazily; carelessly; inexcusably; disagreeably; negligently; objectionably; untidily; hastily; irremediably; terribly; oddly; fantastically; unexpectedly; gaily; perplexingly; inextricably; madly; mischievously; deliberately; inconsiderately; thoughtlessly; heedlessly; wildly; wantonly.

TORCH

adjectives
inverted; bridal; fiery; nuptial; smoldering; flaring; feeble; extemporized; broidered; incandescent; blazing; extemporary; processional.

verbs
apply—; bear—; eclipse—; employ—; extend—; extinguish—; flourish—; obscure—; quench—; screen—; smother—; snuff out—; thrust—; —beams; —chars; —dazzles; —enkindles; —flares; —flashes; —flickers; —gleams; —glimmers; —ignites; —radiates; —scintillates; —scorches; —sheds; —shimmers; —singes; —smoulders.

(See lamp, flame, light.)

TORMENT

adjectives
happy; numberless (pl); invented; abiding; exhausted; human; eternal; haunting; protracted; dreadful; perpetual; exquisite; especial; endless; continual; studied.

verbs
allay—; alleviate—; bear—; dull—; ease—; endure—; experience—; induce—; inflict—; mitigate—; occasion—; suffer—; tolerate—; —agonizes; —crushes; —curses; —galls; —gnaws; —rends; —rings; —shatters; —sours; —wracks.

(See punishment, anguish, itching, torture.)

TORMENT (*v*)

adverbs
constantly; protractedly; exquisitely; endlessly; diabolically; cruelly; heartlessly; unrelentingly; barbarously; devilishly; fiendishly.

(See hurt, pain, torture.)

TORMENTING

adverbs

vaguely; distinctly; mischievously, wantonly; offensively; vexatiously; intolerably; insufferably; unbearably; unwittingly; wilfully; deliberately; intentionally; constantly; unconsciously; purposely; viciously; maliciously; venomously; childishly; youthfully; blithely; continually; consistently; particularly; peculiarly; abominably; detestably; atrociously; facetiously; foolishly.

TORNADO

flounder in—; stagger in—; totter in—; —batters; —blasts; —bowls over; —cripples; —devastates; —ebbs; —effaces; —exterminates; —gyrates; —howls; —levels; —mangles; —plays havoc; —prostrates; —razes; —revolves; —rips over; —roars; —rotates; —scuttles; —smashes; —spends itself; —swamps; —swirls; —topples; —wheezes; —whistles.

(See storm, hurricane, wind.)

TORPID

adverbs

safely; securely; wanly; peculiarly; seasonally; naturally; stupidly; dully; merely; apathetically; terribly; unaccountably; unusually; alarmingly; helplessly; hopelessly; particularly; oddly; peculiarly; uncommonly, mercifully; inertly; contentedly; sluggishly; remarkably; inexplicably; habitually.

TORPOR

adjectives

momentary; guilty; heavy; vegetable; dead; frozen; intellectual; delicious; blank; dazed; death-like.

TORRENT

adjectives

wild; rushing; impetuous; irregular; tempestuous; streaming; furious; fiery; thundering; driving; angry; boiling; muddy; seething; dangerous; racing; living; windy; drenching; rapid, turbid; plunging; instantaneous; silver; deep; narrow; swirling; eddying; restless; tremendous; resistless; noisy; mad; fierce; hushed; flashing; swift; foaming; raging; radical; icy; mountain; descending; lava; turbulent; pent-up.

verbs

check—; dam—; immerse in—; pacify—; slacken—; staunch—; stem—; swell into—; tranquillize—; —batters; —buffets; —cascades; —deluges; —devastates; —foams; —gushes; —inundates; —issues from; —roars; —rolls; —surges; —sweeps; —swirls; —washes; —waves.

(See maelstrom, storm, rain, flood, stream.)

TORRENTIAL

adverbs

unusually; unseasonably; unexpectedly; suddenly; alarmingly; destructively; calamitously; disastrously; violently; viciously; swirlingly; inescapably; windily; frigidly; lamentably; mercilessly; furiously; perilously; frightfully; terribly; indescribably; incomparably; tragically; ominously; positively; actually.

TORRID

adverbs

unpleasantly; unfortunately; mercilessly; cruelly; intolerably; unbearably; parchingly; distressingly; injuriously; disastrously; calamitously; unexpectedly; unseasonably; suddenly; terribly; curiously; oddly; particularly; usually; uncommonly; painfully; inescapably.

TORSO

adjectives

slender; youthful; well-proportioned; antique.

TORTUOUS

adverbs

circuitously; painfully; perplexingly; wonderfully; intricately; unusually; arduously; unnecessarily; craftily; sinuously; deceptively; bewilderingly; distressingly; bothersomely; deliberately; objectionably; unpleasantly; disagreeably; maddeningly; discouragingly; vexatiously; curiously; unreasonably; confusingly; needlessly; terribly; dreadfully; tiresomely.

TORTURE

adjectives

excruciating; bitter; mental; lingering; physical; everlasting; exquisite; measured; hideous; endless; unrepressed; horrible; innate; slow; consuming; supreme; secret; utmost; tightening; eternal; memorable; rational; intense; untold; subtle; curdling; cruel; abominable; righteous; fiendish; burning; showy; grating.

verbs
avert—; contrive—; devise—; endure—; enforce—; palliate—; release from—; submit to—; subject to—; —benumbs; —convulses; —crucifies; —harrows; —lingers; —racks.
(See ordeal, torment, punishment, pain.)

TORTURE (v)

adverbs
excruciatingly; bitterly; lingeringly; physically; hideously; horribly; secretly; irrationally; exquisitely; barbarically; grotesquely.
(See torment, hurt, pain.)

TOSS

adjectives
tremendous; pretty; merry; coquettish; disdainful; careless.

TOSS (v)

adverbs
angrily; carelessly; restlessly; arrogantly; indiscriminately; restively; fretfully; impatiently; pettishly; coyly; coquettishly; disdainfully.
(See hurl, heave.)

TOTAL

adjectives
impressive; alarming; tremendous; enormous; attainable; staggering; incorrect; huge; amazing; erroneous.

verbs
amass—; appraise—; ascertain—; assess—; augment—; balance—; calculate—; check—; compile—; compute—; determine—; dispute —; divulge—; estimate—; integrate—; plumb—; rate—; reckon—; reveal—; underestimate—; weigh—; whittle down—; —aggregates; —astounds; —embraces; —mounts; —soars; —staggers; —totters.
(See amount.)

TOTAL

adverbs
finally; undeniably; grossly; substantially; presumably; indivisably; tentatively; staggeringly; roughly; unconditionally.

TOTTERING

adverbs
tremulously; waveringly; uncertainly; oddly; queerly; agedly; helplessly; pitiably; extremely; effetely; dejectedly.

TOUCH

adjectives
starry; soft; pleading; composing; distinctive; fairy; casual; impassioned; featherlike; caustic; felicitous; innumerable (pl); vivifying; continuous; magic; daughterly; hasty; corroding; subtile; exciting; nurselike; unwonted; polluting; passing; consoling; mortal; mysterious; sophisticated; chilling; dramatic; flexible; quivering; aristocratic; truthful; celestial; pardonable; luxurious; masterly; satiric; humorous; soothing; alien; simplifying; lively; mellow; sensitive; couturier; musical; demoralizing; clinging; crowning; icy; dreamy; uncivil; desperate; glowing; unfelt; ethereal; ironical; sweetest; inspiriting; fascinating; facile; convincing; tainting; finishing; summery; immaculate; all-pervading; immediate; caressing; arch; slight; incautious; simple; deathly; discriminative; abominable; skillful; beastly; plastic; innocent; vulgar; sparkling; superficial; faultless; final; classic; rare; grotesque; lyrical; inimitable; passionate; sophisticated; trial-fire.

verbs
avert—; avoid—; evade—; sense—; sensitize—; —benumbs; —brushes; —chills; —comforts; —contaminates; —defiles; —degrades; —electrifies; —excites; —grazes; —impassions; —petrifies; —pollutes; —reveals; —revolts; —tickles.
(See contact.)

TOUCH (v)

adverbs
delicately; affectionately; lingeringly; reverently; piquantly; inadequately; profoundly; confidingly; genuinely; inexpressibly; angelically; timidly; respectfully; fitfully; cautiously.
(See finger, feel.)

TOUCHDOWN

verbs
achieve—; aim at—; annul—; avert—; bid for—; block—; charge for—; clamor for—; culminate in—; pass to—; pile up—s; plunge for—; prevent—; recall—; score—; sneak over—; stem—; sweep for—; void—; yield—; —climaxes; —demoralizes; —determines.

TOUCHING

adverbs
infinitely; poignantly; extremely; unusually; positively; utterly; tenderly; hauntingly; curiously; pathetically; thrillingly; overwhelmingly; incomparably; unexpectedly; undeniably.

TOUCHY

adverbs
absurdly; unreasonably; vexatiously; significantly; arrogantly; indescribably; nervously; cholerically; churlishly; pugnaciously; curiously; strangely; inexplicably; unaccountably; inherently; naturally; unbecomingly; unpleasantly; disagreeably; atrociously; painfully; distressingly; ridiculously.

TOUGH

adverbs
disagreeably; unpleasantly; unpalatably; inedibly; unwarrantably; inadmissibly; curiously; unreasonably; unpardonably; outrageously; scandalously; shamefully; troublesomely; wantonly; dreadfully; inconceivably; uncommonly; extraordinarily; singularly; particularly; viciously; wickedly; ridiculously.

TOUGHNESS

verbs
acquire—; augment—; boast of—; deplore —; glory in—; mitigate—; preserve—; —affords; —breasts; —defies; —endures; —insures; —protects; —rebuffs; —repels; —resists; —supports; —sustains; —withstands; —yields.
(See strength, tenacity.)

TOUR

adjectives
prolonged; extended; creative; systematic; walking; triumphal; protracted; lecture; expensive; reconnoitering; memorable.

verbs
arrange—; cater for—; conclude—; conduct —; direct—; embark on—; extend—; guide —; map out—; organize—; plan—; project —; protract—; recruit for—; sponsor—; standardize—; —attracts; —broadens; —covers; —embraces; —includes; —provides; —skirts; —touches.
(See journey, trip, voyage, excursion.)

TOUR (*v*)

adverbs
enthusiastically; extendedly; listlessly; hurriedly; drearily; wearily; indefatigably; systematically.
(See travel, visit.)

TOURISTS

adjectives
guileless; romantic; rewarded; listless; hurried; dreary; clever; experienced; wary; weary.

verbs
accommodate—; accompany—; attract—; cater to—; convey—; divert—; entertain—; exploit—; guide—; lecture to—; lure—; shelter—; —consult; —embark; —flock; —marvel at; —mill; —motor; —purchase; —sail; —throng; —view.
(See traveler, passenger.)

TOURNAMENT

adjectives
mock; chivalric; independent; open; national; amateur.

verbs
advance in—; cheer—; color—; compete in —; conduct—; dominate—; emerge from—; engage in—; enter—; judge—; referee—; triumph in—; vie in—; witness—; —excites; —glorifies; —impassions; —publicizes; —rages.
(See contest, game.)

TOWEL

adjectives
ragged; hospitable; cordial; snowy; rough; rubbing; huge; crumpled; soggy.

verbs
begrime—; besmirch—; boil—; defile—; disinfect—; embroider—; employ—; filch—s; launder—; rack—; scour—; spatter—; sully —; swab with—; wrap in—; whip—; —absorbs; —envelops.
(See napkin, handkerchief, cloth.)

TOWER

adjectives
preserved; flying; immortal; quaint; opal; crumbling; meridian; warlike; weird; machicolated; tranquil; nodding; martial-like; impertinent; rent; gigantic; stalagmite; feudal; baroque; temporary; square; leaning; low; tottering; church; strong; top-

less; irregular; showy; flanking; worn; lurching; gleaming; stone; stunted; upper; shattered; slender; ivy-mantled; precipitous; stately; fortified; moldering; massive; overthrown; marshalled; external; shining; turret; skyey; rustic; ecclesiastical; barbaric; cylindrical; movable; tall; time-twin (pl).

verbs
ascend—; assail—; besiege—; clamber up —; convey to—; dismantle—; encompass—; erect—; flank—with; fortify—; hover over —; imprison in—; incarcerate in—; level—; mount—; raze—; repose in—; scale—; storm—; summon to—; surmount—; surround—; topple from—; view from—; —caps; —commemorates; —dominates; —flanks; —frowns; —honors; —looms; —rears; —soars; —symbolizes.

(See pinnacle, peak, mountain, spire.)

TOWER (v)

adverbs
magnificently; sublimely; martially; gigantically; precipitously; massively; awesomely; prodigiously; impressively.

(See rise.)

TOWN

adjectives
mute; quaint; storm-swept; tumultuous; queer; many-languaged; self-respecting; terror-stricken; combustible; seven-faced; drowsy; murmuring; imaginary; scenic; shapeless; provincial; breeding; sedate; everyday; defenseless; cheerful; industrial; bustling; rebel; high-perched; gray; placid; peaceful; beleaguered; adjacent; toiling; natal; inland; pretentious; ragged; haunted; dark; majestic; resurrecting; glittering; adverse; walled; retreating; famished; prosperous; hapless; picturesque; spiry; forest-girdled; benighted; populous; burning; lesser; native; festival; crude; ambitious; abominable; harbor; massive; cosmopolitan; fortified; insignificant; extraordinary; outlying; veritable; fated; colorful; straggling; wondrous; filthy; fascinating; respective; inexorable; thriving; corrupt; dirty; permanent; petty; snow-thatched; grass-grown; bleak.

verbs
abide in—; allude to—; assault—; besiege —; border—; distinguish—; evacuate—; extend—; father—; flank—; forsake—; found —; govern—; guide—; inhabit—; invade—; loot—; make the rounds of—; parade—; people—; potter about—; reclaim—; reconnoiter—; scurry around—; set foot in—; skirt—; sojourn in—; throng—; settle in—; trek across—; trudge around—; wall—; —booms; —flourishes; —s snuggle; —springs up; —thrives; —throngs.

(See city, neighborhood, community, village.)

TOXIC

adverbs
indubitably; truly; dangerously; fatally; alarmingly; curiously; evidently; apparently; immediately; instantly; deeply; palpably; cruelly; usually; irremediably; disturbingly; terribly; incontrovertibly.

TOXIN

verbs
dilute—; dispel—; inject—; liberate—; neutralize—; purge of—; secrete—; succumb to —; —circulates; —envenoms; —s fatigue; —invades; —overruns; —poisons; —pollutes; —s propagate; —ravishes; —taints; —vitiates; —weakens.

(See poison, germ.)

TOY

adjectives
tremulous; rude; lamenting; saccharine; adorable; vulgar; battered; inconstant; amorous; expensive; attractive; fond; imaginative; fairy; trifling; garish.

verbs
absorb in—s; caress—; cherish—; deprive of—s; disburse—s; engross in—s; fondle—; model—; regard—; reward with—s; tempt with—s; tinker with—s; weary of—s; wheedle—s away; —amuses; —beguiles; —cheers; —caricatures; —delights; —distracts; —diverts; —excites; —fascinates; —solaces.

(See rattle, doll.)

TOY (v)

adverbs
valiantly; irresistibly; idly; amorously; vulgarly; triflingly; adoringly; quaintly.

(See play, sport.)

TRACE (v)

adverbs
skillfully; accurately; roughly; laboriously;

painfully; unconsciously; ethnologically; unmistakably; perceptibly.
(See investigate, search.)

TRACEABLE

adverbs
easily; dimly; vaguely; distinctly; reasonably; calculably; obviously; discernibly; hardly; actually; conclusively; manifestly; clearly; allegedly; presumably; vestigially; objectively; psychologically; physically.

TRACES

adjectives
ancient; historical; corroding; abundant; generous; partial; servile; tangled; archaeological; anthropological; ethnological; slight; marked; effacing; sensible; unmistakable; perceptible; undiscovered; phantom; visible; surviving.

verbs
bear—; confirm—; convey—; detect—; dim—; disclose—; discover—; eclipse—; efface—; eradicate—; erase—; examine—; obscure—; obliterate—; outline—; recognize—; record—; reveal—; scent—; scrutinize—; stumble upon—; uncover—; unearth—; veil—; verify—; —disappear; —vanish.
(See evidence, impression, mark, sign, multiply.)

TRACK

adjectives
steep; indelible; foamy; beaten; zigzag; ant; well-chosen; sorrowless; myriad (pl); luminous; resplendent; untraveled; vengeful; receding; shining; adjacent; unending; thirsty; glistening; cloud-swept; solar; suitable; grooved.

verbs
blot out—; careen down—; clear—; deduce from—; efface—; eradicate—; erase—; espy—; expunge—; follow in—; jump—; obliterate—; steal across—; stumble upon—; trace—; uncover—; —s afford; —s bear evidence; —s betoken; —s blaze; —s denote; —enables; —ensnares; —s indicate; —s record; —s reveal.
(See course, groove, trail, trace.)

TRACKLESS

adverbs
bewilderingly; terrifyingly; utterly; hopelessly; completely; incredibly; appallingly; dismally; overwhelmingly; dishearteningly; absolutely.

TRACT

adjectives
inflammable; latent; controversial; much-desired; distributing; uncultivated; wicked; untrodden; considerable; inviting; stifling; dry; missionary; irritable; theologic; marshy; vast; diffusing; humane; alimentary; generous; tender; digestive; adjoining; singular; broad; large; partisan.

verbs
claim—; confine—; cultivate—; enlarge—; entitle to—; expand—; explore—; fence in—; grant—; harrow—; limit—; plow—; reclaim—; sow—; stake out—; till—; work—; —bears; —flourishes; —fructifies; —ranges; —thrives.
(See farm, area, district, field, land.)

TRACTABLE

adverbs
easily; pleasantly; agreeably; conveniently; handily; deceptively; amazingly; unexpectedly; accommodatingly; docilely; surprisingly; dully; quietly; humbly; willingly; happily; fortunately; suddenly; grudgingly; momentarily; amenably; apparently; delightfully; silently; wearily; placidly; tearfully.

TRADE

adjectives
considerable; clandestine; immense; peaceable; savory; melancholy; depressed; dreadful; monstrous; profitable; flourishing; military; lucrative; constant; discordant; penitent; languishing; abominable; essential; harsh; vilest; illicit; wholesale; hereditary; doubtful; permanent; beastly; external; sedentary; diverted; stagnated; unlawful; intermediary; earthly; reciprocal; thriving; frivolous; magnificent.

verbs
abandon—; alienate—; augment—; blockade—; bolster—; cement—; conciliate—; cut into—; decrease—; discontinue—; disrupt—; dominate—; encourage—; endanger—; engage in—; establish—; expand—; facilitate—; foster—; hamper—; impede—; increase—; inspire—; make roads upon—; monopolize—; nurture—; originate—; ply—; promote—; pursue—; regiment—; relinquish—; restrain—; revive—; spur—; stimulate—; strangle—; strengthen—; stymie—; swamp with—; swell—; tackle—;

teach—; threaten—; traffic in—; trample down—; —collapses; —dwindles; —freezes; —jumps up; —lures; —slumps.

(See employment, market, exchange, commerce, industry, calling, business.)

TRADEMARK

verbs

acquaint with—; appropriate—; glorify—; patent—; popularize—; recognize—; stamp —; —attests to; —betokens; —distinguishes; —emblazons; —guarantees; —heralds; —indicates; —insures; —labels; —represents; —symbolizes; —vouches.

(See label, copyright, patent.)

TRADESMEN

verbs

bargain with—; barter with—; dicker with —; cater to—; —deal in; —dispense; —dispose of; —engage in; —haggle; —hawk; —market; —peddle; —ply; —purvey; —retail; —trade; —traffic in; —transact; —vend; —vie.

(See hawker, merchant, salesman.)

TRADITION

adjectives

sacred; mysterious; precise; ancient; soberest; superstitious; venerable; cumulative; social; historic; culinary; inherited; patriotic; simple; saner; time-honored; sentimental; exquisite; ghostly; current; moldy; gentlemanly; ritualistic; intellectual; unscientific; sporting; hospitable; family; high; rare; sweet; dim; hoary; liberal; heroic; aesthetic; untrustworthy; living; remote; medieval; decorous; poetic; remarkable; pleasant; tribal; conventional; popular; established; cherished; imperial; renowned; fine; immutable.

verbs

absorb—; acquire—; adhere to—; annihilate —; authenticate—; "ballyhoo"—; bare—; batter—; better—; bound by—; break down —; cast aside—; carry on—; cherish—; conform to—; continue—; create—; cut loose from—; defend—; derive from—; destroy —; disclose—; discrepit—; disregard—; dissolve—; emancipate—; emasculate—; embody in—; endure—; enrich—; establish —; exist in—; express—; force—; fortify—; found—; glory in—; guard—; honor—; ignore—; illustrate—; imbue—; impair—; imperial—; infuse—; ingrain—; inherit—; "junk"—; limit—s; maintain—; mock—; nourish—; nurture—; observe—; perpetuate —; preserve—; profit by—; rear in—; relate—; relinquish—; repudiate—; revive—; respect—; root in—; saturate with—; shake off—; shatter—; smash—; stand for—; steep in—; stick to—; strangle—; sweep away—; take over—; tinge with—; trace—; undermine—; unfold—; violate—; weld—; —accentuates; —ascribes; —binds; —blinds; —brands; —carries on; —colors; —describes; —determines; —dictates; —enriches; —fetters; —governs; —hands down; —immortalizes; —narrates; —preserves; —persists; —prescribes; —recounts; —regulates; —reports; —rules; —stands; —threatens; —s topple.

(See belief, attitude, culture, habit, custom, usage.)

TRADITIONAL

adverbs

devoutly; deeply; racially; innately; reverently; profoundly; curiously; manifestly; pleasantly; seriously; ineradicably; conventionally; delightfully; apparently; popularly; locally; indestructibly; inflexibly; vaguely; clearly.

TRADUCE (*v*)

adverbs

viciously; scandalously; libelously; hatefully; savagely; vindictively; revengefully.

(See slander, assail.)

TRAFFIC

adjectives

congested; rushing; metropolitan; aerial; dense; heavy; incessant; petty; abominable; ceaseless; roaring; terminate; din-producing; wearisome.

verbs

avert—; check—; choke—; congest—; control—; converge—; direct—; engage in—; escape—; evade—; facilitate—; guide—; hamper—; impede—; jam—; obstruct—; paralyze—; quell—; regulate—; retard—; shun—; speed—; support—; tangle—; —blares; —clogs; —confuses; —converges; —endangers; —flows; —jangles; —jeopardizes; —roars; —surges; —sweeps by; —thunders.

(See intercourse, exchange, commerce.)

TRAGEDY

adjectives

poetic; vast; shocking; unimaginable; derived; inexcusable; bourgeois; radical; unequalled; dark; bombastic; dream; philosophic; classical; bloody; supreme; fantastic; stark; nocturnal; ancient; national; countless (pl); tribal; dismal; terrible; impressive; domestic; timeless; climacteric; successful; terrestrial; world; unavoidable.

verbs
avert—; banish—; bear—; belittle—; bewail—; decry—; deplore—; develop into —; disclose—; facilitate—; heighten—; intensify—; lament—; mourn—; play—; plot—; plunge into—; precipitate—; sense —; shudder at—; skirt the edge of—; stay —; submerge—; suffer—; surmount—; verge on—; —afflicts; —appalls; —bereaves; —curdles; —curses; —deals a blow; —depresses; —descends; —distorts; —excites; —foredooms; —harrows; —haunts; —mows down; —oppresses; —overtakes; —purges; —racks; —rends; —sears; —shakes; —shocks; —sours; —spells; —unfolds; —weighs upon; —wrings.
(See melodrama, atrocity, outrage, calamity, drama, catastrophe.)

TRAGIC

adverbs
overwhelmingly; calamitously; bitterly; cruelly; incredibly; unexpectedly; dismally; appallingly; shockingly; devastatingly; unmitigatedly; hopelessly; unrelievedly; utterly; splendidly; superbly; highly; profoundly; consummately; incalculably; immeasurably.

TRAIL

adjectives
hurrying; downward; sidling; lonesome; traveled; resplendent; recent; dusty; endless; milky; unique; pungent; majestic; arduous; hour-old; winding; sinuous; well-worn; twisting; elusive; spiritual; ancestral.

verbs
blaze—; break—; clarify—; clutter—; construct—; deviate from—; diverge from—; efface—; erase—; explore—; forsake—; illuminate—; jog along—; lay out—; map—; mark—; obliterate—; obscure—; obstruct —; plunge along—; pursue—; scan—; shadow—; skirt—; stir up—; strike into—; veil—; —bewilders; —recedes; —threads its course; —twists; —veers; —winds.
(See track, road, lane.)

TRAIL (v)

adverbs
demurely; faithfully; humbly; tediously; arduously; sinuously; twistingly; elusively; incessantly.
(See follow, trace.)

TRAIN

adjectives
reaper; starry; unparalleled; funeral; illustrious; imperial; crawling; belated; night; retreating; prodigious; express; inferior; gigantic; suburban; shining; grisly; hurtling; fast-flying; virgin; complicated; pointed; harmless; crack; long-laid; additional; pensive; vagrant; incoming; unfeeling; unpainted; gloom-stricken; wooden; immediate; melancholy; haughty; celestial; pompous; sweeping; streamlined.

verbs
assign to—; board—; collide with—; consign to—; convey—; couple—; derail—; flag—; fuel—; hop aboard (colloq.)—; insert in—; launch—; section—; schedule—s; scurry for—; shunt—; signal—; switch—s; transport by—; —bears; —chugs (colloq.); —conveys; —departs; —facilitates; —glides; —plunges; —puffs; —pulls into; —rattles; —rocks; —rolls; —shunts; —shrieks; —steams; —sways; —sweeps away; —thunders; —wheels away; —whistles; —whizzes; —winds its way.
(See automobile, locomotive, trolley-car.)

TRAIN (v)

adverbs
exquisitely; sedulously; scientifically; specially; competently; intellectually; judiciously; technically; adequately; intensively; monastically; academically; arduously; systematically; subtly; theoretically.
(See discipline, teach.)

TRAINED

adverbs
successfully; highly; moderately; skilfully; adequately; recently; well-; badly; inadequately; consummately; carefully; scarcely; cleverly; marvelously; brilliantly; cruelly; mercilessly; patiently; persistently; consistently; effectively; sufficiently; specifically; constantly.

TRAINING

adjectives
continuous; intellectual; judicious; vicious;

elementary; technical; valuable; preparatory; rigid; persistent; watchful; ethical; industrial; disciplinary; adequate; rural; intensive; lifelong; monastic; requisite; vocational; classical; scholarly; precedent; supplementary; arduous; superficial; loving; pious; admirable; secretarial; practical; systematic; rigorous; amatory; leisurely; stabilized; subtle; architectural; theoretical.

verbs
entrust to—; fit for—; imbibe—; persevere with—; prescribe—; relax—; subject to—; undergo—; —accustoms; —breeds; —disciplines; —equips; —forearms; —habituates; —hardens; —impregnates; —inculcates; —infuses; —instils; —inures; —matures; —mellows; —polishes; —prepares; —qualifies; —sharpens; —smooths; —veneers.
(See preparation, education, discipline, exercise.)

TRAIT

adjectives
redeeming; petty; striking; intellectual; boyish; ridiculous; bestial; dominant; overbearing; predominating; advanced; distinguished; outstanding; conspicuous; royal; feminine; multiplex (pl); noble; salient; common; singular; outward; scrupulous; generous; sectional; characteristic; humane; national; essential; desirable; lasting; hereditary; notable; varied (pl); obnoxious; introvert; quantitative; childish; valuable; visible; physiological; ostensible.

verbs
assentuate—; acquire—; breed—s; commend—; cultivate—; discover—s; emphasize—; exhibit—; foster—; illuminate—s; intensify—; manifest—; play a part in—; portray—; relate—; stamp—; value—; —allures; —appears; —attracts; —betokens; —characterizes; —distinguishes; —s etch deeper; —fascinates; —indicates; —individualizes; —s stamp out.
(See characteristic, habit, quality.)

TRAITOR

verbs
accuse—; banish—; denounce—; dub—; exile—; expose—; hiss—; hoot—; ostracize—; outlaw—; proclaim—; pursue—; redeem—; scorn—; sneer at—; spurn—; subdue—; —betrays; —debases; —demeans; —falsifies; —loses caste; —repudiates; —secedes.
(See betrayer, conspirators, plotters, criminal.)

TRAITOROUS

adverbs
despicably; abominably; stealthily; furtively; unbelievably; unexpectedly; suddenly; curiously; detestably; murderously; meretriciously; insidiously; atrociously; odiously; hatefully; venomously; vilely; grossly; ungratefully; confessedly; traceably; evidently; incalculably; cleverly; invidiously; utterly; presumably; allegedly.

TRAJECTION

adjectives
free; limited; swift; uncanny.

TRAMP

adjectives
collier; measured; penniless; steady; dusty; derisible; plashy; echoing; impecunious; dingy; clattering; sullen; beggarly.

TRAMP (v)

adverbs
ruthlessly; vigorously; sullenly; monotonously; dingily; indefatigably; remorselessly.
(See march, trudge.)

TRAMPLE (v)

adverbs
ruthlessly; heedlessly; speedily; cruelly; viciously; contemptuously; heartlessly.
(See tramp, stamp.)

TRANCE

adjectives
spectral; rigid; magic; mystic; compassionate; blissful; icy; stupid; restless; ecstatic; cataleptic; dizzy; spiritual; stilly; lethargic; doleful; speechless; detested.

TRANQUIL

adverbs
sweetly; amazingly; restfully; contentedly; incredibly; suddenly; surprisingly; refreshingly; delightfully; naturally; habitually; always; seldom; enviably; admirably; happily; contentedly; blissfully; extremely; uncommonly.

TRANQUILITY

adjectives
wishless; misty; dignified; well-regulated;

mist-wrapped; divine; magnanimous; honey-sweet; sumptuous; profound; flustered; long-desired; monotonous; perfect; serene; dry; physical; innocent; boresome; empty; dull.

verbs
break—; disturb—; lull into—; recapture —; recollect in—; shatter—; tolerate—; —alleviates; —assuages; —becalms; —chastens; —composes; —deadens; —depresses; —dulcifies; —pacifies; —settles over; —smooths; —smothers; —stagnates; —subdues.
(See calm, apathy, quiet.)

TRANSACT (v)

adverbs
profitably; industriously; efficiently; ethically; momentously; monetarily; fraudulently; spiritually; nefariously; discreditably; philosophically; ephemerally.
(See conduct, negotiate.)

TRANSACTION

adjectives
momentous; mercantile; monetary; notorious; important; fraudulent; clouded; private; flowery; spiritual; extortionate; nefarious; discreditable; philosophical; ritualistic.

verbs
abandon—; bind to—; carry on—; conceal —; conduct—; consummate—; divulge—; draft—; engage in—; endanger—; execute —; facilitate—; insure—; negotiate—; nullify—; outline—; participate in—; plan—; press—; profit by—; promote—; reject—; release from—; rue—; underwrite—; withdraw from—; —obligates; —stipulates.
(See procedure, deal, bargain, intercourse.)

TRANSCEND (v)

adverbs
boundlessly; gloriously; infinitely; obviously; markedly; amazingly; spectacularly.
(See surpass, excel.)

TRANSCENDENTAL

adverbs
presumably; indubitably; impractically; satisfactorily; altogether; curiously; obviously; incalculably; loosely; strictly.

TRANSCRIBE (v)

adverbs
faithfully; diligently; laboriously; patiently; indefatigably; industriously; ambitiously; accurately.
(See copy, write.)

TRANSCRIBED

adverbs
carefully; accurately; usually; responsibly; legally; necessarily; scrupulously; immediately; intelligibly; perfectly; punctiliously; painstakingly; mechanically; scientifically; carelessly; imperfectly.

TRANSFER (v)

adverbs
temporarily; satisfactorily; forcibly; rapidly; professionally; individually.
(See shift, change.)

TRANSFIGURED

adverbs
radiantly; gloriously; celestially; divinely; brilliantly; glowingly; piously; devoutly; unimaginably; incredibly; beauteously; luminously; curiously; brightly; spiritually; idealistically; marvelously; miraculously; supernaturally; utterly; suddenly.

TRANSFORM (v)

adverbs
miraculously; magically; ingeniously; topographically; uniquely; supernaturally; amazingly; extensively; spectacularly.
(See change.)

TRANSFORMATION

adjectives
magical; striking; bucolic; epic; weird; successive (pl); solemn; tremendous; ingenious; unique; supernatural; topographical.

verbs
achieve—; analyze—; condone—; discern —; facilitate—; undergo—; —accentuates; —alters; —deviates; —innovates; —introduces; —modifies; —modulates; —revamps; —swerves from.
(See fermentation, change, alteration, transition.)

TRANSFORMED

adverbs
marvelously; miraculously; suddenly; gloriously; divinely; utterly; luminously;

strangely; peculiarly; oddly; unaccountably; inexplicably; radiantly; grotesquely; palpably; manifestly; unbelievably; undeniably; incredibly.

TRANSGRESS (*v*)

adverbs
outrageously; repetitiously; wantonly; venially; notoriously; incestuously; egregiously.
(See sin, violate.)

TRANSIENT

adverbs
painfully; lamentably; fortunately; fleetingly; merely; pathetically; sadly; tragically; ephemerally; bitterly; meteorically; brilliantly.

TRANSITION

adjectives
ethnological; soft; terrible; quick; hard; sudden; awful; perilous; stormy; violent; delicious; fine; necessary; painful; bitter; swift.

verbs
accomplish—; balk at—; bemoan—; complete—; decry—; denounce—; endure—; necessitate—; smooth—; trace—; undergo —; undertake—; —converts; —involves; —matures; —mellows; —revolutionizes; —ripens.
(See change, modification, transformation.)

TRANSITIONAL

adverbs
expediently; merely; conveniently; practically; feasibly; quickly; profitably; suitably; advantageously; briefly; serviceably; presumably; probably; adaptably; providentially; helpfully; admirably; aptly.

TRANSITORY

adverbs
briefly; ephemerally; impermanently; perishably; sadly; lamentably; unhappily; mortally; evanescently.

TRANSLATE (*v*)

adverbs
literally; fluently; extensively; faithfully; flawlessly; exquisitely; freely; exactly; copiously; skillfully; mentally.
(See interpret, construe.)

TRANSLUCENT

adverbs
mysteriously; strangely; incredibly; scientifically; unbelievably; uncommonly; admirably; commendably; sufficiently; surprisingly; pleasantly; attractively; conveniently; cleverly; agreeably; reasonably; surprisingly; unexpectedly; usefully; practically; satisfactorily.

TRANSPARENT

adverbs
entirely; inconveniently; uncomfortably; delightfully; attractively; unexpectedly; amazingly; conveniently; admirably; commendably; satisfactorily; oddly; comically; absurdly; shamefully; unnecessarily; remarkably; uncommonly; highly; exceptionally; perfectly.

TRANSPLANT (*v*)

adverbs
unceremoniously; agriculturally; patiently; skillfully; ingeniously; successfully; prudently.
(See shift, move, change.)

TRANSPLANTED

adverbs
carelessly; unskilfully; unsuccessfully; seldom; easily; safely; skilfully; carefully; successfully; often; usually; unwisely; clumsily; inexpertly; improperly; properly; experimentally.

TRANSPORT (*v*)

adverbs
swiftly; recklessly; laboriously; dramatically; periodically; annually; regularly; seasonally; continuously; deftly; uniquely.
(See move, ship.)

TRANSPORTATION

adjectives
water; ruined; laborious; swift; air; faultless; reckless.

verbs
accelerate—; afford—; assign—; assure of —; avail of—; block—; cripple—; direct —; disrupt—; expedite—; facilitate—; grant—; hamper—; impede—; manage—; rate—; retard—; slacken—; —cements; —communicates with; —enables; —links; —unites.
(See shipment, conveyance.)

TRAP

adjectives
unyielding; baited; palpable; dramatic; dreaded; ridiculous.

verbs
bait—; circumvent—; elude—; evade—; inveigle into—; lure into—; mask—; spring —; warn of—; —beguiles; —claws; —decoys; —deludes; —dupes; —ensnares; —grasps; —gulls; —hoaxes; —masks; —menaces.
(See pitfall, net, snare, ambush.)

TRAPPED

adverbs
hideously; helplessly; hopelessly; desperately; abominably; maliciously; grimly; unspeakably; utterly; inescapably; fatally; precariously; perilously; permanently; terribly; horribly; frightfuly; appallingly; shockingly; frantically; cleverly; cunningly; finally; ultimately; legally; subtly; adroitly; treacherously.

TRASHY

adverbs
utterly; abominably; terribly; cheaply; worthlessly; horribly; unspeakably; undisguisedly; irretrievably; irredeemably; grossly; crassly; irreclaimably; unacceptably; hopelessly; disagreeably; disgustingly; manifestly; undeniably; arrantly.

TRAVEL

adjectives
earthly; dreary; unknown; riotous; air; irrelevant; tiresome; horseback; prudent; extensive; transient; frequent; equatorial; continental; nomadic; fatiguing.

verbs
afford—; extend—s; facilitate—; forsake —; long for—; modernize—; recall—s; recite—s; recount—s; relinquish—s; widen—s; —acquaints one with; —broadens; —cultivates; —cultures; —edifies; —educates; —endangers; —enlightens; —polishes; —veneers.
(See tour, cruise, adventure, education.)

TRAVEL (*v*)

adverbs
extensively; circuitously; luxuriously; methodically; laboriously; perceptibly; sedately; expensively; advantageously; recklessly.
(See tour, journey.)

TRAVELED

adverbs
widely; highly; broadly; brilliantly; unusually; admirably; wonderfully; far; much; frequently; infrequently; seldom; little; marvelously; extensively.

TRAVELER

adjectives
ephemeral; zealous; wayworn; elegant; weary; cheerful; defenseless; mysterious; unprotected; unwary; desperate; expectant; unprofessional; dawdling; dispirited; shrewd; contemporary; present; thoughtful; economical; colonial; veteran; hoary; storm-tossed; late-arriving; rustic; gaping; sleepless; well-assorted (pl); discriminating; unwilling; fastidious; casual; reputable; disconcerting; arctic; wise; sophisticated; refined; seasoned; epicurean.

verbs
accommodate—; cater to—s; comfort—; enchant—s; enthrall—s; exhaust—; fatigue —; guide—; lecture to—; organize—; plunder—s; route—s; waylay—s; welcome —; —journeys; —lingers; —s mill about; —plans; —prolongs; —protracts; —repairs to; —resides at; —roams; —roves; —views; —wearies of; —wends; —witnesses.
(See marcher, tourists.)

TREACHEROUS

adverbs
abominably; dangerously; alarmingly; ominously; portentously; slyly; smoothly; insidiously; hypocritically; flatteringly; furtively; cleverly; disloyally; despicably; boldly; hideously; subtly; maliciously; grossly; deliberately; adroitly; vilely; astutely; inscrutably; undoubtedly; infinitely; deeply; darkly.

TREACHERY

adjectives
cruel; meditated; base; subtle; signal; bitter.

verbs
condemn—; court-martial for—; disclose—; denounce—; expose—; fear—; frame—; plot—; resort to—; screen—; shroud—; stoop to—; suspect—; uncover—; untangle —; veil—; —baits; —beguiles; —betrays; —debases; —deceives; —decoys; —deludes;

—dishonors; —disillusions; —engulfs; —lures; —lurks; —pollutes; —snares; —stains; —sullies.

(See insincerity, ingratitude, infidelity, betrayal.)

TREAD

adjectives

hasty; quick; elastic; viewless; swinging; limping; winter; victorious; slow; measured; firm; fairy; martial; sacred; monotonous; stately; imperious; stealthy; nervous; delicate; resilient; pointed; scandaled; thundering; persistent; springy; self-assured; conquering; undazzled; muffled; backward; unflinching; cat-like; clanging.

TREAD (*v*)

adverbs

sorrowfully; lightly; boldly; profanely; noiselessly; soundlessly; cautiously; rhythmically; painfully; consciously; gaily; unheedingly; tenderly.

(See walk, proceed.)

TREASON

adjectives

strong; household; detested; pretended; unpardonable; domestic; manifest; ugly; certain; passive; defiant; proud.

verbs

accuse of—; acquit of—; arraign for—; charge with—; cite—; combat—; commit—; condemn for—; confess—; convict of—; deny—; exile for—; indict for—; penalize for—; revenge—; unveil—; uncover—; —betrays; —breaches; —corrupts; —debases; —degrades; —demeans; —dishonors; —stigmatizes.

(See betrayal, crime, treachery.)

TREASONABLE

adverbs

indubitably; utterly; wickedly; admittedly; allegedly; subtly; frankly; assuredly; immeasurably; deliberately; indefeasibly; indefensibly; defiantly; arrantly; unutterably; daringly; boldly; peculiarly; palpably; highly; dangerously; darkly.

TREASURE

adjectives

valued; countless (pl); inexhaustible; sacred; royal; patrimonial; garnered; priceless; celestial; subsequent; vast; portable; precious; costly; heavenly; accursed; lifetime; perishing; dear-bought; self-consuming; chaste; autumn; nobler; numbered (pl); eternal; drainless; sterling; superfluous; golden; accumulated; notable; earthly; ruffling; orphaned; long-lost; sleeping; cherished; unsuspected; dewy; longed-for; purloined; buried.

verbs

accumulate—; adorn—; amass—; appraise—; bury—; cache—; cherish—; disclose—; dispose of—; dive for—; exaggerate—; explore for—; extort—; garner—; harbor—; hoard—; impound—; lavish—upon; pilfer—; reclaim—; reveal—; salvage—; secrete—; seek—; stow away—; swallow—; uncover—; unearth—; —astounds; —dazzles; —enriches.

(See wealth, money.)

TREASURED

adverbs

highly; greatly; carefully; piously; affectionately; fondly; lovingly; tenderly; always; truly; especially; deeply; openly; strangely; oddly; unaccountably; sincerely; nationally; decorously; ceremoniously; insistently.

TREASURY

adjectives

exhaustless; infinite; provincial; veritable; depleted; enfeebled; anemic; national; vest-pocket.

verbs

augment—; bankrupt—; deplete—; divert from—; drain—; embarrass—; embezzle from—; raid—; reinforce—; replenish—; replete—; repose in—; stabilize—; tap—; —accrues; —accumulates; —amasses; —appropriates; —authorizes; —declines; —inflates; —issues; —languishes; —lifts; —mounts; —recalls; —swells; —totters.

(See coffer, bank, reserve.)

TREAT

adjectives

popular; delightful; optical; splendid.

verbs

afford—; extend—; indulge in—; luxuriate in—; offer—; procure—; provide—; relish—; rejoice in—; revel in—; welcome—; yield—; —absorbs; —amuses; —delights; —enlivens; —fascinates; —gladdens; —regales; —solaces; —tickles.

(See dainty, entertainment, feast, repast.)

TREAT (v)

adverbs

rationally; barbarously; circumspectly; humanely; systematically; tenderly; adequately; harshly; elaborately; brutally; deferentially; compassionately; reverently; mercilessly; roughly; histrionically; elaborately; objectively; sympathetically; essentially; hospitably; conscientiously; jocosely; capriciously; contemptuously; surgically; medically; courteously.

(See behave, act.)

TREATISE

adjectives

extensive; erudite; laborious; scholarly; distinguished; lucid; philosophical; pedagogical; far-sighted; important; abstruse; pedantic; musical; celebrated; voluminous; masterly; hard-headed; distinct; elaborate; valuable.

verbs

absorb in—; acclaim—; commend—; comprehend—; condense—; consolidate—; denounce—; illustrate—; peruse—; present—; produce—; publish—; revise—; summarize —; write—; —airs; —boxes; —deals with; —digresses; —discourses; —dissertates; —does justice to; —elaborates on; —exhausts; —extends; —sets forth; —recites; —unfolds; —wearies.

(See dissertation, article, book.)

TREATMENT

adjectives

miraculous; infamous; prompt; acoustical; diabetic; proposed; triple-acting; drastic; abominable; scientific; superficial; dietary; persuasive; bold; thematic; heroic; jocose; intelligent; technical; contemptuous; harsh; pessimistic; realistic; cruel; proper; humane; psychoanalytic; symphonic; affectionate; unjust; preferential; successful; osteopathic; unfilial; inhuman; barbarous; severe; well-considered; judicious; summary; sufficient; axial; statistical; ceiling; appropriate; harmonic; architectural; voluntary; hospitable; routine; cathartic; attentive; torturing; ruthless; reliable; competent; delicate; insolent; surgical; standard; sportive; interior; scandalous; harmonious; remote; beautifying; preferential; perfidious; ungerous; respectful; conscientious; preventive; courteous; hypnotic; capricious; impolite; antiquated; immediate; mosaic; realistic; playful; disrespectful; frank; artistic; original.

verbs

acquaint with—; administer—; adopt—; advise—; advocate—; alter—; apply—; attribute—; carry on—; check—; commence—; conduct—; confer—on; constitute—; consult for—; co-ordinate—; counsel—; discard—; discontinue—; direct—; employ—; endure —; excel in—; expose—; extend—; facilitate —; indicate—; improve—; institute—; modernize—; modify—; neglect—; outline—; place—; prescribe—; prolong—; protract—; pursue—; question—; recommend—; regulate—; render—; repeat—; require—; respond to—; resume—; skill in—; standardize—; subject to—; tolerate—; undergo—; urge—; yield to—; —accomplishes; —allays; —ameliorates; —antidotes; —assuages; —falls; —incenses; —metes out; —misleads; —mitigates; —perseveres; —palliates; —relieves; —remedies; —represents; —varies.

(See cure, method, act, performance, usage.)

TREATY

adjectives

far-sighted; separate; successive (pl); defensive; definitive; supplementary; ambiguous; secret; advantageous; pleasing; monstrous; equitable; obnoxious; outrageous; violated.

verbs

abrogate—; adopt—; comply with—; condition—; condemn—; confirm—; conform to —; contract—; create—; discharge—; disregard—; dissolve—; draft—; frame—; ignore—; infringe upon—; negotiate—; nullify—; observe—; press—; ratify—; repudiate—; rip—; sanction—; scrap—; sign—; trample—; transgress—; violate—; void—; —affords; —aims; —allies; —binds; —cements; —circumvents; —concludes; —embroils; —guarantees; —insures; —leagues; —pledges; —stipulates; —strengthens; —ties; —unites.

(See lease, covenant, agreement.)

TREE

adjectives

rich; ominous; whispering; brittle; cringing; wide-spreading; ragged; overgrown; tropical; trimmed; stately; fledged; interposing; accursed; tangled; wind-swept; well-branched; kindred; assailed; dusty; feathery; tottering; cleft; stunted; hardy; well-cared-for; thread-like; gloomy; embowering; breathless; slender; white-starred; paradise; low; scrubby; dewy-tasseled; resinous; over-hanging; murdered; stretching; mute; shady; patriarchal; tufted; shining-leaved; enticing; notched; waking; unhewn; draped; rejoicing; water-loving; bare; genealogic; unwaving; darling; immortal; blasted; flowering; somber; unguarded; unlawful; lofty; senseless; yielding; parched; pleached; deserted; spectral; exotic; celestial; drooping; attractive; rifled; hoary; sheltering; forbidden; fantastic; stubby; dooryard; deciduous; prostrate; perfect; tempting; pomegranate; coveted; dripping; new-leafed; gnarled; denuded; sturdy; hollow; wayside; virtuous; twisted; interdicted; sprawling; friendly; lusty; gracious; listening; half-budded; slumberous; massive; blossoming; venerable; indigenous; faded; voluptuous; overarching; magnificent; broad-armed; sapient; naked; centennial; hereditary; tortured; undecaying; celestial; waving; fruit-laden; aromatic; bending; long-lived; eldest; full-branched; girdled; gaunt; unbrageous; glittering; gift-bearing; over-leaning; contorted; quivering; luxuriate; antique; trysting; intolerable; shivering; ornamental; pauper; spicy; shadowy; glistening; blessed; unaccustomed; short; majestic; lowering; misshapen; grafted.

verbs
blight—; clamber up—; conserve —s; cultivate —s; dot with —s; fell—; fertilize —s; graft—; hack at—; hew—; label—; level—; nest in—; prune—; raze—; suspend from—; tap—; thin out—; transplant—; uproot—; —affords; —bears; —bends; —blooms; —blossoms; —bows under; —buds; —s cluster; —creaks; —dips; —falls; —flanks; —flourishes; —flowers; —forms; —forsakes; —fructifies; —garlands; —hints; —lashes; —lifts; —loads; —obscures; —occupies; —overspreads; —plunges; —relinquishes; —rises; —rustles; —scourges; —screens; —shades; —sheds; —shelters; —shimmers; —shivers; —shrouds; —soars; —spreads; —s straggle; —sways; —swishes; —thrives; —throws; —thunders; —topples; —totters; —towers; —whips; —whispers; —writhes; —yields.

(See leaf, branch, oak, elm, etc.)

TREMBLE (v)

adverbs
fearsomely; fearfully; violently; inwardly; abominably; visibly; spasmodically; nervously; morbidly; abnormally; agitatedly.

(See shiver, move.)

TREMBLING

adverbs
helplessly; dreadfully; uncertainly; uncontrollably; awkwardly; perceptibly; pitiably; ineptly; paralytically; weakly; feebly.

TREMOR

adjectives
touching; nervous; sharp; immeasurable; emotional; eager; slight; awful; luminous; fierce; earthquake.

verbs
allay —s; excite to —s; inspire—; record—; respond to—; stir with —s; —agitates; —alarms; —convulses; —creeps; —dislodges; —indicates; —jars; —jolts; —jostles; —jounces; —pulsates; —ripples thru; —shocks; —swells; —terrifies; —trickles; —warms; —quivers.

(See agitation, earthquake, shiver, shudder.)

TRENCH

adjectives
slimy; abhorred; trial; current; political; bold; bloody; artificial; flanking; adjacent; defensive; muddy.

TRENCHANT

adverbs
effectively; unusually; famously; remarkably; wonderfully; cleverly; aptly; uncommonly; powerfully; tellingly; savagely; viciously; unmercifully; sarcastically; drolly; brutally; bluntly; sharply.

TRENCHES

verbs
beseige—; blast—; bolster—; bombard—; burrow—; confine to—; excavate—; fortify—; flow from—; lodge in—; maintain—; map—; patrol—; plan—; raid—; repulse from—; scoop out—; straggle to—; stream to—; swarm from—; tunnel—; —afford; —deface; —furrow; —shelter; —shield.

(See ditch, drain, fortification.)

TREND

adjectives
significant; important; radical; philosophic; noticeable; recent; future; mystical; practical; probable; impressive; unhealthy; gambling; significant.

verbs
affect—; approve—; detect—; discern—; divert—; emphasize—; encourage—; foster—; govern—; hail—; herald—; illustrate—; indicate—; influence—; obscure—; promote —; recognize—; regulate—; retard—; reverse—; scotch—; sense—; sway—; warp —; —departs from; —deviates; —inclines toward; —shifts; —signifies; —swerves.
(See mode, fashion, style, tendency.)

TRESPASS (*v*)

adverbs
nefariously; boldly; illegally; brazenly; lawlessly; flagrantly.
(See transgress, intrude.)

TRESPASSER

verbs
admonish—; banish—; bar—; caution—; dispel—; eject—; expel—; inveigh against —; oust—; penalize—; prosecute—; —encroaches on; —infringes on; —intrudes; —invades; —obtrudes; —offends; —oversteps; —violates.
(See aggressor, intruder.)

TRESS

adjectives
raven; ebon; flaming; beauteous; unbound.

TRIAL

adjectives
repeated; fiery; ancient; memorable; ludicrous; harassing; speedy; hurried; religious; gracious; mutual; intensified; terrible; weary; still; bitter; countless (pl); impartial; unnecessary; supreme; petty; amicable; mock; grueling.

verbs
appeal—; arraign for—; arrange for—; bear—; behold—; bias—; challenge to—; conclude—; conduct—; determine—; docket —; judge—; prejudice—; preside over—; protract—; scorn—; summon for—; warrant—; —absolves; —acquits; —airs; —clears; —commences; —discloses; —exculpates; —exonerates; —notorizes; —publicizes; —ventilates; —whitewashes.
(See effort, attempt, endeavor, tribunal, examination.)

TRIBAL

adverbs
ceremonially; strictly; narrowly; originally; characteristically; singularly; peculiarly; exclusively; oddly; actually; apparently; obviously; manifestly; conspicuously.

TRIBE

adjectives
beaten; finny; kindred; rebellious; malignant; predatory; cervine; hostile; crushed; pastoral; illustrious; sylvan; scattered (pl); swarming (pl); cognate; barbarian; unfriendly; neighboring; scaly; contemptible; perishing; indolent; wandering; protected; aboriginal; feline; feathered; unlearned; thriftless; primitive; unnumbered (pl); invisible; swarthy; powerful; fierce; native; carnivorous.

verbs
affiliate with—; ban from—; band in—; cement—; evolve from—; exterminate—; father—; found—; head—; inflame—; mobilize—; muster—; perpetuate—; scatter—; unite—; weld—s; —expands; —multiplies; —ostracizes; —prospers; —survives; —thrives; —vanishes; —wanes.
(See clan, family.)

TRIBULATIONS

verbs
afflict with—; allay—; assuage—; augment —; ease—; encounter—; endure—; experience—; lament—; mitigate—; mourn—; occasion—; palliate—; suffer—; —consume; —distress; —harass; —harrow; —rack; —subdue; —weigh upon.
(See affliction, trouble.)

TRIBUNAL

adjectives
legal; international; judicious; secret; tardy; independent; impartial; peaceful; revolutionary; bustling; arbitral; mock; revolting; supreme; military; just; righteous.

verbs
adjourn—; appeal to—; bias—; convoke—; hamper—; prejudice—; resort to—; —ad-

judicates; —arbitrates; —awards; —brings in a verdict; —confirms; —decides; —determines; —dooms; —evaluates; —judges; —passes an opinion; —proclaims; —reviews; —sentences; —sets aside; —settles.

(See court, jury.)

TRIBUTE

adjectives

tardy; august; odorous; extravagant; sincere; unconscious; significant; fitting; requisite; eloquent; noble; unwilling; touching; impressive; remarkable; manifold (pl); expressive; everlasting; elaborate; grim; extraordinary; floral; stipulated; joyous; sisterly; generous; anonymous; spontaneous; obtrusive; virgin; poetic; personal; russet; complacent; curious; honorable; intuitive; magnificent; whole-hearted.

verbs

accept—; acknowledge—; award—; bestow—; decline—; decry—; demand—; disdain—; extort—; grant—; indulge—; lavish—; levy—; merit—; offer—; owe—; pour—; scorn—; yield—; —acclaims; —compliments; —flatters; —glorifies; —indemnifies; —lauds; —recompenses; —remunerates; —rewards.

(See graft, tax, bribe.)

TRICK

adjectives

psychological; innocent; hideous; juggling; juvenile; perfidious; foremost; scurvy; forgotten; unwarrantable; commercial; ultramontane; pretty; strategic; singular; sardonic; harsh; perverse; ingenious; admiration; momentary; raw; artistic; speeding; ceremonious; unconsidered; shy; mad; fantastical; innate; nasty; extra; cowardly; abominable; ugly; amusing; political; unbecoming; barbarous; stage; trashy; unworthy; fascinating; mathematical; valorous; favorite; villainous; practical.

verbs

concoct—; contrive—; devise—; discern—; disclose—; hatch—; master—; perform—; perpetrate—; practise—; reveal—; spring—; study—; —ambushes; —baffles; —bewilders; —bores; —confounds; —deceives; —defrauds; —deludes; —mystifies; —amuses.

(See puzzle, manipulation, fraud, deceit, magic, mystery.)

TRICK (v)

adverbs

ridiculously; mystifyingly; deftly; unscrupulously; psychologically; perfidiously; singularly; sardonically; ingeniously; amusingly; mathematically; villainously; practically; politically.

(See deceive, fool.)

TRICKERY

adjectives

obvious; successful; low; transparent; base; foreign; shameless.

verbs

disclose—; employ—; fear—; foil—; hint at—; resort to—; scorn—; sense—; surmise—; suspect—; uncover—; unearth—; —baffles; —baits; —bilks; —deceives; —decoys; —defrauds; —deludes; —ensnares; —gulls; —infuriates; —swindles; —victimizes.

(See cunning, hyprocisy, deception, deceit, fraud.)

TRICKSY

adverbs

cleverly; playfully; whimsically; childishly; wildly; uncontrollably; nonsensically; clownishly; roguishly; mischievously; waggishly; comically; laughably; farcically; ludicrously.

TRICKY

adverbs

subtly; cunningly; insidiously; surreptitiously; artfully; slyly; craftily; deceitfully; delightfully; dangerously; cleverly; adroitly; alarmingly; mischievously; playfully; harmlessly; provokingly; disagreeably; plaguedly; foolishly; maneuveringly; underhandedly.

TRIFLE

adjectives

consequential; unspeakable; useless; glittering; laborious; insignificant; nameless; countless (pl); honest; musical; merest; satirical; inconsiderable; inconsequential; important; enchanted; silliest; logical; careless; petty; pedantic.

TRIFLE (v)

adverbs

leeringly; ridiculously; ludicrously; un-

speakably; insignificantly; illogically; inconsequentially; pettishly; pedantically.
(See toy, play.)

TRIFLES

verbs
belittle—; chatter about—; discount—; disregard—; emphasize—; fret over—; ignore—; minimize—; omit—; scrutinize—; shelve—; skim over—; skip—; stress—; underestimate—; —irk; —irritate; —pique; —rile (colloq.); —plague.
(See insignificance, trivialities.)

TRIFLING

adverbs
absurdly; foolishly; facetiously; flippantly; languidly; senselessly; nonsensically; giddily; airily; ridiculously; farcically; clownishly; intolerably; vainly; uncommonly.

TRIGGER

verbs
caress—; cock—; draw—; ease—; finger—; flick—; fondle—; gear—; jam—; jerk—; jiggle—; oil—; lock—; lubricate—; release—; snap—; wedge—; —clicks; —controls; —discharges; —endangers; —menaces; —recedes; —threatens.
(See knob, lever.)

TRIM

adverbs
naturally; pleasantly; agreeably; usually; habitually; unwontedly; stiffly; jauntily; daintily; smoothly; delicately; neatly; unusually; particularly; noticeably; conspicuously; indescribably; painfully; marvelously; delightfully.

TRIM (*v*)

adverbs
cautiously; judiciously; exquisitely; gaudily; garrishly; tastefully; symbolically; neatly; fastidiously.
(See arrange, adjust.)

TRIP

adjectives
fairy; perilous; constant; phantasmagoric; periodic; bridal; shopping; foreign; innumerable (pl); mysterious; ghastly; infernal; stimulating; overland; sight-seeing; curious; delightful; strenuous; previous.

verbs
conclude—; contemplate—; depart on—; embark on—; entrain on—; extend—; journey on—; plan—; prolong—; protract—; sally forth on—; —acquaints one with; —embraces; —enchants; —enlightens; —fatigues; —intrigues; —proceeds; —progresses; —relaxes; —spans; —traverses.
(See flight, journey, excursion, quest, tour.)

TRIP (*v*)

adverbs
rhythmically; gaily; dexterously; lightly; noiselessly; blithely; strenuously; fantastically.
(See dance, move.)

TRIPPING

adverbs
lightly; gaily; merrily; jauntily; blithely; nimbly; tunefully; pleasantly; childishly; girlishly; joyously; happily; beautifully; quickly; buoyantly; ecstatically; melodiously.

TRITE

adverbs
monotonously; tiresomely; vapidly; disagreeably; invariably; trivially; facetiously; fatuously; intolerably; sententiously; uninterestingly; wearily; tediously; flatly; senselessly; vacuously; prosily.

TRIUMPH

adjectives
unworthy; pitiless; crowning; consummate; delusive; melancholy; fiendish; hideous; intoxicating; rare; dawning; gay; paltry; splendid; rhetorical; superficial; turbulent; forensic; ill-concealed; temporary; bitter; assured; absent; unsought; demiurgic; vindictive; final; social; unapproachable; intimate; inimitable; chuckling; strategic; recent; brilliant; nameless; unspeakable; perpetual; wearisome; secure; permanent; malicious; veritable; ultimate; dramatic; awful; debonair; personal; scornful; delirious; ultimate; unmistakable; conscious; passionate; unbroken; remorseless; diplomatic; ceremonial; marvelous; magnificent; peaceful; glorious; melodious; laboring; slight; shameful; contemptible; veritable; bacchanal; temporary.

verbs
acclaim—; attend with—; belittle—; blaze into—; boast—; commemorate—; concede —; congratulate one on—; dilute—; emerge in—; exult in—; foreshadow—; frustrate—; gain—; hail—; mar—; presage—; record —; rejoice in—; return in—; signalize—; sing of—; spur to—; thwart—; witness—; —elates; —emancipates; —flushes; —vanquishes.
(See conquest, ovation.)

TRIUMPH (*v*)

adverbs
markedly; notably; supremely; gloriously; pitilessly; consummately; intoxicatingly; rhetorically; forensically; politically; strategically; ultimately; diplomatically; veritably.
(See win, succeed.)

TRIUMPHANT

adverbs
proudly; elatedly; justly; naturally; exultingly; wholly; gloriously; splendidly; magnificently; happily; radiantly; delightedly; joyously; jubilantly; merrily; laughingly; heartily; mockingly; jeeringly; scoffingly.

TRIVIAL

adverbs
absurdly; foolishly; altogether; wholly; senselessly; nonsensically; ridiculously; intolerably; uncommonly; insignificantly; inconsequentially; particularly; vexatiously; bothersomely; cheaply; childishly.

TRIVIALITIES

verbs
amplify—; babble—; charge with—; clarify —; cloak in—; content with—; discard—; dismiss—; escape—; evade—; flounder on —; magnify—; prate about—; scoff at—; scorn—; shrink from—; —arise; —bore; —crop up; —harass.
(See trifles.)

TROLLEY-CAR

verbs
collide with—; derail—; jam—; man—; outstrip—; pilot—; schedule—s; stream from—; —accelerates; —clatters; —converges on; —crawls along; —disburdens; —jangles by; —jars; —jolts; —lurches; —rumbles; —screeches; —tears.
(See train.)

TROOPING

adverbs
merrily; noisily; gaily; purposefully; sullenly; angrily; boisterously; truculently; pugnaciously; ominously; threateningly; menacingly; mischievously; derisively; happily; shyly; defiantly; resolutely; encouragingly; triumphantly; laughingly.

TROOPS

adjectives
dispirited; sleepy; ragged; shoeless; ill-equipped; mutinous; light-armed; furious; hated; vulgar; servile; available; predatory; parti-colored; raw; flexible; scattered; exhausted; obtained; infectious; radiant; mercenary; wearied; supplementary; fresh; disembarking; organized; disciplined.

verbs
accoutre—; amass—; arm—; assemble—; ban—; conceal—; concentrate—; dispatch —; disperse—; draft—; enhearten—; enlist —; enforce with—; equip—; garrison—; halt—; harry—; mass—; mobilize—; muster —; quarter—; transport—; yield to—; —advance; —beleaguer; —besiege; —bolster; —charge; —coerce; —disband; —drive; —invade; —mutiny; —occupy; —patrol; —pour into; —reconnoitre; —retaliate; —rout; —storm; —throng.
(See brigade, army, besieger, invader, militia.)

TROPHY

adjectives
glorious; grisly; evil-smelling; ghastly; bloody; shining; melancholy; ostentatious.

verbs
acquire—; annex—; attain—; award—; carry off—; cherish—; clinch—; collect—s; compete for—; contend for—; covet—; display—; engrave—; exhibit—; gain—; gather—s; merit—; procure—; recover—; regain—; relinquish—; retain—; retrieve—; treasure—; value—; —commemorates; —elates; —honors; —signifies; —symbolizes.
(See laurels, monument, memorial, medal.)

TROPICAL

adverbs
narrowly; essentially; fundamentally; peculiarly; definitely; scientifically; geographically; preferably; characteristically; distinctly; presumably; unpleasantly; agreeably; intolerably.

TROT (*v*)

adverbs
doggedly; obediently; faithfully; listlessly; monotonously; diligently; jubilantly.
(See gallop, run.)

TROUBLE

adjectives
wretched; associate; endless; unfortunate; personal; perpetual; disciplinary; monetary; annoying; powerful; inflammatory; joyful; intolerable; vague; obscure; major; nocturnal; infinite; lifelong; hesitant; poor; delicious; cruel; constant; garrulous; complex; distressing; pathetic; contagious; invincible; luxurious; measurable.

verbs
afflict with—; anticipate—; arrest—; attend with—; avert—; avoid—; bear—; bewail —; breed—; compensate for—; cure—; diagnose—; endure—; experience—; explore —; foment—; instigate—; lament—; localize—; minimize—; mourn—; pour out—s; probe—; remedy—; repay—; stir up—; undergo—; ward off—; —besets; —blasts; —blights; —crops up; —deranges; —harasses; —haunts; —irks; —irritates; —looms; —lurks; —manifests itself; —originates in; —piques; —preys upon; —rankles; —recurs; —ruffles; —rumples; —seethes; —simmers; —smites; —strikes; —waxes; —weighs upon; —wracks.
(See affliction, hardship, difficulty, adversity, obstacles, tribulation.)

TROUBLE (*v*)

adverbs
impudently; perpetually; vaguely; obscurely; nocturnally; infinitely; distressingly; profoundly.
(See disturb, irritate.)

TROUBLED

adverbs
nervously; frenziedly; unnaturally; laughably; ridiculously; pathetically; lamentably; curiously; abnormally; naturally; touchingly; supremely; unduly; deeply; indescribably; perceptibly; suspiciously; significantly; pitiably; miserably; terribly; tenderly.

TROUBLESOME

adverbs
persistently; increasingly; sometimes; slightly; devilishly; deucedly; perplexingly; mysteriously; conspicuously; palpably; visibly; manifestly; unusually; naturally; particularly; diplomatically; vexatiously; distressingly; painfully; consistently; remarkably; deliberately; despicably; grossly; boldly; defiantly; intentionally; always.

TROUSERS

adjectives
voluminous; baggy; fluttering; plaid; mustard-colored; creaseless; sport.

verbs
alter—; array in—; bare—; divest of—; doff—; don—; drape—; fray—; garb in —; hitch up—; peg—; pleat—; refurbish—; rend—; retrieve—; strip of—; sunder—; tatter—; vest in—; —clothe; —cover; —protect.
(See clothing.)

TRUANT

adverbs
vexatiously; intolerably; deliberately; heedlessly; carelessly; triflingly; negligently; indifferently; worthlessly; incorrigibly; derisively; brazenly; inexplicably; unaccountably; wantonly; unprofitably; unendurably; bafflingly.

TRUCE

adjectives
reasonable; temporary; faithless; broken; perpetual.

verbs
adopt—; agree to—; arrive at—; beseech —; clamor for—; consent to—; declare—; effect—; hail—; hamper—; impede—; invite—; petition for—; plead for—; press for—; proclaim—; project—; refuse—; reject—; rejoice in—; sign—; welcome—; —arrests; —checks; —curtails; —liberates; —lulls; —pacifies; —reprieves; —rescues; —suspends.
(See halt, peace, respite.)

TRUCK

adjectives

rumbling; passing; clattering.

verbs

assign to—; consign to—; fuel—; guide—; license—; lubricate—; manoeuvre—; overhaul—; recondition—; shift—; —bears; —booms; —chugs (colloq.); —clatters; —conveys; —groans; —jars; —jolts; —pounds along; —roars; —rolls; —rumbles; —swerves; —transports.

(See cart, automobile, bus, vehicle.)

TRUCULENT

adverbs

unbearably; offensively; boldly; daringly; intolerably; boorishly; unmistakably; openly; brutally; challengingly; brazenly; grossly; ominously; inordinately; alarmingly; disagreeably; unreasonably; always; sullenly; singularly; curiously; uncommonly; viciously; vengefully; villainously.

TRUDGE (*v*)

adverbs

wearily; monotonously; heavily; tirelessly; lazily; solemnly; indefatigably; bravely; buoyantly; patiently; laboriously.

(See walk, proceed.)

TRUE

adverbs

apparently; positively; unquestionably; avowedly; confessedly; admittedly; professedly; palpably; essentially; obviously; evidently; manifestly; officially; reliably; solemnly; disagreeably; accidentally; fundamentally; profoundly; disgracefully; unpleasantly; horribly; intrinsically; gloriously; unanswerably; painfully; heavily; ironically; shockingly; sublimely; universally.

TRUMPET

adjectives

shattering; martial; hideous; silver; snarling; hostile; fierce; discordant; splitting; unblown.

verbs

flourish—s; hearken to—; sound—; toot—; —alarms; —awakens; —blares; —blasts; —blazes; —calls forth; —deafens; —hails; —heralds; —mobilizes; —musters; —proclaims; —rends; —resounds; —reverberates; —screams; —shatters; —trills.

(See bugle, loudspeaker.)

TRUNK

adjectives

formless; nameless; forest; ungainly; uniform; overhanging; prostrate; silicified; comfortable; quivering; columnar; palpitating; charred; ghostlike; scraggy; knotty; fleshy; decaying; crackling; gnarled; split; ponderous; hoary; fibrous; barky; crashing; moss-grown.

TRUST

adjectives

gentle; boyish; investment; serene; guileless; humble; honorable; unfaltering; blind; changeless; fearless; devoted; stupendous; buoyant; false; unswerving; impious; important; instinctive; delusive; serious; theologic; complete; earnest; human; commercial; implicit; dreadful; sacred; unattainable; ample.

verbs

abuse—; afford—; bestow—; betray—; breach—; breed—; charge with—; cherish—; confide—in; encourage—; entertain—of; fix—; foster—; found—on; inspire—; misplace—; nurse—; nurture—; relinquish—; retain—; root—; rue—; shake—; shatter—; shock out of—; strengthen—; violate—; —crumbles; —falters; —flatters; —reposes in; —wanes; —wavers.

(See hope, assurance, faith, confidence, idealism.)

TRUST (*v*)

adverbs

implicitly; assuredly; fondly; indolently; tacitly; shrewdly; reverentially; credulously; explicitly; guilelessly; delusively; amply; unfalteringly.

(See rely, depend.)

TRUSTFUL

adverbs

innocently; gullibly; overly; wistfully; childishly; foolishly; unwisely; inordinately; singularly; particularly; incredibly; unbelievably; curiously; remarkably; peculiarly; uncommonly; idiotically; touchingly; unaffectedly; pitifully; confidently; terribly; ingenuously; naively.

TRUSTWORTHY

adverbs
admirably; commendably; unusually; exceptionally; absolutely; utterly; uncommonly; singularly; obviously; apparently; undoubtedly; dependably; truly; supposedly; presumably.

TRUTH

adjectives
disagreeable; dual; unlovely; conceivable; accidental; fundamental; invincible; profound; pursuing; abstract; gloomy; clear; hackneyed; striking; delicious; innocent; disgraceful; unpleasant; intense; solemn; transparent; undoubted; distracted; distorted; outspoken; unconscious; searching; fragmentary; absolute; disguised; horrible; bare; consequent; hateful; perfect; sweet; unfaltering; gracious; useful; innate; unequivocal; practical; rigorous; intrinsic; perennial; granite; austere; unadulterated; glorious; crystal; rudimentary; unsophisticated; dramatic; perverting; palpable; historic; objective; unanswerable; demonstrated; religious; astounding; established; magnificent; slighted; moral; painful; remorseless; hideous; burning; lasting; indelible; priceless; unfathomable; domestic; injured; flattering; apparent; immutable; heavenly; benignant; heavy; consolatory; revered; crushing; valid; constant; barbed; naked; substantial; shocking; unornamented; golden; unvarnished; obvious; stretched; serviceable; scattered; droll; general; solid; unique; humbling; unrecognized; melancholy; informing; appalling; sober; relative; heartrending; comparative; dawning; naturalistic; formidable; imageless; irrefragable; physical; maiden; effectual; royal; sacred; essential; precious; unwelcome; bitter; underlying; stately; steadfast; necessary; good; symmetrical; sublime; indestructible; philosophical; extraordinary; approximate; divine; pure; indwelling; guileless; brilliant; strenuous; sensuous; inviolable; poignant; universal.

verbs
accept—; acknowledge—; adumbrate—; affirm—; annihilate—; apprehend—; approach—; arrive at—; ascertain—; assert—; attest to—; blurt out—; cherish—; cloud—; color—; commit to—; communicate—; compromise—; conceal—; consecrate to—; contradict—; convey—; counterfeit—; credit—; demand—; demonstrate—; deny—; determine—; discern—; disclose—; dispute—; distort—; divulge—; dodge—; dress up—; embroider—; emphasize—; establish—; evade—; expose—; face—; falsify—; flinch before—; forecast—; foster—; foreshadow—; garble—; gloss over—; grace with—; grasp—; herald—; imitate—; impart—; inspire—; intermingle with—; misrepresent—; modify—; obscure—; obstruct—; open—; persuade one of—; pervert—; preach—; probe for—; proclaim—; propagate—; question—; re-echo—; reflect on—; refuge in—; reject—; repudiate—; reveal—; seduce from—; seek—; shadow—; shrink at—; simulate—; sift—; skirt—; smother—; stretch—; stumble over—; support—; sustain—; upholster—; utter—; value—; varnish—; verify—; voice—; vouch for—; warp—; welcome—; —blazes; —burns; —dawns upon; —emerges from; —flatters; —looms; —pierces; —prevails; —shines; —triumphs; —vanquishes.

(See gospel, integrity, verity, veracity, sincerity, realism, reality.)

TRUTHFUL

adverbs
dependably; reliably; absolutely; always; altogether; painfully; brutally; fanatically; childishly; completely; dangerously; evidently; reputedly; allegedly; avowedly; inconveniently; usually; notably; fairly; scarcely; faithfully; precisely; literally; glumly; innocently; technically; volubly; statistically; sensationally; frankly; vividly; graphically; impressively; simply; artfully; bluntly; glibly; reluctantly; gravely.

TRY (v)

adverbs
exceedingly; sorely; insistently; surreptitiously; deliberately; variously; perfunctorily; conscientiously; piteously; energetically; manfully; sorely; convulsively; obstinately; blunderingly; elaborately; abominably; faithfully; vainly; nervously; falteringly; guiltily; strenuously.

(See attempt, endeavor.)

TRYST

adjectives
clandestine; childish; bloody; moonlight; amorous; fatal.

verbs
agree upon—; anticipate—; appoint—; cloak—; curtail—; fulfill—; hamper—; impede—; keep—; observe—; plan—; pledge to—; shroud—; suggest—; veil—; —allures; —beguiles; —transgresses; —violates.
(See appointment, place, meeting.)

TUB

adjectives
odious; fermenting; insignificant; daily; refreshing.

verbs
convey in—; dip into—; drain—; emerge from—; ground—; immerse in—; invert—; plug—; plunge into—; propel—; scour—; scuttle—; soak in—; submerge in—; swamp —; swish in—; tap—.
(See kettle, vat, barrel.)

TUBE

adjectives
pneumatic; elegant; ivory; tortuous; magic; hollow; perforated; delicate; slender; golden; railway; twisted.

verbs
coke—; clog—; convolute—; couple—s; dam —; deflate—; dilate—; distend—; drain—; inflate—; insert—; line—; narrow—; obstruct—; penetrate—; perforate—; pierce—; plug—; puncture—; riddle—; seal—; tap—; throttle—; value—; —bursts; —conveys; —expands; —transmits.
(See nozzle, pipe, conduit, tunnel.)

TUBERCULOSIS

verbs
allay—; check—; combat—; contract—; convey—; diagnose as—; predispose to—; succumb to—; tend toward—; wipe out—; —blasts; —blights; —decimates; —devours; —eats; —impairs; —infects; —moulders; —ravages; —saps; —scathes; —taints; —taxes; —undermines; —wastes.
(See consumption, disease.)

TUCK (v)

adverbs
cautiously; mentally; meticulously; picturesquely; snugly; cozily.
(See fold, press.)

TUFT

adjectives
feathery; obligatory; flowery; amber; inky.

TUG (v)

adverbs
hysterically; drowsily; repeatedly; nervously; agitatedly; repetitiously; exasperatingly.
(See pull, draw.)

TUGBOAT

adjectives
vulgar; little; innumerable (pl); straining; squat; sturdy; pug-nosed.

verbs
employ—; guide—; pilot—; ram—; recruit —; —batters; —bestirs; —chugs (colloq.); —draws; —exerts; —s flock about; —hauls; —plies; —puffs; —s retire; —scurries; —snorts; —steams; —strains; —struggles; —s surround; —tows.
(See boat, motor-boat, launch.)

TULIP

adjectives
red; gold; grandiose; lovely; beauteous.

TUMBLE (v)

adverbs
clownishly; comically; clumsily; drunkenly; wretchedly; abruptly; precipitately.
(See fall, heave.)

TUMOR

verbs
confine—; diagnose—; dissolve—; excise—; extirpate—; incise—; reduce—; relieve—; restrict—; treat—; —atrophies; —blocks; —cankers; —compresses; —distends; —enlarges; —expands; —hardens; —invades; —infiltrates; —obstructs; —protrudes; —subsides; —ulcerates.
(See cancer, abscess, growth.)

TUMULT

adjectives
murmuring; fast-gathering; tempestuous; growing; intestinal; formidable; sickening; ensuing; portentous; wild; rolling; surging; internal; inward; passionate; ceaseless; fiery; civic.

verbs
calm—; quell—; restrain—; —bewilders; —breaks loose; —ceases; —dies; —disconcerts; —disorders; —embroils; —ensues; —muddles; —rages; —reigns; —roars; —ruffles; —subsides; —wanes; —waxes.
(See clamor, confusion, disturbance, commotion, noise, turmoil.)

TUMULTUOUS

adverbs
terribly; unmanageably; boisterously; truculently; inordinately; ungovernably; riotously; uproariously; dangerously; dreadfully; fearfully; alarmingly; ominously; significantly; threateningly; lawlessly; defiantly; boldly; grossly; portentously; desperately; derisively; angrily; triumphantly; madly; crazily; deafeningly; hilariously; drunkenly.

TUNE

adjectives
lingering; stirring; plaintive; warbling; fat; fulsome; light; touching; melodious; sentimental; half-remembered; loyal; saucy; enthralling; trivial; tremulous; mysterious; merry; pathetic; greedy; fandango; superfluous; tempting; ecstatic; facile; catchy; pert; lilting; rollicking; romantic.

verbs
accompany—; arrange—; bleat—; carol—; chant—; coax—from; compose—; fake (colloq.)—; fiddle—; harmonize—; hum—; march to—; modulate—; orchestrate—; recall—; render—; score—; strike up—; synchronize—; transpose—; trill—; twitter—; vocalize—; warble—; yodel—; —amuses; —delights; —lilts.
(See ditty, air, incantation, song, music.)

TUNE (*v*)

adverbs
automatically; professionally; skillfully; accurately; melodiously; delicately; deftly.
(See adjust.)

TUNEFUL

adverbs
pleasantly; merrily; happily; melodiously; musically; rhythmically; childishly; naturally; delightfully; simply; sweetly; smoothly; harmoniously; joyously; joyfully; boyishly.

TUNIC

adjectives
sleeveless; spotless; ungirlish; velvet; adamantine; rich; gauzy; revealing.

TUNNEL

adjectives
deep-level; brilliant; unsupported; signaled; clattering; hot; long; snowy; stuffy.

verbs
blast—; blockade—; bore—; burrow—; drive—through; engineer—; gouge out—; guide through—; patrol—; project—; seal—; —couples; —facilitates; —gapes; —links; —pierces; —penetrates; —unites; —yawns.
(See tube, conduit, pipe.)

TURBID

adverbs
peculiarly; singularly; slightly; unfortunately; significantly; unpleasantly; momentarily; temporarily; definitely; particularly; noticeably; obviously.

TURBULENCE

adjectives
licentious; bloody; infantile; bewildering; riotous; frightening; raucous; nasty.

TURBULENT

adverbs
shamefully; riotously; raucously; ruthlessly; desperately; tumultuously; mutinously; uproariously; unmanageably; ungovernably; violently; recklessly; frightfully; implacably; unappeasably; vengefully; brazenly; murderously; unreasoningly; wildly; furiously; madly; dangerously; ominously; significantly.

TURF

adjectives
trodden; moss-inwoven; firm; flowery; frost-bit; close-cropped; wet; spongy; emerald; springing; fine; mountain; ragged; crisp; compact; unscarred.

verbs
corrugate—; delve in—; furrow—; fertilize—; gambol on—; level—; mar—; plow under—; replace—; smooth—; tamp—; trim—; —beautifies; —blankets; —extends; —greens; —mats; —pads; —mow.
(See meadow, grass, tract, ground.)

TURKEY

verbs

carve—; dine on—; domesticate—; gun for —; market—s; pluck—; roast—; savor—; spice—; —dances about; —displays feathers; —s flock; —flutters; —gobbles; —gyrates; —hovers; —preens; —rakes; —ranges; —stirs up; —strokes; —struts; —symbolizes; —wheels.

(See bird, fowl, rooster.)

TURMOIL

adjectives

fierce; urban; destructive; strenuous; stern; bloody; hideous; historic; whizzing; noisy.

verbs

embroil in—; ferment—; foment—; provoke —; quiet—; throw into—; tranquillize—; —accompanies; —agitates; —confuses; —convulses; —deranges; —dishevels; —disquiets; —distracts; —diverts; —follows; —persists; —perturbs; —prevails; —ruffles; —seethes; —tangles.

(See commotion, tumult, confusion.)

TURN

adjectives

romantic; radical; light; extravagant; ostentatious; countless (pl); sensational; administrative; thoughtful; comic; sudden; good; fanciful; melodic; sentimental; epigrammatical; satirical; intimate; unquiet; conversational; unexpected; cynical; artificial; marvelous.

TURN (v)

adverbs

snarlingly; tortuously; petulantly; sinuously; deviously; abruptly; reluctantly; gracefully; deliberately; solemnly; imploringly; exultingly; doggedly; awkwardly; distractedly; insensibly; instinctively; wearily; amiably; insolently; involuntarily; perversely; radiantly; wistfully; simultaneously; disdainfully; capriciously; resolutely; grudgingly; noiselessly; miraculously; indifferently; discreetly; energetically; listlessly; treacherously.

(See spin, revolve.)

TURNING

adjectives

incessant; gentle; fateful; acute; accurate.

TURRET

adjectives

squat; glittering; highest; equal; sequestered; fading; fort.

verbs

armor—; beseige—; command—; festoon—; fortify—; hover over—; imprison in—; level—; mount to—; perch on—; plate—; raze—; surmount—; topple from—; train —s; view from—; —looms; —revolves; —rotates.

(See tower, spire, cannon.)

TURTLE

verbs

capture—; crush—; market—s; relish—; stew—; —s abound; —attains; —breeds; —burrows; —calls; —creeps; —deposits eggs; —exudes; —hibernates; —hisses; —paddles; —perseveres; —protrudes; —snaps at; —snatches; —submerges; —swims; —swishes; —withdraws.

(See reptile.)

TUSKS

adjectives

enormous; ingrown; valuable; sharp; spiral; protective.

TUTOR

adjectives

threadbare; lively; shrewd; deft; skilled; wise; experienced.

TWANG

adjectives

nasal; familiar; peevish; provincial; annoying.

TWANG (v)

adverbs

exasperatingly; nasally; sharply; tunelessly; harshly; hideously; annoyingly; peevishly.

(See sound.)

TWEEDS

adjectives

imported; sturdy; roughish; rugged; inevitable; exquisite; handsome; hand-loomed.

TWIG

adjectives

tired; overhanging; unsightly; fragile; hardwood; insignificant; bleak; upreared;

nervous; gleaming; thorny; threatening; ice-coated; crackling.

verbs
bend—; brace—; burden—; clip—; deform —; gather—s; glean—s; ingraft—; prune —s; restrain—; snip off—; support—; thin out—s; —bears; —projects; —protrudes; —shoots out; —spreads.
(See branch, stem.)

TWILIGHT

adjectives
brightening; silvery; sad; deepening; dark; gruesome; obscure; intermediate; shadowy; cool; brilliant; dubious; rainy; darkling; dim; amber; perpetual; magical; unhurried; blank; uncomfortable; slow-dropping; white; disastrous; sulphurous; mystic; thickening; fading; wintry; gathering; winsome; mournful; ancient; departing; hollow; summer; hot; breathless; hesitant; lingering; hushed; mellow; stilly; dense; chilling; luminous; balmy; sympathetic; beautiful; closing.

verbs
approach—; bathe in—; flicker in—; melt into—; reflect—; twinkle in—; —bedims; —creeps upon; —curtails; —curtains; —declines; —deepens; —descends; —diffuses; —dims; —drapes; —fades; —gathers 'round; —glimmers; —hazes; —obscures; —screens; —shades; —shadows; —veils; —wanes; —wraps; —yields to.
(See night, dusk, evening, light, shadow.)

TWILIGHT

adverbs
faintly; delicately; rosily; dully; dimly; windily; fearsomely; beautifully; seductively; romantically; unforgettably; roseately; coldly; darksomely.

TWIN

adjectives
tributary; fraternal; identical.

adverbs
identically; attractively; apparently; interestingly; affectionately; perplexingly; inseparably.

TWINE (*v*)

adverbs
caressingly; nervously; tortuously; affectionately; complicatedly; intricately; involvedly; abundantly.
(See cling, fasten.)

TWINGE

adjectives
warning; smart; hereditary; conscience; painful.

TWINKLE

adjectives
humorous; rapid; peculiar; vicious; merry; mischievous; lewd.

TWINKLE (*v*)

adverbs
jovially; frostily; softly; luminously; merrily; humorously; peculiarly; mischievously.
(See shimmer, shine.)

TWINKLING

adverbs
brightly; keenly; sharply; affectionately; fondly; mischievously; laughingly; distinctly; irregularly; unmistakably; wittily; brilliantly; intermittently; regularly; indulgently; actually; significantly.

TWIRL (*v*)

adverbs
nonchalantly; languidly; fiercely; gallantly; sophisticatedly; idly; picturesquely.
(See whirl, revolve.)

TWIST

adjectives
infernal; dexterous; restless; worst; spiral; heroic; antique; unusual; brutal.

TWIST (*v*)

adverbs
deftly; drearily; slyly; dexterously; insidiously; craftily; tortuously; superciliously; infernally; ruthlessly; restlessly; brutally; viciously.
(See contort, coil.)

TWIT (*v*)

adverbs
facetiously; vindictively; maliciously; remorselessly; hatefully; spitefully; humorously; comically; blithely; impudently.
(See chide, reproach.)

TWITCH

adjectives

involuntary; vicious; innocent; agonized; virulent.

TWITCH (v)

adverbs

convulsively; weakly; spasmodically; abnormally; morbidly; pathologically; agitatedly; agonizingly.

(See snatch, jerk.)

TWITCHING

adjectives

uneasy; nervous; spasmodic; convulsive.

TWITTER (v)

adverbs

melodiously; sweetly; blithesomely; merrily; innumerably; irritatingly; maddeningly.

(See chirp, sing.)

TWO-FACED

adverbs

despicably; undoubtedly; contemptibly; deceptively; smoothly; smugly; suavely; grossly; subtly; unexpectedly; shamefully; treacherously; disloyally; naturally; craftily; adroitly; artfully; cunningly; slyly.

TYPE

adjectives

innocent; contemplative; existing; rugged; barren; conspicuous; temperamental; severe; shiftless; civilized; austere; myriad (pl); constitutional; conventional; coadequate; psychologic; dominant; nonpareil; sturdy; various (pl); individual; girlish; attentive; established; militant; conceivable; pompous; delicious; feline; ritualist; unchangeable; spirited; aristocratic; unscrupulous; dignified; tender; vulgar; manufactured; dominant; prevalent; fatalistic; chest-heaving; unrealized; faddist; charming; aesthetic; engrossing; delectable; bachelor; evanescent; heroic; spontaneous; gamin; characteristic; unfamiliar; representative; transcendent; malignant; florid; picturesque; myopic; marrying; original; objectionable; intellectual; innumerable (pl); indigenous; ethnic; conceivable; ingenue; lax; crackling; beautiful; primitive; preferred; didactic; elaborate; primeval; favorable; man-hunting; superficial; hideous; perverted; uncanny; consummate; sunny; manifold (pl); lofty.

verbs

breed—; cast—; characterize—; classify—; conceive—; conform to—; denote—; depict—; designate—; determine—; distinguish—; efface—; enact—; exploit—; fall into—; hew—; idealize—; mold—; portray—; register—; reproduce—; revert to—; specify—; warp—; —embodies; —embraces; —includes; —mystifies; —perplexes.

(See symbol, style, class, model, print.)

TYPE (v)

adverbs

individually; swiftly; accurately; originally; consummately; characteristically.

(See represent.)

TYPEWRITER

verbs

bang—; instruct on—; lubricate—; manipulate—; master—; necessitate—; overhaul—; peck at—; pound on—; service—s; silence—; —clicks; —clatters; —disconcerts; —distracts; —disturbs; —eases; —enables; —facilitates; —lightens; —plagues; —rings; —shifts.

TYPHOON

verbs

—abates; —batters; —devastates; —endangers; —howls; —rages; —ravages; —revolves; —roars; —shrieks; —subsides; —sweeps; —topples; —trammels; —uproots; —whirls.

(See hurricane, blizzard, storm.)

TYPICAL

adverbs

absolutely; entirely; truly; accurately; dependably; reliably; substantially; realistically; symbolically; curiously; incidentally; satisfactorily; approximately; exactly; unerringly; distinctly; indicatively; graphically.

TYRANNICAL

adverbs

quietly; adroitly; unendurably; imperiously;

confidently; socially; selfishly; hopelessly; sweetly; gracefully; wantonly; unscrupulously; insupportably; inexorably; cruelly; vindictively; remorselessly; ruthlessly; intolerably; unreasonably; dangerously; viciously; heartlessly; recklessly; outrageously.

TYRANNY

adjectives

municipal; barefaced; odious; clerical; decided; quiet; adroit; unendurable; imperious; worn-out; watchful; confident; social; selfish; hopeless; legal; grinding; sweet; graceful; wanton; petty; unscrupulous; exacting; insupportable.

verbs

exercise—; impose—upon; inflict with—; germinate—; overthrow—; resist—; revolt against—; savor of—; subject to—; —abuses; —crushes; —distresses; —enslaves; —fetters; —harasses; —oppresses; —restricts; —shackles; —tramples; —treads on; —yokes.

(See despotism, domination, persecution.)

TYRANT

adjectives

unpersuaded; professed; inexorable; implacable; early; despotic; cunning; cruel; sportive; petty; vindictive; remorseless; domestic; power-mad; avaricious; guiltiest; benevolent; invaluable; feminine; pious; sanguinary; ambitious; maniacal; haughty; cloud-piercing; usurping.

verbs

oppose—; play—; prove—; rebel against—; repel—; resist—; serve—; submit to—; —administers; —arrogates; —assumes; —beguiles; —butchers; —coerces; —crushes; —dictates; —domineers; —enslaves; —oppresses; —overrides; —persecutes; —subjugates; —tramples; —usurps; —wields; —yokes.

(See dictator, oppressor; monarch; sovereign.)

U

UBIQUITOUS

adverbs
valuably; extraordinarily; comically; importantly; dominantly; aggressively; conspicuously; pompously; curiously; apparently; eagerly; officiously; ostentatiously; undeniably; proudly; quietly; assertively; enterprisingly; busily; actively; patronizingly.

UGLINESS

adjectives
racy; grotesque; ultimate; shapeless; unmitigated; bare; insipid; ferocious; grim; bestial.

verbs
abhor—; accentuate—; aggravate—; deplore—; dispel—; efface—; enhance—; heighten—; lament—; level—; mitigate—; portray—; revolt at—; —blemishes; —defaces; —deforms; —distorts; —embitters; —mars; —pervades; —robs; —sours; —weighs upon.
(See squalor, deformity.)

UGLY

adverbs
awkwardly; fantastically; grotesquely; amusingly; repulsively; pathetically; unbelievably; distressingly; angularly; terribly; horribly; oddly; touchingly; grievously; ludicrously; ridiculously; deplorably; lamentably; singularly; drolly; strangely; queerly; curiously; forbiddingly; frightfully; grossly; clumsily; hideously; grimly; shockingly.

ULCER

verbs
afflict with—s; cauterize—; detect—; expose—; poultice—; probe—; remedy—; salve—; suffer from—; —blemishes; —blights; —cankers; —cicatrizes; —deteriorates; —devours; —disfigures; —erodes; —festers; —infiltrates; —inflames; —rankles; —ravages; —scars; —scathes; —spreads; —taints.
(See abscess, canker, inflammation, blister, sore, cancer.)

ULCEROUS

adverbs
unfortunately; fatally; seriously; slightly; annoyingly; unpleasantly; disagreeably; presumably; obviously; gnawingly; dangerously; alarmingly; chronically; recently; acutely; painfully; disturbingly; distressingly; unaccountably; finally; extremely.

ULTIMATE

verbs
acclaim—; achieve—; afford—; anticipate—; apply—; attain—; dedicate to—; delay—; demand—; determine—; employ—; gain—; necessitate—; proclaim—; seek—; survive—; temporize—; undergo—; waive—; —endures.
(See extreme, goal, aim.)

adverbs
irrevocably; eventually; significantly; tragically; fatally; decisively; unchangeably; hopelessly.

ULTIMATUM

verbs
accede to—; acknowledge—; bow to—; comply with—; contemplate—; contest—; decree—; deliver—; draw up—; enforce—; execute—; file—; ignore—; issue—; reject—; resist—; retract—; slap down—; thunder—; —admonishes; —demands; —impends; —stipulates; —threatens; —warns.
(See warning, demand, challenge, proposition.)

UMBRAGEOUS

adverbs
refreshingly; pleasantly; gloomily; alarmingly; dismally; mysteriously; delightfully; coolly; gratefully; sensitively; curiously; uncommonly; exceptionally; highly; unexpectedly; surprisingly; suddenly; deeply.

UMBRELLA

adjectives
ubiquitous; formidable; protective; leaking.

verbs
arm with—; borrow—; brandish—; discard—; display—; employ—; flourish—; loll under—; mislay—; resort to—; —affords;

—eclipses; —hoods; —insures; —obscures; —obstructs; —screens; —shades; —shelters; —shrouds.

(See pavilion, cane, canopy.)

UMPIRE

verbs

appeal to—; bias—; boo—; bribe—; mob—; prejudice—; protest to—; "razz"—; —admonishes; —arbitrates; —awards; —bars; —confers with; —decides; —determines; —expels; —hands down a decision; —mediates; —penalizes; —referees.

(See judge.)

UNABASHED

adverbs

courageously; frankly; innocently; childishly; boldly; clearly; admirably; surprisingly; entirely; obviously; defiantly; positively; curiously; steadily; strangely; oddly; marvelously; remarkably; fearlessly; calmly; serenely; quietly; composedly; justly; brazenly.

UNACCEPTABLE

adverbs

obviously; cheaply; unfortunately; deplorably; utterly; curiously; vexatiously; embarrassingly; awkwardly; palpably; crudely; shamefully; outrageously; scandalously; seriously; hopelessly.

UNACCOMMODATING

adverbs

gruffly; ungraciously; embarrassingly; grimly; brusquely; crudely; vexatiously; churlishly; sternly; harshly; indifferently; coolly; curiously; strangely; nonchalantly; coldly; cruelly; crisply; bitterly; appraisingly; imperturbably; disturbingly; distressingly; hopelessly; perplexingly; bewilderingly; unconscionably; absurdly; insolently.

UNACCOMPANIED

adverbs

rarely; lonesomely; occasionally; forlornly; courageously; singularly; oddly; preferably; usually; noticeably; obviously; invitingly; manifestly; precariously; embarrassingly; boldly; daringly; challengingly; unfortunately; audaciously; brazenly; oddly; mysteriously; significantly; foolishly; inadvertently.

UNACCOUNTABLE

adverbs

strangely; outlandishly; utterly; perplexingly; bafflingly; apparently; curiously; challengingly.

UNACCUSTOMED

adverbs

apparently; obviously; manifestly; curiously; oddly; significantly; embarrassingly; awkwardly; clearly; appallingly; crudely.

UNADORNED

adverbs

chastely; severely; casually; deliberately; humbly; noticeably; indifferently; carelessly; distinctly; purposely; vexatiously; intentionally; significantly; curiously; remarkably; conspicuously.

UNAIDED

adverbs

surprisingly; obviously; remarkably; utterly; proudly; triumphantly; completely; curiously; manifestly; distinctly; supposedly; presumably; prescriptively; avowedly.

UNALTERABLE

adverbs

deplorably; inconveniently; officially; constitutionally; unfortunately; definitely; presumably; supposedly; luckily; tragically; wretchedly; obviously; regrettably.

UNANIMOUS

adverbs

whole-heartedly; enthusiastically; warmly; practically; absolutely; eagerly; ardently; vociferously; astonishingly; significantly; comfortingly; completely; cheerfully; sensibly; reassuringly; emphatically; impressively; promptly; gladly; miraculously; happily.

UNAPPETIZING

adverbs

dingily; insipidly; colorlessly; miserably; utterly; unfortunately; curiously; unhappily; suddenly; surprisingly; disappointingly; desperately; hopelessly; completely; dismally;

UNAPPROACHABLE

adverbs

sternly; unaccountably; reticently; gloomily;

harshly; cruelly; austerely; pompously; arrogantly; imperially; brutally; coldly; unfortunately; strangely; manifestly; forbiddingly; fearfully; frightfully; gravely; rigorously; unsmilingly; tragically; oddly.

UNASSAILABLE

adverbs
virtuously; pompously; officially; self-righteously; powerfully; imperially; royally; safely; securely; righteously; judicially; constitutionally; happily; arrogantly; presumably; haughtily; hatefully; oddly; monstrously; heartbreakingly; abominably.

UNASSUMING

adverbs
modestly; quietly; demurely; sweetly; shyly; unobtrusively; attractively; charmingly; unaffectedly; delightfully; pleasantly; habitually; naturally; agreeably; artlessly; naively; ingenuously; informally.

UNATTRACTIVE

adverbs
awkwardly; grotesquely; repulsively; unbelievably; pitiably; oddly; angularly; deplorably; strangely; fantastically; pathetically; distressingly; terribly; horridly; touchingly; ridiculously; lamentably; singularly; drolly; queerly: curiously; crudely; painfully.

UNAUTHORIZED

adverbs
blatantly; boldly; brazenly; daringly; unluckily; tragically; foolishly; rashly; recklessly; obviously; palpably; gravely; defiantly; carelessly.

UNAVOIDABLE

adverbs
regrettably; completely; vexatiously; unfortunately; unluckily; awkwardly; embarrassingly; humiliatingly; mortifyingly; incontrovertibly; frankly; fatally; allegedly; manifestly; evidently; obviously; curiously; undoubtedly; legally.

UNAWARE

adverbs
blissfully; innocently; happily; astonishingly; oddly; ironically; curiously; singularly; incredibly; strangely; incongruously; stupidly; carelessly; heedlessly; blithely; nonchalantly; blindly; absurdly.

UNBALANCED

adverbs
dangerously; obviously; palpably; outlandishly; grotesquely; crazily; manifestly; tragically; oddly; singularly; naturally; peculiarly; definitely; presumably; allegedly; unhappily; unfortunately; irresponsibly; curiously; overwhelmingly; incurably; irremediably; deplorably; wretchedly; dangerously; utterly; recently; temporarily.

UNBECOMING

adverbs
utterly; entirely; wholly; frightfully; indecorously; terribly; immodestly; uncommonly; palpably; frankly; awkwardly; exceptionally; discreditably; unworthily; extremely; shamefully; disgracefully.

UNBENDING

adverbs
cruelly; gravely; pompously; austerely; coldly; harshly; severely; bitterly; proudly; taciturnly; implacably; unappeasably; naturally; pridefully; horribly; preposterously; inconceivably; proudly.

UNBIASED

adverbs
delightfully; dependably; truly; actually; sincerely; commendably; admirably; laudably; warrantably; personally; broadly; allegedly; reputedly; avowedly; indisputably; palpably; absolutely; wholly; dispassionately; disinterestedly; fortunately; tolerantly; judiciously; luckily.

UNBURDEN (*v*)

adverbs
deliberately; remorsefully; articulately; freely; faithfully; tremulously; unconsciously.

(See relieve, empty.)

UNBUSINESSLIKE

adverbs
astonishingly; flippantly; astoundingly; disappointingly; surprisingly; curiously; absurdly; disagreeably; disconcertingly; perplexingly; disturbingly; foolishly; seriously; palpably; strangely; unaccountably; remarkably; amazingly; uncommonly; facet-

iously; annoyingly; impractically; suspiciously; evasively; equivocally; shiftily; indecisively; oddly; impossibly.

UNCANNY

adverbs
alarmingly; peculiarly; weirdly; curiously; strangely; inexplicably; unaccountably; harrowingly; oppressively; mysteriously; viciously; vaguely; unreasonably; hauntingly; gloomily; indefinably; obscurely; inescapably; absurdly; inscrutably; eerily.

UNCEREMONIOUS

adverbs
delightfully; independently; casually; pleasantly; brusquely; facetiously; gruffly; hastily; smilingly; nervously; agreeably; portentously; ominously; naturally; usually; remarkably; singularly; unexpectedly; oddly; peculiarly; characteristically; suddenly; marvellously.

UNCERTAIN

adverbs
timidly; clumsily; shyly; tremulously; blindly; feebly; pathetically; curiously; strangely; vexatiously; indecisively; oddly; miserably; wretchedly; terribly; peculiarly; singularly; significantly; awkwardly; nervously.

UNCERTAINTY

adjectives
unconscious; momentary; prevalent; full; horrible; anxious; tremulous; painful; intolerable; pleasing.

verbs
abolish—; consume—; destroy—; dispel—; efface—; erase—; exhibit—; extinguish—; falter in—; flounder in—; hesitate in—; sweep aside—; vacillate in—; wallow in—; waver in—; —clouds; —dogs; —muddles; —perplexes; —persists; —pervades; —plagues; —prevails; —shrouds; —unnerves; —veils.

(See misapprehension, ambiguity, hesitation, doubt.)

UNCHANGEABLE

adverbs
obstinately; stubbornly; obdurately; egotistically; manifestly; obviously; hopelessly; vexatiously; fatefully; dependably; officially; authoritatively; definitely; cruelly; legally; constitutionally; humanly.

UNCHARITABLE

adverbs
selfishly; narrowly; intolerantly; dogmatically; naturally; unfortunately; stubbornly; harshly; thoughtlessly; sternly; abominably; curiously; viciously; disagreeably; coldly; callously; grimly; heartlessly; terribly.

UNCHRISTIAN

adverbs
dreadfully; blatantly; defiantly; definitely; positively; abominably; appallingly; shockingly; boldly; openly; curiously; savagely; barbarously; cruelly; selfishly; flauntingly; gracelessly; indifferently; callously; horribly.

UNCIVIL

adverbs
deliberately; intentionally; significantly; challengingly; rudely; plainly; clearly; inexcusably; unpardonably; contemptibly; arrogantly; crudely; curtly; gruffly; boorishly; churlishly; dangerously; defiantly; boldly; audaciously; curiously; particularly; grossly.

UNCLEAN

adverbs
odiously; squalidly; grossly; obscenely; singularly; indescribably; detestably; abominably; despicably; offensively; disgustingly; impiously; carelessly; arrantly; grievously; scandalously; disastrously; shamefully; infamously; infectiously; horribly; noxiously; deleteriously.

UNCOMFORTABLE

adverbs
definitely; painfully; distressingly; unpleasantly; horribly; dangerously; utterly; coldly; dimly; obscurely; inexcusably; shamefully; uneasily; genuinely; needlessly; extremely; exceedingly; curiously; devilishly; confoundedly; thoroughly; strangely; physically; angrily; embarrassingly; outrageously.

UNCOMMUNICATIVE

adverbs
disagreeably; unsociably; resolutely; doggedly; awkwardly; taciturnly; secretively;

deliberately; stubbornly; loyally; silently; profoundly; determinedly; unpleasantly; desperately; hopelessly; reticently; obstinately; evasively; unflinchingly; exceptionally; immovably; extraordinarily; hopelessly.

UNCOMPLAINING

adverbs
submissively; humbly; curiously; docilely; wisely; fearfully; meekly; singularly; doggedly; resolutely; sullenly; cheerfully; timidly; astutely; craftily; suspiciously; helplessly; shrewdly; patiently; sagaciously; discreetly; cunningly; prudently; knowingly.

UNCOMPLIMENTARY

adverbs
obviously; openly; subtly; maliciously; enviously; terribly; suavely; derisively; cunningly; insidiously; meanly; jealously; smartly; venomously; scandalously; deleteriously; libellously; slightly; highly; unreasonably; curiously; singularly; particularly; smoothly; definitely; contemptibly; deliberately; dreadfully; appallingly; shockingly.

UNCOMPROMISING

adverbs
stiffly; rigidly; unappeasably; obstinately; stubbornly; doctrinally; piously; dogmatically; puritannically; impossibly; terribly; disagreeably; unpleasantly; austerely; severely; sternly; cruelly; brutally; frankly; boldly; truculently; turbulently; gruffly; callously; definitely; indomitably; inexorably; resolutely; fanatically; proudly; arrogantly.

UNCONCERNED

adverbs
indifferently; nonchalantly; blithely; happily; selfishly; thoughtlessly; blindly; ignorantly; pathetically; terribly; deliberately; inconsiderately; curiously; ominously; apparently; singularly; absurdly; strangely; unnaturally; abominably.

UNCONDITIONAL

adverbs
presumably; allegedly; entirely; happily; fortunately; liberally; definitely; constitutionally; practically; generously; broadly; flatly; gloriously; triumphantly; reliably.

UNCONGENIAL

adverbs
unhappily; obviously; bitterly; oddly; surprisingly; helplessly; terribly; dreadfully; intolerably; unfortunately; hopelessly; desperately; singularly; definitely; temperamentally; ominously; fearfully.

UNCONSCIOUS

adverbs
blindly; childishly; selfishly; pathetically; happily; blissfully; momentarily; temporarily; singularly; apparently; obviously; manifestly; presumably; undoubtedly.

UNCONSCIOUSNESS

verbs
approach—; arouse from—; avert—; diagnose—; dope into—; drug into—; fade into —; feign—; hover near—; lapse into—; pretend—; repose in—; shock into—; sink into—; stun into—; —deadens; —endures; —paralyzes; —persists; —seals; —terrifies. (See coma, lethargy.)

UNCONSTITUTIONAL

adverbs
odiously; presumably; flagrantly; supposedly; lamentably; dangerously; daringly; defiantly; trickily; craftily; definitely; manifestly; openly; incontrovertibly; postively; decidedly; flagitiously; unfortunately.

UNCONVENTIONAL

adverbs
absurdly; ridiculously; flauntingly; flagrantly; daringly; slightly; oddly; peculiarly; astonishingly; surprisingly; quaintly; sweetly; singularly; notionally; delightfully; outlandishly; shamefully; purposely; attractively; refreshingly; vexatiously; bewilderingly; unpleasantly; boorishly; crudely.

UNCOUTH

adverbs
rudely; boorishly; naturally; inexcusably; lamentably; awkwardly; fantastically; inordinately; contemptibly; colossally; shockingly; drunkenly; impudently; morosely; unpleasantly; disagreeably; deliberately; boisterously; blatantly; offensively; insufferably; innately; intolerably; unbearably.

UNCOUTHNESS

adjectives
vain; awkward; embarrassing.

UNCOVER (*v*)

adverbs
mercilessly; ruthlessly; searchingly; diligently; fruitfully; formidably; slyly; grimly; cruelly; despotically; cunningly.
(See reveal, disclose.)

UNCTUOUS

adverbs
disgustingly; professionally; pedantically; smugly; blandly; intolerably; obsequiously; submissively; deceptively; ominously; maddeningly; solemnly; softly; persuasively; carefully; properly; ingratiatingly; suavely; adroitly.

UNDAUNTED

adverbs
resolutely; intrepidly; courageously; blithely; gaily; serenely; calmly; curiously; remarkably; gallantly; laughingly; grimly; absurdly; foolishly; daringly; recklessly; apparently; singularly; confidently; amazingly.

UNDECIPHERABLE

adverbs
sadly; strangely; unfortunately; childishly; dimly; curiously; singularly; vexatiously; awkwardly; disappointingly; heartbreakingly; inexcusably; unpardonably; unreasonably; significantly; deliberately; intentionally; craftily; purposely; cruelly.

UNDEMONSTRATIVE

adverbs
habitually; naturally; inherently; significantly; coolly; surprisingly; perplexingly; churlishly; ungratefully; meanly; disappointingly; shyly; bashfully; modestly; awkwardly; demurely; augustly; sternly; forbiddingly; painfully; curiously; oddly; calmly; chillingly; unluckily; unfortunately; temperamentally.

UNDERGO (*v*)

adverbs
heroically; gallantly; stoically; generously; willingly; staunchly; courageously; peacefully.
(See endure, experience.)

UNDERHANDED

adverbs
wickedly; curiously; significantly; nefariously; despicably; detestably; craftily; shrewdly; carefully; mysteriously; cunningly; abominably; adroitly; atrociously; cruelly; disgracefully; basely; viciously; grossly.

UNDERNOURISHED

adverbs
pathetically; cruelly; undeniably; positively; definitely; obviously; miserably; wretchedly; pitiably; dangerously; alarmingly; desperately; helplessly; hopelessly; unconsciously; generally; surprisingly; deplorably; unwisely; impecuniously; dreadfully; terribly; inexcusably; recently; emphatically; bitterly.

UNDERPAID

adverbs
contemptibly; inexcusably; cruelly; terribly; needlessly; obviously; absurdly; remarkably; preposterously; presumably; manifestly; definitely; wretchedly; miserably; unwarrantably; emphatically.

UNDERSCORE (*v*)

adverbs
heavily; blackly; redundantly; indelibly.
(See mark.)

UNDERSELL (*v*)

adverbs
astutely; ethically; secretively; legitimately; momentously; boldly; financially; desperately.
(See transact, win.)

UNDERSTAND (*v*)

adverbs
literally; distinctly; cleverly; dimly; sympathetically; expressly; properly; assuredly; intimately; vaguely; keenly; accurately; theoretically; adequately; subtly; exceptionally; shrewdly; sympathetically; tacitly.
(See comprehend, discern.)

UNDERSTANDING

adjectives
friendly; robust; keen; previous; courteous; prospective; analytical; theoretical; adequate; subtle; slow; unconscious; instinctive; definite; speedy; cynical; cordial; synthetic; useful; retrospective; close; general; comprehensive; masculine; profound; dis-

cursive; exceptional; enlarged; vague; chronic; secret; veiled; barren; shrewd; human; distinct; mutual; kind; sympathetic; furtive; mean; emotional; tacit; verbal; momentary; consummate; full-bodied.

verbs
achieve—; acquire—; arrive at—; attain—; awaken—; blossom into—; chill—; convey to —; demonstrate—; destroy—; display—; engrave on—; enlarge—; enlighten—; enrich —; enter into—; escape—; evince—; feign —; foster—; further—; gain—; grasp—; grope for—; illuminate—; impart—; impede—; inhibit—; lack—; lead to—; manifest—; obtain—; promote—; reflect—; require—; school—; seek—; swell—; temper with—; yield to—; —dawns; —discerns; —discriminates; —harmonizes; —pacifies; —tranquillizes; —triumphs.
(See insight, knowledge, commonsense, intellect, learning.)

adverbs
sympathetically; generously; pleasantly; unusually; remarkably; helpfully; patiently; profoundly; momentarily; marvellously; mercifully; completely.

UNDERTAKE (v)

adverbs
sporadically; rashly; reluctantly; successfully; boldly; ill-advisedly; illicitly; scientifically; desperately; hazardously; perilously; grimly; ridicuously; arduously; financially.
(See assume.)

UNDERTAKING

adjectives
scientific; tangible; desperate; unconnected; momentous; remarkable; bold; spurious; aimless; conciliatory; hazardous; chimerical; illicit; solemn; important; tremendous; munificent; unparalleled; perilous; grim; exciting; ridiculous; involved; arduous; herculean; stupendous; desperate; formidable; financial.

verbs
abandon—; analyze—; bind to—; commend —; conceive—; desert—; encourage—; endanger—; essay—; forego—; forestall—; forsake—; insure—; jeopardize—; laud—; outline—; plan—; relinquish—; promote—; renounce—; tackle—; venture on—; withdraw from—; —embraces; —endeavors; —flourishes; —promises; —thrives.
(See enterprise, plan, deal, program.)

UNDISMAYED

adverbs
gallantly; confidently; optimistically; curiously; admirably; wondrously; apparently; evidently; fortunately; recklessly; pathetically; courageously; singularly; fanatically; zealously; blindly; imperturbably; astonishingly; surprisingly; remarkably; significantly; audaciously; absurdly; arrogantly; brashly.

UNDISTURBED

adverbs
serenely; blindly; stoically; pedantically; witlessly; irresponsibly; calmly; vexatiously; infuriatingly; strangely; amazingly; suspiciously; blandly; unaccountably; surprisingly; philosophically.

UNDULATE (v)

adverbs
restlessly; incessantly; sinuously; gently.
(See wave, curve.)

UNDULATING

adverbs
regularly; smoothly; endlessly; restlessly; dizzily; disturbingly; monotonously; ceaselessly; pleasantly; arably; advantageously; fortunately; crazily; fascinatingly; delightfully; curiously; vastly; extensively; mysteriously; iridescently; colorfully; singularly; marvellously; incessantly; continuously.

UNDUTIFUL

adverbs
curiously; desperately; disagreeably; cruelly; heartbreakingly; incorrigibly; blindly; bitterly; inexcusably; terribly; singularly; coldly; strangely; unquestionably; unbelievably; incredibly; preposterously; shamefully; miserably; unwarrantably; unconcernedly.

UNEASINESS

adjectives
longing; vague; transitory; abrupt; idle; restless; faint; unhappy; growing.

verbs
afflict with—; allay—; assuage—; burden with—; calm—; dispel—; experience—; inspire—; ridicule—; scoff at—; sense—; sweep away—; —accompanies; —distresses;

—dwells in; —envelopes; —gnaws at; —haunts; —oppresses; —persists; —pervades; —prevails; —shrouds; —stabs; —takes hold; —unnerves; —weighs upon; —yields.

(See impatience, discomfort, discontent, anxiety.)

UNEASY

adverbs
naturally; timidly; shyly; unacountably; suddenly; justifiably; unusually; extremely; unnecessarily; needlessly; oddly; ominously; visibly; seriously; obviously; inexplicably; painfully; foolishly; distinctly; inordinately; apparently; profoundly.

UNEDUCATED

adverbs
frankly; unfortunately; academically; supposedly; paradoxically; blessedly; blatantly; strangely; apparently; coarsely; grossly; avowedly; allegedly; manifestly.

UNEMOTIONAL

adverbs
coldly; sternly; gravely; terrifyingly; brutally; harshly; austerely; stoically; unbelievably; unnaturally; abnormally; strangely; singularly; frightfully; ungenerously; stingily; selfishly; terribly; peculiarly; notoriously; reputedly; ostensibly; presumably; conspicuously.

UNEMPLOYED

adverbs
idly; lazily; indolently; unfortunately; miserably; helplessly; inadvertently; unhappily; temporarily; evidently; frequently; manifestly; involuntarily.

UNEMPLOYMENT

adjectives
technological; devastating; partial; continued; nation-wide; artificially-relieved; supposed; appalling; dreaded; frightening.

verbs
absorb—; analyze—; augment—; banish—; bewail—; cancel out—; cause—; check—; decrease—; decry—; deplore—; fear—; increase—; insure against—; legislate against —; lament—; outlaw—; predict—; reduce —; relieve—; remedy—; tackle—; —breeds; —depresses; —deprives; —diminishes; —dwindles; —endangers; —mitigates; —oppresses; —overwhelms; —ravages; —satirizes; —scourges; —shelves; —sweeps; —victimizes.

UNEVEN

adverbs
curiously; perilously; raggedly; roughly; inconveniently; unpleasantly; unjustly; inequitably; unfairly; meanly; disagreeably; absurdly; sadly; crookedly.

UNEVENTFUL

adverbs
tiresomely; dully; flatly; uninterestingly; boresomely; monotonously; curiously; unexpectedly; unpardonably; undeniably; tediously; restfully; fortunately; blessedly; smoothly; conspicuously; placidly; utterly; happily.

UNEXPECTED

adverbs
provokingly; bewilderingly; curiously; utterly; unfeignedly; pitifully; sadly; completely; tragically; suddenly; stunningly; startlingly; terribly; obviously; manifestly; undoubtedly.

UNFAILING

adverbs
blessedly; presumably; generously; usually; reliably; notoriously; reputedly; supposedly; manifestly; miraculously; apparently; conspicuously; notably; dependably; reliably.

UNFAIR

adverbs
manifestly; terribly; openly; flagrantly; abominably; shamefully; cruelly; bitterly; egregiously; despicably; maliciously; unmistakably; daringly; deliberately; dishonorably; uncommonly; secretly; greedily; arrogantly; high-handedly; atrociously.

UNFAIRNESS

verbs
ameliorate—; avenge—; avert—; betray—; condone—; denounce—; deplore—; disclose —; divulge—; mitigate—; rebuke—; remedy—; reveal—; uncover—; —colors; —distorts; —embroiders; —garbles; —glosses over; —taints.

(See injustice, partiality, grievance, wrong.)

UNFAITHFUL

adverbs

notoriously; allegedly; conspicuously; flagrantly; openly; terribly; carelessly; cruelly; irresponsibly; treacherously; curiously; secretly; furtively; actually; presumably; recklessly; undependably; intolerably; abominably; wickedly; viciously; reprehensibly; provokingly; vexatiously; unbearably; unprofitably; deplorably; uselessly; surreptitiously; heinously; wretchedly; miserably; definitely; despicably; detestably; dreadfully; worthlessly; incorrigibly.

UNFAITHFULNESS

verbs

absolve of—; atone for—; avenge—; bear —; breed—; charge—; display—; evince —; expiate—; forgive—; foster—; frown upon—; punish—; regret—; repent—; rue —; —beckons; —disgraces; —dishonors; —tempts.

(See infidelity, insincerity, treachery.)

UNFAMILIAR

adverbs

sadly; embarrassingly; awkwardly; admittedly; evidently; obviously; unconcealably; tragically; helplessly; hopelessly; self-consciously; openly; shamelessly; unsophisticatedly; dreadfully; ineptly; oddly.

UNFASHIONABLE

adverbs

daringly; audaciously; carelessly; slouchily; untidily; dowdily; independently; boldly; recklessly; openly; definitely; admittedly; artistically; strikingly; smartly; ridiculously; bizarrely; ludicrously; intentionally; serenely; indifferently; consciously; naturally; curiously; magnificently; arrogantly; negligently; barbarically; casually; nonchalantly; happily; blithely; thoughtlessly; emphatically; positively; flippantly; notoriously; unashamedly; interestingly; vexatiously; laughingly; foolishly; unwisely.

UNFASTEN (v)

adverbs

readily; automatically; easily; tremblingly; carelessly; artfully; deftly; customarily; strategically.

(See release, relieve.)

UNFATHOMABLE

adverbs

obscurely; mysteriously; darkly; dimly; vaguely; impenetrably; nebulously; perplexingly; eternally; wondrously; abstrusely; muddily; mystically; occultly; inscrutably; puzzlingly; reconditely; unaccountably; unreasonably; irrationally; profoundly; abysmally; infinitely; perpetually; forever.

UNFAVORABLE

adverbs

definitely; unappeasably; uncompromisingly; defiantly; rebelliously; forbiddingly; discouragingly; resolutely; sternly; implacably; emphatically; downright; openly; secretly; surreptitiously; ominously; undeniably; influentially; indifferently; actively; mildly; positively; energetically; dangerously; frankly; expressly; harshly; powerfully; lamentably; fortuitously; stubbornly.

UNFEELING

adverbs

callously; cruelly; coldly; downright; evidently; curiously; strangely; obdurately; implacably; terribly; preposterously; extremely; inexplainably; utterly; harshly; stubbornly; wickedly; brutally; unbelievably; selfishly; incredibly; unimaginably; singularly; viciously; stonily; inhumanly; sternly; austerely; heartlessly.

UNFEIGNED

adverbs

clearly; unquestionably; perceptibly; ingenuously; apparently.

UNFILIAL

adverbs

unnaturally; strangely; horribly; appallingly; incredibly; unreasonably; utterly; unimaginably; astoundingly; justifiably; eventually; sadly; deplorably; wretchedly; miserably; curiously; strangely; remarkably; terribly; inexplicably; ungratefully; inconsiderately; heartbreakingly; surprisingly; stonily; openly.

UNFINISH (v)

adverbs

deservedly; carelessly; sadly; incomprehensibly; unwisely; improvidently.

(See cease, stop.)

UNFIT

adverbs
palpably; altogether; manifestly; allegedly; presumably; ostensibly; utterly; temperamentally; physically; morally; lamentably; deplorably; miserably; wretchedly; curiously; downright.

UNFLINCHING

adverbs
courageously; sturdily; staunchly; boldly; steadily; splendidly; chivalrously; admirably; surprisingly; quietly; imperturbably; firmly; gallantly; heroically; marvellously; magnificently.

UNFOLD (v)

adverbs
beauteously; swiftly; joyously; vividly; prominently; maturely.

(See reveal, uncover.)

UNFORGIVING

adverbs
uncompromisingly; sternly; austerely; seriously; gravely; censoriously; callously; unmercifully; coldly; obdurately; stubbornly; hopelessly; wretchedly; unfortunately; curiously; pharisaically; harshly.

UNFORTUNATE

adverbs
sadly; miserably; tragically; wretchedly; chronically; direly; unexpectedly; suddenly; shamefully; surprisingly; terribly; really; unusually; strangely; oddly; naturally; extremely.

UNFREQUENTED

adverbs
usually; perilously; dangerously; hazardously; notoriously; notably; conspicuously; riskily; unpleasantly; desolately; gloomily; eerily.

UNFRIENDLY

adverbs
cruelly; bitterly; terribly; unreasonably; meanly; hatefully; spitefully; strangely; unwontedly; suddenly; curiously; unwarrantably; disagreeably; snobbishly; inexcusably; churlishly; boorishly; narrow-mindedly; intolerantly; uncharitably; discouragingly; painfully; extremely; uncommonly.

UNFURL (v)

adverbs
automatically; gallantly; awesomely; impressively; picturesquely.

(See release, unfold.)

UNGAINLY

adverbs
miserably; unfortunately; comically; undeniably; terribly; dreadfully; unpleasantly; sadly; curiously; particularly; conspicuously; pathetically; oddly; clumsily; positively; laughably; regrettably; unsuitably; nonchalantly; carelessly; slouchily; indifferently; blandly.

UNGENEROUS

adverbs
surprisingly; suddenly; appallingly; unexpectedly; curiously; unluckily; shockingly; miserably; short-sightedly; foolishly; unwisely; intolerantly; uncharitably; bigotedly; narrowly; terribly; dreadfully; uncommonly.

UNGODLY

adverbs
shamefully; unconscionably; surprisingly; flagrantly; openly; flauntingly; shockingly; appallingly; atrociously; blasphemously; impiously; despicably; offensively; heartbreakingly; viciously; daringly; wickedly; conspicuously; dreadfully; strangely.

UNGOVERNABLE

adverbs
sadly; gracelessly; conspicuously; heinously; highly; inexplicably; atrociously; incomprehensibly; suddenly; sometimes; habitually; boldly; defiantly; mutinously; hopelessly; dreadfully; dangerously; violently; curiously; occasionally; eventually; admittedly; terribly.

UNGRACIOUS

adverbs
curtly; strangely; oddly; significantly; conspicuously; unaccountably; curiously; momentarily; deliberately; intentionally; pointedly; dreadfully; unwontedly; purposely; regrettably; sadly; unfortunately; inadvertently; clumsily; unintentionally; awkwardly; snobbishly.

UNGRATEFUL

adverbs
boorishly; ignorantly; selfishly; indifferently; thoughtlessly; callously; incredibly; unbelievably; oddly; terribly; crassly; grossly; significantly; dreadfully; coldly; stupidly; shamefully; remarkably; unpardonably; astoundingly; cruelly; arrogantly.

UNGUARDED

adverbs
carelessly; inadvertently; momentarily; indifferently; temporarily; insecurely; crassly; strangely; inexplicably; happily; unaccountably; blessedly; advantageously; fortuitously; trustfully; stupidly; incautiously; unexpectedly; seldom; rarely.

UNHANDY

adverbs
deucedly; vexatiously; terribly; foolishly; wastefully; frequently; dreadfully; downright; admittedly; curiously; short-sightedly; extravagantly.

UNHAPPINESS

verbs
bear—; curse with—; dispel—; endure—; evince—; exhibit—; languish in—; lessen—; mitigate—; mollify—; soothe—; suffer—; undergo—; —afflicts; —blasts; —blights; —burdens; —clouds; —crucifies; —dampens; —dejects; —depresses; —desolates; —pervades; —prostrates; —racks; —sprouts; —stabs; —torments; —weighs upon.

(See pathos, distress, misery, sadness.)

UNHAPPY

adverbs
cruelly; bitterly; sadly; desolately; gloomily; moodily; naturally; terribly; dreadfully; unaccountably; inexplicably; curiously; particularly; selfishly; childishly; painfully; admittedly; sullenly; particularly; helplessly; hopelessly; desperately; suddenly; eventually; openly; obviously; frankly; wretchedly; miserably.

UNHEALTHY

adverbs
definitely; terribly; curiously; naturally; apparently; malarially; obviously; manifestly; unfortunately; wickedly; oddly; positively; miserably; wretchedly; congenitally.

UNHOLY

adverbs
frightfully; blasphemously; impiously; terribly; accursedly; profanely; sacrilegiously; wantonly; carelessly; recklessly; appallingly; flippantly; execrably; damnably; dreadfully; horribly.

UNIFORM

adjectives
brilliant; handsome; full; striking; undress; continuous; resplendent; finished; glittering; shabby; outstanding; greasy; practical; gorgeous; dress; gaudy.

verbs
array in—; besmirch—; bestow—s; defile—; discard—; dishonor—; divest of—; don—; espy—; frill—; invest in—; march in—; masquerade in—; recognize—; strip of—; tatter—; —attracts; —denotes; —flatters; —impresses; —symbolizes; —stamps one as; —betokens.

(See tights, clothing, dress.)

adverbs
monotonously; wearisomely; conveniently; adaptably; comfortably; assuredly; pleasantly; tiresomely; flatly; uninterestingly; beautifully; symmetrically; presumably; allegedly; obviously; conspicuously; economically; dependably; reliably; conventionally.

UNIFORM (v)

adverbs
gaudily; gaily; impressively; dramatically; vividly; patriotically; brilliantly; somberly; drably.

(See garb, dress.)

UNION

adjectives
splendid; contingent; mystic; eternal; solemn; incestuous; ultimate; conjugal; habitual; unjust; constant; indissoluble; potent; powerful; fertile; conscious; perpetual; existing; legislative; precipitate; unfathomable; moribund; hurried; illicit; fruitful; visible; labor; celestial; consummate; check-off; complete; substantial; immemorial; perfect; fructifying; loathed; confederated; outstanding.

verbs
band into—; bind into—; consummate—; defend—; destroy—; disrupt—; encourage—; enter into—; foster—; further—; hallow—;

hinder—; impede—; lack—; partition—; preserve—; promote—; protect—; rend—; signify—; solemnize—; sunder—; —affords; —enables; —flourishes; —insures; —strengthens; —suffers.

(See marriage, connection, matrimony, attachment, coalition, combination.)

UNIONS

verbs

affiliate with—; alienate—; ally—; arbitrate—; betray—; cement—; centralize—; combat—; consolidate—; crush—; effect—; enlist in—; enroll in—; dispel—; foster—; head—; install—; league with—; mediate with—; operate—; pacify—; recruit for —; rend—; rule—; scorn—; sympathize with—; —achieve; —band; —call out; —challenge; —clash with; —demand; —embroil; —foment; —link; —merge with; —picket; —preserve; —protect; —strike; —support.

(See strikers, labor.)

UNIT

adjectives

regulatory; myriad (pl); topical; versatile; efficient; functioning; fire-fighting; unmanageable; single; sounding; inseparable; research; harmonious; primary; mechanical; similar; parallactic; potent; political; arbitrary; perfected.

verbs

affiliate with—; amass—; complete—; demolish—; design—; dissolve—; integrate—; isolate—; mould—; partition—; perform as —; rend—; replenish—; shatter—; strengthen—; sunder—; —expands; —swells.

(See cell, property, part.)

UNITE (v)

adverbs

stubbornly; strangely; fraternally; substantially; indissolubly; cordially; subsequently; promptly; unanimously; vigorously; ultimately; dramatically; politically; spiritually; harmoniously; enduringly; strategically; logically; morally; fundamentally; practically.

(See join, ally.)

UNITY

adjectives

distinct; unbroken; political; wielded; necessary; rigorous; dramatic; essential; artistic; pervading; territorial; moral; continental; spiritual; internal; harmonious; enduring; dim; compendious; lasting; brilliant; uncompounded; early; strategic; dramatic; imperial; logical; solid; fundamental; practical; mad.

verbs

accomplish—; achieve—; bind in—; blend in—; clamor for—; commend—; demand—; demolish—; endanger—; foster—; further —; impair—; jeopardize—; lack—; necessitate—; preserve—; promote—; rend—; sunder—; unfold—; verify—; want—; work for—; —enables; —insures; —perpetuates; —persists; —pervades; —prevails; —resists; —rules; —strengthens.

(See harmony, cooperation, agreement.)

UNIVERSAL

adverbs

fundamentally; woefully; universally; significantly; strikingly; curiously; ominously; surprisingly; astonishingly; terribly.

UNIVERSE

adjectives

moral; mad; vast; practical; lampless; useless; illimitable; well-conducted; visible; enduring; conceivable; spiritual; collective; boundless; insubstantial; harmonious; infinite; wise; myriad (pl); expanding; malign; aerial; material; incomprehensible; offensive; effectless; objective; foundering.

verbs

bound—; cloak—; cloud—; comprise—; contemplate—; "debunk"—; dim—; dwell in —; embrace—; encompass—; fathom—; glory in—; govern—; illumine—; impart to —; interpret—; limit—; map—; pervade—; re-create—; regard—; save—; scan—; shroud—; span—; sunder from—; survey—; —acclaims; —evolves from; —links; —mystifies; —mourns; —seethes; —teems; —whirls.

(See creation, life.)

UNIVERSITY

adjectives

studious; sedate; well-rounded; theological; splendid; great; significant; national; state.

verbs

affiliate with—; converge upon—; endow—; enroll in—; enter—; expel from—; found—; guide—; —advances; —breeds; —disciplines; —edifies; —enlightens; —equips; —

facilitates; —fosters; —functions; —furthers; —grounds one in; —honors; —imparts; —instructs; —mothers; —nurtures; —offers; —polishes; —prepares; —primes; —proselytes; —qualifies; —rears; —subsidizes; —verses one in.

(See college, institution, school.)

UNJUST

adverbs

cruelly; bitterly; keenly; unaccountably; unexpectedly; palpably; uncommonly; arrantly; wantonly; intolerably; illogically; vengefully; inexcusably; hatefully; hideously; miserably; wretchedly; incredibly; openly; crassly; stupidly; gravely; seriously; inadvertently; deliberately; intentionally; incredibly; inexplicably; remarkably; incomprehensibly.

UNKEMPT

adverbs

surprisingly; carelessly; deliberately; coolly; nonchalantly; comfortably; provokingly; shamefully; dowdily; embarrassingly; inexcusably; unfortunately; casually; notoriously; conspicuously; unconcealably; horribly; unluckily; deplorably; scandalously; merrily; blowzily; boldly; audaciously; flagrantly.

UNKNOWABLE

adverbs

obscurely; eternally; mysteriously; latently; darkly; dimly; vaguely; impenetratingly; incomprehensibly; perplexingly; wonderfully; mystically; occultly; inscrutably; puzzlingly; elusively; unaccountably; inexplicably; unreasonably; tormentingly; irrationally; profoundly; abysmally; infinitely; perpetually.

UNLAWFUL

adverbs

definitely; implicitly; riskily; perilously; strictly; positively; absurdly; specifically; explicitly; actually; allegedly; presumably; probably; certainly; avowedly; admittedly.

UNLIKELY

adverbs

naturally; utterly; legally; morally; particularly; emphatically; positively.

UNLOCK (v)

adverbs

automatically; readily; rustily; smoothly; easily; temporarily; dexterously.

(See unfasten, release.)

UNMANNERLY

adverbs

strangely; grossly; barbarously; naturally; incredibly; crassly; stupidly; boorishly; cruelly; rustically; provincially; unpleasantly; foolishly; apparently; manifestly; embarrassingly; shamefully; gracelessly; naively; ignorantly; unsophisticatedly; unluckily; wretchedly; unpardonably; oddly; conspicuously; remarkably; highly; uncommonly; unwontedly; disagreeably.

UNMERCIFUL

adverbs

cruelly; coldly; miserably; hatefully; inflexibly; stubbornly; boorishly; brutally; selfishly; unyieldingly; dreadfully; intractably; shamefully; scandalously; wickedly; immovably; sternly; inscrutably; mysteriously; strangely; significantly; remarkably; unwontedly; unaccountably; oddly; surprisingly.

UNMISTAKABLE

adverbs

clearly; explicitly; positively; manifestly; obviously; conspicuously; conveniently; safely; felicitously; fortunately; luckily; happily; definitely; purposely; singularly; designedly.

UNNERVED

adverbs

strangely; naturally; shakily; utterly; oddly; curiously; probably; completely; unreasonably; foolishly; shockingly; palpably; apparently; mysteriously; conspicuously; tremulously; helplessly.

UNOBJECTIONABLE

adverbs

personally; entirely; quite; naturally; pleasantly; harmlessly; manifestly; locally; politically; financially; generally; reasonably; frankly; wholly; fairly; presumably; singularly; altogether.

UNOSTENTATIOUS

adverbs

modestly; quietly; serenely; carefully; calmly; curiously; preferably; always; strangely; shyly; bashfully.

UNPALATABLE

adverbs

strangely; altogether; manifestly; curiously; noxiously; disagreeably; disgustingly; hopelessly; terribly; wretchedly; impossibly; embarrassingly; cruelly; bitterly; disappointingly; outlandishly; dreadfully.

UNPARLIAMENTARY

adverbs

openly; manifestly; wholly; foolishly; ignorantly; boldly; flauntingly; consciously; obstinately; absurdly; entirely; evidently; conspicuously; loosely; casually; carelessly.

UNPERTURBED

adverbs

quietly; strangely; confidently; optimistically; trustfully; curiously; particularly; noticeably; altogether; serenely; certainly; palpably; hopefully.

UNPOPULAR

adverbs

generally; strangely; noticeably; significantly; desperately; currently; terribly; definitely; conspicuously; apparently; manifestly; disturbingly; miserably; mysteriously; curiously; distinctly; emphatically; intensely; seriously; consciously.

UNPREJUDICED

adverbs

admirably; nobly; particularly; admittedly; distinctly; emphatically; curiously; palpably; commendably; dependably; hearteningly; judicially; gravely; honorably; honestly; entirely; wonderfully; happily.

UNPREPARED

adverbs

grossly; carelessly; unpardonably; miserably; palpably; inadvertently; wantonly; financially; socially; wretchedly; undisguisedly; openly; admittedly; unluckily; laughably; comically; tragically; ridiculously; nonchalantly; blithely; merrily.

UNPRESENTABLE

adverbs

horribly; laughably; ridiculously; embarrassingly; muddily; soggily; carelessly; altogether; shamefully; comically; ludicrously; utterly; messily; cruelly; bashfully; obviously; momentarily; always.

UNPROFITABLE

adverbs

disastrously; probably; sadly; extremely; terribly; naturally; seasonally; curiously; suddenly; desperately.

UNQUESTIONABLE

adverbs

utterly; admittedly; luckily; absolutely; momentarily; recognizably; palpably; socially; financially.

UNRAVEL (*v*)

adverbs

persistently; easily; intelligently; patiently; diligently; monotonously.

(See open, reveal.)

UNREAL

adverbs

darkly; abstrusely; obscurely; immaterially; indefinably; chimerically; phantasmally; vaguely; nebulously; evanescently; fantastically; strangely; fabulously; queerly; mystically; insubstantially; virtually; enigmatically; subtly; wildly; spectrally; dimly.

UNREASONABLE

adverbs

foolishly; blunderingly; ridiculously; absurdly; ludicrously; extravagantly; senselessly; egregiously; preposterously; comically; monstrously; fantastically; grotesquely; outlandishly; strangely; manifestly; patently; palpably; perversely; pathetically; grossly; incredibly.

UNREGENERATE

adverbs

obviously; manifestly; evidently; pitiably; stubbornly; obstinately; unfortunately; openly; flagrantly; blasphemously; flippantly; audaciously; impiously; terribly; dreadfully; impenitently.

UNRELENTING

adverbs

wilfully; indomitably; bitterly; sternly; obdurately; pitiably; lamentably; unpardonably; unreasonably; pitilessly; inexorably; obstinately; stubbornly; mulishly; doggedly; perversely; fanatically; pig-headedly; contumaciously; bigotedly; implacably; rancourously; vengefully; ruthlessly; maliciously; cruelly; unmercifully.

UNRELIABLE

adverbs

unfortunately; manifestly; entirely; unluckily; desperately; admittedly; obviously; terribly; actually; furtively; secretly; downright; notoriously; infamously; shamefully; wickedly; palpably; certainly.

UNREST

adjectives

wearisome; secret; political; sickening; unsettled; vain; essential; bitter; ghoulish; eager; sweet.

verbs

allay—; assuage—; calm—; cloak—; cope with—; dispel—; dwell in—; incite—; provoke—; quell—; silence—; still—; stave off—; subdue—; —disconcerts; —gnaws; —irks; —irritates; —racks; —rends; —smoulders; —spreads; —wanes; —weighs upon; —wrings.

(See restlessness, confusion, dissatisfaction, discontent.)

UNRESTRAINED

adverbs

excessively; rakishly; wildly; playfully; wickedly; hilariously; gleefully; joyously; crazily; airily; youthfully; ludicrously; brazenly; monstrously; outlandishly; delightfully; recklessly; wantonly; amazingly; audaciously; impetuously; ardently; heedlessly; indiscreetly.

UNRIGHTEOUS

adverbs

openly; unheedingly; deliberately; heinously; wickedly; impiously; blasphemously; deplorably; wretchedly; miserably; heathenishly.

UNRUFFLED

adverbs

admirably; surprisingly; restrainedly; wonderfully; utterly; calmly; actually; apparently; palpably; evidently; strangely; curiously; fortunately; securely; beautifully.

UNRULY

adverbs

ominously; dreadfully; unmanageably; obstinately; significantly; terribly; oddly; uproariously; boisterously; viciously; politically; truculently; dangerously; violently; unreasonably; ungovernably; obstreperously; jeeringly; designedly; maliciously; viciously; alarmingly; turbulently.

UNSAVORY

adverbs

notoriously; slightly; decidedly; extremely; admittedly; terribly; undisguisedly; dreadfully; manifestly; wickedly.

UNSCATHED

adverbs

mercifully; apparently; blessedly; surprisingly; gloriously; happily; luckily; unexpectedly; blissfully; evidently.

UNSCRUPULOUS

adverbs

notoriously; shamefully; cleverly; astutely; adroitly; infamously; reputedly; allegedly; curiously; terribly; extremely; shamelessly; triumphantly; arrogantly; openly; cruelly; bitterly; desperately; hard-heartedly; greedily; meanly; aggressively; boldly; daringly; criminally; selfishly; hatefully; atrociously.

UNSEASONABLE

adverbs

manifestly; surprisingly; unhealthfully; unprofitably; dangerously; desperately; hazardously; undeniably; highly; uncommonly; curiously; strangely; oddly; significantly; ominously; definitely.

UNSEEMLY

adverbs

desperately; shamefully; unpleasantly; disagreeably; surprisingly; unpardonably; absolutely; inexcusably; indefensibly; daringly; flauntingly; miserably; wantonly; frightfully; horridly; impertinently; blatantly.

UNSELFISH

adverbs

utterly; unnecessarily; ostentatiously; delightfully; remarkably; always; altogether; downright; absurdly; generously; altruistically; charitably; thoughtfully; considerately; graciously; courteously; unexpectedly; usually; naturally; habitually; tenderly; lovingly; extremely; uncommonly; singularly; unexpectedly; unwontedly; sweetly.

UNSETTLED

adverbs

curiously; indecisively; obviously; manifestly; unfortunately; evidently; pitiably; dangerously; temporarily; pathetically; miserably; secretly; confusedly; mentally; financially; sadly; temperamentally; habitually; naturally.

UNSIGHTLY

adverbs

hideously; loathesomely; disgustingly; shabbily; filthily; repulsively; horridly; shockingly; monstrously; gruesomely; dreadfully; positively; terribly; unbearably.

UNSKILFUL

adverbs

naturally; pitiably; awkwardly; clumsily; ineptly; inexpertly; ignorantly; carelessly; heedlessly; pathetically; unacceptably; grossly; undeniably; surprisingly; miserably; terribly; criminally; admittedly; undisguisedly; naively; shyly; self-consciously.

UNSOCIABLE

adverbs

painfully; shyly; disagreeably; terribly; awkwardly; naturally; naively; ungraciously; selfishly; inconsiderately; unwontedly; habitually; unpardonably; miserably; reticently; gravely; surprisingly; unfortunately; pitifully; inexcusably; strangely; offensively.

UNSOPHISTICATED

adverbs

naively; undisguisedly; apparently; palpably; manifestly; ludicrously; ridiculously; embarrassingly; shyly; consciously; painfully; childishly; innocently; awkwardly; clumsily; unhappily; unfortunately; laughably; pathetically.

UNSOUND

adverbs

unfortunately; curiously; inexcusably; untenably; ridiculously; absurdly; dreadfully; wickedly; admittedly; miserably; dangerously; significantly; manifestly; openly; daringly; utterly; unreliably.

UNSPARING

adverbs

sternly; harshly; gravely; unjustly; obstinately; inflexibly; fanatically; narrowly; bigotedly; ridiculously; bitterly; cruelly; unreasoningly; unreasonably; obdurately; gravely; solemnly; frightfully.

UNSTABLE

adverbs

lamentably; deplorably; miserably; ridiculously; obviously; dangerously; alarmingly; ominously; desperately; manifestly; perilously; unpardonably; carelessly; notoriously; flagrantly; unforgivably.

UNSUBSTANTIAL

adverbs

baselessly; fabulously; fantastically; fancifully; suppositiously; virtually; mockingly; illusively; mythically; notionally; romantically; visionarily; quixotically; whimsically; ethereally; tenuously; chimerically.

UNSUITABLE

adverbs

distinctly; positively; altogether; wholly; entirely; incongruously; socially; awkwardly; absurdly; foolishly; extravagantly; unbecomingly; comically; outlandishly; inappropriately; shockingly; crudely; horribly; laughably; singularly.

UNSYSTEMATIC

adverbs

carelessly; bewilderingly; confusingly; chaotically; terribly; unpardonably; inexcusably; criminally; provokingly; irritatingly; inconveniently; vexatiously; ruinously; ignorantly; foolishly; confoundedly; strangely; lazily; negligently; heedlessly; unwarrantably.

UNTENABLE

adverbs

fallibly; unreliably; inaccurately; insubstantially; absolutely; manifestly; carelessly; inconclusively; fallaciously; ultimately; obviously; absurdly; hopelessly; wholly; ridiculously; laughably.

UNTIMELY

adverbs

strangely; obviously; unfortunately; politically; financially; distressingly; terribly.

UNTOUCHED

adverbs

curiously; singularly; momentarily; mercifully; fortunately; blessedly; strangely; absolutely; carefully; providently; luckily; heedfully; apparently; absolutely.

UNTRAMMEL (*v*)

adverbs

entirely; nominally; legally; apparently; obviously.

(See release, free.)

UNTUTORED

adverbs

naively; unbelievably; miraculously; marvelously; curiously; childishly; utterly; obviously; manifestly; miserably; wretchedly; helplessly; distressingly; pathetically; pitiably; fortunately; palpably; blessedly; gloriously; apparently; brilliantly.

UNUSUAL

adverbs

extremely; fortunately; luckily; believably; apparently; obviously; manifestly; gloriously; mercifully; unfortunately; significantly; delightfully; altogether.

UNWARRANTABLE

adverbs

obviously; naturally; altogether; legally; socially; conventionally; decently; judicially; politically; terribly; admittedly; absurdly; ridiculously; ludicrously; wretchedly; miserably; indefensibly; dreadfully; altogether; downright; utterly.

UNWARY

adverbs

youthfully; flippantly; heedlessly; bravely; foolishly; naively; carelessly; ignorantly; wantonly; ridiculously; unbelievably; absurdly; blithely; inconceivably; rashly; witlessly.

UNWEARIED

adverbs

incredibly; fondly; affectionately; helpfully; patriotically; resolutely; intrepidly; unbelievably; miraculously; splendidly; incomprehensibly; lovingly; desperately; marvelously; strangely; oddly; fanatically; amazingly; remarkably.

UNWIELDY

adverbs

awkwardly; clumsily; terribly; unpleasantly; embarrassingly; disagreeably; massively; altogether; manifestly; inconveniently; lumberingly; vexatiously; plaguedly; confoundedly; singularly.

UNWILLINGNESS

adjectives

sheer; dull; deliberate; obstinate; studied.

verbs

acknowledge—; announce—; assert—; aver—; conquer—; contain—; deplore—; discern—; dispel—; display—; dissolve—; emphasize—; express—; indicate—; justify—; maintain—; overcome—; prevail against—; subdue—; surmount—; sweep away—; swerve from—; voice—; —irks; —persists, —piques; —riles (colloq.).

(See indisposition, reluctance.)

UNWISE

adverbs

incredibly; stubbornly; absurdly; habitually; naturally; obstinately; outrageously; palpably; obviously; cruelly; undeniably; flagrantly; fantastically; politically; terribly; utterly; absolutely; bitterly; disastrously; calamitously.

UNWOMANLY

adverbs

strangely; unbelievably; hoydenishly; terribly; lamentably; deplorably; surprisingly; utterly; dreadfully; ungraciously; curiously.

UNWORLDLY

adverbs

curiously; piously; peculiarly; wholly; indubitably; admirably; blessedly; happily; serenely; blandly; truly.

UNWORTHY

adverbs

entirely; deeply; utterly; undeniably; despicably; contemptibly; sadly; selfishly; lamentably; indisputably; peculiarly; particularly; censoriously; outrageously; bitterly.

UPBRAID (v)

adverbs

viciously; vindictively; brutally; obstreperously; laughingly; ferociously; unjustly; volubly; rigorously; paternally; hatefully; jealously.

(See chide, rebuke.)

UPHEAVAL

adjectives

volcanic; economic; religious; devastating; sensuous; business; fatal; passionate; violent; sudden; wild.

verbs

avert—; precipitate—; quash—; quell—; suppress—; —agitates; —arouses; —awakens; —characterizes; —convulses; —dashes; —demolishes; —discloses; —ele-

vates; —jars; —jolts; —jounces; —levels; —prostrates; —razes; —reveals; —revolutionizes; —uncovers.
(See uprising, convulsion, revolution, strike.)

UPHOLD (v)

adverbs
staunchly; faithfully; patiently; patriotically; virtually; solemnly; fiercely; gallantly; extraordinarily; economically; politically; philosophically; metaphysically; nationally.
(See support, defend.)

UPRIGHT

adverbs
splendidly; reputably; admittedly; virtuously; admirably; sincerely; openly; unfailingly; conspicuously; estimably; honorably; boldly; undauntedly; firmly; stably.

UPRISING

adjectives
sudden; armed; courageous; seditious; concerted; marvelous; feared; wide-spread; national; growing .

verbs
annihilate—; blot out—; check—; defeat—; foment—; forestall—; incite—; inspire—; instigate—; provoke—; smash—; squelch —; stem—; subdue—; suppress—; swamp —; —breaks out; —peters out (colloq.); —seethes; —spreads; —violates.
(See upheaval, revolution, strike.)

UPROAR

adjectives
wild; everlasting; positive; stupendous; tremendous; furious; musical; ghastly; stultifying.

verbs
hush—; muffle—; mute—; quash—; quell—; silence—; stifle—; still—; subdue—; suppress—; —abates; —bewilders; —confuses; —deafens; —drowns out; —mounts; —pierces; —rends; —shatters; —splits; —startles; —subsides; —swells; —thunders.
(See clamor, disturbance, din, fracas, roar, rumble.)

UPROARIOUS

adverbs
boisterously; comically; foolishly; hilariously; clownishly; merrily; blithely; gaily; amusingly; divertingly; farcically; fantastically; inimitably; excitedly; hysterically; enthusiastically; jubilantly; exultantly; triumphantly; rampantly; irrepressibly; laughingly.

UPSET

adverbs
peculiarly; utterly; strangely; significantly; inconsolably; grievously; wearily; nervously; physically; mentally; cruelly; miserably; bitterly; oddly; curiously; amazingly; remarkably; mysteriously; unexpectedly; suddenly; inexplicably; unaccountably.

UPSET (v)

adverbs
ultimately; practically; physically; emotionally; incomprehensibly; cruelly; gravely.
(See otherthrow, overpower.)

URBAN

adverbs
smoothly; distinctly; self-consciously; insistantly; ridiculously; scarcely; absurdly; pseudo-; recently; ridiculously; earnestly.

URBANE

adverbs
pleasantly; courteously; unusually; markedly; conspicuously; agreeably; ingratiatingly; skilfully; smoothly; carefully; diplomatically; serenely; complaisantly; graciously; splendidly; elegantly; unfailingly; resolutely; imperturbably; quietly; tolerantly; indulgently.

URGE

adjectives
biological; evolutionary; irresistible; sudden; strong; deep-seated; universal; self-satisfying; demon-like; glandular; swarthy; creative.

verbs
awaken—; check—; choke back—; conquer —; counteract—; dull—; gratify—; quell—; resist—; restrain—; smother—; squelch—; stem—; stifle—; —impels; —overpowers; —overwhelms; —seizes; —swells; intensify —.
(See importunity, desire, impulse.)

URGE (v)

adverbs
diplomatically; passionately; secretly; blandly; disingenuously; plausibly; insolently; ineffectually; blatantly; eloquently; importun-

ately; explicitly; enthusiastically; continually; persistently; ostentatiously; strenuously; powerfully; insidiously; traitorously; clamorously; mutely; irresistibly.

(See impel, incite.)

URGENT

adverbs

vitally; terribly; essentially; immediately; pressingly; personally; sorely; desperately; dreadfully; ominously; significantly; extremely; supremely; singularly; particularly; peculiarly; presumably; conspicuously; momentously; gravely; seriously.

URINE

verbs

acidify—; analyze—; cloud—; contaminate —; convey—; darken—; dilute—; discharge —; drain—; draw off—; egest—; eliminate —; emit—; evacuate—; excrete—; expel—; extract—; purge of—; retain—; saturate with—; secrete—; store—; tap—; vent—; void—; —accumulates; —colors; —concentrates; —emanates; —indicates; —passes; —pollutes; —reeks; —stinks.

(See liquid, odor, excretion.)

USAGE

adjectives

laudable; hereditary; abnormal; pedantic; traditional; general; effective; cruel; diplomatic; sinister; ill; grammatical; established; symphonic; immemorial; dietetic; rough; traditional; troglodytic; social; common.

verbs

accustom to—; approve—; condemn—; condone—; decry—; determine—; encourage—; foster—; govern—; marvel at—; practise—; prescribe—; promote—; rebuke—; recommend—; reproach—; reprove—; set forth —; subject to—; violate—; —infringes; —offends; —persists; —prevails; —sanctions; —violates.

(See procedure, use, custom, fashion, conventionality.)

USE

adjectives

refined; repeated; unsuspected; unspecified; excessive; experimental; inordinate; lavish; economical; amiable; creative; unsparing; assiduous; infrequent; habitual; vain; ignoble; senseless; consistent; occasional; far-reaching; unholy; grave; prolonged; long-continued; brutal; outspoken; diligent; narrow; respective; increased; decorative; metaphorical; unwonted; temporary; transcendent; domestic; particular; remarkable; infinite; ample; imperfect; growing; barren; congenial; valuable; fruitful; effective; uncaged; exclusive; imaginative; specific; instinctive; unreasoning; judicious; singular; delicate; efficient; dexterous; brilliant; constant; immediate; charitable; plentiful; deliberate; recurrent; varied (pl); concealed; common; accepted; mandatory; precocious; subordinate; unauthorized; industrious; ultimate; indiscriminate; immoderate; unnatural; voluntary; homespun.

verbs

accede to—; addict to—; advance—; advocate—; approve—; assure of—; authorize —; begrudge—; bid for—; concede—; condemn—; confer upon—; confine—to; consider—; counsel—; crave—; cultivate—; curb—; curtail—; debar—; debase—; decline—; decry—; deprecate—; design for—; develop—; disclaim—; discontinue—; discourage—; encourage—; enforce—; enjoin from—; exhort—; facilitate—; foster—; frown upon—; grant—; guide—; impair—; impede—; induce—; inspire—; involve—; master—; obviate—; offer—; outlive—; petition for—; pledge—; ponder—; press to—; prolong—; prompt—; propose—; provoke—; protest—; recommend—; request—; resort to—; restrain—; restrict—; ridicule —; suppress—; tender—; —dishonors; —entails; —facilitates; —habituates; —hardens; —insures.

(See service, need, employment, application.)

USE (v)

adverbs

indiscriminately; similarly; mercifully; promiscuously; universally; exclusively; extensively; lavishly; chiefly; conspicuously; intermittently; ostentatiously; effectively; officially; simultaneously; artfully; deftly; tenderly; ethically; magnanimously; economically; creatively; assiduously; consistently; diligently; domestically; congenially; singularly; judiciously; dexterously; ultimately; voluntarily.

(See employ, utilize.)

USEFUL

adverbs

conveniently; constantly; wholly; unusually;

particularly; specially; peculiarly; amazingly; wonderfully; admirably; curiously; frequently; remarkably; unexpectedly; politically; suddenly; actually; extremely; marvellously; socially; adaptably; invariably; dependably; downright.

USEFULNESS

adjectives
sheer; varied; desultory; partial; increased; high; conspicuous; extraordinary; practical; lively; prodigious; preeminent.

verbs
acclaim—; acquire—; appreciate—; augment—; belittle—; commend—; consider—; contemplate—; discern—; disclose—; hamper—; heighten—; impair—; judge—; lack—; laud—; measure—; minimize—; outlive—; recognize—; regard—; reveal—; weigh—; —ceases; —ebbs; —impresses.

(See value, advantage, benefit.)

USELESS

adverbs
eventually; definitely; utterly; absolutely; probably; finally; ultimately; absurdly; certainly; fantastically; ridiculously; possibly; undoubtedly; completely; pathetically; admittedly; unaccountably; manifestly; obviously.

USELESSNESS

verbs
decry—; deplore—; disclose—; fall into—; inveigh against—; overcome—; rebuke—; scoff at—; set forth—; —burdens; —irks; —irritates; —oppresses; —riles (colloq.); —stigmatizes; —vexes; —weighs upon.

(See futility, waste.)

USHER (*v*)

adverbs
hospitably; gallantly; politely; formally; habitually; professionally.

(See escort, introduce.)

USUAL

adverbs
altogether; scarcely; quite; absolutely; too; rather; admittedly.

USURP (*v*)

adverbs
treacherously; violently; murderously; dictatorially; tyrannically; illegally; sternly; vigorously; politically; arbitrarily.

(See seize, take.)

UTENSIL

adjectives
washing; primitive; cooking; valuable; practical.

verbs
blacken—; cleanse—; discard—; edge—; employ—; encumber—; equip with—s; exhibit—; fashion—; grind—; pilfer—; plate—; polish—; renew—; rinse—; scour—; scrape—; sharpen—; soak—; —enables; —facilitates.

(See instrument, knife, fork, cup, kettle, tool.)

UTILITARIAN

adverbs
handsomely; truly; altogether; sordidly; plainly; entirely; possibly; conveniently; admittedly; warrantably; sensibly; obviously; distinctly.

UTILITY
(*general*)

adjectives
respectable; universal; industrial; misconceived; practical; social; ultimate; heartless; essential; vulgar; definite; wide; obvious.

UTILITY
(*public utility*)

verbs
cater to—; charge—with; dance attendance to—; enrich—; govern—; head—; inveigh against—; investigate—; legislate against—; regulate—; tax—; —s amass; —bribes; —s "crack"; —s crack up (colloq.); —s facilitate; —s function; —s grind; —s lobby; —s perform; —s profit; —s rule; —serves; —s subserve; —tyrannizes.

(See power, company.)

UTILIZE (*v*)

adverbs
economically; effectively; politically; strategically; heartlessly; obviously; essentially; prodigiously; potently.

(See use, employ.)

UTOPIA

adjectives
mechanistic; economic; incorrigible; long-awaited; planned.

verbs
abide in—; cherish—; contrive—; depict—;

desert—; desire—; dream of—; dwell in—; fancy—; forsake—; gain—; hail—; imagine—; inspire—; picture—; portray—; predict—; proclaim—; promise—; quit—; relinquish—; renounce—; reside in—; strive for—; struggle for—.

(See heaven, perfection, ideal.)

UTOPIAN

adverbs

brightly; cheerfully; desirably; airily; illusively; promisingly; elusively; roseately; romantically; fancifully; phantasmally; hopefully; optimistically; whimsically; seriously; boldly; fallaciously; fantastically; notionally; chimerically; ingeniously.

UTTER (v)

adverbs

drolly; involuntarily; tremulously; decisively; articulately; prophetically; disparagingly; foolishly; coaxingly; mechanically; inarticulately; impassionately; lyrically; incisively; exquisitely; indiscriminately; voluntarily; specifically; delicately; deliberately.

(See speak, say.)

UTTERANCE

adjectives

bare; mordant; effective; unblushing; rapid; impassioned; mere; audible; rhythmical; graphic; broken; ill-considered; discouraging; homogeneous; full; characteristic; rending; death-defying; articulate; private; prophetic; premature; lyrical; exquisite; lofty; historic; incisive; noble; perfect; calm; lively; spontaneous; loving; imperfect; unheard; monotonous; mastered; public; hearty; numberless (pl); recent; glowing; rapid; fiery; supreme; impressive; simulated; intimate; recorded; luminous; harmonized; caustic; practical; injudicious; brute; spasmodic; simple; indistinct; expansive; vivid; roseate; important; grave; reasonable; powerful; weighty; precise.

verbs

acclaim—; clarify—; clothe—; condense—; deprecate—; magnify—; muffle—; mumble —; mute—; mutter—; rue—; silence—; smother—; stifle—; still—; voice—; weigh —; —astounds; —electrifies; —irks; —perplexes; —rings out; —sears; —shocks; —startles; —stuns.

(See exclamation, drawl, expression, statement.)

UXORIOUS

adverbs

noticeably; absurdly; notoriously; openly; absurdly; ridiculously; conspicuously; foolishly; outlandishly; obviously; ludicrously.

V

VACANCY

adjectives
dull; prospective; stony; rectangular; soundless; blank; utter; absolute; astounding; complete.

VACANT

adverbs
apparently; recently; obviously; coldly; mysteriously; forbiddingly; dismally; unexpectedly; gloriously; opportunely; actually; presumably; allegedly; seldom; happily; fortunately; unfortunately; unprofitably; gloomily; blankly; seasonally; temporarily; frequently.

VACATION

adjectives
memorable; peaceful; unspoiled; thorough; complete; thrilling; never-to-be-forgotten; carefree; summer; inclusive; unique; pictorial; glorious; frequent (pl); restful; giddy; wild; joyous; longed-for; wonderful.

verbs
advise—; conclude—; counsel—; crave—; curtail—; depart on—; extend—; grant—; loll on—; lounge on—; merit—; necessitate —; prolong—; protract—; recommend—; reward with—; terminate—; warrant—; yearn for—; —distracts; —diverts; —reanimates; —refreshes; —relaxes; —renews; —restores; —unbends; —vivifies; —wanes.
(See recess, rest, respite.)

VACATION (v)

adverbs
luxuriously; jovially; sumptuously; fraternally; memorably; peacefully; thrillingly; uniquely; gloriously; giddily; joyously; exquisitely.
(See refresh, travel.)

VACCINATION

verbs
advise—; compel—; employ—; prescribe—; procure—; submit to—; undergo—; —assures; —benefits; —discommodes; —erases; —erupts; —immunizes; —inflames; —insures; —modifies; —safeguards; —scars; —stamps out.
(See operation, serum.)

VACCINE

verbs
assimilate—; diffuse—; dispense; —glycerinate—; inject—; inoculate with—; insert —; introduce—; prepare—; prescribe—; sensitize—; utilize—; —builds up; —exempts; —immunizes; —induces; —inflames; —insures; —irritates; —modifies; —protects; —resists; —safeguards; —stimulates.

VACILLATE (v)

adverbs
irresolutely; weakly; pusillanimously; irrationally; indecisively; desultorily; improvidently.
(See sway, waver.)

VACILLATING

adverbs
vexatiously; hopelessly; indecisively; wantonly; intolerably; foolishly; incorrigibly; habitually; strangely; absurdly; mindlessly; incurably; naturally; inherently; irresolutely; deplorably; unfortunately; sluggishly; helplessly; lamentably; feebly; witlessly; remarkably; inordinately; unreasonably; unbearably; disgustingly.

VACUOUS

adverbs
deplorably; wantonly; sluggishly; lamentably; irremediably; irrecoverably; helplessly; pitiably; strangely; mysteriously; unaccountably; suddenly; unintelligibly; irresponsibly; evidently; manifestly; curiously; grotesquely; miserably; wretchedly.

VACUUM

adjectives
luminous; sterile; dreary; absolute.

verbs
achieve—; create—; employ—; exhaust to —; fill—; induce—; obtain—; reduce to—; require—; seal—; utilize—; valve—; —fails; —retains; —preserves.

VAGABOND

adjectives
incorrigible; royal; nondescript; seedy; precious; wandering; romantic; clever-appearing; lazy; roaming; alluring.

adverbs
delightfully; whimsically; foolishly; notionally; irresponsibly; crazily; elfishly; irrepressibly; merrily; blithely; wholesomely; gaily; happily; uncontrollably; wittily; affably; genially.

VAGARIES

adjectives
superstitious; metaphysical; strange; queer; unusual; wild.

VAGINA

verbs
abscess—; dilate—; distend—; drain—; examine—; explore—; incise—; infect—; inflame—; inseminate—; insert into—; invade—; irritate—; lacerate—; line—; obstruct—; occlude—; plug—; probe—; suppurate—; syringe—; —discharges; —emits.

VAGRANT

adjectives
scattered (pl); undeveloped; apprehended; arrested.

adverbs
blithely; gaily; jauntily; happily; carelessly; irresponsibly; suspiciously; joyously; alertly; profitably; enviably; inconveniently; selfishly; luxuriously; habitually; pleasantly; nervously; furtively; stealthily; merrily; nonchalantly; delightfully; wretchedly; uncertainly; miserably; lonesomely; preferably; hazardously; independently; innocently; harmlessly.

VAGUE

adverbs
intentionally; perplexingly; embarrassingly; obscurely; dimly; stupidly; precariously; ambiguously; unintelligibly; distressingly; mysteriously; unwisely; uncertainly; casually; airily; delusively; evasively; subtly; inconclusively; darkly; abstrusely; impenetrably; remotely; unwarrantably; foolishly; speciously; misleadingly; tenuously; terribly; nonsensically; senselessly; completely; perilously; fearfully; alarmingly; ominously; significantly; fantastically; needlessly; unreliably.

VAGUENESS

adjectives
mysterious; comprehensible; voluptuous; studied; calculated; intentional.

VAIN

adverbs
awkwardly; fantastically; inordinately; offensively; contemptibly; amusingly; artlessly; morbidly; prodigiously; complacently; colossally; tediously.

VAINGLORIOUS

adverbs
bombastically; egregiously; incredibly; disgustingly; curiously; unreasonably; absurdly; insanely; harmlessly; ridiculously; ludicrously; laughably; sadly; extremely; manifestly; blindly; pompously; fantastically; preposterously; singularly.

VALE

adjectives
hopeless; melancholy; pleasant; fast-filling; sequestered; horrid; well-watered; hollow; simmering; shadowy; sunny; dimpling; dimmer; grassy; tuneful; gloomy; lonely; wondrous; intervening; dewy; spicy; luxuriant; smooth; sinuous; dreary; long; lit; deep.

verbs
(See valley, dale.)

VALEDICTORY

adverbs
sadly; seriously; appraisingly; analytically; admonitory; complimentarily; apparently; manifestly; obviously; warningly; critically; bitterly; affectionately; fondly; touchingly; affectingly; conventionally; comprehensively.

VALET

adjectives
inestimable; obsequious; bowing; quiet; effective; artful; deft; efficient; silk-hosed.

VALIANT

adverbs
resolutely; steadily; unfalteringly; boldly; admirably; wonderfully; marvellously; particularly; amazingly; gloriously; notably; surpassingly; incomparably; immeasurably; indescribably; intrepidly; superhumanly; superbly; splendidly; magnificently; unforgettably; fearlessly; supremely.

VALID

adverbs
reasonably; undoubtedly; assuredly; legally; financially; manifestly; obviously; evi-

dently; reputably; presumably; probably; unquestionably; altogether; substantially; effectively; curiously; definitely.

VALIDITY

adjectives
incontestable; legal; objective; eternal; supreme; scientific; independent; demonstrated; definite.

verbs
analyze—; attack—; avow—; challenge—; defend—; destroy—; discuss—; dispute—; emphasize—; endanger—; exhibit—; honor —; imperil—; impugn—; interfere with—; jeopardize—; maintain—; preserve—; question—; respect—; stamp with—; sustain—; test—; view—; —signifies; —stands.
(See value, position.)

VALLEY

adjectives
fantastic; stretching; fertile; overshadowed; precipitous; placid; solitary; sun-baked; pleasant; delectable; tributary; lofty; rugged; canyon-like; seductive; miserable; heated; copse-clad; picturesque; fabled; serene; blooming; fog-obscured; profound; irregular; branching; beautiful; breathless; solitary; pastoral; fruitful; wooded; flowering; watered; lovely; nest-like; desolate; immense; widening; conspicuous; shallow; redolent; grassy; oblivious; receding; haystack-dotted; verdant; cozy; little; terrible; formless; tiny; untenable; hill-beholden; flat-bottomed; dizzy; lonely; mountain; dusky; southern; imperial; winding; viewless; pathless.

verbs
command—; dash to—; devastate—; discern —; dot—; dwell in—; fill—; haunt—; inhabit—; overrun—; overspread—; penetrate —; people—; permeate—; pervade—; revisit—; ring through—; settle in—; view—; —awakes; —bestirs; —blossoms; —bristles; —dozes; —endures; —glistens; —inspires; —sleeps; —snuggles; —thickens; —waxes; —winds.
(See plain, dale, dell.)

VALOR

adjectives
deliberated; heroic; exceeding; unquestioned; unaffected; loyal; naked; idealized; sheer; free; honorable; bloody; dormouse; personal; distinguished; approved; deliberate; self-respecting; desperate; redoubled; unsurpassed; truculent; mock; reverend; true; frantic; indomitable; patient; pristine; individual; splendid.

verbs
awaken—; call forth—; confirm—; consecrate—; counterfeit—; dedicate to—; discard—; dispense with—; display—; endow with—; gape at—; herald—; impeach—; impugn—; marvel at—; practise—; proclaim—; report—; reward—; tax—; —beggars description; —bewilders; —confounds; —dazzles; —figures; —vanishes.
(See courage, heroism, morale.)

VALOROUS

adverbs
highly; wonderfully; intrepidly; amazingly; commendably; unusually; uncommonly; admirably; tremendously; brilliantly; resolutely; stubbornly; incredibly; invincibly; remarkably.

VALUABLE

adverbs
curiously; exceptionably; exceptionally; extremely; marvellously; seriously; magnificently; incredibly; incalculably; immeasurably; unbelievably; significantly; wonderfully; oddly; unexpectedly; rarely; immensely; enormously; suddenly; immediately; absurdly; fabulously; extraordinarily.

VALUATION

adjectives
false; mental; cordial; fair; common; altered; assessed; improper; reduced.

VALUE

adjectives
historical; rental; thrilling; artistic; independent; priceless; desirable; anticipatory; investment; inestimable; speculative; apologetic; determining; relative; unjust; intrinsic; unescapable; additional; material; positive; restorative; fictitious; sacred; tremendous; incalculable; opposite; symbolic; demonstrated; excellent; amazing; therapeutic; important; outstanding; fundamental; remarkable; heating; exchange; retail; sheer; energy-yielding; sound; uniform; decorative; grand; verified; memorable; prime; essential; food; big; extraordinary; aesthetic; compensating; monetary; unappreciable; local; caloric; asserted; intellectual; independent; prodigious; aggregate; annual;

potential; comparative; vitamin; immeasurable; psychological; paper; survival; practical; marvelous; rare; half-mystical; chief; extra; cultural; reasonable; literary; scientific; full; proper; sensational; nominal; numerical; psychopathic; ultimate; property; fallacious; thrifty; fancy; representative; mere; sentimental; emotional; educational; uncertain; needful; economic; nutritional; permanent; enormous; corresponding; distinct; immense; determinate; splendid; exciting; enduring; customary; specific; beneficial; affective; expressive; unprecedented; conducive; consequent; ethical; critical; diagnostic; refrigerating; social; sacred; unexpected; varying; unrivaled; cherished; additive; face; fluctuating; surprise; moral; extrinsic; compelling; unbelievable; irresistible; exceptional; unbeatable; good; true; unmatchable; surpassed; supreme; entire; lasting; questionable; documentary; exquisite; cash; insulation; top; conspicuous; negotiable; rachitic; fabulous; honest; eye; experimental; brighter; market; dollar; unusual; quality; heart-warming; transcendental; crowning; genuine; scarcity; specified; delusive; peculiar.

verbs
abuse—; advance—; advertise—; analyze —; appraise—; ascertain—; ascribe—to; assess—; attach—to; atribute—to; audit—; authenticate—; belittle—; bolster—; boast —; broadcast—; calculate—; certify—; cite —; comprehend—; compute—; contribute—; debase—; declare—; deflate—; demonstrate —; depreciate—; depress—; determine—; detract from—; dilute—; discount—; dispute—; distort—; dwell upon—; emasculate —; enhance—; establish—; estimate—; exploit—; fathom—; grasp—; impair—; intensify—; judge—; maintain—; misjudge—; negate—; overestimate—; predetermine—; preserve—; proclaim—; rate—; readjust—; reckon—; recognize—; repudiate—; salvage —; sense—; share—; stress—; substantiate —; tender—; testify to—; verify—; vindicate—; weigh—; yield—; —dawns upon; —diminishes; —enriches; —fluctuates; —hurtles; —inheres; —leaps; —melts away; —mounts; —shrivels; —soars.
(See esteem, usefulness, worth, significance, importance.)

VALUE (v)

adverbs
inordinately; adequately; artistically; historically; pricelessly; sacredly; symbolically; extraordinarily; aesthetically; locally; potentially; immeasurably; psychologically; scientifically; emotionally; economically; politically; ethically; critically; morally; transcendentally; genuinely.
(See estimate, prize.)

VANDAL

adjectives
arrogant; literary; lawless.

VANISH (v)

adverbs
ultimately; mysteriously; utterly; simultaneously; noiselessly; speedily; swiftly; wholly; magically; completely.
(See disappear.)

VANISHING

adverbs
mysteriously; inconsiderately; strangely; inconveniently; magically; outlandishly; deliberately; curiously; strangely; suddenly; unaccountably; mischievously; fantastically; impishly; selfishly.

VANITY

adjectives
flattering; awkward; fantastic; soothed; foolish; petty; violent; generous; roused; racial; inordinate; mundane; unpunctured; courageous; offensive; contemptible; amusing; ingenuous; artless; punctured; insatiable; reawakened; earthly; morbid; literary; innocent; wounded; motherly; restless; complacent; professed; chargeable; prodigious; colossal; selfish; sanguine; ingenious; offended; sheer; masculine; outworn; trampled; tedious; unconscious; ill-bred.

verbs
appease—; betray—; cater to—; conceal—; counteract—; down—; eradicate—; exhibit —; gratify—; humble—; indulge—; irritate —; loathe—; measure—; mollify—; pander to—; prick—; puncture—; ridicule—; ruffle —; satirize—; tickle—; yield to—; —angers; —cloys; —despoils; —diminishes; —functions; —nauseates; —operates; —repulses; —singes; —stirs.
(See egotism, conceit, pedantry, futility.)

VAPID

adverbs
disappointingly; disagreeably; hopelessly; unbelievably; utterly; strangely; unexpect-

edly; hopelessly; monotonously; uninterestingly; curiously; horribly.

VAPOR

adjectives
oracular; sulphurous; obscuring; aqueous; portentous; black; deathly; foul; gross; swimming; sealike; miasmatic; sunless; steaming; impalpable; misty; sympathetic; poisonous; smoke; soothing; relieving; oracular; radiant; noxious; agitated; rent; gaseous; invisible; stifling; gloomy; midnight; wintry; milky; hideous; imponderable; unctuous; quivering; dim; noontide; suffocating; temperate; corrosive; mercury; ghostly; pale; murky; noxious; alcoholic; quick; evil; diaphanous; motionless.

verbs
diffuse—; distill—; emit—; exhale—; free —; inhale—; liquefy—; —arises; —asphyxiates; —bedims; —befogs; —clouds; —condenses; —eddies; —explodes; —floats; —fumes; —hovers over; —infiltrates; —melts; —obscures; —offends; —permeates; —reeks; —rises; —shrouds; —smothers; —vanishes; —veils.

(See haze, fog, fume, mist, moisture.)

VAPOROUS

adverbs
curiously; strangely; terribly; confusingly; alarmingly; insecurely; mysteriously; intensely; foggily; mistily; steamily; bewilderingly; unhealthfully; dankly; hotly; suffocatingly; mustily.

VARIABLE

adverbs
vexatiously; mysteriously; irritatingly; unpredictably; strangely; unreasonably; mischievously; absurdly; inexplicably; unwarrantably; unstably; unreliably; provokingly; remarkably; unaccountably; intensely; inconveniently; uncomfortably; uselessly; unnecessarily.

VARIANCE

adjectives
internal; usual; perpetual; wide; noticeable.

VARIATION

adjectives
graceful; periodic; momentary; secular; diurnal; visible; sure; divers (pl); incessant; discreet; seasonal; occasional; skillful; fantastic; pyro-technical; erratic; verbal; slight; injurious; pleasing; distracting; endless; beneficial; numerous (pl); dignified; appreciable; perpetual; transient; emotional.

verbs
account for—; afford—; ascertain—; augment—; calculate—; check—; condone—; correct—; countenance—; decry—; determine—; discern—; disclose—; discount—; dispel—; evolve—; record—; register—; result in—; welcome—; —arises; —deviates; —modifies; —modulates; —occurs.

(See difference, discrepancy, deviation, change, alteration, modification.)

VARIEGATED

adverbs
beautifully; iridescently; colorfully; opalescently; constantly; unpredictably; remarkably; amazingly; curiously; unusually; mysteriously; handsomely.

VARIETY

adjectives
extraordinary; unmotived; improved; dominant; endless; interesting; considerable; immense; amazing; enchanting; distinct; natural; delicious; continental; boundless; manifold (pl); impressive; multiform (pl); infinite; internal; cultivated; epileptic; sportive; splendid; tubular; crafty; graceful; multifarious (pl); bewildering; coarse; picturesque; aquatic; stout; rich; external; embarrassing; tumultuous; stubborn; inordinate; fresh; dull; conceivable; hideous; gorgeous; agreeable; clinging; remarkable; accurate; distinct; limited; wide; colorful.

verbs
achieve—; afford—; crave—; demand—; display—; distinguish by—; encourage—; foster—; indulge in—; infuse—; inspire—; lack—; offer—; procure—; value—; want —; yield—; —animates; —dazes; —diversifies; —diverts; —enlivens; —entertains; —seasons; —spices.

(See collection, change, violation.)

VARLET

adjectives
wicked; abominable; graceless; crimson; incontinent; naughty.

VARNISH (*v*)

adverbs
sickly; sleekly; luxuriously; thickly; lustrously; smoothly.

(See polish, shine.)

VARY (v)

adverbs
widely; radically; infinitely; indefinitely; heterogeneously; periodically; incessantly; bewilderingly; distinctly.
(See charge, modify.)

VASE

adjectives
exquisite; ponderous; cloisonne; priceless; broken; patched; inimitable.

VASSAL

adjectives
rebellious; gallant; skillful; tributary; belligerent; dreaded; duteous; humble; obsequious.

VASSALAGE

adjectives
commercial; hereditary; economic; complete; effectual.

VAST

adjectives
populous; current; fathomless; boundless; unimagined.

adverbs
enormously; mysteriously; stupendously; impossibly; overwhelmingly; strangely; colossally; prodigiously; astonishingly; marvellously; extraordinarily; miraculously.

VASTNESS

adjectives
tangled; mysterious; encircling; physical; unending.

verbs
bridge—; comprehend—; explore—; measure—; scale—; scan—; span—; survey—; —affords; —allows; —astounds; —awes; —bewilders; —bulks large; —cows; —embraces; —enraptures; —extends; —fascinates; —impresses; —inspires; —intrigues; —looms; —overawes; —overwhelms; —staggers; —stuns; —transcends.
(See spaciousness, magnitude, size.)

VAT

verbs
age in—; char—; contaminate—; deplete—; drain—; ferment in—; immerse in—; label —; plunge into—; replenish—; store in—; submerge in—; tap—; —diffuses; —emits; —preserves; —reeks.
(See kettle, tub.)

VAULT

adjectives
choked-up; adjoining; gloomy; intersecting; unribbed; majestic; lurid; heavenly; deep; midnight; opaque; celestial; noxious; sinuous; fathomless; wintry; starry; measurable; lofty; inexhaustible; resounding; dungeon-like; imbowered; azure; ebon; dankish; flaming; funereal.

verbs
amass in—; consign to—; defile—; deposit in—; desecrate—; engrave on—; entomb in —; filch from—; haunt—; inscribe on—; inter in—; invade—; pillage—; plunder—; repose in—; seal—; store in—; stow in—; —depresses; —honors; —insures; —muffles; —receives; —reeks; —resounds; —safeguards.
(See cellar, tomb, box.)

VAULT (v)

adverbs
agilely; skillfully; precipitately; rashly; vigorously; lightly; thrillingly.
(See jump, spring.)

VAULTED

adverbs
ethereally; beautifully; immensely; magnificently; splendidly; brilliantly; safely; closely; tightly; securely.

VAUNT

adjectives
obligatory; vainglorious; ostentatious; nauseating.

VAUNT (v)

adverbs
arrogantly; unduly; obstreperously; vaingloriously; ostentatiously; belligerently; verbally.
(See boast, extol.)

VAUNTING

adjectives
compulsory; idle; boastful.

VEGETABLES

adjectives
frozen; thriving; indigenous; succulent; un-

palatable; flabby; shade-living; out-of-season; fresh; raw; green.

verbs
bed out—; broil—; consume—; cultivate—; delve among—; fertilize—; hawk—; husband—; label—; market—; partake of—; pluck—; nurse—; prize—; purvey—; reap —; —relish—; savor—; sow—; sprout—; steam—; transplant—.
(See peanut, plant, fruit, food, peas, etc.)

VEGETATION

adjectives
spontaneous; riotous; luxuriant; decaying; exuberant; tropical; treacherous; aboreal; delicate; objectionable; reeking; thriving; velvet; noxious; spiteful; repulsive; slumbering; coarse; variegated; vigorous.

verbs
tame—; —bourgeons; —buds; —bursts forth; —chokes; —curtains; —eclipses; —flourishes; —flowers; —germinates; —mantles; —obscures; —overruns; —overspreads; —pullulates; —screens; —shades; —shadows; —shoots up; —smothers; —sprouts; —strangles; —thickens; —veils.
(See vegetables.)

VEHEMENCE

adjectives
noisy; unaccountable; petitionary; earnest; suppressed; essential; passionate; excessive; sudden; lively; hasty; wild; corresponding; equal.

VEHEMENT

adverbs
unnecessarily; absurdly; laughably; earnestly; foolishly; wildly; loudly; enthusiastically; zealously; ridiculously; gravely; seriously; passionately; forcibly; energetically; pleadingly; fanatically; oddly; singularly; dogmatically; unwisely; vexatiously.

VEHICLE

adjectives
muddled; passing; appropriate; gleaming; favored; poor; groaning; abused; motor; wind-driven; fluid; mechanical; propelled; nominal; crazy; festive; lumbering; sole; back-country; humble; mimic; commonplace; up-to-date; moldering.

verbs
accelerate—; brake—; draw—; fuel—; guide—; impair—; lubricate—; park—; pilot—; —bears; —conveys; —jars; —jolts; —jounces; —rattles; —roars by; —trundles; —whizzes by.
(See cart, conveyance, carriage, chariot, truck.)

VEIL

adjectives
emerald; snowy; inmost; pitchy; misty; dusky; leafy; gloomy; intervening; star-studded; lucid; ugly; solemnizing; gauzy; impenetrable; twilight; obligatory; tangled; mystic; turbid; close-spun; diaphanous; hieroglyphic; sinuous; overhanging; filmy; trembling; fluttering; raw; golden-tissued; borrowed; adamantine; amethystine; fleecy; fearful; maiden.

verbs
bare—; bedeck with—; cast off—; discard —; dispel—; divest of—; doff—; don—; drape—over; draw—; envelop in—; maintain—; penetrate—; rend—; suspend—over; withdraw—; —beguiles; —billows behind; —conceals; —curtains; —deceives; —deludes; —dims; —disguises; —eclipses; —mantles; —muffles; —obstructs; —obscures; —screens; —shades; —shadows.
(See mask, cloak, disguise, fabric, cloth.)

VEIL (v)

adverbs
curiously; unconsciously; impenetrably; skillfully; gloomily; mystically; diaphanously.
(See conceal, hide.)

VEILED

adverbs
beautifully; closely; msyteriously; heavily; luminously; colorfully; provocatively; secretly; furtively; remarkably; marvellously; splendidly; lightly; thinly; deeply; mystically; symbolically; resolutely; exotically.

VEINS

adjectives
hepatic; freezing; moralizing; throbbing; masterful; aging; scorching; rapid; sap-transmitting; sacred; flushed; sanguine; philosophical; prevalent; cloven; idealistic; empty; azure; agreeable; languid; strenuous; whimsical; merry; swollen; fluent; purple-pulsing; translucent; humorous; dra-

matic; varicose; heroic; melodic; equivocating; contaminated; superstitious; prominent; benignant; enamored; prolific; satirical; sluggish; indurated; furtive; rich; laboring; reminiscent; didactic.

verbs
abscess—; attack—; block—; calcify—; compress—; constrict—; dilate—; disperse through—; distend—; drain—; inflame—; inject into—; issue from—; ligature—; occlude—; puncture—; stir in—; tap—; traverse—; trickle through—; —anastomose; —atrophy; —branch off; —clot; —convey; —degenerate; —harden; —proliferate; —pulsate; —thicken; —ulcerate.
(See blood-vessel, artery.)

VELOCITY

adjectives
high; angular; extraneous; extravagant; accentuated; unrelaxed; inconceivable; ascertained; elliptic; linear; standard; undetermined.

verbs
accelerate—; ascertain—; attain—; check—; determine—; diminish—; gain—; heighten—; measure—; stablize—; —abates; —declines; —dwindles; —ebbs; —endangers; —fluctuates; —subsides; —vacillates; —wanes.
(See momentum, speed.)

VELVET

adjectives
prodigious; slashed; fawn-tinted; transparent; smooth; ruffled; regal; wrinkled; flattering.

verbs
array in—; attire in—; bask on—; crumple—; divest of—; garb in—; lounge in—; ruffle—; rumple—; swathe in—; upholster in—; —adds; —colors; —enhances; —enriches; —signifies; —symbolizes.
(See linen, silk.)

VENDIBLE

adverbs
readily; conveniently; easily; profitably; remarkably; extremely; universally; marvellously; incredibly.

VENERABLE

adverbs
ripely; reputably; extraordinarily; signally; conspicuously; notoriously; estimably; distinctly; nobly; justly; illustriously; virtuously; splendidly; eminently.

VENERATE (*v*)

adverbs
highly; deeply; religiously; superstitiously; profoundly; obsequiously; humbly; abjectly.
(See respect, esteem.)

VENERATION

adjectives
superstitious; unsympathetic; striking; partial; profound; defective; high; special; deep; remarkable.

VENGEANCE

adjectives
savage; hoarded; gratified; eternal; heroic; bloody; dark; spiteful; cowardly; exemplary; political; vulgar; dastardly; brooding; ample; summary; popular; kindred; pleasing; fiery; worthy; wreakful; satisfied; instant; indiscriminate; gloomy; legal; ripened.

verbs
achieve—; bear—; claim—; clamor for—; conspire—; crave—; demand—; enact—; exact—; forego—; pledge—; press for—; promise—; pursue—; rain—on; seek—; swear—; vow—; wreak—; yield—; —overtakes.
(See revenge, retribution.)

VENGEFUL

adverbs
openly; notoriously; spitefully; murderously; naturally; temperamentally; remarkably; cruelly; bitterly; unrestrainedly; dangerously; secretly; alarmingly; fanatically; wickedly; unforgivingly; reprehensibly; curiously; outrageously; furtively; stealthily; savagely.

VENOM

adjectives
subtle; palsying; spider; lasting; rank.

verbs
anoint with—; antidote—; assimilate—; extract—; immunize to—; infuse—; inject—; neutralize—; resist—; steep in—; succumb to—; suck up—; weaken—; —courses through; —deadens; —overcomes; —paralyzes; —rankles; —seeps through; —stuns.
(See poison, toxin.)

VENOMOUS

adverbs

notoriously; incredibly; hatefully; unfortunately; incurably; fatally; mortally; naturally; terribly; manifestly; horribly; fearfully; conspicuously; outrageously; reprehensibly; uncommonly; highly; intensely.

VENTILATE (*v*)

adverbs

adequately; thoroughly; defectively; healthfully; beneficially; automatically.

VENTILATION

adjectives

controlled; defective; adequate; automatic; necessary; healthful.

verbs

accomplish—; adjust—; afford—; allow—; facilitate—; furnish—; impair—; lack—; offer—; prescribe—; prevent—; promote—; require—; stabilize—; starve for—; systematize—; want—; —reanimates; —refreshes; —restores; —revivifies.

(See breathing, respiration.)

VENTURE

adjectives

advantageous; revolutionary; maiden; disillusioning; successful; uncertain; amateur; scientific; short-lived; private; matrimonial; speculative; prodigious; fruitful; maritime; succeeding; money-making; biographical; profitable.

verbs

abandon—; acclaim—; back—; contemplate —; decry—; defeat—; denounce—; disclose —; embark on—; encourage—; endanger—; eye—; finance—; forsake—; further—; gamble on—; imperil—; insure—; menace —; promote—; pursue—; relinquish—; threaten—; undertake—; stake on—; withdraw from—; —crashes; —entails; —flourishes; —tempts; —thrives.

(See effort, enterprise, project, undertaking.)

VENTURE (*v*)

adverbs

buoyantly; soothingly; boldly; timidly; hazardously; trustfully; wistfully; occasionally; cautiously; oracularly; imperiously; openly; solemnly; daringly; rashly; madly; sullenly; complacently; tactfully; timorously; fruitlessly; profitably.

(See dare, risk.)

VENTURESOME

adverbs

distressingly; boyishly; joyously; fantastically; disturbingly; unaccountably; alarmingly; colossally; terribly; dramatically; crazily; spectacularly; notoriously; strangely; singularly; amazingly; recklessly; incredibly; foolishly; boldly; bravely; audaciously; romantically; vicariously; courageously; unnecessarily; disconcertingly; ostentatiously; showily; daringly.

VERACIOUS

adverbs

naturally; habitually; dependably; utterly; absolutely; reliably; strictly; wholly; courageously; boldly; defiantly.

VERACITY

adjectives

scrupulous; attested; unalloyed; simple; inflexible; proved; innate.

verbs

affirm—; assure of—; authenticate—; confirm—; contravene—; demand—; discipline to—; dispute—; doubt—; gainsay—; impugn —; insure of—; maintain—; profess—; question—; reassert—; rebut—; refute—; regard—; repudiate—; swear to—; trust—; vow to—.

(See honesty, truth, frankness.)

VERANDA

adjectives

spreading; glass-enclosed; canvas-covered; sunken; shady; cool.

VERB

verbs

abuse—; accentuate—; adorn with—; avoid —; bandy—s; bristle with—; classify—; choose—; coin—; condense—; conjugate—; corrupt—; cull—s; decide on—; dedicate —; discard—; dispense with—; elect—; eliminate—; employ—; encounter—; eschew —; espouse—s; examine—s; exclude—s; explore—; fancy—; fix upon—; gasp at—; gather—; go in quest of—; grind out—s; identify—; indulge in—; inspire—; intone—; lavish—; manipulate—; marvel at—; misemploy—; modify—; overwork—; pluck—; prefer—; probe—; reel off—s; reject—; repudiate—s; sanction—; search for—; scrutinize—; seek—; select—; shun—; tabulate —s; thirst for—; —accomplishes; —achieves; —alludes to; —animates; —appeals; —asserts; —bites; —caps; —carries out; —colors; —compels; —complements; —completes; —connotes; —consummates; —controls; —conveys; —crowns; —crystallizes; —declares; —defines; —delineates; —depicts; —derives from; —denotes; —distorts; —drives home; —effects; —energizes; —enlivens; —enriches; —exaggerates; —expresses; —frolics; —fulfills; —gyrates; —impels; —implies; —imports; —improves; —indicates; —informs; —interprets; —invigorates; —kindles; —maintains; —moves; —overshadows; —penetrates; —perfects; —performs; —s plunge into; —portrays; —predicates; —provokes; —renders complete; —responds; —rounds out; —rouses; —seals; —s seethe with; —signifies; —s spring into; —states; —stimulates; —strengthens; —suggests; —supplies action; —swings into action; —urges; —wages; analyzes—; —purports.

VERBOSE

adverbs
incurably; tiresomely; inveterately; monotonously; wearisomely; awkwardly; unexpectedly; grossly; crassly; ineptly; clumsily; childishly; garrulously; fulsomely; terribly; extravagantly; unacceptably; unfortunately.

VERDANT

adverbs
delightfully; luxuriantly; invitingly; alluringly; lushly; properly; unexpectedly; gratifyingly; brilliantly; remarkably; unusually; beautifully.

VERDICT

adjectives
lawful; unanimous; manic-depressive; inevitable; consistent; emphatic; intelligent; differing; favorable; adverse; contrary; just; preposterous; fair; inexplicable.

verbs
affect—; appeal—; arrive at—; bias—; carry—; cast—; clarify—; confirm—; contest—; dally with—; deliver—; denounce—; determine—; disclose—; dispute—; elicit—; enter—; evolve—; influence—; justify—; maintain—; ponder—; prejudice—; present —; pronounce—; propound—; question—; render—; return—; reverse—; secure—; sustain—; venture—; verify—; voice—; warrant—; —awards; —dooms; —involves; —misjudges; —startles.

(See judgment, award, finding, decision.)

VERDURE

adjectives
lush; perpetual; profuse; deepening; rank; gloomy; restful; living; perennial; vigorous; tropical; virgin; black; complex; endless; vivid; close-cropped; unchanging.

verbs
clothe in—; prune—; reflect—; thin out—; trim—; —blankets; —cloaks; —colors; —curtains; —flourishes; —freshens; —mantles; —obscures; —overspreads; —screens; —shades; —smothers; —veils.

(See grass, vegetation.)

VERGE

adjectives
utmost; inclusive; uppermost; farthest; beetling; extreme; outward.

verbs
achieve—; ascend to—; approach—; attain —; skirt—; steer to—; tread on—; —borders; —bounds; —encloses.

(See boundary, edge.)

VERIFICATION

adjectives
official; decisive; experimental; attempted.

VERIFY (*v*)

adverbs
unaccountably; accurately; substantially; impartially; officially; experimentally; decisively; specifically.

(See confirm, prove.)

VERITY

adjectives
continual; intense; eternal; conditional; fundamental; bitter; faithful.

verbs
acclaim—; adulterate—; apprehend—; arm with—; demonstrate—; deny—; establish—; evidence—; garble—; ponder—; proclaim —; pronounce—; realize—; reveal—; substantiate—; sustain—; testify to—; unfold —; utter—; voice—.

(See veracity, reality.)

VERMIN

adjectives
creeping; invisible; filthy; parasitic; unpleasant.

verbs
abhor—; breed—; dispel—; eradicate—; exterminate—; swarm with—; —abound; —carry; —contaminate; —defile; —endanger; —infect; —infest; —nauseate; —offend; —overrun; —plague; —pollute; —thrive.
(See insects, cockroach, bug.)

VERMINOUS

adverbs
dangerously; filthily; disgustingly; deplorably; hopelessly; unhealthfully; unsanitarily; unfortunately; damnably; grossly; terribly; dreadfully; unspeakably; indescribably; irremediably; foully; revoltingly; awfully; incredibly.

VERSATILE

adverbs
delightfully; amazingly; charmingly; curiously; admirably; surprisingly; incredibly; marvellously; unbelievably; eminently; illustriously; uncommonly; distinctly; conspicuously; consummately; remarkably; highly.

VERSATILITY

adjectives
vivacious; enormous; characteristic; established; apparent.

verbs
acclaim—; acquire—; appreciate—; attain—; commend—; display—; evince—; exhibit—; marvel at—; value—; —affords; —amazes; —astounds; —embraces; —enables; —excels; —staggers.
(See skill, ability.)

VERSE

adjectives
unpremeditated; mature; evocative; ironic; abominable; flower-sweet; golden; deathless; luxurious; dramatic; magnificent; prosaic; little; magnanimous; well-cadenced; jolly; metaphysical; immortal; marvellous; graceful; introspective; devotional; macaronic; malicious; supererogatory; graceful; slumberous; polished; society; various (pl); measured; heroic; flattering; homely; blank; realistic; faultless; exquisite; sonorous; caustic; singable; sanguinary; halting; rustic; numerous (pl); neglected; faltering; patriotic; poetic; fascinating; goodly; doggerel; trashy; matchless; piercing; common; undistinguished; musical; balanced; classical; mournful; distinctive; satiric; quillwrit; soothing; galloping; insulting; delicate; melodious; non-dramatic; sorrowful; alliterative; inspired; tolerable; ennobling; clever; octosyllabic; circulated; mechanical; commonplace; comic; unfinished; coarse; outstanding; ridiculous; assonanced; occasional.

verbs
bawl—; carol—; compose—; dash off—; declaim—; divide into—s; enumerate—s; inscribe—on; improvise—; measure—; memorize—; peruse—; polish—; quote—; render—; scan—; scrawl—; sing—; —delights; —effloresces; —eulogizes; —proclaims; —rhymes; —sings of.
(See poetry, poem.)

VERSED

adverbs
well; remarkably; consummately; learnedly; completely; unusually; extraordinarily; supremely; distinctly; effectively.

VERSIFIER

adjectives
ingenious; skillful; mere; melodious.

VERSIFY (*v*)

adverbs
wittily; cleverly; beautifully; exquisitely; scurrilously; ingeniously; melodiously; skillfully.
(See write, compose.)

VERSION

adjectives
corrected; discordant; condensed; spirited; difficult; vamped-up; coarse; dramatic; rhymed; brisk; virulent; defunct; trimmed-down; garbled; thrilling; pedantic; useful; varying (pl); different; radical; scurrilous; casual; faithful; authorized; modified; artistic; classic; exaggerated; improved; authentic; appealing.

verbs
afford—; authenticate—; color—; confirm—; dash off—; distort—; garble—; illustrate—; maintain—; modify—; offer—; pervert—; simplify—; sustain—; unearth—; varnish—; verify—; —s conflict; —contradicts; —differs; —falsifies; —glosses over;

—interprets; —misrepresents; —slanders.
(See comparison, description, meaning.)

VESICAL

verbs
compress—; contract—; dilate—; distend—; drain—; excise—; incise—; inflame—; irritate—; occlude—; pierce—; puncture—; strangulate—; tap—; —bursts; —dries up; —expands; —protrudes; —shrinks; —shrivels.
(See cell, cavity, sac.)

VESSEL
(boat)

verbs
abandon—; batter—; buffet—; captain—; embark on—; equip—; fit out—; fuel—; ground—; helm—; man—; moor—; navigate—; pilot—; punt—; rig out—; scull—; strand—; waft—; —conveys; —departs; —plies; —plows; —sallies forth; —scuds; —shoves off; —skims; —straggles in; —tosses; —weighs anchor.
(See launch, boat, motor-boat, ship.)

VESSEL
(general)

adjectives
primitive; anchored; ship-wrecked; surrendered; tossing; precious; perished; contaminated; rowing; excretory; convenient; rich-laden; populous; disabled; earthen; effective; weather-beaten; superb; foundering; communicating; fragile; overcrowded; capillary; half-empty; sacred; lymphatic; puny; puffing; staggering; seaworthy; gentle; endangered; straggling; suspicious; suitable.

VEST

adjectives
jeweled; warm; bedecked; plain; stylish.

VEST (v)

adverbs
exclusively; specifically; diplomatically; legislatively; religiously; temporarily.
(See invest.)

VESTIBULE

adjectives
crowded; well-designed; monumental.

VESTIGE

adjectives
last; remaining; enormous; lone.

verbs
bear—; discern—; disclose—; display—; exhibit—; mark—; recognize—; reveal—; stamp out—; uncover—; unearth—; —betokens; —evidences; —fades; —indicates; —remains; —survives; —tesifies to.
(See sign, mark, trace, remnant, remains.)

VESTIGIAL

adverbs
probably; undoubtedly; apparently; manifestly; unmistakably; possibly; credibly; curiously; interestingly; traceably; definitely.

VESTMENT

adjectives
gorgeous; coarse; tattered; purchasable; antique; glorious; somber.

VESTURE

adjectives
imperfect; muddy; pretty; mechanic; napless; choral; pompous; linen; fatal.

VETERAN

adjectives
shoeless; surviving; wary; old; experienced; seasoned; war-worn; gallant; right-minded; decrepit; battered; stalwart; invalided; grim-visaged; hardy; callous.

VETO

adjectives
suspensive; exasperating; equivocal; final; overruled.

verbs
anticipate—; clamp down—; exercise—; fear—; override—; sustain—; table—; —annuls; —checks; —curtails; —dashes the hopes; —debars; —declines; —excludes; —nullifies; —overrides; —overrules; —quashes; —quells; —rejects; —sets aside; —stems; —voids; —withholds.
(See vote, restriction, prohibition.)

VEX (v)

adverbs
intolerably; shrewdly; exceedingly; maddeningly; bitterly; ceaselessly; mutely; horridly; violently; mentally; fiercely; tryingly.
(See irritate, annoy.)

VEXATION

adjectives
silent; resentful; mutual; insupportable; horrid; extreme; evident; puzzled; fierce;

tearful; violent; mental; bitter; trying.

verbs
allay—; arouse—; bear—; conceal—; conciliate—; disclose—; display—; evince—; exhibit—; feign—; foment—; fret in—; incite—; induce—; occasion—; overcome—; palliate—; provoke—; restrain—; writhe in—; —cankers; —irks; —gnaws at; —riles (colloq.); —ruffles; —sours.

(See anger, annoyance, displeasure, irritation, ire, chagrin.)

VEXATIOUS

adverbs
especially; unusually; naturally; occasionally; recently; particularly; monotonously; pettily; terribly; inopportunely; plaguedly; deucedly; intolerably; unfortunately; unimaginably; horribly.

VEXED

adverbs
definitely; unreasonably; foolishly; senselessly; unfairly; deeply; unjustly; distinctly; quickly; easily; unhappily; miserably; wretchedly; ill-temperedly; annoyingly; bitterly; plaguedly; pathetically; sorely; grievously; frightfully; intolerably; distressingly; unbearably; furiously; mightily; hotly.

VIAL

adjectives
wrathful; blasting; tiny; bitter; poisonous.

verbs
analyze—; charge—; despatch—; drain—; eject—; filter—; imbibe from—; inhale from —; label—; quaff from—; seal—; snuff up from—; sterilize—; swill—; uncork—; —befuddles; —enlivens; —envenoms; —paralyzes.

(See medicine, glass bottle.)

VIANDS

adjectives
ruder; exotic; mortal; dainty; ready-baked; tasty; savory.

verbs
bolt—; despatch—; devour—; display—; do justice to—; fall to—; gobble—; gulp—; market—; nibble—; preserve—; purvey—; regale with—; relish—; savor—; tuck in—; —nourish; —revive; —tempt.

(See food, victuals, provisions, fare.)

VIBRATE (v)

adverbs
resonantly; discordantly; tunelessly; curiously; rhythmically; mournfully; audibly; sonorously; tremulously; mysteriously.

(See swing, vacillate.)

VIBRATING

adverbs
constantly; thunderously; regularly; tremulously; sympathetically; rapidly; curiously; magically; tunefully; mysteriously; noisily; silently; strangely; secretly; incomprehensibly; dependably; inexplicably; ominously; steadily.

VIBRATION

adjectives
stimulating; rhythmical; deep; touching; braced; nervous; constant; superimposed; mysterious; longitudinal; brave; mournful; audible; sonorous; heart-quaking; rapid; tremulous; ravishing; isochronous; uncomfortable; definite.

verbs
avert—; curb—; record—s; transmit—; —agitates; —ceases; —churns; —disconcerts; —disquiets; —jars; —jiggles; —joggles; —jolts; —jostles; —jounces; —oscillates; —perturbs; —pitches; —pulsates; —rocks; —throbs.

(See pulse, earthquake.)

VICARIOUS

adverbs
altogether; comfortably; perilously; wholly; strangely; generously; curiously; merely.

VICE

adjectives
solemn; enemy; ultimate; incurable; selfish; discordant; encroaching; virtuous; kindred; respective; disgusting; monstrous; gilded; beneficial; hereditary; distinguished; black; ineffable; distorted; plausible; infamous; searing; overshadowing; ruling; alluring; reckless; engendering; unmarred; trivial; heathen; distressing; deliberate; fashionable; supreme; depicting; abstract; notorious; hateful; gross; coarse; bold; reputed; solitary; ingrained; popular; essential; embodied; walking; redeeming; filthy.

verbs
abandon—; addict to—; campaign against check—; clothe in—; combat—; commercial-

ize—; condemn—; condone—; confess—; crusade against—; curb—; cure—; denounce —; expose—; fall into—; forsake—; foster —; indulge in—; renounce—; reveal—; smack of—; sow—; stem—; stray into—; succumb to—; uncover—; weed out—; —corrupts; —debauches; —demoralizes; —depraves; —desecrates; —flourishes; —fouls; —perverts; —stains; —sullies; —taints; lapse into—.

(See knavery, lawlessness, licentiousness, crime.)

VICINITY

adjectives

immediate; apogeal; perilous; proximate.

verbs

abandon—; acquaint one with—; adjoin—; approach—; betake oneself to—; border—; comb—; converge on—; denude—; devastate—; drift to—; encircle—; encompass—; expel from—; flank—; forsake—; frequent —; guard—; patrol—; picket—; prowl about—; ramble about—; roam—; rove—; screen—; shroud—; skirt—; stroll about—.

(See locality, neighborhood.)

VICIOUS

adverbs

notoriously; famously; incomparably; alarmingly; criminally; heinously; nefariously; brutally; incredibly; indescribably; incomparably; wholly; politically; obviously; deplorably; manifestly; terribly; basely; grossly; obscenely; morally; notably; indefensibly; dangerously; intolerably.

VICIOUSNESS

adjectives

inherent; senile; compounded; essential; natural; characteristic.

VICISSITUDES

adjectives

myriad; sublime; sweet; sudden; mortal; sad; strange.

verbs

acquaint one with—; avert—; control—; decry—; denounce—; deplore—; dwell upon —; forecast—; forestall—; foretell—; hazard—; meet—; prepare for—; prophesy—; risk—; suffer—; welcome—; —alter; —imperil; —jeopardize; —revolutionize; —threaten.

(See change, misfortune.)

VICTIM

adjectives

unsuspicious; noble; unfortunate; struggling; hapless; miserable; desirable; ulster-clad; prospective; unspotted; penitent; wretched; choking; immediate; bridal; potential; slaughtered; unresisting; deluded; hunted; illustrious; innumerable (pl); unthinking; contemptible; cowering; countless (pl); unshriven; unnamed; supposed; ingenuous; mutilated; livid; squalid; multifarious (pl).

verbs

avenge—; bait—; beguile—; bilk—; console—; decoy—; defraud—; dupe—; ease —; ensnare—; entice—; exonerate—; goad —; harass—; harrow—; lure—; maim—; martyrize—; sacrifice—; snare—; solicit—s; succor—s; trap—; wrack—; wring—; —bewails; —decries; —despairs; —endures; —grieves; —laments; —languishes; —mourns; —pines; —suffers; —testifies; —tolerates; —succumbs to.

(See prey, quarry, amateur.)

VICTOR

adjectives

laurel-crowned; joyless; loving; upborne; modest.

VICTORIOUS

adverbs

ultimately; finally; eventually; immediately; recently; grandly; brilliantly; magnificently; gloriously; splendidly; royally; modestly; triumphantly; quietly; logically; reasonably; suddenly; unexpectedly; deservedly; happily; luckily; blessedly; utterly.

VICTORY

adjectives

smashing; splendid; subsequent; glorious; brilliant; dialectic; decisive; barren; undeclining; approaching; partisan; ultimate; triumphant; sweeping; marvelous; inevitable; overwhelming; publicized; enormous; fresh; unvarying; superb; prospective; world-famous; ineffective; self-assured; bloody; wholesome; retributive; manifold (pl); signal; endless; speedy; secret; obligatory; gladsome; strategic; Pyrrhic.

verbs

acclaim—; achieve—; advance to—; anticipate—; assure of—; botch—; celebrate—; chalk up—; clinch—; commemorate—;

crown with—; emerge with—; eventuate in —; fall short of—; gain—; glorify—; goad to—; grace—; grind out—; guide to—; hail —; inspire—; insure—; magnify—; pledge to—; proclaim—; promise—; purchase—; radiate—; rob of—; romp to—; result in—; salute—; score—; seal—; sense—; signify —; snatch—; spur to—; sweep to—; temper —; wreathe in—; wrest—from; —demoralizes; —eludes; —evades; —overwhelms; —routs; —vanquishes.

(See conquest, advantage, triumph, success, supremacy.)

VICTUALS

verbs

bolt—; consume—; deluge with—; deplete —; despatch—; devour—; dispense—; furnish with—; gobble—; gorge—; gulp—; laud—; munch—; praise—; preserve—; prepare—; provide—; purvey—; refrigerate—; relish—; replenish—; savor—; stint on—; stock with—; —attract; —lure; —nourish; —refresh; —renew; —restore; —tempt.

(See food, viands.)

VIEW
(*general*)

adjectives

extensive; provincial; splendid; comprehensive; topographical; modern; regimentalist; historical; respective (pl); foregoing; definite; monarchical; wide; representative; personal; broad; solemn; reiterated; clashing; enlarged; spiritual; systematized; theological; religious; divergent; masculine; gloomy; prehistoric; realistic; bloody; rationalist; stereopticon; philosophic; dismayed; differing; pessimistic; magnificent; distinct; enchanting; optimistic; perspective; dubious; architectural; humanistic; infinite; dynamic; trustworthy; lucid; celebrated; exaggerated; prophetic; benighted; interesting; experimental; anti-democratic; vivid; complete; unmitigated; intensive; spectacular; elaborate; successive (pl); deliberate; panoramic; dissolving; sentimental; esthetic; superb; metaphysical; charitable; illuminated; individualistic; unbounded; intellectual; peculiar; unwashed; liberal; nihilistic; sudden; injurious; aberrant; unobstructed; continuous; partial; stable; mischievous; worldly; unfavorable; glorious; luminous; lofty; idealistic; impressive; practical; prevalent; ample; mechanical; cynic; human; similar; mystical; sharp; clear; orthodox; believing; angelic; erroneous; nerve-trying; subjective; romantic; beautiful; shuddering; hopeless; dismal; sympathetic; primitive; cheerful; gorgeous; old-fashioned; superficial; many-sided; fascinating; mortal; rosy; undulating; startled; disparaging; dignified; prudent; calm; sanguine; deep; advanced; materialistic; despairing; evolutionary; irresponsible; investigating; charming; disheartened; constitutional; rational; especial; collateral; dissolving; limited; pecuniary; tenable; straining; benevolent; theoretic; matured; retrospective; unfair; uninterrupted; rigid; indescribable; dissolving; sightless; enlightened; melancholy; cross-section; partial; stately; conservative; top-lofty; settled; picturesque; disputed; world-famous; thrilling; splendid; skyline; river; exceptional; overpowering; orthodox.

VIEW
(*intellectual*)

verbs

advertise—; air—; alter—; analyze—; arrive at—; balance—; bias—; bolster—; broaden—; cancel—; cherish—; clarify—; color—; conceive—; conciliate—; confide—; confirm—; countenance—; credit—; demonstrate—; dispute—; distort—; embrace—; entertain—; establish—; evaluate—; exchange—s; expose—s; expound—; falsify—; fix—; formulate—; grasp—; illustrate—; inculcate—; indoctrinate—; indorse—; influence—; inspire—; integrate—s; interpret —; justify—; lack—; maintain—; narrow —; nurse—; object to—; oppose—; originate —; present—; proclaim—; profess—; reconsider—; repudiate—; retain—; reveal—; set forth—; shape—; share—; shift—; substantiate—; sum up—; support—; sustain—; thwart—; uphold—; voice—; warp—; warrant—; —prevails; —shocks.

(See belief, aim, mission, notion, aspect, perspective, perception, opinion.)

VIEW
(*landscape, sight, etc.*)

verbs

afford—; bare to—; beautify—; blemish—; cloud—; command—; contemplate—; deface —; distort—; dull—; emblazon—; enjoy—; exalt—; frame—; gaze at—; glimpse—; mar—; obliterate—; obscure—; obstruct—; photograph—; pop into—; portray—; preserve—; rivet upon—; screen—; shade—; sketch—; telescope—; vanish from—; —

blurs; —dazzles; —enchants; —enkindles; —enraptures; —enthralls; —impassions; —impresses; —inspires; —petrifies; —unfolds.
(See sight, scene, prospect, panorama, landscape.)

VIEW (v)

adverbs
regretfully; historically; cynically; sardonically; incessantly; dispassionately; faintly; fitfully; hastily; curiously; extensively; solemnly; philosophically; optimistically; charitably; idealistically; subjectively; sympathetically; objectively; theoretically; panoramically.
(See regard, see.)

VIEWPOINT

adjectives
hard-boiled; short-sighted; national; practical; impersonal; unbiased; fresh; optimistic; evolutionistic; customary; universal; sociological; pessimistic; prejudiced.

VIGIL

adjectives
tearless; lone; late; bitter; dangerous; heart-chilling; weary; solemn; unhallowed; anxious; tongueless.

verbs
allay—; arrest—; curtail—; dread—; ease—; eke out—; endure—; interrupt—; maintain—; necessitate—; prolong—; protract—; relax—; relinquish—; resume—; slacken—; survive—; suspend—; sustain—; terminate—; —fatigues; —tells; —weakens; —wearies; —weighs upon.
(See vigilance, interest, watch, scrutiny.)

VIGILANCE

adjectives
eternal; remarkable; utmost; constant; increasing; unceasing; determined; extraordinary; redoubled; jealous; habitual; stern.

verbs
admonish—; circumvent—; ease—; enforce—; escape—; exhort—; heighten—; intensify—; lighten—; maintain—; mitigate—; necessitate—; reduce—; relax—; sharpen—; slacken—; —declines; —discovers; —insures; —lapses; —safeguards; —subsides; —wanes; —wearies.
(See interest, vigil, caution.)

VIGILANT

adverbs
eternally; constantly; unrelentingly; carefully; intelligently; ordinarily; usually; uncommonly; especially; particularly; unremittingly; cruelly; lovingly; fondly; affectionately; gently; anxiously; fearfully; timidly; nervously; sternly; harshly; curiously; inquisitively; inexcusably; vexatiously; inescapably.

VIGNETTE

verbs
adorn with—s; dash off—; embellish with—s; enamel—; etch—; execute—; frame—; impress—; print—; sketch—; stipple—; varnish—; —delineates; —depicts; —describes; —illustrates; —ornaments; —pictures; —portrays.
(See portrait, picture, sketch.)

VIGOR

adjectives
mortal; ethereal; disciplined; hybrid; prime; uninterrupted; florid; excessive; tireless; sinewy; remarkable; accustomed; terse; quickened; coarse; wild; dramatic; muscular; athletic; wonted; intellectual; pristine; furious; rude; aggressive; manly; plastic; incisive; contrary; bodily; selfish; incredible; extraordinary; original; renewing; increased; peristaltic; conscious; customary; dynamic; remorseless; emulating; recuperative; glorious; determined; rustic; redoubled; lusty; classic; especial; elastic; hardy; graceful; masculine; mighty; purposeful; youthful; mental; terrible; unabated; astonishing; superabundant; full; sudden; original; unimpaired; native; offhand; renovated.

verbs
acquire—; demand—; deplete—; display—; endow with—; enhance—; exert—; exhibit—; infuse—; inject—; instill—; lessen—; maintain—; perform with—; preserve—; radiate—; renew—; retain—; restore—; sap up—; stimulate—; store up—; sustain—; —buttresses; —fades; —fortifies.
(See force, energy, "pep", strength.)

VIGOROUS

adverbs
splendidly; sufficiently; brawnily; healthily; warrantably; actually; fortunately; necessarily; apparently; mysteriously; manifestly; uncommonly; remarkably; luckily.

VILIFY (*v*)

adverbs
blackly; wrathfully; maliciously; malignantly; cruelly; viciously; jealously; furiously; terribly; coarsely; rudely; hatefully; grossly.
(See slander, traduce.)

VILLA

adjectives
glittering; enchanting; expensive; commodious; peaceful; dainty; restful; gaudy; handsome; spacious; suburban; voluptuous; sumptuous; medieval.

VILLAGE

adjectives
smiling; toy-like; poverty-stricken; cool; shady; damp; worn-out; patriarchal; incurious; straggling; dependent; adjacent; innumerable (pl); obscure; rustic; neighboring; ordinary; provincial; whitewashed; poor; dusky; ghost-like; pathetic; retired; pleasant; well-ordered; preoccupied; miserable; insensible; rural; native; deserted; squalid; insignificant; forsaken; producing; self-supporting; isolated; delightful; stupid-looking; little; stony; picturesque; manufacturing; sprawling; embowered; remote; shabby; lovely; sweet; smiling; red-roofed; helpless; pastoral; benighted.

verbs
abide in—; arouse—; border—; commute from—; desert—; devastate—; dot with—s; ensconce in—; flank—; forsake—; frequent —; inhabit—; lull—; nestle in—; quarter in—; raze—; repair to—; skirt—; storm—; —expands; —flourishes; —hums; —straggles; —thrives.
(See neighborhood, community, town, city.)

VILLAGER

verbs
alarm—; beseech—; bilk—; dominate—; educate—; enslave—; harangue—; plague —; rook—; rouse—; summon—; swindle —; tax—; —bands; —commutes; —cultivates; —descends upon; —flocks to; —markets; —prospers; —rises; —scatters; —thwarts.
(See citizen, individual, inhabitant, taxpayer, public.)

VILLAIN

adjectives
plain-dealing; replenished; ungrateful; dissembling; precise; white; sweet; monstrous; soulless; repulsive; murdering; rich; senseless; false; infernal; cursed; notorious; prodigious; wicked; skulking; accomplished; penurious; scheming; murderous; shag-haired; fine; hoary; inflexible; trusty; honorable; abandoned; atrocious; deliberate; cool.

verbs
apprehend—; banish—; band—; condemn —; curtail—; denounce—; expose—; ferret out—; incarcerate—; inveigh against—; jail—; portray—; prosecute—; reveal—; scourge—; seize—; sniff out—; —s band; —betrays; —confesses; —conspires; —defiles; —desecrates; —eludes; —evades; —plots; —seduces; —slanders; —transgresses.
(See profligate, actor, scoundrel, criminal, monster, character.)

VILLAINOUS

adverbs
unmistakably; utterly; despicably; unhappily; terribly; dreadfully; unspeakably; infamously; conspicuously; incredibly; unimaginably; remarkably; contemptibly; defiantly; openly; secretly; blandly; actually; manifestly.

VILLAINY

adjectives
cold-blooded; multiplying; deliberate; unusual; naked; superfluous; reeking; systematic; stupendous; vocal; sensual; deliberate; demoniacal; subtle.

verbs
accuse of—; charge with—; denounce—; deplore—; detect—; disclose—; expose—; forsake—; involve—; lapse into—; practise—; punish—; renounce—; resort to—; reveal —; rue—; sink into—; turn from—; uncover —; —defames; —degrades.
(See sin, wickedness, crime.)

VINDICATE (*v*)

adverbs
amply; sufficiently; triumphantly; gallantly; honorably; magnanimously; heroically; creditably; ingeniously; simply.
(See justify, correct.)

VINDICATION

adjectives
alleged; gloomy; culminating; prompt; attempted; triumphant; labored; simple; cred-

itable; vicarious; ingenious; mischievous; pampered.

VINDICTIVE

adverbs
utterly; openly; secretly; defiantly; violently; dangerously; furtively; alarmingly; portentously; ominously; oddly; peculiarly; smoothly; cruelly; bitterly; brutally.

VINDICTIVENESS

adjectives
satanic; detestable; vicious; spiteful; hateful.

verbs
appease—; assert—; assuage—; calm—; dispose toward—; ease—; express—; indulge in—; justify—; harbor—; quell—; relax—; relent—; reveal—; satisfy—; temper—; tranquillize—; warrant—; —grows; —subsides; —wanes; —wakes.

(See hatred, animosity, contempt.)

VINE

adjectives
withering; never-flowering; gadding; tangled; clinging; trellised; scented; delicate; springing; arching; thorny; sovereign; trailing; delicious; intricate; clustering; bordering; ambitious; well-pruned; perfume-breathing; flaming; riotous; luxuriant; creeping; strangling; ambrosial; cloistral; rose-flecked; immense; parasitic; sweet; breathed; interwoven; twisted; choice.

verbs
bunch on—; graft into—; husband—; load—; lop—; prune—; screen with—s; smother in—s; support—; transplant—; —bears; —bows with; —clambers; —clings; —creeps; —embowers; —enriches; —entwines; —flourishes; —overspreads; —scents; —thickens; —thrives; —trails; —yields.

(See honeysuckle, etc.)

VINEYARD

adjectives
sloping; blood-tinctured; terraced; luscious; productive.

VIOLATE (*v*)

adverbs
flagrantly; expressly; palpably; basely; grossly; flatly; wickedly; persistently; undisguisedly; expressly; criminally; spiritually.

(See transgress, trespass.)

VIOLATION

adjectives
gross; flat; denouncing; wide-spread; wicked; conscious; signal; persistent; undisguised; express.

verbs
condone—; constitute—; disapprove of—; disclose—; dismiss for—; frown on—; ignore—; justify—; penalize—; protest—; wink at—; —desecrates; —encroaches upon; —infringes; —nullifies; —ostracizes; —piques; —repudiates; —riles (colloq.); —tramples; —transgresses; —voids.

(See breach, infringement, infraction.)

VIOLATOR

adjectives
apparent; sacrilegious.

verbs
apprehend—; check—; denounce—; disclose—; exile—; fine—; jail—; "nab"—; pounce upon—; punish—; seize—; trail—; —abuses; —baffles; —breaks; —despoils; —disregards; —eludes; —encroaches; —evades; —infringes; —mulcts; —profanes; —ravishes.

(See criminal.)

VIOLENCE

adjectives
frightful; murderous; unlooked-for; sheer; spontaneous; physical; reckless; passionate; high-handed; unwonted; brutal; unjustifiable; glorious; unscrupulous; theatric; impetuous; irreconcilable; ghostly; gentle; midnight; unreasoning; swift; bloody; needful; uncommon; loud; extreme; odious; meditated; irregular; personal; momentary; aggressive; stunning; sacrilegious; devilish; cowardly; invisible; undiminished; occasional; tragic; threatening; restless; increasing; quiet.

verbs
advocate—; allay—; avert—; balk at—; bar—; burst into—; condone—; cow by—; curb—; denounce—; deplore—; deprecate—; discountenance—; employ—; foment—; frustrate—; incite—; indulge in—; inflame to—; instigate—; lull—; pacify—; precipi-

tate—; provoke—; quell—; resort to—; restrain—; subdue—; —erupts; —rages.

(See malice, impetuosity, indignation, intensify, fury, anger.)

VIOLENT

adverbs

ungovernably; dangerously; lawlessly; youthfully; heedlessly; lamentably; deplorably; openly; actively; defiantly; insurgently; restively; mutinously; rebelliously; tumultuously; treasonably; incorrigibly; persistently; obstinately.

VIOLET

adjectives

glowing; blue-veined; royal; nodding; shrinking; purple; dewy; first; blown; lucid.

VIOLIN

adjectives

alto; beautiful; masterful; priceless.

VIPER

adjectives

universal; jumping; startled.

VIRGIN

adjectives

wily; white-robed; young; budding; vestal; regarded; pale-eyed; poor; learned; powerful; ill-drawn; ultimate; charming; bashful; blushing.

verbs

befit—; bestow upon—; defile—; deflower—; despoil—; esteem—; play the—; respect—; revere—; seduce—; sully—; touch—; —binds; —brags; —captives; —exults; —flaunts; —flouts; —glories; —scolds; —stifles.

(See girl, woman, wife.)

VIRGINITY

adjectives

pretty; irrevocable; indestructible; antiquated; long-preserved.

verbs

acknowledge—; ascribe—; blemish—; dignify—; preserve—; pride oneself on—; profess—; question—; stain—; taint—; take—; tarnish—; threaten—; violate—; worship—; —imparts.

(See chastity, purity, virtue.)

VIRTUE

adjectives

disinterested; hereditary; acquired; slender; manly; unselfish; self-abnegating; conscious; commonplace; attractive; negative; imputed; stellar; domestic; sounding; sterling; vestal; infinite; peculiar; rigid; heroic; admirable; rare; impregnable; barbaric; paltry; distinguished; new-built; abstract; consummate; sober; well-known; surface; unassailable; exemplary; external; unpretending; perfect; unquestionable; diuretic; delightful; dominant; fanciful; honorable; active; ennobling; illustrious; beaming; wondrous; proud; suffering; healing; probable; proverbial; outraged; distressed; aromatic; contradictory; magnetic; outstanding; prime; redeeming; humble; lofty; wearied; beatific; grateful; possible; personal; ever-flourishing; supposed; unique; political; simple; superstitious; thoughtful; godlike; chief; inimitable; boasted; excellent; artificial; manifold (pl); legitimate; proper; nameless; eminent; high; spirited; preserved; knightly; intrinsic; certain; sublime; eclipsed; natural; unbecoming; old-fashioned; healing; ruining; comely; sweet; rude; ruffled; right; strict; sober; solid; public; prosaic; pure; nectarous; disputable; injurious; liberal; politic; cardinal; low; succored; religious; infant; medicinal; flowering; severe; reawakening; moral; middle; untainted; fundamental; marvelous; tangible; loving; aristocratic; definite; traditionary; boasted; small; philanthropic; powerful; cheap; incessant; rural; befriending; feminine; bastard; sundry (pl); leading; private; uncertain; amiable; grand; special; soporific; prodigious; ignominious.

verbs

acclaim—s; blot out—; commend—; cultivate—s; defend—; delight in—; embody—s; emphasize—s; esteem—; exemplify—; extol—s; forsake—; foster—; hail—; impart—to; implant—; incarnate—s; inculcate—; instil—; magnify—s; nurture—; observe—s; preserve—; proclaim—s; question—; recognize—s; redeem—; relinquish—; reward—; scoff at—; scorn—; sing—s; stray from—;

sustain—; —distinguishes; —prevails; —triumphs; —uplifts; embrace—.

(See chastity, integrity, morality, courage, prudence, honesty, fortitude, temperance, justice.)

VIRTUOUS

adverbs

pretentiously; unctuously; pharasaically; ostentatiously; actually; notably; entirely; conspicuously; apparently; supposedly; utterly; unquestionably; manifestly; palpably; definitely; remarkably; honestly; sincerely.

VIRULENT

adverbs

disastrously; unfortunately; cruelly; bitterly; admittedly; unusually; terribly; remarkably; insidiously; unbelievably; uncommonly; highly; dreadfully; dangerously.

VIRUS

verbs

allay—; antidote—; check—; combat—; confine—; counteract—; immunize to—; inactivate—; infect with—; inject—; isolate—; neutralize—; weaken—; —attacks; —consumes; —devastates; —inflames; —invades; —paralyzes; —prostrates; —ravages.

(See germ, disease, poison, venom.)

VISAGE

adjectives

grotesque; tawny; shattered; unmutilated; gory; grim; great; bloody; impassive; wrinkled; puckered; swarthy; fierce; monstrous; storied; infernal; importing; bleared; silver; favored; borrowed; illuminated; horrent; ironical; sickly; grotesque; hard-favored; glimmering; revolting; saintly; unrepentant; dark; passionless; weather-beaten; leathery; pale; choleric; ancient; coppery.

VISIBLE

adverbs

easily; undoubtedly; dimly; clearly; usually; wholly; completely; faintly; brightly; obscurely; distinctly; conspicuously; embarrassingly; inadvertently; unavoidably; purposely; inconveniently; awkwardly.

VISION
(*eyesight, etc.*)

verbs

astigmatize—; augment—; blur—; cloud—; conserve—; correct—; dazzle—; deprive of —; dim—; distort—; dull—; eclipse—; focus—upon; impair—; infract—; measure —; obscure—; obstruct—; preserve—; quicken—; ravage—; refract—; scathe—; screen—; sharpen—; shield from—; value —; veil—; warp—.

(See sight.)

VISION
(*general*)

adjectives

sudden; frightful; telescopic; sun-compelling; moral; transitory; tender; ravishing; foregone; delightful; alleged; vivid; specialized; remarkable; appointed; angelic; sweet; light; radiant; rectified; fresh; stunted; mental; early; concentrated; failing; gloomy; spiritual; horrible; calm; relentless; prophetic; useful; disturbing; embodied; unremembered; anxious; uncertain; harassing; artless; dying; frightful; dreadful; singular; ecstatic; tranced; charmed; skyey; world; unforgettable; transcendent; myopic; subjective; halting; transient; dim; fatal; chill; airy; baseless; blissful; narrating; painful; unreal; troubled; mysterious; culminating; morning; earthly; infinite; subtle; alluring; enchanted; unsubstantial; heavenly; saintly; rapturous; entrancing; hawk-like; glorious; cosmic; aesthetic; imaginary; extended; inspiring; subsequent; importunate; cold; confused; delirious; paradisical; impaired; encompassed; tranquil; ominous; pleasing; beautiful; long-promised; discriminating; beatific; downcast; obscure; lucid; hallowed; intellectual; unaided; creative; crystal; cradled; mental; clear; midday; pious; unclouded; overwhelming; singular; bored; sweet; rare; yearning; everlasting; earth-dimmed; defective; philosophical; vague; sun; window; fruitless; far-seeing; apocalyptic.

VISION
(*imagination*)

verbs

blur—; cherish—; conjure up—; fire by—; flirt with—; fulfill—; resolve—; reveal—; shake off—; train on—; —appears; —arises; —dances; —dawns upon; —dazes; —departs; —fascinates; —flashes before; —flees; —flits; —foretells; —haunts; —materializes; —prophesies.

(See imagination, phantom, dream, phantasy, mirage, nightmare, image.)

VISIONARY

adverbs
fantastically; quixotically; chimerically; ephemerally; unsubstantially; imponderably; tenuously; mystically; mythically; fancifully; uncommonly; highly; inanely; vacuously; airily; blankly; dreamily; groundlessly.

VISIT

adjectives
delightful; dramatic; ultimate; surreptitious; unlooked-for; flying; proffered; cordial; doubtful; courteous; unceremonious; yearly; imperial; casual; frequent (pl); distinguished; intended; transient; extraordinary; dreaded; volunteered; ill-timed; agreeable; unavailing; momentous; intemperate; meditated; unwelcome; gentle; prolonged; approaching; parochial; wonted; flying; last-mentioned; hurried; occasional; untimely; perfunctory; domiciliary; impending; stated; cool; comfortable; quiet; happy; pleasant; well-rounded.

verbs
abbreviate—; alternate—; cancel—; close—; conclude—; curtail—; defer—; depart on—; draw out—; extend—; plan—; prolong—; protract—; reciprocate—; resume—; return—; season—; schedule—; terminate—; welcome—; —delights; —wearies.
(See vacation, interview.)

VISIT (*v*)

adverbs
habitually; customarily; traditionally; periodically; seasonally; surreptitiously; cordially; courteously; ceremoniously; annually; imperially; agreeably; momentously; intemperately.
(See call, journey.)

VISITANT

adjectives
ghostly; weird; undesirable; strange.

VISITATION

adjectives
wide-spread; loving; gentle; transient; providential; heavenly; supernatural; troublesome; undeserved; nightly; sudden.

VISITING

adjectives
compunctious; continual; yearly; routine.

VISITORS

adjectives
transient; assiduous; unseen; anonymous; favored; struggling; nightly; distraught; gaping; pedestrian; enthusiastic; transcendental; dwindling; prominent; casual; uninitiated; wondering; gentle; frequent; haggard; savage; constant; distinguished; celestial; wandering; pauper; ordinary; belated; time-stealing; transitory; accustomed; dreadful; unwelcome.

verbs
amuse—; anticipate—; ban—; bar—; beam at—; confront—; discourage—; elude—; embrace—; entertain—; exclude—; greet—; hail—; ignore—; limit—; receive—; regale—; salute—; shun—; welcome—; —bore; —distract; —divert; —interrupt; —stream in; —surge in; —throng; —weary.
(See guest, listener.)

VISTA

adjectives
economic; pillared; enticing; distant; boundless; backward; frequent; mental; stately; unexpected; spectral.

verbs
cloud—; gaze at—; glory in—; obscure—; pore over—; rivet upon—; scan—; screen—; stare at—; survey—; —dazzles; —enraptures; —enthralls; —extends; —glitters; —opens before; —yawns.
(See view, landscape.)

VITAL

adverbs
obviously; indisputably; clearly; admittedly; curiously; strangely; significantly; particularly; absolutely; fundamentally; palpably; manifestly; remarkably.

VITALITY

adjectives
undreamed-of; intellectual; sportive; hilarious; protracted; restless; aggressive; creative; genuine; lingering; sparkling; continued; departing; brisk; enfeebled; abounding; mental; characteristic; inherent; forgotten; enormous; subterranean; unfailing; immaculate; vigorous; dimensional; glorious; unrivaled; inexhaustible; persistent; overpowering; brutal; miserable; great; low.

verbs
absorb—; acquire—; brim with—; build—; charge with—; concentrate—; conserve—; deprive of—; destroy—; detract from—; dull—; endow with—; exhaust—; glow with —; impair—; instil—; invest with—; lack —; maintain—; preserve—; recruit—; reduce—; reinforce—; renew—; rob of—; retain—; sap—; spare—; sustain—; throb with—; undermine—; —ebbs; —endures; —wanes; —wavers.
(See strength, health.)

VITAMINS

adjectives
toxic; essential; prevailing; helpful; overemphasized.

verbs
classify—; condense—; demand—; despatch —; enrich in—; instil—; lack—; measure —; necessitate—; prate of—; require—; rob of—; —build resistance; —deteriorate; —immunize; —nourish; —sustain.
(See nourishment, food.)

VITUPERATE (*v*)

adverbs
bitterly; cruelly; insidiously; vitriolically; personally; emotionally; exceedingly; viciously; craftily; savagely; sardonically; snarlingly; horribly; jubilantly; shrilly; stridently; vulgarly; unspeakably.
(See vilify, slander.)

VITUPERATION

adjectives
personal; emotional; nasty; vitriolic.

VITUPERATIVE

adverbs
profanely; obscenely; loudly; blatantly; boisterously; insanely; furiously; justly; unreasonably; terribly; unjustly; coarsely; openly; particularly; shamefully; blisteringly; brutally; unspeakably; incredibly; noisily; shamelessly; publicly; scathingly.

VIVACIOUS

adverbs
delightfully; pleasantly; merrily; nonsensically; comically; entertainingly; divertingly; extremely; uncommonly; highly; amusingly; excitably; enthusiastically; briskly; restlessly; alertly.

VIVACITY

adjectives
violent; nervous; ingenuous; high; unflagging; immense; unsurpassable; unabated; exuberant; sparkling; pert; artificial; unbelievable.

verbs
awaken—; cultivate—; destroy—; display —; lack—; preserve—; recapture—; value —; —animates; —bubbles; —cheers; —declines; —delights; —enlivens; —endears; —exhilarates; —gladdens; —infects; —inspirits; —refreshes; —tires; —vivifies; —wanes.
(See gayety, liveliness, animation.)

VIVID

adverbs
extremely; supernaturally; terribly; frightfully; beautifully; admirably; commendably; unusually; splendidly; wonderfully; miraculously; unbelievably; uncommonly; particularly; peculiarly; curiously; mysteriously; delightfully.

VIVIDNESS

adjectives
shocking; painful; tremendous; transparent; burning; bright; startling; journalistic.

VIXENISH

adverbs
impishly; comically; childishly; significantly; portentously; unbecomingly; ridiculously; unwarrantably; inexplicably; suddenly; hysterically; violently; surprisingly; unwontedly; alarmingly; dreadfully; momentarily.

VOCABULARY

adjectives
lurid; workable; adequate; copious; fundamental; enormous; scientific; picturesque; fashionable; full; varied; working; reading; reserve; valuable; speaking; built-up; stimulated; choice; wide; notable; well-balanced; normal; brilliant; scant; lively; rich; racy; saucy; unusual.

verbs
acquire—; add to—; adopt—; aggrandize —; amass—; analyze—; arrange—; augment—; better—; broaden—; build—; color —; compare—; compile—; contrast—; criticize—; cultivate—; culture—; derive—; develop—; display—; eliminate from—; employ—; enhance—; enlarge—; enrich—; ex-

amine—; exhaust—; familiarize oneself with —; furnish with—; gather—; improve—; increase—; limit—; make—active; mature —; narrow—; ransack—; refine—; require —; retain—; select—; simplify—; strengthen—; swell—; vary—; vulgarize—; weaken —; —accrrues; —aids; —amazes; —astounds; —colors; —derives from; —embraces; —equips; —excels; —expresses; —flowers; —fructifies; —grows; —includes; —indicates; —insures; —invigorates; —multiplies; —provides; —ranges; —reveals.

VOCAL CHORDS

verbs
discipline—; distend—; ease—; elongate—; impair—; injure—; irritate—; rasp—; soothe—; strain—; tax—; tighten—; train —; trap—; weaken—; —change; —contract; —emit; —lengthen; —quiver; —utter; —vibrate.

VOCALIST

adjectives
eminent; prominent; wonderful; thrilling.

verbs
acclaim—; accompany—; applaud—; arrange for—; laud—; train—; —carols; —enraptures; —enthralls; —entrances; —executes; —improvises; —intones; —lilts; —quavers; —records; —renders; —scales; —thrills; —trills; —twitters.

(See singer, soprano, choir.)

VOCALIZATION

adjectives
enormous; delicious; picturesque; proper.

VOCATION

adjectives
perilous; sane; sacred; legitimate; peaceful; lifelong.

verbs
desert—; employ in—; enter—; fit for—; forsake—; master—; overcrowd—; prepare for—; pursue—; qualify for—; skill in—; —allures; —attracts; —beckons; —demands; —exacts; —fascinates; —interests; —necessitates; —requires; —treats of.

(See hobby, employment, industry, calling, teaching, law, etc.)

VOCIFERATION

adjectives
harsh; ferocious; raging.

VOCIFEROUS

adverbs
unnecessarily; comically; naturally; earnestly; excitedly; hysterically; enthusiastically; riotously; shrilly; clamorously; inexcusably; disagreeably; unbecomingly; coarsely; surprisingly; grossly; foolishly; unfortunately.

VOGUE

adjectives
instigated; appreciable; tremendous; immense; decorative; fashionable.

verbs
adhere to—; alter—; create—; design—; devise—; dictate—; dignify—; emulate—; establish—; exalt—; fashion—; foster—; glorify—; maintain—; outlive—; popularize —; —dies; —diminishes; —fades; —glitters; —persists; —prevails; —wanes.

(See mode, fashion.)

VOICE

adjectives
able; abrupt; accusing; admirable; admonishing; affectionate; agonized; agitated; airy; alarmed; alien; angelic; angry; antagonistic; anxious; apocalyptic; apologetic; appropriate; arbitrary; assuring; audible; authoritative; awe-struck; babbling; baritone; barren; base; bass; beautiful; beguiling; bellowing; beloved; bemused; bewildered; bitter; blatant; bleating; bluff; blunt; blurred; booming; breathless; brisk; buzzing; broken; calm; caressing; carrying; cavernous; celestial; charming; checked; cheerful; cheering; childish; choked; clamoring; clarion; clashing; clear; clinging; cold; collective; commanding; compelling; complete; concentrated; contentious; controlling; convinced; corrupted; courteous; cracked; crashing; crisp; croaking; darkening; deceptive; decisive; decorous; deep; deferential; deliberate; demoniac; desired; determined; dictatorial; discordant; disembodied; dispassionate; dissentient; dissenting; distant; distinct; divine; doleful; dominant; dragging; dreaded; droning; drunken; dry; dull; eager; ear-deafening; earnest; easy; effective; elegant; eloquent; embarrassed; erect; exasperating; excited; exhilarating; expressionless; exquisite; extinguished; extraordinary; exultant; faint; false; falsetto;

faltering; familiar; far-away; far-off; far-ringing; fascinating; fearful; fear-struck; feeble; feigned; feminine; fiendish; fine; firm; flexible; flowing; flute-like; fluttering; foghorn; frequent; fretful; fresh; frightened; full; functioning; gentle; ghostly; gibing; gleeful; glorious; godly; good; gorgeous; gracious; great; growling; gruff; guiding; guttural; habitual; half-hesitant; half-whispered; hard; harsh; harmonious; hearty; heathen; heavenly; heavy; helpless; high; high-pitched; hoarse; hollow; horrible; hurried; hushed; husky; icy; ignorant; imaginary; impassioned; impressive; improved; impelling; imperative; inarticulate; inaudible; incarnate; incessant; incisive; independent; indistinct; ineffectual; inexorable; infallible; inflexible; inner; insinuating; insolent; inward; iron; irritable; jerky; jubilant; labored; languid; languorous; laughing; lazy; leafy; level; lifeless; lifted; lingering; lisping; living; loathing; loud; loving; low; lowered; low-keyed; low-pitched; lusty; magnificent; magniloquent; majestic; manful; manly; masculine; matchless; maudlin; measured; meek; melancholy; mellifluous; mellow; melodious; melting; merciless; metallic; meteoric; mighty; mingled (pl); mirthful; modulated; monotonous; monstrous; mortal; motherly; mournful; multitudinous (pl); muffled; mumbling; murmuring; musical; mute; myriad (pl); mysterious; nagging; nasal; native; natural; odious; offended; oily; omniscient; ominous; painful; palpitant; parrot-like; passionate; patient; patriotic; peaceful; peevish; penetrating; perpetual; pertinent; pettish; petulant; phantom-like; piercing; piping; pitying; placating; plaining; plaintive; playful; pleading; pleasant; polite; powerful; prodigious; purring; puzzled; quarreling; quavering; querulous; questioning; quiet; quivering; rapid; raised; rasping; raucous; reckless; recognized; reedy; remarkable; reminiscent; reprehensible; reproachful; resonant; respectful; responsive; reverential; ringing; rough; rowdy; rusty; sacred; sad; salutary; sardonic; savage; secret; seductive; sepulchral; seraphic; serious; shaken; sharp; short-breathed; shrieking; shrill; silky; silvery; singsong; sleep-thick; slender; slow; slurring; smooth; smothered; snapping; snarling; snuffling; sobbing; soft; solemn; sonorous; soothing; sorrowful; soul-piercing; soul-subduing; sprightly; stammering; stately; stationary; steady; stentorian; stern; stifled; still; stirring; strained; strange; strangled; stricken; strident; strong; stumbling; stupendous; subdued; subterranean; sudden; suitable; suppressed; surmounting; suspicious; sweet; swelled; synchronized; taunting; tearful; tender; tentative; tenuous; thick; thin; thundering; tiny; toneless; tottering; tragic; tranquil; transcendent; transformed; transported; trembling; tremulous; triumphant; troubled; trumpeting; tyrannical; uncertain; unctuous; uneducated; unearthly; unheeded; universal; unmistakable; unmodulated; unmoved; unrestrained; unruffled; unruly; unshaded; unshaken; unsteady; unsyllabic; uttered; vacuous; vague; velvet; venal; venomous; veritable; vigorous; virgin; vociferous; vulgar; wailing; warbled; warning; weary; welcoming; well-attuned; well-bred; well-known; well-modulated; well-tuned; wheedling; whining; whispering; wistful; wondering; woodland; wondrous; wretched; yawning; yearning; young; impatient; impersonal.

verbs
acclaim—; attune to—; blot out—; candy —; choke—; control—; dampen—; discipline—; disguise—; drop—; drown out—; dull—; echo—; exercise—; guard—; harken to—; heed—; hush—; irritate—; laud —; lift—; mellow—; modulate—; muffle —; mute—; muzzle—; pitch—; place—; recognize—; silence—; still—; strain—; study —; sugar—; sweeten—; thrill to—; throttle —; tinge—; train—; —awakens; —bawls; —beguiles; —booms; —breaks; —carols; —carries; —censures; —changes; —charms; —chokes; —cracks; —cuts; —deepens; —drones on; —dwindles; —enraptures; —fascinates; —flags; —flames; —floats up; —lashes; —murmurs; —palpitates; —penetrates; —pierces; —quavers; —ranges; —rasps; —registers; —resounds; —rings out; —rises; —rolls; —sharpens; —slurs; —squeaks; —stirs; —swells; —thickens; —throbs; —thunders; —tightens; —trails off; —trembles; —twitters; —vibrates; —warms; —wavers; —wheedles; —whines; —whispers; —wracks; —wrings.

(See sound, utterance, tone.)

VOICE (v)

adverbs
tenderly; harmoniously; accusingly; antagonistically; anxiously; authoritatively; bluntly; exultantly; ominously; sternly; patriotically; lustily; audibly; monotonously; petu-

lantly; raucously; reproachfully; sepulchrally; vulgarly; vigorously; vociferously; venomously.

(See express, say.)

VOID

adjectives

trackless; foggy; pale; bare; absolute; mysterious; boundless; populous; fathomless; immeasurable; illimitable; blank.

adverbs

legally; unluckily; apparently; manifestly; unfortunately; blessedly; fortunately; utterly; recently; temporarily; hopelessly; undeniably; definitely; curiously.

VOLCANO

adjectives

extinct; perilous; concealed; slumbering; barren; drowned; spiritual; smoldering.

verbs

fling into—; gaze into—; pacify—; placate—; toss into—; —activates; —awakens; —belches; —buries; —chokes; —destroys; —devastates; —discharges; —ejects; —embroils; —emits; —endangers; —erupts; —flows; —foments; —fulminates; —fumes; —lies dormant; —looms; —quiets; —rampages; —rises; —roars; —rumbles; —seethes; —simmers; —sleeps; —smoulders; —spews forth; —strangles; —streams over; —threatens; —vents.

(See eruption, crater.)

VOLITION

adjectives

distinct; special; true; passionate; conscious; particular.

VOLLEY

adjectives

severe; fine; bombastic; pyrotechnic; instantaneous; incessant; intermitting; useless; deafening.

verbs

blast—; discharge—; flash—; fulminate—; prolong—; renew—; —assaults; —bombards; —crashes; —decimates; —destroys; —detonates; —devastates; —echoes; —flares; —levels; —rattles; —razes; —rends; —resounds; —rings out; —roars; —rolls; —rumbles; —shatters; —splits; —thunders; —wreaks.

(See gun-fire, shots, fussilade.)

VOLUBILITY

adjectives

startling; accustomed; infinite; fierce.

VOLUBLE

adverbs

usually; habitually; comically; chattily; torrentially; ridiculously; unnecessarily; peculiarly; characteristically; momentarily; unusually; hysterically; excitedly; officiously; vexatiously; intolerably; amusingly.

VOLUME

adjectives

separate; immense; added; record; sympathetic; respective; published; comfortable; ambitious; increasing; unprecedented; random; dusky; ragged; penultimate; inexhaustible; thumb-scarred; pale; magnificent; enormous; arid; precious; attractive; ponderous; endless; unlimited; growing; rushing; valuable; library; thundering; remarkable; swelling; respectable; charming; solemn; supplementary; worthless; far-reaching; poetic; tasteful; long-coveted; subsequent; forthcoming; dog-eared; serried (pl); tremendous; substantial; collected; thrilling; proud; pathetic; posthumous; universal; fascinating; masterful; brilliant; momentous; sturdy; vast; venerable; splendid; printed; blinding; mere; bulky; sulphurous; enormous; weighty; instructive; stray; odd; scholarly; sumptuous; inspired; comprehensive.

verbs

author—; autograph—; bind—; browse through—; compile—; con—; confiscate—; consult—; curtail—; delve into—; display—; entitle—; fray—; illustrate—; immerse in—; interpret—; peruse—; ponder—; prepare—; prize—; publish—; review—; revise—; scan—; skim over—; summarize—; tackle—; value—; —airs; —circulates; —condemns; —deals with; —discourses on; —dissertates; —diverts; —exposes; —libels; —narrates; —plagiarizes; —recites; —recounts; —relates; —slanders; —treats of; —unfolds; —ventilates; devote—to.

(See book, manuscript, story, work, tome.)

VOLUMINOUS

adverbs

overwhelmingly; stupendously; inclusively; pedantically; ambitiously; monumentally; sufficiently; immensely; manifestly; absurdly; unnecessarily.

VOLUNTARY

adverbs

freely; generously; impetuously; eagerly; earnestly; energetically; emphatically; unmistakably; undoubtedly; unquestionably; usually; frankly; necessarily; amicably; delightfully; completely.

VOLUNTEERS

adjectives

raw; devoted; zealous; tireless; fanatic; susceptible; doughty; brave.

verbs

acclaim—; arm—; command—; compose of —; discipline—; equip—; furnish—; honor —; laud—; plead for—; quarter—; recruit —; rig out—; train—; transport—; —bid for; —brave; —comprise; —defend; —disband; —enlist; —offer; —proffer; —serve; —storm; —tackle; —tender.

(See soldier, recruit.)

VOLUPTUARY

adjectives

cautious; refined; hedonistic.

VOLUPTUOUS

adverbs

pleasantly; buxomly; luxuriously; delightedly; naturally; habitually; notoriously; conspicuously; openly; utterly; unmistakably.

VOLUPTUOUSNESS

adjectives

inebriating; supposed; gorgeous.

VOMIT (v)

adverbs

nauseatingly; sickeningly; disgustingly; recurringly; drunkenly.

VOMITING

verbs

allay—; ameliorate—; check—; curtail—; diagnose—; encourage—; force—; forestall—; induce—; produce—; stem—; stimulate to—; —cleanses; —dislodges; —eases; —ejects; —eliminates; —endangers; —expels; —indicates; —purges; —sheds; —unburdens; —vents; —weakens.

(See nausea.)

VORACIOUS

adverbs

overweeningly; rabidly; insatiately; incredibly; dreadfully; unspeakably; frightfully; unbelievably; wolfishly; bestially.

VORACITY

adjectives

impotent; insatiable; unscrupulous.

VORTEX

verbs

form—; sweep into—; tumble into—; —agitates; —billows; —boils; —churns; —circumvolutes; —convolutes; —eddies; —engulfs; —expands; —foams; —gyrates; —immerses; —pirouettes; —revolves; —ripples; —rotates; —submerges; —surges; —swells; —swirls; —trundles; —twirls; —whirls.

(See whirlpool, maelstrom.)

VOTARY

adjectives

boyish; dull; firm; mistaken.

VOTE

adjectives

majority; overhanging; overwhelming; disputed; injudicious; unanimous; purchasable; direct; negative; reluctant; decisive; ignorant; appalling; valid; dissenting; simple; plurality; deciding; heavy; loyal; crooked.

VOTE (v)

adverbs

unanimously; progressively; overwhelmingly; democratically; inconsistently; regularly; affirmatively; loyally; intelligently; legally; judiciously; ignorantly; decisively.

(See elect, declare.)

VOTERS

adjectives

independent-minded; submissive; patient; stupid; blinded; purchased; intelligent; thinking.

verbs

address—; appeal to—; assure—; beguile —; coerce—; dictate to—; divide—; harangue—; pledge to—; poll—; promise—; sway—; woo—; —acknowledge; —approve; —ballot; —choose; —determine; —elect; —endorse; —overwhelm; —reign; —rule; —select; —stream to; —subscribe to; —support; —sustain; —vacillate; —voice.

(See constituent, public, citizen.)

VOTES

verbs
aggregate—; alienate—; amass—; angle for —; apportion—; assure of—; bag—; bias —; calculate—; campaign for—; compute —; conciliate—; corral—; gain—; gather —; guarantee—; hazard—; imperil—; influence—; insure—; jeopardize—; line up —; muster—; poll—; procure—; promise—; record—; recount—; register—; risk—; separate—; sew up—; split—; sway—; swing —; void—; win—; —determine; —pile up; —pour in.
(See election, nomination, plurality, ballot.)

VOTIVE

adverbs
sacredly; sacrificially; devoutly; undeniably; apparently; sincerely; truly; completely; contritely.

VOW

adjectives
earthly; capricious; rash; musical; unheedful; violated; truant; passionate; unbroken; moist; bridal; ardent; intermingled; sainted; hollow; frail; noble; slighted; monastic; limber; monkish; solemn; marital; sacred; dread; grateful; self-imposed; idle; generous; heavenly; serviceable.

verbs
annul—; breathe—; commit to—; comply with—; contract—; declare—; desecrate—; discharge from—; divorce from—; embody in—; enforce—; forfeit—; fulfill—; heed—; ignore—; infringe—; liberate from—; maintain—; observe—; pursue—; register—; relax—; respect—; sanctify—; slacken—; solemnize—; swear to—; undertake—; violate—; —binds; —burdens; —chains; —fetters; —pledges; —prohibits; —restrains; —restricts; —weighs upon.
(See pledge, oath, promise, contract.)

VOW (*v*)

adverbs
patiently; passionately; languidly; capriciously; rashly; ardently; nobly; magnanimously; monastically; sacredly; generously; maritally.
(See promise, swear.)

VOWEL

adjectives
open; various (pl); softening; euphonious; nasalized; drawled; guttural; mispronounced; throaty.

verbs
ablaut—; accent—; accentuate—; articulate —; discard—; economize on—s; emphasize —; employ—; lengthen—; misuse—; pronounce—; silence—; shorten—; stress—; umlaut—; trip up on—s; —changes; —sharpens.
(See sound.)

VOYAGE

adjectives
prosperous; loving; projected; aimless; tedious; eventful; magnificent; determinate; stormy; tempestuous; ill-fated; frequent (pl); uncertain; romantic; perilous; mysterious; homeward.

verbs
brave—; chart—; conclude—; curtail—; delay—; deviate from—; embark on—; extend —; hazard—; plan—; prolong—; protract —; set forth on—; terminate—; venture upon—; —broadens; —embraces; —fascinates; —lures; —intrigues; —refreshes; —relaxes; —touches upon; —tranquillizes.
(See journey, trip.)

VOYAGER

adjectives
dusty-throated; battered; uninstructed; seasick.

VULGAR

adverbs
incredibly; strangely; habitually; unwontedly; grossly; boorishly; defiantly; crassly; strangely; purposely; arrantly; definitely; openly; conspicuously; shamefully; carelessly; unmistakably; singularly; surprisingly; intentionally; deliberately; flagrantly.

VULGARITY

adjectives
patent; hideous; rude; vigorous; impertinent; unutterable; innumerable (pl); purse-proud; finished; pathetic; stupid; private; blatant; odious; intense; superlative; petty; universal; studied.

verbs
abhor—; blush at—; breed—; countenance —; deplore—; descend to—; exhibit—; flaunt—; frown upon—; recoil from—; —

coarsens; —debases; —degrades; —irks; —mortifies; —ostracizes; —repels; —shocks; —surrounds.

(See coarseness.)

VULNERABLE

adverbs

sadly; unfortunately; admittedly; wretchedly; miserably; probably; unluckily; terribly; alarmingly; portentously; ominously; significantly; dangerously; perilously; carelessly; incautiously; criminally; dreadfully; unbelievably; unforgivably; negligently; unhappily.

VULTURE

adjectives

famished; gnawing; carrion; hovering; greedy; swooping; ugly.

verbs

—circles; —clutches; —descends; —devours; —dives; —divests; —flutters; —glides; —gorges; —hisses; —hovers over; —picks clean; —plucks; —pounces upon; —preys upon; —ravishes; —regurgitates; —scales; —scavenges; —seizes; —soars; —shrieks; —subsists; —swoops down; —whirls.

(See bird, eagle, hawk.)

W

WADE (*v*)

adverbs
laboriously; conscientiously; cautiously; fastidiously; carefully.
(See swim.)

WAFT (*v*)

adverbs
delicately; pungently; insidiously; gently; capriciously.
(See carry, float.)

WAG (*v*)

adverbs
humorously; sardonically; slowly; feebly; mutely; wordlessly; sagely; cryptically.
(See nod, move.)

WAGE

adjectives
preposterous; satisfactory; aggregate; hard-earned; comparative; prevailing; monetary; actual; scanty; unsteady; uncertain; exorbitant; inflated; youthful; daily; living.

WAGER

verbs
accept—; agree upon—; cast—; chance—; claim—; contest—; decide—; determine—; force—; frame—; gamble on—; lay—; propose—; record—; release from—; speculate on—; stake—on; transact—; venture—; —challenges; —hazards; —pledges.
(See bet, gambling.)

WAGES

verbs
advance—; boost—; default—; determine—; distribute—; engage for—; expend—; fix—; forfeit—; grudge—; halve—; increase—; invest—; level—; lift—; proportion—; raise—; rate—; realize—; reap—; reduce—; regulate—; scale—; scorn—; serve for—; slash—; squander—; step up—; stimulate—; supplement—; tabulate—; withhold—; —compensate; —conform; —decline; —indemnify; —remunerate; —reward; —soar.
(See income, earnings, fee, pittance, living, livelihood.)

WAGGISH

adverbs
jocosely; facetiously; fatuously; banteringly; boastfully; drolly; clownishly; pleasantly; foolishly; playfully; intolerably; disagreeably; smartly; conceitedly; whimsically; fantastically; vexatiously; disgustingly; merrily; mischievously.

WAGON

adjectives
ancient; lumbering; serviceable; jolting; creaking; wobbling; emigrant; clanking; broken-down; hooded; ramshackle; vengeful.

verbs
brake—; cart on—; convoy—; dispatch—; draw—; harness to—; hitch—; journey by—; —conveys; —creeps along; —draws up; —jolts; —jounces; —rattles; —rolls; —transports.
(See caravan, automobile, cart, vehicle.)

WAIL

adjectives
piteous; faint; infantile; obstreperous; lusty; articulate; windy; inward; melodramatic; thin; fretful; dismal; doleful; dying; hideous; damned; confused; heartbroken; young; passionate; patriotic; pathetic; murmured; tender; moaning; wild; liquid; weird; far-off; mournful; amazed; angry; nightly; flute-like.

verbs
emit—; prolong—; set up—; shrill—; utter—; —complains of; —deplores; —deprecates; —grieves; —laments; —mourns; —pierces; —rends; —rings out; —rises; —wrings.
(See cry, howl, lamentation.)

WAIL (*v*)

adverbs
distressfully; mournfully; dismally; piteously; inarticulately; fretfully; dolefully; passionately; wildly; weirdly; mournfully; lustily; obstreperously.
(See moan, lament.)

WAILING

adverbs

mournfully; incessantly; continually; intermittently; hopefully; piously; confoundedly; petulantly; disagreeably; feebly; vociferously; loudly; wistfully; ostentatiously; pitifully; hungrily; sleepily; drowsily; insincerely; tiresomely; monotonously; desperately; vexatiously; pettishly.

WAIST

adjectives

snug; thickening; imperceptible; tapering; enormous; collective; trackless; slender; winsome; wasplike; well-fitting; capacious.

WAIT (*v*)

adverbs

breathlessly; passively; sadly; reverently; anxiously; exultantly; mutely; devotedly; placidly; instinctively; calmly; apprehensively; boldly; hungrily; morbidly; disastrously; indecisively; tensely.

(See pause, delay.)

WAITER

adjectives

smug; oblivious; rowdy; obsequious; swarthy; corpulent; stately; efficient.

verbs

beckon to—; bid—; bow—out; employ—; engage—; rebuke—; reproach—; ring for —; signal—; summon—; tip—; uniform—; —announces; —approaches; —attends; —directs to; —fumbles; —hovers near; —informs; —recommends; —serves; —suggests.

(See matron, nurse, servant.)

WAITING

adverbs

silently; doggedly; resolutely; hopelessly; helplessly; intolerably; restlessly; feverishly; optimistically; trustfully; happily; forlornly; eagerly; boisterously; cruelly; miserably; interminably; insistently.

WAIVE (*v*)

adverbs

magnanimously; willingly; voluntarily; deliberately; nobly; generously; affectionately; informally.

(See dispense, relinquish.)

WAKEFUL

adverbs

nervously; mysteriously; alertly; anxiously; miserably; wretchedly; vigilantly; habitually; watchfully; unnaturally; peculiarly; strangely; significantly; fortunately; luckily; suddenly; feverishly; comfortably.

WALK (*general*)

adjectives

solar; winding; strenuous; long; sunken; gravel; aimless; sanguine; flagged; exhilarating; cheerful; moderate; cloistered; lumbering; obscure; sunny; rough; windy; fatiguing; leisurely; lingering; tangling; cultured; mincing; haphazard; laurel; solitary; hedge-lined; contemplative; rampart; willowy; shady; slow; undulating; rhythmic; moonlight; enrapturing; roaming; royal; humble; swarming; tremendous; silent; visionary; smart; mind-clearing; dark; night; restless; glorious; opposite; spacious; sequestered; imposing; tangling; lazy; murmuring; substantial; oval; umbrageous.

WALK (*path*)

verbs

beautify—; border—; block—; bound—; circle—; designate—; elevate—; enclose—; fence in—; flank—; intersect—; occupy—; parallel—; pave—; plank—; promenade—; repair—; run up—; seclude—; shade—; skirt—.

(See lane, alley, path.)

WALK (*v*)

adverbs

cavalierly; gingerly; sprightly; blindly; spirally; deliberately; defiantly; meekly; humbly; unsteadily; characteristically; mutely; monotonously; untiringly; tempestuously; stealthily; strenuously; musingly; restlessly; languidly; foppishly; aimlessly; wantonly; reflectively; defiantly; jauntily; calmly; briskly; warily; abstractedly; sedately; haphazardly; contemplatively; lazily.

(See trudge, stroll.)

WALLET

verbs

adorn—; appropriate—; cram—; emboss—; engrave—; examine—; filch—; guard—; lift—; mulct of—; palm—; pilfer—; prize —; protrude from—; rifle—; stuff—; swell —; thrust into—; —bulges; —wears.

(See bag, purse.)

WALLOW (v)

adverbs
bestially; voluptuously; hoggishly; disgustingly; revoltingly; carnally; lewdly; insatiably; vulgarly.
(See flounder, grovel.)

WALLS

adjectives
naked; massive; rugged; crannied; crumbling; shattered; eloquent; high; espaliered; garden; bartizan; sapphire; gloomy; adamantine; tired; thick; crenelated; staring; tinted; forsaken; weltering; well-built; verdurous; unsurmounted; emblazoned; proscenium; continuous; impregnable; imperial; pretty; impassable; forested; outward; obliterated; impenetrable; celestial; beauteous; ruined; munimental; abdominal; dignified; flaming; expressionless; far-reaching; buttressed; decaying; wicked; dainty; trembling; moldering; ancient; ruinous; humid; courteous; chancel; battlemented; venerable; dungeon; illuminated; exterior; everlasting; dull; damp; fluttering; roofless; low; unplastered; paneled; high-jutting; pictured; dark; grimy; prison; frowning; fortress; tottering; inaccessible; protecting; sheer; remote; unbroken; leafy-bannered; conventual; vertical; steep; jointed; rocky; lengthy; living; soft; evenly-tinted; gleaming; mossy; shiny; sunny; yonder; wailing; rose-bannered; garden; wind-proofed; austered; cerulean; majestic; towering; girdling; unornamented; unfinished; moaning; mountain; lofty; protecting; silver-seamed; somber; melted; unpeopled; projecting; brazen; eternal; intervening; triple; leprous; lateral; beloved; multitudinous; blistered; fragmentary; rustling; weathered; ageless; scarped; confining; mirrored; moss-covered; dingy; distempered.

verbs
barricade behind—; batter down—; bedaub —; clamber over—; decorate—; deface—; drape—; drive to—; emboss—; erect—; flank—; fortify—; fresco—; harbor within —; mount—; paper—; pierce—; rib—; scale—; scan—; smite—; surmount—; vault—; —arise; —confine; —crumble; —defend; —enclose; —envelop; —gird; —impede; —partition; —obscure; —shelter; —shield; —shoulder; —surround.
(See fence, barricade, fortification.)

WALTZ

adjectives
lilting; wheeling; ingratiating; old-fashioned; whirling; graceful; appealing.

verbs
compose—; embrace in—; enjoy—; fling into—; introduce—; popularize—; portray —; sway to—; whirl in—; —calms; —enthralls; —entrances; —graces; —gyrates; —relaxes; —revolves; —rolls; —survives; —thrills.
(See dance, minuet.)

WALTZ (v)

adverbs
gracefully; harmoniously; deftly; energetically; charmingly; seductively; rhythmically; liltingly; ingratiatingly; appealingly.
(See dance, trip.)

WAN

adverbs
pitifully; unfortunately; alarmingly; miserably; feebly; unhealthily; wretchedly; dreadfully; unaccountably; unusually; naturally; strangely; curiously; unnaturally; ghastly.

WAND

adjectives
opiate; streaked; potent; scribbling; snake-encircled; certain; sable.

verbs
bear—; brandish—; cleave—; endow—; fashion—; flex—; flourish—; magnetize—; ply—; smite with—; splinter—; split—; strike with—; stroke—; tip—; whittle—; —charms; —chastises; —enchants; —guides; —mesmerizes; —mystifies; —symbolizes.
(See baton, cane, scepter, twig.)

WANDER (v)

adverbs
desolately; erratically; deviously; dilatorily; errantly; listlessly; aimlessly; disconsolately; blindly; ruefully; stupidly; hopelessly; promiscuously; rashly; wearily.
(See roam, ramble.)

WANDERER

adjectives
bodiless; fantastic; forlorn; night; weary; unwilling; immortal; archetypical; blithe; half-frozen; long-lost; undisciplined.

WANDERING

adjectives
eccentric; devious; difficult; weary; sleepless; restless; vague; unquiet; aimless; accidental; dream-led; enfranchised; much; occasional.

adverbs
inanely; fruitlessly; incessantly; doggedly; hopefully; idly; actually; mentally; confusedly; nervously; nonchalantly; irresponsibly.

WANDERINGS

verbs
cease—; chart—; color—; condemn to—; describe—; embark on—; experience in—; extend—; narrate—; prolong—; protract—; record—; relate—; retire from—; unfold—; weary of—; —aberrate; —age; —amuse; —embrace; —interest; —thrill.
(See travel, voyage.)

WANDERLUST

adjectives
unconquerable; reoccurring; uncontrollable.

verbs
extinguish—; nip—; obey—; quash—; quell—; quench—; resist—; stamp out—; subdue—; succumb to—; surrender to—; yield to—; suppress—; —fires; —grips; —impels; —overwhelms; —perishes; —prods; —pushes; —seizes; —urges.
(See desire, longing, impulse.)

WANT

adjectives
abject; burning; thirsty; fiery; gnawing; acute; actual; spontaneous; unreflected; needful; artificial; common; utter; frank; fearless; passionate; respective; material; immediate; total; unpardonable; unbounded; shameful; endless; wondrous; tender; squalid; divine; present; narrow; curious; presumptive; ripe; absolute; modest; lower; spiritual; conscious; returning; sufficient.

verbs
administer to—s; anticipate—s; come to—; consult—s; correct—; diminish—s; discharge—s; express—; gratify—; impoverish with—; intensify—; mark by—; occasion—; provide for—s; reduce to—; subject to—; suffer—; —blemishes; —goads on; —s multiply.
(See need, lack, necessity, destitution.)

WANT (*v*)

adverbs
desperately; distressingly; intensely; vaguely; immediately; manifestly; particularly; shamelessly; absolutely; immodestly; spiritually; wistfully; conspicuously; abjectly; passionately.
(See need, desire.)

WANTON

adverbs
recklessly; playfully; immorally; irrepressibly; loosely; unrestrainedly; wickedly; provocatively; delightedly; hilariously; drunkenly; airily; emotionally; insanely; crazily; childishly; ludicrously; pitiably; brazenly; audaciously; heedlessly; imprudently; incorrigibly; eccentrically; monstrously; lawlessly; outlandishly; unwontedly; bafflingly.

WAR

adjectives
suicidal; glorious; brooding; vigorous; impious; exhausting; guerrilla; diabolical; ruthless; expensive; aggressive; ferocious; defensive; internecine; offensive; desolating; mimic; mustering; bitter; grim; impending; universal; increasing; horrible; aboriginal; glorified; inevitable; imminent; classical; barbarous; undeclared; virtuous; fratricidal; open; manful; cormorant; victorious; fearful; intrepid; successive (pl); deadly; successful; tribal; unearthly; meritorious; righteous; unholy; interminable; raging; ensuing; disastrous; banded; brutal; pelting; unvanquished; unjust; incessant; rebellious; devastating; nonsparing; silvan; plangent; elemental; imperialist; contemplated; ghastly; mercenary; renewed; silent; sanguinary; strenuous; social; servile; innocent; irrepressible; intellectual; contumelious; beastly; mad-brained; realistic; fierce; courageous; petty; theologic; religious; witching; tremendous; passive.

verbs
abstain from—; aggravate—; anticipate—; avert—; banish—; cease—; control—; dedicate to—; determine—; dramatize—; dread—; drift into—; embrace—; entangle in—; enter—; envisage—; fend off—; flame into—; foment—; gird for—; halt—; launch—; localize—; muster for—; outlaw—; plunge into—; prolong—; promote—; provoke—; resort to—; romanticize—; stage—; stave off—; stem—; survive—; taboo—; throttle

—; vilify—; wage—; witness—; —arises; —bestializes; —blasts; —bristles; —drags on; —endangers; —entangles; —looms; —overclouds; —overshadows; —progresses; —rages; —ravages; —runs rampant; —sunders; —terminates; —vilifies.

(See fight, combat, battle, warfare.)

WARD

adjectives

unguarded; close; legitimate; hard; slow-turning; airy; intricate; mutinous; surgical; gracious.

WARDROBE

adjectives

sophisticated; natty; all-occasion; personalized; endless; summer; outdoor; holiday.

verbs

attain—; augment—; complete—; delete—; envy—; equip with—; expend on—; fit out with—; luxuriate in—; mend—; mutilate—; perfect—; provide—; purchase—; renew—; repair—; replenish—; restore—; —suffers; —suffices.

(See clothing, apparel.)

WARE

adjectives

varnished; universal; tawdry; gaudy.

WARES

verbs

auction—; bargain for—; bid for—; cheapen—; dispense—; display—; dispose of—; examine—; hawk—; inflate—; inspect—; liquidate—; loot—; market—; peddle—; pilfer—; proclaim—; purvey—; put—under the hammer; retail—; scatter—; test—; undersell—; vend—; —allure; —depreciate.

(See merchandise, product.)

WARFARE

adjectives

manful; curious; dulcet; cruel; chivalrous; incessant; nightly; friendless; deadly; desperate; foreign; unceasing; offensive; tremendous; unrelenting; eternal; aggressive; wanton; devastating; hopeless; internecine; sylvan; perpetual; unsuccessful; bloody; critical; protracted; vigorous; disjointed; impending; predatory; guerrilla; mimic; licentious; partisan; heartrending.

verbs

abolish—; arm for—; array for—; balk at—; carry on—; conclude—; decry—; engage in—; force into—; incite—; inflame to—; initiate into—; instigate—; kindle—; light the torch of—; mobilize for—; precipitate into—; resign to—; revolt at—; threaten—; train for—; —devastates; —exterminates; —menaces; —pillages; —plunders; —seethes; —takes toll: —undermines: —wreaks.

(See hostility, war, struggle, conflict.)

WARLIKE

adverbs

insatiably; recklessly; criminally; bestially; flagrantly; viciously; inherently; foully; systematically; abominably; inhumanly; atrociously; brutally; infamously; iniquitously; nefariously; scandalously; savagely; ferociously; vilely; wickedly; barbarously; incorrigibly; unfeelingly; sinfully; horribly; unspeakably; fiendishly; flagitiously; villainously; needlessly; indecently.

WARM

adverbs

unseasonably; uncomfortably; unreasonably; curiously; terribly; comfortably; securely; gratefully; surprisingly; slightly; dreadfully; suffocatingly; unnecessarily; extremely; sufficiently; pleasantly.

WARM (*v*)

adverbs

perceptibly; appreciably; uncomfortably; frightfully; dangerously; significantly.

(See heat, arouse.)

WARM-HEARTED

adverbs

delightfully; impulsively; lovingly; generously; philanthropically; naturally; dependably; especially; marvelously; pleasantly; wonderfully; altruistically; cordially; hospitably; unusually; uncommonly; sincerely; conspicuously; genuinely; really; truly; always; frankly; earnestly.

WARMTH

adjectives

genial; comfortable; thrilling; redolent; juvenile; life-giving; personal; soft; native; grateful; bright; added; balmy; considerable; unseemly; vivacious; trustworthy; deceitful; feeble; loathy; refreshing; virile; varying; peculiar; ethereal; brooding; passionate; heartfelt; tongueless; friendly; dissolving; tingling; true; human; added; eccentric; rugged; confiding; voluptuous; fostering; utmost.

verbs
accustom to—; afford—; bask in—; diffuse —; drowse in—; enjoy—; excite—; exude —; glow with—; impart—; inhale—; provide—; radiate—; regain—; retain—; sense —; swelter in—; temper with—; welcome—; —animates; —chafes; —comforts; —flushes; —fuses; —lingers; —pervades; —renews; —revives; —revivifies; —thaws.
(See glow, geniality, fervor, ardor, heat.)

WARN (*v*)
adverbs
providentially; solemnly; amply; sufficiently; grimly; prophetically; urgently; graciously; forcefully; subtly; soberly; earnestly; faithfully.
(See admonish.)

WARNING
adjectives
grim; prophetic; ecclesiastical; celestial; competent; sundry (pl); gracious; urgent; open; preliminary; startling; eternal; slender; forceful; important; hoarse; subtle; timely; anonymous; displeasing; terrible; anxious; secular; fair; pathetic; sober; earnest; paradoxical.

verbs
accept—; broadcast—; convey—; disregard —; distribute—s; explode—; furnish—; heed—; ignore—; issue—; protest—; regard —; rumble—; signal—; sound—; stress—; tender—; voice—; yield to—; —alarms; —impends; —terrifies.
(See counsel, portent, admonition.)

WARRANT
adjectives
external; lawful; bloody; sufficient; seeming; scriptural; doubtful; valid; avowed; infallible; further.

verbs
arm with—; draw up—; exercise—; flourish —; issue—; procure—; resort to—; retain on—; swear out—; wield—; —accredits; —apprehends; —authorizes; —commissions; —delegates; —deputizes; —empowers; —permits; —pledges; —proclaims; —protects.
(See authority, mandate, summons.)

WARRANTABLE
adverbs
thoroughly; entirely; soundly; altogether; wholly; justly; properly; safely; reasonably; sufficiently; probably; presumably; supposedly; definitely.

WARRIOR
adjectives
sullen; painful; intrepid; inferior; flaming; simple-minded; charging; care-stricken; delighted; naked; redoubtable; savage; struggling; indefatigable; stern-faced; discomfited; long-dead; gloomy-looking; veteran; fierce; illustrious; exhausted; devilish; magnificent; invincible; tiny; dauntless; fell-handed.

verbs
acclaim—; arm—; beribbon—; commemorate—; conciliate—; confer upon—; decorate—; dedicate to—; distinguish—; draft —; elevate—; emulate—; ennoble—; enshrine—; esteem—; exalt—; exhort—; glorify—; hail—; honor—; idealize—; immortalize—; knight—; laud—; lionize—; pacify —; pay homage to—; rank—; revere—; reward—; salute—; worship—; —combats; —engages; —intrenches; —s mobilize; —parries; —perishes; —repels; —sheathes; —wields.
(See soldier, fighter, hero.)

WARSHIP
verbs
anchor—; bomb—; command—; confine on —; engage—; evade—; dodge—; scale—; —blockades; —bombards; —conveys; —convoys; —founders; —hems in; —maneuvers; —s mass; —patrols; —plies; —raids; —rakes; —rams; —retaliates; —rolls; —rushes; —sallies; —shells; —threatens; —transports.
(See boat, ship, army.)

WART
verbs
apply to—; burn—; cauterize—; cut—; daub on—; detach—; dissect—; excise—s; grease—; incise—; patch—s; peel—; remove—; salve—; sever—; subject to—s; treat—; —appears; —blemishes; —bulges; —s develop; —disfigures; —erupts; —flattens; —maligns; —mars; —protrudes; —swells; —thickens; —vanishes.
(See sore, wound.)

WARY

adverbs
habitually; constantly; necessarily; alertly; uncommonly; significantly; extraordinarily; noticeably; nervously; wisely; ordinarily; curiously; tiresomely; conspicuously; timidly; sagaciously; deliberately; anxiously; admirably.

WASH (v)

adverbs
surreptitiously; scrupulously; listlessly; fastidiously; habitually; laboriously; deliberately.
(See clean, scrub.)

WASHING

verbs
obviate—; require—; subject to—; —ablutes; —cleanses; —deodorizes; —deterges; —disinfects; —elutriates; —expurgates; —eliminates; —laves; —lixiviates; —purges; —purifies; —refreshes; —renews; —vivifies.
(See bath, water.)

WASPS

adjectives
injurious; stinging; buzzing; rowdy.

verbs
avoid—; classify—; —barb; —burrow; —buzz; —dig; —excavate; —hum; —flit; —molest; —nest; —paralyze; —poison; —provision; —pursue; —snare; —sting; —store; —tunnel; —wing.
(See hornet, insect, bee.)

WASTE

adjectives
unbridled; trackless; wandering; sinful; deliberate; dismal; encompassing; watery; woeful; colorless; indeterminate; gloomy; senseless; vast; thriftless; solemn-sounding; stupendous; unnecessary; terrible; inexcusable; wintry; glimmering; unproductive; arctic; barren; widening; sprinkled; spiritual; lonely; putrid; melancholy; simple; premature; colossal; tragic; aching; positive; nitrogenous; inward; desolate; hurried; remote; snowy; frightful; hopeless; burning; pathless; muscular; weltering; garden; flowering; sanctuary; shoreless; lavish; unpardonable; fruitless; boundless; ruinous; digestive; uninhabited; woodland; full; sandy; merciless; monstrous; howling; arid; frozen; turbid; war-worn; useless; dreary; dangerous; sterile; insidious; desert; wanton; verdant; enormous; tedious; billowy; illimitable; untamed; profligate; dread; moldering.

verbs
abate—; bewail—; check—; countenance—; curb—; curtail—; decry—; detect—; diminish—; discharge—; eliminate—; excrete—; harvest—; imply—; incur—; manufacture —; rebuke for—; reproach for—; restore —; result in—; retrieve—; rid of—; upbraid for—; wipe out—; withdraw—; —abuses; —accumulates; —appals; —declines; —denudes; —desecrates; —diminishes; —dissipates; —endangers; —shrinks; —squanders; —threatens.
(See junk, mess, garbage, extravagance.)

WASTE (v)

adverbs
unprofitably; improvidently; rashly; carelessly; heedlessly; deliberately; woefully; senselessly; stupendously; unnecessarily; unproductively; spiritually; ruthlessly; fruitlessly; wantonly; profligately.
(See sqaunder, dissipate.)

WASTE-BASKET

verbs
cast into—; consign to—; cram into—; deluge—; empty—; find in—; mouse around —; relegate to—; stuff—; —provides; —serves; —overflows.
(See basket.)

WASTED
(emaciated)

adverbs
pitiably; remarkably; haggardly; gauntly; helplessly; lankly; feebly; desperately; wretchedly; extremely.

WASTEFUL

adverbs
criminally; wickedly; extremely; wantonly; thoughtlessly; inconsiderately; immoderately; terribly; carelessly; negligently; foolishly; enormously; indolently; improvidently; ignorantly; crazily; unconscionably; inordinately; egregiously; atrociously; incredibly; miserably; extremely; imprudently; wretchedly.

WATCH

adjectives
happy; railroad; neglected; solitary; clam-

orous; fierce; advised; adventuring; vigilant; tireless; celestial; sympathetic; expensive; airy; couchant; brotherly; breathless; unnatural; strict; unceasing; patient; furtive; incessant; faithful; thrilling.

verbs
adjust—; check—; consult—; embellish—; engrave—; fondle—; illuminate—; jewel—; lubricate—; observe—; overwind—; pawn—; refer to—; regulate—; rely upon—; repair—; set—; snatch—; value—; wind—; —fails; —informs; —reminds; —runs down.
(See dial, clock.)

WATCH (v)

adverbs
vigilantly; anxiously; surreptitiously; sullenly; furtively; narrowly; assiduously; disconsolately; absently; minutely; keenly; vaguely; listlessly; slyly; idly; breathlessly; wistfully; apprehensively; attentively; stealthily; greedily; incessantly; moodily; covertly; defiantly; somberly; pensively; lazily; faithfully.
(See observe, scrutinize.)

WATCHER

adjectives
indolent; wingless; unsuspected; lone; sleepless.

WATCHFUL

adverbs
carefully; cautiously; responsibly; properly; stingily; greedily; hungrily; coldly; slyly; alertly; wisely; justifiably; sagaciously; inquisitively; curiously; maliciously; fondly; devotedly; jealously; enviously; constantly; anxiously; timidly.

WATCHFULNESS

adjectives
incumbent; calm; heavy; stealthy; constant; suspicious; assiduous; sharp; alert; silent; strenuous.

WATER

adjectives
poisonous; murky; wrinkled; brackish; gentle; golden; pellucid; swishing; impounded; shining; marching; sunny; purplish; winding; honeyed; unshaken; precious; steaming; greasy; saline; putrid; bitter; gliding; hidden; rampant; sky-hued; limpid; rocking; darkening; stagnant; shadowless; hurrying; clear; sparkling; hot; glittering; silvery; seaward; surplus; numberless (pl); glistening; emerald; thundering; sleepy; blessed; ready; burning; blue-bosomed; streaming; muddy; invisible; huddling; climbing; living; wind-swept; lonely; reflecting; cleansing; ornamental; brooding; yielding; insipid; weary; swollen; navigable; transparent; festering; reef-strewn; trackless; starlit; moving; virgin; shoal-impatient; swift; giddy; annihilating; quivering; seething; placid; rose-white; glaring; restless; heaving; meager; dropping; sluggish; bickering; reviving; ebbing; imprisoned; dreamy; land-locked; crystal; flowing; gloomy; turbid; broken; perilous; vivifying; healing; moon-clear; tepid; enchanted; cloistered; sunshiny; fetid; dreary; azure; fastflowing; moon-lit; angry; wasteful; perennial; pliant; unsuspected; hydrant; chanting; loathsome; abundant; fluvial; smooth; idle; silent; booming; still; wide; sweltering; distilled; darkling; inviolable; flashing; scalding; treacherous; devouring; circumfluous; glorious; mysterious; dimpled; surging; life-giving; purling; fleecy; sweet; trickling; blushing; journalistic; tree-fringed; bleak; deep; cold; tributary; bubbling; warm; slow-moving; filthy; odorous; spreading; stormy; nearing; glorious; unclean; distant; glassy; roaring; wild; troubled; retreating; glimmering; western; fleeting; imprisoned; mountainous; jumbled; brilliant; benevolent; green; unknown; unstirring; august; tangy; medicinal; forest; fretting; polished; fatal; sharked; slimy; resistant; rushing; lisping; peaceful; smitten; milky; calm; sliding; tormented; rippling; tideless; running; unruffled; teeming; inundating; mute; destined; faint; black; turbulent; adjacent; fragrant; phosphorescent; unflinching; invisible; frothy.

verbs
administer—; agitate—; cart—; cast upon—; chart—; contaminate—; dabble in—; dam up—; dilute with—; distil—; disturb—; draw—; excrete—; filter—; frisk in—; gaze upon—; harness—; immerse in—; infest—; ingest—; pacify—; partake of—; plod through—; plunge into—; ply with—; pollute—; resort to—; saturate with—; slither into—; slash—; smooth—; steep in—; submerge in—; suck up—; —babbles; —drenches; —dribbles; —drips; —engulfs; —evaporates; —glimmers; —gurgles; —

gushes; —invigorates; —laps; —lashes; —murmurs; —oozes out; —penetrates; —precipitates; —quenches; —recedes; —ripples; —roars; —seeps in; —simmers; —snuffs out; —spurts; —stagnates; —subsides; —surges; —stains; —swells; —swirls; —trickles in.

(See moisture, bath, liquid, pond, juice, lava.)

WATER (*v*)

adverbs

diligently; literally; faithfully; daily; constantly; superfluously; patiently.

(See refresh, supply.)

WATERFALL

adjectives

ethereal; sheeted; distant; babbling; misty; overhanging; sudden; blazing; dashing; living; roaring; gamboling; rainbowed; graceful.

verbs

approach—; bridge—; erode into—; span —; view—; —cascades; —churns; —deluges; —descends; —endangers; —froths; —gurgles; —s lace; —leaps; —pitches; —roars; —rolls; —rumbles; —scuds over; —sprays; —threatens; —thunders; —tinkles.

(See cataract, spray, mist.)

WAVE

adjectives

sanguine; dark; voiceless; weltering; moon-whitened; tremendous; accompanying; playful; petulant; warring; transcendent; plunging; troubled; unnumbered (pl); sloping; foaming; sordid; successive (pl); tidal; glowing; bounteous; scornful; long; throbbing; turbid; surging; bright; translucent; dignified; furious; lava; fleecy; towering; gliding; rugged; all-powerful; rolling; never-tiring; feathery; lustrous; charming; fluctuating; delicate; glittering; eternal; greedy; burning; whirling; immeasurable; lapsing; flashing; drunken; dividual (pl); yeasty; sparkling; fierce; green; wintry; dull; monstrous; amber; petrified; vivid; haunted; oblivious; rippling; inveterate; hurrying; turbulent; startled; bellowing; rebellious; reckless; inflated; chilly; mounting; softening; impressive; weltering; painted; great; white-crested; pent; impetuous; flinging; whispering; hiding; fiery; yellow; breaking; indented; wobbly; uneven; glossy; frolicsome; audacious; gleaming; lasting; tempestuous; surf; glooming; dissolving; sheltering; dashing; sullen; conquered; starry; blackening; high-rolling; engulfing; melodious; wireless; caressing; calm; ruthless; careless; moon-lit; mirrored; full-flushed; late; rhythmical; curling; ever-deepening; undulating; tossing; wide-wallowing; blind; restless; migratory; lustrous; tractable; bounding; peaceful; dashing; refluent; shattered; wan; slumberous; sparkling; tepid; intermingled (pl); electric; brimming; peaked; mountainous; slimy; salt; wandering; pandemic; infinitesimal; frantic; breaking; foam-figured; whistling; slight; creative; lambent; thin-edged; unfathomable; lonely; mournful; eerie; uncharted; rival; enormous; conflicting; angry; burnished; grassy; conciliatory; crisp; dimpled; quivering; advancing; sable; sympathetic; spent; implacable; ruffled; alarming; loyal; urgent; wildered; jostling; rising; shallow; fretting; mighty; mimic; sonorous; receding; gurgling; siren-haunted; sun-kissed; charmed; frothy; inconstant; unsullied; raging; heaving; peristaltic; stormy; summer; western; blind.

WAVE (*v*)

adverbs

gaily; gracefully; magically; helplessly; frantically; amicably; cheerfully; energetically; desolately; tremulously; rhythmically; constantly; languidly; erratically; impudently; mournfully; eloquently; gently; contemptuously; surreptitiously.

(See flaunt, brandish.)

WAVER (*v*)

adverbs

indecisively; irresolutely; weakly; morbidly; vacillatingly; erratically; doubtfully.

(See vacillate.)

WAVERING

adverbs

feebly; decrepitly; indecisively; hesitantly; weakly; finally; seldom; vexatiously; foolishly; irresponsibly; weakly; shyly; timidly; terribly; anxiously; strangely.

WAVES

verbs

breast—; command—; launch upon—; ride —; stem—; walk upon—; —batter; —beat; —break; —buffet; —chant; —dance; —dash; —emanate; —fall; —fizzle; —foam; —lap; —lash; —lift their heads; —lull;

—pound; —rage; —recede; —ripple; —rise; —show their teeth; —sigh; —slap; —slop; —swamp; —toss their manes; —tremble; —tumble; —vibrate.

(See ocean, breaker, billow, maelstrom.)

WAX

adjectives

yielding; incorruptible; plastic; soft; dental.

verbs

accumulate—; bleach—; candle—; collect—; derive—; extract—; fuse—; impress on—; model in—; mould—; plug with—; scrape—; seal with—; secrete—; wick—; yield—; —adheres; —melts; —polishes; —seals; —smooths; —waterproofs.

(See candle, putty.)

WAX (v)

adverbs

mightily; indignantly; boisterously; prodigiously; abnormally; spectacularly.

(See grow, increase.)

WAY

adjectives

abnormal; absolute; admirable; abstract; accommodating; admonitory; adroit; advantageous; agitated; agreeable; aimless; airy; allegorical; ancient; ambitious; amorous; applauded; arched; appointed; artful; assured; astounding; avoidable; bachelor; busy; calculating; caressing; categorical; celestial; challenged; chance; characteristic; charming; cheap; cheerful; childish; comical; circuitous; cold; comfortable; compact; companionable; comparative; complete; composed; comradely; confidential; convenient; cordial; creative; critical; cynical; dank; dark; darkling; dauntless; defiant; deep; delicate; delicious; delightful; depreciating; desolate; desultory; devious; dignified; dim; direct; disagreeable; dishonest; disorderly; distant; distempered; divers (pl); divine; dogged; dolorous; doubtful; doubtless; dreamy; dull; dusty; easy; eccentric; effective; endearing; egoistic; elaborate; enigmatical; enlightened; erring; everlasting; existing; execrable; expeditious; expensive; explicable; expressive; false; fantastic; farthest; fathomable; fiery; flaming; flowered; foul; fumbling; genial; glib; gloomy; good-humored; gracious; gratifying; grave; grim; guileless; happy; half-frightened; hateful; hearty; heavenward; heavy-hearted; heedful; heterogeneous; hilarious; honorable; humble; idiomatic; idle; illogical; immortal; imperious; impersonal; impetuous; impregnable; incomprehensible; inconsequent; indefinite; indifferent; indirect; inexplicable; infinite; inflexible; ingenious; inscrutable; insolent; insular; inspired; intimate; introverted; irregular; invisible; irresistible; irritating; jerky; jostling; kind; laborious; lampless; labyrinthine; languid; last; laudable; lawful; leafy; learned; legendary; leisure; listless; lofty; loitering; lonely; luxurious; magical; marvelous; melancholy; mild; military; mischievous; modern; monstrous; moon-lit; muddled; murderous; muffled; mysterious; mystical; narrow; nasty; negative; noiseless; objective; night-wandering; nudging; obscure; obedient; offensive; oily; old; organic; original; ostentatious; outmoded; over-darkened; particular; peaceable; passive; paved; pebbly; peculiar; penetrating; peremptory; perfunctory; perilous; perplexing; picturesque; pilgrim; plausible; practical; prefatory; preoccupied; priestly; primrose; privy; promiscuous; promising; prosperous; provincial; provoking; prudent; public; quaint; queer; quick; rakish; random; rational; ready; realistic; reasonable; reassuring; reckless; reflective; respected; restless; restrained; restricted; roundabout; rude; rugged; safe; satisfactory; scaly; scornful; scrupulous; secret; self-chosen; self-made; self-pleasing; servile; shameful; facile; sharp; sheepish; shy; silly; sinuous; slimy; slippery; sodden; soft; solitary; sophisticated; sound; spasmodic; special; spectacular; spiky; spirited; sporadic; spring; squalid; starry; steadfast; stiff-necked; stolid; strange; stylish; sublime; subterranean; successful; sunken; supernatural; suspicious; symmetrical; sympathetic; systematic; temporary; tainted; tentative; theological; thorny; toilsome; tortuous; trackless; tranquil; treacherous; tricky; tumultuous; unaccountable; unceremonious; unchristian; uncompromising; uncouth; undynamic; unemotional; unerring; unexpected; uneven; unfriendly; ungenerous; ungracious; unhandsome; unimpassioned; unique; unkindled; unknown; unmeaning; unmerciful; unmistakable; unmitigated; unobtrusive; unpremeditated; unskilled; unslackened; unsuspected; untrodden; untutored; unwithered; upland; varied; venturous; vigorous; vulgar; wandering; wanton; wary; weary; weedy; whimsical; wildering; willowy; winding; woodland; workable; conscientious; constrained; contrary; half-fascinated.

verbs
adapt to—s; bar—; betray—; block—; bluff —; clutter—; contemplate—; demonstrate —; designate—; devise—; discern—; disclose—; elbow—; emulate—s; err in—; explore—; forge—; forsake—s; grope—; guide—; hew—; illumine—; inaugurate—; initiate in—s; inspire—; interpret—; lurk along—; mark—; mend—s; muddle—; pave —; pick—; plod—; plow—; point out—; pursue—; renounce—s; retrace—; smash—; smooth—; stray from—; strew—; thread—; veer from—; wangle—; welter—; wend—; worm—; yield—.

(See fashion, highway, gate, alley, avenue, manner, course, habit, lane.)

WAYWARD

adverbs
reprehensibly; heartbreakingly; incredibly; miserably; wretchedly; pitiably; curiously; remarkably; unaccountably; unmanageably; incorrigibly; strangely; haplessly; peculiarly; unfortunately; uncommonly; singularly; hopelessly; desperately; childishly.

WAYWORN

adverbs
terribly; weakly; feebly; pitiably; pathetically; undoubtedly; naturally; credibly; extremely; completely; utterly; ominously; momentarily; dreadfully.

WEAK

adverbs
pathetically; terribly; unusually; naturally; extremely; inordinately; significantly; palpably; languidly; remarkably; strangely; curiously; unexpectedly; surprisingly; unaccountably; distressingly; disappointingly; fatally; mortally; alarmingly; unfortunately.

WEAKEN (v)

adverbs
painfully; constitutionally; unsuspectedly; alarmingly; tragically; treacherously; precipitately; materially; basically; ostensibly; insidiously.

(See impair, decline.)

WEAKNESS

adjectives
cold-pale; youthful; normal; mortal; anarchical; potential; veriest; hereditary; childish; extraordinary; disordered; bodily; relative; physical; endearing; momentary; incurable; inherent; curious; unworthy; progressive; absolute; overmastering; confessed; extreme; deadly; amiable; earthly; intellectual; fatal; permanent; contemptible; prevalent; inborn; hollow.

verbs
arise from—; betray—; bewail—; blame—; confess to—; conquer—; deride—; dress up —; exploit—; increase—; indicate—; lament —; overcome—; pander to—; parade—; produce—; redeem—; reproach for—; speculate upon—; spurn—; —assails; —forfeits; —impairs; —prostrates; —thwarts; induce —.

(See infirmity, inability, disability, impotence, frailty, helplessness.)

WEAL

adjectives
common; public; universal; all-embracing.

WEALTH

adjectives
incipient; personal; incalculable; flowing; estimated; melodic; comparative; boundless; enormous; wanton; ill-gotten; unlimited; diminished; fabulous; proverbial; maiden; undeveloped; mineral; independent; movable; sole; hoarded; substantive; intellectual; growing; concentrated; complacent; monopolistic; lavished; priceless; crystal; progressive; natural; tremendous; material; conspicuous; squandering; magic; unwieldy; veritable; many-sided; lacteal; emotional; religious; disregarded; physical; inherited; immense; spiritual; available; gleaned; sparkling.

verbs
accumulate—; affect—; apportion—; attain —; confer—; confiscate—; consume—; destroy—; diffuse—; dissipate—; drain—; efface—; euphemize—; forfeit—; gather—; groan with—; hoard—; labor for—; lavish —; load with—; lust for—; obviate—; plunder—; redistribute—; reject—; roll in—; scatter—; scramble for—; squander—; tap —; tax—; toil for—; winnow—; —destines; —menaces; —multiplies; —surpasses.

(See fortune, affluence, legacy, capital, luxury, money, riches, plenty.)

WEALTHY

adverbs

gorgeously; enormously; comfortably; fortunately; pleasantly; agreeably; serenely; snugly; enviably; complacently; sufficiently; smugly; graciously; fabulously; independently; substantially; tremendously; conspicuously; immensely; crassly; excessively; fairly.

WEAPON

adjectives

slight; spiritual; enticing; ancipital; lethal; unsheathed; respectable; resistless; fierce; habitual; mimic; economic; inadequate; ceremonial; saintly; climatic; pitiless; prohibited; keen; formidable; devastating; ghastly; idle; defensive; fatal; blood-tipped; effective; primitive; death-dealing; trusty; lavish; dripping; heroic; dangerous; imperial; competent.

verbs

brandish—; conceal—; devise—; discredit —; display—; draw—; flourish—; forge—; furnish with—; resort to—; scorn—; sheathe —; stroke—; shield from—; temper—; wield—; wrest—; —s clang; —s clash; —cracks; —s crash; —flashes; —intimidates; —roars; —coerces.

(See arms, cannon, bow, cutlass, dagger, missile, gun, sword.)

WEAR

adjectives

abundant; minimum; worthy; immediate; superfluous; forcible; fashionable; prolonging; satisfactory.

WEAR (*v*)

adverbs

habitually; absurdly; customarily; religiously; gracefully; conventionally; invariably; jauntily; loosely; haughtily; superfluously; fashionably.

(See use, sport.)

WEARINESS

adjectives

elemental; humble; delicious; despairing; simple; utter; exasperated; satisfied; sheer; mortal; everlasting; blissful; silent; colossal; never-ending; eternal.

verbs

allay—; alleviate—; assuage—; augment—; complain of—; endure—; induce—; mitigate —; relieve—; result in—; succumb to—; —besets; —consumes; —creeps; —deters; —diminishes; —drags; —engulfs; —irks; —irritates; —oppresses; —overtakes; —overwhelms.

(See impotence, fatigue, languor, exhaustion, lassitude, lethargy, ennui.)

WEARISOME

adverbs

intolerably; tediously; monotonously; profoundly; irksomely; terribly; inordinately; exhaustingly; prosily; disgustingly; unbearably; stupidly; vexatiously; annoyingly; excessively; utterly; painfully; dreadfully.

WEARY

adverbs

naturally; inordinately; terribly; utterly; strangely; pitifully; forlornly; physically; nervously; unutterably; immeasurably; profoundly; extremely; mortally; inexpressibly; distressingly; pathetically; sadly.

WEASEL

verbs

—claws; —climbs; —constructs; —defends; —deposits; —inhabits; —pillages; —preys on; —plunders; —slays; —swims.

(See animal.)

WEATHER

adjectives

fair; green; heavy; high; windy; frosty; prized; harsh; inclement; bitter; portentous; overhung; unsullied; thick; warm; sunshiny; damp; foggy; sticky; summer; capricious; foul; whirling; militant; ripening; bright; hard; glad; wintry; unseasonable; darkening; somber; common; extreme; unfavorable; sultry; gypsy; mild; blue; rough; oppressive; humid; starless; unsettled; loud; delicious; glorious; golden; wilting; surface; tough; ripening; gusty; blusterous; unpropitious; cloudless; feverish; detestable; intemperate; singing.

verbs

anticipate—; bare to—; bear—; becloud—; chart—; conjecture on—; converse about—; endure—; expose to—; exult in—; forecast —; predict—; prophesy—; stomach—; unsettle—; —affects; —brightens; —clears; —damages; —dejects; —demoralizes; —depresses; —discourages; —disheartens; —en-

livens; —frowns; —hovers; —invigorates; —limits; —modifies; —permits; —thickens.
(See climate, cold, heat.)

WEATHER-BEATEN

adverbs
curiously; hopelessly; sturdily; dingily; apparently; admittedly; probably; naturally; obviously; palpably; manifestly; laughingly; harmlessly; oddly; shabbily; dingily.

WEATHERED

adverbs
decrepitly; invincibly; sturdily; anciently; admirably; pitifully; languidly; outrageously; definitely; agedly; gauntly; desperately; hopelessly.

WEAVE (v)

adverbs
deceptively; coarsely; subtly; laboriously; ingeniously; inextricably; deftly; skillfully; dexterously; artfully.
(See braid, fabricate.)

WEB

adjectives
singularly-formed; mysterious; bandana; tangled; dark; illuminated; contrapuntal; atrocious; unfinished; intricate; thick-spun; frail; luminous; wondrous; graceful-looking; braided.

verbs
avoid—; elude—; escape—; evade—; spin —; weave—; wreathe—; —ambushes; —attracts; —baits; —beguiles; —convolutes; —curves; —decussates; —enmeshes; —entangles; —entwines; —intersects; —lures; —reticulates; —snares; —traps; —vibrates.
(See cobweb, trap, net.)

WED (v)

adverbs
auspiciously; admirably; happily; gaily; blissfully; genially; perfunctorily; passionately.
(See marry, unite.)

WEDDING

verbs
approve of—; attend—; bar from—; bless —; celebrate—; ceremonialize—; contemplate—; entertain at—; feast at—; officiate at—; perform—; ritualize—; witness—; —binds; —cements; —contracts; —joins; —pledges; —ties; —unites.
(See nuptials, matrimony, marriage.)

WEEDS

adjectives
hardy; pageant; luxuriant; offensive; sea; bladdery; troublesome; unwholesome; mourning; coarse; brittle; silver-budded; fancy; rank; dank; valueless; wretched-looking; little; scented; flowerless; loathed; huddling; clinging; convent; blossoming; amphibious; bending; noisome; fragrant; deleterious; undulating; ineradicable; wasting; encumbering; swaying; thin; choking; noxious; unsightly; berry-spotted.

verbs
clear of—; exterminate—; eradicate—; nip —; pluck—; sever—; suffocate by—; teem with—; —attain; —choke; —crowd; —cumber; —deprive; —destroy; —entwine; —fringe; —hamper; —hinder; —overgrow; —parch; —strangle.
(See grass, plant.)

WEEDY

adverbs
excessively; horribly; hopelessly; inordinately; extraordinarily; naturally; offensively; vexatiously; terribly; unnecessarily; inexcusably; carelessly; hideously; rankly; unwholesomely; disgustingly; discouragingly.

WEEK

adjectives
consecutive (pl); bewildering; tempestuous; momentous; previous; ensuing; successive (pl); eventful; disturbing; dreary; happy; intoxicating; long; tedious; weary.

verbs
abide—; beguile—; celebrate—; commemorate—; endure—; extend—; fix—; forecast —; fritter away—; gain—; outlast—; prolong—; reckon—s; remain—; survive—; terminate—; tolerate for—; while away—; —elapses; —expires; —inaugurates; —lapses; —marks; —s stretch.
(See month, day, hour, time.)

WEEP (v)

adverbs
pitifully; plaintively; piteously; bitterly; wildly; tumultuously; sentimentally; pathetically; intermittently; stormily; hysterically; abundantly; furiously; copiously; ludicrously; sympathetically.
(See lament, moan.)

WEEPING

adjectives
responsive; mysterious; incessant; hysterical; violent; passionate; continual; ludicrous; sore; chronic; wild; focused; untimely.

WEIGH (*v*)

adverbs
gravely; judiciously; reflectively; empirically; correctly; onerously; heavily; minutely; momentously; ponderously.

(See balance, estimate.)

WEIGHT

adjectives
nightmare; slumberous; undue; soft; dark; mass; excess; increasing; overwhelming; panting; superior; sweet; enormous; withering; unsolicited; panting; patent; caressing; portcullis; co-extensive; lesser; dead; comfortable; unaccustomed; hard; icy; noticeable; prodigal; definite; descending; weary; augmented; emotional; specific; idle; crushing; finite; momentous; ponderous; relative; surplus; massive; cruel; exceptional; light; sufficient; combined.

verbs
adjust—; ascertain—; attain—; bear—; carry—; cast off—; convey—; determine—; exert—; flounder under—; groan under—; manipulate—; match—; modify—; propel —; regulate—; shoulder—; support—; suspend—; unburden—; vary in—; —balances; —bruises; —burdens; —compresses; —constricts; —crumples; —crushes; —descends; —diminishes; —fatigues; —oppresses; —overwhelms; —submerges.

(See load, heaviness, burden.)

WEIRD

adverbs
strangely; gloomily; uncannily; terribly; dismally; fearfully; mysteriously; darkly; curiously; fantastically; grotesquely; incomprehensibly; unpleasantly; disagreeably; peculiarly; eerily.

WELCOME

adjectives
formal; courteous; healthful; comfortless; chill; familiar; tepid; hearty; smiling; preposterous; cordial; awkward; unclouded; pathetic; homely; triumphant; pure; majestic; friendly; noisy; kindred; heart-sped; royal; dismal; generous; intuitive; gracious; unquestioned; premeditated; scant; boisterous; kindly; languid; urbane; immemorial; unostentatious; frank; energetic; extraordinary; joyous; hospitable; genial; cheerful; reverend; warm; lavish; frolic.

verbs
assure—; bark—; bid—; bow—; embrace in—; extend—; greet with—; hail—; insure —; nod—; offer—; overstay—; rejoice in—; roar—; salute—; shout—; smile—; thunder —; win—; —cools; —flatters; —greets; —heartens; —rings.

(See greeting, friendship.)

adverbs
gratefully; refreshingly; cordially; sincerely; hospitably; warmly; truly; unexpectedly; supremely; encouragingly; frankly; acceptably; pleasantly; genially; graciously.

WELCOME (*v*)

adverbs
smilingly; spaciously; hospitably; enthusiastically; fondly; heartily; affectionately; ecstatically; gleefully; courteously; majestically; generously; languidly; urbanely; ostentatiously; frankly; energetically; joyously; genially; lavishly.

(See greet, hail.)

WELD (*v*)

adverbs
electrically; sturdily; staunchly; firmly.

WELDING

adjectives
intimate; sturdy; gradual; necessary.

WELFARE

adjectives
immediate; bodily; real; general; human; material; permanent; spiritual; financial; commercial; national; eternal.

verbs
administer—; advance—; aid—; concern—; consider—; consult—; contribute to—; determine—; devote to—; disregard—; encourage —; endanger—; forward—; foster—; further—; ignore—; impair—; improve—; jeopardize—; neglect—; overlook—; plan —; promote—; raise—; regard—; respect —; sacrifice—; safeguard—; seek—; serve —; study—; threaten—; —ascends; —flourishes; —thrives.

(See good, health, happiness, well-being.)

WELL

adjectives
deep; calm; handsome; stone; decorated; poisoned; projected; fathomable; crystal; transparent; mossy; extreme; babbling; connected; polluted; harmonious; bubbling.

verbs
bare—; case—; contaminate—; drain—; drill—; emanate from—; excavate—; issue from—; line—; pollute—; probe—; pump from—; sink—; sound—; submerge in—; tap—; test—; —affords; —bubbles; —facilitates; —offers; —overflows; —springs up; —yields.
(See spring, shaft, source, fountain, volcano.)

adverbs
gloriously; splendidly; magnificently; wholly; gaily; entirely; seldom; recently; finally; radiantly; miraculously; happily; fortunately; luckily; naturally; surprisingly; extremely; incomparably; sturdily; rosily.

WELL-BEING

verbs
administer to—; advance—; afford—; bask in—; contribute toward—; desire—; discern —; encourage—; envy—; indicate—; jeopardize—; promote—; sense—; serve—; threaten—; wrap up in—; —flourishes; —permeates; —pervades; —prospers; —thrives.
(See welfare.)

WELL-BRED

adverbs
extremely; satisfactorily; gratifyingly; acceptably; unusually; delightfully; extraordinarily; beautifully; marvelously; surprisingly; unexpectedly; obviously; manifestly; meticulously; charmingly; naturally.

WELL-INFORMED

adverbs
remarkably; eminently; illustriously; exceptionally; consummately; distinctly; particularly; marvelously; wonderfully; profoundly; incredibly; surprisingly; undeniably; intelligently; unusually; certainly; impressively.

WELL-MEANING

adverbs
possibly; probably; apparently; evidently; manifestly; painfully; obviously; hopefully; awkwardly; clumsily; sufficiently.

WEST

adjectives
sublimated; faded; bountiful; infinite; flameless; unfooted; shadowy; vagrant; rich; glowing; fiery; crimson; bloody.

verbs
determine—; drift to—; establish in—; filter into—; invade—; migrate to—; penetrate—; pioneer—; settle in—; —absorbs; —attracts; —beckons; —calls; —flourishes; —importunes; —invites; —lures; —offers; —retreats; —thrives.
(See territory, country, region, locality.)

WET

adverbs
terribly; obnoxiously; unwholesomely; soppily; hopelessly; unseasonably; swampily; quaggily; mysteriously; strangely; disgustingly; unpleasantly; unhealthfully; utterly.

WETNESS

adjectives
dripping; sticky; red; annoying; permanent.

WETTING

adjectives
hearty; customary; voluntary; necessary.

WHALE

adjectives
wanton; large-finned; awkward; belching; monstrous; trained.

verbs
conserve—; derive from—s; dissect—; encounter—; exterminate—; glimpse—; harpoon—; haul in—; land—; market—; pursue—; sight—; spot—; strand—; strip—; value—; —s frequent; —gives battle; —s haunt; —inhabits; —looms; —plunges; —preys upon; —spouts; —submerges; —tows; —yields.
(See shark, fish, animal.)

WHEAT

adjectives
fruitless; scythed; yellowing; tender; nodding; ripe; whole; cracked; ground; bleached.

verbs
attack—; consume—; convert—; cultivate—; enrich—; glean—; grind—; harvest—; import—; market—; mill—; pulverize—; sow —; thresh—; trade in—; winnow the chaff

from—; —booms; —fails; —flourishes; —fluctuates; —germinates; —matures; —ripens; —ripples; —thrives.
(See crop, harvest, grain, cereal, grass, plant.)

WHEEDLING

adverbs
teasingly; coaxingly; flatteringly; fondly; carefully; foxily; tenderly; persistently; successfully; constantly.

WHEEL

adjectives
ardent; muffled; toothed; sentient; tardy; interior; flaming; buckled; whirling; fervid; humming; formidable; jarring; worm-eaten; gilded; living; westering; broad-tired; massive; shining; wobbling; rolling; restless; ponderous; creaking; glowing; retreating; worn-out; waggly; spinning; whirring; gambling.

verbs
derail—; grip—; lubricate—; maneuver—; pad—; realign—s; shatter—; tread—; trundle—; twirl—; —clicks; —creaks; —deviates; —drones; —encompasses; —encircles; —girdles; —facilitates; —gyrates; —lurches; —jars; —jolts; —jounces; —pivots on; —recoils; —responds; —revolves; —rumbles; —spins; —swerves; —twirls; —whirls.
(See helm, cycle.)

WHEEL (v)

adverbs
automatically; serenely; sharply; swiftly; dizzily; drunkenly; mechanically; ceaselessly; whirringly; smoothly.
(See roll, move.)

WHEREABOUTS

verbs
allude to—; ascertain—; bare—; betray—; bring to light—; conceal—; confirm—; determine—; discern—; disclose—; discover—; divulge—; establish—; expose—; fix—; inform of—; report—; reveal—; screen—; solve—; trace—; unearth—; veil—; verify—; —baffles; —creeps out; —mystifies.
(See existence, position, place.)

WHIFF

adjectives
jealous; subtle; odorous; suggestive; gentle.

WHIM

adjectives
wild; eccentric; epicurean; delightful; illogical; abrupt; mere; ornamental; arbitrary; idle; anti-social; inconvenient; humorous; arrant; curious; mad; silly.

verbs
accede to—; conceive—; deny—; deplore—; discard—; dismiss as—; excite—; grant—; gratify—; humor—; indulge in—; outgrow—; play up to—; provoke—; satisfy—; smother—; yield to—; —intoxicates; —irritates; —piques; —riles (colloq.); —seizes.
(See humor, fad, fancy, caprice.)

WHIMPER (v)

adverbs
fretfully; distractedly; pusillanimously; reproachfully; feebly; pitifully; nervously; weakly; brokenly; hysterically; fruitlessly.
(See weep, cry.)

WHIMPERING

adjectives
nervous; secret; everlasting; continual; frightened; pitiful.

WHIMSICAL

adverbs
ludicrously; fancifully; fantastically; amusingly; pleasantly; cleverly; subtly; agreeably; fascinatingly; charmingly; grotesquely; outlandishly; delightfully; immensely; absurdly; unusually; oddly.

WHINE

adjectives
shrill; pusillanimous; friendly; cracked; peculiar; hungry; begging.

verbs
choke back—; discern—; elicit—; emit—; provoke—; restrain—; smother—; stifle—; subdue—; —distresses; —expresses; —irks; —irritates; —laments; —moves; —riles (colloq.); —s subside; —touches.
(See moan, sob, complaint.)

WHINE (v)

adverbs
piteously; wretchedly; churlishly; shrilly; pusillanimously; beggingly; mournfully; intolerably; hungrily.
(See whimper, cry.)

WHINNY

adjectives
colt-like; shrill; nervous; excited.

WHIP

adjectives
gigantic; remorseless; cutting; keen; deadly; brutal.

verbs
apply—; brandish—; crack—; cut with—; flick—; flog with—; lay on—; prod with—; utilize—; yield to—; —accelerates; —belabors; —bestirs; —coerces; —crackles; —cracks; —flays; —cuts; —impels; —induces; —lashes; —pricks; —reddens; —scourges; —spurs; —stimulates; —stings; —urges; —goads.

WHIP (*v*)

adverbs
unmercifully; deservedly; savagely; brutally; remorselessly; viciously.
(See beat, thrash.)

WHIPPOORWILL

verbs
—calls; —moans; —reiterates; —vociferates; —wails.
(See bird.)

WHIRL

adjectives
little; powdery; foamy; continuous; social; giddy.

WHIRL (*v*)

adverbs
crazily; dizzily; madly; gaily; joyously; incessantly; furiously; giddily; continuously.
(See revolve, swirl.)

WHIRLPOOL

adjectives
everlasting; continued; foamy; fatal; heartless.

verbs
avoid—; drift into—; escape—; ferment—; flounder in—; quiver in—; sweep into—; yield to—; —agitates; —batters; —boils; —buffets; —churns; —dashes; —eddies; —endangers; —foams; —froths; —gyrates; —imperils; —jostles; —jounces; —menaces; —plays; —roars; —seethes; —spouts; —sucks; —swirls; —threatens; —whips.
(See maelstrom, vortex, waves.)

WHIRLWIND

adjectives
drear; cloudy; weltering; dark; awful; rending; eddying; good; undulating; toying; fatal; unexpected.

WHISK (*v*)

adverbs
deftly; cleverly; eagerly; abruptly; resolutely; noiselessly; cunningly.
(See sweep, whirl.)

WHISKERS

adjectives
solitary; grizzled; sere; miserable; half-starved; shaggy; educated; combed; closely-cropped; bushy; unruly; optimistic; huge; fuzzy; bountiful; unkempt; ingrown.

verbs
affect—; clip—; crop—; cultivate—; discard—; lop off—; pluck—; respect—; ruffle—; rumple—; shag—; shampoo—; shear—; smooth—; stroke—; thin out—; trim—; —adorn; —cloak; —disguise; —fringe; —gray; —quiver; —transform; —tuft.
(See moustache, mane, hair, beard.)

WHISKEY

adjectives
indispensable; hot; commissary; straight; blended; bonded; young; medicinal; cheap; smooth; fiery; burning; synthetic.

verbs
abstain from—; addict to—; age—; assimilate—; bond—; bootleg—; bottle—; consume—; dispatch—; distil—; drain—; inure to—; legalize—; prohibit—; quaff—; refine—; sip—; swill—; tax—; value—; —anaesthetizes; —befogs; —deadens; —dulls; —enlivens; —flows; —flings down; —inebriates; —enslaves; —intoxicates; —narcotizes; —perverts; —revives; swig—.
(See brandy, liquor, alcohol, gin, wine.)

WHISPER

adjectives
delightful; gentle; sullen; friendly; dainty; icy; sibilant; soothing; awe-stricken; stirring; naked; subdued; ragged; little; rapid; hysteric; broken; persuasive; insistent; stage; imperturbable; laughing; silken;

stealthy; confidential; frantic; resolute; ceaseless; indolent; answering; intense; solemn; unnatural; keen; wheezing; busy; blasphemous; significant; low; muttered; hoarse; failing; vibrating; swelling; precautionary; benignant; bearded; husky; multitudinous (pl); fierce; tragic; hollow; ghostly; hideous; bass; audible; hurried; frightened; serene; overt; eloquent; agonized; strained; occasional; caressing; complaining; fanatical; distressed.

verbs
amplify—; conspire in—s; converse in—s; convey in—; drown out—; emit—; harken to—; hush—; inform in—; muffle—; overhear—; raise above—; reduce to—; resort to—; revive—; stifle—; suppress—; —beckons; —buzzes; —dies; —distracts; —diverts; —hints; —prompts; —quavers; —rebukes; —sears; still—.

(See sound, tone, noise, hum.)

WHISPER (v)

adverbs
hoarsely; treasonably; brokenly; passionately; impressively; eagerly; tremulously; urgently; mysteriously; audibly; affectionately; discreetly; petulantly; breathlessly; fiercely; savagely; feebly; defiantly; appealingly; compassionately; insidiously; vehemently; feverishly; stealthily; overtly; eloquently; impressively.

(See gossip, speak.)

WHISTLE

adjectives
noiseless; plaintive; hoarse; careless; expressive; fierce; denouncing; shrill; incessant; congratulatory; occasional.

verbs
blow on—; toot—; —alarms; —announces; —awakens; —beckons; —deafens; —distracts; —drowns out; —pierces; —proclaims; —rends; —screams; —shrieks; —shrills; —signals; —sounds; —splits; —startles; —wails; —warns.

(See warning, flute, note, scream.)

WHISTLE (v)

adverbs
sharply; briskly; piercingly; incisively; warningly; desperately; weirdly; thinly; tunelessly; mockingly; gently; repetitiously; melodiously; plaintively.

(See sound, sing.)

WHITE

adjectives
pure; new; snow; artemisia; frosty; clinging; unendurable; moon-washed; brilliant; beach; billowy; delicate; silvery; translucent; uncanny; popular; smart; plain; wanted; smooth; dazzling; creamy; foaming; shining; whirling; argent; deadly; immaculate; bloodless; slashing; luminous.

adverbs
ghastly; utterly; suddenly; brilliantly; dingily; dustily; dully; nervously; sickly; frightfully; gleamingly; blazingly; chalkily; ghostly; surprisingly; inappropriately; startlingly.

WHITE-LIVERED

adverbs
disgustingly; foolishly; shamefully; terribly; despicably; contemptibly; obviously; manifestly; notoriously; infamously; unusually; spinelessly; abjectly; helplessly; undisguisedly; hideously; terribly.

WHITENESS

adjectives
dazzling; splendid; immaculate; gleaming; downy; pristine; spotless; ghastly; unbroken; chalky; silent; bony; evanescent; dead; odious.

WHITEWASHED

adverbs
neatly; gleamingly; recently; tidily; sanitarily; pleasantly; conveniently; hilariously; quickly; diplomatically; wisely; cheaply; delightfully; cheerfully; ingeniously; thoughtfully; carefully; deceptively; artistically.

WHOLE

adjectives
consistent; magnificent; stupendous; homogeneous; coherent; immeasurable; complete; great; weltering.

WHOLESOME

adverbs
pleasantly; delightfully; palatably; tastily; notably; admittedly; soundly; nutritiously; splendidly; happily; admirably; commendably; attractively; smilingly; rosily; sturdily.

WHOOP (v)

adverbs
hideously; madly; wildly; insanely; barbar-

ously; terrifyingly; viciously; insistently; hysterically.
(See cry, yell.)

WICK

adjectives
flaring; homemade; burned; cotton; low.

verbs
enkindle—; ignite—; immerse—; lower—; raise—; renew—; saturate—; smother—; snuff out—; soak—; —blazes; —diffuses; —flares; —flickers; —flutters; —glimmers; —glows; —illumines; —radiates; —scintillates; —sears; —singes; —sparkles.
(See candle.)

WICKED

adverbs
scarcely; slightly; interestingly; alluringly; terribly; brutally; heinously; undeniably; palpably; manifestly; nefariously; unspeakably; inexpressibly; dreadfully; obscenely; conspicuously; notoriously; infamously.

WICKEDNESS

adjectives
loathsome; idolatrous; flagrant; unforgivable; exceeding.

verbs
acquit of—; atone for—; breed—; condone—; convert from—; denounce—; deplore—; disclose—; do penance for—; expiate—; expose—; extirpate—; forsake—; impute—to; inveigh against—; paint—; purge of—; renounce—; repent—; reproach for—; reveal—; rue—; shrive of—; stamp out—; stew in—; work—; —corrupts; —prevails; —reigns; —taints.
(See lawlessness, abomination, iniquity, licentiousness, immorality, evil.)

WIDE

adverbs
amply; sufficiently; generously; unexpectedly; capaciously; voluminously; exceptionally; particularly; peculiarly; conveniently; commodiously; spaciously; advantageously; tremendously; immensely; adequately; suitably; properly; fortunately; outlandishly; unnecessarily.

WIDEN (v)

adverbs
perceptibly; appreciably; gradually; markedly; proportionately; sufficiently; immeasurably; illimitably.
(See broaden, increase.)

WIDE-SPREAD

adverbs
unfortunately; manifestly; remarkably; amazingly; alarmingly; fearfully; luckily; dangerously; profitably; ineradicably; presumably; allegedly; fantastically; curiously.

WIDOW

adjectives
charming; agreeable; disconsolate; brokenhearted; wanton; childless; perverse; loving; pious; sentimental; virginal; lusty; unpensioned; polygamous; intrepid; austere; superabundant (pl).

WIELD (v)

adverbs
magically; potently; honorably; viciously; dictatorially; tyrannically; cunningly; dangerously; slyly; hatefully; deceitfully; craftily; subtly; ambitiously; ambiguously; virtuously; vigorously; powerfully; ruthlessly.
(See employ, use.)

WIFE

adjectives
shrewish; meek-eyed; worthy; tearful; disrespectful; legitimate; stainless; delicate; profligate; faithless; high-corseted; prideful; sprightly; bejeweled; coquettish; devoted; high-spirited; splendid; querulous; flattered; unsustained; exemplary; playful; dutiful; burdensome; slovenly; frantic; respective (pl); conquering; affectionate; trustful; sainted; temporary; spotless; forward; churchly; begotten; bullied; gracious; beaten; affianced; patient; sweet; virtuous; pale-faced; murdered; undivorced; unalienable; whimpering; smooth-haired; celebrated; amiable; strong-willed; tyrannical; diminutive; mercenary; constant; lewd-tongued; chaste; lawful; attractive; innocent; young; execrable; shameless; nervous; simple; common-law; slippery; perjured; aristocratic; pale-cheeked; tender; prudent; pining.

verbs
adore—; alienate—; caress—; choose—; cohabit with—; court—; desert—; embrace—; escort—; estrange from—; extol—; forsake—; intimidate—; seduce—; seek—; slander

—; strike—; take—; win—; —begets; —betrays; —comforts; —conceives; —haggles; —inspires; —mothers; —nags; —presides over; —rails; —shares.

(See mate, husband, mistress.)

WIG

adjectives

glossy; curly; formidable; elastic; frizzled; obvious; tangled; little; flaxen; towering; comical-looking.

WILD

adjectives

vast; impenetrable; sequestered; hidden; unapprehensive; dawning; fretted; luscious; untrodden; dreary.

adverbs

apparently; terribly; unmanageably; rankly; rampantly; fantastically; outrageously; outlandishly; savagely; ungovernably; naturally; inexpressibly; inordinately; boisterously; crazily; frantically; unconscionably; inveterately; hopelessly; manifestly; extraordinarily; pestiferously.

WILDCAT

adjectives

docile; cunning; vicious; sly; dangerous.

verbs

encounter—; skin—; trap—; —carries away; —claws; —depredates; —devours; —glares; —growls; —preys on; —roams; —slinks; —springs; —stalks.

(See animal.)

WILDERNESS

adjectives

vast; sub-arctic; intricate; unwithered; howling; watery; uneasy; rough; trackless; ancient; woody; indiscriminate; equal; untamed; obscure; pristine; remote; reluctant; barren; virgin; leafy; boundless; tangled; lonely; glowing; native; world-wide; unsettled; death-fraught; untrodden; broad; wild; shadowed; frozen; tangled; snowy; intricate; fertile; wasteful; uninhabited; untraveled; savage; measureless; constellated; adoring; interminable; pathless; untamable; marshy; inquiring; parched; arid.

verbs

brave—; circumvent—; clear—; dare—; explore—; fertilize—; flee into—; forsake—; frequent—; infest—; inhabit—; issue from —; level—; penetrate into—; pioneer into —; plunge into—; range—; retire to—; roam—; skirt—; subdue—; tame—; tangle in—; traverse—; venture into—; —beckons; —broods; —cloaks; —extends; —fascinates; —lures; —screens; —shrouds; invade—.

(See jungle, forest, desert.)

WILDNESS

adjectives

dreaming; wailing; graceful.

WILES

adjectives

intrinsic; instinctive; wanton; insidious; manifold; feminine; endearing; imaginary; winning; subtle; deceitful; crafty.

verbs

discern—; disguise—; fall victim to—; pierce—; resist—; resort to—; succumb to —; yield to—; —allure; —attract; —bait; —deceive; —defraud; —delude; —dupe; —ensnare; —entangle; —gull; —hook; —inveigle; —lure; —seduce; —succeed; —trap.

(See trick, deception, ruse, cunning.)

WILFUL

adverbs

naturally; inveterately; uncontrollably; notoriously; wickedly; stubbornly; foolishly; unreasonably; unmanageably; erratically; fanatically; impudently; inconsiderately; ungraciously; rudely; grossly; brutally; selfishly.

WILL
(*document*)

verbs

abide by—; attest to—; comply with—; contest—; direct in—; discharge—; dispute—; evidence—; execute—; file—; invalidate—; negate—; nullify—; observe—; probate—; seal—; set aside—; stipulate in—; witness —; wrangle over—; —assigns; —bequeaths; —bestows upon; —confers on; —consigns; —contributes to; —declares; —decrees; —discloses; —dispenses; —disposes of; —doles out; —endows; —enriches; —entrusts with; —estranges; —grants; —invests; —metes out; —restores; —settles; —subsidizes; —transfers.

(See contract, legacy, document.)

WILL

(*general*)

adjectives

passionless; individual; vulgar; overmastering; ambitious; cheerful; irresistible; unstable; grumbling; ill; intense; fiery; gracious; incorporated; inexorable; virtuous; devilish; firm-set; indomitable; unconquerable; holy; rational; never-daunted; vigorous; strenuous; inscrutable; powerful; regenerate; hindering; sturdy; unreined; invincible; tyrant; fallible; tormenting; idiotic; uncontrolled; dauntless; overruling; nerveless; natural; arbitrary; potent; genuine; good; lordly; sublime; basic; universal; arch-imperial; opposing; mutual; imperious; cruel; incorruptible; sensory; sovereign; sanguine; self-determined; undivided; sacred; honest; expressive; tremendous; lawless; clearly-expressed; tempered; despotic; tyrannic; benumbed; entangled; tendril-like; royal; imperative; imminent; unrelaxing; gracious.

verbs

accede to—; annihilate—; assert—; bend to —; blind—; blunt—; control—; curb—; effect—; energize—; enforce—; exercise—; express—; flout—; harden—; impose—; ignore—; liberate—; mold to—; obey—; oppose—; perform—; restore—; subject to—; subjugate—; subordinate—; weaken—; work—; yield to—; —s clash; —moves; —prevails; indulge—.

(See preference, desire, determination, willpower.)

WILLFULNESS

verbs

brook—; curb—; decry—; denounce—; deplore—; dispel—; dispose toward—; dissolve—; endure—; govern by—; incline toward—; put up with—; relax—; relent—; repent—; rue—; tolerate—; —irks; —irritates; —piques; —riles (colloq.); —succumbs to; —yields to.

(See perversity, obstinacy, stubbornness.)

WILLING

adverbs

usually; graciously; politely; considerately; indulgently; generously; agreeably; pleasantly; helpfully; indifferently; enthusiastically; surprisingly; suspiciously; curiously; generously; unexpectedly.

WILLINGNESS

adjectives

gruff; repeated; obvious; ready; surface.

WILLOW

adjectives

idling; silken; sprouting; shivery; weeping; slender.

WILLPOWER

verbs

breed—; cultivate—; discern—; display—; evince—; exhibit—; foster—; inherit—; lack —; lower—; necessitate—; rejuvenate—; require—; stimulate—; test—; want—; weaken—; —banishes; —curbs; —determines; —directs; —dominates; —droops; —flags; —flinches; —perseveres; —rebels; —rejects; —relaxes; —resists; —swerves; —wavers.

(See will, strength, desire, power.)

WIN (*v*)

adverbs

strategically; decisively; effectually; spectacularly; phenomenally; competitively; gallantly; substantially; intrepidly; treacherously.

(See triumph, achieve.)

WINCE (*v*)

adverbs

visibly; perceptibly; markedly; painfully; abruptly; revealingly; guiltily.

(See recoil, shrink.)

WINCING

adverbs

fearfully; constantly; suddenly; significantly; tremulously; painfully; haggardly; arrantly; senselessly; timidly; abjectly; indescribably; secretly; inwardly; openly; miserably; wretchedly; timorously; dreadfully; pathetically; curiously.

WIND

adjectives

crannying; worldly; southerly; good; swift; ill; cruel; biting; wandering; whispering; boisterous; hurtling; rolling; rough; poisonous; shrill; mad; curdling; dew-impearled; wild; chilling; whimsical; ocean; continuous; noiseless; streaming; sharp; rising; wailing; wanton; rude; nimble; special; spleenless; contrary; passing; foul; bleak; whitening; viewless; red-hot; roaring; crackling; fierce; gentle; dirty; sunny; bitter; keen; merry; favoring; shifting; restless; sleepy; sudden; sleety; gusty; cutting; whistling; murderous; dirgeful; pensive; uplifting; soughing; dying; wrinkling; wooing; weighty; unwilling; intricate; doleful; dead; hollow; moaning; mysterious; lulled; light; baffling; fabulous; azure; listening; inanimate; wintry; desert; woven; ferocious; delicate; fresh; panting; ravishing; hurricane; amorous; luscious; weak; tearing; felon; sportive; driving; boisterous; impetuous; mournful; adverse; piercing; tempestuous; contending; baleful; perverse; thirsty; ill-dispersing; tossing; monotonous; soothing; bracing; rustling; throwing; contrary; supple; wrecking; careless; bone-piercing; prevailing; serviceable; sighing; beating; impotent; fitful; quickening; petulant; winged; clinging; weary; lowered; treacherous; awakening; billowy; warring; fickle; life-breathing; unseen; frolic; screaming; dull; illuminated; sole; buffeting; eddying; gathering; marsh-bred; evil; murmuring; swift-winged; merciful; idle; sounding; sweeping; false; rainless; hot; stormy; furious; powerful; withering; warbling; frosty; surly; wave-building; parching; burdened; ungovernable; suffocating; burning; shrieking; repining; stray; drying; unwholesome; inconstant; soothed; mighty; worn-out; unfettered; prophetic; rushing; unbreathed; vagrant; lazy; summer; icy; unleashed; pious; relentless; hungry; odorous; cold; riotous; mounting; intermitting; lapsing; insulting; invisible; laughing; morning; voiceless; howling; translucent; stifling; lifting; visiting; speaking; wicked; tainted; chainless; forgetting; nimble; noble; envious; endless; blustering; mindless; melodious; life-breathing.

verbs

bear on— breast—; expose to—; harness—; ride—; ripple in—; sniff—; soar on—; still —; —abates; —assails; —bites; —blasts; —blusters; —breathes; —buffets; —caresses; —chants; —chills; —s conflict; —cuts; —dallies; —diminishes; —disturbs; —enfolds; —etches; —extinguishes; —grieves; —howls; —hums; —knifes; —lashes; —moans; —mourns; —murmurs; —rages; —rakes; —ranges; —rattles; —roars; —ruffles; —rustles; —scatters; —scourges; —shrieks; —sighs; —sings; —slaps; —slashes; —smites; —snaps; —soughs; —stings; —strips; —sweeps; —swells; —swirls; —threatens; —tugs; —twists; —uproots; —veers; —wafts; —wails; —wanders; —whines; —whips; —whispers; —whistles; —winnows; shelter from—.

(See gale, blizzard, air, breeze.)

WIND (v)

adverbs

tortuously; sinuously; picturesquely; intricately; monotonously; incessantly.

(See coil, curve.)

WINDMILL

verbs

agitate—; becalm—; drive—; employ—; outmode—; —churns; —circumvolves; —clatters; —s dot; —flaps; —gyrates; —quivers; —revolves; —rotates; —spins; —swirls; —twirls; —whirls.

(See propeller.)

WINDOW

adjectives

embayed; downy; hallowed; eye-like; stained-glass; pictured; foul; shattered; gaping; modern; prominent; bay; oriel; goggle-eyed; mullioned; iron-barred; steamy; irregular; lofty; filmy; diamond-paned; jeweled; dusky; glittering; dark; eastern; grimy; shuttered; thick; curtained; heat-clouded; latticed; emblazoned; delicate; panoramic; countrified; translucent; unglazed; scullery; fading; outjutting; shop; showy; fitted; rusty; iron-grilled; arched; tight; shut; barred; dingy; transparent; panting; regular; memorial; well-glazed; viewless; moon-lit.

verbs

beat on—; besiege—s; besmirch—; besmudge—; confront—; curtain—; drum on —; frame—; glower through—; jimmy—; peep out—; peer through—; pelt—; pour through—; putty—; rap on—; scour—; screen—; scrutinize through—; seal—; shade—; shatter—; spatter—; view from —; weatherstrip—; yank up (colloq.)—; —admits; —affords; —discloses; —glitters; —rattles; —vents; —ventilates.

(See glass, opening.)

WINDOW-PANE

adjectives

shining; grimy; well-fitted; dirt-streaked.

WINDY

adverbs

gustily; terribly; fatally; alarmingly; ominously; frigidly; freezingly; hotly; bitterly;

scorchingly; dreadfully; curiously; increasingly; cruelly; bitterly; bitingly; cuttingly; deucedly; plaguedly; infernally.

WINE

adjectives
diluted; sepulchral; generous; home-brewed; scuppernong; fierce; costly; agitated; raging; nectareous; new; copious; opulent; thick-purpled; straining; windy; heady; wholesome; fermented; medicated; mirthful; remembering; resplendent; inspiring; split; murmuring; heart-warming; splashing; foaming; frothing; forbearing; glimmering; palmy; enchanted; unmingled; fiery.

verbs
age—; brew—; chill—; cure in—; derive —from; distil—; ferment into—; gulp—; guzzle—; heat with—; imbibe—; ply with —; quaff—; reek of—; regale with—; savor —; sip—; sour—; swill—; value—; —animates; —dulls; —enlivens; —exhilarates; —flows; —flushes; —heats; —inflames; —inspires; —inspirits; —putrefies; —relaxes; —revives; —stimulates; —tempts; —warms; —intoxicates.

(See beverage, alcohol, liquor, champagne, beer.)

WING (*v*)

adverbs
gaily; sublimely; tirelessly; gracefully; joyously; unflaggingly; angelically; serenely; powerfully.

(See fly, float.)

WINGS
(*general*)

adjectives
leathern; curbed; trustless; joyous; fiery; hovering; glad; crumpled; snowy; divine; speckled; untiring; budding; light; steady; spacious; gleaming; huge; shadowy; flagging; redoubled; errant; overhanging; vibrating; folded; fateful; peaceful; rushing; silken; scare-crow; glowing; restless; futile; celestial; peerless; feeble; odoriferous; linen; fluttering; expanded; wide-open; invisible; noiseless; slow; laboring; winnowing; swift-rushing; feathered; untried; reverberate; mighty; motionless; fearless; aggressive; plume-plucked; sumptuous; wandering; wavering; dusky; sheltering; grisly; joyful; dawn-white; intended; outspread; rich; ruffled; viewless; hurrying; trembling; filmy; ebon; languid; nimble; dewy; aerial; twinkling; fanning; aurora; oaring; angelic; cherubic; parental; luminous; airy; unhallowed; immortal; overshadowing; gelid; moving; murmurous; gorgeous; quivering; outstretched; healing; unsustaining; enchanted; gauzy; jealous; unconquerable; multicolored; daedal; drooping; serene; expanded; inconstant; sunny; shower-struck; thunderous; rugged; sounding; unfledged; mealy; gaudy; velvet; fairy; shadowing; glassy; parted; tremulous; glossy; imprisoned; downy; sportive; swift; wheeling; laden; clanking; dye-dusty; unconfined; quickening; mutable; radiant; shrouding; rustling; bruised; agile; dipping; merciful; melancholy; blessed; shivering; glancing; quivering.

verbs
clip—; disable—; flap—; flit on—; fracture —; gather beneath—; hover on—; lend—; pluck—; preen—; prune—; singe—; soar on—; sprout—; strengthen—; take to—; try —; tuck under—; waft on—; —beat; —droop; —enable; —enfold; —flag; —flutter; —liberate; —quiver; —rustle; —wither.

WINGS
(*parts of a building*)

verbs
add—; explore—; extend into—; face—; flank—; gain access to—; haunt—; install —; level—; partition—; raze—; renovate —; restore—; seal—; shout from—; skirt —; skulk in—; view from—; —adjoin; —annex; —append; —project; —supplement.

(See passage, addition.)

WINK

adjectives
single; significant; unfatherly; lasting; cunning; impudent; sly; furtive; suggestive; pitying.

verbs
burlesque—; discern—; exaggerate—; exchange—s; swap—s (colloq.); tip—to; —allures; —amuses; —beckons; —beguiles; —betokens; —conveys; —denotes; —discloses; —distorts; —distracts; —entices; —expresses; —flirts; —indicates; —lures; —passes between; —prompts; —warns.

(See look, grin.)

WINK (v)

adverbs

coyly; triumphantly; significantly; wickedly; broadly; saucily; cunningly; impudently: furtively; suggestively.

(See blink, overlook.)

WINNER

adjectives

outstanding; capable; bread; practical; consistent.

verbs

acclaim—; announce—; applaud—; award to—; crown—; declare—; dispute—; emerge —; entertain—; fete—; glorify—; hail—; herald—; honor—; judge—; proclaim—; publicize—; reward—; —annexes; —profits; —reaps; —surmounts.

(See champion, hero, conqueror.)

WINSOME

adverbs

bonnily; sweetly; consciously; happily; merrily; rosily; graciously; innocently; childishly; youthfully; quietly; laughingly; irresistibly; wholly; alluringly; incomparably; daintily; airily; blithely; wholesomely; truly.

WINTER

adjectives

withered; rough; tedious; semi-arctic; dreadful; belated; rude; terrible; dreary; oblivious; laggard; bitter; brown; collapsing; stern; grand; dumb; dogged; brilliant; fatal; weeping; immortalizing; veritable; polar; trembling; monstrous; cheerless; unearthly; oppressive.

verbs

approach—; evade—; survive—; usher in —; —benumbs; —bites; —blankets; —blasts; —blights; —cloaks; —continues; —declines; —exterminates; —frosts; —glistens; —grips; —impoverishes; —nips; —persists; —presses; —relaxes; —roars; —wanes; —whips across.

(See cold, blizzard, storm, fall.)

WINTRY

adverbs

bracingly; bitterly; invigoratingly; snappily; nippingly; frigidly; delightfully; pleasantly; gloriously; picturesquely; delightfully; freezingly; unpleasantly; bleakly; barely.

WIPE (v)

adverbs

gently; timidly; sedately; quietly; hastily; mechanically; cautiously; medicinally.

(See whisk, obliterate.)

WIRE

adjectives

vertical; braided; flaxen; silver; tattered; telephone; leased; old-fashioned; singing; magnetic; envious; flexible; gilded; cunning.

verbs

base—; coat—; encase—; entwine—; fish with—; insulate—; tape—; —binds; —braces; —communicates with; —conveys; —electrifies; —furnishes; —hums; —reinforces; —transmits; —vibrates.

(See cable.)

WIRY

adverbs

inexhaustibly; sturdily; huskily; indefatigably; untiringly; dependably; wonderfully; amazingly; unbelievably; marvellously.

WISDOM

adjectives

divine; slow; memorable; infinite; wasted; practical; united; quaint; astute; stupendous; assimilable; incomparable; weighty; unseasonable; smiling; ancient; surpassing; calculating; revered; peculiar; limitless; protecting; profound; powerless; worldly; polished; political; moral; heavenly; determined; rich; presumptuous; ripe; deep; aphoristic; sufficient; Magian; supreme; collective; gnomic; honest; dark; musical; parabolical; selfsame; cunning; divine; mature; inner; magisterial; earthly; passion-starved; sifted; ruthless; superhuman; eternal; detestable; conceited; whimsy; sinister; crooked; undefiled; incomprehensible; pointed; prophetic; modest; housewifey; vulgar; fair; just.

verbs

accumulate—; belittle—; bow to—; challenge—; cloak—; conceal—; disclose—; distil—from; doubt—; enthrone in—; garner—; impugn—; inspire with—; invoke—; judge—; lack—; manifest—; partake of—; require—; school in—; seek—; simulate—; steep in—; temper with—; unfold—; yield to—; —decrees; —guides; —ripens; —rules; —warns.

(See information, philosophy, erudition, learning, intelligence, enlightenment, knowledge.)

WISE

adverbs

infinitely; unassailably; astutely; incomparably; surpassingly; particularly; ripely; expertly; sufficiently; supremely; honestly; darkly; cunningly; cleverly; divinely; magisterially; genially; ruthlessly; eternally; detestably; whimsically; significantly; pointedly; prophetically; affectionately; modestly; indubitably; scarcely; financially; discreetly; practically; profoundly; politically; usually; selfishly; surprisingly; undeniably; instinctively; intuitively; sensibly; judicially; capably; sagaciously; acutely; intelligently; sagely; cannily; coolly; equitably; solidly; discerningly.

WISE-CRACKING

adverbs

ridiculously; entertainingly; divertingly; amusingly; cleverly; nonsensically; comically; continually; crazily; smartly; clownishly; drolly; ludicrously; facetiously; waggishly; ridiculously.

WISH

adjectives

ardent; pious; gnawing; lifelong; reasonable; earnest; idle; faint; conscious; homicidal; audible; changing; vague; unrealized; cruel; forbidden; utmost; eager; doleful; docile; distinct; avaricious; fondest; irreconcilable; unaccomplished; slight; irrational; lawless; humble; incestuous; willful; repressed; poor; petty; inordinate; dignified; urgent; ambitious; sensual; venturous; fervent; careless; vehement; added; repressed; ardent; fleeting; anxious; dying; granted; dominant; feeble; foolish; dubious; helpless; passing; pious.

verbs

abandon—; accede to—; achieve—; acquiesce to—; anticipate—; assent to—; betray—; cater to—s; comply with—; conceive—; convey—; defy—s; disclose—; entertain—; express—; favor—; fulfill—; govern—; grant—; gratify—; harbor—; honor—; indicate—; indulge—; inform of —; manifest—; mask—; override—; realize—; repress—; satisfy—; submit to—; subordinate—; uphold—; voice—; yield to —; —consumes; —materializes; —prevails.

(See desire, want, need.)

WISH (*v*)

adverbs

heartily; devoutly; earnestly; ardently; solemnly; fervently; craftily; seriously; deliberately; viciously; conscientiously; piously; fondly; irrationally; vehemently; foolishly; vainly.

(See desire, want.)

WISP

adjectives

stringy; dewy; lazy.

WISTFULNESS

adjectives

pathetic; queer; tearful.

WIT

adjectives

licentious; shallow; out-of-fashion; undergraduate; blunted; scholarly; fresh; mellow; simple; bitter; obscene; mighty; sarcastic; keen; sprightly; mobile; caustic; courteous; admirable; perplexed; mixed; sparkling; comic; foolish; open; fastidious; paradoxical; sparkling; prodigal; unstrained; inexhaustible; insidious; conversational; vigorous; shrewd; homely; quick; trenchant; various (pl); inimitable; threadbare; human; metaphysic; crack-brained; unseasonable; native; loyal; microscopic; shattered; merciless; strayed; rude; aimless; sharpened; diabolic; assured; fouled; fogged; worthless; acidulous; sluggish; sudden; acute; dextrous; light; confounded; spontaneous; verbal; alert; subtle; delicate; unpremeditated; ebullient; satirical; airy; incomparable; exhilarating; eminent; unmatched; vulgar; ready.

verbs

clothe in—; dampen—; display—; draw—; dull—; exhibit—; grasp—; infuse—; inject —; kindle—; match—; pervert—; refine—; scatter—; sharpen—; tinge with—; —amuses; —beguiles; —bores; —cuts; —delights; —flashes; —flourishes; —flowers; —flows; —penetrates; —rebounds; —scathes; —scintillates; —shines; —sparkles; —totters; —victimizes.

(See understanding, humor, banter, repartee, witticism.)

WITCH

adjectives
soul-killing; potent; wrinkled; foul; reputed.

WITCHCRAFT

verbs
charge with—; condemn—; delve into—; embrace—; employ—; exercise—; explode —; hang for—; practise—; resort to—; suspect of—; —bewitches; —charms; —conjures up; —enchants; —flourishes; —intrigues; —mesmerizes; —presages; employ—; exercise—.
(See enchantment, magic, mysticism.)

WITCHERY

adjectives
dear; languorous; traditional; strange; romantic.

WITHDRAW (*v*)

adverbs
honorably; modestly; steadily; definitely; hostilely; apologetically; involuntarily; mysteriously; courteously; formally; gracefully; shamefacedly; noiselessly; precipitately; unmolestedly; pusillanimously.
(See retreat, retract.)

WITHDRAWAL

adjectives
timely; unmolested; contemporaneous; early.

verbs
advise—; advocate—; announce—; attend —; begrudge—; contemplate—; consider—; curtail—; promote—; recommend—; regard —; shrink from—; subject to—; —closes; —devoids; —disturbs; —ebbs; —evacuates; —strains; —taxes.
(See removal, departure, evacuation.)

WITHERED

adverbs
pitiably; helplessly; remarkably; surprisingly; gauntly; desperately; paralytically; perceptibly.

WITHHOLD (*v*)

adverbs
deliberately; purposely; mystically; insidiously; venomously; hatefully; relentlessly; tenaciously; perfidiously.
(See deny, refuse.)

WITHSTAND (*v*)

adverbs
manfully; gallantly; vigorously; staunchly; stalwartly; admirably; perpetually; economically; boldly.
(See resist, oppose.)

WITLESS

adverbs
provokingly; utterly; absolutely; helplessly; crazily; pitiably; pathetically; miserably; wretchedly; piteously; allegedly; vexatiously.

WITNESS

adjectives
mute; trustworthy; laughing; material; missing; singular; actual; striking; eloquent; perjured; divers (pl); long-lost; perpetual; impartial; terror-stricken; awful; creditable; reluctant; silent; surviving; all-judging; eternal; too-willing; followed; crushing; credible; thorough; steadfast; relentless; petrified; sympathizing.

verbs
bear—; bias—; bribe—; cite—; coach—; confront with—; contradict—; cross-examine —; intimidate—; introduce—; prejudice—; present—; produce—; rake up—s; suborn —; subpoena—; summon—; —acknowledges; —alleges; —attests to; —authenticates; —avers; —bears on; —beholds; —certifies; —confesses; —confirms; —contends; —contradicts; —corroborates; —damns; —endorses; —evidences; —falsifies; —impugns; —perjures; —pictures; —pleads; —records; —reports; —reveals; —seals; —signs; —substantiates; —supports; —testifies; —upholds; —verifies; —views; —vouches for; —vows.
(See observer, bystander, evidence.)

WITTICISM

adjectives
characteristic; pert; neat; coarse; constrained; obscene; painful; withering.

verbs
banter—s; evoke—; exchange—s; flash—; indulge in—s; roar at—; trade—s; —bites; —glitters; —retorts; —salts; —scintillates; —sparkles; —spices; —stings.
(See wit, joke, jest, humor.)

WITTY

adverbs

profoundly; divertingly; amusingly; delightfully; uncommonly; extremely; mischievously; comically; roguishly; mischievously; scintillatingly; brilliantly; splendidly; unusually; broadly; drolly; facetiously; fatuously; pleasantly; smartly; whimsically; waggishly; cruelly; merrily; fantastically; sparklingly.

WIZARD

adjectives

reputed; doting; egregious; glancing; baffled; bounteous; aged.

WOE

adjectives

silent; unavailing; gloomy; unwieldy; unutterable; comic; lesser; intolerable; outward; imaginative; holy; speechless; bitter; endless; tedious; unreposing; human; immedicable; life-consuming; harboring; guilty; pious; tedious; immortal; irredeemable; wearied; earthly; conscious; unprevailing; nameless; imaginary; discordant; impending; eternal; black; worthless; outward; everlasting; mortal; incommunicable; ending; thankless; stagnant; perplexing; lofty; great; rank; inexpressible; constant; wanton; insuperable.

verbs

afflict with—; allay—; alleviate—; babble —; bewail—; bow in—; burden with—; ease—; exclaim—; hide—; induce—; nurse —; occasion—; overcome with—; palliate —; predict—; recompense for—; remedy—; sink into—; spin out—; suffer—; triumph over—; whimper of—; —curses; —lacerates; —overwhelms; —rends; —saddens; —sours; —wracks; —wrings.

(See grief, sadness, sorrow.)

WOEFUL

adverbs

sadly; dolefully; habitually; utterly; wretchedly; helplessly; terribly; naturally; pathetically; pitiably.

WOLF

verbs

pay a bounty on—s; —s assemble; —s chase; —s devastate; —s infest; —s overpower; —preys on; —prowls; —pursues; —ranges; —runs down; —skulks; —slinks; —snarls; —stalks; —s terrorize; —s troop; —s visit.

(See animal.)

WOLVES

adjectives

famished; snapping; snarling; mangled; bloodless; shrewd; rabid; human; ravenous; fearful; genteel; universal.

WOMAN

adjectives

abject; accomplished; admirable; affected; affectionate; aggressive; ambitious; amiable; appealing; aproned; artful; ashy-hued; attractive; beautiful; awe-stricken; baby-faced; bedraggled; bedridden; bent; bewitching; brawny; bread-winning; brilliant; broken-hearted; bustling; careworn; celebrated; charming; chaste; childless; clear-eyed; clear-headed; clever; clinging; comely; compassionate; composed; consonant; corpulent; courageous; crabby; crisp; cruel; curious; cynical; decent; decrepit; defenseless; delicate; desireful; determined; devout; discontented; distinguished; dutiful; dowdyish; dressed; earthly; economical; ecstatic; elaborate; elegant; embroidering; emerging; enduring; energetic; equable; erring; estimable; excellent; exemplary; fair-faced; fanatic; fantastic; fascinating; fashionable; fervent; feverish; flashy; flat; foolish; forsaken; fragile; frantic; frightened; fruitful; frigid; frowsy; full-blossomed; garrulous; gaunt; ghastly; glamorous; glittering; gray; grim; grizzled; handsome; happy; hard-faced; hard-worked; headstrong; haughty; heartless; helpless; heroic; hesitating; high-minded; home-keeping; home-loving; hypersensitive; hysterical; idealistic; illiterate; imperious; impish; implacable; importunate; impressible; incorrigible; indefatigable; independent; indigent; industrious; infidel; informal; insipid; intelligent; intrepid; jealous; jocose; large-souled; lewd; limping; listless; lithe; little; lonely; loitering; long; loose; loquacious; lovely; lumpish; lustful; managing; marble-limbed; mean; middle-aged; mincing; miserable; miserly; modern; modest; morbid; mortal; motherly; much-loved; mulatto; mystic; new; nice; noble; observant; odious; old; over-virtuous; over-worked; overwrought; pale; perfidious; perjured; pernicious; pinched; pitiless; plain-featured; plainly-dressed; plump; poor; preeminent; presumptuous; pretty; promiscuous; prosaic;

prosperous; proud; prudent; querulous; radiant; rapacious; remarkable; repentant; resolute; respected; reticent; rheumatic; romantic; sad-eyed; scrawny; seductive; self-loving; sensible; sensitive; serene-eyed; serious; shabby; shadowy; shallow; showy; shrewd; shriveled; silken-tressed; silly; slatternly; slender; slim; smooth-limbed; sorrowful; sour-faced; sporting; spotless; square-browed; stalwart; stout; striking; sumptuous; super-annuated; superior; sweet; sweet-voiced; tactful; tattling; tawdry; tenacious; tender; terrified; timid; timorous; tremendous; tremulous; unconstant; uncultivated; uncultured; unenlightened; unescorted; unkempt; unprotected; unworldly; vain; versatile; virtuous; vivacious; warm-hearted; wayside; wayward; weak-willed; wearied; wearisome; weeping; weird; well-dressed; well-favored; white-faced; wilted; witchlike; withered; witty; wooden; worldly; wretched; wrinkled; young.

WOMANLY

adverbs

truly; sweetly; graciously; delightfully; comfortingly; quietly; gracefully; compassionately; serenely; gently; hospitably; pleasantly; naturally; unusually; particularly; remarkably; surprisingly; unexpectedly; attractively; extremely.

WOMB

adjectives

solemn; hollow; tortured; unfathomed; shuddering; fruitful.

verbs

abscess—; develop in—; displace—; empty—; enter—; infect—; incise—; lacerate—; manipulate—; retain in—; support—; ulcerate—; —atrophies; —bends; —contracts; —discharges; —dilates; —dislodges; —distends; —encloses; —engenders; —enlarges; —expels; —falls; —involutes; —manipulates; —pulsates; —quickens; —relaxes; —sags; —yields.

WOMEN

verbs

appeal to—; ban—; bar—; cater to—; charm—; consort with—; defame—; defile—; degrade—; disparage—; emancipate—; enchant—; enfranchise—; enlighten—; liberate—; persecute—; rally—; rape—; ravish—; spurn—; sway—; typify—; uplift—; —bear; —beget; —beguile; —charm; —conceive; —flock about; —inflame; —labor; —mature; —provide; —nag; —scold.

(See damsel, girl, daughter.)

WONDER

adjectives

natural; varied (pl); small; breathing; envious; utmost; ignorant; lying; listening; breathless; midnight; despairing; sickened; perplexed; sullen; admiring; prodigious; curling; universal; elderly; loving; ornithological; vague; admiring; scornful; peerless; unreasoning; troubled; stupid; reverent; unimaginative; dramatic; lustrous; incredulous; estimable; unearthed; perpetual; isolated; speculative; special; snaky; late; scientific; supernatural; overwhelming; comedy; half-reproachful; silent; effusive.

verbs

acclaim—; bare—s; delve into—s; disclose—s; excite—; explore—s; gain—; gape at—; hail—; inspire—; marvel at—; occasion—; overcome with—; reveal—; stare with—; strike with—; —allures; —amazes; —astounds; —awes; —baffles; —bewilders; —dazzles; —dumbfounds; —mystifies; —petrifies; —startles.

(See curiosity, astonishment, incredulity, admiration, miracle, marvel.)

WONDER (v)

adverbs

confusedly; desperately; wistfully; anxiously; idly; uneasily; vaguely; irrelevantly; distractedly; detachedly; abjectly; capriciously; gloomily; blindly; ironically; uncomfortably; dazedly; sneeringly; miserably; enviously.

(See marvel, amaze.)

WONDERFUL

adverbs

utterly; amazingly; spectacularly; mysteriously; magically; unsurpassably; incredibly; fantastically.

WOO (v)

adverbs

roughly; affectionately; tenderly; timorously; ardently; vigorously; genially; subtly; lackadaisically; abortively; eloquently; earnestly; amusingly.

(See court, love.)

WOOD
(forest)

verbs

comb—; encamp in—; flank—; forsake—; frequent—; infest—; inhabit—; nest in—; prowl—; roam—; rove—; scour—; shelter in—; skirt—; thread through—; —blooms; —extends; —flowers; —obscures; —ranges; —screens; —shades; —shadows; —veils.

(See jungle, forest.)

WOOD
(general)

adjectives

sheltering; bushy; stormy; untrodden; boundless; split; green; tangled; sportive; intricate; wild; solemn; extensive; rippling; swampy; sonorous; violet; echoing; odorous; interminable; scented; ancient; plundered; darkling; dense; vernal; thorny; glowing; gloomy; snow-choked; mistrustful; rooky; soft-textured; crimson; sleeping; unfrequented; pathless; stilly; tuneful; dusky; rare; volumned; native; visionless; round-bosomed; primitive; fragrant; budding; naked; shaded; resinous; haughty; high; beechen; desolate; shining; wet; wide-stretching; sun-bedappled; trackless; dim-seen; distant; unshorn; ragged; aromatic; branching; rank; intervening; thick; ruined; gray-colored; delightsome; changing; hanging; whispering; shaggy; surrounding; dewy; variegated; chestnut; prehistoric; waving; precious; mazy; legendary; oracular; musical; autumnal; pheasant; inaccessible; ruthless; vast; competing; dreadful; deaf; dull; virgin; fatal; magnificent; wild; primeval.

WOOD
(material)

verbs

bevel—; carve in—; char—; chisel—; compress—; debark—; enkindle—; hack—; hew —; gather—; glean—; level—; model in—; plan—; sand—; sear—; shatter—; shave—; splinter—; whittle—; —blazes; —braces; —erodes; —hardens; —petrifies; —rots; —supports.

(See forest, carpenter, board, log, timber.)

WOODCHUCK

verbs

—hole; —burrows; —claws; —damages; —defends; —digs; —holes up; —pops into its hole; —preys on; —pursues; —rips; —tears; —slays; —snatches; —waddles away.

(See animal.)

WOODCOCK

verbs

bag—; decoy—; gun for—; —booms;—defies; —flits; —flocks; —glides; —honks; —inflates; —nips; —probes; —squats; —whirs; —zigzags.

(See bird.)

WOODED

adverbs

densely; thickly; valuably; wonderfully; profitably; beautifully; venerably; gently; sparsely; thinly; carefully; scientifically; intelligently; selectively; variously; impenetrably; gratefully; pleasantly.

WOODPECKER

verbs

—axes; —bores; —chisels; —clings; —digs; —hammers; —laps; —pecks; —prevents; —protects; —taps.

(See bird.)

WOOL

adjectives

soft; unbleached; mineral; ticklish; prickly.

verbs

bear—; brush—; card—; comb—; line with —; market—; oil—; rumple—; shear—; sort—; value—; weave of—; yield—; —affords; —comforts; —frays; —insures; —shelters; —shields.

(See cloth, leather, cotton.)

WORD

adjectives

abhorred; abounding; abrupt; abused: action; agonizing; altered; amazing; ambiguous; amusing; angry; appropriate; archaic; ardent; articulate; astonishing; audible; balanced; barbarous; barbed; bare; barren; bawled; biographical; biting; bitter; blameful; bland; blasphemous; blazing; blessed; bludgeoning; blundering; blunt; boastful; brave; bracketed; brawling; brotherly; brief; broken; burning; cabalistic; careless; caressing; casual; celebrated; certain; ceremonial; chanted; cheering; cherished; choice; choleric; coarse; coaxing; coined; comfortable; comforted; common-sense; comprehensive; conciliatory; conquering; considerate; consoling; constructive; contumelious; conventional; cordial; courteous; cruel; cunning; cutting; dainty; dangerous; daring; deadly; deathful; deathless; debasing; defensive; deliberate; delicate; deprecatory; derisive; descriptive; devastating; devout; dismal; disputatious; distinct; distracted; divided; doubtful; dread; dreadful; dying; eager; earnest; eloquent; elusive; emotional; emphatic; empty; encouraging; endearing; enriched; equivocal; eternal; explanatory; excusing; exotic; evangelical; explicit; extended; exultant; faithful; faltering; famed; fancy; farewell; fatal; favorite; feeble; fervent; fiery; fitting; flaming; flat; flattering; flowery; flying; foul; frequent; frivolous; futile; general; generous; gentle; genial; gigantic; glorious; glowing; golden; good; Gordian; graceful; gracious; grand; grateful; grave; great; half-extinguished; happy; hard; harsh; hasty; healing; heart-easing; heartrending; hesitant; hideous; high; high-born; homely; honest; honeyed; honorable; honored; hopeful; horrible; hot; household; hyphenated; identical (pl); idle; ill; imbedded; impious; imposing; impressive; inappropriate; inarticulate; incarnate; incautious; incoherent; incongruous; indignant; inexcusable; insane; inspiring; insulated; insulting; interchangeable; interrogative; iron; irrevocable; irritable; isolated; jeering; joking; just; keenly-felt; light; lilting; liquid; living; loved; loving; low-pitched; low-spoken; low-toned; luminous; lying; magic; magnanimous; majestic; matchless; meandering; meaningful; measured; meditated; mellifluous; mellow; melting; memorable; merciful; mere; metaphorical; meticulous; mighty; modified; momentary; momentous; monosyllabic; monotonous; moral; mortal; motherly; moving; much-abused; musical; muttered; mystic; naive; naughty; nauseous; nice; necromantic; noble; noisy; noted; obscure; obsolete; odd; odious; offending; oft-repeated; ominous; oppressive; orthodox; overpowering; passing; passionate; pathetic; peerless; perennial; persuasive; petulant; pithy; pitiful; plain; plausible; pleading; plighted; plump; plundered; poetic; poignant; polysyllable; pompous; portentous; potent; precious; precise; pregnant; provocative; quaint; qualified; queer; quenchless; quick; quickening; quiet; rabble-rousing; racy; radical; ragged; rallying; rapturous; rare; rash; ravishing; ready; reasoning; reconciling; recreative; reread; reproachful; repulsive; resonant; restless; revengeful; ringing; rough; rude; sacred; scientific; scornful; scurrilous; seafaring; sea-going; senseless; serious; serviceable; shy; shameful; sharp; significant; simple; simple-seeming; single; smooth; sneering; sober; soft; soggy; solemn; soothing; soulful; spoken; standardized; stemmed; stifled; stinging; stirring; stormy; strange; strong; stumbling; submissive; successful; sugared; sulphurous; sumptuous; superfluous; sweet; swelling; sympathetic; talismanic; tender; thick; thin; thoughtful; thought-up; threatening; torrential; touching; transparent; tremulous; trite; trenchant; tricky; tumbled; twanging; ugly; unalterable; unchosen; uncomprehended; uncompromising; undecided; understandable; unfamiliar; unfeeling; unflattering; unforgettable; ungrateful; unhappy; unheeded; universal; unkind; unlucky; unmistakable; unmodest; unmodulated; unmoving; unpleasant; unspeakable; unusual; unmuttered; unwinged; unwonted; useless; uttered; vague; veritable; vilified; vituperative; vivid; vulgar; wandering; warning; weak; weird; whirling; whispering; wild; wily; wise; witty; woeful; wondrous; woolly; worthless; woven; written; yearning; superlative; suppliant; suspicious.

WORD (v)

adverbs

courteously; succinctly; cautiously; ingeniously; deftly; insidiously; theoretically; meticulously; religiously; musically; quaintly; modestly; vaguely; vividly; sulphurously.

(See express, speak.)

WORDS

verbs

accept—; amend—; blink at—; boggle over —; breathe—; burble (colloq.)—; clip—; coax—; comprehend—; confirm—; conjure up —; contradict—; convey—; coo—; coin —; cram—; crowd—; cull—; debase—; decipher—; define—; derive—; detect—; digest—; discharge—; dissect—; distort—; dog—; drawl—; drink—; emphasize—; employ—; encounter—; enunciate—; epitomize—; exchange—; exemplify—; fear—; flounder for—; fondle—; forge—; fumble with—; grasp—; grope for—; hang on—; hum—; hurl—; interpose—; interpret—; interrupt—; loose—; measure—; meditate upon—; mince—; misuse—; modify—; mould—; mouth—; muffle—; mumble—; play on—; ponder—; prune down—; quote

—; recall—; record—; reject—; relay—; retract—; rob of—; scrutinize—; search for —; seek—; set forth—; shun—; shy at—; snap at—; snarl—; span—; speak—; spread —; stem—; strain—; string—; stumble through—; swallow—; sweep—; tangle—; tap—; trade—; toss—; toy with—; transcribe—; utter—; verify—; voice—; weave —; weigh—; wrench—; —add; —arrest; —awaken; —boom; —burst; —cluster; —come forth; —crash; —designate; —drift; —drone; —echo; —elude; —embed; —embody; —escape; —expound; —express; —fail; —filter; —flash; —fling; —float; —flow; —gull; —haunt; —imply; —imprison; —inspire; —leak out; —make sense; —overwhelm; —play; —pour; —rebound; —resuscitate; —ring; —rise; —salve; —set forth; —signify; —shower; —slur; —stab; —stare; —sting; —storm; —strangle; —suggest; —surge; —sweep; —symbolize; —toll; —trail; —trickle out; —vibrate; —waft; —wing; —drip.

(See idiom, metaphor, derivative, expression, thought.)

WORDY

adverbs

endlessly; tiresomely; inexpertly; grossly; intolerably; disappointingly; incomprehensibly; monotonously; wearisomely; impossibly; tediously; repetitiously; vilely; confoundedly; unsatisfactorily; crudely.

WORK

adjectives

able; abortive; absurd; accessible; accomplished; admired; aesthetic; aggressive; airy; alleged; ambitious; analogous; anatomical; architectural; arduous; artistic; authentic; authoritative; barbarous; beneficent; biographical; blessed; blundering; brain-directed; celebrated; bread-winning; calamitous; caretaking; catalogue; chamber; changeless; characteristic; charming; cherished; choicest; clean; clerical; colossal; commemorative; compassionate; comprehensive; conscienceless; conscientous; conspicuous; constructive; contemporary; continued; creative; creditable; critical; damp; defective; dental; desolate; destructive; desultory; development; dignified; diplomatic; diversified; domestic; dramatic; dreary; drudgery; durable; easy; ecclesiastical; editorial; egocentric; elaborate; elegant; embroidered; entertaining; epoch-making; exact; executive; exhaustive; experimental; explicable; expressive; exquisite; extemporaneous; extension; exterior; extravagant; fanciful; fascinating; fatiguing; fiendish; finicky; flourishing; free-lance; frenzied; ghastly; gigantic; graceful; grim; hand; harassing; hard; harmonious; hasty; hazardous; heartbreaking; helpless; home; hospital; humblest; humorous; idealistic; immediate; immoral; immortal; impassioned; imperishable; important; imposing; impressive; incomparable; indifferent; individual; ingenious; inimitable; inner; intellectual; intensive; interesting; irregular; irreligious; irreproachable; journalistic; laboratory; laborious; lacework; lax; licentious; literary; lofty; long-baffled; luminous; lyrical; majestic; makeshift; manifold (pl); masterful; masterly; mature; mechanical; memorable; menial; meretricious; meritorious; merry; monumental; multitudinous (pl); mystical; mythological; nefarious; new; noble; noted; noteworthy; objective; operative; orchestral; ornamental; outer; painful; patriotic; peaceful; permanent; perpendicular; persistent; philanthropic; philosophic; photographic; pianoforte; pioneer; piquant; pleasant; ponderous; popular; practical; profitable; prose; radiant; redeeming; regretful; remarkable; remunerate; reposing; representative; reproductive; risky; rhapsodical; routine; rudimentary; ruinous; rural; scandalous; sensational; sensitive; serious; sham; shielding; short; shriving; significant; sinful; sinless; solid; solitary; spontaneous; startling; statistical; steady; stellar; stern; subsequent; straightforward; stupendous; substantial; subtle; superficial; supplementary; suspended; symbolic; symphonic; systematic; tasteful; tawdry; technical; tedious; theological; theoretical; ticklish; tiring; titanic; toilsome; tolerable; unaccountable; tragic; unfruitful; unhallowed; uniting; unnecessary; unremitting; unsatisfactory; unstinted; unworthy; uplifting; urgent; valorous; variegated; valuable; vigorous; vital; vocal; voluntary; wearisome; well-composed; wholesome; winter; wondrous; worldly; master.

verbs

abandon—; acclaim—; accomplish—; buckle down to—; carry on—; christen—; comprehend—; conceive—; conclude—; delegate—; deprive of—; detail—; differentiate—; digest—; discredit—; distinguish—; dive into—; drug with—; efface—; embark upon

—; enlarge—; execute—; flinch at—; force —; foster—; fulfill—; hamper—; hinder—; immerse in—; impair—; improve—; investigate—; issue—; knock off—; mar—; master —; merge—; minimize—; nurture—; outdo —; perfect—; perform—; pigeonhole—; prosecute—; provide—; reconstruct—; recount—; regulate—; remunerate for—; retard—; shirk—; simplify—; submit—; supplement—; suspend from—; swamp with —; terminate—; thrive on—; undo—; wind up with—; wrestle with—; —blunts; —ceases; —commences; —confirms; —confounds; —constitutes; —devolves; —eases; —encumbers; —engrosses; —ennobles; —entails; —exacts; —extolls; —galls; —glorifies; —honors; —imbeds; —involves; —inspires; —overwhelms; —rectifies; —suspends.

(See drudgery, duty, enterprise, job, labor, occupation, business, grind.)

WORK (v)

adverbs

diligently; feverishly; passionately; energetically; zealously; automatically; faithfully; diurnally; persistently; furiously; simultaneously; concertedly; strenuously; indefatigably; minutely; assiduously; prodigiously; unremittingly; sedulously; spasmodically; continuously; effectually; exquisitely; harmoniously; independently; conscientiously; competently; listlessly.

(See labor, toil.)

WORKABLE

adverbs

splendidly; altogether; happily; practically; conveniently; opportunely; entirely; absolutely; easily; satisfactorily; adequately; actually; readily; luckily.

WORKERS

adjectives

energetic; subservient; mechanical; brisk; overburdened; copious; deceased; eligible; subtle; indefatigable; zealous; offending; routine; faithful; prodigious; bunchy; conservative; inert; chosen; ardent; methodical; swarming; migratory; rotund; rosy; noble; able-bodied; relief.

verbs

address—; battle—; bind—; discharge—; engage—; entitle—; exhaust—; exploit—; fag—; fatigue—; ferret out—; goad—; harangue—; house—; incite—; inveigle—; lock out—; master—; oust—; oversee—; prod —; refresh—; regiment—; reimburse—; reinstate—; reward—; ride—; speed—; spur —; superintend—; —accomplish; —arbitrate; —contribute; —lag; —parade; —pile into; —plunge into; —relax; —strain; —strike; —toil; —unionize; —weary.

(See labor, employee, striker.)

WORKMANSHIP

adjectives

exquisite; impeccable; intricate; meticulous; domestic; experienced; sterling; intrinsic; reliable; perfect; exacting; gossamer-like; cumbrous; competent; masterly; expert; cunning; delicate; fine; highest; elaborate; artistic; crude.

WORLD

adjectives

giddy; operatic; expectant; epicurean; outside; drowsy; immense; custom-laden; organic; humming; polite; gloomy; tolerant; good-tempered; well-breeding; impure; industrial; pagan; demolished; shadowy; unspotted; mighty; unsympathizing; noisy; unending; suffering; romantic; naughty; dim-eyed; injurious; contemporary; insulted; innumerable (pl); interminable; mundane; fantastic; unconscious; dissolving; pitiful; countless (pl); frozen; bustling; spiritual; intellectual; candid; uncounted (pl); disordered; supernatural; financial; dense; degenerate; commonplace; everyday; sensual; untraveled; breathing; diagrammed; wondering; invisible; hollow-hearted; crashing; assembled; unimaginable; fictitious; globular; convex; boisterous; workaday; clamorous; grieved; shaggy; material; flaming; unseen; busy; turbulent; alien; dingy; congregated; sorrowful; exclusive; neglected; seething; limited; conscious; benighted; listening; intelligible; contradictory; pulseless; writhing; famous; teeming; spacious; thinking; unusual; busy; witty; recreant; pendant; frantic; recorded; lazy; working; manifold; extraordinary; falling; unfamiliar; new-born; atheistic; chilling; arduous; contemptible; snowy; approving; archetypal; war-convulsed; desert; heaving; unbelieving; quivering; false; monstrous; selfish; despicable; contumelious; fashionable; angry; inexpressive; rain-wet; fast; moving; distasteful; decomposed; ever-advancing; godless; hero-worshipping; fighting; monotonous; corrupted; sin-bound; sympathizing; unremembered; celestial; hoary; altered; heartless; obscure; splendor-winged; divided; fascinating; undiscriminating; literary; careless; censorious; enduring; undisparaged; undespoiled; amphibious; merciless; unfriendly; insipid; infinite; watery; artistic; insecure; imaginative; unfathomable; sphered; warring; carping; commercial; merry; interdependent; well-loved; beautiful; beggared; distraught; sacrilegious; insurgent; shabby; golden; unsteady; dim; mazed; beseiged; offended; ancient; waiting; rough; eugenic; supernatural; external; mechanized; enlightened; white; voiceless; antique; vegetable; unappreciative; practical; ranking; inaccessible; united; boundless; imperfect; mechanistic; resplendent; civilized; panicky; indifferent; simple; violent; unstable; perfumed; ghostly; somber; dream; cautious; feminized; surrounding; spacious; groaning; resplendent; primeval; renovated; too-busy; sublime; thankless; faithless; wide; lampless; apostate; unroofed; war-pliant; hostile; fallen; imperfect; ungoverned.

verbs
bedevil—; befuddle—; benefit—; bestride —; blight—; confront—; consolidate—; contemplate—; convulse—; disease—; dislocate—; doom—; dwarf—; encompass—; enrich—; entangle—; flood—; grace—; heal —; hide from—; ignore—; isolate from—; people—; present to—; proclaim to—; redeem—; reform—; renounce—; revolutionize—; roam—; rock—; shape—; stir—; storm—; struggle with—; survey—; trample on—; transfigure—; triumph over—; withdraw from—; —acclaims; —acknowledges; —collapses; —crumbles; —rejects; —revolves; —slumbers; —teems with; —turns.

(See mankind, humanity, individual, globe, earth, creation, universe.)

WORLDLINESS

verbs
abhor—; achieve—; attain—; declaim—; decry—; denounce—; deplore—; envelop in —; exhibit—; feign—; forsake—; gain—; pretend—; purge of—; quit—; reject—; renounce—; supplant—; wrap in—; —callouses; —centers; —cloaks; —doubts; —hardens; —polishes; —questions; —veneers.

(See erudition, ambition, cynicism, experience.)

WORLDLY

adverbs
godlessly; selfishly; egotistically; covetously; immensely; pitiably; extraordinarily; lazily; contemptibly; deplorably; monstrously; heartlessly; gracelessly; stubbornly; callously; mercenarily; inexplicably; unreasonably; irritatingly; insensately; irreligiously; sacrilegiously; atheistically; irreverently; irrevocably; apostately; horribly; impiously; perversely; fanatically; recklessly; avowedly; blasphemously; profanely; heartbreakingly; grievously; obstinately; obdurately; unhappily; irrationally; unreasonably; openly.

WORM

adjectives
destitute; surfeited; unwholesome; obscene; invisible; lowly; humble; pollution-nourished; sluggish; nameless; voracious; resuscitated; venomous; reluctant; fiery; trodden; dead; crawling; lucky; worthless; velvet; vile.

verbs
angle with—; attract—s; bait with—; crush —; dig for—; excavate for—; hook—; impale—; —s annihilate; —attacks; —bores; —burrows; —creeps; —gnaws; —infects; —pupates; —screws; —slithers; —spirals; —symbolizes; —wriggles.

(See bait, animal.)

WORN

adverbs
shabbily; uselessly; irrecoverably; terribly; naturally; utterly; dingily; undesirably; utterly; pitifully; miserably; dreadfully.

WORRIED

adverbs
unnaturally; nervously; excitedly; terribly; miserably; frantically; pitiably; keenly; significantly; perceptibly; indescribably; deeply; unduly; touchingly; abnormally; naturally; curiously; lamentably; pathetically; ridiculously; ludicrously.

WORRY

adjectives
manifold (pl); mental; faint; territorial; eternal; death-dealing.

verbs
afflict with—; allay—; bear—; beset with —; betray—; dispel—; drown—; experience

—; immerse in—; induce—; occasion—; plunge into—; relieve of—; submerge in—; imburden—; —harasses; —harrows; —haunts; —hounds; —lashes; —oppresses; —plagues; —preys upon; —racks; —rends; —retards; —rings; —shatters; —weighs upon.

(See **anxiety, misgivings, liability, care.**)

WORRY (v)

adverbs

morbidly; miserably; neurotically; perpetually; abnormally; needlessly; desperately.

(See **fret, vex.**)

WORSHIP

adjectives

pagan; outward; astral; mystical; inhuman; spiritual; reverent; sane; idealistic; silent; cynical; imploring; coterie; divine; passionate; reverential; ardent; worthy; unhesitating; continual; interrupted; lifelong.

verbs

bow in—; chant—; congregate for—; defile—; desecrate—; dogmatize—; exalt—; intone—; join in—; kneel in—; lead—; perform—; persecute—; rejoice in—; renounce—; ridicule—; ritualize—; scorn—; sing—; —deifies; —exalts; —glorifies; —idolizes; —invokes; —lauds; —supplicates; —survives.

(See **cult, devotion, adoration, love, prayer, mass.**)

WORSHIP (v)

adverbs

blindly; inconsistently; religiously; solemnly; idolatrously; mystically; reverently; silently; passionately; ardently; continually.

(See **adore, reverence.**)

WORSHIPERS

adjectives

insensate; false; frenzied; vulgar; idol; heathen; devout.

verbs

address—; awe—; convoke—; electrify—; elevate—; hallow—; inspire—; preach to—; —adore; —beseech; —bow; —deify; —enshrine; —give thanks; —glorify; —invoke; —kneel; —pay homage; —pay tribute; —petition; —prostrate; —revere; —sacrifice; —supplicate; —vow.

(See **church-goers, priest, minister.**)

WORSHIPFUL

adverbs

fatuously; foolishly; obviously; conspicuously; devotedly; devoutly; faithfully; fanatically; sincerely; gloriously; admirably; ostentatiously; unctuously; smugly; blandly; truly; laudably; pharasaically; humbly; abjectly; adoringly; meekly.

WORTH

adjectives

transcendent; priceless; individual; passing; inestimable; artistic; imaginary; venerable; intrinsic; known; matchless; martial; nameless; sterling; high; unspeakable; additional; spiritual; reverend; divine; ultimate; genuine.

verbs

appraise—; appreciate—; ascertain—; assert—; assess—; attest to—; challenge—; degrade—; derive—from; determine—; disclose—; display—; endow with—; establish—; estimate—; exhibit—; gauge—; judge—; measure—; probe—; prove—; question—; reflect upon—; signify—; stamp—; weigh—; —ascends; —depreciates; —mounts; —skyrockets.

(See **value, merit, ability.**)

WORTHLESS

adverbs

terribly; undeniably; altogether; absolutely; hopelessly; scandalously; abominably; curiously; peculiarly; outlandishly; trashily; shabbily; miserably; wretchedly; atrociously; completely; contemptibly.

WORTHLESSNESS

verbs

acknowledge—; admit—; balance—; bare—; bemoan—; betray—; bewail—; concede—; consider—; contemplate—; decry—; denounce—; deplore—; divulge—; evidence—; expose—; inveigh against—; lapse into—; mask—; regard—; reveal—; ridicule—; scoff at—; scorn—; stray into—; unveil—.

(See **futility, inferiority, inefficiency, mediocrity, stupidity.**)

WORTHY

adverbs

completely; utterly; laudably; meritoriously; notably; conspicuously; sincerely; truly; incomparably; surpassingly; extraordinarily; amazingly; obviously; recognizably; manifestly; singularly.

WOUND

adjectives
sharp; starched; gaping; unprobed; obstinate; desperate; lifelong; unhealed; sterile; sharp; unadvised; stiffening; self-inflicted; dark; bleeding; ancient; external; immedicable; ghastly; fatal; infected; punctured; lacerated; mortal; grievous; suppurating; cruel; serious; aching; frightful; reeking; recurring; raw; numerous (pl); surface; immediate; hideous; disastrous; severe.

verbs
allay—; alleviate—; assuage—; balm—; caress—; cauterize—; cleanse—; disinfect —; drain—; dress—; inflict—; irrigate—; pack—; probe—; soothe—; staunch—; suck —; swab—; weather—; —bleeds; —punctures; —scars.

(See cut, laceration, injury.)

WOUND (v)

adverbs
indirectly; mortally; spiritually; dangerously; frightfully; cruelly; seriously; severely; critically; sorely; fatally; internally; grievously; hideously; disastrously.

(See hurt, injure.)

WRAITH

adjectives
meek; likely; unusual.

WRANGLE

adjectives
bloody; vestry; conjugal; political; brutal.

verbs
arbitrate—; avert—; curb—; curtail—; engage in—; incite—; instigate—; quell—; subdue—; —annoys; —arises; —bickers; —breaches; —clashes; —disputes; —distracts; —diverts; —ebbs; —embroils; —estranges; —jars; —jolts; —shocks; —wanes.

(See brawl, dispute, argument, quarrel.)

WRANGLE (v)

adverbs
stridently; vociferously; indignantly; furiously; conjugally; politically; brutally; viciously; vindictively; heatedly; incessantly; jealously; pettishly; argumentatively.

(See quarrel, argue.)

WRAP (v)

adverbs
snugly; clumsily; punctiliously; impeccably; festively; meticulously; competently; artistically; crudely.

(See cover, conceal.)

WRAPPER

adjectives
protective; formless; holiday.

verbs
bind—; cast off—; divest of—; enclose in —; husk—; invest in—; package in—s; penetrate—; pierce—; seal—; shed—; strip off—; superimpose—; —affords; —armors; —envelops; —girds; —insures; —preserves; — protects; —safeguards; —shelters; —shields; —swathes.

(See envelope, lining, cover.)

WRATH

adjectives
tiger-like; indignant; dead; volcanic; infinite; jealous; immoderate; swollen; righteous; unconscious; intolerable; glutinous; treacherous; mingled; passionate; desolating; whimsical; vindictive; drunken; popular; fiercest; uncaged; chastening; scornful; patient; ill-suppressed; silent; bitter; naked; envious; stormy; celestial; crazy; awakened; relentless; intense; mysterious; helpless; deathless; senile; destructive; parental; eternal; reproachful; unholy; headlong; foolish; revengeful; celebrated; threatening; righteous.

verbs
appease—; brave—; bring to—; burst into —; dampen—; draw—; encounter—; endure—; escape—; explode in—; fire with —; incur—; mollify—; move to—; pacify —; placate—; provoke—; repent—; rouse —; slake—; uncork—; vent—; —abates; —abuses; —bites; —blazes —clouds; —descends upon; —melts; —oppresses; —smoulders.

(See ire, anger, indignation, rage.)

WRATHFUL

adverbs
desperately; dangerously; inordinately; brutally; ominously; portentously; alarmingly; terribly; frightfully; unusually; unmitigably; unreasoningly; insensately; senselessly.

WREATH

adjectives
wanton; flavored; branching; rosy; light; variegated; flimsy; summer; noble; festal; odorous; bridal.

WRECK

adjectives
isolated; passive; sunken; pensile; irredeemable; silent; human; stunted; profitable; dilapidated; emotional; colossal; leafless; pulverized; shattered; crimson; moral; mangled; horrid; centennial; complicated; dreaded; ghastly; pitiable.

verbs
avert—; avoid—; escape—; explore—; glean from—; investigate—; perish in—; probe—; rummage through—; salvage—; survive—; —annihilates; —blights; —defaces; —demolishes; —devastates; —disheartens; —encumbers; —impairs; —impedes; —mars; —obstructs; —scars; —scathes; —strews.

(See ruins, debris, remains, accident.)

WRECK (*v*)

adverbs
deliberately; wantonly; revengefully; vindictively; desperately; hideously; disastrously; spiritually; destructively; insanely; treacherously.

(See destroy, ruin.)

WREN

verbs
—bubbles along; —busies; —chatters; —cheers; —cuddles; —dances; —hops; —peeps; —runs; —skips; —warms.

(See bird.)

WRENCH (*v*)

adverbs
violently; abruptly; distressfully; simultaneously; drastically; fiercely; disastrously; diabolically; rudely.

(See seize, grasp.)

WRESTLE (*v*)

adverbs
persuasively; religiously; prodigiously; arduously; ignominiously; industrially; economically; politically; wrathfully; fanatically; fiercely.

(See contend, fight.)

WRESTLER

verbs
coach—; manage—; train—; —batters; —buffets; —contends; —crouches; —dives; —engages; —fends; —flattens; —flings; —feints; —grapples; —groans; —grunts; —hugs; —hurls; —locks; —pancakes; —pinions; —rams; —scrambles; —spread-eagles; —strains; —strips; —tackles; —trains; —tussles; —vies for; —wards off.

WRETCH

adjectives
wondrous; mutinous; timorous; base; despairing; stupid; extreme; trembling; pretty; utter; short-sighted; imperturbable; tame; hollow-eyed; miserable; pitied; profligate; loathed; restless; fanatical; scandalous; enormous; self-nurtured; abandoned; nameless; barbarous; famishing; hunted; ephemeral; execrable; caitiff; shattered; delicate; disobedient; cruel; disabled; cowering; intense; fond; tortured; rude; miserable; famished; dishonest; drunken; jealous; deceptive; violent; sodden; smoky; inhuman; stupid; dew-bedabbled; conscious-stricken; odious; needy; houseless; irreparable; filthy.

WRETCHED

adverbs
miserably; pitiably; wordlessly; silently; utterly; inexpressibly; unspeakably; helplessly; feebly; hopelessly; cruelly; bitterly; singularly; inconsolably; disconsolately.

WRIGGLE (*v*)

adverbs
ecstatically; uncomfortably; uneasily; nervously; oppressively; distressfully; impatiently; impulsively; slickly; deftly; slyly.

(See move, writhe.)

WRING (*v*)

adverbs
fiercely; hysterically; vehemently; imperiously; convulsively; wildly; demoniacally; jubilantly; barbarically; sickeningly; fiendishly; iniquitously.

(See clutch, grasp.)

WRINKLE (*v*)

adverbs
carelessly; furiously; curiously; impatiently; prematurely; superciliously; fastidiously; scornfully.

(See pucker, crease.)

WRINKLED

adverbs
oddly; deeply; remarkably; excessively; terribly; merrily; agedly; uncommonly; curiously; noticeably; surprisingly; perceptibly.

WRINKLES

adjectives
upright; facial; weeping; frown-caused.

verbs
acquire—; avoid—; decry—; deplore—; knead—; smooth—; —appear; —blemish; —corrugate; —crease; —deepen; —disfigure; —distress; —furrow; —line; —mar; —ruffle.

WRISTS

adjectives
fettered; limp; blue-veined; gallant; compact; slim; strong.

verbs
adorn—; band—; bare—; benumb—; bind —; brace—; bruise—; dislocate—; distort —; encircle—; extend—; flex—; fracture —; grasp—; handcuff—; lacerate—; manipulate—; misshape—; paralyze—; prick —; seize by—; sprain—.
(See arm, hand, joint.)

WRIT

adjectives
ingenious; hallowed; apostolic; moving; deathless; legal.

verbs
apply for—; draw up—; file—; grant—; honor—; refuse—; respect—; —absolves; —accords; —allows; —authorizes; —confirms; —decrees; —disposes; —empowers; —evicts; —exempts; —exonerates; —immunizes; —informs; —legalizes; —pardons; —privileges; —releases; —sanctions; —summons; —verifies.
(See decree, award, decision, edict, order.)

WRITE (v)

adverbs
diplomatically; admirably; bombastically; trenchantly; graphically; crudely; barbarously; devastatingly; convincingly; pornographically; scintillatingly; profusely; magnanimously; scientifically; laboriously; ironically; irresolutely; irresistibly; pretentiously; tremulously; elegantly; desultorily; anonymously; satirically; hypothetically; harshly; affectionately; expressly; faultlessly; industriously; legibly; prosaically; salaciously; erotically; sensuously; contemporaneously; authoritatively; genially; avidly; solemnly; incoherently; vigorously; urgently; dogmatically; didactically; eclectically; voluminously; inscrutably; realistically; cynically.
(See compose, inscribe.)

WRITER

adjectives
outstanding; foremost; verbose; nature; world-famous; fatigued; controversial; credible; ancient; profane; neo-romantic; prolific; theoretic; travel; authoritative; ecclesiastical; illustrious; distinguished; public; opera; miscellaneous; quaint; sociological; sensational; inspiring; discouraged; unscientific; impressionistic; well-known; promising; juvenile; wretched; designing; seduced; eminent; vivacious; historical; roguish; original; anonymous; polemical; tragic; imaginative; convincing; passionate; discriminating; splendid; creative; influential; monkish; native; fertile; talented; thoughtful; philosophical; early; copious; ghost; practised; vigorous; estimable; nondescript; classic; revolutionary; charming; meritorious; previous; prose; diestical; voluminous; reputed; embryo; entertaining.

verbs
acclaim—; honor—; immortalize—; inspire —; laud—; —climaxes; —clothes in; —colors; —composes; —concocts; —couches in; —dashes off; —decries; —depicts; —elucidates; —eulogizes; —fabricates; —fascinates; —infers; —interprets; —libels; —molds; —narrates; —pens; —plagiarizes; —portrays; —recounts; —relates; —reports; —slanders; —soliloquizes; —styles; —unfolds; —vitalizes; —voices; —weaves.
(See dramatist, novelist, journalist, author, poet.)

WRITHE (v)

adverbs
spiritually; convulsively; sickeningly; agonizingly; pitiably.
(See wriggle, struggle.)

WRITHING

adjectives
mental; gnarled; imaginative; splendid; ignominious.

WRITINGS

adjectives

superb; first-class; breezy; contrapuntal; philosophical; epistolary; biographical; voluminous; humorous; undecipherable; wedge-shaped; hieroglyphic; tropical; free-lance; controversial; metaphorical; foremost; impressive; contemporary; descriptive; elaborate; clear; ghost; imaginative; copious; tragic; historical; propagandist; theoretical; inter-twisted; classic; commercial; prophetical; pernicious; dimmed; superb; representative; figurative; straightforward; unfinished; undistinguished; phonetic; miscellaneous; clerkly; distinct; admirable; sacred; cryptic; dramatic; poignant; unacademic; unpublished; excellent; lucid; scholarly; stylistic.

verbs

abridge—; acclaim—; analyze—; ban—; comprehend—; dissect—; disseminate—; engross in—; ferret out—; herald—; immortalize—; interpret—; laud—; permeate—; peruse—; pervade—; pervert—; probe—; prostitute—; publish—; rival—; —air; —dissertate; —embody; —embrace; —enthrall; —impassion; —inspire; —live; —particularize; —treat of; —ventilate.

(See editorial, epistle, epigram, handwriting, literature, prose, poetry.)

WRONG

adjectives

avenged; uncomplaining; revenging; cruel; deadly; great; bitter; ruthless; grievous; deep; hideous; fancied; intrinsic; culminating; enforced; irrevocable; willful; private; petty; perfidious; inevitable; early; fierce; trifling; illegal; foul; heinous; hoarded; irreparable; unredeemed; diabolic; mutual; deplored; inexpiable; accumulated; brazen; abstract; secret; drastic.

verbs

amend—; avenge—; challenge—; combat—; defeat—; denounce—; discern—; efface—; expose—; extenuate—; heal—; implant—; intend—; perpetuate—; redress—; reform—; remedy—; repent—; reproach—; reveal—; sustain—; —blemishes; —blots; —corrupts; —harasses; —injures; —mars; —offends; —oppresses; —weighs upon.

(See guilt, evil, injustice, grievance, crime.)

adverbs

utterly; absolutely; altogether; singularly; curiously; completely; wickedly; mischievously; deliberately; blunderingly; knowingly; outrageously; scandalously; brutally; cruelly; fatally.

WRONG (v)

adverbs

grievously; irreparably; deeply; grossly; iniquitously; ignominiously; insidiously; dishonestly; treacherously; egregiously; ruthlessly; diabolically; secretly.

(See deceive, trick.)

WRONG-DOING

verbs

ameliorate—; atone for—; avert—; campaign against—; check—; condone—; countenance—; decry—; deplore—; expiate—; inveigh against—; penalize—; quell—; reprove—; —despoils; —embitters; —invalidates; —saps; —undermines.

(See wrong, crime, sin.)

WRY

adverbs

fantastically; comically; decrepitly; curiously; cynically; pathetically; congenitally; pitiably; miserably; tragically; hopelessly; irremediably; permanently.

X

X-RAY

verbs

blur—; diagnose by—; dim—; examine under—; employ—; introduce—; observe—; resort to—; scrutinize—; study—; —delineates; —depicts; —discloses; —outlines; —photographs; —reveals; —shadows; —traces.

(See picture, microscope, photograph.)

Y

YACHT

adjectives
graceful; magnificent; furtive; converted.

verbs
batter—; board—; buffet—; captain—; christen—; collide with—; dock—; ground—; guide—; lash—; launch—; luxuriate on—; navigate—; pilot—; provision—; quarter on—; ram—; refurbish—; salvage—; scuttle—; swamp—; waft—; —flounders; —reels; —signals.
(See launch, boat, motor-boat, ship.)

YAMMERING

adverbs
hungrily; excitedly; pathetically; pitifully; pitiably; miserably; touchingly; affectingly; heartbreakingly; agonizedly; painfully; distressingly; pleadingly; wretchedly; hopefully; clamorously; feebly; despairingly; madly; dolefully; exhaustedly.

YAPPING

adverbs
spitefully; derisively; threateningly; disagreeably; noisily; clamorously; unpleasantly; grossly; coarsely; excitedly; viciously; eagerly; uncontrollably; unmanageably; alarmingly; snappishly; menacingly; fearfully.

YARD

adjectives
bustling; spacious; industrial; back; snowy; discreet; embowered; obscure; diminutive.

verbs
border—; bound—; circumscribe—; clutter—; confine to—; embrace—; encamp in—; enclose—; fence—; festoon—; flank—; garland—; litter—; provision—; restock—; romp in—; skirt—; span—; survey—; —affords; —extends.
(See area, garden, park.)

YARN
(colloq.)
(tale)

verbs
blast—; climax—; color—; debunk—; digress from—; embroider—; exaggerate—; explode—; fabricate—; magnify—; narrate—; recite—; recount—; relate—; retail—; spin—; stretch—; swap—s; terminate—; unfold—; varnish—; weave—; —delights; —distracts; —enthralls; —thrills.
(See story, tale.)

YARN
(general)

adjectives
mingled; rollicking; mystical; interminable; periodic; unlikely.

YARN
(thread)

verbs
arrange—; baste—; chain with—; entwine in—; fabricate—; interlace—; knit with—; pad with—; rend—; spin—; tack with—; twist—; unravel—; unsnarl—; unwind—; weave—; web—.
(See knitting, thread.)

YAWN

adjectives
smothered; suppressed; slight; prodigious; prolonged; imitative.

verbs
camouflage—; choke back—; conceal—; gag—; interpret—; muzzle—; restrain—; smother—; stifle—; suppress—; veil—; —betrays; —implies; —indicates; —insults; —masks; —silences; —widens.

YAWN (v)

adverbs
ferociously; prodigiously; drowsily; audibly; lazily; dreamily; surreptitiously; furtively; secretly; imitatively.

YAWNING

adverbs
embarrassingly; uncontrollably; significantly; undisguisedly; openly; unaccountably; impolitely; discourteously; deliberately; suggestively; unconscionably; wearily; drowsily; sleepily; oddly; continually; prodigiously; nonchalantly; indifferently; audibly; monstrously; loudly; ridiculously; cavernously; frankly; purposely; unconsciously; inadvertently.

YEAR

adjectives

virgin; elder; young; declining; golden; eternal; blighted; fineless (pl); desolate; vanished; studious; early; tender; childish; dying; successful; important; dangerous; unripe; formative; mature; short; undawned; magnificent; allotted; varied; revolving; troublous; mellowed; plenteous; good; healing; quiet; ominous; countless (pl); reluctant; exasperating; imperial; creeping; cruel; revealing; experimental; enormous; unfulfilling; previous; mighty; mournful; blessed; blooming; arduous; impatient; unique; gilded; rolling (pl); adolescent; ensuing; silent; rare; beauteous; endless; far; distant; synodical; sidereal; peaceful; sanguine; weary; infinite; rapid; dreary; advancing; active; green; inverted; vernal; hopeless; innocent; tempestuous; sleeping; gracious; darkling; hallowed; ravaged; subsequent; trembling; iron-footed; fleeting; flying; rolling; slanting; lengthened; lapsing; strong; bitter; impending; heavy-footed; paltry; dreaded; long-vanished; grueling; extinguished; unreluctant; soon-ended; envenomed; recent (pl); peaceful; precious; disastrous; lying; moldering; turbulent; successive (pl); achieving; consecutive (pl); troubled; illimitable; pregnant; alternate (pl); merry; blissful; absent; industrious; memorable; probationary; unreckoned; columned; bountiful; swelling; long-buried; departed; eventful; canceled; straitened; ill-starred; terrible; innumerable (pl); ragged; blurred; laborious; fabulous; ripened; hoarded; changing; wasted; withering; fiscal; plenteous; execrated.

YEARN (v)

adverbs

vaguely; tenderly; passionately; pensively; compassionately; ineffably; deeply; honestly; restlessly; mutely; inchoately.

(See desire, wish.)

YEARNING

adjectives

rhythmical; passionate; affectionate; anguished; nebulous; poignant; strange; heavenly; pitiful; keen; mortal; tender; intense; silent; precious; innermost; moral; equal; double; inchoate; naive; ineffable; restless; awful; natural; deep; honest; earnest.

verbs

allay—; cherish—; crush—; disclose—; dull—; ease—; gratify—; intensify—; mitigate—; palliate—; quell—; quench—; reveal—; satiate—; satisfy—; slake—; smother—; stifle—; suppress—; —intoxicates; —overwhelms; —seizes.

(See craving, longing.)

adverbs

anxiously; affectionately; fondly; lovingly; amorously; solicitously; hungrily; wearily; eagerly; manifestly; ambitiously; politically; conspicuously; obviously.

YEARS

verbs

advance in—; blank out—; curtail—; devote—to; dream away—; ease—; enliven—; enumerate—; extend—; forsee—; order—; prolong—; record—; rob of—; romp through—; shorten—; span—; survive—; —accumulate; —age; —creep by; —dim; —expire; —file by; —fly; —gnarl; —intervene; —lapse; —mature; —mellow; —parch; —race by; —ripen; —sear; —shrivel; —steal by; —twist.

(See months, time.)

YELL

adjectives

mingled (pl); incessant; long-drawn; simultaneous; fiendish; exultant; doleful; demoniac; jubilant; sickening; frantic; mocking; responsive; excited; deafening; barbaric; fierce; clamorous; triumphant; taunting; distressful; shrill; blood-curdling.

verbs

emit—; muffle—; mute—; muzzle—; restrain—; smother—; stifle—; suppress—; —agonizes; —alarms; —betrays; —discloses; —echoes; —penetrates; —pierces; —rends; —rings out; —shatters; —shrills; —startles.

(See shout, shriek, cry.)

YELL (v)

adverbs

stridently; enthusiastically; violently; furiously; barbarically; viciously; mockingly; demoniacally; fiercely; clamorously; triumphantly; tauntingly; fiendishly; jubilantly; exultantly.

(See cry, bellow.)

YELLOW

adjectives
dazzling; brass; gay; soft; durable; rich; canary; cheerful; bright; eye-taking.

YELLOWED

adverbs
dreadfully; deeply; uncommonly; perceptibly; agedly; significantly; ominously; sadly; sorrily; darkly; biliously; mopishly; desperately.

YELP

adjectives
throaty; deep; hot; unmistakable; hostile.

YEW

adjectives
pyramidal; gigantic.

YIELD

adjectives
excellent; abundant; desired; glorious; astounding; bloodless; remarkable; reassuring; prosperous; fabulous.

verbs
conserve—; consume—; curtail—; augment—; deplete—; disperse—; enhance—; estimate—; exhaust—; forecast—; garner—; market—; multiply—; squander—; treasure—; value—; —accrues; —ascends; —descends; —exceeds; —floods; —gluts; —mounts; —replenishes; —soars; —swells.

(See harvest, crop.)

YIELD (*v*)

adverbs
unequivocally; copiously; ostensibly; dejectedly; reluctantly; submissively; unwillingly; gracefully; blindly; prudently; begrudgingly; heroically; gallantly; abundantly; pusillanimously; gloriously.

(See submit, surrender.)

YIELDING

adverbs
suddenly; warmly; reluctantly; ardently; eagerly; agreeably; politely; courteously; finally; grudgingly; inconsistently; unwillingly; voluntarily; eventually; harmoniously; helpfully; pleasantly; suavely; urbanly.

YOKE

adjectives
unsought; galling; oppressive; detested; equal; brazen; chafing; heavy; bloody; tyrannical; cruel; servile; insufferable; harnessed.

verbs
bow to—; cast off—; deliver from—; ease—; emancipate from—; endure—; escape—; evade—; harness to—; liberate from—; rend—; sever—; subject to—; throw off—; tolerate—; unburden—; —couples; —curbs; —detains; —enslaves; —fetters; —irritates; —limits; —manacles; —restrains; —restricts; —shackles; —subjugates; —tethers.

(See manacle, chain, authority, band, tyranny.)

YOUNG

verbs
beget—; befriend—; cherish—; conceive—; defend—; devour—; fledge—; guard—; harass—; mother—; nest—; nurse—; prey upon—; protect—; raise—; restrain—; shield—; succor—; suckle—; teach—; wean—; —mature; —take wings; —test.

(See offspring, child.)

adverbs
adorably; sweetly; refreshingly; ridiculously; ecstatically; rapturously; delightfully; unsuitably; unfortunately; charmingly; appealingly; shyly; absurdly; hopelessly; extremely; wretchedly; terribly; childishly; blithely; happily; joyously; hilariously; infinitely; immortally; unbelievably; excitably; ardently; ingenuously; vividly; gloriously; splendidly; exuberantly; radiantly; blessedly.

YOUNGSTER

adjectives
abashed; sturdy; thoughtless; inquisitive; impatient; irresponsible; vigorous; inexperienced; admiring; sensitive; adolescent; nondescript; impertinent.

verbs
adopt—; amuse—; chasten—; discipline—; divert—; entertain—; guide—; nurse—; scold—; sober—; subdue—; —clambers; —clamors; —naps; —plagues; —questions; —romps; —scampers; —scurries; —wearies.

(See child.)

YOUTH

adjectives
courteous; ardent; home-keeping; poetic; ingenuous; unarmed; dashing; immortal;

glorious; vigorous; ambitious; extreme; unthinking; affected; studious; guarded; sanctimonious; illiterate; splendid; self-enamored; affluent; dazzling; uncouth; philosophical; smiling; malignant; ill-fed; hopeless; facile; mortal; sensitive; foolhardy; venturous; gracious; fragrant; exuberant; fertile; inexperienced; tenacious; timid; sinless; academic; sportive; heroic; everlasting; pensive; busy; handsome; perpetual; romantic; straying; overconfident; thankful; reverend; scorbutic; martial; willful; sweet; disdainful; radiant; burning; early; raucous; unhardened; restless; blessed; mischievous; moonish; unhappy; deflowered; fine; gallant; pretty; saintly; virtuous; bereaved; eager; personable; fresh; ill-kept; afflicted; tranquil; reckless; wasted; self-willed; haughty; extreme; lonely; expanding; refined; obstreperous; thoughtful; consecrated; protracted; shaggy-headed; rustic; lusty; high-spirited; inexplicable; venturesome; bruised; unregenerate; shrinking; soothing; callow; unsociable; unspent; dire; complaining; hapless; scant; loquacious; insensible; impetuous; fair-haired; illustrious; weather-beaten; departed; emulous; lumbering; corrupt; upright; trembling; joyous; tattered; haggard; fadeless; dumb; wooden; dissolute; unfriended; misguided; wretched; passionate; absurd; fantastic; inflammable; ill-boding; dark; irrepressible; yearning; visioning; smirking; emaciated; personable; curly-headed; fervent; handy; flaming; swart; shambling; dapper; post-war; close-lipped; alert.

verbs

attain—; burden—; cherish—; clutch—; commune with—; conscript—; corrupt—; counsel—; curtail—; depict—; discipline—; distress—; exalt—; extend—; exult in—; govern—; guide—; infuse—; inject—; instil —; lecture to—; maintain—; mar—; personify—; prate of—; prepare—; prolong—; quell—; recall—; recapture—; reflect on—; regain—; reminisce of—; reproach—; revel in—; revert to—; ripen into—; rob of—; sacrifice—; stride toward—; struggle to—; survive—; swamp—; symbolize—; —blooms; —emulates; —fades; —fires; —ignites; —impassions; —inspires; —inspirits; —invigorates; —matures; —mellows; —pervades; —reveres; —strays; —surmounts; —sweeps aside; —vaults; —wanes.

(See girl, childhood, maturity.)

YOUTHFUL

adverbs

delightfully; refreshingly; touchingly; wondrously; manifestly; charmingly; surprisingly; unbelievably; ingenuously; alluringly; adorably; artlessly; innocently; joyously; radiantly; blithely; cheerily; rapturously; gloriously; splendidly; adventurously; sweetly; restlessly; mischievously; blessedly; eagerly.

YOUTHFULNESS

adjectives

abounding; joyous; perpetual; mercurial; sparkling.

Z

ZANY

adverbs

amusingly; divertingly; ridiculously; absurdly; nonsensically; utterly; laughably; farcically; clownishly; mischievously; roguishly; playfully; cleverly; ingeniously.

ZEAL

adjectives

untiring; equal; puritan; inconsiderate; unflagging; lofty; cruel; wise; undaunted; peaceful; reformatory; misguided; overtaxed; artistic; benevolent; ancestral; unflinching; high-bred; unselfish; neverwearying; fervent; divine; wavering; accustomed; missionary; indiscreet; plastic; flaming; indomitable; flagging; incredible; hot; ardent; characteristic; solemn; noble; petulant; insensate; unwearied; humble; furious; commendable; religious; pious; upright; immoderate; diminishing.

verbs

attend with—; burn with—; check—; constrain—; cool—; counterfeit—; devote with —; display—; express—; extinguish—; feign—; fire with—; flush with—; heighten —; imbue with—; infuse—; inject—; inspire —; instil—; intensify—; lack—; match—; misguide—; promote—; quench—; regain—; share—; sharpen—; slake—; stimulate—; want—; —blazes; —burns; —consumes; —declines; —ebbs; —goads; —impassions; —melts; —quickens; —spurs; —subsides; —surges; —wanes; —waxes.

(See "pep", ardor, enthusiasm, intensity, fervor, eagerness, energy.)

ZEALOTS

adjectives

religious; wild; fiery; graceless; poetic; crazy-brained; patriotic.

ZEALOUS

adverbs

earnestly; actively; ardently; passionately; energetically; impetuously; eagerly; nervously; excitedly; absurdly; irresistibly; helpfully; extraordinarily; serviceably; delightfully; ridiculously; seriously; devoutly; piously; remarkably; distinctly; efficiently; boldly; willingly; generously.

ZEBRA

verbs

alarm—; cage—; captivate—; cross with—; domesticate—; exterminate—; fetter—; snare—; team with—; thrash—; —abounds in; —balks; —bolts; —bounds; —frequents; —grazes; —herds; —leaps; —pulls; —scurries; —sniffs; —springs.

(See animal, horse.)

ZENITH

verbs

achieve—; ascend to—; attain—; culminate in—; elevate to—; skyrocket to (colloq.)—; toboggan from—; topple from—; whirl to—; —climaxes.

(See height, pinnacle, fame, summit, peak.)

ZEPHYR

adjectives

reckless; delicious; sweet; playful; gracious.

ZERO (*rating*)

verbs

achieve—; bestow—; concede—; degrade to —; dole out—; fling—; impose—; incur—; merit—; rate—; scorn—; solicit—; tender —; threaten—; withdraw—; —confounds; —contradicts; —destroys; —disorders; —strikes.

(See punishment, reward, grade.)

ZEST

adjectives

special; sporting; prodigious; insatiable; inherent; hearty; adventurous; savage; scalping; rollicking; invidious; soldierly; smiling; inextinguishable; exquisite; glorious; hungry; infinite; keen; unflagging; eager; special; cynical; monotonous.

verbs

afford—; arouse—; augment—; curb—; derive—; devour with—; enhance—; excite—; harness—; impart—; inspire—; repress—; savor with—; stimulate—; subdue—; whet —; —animates; —burns; —charms; —ebbs;

—enlivens; —fortifies; —heartens; —invigorates; —pervades; —promotes; —reassures; —refreshes; —restrains; —suffuses; —sustains; —wanes.

(See zeal, ardor, fervor, flavor.)

ZESTFUL

adverbs

eagerly; alertly; happily; earnestly; avidly; energetically; enthusiastically; unusually; marvelously; unexpectedly; remarkably; inordinately; curiously; miraculously; incalculably; splendidly; superbly; joyously; helpfully; ardently; delightfully; boyishly; youthfully; noticeably; unwontedly.

ZIGZAG

adverbs

interestingly; purposely; profitably; curiously; conveniently; oddly; artistically; peculiarly; miserably; clumsily; adroitly; cleverly; intentionally; characteristically; quaintly; disagreeably; attractively; unexpectedly; deliberately.

ZONE

adjectives

temperate; frozen; arctic; inner; verdant; fringed; bodiced; interminable; fortunate; arable; wide-spread.

verbs

amplify—; apportion—; belt—; bisect—; carve out—; chop up—; circumscribe—; detach—; encircle—; encompass—; enlarge—; flank—; incise—; intersect—; invade—; label—; measure—; outline—; overreach—; pare—; patrol—; penetrate—; permeate—; prescribe—; restrict to—; skirt—; slice up —; subdivide—; swerve from—; widen—; —insulates; —isolates; —partitions; —secludes; —segregates.

(See section, neighborhood, area, locality, whereabouts.)